NEW INTERNATIONAL VERSION

COUPLES' DEVOTIONAL *Bible*

NEW INTERNATIONAL VERSION

COUPLES' DEVOTIONAL *Bible*

ZONDERVAN
.com

Published by Zondervan
Grand Rapids, Michigan 49530, U.S.A.

www.zondervan.com

Library of Congress Catalog Card Number 2008930990

Printed in China

---

09 10 11 12 13 /DSC/ 15 14 13 12 11 10 9 8 7 6 5 4 3 2 1

You will be pleased to know that a portion of the purchase price of your new NIV Bible has been provided to International Bible Society to help spread the gospel of Jesus Christ around the world!

International Bible Society
www.ibs.org

The purpose and passion of International Bible Society is to faithfully translate, publish and reach out with God's Word so that people around the world may become disciples of Jesus Christ and members of his Body.

CONTENTS

Contents

WELCOME

Welcome

THE PERFECT WEDDING GIFT

Spring floral bouquets, teal-green bridesmaid dresses with shoes dyed to match, a stunning white satin dress with a handmade veil, upswept hairdos, ushers, organist, singers, preacher; a sit-down dinner reception for the older folks and a boat cruise for the young ones—my daughter had planned it all.

Yet as mother of the bride in this perfect wedding, I was stressed about having to pray in front of the assembled guests. What could I possibly say?

My words gathered strength as I focused on touching God rather than on making an impression. I prayed about how wonderful this wedding was and how much planning had gone into it. Then I said, "In a few hours this will all be over. Then you, Brad and Laura, will be man and wife. And your marriage will begin . . ."

How much time had gone into preparing for *that*? I wish I'd had a copy of the *Couples' Devotional Bible* to hand to the new couple that would help strengthen their union by helping them progress through the Word of God with daily devotionals and weekend assessments and activities. I wish they could have immersed themselves in this Bible with a sense of wonder at how rich and deep and wide its lessons are for marriage: How much God loves and honors the love between a man and a woman in a lifetime commitment; how diligently his commandments protect fidelity and honesty and transparency in two who have become one flesh; how stern his warnings are against infidelity and other hurtful sins.

For you who are about to marry, are newly married or have been at this for awhile, I highly recommend the *Couples' Devotional Bible* to help you walk together through various challenges of life, such as interfering in-laws, stepparenting, infertility, debt, sickness, relocating, finding a church, fighting fair, living with regrets, guilt, whatever. There isn't a problem in your relationship that the Word of God does not address. This Bible will help you walk with each other in the Lord. And, as Ecclesiastes 4:12 says, "A cord of three strands is not quickly broken."

May God bless you as much as he has me through this Bible. I think I will still give Laura and Brad a copy. My son, too, who recently married. And every other couple whose wedding I am privileged to attend, praying, "May God bless this man and woman as they become husband and wife. May he help the two become one flesh as they walk through life. May they work through difficulties with honesty, diligence and grace. May they stick with each other through God's help. For as Jesus himself stated, 'What God has joined together, let man not separate'" (Mark 10:9).

—PHYLLIS TEN ELSHOF
2007

HOW TO USE THIS BIBLE

How to Use This Bible

LET'S GET STARTED!

Welcome to the revised *Couples' Devotional Bible*. Within this Bible you'll find features specifically designed to help you nurture and develop your devotional life as a couple. The next few pages will describe the different elements of this Bible, giving you an idea of how to get the most out of your time with God.

NEW INTERNATIONAL VERSION OF THE BIBLE (NIV)

The *New International Version* is today's most read, most trusted translation. For more on the NIV, see "Preface to the NIV," page xii.

260 DEVOTIONS, ONE FOR EACH WEEKDAY OF THE YEAR

All of the daily devotions were written by godly Christian writers who provide insight into the Scriptures and relate the Bible to married life. Many share their own stories or use illustrations from the lives of other couples to ensure the principles they set forth from Scripture are clearly explained. Each devotion concludes with a series of thought-provoking questions to encourage reflection and enhance a couples' communication.

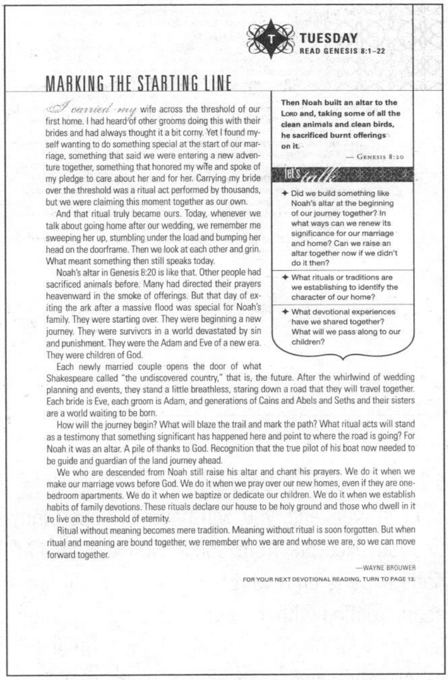
TUESDAY
READ GENESIS 8:1–22

MARKING THE STARTING LINE

I carried my wife across the threshold of our first home. I had heard of other grooms doing this with their brides and had always thought it a bit corny. Yet I found myself wanting to do something special at the start of our marriage, something that said we were entering a new adventure together, something that honored my wife and spoke of my pledge to care about her and for her. Carrying my bride over the threshold was a ritual act performed by thousands, but we were claiming this moment together as our own.

And that ritual truly became ours. Today, whenever we talk about going home after our wedding, we remember me sweeping her up, stumbling under the load and bumping her head on the doorframe. Then we look at each other and grin. What meant something then still speaks today.

Noah's altar in Genesis 8:20 is like that. Other people had sacrificed animals before. Many had directed their prayers heavenward in the smoke of offerings. But that day of exiting the ark after a massive flood was special for Noah's family. They were starting over. They were beginning a new journey. They were survivors in a world devastated by sin and punishment. They were the Adam and Eve of a new era. They were children of God.

Each newly married couple opens the door of what Shakespeare called "the undiscovered country," that is, the future. After the whirlwind of wedding planning and events, they stand a little breathless, staring down a road that they will travel together. Each bride is Eve, each groom is Adam, and generations of Cains and Abels and Seths and their sisters are a world waiting to be born.

How will the journey begin? What will blaze the trail and mark the path? What ritual acts will stand as a testimony that something significant has happened here and point to where the road is going? For Noah it was an altar. A pile of thanks to God. Recognition that the true pilot of his boat now needed to be guide and guardian of the land journey ahead.

We who are descended from Noah still raise his altar and chant his prayers. We do it when we make our marriage vows before God. We do it when we pray over our new homes, even if they are one-bedroom apartments. We do it when we baptize or dedicate our children. We do it when we establish habits of family devotions. These rituals declare our house to be holy ground and those who dwell in it to live on the threshold of eternity.

Ritual without meaning becomes mere tradition. Meaning without ritual is soon forgotten. But when ritual and meaning are bound together, we remember who we are and whose we are, so we can move forward together.

—WAYNE BROUWER

Then Noah built an altar to the LORD and, taking some of all the clean animals and clean birds, he sacrificed burnt offerings on it.

— GENESIS 8:20

let's talk

✦ Did we build something like Noah's altar at the beginning of our journey together? In what ways can we renew its significance for our marriage and home? Can we raise an altar together now if we didn't do it then?

✦ What rituals or traditions are we establishing to identify the character of our home?

✦ What devotional experiences have we shared together? What will we pass along to our children?

FOR YOUR NEXT DEVOTIONAL READING, TURN TO PAGE 13.

The devotions follow the days of the week, so no matter what day of the week you begin reading, simply turn to that devotion. For example, if you start on a Tuesday, just turn to the first "Tuesday" devotion in the book of Genesis. The page number for the next reading will be listed at the bottom of the page.

WEEKEND

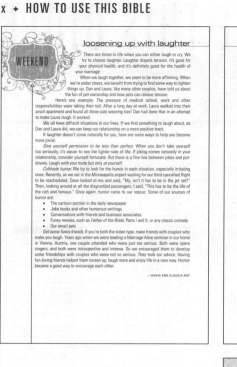

loosening up with laughter

There are times in life when you can either laugh or cry. We try to choose laughter. Laughter dispels tension. It's good for your physical health, and it's definitely good for the health of your marriage.

When we laugh together, we seem to be more affirming. When we're under stress, we benefit from trying to find some way to lighten things up. Dan and Laura, like many other couples, have told us about the fun of pet ownership and how pets can relieve tension.

Here's one example. The pressure of medical school, work and other responsibilities were taking their toll. After a long day at work, Laura walked into their small apartment and found all three cats wearing ties! Dan had done that in an attempt to make Laura laugh. It worked.

We all have difficult situations in our lives. If we find something to laugh about, as Dan and Laura did, we can keep our relationship on a more positive track.

If laughter doesn't come naturally for you, here are some ways to help you become more jovial.

Give yourself permission to be less than perfect. When you don't take yourself too seriously, it's easier to see the lighter side of life. If joking comes naturally in your relationship, consider yourself fortunate. But there is a fine line between jokes and put-downs. Laugh *with* your mate but only *at* yourself.

Cultivate humor. We try to look for the humor in each situation, especially irritating ones. Recently, as we sat in the Minneapolis airport waiting for our third cancelled flight to be rescheduled, Dave looked at me and said, "My, isn't it fun to be in the jet set?" Then, looking around at all the disgruntled passengers, I said, "This has to be the life of the rich and famous." Once again, humor came to our rescue. Some of our sources of humor are:

- The cartoon section in the daily newspaper
- Joke books and other humorous writings
- Conversations with friends and business associates
- Funny movies, such as *Father of the Bride*, Parts I and II, or any classic comedy
- Our email pals

Get some funny friends. If you're both the sober type, make friends with couples who make you laugh. Years ago when we were leading a Marriage Alive seminar in our home in Vienna, Austria, one couple attended who were just too serious. Both were opera singers, and both were introspective and intense. So we encouraged them to develop some friendships with couples who were not so serious. They took our advice. Having fun-loving friends helped them loosen up, laugh more and enjoy life in a new way. Humor became a good way to encourage each other.

—DAVID AND CLAUDIA ARP

HOW ARE WE DOING?

learning to laugh

Laughter is not only good medicine, but it also can be a cure for stress. If you can find something that's funny in any situation, you'll defuse anxiety and decrease your stress. Discuss the following situations with your spouse (or enlist a funny friend if you must) and find something humorous in each scenario. Remember, you're using humor to encourage each other, not to laugh at each other, so find ways to be funny and supportive!

1. You're on the way to a big job interview and as you get out of the car you realize you're wearing one black sock and one navy blue sock. You laugh. What's so funny?
2. You wanted a nice weekend at home relaxing and doing nothing around the house; then your mother-in-law calls to say she is coming for the weekend. What's so funny?
3. Traffic is worse than you've seen it in months. As you wait out another light change without moving forward, you look at the faces of the drivers around you. What's so funny?
4. You show up at a party and you're wearing the same dress as the hostess. What's so funny?
5. You twisted your ankle and the doctor says you have to stay off it and keep it elevated for three days. What's so funny?
6. There was a closeout sale on specialty paint so you decided to surprise your spouse and spruce up the bedroom. Half way through the project, you realize you don't have enough paint. What's so funny?
7. You've been asked to speak in church and right before you go up, the heel comes off your shoe. What's so funny?
8. Your two-year-old lost her diaper—in the grocery store. What's so funny?

let's make a DATE *date*

HUMOR ME!

Go to a local comedy club (try to check out the content first), rent a classic comedy or watch a comedian on TV. Afterward, try to make each other laugh. Tell that one story that always makes her giggle (complete with impersonations!). Notice what happens to your intimacy level when you start laughing together. Collect jokes or cartoons that are sure to make him chuckle and share them with him. Maybe the two of you can start a joke box for your favorite funnies. Secretly fill it with stories, jokes, cartoons, pictures or whatever will bring a smile to your spouse's face. The next time you need a laugh, take the lid off and enjoy.

FOR YOUR NEXT DEVOTIONAL READING, TURN TO PAGE 28.

LESSONS FROM THE *Bible*

Though laughter isn't mentioned much in the Bible, one couple in particular is known for their laughter. Check out Abraham and Sarah's story in Genesis 17:16–17; 18:1–15; 21:1–7 and discuss why the couple laughed and what God did in response. When is laughter appropriate and when is it not?

52 WEEKEND DEVOTIONS

Each weekend, you will have an opportunity to read excerpts from some well-known marriage experts on a variety of topics. You'll learn about dealing with in-laws, incorporating laughter into your marriage, forgiving each other, enjoying your blended family, and much more. Each weekend devotion includes an assessment, "How Are We Doing?" to make the topic applicable to your own marriage and give you both a chance to share with each other. "Lessons From the Bible" relates the topic to Scripture. Often, Bible couples are used as examples or relevant passages of Scripture are included. Finally, "Let's Make a Date" make the topic fun. Each weekend devotion includes an idea for making a date together to reconnect and enjoy one another.

BOOK INTRODUCTIONS

Each book of the Bible begins with a book introduction to give you some quick factual information about the book. Then a short introduction provides a window into the themes, backgrounds and other important aspects of the book, and often gives a short application.

GENESIS

Genesis

QUICK FACTS

AUTHOR Moses

AUDIENCE The people of Israel

DATE Between 1446 and 1406 B.C.

SETTING The area known today as the Middle East

Genesis is the book of beginnings. It documents the beginning of Earth, of animals roaming in the forest, of critters splashing in the sea and of plants growing in the dirt. It also recounts the beginning of the human race: how man and woman were made for each other to work, play, eat, reproduce and commune with God, and how they broke unity with him and each other by sinning.

That first sin led to many more—the first murder, the first lie, the first worldwide wickedness, the first attempt of humanity to usurp God's place. But in that darkness also came two great things: the first hint of a promised Savior who would one day defeat evil (see Genesis 3:14–15), and the first covenant promise that God would make a great nation of Abraham through whom all the nations of the earth would be blessed (see Genesis 12:1–3).

In addition, Genesis is also a book of relationships: Adam and Eve, Abraham and Sarah, Isaac and Rebekah, Jacob and Rachel and Leah. Through these first husband-wife relationships, we can gather many powerful lessons for marriage, including how couples struggle in a fallen world—with issues of infertility, jealousy, betrayal, sibling rivalry and more—yet somehow keep going because God, whose hand is on them, will not let them go.

SUBJECT INDEX

This useful tool, located in the back of the Bible, lists a wide variety of subjects and points you to features in the Bible that deal with each topic.

SUBJECT INDEX

Subject Index

PREFACE TO THE NIV

Preface to the NIV

THE NEW INTERNATIONAL VERSION is a completely new translation of the Holy Bible made by over a hundred scholars working directly from the best available Hebrew, Aramaic and Greek texts. It had its beginning in 1965 when, after several years of exploratory study by committees from the Christian Reformed Church and the National Association of Evangelicals, a group of scholars met at Palos Heights, Illinois, and concurred in the need for a new translation of the Bible in contemporary English. This group, though not made up of official church representatives, was transdenominational. Its conclusion was endorsed by a large number of leaders from many denominations who met in Chicago in 1966.

Responsibility for the new version was delegated by the Palos Heights group to a self-governing body of fifteen, the Committee on Bible Translation, composed for the most part of Biblical scholars from colleges, universities and seminaries. In 1967 the New York Bible Society (now the International Bible Society) generously undertook the financial sponsorship of the project—a sponsorship that made it possible to enlist the help of many distinguished scholars. The fact that participants from the United States, Great Britain, Canada, Australia and New Zealand worked together gave the project its international scope. That they were from many denominations—including Anglican, Assemblies of God, Baptist, Brethren, Christian Reformed, Church of Christ, Evangelical Free, Lutheran, Mennonite, Methodist, Nazarene, Presbyterian, Wesleyan and other churches—helped to safeguard the translation from sectarian bias.

How it was made helps to give the New International Version its distinctiveness. The translation of each book was assigned to a team of scholars. Next, one of the Intermediate Editorial Committees revised the initial translation, with constant reference to the Hebrew, Aramaic or Greek. Their work then went to one of the General Editorial Committees, which checked it in detail and made another thorough revision. This revision in turn was carefully reviewed by the Committee on Bible Translation, which made further changes and then released the final version for publication. In this way the entire Bible underwent three revisions, during each of which the translation was examined for its faithfulness to the original languages and for its English style.

All this involved many thousands of hours of research and discussion regarding the meaning of the texts and the precise way of putting them into English. It may well be that no other translation has been made by a more thorough process of review and revision from committee to committee than this one.

From the beginning of the project, the Committee on Bible Translation held to certain goals for the New International Version: that it would be an accurate translation and one that would have clarity and literary quality and so prove suitable for public and private reading, teaching, preaching, memorizing and liturgical use. The Committee also sought to preserve some measure of continuity with the long tradition of translating the Scriptures into English.

In working toward these goals, the translators were united in their commitment to the authority and infallibility of the Bible as God's Word in written form. They believe that it contains the divine answer to the deepest needs of humanity, that it sheds unique light on our path in a dark world, and that it sets forth the way to our eternal well-being.

The first concern of the translators has been the accuracy of the translation and its fidelity to the thought of the Biblical writers. They have weighed the significance of the lexical and grammatical details of the Hebrew, Aramaic and Greek texts. At the same time, they have striven for more than a word-for-word translation. Because thought patterns and syntax differ from language to language, faithful communication of the meaning of the writers of the Bible demands frequent modifications in sentence structure and constant regard for the contextual meanings of words.

A sensitive feeling for style does not always accompany scholarship. Accordingly the Committee on Bible Translation submitted the developing version to a number of stylistic consultants. Two of them read every book of both Old and New Testaments twice—once before and once after the last major revision—and made invaluable suggestions. Samples of the translation were tested for clarity and ease of reading by various kinds of people—young and old, highly educated and less well educated, ministers and laymen.

Concern for clear and natural English—that the New International Version should be idiomatic but not idiosyncratic, contemporary but not dated—motivated the translators and consultants. At the same time, they tried to reflect the differing styles of the Biblical writers. In view of the international use of English, the translators sought to avoid obvious Americanisms on the one hand and obvious Anglicisms on the other. A British edition reflects the comparatively few differences of significant idiom and of spelling.

As for the traditional pronouns "thou," "thee" and "thine" in reference to the Deity, the translators judged that to use these archaisms (along with the old verb forms such as "doest," "wouldest" and "hadst") would violate accuracy in translation. Neither Hebrew, Aramaic nor Greek uses special pronouns for the persons of the Godhead. A present-day translation is not enhanced by forms that in the time of the King James Version were used in everyday speech, whether referring to God or man.

For the Old Testament the standard Hebrew text, the Masoretic Text as published in the latest editions of *Biblia Hebraica,* was used throughout. The Dead Sea Scrolls contain material bearing on an earlier stage of the Hebrew text. They were consulted, as were the Samaritan Pentateuch and the ancient scribal traditions relating to textual changes. Sometimes a variant Hebrew reading in the margin of the Masoretic Text was followed instead of the text itself. Such instances, being variants within the Masoretic tradition, are not specified by footnotes. In rare cases, words in the consonantal text were divided differently from the way they appear in the Masoretic Text. Footnotes indicate this. The translators also consulted the more important early versions—the Septuagint; Aquila, Symmachus and Theodotion; the Vulgate; the Syriac Peshitta; the Targums; and for the Psalms the *Juxta Hebraica* of Jerome. Readings from these versions were occasionally followed where the Masoretic Text seemed doubtful and where accepted principles of textual criticism showed that one or more of these textual witnesses appeared to provide the correct reading. Such instances are footnoted. Sometimes vowel letters and vowel signs did not, in the judgment of the translators, represent the correct vowels for the original consonantal text. Accordingly some words were read with a different set of vowels. These instances are usually not indicated by footnotes.

The Greek text used in translating the New Testament was an eclectic one. No other piece of ancient literature has such an abundance of manuscript witnesses as does the New Testament. Where existing manuscripts differ, the translators made their choice of readings according to accepted principles of New Testament textual criticism. Footnotes call attention to places where there was uncertainty about what the original text was. The best current printed texts of the Greek New Testament were used.

There is a sense in which the work of translation is never wholly finished. This applies to all great literature and uniquely so to the Bible. In 1973 the New Testament in the New International Version was published. Since then, suggestions for corrections and revisions have been received from various sources. The Committee on Bible Translation carefully considered the suggestions and adopted a number of them. These were incorporated in the first printing of the entire Bible in 1978. Additional revisions were made by the Committee on Bible Translation in 1983 and appear in printings after that date.

As in other ancient documents, the precise meaning of the Biblical texts is sometimes uncertain. This is more often the case with the Hebrew and Aramaic texts than with the Greek text. Although archaeological and linguistic discoveries in this century aid in understanding difficult passages, some uncertainties remain. The more significant of these have been called to the reader's attention in the footnotes.

In regard to the divine name *YHWH,* commonly referred to as the *Tetragrammaton,* the translators adopted the device used in most English versions of rendering that name as "LORD" in capital letters to distinguish it from *Adonai,* another Hebrew word rendered "Lord," for which small letters are used. Wherever the two names stand together in the Old Testament as a compound name of God, they are rendered "Sovereign LORD."

Because for most readers today the phrases "the LORD of hosts" and "God of hosts" have little meaning, this version renders them "the LORD Almighty" and "God Almighty." These renderings convey the sense of the Hebrew, namely, "he who is sovereign over all the 'hosts' (powers) in heaven and on earth, especially over the 'hosts' (armies) of Israel." For readers unacquainted with Hebrew this does not make clear the distinction between *Sabaoth* ("hosts" or "Almighty") and *Shaddai* (which can also be translated "Almighty"), but the latter occurs infrequently and is always footnoted. When *Adonai* and *YHWH Sabaoth* occur together, they are rendered "the Lord, the LORD Almighty."

As for other proper nouns, the familiar spellings of the King James Version are generally retained. Names traditionally spelled with "ch," except where it is final, are usually spelled in this translation with "k" or "c," since the Biblical languages do not have the sound that "ch" frequently indicates in English—for example, in *chant.* For well-known names such as Zechariah, however, the traditional spelling has been retained. Variation in the spelling of names in the original languages has usually not been indicated. Where a person or place has two or more different names in the Hebrew, Aramaic or Greek texts, the more familiar one has generally been used, with footnotes where needed.

To achieve clarity the translators sometimes supplied words not in the original texts but required by the context. If there was uncertainty about such material, it is enclosed in brackets. Also for the sake of clarity or style, nouns, including some proper nouns, are sometimes substituted for pronouns, and vice versa. And though the Hebrew writers often shifted back and forth between first, second and third personal pronouns without change of antecedent, this translation often makes them uniform, in accordance with English style and without the use of footnotes.

Poetical passages are printed as poetry, that is, with indentation of lines and with separate stanzas. These are generally designed to reflect the structure of Hebrew poetry. This poetry is normally characterized by parallelism in balanced lines. Most of the poetry in the Bible is in the Old Testament, and scholars differ regarding the scansion of Hebrew lines. The translators determined the stanza divisions for the most part by analysis of the subject matter. The stanzas therefore serve as poetic paragraphs.

As an aid to the reader, italicized sectional headings are inserted in most of the books. They are not to be regarded as part of the NIV text, are not for oral reading, and are not intended to dictate the interpretation of the sections they head.

The footnotes in this version are of several kinds, most of which need no explanation. Those giving alternative translations begin with "Or" and generally introduce the alternative with the last word preceding it in the text, except when it is a single-word alternative; in poetry quoted in a footnote a slant mark indicates a line division. Footnotes introduced by "Or" do not have uniform significance. In some cases two possible translations were considered to have about equal validity. In other cases, though the translators were convinced that the translation in the text was correct, they judged that another interpretation was possible and of sufficient importance to be represented in a footnote.

In the New Testament, footnotes that refer to uncertainty regarding the original text are introduced by "Some manuscripts" or similar expressions. In the Old Testament, evidence for the reading chosen is given first and evidence for the alternative is added after a semicolon (for example: Septuagint; Hebrew *father*). In such notes the term "Hebrew" refers to the Masoretic Text.

It should be noted that minerals, flora and fauna, architectural details, articles of clothing and jewelry, musical instruments and other articles cannot always be identified with precision. Also measures of capacity in the Biblical period are particularly uncertain (see the table of weights and measures following the text).

Like all translations of the Bible, made as they are by imperfect man, this one undoubtedly falls short of its goals. Yet we are grateful to God for the extent to which he has enabled us to realize these goals and for the strength he has given us and our colleagues to complete our task. We offer this version of the Bible to him in whose name and for whose glory it has been made. We pray that it will lead many into a better understanding of the Holy Scriptures and a fuller knowledge of Jesus Christ the incarnate Word, of whom the Scriptures so faithfully testify.

The Committee on Bible Translation

June 1978
(Revised August 1983)

Names of the translators and editors may be secured from the International Bible Society, translation sponsors of the New International Version, 1820 Jet Stream Drive, Colorado Springs, Colorado 80921-3696 U.S.A.

THE OLD TESTAMENT

GENESIS

Genesis

QUICK FACTS

AUTHOR Moses

AUDIENCE The people of Israel

DATE Between 1446 and 1406 B.C.

SETTING The area known today as the Middle East

Genesis is the book of beginnings. It documents the beginning of Earth, of animals roaming in the forest, of critters splashing in the sea and of plants growing in the dirt. It also recounts the beginning of the human race: how man and woman were made for each other to work, play, eat, reproduce and commune with God, and how they broke unity with him and each other by sinning.

That first sin led to many more—the first murder, the first lie, the first worldwide wickedness, the first attempt of humanity to usurp God's place. But in that darkness also came two great things: the first hint of a promised Savior who would one day defeat evil (see Genesis 3:14–15), and the first covenant promise that God would make a great nation of Abraham through whom all the nations of the earth would be blessed (see Genesis 12:1–3).

In addition, Genesis is also a book of relationships: Adam and Eve, Abraham and Sarah, Isaac and Rebekah, Jacob and Rachel and Leah. Through these first husband-wife relationships, we can gather many powerful lessons for marriage, including how couples struggle in a fallen world—with issues of infertility, jealousy, betrayal, sibling rivalry and more—yet somehow keep going because God, whose hand is on them, will not let them go.

The Beginning

1 In the beginning God created the
heavens and the earth. 2 Now the earth
was[a] formless and empty, darkness was
over the surface of the deep, and the
Spirit of God was hovering over the waters.

3 And God said, "Let there be light," and
there was light. 4 God saw that the light
was good, and he separated the light
from the darkness. 5 God called the light
"day," and the darkness he called "night."
And there was evening, and there was
morning—the first day.
6 And God said, "Let there be an expanse between the waters to separate water from
water." 7 So God made the expanse and
separated the water under the expanse
from the water above it. And it was so.
8 God called the expanse "sky." And there
was evening, and there was morning—
the second day.
9 And God said, "Let the water under the
sky be gathered to one place, and let dry
ground appear." And it was so. 10 God
called the dry ground "land," and the
gathered waters he called "seas." And
God saw that it was good.
11 Then God said, "Let the land produce vegetation: seed-bearing plants and
trees on the land that bear fruit with seed
in it, according to their various kinds."
And it was so. 12 The land produced vegetation: plants bearing seed according to
their kinds and trees bearing fruit with
seed in it according to their kinds. And
God saw that it was good. 13 And there
was evening, and there was morning—
the third day.
14 And God said, "Let there be lights in the
expanse of the sky to separate the day
from the night, and let them serve as
signs to mark seasons and days and
years, 15 and let them be lights in the
expanse of the sky to give light on the
earth." And it was so. 16 God made two
great lights—the greater light to govern
the day and the lesser light to govern the
night. He also made the stars. 17 God set
them in the expanse of the sky to give
light on the earth, 18 to govern the day
and the night, and to separate light from
darkness. And God saw that it was good.
19 And there was evening, and there was
morning—the fourth day.
20 And God said, "Let the water teem with living creatures, and let birds fly above the
earth across the expanse of the sky." 21 So
God created the great creatures of the
sea and every living and moving thing
with which the water teems, according
to their kinds, and every winged bird according to its kind. And God saw that it
was good. 22 God blessed them and said,
"Be fruitful and increase in number and
fill the water in the seas, and let the birds
increase on the earth." 23 And there was
evening, and there was morning—the
fifth day.
24 And God said, "Let the land produce living creatures according to their kinds:
livestock, creatures that move along the
ground, and wild animals, each according to its kind." And it was so. 25 God
made the wild animals according to their
kinds, the livestock according to their
kinds, and all the creatures that move
along the ground according to their
kinds. And God saw that it was good.
26 Then God said, "Let us make man
in our image, in our likeness, and let
them rule over the fish of the sea and the
birds of the air, over the livestock, over
all the earth,[b] and over all the creatures
that move along the ground."

27 So God created man in his own image,
in the image of God he created him;
male and female he created them.

28 God blessed them and said to them,
"Be fruitful and increase in number; fill
the earth and subdue it. Rule over the
fish of the sea and the birds of the air and
over every living creature that moves on
the ground."
29 Then God said, "I give you every seed-bearing plant on the face of
the whole earth and every tree that
has fruit with seed in it. They will be
yours for food. 30 And to all the beasts
of the earth and all the birds of the air
and all the creatures that move on the
ground—everything that has the breath
of life in it—I give every green plant for
food." And it was so.
31 God saw all that he had made, and
it was very good. And there was evening,
and there was morning—the sixth day.

---

[a] 2 Or possibly *became* [b] 26 Hebrew; Syriac *all the wild animals*

2 Thus the heavens and the earth were
completed in all their vast array.
2 By the seventh day God had finished the
work he had been doing; so on the seventh day he rested[a] from all his work.
3 And God blessed the seventh day and
made it holy, because on it he rested
from all the work of creating that he had
done.

Adam and Eve

4 This is the account of the heavens and the
earth when they were created.

When the LORD God made the earth and
the heavens— 5 and no shrub of the field had
yet appeared on the earth[b] and no plant of the
field had yet sprung up, for the LORD God had
not sent rain on the earth[b] and there was no
man to work the ground, 6 but streams[c] came
up from the earth and watered the whole surface of the ground— 7 the LORD God formed
the man[d] from the dust of the ground and
breathed into his nostrils the breath of life,
and the man became a living being.
8 Now the LORD God had planted a garden
in the east, in Eden; and there he put the man
he had formed. 9 And the LORD God made all
kinds of trees grow out of the ground—trees
that were pleasing to the eye and good for food.
In the middle of the garden were the tree of life
and the tree of the knowledge of good and evil.
10 A river watering the garden flowed from
Eden; from there it was separated into four
headwaters. 11 The name of the first is the Pi-
shon; it winds through the entire land of Havilah, where there is gold. 12 (The gold of that
land is good; aromatic resin[e] and onyx are
also there.) 13 The name of the second river is
the Gihon; it winds through the entire land of
Cush.[f] 14 The name of the third river is the Tigris; it runs along the east side of Asshur. And
the fourth river is the Euphrates.
15 The LORD God took the man and put him
in the Garden of Eden to work it and take care
of it. 16 And the LORD God commanded the
man, "You are free to eat from any tree in the
garden; 17 but you must not eat from the tree
of the knowledge of good and evil, for when
you eat of it you will surely die."
18 The LORD God said, "It is not good for
the man to be alone. I will make a helper suitable for him."
19 Now the LORD God had formed out of
the ground all the beasts of the field and all
the birds of the air. He brought them to the
man to see what he would name them; and
whatever the man called each living creature,
that was its name. 20 So the man gave names to
all the livestock, the birds of the air and all the
beasts of the field.
But for Adam[g] no suitable helper was
found. 21 So the LORD God caused the man to
fall into a deep sleep; and while he was sleeping, he took one of the man's ribs[h] and closed
up the place with flesh. 22 Then the LORD God
made a woman from the rib[i] he had taken out
of the man, and he brought her to the man.
23 The man said,

"This is now bone of my bones
 and flesh of my flesh;
she shall be called 'woman,[j]'
 for she was taken out of man."

24 For this reason a man will leave his father
and mother and be united to his wife, and
they will become one flesh.
25 The man and his wife were both naked,
and they felt no shame.

The Fall of Man

3 Now the serpent was more crafty than any
of the wild animals the LORD God had
made. He said to the woman, "Did God
really say, 'You must not eat from any tree in
the garden'?"
2 The woman said to the serpent, "We may
eat fruit from the trees in the garden, 3 but
God did say, 'You must not eat fruit from the
tree that is in the middle of the garden, and
you must not touch it, or you will die.' "
4 "You will not surely die," the serpent said
to the woman. 5 "For God knows that when
you eat of it your eyes will be opened, and you
will be like God, knowing good and evil."
6 When the woman saw that the fruit of the
tree was good for food and pleasing to the eye,
and also desirable for gaining wisdom, she
took some and ate it. She also gave some to
her husband, who was with her, and he ate it.
7 Then the eyes of both of them were opened,
and they realized they were naked; so they
sewed fig leaves together and made coverings
for themselves.
8 Then the man and his wife heard the
sound of the LORD God as he was walking in

[a] 2 Or *ceased*; also in verse 3 [b] 5 Or *land*; also in verse 6 [c] 6 Or *mist* [d] 7 The Hebrew for *man (adam)* sounds like and may be related to the Hebrew for *ground (adamah)*; it is also the name *Adam* (see Gen. 2:20). [e] 12 Or *good; pearls* [f] 13 Possibly southeast Mesopotamia [g] 20 Or *the man* [h] 21 Or *took part of the man's side* [i] 22 Or *part* [j] 23 The Hebrew for *woman* sounds like the Hebrew for *man*.

MONDAY
READ GENESIS 2:4–25

LOVING OUR DIFFERENCES

> **The LORD God said, "It is not good for the man to be alone. I will make a helper suitable for him."**
>
> — GENESIS 2:18

In the beginning God created the heavens and the earth, complete with a vast array of flying, creeping, crawling things; shining lights in the sky; teeming waters; green plants and seed-bearing trees. And for the finishing touch, he made a human man in his own image, with a soul that would live forever.

But as great as all that was, it wasn't enough. God, who had declared "good" everything that he had made thus far, realized it was "not good" for the man to be alone. So God put the man into a deep sleep, took a bone out of his side and created a creature so exquisite, so mind-boggling, so new and yet so familiar that when Adam woke to find Eve next to him, he exclaimed, "This is now bone of my bones and flesh of my flesh" (Genesis 2:23).

They fit so beautifully together, these two, that their lives intertwined. One can only imagine the special times they shared: the first time they made love, their first sunrise together, their late-night walks through the garden. How God must have delighted in these creatures he had made to expand the harmonious, loving relationship enjoyed by the Trinity itself!

Still, there were differences. Beyond the obvious anatomical distinctives, which made being together so pleasurable, there were differences built into the very DNA of this man and woman, such as how they showed their feelings, how they valued relationships, and how they solved problems. But the Creator God had designed those differences—not just the sexual ones—to bring man and woman together.

In the first blush of love, we too are intrigued by our differences. She loves his take-charge authority; he is intrigued by her emotional vulnerability. She is impressed by his concern for others; he admires her dedication to her job. He loves the sound of her voice; she loves his willingness to listen.

Still, in time, as love settles into the everyday intimacy of marriage, those very differences may begin to annoy us. And the more we dwell on those differences, the more power they have to separate and divide us. She talks too much; he never listens. She's a workaholic; he's too into his friends. He's a control freak; she falls apart with the slightest challenge.

Our marriage vows challenge us to work through those differences. They remind us that no matter what threatens to divide and conquer us—chronic sickness, job changes, cross-country moves, recurrent infertility, pornography addiction, overspending—we will give our best effort to hang in there together, loving, honoring and obeying each other.

We can't do that alone, however. The superglue that holds us together when everything threatens to push us apart is the God before whom we made our marriage vows. Through the power of his saving love, he can so transform us that we become more like him—and, amazingly, for all our differences, more like each other. And in that oneness, we become, as Ecclesiastes 4:12 says, "a cord of three strands," which is not easily broken.

—PHYLLIS TEN ELSHOF

let's talk

- What are some things that attracted us to each other in the beginning? What did I most admire in you? What did you find irresistible in me?
- What are some of our pet gripes about each other today? Are these in any way related to what we initially found attractive?
- What are some differences that have actually helped improve and strengthen us? How does appreciating those differences make us more willing to accept differences in other people?

FOR YOUR NEXT DEVOTIONAL READING, TURN TO PAGE 9.

the garden in the cool of the day, and they hid
from the LORD God among the trees of the
garden. 9But the LORD God called to the man,
"Where are you?"
10He answered, "I heard you in the garden, and I was afraid because I was naked; so
I hid."
11And he said, "Who told you that you
were naked? Have you eaten from the tree that
I commanded you not to eat from?"
12The man said, "The woman you put here
with me—she gave me some fruit from the
tree, and I ate it."
13Then the LORD God said to the woman,
"What is this you have done?"
The woman said, "The serpent deceived
me, and I ate."
14So the LORD God said to the serpent,
"Because you have done this,

"Cursed are you above all the livestock
and all the wild animals!
You will crawl on your belly
and you will eat dust
all the days of your life.
15And I will put enmity
between you and the woman,
and between your offspring[a] and hers;
he will crush[b] your head,
and you will strike his heel."

16To the woman he said,

"I will greatly increase your pains in
childbearing;
with pain you will give birth to
children.
Your desire will be for your husband,
and he will rule over you."

17To Adam he said, "Because you listened
to your wife and ate from the tree about which
I commanded you, 'You must not eat of it,'

"Cursed is the ground because of you;
through painful toil you will eat of it
all the days of your life.
18It will produce thorns and thistles for you,
and you will eat the plants of the field.
19By the sweat of your brow
you will eat your food
until you return to the ground,
since from it you were taken;
for dust you are
and to dust you will return."

20Adam[c] named his wife Eve,[d] because she
would become the mother of all the living.
21The LORD God made garments of skin
for Adam and his wife and clothed them.
22And the LORD God said, "The man has
now become like one of us, knowing good
and evil. He must not be allowed to reach
out his hand and take also from the tree of
life and eat, and live forever." 23So the LORD
God banished him from the Garden of Eden
to work the ground from which he had
been taken. 24After he drove the man out,
he placed on the east side[e] of the Garden of
Eden cherubim and a flaming sword flashing
back and forth to guard the way to the tree
of life.

Cain and Abel

4 Adam[c] lay with his wife Eve, and she became pregnant and gave birth to Cain.[f]
She said, "With the help of the LORD I
have brought forth[g] a man." 2Later she gave
birth to his brother Abel.
Now Abel kept flocks, and Cain worked the
soil. 3In the course of time Cain brought some
of the fruits of the soil as an offering to the
LORD. 4But Abel brought fat portions from
some of the firstborn of his flock. The LORD
looked with favor on Abel and his offering,
5but on Cain and his offering he did not look
with favor. So Cain was very angry, and his
face was downcast.
6Then the LORD said to Cain, "Why are
you angry? Why is your face downcast? 7If you
do what is right, will you not be accepted? But
if you do not do what is right, sin is crouching
at your door; it desires to have you, but you
must master it."
8Now Cain said to his brother Abel, "Let's
go out to the field."[h] And while they were in
the field, Cain attacked his brother Abel and
killed him.
9Then the LORD said to Cain, "Where is
your brother Abel?"
"I don't know," he replied. "Am I my brother's keeper?"
10The LORD said, "What have you done?
Listen! Your brother's blood cries out to me
from the ground. 11Now you are under a curse
and driven from the ground, which opened its
mouth to receive your brother's blood from
your hand. 12When you work the ground, it
will no longer yield its crops for you. You will
be a restless wanderer on the earth."

---

[a] 15 Or *seed* [b] 15 Or *strike* [c] 20,1 Or *The man* [d] 20 *Eve* probably means *living.* [e] 24 Or *placed in front* [f] 1 *Cain* sounds like the Hebrew for *brought forth* or *acquired.* [g] 1 Or *have acquired* [h] 8 Samaritan Pentateuch, Septuagint, Vulgate and Syriac; Masoretic Text does not have *"Let's go out to the field."*

13 Cain said to the LORD, "My punishment is more than I can bear. 14 Today you are driving me from the land, and I will be hidden from your presence; I will be a restless wanderer on the earth, and whoever finds me will kill me."

15 But the LORD said to him, "Not so[a]; if anyone kills Cain, he will suffer vengeance seven times over." Then the LORD put a mark on Cain so that no one who found him would kill him. 16 So Cain went out from the LORD's presence and lived in the land of Nod,[b] east of Eden.

17 Cain lay with his wife, and she became pregnant and gave birth to Enoch. Cain was then building a city, and he named it after his son Enoch. 18 To Enoch was born Irad, and Irad was the father of Mehujael, and Mehujael was the father of Methushael, and Methushael was the father of Lamech.

19 Lamech married two women, one named Adah and the other Zillah. 20 Adah gave birth to Jabal; he was the father of those who live in tents and raise livestock. 21 His brother's name was Jubal; he was the father of all who play the harp and flute. 22 Zillah also had a son, Tubal-Cain, who forged all kinds of tools out of[c] bronze and iron. Tubal-Cain's sister was Naamah.

23 Lamech said to his wives,

"Adah and Zillah, listen to me;
 wives of Lamech, hear my words.
I have killed[d] a man for wounding me,
 a young man for injuring me.
24 If Cain is avenged seven times,
 then Lamech seventy-seven times."

25 Adam lay with his wife again, and she gave birth to a son and named him Seth,[e] saying, "God has granted me another child in place of Abel, since Cain killed him." 26 Seth also had a son, and he named him Enosh.

At that time men began to call on[f] the name of the LORD.

From Adam to Noah

5 This is the written account of Adam's line.

When God created man, he made him in the likeness of God. 2 He created them male and female and blessed them. And when they were created, he called them "man.[g]"

3 When Adam had lived 130 years, he had a son in his own likeness, in his own image; and he named him Seth. 4 After Seth was born, Adam lived 800 years and had other sons and daughters. 5 Altogether, Adam lived 930 years, and then he died.

6 When Seth had lived 105 years, he became the father[h] of Enosh. 7 And after he became the father of Enosh, Seth lived 807 years and had other sons and daughters. 8 Altogether, Seth lived 912 years, and then he died.

9 When Enosh had lived 90 years, he became the father of Kenan. 10 And after he became the father of Kenan, Enosh lived 815 years and had other sons and daughters. 11 Altogether, Enosh lived 905 years, and then he died.

12 When Kenan had lived 70 years, he became the father of Mahalalel. 13 And after he became the father of Mahalalel, Kenan lived 840 years and had other sons and daughters. 14 Altogether, Kenan lived 910 years, and then he died.

15 When Mahalalel had lived 65 years, he became the father of Jared. 16 And after he became the father of Jared, Mahalalel lived 830 years and had other sons and daughters. 17 Altogether, Mahalalel lived 895 years, and then he died.

18 When Jared had lived 162 years, he became the father of Enoch. 19 And after he became the father of Enoch, Jared lived 800 years and had other sons and daughters. 20 Altogether, Jared lived 962 years, and then he died.

21 When Enoch had lived 65 years, he became the father of Methuselah. 22 And after he became the father of Methuselah, Enoch walked with God 300 years and had other sons and daughters. 23 Altogether, Enoch lived 365 years. 24 Enoch walked with God; then he was no more, because God took him away.

25 When Methuselah had lived 187 years, he became the father of Lamech. 26 And after he became the father of Lamech, Methuselah lived 782 years and had other sons and daughters. 27 Altogether, Methuselah lived 969 years, and then he died.

28 When Lamech had lived 182 years, he had a son. 29 He named him Noah[i] and said, "He will comfort us in the labor and painful toil of our hands caused by the ground the LORD has cursed." 30 After Noah was born, Lamech lived 595 years and had other sons and

---

[a] 15 Septuagint, Vulgate and Syriac; Hebrew *Very well* [b] 16 *Nod* means *wandering* (see verses 12 and 14). [c] 22 Or *who instructed all who work in* [d] 23 Or *I will kill* [e] 25 *Seth* probably means *granted.* [f] 26 Or *to proclaim* [g] 2 Hebrew *adam* [h] 6 *Father* may mean *ancestor*; also in verses 7-26. [i] 29 *Noah* sounds like the Hebrew for *comfort.*

daughters. 31 Altogether, Lamech lived 777 years, and then he died.

32 After Noah was 500 years old, he became the father of Shem, Ham and Japheth.

The Flood

6 When men began to increase in number on the earth and daughters were born to them, 2 the sons of God saw that the daughters of men were beautiful, and they married any of them they chose. 3 Then the LORD said, "My Spirit will not contend with[a] man forever, for he is mortal[b]; his days will be a hundred and twenty years."

4 The Nephilim were on the earth in those days—and also afterward—when the sons of God went to the daughters of men and had children by them. They were the heroes of old, men of renown.

5 The LORD saw how great man's wickedness on the earth had become, and that every inclination of the thoughts of his heart was only evil all the time. 6 The LORD was grieved that he had made man on the earth, and his heart was filled with pain. 7 So the LORD said, "I will wipe mankind, whom I have created, from the face of the earth—men and animals, and creatures that move along the ground, and birds of the air—for I am grieved that I have made them." 8 But Noah found favor in the eyes of the LORD.

9 This is the account of Noah.

Noah was a righteous man, blameless among the people of his time, and he walked with God. 10 Noah had three sons: Shem, Ham and Japheth.

11 Now the earth was corrupt in God's sight and was full of violence. 12 God saw how corrupt the earth had become, for all the people on earth had corrupted their ways. 13 So God said to Noah, "I am going to put an end to all people, for the earth is filled with violence because of them. I am surely going to destroy both them and the earth. 14 So make yourself an ark of cypress[c] wood; make rooms in it and coat it with pitch inside and out. 15 This is how you are to build it: The ark is to be 450 feet long, 75 feet wide and 45 feet high.[d] 16 Make a roof for it and finish[e] the ark to within 18 inches[f] of the top. Put a door in the side of the ark and make lower, middle and upper decks. 17 I am going to bring floodwaters on the earth to destroy all life under the heavens, every creature that has the breath of life in it. Everything on earth will perish. 18 But I will establish my covenant with you, and you will enter the ark—you and your sons and your wife and your sons' wives with you. 19 You are to bring into the ark two of all living creatures, male and female, to keep them alive with you. 20 Two of every kind of bird, of every kind of animal and of every kind of creature that moves along the ground will come to you to be kept alive. 21 You are to take every kind of food that is to be eaten and store it away as food for you and for them."

22 Noah did everything just as God commanded him.

7 The LORD then said to Noah, "Go into the ark, you and your whole family, because I have found you righteous in this generation. 2 Take with you seven[g] of every kind of clean animal, a male and its mate, and two of every kind of unclean animal, a male and its mate, 3 and also seven of every kind of bird, male and female, to keep their various kinds alive throughout the earth. 4 Seven days from now I will send rain on the earth for forty days and forty nights, and I will wipe from the face of the earth every living creature I have made."

5 And Noah did all that the LORD commanded him.

6 Noah was six hundred years old when the floodwaters came on the earth. 7 And Noah and his sons and his wife and his sons' wives entered the ark to escape the waters of the flood. 8 Pairs of clean and unclean animals, of birds and of all creatures that move along the ground, 9 male and female, came to Noah and entered the ark, as God had commanded Noah. 10 And after the seven days the floodwaters came on the earth.

11 In the six hundredth year of Noah's life, on the seventeenth day of the second month—on that day all the springs of the great deep burst forth, and the floodgates of the heavens were opened. 12 And rain fell on the earth forty days and forty nights.

13 On that very day Noah and his sons, Shem, Ham and Japheth, together with his wife and the wives of his three sons, entered the ark. 14 They had with them every wild animal according to its kind, all livestock according to their kinds, every creature that moves along the ground according to its kind and

---

[a] 3 Or *My spirit will not remain in* [b] 3 Or *corrupt* [c] 14 The meaning of the Hebrew for this word is uncertain. [d] 15 Hebrew *300 cubits long, 50 cubits wide and 30 cubits high* (about 140 meters long, 23 meters wide and 13.5 meters high) [e] 16 Or *Make an opening for light by finishing* [f] 16 Hebrew *a cubit* (about 0.5 meter) [g] 2 Or *seven pairs*; also in verse 3

every bird according to its kind, everything
with wings. [15]Pairs of all creatures that have
the breath of life in them came to Noah and
entered the ark. [16]The animals going in were
male and female of every living thing, as God
had commanded Noah. Then the LORD shut
him in.

[17]For forty days the flood kept coming on
the earth, and as the waters increased they
lifted the ark high above the earth. [18]The waters rose and increased greatly on the earth,
and the ark floated on the surface of the water. [19]They rose greatly on the earth, and all
the high mountains under the entire heavens
were covered. [20]The waters rose and covered
the mountains to a depth of more than twenty feet.[a,b] [21]Every living thing that moved
on the earth perished—birds, livestock, wild
animals, all the creatures that swarm over the
earth, and all mankind. [22]Everything on dry
land that had the breath of life in its nostrils
died. [23]Every living thing on the face of the
earth was wiped out; men and animals and
the creatures that move along the ground and
the birds of the air were wiped from the earth.
Only Noah was left, and those with him in
the ark.

[24]The waters flooded the earth for a hundred and fifty days.

8 But God remembered Noah and all
the wild animals and the livestock that
were with him in the ark, and he sent a
wind over the earth, and the waters receded. [2]Now the springs of the deep and the
floodgates of the heavens had been closed,
and the rain had stopped falling from the
sky. [3]The water receded steadily from the
earth. At the end of the hundred and fifty
days the water had gone down, [4]and on the
seventeenth day of the seventh month the
ark came to rest on the mountains of Ararat. [5]The waters continued to recede until
the tenth month, and on the first day of the
tenth month the tops of the mountains became visible.

[6]After forty days Noah opened the window
he had made in the ark [7]and sent out a raven, and it kept flying back and forth until
the water had dried up from the earth. [8]Then
he sent out a dove to see if the water had receded from the surface of the ground. [9]But
the dove could find no place to set its feet
because there was water over all the surface
of the earth; so it returned to Noah in the
ark. He reached out his hand and took the
dove and brought it back to himself in the
ark. [10]He waited seven more days and again
sent out the dove from the ark. [11]When the
dove returned to him in the evening, there in
its beak was a freshly plucked olive leaf! Then
Noah knew that the water had receded from
the earth. [12]He waited seven more days and
sent the dove out again, but this time it did
not return to him.

[13]By the first day of the first month of Noah's six hundred and first year, the water had
dried up from the earth. Noah then removed
the covering from the ark and saw that the
surface of the ground was dry. [14]By the twenty-seventh day of the second month the earth
was completely dry.

[15]Then God said to Noah, [16]"Come out of
the ark, you and your wife and your sons and
their wives. [17]Bring out every kind of living
creature that is with you—the birds, the animals, and all the creatures that move along
the ground—so they can multiply on the
earth and be fruitful and increase in number
upon it."

[18]So Noah came out, together with his sons
and his wife and his sons' wives. [19]All the animals and all the creatures that move along
the ground and all the birds—everything that
moves on the earth—came out of the ark, one
kind after another.

[20]Then Noah built an altar to the LORD
and, taking some of all the clean animals and
clean birds, he sacrificed burnt offerings on it.
[21]The LORD smelled the pleasing aroma and
said in his heart: "Never again will I curse the
ground because of man, even though[c] every
inclination of his heart is evil from childhood.
And never again will I destroy all living creatures, as I have done.

[22]"As long as the earth endures,
seedtime and harvest,
cold and heat,
summer and winter,
day and night
will never cease."

God's Covenant With Noah

9 Then God blessed Noah and his sons, saying to them, "Be fruitful and increase in
number and fill the earth. [2]The fear and
dread of you will fall upon all the beasts of
the earth and all the birds of the air, upon every creature that moves along the ground, and
upon all the fish of the sea; they are given into

[a] 20 Hebrew *fifteen cubits* (about 6.9 meters) [b] 20 Or *rose more than twenty feet, and the mountains were covered*
[c] 21 Or *man, for*

MARKING THE STARTING LINE

> **Then Noah built an altar to the LORD and, taking some of all the clean animals and clean birds, he sacrificed burnt offerings on it.**
>
> —GENESIS 8:20

I carried my wife across the threshold of our first home. I had heard of other grooms doing this with their brides and had always thought it a bit corny. Yet I found myself wanting to do something special at the start of our marriage, something that said we were entering a new adventure together, something that honored my wife and spoke of my pledge to care about her and for her. Carrying my bride over the threshold was a ritual act performed by thousands, but we were claiming this moment together as our own.

And that ritual truly became ours. Today, whenever we talk about going home after our wedding, we remember me sweeping her up, stumbling under the load and bumping her head on the doorframe. Then we look at each other and grin. What meant something then still speaks today.

Noah's altar in Genesis 8:20 is like that. Other people had sacrificed animals before. Many had directed their prayers heavenward in the smoke of offerings. But that day of exiting the ark after a massive flood was special for Noah's family. They were starting over. They were beginning a new journey. They were survivors in a world devastated by sin and punishment. They were the Adam and Eve of a new era. They were children of God.

Each newly married couple opens the door of what Shakespeare called "the undiscovered country," that is, the future. After the whirlwind of wedding planning and events, they stand a little breathless, staring down a road that they will travel together. Each bride is Eve, each groom is Adam, and generations of Cains and Abels and Seths and their sisters are a world waiting to be born.

How will the journey begin? What will blaze the trail and mark the path? What ritual acts will stand as a testimony that something significant has happened here and point to where the road is going? For Noah it was an altar. A pile of thanks to God. Recognition that the true pilot of his boat now needed to be guide and guardian of the land journey ahead.

We who are descended from Noah still raise his altar and chant his prayers. We do it when we make our marriage vows before God. We do it when we pray over our new homes, even if they are one-bedroom apartments. We do it when we baptize or dedicate our children. We do it when we establish habits of family devotions. These rituals declare our house to be holy ground and those who dwell in it to live on the threshold of eternity.

Ritual without meaning becomes mere tradition. Meaning without ritual is soon forgotten. But when ritual and meaning are bound together, we remember who we are and whose we are, so we can move forward together.

—WAYNE BROUWER

let's talk

- Did we build something like Noah's altar at the beginning of our journey together? In what ways can we renew its significance for our marriage and home? Can we raise an altar together now if we didn't do it then?
- What rituals or traditions are we establishing to identify the character of our home?
- What devotional experiences have we shared together? What will we pass along to our children?

FOR YOUR NEXT DEVOTIONAL READING, TURN TO PAGE 13.

your hands. 3Everything that lives and moves
will be food for you. Just as I gave you the
green plants, I now give you everything.
4"But you must not eat meat that has its
lifeblood still in it. 5And for your lifeblood I
will surely demand an accounting. I will demand an accounting from every animal. And
from each man, too, I will demand an accounting for the life of his fellow man.

6"Whoever sheds the blood of man,
by man shall his blood be shed;
for in the image of God
has God made man.

7As for you, be fruitful and increase in number;
multiply on the earth and increase upon it."
8Then God said to Noah and to his sons
with him: 9"I now establish my covenant
with you and with your descendants after you
10and with every living creature that was with
you—the birds, the livestock and all the wild
animals, all those that came out of the ark
with you—every living creature on earth. 11I
establish my covenant with you: Never again
will all life be cut off by the waters of a flood;
never again will there be a flood to destroy the
earth."
12And God said, "This is the sign of the
covenant I am making between me and you
and every living creature with you, a covenant for all generations to come: 13I have
set my rainbow in the clouds, and it will be
the sign of the covenant between me and the
earth. 14Whenever I bring clouds over the
earth and the rainbow appears in the clouds,
15I will remember my covenant between
me and you and all living creatures of every
kind. Never again will the waters become a
flood to destroy all life. 16Whenever the rainbow appears in the clouds, I will see it and
remember the everlasting covenant between
God and all living creatures of every kind on
the earth."
17So God said to Noah, "This is the sign of
the covenant I have established between me
and all life on the earth."

The Sons of Noah

18The sons of Noah who came out of the
ark were Shem, Ham and Japheth. (Ham was
the father of Canaan.) 19These were the three
sons of Noah, and from them came the people
who were scattered over the earth.
20Noah, a man of the soil, proceeded[a] to
plant a vineyard. 21When he drank some of
its wine, he became drunk and lay uncovered
inside his tent. 22Ham, the father of Canaan,
saw his father's nakedness and told his two
brothers outside. 23But Shem and Japheth
took a garment and laid it across their shoulders; then they walked in backward and covered their father's nakedness. Their faces were
turned the other way so that they would not
see their father's nakedness.
24When Noah awoke from his wine and
found out what his youngest son had done to
him, 25he said,

"Cursed be Canaan!
The lowest of slaves
will he be to his brothers."

26He also said,

"Blessed be the LORD, the God of Shem!
May Canaan be the slave of Shem.[b]
27May God extend the territory of Japheth[c];
may Japheth live in the tents of Shem,
and may Canaan be his[d] slave."

28After the flood Noah lived 350 years.
29Altogether, Noah lived 950 years, and then
he died.

The Table of Nations

10 This is the account of Shem, Ham and
Japheth, Noah's sons, who themselves
had sons after the flood.

The Japhethites

2The sons[e] of Japheth:
Gomer, Magog, Madai, Javan, Tubal,
Meshech and Tiras.
3The sons of Gomer:
Ashkenaz, Riphath and Togarmah.
4The sons of Javan:
Elishah, Tarshish, the Kittim and the
Rodanim.[f] 5(From these the maritime
peoples spread out into their territories by their clans within their nations,
each with its own language.)

The Hamites

6The sons of Ham:
Cush, Mizraim,[g] Put and Canaan.
7The sons of Cush:
Seba, Havilah, Sabtah, Raamah and
Sabteca.

---

[a] 20 Or *soil, was the first* [b] 26 Or *be his slave* [c] 27 *Japheth* sounds like the Hebrew for *extend.* [d] 27 Or *their* [e] 2 *Sons* may mean *descendants* or *successors* or *nations*; also in verses 3, 4, 6, 7, 20-23, 29 and 31. [f] 4 Some manuscripts of the Masoretic Text and Samaritan Pentateuch (see also Septuagint and 1 Chron. 1:7); most manuscripts of the Masoretic Text *Dodanim* [g] 6 That is, Egypt; also in verse 13

The sons of Raamah:
Sheba and Dedan.

8Cush was the father[a] of Nimrod, who grew
to be a mighty warrior on the earth. 9He was a
mighty hunter before the LORD; that is why it
is said, "Like Nimrod, a mighty hunter before
the LORD." 10The first centers of his kingdom
were Babylon, Erech, Akkad and Calneh, in[b]
Shinar.[c] 11From that land he went to Assyria,
where he built Nineveh, Rehoboth Ir,[d] Calah
12and Resen, which is between Nineveh and
Calah; that is the great city.

13Mizraim was the father of
the Ludites, Anamites, Lehabites,
Naphtuhites, 14Pathrusites, Casluhites
(from whom the Philistines came) and
Caphtorites.

15Canaan was the father of
Sidon his firstborn,[e] and of the Hittites, 16Jebusites, Amorites, Girgashites, 17Hivites, Arkites, Sinites, 18Ar-
vadites, Zemarites and Hamathites.

Later the Canaanite clans scattered 19and
the borders of Canaan reached from Sidon toward Gerar as far as Gaza, and then toward
Sodom, Gomorrah, Admah and Zeboiim, as
far as Lasha.

20These are the sons of Ham by their clans
and languages, in their territories and nations.

The Semites

21Sons were also born to Shem, whose older
brother was[f] Japheth; Shem was the ancestor
of all the sons of Eber.

22The sons of Shem:
Elam, Asshur, Arphaxad, Lud and
Aram.

23The sons of Aram:
Uz, Hul, Gether and Meshech.[g]

24Arphaxad was the father of[h] Shelah,
and Shelah the father of Eber.

25Two sons were born to Eber:
One was named Peleg,[i] because in his
time the earth was divided; his brother
was named Joktan.

26Joktan was the father of
Almodad, Sheleph, Hazarmaveth, Je-
rah, 27Hadoram, Uzal, Diklah, 28Obal,
Abimael, Sheba, 29Ophir, Havilah and
Jobab. All these were sons of Joktan.

30The region where they lived stretched from
Mesha toward Sephar, in the eastern hill country.

31These are the sons of Shem by their clans
and languages, in their territories and nations.

32These are the clans of Noah's sons, according to their lines of descent, within their nations. From these the nations spread out over
the earth after the flood.

The Tower of Babel

11 Now the whole world had one language
and a common speech. 2As men moved
eastward,[j] they found a plain in Shinar[c]
and settled there.

3They said to each other, "Come, let's make
bricks and bake them thoroughly." They used
brick instead of stone, and tar for mortar.
4Then they said, "Come, let us build ourselves
a city, with a tower that reaches to the heavens, so that we may make a name for ourselves
and not be scattered over the face of the whole
earth."

5But the LORD came down to see the city
and the tower that the men were building.
6The LORD said, "If as one people speaking
the same language they have begun to do this,
then nothing they plan to do will be impossible for them. 7Come, let us go down and confuse their language so they will not understand
each other."

8So the LORD scattered them from there
over all the earth, and they stopped building
the city. 9That is why it was called Babel[k]—because there the LORD confused the language of
the whole world. From there the LORD scattered them over the face of the whole earth.

From Shem to Abram

10This is the account of Shem.

Two years after the flood, when Shem was
100 years old, he became the father[l] of Arphaxad. 11And after he became the father of
Arphaxad, Shem lived 500 years and had other sons and daughters.

12When Arphaxad had lived 35 years, he
became the father of Shelah. 13And after he

---

a 8 *Father* may mean *ancestor* or *predecessor* or *founder*; also in verses 13, 15, 24 and 26. b 10 Or *Erech and Akkad—all of them in* c 10,2 That is, Babylonia d 11 Or *Nineveh with its city squares* e 15 Or *of the Sidonians, the foremost* f 21 Or *Shem, the older brother of* g 23 See Septuagint and 1 Chron. 1:17; Hebrew *Mash* h 24 Hebrew; Septuagint *father of Cainan, and Cainan was the father of* i 25 *Peleg* means *division.* j 2 Or *from the east*; or *in the east* k 9 That is, Babylon; *Babel* sounds like the Hebrew for *confused.* l 10 *Father* may mean *ancestor*; also in verses 11-25.

became the father of Shelah, Arphaxad lived 403 years and had other sons and daughters.[a]

14When Shelah had lived 30 years, he became the father of Eber. 15And after he became the father of Eber, Shelah lived 403 years and had other sons and daughters.

16When Eber had lived 34 years, he became the father of Peleg. 17And after he became the father of Peleg, Eber lived 430 years and had other sons and daughters.

18When Peleg had lived 30 years, he became the father of Reu. 19And after he became the father of Reu, Peleg lived 209 years and had other sons and daughters.

20When Reu had lived 32 years, he became the father of Serug. 21And after he became the father of Serug, Reu lived 207 years and had other sons and daughters.

22When Serug had lived 30 years, he became the father of Nahor. 23And after he became the father of Nahor, Serug lived 200 years and had other sons and daughters.

24When Nahor had lived 29 years, he became the father of Terah. 25And after he became the father of Terah, Nahor lived 119 years and had other sons and daughters.

26After Terah had lived 70 years, he became the father of Abram, Nahor and Haran.

27This is the account of Terah.

Terah became the father of Abram, Nahor and Haran. And Haran became the father of Lot. 28While his father Terah was still alive, Haran died in Ur of the Chaldeans, in the land of his birth. 29Abram and Nahor both married. The name of Abram's wife was Sarai, and the name of Nahor's wife was Milcah; she was the daughter of Haran, the father of both Milcah and Iscah. 30Now Sarai was barren; she had no children.

31Terah took his son Abram, his grandson Lot son of Haran, and his daughter-in-law Sarai, the wife of his son Abram, and together they set out from Ur of the Chaldeans to go to Canaan. But when they came to Haran, they settled there.

32Terah lived 205 years, and he died in Haran.

The Call of Abram

12 The LORD had said to Abram, "Leave your country, your people and your father's household and go to the land I will show you.

2"I will make you into a great nation
  and I will bless you;
I will make your name great,
  and you will be a blessing.
3I will bless those who bless you,
  and whoever curses you I will curse;
and all peoples on earth
  will be blessed through you."

4So Abram left, as the LORD had told him; and Lot went with him. Abram was seventy-five years old when he set out from Haran. 5He took his wife Sarai, his nephew Lot, all the possessions they had accumulated and the people they had acquired in Haran, and they set out for the land of Canaan, and they arrived there.

6Abram traveled through the land as far as the site of the great tree of Moreh at Shechem. At that time the Canaanites were in the land. 7The LORD appeared to Abram and said, "To your offspring[b] I will give this land." So he built an altar there to the LORD, who had appeared to him.

8From there he went on toward the hills east of Bethel and pitched his tent, with Bethel on the west and Ai on the east. There he built an altar to the LORD and called on the name of the LORD. 9Then Abram set out and continued toward the Negev.

Abram in Egypt

10Now there was a famine in the land, and Abram went down to Egypt to live there for a while because the famine was severe. 11As he was about to enter Egypt, he said to his wife Sarai, "I know what a beautiful woman you are. 12When the Egyptians see you, they will say, 'This is his wife.' Then they will kill me but will let you live. 13Say you are my sister, so that I will be treated well for your sake and my life will be spared because of you."

14When Abram came to Egypt, the Egyptians saw that she was a very beautiful woman. 15And when Pharaoh's officials saw her, they praised her to Pharaoh, and she was taken into his palace. 16He treated Abram well for her sake, and Abram acquired sheep and cattle,

[a] 12,13 Hebrew; Septuagint (see also Luke 3:35, 36 and note at Gen. 10:24) *35 years, he became the father of Cainan.* [13]*And after he became the father of Cainan, Arphaxad lived 430 years and had other sons and daughters, and then he died. When Cainan had lived 130 years, he became the father of Shelah. And after he became the father of Shelah, Cainan lived 330 years and had other sons and daughters*
[b] 7 Or *seed*

WEDNESDAY
READ GENESIS 12:10–20

THE NEED FOR RESPECT

Life can present a married couple with tough choices. Do you take the promotion at work if it means traveling with business associates who have no scruples? Do you keep having lunches with your friend of the opposite sex if it makes your spouse uncomfortable? The list goes on.

So it was with Abram and Sarai. Famine in the land put them into crisis: move or die of starvation. So the couple relocated to Egypt to find food. But Abram made some poor choices there. Sarai was so beautiful that she was sure to attract the attention of Egyptian rulers who wouldn't hesitate to kill Abram to get his wife. So Abram told his wife to say she was his sister. After all, it was partly true; Sarai was his half sister (see Genesis 20:12). And Abram did need to survive for the covenant promises of God to come true, right?

According to the prevailing pattern for women in that era, Sarai had no say about the arrangement. But how do you think she felt about a husband who feared more for his own skin than for hers? Could you trust your spouse after being misrepresented as someone you're not? That kind of betrayal can drive a wedge between a couple that only widens over time.

"Say you are my sister, so that I will be treated well for your sake and my life will be spared because of you."

— Genesis 12:13

let's *talk*

- Given the cultural and gender roles of his time, should Abram have apologized to his wife for his treatment of her? What might have happened as a result?
- Can telling all the truth in a situation also be a form of using each other? How far should we go in telling the truth?
- Do we agree or disagree with the statement "Love means never having to say you're sorry"?

In the movie *Love Story*, Oliver tells his girlfriend, Jennifer, "Love means never having to say you're sorry." Maybe that's what Abram thought after telling a lie about his wife. Sure enough, the Egyptians praised her to Pharaoh, and Sarai was taken into Pharaoh's palace. But God rescued Sarai out of that difficult situation by afflicting Pharaoh and his family with such serious diseases that Sarai was sent back to her husband—and Abram even got to keep the livestock and servants he had acquired in the process.

One problem with never saying you're sorry after wronging your spouse is that you are then inclined to repeat your behavior. That's exactly what happened. Some years later, Abram once more passed off his wife as his sister, this time to Abimelek, the king of Gerar (see Genesis 20). And years after that, Abram and Sarai's son, Isaac, did the same thing with his wife, Rebekah (see Genesis 26). So one wrong left unresolved between a couple only succeeded in perpetuating the abuse, threatening the very calling of Abram to be the father of many nations.

The poor choices that Abram made affected his marriage and his future. A Christian married couple can learn from Abram's life that choices have long-lasting ramifications. To deal with poor choices, own up to any misuse or disrespect of each other. Deal openly and quickly with the sin; come clean with each other and the Lord, and ask each other and God for forgiveness. Then resolve not to repeat the offense.

—JOHN R. THROOP

FOR YOUR NEXT DEVOTIONAL READING, TURN TO PAGE 17.

male and female donkeys, menservants and
maidservants, and camels.
17But the LORD inflicted serious diseases on Pharaoh and his household because of
Abram's wife Sarai. 18So Pharaoh summoned
Abram. "What have you done to me?" he said.
"Why didn't you tell me she was your wife?
19Why did you say, 'She is my sister,' so that
I took her to be my wife? Now then, here is
your wife. Take her and go!" 20Then Pharaoh
gave orders about Abram to his men, and they
sent him on his way, with his wife and everything he had.

Abram and Lot Separate

13 So Abram went up from Egypt to the
Negev, with his wife and everything he
had, and Lot went with him. 2Abram
had become very wealthy in livestock and in
silver and gold.
3From the Negev he went from place to
place until he came to Bethel, to the place
between Bethel and Ai where his tent had
been earlier 4and where he had first built an
altar. There Abram called on the name of the
LORD.
5Now Lot, who was moving about with
Abram, also had flocks and herds and tents.
6But the land could not support them while
they stayed together, for their possessions were
so great that they were not able to stay together. 7And quarreling arose between Abram's
herdsmen and the herdsmen of Lot. The Canaanites and Perizzites were also living in the
land at that time.
8So Abram said to Lot, "Let's not have any
quarreling between you and me, or between
your herdsmen and mine, for we are brothers. 9Is not the whole land before you? Let's
part company. If you go to the left, I'll go to
the right; if you go to the right, I'll go to the
left."
10Lot looked up and saw that the whole
plain of the Jordan was well watered, like
the garden of the LORD, like the land of
Egypt, toward Zoar. (This was before the
LORD destroyed Sodom and Gomorrah.)
11So Lot chose for himself the whole plain of
the Jordan and set out toward the east. The
two men parted company: 12Abram lived in
the land of Canaan, while Lot lived among
the cities of the plain and pitched his tents
near Sodom. 13Now the men of Sodom were
wicked and were sinning greatly against the
LORD.
14The LORD said to Abram after Lot had
parted from him, "Lift up your eyes from
where you are and look north and south, east
and west. 15All the land that you see I will give
to you and your offspring[a] forever. 16I will
make your offspring like the dust of the earth,
so that if anyone could count the dust, then
your offspring could be counted. 17Go, walk
through the length and breadth of the land,
for I am giving it to you."
18So Abram moved his tents and went to
live near the great trees of Mamre at Hebron,
where he built an altar to the LORD.

Abram Rescues Lot

14 At this time Amraphel king of Shinar,[b]
Arioch king of Ellasar, Kedorlaomer
king of Elam and Tidal king of Goiim
2went to war against Bera king of Sodom,
Birsha king of Gomorrah, Shinab king of Admah, Shemeber king of Zeboiim, and the king
of Bela (that is, Zoar). 3All these latter kings
joined forces in the Valley of Siddim (the Salt
Sea[c]). 4For twelve years they had been subject
to Kedorlaomer, but in the thirteenth year
they rebelled.
5In the fourteenth year, Kedorlaomer and
the kings allied with him went out and defeated the Rephaites in Ashteroth Karnaim,
the Zuzites in Ham, the Emites in Shaveh
Kiriathaim 6and the Horites in the hill country of Seir, as far as El Paran near the desert.
7Then they turned back and went to En Mish-
pat (that is, Kadesh), and they conquered the
whole territory of the Amalekites, as well as
the Amorites who were living in Hazazon Tamar.
8Then the king of Sodom, the king of Gomorrah, the king of Admah, the king of Zeboiim and the king of Bela (that is, Zoar)
marched out and drew up their battle lines
in the Valley of Siddim 9against Kedorlaomer
king of Elam, Tidal king of Goiim, Amraphel king of Shinar and Arioch king of Ellasar—four kings against five. 10Now the Valley
of Siddim was full of tar pits, and when the
kings of Sodom and Gomorrah fled, some
of the men fell into them and the rest fled to
the hills. 11The four kings seized all the goods
of Sodom and Gomorrah and all their food;
then they went away. 12They also carried off
Abram's nephew Lot and his possessions, since
he was living in Sodom.
13One who had escaped came and reported this to Abram the Hebrew. Now Abram

---

a *15* Or *seed*; also in verse 16 b *1* That is, Babylonia; also in verse 9 c *3* That is, the Dead Sea

was living near the great trees of Mamre the
Amorite, a brother[a] of Eshcol and Aner, all
of whom were allied with Abram. 14When
Abram heard that his relative had been tak-
en captive, he called out the 318 trained men
born in his household and went in pursuit
as far as Dan. 15During the night Abram divided his men to attack them and he routed
them, pursuing them as far as Hobah, north
of Damascus. 16He recovered all the goods
and brought back his relative Lot and his possessions, together with the women and the
other people.

17After Abram returned from defeating
Kedorlaomer and the kings allied with him,
the king of Sodom came out to meet him in
the Valley of Shaveh (that is, the King's Valley).

18Then Melchizedek king of Salem[b]
brought out bread and wine. He was priest
of God Most High, 19and he blessed Abram,
saying,

"Blessed be Abram by God Most High,
Creator[c] of heaven and earth.
20And blessed be[d] God Most High,
who delivered your enemies into your
hand."

Then Abram gave him a tenth of everything.

21The king of Sodom said to Abram, "Give
me the people and keep the goods for yourself."

22But Abram said to the king of Sodom, "I
have raised my hand to the LORD, God Most
High, Creator of heaven and earth, and have
taken an oath 23that I will accept nothing belonging to you, not even a thread or the thong
of a sandal, so that you will never be able to
say, 'I made Abram rich.' 24I will accept nothing but what my men have eaten and the share
that belongs to the men who went with me—
to Aner, Eshcol and Mamre. Let them have
their share."

God's Covenant With Abram

15 After this, the word of the LORD came to
Abram in a vision:

"Do not be afraid, Abram.
I am your shield,[e]
your very great reward.[f]"

2But Abram said, "O Sovereign LORD, what
can you give me since I remain childless and
the one who will inherit[g] my estate is Eliezer of Damascus?" 3And Abram said, "You
have given me no children; so a servant in my
household will be my heir."

4Then the word of the LORD came to him:
"This man will not be your heir, but a son
coming from your own body will be your
heir." 5He took him outside and said, "Look
up at the heavens and count the stars—if indeed you can count them." Then he said to
him, "So shall your offspring be."

6Abram believed the LORD, and he credited
it to him as righteousness.

7He also said to him, "I am the LORD, who
brought you out of Ur of the Chaldeans to
give you this land to take possession of it."

8But Abram said, "O Sovereign LORD, how
can I know that I will gain possession of it?"

9So the LORD said to him, "Bring me a
heifer, a goat and a ram, each three years old,
along with a dove and a young pigeon."

10Abram brought all these to him, cut them
in two and arranged the halves opposite each
other; the birds, however, he did not cut in
half. 11Then birds of prey came down on the
carcasses, but Abram drove them away.

12As the sun was setting, Abram fell into a
deep sleep, and a thick and dreadful darkness
came over him. 13Then the LORD said to him,
"Know for certain that your descendants will
be strangers in a country not their own, and
they will be enslaved and mistreated four hundred years. 14But I will punish the nation they
serve as slaves, and afterward they will come
out with great possessions. 15You, however,
will go to your fathers in peace and be buried
at a good old age. 16In the fourth generation
your descendants will come back here, for the
sin of the Amorites has not yet reached its full
measure."

17When the sun had set and darkness
had fallen, a smoking firepot with a blazing
torch appeared and passed between the pieces. 18On that day the LORD made a covenant
with Abram and said, "To your descendants I
give this land, from the river[h] of Egypt to the
great river, the Euphrates— 19the land of the
Kenites, Kenizzites, Kadmonites, 20Hittites,
Perizzites, Rephaites, 21Amorites, Canaanites,
Girgashites and Jebusites."

a 13 Or *a relative;* or *an ally* *b* 18 That is, Jerusalem *c* 19 Or *Possessor;* also in verse 22 *d* 20 Or *And praise be to* *e* 1 Or *sovereign*
f 1 Or *shield; / your reward will be very great* *g* 2 The meaning of the Hebrew for this phrase is uncertain. *h* 18 Or *Wadi*

Hagar and Ishmael

16 Now Sarai, Abram's wife, had borne him no children. But she had an Egyptian maidservant named Hagar; 2so she said to Abram, "The LORD has kept me from having children. Go, sleep with my maidservant; perhaps I can build a family through her."

Abram agreed to what Sarai said. 3So after Abram had been living in Canaan ten years, Sarai his wife took her Egyptian maidservant Hagar and gave her to her husband to be his wife. 4He slept with Hagar, and she conceived.

When she knew she was pregnant, she began to despise her mistress. 5Then Sarai said to Abram, "You are responsible for the wrong I am suffering. I put my servant in your arms, and now that she knows she is pregnant, she despises me. May the LORD judge between you and me."

6"Your servant is in your hands," Abram said. "Do with her whatever you think best." Then Sarai mistreated Hagar; so she fled from her.

7The angel of the LORD found Hagar near a spring in the desert; it was the spring that is beside the road to Shur. 8And he said, "Hagar, servant of Sarai, where have you come from, and where are you going?"

"I'm running away from my mistress Sarai," she answered.

9Then the angel of the LORD told her, "Go back to your mistress and submit to her." 10The angel added, "I will so increase your descendants that they will be too numerous to count."

11The angel of the LORD also said to her:

"You are now with child
  and you will have a son.
You shall name him Ishmael,[a]
  for the LORD has heard of your misery.
12He will be a wild donkey of a man;
  his hand will be against everyone
  and everyone's hand against him,
and he will live in hostility
  toward[b] all his brothers."

13She gave this name to the LORD who spoke to her: "You are the God who sees me," for she said, "I have now seen[c] the One who sees me." 14That is why the well was called Beer Lahai Roi[d]; it is still there, between Kadesh and Bered.

15So Hagar bore Abram a son, and Abram gave the name Ishmael to the son she had borne. 16Abram was eighty-six years old when Hagar bore him Ishmael.

The Covenant of Circumcision

17 When Abram was ninety-nine years old, the LORD appeared to him and said, "I am God Almighty[e]; walk before me and be blameless. 2I will confirm my covenant between me and you and will greatly increase your numbers."

3Abram fell facedown, and God said to him, 4"As for me, this is my covenant with you: You will be the father of many nations. 5No longer will you be called Abram[f]; your name will be Abraham,[g] for I have made you a father of many nations. 6I will make you very fruitful; I will make nations of you, and kings will come from you. 7I will establish my covenant as an everlasting covenant between me and you and your descendants after you for the generations to come, to be your God and the God of your descendants after you. 8The whole land of Canaan, where you are now an alien, I will give as an everlasting possession to you and your descendants after you; and I will be their God."

9Then God said to Abraham, "As for you, you must keep my covenant, you and your descendants after you for the generations to come. 10This is my covenant with you and your descendants after you, the covenant you are to keep: Every male among you shall be circumcised. 11You are to undergo circumcision, and it will be the sign of the covenant between me and you. 12For the generations to come every male among you who is eight days old must be circumcised, including those born in your household or bought with money from a foreigner—those who are not your offspring. 13Whether born in your household or bought with your money, they must be circumcised. My covenant in your flesh is to be an everlasting covenant. 14Any uncircumcised male, who has not been circumcised in the flesh, will be cut off from his people; he has broken my covenant."

15God also said to Abraham, "As for Sarai your wife, you are no longer to call her Sarai; her name will be Sarah. 16I will bless her and will surely give you a son by her. I will bless her so that she will be the mother of nations; kings of peoples will come from her."

17Abraham fell facedown; he laughed and said to himself, "Will a son be born to a man

---

[a] 11 *Ishmael* means *God hears.* [b] 12 Or *live to the east / of* [c] 13 Or *seen the back of* [d] 14 *Beer Lahai Roi* means *well of the Living One who sees me.* [e] 1 Hebrew *El-Shaddai* [f] 5 *Abram* means *exalted father.* [g] 5 *Abraham* means *father of many.*

THURSDAY

READ GENESIS 16:1–16

HOW FAR TO GO TO HAVE A BABY

> **"The LORD has kept me from having children. Go, sleep with my maidservant; perhaps I can build a family through her."**
>
> — GENESIS 16:2

let's talk

- Is using an infertility treatment an example of taking matters into our own hands? Why or why not?
- How can infertility treatments be considered a part of God's plan?
- If I promised you something and ten years later you still hadn't gotten it, what might you be tempted to do? How does that compare with your response to God's delays?

When the Lord first called Abram, he said he would make him "into a great nation" (Genesis 12:2). Later God clearly promised Abram that he would have a child. He said that Abram would have an heir, a son from his own body, and that his descendants would be as numerous as the stars (see Genesis 15:4–5). But ten years after God's initial promise and Abram's call, Sarai was still childless. She decided that maybe God's plan of producing a child was other than through her and Abram.

Sarai approached Abram and suggested that he sleep with her maidservant Hagar in hopes that Hagar would get pregnant. To modern readers this sounds illicit, but it was an accepted practice of that day. The servant would give birth and the mistress could adopt the child as her own.

How far would you go to have a child? For many couples diagnosed with infertility problems, the answer is, "We'll do whatever the doctor recommends." As technology has progressed, so have the options. Various therapies, including drugs, herbal supplements and surgery can be used to stimulate a stalled reproductive system. Sperm can be injected directly into the uterus. Or sperm and ova can be brought together outside the womb and the fertilized eggs then implanted into the womb. Sometimes an infertile couple decides to pay a surrogate to bear a child for them.

What does God's Word say about such choices? The Bible doesn't comment directly on modern medical treatments, and even well-meaning Christian scholars can disagree on what a couple should do. Thus, many couples are confused as to what is right and wrong in God's eyes. But Sarai's story helps us to understand one of the basic principles of God's Word: Faith in God, even if it means waiting a long time for him to act, is better than taking matters into our own hands.

If you long for a baby—or anything else for that matter—seek God's will as a couple, search the Scriptures and then pray together, asking God what to do. One couple we know became so stressed by doctor visits and infertility treatments that they decided to take a break and leave everything to God. To their surprise they soon learned they would have a child. Another couple wrestled with infertility options and felt led by God to go with in vitro fertilization, partly because pregnancy would help alleviate the wife's endometriosis. Still another decided to pursue adoption rather than fertility treatments.

What's the right choice for you? That depends on how God leads you. But whatever you decide, be sure that you both agree on what you see as God's will for you. If one of you wants to pursue an action and the other doesn't, seek out advice from professionals if necessary, as well as a pastor or Christian counselor to help you both come to an agreement. The challenge of infertility can be a time of building unity in your marriage as you face the decisions, struggles and pain together.

Also, make sure you do your homework. Explore the options available to you, and take plenty of time to discuss their moral, ethical and spiritual implications. And keep praying, together asking God to clearly make his will known.

—JENNIFER SCHUCHMANN

FOR YOUR NEXT DEVOTIONAL READING, TURN TO PAGE 20.

a hundred years old? Will Sarah bear a child at the age of ninety?" 18And Abraham said to God, "If only Ishmael might live under your blessing!"

19Then God said, "Yes, but your wife Sarah will bear you a son, and you will call him Isaac.[a] I will establish my covenant with him as an everlasting covenant for his descendants after him. 20And as for Ishmael, I have heard you: I will surely bless him; I will make him fruitful and will greatly increase his numbers. He will be the father of twelve rulers, and I will make him into a great nation. 21But my covenant I will establish with Isaac, whom Sarah will bear to you by this time next year." 22When he had finished speaking with Abraham, God went up from him.

23On that very day Abraham took his son Ishmael and all those born in his household or bought with his money, every male in his household, and circumcised them, as God told him. 24Abraham was ninety-nine years old when he was circumcised, 25and his son Ishmael was thirteen; 26Abraham and his son Ishmael were both circumcised on that same day. 27And every male in Abraham's household, including those born in his household or bought from a foreigner, was circumcised with him.

The Three Visitors

18 The LORD appeared to Abraham near the great trees of Mamre while he was sitting at the entrance to his tent in the heat of the day. 2Abraham looked up and saw three men standing nearby. When he saw them, he hurried from the entrance of his tent to meet them and bowed low to the ground.

3He said, "If I have found favor in your eyes, my lord,[b] do not pass your servant by. 4Let a little water be brought, and then you may all wash your feet and rest under this tree. 5Let me get you something to eat, so you can be refreshed and then go on your way—now that you have come to your servant."

"Very well," they answered, "do as you say."

6So Abraham hurried into the tent to Sarah. "Quick," he said, "get three seahs[c] of fine flour and knead it and bake some bread."

7Then he ran to the herd and selected a choice, tender calf and gave it to a servant, who hurried to prepare it. 8He then brought some curds and milk and the calf that had been prepared, and set these before them. While they ate, he stood near them under a tree.

9"Where is your wife Sarah?" they asked him.

"There, in the tent," he said.

10Then the LORD[d] said, "I will surely return to you about this time next year, and Sarah your wife will have a son."

Now Sarah was listening at the entrance to the tent, which was behind him. 11Abraham and Sarah were already old and well advanced in years, and Sarah was past the age of childbearing. 12So Sarah laughed to herself as she thought, "After I am worn out and my master[e] is old, will I now have this pleasure?"

13Then the LORD said to Abraham, "Why did Sarah laugh and say, 'Will I really have a child, now that I am old?' 14Is anything too hard for the LORD? I will return to you at the appointed time next year and Sarah will have a son."

15Sarah was afraid, so she lied and said, "I did not laugh."

But he said, "Yes, you did laugh."

Abraham Pleads for Sodom

16When the men got up to leave, they looked down toward Sodom, and Abraham walked along with them to see them on their way. 17Then the LORD said, "Shall I hide from Abraham what I am about to do? 18Abraham will surely become a great and powerful nation, and all nations on earth will be blessed through him. 19For I have chosen him, so that he will direct his children and his household after him to keep the way of the LORD by doing what is right and just, so that the LORD will bring about for Abraham what he has promised him."

20Then the LORD said, "The outcry against Sodom and Gomorrah is so great and their sin so grievous 21that I will go down and see if what they have done is as bad as the outcry that has reached me. If not, I will know."

22The men turned away and went toward Sodom, but Abraham remained standing before the LORD.[f] 23Then Abraham approached him and said: "Will you sweep away the righteous with the wicked? 24What if there are fifty righteous people in the city? Will you really sweep it away and not spare[g] the place for the sake of the fifty righteous people in it? 25Far be it from you to do such a thing—to kill the righteous with the wicked, treating the righ-

---

[a] 19 *Isaac* means *he laughs.* [b] 3 Or *O Lord* [c] 6 That is, probably about 20 quarts (about 22 liters) [d] 10 Hebrew *Then he*
[e] 12 Or *husband* [f] 22 Masoretic Text; an ancient Hebrew scribal tradition *but the LORD remained standing before Abraham*
[g] 24 Or *forgive*; also in verse 26

teous and the wicked alike. Far be it from you!
Will not the Judge[a] of all the earth do right?"
26The LORD said, "If I find fifty righteous
people in the city of Sodom, I will spare the
whole place for their sake."
27Then Abraham spoke up again: "Now
that I have been so bold as to speak to the
Lord, though I am nothing but dust and ashes, 28what if the number of the righteous is
five less than fifty? Will you destroy the whole
city because of five people?"
"If I find forty-five there," he said, "I will
not destroy it."
29Once again he spoke to him, "What if
only forty are found there?"
He said, "For the sake of forty, I will not
do it."
30Then he said, "May the Lord not be angry, but let me speak. What if only thirty can
be found there?"
He answered, "I will not do it if I find thirty there."
31Abraham said, "Now that I have been
so bold as to speak to the Lord, what if only
twenty can be found there?"
He said, "For the sake of twenty, I will not
destroy it."
32Then he said, "May the Lord not be angry, but let me speak just once more. What if
only ten can be found there?"
He answered, "For the sake of ten, I will
not destroy it."
33When the LORD had finished speaking
with Abraham, he left, and Abraham returned
home.

Sodom and Gomorrah Destroyed

19 The two angels arrived at Sodom in the
evening, and Lot was sitting in the gateway of the city. When he saw them, he
got up to meet them and bowed down with
his face to the ground. 2"My lords," he said,
"please turn aside to your servant's house. You
can wash your feet and spend the night and
then go on your way early in the morning."
"No," they answered, "we will spend the
night in the square."
3But he insisted so strongly that they did
go with him and entered his house. He prepared a meal for them, baking bread without
yeast, and they ate. 4Before they had gone to
bed, all the men from every part of the city
of Sodom—both young and old—surrounded
the house. 5They called to Lot, "Where are the
men who came to you tonight? Bring them
out to us so that we can have sex with them."
6Lot went outside to meet them and shut
the door behind him 7and said, "No, my
friends. Don't do this wicked thing. 8Look, I
have two daughters who have never slept with
a man. Let me bring them out to you, and you
can do what you like with them. But don't do
anything to these men, for they have come under the protection of my roof."
9"Get out of our way," they replied. And
they said, "This fellow came here as an alien,
and now he wants to play the judge! We'll
treat you worse than them." They kept bringing pressure on Lot and moved forward to
break down the door.
10But the men inside reached out and pulled
Lot back into the house and shut the door.
11Then they struck the men who were at the
door of the house, young and old, with blindness so that they could not find the door.
12The two men said to Lot, "Do you have
anyone else here—sons-in-law, sons or daughters, or anyone else in the city who belongs to
you? Get them out of here, 13because we are
going to destroy this place. The outcry to the
LORD against its people is so great that he has
sent us to destroy it."
14So Lot went out and spoke to his sons-in-
law, who were pledged to marry[b] his daughters. He said, "Hurry and get out of this place,
because the LORD is about to destroy the city!"
But his sons-in-law thought he was joking.
15With the coming of dawn, the angels
urged Lot, saying, "Hurry! Take your wife and
your two daughters who are here, or you will
be swept away when the city is punished."
16When he hesitated, the men grasped his
hand and the hands of his wife and of his two
daughters and led them safely out of the city,
for the LORD was merciful to them. 17As soon
as they had brought them out, one of them
said, "Flee for your lives! Don't look back, and
don't stop anywhere in the plain! Flee to the
mountains or you will be swept away!"
18But Lot said to them, "No, my lords,[c]
please! 19Your[d] servant has found favor in
your[d] eyes, and you[d] have shown great kindness to me in sparing my life. But I can't flee
to the mountains; this disaster will overtake
me, and I'll die. 20Look, here is a town near
enough to run to, and it is small. Let me flee
to it—it is very small, isn't it? Then my life
will be spared."
21He said to him, "Very well, I will grant

[a] 25 Or *Ruler* [b] 14 Or *were married to* [c] 18 Or *No, Lord*; or *No, my lord* [d] 19 The Hebrew is singular.

FRIDAY
READ GENESIS 19:1–29

CONQUERING REGRETS

If only we hadn't married so soon. If only we had more money. If only I had married Jake instead of John. Regrets in marriage are damaging. They keep our eyes fixed on the rearview mirror instead of on the road ahead. While reviewing the past and assessing what we've learned through mistakes can be a healthy exercise, regretting the past only serves to fuel discontentment and impede growth.

When Dan and I decided to close a three-year-old business, I struggled with regret. I had used up all of our nest egg to pursue a business venture I had believed in. When the business failed, I regretted so many decisions I had made, especially not listening to Dan's advice along the way. My failure meant that we would be struggling financially again after having enjoyed several years of monetary comfort. Even though I knew God had walked us through this difficult time and taught us invaluable lessons, it was tempting to think, "If I hadn't tried to start that new business, we'd be financially set right now." Instead of keeping my eyes focused on God's plan for my life, I chose to get stuck in my tracks with if-only thinking.

"Flee for your lives! Don't look back, and don't stop anywhere in the plain! Flee to the mountains or you will be swept away!"

— GENESIS 19:17

let's talk

- What, if any, regrets do either of us have in our lives?
- What unmet need might those regrets indicate?
- How might we use regrets to improve our relationship with each other? What do we need to entrust to God to move forward in our marriage?

Lot's wife had a similar problem. She and her husband were running for their lives from Sodom and Gomorrah, knowing that God had judged the culture they were living in and was about to decimate everything they had ever known. While Lot was running full steam ahead, his wife kept looking over her shoulder. Eventually, the distance between them became so great that Lot literally left his wife in the dust.

Regret is like that. We keep looking over our shoulder, wondering if what we've left behind might have been better than what we're moving toward. God's angel warned Lot and his wife not to look back, and it's a warning for us too.

If you routinely catch yourself starting a sentence with "If only," regret may be an issue you need to deal with. While dwelling on what might have been is never healthy, regret can be an important signal to stop and examine your emotions. For instance, if you catch yourself thinking, "If only I had married Jake instead of John," it may be time to evaluate why John isn't measuring up. In your private time with God, pray about the emotions you're experiencing. Perhaps you'll discover that your disappointment is springing from unmet needs. With these needs clarified, you can then have a forward-thinking conversation with your spouse about how to improve your relationship.

When I caught myself saying, "If only I hadn't tried to start this business," I realized that my fear of God's inability to meet our needs in the future was driving my regret. Once I discovered that, I could stop looking to the past and begin focusing on a vision for what God might accomplish in our future.

—MARIAN V. LIAUTAUD

FOR YOUR NEXT DEVOTIONAL READING, TURN TO PAGE 24.

this request too; I will not overthrow the town you speak of. 22But flee there quickly, because I cannot do anything until you reach it." (That is why the town was called Zoar.[a])

23By the time Lot reached Zoar, the sun had risen over the land. 24Then the LORD rained down burning sulfur on Sodom and Gomorrah—from the LORD out of the heavens. 25Thus he overthrew those cities and the entire plain, including all those living in the cities—and also the vegetation in the land. 26But Lot's wife looked back, and she became a pillar of salt.

27Early the next morning Abraham got up and returned to the place where he had stood before the LORD. 28He looked down toward Sodom and Gomorrah, toward all the land of the plain, and he saw dense smoke rising from the land, like smoke from a furnace.

29So when God destroyed the cities of the plain, he remembered Abraham, and he brought Lot out of the catastrophe that overthrew the cities where Lot had lived.

Lot and His Daughters

30Lot and his two daughters left Zoar and settled in the mountains, for he was afraid to stay in Zoar. He and his two daughters lived in a cave. 31One day the older daughter said to the younger, "Our father is old, and there is no man around here to lie with us, as is the custom all over the earth. 32Let's get our father to drink wine and then lie with him and preserve our family line through our father."

33That night they got their father to drink wine, and the older daughter went in and lay with him. He was not aware of it when she lay down or when she got up.

34The next day the older daughter said to the younger, "Last night I lay with my father. Let's get him to drink wine again tonight, and you go in and lie with him so we can preserve our family line through our father." 35So they got their father to drink wine that night also, and the younger daughter went and lay with him. Again he was not aware of it when she lay down or when she got up.

36So both of Lot's daughters became pregnant by their father. 37The older daughter had a son, and she named him Moab[b]; he is the father of the Moabites of today. 38The younger daughter also had a son, and she named him Ben-Ammi[c]; he is the father of the Ammonites of today.

Abraham and Abimelech

20 Now Abraham moved on from there into the region of the Negev and lived between Kadesh and Shur. For a while he stayed in Gerar, 2and there Abraham said of his wife Sarah, "She is my sister." Then Abimelech king of Gerar sent for Sarah and took her.

3But God came to Abimelech in a dream one night and said to him, "You are as good as dead because of the woman you have taken; she is a married woman."

4Now Abimelech had not gone near her, so he said, "Lord, will you destroy an innocent nation? 5Did he not say to me, 'She is my sister,' and didn't she also say, 'He is my brother'? I have done this with a clear conscience and clean hands."

6Then God said to him in the dream, "Yes, I know you did this with a clear conscience, and so I have kept you from sinning against me. That is why I did not let you touch her. 7Now return the man's wife, for he is a prophet, and he will pray for you and you will live. But if you do not return her, you may be sure that you and all yours will die."

8Early the next morning Abimelech summoned all his officials, and when he told them all that had happened, they were very much afraid. 9Then Abimelech called Abraham in and said, "What have you done to us? How have I wronged you that you have brought such great guilt upon me and my kingdom? You have done things to me that should not be done." 10And Abimelech asked Abraham, "What was your reason for doing this?"

11Abraham replied, "I said to myself, 'There is surely no fear of God in this place, and they will kill me because of my wife.' 12Besides, she really is my sister, the daughter of my father though not of my mother; and she became my wife. 13And when God had me wander from my father's household, I said to her, 'This is how you can show your love to me: Everywhere we go, say of me, "He is my brother." ' "

14Then Abimelech brought sheep and cattle and male and female slaves and gave them to Abraham, and he returned Sarah his wife to him. 15And Abimelech said, "My land is before you; live wherever you like."

16To Sarah he said, "I am giving your brother a thousand shekels[d] of silver. This is to cover the offense against you before all who are with you; you are completely vindicated."

[a] 22 *Zoar* means *small.* [b] 37 *Moab* sounds like the Hebrew for *from father.* [c] 38 *Ben-Ammi* means *son of my people.* [d] 16 That is, about 25 pounds (about 11.5 kilograms)

[17]Then Abraham prayed to God, and God
healed Abimelech, his wife and his slave girls
so they could have children again, [18]for the
Lord had closed up every womb in Abimelech's household because of Abraham's wife
Sarah.

The Birth of Isaac

21 Now the Lord was gracious to Sarah as
he had said, and the Lord did for Sarah
what he had promised. [2]Sarah became
pregnant and bore a son to Abraham in his old
age, at the very time God had promised him.
[3]Abraham gave the name Isaac[a] to the son Sarah bore him. [4]When his son Isaac was eight
days old, Abraham circumcised him, as God
commanded him. [5]Abraham was a hundred
years old when his son Isaac was born to him.

[6]Sarah said, "God has brought me laughter,
and everyone who hears about this will laugh
with me." [7]And she added, "Who would have
said to Abraham that Sarah would nurse children? Yet I have borne him a son in his old
age."

Hagar and Ishmael Sent Away

[8]The child grew and was weaned, and on
the day Isaac was weaned Abraham held a
great feast. [9]But Sarah saw that the son whom
Hagar the Egyptian had borne to Abraham
was mocking, [10]and she said to Abraham,
"Get rid of that slave woman and her son, for
that slave woman's son will never share in the
inheritance with my son Isaac."

[11]The matter distressed Abraham greatly
because it concerned his son. [12]But God said
to him, "Do not be so distressed about the
boy and your maidservant. Listen to whatever Sarah tells you, because it is through Isaac
that your offspring[b] will be reckoned. [13]I will
make the son of the maidservant into a nation
also, because he is your offspring."

[14]Early the next morning Abraham took
some food and a skin of water and gave them
to Hagar. He set them on her shoulders and
then sent her off with the boy. She went on her
way and wandered in the desert of Beersheba.

[15]When the water in the skin was gone, she
put the boy under one of the bushes. [16]Then
she went off and sat down nearby, about a
bowshot away, for she thought, "I cannot
watch the boy die." And as she sat there nearby, she[c] began to sob.

[17]God heard the boy crying, and the angel
of God called to Hagar from heaven and said
to her, "What is the matter, Hagar? Do not
be afraid; God has heard the boy crying as he
lies there. [18]Lift the boy up and take him by
the hand, for I will make him into a great nation."

[19]Then God opened her eyes and she saw a
well of water. So she went and filled the skin
with water and gave the boy a drink.

[20]God was with the boy as he grew up.
He lived in the desert and became an archer.
[21]While he was living in the Desert of Paran,
his mother got a wife for him from Egypt.

The Treaty at Beersheba

[22]At that time Abimelech and Phicol the
commander of his forces said to Abraham,
"God is with you in everything you do. [23]Now
swear to me here before God that you will not
deal falsely with me or my children or my descendants. Show to me and the country where
you are living as an alien the same kindness I
have shown to you."

[24]Abraham said, "I swear it."

[25]Then Abraham complained to Abimelech
about a well of water that Abimelech's servants
had seized. [26]But Abimelech said, "I don't
know who has done this. You did not tell me,
and I heard about it only today."

[27]So Abraham brought sheep and cattle
and gave them to Abimelech, and the two
men made a treaty. [28]Abraham set apart sev-
en ewe lambs from the flock, [29]and Abimelech asked Abraham, "What is the meaning of
these seven ewe lambs you have set apart by
themselves?"

[30]He replied, "Accept these seven lambs from
my hand as a witness that I dug this well."

[31]So that place was called Beersheba,[d] because the two men swore an oath there.

[32]After the treaty had been made at Beersheba, Abimelech and Phicol the commander
of his forces returned to the land of the Philistines. [33]Abraham planted a tamarisk tree in
Beersheba, and there he called upon the name
of the Lord, the Eternal God. [34]And Abraham stayed in the land of the Philistines for
a long time.

Abraham Tested

22 Some time later God tested Abraham.
He said to him, "Abraham!"
"Here I am," he replied.

[2]Then God said, "Take your son, your only
son, Isaac, whom you love, and go to the region of Moriah. Sacrifice him there as a burnt

---

[a] 3 *Isaac* means *he laughs.* [b] 12 Or *seed* [c] 16 Hebrew; Septuagint *the child* [d] 31 *Beersheba* can mean *well of seven* or *well of the oath.*

offering on one of the mountains I will tell you about."

[3]Early the next morning Abraham got up and saddled his donkey. He took with him two of his servants and his son Isaac. When he had cut enough wood for the burnt offering, he set out for the place God had told him about. [4]On the third day Abraham looked up and saw the place in the distance. [5]He said to his servants, "Stay here with the donkey while I and the boy go over there. We will worship and then we will come back to you."

[6]Abraham took the wood for the burnt offering and placed it on his son Isaac, and he himself carried the fire and the knife. As the two of them went on together, [7]Isaac spoke up and said to his father Abraham, "Father?"

"Yes, my son?" Abraham replied.

"The fire and wood are here," Isaac said, "but where is the lamb for the burnt offering?"

[8]Abraham answered, "God himself will provide the lamb for the burnt offering, my son." And the two of them went on together.

[9]When they reached the place God had told him about, Abraham built an altar there and arranged the wood on it. He bound his son Isaac and laid him on the altar, on top of the wood. [10]Then he reached out his hand and took the knife to slay his son. [11]But the angel of the LORD called out to him from heaven, "Abraham! Abraham!"

"Here I am," he replied.

[12]"Do not lay a hand on the boy," he said. "Do not do anything to him. Now I know that you fear God, because you have not withheld from me your son, your only son."

[13]Abraham looked up and there in a thicket he saw a ram[a] caught by its horns. He went over and took the ram and sacrificed it as a burnt offering instead of his son. [14]So Abraham called that place The LORD Will Provide. And to this day it is said, "On the mountain of the LORD it will be provided."

[15]The angel of the LORD called to Abraham from heaven a second time [16]and said, "I swear by myself, declares the LORD, that because you have done this and have not withheld your son, your only son, [17]I will surely bless you and make your descendants as numerous as the stars in the sky and as the sand on the seashore. Your descendants will take possession of the cities of their enemies, [18]and through your offspring[b] all nations on earth will be blessed, because you have obeyed me."

[19]Then Abraham returned to his servants, and they set off together for Beersheba. And Abraham stayed in Beersheba.

Nahor's Sons

[20]Some time later Abraham was told, "Milcah is also a mother; she has borne sons to your brother Nahor: [21]Uz the firstborn, Buz his brother, Kemuel (the father of Aram), [22]Kesed, Hazo, Pildash, Jidlaph and Bethuel." [23]Bethuel became the father of Rebekah. Milcah bore these eight sons to Abraham's brother Nahor. [24]His concubine, whose name was Reumah, also had sons: Tebah, Gaham, Tahash and Maacah.

The Death of Sarah

23 Sarah lived to be a hundred and twenty-seven years old. [2]She died at Kiriath Arba (that is, Hebron) in the land of Canaan, and Abraham went to mourn for Sarah and to weep over her.

[3]Then Abraham rose from beside his dead wife and spoke to the Hittites.[c] He said, [4]"I am an alien and a stranger among you. Sell me some property for a burial site here so I can bury my dead."

[5]The Hittites replied to Abraham, [6]"Sir, listen to us. You are a mighty prince among us. Bury your dead in the choicest of our tombs. None of us will refuse you his tomb for burying your dead."

[7]Then Abraham rose and bowed down before the people of the land, the Hittites. [8]He said to them, "If you are willing to let me bury my dead, then listen to me and intercede with Ephron son of Zohar on my behalf [9]so he will sell me the cave of Machpelah, which belongs to him and is at the end of his field. Ask him to sell it to me for the full price as a burial site among you."

[10]Ephron the Hittite was sitting among his people and he replied to Abraham in the hearing of all the Hittites who had come to the gate of his city. [11]"No, my lord," he said. "Listen to me; I give[d] you the field, and I give[d] you the cave that is in it. I give[d] it to you in the presence of my people. Bury your dead."

[12]Again Abraham bowed down before the people of the land [13]and he said to Ephron in their hearing, "Listen to me, if you will. I will pay the price of the field. Accept it from me so I can bury my dead there."

[14]Ephron answered Abraham, [15]"Listen to me, my lord; the land is worth four hundred

---

[a] *13* Many manuscripts of the Masoretic Text, Samaritan Pentateuch, Septuagint and Syriac; most manuscripts of the Masoretic Text *a ram behind* ⌊*him*⌋ [b] *18* Or *seed* [c] *3* Or *the sons of Heth*; also in verses 5, 7, 10, 16, 18 and 20 [d] *11* Or *sell*

WEEKEND

loosening up with laughter

There are times in life when you can either laugh or cry. We try to choose laughter. Laughter dispels tension. It's good for your physical health, and it's definitely good for the health of your marriage.

When we laugh together, we seem to be more affirming. When we're under stress, we benefit from trying to find some way to lighten things up. Dan and Laura, like many other couples, have told us about the fun of pet ownership and how pets can relieve tension.

Here's one example. The pressure of medical school, work and other responsibilities were taking their toll. After a long day at work, Laura walked into their small apartment and found all three cats wearing ties! Dan had done that in an attempt to make Laura laugh. It worked.

We all have difficult situations in our lives. If we find something to laugh about, as Dan and Laura did, we can keep our relationship on a more positive track.

If laughter doesn't come naturally for you, here are some ways to help you become more jovial.

Give yourself permission to be less than perfect. When you don't take yourself too seriously, it's easier to see the lighter side of life. If joking comes naturally in your relationship, consider yourself fortunate. But there is a fine line between jokes and put-downs. Laugh *with* your mate but only *at* yourself.

Cultivate humor. We try to look for the humor in each situation, especially irritating ones. Recently, as we sat in the Minneapolis airport waiting for our third cancelled flight to be rescheduled, Dave looked at me and said, "My, isn't it fun to be in the jet set?" Then, looking around at all the disgruntled passengers, I said, "This has to be the life of the rich and famous." Once again, humor came to our rescue. Some of our sources of humor are:

- The cartoon section in the daily newspaper
- Joke books and other humorous writings
- Conversations with friends and business associates
- Funny movies, such as *Father of the Bride*, Parts I and II, or any classic comedy
- Our email pals

Get some funny friends. If you're both the sober type, make friends with couples who make you laugh. Years ago when we were leading a Marriage Alive seminar in our home in Vienna, Austria, one couple attended who were just too serious. Both were opera singers, and both were introspective and intense. So we encouraged them to develop some friendships with couples who were not so serious. They took our advice. Having fun-loving friends helped them loosen up, laugh more and enjoy life in a new way. Humor became a good way to encourage each other.

—DAVID AND CLAUDIA ARP

HOW ARE WE DOING?

learning to laugh

Laughter is not only good medicine, but it also can be a cure for stress. If you can find something that's funny in any situation, you'll defuse anxiety and decrease your stress. Discuss the following situations with your spouse (or enlist a funny friend if you must) and find something humorous in each scenario. Remember, you're using humor to encourage each other, not to laugh at each other, so find ways to be funny and supportive!

1. You're on the way to a big job interview and as you get out of the car you realize you're wearing one black sock and one navy blue sock. You laugh. What's so funny?
2. You wanted a nice weekend at home relaxing and doing nothing around the house; then your mother-in-law calls to say she is coming for the weekend. What's so funny?
3. Traffic is worse than you've seen it in months. As you wait out another light change without moving forward, you look at the faces of the drivers around you. What's so funny?
4. You show up at a party and you're wearing the same dress as the hostess. What's so funny?
5. You twisted your ankle and the doctor says you have to stay off it and keep it elevated for three days. What's so funny?
6. There was a closeout sale on specialty paint so you decided to surprise your spouse and spruce up the bedroom. Half way through the project, you realize you don't have enough paint. What's so funny?
7. You've been asked to speak in church and right before you go up, the heel comes off your shoe. What's so funny?
8. Your two-year-old lost her diaper—in the grocery store. What's so funny?

let's make a DATE

HUMOR ME!

Go to a local comedy club (try to check out the content first), rent a classic comedy or watch a comedian on TV. Afterward, try to make each other laugh. Tell that one story that always makes her giggle (complete with impersonations!). Notice what happens to your intimacy level when you start laughing together. Collect jokes or cartoons that are sure to make him chuckle and share them with him. Maybe the two of you can start a joke box for your favorite funnies. Secretly fill it with stories, jokes, cartoons, pictures or whatever will bring a smile to your spouse's face. The next time you need a laugh, take the lid off and enjoy.

FOR YOUR NEXT DEVOTIONAL READING, TURN TO PAGE 28.

LESSONS FROM THE *Bible*

Though laughter isn't mentioned much in the Bible, one couple in particular is known for their laughter. Check out Abraham and Sarah's story in Genesis 17:16–17; 18:1–15; 21:1–7 and discuss why the couple laughed and what God did in response. When is laughter appropriate and when is it not?

shekels[a] of silver, but what is that between me and you? Bury your dead."

16 Abraham agreed to Ephron's terms and weighed out for him the price he had named in the hearing of the Hittites: four hundred shekels of silver, according to the weight current among the merchants.

17 So Ephron's field in Machpelah near Mamre—both the field and the cave in it, and all the trees within the borders of the field—was deeded 18 to Abraham as his property in the presence of all the Hittites who had come to the gate of the city. 19 Afterward Abraham buried his wife Sarah in the cave in the field of Machpelah near Mamre (which is at Hebron) in the land of Canaan. 20 So the field and the cave in it were deeded to Abraham by the Hittites as a burial site.

Isaac and Rebekah

24 Abraham was now old and well advanced in years, and the LORD had blessed him in every way. 2 He said to the chief[b] servant in his household, the one in charge of all that he had, "Put your hand under my thigh. 3 I want you to swear by the LORD, the God of heaven and the God of earth, that you will not get a wife for my son from the daughters of the Canaanites, among whom I am living, 4 but will go to my country and my own relatives and get a wife for my son Isaac."

5 The servant asked him, "What if the woman is unwilling to come back with me to this land? Shall I then take your son back to the country you came from?"

6 "Make sure that you do not take my son back there," Abraham said. 7 "The LORD, the God of heaven, who brought me out of my father's household and my native land and who spoke to me and promised me on oath, saying, 'To your offspring[c] I will give this land'—he will send his angel before you so that you can get a wife for my son from there. 8 If the woman is unwilling to come back with you, then you will be released from this oath of mine. Only do not take my son back there." 9 So the servant put his hand under the thigh of his master Abraham and swore an oath to him concerning this matter.

10 Then the servant took ten of his master's camels and left, taking with him all kinds of good things from his master. He set out for Aram Naharaim[d] and made his way to the town of Nahor. 11 He had the camels kneel down near the well outside the town; it was toward evening, the time the women go out to draw water.

12 Then he prayed, "O LORD, God of my master Abraham, give me success today, and show kindness to my master Abraham. 13 See, I am standing beside this spring, and the daughters of the townspeople are coming out to draw water. 14 May it be that when I say to a girl, 'Please let down your jar that I may have a drink,' and she says, 'Drink, and I'll water your camels too'—let her be the one you have chosen for your servant Isaac. By this I will know that you have shown kindness to my master."

15 Before he had finished praying, Rebekah came out with her jar on her shoulder. She was the daughter of Bethuel son of Milcah, who was the wife of Abraham's brother Nahor. 16 The girl was very beautiful, a virgin; no man had ever lain with her. She went down to the spring, filled her jar and came up again.

17 The servant hurried to meet her and said, "Please give me a little water from your jar."

18 "Drink, my lord," she said, and quickly lowered the jar to her hands and gave him a drink.

19 After she had given him a drink, she said, "I'll draw water for your camels too, until they have finished drinking." 20 So she quickly emptied her jar into the trough, ran back to the well to draw more water, and drew enough for all his camels. 21 Without saying a word, the man watched her closely to learn whether or not the LORD had made his journey successful.

22 When the camels had finished drinking, the man took out a gold nose ring weighing a beka[e] and two gold bracelets weighing ten shekels.[f] 23 Then he asked, "Whose daughter are you? Please tell me, is there room in your father's house for us to spend the night?"

24 She answered him, "I am the daughter of Bethuel, the son that Milcah bore to Nahor." 25 And she added, "We have plenty of straw and fodder, as well as room for you to spend the night."

26 Then the man bowed down and worshiped the LORD, 27 saying, "Praise be to the LORD, the God of my master Abraham, who has not abandoned his kindness and faithfulness to my master. As for me, the LORD has led me on the journey to the house of my master's relatives."

28 The girl ran and told her mother's household about these things. 29 Now Rebekah had

[a] *15* That is, about 10 pounds (about 4.5 kilograms) [b] *2* Or *oldest* [c] *7* Or *seed* [d] *10* That is, Northwest Mesopotamia [e] *22* That is, about 1/5 ounce (about 5.5 grams) [f] *22* That is, about 4 ounces (about 110 grams)

a brother named Laban, and he hurried out to the man at the spring. 30As soon as he had seen the nose ring, and the bracelets on his sister's arms, and had heard Rebekah tell what the man said to her, he went out to the man and found him standing by the camels near the spring. 31"Come, you who are blessed by the Lord," he said. "Why are you standing out here? I have prepared the house and a place for the camels."

32So the man went to the house, and the camels were unloaded. Straw and fodder were brought for the camels, and water for him and his men to wash their feet. 33Then food was set before him, but he said, "I will not eat until I have told you what I have to say."

"Then tell us," ⌊Laban⌋ said.

34So he said, "I am Abraham's servant. 35The Lord has blessed my master abundantly, and he has become wealthy. He has given him sheep and cattle, silver and gold, menservants and maidservants, and camels and donkeys. 36My master's wife Sarah has borne him a son in her[a] old age, and he has given him everything he owns. 37And my master made me swear an oath, and said, 'You must not get a wife for my son from the daughters of the Canaanites, in whose land I live, 38but go to my father's family and to my own clan, and get a wife for my son.'

39"Then I asked my master, 'What if the woman will not come back with me?'

40"He replied, 'The Lord, before whom I have walked, will send his angel with you and make your journey a success, so that you can get a wife for my son from my own clan and from my father's family. 41Then, when you go to my clan, you will be released from my oath even if they refuse to give her to you—you will be released from my oath.'

42"When I came to the spring today, I said, 'O Lord, God of my master Abraham, if you will, please grant success to the journey on which I have come. 43See, I am standing beside this spring; if a maiden comes out to draw water and I say to her, "Please let me drink a little water from your jar," 44and if she says to me, "Drink, and I'll draw water for your camels too," let her be the one the Lord has chosen for my master's son.'

45"Before I finished praying in my heart, Rebekah came out, with her jar on her shoulder. She went down to the spring and drew water, and I said to her, 'Please give me a drink.'

46"She quickly lowered her jar from her shoulder and said, 'Drink, and I'll water your camels too.' So I drank, and she watered the camels also.

47"I asked her, 'Whose daughter are you?'

"She said, 'The daughter of Bethuel son of Nahor, whom Milcah bore to him.'

"Then I put the ring in her nose and the bracelets on her arms, 48and I bowed down and worshiped the Lord. I praised the Lord, the God of my master Abraham, who had led me on the right road to get the granddaughter of my master's brother for his son. 49Now if you will show kindness and faithfulness to my master, tell me; and if not, tell me, so I may know which way to turn."

50Laban and Bethuel answered, "This is from the Lord; we can say nothing to you one way or the other. 51Here is Rebekah; take her and go, and let her become the wife of your master's son, as the Lord has directed."

52When Abraham's servant heard what they said, he bowed down to the ground before the Lord. 53Then the servant brought out gold and silver jewelry and articles of clothing and gave them to Rebekah; he also gave costly gifts to her brother and to her mother. 54Then he and the men who were with him ate and drank and spent the night there.

When they got up the next morning, he said, "Send me on my way to my master."

55But her brother and her mother replied, "Let the girl remain with us ten days or so; then you[b] may go."

56But he said to them, "Do not detain me, now that the Lord has granted success to my journey. Send me on my way so I may go to my master."

57Then they said, "Let's call the girl and ask her about it." 58So they called Rebekah and asked her, "Will you go with this man?"

"I will go," she said.

59So they sent their sister Rebekah on her way, along with her nurse and Abraham's servant and his men. 60And they blessed Rebekah and said to her,

"Our sister, may you increase
  to thousands upon thousands;
may your offspring possess
  the gates of their enemies."

61Then Rebekah and her maids got ready and mounted their camels and went back with the man. So the servant took Rebekah and left.

---

[a] 36 Or *his* [b] 55 Or *she*

PRINCIPLES OF A GOOD MATCH

Laban and Bethuel answered, "This is from the LORD; we can say nothing to you one way or the other. Here is Rebekah; take her and go, and let her become the wife of your master's son, as the LORD has directed."

— GENESIS 24:50–51

The story of Abraham sending his servant to find a wife for his son Isaac illustrates several Biblical principles for marriage.

The first principle is that prayer is important in all stages and in all decisions regarding marriage. Abraham's servant prayed that he would find the right wife for his master's son. Instead of relying on his own judgment or opinion, the servant let God guide his actions. And the Lord gave him success, leading him to Rebekah.

A second principle, one that Abraham insisted upon, is that we should marry a person who shares our beliefs. Abraham sent his servant hundreds of miles away to find a wife for his son Isaac among his family, knowing that would be the best place to find a woman who would share Isaac's faith. Today, we know that God wants Christians to marry those who also follow Christ.

But even when we fail to heed that principle, God can still work in marriage. He did in my life, since I was an unbeliever when my husband, Grey, proposed to me. Grey said he sensed I was seeking Christ, but that's not how I remember it. It was God's grace alone that brought me to Jesus. Still, I doubt Grey and I would still be married had I not become a believer.

A third principle of marriage displayed here is that commitment is crucial. Amazingly, Rebekah agreed to marry Isaac without ever having met him. She didn't say, "Well, I'll see if I like him" or "I'll give it a try." She made a commitment and stuck with it.

I once heard marriage compared to buying a car. If you know this is the only car you will ever have, you will take very good care of it. If, on the other hand, you buy the car thinking you can always junk it and get another one, you're less likely to change the oil and pay attention to the warning lights on the console.

While we want to heed the Bible's principles on marriage, we don't have to follow some of its customs, such as arranged marriages. In American culture we value individual choice and generally shun matchmaking, unless it's on the Internet and we control the criteria. In finding a spouse for his son, Abraham would have listed such requirements as "relative" and "follower of God." His servant might have added "kind, generous and hardworking"—someone who would respond to his request for water by providing enough for him and his camels to drink.

Whether or not you're sure you married the one and only person in the world for you, once you're married, that person becomes your one and only. Once the choice is made, all other choices are off the table. No matter how you and your partner came together, you are now one flesh, a unit, a team. Let God help your marriage become all that it can be.

—MARY ANN JEFFREYS

let's *talk*

- ✦ Some people think there is only one right person to marry. In what ways do we agree with that? Disagree? Why?
- ✦ How does being committed for life to someone influence our actions toward each other?
- ✦ Before we met each other, what ingredients did we think were essential in a person before we'd consider marrying him or her? Which of those "essentials" were no longer important when we fell in love with each other? What caused the shift?

FOR YOUR NEXT DEVOTIONAL READING, TURN TO PAGE 34.

62Now Isaac had come from Beer Lahai Roi, for he was living in the Negev. 63He went out to the field one evening to meditate,[a] and as he looked up, he saw camels approaching. 64Rebekah also looked up and saw Isaac. She got down from her camel 65and asked the servant, "Who is that man in the field coming to meet us?"

"He is my master," the servant answered. So she took her veil and covered herself.

66Then the servant told Isaac all he had done. 67Isaac brought her into the tent of his mother Sarah, and he married Rebekah. So she became his wife, and he loved her; and Isaac was comforted after his mother's death.

The Death of Abraham

25 Abraham took[b] another wife, whose name was Keturah. 2She bore him Zimran, Jokshan, Medan, Midian, Ishbak and Shuah. 3Jokshan was the father of Sheba and Dedan; the descendants of Dedan were the Asshurites, the Letushites and the Leummites. 4The sons of Midian were Ephah, Epher, Hanoch, Abida and Eldaah. All these were descendants of Keturah.

5Abraham left everything he owned to Isaac. 6But while he was still living, he gave gifts to the sons of his concubines and sent them away from his son Isaac to the land of the east.

7Altogether, Abraham lived a hundred and seventy-five years. 8Then Abraham breathed his last and died at a good old age, an old man and full of years; and he was gathered to his people. 9His sons Isaac and Ishmael buried him in the cave of Machpelah near Mamre, in the field of Ephron son of Zohar the Hittite, 10the field Abraham had bought from the Hittites.[c] There Abraham was buried with his wife Sarah. 11After Abraham's death, God blessed his son Isaac, who then lived near Beer Lahai Roi.

Ishmael's Sons

12This is the account of Abraham's son Ishmael, whom Sarah's maidservant, Hagar the Egyptian, bore to Abraham.

13These are the names of the sons of Ishmael, listed in the order of their birth: Nebaioth the firstborn of Ishmael, Kedar, Adbeel, Mibsam, 14Mishma, Dumah, Massa, 15Hadad, Tema, Jetur, Naphish and Kedemah. 16These were the sons of Ishmael, and these are the names of the twelve tribal rulers according to their settlements and camps. 17Altogether, Ishmael lived a hundred and thirty-seven years. He breathed his last and died, and he was gathered to his people. 18His descendants settled in the area from Havilah to Shur, near the border of Egypt, as you go toward Asshur. And they lived in hostility toward[d] all their brothers.

Jacob and Esau

19This is the account of Abraham's son Isaac.

Abraham became the father of Isaac, 20and Isaac was forty years old when he married Rebekah daughter of Bethuel the Aramean from Paddan Aram[e] and sister of Laban the Aramean.

21Isaac prayed to the LORD on behalf of his wife, because she was barren. The LORD answered his prayer, and his wife Rebekah became pregnant. 22The babies jostled each other within her, and she said, "Why is this happening to me?" So she went to inquire of the LORD.

23The LORD said to her,

"Two nations are in your womb,
and two peoples from within you will be separated;
one people will be stronger than the other,
and the older will serve the younger."

24When the time came for her to give birth, there were twin boys in her womb. 25The first to come out was red, and his whole body was like a hairy garment; so they named him Esau.[f] 26After this, his brother came out, with his hand grasping Esau's heel; so he was named Jacob.[g] Isaac was sixty years old when Rebekah gave birth to them.

27The boys grew up, and Esau became a skillful hunter, a man of the open country, while Jacob was a quiet man, staying among the tents. 28Isaac, who had a taste for wild game, loved Esau, but Rebekah loved Jacob.

29Once when Jacob was cooking some stew, Esau came in from the open country, famished. 30He said to Jacob, "Quick, let me have some of that red stew! I'm famished!" (That is why he was also called Edom.[h])

31Jacob replied, "First sell me your birthright."

32"Look, I am about to die," Esau said. "What good is the birthright to me?"

---

[a] 63 The meaning of the Hebrew for this word is uncertain. [b] 1 Or *had taken* [c] 10 Or *the sons of Heth* [d] 18 Or *lived to the east of* [e] 20 That is, Northwest Mesopotamia [f] 25 *Esau* may mean *hairy*; he was also called Edom, which means *red.* [g] 26 *Jacob* means *he grasps the heel* (figuratively, *he deceives*). [h] 30 *Edom* means *red.*

33But Jacob said, "Swear to me first." So he
swore an oath to him, selling his birthright to
Jacob.
34Then Jacob gave Esau some bread and
some lentil stew. He ate and drank, and then
got up and left.
So Esau despised his birthright.

Isaac and Abimelech

26 Now there was a famine in the land—
besides the earlier famine of Abraham's
time—and Isaac went to Abimelech
king of the Philistines in Gerar. 2The LORD
appeared to Isaac and said, "Do not go down
to Egypt; live in the land where I tell you to
live. 3Stay in this land for a while, and I will
be with you and will bless you. For to you and
your descendants I will give all these lands
and will confirm the oath I swore to your father Abraham. 4I will make your descendants
as numerous as the stars in the sky and will
give them all these lands, and through your
offspring[a] all nations on earth will be blessed,
5because Abraham obeyed me and kept my requirements, my commands, my decrees and
my laws." 6So Isaac stayed in Gerar.
7When the men of that place asked him
about his wife, he said, "She is my sister," because he was afraid to say, "She is my wife."
He thought, "The men of this place might
kill me on account of Rebekah, because she
is beautiful."
8When Isaac had been there a long time,
Abimelech king of the Philistines looked
down from a window and saw Isaac caressing
his wife Rebekah. 9So Abimelech summoned
Isaac and said, "She is really your wife! Why
did you say, 'She is my sister'?"
Isaac answered him, "Because I thought I
might lose my life on account of her."
10Then Abimelech said, "What is this you
have done to us? One of the men might well
have slept with your wife, and you would have
brought guilt upon us."
11So Abimelech gave orders to all the people: "Anyone who molests this man or his wife
shall surely be put to death."
12Isaac planted crops in that land and the
same year reaped a hundredfold, because the
LORD blessed him. 13The man became rich,
and his wealth continued to grow until he became very wealthy. 14He had so many flocks
and herds and servants that the Philistines envied him. 15So all the wells that his father's servants had dug in the time of his father Abraham, the Philistines stopped up, filling them
with earth.
16Then Abimelech said to Isaac, "Move
away from us; you have become too powerful
for us."
17So Isaac moved away from there and
encamped in the Valley of Gerar and settled
there. 18Isaac reopened the wells that had been
dug in the time of his father Abraham, which
the Philistines had stopped up after Abraham
died, and he gave them the same names his
father had given them.
19Isaac's servants dug in the valley and
discovered a well of fresh water there. 20But
the herdsmen of Gerar quarreled with Isaac's
herdsmen and said, "The water is ours!" So he
named the well Esek,[b] because they disputed
with him. 21Then they dug another well, but
they quarreled over that one also; so he named
it Sitnah.[c] 22He moved on from there and dug
another well, and no one quarreled over it. He
named it Rehoboth,[d] saying, "Now the LORD
has given us room and we will flourish in the
land."
23From there he went up to Beersheba.
24That night the LORD appeared to him and
said, "I am the God of your father Abraham.
Do not be afraid, for I am with you; I will
bless you and will increase the number of your
descendants for the sake of my servant Abraham."
25Isaac built an altar there and called on the
name of the LORD. There he pitched his tent,
and there his servants dug a well.
26Meanwhile, Abimelech had come to him
from Gerar, with Ahuzzath his personal adviser and Phicol the commander of his forces.
27Isaac asked them, "Why have you come to
me, since you were hostile to me and sent me
away?"
28They answered, "We saw clearly that the
LORD was with you; so we said, 'There ought
to be a sworn agreement between us'—between us and you. Let us make a treaty with
you 29that you will do us no harm, just as we
did not molest you but always treated you well
and sent you away in peace. And now you are
blessed by the LORD."
30Isaac then made a feast for them, and they
ate and drank. 31Early the next morning the
men swore an oath to each other. Then Isaac
sent them on their way, and they left him in
peace.
32That day Isaac's servants came and told
him about the well they had dug. They said,

[a] 4 Or *seed* [b] 20 *Esek* means *dispute.* [c] 21 *Sitnah* means *opposition.* [d] 22 *Rehoboth* means *room.*

"We've found water!" 33He called it Shibah,[a]
and to this day the name of the town has been
Beersheba.[b]

34When Esau was forty years old, he married Judith daughter of Beeri the Hittite, and
also Basemath daughter of Elon the Hittite.
35They were a source of grief to Isaac and Rebekah.

Jacob Gets Isaac's Blessing

27 When Isaac was old and his eyes were
so weak that he could no longer see, he
called for Esau his older son and said to
him, "My son."

"Here I am," he answered.

2Isaac said, "I am now an old man and don't
know the day of my death. 3Now then, get
your weapons—your quiver and bow—and
go out to the open country to hunt some wild
game for me. 4Prepare me the kind of tasty
food I like and bring it to me to eat, so that I
may give you my blessing before I die."

5Now Rebekah was listening as Isaac spoke
to his son Esau. When Esau left for the open
country to hunt game and bring it back, 6Re-
bekah said to her son Jacob, "Look, I overheard
your father say to your brother Esau, 7'Bring
me some game and prepare me some tasty
food to eat, so that I may give you my blessing in the presence of the LORD before I die.'
8Now, my son, listen carefully and do what I
tell you: 9Go out to the flock and bring me two
choice young goats, so I can prepare some tasty
food for your father, just the way he likes it.
10Then take it to your father to eat, so that he
may give you his blessing before he dies."

11Jacob said to Rebekah his mother, "But
my brother Esau is a hairy man, and I'm a
man with smooth skin. 12What if my father
touches me? I would appear to be tricking him
and would bring down a curse on myself rather than a blessing."

13His mother said to him, "My son, let the
curse fall on me. Just do what I say; go and get
them for me."

14So he went and got them and brought
them to his mother, and she prepared some
tasty food, just the way his father liked it.
15Then Rebekah took the best clothes of Esau
her older son, which she had in the house, and
put them on her younger son Jacob. 16She also
covered his hands and the smooth part of his
neck with the goatskins. 17Then she handed
to her son Jacob the tasty food and the bread
she had made.

18He went to his father and said, "My father."

"Yes, my son," he answered. "Who is it?"

19Jacob said to his father, "I am Esau your
firstborn. I have done as you told me. Please
sit up and eat some of my game so that you
may give me your blessing."

20Isaac asked his son, "How did you find it
so quickly, my son?"

"The LORD your God gave me success," he
replied.

21Then Isaac said to Jacob, "Come near so I
can touch you, my son, to know whether you
really are my son Esau or not."

22Jacob went close to his father Isaac, who
touched him and said, "The voice is the voice
of Jacob, but the hands are the hands of Esau."
23He did not recognize him, for his hands
were hairy like those of his brother Esau; so he
blessed him. 24"Are you really my son Esau?"
he asked.

"I am," he replied.

25Then he said, "My son, bring me some of
your game to eat, so that I may give you my
blessing."

Jacob brought it to him and he ate; and he
brought some wine and he drank. 26Then his
father Isaac said to him, "Come here, my son,
and kiss me."

27So he went to him and kissed him. When
Isaac caught the smell of his clothes, he blessed
him and said,

"Ah, the smell of my son
  is like the smell of a field
  that the LORD has blessed.
28 May God give you of heaven's dew
  and of earth's richness—
  an abundance of grain and new wine.
29 May nations serve you
  and peoples bow down to you.
Be lord over your brothers,
  and may the sons of your mother bow
    down to you.
May those who curse you be cursed
  and those who bless you be blessed."

30After Isaac finished blessing him and Jacob had scarcely left his father's presence, his
brother Esau came in from hunting. 31He too
prepared some tasty food and brought it to his
father. Then he said to him, "My father, sit up
and eat some of my game, so that you may
give me your blessing."

32His father Isaac asked him, "Who are
you?"

---

[a] 33 *Shibah* can mean *oath* or *seven.* [b] 33 *Beersheba* can mean *well of the oath* or *well of seven.*

"I am your son," he answered, "your firstborn, Esau."
33Isaac trembled violently and said, "Who
was it, then, that hunted game and brought
it to me? I ate it just before you came and I
blessed him—and indeed he will be blessed!"
34When Esau heard his father's words, he
burst out with a loud and bitter cry and said to
his father, "Bless me—me too, my father!"
35But he said, "Your brother came deceitfully and took your blessing."
36Esau said, "Isn't he rightly named Jacob[a]?
He has deceived me these two times: He took
my birthright, and now he's taken my blessing!" Then he asked, "Haven't you reserved
any blessing for me?"
37Isaac answered Esau, "I have made him
lord over you and have made all his relatives
his servants, and I have sustained him with
grain and new wine. So what can I possibly do
for you, my son?"
38Esau said to his father, "Do you have only
one blessing, my father? Bless me too, my father!" Then Esau wept aloud.
39His father Isaac answered him,

"Your dwelling will be
away from the earth's richness,
away from the dew of heaven above.
40You will live by the sword
and you will serve your brother.
But when you grow restless,
you will throw his yoke
from off your neck."

Jacob Flees to Laban

41Esau held a grudge against Jacob because
of the blessing his father had given him. He
said to himself, "The days of mourning for my
father are near; then I will kill my brother Jacob."
42When Rebekah was told what her older
son Esau had said, she sent for her younger
son Jacob and said to him, "Your brother Esau
is consoling himself with the thought of killing you. 43Now then, my son, do what I say:
Flee at once to my brother Laban in Haran.
44Stay with him for a while until your brother's fury subsides. 45When your brother is no
longer angry with you and forgets what you
did to him, I'll send word for you to come
back from there. Why should I lose both of
you in one day?"
46Then Rebekah said to Isaac, "I'm disgust-
ed with living because of these Hittite women.
If Jacob takes a wife from among the women
of this land, from Hittite women like these,
my life will not be worth living."

28 So Isaac called for Jacob and blessed[b]
him and commanded him: "Do not
marry a Canaanite woman. 2Go at once
to Paddan Aram,[c] to the house of your mother's father Bethuel. Take a wife for yourself
there, from among the daughters of Laban,
your mother's brother. 3May God Almighty[d]
bless you and make you fruitful and increase
your numbers until you become a community
of peoples. 4May he give you and your descendants the blessing given to Abraham, so that
you may take possession of the land where
you now live as an alien, the land God gave to
Abraham." 5Then Isaac sent Jacob on his way,
and he went to Paddan Aram, to Laban son of
Bethuel the Aramean, the brother of Rebekah,
who was the mother of Jacob and Esau.
6Now Esau learned that Isaac had blessed
Jacob and had sent him to Paddan Aram to
take a wife from there, and that when he
blessed him he commanded him, "Do not
marry a Canaanite woman," 7and that Jacob
had obeyed his father and mother and had
gone to Paddan Aram. 8Esau then realized
how displeasing the Canaanite women were
to his father Isaac; 9so he went to Ishmael and
married Mahalath, the sister of Nebaioth and
daughter of Ishmael son of Abraham, in addition to the wives he already had.

Jacob's Dream at Bethel

10Jacob left Beersheba and set out for Haran.
11When he reached a certain place, he stopped
for the night because the sun had set. Taking
one of the stones there, he put it under his
head and lay down to sleep. 12He had a dream
in which he saw a stairway[e] resting on the
earth, with its top reaching to heaven, and the
angels of God were ascending and descending
on it. 13There above it[f] stood the LORD, and
he said: "I am the LORD, the God of your father Abraham and the God of Isaac. I will give
you and your descendants the land on which
you are lying. 14Your descendants will be like
the dust of the earth, and you will spread out
to the west and to the east, to the north and to
the south. All peoples on earth will be blessed
through you and your offspring. 15I am with
you and will watch over you wherever you go,
and I will bring you back to this land. I will
not leave you until I have done what I have
promised you."

---

[a] 36 *Jacob* means *he grasps the heel* (figuratively, *he deceives*). [b] 1 Or *greeted* [c] 2 That is, Northwest Mesopotamia; also in verses 5, 6 and 7 [d] 3 Hebrew *El-Shaddai* [e] 12 Or *ladder* [f] 13 Or *There beside him*

16 When Jacob awoke from his sleep, he
thought, "Surely the LORD is in this place, and
I was not aware of it." 17 He was afraid and
said, "How awesome is this place! This is none
other than the house of God; this is the gate
of heaven."
18 Early the next morning Jacob took the
stone he had placed under his head and set it
up as a pillar and poured oil on top of it. 19 He
called that place Bethel,[a] though the city used
to be called Luz.
20 Then Jacob made a vow, saying, "If God
will be with me and will watch over me on this
journey I am taking and will give me food to
eat and clothes to wear 21 so that I return safely
to my father's house, then the LORD[b] will be
my God 22 and[c] this stone that I have set up as
a pillar will be God's house, and of all that you
give me I will give you a tenth."

Jacob Arrives in Paddan Aram

29 Then Jacob continued on his journey
and came to the land of the eastern peoples. 2 There he saw a well in the field,
with three flocks of sheep lying near it because
the flocks were watered from that well. The
stone over the mouth of the well was large.
3 When all the flocks were gathered there, the
shepherds would roll the stone away from the
well's mouth and water the sheep. Then they
would return the stone to its place over the
mouth of the well.
4 Jacob asked the shepherds, "My brothers,
where are you from?"
"We're from Haran," they replied.
5 He said to them, "Do you know Laban,
Nahor's grandson?"
"Yes, we know him," they answered.
6 Then Jacob asked them, "Is he well?"
"Yes, he is," they said, "and here comes his
daughter Rachel with the sheep."
7 "Look," he said, "the sun is still high; it is
not time for the flocks to be gathered. Water
the sheep and take them back to pasture."
8 "We can't," they replied, "until all the
flocks are gathered and the stone has been
rolled away from the mouth of the well. Then
we will water the sheep."
9 While he was still talking with them, Rachel came with her father's sheep, for she was a
shepherdess. 10 When Jacob saw Rachel daughter of Laban, his mother's brother, and Laban's
sheep, he went over and rolled the stone away
from the mouth of the well and watered his
uncle's sheep. 11 Then Jacob kissed Rachel and
began to weep aloud. 12 He had told Rachel
that he was a relative of her father and a son of
Rebekah. So she ran and told her father.
13 As soon as Laban heard the news about
Jacob, his sister's son, he hurried to meet him.
He embraced him and kissed him and brought
him to his home, and there Jacob told him all
these things. 14 Then Laban said to him, "You
are my own flesh and blood."

Jacob Marries Leah and Rachel

After Jacob had stayed with him for a whole
month, 15 Laban said to him, "Just because
you are a relative of mine, should you work
for me for nothing? Tell me what your wages
should be."
16 Now Laban had two daughters; the name
of the older was Leah, and the name of the
younger was Rachel. 17 Leah had weak[d] eyes,
but Rachel was lovely in form, and beautiful.
18 Jacob was in love with Rachel and said, "I'll
work for you seven years in return for your
younger daughter Rachel."
19 Laban said, "It's better that I give her to
you than to some other man. Stay here with
me." 20 So Jacob served seven years to get Rachel, but they seemed like only a few days to
him because of his love for her.
21 Then Jacob said to Laban, "Give me my
wife. My time is completed, and I want to lie
with her."
22 So Laban brought together all the people of the place and gave a feast. 23 But when
evening came, he took his daughter Leah and
gave her to Jacob, and Jacob lay with her.
24 And Laban gave his servant girl Zilpah to
his daughter as her maidservant.
25 When morning came, there was Leah! So
Jacob said to Laban, "What is this you have
done to me? I served you for Rachel, didn't I?
Why have you deceived me?"
26 Laban replied, "It is not our custom here
to give the younger daughter in marriage before the older one. 27 Finish this daughter's
bridal week; then we will give you the younger
one also, in return for another seven years of
work."
28 And Jacob did so. He finished the week
with Leah, and then Laban gave him his
daughter Rachel to be his wife. 29 Laban gave
his servant girl Bilhah to his daughter Rachel as
her maidservant. 30 Jacob lay with Rachel also,
and he loved Rachel more than Leah. And he
worked for Laban another seven years.

---

[a] 19 *Bethel* means *house of God.* [b] 20,21 Or *Since God . . . father's house, the* LORD [c] 21,22 Or *house, and the* LORD *will be my God,* *22then* [d] 17 Or *delicate*

TUESDAY
READ GENESIS 29:16–30

LOVE THE SECOND TIME AROUND

Is there a deceased spouse, an ex or even a high school sweetheart who lives on as your competitor in family folklore? Do you occasionally feel less smart, funny or sexy than the former love of your spouse?

Each of us wants a spouse who has loved only us, but, statistically speaking, that is becoming less likely. Experts estimate that 43 percent of all marriages are remarriages for one or both partners. Second loves can add additional levels of stress, especially when one partner, justifiably or not, feels unable to live up to standards set by someone else. Such comparisons leave us feeling bitter, jealous and unloved.

Leah, the unloved sister referred to in today's Scripture reading, could relate. Her name means "wild cow," and she is described as having "weak eyes." Contrast that with her younger sister Rachel, whose name means "lamb or ewe," and who is described as being "lovely in form" and "beautiful" (Genesis 29:17).

The first time Jacob saw Rachel, he was so blown away by her beauty that he single-handedly rolled a huge stone cover off a well, kissed her and began to weep. Jacob then agreed to work for Rachel's father, Laban, for seven years in exchange for his daughter's hand in marriage. But at the wedding, Laban didn't keep his end of the bargain. Instead of giving Rachel to Jacob, he substituted his oldest daughter, Leah.

Imagine Leah's pain that night. It would have been dark when she unveiled herself. Jacob would not have known who she was. Perhaps a tear slid down her cheek when he nestled his face in her hair and whispered, "I love you, Rachel, more than anyone else in this world." How Leah must have feared the sunrise. How did Leah react when Jacob discovered she wasn't Rachel? Did she quietly try to please him? Did she fantasize that Jacob loved her now instead of Rachel?

If your spouse has had a previous relationship, you may feel like Leah at times. But you are not in her situation. Leah's status as a wife was a result of her father's trickery. Your marriage is based on choice, not deceit. You have chosen each other in love, regardless of your pasts. You can both learn to work through the inevitable mixed feelings, comparisons and difficult situations that arise when two people make a new life together.

Though Leah felt second best most of her marriage, she learned to pour out her heart to God, as we see in the way she chose her children's names. During times of insecurity or hurt feelings, God can soothe your soul too. Take your feelings to him. Then bring your concerns to your spouse and talk through the situation, so that the two of you may grow closer and learn more about each other over time.

—JENNIFER SCHUCHMANN

Jacob lay with Rachel also, and he loved Rachel more than Leah. And he worked for Laban another seven years.

— GENESIS 29:30

let's talk

- ✦ How do we feel about relationships in our pasts? Are there feelings or situations we need to talk through?
- ✦ Leah and Rachel's relationship was marked by competition, jealousy and bitterness. What caused this and what could have changed it?
- ✦ Check out the names Leah gave to her children (see Genesis 29:31–35; 30:16–21). What do they say about her relationship with God?

FOR YOUR NEXT DEVOTIONAL READING, TURN TO PAGE 45.

Jacob's Children

31 When the LORD saw that Leah was not loved, he opened her womb, but Rachel was barren. 32 Leah became pregnant and gave birth to a son. She named him Reuben,[a] for she said, "It is because the LORD has seen my misery. Surely my husband will love me now."

33 She conceived again, and when she gave birth to a son she said, "Because the LORD heard that I am not loved, he gave me this one too." So she named him Simeon.[b]

34 Again she conceived, and when she gave birth to a son she said, "Now at last my husband will become attached to me, because I have borne him three sons." So he was named Levi.[c]

35 She conceived again, and when she gave birth to a son she said, "This time I will praise the LORD." So she named him Judah.[d] Then she stopped having children.

30 When Rachel saw that she was not bearing Jacob any children, she became jealous of her sister. So she said to Jacob, "Give me children, or I'll die!"

2 Jacob became angry with her and said, "Am I in the place of God, who has kept you from having children?"

3 Then she said, "Here is Bilhah, my maidservant. Sleep with her so that she can bear children for me and that through her I too can build a family."

4 So she gave him her servant Bilhah as a wife. Jacob slept with her, 5 and she became pregnant and bore him a son. 6 Then Rachel said, "God has vindicated me; he has listened to my plea and given me a son." Because of this she named him Dan.[e]

7 Rachel's servant Bilhah conceived again and bore Jacob a second son. 8 Then Rachel said, "I have had a great struggle with my sister, and I have won." So she named him Naphtali.[f]

9 When Leah saw that she had stopped having children, she took her maidservant Zilpah and gave her to Jacob as a wife. 10 Leah's servant Zilpah bore Jacob a son. 11 Then Leah said, "What good fortune!"[g] So she named him Gad.[h]

12 Leah's servant Zilpah bore Jacob a second son. 13 Then Leah said, "How happy I am! The women will call me happy." So she named him Asher.[i]

14 During wheat harvest, Reuben went out into the fields and found some mandrake plants, which he brought to his mother Leah. Rachel said to Leah, "Please give me some of your son's mandrakes."

15 But she said to her, "Wasn't it enough that you took away my husband? Will you take my son's mandrakes too?"

"Very well," Rachel said, "he can sleep with you tonight in return for your son's mandrakes."

16 So when Jacob came in from the fields that evening, Leah went out to meet him. "You must sleep with me," she said. "I have hired you with my son's mandrakes." So he slept with her that night.

17 God listened to Leah, and she became pregnant and bore Jacob a fifth son. 18 Then Leah said, "God has rewarded me for giving my maidservant to my husband." So she named him Issachar.[j]

19 Leah conceived again and bore Jacob a sixth son. 20 Then Leah said, "God has presented me with a precious gift. This time my husband will treat me with honor, because I have borne him six sons." So she named him Zebulun.[k]

21 Some time later she gave birth to a daughter and named her Dinah.

22 Then God remembered Rachel; he listened to her and opened her womb. 23 She became pregnant and gave birth to a son and said, "God has taken away my disgrace." 24 She named him Joseph,[l] and said, "May the LORD add to me another son."

Jacob's Flocks Increase

25 After Rachel gave birth to Joseph, Jacob said to Laban, "Send me on my way so I can go back to my own homeland. 26 Give me my wives and children, for whom I have served you, and I will be on my way. You know how much work I've done for you."

27 But Laban said to him, "If I have found favor in your eyes, please stay. I have learned by divination that[m] the LORD has blessed me because of you." 28 He added, "Name your wages, and I will pay them."

29 Jacob said to him, "You know how I have worked for you and how your livestock has fared under my care. 30 The little you had

---

[a] *32 Reuben* sounds like the Hebrew for *he has seen my misery*; the name means *see, a son.* [b] *33 Simeon* probably means *one who hears.* [c] *34 Levi* sounds like and may be derived from the Hebrew for *attached.* [d] *35 Judah* sounds like and may be derived from the Hebrew for *praise.* [e] *6 Dan* here means *he has vindicated.* [f] *8 Naphtali* means *my struggle.* [g] *11* Or *"A troop is coming!"* [h] *11 Gad* can mean *good fortune* or *a troop.* [i] *13 Asher* means *happy.* [j] *18 Issachar* sounds like the Hebrew for *reward.* [k] *20 Zebulun* probably means *honor.* [l] *24 Joseph* means *may he add.* [m] *27* Or possibly *have become rich and*

before I came has increased greatly, and the LORD has blessed you wherever I have been. But now, when may I do something for my own household?"

31"What shall I give you?" he asked.

"Don't give me anything," Jacob replied. "But if you will do this one thing for me, I will go on tending your flocks and watching over them: 32Let me go through all your flocks today and remove from them every speckled or spotted sheep, every dark-colored lamb and every spotted or speckled goat. They will be my wages. 33And my honesty will testify for me in the future, whenever you check on the wages you have paid me. Any goat in my possession that is not speckled or spotted, or any lamb that is not dark-colored, will be considered stolen."

34"Agreed," said Laban. "Let it be as you have said." 35That same day he removed all the male goats that were streaked or spotted, and all the speckled or spotted female goats (all that had white on them) and all the dark-colored lambs, and he placed them in the care of his sons. 36Then he put a three-day journey between himself and Jacob, while Jacob continued to tend the rest of Laban's flocks.

37Jacob, however, took fresh-cut branches from poplar, almond and plane trees and made white stripes on them by peeling the bark and exposing the white inner wood of the branches. 38Then he placed the peeled branches in all the watering troughs, so that they would be directly in front of the flocks when they came to drink. When the flocks were in heat and came to drink, 39they mated in front of the branches. And they bore young that were streaked or speckled or spotted. 40Jacob set apart the young of the flock by themselves, but made the rest face the streaked and dark-colored animals that belonged to Laban. Thus he made separate flocks for himself and did not put them with Laban's animals. 41Whenever the stronger females were in heat, Jacob would place the branches in the troughs in front of the animals so they would mate near the branches, 42but if the animals were weak, he would not place them there. So the weak animals went to Laban and the strong ones to Jacob. 43In this way the man grew exceedingly prosperous and came to own large flocks, and maidservants and menservants, and camels and donkeys.

Jacob Flees From Laban

31 Jacob heard that Laban's sons were saying, "Jacob has taken everything our father owned and has gained all this wealth from what belonged to our father." 2And Jacob noticed that Laban's attitude toward him was not what it had been.

3Then the LORD said to Jacob, "Go back to the land of your fathers and to your relatives, and I will be with you."

4So Jacob sent word to Rachel and Leah to come out to the fields where his flocks were. 5He said to them, "I see that your father's attitude toward me is not what it was before, but the God of my father has been with me. 6You know that I've worked for your father with all my strength, 7yet your father has cheated me by changing my wages ten times. However, God has not allowed him to harm me. 8If he said, 'The speckled ones will be your wages,' then all the flocks gave birth to speckled young; and if he said, 'The streaked ones will be your wages,' then all the flocks bore streaked young. 9So God has taken away your father's livestock and has given them to me.

10"In breeding season I once had a dream in which I looked up and saw that the male goats mating with the flock were streaked, speckled or spotted. 11The angel of God said to me in the dream, 'Jacob.' I answered, 'Here I am.' 12And he said, 'Look up and see that all the male goats mating with the flock are streaked, speckled or spotted, for I have seen all that Laban has been doing to you. 13I am the God of Bethel, where you anointed a pillar and where you made a vow to me. Now leave this land at once and go back to your native land.' "

14Then Rachel and Leah replied, "Do we still have any share in the inheritance of our father's estate? 15Does he not regard us as foreigners? Not only has he sold us, but he has used up what was paid for us. 16Surely all the wealth that God took away from our father belongs to us and our children. So do whatever God has told you."

17Then Jacob put his children and his wives on camels, 18and he drove all his livestock ahead of him, along with all the goods he had accumulated in Paddan Aram,[a] to go to his father Isaac in the land of Canaan.

19When Laban had gone to shear his sheep, Rachel stole her father's household gods. 20Moreover, Jacob deceived Laban the Aramean by not telling him he was running

a *18* That is, Northwest Mesopotamia

away. [21]So he fled with all he had, and crossing the River,[a] he headed for the hill country of Gilead.

Laban Pursues Jacob

[22]On the third day Laban was told that Jacob had fled. [23]Taking his relatives with him, he pursued Jacob for seven days and caught up with him in the hill country of Gilead. [24]Then God came to Laban the Aramean in a dream at night and said to him, "Be careful not to say anything to Jacob, either good or bad."

[25]Jacob had pitched his tent in the hill country of Gilead when Laban overtook him, and Laban and his relatives camped there too. [26]Then Laban said to Jacob, "What have you done? You've deceived me, and you've carried off my daughters like captives in war. [27]Why did you run off secretly and deceive me? Why didn't you tell me, so I could send you away with joy and singing to the music of tambourines and harps? [28]You didn't even let me kiss my grandchildren and my daughters good-by. You have done a foolish thing. [29]I have the power to harm you; but last night the God of your father said to me, 'Be careful not to say anything to Jacob, either good or bad.' [30]Now you have gone off because you longed to return to your father's house. But why did you steal my gods?"

[31]Jacob answered Laban, "I was afraid, because I thought you would take your daughters away from me by force. [32]But if you find anyone who has your gods, he shall not live. In the presence of our relatives, see for yourself whether there is anything of yours here with me; and if so, take it." Now Jacob did not know that Rachel had stolen the gods.

[33]So Laban went into Jacob's tent and into Leah's tent and into the tent of the two maidservants, but he found nothing. After he came out of Leah's tent, he entered Rachel's tent. [34]Now Rachel had taken the household gods and put them inside her camel's saddle and was sitting on them. Laban searched through everything in the tent but found nothing.

[35]Rachel said to her father, "Don't be angry, my lord, that I cannot stand up in your presence; I'm having my period." So he searched but could not find the household gods.

[36]Jacob was angry and took Laban to task. "What is my crime?" he asked Laban. "What sin have I committed that you hunt me down? [37]Now that you have searched through all my goods, what have you found that belongs to your household? Put it here in front of your relatives and mine, and let them judge between the two of us.

[38]"I have been with you for twenty years now. Your sheep and goats have not miscarried, nor have I eaten rams from your flocks. [39]I did not bring you animals torn by wild beasts; I bore the loss myself. And you demanded payment from me for whatever was stolen by day or night. [40]This was my situation: The heat consumed me in the daytime and the cold at night, and sleep fled from my eyes. [41]It was like this for the twenty years I was in your household. I worked for you fourteen years for your two daughters and six years for your flocks, and you changed my wages ten times. [42]If the God of my father, the God of Abraham and the Fear of Isaac, had not been with me, you would surely have sent me away empty-handed. But God has seen my hardship and the toil of my hands, and last night he rebuked you."

[43]Laban answered Jacob, "The women are my daughters, the children are my children, and the flocks are my flocks. All you see is mine. Yet what can I do today about these daughters of mine, or about the children they have borne? [44]Come now, let's make a covenant, you and I, and let it serve as a witness between us."

[45]So Jacob took a stone and set it up as a pillar. [46]He said to his relatives, "Gather some stones." So they took stones and piled them in a heap, and they ate there by the heap. [47]Laban called it Jegar Sahadutha,[b] and Jacob called it Galeed.[c]

[48]Laban said, "This heap is a witness between you and me today." That is why it was called Galeed. [49]It was also called Mizpah,[d] because he said, "May the LORD keep watch between you and me when we are away from each other. [50]If you mistreat my daughters or if you take any wives besides my daughters, even though no one is with us, remember that God is a witness between you and me."

[51]Laban also said to Jacob, "Here is this heap, and here is this pillar I have set up between you and me. [52]This heap is a witness, and this pillar is a witness, that I will not go past this heap to your side to harm you and that you will not go past this heap and pillar to my side to harm me. [53]May the God of Abraham and the God of Nahor, the God of their father, judge between us."

So Jacob took an oath in the name of the

---

[a] 21 That is, the Euphrates [b] 47 The Aramaic *Jegar Sahadutha* means *witness heap.* [c] 47 The Hebrew *Galeed* means *witness heap.*
[d] 49 *Mizpah* means *watchtower.*

Fear of his father Isaac. 54He offered a sacrifice there in the hill country and invited his relatives to a meal. After they had eaten, they spent the night there.

55Early the next morning Laban kissed his grandchildren and his daughters and blessed them. Then he left and returned home.

Jacob Prepares to Meet Esau

32 Jacob also went on his way, and the angels of God met him. 2When Jacob saw them, he said, "This is the camp of God!" So he named that place Mahanaim.[a]

3Jacob sent messengers ahead of him to his brother Esau in the land of Seir, the country of Edom. 4He instructed them: "This is what you are to say to my master Esau: 'Your servant Jacob says, I have been staying with Laban and have remained there till now. 5I have cattle and donkeys, sheep and goats, menservants and maidservants. Now I am sending this message to my lord, that I may find favor in your eyes.' "

6When the messengers returned to Jacob, they said, "We went to your brother Esau, and now he is coming to meet you, and four hundred men are with him."

7In great fear and distress Jacob divided the people who were with him into two groups,[b] and the flocks and herds and camels as well. 8He thought, "If Esau comes and attacks one group,[c] the group[c] that is left may escape."

9Then Jacob prayed, "O God of my father Abraham, God of my father Isaac, O LORD, who said to me, 'Go back to your country and your relatives, and I will make you prosper,' 10I am unworthy of all the kindness and faithfulness you have shown your servant. I had only my staff when I crossed this Jordan, but now I have become two groups. 11Save me, I pray, from the hand of my brother Esau, for I am afraid he will come and attack me, and also the mothers with their children. 12But you have said, 'I will surely make you prosper and will make your descendants like the sand of the sea, which cannot be counted.' "

13He spent the night there, and from what he had with him he selected a gift for his brother Esau: 14two hundred female goats and twenty male goats, two hundred ewes and twenty rams, 15thirty female camels with their young, forty cows and ten bulls, and twenty female donkeys and ten male donkeys. 16He put them in the care of his servants, each herd by itself, and said to his servants, "Go ahead of me, and keep some space between the herds."

17He instructed the one in the lead: "When my brother Esau meets you and asks, 'To whom do you belong, and where are you going, and who owns all these animals in front of you?' 18then you are to say, 'They belong to your servant Jacob. They are a gift sent to my lord Esau, and he is coming behind us.' "

19He also instructed the second, the third and all the others who followed the herds: "You are to say the same thing to Esau when you meet him. 20And be sure to say, 'Your servant Jacob is coming behind us.' " For he thought, "I will pacify him with these gifts I am sending on ahead; later, when I see him, perhaps he will receive me." 21So Jacob's gifts went on ahead of him, but he himself spent the night in the camp.

Jacob Wrestles With God

22That night Jacob got up and took his two wives, his two maidservants and his eleven sons and crossed the ford of the Jabbok. 23After he had sent them across the stream, he sent over all his possessions. 24So Jacob was left alone, and a man wrestled with him till daybreak. 25When the man saw that he could not overpower him, he touched the socket of Jacob's hip so that his hip was wrenched as he wrestled with the man. 26Then the man said, "Let me go, for it is daybreak."

But Jacob replied, "I will not let you go unless you bless me."

27The man asked him, "What is your name?"

"Jacob," he answered.

28Then the man said, "Your name will no longer be Jacob, but Israel,[d] because you have struggled with God and with men and have overcome."

29Jacob said, "Please tell me your name."

But he replied, "Why do you ask my name?" Then he blessed him there.

30So Jacob called the place Peniel,[e] saying, "It is because I saw God face to face, and yet my life was spared."

31The sun rose above him as he passed Peniel,[f] and he was limping because of his hip. 32Therefore to this day the Israelites do not eat the tendon attached to the socket of the hip, because the socket of Jacob's hip was touched near the tendon.

---

[a] 2 *Mahanaim* means *two camps.* [b] 7 Or *camps*; also in verse 10 [c] 8 Or *camp* [d] 28 *Israel* means *he struggles with God.*
[e] 30 *Peniel* means *face of God.* [f] 31 Hebrew *Penuel,* a variant of *Peniel*

Jacob Meets Esau

33 Jacob looked up and there was Esau,
coming with his four hundred men; so
he divided the children among Leah,
Rachel and the two maidservants. 2He put the
maidservants and their children in front, Leah
and her children next, and Rachel and Joseph
in the rear. 3He himself went on ahead and
bowed down to the ground seven times as he
approached his brother.
4But Esau ran to meet Jacob and embraced
him; he threw his arms around his neck
and kissed him. And they wept. 5Then Esau
looked up and saw the women and children.
"Who are these with you?" he asked.
Jacob answered, "They are the children God
has graciously given your servant."
6Then the maidservants and their children
approached and bowed down. 7Next, Leah
and her children came and bowed down. Last
of all came Joseph and Rachel, and they too
bowed down.
8Esau asked, "What do you mean by all
these droves I met?"
"To find favor in your eyes, my lord," he
said.
9But Esau said, "I already have plenty, my
brother. Keep what you have for yourself."
10"No, please!" said Jacob. "If I have found
favor in your eyes, accept this gift from me.
For to see your face is like seeing the face of
God, now that you have received me favorably. 11Please accept the present that was
brought to you, for God has been gracious to
me and I have all I need." And because Jacob
insisted, Esau accepted it.
12Then Esau said, "Let us be on our way; I'll
accompany you."
13But Jacob said to him, "My lord knows
that the children are tender and that I must
care for the ewes and cows that are nursing
their young. If they are driven hard just one
day, all the animals will die. 14So let my lord
go on ahead of his servant, while I move along
slowly at the pace of the droves before me and
that of the children, until I come to my lord
in Seir."
15Esau said, "Then let me leave some of my
men with you."
"But why do that?" Jacob asked. "Just let
me find favor in the eyes of my lord."
16So that day Esau started on his way back
to Seir. 17Jacob, however, went to Succoth,
where he built a place for himself and made
shelters for his livestock. That is why the place
is called Succoth.[a]
18After Jacob came from Paddan Aram,[b]
he arrived safely at the[c] city of Shechem in
Canaan and camped within sight of the city.
19For a hundred pieces of silver,[d] he bought
from the sons of Hamor, the father of Shechem, the plot of ground where he pitched his
tent. 20There he set up an altar and called it El
Elohe Israel.[e]

Dinah and the Shechemites

34 Now Dinah, the daughter Leah had
borne to Jacob, went out to visit the
women of the land. 2When Shechem
son of Hamor the Hivite, the ruler of that
area, saw her, he took her and violated her.
3His heart was drawn to Dinah daughter of
Jacob, and he loved the girl and spoke tenderly
to her. 4And Shechem said to his father Hamor, "Get me this girl as my wife."
5When Jacob heard that his daughter Dinah had been defiled, his sons were in the
fields with his livestock; so he kept quiet about
it until they came home.
6Then Shechem's father Hamor went out
to talk with Jacob. 7Now Jacob's sons had
come in from the fields as soon as they heard
what had happened. They were filled with
grief and fury, because Shechem had done a
disgraceful thing in[f] Israel by lying with Jacob's daughter—a thing that should not be
done.
8But Hamor said to them, "My son Shechem has his heart set on your daughter. Please
give her to him as his wife. 9Intermarry with
us; give us your daughters and take our daughters for yourselves. 10You can settle among us;
the land is open to you. Live in it, trade[g] in it,
and acquire property in it."
11Then Shechem said to Dinah's father and
brothers, "Let me find favor in your eyes, and
I will give you whatever you ask. 12Make the
price for the bride and the gift I am to bring as
great as you like, and I'll pay whatever you ask
me. Only give me the girl as my wife."
13Because their sister Dinah had been defiled, Jacob's sons replied deceitfully as they
spoke to Shechem and his father Hamor.
14They said to them, "We can't do such a
thing; we can't give our sister to a man who
is not circumcised. That would be a disgrace
to us. 15We will give our consent to you on
one condition only: that you become like us

---

[a] *17 Succoth* means *shelters.* [b] *18* That is, Northwest Mesopotamia [c] *18* Or *arrived at Shalem, a* [d] *19* Hebrew *hundred kesitahs;* a kesitah was a unit of money of unknown weight and value. [e] *20 El Elohe Israel* can mean *God, the God of Israel* or *mighty is the God of Israel.* [f] *7* Or *against* [g] *10* Or *move about freely;* also in verse 21

by circumcising all your males. 16Then we will
give you our daughters and take your daughters for ourselves. We'll settle among you and
become one people with you. 17But if you will
not agree to be circumcised, we'll take our sister[a] and go."
18Their proposal seemed good to Hamor
and his son Shechem. 19The young man,
who was the most honored of all his father's
household, lost no time in doing what they
said, because he was delighted with Jacob's
daughter. 20So Hamor and his son Shechem
went to the gate of their city to speak to their
fellow townsmen. 21"These men are friendly
toward us," they said. "Let them live in our
land and trade in it; the land has plenty of
room for them. We can marry their daughters and they can marry ours. 22But the men
will consent to live with us as one people
only on the condition that our males be circumcised, as they themselves are. 23Won't
their livestock, their property and all their
other animals become ours? So let us give
our consent to them, and they will settle
among us."
24All the men who went out of the city gate
agreed with Hamor and his son Shechem, and
every male in the city was circumcised.
25Three days later, while all of them were
still in pain, two of Jacob's sons, Simeon and
Levi, Dinah's brothers, took their swords and
attacked the unsuspecting city, killing every
male. 26They put Hamor and his son Shechem
to the sword and took Dinah from Shechem's
house and left. 27The sons of Jacob came upon
the dead bodies and looted the city where[b]
their sister had been defiled. 28They seized
their flocks and herds and donkeys and everything else of theirs in the city and out in the
fields. 29They carried off all their wealth and
all their women and children, taking as plunder everything in the houses.
30Then Jacob said to Simeon and Levi,
"You have brought trouble on me by making
me a stench to the Canaanites and Perizzites,
the people living in this land. We are few in
number, and if they join forces against me
and attack me, I and my household will be
destroyed."
31But they replied, "Should he have treated
our sister like a prostitute?"

Jacob Returns to Bethel

35 Then God said to Jacob, "Go up to
Bethel and settle there, and build an
altar there to God, who appeared to
you when you were fleeing from your brother
Esau."
2So Jacob said to his household and to all
who were with him, "Get rid of the foreign
gods you have with you, and purify yourselves
and change your clothes. 3Then come, let us
go up to Bethel, where I will build an altar
to God, who answered me in the day of my
distress and who has been with me wherever I
have gone." 4So they gave Jacob all the foreign
gods they had and the rings in their ears, and
Jacob buried them under the oak at Shechem.
5Then they set out, and the terror of God fell
upon the towns all around them so that no
one pursued them.
6Jacob and all the people with him came
to Luz (that is, Bethel) in the land of Canaan.
7There he built an altar, and he called the place
El Bethel,[c] because it was there that God revealed himself to him when he was fleeing
from his brother.
8Now Deborah, Rebekah's nurse, died and
was buried under the oak below Bethel. So it
was named Allon Bacuth.[d]
9After Jacob returned from Paddan Aram,[e]
God appeared to him again and blessed him.
10God said to him, "Your name is Jacob,[f] but
you will no longer be called Jacob; your name
will be Israel.[g]" So he named him Israel.
11And God said to him, "I am God Almighty[h]; be fruitful and increase in number.
A nation and a community of nations will
come from you, and kings will come from
your body. 12The land I gave to Abraham and
Isaac I also give to you, and I will give this
land to your descendants after you." 13Then
God went up from him at the place where he
had talked with him.
14Jacob set up a stone pillar at the place
where God had talked with him, and he
poured out a drink offering on it; he also
poured oil on it. 15Jacob called the place where
God had talked with him Bethel.[i]

The Deaths of Rachel and Isaac

16Then they moved on from Bethel. While
they were still some distance from Ephrath,
Rachel began to give birth and had great difficulty. 17And as she was having great difficulty
in childbirth, the midwife said to her, "Don't

[a] 17 Hebrew *daughter* [b] 27 Or *because* [c] 7 *El Bethel* means *God of Bethel.* [d] 8 *Allon Bacuth* means *oak of weeping.* [e] 9 That is, Northwest Mesopotamia; also in verse 26 [f] 10 *Jacob* means *he grasps the heel* (figuratively, *he deceives*). [g] 10 *Israel* means *he struggles with God.* [h] 11 Hebrew *El-Shaddai* [i] 15 *Bethel* means *house of God.*

be afraid, for you have another son." 18As she
breathed her last—for she was dying—she
named her son Ben-Oni.[a] But his father
named him Benjamin.[b]
19So Rachel died and was buried on the way
to Ephrath (that is, Bethlehem). 20Over her
tomb Jacob set up a pillar, and to this day that
pillar marks Rachel's tomb.
21Israel moved on again and pitched his
tent beyond Migdal Eder. 22While Israel was
living in that region, Reuben went in and slept
with his father's concubine Bilhah, and Israel
heard of it.

Jacob had twelve sons:
23The sons of Leah:
Reuben the firstborn of Jacob,
Simeon, Levi, Judah, Issachar and
Zebulun.
24The sons of Rachel:
Joseph and Benjamin.
25The sons of Rachel's maidservant Bilhah:
Dan and Naphtali.
26The sons of Leah's maidservant Zilpah:
Gad and Asher.
These were the sons of Jacob, who were
born to him in Paddan Aram.

27Jacob came home to his father Isaac in
Mamre, near Kiriath Arba (that is, Hebron),
where Abraham and Isaac had stayed. 28Isaac
lived a hundred and eighty years. 29Then he
breathed his last and died and was gathered to
his people, old and full of years. And his sons
Esau and Jacob buried him.

Esau's Descendants

36 This is the account of Esau (that is,
Edom).
2Esau took his wives from the wom-
en of Canaan: Adah daughter of Elon the
Hittite, and Oholibamah daughter of
Anah and granddaughter of Zibeon the
Hivite— 3also Basemath daughter of Ishmael and sister of Nebaioth.
4Adah bore Eliphaz to Esau, Basemath
bore Reuel, 5and Oholibamah bore Jeush,
Jalam and Korah. These were the sons of
Esau, who were born to him in Canaan.
6Esau took his wives and sons and
daughters and all the members of his
household, as well as his livestock and
all his other animals and all the goods he
had acquired in Canaan, and moved to a
land some distance from his brother Jacob. 7Their possessions were too great for
them to remain together; the land where
they were staying could not support them
both because of their livestock. 8So Esau
(that is, Edom) settled in the hill country
of Seir.

9This is the account of Esau the father of
the Edomites in the hill country of Seir.
10These are the names of Esau's sons:
Eliphaz, the son of Esau's wife Adah,
and Reuel, the son of Esau's wife Basemath.
11The sons of Eliphaz:
Teman, Omar, Zepho, Gatam and Kenaz.
12Esau's son Eliphaz also had a concubine named Timna, who bore him
Amalek. These were grandsons of
Esau's wife Adah.
13The sons of Reuel:
Nahath, Zerah, Shammah and Mizzah. These were grandsons of Esau's
wife Basemath.
14The sons of Esau's wife Oholibamah
daughter of Anah and granddaughter of
Zibeon, whom she bore to Esau:
Jeush, Jalam and Korah.

15These were the chiefs among Esau's descendants:
The sons of Eliphaz the firstborn of
Esau:
Chiefs Teman, Omar, Zepho, Kenaz,
16Korah,[c] Gatam and Amalek. These
were the chiefs descended from Eliphaz in Edom; they were grandsons of
Adah.
17The sons of Esau's son Reuel:
Chiefs Nahath, Zerah, Shammah and
Mizzah. These were the chiefs descended from Reuel in Edom; they were
grandsons of Esau's wife Basemath.
18The sons of Esau's wife Oholibamah:
Chiefs Jeush, Jalam and Korah. These
were the chiefs descended from Esau's
wife Oholibamah daughter of Anah.
19These were the sons of Esau (that is,
Edom), and these were their chiefs.

20These were the sons of Seir the Horite,
who were living in the region:
Lotan, Shobal, Zibeon, Anah, 21Di-
shon, Ezer and Dishan. These sons of
Seir in Edom were Horite chiefs.
22The sons of Lotan:

---

[a] 18 *Ben-Oni* means *son of my trouble.* [b] 18 *Benjamin* means *son of my right hand.* [c] 16 Masoretic Text; Samaritan Pentateuch (see also Gen. 36:11 and 1 Chron. 1:36) does not have *Korah.*

Hori and Homam.[a] Timna was Lotan's sister.
23 The sons of Shobal:
Alvan, Manahath, Ebal, Shepho and Onam.
24 The sons of Zibeon:
Aiah and Anah. This is the Anah who discovered the hot springs[b] in the desert while he was grazing the donkeys of his father Zibeon.
25 The children of Anah:
Dishon and Oholibamah daughter of Anah.
26 The sons of Dishon[c]:
Hemdan, Eshban, Ithran and Keran.
27 The sons of Ezer:
Bilhan, Zaavan and Akan.
28 The sons of Dishan:
Uz and Aran.
29 These were the Horite chiefs:
Lotan, Shobal, Zibeon, Anah, 30 Dishon, Ezer and Dishan. These were the Horite chiefs, according to their divisions, in the land of Seir.

The Rulers of Edom

31 These were the kings who reigned in Edom before any Israelite king reigned[d]:
32 Bela son of Beor became king of Edom. His city was named Dinhabah.
33 When Bela died, Jobab son of Zerah from Bozrah succeeded him as king.
34 When Jobab died, Husham from the land of the Temanites succeeded him as king.
35 When Husham died, Hadad son of Bedad, who defeated Midian in the country of Moab, succeeded him as king. His city was named Avith.
36 When Hadad died, Samlah from Masrekah succeeded him as king.
37 When Samlah died, Shaul from Rehoboth on the river[e] succeeded him as king.
38 When Shaul died, Baal-Hanan son of Acbor succeeded him as king.
39 When Baal-Hanan son of Acbor died, Hadad[f] succeeded him as king. His city was named Pau, and his wife's name was Mehetabel daughter of Matred, the daughter of Me-Zahab.

40 These were the chiefs descended from Esau, by name, according to their clans and regions:
Timna, Alvah, Jetheth, 41 Oholibamah, Elah, Pinon, 42 Kenaz, Teman, Mibzar, 43 Magdiel and Iram. These were the chiefs of Edom, according to their settlements in the land they occupied.

This was Esau the father of the Edomites.

Joseph's Dreams

37 Jacob lived in the land where his father had stayed, the land of Canaan.

2 This is the account of Jacob.

Joseph, a young man of seventeen, was tending the flocks with his brothers, the sons of Bilhah and the sons of Zilpah, his father's wives, and he brought their father a bad report about them.
3 Now Israel loved Joseph more than any of his other sons, because he had been born to him in his old age; and he made a richly ornamented[g] robe for him. 4 When his brothers saw that their father loved him more than any of them, they hated him and could not speak a kind word to him.
5 Joseph had a dream, and when he told it to his brothers, they hated him all the more.
6 He said to them, "Listen to this dream I had:
7 We were binding sheaves of grain out in the field when suddenly my sheaf rose and stood upright, while your sheaves gathered around mine and bowed down to it."
8 His brothers said to him, "Do you intend to reign over us? Will you actually rule us?" And they hated him all the more because of his dream and what he had said.
9 Then he had another dream, and he told it to his brothers. "Listen," he said, "I had another dream, and this time the sun and moon and eleven stars were bowing down to me."
10 When he told his father as well as his brothers, his father rebuked him and said, "What is this dream you had? Will your mother and I and your brothers actually come and bow down to the ground before you?" 11 His brothers were jealous of him, but his father kept the matter in mind.

Joseph Sold by His Brothers

12 Now his brothers had gone to graze their father's flocks near Shechem, 13 and Israel said

[a] 22 Hebrew *Hemam,* a variant of *Homam* (see 1 Chron. 1:39) [b] 24 Vulgate; Syriac *discovered water;* the meaning of the Hebrew for this word is uncertain. [c] 26 Hebrew *Dishan,* a variant of *Dishon* [d] 31 Or *before an Israelite king reigned over them* [e] 37 Possibly the Euphrates [f] 39 Many manuscripts of the Masoretic Text, Samaritan Pentateuch and Syriac (see also 1 Chron. 1:50); most manuscripts of the Masoretic Text *Hadar* [g] 3 The meaning of the Hebrew for *richly ornamented* is uncertain; also in verses 23 and 32.

to Joseph, "As you know, your brothers are
grazing the flocks near Shechem. Come, I am
going to send you to them."
"Very well," he replied.
14So he said to him, "Go and see if all is
well with your brothers and with the flocks,
and bring word back to me." Then he sent him
off from the Valley of Hebron.
When Joseph arrived at Shechem, 15a man
found him wandering around in the fields and
asked him, "What are you looking for?"
16He replied, "I'm looking for my brothers.
Can you tell me where they are grazing their
flocks?"
17"They have moved on from here," the
man answered. "I heard them say, 'Let's go to
Dothan.' "
So Joseph went after his brothers and found
them near Dothan. 18But they saw him in the
distance, and before he reached them, they
plotted to kill him.
19"Here comes that dreamer!" they said to
each other. 20"Come now, let's kill him and
throw him into one of these cisterns and say
that a ferocious animal devoured him. Then
we'll see what comes of his dreams."
21When Reuben heard this, he tried to rescue him from their hands. "Let's not take his
life," he said. 22"Don't shed any blood. Throw
him into this cistern here in the desert, but
don't lay a hand on him." Reuben said this to
rescue him from them and take him back to
his father.
23So when Joseph came to his brothers,
they stripped him of his robe—the richly ornamented robe he was wearing— 24and they
took him and threw him into the cistern.
Now the cistern was empty; there was no water in it.
25As they sat down to eat their meal, they
looked up and saw a caravan of Ishmaelites
coming from Gilead. Their camels were loaded with spices, balm and myrrh, and they were
on their way to take them down to Egypt.
26Judah said to his brothers, "What will we
gain if we kill our brother and cover up his
blood? 27Come, let's sell him to the Ishmaelites and not lay our hands on him; after all, he
is our brother, our own flesh and blood." His
brothers agreed.
28So when the Midianite merchants came
by, his brothers pulled Joseph up out of the cistern and sold him for twenty shekels[a] of silver
to the Ishmaelites, who took him to Egypt.
29When Reuben returned to the cistern
and saw that Joseph was not there, he tore his
clothes. 30He went back to his brothers and
said, "The boy isn't there! Where can I turn
now?"
31Then they got Joseph's robe, slaughtered a
goat and dipped the robe in the blood. 32They
took the ornamented robe back to their father
and said, "We found this. Examine it to see
whether it is your son's robe."
33He recognized it and said, "It is my son's
robe! Some ferocious animal has devoured
him. Joseph has surely been torn to pieces."
34Then Jacob tore his clothes, put on sackcloth and mourned for his son many days. 35All
his sons and daughters came to comfort him,
but he refused to be comforted. "No," he said,
"in mourning will I go down to the grave[b] to
my son." So his father wept for him.
36Meanwhile, the Midianites[c] sold Joseph
in Egypt to Potiphar, one of Pharaoh's officials, the captain of the guard.

Judah and Tamar

38 At that time, Judah left his brothers
and went down to stay with a man of
Adullam named Hirah. 2There Judah
met the daughter of a Canaanite man named
Shua. He married her and lay with her; 3she
became pregnant and gave birth to a son, who
was named Er. 4She conceived again and gave
birth to a son and named him Onan. 5She
gave birth to still another son and named him
Shelah. It was at Kezib that she gave birth to
him.
6Judah got a wife for Er, his firstborn, and
her name was Tamar. 7But Er, Judah's firstborn, was wicked in the LORD's sight; so the
LORD put him to death.
8Then Judah said to Onan, "Lie with
your brother's wife and fulfill your duty to
her as a brother-in-law to produce offspring
for your brother." 9But Onan knew that the
offspring would not be his; so whenever he
lay with his brother's wife, he spilled his semen on the ground to keep from producing
offspring for his brother. 10What he did was
wicked in the LORD's sight; so he put him to
death also.
11Judah then said to his daughter-in-law
Tamar, "Live as a widow in your father's house
until my son Shelah grows up." For he thought,
"He may die too, just like his brothers." So Tamar went to live in her father's house.
12After a long time Judah's wife, the daughter of Shua, died. When Judah had recovered

[a] *28* That is, about 8 ounces (about 0.2 kilogram) [b] *35* Hebrew *Sheol* [c] *36* Samaritan Pentateuch, Septuagint, Vulgate and Syriac (see also verse 28); Masoretic Text *Medanites*

from his grief, he went up to Timnah, to the
men who were shearing his sheep, and his
friend Hirah the Adullamite went with him.
13When Tamar was told, "Your father-
in-law is on his way to Timnah to shear his
sheep," 14she took off her widow's clothes,
covered herself with a veil to disguise herself,
and then sat down at the entrance to Enaim,
which is on the road to Timnah. For she saw
that, though Shelah had now grown up, she
had not been given to him as his wife.
15When Judah saw her, he thought she
was a prostitute, for she had covered her face.
16Not realizing that she was his daughter-in-
law, he went over to her by the roadside and
said, "Come now, let me sleep with you."

"And what will you give me to sleep with
you?" she asked.

17"I'll send you a young goat from my
flock," he said.

"Will you give me something as a pledge
until you send it?" she asked.

18He said, "What pledge should I give
you?"

"Your seal and its cord, and the staff in your
hand," she answered. So he gave them to her
and slept with her, and she became pregnant
by him. 19After she left, she took off her veil
and put on her widow's clothes again.
20Meanwhile Judah sent the young goat by
his friend the Adullamite in order to get his
pledge back from the woman, but he did not
find her. 21He asked the men who lived there,
"Where is the shrine prostitute who was beside the road at Enaim?"

"There hasn't been any shrine prostitute
here," they said.

22So he went back to Judah and said, "I
didn't find her. Besides, the men who lived
there said, 'There hasn't been any shrine prostitute here.' "

23Then Judah said, "Let her keep what she
has, or we will become a laughingstock. After
all, I did send her this young goat, but you
didn't find her."

24About three months later Judah was told,
"Your daughter-in-law Tamar is guilty of prostitution, and as a result she is now pregnant."

Judah said, "Bring her out and have her
burned to death!"

25As she was being brought out, she sent a
message to her father-in-law. "I am pregnant
by the man who owns these," she said. And
she added, "See if you recognize whose seal
and cord and staff these are."

26Judah recognized them and said, "She is
more righteous than I, since I wouldn't give
her to my son Shelah." And he did not sleep
with her again.

27When the time came for her to give birth,
there were twin boys in her womb. 28As she
was giving birth, one of them put out his
hand; so the midwife took a scarlet thread and
tied it on his wrist and said, "This one came
out first." 29But when he drew back his hand,
his brother came out, and she said, "So this is
how you have broken out!" And he was named
Perez.[a] 30Then his brother, who had the scarlet thread on his wrist, came out and he was
given the name Zerah.[b]

Joseph and Potiphar's Wife

39 Now Joseph had been taken down to
Egypt. Potiphar, an Egyptian who was
one of Pharaoh's officials, the captain of
the guard, bought him from the Ishmaelites
who had taken him there.

2The LORD was with Joseph and he prospered, and he lived in the house of his Egyptian
master. 3When his master saw that the LORD
was with him and that the LORD gave him success in everything he did, 4Joseph found favor
in his eyes and became his attendant. Potiphar
put him in charge of his household, and he
entrusted to his care everything he owned.
5From the time he put him in charge of his
household and of all that he owned, the LORD
blessed the household of the Egyptian because
of Joseph. The blessing of the LORD was on
everything Potiphar had, both in the house
and in the field. 6So he left in Joseph's care
everything he had; with Joseph in charge, he
did not concern himself with anything except
the food he ate.

Now Joseph was well-built and handsome,
7and after a while his master's wife took notice
of Joseph and said, "Come to bed with me!"

8But he refused. "With me in charge," he
told her, "my master does not concern himself with anything in the house; everything he
owns he has entrusted to my care. 9No one
is greater in this house than I am. My master has withheld nothing from me except you,
because you are his wife. How then could I
do such a wicked thing and sin against God?"
10And though she spoke to Joseph day after
day, he refused to go to bed with her or even
be with her.

11One day he went into the house to attend to his duties, and none of the household

[a] 29 *Perez* means *breaking out.* [b] 30 *Zerah* can mean *scarlet* or *brightness.*

SAFEGUARDING YOUR MARRIAGE

> **"My master has withheld nothing from me except you, because you are his wife. How then could I do such a wicked thing and sin against God?"**
>
> — Genesis 39:9

let's talk

- When do we feel vulnerable and attracted to others?
- Other than each other, who are our closest friends? In what ways are these people helpful to our marriage? In what ways are they not?
- How can we build inner strength to deal with those times when our emotions beg us to seek comfort in others?

The pastor and his wife thought infidelity was a problem for others, not them. They were devoted to each other and had two lovely daughters. They helped other couples prepare for marriage. They counseled those having marital problems on how to get back together.

But then she had an affair with the chairman of the church board. While her husband was out making calls on people in distress, she was at home in bed with his closest friend.

Everybody was dumbfounded. It didn't make sense!

But maybe it did. Think of Potiphar's wife, a vibrant woman left home too often by an important husband. She got the leftovers of his energy after he had given his best to those who paid his salary. Feeling unsatisfied, she was attracted to someone new, young and good-looking—someone who reminded her that something was missing in her life.

So too with the pastor's wife. When she and her husband took the call to this new congregation, the board chairman paid special attention to their relocation concerns. He became fast friends with the new pastor. He went out of his way to ensure that the pastor's wife was settling in well. While the pastor's star rose, his wife and the board chairman did a little dance of kindness with each other.

All three played a part in the infidelity. The pastor should have paid more attention to his wife. The wife should have been aware of the danger of coffees and lunches with the chairman. And the chairman should have stayed within appropriate boundaries instead of flitting lightly across them.

Infidelity can happen to any couple—even those devoted to spiritual pursuits. For God has made us fully human and fully alive, and we often feel it most in our sexuality.

How does a couple deal with sexual temptations? First, develop a healthy self-awareness and a clear sense of moral boundaries. Joseph knew who he was and what his place was in Egyptian society. Potiphar's wife, on the other hand, helped herself to whatever she wanted, regardless of whether it was right or wrong.

Second, have an exit strategy for situations that seem overpowering. Be like Joseph, who knew when to get out of a morally suspect position. Potiphar's wife made Joseph's life miserable after he resisted her, but imprisonment was nothing compared to the spiritual cost of an affair.

Third, don't deny your vulnerability. We are all prey to temptation. So talk to your spouse about problems such as overwork, loneliness and time with others before they become excuses for an affair. Build a wall of protection around your relationship before you begin to drift apart.

—WAYNE BROUWER

FOR YOUR NEXT DEVOTIONAL READING, TURN TO PAGE 49.

servants was inside. 12She caught him by his
cloak and said, "Come to bed with me!" But
he left his cloak in her hand and ran out of
the house.
13When she saw that he had left his cloak in
her hand and had run out of the house, 14she
called her household servants. "Look," she said
to them, "this Hebrew has been brought to us
to make sport of us! He came in here to sleep
with me, but I screamed. 15When he heard me
scream for help, he left his cloak beside me
and ran out of the house."
16She kept his cloak beside her until his
master came home. 17Then she told him this
story: "That Hebrew slave you brought us
came to me to make sport of me. 18But as
soon as I screamed for help, he left his cloak
beside me and ran out of the house."
19When his master heard the story his wife
told him, saying, "This is how your slave treated me," he burned with anger. 20Joseph's master took him and put him in prison, the place
where the king's prisoners were confined.
But while Joseph was there in the prison,
21the LORD was with him; he showed him
kindness and granted him favor in the eyes of
the prison warden. 22So the warden put Joseph in charge of all those held in the prison,
and he was made responsible for all that was
done there. 23The warden paid no attention
to anything under Joseph's care, because the
LORD was with Joseph and gave him success
in whatever he did.

The Cupbearer and the Baker

40 Some time later, the cupbearer and the
baker of the king of Egypt offended
their master, the king of Egypt. 2Phar-
aoh was angry with his two officials, the chief
cupbearer and the chief baker, 3and put them
in custody in the house of the captain of the
guard, in the same prison where Joseph was
confined. 4The captain of the guard assigned
them to Joseph, and he attended them.
After they had been in custody for some
time, 5each of the two men—the cupbearer
and the baker of the king of Egypt, who were
being held in prison—had a dream the same
night, and each dream had a meaning of its
own.
6When Joseph came to them the next
morning, he saw that they were dejected. 7So
he asked Pharaoh's officials who were in custody with him in his master's house, "Why are
your faces so sad today?"
8"We both had dreams," they answered,
"but there is no one to interpret them."
Then Joseph said to them, "Do not interpretations belong to God? Tell me your
dreams."
9So the chief cupbearer told Joseph his
dream. He said to him, "In my dream I saw
a vine in front of me, 10and on the vine were
three branches. As soon as it budded, it blossomed, and its clusters ripened into grapes.
11Pharaoh's cup was in my hand, and I took
the grapes, squeezed them into Pharaoh's cup
and put the cup in his hand."
12"This is what it means," Joseph said to
him. "The three branches are three days.
13Within three days Pharaoh will lift up
your head and restore you to your position,
and you will put Pharaoh's cup in his hand,
just as you used to do when you were his
cupbearer. 14But when all goes well with
you, remember me and show me kindness;
mention me to Pharaoh and get me out of
this prison. 15For I was forcibly carried off
from the land of the Hebrews, and even here
I have done nothing to deserve being put in
a dungeon."
16When the chief baker saw that Joseph
had given a favorable interpretation, he said
to Joseph, "I too had a dream: On my head
were three baskets of bread.[a] 17In the top basket were all kinds of baked goods for Pharaoh,
but the birds were eating them out of the basket on my head."
18"This is what it means," Joseph said. "The
three baskets are three days. 19Within three
days Pharaoh will lift off your head and hang
you on a tree.[b] And the birds will eat away
your flesh."
20Now the third day was Pharaoh's birthday, and he gave a feast for all his officials. He
lifted up the heads of the chief cupbearer and
the chief baker in the presence of his officials:
21He restored the chief cupbearer to his position, so that he once again put the cup into
Pharaoh's hand, 22but he hanged[c] the chief
baker, just as Joseph had said to them in his
interpretation.
23The chief cupbearer, however, did not remember Joseph; he forgot him.

Pharaoh's Dreams

41 When two full years had passed, Pharaoh had a dream: He was standing by
the Nile, 2when out of the river there
came up seven cows, sleek and fat, and they

[a] 16 Or *three wicker baskets* [b] 19 Or *and impale you on a pole* [c] 22 Or *impaled*

grazed among the reeds. 3After them, seven
other cows, ugly and gaunt, came up out of
the Nile and stood beside those on the river-
bank. 4And the cows that were ugly and gaunt
ate up the seven sleek, fat cows. Then Pharaoh
woke up.
5He fell asleep again and had a second
dream: Seven heads of grain, healthy and good,
were growing on a single stalk. 6After them,
seven other heads of grain sprouted—thin and
scorched by the east wind. 7The thin heads of
grain swallowed up the seven healthy, full heads.
Then Pharaoh woke up; it had been a dream.
8In the morning his mind was troubled, so
he sent for all the magicians and wise men of
Egypt. Pharaoh told them his dreams, but no
one could interpret them for him.
9Then the chief cupbearer said to Pharaoh,
"Today I am reminded of my shortcomings.
10Pharaoh was once angry with his servants,
and he imprisoned me and the chief baker in
the house of the captain of the guard. 11Each
of us had a dream the same night, and each
dream had a meaning of its own. 12Now a
young Hebrew was there with us, a servant
of the captain of the guard. We told him our
dreams, and he interpreted them for us, giving each man the interpretation of his dream.
13And things turned out exactly as he interpreted them to us: I was restored to my position, and the other man was hanged.[a]"
14So Pharaoh sent for Joseph, and he was
quickly brought from the dungeon. When he
had shaved and changed his clothes, he came
before Pharaoh.
15Pharaoh said to Joseph, "I had a dream,
and no one can interpret it. But I have heard
it said of you that when you hear a dream you
can interpret it."
16"I cannot do it," Joseph replied to Pharaoh, "but God will give Pharaoh the answer
he desires."
17Then Pharaoh said to Joseph, "In my
dream I was standing on the bank of the Nile,
18when out of the river there came up seven
cows, fat and sleek, and they grazed among
the reeds. 19After them, seven other cows
came up—scrawny and very ugly and lean. I
had never seen such ugly cows in all the land
of Egypt. 20The lean, ugly cows ate up the sev-
en fat cows that came up first. 21But even after they ate them, no one could tell that they
had done so; they looked just as ugly as before.
Then I woke up.
22"In my dreams I also saw seven heads
of grain, full and good, growing on a single
stalk. 23After them, seven other heads sprouted—withered and thin and scorched by the
east wind. 24The thin heads of grain swallowed
up the seven good heads. I told this to the magicians, but none could explain it to me."
25Then Joseph said to Pharaoh, "The
dreams of Pharaoh are one and the same. God
has revealed to Pharaoh what he is about to
do. 26The seven good cows are seven years, and
the seven good heads of grain are seven years;
it is one and the same dream. 27The seven lean,
ugly cows that came up afterward are seven
years, and so are the seven worthless heads of
grain scorched by the east wind: They are sev-
en years of famine.
28"It is just as I said to Pharaoh: God
has shown Pharaoh what he is about to do.
29Seven years of great abundance are coming
throughout the land of Egypt, 30but seven
years of famine will follow them. Then all the
abundance in Egypt will be forgotten, and the
famine will ravage the land. 31The abundance
in the land will not be remembered, because
the famine that follows it will be so severe.
32The reason the dream was given to Pharaoh
in two forms is that the matter has been firmly
decided by God, and God will do it soon.
33"And now let Pharaoh look for a discerning and wise man and put him in charge
of the land of Egypt. 34Let Pharaoh appoint
commissioners over the land to take a fifth of
the harvest of Egypt during the seven years of
abundance. 35They should collect all the food
of these good years that are coming and store
up the grain under the authority of Pharaoh,
to be kept in the cities for food. 36This food
should be held in reserve for the country, to be
used during the seven years of famine that will
come upon Egypt, so that the country may
not be ruined by the famine."
37The plan seemed good to Pharaoh and
to all his officials. 38So Pharaoh asked them,
"Can we find anyone like this man, one in
whom is the spirit of God[b]?"
39Then Pharaoh said to Joseph, "Since God
has made all this known to you, there is no one
so discerning and wise as you. 40You shall be
in charge of my palace, and all my people are
to submit to your orders. Only with respect to
the throne will I be greater than you."

Joseph in Charge of Egypt

41So Pharaoh said to Joseph, "I hereby put
you in charge of the whole land of Egypt."

[a] 13 Or *impaled* [b] 38 Or *of the gods*

42Then Pharaoh took his signet ring from his finger and put it on Joseph's finger. He dressed him in robes of fine linen and put a gold chain around his neck. 43He had him ride in a chariot as his second-in-command,[a] and men shouted before him, "Make way[b]!" Thus he put him in charge of the whole land of Egypt.

44Then Pharaoh said to Joseph, "I am Pharaoh, but without your word no one will lift hand or foot in all Egypt." 45Pharaoh gave Joseph the name Zaphenath-Paneah and gave him Asenath daughter of Potiphera, priest of On,[c] to be his wife. And Joseph went throughout the land of Egypt.

46Joseph was thirty years old when he entered the service of Pharaoh king of Egypt. And Joseph went out from Pharaoh's presence and traveled throughout Egypt. 47During the seven years of abundance the land produced plentifully. 48Joseph collected all the food produced in those seven years of abundance in Egypt and stored it in the cities. In each city he put the food grown in the fields surrounding it. 49Joseph stored up huge quantities of grain, like the sand of the sea; it was so much that he stopped keeping records because it was beyond measure.

50Before the years of famine came, two sons were born to Joseph by Asenath daughter of Potiphera, priest of On. 51Joseph named his firstborn Manasseh[d] and said, "It is because God has made me forget all my trouble and all my father's household." 52The second son he named Ephraim[e] and said, "It is because God has made me fruitful in the land of my suffering."

53The seven years of abundance in Egypt came to an end, 54and the seven years of famine began, just as Joseph had said. There was famine in all the other lands, but in the whole land of Egypt there was food. 55When all Egypt began to feel the famine, the people cried to Pharaoh for food. Then Pharaoh told all the Egyptians, "Go to Joseph and do what he tells you."

56When the famine had spread over the whole country, Joseph opened the storehouses and sold grain to the Egyptians, for the famine was severe throughout Egypt. 57And all the countries came to Egypt to buy grain from Joseph, because the famine was severe in all the world.

Joseph's Brothers Go to Egypt

42 When Jacob learned that there was grain in Egypt, he said to his sons, "Why do you just keep looking at each other?" 2He continued, "I have heard that there is grain in Egypt. Go down there and buy some for us, so that we may live and not die."

3Then ten of Joseph's brothers went down to buy grain from Egypt. 4But Jacob did not send Benjamin, Joseph's brother, with the others, because he was afraid that harm might come to him. 5So Israel's sons were among those who went to buy grain, for the famine was in the land of Canaan also.

6Now Joseph was the governor of the land, the one who sold grain to all its people. So when Joseph's brothers arrived, they bowed down to him with their faces to the ground. 7As soon as Joseph saw his brothers, he recognized them, but he pretended to be a stranger and spoke harshly to them. "Where do you come from?" he asked.

"From the land of Canaan," they replied, "to buy food."

8Although Joseph recognized his brothers, they did not recognize him. 9Then he remembered his dreams about them and said to them, "You are spies! You have come to see where our land is unprotected."

10"No, my lord," they answered. "Your servants have come to buy food. 11We are all the sons of one man. Your servants are honest men, not spies."

12"No!" he said to them. "You have come to see where our land is unprotected."

13But they replied, "Your servants were twelve brothers, the sons of one man, who lives in the land of Canaan. The youngest is now with our father, and one is no more."

14Joseph said to them, "It is just as I told you: You are spies! 15And this is how you will be tested: As surely as Pharaoh lives, you will not leave this place unless your youngest brother comes here. 16Send one of your number to get your brother; the rest of you will be kept in prison, so that your words may be tested to see if you are telling the truth. If you are not, then as surely as Pharaoh lives, you are spies!" 17And he put them all in custody for three days.

18On the third day, Joseph said to them, "Do this and you will live, for I fear God: 19If you are honest men, let one of your brothers stay here in prison, while the rest of you go and take grain back for your starving house-

[a] 43 Or *in the chariot of his second-in-command*; or *in his second chariot* [b] 43 Or *Bow down* [c] 45 That is, Heliopolis; also in verse 50
[d] 51 *Manasseh* sounds like and may be derived from the Hebrew for *forget.* [e] 52 *Ephraim* sounds like the Hebrew for *twice fruitful.*

THURSDAY
READ GENESIS 41:41–52

AN UNBELIEVING SPOUSE AND GOD'S PLAN

Pharaoh gave Joseph the name Zaphenath-Paneah and gave him Asenath daughter of Potiphera, priest of On, to be his wife.

— Genesis 41:45

We would all like to have an Einstein, a Tchaikovsky or a Rosa Parks in the family lineage. We're less proud of the "rebels" in the family—and every family has at least one or two of those.

Joseph introduced a whopper into his lineage when he married a pagan woman. Granted, she was given to him by his boss, Egypt's pharaoh. Granted, Joseph lived a couple hundred miles away from people who believed in the one true God. But he really went out on a limb when he married this woman: Asenath, daughter of the priest of On in the cult of Ra, the sun god of Egypt.

The wonder is that God can work through anyone, redeeming families regardless of ancestry, poor choices and bad marriages. For example, my brother and his wife were used by God to redeem the marriages of two of their children. When my brother's two sons chose unbelieving wives and conceived babies before the weddings, my brother chose not to condemn them. Instead, he purposefully spent days with each couple, offering them the opportunity to accept God's grace, be forgiven and start their marriages on the right track.

As a result, both wives became Christians. We don't yet see the long-term implications of those redemptions, but we know that the six children of those marriages are being given a Christian upbringing. What if the wives had not become believers? It would have been more difficult, but still important, for the believing husbands to have introduced their children to Christ.

Joseph knew Yahweh was the one true God. He was taught that in his childhood. But because his brothers had sold him into slavery, Joseph spent the rest of his life in Egypt, surrounded by unbelievers. When Joseph was given a wife by the ruler of Egypt, he could hardly have refused.

God works his plan, no matter what. Joseph had two sons with Asenath: Manasseh and Ephraim. We know Joseph raised his children to follow God because their descendants were ultimately welcomed into the tribes of Israel. By the time the Israelites entered the promised land, the census of men in the tribe of Manasseh who were able to serve in the army numbered 52,700 (see Numbers 26:34). Some of the daughters of that tribe successfully crusaded for the right to receive land as their inheritance (see Numbers 27:1–11). Ephraim's big claim to fame, although it took 400 years to come about, was producing Joshua (see 1 Chronicles 7:20–27), who led the Israelites into the promised land.

Families matter because all people matter to God. And yet God redeems people one by one, working his plan throughout generations. The children God gives us today will play roles in the future that we can't even imagine. Like Joseph, our job is to raise our children to know and trust the one true God. It is also our responsibility to lead them to salvation through faith in Jesus Christ, God's only Son. There is no better legacy to give to future generations.

—MARY ANN JEFFREYS

let's talk

- ✦ Name some people in our families who were instrumental in leading us to salvation through faith in Jesus Christ. In what ways did they influence us?
- ✦ What other people helped nurture our faith?
- ✦ What people in our families remain distanced from God? What are some things we might do to bring them to the Lord?

FOR YOUR NEXT DEVOTIONAL READING, TURN TO PAGE 63.

holds. 20But you must bring your youngest
brother to me, so that your words may be
verified and that you may not die." This they
proceeded to do.
21They said to one another, "Surely we are
being punished because of our brother. We
saw how distressed he was when he pleaded
with us for his life, but we would not listen;
that's why this distress has come upon us."
22Reuben replied, "Didn't I tell you not
to sin against the boy? But you wouldn't listen! Now we must give an accounting for his
blood." 23They did not realize that Joseph
could understand them, since he was using an
interpreter.
24He turned away from them and began
to weep, but then turned back and spoke to
them again. He had Simeon taken from them
and bound before their eyes.
25Joseph gave orders to fill their bags with
grain, to put each man's silver back in his sack,
and to give them provisions for their journey.
After this was done for them, 26they loaded
their grain on their donkeys and left.
27At the place where they stopped for the
night one of them opened his sack to get feed
for his donkey, and he saw his silver in the
mouth of his sack. 28"My silver has been returned," he said to his brothers. "Here it is in
my sack."
Their hearts sank and they turned to each
other trembling and said, "What is this that
God has done to us?"
29When they came to their father Jacob in
the land of Canaan, they told him all that had
happened to them. They said, 30"The man
who is lord over the land spoke harshly to us
and treated us as though we were spying on
the land. 31But we said to him, 'We are honest men; we are not spies. 32We were twelve
brothers, sons of one father. One is no more,
and the youngest is now with our father in Canaan.'
33"Then the man who is lord over the land
said to us, 'This is how I will know whether you are honest men: Leave one of your
brothers here with me, and take food for your
starving households and go. 34But bring your
youngest brother to me so I will know that
you are not spies but honest men. Then I will
give your brother back to you, and you can
trade[a] in the land.' "
35As they were emptying their sacks, there
in each man's sack was his pouch of silver!
When they and their father saw the money
pouches, they were frightened. 36Their father
Jacob said to them, "You have deprived me of
my children. Joseph is no more and Simeon
is no more, and now you want to take Benjamin. Everything is against me!"
37Then Reuben said to his father, "You may
put both of my sons to death if I do not bring
him back to you. Entrust him to my care, and
I will bring him back."
38But Jacob said, "My son will not go down
there with you; his brother is dead and he is
the only one left. If harm comes to him on the
journey you are taking, you will bring my gray
head down to the grave[b] in sorrow."

The Second Journey to Egypt

43 Now the famine was still severe in the
land. 2So when they had eaten all the
grain they had brought from Egypt,
their father said to them, "Go back and buy
us a little more food."
3But Judah said to him, "The man warned
us solemnly, 'You will not see my face again
unless your brother is with you.' 4If you will
send our brother along with us, we will go
down and buy food for you. 5But if you will
not send him, we will not go down, because
the man said to us, 'You will not see my face
again unless your brother is with you.' "
6Israel asked, "Why did you bring this trouble on me by telling the man you had another
brother?"
7They replied, "The man questioned us
closely about ourselves and our family. 'Is your
father still living?' he asked us. 'Do you have
another brother?' We simply answered his
questions. How were we to know he would
say, 'Bring your brother down here'?"
8Then Judah said to Israel his father, "Send
the boy along with me and we will go at once,
so that we and you and our children may live
and not die. 9I myself will guarantee his safety; you can hold me personally responsible
for him. If I do not bring him back to you
and set him here before you, I will bear the
blame before you all my life. 10As it is, if we
had not delayed, we could have gone and returned twice."
11Then their father Israel said to them,
"If it must be, then do this: Put some of the
best products of the land in your bags and
take them down to the man as a gift—a little balm and a little honey, some spices and
myrrh, some pistachio nuts and almonds.
12Take double the amount of silver with you,

[a] 34 Or *move about freely* [b] 38 Hebrew *Sheol*

for you must return the silver that was put
back into the mouths of your sacks. Perhaps
it was a mistake. 13 Take your brother also and
go back to the man at once. 14 And may God
Almighty[a] grant you mercy before the man so
that he will let your other brother and Benjamin come back with you. As for me, if I am
bereaved, I am bereaved."

15 So the men took the gifts and double the
amount of silver, and Benjamin also. They
hurried down to Egypt and presented themselves to Joseph. 16 When Joseph saw Benjamin with them, he said to the steward of his
house, "Take these men to my house, slaughter an animal and prepare dinner; they are to
eat with me at noon."

17 The man did as Joseph told him and took
the men to Joseph's house. 18 Now the men
were frightened when they were taken to his
house. They thought, "We were brought here
because of the silver that was put back into our
sacks the first time. He wants to attack us and
overpower us and seize us as slaves and take
our donkeys."

19 So they went up to Joseph's steward and
spoke to him at the entrance to the house.
20 "Please, sir," they said, "we came down here
the first time to buy food. 21 But at the place
where we stopped for the night we opened
our sacks and each of us found his silver—the
exact weight—in the mouth of his sack. So
we have brought it back with us. 22 We have
also brought additional silver with us to buy
food. We don't know who put our silver in our
sacks."

23 "It's all right," he said. "Don't be afraid.
Your God, the God of your father, has given
you treasure in your sacks; I received your silver." Then he brought Simeon out to them.

24 The steward took the men into Joseph's
house, gave them water to wash their feet and
provided fodder for their donkeys. 25 They prepared their gifts for Joseph's arrival at noon,
because they had heard that they were to eat
there.

26 When Joseph came home, they presented to him the gifts they had brought into the
house, and they bowed down before him to
the ground. 27 He asked them how they were,
and then he said, "How is your aged father
you told me about? Is he still living?"

28 They replied, "Your servant our father is
still alive and well." And they bowed low to
pay him honor.

29 As he looked about and saw his brother
Benjamin, his own mother's son, he asked, "Is
this your youngest brother, the one you told
me about?" And he said, "God be gracious to
you, my son." 30 Deeply moved at the sight of
his brother, Joseph hurried out and looked for
a place to weep. He went into his private room
and wept there.

31 After he had washed his face, he came
out and, controlling himself, said, "Serve the
food."

32 They served him by himself, the brothers by themselves, and the Egyptians who ate
with him by themselves, because Egyptians
could not eat with Hebrews, for that is detestable to Egyptians. 33 The men had been seated before him in the order of their ages, from
the firstborn to the youngest; and they looked
at each other in astonishment. 34 When portions were served to them from Joseph's table,
Benjamin's portion was five times as much as
anyone else's. So they feasted and drank freely
with him.

A Silver Cup in a Sack

44 Now Joseph gave these instructions to
the steward of his house: "Fill the men's
sacks with as much food as they can carry, and put each man's silver in the mouth of
his sack. 2 Then put my cup, the silver one, in
the mouth of the youngest one's sack, along
with the silver for his grain." And he did as
Joseph said.

3 As morning dawned, the men were sent
on their way with their donkeys. 4 They had
not gone far from the city when Joseph said to
his steward, "Go after those men at once, and
when you catch up with them, say to them,
'Why have you repaid good with evil? 5 Isn't
this the cup my master drinks from and also
uses for divination? This is a wicked thing you
have done.' "

6 When he caught up with them, he repeated these words to them. 7 But they said to him,
"Why does my lord say such things? Far be it
from your servants to do anything like that!
8 We even brought back to you from the land of
Canaan the silver we found inside the mouths
of our sacks. So why would we steal silver or
gold from your master's house? 9 If any of your
servants is found to have it, he will die; and the
rest of us will become my lord's slaves."

10 "Very well, then," he said, "let it be as you
say. Whoever is found to have it will become
my slave; the rest of you will be free from
blame."

[a] 14 Hebrew *El-Shaddai*

11Each of them quickly lowered his sack to the ground and opened it. 12Then the steward proceeded to search, beginning with the oldest and ending with the youngest. And the cup was found in Benjamin's sack. 13At this, they tore their clothes. Then they all loaded their donkeys and returned to the city.

14Joseph was still in the house when Judah and his brothers came in, and they threw themselves to the ground before him. 15Joseph said to them, "What is this you have done? Don't you know that a man like me can find things out by divination?"

16"What can we say to my lord?" Judah replied. "What can we say? How can we prove our innocence? God has uncovered your servants' guilt. We are now my lord's slaves—we ourselves and the one who was found to have the cup."

17But Joseph said, "Far be it from me to do such a thing! Only the man who was found to have the cup will become my slave. The rest of you, go back to your father in peace."

18Then Judah went up to him and said: "Please, my lord, let your servant speak a word to my lord. Do not be angry with your servant, though you are equal to Pharaoh himself. 19My lord asked his servants, 'Do you have a father or a brother?' 20And we answered, 'We have an aged father, and there is a young son born to him in his old age. His brother is dead, and he is the only one of his mother's sons left, and his father loves him.'

21"Then you said to your servants, 'Bring him down to me so I can see him for myself.' 22And we said to my lord, 'The boy cannot leave his father; if he leaves him, his father will die.' 23But you told your servants, 'Unless your youngest brother comes down with you, you will not see my face again.' 24When we went back to your servant my father, we told him what my lord had said.

25"Then our father said, 'Go back and buy a little more food.' 26But we said, 'We cannot go down. Only if our youngest brother is with us will we go. We cannot see the man's face unless our youngest brother is with us.'

27"Your servant my father said to us, 'You know that my wife bore me two sons. 28One of them went away from me, and I said, "He has surely been torn to pieces." And I have not seen him since. 29If you take this one from me too and harm comes to him, you will bring my gray head down to the grave[a] in misery.'

30"So now, if the boy is not with us when I go back to your servant my father and if my father, whose life is closely bound up with the boy's life, 31sees that the boy isn't there, he will die. Your servants will bring the gray head of our father down to the grave in sorrow. 32Your servant guaranteed the boy's safety to my father. I said, 'If I do not bring him back to you, I will bear the blame before you, my father, all my life!'

33"Now then, please let your servant remain here as my lord's slave in place of the boy, and let the boy return with his brothers. 34How can I go back to my father if the boy is not with me? No! Do not let me see the misery that would come upon my father."

Joseph Makes Himself Known

45 Then Joseph could no longer control himself before all his attendants, and he cried out, "Have everyone leave my presence!" So there was no one with Joseph when he made himself known to his brothers. 2And he wept so loudly that the Egyptians heard him, and Pharaoh's household heard about it.

3Joseph said to his brothers, "I am Joseph! Is my father still living?" But his brothers were not able to answer him, because they were terrified at his presence.

4Then Joseph said to his brothers, "Come close to me." When they had done so, he said, "I am your brother Joseph, the one you sold into Egypt! 5And now, do not be distressed and do not be angry with yourselves for selling me here, because it was to save lives that God sent me ahead of you. 6For two years now there has been famine in the land, and for the next five years there will not be plowing and reaping. 7But God sent me ahead of you to preserve for you a remnant on earth and to save your lives by a great deliverance.[b]

8"So then, it was not you who sent me here, but God. He made me father to Pharaoh, lord of his entire household and ruler of all Egypt. 9Now hurry back to my father and say to him, 'This is what your son Joseph says: God has made me lord of all Egypt. Come down to me; don't delay. 10You shall live in the region of Goshen and be near me—you, your children and grandchildren, your flocks and herds, and all you have. 11I will provide for you there, because five years of famine are still to come. Otherwise you and your household and all who belong to you will become destitute.'

12"You can see for yourselves, and so can

[a] 29 Hebrew *Sheol*; also in verse 31 [b] 7 Or *save you as a great band of survivors*

my brother Benjamin, that it is really I who
am speaking to you. 13Tell my father about all
the honor accorded me in Egypt and about everything you have seen. And bring my father
down here quickly."
14Then he threw his arms around his brother Benjamin and wept, and Benjamin embraced him, weeping. 15And he kissed all his
brothers and wept over them. Afterward his
brothers talked with him.
16When the news reached Pharaoh's palace
that Joseph's brothers had come, Pharaoh and
all his officials were pleased. 17Pharaoh said
to Joseph, "Tell your brothers, 'Do this: Load
your animals and return to the land of Canaan,
18and bring your father and your families back
to me. I will give you the best of the land of
Egypt and you can enjoy the fat of the land.'
19"You are also directed to tell them, 'Do
this: Take some carts from Egypt for your children and your wives, and get your father and
come. 20Never mind about your belongings,
because the best of all Egypt will be yours.' "
21So the sons of Israel did this. Joseph gave
them carts, as Pharaoh had commanded, and
he also gave them provisions for their journey.
22To each of them he gave new clothing, but
to Benjamin he gave three hundred shekels[a]
of silver and five sets of clothes. 23And this is
what he sent to his father: ten donkeys loaded
with the best things of Egypt, and ten female
donkeys loaded with grain and bread and other provisions for his journey. 24Then he sent
his brothers away, and as they were leaving he
said to them, "Don't quarrel on the way!"
25So they went up out of Egypt and came
to their father Jacob in the land of Canaan.
26They told him, "Joseph is still alive! In fact,
he is ruler of all Egypt." Jacob was stunned; he
did not believe them. 27But when they told
him everything Joseph had said to them, and
when he saw the carts Joseph had sent to carry
him back, the spirit of their father Jacob revived. 28And Israel said, "I'm convinced! My
son Joseph is still alive. I will go and see him
before I die."

Jacob Goes to Egypt

46 So Israel set out with all that was his,
and when he reached Beersheba, he offered sacrifices to the God of his father
Isaac.
2And God spoke to Israel in a vision at
night and said, "Jacob! Jacob!"
"Here I am," he replied.
3"I am God, the God of your father," he
said. "Do not be afraid to go down to Egypt,
for I will make you into a great nation there.
4I will go down to Egypt with you, and I will
surely bring you back again. And Joseph's own
hand will close your eyes."
5Then Jacob left Beersheba, and Israel's sons
took their father Jacob and their children and
their wives in the carts that Pharaoh had sent
to transport him. 6They also took with them
their livestock and the possessions they had
acquired in Canaan, and Jacob and all his offspring went to Egypt. 7He took with him to
Egypt his sons and grandsons and his daughters and granddaughters—all his offspring.
8These are the names of the sons of Israel (Jacob and his descendants) who went to
Egypt:

Reuben the firstborn of Jacob.
9 The sons of Reuben:
Hanoch, Pallu, Hezron and Carmi.
10 The sons of Simeon:
Jemuel, Jamin, Ohad, Jakin, Zohar and
Shaul the son of a Canaanite woman.
11 The sons of Levi:
Gershon, Kohath and Merari.
12 The sons of Judah:
Er, Onan, Shelah, Perez and Zerah
(but Er and Onan had died in the land
of Canaan).
The sons of Perez:
Hezron and Hamul.
13 The sons of Issachar:
Tola, Puah,[b] Jashub[c] and Shimron.
14 The sons of Zebulun:
Sered, Elon and Jahleel.
15These were the sons Leah bore to Jacob in
Paddan Aram,[d] besides his daughter Dinah.
These sons and daughters of his were thirty-
three in all.

16 The sons of Gad:
Zephon,[e] Haggi, Shuni, Ezbon, Eri,
Arodi and Areli.
17 The sons of Asher:
Imnah, Ishvah, Ishvi and Beriah.
Their sister was Serah.
The sons of Beriah:
Heber and Malkiel.
18These were the children born to Jacob by
Zilpah, whom Laban had given to his daugh-
ter Leah—sixteen in all.

a 22 That is, about 7 1/2 pounds (about 3.5 kilograms) *b 13* Samaritan Pentateuch and Syriac (see also 1 Chron. 7:1); Masoretic Text *Puvah* *c 13* Samaritan Pentateuch and some Septuagint manuscripts (see also Num. 26:24 and 1 Chron. 7:1); Masoretic Text *Iob* *d 15* That is, Northwest Mesopotamia *e 16* Samaritan Pentateuch and Septuagint (see also Num. 26:15); Masoretic Text *Ziphion*

19 The sons of Jacob's wife Rachel:
Joseph and Benjamin. 20 In Egypt,
Manasseh and Ephraim were born to
Joseph by Asenath daughter of Potiph-
era, priest of On.[a]
21 The sons of Benjamin:
Bela, Beker, Ashbel, Gera, Naaman,
Ehi, Rosh, Muppim, Huppim and
Ard.
22 These were the sons of Rachel who were
born to Jacob—fourteen in all.

23 The son of Dan:
Hushim.
24 The sons of Naphtali:
Jahziel, Guni, Jezer and Shillem.
25 These were the sons born to Jacob by Bilhah, whom Laban had given to his daughter
Rachel—seven in all.

26 All those who went to Egypt with Jacob—those who were his direct descendants,
not counting his sons' wives—numbered sixty-six persons. 27 With the two sons[b] who had
been born to Joseph in Egypt, the members
of Jacob's family, which went to Egypt, were
seventy[c] in all.

28 Now Jacob sent Judah ahead of him to Joseph to get directions to Goshen. When they
arrived in the region of Goshen, 29 Joseph had
his chariot made ready and went to Goshen to
meet his father Israel. As soon as Joseph appeared before him, he threw his arms around
his father[d] and wept for a long time.
30 Israel said to Joseph, "Now I am ready to
die, since I have seen for myself that you are
still alive."
31 Then Joseph said to his brothers and to
his father's household, "I will go up and speak
to Pharaoh and will say to him, 'My brothers
and my father's household, who were living in
the land of Canaan, have come to me. 32 The
men are shepherds; they tend livestock, and
they have brought along their flocks and herds
and everything they own.' 33 When Pharaoh
calls you in and asks, 'What is your occupation?' 34 you should answer, 'Your servants
have tended livestock from our boyhood on,
just as our fathers did.' Then you will be allowed to settle in the region of Goshen, for all
shepherds are detestable to the Egyptians."

47 Joseph went and told Pharaoh, "My father and brothers, with their flocks and
herds and everything they own, have
come from the land of Canaan and are now
in Goshen." 2 He chose five of his brothers and
presented them before Pharaoh.
3 Pharaoh asked the brothers, "What is your
occupation?"
"Your servants are shepherds," they replied
to Pharaoh, "just as our fathers were." 4 They
also said to him, "We have come to live here
awhile, because the famine is severe in Canaan
and your servants' flocks have no pasture. So
now, please let your servants settle in Goshen."
5 Pharaoh said to Joseph, "Your father and
your brothers have come to you, 6 and the land
of Egypt is before you; settle your father and
your brothers in the best part of the land. Let
them live in Goshen. And if you know of any
among them with special ability, put them in
charge of my own livestock."
7 Then Joseph brought his father Jacob in
and presented him before Pharaoh. After Jacob blessed[e] Pharaoh, 8 Pharaoh asked him,
"How old are you?"
9 And Jacob said to Pharaoh, "The years of
my pilgrimage are a hundred and thirty. My
years have been few and difficult, and they do
not equal the years of the pilgrimage of my
fathers." 10 Then Jacob blessed[f] Pharaoh and
went out from his presence.
11 So Joseph settled his father and his brothers in Egypt and gave them property in the
best part of the land, the district of Rameses,
as Pharaoh directed. 12 Joseph also provided
his father and his brothers and all his father's
household with food, according to the number of their children.

Joseph and the Famine

13 There was no food, however, in the whole
region because the famine was severe; both
Egypt and Canaan wasted away because of
the famine. 14 Joseph collected all the money
that was to be found in Egypt and Canaan in
payment for the grain they were buying, and
he brought it to Pharaoh's palace. 15 When the
money of the people of Egypt and Canaan was
gone, all Egypt came to Joseph and said, "Give
us food. Why should we die before your eyes?
Our money is used up."
16 "Then bring your livestock," said Joseph.
"I will sell you food in exchange for your livestock, since your money is gone." 17 So they
brought their livestock to Joseph, and he gave
them food in exchange for their horses, their
sheep and goats, their cattle and donkeys. And

[a] *20* That is, Heliopolis [b] *27* Hebrew; Septuagint *the nine children* [c] *27* Hebrew (see also Exodus 1:5 and footnote); Septuagint (see also Acts 7:14) *seventy-five* [d] *29* Hebrew *around him* [e] *7* Or *greeted* [f] *10* Or *said farewell to*

he brought them through that year with food
in exchange for all their livestock.
18When that year was over, they came to
him the following year and said, "We cannot hide from our lord the fact that since our
money is gone and our livestock belongs to
you, there is nothing left for our lord except
our bodies and our land. 19Why should we
perish before your eyes—we and our land as
well? Buy us and our land in exchange for
food, and we with our land will be in bondage
to Pharaoh. Give us seed so that we may live
and not die, and that the land may not become desolate."
20So Joseph bought all the land in Egypt
for Pharaoh. The Egyptians, one and all, sold
their fields, because the famine was too severe
for them. The land became Pharaoh's, 21and
Joseph reduced the people to servitude,[a] from
one end of Egypt to the other. 22However, he
did not buy the land of the priests, because
they received a regular allotment from Pharaoh and had food enough from the allotment
Pharaoh gave them. That is why they did not
sell their land.
23Joseph said to the people, "Now that
I have bought you and your land today for
Pharaoh, here is seed for you so you can plant
the ground. 24But when the crop comes in,
give a fifth of it to Pharaoh. The other four-
fifths you may keep as seed for the fields and as
food for yourselves and your households and
your children."
25"You have saved our lives," they said.
"May we find favor in the eyes of our lord; we
will be in bondage to Pharaoh."
26So Joseph established it as a law concerning land in Egypt—still in force today—that
a fifth of the produce belongs to Pharaoh. It
was only the land of the priests that did not
become Pharaoh's.
27Now the Israelites settled in Egypt in the
region of Goshen. They acquired property
there and were fruitful and increased greatly
in number.
28Jacob lived in Egypt seventeen years, and
the years of his life were a hundred and forty-
seven. 29When the time drew near for Israel
to die, he called for his son Joseph and said to
him, "If I have found favor in your eyes, put
your hand under my thigh and promise that
you will show me kindness and faithfulness.
Do not bury me in Egypt, 30but when I rest
with my fathers, carry me out of Egypt and
bury me where they are buried."
"I will do as you say," he said.
31"Swear to me," he said. Then Joseph swore
to him, and Israel worshiped as he leaned on
the top of his staff.[b]

Manasseh and Ephraim

48 Some time later Joseph was told, "Your
father is ill." So he took his two sons
Manasseh and Ephraim along with him.
2When Jacob was told, "Your son Joseph has
come to you," Israel rallied his strength and sat
up on the bed.
3Jacob said to Joseph, "God Almighty[c] appeared to me at Luz in the land of Canaan,
and there he blessed me 4and said to me, 'I am
going to make you fruitful and will increase
your numbers. I will make you a community of peoples, and I will give this land as an
everlasting possession to your descendants after you.'
5"Now then, your two sons born to you in
Egypt before I came to you here will be reckoned as mine; Ephraim and Manasseh will be
mine, just as Reuben and Simeon are mine.
6Any children born to you after them will be
yours; in the territory they inherit they will be
reckoned under the names of their brothers.
7As I was returning from Paddan,[d] to my sorrow Rachel died in the land of Canaan while
we were still on the way, a little distance from
Ephrath. So I buried her there beside the road
to Ephrath" (that is, Bethlehem).
8When Israel saw the sons of Joseph, he
asked, "Who are these?"
9"They are the sons God has given me here,"
Joseph said to his father.
Then Israel said, "Bring them to me so I
may bless them."
10Now Israel's eyes were failing because of
old age, and he could hardly see. So Joseph
brought his sons close to him, and his father
kissed them and embraced them.
11Israel said to Joseph, "I never expected to
see your face again, and now God has allowed
me to see your children too."
12Then Joseph removed them from Israel's knees and bowed down with his face to
the ground. 13And Joseph took both of them,
Ephraim on his right toward Israel's left hand
and Manasseh on his left toward Israel's right
hand, and brought them close to him. 14But
Israel reached out his right hand and put it on
Ephraim's head, though he was the younger,
and crossing his arms, he put his left hand on

---

a 21 Samaritan Pentateuch and Septuagint (see also Vulgate); Masoretic Text *and he moved the people into the cities* *b* 31 Or *Israel bowed down at the head of his bed* *c* 3 Hebrew *El-Shaddai* *d* 7 That is, Northwest Mesopotamia

Manasseh's head, even though Manasseh was the firstborn.
15 Then he blessed Joseph and said,

"May the God before whom my fathers
Abraham and Isaac walked,
the God who has been my shepherd
all my life to this day,
16 the Angel who has delivered me from all
harm
—may he bless these boys.
May they be called by my name
and the names of my fathers Abraham
and Isaac,
and may they increase greatly
upon the earth."

17 When Joseph saw his father placing his
right hand on Ephraim's head he was displeased; so he took hold of his father's hand to move it from Ephraim's head to Manasseh's
head. 18 Joseph said to him, "No, my father, this one is the firstborn; put your right hand on his head."
19 But his father refused and said, "I know, my son, I know. He too will become a people, and he too will become great. Nevertheless, his younger brother will be greater than he, and his descendants will become a group
of nations." 20 He blessed them that day and said,

"In your[a] name will Israel pronounce this
blessing:
'May God make you like Ephraim and
Manasseh.' "

So he put Ephraim ahead of Manasseh.
21 Then Israel said to Joseph, "I am about to die, but God will be with you[b] and take you[b] back to the land of your[b] fathers. 22 And to you, as one who is over your brothers, I give the ridge of land[c] I took from the Amorites with my sword and my bow."

Jacob Blesses His Sons

49 Then Jacob called for his sons and said: "Gather around so I can tell you what will happen to you in days to come.

2 "Assemble and listen, sons of Jacob;
listen to your father Israel.

3 "Reuben, you are my firstborn,
my might, the first sign of my strength,
excelling in honor, excelling in power.
4 Turbulent as the waters, you will no longer
excel,
for you went up onto your father's bed,
onto my couch and defiled it.

5 "Simeon and Levi are brothers—
their swords[d] are weapons of violence.
6 Let me not enter their council,
let me not join their assembly,
for they have killed men in their anger
and hamstrung oxen as they pleased.
7 Cursed be their anger, so fierce,
and their fury, so cruel!
I will scatter them in Jacob
and disperse them in Israel.

8 "Judah,[e] your brothers will praise you;
your hand will be on the neck of your
enemies;
your father's sons will bow down to
you.
9 You are a lion's cub, O Judah;
you return from the prey, my son.
Like a lion he crouches and lies down,
like a lioness—who dares to rouse him?
10 The scepter will not depart from Judah,
nor the ruler's staff from between his
feet,
until he comes to whom it belongs[f]
and the obedience of the nations is his.
11 He will tether his donkey to a vine,
his colt to the choicest branch;
he will wash his garments in wine,
his robes in the blood of grapes.
12 His eyes will be darker than wine,
his teeth whiter than milk.[g]

13 "Zebulun will live by the seashore
and become a haven for ships;
his border will extend toward Sidon.

14 "Issachar is a rawboned[h] donkey
lying down between two saddlebags.[i]
15 When he sees how good is his resting place
and how pleasant is his land,
he will bend his shoulder to the burden
and submit to forced labor.

16 "Dan[j] will provide justice for his people
as one of the tribes of Israel.
17 Dan will be a serpent by the roadside,
a viper along the path,
that bites the horse's heels
so that its rider tumbles backward.

18 "I look for your deliverance, O LORD.

---

a 20 The Hebrew is singular. b 21 The Hebrew is plural. c 22 Or *And to you I give one portion more than to your brothers—the portion* d 5 The meaning of the Hebrew for this word is uncertain. e 8 *Judah* sounds like and may be derived from the Hebrew for *praise.* f 10 Or *until Shiloh comes*; or *until he comes to whom tribute belongs* g 12 Or *will be dull from wine, / his teeth white from milk* h 14 Or *strong* i 14 Or *campfires* j 16 *Dan* here means *he provides justice.*

19 "Gad[a] will be attacked by a band of
raiders,
but he will attack them at their heels.

20 "Asher's food will be rich;
he will provide delicacies fit for a king.

21 "Naphtali is a doe set free
that bears beautiful fawns.[b]

22 "Joseph is a fruitful vine,
a fruitful vine near a spring,
whose branches climb over a wall.[c]
23 With bitterness archers attacked him;
they shot at him with hostility.
24 But his bow remained steady,
his strong arms stayed[d] limber,
because of the hand of the Mighty One of
Jacob,
because of the Shepherd, the Rock of
Israel,
25 because of your father's God, who helps
you,
because of the Almighty,[e] who blesses
you
with blessings of the heavens above,
blessings of the deep that lies below,
blessings of the breast and womb.
26 Your father's blessings are greater
than the blessings of the ancient
mountains,
than[f] the bounty of the age-old hills.
Let all these rest on the head of Joseph,
on the brow of the prince among[g] his
brothers.

27 "Benjamin is a ravenous wolf;
in the morning he devours the prey,
in the evening he divides the plunder."

28 All these are the twelve tribes of Israel,
and this is what their father said to them when
he blessed them, giving each the blessing appropriate to him.

The Death of Jacob

29 Then he gave them these instructions: "I
am about to be gathered to my people. Bury
me with my fathers in the cave in the field of
Ephron the Hittite, 30 the cave in the field of
Machpelah, near Mamre in Canaan, which
Abraham bought as a burial place from Ephron
the Hittite, along with the field. 31 There Abraham and his wife Sarah were buried, there
Isaac and his wife Rebekah were buried, and
there I buried Leah. 32 The field and the cave in
it were bought from the Hittites.[h]"

33 When Jacob had finished giving instructions to his sons, he drew his feet up into the
bed, breathed his last and was gathered to his
people.

50 Joseph threw himself upon his father
and wept over him and kissed him.
2 Then Joseph directed the physicians in
his service to embalm his father Israel. So the
physicians embalmed him, 3 taking a full forty
days, for that was the time required for em-
balming. And the Egyptians mourned for him
seventy days.

4 When the days of mourning had passed,
Joseph said to Pharaoh's court, "If I have
found favor in your eyes, speak to Pharaoh for
me. Tell him, 5 'My father made me swear an
oath and said, "I am about to die; bury me in
the tomb I dug for myself in the land of Canaan." Now let me go up and bury my father;
then I will return.' "

6 Pharaoh said, "Go up and bury your father, as he made you swear to do."

7 So Joseph went up to bury his father. All
Pharaoh's officials accompanied him—the dignitaries of his court and all the dignitaries of
Egypt— 8 besides all the members of Joseph's
household and his brothers and those belonging to his father's household. Only their children and their flocks and herds were left in
Goshen. 9 Chariots and horsemen[i] also went
up with him. It was a very large company.

10 When they reached the threshing floor
of Atad, near the Jordan, they lamented loudly and bitterly; and there Joseph observed a
seven-day period of mourning for his father.
11 When the Canaanites who lived there saw
the mourning at the threshing floor of Atad,
they said, "The Egyptians are holding a solemn ceremony of mourning." That is why that
place near the Jordan is called Abel Mizraim.[j]

12 So Jacob's sons did as he had commanded
them: 13 They carried him to the land of Canaan and buried him in the cave in the field
of Machpelah, near Mamre, which Abraham
had bought as a burial place from Ephron the
Hittite, along with the field. 14 After burying
his father, Joseph returned to Egypt, together
with his brothers and all the others who had
gone with him to bury his father.

---

[a] *19* Gad can mean *attack* and *band of raiders.* [b] *21* Or *free; / he utters beautiful words* [c] *22* Or *Joseph is a wild colt, / a wild colt near a spring, / a wild donkey on a terraced hill* [d] *23,24* Or *archers will attack . . . will shoot . . . will remain . . . will stay* [e] *25* Hebrew *Shaddai* [f] *26* Or *of my progenitors, / as great as* [g] *26* Or *the one separated from* [h] *32* Or *the sons of Heth* [i] *9* Or *charioteers*
[j] *11* *Abel Mizraim* means *mourning of the Egyptians.*

Joseph Reassures His Brothers

15When Joseph's brothers saw that their
father was dead, they said, "What if Joseph
holds a grudge against us and pays us back for
all the wrongs we did to him?" 16So they sent
word to Joseph, saying, "Your father left these
instructions before he died: 17'This is what you
are to say to Joseph: I ask you to forgive your
brothers the sins and the wrongs they committed in treating you so badly.' Now please
forgive the sins of the servants of the God of
your father." When their message came to
him, Joseph wept.
18His brothers then came and threw themselves down before him. "We are your slaves,"
they said.
19But Joseph said to them, "Don't be afraid.
Am I in the place of God? 20You intended to
harm me, but God intended it for good to accomplish what is now being done, the saving
of many lives. 21So then, don't be afraid. I will
provide for you and your children." And he
reassured them and spoke kindly to them.

The Death of Joseph

22Joseph stayed in Egypt, along with all his
father's family. He lived a hundred and ten
years 23and saw the third generation of Ephraim's children. Also the children of Makir son
of Manasseh were placed at birth on Joseph's
knees.[a]
24Then Joseph said to his brothers, "I am
about to die. But God will surely come to your
aid and take you up out of this land to the
land he promised on oath to Abraham, Isaac
and Jacob." 25And Joseph made the sons of Israel swear an oath and said, "God will surely
come to your aid, and then you must carry my
bones up from this place."
26So Joseph died at the age of a hundred
and ten. And after they embalmed him, he
was placed in a coffin in Egypt.

---

[a] *23* That is, were counted as his

EXODUS

Exodus

QUICK FACTS

AUTHOR Moses

AUDIENCE The people of Israel

DATE Between 1446 and 1406 B.C.

SETTING Opening scenes are in Egypt. The plot then moves to the region of the Sinai peninsula.

Exodus, which means "a way out," is the story of the Israelites' miraculous deliverance from slavery. Abraham's descendants, who had moved to Egypt to escape famine, became a great nation. But they also became slaves, and at one point, the pharaoh of Egypt ordered that their baby boys be drowned as a method of population control.

One of those babies, Moses, was rescued, raised in an Egyptian palace and disciplined in the desert until he was called to lead God's chosen people out of Egypt. Along the way God provided several miraculous signs of his presence: a burning bush, a staff that turned into a snake, ten plagues that broke the resistance of Egypt's pharaoh to free the Israelites, and a body of water that parted for the escaping people.

The Passover, the giving of the Law at Mount Sinai and the construction of the tabernacle, which taught God's people how to live in relationship with him, serve as reminders for us today. As we read of God's desire to care for and rescue his people, his love for them and his yearning to live among them, we are reminded of God's love for us. Even though life and love may, at times, lose their brilliance in the daily drudgery of working, paying bills and keeping the house clean, there is always a beacon of hope provided by God, who dwells among us.

The Israelites Oppressed

1 These are the names of the sons of Israel who went to Egypt with Jacob, each with his family: [2]Reuben, Simeon, Levi and Judah; [3]Issachar, Zebulun and Benjamin; [4]Dan and Naphtali; Gad and Asher. [5]The descendants of Jacob numbered seventy[a] in all; Joseph was already in Egypt.

[6]Now Joseph and all his brothers and all that generation died, [7]but the Israelites were fruitful and multiplied greatly and became exceedingly numerous, so that the land was filled with them.

[8]Then a new king, who did not know about Joseph, came to power in Egypt. [9]"Look," he said to his people, "the Israelites have become much too numerous for us. [10]Come, we must deal shrewdly with them or they will become even more numerous and, if war breaks out, will join our enemies, fight against us and leave the country."

[11]So they put slave masters over them to oppress them with forced labor, and they built Pithom and Rameses as store cities for Pharaoh. [12]But the more they were oppressed, the more they multiplied and spread; so the Egyptians came to dread the Israelites [13]and worked them ruthlessly. [14]They made their lives bitter with hard labor in brick and mortar and with all kinds of work in the fields; in all their hard labor the Egyptians used them ruthlessly.

[15]The king of Egypt said to the Hebrew midwives, whose names were Shiphrah and Puah, [16]"When you help the Hebrew women in childbirth and observe them on the delivery stool, if it is a boy, kill him; but if it is a girl, let her live." [17]The midwives, however, feared God and did not do what the king of Egypt had told them to do; they let the boys live. [18]Then the king of Egypt summoned the midwives and asked them, "Why have you done this? Why have you let the boys live?"

[19]The midwives answered Pharaoh, "Hebrew women are not like Egyptian women; they are vigorous and give birth before the midwives arrive."

[20]So God was kind to the midwives and the people increased and became even more numerous. [21]And because the midwives feared God, he gave them families of their own.

[22]Then Pharaoh gave this order to all his people: "Every boy that is born[b] you must throw into the Nile, but let every girl live."

The Birth of Moses

2 Now a man of the house of Levi married a Levite woman, [2]and she became pregnant and gave birth to a son. When she saw that he was a fine child, she hid him for three months. [3]But when she could hide him no longer, she got a papyrus basket for him and coated it with tar and pitch. Then she placed the child in it and put it among the reeds along the bank of the Nile. [4]His sister stood at a distance to see what would happen to him.

[5]Then Pharaoh's daughter went down to the Nile to bathe, and her attendants were walking along the river bank. She saw the basket among the reeds and sent her slave girl to get it. [6]She opened it and saw the baby. He was crying, and she felt sorry for him. "This is one of the Hebrew babies," she said.

[7]Then his sister asked Pharaoh's daughter, "Shall I go and get one of the Hebrew women to nurse the baby for you?"

[8]"Yes, go," she answered. And the girl went and got the baby's mother. [9]Pharaoh's daughter said to her, "Take this baby and nurse him for me, and I will pay you." So the woman took the baby and nursed him. [10]When the child grew older, she took him to Pharaoh's daughter and he became her son. She named him Moses,[c] saying, "I drew him out of the water."

Moses Flees to Midian

[11]One day, after Moses had grown up, he went out to where his own people were and watched them at their hard labor. He saw an Egyptian beating a Hebrew, one of his own people. [12]Glancing this way and that and seeing no one, he killed the Egyptian and hid him in the sand. [13]The next day he went out and saw two Hebrews fighting. He asked the one in the wrong, "Why are you hitting your fellow Hebrew?"

[14]The man said, "Who made you ruler and judge over us? Are you thinking of killing me as you killed the Egyptian?" Then Moses was afraid and thought, "What I did must have become known."

[15]When Pharaoh heard of this, he tried to kill Moses, but Moses fled from Pharaoh and went to live in Midian, where he sat down by a well. [16]Now a priest of Midian had seven daughters, and they came to draw water and fill the troughs to water their father's flock.

[a] 5 Masoretic Text (see also Gen. 46:27); Dead Sea Scrolls and Septuagint (see also Acts 7:14 and note at Gen. 46:27) *seventy-five*
[b] 22 Masoretic Text; Samaritan Pentateuch, Septuagint and Targums *born to the Hebrews* [c] 10 *Moses* sounds like the Hebrew for *draw out.*

17 Some shepherds came along and drove them
away, but Moses got up and came to their rescue and watered their flock.
18 When the girls returned to Reuel their father, he asked them, "Why have you returned
so early today?"
19 They answered, "An Egyptian rescued us
from the shepherds. He even drew water for us
and watered the flock."
20 "And where is he?" he asked his daughters. "Why did you leave him? Invite him to
have something to eat."
21 Moses agreed to stay with the man, who
gave his daughter Zipporah to Moses in marriage. 22 Zipporah gave birth to a son, and
Moses named him Gershom,[a] saying, "I have
become an alien in a foreign land."
23 During that long period, the king of
Egypt died. The Israelites groaned in their
slavery and cried out, and their cry for help because of their slavery went up to God. 24 God
heard their groaning and he remembered his
covenant with Abraham, with Isaac and with
Jacob. 25 So God looked on the Israelites and
was concerned about them.

Moses and the Burning Bush

3 Now Moses was tending the flock of Jethro
his father-in-law, the priest of Midian, and
he led the flock to the far side of the desert and came to Horeb, the mountain of God.
2 There the angel of the LORD appeared to him
in flames of fire from within a bush. Moses
saw that though the bush was on fire it did
not burn up. 3 So Moses thought, "I will go
over and see this strange sight—why the bush
does not burn up."
4 When the LORD saw that he had gone over
to look, God called to him from within the
bush, "Moses! Moses!"
And Moses said, "Here I am."
5 "Do not come any closer," God said. "Take
off your sandals, for the place where you are
standing is holy ground." 6 Then he said, "I am
the God of your father, the God of Abraham,
the God of Isaac and the God of Jacob." At
this, Moses hid his face, because he was afraid
to look at God.
7 The LORD said, "I have indeed seen the
misery of my people in Egypt. I have heard
them crying out because of their slave drivers,
and I am concerned about their suffering. 8 So
I have come down to rescue them from the
hand of the Egyptians and to bring them up
out of that land into a good and spacious land,
a land flowing with milk and honey—the
home of the Canaanites, Hittites, Amorites,
Perizzites, Hivites and Jebusites. 9 And now
the cry of the Israelites has reached me, and I
have seen the way the Egyptians are oppressing them. 10 So now, go. I am sending you to
Pharaoh to bring my people the Israelites out
of Egypt."
11 But Moses said to God, "Who am I, that
I should go to Pharaoh and bring the Israelites
out of Egypt?"
12 And God said, "I will be with you. And
this will be the sign to you that it is I who have
sent you: When you have brought the people
out of Egypt, you[b] will worship God on this
mountain."
13 Moses said to God, "Suppose I go to the
Israelites and say to them, 'The God of your
fathers has sent me to you,' and they ask me,
'What is his name?' Then what shall I tell
them?"
14 God said to Moses, "I AM WHO I AM.[c]
This is what you are to say to the Israelites: 'I
AM has sent me to you.' "
15 God also said to Moses, "Say to the Israelites, 'The LORD,[d] the God of your fathers—
the God of Abraham, the God of Isaac and
the God of Jacob—has sent me to you.' This
is my name forever, the name by which I am
to be remembered from generation to generation.
16 "Go, assemble the elders of Israel and
say to them, 'The LORD, the God of your
fathers—the God of Abraham, Isaac and Jacob—appeared to me and said: I have watched
over you and have seen what has been done to
you in Egypt. 17 And I have promised to bring
you up out of your misery in Egypt into the
land of the Canaanites, Hittites, Amorites,
Perizzites, Hivites and Jebusites—a land flowing with milk and honey.'
18 "The elders of Israel will listen to you.
Then you and the elders are to go to the king
of Egypt and say to him, 'The LORD, the God
of the Hebrews, has met with us. Let us take a
three-day journey into the desert to offer sacrifices to the LORD our God.' 19 But I know that
the king of Egypt will not let you go unless a
mighty hand compels him. 20 So I will stretch
out my hand and strike the Egyptians with all
the wonders that I will perform among them.
After that, he will let you go.
21 "And I will make the Egyptians favorably
disposed toward this people, so that when you
leave you will not go empty-handed. 22 Every

[a] *22* *Gershom* sounds like the Hebrew for *an alien there.* [b] *12* The Hebrew is plural. [c] *14* Or *I WILL BE WHAT I WILL BE*
[d] *15* The Hebrew for *LORD* sounds like and may be derived from the Hebrew for *I AM* in verse 14.

woman is to ask her neighbor and any woman living in her house for articles of silver and gold and for clothing, which you will put on your sons and daughters. And so you will plunder the Egyptians."

Signs for Moses

4 Moses answered, "What if they do not believe me or listen to me and say, 'The LORD did not appear to you'?"

2Then the LORD said to him, "What is that in your hand?"

"A staff," he replied.

3The LORD said, "Throw it on the ground."

Moses threw it on the ground and it became a snake, and he ran from it. 4Then the LORD said to him, "Reach out your hand and take it by the tail." So Moses reached out and took hold of the snake and it turned back into a staff in his hand. 5"This," said the LORD, "is so that they may believe that the LORD, the God of their fathers—the God of Abraham, the God of Isaac and the God of Jacob—has appeared to you."

6Then the LORD said, "Put your hand inside your cloak." So Moses put his hand into his cloak, and when he took it out, it was leprous,[a] like snow.

7"Now put it back into your cloak," he said. So Moses put his hand back into his cloak, and when he took it out, it was restored, like the rest of his flesh.

8Then the LORD said, "If they do not believe you or pay attention to the first miraculous sign, they may believe the second. 9But if they do not believe these two signs or listen to you, take some water from the Nile and pour it on the dry ground. The water you take from the river will become blood on the ground."

10Moses said to the LORD, "O Lord, I have never been eloquent, neither in the past nor since you have spoken to your servant. I am slow of speech and tongue."

11The LORD said to him, "Who gave man his mouth? Who makes him deaf or mute? Who gives him sight or makes him blind? Is it not I, the LORD? 12Now go; I will help you speak and will teach you what to say."

13But Moses said, "O Lord, please send someone else to do it."

14Then the LORD's anger burned against Moses and he said, "What about your brother, Aaron the Levite? I know he can speak well. He is already on his way to meet you, and his heart will be glad when he sees you. 15You shall speak to him and put words in his mouth; I will help both of you speak and will teach you what to do. 16He will speak to the people for you, and it will be as if he were your mouth and as if you were God to him. 17But take this staff in your hand so you can perform miraculous signs with it."

Moses Returns to Egypt

18Then Moses went back to Jethro his father-in-law and said to him, "Let me go back to my own people in Egypt to see if any of them are still alive."

Jethro said, "Go, and I wish you well."

19Now the LORD had said to Moses in Midian, "Go back to Egypt, for all the men who wanted to kill you are dead." 20So Moses took his wife and sons, put them on a donkey and started back to Egypt. And he took the staff of God in his hand.

21The LORD said to Moses, "When you return to Egypt, see that you perform before Pharaoh all the wonders I have given you the power to do. But I will harden his heart so that he will not let the people go. 22Then say to Pharaoh, 'This is what the LORD says: Israel is my firstborn son, 23and I told you, "Let my son go, so he may worship me." But you refused to let him go; so I will kill your firstborn son.' "

24At a lodging place on the way, the LORD met ⌊Moses⌋[b] and was about to kill him. 25But Zipporah took a flint knife, cut off her son's foreskin and touched ⌊Moses'⌋ feet with it.[c] "Surely you are a bridegroom of blood to me," she said. 26So the LORD let him alone. (At that time she said "bridegroom of blood," referring to circumcision.)

27The LORD said to Aaron, "Go into the desert to meet Moses." So he met Moses at the mountain of God and kissed him. 28Then Moses told Aaron everything the LORD had sent him to say, and also about all the miraculous signs he had commanded him to perform.

29Moses and Aaron brought together all the elders of the Israelites, 30and Aaron told them everything the LORD had said to Moses. He also performed the signs before the people, 31and they believed. And when they heard that the LORD was concerned about them and had seen their misery, they bowed down and worshiped.

---

[a] *6* The Hebrew word was used for various diseases affecting the skin—not necessarily leprosy. [b] *24* Or ⌊*Moses' son*⌋; Hebrew *him*
[c] *25* Or *and drew near* ⌊*Moses'*⌋ *feet*

FRIDAY
READ EXODUS 4:24–26

MAKING PEACE WITH EACH OTHER

But Zipporah took a flint knife, cut off her son's foreskin and touched ⌞Moses'⌟ feet with it. "Surely you are a bridegroom of blood to me," she said.

— Exodus 4:25

let's talk

- Is there some area of our marriage in which we feel that one of us has unmet expectations? Let's talk about some of those expectations.
- When one of us gets angry, do our arguments quickly get out of hand? How can we put a stop to that pattern?
- Let's try a pen-passing conversation on a nonthreatening topic. How does that approach differ from the way we usually try to resolve a problem? In what ways could this approach help?

Zipporah performed hasty surgery on her son when she realized God was about to kill her husband, Moses. While it isn't stated, evidently God was about to destroy Moses because he had failed to circumcise his son. Zipporah took the situation into her own hands, completing the act of obedience Moses had neglected to do.

But there seems to be an air of resentment in her abrupt actions. Perhaps she was angry at her husband for shirking his fatherly duties. Or maybe Zipporah resented having to perform a spiritual rite she herself didn't believe in.

Whatever the details of a disagreement, resulting feelings can drive a wedge between spouses. Resentment can lead to barbed words, sarcastic comments and actions that undercut one another. For example, children came early in our marriage. I used to get so angry when Dan would nudge me to get out of bed in the middle of the night because the baby was crying. Both Dan and I desperately needed sleep, but I resented the assumption that it was my responsibility to get up with the baby. Lack of sleep, combined with my expectation that Dan share in the 3:00 A.M. feedings, fueled resentment in me. In a huff, I would perform my motherly duties, seething silently as Dan snored and I rocked a cranky baby. It didn't take too many sleepless nights like that before we had built walls of anger between us.

When you notice resentment creeping in or a disagreement escalating in your relationship, admit your anger and call an immediate cease-fire. Take some advice from marriage counselor Scott M. Stanley (*Marriage Partnership*, Fall 1995). Agree on a specific time when you can talk. Then sit down together and use a small object, such as a pen, to indicate who has the floor. The person holding the pen is the speaker. When the pen changes hands, the roles change. The speaker's job is to get his or her point across. The listener's job is to absorb information and give feedback by paraphrasing what the other has just said.

While this approach feels somewhat artificial, it greatly enhances communication by slowing things down and emphasizing listening and working together. It helps you, as James 1:19 says, to be "quick to listen, slow to speak and slow to become angry." It's a great tool for aiding interaction and understanding. And it helps to insure that resentments don't fester or turn into full-blown arguments.

When you sense resentment growing within you, ask yourself what expectations you have of your spouse, particularly in a situation that's brewing trouble between you. Very often, resentment grows from unmet expectations. Zipporah expected something from Moses. I expected something of Dan. Recognizing what your expectations are is the first step toward resolving resentment.

—MARIAN V. LIAUTAUD

FOR YOUR NEXT DEVOTIONAL READING, TURN TO PAGE 68.

Bricks Without Straw

5 Afterward Moses and Aaron went to Pharaoh and said, "This is what the LORD, the God of Israel, says: 'Let my people go, so that they may hold a festival to me in the desert.' "

2 Pharaoh said, "Who is the LORD, that I should obey him and let Israel go? I do not know the LORD and I will not let Israel go."

3 Then they said, "The God of the Hebrews has met with us. Now let us take a three-day journey into the desert to offer sacrifices to the LORD our God, or he may strike us with plagues or with the sword."

4 But the king of Egypt said, "Moses and Aaron, why are you taking the people away from their labor? Get back to your work!" 5 Then Pharaoh said, "Look, the people of the land are now numerous, and you are stopping them from working."

6 That same day Pharaoh gave this order to the slave drivers and foremen in charge of the people: 7 "You are no longer to supply the people with straw for making bricks; let them go and gather their own straw. 8 But require them to make the same number of bricks as before; don't reduce the quota. They are lazy; that is why they are crying out, 'Let us go and sacrifice to our God.' 9 Make the work harder for the men so that they keep working and pay no attention to lies."

10 Then the slave drivers and the foremen went out and said to the people, "This is what Pharaoh says: 'I will not give you any more straw. 11 Go and get your own straw wherever you can find it, but your work will not be reduced at all.' " 12 So the people scattered all over Egypt to gather stubble to use for straw. 13 The slave drivers kept pressing them, saying, "Complete the work required of you for each day, just as when you had straw." 14 The Israelite foremen appointed by Pharaoh's slave drivers were beaten and were asked, "Why didn't you meet your quota of bricks yesterday or today, as before?"

15 Then the Israelite foremen went and appealed to Pharaoh: "Why have you treated your servants this way? 16 Your servants are given no straw, yet we are told, 'Make bricks!' Your servants are being beaten, but the fault is with your own people."

17 Pharaoh said, "Lazy, that's what you are—lazy! That is why you keep saying, 'Let us go and sacrifice to the LORD.' 18 Now get to work. You will not be given any straw, yet you must produce your full quota of bricks."

19 The Israelite foremen realized they were in trouble when they were told, "You are not to reduce the number of bricks required of you for each day." 20 When they left Pharaoh, they found Moses and Aaron waiting to meet them, 21 and they said, "May the LORD look upon you and judge you! You have made us a stench to Pharaoh and his officials and have put a sword in their hand to kill us."

God Promises Deliverance

22 Moses returned to the LORD and said, "O Lord, why have you brought trouble upon this people? Is this why you sent me? 23 Ever since I went to Pharaoh to speak in your name, he has brought trouble upon this people, and you have not rescued your people at all."

6 Then the LORD said to Moses, "Now you will see what I will do to Pharaoh: Because of my mighty hand he will let them go; because of my mighty hand he will drive them out of his country."

2 God also said to Moses, "I am the LORD. 3 I appeared to Abraham, to Isaac and to Jacob as God Almighty,[a] but by my name the LORD[b] I did not make myself known to them.[c] 4 I also established my covenant with them to give them the land of Canaan, where they lived as aliens. 5 Moreover, I have heard the groaning of the Israelites, whom the Egyptians are enslaving, and I have remembered my covenant.

6 "Therefore, say to the Israelites: 'I am the LORD, and I will bring you out from under the yoke of the Egyptians. I will free you from being slaves to them, and I will redeem you with an outstretched arm and with mighty acts of judgment. 7 I will take you as my own people, and I will be your God. Then you will know that I am the LORD your God, who brought you out from under the yoke of the Egyptians. 8 And I will bring you to the land I swore with uplifted hand to give to Abraham, to Isaac and to Jacob. I will give it to you as a possession. I am the LORD.' "

9 Moses reported this to the Israelites, but they did not listen to him because of their discouragement and cruel bondage.

10 Then the LORD said to Moses, 11 "Go, tell Pharaoh king of Egypt to let the Israelites go out of his country."

12 But Moses said to the LORD, "If the Israelites will not listen to me, why would Phar-

---

[a] 3 Hebrew *El-Shaddai* [b] 3 See note at Exodus 3:15. [c] 3 Or *Almighty, and by my name the LORD did I not let myself be known to them?*

aoh listen to me, since I speak with faltering lips[a]?"

Family Record of Moses and Aaron

13Now the LORD spoke to Moses and Aaron about the Israelites and Pharaoh king of Egypt, and he commanded them to bring the Israelites out of Egypt.

14These were the heads of their families[b]:

The sons of Reuben the firstborn son of Israel were Hanoch and Pallu, Hezron and Carmi. These were the clans of Reuben.

15The sons of Simeon were Jemuel, Jamin, Ohad, Jakin, Zohar and Shaul the son of a Canaanite woman. These were the clans of Simeon.

16These were the names of the sons of Levi according to their records: Gershon, Kohath and Merari. Levi lived 137 years.

17The sons of Gershon, by clans, were Libni and Shimei.

18The sons of Kohath were Amram, Izhar, Hebron and Uzziel. Kohath lived 133 years.

19The sons of Merari were Mahli and Mushi.

These were the clans of Levi according to their records.

20Amram married his father's sister Jochebed, who bore him Aaron and Moses. Amram lived 137 years.

21The sons of Izhar were Korah, Nepheg and Zicri.

22The sons of Uzziel were Mishael, Elzaphan and Sithri.

23Aaron married Elisheba, daughter of Amminadab and sister of Nahshon, and she bore him Nadab and Abihu, Eleazar and Ithamar.

24The sons of Korah were Assir, Elkanah and Abiasaph. These were the Korahite clans.

25Eleazar son of Aaron married one of the daughters of Putiel, and she bore him Phinehas.

These were the heads of the Levite families, clan by clan.

26It was this same Aaron and Moses to whom the LORD said, "Bring the Israelites out of Egypt by their divisions." 27They were the ones who spoke to Pharaoh king of Egypt about bringing the Israelites out of Egypt. It was the same Moses and Aaron.

Aaron to Speak for Moses

28Now when the LORD spoke to Moses in Egypt, 29he said to him, "I am the LORD. Tell Pharaoh king of Egypt everything I tell you."

30But Moses said to the LORD, "Since I speak with faltering lips, why would Pharaoh listen to me?"

7 Then the LORD said to Moses, "See, I have made you like God to Pharaoh, and your brother Aaron will be your prophet. 2You are to say everything I command you, and your brother Aaron is to tell Pharaoh to let the Israelites go out of his country. 3But I will harden Pharaoh's heart, and though I multiply my miraculous signs and wonders in Egypt, 4he will not listen to you. Then I will lay my hand on Egypt and with mighty acts of judgment I will bring out my divisions, my people the Israelites. 5And the Egyptians will know that I am the LORD when I stretch out my hand against Egypt and bring the Israelites out of it."

6Moses and Aaron did just as the LORD commanded them. 7Moses was eighty years old and Aaron eighty-three when they spoke to Pharaoh.

Aaron's Staff Becomes a Snake

8The LORD said to Moses and Aaron, 9"When Pharaoh says to you, 'Perform a miracle,' then say to Aaron, 'Take your staff and throw it down before Pharaoh,' and it will become a snake."

10So Moses and Aaron went to Pharaoh and did just as the LORD commanded. Aaron threw his staff down in front of Pharaoh and his officials, and it became a snake. 11Pharaoh then summoned wise men and sorcerers, and the Egyptian magicians also did the same things by their secret arts: 12Each one threw down his staff and it became a snake. But Aaron's staff swallowed up their staffs. 13Yet Pharaoh's heart became hard and he would not listen to them, just as the LORD had said.

The Plague of Blood

14Then the LORD said to Moses, "Pharaoh's heart is unyielding; he refuses to let the people go. 15Go to Pharaoh in the morning as he goes out to the water. Wait on the bank of the Nile to meet him, and take in your hand the

[a] 12 Hebrew *I am uncircumcised of lips*; also in verse 30 [b] 14 The Hebrew for *families* here and in verse 25 refers to units larger than clans.

staff that was changed into a snake. [16]Then say to him, 'The LORD, the God of the Hebrews, has sent me to say to you: Let my people go, so that they may worship me in the desert. But until now you have not listened. [17]This is what the LORD says: By this you will know that I am the LORD: With the staff that is in my hand I will strike the water of the Nile, and it will be changed into blood. [18]The fish in the Nile will die, and the river will stink; the Egyptians will not be able to drink its water.' "

[19]The LORD said to Moses, "Tell Aaron, 'Take your staff and stretch out your hand over the waters of Egypt—over the streams and canals, over the ponds and all the reservoirs'—and they will turn to blood. Blood will be everywhere in Egypt, even in the wooden buckets and stone jars."

[20]Moses and Aaron did just as the LORD had commanded. He raised his staff in the presence of Pharaoh and his officials and struck the water of the Nile, and all the water was changed into blood. [21]The fish in the Nile died, and the river smelled so bad that the Egyptians could not drink its water. Blood was everywhere in Egypt.

[22]But the Egyptian magicians did the same things by their secret arts, and Pharaoh's heart became hard; he would not listen to Moses and Aaron, just as the LORD had said. [23]Instead, he turned and went into his palace, and did not take even this to heart. [24]And all the Egyptians dug along the Nile to get drinking water, because they could not drink the water of the river.

The Plague of Frogs

[25]Seven days passed after the LORD struck

8 the Nile. [1]Then the LORD said to Moses, "Go to Pharaoh and say to him, 'This is what the LORD says: Let my people go, so that they may worship me. [2]If you refuse to let them go, I will plague your whole country with frogs. [3]The Nile will teem with frogs. They will come up into your palace and your bedroom and onto your bed, into the houses of your officials and on your people, and into your ovens and kneading troughs. [4]The frogs will go up on you and your people and all your officials.' "

[5]Then the LORD said to Moses, "Tell Aaron, 'Stretch out your hand with your staff over the streams and canals and ponds, and make frogs come up on the land of Egypt.' "

[6]So Aaron stretched out his hand over the waters of Egypt, and the frogs came up and covered the land. [7]But the magicians did the same things by their secret arts; they also made frogs come up on the land of Egypt.

[8]Pharaoh summoned Moses and Aaron and said, "Pray to the LORD to take the frogs away from me and my people, and I will let your people go to offer sacrifices to the LORD."

[9]Moses said to Pharaoh, "I leave to you the honor of setting the time for me to pray for you and your officials and your people that you and your houses may be rid of the frogs, except for those that remain in the Nile."

[10]"Tomorrow," Pharaoh said.

Moses replied, "It will be as you say, so that you may know there is no one like the LORD our God. [11]The frogs will leave you and your houses, your officials and your people; they will remain only in the Nile."

[12]After Moses and Aaron left Pharaoh, Moses cried out to the LORD about the frogs he had brought on Pharaoh. [13]And the LORD did what Moses asked. The frogs died in the houses, in the courtyards and in the fields. [14]They were piled into heaps, and the land reeked of them. [15]But when Pharaoh saw that there was relief, he hardened his heart and would not listen to Moses and Aaron, just as the LORD had said.

The Plague of Gnats

[16]Then the LORD said to Moses, "Tell Aaron, 'Stretch out your staff and strike the dust of the ground,' and throughout the land of Egypt the dust will become gnats." [17]They did this, and when Aaron stretched out his hand with the staff and struck the dust of the ground, gnats came upon men and animals. All the dust throughout the land of Egypt became gnats. [18]But when the magicians tried to produce gnats by their secret arts, they could not. And the gnats were on men and animals.

[19]The magicians said to Pharaoh, "This is the finger of God." But Pharaoh's heart was hard and he would not listen, just as the LORD had said.

The Plague of Flies

[20]Then the LORD said to Moses, "Get up early in the morning and confront Pharaoh as he goes to the water and say to him, 'This is what the LORD says: Let my people go, so that they may worship me. [21]If you do not let my people go, I will send swarms of flies on you and your officials, on your people and into your houses. The houses of the Egyptians

will be full of flies, and even the ground where
they are.
22" 'But on that day I will deal differently
with the land of Goshen, where my people
live; no swarms of flies will be there, so that
you will know that I, the LORD, am in this
land. 23I will make a distinction[a] between my
people and your people. This miraculous sign
will occur tomorrow.' "
24And the LORD did this. Dense swarms of
flies poured into Pharaoh's palace and into the
houses of his officials, and throughout Egypt
the land was ruined by the flies.
25Then Pharaoh summoned Moses and
Aaron and said, "Go, sacrifice to your God
here in the land."
26But Moses said, "That would not be right.
The sacrifices we offer the LORD our God
would be detestable to the Egyptians. And if
we offer sacrifices that are detestable in their
eyes, will they not stone us? 27We must take
a three-day journey into the desert to offer
sacrifices to the LORD our God, as he commands us."
28Pharaoh said, "I will let you go to offer
sacrifices to the LORD your God in the desert, but you must not go very far. Now pray
for me."
29Moses answered, "As soon as I leave you, I
will pray to the LORD, and tomorrow the flies
will leave Pharaoh and his officials and his
people. Only be sure that Pharaoh does not
act deceitfully again by not letting the people
go to offer sacrifices to the LORD."
30Then Moses left Pharaoh and prayed to
the LORD, 31and the LORD did what Moses
asked: The flies left Pharaoh and his officials
and his people; not a fly remained. 32But this
time also Pharaoh hardened his heart and
would not let the people go.

The Plague on Livestock

9 Then the LORD said to Moses, "Go to
Pharaoh and say to him, 'This is what the
LORD, the God of the Hebrews, says: "Let
my people go, so that they may worship me."
2If you refuse to let them go and continue to
hold them back, 3the hand of the LORD will
bring a terrible plague on your livestock in the
field—on your horses and donkeys and camels
and on your cattle and sheep and goats. 4But
the LORD will make a distinction between the
livestock of Israel and that of Egypt, so that no
animal belonging to the Israelites will die.' "
5The LORD set a time and said, "Tomorrow
the LORD will do this in the land." 6And the
next day the LORD did it: All the livestock of
the Egyptians died, but not one animal belonging to the Israelites died. 7Pharaoh sent
men to investigate and found that not even
one of the animals of the Israelites had died.
Yet his heart was unyielding and he would not
let the people go.

The Plague of Boils

8Then the LORD said to Moses and Aaron,
"Take handfuls of soot from a furnace and
have Moses toss it into the air in the presence
of Pharaoh. 9It will become fine dust over the
whole land of Egypt, and festering boils will
break out on men and animals throughout the
land."
10So they took soot from a furnace and
stood before Pharaoh. Moses tossed it into
the air, and festering boils broke out on men
and animals. 11The magicians could not stand
before Moses because of the boils that were
on them and on all the Egyptians. 12But the
LORD hardened Pharaoh's heart and he would
not listen to Moses and Aaron, just as the
LORD had said to Moses.

The Plague of Hail

13Then the LORD said to Moses, "Get up
early in the morning, confront Pharaoh and
say to him, 'This is what the LORD, the God
of the Hebrews, says: Let my people go, so
that they may worship me, 14or this time I
will send the full force of my plagues against
you and against your officials and your people, so you may know that there is no one like
me in all the earth. 15For by now I could have
stretched out my hand and struck you and
your people with a plague that would have
wiped you off the earth. 16But I have raised
you up[b] for this very purpose, that I might
show you my power and that my name might
be proclaimed in all the earth. 17You still set
yourself against my people and will not let
them go. 18Therefore, at this time tomorrow
I will send the worst hailstorm that has ever
fallen on Egypt, from the day it was founded
till now. 19Give an order now to bring your
livestock and everything you have in the field
to a place of shelter, because the hail will fall
on every man and animal that has not been
brought in and is still out in the field, and
they will die.' "
20Those officials of Pharaoh who feared the
word of the LORD hurried to bring their slaves

a 23 Septuagint and Vulgate; Hebrew *will put a deliverance* *b* 16 Or *have spared you*

WEEKEND

building our strengths

Jim stared silently at the television set while Carol ached inside, wondering why he was angry at her. They had only been married a year, and Carol could already see their relationship deteriorating. She couldn't help wonder if she would soon join the millions of other couples whose marriage had ended in divorce. When she finally asked Jim what was wrong, he refused to answer. Hurting for a few minutes, she repeated the question. His response wounded her so deeply she began to doubt her adequacy as a wife.

He said, "I'm sick and tired of you taking everything so seriously. You're just too sensitive! If I had known you were this emotional, I probably never would have married you. But since we are married, I think you need to do your part. Cut the overreacting and stop being so touchy about what I say and do. If we're going to have any kind of marriage, you have to stop being so childish!"

Sound familiar? With these harsh words, Jim unknowingly has set their relationship on a destructive path leading to some very unattractive changes—changes that could lead to the ultimate disintegration of their relationship. Jim's main problem, shared by thousands of other husbands, is that he fails to understand the basic difference between the natures of men and women. Jim has taken two of his wife's greatest natural strengths, her sensitivity and intuitive awareness of life, and labeled them weaknesses. In response to Jim's reproof, Carol, like thousands of other wives, will begin to form a calloused, hardened attitude toward life in general and Jim in particular.

If their marriage lasts more than a few years, Jim will find to his dismay that Carol's sensitivity has finally been subdued and that he has lost most or all of his attraction to her. If only he could remember that her sensitivity was one of the first things that attracted him. If only he understood that her alertness was one of her greatest strengths and began treating her with tenderness, gentleness and kindness, their relationship would grow stronger and more fulfilling.

It is typical for a man to marry without knowing *how* to talk to his wife. Some men don't even know that their wives *need* intimate communication. Often a man is completely unaware of his wife's sensitive nature. He doesn't know that things he considers trivial can be extremely important to her—things like anniversaries and holidays. Nor does he realize why such things *are* special to her, so he is unable to meet her needs.

Many women step into marriage equally handicapped. They don't understand that admiration is to a man what romance is to a woman. They don't realize that a man generally relies on reasoning rather than intuitive sensitivity.

If both husband and wife lack the vital knowledge and skills to meet each other's needs, their needs will go unmet. One of the great psychiatrists of our time, Dr. Karl Menninger, said that when our basic needs are not met, we move in one of two directions. We either withdraw in "flight" or turn to "fight." The woman who takes the "flight" approach is not escaping her problems. As she runs, she begins to doubt her self-worth. On the other hand, if she takes the "fight" approach, she may become an unattractive nag to her husband.

I believe the ideal marriage evolves when the wife concentrates on meeting her husband's needs and the husband concentrates on meeting his wife's needs. That combination builds the lasting qualities of relationship.

—GARY SMALLEY

what are your needs?

How good are you at recognizing your spouse's needs or your own? Below is a list of needs. Which ones are his needs? Which ones are hers? Which do you both share?

1. I need you to understand me.
2. I need you to listen to me without trying to solve problems.
3. I need for us to spend time together as a couple.
4. I need you to nag less.
5. I need you to say, "I love you."
6. I need to pray with you.
7. I need to talk about stuff so I know what I think.
8. I need to think about stuff on my own.
9. I need physical touch.
10. I need you to be more spontaneous about sex.
11. I need you to remember special occasions.
12. I need a weekend away with you.
13. I need more sleep.
14. I need you to help around the house.
15. I need you to open up more.
16. I need more alone time.
17. I need you to travel less.
18. I need you to go to bed when I go to bed.
19. I need you to take care of your health.
20. I need you.

HOW ARE WE DOING?

let's make a DATE

MEET SOMEONE ELSE'S NEEDS

This weekend, volunteer to help meet someone else's needs by working at a local soup kitchen, homeless shelter or Habitat for Humanity building site. Or bring a dessert to a person in a retirement home. Or call on someone in the hospital. Have fun meeting someone else's needs and see how many of yours get met in the process.

FOR YOUR NEXT DEVOTIONAL READING, TURN TO PAGE 77.

LESSONS FROM THE *Bible*

How do you think Priscilla and Aquila met each other's needs as they worked together? See Acts 18:1–26; Romans 16:3–4; 1 Corinthians 16:19.

and their livestock inside. [21]But those who ignored the word of the LORD left their slaves
and livestock in the field.
[22]Then the LORD said to Moses, "Stretch
out your hand toward the sky so that hail will
fall all over Egypt—on men and animals and
on everything growing in the fields of Egypt."
[23]When Moses stretched out his staff toward
the sky, the LORD sent thunder and hail, and
lightning flashed down to the ground. So the
LORD rained hail on the land of Egypt; [24]hail
fell and lightning flashed back and forth. It was
the worst storm in all the land of Egypt since
it had become a nation. [25]Throughout Egypt
hail struck everything in the fields—both men
and animals; it beat down everything growing in the fields and stripped every tree. [26]The
only place it did not hail was the land of Goshen, where the Israelites were.
[27]Then Pharaoh summoned Moses and
Aaron. "This time I have sinned," he said to
them. "The LORD is in the right, and I and my
people are in the wrong. [28]Pray to the LORD,
for we have had enough thunder and hail. I
will let you go; you don't have to stay any longer."
[29]Moses replied, "When I have gone out of
the city, I will spread out my hands in prayer
to the LORD. The thunder will stop and there
will be no more hail, so you may know that
the earth is the LORD's. [30]But I know that you
and your officials still do not fear the LORD
God."
[31](The flax and barley were destroyed, since
the barley had headed and the flax was in
bloom. [32]The wheat and spelt, however, were
not destroyed, because they ripen later.)
[33]Then Moses left Pharaoh and went out
of the city. He spread out his hands toward
the LORD; the thunder and hail stopped, and
the rain no longer poured down on the land.
[34]When Pharaoh saw that the rain and hail
and thunder had stopped, he sinned again:
He and his officials hardened their hearts.
[35]So Pharaoh's heart was hard and he would
not let the Israelites go, just as the LORD had
said through Moses.

The Plague of Locusts

10 Then the LORD said to Moses, "Go to
Pharaoh, for I have hardened his heart
and the hearts of his officials so that I
may perform these miraculous signs of mine
among them [2]that you may tell your children
and grandchildren how I dealt harshly with
the Egyptians and how I performed my signs
among them, and that you may know that I
am the LORD."
[3]So Moses and Aaron went to Pharaoh and
said to him, "This is what the LORD, the God
of the Hebrews, says: 'How long will you refuse to humble yourself before me? Let my
people go, so that they may worship me. [4]If
you refuse to let them go, I will bring locusts
into your country tomorrow. [5]They will cover the face of the ground so that it cannot be
seen. They will devour what little you have left
after the hail, including every tree that is growing in your fields. [6]They will fill your houses
and those of all your officials and all the Egyptians—something neither your fathers nor
your forefathers have ever seen from the day
they settled in this land till now.' " Then Moses turned and left Pharaoh.
[7]Pharaoh's officials said to him, "How long
will this man be a snare to us? Let the people
go, so that they may worship the LORD their
God. Do you not yet realize that Egypt is ruined?"
[8]Then Moses and Aaron were brought back
to Pharaoh. "Go, worship the LORD your
God," he said. "But just who will be going?"
[9]Moses answered, "We will go with our
young and old, with our sons and daughters,
and with our flocks and herds, because we are
to celebrate a festival to the LORD."
[10]Pharaoh said, "The LORD be with you—
if I let you go, along with your women and
children! Clearly you are bent on evil.[a] [11]No!
Have only the men go; and worship the LORD,
since that's what you have been asking for."
Then Moses and Aaron were driven out of
Pharaoh's presence.
[12]And the LORD said to Moses, "Stretch out
your hand over Egypt so that locusts will swarm
over the land and devour everything growing
in the fields, everything left by the hail."
[13]So Moses stretched out his staff over
Egypt, and the LORD made an east wind blow
across the land all that day and all that night.
By morning the wind had brought the locusts;
[14]they invaded all Egypt and settled down in
every area of the country in great numbers.
Never before had there been such a plague of
locusts, nor will there ever be again. [15]They
covered all the ground until it was black. They
devoured all that was left after the hail—everything growing in the fields and the fruit on
the trees. Nothing green remained on tree or
plant in all the land of Egypt.

[a] 10 Or *Be careful, trouble is in store for you!*

16 Pharaoh quickly summoned Moses and Aaron and said, "I have sinned against the LORD your God and against you. 17 Now forgive my sin once more and pray to the LORD your God to take this deadly plague away from me."

18 Moses then left Pharaoh and prayed to the LORD. 19 And the LORD changed the wind to a very strong west wind, which caught up the locusts and carried them into the Red Sea.[a] Not a locust was left anywhere in Egypt. 20 But the LORD hardened Pharaoh's heart, and he would not let the Israelites go.

The Plague of Darkness

21 Then the LORD said to Moses, "Stretch out your hand toward the sky so that darkness will spread over Egypt—darkness that can be felt." 22 So Moses stretched out his hand toward the sky, and total darkness covered all Egypt for three days. 23 No one could see anyone else or leave his place for three days. Yet all the Israelites had light in the places where they lived.

24 Then Pharaoh summoned Moses and said, "Go, worship the LORD. Even your women and children may go with you; only leave your flocks and herds behind."

25 But Moses said, "You must allow us to have sacrifices and burnt offerings to present to the LORD our God. 26 Our livestock too must go with us; not a hoof is to be left behind. We have to use some of them in worshiping the LORD our God, and until we get there we will not know what we are to use to worship the LORD."

27 But the LORD hardened Pharaoh's heart, and he was not willing to let them go. 28 Pharaoh said to Moses, "Get out of my sight! Make sure you do not appear before me again! The day you see my face you will die."

29 "Just as you say," Moses replied, "I will never appear before you again."

The Plague on the Firstborn

11 Now the LORD had said to Moses, "I will bring one more plague on Pharaoh and on Egypt. After that, he will let you go from here, and when he does, he will drive you out completely. 2 Tell the people that men and women alike are to ask their neighbors for articles of silver and gold." 3 (The LORD made the Egyptians favorably disposed toward the people, and Moses himself was highly regarded in Egypt by Pharaoh's officials and by the people.)

4 So Moses said, "This is what the LORD says: 'About midnight I will go throughout Egypt. 5 Every firstborn son in Egypt will die, from the firstborn son of Pharaoh, who sits on the throne, to the firstborn son of the slave girl, who is at her hand mill, and all the firstborn of the cattle as well. 6 There will be loud wailing throughout Egypt—worse than there has ever been or ever will be again. 7 But among the Israelites not a dog will bark at any man or animal.' Then you will know that the LORD makes a distinction between Egypt and Israel. 8 All these officials of yours will come to me, bowing down before me and saying, 'Go, you and all the people who follow you!' After that I will leave." Then Moses, hot with anger, left Pharaoh.

9 The LORD had said to Moses, "Pharaoh will refuse to listen to you—so that my wonders may be multiplied in Egypt." 10 Moses and Aaron performed all these wonders before Pharaoh, but the LORD hardened Pharaoh's heart, and he would not let the Israelites go out of his country.

The Passover

12 The LORD said to Moses and Aaron in Egypt, 2 "This month is to be for you the first month, the first month of your year. 3 Tell the whole community of Israel that on the tenth day of this month each man is to take a lamb[b] for his family, one for each household. 4 If any household is too small for a whole lamb, they must share one with their nearest neighbor, having taken into account the number of people there are. You are to determine the amount of lamb needed in accordance with what each person will eat. 5 The animals you choose must be year-old males without defect, and you may take them from the sheep or the goats. 6 Take care of them until the fourteenth day of the month, when all the people of the community of Israel must slaughter them at twilight. 7 Then they are to take some of the blood and put it on the sides and tops of the doorframes of the houses where they eat the lambs. 8 That same night they are to eat the meat roasted over the fire, along with bitter herbs, and bread made without yeast. 9 Do not eat the meat raw or cooked in water, but roast it over the fire—head, legs and inner parts. 10 Do not leave any of it till morning; if some is left till morning, you must burn it. 11 This is how you are to eat it: with

---

a 19 Hebrew *Yam Suph*; that is, Sea of Reeds *b* 3 The Hebrew word can mean *lamb* or *kid*; also in verse 4.

your cloak tucked into your belt, your sandals
on your feet and your staff in your hand. Eat
it in haste; it is the LORD's Passover.
12"On that same night I will pass through
Egypt and strike down every firstborn—both
men and animals—and I will bring judgment
on all the gods of Egypt. I am the LORD. 13The
blood will be a sign for you on the houses
where you are; and when I see the blood, I
will pass over you. No destructive plague will
touch you when I strike Egypt.
14"This is a day you are to commemorate; for
the generations to come you shall celebrate it
as a festival to the LORD—a lasting ordinance.
15For seven days you are to eat bread made
without yeast. On the first day remove the
yeast from your houses, for whoever eats anything with yeast in it from the first day through
the seventh must be cut off from Israel. 16On
the first day hold a sacred assembly, and another one on the seventh day. Do no work at all on
these days, except to prepare food for everyone
to eat—that is all you may do.
17"Celebrate the Feast of Unleavened Bread,
because it was on this very day that I brought
your divisions out of Egypt. Celebrate this day
as a lasting ordinance for the generations to
come. 18In the first month you are to eat bread
made without yeast, from the evening of the
fourteenth day until the evening of the twenty-first day. 19For seven days no yeast is to be
found in your houses. And whoever eats anything with yeast in it must be cut off from the
community of Israel, whether he is an alien or
native-born. 20Eat nothing made with yeast.
Wherever you live, you must eat unleavened
bread."
21Then Moses summoned all the elders of
Israel and said to them, "Go at once and select
the animals for your families and slaughter the
Passover lamb. 22Take a bunch of hyssop, dip
it into the blood in the basin and put some of
the blood on the top and on both sides of the
doorframe. Not one of you shall go out the
door of his house until morning. 23When the
LORD goes through the land to strike down
the Egyptians, he will see the blood on the
top and sides of the doorframe and will pass
over that doorway, and he will not permit the
destroyer to enter your houses and strike you
down.
24"Obey these instructions as a lasting ordinance for you and your descendants. 25When
you enter the land that the LORD will give you
as he promised, observe this ceremony. 26And
when your children ask you, 'What does this
ceremony mean to you?' 27then tell them, 'It is
the Passover sacrifice to the LORD, who passed
over the houses of the Israelites in Egypt and
spared our homes when he struck down the
Egyptians.'" Then the people bowed down
and worshiped. 28The Israelites did just what
the LORD commanded Moses and Aaron.
29At midnight the LORD struck down all the
firstborn in Egypt, from the firstborn of Pharaoh, who sat on the throne, to the firstborn of
the prisoner, who was in the dungeon, and the
firstborn of all the livestock as well. 30Phar-
aoh and all his officials and all the Egyptians
got up during the night, and there was loud
wailing in Egypt, for there was not a house
without someone dead.

The Exodus

31During the night Pharaoh summoned
Moses and Aaron and said, "Up! Leave my
people, you and the Israelites! Go, worship
the LORD as you have requested. 32Take your
flocks and herds, as you have said, and go.
And also bless me."
33The Egyptians urged the people to hurry and leave the country. "For otherwise,"
they said, "we will all die!" 34So the people
took their dough before the yeast was added,
and carried it on their shoulders in kneading
troughs wrapped in clothing. 35The Israelites
did as Moses instructed and asked the Egyptians for articles of silver and gold and for
clothing. 36The LORD had made the Egyptians
favorably disposed toward the people, and
they gave them what they asked for; so they
plundered the Egyptians.
37The Israelites journeyed from Rameses
to Succoth. There were about six hundred
thousand men on foot, besides women and
children. 38Many other people went up with
them, as well as large droves of livestock, both
flocks and herds. 39With the dough they had
brought from Egypt, they baked cakes of unleavened bread. The dough was without yeast
because they had been driven out of Egypt
and did not have time to prepare food for
themselves.
40Now the length of time the Israelite people lived in Egypt[a] was 430 years. 41At the end
of the 430 years, to the very day, all the LORD's
divisions left Egypt. 42Because the LORD kept
vigil that night to bring them out of Egypt, on
this night all the Israelites are to keep vigil to
honor the LORD for the generations to come.

[a] 40 Masoretic Text; Samaritan Pentateuch and Septuagint *Egypt and Canaan*

Passover Restrictions

43The LORD said to Moses and Aaron,
"These are the regulations for the Passover:
"No foreigner is to eat of it. 44Any slave you
have bought may eat of it after you have circumcised him, 45but a temporary resident and
a hired worker may not eat of it.
46"It must be eaten inside one house; take
none of the meat outside the house. Do not
break any of the bones. 47The whole community of Israel must celebrate it.
48"An alien living among you who wants to
celebrate the LORD's Passover must have all the
males in his household circumcised; then he
may take part like one born in the land. No
uncircumcised male may eat of it. 49The same
law applies to the native-born and to the alien
living among you."

50All the Israelites did just what the LORD
had commanded Moses and Aaron. 51And on
that very day the LORD brought the Israelites
out of Egypt by their divisions.

Consecration of the Firstborn

13 The LORD said to Moses, 2"Consecrate
to me every firstborn male. The first offspring of every womb among the Israelites belongs to me, whether man or animal."
3Then Moses said to the people, "Commemorate this day, the day you came out of
Egypt, out of the land of slavery, because the
LORD brought you out of it with a mighty
hand. Eat nothing containing yeast. 4Today,
in the month of Abib, you are leaving. 5When
the LORD brings you into the land of the Canaanites, Hittites, Amorites, Hivites and Jebusites—the land he swore to your forefathers
to give you, a land flowing with milk and
honey—you are to observe this ceremony in
this month: 6For seven days eat bread made
without yeast and on the seventh day hold a
festival to the LORD. 7Eat unleavened bread
during those seven days; nothing with yeast in
it is to be seen among you, nor shall any yeast
be seen anywhere within your borders. 8On
that day tell your son, 'I do this because of
what the LORD did for me when I came out of
Egypt.' 9This observance will be for you like
a sign on your hand and a reminder on your
forehead that the law of the LORD is to be on
your lips. For the LORD brought you out of
Egypt with his mighty hand. 10You must keep
this ordinance at the appointed time year after year.
11"After the LORD brings you into the land
of the Canaanites and gives it to you, as he
promised on oath to you and your forefathers,
12you are to give over to the LORD the first offspring of every womb. All the firstborn males
of your livestock belong to the LORD. 13Re-
deem with a lamb every firstborn donkey, but
if you do not redeem it, break its neck. Redeem every firstborn among your sons.
14"In days to come, when your son asks
you, 'What does this mean?' say to him, 'With
a mighty hand the LORD brought us out of
Egypt, out of the land of slavery. 15When
Pharaoh stubbornly refused to let us go, the
LORD killed every firstborn in Egypt, both
man and animal. This is why I sacrifice to the
LORD the first male offspring of every womb
and redeem each of my firstborn sons.' 16And
it will be like a sign on your hand and a symbol on your forehead that the LORD brought
us out of Egypt with his mighty hand."

Crossing the Sea

17When Pharaoh let the people go, God did
not lead them on the road through the Philistine country, though that was shorter. For
God said, "If they face war, they might change
their minds and return to Egypt." 18So God
led the people around by the desert road toward the Red Sea.[a] The Israelites went up out
of Egypt armed for battle.
19Moses took the bones of Joseph with him
because Joseph had made the sons of Israel
swear an oath. He had said, "God will surely
come to your aid, and then you must carry my
bones up with you from this place."[b]
20After leaving Succoth they camped at
Etham on the edge of the desert. 21By day the
LORD went ahead of them in a pillar of cloud
to guide them on their way and by night in a
pillar of fire to give them light, so that they
could travel by day or night. 22Neither the pillar of cloud by day nor the pillar of fire by
night left its place in front of the people.
14 Then the LORD said to Moses, 2"Tell
the Israelites to turn back and encamp
near Pi Hahiroth, between Migdol and
the sea. They are to encamp by the sea, directly opposite Baal Zephon. 3Pharaoh will
think, 'The Israelites are wandering around
the land in confusion, hemmed in by the desert.' 4And I will harden Pharaoh's heart, and
he will pursue them. But I will gain glory for
myself through Pharaoh and all his army, and
the Egyptians will know that I am the LORD."
So the Israelites did this.

[a] 18 Hebrew *Yam Suph*; that is, Sea of Reeds [b] 19 See Gen. 50:25.

5When the king of Egypt was told that the people had fled, Pharaoh and his officials changed their minds about them and said, "What have we done? We have let the Israelites go and have lost their services!" 6So he had his chariot made ready and took his army with him. 7He took six hundred of the best chariots, along with all the other chariots of Egypt, with officers over all of them. 8The LORD hardened the heart of Pharaoh king of Egypt, so that he pursued the Israelites, who were marching out boldly. 9The Egyptians—all Pharaoh's horses and chariots, horsemen[a] and troops—pursued the Israelites and overtook them as they camped by the sea near Pi Hahiroth, opposite Baal Zephon.

10As Pharaoh approached, the Israelites looked up, and there were the Egyptians, marching after them. They were terrified and cried out to the LORD. 11They said to Moses, "Was it because there were no graves in Egypt that you brought us to the desert to die? What have you done to us by bringing us out of Egypt? 12Didn't we say to you in Egypt, 'Leave us alone; let us serve the Egyptians'? It would have been better for us to serve the Egyptians than to die in the desert!"

13Moses answered the people, "Do not be afraid. Stand firm and you will see the deliverance the LORD will bring you today. The Egyptians you see today you will never see again. 14The LORD will fight for you; you need only to be still."

15Then the LORD said to Moses, "Why are you crying out to me? Tell the Israelites to move on. 16Raise your staff and stretch out your hand over the sea to divide the water so that the Israelites can go through the sea on dry ground. 17I will harden the hearts of the Egyptians so that they will go in after them. And I will gain glory through Pharaoh and all his army, through his chariots and his horsemen. 18The Egyptians will know that I am the LORD when I gain glory through Pharaoh, his chariots and his horsemen."

19Then the angel of God, who had been traveling in front of Israel's army, withdrew and went behind them. The pillar of cloud also moved from in front and stood behind them, 20coming between the armies of Egypt and Israel. Throughout the night the cloud brought darkness to the one side and light to the other side; so neither went near the other all night long.

21Then Moses stretched out his hand over the sea, and all that night the LORD drove the sea back with a strong east wind and turned it into dry land. The waters were divided, 22and the Israelites went through the sea on dry ground, with a wall of water on their right and on their left.

23The Egyptians pursued them, and all Pharaoh's horses and chariots and horsemen followed them into the sea. 24During the last watch of the night the LORD looked down from the pillar of fire and cloud at the Egyptian army and threw it into confusion. 25He made the wheels of their chariots come off[b] so that they had difficulty driving. And the Egyptians said, "Let's get away from the Israelites! The LORD is fighting for them against Egypt."

26Then the LORD said to Moses, "Stretch out your hand over the sea so that the waters may flow back over the Egyptians and their chariots and horsemen." 27Moses stretched out his hand over the sea, and at daybreak the sea went back to its place. The Egyptians were fleeing toward[c] it, and the LORD swept them into the sea. 28The water flowed back and covered the chariots and horsemen—the entire army of Pharaoh that had followed the Israelites into the sea. Not one of them survived.

29But the Israelites went through the sea on dry ground, with a wall of water on their right and on their left. 30That day the LORD saved Israel from the hands of the Egyptians, and Israel saw the Egyptians lying dead on the shore. 31And when the Israelites saw the great power the LORD displayed against the Egyptians, the people feared the LORD and put their trust in him and in Moses his servant.

The Song of Moses and Miriam

15 Then Moses and the Israelites sang this song to the LORD:

"I will sing to the LORD,
  for he is highly exalted.
The horse and its rider
  he has hurled into the sea.
2The LORD is my strength and my song;
  he has become my salvation.
He is my God, and I will praise him,
  my father's God, and I will exalt him.
3The LORD is a warrior;
  the LORD is his name.
4Pharaoh's chariots and his army
  he has hurled into the sea.

[a] 9 Or *charioteers*; also in verses 17, 18, 23, 26 and 28 [b] 25 Or *He jammed the wheels of their chariots* (see Samaritan Pentateuch, Septuagint and Syriac) [c] 27 Or *from*

The best of Pharaoh's officers
are drowned in the Red Sea.[a]
5 The deep waters have covered them;
they sank to the depths like a stone.

6 "Your right hand, O LORD,
was majestic in power.
Your right hand, O LORD,
shattered the enemy.
7 In the greatness of your majesty
you threw down those who opposed
you.
You unleashed your burning anger;
it consumed them like stubble.
8 By the blast of your nostrils
the waters piled up.
The surging waters stood firm like a wall;
the deep waters congealed in the heart
of the sea.

9 "The enemy boasted,
'I will pursue, I will overtake them.
I will divide the spoils;
I will gorge myself on them.
I will draw my sword
and my hand will destroy them.'
10 But you blew with your breath,
and the sea covered them.
They sank like lead
in the mighty waters.

11 "Who among the gods is like you,
O LORD?
Who is like you—
majestic in holiness,
awesome in glory,
working wonders?
12 You stretched out your right hand
and the earth swallowed them.

13 "In your unfailing love you will lead
the people you have redeemed.
In your strength you will guide them
to your holy dwelling.
14 The nations will hear and tremble;
anguish will grip the people of
Philistia.
15 The chiefs of Edom will be terrified,
the leaders of Moab will be seized with
trembling,
the people[b] of Canaan will melt away;
16 terror and dread will fall upon them.
By the power of your arm
they will be as still as a stone—
until your people pass by, O LORD,
until the people you bought[c] pass by.
17 You will bring them in and plant them
on the mountain of your inheritance—
the place, O LORD, you made for your
dwelling,
the sanctuary, O Lord, your hands
established.
18 The LORD will reign
for ever and ever."

19 When Pharaoh's horses, chariots and
horsemen[d] went into the sea, the LORD
brought the waters of the sea back over them,
but the Israelites walked through the sea on
dry ground. 20 Then Miriam the prophetess,
Aaron's sister, took a tambourine in her hand,
and all the women followed her, with tambourines and dancing. 21 Miriam sang to them:

"Sing to the LORD,
for he is highly exalted.
The horse and its rider
he has hurled into the sea."

The Waters of Marah and Elim

22 Then Moses led Israel from the Red Sea
and they went into the Desert of Shur. For
three days they traveled in the desert without
finding water. 23 When they came to Marah,
they could not drink its water because it was
bitter. (That is why the place is called Marah.[e])
24 So the people grumbled against Moses, saying, "What are we to drink?"
25 Then Moses cried out to the LORD, and
the LORD showed him a piece of wood. He
threw it into the water, and the water became
sweet.

There the LORD made a decree and a law for
them, and there he tested them. 26 He said, "If
you listen carefully to the voice of the LORD
your God and do what is right in his eyes, if
you pay attention to his commands and keep
all his decrees, I will not bring on you any of
the diseases I brought on the Egyptians, for I
am the LORD, who heals you."
27 Then they came to Elim, where there
were twelve springs and seventy palm trees,
and they camped there near the water.

Manna and Quail

16 The whole Israelite community set out
from Elim and came to the Desert of
Sin, which is between Elim and Sinai,
on the fifteenth day of the second month after
they had come out of Egypt. 2 In the desert
the whole community grumbled against Moses and Aaron. 3 The Israelites said to them, "If
only we had died by the LORD's hand in Egypt!

[a] 4 Hebrew *Yam Suph*; that is, Sea of Reeds; also in verse 22 [b] 15 Or *rulers* [c] 16 Or *created* [d] 19 Or *charioteers* [e] 23 *Marah* means *bitter.*

There we sat around pots of meat and ate all
the food we wanted, but you have brought us
out into this desert to starve this entire assembly to death."

4Then the LORD said to Moses, "I will rain
down bread from heaven for you. The people
are to go out each day and gather enough for
that day. In this way I will test them and see
whether they will follow my instructions. 5On
the sixth day they are to prepare what they
bring in, and that is to be twice as much as
they gather on the other days."

6So Moses and Aaron said to all the Israelites, "In the evening you will know that it was
the LORD who brought you out of Egypt, 7and
in the morning you will see the glory of the
LORD, because he has heard your grumbling
against him. Who are we, that you should
grumble against us?" 8Moses also said, "You
will know that it was the LORD when he gives
you meat to eat in the evening and all the
bread you want in the morning, because he
has heard your grumbling against him. Who
are we? You are not grumbling against us, but
against the LORD."

9Then Moses told Aaron, "Say to the entire
Israelite community, 'Come before the LORD,
for he has heard your grumbling.' "

10While Aaron was speaking to the whole
Israelite community, they looked toward the
desert, and there was the glory of the LORD
appearing in the cloud.

11The LORD said to Moses, 12"I have heard
the grumbling of the Israelites. Tell them, 'At
twilight you will eat meat, and in the morning
you will be filled with bread. Then you will
know that I am the LORD your God.' "

13That evening quail came and covered the
camp, and in the morning there was a layer of
dew around the camp. 14When the dew was
gone, thin flakes like frost on the ground appeared on the desert floor. 15When the Israelites saw it, they said to each other, "What is
it?" For they did not know what it was.

Moses said to them, "It is the bread the
LORD has given you to eat. 16This is what the
LORD has commanded: 'Each one is to gather
as much as he needs. Take an omer[a] for each
person you have in your tent.' "

17The Israelites did as they were told; some
gathered much, some little. 18And when they
measured it by the omer, he who gathered
much did not have too much, and he who
gathered little did not have too little. Each one
gathered as much as he needed.

19Then Moses said to them, "No one is to
keep any of it until morning."

20However, some of them paid no attention
to Moses; they kept part of it until morning,
but it was full of maggots and began to smell.
So Moses was angry with them.

21Each morning everyone gathered as much
as he needed, and when the sun grew hot, it
melted away. 22On the sixth day, they gathered twice as much—two omers[b] for each person—and the leaders of the community came
and reported this to Moses. 23He said to them,
"This is what the LORD commanded: 'Tomorrow is to be a day of rest, a holy Sabbath to
the LORD. So bake what you want to bake and
boil what you want to boil. Save whatever is
left and keep it until morning.' "

24So they saved it until morning, as Moses
commanded, and it did not stink or get maggots in it. 25"Eat it today," Moses said, "because today is a Sabbath to the LORD. You will
not find any of it on the ground today. 26Six
days you are to gather it, but on the seventh
day, the Sabbath, there will not be any."

27Nevertheless, some of the people went
out on the seventh day to gather it, but they
found none. 28Then the LORD said to Moses,
"How long will you[c] refuse to keep my commands and my instructions? 29Bear in mind
that the LORD has given you the Sabbath; that
is why on the sixth day he gives you bread for
two days. Everyone is to stay where he is on
the seventh day; no one is to go out." 30So the
people rested on the seventh day.

31The people of Israel called the bread
manna.[d] It was white like coriander seed and
tasted like wafers made with honey. 32Moses
said, "This is what the LORD has commanded:
'Take an omer of manna and keep it for the
generations to come, so they can see the bread
I gave you to eat in the desert when I brought
you out of Egypt.' "

33So Moses said to Aaron, "Take a jar and
put an omer of manna in it. Then place it before the LORD to be kept for the generations
to come."

34As the LORD commanded Moses, Aaron
put the manna in front of the Testimony, that
it might be kept. 35The Israelites ate manna
forty years, until they came to a land that was
settled; they ate manna until they reached the
border of Canaan.

36(An omer is one tenth of an ephah.)

---

[a] *16* That is, probably about 2 quarts (about 2 liters); also in verses 18, 32, 33 and 36 [b] *22* That is, probably about 4 quarts (about 4.5 liters) [c] *28* The Hebrew is plural. [d] *31* *Manna* means *What is it?* (see verse 15).

WANTING MORE

An older couple was looking for a piece of property in a neighborhood dotted with brand-new, expensive homes. Through careful planning, the couple had paid off their first home and put their kids through college. Now they wanted to build their dream home in which to retire.

As they drove around the subdivision, the husband was impressed with the number of young families living in the neighborhood. He noticed they all had nice cars. He was curious because the local economy was suffering. "How can these young people afford such nice houses?" he asked the realtor.

"Many of them can't," the realtor responded. "They've got adjustable rate mortgages so their payments are low now, but they won't be able to afford the payments when interest rates rise. They also bought cars with low-interest loans. They're funding their lifestyle through credit card debt." He thought for a moment and then added, "I think a lot of them grew up in nice homes. They think they deserve everything their parents have even though their parents worked for years to get it."

The Israelites may have felt a similar sense of entitlement. They were wandering in the desert. There were no crops or livestock; they gathered their own food. But miraculously, God provided for them each day with a flakelike substance that was called *manna*, or "bread from heaven." The people were warned not to take more manna than they needed for the day, and under no conditions were they to store it until morning. The only exception was on the sixth day, when they were allowed to gather two days' worth to provide for the Sabbath.

But some of the Israelites didn't listen. They gathered more manna than they needed and stored it. In the morning, the bread was full of maggots and began to smell. Soon everyone knew they had disobeyed because of the stench of the rotting manna.

Some of those young couples in the affluent neighborhood may find themselves in a similar embarrassing situation. Using creative financing, they are taking what they want. One day they will awaken to find that the new-house and new-car smell has been replaced by the stench of unpaid credit card bills. Their secret will be discovered when the foreclosure sign is placed on the lawn of their luxury house.

It's true that God wants to bless us, but sometimes we think that means we should get stuff that we want right now. God told the Israelites to take only what they needed because he wanted to teach them daily dependence on him. Later Jesus taught his disciples to pray for their "daily bread" (Matthew 6:11). Growing closer to God means knowing the difference between our wants and our needs, and understanding that God's blessings aren't necessarily monetary. As we trust God to meet our desires, our wants and needs may change.

—JENNIFER SCHUCHMANN

"Each one is to gather as much as he needs. Take an omer for each person you have in your tent."

— Exodus 16:16

let's talk

- ✦ To some it may have seemed wise for the Israelites to gather extra manna and save it "just in case." What's the difference between smart financial planning and trusting God to provide for our needs—both now and into the future?
- ✦ What are our daily needs? How is God providing for them? In what ways do we feel dissatisfied with what God's given us?
- ✦ How should we save for retirement? When do we cross the line between relying on our own efforts to provide for the future and trusting God (or the government) to do that for us?

FOR YOUR NEXT DEVOTIONAL READING, TURN TO PAGE 79.

Water From the Rock

17 The whole Israelite community set out
from the Desert of Sin, traveling from
place to place as the LORD commanded.
They camped at Rephidim, but there was no
water for the people to drink. 2So they quarreled with Moses and said, "Give us water to
drink."
Moses replied, "Why do you quarrel with
me? Why do you put the LORD to the test?"
3But the people were thirsty for water there,
and they grumbled against Moses. They said,
"Why did you bring us up out of Egypt to
make us and our children and livestock die of
thirst?"
4Then Moses cried out to the LORD, "What
am I to do with these people? They are almost
ready to stone me."
5The LORD answered Moses, "Walk on
ahead of the people. Take with you some of
the elders of Israel and take in your hand the
staff with which you struck the Nile, and go.
6I will stand there before you by the rock at
Horeb. Strike the rock, and water will come
out of it for the people to drink." So Moses
did this in the sight of the elders of Israel.
7And he called the place Massah[a] and Meribah[b] because the Israelites quarreled and
because they tested the LORD saying, "Is the
LORD among us or not?"

The Amalekites Defeated

8The Amalekites came and attacked the
Israelites at Rephidim. 9Moses said to Joshua, "Choose some of our men and go out to
fight the Amalekites. Tomorrow I will stand
on top of the hill with the staff of God in my
hands."
10So Joshua fought the Amalekites as Moses had ordered, and Moses, Aaron and Hur
went to the top of the hill. 11As long as Moses
held up his hands, the Israelites were winning,
but whenever he lowered his hands, the Amalekites were winning. 12When Moses' hands
grew tired, they took a stone and put it under
him and he sat on it. Aaron and Hur held his
hands up—one on one side, one on the other—so that his hands remained steady till sunset. 13So Joshua overcame the Amalekite army
with the sword.
14Then the LORD said to Moses, "Write this
on a scroll as something to be remembered
and make sure that Joshua hears it, because I
will completely blot out the memory of Amalek from under heaven."
15Moses built an altar and called it The
LORD is my Banner. 16He said, "For hands
were lifted up to the throne of the LORD. The[c]
LORD will be at war against the Amalekites
from generation to generation."

Jethro Visits Moses

18 Now Jethro, the priest of Midian and
father-in-law of Moses, heard of everything God had done for Moses and
for his people Israel, and how the LORD had
brought Israel out of Egypt.
2After Moses had sent away his wife Zipporah, his father-in-law Jethro received her 3and
her two sons. One son was named Gershom,[d]
for Moses said, "I have become an alien in a
foreign land"; 4and the other was named Eliezer,[e] for he said, "My father's God was my
helper; he saved me from the sword of Pharaoh."
5Jethro, Moses' father-in-law, together with
Moses' sons and wife, came to him in the desert, where he was camped near the mountain
of God. 6Jethro had sent word to him, "I, your
father-in-law Jethro, am coming to you with
your wife and her two sons."
7So Moses went out to meet his father-in-
law and bowed down and kissed him. They
greeted each other and then went into the
tent. 8Moses told his father-in-law about everything the LORD had done to Pharaoh and
the Egyptians for Israel's sake and about all
the hardships they had met along the way and
how the LORD had saved them.
9Jethro was delighted to hear about all the
good things the LORD had done for Israel in
rescuing them from the hand of the Egyptians.
10He said, "Praise be to the LORD, who rescued you from the hand of the Egyptians and
of Pharaoh, and who rescued the people from
the hand of the Egyptians. 11Now I know that
the LORD is greater than all other gods, for he
did this to those who had treated Israel arrogantly." 12Then Jethro, Moses' father-in-law,
brought a burnt offering and other sacrifices
to God, and Aaron came with all the elders of
Israel to eat bread with Moses' father-in-law in
the presence of God.
13The next day Moses took his seat to serve
as judge for the people, and they stood around
him from morning till evening. 14When his
father-in-law saw all that Moses was doing for
the people, he said, "What is this you are doing for the people? Why do you alone sit as

---

[a] 7 *Massah* means *testing.* [b] 7 *Meribah* means *quarreling.* [c] 16 Or *"Because a hand was against the throne of the LORD, the*
[d] 3 *Gershom* sounds like the Hebrew for *an alien there.* [e] 4 *Eliezer* means *my God is helper.*

TUESDAY

READ EXODUS 18:5–27

LEARNING FROM THE IN-LAWS

When my friend Craig turned 40, most of the guests at his birthday party were his age, but several couples appeared much older, perhaps in their 60s or 70s. The older couples participated in the festivities along with the younger crowd, and everyone seemed to have a good time. Later, I learned these older couples were Craig's parents and in-laws and the parents and in-laws of his best friend, Dave.

It was refreshing to see my friends having a good time with their in-laws. Usually we just hear in-law horror stories. When it comes to getting along with in-laws, Moses set a great example of how to do it right. Though Moses was undoubtedly the busiest man in Israel, he dropped everything to go out and meet his father-in-law. He bowed to Jethro and greeted him with a kiss.

In that time and culture bowing showed respect, but kissing was a sign of friendship. This is one of a very few recorded incidents in the Bible in which bowing and kissing both occur. We might infer from this that not only did Moses respect his father-in-law but he also considered him a friend. When was the last time you considered an in-law your friend?

Moses listened to his father-in-law and did everything he said.

— Exodus 18:24

let's talk

- Moses treated his father-in-law with respect and as a friend. What can this passage teach us about relating to our in-laws? What if our in-laws aren't particularly friend-worthy? What are some ways we can still have a positive relationship with them?
- Jethro earned the right to give advice to Moses. What are some ways we can allow that kind of process to happen with our in-laws?
- Do you think God used Jethro to get a message to Moses? Why didn't God deliver that message directly?

Perhaps the biggest complaint about in-laws is that they tend to stick their noses where they don't belong. Jethro appeared to be doing that, at least initially. Jethro knew that Moses had a direct connection to God, but he still dared to offer him advice. And, amazingly, Moses listened to his father-in-law and implemented his advice.

We'll never know for sure why Moses was so open to Jethro—perhaps it was part of Moses' meekness that led him to listen to others—but we can learn from Jethro how to make others more receptive to listening.

First, Jethro observed Moses. He didn't jump into Moses' business with an uninformed opinion; he expressed an opinion only after sitting with Moses through a long day of settling disputes.

Second, Jethro asked questions to understand why Moses did things the way he did. And third, when Jethro offered advice, he made sure Moses understood that it was given out of love. He didn't say, "You need to follow my advice so you will be a better husband and father." Instead, he expressed concern that Moses would wear himself out. Fourth, Jethro was a believer. When he offered advice, Moses knew it came from someone who worshiped the same God that he did. And when Jethro gave Moses solid, practical advice, he told Moses to follow it only if God agreed or commanded it.

Thousands of years later, Jethro's words are still considered sound management advice. Perhaps their value remains not only because of their content but also because Moses wasn't afraid to listen to an in-law who had become his friend.

—JENNIFER SCHUCHMANN

FOR YOUR NEXT DEVOTIONAL READING, TURN TO PAGE 82.

judge, while all these people stand around you
from morning till evening?"
[15]Moses answered him, "Because the people come to me to seek God's will. [16]Whenev-
er they have a dispute, it is brought to me, and
I decide between the parties and inform them
of God's decrees and laws."
[17]Moses' father-in-law replied, "What you
are doing is not good. [18]You and these people
who come to you will only wear yourselves
out. The work is too heavy for you; you cannot handle it alone. [19]Listen now to me and
I will give you some advice, and may God be
with you. You must be the people's representative before God and bring their disputes
to him. [20]Teach them the decrees and laws,
and show them the way to live and the duties they are to perform. [21]But select capable
men from all the people—men who fear God,
trustworthy men who hate dishonest gain—
and appoint them as officials over thousands,
hundreds, fifties and tens. [22]Have them serve
as judges for the people at all times, but have
them bring every difficult case to you; the
simple cases they can decide themselves. That
will make your load lighter, because they will
share it with you. [23]If you do this and God
so commands, you will be able to stand the
strain, and all these people will go home satisfied."
[24]Moses listened to his father-in-law and
did everything he said. [25]He chose capable
men from all Israel and made them leaders of
the people, officials over thousands, hundreds,
fifties and tens. [26]They served as judges for
the people at all times. The difficult cases they
brought to Moses, but the simple ones they
decided themselves.
[27]Then Moses sent his father-in-law on his
way, and Jethro returned to his own country.

At Mount Sinai

19 In the third month after the Israelites
left Egypt—on the very day—they came
to the Desert of Sinai. [2]After they set
out from Rephidim, they entered the Desert
of Sinai, and Israel camped there in the desert
in front of the mountain.
[3]Then Moses went up to God, and the
LORD called to him from the mountain and
said, "This is what you are to say to the house
of Jacob and what you are to tell the people of
Israel: [4]'You yourselves have seen what I did to
Egypt, and how I carried you on eagles' wings
and brought you to myself. [5]Now if you obey
me fully and keep my covenant, then out of
all nations you will be my treasured possession. Although the whole earth is mine, [6]you[a]
will be for me a kingdom of priests and a holy
nation.' These are the words you are to speak
to the Israelites."
[7]So Moses went back and summoned the
elders of the people and set before them all
the words the LORD had commanded him to
speak. [8]The people all responded together,
"We will do everything the LORD has said."
So Moses brought their answer back to the
LORD.
[9]The LORD said to Moses, "I am going to
come to you in a dense cloud, so that the people will hear me speaking with you and will always put their trust in you." Then Moses told
the LORD what the people had said.
[10]And the LORD said to Moses, "Go to the
people and consecrate them today and tomorrow. Have them wash their clothes [11]and
be ready by the third day, because on that
day the LORD will come down on Mount Sinai in the sight of all the people. [12]Put limits for the people around the mountain and
tell them, 'Be careful that you do not go up
the mountain or touch the foot of it. Whoever touches the mountain shall surely be
put to death. [13]He shall surely be stoned or
shot with arrows; not a hand is to be laid on
him. Whether man or animal, he shall not
be permitted to live.' Only when the ram's
horn sounds a long blast may they go up to
the mountain."
[14]After Moses had gone down the mountain to the people, he consecrated them, and
they washed their clothes. [15]Then he said to
the people, "Prepare yourselves for the third
day. Abstain from sexual relations."
[16]On the morning of the third day there
was thunder and lightning, with a thick cloud
over the mountain, and a very loud trumpet
blast. Everyone in the camp trembled. [17]Then
Moses led the people out of the camp to meet
with God, and they stood at the foot of the
mountain. [18]Mount Sinai was covered with
smoke, because the LORD descended on it in
fire. The smoke billowed up from it like smoke
from a furnace, the whole mountain[b] trembled violently, [19]and the sound of the trumpet
grew louder and louder. Then Moses spoke
and the voice of God answered him.[c]
[20]The LORD descended to the top of Mount
Sinai and called Moses to the top of the
mountain. So Moses went up [21]and the LORD

[a] 5,6 Or *possession, for the whole earth is mine.* [6]*You* [b] 18 Most Hebrew manuscripts; a few Hebrew manuscripts and Septuagint *all the people* [c] 19 Or *and God answered him with thunder*

said to him, "Go down and warn the people so
they do not force their way through to see the
LORD and many of them perish. 22Even the
priests, who approach the LORD, must consecrate themselves, or the LORD will break out
against them."

23Moses said to the LORD, "The people cannot come up Mount Sinai, because you yourself warned us, 'Put limits around the mountain and set it apart as holy.'"

24The LORD replied, "Go down and bring
Aaron up with you. But the priests and the
people must not force their way through to
come up to the LORD, or he will break out
against them."

25So Moses went down to the people and
told them.

The Ten Commandments

20 And God spoke all these words:

2"I am the LORD your God, who brought you out of Egypt, out of the land of slavery.

3"You shall have no other gods before[a] me.

4"You shall not make for yourself an idol in the form of anything in heaven above or on the earth beneath or in the waters below. 5You shall not bow down to them or worship them; for I, the LORD your God, am a jealous God, punishing the children for the sin of the fathers to the third and fourth generation of those who hate me, 6but showing love to a thousand ⌊generations⌋ of those who love me and keep my commandments.

7"You shall not misuse the name of the LORD your God, for the LORD will not hold anyone guiltless who misuses his name.

8"Remember the Sabbath day by keeping it holy. 9Six days you shall labor and do all your work, 10but the seventh day is a Sabbath to the LORD your God. On it you shall not do any work, neither you, nor your son or daughter, nor your manservant or maidservant, nor your animals, nor the alien within your gates. 11For in six days the LORD made the heavens and the earth, the sea, and all that is in them, but he rested on the seventh day. Therefore the LORD blessed the Sabbath day and made it holy.

12"Honor your father and your mother, so that you may live long in the land the LORD your God is giving you.

13"You shall not murder.

14"You shall not commit adultery.

15"You shall not steal.

16"You shall not give false testimony against your neighbor.

17"You shall not covet your neighbor's house. You shall not covet your neighbor's wife, or his manservant or maidservant, his ox or donkey, or anything that belongs to your neighbor."

18When the people saw the thunder and
lightning and heard the trumpet and saw the
mountain in smoke, they trembled with fear.
They stayed at a distance 19and said to Moses,
"Speak to us yourself and we will listen. But
do not have God speak to us or we will die."

20Moses said to the people, "Do not be
afraid. God has come to test you, so that the
fear of God will be with you to keep you from
sinning."

21The people remained at a distance, while
Moses approached the thick darkness where
God was.

Idols and Altars

22Then the LORD said to Moses, "Tell the
Israelites this: 'You have seen for yourselves
that I have spoken to you from heaven: 23Do
not make any gods to be alongside me; do not
make for yourselves gods of silver or gods of
gold.

24" 'Make an altar of earth for me and sacrifice on it your burnt offerings and fellowship
offerings,[b] your sheep and goats and your
cattle. Wherever I cause my name to be honored, I will come to you and bless you. 25If
you make an altar of stones for me, do not
build it with dressed stones, for you will defile
it if you use a tool on it. 26And do not go up
to my altar on steps, lest your nakedness be
exposed on it.'

21 "These are the laws you are to set before them:

Hebrew Servants

2"If you buy a Hebrew servant, he is to
serve you for six years. But in the seventh year,

[a] 3 Or *besides* [b] 24 Traditionally *peace offerings*

WEDNESDAY
READ EXODUS 20:1–17

WHY FAITHFULNESS MATTERS

> **"You shall not commit adultery."**
> — Exodus 20:14

let's talk

- Have we been unfaithful to each other in thoughts, words or deeds? How did that affect our relationship?
- Is it necessary for us to talk about infidelity? Why or why not?
- Why is it especially important for Christians to be faithful in marriage?

Adultery. No couple wants to talk about it. Yet, according to Beth Allen at the University of Denver, adultery is rampant. "Many people who report being in happy marriages commit adultery," she says in "The Roots of Temptation" (*Los Angeles Times*, October 20, 2003). "Those who assume that only bad people in bad marriages cheat can blind themselves to their own risk. They're unprepared for the risky times in their own lives."

Adultery matters so much to God that the penalty for infidelity in Old Testament times was death. Why?

Faithfulness is the heart of covenant relationships. When God made a covenant with his people—first Israel and later the church—faithfulness was the glue that held it together. A covenant depends on the promises made by both parties.

Marriage mirrors God's covenantal relationship with his people. Throughout the Bible, God speaks of his covenant with his people in marriage terms. For example, in Ephesians 5:31–32, Paul explained that the intimacy of marriage is really a picture of Christ's relationship with his bride, the church.

Marriage bonds the spirits of two people. There is soul-deep intimacy. When a husband or wife enters into a romantic, sexual relationship with someone else, the marriage is pulled apart at the seams. The bond between the couple disintegrates; those who were one flesh are torn apart.

Beyond the terrible destruction to the marriage caused by adultery, there is damage done to the victimized spouse, who can no longer trust in the marriage or have any faith in the adulterer. The intense sense of rejection and violation, of failure and loss, is like a death in many ways. The victim must grieve the loss and work through the feelings of pain, anger and sorrow.

God forbids adultery because he loves us, and adultery is like swallowing a grenade that will blow us and our home to pieces. Faithfulness, on the other hand, cultivates love and trust deep within our hearts. Fidelity is hard sometimes, but it is at these very points of stress that love matures and deepens and becomes more like God's love for us. Faithfulness, especially when it is difficult, shapes us into the image of Christ.

When loving is difficult, we can turn to God, asking for grace to forgive what we cannot forgive on our own, wisdom to know how to love, and perseverance when there is little improvement in our relationship. In times when love is broken by adultery, God can build faithful love back into our lives. When we love despite the hurt, we reflect our Master.

In *The Little Brown Book of Anecdotes* (Little, Brown & Co., 1985), Clifton Fadiman writes about Daniel Webster, a nineteenth-century lawyer and statesman, who was courting his wife-to-be, Grace Fletcher. As Daniel held skeins of silk thread for Grace, he said, "Grace, we've been engaged in untying knots; let us see if we can tie a knot that will not untie for a lifetime."

They tied a silk knot then and there. Grace accepted Daniel's proposal. After the couple passed from this world, their children found a little box marked "Precious Documents." Among the contents were letters of courtship and a tiny silk knot that had never been untied.

—LEE ECLOV

FOR YOUR NEXT DEVOTIONAL READING, TURN TO PAGE 93.

he shall go free, without paying anything. 3If he comes alone, he is to go free alone; but if he has a wife when he comes, she is to go with him. 4If his master gives him a wife and she bears him sons or daughters, the woman and her children shall belong to her master, and only the man shall go free.

5"But if the servant declares, 'I love my master and my wife and children and do not want to go free,' 6then his master must take him before the judges.[a] He shall take him to the door or the doorpost and pierce his ear with an awl. Then he will be his servant for life.

7"If a man sells his daughter as a servant, she is not to go free as menservants do. 8If she does not please the master who has selected her for himself,[b] he must let her be redeemed. He has no right to sell her to foreigners, because he has broken faith with her. 9If he selects her for his son, he must grant her the rights of a daughter. 10If he marries another woman, he must not deprive the first one of her food, clothing and marital rights. 11If he does not provide her with these three things, she is to go free, without any payment of money.

Personal Injuries

12"Anyone who strikes a man and kills him shall surely be put to death. 13However, if he does not do it intentionally, but God lets it happen, he is to flee to a place I will designate. 14But if a man schemes and kills another man deliberately, take him away from my altar and put him to death.

15"Anyone who attacks[c] his father or his mother must be put to death.

16"Anyone who kidnaps another and either sells him or still has him when he is caught must be put to death.

17"Anyone who curses his father or mother must be put to death.

18"If men quarrel and one hits the other with a stone or with his fist[d] and he does not die but is confined to bed, 19the one who struck the blow will not be held responsible if the other gets up and walks around outside with his staff; however, he must pay the injured man for the loss of his time and see that he is completely healed.

20"If a man beats his male or female slave with a rod and the slave dies as a direct result, he must be punished, 21but he is not to be punished if the slave gets up after a day or two, since the slave is his property.

22"If men who are fighting hit a pregnant woman and she gives birth prematurely[e] but there is no serious injury, the offender must be fined whatever the woman's husband demands and the court allows. 23But if there is serious injury, you are to take life for life, 24eye for eye, tooth for tooth, hand for hand, foot for foot, 25burn for burn, wound for wound, bruise for bruise.

26"If a man hits a manservant or maidservant in the eye and destroys it, he must let the servant go free to compensate for the eye. 27And if he knocks out the tooth of a manservant or maidservant, he must let the servant go free to compensate for the tooth.

28"If a bull gores a man or a woman to death, the bull must be stoned to death, and its meat must not be eaten. But the owner of the bull will not be held responsible. 29If, however, the bull has had the habit of goring and the owner has been warned but has not kept it penned up and it kills a man or woman, the bull must be stoned and the owner also must be put to death. 30However, if payment is demanded of him, he may redeem his life by paying whatever is demanded. 31This law also applies if the bull gores a son or daughter. 32If the bull gores a male or female slave, the owner must pay thirty shekels[f] of silver to the master of the slave, and the bull must be stoned.

33"If a man uncovers a pit or digs one and fails to cover it and an ox or a donkey falls into it, 34the owner of the pit must pay for the loss; he must pay its owner, and the dead animal will be his.

35"If a man's bull injures the bull of another and it dies, they are to sell the live one and divide both the money and the dead animal equally. 36However, if it was known that the bull had the habit of goring, yet the owner did not keep it penned up, the owner must pay, animal for animal, and the dead animal will be his.

Protection of Property

22 "If a man steals an ox or a sheep and slaughters it or sells it, he must pay back five head of cattle for the ox and four sheep for the sheep.

2"If a thief is caught breaking in and is struck so that he dies, the defender is not guilty of bloodshed; 3but if it happens[g] after sunrise, he is guilty of bloodshed.

"A thief must certainly make restitution,

[a] 6 Or *before God* [b] 8 Or *master so that he does not choose her* [c] 15 Or *kills* [d] 18 Or *with a tool* [e] 22 Or *she has a miscarriage*
[f] 32 That is, about 12 ounces (about 0.3 kilogram) [g] 3 Or *if he strikes him*

but if he has nothing, he must be sold to pay for his theft.

4“If the stolen animal is found alive in his possession—whether ox or donkey or sheep—he must pay back double.

5“If a man grazes his livestock in a field or vineyard and lets them stray and they graze in another man’s field, he must make restitution from the best of his own field or vineyard.

6“If a fire breaks out and spreads into thornbushes so that it burns shocks of grain or standing grain or the whole field, the one who started the fire must make restitution.

7“If a man gives his neighbor silver or goods for safekeeping and they are stolen from the neighbor’s house, the thief, if he is caught, must pay back double. 8But if the thief is not found, the owner of the house must appear before the judges[a] to determine whether he has laid his hands on the other man’s property. 9In all cases of illegal possession of an ox, a donkey, a sheep, a garment, or any other lost property about which somebody says, ‘This is mine,’ both parties are to bring their cases before the judges. The one whom the judges declare[b] guilty must pay back double to his neighbor.

10“If a man gives a donkey, an ox, a sheep or any other animal to his neighbor for safekeeping and it dies or is injured or is taken away while no one is looking, 11the issue between them will be settled by the taking of an oath before the Lord that the neighbor did not lay hands on the other person’s property. The owner is to accept this, and no restitution is required. 12But if the animal was stolen from the neighbor, he must make restitution to the owner. 13If it was torn to pieces by a wild animal, he shall bring in the remains as evidence and he will not be required to pay for the torn animal.

14“If a man borrows an animal from his neighbor and it is injured or dies while the owner is not present, he must make restitution. 15But if the owner is with the animal, the borrower will not have to pay. If the animal was hired, the money paid for the hire covers the loss.

Social Responsibility

16“If a man seduces a virgin who is not pledged to be married and sleeps with her, he must pay the bride-price, and she shall be his wife. 17If her father absolutely refuses to give her to him, he must still pay the bride-price for virgins.

18“Do not allow a sorceress to live.

19“Anyone who has sexual relations with an animal must be put to death.

20“Whoever sacrifices to any god other than the Lord must be destroyed.[c]

21“Do not mistreat an alien or oppress him, for you were aliens in Egypt.

22“Do not take advantage of a widow or an orphan. 23If you do and they cry out to me, I will certainly hear their cry. 24My anger will be aroused, and I will kill you with the sword; your wives will become widows and your children fatherless.

25“If you lend money to one of my people among you who is needy, do not be like a moneylender; charge him no interest.[d] 26If you take your neighbor’s cloak as a pledge, return it to him by sunset, 27because his cloak is the only covering he has for his body. What else will he sleep in? When he cries out to me, I will hear, for I am compassionate.

28“Do not blaspheme God[e] or curse the ruler of your people.

29“Do not hold back offerings from your granaries or your vats.[f]

“You must give me the firstborn of your sons. 30Do the same with your cattle and your sheep. Let them stay with their mothers for seven days, but give them to me on the eighth day.

31“You are to be my holy people. So do not eat the meat of an animal torn by wild beasts; throw it to the dogs.

Laws of Justice and Mercy

23 “Do not spread false reports. Do not help a wicked man by being a malicious witness.

2“Do not follow the crowd in doing wrong. When you give testimony in a lawsuit, do not pervert justice by siding with the crowd, 3and do not show favoritism to a poor man in his lawsuit.

4“If you come across your enemy’s ox or donkey wandering off, be sure to take it back to him. 5If you see the donkey of someone who hates you fallen down under its load, do not leave it there; be sure you help him with it.

6“Do not deny justice to your poor people in their lawsuits. 7Have nothing to do with a false charge and do not put an innocent or

[a] 8 Or *before God*; also in verse 9 [b] 9 Or *whom God declares* [c] 20 The Hebrew term refers to the irrevocable giving over of things or persons to the Lord, often by totally destroying them. [d] 25 Or *excessive interest* [e] 28 Or *Do not revile the judges* [f] 29 The meaning of the Hebrew for this phrase is uncertain.

honest person to death, for I will not acquit
the guilty.
8“Do not accept a bribe, for a bribe blinds
those who see and twists the words of the righteous.
9“Do not oppress an alien; you yourselves
know how it feels to be aliens, because you
were aliens in Egypt.

Sabbath Laws

10“For six years you are to sow your fields
and harvest the crops, 11but during the seventh year let the land lie unplowed and un-
used. Then the poor among your people may
get food from it, and the wild animals may eat
what they leave. Do the same with your vineyard and your olive grove.
12“Six days do your work, but on the seventh day do not work, so that your ox and
your donkey may rest and the slave born in
your household, and the alien as well, may be
refreshed.
13“Be careful to do everything I have said to
you. Do not invoke the names of other gods;
do not let them be heard on your lips.

The Three Annual Festivals

14“Three times a year you are to celebrate a
festival to me.
15“Celebrate the Feast of Unleavened Bread;
for seven days eat bread made without yeast,
as I commanded you. Do this at the appointed
time in the month of Abib, for in that month
you came out of Egypt.
“No one is to appear before me empty-
handed.
16“Celebrate the Feast of Harvest with the
firstfruits of the crops you sow in your field.
“Celebrate the Feast of Ingathering at the
end of the year, when you gather in your crops
from the field.
17“Three times a year all the men are to appear before the Sovereign LORD.
18“Do not offer the blood of a sacrifice to
me along with anything containing yeast.
“The fat of my festival offerings must not be
kept until morning.
19“Bring the best of the firstfruits of your
soil to the house of the LORD your God.
“Do not cook a young goat in its mother’s
milk.

God’s Angel to Prepare the Way

20“See, I am sending an angel ahead of you
to guard you along the way and to bring you
to the place I have prepared. 21Pay attention
to him and listen to what he says. Do not rebel against him; he will not forgive your rebellion, since my Name is in him. 22If you
listen carefully to what he says and do all that
I say, I will be an enemy to your enemies and
will oppose those who oppose you. 23My angel will go ahead of you and bring you into
the land of the Amorites, Hittites, Perizzites,
Canaanites, Hivites and Jebusites, and I will
wipe them out. 24Do not bow down before
their gods or worship them or follow their
practices. You must demolish them and break
their sacred stones to pieces. 25Worship the
LORD your God, and his blessing will be on
your food and water. I will take away sickness
from among you, 26and none will miscarry or
be barren in your land. I will give you a full
life span.
27“I will send my terror ahead of you and
throw into confusion every nation you encounter. I will make all your enemies turn
their backs and run. 28I will send the hornet
ahead of you to drive the Hivites, Canaanites
and Hittites out of your way. 29But I will not
drive them out in a single year, because the
land would become desolate and the wild animals too numerous for you. 30Little by little
I will drive them out before you, until you
have increased enough to take possession of
the land.
31“I will establish your borders from the
Red Sea[a] to the Sea of the Philistines,[b] and
from the desert to the River.[c] I will hand over
to you the people who live in the land and
you will drive them out before you. 32Do
not make a covenant with them or with their
gods. 33Do not let them live in your land, or
they will cause you to sin against me, because
the worship of their gods will certainly be a
snare to you.”

The Covenant Confirmed

24 Then he said to Moses, “Come up to
the LORD, you and Aaron, Nadab and
Abihu, and seventy of the elders of Israel. You are to worship at a distance, 2but Moses alone is to approach the LORD; the others
must not come near. And the people may not
come up with him.”
3When Moses went and told the people all
the LORD’s words and laws, they responded
with one voice, “Everything the LORD has said
we will do.” 4Moses then wrote down everything the LORD had said.

---

a 31 Hebrew *Yam Suph*; that is, Sea of Reeds   b 31 That is, the Mediterranean   c 31 That is, the Euphrates

He got up early the next morning and built
an altar at the foot of the mountain and set
up twelve stone pillars representing the twelve
tribes of Israel. 5Then he sent young Israelite
men, and they offered burnt offerings and sacrificed young bulls as fellowship offerings[a] to
the LORD. 6Moses took half of the blood and
put it in bowls, and the other half he sprinkled on the altar. 7Then he took the Book of
the Covenant and read it to the people. They
responded, "We will do everything the LORD
has said; we will obey."

8Moses then took the blood, sprinkled it on
the people and said, "This is the blood of the
covenant that the LORD has made with you in
accordance with all these words."

9Moses and Aaron, Nadab and Abihu,
and the seventy elders of Israel went up
10and saw the God of Israel. Under his feet
was something like a pavement made of sapphire,[b] clear as the sky itself. 11But God did
not raise his hand against these leaders of the
Israelites; they saw God, and they ate and
drank.

12The LORD said to Moses, "Come up to
me on the mountain and stay here, and I will
give you the tablets of stone, with the law and
commands I have written for their instruction."

13Then Moses set out with Joshua his aide,
and Moses went up on the mountain of God.
14He said to the elders, "Wait here for us until
we come back to you. Aaron and Hur are with
you, and anyone involved in a dispute can go
to them."

15When Moses went up on the mountain,
the cloud covered it, 16and the glory of the
LORD settled on Mount Sinai. For six days
the cloud covered the mountain, and on the
seventh day the LORD called to Moses from
within the cloud. 17To the Israelites the glory
of the LORD looked like a consuming fire on
top of the mountain. 18Then Moses entered
the cloud as he went on up the mountain.
And he stayed on the mountain forty days and
forty nights.

Offerings for the Tabernacle

25 The LORD said to Moses, 2"Tell the Israelites to bring me an offering. You are
to receive the offering for me from each
man whose heart prompts him to give. 3These
are the offerings you are to receive from them:
gold, silver and bronze; 4blue, purple and scarlet yarn and fine linen; goat hair; 5ram skins
dyed red and hides of sea cows[c]; acacia wood;
6olive oil for the light; spices for the anointing oil and for the fragrant incense; 7and onyx
stones and other gems to be mounted on the
ephod and breastpiece.

8"Then have them make a sanctuary for me,
and I will dwell among them. 9Make this tabernacle and all its furnishings exactly like the
pattern I will show you.

The Ark

10"Have them make a chest of acacia
wood—two and a half cubits long, a cubit
and a half wide, and a cubit and a half high.[d]
11Overlay it with pure gold, both inside and
out, and make a gold molding around it.
12Cast four gold rings for it and fasten them
to its four feet, with two rings on one side and
two rings on the other. 13Then make poles
of acacia wood and overlay them with gold.
14Insert the poles into the rings on the sides of
the chest to carry it. 15The poles are to remain
in the rings of this ark; they are not to be removed. 16Then put in the ark the Testimony,
which I will give you.

17"Make an atonement cover[e] of pure
gold—two and a half cubits long and a cubit
and a half wide.[d] 18And make two cherubim
out of hammered gold at the ends of the cover. 19Make one cherub on one end and the
second cherub on the other; make the cherubim of one piece with the cover, at the two
ends. 20The cherubim are to have their wings
spread upward, overshadowing the cover with
them. The cherubim are to face each other,
looking toward the cover. 21Place the cover on
top of the ark and put in the ark the Testimony, which I will give you. 22There, above
the cover between the two cherubim that are
over the ark of the Testimony, I will meet with
you and give you all my commands for the
Israelites.

The Table

23"Make a table of acacia wood—two cubits long, a cubit wide and a cubit and a half
high.[f] 24Overlay it with pure gold and make a
gold molding around it. 25Also make around
it a rim a handbreadth[g] wide and put a gold
molding on the rim. 26Make four gold rings
for the table and fasten them to the four corners, where the four legs are. 27The rings are to
be close to the rim to hold the poles used in

[a] 5 Traditionally *peace offerings* [b] *10* Or *lapis lazuli* [c] *5* That is, dugongs [d] *10,17* That is, about 3 3/4 feet (about 1.1 meters) long and 2 1/4 feet (about 0.7 meter) wide and high [e] *17* Traditionally *a mercy seat* [f] *23* That is, about 3 feet (about 0.9 meter) long and 1 1/2 feet (about 0.5 meter) wide and 2 1/4 feet (about 0.7 meter) high [g] *25* That is, about 3 inches (about 8 centimeters)

carrying the table. 28Make the poles of acacia
wood, overlay them with gold and carry the
table with them. 29And make its plates and
dishes of pure gold, as well as its pitchers and
bowls for the pouring out of offerings. 30Put
the bread of the Presence on this table to be
before me at all times.

The Lampstand

31"Make a lampstand of pure gold and
hammer it out, base and shaft; its flowerlike
cups, buds and blossoms shall be of one piece
with it. 32Six branches are to extend from the
sides of the lampstand—three on one side
and three on the other. 33Three cups shaped
like almond flowers with buds and blossoms
are to be on one branch, three on the next
branch, and the same for all six branches extending from the lampstand. 34And on the
lampstand there are to be four cups shaped
like almond flowers with buds and blossoms.
35One bud shall be under the first pair of
branches extending from the lampstand, a
second bud under the second pair, and a third
bud under the third pair—six branches in all.
36The buds and branches shall all be of one
piece with the lampstand, hammered out of
pure gold.

37"Then make its seven lamps and set them
up on it so that they light the space in front
of it. 38Its wick trimmers and trays are to be
of pure gold. 39A talent[a] of pure gold is to be
used for the lampstand and all these accessories. 40See that you make them according to
the pattern shown you on the mountain.

The Tabernacle

26 "Make the tabernacle with ten curtains
of finely twisted linen and blue, purple
and scarlet yarn, with cherubim worked
into them by a skilled craftsman. 2All the curtains are to be the same size—twenty-eight
cubits long and four cubits wide.[b] 3Join five
of the curtains together, and do the same with
the other five. 4Make loops of blue material
along the edge of the end curtain in one set,
and do the same with the end curtain in the
other set. 5Make fifty loops on one curtain
and fifty loops on the end curtain of the other
set, with the loops opposite each other. 6Then
make fifty gold clasps and use them to fasten
the curtains together so that the tabernacle is
a unit.

7"Make curtains of goat hair for the tent
over the tabernacle—eleven altogether. 8All
eleven curtains are to be the same size—thirty
cubits long and four cubits wide.[c] 9Join five
of the curtains together into one set and the
other six into another set. Fold the sixth curtain double at the front of the tent. 10Make
fifty loops along the edge of the end curtain in
one set and also along the edge of the end curtain in the other set. 11Then make fifty bronze
clasps and put them in the loops to fasten the
tent together as a unit. 12As for the additional length of the tent curtains, the half curtain
that is left over is to hang down at the rear of
the tabernacle. 13The tent curtains will be a
cubit[d] longer on both sides; what is left will
hang over the sides of the tabernacle so as to
cover it. 14Make for the tent a covering of ram
skins dyed red, and over that a covering of
hides of sea cows.[e]

15"Make upright frames of acacia wood for
the tabernacle. 16Each frame is to be ten cubits long and a cubit and a half wide,[f] 17with
two projections set parallel to each other.
Make all the frames of the tabernacle in this
way. 18Make twenty frames for the south
side of the tabernacle 19and make forty silver bases to go under them—two bases for
each frame, one under each projection. 20For
the other side, the north side of the tabernacle, make twenty frames 21and forty silver
bases—two under each frame. 22Make six
frames for the far end, that is, the west end
of the tabernacle, 23and make two frames for
the corners at the far end. 24At these two corners they must be double from the bottom
all the way to the top, and fitted into a single
ring; both shall be like that. 25So there will
be eight frames and sixteen silver bases—two
under each frame.

26"Also make crossbars of acacia wood: five
for the frames on one side of the tabernacle,
27five for those on the other side, and five for
the frames on the west, at the far end of the
tabernacle. 28The center crossbar is to extend
from end to end at the middle of the frames.
29Overlay the frames with gold and make gold
rings to hold the crossbars. Also overlay the
crossbars with gold.

30"Set up the tabernacle according to the
plan shown you on the mountain.

31"Make a curtain of blue, purple and scarlet yarn and finely twisted linen, with cherubim worked into it by a skilled craftsman.
32Hang it with gold hooks on four posts of

---

[a] *39* That is, about 75 pounds (about 34 kilograms) [b] *2* That is, about 42 feet (about 12.5 meters) long and 6 feet (about 1.8 meters) wide [c] *8* That is, about 45 feet (about 13.5 meters) long and 6 feet (about 1.8 meters) wide [d] *13* That is, about 1 1/2 feet (about 0.5 meter) [e] *14* That is, dugongs [f] *16* That is, about 15 feet (about 4.5 meters) long and 2 1/4 feet (about 0.7 meter) wide

acacia wood overlaid with gold and standing on four silver bases. [33]Hang the curtain from the clasps and place the ark of the Testimony behind the curtain. The curtain will separate the Holy Place from the Most Holy Place. [34]Put the atonement cover on the ark of the Testimony in the Most Holy Place. [35]Place the table outside the curtain on the north side of the tabernacle and put the lampstand opposite it on the south side.

[36]"For the entrance to the tent make a curtain of blue, purple and scarlet yarn and finely twisted linen—the work of an embroiderer. [37]Make gold hooks for this curtain and five posts of acacia wood overlaid with gold. And cast five bronze bases for them.

The Altar of Burnt Offering

27 "Build an altar of acacia wood, three cubits[a] high; it is to be square, five cubits long and five cubits wide.[b] [2]Make a horn at each of the four corners, so that the horns and the altar are of one piece, and overlay the altar with bronze. [3]Make all its utensils of bronze—its pots to remove the ashes, and its shovels, sprinkling bowls, meat forks and firepans. [4]Make a grating for it, a bronze network, and make a bronze ring at each of the four corners of the network. [5]Put it under the ledge of the altar so that it is halfway up the altar. [6]Make poles of acacia wood for the altar and overlay them with bronze. [7]The poles are to be inserted into the rings so they will be on two sides of the altar when it is carried. [8]Make the altar hollow, out of boards. It is to be made just as you were shown on the mountain.

The Courtyard

[9]"Make a courtyard for the tabernacle. The south side shall be a hundred cubits[c] long and is to have curtains of finely twisted linen, [10]with twenty posts and twenty bronze bases and with silver hooks and bands on the posts. [11]The north side shall also be a hundred cubits long and is to have curtains, with twenty posts and twenty bronze bases and with silver hooks and bands on the posts.

[12]"The west end of the courtyard shall be fifty cubits[d] wide and have curtains, with ten posts and ten bases. [13]On the east end, toward the sunrise, the courtyard shall also be fifty cubits wide. [14]Curtains fifteen cubits[e] long are to be on one side of the entrance, with three posts and three bases, [15]and curtains fifteen cubits long are to be on the other side, with three posts and three bases.

[16]"For the entrance to the courtyard, provide a curtain twenty cubits[f] long, of blue, purple and scarlet yarn and finely twisted linen—the work of an embroiderer—with four posts and four bases. [17]All the posts around the courtyard are to have silver bands and hooks, and bronze bases. [18]The courtyard shall be a hundred cubits long and fifty cubits wide,[g] with curtains of finely twisted linen five cubits[h] high, and with bronze bases. [19]All the other articles used in the service of the tabernacle, whatever their function, including all the tent pegs for it and those for the courtyard, are to be of bronze.

Oil for the Lampstand

[20]"Command the Israelites to bring you clear oil of pressed olives for the light so that the lamps may be kept burning. [21]In the Tent of Meeting, outside the curtain that is in front of the Testimony, Aaron and his sons are to keep the lamps burning before the LORD from evening till morning. This is to be a lasting ordinance among the Israelites for the generations to come.

The Priestly Garments

28 "Have Aaron your brother brought to you from among the Israelites, along with his sons Nadab and Abihu, Eleazar and Ithamar, so they may serve me as priests. [2]Make sacred garments for your brother Aaron, to give him dignity and honor. [3]Tell all the skilled men to whom I have given wisdom in such matters that they are to make garments for Aaron, for his consecration, so he may serve me as priest. [4]These are the garments they are to make: a breastpiece, an ephod, a robe, a woven tunic, a turban and a sash. They are to make these sacred garments for your brother Aaron and his sons, so they may serve me as priests. [5]Have them use gold, and blue, purple and scarlet yarn, and fine linen.

The Ephod

[6]"Make the ephod of gold, and of blue, purple and scarlet yarn, and of finely twisted linen—the work of a skilled craftsman. [7]It is

[a] *1* That is, about 4 1/2 feet (about 1.3 meters) [b] *1* That is, about 7 1/2 feet (about 2.3 meters) long and wide [c] *9* That is, about 150 feet (about 46 meters); also in verse 11 [d] *12* That is, about 75 feet (about 23 meters); also in verse 13 [e] *14* That is, about 22 1/2 feet (about 6.9 meters); also in verse 15 [f] *16* That is, about 30 feet (about 9 meters) [g] *18* That is, about 150 feet (about 46 meters) long and 75 feet (about 23 meters) wide [h] *18* That is, about 7 1/2 feet (about 2.3 meters)

to have two shoulder pieces attached to two of its corners, so it can be fastened. 8Its skillfully woven waistband is to be like it—of one piece with the ephod and made with gold, and with blue, purple and scarlet yarn, and with finely twisted linen.

9"Take two onyx stones and engrave on them the names of the sons of Israel 10in the order of their birth—six names on one stone and the remaining six on the other. 11Engrave the names of the sons of Israel on the two stones the way a gem cutter engraves a seal. Then mount the stones in gold filigree settings 12and fasten them on the shoulder pieces of the ephod as memorial stones for the sons of Israel. Aaron is to bear the names on his shoulders as a memorial before the LORD. 13Make gold filigree settings 14and two braided chains of pure gold, like a rope, and attach the chains to the settings.

The Breastpiece

15"Fashion a breastpiece for making decisions—the work of a skilled craftsman. Make it like the ephod: of gold, and of blue, purple and scarlet yarn, and of finely twisted linen. 16It is to be square—a span[a] long and a span wide—and folded double. 17Then mount four rows of precious stones on it. In the first row there shall be a ruby, a topaz and a beryl; 18in the second row a turquoise, a sapphire[b] and an emerald; 19in the third row a jacinth, an agate and an amethyst; 20in the fourth row a chrysolite, an onyx and a jasper.[c] Mount them in gold filigree settings. 21There are to be twelve stones, one for each of the names of the sons of Israel, each engraved like a seal with the name of one of the twelve tribes.

22"For the breastpiece make braided chains of pure gold, like a rope. 23Make two gold rings for it and fasten them to two corners of the breastpiece. 24Fasten the two gold chains to the rings at the corners of the breastpiece, 25and the other ends of the chains to the two settings, attaching them to the shoulder pieces of the ephod at the front. 26Make two gold rings and attach them to the other two corners of the breastpiece on the inside edge next to the ephod. 27Make two more gold rings and attach them to the bottom of the shoulder pieces on the front of the ephod, close to the seam just above the waistband of the ephod. 28The rings of the breastpiece are to be tied to the rings of the ephod with blue cord, connecting it to the waistband, so that the breastpiece will not swing out from the ephod.

29"Whenever Aaron enters the Holy Place, he will bear the names of the sons of Israel over his heart on the breastpiece of decision as a continuing memorial before the LORD. 30Also put the Urim and the Thummim in the breastpiece, so they may be over Aaron's heart whenever he enters the presence of the LORD. Thus Aaron will always bear the means of making decisions for the Israelites over his heart before the LORD.

Other Priestly Garments

31"Make the robe of the ephod entirely of blue cloth, 32with an opening for the head in its center. There shall be a woven edge like a collar[d] around this opening, so that it will not tear. 33Make pomegranates of blue, purple and scarlet yarn around the hem of the robe, with gold bells between them. 34The gold bells and the pomegranates are to alternate around the hem of the robe. 35Aaron must wear it when he ministers. The sound of the bells will be heard when he enters the Holy Place before the LORD and when he comes out, so that he will not die.

36"Make a plate of pure gold and engrave on it as on a seal: HOLY TO THE LORD. 37Fasten a blue cord to it to attach it to the turban; it is to be on the front of the turban. 38It will be on Aaron's forehead, and he will bear the guilt involved in the sacred gifts the Israelites consecrate, whatever their gifts may be. It will be on Aaron's forehead continually so that they will be acceptable to the LORD.

39"Weave the tunic of fine linen and make the turban of fine linen. The sash is to be the work of an embroiderer. 40Make tunics, sashes and headbands for Aaron's sons, to give them dignity and honor. 41After you put these clothes on your brother Aaron and his sons, anoint and ordain them. Consecrate them so they may serve me as priests.

42"Make linen undergarments as a covering for the body, reaching from the waist to the thigh. 43Aaron and his sons must wear them whenever they enter the Tent of Meeting or approach the altar to minister in the Holy Place, so that they will not incur guilt and die.

"This is to be a lasting ordinance for Aaron and his descendants.

---

[a] *16* That is, about 9 inches (about 22 centimeters) [b] *18* Or *lapis lazuli* [c] *20* The precise identification of some of these precious stones is uncertain. [d] *32* The meaning of the Hebrew for this word is uncertain.

Consecration of the Priests

29 "This is what you are to do to consecrate
them, so they may serve me as priests:
Take a young bull and two rams without defect. 2And from fine wheat flour, without yeast, make bread, and cakes mixed with
oil, and wafers spread with oil. 3Put them in
a basket and present them in it—along with
the bull and the two rams. 4Then bring Aaron and his sons to the entrance to the Tent
of Meeting and wash them with water. 5Take
the garments and dress Aaron with the tunic,
the robe of the ephod, the ephod itself and
the breastpiece. Fasten the ephod on him by
its skillfully woven waistband. 6Put the turban
on his head and attach the sacred diadem to
the turban. 7Take the anointing oil and anoint
him by pouring it on his head. 8Bring his sons
and dress them in tunics 9and put headbands
on them. Then tie sashes on Aaron and his
sons.[a] The priesthood is theirs by a lasting ordinance. In this way you shall ordain Aaron
and his sons.

10"Bring the bull to the front of the Tent
of Meeting, and Aaron and his sons shall lay
their hands on its head. 11Slaughter it in the
LORD's presence at the entrance to the Tent of
Meeting. 12Take some of the bull's blood and
put it on the horns of the altar with your finger, and pour out the rest of it at the base of
the altar. 13Then take all the fat around the
inner parts, the covering of the liver, and both
kidneys with the fat on them, and burn them
on the altar. 14But burn the bull's flesh and its
hide and its offal outside the camp. It is a sin
offering.

15"Take one of the rams, and Aaron and his
sons shall lay their hands on its head. 16Slaugh-
ter it and take the blood and sprinkle it against
the altar on all sides. 17Cut the ram into pieces and wash the inner parts and the legs, putting them with the head and the other pieces.
18Then burn the entire ram on the altar. It is a
burnt offering to the LORD, a pleasing aroma,
an offering made to the LORD by fire.

19"Take the other ram, and Aaron and his
sons shall lay their hands on its head. 20Slaugh-
ter it, take some of its blood and put it on the
lobes of the right ears of Aaron and his sons,
on the thumbs of their right hands, and on
the big toes of their right feet. Then sprinkle
blood against the altar on all sides. 21And take
some of the blood on the altar and some of the
anointing oil and sprinkle it on Aaron and his
garments and on his sons and their garments.
Then he and his sons and their garments will
be consecrated.

22"Take from this ram the fat, the fat tail,
the fat around the inner parts, the covering of
the liver, both kidneys with the fat on them,
and the right thigh. (This is the ram for the
ordination.) 23From the basket of bread made
without yeast, which is before the LORD, take
a loaf, and a cake made with oil, and a wafer. 24Put all these in the hands of Aaron and
his sons and wave them before the LORD as
a wave offering. 25Then take them from their
hands and burn them on the altar along with
the burnt offering for a pleasing aroma to the
LORD, an offering made to the LORD by fire.
26After you take the breast of the ram for Aaron's ordination, wave it before the LORD as a
wave offering, and it will be your share.

27"Consecrate those parts of the ordination ram that belong to Aaron and his sons:
the breast that was waved and the thigh that
was presented. 28This is always to be the regular share from the Israelites for Aaron and his
sons. It is the contribution the Israelites are to
make to the LORD from their fellowship offerings.[b]

29"Aaron's sacred garments will belong to
his descendants so that they can be anointed
and ordained in them. 30The son who succeeds him as priest and comes to the Tent of
Meeting to minister in the Holy Place is to
wear them seven days.

31"Take the ram for the ordination and
cook the meat in a sacred place. 32At the entrance to the Tent of Meeting, Aaron and his
sons are to eat the meat of the ram and the
bread that is in the basket. 33They are to eat
these offerings by which atonement was made
for their ordination and consecration. But no
one else may eat them, because they are sacred. 34And if any of the meat of the ordination ram or any bread is left over till morning,
burn it up. It must not be eaten, because it
is sacred.

35"Do for Aaron and his sons everything I
have commanded you, taking seven days to
ordain them. 36Sacrifice a bull each day as a
sin offering to make atonement. Purify the altar by making atonement for it, and anoint it
to consecrate it. 37For seven days make atonement for the altar and consecrate it. Then the
altar will be most holy, and whatever touches
it will be holy.

38"This is what you are to offer on the altar regularly each day: two lambs a year old.

---

[a] 9 Hebrew; Septuagint *on them* [b] 28 Traditionally *peace offerings*

39Offer one in the morning and the other at
twilight. 40With the first lamb offer a tenth
of an ephah[a] of fine flour mixed with a quarter of a hin[b] of oil from pressed olives, and a
quarter of a hin of wine as a drink offering.
41Sacrifice the other lamb at twilight with the
same grain offering and its drink offering as in
the morning—a pleasing aroma, an offering
made to the LORD by fire.

42"For the generations to come this burnt
offering is to be made regularly at the entrance
to the Tent of Meeting before the LORD. There
I will meet you and speak to you; 43there also I
will meet with the Israelites, and the place will
be consecrated by my glory.

44"So I will consecrate the Tent of Meeting
and the altar and will consecrate Aaron and
his sons to serve me as priests. 45Then I will
dwell among the Israelites and be their God.
46They will know that I am the LORD their
God, who brought them out of Egypt so that
I might dwell among them. I am the LORD
their God.

The Altar of Incense

30 "Make an altar of acacia wood for burning incense. 2It is to be square, a cubit
long and a cubit wide, and two cubits
high[c]—its horns of one piece with it. 3Over-
lay the top and all the sides and the horns with
pure gold, and make a gold molding around
it. 4Make two gold rings for the altar below
the molding—two on opposite sides—to hold
the poles used to carry it. 5Make the poles of
acacia wood and overlay them with gold. 6Put
the altar in front of the curtain that is before
the ark of the Testimony—before the atonement cover that is over the Testimony—where
I will meet with you.

7"Aaron must burn fragrant incense on the
altar every morning when he tends the lamps.
8He must burn incense again when he lights
the lamps at twilight so incense will burn regularly before the LORD for the generations to
come. 9Do not offer on this altar any other
incense or any burnt offering or grain offering, and do not pour a drink offering on it.
10Once a year Aaron shall make atonement
on its horns. This annual atonement must be
made with the blood of the atoning sin offering for the generations to come. It is most
holy to the LORD."

Atonement Money

11Then the LORD said to Moses, 12"When
you take a census of the Israelites to count
them, each one must pay the LORD a ransom
for his life at the time he is counted. Then no
plague will come on them when you number
them. 13Each one who crosses over to those
already counted is to give a half shekel,[d] according to the sanctuary shekel, which weighs
twenty gerahs. This half shekel is an offering
to the LORD. 14All who cross over, those twenty years old or more, are to give an offering
to the LORD. 15The rich are not to give more
than a half shekel and the poor are not to give
less when you make the offering to the LORD
to atone for your lives. 16Receive the atonement money from the Israelites and use it for
the service of the Tent of Meeting. It will be a
memorial for the Israelites before the LORD,
making atonement for your lives."

Basin for Washing

17Then the LORD said to Moses, 18"Make a
bronze basin, with its bronze stand, for washing. Place it between the Tent of Meeting and
the altar, and put water in it. 19Aaron and his
sons are to wash their hands and feet with water from it. 20Whenever they enter the Tent of
Meeting, they shall wash with water so that
they will not die. Also, when they approach
the altar to minister by presenting an offering
made to the LORD by fire, 21they shall wash
their hands and feet so that they will not die.
This is to be a lasting ordinance for Aaron and
his descendants for the generations to come."

Anointing Oil

22Then the LORD said to Moses, 23"Take
the following fine spices: 500 shekels[e] of liquid myrrh, half as much (that is, 250 shekels)
of fragrant cinnamon, 250 shekels of fragrant
cane, 24500 shekels of cassia—all according
to the sanctuary shekel—and a hin[f] of olive
oil. 25Make these into a sacred anointing oil,
a fragrant blend, the work of a perfumer. It
will be the sacred anointing oil. 26Then use it
to anoint the Tent of Meeting, the ark of the
Testimony, 27the table and all its articles, the
lampstand and its accessories, the altar of incense, 28the altar of burnt offering and all its
utensils, and the basin with its stand. 29You
shall consecrate them so they will be most
holy, and whatever touches them will be holy.
30"Anoint Aaron and his sons and conse-

a 40 That is, probably about 2 quarts (about 2 liters) *b 40* That is, probably about 1 quart (about 1 liter) *c 2* That is, about 1 1/2 feet (about 0.5 meter) long and wide and about 3 feet (about 0.9 meter) high *d 13* That is, about 1/5 ounce (about 6 grams); also in verse 15 *e 23* That is, about 12 1/2 pounds (about 6 kilograms) *f 24* That is, probably about 4 quarts (about 4 liters)

crate them so they may serve me as priests.
31Say to the Israelites, 'This is to be my sacred
anointing oil for the generations to come.
32Do not pour it on men's bodies and do not
make any oil with the same formula. It is sacred, and you are to consider it sacred. 33Who-
ever makes perfume like it and whoever puts it
on anyone other than a priest must be cut off
from his people.' "

Incense

34Then the LORD said to Moses, "Take
fragrant spices—gum resin, onycha and gal-
banum—and pure frankincense, all in equal
amounts, 35and make a fragrant blend of incense, the work of a perfumer. It is to be salted and pure and sacred. 36Grind some of it to
powder and place it in front of the Testimony
in the Tent of Meeting, where I will meet with
you. It shall be most holy to you. 37Do not
make any incense with this formula for yourselves; consider it holy to the LORD. 38Whoev-
er makes any like it to enjoy its fragrance must
be cut off from his people."

Bezalel and Oholiab

31 Then the LORD said to Moses, 2"See, I
have chosen Bezalel son of Uri, the son
of Hur, of the tribe of Judah, 3and I
have filled him with the Spirit of God, with
skill, ability and knowledge in all kinds of
crafts— 4to make artistic designs for work in
gold, silver and bronze, 5to cut and set stones,
to work in wood, and to engage in all kinds
of craftsmanship. 6Moreover, I have appointed Oholiab son of Ahisamach, of the tribe of
Dan, to help him. Also I have given skill to
all the craftsmen to make everything I have
commanded you: 7the Tent of Meeting, the
ark of the Testimony with the atonement cover on it, and all the other furnishings of the
tent— 8the table and its articles, the pure gold
lampstand and all its accessories, the altar of
incense, 9the altar of burnt offering and all
its utensils, the basin with its stand— 10and
also the woven garments, both the sacred garments for Aaron the priest and the garments
for his sons when they serve as priests, 11and
the anointing oil and fragrant incense for the
Holy Place. They are to make them just as I
commanded you."

The Sabbath

12Then the LORD said to Moses, 13"Say to
the Israelites, 'You must observe my Sabbaths.
This will be a sign between me and you for the
generations to come, so you may know that I
am the LORD, who makes you holy.[a]
14" 'Observe the Sabbath, because it is holy
to you. Anyone who desecrates it must be put
to death; whoever does any work on that day
must be cut off from his people. 15For six days,
work is to be done, but the seventh day is a
Sabbath of rest, holy to the LORD. Whoever
does any work on the Sabbath day must be
put to death. 16The Israelites are to observe
the Sabbath, celebrating it for the generations
to come as a lasting covenant. 17It will be a
sign between me and the Israelites forever, for
in six days the LORD made the heavens and
the earth, and on the seventh day he abstained
from work and rested.' "
18When the LORD finished speaking to
Moses on Mount Sinai, he gave him the two
tablets of the Testimony, the tablets of stone
inscribed by the finger of God.

The Golden Calf

32 When the people saw that Moses was so
long in coming down from the mountain, they gathered around Aaron and
said, "Come, make us gods[b] who will go before us. As for this fellow Moses who brought
us up out of Egypt, we don't know what has
happened to him."
2Aaron answered them, "Take off the gold
earrings that your wives, your sons and your
daughters are wearing, and bring them to me."
3So all the people took off their earrings and
brought them to Aaron. 4He took what they
handed him and made it into an idol cast in
the shape of a calf, fashioning it with a tool.
Then they said, "These are your gods,[c] O Israel, who brought you up out of Egypt."
5When Aaron saw this, he built an altar in
front of the calf and announced, "Tomorrow
there will be a festival to the LORD." 6So the
next day the people rose early and sacrificed
burnt offerings and presented fellowship offerings.[d] Afterward they sat down to eat and
drink and got up to indulge in revelry.
7Then the LORD said to Moses, "Go down,
because your people, whom you brought up
out of Egypt, have become corrupt. 8They
have been quick to turn away from what I
commanded them and have made themselves
an idol cast in the shape of a calf. They have
bowed down to it and sacrificed to it and
have said, 'These are your gods, O Israel, who
brought you up out of Egypt.'

[a] 13 Or *who sanctifies you*; or *who sets you apart as holy* [b] 1 Or *a god*; also in verses 23 and 31 [c] 4 Or *This is your god*; also in verse 8 [d] 6 Traditionally *peace offerings*

THURSDAY
READ EXODUS 31:12–17

A MODERN SABBATH

As husbands and wives, we are overwhelmed with things to do. Although time was given to us by God as a resource for us to manage, it often seems we can't disconnect from the tyranny of time. In our busy lives, sometimes we find that time is managing us rather than the other way around.

Our trouble with time begins when we start from the wrong place: First we plan our weekdays of work, family responsibilities, household chores, shopping and countless other tasks. Then we approach the weekends with a giant to-do list that further overwhelms us. We have to hit the supermarket, the home center, the shopping mall, soccer practice, the gym. Rest—are you kidding? We have too much to do.

When God created time, he established the Sabbath as an interlude in the bustle of daily life. The Sabbath was the regular, weekly time for the Israelites to remember that God had made them a holy people. On this day they were to connect with God in worship and prayer, meditation, physical rest and family enjoyment. On this day they were to knit themselves together with God in fellowship and refreshment, and to one another in loving, nurturing relationships.

"You must observe my Sabbaths. This will be a sign between me and you for the generations to come, so you may know that I am the LORD, who makes you holy."

— EXODUS 31:13

let's talk

- How can putting aside a day of Sabbath rest first help us plan the rest of our week?
- What problems do we need to address to put the Sabbath first?
- What are some temptations and demands we must overcome to keep the Sabbath a priority? How can we pray for holiness in the use of our time?

The Sabbath was established and regulated by Old Testament laws; today most of us worship on Sunday, as it appears believers did in the early church (see Acts 20:7; 1 Corinthians 16:2), and then struggle to figure out what we are and are not "supposed" to do with the rest of the day. How do we make the Old Testament concept of Sabbath rest relevant to our lives today? For starters, we need to decide together as Christian families that our Sabbath day is the most important day of the week. It is first and foremost a day set aside as special, different, holy. It is a day of rest and refreshment. It is a day when we gather with other believers to worship our Maker and Redeemer. It is a day that we devote to God for seeking his will for the rest of the week—and the rest of life. Instead of a list of dos and don'ts, we need to focus on the purpose of the day, and then make our decisions based on that perspective.

It is so important—especially in the beginning of marriage, when we're establishing lifetime habits—to plan our lives beginning with a Sabbath. That's what the Israelites did. In observing the Sabbath, the Israelites showed that they had a unique relationship with the Lord and were obedient to his command. The command was not to be a burden; it was to be a gift from God. We can likewise orient our time to the Lord's Day so we can enjoy the Sabbath, not as a leftover time squeezed between other weekday priorities, but as the special day of every week that anchors us in God and sets the pace for each week—as well as eternity.

—JOHN R. THROOP

FOR YOUR NEXT DEVOTIONAL READING, TURN TO PAGE 107.

9“I have seen these people,” the LORD said to Moses, “and they are a stiff-necked people. 10Now leave me alone so that my anger may burn against them and that I may destroy them. Then I will make you into a great nation.”

11But Moses sought the favor of the LORD his God. “O LORD,” he said, “why should your anger burn against your people, whom you brought out of Egypt with great power and a mighty hand? 12Why should the Egyptians say, ‘It was with evil intent that he brought them out, to kill them in the mountains and to wipe them off the face of the earth’? Turn from your fierce anger; relent and do not bring disaster on your people. 13Remember your servants Abraham, Isaac and Israel, to whom you swore by your own self: ‘I will make your descendants as numerous as the stars in the sky and I will give your descendants all this land I promised them, and it will be their inheritance forever.’ ” 14Then the LORD relented and did not bring on his people the disaster he had threatened.

15Moses turned and went down the mountain with the two tablets of the Testimony in his hands. They were inscribed on both sides, front and back. 16The tablets were the work of God; the writing was the writing of God, engraved on the tablets.

17When Joshua heard the noise of the people shouting, he said to Moses, “There is the sound of war in the camp.”

18Moses replied:

“It is not the sound of victory,
  it is not the sound of defeat;
  it is the sound of singing that I hear.”

19When Moses approached the camp and saw the calf and the dancing, his anger burned and he threw the tablets out of his hands, breaking them to pieces at the foot of the mountain. 20And he took the calf they had made and burned it in the fire; then he ground it to powder, scattered it on the water and made the Israelites drink it.

21He said to Aaron, “What did these people do to you, that you led them into such great sin?”

22“Do not be angry, my lord,” Aaron answered. “You know how prone these people are to evil. 23They said to me, ‘Make us gods who will go before us. As for this fellow Moses who brought us up out of Egypt, we don’t know what has happened to him.’ 24So I told them, ‘Whoever has any gold jewelry, take it off.’ Then they gave me the gold, and I threw it into the fire, and out came this calf!”

25Moses saw that the people were running wild and that Aaron had let them get out of control and so become a laughingstock to their enemies. 26So he stood at the entrance to the camp and said, “Whoever is for the LORD, come to me.” And all the Levites rallied to him.

27Then he said to them, “This is what the LORD, the God of Israel, says: ‘Each man strap a sword to his side. Go back and forth through the camp from one end to the other, each killing his brother and friend and neighbor.’ ” 28The Levites did as Moses commanded, and that day about three thousand of the people died. 29Then Moses said, “You have been set apart to the LORD today, for you were against your own sons and brothers, and he has blessed you this day.”

30The next day Moses said to the people, “You have committed a great sin. But now I will go up to the LORD; perhaps I can make atonement for your sin.”

31So Moses went back to the LORD and said, “Oh, what a great sin these people have committed! They have made themselves gods of gold. 32But now, please forgive their sin—but if not, then blot me out of the book you have written.”

33The LORD replied to Moses, “Whoever has sinned against me I will blot out of my book. 34Now go, lead the people to the place I spoke of, and my angel will go before you. However, when the time comes for me to punish, I will punish them for their sin.”

35And the LORD struck the people with a plague because of what they did with the calf Aaron had made.

33 Then the LORD said to Moses, “Leave this place, you and the people you brought up out of Egypt, and go up to the land I promised on oath to Abraham, Isaac and Jacob, saying, ‘I will give it to your descendants.’ 2I will send an angel before you and drive out the Canaanites, Amorites, Hittites, Perizzites, Hivites and Jebusites. 3Go up to the land flowing with milk and honey. But I will not go with you, because you are a stiff-necked people and I might destroy you on the way.”

4When the people heard these distressing words, they began to mourn and no one put on any ornaments. 5For the LORD had said to Moses, “Tell the Israelites, ‘You are a stiff-necked people. If I were to go with you even for a moment, I might destroy you. Now take off your ornaments and I will decide what to do with you.’ ” 6So the Israelites stripped off their ornaments at Mount Horeb.

The Tent of Meeting

7Now Moses used to take a tent and pitch
it outside the camp some distance away, calling it the "tent of meeting." Anyone inquiring
of the LORD would go to the tent of meeting
outside the camp. 8And whenever Moses went
out to the tent, all the people rose and stood
at the entrances to their tents, watching Moses
until he entered the tent. 9As Moses went into
the tent, the pillar of cloud would come down
and stay at the entrance, while the LORD spoke
with Moses. 10Whenever the people saw the
pillar of cloud standing at the entrance to the
tent, they all stood and worshiped, each at the
entrance to his tent. 11The LORD would speak
to Moses face to face, as a man speaks with his
friend. Then Moses would return to the camp,
but his young aide Joshua son of Nun did not
leave the tent.

Moses and the Glory of the LORD

12Moses said to the LORD, "You have been
telling me, 'Lead these people,' but you have
not let me know whom you will send with me.
You have said, 'I know you by name and you
have found favor with me.' 13If you are pleased
with me, teach me your ways so I may know
you and continue to find favor with you. Remember that this nation is your people."

14The LORD replied, "My Presence will go
with you, and I will give you rest."

15Then Moses said to him, "If your Presence does not go with us, do not send us up
from here. 16How will anyone know that you
are pleased with me and with your people unless you go with us? What else will distinguish
me and your people from all the other people
on the face of the earth?"

17And the LORD said to Moses, "I will do
the very thing you have asked, because I am
pleased with you and I know you by name."

18Then Moses said, "Now show me your
glory."

19And the LORD said, "I will cause all my
goodness to pass in front of you, and I will
proclaim my name, the LORD, in your presence. I will have mercy on whom I will have
mercy, and I will have compassion on whom
I will have compassion. 20But," he said, "you
cannot see my face, for no one may see me
and live."

21Then the LORD said, "There is a place near
me where you may stand on a rock. 22When
my glory passes by, I will put you in a cleft in
the rock and cover you with my hand until I
have passed by. 23Then I will remove my hand
and you will see my back; but my face must
not be seen."

The New Stone Tablets

34 The LORD said to Moses, "Chisel out
two stone tablets like the first ones,
and I will write on them the words that
were on the first tablets, which you broke. 2Be
ready in the morning, and then come up on
Mount Sinai. Present yourself to me there on
top of the mountain. 3No one is to come with
you or be seen anywhere on the mountain; not
even the flocks and herds may graze in front of
the mountain."

4So Moses chiseled out two stone tablets
like the first ones and went up Mount Sinai
early in the morning, as the LORD had commanded him; and he carried the two stone
tablets in his hands. 5Then the LORD came
down in the cloud and stood there with him
and proclaimed his name, the LORD. 6And he
passed in front of Moses, proclaiming, "The
LORD, the LORD, the compassionate and gracious God, slow to anger, abounding in love
and faithfulness, 7maintaining love to thousands, and forgiving wickedness, rebellion and
sin. Yet he does not leave the guilty unpunished; he punishes the children and their children for the sin of the fathers to the third and
fourth generation."

8Moses bowed to the ground at once and
worshiped. 9"O Lord, if I have found favor in
your eyes," he said, "then let the Lord go with
us. Although this is a stiff-necked people, forgive our wickedness and our sin, and take us
as your inheritance."

10Then the LORD said: "I am making a covenant with you. Before all your people I will
do wonders never before done in any nation
in all the world. The people you live among
will see how awesome is the work that I, the
LORD, will do for you. 11Obey what I command you today. I will drive out before you
the Amorites, Canaanites, Hittites, Perizzites,
Hivites and Jebusites. 12Be careful not to make
a treaty with those who live in the land where
you are going, or they will be a snare among
you. 13Break down their altars, smash their sacred stones and cut down their Asherah poles.[a]
14Do not worship any other god, for the LORD,
whose name is Jealous, is a jealous God.

15"Be careful not to make a treaty with those
who live in the land; for when they prostitute
themselves to their gods and sacrifice to them,

---

a *13* That is, symbols of the goddess Asherah

they will invite you and you will eat their sacrifices. 16And when you choose some of their
daughters as wives for your sons and those
daughters prostitute themselves to their gods,
they will lead your sons to do the same.
17"Do not make cast idols.
18"Celebrate the Feast of Unleavened Bread.
For seven days eat bread made without yeast,
as I commanded you. Do this at the appointed
time in the month of Abib, for in that month
you came out of Egypt.
19"The first offspring of every womb belongs to me, including all the firstborn males
of your livestock, whether from herd or flock.
20Redeem the firstborn donkey with a lamb,
but if you do not redeem it, break its neck.
Redeem all your firstborn sons.
"No one is to appear before me empty-
handed.
21"Six days you shall labor, but on the seventh day you shall rest; even during the plowing season and harvest you must rest.
22"Celebrate the Feast of Weeks with the
firstfruits of the wheat harvest, and the Feast
of Ingathering at the turn of the year.[a] 23Three
times a year all your men are to appear before the Sovereign LORD, the God of Israel. 24I
will drive out nations before you and enlarge
your territory, and no one will covet your land
when you go up three times each year to appear before the LORD your God.
25"Do not offer the blood of a sacrifice to
me along with anything containing yeast, and
do not let any of the sacrifice from the Passover Feast remain until morning.
26"Bring the best of the firstfruits of your
soil to the house of the LORD your God.
"Do not cook a young goat in its mother's
milk."
27Then the LORD said to Moses, "Write
down these words, for in accordance with
these words I have made a covenant with you
and with Israel." 28Moses was there with the
LORD forty days and forty nights without eating bread or drinking water. And he wrote on
the tablets the words of the covenant—the
Ten Commandments.

The Radiant Face of Moses

29When Moses came down from Mount Sinai with the two tablets of the Testimony in
his hands, he was not aware that his face was
radiant because he had spoken with the LORD.
30When Aaron and all the Israelites saw Moses, his face was radiant, and they were afraid
to come near him. 31But Moses called to them;
so Aaron and all the leaders of the community came back to him, and he spoke to them.
32Afterward all the Israelites came near him,
and he gave them all the commands the LORD
had given him on Mount Sinai.
33When Moses finished speaking to them,
he put a veil over his face. 34But whenever
he entered the LORD's presence to speak with
him, he removed the veil until he came out.
And when he came out and told the Israelites what he had been commanded, 35they saw
that his face was radiant. Then Moses would
put the veil back over his face until he went in
to speak with the LORD.

Sabbath Regulations

35 Moses assembled the whole Israelite
community and said to them, "These
are the things the LORD has command-
ed you to do: 2For six days, work is to be done,
but the seventh day shall be your holy day, a
Sabbath of rest to the LORD. Whoever does
any work on it must be put to death. 3Do not
light a fire in any of your dwellings on the Sabbath day."

Materials for the Tabernacle

4Moses said to the whole Israelite community, "This is what the LORD has commanded: 5From what you have, take an offering
for the LORD. Everyone who is willing is to
bring to the LORD an offering of gold, silver
and bronze; 6blue, purple and scarlet yarn and
fine linen; goat hair; 7ram skins dyed red and
hides of sea cows[b]; acacia wood; 8olive oil for
the light; spices for the anointing oil and for
the fragrant incense; 9and onyx stones and
other gems to be mounted on the ephod and
breastpiece.
10"All who are skilled among you are to
come and make everything the LORD has
commanded: 11the tabernacle with its tent
and its covering, clasps, frames, crossbars,
posts and bases; 12the ark with its poles and
the atonement cover and the curtain that
shields it; 13the table with its poles and all its
articles and the bread of the Presence; 14the
lampstand that is for light with its accessories, lamps and oil for the light; 15the altar of
incense with its poles, the anointing oil and
the fragrant incense; the curtain for the doorway at the entrance to the tabernacle; 16the
altar of burnt offering with its bronze grating,
its poles and all its utensils; the bronze ba-

[a] 22 That is, in the fall [b] 7 That is, dugongs; also in verse 23

sin with its stand; 17the curtains of the courtyard with its posts and bases, and the curtain
for the entrance to the courtyard; 18the tent
pegs for the tabernacle and for the courtyard, and their ropes; 19the woven garments
worn for ministering in the sanctuary—both
the sacred garments for Aaron the priest and
the garments for his sons when they serve as
priests."

20Then the whole Israelite community
withdrew from Moses' presence, 21and everyone who was willing and whose heart
moved him came and brought an offering to
the LORD for the work on the Tent of Meeting, for all its service, and for the sacred
garments. 22All who were willing, men and
women alike, came and brought gold jewelry of all kinds: brooches, earrings, rings and
ornaments. They all presented their gold as a
wave offering to the LORD. 23Everyone who
had blue, purple or scarlet yarn or fine lin-
en, or goat hair, ram skins dyed red or hides
of sea cows brought them. 24Those presenting
an offering of silver or bronze brought it as an
offering to the LORD, and everyone who had
acacia wood for any part of the work brought
it. 25Every skilled woman spun with her
hands and brought what she had spun—blue,
purple or scarlet yarn or fine linen. 26And all
the women who were willing and had the skill
spun the goat hair. 27The leaders brought onyx
stones and other gems to be mounted on the
ephod and breastpiece. 28They also brought
spices and olive oil for the light and for the
anointing oil and for the fragrant incense.
29All the Israelite men and women who were
willing brought to the LORD freewill offerings
for all the work the LORD through Moses had
commanded them to do.

Bezalel and Oholiab

30Then Moses said to the Israelites, "See, the
LORD has chosen Bezalel son of Uri, the son of
Hur, of the tribe of Judah, 31and he has filled
him with the Spirit of God, with skill, ability and knowledge in all kinds of crafts— 32to
make artistic designs for work in gold, silver
and bronze, 33to cut and set stones, to work
in wood and to engage in all kinds of artistic
craftsmanship. 34And he has given both him
and Oholiab son of Ahisamach, of the tribe
of Dan, the ability to teach others. 35He has
filled them with skill to do all kinds of work
as craftsmen, designers, embroiderers in blue,
purple and scarlet yarn and fine linen, and
weavers—all of them master craftsmen and
36 designers. 1So Bezalel, Oholiab and every skilled person to whom the LORD
has given skill and ability to know how
to carry out all the work of constructing the
sanctuary are to do the work just as the LORD
has commanded."

2Then Moses summoned Bezalel and Oholiab and every skilled person to whom the LORD
had given ability and who was willing to come
and do the work. 3They received from Moses
all the offerings the Israelites had brought to
carry out the work of constructing the sanctuary. And the people continued to bring freewill offerings morning after morning. 4So all
the skilled craftsmen who were doing all the
work on the sanctuary left their work 5and
said to Moses, "The people are bringing more
than enough for doing the work the LORD
commanded to be done."

6Then Moses gave an order and they sent
this word throughout the camp: "No man or
woman is to make anything else as an offering
for the sanctuary." And so the people were restrained from bringing more, 7because what
they already had was more than enough to do
all the work.

The Tabernacle

8All the skilled men among the workmen
made the tabernacle with ten curtains of finely twisted linen and blue, purple and scarlet
yarn, with cherubim worked into them by a
skilled craftsman. 9All the curtains were the
same size—twenty-eight cubits long and four
cubits wide.[a] 10They joined five of the curtains together and did the same with the other
five. 11Then they made loops of blue material
along the edge of the end curtain in one set,
and the same was done with the end curtain in
the other set. 12They also made fifty loops on
one curtain and fifty loops on the end curtain
of the other set, with the loops opposite each
other. 13Then they made fifty gold clasps and
used them to fasten the two sets of curtains together so that the tabernacle was a unit.

14They made curtains of goat hair for the
tent over the tabernacle—eleven altogether.
15All eleven curtains were the same size—thirty cubits long and four cubits wide.[b] 16They
joined five of the curtains into one set and the
other six into another set. 17Then they made
fifty loops along the edge of the end curtain
in one set and also along the edge of the end

[a] *9* That is, about 42 feet (about 12.5 meters) long and 6 feet (about 1.8 meters) wide [b] *15* That is, about 45 feet (about 13.5 meters) long and 6 feet (about 1.8 meters) wide

curtain in the other set. 18They made fifty
bronze clasps to fasten the tent together as a
unit. 19Then they made for the tent a covering
of ram skins dyed red, and over that a covering
of hides of sea cows.[a]
20They made upright frames of acacia wood
for the tabernacle. 21Each frame was ten cubits long and a cubit and a half wide,[b] 22with
two projections set parallel to each other. They
made all the frames of the tabernacle in this
way. 23They made twenty frames for the south
side of the tabernacle 24and made forty silver
bases to go under them—two bases for each
frame, one under each projection. 25For the
other side, the north side of the tabernacle,
they made twenty frames 26and forty silver
bases—two under each frame. 27They made
six frames for the far end, that is, the west end
of the tabernacle, 28and two frames were made
for the corners of the tabernacle at the far end.
29At these two corners the frames were double
from the bottom all the way to the top and
fitted into a single ring; both were made alike.
30So there were eight frames and sixteen silver
bases—two under each frame.
31They also made crossbars of acacia wood:
five for the frames on one side of the tabernacle, 32five for those on the other side, and five
for the frames on the west, at the far end of
the tabernacle. 33They made the center crossbar so that it extended from end to end at
the middle of the frames. 34They overlaid the
frames with gold and made gold rings to hold
the crossbars. They also overlaid the crossbars
with gold.
35They made the curtain of blue, purple
and scarlet yarn and finely twisted linen, with
cherubim worked into it by a skilled craftsman. 36They made four posts of acacia wood
for it and overlaid them with gold. They made
gold hooks for them and cast their four silver
bases. 37For the entrance to the tent they made
a curtain of blue, purple and scarlet yarn and
finely twisted linen—the work of an embroiderer; 38and they made five posts with hooks
for them. They overlaid the tops of the posts
and their bands with gold and made their five
bases of bronze.

The Ark

37 Bezalel made the ark of acacia wood—
two and a half cubits long, a cubit and a
half wide, and a cubit and a half high.[c]
2He overlaid it with pure gold, both inside and
out, and made a gold molding around it. 3He
cast four gold rings for it and fastened them to
its four feet, with two rings on one side and
two rings on the other. 4Then he made poles
of acacia wood and overlaid them with gold.
5And he inserted the poles into the rings on
the sides of the ark to carry it.
6He made the atonement cover of pure
gold—two and a half cubits long and a cubit
and a half wide.[d] 7Then he made two cherubim out of hammered gold at the ends of
the cover. 8He made one cherub on one end
and the second cherub on the other; at the
two ends he made them of one piece with the
cover. 9The cherubim had their wings spread
upward, overshadowing the cover with them.
The cherubim faced each other, looking toward the cover.

The Table

10They[e] made the table of acacia wood—
two cubits long, a cubit wide, and a cubit
and a half high.[f] 11Then they overlaid it with
pure gold and made a gold molding around
it. 12They also made around it a rim a handbreadth[g] wide and put a gold molding on the
rim. 13They cast four gold rings for the table
and fastened them to the four corners, where
the four legs were. 14The rings were put close
to the rim to hold the poles used in carrying
the table. 15The poles for carrying the table
were made of acacia wood and were overlaid
with gold. 16And they made from pure gold
the articles for the table—its plates and dishes
and bowls and its pitchers for the pouring out
of drink offerings.

The Lampstand

17They made the lampstand of pure gold
and hammered it out, base and shaft; its flowerlike cups, buds and blossoms were of one
piece with it. 18Six branches extended from
the sides of the lampstand—three on one side
and three on the other. 19Three cups shaped
like almond flowers with buds and blossoms
were on one branch, three on the next branch
and the same for all six branches extending
from the lampstand. 20And on the lampstand
were four cups shaped like almond flowers
with buds and blossoms. 21One bud was under the first pair of branches extending from
the lampstand, a second bud under the second

[a] *19* That is, dugongs [b] *21* That is, about 15 feet (about 4.5 meters) long and 2 1/4 feet (about 0.7 meter) wide [c] *1* That is, about 3 3/4 feet (about 1.1 meters) long and 2 1/4 feet (about 0.7 meter) wide and high [d] *6* That is, about 3 3/4 feet (about 1.1 meters) long and 2 1/4 feet (about 0.7 meter) wide [e] *10* Or *He*; also in verses 11-29 [f] *10* That is, about 3 feet (about 0.9 meter) long, 1 1/2 feet (about 0.5 meter) wide, and 2 1/4 feet (about 0.7 meter) high [g] *12* That is, about 3 inches (about 8 centimeters)

pair, and a third bud under the third pair—six
branches in all. 22The buds and the branches were all of one piece with the lampstand,
hammered out of pure gold.
23They made its seven lamps, as well as its
wick trimmers and trays, of pure gold. 24They
made the lampstand and all its accessories
from one talent[a] of pure gold.

The Altar of Incense

25They made the altar of incense out of acacia wood. It was square, a cubit long and a
cubit wide, and two cubits high[b]—its horns
of one piece with it. 26They overlaid the top
and all the sides and the horns with pure gold,
and made a gold molding around it. 27They
made two gold rings below the molding—two
on opposite sides—to hold the poles used to
carry it. 28They made the poles of acacia wood
and overlaid them with gold.
29They also made the sacred anointing oil
and the pure, fragrant incense—the work of
a perfumer.

The Altar of Burnt Offering

38 They[c] built the altar of burnt offering
of acacia wood, three cubits[d] high; it
was square, five cubits long and five cubits wide.[e] 2They made a horn at each of the
four corners, so that the horns and the altar
were of one piece, and they overlaid the altar with bronze. 3They made all its utensils of
bronze—its pots, shovels, sprinkling bowls,
meat forks and firepans. 4They made a grating
for the altar, a bronze network, to be under its
ledge, halfway up the altar. 5They cast bronze
rings to hold the poles for the four corners of
the bronze grating. 6They made the poles of
acacia wood and overlaid them with bronze.
7They inserted the poles into the rings so they
would be on the sides of the altar for carrying
it. They made it hollow, out of boards.

Basin for Washing

8They made the bronze basin and its bronze
stand from the mirrors of the women who
served at the entrance to the Tent of Meeting.

The Courtyard

9Next they made the courtyard. The south
side was a hundred cubits[f] long and had curtains of finely twisted linen, 10with twenty
posts and twenty bronze bases, and with silver hooks and bands on the posts. 11The north
side was also a hundred cubits long and had
twenty posts and twenty bronze bases, with
silver hooks and bands on the posts.
12The west end was fifty cubits[g] wide and
had curtains, with ten posts and ten bases,
with silver hooks and bands on the posts.
13The east end, toward the sunrise, was also
fifty cubits wide. 14Curtains fifteen cubits[h]
long were on one side of the entrance, with
three posts and three bases, 15and curtains fifteen cubits long were on the other side of the
entrance to the courtyard, with three posts
and three bases. 16All the curtains around the
courtyard were of finely twisted linen. 17The
bases for the posts were bronze. The hooks and
bands on the posts were silver, and their tops
were overlaid with silver; so all the posts of the
courtyard had silver bands.
18The curtain for the entrance to the courtyard was of blue, purple and scarlet yarn and
finely twisted linen—the work of an embroiderer. It was twenty cubits[i] long and, like the
curtains of the courtyard, five cubits[j] high,
19with four posts and four bronze bases. Their
hooks and bands were silver, and their tops
were overlaid with silver. 20All the tent pegs of
the tabernacle and of the surrounding courtyard were bronze.

The Materials Used

21These are the amounts of the materials
used for the tabernacle, the tabernacle of the
Testimony, which were recorded at Moses'
command by the Levites under the direction
of Ithamar son of Aaron, the priest. 22(Bezalel
son of Uri, the son of Hur, of the tribe of Judah, made everything the LORD commanded
Moses; 23with him was Oholiab son of Ahisamach, of the tribe of Dan—a craftsman and
designer, and an embroiderer in blue, purple
and scarlet yarn and fine linen.) 24The total
amount of the gold from the wave offering
used for all the work on the sanctuary was
29 talents and 730 shekels,[k] according to the
sanctuary shekel.
25The silver obtained from those of the
community who were counted in the census was 100 talents and 1,775 shekels,[l] according to the sanctuary shekel— 26one beka
per person, that is, half a shekel,[m] according

[a] *24* That is, about 75 pounds (about 34 kilograms) [b] *25* That is, about 1 1/2 feet (about 0.5 meter) long and wide, and about 3 feet (about 0.9 meter) high [c] *1* Or *He*; also in verses 2-9 [d] *1* That is, about 4 1/2 feet (about 1.3 meters) [e] *1* That is, about 7 1/2 feet (about 2.3 meters) long and wide [f] *9* That is, about 150 feet (about 46 meters) [g] *12* That is, about 75 feet (about 23 meters) [h] *14* That is, about 22 1/2 feet (about 6.9 meters) [i] *18* That is, about 30 feet (about 9 meters) [j] *18* That is, about 7 1/2 feet (about 2.3 meters) [k] *24* The weight of the gold was a little over one ton (about 1 metric ton). [l] *25* The weight of the silver was a little over 3 3/4 tons (about 3.4 metric tons). [m] *26* That is, about 1/5 ounce (about 5.5 grams)

to the sanctuary shekel, from everyone who
had crossed over to those counted, twenty
years old or more, a total of 603,550 men.
27 The 100 talents[a] of silver were used to cast
the bases for the sanctuary and for the curtain—100 bases from the 100 talents, one
talent for each base. 28 They used the 1,775
shekels[b] to make the hooks for the posts, to
overlay the tops of the posts, and to make
their bands.

29 The bronze from the wave offering was 70
talents and 2,400 shekels.[c] 30 They used it to
make the bases for the entrance to the Tent
of Meeting, the bronze altar with its bronze
grating and all its utensils, 31 the bases for the
surrounding courtyard and those for its entrance and all the tent pegs for the tabernacle
and those for the surrounding courtyard.

The Priestly Garments

39 From the blue, purple and scarlet yarn
they made woven garments for ministering in the sanctuary. They also made
sacred garments for Aaron, as the LORD commanded Moses.

The Ephod

2 They[d] made the ephod of gold, and of
blue, purple and scarlet yarn, and of finely twisted linen. 3 They hammered out thin
sheets of gold and cut strands to be worked
into the blue, purple and scarlet yarn and fine
linen—the work of a skilled craftsman. 4 They
made shoulder pieces for the ephod, which
were attached to two of its corners, so it could
be fastened. 5 Its skillfully woven waistband
was like it—of one piece with the ephod and
made with gold, and with blue, purple and
scarlet yarn, and with finely twisted linen, as
the LORD commanded Moses.

6 They mounted the onyx stones in gold
filigree settings and engraved them like a seal
with the names of the sons of Israel. 7 Then
they fastened them on the shoulder pieces of
the ephod as memorial stones for the sons of
Israel, as the LORD commanded Moses.

The Breastpiece

8 They fashioned the breastpiece—the work
of a skilled craftsman. They made it like the
ephod: of gold, and of blue, purple and scarlet yarn, and of finely twisted linen. 9 It was
square—a span[e] long and a span wide—and
folded double. 10 Then they mounted four
rows of precious stones on it. In the first row
there was a ruby, a topaz and a beryl; 11 in
the second row a turquoise, a sapphire[f] and
an emerald; 12 in the third row a jacinth, an
agate and an amethyst; 13 in the fourth row a
chrysolite, an onyx and a jasper.[g] They were
mounted in gold filigree settings. 14 There were
twelve stones, one for each of the names of the
sons of Israel, each engraved like a seal with
the name of one of the twelve tribes.

15 For the breastpiece they made braided
chains of pure gold, like a rope. 16 They made
two gold filigree settings and two gold rings,
and fastened the rings to two of the corners of
the breastpiece. 17 They fastened the two gold
chains to the rings at the corners of the breastpiece, 18 and the other ends of the chains to the
two settings, attaching them to the shoulder
pieces of the ephod at the front. 19 They made
two gold rings and attached them to the other
two corners of the breastpiece on the inside
edge next to the ephod. 20 Then they made two
more gold rings and attached them to the bottom of the shoulder pieces on the front of the
ephod, close to the seam just above the waistband of the ephod. 21 They tied the rings of the
breastpiece to the rings of the ephod with blue
cord, connecting it to the waistband so that
the breastpiece would not swing out from the
ephod—as the LORD commanded Moses.

Other Priestly Garments

22 They made the robe of the ephod entirely
of blue cloth—the work of a weaver— 23 with
an opening in the center of the robe like the
opening of a collar,[h] and a band around this
opening, so that it would not tear. 24 They
made pomegranates of blue, purple and scarlet yarn and finely twisted linen around the
hem of the robe. 25 And they made bells of
pure gold and attached them around the hem
between the pomegranates. 26 The bells and
pomegranates alternated around the hem of
the robe to be worn for ministering, as the
LORD commanded Moses.

27 For Aaron and his sons, they made tunics
of fine linen—the work of a weaver— 28 and
the turban of fine linen, the linen headbands
and the undergarments of finely twisted linen.
29 The sash was of finely twisted linen and blue,
purple and scarlet yarn—the work of an embroiderer—as the LORD commanded Moses.

---

a 27 That is, about 3 3/4 tons (about 3.4 metric tons) b 28 That is, about 45 pounds (about 20 kilograms) c 29 The weight of the bronze was about 2 1/2 tons (about 2.4 metric tons). d 2 Or *He*; also in verses 7, 8 and 22 e 9 That is, about 9 inches (about 22 centimeters) f 11 Or *lapis lazuli* g 13 The precise identification of some of these precious stones is uncertain. h 23 The meaning of the Hebrew for this word is uncertain.

30They made the plate, the sacred diadem,
out of pure gold and engraved on it, like an inscription on a seal: HOLY TO THE LORD. 31Then
they fastened a blue cord to it to attach it to
the turban, as the LORD commanded Moses.

Moses Inspects the Tabernacle

32So all the work on the tabernacle, the
Tent of Meeting, was completed. The Israelites
did everything just as the LORD commanded
Moses. 33Then they brought the tabernacle
to Moses: the tent and all its furnishings, its
clasps, frames, crossbars, posts and bases; 34the
covering of ram skins dyed red, the covering of
hides of sea cows[a] and the shielding curtain;
35the ark of the Testimony with its poles and
the atonement cover; 36the table with all its articles and the bread of the Presence; 37the pure
gold lampstand with its row of lamps and all
its accessories, and the oil for the light; 38the
gold altar, the anointing oil, the fragrant incense, and the curtain for the entrance to the
tent; 39the bronze altar with its bronze grating,
its poles and all its utensils; the basin with its
stand; 40the curtains of the courtyard with its
posts and bases, and the curtain for the entrance to the courtyard; the ropes and tent
pegs for the courtyard; all the furnishings for
the tabernacle, the Tent of Meeting; 41and the
woven garments worn for ministering in the
sanctuary, both the sacred garments for Aaron
the priest and the garments for his sons when
serving as priests.

42The Israelites had done all the work just
as the LORD had commanded Moses. 43Mo-
ses inspected the work and saw that they had
done it just as the LORD had commanded. So
Moses blessed them.

Setting Up the Tabernacle

40 Then the LORD said to Moses: 2"Set up
the tabernacle, the Tent of Meeting, on
the first day of the first month. 3Place
the ark of the Testimony in it and shield the
ark with the curtain. 4Bring in the table and
set out what belongs on it. Then bring in the
lampstand and set up its lamps. 5Place the
gold altar of incense in front of the ark of the
Testimony and put the curtain at the entrance
to the tabernacle.

6"Place the altar of burnt offering in front
of the entrance to the tabernacle, the Tent of
Meeting; 7place the basin between the Tent of
Meeting and the altar and put water in it. 8Set
up the courtyard around it and put the curtain
at the entrance to the courtyard.

9"Take the anointing oil and anoint the
tabernacle and everything in it; consecrate
it and all its furnishings, and it will be holy.
10Then anoint the altar of burnt offering and
all its utensils; consecrate the altar, and it will
be most holy. 11Anoint the basin and its stand
and consecrate them.

12"Bring Aaron and his sons to the entrance
to the Tent of Meeting and wash them with
water. 13Then dress Aaron in the sacred garments, anoint him and consecrate him so he
may serve me as priest. 14Bring his sons and
dress them in tunics. 15Anoint them just as
you anointed their father, so they may serve
me as priests. Their anointing will be to a
priesthood that will continue for all generations to come." 16Moses did everything just as
the LORD commanded him.

17So the tabernacle was set up on the first
day of the first month in the second year.
18When Moses set up the tabernacle, he put
the bases in place, erected the frames, inserted the crossbars and set up the posts. 19Then
he spread the tent over the tabernacle and put
the covering over the tent, as the LORD commanded him.

20He took the Testimony and placed it
in the ark, attached the poles to the ark and
put the atonement cover over it. 21Then he
brought the ark into the tabernacle and hung
the shielding curtain and shielded the ark of
the Testimony, as the LORD commanded him.

22Moses placed the table in the Tent of Meeting on the north side of the tabernacle outside
the curtain 23and set out the bread on it before
the LORD, as the LORD commanded him.

24He placed the lampstand in the Tent of
Meeting opposite the table on the south side
of the tabernacle 25and set up the lamps before
the LORD, as the LORD commanded him.

26Moses placed the gold altar in the Tent of
Meeting in front of the curtain 27and burned
fragrant incense on it, as the LORD commanded him. 28Then he put up the curtain at the
entrance to the tabernacle.

29He set the altar of burnt offering near the
entrance to the tabernacle, the Tent of Meeting, and offered on it burnt offerings and grain
offerings, as the LORD commanded him.

30He placed the basin between the Tent of
Meeting and the altar and put water in it for
washing, 31and Moses and Aaron and his sons
used it to wash their hands and feet. 32They

---

a 34 That is, dugongs

washed whenever they entered the Tent of
Meeting or approached the altar, as the LORD
commanded Moses.

33Then Moses set up the courtyard around
the tabernacle and altar and put up the curtain
at the entrance to the courtyard. And so Moses finished the work.

The Glory of the LORD

34Then the cloud covered the Tent of Meeting, and the glory of the LORD filled the tabernacle. 35Moses could not enter the Tent of
Meeting because the cloud had settled upon it,
and the glory of the LORD filled the tabernacle.

36In all the travels of the Israelites, whenever the cloud lifted from above the tabernacle,
they would set out; 37but if the cloud did not
lift, they did not set out—until the day it lifted. 38So the cloud of the LORD was over the
tabernacle by day, and fire was in the cloud
by night, in the sight of all the house of Israel
during all their travels.

LEVITICUS

Leviticus

QUICK FACTS

AUTHOR Moses

AUDIENCE The people of Israel

DATE Between 1446 and 1406 B.C.

SETTING The foot of Mount Sinai, where God introduced laws for living

Leviticus is about the nitty-gritty of living as the people of God. In addition to detailed regulations about offering sacrifices to God—in thanks, in atonement for sin, in worship, in devotion—and instructions on how to celebrate festivals and other sacred days, the book delves into the finer points of life.

When we read this book today, the information—what makes an animal clean or unclean, how priests were to be anointed, and how people were to purify themselves before worshiping God—may seem irrelevant to us. But the overarching lesson, particularly in regard to marriage, is that God cares about every aspect of our lives—how we greet each other in the morning, what we do to show respect for one another, how we groom our bodies, how we make a living, how we love one another and, most important, how we worship God and serve him together. Everything we do matters to God.

The Burnt Offering

1 The LORD called to Moses and spoke to him from the Tent of Meeting. He said, 2"Speak to the Israelites and say to them: 'When any of you brings an offering to the LORD, bring as your offering an animal from either the herd or the flock.

3" 'If the offering is a burnt offering from the herd, he is to offer a male without defect. He must present it at the entrance to the Tent of Meeting so that it[a] will be acceptable to the LORD. 4He is to lay his hand on the head of the burnt offering, and it will be accepted on his behalf to make atonement for him. 5He is to slaughter the young bull before the LORD, and then Aaron's sons the priests shall bring the blood and sprinkle it against the altar on all sides at the entrance to the Tent of Meeting. 6He is to skin the burnt offering and cut it into pieces. 7The sons of Aaron the priest are to put fire on the altar and arrange wood on the fire. 8Then Aaron's sons the priests shall arrange the pieces, including the head and the fat, on the burning wood that is on the altar. 9He is to wash the inner parts and the legs with water, and the priest is to burn all of it on the altar. It is a burnt offering, an offering made by fire, an aroma pleasing to the LORD.

10" 'If the offering is a burnt offering from the flock, from either the sheep or the goats, he is to offer a male without defect. 11He is to slaughter it at the north side of the altar before the LORD, and Aaron's sons the priests shall sprinkle its blood against the altar on all sides. 12He is to cut it into pieces, and the priest shall arrange them, including the head and the fat, on the burning wood that is on the altar. 13He is to wash the inner parts and the legs with water, and the priest is to bring all of it and burn it on the altar. It is a burnt offering, an offering made by fire, an aroma pleasing to the LORD.

14" 'If the offering to the LORD is a burnt offering of birds, he is to offer a dove or a young pigeon. 15The priest shall bring it to the altar, wring off the head and burn it on the altar; its blood shall be drained out on the side of the altar. 16He is to remove the crop with its contents[b] and throw it to the east side of the altar, where the ashes are. 17He shall tear it open by the wings, not severing it completely, and then the priest shall burn it on the wood that is on the fire on the altar. It is a burnt offering, an offering made by fire, an aroma pleasing to the LORD.

The Grain Offering

2 " 'When someone brings a grain offering to the LORD, his offering is to be of fine flour. He is to pour oil on it, put incense on it 2and take it to Aaron's sons the priests. The priest shall take a handful of the fine flour and oil, together with all the incense, and burn this as a memorial portion on the altar, an offering made by fire, an aroma pleasing to the LORD. 3The rest of the grain offering belongs to Aaron and his sons; it is a most holy part of the offerings made to the LORD by fire.

4" 'If you bring a grain offering baked in an oven, it is to consist of fine flour: cakes made without yeast and mixed with oil, or[c] wafers made without yeast and spread with oil. 5If your grain offering is prepared on a griddle, it is to be made of fine flour mixed with oil, and without yeast. 6Crumble it and pour oil on it; it is a grain offering. 7If your grain offering is cooked in a pan, it is to be made of fine flour and oil. 8Bring the grain offering made of these things to the LORD; present it to the priest, who shall take it to the altar. 9He shall take out the memorial portion from the grain offering and burn it on the altar as an offering made by fire, an aroma pleasing to the LORD. 10The rest of the grain offering belongs to Aaron and his sons; it is a most holy part of the offerings made to the LORD by fire.

11" 'Every grain offering you bring to the LORD must be made without yeast, for you are not to burn any yeast or honey in an offering made to the LORD by fire. 12You may bring them to the LORD as an offering of the firstfruits, but they are not to be offered on the altar as a pleasing aroma. 13Season all your grain offerings with salt. Do not leave the salt of the covenant of your God out of your grain offerings; add salt to all your offerings.

14" 'If you bring a grain offering of firstfruits to the LORD, offer crushed heads of new grain roasted in the fire. 15Put oil and incense on it; it is a grain offering. 16The priest shall burn the memorial portion of the crushed grain and the oil, together with all the incense, as an offering made to the LORD by fire.

The Fellowship Offering

3 " 'If someone's offering is a fellowship offering,[d] and he offers an animal from the herd, whether male or female, he is to present before the LORD an animal without defect. 2He is to lay his hand on the head of his offering and slaughter it at the entrance to the

[a] 3 Or *he* [b] 16 Or *crop and the feathers*; the meaning of the Hebrew for this word is uncertain. [c] 4 Or *and* [d] 1 Traditionally *peace offering*; also in verses 3, 6 and 9

Tent of Meeting. Then Aaron's sons the priests
shall sprinkle the blood against the altar on all
sides. 3From the fellowship offering he is to
bring a sacrifice made to the LORD by fire: all
the fat that covers the inner parts or is connected to them, 4both kidneys with the fat on
them near the loins, and the covering of the
liver, which he will remove with the kidneys.
5Then Aaron's sons are to burn it on the altar on top of the burnt offering that is on the
burning wood, as an offering made by fire, an
aroma pleasing to the LORD.

6" 'If he offers an animal from the flock as a
fellowship offering to the LORD, he is to offer
a male or female without defect. 7If he offers
a lamb, he is to present it before the LORD.
8He is to lay his hand on the head of his offering and slaughter it in front of the Tent of
Meeting. Then Aaron's sons shall sprinkle its
blood against the altar on all sides. 9From the
fellowship offering he is to bring a sacrifice
made to the LORD by fire: its fat, the entire
fat tail cut off close to the backbone, all the
fat that covers the inner parts or is connected
to them, 10both kidneys with the fat on them
near the loins, and the covering of the liver,
which he will remove with the kidneys. 11The
priest shall burn them on the altar as food, an
offering made to the LORD by fire.

12" 'If his offering is a goat, he is to present
it before the LORD. 13He is to lay his hand on
its head and slaughter it in front of the Tent
of Meeting. Then Aaron's sons shall sprinkle
its blood against the altar on all sides. 14From
what he offers he is to make this offering to
the LORD by fire: all the fat that covers the inner parts or is connected to them, 15both kidneys with the fat on them near the loins, and
the covering of the liver, which he will remove
with the kidneys. 16The priest shall burn them
on the altar as food, an offering made by fire, a
pleasing aroma. All the fat is the LORD's.

17" 'This is a lasting ordinance for the generations to come, wherever you live: You must
not eat any fat or any blood.' "

The Sin Offering

4 The LORD said to Moses, 2"Say to the Israelites: 'When anyone sins unintentionally
and does what is forbidden in any of the
LORD's commands—

3" 'If the anointed priest sins, bringing guilt
on the people, he must bring to the LORD a
young bull without defect as a sin offering for
the sin he has committed. 4He is to present
the bull at the entrance to the Tent of Meeting before the LORD. He is to lay his hand
on its head and slaughter it before the LORD.
5Then the anointed priest shall take some of
the bull's blood and carry it into the Tent
of Meeting. 6He is to dip his finger into the
blood and sprinkle some of it seven times before the LORD, in front of the curtain of the
sanctuary. 7The priest shall then put some of
the blood on the horns of the altar of fragrant
incense that is before the LORD in the Tent of
Meeting. The rest of the bull's blood he shall
pour out at the base of the altar of burnt offering at the entrance to the Tent of Meeting.
8He shall remove all the fat from the bull of
the sin offering—the fat that covers the inner
parts or is connected to them, 9both kidneys
with the fat on them near the loins, and the
covering of the liver, which he will remove
with the kidneys— 10just as the fat is removed
from the ox[a] sacrificed as a fellowship offering.[b] Then the priest shall burn them on the
altar of burnt offering. 11But the hide of the
bull and all its flesh, as well as the head and
legs, the inner parts and offal— 12that is, all
the rest of the bull—he must take outside the
camp to a place ceremonially clean, where the
ashes are thrown, and burn it in a wood fire
on the ash heap.

13" 'If the whole Israelite community sins
unintentionally and does what is forbidden
in any of the LORD's commands, even though
the community is unaware of the matter, they
are guilty. 14When they become aware of the
sin they committed, the assembly must bring
a young bull as a sin offering and present it
before the Tent of Meeting. 15The elders of
the community are to lay their hands on the
bull's head before the LORD, and the bull shall
be slaughtered before the LORD. 16Then the
anointed priest is to take some of the bull's
blood into the Tent of Meeting. 17He shall dip
his finger into the blood and sprinkle it before
the LORD seven times in front of the curtain.
18He is to put some of the blood on the horns
of the altar that is before the LORD in the Tent
of Meeting. The rest of the blood he shall pour
out at the base of the altar of burnt offering
at the entrance to the Tent of Meeting. 19He
shall remove all the fat from it and burn it on
the altar, 20and do with this bull just as he did
with the bull for the sin offering. In this way
the priest will make atonement for them, and
they will be forgiven. 21Then he shall take
the bull outside the camp and burn it as he

[a] 10 The Hebrew word can include both male and female. [b] 10 Traditionally *peace offering*; also in verses 26, 31 and 35

burned the first bull. This is the sin offering
for the community.

22“ ‘When a leader sins unintentionally and does what is forbidden in any of the
commands of the LORD his God, he is guilty.
23When he is made aware of the sin he committed, he must bring as his offering a male
goat without defect. 24He is to lay his hand
on the goat’s head and slaughter it at the place
where the burnt offering is slaughtered before
the LORD. It is a sin offering. 25Then the priest
shall take some of the blood of the sin offering
with his finger and put it on the horns of the
altar of burnt offering and pour out the rest of
the blood at the base of the altar. 26He shall
burn all the fat on the altar as he burned the
fat of the fellowship offering. In this way the
priest will make atonement for the man’s sin,
and he will be forgiven.

27“ ‘If a member of the community sins
unintentionally and does what is forbidden
in any of the LORD’s commands, he is guilty.
28When he is made aware of the sin he committed, he must bring as his offering for the
sin he committed a female goat without defect. 29He is to lay his hand on the head of
the sin offering and slaughter it at the place
of the burnt offering. 30Then the priest is to
take some of the blood with his finger and put
it on the horns of the altar of burnt offering
and pour out the rest of the blood at the base
of the altar. 31He shall remove all the fat, just
as the fat is removed from the fellowship offering, and the priest shall burn it on the altar
as an aroma pleasing to the LORD. In this way
the priest will make atonement for him, and
he will be forgiven.
32“ ‘If he brings a lamb as his sin offering,
he is to bring a female without defect. 33He
is to lay his hand on its head and slaughter it
for a sin offering at the place where the burnt
offering is slaughtered. 34Then the priest shall
take some of the blood of the sin offering with
his finger and put it on the horns of the altar of burnt offering and pour out the rest of
the blood at the base of the altar. 35He shall
remove all the fat, just as the fat is removed
from the lamb of the fellowship offering, and
the priest shall burn it on the altar on top of
the offerings made to the LORD by fire. In this
way the priest will make atonement for him
for the sin he has committed, and he will be
forgiven.

5 “ ‘If a person sins because he does not speak
up when he hears a public charge to testify
regarding something he has seen or learned
about, he will be held responsible.
2“ ‘Or if a person touches anything ceremonially unclean—whether the carcasses of
unclean wild animals or of unclean livestock
or of unclean creatures that move along the
ground—even though he is unaware of it, he
has become unclean and is guilty.
3“ ‘Or if he touches human uncleanness—
anything that would make him unclean—even
though he is unaware of it, when he learns of
it he will be guilty.
4“ ‘Or if a person thoughtlessly takes an
oath to do anything, whether good or evil—
in any matter one might carelessly swear
about—even though he is unaware of it, in
any case when he learns of it he will be guilty.
5“ ‘When anyone is guilty in any of these
ways, he must confess in what way he has
sinned 6and, as a penalty for the sin he has
committed, he must bring to the LORD a female lamb or goat from the flock as a sin offering; and the priest shall make atonement for
him for his sin.
7“ ‘If he cannot afford a lamb, he is to bring
two doves or two young pigeons to the LORD
as a penalty for his sin—one for a sin offering
and the other for a burnt offering. 8He is to
bring them to the priest, who shall first offer
the one for the sin offering. He is to wring its
head from its neck, not severing it completely,
9and is to sprinkle some of the blood of the sin
offering against the side of the altar; the rest of
the blood must be drained out at the base of
the altar. It is a sin offering. 10The priest shall
then offer the other as a burnt offering in the
prescribed way and make atonement for him
for the sin he has committed, and he will be
forgiven.
11“ ‘If, however, he cannot afford two doves
or two young pigeons, he is to bring as an offering for his sin a tenth of an ephah[a] of fine
flour for a sin offering. He must not put oil or
incense on it, because it is a sin offering. 12He
is to bring it to the priest, who shall take a
handful of it as a memorial portion and burn
it on the altar on top of the offerings made to
the LORD by fire. It is a sin offering. 13In this
way the priest will make atonement for him
for any of these sins he has committed, and he
will be forgiven. The rest of the offering will
belong to the priest, as in the case of the grain
offering.’ ”

---

a 11 That is, probably about 2 quarts (about 2 liters)

DON'T-MEAN-IT SINS

If a member of the community sins unintentionally and does what is forbidden in any of the LORD's commands, he is guilty. When he is made aware of the sin he committed, he must bring as his offering for the sin he committed a female goat without defect.

— LEVITICUS 4:27–28

Everyone roared with laughter at Maggie's story about Brad's klutziness in fixing the car. Brad was mortified.

Thad had been paying bills online and then, without ever really planning to, he found himself deep in pornography. Melanie walked in and found him viewing images he had no business seeing.

Arthur and Gabriela thought they were just getting together with some friends from church, but then they found themselves caught up in an angry coup to get rid of the pastor. Six months later, the church was in shambles, and Arthur and Gabriela were wondering how they let themselves get involved in the mess.

Sometimes we sin without meaning to. We aim for righteousness, honor and wisdom, but we miss by a mile. Leviticus 4:2 introduces a Hebrew word for sin that means "to miss the mark." George R. Knight, professor of church history at Andrews University Theological Seminary (Berrien Springs, Michigan), explains, "You have missed, not because you are wicked, but because you are stupid, silly, careless, inattentive, perhaps lazy, or more probably because you do not possess the proper aim in life."

Add to that Hebrew word for sin the word "unintentionally," and it suggests someone wandering away like a silly sheep or someone who isn't thinking. We sometimes feel we ought to be given a break if we didn't really mean to sin. But the Bible doesn't cut us any slack. Whether we mean it or not, sin damages our relationship with God and with others. Anyone who is married knows that unintentional hurts, such as teasing about someone's weaknesses or being chronically late or missing a birthday, can do a lot of harm.

Leviticus 4 shows that God takes unintentional sins seriously. Forgiveness is available, but it doesn't come cheap. No quick, "Oops, sorry. Guess I wasn't thinking." Specific instructions were given in Leviticus 4 for how different groups were to deal with these kinds of sins. While the details differed a little from one group to another, the basic corrective steps were the same for each situation: bring an offering, then have it sacrificed to atone for the sin.

Today, we who confess Jesus Christ as Savior are grateful that we don't have to go through the laborious and gruesome atonement rituals of the Old Testament. Still, as we read through the requirements in Leviticus, we realize how the sacrificial system illustrates the seriousness of sin. These sin sacrifices did not overdramatize the sinner's situation; rather, they underdramatized it. The blood of animals could never pay for sin, whether unintentional or not. God mercifully accepted such sacrifices until his plan could be carried out to give his one and only Son, Jesus, as the complete sacrifice for sin.

Sin is terrible—even when it's unintentional. Praise God that Christ's death provides forgiveness for us and that his indwelling Spirit gives us the strength to aim straight at godliness.

—LEE ECLOV

let's *talk*

- ✦ What unintentional sins have we committed that proved our aim was way off?
- ✦ What happens when we do not take such sins as seriously as God does?
- ✦ As we read Leviticus 4:27–35, let's imagine doing each corrective step. What would it feel like? How would we be affected?

FOR YOUR NEXT DEVOTIONAL READING, TURN TO PAGE 110.

The Guilt Offering

14 The LORD said to Moses: 15 "When a person commits a violation and sins unintentionally in regard to any of the LORD's holy things, he is to bring to the LORD as a penalty a ram from the flock, one without defect and of the proper value in silver, according to the sanctuary shekel.[a] It is a guilt offering. 16 He must make restitution for what he has failed to do in regard to the holy things, add a fifth of the value to that and give it all to the priest, who will make atonement for him with the ram as a guilt offering, and he will be forgiven.

17 "If a person sins and does what is forbidden in any of the LORD's commands, even though he does not know it, he is guilty and will be held responsible. 18 He is to bring to the priest as a guilt offering a ram from the flock, one without defect and of the proper value. In this way the priest will make atonement for him for the wrong he has committed unintentionally, and he will be forgiven. 19 It is a guilt offering; he has been guilty of[b] wrongdoing against the LORD."

6 The LORD said to Moses: 2 "If anyone sins and is unfaithful to the LORD by deceiving his neighbor about something entrusted to him or left in his care or stolen, or if he cheats him, 3 or if he finds lost property and lies about it, or if he swears falsely, or if he commits any such sin that people may do— 4 when he thus sins and becomes guilty, he must return what he has stolen or taken by extortion, or what was entrusted to him, or the lost property he found, 5 or whatever it was he swore falsely about. He must make restitution in full, add a fifth of the value to it and give it all to the owner on the day he presents his guilt offering. 6 And as a penalty he must bring to the priest, that is, to the LORD, his guilt offering, a ram from the flock, one without defect and of the proper value. 7 In this way the priest will make atonement for him before the LORD, and he will be forgiven for any of these things he did that made him guilty."

The Burnt Offering

8 The LORD said to Moses: 9 "Give Aaron and his sons this command: 'These are the regulations for the burnt offering: The burnt offering is to remain on the altar hearth throughout the night, till morning, and the fire must be kept burning on the altar. 10 The priest shall then put on his linen clothes, with linen undergarments next to his body, and shall remove the ashes of the burnt offering that the fire has consumed on the altar and place them beside the altar. 11 Then he is to take off these clothes and put on others, and carry the ashes outside the camp to a place that is ceremonially clean. 12 The fire on the altar must be kept burning; it must not go out. Every morning the priest is to add firewood and arrange the burnt offering on the fire and burn the fat of the fellowship offerings[c] on it. 13 The fire must be kept burning on the altar continuously; it must not go out.

The Grain Offering

14 " 'These are the regulations for the grain offering: Aaron's sons are to bring it before the LORD, in front of the altar. 15 The priest is to take a handful of fine flour and oil, together with all the incense on the grain offering, and burn the memorial portion on the altar as an aroma pleasing to the LORD. 16 Aaron and his sons shall eat the rest of it, but it is to be eaten without yeast in a holy place; they are to eat it in the courtyard of the Tent of Meeting. 17 It must not be baked with yeast; I have given it as their share of the offerings made to me by fire. Like the sin offering and the guilt offering, it is most holy. 18 Any male descendant of Aaron may eat it. It is his regular share of the offerings made to the LORD by fire for the generations to come. Whatever touches them will become holy.[d] ' "

19 The LORD also said to Moses, 20 "This is the offering Aaron and his sons are to bring to the LORD on the day he[e] is anointed: a tenth of an ephah[f] of fine flour as a regular grain offering, half of it in the morning and half in the evening. 21 Prepare it with oil on a griddle; bring it well-mixed and present the grain offering broken[g] in pieces as an aroma pleasing to the LORD. 22 The son who is to succeed him as anointed priest shall prepare it. It is the LORD's regular share and is to be burned completely. 23 Every grain offering of a priest shall be burned completely; it must not be eaten."

The Sin Offering

24 The LORD said to Moses, 25 "Say to Aaron and his sons: 'These are the regulations for the sin offering: The sin offering is to be slaughtered before the LORD in the place the burnt offering is slaughtered; it is most holy. 26 The priest who offers it shall eat it; it is to

---

a 15 That is, about 2/5 ounce (about 11.5 grams) *b 19* Or *has made full expiation for his* *c 12* Traditionally *peace offerings*
d 18 Or *Whoever touches them must be holy*; similarly in verse 27 *e 20* Or *each* *f 20* That is, probably about 2 quarts (about 2 liters)
g 21 The meaning of the Hebrew for this word is uncertain.

be eaten in a holy place, in the courtyard of the Tent of Meeting. 27Whatever touches any of the flesh will become holy, and if any of the blood is spattered on a garment, you must wash it in a holy place. 28The clay pot the meat is cooked in must be broken; but if it is cooked in a bronze pot, the pot is to be scoured and rinsed with water. 29Any male in a priest's family may eat it; it is most holy. 30But any sin offering whose blood is brought into the Tent of Meeting to make atonement in the Holy Place must not be eaten; it must be burned.

The Guilt Offering

7 " 'These are the regulations for the guilt offering, which is most holy: 2The guilt offering is to be slaughtered in the place where the burnt offering is slaughtered, and its blood is to be sprinkled against the altar on all sides. 3All its fat shall be offered: the fat tail and the fat that covers the inner parts, 4both kidneys with the fat on them near the loins, and the covering of the liver, which is to be removed with the kidneys. 5The priest shall burn them on the altar as an offering made to the LORD by fire. It is a guilt offering. 6Any male in a priest's family may eat it, but it must be eaten in a holy place; it is most holy.

7" 'The same law applies to both the sin offering and the guilt offering: They belong to the priest who makes atonement with them. 8The priest who offers a burnt offering for anyone may keep its hide for himself. 9Every grain offering baked in an oven or cooked in a pan or on a griddle belongs to the priest who offers it, 10and every grain offering, whether mixed with oil or dry, belongs equally to all the sons of Aaron.

The Fellowship Offering

11" 'These are the regulations for the fellowship offering[a] a person may present to the LORD:

12" 'If he offers it as an expression of thankfulness, then along with this thank offering he is to offer cakes of bread made without yeast and mixed with oil, wafers made without yeast and spread with oil, and cakes of fine flour well-kneaded and mixed with oil. 13Along with his fellowship offering of thanksgiving he is to present an offering with cakes of bread made with yeast. 14He is to bring one of each kind as an offering, a contribution to the LORD; it belongs to the priest who sprinkles the blood of the fellowship offerings. 15The meat of his fellowship offering of thanksgiving must be eaten on the day it is offered; he must leave none of it till morning.

16" 'If, however, his offering is the result of a vow or is a freewill offering, the sacrifice shall be eaten on the day he offers it, but anything left over may be eaten on the next day. 17Any meat of the sacrifice left over till the third day must be burned up. 18If any meat of the fellowship offering is eaten on the third day, it will not be accepted. It will not be credited to the one who offered it, for it is impure; the person who eats any of it will be held responsible.

19" 'Meat that touches anything ceremonially unclean must not be eaten; it must be burned up. As for other meat, anyone ceremonially clean may eat it. 20But if anyone who is unclean eats any meat of the fellowship offering belonging to the LORD, that person must be cut off from his people. 21If anyone touches something unclean—whether human uncleanness or an unclean animal or any unclean, detestable thing—and then eats any of the meat of the fellowship offering belonging to the LORD, that person must be cut off from his people.' "

Eating Fat and Blood Forbidden

22The LORD said to Moses, 23"Say to the Israelites: 'Do not eat any of the fat of cattle, sheep or goats. 24The fat of an animal found dead or torn by wild animals may be used for any other purpose, but you must not eat it. 25Anyone who eats the fat of an animal from which an offering by fire may be[b] made to the LORD must be cut off from his people. 26And wherever you live, you must not eat the blood of any bird or animal. 27If anyone eats blood, that person must be cut off from his people.' "

The Priests' Share

28The LORD said to Moses, 29"Say to the Israelites: 'Anyone who brings a fellowship offering to the LORD is to bring part of it as his sacrifice to the LORD. 30With his own hands he is to bring the offering made to the LORD by fire; he is to bring the fat, together with the breast, and wave the breast before the LORD as a wave offering. 31The priest shall burn the fat on the altar, but the breast belongs to Aaron and his sons. 32You are to give the right thigh

a *11* Traditionally *peace offering;* also in verses 13-37 *b* *25* Or *fire is*

WEEKEND

discussing sex

Sex is the world's most exciting subject, yet most people find it embarrassing to discuss. That is particularly true of married partners unless they begin immediately—on their honeymoon or shortly after. We suggest taking the following steps:

1. Pray for God's leading and direction.
2. Set a good time for your partner when you are not rushed and will not be interrupted.
3. Assure him or her of your basic love, then kindly state your true feelings—that you think something is missing in your love life and you would like to talk about it.
4. The giant step in working things out is for both partners to admit to a problem. In all likelihood, if you find sex difficult to discuss, you probably find it difficult to communicate about many things.
5. Try to get your partner to read [a book on sex] and hopefully discuss it with you.
6. Anticipate a solution—don't present an overly bleak picture; you *can* overcome this problem with God's help (Philippians 4:13).
7. If difficulties persist, make an appointment to consult your minister [or a Christian counselor] together.

When I ask about my husband's long time (four to six weeks) without sex, he merely says he's been too busy. Is this normal?

Once every four to six weeks is certainly less than the average recorded in our survey. Sex organs need to be used regularly to function at their best. Talk to him frankly; if nothing happens, he should get a checkup from a doctor.

How do you make men understand that a woman's passions rise and fall according to the cares and problems of the day and that their tiredness and lack of passion are in no way a rejection of their husbands?

By telling them so—gently—seasoned with love. Make sure you don't use "tiredness" as a cop-out. Do you take a nap before your husband comes home? If you are too tired to make love a majority of the time he desires it, you *are* too tired. You may need a medical checkup, vitamins, exercise, more rest or curtailment of some of your activities.

To what extent should a couple talk about previous relationships (some perverted)?

Almost none. The Bible teaches us to forget "what is behind" (Philippians 3:13) and think of those things that are pure (Philippians 4:8). Force your mind to think only of the good things of life, particularly those things that relate to love with your partner.

How can the sexual relationship be a spiritual experience also?

Everything a Christ-controlled Christian does is spiritual. That includes eating, elimination, spanking children or emptying the trash. Why isolate sex in marriage as if it were in a category all by itself? Many spiritual Christians pray before going to bed, then in a matter of minutes engage each other in foreplay, stimulation, coitus and finally orgasm. Why isn't that just as spiritual as anything else couples do? In fact, we believe that the more truly spiritual they are, the more loving and affectionate they will be with each other and consequently the more frequently they will make love. Actually, coitus should be the ultimate expression of a rich spiritual experience that continues to enrich the couple's relationship.

—TIM AND BEVERLY LAHAYE

let's talk

Talking about sex can be uncomfortable, even in the closest of relationships, but learning how to communicate about this topic from the beginning of your marriage will ensure that problems aren't allowed to fester and are resolved quickly. In order to facilitate communication about sex, we've listed 15 sentence starters. Finish the sentences for each statement and ask your spouse to do the same. Then discuss your answers.

Remember, there is no right or wrong answer; you only get points for answering honestly.

1. Talking about sex makes me feel . . .
2. What I like best about our sex life is . . .
3. The area of our sex life that I think needs some improvement is . . .
4. One thing in our sex life that has changed since we got married is . . .
5. If I could try anything in bed with my partner, it would be . . .
6. Sometimes I worry that I don't . . .
7. I fear that someday my partner might . . .
8. I like to be kissed . . .
9. My favorite thing to do before making love is . . .
10. My favorite thing to do after making love is . . .
11. To get me in the mood, all my partner has to do is . . .
12. The best romantic advice I've ever gotten is . . .
13. The romantic advice I wish my partner would follow is . . .
14. For me, the perfect place in which to make love to my partner is . . .
15. The three things I like best about my partner are . . .

HOW ARE WE DOING?

let's make a DATE

OOO LA LA!

Buy or borrow a French cookbook and make an extravagant French dinner at home. Or eat out at a French restaurant of your choice and then come home and make crepes for dessert. Put on a romantic French film and take turns reading the subtitles to each other. What if one of you doesn't like subtitles? Well, there is always French-kissing instead!

FOR YOUR NEXT DEVOTIONAL READING, TURN TO PAGE 113.

LESSONS FROM THE *Bible*

What do these passages tell you about marriage? Discuss God's teachings with each other.

1. A man and the wife of his youth (Proverbs 5:15–20)
2. Husbands and wives (Ephesians 5:21–33)

of your fellowship offerings to the priest as a contribution. 33The son of Aaron who offers the blood and the fat of the fellowship offering shall have the right thigh as his share. 34From the fellowship offerings of the Israelites, I have taken the breast that is waved and the thigh that is presented and have given them to Aaron the priest and his sons as their regular share from the Israelites.' "

35This is the portion of the offerings made to the LORD by fire that were allotted to Aaron and his sons on the day they were presented to serve the LORD as priests. 36On the day they were anointed, the LORD commanded that the Israelites give this to them as their regular share for the generations to come.

37These, then, are the regulations for the burnt offering, the grain offering, the sin offering, the guilt offering, the ordination offering and the fellowship offering, 38which the LORD gave Moses on Mount Sinai on the day he commanded the Israelites to bring their offerings to the LORD, in the Desert of Sinai.

The Ordination of Aaron and His Sons

8 The LORD said to Moses, 2"Bring Aaron and his sons, their garments, the anointing oil, the bull for the sin offering, the two rams and the basket containing bread made without yeast, 3and gather the entire assembly at the entrance to the Tent of Meeting." 4Moses did as the LORD commanded him, and the assembly gathered at the entrance to the Tent of Meeting.

5Moses said to the assembly, "This is what the LORD has commanded to be done." 6Then Moses brought Aaron and his sons forward and washed them with water. 7He put the tunic on Aaron, tied the sash around him, clothed him with the robe and put the ephod on him. He also tied the ephod to him by its skillfully woven waistband; so it was fastened on him. 8He placed the breastpiece on him and put the Urim and Thummim in the breastpiece. 9Then he placed the turban on Aaron's head and set the gold plate, the sacred diadem, on the front of it, as the LORD commanded Moses.

10Then Moses took the anointing oil and anointed the tabernacle and everything in it, and so consecrated them. 11He sprinkled some of the oil on the altar seven times, anointing the altar and all its utensils and the basin with its stand, to consecrate them. 12He poured some of the anointing oil on Aaron's head and anointed him to consecrate him. 13Then he brought Aaron's sons forward, put tunics on them, tied sashes around them and put headbands on them, as the LORD commanded Moses.

14He then presented the bull for the sin offering, and Aaron and his sons laid their hands on its head. 15Moses slaughtered the bull and took some of the blood, and with his finger he put it on all the horns of the altar to purify the altar. He poured out the rest of the blood at the base of the altar. So he consecrated it to make atonement for it. 16Moses also took all the fat around the inner parts, the covering of the liver, and both kidneys and their fat, and burned it on the altar. 17But the bull with its hide and its flesh and its offal he burned up outside the camp, as the LORD commanded Moses.

18He then presented the ram for the burnt offering, and Aaron and his sons laid their hands on its head. 19Then Moses slaughtered the ram and sprinkled the blood against the altar on all sides. 20He cut the ram into pieces and burned the head, the pieces and the fat. 21He washed the inner parts and the legs with water and burned the whole ram on the altar as a burnt offering, a pleasing aroma, an offering made to the LORD by fire, as the LORD commanded Moses.

22He then presented the other ram, the ram for the ordination, and Aaron and his sons laid their hands on its head. 23Moses slaughtered the ram and took some of its blood and put it on the lobe of Aaron's right ear, on the thumb of his right hand and on the big toe of his right foot. 24Moses also brought Aaron's sons forward and put some of the blood on the lobes of their right ears, on the thumbs of their right hands and on the big toes of their right feet. Then he sprinkled blood against the altar on all sides. 25He took the fat, the fat tail, all the fat around the inner parts, the covering of the liver, both kidneys and their fat and the right thigh. 26Then from the basket of bread made without yeast, which was before the LORD, he took a cake of bread, and one made with oil, and a wafer; he put these on the fat portions and on the right thigh. 27He put all these in the hands of Aaron and his sons and waved them before the LORD as a wave offering. 28Then Moses took them from their hands and burned them on the altar on top of the burnt offering as an ordination offering, a pleasing aroma, an offering made to the LORD by fire. 29He also took the breast—Moses' share of the ordination ram—and waved it be-

THANK OFFERINGS

Remember the musical, Fiddler on the Roof, when Tevye sang "Tradition"? Tevye, the Jewish father of three daughters, knew how essential religious traditions were for holding a family together while living in the hostile culture of pre-Revolution Russia.

This idea comes right out of the Old Testament. While the Israelites were wandering in the wilderness, God was forming them into a community holy and set apart. The people were about to enter a land where the inhabitants were steeped in paganism and idol worship. So God through Moses shared with the people holy habits, such as practicing proper diet and hygiene, setting aside days of remembrance, and worshiping God through sacrifices.

In Leviticus 7:11–21, for instance, we read about the regulations for three kinds of "fellowship offerings": thank offerings, freewill offerings and offerings as the result of a vow. How does a twenty-first-century non-Israelite couple apply ancient instructions like these to their own lives? The apostle Paul gives us a clue in Romans 12:1 where he says we should offer "[our] bodies as living sacrifices, holy and pleasing to God." Simply put, we can show our dedication to God by offering him ourselves, our desires, our interests, our yearnings, our relationships and our futures. We can offer those in gratitude for the benefits of living, by God's grace, in a marriage that pleases God.

Along with his fellowship offering of thanksgiving he is to present an offering with cakes of bread made with yeast. He is to bring one of each kind as an offering, a contribution to the Lord.

— Leviticus 7:13–14

let's talk

- What individual hobbies or activities do we participate in? Are there any that we feel we need to give up to spend more time with each other?
- Let's list some things that we're doing now that we might not have experienced had it not been for each other. How do each of our individual interests add to our lives together as a couple?
- How does sacrificing something strengthen our relationship?

As believers, husbands and wives also offer themselves to each other. Make no mistake; it is not easy to crawl up on the sacrificial altar and leave a part of yourself there so that your marriage can thrive. My husband, Grey, sacrificed his hobby of flying gliders every Saturday because I was not able to join him in it. I gave up my hobby of fly-fishing for the same reason, although I'm still working on him to give it a try.

I believe the key to making such sacrifices is thankfulness. We are grateful for each other, and we want to do things together more than we want to engage in individual hobbies. We didn't demand that the other give up these hobbies; we each willingly and voluntarily set aside something that was taking us away from each other.

Being thankful can ward off many temptations to sin. If I'm thankful for my spouse, I will not be looking for sexual pleasure or affirmation from other men. If I'm offering thanks for his job, I will be less willing to be envious of my friend's bigger house or nicer car. Making sacrificial offerings of self in thanksgiving for our relationship makes us look to each other and to God for joy rather than to other people or more stuff.

—MARY ANN JEFFREYS

FOR YOUR NEXT DEVOTIONAL READING, TURN TO PAGE 126.

fore the LORD as a wave offering, as the LORD
commanded Moses.
30 Then Moses took some of the anointing
oil and some of the blood from the altar and
sprinkled them on Aaron and his garments
and on his sons and their garments. So he consecrated Aaron and his garments and his sons
and their garments.
31 Moses then said to Aaron and his sons,
"Cook the meat at the entrance to the Tent of
Meeting and eat it there with the bread from
the basket of ordination offerings, as I commanded, saying,[a] 'Aaron and his sons are to
eat it.' 32 Then burn up the rest of the meat and
the bread. 33 Do not leave the entrance to the
Tent of Meeting for seven days, until the days
of your ordination are completed, for your ordination will last seven days. 34 What has been
done today was commanded by the LORD to
make atonement for you. 35 You must stay at
the entrance to the Tent of Meeting day and
night for seven days and do what the LORD
requires, so you will not die; for that is what
I have been commanded." 36 So Aaron and his
sons did everything the LORD commanded
through Moses.

The Priests Begin Their Ministry

9 On the eighth day Moses summoned Aaron and his sons and the elders of Israel. 2 He
said to Aaron, "Take a bull calf for your
sin offering and a ram for your burnt offering, both without defect, and present them
before the LORD. 3 Then say to the Israelites:
'Take a male goat for a sin offering, a calf
and a lamb—both a year old and without defect—for a burnt offering, 4 and an ox[b] and a
ram for a fellowship offering[c] to sacrifice before the LORD, together with a grain offering
mixed with oil. For today the LORD will appear to you.' "
5 They took the things Moses commanded
to the front of the Tent of Meeting, and the
entire assembly came near and stood before
the LORD. 6 Then Moses said, "This is what the
LORD has commanded you to do, so that the
glory of the LORD may appear to you."
7 Moses said to Aaron, "Come to the altar
and sacrifice your sin offering and your burnt
offering and make atonement for yourself and
the people; sacrifice the offering that is for the
people and make atonement for them, as the
LORD has commanded."
8 So Aaron came to the altar and slaughtered
the calf as a sin offering for himself. 9 His sons
brought the blood to him, and he dipped his
finger into the blood and put it on the horns
of the altar; the rest of the blood he poured
out at the base of the altar. 10 On the altar he
burned the fat, the kidneys and the covering
of the liver from the sin offering, as the LORD
commanded Moses; 11 the flesh and the hide
he burned up outside the camp.
12 Then he slaughtered the burnt offering.
His sons handed him the blood, and he sprinkled it against the altar on all sides. 13 They
handed him the burnt offering piece by piece,
including the head, and he burned them on
the altar. 14 He washed the inner parts and the
legs and burned them on top of the burnt offering on the altar.
15 Aaron then brought the offering that
was for the people. He took the goat for the
people's sin offering and slaughtered it and offered it for a sin offering as he did with the
first one.
16 He brought the burnt offering and offered
it in the prescribed way. 17 He also brought the
grain offering, took a handful of it and burned
it on the altar in addition to the morning's
burnt offering.
18 He slaughtered the ox and the ram as
the fellowship offering for the people. His
sons handed him the blood, and he sprinkled
it against the altar on all sides. 19 But the fat
portions of the ox and the ram—the fat tail,
the layer of fat, the kidneys and the covering
of the liver— 20 these they laid on the breasts,
and then Aaron burned the fat on the altar.
21 Aaron waved the breasts and the right thigh
before the LORD as a wave offering, as Moses
commanded.
22 Then Aaron lifted his hands toward the
people and blessed them. And having sacrificed the sin offering, the burnt offering and
the fellowship offering, he stepped down.
23 Moses and Aaron then went into the
Tent of Meeting. When they came out, they
blessed the people; and the glory of the LORD
appeared to all the people. 24 Fire came out
from the presence of the LORD and consumed
the burnt offering and the fat portions on the
altar. And when all the people saw it, they
shouted for joy and fell facedown.

The Death of Nadab and Abihu

10 Aaron's sons Nadab and Abihu took
their censers, put fire in them and added
incense; and they offered unauthorized
fire before the LORD, contrary to his com-

[a] *31* Or *I was commanded:* [b] *4* The Hebrew word can include both male and female; also in verses 18 and 19. [c] *4* Traditionally *peace offering;* also in verses 18 and 22

mand. 2So fire came out from the presence
of the LORD and consumed them, and they
died before the LORD. 3Moses then said to
Aaron, "This is what the LORD spoke of when
he said:

" 'Among those who approach me
I will show myself holy;
in the sight of all the people
I will be honored.' "

Aaron remained silent.
4Moses summoned Mishael and Elzaphan,
sons of Aaron's uncle Uzziel, and said to
them, "Come here; carry your cousins outside the camp, away from the front of the
sanctuary." 5So they came and carried them,
still in their tunics, outside the camp, as Moses ordered.
6Then Moses said to Aaron and his sons Eleazar and Ithamar, "Do not let your hair become unkempt,[a] and do not tear your clothes,
or you will die and the LORD will be angry
with the whole community. But your relatives,
all the house of Israel, may mourn for those
the LORD has destroyed by fire. 7Do not leave
the entrance to the Tent of Meeting or you
will die, because the LORD's anointing oil is on
you." So they did as Moses said.
8Then the LORD said to Aaron, 9"You and
your sons are not to drink wine or other fermented drink whenever you go into the Tent
of Meeting, or you will die. This is a lasting
ordinance for the generations to come. 10You
must distinguish between the holy and the
common, between the unclean and the clean,
11and you must teach the Israelites all the decrees the LORD has given them through Moses."
12Moses said to Aaron and his remaining
sons, Eleazar and Ithamar, "Take the grain offering left over from the offerings made to the
LORD by fire and eat it prepared without yeast
beside the altar, for it is most holy. 13Eat it in
a holy place, because it is your share and your
sons' share of the offerings made to the LORD
by fire; for so I have been commanded. 14But
you and your sons and your daughters may
eat the breast that was waved and the thigh
that was presented. Eat them in a ceremonially clean place; they have been given to you
and your children as your share of the Israelites' fellowship offerings.[b] 15The thigh that
was presented and the breast that was waved
must be brought with the fat portions of the
offerings made by fire, to be waved before the
LORD as a wave offering. This will be the regular share for you and your children, as the
LORD has commanded."
16When Moses inquired about the goat of
the sin offering and found that it had been
burned up, he was angry with Eleazar and
Ithamar, Aaron's remaining sons, and asked,
17"Why didn't you eat the sin offering in the
sanctuary area? It is most holy; it was given
to you to take away the guilt of the community by making atonement for them before
the LORD. 18Since its blood was not taken
into the Holy Place, you should have eat-
en the goat in the sanctuary area, as I commanded."
19Aaron replied to Moses, "Today they sacrificed their sin offering and their burnt offering before the LORD, but such things as this
have happened to me. Would the LORD have
been pleased if I had eaten the sin offering today?" 20When Moses heard this, he was satisfied.

Clean and Unclean Food

11 The LORD said to Moses and Aaron,
2"Say to the Israelites: 'Of all the animals that live on land, these are the ones
you may eat: 3You may eat any animal that
has a split hoof completely divided and that
chews the cud.
4" 'There are some that only chew the cud
or only have a split hoof, but you must not
eat them. The camel, though it chews the cud,
does not have a split hoof; it is ceremonially
unclean for you. 5The coney,[c] though it chews
the cud, does not have a split hoof; it is unclean for you. 6The rabbit, though it chews the
cud, does not have a split hoof; it is unclean
for you. 7And the pig, though it has a split
hoof completely divided, does not chew the
cud; it is unclean for you. 8You must not eat
their meat or touch their carcasses; they are
unclean for you.
9" 'Of all the creatures living in the water
of the seas and the streams, you may eat any
that have fins and scales. 10But all creatures
in the seas or streams that do not have fins
and scales—whether among all the swarm-
ing things or among all the other living creatures in the water—you are to detest. 11And
since you are to detest them, you must not eat
their meat and you must detest their carcasses. 12Anything living in the water that does
not have fins and scales is to be detestable to
you.

[a] 6 Or *Do not uncover your heads* [b] 14 Traditionally *peace offerings* [c] 5 That is, the hyrax or rock badger

13“ ‘These are the birds you are to detest and
not eat because they are detestable: the eagle,
the vulture, the black vulture, 14the red kite,
any kind of black kite, 15any kind of raven,
16the horned owl, the screech owl, the gull,
any kind of hawk, 17the little owl, the cormorant, the great owl, 18the white owl, the desert
owl, the osprey, 19the stork, any kind of heron,
the hoopoe and the bat.[a]

20“ ‘All flying insects that walk on all fours
are to be detestable to you. 21There are, however, some winged creatures that walk on all
fours that you may eat: those that have joint-
ed legs for hopping on the ground. 22Of these
you may eat any kind of locust, katydid, crick-
et or grasshopper. 23But all other winged creatures that have four legs you are to detest.

24“ ‘You will make yourselves unclean by
these; whoever touches their carcasses will be
unclean till evening. 25Whoever picks up one
of their carcasses must wash his clothes, and
he will be unclean till evening.

26“ ‘Every animal that has a split hoof not
completely divided or that does not chew the
cud is unclean for you; whoever touches ⌞the
carcass of⌟ any of them will be unclean. 27Of
all the animals that walk on all fours, those
that walk on their paws are unclean for you;
whoever touches their carcasses will be unclean till evening. 28Anyone who picks up
their carcasses must wash his clothes, and he
will be unclean till evening. They are unclean
for you.

29“ ‘Of the animals that move about on the
ground, these are unclean for you: the weasel,
the rat, any kind of great lizard, 30the gecko,
the monitor lizard, the wall lizard, the skink
and the chameleon. 31Of all those that move
along the ground, these are unclean for you.
Whoever touches them when they are dead
will be unclean till evening. 32When one of
them dies and falls on something, that article,
whatever its use, will be unclean, whether it is
made of wood, cloth, hide or sackcloth. Put
it in water; it will be unclean till evening, and
then it will be clean. 33If one of them falls into
a clay pot, everything in it will be unclean,
and you must break the pot. 34Any food that
could be eaten but has water on it from such
a pot is unclean, and any liquid that could be
drunk from it is unclean. 35Anything that one
of their carcasses falls on becomes unclean;
an oven or cooking pot must be broken up.
They are unclean, and you are to regard them
as unclean. 36A spring, however, or a cistern
for collecting water remains clean, but anyone
who touches one of these carcasses is unclean.
37If a carcass falls on any seeds that are to be
planted, they remain clean. 38But if water has
been put on the seed and a carcass falls on it,
it is unclean for you.

39“ ‘If an animal that you are allowed to eat
dies, anyone who touches the carcass will be
unclean till evening. 40Anyone who eats some
of the carcass must wash his clothes, and he
will be unclean till evening. Anyone who picks
up the carcass must wash his clothes, and he
will be unclean till evening.

41“ ‘Every creature that moves about on
the ground is detestable; it is not to be eaten.
42You are not to eat any creature that moves
about on the ground, whether it moves on its
belly or walks on all fours or on many feet;
it is detestable. 43Do not defile yourselves by
any of these creatures. Do not make yourselves unclean by means of them or be made
unclean by them. 44I am the LORD your God;
consecrate yourselves and be holy, because I
am holy. Do not make yourselves unclean by
any creature that moves about on the ground.
45I am the LORD who brought you up out of
Egypt to be your God; therefore be holy, because I am holy.

46“ ‘These are the regulations concerning
animals, birds, every living thing that moves
in the water and every creature that moves
about on the ground. 47You must distinguish
between the unclean and the clean, between
living creatures that may be eaten and those
that may not be eaten.’ ”

Purification After Childbirth

12 The LORD said to Moses, 2“Say to the
Israelites: ‘A woman who becomes pregnant and gives birth to a son will be ceremonially unclean for seven days, just as she
is unclean during her monthly period. 3On
the eighth day the boy is to be circumcised.
4Then the woman must wait thirty-three days
to be purified from her bleeding. She must not
touch anything sacred or go to the sanctuary
until the days of her purification are over. 5If
she gives birth to a daughter, for two weeks the
woman will be unclean, as during her period.
Then she must wait sixty-six days to be purified from her bleeding.

6“ ‘When the days of her purification for a
son or daughter are over, she is to bring to the
priest at the entrance to the Tent of Meeting a
year-old lamb for a burnt offering and a young

a *19* The precise identification of some of the birds, insects and animals in this chapter is uncertain.

pigeon or a dove for a sin offering. 7He shall
offer them before the LORD to make atonement for her, and then she will be ceremonially clean from her flow of blood.
" 'These are the regulations for the woman
who gives birth to a boy or a girl. 8If she cannot afford a lamb, she is to bring two doves or
two young pigeons, one for a burnt offering
and the other for a sin offering. In this way
the priest will make atonement for her, and
she will be clean.' "

Regulations About Infectious Skin Diseases

13 The LORD said to Moses and Aaron,
2"When anyone has a swelling or a rash
or a bright spot on his skin that may
become an infectious skin disease,[a] he must
be brought to Aaron the priest or to one of his
sons[b] who is a priest. 3The priest is to examine the sore on his skin, and if the hair in the
sore has turned white and the sore appears to
be more than skin deep,[c] it is an infectious
skin disease. When the priest examines him,
he shall pronounce him ceremonially unclean. 4If the spot on his skin is white but
does not appear to be more than skin deep
and the hair in it has not turned white, the
priest is to put the infected person in isolation
for seven days. 5On the seventh day the priest
is to examine him, and if he sees that the sore
is unchanged and has not spread in the skin,
he is to keep him in isolation another seven
days. 6On the seventh day the priest is to examine him again, and if the sore has faded
and has not spread in the skin, the priest shall
pronounce him clean; it is only a rash. The
man must wash his clothes, and he will be
clean. 7But if the rash does spread in his skin
after he has shown himself to the priest to be
pronounced clean, he must appear before the
priest again. 8The priest is to examine him,
and if the rash has spread in the skin, he shall
pronounce him unclean; it is an infectious
disease.

9"When anyone has an infectious skin
disease, he must be brought to the priest.
10The priest is to examine him, and if there
is a white swelling in the skin that has turned
the hair white and if there is raw flesh in the
swelling, 11it is a chronic skin disease and the
priest shall pronounce him unclean. He is not
to put him in isolation, because he is already
unclean.

12"If the disease breaks out all over his skin
and, so far as the priest can see, it covers all
the skin of the infected person from head to
foot, 13the priest is to examine him, and if the
disease has covered his whole body, he shall
pronounce that person clean. Since it has all
turned white, he is clean. 14But whenever
raw flesh appears on him, he will be unclean.
15When the priest sees the raw flesh, he shall
pronounce him unclean. The raw flesh is unclean; he has an infectious disease. 16Should
the raw flesh change and turn white, he must
go to the priest. 17The priest is to examine
him, and if the sores have turned white, the
priest shall pronounce the infected person
clean; then he will be clean.

18"When someone has a boil on his skin
and it heals, 19and in the place where the boil
was, a white swelling or reddish-white spot appears, he must present himself to the priest.
20The priest is to examine it, and if it appears
to be more than skin deep and the hair in it has
turned white, the priest shall pronounce him
unclean. It is an infectious skin disease that
has broken out where the boil was. 21But if,
when the priest examines it, there is no white
hair in it and it is not more than skin deep
and has faded, then the priest is to put him in
isolation for seven days. 22If it is spreading in
the skin, the priest shall pronounce him unclean; it is infectious. 23But if the spot is unchanged and has not spread, it is only a scar
from the boil, and the priest shall pronounce
him clean.

24"When someone has a burn on his skin
and a reddish-white or white spot appears in
the raw flesh of the burn, 25the priest is to examine the spot, and if the hair in it has turned
white, and it appears to be more than skin
deep, it is an infectious disease that has broken
out in the burn. The priest shall pronounce
him unclean; it is an infectious skin disease.
26But if the priest examines it and there is no
white hair in the spot and if it is not more
than skin deep and has faded, then the priest
is to put him in isolation for seven days. 27On
the seventh day the priest is to examine him,
and if it is spreading in the skin, the priest
shall pronounce him unclean; it is an infectious skin disease. 28If, however, the spot is
unchanged and has not spread in the skin but
has faded, it is a swelling from the burn, and
the priest shall pronounce him clean; it is only
a scar from the burn.

29"If a man or woman has a sore on the
head or on the chin, 30the priest is to examine
the sore, and if it appears to be more than skin

[a] 2 Traditionally *leprosy*; the Hebrew word was used for various diseases affecting the skin—not necessarily leprosy; also elsewhere in this chapter. [b] 2 Or *descendants* [c] 3 Or *be lower than the rest of the skin*; also elsewhere in this chapter

deep and the hair in it is yellow and thin, the
priest shall pronounce that person unclean; it
is an itch, an infectious disease of the head or
chin. 31But if, when the priest examines this
kind of sore, it does not seem to be more than
skin deep and there is no black hair in it, then
the priest is to put the infected person in isolation for seven days. 32On the seventh day the
priest is to examine the sore, and if the itch has
not spread and there is no yellow hair in it and
it does not appear to be more than skin deep,
33he must be shaved except for the diseased
area, and the priest is to keep him in isolation
another seven days. 34On the seventh day the
priest is to examine the itch, and if it has not
spread in the skin and appears to be no more
than skin deep, the priest shall pronounce him
clean. He must wash his clothes, and he will be
clean. 35But if the itch does spread in the skin
after he is pronounced clean, 36the priest is to
examine him, and if the itch has spread in the
skin, the priest does not need to look for yellow hair; the person is unclean. 37If, however,
in his judgment it is unchanged and black hair
has grown in it, the itch is healed. He is clean,
and the priest shall pronounce him clean.

38"When a man or woman has white spots
on the skin, 39the priest is to examine them,
and if the spots are dull white, it is a harmless
rash that has broken out on the skin; that person is clean.

40"When a man has lost his hair and is bald,
he is clean. 41If he has lost his hair from the
front of his scalp and has a bald forehead, he
is clean. 42But if he has a reddish-white sore
on his bald head or forehead, it is an infectious disease breaking out on his head or forehead. 43The priest is to examine him, and if
the swollen sore on his head or forehead is
reddish-white like an infectious skin disease,
44the man is diseased and is unclean. The
priest shall pronounce him unclean because of
the sore on his head.

45"The person with such an infectious disease must wear torn clothes, let his hair be unkempt,[a] cover the lower part of his face and
cry out, 'Unclean! Unclean!' 46As long as he
has the infection he remains unclean. He must
live alone; he must live outside the camp.

Regulations About Mildew

47"If any clothing is contaminated with
mildew—any woolen or linen clothing, 48any
woven or knitted material of linen or wool,
any leather or anything made of leather—
49and if the contamination in the clothing, or
leather, or woven or knitted material, or any
leather article, is greenish or reddish, it is a
spreading mildew and must be shown to the
priest. 50The priest is to examine the mildew
and isolate the affected article for seven days.
51On the seventh day he is to examine it, and
if the mildew has spread in the clothing, or
the woven or knitted material, or the leather, whatever its use, it is a destructive mildew;
the article is unclean. 52He must burn up the
clothing, or the woven or knitted material of
wool or linen, or any leather article that has
the contamination in it, because the mildew is
destructive; the article must be burned up.

53"But if, when the priest examines it, the
mildew has not spread in the clothing, or the
woven or knitted material, or the leather article, 54he shall order that the contaminated
article be washed. Then he is to isolate it for
another seven days. 55After the affected article has been washed, the priest is to examine
it, and if the mildew has not changed its appearance, even though it has not spread, it is
unclean. Burn it with fire, whether the mildew
has affected one side or the other. 56If, when
the priest examines it, the mildew has faded
after the article has been washed, he is to tear
the contaminated part out of the clothing, or
the leather, or the woven or knitted material.
57But if it reappears in the clothing, or in the
woven or knitted material, or in the leather
article, it is spreading, and whatever has the
mildew must be burned with fire. 58The clothing, or the woven or knitted material, or any
leather article that has been washed and is rid
of the mildew, must be washed again, and it
will be clean."

59These are the regulations concerning
contamination by mildew in woolen or linen
clothing, woven or knitted material, or any
leather article, for pronouncing them clean or
unclean.

Cleansing From Infectious Skin Diseases

14 The LORD said to Moses, 2"These are
the regulations for the diseased person
at the time of his ceremonial cleansing,
when he is brought to the priest: 3The priest
is to go outside the camp and examine him.
If the person has been healed of his infectious
skin disease,[b] 4the priest shall order that two
live clean birds and some cedar wood, scarlet
yarn and hyssop be brought for the one to be
cleansed. 5Then the priest shall order that one

[a] 45 Or *clothes, uncover his head* [b] 3 Traditionally *leprosy*; the Hebrew word was used for various diseases affecting the skin—not necessarily leprosy; also elsewhere in this chapter.

of the birds be killed over fresh water in a clay
pot. 6He is then to take the live bird and dip
it, together with the cedar wood, the scarlet
yarn and the hyssop, into the blood of the bird
that was killed over the fresh water. 7Seven
times he shall sprinkle the one to be cleansed
of the infectious disease and pronounce him
clean. Then he is to release the live bird in the
open fields.

8"The person to be cleansed must wash his
clothes, shave off all his hair and bathe with
water; then he will be ceremonially clean. After this he may come into the camp, but he
must stay outside his tent for seven days. 9On
the seventh day he must shave off all his hair;
he must shave his head, his beard, his eyebrows and the rest of his hair. He must wash
his clothes and bathe himself with water, and
he will be clean.

10"On the eighth day he must bring two
male lambs and one ewe lamb a year old,
each without defect, along with three-tenths
of an ephah[a] of fine flour mixed with oil for
a grain offering, and one log[b] of oil. 11The
priest who pronounces him clean shall present both the one to be cleansed and his offerings before the LORD at the entrance to the
Tent of Meeting.

12"Then the priest is to take one of the
male lambs and offer it as a guilt offering,
along with the log of oil; he shall wave them
before the LORD as a wave offering. 13He is
to slaughter the lamb in the holy place where
the sin offering and the burnt offering are
slaughtered. Like the sin offering, the guilt
offering belongs to the priest; it is most holy.
14The priest is to take some of the blood of
the guilt offering and put it on the lobe of
the right ear of the one to be cleansed, on the
thumb of his right hand and on the big toe
of his right foot. 15The priest shall then take
some of the log of oil, pour it in the palm of
his own left hand, 16dip his right forefinger
into the oil in his palm, and with his finger sprinkle some of it before the LORD seven times. 17The priest is to put some of the
oil remaining in his palm on the lobe of the
right ear of the one to be cleansed, on the
thumb of his right hand and on the big toe of
his right foot, on top of the blood of the guilt
offering. 18The rest of the oil in his palm the
priest shall put on the head of the one to be
cleansed and make atonement for him before
the LORD.

19"Then the priest is to sacrifice the sin offering and make atonement for the one to be
cleansed from his uncleanness. After that, the
priest shall slaughter the burnt offering 20and
offer it on the altar, together with the grain
offering, and make atonement for him, and
he will be clean.

21"If, however, he is poor and cannot afford
these, he must take one male lamb as a guilt
offering to be waved to make atonement for
him, together with a tenth of an ephah[c] of
fine flour mixed with oil for a grain offering,
a log of oil, 22and two doves or two young pigeons, which he can afford, one for a sin offering and the other for a burnt offering.

23"On the eighth day he must bring them
for his cleansing to the priest at the entrance to
the Tent of Meeting, before the LORD. 24The
priest is to take the lamb for the guilt offering,
together with the log of oil, and wave them
before the LORD as a wave offering. 25He shall
slaughter the lamb for the guilt offering and
take some of its blood and put it on the lobe
of the right ear of the one to be cleansed, on
the thumb of his right hand and on the big toe
of his right foot. 26The priest is to pour some
of the oil into the palm of his own left hand,
27and with his right forefinger sprinkle some
of the oil from his palm seven times before
the LORD. 28Some of the oil in his palm he
is to put on the same places he put the blood
of the guilt offering—on the lobe of the right
ear of the one to be cleansed, on the thumb
of his right hand and on the big toe of his
right foot. 29The rest of the oil in his palm the
priest shall put on the head of the one to be
cleansed, to make atonement for him before
the LORD. 30Then he shall sacrifice the doves
or the young pigeons, which the person can
afford, 31one[d] as a sin offering and the other
as a burnt offering, together with the grain offering. In this way the priest will make atonement before the LORD on behalf of the one to
be cleansed."

32These are the regulations for anyone who
has an infectious skin disease and who cannot
afford the regular offerings for his cleansing.

Cleansing From Mildew

33The LORD said to Moses and Aaron,
34"When you enter the land of Canaan, which
I am giving you as your possession, and I put
a spreading mildew in a house in that land,
35the owner of the house must go and tell the

a 10 That is, probably about 6 quarts (about 6.5 liters) *b 10* That is, probably about 2/3 pint (about 0.3 liter); also in verses 12, 15, 21 and 24 *c 21* That is, probably about 2 quarts (about 2 liters) *d 31* Septuagint and Syriac; Hebrew [31]*such as the person can afford, one*

priest, 'I have seen something that looks like
mildew in my house.' 36The priest is to order
the house to be emptied before he goes in to
examine the mildew, so that nothing in the
house will be pronounced unclean. After this
the priest is to go in and inspect the house.
37He is to examine the mildew on the walls,
and if it has greenish or reddish depressions
that appear to be deeper than the surface of
the wall, 38the priest shall go out the doorway
of the house and close it up for seven days.
39On the seventh day the priest shall return to
inspect the house. If the mildew has spread on
the walls, 40he is to order that the contaminated stones be torn out and thrown into an unclean place outside the town. 41He must have
all the inside walls of the house scraped and
the material that is scraped off dumped into
an unclean place outside the town. 42Then
they are to take other stones to replace these
and take new clay and plaster the house.

43"If the mildew reappears in the house after the stones have been torn out and the house
scraped and plastered, 44the priest is to go and
examine it and, if the mildew has spread in the
house, it is a destructive mildew; the house is
unclean. 45It must be torn down—its stones,
timbers and all the plaster—and taken out of
the town to an unclean place.

46"Anyone who goes into the house while
it is closed up will be unclean till evening.
47Anyone who sleeps or eats in the house must
wash his clothes.

48"But if the priest comes to examine it and
the mildew has not spread after the house has
been plastered, he shall pronounce the house
clean, because the mildew is gone. 49To purify the house he is to take two birds and some
cedar wood, scarlet yarn and hyssop. 50He
shall kill one of the birds over fresh water in a
clay pot. 51Then he is to take the cedar wood,
the hyssop, the scarlet yarn and the live bird,
dip them into the blood of the dead bird and
the fresh water, and sprinkle the house seven
times. 52He shall purify the house with the
bird's blood, the fresh water, the live bird, the
cedar wood, the hyssop and the scarlet yarn.
53Then he is to release the live bird in the open
fields outside the town. In this way he will
make atonement for the house, and it will be
clean."

54These are the regulations for any infectious skin disease, for an itch, 55for mildew in
clothing or in a house, 56and for a swelling,
a rash or a bright spot, 57to determine when
something is clean or unclean.

These are the regulations for infectious skin
diseases and mildew.

Discharges Causing Uncleanness

15 The LORD said to Moses and Aaron,
2"Speak to the Israelites and say to them:
'When any man has a bodily discharge,
the discharge is unclean. 3Whether it continues flowing from his body or is blocked, it will
make him unclean. This is how his discharge
will bring about uncleanness:

4" 'Any bed the man with a discharge lies
on will be unclean, and anything he sits on
will be unclean. 5Anyone who touches his bed
must wash his clothes and bathe with water,
and he will be unclean till evening. 6Whoever
sits on anything that the man with a discharge
sat on must wash his clothes and bathe with
water, and he will be unclean till evening.

7" 'Whoever touches the man who has a discharge must wash his clothes and bathe with
water, and he will be unclean till evening.

8" 'If the man with the discharge spits on
someone who is clean, that person must wash
his clothes and bathe with water, and he will
be unclean till evening.

9" 'Everything the man sits on when riding
will be unclean, 10and whoever touches any of
the things that were under him will be unclean
till evening; whoever picks up those things
must wash his clothes and bathe with water,
and he will be unclean till evening.

11" 'Anyone the man with a discharge
touches without rinsing his hands with water
must wash his clothes and bathe with water,
and he will be unclean till evening.

12" 'A clay pot that the man touches must
be broken, and any wooden article is to be
rinsed with water.

13" 'When a man is cleansed from his discharge, he is to count off seven days for his
ceremonial cleansing; he must wash his clothes
and bathe himself with fresh water, and he will
be clean. 14On the eighth day he must take
two doves or two young pigeons and come
before the LORD to the entrance to the Tent
of Meeting and give them to the priest. 15The
priest is to sacrifice them, the one for a sin offering and the other for a burnt offering. In
this way he will make atonement before the
LORD for the man because of his discharge.

16" 'When a man has an emission of semen,
he must bathe his whole body with water, and
he will be unclean till evening. 17Any clothing
or leather that has semen on it must be washed
with water, and it will be unclean till evening.
18When a man lies with a woman and there is

an emission of semen, both must bathe with
water, and they will be unclean till evening.
19“ ‘When a woman has her regular flow
of blood, the impurity of her monthly period
will last seven days, and anyone who touches
her will be unclean till evening.
20“ ‘Anything she lies on during her period
will be unclean, and anything she sits on will
be unclean. 21Whoever touches her bed must
wash his clothes and bathe with water, and he
will be unclean till evening. 22Whoever touches anything she sits on must wash his clothes
and bathe with water, and he will be unclean
till evening. 23Whether it is the bed or anything she was sitting on, when anyone touches
it, he will be unclean till evening.
24“ ‘If a man lies with her and her monthly
flow touches him, he will be unclean for seven
days; any bed he lies on will be unclean.
25“ ‘When a woman has a discharge of
blood for many days at a time other than her
monthly period or has a discharge that continues beyond her period, she will be unclean
as long as she has the discharge, just as in the
days of her period. 26Any bed she lies on while
her discharge continues will be unclean, as is
her bed during her monthly period, and anything she sits on will be unclean, as during
her period. 27Whoever touches them will be
unclean; he must wash his clothes and bathe
with water, and he will be unclean till evening.
28“ ‘When she is cleansed from her discharge, she must count off seven days, and
after that she will be ceremonially clean.
29On the eighth day she must take two doves
or two young pigeons and bring them to the
priest at the entrance to the Tent of Meeting. 30The priest is to sacrifice one for a sin
offering and the other for a burnt offering.
In this way he will make atonement for her
before the LORD for the uncleanness of her
discharge.
31“ ‘You must keep the Israelites separate from things that make them unclean,
so they will not die in their uncleanness for
defiling my dwelling place,[a] which is among
them.’ ”
32These are the regulations for a man with
a discharge, for anyone made unclean by an
emission of semen, 33for a woman in her
monthly period, for a man or a woman with a
discharge, and for a man who lies with a woman who is ceremonially unclean.

The Day of Atonement

16 The LORD spoke to Moses after the
death of the two sons of Aaron who died
when they approached the LORD. 2The
LORD said to Moses: “Tell your brother Aaron not to come whenever he chooses into the
Most Holy Place behind the curtain in front
of the atonement cover on the ark, or else he
will die, because I appear in the cloud over the
atonement cover.
3“This is how Aaron is to enter the sanctuary area: with a young bull for a sin offering
and a ram for a burnt offering. 4He is to put
on the sacred linen tunic, with linen undergarments next to his body; he is to tie the linen
sash around him and put on the linen turban.
These are sacred garments; so he must bathe
himself with water before he puts them on.
5From the Israelite community he is to take
two male goats for a sin offering and a ram for
a burnt offering.
6“Aaron is to offer the bull for his own sin
offering to make atonement for himself and
his household. 7Then he is to take the two
goats and present them before the LORD at
the entrance to the Tent of Meeting. 8He is
to cast lots for the two goats—one lot for the
LORD and the other for the scapegoat.[b] 9Aar-
on shall bring the goat whose lot falls to the
LORD and sacrifice it for a sin offering. 10But
the goat chosen by lot as the scapegoat shall
be presented alive before the LORD to be used
for making atonement by sending it into the
desert as a scapegoat.
11“Aaron shall bring the bull for his own
sin offering to make atonement for himself
and his household, and he is to slaughter the
bull for his own sin offering. 12He is to take
a censer full of burning coals from the altar
before the LORD and two handfuls of finely
ground fragrant incense and take them behind
the curtain. 13He is to put the incense on the
fire before the LORD, and the smoke of the incense will conceal the atonement cover above
the Testimony, so that he will not die. 14He is
to take some of the bull’s blood and with his
finger sprinkle it on the front of the atonement cover; then he shall sprinkle some of it
with his finger seven times before the atonement cover.
15“He shall then slaughter the goat for the
sin offering for the people and take its blood
behind the curtain and do with it as he did
with the bull’s blood: He shall sprinkle it on
the atonement cover and in front of it. 16In

[a] 31 Or *my tabernacle* [b] 8 That is, the goat of removal; Hebrew *azazel*; also in verses 10 and 26

this way he will make atonement for the Most
Holy Place because of the uncleanness and
rebellion of the Israelites, whatever their sins
have been. He is to do the same for the Tent
of Meeting, which is among them in the midst
of their uncleanness. 17 No one is to be in the
Tent of Meeting from the time Aaron goes in
to make atonement in the Most Holy Place
until he comes out, having made atonement
for himself, his household and the whole community of Israel.

18 "Then he shall come out to the altar that
is before the LORD and make atonement for
it. He shall take some of the bull's blood and
some of the goat's blood and put it on all the
horns of the altar. 19 He shall sprinkle some of
the blood on it with his finger seven times to
cleanse it and to consecrate it from the uncleanness of the Israelites.

20 "When Aaron has finished making atonement for the Most Holy Place, the Tent of
Meeting and the altar, he shall bring forward
the live goat. 21 He is to lay both hands on the
head of the live goat and confess over it all the
wickedness and rebellion of the Israelites—all
their sins—and put them on the goat's head.
He shall send the goat away into the desert
in the care of a man appointed for the task.
22 The goat will carry on itself all their sins to
a solitary place; and the man shall release it in
the desert.

23 "Then Aaron is to go into the Tent of
Meeting and take off the linen garments he
put on before he entered the Most Holy Place,
and he is to leave them there. 24 He shall bathe
himself with water in a holy place and put on
his regular garments. Then he shall come out
and sacrifice the burnt offering for himself
and the burnt offering for the people, to make
atonement for himself and for the people.
25 He shall also burn the fat of the sin offering
on the altar.

26 "The man who releases the goat as a scapegoat must wash his clothes and bathe himself
with water; afterward he may come into the
camp. 27 The bull and the goat for the sin offerings, whose blood was brought into the Most
Holy Place to make atonement, must be taken
outside the camp; their hides, flesh and offal
are to be burned up. 28 The man who burns
them must wash his clothes and bathe himself with water; afterward he may come into
the camp.

29 "This is to be a lasting ordinance for you:
On the tenth day of the seventh month
you must deny yourselves[a] and not do any
work—whether native-born or an alien living
among you— 30 because on this day atonement will be made for you, to cleanse you.
Then, before the LORD, you will be clean from
all your sins. 31 It is a sabbath of rest, and you
must deny yourselves; it is a lasting ordinance.
32 The priest who is anointed and ordained to
succeed his father as high priest is to make
atonement. He is to put on the sacred linen
garments 33 and make atonement for the Most
Holy Place, for the Tent of Meeting and the
altar, and for the priests and all the people of
the community.

34 "This is to be a lasting ordinance for you:
Atonement is to be made once a year for all
the sins of the Israelites."

And it was done, as the LORD commanded
Moses.

Eating Blood Forbidden

17 The LORD said to Moses, 2 "Speak to
Aaron and his sons and to all the Israelites and say to them: 'This is what the
LORD has commanded: 3 Any Israelite who
sacrifices an ox,[b] a lamb or a goat in the camp
or outside of it 4 instead of bringing it to the
entrance to the Tent of Meeting to present it
as an offering to the LORD in front of the tabernacle of the LORD—that man shall be considered guilty of bloodshed; he has shed blood
and must be cut off from his people. 5 This is
so the Israelites will bring to the LORD the sacrifices they are now making in the open fields.
They must bring them to the priest, that is, to
the LORD, at the entrance to the Tent of Meeting and sacrifice them as fellowship offerings.[c]
6 The priest is to sprinkle the blood against
the altar of the LORD at the entrance to the
Tent of Meeting and burn the fat as an aroma
pleasing to the LORD. 7 They must no longer
offer any of their sacrifices to the goat idols[d]
to whom they prostitute themselves. This is to
be a lasting ordinance for them and for the
generations to come.'

8 "Say to them: 'Any Israelite or any alien
living among them who offers a burnt offering or sacrifice 9 and does not bring it to the
entrance to the Tent of Meeting to sacrifice it
to the LORD—that man must be cut off from
his people.

10 " 'Any Israelite or any alien living among
them who eats any blood—I will set my face

[a] 29 Or *must fast*; also in verse 31 [b] 3 The Hebrew word can include both male and female. [c] 5 Traditionally *peace offerings*
[d] 7 Or *demons*

against that person who eats blood and will cut him off from his people. 11For the life of a creature is in the blood, and I have given it to you to make atonement for yourselves on the altar; it is the blood that makes atonement for one's life. 12Therefore I say to the Israelites, "None of you may eat blood, nor may an alien living among you eat blood."

13" 'Any Israelite or any alien living among you who hunts any animal or bird that may be eaten must drain out the blood and cover it with earth, 14because the life of every creature is its blood. That is why I have said to the Israelites, "You must not eat the blood of any creature, because the life of every creature is its blood; anyone who eats it must be cut off."

15" 'Anyone, whether native-born or alien, who eats anything found dead or torn by wild animals must wash his clothes and bathe with water, and he will be ceremonially unclean till evening; then he will be clean. 16But if he does not wash his clothes and bathe himself, he will be held responsible.' "

Unlawful Sexual Relations

18 The LORD said to Moses, 2"Speak to the Israelites and say to them: 'I am the LORD your God. 3You must not do as they do in Egypt, where you used to live, and you must not do as they do in the land of Canaan, where I am bringing you. Do not follow their practices. 4You must obey my laws and be careful to follow my decrees. I am the LORD your God. 5Keep my decrees and laws, for the man who obeys them will live by them. I am the LORD.

6" 'No one is to approach any close relative to have sexual relations. I am the LORD.

7" 'Do not dishonor your father by having sexual relations with your mother. She is your mother; do not have relations with her.

8" 'Do not have sexual relations with your father's wife; that would dishonor your father.

9" 'Do not have sexual relations with your sister, either your father's daughter or your mother's daughter, whether she was born in the same home or elsewhere.

10" 'Do not have sexual relations with your son's daughter or your daughter's daughter; that would dishonor you.

11" 'Do not have sexual relations with the daughter of your father's wife, born to your father; she is your sister.

12" 'Do not have sexual relations with your father's sister; she is your father's close relative.

13" 'Do not have sexual relations with your mother's sister, because she is your mother's close relative.

14" 'Do not dishonor your father's brother by approaching his wife to have sexual relations; she is your aunt.

15" 'Do not have sexual relations with your daughter-in-law. She is your son's wife; do not have relations with her.

16" 'Do not have sexual relations with your brother's wife; that would dishonor your brother.

17" 'Do not have sexual relations with both a woman and her daughter. Do not have sexual relations with either her son's daughter or her daughter's daughter; they are her close relatives. That is wickedness.

18" 'Do not take your wife's sister as a rival wife and have sexual relations with her while your wife is living.

19" 'Do not approach a woman to have sexual relations during the uncleanness of her monthly period.

20" 'Do not have sexual relations with your neighbor's wife and defile yourself with her.

21" 'Do not give any of your children to be sacrificed[a] to Molech, for you must not profane the name of your God. I am the LORD.

22" 'Do not lie with a man as one lies with a woman; that is detestable.

23" 'Do not have sexual relations with an animal and defile yourself with it. A woman must not present herself to an animal to have sexual relations with it; that is a perversion.

24" 'Do not defile yourselves in any of these ways, because this is how the nations that I am going to drive out before you became defiled. 25Even the land was defiled; so I punished it for its sin, and the land vomited out its inhabitants. 26But you must keep my decrees and my laws. The native-born and the aliens living among you must not do any of these detestable things, 27for all these things were done by the people who lived in the land before you, and the land became defiled. 28And if you defile the land, it will vomit you out as it vomited out the nations that were before you.

29" 'Everyone who does any of these detestable things—such persons must be cut off from their people. 30Keep my requirements and do not follow any of the detestable customs that were practiced before you came and

---

a 21 Or to be passed through ⌊the fire⌋

do not defile yourselves with them. I am the LORD your God.’ ”

Various Laws

19 The LORD said to Moses, 2“Speak to the entire assembly of Israel and say to them: ‘Be holy because I, the LORD your God, am holy.

3“ ‘Each of you must respect his mother and father, and you must observe my Sabbaths. I am the LORD your God.

4“ ‘Do not turn to idols or make gods of cast metal for yourselves. I am the LORD your God.

5“ ‘When you sacrifice a fellowship offering[a] to the LORD, sacrifice it in such a way that it will be accepted on your behalf. 6It shall be eaten on the day you sacrifice it or on the next day; anything left over until the third day must be burned up. 7If any of it is eaten on the third day, it is impure and will not be accepted. 8Whoever eats it will be held responsible because he has desecrated what is holy to the LORD; that person must be cut off from his people.

9“ ‘When you reap the harvest of your land, do not reap to the very edges of your field or gather the gleanings of your harvest. 10Do not go over your vineyard a second time or pick up the grapes that have fallen. Leave them for the poor and the alien. I am the LORD your God.

11“ ‘Do not steal.

“ ‘Do not lie.

“ ‘Do not deceive one another.

12“ ‘Do not swear falsely by my name and so profane the name of your God. I am the LORD.

13“ ‘Do not defraud your neighbor or rob him.

“ ‘Do not hold back the wages of a hired man overnight.

14“ ‘Do not curse the deaf or put a stumbling block in front of the blind, but fear your God. I am the LORD.

15“ ‘Do not pervert justice; do not show partiality to the poor or favoritism to the great, but judge your neighbor fairly.

16“ ‘Do not go about spreading slander among your people.

“ ‘Do not do anything that endangers your neighbor’s life. I am the LORD.

17“ ‘Do not hate your brother in your heart. Rebuke your neighbor frankly so you will not share in his guilt.

18“ ‘Do not seek revenge or bear a grudge against one of your people, but love your neighbor as yourself. I am the LORD.

19“ ‘Keep my decrees.

“ ‘Do not mate different kinds of animals.

“ ‘Do not plant your field with two kinds of seed.

“ ‘Do not wear clothing woven of two kinds of material.

20“ ‘If a man sleeps with a woman who is a slave girl promised to another man but who has not been ransomed or given her freedom, there must be due punishment. Yet they are not to be put to death, because she had not been freed. 21The man, however, must bring a ram to the entrance to the Tent of Meeting for a guilt offering to the LORD. 22With the ram of the guilt offering the priest is to make atonement for him before the LORD for the sin he has committed, and his sin will be forgiven.

23“ ‘When you enter the land and plant any kind of fruit tree, regard its fruit as forbidden.[b] For three years you are to consider it forbidden[b]; it must not be eaten. 24In the fourth year all its fruit will be holy, an offering of praise to the LORD. 25But in the fifth year you may eat its fruit. In this way your harvest will be increased. I am the LORD your God.

26“ ‘Do not eat any meat with the blood still in it.

“ ‘Do not practice divination or sorcery.

27“ ‘Do not cut the hair at the sides of your head or clip off the edges of your beard.

28“ ‘Do not cut your bodies for the dead or put tattoo marks on yourselves. I am the LORD.

29“ ‘Do not degrade your daughter by making her a prostitute, or the land will turn to prostitution and be filled with wickedness.

30“ ‘Observe my Sabbaths and have reverence for my sanctuary. I am the LORD.

31“ ‘Do not turn to mediums or seek out spiritists, for you will be defiled by them. I am the LORD your God.

32“ ‘Rise in the presence of the aged, show respect for the elderly and revere your God. I am the LORD.

33“ ‘When an alien lives with you in your land, do not mistreat him. 34The alien living with you must be treated as one of your native-born. Love him as yourself, for you were aliens in Egypt. I am the LORD your God.

35“ ‘Do not use dishonest standards when measuring length, weight or quantity. 36Use

[a] 5 Traditionally *peace offering* [b] 23 Hebrew *uncircumcised*

honest scales and honest weights, an honest
ephah[a] and an honest hin.[b] I am the LORD
your God, who brought you out of Egypt.
37 " 'Keep all my decrees and all my laws
and follow them. I am the LORD.' "

Punishments for Sin

20 The LORD said to Moses, 2 "Say to the Israelites: 'Any Israelite or any alien living
in Israel who gives[c] any of his children
to Molech must be put to death. The people
of the community are to stone him. 3 I will set
my face against that man and I will cut him
off from his people; for by giving his children
to Molech, he has defiled my sanctuary and
profaned my holy name. 4 If the people of the
community close their eyes when that man
gives one of his children to Molech and they
fail to put him to death, 5 I will set my face
against that man and his family and will cut
off from their people both him and all who
follow him in prostituting themselves to Molech.
6 " 'I will set my face against the person who
turns to mediums and spiritists to prostitute
himself by following them, and I will cut him
off from his people.
7 " 'Consecrate yourselves and be holy, because I am the LORD your God. 8 Keep my decrees and follow them. I am the LORD, who
makes you holy.[d]
9 " 'If anyone curses his father or mother, he
must be put to death. He has cursed his father
or his mother, and his blood will be on his
own head.
10 " 'If a man commits adultery with another man's wife—with the wife of his neighbor—both the adulterer and the adulteress
must be put to death.
11 " 'If a man sleeps with his father's wife, he
has dishonored his father. Both the man and
the woman must be put to death; their blood
will be on their own heads.
12 " 'If a man sleeps with his daughter-in-
law, both of them must be put to death. What
they have done is a perversion; their blood will
be on their own heads.
13 " 'If a man lies with a man as one lies
with a woman, both of them have done what
is detestable. They must be put to death; their
blood will be on their own heads.
14 " 'If a man marries both a woman and her
mother, it is wicked. Both he and they must
be burned in the fire, so that no wickedness
will be among you.
15 " 'If a man has sexual relations with an
animal, he must be put to death, and you
must kill the animal.
16 " 'If a woman approaches an animal to
have sexual relations with it, kill both the
woman and the animal. They must be put
to death; their blood will be on their own
heads.
17 " 'If a man marries his sister, the daughter of either his father or his mother, and they
have sexual relations, it is a disgrace. They
must be cut off before the eyes of their people.
He has dishonored his sister and will be held
responsible.
18 " 'If a man lies with a woman during her
monthly period and has sexual relations with
her, he has exposed the source of her flow, and
she has also uncovered it. Both of them must
be cut off from their people.
19 " 'Do not have sexual relations with the
sister of either your mother or your father, for
that would dishonor a close relative; both of
you would be held responsible.
20 " 'If a man sleeps with his aunt, he has
dishonored his uncle. They will be held responsible; they will die childless.
21 " 'If a man marries his brother's wife, it
is an act of impurity; he has dishonored his
brother. They will be childless.
22 " 'Keep all my decrees and laws and follow them, so that the land where I am bringing you to live may not vomit you out. 23 You
must not live according to the customs of the
nations I am going to drive out before you.
Because they did all these things, I abhorred
them. 24 But I said to you, "You will possess
their land; I will give it to you as an inheritance, a land flowing with milk and honey." I
am the LORD your God, who has set you apart
from the nations.
25 " 'You must therefore make a distinction
between clean and unclean animals and between unclean and clean birds. Do not defile
yourselves by any animal or bird or anything
that moves along the ground—those which I
have set apart as unclean for you. 26 You are to
be holy to me[e] because I, the LORD, am holy,
and I have set you apart from the nations to
be my own.
27 " 'A man or woman who is a medium or
spiritist among you must be put to death. You
are to stone them; their blood will be on their
own heads.' "

[a] 36 An ephah was a dry measure. [b] 36 A hin was a liquid measure. [c] 2 Or *sacrifices*; also in verses 3 and 4 [d] 8 Or *who sanctifies you*; or *who sets you apart as holy* [e] 26 Or *be my holy ones*

TUESDAY
READ LEVITICUS 20:6–8

EXTENDING THE BENEFITS OF MARRIAGE

Remember when you were engaged and imagining your life together? You probably envisioned cozy dinners at home, quiet evenings snuggled up on the couch, lazy Saturday mornings drinking coffee together and sharing the newspaper.

But if you have been married for more than, oh, five minutes, you know that it doesn't take long for those romantic dreams to fade when reality sets in. That cozy dinner becomes a quick bite squeezed in between work and a meeting. Snuggling on the couch becomes snoozing on the couch. And those lazy mornings? Who has the time?

It's easy for marriage to become little more than a series of routines—a kiss before work, a quick call during lunch, a rote conversation over dinner, a perfunctory smooch at bedtime. That's why the best marriages are about more than romantic dreams. The best marriages are about working together to share God's love with the world.

There are days—and sometimes weeks—when my husband drives me nuts. He would certainly say the same about me. But what gets us through those times is the belief that our marriage is meant for something greater than our happiness.

Every other week we host a small group at our house. To be honest, this involves a lot of work for us. We clean the house, make dinner for 20 people, and end up with an incredibly messy kitchen when it's over.

Some weeks I wish we could skip the rigmarole. But my husband believes strongly that Christian community is an essential practice of our faith and that this small group is a lifeline for the people who come each week. And he's right. Every week, even as I put the umpteenth plate in the dishwasher, I know we have made a difference in the lives of these friends and that they have made a difference in ours.

When something is consecrated, it means it has been dedicated to a divine purpose. A key theme in the book of Leviticus is holiness, and in this book God tells the Israelites how to be a holy people, set apart to be used by God for his glory. In our lives, we do not need to follow each and every law listed here, but we can apply the principles of Leviticus to our lives by thinking through how we can be used by God for his glory.

So try thinking of your marriage as something God can use in the lives of others. That simple shift in perspective can keep you from feeling stuck in the daily grind of living together and can instead inspire you to let your marriage be one of God's great gifts to the world.

—CARLA BARNHILL

"Consecrate yourselves and be holy, because I am the LORD your God."

— LEVITICUS 20:7

let's *talk*

- ✦ What gifts do we each have and how can we team up to be living examples of God's love? Could we open our home to a friend who needs a temporary place to live? Could we help out a single parent or an elderly neighbor?
- ✦ How do our gifts, talents and passions complement each other? Does either of us have dreams of a specific kind of ministry: working with the church's youth group, leading a neighborhood Bible study? How can we work together to make this dream a reality?
- ✦ Let's each make a list of at least five ways we can help each other grow personally. The next time one of us drives the other crazy, we'll break out the list and remember one way God has uniquely gifted us for each other.

FOR YOUR NEXT DEVOTIONAL READING, TURN TO PAGE 131.

Rules for Priests

21 The LORD said to Moses, "Speak to the priests, the sons of Aaron, and say to them: 'A priest must not make himself ceremonially unclean for any of his people who die, 2except for a close relative, such as his mother or father, his son or daughter, his brother, 3or an unmarried sister who is dependent on him since she has no husband—for her he may make himself unclean. 4He must not make himself unclean for people related to him by marriage,[a] and so defile himself.

5" 'Priests must not shave their heads or shave off the edges of their beards or cut their bodies. 6They must be holy to their God and must not profane the name of their God. Because they present the offerings made to the LORD by fire, the food of their God, they are to be holy.

7" 'They must not marry women defiled by prostitution or divorced from their husbands, because priests are holy to their God. 8Regard them as holy, because they offer up the food of your God. Consider them holy, because I the LORD am holy—I who make you holy.[b]

9" 'If a priest's daughter defiles herself by becoming a prostitute, she disgraces her father; she must be burned in the fire.

10" 'The high priest, the one among his brothers who has had the anointing oil poured on his head and who has been ordained to wear the priestly garments, must not let his hair become unkempt[c] or tear his clothes. 11He must not enter a place where there is a dead body. He must not make himself unclean, even for his father or mother, 12nor leave the sanctuary of his God or desecrate it, because he has been dedicated by the anointing oil of his God. I am the LORD.

13" 'The woman he marries must be a virgin. 14He must not marry a widow, a divorced woman, or a woman defiled by prostitution, but only a virgin from his own people, 15so he will not defile his offspring among his people. I am the LORD, who makes him holy.[d]' "

16The LORD said to Moses, 17"Say to Aaron: 'For the generations to come none of your descendants who has a defect may come near to offer the food of his God. 18No man who has any defect may come near: no man who is blind or lame, disfigured or deformed; 19no man with a crippled foot or hand, 20or who is hunchbacked or dwarfed, or who has any eye defect, or who has festering or running sores or damaged testicles. 21No descendant of Aaron the priest who has any defect is to come near to present the offerings made to the LORD by fire. He has a defect; he must not come near to offer the food of his God. 22He may eat the most holy food of his God, as well as the holy food; 23yet because of his defect, he must not go near the curtain or approach the altar, and so desecrate my sanctuary. I am the LORD, who makes them holy.[e]' "

24So Moses told this to Aaron and his sons and to all the Israelites.

22 The LORD said to Moses, 2"Tell Aaron and his sons to treat with respect the sacred offerings the Israelites consecrate to me, so they will not profane my holy name. I am the LORD.

3"Say to them: 'For the generations to come, if any of your descendants is ceremonially unclean and yet comes near the sacred offerings that the Israelites consecrate to the LORD, that person must be cut off from my presence. I am the LORD.

4" 'If a descendant of Aaron has an infectious skin disease[f] or a bodily discharge, he may not eat the sacred offerings until he is cleansed. He will also be unclean if he touches something defiled by a corpse or by anyone who has an emission of semen, 5or if he touches any crawling thing that makes him unclean, or any person who makes him unclean, whatever the uncleanness may be. 6The one who touches any such thing will be unclean till evening. He must not eat any of the sacred offerings unless he has bathed himself with water. 7When the sun goes down, he will be clean, and after that he may eat the sacred offerings, for they are his food. 8He must not eat anything found dead or torn by wild animals, and so become unclean through it. I am the LORD.

9" 'The priests are to keep my requirements so that they do not become guilty and die for treating them with contempt. I am the LORD, who makes them holy.[g]

10" 'No one outside a priest's family may eat the sacred offering, nor may the guest of a priest or his hired worker eat it. 11But if a priest buys a slave with money, or if a slave is born in his household, that slave may eat his

---

[a] 4 Or *unclean as a leader among his people* [b] 8 Or *who sanctify you*; or *who set you apart as holy* [c] 10 Or *not uncover his head* [d] 15 Or *who sanctifies him*; or *who sets him apart as holy* [e] 23 Or *who sanctifies them*; or *who sets them apart as holy*
[f] 4 Traditionally *leprosy*; the Hebrew word was used for various diseases affecting the skin—not necessarily leprosy. [g] 9 Or *who sanctifies them*; or *who sets them apart as holy*; also in verse 16

food. 12If a priest's daughter marries anyone other than a priest, she may not eat any of the sacred contributions. 13But if a priest's daughter becomes a widow or is divorced, yet has no children, and she returns to live in her father's house as in her youth, she may eat of her father's food. No unauthorized person, however, may eat any of it.

14" 'If anyone eats a sacred offering by mistake, he must make restitution to the priest for the offering and add a fifth of the value to it. 15The priests must not desecrate the sacred offerings the Israelites present to the LORD 16by allowing them to eat the sacred offerings and so bring upon them guilt requiring payment. I am the LORD, who makes them holy.' "

Unacceptable Sacrifices

17The LORD said to Moses, 18"Speak to Aaron and his sons and to all the Israelites and say to them: 'If any of you—either an Israelite or an alien living in Israel—presents a gift for a burnt offering to the LORD, either to fulfill a vow or as a freewill offering, 19you must present a male without defect from the cattle, sheep or goats in order that it may be accepted on your behalf. 20Do not bring anything with a defect, because it will not be accepted on your behalf. 21When anyone brings from the herd or flock a fellowship offering[a] to the LORD to fulfill a special vow or as a freewill offering, it must be without defect or blemish to be acceptable. 22Do not offer to the LORD the blind, the injured or the maimed, or anything with warts or festering or running sores. Do not place any of these on the altar as an offering made to the LORD by fire. 23You may, however, present as a freewill offering an ox[b] or a sheep that is deformed or stunted, but it will not be accepted in fulfillment of a vow. 24You must not offer to the LORD an animal whose testicles are bruised, crushed, torn or cut. You must not do this in your own land, 25and you must not accept such animals from the hand of a foreigner and offer them as the food of your God. They will not be accepted on your behalf, because they are deformed and have defects.' "

26The LORD said to Moses, 27"When a calf, a lamb or a goat is born, it is to remain with its mother for seven days. From the eighth day on, it will be acceptable as an offering made to the LORD by fire. 28Do not slaughter a cow or a sheep and its young on the same day.

29"When you sacrifice a thank offering to the LORD, sacrifice it in such a way that it will be accepted on your behalf. 30It must be eaten that same day; leave none of it till morning. I am the LORD.

31"Keep my commands and follow them. I am the LORD. 32Do not profane my holy name. I must be acknowledged as holy by the Israelites. I am the LORD, who makes[c] you holy[d] 33and who brought you out of Egypt to be your God. I am the LORD."

23 The LORD said to Moses, 2"Speak to the Israelites and say to them: 'These are my appointed feasts, the appointed feasts of the LORD, which you are to proclaim as sacred assemblies.

The Sabbath

3" 'There are six days when you may work, but the seventh day is a Sabbath of rest, a day of sacred assembly. You are not to do any work; wherever you live, it is a Sabbath to the LORD.

The Passover and Unleavened Bread

4" 'These are the LORD's appointed feasts, the sacred assemblies you are to proclaim at their appointed times: 5The LORD's Passover begins at twilight on the fourteenth day of the first month. 6On the fifteenth day of that month the LORD's Feast of Unleavened Bread begins; for seven days you must eat bread made without yeast. 7On the first day hold a sacred assembly and do no regular work. 8For seven days present an offering made to the LORD by fire. And on the seventh day hold a sacred assembly and do no regular work.' "

Firstfruits

9The LORD said to Moses, 10"Speak to the Israelites and say to them: 'When you enter the land I am going to give you and you reap its harvest, bring to the priest a sheaf of the first grain you harvest. 11He is to wave the sheaf before the LORD so it will be accepted on your behalf; the priest is to wave it on the day after the Sabbath. 12On the day you wave the sheaf, you must sacrifice as a burnt offering to the LORD a lamb a year old without defect, 13together with its grain offering of two-tenths of an ephah[e] of fine flour mixed with oil—an offering made to the LORD by fire, a pleasing aroma—and its drink offering of a quarter of a hin[f] of wine.

[a] 21 Traditionally *peace offering* [b] 23 The Hebrew word can include both male and female. [c] 32 Or *made* [d] 32 Or *who sanctifies you*; or *who sets you apart as holy* [e] 13 That is, probably about 4 quarts (about 4.5 liters); also in verse 17 [f] 13 That is, probably about 1 quart (about 1 liter)

14You must not eat any bread, or roasted or
new grain, until the very day you bring this
offering to your God. This is to be a lasting
ordinance for the generations to come, wherever you live.

Feast of Weeks

15" 'From the day after the Sabbath, the day
you brought the sheaf of the wave offering,
count off seven full weeks. 16Count off fifty
days up to the day after the seventh Sabbath,
and then present an offering of new grain to
the LORD. 17From wherever you live, bring
two loaves made of two-tenths of an ephah of
fine flour, baked with yeast, as a wave offering
of firstfruits to the LORD. 18Present with this
bread seven male lambs, each a year old and
without defect, one young bull and two rams.
They will be a burnt offering to the LORD,
together with their grain offerings and drink
offerings—an offering made by fire, an aroma pleasing to the LORD. 19Then sacrifice one
male goat for a sin offering and two lambs,
each a year old, for a fellowship offering.[a]
20The priest is to wave the two lambs before
the LORD as a wave offering, together with the
bread of the firstfruits. They are a sacred offering to the LORD for the priest. 21On that same
day you are to proclaim a sacred assembly and
do no regular work. This is to be a lasting ordinance for the generations to come, wherever
you live.

22" 'When you reap the harvest of your
land, do not reap to the very edges of your
field or gather the gleanings of your harvest.
Leave them for the poor and the alien. I am
the LORD your God.' "

Feast of Trumpets

23The LORD said to Moses, 24"Say to the Israelites: 'On the first day of the seventh month
you are to have a day of rest, a sacred assembly
commemorated with trumpet blasts. 25Do no
regular work, but present an offering made to
the LORD by fire.' "

Day of Atonement

26The LORD said to Moses, 27"The tenth
day of this seventh month is the Day of
Atonement. Hold a sacred assembly and deny
yourselves,[b] and present an offering made to
the LORD by fire. 28Do no work on that day,
because it is the Day of Atonement, when
atonement is made for you before the LORD
your God. 29Anyone who does not deny himself on that day must be cut off from his people. 30I will destroy from among his people
anyone who does any work on that day. 31You
shall do no work at all. This is to be a lasting ordinance for the generations to come,
wherever you live. 32It is a sabbath of rest for
you, and you must deny yourselves. From the
evening of the ninth day of the month until
the following evening you are to observe your
sabbath."

Feast of Tabernacles

33The LORD said to Moses, 34"Say to the Israelites: 'On the fifteenth day of the seventh
month the LORD's Feast of Tabernacles begins,
and it lasts for seven days. 35The first day is
a sacred assembly; do no regular work. 36For
seven days present offerings made to the LORD
by fire, and on the eighth day hold a sacred
assembly and present an offering made to the
LORD by fire. It is the closing assembly; do no
regular work.

37(" 'These are the LORD's appointed feasts,
which you are to proclaim as sacred assemblies
for bringing offerings made to the LORD by
fire—the burnt offerings and grain offerings,
sacrifices and drink offerings required for each
day. 38These offerings are in addition to those
for the LORD's Sabbaths and[c] in addition
to your gifts and whatever you have vowed
and all the freewill offerings you give to the
LORD.)

39" 'So beginning with the fifteenth day of
the seventh month, after you have gathered
the crops of the land, celebrate the festival to
the LORD for seven days; the first day is a day
of rest, and the eighth day also is a day of
rest. 40On the first day you are to take choice
fruit from the trees, and palm fronds, leafy
branches and poplars, and rejoice before the
LORD your God for seven days. 41Celebrate
this as a festival to the LORD for seven days
each year. This is to be a lasting ordinance
for the generations to come; celebrate it in
the seventh month. 42Live in booths for sev-
en days: All native-born Israelites are to live
in booths 43so your descendants will know
that I had the Israelites live in booths when
I brought them out of Egypt. I am the LORD
your God.' "

44So Moses announced to the Israelites the
appointed feasts of the LORD.

---

a 19 Traditionally *peace offering* *b* 27 Or *and fast;* also in verses 29 and 32 *c* 38 Or *These feasts are in addition to the LORD's Sabbaths, and these offerings are*

Oil and Bread Set Before the LORD

24 The LORD said to Moses, 2“Command the Israelites to bring you clear oil of pressed olives for the light so that the lamps may be kept burning continually. 3Outside the curtain of the Testimony in the Tent of Meeting, Aaron is to tend the lamps before the LORD from evening till morning, continually. This is to be a lasting ordinance for the generations to come. 4The lamps on the pure gold lampstand before the LORD must be tended continually.

5“Take fine flour and bake twelve loaves of bread, using two-tenths of an ephah[a] for each loaf. 6Set them in two rows, six in each row, on the table of pure gold before the LORD. 7Along each row put some pure incense as a memorial portion to represent the bread and to be an offering made to the LORD by fire. 8This bread is to be set out before the LORD regularly, Sabbath after Sabbath, on behalf of the Israelites, as a lasting covenant. 9It belongs to Aaron and his sons, who are to eat it in a holy place, because it is a most holy part of their regular share of the offerings made to the LORD by fire.”

A Blasphemer Stoned

10Now the son of an Israelite mother and an Egyptian father went out among the Israelites, and a fight broke out in the camp between him and an Israelite. 11The son of the Israelite woman blasphemed the Name with a curse; so they brought him to Moses. (His mother’s name was Shelomith, the daughter of Dibri the Danite.) 12They put him in custody until the will of the LORD should be made clear to them.

13Then the LORD said to Moses: 14“Take the blasphemer outside the camp. All those who heard him are to lay their hands on his head, and the entire assembly is to stone him. 15Say to the Israelites: ‘If anyone curses his God, he will be held responsible; 16anyone who blasphemes the name of the LORD must be put to death. The entire assembly must stone him. Whether an alien or native-born, when he blasphemes the Name, he must be put to death.

17“ ‘If anyone takes the life of a human being, he must be put to death. 18Anyone who takes the life of someone’s animal must make restitution—life for life. 19If anyone injures his neighbor, whatever he has done must be done to him: 20fracture for fracture, eye for eye, tooth for tooth. As he has injured the other, so he is to be injured. 21Whoever kills an animal must make restitution, but whoever kills a man must be put to death. 22You are to have the same law for the alien and the native-born. I am the LORD your God.’ ”

23Then Moses spoke to the Israelites, and they took the blasphemer outside the camp and stoned him. The Israelites did as the LORD commanded Moses.

The Sabbath Year

25 The LORD said to Moses on Mount Sinai, 2“Speak to the Israelites and say to them: ‘When you enter the land I am going to give you, the land itself must observe a sabbath to the LORD. 3For six years sow your fields, and for six years prune your vineyards and gather their crops. 4But in the seventh year the land is to have a sabbath of rest, a sabbath to the LORD. Do not sow your fields or prune your vineyards. 5Do not reap what grows of itself or harvest the grapes of your untended vines. The land is to have a year of rest. 6Whatever the land yields during the sabbath year will be food for you—for yourself, your manservant and maidservant, and the hired worker and temporary resident who live among you, 7as well as for your livestock and the wild animals in your land. Whatever the land produces may be eaten.

The Year of Jubilee

8“ ‘Count off seven sabbaths of years—seven times seven years—so that the seven sabbaths of years amount to a period of forty-nine years. 9Then have the trumpet sounded everywhere on the tenth day of the seventh month; on the Day of Atonement sound the trumpet throughout your land. 10Consecrate the fiftieth year and proclaim liberty throughout the land to all its inhabitants. It shall be a jubilee for you; each one of you is to return to his family property and each to his own clan. 11The fiftieth year shall be a jubilee for you; do not sow and do not reap what grows of itself or harvest the untended vines. 12For it is a jubilee and is to be holy for you; eat only what is taken directly from the fields.

13“ ‘In this Year of Jubilee everyone is to return to his own property.

14“ ‘If you sell land to one of your countrymen or buy any from him, do not take advantage of each other. 15You are to buy from your countryman on the basis of the number

[a] 5 That is, probably about 4 quarts (about 4.5 liters)

MAKING A FRESH START

My friend Christine's husband has a new job, so next week they'll be packing up and moving into a brand-new home that's been freshly painted and carpeted. "Ten minutes; that's how long it'll stay clean," she tells me, thinking of her six active children. "But I'm going to enjoy those ten minutes!"

A fresh start has its appeal. I have a daydream of my own in which I fling open the attic windows and begin hurling our stuff out onto the driveway. It would be lovely to see the attic floor again. Here's another fantasy: It's monthly bill-paying time and—lo and behold!—we have no debts to pay. No student loans or consumer debt. Not even a mortgage payment!

These are the kinds of dreams that came true for the Israelite people because of God's Jubilee plan. In the same way that God built Sabbath rest into the Israelites' weekly schedule, he planned times of labor and financial relief into their community and business life. The Year of Jubilee was a time when crop-bearing fields rested, debts were forgiven and indentured servants were released from their obligation. The Israelites were instructed to use that entire year for worshiping and building their family and community life. During that time they had to depend on God to sustain their lives because they weren't actively working to provide for themselves.

I can't take a shovel to the stuff in the attic; after all, it's mostly my husband's stuff up there. And as long as our kids require a roof over their heads, we'll keep making that mortgage payment. But there are ways I can bring a Jubilee-type freedom and celebration into my marriage. I can throw away the scorecard, for starters, and quit worrying about who's working harder (at home or away) or who's changed the most dreadful diapers. With a Jubilee mentality, David doesn't owe me a certain number of hours of vacuuming or lawn mowing.

Another way for our relationship to stay debt free is for me to put away old hurts and disagreements, not bringing them up when I'm angry or holding them against David in today's interactions. Every relationship benefits from emotional fresh starts.

Family life is financially draining, and it's easy for David and me to give priority to his career and to moneymaking projects. The tasks that come with our ministry commitments take a large portion of our time and attention. But whether or not we think we can afford travel and hotels for an actual getaway, we're trying occasionally to put aside work to make time to enjoy our relationship.

These are my everyday Jubilee practices. I need them because I can't afford to wait 50 years to build some Jubilee into our relationship!

—ANNETTE LAPLACA

The fiftieth year shall be a jubilee for you; do not sow and do not reap what grows of itself or harvest the untended vines.

— LEVITICUS 25:11

let's talk

- How does our calendar reflect the time we spend on work and obligations? Can we build in some Jubilee time for marriage building and fun?
- When do we fall into scorekeeping mode, feeling that we "owe" each other something?
- What relationship debts between us could be released or forgiven?

FOR YOUR NEXT DEVOTIONAL READING, TURN TO PAGE 143.

of years since the Jubilee. And he is to sell to
you on the basis of the number of years left for
harvesting crops. 16When the years are many,
you are to increase the price, and when the
years are few, you are to decrease the price, because what he is really selling you is the number of crops. 17Do not take advantage of each
other, but fear your God. I am the LORD your
God.

18" 'Follow my decrees and be careful to
obey my laws, and you will live safely in the
land. 19Then the land will yield its fruit, and
you will eat your fill and live there in safety.
20You may ask, "What will we eat in the seventh year if we do not plant or harvest our
crops?" 21I will send you such a blessing in
the sixth year that the land will yield enough
for three years. 22While you plant during the
eighth year, you will eat from the old crop and
will continue to eat from it until the harvest of
the ninth year comes in.

23" 'The land must not be sold permanently,
because the land is mine and you are but aliens
and my tenants. 24Throughout the country
that you hold as a possession, you must provide for the redemption of the land.

25" 'If one of your countrymen becomes
poor and sells some of his property, his nearest relative is to come and redeem what his
countryman has sold. 26If, however, a man has
no one to redeem it for him but he himself
prospers and acquires sufficient means to redeem it, 27he is to determine the value for the
years since he sold it and refund the balance
to the man to whom he sold it; he can then
go back to his own property. 28But if he does
not acquire the means to repay him, what he
sold will remain in the possession of the buyer
until the Year of Jubilee. It will be returned
in the Jubilee, and he can then go back to his
property.

29" 'If a man sells a house in a walled city,
he retains the right of redemption a full year
after its sale. During that time he may redeem
it. 30If it is not redeemed before a full year has
passed, the house in the walled city shall belong permanently to the buyer and his descendants. It is not to be returned in the Jubilee.
31But houses in villages without walls around
them are to be considered as open country.
They can be redeemed, and they are to be returned in the Jubilee.

32" 'The Levites always have the right to
redeem their houses in the Levitical towns,
which they possess. 33So the property of the
Levites is redeemable—that is, a house sold in
any town they hold—and is to be returned in
the Jubilee, because the houses in the towns of
the Levites are their property among the Israelites. 34But the pastureland belonging to their
towns must not be sold; it is their permanent
possession.

35" 'If one of your countrymen becomes
poor and is unable to support himself among
you, help him as you would an alien or a temporary resident, so he can continue to live
among you. 36Do not take interest of any
kind[a] from him, but fear your God, so that
your countryman may continue to live among
you. 37You must not lend him money at interest or sell him food at a profit. 38I am the
LORD your God, who brought you out of
Egypt to give you the land of Canaan and to
be your God.

39" 'If one of your countrymen becomes
poor among you and sells himself to you, do
not make him work as a slave. 40He is to be
treated as a hired worker or a temporary resident among you; he is to work for you until
the Year of Jubilee. 41Then he and his children
are to be released, and he will go back to his
own clan and to the property of his forefathers.
42Because the Israelites are my servants, whom
I brought out of Egypt, they must not be sold
as slaves. 43Do not rule over them ruthlessly,
but fear your God.

44" 'Your male and female slaves are to come
from the nations around you; from them you
may buy slaves. 45You may also buy some of
the temporary residents living among you and
members of their clans born in your country,
and they will become your property. 46You can
will them to your children as inherited property and can make them slaves for life, but
you must not rule over your fellow Israelites
ruthlessly.

47" 'If an alien or a temporary resident
among you becomes rich and one of your
countrymen becomes poor and sells himself
to the alien living among you or to a member of the alien's clan, 48he retains the right
of redemption after he has sold himself. One
of his relatives may redeem him: 49An uncle
or a cousin or any blood relative in his clan
may redeem him. Or if he prospers, he may
redeem himself. 50He and his buyer are to
count the time from the year he sold himself up to the Year of Jubilee. The price for
his release is to be based on the rate paid to
a hired man for that number of years. 51If

---

[a] 36 Or *take excessive interest*; similarly in verse 37

many years remain, he must pay for his redemption a larger share of the price paid for
him. 52If only a few years remain until the
Year of Jubilee, he is to compute that and pay
for his redemption accordingly. 53He is to be
treated as a man hired from year to year; you
must see to it that his owner does not rule
over him ruthlessly.
54" 'Even if he is not redeemed in any of
these ways, he and his children are to be released in the Year of Jubilee, 55for the Israelites
belong to me as servants. They are my servants, whom I brought out of Egypt. I am the
LORD your God.

Reward for Obedience

26 " 'Do not make idols or set up an image or a sacred stone for yourselves, and
do not place a carved stone in your land
to bow down before it. I am the LORD your
God.
2" 'Observe my Sabbaths and have reverence for my sanctuary. I am the LORD.
3" 'If you follow my decrees and are careful to obey my commands, 4I will send you
rain in its season, and the ground will yield
its crops and the trees of the field their fruit.
5Your threshing will continue until grape harvest and the grape harvest will continue until planting, and you will eat all the food you
want and live in safety in your land.
6" 'I will grant peace in the land, and you
will lie down and no one will make you afraid.
I will remove savage beasts from the land, and
the sword will not pass through your country.
7You will pursue your enemies, and they will
fall by the sword before you. 8Five of you will
chase a hundred, and a hundred of you will
chase ten thousand, and your enemies will fall
by the sword before you.
9" 'I will look on you with favor and make
you fruitful and increase your numbers, and
I will keep my covenant with you. 10You will
still be eating last year's harvest when you will
have to move it out to make room for the new.
11I will put my dwelling place[a] among you,
and I will not abhor you. 12I will walk among
you and be your God, and you will be my people. 13I am the LORD your God, who brought
you out of Egypt so that you would no longer
be slaves to the Egyptians; I broke the bars of
your yoke and enabled you to walk with heads
held high.

Punishment for Disobedience

14" 'But if you will not listen to me and carry out all these commands, 15and if you reject my decrees and abhor my laws and fail
to carry out all my commands and so violate
my covenant, 16then I will do this to you: I
will bring upon you sudden terror, wasting
diseases and fever that will destroy your sight
and drain away your life. You will plant seed
in vain, because your enemies will eat it. 17I
will set my face against you so that you will be
defeated by your enemies; those who hate you
will rule over you, and you will flee even when
no one is pursuing you.
18" 'If after all this you will not listen to
me, I will punish you for your sins seven times
over. 19I will break down your stubborn pride
and make the sky above you like iron and
the ground beneath you like bronze. 20Your
strength will be spent in vain, because your
soil will not yield its crops, nor will the trees
of the land yield their fruit.
21" 'If you remain hostile toward me and refuse to listen to me, I will multiply your afflictions seven times over, as your sins deserve. 22I
will send wild animals against you, and they
will rob you of your children, destroy your
cattle and make you so few in number that
your roads will be deserted.
23" 'If in spite of these things you do not
accept my correction but continue to be hostile toward me, 24I myself will be hostile toward you and will afflict you for your sins sev-
en times over. 25And I will bring the sword
upon you to avenge the breaking of the covenant. When you withdraw into your cities,
I will send a plague among you, and you will
be given into enemy hands. 26When I cut off
your supply of bread, ten women will be able
to bake your bread in one oven, and they will
dole out the bread by weight. You will eat, but
you will not be satisfied.
27" 'If in spite of this you still do not listen
to me but continue to be hostile toward me,
28then in my anger I will be hostile toward
you, and I myself will punish you for your
sins seven times over. 29You will eat the flesh
of your sons and the flesh of your daughters.
30I will destroy your high places, cut down
your incense altars and pile your dead bodies
on the lifeless forms of your idols, and I will
abhor you. 31I will turn your cities into ruins
and lay waste your sanctuaries, and I will take
no delight in the pleasing aroma of your offerings. 32I will lay waste the land, so that your

[a] *11* Or *my tabernacle*

enemies who live there will be appalled. 33I will scatter you among the nations and will draw out my sword and pursue you. Your land will be laid waste, and your cities will lie in ruins. 34Then the land will enjoy its sabbath years all the time that it lies desolate and you are in the country of your enemies; then the land will rest and enjoy its sabbaths. 35All the time that it lies desolate, the land will have the rest it did not have during the sabbaths you lived in it.

36" 'As for those of you who are left, I will make their hearts so fearful in the lands of their enemies that the sound of a windblown leaf will put them to flight. They will run as though fleeing from the sword, and they will fall, even though no one is pursuing them. 37They will stumble over one another as though fleeing from the sword, even though no one is pursuing them. So you will not be able to stand before your enemies. 38You will perish among the nations; the land of your enemies will devour you. 39Those of you who are left will waste away in the lands of their enemies because of their sins; also because of their fathers' sins they will waste away.

40" 'But if they will confess their sins and the sins of their fathers—their treachery against me and their hostility toward me, 41which made me hostile toward them so that I sent them into the land of their enemies—then when their uncircumcised hearts are humbled and they pay for their sin, 42I will remember my covenant with Jacob and my covenant with Isaac and my covenant with Abraham, and I will remember the land. 43For the land will be deserted by them and will enjoy its sabbaths while it lies desolate without them. They will pay for their sins because they rejected my laws and abhorred my decrees. 44Yet in spite of this, when they are in the land of their enemies, I will not reject them or abhor them so as to destroy them completely, breaking my covenant with them. I am the LORD their God. 45But for their sake I will remember the covenant with their ancestors whom I brought out of Egypt in the sight of the nations to be their God. I am the LORD.' "

46These are the decrees, the laws and the regulations that the LORD established on Mount Sinai between himself and the Israelites through Moses.

Redeeming What Is the LORD's

27 The LORD said to Moses, 2"Speak to the Israelites and say to them: 'If anyone makes a special vow to dedicate persons to the LORD by giving equivalent values, 3set the value of a male between the ages of twenty and sixty at fifty shekels[a] of silver, according to the sanctuary shekel[b]; 4and if it is a female, set her value at thirty shekels.[c] 5If it is a person between the ages of five and twenty, set the value of a male at twenty shekels[d] and of a female at ten shekels.[e] 6If it is a person between one month and five years, set the value of a male at five shekels[f] of silver and that of a female at three shekels[g] of silver. 7If it is a person sixty years old or more, set the value of a male at fifteen shekels[h] and of a female at ten shekels. 8If anyone making the vow is too poor to pay the specified amount, he is to present the person to the priest, who will set the value for him according to what the man making the vow can afford.

9" 'If what he vowed is an animal that is acceptable as an offering to the LORD, such an animal given to the LORD becomes holy. 10He must not exchange it or substitute a good one for a bad one, or a bad one for a good one; if he should substitute one animal for another, both it and the substitute become holy. 11If what he vowed is a ceremonially unclean animal—one that is not acceptable as an offering to the LORD—the animal must be presented to the priest, 12who will judge its quality as good or bad. Whatever value the priest then sets, that is what it will be. 13If the owner wishes to redeem the animal, he must add a fifth to its value.

14" 'If a man dedicates his house as something holy to the LORD, the priest will judge its quality as good or bad. Whatever value the priest then sets, so it will remain. 15If the man who dedicates his house redeems it, he must add a fifth to its value, and the house will again become his.

16" 'If a man dedicates to the LORD part of his family land, its value is to be set according to the amount of seed required for it—fifty shekels of silver to a homer[i] of barley seed. 17If he dedicates his field during the Year of Jubilee, the value that has been set remains. 18But if he dedicates his field after the Jubilee, the priest will determine the value according to the number of years that remain until the

[a] *3* That is, about 1 1/4 pounds (about 0.6 kilogram); also in verse 16 [b] *3* That is, about 2/5 ounce (about 11.5 grams); also in verse 25 [c] *4* That is, about 12 ounces (about 0.3 kilogram) [d] *5* That is, about 8 ounces (about 0.2 kilogram) [e] *5* That is, about 4 ounces (about 110 grams); also in verse 7 [f] *6* That is, about 2 ounces (about 55 grams) [g] *6* That is, about 1 1/4 ounces (about 35 grams) [h] *7* That is, about 6 ounces (about 170 grams) [i] *16* That is, probably about 6 bushels (about 220 liters)

next Year of Jubilee, and its set value will be
reduced. 19If the man who dedicates the field
wishes to redeem it, he must add a fifth to its
value, and the field will again become his. 20If,
however, he does not redeem the field, or if
he has sold it to someone else, it can never be
redeemed. 21When the field is released in the
Jubilee, it will become holy, like a field devoted to the LORD; it will become the property of
the priests.[a]

22" 'If a man dedicates to the LORD a field
he has bought, which is not part of his family
land, 23the priest will determine its value up
to the Year of Jubilee, and the man must pay
its value on that day as something holy to the
LORD. 24In the Year of Jubilee the field will
revert to the person from whom he bought it,
the one whose land it was. 25Every value is to
be set according to the sanctuary shekel, twenty gerahs to the shekel.

26" 'No one, however, may dedicate the
firstborn of an animal, since the firstborn already belongs to the LORD; whether an ox[b]
or a sheep, it is the LORD's. 27If it is one of
the unclean animals, he may buy it back at
its set value, adding a fifth of the value to it.
If he does not redeem it, it is to be sold at its
set value.

28" 'But nothing that a man owns and de-
votes[c] to the LORD—whether man or animal
or family land—may be sold or redeemed; everything so devoted is most holy to the LORD.

29" 'No person devoted to destruction[d]
may be ransomed; he must be put to death.

30" 'A tithe of everything from the land,
whether grain from the soil or fruit from the
trees, belongs to the LORD; it is holy to the
LORD. 31If a man redeems any of his tithe, he
must add a fifth of the value to it. 32The entire
tithe of the herd and flock—every tenth animal that passes under the shepherd's rod—will
be holy to the LORD. 33He must not pick out
the good from the bad or make any substitution. If he does make a substitution, both
the animal and its substitute become holy and
cannot be redeemed.' "

34These are the commands the LORD gave
Moses on Mount Sinai for the Israelites.

---

[a] *21* Or *priest* [b] *26* The Hebrew word can include both male and female. [c] *28* The Hebrew term refers to the irrevocable giving over of things or persons to the LORD. [d] *29* The Hebrew term refers to the irrevocable giving over of things or persons to the LORD, often by totally destroying them.

NUMBERS

Numbers

QUICK FACTS

AUTHOR Moses

AUDIENCE The people of Israel

DATE Between 1446 and 1406 B.C.

SETTING After a year in the Desert of Sinai, a census is taken. Then the people continue onward toward Canaan and 39 more years of wandering in the wilderness.

The book of Numbers begins with a census of the people of Israel according to their clans and families. However, the people whom God had rescued from slavery did not rejoice in the freedom God had granted. Rather, they griped about what they weren't getting.

They complained about tasteless food, lack of water, Moses' leadership and the giantlike people of Canaan who seemed impossible to conquer. "We should go back to Egypt," they told Moses. For their lack of faith and ingratitude, they would spend 40 more years wandering in the wilderness. No one 20 years old or older (except two spies, Joshua and Caleb, who trusted God) would enter the promised land.

Still, God cared for his people in the wilderness, providing them with food and water, clothes that didn't wear out and feet that didn't swell (see Deuteronomy 8:2–4). And after 40 years of learning to be grateful to God for their daily provision, God's people gathered once more to enter Canaan.

Complaining is a natural, human tendency. We grumble about bosses, sermons, food and friends. And when our marriages become difficult, we whine about our spouses too. Before succumbing to ingratitude, consider what happened to the Israelites, and think of how much better life became when they praised God for what he had done for them instead of complaining about what he hadn't done!

The Census

1 The LORD spoke to Moses in the Tent of
Meeting in the Desert of Sinai on the first
day of the second month of the second year
after the Israelites came out of Egypt. He said:
2"Take a census of the whole Israelite community by their clans and families, listing every
man by name, one by one. 3You and Aaron
are to number by their divisions all the men
in Israel twenty years old or more who are able
to serve in the army. 4One man from each
tribe, each the head of his family, is to help
you. 5These are the names of the men who are
to assist you:

from Reuben, Elizur son of Shedeur;
6 from Simeon, Shelumiel son of Zurishaddai;
7 from Judah, Nahshon son of Amminadab;
8 from Issachar, Nethanel son of Zuar;
9 from Zebulun, Eliab son of Helon;
10 from the sons of Joseph:
from Ephraim, Elishama son of Ammihud;
from Manasseh, Gamaliel son of Pedahzur;
11 from Benjamin, Abidan son of Gideoni;
12 from Dan, Ahiezer son of Ammishaddai;
13 from Asher, Pagiel son of Ocran;
14 from Gad, Eliasaph son of Deuel;
15 from Naphtali, Ahira son of Enan."

16These were the men appointed from the
community, the leaders of their ancestral
tribes. They were the heads of the clans of Israel.
17Moses and Aaron took these men whose
names had been given, 18and they called the
whole community together on the first day of
the second month. The people indicated their
ancestry by their clans and families, and the
men twenty years old or more were listed by
name, one by one, 19as the LORD commanded
Moses. And so he counted them in the Desert
of Sinai:

20From the descendants of Reuben the firstborn son of Israel:
All the men twenty years old or more
who were able to serve in the army
were listed by name, one by one, according to the records of their clans
and families. 21The number from the
tribe of Reuben was 46,500.

22From the descendants of Simeon:
All the men twenty years old or more
who were able to serve in the army
were counted and listed by name, one
by one, according to the records of
their clans and families. 23The number
from the tribe of Simeon was 59,300.

24From the descendants of Gad:
All the men twenty years old or more
who were able to serve in the army
were listed by name, according to the
records of their clans and families.
25The number from the tribe of Gad
was 45,650.

26From the descendants of Judah:
All the men twenty years old or more
who were able to serve in the army
were listed by name, according to the
records of their clans and families.
27The number from the tribe of Judah
was 74,600.

28From the descendants of Issachar:
All the men twenty years old or more
who were able to serve in the army
were listed by name, according to the
records of their clans and families.
29The number from the tribe of Issachar was 54,400.

30From the descendants of Zebulun:
All the men twenty years old or more
who were able to serve in the army
were listed by name, according to the
records of their clans and families.
31The number from the tribe of Zebulun was 57,400.

32From the sons of Joseph:
From the descendants of Ephraim:
All the men twenty years old or more
who were able to serve in the army
were listed by name, according to the
records of their clans and families.
33The number from the tribe of Ephraim was 40,500.

34From the descendants of Manasseh:
All the men twenty years old or more
who were able to serve in the army
were listed by name, according to the
records of their clans and families.
35The number from the tribe of Manasseh was 32,200.

36From the descendants of Benjamin:
All the men twenty years old or more
who were able to serve in the army
were listed by name, according to the
records of their clans and families.
37The number from the tribe of Benjamin was 35,400.

38From the descendants of Dan:

All the men twenty years old or more who were able to serve in the army were listed by name, according to the records of their clans and families. 39The number from the tribe of Dan was 62,700.

40From the descendants of Asher:

All the men twenty years old or more who were able to serve in the army were listed by name, according to the records of their clans and families. 41The number from the tribe of Asher was 41,500.

42From the descendants of Naphtali:

All the men twenty years old or more who were able to serve in the army were listed by name, according to the records of their clans and families. 43The number from the tribe of Naphtali was 53,400.

44These were the men counted by Moses and Aaron and the twelve leaders of Israel, each one representing his family. 45All the Israelites twenty years old or more who were able to serve in Israel's army were counted according to their families. 46The total number was 603,550.

47The families of the tribe of Levi, however, were not counted along with the others. 48The LORD had said to Moses: 49"You must not count the tribe of Levi or include them in the census of the other Israelites. 50Instead, appoint the Levites to be in charge of the tabernacle of the Testimony—over all its furnishings and everything belonging to it. They are to carry the tabernacle and all its furnishings; they are to take care of it and encamp around it. 51Whenever the tabernacle is to move, the Levites are to take it down, and whenever the tabernacle is to be set up, the Levites shall do it. Anyone else who goes near it shall be put to death. 52The Israelites are to set up their tents by divisions, each man in his own camp under his own standard. 53The Levites, however, are to set up their tents around the tabernacle of the Testimony so that wrath will not fall on the Israelite community. The Levites are to be responsible for the care of the tabernacle of the Testimony."

54The Israelites did all this just as the LORD commanded Moses.

The Arrangement of the Tribal Camps

2 The LORD said to Moses and Aaron: 2"The Israelites are to camp around the Tent of Meeting some distance from it, each man under his standard with the banners of his family."

3On the east, toward the sunrise, the divisions of the camp of Judah are to encamp under their standard. The leader of the people of Judah is Nahshon son of Amminadab. 4His division numbers 74,600.

5The tribe of Issachar will camp next to them. The leader of the people of Issachar is Nethanel son of Zuar. 6His division numbers 54,400.

7The tribe of Zebulun will be next. The leader of the people of Zebulun is Eliab son of Helon. 8His division numbers 57,400.

9All the men assigned to the camp of Judah, according to their divisions, number 186,400. They will set out first.

10On the south will be the divisions of the camp of Reuben under their standard. The leader of the people of Reuben is Elizur son of Shedeur. 11His division numbers 46,500.

12The tribe of Simeon will camp next to them. The leader of the people of Simeon is Shelumiel son of Zurishaddai. 13His division numbers 59,300.

14The tribe of Gad will be next. The leader of the people of Gad is Eliasaph son of Deuel.[a] 15His division numbers 45,650.

16All the men assigned to the camp of Reuben, according to their divisions, number 151,450. They will set out second.

17Then the Tent of Meeting and the camp of the Levites will set out in the middle of the camps. They will set out in the same order as they encamp, each in his own place under his standard.

18On the west will be the divisions of the camp of Ephraim under their standard. The leader of the people of Ephraim is Elishama son of Ammihud. 19His division numbers 40,500.

20The tribe of Manasseh will be next to them. The leader of the people of Manasseh is Gamaliel son of Pedahzur. 21His division numbers 32,200.

---

a 14 Many manuscripts of the Masoretic Text, Samaritan Pentateuch and Vulgate (see also Num. 1:14); most manuscripts of the Masoretic Text *Reuel*

22The tribe of Benjamin will be next.
The leader of the people of Benjamin is
Abidan son of Gideoni. 23His division
numbers 35,400.
24All the men assigned to the camp
of Ephraim, according to their divisions, number 108,100. They will set out
third.

25On the north will be the divisions of
the camp of Dan, under their standard.
The leader of the people of Dan is Ahiezer son of Ammishaddai. 26His division
numbers 62,700.
27The tribe of Asher will camp next to
them. The leader of the people of Asher is
Pagiel son of Ocran. 28His division numbers 41,500.
29The tribe of Naphtali will be next.
The leader of the people of Naphtali is
Ahira son of Enan. 30His division numbers 53,400.
31All the men assigned to the camp of
Dan number 157,600. They will set out
last, under their standards.

32These are the Israelites, counted according to their families. All those in
the camps, by their divisions, number
603,550. 33The Levites, however, were
not counted along with the other Israelites, as the LORD commanded Moses.

34So the Israelites did everything the LORD
commanded Moses; that is the way they encamped under their standards, and that is the
way they set out, each with his clan and family.

The Levites

3 This is the account of the family of Aaron and Moses at the time the LORD talked
with Moses on Mount Sinai.
2The names of the sons of Aaron were Nadab the firstborn and Abihu, Eleazar and Ithamar. 3Those were the names of Aaron's sons,
the anointed priests, who were ordained to
serve as priests. 4Nadab and Abihu, however,
fell dead before the LORD when they made an
offering with unauthorized fire before him in
the Desert of Sinai. They had no sons; so only
Eleazar and Ithamar served as priests during
the lifetime of their father Aaron.
5The LORD said to Moses, 6"Bring the tribe
of Levi and present them to Aaron the priest
to assist him. 7They are to perform duties for
him and for the whole community at the Tent
of Meeting by doing the work of the tabernacle. 8They are to take care of all the furnishings of the Tent of Meeting, fulfilling the obligations of the Israelites by doing the work
of the tabernacle. 9Give the Levites to Aaron
and his sons; they are the Israelites who are
to be given wholly to him.[a] 10Appoint Aaron
and his sons to serve as priests; anyone else
who approaches the sanctuary must be put to
death."
11The LORD also said to Moses, 12"I have
taken the Levites from among the Israelites in
place of the first male offspring of every Israelite woman. The Levites are mine, 13for all the
firstborn are mine. When I struck down all the
firstborn in Egypt, I set apart for myself every firstborn in Israel, whether man or animal.
They are to be mine. I am the LORD."
14The LORD said to Moses in the Desert of
Sinai, 15"Count the Levites by their families
and clans. Count every male a month old or
more." 16So Moses counted them, as he was
commanded by the word of the LORD.
17These were the names of the sons of
Levi:
Gershon, Kohath and Merari.
18These were the names of the Gershonite
clans:
Libni and Shimei.
19The Kohathite clans:
Amram, Izhar, Hebron and Uzziel.
20The Merarite clans:
Mahli and Mushi.
These were the Levite clans, according to
their families.

21To Gershon belonged the clans of the Lib-
nites and Shimeites; these were the Gershonite
clans. 22The number of all the males a month
old or more who were counted was 7,500.
23The Gershonite clans were to camp on the
west, behind the tabernacle. 24The leader of
the families of the Gershonites was Eliasaph
son of Lael. 25At the Tent of Meeting the Gershonites were responsible for the care of the
tabernacle and tent, its coverings, the curtain
at the entrance to the Tent of Meeting, 26the
curtains of the courtyard, the curtain at the
entrance to the courtyard surrounding the
tabernacle and altar, and the ropes—and everything related to their use.

27To Kohath belonged the clans of the
Amramites, Izharites, Hebronites and Uzzi-

---

[a] 9 Most manuscripts of the Masoretic Text; some manuscripts of the Masoretic Text, Samaritan Pentateuch and Septuagint (see also Num. 8:16) *to me*

elites; these were the Kohathite clans. [28]The number of all the males a month old or more was 8,600.[a] The Kohathites were responsible for the care of the sanctuary. [29]The Kohathite clans were to camp on the south side of the tabernacle. [30]The leader of the families of the Kohathite clans was Elizaphan son of Uzziel. [31]They were responsible for the care of the ark, the table, the lampstand, the altars, the articles of the sanctuary used in ministering, the curtain, and everything related to their use. [32]The chief leader of the Levites was Eleazar son of Aaron, the priest. He was appointed over those who were responsible for the care of the sanctuary.

[33]To Merari belonged the clans of the Mahlites and the Mushites; these were the Merarite clans. [34]The number of all the males a month old or more who were counted was 6,200. [35]The leader of the families of the Merarite clans was Zuriel son of Abihail; they were to camp on the north side of the tabernacle. [36]The Merarites were appointed to take care of the frames of the tabernacle, its crossbars, posts, bases, all its equipment, and everything related to their use, [37]as well as the posts of the surrounding courtyard with their bases, tent pegs and ropes.

[38]Moses and Aaron and his sons were to camp to the east of the tabernacle, toward the sunrise, in front of the Tent of Meeting. They were responsible for the care of the sanctuary on behalf of the Israelites. Anyone else who approached the sanctuary was to be put to death.

[39]The total number of Levites counted at the LORD's command by Moses and Aaron according to their clans, including every male a month old or more, was 22,000.

[40]The LORD said to Moses, "Count all the firstborn Israelite males who are a month old or more and make a list of their names. [41]Take the Levites for me in place of all the firstborn of the Israelites, and the livestock of the Levites in place of all the firstborn of the livestock of the Israelites. I am the LORD."

[42]So Moses counted all the firstborn of the Israelites, as the LORD commanded him. [43]The total number of firstborn males a month old or more, listed by name, was 22,273.

[44]The LORD also said to Moses, [45]"Take the Levites in place of all the firstborn of Israel, and the livestock of the Levites in place of their livestock. The Levites are to be mine. I am the LORD. [46]To redeem the 273 firstborn Israelites who exceed the number of the Levites, [47]collect five shekels[b] for each one, according to the sanctuary shekel, which weighs twenty gerahs. [48]Give the money for the redemption of the additional Israelites to Aaron and his sons."

[49]So Moses collected the redemption money from those who exceeded the number redeemed by the Levites. [50]From the firstborn of the Israelites he collected silver weighing 1,365 shekels,[c] according to the sanctuary shekel. [51]Moses gave the redemption money to Aaron and his sons, as he was commanded by the word of the LORD.

The Kohathites

4 The LORD said to Moses and Aaron: [2]"Take a census of the Kohathite branch of the Levites by their clans and families. [3]Count all the men from thirty to fifty years of age who come to serve in the work in the Tent of Meeting.

[4]"This is the work of the Kohathites in the Tent of Meeting: the care of the most holy things. [5]When the camp is to move, Aaron and his sons are to go in and take down the shielding curtain and cover the ark of the Testimony with it. [6]Then they are to cover this with hides of sea cows,[d] spread a cloth of solid blue over that and put the poles in place.

[7]"Over the table of the Presence they are to spread a blue cloth and put on it the plates, dishes and bowls, and the jars for drink offerings; the bread that is continually there is to remain on it. [8]Over these they are to spread a scarlet cloth, cover that with hides of sea cows and put its poles in place.

[9]"They are to take a blue cloth and cover the lampstand that is for light, together with its lamps, its wick trimmers and trays, and all its jars for the oil used to supply it. [10]Then they are to wrap it and all its accessories in a covering of hides of sea cows and put it on a carrying frame.

[11]"Over the gold altar they are to spread a blue cloth and cover that with hides of sea cows and put its poles in place.

[12]"They are to take all the articles used for ministering in the sanctuary, wrap them in a

[a] *28* Hebrew; some Septuagint manuscripts *8,300* [b] *47* That is, about 2 ounces (about 55 grams) [c] *50* That is, about 35 pounds (about 15.5 kilograms) [d] *6* That is, dugongs; also in verses 8, 10, 11, 12, 14 and 25

blue cloth, cover that with hides of sea cows and put them on a carrying frame.

13“They are to remove the ashes from the bronze altar and spread a purple cloth over it. 14Then they are to place on it all the utensils used for ministering at the altar, including the firepans, meat forks, shovels and sprinkling bowls. Over it they are to spread a covering of hides of sea cows and put its poles in place.

15“After Aaron and his sons have finished covering the holy furnishings and all the holy articles, and when the camp is ready to move, the Kohathites are to come to do the carrying. But they must not touch the holy things or they will die. The Kohathites are to carry those things that are in the Tent of Meeting.

16“Eleazar son of Aaron, the priest, is to have charge of the oil for the light, the fragrant incense, the regular grain offering and the anointing oil. He is to be in charge of the entire tabernacle and everything in it, including its holy furnishings and articles.”

17The LORD said to Moses and Aaron, 18“See that the Kohathite tribal clans are not cut off from the Levites. 19So that they may live and not die when they come near the most holy things, do this for them: Aaron and his sons are to go into the sanctuary and assign to each man his work and what he is to carry. 20But the Kohathites must not go in to look at the holy things, even for a moment, or they will die.”

The Gershonites

21The LORD said to Moses, 22“Take a census also of the Gershonites by their families and clans. 23Count all the men from thirty to fifty years of age who come to serve in the work at the Tent of Meeting.

24“This is the service of the Gershonite clans as they work and carry burdens: 25They are to carry the curtains of the tabernacle, the Tent of Meeting, its covering and the outer covering of hides of sea cows, the curtains for the entrance to the Tent of Meeting, 26the curtains of the courtyard surrounding the tabernacle and altar, the curtain for the entrance, the ropes and all the equipment used in its service. The Gershonites are to do all that needs to be done with these things. 27All their service, whether carrying or doing other work, is to be done under the direction of Aaron and his sons. You shall assign to them as their responsibility all they are to carry. 28This is the service of the Gershonite clans at the Tent of Meeting. Their duties are to be under the direction of Ithamar son of Aaron, the priest.

The Merarites

29“Count the Merarites by their clans and families. 30Count all the men from thirty to fifty years of age who come to serve in the work at the Tent of Meeting. 31This is their duty as they perform service at the Tent of Meeting: to carry the frames of the tabernacle, its crossbars, posts and bases, 32as well as the posts of the surrounding courtyard with their bases, tent pegs, ropes, all their equipment and everything related to their use. Assign to each man the specific things he is to carry. 33This is the service of the Merarite clans as they work at the Tent of Meeting under the direction of Ithamar son of Aaron, the priest.”

The Numbering of the Levite Clans

34Moses, Aaron and the leaders of the community counted the Kohathites by their clans and families. 35All the men from thirty to fifty years of age who came to serve in the work in the Tent of Meeting, 36counted by clans, were 2,750. 37This was the total of all those in the Kohathite clans who served in the Tent of Meeting. Moses and Aaron counted them according to the LORD’s command through Moses.

38The Gershonites were counted by their clans and families. 39All the men from thirty to fifty years of age who came to serve in the work at the Tent of Meeting, 40counted by their clans and families, were 2,630. 41This was the total of those in the Gershonite clans who served at the Tent of Meeting. Moses and Aaron counted them according to the LORD’s command.

42The Merarites were counted by their clans and families. 43All the men from thirty to fifty years of age who came to serve in the work at the Tent of Meeting, 44counted by their clans, were 3,200. 45This was the total of those in the Merarite clans. Moses and Aaron counted them according to the LORD’s command through Moses.

46So Moses, Aaron and the leaders of Israel counted all the Levites by their clans and families. 47All the men from thirty to fifty years of age who came to do the work of serving and carrying the Tent of Meeting 48numbered 8,580. 49At the LORD’s command through Moses, each was assigned his work and told what to carry.

Thus they were counted, as the LORD commanded Moses.

The Purity of the Camp

5 The LORD said to Moses, 2“Command the
Israelites to send away from the camp anyone who has an infectious skin disease[a] or
a discharge of any kind, or who is ceremonially unclean because of a dead body. 3Send away
male and female alike; send them outside the
camp so they will not defile their camp, where
I dwell among them.” 4The Israelites did this;
they sent them outside the camp. They did
just as the LORD had instructed Moses.

Restitution for Wrongs

5The LORD said to Moses, 6“Say to the Israelites: ‘When a man or woman wrongs another in any way[b] and so is unfaithful to the
LORD, that person is guilty 7and must confess
the sin he has committed. He must make full
restitution for his wrong, add one fifth to it
and give it all to the person he has wronged.
8But if that person has no close relative to
whom restitution can be made for the wrong,
the restitution belongs to the LORD and must
be given to the priest, along with the ram with
which atonement is made for him. 9All the
sacred contributions the Israelites bring to a
priest will belong to him. 10Each man’s sacred gifts are his own, but what he gives to the
priest will belong to the priest.’ ”

The Test for an Unfaithful Wife

11Then the LORD said to Moses, 12“Speak to
the Israelites and say to them: ‘If a man’s wife
goes astray and is unfaithful to him 13by sleeping with another man, and this is hidden from
her husband and her impurity is undetected
(since there is no witness against her and she
has not been caught in the act), 14and if feelings of jealousy come over her husband and
he suspects his wife and she is impure—or if
he is jealous and suspects her even though she
is not impure— 15then he is to take his wife
to the priest. He must also take an offering
of a tenth of an ephah[c] of barley flour on her
behalf. He must not pour oil on it or put incense on it, because it is a grain offering for
jealousy, a reminder offering to draw attention
to guilt.
16“ ‘The priest shall bring her and have her
stand before the LORD. 17Then he shall take
some holy water in a clay jar and put some
dust from the tabernacle floor into the water.
18After the priest has had the woman stand
before the LORD, he shall loosen her hair and
place in her hands the reminder offering, the
grain offering for jealousy, while he himself
holds the bitter water that brings a curse.
19Then the priest shall put the woman under
oath and say to her, “If no other man has slept
with you and you have not gone astray and
become impure while married to your husband, may this bitter water that brings a curse
not harm you. 20But if you have gone astray
while married to your husband and you have
defiled yourself by sleeping with a man other
than your husband”— 21here the priest is to
put the woman under this curse of the oath—
“may the LORD cause your people to curse
and denounce you when he causes your thigh
to waste away and your abdomen to swell.[d]
22May this water that brings a curse enter your
body so that your abdomen swells and your
thigh wastes away.[e]”
“ ‘Then the woman is to say, “Amen. So
be it.”
23“ ‘The priest is to write these curses on a
scroll and then wash them off into the bitter
water. 24He shall have the woman drink the
bitter water that brings a curse, and this water
will enter her and cause bitter suffering. 25The
priest is to take from her hands the grain offering for jealousy, wave it before the LORD and
bring it to the altar. 26The priest is then to take
a handful of the grain offering as a memorial
offering and burn it on the altar; after that, he
is to have the woman drink the water. 27If she
has defiled herself and been unfaithful to her
husband, then when she is made to drink the
water that brings a curse, it will go into her and
cause bitter suffering; her abdomen will swell
and her thigh waste away,[f] and she will become
accursed among her people. 28If, however, the
woman has not defiled herself and is free from
impurity, she will be cleared of guilt and will be
able to have children.
29“ ‘This, then, is the law of jealousy when
a woman goes astray and defiles herself while
married to her husband, 30or when feelings of
jealousy come over a man because he suspects
his wife. The priest is to have her stand before
the LORD and is to apply this entire law to her.
31The husband will be innocent of any wrongdoing, but the woman will bear the consequences of her sin.’ ”

---

[a] 2 Traditionally *leprosy*; the Hebrew word was used for various diseases affecting the skin—not necessarily leprosy. [b] 6 Or *woman commits any wrong common to mankind* [c] 15 That is, probably about 2 quarts (about 2 liters) [d] 21 Or *causes you to have a miscarrying womb and barrenness* [e] 22 Or *body and cause you to be barren and have a miscarrying womb* [f] 27 Or *suffering; she will have barrenness and a miscarrying womb*

THURSDAY
READ NUMBERS 5:11–28

FIDELITY CHECK

Then he is to take his wife to the priest. He must also take an offering of a tenth of an ephah of barley flour on her behalf. He must not pour oil on it or put incense on it, because it is a grain offering for jealousy, a reminder offering to draw attention to guilt.

— Numbers 5:15

When Anya suspected her husband, Ron, was having an affair, her antennae went up. She began watching for evidence—receipts, long-distance phone calls, email—to confirm her suspicion: Over time, the evidence was clear: Ron was cheating on her.

When Anya confronted her husband, however, he told her she was crazy for thinking that way. Ron's words cut her to the core. Not only did his vehement denial magnify his guilt, but his demeaning words reinforced what she was already feeling—that she was losing her mind. Jealousy and suspicion were taking over her life.

Anya decided to meet with her pastor. She shared her suspicion and the evidence that pointed to her husband's guilt. Anya hoped this respected leader would come alongside her to intervene. She knew that her husband was lying about his affair. She also knew the public revelation of his affair would be devastating to his career and to the woman he was involved with. Unfortunately, Anya's pastor didn't believe her claims and dismissed her fears. Anya left the pastor's office feeling utterly rejected. She had to deal with her overwhelming feelings of suspicion, jealousy, rejection and anger on her own.

At some point, every couple will experience feelings of jealousy and suspicion. While we might not have a modern-day equivalent to the bitter-water litmus test of Numbers 5:11–31, there are some practical steps we can take to deal with fears of infidelity and to restore trust once it has been broken by an affair.

For starters, we can pray daily for a hedge of protection around our marriage. Jerry Jenkins explains how this works in his book *Hedges* (Good News/Crossway, 2005). No one is immune from the possibility of committing adultery. At no point in our marriage are any of us safe from this sin. Recognizing this fact is our first defense.

Second, we can build a climate of trust with our partner through open communication and checkpoints that give our partner windows into our world. Without allowing it to become controlling, there's nothing wrong with setting up checkpoints that verify our whereabouts, our communications with others (especially online), and what we do when we're alone. For example, ever since Lyla developed a romantic relationship with a man she met on the Internet, her husband, Phil, has needed reassurance that she is being faithful to him now that the relationship has ended. Lyla and Phil now keep a shared email address. Occasionally Phil checks Lyla's mail. Lyla doesn't argue about those checkups, knowing that accountability to her husband is a good way to rebuild the trust she compromised.

For some time in our marriage, I saw this kind of accountability as invasive and demeaning. What difference did it make if I took a different route to work than Dan thought? Over time, though, I've come to see that by giving Dan my daily itinerary, I'm letting him peek into my world. It's a safeguard for our marriage. Building hedges around each other goes a long way toward protecting us from infidelity, and it also alleviates the fear of infidelity once trust has been broken.

—MARIAN V. LIAUTAUD

let's *talk*

- ✦ What kinds of checkpoints do we have in our marriage? Are we open about our emails, lunch dates and daily schedules?
- ✦ What are some ways we can deal with jealousy or suspicion should they occur in our marriage?
- ✦ What kinds of accountability would be helpful in creating a climate of trust in our marriage?

FOR YOUR NEXT DEVOTIONAL READING, TURN TO PAGE 149.

The Nazirite

6 The LORD said to Moses, 2“Speak to the Israelites and say to them: ‘If a man or woman wants to make a special vow, a vow of
separation to the LORD as a Nazirite, 3he must
abstain from wine and other fermented drink
and must not drink vinegar made from wine
or from other fermented drink. He must not
drink grape juice or eat grapes or raisins. 4As
long as he is a Nazirite, he must not eat anything that comes from the grapevine, not even
the seeds or skins.
5“ ‘During the entire period of his vow of
separation no razor may be used on his head.
He must be holy until the period of his separation to the LORD is over; he must let the hair
of his head grow long. 6Throughout the period of his separation to the LORD he must not
go near a dead body. 7Even if his own father
or mother or brother or sister dies, he must
not make himself ceremonially unclean on account of them, because the symbol of his separation to God is on his head. 8Throughout
the period of his separation he is consecrated
to the LORD.
9“ ‘If someone dies suddenly in his presence, thus defiling the hair he has dedicated, he must shave his head on the day of his
cleansing—the seventh day. 10Then on the
eighth day he must bring two doves or two
young pigeons to the priest at the entrance
to the Tent of Meeting. 11The priest is to offer one as a sin offering and the other as a
burnt offering to make atonement for him
because he sinned by being in the presence of
the dead body. That same day he is to consecrate his head. 12He must dedicate himself to
the LORD for the period of his separation and
must bring a year-old male lamb as a guilt
offering. The previous days do not count,
because he became defiled during his separation.
13“ ‘Now this is the law for the Nazirite
when the period of his separation is over. He
is to be brought to the entrance to the Tent
of Meeting. 14There he is to present his offerings to the LORD: a year-old male lamb without defect for a burnt offering, a year-old ewe
lamb without defect for a sin offering, a ram
without defect for a fellowship offering,[a] 15to-
gether with their grain offerings and drink offerings, and a basket of bread made without
yeast—cakes made of fine flour mixed with
oil, and wafers spread with oil.
16“ ‘The priest is to present them before the
LORD and make the sin offering and the burnt
offering. 17He is to present the basket of unleavened bread and is to sacrifice the ram as a
fellowship offering to the LORD, together with
its grain offering and drink offering.
18“ ‘Then at the entrance to the Tent of
Meeting, the Nazirite must shave off the hair
that he dedicated. He is to take the hair and
put it in the fire that is under the sacrifice of
the fellowship offering.
19“ ‘After the Nazirite has shaved off the hair
of his dedication, the priest is to place in his
hands a boiled shoulder of the ram, and a cake
and a wafer from the basket, both made without yeast. 20The priest shall then wave them
before the LORD as a wave offering; they are
holy and belong to the priest, together with
the breast that was waved and the thigh that
was presented. After that, the Nazirite may
drink wine.
21“ ‘This is the law of the Nazirite who vows
his offering to the LORD in accordance with
his separation, in addition to whatever else
he can afford. He must fulfill the vow he has
made, according to the law of the Nazirite.’ ”

The Priestly Blessing

22The LORD said to Moses, 23“Tell Aaron
and his sons, ‘This is how you are to bless the
Israelites. Say to them:

24“ ‘ “The LORD bless you
  and keep you;
25the LORD make his face shine upon you
  and be gracious to you;
26the LORD turn his face toward you
  and give you peace.” ’

27“So they will put my name on the Israelites, and I will bless them.”

Offerings at the Dedication of the Tabernacle

7 When Moses finished setting up the tabernacle, he anointed it and consecrated it and
all its furnishings. He also anointed and
consecrated the altar and all its utensils. 2Then
the leaders of Israel, the heads of families who
were the tribal leaders in charge of those who
were counted, made offerings. 3They brought
as their gifts before the LORD six covered carts
and twelve oxen—an ox from each leader and
a cart from every two. These they presented
before the tabernacle.
4The LORD said to Moses, 5“Accept these
from them, that they may be used in the work

[a] *14* Traditionally *peace offering;* also in verses 17 and 18

at the Tent of Meeting. Give them to the Levites as each man's work requires."

6So Moses took the carts and oxen and gave
them to the Levites. 7He gave two carts and
four oxen to the Gershonites, as their work required, 8and he gave four carts and eight oxen
to the Merarites, as their work required. They
were all under the direction of Ithamar son of
Aaron, the priest. 9But Moses did not give any
to the Kohathites, because they were to carry
on their shoulders the holy things, for which
they were responsible.

10When the altar was anointed, the leaders brought their offerings for its dedication
and presented them before the altar. 11For the
LORD had said to Moses, "Each day one leader
is to bring his offering for the dedication of
the altar."

12The one who brought his offering on the
first day was Nahshon son of Amminadab of
the tribe of Judah.

13His offering was one silver plate weighing a hundred and thirty shekels,[a] and
one silver sprinkling bowl weighing seventy shekels,[b] both according to the
sanctuary shekel, each filled with fine
flour mixed with oil as a grain offering;
14one gold dish weighing ten shekels,[c]
filled with incense; 15one young bull, one
ram and one male lamb a year old, for a
burnt offering; 16one male goat for a sin
offering; 17and two oxen, five rams, five
male goats and five male lambs a year old,
to be sacrificed as a fellowship offering.[d]
This was the offering of Nahshon son of
Amminadab.

18On the second day Nethanel son of Zuar,
the leader of Issachar, brought his offering.

19The offering he brought was one silver plate weighing a hundred and thirty
shekels, and one silver sprinkling bowl
weighing seventy shekels, both according
to the sanctuary shekel, each filled with
fine flour mixed with oil as a grain offering; 20one gold dish weighing ten shekels,
filled with incense; 21one young bull, one
ram and one male lamb a year old, for a
burnt offering; 22one male goat for a sin
offering; 23and two oxen, five rams, five
male goats and five male lambs a year old,
to be sacrificed as a fellowship offering.
This was the offering of Nethanel son of
Zuar.

24On the third day, Eliab son of Helon, the
leader of the people of Zebulun, brought his
offering.

25His offering was one silver plate weighing a hundred and thirty shekels, and one
silver sprinkling bowl weighing seventy
shekels, both according to the sanctuary
shekel, each filled with fine flour mixed
with oil as a grain offering; 26one gold
dish weighing ten shekels, filled with incense; 27one young bull, one ram and one
male lamb a year old, for a burnt offering;
28one male goat for a sin offering; 29and
two oxen, five rams, five male goats and
five male lambs a year old, to be sacrificed
as a fellowship offering. This was the offering of Eliab son of Helon.

30On the fourth day Elizur son of Shedeur, the
leader of the people of Reuben, brought his
offering.

31His offering was one silver plate weighing a hundred and thirty shekels, and
one silver sprinkling bowl weighing seventy shekels, both according to the sanctuary shekel, each filled with fine flour
mixed with oil as a grain offering; 32one
gold dish weighing ten shekels, filled
with incense; 33one young bull, one ram
and one male lamb a year old, for a burnt
offering; 34one male goat for a sin offering; 35and two oxen, five rams, five male
goats and five male lambs a year old, to
be sacrificed as a fellowship offering. This
was the offering of Elizur son of Shedeur.

36On the fifth day Shelumiel son of Zurishaddai, the leader of the people of Simeon,
brought his offering.

37His offering was one silver plate weighing a hundred and thirty shekels, and
one silver sprinkling bowl weighing seventy shekels, both according to the sanctuary shekel, each filled with fine flour
mixed with oil as a grain offering; 38one
gold dish weighing ten shekels, filled
with incense; 39one young bull, one ram
and one male lamb a year old, for a burnt
offering; 40one male goat for a sin offering; 41and two oxen, five rams, five male
goats and five male lambs a year old, to
be sacrificed as a fellowship offering. This
was the offering of Shelumiel son of Zurishaddai.

---

a *13* That is, about 3 1/4 pounds (about 1.5 kilograms); also elsewhere in this chapter *b* *13* That is, about 1 3/4 pounds (about 0.8 kilogram); also elsewhere in this chapter *c* *14* That is, about 4 ounces (about 110 grams); also elsewhere in this chapter
d *17* Traditionally *peace offering*; also elsewhere in this chapter

42On the sixth day Eliasaph son of Deuel, the
leader of the people of Gad, brought his offering.
43His offering was one silver plate weighing a hundred and thirty shekels, and one
silver sprinkling bowl weighing seventy
shekels, both according to the sanctuary
shekel, each filled with fine flour mixed
with oil as a grain offering; 44one gold
dish weighing ten shekels, filled with incense; 45one young bull, one ram and one
male lamb a year old, for a burnt offering;
46one male goat for a sin offering; 47and
two oxen, five rams, five male goats and
five male lambs a year old, to be sacrificed
as a fellowship offering. This was the offering of Eliasaph son of Deuel.

48On the seventh day Elishama son of Ammihud, the leader of the people of Ephraim,
brought his offering.
49His offering was one silver plate weighing a hundred and thirty shekels, and
one silver sprinkling bowl weighing seventy shekels, both according to the sanctuary shekel, each filled with fine flour
mixed with oil as a grain offering; 50one
gold dish weighing ten shekels, filled
with incense; 51one young bull, one ram
and one male lamb a year old, for a burnt
offering; 52one male goat for a sin offering; 53and two oxen, five rams, five male
goats and five male lambs a year old, to
be sacrificed as a fellowship offering. This
was the offering of Elishama son of Ammihud.

54On the eighth day Gamaliel son of Pedahzur, the leader of the people of Manasseh,
brought his offering.
55His offering was one silver plate weighing a hundred and thirty shekels, and
one silver sprinkling bowl weighing seventy shekels, both according to the sanctuary shekel, each filled with fine flour
mixed with oil as a grain offering; 56one
gold dish weighing ten shekels, filled
with incense; 57one young bull, one ram
and one male lamb a year old, for a burnt
offering; 58one male goat for a sin offering; 59and two oxen, five rams, five male
goats and five male lambs a year old, to
be sacrificed as a fellowship offering. This
was the offering of Gamaliel son of Pedahzur.

60On the ninth day Abidan son of Gideoni,
the leader of the people of Benjamin, brought
his offering.
61His offering was one silver plate weighing a hundred and thirty shekels, and one
silver sprinkling bowl weighing seventy
shekels, both according to the sanctuary
shekel, each filled with fine flour mixed
with oil as a grain offering; 62one gold
dish weighing ten shekels, filled with incense; 63one young bull, one ram and one
male lamb a year old, for a burnt offering;
64one male goat for a sin offering; 65and
two oxen, five rams, five male goats and
five male lambs a year old, to be sacrificed
as a fellowship offering. This was the offering of Abidan son of Gideoni.

66On the tenth day Ahiezer son of Ammishaddai, the leader of the people of Dan, brought
his offering.
67His offering was one silver plate weighing a hundred and thirty shekels, and one
silver sprinkling bowl weighing seventy
shekels, both according to the sanctuary
shekel, each filled with fine flour mixed
with oil as a grain offering; 68one gold
dish weighing ten shekels, filled with
incense; 69one young bull, one ram and
one male lamb a year old, for a burnt
offering; 70one male goat for a sin offering; 71and two oxen, five rams, five male
goats and five male lambs a year old, to
be sacrificed as a fellowship offering. This
was the offering of Ahiezer son of Ammishaddai.

72On the eleventh day Pagiel son of Ocran,
the leader of the people of Asher, brought his
offering.
73His offering was one silver plate weighing a hundred and thirty shekels, and
one silver sprinkling bowl weighing seventy shekels, both according to the sanctuary shekel, each filled with fine flour
mixed with oil as a grain offering; 74one
gold dish weighing ten shekels, filled
with incense; 75one young bull, one
ram and one male lamb a year old, for
a burnt offering; 76one male goat for a
sin offering; 77and two oxen, five rams,
five male goats and five male lambs a
year old, to be sacrificed as a fellowship
offering. This was the offering of Pagiel
son of Ocran.

78On the twelfth day Ahira son of Enan, the
leader of the people of Naphtali, brought his
offering.

79His offering was one silver plate weighing a hundred and thirty shekels, and one silver sprinkling bowl weighing seventy shekels, both according to the sanctuary shekel, each filled with fine flour mixed with oil as a grain offering; 80one gold dish weighing ten shekels, filled with incense; 81one young bull, one ram and one male lamb a year old, for a burnt offering; 82one male goat for a sin offering; 83and two oxen, five rams, five male goats and five male lambs a year old, to be sacrificed as a fellowship offering. This was the offering of Ahira son of Enan.

84These were the offerings of the Israelite leaders for the dedication of the altar when it was anointed: twelve silver plates, twelve silver sprinkling bowls and twelve gold dishes. 85Each silver plate weighed a hundred and thirty shekels, and each sprinkling bowl seventy shekels. Altogether, the silver dishes weighed two thousand four hundred shekels,[a] according to the sanctuary shekel. 86The twelve gold dishes filled with incense weighed ten shekels each, according to the sanctuary shekel. Altogether, the gold dishes weighed a hundred and twenty shekels.[b] 87The total number of animals for the burnt offering came to twelve young bulls, twelve rams and twelve male lambs a year old, together with their grain offering. Twelve male goats were used for the sin offering. 88The total number of animals for the sacrifice of the fellowship offering came to twenty-four oxen, sixty rams, sixty male goats and sixty male lambs a year old. These were the offerings for the dedication of the altar after it was anointed.

89When Moses entered the Tent of Meeting to speak with the LORD, he heard the voice speaking to him from between the two cherubim above the atonement cover on the ark of the Testimony. And he spoke with him.

Setting Up the Lamps

8 The LORD said to Moses, 2"Speak to Aaron and say to him, 'When you set up the seven lamps, they are to light the area in front of the lampstand.' "

3Aaron did so; he set up the lamps so that they faced forward on the lampstand, just as the LORD commanded Moses. 4This is how the lampstand was made: It was made of hammered gold—from its base to its blossoms. The lampstand was made exactly like the pattern the LORD had shown Moses.

The Setting Apart of the Levites

5The LORD said to Moses: 6"Take the Levites from among the other Israelites and make them ceremonially clean. 7To purify them, do this: Sprinkle the water of cleansing on them; then have them shave their whole bodies and wash their clothes, and so purify themselves. 8Have them take a young bull with its grain offering of fine flour mixed with oil; then you are to take a second young bull for a sin offering. 9Bring the Levites to the front of the Tent of Meeting and assemble the whole Israelite community. 10You are to bring the Levites before the LORD, and the Israelites are to lay their hands on them. 11Aaron is to present the Levites before the LORD as a wave offering from the Israelites, so that they may be ready to do the work of the LORD.

12"After the Levites lay their hands on the heads of the bulls, use the one for a sin offering to the LORD and the other for a burnt offering, to make atonement for the Levites. 13Have the Levites stand in front of Aaron and his sons and then present them as a wave offering to the LORD. 14In this way you are to set the Levites apart from the other Israelites, and the Levites will be mine.

15"After you have purified the Levites and presented them as a wave offering, they are to come to do their work at the Tent of Meeting. 16They are the Israelites who are to be given wholly to me. I have taken them as my own in place of the firstborn, the first male offspring from every Israelite woman. 17Every firstborn male in Israel, whether man or animal, is mine. When I struck down all the firstborn in Egypt, I set them apart for myself. 18And I have taken the Levites in place of all the firstborn sons in Israel. 19Of all the Israelites, I have given the Levites as gifts to Aaron and his sons to do the work at the Tent of Meeting on behalf of the Israelites and to make atonement for them so that no plague will strike the Israelites when they go near the sanctuary."

20Moses, Aaron and the whole Israelite community did with the Levites just as the LORD commanded Moses. 21The Levites purified themselves and washed their clothes. Then Aaron presented them as a wave offering before the LORD and made atonement for them to purify them. 22After that, the Levites came to do their work at the Tent of Meeting under the supervision of Aaron and his sons.

---

a 85 That is, about 60 pounds (about 28 kilograms) *b* 86 That is, about 3 pounds (about 1.4 kilograms)

They did with the Levites just as the LORD
commanded Moses.
23The LORD said to Moses, 24"This applies
to the Levites: Men twenty-five years old or
more shall come to take part in the work at
the Tent of Meeting, 25but at the age of fifty,
they must retire from their regular service and
work no longer. 26They may assist their brothers in performing their duties at the Tent of
Meeting, but they themselves must not do the
work. This, then, is how you are to assign the
responsibilities of the Levites."

The Passover

9 The LORD spoke to Moses in the Desert
of Sinai in the first month of the second
year after they came out of Egypt. He said,
2"Have the Israelites celebrate the Passover at
the appointed time. 3Celebrate it at the appointed time, at twilight on the fourteenth
day of this month, in accordance with all its
rules and regulations."
4So Moses told the Israelites to celebrate the
Passover, 5and they did so in the Desert of Sinai at twilight on the fourteenth day of the
first month. The Israelites did everything just
as the LORD commanded Moses.
6But some of them could not celebrate the
Passover on that day because they were ceremonially unclean on account of a dead body.
So they came to Moses and Aaron that same
day 7and said to Moses, "We have become unclean because of a dead body, but why should
we be kept from presenting the LORD's offering with the other Israelites at the appointed
time?"
8Moses answered them, "Wait until I find
out what the LORD commands concerning
you."
9Then the LORD said to Moses, 10"Tell the
Israelites: 'When any of you or your descendants are unclean because of a dead body or
are away on a journey, they may still celebrate
the LORD's Passover. 11They are to celebrate it
on the fourteenth day of the second month
at twilight. They are to eat the lamb, together with unleavened bread and bitter herbs.
12They must not leave any of it till morning or
break any of its bones. When they celebrate the
Passover, they must follow all the regulations.
13But if a man who is ceremonially clean and
not on a journey fails to celebrate the Passover,
that person must be cut off from his people
because he did not present the LORD's offering
at the appointed time. That man will bear the
consequences of his sin.
14" 'An alien living among you who wants
to celebrate the LORD's Passover must do so in
accordance with its rules and regulations. You
must have the same regulations for the alien
and the native-born.' "

The Cloud Above the Tabernacle

15On the day the tabernacle, the Tent of the
Testimony, was set up, the cloud covered it.
From evening till morning the cloud above
the tabernacle looked like fire. 16That is how it
continued to be; the cloud covered it, and at
night it looked like fire. 17Whenever the cloud
lifted from above the Tent, the Israelites set
out; wherever the cloud settled, the Israelites
encamped. 18At the LORD's command the Israelites set out, and at his command they encamped. As long as the cloud stayed over the
tabernacle, they remained in camp. 19When
the cloud remained over the tabernacle a long
time, the Israelites obeyed the LORD's order
and did not set out. 20Sometimes the cloud
was over the tabernacle only a few days; at
the LORD's command they would encamp,
and then at his command they would set out.
21Sometimes the cloud stayed only from evening till morning, and when it lifted in the
morning, they set out. Whether by day or by
night, whenever the cloud lifted, they set out.
22Whether the cloud stayed over the tabernacle for two days or a month or a year, the Israelites would remain in camp and not set out;
but when it lifted, they would set out. 23At the
LORD's command they encamped, and at the
LORD's command they set out. They obeyed
the LORD's order, in accordance with his command through Moses.

The Silver Trumpets

10 The LORD said to Moses: 2"Make two
trumpets of hammered silver, and use
them for calling the community together and for having the camps set out. 3When
both are sounded, the whole community is to
assemble before you at the entrance to the Tent
of Meeting. 4If only one is sounded, the leaders—the heads of the clans of Israel—are to
assemble before you. 5When a trumpet blast is
sounded, the tribes camping on the east are to
set out. 6At the sounding of a second blast, the
camps on the south are to set out. The blast
will be the signal for setting out. 7To gather
the assembly, blow the trumpets, but not with
the same signal.
8"The sons of Aaron, the priests, are to blow
the trumpets. This is to be a lasting ordinance
for you and the generations to come. 9When
you go into battle in your own land against an

FRIDAY
READ NUMBERS 9:15–23

WAITING FOR A SIGN

So often, married life feels like little more than a series of decisions: Should we buy that house? Is it the right time to start a family? Do we need to save more money for the future? So often, we look to God for some kind of clear answer telling us just what to do.

Early in our marriage, my husband began looking for a job closer to our home. He happened upon a job opening at a social service agency just a few blocks from our apartment. Not only was the job close, but it was the kind of work he was passionate about at the kind of organization he'd wanted to work for. The company was even willing to let him work flexible hours so he could be home with our baby part of the day.

My husband sailed through his interview and was offered the job right away. Before he said yes, we talked briefly about the wisdom of taking the job. As we reviewed the circumstances it seemed that God had dropped this opportunity in his lap. We didn't need to discuss the issue for long. We felt God's leading very clearly.

While wandering through the wilderness, the people of Israel knew when to move and when to stay put because God gave them a sign: if the cloud that covered the tabernacle stayed put, they were to do likewise; when the cloud moved, they were to move. In our situation, we felt that the "cloud" had moved, and that my husband should take the job.

But we don't always get a clear sign from God. There have been many, many times when we have prayed, sought the advice of friends and family, and waited for God to point us in the right direction, only to get . . . nothing. For example, when I was trying to decide whether I should quit my job, I agonized for months with no sense of what God wanted me to do. Where was our sign?

The truth is, God doesn't always move the clouds to show us which way to go. Instead, God asks us to be faithful, to make choices with our lives that honor him. He asks us to get our priorities in order, to turn away from worldly standards of success and achievement and to bend our will to that of our Lord and Savior, Jesus Christ. And as we follow his example, walking in his ways, we begin to think more like him. Paul tells us in Romans 12:2: "Do not conform any longer to the pattern of this world, but be transformed by the renewing of your mind. Then you will be able to test and approve what God's will is—his good, pleasing and perfect will."

We will make our share of mistakes in life decisions. At times, we will undoubtedly go when we should stay and stay when we should go. But the promise that God gives us is that no matter where we go—to a new state, to a new job, to a new stage of family life—our God goes with us.

—CARLA BARNHILL

FOR YOUR NEXT DEVOTIONAL READING, TURN TO PAGE 152.

Whenever the cloud lifted from above the Tent, the Israelites set out; wherever the cloud settled, the Israelites encamped.

— NUMBERS 9:17

let's talk

- What choices have we made as a couple? Has there been a time when we've had to step out in faith without a clear sense of what the right choice was? How was God present with us in that uncertain situation?
- What kind of decision-makers are we? What are some ways we can show each other support and respect when we have a difficult decision to make?
- What people do we trust to help us think through difficult decisions? If we can't think of anyone, maybe we should develop deeper relationships with a few other couples from church.

enemy who is oppressing you, sound a blast on
the trumpets. Then you will be remembered
by the LORD your God and rescued from your
enemies. 10Also at your times of rejoicing—
your appointed feasts and New Moon festivals—you are to sound the trumpets over your
burnt offerings and fellowship offerings,[a] and
they will be a memorial for you before your
God. I am the LORD your God."

The Israelites Leave Sinai

11On the twentieth day of the second
month of the second year, the cloud lifted
from above the tabernacle of the Testimony.
12Then the Israelites set out from the Desert
of Sinai and traveled from place to place until
the cloud came to rest in the Desert of Paran.
13They set out, this first time, at the LORD's
command through Moses.

14The divisions of the camp of Judah went
first, under their standard. Nahshon son of
Amminadab was in command. 15Nethan-
el son of Zuar was over the division of the
tribe of Issachar, 16and Eliab son of Helon
was over the division of the tribe of Zebulun.
17Then the tabernacle was taken down, and
the Gershonites and Merarites, who carried
it, set out.

18The divisions of the camp of Reuben went
next, under their standard. Elizur son of Shedeur was in command. 19Shelumiel son of Zurishaddai was over the division of the tribe of
Simeon, 20and Eliasaph son of Deuel was over
the division of the tribe of Gad. 21Then the
Kohathites set out, carrying the holy things.
The tabernacle was to be set up before they
arrived.

22The divisions of the camp of Ephraim
went next, under their standard. Elishama
son of Ammihud was in command. 23Gama-
liel son of Pedahzur was over the division of
the tribe of Manasseh, 24and Abidan son of
Gideoni was over the division of the tribe of
Benjamin.

25Finally, as the rear guard for all the units,
the divisions of the camp of Dan set out, under their standard. Ahiezer son of Ammishaddai was in command. 26Pagiel son of Ocran
was over the division of the tribe of Asher,
27and Ahira son of Enan was over the division
of the tribe of Naphtali. 28This was the order
of march for the Israelite divisions as they set
out.

29Now Moses said to Hobab son of Reuel the Midianite, Moses' father-in-law, "We
are setting out for the place about which the
LORD said, 'I will give it to you.' Come with
us and we will treat you well, for the LORD has
promised good things to Israel."

30He answered, "No, I will not go; I am going back to my own land and my own people."

31But Moses said, "Please do not leave us.
You know where we should camp in the desert, and you can be our eyes. 32If you come
with us, we will share with you whatever good
things the LORD gives us."

33So they set out from the mountain of the
LORD and traveled for three days. The ark of
the covenant of the LORD went before them
during those three days to find them a place to
rest. 34The cloud of the LORD was over them
by day when they set out from the camp.

35Whenever the ark set out, Moses said,

"Rise up, O LORD!
May your enemies be scattered;
may your foes flee before you."

36Whenever it came to rest, he said,

"Return, O LORD,
to the countless thousands of Israel."

Fire From the LORD

11 Now the people complained about their
hardships in the hearing of the LORD,
and when he heard them his anger was
aroused. Then fire from the LORD burned
among them and consumed some of the outskirts of the camp. 2When the people cried
out to Moses, he prayed to the LORD and the
fire died down. 3So that place was called Taberah,[b] because fire from the LORD had burned
among them.

Quail From the LORD

4The rabble with them began to crave other
food, and again the Israelites started wailing
and said, "If only we had meat to eat! 5We remember the fish we ate in Egypt at no cost—
also the cucumbers, melons, leeks, onions and
garlic. 6But now we have lost our appetite; we
never see anything but this manna!"

7The manna was like coriander seed and
looked like resin. 8The people went around
gathering it, and then ground it in a handmill
or crushed it in a mortar. They cooked it in a
pot or made it into cakes. And it tasted like
something made with olive oil. 9When the
dew settled on the camp at night, the manna
also came down.

---

[a] *10* Traditionally *peace offerings* [b] *3* *Taberah* means *burning.*

10 Moses heard the people of every family wailing, each at the entrance to his tent. The LORD became exceedingly angry, and Moses was troubled. 11 He asked the LORD, "Why have you brought this trouble on your servant? What have I done to displease you that you put the burden of all these people on me? 12 Did I conceive all these people? Did I give them birth? Why do you tell me to carry them in my arms, as a nurse carries an infant, to the land you promised on oath to their forefathers? 13 Where can I get meat for all these people? They keep wailing to me, 'Give us meat to eat!' 14 I cannot carry all these people by myself; the burden is too heavy for me. 15 If this is how you are going to treat me, put me to death right now—if I have found favor in your eyes—and do not let me face my own ruin."

16 The LORD said to Moses: "Bring me seventy of Israel's elders who are known to you as leaders and officials among the people. Have them come to the Tent of Meeting, that they may stand there with you. 17 I will come down and speak with you there, and I will take of the Spirit that is on you and put the Spirit on them. They will help you carry the burden of the people so that you will not have to carry it alone.

18 "Tell the people: 'Consecrate yourselves in preparation for tomorrow, when you will eat meat. The LORD heard you when you wailed, "If only we had meat to eat! We were better off in Egypt!" Now the LORD will give you meat, and you will eat it. 19 You will not eat it for just one day, or two days, or five, ten or twenty days, 20 but for a whole month—until it comes out of your nostrils and you loathe it—because you have rejected the LORD, who is among you, and have wailed before him, saying, "Why did we ever leave Egypt?" ' "

21 But Moses said, "Here I am among six hundred thousand men on foot, and you say, 'I will give them meat to eat for a whole month!' 22 Would they have enough if flocks and herds were slaughtered for them? Would they have enough if all the fish in the sea were caught for them?"

23 The LORD answered Moses, "Is the LORD's arm too short? You will now see whether or not what I say will come true for you."

24 So Moses went out and told the people what the LORD had said. He brought together seventy of their elders and had them stand around the Tent. 25 Then the LORD came down in the cloud and spoke with him, and he took of the Spirit that was on him and put the Spirit on the seventy elders. When the Spirit rested on them, they prophesied, but they did not do so again.[a]

26 However, two men, whose names were Eldad and Medad, had remained in the camp. They were listed among the elders, but did not go out to the Tent. Yet the Spirit also rested on them, and they prophesied in the camp. 27 A young man ran and told Moses, "Eldad and Medad are prophesying in the camp."

28 Joshua son of Nun, who had been Moses' aide since youth, spoke up and said, "Moses, my lord, stop them!"

29 But Moses replied, "Are you jealous for my sake? I wish that all the LORD's people were prophets and that the LORD would put his Spirit on them!" 30 Then Moses and the elders of Israel returned to the camp.

31 Now a wind went out from the LORD and drove quail in from the sea. It brought them[b] down all around the camp to about three feet[c] above the ground, as far as a day's walk in any direction. 32 All that day and night and all the next day the people went out and gathered quail. No one gathered less than ten homers.[d] Then they spread them out all around the camp. 33 But while the meat was still between their teeth and before it could be consumed, the anger of the LORD burned against the people, and he struck them with a severe plague. 34 Therefore the place was named Kibroth Hattaavah,[e] because there they buried the people who had craved other food.

35 From Kibroth Hattaavah the people traveled to Hazeroth and stayed there.

Miriam and Aaron Oppose Moses

12 Miriam and Aaron began to talk against Moses because of his Cushite wife, for he had married a Cushite. 2 "Has the LORD spoken only through Moses?" they asked. "Hasn't he also spoken through us?" And the LORD heard this.

3 (Now Moses was a very humble man, more humble than anyone else on the face of the earth.)

4 At once the LORD said to Moses, Aaron and Miriam, "Come out to the Tent of Meeting, all three of you." So the three of them came out. 5 Then the LORD came down in a pillar of cloud; he stood at the entrance to

---

[a] 25 Or *prophesied and continued to do so* [b] 31 Or *They flew* [c] 31 Hebrew *two cubits* (about 1 meter) [d] 32 That is, probably about 60 bushels (about 2.2 kiloliters) [e] 34 *Kibroth Hattaavah* means *graves of craving.*

WEEKEND

facts or feelings

"It looks like this meeting is going to end early—can you pick me up?" Steve asked.

"Okay, I think I'll take I-90," said Patti. "Linda told me about these new lights in the tunnel. I guess they're really cool—like space-age or something."

"I just checked the traffic report five minutes ago, and I-90 is backed up, so the 202 is definitely the way to get here," Steve said.

"That's sweet, babe, but I never have problems on I-90, so don't worry about it."

"What?" asked Steve. "I just told you you've got to take the 202 or you'll run into traffic. Are you listening to me? I don't want to be waiting around after this meeting. Take the 202. It has less traffic, plus they're doing road construction on I-90. The facts speak for themselves."

"Oh, remind me to tell you about my conversation with Tina today. You're going to love this one."

"Patti, we can talk about all that when you get here. Just take the 202!"

"Stevie, I'm leaving right now—I love you."

Here's a couple at opposite ends of the Influence Scale. Steve influences with facts while Patti is all about feelings. She's animated rather than analytical. She's optimistic rather than objective. Her fear factor is losing the approval of others—especially Steve's. But unwittingly, that is exactly what she does here.

"Hey, babe, have you been waiting long?" Patti asks as she pulls up to the curb where Steve is standing. "You have to see the new lights in the tunnel—they are amazing!"

Steve grunts.

"How was the meeting?"

"Fine," Steve sighs.

"I got you a double-shot latte. It's there in the cup holder."

Steve sits silent, eyes on the road.

"Stevie, what's wrong?"

"You know what's wrong."

And so do you. Steve laid out the facts to Patti as plain as day. He wanted her to take the fastest route and not leave him stranded. He's a critical thinker, not swayed by emotion. He doesn't care if the lights in the tunnel are great or if he's going to get a cup of coffee. He wanted to be picked up on time and Patti needed to take the 202 to do so. Because she didn't, he feels like Patti doesn't listen to him or care about his opinion.

Are Patti and Steve doomed to crisscrossed communications? Absolutely not. They have huge potential to make a great team once they understand each other's style. This understanding will help them to see how invaluable they are to each other. Patti needs Steve's logical questions, and Steve needs Patti's fun-loving perspective.

Chances are your hardwiring for being influenced more by facts or more by feelings was passed down from your family. It's in your hardwiring. And that's exactly why understanding your partner's hardwiring on this dimension is vital to improving your communication.

—DR. LES PARROTT III AND DR. LESLIE PARROTT

check your style

Take this quiz to determine whether you're more influenced by facts or feelings. Ask your spouse do the same and then have fun comparing your answers.

1. You're facing a potentially life-changing decision. You say:
   a. "Trust me. This will all work out."
   b. "After a careful study of the evidence, I think we should . . ."
2. You need a new babysitter for your two-year-old. You:
   a. Talk to some friends and trust your instincts about their recommendations.
   b. Interview. Call for references. Do background checks.
3. The meeting has been moved up and there is no way to finish your presentation on time. You:
   a. Grab everything you've got, throw it together and just pray that it works.
   b. Get really down, wondering how this happened to you.
4. Your spouse proposes a new budget. You:
   a. Find it hard to put your spouse's suggestions into practice because you forget what your spouse said.
   b. Don't say anything. The record shows budgeting doesn't work.
5. Would others describe you as:
   a. Optimistic, friendly, outgoing and inspiring.
   b. Realistic, logical, reflective and calm.
6. When you take a quiz like this, you think:
   a. Even if it's not accurate, it's fun and I'm learning something about myself.
   b. Who writes these things anyway? They don't know what they're doing.

Scoring: If you chose more *a*'s than *b*'s, you influence people with feelings. If you chose more *b*'s than *a*'s, facts are what matter most to you; unfortunately, we don't have the science to back up this claim, so you probably won't buy it.

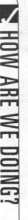

HOW ARE WE DOING?

date

let's make a DATE

CHECK OUT THE FAMILY TREE

Together work on researching and putting together family trees for both of your families. The facts-based spouse can track down data such as dates, birth information and burial locations. He or she can then organize the data into a computer program. The feelings-based spouse can use this opportunity to interview relatives, record stories and create a special album of family memories.

FOR YOUR NEXT DEVOTIONAL READING, TURN TO PAGE 155.

LESSONS FROM THE *Bible*

Facts and feelings probably made a difference in the lives of these two Bible couples. How do you think these couples related? How do you see facts or feelings affecting what happened in their relationships?

1. Samson and Delilah (Judges 16:1–22)
2. Ahab and Jezebel (1 Kings 21:1–29)

the Tent and summoned Aaron and Miriam. When both of them stepped forward, 6he said, "Listen to my words:

"When a prophet of the LORD is among
you,
I reveal myself to him in visions,
I speak to him in dreams.
7 But this is not true of my servant Moses;
he is faithful in all my house.
8 With him I speak face to face,
clearly and not in riddles;
he sees the form of the LORD.
Why then were you not afraid
to speak against my servant Moses?"

9The anger of the LORD burned against them, and he left them.
10When the cloud lifted from above the Tent, there stood Miriam—leprous,[a] like snow. Aaron turned toward her and saw that she had leprosy; 11and he said to Moses, "Please, my lord, do not hold against us the sin we have so foolishly committed. 12Do not let her be like a stillborn infant coming from its mother's womb with its flesh half eaten away."
13So Moses cried out to the LORD, "O God, please heal her!"
14The LORD replied to Moses, "If her father had spit in her face, would she not have been in disgrace for seven days? Confine her outside the camp for seven days; after that she can be brought back." 15So Miriam was confined outside the camp for seven days, and the people did not move on till she was brought back.
16After that, the people left Hazeroth and encamped in the Desert of Paran.

Exploring Canaan

13 The LORD said to Moses, 2"Send some men to explore the land of Canaan, which I am giving to the Israelites. From each ancestral tribe send one of its leaders."
3So at the LORD's command Moses sent them out from the Desert of Paran. All of them were leaders of the Israelites. 4These are their names:

from the tribe of Reuben, Shammua son
of Zaccur;
5 from the tribe of Simeon, Shaphat son of
Hori;
6 from the tribe of Judah, Caleb son of Jephunneh;
7 from the tribe of Issachar, Igal son of Joseph;
8 from the tribe of Ephraim, Hoshea son of
Nun;
9 from the tribe of Benjamin, Palti son of
Raphu;
10 from the tribe of Zebulun, Gaddiel son
of Sodi;
11 from the tribe of Manasseh (a tribe of Joseph), Gaddi son of Susi;
12 from the tribe of Dan, Ammiel son of
Gemalli;
13 from the tribe of Asher, Sethur son of Michael;
14 from the tribe of Naphtali, Nahbi son of
Vophsi;
15 from the tribe of Gad, Geuel son of
Maki.

16These are the names of the men Moses sent to explore the land. (Moses gave Hoshea son of Nun the name Joshua.)
17When Moses sent them to explore Canaan, he said, "Go up through the Negev and on into the hill country. 18See what the land is like and whether the people who live there are strong or weak, few or many. 19What kind of land do they live in? Is it good or bad? What kind of towns do they live in? Are they unwalled or fortified? 20How is the soil? Is it fertile or poor? Are there trees on it or not? Do your best to bring back some of the fruit of the land." (It was the season for the first ripe grapes.)
21So they went up and explored the land from the Desert of Zin as far as Rehob, toward Lebo[b] Hamath. 22They went up through the Negev and came to Hebron, where Ahiman, Sheshai and Talmai, the descendants of Anak, lived. (Hebron had been built seven years before Zoan in Egypt.) 23When they reached the Valley of Eshcol,[c] they cut off a branch bearing a single cluster of grapes. Two of them carried it on a pole between them, along with some pomegranates and figs. 24That place was called the Valley of Eshcol because of the cluster of grapes the Israelites cut off there. 25At the end of forty days they returned from exploring the land.

Report on the Exploration

26They came back to Moses and Aaron and the whole Israelite community at Kadesh in the Desert of Paran. There they reported to them and to the whole assembly and showed

[a] *10* The Hebrew word was used for various diseases affecting the skin—not necessarily leprosy. [b] *21* Or *toward the entrance to*
[c] *23* *Eshcol* means *cluster*; also in verse 24.

THE WAY WE FIGHT

But the men who had gone up with him said, "We can't attack those people; they are stronger than we are." And they spread among the Israelites a bad report about the land they had explored.

— NUMBERS 13:31–32

The Israelites had good reason to be afraid. The land they were moving toward was home to a hostile people who might destroy them. As word spread of the danger that lay ahead, the Israelites lost their faith in God's promise to bring them into that land of milk and honey. Even though God had carried them safely up to that point, the dangerous reality of fighting people stronger than themselves pushed their faith aside and replaced it with doubt.

Most of us can relate to the Israelites. We know how it feels to struggle with feelings of fear and doubt, especially if we're confronting problems that appear bigger than we can handle. We also know how tempting it is to turn our fears into negativity and grumbling in an effort to avoid the thing we fear. Yet as normal as it is to see the negative side of life, doing so can rob us of the ability to enjoy the good things that God has given us.

One of the issues we deal with in our house is how to manage conflict. My husband grew up with parents who fought a lot. My parents rarely fought, or at least rarely fought in front of me.

My husband and I approach conflict somewhere in the middle of those two approaches. Yet, because of our experiences with our parents, I think we fight far too much, while my husband thinks we hardly ever fight. So we often find ourselves fighting about how much we fight!

On our best days, we can resolve conflict fairly quickly. But there are times when I can't get past a disagreement. As I focus more and more on the problem, I start to see our whole marriage as a big mistake simply because we argue more than I think a happy couple should. Once that negativity sets in, it becomes the lens through which I view my husband and our entire life together. Fear and doubt prevent me from seeing the great things about my spouse that attracted me to him in the first place. And negative thinking blocks me from appreciating the ways in which our marriage works well.

Any couple can become caught in the trap of doubt. Like the Israelites, when we let our fears take over, we lose sight of the goodness that's all around us. We forget about God's promise to walk with us through life's ups and downs. Thankfully, we have a God who cares for us and loves us despite our sins and shortcomings, and One to whom we can turn to help us overcome our greatest fears. When we turn our negative feelings over to God, through his Word he can guide us to a clearer view of our marriage.

—CARLA BARNHILL

let's talk

- ✦ What are some things we grumble about? What fears might be at the heart of those negative feelings?
- ✦ Are there ways in which fears about the future hold us back in our marriage? What are some of those fears?
- ✦ What would be the cost of addressing these fears? What would be the benefit? Is it worth the risk if it forges a deeper relationship between us?

FOR YOUR NEXT DEVOTIONAL READING, TURN TO PAGE 163.

them the fruit of the land. 27They gave Moses
this account: "We went into the land to which
you sent us, and it does flow with milk and
honey! Here is its fruit. 28But the people who
live there are powerful, and the cities are fortified and very large. We even saw descendants
of Anak there. 29The Amalekites live in the
Negev; the Hittites, Jebusites and Amorites
live in the hill country; and the Canaanites
live near the sea and along the Jordan."

30Then Caleb silenced the people before
Moses and said, "We should go up and take
possession of the land, for we can certainly
do it."

31But the men who had gone up with him
said, "We can't attack those people; they are
stronger than we are." 32And they spread
among the Israelites a bad report about the
land they had explored. They said, "The land
we explored devours those living in it. All the
people we saw there are of great size. 33We saw
the Nephilim there (the descendants of Anak
come from the Nephilim). We seemed like
grasshoppers in our own eyes, and we looked
the same to them."

The People Rebel

14 That night all the people of the community raised their voices and wept aloud.
2All the Israelites grumbled against Moses and Aaron, and the whole assembly said
to them, "If only we had died in Egypt! Or
in this desert! 3Why is the LORD bringing us
to this land only to let us fall by the sword?
Our wives and children will be taken as plunder. Wouldn't it be better for us to go back
to Egypt?" 4And they said to each other,
"We should choose a leader and go back to
Egypt."

5Then Moses and Aaron fell facedown in
front of the whole Israelite assembly gathered
there. 6Joshua son of Nun and Caleb son of
Jephunneh, who were among those who had
explored the land, tore their clothes 7and said
to the entire Israelite assembly, "The land we
passed through and explored is exceedingly good. 8If the LORD is pleased with us, he
will lead us into that land, a land flowing with
milk and honey, and will give it to us. 9Only
do not rebel against the LORD. And do not
be afraid of the people of the land, because
we will swallow them up. Their protection
is gone, but the LORD is with us. Do not be
afraid of them."

10But the whole assembly talked about
stoning them. Then the glory of the LORD appeared at the Tent of Meeting to all the Israelites. 11The LORD said to Moses, "How long
will these people treat me with contempt?
How long will they refuse to believe in me,
in spite of all the miraculous signs I have
performed among them? 12I will strike them
down with a plague and destroy them, but I
will make you into a nation greater and stronger than they."

13Moses said to the LORD, "Then the
Egyptians will hear about it! By your power you brought these people up from among
them. 14And they will tell the inhabitants
of this land about it. They have already heard
that you, O LORD, are with these people
and that you, O LORD, have been seen face to
face, that your cloud stays over them, and that
you go before them in a pillar of cloud by day
and a pillar of fire by night. 15If you put these
people to death all at one time, the nations
who have heard this report about you will say,
16'The LORD was not able to bring these people into the land he promised them on oath;
so he slaughtered them in the desert.'

17"Now may the Lord's strength be displayed, just as you have declared: 18'The LORD
is slow to anger, abounding in love and forgiving sin and rebellion. Yet he does not leave
the guilty unpunished; he punishes the children for the sin of the fathers to the third and
fourth generation.' 19In accordance with your
great love, forgive the sin of these people, just
as you have pardoned them from the time
they left Egypt until now."

20The LORD replied, "I have forgiven them,
as you asked. 21Nevertheless, as surely as I live
and as surely as the glory of the LORD fills the
whole earth, 22not one of the men who saw my
glory and the miraculous signs I performed in
Egypt and in the desert but who disobeyed me
and tested me ten times— 23not one of them
will ever see the land I promised on oath to
their forefathers. No one who has treated me
with contempt will ever see it. 24But because
my servant Caleb has a different spirit and follows me wholeheartedly, I will bring him into
the land he went to, and his descendants will
inherit it. 25Since the Amalekites and Canaanites are living in the valleys, turn back tomorrow and set out toward the desert along the
route to the Red Sea.[a]"

26The LORD said to Moses and Aaron:
27"How long will this wicked community
grumble against me? I have heard the com-

---

[a] 25 Hebrew *Yam Suph*; that is, Sea of Reeds

plaints of these grumbling Israelites. 28So tell
them, 'As surely as I live, declares the LORD, I
will do to you the very things I heard you say:
29In this desert your bodies will fall—every
one of you twenty years old or more who was
counted in the census and who has grumbled
against me. 30Not one of you will enter the
land I swore with uplifted hand to make your
home, except Caleb son of Jephunneh and
Joshua son of Nun. 31As for your children
that you said would be taken as plunder, I
will bring them in to enjoy the land you have
rejected. 32But you—your bodies will fall
in this desert. 33Your children will be shepherds here for forty years, suffering for your
unfaithfulness, until the last of your bodies
lies in the desert. 34For forty years—one year
for each of the forty days you explored the
land—you will suffer for your sins and know
what it is like to have me against you.' 35I,
the LORD, have spoken, and I will surely do
these things to this whole wicked community,
which has banded together against me. They
will meet their end in this desert; here they
will die."

36So the men Moses had sent to explore the
land, who returned and made the whole community grumble against him by spreading a
bad report about it— 37these men responsible
for spreading the bad report about the land
were struck down and died of a plague before
the LORD. 38Of the men who went to explore
the land, only Joshua son of Nun and Caleb
son of Jephunneh survived.

39When Moses reported this to all the Israelites, they mourned bitterly. 40Early the
next morning they went up toward the high
hill country. "We have sinned," they said. "We
will go up to the place the LORD promised."

41But Moses said, "Why are you disobeying
the LORD's command? This will not succeed!
42Do not go up, because the LORD is not with
you. You will be defeated by your enemies,
43for the Amalekites and Canaanites will face
you there. Because you have turned away from
the LORD, he will not be with you and you will
fall by the sword."

44Nevertheless, in their presumption they
went up toward the high hill country, though
neither Moses nor the ark of the LORD's covenant moved from the camp. 45Then the Amalekites and Canaanites who lived in that hill
country came down and attacked them and
beat them down all the way to Hormah.

Supplementary Offerings

15 The LORD said to Moses, 2"Speak to the
Israelites and say to them: 'After you enter the land I am giving you as a home
3and you present to the LORD offerings made
by fire, from the herd or the flock, as an aroma
pleasing to the LORD—whether burnt offerings or sacrifices, for special vows or freewill
offerings or festival offerings— 4then the one
who brings his offering shall present to the
LORD a grain offering of a tenth of an ephah[a]
of fine flour mixed with a quarter of a hin[b] of
oil. 5With each lamb for the burnt offering or
the sacrifice, prepare a quarter of a hin of wine
as a drink offering.

6" 'With a ram prepare a grain offering of
two-tenths of an ephah[c] of fine flour mixed
with a third of a hin[d] of oil, 7and a third of a
hin of wine as a drink offering. Offer it as an
aroma pleasing to the LORD.

8" 'When you prepare a young bull as a
burnt offering or sacrifice, for a special vow
or a fellowship offering[e] to the LORD, 9bring
with the bull a grain offering of three-tenths
of an ephah[f] of fine flour mixed with half a
hin[g] of oil. 10Also bring half a hin of wine as a
drink offering. It will be an offering made by
fire, an aroma pleasing to the LORD. 11Each
bull or ram, each lamb or young goat, is to be
prepared in this manner. 12Do this for each
one, for as many as you prepare.

13" 'Everyone who is native-born must do
these things in this way when he brings an offering made by fire as an aroma pleasing to the
LORD. 14For the generations to come, whenever an alien or anyone else living among you
presents an offering made by fire as an aroma
pleasing to the LORD, he must do exactly as
you do. 15The community is to have the same
rules for you and for the alien living among
you; this is a lasting ordinance for the generations to come. You and the alien shall be the
same before the LORD: 16The same laws and
regulations will apply both to you and to the
alien living among you.' "

17The LORD said to Moses, 18"Speak to the
Israelites and say to them: 'When you enter
the land to which I am taking you 19and you
eat the food of the land, present a portion
as an offering to the LORD. 20Present a cake

[a] *4* That is, probably about 2 quarts (about 2 liters) [b] *4* That is, probably about 1 quart (about 1 liter); also in verse 5 [c] *6* That is, probably about 4 quarts (about 4.5 liters) [d] *6* That is, probably about 1 1/4 quarts (about 1.2 liters); also in verse 7 [e] *8* Traditionally *peace offering* [f] *9* That is, probably about 6 quarts (about 6.5 liters) [g] *9* That is, probably about 2 quarts (about 2 liters); also in verse 10

from the first of your ground meal and present it as an offering from the threshing floor.
21Throughout the generations to come you are
to give this offering to the LORD from the first
of your ground meal.

Offerings for Unintentional Sins

22“ ‘Now if you unintentionally fail to keep
any of these commands the LORD gave Moses— 23any of the LORD’s commands to you
through him, from the day the LORD gave
them and continuing through the generations
to come— 24and if this is done unintentionally without the community being aware of it,
then the whole community is to offer a young
bull for a burnt offering as an aroma pleasing to the LORD, along with its prescribed
grain offering and drink offering, and a male
goat for a sin offering. 25The priest is to make
atonement for the whole Israelite community,
and they will be forgiven, for it was not intentional and they have brought to the LORD for
their wrong an offering made by fire and a sin
offering. 26The whole Israelite community and
the aliens living among them will be forgiven,
because all the people were involved in the unintentional wrong.

27“ ‘But if just one person sins unintentionally, he must bring a year-old female goat for a
sin offering. 28The priest is to make atonement
before the LORD for the one who erred by sinning unintentionally, and when atonement
has been made for him, he will be forgiven.
29One and the same law applies to everyone
who sins unintentionally, whether he is a native-born Israelite or an alien.

30“ ‘But anyone who sins defiantly, whether native-born or alien, blasphemes the LORD,
and that person must be cut off from his people. 31Because he has despised the LORD’s word
and broken his commands, that person must
surely be cut off; his guilt remains on him.’ ”

The Sabbath-Breaker Put to Death

32While the Israelites were in the desert, a
man was found gathering wood on the Sabbath day. 33Those who found him gathering
wood brought him to Moses and Aaron and
the whole assembly, 34and they kept him in
custody, because it was not clear what should
be done to him. 35Then the LORD said to Moses, “The man must die. The whole assembly must stone him outside the camp.” 36So
the assembly took him outside the camp and
stoned him to death, as the LORD commanded Moses.

Tassels on Garments

37The LORD said to Moses, 38“Speak to the
Israelites and say to them: ‘Throughout the
generations to come you are to make tassels on
the corners of your garments, with a blue cord
on each tassel. 39You will have these tassels to
look at and so you will remember all the commands of the LORD, that you may obey them
and not prostitute yourselves by going after
the lusts of your own hearts and eyes. 40Then
you will remember to obey all my commands
and will be consecrated to your God. 41I am
the LORD your God, who brought you out of
Egypt to be your God. I am the LORD your
God.’ ”

Korah, Dathan and Abiram

16 Korah son of Izhar, the son of Kohath,
the son of Levi, and certain Reubenites—Dathan and Abiram, sons of Eliab, and On son of Peleth—became insolent[a]
2and rose up against Moses. With them were
250 Israelite men, well-known community
leaders who had been appointed members
of the council. 3They came as a group to oppose Moses and Aaron and said to them, “You
have gone too far! The whole community is
holy, every one of them, and the LORD is with
them. Why then do you set yourselves above
the LORD’s assembly?”

4When Moses heard this, he fell facedown.
5Then he said to Korah and all his followers:
“In the morning the LORD will show who
belongs to him and who is holy, and he will
have that person come near him. The man he
chooses he will cause to come near him. 6You,
Korah, and all your followers are to do this:
Take censers 7and tomorrow put fire and incense in them before the LORD. The man the
LORD chooses will be the one who is holy. You
Levites have gone too far!”

8Moses also said to Korah, “Now listen, you
Levites! 9Isn’t it enough for you that the God
of Israel has separated you from the rest of the
Israelite community and brought you near
himself to do the work at the LORD’s tabernacle and to stand before the community and
minister to them? 10He has brought you and
all your fellow Levites near himself, but now
you are trying to get the priesthood too. 11It is
against the LORD that you and all your follow-

[a] 1 Or *Peleth—took* ⌞*men*⌟

fered to the LORD is yours. But you must redeem every firstborn son and every firstborn
male of unclean animals. 16When they are a
month old, you must redeem them at the redemption price set at five shekels[a] of silver, according to the sanctuary shekel, which weighs
twenty gerahs.
17"But you must not redeem the firstborn of
an ox, a sheep or a goat; they are holy. Sprinkle
their blood on the altar and burn their fat as
an offering made by fire, an aroma pleasing to
the LORD. 18Their meat is to be yours, just as
the breast of the wave offering and the right
thigh are yours. 19Whatever is set aside from
the holy offerings the Israelites present to the
LORD I give to you and your sons and daughters as your regular share. It is an everlasting
covenant of salt before the LORD for both you
and your offspring."
20The LORD said to Aaron, "You will have
no inheritance in their land, nor will you have
any share among them; I am your share and
your inheritance among the Israelites.
21"I give to the Levites all the tithes in Israel as their inheritance in return for the work
they do while serving at the Tent of Meeting.
22From now on the Israelites must not go near
the Tent of Meeting, or they will bear the consequences of their sin and will die. 23It is the
Levites who are to do the work at the Tent of
Meeting and bear the responsibility for offenses against it. This is a lasting ordinance
for the generations to come. They will receive
no inheritance among the Israelites. 24Instead,
I give to the Levites as their inheritance the
tithes that the Israelites present as an offering
to the LORD. That is why I said concerning
them: 'They will have no inheritance among
the Israelites.' "
25The LORD said to Moses, 26"Speak to
the Levites and say to them: 'When you receive from the Israelites the tithe I give you
as your inheritance, you must present a tenth
of that tithe as the LORD's offering. 27Your offering will be reckoned to you as grain from
the threshing floor or juice from the winepress. 28In this way you also will present an
offering to the LORD from all the tithes you
receive from the Israelites. From these tithes
you must give the LORD's portion to Aaron
the priest. 29You must present as the LORD's
portion the best and holiest part of everything
given to you.'
30"Say to the Levites: 'When you present
the best part, it will be reckoned to you as the
product of the threshing floor or the winepress. 31You and your households may eat the
rest of it anywhere, for it is your wages for your
work at the Tent of Meeting. 32By presenting
the best part of it you will not be guilty in this
matter; then you will not defile the holy offerings of the Israelites, and you will not die.' "

The Water of Cleansing

19 The LORD said to Moses and Aaron:
2"This is a requirement of the law that
the LORD has commanded: Tell the Israelites to bring you a red heifer without defect
or blemish and that has never been under a
yoke. 3Give it to Eleazar the priest; it is to be
taken outside the camp and slaughtered in his
presence. 4Then Eleazar the priest is to take
some of its blood on his finger and sprinkle
it seven times toward the front of the Tent
of Meeting. 5While he watches, the heifer is
to be burned—its hide, flesh, blood and offal. 6The priest is to take some cedar wood,
hyssop and scarlet wool and throw them onto
the burning heifer. 7After that, the priest must
wash his clothes and bathe himself with water. He may then come into the camp, but he
will be ceremonially unclean till evening. 8The
man who burns it must also wash his clothes
and bathe with water, and he too will be unclean till evening.
9"A man who is clean shall gather up the
ashes of the heifer and put them in a ceremonially clean place outside the camp. They shall
be kept by the Israelite community for use in
the water of cleansing; it is for purification
from sin. 10The man who gathers up the ashes
of the heifer must also wash his clothes, and
he too will be unclean till evening. This will be
a lasting ordinance both for the Israelites and
for the aliens living among them.
11"Whoever touches the dead body of anyone will be unclean for seven days. 12He must
purify himself with the water on the third day
and on the seventh day; then he will be clean.
But if he does not purify himself on the third
and seventh days, he will not be clean. 13Who-
ever touches the dead body of anyone and fails
to purify himself defiles the LORD's tabernacle. That person must be cut off from Israel.
Because the water of cleansing has not been
sprinkled on him, he is unclean; his uncleanness remains on him.
14"This is the law that applies when a person dies in a tent: Anyone who enters the tent
and anyone who is in it will be unclean for

b 16 That is, about 2 ounces (about 55 grams)

seven days, [15]and every open container without a lid fastened on it will be unclean.

[16]"Anyone out in the open who touches someone who has been killed with a sword or someone who has died a natural death, or anyone who touches a human bone or a grave, will be unclean for seven days.

[17]"For the unclean person, put some ashes from the burned purification offering into a jar and pour fresh water over them. [18]Then a man who is ceremonially clean is to take some hyssop, dip it in the water and sprinkle the tent and all the furnishings and the people who were there. He must also sprinkle anyone who has touched a human bone or a grave or someone who has been killed or someone who has died a natural death. [19]The man who is clean is to sprinkle the unclean person on the third and seventh days, and on the seventh day he is to purify him. The person being cleansed must wash his clothes and bathe with water, and that evening he will be clean. [20]But if a person who is unclean does not purify himself, he must be cut off from the community, because he has defiled the sanctuary of the LORD. The water of cleansing has not been sprinkled on him, and he is unclean. [21]This is a lasting ordinance for them.

"The man who sprinkles the water of cleansing must also wash his clothes, and anyone who touches the water of cleansing will be unclean till evening. [22]Anything that an unclean person touches becomes unclean, and anyone who touches it becomes unclean till evening."

Water From the Rock

20 In the first month the whole Israelite community arrived at the Desert of Zin, and they stayed at Kadesh. There Miriam died and was buried.

[2]Now there was no water for the community, and the people gathered in opposition to Moses and Aaron. [3]They quarreled with Moses and said, "If only we had died when our brothers fell dead before the LORD! [4]Why did you bring the LORD's community into this desert, that we and our livestock should die here? [5]Why did you bring us up out of Egypt to this terrible place? It has no grain or figs, grapevines or pomegranates. And there is no water to drink!"

[6]Moses and Aaron went from the assembly to the entrance to the Tent of Meeting and fell facedown, and the glory of the LORD appeared to them. [7]The LORD said to Moses, [8]"Take the staff, and you and your brother Aaron gather the assembly together. Speak to that rock before their eyes and it will pour out its water. You will bring water out of the rock for the community so they and their livestock can drink."

[9]So Moses took the staff from the LORD's presence, just as he commanded him. [10]He and Aaron gathered the assembly together in front of the rock and Moses said to them, "Listen, you rebels, must we bring you water out of this rock?" [11]Then Moses raised his arm and struck the rock twice with his staff. Water gushed out, and the community and their livestock drank.

[12]But the LORD said to Moses and Aaron, "Because you did not trust in me enough to honor me as holy in the sight of the Israelites, you will not bring this community into the land I give them."

[13]These were the waters of Meribah,[a] where the Israelites quarreled with the LORD and where he showed himself holy among them.

Edom Denies Israel Passage

[14]Moses sent messengers from Kadesh to the king of Edom, saying:

> "This is what your brother Israel says: You know about all the hardships that have come upon us. [15]Our forefathers went down into Egypt, and we lived there many years. The Egyptians mistreated us and our fathers, [16]but when we cried out to the LORD, he heard our cry and sent an angel and brought us out of Egypt.
>
> "Now we are here at Kadesh, a town on the edge of your territory. [17]Please let us pass through your country. We will not go through any field or vineyard, or drink water from any well. We will travel along the king's highway and not turn to the right or to the left until we have passed through your territory."

[18]But Edom answered:

> "You may not pass through here; if you try, we will march out and attack you with the sword."

[19]The Israelites replied:

> "We will go along the main road, and if we or our livestock drink any of your

---

[a] 13 *Meribah* means *quarreling.*

TUESDAY
READ NUMBERS 20:1–13

EXPRESSING ANGER

> **Then Moses raised his arm and struck the rock twice with his staff. Water gushed out, and the community and their livestock drank.**
>
> — NUMBERS 20:11

let's talk

- What are our individual styles of expressing anger? Do we individually "flash and burn" or "simmer and stew"?
- How can each style lead to sin? What are some ways to keep anger from leading to sin?
- What ground rules can we set for future disagreements?

A young, thirsty lion and an equally thirsty cougar arrived at their usual watering hole at the same time. Immediately, they began arguing about who should drink first.

Their argument quickly escalated into rage, and the animals started clawing at one another. However, the fight was interrupted when the lion and cougar caught sight of vultures circling overhead, waiting for the loser to fall. The thought of being eaten was enough for the lion and cougar to end their fight.

Anger destroys people and relationships. Cain, the son of Adam and Eve, committed the world's first murder when in anger he killed his brother Abel. Today, jails, hospitals, abuse shelters and divorce courts are filled with the evidence of anger's destructive power. However, anger itself isn't bad. Ephesians 4:26 doesn't condemn anger; rather, it says, "In your anger do not sin."

Moses knew the consequences of letting anger lead to sin. At age 40, Moses became so angry when he saw an Egyptian beating a Hebrew that he killed the Egyptian (see Acts 7:23–24). Then Moses had to flee for his life, remaining in exile for 40 years (see Acts 7:30). Then, 40 years after Moses led the Hebrews out of Egypt, Moses' anger got him into trouble again. The wandering Israelites complained bitterly about their thirst to Moses, blaming him for their discomfort and hardships. So God instructed Moses, "Speak to that rock before their eyes and it will pour out its water" (Numbers 20:8). Instead, Moses angrily struck the rock with his staff. That disobedience against God cost Moses entrance into the promised land (see verse 12).

Anger in marriage isn't wrong. In "Anger and a Good Marriage" (Together in His Grace, *Heartlight Magazine*, September 19, 2005), Byron Ware says that anger is inevitable, and the healthy expression of it is a testimony to the strength of a marriage. "Relationships that don't acknowledge or express anger are usually fragile, unstable, and anemic," he writes. "For anger not to be expressed suggests that the couple isn't secure enough or the marriage isn't strong enough to handle disagreement."

Not expressing anger leads to the stockpiling of bitterness and resentment; it leads to cold shoulders and cold wars. On the other end of the spectrum is out-of-control anger that is expressed through name-calling, profanity, belittling, intimidation, character assassination and even physical violence. Both extremes are costly to a marriage, undermining intimacy and trust. At its most extreme, unrestrained anger can cost one or both partners their very lives.

In a marriage, respect is key to expressing anger. When anger flares, respect will lead to a discussion of the anger rather than one spouse swallowing their anger in silence. Respect will also guide the expression of anger so that actions are kept within boundaries when tempers blaze. Respect leads to spouses treating each other as helpers and advocates, not as adversaries. And when that happens, the vultures retreat and no one gets eaten.

—NANCY KENNEDY

FOR YOUR NEXT DEVOTIONAL READING, TURN TO PAGE 179.

water, we will pay for it. We only want to pass through on foot—nothing else."

[20]Again they answered:

"You may not pass through."

Then Edom came out against them with a large and powerful army. [21]Since Edom refused to let them go through their territory, Israel turned away from them.

The Death of Aaron

[22]The whole Israelite community set out from Kadesh and came to Mount Hor. [23]At Mount Hor, near the border of Edom, the LORD said to Moses and Aaron, [24]"Aaron will be gathered to his people. He will not enter the land I give the Israelites, because both of you rebelled against my command at the waters of Meribah. [25]Get Aaron and his son Eleazar and take them up Mount Hor. [26]Remove Aaron's garments and put them on his son Eleazar, for Aaron will be gathered to his people; he will die there."

[27]Moses did as the LORD commanded: They went up Mount Hor in the sight of the whole community. [28]Moses removed Aaron's garments and put them on his son Eleazar. And Aaron died there on top of the mountain. Then Moses and Eleazar came down from the mountain, [29]and when the whole community learned that Aaron had died, the entire house of Israel mourned for him thirty days.

Arad Destroyed

21 When the Canaanite king of Arad, who lived in the Negev, heard that Israel was coming along the road to Atharim, he attacked the Israelites and captured some of them. [2]Then Israel made this vow to the LORD: "If you will deliver these people into our hands, we will totally destroy[a] their cities." [3]The LORD listened to Israel's plea and gave the Canaanites over to them. They completely destroyed them and their towns; so the place was named Hormah.[b]

The Bronze Snake

[4]They traveled from Mount Hor along the route to the Red Sea,[c] to go around Edom. But the people grew impatient on the way; [5]they spoke against God and against Moses, and said, "Why have you brought us up out of Egypt to die in the desert? There is no bread! There is no water! And we detest this miserable food!"

[6]Then the LORD sent venomous snakes among them; they bit the people and many Israelites died. [7]The people came to Moses and said, "We sinned when we spoke against the LORD and against you. Pray that the LORD will take the snakes away from us." So Moses prayed for the people.

[8]The LORD said to Moses, "Make a snake and put it up on a pole; anyone who is bitten can look at it and live." [9]So Moses made a bronze snake and put it up on a pole. Then when anyone was bitten by a snake and looked at the bronze snake, he lived.

The Journey to Moab

[10]The Israelites moved on and camped at Oboth. [11]Then they set out from Oboth and camped in Iye Abarim, in the desert that faces Moab toward the sunrise. [12]From there they moved on and camped in the Zered Valley. [13]They set out from there and camped alongside the Arnon, which is in the desert extending into Amorite territory. The Arnon is the border of Moab, between Moab and the Amorites. [14]That is why the Book of the Wars of the LORD says:

". . . Waheb in Suphah[d] and the ravines,
  the Arnon [15]and[e] the slopes of the
    ravines
that lead to the site of Ar
  and lie along the border of Moab."

[16]From there they continued on to Beer, the well where the LORD said to Moses, "Gather the people together and I will give them water."

[17]Then Israel sang this song:

"Spring up, O well!
  Sing about it,
[18]about the well that the princes dug,
  that the nobles of the people sank—
  the nobles with scepters and staffs."

Then they went from the desert to Mattanah, [19]from Mattanah to Nahaliel, from Nahaliel to Bamoth, [20]and from Bamoth to the valley in Moab where the top of Pisgah overlooks the wasteland.

Defeat of Sihon and Og

[21]Israel sent messengers to say to Sihon king of the Amorites:

---

[a] 2 The Hebrew term refers to the irrevocable giving over of things or persons to the LORD, often by totally destroying them; also in verse 3. [b] 3 *Hormah* means *destruction.* [c] 4 Hebrew *Yam Suph*; that is, Sea of Reeds [d] 14 The meaning of the Hebrew for this phrase is uncertain. [e] 14,15 Or *"I have been given from Suphah and the ravines / of the Arnon [15]to*

22“Let us pass through your country.
We will not turn aside into any field or
vineyard, or drink water from any well.
We will travel along the king’s highway
until we have passed through your territory.”

23But Sihon would not let Israel pass
through his territory. He mustered his entire
army and marched out into the desert against
Israel. When he reached Jahaz, he fought
with Israel. 24Israel, however, put him to the
sword and took over his land from the Arnon
to the Jabbok, but only as far as the Ammonites, because their border was fortified. 25Israel
captured all the cities of the Amorites and occupied them, including Heshbon and all its
surrounding settlements. 26Heshbon was the
city of Sihon king of the Amorites, who had
fought against the former king of Moab and
had taken from him all his land as far as the
Arnon.
27That is why the poets say:

“Come to Heshbon and let it be rebuilt;
let Sihon’s city be restored.

28 “Fire went out from Heshbon,
a blaze from the city of Sihon.
It consumed Ar of Moab,
the citizens of Arnon’s heights.
29 Woe to you, O Moab!
You are destroyed, O people of
Chemosh!
He has given up his sons as fugitives
and his daughters as captives
to Sihon king of the Amorites.

30 “But we have overthrown them;
Heshbon is destroyed all the way to
Dibon.
We have demolished them as far as
Nophah,
which extends to Medeba.”

31So Israel settled in the land of the Amorites.
32After Moses had sent spies to Jazer, the
Israelites captured its surrounding settlements
and drove out the Amorites who were there.
33Then they turned and went up along the
road toward Bashan, and Og king of Bashan
and his whole army marched out to meet
them in battle at Edrei.
34The LORD said to Moses, “Do not be
afraid of him, for I have handed him over to
you, with his whole army and his land. Do to
him what you did to Sihon king of the Amorites, who reigned in Heshbon.”
35So they struck him down, together with
his sons and his whole army, leaving them
no survivors. And they took possession of his
land.

Balak Summons Balaam

22 Then the Israelites traveled to the plains
of Moab and camped along the Jordan
across from Jericho.[a]
2Now Balak son of Zippor saw all that Israel had done to the Amorites, 3and Moab was
terrified because there were so many people.
Indeed, Moab was filled with dread because
of the Israelites.
4The Moabites said to the elders of Midian, “This horde is going to lick up everything
around us, as an ox licks up the grass of the
field.”
So Balak son of Zippor, who was king of
Moab at that time, 5sent messengers to summon Balaam son of Beor, who was at Pethor,
near the River,[b] in his native land. Balak said:

“A people has come out of Egypt; they
cover the face of the land and have settled
next to me. 6Now come and put a curse
on these people, because they are too
powerful for me. Perhaps then I will be
able to defeat them and drive them out
of the country. For I know that those you
bless are blessed, and those you curse are
cursed.”

7The elders of Moab and Midian left, taking with them the fee for divination. When
they came to Balaam, they told him what Balak had said.
8“Spend the night here,” Balaam said to
them, “and I will bring you back the answer
the LORD gives me.” So the Moabite princes
stayed with him.
9God came to Balaam and asked, “Who are
these men with you?”
10Balaam said to God, “Balak son of Zippor, king of Moab, sent me this message: 11‘A
people that has come out of Egypt covers the
face of the land. Now come and put a curse
on them for me. Perhaps then I will be able to
fight them and drive them away.’ ”
12But God said to Balaam, “Do not go with
them. You must not put a curse on those people, because they are blessed.”
13The next morning Balaam got up and
said to Balak’s princes, “Go back to your own

[a] 1 Hebrew *Jordan of Jericho*; possibly an ancient name for the Jordan River [b] 5 That is, the Euphrates

country, for the LORD has refused to let me go with you."

14So the Moabite princes returned to Balak and said, "Balaam refused to come with us."

15Then Balak sent other princes, more numerous and more distinguished than the first. 16They came to Balaam and said:

> "This is what Balak son of Zippor says: Do not let anything keep you from coming to me, 17because I will reward you handsomely and do whatever you say. Come and put a curse on these people for me."

18But Balaam answered them, "Even if Balak gave me his palace filled with silver and gold, I could not do anything great or small to go beyond the command of the LORD my God. 19Now stay here tonight as the others did, and I will find out what else the LORD will tell me."

20That night God came to Balaam and said, "Since these men have come to summon you, go with them, but do only what I tell you."

Balaam's Donkey

21Balaam got up in the morning, saddled his donkey and went with the princes of Moab. 22But God was very angry when he went, and the angel of the LORD stood in the road to oppose him. Balaam was riding on his donkey, and his two servants were with him. 23When the donkey saw the angel of the LORD standing in the road with a drawn sword in his hand, she turned off the road into a field. Balaam beat her to get her back on the road.

24Then the angel of the LORD stood in a narrow path between two vineyards, with walls on both sides. 25When the donkey saw the angel of the LORD, she pressed close to the wall, crushing Balaam's foot against it. So he beat her again.

26Then the angel of the LORD moved on ahead and stood in a narrow place where there was no room to turn, either to the right or to the left. 27When the donkey saw the angel of the LORD, she lay down under Balaam, and he was angry and beat her with his staff. 28Then the LORD opened the donkey's mouth, and she said to Balaam, "What have I done to you to make you beat me these three times?"

29Balaam answered the donkey, "You have made a fool of me! If I had a sword in my hand, I would kill you right now."

30The donkey said to Balaam, "Am I not your own donkey, which you have always ridden, to this day? Have I been in the habit of doing this to you?"

"No," he said.

31Then the LORD opened Balaam's eyes, and he saw the angel of the LORD standing in the road with his sword drawn. So he bowed low and fell facedown.

32The angel of the LORD asked him, "Why have you beaten your donkey these three times? I have come here to oppose you because your path is a reckless one before me.[a] 33The donkey saw me and turned away from me these three times. If she had not turned away, I would certainly have killed you by now, but I would have spared her."

34Balaam said to the angel of the LORD, "I have sinned. I did not realize you were standing in the road to oppose me. Now if you are displeased, I will go back."

35The angel of the LORD said to Balaam, "Go with the men, but speak only what I tell you." So Balaam went with the princes of Balak.

36When Balak heard that Balaam was coming, he went out to meet him at the Moabite town on the Arnon border, at the edge of his territory. 37Balak said to Balaam, "Did I not send you an urgent summons? Why didn't you come to me? Am I really not able to reward you?"

38"Well, I have come to you now," Balaam replied. "But can I say just anything? I must speak only what God puts in my mouth."

39Then Balaam went with Balak to Kiriath Huzoth. 40Balak sacrificed cattle and sheep, and gave some to Balaam and the princes who were with him. 41The next morning Balak took Balaam up to Bamoth Baal, and from there he saw part of the people.

Balaam's First Oracle

23 Balaam said, "Build me seven altars here, and prepare seven bulls and seven rams for me." 2Balak did as Balaam said, and the two of them offered a bull and a ram on each altar.

3Then Balaam said to Balak, "Stay here beside your offering while I go aside. Perhaps the LORD will come to meet with me. Whatever he reveals to me I will tell you." Then he went off to a barren height.

4God met with him, and Balaam said, "I

---

a 32 The meaning of the Hebrew for this clause is uncertain.

have prepared seven altars, and on each altar I have offered a bull and a ram."

5The LORD put a message in Balaam's mouth and said, "Go back to Balak and give him this message."

6So he went back to him and found him standing beside his offering, with all the princes of Moab. 7Then Balaam uttered his oracle:

"Balak brought me from Aram,
the king of Moab from the eastern mountains.
'Come,' he said, 'curse Jacob for me;
come, denounce Israel.'
8 How can I curse
those whom God has not cursed?
How can I denounce
those whom the LORD has not denounced?
9 From the rocky peaks I see them,
from the heights I view them.
I see a people who live apart
and do not consider themselves one of the nations.
10 Who can count the dust of Jacob
or number the fourth part of Israel?
Let me die the death of the righteous,
and may my end be like theirs!"

11Balak said to Balaam, "What have you done to me? I brought you to curse my enemies, but you have done nothing but bless them!"

12He answered, "Must I not speak what the LORD puts in my mouth?"

Balaam's Second Oracle

13Then Balak said to him, "Come with me to another place where you can see them; you will see only a part but not all of them. And from there, curse them for me." 14So he took him to the field of Zophim on the top of Pisgah, and there he built seven altars and offered a bull and a ram on each altar.

15Balaam said to Balak, "Stay here beside your offering while I meet with him over there."

16The LORD met with Balaam and put a message in his mouth and said, "Go back to Balak and give him this message."

17So he went to him and found him standing beside his offering, with the princes of Moab. Balak asked him, "What did the LORD say?"

18Then he uttered his oracle:

"Arise, Balak, and listen;
hear me, son of Zippor.
19 God is not a man, that he should lie,
nor a son of man, that he should change his mind.
Does he speak and then not act?
Does he promise and not fulfill?
20 I have received a command to bless;
he has blessed, and I cannot change it.

21 "No misfortune is seen in Jacob,
no misery observed in Israel.[a]
The LORD their God is with them;
the shout of the King is among them.
22 God brought them out of Egypt;
they have the strength of a wild ox.
23 There is no sorcery against Jacob,
no divination against Israel.
It will now be said of Jacob
and of Israel, 'See what God has done!'
24 The people rise like a lioness;
they rouse themselves like a lion
that does not rest till he devours his prey
and drinks the blood of his victims."

25Then Balak said to Balaam, "Neither curse them at all nor bless them at all!"

26Balaam answered, "Did I not tell you I must do whatever the LORD says?"

Balaam's Third Oracle

27Then Balak said to Balaam, "Come, let me take you to another place. Perhaps it will please God to let you curse them for me from there." 28And Balak took Balaam to the top of Peor, overlooking the wasteland.

29Balaam said, "Build me seven altars here, and prepare seven bulls and seven rams for me." 30Balak did as Balaam had said, and offered a bull and a ram on each altar.

24 Now when Balaam saw that it pleased the LORD to bless Israel, he did not resort to sorcery as at other times, but turned his face toward the desert. 2When Balaam looked out and saw Israel encamped tribe by tribe, the Spirit of God came upon him 3and he uttered his oracle:

"The oracle of Balaam son of Beor,
the oracle of one whose eye sees clearly,
4 the oracle of one who hears the words of God,
who sees a vision from the Almighty,[b]
who falls prostrate, and whose eyes are opened:

[a] 21 Or *He has not looked on Jacob's offenses / or on the wrongs found in Israel.* [b] 4 Hebrew *Shaddai*; also in verse 16

5 "How beautiful are your tents, O Jacob,
your dwelling places, O Israel!

6 "Like valleys they spread out,
like gardens beside a river,
like aloes planted by the LORD,
like cedars beside the waters.
7 Water will flow from their buckets;
their seed will have abundant water.

"Their king will be greater than Agag;
their kingdom will be exalted.

8 "God brought them out of Egypt;
they have the strength of a wild ox.
They devour hostile nations
and break their bones in pieces;
with their arrows they pierce them.
9 Like a lion they crouch and lie down,
like a lioness—who dares to rouse
them?

"May those who bless you be blessed
and those who curse you be cursed!"

10 Then Balak's anger burned against Balaam. He struck his hands together and said to
him, "I summoned you to curse my enemies,
but you have blessed them these three times.
11 Now leave at once and go home! I said I
would reward you handsomely, but the LORD
has kept you from being rewarded."
12 Balaam answered Balak, "Did I not tell
the messengers you sent me, 13 'Even if Balak
gave me his palace filled with silver and gold,
I could not do anything of my own accord,
good or bad, to go beyond the command
of the LORD—and I must say only what the
LORD says'? 14 Now I am going back to my
people, but come, let me warn you of what
this people will do to your people in days to
come."

Balaam's Fourth Oracle

15 Then he uttered his oracle:

"The oracle of Balaam son of Beor,
the oracle of one whose eye sees
clearly,
16 the oracle of one who hears the words of
God,
who has knowledge from the Most
High,
who sees a vision from the Almighty,
who falls prostrate, and whose eyes are
opened:

17 "I see him, but not now;
I behold him, but not near.
A star will come out of Jacob;
a scepter will rise out of Israel.
He will crush the foreheads of Moab,
the skulls[a] of[b] all the sons of Sheth.[c]
18 Edom will be conquered;
Seir, his enemy, will be conquered,
but Israel will grow strong.
19 A ruler will come out of Jacob
and destroy the survivors of the city."

Balaam's Final Oracles

20 Then Balaam saw Amalek and uttered his
oracle:

"Amalek was first among the nations,
but he will come to ruin at last."

21 Then he saw the Kenites and uttered his
oracle:

"Your dwelling place is secure,
your nest is set in a rock;
22 yet you Kenites will be destroyed
when Asshur takes you captive."

23 Then he uttered his oracle:

"Ah, who can live when God does this?[d]
24 Ships will come from the shores of
Kittim;
they will subdue Asshur and Eber,
but they too will come to ruin."

25 Then Balaam got up and returned home
and Balak went his own way.

Moab Seduces Israel

25 While Israel was staying in Shittim,
the men began to indulge in sexual immorality with Moabite women, 2 who
invited them to the sacrifices to their gods.
The people ate and bowed down before these
gods. 3 So Israel joined in worshiping the Baal
of Peor. And the LORD's anger burned against
them.
4 The LORD said to Moses, "Take all the
leaders of these people, kill them and expose
them in broad daylight before the LORD, so
that the LORD's fierce anger may turn away
from Israel."
5 So Moses said to Israel's judges, "Each of
you must put to death those of your men who
have joined in worshiping the Baal of Peor."
6 Then an Israelite man brought to his family a Midianite woman right before the eyes of

---

[a] 17 Samaritan Pentateuch (see also Jer. 48:45); the meaning of the word in the Masoretic Text is uncertain. [b] 17 Or possibly *Moab, / batter* [c] 17 Or *all the noisy boasters* [d] 23 Masoretic Text; with a different word division of the Hebrew *A people will gather from the north.*

Moses and the whole assembly of Israel while they were weeping at the entrance to the Tent of Meeting. 7When Phinehas son of Eleazar, the son of Aaron, the priest, saw this, he left the assembly, took a spear in his hand 8and followed the Israelite into the tent. He drove the spear through both of them—through the Israelite and into the woman's body. Then the plague against the Israelites was stopped; 9but those who died in the plague numbered 24,000.

10The LORD said to Moses, 11"Phinehas son of Eleazar, the son of Aaron, the priest, has turned my anger away from the Israelites; for he was as zealous as I am for my honor among them, so that in my zeal I did not put an end to them. 12Therefore tell him I am making my covenant of peace with him. 13He and his descendants will have a covenant of a lasting priesthood, because he was zealous for the honor of his God and made atonement for the Israelites."

14The name of the Israelite who was killed with the Midianite woman was Zimri son of Salu, the leader of a Simeonite family. 15And the name of the Midianite woman who was put to death was Cozbi daughter of Zur, a tribal chief of a Midianite family.

16The LORD said to Moses, 17"Treat the Midianites as enemies and kill them, 18because they treated you as enemies when they deceived you in the affair of Peor and their sister Cozbi, the daughter of a Midianite leader, the woman who was killed when the plague came as a result of Peor."

The Second Census

26 After the plague the LORD said to Moses and Eleazar son of Aaron, the priest, 2"Take a census of the whole Israelite community by families—all those twenty years old or more who are able to serve in the army of Israel." 3So on the plains of Moab by the Jordan across from Jericho,[a] Moses and Eleazar the priest spoke with them and said, 4"Take a census of the men twenty years old or more, as the LORD commanded Moses."

These were the Israelites who came out of Egypt:

5The descendants of Reuben, the firstborn son of Israel, were:
through Hanoch, the Hanochite clan;
through Pallu, the Palluite clan;
6through Hezron, the Hezronite clan;
through Carmi, the Carmite clan.
7These were the clans of Reuben; those numbered were 43,730.

8The son of Pallu was Eliab, 9and the sons of Eliab were Nemuel, Dathan and Abiram. The same Dathan and Abiram were the community officials who rebelled against Moses and Aaron and were among Korah's followers when they rebelled against the LORD. 10The earth opened its mouth and swallowed them along with Korah, whose followers died when the fire devoured the 250 men. And they served as a warning sign. 11The line of Korah, however, did not die out.

12The descendants of Simeon by their clans were:
through Nemuel, the Nemuelite clan;
through Jamin, the Jaminite clan;
through Jakin, the Jakinite clan;
13through Zerah, the Zerahite clan;
through Shaul, the Shaulite clan.
14These were the clans of Simeon; there were 22,200 men.

15The descendants of Gad by their clans were:
through Zephon, the Zephonite clan;
through Haggi, the Haggite clan;
through Shuni, the Shunite clan;
16through Ozni, the Oznite clan;
through Eri, the Erite clan;
17through Arodi,[b] the Arodite clan;
through Areli, the Arelite clan.
18These were the clans of Gad; those numbered were 40,500.

19Er and Onan were sons of Judah, but they died in Canaan.
20The descendants of Judah by their clans were:
through Shelah, the Shelanite clan;
through Perez, the Perezite clan;
through Zerah, the Zerahite clan.
21The descendants of Perez were:
through Hezron, the Hezronite clan;
through Hamul, the Hamulite clan.
22These were the clans of Judah; those numbered were 76,500.

23The descendants of Issachar by their clans were:
through Tola, the Tolaite clan;
through Puah, the Puite[c] clan;
24through Jashub, the Jashubite clan;
through Shimron, the Shimronite clan.

---

[a] 3 Hebrew *Jordan of Jericho*; possibly an ancient name for the Jordan River; also in verse 63 [b] 17 Samaritan Pentateuch and Syriac (see also Gen. 46:16); Masoretic Text *Arod* [c] 23 Samaritan Pentateuch, Septuagint, Vulgate and Syriac (see also 1 Chron. 7:1); Masoretic Text *through Puvah, the Punite*

25These were the clans of Issachar; those numbered were 64,300.

26The descendants of Zebulun by their clans were:
through Sered, the Seredite clan;
through Elon, the Elonite clan;
through Jahleel, the Jahleelite clan.
27These were the clans of Zebulun; those numbered were 60,500.

28The descendants of Joseph by their clans through Manasseh and Ephraim were:

29The descendants of Manasseh:
through Makir, the Makirite clan (Makir was the father of Gilead);
through Gilead, the Gileadite clan.
30These were the descendants of Gilead:
through Iezer, the Iezerite clan;
through Helek, the Helekite clan;
31through Asriel, the Asrielite clan;
through Shechem, the Shechemite clan;
32through Shemida, the Shemidaite clan;
through Hepher, the Hepherite clan.
33(Zelophehad son of Hepher had no sons; he had only daughters, whose names were Mahlah, Noah, Hoglah, Milcah and Tirzah.)
34These were the clans of Manasseh; those numbered were 52,700.

35These were the descendants of Ephraim by their clans:
through Shuthelah, the Shuthelahite clan;
through Beker, the Bekerite clan;
through Tahan, the Tahanite clan.
36These were the descendants of Shuthelah:
through Eran, the Eranite clan.
37These were the clans of Ephraim; those numbered were 32,500.

These were the descendants of Joseph by their clans.

38The descendants of Benjamin by their clans were:
through Bela, the Belaite clan;
through Ashbel, the Ashbelite clan;
through Ahiram, the Ahiramite clan;
39through Shupham,[a] the Shuphamite clan;
through Hupham, the Huphamite clan.
40The descendants of Bela through Ard and Naaman were:
through Ard,[b] the Ardite clan;
through Naaman, the Naamite clan.
41These were the clans of Benjamin; those numbered were 45,600.

42These were the descendants of Dan by their clans:
through Shuham, the Shuhamite clan.
These were the clans of Dan: 43All of them were Shuhamite clans; and those numbered were 64,400.

44The descendants of Asher by their clans were:
through Imnah, the Imnite clan;
through Ishvi, the Ishvite clan;
through Beriah, the Beriite clan;
45and through the descendants of Beriah:
through Heber, the Heberite clan;
through Malkiel, the Malkielite clan.
46(Asher had a daughter named Serah.)
47These were the clans of Asher; those numbered were 53,400.

48The descendants of Naphtali by their clans were:
through Jahzeel, the Jahzeelite clan;
through Guni, the Gunite clan;
49through Jezer, the Jezerite clan;
through Shillem, the Shillemite clan.
50These were the clans of Naphtali; those numbered were 45,400.

51The total number of the men of Israel was 601,730.

52The LORD said to Moses, 53"The land is to
be allotted to them as an inheritance based on
the number of names. 54To a larger group give
a larger inheritance, and to a smaller group a
smaller one; each is to receive its inheritance
according to the number of those listed. 55Be
sure that the land is distributed by lot. What
each group inherits will be according to the
names for its ancestral tribe. 56Each inheritance is to be distributed by lot among the
larger and smaller groups."

57These were the Levites who were counted by their clans:
through Gershon, the Gershonite clan;
through Kohath, the Kohathite clan;
through Merari, the Merarite clan.
58These also were Levite clans:

[a] 39 A few manuscripts of the Masoretic Text, Samaritan Pentateuch, Vulgate and Syriac (see also Septuagint); most manuscripts of the Masoretic Text *Shephupham* [b] 40 Samaritan Pentateuch and Vulgate (see also Septuagint); Masoretic Text does not have *through Ard.*

the Libnite clan,
the Hebronite clan,
the Mahlite clan,
the Mushite clan,
the Korahite clan.
(Kohath was the forefather of Amram; 59the name of Amram's wife was Jochebed, a descendant of Levi, who was born to the Levites[a] in Egypt. To Amram she bore Aaron, Moses and their sister Miriam. 60Aaron was the father of Nadab and Abihu, Eleazar and Ithamar. 61But Nadab and Abihu died when they made an offering before the LORD with unauthorized fire.)

62All the male Levites a month old or more numbered 23,000. They were not counted along with the other Israelites because they received no inheritance among them.

63These are the ones counted by Moses and Eleazar the priest when they counted the Israelites on the plains of Moab by the Jordan across from Jericho. 64Not one of them was among those counted by Moses and Aaron the priest when they counted the Israelites in the Desert of Sinai. 65For the LORD had told those Israelites they would surely die in the desert, and not one of them was left except Caleb son of Jephunneh and Joshua son of Nun.

Zelophehad's Daughters

27 The daughters of Zelophehad son of Hepher, the son of Gilead, the son of Makir, the son of Manasseh, belonged to the clans of Manasseh son of Joseph. The names of the daughters were Mahlah, Noah, Hoglah, Milcah and Tirzah. They approached 2the entrance to the Tent of Meeting and stood before Moses, Eleazar the priest, the leaders and the whole assembly, and said, 3"Our father died in the desert. He was not among Korah's followers, who banded together against the LORD, but he died for his own sin and left no sons. 4Why should our father's name disappear from his clan because he had no son? Give us property among our father's relatives."

5So Moses brought their case before the LORD 6and the LORD said to him, 7"What Zelophehad's daughters are saying is right. You must certainly give them property as an inheritance among their father's relatives and turn their father's inheritance over to them.

8"Say to the Israelites, 'If a man dies and leaves no son, turn his inheritance over to his daughter. 9If he has no daughter, give his inheritance to his brothers. 10If he has no brothers, give his inheritance to his father's brothers. 11If his father had no brothers, give his inheritance to the nearest relative in his clan, that he may possess it. This is to be a legal requirement for the Israelites, as the LORD commanded Moses.' "

Joshua to Succeed Moses

12Then the LORD said to Moses, "Go up this mountain in the Abarim range and see the land I have given the Israelites. 13After you have seen it, you too will be gathered to your people, as your brother Aaron was, 14for when the community rebelled at the waters in the Desert of Zin, both of you disobeyed my command to honor me as holy before their eyes." (These were the waters of Meribah Kadesh, in the Desert of Zin.)

15Moses said to the LORD, 16"May the LORD, the God of the spirits of all mankind, appoint a man over this community 17to go out and come in before them, one who will lead them out and bring them in, so the LORD's people will not be like sheep without a shepherd."

18So the LORD said to Moses, "Take Joshua son of Nun, a man in whom is the spirit,[b] and lay your hand on him. 19Have him stand before Eleazar the priest and the entire assembly and commission him in their presence. 20Give him some of your authority so the whole Israelite community will obey him. 21He is to stand before Eleazar the priest, who will obtain decisions for him by inquiring of the Urim before the LORD. At his command he and the entire community of the Israelites will go out, and at his command they will come in."

22Moses did as the LORD commanded him. He took Joshua and had him stand before Eleazar the priest and the whole assembly. 23Then he laid his hands on him and commissioned him, as the LORD instructed through Moses.

Daily Offerings

28 The LORD said to Moses, 2"Give this command to the Israelites and say to them: 'See that you present to me at the appointed time the food for my offerings made by fire, as an aroma pleasing to me.' 3Say to them: 'This is the offering made by fire that you are to present to the LORD: two

---

[a] 59 Or *Jochebed, a daughter of Levi, who was born to Levi* [b] 18 Or *Spirit*

lambs a year old without defect, as a regular
burnt offering each day. 4Prepare one lamb in
the morning and the other at twilight, 5to-
gether with a grain offering of a tenth of an
ephah[a] of fine flour mixed with a quarter of
a hin[b] of oil from pressed olives. 6This is the
regular burnt offering instituted at Mount Sinai as a pleasing aroma, an offering made to
the LORD by fire. 7The accompanying drink
offering is to be a quarter of a hin of fermented drink with each lamb. Pour out the drink
offering to the LORD at the sanctuary. 8Pre-
pare the second lamb at twilight, along with
the same kind of grain offering and drink offering that you prepare in the morning. This
is an offering made by fire, an aroma pleasing
to the LORD.

Sabbath Offerings

9" 'On the Sabbath day, make an offering of
two lambs a year old without defect, together
with its drink offering and a grain offering of
two-tenths of an ephah[c] of fine flour mixed
with oil. 10This is the burnt offering for every
Sabbath, in addition to the regular burnt offering and its drink offering.

Monthly Offerings

11" 'On the first of every month, present to
the LORD a burnt offering of two young bulls,
one ram and seven male lambs a year old, all
without defect. 12With each bull there is to be
a grain offering of three-tenths of an ephah[d]
of fine flour mixed with oil; with the ram, a
grain offering of two-tenths of an ephah of
fine flour mixed with oil; 13and with each
lamb, a grain offering of a tenth of an ephah
of fine flour mixed with oil. This is for a burnt
offering, a pleasing aroma, an offering made
to the LORD by fire. 14With each bull there is
to be a drink offering of half a hin[e] of wine;
with the ram, a third of a hin[f]; and with each
lamb, a quarter of a hin. This is the monthly
burnt offering to be made at each new moon
during the year. 15Besides the regular burnt
offering with its drink offering, one male goat
is to be presented to the LORD as a sin offering.

The Passover

16" 'On the fourteenth day of the first
month the LORD's Passover is to be held.
17On the fifteenth day of this month there
is to be a festival; for seven days eat bread
made without yeast. 18On the first day hold
a sacred assembly and do no regular work.
19Present to the LORD an offering made by
fire, a burnt offering of two young bulls,
one ram and seven male lambs a year old, all
without defect. 20With each bull prepare a
grain offering of three-tenths of an ephah of
fine flour mixed with oil; with the ram, two-
tenths; 21and with each of the seven lambs,
one-tenth. 22Include one male goat as a sin
offering to make atonement for you. 23Pre-
pare these in addition to the regular morning
burnt offering. 24In this way prepare the food
for the offering made by fire every day for
seven days as an aroma pleasing to the LORD;
it is to be prepared in addition to the regular
burnt offering and its drink offering. 25On
the seventh day hold a sacred assembly and
do no regular work.

Feast of Weeks

26" 'On the day of firstfruits, when you
present to the LORD an offering of new grain
during the Feast of Weeks, hold a sacred assembly and do no regular work. 27Present a
burnt offering of two young bulls, one ram
and seven male lambs a year old as an aroma pleasing to the LORD. 28With each bull
there is to be a grain offering of three-tenths
of an ephah of fine flour mixed with oil; with
the ram, two-tenths; 29and with each of the
seven lambs, one-tenth. 30Include one male
goat to make atonement for you. 31Prepare
these together with their drink offerings, in
addition to the regular burnt offering and its
grain offering. Be sure the animals are without defect.

Feast of Trumpets

29 " 'On the first day of the seventh
month hold a sacred assembly and do
no regular work. It is a day for you to
sound the trumpets. 2As an aroma pleasing
to the LORD, prepare a burnt offering of one
young bull, one ram and seven male lambs a
year old, all without defect. 3With the bull
prepare a grain offering of three-tenths of an
ephah[g] of fine flour mixed with oil; with the
ram, two-tenths[h]; 4and with each of the sev-
en lambs, one-tenth.[i] 5Include one male goat

[a] *5* That is, probably about 2 quarts (about 2 liters); also in verses 13, 21 and 29 [b] *5* That is, probably about 1 quart (about 1 liter); also in verses 7 and 14 [c] *9* That is, probably about 4 quarts (about 4.5 liters); also in verses 12, 20 and 28 [d] *12* That is, probably about 6 quarts (about 6.5 liters); also in verses 20 and 28 [e] *14* That is, probably about 2 quarts (about 2 liters) [f] *14* That is, probably about 1 1/4 quarts (about 1.2 liters) [g] *3* That is, probably about 6 quarts (about 6.5 liters); also in verses 9 and 14 [h] *3* That is, probably about 4 quarts (about 4.5 liters); also in verses 9 and 14 [i] *4* That is, probably about 2 quarts (about 2 liters); also in verses 10 and 15

as a sin offering to make atonement for you.
6These are in addition to the monthly and
daily burnt offerings with their grain offerings and drink offerings as specified. They are
offerings made to the LORD by fire—a pleasing aroma.

Day of Atonement

7“ ‘On the tenth day of this seventh month
hold a sacred assembly. You must deny yourselves[a] and do no work. 8Present as an aroma
pleasing to the LORD a burnt offering of one
young bull, one ram and seven male lambs a
year old, all without defect. 9With the bull
prepare a grain offering of three-tenths of an
ephah of fine flour mixed with oil; with the
ram, two-tenths; 10and with each of the seven
lambs, one-tenth. 11Include one male goat as
a sin offering, in addition to the sin offering
for atonement and the regular burnt offering
with its grain offering, and their drink offerings.

Feast of Tabernacles

12“ ‘On the fifteenth day of the seventh
month, hold a sacred assembly and do no regular work. Celebrate a festival to the LORD for
seven days. 13Present an offering made by fire
as an aroma pleasing to the LORD, a burnt offering of thirteen young bulls, two rams and
fourteen male lambs a year old, all without defect. 14With each of the thirteen bulls prepare
a grain offering of three-tenths of an ephah of
fine flour mixed with oil; with each of the two
rams, two-tenths; 15and with each of the fourteen lambs, one-tenth. 16Include one male
goat as a sin offering, in addition to the regular burnt offering with its grain offering and
drink offering.

17“ ‘On the second day prepare twelve
young bulls, two rams and fourteen male
lambs a year old, all without defect. 18With
the bulls, rams and lambs, prepare their grain
offerings and drink offerings according to the
number specified. 19Include one male goat as
a sin offering, in addition to the regular burnt
offering with its grain offering, and their drink
offerings.

20“ ‘On the third day prepare eleven bulls,
two rams and fourteen male lambs a year old,
all without defect. 21With the bulls, rams and
lambs, prepare their grain offerings and drink
offerings according to the number specified.
22Include one male goat as a sin offering, in
addition to the regular burnt offering with its
grain offering and drink offering.

23“ ‘On the fourth day prepare ten bulls,
two rams and fourteen male lambs a year old,
all without defect. 24With the bulls, rams and
lambs, prepare their grain offerings and drink
offerings according to the number specified.
25Include one male goat as a sin offering, in
addition to the regular burnt offering with its
grain offering and drink offering.

26“ ‘On the fifth day prepare nine bulls, two
rams and fourteen male lambs a year old, all
without defect. 27With the bulls, rams and
lambs, prepare their grain offerings and drink
offerings according to the number specified.
28Include one male goat as a sin offering, in
addition to the regular burnt offering with its
grain offering and drink offering.

29“ ‘On the sixth day prepare eight bulls,
two rams and fourteen male lambs a year old,
all without defect. 30With the bulls, rams and
lambs, prepare their grain offerings and drink
offerings according to the number specified.
31Include one male goat as a sin offering, in
addition to the regular burnt offering with its
grain offering and drink offering.

32“ ‘On the seventh day prepare seven bulls,
two rams and fourteen male lambs a year old,
all without defect. 33With the bulls, rams and
lambs, prepare their grain offerings and drink
offerings according to the number specified.
34Include one male goat as a sin offering, in
addition to the regular burnt offering with its
grain offering and drink offering.

35“ ‘On the eighth day hold an assembly
and do no regular work. 36Present an offering
made by fire as an aroma pleasing to the LORD,
a burnt offering of one bull, one ram and sev-
en male lambs a year old, all without defect.
37With the bull, the ram and the lambs, prepare their grain offerings and drink offerings
according to the number specified. 38Include
one male goat as a sin offering, in addition to
the regular burnt offering with its grain offering and drink offering.

39“ ‘In addition to what you vow and your
freewill offerings, prepare these for the LORD
at your appointed feasts: your burnt offerings,
grain offerings, drink offerings and fellowship
offerings.[b]’ ”

40Moses told the Israelites all that the LORD
commanded him.

---

[a] 7 Or *must fast* [b] 39 Traditionally *peace offerings*

Vows

30 Moses said to the heads of the tribes of Israel: "This is what the LORD commands: 2When a man makes a vow to the LORD or takes an oath to obligate himself by a pledge, he must not break his word but must do everything he said.

3"When a young woman still living in her father's house makes a vow to the LORD or obligates herself by a pledge 4and her father hears about her vow or pledge but says nothing to her, then all her vows and every pledge by which she obligated herself will stand. 5But if her father forbids her when he hears about it, none of her vows or the pledges by which she obligated herself will stand; the LORD will release her because her father has forbidden her.

6"If she marries after she makes a vow or after her lips utter a rash promise by which she obligates herself 7and her husband hears about it but says nothing to her, then her vows or the pledges by which she obligated herself will stand. 8But if her husband forbids her when he hears about it, he nullifies the vow that obligates her or the rash promise by which she obligates herself, and the LORD will release her.

9"Any vow or obligation taken by a widow or divorced woman will be binding on her.

10"If a woman living with her husband makes a vow or obligates herself by a pledge under oath 11and her husband hears about it but says nothing to her and does not forbid her, then all her vows or the pledges by which she obligated herself will stand. 12But if her husband nullifies them when he hears about them, then none of the vows or pledges that came from her lips will stand. Her husband has nullified them, and the LORD will release her. 13Her husband may confirm or nullify any vow she makes or any sworn pledge to deny herself. 14But if her husband says nothing to her about it from day to day, then he confirms all her vows or the pledges binding on her. He confirms them by saying nothing to her when he hears about them. 15If, however, he nullifies them some time after he hears about them, then he is responsible for her guilt."

16These are the regulations the LORD gave Moses concerning relationships between a man and his wife, and between a father and his young daughter still living in his house.

Vengeance on the Midianites

31 The LORD said to Moses, 2"Take vengeance on the Midianites for the Israelites. After that, you will be gathered to your people."

3So Moses said to the people, "Arm some of your men to go to war against the Midianites and to carry out the LORD's vengeance on them. 4Send into battle a thousand men from each of the tribes of Israel." 5So twelve thousand men armed for battle, a thousand from each tribe, were supplied from the clans of Israel. 6Moses sent them into battle, a thousand from each tribe, along with Phinehas son of Eleazar, the priest, who took with him articles from the sanctuary and the trumpets for signaling.

7They fought against Midian, as the LORD commanded Moses, and killed every man. 8Among their victims were Evi, Rekem, Zur, Hur and Reba—the five kings of Midian. They also killed Balaam son of Beor with the sword. 9The Israelites captured the Midianite women and children and took all the Midianite herds, flocks and goods as plunder. 10They burned all the towns where the Midianites had settled, as well as all their camps. 11They took all the plunder and spoils, including the people and animals, 12and brought the captives, spoils and plunder to Moses and Eleazar the priest and the Israelite assembly at their camp on the plains of Moab, by the Jordan across from Jericho.[a]

13Moses, Eleazar the priest and all the leaders of the community went to meet them outside the camp. 14Moses was angry with the officers of the army—the commanders of thousands and commanders of hundreds—who returned from the battle.

15"Have you allowed all the women to live?" he asked them. 16"They were the ones who followed Balaam's advice and were the means of turning the Israelites away from the LORD in what happened at Peor, so that a plague struck the LORD's people. 17Now kill all the boys. And kill every woman who has slept with a man, 18but save for yourselves every girl who has never slept with a man.

19"All of you who have killed anyone or touched anyone who was killed must stay outside the camp seven days. On the third and seventh days you must purify yourselves and your captives. 20Purify every garment as well

---

a 12 Hebrew *Jordan of Jericho*; possibly an ancient name for the Jordan River

as everything made of leather, goat hair or
wood."
[21]Then Eleazar the priest said to the soldiers
who had gone into battle, "This is the requirement of the law that the LORD gave Moses:
[22]Gold, silver, bronze, iron, tin, lead [23]and
anything else that can withstand fire must be
put through the fire, and then it will be clean.
But it must also be purified with the water of
cleansing. And whatever cannot withstand fire
must be put through that water. [24]On the seventh day wash your clothes and you will be
clean. Then you may come into the camp."

Dividing the Spoils

[25]The LORD said to Moses, [26]"You and Eleazar the priest and the family heads of the
community are to count all the people and animals that were captured. [27]Divide the spoils
between the soldiers who took part in the battle and the rest of the community. [28]From the
soldiers who fought in the battle, set apart as
tribute for the LORD one out of every five hundred, whether persons, cattle, donkeys, sheep
or goats. [29]Take this tribute from their half
share and give it to Eleazar the priest as the
LORD's part. [30]From the Israelites' half, select
one out of every fifty, whether persons, cattle,
donkeys, sheep, goats or other animals. Give
them to the Levites, who are responsible for
the care of the LORD's tabernacle." [31]So Moses
and Eleazar the priest did as the LORD commanded Moses.
[32]The plunder remaining from the spoils
that the soldiers took was 675,000 sheep,
[33]72,000 cattle, [34]61,000 donkeys [35]and
32,000 women who had never slept with a
man.
[36]The half share of those who fought in the
battle was:

337,500 sheep, [37]of which the tribute for the LORD was 675;
[38]36,000 cattle, of which the tribute for the LORD was 72;
[39]30,500 donkeys, of which the tribute for the LORD was 61;
[40]16,000 people, of which the tribute for the LORD was 32.

[41]Moses gave the tribute to Eleazar the
priest as the LORD's part, as the LORD commanded Moses.
[42]The half belonging to the Israelites, which
Moses set apart from that of the fighting
men— [43]the community's half—was 337,500
sheep, [44]36,000 cattle, [45]30,500 donkeys
[46]and 16,000 people. [47]From the Israelites'
half, Moses selected one out of every fifty persons and animals, as the LORD commanded
him, and gave them to the Levites, who were
responsible for the care of the LORD's tabernacle.
[48]Then the officers who were over the units
of the army—the commanders of thousands
and commanders of hundreds—went to Moses [49]and said to him, "Your servants have
counted the soldiers under our command, and
not one is missing. [50]So we have brought as an
offering to the LORD the gold articles each of
us acquired—armlets, bracelets, signet rings,
earrings and necklaces—to make atonement
for ourselves before the LORD."
[51]Moses and Eleazar the priest accepted
from them the gold—all the crafted articles.
[52]All the gold from the commanders of thousands and commanders of hundreds that Moses and Eleazar presented as a gift to the LORD
weighed 16,750 shekels.[a] [53]Each soldier had
taken plunder for himself. [54]Moses and Eleazar the priest accepted the gold from the
commanders of thousands and commanders
of hundreds and brought it into the Tent of
Meeting as a memorial for the Israelites before
the LORD.

The Transjordan Tribes

32 The Reubenites and Gadites, who had
very large herds and flocks, saw that
the lands of Jazer and Gilead were suitable for livestock. [2]So they came to Moses
and Eleazar the priest and to the leaders of
the community, and said, [3]"Ataroth, Dibon,
Jazer, Nimrah, Heshbon, Elealeh, Sebam,
Nebo and Beon— [4]the land the LORD subdued before the people of Israel—are suitable
for livestock, and your servants have livestock. [5]If we have found favor in your eyes,"
they said, "let this land be given to your servants as our possession. Do not make us cross
the Jordan."
[6]Moses said to the Gadites and Reubenites,
"Shall your countrymen go to war while you
sit here? [7]Why do you discourage the Israelites from going over into the land the LORD
has given them? [8]This is what your fathers
did when I sent them from Kadesh Barnea
to look over the land. [9]After they went up to
the Valley of Eshcol and viewed the land, they
discouraged the Israelites from entering the
land the LORD had given them. [10]The LORD's

[a] *52* That is, about 420 pounds (about 190 kilograms)

anger was aroused that day and he swore this oath: 11‘Because they have not followed me wholeheartedly, not one of the men twenty years old or more who came up out of Egypt will see the land I promised on oath to Abraham, Isaac and Jacob— 12not one except Caleb son of Jephunneh the Kenizzite and Joshua son of Nun, for they followed the LORD wholeheartedly.’ 13The LORD’s anger burned against Israel and he made them wander in the desert forty years, until the whole generation of those who had done evil in his sight was gone.

14“And here you are, a brood of sinners, standing in the place of your fathers and making the LORD even more angry with Israel. 15If you turn away from following him, he will again leave all this people in the desert, and you will be the cause of their destruction.”

16Then they came up to him and said, “We would like to build pens here for our livestock and cities for our women and children. 17But we are ready to arm ourselves and go ahead of the Israelites until we have brought them to their place. Meanwhile our women and children will live in fortified cities, for protection from the inhabitants of the land. 18We will not return to our homes until every Israelite has received his inheritance. 19We will not receive any inheritance with them on the other side of the Jordan, because our inheritance has come to us on the east side of the Jordan.”

20Then Moses said to them, “If you will do this—if you will arm yourselves before the LORD for battle, 21and if all of you will go armed over the Jordan before the LORD until he has driven his enemies out before him— 22then when the land is subdued before the LORD, you may return and be free from your obligation to the LORD and to Israel. And this land will be your possession before the LORD.

23“But if you fail to do this, you will be sinning against the LORD; and you may be sure that your sin will find you out. 24Build cities for your women and children, and pens for your flocks, but do what you have promised.”

25The Gadites and Reubenites said to Moses, “We your servants will do as our lord commands. 26Our children and wives, our flocks and herds will remain here in the cities of Gilead. 27But your servants, every man armed for battle, will cross over to fight before the LORD, just as our lord says.”

28Then Moses gave orders about them to Eleazar the priest and Joshua son of Nun and to the family heads of the Israelite tribes. 29He said to them, “If the Gadites and Reubenites, every man armed for battle, cross over the Jordan with you before the LORD, then when the land is subdued before you, give them the land of Gilead as their possession. 30But if they do not cross over with you armed, they must accept their possession with you in Canaan.”

31The Gadites and Reubenites answered, “Your servants will do what the LORD has said. 32We will cross over before the LORD into Canaan armed, but the property we inherit will be on this side of the Jordan.”

33Then Moses gave to the Gadites, the Reubenites and the half-tribe of Manasseh son of Joseph the kingdom of Sihon king of the Amorites and the kingdom of Og king of Bashan—the whole land with its cities and the territory around them.

34The Gadites built up Dibon, Ataroth, Aroer, 35Atroth Shophan, Jazer, Jogbehah, 36Beth Nimrah and Beth Haran as fortified cities, and built pens for their flocks. 37And the Reubenites rebuilt Heshbon, Elealeh and Kiriathaim, 38as well as Nebo and Baal Meon (these names were changed) and Sibmah. They gave names to the cities they rebuilt.

39The descendants of Makir son of Manasseh went to Gilead, captured it and drove out the Amorites who were there. 40So Moses gave Gilead to the Makirites, the descendants of Manasseh, and they settled there. 41Jair, a descendant of Manasseh, captured their settlements and called them Havvoth Jair.[a] 42And Nobah captured Kenath and its surrounding settlements and called it Nobah after himself.

Stages in Israel’s Journey

33 Here are the stages in the journey of the Israelites when they came out of Egypt by divisions under the leadership of Moses and Aaron. 2At the LORD’s command Moses recorded the stages in their journey. This is their journey by stages:

3The Israelites set out from Rameses
on the fifteenth day of the first month,
the day after the Passover. They marched
out boldly in full view of all the Egyptians,
4who were burying all their firstborn,
whom the LORD had struck down
among them; for the LORD had brought
judgment on their gods.

a 41 Or *them the settlements of Jair*

[5]The Israelites left Rameses and camped at Succoth.

[6]They left Succoth and camped at Etham, on the edge of the desert.

[7]They left Etham, turned back to Pi Hahiroth, to the east of Baal Zephon, and camped near Migdol.

[8]They left Pi Hahiroth [a] and passed through the sea into the desert, and when they had traveled for three days in the Desert of Etham, they camped at Marah.

[9]They left Marah and went to Elim, where there were twelve springs and seventy palm trees, and they camped there.

[10]They left Elim and camped by the Red Sea. [b]

[11]They left the Red Sea and camped in the Desert of Sin.

[12]They left the Desert of Sin and camped at Dophkah.

[13]They left Dophkah and camped at Alush.

[14]They left Alush and camped at Rephidim, where there was no water for the people to drink.

[15]They left Rephidim and camped in the Desert of Sinai.

[16]They left the Desert of Sinai and camped at Kibroth Hattaavah.

[17]They left Kibroth Hattaavah and camped at Hazeroth.

[18]They left Hazeroth and camped at Rithmah.

[19]They left Rithmah and camped at Rimmon Perez.

[20]They left Rimmon Perez and camped at Libnah.

[21]They left Libnah and camped at Rissah.

[22]They left Rissah and camped at Kehelathah.

[23]They left Kehelathah and camped at Mount Shepher.

[24]They left Mount Shepher and camped at Haradah.

[25]They left Haradah and camped at Makheloth.

[26]They left Makheloth and camped at Tahath.

[27]They left Tahath and camped at Terah.

[28]They left Terah and camped at Mithcah.

[29]They left Mithcah and camped at Hashmonah.

[30]They left Hashmonah and camped at Moseroth.

[31]They left Moseroth and camped at Bene Jaakan.

[32]They left Bene Jaakan and camped at Hor Haggidgad.

[33]They left Hor Haggidgad and camped at Jotbathah.

[34]They left Jotbathah and camped at Abronah.

[35]They left Abronah and camped at Ezion Geber.

[36]They left Ezion Geber and camped at Kadesh, in the Desert of Zin.

[37]They left Kadesh and camped at Mount Hor, on the border of Edom.
[38]At the LORD's command Aaron the priest went up Mount Hor, where he died on the first day of the fifth month of the fortieth year after the Israelites came out of Egypt. [39]Aaron was a hundred and twenty-three years old when he died on Mount Hor.

[40]The Canaanite king of Arad, who lived in the Negev of Canaan, heard that the Israelites were coming.

[41]They left Mount Hor and camped at Zalmonah.

[42]They left Zalmonah and camped at Punon.

[43]They left Punon and camped at Oboth.

[44]They left Oboth and camped at Iye Abarim, on the border of Moab.

[45]They left Iyim [c] and camped at Dibon Gad.

[46]They left Dibon Gad and camped at Almon Diblathaim.

[47]They left Almon Diblathaim and camped in the mountains of Abarim, near Nebo.

[48]They left the mountains of Abarim and camped on the plains of Moab by the Jordan across from Jericho. [d] [49]There on the plains of Moab they camped along the Jordan from Beth Jeshimoth to Abel Shittim.

[50]On the plains of Moab by the Jordan across from Jericho the LORD said to Moses,
[51]"Speak to the Israelites and say to them: 'When you cross the Jordan into Canaan,
[52]drive out all the inhabitants of the land be-

[a] *8* Many manuscripts of the Masoretic Text, Samaritan Pentateuch and Vulgate; most manuscripts of the Masoretic Text *left from before Hahiroth* [b] *10* Hebrew *Yam Suph*; that is, Sea of Reeds; also in verse 11 [c] *45* That is, Iye Abarim [d] *48* Hebrew *Jordan of Jericho*; possibly an ancient name for the Jordan River; also in verse 50

fore you. Destroy all their carved images and
their cast idols, and demolish all their high
places. 53Take possession of the land and settle in it, for I have given you the land to possess. 54Distribute the land by lot, according
to your clans. To a larger group give a larger
inheritance, and to a smaller group a smaller one. Whatever falls to them by lot will be
theirs. Distribute it according to your ancestral tribes.

55" 'But if you do not drive out the inhabitants of the land, those you allow to remain
will become barbs in your eyes and thorns in
your sides. They will give you trouble in the
land where you will live. 56And then I will do
to you what I plan to do to them.' "

Boundaries of Canaan

34 The LORD said to Moses, 2"Command
the Israelites and say to them: 'When
you enter Canaan, the land that will
be allotted to you as an inheritance will have
these boundaries:

3" 'Your southern side will include some of
the Desert of Zin along the border of Edom.
On the east, your southern boundary will start
from the end of the Salt Sea,[a] 4cross south of
Scorpion[b] Pass, continue on to Zin and go
south of Kadesh Barnea. Then it will go to
Hazar Addar and over to Azmon, 5where it
will turn, join the Wadi of Egypt and end at
the Sea.[c]

6" 'Your western boundary will be the coast
of the Great Sea. This will be your boundary
on the west.

7" 'For your northern boundary, run a
line from the Great Sea to Mount Hor 8and
from Mount Hor to Lebo[d] Hamath. Then
the boundary will go to Zedad, 9continue to
Ziphron and end at Hazar Enan. This will be
your boundary on the north.

10" 'For your eastern boundary, run a line
from Hazar Enan to Shepham. 11The boundary will go down from Shepham to Riblah on
the east side of Ain and continue along the
slopes east of the Sea of Kinnereth.[e] 12Then
the boundary will go down along the Jordan
and end at the Salt Sea.

" 'This will be your land, with its boundaries on every side.' "

13Moses commanded the Israelites: "Assign
this land by lot as an inheritance. The LORD
has ordered that it be given to the nine and a
half tribes, 14because the families of the tribe
of Reuben, the tribe of Gad and the half-tribe
of Manasseh have received their inheritance.
15These two and a half tribes have received
their inheritance on the east side of the Jordan
of Jericho,[f] toward the sunrise."

16The LORD said to Moses, 17"These are the
names of the men who are to assign the land
for you as an inheritance: Eleazar the priest
and Joshua son of Nun. 18And appoint one
leader from each tribe to help assign the land.
19These are their names:

Caleb son of Jephunneh,
from the tribe of Judah;
20 Shemuel son of Ammihud,
from the tribe of Simeon;
21 Elidad son of Kislon,
from the tribe of Benjamin;
22 Bukki son of Jogli,
the leader from the tribe of Dan;
23 Hanniel son of Ephod,
the leader from the tribe of Manasseh
son of Joseph;
24 Kemuel son of Shiphtan,
the leader from the tribe of Ephraim
son of Joseph;
25 Elizaphan son of Parnach,
the leader from the tribe of Zebulun;
26 Paltiel son of Azzan,
the leader from the tribe of Issachar;
27 Ahihud son of Shelomi,
the leader from the tribe of Asher;
28 Pedahel son of Ammihud,
the leader from the tribe of Naphtali."

29These are the men the LORD commanded
to assign the inheritance to the Israelites in the
land of Canaan.

Towns for the Levites

35 On the plains of Moab by the Jordan
across from Jericho,[g] the LORD said to
Moses, 2"Command the Israelites to
give the Levites towns to live in from the inheritance the Israelites will possess. And give
them pasturelands around the towns. 3Then
they will have towns to live in and pasturelands for their cattle, flocks and all their other
livestock.

4"The pasturelands around the towns that
you give the Levites will extend out fifteen
hundred feet[h] from the town wall. 5Outside
the town, measure three thousand feet[i] on the
east side, three thousand on the south side,

[a] 3 That is, the Dead Sea; also in verse 12 [b] 4 Hebrew *Akrabbim* [c] 5 That is, the Mediterranean; also in verses 6 and 7 [d] 8 Or *to the entrance to* [e] 11 That is, Galilee [f] 15 *Jordan of Jericho* was possibly an ancient name for the Jordan River. [g] 1 Hebrew *Jordan of Jericho*; possibly an ancient name for the Jordan River [h] 4 Hebrew *a thousand cubits* (about 450 meters) [i] 5 Hebrew *two thousand cubits* (about 900 meters)

W

WEDNESDAY
READ NUMBERS 33:50–56

PLANNING A MARRIAGE

In the months, weeks and days leading up to our wedding, we were blown away by the amount of work it took to pull off that single day of celebration. But we also remember the irony that struck us when we first started to settle into our new life together: besides a half dozen sessions of pre-marital counseling, we had done very little planning for our life beyond our first week together.

Now imagine for a moment the excitement of the Israelites who, after a 40-year journey, were finally preparing to enter the land long promised to them by God. God had led them through the desert, and now everything was culminating in this final conquest.

On the eve of this momentous invasion came a sobering message from God (see Numbers 33:50–54). God said that when his people took possession of the land, they were to run off the inhabitants of the land and destroy their religious symbols.

Why would God utter such harsh words and follow them up with such a harsh warning (see verses 55–56) in the middle of all the joy and excitement? The answer is simple: The Israelites' emotional excitement about moving into the promised land had made them nearsighted. They weren't thinking about ensuring their longevity and blessings in the beautiful land—they weren't thinking that far ahead.

God remained farsighted, however. And what he saw made him warn his children about the dangers that could have devastating effects on their devotion to him. God didn't advise the Israelites to just politely address the issue; he commanded them to deal with it violently and dramatically.

God is similarly farsighted on our behalf when it comes to marriage. When we join God in taking the long view of our marriage, we begin to see that amidst the excitement and joy of wedding festivities, we have a serious calling. We must address marital stumbling blocks such as bitterness over past hurts, dysfunctional relationships with our parents, critical attitudes, memories of sexual sins, or unhealthy habits and addictions. We need to meet those stumbling blocks head on.

One night our friend Sarah called us in tears. She had just found out that her husband, Michael, was addicted to Internet pornography. At first Sarah seriously considered separating from her husband. But over the next few weeks, she watched as Michael changed from a guilty, defeated, self-proclaimed loser into a warrior. With great courage, Michael took dramatic steps to fight his battle with pornography. He spoke frankly with his pastor and asked to be held accountable. He installed pornography-blocking software on his computer. And he began intensive professional Christian counseling every week.

A few months later, Sarah again called us in tears, but this time was different. "I love Michael so much more now than I ever did before," she said. "Seeing his courage and his passion to fight hard for our marriage has made us so much closer. I know this sounds corny, but I mean it: Now he truly is my knight in shining armor."

—DAVID AND KELLI TRUJILLO

"But if you do not drive out the inhabitants of the land, those you allow to remain will become barbs in your eyes and thorns in your sides. They will give you trouble in the land where you will live. And then I will do to you what I plan to do to them."

— NUMBERS 33:55–56

let's talk

- ✦ What are some potential stumbling blocks for us in our relationship? In what ways should we confront them?
- ✦ What are some of the unique challenges we face as a couple? Are there experiences or patterns from our past that might be threats to the health of our marriage?
- ✦ What dramatic action should we take to address these issues to ensure the longevity of our marriage?

FOR YOUR NEXT DEVOTIONAL READING, TURN TO PAGE 190.

three thousand on the west and three thousand on the north, with the town in the center. They will have this area as pastureland for the towns.

Cities of Refuge

6"Six of the towns you give the Levites will be cities of refuge, to which a person who has killed someone may flee. In addition, give them forty-two other towns. 7In all you must give the Levites forty-eight towns, together with their pasturelands. 8The towns you give the Levites from the land the Israelites possess are to be given in proportion to the inheritance of each tribe: Take many towns from a tribe that has many, but few from one that has few."

9Then the LORD said to Moses: 10"Speak to the Israelites and say to them: 'When you cross the Jordan into Canaan, 11select some towns to be your cities of refuge, to which a person who has killed someone accidentally may flee. 12They will be places of refuge from the avenger, so that a person accused of murder may not die before he stands trial before the assembly. 13These six towns you give will be your cities of refuge. 14Give three on this side of the Jordan and three in Canaan as cities of refuge. 15These six towns will be a place of refuge for Israelites, aliens and any other people living among them, so that anyone who has killed another accidentally can flee there.

16" 'If a man strikes someone with an iron object so that he dies, he is a murderer; the murderer shall be put to death. 17Or if anyone has a stone in his hand that could kill, and he strikes someone so that he dies, he is a murderer; the murderer shall be put to death. 18Or if anyone has a wooden object in his hand that could kill, and he hits someone so that he dies, he is a murderer; the murderer shall be put to death. 19The avenger of blood shall put the murderer to death; when he meets him, he shall put him to death. 20If anyone with malice aforethought shoves another or throws something at him intentionally so that he dies 21or if in hostility he hits him with his fist so that he dies, that person shall be put to death; he is a murderer. The avenger of blood shall put the murderer to death when he meets him.

22" 'But if without hostility someone suddenly shoves another or throws something at him unintentionally 23or, without seeing him, drops a stone on him that could kill him, and he dies, then since he was not his enemy and he did not intend to harm him, 24the assembly must judge between him and the avenger of blood according to these regulations. 25The assembly must protect the one accused of murder from the avenger of blood and send him back to the city of refuge to which he fled. He must stay there until the death of the high priest, who was anointed with the holy oil.

26" 'But if the accused ever goes outside the limits of the city of refuge to which he has fled 27and the avenger of blood finds him outside the city, the avenger of blood may kill the accused without being guilty of murder. 28The accused must stay in his city of refuge until the death of the high priest; only after the death of the high priest may he return to his own property.

29" 'These are to be legal requirements for you throughout the generations to come, wherever you live.

30" 'Anyone who kills a person is to be put to death as a murderer only on the testimony of witnesses. But no one is to be put to death on the testimony of only one witness.

31" 'Do not accept a ransom for the life of a murderer, who deserves to die. He must surely be put to death.

32" 'Do not accept a ransom for anyone who has fled to a city of refuge and so allow him to go back and live on his own land before the death of the high priest.

33" 'Do not pollute the land where you are. Bloodshed pollutes the land, and atonement cannot be made for the land on which blood has been shed, except by the blood of the one who shed it. 34Do not defile the land where you live and where I dwell, for I, the LORD, dwell among the Israelites.' "

Inheritance of Zelophehad's Daughters

36 The family heads of the clan of Gilead son of Makir, the son of Manasseh, who were from the clans of the descendants of Joseph, came and spoke before Moses and the leaders, the heads of the Israelite families. 2They said, "When the LORD commanded my lord to give the land as an inheritance to the Israelites by lot, he ordered you to give the inheritance of our brother Zelophehad to his daughters. 3Now suppose they marry men from other Israelite tribes; then their inheritance will be taken from our ancestral inheritance and added to that of the tribe they marry into. And so part of the inheritance allotted to us will be taken away. 4When the Year of Jubilee for the Israelites comes, their inheri-

tance will be added to that of the tribe into
which they marry, and their property will be
taken from the tribal inheritance of our forefathers."
5Then at the LORD's command Moses gave
this order to the Israelites: "What the tribe of
the descendants of Joseph is saying is right.
6This is what the LORD commands for Zelophehad's daughters: They may marry anyone
they please as long as they marry within the
tribal clan of their father. 7No inheritance in
Israel is to pass from tribe to tribe, for every
Israelite shall keep the tribal land inherited
from his forefathers. 8Every daughter who inherits land in any Israelite tribe must marry
someone in her father's tribal clan, so that every Israelite will possess the inheritance of his
fathers. 9No inheritance may pass from tribe
to tribe, for each Israelite tribe is to keep the
land it inherits."
10So Zelophehad's daughters did as the
LORD commanded Moses. 11Zelophehad's
daughters—Mahlah, Tirzah, Hoglah, Milcah
and Noah—married their cousins on their father's side. 12They married within the clans of
the descendants of Manasseh son of Joseph,
and their inheritance remained in their father's
clan and tribe.

13These are the commands and regulations
the LORD gave through Moses to the Israelites
on the plains of Moab by the Jordan across
from Jericho.[a]

---

a 13 Hebrew *Jordan of Jericho*; possibly an ancient name for the Jordan River

DEUTERONOMY

QUICK FACTS

AUTHOR Moses

AUDIENCE The people of Israel

DATE About 1406 B.C.

SETTING Front row seats to the promised land

The book of Deuteronomy is a collection of farewell speeches that Moses gave to the people of Israel. In these addresses he reviewed the history of Israel. He recited the laws given at Mount Sinai for worshiping God and living in community. He repeated detailed warnings against marriage violations, such as promiscuity and adultery, and discouraged easy divorce. He reminded the people of God's faithfulness and urged them to be obedient to God's commands.

The first four books of the Bible are about God choosing his people; Deuteronomy is about God challenging his people to choose him and his ways. Moses told them, "Keep his decrees and commands . . . that it may go well with you and your children after you and that you may live long in the land the LORD your God gives you for all time" (Deuteronomy 4:40).

Obedience is crucial for marriage today. We cannot fully live up to our promises to love, honor and submit to each other if we do not first obey God. As Moses said to his people, "Choose life, so that you and your children may live" (Deuteronomy 30:19).

The Command to Leave Horeb

1 These are the words Moses spoke to all Israel in the desert east of the Jordan—that
is, in the Arabah—opposite Suph, between
Paran and Tophel, Laban, Hazeroth and Diza-
hab. 2(It takes eleven days to go from Horeb to
Kadesh Barnea by the Mount Seir road.)
3In the fortieth year, on the first day of the
eleventh month, Moses proclaimed to the
Israelites all that the LORD had commanded him concerning them. 4This was after he
had defeated Sihon king of the Amorites, who
reigned in Heshbon, and at Edrei had defeated Og king of Bashan, who reigned in Ashtaroth.
5East of the Jordan in the territory of Moab,
Moses began to expound this law, saying:

6The LORD our God said to us at Horeb,
"You have stayed long enough at this mountain. 7Break camp and advance into the hill
country of the Amorites; go to all the neighboring peoples in the Arabah, in the mountains, in the western foothills, in the Negev and
along the coast, to the land of the Canaanites
and to Lebanon, as far as the great river, the
Euphrates. 8See, I have given you this land.
Go in and take possession of the land that the
LORD swore he would give to your fathers—to
Abraham, Isaac and Jacob—and to their descendants after them."

The Appointment of Leaders

9At that time I said to you, "You are too
heavy a burden for me to carry alone. 10The
LORD your God has increased your numbers
so that today you are as many as the stars in
the sky. 11May the LORD, the God of your fathers, increase you a thousand times and bless
you as he has promised! 12But how can I bear
your problems and your burdens and your disputes all by myself? 13Choose some wise, understanding and respected men from each of
your tribes, and I will set them over you."
14You answered me, "What you propose to
do is good."
15So I took the leading men of your tribes,
wise and respected men, and appointed them
to have authority over you—as commanders
of thousands, of hundreds, of fifties and of
tens and as tribal officials. 16And I charged
your judges at that time: Hear the disputes
between your brothers and judge fairly,
whether the case is between brother Israelites
or between one of them and an alien. 17Do
not show partiality in judging; hear both
small and great alike. Do not be afraid of any
man, for judgment belongs to God. Bring me
any case too hard for you, and I will hear it.
18And at that time I told you everything you
were to do.

Spies Sent Out

19Then, as the LORD our God commanded
us, we set out from Horeb and went toward
the hill country of the Amorites through all
that vast and dreadful desert that you have
seen, and so we reached Kadesh Barnea.
20Then I said to you, "You have reached the
hill country of the Amorites, which the LORD
our God is giving us. 21See, the LORD your
God has given you the land. Go up and take
possession of it as the LORD, the God of your
fathers, told you. Do not be afraid; do not be
discouraged."
22Then all of you came to me and said, "Let
us send men ahead to spy out the land for us
and bring back a report about the route we are
to take and the towns we will come to."
23The idea seemed good to me; so I selected twelve of you, one man from each tribe.
24They left and went up into the hill country,
and came to the Valley of Eshcol and explored
it. 25Taking with them some of the fruit of the
land, they brought it down to us and reported, "It is a good land that the LORD our God
is giving us."

Rebellion Against the LORD

26But you were unwilling to go up; you rebelled against the command of the LORD your
God. 27You grumbled in your tents and said,
"The LORD hates us; so he brought us out of
Egypt to deliver us into the hands of the Amorites to destroy us. 28Where can we go? Our
brothers have made us lose heart. They say,
'The people are stronger and taller than we are;
the cities are large, with walls up to the sky.
We even saw the Anakites there.' "
29Then I said to you, "Do not be terrified;
do not be afraid of them. 30The LORD your
God, who is going before you, will fight for
you, as he did for you in Egypt, before your
very eyes, 31and in the desert. There you saw
how the LORD your God carried you, as a father carries his son, all the way you went until
you reached this place."
32In spite of this, you did not trust in the
LORD your God, 33who went ahead of you on
your journey, in fire by night and in a cloud by
day, to search out places for you to camp and
to show you the way you should go.
34When the LORD heard what you said,
he was angry and solemnly swore: 35"Not a

man of this evil generation shall see the good
land I swore to give your forefathers, 36except
Caleb son of Jephunneh. He will see it, and I
will give him and his descendants the land he
set his feet on, because he followed the LORD
wholeheartedly."
37Because of you the LORD became angry
with me also and said, "You shall not enter
it, either. 38But your assistant, Joshua son of
Nun, will enter it. Encourage him, because
he will lead Israel to inherit it. 39And the little ones that you said would be taken captive,
your children who do not yet know good from
bad—they will enter the land. I will give it to
them and they will take possession of it. 40But
as for you, turn around and set out toward the
desert along the route to the Red Sea. [a]"
41Then you replied, "We have sinned
against the LORD. We will go up and fight, as
the LORD our God commanded us." So every
one of you put on his weapons, thinking it
easy to go up into the hill country.
42But the LORD said to me, "Tell them, 'Do
not go up and fight, because I will not be with
you. You will be defeated by your enemies.' "
43So I told you, but you would not listen.
You rebelled against the LORD's command
and in your arrogance you marched up into
the hill country. 44The Amorites who lived in
those hills came out against you; they chased
you like a swarm of bees and beat you down
from Seir all the way to Hormah. 45You came
back and wept before the LORD, but he paid
no attention to your weeping and turned a
deaf ear to you. 46And so you stayed in Kadesh
many days—all the time you spent there.

Wanderings in the Desert

2 Then we turned back and set out toward
the desert along the route to the Red Sea, [a]
as the LORD had directed me. For a long
time we made our way around the hill country of Seir.
2Then the LORD said to me, 3"You have
made your way around this hill country long
enough; now turn north. 4Give the people
these orders: 'You are about to pass through
the territory of your brothers the descendants
of Esau, who live in Seir. They will be afraid
of you, but be very careful. 5Do not provoke
them to war, for I will not give you any of
their land, not even enough to put your foot
on. I have given Esau the hill country of Seir
as his own. 6You are to pay them in silver for
the food you eat and the water you drink.' "
7The LORD your God has blessed you in all
the work of your hands. He has watched over
your journey through this vast desert. These
forty years the LORD your God has been with
you, and you have not lacked anything.
8So we went on past our brothers the descendants of Esau, who live in Seir. We turned
from the Arabah road, which comes up from
Elath and Ezion Geber, and traveled along the
desert road of Moab.
9Then the LORD said to me, "Do not harass the Moabites or provoke them to war, for
I will not give you any part of their land. I
have given Ar to the descendants of Lot as a
possession."
10(The Emites used to live there—a people strong and numerous, and as tall as the
Anakites. 11Like the Anakites, they too were
considered Rephaites, but the Moabites called
them Emites. 12Horites used to live in Seir,
but the descendants of Esau drove them out.
They destroyed the Horites from before them
and settled in their place, just as Israel did in
the land the LORD gave them as their possession.)
13And the LORD said, "Now get up and
cross the Zered Valley." So we crossed the valley.
14Thirty-eight years passed from the time
we left Kadesh Barnea until we crossed the
Zered Valley. By then, that entire generation
of fighting men had perished from the camp,
as the LORD had sworn to them. 15The LORD's
hand was against them until he had completely eliminated them from the camp.
16Now when the last of these fighting men
among the people had died, 17the LORD said
to me, 18"Today you are to pass by the region
of Moab at Ar. 19When you come to the Ammonites, do not harass them or provoke them
to war, for I will not give you possession of
any land belonging to the Ammonites. I have
given it as a possession to the descendants of
Lot."
20(That too was considered a land of the
Rephaites, who used to live there; but the Ammonites called them Zamzummites. 21They
were a people strong and numerous, and as
tall as the Anakites. The LORD destroyed them
from before the Ammonites, who drove them
out and settled in their place. 22The LORD had
done the same for the descendants of Esau,
who lived in Seir, when he destroyed the Horites from before them. They drove them out
and have lived in their place to this day. 23And

a 40,1 Hebrew *Yam Suph*; that is, Sea of Reeds

as for the Avvites who lived in villages as far
as Gaza, the Caphtorites coming out from
Caphtor[a] destroyed them and settled in their
place.)

Defeat of Sihon King of Heshbon

24“Set out now and cross the Arnon Gorge.
See, I have given into your hand Sihon the
Amorite, king of Heshbon, and his country.
Begin to take possession of it and engage him
in battle. 25This very day I will begin to put
the terror and fear of you on all the nations
under heaven. They will hear reports of you
and will tremble and be in anguish because of
you.”

26From the desert of Kedemoth I sent messengers to Sihon king of Heshbon offering
peace and saying, 27“Let us pass through your
country. We will stay on the main road; we
will not turn aside to the right or to the left.
28Sell us food to eat and water to drink for
their price in silver. Only let us pass through
on foot— 29as the descendants of Esau, who
live in Seir, and the Moabites, who live in Ar,
did for us—until we cross the Jordan into the
land the LORD our God is giving us.” 30But
Sihon king of Heshbon refused to let us pass
through. For the LORD your God had made
his spirit stubborn and his heart obstinate in
order to give him into your hands, as he has
now done.

31The LORD said to me, “See, I have begun
to deliver Sihon and his country over to you.
Now begin to conquer and possess his land.”

32When Sihon and all his army came out to
meet us in battle at Jahaz, 33the LORD our God
delivered him over to us and we struck him
down, together with his sons and his whole
army. 34At that time we took all his towns and
completely destroyed[b] them—men, wom-
en and children. We left no survivors. 35But
the livestock and the plunder from the towns
we had captured we carried off for ourselves.
36From Aroer on the rim of the Arnon Gorge,
and from the town in the gorge, even as far as
Gilead, not one town was too strong for us.
The LORD our God gave us all of them. 37But
in accordance with the command of the LORD
our God, you did not encroach on any of the
land of the Ammonites, neither the land along
the course of the Jabbok nor that around the
towns in the hills.

Defeat of Og King of Bashan

3 Next we turned and went up along the road
toward Bashan, and Og king of Bashan
with his whole army marched out to meet
us in battle at Edrei. 2The LORD said to me,
“Do not be afraid of him, for I have handed
him over to you with his whole army and his
land. Do to him what you did to Sihon king
of the Amorites, who reigned in Heshbon.”

3So the LORD our God also gave into our
hands Og king of Bashan and all his army. We
struck them down, leaving no survivors. 4At
that time we took all his cities. There was not
one of the sixty cities that we did not take from
them—the whole region of Argob, Og’s kingdom in Bashan. 5All these cities were fortified
with high walls and with gates and bars, and
there were also a great many unwalled villages.
6We completely destroyed[b] them, as we had
done with Sihon king of Heshbon, destroying[b] every city—men, women and children.
7But all the livestock and the plunder from
their cities we carried off for ourselves.

8So at that time we took from these two
kings of the Amorites the territory east of the
Jordan, from the Arnon Gorge as far as Mount
Hermon. 9(Hermon is called Sirion by the Sidonians; the Amorites call it Senir.) 10We took
all the towns on the plateau, and all Gilead,
and all Bashan as far as Salecah and Edrei,
towns of Og’s kingdom in Bashan. 11(Only
Og king of Bashan was left of the remnant of
the Rephaites. His bed[c] was made of iron and
was more than thirteen feet long and six feet
wide.[d] It is still in Rabbah of the Ammonites.)

Division of the Land

12Of the land that we took over at that time,
I gave the Reubenites and the Gadites the territory north of Aroer by the Arnon Gorge, including half the hill country of Gilead, together with its towns. 13The rest of Gilead and also
all of Bashan, the kingdom of Og, I gave to
the half-tribe of Manasseh. (The whole region
of Argob in Bashan used to be known as a land
of the Rephaites. 14Jair, a descendant of Manasseh, took the whole region of Argob as far
as the border of the Geshurites and the Maac-
athites; it was named after him, so that to this
day Bashan is called Havvoth Jair.[e]) 15And I
gave Gilead to Makir. 16But to the Reubenites
and the Gadites I gave the territory extending
from Gilead down to the Arnon Gorge (the

[a] *23* That is, Crete [b] *34,6* The Hebrew term refers to the irrevocable giving over of things or persons to the LORD, often by totally destroying them. [c] *11* Or *sarcophagus* [d] *11* Hebrew *nine cubits long and four cubits wide* (about 4 meters long and 1.8 meters wide)
[e] *14* Or *called the settlements of Jair*

middle of the gorge being the border) and out to the Jabbok River, which is the border of the Ammonites. [17]Its western border was the Jordan in the Arabah, from Kinnereth to the Sea of the Arabah (the Salt Sea[a]), below the slopes of Pisgah.

[18]I commanded you at that time: "The Lord your God has given you this land to take possession of it. But all your able-bodied men, armed for battle, must cross over ahead of your brother Israelites. [19]However, your wives, your children and your livestock (I know you have much livestock) may stay in the towns I have given you, [20]until the Lord gives rest to your brothers as he has to you, and they too have taken over the land that the Lord your God is giving them, across the Jordan. After that, each of you may go back to the possession I have given you."

Moses Forbidden to Cross the Jordan

[21]At that time I commanded Joshua: "You have seen with your own eyes all that the Lord your God has done to these two kings. The Lord will do the same to all the kingdoms over there where you are going. [22]Do not be afraid of them; the Lord your God himself will fight for you."

[23]At that time I pleaded with the Lord: [24]"O Sovereign Lord, you have begun to show to your servant your greatness and your strong hand. For what god is there in heaven or on earth who can do the deeds and mighty works you do? [25]Let me go over and see the good land beyond the Jordan—that fine hill country and Lebanon."

[26]But because of you the Lord was angry with me and would not listen to me. "That is enough," the Lord said. "Do not speak to me anymore about this matter. [27]Go up to the top of Pisgah and look west and north and south and east. Look at the land with your own eyes, since you are not going to cross this Jordan. [28]But commission Joshua, and encourage and strengthen him, for he will lead this people across and will cause them to inherit the land that you will see." [29]So we stayed in the valley near Beth Peor.

Obedience Commanded

4 Hear now, O Israel, the decrees and laws I am about to teach you. Follow them so that you may live and may go in and take possession of the land that the Lord, the God of your fathers, is giving you. [2]Do not add to what I command you and do not subtract from it, but keep the commands of the Lord your God that I give you.

[3]You saw with your own eyes what the Lord did at Baal Peor. The Lord your God destroyed from among you everyone who followed the Baal of Peor, [4]but all of you who held fast to the Lord your God are still alive today.

[5]See, I have taught you decrees and laws as the Lord my God commanded me, so that you may follow them in the land you are entering to take possession of it. [6]Observe them carefully, for this will show your wisdom and understanding to the nations, who will hear about all these decrees and say, "Surely this great nation is a wise and understanding people." [7]What other nation is so great as to have their gods near them the way the Lord our God is near us whenever we pray to him? [8]And what other nation is so great as to have such righteous decrees and laws as this body of laws I am setting before you today?

[9]Only be careful, and watch yourselves closely so that you do not forget the things your eyes have seen or let them slip from your heart as long as you live. Teach them to your children and to their children after them. [10]Remember the day you stood before the Lord your God at Horeb, when he said to me, "Assemble the people before me to hear my words so that they may learn to revere me as long as they live in the land and may teach them to their children." [11]You came near and stood at the foot of the mountain while it blazed with fire to the very heavens, with black clouds and deep darkness. [12]Then the Lord spoke to you out of the fire. You heard the sound of words but saw no form; there was only a voice. [13]He declared to you his covenant, the Ten Commandments, which he commanded you to follow and then wrote them on two stone tablets. [14]And the Lord directed me at that time to teach you the decrees and laws you are to follow in the land that you are crossing the Jordan to possess.

Idolatry Forbidden

[15]You saw no form of any kind the day the Lord spoke to you at Horeb out of the fire. Therefore watch yourselves very carefully, [16]so that you do not become corrupt and make for yourselves an idol, an image of any shape, whether formed like a man or a woman, [17]or like any animal on earth or any bird that flies in the air, [18]or like any creature that moves along

[a] *17* That is, the Dead Sea

the ground or any fish in the waters below. 19And when you look up to the sky and see the sun, the moon and the stars—all the heavenly array—do not be enticed into bowing down to them and worshiping things the LORD your God has apportioned to all the nations under heaven. 20But as for you, the LORD took you and brought you out of the iron-smelting furnace, out of Egypt, to be the people of his inheritance, as you now are.

21The LORD was angry with me because of you, and he solemnly swore that I would not cross the Jordan and enter the good land the LORD your God is giving you as your inheritance. 22I will die in this land; I will not cross the Jordan; but you are about to cross over and take possession of that good land. 23Be careful not to forget the covenant of the LORD your God that he made with you; do not make for yourselves an idol in the form of anything the LORD your God has forbidden. 24For the LORD your God is a consuming fire, a jealous God.

25After you have had children and grandchildren and have lived in the land a long time—if you then become corrupt and make any kind of idol, doing evil in the eyes of the LORD your God and provoking him to anger, 26I call heaven and earth as witnesses against you this day that you will quickly perish from the land that you are crossing the Jordan to possess. You will not live there long but will certainly be destroyed. 27The LORD will scatter you among the peoples, and only a few of you will survive among the nations to which the LORD will drive you. 28There you will worship man-made gods of wood and stone, which cannot see or hear or eat or smell. 29But if from there you seek the LORD your God, you will find him if you look for him with all your heart and with all your soul. 30When you are in distress and all these things have happened to you, then in later days you will return to the LORD your God and obey him. 31For the LORD your God is a merciful God; he will not abandon or destroy you or forget the covenant with your forefathers, which he confirmed to them by oath.

The LORD Is God

32Ask now about the former days, long before your time, from the day God created man on the earth; ask from one end of the heavens to the other. Has anything so great as this ever happened, or has anything like it ever been heard of? 33Has any other people heard the voice of God[a] speaking out of fire, as you have, and lived? 34Has any god ever tried to take for himself one nation out of another nation, by testings, by miraculous signs and wonders, by war, by a mighty hand and an outstretched arm, or by great and awesome deeds, like all the things the LORD your God did for you in Egypt before your very eyes?

35You were shown these things so that you might know that the LORD is God; besides him there is no other. 36From heaven he made you hear his voice to discipline you. On earth he showed you his great fire, and you heard his words from out of the fire. 37Because he loved your forefathers and chose their descendants after them, he brought you out of Egypt by his Presence and his great strength, 38to drive out before you nations greater and stronger than you and to bring you into their land to give it to you for your inheritance, as it is today.

39Acknowledge and take to heart this day that the LORD is God in heaven above and on the earth below. There is no other. 40Keep his decrees and commands, which I am giving you today, so that it may go well with you and your children after you and that you may live long in the land the LORD your God gives you for all time.

Cities of Refuge

41Then Moses set aside three cities east of the Jordan, 42to which anyone who had killed a person could flee if he had unintentionally killed his neighbor without malice aforethought. He could flee into one of these cities and save his life. 43The cities were these: Bezer in the desert plateau, for the Reubenites; Ramoth in Gilead, for the Gadites; and Golan in Bashan, for the Manassites.

Introduction to the Law

44This is the law Moses set before the Israelites. 45These are the stipulations, decrees and laws Moses gave them when they came out of Egypt 46and were in the valley near Beth Peor east of the Jordan, in the land of Sihon king of the Amorites, who reigned in Heshbon and was defeated by Moses and the Israelites as they came out of Egypt. 47They took possession of his land and the land of Og king of Bashan, the two Amorite kings east of the Jordan. 48This land extended from Aroer on the rim of the Arnon Gorge to Mount Siyon[b] (that is, Hermon), 49and included all the Arabah east of the Jordan, as far as the Sea of the Arabah,[c] below the slopes of Pisgah.

---

[a] 33 Or *of a god* [b] 48 Hebrew; Syriac (see also Deut. 3:9) *Sirion* [c] 49 That is, the Dead Sea

The Ten Commandments

5 Moses summoned all Israel and said:
Hear, O Israel, the decrees and laws I declare in your hearing today. Learn them
and be sure to follow them. 2The LORD our
God made a covenant with us at Horeb. 3It
was not with our fathers that the LORD made
this covenant, but with us, with all of us who
are alive here today. 4The LORD spoke to you
face to face out of the fire on the mountain.
5(At that time I stood between the LORD and
you to declare to you the word of the LORD,
because you were afraid of the fire and did not
go up the mountain.) And he said:

6"I am the LORD your God, who
brought you out of Egypt, out of
the land of slavery.
7"You shall have no other gods before[a] me.
8"You shall not make for yourself an idol
in the form of anything in heaven
above or on the earth beneath or in
the waters below. 9You shall not bow
down to them or worship them; for
I, the LORD your God, am a jealous
God, punishing the children for the
sin of the fathers to the third and
fourth generation of those who hate
me, 10but showing love to a thousand ⌊generations⌋ of those who love
me and keep my commandments.
11"You shall not misuse the name of the
LORD your God, for the LORD will
not hold anyone guiltless who misuses his name.
12"Observe the Sabbath day by keeping
it holy, as the LORD your God has
commanded you. 13Six days you
shall labor and do all your work,
14but the seventh day is a Sabbath
to the LORD your God. On it you
shall not do any work, neither you,
nor your son or daughter, nor your
manservant or maidservant, nor
your ox, your donkey or any of your
animals, nor the alien within your
gates, so that your manservant and
maidservant may rest, as you do.
15Remember that you were slaves
in Egypt and that the LORD your
God brought you out of there with
a mighty hand and an outstretched
arm. Therefore the LORD your God
has commanded you to observe the
Sabbath day.
16"Honor your father and your mother, as
the LORD your God has command-
ed you, so that you may live long
and that it may go well with you in
the land the LORD your God is giving you.
17"You shall not murder.
18"You shall not commit adultery.
19"You shall not steal.
20"You shall not give false testimony against
your neighbor.
21"You shall not covet your neighbor's wife.
You shall not set your desire on your
neighbor's house or land, his manservant or maidservant, his ox or
donkey, or anything that belongs to
your neighbor."

22These are the commandments the LORD
proclaimed in a loud voice to your whole assembly there on the mountain from out of the
fire, the cloud and the deep darkness; and he
added nothing more. Then he wrote them on
two stone tablets and gave them to me.

23When you heard the voice out of the
darkness, while the mountain was ablaze with
fire, all the leading men of your tribes and
your elders came to me. 24And you said, "The
LORD our God has shown us his glory and
his majesty, and we have heard his voice from
the fire. Today we have seen that a man can
live even if God speaks with him. 25But now,
why should we die? This great fire will consume us, and we will die if we hear the voice
of the LORD our God any longer. 26For what
mortal man has ever heard the voice of the
living God speaking out of fire, as we have,
and survived? 27Go near and listen to all that
the LORD our God says. Then tell us whatever
the LORD our God tells you. We will listen
and obey."

28The LORD heard you when you spoke to
me and the LORD said to me, "I have heard
what this people said to you. Everything they
said was good. 29Oh, that their hearts would
be inclined to fear me and keep all my commands always, so that it might go well with
them and their children forever!

30"Go, tell them to return to their tents.
31But you stay here with me so that I may give
you all the commands, decrees and laws you
are to teach them to follow in the land I am
giving them to possess."

32So be careful to do what the LORD your
God has commanded you; do not turn aside
to the right or to the left. 33Walk in all the

[a] 7 Or *besides*

way that the LORD your God has commanded you, so that you may live and prosper and
prolong your days in the land that you will
possess.

Love the LORD Your God

6 These are the commands, decrees and laws
the LORD your God directed me to teach
you to observe in the land that you are
crossing the Jordan to possess, 2so that you,
your children and their children after them
may fear the LORD your God as long as you
live by keeping all his decrees and commands
that I give you, and so that you may enjoy long
life. 3Hear, O Israel, and be careful to obey so
that it may go well with you and that you may
increase greatly in a land flowing with milk
and honey, just as the LORD, the God of your
fathers, promised you.
4Hear, O Israel: The LORD our God, the
LORD is one.[a] 5Love the LORD your God with
all your heart and with all your soul and with
all your strength. 6These commandments that
I give you today are to be upon your hearts.
7Impress them on your children. Talk about
them when you sit at home and when you
walk along the road, when you lie down and
when you get up. 8Tie them as symbols on
your hands and bind them on your foreheads.
9Write them on the doorframes of your houses
and on your gates.
10When the LORD your God brings you
into the land he swore to your fathers, to
Abraham, Isaac and Jacob, to give you—a
land with large, flourishing cities you did not
build, 11houses filled with all kinds of good
things you did not provide, wells you did not
dig, and vineyards and olive groves you did
not plant—then when you eat and are satisfied, 12be careful that you do not forget the
LORD, who brought you out of Egypt, out of
the land of slavery.
13Fear the LORD your God, serve him only
and take your oaths in his name. 14Do not follow other gods, the gods of the peoples around
you; 15for the LORD your God, who is among
you, is a jealous God and his anger will burn
against you, and he will destroy you from the
face of the land. 16Do not test the LORD your
God as you did at Massah. 17Be sure to keep
the commands of the LORD your God and
the stipulations and decrees he has given you.
18Do what is right and good in the LORD's
sight, so that it may go well with you and you
may go in and take over the good land that the
LORD promised on oath to your forefathers,
19thrusting out all your enemies before you, as
the LORD said.
20In the future, when your son asks you,
"What is the meaning of the stipulations, decrees and laws the LORD our God has commanded you?" 21tell him: "We were slaves of
Pharaoh in Egypt, but the LORD brought us
out of Egypt with a mighty hand. 22Before our
eyes the LORD sent miraculous signs and wonders—great and terrible—upon Egypt and
Pharaoh and his whole household. 23But he
brought us out from there to bring us in and
give us the land that he promised on oath to
our forefathers. 24The LORD commanded us to
obey all these decrees and to fear the LORD our
God, so that we might always prosper and be
kept alive, as is the case today. 25And if we are
careful to obey all this law before the LORD
our God, as he has commanded us, that will
be our righteousness."

Driving Out the Nations

7 When the LORD your God brings you into
the land you are entering to possess and
drives out before you many nations—the
Hittites, Girgashites, Amorites, Canaanites,
Perizzites, Hivites and Jebusites, seven nations larger and stronger than you— 2and
when the LORD your God has delivered them
over to you and you have defeated them,
then you must destroy them totally.[b] Make
no treaty with them, and show them no mercy. 3Do not intermarry with them. Do not
give your daughters to their sons or take their
daughters for your sons, 4for they will turn
your sons away from following me to serve
other gods, and the LORD's anger will burn
against you and will quickly destroy you.
5This is what you are to do to them: Break
down their altars, smash their sacred stones,
cut down their Asherah poles[c] and burn their
idols in the fire. 6For you are a people holy
to the LORD your God. The LORD your God
has chosen you out of all the peoples on the
face of the earth to be his people, his treasured possession.
7The LORD did not set his affection on you
and choose you because you were more numerous than other peoples, for you were the
fewest of all peoples. 8But it was because the
LORD loved you and kept the oath he swore
to your forefathers that he brought you out

[a] 4 Or *The LORD our God is one LORD*; or *The LORD is our God, the LORD is one*; or *The LORD is our God, the LORD alone*
[b] 2 The Hebrew term refers to the irrevocable giving over of things or persons to the LORD, often by totally destroying them; also in verse 26. [c] 5 That is, symbols of the goddess Asherah; here and elsewhere in Deuteronomy

THURSDAY
READ DEUTERONOMY 7:1–11

TAKE-IT-OR-LEAVE-IT ADVICE

> **The Lord did not set his affection on you and choose you because you were more numerous than other peoples, for you were the fewest of all peoples. But it was because the Lord loved you and kept the oath he swore to your forefathers . . .**
>
> — Deuteronomy 7:7–8

Before we got married, we received a lot of advice from friends and family, and we read a lot of books on marriage that offered counsel—how to keep the romance alive, how to handle finances, how to define success in marriage, how to deal with conflict, and even detailed suggestions about how to approach the wedding night. Some of the advice was good and some of it was . . . not.

Let's be honest: almost everyone feels the urge to offer engaged couples wisdom on marriage, even if it's unwanted. For me (Kelli), my views on marriage were influenced most significantly by two people who didn't share their opinions in words. During our wedding ceremony, I looked at my parents, who had been faithfully committed to one another for 30 years. Their example was the most powerful statement about marriage in my life.

If you're looking for advice on marriage, God's Word contains the best information and advice. And God's unconditional, enduring love and commitment to his people is a great model for human marriage. It is the most profound example we could ever look to. It trumps even the best marriage advice. It is amazing to think about God's unswerving commitment to his people as a model for marriage.

Throughout Scripture, God's relationship with his people is described in beautiful and poetic language. For example, God's words to the Israelites in Deuteronomy 7:6–9 are riddled with phrases reminiscent of marriage: The Israelites were a "people holy [set apart] to the Lord" (verse 6). God "set his affection on [them]" (verse 7) and chose them (see verse 7). He "loved [them] and kept the oath he swore" (verse 8). And they were to know that God is "the faithful God" (verse 9). Look at some of the other marriage talk in the Bible: we are the "bride" of Christ (Revelation 19:7), and we will celebrate the "wedding supper of the Lamb" in heaven (Revelation 19:9).

A good, healthy marriage can reveal the depth of God's love for us in profound and even overwhelming ways. We were struck by this truth when we had a double date with our church friends Willis and Betty. This wasn't your normal double date; it involved watching a rather cheesy video and having a hymn-sing with an accordion. You see, Willis and Betty were in their 90s; they had been married for more than 70 years. As we watched them finish each other's sentences, chuckle with laughter together, and give each other a light kiss on the cheek, we came away with a revolutionized understanding of romance. This was real love—this was the way God loves. It was determined, unwavering love for a lifetime . . . and beyond.

Whether you've been married for 70 years or just 70 days, your earthly marriage can serve as a concrete example of God's passionate and determined commitment to his people.

Want some good marriage advice? Seek to love your spouse the way God loves you.

—DAVID AND KELLI TRUJILLO

let's *talk*

- ✦ How does marriage between a man and a woman illustrate the relationship between God and his people? Whose marriage has been a profound example for us?
- ✦ What are some ways that our marriage reflects God's attitude toward his people? What are some ways that our commitment doesn't reflect this?
- ✦ How will we personally commit to love each other in a way that reflects God's love for his people?

FOR YOUR NEXT DEVOTIONAL READING, TURN TO PAGE 198.

with a mighty hand and redeemed you from the land of slavery, from the power of Pharaoh king of Egypt. 9Know therefore that the LORD your God is God; he is the faithful God, keeping his covenant of love to a thousand generations of those who love him and keep his commands. 10But

those who hate him he will repay to their
face by destruction;
he will not be slow to repay to their
face those who hate him.

11Therefore, take care to follow the commands, decrees and laws I give you today.

12If you pay attention to these laws and are careful to follow them, then the LORD your God will keep his covenant of love with you, as he swore to your forefathers. 13He will love you and bless you and increase your numbers. He will bless the fruit of your womb, the crops of your land—your grain, new wine and oil—the calves of your herds and the lambs of your flocks in the land that he swore to your forefathers to give you. 14You will be blessed more than any other people; none of your men or women will be childless, nor any of your livestock without young. 15The LORD will keep you free from every disease. He will not inflict on you the horrible diseases you knew in Egypt, but he will inflict them on all who hate you. 16You must destroy all the peoples the LORD your God gives over to you. Do not look on them with pity and do not serve their gods, for that will be a snare to you.

17You may say to yourselves, "These nations are stronger than we are. How can we drive them out?" 18But do not be afraid of them; remember well what the LORD your God did to Pharaoh and to all Egypt. 19You saw with your own eyes the great trials, the miraculous signs and wonders, the mighty hand and outstretched arm, with which the LORD your God brought you out. The LORD your God will do the same to all the peoples you now fear. 20Moreover, the LORD your God will send the hornet among them until even the survivors who hide from you have perished. 21Do not be terrified by them, for the LORD your God, who is among you, is a great and awesome God. 22The LORD your God will drive out those nations before you, little by little. You will not be allowed to eliminate them all at once, or the wild animals will multiply around you. 23But the LORD your God will deliver them over to you, throwing them into great confusion until they are destroyed. 24He will give their kings into your hand, and you will wipe out their names from under heaven. No one will be able to stand up against you; you will destroy them. 25The images of their gods you are to burn in the fire. Do not covet the silver and gold on them, and do not take it for yourselves, or you will be ensnared by it, for it is detestable to the LORD your God. 26Do not bring a detestable thing into your house or you, like it, will be set apart for destruction. Utterly abhor and detest it, for it is set apart for destruction.

Do Not Forget the LORD

8 Be careful to follow every command I am giving you today, so that you may live and increase and may enter and possess the land that the LORD promised on oath to your forefathers. 2Remember how the LORD your God led you all the way in the desert these forty years, to humble you and to test you in order to know what was in your heart, whether or not you would keep his commands. 3He humbled you, causing you to hunger and then feeding you with manna, which neither you nor your fathers had known, to teach you that man does not live on bread alone but on every word that comes from the mouth of the LORD. 4Your clothes did not wear out and your feet did not swell during these forty years. 5Know then in your heart that as a man disciplines his son, so the LORD your God disciplines you.

6Observe the commands of the LORD your God, walking in his ways and revering him. 7For the LORD your God is bringing you into a good land—a land with streams and pools of water, with springs flowing in the valleys and hills; 8a land with wheat and barley, vines and fig trees, pomegranates, olive oil and honey; 9a land where bread will not be scarce and you will lack nothing; a land where the rocks are iron and you can dig copper out of the hills.

10When you have eaten and are satisfied, praise the LORD your God for the good land he has given you. 11Be careful that you do not forget the LORD your God, failing to observe his commands, his laws and his decrees that I am giving you this day. 12Otherwise, when you eat and are satisfied, when you build fine houses and settle down, 13and when your herds and flocks grow large and your silver and gold increase and all you have is multiplied, 14then your heart will become proud and you will forget the LORD your God, who brought you out of Egypt, out of the land of slavery. 15He led you through the vast and dreadful desert, that thirsty and waterless land, with its venomous snakes and scorpions. He brought you water out of hard rock. 16He gave you manna to eat in the desert, something your fathers had never known, to humble and to test you so that in the end it might go well with you. 17You may say to yourself, "My power and the strength of my hands have produced this wealth for me." 18But remember the LORD your God, for it is he who gives you the ability to produce wealth, and so confirms his covenant, which he swore to your forefathers, as it is today.

19If you ever forget the LORD your God and follow other gods and worship and bow down to them, I testify against you today that you will surely be destroyed. 20Like the nations the LORD destroyed before you, so you will be destroyed for not obeying the LORD your God.

Not Because of Israel's Righteousness

9 Hear, O Israel. You are now about to cross the Jordan to go in and dispossess nations greater and stronger than you, with large cities that have walls up to the sky. 2The people are strong and tall—Anakites! You know about them and have heard it said: "Who can stand up against the Anakites?" 3But be assured today that the LORD your God is the one who goes across ahead of you like a devouring fire. He will destroy them; he will subdue them before you. And you will drive them out and annihilate them quickly, as the LORD has promised you.

4After the LORD your God has driven them out before you, do not say to yourself, "The LORD has brought me here to take possession of this land because of my righteousness." No, it is on account of the wickedness of these nations that the LORD is going to drive them out before you. 5It is not because of your righteousness or your integrity that you are going in to take possession of their land; but on account of the wickedness of these nations, the LORD your God will drive them out before you, to accomplish what he swore to your fathers, to Abraham, Isaac and Jacob. 6Understand, then, that it is not because of your righteousness that the LORD your God is giving you this good land to possess, for you are a stiff-necked people.

The Golden Calf

7Remember this and never forget how you provoked the LORD your God to anger in the desert. From the day you left Egypt until you arrived here, you have been rebellious against the LORD. 8At Horeb you aroused the LORD's wrath so that he was angry enough to destroy you. 9When I went up on the mountain to receive the tablets of stone, the tablets of the covenant that the LORD had made with you, I stayed on the mountain forty days and forty nights; I ate no bread and drank no water. 10The LORD gave me two stone tablets inscribed by the finger of God. On them were all the commandments the LORD proclaimed to you on the mountain out of the fire, on the day of the assembly.

11At the end of the forty days and forty nights, the LORD gave me the two stone tablets, the tablets of the covenant. 12Then the LORD told me, "Go down from here at once, because your people whom you brought out of Egypt have become corrupt. They have turned away quickly from what I commanded them and have made a cast idol for themselves."

13And the LORD said to me, "I have seen this people, and they are a stiff-necked people indeed! 14Let me alone, so that I may destroy them and blot out their name from under heaven. And I will make you into a nation stronger and more numerous than they."

15So I turned and went down from the mountain while it was ablaze with fire. And the two tablets of the covenant were in my hands.[a] 16When I looked, I saw that you had sinned against the LORD your God; you had made for yourselves an idol cast in the shape of a calf. You had turned aside quickly from the way that the LORD had commanded you. 17So I took the two tablets and threw them out of my hands, breaking them to pieces before your eyes.

18Then once again I fell prostrate before the LORD for forty days and forty nights; I ate no bread and drank no water, because of all the sin you had committed, doing what was evil in the LORD's sight and so provoking him to anger. 19I feared the anger and wrath of the LORD, for he was angry enough with you to destroy you. But again the LORD listened to me. 20And the LORD was angry enough with Aaron to destroy him, but at that time I prayed for Aaron too. 21Also I took that sinful thing of yours, the calf you had made, and burned it in the fire. Then I crushed it and ground it to powder as fine as dust and threw the dust into a stream that flowed down the mountain.

22You also made the LORD angry at Taberah, at Massah and at Kibroth Hattaavah.

---

[a] 15 Or *And I had the two tablets of the covenant with me, one in each hand*

23And when the LORD sent you out from
Kadesh Barnea, he said, "Go up and take possession of the land I have given you." But you
rebelled against the command of the LORD
your God. You did not trust him or obey him.
24You have been rebellious against the LORD
ever since I have known you.

25I lay prostrate before the LORD those forty
days and forty nights because the LORD had
said he would destroy you. 26I prayed to the
LORD and said, "O Sovereign LORD, do not
destroy your people, your own inheritance
that you redeemed by your great power and
brought out of Egypt with a mighty hand.
27Remember your servants Abraham, Isaac
and Jacob. Overlook the stubbornness of this
people, their wickedness and their sin. 28Oth-
erwise, the country from which you brought
us will say, 'Because the LORD was not able
to take them into the land he had promised
them, and because he hated them, he brought
them out to put them to death in the desert.'
29But they are your people, your inheritance
that you brought out by your great power and
your outstretched arm."

Tablets Like the First Ones

10 At that time the LORD said to me, "Chisel out two stone tablets like the first ones
and come up to me on the mountain.
Also make a wooden chest.[a] 2I will write on
the tablets the words that were on the first
tablets, which you broke. Then you are to put
them in the chest."

3So I made the ark out of acacia wood and
chiseled out two stone tablets like the first ones,
and I went up on the mountain with the two
tablets in my hands. 4The LORD wrote on these
tablets what he had written before, the Ten
Commandments he had proclaimed to you
on the mountain, out of the fire, on the day of
the assembly. And the LORD gave them to me.
5Then I came back down the mountain and put
the tablets in the ark I had made, as the LORD
commanded me, and they are there now.

6(The Israelites traveled from the wells of
the Jaakanites to Moserah. There Aaron died
and was buried, and Eleazar his son succeeded him as priest. 7From there they traveled to
Gudgodah and on to Jotbathah, a land with
streams of water. 8At that time the LORD set
apart the tribe of Levi to carry the ark of the
covenant of the LORD, to stand before the
LORD to minister and to pronounce blessings
in his name, as they still do today. 9That is
why the Levites have no share or inheritance
among their brothers; the LORD is their inheritance, as the LORD your God told them.)

10Now I had stayed on the mountain forty
days and nights, as I did the first time, and the
LORD listened to me at this time also. It was
not his will to destroy you. 11"Go," the LORD
said to me, "and lead the people on their way,
so that they may enter and possess the land
that I swore to their fathers to give them."

Fear the LORD

12And now, O Israel, what does the LORD
your God ask of you but to fear the LORD your
God, to walk in all his ways, to love him, to
serve the LORD your God with all your heart
and with all your soul, 13and to observe the
LORD's commands and decrees that I am giving you today for your own good?

14To the LORD your God belong the heavens, even the highest heavens, the earth and
everything in it. 15Yet the LORD set his affection on your forefathers and loved them, and
he chose you, their descendants, above all
the nations, as it is today. 16Circumcise your
hearts, therefore, and do not be stiff-necked
any longer. 17For the LORD your God is God
of gods and Lord of lords, the great God,
mighty and awesome, who shows no partiality
and accepts no bribes. 18He defends the cause
of the fatherless and the widow, and loves the
alien, giving him food and clothing. 19And
you are to love those who are aliens, for you
yourselves were aliens in Egypt. 20Fear the
LORD your God and serve him. Hold fast to
him and take your oaths in his name. 21He is
your praise; he is your God, who performed
for you those great and awesome wonders you
saw with your own eyes. 22Your forefathers
who went down into Egypt were seventy in
all, and now the LORD your God has made
you as numerous as the stars in the sky.

Love and Obey the LORD

11 Love the LORD your God and keep his
requirements, his decrees, his laws and
his commands always. 2Remember today that your children were not the ones who
saw and experienced the discipline of the LORD
your God: his majesty, his mighty hand, his
outstretched arm; 3the signs he performed and
the things he did in the heart of Egypt, both to
Pharaoh king of Egypt and to his whole country; 4what he did to the Egyptian army, to
its horses and chariots, how he overwhelmed

a 1 That is, an ark

them with the waters of the Red Sea[a] as they were pursuing you, and how the LORD brought lasting ruin on them. 5It was not your children who saw what he did for you in the desert until you arrived at this place, 6and what he did to Dathan and Abiram, sons of Eliab the Reubenite, when the earth opened its mouth right in the middle of all Israel and swallowed them up with their households, their tents and every living thing that belonged to them. 7But it was your own eyes that saw all these great things the LORD has done.

8Observe therefore all the commands I am giving you today, so that you may have the strength to go in and take over the land that you are crossing the Jordan to possess, 9and so that you may live long in the land that the LORD swore to your forefathers to give to them and their descendants, a land flowing with milk and honey. 10The land you are entering to take over is not like the land of Egypt, from which you have come, where you planted your seed and irrigated it by foot as in a vegetable garden. 11But the land you are crossing the Jordan to take possession of is a land of mountains and valleys that drinks rain from heaven. 12It is a land the LORD your God cares for; the eyes of the LORD your God are continually on it from the beginning of the year to its end.

13So if you faithfully obey the commands I am giving you today—to love the LORD your God and to serve him with all your heart and with all your soul— 14then I will send rain on your land in its season, both autumn and spring rains, so that you may gather in your grain, new wine and oil. 15I will provide grass in the fields for your cattle, and you will eat and be satisfied.

16Be careful, or you will be enticed to turn away and worship other gods and bow down to them. 17Then the LORD's anger will burn against you, and he will shut the heavens so that it will not rain and the ground will yield no produce, and you will soon perish from the good land the LORD is giving you. 18Fix these words of mine in your hearts and minds; tie them as symbols on your hands and bind them on your foreheads. 19Teach them to your children, talking about them when you sit at home and when you walk along the road, when you lie down and when you get up. 20Write them on the doorframes of your houses and on your gates, 21so that your days and the days of your children may be many in the land that the LORD swore to give your forefathers, as many as the days that the heavens are above the earth.

22If you carefully observe all these commands I am giving you to follow—to love the LORD your God, to walk in all his ways and to hold fast to him— 23then the LORD will drive out all these nations before you, and you will dispossess nations larger and stronger than you. 24Every place where you set your foot will be yours: Your territory will extend from the desert to Lebanon, and from the Euphrates River to the western sea.[b] 25No man will be able to stand against you. The LORD your God, as he promised you, will put the terror and fear of you on the whole land, wherever you go.

26See, I am setting before you today a blessing and a curse— 27the blessing if you obey the commands of the LORD your God that I am giving you today; 28the curse if you disobey the commands of the LORD your God and turn from the way that I command you today by following other gods, which you have not known. 29When the LORD your God has brought you into the land you are entering to possess, you are to proclaim on Mount Gerizim the blessings, and on Mount Ebal the curses. 30As you know, these mountains are across the Jordan, west of the road,[c] toward the setting sun, near the great trees of Moreh, in the territory of those Canaanites living in the Arabah in the vicinity of Gilgal. 31You are about to cross the Jordan to enter and take possession of the land the LORD your God is giving you. When you have taken it over and are living there, 32be sure that you obey all the decrees and laws I am setting before you today.

The One Place of Worship

12 These are the decrees and laws you must be careful to follow in the land that the LORD, the God of your fathers, has given you to possess—as long as you live in the land. 2Destroy completely all the places on the high mountains and on the hills and under every spreading tree where the nations you are dispossessing worship their gods. 3Break down their altars, smash their sacred stones and burn their Asherah poles in the fire; cut down the idols of their gods and wipe out their names from those places.

4You must not worship the LORD your God in their way. 5But you are to seek the place the LORD your God will choose from among all your tribes to put his Name there for his dwelling. To that place you must go; 6there

[a] 4 Hebrew *Yam Suph*; that is, Sea of Reeds [b] 24 That is, the Mediterranean [c] 30 Or *Jordan, westward*

bring your burnt offerings and sacrifices, your
tithes and special gifts, what you have vowed
to give and your freewill offerings, and the
firstborn of your herds and flocks. 7There, in
the presence of the LORD your God, you and
your families shall eat and shall rejoice in everything you have put your hand to, because
the LORD your God has blessed you.

8You are not to do as we do here today, everyone as he sees fit, 9since you have not yet
reached the resting place and the inheritance
the LORD your God is giving you. 10But you
will cross the Jordan and settle in the land
the LORD your God is giving you as an inheritance, and he will give you rest from all
your enemies around you so that you will live
in safety. 11Then to the place the LORD your
God will choose as a dwelling for his Name—
there you are to bring everything I command
you: your burnt offerings and sacrifices, your
tithes and special gifts, and all the choice possessions you have vowed to the LORD. 12And
there rejoice before the LORD your God, you,
your sons and daughters, your menservants
and maidservants, and the Levites from your
towns, who have no allotment or inheritance
of their own. 13Be careful not to sacrifice your
burnt offerings anywhere you please. 14Offer
them only at the place the LORD will choose
in one of your tribes, and there observe everything I command you.

15Nevertheless, you may slaughter your animals in any of your towns and eat as much of
the meat as you want, as if it were gazelle or
deer, according to the blessing the LORD your
God gives you. Both the ceremonially unclean
and the clean may eat it. 16But you must not
eat the blood; pour it out on the ground like
water. 17You must not eat in your own towns
the tithe of your grain and new wine and oil,
or the firstborn of your herds and flocks, or
whatever you have vowed to give, or your freewill offerings or special gifts. 18Instead, you
are to eat them in the presence of the LORD
your God at the place the LORD your God will
choose—you, your sons and daughters, your
menservants and maidservants, and the Levites from your towns—and you are to rejoice
before the LORD your God in everything you
put your hand to. 19Be careful not to neglect
the Levites as long as you live in your land.

20When the LORD your God has enlarged
your territory as he promised you, and you
crave meat and say, "I would like some meat,"
then you may eat as much of it as you want.
21If the place where the LORD your God chooses to put his Name is too far away from you,
you may slaughter animals from the herds and
flocks the LORD has given you, as I have commanded you, and in your own towns you may
eat as much of them as you want. 22Eat them
as you would gazelle or deer. Both the ceremonially unclean and the clean may eat. 23But
be sure you do not eat the blood, because the
blood is the life, and you must not eat the life
with the meat. 24You must not eat the blood;
pour it out on the ground like water. 25Do not
eat it, so that it may go well with you and your
children after you, because you will be doing
what is right in the eyes of the LORD.

26But take your consecrated things and
whatever you have vowed to give, and go to
the place the LORD will choose. 27Present your
burnt offerings on the altar of the LORD your
God, both the meat and the blood. The blood
of your sacrifices must be poured beside the
altar of the LORD your God, but you may eat
the meat. 28Be careful to obey all these regulations I am giving you, so that it may always
go well with you and your children after you,
because you will be doing what is good and
right in the eyes of the LORD your God.

29The LORD your God will cut off before
you the nations you are about to invade and
dispossess. But when you have driven them
out and settled in their land, 30and after they
have been destroyed before you, be careful
not to be ensnared by inquiring about their
gods, saying, "How do these nations serve
their gods? We will do the same." 31You must
not worship the LORD your God in their way,
because in worshiping their gods, they do all
kinds of detestable things the LORD hates.
They even burn their sons and daughters in
the fire as sacrifices to their gods.

32See that you do all I command you; do
not add to it or take away from it.

Worshiping Other Gods

13 If a prophet, or one who foretells by
dreams, appears among you and announces to you a miraculous sign or
wonder, 2and if the sign or wonder of which
he has spoken takes place, and he says, "Let us
follow other gods" (gods you have not known)
"and let us worship them," 3you must not listen to the words of that prophet or dreamer.
The LORD your God is testing you to find out
whether you love him with all your heart and
with all your soul. 4It is the LORD your God
you must follow, and him you must revere.
Keep his commands and obey him; serve him
and hold fast to him. 5That prophet or dreamer must be put to death, because he preached

rebellion against the LORD your God, who
brought you out of Egypt and redeemed you
from the land of slavery; he has tried to turn
you from the way the LORD your God commanded you to follow. You must purge the
evil from among you.
6If your very own brother, or your son or
daughter, or the wife you love, or your closest friend secretly entices you, saying, "Let us
go and worship other gods" (gods that neither
you nor your fathers have known, 7gods of
the peoples around you, whether near or far,
from one end of the land to the other), 8do
not yield to him or listen to him. Show him
no pity. Do not spare him or shield him. 9You
must certainly put him to death. Your hand
must be the first in putting him to death,
and then the hands of all the people. 10Stone
him to death, because he tried to turn you
away from the LORD your God, who brought
you out of Egypt, out of the land of slavery.
11Then all Israel will hear and be afraid, and
no one among you will do such an evil thing
again.
12If you hear it said about one of the towns
the LORD your God is giving you to live in
13that wicked men have arisen among you
and have led the people of their town astray,
saying, "Let us go and worship other gods"
(gods you have not known), 14then you must
inquire, probe and investigate it thoroughly.
And if it is true and it has been proved that
this detestable thing has been done among
you, 15you must certainly put to the sword all
who live in that town. Destroy it completely,[a]
both its people and its livestock. 16Gather all
the plunder of the town into the middle of the
public square and completely burn the town
and all its plunder as a whole burnt offering to
the LORD your God. It is to remain a ruin forever, never to be rebuilt. 17None of those condemned things[a] shall be found in your hands,
so that the LORD will turn from his fierce
anger; he will show you mercy, have compassion on you, and increase your numbers, as
he promised on oath to your forefathers, 18be-
cause you obey the LORD your God, keeping
all his commands that I am giving you today
and doing what is right in his eyes.

Clean and Unclean Food

14 You are the children of the LORD your
God. Do not cut yourselves or shave the
front of your heads for the dead, 2for
you are a people holy to the LORD your God.
Out of all the peoples on the face of the earth,
the LORD has chosen you to be his treasured
possession.
3Do not eat any detestable thing. 4These are
the animals you may eat: the ox, the sheep,
the goat, 5the deer, the gazelle, the roe deer,
the wild goat, the ibex, the antelope and the
mountain sheep.[b] 6You may eat any animal
that has a split hoof divided in two and that
chews the cud. 7However, of those that chew
the cud or that have a split hoof completely
divided you may not eat the camel, the rabbit
or the coney.[c] Although they chew the cud,
they do not have a split hoof; they are ceremonially unclean for you. 8The pig is also unclean; although it has a split hoof, it does not
chew the cud. You are not to eat their meat or
touch their carcasses.
9Of all the creatures living in the water, you
may eat any that has fins and scales. 10But anything that does not have fins and scales you
may not eat; for you it is unclean.
11You may eat any clean bird. 12But these
you may not eat: the eagle, the vulture, the
black vulture, 13the red kite, the black kite,
any kind of falcon, 14any kind of raven, 15the
horned owl, the screech owl, the gull, any
kind of hawk, 16the little owl, the great owl,
the white owl, 17the desert owl, the osprey, the
cormorant, 18the stork, any kind of heron, the
hoopoe and the bat.
19All flying insects that swarm are unclean
to you; do not eat them. 20But any winged
creature that is clean you may eat.
21Do not eat anything you find already
dead. You may give it to an alien living in any
of your towns, and he may eat it, or you may
sell it to a foreigner. But you are a people holy
to the LORD your God.
Do not cook a young goat in its mother's
milk.

Tithes

22Be sure to set aside a tenth of all that your
fields produce each year. 23Eat the tithe of
your grain, new wine and oil, and the firstborn of your herds and flocks in the presence of the LORD your God at the place he
will choose as a dwelling for his Name, so
that you may learn to revere the LORD your
God always. 24But if that place is too distant
and you have been blessed by the LORD your
God and cannot carry your tithe (because the
place where the LORD will choose to put his
Name is so far away), 25then exchange your

[a] *15,17* The Hebrew term refers to the irrevocable giving over of things or persons to the LORD, often by totally destroying them.
[b] *5* The precise identification of some of the birds and animals in this chapter is uncertain. [c] *7* That is, the hyrax or rock badger

tithe for silver, and take the silver with you
and go to the place the LORD your God will
choose. 26Use the silver to buy whatever you
like: cattle, sheep, wine or other fermented
drink, or anything you wish. Then you and
your household shall eat there in the presence
of the LORD your God and rejoice. 27And do
not neglect the Levites living in your towns,
for they have no allotment or inheritance of
their own.

28At the end of every three years, bring all
the tithes of that year's produce and store it in
your towns, 29so that the Levites (who have no
allotment or inheritance of their own) and the
aliens, the fatherless and the widows who live
in your towns may come and eat and be satisfied, and so that the LORD your God may bless
you in all the work of your hands.

The Year for Canceling Debts

15 At the end of every seven years you must
cancel debts. 2This is how it is to be done:
Every creditor shall cancel the loan he
has made to his fellow Israelite. He shall not
require payment from his fellow Israelite or
brother, because the LORD's time for canceling
debts has been proclaimed. 3You may require
payment from a foreigner, but you must cancel any debt your brother owes you. 4Howev-
er, there should be no poor among you, for in
the land the LORD your God is giving you to
possess as your inheritance, he will richly bless
you, 5if only you fully obey the LORD your
God and are careful to follow all these commands I am giving you today. 6For the LORD
your God will bless you as he has promised,
and you will lend to many nations but will
borrow from none. You will rule over many
nations but none will rule over you.

7If there is a poor man among your brothers
in any of the towns of the land that the LORD
your God is giving you, do not be hardheart-
ed or tightfisted toward your poor brother.
8Rather be openhanded and freely lend him
whatever he needs. 9Be careful not to harbor
this wicked thought: "The seventh year, the
year for canceling debts, is near," so that you
do not show ill will toward your needy brother
and give him nothing. He may then appeal to
the LORD against you, and you will be found
guilty of sin. 10Give generously to him and
do so without a grudging heart; then because
of this the LORD your God will bless you in
all your work and in everything you put your
hand to. 11There will always be poor people
in the land. Therefore I command you to be
openhanded toward your brothers and toward
the poor and needy in your land.

Freeing Servants

12If a fellow Hebrew, a man or a woman,
sells himself to you and serves you six years,
in the seventh year you must let him go free.
13And when you release him, do not send him
away empty-handed. 14Supply him liberally
from your flock, your threshing floor and your
winepress. Give to him as the LORD your God
has blessed you. 15Remember that you were
slaves in Egypt and the LORD your God redeemed you. That is why I give you this command today.

16But if your servant says to you, "I do not
want to leave you," because he loves you and
your family and is well off with you, 17then
take an awl and push it through his ear lobe
into the door, and he will become your servant
for life. Do the same for your maidservant.

18Do not consider it a hardship to set your
servant free, because his service to you these
six years has been worth twice as much as that
of a hired hand. And the LORD your God will
bless you in everything you do.

The Firstborn Animals

19Set apart for the LORD your God every
firstborn male of your herds and flocks. Do
not put the firstborn of your oxen to work,
and do not shear the firstborn of your sheep.
20Each year you and your family are to eat
them in the presence of the LORD your God
at the place he will choose. 21If an animal has
a defect, is lame or blind, or has any serious
flaw, you must not sacrifice it to the LORD
your God. 22You are to eat it in your own
towns. Both the ceremonially unclean and the
clean may eat it, as if it were gazelle or deer.
23But you must not eat the blood; pour it out
on the ground like water.

Passover

16 Observe the month of Abib and celebrate the Passover of the LORD your
God, because in the month of Abib he
brought you out of Egypt by night. 2Sacrifice
as the Passover to the LORD your God an animal from your flock or herd at the place the
LORD will choose as a dwelling for his Name.
3Do not eat it with bread made with yeast,
but for seven days eat unleavened bread, the
bread of affliction, because you left Egypt in
haste—so that all the days of your life you may
remember the time of your departure from
Egypt. 4Let no yeast be found in your posses-

FRIDAY
READ DEUTERONOMY 15:1–11

GIVING WITH GRACE

Give generously to him and do so without a grudging heart; then because of this the LORD your God will bless you in all your work and in everything you put your hand to.

— DEUTERONOMY 15:10

let's talk

- In what ways has God blessed us as a couple? In what ways are we tightfisted about sharing what we have? How can we make our spending and giving reflect our values?
- Who are some generous people who have helped us along the way? What have we learned from them? How are we becoming like them?
- What did we learn about money and generosity from our parents? Were these good or bad lessons? What will our children learn from us?

Years ago I said something that still bothers me when I think about it. I had led a young couple to faith in Jesus. The husband earned a good living in his hairstyling salon. In the basement of their home he kept the barber's chair that his deceased father had once used in a shop in another town.

His father's chair was more than an item of nostalgia, however. My friend used the chair in his basement two evenings and part of Saturday each week to seat customers who couldn't afford to see him in his shop. In this homey room my friend clipped and snipped the hair of the poor. Some, like me, he charged a nominal fee; others he waved out the door with a smile.

After one splendid haircut, I pulled out my wallet and handed him a note that was twice what he normally charged me. It was my smallest note, but he had no change. "Just keep it," I said. "Next time I won't have to pay anything."

Indeed, as I stepped out of the chair after my next grooming session and reached for my wallet, my friend said, "Wait! You've already paid for this one!"

It was then that I said some horrible words: "If you had remembered that earlier," I teased, "you wouldn't have done such a good job, would you?"

A slight grimace furrowed my friend's brow before he caught himself and laughed. He was a generous man, and I had treated his kindness flippantly by joking that mercenary demons drove his heart.

It seems like materialism is all around us, and it is not uncommon for people to be driven by need and greed. During the lean years that many of us experience early in marriage, we can become selfish and cheap. Those attitudes can stick, even when resources grow and demands diminish.

God built safeguards into Israelite society so that debt wouldn't dehumanize those who became trapped in it. But God also knew that some people would try to manipulate handouts and bailouts and other kinds of welfare for their own cunning ends. So he asked his people to be generous to the poor, even if the poor appeared to be abusing the gifts.

Generosity and graciousness are learned qualities. They must be caught from the example of big-hearted souls. Like God. Like the widow who gave two very small copper coins—all she had to live on (see Mark 12:41–44). Like the disciples who shared their lunch with a crowd (see Matthew 15:29–39). Like my barber.

We must practice giving so that generosity becomes an essential part of who we are. And when we give, we'll find that our generosity is rewarded by God, who will "throw open the floodgates of heaven and pour out so much blessing that you will not have room enough for it" (Malachi 3:10).

—WAYNE BROUWER

FOR YOUR NEXT DEVOTIONAL READING, TURN TO PAGE 202.

sion in all your land for seven days. Do not let
any of the meat you sacrifice on the evening of
the first day remain until morning.
5You must not sacrifice the Passover in any
town the LORD your God gives you 6except in
the place he will choose as a dwelling for his
Name. There you must sacrifice the Passover in
the evening, when the sun goes down, on the
anniversary[a] of your departure from Egypt.
7Roast it and eat it at the place the LORD your
God will choose. Then in the morning return
to your tents. 8For six days eat unleavened
bread and on the seventh day hold an assembly to the LORD your God and do no work.

Feast of Weeks

9Count off seven weeks from the time you
begin to put the sickle to the standing grain.
10Then celebrate the Feast of Weeks to the
LORD your God by giving a freewill offering
in proportion to the blessings the LORD your
God has given you. 11And rejoice before the
LORD your God at the place he will choose
as a dwelling for his Name—you, your sons
and daughters, your menservants and maidservants, the Levites in your towns, and the
aliens, the fatherless and the widows living
among you. 12Remember that you were slaves
in Egypt, and follow carefully these decrees.

Feast of Tabernacles

13Celebrate the Feast of Tabernacles for sev-
en days after you have gathered the produce
of your threshing floor and your winepress.
14Be joyful at your Feast—you, your sons and
daughters, your menservants and maidservants, and the Levites, the aliens, the fatherless
and the widows who live in your towns. 15For
seven days celebrate the Feast to the LORD
your God at the place the LORD will choose.
For the LORD your God will bless you in all
your harvest and in all the work of your hands,
and your joy will be complete.
16Three times a year all your men must appear before the LORD your God at the place he
will choose: at the Feast of Unleavened Bread,
the Feast of Weeks and the Feast of Tabernacles. No man should appear before the LORD
empty-handed: 17Each of you must bring a
gift in proportion to the way the LORD your
God has blessed you.

Judges

18Appoint judges and officials for each of
your tribes in every town the LORD your God
is giving you, and they shall judge the people
fairly. 19Do not pervert justice or show partiality. Do not accept a bribe, for a bribe blinds
the eyes of the wise and twists the words of the
righteous. 20Follow justice and justice alone,
so that you may live and possess the land the
LORD your God is giving you.

Worshiping Other Gods

21Do not set up any wooden Asherah pole[b]
beside the altar you build to the LORD your
God, 22and do not erect a sacred stone, for
these the LORD your God hates.

17 Do not sacrifice to the LORD your God
an ox or a sheep that has any defect or
flaw in it, for that would be detestable
to him.
2If a man or woman living among you in
one of the towns the LORD gives you is found
doing evil in the eyes of the LORD your God in
violation of his covenant, 3and contrary to my
command has worshiped other gods, bowing
down to them or to the sun or the moon or
the stars of the sky, 4and this has been brought
to your attention, then you must investigate it
thoroughly. If it is true and it has been proved
that this detestable thing has been done in Israel, 5take the man or woman who has done
this evil deed to your city gate and stone that
person to death. 6On the testimony of two or
three witnesses a man shall be put to death,
but no one shall be put to death on the testimony of only one witness. 7The hands of the
witnesses must be the first in putting him to
death, and then the hands of all the people.
You must purge the evil from among you.

Law Courts

8If cases come before your courts that are
too difficult for you to judge—whether bloodshed, lawsuits or assaults—take them to the
place the LORD your God will choose. 9Go to
the priests, who are Levites, and to the judge
who is in office at that time. Inquire of them
and they will give you the verdict. 10You must
act according to the decisions they give you at
the place the LORD will choose. Be careful to
do everything they direct you to do. 11Act according to the law they teach you and the decisions they give you. Do not turn aside from
what they tell you, to the right or to the left.
12The man who shows contempt for the judge
or for the priest who stands ministering there
to the LORD your God must be put to death.
You must purge the evil from Israel. 13All the

[a] 6 Or *down, at the time of day* [b] 21 Or *Do not plant any tree dedicated to Asherah*

people will hear and be afraid, and will not be
contemptuous again.

The King

14When you enter the land the LORD your
God is giving you and have taken possession
of it and settled in it, and you say, "Let us set
a king over us like all the nations around us,"
15be sure to appoint over you the king the LORD
your God chooses. He must be from among
your own brothers. Do not place a foreigner
over you, one who is not a brother Israelite.
16The king, moreover, must not acquire great
numbers of horses for himself or make the people return to Egypt to get more of them, for the
LORD has told you, "You are not to go back that
way again." 17He must not take many wives, or
his heart will be led astray. He must not accumulate large amounts of silver and gold.

18When he takes the throne of his kingdom,
he is to write for himself on a scroll a copy of
this law, taken from that of the priests, who
are Levites. 19It is to be with him, and he is
to read it all the days of his life so that he may
learn to revere the LORD his God and follow
carefully all the words of this law and these
decrees 20and not consider himself better than
his brothers and turn from the law to the right
or to the left. Then he and his descendants will
reign a long time over his kingdom in Israel.

Offerings for Priests and Levites

18 The priests, who are Levites—indeed
the whole tribe of Levi—are to have
no allotment or inheritance with Israel. They shall live on the offerings made to
the LORD by fire, for that is their inheritance.
2They shall have no inheritance among their
brothers; the LORD is their inheritance, as he
promised them.

3This is the share due the priests from the
people who sacrifice a bull or a sheep: the
shoulder, the jowls and the inner parts. 4You
are to give them the firstfruits of your grain,
new wine and oil, and the first wool from the
shearing of your sheep, 5for the LORD your
God has chosen them and their descendants
out of all your tribes to stand and minister in
the LORD's name always.

6If a Levite moves from one of your towns
anywhere in Israel where he is living, and
comes in all earnestness to the place the LORD
will choose, 7he may minister in the name of
the LORD his God like all his fellow Levites
who serve there in the presence of the LORD.
8He is to share equally in their benefits, even
though he has received money from the sale of
family possessions.

Detestable Practices

9When you enter the land the LORD your
God is giving you, do not learn to imitate the
detestable ways of the nations there. 10Let no
one be found among you who sacrifices his
son or daughter in[a] the fire, who practices
divination or sorcery, interprets omens, engag-
es in witchcraft, 11or casts spells, or who is a
medium or spiritist or who consults the dead.
12Anyone who does these things is detestable
to the LORD, and because of these detestable practices the LORD your God will drive
out those nations before you. 13You must be
blameless before the LORD your God.

The Prophet

14The nations you will dispossess listen to
those who practice sorcery or divination. But
as for you, the LORD your God has not permitted you to do so. 15The LORD your God
will raise up for you a prophet like me from
among your own brothers. You must listen to
him. 16For this is what you asked of the LORD
your God at Horeb on the day of the assembly
when you said, "Let us not hear the voice of
the LORD our God nor see this great fire anymore, or we will die."

17The LORD said to me: "What they say is
good. 18I will raise up for them a prophet like
you from among their brothers; I will put my
words in his mouth, and he will tell them everything I command him. 19If anyone does
not listen to my words that the prophet speaks
in my name, I myself will call him to account.
20But a prophet who presumes to speak in my
name anything I have not commanded him to
say, or a prophet who speaks in the name of
other gods, must be put to death."

21You may say to yourselves, "How can we
know when a message has not been spoken by
the LORD?" 22If what a prophet proclaims in
the name of the LORD does not take place or
come true, that is a message the LORD has not
spoken. That prophet has spoken presumptu-
ously. Do not be afraid of him.

Cities of Refuge

19 When the LORD your God has destroyed
the nations whose land he is giving you,
and when you have driven them out
and settled in their towns and houses, 2then

[a] 10 Or *who makes his son or daughter pass through*

set aside for yourselves three cities centrally located in the land the LORD your God is giving
you to possess. 3Build roads to them and divide into three parts the land the LORD your
God is giving you as an inheritance, so that
anyone who kills a man may flee there.
4This is the rule concerning the man who
kills another and flees there to save his life—
one who kills his neighbor unintentionally,
without malice aforethought. 5For instance, a
man may go into the forest with his neighbor
to cut wood, and as he swings his ax to fell a
tree, the head may fly off and hit his neighbor and kill him. That man may flee to one of
these cities and save his life. 6Otherwise, the
avenger of blood might pursue him in a rage,
overtake him if the distance is too great, and
kill him even though he is not deserving of
death, since he did it to his neighbor without
malice aforethought. 7This is why I command
you to set aside for yourselves three cities.
8If the LORD your God enlarges your territory, as he promised on oath to your forefathers, and gives you the whole land he promised them, 9because you carefully follow all
these laws I command you today—to love
the LORD your God and to walk always in his
ways—then you are to set aside three more cities. 10Do this so that innocent blood will not
be shed in your land, which the LORD your
God is giving you as your inheritance, and so
that you will not be guilty of bloodshed.
11But if a man hates his neighbor and lies in
wait for him, assaults and kills him, and then
flees to one of these cities, 12the elders of his
town shall send for him, bring him back from
the city, and hand him over to the avenger of
blood to die. 13Show him no pity. You must
purge from Israel the guilt of shedding innocent blood, so that it may go well with you.
14Do not move your neighbor's boundary
stone set up by your predecessors in the inheritance you receive in the land the LORD your
God is giving you to possess.

Witnesses

15One witness is not enough to convict a
man accused of any crime or offense he may
have committed. A matter must be established
by the testimony of two or three witnesses.
16If a malicious witness takes the stand to
accuse a man of a crime, 17the two men involved in the dispute must stand in the presence of the LORD before the priests and the
judges who are in office at the time. 18The
judges must make a thorough investigation,
and if the witness proves to be a liar, giving
false testimony against his brother, 19then do
to him as he intended to do to his brother.
You must purge the evil from among you.
20The rest of the people will hear of this and
be afraid, and never again will such an evil
thing be done among you. 21Show no pity:
life for life, eye for eye, tooth for tooth, hand
for hand, foot for foot.

Going to War

20 When you go to war against your enemies and see horses and chariots and
an army greater than yours, do not be
afraid of them, because the LORD your God,
who brought you up out of Egypt, will be with
you. 2When you are about to go into battle,
the priest shall come forward and address the
army. 3He shall say: "Hear, O Israel, today you
are going into battle against your enemies. Do
not be fainthearted or afraid; do not be terrified or give way to panic before them. 4For the
LORD your God is the one who goes with you
to fight for you against your enemies to give
you victory."
5The officers shall say to the army: "Has
anyone built a new house and not dedicated
it? Let him go home, or he may die in battle
and someone else may dedicate it. 6Has anyone planted a vineyard and not begun to enjoy
it? Let him go home, or he may die in battle
and someone else enjoy it. 7Has anyone become pledged to a woman and not married
her? Let him go home, or he may die in battle
and someone else marry her." 8Then the officers shall add, "Is any man afraid or fainthearted? Let him go home so that his brothers
will not become disheartened too." 9When the
officers have finished speaking to the army,
they shall appoint commanders over it.
10When you march up to attack a city,
make its people an offer of peace. 11If they accept and open their gates, all the people in it
shall be subject to forced labor and shall work
for you. 12If they refuse to make peace and
they engage you in battle, lay siege to that city.
13When the LORD your God delivers it into
your hand, put to the sword all the men in
it. 14As for the women, the children, the livestock and everything else in the city, you may
take these as plunder for yourselves. And you
may use the plunder the LORD your God gives
you from your enemies. 15This is how you are
to treat all the cities that are at a distance from
you and do not belong to the nations nearby.
16However, in the cities of the nations
the LORD your God is giving you as an inheritance, do not leave alive anything that

WEEKEND

the purpose of marriage

To spiritually benefit from a marriage, we have to be honest. We have to look at our disappointments, own up to our ugly attitudes, and confront our selfishness. We also have to rid ourselves of the notion that difficulties of a marriage can be overcome if we simply pray harder or learn a few simple principles. Most of us have discovered that these "simple steps" work only on a superficial level. Why is this? Because there's a deeper question that needs to be addressed beyond how we can "improve" our marriage: What if God didn't design marriage to be "easier"? What if God had an end in mind that went beyond our happiness, our comfort and our desire to be infatuated and happy, as if the world were a perfect place?

What if God designed marriage to make us holy more than to make us happy?

You've probably already realized that there was a purpose for your marriage that went beyond happiness. You might not have chosen the word *holiness* to express it, but you understood there was a transcendent truth beyond the superficial romance depicted in popular culture.

When marriage becomes our primary pursuit, our delight in the relationship will be crippled by fear, possessiveness and self-centeredness. We were made to admire, respect and love someone who has a purpose bigger than ourselves, a purpose centered on God's untiring work of calling his people home to his heart of love.

Looking beyond the marriage relationship is necessary because marriage itself is not eternal. When God provides us with a mate, there is no guarantee that this mate will be with us for life. We certainly hope this will be the case, but very few marriages end in simultaneous death.

We allow marriage to point beyond itself when we accept two central missions: becoming the people God created us to be and doing the work God has given us to do. If we embrace—not just accept, but actively embrace—these two missions, we will have a full life, a rich life, a meaningful life, and a successful life. The irony is we will probably also have a happy marriage, but that will come as a blessed by-product of putting everything else in order.

Is it true? Marriage is about finding your soul mate and committing to him or her for the rest of your life. It's about finding love and then growing that love from a romantic spark to a happy and fulfilled life that has relatively few problems. It's about being filled up by the presence and love of an understanding spouse who is by your side until death do you part.

A better view: Marriage is the second most intimate relationship we will ever have. The first is with our Lord, our Creator and our Savior. Marriage teaches us about our self; our strengths, our weaknesses, and our ability to relate to someone else so that we can better relate to our God. Marriage helps us to strip away the pretenses and clearly see who we are. The joys we experience in marriage are but a glimpse of the life we will have when we are finally united with our ultimate lover Jesus Christ.

—GARY THOMAS

working through it

Spend a few minutes discussing how each situation would make you unhappy and then how you might work through it to find happiness and holiness.

1. Your mother-in-law can't take care of herself anymore. You and your spouse must decide whether to put her in a nursing home or keep her in yours.
2. The day of your long-awaited vacation has finally come, but your flight is cancelled due to bad weather.
3. The neighbors next door are really terrific, but they don't know that their teen son is throwing wild parties whenever they leave town.
4. You throw a surprise birthday party for me. I hate surprises.
5. You just cleaned the house, and when you return from work, you find dirty clothes on the floor.
6. You correct me in front of other people.
7. A promotion at work brings an increased salary and more vacation days but requires you to travel two or three nights a week.
8. We just purchased our first home. It's a fixer-upper, and we don't have much money.
9. We've been asked to teach a Sunday school class together. All fifteen of our new students are under the age of four.
10. You agreed to volunteer at a homeless shelter. That's great, but I feel that we're already too busy.

HOW ARE WE DOING?

date

let's make a DATE

SKATE DATE

Go roller-skating. Find a rink with open skating hours for adults. Ask the DJ to put on your favorite song or bring along your iPod and dual headphones. Then hold hands with your spouse while you skate to "your song."

Or skate outside. Pick up a pair of inline skates at the local discount store (or rent skates), along with the necessary safety equipment. Pack a picnic and head to the local park. Look for ways that happiness and holiness combine in God's creation.

FOR YOUR NEXT DEVOTIONAL READING, TURN TO PAGE 205.

LESSONS FROM THE *Bible*

What do Job and his wife teach us about happiness and holiness? See Job 1:1–5,13–22; 2:7–10; 42:12–17.

breathes. 17Completely destroy[a] them—the Hittites, Amorites, Canaanites, Perizzites, Hivites and Jebusites—as the LORD your God has commanded you. 18Otherwise, they will teach you to follow all the detestable things they do in worshiping their gods, and you will sin against the LORD your God.

19When you lay siege to a city for a long time, fighting against it to capture it, do not destroy its trees by putting an ax to them, because you can eat their fruit. Do not cut them down. Are the trees of the field people, that you should besiege them?[b] 20However, you may cut down trees that you know are not fruit trees and use them to build siege works until the city at war with you falls.

Atonement for an Unsolved Murder

21 If a man is found slain, lying in a field in the land the LORD your God is giving you to possess, and it is not known who killed him, 2your elders and judges shall go out and measure the distance from the body to the neighboring towns. 3Then the elders of the town nearest the body shall take a heifer that has never been worked and has never worn a yoke 4and lead her down to a valley that has not been plowed or planted and where there is a flowing stream. There in the valley they are to break the heifer's neck. 5The priests, the sons of Levi, shall step forward, for the LORD your God has chosen them to minister and to pronounce blessings in the name of the LORD and to decide all cases of dispute and assault. 6Then all the elders of the town nearest the body shall wash their hands over the heifer whose neck was broken in the valley, 7and they shall declare: "Our hands did not shed this blood, nor did our eyes see it done. 8Accept this atonement for your people Israel, whom you have redeemed, O LORD, and do not hold your people guilty of the blood of an innocent man." And the bloodshed will be atoned for. 9So you will purge from yourselves the guilt of shedding innocent blood, since you have done what is right in the eyes of the LORD.

Marrying a Captive Woman

10When you go to war against your enemies and the LORD your God delivers them into your hands and you take captives, 11if you notice among the captives a beautiful woman and are attracted to her, you may take her as your wife. 12Bring her into your home and have her shave her head, trim her nails 13and put aside the clothes she was wearing when captured. After she has lived in your house and mourned her father and mother for a full month, then you may go to her and be her husband and she shall be your wife. 14If you are not pleased with her, let her go wherever she wishes. You must not sell her or treat her as a slave, since you have dishonored her.

The Right of the Firstborn

15If a man has two wives, and he loves one but not the other, and both bear him sons but the firstborn is the son of the wife he does not love, 16when he wills his property to his sons, he must not give the rights of the firstborn to the son of the wife he loves in preference to his actual firstborn, the son of the wife he does not love. 17He must acknowledge the son of his unloved wife as the firstborn by giving him a double share of all he has. That son is the first sign of his father's strength. The right of the firstborn belongs to him.

A Rebellious Son

18If a man has a stubborn and rebellious son who does not obey his father and mother and will not listen to them when they discipline him, 19his father and mother shall take hold of him and bring him to the elders at the gate of his town. 20They shall say to the elders, "This son of ours is stubborn and rebellious. He will not obey us. He is a profligate and a drunkard." 21Then all the men of his town shall stone him to death. You must purge the evil from among you. All Israel will hear of it and be afraid.

Various Laws

22If a man guilty of a capital offense is put to death and his body is hung on a tree, 23you must not leave his body on the tree overnight. Be sure to bury him that same day, because anyone who is hung on a tree is under God's curse. You must not desecrate the land the LORD your God is giving you as an inheritance.

22 If you see your brother's ox or sheep straying, do not ignore it but be sure to take it back to him. 2If the brother does not live near you or if you do not know who he is, take it home with you and keep it until he comes looking for it. Then give it back to him. 3Do the same if you find your brother's donkey or his cloak or anything he loses. Do not ignore it.

---

[a] *17* The Hebrew term refers to the irrevocable giving over of things or persons to the LORD, often by totally destroying them.
[b] *19* Or *down to use in the siege, for the fruit trees are for the benefit of man.*

MONDAY
READ
DEUTERONOMY 21:15–17

BEING FAIR IN A BLENDED FAMILY

> **If a man has two wives, and he loves one but not the other, and both bear him sons but the firstborn is the son of the wife he does not love, when he wills his property to his sons, he must not give the rights of the firstborn to the son of the wife he loves in preference to his actual firstborn, the son of the wife he does not love.**
>
> — DEUTERONOMY 21:15–16

Polygamy is illegal in our society, yet this verse speaks to the complicated relationships often found within families today. Many couples have been married, divorced and are now remarried. For various reasons, we have family situations in which a person may have had more than one wife or husband, or there are children in the family from different relationships. The emotional difficulties caused by multiple marriages can be complicated indeed.

In ancient Israel, a firstborn son had special rights of inheritance. A man could not will his property to the son of the wife he loved and provide nothing for the son of the unloved wife; a firstborn was first in line for the inheritance, regardless of how the parent felt about the situation.

Today, people with previous marriages have tangled emotional issues, especially when it comes to their children. Children of divorce can feel abandoned or forgotten when their parents no longer love each other, and they may especially have a difficult time when their father or mother remarries. Children in a blended family may feel like second-class citizens when a new brother or sister comes along. Stepbrothers and stepsisters may compete for parental love and attention when a parent is alive as well as for property and possessions when a parent dies.

Deuteronomy 21 says that even if a wife was unloved, her firstborn son had certain indisputable rights to the property of his parents. Today, a firstborn child doesn't necessarily have inheritance rights; however, this passage is relevant in that it reminds parents to be fair and evenhanded with all the children in a family, as difficult as that may be. Fair and loving treatment is the first sign of a parent's strength (or a stepmother or stepfather's strength). To do right by our children, whether they are our biological children or not, is to honor the Lord.

When preparing a young couple for marriage, I asked the young woman about growing up as a child of divorced parents. "It was very hard, and I wish that my mom and dad could have stayed together," she said. "But they did the best they could for me and my brothers and sisters. So now I feel like I have two moms and two dads who love me."

Evenhanded love is a sign of the strength of these parents and stepparents. It's a lesson that will undoubtedly take root and grow into the next generation.

—JOHN R. THROOP

let's *talk*

- What are some ways we can show fairness to all of our children? How can we provide for their emotional welfare?
- In what ways can we support the faith of our children?
- If we have not experienced a blended family situation, how can we support and strengthen our friends who face some of these circumstances?

FOR YOUR NEXT DEVOTIONAL READING, TURN TO PAGE 208.

4If you see your brother's donkey or his ox
fallen on the road, do not ignore it. Help him
get it to its feet.
5A woman must not wear men's clothing,
nor a man wear women's clothing, for the
LORD your God detests anyone who does
this.
6If you come across a bird's nest beside the
road, either in a tree or on the ground, and
the mother is sitting on the young or on the
eggs, do not take the mother with the young.
7You may take the young, but be sure to let
the mother go, so that it may go well with you
and you may have a long life.
8When you build a new house, make a parapet around your roof so that you may not
bring the guilt of bloodshed on your house if
someone falls from the roof.
9Do not plant two kinds of seed in your
vineyard; if you do, not only the crops you
plant but also the fruit of the vineyard will be
defiled.[a]
10Do not plow with an ox and a donkey
yoked together.
11Do not wear clothes of wool and linen
woven together.
12Make tassels on the four corners of the
cloak you wear.

Marriage Violations

13If a man takes a wife and, after lying with
her, dislikes her 14and slanders her and gives
her a bad name, saying, "I married this woman, but when I approached her, I did not find
proof of her virginity," 15then the girl's father
and mother shall bring proof that she was a
virgin to the town elders at the gate. 16The
girl's father will say to the elders, "I gave my
daughter in marriage to this man, but he dislikes her. 17Now he has slandered her and said,
'I did not find your daughter to be a virgin.'
But here is the proof of my daughter's virginity." Then her parents shall display the cloth
before the elders of the town, 18and the elders
shall take the man and punish him. 19They
shall fine him a hundred shekels of silver[b] and
give them to the girl's father, because this man
has given an Israelite virgin a bad name. She
shall continue to be his wife; he must not divorce her as long as he lives.
20If, however, the charge is true and no
proof of the girl's virginity can be found, 21she
shall be brought to the door of her father's
house and there the men of her town shall
stone her to death. She has done a disgraceful thing in Israel by being promiscuous while
still in her father's house. You must purge the
evil from among you.
22If a man is found sleeping with another
man's wife, both the man who slept with her
and the woman must die. You must purge the
evil from Israel.
23If a man happens to meet in a town a virgin pledged to be married and he sleeps with
her, 24you shall take both of them to the gate
of that town and stone them to death—the
girl because she was in a town and did not
scream for help, and the man because he violated another man's wife. You must purge the
evil from among you.
25But if out in the country a man happens
to meet a girl pledged to be married and rapes
her, only the man who has done this shall die.
26Do nothing to the girl; she has committed no sin deserving death. This case is like
that of someone who attacks and murders his
neighbor, 27for the man found the girl out in
the country, and though the betrothed girl
screamed, there was no one to rescue her.
28If a man happens to meet a virgin who is
not pledged to be married and rapes her and
they are discovered, 29he shall pay the girl's father fifty shekels of silver.[c] He must marry the
girl, for he has violated her. He can never divorce her as long as he lives.
30A man is not to marry his father's wife; he
must not dishonor his father's bed.

Exclusion From the Assembly

23 No one who has been emasculated by
crushing or cutting may enter the assembly of the LORD.
2No one born of a forbidden marriage[d] nor
any of his descendants may enter the assembly
of the LORD, even down to the tenth generation.
3No Ammonite or Moabite or any of his descendants may enter the assembly of the LORD,
even down to the tenth generation. 4For they
did not come to meet you with bread and water on your way when you came out of Egypt,
and they hired Balaam son of Beor from Pethor in Aram Naharaim[e] to pronounce a curse
on you. 5However, the LORD your God would
not listen to Balaam but turned the curse into
a blessing for you, because the LORD your God
loves you. 6Do not seek a treaty of friendship
with them as long as you live.

---

[a] 9 Or *be forfeited to the sanctuary* [b] 19 That is, about 2 1/2 pounds (about 1 kilogram) [c] 29 That is, about 1 1/4 pounds (about 0.6 kilogram) [d] 2 Or *one of illegitimate birth* [e] 4 That is, Northwest Mesopotamia

7Do not abhor an Edomite, for he is your
brother. Do not abhor an Egyptian, because
you lived as an alien in his country. 8The third
generation of children born to them may enter the assembly of the LORD.

Uncleanness in the Camp

9When you are encamped against your enemies, keep away from everything impure. 10If
one of your men is unclean because of a noc-
turnal emission, he is to go outside the camp
and stay there. 11But as evening approaches he
is to wash himself, and at sunset he may return
to the camp.
12Designate a place outside the camp where
you can go to relieve yourself. 13As part of
your equipment have something to dig with,
and when you relieve yourself, dig a hole and
cover up your excrement. 14For the LORD your
God moves about in your camp to protect you
and to deliver your enemies to you. Your camp
must be holy, so that he will not see among
you anything indecent and turn away from
you.

Miscellaneous Laws

15If a slave has taken refuge with you, do
not hand him over to his master. 16Let him
live among you wherever he likes and in whatever town he chooses. Do not oppress him.
17No Israelite man or woman is to become
a shrine prostitute. 18You must not bring the
earnings of a female prostitute or of a male
prostitute[a] into the house of the LORD your
God to pay any vow, because the LORD your
God detests them both.
19Do not charge your brother interest,
whether on money or food or anything else
that may earn interest. 20You may charge a foreigner interest, but not a brother Israelite, so
that the LORD your God may bless you in everything you put your hand to in the land you
are entering to possess.
21If you make a vow to the LORD your God,
do not be slow to pay it, for the LORD your
God will certainly demand it of you and you
will be guilty of sin. 22But if you refrain from
making a vow, you will not be guilty. 23What-
ever your lips utter you must be sure to do,
because you made your vow freely to the LORD
your God with your own mouth.
24If you enter your neighbor's vineyard, you
may eat all the grapes you want, but do not
put any in your basket. 25If you enter your
neighbor's grainfield, you may pick kernels
with your hands, but you must not put a sickle to his standing grain.

24 If a man marries a woman who becomes
displeasing to him because he finds
something indecent about her, and he
writes her a certificate of divorce, gives it to
her and sends her from his house, 2and if after
she leaves his house she becomes the wife of
another man, 3and her second husband dislikes her and writes her a certificate of divorce,
gives it to her and sends her from his house,
or if he dies, 4then her first husband, who divorced her, is not allowed to marry her again
after she has been defiled. That would be detestable in the eyes of the LORD. Do not bring
sin upon the land the LORD your God is giving you as an inheritance.
5If a man has recently married, he must not
be sent to war or have any other duty laid on
him. For one year he is to be free to stay at
home and bring happiness to the wife he has
married.
6Do not take a pair of millstones—not even
the upper one—as security for a debt, because
that would be taking a man's livelihood as security.
7If a man is caught kidnapping one of his
brother Israelites and treats him as a slave or
sells him, the kidnapper must die. You must
purge the evil from among you.
8In cases of leprous[b] diseases be very careful
to do exactly as the priests, who are Levites,
instruct you. You must follow carefully what I
have commanded them. 9Remember what the
LORD your God did to Miriam along the way
after you came out of Egypt.
10When you make a loan of any kind to
your neighbor, do not go into his house to
get what he is offering as a pledge. 11Stay outside and let the man to whom you are making the loan bring the pledge out to you. 12If
the man is poor, do not go to sleep with his
pledge in your possession. 13Return his cloak
to him by sunset so that he may sleep in it.
Then he will thank you, and it will be regarded as a righteous act in the sight of the LORD
your God.
14Do not take advantage of a hired man
who is poor and needy, whether he is a brother Israelite or an alien living in one of your
towns. 15Pay him his wages each day before
sunset, because he is poor and is counting on
it. Otherwise he may cry to the LORD against
you, and you will be guilty of sin.
16Fathers shall not be put to death for their

[a] 18 Hebrew *of a dog* [b] 8 The Hebrew word was used for various diseases affecting the skin—not necessarily leprosy.

TUESDAY
READ DEUTERONOMY 24:1–5

A YEAR FOR EACH OTHER

> **If a man has recently married, he must not be sent to war or have any other duty laid on him. For one year he is to be free to stay at home and bring happiness to the wife he has married.**
>
> — Deuteronomy 24:5

At different stages in married life, the relationship between a husband and wife needs a lot of time and attention. But marriage building is especially critical in the beginning, when two people who love each other and are committed before God to make their union work are finding out how much time and effort it really takes.

In Deuteronomy 24:5, Moses instructed the elders of Israel to give a newly married man an exemption from military duty so that he could have time to be with his wife. Israel needed young men for battle, but in God's design, new wives needed their husbands more. In God's plan, couples need time for togetherness after the wedding; they need a strong foundation on which to build a platform to endure life's challenges. God determined that a couple needs an entire year to be together and to make their marriage their first priority.

In our culture, how do we approach the first year of marriage? We are certainly all busy people: often both husband and wife have demanding full-time jobs and careers, and responsibilities to extended families can take up free time after work. We fill up our days with obligations to our church, pursuing a degree or maintaining our relationships with our friends. And people are still needed to fight wars today. Some are called into the military just days after being married. Wives (and husbands) are left on their own. Any of these activities can distract us from marriage building or hinder our first attempts to build a life together.

In the beginning days of marriage, you might heed God's gracious command to spend at least a year together before getting overly involved with other commitments. Look over your schedules and make decisions together regarding what outside obligations to undertake. Discuss how much overtime or work-related travel you are both comfortable with. Take God's words to heart and take it easy that first year. It could have a lasting effect on your marriage.

—JOHN R. THROOP

let's *talk*

- What were some of the positive results of God's command for newly married men to have a year off from war?
- What are some of the demanding commitments we face in our marriage? What steps can we take to find time to make life together our priority?
- What engaged or newly married couple do we know whom we could encourage to apply the principle of Deuteronomy 24:5?

FOR YOUR NEXT DEVOTIONAL READING, TURN TO PAGE 214.

children, nor children put to death for their
fathers; each is to die for his own sin.
17Do not deprive the alien or the fatherless
of justice, or take the cloak of the widow as a
pledge. 18Remember that you were slaves in
Egypt and the LORD your God redeemed you
from there. That is why I command you to
do this.
19When you are harvesting in your field and
you overlook a sheaf, do not go back to get it.
Leave it for the alien, the fatherless and the
widow, so that the LORD your God may bless
you in all the work of your hands. 20When
you beat the olives from your trees, do not go
over the branches a second time. Leave what
remains for the alien, the fatherless and the
widow. 21When you harvest the grapes in your
vineyard, do not go over the vines again. Leave
what remains for the alien, the fatherless and
the widow. 22Remember that you were slaves
in Egypt. That is why I command you to do
this.

25 When men have a dispute, they are to
take it to court and the judges will decide the case, acquitting the innocent
and condemning the guilty. 2If the guilty man
deserves to be beaten, the judge shall make
him lie down and have him flogged in his
presence with the number of lashes his crime
deserves, 3but he must not give him more than
forty lashes. If he is flogged more than that,
your brother will be degraded in your eyes.
4Do not muzzle an ox while it is treading
out the grain.
5If brothers are living together and one
of them dies without a son, his widow must
not marry outside the family. Her husband's
brother shall take her and marry her and fulfill
the duty of a brother-in-law to her. 6The first
son she bears shall carry on the name of the
dead brother so that his name will not be blotted out from Israel.
7However, if a man does not want to marry
his brother's wife, she shall go to the elders at
the town gate and say, "My husband's brother
refuses to carry on his brother's name in Israel. He will not fulfill the duty of a brother-in-
law to me." 8Then the elders of his town shall
summon him and talk to him. If he persists
in saying, "I do not want to marry her," 9his
brother's widow shall go up to him in the presence of the elders, take off one of his sandals,
spit in his face and say, "This is what is done
to the man who will not build up his brother's
family line." 10That man's line shall be known
in Israel as The Family of the Unsandaled.
11If two men are fighting and the wife of
one of them comes to rescue her husband
from his assailant, and she reaches out and
seizes him by his private parts, 12you shall cut
off her hand. Show her no pity.
13Do not have two differing weights in your
bag—one heavy, one light. 14Do not have two
differing measures in your house—one large,
one small. 15You must have accurate and honest weights and measures, so that you may live
long in the land the LORD your God is giving
you. 16For the LORD your God detests anyone
who does these things, anyone who deals dis-
honestly.
17Remember what the Amalekites did to
you along the way when you came out of
Egypt. 18When you were weary and worn out,
they met you on your journey and cut off all
who were lagging behind; they had no fear of
God. 19When the LORD your God gives you
rest from all the enemies around you in the
land he is giving you to possess as an inheritance, you shall blot out the memory of Amalek from under heaven. Do not forget!

Firstfruits and Tithes

26 When you have entered the land the
LORD your God is giving you as an inheritance and have taken possession of
it and settled in it, 2take some of the firstfruits
of all that you produce from the soil of the
land the LORD your God is giving you and
put them in a basket. Then go to the place the
LORD your God will choose as a dwelling for
his Name 3and say to the priest in office at the
time, "I declare today to the LORD your God
that I have come to the land the LORD swore
to our forefathers to give us." 4The priest shall
take the basket from your hands and set it down
in front of the altar of the LORD your God.
5Then you shall declare before the LORD your
God: "My father was a wandering Aramean,
and he went down into Egypt with a few people and lived there and became a great nation,
powerful and numerous. 6But the Egyptians
mistreated us and made us suffer, putting us
to hard labor. 7Then we cried out to the LORD,
the God of our fathers, and the LORD heard
our voice and saw our misery, toil and oppression. 8So the LORD brought us out of Egypt
with a mighty hand and an outstretched arm,
with great terror and with miraculous signs
and wonders. 9He brought us to this place and
gave us this land, a land flowing with milk and
honey; 10and now I bring the firstfruits of the
soil that you, O LORD, have given me." Place
the basket before the LORD your God and bow
down before him. 11And you and the Levites

and the aliens among you shall rejoice in all
the good things the LORD your God has given
to you and your household.
12When you have finished setting aside a
tenth of all your produce in the third year,
the year of the tithe, you shall give it to the
Levite, the alien, the fatherless and the widow, so that they may eat in your towns and be
satisfied. 13Then say to the LORD your God:
"I have removed from my house the sacred
portion and have given it to the Levite, the
alien, the fatherless and the widow, according to all you commanded. I have not turned
aside from your commands nor have I forgotten any of them. 14I have not eaten any of the
sacred portion while I was in mourning, nor
have I removed any of it while I was unclean,
nor have I offered any of it to the dead. I have
obeyed the LORD my God; I have done everything you commanded me. 15Look down
from heaven, your holy dwelling place, and
bless your people Israel and the land you have
given us as you promised on oath to our forefathers, a land flowing with milk and honey."

Follow the LORD's Commands

16The LORD your God commands you this
day to follow these decrees and laws; carefully
observe them with all your heart and with all
your soul. 17You have declared this day that the
LORD is your God and that you will walk in his
ways, that you will keep his decrees, commands
and laws, and that you will obey him. 18And
the LORD has declared this day that you are his
people, his treasured possession as he promised,
and that you are to keep all his commands.
19He has declared that he will set you in praise,
fame and honor high above all the nations he
has made and that you will be a people holy to
the LORD your God, as he promised.

The Altar on Mount Ebal

27 Moses and the elders of Israel commanded the people: "Keep all these commands
that I give you today. 2When you have
crossed the Jordan into the land the LORD your
God is giving you, set up some large stones and
coat them with plaster. 3Write on them all the
words of this law when you have crossed over
to enter the land the LORD your God is giving
you, a land flowing with milk and honey, just
as the LORD, the God of your fathers, promised
you. 4And when you have crossed the Jordan,
set up these stones on Mount Ebal, as I command you today, and coat them with plaster.
5Build there an altar to the LORD your God, an
altar of stones. Do not use any iron tool upon
them. 6Build the altar of the LORD your God
with fieldstones and offer burnt offerings on it
to the LORD your God. 7Sacrifice fellowship offerings[a] there, eating them and rejoicing in the
presence of the LORD your God. 8And you shall
write very clearly all the words of this law on
these stones you have set up."

Curses From Mount Ebal

9Then Moses and the priests, who are Levites, said to all Israel, "Be silent, O Israel, and
listen! You have now become the people of the
LORD your God. 10Obey the LORD your God
and follow his commands and decrees that I
give you today."
11On the same day Moses commanded the
people:
12When you have crossed the Jordan, these
tribes shall stand on Mount Gerizim to bless the
people: Simeon, Levi, Judah, Issachar, Joseph
and Benjamin. 13And these tribes shall stand
on Mount Ebal to pronounce curses: Reuben,
Gad, Asher, Zebulun, Dan and Naphtali.
14The Levites shall recite to all the people of
Israel in a loud voice:

15"Cursed is the man who carves an
image or casts an idol—a thing detestable
to the LORD, the work of the craftsman's
hands—and sets it up in secret."
Then all the people shall say,
"Amen!"
16"Cursed is the man who dishonors
his father or his mother."
Then all the people shall say,
"Amen!"
17"Cursed is the man who moves his
neighbor's boundary stone."
Then all the people shall say,
"Amen!"
18"Cursed is the man who leads the
blind astray on the road."
Then all the people shall say,
"Amen!"
19"Cursed is the man who withholds
justice from the alien, the fatherless or
the widow."
Then all the people shall say,
"Amen!"
20"Cursed is the man who sleeps with
his father's wife, for he dishonors his father's bed."
Then all the people shall say,
"Amen!"

---

a 7 Traditionally *peace offerings*

21“Cursed is the man who has sexual
relations with any animal.”
Then all the people shall say,
“Amen!”
22“Cursed is the man who sleeps with
his sister, the daughter of his father or the
daughter of his mother.”
Then all the people shall say,
“Amen!”
23“Cursed is the man who sleeps with
his mother-in-law.”
Then all the people shall say,
“Amen!”
24“Cursed is the man who kills his
neighbor secretly.”
Then all the people shall say,
“Amen!”
25“Cursed is the man who accepts a
bribe to kill an innocent person.”
Then all the people shall say,
“Amen!”
26“Cursed is the man who does not
uphold the words of this law by carrying
them out.”
Then all the people shall say,
“Amen!”

Blessings for Obedience

28 If you fully obey the LORD your God and
carefully follow all his commands I give
you today, the LORD your God will set
you high above all the nations on earth. 2All
these blessings will come upon you and accompany you if you obey the LORD your God:

3You will be blessed in the city and
blessed in the country.
4The fruit of your womb will be blessed,
and the crops of your land and the young
of your livestock—the calves of your herds
and the lambs of your flocks.
5Your basket and your kneading trough
will be blessed.
6You will be blessed when you come in
and blessed when you go out.

7The LORD will grant that the enemies who
rise up against you will be defeated before you.
They will come at you from one direction but
flee from you in seven.
8The LORD will send a blessing on your
barns and on everything you put your hand
to. The LORD your God will bless you in the
land he is giving you.
9The LORD will establish you as his holy
people, as he promised you on oath, if you
keep the commands of the LORD your God
and walk in his ways. 10Then all the peoples on
earth will see that you are called by the name
of the LORD, and they will fear you. 11The
LORD will grant you abundant prosperity—in
the fruit of your womb, the young of your livestock and the crops of your ground—in the
land he swore to your forefathers to give you.
12The LORD will open the heavens, the storehouse of his bounty, to send rain on your land
in season and to bless all the work of your
hands. You will lend to many nations but will
borrow from none. 13The LORD will make you
the head, not the tail. If you pay attention to
the commands of the LORD your God that I
give you this day and carefully follow them, you
will always be at the top, never at the bottom.
14Do not turn aside from any of the commands
I give you today, to the right or to the left, following other gods and serving them.

Curses for Disobedience

15However, if you do not obey the LORD
your God and do not carefully follow all his
commands and decrees I am giving you today,
all these curses will come upon you and overtake you:

16You will be cursed in the city and
cursed in the country.
17Your basket and your kneading
trough will be cursed.
18The fruit of your womb will be
cursed, and the crops of your land, and
the calves of your herds and the lambs of
your flocks.
19You will be cursed when you come in
and cursed when you go out.

20The LORD will send on you curses, confusion and rebuke in everything you put your
hand to, until you are destroyed and come to
sudden ruin because of the evil you have done
in forsaking him.[a] 21The LORD will plague you
with diseases until he has destroyed you from
the land you are entering to possess. 22The
LORD will strike you with wasting disease, with
fever and inflammation, with scorching heat
and drought, with blight and mildew, which
will plague you until you perish. 23The sky over
your head will be bronze, the ground beneath
you iron. 24The LORD will turn the rain of your
country into dust and powder; it will come
down from the skies until you are destroyed.
25The LORD will cause you to be defeated
before your enemies. You will come at them

a 20 Hebrew *me*

from one direction but flee from them in seven, and you will become a thing of horror to all the kingdoms on earth. 26Your carcasses will be food for all the birds of the air and the beasts of the earth, and there will be no one to frighten them away. 27The LORD will afflict you with the boils of Egypt and with tumors, festering sores and the itch, from which you cannot be cured. 28The LORD will afflict you with madness, blindness and confusion of mind. 29At midday you will grope about like a blind man in the dark. You will be unsuccessful in everything you do; day after day you will be oppressed and robbed, with no one to rescue you.

30You will be pledged to be married to a woman, but another will take her and ravish her. You will build a house, but you will not live in it. You will plant a vineyard, but you will not even begin to enjoy its fruit. 31Your ox will be slaughtered before your eyes, but you will eat none of it. Your donkey will be forcibly taken from you and will not be returned. Your sheep will be given to your enemies, and no one will rescue them. 32Your sons and daughters will be given to another nation, and you will wear out your eyes watching for them day after day, powerless to lift a hand. 33A people that you do not know will eat what your land and labor produce, and you will have nothing but cruel oppression all your days. 34The sights you see will drive you mad. 35The LORD will afflict your knees and legs with painful boils that cannot be cured, spreading from the soles of your feet to the top of your head.

36The LORD will drive you and the king you set over you to a nation unknown to you or your fathers. There you will worship other gods, gods of wood and stone. 37You will become a thing of horror and an object of scorn and ridicule to all the nations where the LORD will drive you.

38You will sow much seed in the field but you will harvest little, because locusts will devour it. 39You will plant vineyards and cultivate them but you will not drink the wine or gather the grapes, because worms will eat them. 40You will have olive trees throughout your country but you will not use the oil, because the olives will drop off. 41You will have sons and daughters but you will not keep them, because they will go into captivity. 42Swarms of locusts will take over all your trees and the crops of your land.

43The alien who lives among you will rise above you higher and higher, but you will sink lower and lower. 44He will lend to you, but you will not lend to him. He will be the head, but you will be the tail.

45All these curses will come upon you. They will pursue you and overtake you until you are destroyed, because you did not obey the LORD your God and observe the commands and decrees he gave you. 46They will be a sign and a wonder to you and your descendants forever. 47Because you did not serve the LORD your God joyfully and gladly in the time of prosperity, 48therefore in hunger and thirst, in nakedness and dire poverty, you will serve the enemies the LORD sends against you. He will put an iron yoke on your neck until he has destroyed you.

49The LORD will bring a nation against you from far away, from the ends of the earth, like an eagle swooping down, a nation whose language you will not understand, 50a fierce-looking nation without respect for the old or pity for the young. 51They will devour the young of your livestock and the crops of your land until you are destroyed. They will leave you no grain, new wine or oil, nor any calves of your herds or lambs of your flocks until you are ruined. 52They will lay siege to all the cities throughout your land until the high fortified walls in which you trust fall down. They will besiege all the cities throughout the land the LORD your God is giving you.

53Because of the suffering that your enemy will inflict on you during the siege, you will eat the fruit of the womb, the flesh of the sons and daughters the LORD your God has given you. 54Even the most gentle and sensitive man among you will have no compassion on his own brother or the wife he loves or his surviving children, 55and he will not give to one of them any of the flesh of his children that he is eating. It will be all he has left because of the suffering your enemy will inflict on you during the siege of all your cities. 56The most gentle and sensitive woman among you—so sensitive and gentle that she would not venture to touch the ground with the sole of her foot—will begrudge the husband she loves and her own son or daughter 57the afterbirth from her womb and the children she bears. For she intends to eat them secretly during the siege and in the distress that your enemy will inflict on you in your cities.

58If you do not carefully follow all the words of this law, which are written in this book, and do not revere this glorious and awesome name—the LORD your God— 59the LORD will send fearful plagues on you and your descendants, harsh and prolonged disasters, and severe and lingering illnesses. 60He will bring upon you all the diseases of Egypt

that you dreaded, and they will cling to you.
61The LORD will also bring on you every kind
of sickness and disaster not recorded in this
Book of the Law, until you are destroyed.
62You who were as numerous as the stars in
the sky will be left but few in number, because
you did not obey the LORD your God. 63Just
as it pleased the LORD to make you prosper
and increase in number, so it will please him
to ruin and destroy you. You will be uprooted
from the land you are entering to possess.

64Then the LORD will scatter you among all
nations, from one end of the earth to the other. There you will worship other gods—gods
of wood and stone, which neither you nor
your fathers have known. 65Among those nations you will find no repose, no resting place
for the sole of your foot. There the LORD will
give you an anxious mind, eyes weary with
longing, and a despairing heart. 66You will
live in constant suspense, filled with dread
both night and day, never sure of your life.
67In the morning you will say, "If only it were
evening!" and in the evening, "If only it were
morning!"—because of the terror that will fill
your hearts and the sights that your eyes will
see. 68The LORD will send you back in ships
to Egypt on a journey I said you should never
make again. There you will offer yourselves for
sale to your enemies as male and female slaves,
but no one will buy you.

Renewal of the Covenant

29 These are the terms of the covenant the
LORD commanded Moses to make with
the Israelites in Moab, in addition to the
covenant he had made with them at Horeb.

2Moses summoned all the Israelites and
said to them:

Your eyes have seen all that the LORD did
in Egypt to Pharaoh, to all his officials and
to all his land. 3With your own eyes you saw
those great trials, those miraculous signs and
great wonders. 4But to this day the LORD has
not given you a mind that understands or eyes
that see or ears that hear. 5During the forty
years that I led you through the desert, your
clothes did not wear out, nor did the sandals
on your feet. 6You ate no bread and drank no
wine or other fermented drink. I did this so
that you might know that I am the LORD your
God.

7When you reached this place, Sihon king
of Heshbon and Og king of Bashan came out
to fight against us, but we defeated them. 8We
took their land and gave it as an inheritance to
the Reubenites, the Gadites and the half-tribe
of Manasseh.

9Carefully follow the terms of this covenant,
so that you may prosper in everything you do.
10All of you are standing today in the presence of the LORD your God—your leaders and
chief men, your elders and officials, and all the
other men of Israel, 11together with your children and your wives, and the aliens living in
your camps who chop your wood and carry
your water. 12You are standing here in order
to enter into a covenant with the LORD your
God, a covenant the LORD is making with you
this day and sealing with an oath, 13to confirm you this day as his people, that he may be
your God as he promised you and as he swore
to your fathers, Abraham, Isaac and Jacob. 14I
am making this covenant, with its oath, not
only with you 15who are standing here with
us today in the presence of the LORD our God
but also with those who are not here today.

16You yourselves know how we lived in
Egypt and how we passed through the countries on the way here. 17You saw among them
their detestable images and idols of wood and
stone, of silver and gold. 18Make sure there is
no man or woman, clan or tribe among you
today whose heart turns away from the LORD
our God to go and worship the gods of those
nations; make sure there is no root among you
that produces such bitter poison.

19When such a person hears the words of
this oath, he invokes a blessing on himself and
therefore thinks, "I will be safe, even though I
persist in going my own way." This will bring
disaster on the watered land as well as the
dry.[a] 20The LORD will never be willing to forgive him; his wrath and zeal will burn against
that man. All the curses written in this book
will fall upon him, and the LORD will blot out
his name from under heaven. 21The LORD will
single him out from all the tribes of Israel for
disaster, according to all the curses of the covenant written in this Book of the Law.

22Your children who follow you in later
generations and foreigners who come from
distant lands will see the calamities that have
fallen on the land and the diseases with which
the LORD has afflicted it. 23The whole land will
be a burning waste of salt and sulfur—nothing planted, nothing sprouting, no vegetation
growing on it. It will be like the destruction
of Sodom and Gomorrah, Admah and Zeboiim, which the LORD overthrew in fierce anger.

a 19 Or *way, in order to add drunkenness to thirst."*

WEDNESDAY
READ DEUTERONOMY 29:2–6

OUR FAVORITE YEAR

During the forty years that I led you through the desert, your clothes did not wear out, nor did the sandals on your feet. You ate no bread and drank no wine or other fermented drink. I did this so that you might know that I am the LORD your God.

— DEUTERONOMY 29:5–6

To celebrate our anniversary, my husband and I splurged on an Italian feast. Over an appetizer, David startled me by asking, "What has been your favorite year since we married?" I really had to think about that. I'm not sure I can choose one specific year even now.

My first instinct was to look back, way back, because recent years have been fraught with painful experiences. My father died, David's work situation fell apart and our church suffered a long period of conflict. Yet God was amazingly near to us during our heartbreak, during our waiting, during our healing. Recent years were awful years, but they convinced us that God is sovereign and that he is good.

As for those early years, we were so broke! David was going to school, and we were trying to pay off school debts at the same time. We drove a little tin can on wheels. David stuck cardboard in his loafers to cover the holes in the soles. We turned the channels on our $10 black-and-white TV with a pliers and spent a lot of time in our bedroom—the only room we could afford to cool. From our honeymoon until our first anniversary, we didn't set foot in a restaurant, not even for fast food. And we loved it. Month after month, we paid the bills. Those early years convinced us that God would provide.

Marriage statistics report that the years of raising young children rank lowest for marital satisfaction. We're still dealing with dirty diapers, sleepless nights, constant noise and toys, and an overload of personalities in the house. Yet, it's been incredible to see God create four whole new people, using us. These years have been tough, but God has built our marriage by drawing us together as we made crucial parenting decisions.

You see? It's impossible to settle on a "best year yet." But as I look back, I see that God has been with us, and he's always been good.

God disciplined his chosen people by making them spend 40 years wandering in the wilderness. The Israelites didn't get closer to their goal of the promised land. But God had a purpose for those 40 years. God made sure that his children had enough to eat and that their clothes didn't wear out. The Israelites didn't need to grow wheat for bread or grapes for wine; God miraculously provided them with manna and water instead. They were free of the distractions of careers and earning money for life's basic needs. They had more time to consider this truth: God is Lord.

The truth that God is the Master, the Creator, the One to worship and adore, the One to build a lifetime on was so important that God didn't mind taking 40 years to teach it to his people.

David and I are learning that now, as we did in every one of the 16 years of our marriage.

—ANNETTE LAPLACA

let's talk

- ✦ Could we pick a favorite year of our married life? Which would it be and why?
- ✦ How has God shown himself to us in different ways at different stages of our life together?
- ✦ How does our marriage reflect that God is Lord?

FOR YOUR NEXT DEVOTIONAL READING, TURN TO PAGE 224.

24All the nations will ask: "Why has the LORD
done this to this land? Why this fierce, burning anger?"
25And the answer will be: "It is because this
people abandoned the covenant of the LORD,
the God of their fathers, the covenant he
made with them when he brought them out
of Egypt. 26They went off and worshiped other gods and bowed down to them, gods they
did not know, gods he had not given them.
27Therefore the LORD's anger burned against
this land, so that he brought on it all the curses written in this book. 28In furious anger and
in great wrath the LORD uprooted them from
their land and thrust them into another land,
as it is now."
29The secret things belong to the LORD our
God, but the things revealed belong to us and
to our children forever, that we may follow all
the words of this law.

Prosperity After Turning to the LORD

30 When all these blessings and curses I
have set before you come upon you
and you take them to heart wherever
the LORD your God disperses you among the
nations, 2and when you and your children
return to the LORD your God and obey him
with all your heart and with all your soul according to everything I command you today,
3then the LORD your God will restore your
fortunes[a] and have compassion on you and
gather you again from all the nations where
he scattered you. 4Even if you have been
banished to the most distant land under the
heavens, from there the LORD your God will
gather you and bring you back. 5He will
bring you to the land that belonged to your
fathers, and you will take possession of it. He
will make you more prosperous and numerous than your fathers. 6The LORD your God
will circumcise your hearts and the hearts of
your descendants, so that you may love him
with all your heart and with all your soul, and
live. 7The LORD your God will put all these
curses on your enemies who hate and persecute you. 8You will again obey the LORD and
follow all his commands I am giving you today. 9Then the LORD your God will make you
most prosperous in all the work of your hands
and in the fruit of your womb, the young of
your livestock and the crops of your land. The
LORD will again delight in you and make you
prosperous, just as he delighted in your fathers, 10if you obey the LORD your God and
keep his commands and decrees that are written in this Book of the Law and turn to the
LORD your God with all your heart and with
all your soul.

The Offer of Life or Death

11Now what I am commanding you today
is not too difficult for you or beyond your
reach. 12It is not up in heaven, so that you
have to ask, "Who will ascend into heaven to
get it and proclaim it to us so we may obey it?"
13Nor is it beyond the sea, so that you have to
ask, "Who will cross the sea to get it and proclaim it to us so we may obey it?" 14No, the
word is very near you; it is in your mouth and
in your heart so you may obey it.
15See, I set before you today life and prosperity, death and destruction. 16For I command
you today to love the LORD your God, to walk
in his ways, and to keep his commands, decrees and laws; then you will live and increase,
and the LORD your God will bless you in the
land you are entering to possess.
17But if your heart turns away and you are
not obedient, and if you are drawn away to
bow down to other gods and worship them,
18I declare to you this day that you will certainly be destroyed. You will not live long in
the land you are crossing the Jordan to enter
and possess.
19This day I call heaven and earth as witnesses against you that I have set before you
life and death, blessings and curses. Now
choose life, so that you and your children may
live 20and that you may love the LORD your
God, listen to his voice, and hold fast to him.
For the LORD is your life, and he will give you
many years in the land he swore to give to
your fathers, Abraham, Isaac and Jacob.

Joshua to Succeed Moses

31 Then Moses went out and spoke these
words to all Israel: 2"I am now a hundred and twenty years old and I am no
longer able to lead you. The LORD has said
to me, 'You shall not cross the Jordan.' 3The
LORD your God himself will cross over ahead
of you. He will destroy these nations before
you, and you will take possession of their land.
Joshua also will cross over ahead of you, as the
LORD said. 4And the LORD will do to them
what he did to Sihon and Og, the kings of
the Amorites, whom he destroyed along with
their land. 5The LORD will deliver them to
you, and you must do to them all that I have

---

a 3 Or *will bring you back from captivity*

commanded you. 6Be strong and courageous.
Do not be afraid or terrified because of them,
for the LORD your God goes with you; he will
never leave you nor forsake you."
7Then Moses summoned Joshua and said
to him in the presence of all Israel, "Be strong
and courageous, for you must go with this people into the land that the LORD swore to their
forefathers to give them, and you must divide
it among them as their inheritance. 8The LORD
himself goes before you and will be with you;
he will never leave you nor forsake you. Do
not be afraid; do not be discouraged."

The Reading of the Law

9So Moses wrote down this law and gave
it to the priests, the sons of Levi, who carried
the ark of the covenant of the LORD, and to all
the elders of Israel. 10Then Moses commanded
them: "At the end of every seven years, in the
year for canceling debts, during the Feast of
Tabernacles, 11when all Israel comes to appear
before the LORD your God at the place he will
choose, you shall read this law before them in
their hearing. 12Assemble the people—men,
women and children, and the aliens living in
your towns—so they can listen and learn to
fear the LORD your God and follow carefully all the words of this law. 13Their children,
who do not know this law, must hear it and
learn to fear the LORD your God as long as
you live in the land you are crossing the Jordan to possess."

Israel's Rebellion Predicted

14The LORD said to Moses, "Now the day
of your death is near. Call Joshua and present
yourselves at the Tent of Meeting, where I will
commission him." So Moses and Joshua came
and presented themselves at the Tent of Meeting.
15Then the LORD appeared at the Tent in a
pillar of cloud, and the cloud stood over the entrance to the Tent. 16And the LORD said to Moses: "You are going to rest with your fathers, and
these people will soon prostitute themselves to
the foreign gods of the land they are entering.
They will forsake me and break the covenant I
made with them. 17On that day I will become
angry with them and forsake them; I will hide
my face from them, and they will be destroyed.
Many disasters and difficulties will come upon
them, and on that day they will ask, 'Have not
these disasters come upon us because our God
is not with us?' 18And I will certainly hide my
face on that day because of all their wickedness
in turning to other gods.
19"Now write down for yourselves this song
and teach it to the Israelites and have them sing
it, so that it may be a witness for me against
them. 20When I have brought them into the
land flowing with milk and honey, the land I
promised on oath to their forefathers, and when
they eat their fill and thrive, they will turn to
other gods and worship them, rejecting me
and breaking my covenant. 21And when many
disasters and difficulties come upon them, this
song will testify against them, because it will
not be forgotten by their descendants. I know
what they are disposed to do, even before I
bring them into the land I promised them on
oath." 22So Moses wrote down this song that
day and taught it to the Israelites.
23The LORD gave this command to Joshua son of Nun: "Be strong and courageous,
for you will bring the Israelites into the land I
promised them on oath, and I myself will be
with you."
24After Moses finished writing in a book
the words of this law from beginning to end,
25he gave this command to the Levites who
carried the ark of the covenant of the LORD:
26"Take this Book of the Law and place it
beside the ark of the covenant of the LORD
your God. There it will remain as a witness
against you. 27For I know how rebellious and
stiff-necked you are. If you have been rebellious against the LORD while I am still alive
and with you, how much more will you rebel
after I die! 28Assemble before me all the elders
of your tribes and all your officials, so that I
can speak these words in their hearing and call
heaven and earth to testify against them. 29For
I know that after my death you are sure to become utterly corrupt and to turn from the way
I have commanded you. In days to come, disaster will fall upon you because you will do
evil in the sight of the LORD and provoke him
to anger by what your hands have made."

The Song of Moses

30And Moses recited the words of this song
from beginning to end in the hearing of the
whole assembly of Israel:

32 Listen, O heavens, and I will speak;
hear, O earth, the words of my mouth.
2 Let my teaching fall like rain
and my words descend like dew,
like showers on new grass,
like abundant rain on tender plants.

3 I will proclaim the name of the LORD.
Oh, praise the greatness of our God!
4 He is the Rock, his works are perfect,

and all his ways are just.
A faithful God who does no wrong,
upright and just is he.

5 They have acted corruptly toward him;
to their shame they are no longer his children,
but a warped and crooked generation.[a]
6 Is this the way you repay the LORD,
O foolish and unwise people?
Is he not your Father, your Creator,[b]
who made you and formed you?

7 Remember the days of old;
consider the generations long past.
Ask your father and he will tell you,
your elders, and they will explain to you.
8 When the Most High gave the nations their inheritance,
when he divided all mankind,
he set up boundaries for the peoples
according to the number of the sons of Israel.[c]
9 For the LORD's portion is his people,
Jacob his allotted inheritance.

10 In a desert land he found him,
in a barren and howling waste.
He shielded him and cared for him;
he guarded him as the apple of his eye,
11 like an eagle that stirs up its nest
and hovers over its young,
that spreads its wings to catch them
and carries them on its pinions.
12 The LORD alone led him;
no foreign god was with him.

13 He made him ride on the heights of the land
and fed him with the fruit of the fields.
He nourished him with honey from the rock,
and with oil from the flinty crag,
14 with curds and milk from herd and flock
and with fattened lambs and goats,
with choice rams of Bashan
and the finest kernels of wheat.
You drank the foaming blood of the grape.

15 Jeshurun[d] grew fat and kicked;
filled with food, he became heavy and sleek.
He abandoned the God who made him
and rejected the Rock his Savior.
16 They made him jealous with their foreign gods
and angered him with their detestable idols.
17 They sacrificed to demons, which are not God—
gods they had not known,
gods that recently appeared,
gods your fathers did not fear.
18 You deserted the Rock, who fathered you;
you forgot the God who gave you birth.

19 The LORD saw this and rejected them
because he was angered by his sons and daughters.
20 "I will hide my face from them," he said,
"and see what their end will be;
for they are a perverse generation,
children who are unfaithful.
21 They made me jealous by what is no god
and angered me with their worthless idols.
I will make them envious by those who are not a people;
I will make them angry by a nation that has no understanding.
22 For a fire has been kindled by my wrath,
one that burns to the realm of death[e] below.
It will devour the earth and its harvests
and set afire the foundations of the mountains.

23 "I will heap calamities upon them
and spend my arrows against them.
24 I will send wasting famine against them,
consuming pestilence and deadly plague;
I will send against them the fangs of wild beasts,
the venom of vipers that glide in the dust.
25 In the street the sword will make them childless;
in their homes terror will reign.
Young men and young women will perish,
infants and gray-haired men.
26 I said I would scatter them
and blot out their memory from mankind,
27 but I dreaded the taunt of the enemy,
lest the adversary misunderstand
and say, 'Our hand has triumphed;
the LORD has not done all this.' "

[a] 5 Or *Corrupt are they and not his children, / a generation warped and twisted to their shame* [b] 6 Or *Father, who bought you* [c] 8 Masoretic Text; Dead Sea Scrolls (see also Septuagint) *sons of God* [d] 15 *Jeshurun* means *the upright one,* that is, Israel. [e] 22 Hebrew *to Sheol*

28 They are a nation without sense,
there is no discernment in them.
29 If only they were wise and would
understand this
and discern what their end will be!
30 How could one man chase a thousand,
or two put ten thousand to flight,
unless their Rock had sold them,
unless the LORD had given them up?
31 For their rock is not like our Rock,
as even our enemies concede.
32 Their vine comes from the vine of Sodom
and from the fields of Gomorrah.
Their grapes are filled with poison,
and their clusters with bitterness.
33 Their wine is the venom of serpents,
the deadly poison of cobras.

34 "Have I not kept this in reserve
and sealed it in my vaults?
35 It is mine to avenge; I will repay.
In due time their foot will slip;
their day of disaster is near
and their doom rushes upon them."

36 The LORD will judge his people
and have compassion on his servants
when he sees their strength is gone
and no one is left, slave or free.
37 He will say: "Now where are their gods,
the rock they took refuge in,
38 the gods who ate the fat of their sacrifices
and drank the wine of their drink
offerings?
Let them rise up to help you!
Let them give you shelter!

39 "See now that I myself am He!
There is no god besides me.
I put to death and I bring to life,
I have wounded and I will heal,
and no one can deliver out of my hand.
40 I lift my hand to heaven and declare:
As surely as I live forever,
41 when I sharpen my flashing sword
and my hand grasps it in judgment,
I will take vengeance on my adversaries
and repay those who hate me.
42 I will make my arrows drunk with blood,
while my sword devours flesh:
the blood of the slain and the captives,
the heads of the enemy leaders."

43 Rejoice, O nations, with his people,[a, b]
for he will avenge the blood of his
servants;
he will take vengeance on his enemies
and make atonement for his land and
people.

44 Moses came with Joshua[c] son of Nun and
spoke all the words of this song in the hearing
of the people. 45 When Moses finished reciting
all these words to all Israel, 46 he said to them,
"Take to heart all the words I have solemnly declared to you this day, so that you may
command your children to obey carefully all
the words of this law. 47 They are not just idle
words for you—they are your life. By them
you will live long in the land you are crossing
the Jordan to possess."

Moses to Die on Mount Nebo

48 On that same day the LORD told Moses,
49 "Go up into the Abarim Range to Mount
Nebo in Moab, across from Jericho, and view
Canaan, the land I am giving the Israelites as
their own possession. 50 There on the mountain that you have climbed you will die and be
gathered to your people, just as your brother
Aaron died on Mount Hor and was gathered
to his people. 51 This is because both of you
broke faith with me in the presence of the Israelites at the waters of Meribah Kadesh in the
Desert of Zin and because you did not uphold
my holiness among the Israelites. 52 Therefore,
you will see the land only from a distance; you
will not enter the land I am giving to the people of Israel."

Moses Blesses the Tribes

33 This is the blessing that Moses the man
of God pronounced on the Israelites before his death. 2 He said:

"The LORD came from Sinai
and dawned over them from Seir;
he shone forth from Mount Paran.
He came with[d] myriads of holy ones
from the south, from his mountain
slopes.[e]
3 Surely it is you who love the people;
all the holy ones are in your hand.
At your feet they all bow down,
and from you receive instruction,
4 the law that Moses gave us,
the possession of the assembly of Jacob.
5 He was king over Jeshurun[f]
when the leaders of the people
assembled,
along with the tribes of Israel.

[a] 43 Or *Make his people rejoice, O nations* [b] 43 Masoretic Text; Dead Sea Scrolls (see also Septuagint) *people, / and let all the angels worship him /* [c] 44 Hebrew *Hoshea,* a variant of *Joshua* [d] 2 Or *from* [e] 2 The meaning of the Hebrew for this phrase is uncertain.
[f] 5 *Jeshurun* means *the upright one,* that is, Israel; also in verse 26.

6 "Let Reuben live and not die,
nor[a] his men be few."

7 And this he said about Judah:

"Hear, O LORD, the cry of Judah;
bring him to his people.
With his own hands he defends his cause.
Oh, be his help against his foes!"

8 About Levi he said:

"Your Thummim and Urim belong
to the man you favored.
You tested him at Massah;
you contended with him at the waters of Meribah.
9 He said of his father and mother,
'I have no regard for them.'
He did not recognize his brothers
or acknowledge his own children,
but he watched over your word
and guarded your covenant.
10 He teaches your precepts to Jacob
and your law to Israel.
He offers incense before you
and whole burnt offerings on your altar.
11 Bless all his skills, O LORD,
and be pleased with the work of his hands.
Smite the loins of those who rise up against him;
strike his foes till they rise no more."

12 About Benjamin he said:

"Let the beloved of the LORD rest secure in him,
for he shields him all day long,
and the one the LORD loves rests between his shoulders."

13 About Joseph he said:

"May the LORD bless his land
with the precious dew from heaven above
and with the deep waters that lie below;
14 with the best the sun brings forth
and the finest the moon can yield;
15 with the choicest gifts of the ancient mountains
and the fruitfulness of the everlasting hills;
16 with the best gifts of the earth and its fullness
and the favor of him who dwelt in the burning bush.
Let all these rest on the head of Joseph,
on the brow of the prince among[b] his brothers.
17 In majesty he is like a firstborn bull;
his horns are the horns of a wild ox.
With them he will gore the nations,
even those at the ends of the earth.
Such are the ten thousands of Ephraim;
such are the thousands of Manasseh."

18 About Zebulun he said:

"Rejoice, Zebulun, in your going out,
and you, Issachar, in your tents.
19 They will summon peoples to the mountain
and there offer sacrifices of righteousness;
they will feast on the abundance of the seas,
on the treasures hidden in the sand."

20 About Gad he said:

"Blessed is he who enlarges Gad's domain!
Gad lives there like a lion,
tearing at arm or head.
21 He chose the best land for himself;
the leader's portion was kept for him.
When the heads of the people assembled,
he carried out the LORD's righteous will,
and his judgments concerning Israel."

22 About Dan he said:

"Dan is a lion's cub,
springing out of Bashan."

23 About Naphtali he said:

"Naphtali is abounding with the favor of the LORD
and is full of his blessing;
he will inherit southward to the lake."

24 About Asher he said:

"Most blessed of sons is Asher;
let him be favored by his brothers,
and let him bathe his feet in oil.
25 The bolts of your gates will be iron and bronze,
and your strength will equal your days.

26 "There is no one like the God of Jeshurun,
who rides on the heavens to help you
and on the clouds in his majesty.
27 The eternal God is your refuge,
and underneath are the everlasting arms.

[a] 6 Or *but let* [b] 16 Or *of the one separated from*

He will drive out your enemy before you,
saying, 'Destroy him!'
28 So Israel will live in safety alone;
Jacob's spring is secure
in a land of grain and new wine,
where the heavens drop dew.
29 Blessed are you, O Israel!
Who is like you,
a people saved by the LORD?
He is your shield and helper
and your glorious sword.
Your enemies will cower before you,
and you will trample down their high
places.[a]"

The Death of Moses

34 Then Moses climbed Mount Nebo from
the plains of Moab to the top of Pisgah,
across from Jericho. There the LORD
showed him the whole land—from Gilead to
Dan, 2all of Naphtali, the territory of Ephraim
and Manasseh, all the land of Judah as far as the
western sea,[b] 3the Negev and the whole region
from the Valley of Jericho, the City of Palms, as
far as Zoar. 4Then the LORD said to him, "This is
the land I promised on oath to Abraham, Isaac
and Jacob when I said, 'I will give it to your descendants.' I have let you see it with your eyes,
but you will not cross over into it."

5And Moses the servant of the LORD died
there in Moab, as the LORD had said. 6He
buried him[c] in Moab, in the valley opposite
Beth Peor, but to this day no one knows where
his grave is. 7Moses was a hundred and twenty years old when he died, yet his eyes were
not weak nor his strength gone. 8The Israelites
grieved for Moses in the plains of Moab thirty
days, until the time of weeping and mourning
was over.

9Now Joshua son of Nun was filled with
the spirit[d] of wisdom because Moses had laid
his hands on him. So the Israelites listened to
him and did what the LORD had commanded
Moses.

10Since then, no prophet has risen in Israel
like Moses, whom the LORD knew face to face,
11who did all those miraculous signs and wonders the LORD sent him to do in Egypt—to
Pharaoh and to all his officials and to his whole
land. 12For no one has ever shown the mighty
power or performed the awesome deeds that
Moses did in the sight of all Israel.

[a] 29 Or *will tread upon their bodies* [b] 2 That is, the Mediterranean [c] 6 Or *He was buried* [d] 9 Or *Spirit*

JOSHUA

Joshua

QUICK FACTS

AUTHOR Joshua likely wrote much of the book in its earliest form.

AUDIENCE The Israelites who settled in the promised land

DATE Most of the book was probably written near the time of Joshua's death, about 1390 B.C.

SETTING Crossing the Jordan River and entering the promised land (Canaan)

Before Moses died, he commissioned and laid hands on his successor, Joshua, one of two spies who had seen Canaan and trusted God to help the Israelites conquer it. In the book of Joshua, we see God instructing Joshua to finish the job started by Moses and lead the people into the promised land. "Be strong and very courageous," God charged Joshua. "Be careful to obey all the law my servant Moses gave you" (Joshua 1:7).

So Joshua led the people, first by presenting them with a new intelligence report of the enemy's morale: "All who live in this country are melting in fear because of you" (Joshua 2:9), and then by leading them through the floodwaters of the Jordan River, around the city of Jericho till its walls collapsed, and into the promised land, destroying wicked kings, people and pagan practices as they went. Along the way the people of Israel learned several powerful lessons: Battles were won by God's strength, not their own. One man's greed could cause massive defeat. A treaty made without God's direction could be costly. God would divide Canaan among them.

In many ways, marriage can be like a promised land that we enter with trembling hearts. The joys are so alluring, yet the challenges so great. But like Joshua and the Israelites, we can go forward in victory if we together hold fast to the Lord, trusting him to lead us and give us the courage and strength we need.

The LORD Commands Joshua

1 After the death of Moses the servant of the LORD, the LORD said to Joshua son of Nun, Moses' aide: 2“Moses my servant is dead. Now then, you and all these people, get ready to cross the Jordan River into the land I am about to give to them—to the Israelites. 3I will give you every place where you set your foot, as I promised Moses. 4Your territory will extend from the desert to Lebanon, and from the great river, the Euphrates—all the Hittite country—to the Great Sea[a] on the west. 5No one will be able to stand up against you all the days of your life. As I was with Moses, so I will be with you; I will never leave you nor forsake you.

6“Be strong and courageous, because you will lead these people to inherit the land I swore to their forefathers to give them. 7Be strong and very courageous. Be careful to obey all the law my servant Moses gave you; do not turn from it to the right or to the left, that you may be successful wherever you go. 8Do not let this Book of the Law depart from your mouth; meditate on it day and night, so that you may be careful to do everything written in it. Then you will be prosperous and successful. 9Have I not commanded you? Be strong and courageous. Do not be terrified; do not be discouraged, for the LORD your God will be with you wherever you go.”

10So Joshua ordered the officers of the people: 11“Go through the camp and tell the people, ‘Get your supplies ready. Three days from now you will cross the Jordan here to go in and take possession of the land the LORD your God is giving you for your own.’ ”

12But to the Reubenites, the Gadites and the half-tribe of Manasseh, Joshua said, 13“Remember the command that Moses the servant of the LORD gave you: ‘The LORD your God is giving you rest and has granted you this land.’ 14Your wives, your children and your livestock may stay in the land that Moses gave you east of the Jordan, but all your fighting men, fully armed, must cross over ahead of your brothers. You are to help your brothers 15until the LORD gives them rest, as he has done for you, and until they too have taken possession of the land that the LORD your God is giving them. After that, you may go back and occupy your own land, which Moses the servant of the LORD gave you east of the Jordan toward the sunrise.”

16Then they answered Joshua, “Whatever you have commanded us we will do, and wherever you send us we will go. 17Just as we fully obeyed Moses, so we will obey you. Only may the LORD your God be with you as he was with Moses. 18Whoever rebels against your word and does not obey your words, whatever you may command them, will be put to death. Only be strong and courageous!”

Rahab and the Spies

2 Then Joshua son of Nun secretly sent two spies from Shittim. “Go, look over the land,” he said, “especially Jericho.” So they went and entered the house of a prostitute[b] named Rahab and stayed there.

2The king of Jericho was told, “Look! Some of the Israelites have come here tonight to spy out the land.” 3So the king of Jericho sent this message to Rahab: “Bring out the men who came to you and entered your house, because they have come to spy out the whole land.”

4But the woman had taken the two men and hidden them. She said, “Yes, the men came to me, but I did not know where they had come from. 5At dusk, when it was time to close the city gate, the men left. I don't know which way they went. Go after them quickly. You may catch up with them.” 6(But she had taken them up to the roof and hidden them under the stalks of flax she had laid out on the roof.) 7So the men set out in pursuit of the spies on the road that leads to the fords of the Jordan, and as soon as the pursuers had gone out, the gate was shut.

8Before the spies lay down for the night, she went up on the roof 9and said to them, “I know that the LORD has given this land to you and that a great fear of you has fallen on us, so that all who live in this country are melting in fear because of you. 10We have heard how the LORD dried up the water of the Red Sea[c] for you when you came out of Egypt, and what you did to Sihon and Og, the two kings of the Amorites east of the Jordan, whom you completely destroyed.[d] 11When we heard of it, our hearts melted and everyone's courage failed because of you, for the LORD your God is God in heaven above and on the earth below. 12Now then, please swear to me by the LORD that you will show kindness to my family, because I have shown kindness to you. Give me a sure sign 13that you will spare the lives of my father and mother, my brothers and sisters, and all

[a] 4 That is, the Mediterranean [b] 1 Or possibly *an innkeeper* [c] 10 Hebrew *Yam Suph*; that is, Sea of Reeds [d] 10 The Hebrew term refers to the irrevocable giving over of things or persons to the LORD, often by totally destroying them.

who belong to them, and that you will save
us from death.”
14“Our lives for your lives!” the men assured her. “If you don’t tell what we are doing,
we will treat you kindly and faithfully when
the LORD gives us the land.”
15So she let them down by a rope through
the window, for the house she lived in was part
of the city wall. 16Now she had said to them,
“Go to the hills so the pursuers will not find
you. Hide yourselves there three days until
they return, and then go on your way.”
17The men said to her, “This oath you made
us swear will not be binding on us 18unless,
when we enter the land, you have tied this
scarlet cord in the window through which you
let us down, and unless you have brought your
father and mother, your brothers and all your
family into your house. 19If anyone goes outside your house into the street, his blood will
be on his own head; we will not be responsible. As for anyone who is in the house with
you, his blood will be on our head if a hand
is laid on him. 20But if you tell what we are
doing, we will be released from the oath you
made us swear.”
21“Agreed,” she replied. “Let it be as you
say.” So she sent them away and they departed.
And she tied the scarlet cord in the window.
22When they left, they went into the hills
and stayed there three days, until the pursuers
had searched all along the road and returned
without finding them. 23Then the two men
started back. They went down out of the hills,
forded the river and came to Joshua son of
Nun and told him everything that had happened to them. 24They said to Joshua, “The
LORD has surely given the whole land into our
hands; all the people are melting in fear because of us.”

Crossing the Jordan

3 Early in the morning Joshua and all the
Israelites set out from Shittim and went
to the Jordan, where they camped before
crossing over. 2After three days the officers
went throughout the camp, 3giving orders to
the people: “When you see the ark of the covenant of the LORD your God, and the priests,
who are Levites, carrying it, you are to move
out from your positions and follow it. 4Then
you will know which way to go, since you
have never been this way before. But keep a
distance of about a thousand yards[a] between
you and the ark; do not go near it.”
5Joshua told the people, “Consecrate yourselves, for tomorrow the LORD will do amazing things among you.”
6Joshua said to the priests, “Take up the
ark of the covenant and pass on ahead of the
people.” So they took it up and went ahead
of them.
7And the LORD said to Joshua, “Today I
will begin to exalt you in the eyes of all Israel, so they may know that I am with you as
I was with Moses. 8Tell the priests who carry
the ark of the covenant: ‘When you reach the
edge of the Jordan’s waters, go and stand in
the river.’ ”
9Joshua said to the Israelites, “Come here
and listen to the words of the LORD your God.
10This is how you will know that the living
God is among you and that he will certainly
drive out before you the Canaanites, Hittites,
Hivites, Perizzites, Girgashites, Amorites and
Jebusites. 11See, the ark of the covenant of
the Lord of all the earth will go into the Jordan ahead of you. 12Now then, choose twelve
men from the tribes of Israel, one from each
tribe. 13And as soon as the priests who carry the ark of the LORD—the Lord of all the
earth—set foot in the Jordan, its waters flowing downstream will be cut off and stand up
in a heap.”
14So when the people broke camp to cross
the Jordan, the priests carrying the ark of the
covenant went ahead of them. 15Now the Jordan is at flood stage all during harvest. Yet
as soon as the priests who carried the ark
reached the Jordan and their feet touched
the water’s edge, 16the water from upstream
stopped flowing. It piled up in a heap a great
distance away, at a town called Adam in the
vicinity of Zarethan, while the water flowing
down to the Sea of the Arabah (the Salt Sea[b])
was completely cut off. So the people crossed
over opposite Jericho. 17The priests who carried the ark of the covenant of the LORD
stood firm on dry ground in the middle of
the Jordan, while all Israel passed by until the
whole nation had completed the crossing on
dry ground.
4 When the whole nation had finished crossing the Jordan, the LORD said to Joshua,
2“Choose twelve men from among the
people, one from each tribe, 3and tell them
to take up twelve stones from the middle of
the Jordan from right where the priests stood
and to carry them over with you and put them
down at the place where you stay tonight.”

---

[a] 4 Hebrew *about two thousand cubits* (about 900 meters) [b] 16 That is, the Dead Sea

THURSDAY
READ JOSHUA 4:1–9

MEMORY STONE COLLECTION

We have a plate hanging on the wall just above the light switch in our bedroom. It's one of those commemorative plates with the date of our wedding. Every time we turn on the light, we're reminded of our wedding day.

Reminders of significant events accomplish a variety of purposes. God directed Joshua to set up a pile of stones taken from the Jordan River after the children of Israel crossed the river on dry ground. The stones served as a reminder that God had brought his people into the promised land. The stones also functioned as a device that would encourage the next generation of Israelites to ask their parents what the stones meant. The Israelite parents were to respond by telling their children how God had miraculously ushered them into Canaan, just as he had miraculously delivered them from Pharaoh when they crossed the Red Sea.

My wife and I are well served by the plate that hangs on our wall. It reminds us that we have committed to live together as husband and wife. We have been doing so for more than 40 years.

"Each of you is to take up a stone on his shoulder, according to the number of the tribes of the Israelites, to serve as a sign among you."

— Joshua 4:5–6

let's *talk*

- ✦ What reminders do we have of our wedding or life together? Why are they important to us?
- ✦ What "memory stones" have we specifically created to remind us of what God has done for us?
- ✦ What do we say when our children or others ask us about our reminders?

In our society we need reminders that in marriage we have pledged to be faithful to each other for as long as we live. My wedding band does the same thing as the wedding plate: It reminds me that I am married. It reminds me that I have pledged myself to be faithful to my wife. I find these reminders helpful; they keep my mind on what is important in the midst of the daily routines of life.

I am sure the people of Israel found reminders helpful as well. If you have children, you know that they can ask multitudes of questions. Just about anything can set off a barrage of questions. No doubt children in ancient Israel behaved in the same way. The stones from the Jordan River were not just artifacts of history; they served as a reminder of God's mighty acts. The pile of stones provided fathers and mothers an opportunity to explain to their children *what* God had done, *how* God had delivered his people, and *why* he had done this—because he was their Redeemer.

When I look at the plate hanging on my wall, I remember that I'm married. Even more important, I remember that my wife and I are to live together as those redeemed by God and brought together to live for his glory.

We all need reminders of our marriage. We also need to remember that Christian marriage is unique. We live for one another, but together we also live for our Lord and Savior, Jesus Christ. The next time you look at your wedding band, remember how God brought you and your spouse together to serve him as a couple. If you have kids and they ask you why you wear your ring, tell them how Jesus is the center of your relationship. Then tell them about Jesus.

—ALLEN CURRY

FOR YOUR NEXT DEVOTIONAL READING, TURN TO PAGE 228.

4So Joshua called together the twelve men he had appointed from the Israelites, one from each tribe, 5and said to them, "Go over before the ark of the LORD your God into the middle of the Jordan. Each of you is to take up a stone on his shoulder, according to the number of the tribes of the Israelites, 6to serve as a sign among you. In the future, when your children ask you, 'What do these stones mean?' 7tell them that the flow of the Jordan was cut off before the ark of the covenant of the LORD. When it crossed the Jordan, the waters of the Jordan were cut off. These stones are to be a memorial to the people of Israel forever."

8So the Israelites did as Joshua commanded them. They took twelve stones from the middle of the Jordan, according to the number of the tribes of the Israelites, as the LORD had told Joshua; and they carried them over with them to their camp, where they put them down. 9Joshua set up the twelve stones that had been[a] in the middle of the Jordan at the spot where the priests who carried the ark of the covenant had stood. And they are there to this day.

10Now the priests who carried the ark remained standing in the middle of the Jordan until everything the LORD had commanded Joshua was done by the people, just as Moses had directed Joshua. The people hurried over, 11and as soon as all of them had crossed, the ark of the LORD and the priests came to the other side while the people watched. 12The men of Reuben, Gad and the half-tribe of Manasseh crossed over, armed, in front of the Israelites, as Moses had directed them. 13About forty thousand armed for battle crossed over before the LORD to the plains of Jericho for war.

14That day the LORD exalted Joshua in the sight of all Israel; and they revered him all the days of his life, just as they had revered Moses.

15Then the LORD said to Joshua, 16"Command the priests carrying the ark of the Testimony to come up out of the Jordan."

17So Joshua commanded the priests, "Come up out of the Jordan."

18And the priests came up out of the river carrying the ark of the covenant of the LORD. No sooner had they set their feet on the dry ground than the waters of the Jordan returned to their place and ran at flood stage as before.

19On the tenth day of the first month the people went up from the Jordan and camped at Gilgal on the eastern border of Jericho. 20And Joshua set up at Gilgal the twelve stones they had taken out of the Jordan. 21He said to the Israelites, "In the future when your descendants ask their fathers, 'What do these stones mean?' 22tell them, 'Israel crossed the Jordan on dry ground.' 23For the LORD your God dried up the Jordan before you until you had crossed over. The LORD your God did to the Jordan just what he had done to the Red Sea[b] when he dried it up before us until we had crossed over. 24He did this so that all the peoples of the earth might know that the hand of the LORD is powerful and so that you might always fear the LORD your God."

Circumcision at Gilgal

5 Now when all the Amorite kings west of the Jordan and all the Canaanite kings along the coast heard how the LORD had dried up the Jordan before the Israelites until we had crossed over, their hearts melted and they no longer had the courage to face the Israelites.

2At that time the LORD said to Joshua, "Make flint knives and circumcise the Israelites again." 3So Joshua made flint knives and circumcised the Israelites at Gibeath Haaraloth.[c]

4Now this is why he did so: All those who came out of Egypt—all the men of military age—died in the desert on the way after leaving Egypt. 5All the people that came out had been circumcised, but all the people born in the desert during the journey from Egypt had not. 6The Israelites had moved about in the desert forty years until all the men who were of military age when they left Egypt had died, since they had not obeyed the LORD. For the LORD had sworn to them that they would not see the land that he had solemnly promised their fathers to give us, a land flowing with milk and honey. 7So he raised up their sons in their place, and these were the ones Joshua circumcised. They were still uncircumcised because they had not been circumcised on the way. 8And after the whole nation had been circumcised, they remained where they were in camp until they were healed.

9Then the LORD said to Joshua, "Today I have rolled away the reproach of Egypt from you." So the place has been called Gilgal[d] to this day.

[a] 9 Or *Joshua also set up twelve stones* [b] 23 Hebrew *Yam Suph*; that is, Sea of Reeds [c] 3 *Gibeath Haaraloth* means *hill of foreskins.*
[d] 9 *Gilgal* sounds like the Hebrew for *roll.*

10 On the evening of the fourteenth day of
the month, while camped at Gilgal on the
plains of Jericho, the Israelites celebrated the
Passover. 11 The day after the Passover, that
very day, they ate some of the produce of the
land: unleavened bread and roasted grain.
12 The manna stopped the day after[a] they ate
this food from the land; there was no longer
any manna for the Israelites, but that year they
ate of the produce of Canaan.

The Fall of Jericho

13 Now when Joshua was near Jericho, he
looked up and saw a man standing in front of
him with a drawn sword in his hand. Joshua
went up to him and asked, "Are you for us or
for our enemies?"

14 "Neither," he replied, "but as commander
of the army of the LORD I have now come."
Then Joshua fell facedown to the ground in
reverence, and asked him, "What message
does my Lord[b] have for his servant?"

15 The commander of the LORD's army replied, "Take off your sandals, for the place
where you are standing is holy." And Joshua
did so.

6 Now Jericho was tightly shut up because
of the Israelites. No one went out and no
one came in.

2 Then the LORD said to Joshua, "See, I have
delivered Jericho into your hands, along with
its king and its fighting men. 3 March around
the city once with all the armed men. Do this
for six days. 4 Have seven priests carry trumpets of rams' horns in front of the ark. On
the seventh day, march around the city seven
times, with the priests blowing the trumpets.
5 When you hear them sound a long blast
on the trumpets, have all the people give a
loud shout; then the wall of the city will collapse and the people will go up, every man
straight in."

6 So Joshua son of Nun called the priests
and said to them, "Take up the ark of the covenant of the LORD and have seven priests carry
trumpets in front of it." 7 And he ordered the
people, "Advance! March around the city, with
the armed guard going ahead of the ark of the
LORD."

8 When Joshua had spoken to the people,
the seven priests carrying the seven trumpets
before the LORD went forward, blowing their
trumpets, and the ark of the LORD's covenant
followed them. 9 The armed guard marched
ahead of the priests who blew the trumpets,
and the rear guard followed the ark. All this
time the trumpets were sounding. 10 But Joshua had commanded the people, "Do not give
a war cry, do not raise your voices, do not say
a word until the day I tell you to shout. Then
shout!" 11 So he had the ark of the LORD carried around the city, circling it once. Then the
people returned to camp and spent the night
there.

12 Joshua got up early the next morning and
the priests took up the ark of the LORD. 13 The
seven priests carrying the seven trumpets went
forward, marching before the ark of the LORD
and blowing the trumpets. The armed men
went ahead of them and the rear guard followed the ark of the LORD, while the trumpets
kept sounding. 14 So on the second day they
marched around the city once and returned to
the camp. They did this for six days.

15 On the seventh day, they got up at daybreak and marched around the city seven
times in the same manner, except that on that
day they circled the city seven times. 16 The
seventh time around, when the priests sounded the trumpet blast, Joshua commanded the
people, "Shout! For the LORD has given you
the city! 17 The city and all that is in it are to be
devoted[c] to the LORD. Only Rahab the prostitute[d] and all who are with her in her house
shall be spared, because she hid the spies
we sent. 18 But keep away from the devoted
things, so that you will not bring about your
own destruction by taking any of them. Otherwise you will make the camp of Israel liable
to destruction and bring trouble on it. 19 All
the silver and gold and the articles of bronze
and iron are sacred to the LORD and must go
into his treasury."

20 When the trumpets sounded, the people shouted, and at the sound of the trumpet, when the people gave a loud shout, the
wall collapsed; so every man charged straight
in, and they took the city. 21 They devoted the
city to the LORD and destroyed with the sword
every living thing in it—men and women,
young and old, cattle, sheep and donkeys.

22 Joshua said to the two men who had spied
out the land, "Go into the prostitute's house
and bring her out and all who belong to her,
in accordance with your oath to her." 23 So the
young men who had done the spying went in
and brought out Rahab, her father and mother and brothers and all who belonged to her.
They brought out her entire family and put
them in a place outside the camp of Israel.

[a] *12* Or *the day* [b] *14* Or *lord* [c] *17* The Hebrew term refers to the irrevocable giving over of things or persons to the LORD, often by totally destroying them; also in verses 18 and 21. [d] *17* Or possibly *innkeeper*; also in verses 22 and 25

24 Then they burned the whole city and everything in it, but they put the silver and gold
and the articles of bronze and iron into the
treasury of the LORD's house. 25 But Joshua
spared Rahab the prostitute, with her family and all who belonged to her, because she
hid the men Joshua had sent as spies to Jericho—and she lives among the Israelites to
this day.
26 At that time Joshua pronounced this solemn oath: "Cursed before the LORD is the man
who undertakes to rebuild this city, Jericho:

"At the cost of his firstborn son
  will he lay its foundations;
at the cost of his youngest
  will he set up its gates."

27 So the LORD was with Joshua, and his
fame spread throughout the land.

Achan's Sin

7 But the Israelites acted unfaithfully in regard to the devoted things[a]; Achan son of
Carmi, the son of Zimri,[b] the son of Zerah, of the tribe of Judah, took some of them.
So the LORD's anger burned against Israel.
2 Now Joshua sent men from Jericho to Ai,
which is near Beth Aven to the east of Bethel,
and told them, "Go up and spy out the region." So the men went up and spied out Ai.
3 When they returned to Joshua, they said,
"Not all the people will have to go up against
Ai. Send two or three thousand men to take it
and do not weary all the people, for only a few
men are there." 4 So about three thousand men
went up; but they were routed by the men of
Ai, 5 who killed about thirty-six of them. They
chased the Israelites from the city gate as far
as the stone quarries[c] and struck them down
on the slopes. At this the hearts of the people
melted and became like water.
6 Then Joshua tore his clothes and fell
facedown to the ground before the ark of
the LORD, remaining there till evening. The
elders of Israel did the same, and sprinkled
dust on their heads. 7 And Joshua said, "Ah,
Sovereign LORD, why did you ever bring this
people across the Jordan to deliver us into the
hands of the Amorites to destroy us? If only
we had been content to stay on the other side
of the Jordan! 8 O Lord, what can I say, now
that Israel has been routed by its enemies?
9 The Canaanites and the other people of the
country will hear about this and they will surround us and wipe out our name from the
earth. What then will you do for your own
great name?"
10 The LORD said to Joshua, "Stand up! What
are you doing down on your face? 11 Israel has
sinned; they have violated my covenant, which
I commanded them to keep. They have taken
some of the devoted things; they have stolen,
they have lied, they have put them with their
own possessions. 12 That is why the Israelites
cannot stand against their enemies; they turn
their backs and run because they have been
made liable to destruction. I will not be with
you anymore unless you destroy whatever
among you is devoted to destruction.
13 "Go, consecrate the people. Tell them,
'Consecrate yourselves in preparation for tomorrow; for this is what the LORD, the God
of Israel, says: That which is devoted is among
you, O Israel. You cannot stand against your
enemies until you remove it.
14 " 'In the morning, present yourselves
tribe by tribe. The tribe that the LORD takes
shall come forward clan by clan; the clan that
the LORD takes shall come forward family by
family; and the family that the LORD takes
shall come forward man by man. 15 He who
is caught with the devoted things shall be destroyed by fire, along with all that belongs to
him. He has violated the covenant of the LORD
and has done a disgraceful thing in Israel!' "
16 Early the next morning Joshua had Israel
come forward by tribes, and Judah was tak-
en. 17 The clans of Judah came forward, and he
took the Zerahites. He had the clan of the Zerahites come forward by families, and Zimri
was taken. 18 Joshua had his family come forward man by man, and Achan son of Carmi,
the son of Zimri, the son of Zerah, of the tribe
of Judah, was taken.
19 Then Joshua said to Achan, "My son, give
glory to the LORD,[d] the God of Israel, and
give him the praise.[e] Tell me what you have
done; do not hide it from me."
20 Achan replied, "It is true! I have sinned
against the LORD, the God of Israel. This is
what I have done: 21 When I saw in the plunder a beautiful robe from Babylonia,[f] two
hundred shekels[g] of silver and a wedge of gold
weighing fifty shekels,[h] I coveted them and
took them. They are hidden in the ground inside my tent, with the silver underneath."

---

a 1 The Hebrew term refers to the irrevocable giving over of things or persons to the LORD, often by totally destroying them; also in verses 11, 12, 13 and 15. *b 1* See Septuagint and 1 Chron. 2:6; Hebrew *Zabdi*; also in verses 17 and 18. *c 5* Or *as far as Shebarim* *d 19* A solemn charge to tell the truth *e 19* Or *and confess to him* *f 21* Hebrew *Shinar* *g 21* That is, about 5 pounds (about 2.3 kilograms) *h 21* That is, about 1 1/4 pounds (about 0.6 kilogram)

FRIDAY
READ JOSHUA 7:1–26

DIGGING OUT OF A LITTLE SIN

I'm tempted to cry, "Not fair!" upon reading the story of Achan. First, it doesn't seem like that big of a deal for him to have taken some treasure as reward for victory in battle. And second, all of the Israelites were held responsible for the sin of one man who had stolen and hidden plunder after the battle of Jericho against God's direct command. Because of the "small" sin of one man, God punished all of Israel by withdrawing his blessing and allowing the people to be humiliated and defeated at the battle of Ai.

I remember when my young children would complain that a punishment was too harsh for their "teeny" disobedience. I'd bring up Adam and Eve's teeny bite of the forbidden fruit. I'd ask them how many bites of the fruit it would have taken to become a punishable act. They got it—that it's not the size of the disobedience but the meaning behind it that's the problem. Like with Achan, Adam and Eve disrespected God by their disobedience.

Likewise, in marriage, individual actions reflect one's commitment to the marriage covenant. When I'm tempted to do something selfish, I ask myself two questions: (1) "How would I feel if Grey did this?" and (2) "How would I feel if our children found out?" I'm stopped in my tracks every time. So, something like an "innocent" email exchange with an old flame is now revealed to my own heart for what it is: betrayal.

"Israel has sinned; they have violated my covenant, which I commanded them to keep. They have taken some of the devoted things; they have stolen, they have lied, they have put them with their own possessions."

— JOSHUA 7:11

let's *talk*

✦ What steps will we take to stay honest with each other about money, friends, recreational activities? In what areas have we been less than fully honest?

✦ What effect might "hidden" sins have on our marriage if we continue doing them for several months or even years?

✦ What "no big deal" sins are we willing to overlook in our relationship? If we continue doing them, what or who might then bring them to light?

Sin in marriage is not an individual issue. It affects the marriage relationship, the wider family and also the entire community. Who would deny that infidelity and divorce have wreaked havoc upon millions of children and ripped the fabric of our society? In the same way, Achan's selfish act ripped the fabric of Israel's relationship with God.

Achan's other sin was the cover-up; he deceitfully hid the plunder he had stolen. But eventually the truth was revealed, just as it is in twenty-first-century families. A woman writes in her journal about her intimate relationship with another man. She thinks no one will ever know. But one day her husband does the unthinkable; he decides to clean all the books on the bookshelf and discovers the diary behind the dusty volumes. Or a husband thinks he can cover his gambling losses by taking greater risks that promise bigger payoffs. But when the bank statement arrives with a negative balance—and his wife gets the mail—the whole family suffers the painful consequences of financial loss.

Achan's lesson still holds true: Everyone loses in the sin game.

—MARY ANN JEFFREYS

FOR YOUR NEXT DEVOTIONAL READING, TURN TO PAGE 234.

22So Joshua sent messengers, and they ran
to the tent, and there it was, hidden in his
tent, with the silver underneath. 23They took
the things from the tent, brought them to
Joshua and all the Israelites and spread them
out before the LORD.

24Then Joshua, together with all Israel, took
Achan son of Zerah, the silver, the robe, the
gold wedge, his sons and daughters, his cattle, donkeys and sheep, his tent and all that
he had, to the Valley of Achor. 25Joshua said,
"Why have you brought this trouble on us?
The LORD will bring trouble on you today."

Then all Israel stoned him, and after they
had stoned the rest, they burned them. 26Over
Achan they heaped up a large pile of rocks,
which remains to this day. Then the LORD
turned from his fierce anger. Therefore that
place has been called the Valley of Achor[a] ever
since.

Ai Destroyed

8 Then the LORD said to Joshua, "Do not
be afraid; do not be discouraged. Take the
whole army with you, and go up and attack
Ai. For I have delivered into your hands the
king of Ai, his people, his city and his land.
2You shall do to Ai and its king as you did to
Jericho and its king, except that you may carry
off their plunder and livestock for yourselves.
Set an ambush behind the city."

3So Joshua and the whole army moved out
to attack Ai. He chose thirty thousand of his
best fighting men and sent them out at night
4with these orders: "Listen carefully. You are to
set an ambush behind the city. Don't go very
far from it. All of you be on the alert. 5I and
all those with me will advance on the city, and
when the men come out against us, as they did
before, we will flee from them. 6They will pursue us until we have lured them away from the
city, for they will say, 'They are running away
from us as they did before.' So when we flee
from them, 7you are to rise up from ambush
and take the city. The LORD your God will
give it into your hand. 8When you have taken
the city, set it on fire. Do what the LORD has
commanded. See to it; you have my orders."

9Then Joshua sent them off, and they went
to the place of ambush and lay in wait between Bethel and Ai, to the west of Ai—but
Joshua spent that night with the people.

10Early the next morning Joshua mustered his men, and he and the leaders of Israel marched before them to Ai. 11The entire
force that was with him marched up and approached the city and arrived in front of it.
They set up camp north of Ai, with the valley
between them and the city. 12Joshua had tak-
en about five thousand men and set them in
ambush between Bethel and Ai, to the west of
the city. 13They had the soldiers take up their
positions—all those in the camp to the north
of the city and the ambush to the west of it.
That night Joshua went into the valley.

14When the king of Ai saw this, he and all
the men of the city hurried out early in the
morning to meet Israel in battle at a certain
place overlooking the Arabah. But he did not
know that an ambush had been set against
him behind the city. 15Joshua and all Israel let
themselves be driven back before them, and
they fled toward the desert. 16All the men of
Ai were called to pursue them, and they pursued Joshua and were lured away from the
city. 17Not a man remained in Ai or Bethel
who did not go after Israel. They left the city
open and went in pursuit of Israel.

18Then the LORD said to Joshua, "Hold out
toward Ai the javelin that is in your hand, for
into your hand I will deliver the city." So Joshua held out his javelin toward Ai. 19As soon
as he did this, the men in the ambush rose
quickly from their position and rushed forward. They entered the city and captured it
and quickly set it on fire.

20The men of Ai looked back and saw the
smoke of the city rising against the sky, but
they had no chance to escape in any direction,
for the Israelites who had been fleeing toward
the desert had turned back against their pursuers. 21For when Joshua and all Israel saw
that the ambush had taken the city and that
smoke was going up from the city, they turned
around and attacked the men of Ai. 22The
men of the ambush also came out of the city
against them, so that they were caught in the
middle, with Israelites on both sides. Israel cut
them down, leaving them neither survivors
nor fugitives. 23But they took the king of Ai
alive and brought him to Joshua.

24When Israel had finished killing all the
men of Ai in the fields and in the desert where
they had chased them, and when every one of
them had been put to the sword, all the Israelites returned to Ai and killed those who were
in it. 25Twelve thousand men and women fell
that day—all the people of Ai. 26For Joshua
did not draw back the hand that held out his
javelin until he had destroyed[b] all who lived in

---

[a] 26 *Achor* means *trouble.* [b] 26 The Hebrew term refers to the irrevocable giving over of things or persons to the LORD, often by totally destroying them.

Ai. 27But Israel did carry off for themselves the livestock and plunder of this city, as the LORD had instructed Joshua.

28So Joshua burned Ai and made it a permanent heap of ruins, a desolate place to this day. 29He hung the king of Ai on a tree and left him there until evening. At sunset, Joshua ordered them to take his body from the tree and throw it down at the entrance of the city gate. And they raised a large pile of rocks over it, which remains to this day.

The Covenant Renewed at Mount Ebal

30Then Joshua built on Mount Ebal an altar to the LORD, the God of Israel, 31as Moses the servant of the LORD had commanded the Israelites. He built it according to what is written in the Book of the Law of Moses—an altar of uncut stones, on which no iron tool had been used. On it they offered to the LORD burnt offerings and sacrificed fellowship offerings.[a] 32There, in the presence of the Israelites, Joshua copied on stones the law of Moses, which he had written. 33All Israel, aliens and citizens alike, with their elders, officials and judges, were standing on both sides of the ark of the covenant of the LORD, facing those who carried it—the priests, who were Levites. Half of the people stood in front of Mount Gerizim and half of them in front of Mount Ebal, as Moses the servant of the LORD had formerly commanded when he gave instructions to bless the people of Israel.

34Afterward, Joshua read all the words of the law—the blessings and the curses—just as it is written in the Book of the Law. 35There was not a word of all that Moses had commanded that Joshua did not read to the whole assembly of Israel, including the women and children, and the aliens who lived among them.

The Gibeonite Deception

9 Now when all the kings west of the Jordan heard about these things—those in the hill country, in the western foothills, and along the entire coast of the Great Sea[b] as far as Lebanon (the kings of the Hittites, Amorites, Canaanites, Perizzites, Hivites and Jebusites)— 2they came together to make war against Joshua and Israel.

3However, when the people of Gibeon heard what Joshua had done to Jericho and Ai, 4they resorted to a ruse: They went as a delegation whose donkeys were loaded[c] with worn-out sacks and old wineskins, cracked and mended. 5The men put worn and patched sandals on their feet and wore old clothes. All the bread of their food supply was dry and moldy. 6Then they went to Joshua in the camp at Gilgal and said to him and the men of Israel, "We have come from a distant country; make a treaty with us."

7The men of Israel said to the Hivites, "But perhaps you live near us. How then can we make a treaty with you?"

8"We are your servants," they said to Joshua.

But Joshua asked, "Who are you and where do you come from?"

9They answered: "Your servants have come from a very distant country because of the fame of the LORD your God. For we have heard reports of him: all that he did in Egypt, 10and all that he did to the two kings of the Amorites east of the Jordan—Sihon king of Heshbon, and Og king of Bashan, who reigned in Ashtaroth. 11And our elders and all those living in our country said to us, 'Take provisions for your journey; go and meet them and say to them, "We are your servants; make a treaty with us." ' 12This bread of ours was warm when we packed it at home on the day we left to come to you. But now see how dry and moldy it is. 13And these wineskins that we filled were new, but see how cracked they are. And our clothes and sandals are worn out by the very long journey."

14The men of Israel sampled their provisions but did not inquire of the LORD. 15Then Joshua made a treaty of peace with them to let them live, and the leaders of the assembly ratified it by oath.

16Three days after they made the treaty with the Gibeonites, the Israelites heard that they were neighbors, living near them. 17So the Israelites set out and on the third day came to their cities: Gibeon, Kephirah, Beeroth and Kiriath Jearim. 18But the Israelites did not attack them, because the leaders of the assembly had sworn an oath to them by the LORD, the God of Israel.

The whole assembly grumbled against the leaders, 19but all the leaders answered, "We have given them our oath by the LORD, the God of Israel, and we cannot touch them now. 20This is what we will do to them: We will let them live, so that wrath will not fall on us for breaking the oath we swore to them." 21They

[a] *31* Traditionally *peace offerings* [b] *1* That is, the Mediterranean [c] *4* Most Hebrew manuscripts; some Hebrew manuscripts, Vulgate and Syriac (see also Septuagint) *They prepared provisions and loaded their donkeys*

continued, "Let them live, but let them be woodcutters and water carriers for the entire community." So the leaders' promise to them was kept.

22 Then Joshua summoned the Gibeonites and said, "Why did you deceive us by saying, 'We live a long way from you,' while actually you live near us? 23 You are now under a curse: You will never cease to serve as woodcutters and water carriers for the house of my God."

24 They answered Joshua, "Your servants were clearly told how the LORD your God had commanded his servant Moses to give you the whole land and to wipe out all its inhabitants from before you. So we feared for our lives because of you, and that is why we did this. 25 We are now in your hands. Do to us whatever seems good and right to you."

26 So Joshua saved them from the Israelites, and they did not kill them. 27 That day he made the Gibeonites woodcutters and water carriers for the community and for the altar of the LORD at the place the LORD would choose. And that is what they are to this day.

The Sun Stands Still

10 Now Adoni-Zedek king of Jerusalem heard that Joshua had taken Ai and totally destroyed[a] it, doing to Ai and its king as he had done to Jericho and its king, and that the people of Gibeon had made a treaty of peace with Israel and were living near them. 2 He and his people were very much alarmed at this, because Gibeon was an important city, like one of the royal cities; it was larger than Ai, and all its men were good fighters. 3 So Adoni-Zedek king of Jerusalem appealed to Hoham king of Hebron, Piram king of Jarmuth, Japhia king of Lachish and Debir king of Eglon. 4 "Come up and help me attack Gibeon," he said, "because it has made peace with Joshua and the Israelites."

5 Then the five kings of the Amorites—the kings of Jerusalem, Hebron, Jarmuth, Lachish and Eglon—joined forces. They moved up with all their troops and took up positions against Gibeon and attacked it.

6 The Gibeonites then sent word to Joshua in the camp at Gilgal: "Do not abandon your servants. Come up to us quickly and save us! Help us, because all the Amorite kings from the hill country have joined forces against us."

7 So Joshua marched up from Gilgal with his entire army, including all the best fighting men. 8 The LORD said to Joshua, "Do not be afraid of them; I have given them into your hand. Not one of them will be able to withstand you."

9 After an all-night march from Gilgal, Joshua took them by surprise. 10 The LORD threw them into confusion before Israel, who defeated them in a great victory at Gibeon. Israel pursued them along the road going up to Beth Horon and cut them down all the way to Azekah and Makkedah. 11 As they fled before Israel on the road down from Beth Horon to Azekah, the LORD hurled large hailstones down on them from the sky, and more of them died from the hailstones than were killed by the swords of the Israelites.

12 On the day the LORD gave the Amorites over to Israel, Joshua said to the LORD in the presence of Israel:

"O sun, stand still over Gibeon,
  O moon, over the Valley of Aijalon."
13 So the sun stood still,
  and the moon stopped,
  till the nation avenged itself on[b] its
    enemies,

as it is written in the Book of Jashar.

The sun stopped in the middle of the sky and delayed going down about a full day. 14 There has never been a day like it before or since, a day when the LORD listened to a man. Surely the LORD was fighting for Israel!

15 Then Joshua returned with all Israel to the camp at Gilgal.

Five Amorite Kings Killed

16 Now the five kings had fled and hidden in the cave at Makkedah. 17 When Joshua was told that the five kings had been found hiding in the cave at Makkedah, 18 he said, "Roll large rocks up to the mouth of the cave, and post some men there to guard it. 19 But don't stop! Pursue your enemies, attack them from the rear and don't let them reach their cities, for the LORD your God has given them into your hand."

20 So Joshua and the Israelites destroyed them completely—almost to a man—but the few who were left reached their fortified cities. 21 The whole army then returned safely to Joshua in the camp at Makkedah, and no one uttered a word against the Israelites.

22 Joshua said, "Open the mouth of the cave

---

[a] *1* The Hebrew term refers to the irrevocable giving over of things or persons to the LORD, often by totally destroying them; also in verses 28, 35, 37, 39 and 40. [b] *13* Or *nation triumphed over*

and bring those five kings out to me." 23So
they brought the five kings out of the cave—
the kings of Jerusalem, Hebron, Jarmuth, Lachish and Eglon. 24When they had brought
these kings to Joshua, he summoned all the
men of Israel and said to the army commanders who had come with him, "Come here and
put your feet on the necks of these kings." So
they came forward and placed their feet on
their necks.
25Joshua said to them, "Do not be afraid;
do not be discouraged. Be strong and courageous. This is what the LORD will do to all the
enemies you are going to fight." 26Then Joshua
struck and killed the kings and hung them on
five trees, and they were left hanging on the
trees until evening.
27At sunset Joshua gave the order and they
took them down from the trees and threw
them into the cave where they had been hiding. At the mouth of the cave they placed large
rocks, which are there to this day.
28That day Joshua took Makkedah. He put
the city and its king to the sword and totally
destroyed everyone in it. He left no survivors.
And he did to the king of Makkedah as he had
done to the king of Jericho.

Southern Cities Conquered

29Then Joshua and all Israel with him
moved on from Makkedah to Libnah and attacked it. 30The LORD also gave that city and
its king into Israel's hand. The city and everyone in it Joshua put to the sword. He left no
survivors there. And he did to its king as he
had done to the king of Jericho.
31Then Joshua and all Israel with him
moved on from Libnah to Lachish; he took
up positions against it and attacked it. 32The
LORD handed Lachish over to Israel, and Joshua took it on the second day. The city and everyone in it he put to the sword, just as he had
done to Libnah. 33Meanwhile, Horam king
of Gezer had come up to help Lachish, but
Joshua defeated him and his army—until no
survivors were left.
34Then Joshua and all Israel with him
moved on from Lachish to Eglon; they took
up positions against it and attacked it. 35They
captured it that same day and put it to the
sword and totally destroyed everyone in it, just
as they had done to Lachish.
36Then Joshua and all Israel with him went
up from Eglon to Hebron and attacked it.
37They took the city and put it to the sword,
together with its king, its villages and everyone in it. They left no survivors. Just as at
Eglon, they totally destroyed it and everyone
in it.
38Then Joshua and all Israel with him
turned around and attacked Debir. 39They
took the city, its king and its villages, and put
them to the sword. Everyone in it they totally
destroyed. They left no survivors. They did to
Debir and its king as they had done to Libnah
and its king and to Hebron.
40So Joshua subdued the whole region, including the hill country, the Negev, the western foothills and the mountain slopes, together with all their kings. He left no survivors.
He totally destroyed all who breathed, just as
the LORD, the God of Israel, had commanded.
41Joshua subdued them from Kadesh Barnea
to Gaza and from the whole region of Goshen to Gibeon. 42All these kings and their
lands Joshua conquered in one campaign, because the LORD, the God of Israel, fought for
Israel.
43Then Joshua returned with all Israel to the
camp at Gilgal.

Northern Kings Defeated

11 When Jabin king of Hazor heard of this,
he sent word to Jobab king of Madon,
to the kings of Shimron and Acshaph,
2and to the northern kings who were in the
mountains, in the Arabah south of Kinnereth, in the western foothills and in Naphoth
Dor[a] on the west; 3to the Canaanites in the
east and west; to the Amorites, Hittites, Perizzites and Jebusites in the hill country; and
to the Hivites below Hermon in the region of
Mizpah. 4They came out with all their troops
and a large number of horses and chariots—a
huge army, as numerous as the sand on the
seashore. 5All these kings joined forces and
made camp together at the Waters of Merom,
to fight against Israel.
6The LORD said to Joshua, "Do not be
afraid of them, because by this time tomorrow
I will hand all of them over to Israel, slain. You
are to hamstring their horses and burn their
chariots."
7So Joshua and his whole army came
against them suddenly at the Waters of Merom and attacked them, 8and the LORD gave
them into the hand of Israel. They defeated
them and pursued them all the way to Greater
Sidon, to Misrephoth Maim, and to the Valley
of Mizpah on the east, until no survivors were

a 2 Or *in the heights of Dor*

left. 9Joshua did to them as the LORD had directed: He hamstrung their horses and burned
their chariots.
10At that time Joshua turned back and captured Hazor and put its king to the sword.
(Hazor had been the head of all these kingdoms.) 11Everyone in it they put to the sword.
They totally destroyed[a] them, not sparing
anything that breathed, and he burned up
Hazor itself.
12Joshua took all these royal cities and
their kings and put them to the sword. He
totally destroyed them, as Moses the servant of the LORD had commanded. 13Yet Israel did not burn any of the cities built on
their mounds—except Hazor, which Joshua
burned. 14The Israelites carried off for themselves all the plunder and livestock of these
cities, but all the people they put to the sword
until they completely destroyed them, not
sparing anyone that breathed. 15As the LORD
commanded his servant Moses, so Moses
commanded Joshua, and Joshua did it; he left
nothing undone of all that the LORD commanded Moses.
16So Joshua took this entire land: the hill
country, all the Negev, the whole region of
Goshen, the western foothills, the Arabah and
the mountains of Israel with their foothills,
17from Mount Halak, which rises toward Seir,
to Baal Gad in the Valley of Lebanon below
Mount Hermon. He captured all their kings
and struck them down, putting them to death.
18Joshua waged war against all these kings for
a long time. 19Except for the Hivites living in
Gibeon, not one city made a treaty of peace
with the Israelites, who took them all in battle.
20For it was the LORD himself who hardened
their hearts to wage war against Israel, so that
he might destroy them totally, exterminating
them without mercy, as the LORD had commanded Moses.
21At that time Joshua went and destroyed
the Anakites from the hill country: from Hebron, Debir and Anab, from all the hill country of Judah, and from all the hill country of
Israel. Joshua totally destroyed them and their
towns. 22No Anakites were left in Israelite territory; only in Gaza, Gath and Ashdod did
any survive. 23So Joshua took the entire land,
just as the LORD had directed Moses, and he
gave it as an inheritance to Israel according to
their tribal divisions.

Then the land had rest from war.

List of Defeated Kings

12 These are the kings of the land whom the
Israelites had defeated and whose territory they took over east of the Jordan,
from the Arnon Gorge to Mount Hermon, including all the eastern side of the Arabah:

2Sihon king of the Amorites,
who reigned in Heshbon. He ruled
from Aroer on the rim of the Arnon
Gorge—from the middle of the gorge—to
the Jabbok River, which is the border of
the Ammonites. This included half of
Gilead. 3He also ruled over the eastern
Arabah from the Sea of Kinnereth[b] to
the Sea of the Arabah (the Salt Sea[c]), to
Beth Jeshimoth, and then southward below the slopes of Pisgah.

4And the territory of Og king of Bashan,
one of the last of the Rephaites, who
reigned in Ashtaroth and Edrei. 5He
ruled over Mount Hermon, Salecah, all
of Bashan to the border of the people of
Geshur and Maacah, and half of Gilead
to the border of Sihon king of Heshbon.

6Moses, the servant of the LORD, and the
Israelites conquered them. And Moses the servant of the LORD gave their land to the Reubenites, the Gadites and the half-tribe of Manasseh to be their possession.
7These are the kings of the land that Joshua
and the Israelites conquered on the west side
of the Jordan, from Baal Gad in the Valley of
Lebanon to Mount Halak, which rises toward
Seir (their lands Joshua gave as an inheritance
to the tribes of Israel according to their tribal divisions— 8the hill country, the western
foothills, the Arabah, the mountain slopes, the
desert and the Negev—the lands of the Hittites, Amorites, Canaanites, Perizzites, Hivites
and Jebusites):

9 the king of Jericho — one
the king of Ai (near Bethel) — one
10 the king of Jerusalem — one
the king of Hebron — one
11 the king of Jarmuth — one
the king of Lachish — one
12 the king of Eglon — one
the king of Gezer — one
13 the king of Debir — one
the king of Geder — one
14 the king of Hormah — one
the king of Arad — one

[a] *11* The Hebrew term refers to the irrevocable giving over of things or persons to the LORD, often by totally destroying them; also in verses 12, 20 and 21. [b] *3* That is, Galilee [c] *3* That is, the Dead Sea

WEEKEND

let's talk

In 1997, the Washington Capitals was one of the hottest hockey teams on ice; they were skating their way into the Stanley Cup finals. But by the fall of 1999, they had slipped to the brink of disaster with one of the worst records in the NHL. Coach Ron Wilson decided drastic measures were necessary and quickly changed their strategy. Yet injuries abounded, and the losses mounted. The team couldn't figure out what was wrong.

Just before Christmas, the team took a late-night, seven-hour flight home from Vancouver and did what they typically do on such a flight: They popped in a movie to pass the time. To unwind. To lick their wounds. That's when the unexpected happened. The VCR froze—there would be no movie on this flight.

As the plane winged its way through the evening sky, one by one the players started talking with each other. They talked strategy. Obstacles. Key plays. Out of necessity, they rediscovered the ancient art of conversation. By the time the plane touched down, the Capitals had picked apart their game and knew what needed to be done.

In the weeks that followed, they became virtually unstoppable, going on an eleven-game winning streak. Goal tender Olaf Kolzig reflected, "Maybe it was fate the VCR didn't work. It gave us a chance to just roam about the plane and talk. It was a good way to clear the air."

Many husbands and wives have become out-of-breath companions, racing around to catch up with their schedules (as well as their children's). Even our sentences are peppered with such words as *time crunch, fast food, rush hour, frequent flyer, expressway* and *rapid transit*. We use cell phones managed by Sprint, do our finances on Quicken, schedule appointments in our DayRunner, diet with SlimFast. Whew! We're all in a hurry and anything that slows us down becomes the equivalent of road-kill—including our most important relationships.

That's why we are compelled to state the obvious: good communication requires time to talk. A good conversation simply doesn't happen while traveling at breakneck speed. So cure your hurry sickness, take a deep breath, and obey the speed limit of human connection. If you want to improve your communication, you must ruthlessly eliminate hurry from your conversations. You can accomplish this the old-fashioned way: sitting still without multitasking, lingering over your dinner conversation, taking advantage of a quiet house when the kids are in bed before you fall asleep, turning off the radio when you are driving in the car, or turning off the TV when it is simply background noise—so you can talk.

—DR. LES PARROTT III AND DR. LESLIE PARROTT

how we communicate

Which of these communication situations best describes you and your partner?

1. When you talk, your partner's eyes:
   a. Are shut
   b. Are glued on you
   c. Occasionally glance up from reading
2. How often do you and your partner talk?
   a. When forced by court order
   b. Every hour
   c. Counting grunts, at least twice a day
3. Finish this sentence: "The part I like best about talking with my partner is . . ."
   a. The part when it's over
   b. The part where we share our innermost needs and brainstorm ways we can meet them for each other
   c. The part where we move past the days events to talk about something more interesting
4. If your partner wakes you up in the middle of the night to talk:
   a. It means the argument still isn't over
   b. You think it is so sweet because you also wanted to talk but didn't want to wake your partner
   c. It's a euphemism for "I want sex—now"
5. To you, a productive conversation is one that:
   a. Ends quickly
   b. Never ends
   c. Ends with "and don't forget the milk!"

How to score:

Mostly *a*'s: You need more than this couple's Bible; you need couple therapy. Spend more time talking. Begin by discussing your answers on this quiz.

Mostly *b*'s: What are you reading this for? You could have written it, that is, if you weren't so busy talking.

Mostly *c*'s: You communicate regularly but often while doing something else. Focus only on your partner the next time you talk.

Ultimately, your score doesn't matter, but talking about it could!

HOW ARE WE DOING?

let's make a DATE

WHAT DO YOU WANT TO TALK ABOUT?

This weekend, each of you take nine slips of paper and write down three times of day you like to talk, three things you'd like to talk about (that don't have to do with finances, chores or kids), and three places you like to talk. Put the slips into three separate jars (there should be six in each jar) and randomly draw one slip from each jar. Then do your best to make it happen. The fun happens as you have random conversations like "7 A.M. in the bathtub, discussing third world poverty" or "midnight on your favorite hiking path, discussing your partner's childhood."

FOR YOUR NEXT DEVOTIONAL READING, TURN TO PAGE 238.

LESSONS FROM THE *Bible*

Discuss what Joseph and Mary may have talked about:
1. On their way to Bethlehem (see Luke 2:1–6)
2. After Jesus was born (see Luke 2:7)
3. After they found their missing son in the temple (see Luke 2:41–50)

15 the king of Libnah one
the king of Adullam one
16 the king of Makkedah one
the king of Bethel one
17 the king of Tappuah one
the king of Hepher one
18 the king of Aphek one
the king of Lasharon one
19 the king of Madon one
the king of Hazor one
20 the king of Shimron Meron one
the king of Acshaph one
21 the king of Taanach one
the king of Megiddo one
22 the king of Kedesh one
the king of Jokneam in Carmel one
23 the king of Dor (in Naphoth
Dor[a]) one
the king of Goyim in Gilgal one
24 the king of Tirzah one
thirty-one kings in all.

Land Still to Be Taken

13 When Joshua was old and well advanced
in years, the LORD said to him, "You are
very old, and there are still very large areas of land to be taken over.

2 "This is the land that remains: all the
regions of the Philistines and Geshurites: 3 from the Shihor River on the east
of Egypt to the territory of Ekron on
the north, all of it counted as Canaanite (the territory of the five Philistine
rulers in Gaza, Ashdod, Ashkelon, Gath
and Ekron—that of the Avvites); 4 from
the south, all the land of the Canaanites, from Arah of the Sidonians as far as
Aphek, the region of the Amorites, 5 the
area of the Gebalites[b]; and all Lebanon
to the east, from Baal Gad below Mount
Hermon to Lebo[c] Hamath.

6 "As for all the inhabitants of the mountain
regions from Lebanon to Misrephoth Maim,
that is, all the Sidonians, I myself will drive
them out before the Israelites. Be sure to allocate this land to Israel for an inheritance, as I
have instructed you, 7 and divide it as an inheritance among the nine tribes and half of the
tribe of Manasseh."

Division of the Land East of the Jordan

8 The other half of Manasseh,[d] the Reubenites
and the Gadites had received the inheritance
that Moses had given them east of the Jordan,
as he, the servant of the LORD, had assigned
it to them.

9 It extended from Aroer on the rim of
the Arnon Gorge, and from the town
in the middle of the gorge, and included the whole plateau of Medeba as far as
Dibon, 10 and all the towns of Sihon king
of the Amorites, who ruled in Heshbon,
out to the border of the Ammonites. 11 It
also included Gilead, the territory of the
people of Geshur and Maacah, all of
Mount Hermon and all Bashan as far as
Salecah— 12 that is, the whole kingdom
of Og in Bashan, who had reigned in
Ashtaroth and Edrei and had survived as
one of the last of the Rephaites. Moses
had defeated them and taken over their
land. 13 But the Israelites did not drive
out the people of Geshur and Maacah, so
they continue to live among the Israelites
to this day.

14 But to the tribe of Levi he gave no inheritance, since the offerings made by fire to the
LORD, the God of Israel, are their inheritance,
as he promised them.

15 This is what Moses had given to the tribe of
Reuben, clan by clan:

16 The territory from Aroer on the rim of
the Arnon Gorge, and from the town in
the middle of the gorge, and the whole
plateau past Medeba 17 to Heshbon and
all its towns on the plateau, including Dibon, Bamoth Baal, Beth Baal Meon, 18 Jahaz, Kedemoth, Mephaath, 19 Kiriathaim,
Sibmah, Zereth Shahar on the hill in the
valley, 20 Beth Peor, the slopes of Pisgah,
and Beth Jeshimoth— 21 all the towns on
the plateau and the entire realm of Sihon king of the Amorites, who ruled at
Heshbon. Moses had defeated him and
the Midianite chiefs, Evi, Rekem, Zur,
Hur and Reba—princes allied with Sihon—who lived in that country. 22 In
addition to those slain in battle, the Israelites had put to the sword Balaam son
of Beor, who practiced divination. 23 The
boundary of the Reubenites was the bank
of the Jordan. These towns and their villages were the inheritance of the Reubenites, clan by clan.

24 This is what Moses had given to the tribe of
Gad, clan by clan:

---

[a] 23 Or *in the heights of Dor* [b] 5 That is, the area of Byblos [c] 5 Or *to the entrance to* [d] 8 Hebrew *With it* (that is, with the other half of Manasseh)

25 The territory of Jazer, all the towns of
Gilead and half the Ammonite country
as far as Aroer, near Rabbah; 26 and from
Heshbon to Ramath Mizpah and Beto-
nim, and from Mahanaim to the territory
of Debir; 27 and in the valley, Beth Ha-
ram, Beth Nimrah, Succoth and Zaphon
with the rest of the realm of Sihon king
of Heshbon (the east side of the Jordan,
the territory up to the end of the Sea of
Kinnereth[a]). 28 These towns and their villages were the inheritance of the Gadites,
clan by clan.

29 This is what Moses had given to the half-
tribe of Manasseh, that is, to half the family of
the descendants of Manasseh, clan by clan:

30 The territory extending from Mahanaim and including all of Bashan, the entire
realm of Og king of Bashan—all the settlements of Jair in Bashan, sixty towns,
31 half of Gilead, and Ashtaroth and Edrei
(the royal cities of Og in Bashan). This
was for the descendants of Makir son of
Manasseh—for half of the sons of Makir,
clan by clan.

32 This is the inheritance Moses had giv-
en when he was in the plains of Moab across
the Jordan east of Jericho. 33 But to the tribe
of Levi, Moses had given no inheritance; the
LORD, the God of Israel, is their inheritance,
as he promised them.

Division of the Land West of the Jordan

14 Now these are the areas the Israelites received as an inheritance in the land of
Canaan, which Eleazar the priest, Joshua son of Nun and the heads of the tribal clans
of Israel allotted to them. 2 Their inheritances were assigned by lot to the nine-and-a-half
tribes, as the LORD had commanded through
Moses. 3 Moses had granted the two-and-a-
half tribes their inheritance east of the Jordan
but had not granted the Levites an inheritance
among the rest, 4 for the sons of Joseph had
become two tribes—Manasseh and Ephraim.
The Levites received no share of the land but
only towns to live in, with pasturelands for
their flocks and herds. 5 So the Israelites divided the land, just as the LORD had commanded
Moses.

Hebron Given to Caleb

6 Now the men of Judah approached Joshua at Gilgal, and Caleb son of Jephunneh the
Kenizzite said to him, "You know what the
LORD said to Moses the man of God at Kadesh Barnea about you and me. 7 I was forty
years old when Moses the servant of the LORD
sent me from Kadesh Barnea to explore the
land. And I brought him back a report according to my convictions, 8 but my brothers
who went up with me made the hearts of the
people melt with fear. I, however, followed the
LORD my God wholeheartedly. 9 So on that
day Moses swore to me, 'The land on which
your feet have walked will be your inheritance
and that of your children forever, because you
have followed the LORD my God wholeheartedly.'[b]

10 "Now then, just as the LORD promised,
he has kept me alive for forty-five years since
the time he said this to Moses, while Israel
moved about in the desert. So here I am today, eighty-five years old! 11 I am still as strong
today as the day Moses sent me out; I'm just
as vigorous to go out to battle now as I was
then. 12 Now give me this hill country that
the LORD promised me that day. You yourself
heard then that the Anakites were there and
their cities were large and fortified, but, the
LORD helping me, I will drive them out just
as he said."

13 Then Joshua blessed Caleb son of Jephunneh and gave him Hebron as his inheritance.
14 So Hebron has belonged to Caleb son of Jephunneh the Kenizzite ever since, because he
followed the LORD, the God of Israel, wholeheartedly. 15 (Hebron used to be called Kiriath
Arba after Arba, who was the greatest man
among the Anakites.)

Then the land had rest from war.

Allotment for Judah

15 The allotment for the tribe of Judah,
clan by clan, extended down to the territory of Edom, to the Desert of Zin in
the extreme south.

2 Their southern boundary started from
the bay at the southern end of the Salt
Sea,[c] 3 crossed south of Scorpion[d] Pass,
continued on to Zin and went over to the
south of Kadesh Barnea. Then it ran past
Hezron up to Addar and curved around
to Karka. 4 It then passed along to Azmon
and joined the Wadi of Egypt, ending at
the sea. This is their[e] southern boundary.

5 The eastern boundary is the Salt Sea
as far as the mouth of the Jordan.

---

a 27 That is, Galilee *b* 9 Deut. 1:36 *c* 2 That is, the Dead Sea; also in verse 5 *d* 3 Hebrew *Akrabbim* *e* 4 Hebrew *your*

M **MONDAY**
READ JOSHUA 14:6–15

KEEPING PROMISES

> **"Now give me this hill country that the LORD promised me that day."**
>
> — JOSHUA 14:12

let's talk

- What promises did we make to each other before we got married? What promises did we make in our wedding vows?
- How have we lived up to those promises? Which ones have been the most difficult to keep? Which ones have been the easiest to keep? Which ones are still testing us?
- How have we seen God keep his promises to us in our life together?

Caleb waited 45 years to get his promised inheritance from God. That's a long time to wait.

As I write this, I realize that my wife and I have been married nearly as long as Caleb waited to get his promised parcel of land. I remember when Marilyn walked down the aisle toward me. I remember how she looked at me and promised to "love, honor and obey" me. Like Caleb, I have cherished and depended on those promises for a long time.

Contrary to much of what we hear today, promises are made to be kept, not broken. Marilyn has kept her promises to me, and that is a source of great comfort and happiness. Marriage works best when people keep their promises.

When we marry, we make promises to one another. But we also depend on the promises God makes about marriage. Just as God promised Caleb that he would get an inheritance, God promises Christians that he will bless their marriages. Some couples wait a long time to experience the fulfillment of that promise. And many marriages seem to have so much wrong with them.

When you and your spouse experience conflict, emptiness, dissatisfaction or hopelessness in your marriage, it's time to remember God's promises. He doesn't do things on our timetable; he does them on his own. Because he is a perfect God, his timetable is perfect.

Caleb understood that. He forthrightly reminded God of his promises and explained how he had been faithful to God when most of the other spies had not been. Caleb did not doubt that God would do what he had promised. And guess what? God was faithful; he gave Hebron to Caleb.

I need to follow the pattern God set when he made his promise to Caleb. I need to keep my promises, especially the promises I made to Marilyn many years ago. But even when I'm a promise-breaker, I need to remember that God is not. I can honestly testify that God has played a role in our marriage. He has kept us together. He has blessed us as we've grown old together.

Our marriage will end someday when one of us dies. I dread the thought of it. Nonetheless, I can bear it because I have the promise of Jesus that he has gone to prepare a place for both of us and we will go to be with him (see John 14:1–3). Caleb waited 45 years to see God keep his promise. I see his promises fulfilled every day. How about you?

—ALLEN CURRY

FOR YOUR NEXT DEVOTIONAL READING, TURN TO PAGE 244.

the Israelites grew stronger, they subjected the
Canaanites to forced labor but did not drive
them out completely.
14 The people of Joseph said to Joshua,
"Why have you given us only one allotment
and one portion for an inheritance? We are a
numerous people and the LORD has blessed us
abundantly."
15 "If you are so numerous," Joshua answered, "and if the hill country of Ephraim is
too small for you, go up into the forest and
clear land for yourselves there in the land of
the Perizzites and Rephaites."
16 The people of Joseph replied, "The hill
country is not enough for us, and all the Canaanites who live in the plain have iron chariots, both those in Beth Shan and its settlements and those in the Valley of Jezreel."
17 But Joshua said to the house of Joseph—
to Ephraim and Manasseh—"You are numerous and very powerful. You will have not only
one allotment 18 but the forested hill country
as well. Clear it, and its farthest limits will be
yours; though the Canaanites have iron chariots and though they are strong, you can drive
them out."

Division of the Rest of the Land

18 The whole assembly of the Israelites
gathered at Shiloh and set up the Tent of
Meeting there. The country was brought
under their control, 2 but there were still seven
Israelite tribes who had not yet received their
inheritance.
3 So Joshua said to the Israelites: "How
long will you wait before you begin to take
possession of the land that the LORD, the
God of your fathers, has given you? 4 Appoint three men from each tribe. I will send
them out to make a survey of the land and
to write a description of it, according to the
inheritance of each. Then they will return to
me. 5 You are to divide the land into seven
parts. Judah is to remain in its territory on
the south and the house of Joseph in its territory on the north. 6 After you have written
descriptions of the seven parts of the land,
bring them here to me and I will cast lots for
you in the presence of the LORD our God.
7 The Levites, however, do not get a portion
among you, because the priestly service of the
LORD is their inheritance. And Gad, Reuben
and the half-tribe of Manasseh have already
received their inheritance on the east side of
the Jordan. Moses the servant of the LORD
gave it to them."
8 As the men started on their way to map
out the land, Joshua instructed them, "Go and
make a survey of the land and write a description of it. Then return to me, and I will cast
lots for you here at Shiloh in the presence of
the LORD." 9 So the men left and went through
the land. They wrote its description on a scroll,
town by town, in seven parts, and returned to
Joshua in the camp at Shiloh. 10 Joshua then
cast lots for them in Shiloh in the presence of
the LORD, and there he distributed the land
to the Israelites according to their tribal divisions.

Allotment for Benjamin

11 The lot came up for the tribe of Benjamin,
clan by clan. Their allotted territory lay between the tribes of Judah and Joseph:
12 On the north side their boundary
began at the Jordan, passed the northern
slope of Jericho and headed west into the
hill country, coming out at the desert of
Beth Aven. 13 From there it crossed to the
south slope of Luz (that is, Bethel) and
went down to Ataroth Addar on the hill
south of Lower Beth Horon.
14 From the hill facing Beth Horon
on the south the boundary turned south
along the western side and came out at
Kiriath Baal (that is, Kiriath Jearim), a
town of the people of Judah. This was the
western side.
15 The southern side began at the outskirts of Kiriath Jearim on the west, and
the boundary came out at the spring of
the waters of Nephtoah. 16 The boundary
went down to the foot of the hill facing
the Valley of Ben Hinnom, north of the
Valley of Rephaim. It continued down
the Hinnom Valley along the southern slope of the Jebusite city and so to
En Rogel. 17 It then curved north, went
to En Shemesh, continued to Geliloth,
which faces the Pass of Adummim, and
ran down to the Stone of Bohan son of
Reuben. 18 It continued to the northern
slope of Beth Arabah[a] and on down into
the Arabah. 19 It then went to the northern slope of Beth Hoglah and came out at
the northern bay of the Salt Sea,[b] at the
mouth of the Jordan in the south. This
was the southern boundary.

[a] 18 Septuagint; Hebrew *slope facing the Arabah* [b] 19 That is, the Dead Sea

[20]The Jordan formed the boundary on
the eastern side.
These were the boundaries that marked out
the inheritance of the clans of Benjamin on
all sides.

[21]The tribe of Benjamin, clan by clan, had the
following cities:
Jericho, Beth Hoglah, Emek Keziz,
[22]Beth Arabah, Zemaraim, Bethel, [23]Av-
vim, Parah, Ophrah, [24]Kephar Ammo-
ni, Ophni and Geba—twelve towns and
their villages.
[25]Gibeon, Ramah, Beeroth, [26]Mizpah,
Kephirah, Mozah, [27]Rekem, Irpeel, Tar-
alah, [28]Zelah, Haeleph, the Jebusite city
(that is, Jerusalem), Gibeah and Kiriath—fourteen towns and their villages.
This was the inheritance of Benjamin for its
clans.

Allotment for Simeon

19 The second lot came out for the tribe of
Simeon, clan by clan. Their inheritance
lay within the territory of Judah. [2]It included:
Beersheba (or Sheba),[a] Moladah, [3]Ha-
zar Shual, Balah, Ezem, [4]Eltolad, Beth-
ul, Hormah, [5]Ziklag, Beth Marcaboth,
Hazar Susah, [6]Beth Lebaoth and Sharu-
hen—thirteen towns and their villages;
[7]Ain, Rimmon, Ether and Ashan—four
towns and their villages— [8]and all the
villages around these towns as far as Baalath Beer (Ramah in the Negev).
This was the inheritance of the tribe of the
Simeonites, clan by clan. [9]The inheritance
of the Simeonites was taken from the share
of Judah, because Judah's portion was more
than they needed. So the Simeonites received
their inheritance within the territory of Judah.

Allotment for Zebulun

[10]The third lot came up for Zebulun, clan by
clan:
The boundary of their inheritance
went as far as Sarid. [11]Going west it ran
to Maralah, touched Dabbesheth, and
extended to the ravine near Jokneam. [12]It
turned east from Sarid toward the sunrise
to the territory of Kisloth Tabor and went
on to Daberath and up to Japhia. [13]Then
it continued eastward to Gath Hepher
and Eth Kazin; it came out at Rimmon
and turned toward Neah. [14]There the
boundary went around on the north to
Hannathon and ended at the Valley of
Iphtah El. [15]Included were Kattath, Nahalal, Shimron, Idalah and Bethlehem.
There were twelve towns and their villages.
[16]These towns and their villages were the inheritance of Zebulun, clan by clan.

Allotment for Issachar

[17]The fourth lot came out for Issachar, clan by
clan. [18]Their territory included:
Jezreel, Kesulloth, Shunem, [19]Haph-
araim, Shion, Anaharath, [20]Rabbith,
Kishion, Ebez, [21]Remeth, En Gannim,
En Haddah and Beth Pazzez. [22]The
boundary touched Tabor, Shahazumah
and Beth Shemesh, and ended at the Jordan. There were sixteen towns and their
villages.
[23]These towns and their villages were the inheritance of the tribe of Issachar, clan by clan.

Allotment for Asher

[24]The fifth lot came out for the tribe of Asher,
clan by clan. [25]Their territory included:
Helkath, Hali, Beten, Acshaph, [26]Al-
lammelech, Amad and Mishal. On the
west the boundary touched Carmel and
Shihor Libnath. [27]It then turned east toward Beth Dagon, touched Zebulun and
the Valley of Iphtah El, and went north
to Beth Emek and Neiel, passing Cabul
on the left. [28]It went to Abdon,[b] Rehob,
Hammon and Kanah, as far as Greater
Sidon. [29]The boundary then turned back
toward Ramah and went to the fortified
city of Tyre, turned toward Hosah and
came out at the sea in the region of Aczib, [30]Ummah, Aphek and Rehob. There
were twenty-two towns and their villages.
[31]These towns and their villages were the inheritance of the tribe of Asher, clan by clan.

Allotment for Naphtali

[32]The sixth lot came out for Naphtali, clan by
clan:
[33]Their boundary went from Heleph
and the large tree in Zaanannim, passing
Adami Nekeb and Jabneel to Lakkum
and ending at the Jordan. [34]The boundary ran west through Aznoth Tabor and
came out at Hukkok. It touched Zebu-

[a] 2 Or *Beersheba, Sheba*; 1 Chron. 4:28 does not have *Sheba*. [b] 28 Some Hebrew manuscripts (see also Joshua 21:30); most Hebrew manuscripts *Ebron*

lun on the south, Asher on the west and
the Jordan[a] on the east. 35The fortified
cities were Ziddim, Zer, Hammath, Rak-
kath, Kinnereth, 36Adamah, Ramah, Hazor, 37Kedesh, Edrei, En Hazor, 38Iron,
Migdal El, Horem, Beth Anath and Beth
Shemesh. There were nineteen towns and
their villages.
39These towns and their villages were the inheritance of the tribe of Naphtali, clan by
clan.

Allotment for Dan

40The seventh lot came out for the tribe of
Dan, clan by clan. 41The territory of their inheritance included:
Zorah, Eshtaol, Ir Shemesh, 42Shaa-
labbin, Aijalon, Ithlah, 43Elon, Timnah,
Ekron, 44Eltekeh, Gibbethon, Baalath,
45Jehud, Bene Berak, Gath Rimmon,
46Me Jarkon and Rakkon, with the area
facing Joppa.
47(But the Danites had difficulty taking
possession of their territory, so they went up
and attacked Leshem, took it, put it to the
sword and occupied it. They settled in Leshem
and named it Dan after their forefather.)
48These towns and their villages were the inheritance of the tribe of Dan, clan by clan.

Allotment for Joshua

49When they had finished dividing the
land into its allotted portions, the Israelites
gave Joshua son of Nun an inheritance among
them, 50as the LORD had commanded. They
gave him the town he asked for—Timnath Serah[b] in the hill country of Ephraim. And he
built up the town and settled there.
51These are the territories that Eleazar the
priest, Joshua son of Nun and the heads of the
tribal clans of Israel assigned by lot at Shiloh
in the presence of the LORD at the entrance
to the Tent of Meeting. And so they finished
dividing the land.

Cities of Refuge

20 Then the LORD said to Joshua: 2"Tell
the Israelites to designate the cities of
refuge, as I instructed you through
Moses, 3so that anyone who kills a person
accidentally and unintentionally may flee
there and find protection from the avenger
of blood.
4"When he flees to one of these cities, he is
to stand in the entrance of the city gate and
state his case before the elders of that city.
Then they are to admit him into their city
and give him a place to live with them. 5If
the avenger of blood pursues him, they must
not surrender the one accused, because he
killed his neighbor unintentionally and without malice aforethought. 6He is to stay in that
city until he has stood trial before the assembly and until the death of the high priest who
is serving at that time. Then he may go back
to his own home in the town from which he
fled."
7So they set apart Kedesh in Galilee in the
hill country of Naphtali, Shechem in the hill
country of Ephraim, and Kiriath Arba (that
is, Hebron) in the hill country of Judah. 8On
the east side of the Jordan of Jericho[c] they
designated Bezer in the desert on the plateau
in the tribe of Reuben, Ramoth in Gilead
in the tribe of Gad, and Golan in Bashan in
the tribe of Manasseh. 9Any of the Israelites
or any alien living among them who killed
someone accidentally could flee to these designated cities and not be killed by the avenger of blood prior to standing trial before the
assembly.

Towns for the Levites

21 Now the family heads of the Levites
approached Eleazar the priest, Joshua
son of Nun, and the heads of the other
tribal families of Israel 2at Shiloh in Canaan
and said to them, "The LORD commanded
through Moses that you give us towns to live
in, with pasturelands for our livestock." 3So, as
the LORD had commanded, the Israelites gave
the Levites the following towns and pasturelands out of their own inheritance:
4The first lot came out for the Kohathites,
clan by clan. The Levites who were descendants of Aaron the priest were allotted thirteen towns from the tribes of Judah, Simeon
and Benjamin. 5The rest of Kohath's descendants were allotted ten towns from the clans
of the tribes of Ephraim, Dan and half of Manasseh.
6The descendants of Gershon were allotted
thirteen towns from the clans of the tribes of
Issachar, Asher, Naphtali and the half-tribe of
Manasseh in Bashan.
7The descendants of Merari, clan by clan,
received twelve towns from the tribes of Reuben, Gad and Zebulun.
8So the Israelites allotted to the Levites these

[a] *34* Septuagint; Hebrew *west, and Judah, the Jordan,* [b] *50* Also known as *Timnath Heres* (see Judges 2:9) [c] *8* *Jordan of Jericho* was possibly an ancient name for the Jordan River.

TUESDAY

READ JOSHUA 20:1–9

A SAFE PLACE TO RECOVER

When a marriage suffers an accidental or unintentional tragedy, especially if one or both partners were responsible even in a minor way, a husband and wife have an opportunity to enrich the relationship, not abandon it. But where can they find safety while they pursue healing and restoration?

The story of the Israelite cities of refuge gives us some principles we can apply when our marriage suffers a deep wound such as the death of a child, a serious illness or financial ruin.

First, we can cling to hope. For example, not many things are more devastating to a marriage than the death of a child. For people who have experienced this tragedy, there are refuges where couples can find comfort in their grief. According to the organization, The Compassionate Friends, Inc. (TCF), the most helpful refuges are family and clergy. But their website also provides an entry to other refuges: Mothers Against Drunk Drivers (MADD), Sudden Infant Death Alliance (SIDS Alliance) and Parents of Murdered Children. As the Israelites stated their case before the elders of the city (see Joshua 20:4), parents can also share their story, their grief, even their tendency to blame the other spouse. And contrary to widely publicized high divorce statistics, only one of four couples who divorced after a tragedy said the death of their child contributed to their divorce.

Then the LORD said to Joshua, "Tell the Israelites to designate the cities of refuge, as I instructed you through Moses, so that anyone who kills a person accidentally and unintentionally may flee there and find protection from the avenger of blood."

—JOSHUA 20:1–3

let's talk

- What unhealthy or unhelpful refuges do we retreat to in marital crises? What are some healthy or helpful refuges?
- How can we be patient with each other during a crisis? How can we support each other?
- Who are some people we could trust for counsel during a family tragedy? In what ways are they safe? In what ways are they not safe?

When our 13-year-old daughter was diagnosed with curvature of the spine, my husband initially sought refuge in solitude and denial. But his absence was not helpful to our daughter or our marriage. I sought refuge by seeking the counsel of a pediatric surgeon and figuring out what to do. When Grey saw the S curve on the X-ray, he returned to reality and Suzanne had spinal surgery.

When crises come in marriage, we can't avoid them or flee aimlessly from them. As King David and other psalmists proclaimed over 40 times in Psalms, our best, strongest, most faithful refuge is God. He is the first place we should seek refuge. "The LORD is a refuge for the oppressed, a stronghold in times of trouble" (Psalm 9:9). Likewise, the widow Ruth was commended to "the God of Israel, under whose wings you have come to take refuge" (Ruth 2:12).

Why was an Israelite who had fled to a city of refuge instructed to wait until the death of the high priest before returning to his home (see Joshua 20:6)? Could it have been to allow time to pass and wounds to heal? I think so. Likewise, when a marital tragedy strikes us to our core, perhaps patience and time are the best salves to apply to the wound. With the passing of time comes a measure of healing. Whether it's death, financial loss, foolishness, indiscretion or something else, we need time to stem the bleeding and set broken parts before we have the strength to dig deeper into its cause and effect on our marriage.

—MARY ANN JEFFREYS

FOR YOUR NEXT DEVOTIONAL READING, TURN TO PAGE 252.

towns and their pasturelands, as the LORD had commanded through Moses.

[9]From the tribes of Judah and Simeon they allotted the following towns by name [10](these towns were assigned to the descendants of Aaron who were from the Kohathite clans of the Levites, because the first lot fell to them):

[11]They gave them Kiriath Arba (that is, Hebron), with its surrounding pastureland, in the hill country of Judah. (Arba was the forefather of Anak.) [12]But the fields and villages around the city they had given to Caleb son of Jephunneh as his possession.

[13]So to the descendants of Aaron the priest they gave Hebron (a city of refuge for one accused of murder), Libnah, [14]Jattir, Eshtemoa, [15]Holon, Debir, [16]Ain, Juttah and Beth Shemesh, together with their pasturelands—nine towns from these two tribes.

[17]And from the tribe of Benjamin they gave them Gibeon, Geba, [18]Anathoth and Almon, together with their pasturelands—four towns.

[19]All the towns for the priests, the descendants of Aaron, were thirteen, together with their pasturelands.

[20]The rest of the Kohathite clans of the Levites were allotted towns from the tribe of Ephraim:

[21]In the hill country of Ephraim they were given Shechem (a city of refuge for one accused of murder) and Gezer, [22]Kibzaim and Beth Horon, together with their pasturelands—four towns.

[23]Also from the tribe of Dan they received Eltekeh, Gibbethon, [24]Aijalon and Gath Rimmon, together with their pasturelands—four towns.

[25]From half the tribe of Manasseh they received Taanach and Gath Rimmon, together with their pasturelands—two towns.

[26]All these ten towns and their pasturelands were given to the rest of the Kohathite clans.

[27]The Levite clans of the Gershonites were given:

from the half-tribe of Manasseh,
Golan in Bashan (a city of refuge for one accused of murder) and Be Eshtarah, together with their pasturelands—two towns;

[28]from the tribe of Issachar,
Kishion, Daberath, [29]Jarmuth and En Gannim, together with their pasturelands—four towns;

[30]from the tribe of Asher,
Mishal, Abdon, [31]Helkath and Rehob, together with their pasturelands—four towns;

[32]from the tribe of Naphtali,
Kedesh in Galilee (a city of refuge for one accused of murder), Hammoth Dor and Kartan, together with their pasturelands—three towns.

[33]All the towns of the Gershonite clans were thirteen, together with their pasturelands.

[34]The Merarite clans (the rest of the Levites) were given:

from the tribe of Zebulun,
Jokneam, Kartah, [35]Dimnah and Nahalal, together with their pasturelands—four towns;

[36]from the tribe of Reuben,
Bezer, Jahaz, [37]Kedemoth and Mephaath, together with their pasturelands—four towns;

[38]from the tribe of Gad,
Ramoth in Gilead (a city of refuge for one accused of murder), Mahanaim, [39]Heshbon and Jazer, together with their pasturelands—four towns in all.

[40]All the towns allotted to the Merarite clans, who were the rest of the Levites, were twelve.

[41]The towns of the Levites in the territory held by the Israelites were forty-eight in all, together with their pasturelands. [42]Each of these towns had pasturelands surrounding it; this was true for all these towns.

[43]So the LORD gave Israel all the land he had sworn to give their forefathers, and they took possession of it and settled there. [44]The LORD gave them rest on every side, just as he had sworn to their forefathers. Not one of their enemies withstood them; the LORD handed all their enemies over to them. [45]Not one of all the LORD's good promises to the house of Israel failed; every one was fulfilled.

Eastern Tribes Return Home

22 Then Joshua summoned the Reubenites, the Gadites and the half-tribe of Manasseh [2]and said to them, "You have done all that Moses the servant of the LORD commanded, and you have obeyed me in everything I commanded. [3]For a long time now—to this very day—you have not deserted your brothers but have carried out the mission

the Lord your God gave you. 4Now that the
Lord your God has given your brothers rest as
he promised, return to your homes in the land
that Moses the servant of the Lord gave you
on the other side of the Jordan. 5But be very
careful to keep the commandment and the law
that Moses the servant of the Lord gave you:
to love the Lord your God, to walk in all his
ways, to obey his commands, to hold fast to
him and to serve him with all your heart and
all your soul."

6Then Joshua blessed them and sent them
away, and they went to their homes. 7(To the
half-tribe of Manasseh Moses had given land
in Bashan, and to the other half of the tribe
Joshua gave land on the west side of the Jordan with their brothers.) When Joshua sent
them home, he blessed them, 8saying, "Return
to your homes with your great wealth—with
large herds of livestock, with silver, gold,
bronze and iron, and a great quantity of clothing—and divide with your brothers the plunder from your enemies."

9So the Reubenites, the Gadites and the
half-tribe of Manasseh left the Israelites at Shiloh in Canaan to return to Gilead, their own
land, which they had acquired in accordance
with the command of the Lord through Moses.

10When they came to Geliloth near the Jordan in the land of Canaan, the Reubenites, the
Gadites and the half-tribe of Manasseh built
an imposing altar there by the Jordan. 11And
when the Israelites heard that they had built
the altar on the border of Canaan at Geliloth
near the Jordan on the Israelite side, 12the
whole assembly of Israel gathered at Shiloh to
go to war against them.

13So the Israelites sent Phinehas son of Eleazar, the priest, to the land of Gilead—to
Reuben, Gad and the half-tribe of Manasseh.
14With him they sent ten of the chief men,
one for each of the tribes of Israel, each the
head of a family division among the Israelite
clans.

15When they went to Gilead—to Reuben,
Gad and the half-tribe of Manasseh—they
said to them: 16"The whole assembly of the
Lord says: 'How could you break faith with
the God of Israel like this? How could you
turn away from the Lord and build yourselves an altar in rebellion against him now?
17Was not the sin of Peor enough for us? Up
to this very day we have not cleansed ourselves
from that sin, even though a plague fell on the
community of the Lord! 18And are you now
turning away from the Lord?

" 'If you rebel against the Lord today, tomorrow he will be angry with the whole community of Israel. 19If the land you possess is
defiled, come over to the Lord's land, where
the Lord's tabernacle stands, and share the
land with us. But do not rebel against the
Lord or against us by building an altar for
yourselves, other than the altar of the Lord
our God. 20When Achan son of Zerah acted
unfaithfully regarding the devoted things,[a]
did not wrath come upon the whole community of Israel? He was not the only one who
died for his sin.' "

21Then Reuben, Gad and the half-tribe of
Manasseh replied to the heads of the clans of
Israel: 22"The Mighty One, God, the Lord!
The Mighty One, God, the Lord! He knows!
And let Israel know! If this has been in rebellion or disobedience to the Lord, do not spare
us this day. 23If we have built our own altar to
turn away from the Lord and to offer burnt
offerings and grain offerings, or to sacrifice fellowship offerings[b] on it, may the Lord himself call us to account.

24"No! We did it for fear that some day
your descendants might say to ours, 'What
do you have to do with the Lord, the God
of Israel? 25The Lord has made the Jordan
a boundary between us and you—you Reubenites and Gadites! You have no share in the
Lord.' So your descendants might cause ours
to stop fearing the Lord.

26"That is why we said, 'Let us get ready and
build an altar—but not for burnt offerings or
sacrifices.' 27On the contrary, it is to be a witness between us and you and the generations
that follow, that we will worship the Lord at
his sanctuary with our burnt offerings, sacrifices and fellowship offerings. Then in the future your descendants will not be able to say to
ours, 'You have no share in the Lord.'

28"And we said, 'If they ever say this to us,
or to our descendants, we will answer: Look
at the replica of the Lord's altar, which our
fathers built, not for burnt offerings and sacrifices, but as a witness between us and you.'

29"Far be it from us to rebel against the
Lord and turn away from him today by building an altar for burnt offerings, grain offerings
and sacrifices, other than the altar of the Lord
our God that stands before his tabernacle."

[a] 20 The Hebrew term refers to the irrevocable giving over of things or persons to the Lord, often by totally destroying them.
[b] 23 Traditionally *peace offerings*; also in verse 27

30 When Phinehas the priest and the leaders of the community—the heads of the clans
of the Israelites—heard what Reuben, Gad
and Manasseh had to say, they were pleased.
31 And Phinehas son of Eleazar, the priest, said
to Reuben, Gad and Manasseh, "Today we
know that the LORD is with us, because you
have not acted unfaithfully toward the LORD
in this matter. Now you have rescued the Israelites from the LORD's hand."

32 Then Phinehas son of Eleazar, the priest,
and the leaders returned to Canaan from their
meeting with the Reubenites and Gadites in
Gilead and reported to the Israelites. 33 They
were glad to hear the report and praised God.
And they talked no more about going to war
against them to devastate the country where
the Reubenites and the Gadites lived.

34 And the Reubenites and the Gadites gave
the altar this name: A Witness Between Us
that the LORD is God.

Joshua's Farewell to the Leaders

23 After a long time had passed and the
LORD had given Israel rest from all their
enemies around them, Joshua, by then
old and well advanced in years, 2 summoned
all Israel—their elders, leaders, judges and officials—and said to them: "I am old and well
advanced in years. 3 You yourselves have seen
everything the LORD your God has done to all
these nations for your sake; it was the LORD
your God who fought for you. 4 Remember
how I have allotted as an inheritance for your
tribes all the land of the nations that remain—
the nations I conquered—between the Jordan
and the Great Sea[a] in the west. 5 The LORD
your God himself will drive them out of your
way. He will push them out before you, and
you will take possession of their land, as the
LORD your God promised you.

6 "Be very strong; be careful to obey all that
is written in the Book of the Law of Moses,
without turning aside to the right or to the
left. 7 Do not associate with these nations that
remain among you; do not invoke the names
of their gods or swear by them. You must not
serve them or bow down to them. 8 But you
are to hold fast to the LORD your God, as you
have until now.

9 "The LORD has driven out before you great
and powerful nations; to this day no one has
been able to withstand you. 10 One of you
routs a thousand, because the LORD your God
fights for you, just as he promised. 11 So be
very careful to love the LORD your God.

12 "But if you turn away and ally yourselves
with the survivors of these nations that remain
among you and if you intermarry with them
and associate with them, 13 then you may be
sure that the LORD your God will no longer
drive out these nations before you. Instead,
they will become snares and traps for you,
whips on your backs and thorns in your eyes,
until you perish from this good land, which
the LORD your God has given you.

14 "Now I am about to go the way of all the
earth. You know with all your heart and soul
that not one of all the good promises the LORD
your God gave you has failed. Every promise
has been fulfilled; not one has failed. 15 But
just as every good promise of the LORD your
God has come true, so the LORD will bring
on you all the evil he has threatened, until he
has destroyed you from this good land he has
given you. 16 If you violate the covenant of the
LORD your God, which he commanded you,
and go and serve other gods and bow down to
them, the LORD's anger will burn against you,
and you will quickly perish from the good
land he has given you."

The Covenant Renewed at Shechem

24 Then Joshua assembled all the tribes of
Israel at Shechem. He summoned the
elders, leaders, judges and officials of
Israel, and they presented themselves before
God.

2 Joshua said to all the people, "This is what
the LORD, the God of Israel, says: 'Long ago
your forefathers, including Terah the father of
Abraham and Nahor, lived beyond the River[b]
and worshiped other gods. 3 But I took your
father Abraham from the land beyond the
River and led him throughout Canaan and
gave him many descendants. I gave him Isaac,
4 and to Isaac I gave Jacob and Esau. I assigned
the hill country of Seir to Esau, but Jacob and
his sons went down to Egypt.

5 " 'Then I sent Moses and Aaron, and I afflicted the Egyptians by what I did there, and
I brought you out. 6 When I brought your fathers out of Egypt, you came to the sea, and
the Egyptians pursued them with chariots
and horsemen[c] as far as the Red Sea.[d] 7 But
they cried to the LORD for help, and he put
darkness between you and the Egyptians; he
brought the sea over them and covered them.

[a] 4 That is, the Mediterranean [b] 2 That is, the Euphrates; also in verses 3, 14 and 15 [c] 6 Or *charioteers* [d] 6 Hebrew *Yam Suph*; that is, Sea of Reeds

You saw with your own eyes what I did to the Egyptians. Then you lived in the desert for a long time.

8" 'I brought you to the land of the Amorites who lived east of the Jordan. They fought against you, but I gave them into your hands. I destroyed them from before you, and you took possession of their land. 9When Balak son of Zippor, the king of Moab, prepared to fight against Israel, he sent for Balaam son of Beor to put a curse on you. 10But I would not listen to Balaam, so he blessed you again and again, and I delivered you out of his hand.

11" 'Then you crossed the Jordan and came to Jericho. The citizens of Jericho fought against you, as did also the Amorites, Perizzites, Canaanites, Hittites, Girgashites, Hivites and Jebusites, but I gave them into your hands. 12I sent the hornet ahead of you, which drove them out before you—also the two Amorite kings. You did not do it with your own sword and bow. 13So I gave you a land on which you did not toil and cities you did not build; and you live in them and eat from vineyards and olive groves that you did not plant.'

14"Now fear the LORD and serve him with all faithfulness. Throw away the gods your forefathers worshiped beyond the River and in Egypt, and serve the LORD. 15But if serving the LORD seems undesirable to you, then choose for yourselves this day whom you will serve, whether the gods your forefathers served beyond the River, or the gods of the Amorites, in whose land you are living. But as for me and my household, we will serve the LORD."

16Then the people answered, "Far be it from us to forsake the LORD to serve other gods! 17It was the LORD our God himself who brought us and our fathers up out of Egypt, from that land of slavery, and performed those great signs before our eyes. He protected us on our entire journey and among all the nations through which we traveled. 18And the LORD drove out before us all the nations, including the Amorites, who lived in the land. We too will serve the LORD, because he is our God."

19Joshua said to the people, "You are not able to serve the LORD. He is a holy God; he is a jealous God. He will not forgive your rebellion and your sins. 20If you forsake the LORD and serve foreign gods, he will turn and bring disaster on you and make an end of you, after he has been good to you."

21But the people said to Joshua, "No! We will serve the LORD."

22Then Joshua said, "You are witnesses against yourselves that you have chosen to serve the LORD."

"Yes, we are witnesses," they replied.

23"Now then," said Joshua, "throw away the foreign gods that are among you and yield your hearts to the LORD, the God of Israel."

24And the people said to Joshua, "We will serve the LORD our God and obey him."

25On that day Joshua made a covenant for the people, and there at Shechem he drew up for them decrees and laws. 26And Joshua recorded these things in the Book of the Law of God. Then he took a large stone and set it up there under the oak near the holy place of the LORD.

27"See!" he said to all the people. "This stone will be a witness against us. It has heard all the words the LORD has said to us. It will be a witness against you if you are untrue to your God."

Buried in the Promised Land

28Then Joshua sent the people away, each to his own inheritance.

29After these things, Joshua son of Nun, the servant of the LORD, died at the age of a hundred and ten. 30And they buried him in the land of his inheritance, at Timnath Serah[a] in the hill country of Ephraim, north of Mount Gaash.

31Israel served the LORD throughout the lifetime of Joshua and of the elders who outlived him and who had experienced everything the LORD had done for Israel.

32And Joseph's bones, which the Israelites had brought up from Egypt, were buried at Shechem in the tract of land that Jacob bought for a hundred pieces of silver[b] from the sons of Hamor, the father of Shechem. This became the inheritance of Joseph's descendants.

33And Eleazar son of Aaron died and was buried at Gibeah, which had been allotted to his son Phinehas in the hill country of Ephraim.

[a] 30 Also known as *Timnath Heres* (see Judges 2:9) [b] 32 Hebrew *hundred kesitahs*; a kesitah was a unit of money of unknown weight and value.

JUDGES

QUICK FACTS

AUTHOR Possibly Samuel

AUDIENCE The Israelites living in the promised land

DATE Around 1000 B.C.

SETTING Israel's ups and (mostly) downs after the time of Joshua

The book of Judges recounts the years when the Israelites were in Canaan but hadn't fully expelled the residents and occupied the land. The book is a sad saga of what happened as a result: "The Israelites did evil in the eyes of the LORD" (Judges 2:11), worshiping the gods of the people around them. So God handed them over to their enemies, who plundered them. When the people cried out to the Lord for relief, God raised up "judges"—leaders such as Deborah, Gideon and Samson—who rescued them from their oppressors. When each judge died, however, the people returned to their idolatry, and the cycle started over again.

In the end, the judges failed to motivate the people do what they were commanded to do: work together to drive out the Canaanites and live as God's chosen people. Instead, the Israelites immersed themselves in the culture around them; they intermarried with the Canaanites and followed their worship practices. The book of Judges closes with the haunting refrain: "In those days Israel had no king; everyone did as he saw fit" (Judges 21:25).

That same refrain can be used to describe today's culture as well. Christian couples today face many of the same challenges that the Israelites encountered in resisting the pressures and practices of the world around them. But unlike any judge in Israel's time, we have an eternal King who helps us bond and grow so we can live the holy, God-centered lives he has intended for us to live.

Israel Fights the Remaining Canaanites

1 After the death of Joshua, the Israelites asked the LORD, "Who will be the first to go up and fight for us against the Canaanites?"

2 The LORD answered, "Judah is to go; I have given the land into their hands."

3 Then the men of Judah said to the Simeonites their brothers, "Come up with us into the territory allotted to us, to fight against the Canaanites. We in turn will go with you into yours." So the Simeonites went with them.

4 When Judah attacked, the LORD gave the Canaanites and Perizzites into their hands and they struck down ten thousand men at Bezek. 5 It was there that they found Adoni-Bezek and fought against him, putting to rout the Canaanites and Perizzites. 6 Adoni-Bezek fled, but they chased him and caught him, and cut off his thumbs and big toes.

7 Then Adoni-Bezek said, "Seventy kings with their thumbs and big toes cut off have picked up scraps under my table. Now God has paid me back for what I did to them." They brought him to Jerusalem, and he died there.

8 The men of Judah attacked Jerusalem also and took it. They put the city to the sword and set it on fire.

9 After that, the men of Judah went down to fight against the Canaanites living in the hill country, the Negev and the western foothills. 10 They advanced against the Canaanites living in Hebron (formerly called Kiriath Arba) and defeated Sheshai, Ahiman and Talmai.

11 From there they advanced against the people living in Debir (formerly called Kiriath Sepher). 12 And Caleb said, "I will give my daughter Acsah in marriage to the man who attacks and captures Kiriath Sepher." 13 Othniel son of Kenaz, Caleb's younger brother, took it; so Caleb gave his daughter Acsah to him in marriage.

14 One day when she came to Othniel, she urged him[a] to ask her father for a field. When she got off her donkey, Caleb asked her, "What can I do for you?"

15 She replied, "Do me a special favor. Since you have given me land in the Negev, give me also springs of water." Then Caleb gave her the upper and lower springs.

16 The descendants of Moses' father-in-law, the Kenite, went up from the City of Palms[b] with the men of Judah to live among the people of the Desert of Judah in the Negev near Arad.

17 Then the men of Judah went with the Simeonites their brothers and attacked the Canaanites living in Zephath, and they totally destroyed[c] the city. Therefore it was called Hormah.[d] 18 The men of Judah also took[e] Gaza, Ashkelon and Ekron—each city with its territory.

19 The LORD was with the men of Judah. They took possession of the hill country, but they were unable to drive the people from the plains, because they had iron chariots. 20 As Moses had promised, Hebron was given to Caleb, who drove from it the three sons of Anak. 21 The Benjamites, however, failed to dislodge the Jebusites, who were living in Jerusalem; to this day the Jebusites live there with the Benjamites.

22 Now the house of Joseph attacked Bethel, and the LORD was with them. 23 When they sent men to spy out Bethel (formerly called Luz), 24 the spies saw a man coming out of the city and they said to him, "Show us how to get into the city and we will see that you are treated well." 25 So he showed them, and they put the city to the sword but spared the man and his whole family. 26 He then went to the land of the Hittites, where he built a city and called it Luz, which is its name to this day.

27 But Manasseh did not drive out the people of Beth Shan or Taanach or Dor or Ibleam or Megiddo and their surrounding settlements, for the Canaanites were determined to live in that land. 28 When Israel became strong, they pressed the Canaanites into forced labor but never drove them out completely. 29 Nor did Ephraim drive out the Canaanites living in Gezer, but the Canaanites continued to live there among them. 30 Neither did Zebulun drive out the Canaanites living in Kitron or Nahalol, who remained among them; but they did subject them to forced labor. 31 Nor did Asher drive out those living in Acco or Sidon or Ahlab or Aczib or Helbah or Aphek or Rehob, 32 and because of this the people of Asher lived among the Canaanite inhabitants of the land. 33 Neither did Naphtali drive out those living in Beth Shemesh or Beth Anath; but the Naphtalites too lived among the Canaanite inhabitants of the land, and those living in Beth Shemesh and Beth Anath became forced laborers for them. 34 The Amorites confined

---

[a] *14* Hebrew; Septuagint and Vulgate *Othniel, he urged her* [b] *16* That is, Jericho [c] *17* The Hebrew term refers to the irrevocable giving over of things or persons to the LORD, often by totally destroying them. [d] *17* *Hormah* means *destruction.* [e] *18* Hebrew; Septuagint *Judah did not take*

the Danites to the hill country, not allowing them to come down into the plain. 35And the Amorites were determined also to hold out in Mount Heres, Aijalon and Shaalbim, but when the power of the house of Joseph increased, they too were pressed into forced labor. 36The boundary of the Amorites was from Scorpion[a] Pass to Sela and beyond.

The Angel of the LORD at Bokim

2 The angel of the LORD went up from Gilgal to Bokim and said, "I brought you up out of Egypt and led you into the land that I swore to give to your forefathers. I said, 'I will never break my covenant with you, 2and you shall not make a covenant with the people of this land, but you shall break down their altars.' Yet you have disobeyed me. Why have you done this? 3Now therefore I tell you that I will not drive them out before you; they will be ⌞thorns⌟ in your sides and their gods will be a snare to you."

4When the angel of the LORD had spoken these things to all the Israelites, the people wept aloud, 5and they called that place Bokim.[b] There they offered sacrifices to the LORD.

Disobedience and Defeat

6After Joshua had dismissed the Israelites, they went to take possession of the land, each to his own inheritance. 7The people served the LORD throughout the lifetime of Joshua and of the elders who outlived him and who had seen all the great things the LORD had done for Israel.

8Joshua son of Nun, the servant of the LORD, died at the age of a hundred and ten. 9And they buried him in the land of his inheritance, at Timnath Heres[c] in the hill country of Ephraim, north of Mount Gaash.

10After that whole generation had been gathered to their fathers, another generation grew up, who knew neither the LORD nor what he had done for Israel. 11Then the Israelites did evil in the eyes of the LORD and served the Baals. 12They forsook the LORD, the God of their fathers, who had brought them out of Egypt. They followed and worshiped various gods of the peoples around them. They provoked the LORD to anger 13because they forsook him and served Baal and the Ashtoreths. 14In his anger against Israel the LORD handed them over to raiders who plundered them. He sold them to their enemies all around, whom they were no longer able to resist. 15Whenever Israel went out to fight, the hand of the LORD was against them to defeat them, just as he had sworn to them. They were in great distress.

16Then the LORD raised up judges,[d] who saved them out of the hands of these raiders. 17Yet they would not listen to their judges but prostituted themselves to other gods and worshiped them. Unlike their fathers, they quickly turned from the way in which their fathers had walked, the way of obedience to the LORD's commands. 18Whenever the LORD raised up a judge for them, he was with the judge and saved them out of the hands of their enemies as long as the judge lived; for the LORD had compassion on them as they groaned under those who oppressed and afflicted them. 19But when the judge died, the people returned to ways even more corrupt than those of their fathers, following other gods and serving and worshiping them. They refused to give up their evil practices and stubborn ways.

20Therefore the LORD was very angry with Israel and said, "Because this nation has violated the covenant that I laid down for their forefathers and has not listened to me, 21I will no longer drive out before them any of the nations Joshua left when he died. 22I will use them to test Israel and see whether they will keep the way of the LORD and walk in it as their forefathers did." 23The LORD had allowed those nations to remain; he did not drive them out at once by giving them into the hands of Joshua.

3 These are the nations the LORD left to test all those Israelites who had not experienced any of the wars in Canaan 2(he did this only to teach warfare to the descendants of the Israelites who had not had previous battle experience): 3the five rulers of the Philistines, all the Canaanites, the Sidonians, and the Hivites living in the Lebanon mountains from Mount Baal Hermon to Lebo[e] Hamath. 4They were left to test the Israelites to see whether they would obey the LORD's commands, which he had given their forefathers through Moses.

5The Israelites lived among the Canaanites, Hittites, Amorites, Perizzites, Hivites and Jebusites. 6They took their daughters in marriage and gave their own daughters to their sons, and served their gods.

Othniel

7The Israelites did evil in the eyes of the LORD; they forgot the LORD their God and

---

[a] *36* Hebrew *Akrabbim* [b] *5* *Bokim* means *weepers.* [c] *9* Also known as *Timnath Serah* (see Joshua 19:50 and 24:30) [d] *16* Or *leaders;* similarly in verses 17-19 [e] *3* Or *to the entrance to*

WEDNESDAY
READ JUDGES 2:6–19

THE IMPORTANCE OF REMEMBERING

After that whole generation had been gathered to their fathers, another generation grew up, who knew neither the LORD nor what he had done for Israel.

— JUDGES 2:10

Some time ago my mail carrier brought me a package wrapped in brown paper. Inside I found a book that I thought I had lost. A note of apology solved the mystery. One of my college buddies had borrowed the book and only recently had rediscovered it. His regret was profuse and reminded me of what Sir Walter Scott said: "Although my friends are very bad at arithmetic, they tend to be very excellent at bookkeeping."

Books have a way of wandering. I went back to a former congregation to preach and found a stack of 11 books with my name in them on the table in the room where we met for preservice prayer. No one told me who put the books there, but the elders urged me to take the books home before they vanished again. Another time I visited a widow whose husband had been a great friend of mine. She pulled out a book and said, "I found this in John's things and thought you might want it back." Although I'm glad for the book, I wish I could have John instead.

Forgetfulness is a great human weakness. The most pervasive New Year's resolution in ancient Babylon was a commitment to return borrowed tools and utensils to their rightful owners.

One marriage counselor says that forgetfulness is the greatest trigger to marriage failure. He has worked with many couples who became so caught up in skirmishes about recent hurts that they forgot why they had married in the first place. When we lose our bearings in the fog of petty gripes, they can mushroom into a cloud of despair that hides us from wonderful safe harbors, magnificent marriage destinations and the joy of traveling well.

The writer of Judges seems to have had something like that in mind when he wrote the difficult words of Judges 2:10. The writer offered a sad commentary about repeated unfaithfulness, saying that the generation succeeding Joshua and his contemporaries knew nothing about God or what he had done for Israel.

Forgetfulness may be humorous or embarrassing on occasion, but when we forget our relationship with God and fail to pass on truths about his goodness to each other and our children, the results are tragic. The very foundation of our marriage crumbles. Family life fractures. And eventually the children whose we failed to bring up in the ways of the Lord become a generation that knows nothing about him.

let's talk

- What aids to memory are we using to nurture each other in our home? What symbols are visible? What devotional practices are becoming habits?
- How does the rhythm of our lives encourage spiritual memories? How are our practices of church participation, of service, and of the tithing of our time and money a reflection of our faith?
- How will we pass along to our children and grandchildren the foundations and markers of faith? What actions do we need to take now to ensure that these will be present during the years ahead?

—WAYNE BROUWER

FOR YOUR NEXT DEVOTIONAL READING, TURN TO PAGE 256.

served the Baals and the Asherahs. 8The anger of the LORD burned against Israel so that he sold them into the hands of Cushan-Rishathaim king of Aram Naharaim,[a] to whom the Israelites were subject for eight years. 9But when they cried out to the LORD, he raised up for them a deliverer, Othniel son of Kenaz, Caleb's younger brother, who saved them. 10The Spirit of the LORD came upon him, so that he became Israel's judge[b] and went to war. The LORD gave Cushan-Rishathaim king of Aram into the hands of Othniel, who overpowered him. 11So the land had peace for forty years, until Othniel son of Kenaz died.

Ehud

12Once again the Israelites did evil in the eyes of the LORD, and because they did this evil the LORD gave Eglon king of Moab power over Israel. 13Getting the Ammonites and Amalekites to join him, Eglon came and attacked Israel, and they took possession of the City of Palms.[c] 14The Israelites were subject to Eglon king of Moab for eighteen years.

15Again the Israelites cried out to the LORD, and he gave them a deliverer—Ehud, a left-handed man, the son of Gera the Benjamite. The Israelites sent him with tribute to Eglon king of Moab. 16Now Ehud had made a double-edged sword about a foot and a half[d] long, which he strapped to his right thigh under his clothing. 17He presented the tribute to Eglon king of Moab, who was a very fat man. 18After Ehud had presented the tribute, he sent on their way the men who had carried it. 19At the idols[e] near Gilgal he himself turned back and said, "I have a secret message for you, O king."

The king said, "Quiet!" And all his attendants left him.

20Ehud then approached him while he was sitting alone in the upper room of his summer palace[f] and said, "I have a message from God for you." As the king rose from his seat, 21Ehud reached with his left hand, drew the sword from his right thigh and plunged it into the king's belly. 22Even the handle sank in after the blade, which came out his back. Ehud did not pull the sword out, and the fat closed in over it. 23Then Ehud went out to the porch[g]; he shut the doors of the upper room behind him and locked them.

24After he had gone, the servants came and found the doors of the upper room locked. They said, "He must be relieving himself in the inner room of the house." 25They waited to the point of embarrassment, but when he did not open the doors of the room, they took a key and unlocked them. There they saw their lord fallen to the floor, dead.

26While they waited, Ehud got away. He passed by the idols and escaped to Seirah. 27When he arrived there, he blew a trumpet in the hill country of Ephraim, and the Israelites went down with him from the hills, with him leading them.

28"Follow me," he ordered, "for the LORD has given Moab, your enemy, into your hands." So they followed him down and, taking possession of the fords of the Jordan that led to Moab, they allowed no one to cross over. 29At that time they struck down about ten thousand Moabites, all vigorous and strong; not a man escaped. 30That day Moab was made subject to Israel, and the land had peace for eighty years.

Shamgar

31After Ehud came Shamgar son of Anath, who struck down six hundred Philistines with an oxgoad. He too saved Israel.

Deborah

4 After Ehud died, the Israelites once again did evil in the eyes of the LORD. 2So the LORD sold them into the hands of Jabin, a king of Canaan, who reigned in Hazor. The commander of his army was Sisera, who lived in Harosheth Haggoyim. 3Because he had nine hundred iron chariots and had cruelly oppressed the Israelites for twenty years, they cried to the LORD for help.

4Deborah, a prophetess, the wife of Lappidoth, was leading[h] Israel at that time. 5She held court under the Palm of Deborah between Ramah and Bethel in the hill country of Ephraim, and the Israelites came to her to have their disputes decided. 6She sent for Barak son of Abinoam from Kedesh in Naphtali and said to him, "The LORD, the God of Israel, commands you: 'Go, take with you ten thousand men of Naphtali and Zebulun and lead the way to Mount Tabor. 7I will lure Sisera, the commander of Jabin's army, with his chariots and his troops to the Kishon River and give him into your hands.' "

---

[a] *8* That is, Northwest Mesopotamia [b] *10* Or *leader* [c] *13* That is, Jericho [d] *16* Hebrew *a cubit* (about 0.5 meter) [e] *19* Or *the stone quarries*; also in verse 26 [f] *20* The meaning of the Hebrew for this phrase is uncertain. [g] *23* The meaning of the Hebrew for this word is uncertain. [h] *4* Traditionally *judging*

8 Barak said to her, "If you go with me, I will
go; but if you don't go with me, I won't go."
9 "Very well," Deborah said, "I will go with
you. But because of the way you are going
about this,[a] the honor will not be yours, for
the LORD will hand Sisera over to a woman." So Deborah went with Barak to Kedesh,
10 where he summoned Zebulun and Naphtali.
Ten thousand men followed him, and Deborah also went with him.
11 Now Heber the Kenite had left the other Kenites, the descendants of Hobab, Moses'
brother-in-law,[b] and pitched his tent by the
great tree in Zaanannim near Kedesh.
12 When they told Sisera that Barak son of
Abinoam had gone up to Mount Tabor, 13 Sisera gathered together his nine hundred iron
chariots and all the men with him, from Harosheth Haggoyim to the Kishon River.
14 Then Deborah said to Barak, "Go! This
is the day the LORD has given Sisera into your
hands. Has not the LORD gone ahead of you?"
So Barak went down Mount Tabor, followed
by ten thousand men. 15 At Barak's advance,
the LORD routed Sisera and all his chariots
and army by the sword, and Sisera abandoned
his chariot and fled on foot. 16 But Barak pursued the chariots and army as far as Harosheth
Haggoyim. All the troops of Sisera fell by the
sword; not a man was left.
17 Sisera, however, fled on foot to the tent
of Jael, the wife of Heber the Kenite, because
there were friendly relations between Jabin king
of Hazor and the clan of Heber the Kenite.
18 Jael went out to meet Sisera and said to
him, "Come, my lord, come right in. Don't be
afraid." So he entered her tent, and she put a
covering over him.
19 "I'm thirsty," he said. "Please give me
some water." She opened a skin of milk, gave
him a drink, and covered him up.
20 "Stand in the doorway of the tent," he
told her. "If someone comes by and asks you,
'Is anyone here?' say 'No.' "
21 But Jael, Heber's wife, picked up a tent
peg and a hammer and went quietly to him
while he lay fast asleep, exhausted. She drove
the peg through his temple into the ground,
and he died.
22 Barak came by in pursuit of Sisera, and
Jael went out to meet him. "Come," she said,
"I will show you the man you're looking for."
So he went in with her, and there lay Sisera
with the tent peg through his temple—dead.
23 On that day God subdued Jabin, the Canaanite king, before the Israelites. 24 And the
hand of the Israelites grew stronger and stronger against Jabin, the Canaanite king, until
they destroyed him.

The Song of Deborah

5 On that day Deborah and Barak son of
Abinoam sang this song:

2 "When the princes in Israel take the lead,
when the people willingly offer
themselves—
praise the LORD!

3 "Hear this, you kings! Listen, you rulers!
I will sing to[c] the LORD, I will sing;
I will make music to[d] the LORD, the
God of Israel.

4 "O LORD, when you went out from Seir,
when you marched from the land of
Edom,
the earth shook, the heavens poured,
the clouds poured down water.
5 The mountains quaked before the LORD,
the One of Sinai,
before the LORD, the God of Israel.

6 "In the days of Shamgar son of Anath,
in the days of Jael, the roads were
abandoned;
travelers took to winding paths.
7 Village life[e] in Israel ceased,
ceased until I,[f] Deborah, arose,
arose a mother in Israel.
8 When they chose new gods,
war came to the city gates,
and not a shield or spear was seen
among forty thousand in Israel.
9 My heart is with Israel's princes,
with the willing volunteers among the
people.
Praise the LORD!

10 "You who ride on white donkeys,
sitting on your saddle blankets,
and you who walk along the road,
consider 11 the voice of the singers[g] at the
watering places.
They recite the righteous acts of the
LORD,
the righteous acts of his warriors[h] in
Israel.

"Then the people of the LORD
went down to the city gates.
12 'Wake up, wake up, Deborah!

[a] 9 Or *But on the expedition you are undertaking* [b] 11 Or *father-in-law* [c] 3 Or *of* [d] 3 Or / *with song I will praise* [e] 7 Or *Warriors*
[f] 7 Or *you* [g] 11 Or *archers*; the meaning of the Hebrew for this word is uncertain. [h] 11 Or *villagers*

Wake up, wake up, break out in song!
Arise, O Barak!
Take captive your captives, O son of Abinoam.'

13 "Then the men who were left
came down to the nobles;
the people of the LORD
came to me with the mighty.
14 Some came from Ephraim, whose roots were in Amalek;
Benjamin was with the people who followed you.
From Makir captains came down,
from Zebulun those who bear a commander's staff.
15 The princes of Issachar were with Deborah;
yes, Issachar was with Barak,
rushing after him into the valley.
In the districts of Reuben
there was much searching of heart.
16 Why did you stay among the campfires[a]
to hear the whistling for the flocks?
In the districts of Reuben
there was much searching of heart.
17 Gilead stayed beyond the Jordan.
And Dan, why did he linger by the ships?
Asher remained on the coast
and stayed in his coves.
18 The people of Zebulun risked their very lives;
so did Naphtali on the heights of the field.

19 "Kings came, they fought;
the kings of Canaan fought
at Taanach by the waters of Megiddo,
but they carried off no silver, no plunder.
20 From the heavens the stars fought,
from their courses they fought against Sisera.
21 The river Kishon swept them away,
the age-old river, the river Kishon.
March on, my soul; be strong!
22 Then thundered the horses' hoofs—
galloping, galloping go his mighty steeds.
23 'Curse Meroz,' said the angel of the LORD.
'Curse its people bitterly,
because they did not come to help the LORD,
to help the LORD against the mighty.'

24 "Most blessed of women be Jael,
the wife of Heber the Kenite,
most blessed of tent-dwelling women.
25 He asked for water, and she gave him milk;
in a bowl fit for nobles she brought him curdled milk.
26 Her hand reached for the tent peg,
her right hand for the workman's hammer.
She struck Sisera, she crushed his head,
she shattered and pierced his temple.
27 At her feet he sank,
he fell; there he lay.
At her feet he sank, he fell;
where he sank, there he fell—dead.

28 "Through the window peered Sisera's mother;
behind the lattice she cried out,
'Why is his chariot so long in coming?
Why is the clatter of his chariots delayed?'
29 The wisest of her ladies answer her;
indeed, she keeps saying to herself,
30 'Are they not finding and dividing the spoils:
a girl or two for each man,
colorful garments as plunder for Sisera,
colorful garments embroidered,
highly embroidered garments for my neck—
all this as plunder?'

31 "So may all your enemies perish, O LORD!
But may they who love you be like the sun
when it rises in its strength."

Then the land had peace forty years.

Gideon

6 Again the Israelites did evil in the eyes of the
LORD, and for seven years he gave them into
the hands of the Midianites. 2 Because the
power of Midian was so oppressive, the Israelites prepared shelters for themselves in mountain clefts, caves and strongholds. 3 Whenever
the Israelites planted their crops, the Midianites, Amalekites and other eastern peoples invaded the country. 4 They camped on the land
and ruined the crops all the way to Gaza and
did not spare a living thing for Israel, neither
sheep nor cattle nor donkeys. 5 They came up
with their livestock and their tents like swarms
of locusts. It was impossible to count the men
and their camels; they invaded the land to ravage it. 6 Midian so impoverished the Israelites
that they cried out to the LORD for help.

[a] 16 Or *saddlebags*

THURSDAY
READ JUDGES 6:1–27

WHEN EXCUSES WON'T DO

Isn't God amazing? Throughout the Bible he patiently works with complainers, self-doubters and rebels. And not only that, but God also works his plan through truly weak people, like Gideon—or like a man and woman in marriage.

Gideon had good reason to fear an assignment from God to deliver the children of Israel from the oppression of the Midianites. His faith and his clan were weak, and the Israelites were mixing Baal worship with God worship. Even just talking to the Lord must have struck fear in Gideon's heart: Didn't he also deserve to be punished for failing to worship God with his whole heart?

Gideon thought his conversation with God was all about him. But, as we find out, Gideon came to realize he was just a player in God's story, and God was the One with the power to save Israel. God patiently worked with Gideon to remove his doubts and to make him aware that God alone was his strength, telling him in verse 16, "I will be with you."

"But Lord," Gideon asked, "how can I save Israel? My clan is the weakest in Manasseh, and I am the least in my family."

— JUDGES 6:15

let's *talk*

- ✦ What are some methods God uses to lead our decision making in marriage?
- ✦ How do we distinguish God's leading from our own desires and goals?
- ✦ When we sense God leading each of us in different directions, how can we come to agreement?

So how do we complainers, self-doubters and rebels respond when we encounter God's assignments in our married life? The first challenge is that there are two of us for God to deal with. Since God established the marriage covenant, he's not inclined to undermine it by leading a husband and wife in different directions.

When my husband, Grey, and I were ending a one-year overseas mission assignment, the director of the mission agency challenged us to return as career workers. Grey was game, but I was unwilling to commit because I didn't want to take on the challenge of raising financial support. We had funded one year of mission work with our own savings, but relying on God to lead people to support us caused me great anxiety.

While Grey stayed steady in his commitment to return to the mission field, I, like Gideon, whined about it and then asked God for a sign. When the first sign came (I encouraged Grey to look for a job in the United States, but all those career doors closed), I asked for another sign. Gideon-like, I was setting up my own fleece experiments.

This time God's response was unmistakable. People started giving to us. Check after check finally brought me to the conclusion that God wanted to use us, ordinary people, to do his work overseas. We were nothing special, but raising support went well. We went back to the field for nine more years.

Gideon's story, and the whole Bible, is full of principles we can apply to our lives today. Each day of marriage we can recall God's blessings to us, be assured that he is with us—even in our weaknesses—and believe that he has work for us to do.

—MARY ANN JEFFREYS

FOR YOUR NEXT DEVOTIONAL READING, TURN TO PAGE 267.

7When the Israelites cried to the LORD because of Midian, 8he sent them a prophet,
who said, "This is what the LORD, the God of
Israel, says: I brought you up out of Egypt, out
of the land of slavery. 9I snatched you from the
power of Egypt and from the hand of all your
oppressors. I drove them from before you and
gave you their land. 10I said to you, 'I am the
LORD your God; do not worship the gods of
the Amorites, in whose land you live.' But you
have not listened to me."

11The angel of the LORD came and sat down
under the oak in Ophrah that belonged to Joash the Abiezrite, where his son Gideon was
threshing wheat in a winepress to keep it from
the Midianites. 12When the angel of the LORD
appeared to Gideon, he said, "The LORD is
with you, mighty warrior."

13"But sir," Gideon replied, "if the LORD
is with us, why has all this happened to us?
Where are all his wonders that our fathers told
us about when they said, 'Did not the LORD
bring us up out of Egypt?' But now the LORD
has abandoned us and put us into the hand
of Midian."

14The LORD turned to him and said, "Go
in the strength you have and save Israel out of
Midian's hand. Am I not sending you?"

15"But Lord,[a]" Gideon asked, "how can I
save Israel? My clan is the weakest in Manasseh, and I am the least in my family."

16The LORD answered, "I will be with you,
and you will strike down all the Midianites together."

17Gideon replied, "If now I have found favor in your eyes, give me a sign that it is really
you talking to me. 18Please do not go away
until I come back and bring my offering and
set it before you."

And the LORD said, "I will wait until you
return."

19Gideon went in, prepared a young goat,
and from an ephah[b] of flour he made bread
without yeast. Putting the meat in a basket
and its broth in a pot, he brought them out
and offered them to him under the oak.

20The angel of God said to him, "Take the
meat and the unleavened bread, place them on
this rock, and pour out the broth." And Gideon did so. 21With the tip of the staff that was
in his hand, the angel of the LORD touched
the meat and the unleavened bread. Fire flared
from the rock, consuming the meat and the
bread. And the angel of the LORD disappeared.
22When Gideon realized that it was the angel of the LORD, he exclaimed, "Ah, Sovereign
LORD! I have seen the angel of the LORD face
to face!"

23But the LORD said to him, "Peace! Do not
be afraid. You are not going to die."

24So Gideon built an altar to the LORD
there and called it The LORD is Peace. To this
day it stands in Ophrah of the Abiezrites.

25That same night the LORD said to him,
"Take the second bull from your father's herd,
the one seven years old.[c] Tear down your father's altar to Baal and cut down the Asherah
pole[d] beside it. 26Then build a proper kind of[e]
altar to the LORD your God on the top of this
height. Using the wood of the Asherah pole
that you cut down, offer the second[f] bull as a
burnt offering."

27So Gideon took ten of his servants and
did as the LORD told him. But because he was
afraid of his family and the men of the town,
he did it at night rather than in the daytime.

28In the morning when the men of the town
got up, there was Baal's altar, demolished, with
the Asherah pole beside it cut down and the
second bull sacrificed on the newly built altar!

29They asked each other, "Who did this?"

When they carefully investigated, they were
told, "Gideon son of Joash did it."

30The men of the town demanded of Joash,
"Bring out your son. He must die, because he
has broken down Baal's altar and cut down the
Asherah pole beside it."

31But Joash replied to the hostile crowd
around him, "Are you going to plead Baal's
cause? Are you trying to save him? Whoever fights for him shall be put to death by
morning! If Baal really is a god, he can defend
himself when someone breaks down his altar." 32So that day they called Gideon "Jerub-
Baal,[g]" saying, "Let Baal contend with him,"
because he broke down Baal's altar.

33Now all the Midianites, Amalekites and
other eastern peoples joined forces and crossed
over the Jordan and camped in the Valley of
Jezreel. 34Then the Spirit of the LORD came
upon Gideon, and he blew a trumpet, summoning the Abiezrites to follow him. 35He
sent messengers throughout Manasseh, calling them to arms, and also into Asher, Zebulun and Naphtali, so that they too went up
to meet them.

36Gideon said to God, "If you will save Isra-

---

a 15 Or *sir* *b* 19 That is, probably about 3/5 bushel (about 22 liters) *c* 25 Or *Take a full-grown, mature bull from your father's herd* *d* 25 That is, a symbol of the goddess Asherah; here and elsewhere in Judges *e* 26 Or *build with layers of stone an* *f* 26 Or *full-grown*; also in verse 28 *g* 32 *Jerub-Baal* means *let Baal contend.*

el by my hand as you have promised— 37look, I will place a wool fleece on the threshing floor. If there is dew only on the fleece and all the ground is dry, then I will know that you will save Israel by my hand, as you said." 38And that is what happened. Gideon rose early the next day; he squeezed the fleece and wrung out the dew—a bowlful of water.

39Then Gideon said to God, "Do not be angry with me. Let me make just one more request. Allow me one more test with the fleece. This time make the fleece dry and the ground covered with dew." 40That night God did so. Only the fleece was dry; all the ground was covered with dew.

Gideon Defeats the Midianites

7 Early in the morning, Jerub-Baal (that is, Gideon) and all his men camped at the spring of Harod. The camp of Midian was north of them in the valley near the hill of Moreh. 2The LORD said to Gideon, "You have too many men for me to deliver Midian into their hands. In order that Israel may not boast against me that her own strength has saved her, 3announce now to the people, 'Anyone who trembles with fear may turn back and leave Mount Gilead.' " So twenty-two thousand men left, while ten thousand remained.

4But the LORD said to Gideon, "There are still too many men. Take them down to the water, and I will sift them for you there. If I say, 'This one shall go with you,' he shall go; but if I say, 'This one shall not go with you,' he shall not go."

5So Gideon took the men down to the water. There the LORD told him, "Separate those who lap the water with their tongues like a dog from those who kneel down to drink." 6Three hundred men lapped with their hands to their mouths. All the rest got down on their knees to drink.

7The LORD said to Gideon, "With the three hundred men that lapped I will save you and give the Midianites into your hands. Let all the other men go, each to his own place." 8So Gideon sent the rest of the Israelites to their tents but kept the three hundred, who took over the provisions and trumpets of the others.

Now the camp of Midian lay below him in the valley. 9During that night the LORD said to Gideon, "Get up, go down against the camp, because I am going to give it into your hands. 10If you are afraid to attack, go down to the camp with your servant Purah 11and listen to what they are saying. Afterward, you will be encouraged to attack the camp." So he and Purah his servant went down to the outposts of the camp. 12The Midianites, the Amalekites and all the other eastern peoples had settled in the valley, thick as locusts. Their camels could no more be counted than the sand on the seashore.

13Gideon arrived just as a man was telling a friend his dream. "I had a dream," he was saying. "A round loaf of barley bread came tumbling into the Midianite camp. It struck the tent with such force that the tent overturned and collapsed."

14His friend responded, "This can be nothing other than the sword of Gideon son of Joash, the Israelite. God has given the Midianites and the whole camp into his hands."

15When Gideon heard the dream and its interpretation, he worshiped God. He returned to the camp of Israel and called out, "Get up! The LORD has given the Midianite camp into your hands." 16Dividing the three hundred men into three companies, he placed trumpets and empty jars in the hands of all of them, with torches inside.

17"Watch me," he told them. "Follow my lead. When I get to the edge of the camp, do exactly as I do. 18When I and all who are with me blow our trumpets, then from all around the camp blow yours and shout, 'For the LORD and for Gideon.' "

19Gideon and the hundred men with him reached the edge of the camp at the beginning of the middle watch, just after they had changed the guard. They blew their trumpets and broke the jars that were in their hands. 20The three companies blew the trumpets and smashed the jars. Grasping the torches in their left hands and holding in their right hands the trumpets they were to blow, they shouted, "A sword for the LORD and for Gideon!" 21While each man held his position around the camp, all the Midianites ran, crying out as they fled.

22When the three hundred trumpets sounded, the LORD caused the men throughout the camp to turn on each other with their swords. The army fled to Beth Shittah toward Zererah as far as the border of Abel Meholah near Tabbath. 23Israelites from Naphtali, Asher and all Manasseh were called out, and they pursued the Midianites. 24Gideon sent messengers throughout the hill country of Ephraim, saying, "Come down against the Midianites and seize the waters of the Jordan ahead of them as far as Beth Barah."

So all the men of Ephraim were called out and they took the waters of the Jordan as far as Beth Barah. 25They also captured two of the Midianite leaders, Oreb and Zeeb. They killed Oreb at the rock of Oreb, and Zeeb at the winepress of Zeeb. They pursued the Midianites and brought the heads of Oreb and Zeeb to Gideon, who was by the Jordan.

Zebah and Zalmunna

8 Now the Ephraimites asked Gideon, "Why have you treated us like this? Why didn't you call us when you went to fight Midian?" And they criticized him sharply.

2But he answered them, "What have I accomplished compared to you? Aren't the gleanings of Ephraim's grapes better than the full grape harvest of Abiezer? 3God gave Oreb and Zeeb, the Midianite leaders, into your hands. What was I able to do compared to you?" At this, their resentment against him subsided.

4Gideon and his three hundred men, exhausted yet keeping up the pursuit, came to the Jordan and crossed it. 5He said to the men of Succoth, "Give my troops some bread; they are worn out, and I am still pursuing Zebah and Zalmunna, the kings of Midian."

6But the officials of Succoth said, "Do you already have the hands of Zebah and Zalmunna in your possession? Why should we give bread to your troops?"

7Then Gideon replied, "Just for that, when the LORD has given Zebah and Zalmunna into my hand, I will tear your flesh with desert thorns and briers."

8From there he went up to Peniel[a] and made the same request of them, but they answered as the men of Succoth had. 9So he said to the men of Peniel, "When I return in triumph, I will tear down this tower."

10Now Zebah and Zalmunna were in Karkor with a force of about fifteen thousand men, all that were left of the armies of the eastern peoples; a hundred and twenty thousand swordsmen had fallen. 11Gideon went up by the route of the nomads east of Nobah and Jogbehah and fell upon the unsuspecting army. 12Zebah and Zalmunna, the two kings of Midian, fled, but he pursued them and captured them, routing their entire army.

13Gideon son of Joash then returned from the battle by the Pass of Heres. 14He caught a young man of Succoth and questioned him, and the young man wrote down for him the names of the seventy-seven officials of Succoth, the elders of the town. 15Then Gideon came and said to the men of Succoth, "Here are Zebah and Zalmunna, about whom you taunted me by saying, 'Do you already have the hands of Zebah and Zalmunna in your possession? Why should we give bread to your exhausted men?' " 16He took the elders of the town and taught the men of Succoth a lesson by punishing them with desert thorns and briers. 17He also pulled down the tower of Peniel and killed the men of the town.

18Then he asked Zebah and Zalmunna, "What kind of men did you kill at Tabor?"

"Men like you," they answered, "each one with the bearing of a prince."

19Gideon replied, "Those were my brothers, the sons of my own mother. As surely as the LORD lives, if you had spared their lives, I would not kill you." 20Turning to Jether, his oldest son, he said, "Kill them!" But Jether did not draw his sword, because he was only a boy and was afraid.

21Zebah and Zalmunna said, "Come, do it yourself. 'As is the man, so is his strength.' " So Gideon stepped forward and killed them, and took the ornaments off their camels' necks.

Gideon's Ephod

22The Israelites said to Gideon, "Rule over us—you, your son and your grandson—because you have saved us out of the hand of Midian."

23But Gideon told them, "I will not rule over you, nor will my son rule over you. The LORD will rule over you." 24And he said, "I do have one request, that each of you give me an earring from your share of the plunder." (It was the custom of the Ishmaelites to wear gold earrings.)

25They answered, "We'll be glad to give them." So they spread out a garment, and each man threw a ring from his plunder onto it. 26The weight of the gold rings he asked for came to seventeen hundred shekels,[b] not counting the ornaments, the pendants and the purple garments worn by the kings of Midian or the chains that were on their camels' necks. 27Gideon made the gold into an ephod, which he placed in Ophrah, his town. All Israel prostituted themselves by worshiping it there, and it became a snare to Gideon and his family.

Gideon's Death

28Thus Midian was subdued before the Israelites and did not raise its head again. Dur-

[a] 8 Hebrew *Penuel,* a variant of *Peniel;* also in verses 9 and 17 [b] 26 That is, about 43 pounds (about 19.5 kilograms)

ing Gideon's lifetime, the land enjoyed peace
forty years.
29Jerub-Baal son of Joash went back home
to live. 30He had seventy sons of his own, for
he had many wives. 31His concubine, who
lived in Shechem, also bore him a son, whom
he named Abimelech. 32Gideon son of Joash
died at a good old age and was buried in the
tomb of his father Joash in Ophrah of the Abiezrites.
33No sooner had Gideon died than the Israelites again prostituted themselves to the
Baals. They set up Baal-Berith as their god
34and did not remember the LORD their God,
who had rescued them from the hands of all
their enemies on every side. 35They also failed
to show kindness to the family of Jerub-Baal
(that is, Gideon) for all the good things he had
done for them.

Abimelech

9 Abimelech son of Jerub-Baal went to his
mother's brothers in Shechem and said to
them and to all his mother's clan, 2"Ask all
the citizens of Shechem, 'Which is better for
you: to have all seventy of Jerub-Baal's sons
rule over you, or just one man?' Remember, I
am your flesh and blood."
3When the brothers repeated all this to the
citizens of Shechem, they were inclined to
follow Abimelech, for they said, "He is our
brother." 4They gave him seventy shekels[a]
of silver from the temple of Baal-Berith, and
Abimelech used it to hire reckless adventurers, who became his followers. 5He went to
his father's home in Ophrah and on one stone
murdered his seventy brothers, the sons of
Jerub-Baal. But Jotham, the youngest son of
Jerub-Baal, escaped by hiding. 6Then all the
citizens of Shechem and Beth Millo gathered
beside the great tree at the pillar in Shechem
to crown Abimelech king.
7When Jotham was told about this, he
climbed up on the top of Mount Gerizim
and shouted to them, "Listen to me, citizens
of Shechem, so that God may listen to you.
8One day the trees went out to anoint a king
for themselves. They said to the olive tree, 'Be
our king.'
9"But the olive tree answered, 'Should I
give up my oil, by which both gods and men
are honored, to hold sway over the trees?'
10"Next, the trees said to the fig tree, 'Come
and be our king.'
11"But the fig tree replied, 'Should I give
up my fruit, so good and sweet, to hold sway
over the trees?'
12"Then the trees said to the vine, 'Come
and be our king.'
13"But the vine answered, 'Should I give up
my wine, which cheers both gods and men, to
hold sway over the trees?'
14"Finally all the trees said to the thornbush, 'Come and be our king.'
15"The thornbush said to the trees, 'If you
really want to anoint me king over you, come
and take refuge in my shade; but if not, then
let fire come out of the thornbush and consume the cedars of Lebanon!'
16"Now if you have acted honorably and in
good faith when you made Abimelech king,
and if you have been fair to Jerub-Baal and his
family, and if you have treated him as he deserves— 17and to think that my father fought
for you, risked his life to rescue you from the
hand of Midian 18(but today you have revolted
against my father's family, murdered his seventy sons on a single stone, and made Abimelech, the son of his slave girl, king over the
citizens of Shechem because he is your brother)— 19if then you have acted honorably and
in good faith toward Jerub-Baal and his family
today, may Abimelech be your joy, and may
you be his, too! 20But if you have not, let fire
come out from Abimelech and consume you,
citizens of Shechem and Beth Millo, and let
fire come out from you, citizens of Shechem
and Beth Millo, and consume Abimelech!"
21Then Jotham fled, escaping to Beer, and
he lived there because he was afraid of his
brother Abimelech.
22After Abimelech had governed Israel
three years, 23God sent an evil spirit between
Abimelech and the citizens of Shechem, who
acted treacherously against Abimelech. 24God
did this in order that the crime against Jerub-Baal's seventy sons, the shedding of their
blood, might be avenged on their brother
Abimelech and on the citizens of Shechem,
who had helped him murder his brothers. 25In
opposition to him these citizens of Shechem
set men on the hilltops to ambush and rob everyone who passed by, and this was reported
to Abimelech.
26Now Gaal son of Ebed moved with his
brothers into Shechem, and its citizens put
their confidence in him. 27After they had
gone out into the fields and gathered the
grapes and trodden them, they held a festival
in the temple of their god. While they were

[a] 4 That is, about 1 3/4 pounds (about 0.8 kilogram)

eating and drinking, they cursed Abimelech.
[28]Then Gaal son of Ebed said, "Who is Abimelech, and who is Shechem, that we should be
subject to him? Isn't he Jerub-Baal's son, and
isn't Zebul his deputy? Serve the men of Hamor, Shechem's father! Why should we serve
Abimelech? [29]If only this people were under
my command! Then I would get rid of him. I
would say to Abimelech, 'Call out your whole
army!' "[a]
[30]When Zebul the governor of the city
heard what Gaal son of Ebed said, he was very
angry. [31]Under cover he sent messengers to
Abimelech, saying, "Gaal son of Ebed and his
brothers have come to Shechem and are stirring up the city against you. [32]Now then, during the night you and your men should come
and lie in wait in the fields. [33]In the morning at sunrise, advance against the city. When
Gaal and his men come out against you, do
whatever your hand finds to do."
[34]So Abimelech and all his troops set out
by night and took up concealed positions near
Shechem in four companies. [35]Now Gaal son
of Ebed had gone out and was standing at the
entrance to the city gate just as Abimelech and
his soldiers came out from their hiding place.
[36]When Gaal saw them, he said to Zebul,
"Look, people are coming down from the tops
of the mountains!"

Zebul replied, "You mistake the shadows of
the mountains for men."
[37]But Gaal spoke up again: "Look, people
are coming down from the center of the land,
and a company is coming from the direction
of the soothsayers' tree."
[38]Then Zebul said to him, "Where is your
big talk now, you who said, 'Who is Abimelech that we should be subject to him?' Aren't
these the men you ridiculed? Go out and fight
them!"
[39]So Gaal led out[b] the citizens of Shechem
and fought Abimelech. [40]Abimelech chased
him, and many fell wounded in the flight—all
the way to the entrance to the gate. [41]Abime-
lech stayed in Arumah, and Zebul drove Gaal
and his brothers out of Shechem.
[42]The next day the people of Shechem
went out to the fields, and this was reported
to Abimelech. [43]So he took his men, divided
them into three companies and set an ambush
in the fields. When he saw the people coming
out of the city, he rose to attack them. [44]Abim-
elech and the companies with him rushed forward to a position at the entrance to the city
gate. Then two companies rushed upon those
in the fields and struck them down. [45]All that
day Abimelech pressed his attack against the
city until he had captured it and killed its people. Then he destroyed the city and scattered
salt over it.
[46]On hearing this, the citizens in the tower of Shechem went into the stronghold of
the temple of El-Berith. [47]When Abimelech
heard that they had assembled there, [48]he and
all his men went up Mount Zalmon. He took
an ax and cut off some branches, which he
lifted to his shoulders. He ordered the men
with him, "Quick! Do what you have seen
me do!" [49]So all the men cut branches and
followed Abimelech. They piled them against
the stronghold and set it on fire over the people inside. So all the people in the tower of
Shechem, about a thousand men and wom-
en, also died.
[50]Next Abimelech went to Thebez and besieged it and captured it. [51]Inside the city,
however, was a strong tower, to which all the
men and women—all the people of the city—
fled. They locked themselves in and climbed
up on the tower roof. [52]Abimelech went to the
tower and stormed it. But as he approached
the entrance to the tower to set it on fire, [53]a
woman dropped an upper millstone on his
head and cracked his skull.
[54]Hurriedly he called to his armor-bearer,
"Draw your sword and kill me, so that they
can't say, 'A woman killed him.' " So his servant ran him through, and he died. [55]When
the Israelites saw that Abimelech was dead,
they went home.
[56]Thus God repaid the wickedness that
Abimelech had done to his father by murdering his seventy brothers. [57]God also made the
men of Shechem pay for all their wickedness.
The curse of Jotham son of Jerub-Baal came
on them.

Tola

10 After the time of Abimelech a man of
Issachar, Tola son of Puah, the son of
Dodo, rose to save Israel. He lived in
Shamir, in the hill country of Ephraim. [2]He
led[c] Israel twenty-three years; then he died,
and was buried in Shamir.

Jair

[3]He was followed by Jair of Gilead, who led
Israel twenty-two years. [4]He had thirty sons,
who rode thirty donkeys. They controlled

[a] 29 Septuagint; Hebrew *him." Then he said to Abimelech, "Call out your whole army!"* [b] 39 Or *Gaal went out in the sight of*
[c] 2 Traditionally *judged;* also in verse 3

thirty towns in Gilead, which to this day are
called Havvoth Jair.[a] 5When Jair died, he was
buried in Kamon.

Jephthah

6Again the Israelites did evil in the eyes
of the LORD. They served the Baals and the
Ashtoreths, and the gods of Aram, the gods
of Sidon, the gods of Moab, the gods of the
Ammonites and the gods of the Philistines.
And because the Israelites forsook the LORD
and no longer served him, 7he became angry
with them. He sold them into the hands of
the Philistines and the Ammonites, 8who that
year shattered and crushed them. For eighteen
years they oppressed all the Israelites on the
east side of the Jordan in Gilead, the land of
the Amorites. 9The Ammonites also crossed
the Jordan to fight against Judah, Benjamin
and the house of Ephraim; and Israel was in
great distress. 10Then the Israelites cried out to
the LORD, "We have sinned against you, forsaking our God and serving the Baals."

11The LORD replied, "When the Egyptians,
the Amorites, the Ammonites, the Philistines,
12the Sidonians, the Amalekites and the Ma-
onites[b] oppressed you and you cried to me
for help, did I not save you from their hands?
13But you have forsaken me and served other
gods, so I will no longer save you. 14Go and
cry out to the gods you have chosen. Let them
save you when you are in trouble!"

15But the Israelites said to the LORD, "We
have sinned. Do with us whatever you think
best, but please rescue us now." 16Then they
got rid of the foreign gods among them and
served the LORD. And he could bear Israel's
misery no longer.

17When the Ammonites were called to arms
and camped in Gilead, the Israelites assembled
and camped at Mizpah. 18The leaders of the
people of Gilead said to each other, "Whoever
will launch the attack against the Ammonites
will be the head of all those living in Gilead."

11 Jephthah the Gileadite was a mighty
warrior. His father was Gilead; his
mother was a prostitute. 2Gilead's wife
also bore him sons, and when they were grown
up, they drove Jephthah away. "You are not
going to get any inheritance in our family,"
they said, "because you are the son of another
woman." 3So Jephthah fled from his brothers
and settled in the land of Tob, where a group
of adventurers gathered around him and followed him.

4Some time later, when the Ammonites
made war on Israel, 5the elders of Gilead
went to get Jephthah from the land of Tob.
6"Come," they said, "be our commander, so
we can fight the Ammonites."

7Jephthah said to them, "Didn't you hate
me and drive me from my father's house? Why
do you come to me now, when you're in trouble?"

8The elders of Gilead said to him, "Nevertheless, we are turning to you now; come with
us to fight the Ammonites, and you will be
our head over all who live in Gilead."

9Jephthah answered, "Suppose you take
me back to fight the Ammonites and the
LORD gives them to me—will I really be your
head?"

10The elders of Gilead replied, "The LORD
is our witness; we will certainly do as you say."
11So Jephthah went with the elders of Gilead, and the people made him head and commander over them. And he repeated all his
words before the LORD in Mizpah.

12Then Jephthah sent messengers to the
Ammonite king with the question: "What do
you have against us that you have attacked our
country?"

13The king of the Ammonites answered
Jephthah's messengers, "When Israel came up
out of Egypt, they took away my land from
the Arnon to the Jabbok, all the way to the
Jordan. Now give it back peaceably."

14Jephthah sent back messengers to the
Ammonite king, 15saying:

> "This is what Jephthah says: Israel did
> not take the land of Moab or the land of
> the Ammonites. 16But when they came
> up out of Egypt, Israel went through the
> desert to the Red Sea[c] and on to Kadesh.
> 17Then Israel sent messengers to the king
> of Edom, saying, 'Give us permission to
> go through your country,' but the king
> of Edom would not listen. They sent also
> to the king of Moab, and he refused. So
> Israel stayed at Kadesh.
>
> 18"Next they traveled through the des-
> ert, skirted the lands of Edom and Moab,
> passed along the eastern side of the coun-
> try of Moab, and camped on the other
> side of the Arnon. They did not enter the
> territory of Moab, for the Arnon was its
> border.
>
> 19"Then Israel sent messengers to Si-
> hon king of the Amorites, who ruled in

---

[a] 4 Or *called the settlements of Jair* [b] 12 Hebrew; some Septuagint manuscripts *Midianites* [c] 16 Hebrew *Yam Suph*; that is, Sea of Reeds

Heshbon, and said to him, 'Let us pass
through your country to our own place.'
20Sihon, however, did not trust Israel[a] to
pass through his territory. He mustered
all his men and encamped at Jahaz and
fought with Israel.
21"Then the LORD, the God of Israel,
gave Sihon and all his men into Israel's
hands, and they defeated them. Israel
took over all the land of the Amorites
who lived in that country, 22capturing all
of it from the Arnon to the Jabbok and
from the desert to the Jordan.
23"Now since the LORD, the God of Israel, has driven the Amorites out before
his people Israel, what right have you to
take it over? 24Will you not take what
your god Chemosh gives you? Likewise,
whatever the LORD our God has given
us, we will possess. 25Are you better than
Balak son of Zippor, king of Moab? Did
he ever quarrel with Israel or fight with
them? 26For three hundred years Israel
occupied Heshbon, Aroer, the surrounding settlements and all the towns along
the Arnon. Why didn't you retake them
during that time? 27I have not wronged
you, but you are doing me wrong by waging war against me. Let the LORD, the
Judge,[b] decide the dispute this day between the Israelites and the Ammonites."

28The king of Ammon, however, paid no attention to the message Jephthah sent him.
29Then the Spirit of the LORD came upon
Jephthah. He crossed Gilead and Manasseh,
passed through Mizpah of Gilead, and from
there he advanced against the Ammonites.
30And Jephthah made a vow to the LORD:
"If you give the Ammonites into my hands,
31whatever comes out of the door of my house
to meet me when I return in triumph from
the Ammonites will be the LORD's, and I will
sacrifice it as a burnt offering."
32Then Jephthah went over to fight the
Ammonites, and the LORD gave them into his
hands. 33He devastated twenty towns from
Aroer to the vicinity of Minnith, as far as Abel
Keramim. Thus Israel subdued Ammon.
34When Jephthah returned to his home
in Mizpah, who should come out to meet
him but his daughter, dancing to the sound
of tambourines! She was an only child. Except for her he had neither son nor daughter.
35When he saw her, he tore his clothes and
cried, "Oh! My daughter! You have made me
miserable and wretched, because I have made
a vow to the LORD that I cannot break."
36"My father," she replied, "you have given
your word to the LORD. Do to me just as you
promised, now that the LORD has avenged you
of your enemies, the Ammonites. 37But grant
me this one request," she said. "Give me two
months to roam the hills and weep with my
friends, because I will never marry."
38"You may go," he said. And he let her go
for two months. She and the girls went into
the hills and wept because she would never
marry. 39After the two months, she returned
to her father and he did to her as he had
vowed. And she was a virgin.
From this comes the Israelite custom 40that
each year the young women of Israel go out
for four days to commemorate the daughter
of Jephthah the Gileadite.

Jephthah and Ephraim

12 The men of Ephraim called out their
forces, crossed over to Zaphon and said
to Jephthah, "Why did you go to fight
the Ammonites without calling us to go with
you? We're going to burn down your house
over your head."
2Jephthah answered, "I and my people were
engaged in a great struggle with the Ammonites, and although I called, you didn't save
me out of their hands. 3When I saw that you
wouldn't help, I took my life in my hands and
crossed over to fight the Ammonites, and the
LORD gave me the victory over them. Now
why have you come up today to fight me?"
4Jephthah then called together the men of
Gilead and fought against Ephraim. The Gileadites struck them down because the Ephraimites had said, "You Gileadites are renegades
from Ephraim and Manasseh." 5The Gileadites captured the fords of the Jordan leading to
Ephraim, and whenever a survivor of Ephraim
said, "Let me cross over," the men of Gilead
asked him, "Are you an Ephraimite?" If he replied, "No," 6they said, "All right, say 'Shib-
boleth.' " If he said, "Sibboleth," because he
could not pronounce the word correctly, they
seized him and killed him at the fords of the
Jordan. Forty-two thousand Ephraimites were
killed at that time.
7Jephthah led[c] Israel six years. Then Jephthah the Gileadite died, and was buried in a
town in Gilead.

[a] 20 Or *however, would not make an agreement for Israel* [b] 27 Or *Ruler* [c] 7 Traditionally *judged*; also in verses 8-14

Ibzan, Elon and Abdon

[8]After him, Ibzan of Bethlehem led Israel.
[9]He had thirty sons and thirty daughters. He
gave his daughters away in marriage to those
outside his clan, and for his sons he brought in
thirty young women as wives from outside his
clan. Ibzan led Israel seven years. [10]Then Ibzan
died, and was buried in Bethlehem.
[11]After him, Elon the Zebulunite led Israel
ten years. [12]Then Elon died, and was buried in
Aijalon in the land of Zebulun.
[13]After him, Abdon son of Hillel, from Pirathon, led Israel. [14]He had forty sons and thirty grandsons, who rode on seventy donkeys.
He led Israel eight years. [15]Then Abdon son
of Hillel died, and was buried at Pirathon in
Ephraim, in the hill country of the Amalekites.

The Birth of Samson

13 Again the Israelites did evil in the eyes of
the LORD, so the LORD delivered them
into the hands of the Philistines for forty years.
[2]A certain man of Zorah, named Manoah, from the clan of the Danites, had a wife
who was sterile and remained childless. [3]The
angel of the LORD appeared to her and said,
"You are sterile and childless, but you are going to conceive and have a son. [4]Now see to
it that you drink no wine or other fermented drink and that you do not eat anything
unclean, [5]because you will conceive and give
birth to a son. No razor may be used on his
head, because the boy is to be a Nazirite, set
apart to God from birth, and he will begin
the deliverance of Israel from the hands of the
Philistines."
[6]Then the woman went to her husband and
told him, "A man of God came to me. He
looked like an angel of God, very awesome.
I didn't ask him where he came from, and he
didn't tell me his name. [7]But he said to me,
'You will conceive and give birth to a son.
Now then, drink no wine or other fermented
drink and do not eat anything unclean, because the boy will be a Nazirite of God from
birth until the day of his death.' "
[8]Then Manoah prayed to the LORD:
"O Lord, I beg you, let the man of God you
sent to us come again to teach us how to bring
up the boy who is to be born."
[9]God heard Manoah, and the angel of God
came again to the woman while she was out
in the field; but her husband Manoah was not
with her. [10]The woman hurried to tell her husband, "He's here! The man who appeared to
me the other day!"
[11]Manoah got up and followed his wife.
When he came to the man, he said, "Are you
the one who talked to my wife?"
"I am," he said.
[12]So Manoah asked him, "When your
words are fulfilled, what is to be the rule for
the boy's life and work?"
[13]The angel of the LORD answered, "Your
wife must do all that I have told her. [14]She
must not eat anything that comes from the
grapevine, nor drink any wine or other fermented drink nor eat anything unclean. She
must do everything I have commanded her."
[15]Manoah said to the angel of the LORD,
"We would like you to stay until we prepare a
young goat for you."
[16]The angel of the LORD replied, "Even
though you detain me, I will not eat any of
your food. But if you prepare a burnt offering,
offer it to the LORD." (Manoah did not realize
that it was the angel of the LORD.)
[17]Then Manoah inquired of the angel of the
LORD, "What is your name, so that we may
honor you when your word comes true?"
[18]He replied, "Why do you ask my name?
It is beyond understanding.[a]" [19]Then Manoah took a young goat, together with the grain
offering, and sacrificed it on a rock to the
LORD. And the LORD did an amazing thing
while Manoah and his wife watched: [20]As the
flame blazed up from the altar toward heaven,
the angel of the LORD ascended in the flame.
Seeing this, Manoah and his wife fell with
their faces to the ground. [21]When the angel of
the LORD did not show himself again to Manoah and his wife, Manoah realized that it was
the angel of the LORD.
[22]"We are doomed to die!" he said to his
wife. "We have seen God!"
[23]But his wife answered, "If the LORD had
meant to kill us, he would not have accepted
a burnt offering and grain offering from our
hands, nor shown us all these things or now
told us this."
[24]The woman gave birth to a boy and
named him Samson. He grew and the LORD
blessed him, [25]and the Spirit of the LORD began to stir him while he was in Mahaneh Dan,
between Zorah and Eshtaol.

---

a 18 Or *is wonderful*

Samson's Marriage

14 Samson went down to Timnah and saw
there a young Philistine woman. 2When
he returned, he said to his father and
mother, "I have seen a Philistine woman in
Timnah; now get her for me as my wife."
3His father and mother replied, "Isn't there
an acceptable woman among your relatives or
among all our people? Must you go to the uncircumcised Philistines to get a wife?"
But Samson said to his father, "Get her for
me. She's the right one for me." 4(His parents
did not know that this was from the LORD,
who was seeking an occasion to confront the
Philistines; for at that time they were ruling
over Israel.) 5Samson went down to Timnah
together with his father and mother. As they
approached the vineyards of Timnah, suddenly a young lion came roaring toward him. 6The
Spirit of the LORD came upon him in power so
that he tore the lion apart with his bare hands
as he might have torn a young goat. But he
told neither his father nor his mother what
he had done. 7Then he went down and talked
with the woman, and he liked her.
8Some time later, when he went back to
marry her, he turned aside to look at the lion's
carcass. In it was a swarm of bees and some
honey, 9which he scooped out with his hands
and ate as he went along. When he rejoined
his parents, he gave them some, and they too
ate it. But he did not tell them that he had tak-
en the honey from the lion's carcass.
10Now his father went down to see the
woman. And Samson made a feast there, as
was customary for bridegrooms. 11When he
appeared, he was given thirty companions.
12"Let me tell you a riddle," Samson said to
them. "If you can give me the answer within
the seven days of the feast, I will give you thirty linen garments and thirty sets of clothes.
13If you can't tell me the answer, you must
give me thirty linen garments and thirty sets
of clothes."
"Tell us your riddle," they said. "Let's
hear it."
14He replied,

"Out of the eater, something to eat;
out of the strong, something sweet."

For three days they could not give the answer.
15On the fourth[a] day, they said to Samson's
wife, "Coax your husband into explaining the
riddle for us, or we will burn you and your
father's household to death. Did you invite us
here to rob us?"
16Then Samson's wife threw herself on him,
sobbing, "You hate me! You don't really love
me. You've given my people a riddle, but you
haven't told me the answer."
"I haven't even explained it to my father or
mother," he replied, "so why should I explain
it to you?" 17She cried the whole seven days of
the feast. So on the seventh day he finally told
her, because she continued to press him. She
in turn explained the riddle to her people.
18Before sunset on the seventh day the men
of the town said to him,

"What is sweeter than honey?
What is stronger than a lion?"

Samson said to them,

"If you had not plowed with my heifer,
you would not have solved my riddle."

19Then the Spirit of the LORD came upon
him in power. He went down to Ashkelon,
struck down thirty of their men, stripped them
of their belongings and gave their clothes to
those who had explained the riddle. Burning
with anger, he went up to his father's house.
20And Samson's wife was given to the friend
who had attended him at his wedding.

Samson's Vengeance on the Philistines

15 Later on, at the time of wheat harvest,
Samson took a young goat and went to
visit his wife. He said, "I'm going to my
wife's room." But her father would not let him
go in.
2"I was so sure you thoroughly hated her,"
he said, "that I gave her to your friend. Isn't
her younger sister more attractive? Take her
instead."
3Samson said to them, "This time I have a
right to get even with the Philistines; I will
really harm them." 4So he went out and caught
three hundred foxes and tied them tail to tail
in pairs. He then fastened a torch to every pair
of tails, 5lit the torches and let the foxes loose
in the standing grain of the Philistines. He
burned up the shocks and standing grain, together with the vineyards and olive groves.
6When the Philistines asked, "Who did
this?" they were told, "Samson, the Timnite's
son-in-law, because his wife was given to his
friend."
So the Philistines went up and burned her
and her father to death. 7Samson said to them,

a 15 Some Septuagint manuscripts and Syriac; Hebrew *seventh*

"Since you've acted like this, I won't stop until
I get my revenge on you." [8]He attacked them
viciously and slaughtered many of them. Then
he went down and stayed in a cave in the rock
of Etam.
[9]The Philistines went up and camped in Judah, spreading out near Lehi. [10]The men of Judah asked, "Why have you come to fight us?"
"We have come to take Samson prisoner,"
they answered, "to do to him as he did to us."
[11]Then three thousand men from Judah
went down to the cave in the rock of Etam
and said to Samson, "Don't you realize that
the Philistines are rulers over us? What have
you done to us?"
He answered, "I merely did to them what
they did to me."
[12]They said to him, "We've come to tie you
up and hand you over to the Philistines."
Samson said, "Swear to me that you won't
kill me yourselves."
[13]"Agreed," they answered. "We will only
tie you up and hand you over to them. We
will not kill you." So they bound him with
two new ropes and led him up from the rock.
[14]As he approached Lehi, the Philistines came
toward him shouting. The Spirit of the LORD
came upon him in power. The ropes on his
arms became like charred flax, and the bind-
ings dropped from his hands. [15]Finding a fresh
jawbone of a donkey, he grabbed it and struck
down a thousand men.
[16]Then Samson said,

"With a donkey's jawbone
I have made donkeys of them.[a]
With a donkey's jawbone
I have killed a thousand men."

[17]When he finished speaking, he threw away
the jawbone; and the place was called Ramath
Lehi.[b]
[18]Because he was very thirsty, he cried out
to the LORD, "You have given your servant this
great victory. Must I now die of thirst and fall
into the hands of the uncircumcised?" [19]Then
God opened up the hollow place in Lehi, and
water came out of it. When Samson drank,
his strength returned and he revived. So the
spring was called En Hakkore,[c] and it is still
there in Lehi.
[20]Samson led[d] Israel for twenty years in the
days of the Philistines.

Samson and Delilah

16 One day Samson went to Gaza, where
he saw a prostitute. He went in to spend
the night with her. [2]The people of Gaza
were told, "Samson is here!" So they surrounded the place and lay in wait for him all night at
the city gate. They made no move during the
night, saying, "At dawn we'll kill him."
[3]But Samson lay there only until the middle of the night. Then he got up and took hold
of the doors of the city gate, together with the
two posts, and tore them loose, bar and all. He
lifted them to his shoulders and carried them
to the top of the hill that faces Hebron.
[4]Some time later, he fell in love with a
woman in the Valley of Sorek whose name was
Delilah. [5]The rulers of the Philistines went to
her and said, "See if you can lure him into
showing you the secret of his great strength
and how we can overpower him so we may tie
him up and subdue him. Each one of us will
give you eleven hundred shekels[e] of silver."
[6]So Delilah said to Samson, "Tell me the
secret of your great strength and how you can
be tied up and subdued."
[7]Samson answered her, "If anyone ties me
with seven fresh thongs[f] that have not been
dried, I'll become as weak as any other man."
[8]Then the rulers of the Philistines brought
her seven fresh thongs that had not been dried,
and she tied him with them. [9]With men hidden in the room, she called to him, "Samson,
the Philistines are upon you!" But he snapped
the thongs as easily as a piece of string snaps
when it comes close to a flame. So the secret of
his strength was not discovered.
[10]Then Delilah said to Samson, "You have
made a fool of me; you lied to me. Come now,
tell me how you can be tied."
[11]He said, "If anyone ties me securely with
new ropes that have never been used, I'll become as weak as any other man."
[12]So Delilah took new ropes and tied him
with them. Then, with men hidden in the
room, she called to him, "Samson, the Philistines are upon you!" But he snapped the ropes
off his arms as if they were threads.
[13]Delilah then said to Samson, "Until now,
you have been making a fool of me and lying
to me. Tell me how you can be tied."
He replied, "If you weave the seven braids
of my head into the fabric ⌞on the loom⌟ and
tighten it with the pin, I'll become as weak as
any other man." So while he was sleeping, De-

a 16 Or *made a heap or two*; the Hebrew for *donkey* sounds like the Hebrew for *heap.* *b* 17 *Ramath Lehi* means *jawbone hill.* *c* 19 *En Hakkore* means *caller's spring.* *d* 20 Traditionally *judged* *e* 5 That is, about 28 pounds (about 13 kilograms) *f* 7 Or *bowstrings*; also in verses 8 and 9

F **FRIDAY**
READ JUDGES 16:1–21

THE BIG EFFECT OF LITTLE CHOICES

Samson seemed to have all the right stuff. An angel announced his birth and instructed his parents to raise him to live as a lifelong Nazirite, a person set apart by God. As a result of his standing, he was to abstain from grape products, have no contact with dead bodies and forego haircuts (see Numbers 6:1–8). Samson grew up with godly parents who loved him. He was given a life purpose—to begin to deliver Israel from the Philistines—and an incredible strength to help him achieve the task.

But Samson's privileged beginnings didn't automatically endow him with moral integrity. Over the course of his life, he deliberately participated in the things he and his parents had promised not to do. He ate honey from a lion's carcass, violating his Nazirite vow in order to delight himself with something sweet (see Judges 14:8–9). Instead of being a great warrior against the Philistines, Samson's crusades were often spurred by personal vendettas. And he had an insatiable appetite for Philistine women. Ultimately, one of those women, Delilah, learned the secret of Samson's strength and traded that knowledge for a large sum of money.

Some time later, he fell in love with a woman in the Valley of Sorek whose name was Delilah.

— JUDGES 16:4

let's talk

- ✦ Beginning with Samson's birth in Judges 13, examine the decisions that Samson made in his life. Which ones led him to God? Which ones separated him from God?
- ✦ What were the costs Samson paid for his decisions?
- ✦ As a Nazirite, Samson had specific things that set him apart for God. What things set us apart for God? What sets our marriage apart as a Christian marriage?

Maybe you remember learning in church school that Samson was strong because he had long hair. Actually, Samson's strength wasn't in his hair but in his relationship with God. When his head was shaved, it was merely an outward indication of what he had already lost inside.

Ultimately Samson was unable to fully realize his potential or use the gifts God had given him. This is true of many of us. Though God has uniquely gifted us for his purpose, we are unable to live up to our potential because we continually fall victim to our sinful nature.

Samson didn't turn toward sin in one grand decision. A lifetime of little choices resulted in Samson's demise. Similarly, it isn't the politician's final bribe, but rather his early career decisions to bend the rules, that leads to his downfall. It isn't the public moral failing of the religious leader, but the many unconfessed sins that preceded it, that brings him down. It's not the addiction, but the little indulgences that fed the addiction, that kills a family.

This principle also applies to our marriages. Most Christians don't wake up one day and decide to throw their marriage and family away with one grand affair. The separation begins with participating in a bit of seemingly innocent flirting at work or sending an innocuous email to an old friend or confiding a bit of unhappiness with one's spouse to a sympathetic friend.

Before making what appears to be a harmless decision, stop and evaluate the cost. Success is less about having the right stuff than it is about choosing the right way. A lot of little choices done God's way will add up to a lifetime of purpose.

—JENNIFER SCHUCHMANN

FOR YOUR NEXT DEVOTIONAL READING, TURN TO PAGE 272.

lilah took the seven braids of his head, wove
them into the fabric 14and[a] tightened it with
the pin.

Again she called to him, "Samson, the Philistines are upon you!" He awoke from his
sleep and pulled up the pin and the loom,
with the fabric.

15Then she said to him, "How can you say,
'I love you,' when you won't confide in me?
This is the third time you have made a fool of
me and haven't told me the secret of your great
strength." 16With such nagging she prodded
him day after day until he was tired to death.

17So he told her everything. "No razor has
ever been used on my head," he said, "because
I have been a Nazirite set apart to God since
birth. If my head were shaved, my strength
would leave me, and I would become as weak
as any other man."

18When Delilah saw that he had told her
everything, she sent word to the rulers of the
Philistines, "Come back once more; he has
told me everything." So the rulers of the Philistines returned with the silver in their hands.
19Having put him to sleep on her lap, she
called a man to shave off the seven braids of
his hair, and so began to subdue him.[b] And
his strength left him.

20Then she called, "Samson, the Philistines
are upon you!"

He awoke from his sleep and thought, "I'll
go out as before and shake myself free." But he
did not know that the LORD had left him.

21Then the Philistines seized him, gouged
out his eyes and took him down to Gaza.
Binding him with bronze shackles, they set
him to grinding in the prison. 22But the hair
on his head began to grow again after it had
been shaved.

The Death of Samson

23Now the rulers of the Philistines assembled to offer a great sacrifice to Dagon their
god and to celebrate, saying, "Our god has delivered Samson, our enemy, into our hands."

24When the people saw him, they praised
their god, saying,

"Our god has delivered our enemy
into our hands,
the one who laid waste our land
and multiplied our slain."

25While they were in high spirits, they
shouted, "Bring out Samson to entertain us."
So they called Samson out of the prison, and
he performed for them.

When they stood him among the pillars,
26Samson said to the servant who held his
hand, "Put me where I can feel the pillars
that support the temple, so that I may lean
against them." 27Now the temple was crowded with men and women; all the rulers of the
Philistines were there, and on the roof were
about three thousand men and women watching Samson perform. 28Then Samson prayed
to the LORD, "O Sovereign LORD, remember
me. O God, please strengthen me just once
more, and let me with one blow get revenge
on the Philistines for my two eyes." 29Then
Samson reached toward the two central pillars
on which the temple stood. Bracing himself
against them, his right hand on the one and
his left hand on the other, 30Samson said, "Let
me die with the Philistines!" Then he pushed
with all his might, and down came the temple
on the rulers and all the people in it. Thus he
killed many more when he died than while he
lived.

31Then his brothers and his father's whole
family went down to get him. They brought
him back and buried him between Zorah and
Eshtaol in the tomb of Manoah his father. He
had led[c] Israel twenty years.

Micah's Idols

17 Now a man named Micah from the hill
country of Ephraim 2said to his mother,
"The eleven hundred shekels[d] of silver
that were taken from you and about which
I heard you utter a curse—I have that silver
with me; I took it."

Then his mother said, "The LORD bless you,
my son!"

3When he returned the eleven hundred
shekels of silver to his mother, she said, "I solemnly consecrate my silver to the LORD for
my son to make a carved image and a cast idol.
I will give it back to you."

4So he returned the silver to his mother,
and she took two hundred shekels[e] of silver
and gave them to a silversmith, who made
them into the image and the idol. And they
were put in Micah's house.

5Now this man Micah had a shrine, and
he made an ephod and some idols and installed one of his sons as his priest. 6In those
days Israel had no king; everyone did as he
saw fit.

---

[a] *13,14* Some Septuagint manuscripts; Hebrew "*⌞I can⌟ if you weave the seven braids of my head into the fabric ⌞on the loom⌟.*" *14So she*
[b] *19* Hebrew; some Septuagint manuscripts *and he began to weaken* [c] *31* Traditionally *judged* [d] *2* That is, about 28 pounds (about 13 kilograms) [e] *4* That is, about 5 pounds (about 2.3 kilograms)

7 A young Levite from Bethlehem in Judah,
who had been living within the clan of Judah,
8 left that town in search of some other place
to stay. On his way[a] he came to Micah's house
in the hill country of Ephraim.
9 Micah asked him, "Where are you from?"
"I'm a Levite from Bethlehem in Judah," he
said, "and I'm looking for a place to stay."
10 Then Micah said to him, "Live with me
and be my father and priest, and I'll give you
ten shekels[b] of silver a year, your clothes and
your food." 11 So the Levite agreed to live
with him, and the young man was to him
like one of his sons. 12 Then Micah installed
the Levite, and the young man became his
priest and lived in his house. 13 And Micah
said, "Now I know that the LORD will be
good to me, since this Levite has become my
priest."

Danites Settle in Laish

18 In those days Israel had no king.
And in those days the tribe of the Danites was seeking a place of their own
where they might settle, because they had
not yet come into an inheritance among the
tribes of Israel. 2 So the Danites sent five warriors from Zorah and Eshtaol to spy out the
land and explore it. These men represented all
their clans. They told them, "Go, explore the
land."
The men entered the hill country of Ephraim and came to the house of Micah, where
they spent the night. 3 When they were near
Micah's house, they recognized the voice of
the young Levite; so they turned in there and
asked him, "Who brought you here? What are
you doing in this place? Why are you here?"
4 He told them what Micah had done for
him, and said, "He has hired me and I am his
priest."
5 Then they said to him, "Please inquire of
God to learn whether our journey will be successful."
6 The priest answered them, "Go in peace.
Your journey has the LORD's approval."
7 So the five men left and came to Laish,
where they saw that the people were living in
safety, like the Sidonians, unsuspecting and
secure. And since their land lacked nothing,
they were prosperous.[c] Also, they lived a long
way from the Sidonians and had no relationship with anyone else.[d]
8 When they returned to Zorah and Eshtaol, their brothers asked them, "How did you
find things?"
9 They answered, "Come on, let's attack
them! We have seen that the land is very good.
Aren't you going to do something? Don't hesitate to go there and take it over. 10 When you
get there, you will find an unsuspecting people and a spacious land that God has put into
your hands, a land that lacks nothing whatever."
11 Then six hundred men from the clan of
the Danites, armed for battle, set out from
Zorah and Eshtaol. 12 On their way they set
up camp near Kiriath Jearim in Judah. This is
why the place west of Kiriath Jearim is called
Mahaneh Dan[e] to this day. 13 From there they
went on to the hill country of Ephraim and
came to Micah's house.
14 Then the five men who had spied out the
land of Laish said to their brothers, "Do you
know that one of these houses has an ephod,
other household gods, a carved image and a
cast idol? Now you know what to do." 15 So
they turned in there and went to the house of
the young Levite at Micah's place and greeted him. 16 The six hundred Danites, armed for
battle, stood at the entrance to the gate. 17 The
five men who had spied out the land went inside and took the carved image, the ephod, the
other household gods and the cast idol while
the priest and the six hundred armed men
stood at the entrance to the gate.
18 When these men went into Micah's house
and took the carved image, the ephod, the
other household gods and the cast idol, the
priest said to them, "What are you doing?"
19 They answered him, "Be quiet! Don't say
a word. Come with us, and be our father and
priest. Isn't it better that you serve a tribe and
clan in Israel as priest rather than just one
man's household?" 20 Then the priest was glad.
He took the ephod, the other household gods
and the carved image and went along with the
people. 21 Putting their little children, their
livestock and their possessions in front of
them, they turned away and left.
22 When they had gone some distance from
Micah's house, the men who lived near Micah
were called together and overtook the Danites. 23 As they shouted after them, the Danites
turned and said to Micah, "What's the matter with you that you called out your men to
fight?"
24 He replied, "You took the gods I made,
and my priest, and went away. What else do

[a] 8 Or *To carry on his profession* [b] 10 That is, about 4 ounces (about 110 grams) [c] 7 The meaning of the Hebrew for this clause is uncertain. [d] 7 Hebrew; some Septuagint manuscripts *with the Arameans* [e] 12 *Mahaneh Dan* means *Dan's camp.*

I have? How can you ask, 'What's the matter with you?' "

[25]The Danites answered, "Don't argue with us, or some hot-tempered men will attack you, and you and your family will lose your lives." [26]So the Danites went their way, and Micah, seeing that they were too strong for him, turned around and went back home.

[27]Then they took what Micah had made, and his priest, and went on to Laish, against a peaceful and unsuspecting people. They attacked them with the sword and burned down their city. [28]There was no one to rescue them because they lived a long way from Sidon and had no relationship with anyone else. The city was in a valley near Beth Rehob.

The Danites rebuilt the city and settled there. [29]They named it Dan after their forefather Dan, who was born to Israel—though the city used to be called Laish. [30]There the Danites set up for themselves the idols, and Jonathan son of Gershom, the son of Moses,[a] and his sons were priests for the tribe of Dan until the time of the captivity of the land. [31]They continued to use the idols Micah had made, all the time the house of God was in Shiloh.

A Levite and His Concubine

19 In those days Israel had no king.

Now a Levite who lived in a remote area in the hill country of Ephraim took a concubine from Bethlehem in Judah. [2]But she was unfaithful to him. She left him and went back to her father's house in Bethlehem, Judah. After she had been there four months, [3]her husband went to her to persuade her to return. He had with him his servant and two donkeys. She took him into her father's house, and when her father saw him, he gladly welcomed him. [4]His father-in-law, the girl's father, prevailed upon him to stay; so he remained with him three days, eating and drinking, and sleeping there.

[5]On the fourth day they got up early and he prepared to leave, but the girl's father said to his son-in-law, "Refresh yourself with something to eat; then you can go." [6]So the two of them sat down to eat and drink together. Afterward the girl's father said, "Please stay tonight and enjoy yourself." [7]And when the man got up to go, his father-in-law persuaded him, so he stayed there that night. [8]On the morning of the fifth day, when he rose to go, the girl's father said, "Refresh yourself. Wait till afternoon!" So the two of them ate together.

[9]Then when the man, with his concubine and his servant, got up to leave, his father-in-law, the girl's father, said, "Now look, it's almost evening. Spend the night here; the day is nearly over. Stay and enjoy yourself. Early tomorrow morning you can get up and be on your way home." [10]But, unwilling to stay another night, the man left and went toward Jebus (that is, Jerusalem), with his two saddled donkeys and his concubine.

[11]When they were near Jebus and the day was almost gone, the servant said to his master, "Come, let's stop at this city of the Jebusites and spend the night."

[12]His master replied, "No. We won't go into an alien city, whose people are not Israelites. We will go on to Gibeah." [13]He added, "Come, let's try to reach Gibeah or Ramah and spend the night in one of those places." [14]So they went on, and the sun set as they neared Gibeah in Benjamin. [15]There they stopped to spend the night. They went and sat in the city square, but no one took them into his home for the night.

[16]That evening an old man from the hill country of Ephraim, who was living in Gibeah (the men of the place were Benjamites), came in from his work in the fields. [17]When he looked and saw the traveler in the city square, the old man asked, "Where are you going? Where did you come from?"

[18]He answered, "We are on our way from Bethlehem in Judah to a remote area in the hill country of Ephraim where I live. I have been to Bethlehem in Judah and now I am going to the house of the LORD. No one has taken me into his house. [19]We have both straw and fodder for our donkeys and bread and wine for ourselves your servants—me, your maidservant, and the young man with us. We don't need anything."

[20]"You are welcome at my house," the old man said. "Let me supply whatever you need. Only don't spend the night in the square." [21]So he took him into his house and fed his donkeys. After they had washed their feet, they had something to eat and drink.

[22]While they were enjoying themselves, some of the wicked men of the city surrounded the house. Pounding on the door, they shouted to the old man who owned the house, "Bring out the man who came to your house so we can have sex with him."

---

[a] 30 An ancient Hebrew scribal tradition, some Septuagint manuscripts and Vulgate; Masoretic Text *Manasseh*

23 The owner of the house went outside
and said to them, "No, my friends, don't be
so vile. Since this man is my guest, don't do
this disgraceful thing. 24 Look, here is my virgin daughter, and his concubine. I will bring
them out to you now, and you can use them
and do to them whatever you wish. But to this
man, don't do such a disgraceful thing."
25 But the men would not listen to him. So
the man took his concubine and sent her outside to them, and they raped her and abused
her throughout the night, and at dawn they
let her go. 26 At daybreak the woman went
back to the house where her master was staying, fell down at the door and lay there until
daylight.
27 When her master got up in the morning
and opened the door of the house and stepped
out to continue on his way, there lay his concubine, fallen in the doorway of the house,
with her hands on the threshold. 28 He said to
her, "Get up; let's go." But there was no answer. Then the man put her on his donkey and
set out for home.
29 When he reached home, he took a knife
and cut up his concubine, limb by limb, into
twelve parts and sent them into all the areas
of Israel. 30 Everyone who saw it said, "Such a
thing has never been seen or done, not since
the day the Israelites came up out of Egypt.
Think about it! Consider it! Tell us what
to do!"

Israelites Fight the Benjamites

20 Then all the Israelites from Dan to Beersheba and from the land of Gilead
came out as one man and assembled
before the LORD in Mizpah. 2 The leaders of
all the people of the tribes of Israel took their
places in the assembly of the people of God,
four hundred thousand soldiers armed with
swords. 3 (The Benjamites heard that the Israelites had gone up to Mizpah.) Then the
Israelites said, "Tell us how this awful thing
happened."
4 So the Levite, the husband of the murdered woman, said, "I and my concubine
came to Gibeah in Benjamin to spend the
night. 5 During the night the men of Gibeah
came after me and surrounded the house, intending to kill me. They raped my concubine,
and she died. 6 I took my concubine, cut her
into pieces and sent one piece to each region
of Israel's inheritance, because they committed this lewd and disgraceful act in Israel.
7 Now, all you Israelites, speak up and give
your verdict."
8 All the people rose as one man, saying,
"None of us will go home. No, not one of us
will return to his house. 9 But now this is what
we'll do to Gibeah: We'll go up against it as
the lot directs. 10 We'll take ten men out of every hundred from all the tribes of Israel, and
a hundred from a thousand, and a thousand
from ten thousand, to get provisions for the
army. Then, when the army arrives at Gibeah[a]
in Benjamin, it can give them what they deserve for all this vileness done in Israel." 11 So
all the men of Israel got together and united as
one man against the city.
12 The tribes of Israel sent men throughout
the tribe of Benjamin, saying, "What about
this awful crime that was committed among
you? 13 Now surrender those wicked men of
Gibeah so that we may put them to death and
purge the evil from Israel."
But the Benjamites would not listen to
their fellow Israelites. 14 From their towns they
came together at Gibeah to fight against the
Israelites. 15 At once the Benjamites mobilized
twenty-six thousand swordsmen from their
towns, in addition to seven hundred chosen
men from those living in Gibeah. 16 Among
all these soldiers there were seven hundred
chosen men who were left-handed, each of
whom could sling a stone at a hair and not
miss.
17 Israel, apart from Benjamin, mustered
four hundred thousand swordsmen, all of
them fighting men.
18 The Israelites went up to Bethel[b] and inquired of God. They said, "Who of us shall go
first to fight against the Benjamites?"
The LORD replied, "Judah shall go first."
19 The next morning the Israelites got up
and pitched camp near Gibeah. 20 The men
of Israel went out to fight the Benjamites and
took up battle positions against them at Gibeah. 21 The Benjamites came out of Gibeah and
cut down twenty-two thousand Israelites on
the battlefield that day. 22 But the men of Israel encouraged one another and again took
up their positions where they had stationed
themselves the first day. 23 The Israelites went
up and wept before the LORD until evening,
and they inquired of the LORD. They said,
"Shall we go up again to battle against the
Benjamites, our brothers?"
The LORD answered, "Go up against
them."

---

[a] *10* One Hebrew manuscript; most Hebrew manuscripts *Geba*, a variant of *Gibeah* [b] *18* Or *to the house of God*; also in verse 26

WEEKEND

marriage skills

We never had premarital counseling, but we spent the first year of our married life in therapy. Once a week, we met with a counselor who helped us iron out the wrinkles we never even saw before getting married. Not that we were in serious trouble. But we had this naïve idea that after our wedding our life would fall naturally into place, and a marriage preparation course or counseling never entered our minds. We had dated for six years before our nine-month engagement, and we had a lot in common (even our first names). We simply thought we would tie the proverbial knot, set up house and, as the fairy tales say, "live happily ever after."

But we didn't. The first years of marriage were difficult right from the start . . . What was it all about, this marriage? Why didn't I feel any different? Who was this person I married, really?

Most engaged couples prepare more for their wedding than they do for their marriage. The $20-billion-a-year wedding industry testifies to that. According to experts, the average two-hundred-guest wedding today costs $15,000 to $30,000. More than one million copies of bridal magazines are sold each month, focusing mainly on wedding ceremonies, honeymoons and home furnishings—but not on marriage itself.

We have learned that living happily ever after is less a mystery than a mastery of certain skills. Although married life will always have its difficulties, you will steadily and dramatically improve your relationship by mastering certain life skills.

Good Skills for Marriage

- Healthy expectations
- Realistic views of love
- Positive attitude
- Communication
- Empathy
- Listening
- Acceptance of gender differences
- Decision-making
- Settling arguments
- Spiritual grounding and goals
- Sense of humor
- Patience

—DR. LES PARROTT III AND DR. LESLIE PARROTT

using your skills

What skills will help you most in the following situations?

1. It's a Saturday morning and the dog needs to be let out. You're both whipped after a busy workweek and just want to sleep.
2. Your spouse has served macaroni and cheese for dinner for the third time this week.
3. Your in-laws are coming to visit this weekend, and you have a one-bedroom apartment.
4. A new church opened in your neighborhood, and your spouse wants to try it.
5. You are so busy at work that you have to work weekends.
6. You've just had a huge argument. You want to go to bed. Your spouse wants to talk about it.
7. On your birthday you open an expensive gift that your spouse has saved for months to buy. You hate it.
8. You try to charge something on your credit card and discover it has been maxed out. You didn't do it.
9. Your spouse has invited a couple that you don't like over for dinner.
10. You want to move to a bigger house. Your spouse doesn't think you can afford it.

HOW ARE WE DOING?

let's make a DATE

LEARN A NEW SKILL

What's a skill you'd like to have? Auto repair? Knitting? CPR? Discuss your interests together and then set aside some time to take a class together. Maybe you both would love to learn woodworking, how to golf or to speak Spanish. Decide the time commitment and price you are comfortable with, and then check out your local community college, parks and rec department, local art studio, etc. See how fun it is to learn something new together.

FOR YOUR NEXT DEVOTIONAL READING, TURN TO PAGE 278.

LESSONS FROM THE *Bible*

Read about Joseph and Asenath in Genesis 41:41–52. Discuss what life skills they might have needed to adapt to marriage in their unique situation.

24Then the Israelites drew near to Benjamin the second day. 25This time, when the Benjamites came out from Gibeah to oppose them, they cut down another eighteen thousand Israelites, all of them armed with swords.

26Then the Israelites, all the people, went up to Bethel, and there they sat weeping before the LORD. They fasted that day until evening and presented burnt offerings and fellowship offerings[a] to the LORD. 27And the Israelites inquired of the LORD. (In those days the ark of the covenant of God was there, 28with Phinehas son of Eleazar, the son of Aaron, ministering before it.) They asked, "Shall we go up again to battle with Benjamin our brother, or not?"

The LORD responded, "Go, for tomorrow I will give them into your hands."

29Then Israel set an ambush around Gibeah. 30They went up against the Benjamites on the third day and took up positions against Gibeah as they had done before. 31The Benjamites came out to meet them and were drawn away from the city. They began to inflict casualties on the Israelites as before, so that about thirty men fell in the open field and on the roads—the one leading to Bethel and the other to Gibeah.

32While the Benjamites were saying, "We are defeating them as before," the Israelites were saying, "Let's retreat and draw them away from the city to the roads."

33All the men of Israel moved from their places and took up positions at Baal Tamar, and the Israelite ambush charged out of its place on the west[b] of Gibeah.[c] 34Then ten thousand of Israel's finest men made a frontal attack on Gibeah. The fighting was so heavy that the Benjamites did not realize how near disaster was. 35The LORD defeated Benjamin before Israel, and on that day the Israelites struck down 25,100 Benjamites, all armed with swords. 36Then the Benjamites saw that they were beaten.

Now the men of Israel had given way before Benjamin, because they relied on the ambush they had set near Gibeah. 37The men who had been in ambush made a sudden dash into Gibeah, spread out and put the whole city to the sword. 38The men of Israel had arranged with the ambush that they should send up a great cloud of smoke from the city, 39and then the men of Israel would turn in the battle.

The Benjamites had begun to inflict casualties on the men of Israel (about thirty), and they said, "We are defeating them as in the first battle." 40But when the column of smoke began to rise from the city, the Benjamites turned and saw the smoke of the whole city going up into the sky. 41Then the men of Israel turned on them, and the men of Benjamin were terrified, because they realized that disaster had come upon them. 42So they fled before the Israelites in the direction of the desert, but they could not escape the battle. And the men of Israel who came out of the towns cut them down there. 43They surrounded the Benjamites, chased them and easily[d] overran them in the vicinity of Gibeah on the east. 44Eighteen thousand Benjamites fell, all of them valiant fighters. 45As they turned and fled toward the desert to the rock of Rimmon, the Israelites cut down five thousand men along the roads. They kept pressing after the Benjamites as far as Gidom and struck down two thousand more.

46On that day twenty-five thousand Benjamite swordsmen fell, all of them valiant fighters. 47But six hundred men turned and fled into the desert to the rock of Rimmon, where they stayed four months. 48The men of Israel went back to Benjamin and put all the towns to the sword, including the animals and everything else they found. All the towns they came across they set on fire.

Wives for the Benjamites

21 The men of Israel had taken an oath at Mizpah: "Not one of us will give his daughter in marriage to a Benjamite."

2The people went to Bethel,[e] where they sat before God until evening, raising their voices and weeping bitterly. 3"O LORD, the God of Israel," they cried, "why has this happened to Israel? Why should one tribe be missing from Israel today?"

4Early the next day the people built an altar and presented burnt offerings and fellowship offerings.[a]

5Then the Israelites asked, "Who from all the tribes of Israel has failed to assemble before the LORD?" For they had taken a solemn oath that anyone who failed to assemble before the LORD at Mizpah should certainly be put to death.

6Now the Israelites grieved for their brothers, the Benjamites. "Today one tribe is cut off from Israel," they said. 7"How can we

---

[a] 26,4 Traditionally *peace offerings* [b] 33 Some Septuagint manuscripts and Vulgate; the meaning of the Hebrew for this word is uncertain. [c] 33 Hebrew *Geba,* a variant of *Gibeah* [d] 43 The meaning of the Hebrew for this word is uncertain. [e] 2 Or *to the house of God*

provide wives for those who are left, since
we have taken an oath by the LORD not to
give them any of our daughters in marriage?”
[8]Then they asked, “Which one of the tribes
of Israel failed to assemble before the LORD at
Mizpah?” They discovered that no one from
Jabesh Gilead had come to the camp for the
assembly. [9]For when they counted the people,
they found that none of the people of Jabesh
Gilead were there.

[10]So the assembly sent twelve thousand
fighting men with instructions to go to Jabesh
Gilead and put to the sword those living there,
including the women and children. [11]“This is
what you are to do,” they said. “Kill every male
and every woman who is not a virgin.” [12]They
found among the people living in Jabesh Gilead four hundred young women who had never
slept with a man, and they took them to the
camp at Shiloh in Canaan.

[13]Then the whole assembly sent an offer of
peace to the Benjamites at the rock of Rimmon. [14]So the Benjamites returned at that
time and were given the women of Jabesh Gilead who had been spared. But there were not
enough for all of them.

[15]The people grieved for Benjamin, because the LORD had made a gap in the tribes
of Israel. [16]And the elders of the assembly said,
“With the women of Benjamin destroyed,
how shall we provide wives for the men who
are left? [17]The Benjamite survivors must have
heirs,” they said, “so that a tribe of Israel will
not be wiped out. [18]We can’t give them our
daughters as wives, since we Israelites have
taken this oath: ‘Cursed be anyone who gives
a wife to a Benjamite.’ [19]But look, there is the
annual festival of the LORD in Shiloh, to the
north of Bethel, and east of the road that goes
from Bethel to Shechem, and to the south of
Lebonah.”

[20]So they instructed the Benjamites, saying,
“Go and hide in the vineyards [21]and watch.
When the girls of Shiloh come out to join in
the dancing, then rush from the vineyards and
each of you seize a wife from the girls of Shiloh and go to the land of Benjamin. [22]When
their fathers or brothers complain to us, we
will say to them, ‘Do us a kindness by helping
them, because we did not get wives for them
during the war, and you are innocent, since
you did not give your daughters to them.’ ”

[23]So that is what the Benjamites did. While
the girls were dancing, each man caught one
and carried her off to be his wife. Then they
returned to their inheritance and rebuilt the
towns and settled in them.

[24]At that time the Israelites left that place
and went home to their tribes and clans, each
to his own inheritance.

[25]In those days Israel had no king; everyone
did as he saw fit.

RUTH

Ruth

QUICK FACTS

AUTHOR Unknown

AUDIENCE The people of Israel

DATE Sometime after David became king in 1010 B.C.

SETTING The period of the judges, at a time when Israel and Moab were at peace

The book of Ruth is a story of faithfulness in everyday life. The story begins at a low point: three women had been left widowed, childless and landless in a society structured around family, heirs and property. The story then follows two of them, Ruth and Naomi, as they struggled to rebuild their lives.

Despite their circumstances, the main characters in this book demonstrated incredible faithfulness: Ruth to her new family, Naomi to her daughters-in-law, Boaz to his extended family, and all of them to God's commands. Much of Scripture records the faith of national leaders; the book of Ruth records the faith of an ordinary family.

At the center of this family was a couple who pursued marriage with faithfulness, selflessness and great respect for their relatives. Ruth and Boaz were remarkable for their commitment to honor God and each other despite life's myriad obligations.

Today, as it was for Ruth and Boaz, many aspects of marriage are unglamorous—navigating family dynamics and social pressures, waking up early and working all day, running errands and caring for others. But we don't need spectacular circumstances to live out our faith. This story teaches us that real faith is everyday faith.

Naomi and Ruth

1 In the days when the judges ruled,[a] there
was a famine in the land, and a man from
Bethlehem in Judah, together with his
wife and two sons, went to live for a while
in the country of Moab. 2The man's name
was Elimelech, his wife's name Naomi, and
the names of his two sons were Mahlon and
Kilion. They were Ephrathites from Bethlehem, Judah. And they went to Moab and
lived there.
3Now Elimelech, Naomi's husband, died,
and she was left with her two sons. 4They
married Moabite women, one named Orpah
and the other Ruth. After they had lived there
about ten years, 5both Mahlon and Kilion
also died, and Naomi was left without her two
sons and her husband.
6When she heard in Moab that the LORD
had come to the aid of his people by providing food for them, Naomi and her daughters-
in-law prepared to return home from there.
7With her two daughters-in-law she left the
place where she had been living and set out
on the road that would take them back to the
land of Judah.
8Then Naomi said to her two daughters-in-
law, "Go back, each of you, to your mother's
home. May the LORD show kindness to you,
as you have shown to your dead and to me.
9May the LORD grant that each of you will
find rest in the home of another husband."
Then she kissed them and they wept aloud
10and said to her, "We will go back with you
to your people."
11But Naomi said, "Return home, my
daughters. Why would you come with me?
Am I going to have any more sons, who could
become your husbands? 12Return home, my
daughters; I am too old to have another husband. Even if I thought there was still hope for
me—even if I had a husband tonight and then
gave birth to sons— 13would you wait until
they grew up? Would you remain unmarried
for them? No, my daughters. It is more bitter
for me than for you, because the LORD's hand
has gone out against me!"
14At this they wept again. Then Orpah
kissed her mother-in-law good-by, but Ruth
clung to her.
15"Look," said Naomi, "your sister-in-law
is going back to her people and her gods. Go
back with her."
16But Ruth replied, "Don't urge me to leave
you or to turn back from you. Where you go
I will go, and where you stay I will stay. Your
people will be my people and your God my
God. 17Where you die I will die, and there I
will be buried. May the LORD deal with me, be
it ever so severely, if anything but death separates you and me." 18When Naomi realized
that Ruth was determined to go with her, she
stopped urging her.
19So the two women went on until they
came to Bethlehem. When they arrived in
Bethlehem, the whole town was stirred because of them, and the women exclaimed,
"Can this be Naomi?"
20"Don't call me Naomi,[b]" she told them.
"Call me Mara,[c] because the Almighty[d] has
made my life very bitter. 21I went away full,
but the LORD has brought me back empty.
Why call me Naomi? The LORD has afflicted[e] me; the Almighty has brought misfortune
upon me."
22So Naomi returned from Moab accompanied by Ruth the Moabitess, her daughter-in-
law, arriving in Bethlehem as the barley harvest was beginning.

Ruth Meets Boaz

2 Now Naomi had a relative on her husband's
side, from the clan of Elimelech, a man of
standing, whose name was Boaz.
2And Ruth the Moabitess said to Naomi,
"Let me go to the fields and pick up the leftover grain behind anyone in whose eyes I find
favor."
Naomi said to her, "Go ahead, my daughter." 3So she went out and began to glean in
the fields behind the harvesters. As it turned
out, she found herself working in a field belonging to Boaz, who was from the clan of
Elimelech.
4Just then Boaz arrived from Bethlehem
and greeted the harvesters, "The LORD be with
you!"
"The LORD bless you!" they called back.
5Boaz asked the foreman of his harvesters,
"Whose young woman is that?"
6The foreman replied, "She is the Moabitess
who came back from Moab with Naomi. 7She
said, 'Please let me glean and gather among
the sheaves behind the harvesters.' She went
into the field and has worked steadily from
morning till now, except for a short rest in the
shelter."
8So Boaz said to Ruth, "My daughter, listen to me. Don't go and glean in another field
and don't go away from here. Stay here with

---

[a] *1* Traditionally *judged* [b] *20* *Naomi* means *pleasant*; also in verse 21. [c] *20* *Mara* means *bitter.* [d] *20* Hebrew *Shaddai*; also in verse 21 [e] *21* Or *has testified against*

MONDAY
READ RUTH 1:1–22

THE BEST WEDDING TEXT

For the first decade of my pastoral ministry, 1 Corinthians 13 and Ruth 1:16 ran a close race as the "sermon" text most often chosen by engaged couples for their weddings. Both passages, of course, are totally inappropriate for that context. When Paul wrote to the Corinthian congregation, he was answering a list of questions the church had sent him. Three chapters (1 Corinthians 12–14) are the apostle's response to people's concerns about how to identify and express spiritual gifts, especially during worship services. Paul hardly had weddings in mind when he wrote that discourse.

Similarly the words of Ruth 1:16 are hardly those of a bride gazing with deep admiration into the loving eyes of her new husband. They are, instead, the almost helpless response of a young widow, Ruth, who needed to make tough choices about how she would spend the rest of her life. The wisest path seemed to be the one suggested by Naomi to both of her widowed daughters-in-law: Go back to your families, grieve for a while, then find new husbands with whom to live out the rest of your days.

Orpah, Ruth's sister-in-law, took Naomi's advice and probably had a rewarding life in her home country of Moab. Ruth chose the path with no guarantees, the journey into uncertainty without an insurance policy. She chose to go with Naomi, a widow who had fewer hopes for a future back in Israel than her daughter-in-law did.

But Ruth replied, "Don't urge me to leave you or to turn back from you. Where you go I will go, and where you stay I will stay. Your people will be my people and your God my God."

— Ruth 1:16

let's talk

- What text did we choose for our marriage vows? What does that mean to us now?
- How do we know that we won't fall out of love? What commitments can we count on from each other? How do we know that?
- If we were to help another couple plan for marriage, what would we tell them about the vows we made to each other and how we've kept them? If they wanted to write their own vows, what guidance would we offer?

Naomi was truly destitute. She had no husband in an age when women had no identity apart from them, and she had no children to function as her old-age welfare and pension system. Naomi was alone in a collapsing universe.

But Naomi couldn't shake Ruth. Ruth promised Naomi that she would remain with her for better, for worse; for richer, for poorer; in sickness and in health; till death parted them. Hmmm . . . That's beginning to sound a lot like marriage vows. Maybe this isn't such a bad wedding text after all!

Ruth 1:16 isn't about courtship but about commitment. Those who make choices in their relationships with others begin to act with divine purpose. They say, "My schedule is unfinished, but I am willing to put your name on every page of my DayPlanner before anything else." They say, "No matter what happens, you can count on me being there with you." They promise, "I cannot be all things to all people, but I will commit to caring about you, no matter what happens."

There is nothing more profound in this uncertain world than to know, first, that your Savior walks with you, and, next, that your spouse is there too. Nothing.

—WAYNE BROUWER

FOR YOUR NEXT DEVOTIONAL READING, TURN TO PAGE 280.

my servant girls. [9]Watch the field where the
men are harvesting, and follow along after
the girls. I have told the men not to touch
you. And whenever you are thirsty, go and
get a drink from the water jars the men have
filled."
[10]At this, she bowed down with her face
to the ground. She exclaimed, "Why have I
found such favor in your eyes that you notice
me—a foreigner?"
[11]Boaz replied, "I've been told all about
what you have done for your mother-in-law
since the death of your husband—how you
left your father and mother and your homeland and came to live with a people you did
not know before. [12]May the LORD repay you
for what you have done. May you be richly rewarded by the LORD, the God of Israel,
under whose wings you have come to take
refuge."
[13]"May I continue to find favor in your
eyes, my lord," she said. "You have given me
comfort and have spoken kindly to your servant—though I do not have the standing of
one of your servant girls."
[14]At mealtime Boaz said to her, "Come over
here. Have some bread and dip it in the wine
vinegar."
When she sat down with the harvesters,
he offered her some roasted grain. She ate all
she wanted and had some left over. [15]As she
got up to glean, Boaz gave orders to his men,
"Even if she gathers among the sheaves, don't
embarrass her. [16]Rather, pull out some stalks
for her from the bundles and leave them for
her to pick up, and don't rebuke her."
[17]So Ruth gleaned in the field until evening.
Then she threshed the barley she had gathered,
and it amounted to about an ephah.[a] [18]She
carried it back to town, and her mother-in-law
saw how much she had gathered. Ruth also
brought out and gave her what she had left
over after she had eaten enough.
[19]Her mother-in-law asked her, "Where did
you glean today? Where did you work? Blessed
be the man who took notice of you!"
Then Ruth told her mother-in-law about
the one at whose place she had been working.
"The name of the man I worked with today is
Boaz," she said.
[20]"The LORD bless him!" Naomi said to her
daughter-in-law. "He has not stopped showing his kindness to the living and the dead."
She added, "That man is our close relative; he
is one of our kinsman-redeemers."
[21]Then Ruth the Moabitess said, "He even
said to me, 'Stay with my workers until they
finish harvesting all my grain.' "
[22]Naomi said to Ruth her daughter-in-law,
"It will be good for you, my daughter, to go
with his girls, because in someone else's field
you might be harmed."
[23]So Ruth stayed close to the servant girls
of Boaz to glean until the barley and wheat
harvests were finished. And she lived with her
mother-in-law.

Ruth and Boaz at the Threshing Floor

3 One day Naomi her mother-in-law said to
her, "My daughter, should I not try to find
a home[b] for you, where you will be well
provided for? [2]Is not Boaz, with whose servant girls you have been, a kinsman of ours?
Tonight he will be winnowing barley on the
threshing floor. [3]Wash and perfume yourself, and put on your best clothes. Then go
down to the threshing floor, but don't let him
know you are there until he has finished eating and drinking. [4]When he lies down, note
the place where he is lying. Then go and uncover his feet and lie down. He will tell you
what to do."
[5]"I will do whatever you say," Ruth answered. [6]So she went down to the threshing
floor and did everything her mother-in-law
told her to do.
[7]When Boaz had finished eating and drinking and was in good spirits, he went over to
lie down at the far end of the grain pile. Ruth
approached quietly, uncovered his feet and lay
down. [8]In the middle of the night something
startled the man, and he turned and discovered a woman lying at his feet.
[9]"Who are you?" he asked.
"I am your servant Ruth," she said. "Spread
the corner of your garment over me, since you
are a kinsman-redeemer."
[10]"The LORD bless you, my daughter," he
replied. "This kindness is greater than that
which you showed earlier: You have not run
after the younger men, whether rich or poor.
[11]And now, my daughter, don't be afraid.
I will do for you all you ask. All my fellow
townsmen know that you are a woman of
noble character. [12]Although it is true that I
am near of kin, there is a kinsman-redeemer
nearer than I. [13]Stay here for the night, and in
the morning if he wants to redeem, good; let
him redeem. But if he is not willing, as surely

---

[a] *17* That is, probably about 3/5 bushel (about 22 liters) [b] *1* Hebrew *find rest* (see Ruth 1:9)

TUESDAY
READ RUTH 2:1—4:22

MARRYING THE MAN OF YOUR CHOICE

While prepping for an interview with the woman who wrote *How to Marry the Man of Your Choice*, I formed a mental impression of this woman who was so confident of wooing a man to the altar that she'd write a book about it. She was probably drop-dead gorgeous, an outrageous flirt and wore a size 2.

I couldn't have been more wrong. Margaret Kent, accompanied by her husband, was warm, witty and outgoing. But she was plainly dressed and definitely not Hollywood's definition of "beautiful." What was evident was that she and her husband were very happy with each other. And Margaret's advice to women seemed to make sense: Don't waste time on men you don't want. Stop trying to change a guy. Know what you want and go after it. Dress to attract a man, not to impress women. Stop chattering and listen—really listen—to him.

Margaret Kent was like Naomi, who advised her daughter-in-law Ruth how to catch the eye of the rich bachelor-farmer Boaz. Granted, Ruth, a poor widow whom Naomi sent out to pick up leftover grain in the fields of nearby farmers, *just happened* to end up in a field owned by Boaz, a close relative of Naomi. And Boaz *just happened* to notice the young woman and kindly offer her his hospitality and protection. And Boaz *just happened* to know about Ruth's great kindness to her mother-in-law, Naomi, in accompanying her to Israel. And Boaz *just happened* to invite Ruth to come back to his fields to glean.

"Go down to the threshing floor, but don't let him know you are there until he has finished eating and drinking. When he lies down, note the place where he is lying. Then go and uncover his feet and lie down. He will tell you what to do."

— Ruth 3:3–4

let's talk

- What did each of us consider important when we were looking for the person we wanted to marry? Did we first decide the attributes and qualities we wanted in a mate, and then go out looking for a person to fit those characteristics? Or was it the other way around?
- If a friend asked our advice on how to find a spouse, what would we say?
- What first attracted us to each other? Are those qualities still drawing us to each other?

The Bible says, "*As it turned out*, [Ruth] found herself working in a field belonging to Boaz" (Ruth 2:3, emphasis added). The truth is that Naomi knew what was really going on. It wasn't a coincidence; Naomi indicated it was the Lord who was orchestrating and working behind the scenes (see Ruth 2:20). So Naomi advised Ruth to bathe and perfume herself and put on her best outfit, and then go after dark to the threshing floor.

"I will do whatever you say," Ruth responded. The outcome was all that Ruth and Naomi had hoped it would be: Boaz recognized Ruth's act as a request for him, as her "family guardian," to marry her and raise up a family to continue the name of her first husband, Mahlon. This was a rightful claim. And Boaz responded as a man of piety, prudence and honor by spreading his garment over the young widow to symbolize his agreement to marry her. Then he made it happen.

Ruth chose to marry Boaz, who also happened to be her mother-in-law's choice for her, and, most important, God's choice for her. And that happy union resulted in incredible blessing, for the son they bore became the grandfather of King David, who was an ancestor of Jesus Christ.

—PHYLLIS TEN ELSHOF

FOR YOUR NEXT DEVOTIONAL READING, TURN TO PAGE 284.

as the LORD lives I will do it. Lie here until
morning."
14So she lay at his feet until morning, but
got up before anyone could be recognized; and
he said, "Don't let it be known that a woman
came to the threshing floor."
15He also said, "Bring me the shawl you are
wearing and hold it out." When she did so, he
poured into it six measures of barley and put it
on her. Then he[a] went back to town.
16When Ruth came to her mother-in-law,
Naomi asked, "How did it go, my daughter?"
Then she told her everything Boaz had
done for her 17and added, "He gave me these
six measures of barley, saying, 'Don't go back
to your mother-in-law empty-handed.' "
18Then Naomi said, "Wait, my daughter,
until you find out what happens. For the man
will not rest until the matter is settled today."

Boaz Marries Ruth

4 Meanwhile Boaz went up to the town gate
and sat there. When the kinsman-redeemer
he had mentioned came along, Boaz said,
"Come over here, my friend, and sit down."
So he went over and sat down.
2Boaz took ten of the elders of the town
and said, "Sit here," and they did so. 3Then
he said to the kinsman-redeemer, "Naomi,
who has come back from Moab, is selling
the piece of land that belonged to our brother Elimelech. 4I thought I should bring the
matter to your attention and suggest that you
buy it in the presence of these seated here and
in the presence of the elders of my people. If
you will redeem it, do so. But if you[b] will
not, tell me, so I will know. For no one has
the right to do it except you, and I am next
in line."
"I will redeem it," he said.
5Then Boaz said, "On the day you buy the
land from Naomi and from Ruth the Moabitess, you acquire[c] the dead man's widow, in
order to maintain the name of the dead with
his property."
6At this, the kinsman-redeemer said, "Then
I cannot redeem it because I might endanger
my own estate. You redeem it yourself. I cannot do it."
7(Now in earlier times in Israel, for the redemption and transfer of property to become
final, one party took off his sandal and gave it
to the other. This was the method of legalizing
transactions in Israel.)
8So the kinsman-redeemer said to Boaz,
"Buy it yourself." And he removed his sandal.
9Then Boaz announced to the elders and
all the people, "Today you are witnesses that
I have bought from Naomi all the property
of Elimelech, Kilion and Mahlon. 10I have
also acquired Ruth the Moabitess, Mahlon's
widow, as my wife, in order to maintain the
name of the dead with his property, so that
his name will not disappear from among his
family or from the town records. Today you
are witnesses!"
11Then the elders and all those at the gate
said, "We are witnesses. May the LORD make
the woman who is coming into your home
like Rachel and Leah, who together built up
the house of Israel. May you have standing
in Ephrathah and be famous in Bethlehem.
12Through the offspring the LORD gives you
by this young woman, may your family be like
that of Perez, whom Tamar bore to Judah."

The Genealogy of David

13So Boaz took Ruth and she became his
wife. Then he went to her, and the LORD enabled her to conceive, and she gave birth to a
son. 14The women said to Naomi: "Praise be
to the LORD, who this day has not left you
without a kinsman-redeemer. May he become
famous throughout Israel! 15He will renew
your life and sustain you in your old age. For
your daughter-in-law, who loves you and who
is better to you than seven sons, has given him
birth."
16Then Naomi took the child, laid him in
her lap and cared for him. 17The women living there said, "Naomi has a son." And they
named him Obed. He was the father of Jesse,
the father of David.
18This, then, is the family line of Perez:

Perez was the father of Hezron,
19 Hezron the father of Ram,
Ram the father of Amminadab,
20 Amminadab the father of Nahshon,
Nahshon the father of Salmon,[d]
21 Salmon the father of Boaz,
Boaz the father of Obed,
22 Obed the father of Jesse,
and Jesse the father of David.

---

a 15 Most Hebrew manuscripts; many Hebrew manuscripts, Vulgate and Syriac *she* *b 4* Many Hebrew manuscripts, Septuagint, Vulgate and Syriac; most Hebrew manuscripts *he* *c 5* Hebrew; Vulgate and Syriac *Naomi, you acquire Ruth the Moabitess,*
d 20 A few Hebrew manuscripts, some Septuagint manuscripts and Vulgate (see also verse 21 and Septuagint of 1 Chron. 2:11); most Hebrew manuscripts *Salma*

1 SAMUEL

1 Samuel

QUICK FACTS

AUTHOR Unknown

AUDIENCE All Israel

DATE Sometime after the division of Israel into the northern and southern kingdoms in 930 B.C.

SETTING The book begins with the birth of Samuel and ends with the death of King Saul, recording Israel's shift from a theocracy to a monarchy.

The three central characters of 1 Samuel are Samuel the prophet, Saul the king and David the warrior. Samuel was the last judge of Israel. He was a very godly judge, but his sons were corrupt. So, under that guise, the people begged Samuel for a king. God gave them Saul, who started out with a promising future but then became prideful and disobedient and finally slipped into madness. Meanwhile, David, who served Saul as a warrior and musician, was a model of faithfulness to God.

As Saul's future was sinking, David's star was rising. His victory over Goliath was only the first of many successes. But the attention that David received stirred Saul's jealousy, so David spent many years running for his life, hiding in desert caves and enemy territory, and—as we know from many psalms—contemplating the character of God.

Two themes stand out in 1 Samuel. The first concerns Saul: "You have not kept the LORD's command" (1 Samuel 13:14). The second describes David: "In everything he did he had great success, because the LORD was with him" (1 Samuel 18:14).

Life today, including marriage, has many challenges. Yet we know from David that any success we have is due to the Lord. Even in the face of Goliath-sized obstacles, we need to remember David's words: "The battle is the LORD's" (1 Samuel 17:47).

The Birth of Samuel

1 There was a certain man from Ramathaim, a Zuphite[a] from the hill country of
Ephraim, whose name was Elkanah son of
Jeroham, the son of Elihu, the son of Tohu,
the son of Zuph, an Ephraimite. 2He had two
wives; one was called Hannah and the other
Peninnah. Peninnah had children, but Hannah had none.
3Year after year this man went up from his
town to worship and sacrifice to the LORD Almighty at Shiloh, where Hophni and Phinehas, the two sons of Eli, were priests of the
LORD. 4Whenever the day came for Elkanah
to sacrifice, he would give portions of the meat
to his wife Peninnah and to all her sons and
daughters. 5But to Hannah he gave a double
portion because he loved her, and the LORD
had closed her womb. 6And because the LORD
had closed her womb, her rival kept provoking her in order to irritate her. 7This went on
year after year. Whenever Hannah went up
to the house of the LORD, her rival provoked
her till she wept and would not eat. 8Elkanah
her husband would say to her, "Hannah, why
are you weeping? Why don't you eat? Why are
you downhearted? Don't I mean more to you
than ten sons?"
9Once when they had finished eating and
drinking in Shiloh, Hannah stood up. Now
Eli the priest was sitting on a chair by the
doorpost of the LORD's temple.[b] 10In bitterness of soul Hannah wept much and prayed
to the LORD. 11And she made a vow, saying,
"O LORD Almighty, if you will only look upon
your servant's misery and remember me, and
not forget your servant but give her a son,
then I will give him to the LORD for all the
days of his life, and no razor will ever be used
on his head."
12As she kept on praying to the LORD, Eli
observed her mouth. 13Hannah was praying
in her heart, and her lips were moving but her
voice was not heard. Eli thought she was drunk
14and said to her, "How long will you keep on
getting drunk? Get rid of your wine."
15"Not so, my lord," Hannah replied, "I am
a woman who is deeply troubled. I have not
been drinking wine or beer; I was pouring out
my soul to the LORD. 16Do not take your servant for a wicked woman; I have been praying
here out of my great anguish and grief."
17Eli answered, "Go in peace, and may the
God of Israel grant you what you have asked
of him."
18She said, "May your servant find favor
in your eyes." Then she went her way and ate
something, and her face was no longer downcast.
19Early the next morning they arose and
worshiped before the LORD and then went
back to their home at Ramah. Elkanah lay
with Hannah his wife, and the LORD remembered her. 20So in the course of time Hannah
conceived and gave birth to a son. She named
him Samuel,[c] saying, "Because I asked the
LORD for him."

Hannah Dedicates Samuel

21When the man Elkanah went up with all
his family to offer the annual sacrifice to the
LORD and to fulfill his vow, 22Hannah did
not go. She said to her husband, "After the
boy is weaned, I will take him and present
him before the LORD, and he will live there
always."
23"Do what seems best to you," Elkanah her
husband told her. "Stay here until you have
weaned him; only may the LORD make good
his[d] word." So the woman stayed at home and
nursed her son until she had weaned him.
24After he was weaned, she took the boy
with her, young as he was, along with a
three-year-old bull,[e] an ephah[f] of flour and a
skin of wine, and brought him to the house of
the LORD at Shiloh. 25When they had slaughtered the bull, they brought the boy to Eli,
26and she said to him, "As surely as you live,
my lord, I am the woman who stood here beside you praying to the LORD. 27I prayed for
this child, and the LORD has granted me what
I asked of him. 28So now I give him to the
LORD. For his whole life he will be given over
to the LORD." And he worshiped the LORD
there.

Hannah's Prayer

2 Then Hannah prayed and said:

"My heart rejoices in the LORD;
in the LORD my horn[g] is lifted high.
My mouth boasts over my enemies,
for I delight in your deliverance.

2"There is no one holy[h] like the LORD;
there is no one besides you;
there is no Rock like our God.

---

[a] 1 Or *from Ramathaim Zuphim* [b] 9 That is, tabernacle [c] 20 *Samuel* sounds like the Hebrew for *heard of God.* [d] 23 Masoretic Text; Dead Sea Scrolls, Septuagint and Syriac *your* [e] 24 Dead Sea Scrolls, Septuagint and Syriac; Masoretic Text *with three bulls* [f] 24 That is, probably about 3/5 bushel (about 22 liters) [g] 1 *Horn* here symbolizes strength; also in verse 10. [h] 2 Or *no Holy One*

WHEN YOUR LOVE ISN'T ENOUGH

> **Elkanah her husband would say to her, "Hannah, why are you weeping? Why don't you eat? Why are you downhearted? Don't I mean more to you than ten sons?"**
>
> — 1 SAMUEL 1:8

About a year ago, my friend Tanya and her husband, Dirk, moved to Colorado from their home in Maine. For the first time, Tanya, a bubbly and social gal who would have been voted "most friendly in the senior class" if she hadn't been home-schooled, found herself having trouble making friends. Oh, there were people from church and her office that she liked well enough, but she hadn't met anyone with whom she felt that instant connection that promises deep friendship.

Dirk might have been hanging out with Elkanah, for when Tanya talked wistfully about the women in Maine whom she missed, Dirk would say, "But you have me! Aren't I enough?"

Elkanah meant well. He realized that his wife was upset and hurting from her inability to get pregnant. Added to that, Hannah had to deal with the daily taunts of Elkanah's other wife, who had plenty of children. Elkanah asked, "Am I not enough? Isn't my wonderful, huge, spilling-over-into-everything love enough?"

Hannah's answer was clear: "No, Elkanah; it's not enough."

let's talk

- ✦ What emotional, spiritual and social needs do we fill for one another?
- ✦ What needs do we fail to fill for each other? How can we have those needs met in appropriate ways?
- ✦ Have either of us ever responded like Elkanah to each other's need? What might have been a better response?

We are so often tempted, like Elkanah, to think that the love we offer in marriage is enough to meet our spouse's every need. We mean well. When our spouse is feeling lonely or has had a bad day at work, we want to fix things. We want our love to take away whatever the hurt is. But people have needs and desires that a spouse can't meet, such as a desire for children, a desire related to a job or a desire for friendship.

Only when Tanya met Cynthia, someone with whom she instantly connected, did Dirk change his tune. "When Tanya would come home from coffee with Cynthia all lit up, I realized how much she needed other friends. Of course I couldn't and shouldn't be her only friend in the whole Mountain Time Zone."

Dirk was also relieved that Tanya had found someone who shared her passion for quilting; now he no longer had to talk about fabrics and patterns every single day. What's more, Tanya and Dirk say their friendship with each other actually deepened as they each made new friends in Colorado. Having other friends took a little pressure off their marriage. Since they no longer were looking to each other to meet *all* their needs, they could relax and enjoy each other more. Dirk even went to an occasional quilting show with Tanya and Cynthia.

When we allow married love to be what it is supposed to be—important but not all-important, meaningful but not all-meaningful, a priority but not the only priority—and when we stop looking to our spouse to be more than he or she can be, then we are better able to appreciate the ways marriage does fulfill us.

—LAUREN WINNER

FOR YOUR NEXT DEVOTIONAL READING, TURN TO PAGE 290.

3 "Do not keep talking so proudly
or let your mouth speak such
arrogance,
for the LORD is a God who knows,
and by him deeds are weighed.

4 "The bows of the warriors are broken,
but those who stumbled are armed with
strength.
5 Those who were full hire themselves out
for food,
but those who were hungry hunger no
more.
She who was barren has borne seven
children,
but she who has had many sons pines
away.

6 "The LORD brings death and makes alive;
he brings down to the grave[a] and raises
up.
7 The LORD sends poverty and wealth;
he humbles and he exalts.
8 He raises the poor from the dust
and lifts the needy from the ash heap;
he seats them with princes
and has them inherit a throne of honor.

"For the foundations of the earth are the
LORD's;
upon them he has set the world.
9 He will guard the feet of his saints,
but the wicked will be silenced in
darkness.

"It is not by strength that one prevails;
10 those who oppose the LORD will be
shattered.
He will thunder against them from
heaven;
the LORD will judge the ends of the
earth.

"He will give strength to his king
and exalt the horn of his anointed."

11 Then Elkanah went home to Ramah, but
the boy ministered before the LORD under Eli
the priest.

Eli's Wicked Sons

12 Eli's sons were wicked men; they had no
regard for the LORD. 13 Now it was the practice
of the priests with the people that whenever
anyone offered a sacrifice and while the meat
was being boiled, the servant of the priest
would come with a three-pronged fork in his
hand. 14 He would plunge it into the pan or
kettle or caldron or pot, and the priest would
take for himself whatever the fork brought up.
This is how they treated all the Israelites who
came to Shiloh. 15 But even before the fat was
burned, the servant of the priest would come
and say to the man who was sacrificing, "Give
the priest some meat to roast; he won't accept
boiled meat from you, but only raw."
16 If the man said to him, "Let the fat be
burned up first, and then take whatever you
want," the servant would then answer, "No,
hand it over now; if you don't, I'll take it by
force."
17 This sin of the young men was very great
in the LORD's sight, for they[b] were treating the
LORD's offering with contempt.
18 But Samuel was ministering before the
LORD—a boy wearing a linen ephod. 19 Each
year his mother made him a little robe and
took it to him when she went up with her husband to offer the annual sacrifice. 20 Eli would
bless Elkanah and his wife, saying, "May the
LORD give you children by this woman to take
the place of the one she prayed for and gave to
the LORD." Then they would go home. 21 And
the LORD was gracious to Hannah; she conceived and gave birth to three sons and two
daughters. Meanwhile, the boy Samuel grew
up in the presence of the LORD.
22 Now Eli, who was very old, heard about
everything his sons were doing to all Israel and
how they slept with the women who served at
the entrance to the Tent of Meeting. 23 So he
said to them, "Why do you do such things?
I hear from all the people about these wicked deeds of yours. 24 No, my sons; it is not a
good report that I hear spreading among the
LORD's people. 25 If a man sins against another man, God[c] may mediate for him; but if a
man sins against the LORD, who will intercede
for him?" His sons, however, did not listen to
their father's rebuke, for it was the LORD's will
to put them to death.
26 And the boy Samuel continued to grow in
stature and in favor with the LORD and with
men.

Prophecy Against the House of Eli

27 Now a man of God came to Eli and said
to him, "This is what the LORD says: 'Did I
not clearly reveal myself to your father's house
when they were in Egypt under Pharaoh? 28 I
chose your father out of all the tribes of Israel
to be my priest, to go up to my altar, to burn
incense, and to wear an ephod in my presence.

[a] 6 Hebrew *Sheol* [b] 17 Or *men* [c] 25 Or *the judges*

I also gave your father's house all the offerings made with fire by the Israelites. 29Why
do you[a] scorn my sacrifice and offering that
I prescribed for my dwelling? Why do you
honor your sons more than me by fattening
yourselves on the choice parts of every offering
made by my people Israel?'
30"Therefore the LORD, the God of Israel,
declares: 'I promised that your house and your
father's house would minister before me forever.' But now the LORD declares: 'Far be it
from me! Those who honor me I will honor,
but those who despise me will be disdained.
31The time is coming when I will cut short
your strength and the strength of your father's
house, so that there will not be an old man in
your family line 32and you will see distress in
my dwelling. Although good will be done to
Israel, in your family line there will never be
an old man. 33Every one of you that I do not
cut off from my altar will be spared only to
blind your eyes with tears and to grieve your
heart, and all your descendants will die in the
prime of life.
34" 'And what happens to your two sons,
Hophni and Phinehas, will be a sign to you—
they will both die on the same day. 35I will
raise up for myself a faithful priest, who will
do according to what is in my heart and mind.
I will firmly establish his house, and he will
minister before my anointed one always.
36Then everyone left in your family line will
come and bow down before him for a piece of
silver and a crust of bread and plead, "Appoint
me to some priestly office so I can have food
to eat." ' "

The LORD Calls Samuel

3 The boy Samuel ministered before the
LORD under Eli. In those days the word of
the LORD was rare; there were not many visions.
2One night Eli, whose eyes were becoming so weak that he could barely see, was lying
down in his usual place. 3The lamp of God had
not yet gone out, and Samuel was lying down
in the temple[b] of the LORD, where the ark of
God was. 4Then the LORD called Samuel.
Samuel answered, "Here I am." 5And he ran
to Eli and said, "Here I am; you called me."
But Eli said, "I did not call; go back and lie
down." So he went and lay down.
6Again the LORD called, "Samuel!" And
Samuel got up and went to Eli and said, "Here
I am; you called me."
"My son," Eli said, "I did not call; go back
and lie down."
7Now Samuel did not yet know the LORD:
The word of the LORD had not yet been revealed to him.
8The LORD called Samuel a third time, and
Samuel got up and went to Eli and said, "Here
I am; you called me."
Then Eli realized that the LORD was calling the boy. 9So Eli told Samuel, "Go and lie
down, and if he calls you, say, 'Speak, LORD,
for your servant is listening.' " So Samuel went
and lay down in his place.
10The LORD came and stood there, calling
as at the other times, "Samuel! Samuel!"
Then Samuel said, "Speak, for your servant
is listening."
11And the LORD said to Samuel: "See, I
am about to do something in Israel that will
make the ears of everyone who hears of it tingle. 12At that time I will carry out against Eli
everything I spoke against his family—from
beginning to end. 13For I told him that I
would judge his family forever because of the
sin he knew about; his sons made themselves
contemptible,[c] and he failed to restrain them.
14Therefore, I swore to the house of Eli, 'The
guilt of Eli's house will never be atoned for by
sacrifice or offering.' "
15Samuel lay down until morning and then
opened the doors of the house of the LORD.
He was afraid to tell Eli the vision, 16but Eli
called him and said, "Samuel, my son."
Samuel answered, "Here I am."
17"What was it he said to you?" Eli asked.
"Do not hide it from me. May God deal with
you, be it ever so severely, if you hide from me
anything he told you." 18So Samuel told him
everything, hiding nothing from him. Then
Eli said, "He is the LORD; let him do what is
good in his eyes."
19The LORD was with Samuel as he grew up,
and he let none of his words fall to the ground.
20And all Israel from Dan to Beersheba recognized that Samuel was attested as a prophet of
the LORD. 21The LORD continued to appear at
Shiloh, and there he revealed himself to Samuel through his word.
4 And Samuel's word came to all Israel.

The Philistines Capture the Ark

Now the Israelites went out to fight against
the Philistines. The Israelites camped at Eben-

[a] 29 The Hebrew is plural. [b] 3 That is, tabernacle [c] 13 Masoretic Text; an ancient Hebrew scribal tradition and Septuagint *sons blasphemed God*

ezer, and the Philistines at Aphek. 2The Philistines deployed their forces to meet Israel, and as the battle spread, Israel was defeated by the Philistines, who killed about four thousand of them on the battlefield. 3When the soldiers returned to camp, the elders of Israel asked, "Why did the LORD bring defeat upon us today before the Philistines? Let us bring the ark of the LORD's covenant from Shiloh, so that it[a] may go with us and save us from the hand of our enemies."

4So the people sent men to Shiloh, and they brought back the ark of the covenant of the LORD Almighty, who is enthroned between the cherubim. And Eli's two sons, Hophni and Phinehas, were there with the ark of the covenant of God.

5When the ark of the LORD's covenant came into the camp, all Israel raised such a great shout that the ground shook. 6Hearing the uproar, the Philistines asked, "What's all this shouting in the Hebrew camp?"

When they learned that the ark of the LORD had come into the camp, 7the Philistines were afraid. "A god has come into the camp," they said. "We're in trouble! Nothing like this has happened before. 8Woe to us! Who will deliver us from the hand of these mighty gods? They are the gods who struck the Egyptians with all kinds of plagues in the desert. 9Be strong, Philistines! Be men, or you will be subject to the Hebrews, as they have been to you. Be men, and fight!"

10So the Philistines fought, and the Israelites were defeated and every man fled to his tent. The slaughter was very great; Israel lost thirty thousand foot soldiers. 11The ark of God was captured, and Eli's two sons, Hophni and Phinehas, died.

Death of Eli

12That same day a Benjamite ran from the battle line and went to Shiloh, his clothes torn and dust on his head. 13When he arrived, there was Eli sitting on his chair by the side of the road, watching, because his heart feared for the ark of God. When the man entered the town and told what had happened, the whole town sent up a cry.

14Eli heard the outcry and asked, "What is the meaning of this uproar?"

The man hurried over to Eli, 15who was ninety-eight years old and whose eyes were set so that he could not see. 16He told Eli, "I have just come from the battle line; I fled from it this very day."

Eli asked, "What happened, my son?"

17The man who brought the news replied, "Israel fled before the Philistines, and the army has suffered heavy losses. Also your two sons, Hophni and Phinehas, are dead, and the ark of God has been captured."

18When he mentioned the ark of God, Eli fell backward off his chair by the side of the gate. His neck was broken and he died, for he was an old man and heavy. He had led[b] Israel forty years.

19His daughter-in-law, the wife of Phinehas, was pregnant and near the time of delivery. When she heard the news that the ark of God had been captured and that her father-in-law and her husband were dead, she went into labor and gave birth, but was overcome by her labor pains. 20As she was dying, the women attending her said, "Don't despair; you have given birth to a son." But she did not respond or pay any attention.

21She named the boy Ichabod,[c] saying, "The glory has departed from Israel"—because of the capture of the ark of God and the deaths of her father-in-law and her husband. 22She said, "The glory has departed from Israel, for the ark of God has been captured."

The Ark in Ashdod and Ekron

5 After the Philistines had captured the ark of God, they took it from Ebenezer to Ashdod. 2Then they carried the ark into Dagon's temple and set it beside Dagon. 3When the people of Ashdod rose early the next day, there was Dagon, fallen on his face on the ground before the ark of the LORD! They took Dagon and put him back in his place. 4But the following morning when they rose, there was Dagon, fallen on his face on the ground before the ark of the LORD! His head and hands had been broken off and were lying on the threshold; only his body remained. 5That is why to this day neither the priests of Dagon nor any others who enter Dagon's temple at Ashdod step on the threshold.

6The LORD's hand was heavy upon the people of Ashdod and its vicinity; he brought devastation upon them and afflicted them with tumors.[d] 7When the men of Ashdod saw what was happening, they said, "The ark of the god of Israel must not stay here with us, because

[a] 3 Or *he* [b] 18 Traditionally *judged* [c] 21 *Ichabod* means *no glory.* [d] 6 Hebrew; Septuagint and Vulgate *tumors. And rats appeared in their land, and death and destruction were throughout the city*

his hand is heavy upon us and upon Dagon our god." [8]So they called together all the rulers of the Philistines and asked them, "What shall we do with the ark of the god of Israel?"

They answered, "Have the ark of the god of Israel moved to Gath." So they moved the ark of the God of Israel.

[9]But after they had moved it, the LORD's hand was against that city, throwing it into a great panic. He afflicted the people of the city, both young and old, with an outbreak of tumors.[a] [10]So they sent the ark of God to Ekron.

As the ark of God was entering Ekron, the people of Ekron cried out, "They have brought the ark of the god of Israel around to us to kill us and our people." [11]So they called together all the rulers of the Philistines and said, "Send the ark of the god of Israel away; let it go back to its own place, or it[b] will kill us and our people." For death had filled the city with panic; God's hand was very heavy upon it. [12]Those who did not die were afflicted with tumors, and the outcry of the city went up to heaven.

The Ark Returned to Israel

6 When the ark of the LORD had been in Philistine territory seven months, [2]the Philistines called for the priests and the diviners and said, "What shall we do with the ark of the LORD? Tell us how we should send it back to its place."

[3]They answered, "If you return the ark of the god of Israel, do not send it away empty, but by all means send a guilt offering to him. Then you will be healed, and you will know why his hand has not been lifted from you."

[4]The Philistines asked, "What guilt offering should we send to him?"

They replied, "Five gold tumors and five gold rats, according to the number of the Philistine rulers, because the same plague has struck both you and your rulers. [5]Make models of the tumors and of the rats that are destroying the country, and pay honor to Israel's god. Perhaps he will lift his hand from you and your gods and your land. [6]Why do you harden your hearts as the Egyptians and Pharaoh did? When he[c] treated them harshly, did they not send the Israelites out so they could go on their way?

[7]"Now then, get a new cart ready, with two cows that have calved and have never been yoked. Hitch the cows to the cart, but take their calves away and pen them up. [8]Take the ark of the LORD and put it on the cart, and in a chest beside it put the gold objects you are sending back to him as a guilt offering. Send it on its way, [9]but keep watching it. If it goes up to its own territory, toward Beth Shemesh, then the LORD has brought this great disaster on us. But if it does not, then we will know that it was not his hand that struck us and that it happened to us by chance."

[10]So they did this. They took two such cows and hitched them to the cart and penned up their calves. [11]They placed the ark of the LORD on the cart and along with it the chest containing the gold rats and the models of the tumors. [12]Then the cows went straight up toward Beth Shemesh, keeping on the road and lowing all the way; they did not turn to the right or to the left. The rulers of the Philistines followed them as far as the border of Beth Shemesh.

[13]Now the people of Beth Shemesh were harvesting their wheat in the valley, and when they looked up and saw the ark, they rejoiced at the sight. [14]The cart came to the field of Joshua of Beth Shemesh, and there it stopped beside a large rock. The people chopped up the wood of the cart and sacrificed the cows as a burnt offering to the LORD. [15]The Levites took down the ark of the LORD, together with the chest containing the gold objects, and placed them on the large rock. On that day the people of Beth Shemesh offered burnt offerings and made sacrifices to the LORD. [16]The five rulers of the Philistines saw all this and then returned that same day to Ekron.

[17]These are the gold tumors the Philistines sent as a guilt offering to the LORD—one each for Ashdod, Gaza, Ashkelon, Gath and Ekron. [18]And the number of the gold rats was according to the number of Philistine towns belonging to the five rulers—the fortified towns with their country villages. The large rock, on which[d] they set the ark of the LORD, is a witness to this day in the field of Joshua of Beth Shemesh.

[19]But God struck down some of the men of Beth Shemesh, putting seventy[e] of them to death because they had looked into the ark of the LORD. The people mourned because of the heavy blow the LORD had dealt them, [20]and the men of Beth Shemesh asked, "Who can stand in the presence of the LORD, this

[a] 9 Or *with tumors in the groin* (see Septuagint) [b] 11 Or *he* [c] 6 That is, God [d] 18 A few Hebrew manuscripts (see also Septuagint); most Hebrew manuscripts *villages as far as Greater Abel, where* [e] 19 A few Hebrew manuscripts; most Hebrew manuscripts and Septuagint *50,070*

holy God? To whom will the ark go up from
here?"
21Then they sent messengers to the people
of Kiriath Jearim, saying, "The Philistines have
returned the ark of the LORD. Come down
7 and take it up to your place." 1So the men
of Kiriath Jearim came and took up the ark
of the LORD. They took it to Abinadab's
house on the hill and consecrated Eleazar his
son to guard the ark of the LORD.

Samuel Subdues the Philistines at Mizpah

2It was a long time, twenty years in all, that
the ark remained at Kiriath Jearim, and all the
people of Israel mourned and sought after the
LORD. 3And Samuel said to the whole house
of Israel, "If you are returning to the LORD
with all your hearts, then rid yourselves of the
foreign gods and the Ashtoreths and commit
yourselves to the LORD and serve him only,
and he will deliver you out of the hand of the
Philistines." 4So the Israelites put away their
Baals and Ashtoreths, and served the LORD
only.
5Then Samuel said, "Assemble all Israel at
Mizpah and I will intercede with the LORD
for you." 6When they had assembled at Mizpah, they drew water and poured it out before
the LORD. On that day they fasted and there
they confessed, "We have sinned against the
LORD." And Samuel was leader[a] of Israel at
Mizpah.
7When the Philistines heard that Israel had
assembled at Mizpah, the rulers of the Philistines came up to attack them. And when
the Israelites heard of it, they were afraid because of the Philistines. 8They said to Samuel, "Do not stop crying out to the LORD our
God for us, that he may rescue us from the
hand of the Philistines." 9Then Samuel took
a suckling lamb and offered it up as a whole
burnt offering to the LORD. He cried out to
the LORD on Israel's behalf, and the LORD answered him.
10While Samuel was sacrificing the burnt
offering, the Philistines drew near to engage
Israel in battle. But that day the LORD thundered with loud thunder against the Philistines and threw them into such a panic that
they were routed before the Israelites. 11The
men of Israel rushed out of Mizpah and pursued the Philistines, slaughtering them along
the way to a point below Beth Car.
12Then Samuel took a stone and set it up
between Mizpah and Shen. He named it Ebenezer,[b] saying, "Thus far has the LORD helped
us." 13So the Philistines were subdued and did
not invade Israelite territory again.
Throughout Samuel's lifetime, the hand of
the LORD was against the Philistines. 14The
towns from Ekron to Gath that the Philistines
had captured from Israel were restored to her,
and Israel delivered the neighboring territory
from the power of the Philistines. And there
was peace between Israel and the Amorites.
15Samuel continued as judge over Israel all
the days of his life. 16From year to year he went
on a circuit from Bethel to Gilgal to Mizpah,
judging Israel in all those places. 17But he always went back to Ramah, where his home
was, and there he also judged Israel. And he
built an altar there to the LORD.

Israel Asks for a King

8 When Samuel grew old, he appointed his
sons as judges for Israel. 2The name of his
firstborn was Joel and the name of his second was Abijah, and they served at Beersheba.
3But his sons did not walk in his ways. They
turned aside after dishonest gain and accepted
bribes and perverted justice.
4So all the elders of Israel gathered together
and came to Samuel at Ramah. 5They said to
him, "You are old, and your sons do not walk
in your ways; now appoint a king to lead[c] us,
such as all the other nations have."
6But when they said, "Give us a king to lead
us," this displeased Samuel; so he prayed to
the LORD. 7And the LORD told him: "Listen
to all that the people are saying to you; it is
not you they have rejected, but they have rejected me as their king. 8As they have done
from the day I brought them up out of Egypt
until this day, forsaking me and serving other
gods, so they are doing to you. 9Now listen to
them; but warn them solemnly and let them
know what the king who will reign over them
will do."
10Samuel told all the words of the LORD to
the people who were asking him for a king.
11He said, "This is what the king who will
reign over you will do: He will take your sons
and make them serve with his chariots and
horses, and they will run in front of his chariots. 12Some he will assign to be commanders
of thousands and commanders of fifties, and
others to plow his ground and reap his harvest, and still others to make weapons of war
and equipment for his chariots. 13He will take
your daughters to be perfumers and cooks and

[a] 6 Traditionally *judge* [b] 12 *Ebenezer* means *stone of help.* [c] 5 Traditionally *judge*; also in verses 6 and 20

THURSDAY
READ 1 SAMUEL 8:1–9

BREAKING BAD FAMILY HABITS

Bad parenting can stem from neglect or abuse, but, more often, parents are simply unaware of their own bad habits, blind spots and personal weaknesses. And they often underestimate the impact their bad parenting can have on their children and subsequent generations.

We don't know why Joel and Abijah turned out to be such terrible men that the elders of Israel (who were looking for an excuse to request a king) refused their leadership. Their father, Samuel, surely had modeled faithfulness as the spiritual and moral leader of the people of Israel. Perhaps somewhere along the way Samuel failed to exercise the kind of fatherly instruction, discipline and training necessary to keep his sons from seeking dishonest gain, accepting bribes and perverting justice.

Perhaps we can understand Samuel's parenting style by looking at how he was raised. Samuel was dedicated to the Lord at a very young age and was given to Eli, Israel's high priest and judge, to raise. Eli had not done a good job of parenting his own two sons; Hophni and Phinehas were so wicked that God had them killed in battle on the same day and took the priesthood away from Eli's family (see 1 Samuel 2:12–36; 4:11).

But his sons did not walk in his ways. They turned aside after dishonest gain and accepted bribes and perverted justice.

— 1 SAMUEL 8:3

let's talk

- What lessons about parenting did we pick up from our moms and dads? Which lessons have been positive? Which ones have led to difficulties for each of us?
- What steps can we take to address any challenges we bring from our parents when it comes to raising our children?
- What might be some evidence of the "Samuel syndrome" in our marriage? How can we break "the law of the generations"?

Perhaps Samuel watched Eli practice bad parenting with his sons. Though Samuel turned out well, he did not learn how to be a good father from watching Eli. Perhaps he was stuck in what Catherine Marshall once called "the law of the generations," in which one generation repeats the behavior of the previous generation.

Our children are watching us—and will repeat behavior that gets the most attention, whether it's good or bad. When they grow into adulthood and become responsible for their own behavior, they may be forced to correct bad habits and practices, but it's possible they may not. And their children will pay the price.

As we become aware of some of the poor practices in our own upbringing (and celebrate the good parenting we did receive), we can help our children to not repeat our mistakes. Husbands and wives come from different families with different styles of child rearing and discipline. One partner can exercise his or her authority through discipline of the children in certain areas, and the other can do the same on another front.

For example, I have had to unlearn poor spending habits that I picked up while growing up. My wife, who has acquired exceptional skills in budgeting and handling money due to great family modeling, has been a great help to me.

She, on the other hand, grew up with weaknesses in the use of her time and talents. In this area my family training was strong. So I found I could offer direction to her and our children in this area.

To help each other in marriage, we must first identify the areas of bad parenting that have affected us. We can then lend our strengths to each other as we learn to overcome personal weaknesses and model the kind of behavior God wants us to pass on to the next generation.

—JOHN R. THROOP

FOR YOUR NEXT DEVOTIONAL READING, TURN TO PAGE 299.

bakers. 14He will take the best of your fields
and vineyards and olive groves and give them
to his attendants. 15He will take a tenth of
your grain and of your vintage and give it to
his officials and attendants. 16Your menservants and maidservants and the best of your
cattle[a] and donkeys he will take for his own
use. 17He will take a tenth of your flocks, and
you yourselves will become his slaves. 18When
that day comes, you will cry out for relief from
the king you have chosen, and the LORD will
not answer you in that day."

19But the people refused to listen to Samuel. "No!" they said. "We want a king over us.
20Then we will be like all the other nations,
with a king to lead us and to go out before us
and fight our battles."

21When Samuel heard all that the people
said, he repeated it before the LORD. 22The
LORD answered, "Listen to them and give
them a king."

Then Samuel said to the men of Israel, "Everyone go back to his town."

Samuel Anoints Saul

9 There was a Benjamite, a man of standing,
whose name was Kish son of Abiel, the son
of Zeror, the son of Becorath, the son of
Aphiah of Benjamin. 2He had a son named
Saul, an impressive young man without equal
among the Israelites—a head taller than any
of the others.

3Now the donkeys belonging to Saul's father
Kish were lost, and Kish said to his son Saul,
"Take one of the servants with you and go and
look for the donkeys." 4So he passed through
the hill country of Ephraim and through the
area around Shalisha, but they did not find
them. They went on into the district of Shaa-
lim, but the donkeys were not there. Then he
passed through the territory of Benjamin, but
they did not find them.

5When they reached the district of Zuph,
Saul said to the servant who was with him,
"Come, let's go back, or my father will stop
thinking about the donkeys and start worrying about us."

6But the servant replied, "Look, in this
town there is a man of God; he is highly respected, and everything he says comes true.
Let's go there now. Perhaps he will tell us what
way to take."

7Saul said to his servant, "If we go, what
can we give the man? The food in our sacks is
gone. We have no gift to take to the man of
God. What do we have?"

8The servant answered him again. "Look,"
he said, "I have a quarter of a shekel[b] of silver.
I will give it to the man of God so that he will
tell us what way to take." 9(Formerly in Israel,
if a man went to inquire of God, he would
say, "Come, let us go to the seer," because the
prophet of today used to be called a seer.)

10"Good," Saul said to his servant. "Come,
let's go." So they set out for the town where
the man of God was.

11As they were going up the hill to the town,
they met some girls coming out to draw water,
and they asked them, "Is the seer here?"

12"He is," they answered. "He's ahead of
you. Hurry now; he has just come to our town
today, for the people have a sacrifice at the
high place. 13As soon as you enter the town,
you will find him before he goes up to the
high place to eat. The people will not begin
eating until he comes, because he must bless
the sacrifice; afterward, those who are invited will eat. Go up now; you should find him
about this time."

14They went up to the town, and as they
were entering it, there was Samuel, coming toward them on his way up to the high place.

15Now the day before Saul came, the LORD
had revealed this to Samuel: 16"About this
time tomorrow I will send you a man from
the land of Benjamin. Anoint him leader
over my people Israel; he will deliver my people from the hand of the Philistines. I have
looked upon my people, for their cry has
reached me."

17When Samuel caught sight of Saul, the
LORD said to him, "This is the man I spoke to
you about; he will govern my people."

18Saul approached Samuel in the gateway
and asked, "Would you please tell me where
the seer's house is?"

19"I am the seer," Samuel replied. "Go up
ahead of me to the high place, for today you
are to eat with me, and in the morning I will
let you go and will tell you all that is in your
heart. 20As for the donkeys you lost three days
ago, do not worry about them; they have been
found. And to whom is all the desire of Israel turned, if not to you and all your father's
family?"

21Saul answered, "But am I not a Benjamite, from the smallest tribe of Israel, and is
not my clan the least of all the clans of the

[a] *16* Septuagint; Hebrew *young men* [b] *8* That is, about 1/10 ounce (about 3 grams)

tribe of Benjamin? Why do you say such a thing to me?"

22Then Samuel brought Saul and his servant into the hall and seated them at the head of those who were invited—about thirty in number. 23Samuel said to the cook, "Bring the piece of meat I gave you, the one I told you to lay aside."

24So the cook took up the leg with what was on it and set it in front of Saul. Samuel said, "Here is what has been kept for you. Eat, because it was set aside for you for this occasion, from the time I said, 'I have invited guests.' " And Saul dined with Samuel that day.

25After they came down from the high place to the town, Samuel talked with Saul on the roof of his house. 26They rose about daybreak and Samuel called to Saul on the roof, "Get ready, and I will send you on your way." When Saul got ready, he and Samuel went outside together. 27As they were going down to the edge of the town, Samuel said to Saul, "Tell the servant to go on ahead of us"—and the servant did so—"but you stay here awhile, so that I may give you a message from God."

10 Then Samuel took a flask of oil and poured it on Saul's head and kissed him, saying, "Has not the LORD anointed you leader over his inheritance?[a] 2When you leave me today, you will meet two men near Rachel's tomb, at Zelzah on the border of Benjamin. They will say to you, 'The donkeys you set out to look for have been found. And now your father has stopped thinking about them and is worried about you. He is asking, "What shall I do about my son?" '

3"Then you will go on from there until you reach the great tree of Tabor. Three men going up to God at Bethel will meet you there. One will be carrying three young goats, another three loaves of bread, and another a skin of wine. 4They will greet you and offer you two loaves of bread, which you will accept from them.

5"After that you will go to Gibeah of God, where there is a Philistine outpost. As you approach the town, you will meet a procession of prophets coming down from the high place with lyres, tambourines, flutes and harps being played before them, and they will be prophesying. 6The Spirit of the LORD will come upon you in power, and you will prophesy with them; and you will be changed into a different person. 7Once these signs are fulfilled, do whatever your hand finds to do, for God is with you.

8"Go down ahead of me to Gilgal. I will surely come down to you to sacrifice burnt offerings and fellowship offerings,[b] but you must wait seven days until I come to you and tell you what you are to do."

Saul Made King

9As Saul turned to leave Samuel, God changed Saul's heart, and all these signs were fulfilled that day. 10When they arrived at Gibeah, a procession of prophets met him; the Spirit of God came upon him in power, and he joined in their prophesying. 11When all those who had formerly known him saw him prophesying with the prophets, they asked each other, "What is this that has happened to the son of Kish? Is Saul also among the prophets?"

12A man who lived there answered, "And who is their father?" So it became a saying: "Is Saul also among the prophets?" 13After Saul stopped prophesying, he went to the high place.

14Now Saul's uncle asked him and his servant, "Where have you been?"

"Looking for the donkeys," he said. "But when we saw they were not to be found, we went to Samuel."

15Saul's uncle said, "Tell me what Samuel said to you."

16Saul replied, "He assured us that the donkeys had been found." But he did not tell his uncle what Samuel had said about the kingship.

17Samuel summoned the people of Israel to the LORD at Mizpah 18and said to them, "This is what the LORD, the God of Israel, says: 'I brought Israel up out of Egypt, and I delivered you from the power of Egypt and all the kingdoms that oppressed you.' 19But you have now rejected your God, who saves you out of all your calamities and distresses. And you have said, 'No, set a king over us.' So now present yourselves before the LORD by your tribes and clans."

20When Samuel brought all the tribes of Israel near, the tribe of Benjamin was chosen. 21Then he brought forward the tribe of Benjamin, clan by clan, and Matri's clan was chosen. Finally Saul son of Kish was chosen. But when they looked for him, he was not to be found.

[a] *1* Hebrew; Septuagint and Vulgate *over his people Israel? You will reign over the LORD's people and save them from the power of their enemies round about. And this will be a sign to you that the LORD has anointed you leader over his inheritance:* [b] *8* Traditionally *peace offerings*

22So they inquired further of the LORD, "Has
the man come here yet?"
And the LORD said, "Yes, he has hidden
himself among the baggage."
23They ran and brought him out, and as he
stood among the people he was a head taller
than any of the others. 24Samuel said to all the
people, "Do you see the man the LORD has
chosen? There is no one like him among all
the people."
Then the people shouted, "Long live the
king!"
25Samuel explained to the people the regulations of the kingship. He wrote them down
on a scroll and deposited it before the LORD.
Then Samuel dismissed the people, each to his
own home.
26Saul also went to his home in Gibeah, accompanied by valiant men whose hearts God
had touched. 27But some troublemakers said,
"How can this fellow save us?" They despised
him and brought him no gifts. But Saul kept
silent.

Saul Rescues the City of Jabesh

11 Nahash the Ammonite went up and besieged Jabesh Gilead. And all the men of
Jabesh said to him, "Make a treaty with
us, and we will be subject to you."
2But Nahash the Ammonite replied, "I will
make a treaty with you only on the condition
that I gouge out the right eye of every one of
you and so bring disgrace on all Israel."
3The elders of Jabesh said to him, "Give us
seven days so we can send messengers throughout Israel; if no one comes to rescue us, we will
surrender to you."
4When the messengers came to Gibeah of
Saul and reported these terms to the people,
they all wept aloud. 5Just then Saul was returning from the fields, behind his oxen, and
he asked, "What is wrong with the people?
Why are they weeping?" Then they repeated
to him what the men of Jabesh had said.
6When Saul heard their words, the Spirit of
God came upon him in power, and he burned
with anger. 7He took a pair of oxen, cut them
into pieces, and sent the pieces by messengers
throughout Israel, proclaiming, "This is what
will be done to the oxen of anyone who does
not follow Saul and Samuel." Then the terror of the LORD fell on the people, and they
turned out as one man. 8When Saul mustered
them at Bezek, the men of Israel numbered
three hundred thousand and the men of Judah
thirty thousand.
9They told the messengers who had come,
"Say to the men of Jabesh Gilead, 'By the time
the sun is hot tomorrow, you will be delivered.'" When the messengers went and reported this to the men of Jabesh, they were
elated. 10They said to the Ammonites, "Tomorrow we will surrender to you, and you can
do to us whatever seems good to you."
11The next day Saul separated his men into
three divisions; during the last watch of the
night they broke into the camp of the Ammonites and slaughtered them until the heat
of the day. Those who survived were scattered,
so that no two of them were left together.

Saul Confirmed as King

12The people then said to Samuel, "Who
was it that asked, 'Shall Saul reign over us?'
Bring these men to us and we will put them
to death."
13But Saul said, "No one shall be put to
death today, for this day the LORD has rescued
Israel."
14Then Samuel said to the people, "Come,
let us go to Gilgal and there reaffirm the kingship." 15So all the people went to Gilgal and
confirmed Saul as king in the presence of the
LORD. There they sacrificed fellowship offerings[a] before the LORD, and Saul and all the
Israelites held a great celebration.

Samuel's Farewell Speech

12 Samuel said to all Israel, "I have listened
to everything you said to me and have
set a king over you. 2Now you have a
king as your leader. As for me, I am old and
gray, and my sons are here with you. I have
been your leader from my youth until this day.
3Here I stand. Testify against me in the presence of the LORD and his anointed. Whose
ox have I taken? Whose donkey have I tak-
en? Whom have I cheated? Whom have I oppressed? From whose hand have I accepted a
bribe to make me shut my eyes? If I have done
any of these, I will make it right."
4"You have not cheated or oppressed us,"
they replied. "You have not taken anything
from anyone's hand."
5Samuel said to them, "The LORD is witness
against you, and also his anointed is witness
this day, that you have not found anything in
my hand."
"He is witness," they said.

---

a *15* Traditionally *peace offerings*

6Then Samuel said to the people, "It is the
LORD who appointed Moses and Aaron and
brought your forefathers up out of Egypt.
7Now then, stand here, because I am going to
confront you with evidence before the LORD
as to all the righteous acts performed by the
LORD for you and your fathers.

8"After Jacob entered Egypt, they cried to
the LORD for help, and the LORD sent Moses
and Aaron, who brought your forefathers out
of Egypt and settled them in this place.

9"But they forgot the LORD their God; so
he sold them into the hand of Sisera, the commander of the army of Hazor, and into the
hands of the Philistines and the king of Moab,
who fought against them. 10They cried out to
the LORD and said, 'We have sinned; we have
forsaken the LORD and served the Baals and
the Ashtoreths. But now deliver us from the
hands of our enemies, and we will serve you.'
11Then the LORD sent Jerub-Baal,[a] Barak,[b]
Jephthah and Samuel,[c] and he delivered you
from the hands of your enemies on every side,
so that you lived securely.

12"But when you saw that Nahash king of
the Ammonites was moving against you, you
said to me, 'No, we want a king to rule over
us'—even though the LORD your God was
your king. 13Now here is the king you have
chosen, the one you asked for; see, the LORD
has set a king over you. 14If you fear the LORD
and serve and obey him and do not rebel
against his commands, and if both you and
the king who reigns over you follow the LORD
your God—good! 15But if you do not obey
the LORD, and if you rebel against his commands, his hand will be against you, as it was
against your fathers.

16"Now then, stand still and see this great
thing the LORD is about to do before your
eyes! 17Is it not wheat harvest now? I will call
upon the LORD to send thunder and rain. And
you will realize what an evil thing you did in
the eyes of the LORD when you asked for a
king."

18Then Samuel called upon the LORD, and
that same day the LORD sent thunder and rain.
So all the people stood in awe of the LORD and
of Samuel.

19The people all said to Samuel, "Pray to
the LORD your God for your servants so that
we will not die, for we have added to all our
other sins the evil of asking for a king."

20"Do not be afraid," Samuel replied. "You
have done all this evil; yet do not turn away
from the LORD, but serve the LORD with all
your heart. 21Do not turn away after useless
idols. They can do you no good, nor can they
rescue you, because they are useless. 22For the
sake of his great name the LORD will not reject his people, because the LORD was pleased
to make you his own. 23As for me, far be it
from me that I should sin against the LORD
by failing to pray for you. And I will teach
you the way that is good and right. 24But be
sure to fear the LORD and serve him faithfully
with all your heart; consider what great things
he has done for you. 25Yet if you persist in
doing evil, both you and your king will be
swept away."

Samuel Rebukes Saul

13 Saul was ⌊thirty⌋[d] years old when he became king, and he reigned over Israel
⌊forty-⌋[e] two years.

2Saul[f] chose three thousand men from Israel; two thousand were with him at Micmash
and in the hill country of Bethel, and a thousand were with Jonathan at Gibeah in Benjamin. The rest of the men he sent back to their
homes.

3Jonathan attacked the Philistine outpost at
Geba, and the Philistines heard about it. Then
Saul had the trumpet blown throughout the
land and said, "Let the Hebrews hear!" 4So all
Israel heard the news: "Saul has attacked the
Philistine outpost, and now Israel has become
a stench to the Philistines." And the people
were summoned to join Saul at Gilgal.

5The Philistines assembled to fight Israel, with three thousand[g] chariots, six thousand charioteers, and soldiers as numerous
as the sand on the seashore. They went up
and camped at Micmash, east of Beth Aven.
6When the men of Israel saw that their situation was critical and that their army was hard
pressed, they hid in caves and thickets, among
the rocks, and in pits and cisterns. 7Some Hebrews even crossed the Jordan to the land of
Gad and Gilead.

Saul remained at Gilgal, and all the troops
with him were quaking with fear. 8He waited seven days, the time set by Samuel; but
Samuel did not come to Gilgal, and Saul's
men began to scatter. 9So he said, "Bring me
the burnt offering and the fellowship offer-

[a] *11* Also called *Gideon* [b] *11* Some Septuagint manuscripts and Syriac; Hebrew *Bedan* [c] *11* Hebrew; some Septuagint manuscripts and Syriac *Samson* [d] *1* A few late manuscripts of the Septuagint; Hebrew does not have *thirty.* [e] *1* See the round number in Acts 13:21; Hebrew does not have *forty-.* [f] *1,2* Or *and when he had reigned over Israel two years, ²he* [g] *5* Some Septuagint manuscripts and Syriac; Hebrew *thirty thousand*

ings.[a]" And Saul offered up the burnt offering. 10Just as he finished making the offering,
Samuel arrived, and Saul went out to greet
him.
11"What have you done?" asked Samuel.
Saul replied, "When I saw that the men
were scattering, and that you did not come at
the set time, and that the Philistines were as-
sembling at Micmash, 12I thought, 'Now the
Philistines will come down against me at Gilgal, and I have not sought the LORD's favor.'
So I felt compelled to offer the burnt offering."
13"You acted foolishly," Samuel said. "You
have not kept the command the LORD your
God gave you; if you had, he would have established your kingdom over Israel for all
time. 14But now your kingdom will not endure; the LORD has sought out a man after his
own heart and appointed him leader of his
people, because you have not kept the LORD's
command."
15Then Samuel left Gilgal[b] and went up
to Gibeah in Benjamin, and Saul counted
the men who were with him. They numbered
about six hundred.

Israel Without Weapons

16Saul and his son Jonathan and the men
with them were staying in Gibeah[c] in Benjamin, while the Philistines camped at Micmash. 17Raiding parties went out from the
Philistine camp in three detachments. One
turned toward Ophrah in the vicinity of Shual, 18another toward Beth Horon, and the
third toward the borderland overlooking the
Valley of Zeboim facing the desert.
19Not a blacksmith could be found in the
whole land of Israel, because the Philistines
had said, "Otherwise the Hebrews will make
swords or spears!" 20So all Israel went down
to the Philistines to have their plowshares,
mattocks, axes and sickles[d] sharpened. 21The
price was two thirds of a shekel[e] for sharpening plowshares and mattocks, and a third of a
shekel[f] for sharpening forks and axes and for
repointing goads.
22So on the day of the battle not a soldier
with Saul and Jonathan had a sword or spear
in his hand; only Saul and his son Jonathan
had them.

Jonathan Attacks the Philistines

23Now a detachment of Philistines had
14 gone out to the pass at Micmash. 1One
day Jonathan son of Saul said to the
young man bearing his armor, "Come,
let's go over to the Philistine outpost on the
other side." But he did not tell his father.
2Saul was staying on the outskirts of Gibeah
under a pomegranate tree in Migron. With him
were about six hundred men, 3among whom
was Ahijah, who was wearing an ephod. He was
a son of Ichabod's brother Ahitub son of Phinehas, the son of Eli, the LORD's priest in Shiloh.
No one was aware that Jonathan had left.
4On each side of the pass that Jonathan intended to cross to reach the Philistine outpost
was a cliff; one was called Bozez, and the other Seneh. 5One cliff stood to the north toward
Micmash, the other to the south toward Geba.
6Jonathan said to his young armor-bearer,
"Come, let's go over to the outpost of those
uncircumcised fellows. Perhaps the LORD will
act in our behalf. Nothing can hinder the
LORD from saving, whether by many or by
few."
7"Do all that you have in mind," his armor-
bearer said. "Go ahead; I am with you heart
and soul."
8Jonathan said, "Come, then; we will cross
over toward the men and let them see us. 9If
they say to us, 'Wait there until we come to
you,' we will stay where we are and not go
up to them. 10But if they say, 'Come up to
us,' we will climb up, because that will be our
sign that the LORD has given them into our
hands."
11So both of them showed themselves to
the Philistine outpost. "Look!" said the Philistines. "The Hebrews are crawling out of the
holes they were hiding in." 12The men of the
outpost shouted to Jonathan and his armor-
bearer, "Come up to us and we'll teach you
a lesson."
So Jonathan said to his armor-bearer,
"Climb up after me; the LORD has given them
into the hand of Israel."
13Jonathan climbed up, using his hands and
feet, with his armor-bearer right behind him.
The Philistines fell before Jonathan, and his
armor-bearer followed and killed behind him.
14In that first attack Jonathan and his armor-
bearer killed some twenty men in an area of
about half an acre.[g]

---

[a] 9 Traditionally *peace offerings* [b] 15 Hebrew; Septuagint *Gilgal and went his way; the rest of the people went after Saul to meet the army, and they went out of Gilgal* [c] 16 Two Hebrew manuscripts; most Hebrew manuscripts *Geba,* a variant of *Gibeah* [d] 20 Septuagint; Hebrew *plowshares* [e] 21 Hebrew *pim*; that is, about 1/4 ounce (about 8 grams) [f] 21 That is, about 1/8 ounce (about 4 grams) [g] 14 Hebrew *half a yoke*; a "yoke" was the land plowed by a yoke of oxen in one day.

Israel Routs the Philistines

15 Then panic struck the whole army—those in the camp and field, and those in the outposts and raiding parties—and the ground shook. It was a panic sent by God.[a]

16 Saul's lookouts at Gibeah in Benjamin saw the army melting away in all directions. 17 Then Saul said to the men who were with him, "Muster the forces and see who has left us." When they did, it was Jonathan and his armor-bearer who were not there.

18 Saul said to Ahijah, "Bring the ark of God." (At that time it was with the Israelites.)[b] 19 While Saul was talking to the priest, the tumult in the Philistine camp increased more and more. So Saul said to the priest, "Withdraw your hand."

20 Then Saul and all his men assembled and went to the battle. They found the Philistines in total confusion, striking each other with their swords. 21 Those Hebrews who had previously been with the Philistines and had gone up with them to their camp went over to the Israelites who were with Saul and Jonathan. 22 When all the Israelites who had hidden in the hill country of Ephraim heard that the Philistines were on the run, they joined the battle in hot pursuit. 23 So the LORD rescued Israel that day, and the battle moved on beyond Beth Aven.

Jonathan Eats Honey

24 Now the men of Israel were in distress that day, because Saul had bound the people under an oath, saying, "Cursed be any man who eats food before evening comes, before I have avenged myself on my enemies!" So none of the troops tasted food.

25 The entire army[c] entered the woods, and there was honey on the ground. 26 When they went into the woods, they saw the honey oozing out, yet no one put his hand to his mouth, because they feared the oath. 27 But Jonathan had not heard that his father had bound the people with the oath, so he reached out the end of the staff that was in his hand and dipped it into the honeycomb. He raised his hand to his mouth, and his eyes brightened.[d] 28 Then one of the soldiers told him, "Your father bound the army under a strict oath, saying, 'Cursed be any man who eats food today!' That is why the men are faint."

29 Jonathan said, "My father has made trouble for the country. See how my eyes brightened[e] when I tasted a little of this honey. 30 How much better it would have been if the men had eaten today some of the plunder they took from their enemies. Would not the slaughter of the Philistines have been even greater?"

31 That day, after the Israelites had struck down the Philistines from Micmash to Aijalon, they were exhausted. 32 They pounced on the plunder and, taking sheep, cattle and calves, they butchered them on the ground and ate them, together with the blood. 33 Then someone said to Saul, "Look, the men are sinning against the LORD by eating meat that has blood in it."

"You have broken faith," he said. "Roll a large stone over here at once." 34 Then he said, "Go out among the men and tell them, 'Each of you bring me your cattle and sheep, and slaughter them here and eat them. Do not sin against the LORD by eating meat with blood still in it.' "

So everyone brought his ox that night and slaughtered it there. 35 Then Saul built an altar to the LORD; it was the first time he had done this.

36 Saul said, "Let us go down after the Philistines by night and plunder them till dawn, and let us not leave one of them alive."

"Do whatever seems best to you," they replied.

But the priest said, "Let us inquire of God here."

37 So Saul asked God, "Shall I go down after the Philistines? Will you give them into Israel's hand?" But God did not answer him that day.

38 Saul therefore said, "Come here, all you who are leaders of the army, and let us find out what sin has been committed today. 39 As surely as the LORD who rescues Israel lives, even if it lies with my son Jonathan, he must die." But not one of the men said a word.

40 Saul then said to all the Israelites, "You stand over there; I and Jonathan my son will stand over here."

"Do what seems best to you," the men replied.

41 Then Saul prayed to the LORD, the God of Israel, "Give me the right answer."[f] And Jonathan and Saul were taken by lot, and the men were cleared. 42 Saul said, "Cast the lot

---

[a] 15 *Or a terrible panic* [b] 18 Hebrew; Septuagint *"Bring the ephod." (At that time he wore the ephod before the Israelites.)* [c] 25 *Or Now all the people of the land* [d] 27 *Or his strength was renewed* [e] 29 *Or my strength was renewed* [f] 41 Hebrew; Septuagint *"Why have you not answered your servant today? If the fault is in me or my son Jonathan, respond with Urim, but if the men of Israel are at fault, respond with Thummim."*

between me and Jonathan my son." And Jonathan was taken.

43 Then Saul said to Jonathan, "Tell me what you have done."

So Jonathan told him, "I merely tasted a little honey with the end of my staff. And now must I die?"

44 Saul said, "May God deal with me, be it ever so severely, if you do not die, Jonathan."

45 But the men said to Saul, "Should Jonathan die—he who has brought about this great deliverance in Israel? Never! As surely as the LORD lives, not a hair of his head will fall to the ground, for he did this today with God's help." So the men rescued Jonathan, and he was not put to death.

46 Then Saul stopped pursuing the Philistines, and they withdrew to their own land.

47 After Saul had assumed rule over Israel, he fought against their enemies on every side: Moab, the Ammonites, Edom, the kings[a] of Zobah, and the Philistines. Wherever he turned, he inflicted punishment on them.[b] 48 He fought valiantly and defeated the Amalekites, delivering Israel from the hands of those who had plundered them.

Saul's Family

49 Saul's sons were Jonathan, Ishvi and Malki-Shua. The name of his older daughter was Merab, and that of the younger was Michal. 50 His wife's name was Ahinoam daughter of Ahimaaz. The name of the commander of Saul's army was Abner son of Ner, and Ner was Saul's uncle. 51 Saul's father Kish and Abner's father Ner were sons of Abiel.

52 All the days of Saul there was bitter war with the Philistines, and whenever Saul saw a mighty or brave man, he took him into his service.

The LORD Rejects Saul as King

15 Samuel said to Saul, "I am the one the LORD sent to anoint you king over his people Israel; so listen now to the message from the LORD. 2 This is what the LORD Almighty says: 'I will punish the Amalekites for what they did to Israel when they waylaid them as they came up from Egypt. 3 Now go, attack the Amalekites and totally destroy[c] everything that belongs to them. Do not spare them; put to death men and women, children and infants, cattle and sheep, camels and donkeys.' "

4 So Saul summoned the men and mustered them at Telaim—two hundred thousand foot soldiers and ten thousand men from Judah. 5 Saul went to the city of Amalek and set an ambush in the ravine. 6 Then he said to the Kenites, "Go away, leave the Amalekites so that I do not destroy you along with them; for you showed kindness to all the Israelites when they came up out of Egypt." So the Kenites moved away from the Amalekites.

7 Then Saul attacked the Amalekites all the way from Havilah to Shur, to the east of Egypt. 8 He took Agag king of the Amalekites alive, and all his people he totally destroyed with the sword. 9 But Saul and the army spared Agag and the best of the sheep and cattle, the fat calves[d] and lambs—everything that was good. These they were unwilling to destroy completely, but everything that was despised and weak they totally destroyed.

10 Then the word of the LORD came to Samuel: 11 "I am grieved that I have made Saul king, because he has turned away from me and has not carried out my instructions." Samuel was troubled, and he cried out to the LORD all that night.

12 Early in the morning Samuel got up and went to meet Saul, but he was told, "Saul has gone to Carmel. There he has set up a monument in his own honor and has turned and gone on down to Gilgal."

13 When Samuel reached him, Saul said, "The LORD bless you! I have carried out the LORD's instructions."

14 But Samuel said, "What then is this bleating of sheep in my ears? What is this lowing of cattle that I hear?"

15 Saul answered, "The soldiers brought them from the Amalekites; they spared the best of the sheep and cattle to sacrifice to the LORD your God, but we totally destroyed the rest."

16 "Stop!" Samuel said to Saul. "Let me tell you what the LORD said to me last night."

"Tell me," Saul replied.

17 Samuel said, "Although you were once small in your own eyes, did you not become the head of the tribes of Israel? The LORD anointed you king over Israel. 18 And he sent you on a mission, saying, 'Go and completely destroy those wicked people, the Amalekites; make war on them until you have wiped them out.' 19 Why did you not obey the LORD? Why

[a] 47 Masoretic Text; Dead Sea Scrolls and Septuagint *king* [b] 47 Hebrew; Septuagint *he was victorious* [c] 3 The Hebrew term refers to the irrevocable giving over of things or persons to the LORD, often by totally destroying them; also in verses 8, 9, 15, 18, 20 and 21.
[d] 9 Or *the grown bulls*; the meaning of the Hebrew for this phrase is uncertain.

did you pounce on the plunder and do evil in
the eyes of the LORD?"
20"But I did obey the LORD," Saul said. "I
went on the mission the LORD assigned me.
I completely destroyed the Amalekites and
brought back Agag their king. 21The soldiers
took sheep and cattle from the plunder, the
best of what was devoted to God, in order to
sacrifice them to the LORD your God at Gilgal."
22But Samuel replied:

"Does the LORD delight in burnt offerings
and sacrifices
as much as in obeying the voice of the
LORD?
To obey is better than sacrifice,
and to heed is better than the fat of
rams.
23 For rebellion is like the sin of divination,
and arrogance like the evil of idolatry.
Because you have rejected the word of the
LORD,
he has rejected you as king."

24Then Saul said to Samuel, "I have sinned.
I violated the LORD's command and your instructions. I was afraid of the people and so
I gave in to them. 25Now I beg you, forgive
my sin and come back with me, so that I may
worship the LORD."
26But Samuel said to him, "I will not go
back with you. You have rejected the word of
the LORD, and the LORD has rejected you as
king over Israel!"
27As Samuel turned to leave, Saul caught
hold of the hem of his robe, and it tore.
28Samuel said to him, "The LORD has torn the
kingdom of Israel from you today and has giv-
en it to one of your neighbors—to one better
than you. 29He who is the Glory of Israel does
not lie or change his mind; for he is not a man,
that he should change his mind."
30Saul replied, "I have sinned. But please
honor me before the elders of my people and
before Israel; come back with me, so that I
may worship the LORD your God." 31So Samuel went back with Saul, and Saul worshiped
the LORD.
32Then Samuel said, "Bring me Agag king
of the Amalekites."
Agag came to him confidently,[a] thinking,
"Surely the bitterness of death is past."
33But Samuel said,

"As your sword has made women childless,
so will your mother be childless among
women."

And Samuel put Agag to death before the
LORD at Gilgal.
34Then Samuel left for Ramah, but Saul
went up to his home in Gibeah of Saul. 35Un-
til the day Samuel died, he did not go to see
Saul again, though Samuel mourned for him.
And the LORD was grieved that he had made
Saul king over Israel.

Samuel Anoints David

16 The LORD said to Samuel, "How long
will you mourn for Saul, since I have rejected him as king over Israel? Fill your
horn with oil and be on your way; I am sending you to Jesse of Bethlehem. I have chosen
one of his sons to be king."
2But Samuel said, "How can I go? Saul will
hear about it and kill me."
The LORD said, "Take a heifer with you and
say, 'I have come to sacrifice to the LORD.' 3In-
vite Jesse to the sacrifice, and I will show you
what to do. You are to anoint for me the one
I indicate."
4Samuel did what the LORD said. When he
arrived at Bethlehem, the elders of the town
trembled when they met him. They asked,
"Do you come in peace?"
5Samuel replied, "Yes, in peace; I have come
to sacrifice to the LORD. Consecrate yourselves
and come to the sacrifice with me." Then he
consecrated Jesse and his sons and invited
them to the sacrifice.
6When they arrived, Samuel saw Eliab and
thought, "Surely the LORD's anointed stands
here before the LORD."
7But the LORD said to Samuel, "Do not
consider his appearance or his height, for I
have rejected him. The LORD does not look
at the things man looks at. Man looks at the
outward appearance, but the LORD looks at
the heart."
8Then Jesse called Abinadab and had him
pass in front of Samuel. But Samuel said, "The
LORD has not chosen this one either." 9Jesse
then had Shammah pass by, but Samuel said,
"Nor has the LORD chosen this one." 10Jesse
had seven of his sons pass before Samuel, but
Samuel said to him, "The LORD has not chosen these." 11So he asked Jesse, "Are these all
the sons you have?"
"There is still the youngest," Jesse answered,
"but he is tending the sheep."

---

a 32 Or *him trembling, yet*

FRIDAY

READ 1 SAMUEL 16:1–13

WHAT WE SEE IN EACH OTHER

> **"The LORD does not look at the things man looks at. Man looks at the outward appearance, but the LORD looks at the heart."**
> — 1 SAMUEL 16:7

let's *talk*

- What characteristics initially attracted us to each other? What qualities do we treasure most today?
- The blind woman never saw her partner's appearance. Like God, she only saw his heart. Would we rather have people look at our appearance or at our heart? Why?
- What steps are we taking to improve our faith, our character and our commitment to God?

Samuel was sent to the house of Jesse to find a new king. When he got there, Samuel saw Eliab, one of Jesse's sons. "Surely, he is the one God has chosen to be the next king," Samuel thought. Evidently, like the previous king, Saul, Eliab was tall and striking. But Eliab was not the one God had in mind.

God warned Samuel not to assess people by their physical appearance. God reminded the old prophet that he doesn't look at the outside; he looks at the inside. So each of Jesse's sons passed before Samuel, but God did not indicate that any of them was the man God had sent him to find. Finally, David, the youngest son, came in from the fields. Then the Lord spoke to Samuel, telling him this was the right one.

When we look at someone's outward appearance, we often fail to see what God sees. This message was clearly illustrated to John Fisher when he was speaking at a seminar. "A couple came in late, and I could see that they were in love," Fisher said. "I couldn't help but notice the woman was very attractive, while the guy was a real nerd.

"What could she see in him?" Fisher wondered. From the outside, this couple didn't look like a match. "Then I realized she was blind," Fisher said.

"What did she see in him? She saw everything that was important in a person. She saw love. While another woman might not have gotten past this man's unimpressive exterior, she was blind to that. She only saw his heart. Blessed are the blind, for they can see people as they really are."

Like Samuel, we often make judgments based on what people look like. But God doesn't use looks as his criteria. He evaluates people by what's in their hearts. He sees their character, their faithfulness and their commitment to him.

During courtship, we can be charmed by someone's good looks, attentiveness or flattery. All of that can be fleeting. Over the course of a marriage, the real person breaks through. Perhaps as your marriage ages, your spouse's outward appearance starts to change. Your spouse grays, loses hair or gains a little weight. Perhaps the two of you fall into a rut, and the special treatment that marked your dating period begins to wane. That's when we need to remember what the Lord said to Samuel about focusing on what's in the heart rather than what's physically noticeable.

The success of a marriage comes, not in finding who we think initially is the "perfect" person for us, but in our willingness to adjust to the real person we married.

—JENNIFER SCHUCHMANN

FOR YOUR NEXT DEVOTIONAL READING, TURN TO PAGE 304.

Samuel said, "Send for him; we will not sit
down[a] until he arrives."
12So he sent and had him brought in. He
was ruddy, with a fine appearance and handsome features.
Then the LORD said, "Rise and anoint him;
he is the one."
13So Samuel took the horn of oil and
anointed him in the presence of his brothers,
and from that day on the Spirit of the LORD
came upon David in power. Samuel then went
to Ramah.

David in Saul's Service

14Now the Spirit of the LORD had departed
from Saul, and an evil[b] spirit from the LORD
tormented him.
15Saul's attendants said to him, "See, an evil
spirit from God is tormenting you. 16Let our
lord command his servants here to search for
someone who can play the harp. He will play
when the evil spirit from God comes upon
you, and you will feel better."
17So Saul said to his attendants, "Find someone who plays well and bring him to me."
18One of the servants answered, "I have
seen a son of Jesse of Bethlehem who knows
how to play the harp. He is a brave man and
a warrior. He speaks well and is a fine-looking
man. And the LORD is with him."
19Then Saul sent messengers to Jesse and
said, "Send me your son David, who is with
the sheep." 20So Jesse took a donkey loaded
with bread, a skin of wine and a young goat
and sent them with his son David to Saul.
21David came to Saul and entered his service. Saul liked him very much, and David
became one of his armor-bearers. 22Then Saul
sent word to Jesse, saying, "Allow David to
remain in my service, for I am pleased with
him."
23Whenever the spirit from God came upon
Saul, David would take his harp and play.
Then relief would come to Saul; he would feel
better, and the evil spirit would leave him.

David and Goliath

17 Now the Philistines gathered their forces for war and assembled at Socoh in Judah. They pitched camp at Ephes Dammim, between Socoh and Azekah. 2Saul and
the Israelites assembled and camped in the
Valley of Elah and drew up their battle line
to meet the Philistines. 3The Philistines occupied one hill and the Israelites another, with
the valley between them.
4A champion named Goliath, who was
from Gath, came out of the Philistine camp.
He was over nine feet[c] tall. 5He had a bronze
helmet on his head and wore a coat of scale
armor of bronze weighing five thousand shekels[d]; 6on his legs he wore bronze greaves, and
a bronze javelin was slung on his back. 7His
spear shaft was like a weaver's rod, and its
iron point weighed six hundred shekels.[e] His
shield bearer went ahead of him.
8Goliath stood and shouted to the ranks of
Israel, "Why do you come out and line up for
battle? Am I not a Philistine, and are you not
the servants of Saul? Choose a man and have
him come down to me. 9If he is able to fight
and kill me, we will become your subjects; but
if I overcome him and kill him, you will become our subjects and serve us." 10Then the
Philistine said, "This day I defy the ranks of
Israel! Give me a man and let us fight each
other." 11On hearing the Philistine's words,
Saul and all the Israelites were dismayed and
terrified.
12Now David was the son of an Ephrath-
ite named Jesse, who was from Bethlehem in
Judah. Jesse had eight sons, and in Saul's time
he was old and well advanced in years. 13Jesse's
three oldest sons had followed Saul to the war:
The firstborn was Eliab; the second, Abinadab; and the third, Shammah. 14David was
the youngest. The three oldest followed Saul,
15but David went back and forth from Saul to
tend his father's sheep at Bethlehem.
16For forty days the Philistine came forward every morning and evening and took his
stand.
17Now Jesse said to his son David, "Take
this ephah[f] of roasted grain and these ten
loaves of bread for your brothers and hurry to
their camp. 18Take along these ten cheeses to
the commander of their unit.[g] See how your
brothers are and bring back some assurance[h]
from them. 19They are with Saul and all the
men of Israel in the Valley of Elah, fighting
against the Philistines."
20Early in the morning David left the flock
with a shepherd, loaded up and set out, as Jesse had directed. He reached the camp as the
army was going out to its battle positions,
shouting the war cry. 21Israel and the Philis-

---

[a] 11 Some Septuagint manuscripts; Hebrew *not gather around* [b] 14 Or *injurious;* also in verses 15, 16 and 23 [c] 4 Hebrew *was six cubits and a span* (about 3 meters) [d] 5 That is, about 125 pounds (about 57 kilograms) [e] 7 That is, about 15 pounds (about 7 kilograms) [f] 17 That is, probably about 3/5 bushel (about 22 liters) [g] 18 Hebrew *thousand* [h] 18 Or *some token;* or *some pledge of spoils*

tines were drawing up their lines facing each
other. 22David left his things with the keeper
of supplies, ran to the battle lines and greeted
his brothers. 23As he was talking with them,
Goliath, the Philistine champion from Gath,
stepped out from his lines and shouted his
usual defiance, and David heard it. 24When
the Israelites saw the man, they all ran from
him in great fear.

25Now the Israelites had been saying, "Do
you see how this man keeps coming out? He
comes out to defy Israel. The king will give
great wealth to the man who kills him. He
will also give him his daughter in marriage
and will exempt his father's family from taxes
in Israel."

26David asked the men standing near him,
"What will be done for the man who kills this
Philistine and removes this disgrace from Israel? Who is this uncircumcised Philistine that
he should defy the armies of the living God?"

27They repeated to him what they had been
saying and told him, "This is what will be
done for the man who kills him."

28When Eliab, David's oldest brother, heard
him speaking with the men, he burned with
anger at him and asked, "Why have you come
down here? And with whom did you leave
those few sheep in the desert? I know how
conceited you are and how wicked your heart
is; you came down only to watch the battle."

29"Now what have I done?" said David.
"Can't I even speak?" 30He then turned away
to someone else and brought up the same
matter, and the men answered him as before.
31What David said was overheard and reported to Saul, and Saul sent for him.

32David said to Saul, "Let no one lose heart
on account of this Philistine; your servant will
go and fight him."

33Saul replied, "You are not able to go out
against this Philistine and fight him; you are
only a boy, and he has been a fighting man
from his youth."

34But David said to Saul, "Your servant has
been keeping his father's sheep. When a lion
or a bear came and carried off a sheep from the
flock, 35I went after it, struck it and rescued
the sheep from its mouth. When it turned on
me, I seized it by its hair, struck it and killed it.
36Your servant has killed both the lion and the
bear; this uncircumcised Philistine will be like
one of them, because he has defied the armies
of the living God. 37The LORD who delivered
me from the paw of the lion and the paw of
the bear will deliver me from the hand of this
Philistine."

Saul said to David, "Go, and the LORD be
with you."

38Then Saul dressed David in his own tunic. He put a coat of armor on him and a
bronze helmet on his head. 39David fastened
on his sword over the tunic and tried walking
around, because he was not used to them.

"I cannot go in these," he said to Saul,
"because I am not used to them." So he took
them off. 40Then he took his staff in his hand,
chose five smooth stones from the stream, put
them in the pouch of his shepherd's bag and,
with his sling in his hand, approached the Philistine.

41Meanwhile, the Philistine, with his shield
bearer in front of him, kept coming closer to
David. 42He looked David over and saw that
he was only a boy, ruddy and handsome, and
he despised him. 43He said to David, "Am I a
dog, that you come at me with sticks?" And the
Philistine cursed David by his gods. 44"Come
here," he said, "and I'll give your flesh to the
birds of the air and the beasts of the field!"

45David said to the Philistine, "You come
against me with sword and spear and javelin, but I come against you in the name of
the LORD Almighty, the God of the armies
of Israel, whom you have defied. 46This day
the LORD will hand you over to me, and I'll
strike you down and cut off your head. Today I will give the carcasses of the Philistine
army to the birds of the air and the beasts
of the earth, and the whole world will know
that there is a God in Israel. 47All those gathered here will know that it is not by sword
or spear that the LORD saves; for the battle
is the LORD's, and he will give all of you into
our hands."

48As the Philistine moved closer to attack
him, David ran quickly toward the battle line
to meet him. 49Reaching into his bag and taking out a stone, he slung it and struck the Philistine on the forehead. The stone sank into
his forehead, and he fell facedown on the
ground.

50So David triumphed over the Philistine
with a sling and a stone; without a sword in
his hand he struck down the Philistine and
killed him.

51David ran and stood over him. He took
hold of the Philistine's sword and drew it from
the scabbard. After he killed him, he cut off
his head with the sword.

When the Philistines saw that their hero was
dead, they turned and ran. 52Then the men of
Israel and Judah surged forward with a shout
and pursued the Philistines to the entrance of

Gath[a] and to the gates of Ekron. Their dead
were strewn along the Shaaraim road to Gath
and Ekron. 53When the Israelites returned
from chasing the Philistines, they plundered
their camp. 54David took the Philistine's head
and brought it to Jerusalem, and he put the
Philistine's weapons in his own tent.
55As Saul watched David going out to meet
the Philistine, he said to Abner, commander
of the army, "Abner, whose son is that young
man?"

Abner replied, "As surely as you live,
O king, I don't know."
56The king said, "Find out whose son this
young man is."
57As soon as David returned from killing
the Philistine, Abner took him and brought
him before Saul, with David still holding the
Philistine's head.
58"Whose son are you, young man?" Saul
asked him.

David said, "I am the son of your servant
Jesse of Bethlehem."

Saul's Jealousy of David

18 After David had finished talking with
Saul, Jonathan became one in spirit with
David, and he loved him as himself.
2From that day Saul kept David with him and
did not let him return to his father's house.
3And Jonathan made a covenant with David
because he loved him as himself. 4Jonathan
took off the robe he was wearing and gave it
to David, along with his tunic, and even his
sword, his bow and his belt.
5Whatever Saul sent him to do, David did
it so successfully[b] that Saul gave him a high
rank in the army. This pleased all the people,
and Saul's officers as well.
6When the men were returning home after David had killed the Philistine, the women
came out from all the towns of Israel to meet
King Saul with singing and dancing, with joyful songs and with tambourines and lutes. 7As
they danced, they sang:

"Saul has slain his thousands,
and David his tens of thousands."

8Saul was very angry; this refrain galled
him. "They have credited David with tens of
thousands," he thought, "but me with only
thousands. What more can he get but the
kingdom?" 9And from that time on Saul kept
a jealous eye on David.
10The next day an evil[c] spirit from God
came forcefully upon Saul. He was prophesying in his house, while David was playing the
harp, as he usually did. Saul had a spear in
his hand 11and he hurled it, saying to himself,
"I'll pin David to the wall." But David eluded
him twice.
12Saul was afraid of David, because the
LORD was with David but had left Saul. 13So
he sent David away from him and gave him
command over a thousand men, and David
led the troops in their campaigns. 14In everything he did he had great success,[d] because the
LORD was with him. 15When Saul saw how
successful[e] he was, he was afraid of him. 16But
all Israel and Judah loved David, because he
led them in their campaigns.
17Saul said to David, "Here is my older daughter Merab. I will give her to you in
marriage; only serve me bravely and fight the
battles of the LORD." For Saul said to himself,
"I will not raise a hand against him. Let the
Philistines do that!"
18But David said to Saul, "Who am I, and
what is my family or my father's clan in Israel,
that I should become the king's son-in-law?"
19So[f] when the time came for Merab, Saul's
daughter, to be given to David, she was given
in marriage to Adriel of Meholah.
20Now Saul's daughter Michal was in love
with David, and when they told Saul about it,
he was pleased. 21"I will give her to him," he
thought, "so that she may be a snare to him
and so that the hand of the Philistines may
be against him." So Saul said to David, "Now
you have a second opportunity to become my
son-in-law."
22Then Saul ordered his attendants: "Speak
to David privately and say, 'Look, the king is
pleased with you, and his attendants all like
you; now become his son-in-law.' "
23They repeated these words to David. But
David said, "Do you think it is a small matter
to become the king's son-in-law? I'm only a
poor man and little known."
24When Saul's servants told him what David
had said, 25Saul replied, "Say to David, 'The
king wants no other price for the bride than a
hundred Philistine foreskins, to take revenge
on his enemies.' " Saul's plan was to have David fall by the hands of the Philistines.
26When the attendants told David these
things, he was pleased to become the king's
son-in-law. So before the allotted time
elapsed, 27David and his men went out and
killed two hundred Philistines. He brought

[a] 52 Some Septuagint manuscripts; Hebrew *a valley* [b] 5 Or *wisely* [c] 10 Or *injurious* [d] 14 Or *he was very wise* [e] 15 Or *wise*
[f] 19 Or *However,*

their foreskins and presented the full number to the king so that he might become the king's son-in-law. Then Saul gave him his daughter Michal in marriage.

28When Saul realized that the LORD was with David and that his daughter Michal loved David, 29Saul became still more afraid of him, and he remained his enemy the rest of his days.

30The Philistine commanders continued to go out to battle, and as often as they did, David met with more success[a] than the rest of Saul's officers, and his name became well known.

Saul Tries to Kill David

19 Saul told his son Jonathan and all the attendants to kill David. But Jonathan was very fond of David 2and warned him, "My father Saul is looking for a chance to kill you. Be on your guard tomorrow morning; go into hiding and stay there. 3I will go out and stand with my father in the field where you are. I'll speak to him about you and will tell you what I find out."

4Jonathan spoke well of David to Saul his father and said to him, "Let not the king do wrong to his servant David; he has not wronged you, and what he has done has benefited you greatly. 5He took his life in his hands when he killed the Philistine. The LORD won a great victory for all Israel, and you saw it and were glad. Why then would you do wrong to an innocent man like David by killing him for no reason?"

6Saul listened to Jonathan and took this oath: "As surely as the LORD lives, David will not be put to death."

7So Jonathan called David and told him the whole conversation. He brought him to Saul, and David was with Saul as before.

8Once more war broke out, and David went out and fought the Philistines. He struck them with such force that they fled before him.

9But an evil[b] spirit from the LORD came upon Saul as he was sitting in his house with his spear in his hand. While David was playing the harp, 10Saul tried to pin him to the wall with his spear, but David eluded him as Saul drove the spear into the wall. That night David made good his escape.

11Saul sent men to David's house to watch it and to kill him in the morning. But Michal, David's wife, warned him, "If you don't run for your life tonight, tomorrow you'll be killed." 12So Michal let David down through a window, and he fled and escaped. 13Then Michal took an idol[c] and laid it on the bed, covering it with a garment and putting some goats' hair at the head.

14When Saul sent the men to capture David, Michal said, "He is ill."

15Then Saul sent the men back to see David and told them, "Bring him up to me in his bed so that I may kill him." 16But when the men entered, there was the idol in the bed, and at the head was some goats' hair.

17Saul said to Michal, "Why did you deceive me like this and send my enemy away so that he escaped?"

Michal told him, "He said to me, 'Let me get away. Why should I kill you?' "

18When David had fled and made his escape, he went to Samuel at Ramah and told him all that Saul had done to him. Then he and Samuel went to Naioth and stayed there. 19Word came to Saul: "David is in Naioth at Ramah"; 20so he sent men to capture him. But when they saw a group of prophets prophesying, with Samuel standing there as their leader, the Spirit of God came upon Saul's men and they also prophesied. 21Saul was told about it, and he sent more men, and they prophesied too. Saul sent men a third time, and they also prophesied. 22Finally, he himself left for Ramah and went to the great cistern at Secu. And he asked, "Where are Samuel and David?"

"Over in Naioth at Ramah," they said.

23So Saul went to Naioth at Ramah. But the Spirit of God came even upon him, and he walked along prophesying until he came to Naioth. 24He stripped off his robes and also prophesied in Samuel's presence. He lay that way all that day and night. This is why people say, "Is Saul also among the prophets?"

David and Jonathan

20 Then David fled from Naioth at Ramah and went to Jonathan and asked, "What have I done? What is my crime? How have I wronged your father, that he is trying to take my life?"

2"Never!" Jonathan replied. "You are not going to die! Look, my father doesn't do anything, great or small, without confiding in me. Why would he hide this from me? It's not so!"

3But David took an oath and said, "Your father knows very well that I have found favor in your eyes, and he has said to himself, 'Jona-

[a] 30 Or *David acted more wisely* [b] 9 Or *injurious* [c] 13 Hebrew *teraphim*; also in verse 16

WEEKEND

becoming best friends

Larry and Lannie were in a counselor's office getting help with their marriage. They were discussing how they tended to treat other people better than each other.

"A perfect example of what we're talking about happened the other night," Lannie began with tears welling up in her eyes. "When we finished dinner at Elaine's house, you got up from the table, helped clear the dishes, and then offered to rinse everything. Elaine said to me later, 'Larry certainly is a wonderful husband. I hope you know how fortunate you are.' "

Lannie said it hurt her deeply that Larry would act like the perfect, concerned, helpful husband when others were watching, but that he hadn't touched a dish or helped clear the table in their own house for over ten years. When Larry responded defensively that he would try to be more helpful at home, Lannie said, "That's not the point. I'm not talking about getting you to be more helpful at home. I'm saying that it hurt me to see you go out of your way to help someone else, but you wouldn't do those things for me. You were considerate of Elaine's needs and not of mine."

It's common. We're on our best behavior when we're out in public. Larry had developed a habit of showing concern for other people and their feelings, but he was no longer working on the relationships in his home.

Being a friend to each other requires decisive action. It necessitates asking oneself questions like, "How can I help this person that I love?" Of course, this applies not just to the big things in life, but also to the little day-to-day things such as dishes, or whatever those little special gestures happen to be.

Gestures of friendship are different for each person. At its best, a gesture of friendship is something that doesn't cost much but has a significant ingredient. It's out of the giver's comfort zone or thinking range. In other words, it's a gesture that the giver would not automatically do or necessarily want in return.

After several counseling sessions Larry and Lannie came into the office, and Lannie announced, "This has been the best week we've had in years! Larry bought me two cards this week that were very affectionate, and he mailed them from his office."

When I asked Larry how he felt about Lannie's reaction to his cards he said, "To tell you the truth, I was shocked at how much they meant to her. After all, these were two cards written by some poet and printed by the thousands. Yet she loved them. I'm sure glad I picked out the right ones!"

"It's not the words in the cards, silly," Lannie said. "It's that you went out of your way to get them for me. I know that cards don't mean much to you, but you got them for me because they mean a lot to me. It's what they represent . . . that you're trying to be my friend."

—ROBERT AND ROSEMARY BARNES

marks of a friend

Deciding to be a friend to your spouse means breaking old lazy habits of taking your spouse and your relationship for granted. Go through the following list, deciding which show the true marks of a friend.

1. You ask what you can do to help with dinner.
2. You tell me I should start working out.
3. You join a book club with me.
4. You take me to a football game.
5. You tell me what I should eat in a restaurant.
6. You go with me to visit a friend in the hospital.
7. You go to bed when I do.
8. You're a morning person, and I'm not, so you make coffee and offer me a cup before making conversation.
9. You switch channels while I'm watching TV.
10. You ask me what I did today and then zone out.
11. You come to me for advice.
12. You tell me how great I look.
13. You tell me my pants are too tight.
14. You're always glad to see me.
15. You sense when I'm upset and ask what's wrong.
16. You plan a huge surprise birthday party for me.
17. You don't have a clue about what I do at work.
18. You wait up for me when I'm out late and then grill me.
19. You change plans if I need you.
20. You pick me up from the airport.

HOW ARE WE DOING?

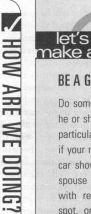

let's make a DATE

BE A GOOD FRIEND

Do something for your spouse that he or she enjoys but that you don't particularly like doing. For example, if your mate enjoys old cars, find a car show to go to. Or maybe your spouse loves sushi. Surprise her with reservations at her favorite spot, or bring home some ready-made sushi for lunch. As you're enjoying your partner's activity, ask him or her about it. What about cars does he like? Which models are his favorite and why? If money were no object, what would he own? What kind of sushi has she tried? What's her favorite? What makes eating at a Japanese restaurant special? Ask each other questions and listen to the answers as if you're finding out about each other for the first time.

FOR YOUR NEXT DEVOTIONAL READING, TURN TO PAGE 311.

LESSONS FROM THE *Bible*

David and Jonathan were best friends. Read their story in 1 Samuel 18:1–4 and 1 Samuel 19–20. What did they do for each other that showed the depth of their friendship? How can their story motivate us to become better friends?

than must not know this or he will be grieved.'
Yet as surely as the LORD lives and as you live,
there is only a step between me and death."
[4]Jonathan said to David, "Whatever you
want me to do, I'll do for you."
[5]So David said, "Look, tomorrow is the
New Moon festival, and I am supposed to
dine with the king; but let me go and hide
in the field until the evening of the day after
tomorrow. [6]If your father misses me at all, tell
him, 'David earnestly asked my permission to
hurry to Bethlehem, his hometown, because
an annual sacrifice is being made there for his
whole clan.' [7]If he says, 'Very well,' then your
servant is safe. But if he loses his temper, you
can be sure that he is determined to harm me.
[8]As for you, show kindness to your servant,
for you have brought him into a covenant
with you before the LORD. If I am guilty, then
kill me yourself! Why hand me over to your
father?"
[9]"Never!" Jonathan said. "If I had the least
inkling that my father was determined to
harm you, wouldn't I tell you?"
[10]David asked, "Who will tell me if your
father answers you harshly?"
[11]"Come," Jonathan said, "let's go out into
the field." So they went there together.
[12]Then Jonathan said to David: "By the
LORD, the God of Israel, I will surely sound
out my father by this time the day after tomorrow! If he is favorably disposed toward
you, will I not send you word and let you
know? [13]But if my father is inclined to harm
you, may the LORD deal with me, be it ever so
severely, if I do not let you know and send you
away safely. May the LORD be with you as he
has been with my father. [14]But show me unfailing kindness like that of the LORD as long
as I live, so that I may not be killed, [15]and do
not ever cut off your kindness from my family—not even when the LORD has cut off every
one of David's enemies from the face of the
earth."
[16]So Jonathan made a covenant with the
house of David, saying, "May the LORD call
David's enemies to account." [17]And Jonathan
had David reaffirm his oath out of love for
him, because he loved him as he loved himself.
[18]Then Jonathan said to David: "Tomorrow
is the New Moon festival. You will be missed,
because your seat will be empty. [19]The day after tomorrow, toward evening, go to the place
where you hid when this trouble began, and
wait by the stone Ezel. [20]I will shoot three arrows to the side of it, as though I were shooting at a target. [21]Then I will send a boy and
say, 'Go, find the arrows.' If I say to him,
'Look, the arrows are on this side of you; bring
them here,' then come, because, as surely as
the LORD lives, you are safe; there is no danger.
[22]But if I say to the boy, 'Look, the arrows are
beyond you,' then you must go, because the
LORD has sent you away. [23]And about the matter you and I discussed—remember, the LORD
is witness between you and me forever."
[24]So David hid in the field, and when the
New Moon festival came, the king sat down
to eat. [25]He sat in his customary place by the
wall, opposite Jonathan,[a] and Abner sat next
to Saul, but David's place was empty. [26]Saul
said nothing that day, for he thought, "Something must have happened to David to make
him ceremonially unclean—surely he is unclean." [27]But the next day, the second day of
the month, David's place was empty again.
Then Saul said to his son Jonathan, "Why
hasn't the son of Jesse come to the meal, either
yesterday or today?"
[28]Jonathan answered, "David earnestly
asked me for permission to go to Bethlehem.
[29]He said, 'Let me go, because our family
is observing a sacrifice in the town and my
brother has ordered me to be there. If I have
found favor in your eyes, let me get away to
see my brothers.' That is why he has not come
to the king's table."
[30]Saul's anger flared up at Jonathan and he
said to him, "You son of a perverse and rebellious woman! Don't I know that you have
sided with the son of Jesse to your own shame
and to the shame of the mother who bore you?
[31]As long as the son of Jesse lives on this earth,
neither you nor your kingdom will be established. Now send and bring him to me, for
he must die!"
[32]"Why should he be put to death? What
has he done?" Jonathan asked his father. [33]But
Saul hurled his spear at him to kill him. Then
Jonathan knew that his father intended to kill
David.
[34]Jonathan got up from the table in fierce
anger; on that second day of the month he did
not eat, because he was grieved at his father's
shameful treatment of David.
[35]In the morning Jonathan went out to the
field for his meeting with David. He had a
small boy with him, [36]and he said to the boy,
"Run and find the arrows I shoot." As the boy

[a] 25 Septuagint; Hebrew *wall. Jonathan arose*

ran, he shot an arrow beyond him. 37When
the boy came to the place where Jonathan's
arrow had fallen, Jonathan called out after
him, "Isn't the arrow beyond you?" 38Then he
shouted, "Hurry! Go quickly! Don't stop!" The
boy picked up the arrow and returned to his
master. 39(The boy knew nothing of all this;
only Jonathan and David knew.) 40Then Jonathan gave his weapons to the boy and said,
"Go, carry them back to town."

41After the boy had gone, David got up
from the south side ⌞of the stone⌟ and bowed
down before Jonathan three times, with his
face to the ground. Then they kissed each other and wept together—but David wept the
most.

42Jonathan said to David, "Go in peace,
for we have sworn friendship with each other
in the name of the LORD, saying, 'The LORD
is witness between you and me, and between
your descendants and my descendants forever.' " Then David left, and Jonathan went back
to the town.

David at Nob

21 David went to Nob, to Ahimelech the
priest. Ahimelech trembled when he
met him, and asked, "Why are you
alone? Why is no one with you?"

2David answered Ahimelech the priest,
"The king charged me with a certain matter
and said to me, 'No one is to know anything
about your mission and your instructions.'
As for my men, I have told them to meet me
at a certain place. 3Now then, what do you
have on hand? Give me five loaves of bread, or
whatever you can find."

4But the priest answered David, "I don't
have any ordinary bread on hand; however,
there is some consecrated bread here—provided the men have kept themselves from
women."

5David replied, "Indeed women have been
kept from us, as usual whenever[a] I set out.
The men's things[b] are holy even on missions
that are not holy. How much more so today!"
6So the priest gave him the consecrated bread,
since there was no bread there except the bread
of the Presence that had been removed from
before the LORD and replaced by hot bread on
the day it was taken away.

7Now one of Saul's servants was there that
day, detained before the LORD; he was Doeg
the Edomite, Saul's head shepherd.

8David asked Ahimelech, "Don't you have
a spear or a sword here? I haven't brought my
sword or any other weapon, because the king's
business was urgent."

9The priest replied, "The sword of Goliath
the Philistine, whom you killed in the Valley
of Elah, is here; it is wrapped in a cloth behind
the ephod. If you want it, take it; there is no
sword here but that one."

David said, "There is none like it; give it
to me."

David at Gath

10That day David fled from Saul and went
to Achish king of Gath. 11But the servants of
Achish said to him, "Isn't this David, the king
of the land? Isn't he the one they sing about in
their dances:

" 'Saul has slain his thousands,
and David his tens of thousands'?"

12David took these words to heart and was
very much afraid of Achish king of Gath. 13So
he pretended to be insane in their presence;
and while he was in their hands he acted like
a madman, making marks on the doors of the
gate and letting saliva run down his beard.

14Achish said to his servants, "Look at the
man! He is insane! Why bring him to me?
15Am I so short of madmen that you have
to bring this fellow here to carry on like this
in front of me? Must this man come into my
house?"

David at Adullam and Mizpah

22 David left Gath and escaped to the cave
of Adullam. When his brothers and his
father's household heard about it, they
went down to him there. 2All those who were
in distress or in debt or discontented gathered around him, and he became their leader.
About four hundred men were with him.

3From there David went to Mizpah in
Moab and said to the king of Moab, "Would
you let my father and mother come and stay
with you until I learn what God will do for
me?" 4So he left them with the king of Moab,
and they stayed with him as long as David was
in the stronghold.

5But the prophet Gad said to David, "Do
not stay in the stronghold. Go into the land
of Judah." So David left and went to the forest
of Hereth.

Saul Kills the Priests of Nob

6Now Saul heard that David and his men

---

[a] 5 Or *from us in the past few days since* [b] 5 Or *bodies*

had been discovered. And Saul, spear in
hand, was seated under the tamarisk tree on
the hill at Gibeah, with all his officials standing around him. [7]Saul said to them, "Listen,
men of Benjamin! Will the son of Jesse give
all of you fields and vineyards? Will he make
all of you commanders of thousands and
commanders of hundreds? [8]Is that why you
have all conspired against me? No one tells
me when my son makes a covenant with the
son of Jesse. None of you is concerned about
me or tells me that my son has incited my
servant to lie in wait for me, as he does today."
[9]But Doeg the Edomite, who was standing
with Saul's officials, said, "I saw the son of Jesse come to Ahimelech son of Ahitub at Nob.
[10]Ahimelech inquired of the LORD for him; he
also gave him provisions and the sword of Goliath the Philistine."
[11]Then the king sent for the priest Ahimelech son of Ahitub and his father's whole family, who were the priests at Nob, and they all
came to the king. [12]Saul said, "Listen now, son
of Ahitub."
"Yes, my lord," he answered.
[13]Saul said to him, "Why have you conspired against me, you and the son of Jesse,
giving him bread and a sword and inquiring of God for him, so that he has rebelled
against me and lies in wait for me, as he does
today?"
[14]Ahimelech answered the king, "Who of
all your servants is as loyal as David, the king's
son-in-law, captain of your bodyguard and
highly respected in your household? [15]Was
that day the first time I inquired of God for
him? Of course not! Let not the king accuse
your servant or any of his father's family, for
your servant knows nothing at all about this
whole affair."
[16]But the king said, "You will surely die,
Ahimelech, you and your father's whole family."
[17]Then the king ordered the guards at his
side: "Turn and kill the priests of the LORD,
because they too have sided with David.
They knew he was fleeing, yet they did not
tell me."
But the king's officials were not willing to
raise a hand to strike the priests of the LORD.
[18]The king then ordered Doeg, "You turn
and strike down the priests." So Doeg the
Edomite turned and struck them down. That
day he killed eighty-five men who wore the
linen ephod. [19]He also put to the sword Nob,
the town of the priests, with its men and
women, its children and infants, and its cattle,
donkeys and sheep.
[20]But Abiathar, a son of Ahimelech son of
Ahitub, escaped and fled to join David. [21]He
told David that Saul had killed the priests
of the LORD. [22]Then David said to Abiathar: "That day, when Doeg the Edomite was
there, I knew he would be sure to tell Saul. I
am responsible for the death of your father's
whole family. [23]Stay with me; don't be afraid;
the man who is seeking your life is seeking
mine also. You will be safe with me."

David Saves Keilah

23 When David was told, "Look, the Philistines are fighting against Keilah and
are looting the threshing floors," [2]he inquired of the LORD, saying, "Shall I go and
attack these Philistines?"
The LORD answered him, "Go, attack the
Philistines and save Keilah."
[3]But David's men said to him, "Here in Judah we are afraid. How much more, then, if
we go to Keilah against the Philistine forces!"
[4]Once again David inquired of the LORD,
and the LORD answered him, "Go down to
Keilah, for I am going to give the Philistines
into your hand." [5]So David and his men went
to Keilah, fought the Philistines and carried
off their livestock. He inflicted heavy losses
on the Philistines and saved the people of Keilah. [6](Now Abiathar son of Ahimelech had
brought the ephod down with him when he
fled to David at Keilah.)

Saul Pursues David

[7]Saul was told that David had gone to Keilah, and he said, "God has handed him over to
me, for David has imprisoned himself by entering a town with gates and bars." [8]And Saul
called up all his forces for battle, to go down to
Keilah to besiege David and his men.
[9]When David learned that Saul was plotting against him, he said to Abiathar the
priest, "Bring the ephod." [10]David said,
"O LORD, God of Israel, your servant has
heard definitely that Saul plans to come to
Keilah and destroy the town on account of
me. [11]Will the citizens of Keilah surrender
me to him? Will Saul come down, as your
servant has heard? O LORD, God of Israel,
tell your servant."
And the LORD said, "He will."
[12]Again David asked, "Will the citizens of
Keilah surrender me and my men to Saul?"
And the LORD said, "They will."
[13]So David and his men, about six hun-

dred in number, left Keilah and kept moving
from place to place. When Saul was told that
David had escaped from Keilah, he did not
go there.
14David stayed in the desert strongholds
and in the hills of the Desert of Ziph. Day
after day Saul searched for him, but God did
not give David into his hands.
15While David was at Horesh in the Desert of Ziph, he learned that Saul had come
out to take his life. 16And Saul's son Jonathan
went to David at Horesh and helped him find
strength in God. 17"Don't be afraid," he said.
"My father Saul will not lay a hand on you.
You will be king over Israel, and I will be second to you. Even my father Saul knows this."
18The two of them made a covenant before the
LORD. Then Jonathan went home, but David
remained at Horesh.
19The Ziphites went up to Saul at Gibeah
and said, "Is not David hiding among us in
the strongholds at Horesh, on the hill of Hakilah, south of Jeshimon? 20Now, O king, come
down whenever it pleases you to do so, and
we will be responsible for handing him over
to the king."
21Saul replied, "The LORD bless you for your
concern for me. 22Go and make further preparation. Find out where David usually goes
and who has seen him there. They tell me he
is very crafty. 23Find out about all the hiding
places he uses and come back to me with definite information.[a] Then I will go with you; if
he is in the area, I will track him down among
all the clans of Judah."
24So they set out and went to Ziph ahead
of Saul. Now David and his men were in the
Desert of Maon, in the Arabah south of Jeshimon. 25Saul and his men began the search,
and when David was told about it, he went
down to the rock and stayed in the Desert of
Maon. When Saul heard this, he went into the
Desert of Maon in pursuit of David.
26Saul was going along one side of the
mountain, and David and his men were on
the other side, hurrying to get away from
Saul. As Saul and his forces were closing in on
David and his men to capture them, 27a messenger came to Saul, saying, "Come quickly!
The Philistines are raiding the land." 28Then
Saul broke off his pursuit of David and went
to meet the Philistines. That is why they call
this place Sela Hammahlekoth.[b] 29And David
went up from there and lived in the strongholds of En Gedi.

David Spares Saul's Life

24 After Saul returned from pursuing the
Philistines, he was told, "David is in the
Desert of En Gedi." 2So Saul took three
thousand chosen men from all Israel and set
out to look for David and his men near the
Crags of the Wild Goats.
3He came to the sheep pens along the way;
a cave was there, and Saul went in to relieve
himself. David and his men were far back in
the cave. 4The men said, "This is the day the
LORD spoke of when he said[c] to you, 'I will
give your enemy into your hands for you to
deal with as you wish.' " Then David crept up
unnoticed and cut off a corner of Saul's robe.
5Afterward, David was conscience-strick-
en for having cut off a corner of his robe.
6He said to his men, "The LORD forbid that
I should do such a thing to my master, the
LORD's anointed, or lift my hand against him;
for he is the anointed of the LORD." 7With
these words David rebuked his men and did
not allow them to attack Saul. And Saul left
the cave and went his way.
8Then David went out of the cave and
called out to Saul, "My lord the king!" When
Saul looked behind him, David bowed down
and prostrated himself with his face to the
ground. 9He said to Saul, "Why do you listen when men say, 'David is bent on harming you'? 10This day you have seen with your
own eyes how the LORD delivered you into
my hands in the cave. Some urged me to kill
you, but I spared you; I said, 'I will not lift
my hand against my master, because he is the
LORD's anointed.' 11See, my father, look at
this piece of your robe in my hand! I cut off
the corner of your robe but did not kill you.
Now understand and recognize that I am not
guilty of wrongdoing or rebellion. I have not
wronged you, but you are hunting me down
to take my life. 12May the LORD judge between you and me. And may the LORD avenge
the wrongs you have done to me, but my hand
will not touch you. 13As the old saying goes,
'From evildoers come evil deeds,' so my hand
will not touch you.
14"Against whom has the king of Israel
come out? Whom are you pursuing? A dead
dog? A flea? 15May the LORD be our judge and
decide between us. May he consider my cause
and uphold it; may he vindicate me by delivering me from your hand."
16When David finished saying this, Saul
asked, "Is that your voice, David my son?"

---

[a] 23 Or *me at Nacon* [b] 28 *Sela Hammahlekoth* means *rock of parting.* [c] 4 Or *"Today the LORD is saying*

And he wept aloud. 17“You are more righteous
than I,” he said. “You have treated me well,
but I have treated you badly. 18You have just
now told me of the good you did to me; the
LORD delivered me into your hands, but you
did not kill me. 19When a man finds his enemy, does he let him get away unharmed? May
the LORD reward you well for the way you
treated me today. 20I know that you will surely
be king and that the kingdom of Israel will
be established in your hands. 21Now swear to
me by the LORD that you will not cut off my
descendants or wipe out my name from my
father’s family.”

22So David gave his oath to Saul. Then Saul
returned home, but David and his men went
up to the stronghold.

David, Nabal and Abigail

25 Now Samuel died, and all Israel assembled and mourned for him; and they
buried him at his home in Ramah.

Then David moved down into the Desert
of Maon.[a] 2A certain man in Maon, who had
property there at Carmel, was very wealthy.
He had a thousand goats and three thousand sheep, which he was shearing in Carmel.
3His name was Nabal and his wife’s name was
Abigail. She was an intelligent and beautiful
woman, but her husband, a Calebite, was sur-
ly and mean in his dealings.

4While David was in the desert, he heard
that Nabal was shearing sheep. 5So he sent ten
young men and said to them, “Go up to Nabal at Carmel and greet him in my name. 6Say
to him: ‘Long life to you! Good health to you
and your household! And good health to all
that is yours!

7“ ‘Now I hear that it is sheep-shearing
time. When your shepherds were with us, we
did not mistreat them, and the whole time
they were at Carmel nothing of theirs was
missing. 8Ask your own servants and they will
tell you. Therefore be favorable toward my
young men, since we come at a festive time.
Please give your servants and your son David
whatever you can find for them.’ ”

9When David’s men arrived, they gave Nabal this message in David’s name. Then they
waited.

10Nabal answered David’s servants, “Who
is this David? Who is this son of Jesse? Many
servants are breaking away from their masters
these days. 11Why should I take my bread and
water, and the meat I have slaughtered for my
shearers, and give it to men coming from who
knows where?”

12David’s men turned around and went
back. When they arrived, they reported every
word. 13David said to his men, “Put on your
swords!” So they put on their swords, and David put on his. About four hundred men went
up with David, while two hundred stayed
with the supplies.

14One of the servants told Nabal’s wife Abigail: “David sent messengers from the desert to
give our master his greetings, but he hurled insults at them. 15Yet these men were very good
to us. They did not mistreat us, and the whole
time we were out in the fields near them nothing was missing. 16Night and day they were a
wall around us all the time we were herding
our sheep near them. 17Now think it over and
see what you can do, because disaster is hanging over our master and his whole household.
He is such a wicked man that no one can talk
to him.”

18Abigail lost no time. She took two hundred loaves of bread, two skins of wine, five
dressed sheep, five seahs[b] of roasted grain, a
hundred cakes of raisins and two hundred
cakes of pressed figs, and loaded them on donkeys. 19Then she told her servants, “Go on
ahead; I’ll follow you.” But she did not tell her
husband Nabal.

20As she came riding her donkey into a
mountain ravine, there were David and his
men descending toward her, and she met
them. 21David had just said, “It’s been useless—all my watching over this fellow’s property in the desert so that nothing of his was
missing. He has paid me back evil for good.
22May God deal with David,[c] be it ever so severely, if by morning I leave alive one male of
all who belong to him!”

23When Abigail saw David, she quickly got
off her donkey and bowed down before David with her face to the ground. 24She fell at
his feet and said: “My lord, let the blame be
on me alone. Please let your servant speak to
you; hear what your servant has to say. 25May
my lord pay no attention to that wicked man
Nabal. He is just like his name—his name is
Fool, and folly goes with him. But as for me,
your servant, I did not see the men my master sent.

26“Now since the LORD has kept you, my
master, from bloodshed and from avenging
yourself with your own hands, as surely as
the LORD lives and as you live, may your en-

[a] *1* Some Septuagint manuscripts; Hebrew *Paran* [b] *18* That is, probably about a bushel (about 37 liters) [c] *22* Some Septuagint manuscripts; Hebrew *with David’s enemies*

MONDAY
READ 1 SAMUEL 25:1–40

WHEN YOUR PARTNER MESSES UP

While in the desert, David and his men spent some time protecting the herds and flocks of a wealthy landowner named Nabal. At sheep-shearing time, David sent ten men to Nabal, in essence to remind him of his debt. It was not an unusual or unreasonable request. Sheep-shearing time was a festive time when the owner of the flock entertained guests and shared his bounty with the poor and outcast. David was not out of line to ask for a share, especially since he and his men had done such a good job of protecting Nabal's assets.

But Nabal refused. When David heard Nabal's response, he was furious. Abigail, Nabal's wife, found out how her husband had wronged David, and she acted quickly. She loaded up donkeys with bread, grain, meat, wine, raisin cakes and fig cakes and went out to meet David. When she reached him, she fell at his feet and expressed great regret for her husband's boorish behavior.

Maybe the actions of someone in your family have affected you negatively. Marriage therapist Leslie Parrot lost a big chunk of her ability to trust men when her father abandoned her mother. "I watched my father decide that his marriage was no longer worth the investment," Parrott said. "I admit that sometimes I fear the same thing could happen to me. I'm tempted to wonder if I'm good enough to prevent my marriage from following the same course as my parents."

"May you be blessed for your good judgment and for keeping me from bloodshed this day and from avenging myself with my own hands."

— 1 Samuel 25:33

let's talk

- ✦ Are either of us struggling with the effects of someone else's bad choices? How can we choose together to work through those effects to learn something or to grow as a couple?
- ✦ Was there a time when one of us was the one making a poor choice that harmed another? How can we grow from that experience?
- ✦ Abigail was willing to do whatever it took to set things right, even though it meant acting without her husband's knowledge. Is it OK to do that in marriage? Why or why not?

Perhaps Abigail, too, wondered if she was good enough to overcome the mistakes made by her husband. Maybe she worried that her actions would never be enough to make up for his meanness and selfishness. But Abigail chose to do what was right, even risking her own life by approaching David as he charged toward his revenge. Abigail did what she could to make up for her husband's failure and to protect her entire household from harm. The result of Abigail's courageous actions? David ceased his murderous mission. Her family and household were spared. And later, when Abigail told Nabal what had happened, he was so shocked that he apparently had a stroke. He died ten days later.

This passage teaches that no matter what another person has done to us, we are responsible for how we respond and for the choices we make. And God can use our good choices to bring about our growth and fulfillment of his plans. Leslie Parrott learned the same lesson. "I now see that my father's decision to leave Mom didn't make me heir to the disease of unfaithfulness," she said. "Their crisis simply brought me face to face with the world's oldest disease: sin. It revealed the hidden crevices of my marriage and gave me courage to face my own unfinished business."

You don't have to live forever with someone else's bad choices. Choose good even when others—including your spouse—choose evil.

—JENNIFER SCHUCHMANN

FOR YOUR NEXT DEVOTIONAL READING, TURN TO PAGE 316.

emies and all who intend to harm my master be like Nabal. 27And let this gift, which your servant has brought to my master, be given to the men who follow you. 28Please forgive your servant's offense, for the LORD will certainly make a lasting dynasty for my master, because he fights the LORD's battles. Let no wrongdoing be found in you as long as you live. 29Even though someone is pursuing you to take your life, the life of my master will be bound securely in the bundle of the living by the LORD your God. But the lives of your enemies he will hurl away as from the pocket of a sling. 30When the LORD has done for my master every good thing he promised concerning him and has appointed him leader over Israel, 31my master will not have on his conscience the staggering burden of needless bloodshed or of having avenged himself. And when the LORD has brought my master success, remember your servant."

32David said to Abigail, "Praise be to the LORD, the God of Israel, who has sent you today to meet me. 33May you be blessed for your good judgment and for keeping me from bloodshed this day and from avenging myself with my own hands. 34Otherwise, as surely as the LORD, the God of Israel, lives, who has kept me from harming you, if you had not come quickly to meet me, not one male belonging to Nabal would have been left alive by daybreak."

35Then David accepted from her hand what she had brought him and said, "Go home in peace. I have heard your words and granted your request."

36When Abigail went to Nabal, he was in the house holding a banquet like that of a king. He was in high spirits and very drunk. So she told him nothing until daybreak. 37Then in the morning, when Nabal was sober, his wife told him all these things, and his heart failed him and he became like a stone. 38About ten days later, the LORD struck Nabal and he died.

39When David heard that Nabal was dead, he said, "Praise be to the LORD, who has upheld my cause against Nabal for treating me with contempt. He has kept his servant from doing wrong and has brought Nabal's wrongdoing down on his own head."

Then David sent word to Abigail, asking her to become his wife. 40His servants went to Carmel and said to Abigail, "David has sent us to you to take you to become his wife."

41She bowed down with her face to the ground and said, "Here is your maidservant, ready to serve you and wash the feet of my master's servants." 42Abigail quickly got on a donkey and, attended by her five maids, went with David's messengers and became his wife. 43David had also married Ahinoam of Jezreel, and they both were his wives. 44But Saul had given his daughter Michal, David's wife, to Paltiel[a] son of Laish, who was from Gallim.

David Again Spares Saul's Life

26 The Ziphites went to Saul at Gibeah and said, "Is not David hiding on the hill of Hakilah, which faces Jeshimon?"

2So Saul went down to the Desert of Ziph, with his three thousand chosen men of Israel, to search there for David. 3Saul made his camp beside the road on the hill of Hakilah facing Jeshimon, but David stayed in the desert. When he saw that Saul had followed him there, 4he sent out scouts and learned that Saul had definitely arrived.[b]

5Then David set out and went to the place where Saul had camped. He saw where Saul and Abner son of Ner, the commander of the army, had lain down. Saul was lying inside the camp, with the army encamped around him.

6David then asked Ahimelech the Hittite and Abishai son of Zeruiah, Joab's brother, "Who will go down into the camp with me to Saul?"

"I'll go with you," said Abishai.

7So David and Abishai went to the army by night, and there was Saul, lying asleep inside the camp with his spear stuck in the ground near his head. Abner and the soldiers were lying around him.

8Abishai said to David, "Today God has delivered your enemy into your hands. Now let me pin him to the ground with one thrust of my spear; I won't strike him twice."

9But David said to Abishai, "Don't destroy him! Who can lay a hand on the LORD's anointed and be guiltless? 10As surely as the LORD lives," he said, "the LORD himself will strike him; either his time will come and he will die, or he will go into battle and perish. 11But the LORD forbid that I should lay a hand on the LORD's anointed. Now get the spear and water jug that are near his head, and let's go."

12So David took the spear and water jug near Saul's head, and they left. No one saw or

[a] 44 Hebrew *Palti,* a variant of *Paltiel* [b] 4 Or *had come to Nacon*

knew about it, nor did anyone wake up. They
were all sleeping, because the LORD had put
them into a deep sleep.
13Then David crossed over to the other side
and stood on top of the hill some distance
away; there was a wide space between them.
14He called out to the army and to Abner son
of Ner, "Aren't you going to answer me, Abner?"
Abner replied, "Who are you who calls to
the king?"
15David said, "You're a man, aren't you?
And who is like you in Israel? Why didn't you
guard your lord the king? Someone came to
destroy your lord the king. 16What you have
done is not good. As surely as the LORD lives,
you and your men deserve to die, because you
did not guard your master, the LORD's anointed. Look around you. Where are the king's
spear and water jug that were near his head?"
17Saul recognized David's voice and said,
"Is that your voice, David my son?"
David replied, "Yes it is, my lord the king."
18And he added, "Why is my lord pursuing
his servant? What have I done, and what
wrong am I guilty of? 19Now let my lord the
king listen to his servant's words. If the LORD
has incited you against me, then may he accept an offering. If, however, men have done
it, may they be cursed before the LORD! They
have now driven me from my share in the
LORD's inheritance and have said, 'Go, serve
other gods.' 20Now do not let my blood fall to
the ground far from the presence of the LORD.
The king of Israel has come out to look for a
flea—as one hunts a partridge in the mountains."
21Then Saul said, "I have sinned. Come
back, David my son. Because you considered
my life precious today, I will not try to harm
you again. Surely I have acted like a fool and
have erred greatly."
22"Here is the king's spear," David answered.
"Let one of your young men come over and
get it. 23The LORD rewards every man for his
righteousness and faithfulness. The LORD delivered you into my hands today, but I would
not lay a hand on the LORD's anointed. 24As
surely as I valued your life today, so may the
LORD value my life and deliver me from all
trouble."
25Then Saul said to David, "May you be
blessed, my son David; you will do great
things and surely triumph."
So David went on his way, and Saul returned home.

David Among the Philistines

27 But David thought to himself, "One
of these days I will be destroyed by the
hand of Saul. The best thing I can do is
to escape to the land of the Philistines. Then
Saul will give up searching for me anywhere in
Israel, and I will slip out of his hand."
2So David and the six hundred men with
him left and went over to Achish son of Ma-
och king of Gath. 3David and his men settled
in Gath with Achish. Each man had his family with him, and David had his two wives:
Ahinoam of Jezreel and Abigail of Carmel, the
widow of Nabal. 4When Saul was told that
David had fled to Gath, he no longer searched
for him.
5Then David said to Achish, "If I have
found favor in your eyes, let a place be assigned to me in one of the country towns, that
I may live there. Why should your servant live
in the royal city with you?"
6So on that day Achish gave him Ziklag,
and it has belonged to the kings of Judah ever
since. 7David lived in Philistine territory a
year and four months.
8Now David and his men went up and
raided the Geshurites, the Girzites and the
Amalekites. (From ancient times these peoples
had lived in the land extending to Shur and
Egypt.) 9Whenever David attacked an area, he
did not leave a man or woman alive, but took
sheep and cattle, donkeys and camels, and
clothes. Then he returned to Achish.
10When Achish asked, "Where did you go
raiding today?" David would say, "Against
the Negev of Judah" or "Against the Negev of
Jerahmeel" or "Against the Negev of the Kenites." 11He did not leave a man or woman
alive to be brought to Gath, for he thought,
"They might inform on us and say, 'This is
what David did.' " And such was his practice as long as he lived in Philistine territory.
12Achish trusted David and said to himself,
"He has become so odious to his people, the
Israelites, that he will be my servant forever."

Saul and the Witch of Endor

28 In those days the Philistines gathered their forces to fight against Israel.
Achish said to David, "You must understand that you and your men will accompany
me in the army."
2David said, "Then you will see for yourself
what your servant can do."
Achish replied, "Very well, I will make you
my bodyguard for life."
3Now Samuel was dead, and all Israel had

mourned for him and buried him in his own
town of Ramah. Saul had expelled the mediums and spiritists from the land.
4 The Philistines assembled and came and
set up camp at Shunem, while Saul gathered
all the Israelites and set up camp at Gilboa.
5 When Saul saw the Philistine army, he was
afraid; terror filled his heart. 6 He inquired of
the LORD, but the LORD did not answer him
by dreams or Urim or prophets. 7 Saul then
said to his attendants, "Find me a woman
who is a medium, so I may go and inquire
of her."
"There is one in Endor," they said.
8 So Saul disguised himself, putting on other clothes, and at night he and two men went
to the woman. "Consult a spirit for me," he
said, "and bring up for me the one I name."
9 But the woman said to him, "Surely you
know what Saul has done. He has cut off the
mediums and spiritists from the land. Why
have you set a trap for my life to bring about
my death?"
10 Saul swore to her by the LORD, "As surely
as the LORD lives, you will not be punished
for this."
11 Then the woman asked, "Whom shall I
bring up for you?"
"Bring up Samuel," he said.
12 When the woman saw Samuel, she cried
out at the top of her voice and said to Saul,
"Why have you deceived me? You are Saul!"
13 The king said to her, "Don't be afraid.
What do you see?"
The woman said, "I see a spirit[a] coming up
out of the ground."
14 "What does he look like?" he asked.
"An old man wearing a robe is coming up,"
she said.
Then Saul knew it was Samuel, and he
bowed down and prostrated himself with his
face to the ground.
15 Samuel said to Saul, "Why have you disturbed me by bringing me up?"
"I am in great distress," Saul said. "The Philistines are fighting against me, and God has
turned away from me. He no longer answers
me, either by prophets or by dreams. So I have
called on you to tell me what to do."
16 Samuel said, "Why do you consult me,
now that the LORD has turned away from
you and become your enemy? 17 The LORD
has done what he predicted through me.
The LORD has torn the kingdom out of your
hands and given it to one of your neighbors—to David. 18 Because you did not obey
the LORD or carry out his fierce wrath against
the Amalekites, the LORD has done this to
you today. 19 The LORD will hand over both
Israel and you to the Philistines, and tomorrow you and your sons will be with me. The
LORD will also hand over the army of Israel to
the Philistines."
20 Immediately Saul fell full length on the
ground, filled with fear because of Samuel's
words. His strength was gone, for he had eaten
nothing all that day and night.
21 When the woman came to Saul and saw
that he was greatly shaken, she said, "Look,
your maidservant has obeyed you. I took my
life in my hands and did what you told me to
do. 22 Now please listen to your servant and let
me give you some food so you may eat and
have the strength to go on your way."
23 He refused and said, "I will not eat."
But his men joined the woman in urging
him, and he listened to them. He got up from
the ground and sat on the couch.
24 The woman had a fattened calf at the
house, which she butchered at once. She took
some flour, kneaded it and baked bread without yeast. 25 Then she set it before Saul and his
men, and they ate. That same night they got
up and left.

Achish Sends David Back to Ziklag

29 The Philistines gathered all their forces at Aphek, and Israel camped by the
spring in Jezreel. 2 As the Philistine rulers marched with their units of hundreds and
thousands, David and his men were marching
at the rear with Achish. 3 The commanders of
the Philistines asked, "What about these Hebrews?"
Achish replied, "Is this not David, who was
an officer of Saul king of Israel? He has already
been with me for over a year, and from the
day he left Saul until now, I have found no
fault in him."
4 But the Philistine commanders were angry
with him and said, "Send the man back, that
he may return to the place you assigned him.
He must not go with us into battle, or he will
turn against us during the fighting. How better could he regain his master's favor than by
taking the heads of our own men? 5 Isn't this
the David they sang about in their dances:

" 'Saul has slain his thousands,
and David his tens of thousands'?"

---
a 13 Or *see spirits*; or *see gods*

6So Achish called David and said to him,
"As surely as the LORD lives, you have been
reliable, and I would be pleased to have you
serve with me in the army. From the day you
came to me until now, I have found no fault in
you, but the rulers don't approve of you. 7Turn
back and go in peace; do nothing to displease
the Philistine rulers."

8"But what have I done?" asked David.
"What have you found against your servant
from the day I came to you until now? Why
can't I go and fight against the enemies of my
lord the king?"

9Achish answered, "I know that you have
been as pleasing in my eyes as an angel of God;
nevertheless, the Philistine commanders have
said, 'He must not go up with us into battle.'
10Now get up early, along with your master's
servants who have come with you, and leave in
the morning as soon as it is light."

11So David and his men got up early in the
morning to go back to the land of the Philistines, and the Philistines went up to Jezreel.

David Destroys the Amalekites

30 David and his men reached Ziklag on
the third day. Now the Amalekites had
raided the Negev and Ziklag. They had
attacked Ziklag and burned it, 2and had tak-
en captive the women and all who were in
it, both young and old. They killed none of
them, but carried them off as they went on
their way.

3When David and his men came to Ziklag, they found it destroyed by fire and their
wives and sons and daughters taken captive.
4So David and his men wept aloud until they
had no strength left to weep. 5David's two
wives had been captured—Ahinoam of Jezreel and Abigail, the widow of Nabal of Carmel. 6David was greatly distressed because
the men were talking of stoning him; each
one was bitter in spirit because of his sons
and daughters. But David found strength in
the LORD his God.

7Then David said to Abiathar the priest, the
son of Ahimelech, "Bring me the ephod." Abiathar brought it to him, 8and David inquired
of the LORD, "Shall I pursue this raiding party? Will I overtake them?"

"Pursue them," he answered. "You will certainly overtake them and succeed in the rescue."

9David and the six hundred men with him
came to the Besor Ravine, where some stayed
behind, 10for two hundred men were too exhausted to cross the ravine. But David and
four hundred men continued the pursuit.

11They found an Egyptian in a field and
brought him to David. They gave him water
to drink and food to eat— 12part of a cake of
pressed figs and two cakes of raisins. He ate
and was revived, for he had not eaten any food
or drunk any water for three days and three
nights.

13David asked him, "To whom do you belong, and where do you come from?"

He said, "I am an Egyptian, the slave of an
Amalekite. My master abandoned me when I
became ill three days ago. 14We raided the Negev of the Kerethites and the territory belonging to Judah and the Negev of Caleb. And we
burned Ziklag."

15David asked him, "Can you lead me
down to this raiding party?"

He answered, "Swear to me before God that
you will not kill me or hand me over to my
master, and I will take you down to them."

16He led David down, and there they were,
scattered over the countryside, eating, drinking and reveling because of the great amount
of plunder they had taken from the land of the
Philistines and from Judah. 17David fought
them from dusk until the evening of the next
day, and none of them got away, except four
hundred young men who rode off on camels
and fled. 18David recovered everything the
Amalekites had taken, including his two wives.
19Nothing was missing: young or old, boy or
girl, plunder or anything else they had taken.
David brought everything back. 20He took all
the flocks and herds, and his men drove them
ahead of the other livestock, saying, "This is
David's plunder."

21Then David came to the two hundred
men who had been too exhausted to follow
him and who were left behind at the Besor Ravine. They came out to meet David and the
people with him. As David and his men approached, he greeted them. 22But all the evil
men and troublemakers among David's followers said, "Because they did not go out with
us, we will not share with them the plunder
we recovered. However, each man may take
his wife and children and go."

23David replied, "No, my brothers, you
must not do that with what the LORD has giv-
en us. He has protected us and handed over to
us the forces that came against us. 24Who will
listen to what you say? The share of the man
who stayed with the supplies is to be the same
as that of him who went down to the battle. All

TUESDAY
READ 1 SAMUEL 30:1–31

LOVING IN THE HARD TIMES

One marriage vow many of us take is to stay together "for better or for worse." Still, we go into marriage counting on the "better" and praying we'll never have to face the "worse."

But the truth is that nearly every couple faces their own version of the "worse" sooner or later. It might be the onset of a debilitating illness, the discovery of infidelity, the death of a child, the loss of a home. These catastrophic events not only threaten faith, but they also threaten marriage.

David's experience at Ziklag offers us hope in such times. David and his men returned from battle to find their homes destroyed and their families stolen. They were devastated and wept bitterly at their loss. But in the face of this tragedy, these men had a choice to make. All of them, apart from David, chose to stay mired in their misery. But for David this terrible turn of events served as a reminder that in God there always is hope. David's faith gave him the strength to trust God to carry him through whatever came next.

When David and his men came to Ziklag, they found it destroyed by fire and their wives and sons and daughters taken captive.

— 1 Samuel 30:3

let's talk

✦ How do we invest in our relationship each day? If we haven't been consistent about this, what are ways to reinforce our bond?

✦ If we are in the midst of a difficult season in our marriage, how can we help each other through this time? Knowing that neither of us might feel strong enough to give much to the other, how can we support each other?

✦ What kind of support network do we have as a couple? What people can we trust to help carry us through a difficult time? If we haven't already, let's invite these people to step into our marriage and walk with us through good times and bad.

My husband, Jim, is a special education teacher who works primarily with students who have behavioral and emotional problems. His first year of teaching was the most difficult year we had as a couple. Each day Jim came home emotionally and physically spent. Needless to say, it was a difficult time for me as well, since I needed him to be emotionally and physically present at home too. By the middle of the school year, it was clear to both of us that something needed to change if we were going to survive as a family. So Jim finished out his school year and took a job with a school that had a better support system for teachers involved in this draining work.

What saved us as a couple was a promise we had made at the beginning of our marriage. We knew that we had to place our relationship above the other priorities in our lives—our jobs, our children, our individual needs. So we made an effort—not always a successful one, mind you!—to deal with conflict right away rather than let it fester. We promised to talk openly and honestly with each other and to pay attention to our relationship, even when it was going well, so that we'd notice when it wasn't. Laying that groundwork early on gave us the firm footing we needed to make our way through a painful year.

David, too, had a firm foundation from which to face his trials. In the midst of suffering, he instinctively turned to God because he had built a foundation of trust in God's love for him. David's efforts to seek God in the good days helped him seek God in the bad days. Likewise, tending to your marriage in the "better" days will strengthen you and prepare you to face the "worse," should it come.

—CARLA BARNHILL

FOR YOUR NEXT DEVOTIONAL READING, TURN TO PAGE 320.

will share alike." 25David made this a statute and ordinance for Israel from that day to this.

26When David arrived in Ziklag, he sent some of the plunder to the elders of Judah, who were his friends, saying, "Here is a present for you from the plunder of the LORD's enemies."

27He sent it to those who were in Bethel, Ramoth Negev and Jattir; 28to those in Aroer, Siphmoth, Eshtemoa 29and Racal; to those in the towns of the Jerahmeelites and the Kenites; 30to those in Hormah, Bor Ashan, Athach 31and Hebron; and to those in all the other places where David and his men had roamed.

Saul Takes His Life

31 Now the Philistines fought against Israel; the Israelites fled before them, and many fell slain on Mount Gilboa. 2The Philistines pressed hard after Saul and his sons, and they killed his sons Jonathan, Abinadab and Malki-Shua. 3The fighting grew fierce around Saul, and when the archers overtook him, they wounded him critically.

4Saul said to his armor-bearer, "Draw your sword and run me through, or these uncircumcised fellows will come and run me through and abuse me."

But his armor-bearer was terrified and would not do it; so Saul took his own sword and fell on it. 5When the armor-bearer saw that Saul was dead, he too fell on his sword and died with him. 6So Saul and his three sons and his armor-bearer and all his men died together that same day.

7When the Israelites along the valley and those across the Jordan saw that the Israelite army had fled and that Saul and his sons had died, they abandoned their towns and fled. And the Philistines came and occupied them.

8The next day, when the Philistines came to strip the dead, they found Saul and his three sons fallen on Mount Gilboa. 9They cut off his head and stripped off his armor, and they sent messengers throughout the land of the Philistines to proclaim the news in the temple of their idols and among their people. 10They put his armor in the temple of the Ashtoreths and fastened his body to the wall of Beth Shan.

11When the people of Jabesh Gilead heard of what the Philistines had done to Saul, 12all their valiant men journeyed through the night to Beth Shan. They took down the bodies of Saul and his sons from the wall of Beth Shan and went to Jabesh, where they burned them. 13Then they took their bones and buried them under a tamarisk tree at Jabesh, and they fasted seven days.

2 SAMUEL

2 Samuel

QUICK FACTS

AUTHOR Unknown

AUDIENCE All Israel

DATE Sometime after the division of Israel into the northern and southern kingdoms in 930 B.C.

SETTING After Saul's death, when David served as Israel's second king

After Saul and three of his four sons died in battle, David came to Hebron, where he was crowned king of Judah. However, the war between the house of Saul and the house of David lasted for many years. Entangled in the struggle were Saul's son Ish-Bosheth and avenging generals Abner and Joab.

Eventually David won the respect of all the tribes, who asked him to be their king. Over the next 33 years David defeated Israel's enemies, securing and expanding the nation's borders. He conquered the Jebusite fortress of Jerusalem and brought the ark of God to Israel's new capital city—the "City of David." This "man after [God's] own heart" united the 12 tribes into one nation under God.

But everything was jeopardized by David's adultery with Bathsheba, which spiraled into deceit and murder. David repented of his sin and was forgiven, but the consequences spread like a fierce fire, first within his own family, then throughout the kingdom.

Like David, as couples we too may have everything going for us. We're deeply in love, passionately committed to each other and giddy with prospects for the future. But as David's life reminds us, everything we work so hard for can quickly be wiped out if we do not remain faithful to God—and to each other.

David Hears of Saul's Death

1 After the death of Saul, David returned
from defeating the Amalekites and stayed
in Ziklag two days. 2On the third day a
man arrived from Saul's camp, with his clothes
torn and with dust on his head. When he
came to David, he fell to the ground to pay
him honor.
3"Where have you come from?" David
asked him.
He answered, "I have escaped from the Israelite camp."
4"What happened?" David asked. "Tell
me."
He said, "The men fled from the battle.
Many of them fell and died. And Saul and his
son Jonathan are dead."
5Then David said to the young man who
brought him the report, "How do you know
that Saul and his son Jonathan are dead?"
6"I happened to be on Mount Gilboa," the
young man said, "and there was Saul, leaning
on his spear, with the chariots and riders almost upon him. 7When he turned around and
saw me, he called out to me, and I said, 'What
can I do?'
8"He asked me, 'Who are you?'
" 'An Amalekite,' I answered.
9"Then he said to me, 'Stand over me and
kill me! I am in the throes of death, but I'm
still alive.'
10"So I stood over him and killed him, because I knew that after he had fallen he could
not survive. And I took the crown that was on
his head and the band on his arm and have
brought them here to my lord."
11Then David and all the men with him
took hold of their clothes and tore them.
12They mourned and wept and fasted till evening for Saul and his son Jonathan, and for
the army of the LORD and the house of Israel,
because they had fallen by the sword.
13David said to the young man who brought
him the report, "Where are you from?"
"I am the son of an alien, an Amalekite,"
he answered.
14David asked him, "Why were you not
afraid to lift your hand to destroy the LORD's
anointed?"
15Then David called one of his men and
said, "Go, strike him down!" So he struck him
down, and he died. 16For David had said to
him, "Your blood be on your own head. Your
own mouth testified against you when you
said, 'I killed the LORD's anointed.' "

David's Lament for Saul and Jonathan

17David took up this lament concerning
Saul and his son Jonathan, 18and ordered that
the men of Judah be taught this lament of the
bow (it is written in the Book of Jashar):

19 "Your glory, O Israel, lies slain on your heights.
How the mighty have fallen!

20 "Tell it not in Gath,
proclaim it not in the streets of Ashkelon,
lest the daughters of the Philistines be glad,
lest the daughters of the uncircumcised rejoice.

21 "O mountains of Gilboa,
may you have neither dew nor rain,
nor fields that yield offerings ⌊of grain⌋.
For there the shield of the mighty was defiled,
the shield of Saul—no longer rubbed with oil.
22 From the blood of the slain,
from the flesh of the mighty,
the bow of Jonathan did not turn back,
the sword of Saul did not return unsatisfied.

23 "Saul and Jonathan—
in life they were loved and gracious,
and in death they were not parted.
They were swifter than eagles,
they were stronger than lions.

24 "O daughters of Israel,
weep for Saul,
who clothed you in scarlet and finery,
who adorned your garments with ornaments of gold.

25 "How the mighty have fallen in battle!
Jonathan lies slain on your heights.
26 I grieve for you, Jonathan my brother;
you were very dear to me.
Your love for me was wonderful,
more wonderful than that of women.

27 "How the mighty have fallen!
The weapons of war have perished!"

David Anointed King Over Judah

2 In the course of time, David inquired of
the LORD. "Shall I go up to one of the
towns of Judah?" he asked.
The LORD said, "Go up."
David asked, "Where shall I go?"
"To Hebron," the LORD answered.

WEDNESDAY
READ 2 SAMUEL 1:1–27

CROSSING THE GENDER GAP

David and Jonathan were alike in so many ways. Though supposedly they were rivals for the kingship of Israel, they were more like brothers who promoted each other rather than themselves. They came to be intimate friends in the royal court and likely fought together in battle. They knew each other so well that they anticipated each other's needs. They worshiped the same God. So when Jonathan died in battle, David was grief stricken. He had lost his soul brother, whose love, he said, was more wonderful than that of a woman.

That doesn't say much about David's relationships with women, most of whom he treated like trophies of war. Still, even today, it can be easier to love a person of the same gender than to relate to a spouse. Despite their hormonal attraction for one another, men and women have different needs, wants, desires and priorities, and they communicate in different ways.

My wife is visually talented; she loves to discuss art, decorating and anything with color in it. She does so with ease with women who think the same way. I, on the other hand, am more sound oriented. I can take apart a piece of music just as I can take apart and reassemble other stuff. I love working on mechanical things with guys, chatting about football at the same time. Cindy gets lost in such conversations, just like I check out when the talk turns to home decorating.

In marriage, a man and a woman cross the great divide of gender differences and are forced to interact in unfamiliar ways. When Zach and Carrie have a problem, for example, Zach tends to assess the situation, reduce it to its essentials, then quickly devise a plan to solve it. Carrie has a more complex approach. She wants to talk about the problem from multiple angles and deal with the emotional issues it generates.

Instead of trying to change each other's approach, a husband and wife would do better to learn from each other. For example, Zach can learn from Carrie to listen more carefully and to express his love and concern while discussing a problem. Carrie could learn from Zach to focus more during a discussion, narrowing the possibilities down to a single solution (with maybe one alternative), closing the issue and getting on with it.

Marriage—if we are called to it—is the primary and most vital human relationship we can have in life. Yes, we need to allow each other time to maintain friendships with people of the same gender. But the greater challenge with the potential for the greatest blessing here on Earth is for two who are different to become so united that they might, in time, say to one another: "Your love for me is wonderful, more wonderful than that of anyone else."

—JOHN R. THROOP

FOR YOUR NEXT DEVOTIONAL READING, TURN TO PAGE 325.

"I grieve for you, Jonathan my brother; you were very dear to me. Your love for me was wonderful, more wonderful than that of women."

— 2 SAMUEL 1:26

let's talk

- What are some of the benefits of letting each other spend time with friends of the same gender? What are some of the drawbacks?
- When do our friendships with others become intrusive on our marriage? How do we find a healthy balance between time together, time alone and time with others?
- In what ways can cultural differences cause misunderstanding about same-gender friendships?

2So David went up there with his two wives,
Ahinoam of Jezreel and Abigail, the widow of
Nabal of Carmel. 3David also took the men
who were with him, each with his family, and
they settled in Hebron and its towns. 4Then
the men of Judah came to Hebron and there
they anointed David king over the house of
Judah.

When David was told that it was the men
of Jabesh Gilead who had buried Saul, 5he sent
messengers to the men of Jabesh Gilead to say
to them, "The LORD bless you for showing this
kindness to Saul your master by burying him.
6May the LORD now show you kindness and
faithfulness, and I too will show you the same
favor because you have done this. 7Now then,
be strong and brave, for Saul your master is
dead, and the house of Judah has anointed me
king over them."

War Between the Houses of David and Saul

8Meanwhile, Abner son of Ner, the commander of Saul's army, had taken Ish-Bosheth
son of Saul and brought him over to Mahanaim. 9He made him king over Gilead, Ashuri[a]
and Jezreel, and also over Ephraim, Benjamin
and all Israel.

10Ish-Bosheth son of Saul was forty years
old when he became king over Israel, and he
reigned two years. The house of Judah, however, followed David. 11The length of time
David was king in Hebron over the house of
Judah was seven years and six months.

12Abner son of Ner, together with the men
of Ish-Bosheth son of Saul, left Mahanaim
and went to Gibeon. 13Joab son of Zeruiah
and David's men went out and met them at
the pool of Gibeon. One group sat down on
one side of the pool and one group on the other side.

14Then Abner said to Joab, "Let's have some
of the young men get up and fight hand to
hand in front of us."

"All right, let them do it," Joab said.

15So they stood up and were counted off—
twelve men for Benjamin and Ish-Bosheth son
of Saul, and twelve for David. 16Then each
man grabbed his opponent by the head and
thrust his dagger into his opponent's side, and
they fell down together. So that place in Gibeon was called Helkath Hazzurim.[b]

17The battle that day was very fierce, and
Abner and the men of Israel were defeated by
David's men.

18The three sons of Zeruiah were there:
Joab, Abishai and Asahel. Now Asahel was
as fleet-footed as a wild gazelle. 19He chased
Abner, turning neither to the right nor to the
left as he pursued him. 20Abner looked behind
him and asked, "Is that you, Asahel?"

"It is," he answered.

21Then Abner said to him, "Turn aside to
the right or to the left; take on one of the
young men and strip him of his weapons." But
Asahel would not stop chasing him.

22Again Abner warned Asahel, "Stop chasing me! Why should I strike you down? How
could I look your brother Joab in the face?"

23But Asahel refused to give up the pursuit;
so Abner thrust the butt of his spear into Asahel's stomach, and the spear came out through
his back. He fell there and died on the spot.
And every man stopped when he came to the
place where Asahel had fallen and died.

24But Joab and Abishai pursued Abner, and
as the sun was setting, they came to the hill of
Ammah, near Giah on the way to the wasteland of Gibeon. 25Then the men of Benjamin
rallied behind Abner. They formed themselves
into a group and took their stand on top of
a hill.

26Abner called out to Joab, "Must the sword
devour forever? Don't you realize that this will
end in bitterness? How long before you order
your men to stop pursuing their brothers?"

27Joab answered, "As surely as God lives,
if you had not spoken, the men would have
continued the pursuit of their brothers until
morning.[c]"

28So Joab blew the trumpet, and all the
men came to a halt; they no longer pursued
Israel, nor did they fight anymore.

29All that night Abner and his men marched
through the Arabah. They crossed the Jordan,
continued through the whole Bithron[d] and
came to Mahanaim.

30Then Joab returned from pursuing Abner and assembled all his men. Besides Asahel,
nineteen of David's men were found missing.
31But David's men had killed three hundred
and sixty Benjamites who were with Abner.
32They took Asahel and buried him in his father's tomb at Bethlehem. Then Joab and his
men marched all night and arrived at Hebron
by daybreak.

---

[a] 9 Or *Asher* [b] 16 *Helkath Hazzurim* means *field of daggers* or *field of hostilities.* [c] 27 Or *spoken this morning, the men would not have taken up the pursuit of their brothers*; or *spoken, the men would have given up the pursuit of their brothers by morning*
[d] 29 Or *morning*; or *ravine*; the meaning of the Hebrew for this word is uncertain.

3 The war between the house of Saul and the house of David lasted a long time. David grew stronger and stronger, while the house of Saul grew weaker and weaker.

2 Sons were born to David in Hebron:
His firstborn was Amnon the son of Ahinoam of Jezreel;
3 his second, Kileab the son of Abigail the widow of Nabal of Carmel;
the third, Absalom the son of Maacah daughter of Talmai king of Geshur;
4 the fourth, Adonijah the son of Haggith;
the fifth, Shephatiah the son of Abital;
5 and the sixth, Ithream the son of David's wife Eglah.
These were born to David in Hebron.

Abner Goes Over to David

6 During the war between the house of Saul and the house of David, Abner had been strengthening his own position in the house of Saul. 7 Now Saul had had a concubine named Rizpah daughter of Aiah. And Ish-Bosheth said to Abner, "Why did you sleep with my father's concubine?"

8 Abner was very angry because of what Ish-Bosheth said and he answered, "Am I a dog's head—on Judah's side? This very day I am loyal to the house of your father Saul and to his family and friends. I haven't handed you over to David. Yet now you accuse me of an offense involving this woman! 9 May God deal with Abner, be it ever so severely, if I do not do for David what the LORD promised him on oath 10 and transfer the kingdom from the house of Saul and establish David's throne over Israel and Judah from Dan to Beersheba." 11 Ish-Bosheth did not dare to say another word to Abner, because he was afraid of him.

12 Then Abner sent messengers on his behalf to say to David, "Whose land is it? Make an agreement with me, and I will help you bring all Israel over to you."

13 "Good," said David. "I will make an agreement with you. But I demand one thing of you: Do not come into my presence unless you bring Michal daughter of Saul when you come to see me." 14 Then David sent messengers to Ish-Bosheth son of Saul, demanding, "Give me my wife Michal, whom I betrothed to myself for the price of a hundred Philistine foreskins."

15 So Ish-Bosheth gave orders and had her taken away from her husband Paltiel son of Laish. 16 Her husband, however, went with her, weeping behind her all the way to Bahurim. Then Abner said to him, "Go back home!" So he went back.

17 Abner conferred with the elders of Israel and said, "For some time you have wanted to make David your king. 18 Now do it! For the LORD promised David, 'By my servant David I will rescue my people Israel from the hand of the Philistines and from the hand of all their enemies.' "

19 Abner also spoke to the Benjamites in person. Then he went to Hebron to tell David everything that Israel and the whole house of Benjamin wanted to do. 20 When Abner, who had twenty men with him, came to David at Hebron, David prepared a feast for him and his men. 21 Then Abner said to David, "Let me go at once and assemble all Israel for my lord the king, so that they may make a compact with you, and that you may rule over all that your heart desires." So David sent Abner away, and he went in peace.

Joab Murders Abner

22 Just then David's men and Joab returned from a raid and brought with them a great deal of plunder. But Abner was no longer with David in Hebron, because David had sent him away, and he had gone in peace. 23 When Joab and all the soldiers with him arrived, he was told that Abner son of Ner had come to the king and that the king had sent him away and that he had gone in peace.

24 So Joab went to the king and said, "What have you done? Look, Abner came to you. Why did you let him go? Now he is gone! 25 You know Abner son of Ner; he came to deceive you and observe your movements and find out everything you are doing."

26 Joab then left David and sent messengers after Abner, and they brought him back from the well of Sirah. But David did not know it. 27 Now when Abner returned to Hebron, Joab took him aside into the gateway, as though to speak with him privately. And there, to avenge the blood of his brother Asahel, Joab stabbed him in the stomach, and he died.

28 Later, when David heard about this, he said, "I and my kingdom are forever innocent before the LORD concerning the blood of Abner son of Ner. 29 May his blood fall upon the head of Joab and upon all his father's house! May Joab's house never be without someone who has a running sore or leprosy[a] or who

[a] *29* The Hebrew word was used for various diseases affecting the skin—not necessarily leprosy.

leans on a crutch or who falls by the sword or
who lacks food."
30(Joab and his brother Abishai murdered
Abner because he had killed their brother Asahel in the battle at Gibeon.)
31Then David said to Joab and all the people with him, "Tear your clothes and put on
sackcloth and walk in mourning in front of
Abner." King David himself walked behind
the bier. 32They buried Abner in Hebron, and
the king wept aloud at Abner's tomb. All the
people wept also.
33The king sang this lament for Abner:

"Should Abner have died as the lawless
die?
34 Your hands were not bound,
your feet were not fettered.
You fell as one falls before wicked men."

And all the people wept over him again.
35Then they all came and urged David to
eat something while it was still day; but David
took an oath, saying, "May God deal with me,
be it ever so severely, if I taste bread or anything else before the sun sets!"
36All the people took note and were pleased;
indeed, everything the king did pleased them.
37So on that day all the people and all Israel
knew that the king had no part in the murder
of Abner son of Ner.
38Then the king said to his men, "Do you
not realize that a prince and a great man has
fallen in Israel this day? 39And today, though
I am the anointed king, I am weak, and these
sons of Zeruiah are too strong for me. May
the LORD repay the evildoer according to his
evil deeds!"

Ish-Bosheth Murdered

4 When Ish-Bosheth son of Saul heard that
Abner had died in Hebron, he lost courage,
and all Israel became alarmed. 2Now Saul's
son had two men who were leaders of raiding bands. One was named Baanah and the
other Recab; they were sons of Rimmon the
Beerothite from the tribe of Benjamin—Beeroth is considered part of Benjamin, 3because
the people of Beeroth fled to Gittaim and have
lived there as aliens to this day.
4(Jonathan son of Saul had a son who was
lame in both feet. He was five years old when
the news about Saul and Jonathan came from
Jezreel. His nurse picked him up and fled, but
as she hurried to leave, he fell and became
crippled. His name was Mephibosheth.)
5Now Recab and Baanah, the sons of Rimmon the Beerothite, set out for the house of
Ish-Bosheth, and they arrived there in the
heat of the day while he was taking his noonday rest. 6They went into the inner part of
the house as if to get some wheat, and they
stabbed him in the stomach. Then Recab and
his brother Baanah slipped away.
7They had gone into the house while he was
lying on the bed in his bedroom. After they
stabbed and killed him, they cut off his head.
Taking it with them, they traveled all night by
way of the Arabah. 8They brought the head of
Ish-Bosheth to David at Hebron and said to
the king, "Here is the head of Ish-Bosheth son
of Saul, your enemy, who tried to take your
life. This day the LORD has avenged my lord
the king against Saul and his offspring."
9David answered Recab and his brother Baanah, the sons of Rimmon the Beerothite, "As
surely as the LORD lives, who has delivered me
out of all trouble, 10when a man told me, 'Saul
is dead,' and thought he was bringing good
news, I seized him and put him to death in
Ziklag. That was the reward I gave him for his
news! 11How much more—when wicked men
have killed an innocent man in his own house
and on his own bed—should I not now demand his blood from your hand and rid the
earth of you!"
12So David gave an order to his men, and
they killed them. They cut off their hands and
feet and hung the bodies by the pool in Hebron. But they took the head of Ish-Bosheth
and buried it in Abner's tomb at Hebron.

David Becomes King Over Israel

5 All the tribes of Israel came to David at Hebron and said, "We are your own flesh and
blood. 2In the past, while Saul was king
over us, you were the one who led Israel on
their military campaigns. And the LORD said
to you, 'You will shepherd my people Israel,
and you will become their ruler.' "
3When all the elders of Israel had come to
King David at Hebron, the king made a compact with them at Hebron before the LORD,
and they anointed David king over Israel.
4David was thirty years old when he became king, and he reigned forty years. 5In Hebron he reigned over Judah seven years and six
months, and in Jerusalem he reigned over all
Israel and Judah thirty-three years.

David Conquers Jerusalem

6The king and his men marched to Jerusalem to attack the Jebusites, who lived there.
The Jebusites said to David, "You will not get
in here; even the blind and the lame can ward

you off." They thought, "David cannot get in here." [7]Nevertheless, David captured the fortress of Zion, the City of David.

[8]On that day, David said, "Anyone who conquers the Jebusites will have to use the water shaft[a] to reach those 'lame and blind' who are David's enemies.[b]" That is why they say, "The 'blind and lame' will not enter the palace."

[9]David then took up residence in the fortress and called it the City of David. He built up the area around it, from the supporting terraces[c] inward. [10]And he became more and more powerful, because the LORD God Almighty was with him.

[11]Now Hiram king of Tyre sent messengers to David, along with cedar logs and carpenters and stonemasons, and they built a palace for David. [12]And David knew that the LORD had established him as king over Israel and had exalted his kingdom for the sake of his people Israel.

[13]After he left Hebron, David took more concubines and wives in Jerusalem, and more sons and daughters were born to him. [14]These are the names of the children born to him there: Shammua, Shobab, Nathan, Solomon, [15]Ibhar, Elishua, Nepheg, Japhia, [16]Elishama, Eliada and Eliphelet.

David Defeats the Philistines

[17]When the Philistines heard that David had been anointed king over Israel, they went up in full force to search for him, but David heard about it and went down to the stronghold. [18]Now the Philistines had come and spread out in the Valley of Rephaim; [19]so David inquired of the LORD, "Shall I go and attack the Philistines? Will you hand them over to me?"

The LORD answered him, "Go, for I will surely hand the Philistines over to you."

[20]So David went to Baal Perazim, and there he defeated them. He said, "As waters break out, the LORD has broken out against my enemies before me." So that place was called Baal Perazim.[d] [21]The Philistines abandoned their idols there, and David and his men carried them off.

[22]Once more the Philistines came up and spread out in the Valley of Rephaim; [23]so David inquired of the LORD, and he answered, "Do not go straight up, but circle around behind them and attack them in front of the balsam trees. [24]As soon as you hear the sound of marching in the tops of the balsam trees, move quickly, because that will mean the LORD has gone out in front of you to strike the Philistine army." [25]So David did as the LORD commanded him, and he struck down the Philistines all the way from Gibeon[e] to Gezer.

The Ark Brought to Jerusalem

6 David again brought together out of Israel chosen men, thirty thousand in all. [2]He and all his men set out from Baalah of Judah[f] to bring up from there the ark of God, which is called by the Name,[g] the name of the LORD Almighty, who is enthroned between the cherubim that are on the ark. [3]They set the ark of God on a new cart and brought it from the house of Abinadab, which was on the hill. Uzzah and Ahio, sons of Abinadab, were guiding the new cart [4]with the ark of God on it,[h] and Ahio was walking in front of it. [5]David and the whole house of Israel were celebrating with all their might before the LORD, with songs[i] and with harps, lyres, tambourines, sistrums and cymbals.

[6]When they came to the threshing floor of Nacon, Uzzah reached out and took hold of the ark of God, because the oxen stumbled. [7]The LORD's anger burned against Uzzah because of his irreverent act; therefore God struck him down and he died there beside the ark of God.

[8]Then David was angry because the LORD's wrath had broken out against Uzzah, and to this day that place is called Perez Uzzah.[j]

[9]David was afraid of the LORD that day and said, "How can the ark of the LORD ever come to me?" [10]He was not willing to take the ark of the LORD to be with him in the City of David. Instead, he took it aside to the house of Obed-Edom the Gittite. [11]The ark of the LORD remained in the house of Obed-Edom the Gittite for three months, and the LORD blessed him and his entire household.

[12]Now King David was told, "The LORD has blessed the household of Obed-Edom and everything he has, because of the ark of God." So David went down and brought up the ark of God from the house of Obed-Edom to the City of David with rejoicing. [13]When those

---

[a] 8 Or *use scaling hooks* [b] 8 Or *are hated by David* [c] 9 Or *the Millo* [d] 20 *Baal Perazim* means *the lord who breaks out.*
[e] 25 Septuagint (see also 1 Chron. 14:16); Hebrew *Geba* [f] 2 That is, Kiriath Jearim; Hebrew *Baale Judah*, a variant of *Baalah of Judah*
[g] 2 Hebrew; Septuagint and Vulgate do not have *the Name.* [h] 3,4 Dead Sea Scrolls and some Septuagint manuscripts; Masoretic Text *cart [4]and they brought it with the ark of God from the house of Abinadab, which was on the hill* [i] 5 See Dead Sea Scrolls, Septuagint and 1 Chronicles 13:8; Masoretic Text *celebrating before the LORD with all kinds of instruments made of pine.* [j] 8 *Perez Uzzah* means *outbreak against Uzzah.*

THURSDAY
READ 2 SAMUEL 6:1–23

CRITICIZING EACH OTHER

As the ark of the LORD was entering the City of David, Michal daughter of Saul watched from a window. And when she saw King David leaping and dancing before the LORD, she despised him in her heart.

— 2 SAMUEL 6:16

Every couple goes through a stage during which they move from "me" to "we." From that point on, couples think in terms of what is best for "us," not just "me." For the most part, this bonding is good and healthy. But sometimes the sense of oneness in marriage can lead us to forget the ways in which we remain unique, separate people.

A few years ago, my husband and I noticed we had a tendency to criticize each other in front of other people. Since neither of us felt good about this, we tried to figure out what was going on. Eventually, we realized that our criticism was a way of distancing ourselves from something the other person was doing that we found embarrassing or annoying. So if I thought Jim was monopolizing a conversation, I'd say something sarcastic about it.

What was really going on was that I was more concerned about what people would think of me than I was about my husband's feelings. I used criticism as a way of siding with other people against my dear husband. As we talked about ways to change this behavior, we recognized that the key was to remember that we aren't the same person. I can let Jim be Jim, knowing that anything he says or does isn't nearly as off-putting to others as watching me take down my husband with a few sharp words. I can still be "me" in the midst of "we"—but only when I remember how important "we" are.

That's a lesson Michal, David's wife, could have used. David and Michal had had a rocky start to their relationship. King Saul had given his daughter Michal to David in marriage for the bride-price of a hundred Philistine foreskins, in the hope that David would be killed in battle (see 1 Samuel 18:17–29). After David fled from Saul, Saul gave Michal to another man. Later, after David had married other women and been crowned king over his own tribe of Judah, David demanded that Michal be returned to him—at least in part for political reasons (see 2 Samuel 3:12–16). While the Bible tells us that Michal loved David before they were married, it's not clear how David felt about her. So while we don't know what kind of bond existed between this man and woman, we see that Michal's initial love wasn't enough to keep her from being embarrassed by her husband's enthusiasm.

We all have moments when we cringe at our spouse's behavior. Sometimes my husband might genuinely be acting inappropriately. Other times, he might just be expressing joy or enthusiasm in a way that seems over-the-top to me. That's when I need to pull back and remember that being "we" means standing side by side with my beloved, even when he embarrasses me.

After all, the beauty of being "we" is having someone who will love you even when it's *your* turn to be embarrassing.

—CARLA BARNHILL

let's talk

- How do we handle situations in which one of us does something that the other finds embarrassing? How can we demonstrate commitment and connection even when we'd rather distance ourselves from each other?
- How are we different in how we express our emotions? How can we learn to appreciate these differences in each other? What can we learn from each other in this area?
- What are some ways we can show each other support when we are with other people and are tempted to disassociate ourselves from each other?

FOR YOUR NEXT DEVOTIONAL READING, TURN TO PAGE 329.

who were carrying the ark of the LORD had
taken six steps, he sacrificed a bull and a fattened calf. 14David, wearing a linen ephod,
danced before the LORD with all his might,
15while he and the entire house of Israel
brought up the ark of the LORD with shouts
and the sound of trumpets.

16As the ark of the LORD was entering
the City of David, Michal daughter of Saul
watched from a window. And when she saw
King David leaping and dancing before the
LORD, she despised him in her heart.

17They brought the ark of the LORD and set
it in its place inside the tent that David had
pitched for it, and David sacrificed burnt offerings and fellowship offerings[a] before the LORD.
18After he had finished sacrificing the burnt
offerings and fellowship offerings, he blessed
the people in the name of the LORD Almighty.
19Then he gave a loaf of bread, a cake of dates
and a cake of raisins to each person in the whole
crowd of Israelites, both men and women. And
all the people went to their homes.

20When David returned home to bless his
household, Michal daughter of Saul came out
to meet him and said, "How the king of Israel
has distinguished himself today, disrobing in
the sight of the slave girls of his servants as any
vulgar fellow would!"

21David said to Michal, "It was before the
LORD, who chose me rather than your father
or anyone from his house when he appointed me ruler over the LORD's people Israel—I
will celebrate before the LORD. 22I will become
even more undignified than this, and I will be
humiliated in my own eyes. But by these slave
girls you spoke of, I will be held in honor."

23And Michal daughter of Saul had no children to the day of her death.

God's Promise to David

7 After the king was settled in his palace and
the LORD had given him rest from all his
enemies around him, 2he said to Nathan
the prophet, "Here I am, living in a palace
of cedar, while the ark of God remains in a
tent."

3Nathan replied to the king, "Whatever
you have in mind, go ahead and do it, for the
LORD is with you."

4That night the word of the LORD came to
Nathan, saying:

5"Go and tell my servant David, 'This
is what the LORD says: Are you the one to
build me a house to dwell in? 6I have not
dwelt in a house from the day I brought
the Israelites up out of Egypt to this day.
I have been moving from place to place
with a tent as my dwelling. 7Wherever
I have moved with all the Israelites, did
I ever say to any of their rulers whom I
commanded to shepherd my people Israel, "Why have you not built me a house
of cedar?" '

8"Now then, tell my servant David,
'This is what the LORD Almighty says: I
took you from the pasture and from following the flock to be ruler over my people Israel. 9I have been with you wherever
you have gone, and I have cut off all your
enemies from before you. Now I will make
your name great, like the names of the
greatest men of the earth. 10And I will provide a place for my people Israel and will
plant them so that they can have a home
of their own and no longer be disturbed.
Wicked people will not oppress them anymore, as they did at the beginning 11and
have done ever since the time I appointed
leaders[b] over my people Israel. I will also
give you rest from all your enemies.

" 'The LORD declares to you that the
LORD himself will establish a house for
you: 12When your days are over and you
rest with your fathers, I will raise up your
offspring to succeed you, who will come
from your own body, and I will establish
his kingdom. 13He is the one who will
build a house for my Name, and I will establish the throne of his kingdom forever.
14I will be his father, and he will be my
son. When he does wrong, I will punish
him with the rod of men, with floggings
inflicted by men. 15But my love will never be taken away from him, as I took it
away from Saul, whom I removed from
before you. 16Your house and your kingdom will endure forever before me[c]; your
throne will be established forever.' "

17Nathan reported to David all the words
of this entire revelation.

David's Prayer

18Then King David went in and sat before
the LORD, and he said:

"Who am I, O Sovereign LORD, and
what is my family, that you have brought
me this far? 19And as if this were not

[a] *17* Traditionally *peace offerings*; also in verse 18 [b] *11* Traditionally *judges* [c] *16* Some Hebrew manuscripts and Septuagint; most Hebrew manuscripts *you*

enough in your sight, O Sovereign LORD,
you have also spoken about the future of
the house of your servant. Is this your
usual way of dealing with man, O Sovereign LORD?
[20]"What more can David say to you?
For you know your servant, O Sovereign
LORD. [21]For the sake of your word and
according to your will, you have done
this great thing and made it known to
your servant.
[22]"How great you are, O Sovereign
LORD! There is no one like you, and there
is no God but you, as we have heard with
our own ears. [23]And who is like your people Israel—the one nation on earth that
God went out to redeem as a people for
himself, and to make a name for himself,
and to perform great and awesome wonders by driving out nations and their gods
from before your people, whom you redeemed from Egypt?[a] [24]You have established your people Israel as your very own
forever, and you, O LORD, have become
their God.
[25]"And now, LORD God, keep forever the promise you have made concerning your servant and his house. Do as
you promised, [26]so that your name will
be great forever. Then men will say, 'The
LORD Almighty is God over Israel!' And
the house of your servant David will be
established before you.
[27]"O LORD Almighty, God of Israel,
you have revealed this to your servant,
saying, 'I will build a house for you.' So
your servant has found courage to offer
you this prayer. [28]O Sovereign LORD, you
are God! Your words are trustworthy, and
you have promised these good things to
your servant. [29]Now be pleased to bless
the house of your servant, that it may
continue forever in your sight; for you,
O Sovereign LORD, have spoken, and
with your blessing the house of your servant will be blessed forever."

David's Victories

8 In the course of time, David defeated the
Philistines and subdued them, and he took
Metheg Ammah from the control of the
Philistines.
[2]David also defeated the Moabites. He
made them lie down on the ground and
measured them off with a length of cord. Every two lengths of them were put to death,
and the third length was allowed to live. So
the Moabites became subject to David and
brought tribute.
[3]Moreover, David fought Hadadezer son
of Rehob, king of Zobah, when he went to
restore his control along the Euphrates River. [4]David captured a thousand of his chariots, seven thousand charioteers[b] and twenty
thousand foot soldiers. He hamstrung all but
a hundred of the chariot horses.
[5]When the Arameans of Damascus came to
help Hadadezer king of Zobah, David struck
down twenty-two thousand of them. [6]He put
garrisons in the Aramean kingdom of Damascus, and the Arameans became subject to him
and brought tribute. The LORD gave David
victory wherever he went.
[7]David took the gold shields that belonged
to the officers of Hadadezer and brought them
to Jerusalem. [8]From Tebah[c] and Berothai,
towns that belonged to Hadadezer, King David took a great quantity of bronze.
[9]When Tou[d] king of Hamath heard that
David had defeated the entire army of Hadadezer, [10]he sent his son Joram[e] to King David
to greet him and congratulate him on his victory in battle over Hadadezer, who had been
at war with Tou. Joram brought with him articles of silver and gold and bronze.
[11]King David dedicated these articles to
the LORD, as he had done with the silver and
gold from all the nations he had subdued:
[12]Edom[f] and Moab, the Ammonites and the
Philistines, and Amalek. He also dedicated the
plunder taken from Hadadezer son of Rehob,
king of Zobah.
[13]And David became famous after he returned from striking down eighteen thousand
Edomites[g] in the Valley of Salt.
[14]He put garrisons throughout Edom, and
all the Edomites became subject to David. The
LORD gave David victory wherever he went.

David's Officials

[15]David reigned over all Israel, doing what
was just and right for all his people. [16]Joab son
of Zeruiah was over the army; Jehoshaphat
son of Ahilud was recorder; [17]Zadok son of

[a] *23* See Septuagint and 1 Chron. 17:21; Hebrew *wonders for your land and before your people, whom you redeemed from Egypt, from the nations and their gods.* [b] *4* Septuagint (see also Dead Sea Scrolls and 1 Chron. 18:4); Masoretic Text *captured seventeen hundred of his charioteers* [c] *8* See some Septuagint manuscripts (see also 1 Chron. 18:8); Hebrew *Betah.* [d] *9* Hebrew *Toi*, a variant of *Tou*; also in verse 10 [e] *10* A variant of *Hadoram* [f] *12* Some Hebrew manuscripts, Septuagint and Syriac (see also 1 Chron. 18:11); most Hebrew manuscripts *Aram* [g] *13* A few Hebrew manuscripts, Septuagint and Syriac (see also 1 Chron. 18:12); most Hebrew manuscripts *Aram* (that is, Arameans)

Ahitub and Ahimelech son of Abiathar were
priests; Seraiah was secretary; 18Benaiah son
of Jehoiada was over the Kerethites and Pelethites; and David's sons were royal advisers.[a]

David and Mephibosheth

9 David asked, "Is there anyone still left of
the house of Saul to whom I can show
kindness for Jonathan's sake?"
2Now there was a servant of Saul's household named Ziba. They called him to appear
before David, and the king said to him, "Are
you Ziba?"
"Your servant," he replied.
3The king asked, "Is there no one still left of
the house of Saul to whom I can show God's
kindness?"
Ziba answered the king, "There is still a son
of Jonathan; he is crippled in both feet."
4"Where is he?" the king asked.
Ziba answered, "He is at the house of Makir son of Ammiel in Lo Debar."
5So King David had him brought from Lo
Debar, from the house of Makir son of Ammiel.
6When Mephibosheth son of Jonathan, the
son of Saul, came to David, he bowed down
to pay him honor.
David said, "Mephibosheth!"
"Your servant," he replied.
7"Don't be afraid," David said to him, "for
I will surely show you kindness for the sake
of your father Jonathan. I will restore to you
all the land that belonged to your grandfather
Saul, and you will always eat at my table."
8Mephibosheth bowed down and said,
"What is your servant, that you should notice
a dead dog like me?"
9Then the king summoned Ziba, Saul's
servant, and said to him, "I have given your
master's grandson everything that belonged to
Saul and his family. 10You and your sons and
your servants are to farm the land for him and
bring in the crops, so that your master's grandson may be provided for. And Mephibosheth,
grandson of your master, will always eat at my
table." (Now Ziba had fifteen sons and twenty
servants.)
11Then Ziba said to the king, "Your servant
will do whatever my lord the king commands
his servant to do." So Mephibosheth ate at
David's[b] table like one of the king's sons.
12Mephibosheth had a young son named
Mica, and all the members of Ziba's household were servants of Mephibosheth. 13And
Mephibosheth lived in Jerusalem, because he
always ate at the king's table, and he was crippled in both feet.

David Defeats the Ammonites

10 In the course of time, the king of the
Ammonites died, and his son Hanun succeeded him as king. 2David
thought, "I will show kindness to Hanun son
of Nahash, just as his father showed kindness to me." So David sent a delegation to
express his sympathy to Hanun concerning
his father.
When David's men came to the land of
the Ammonites, 3the Ammonite nobles said
to Hanun their lord, "Do you think David is
honoring your father by sending men to you
to express sympathy? Hasn't David sent them
to you to explore the city and spy it out and
overthrow it?" 4So Hanun seized David's men,
shaved off half of each man's beard, cut off
their garments in the middle at the buttocks,
and sent them away.
5When David was told about this, he sent
messengers to meet the men, for they were
greatly humiliated. The king said, "Stay at
Jericho till your beards have grown, and then
come back."
6When the Ammonites realized that they
had become a stench in David's nostrils, they
hired twenty thousand Aramean foot soldiers
from Beth Rehob and Zobah, as well as the
king of Maacah with a thousand men, and
also twelve thousand men from Tob.
7On hearing this, David sent Joab out with
the entire army of fighting men. 8The Ammonites came out and drew up in battle formation at the entrance to their city gate, while
the Arameans of Zobah and Rehob and the
men of Tob and Maacah were by themselves
in the open country.
9Joab saw that there were battle lines in
front of him and behind him; so he selected
some of the best troops in Israel and deployed
them against the Arameans. 10He put the rest
of the men under the command of Abishai his
brother and deployed them against the Ammonites. 11Joab said, "If the Arameans are too
strong for me, then you are to come to my
rescue; but if the Ammonites are too strong
for you, then I will come to rescue you. 12Be
strong and let us fight bravely for our people
and the cities of our God. The LORD will do
what is good in his sight."
13Then Joab and the troops with him ad-

[a] *18* Or *were priests* [b] *11* Septuagint; Hebrew *my*

FRIDAY
READ 2 SAMUEL 9:1–13

LOVING THOSE YOU LOVE

Many years after his friend Jonathan died, King David reached out to Jonathan's son Mephibosheth. David restored to Mephibosheth the land that had belonged to his grandfather, King Saul, and David welcomed Mephibosheth to his royal table. Why? Because David loved Jonathan and wanted to do something kind to a member of Saul's household "for Jonathan's sake" (2 Samuel 9:1).

Sometimes, I don't want to extend myself on behalf of anyone else, even my husband. But when we entered into marriage, we committed not just to love each other but also to behave lovingly toward the people we each love. This doesn't mean we necessarily have to like everyone our spouse likes. The Bible, after all, doesn't say whether or not David liked Mephibosheth. What it says is that David and Jonathan had a special love for each other (see 1 Samuel 18:1–4; 20:17; 2 Samuel 1:26); and because David loved Jonathan, he extended kindness to Mephibosheth.

One of the most powerful ways my husband loves me is by loving my sister. To be completely honest, my sister and I don't get along that well. We don't have much in common (except our faces, which are almost identical). When we're together, we seem to regress to childhood, circa 1985, when I was nine and she was sixteen. She tells me what to do, and I bristle. We get tetchy. We pick at each other like hens.

I think Griff and Leanne like each other well enough, though I doubt they would have sought each other out and become friends had not marriage made them siblings-in-law. And it doesn't really matter how much they like each other. What matters is that they extend themselves to one another.

On Wednesday nights, when I have church commitments, Griff eats dinner with Leanne and her family. Griff also volunteers to babysit for my nephew. When I am out of town on business, Leanne calls Griff and checks on him. And though Griff and Leanne do have affection for one another, they make these gestures, I think, less out of affection for one another and more out of love for me. Griff understands that eating dinner with Leanne and her family knits Leanne and me together, even though I am not at the dinner table.

When two people marry, they don't become involved with just one other person. Spouses come with a constellation of families and friends. We can ignore those relationships. We can view them as a threat to our relationship with our spouse and fight them. Or we can lovingly insert ourselves into those relationships and help grow them.

We don't have to develop intimate friendships with all of our spouse's relatives and close friends. But, as David understood, we can best honor, love and serve our spouse by making loving overtures to the people they love.

—LAUREN WINNER

"I will surely show you kindness for the sake of your father Jonathan."

— 2 SAMUEL 9:7

let's talk

- ✦ Who are the people (besides each other and our children) we love best in the world? How have we extended ourselves in love to people in each other's world?
- ✦ Why is it sometimes difficult to love the other people who came with this marriage? Is there someone one of us finds difficult to love? What would happen if we imagined God showing up in our relationships with difficult people?
- ✦ Is there a cherished friend or relative whom we wished had a better relationship with one of us?

FOR YOUR NEXT DEVOTIONAL READING, TURN TO PAGE 332.

vanced to fight the Arameans, and they fled before him. 14When the Ammonites saw that the Arameans were fleeing, they fled before Abishai and went inside the city. So Joab returned from fighting the Ammonites and came to Jerusalem.

15After the Arameans saw that they had been routed by Israel, they regrouped. 16Hadadezer had Arameans brought from beyond the River[a]; they went to Helam, with Shobach the commander of Hadadezer's army leading them.

17When David was told of this, he gathered all Israel, crossed the Jordan and went to Helam. The Arameans formed their battle lines to meet David and fought against him. 18But they fled before Israel, and David killed seven hundred of their charioteers and forty thousand of their foot soldiers.[b] He also struck down Shobach the commander of their army, and he died there. 19When all the kings who were vassals of Hadadezer saw that they had been defeated by Israel, they made peace with the Israelites and became subject to them.

So the Arameans were afraid to help the Ammonites anymore.

David and Bathsheba

11 In the spring, at the time when kings go off to war, David sent Joab out with the king's men and the whole Israelite army. They destroyed the Ammonites and besieged Rabbah. But David remained in Jerusalem.

2One evening David got up from his bed and walked around on the roof of the palace. From the roof he saw a woman bathing. The woman was very beautiful, 3and David sent someone to find out about her. The man said, "Isn't this Bathsheba, the daughter of Eliam and the wife of Uriah the Hittite?" 4Then David sent messengers to get her. She came to him, and he slept with her. (She had purified herself from her uncleanness.) Then[c] she went back home. 5The woman conceived and sent word to David, saying, "I am pregnant."

6So David sent this word to Joab: "Send me Uriah the Hittite." And Joab sent him to David. 7When Uriah came to him, David asked him how Joab was, how the soldiers were and how the war was going. 8Then David said to Uriah, "Go down to your house and wash your feet." So Uriah left the palace, and a gift from the king was sent after him. 9But Uriah slept at the entrance to the palace with all his master's servants and did not go down to his house.

10When David was told, "Uriah did not go home," he asked him, "Haven't you just come from a distance? Why didn't you go home?"

11Uriah said to David, "The ark and Israel and Judah are staying in tents, and my master Joab and my lord's men are camped in the open fields. How could I go to my house to eat and drink and lie with my wife? As surely as you live, I will not do such a thing!"

12Then David said to him, "Stay here one more day, and tomorrow I will send you back." So Uriah remained in Jerusalem that day and the next. 13At David's invitation, he ate and drank with him, and David made him drunk. But in the evening Uriah went out to sleep on his mat among his master's servants; he did not go home.

14In the morning David wrote a letter to Joab and sent it with Uriah. 15In it he wrote, "Put Uriah in the front line where the fighting is fiercest. Then withdraw from him so he will be struck down and die."

16So while Joab had the city under siege, he put Uriah at a place where he knew the strongest defenders were. 17When the men of the city came out and fought against Joab, some of the men in David's army fell; moreover, Uriah the Hittite died.

18Joab sent David a full account of the battle. 19He instructed the messenger: "When you have finished giving the king this account of the battle, 20the king's anger may flare up, and he may ask you, 'Why did you get so close to the city to fight? Didn't you know they would shoot arrows from the wall? 21Who killed Abimelech son of Jerub-Besheth[d]? Didn't a woman throw an upper millstone on him from the wall, so that he died in Thebez? Why did you get so close to the wall?' If he asks you this, then say to him, 'Also, your servant Uriah the Hittite is dead.' "

22The messenger set out, and when he arrived he told David everything Joab had sent him to say. 23The messenger said to David, "The men overpowered us and came out against us in the open, but we drove them back to the entrance to the city gate. 24Then the archers shot arrows at your servants from the wall, and some of the king's men died. Moreover, your servant Uriah the Hittite is dead."

25David told the messenger, "Say this to Joab: 'Don't let this upset you; the sword de-

[a] *16* That is, the Euphrates [b] *18* Some Septuagint manuscripts (see also 1 Chron. 19:18); Hebrew *horsemen* [c] *4* Or *with her. When she purified herself from her uncleanness,* [d] *21* Also known as *Jerub-Baal* (that is, Gideon)

vours one as well as another. Press the attack against the city and destroy it.' Say this to encourage Joab."

26When Uriah's wife heard that her husband was dead, she mourned for him. 27After the time of mourning was over, David had her brought to his house, and she became his wife and bore him a son. But the thing David had done displeased the LORD.

Nathan Rebukes David

12 The LORD sent Nathan to David. When he came to him, he said, "There were two men in a certain town, one rich and the other poor. 2The rich man had a very large number of sheep and cattle, 3but the poor man had nothing except one little ewe lamb he had bought. He raised it, and it grew up with him and his children. It shared his food, drank from his cup and even slept in his arms. It was like a daughter to him.

4"Now a traveler came to the rich man, but the rich man refrained from taking one of his own sheep or cattle to prepare a meal for the traveler who had come to him. Instead, he took the ewe lamb that belonged to the poor man and prepared it for the one who had come to him."

5David burned with anger against the man and said to Nathan, "As surely as the LORD lives, the man who did this deserves to die! 6He must pay for that lamb four times over, because he did such a thing and had no pity."

7Then Nathan said to David, "You are the man! This is what the LORD, the God of Israel, says: 'I anointed you king over Israel, and I delivered you from the hand of Saul. 8I gave your master's house to you, and your master's wives into your arms. I gave you the house of Israel and Judah. And if all this had been too little, I would have given you even more. 9Why did you despise the word of the LORD by doing what is evil in his eyes? You struck down Uriah the Hittite with the sword and took his wife to be your own. You killed him with the sword of the Ammonites. 10Now, therefore, the sword will never depart from your house, because you despised me and took the wife of Uriah the Hittite to be your own.'

11"This is what the LORD says: 'Out of your own household I am going to bring calamity upon you. Before your very eyes I will take your wives and give them to one who is close to you, and he will lie with your wives in broad daylight. 12You did it in secret, but I will do this thing in broad daylight before all Israel.' "

13Then David said to Nathan, "I have sinned against the LORD."

Nathan replied, "The LORD has taken away your sin. You are not going to die. 14But because by doing this you have made the enemies of the LORD show utter contempt,[a] the son born to you will die."

15After Nathan had gone home, the LORD struck the child that Uriah's wife had borne to David, and he became ill. 16David pleaded with God for the child. He fasted and went into his house and spent the nights lying on the ground. 17The elders of his household stood beside him to get him up from the ground, but he refused, and he would not eat any food with them.

18On the seventh day the child died. David's servants were afraid to tell him that the child was dead, for they thought, "While the child was still living, we spoke to David but he would not listen to us. How can we tell him the child is dead? He may do something desperate."

19David noticed that his servants were whispering among themselves and he realized the child was dead. "Is the child dead?" he asked.

"Yes," they replied, "he is dead."

20Then David got up from the ground. After he had washed, put on lotions and changed his clothes, he went into the house of the LORD and worshiped. Then he went to his own house, and at his request they served him food, and he ate.

21His servants asked him, "Why are you acting this way? While the child was alive, you fasted and wept, but now that the child is dead, you get up and eat!"

22He answered, "While the child was still alive, I fasted and wept. I thought, 'Who knows? The LORD may be gracious to me and let the child live.' 23But now that he is dead, why should I fast? Can I bring him back again? I will go to him, but he will not return to me."

24Then David comforted his wife Bathsheba, and he went to her and lay with her. She gave birth to a son, and they named him Solomon. The LORD loved him; 25and because the LORD loved him, he sent word through Nathan the prophet to name him Jedidiah.[b]

26Meanwhile Joab fought against Rabbah of the Ammonites and captured the royal cit-

---

[a] *14* Masoretic Text; an ancient Hebrew scribal tradition *this you have shown utter contempt for the LORD* [b] *25* *Jedidiah* means *loved by the LORD.*

WEEKEND

preventing an affair

An affair is the most arduous course a couple must navigate. The pain of betrayal is devastating. Trust—essential to a vital marriage—is long in the mending. Of course, Satan knows this, so he uses infidelity to try to mortally wound a relationship that was put in place by God. It is essential that Christians work to affair-proof their marriages. Here's how.

1. *Begin with yourself.* Make sure you see your marriage as a covenant, as God does. Acknowledge that vow before God and recommit to it, to your marriage and to your spouse. That vow leaves no room for infidelity. Like Joseph (in Genesis 39), purpose in your heart not to sin against God or defile your marriage. "Wash your mind" often with such passages as Proverbs 5, 1 Thessalonians 4:3–6 and James 1:13–18.
2. *Be honest with each other* about personal needs and marital problems. While sexual addiction, personality disorders or a search for validation can precipitate an affair, most affairs reflect problems in the marriage. The best way to beat temptation is to prevent it from coming. Make sure you're connecting with each other and that appropriate needs are being satisfied at home. Honest discussion shows a commitment to both spouse and marriage. You're willing to take a chance so you and your spouse can address what's important to your marriage's vitality.
3. *Talk frequently and openly with your spouse.* Talk about your relationship, affection, changes (like extra pounds and thinning hair), and failures. Allow your spouse to be open with you. First Peter 3:8–12 has been helpful for us as we navigated the difficulty of honest communication. It's easy to express your unmet needs but far more difficult to hear about your faults.
4. *Monitor priorities.* Don't allow jobs, hobbies, parents, school, church or kids to crowd out the attention that belongs to the marital bond. Not all needs are met at home, but make sure those that should be are.
5. *Be intimate.* Learn what matters to your spouse and make sure it happens. Never discount him or her, and if you do, make sincere amends. Grow together in Christ. Treat your spouse as a precious gift from God. That way you will remain what God has made you—one flesh in his sight.

—DR. TIM AND JULIE CLINTON

setting our rules

We all have rules in our marriages. For example, we expect our spouse to live with us, not with his or her parents, and we don't let our spouse share a hotel room with a coworker of the opposite sex. When both spouses agree to the same rules, the resulting behaviors (even though not strictly forbidden by Scripture) can provide a barrier of protection around the marital relationship.

Consider each of the rules below. Answer "yes" if this is a rule you would agree to, "no" if it is a rule you can't agree to, and "maybe" if you're unsure. Compare answers with your spouse.

1. I will not meet with someone of the opposite sex alone behind closed doors, even at work.
2. All email and Internet activity, such as Web pages surfed and Instant Messaging history is open and available for my spouse to inspect.
3. I will not have a meal alone with someone of the opposite sex (who isn't related to me), unless my spouse knows about it and approves it.
4. In public, I will only say positive and uplifting things about my spouse.
5. I pledge to communicate with my spouse at least once a day while traveling.
6. I surround myself at work with reminders of my spouse and children in the form of pictures, artwork and family mementos.
7. I will have a spiritually mature, same-gender accountability partner and commit to being honest with that person.
8. I commit to spending uninterrupted time with my spouse daily, weekly and annually.
9. I won't discuss marital problems with anyone of the opposite sex.
10. I commit to a no-surprises policy. My spouse will always know where I am going and whom I am with.
11. My spouse will have regular access to all my financial information, including cell phone charges and credit card statements.
12. I commit to reading ___ number of books a year on improving marriage and to attending a marriage retreat, encounter weekend or workshop annually.

HOW ARE WE DOING?

date

let's make a DATE

REVIEW YOUR VOWS

This weekend find an opportunity to read the vows you made when you married, then consider adding new ones. Pick some from the above list, for example. Then, for fun, consider adding vows such as "I promise never to cheer against your favorite team" or "We will be faithful to each other in sickness, in health and during PMS."

Write out all the vows. Then find a place that has special meaning for both of you (a mountain top, a hiking trail, a local park or a secluded church). Exchange your vows privately there.

FOR YOUR NEXT DEVOTIONAL READING, TURN TO PAGE 336.

LESSONS FROM THE *Bible*

What vows might the following couples have made to each other to keep their marriage going?

1. Moses and Zipporah (Exodus 2:11–22)
2. Rahab and Salmon (Joshua 6:22–25; Matthew 1:5)
3. David and Abigail (1 Samuel 25:1–42)

adel. 27 Joab then sent messengers to David, saying, "I have fought against Rabbah and taken its water supply. 28 Now muster the rest of the troops and besiege the city and capture it. Otherwise I will take the city, and it will be named after me."

29 So David mustered the entire army and went to Rabbah, and attacked and captured it. 30 He took the crown from the head of their king[a]—its weight was a talent[b] of gold, and it was set with precious stones—and it was placed on David's head. He took a great quantity of plunder from the city 31 and brought out the people who were there, consigning them to labor with saws and with iron picks and axes, and he made them work at brickmaking.[c] He did this to all the Ammonite towns. Then David and his entire army returned to Jerusalem.

Amnon and Tamar

13 In the course of time, Amnon son of David fell in love with Tamar, the beautiful sister of Absalom son of David.

2 Amnon became frustrated to the point of illness on account of his sister Tamar, for she was a virgin, and it seemed impossible for him to do anything to her.

3 Now Amnon had a friend named Jonadab son of Shimeah, David's brother. Jonadab was a very shrewd man. 4 He asked Amnon, "Why do you, the king's son, look so haggard morning after morning? Won't you tell me?"

Amnon said to him, "I'm in love with Tamar, my brother Absalom's sister."

5 "Go to bed and pretend to be ill," Jonadab said. "When your father comes to see you, say to him, 'I would like my sister Tamar to come and give me something to eat. Let her prepare the food in my sight so I may watch her and then eat it from her hand.' "

6 So Amnon lay down and pretended to be ill. When the king came to see him, Amnon said to him, "I would like my sister Tamar to come and make some special bread in my sight, so I may eat from her hand."

7 David sent word to Tamar at the palace: "Go to the house of your brother Amnon and prepare some food for him." 8 So Tamar went to the house of her brother Amnon, who was lying down. She took some dough, kneaded it, made the bread in his sight and baked it. 9 Then she took the pan and served him the bread, but he refused to eat.

"Send everyone out of here," Amnon said. So everyone left him. 10 Then Amnon said to Tamar, "Bring the food here into my bedroom so I may eat from your hand." And Tamar took the bread she had prepared and brought it to her brother Amnon in his bedroom. 11 But when she took it to him to eat, he grabbed her and said, "Come to bed with me, my sister."

12 "Don't, my brother!" she said to him. "Don't force me. Such a thing should not be done in Israel! Don't do this wicked thing. 13 What about me? Where could I get rid of my disgrace? And what about you? You would be like one of the wicked fools in Israel. Please speak to the king; he will not keep me from being married to you." 14 But he refused to listen to her, and since he was stronger than she, he raped her.

15 Then Amnon hated her with intense hatred. In fact, he hated her more than he had loved her. Amnon said to her, "Get up and get out!"

16 "No!" she said to him. "Sending me away would be a greater wrong than what you have already done to me."

But he refused to listen to her. 17 He called his personal servant and said, "Get this woman out of here and bolt the door after her." 18 So his servant put her out and bolted the door after her. She was wearing a richly ornamented[d] robe, for this was the kind of garment the virgin daughters of the king wore. 19 Tamar put ashes on her head and tore the ornamented[e] robe she was wearing. She put her hand on her head and went away, weeping aloud as she went.

20 Her brother Absalom said to her, "Has that Amnon, your brother, been with you? Be quiet now, my sister; he is your brother. Don't take this thing to heart." And Tamar lived in her brother Absalom's house, a desolate woman.

21 When King David heard all this, he was furious. 22 Absalom never said a word to Amnon, either good or bad; he hated Amnon because he had disgraced his sister Tamar.

Absalom Kills Amnon

23 Two years later, when Absalom's sheepshearers were at Baal Hazor near the border of Ephraim, he invited all the king's sons to come there. 24 Absalom went to the king and said,

[a] *30* Or *of Milcom* (that is, Molech) [b] *30* That is, about 75 pounds (about 34 kilograms) [c] *31* The meaning of the Hebrew for this clause is uncertain. [d] *18* The meaning of the Hebrew for this phrase is uncertain. [e] *19* The meaning of the Hebrew for this word is uncertain.

"Your servant has had shearers come. Will the
king and his officials please join me?"
25"No, my son," the king replied. "All of us
should not go; we would only be a burden to
you." Although Absalom urged him, he still
refused to go, but gave him his blessing.
26Then Absalom said, "If not, please let my
brother Amnon come with us."
The king asked him, "Why should he go
with you?" 27But Absalom urged him, so he
sent with him Amnon and the rest of the
king's sons.
28Absalom ordered his men, "Listen! When
Amnon is in high spirits from drinking wine
and I say to you, 'Strike Amnon down,' then
kill him. Don't be afraid. Have not I given
you this order? Be strong and brave." 29So
Absalom's men did to Amnon what Absalom
had ordered. Then all the king's sons got up,
mounted their mules and fled.
30While they were on their way, the report
came to David: "Absalom has struck down all
the king's sons; not one of them is left." 31The
king stood up, tore his clothes and lay down
on the ground; and all his servants stood by
with their clothes torn.
32But Jonadab son of Shimeah, David's
brother, said, "My lord should not think that
they killed all the princes; only Amnon is
dead. This has been Absalom's expressed intention ever since the day Amnon raped his
sister Tamar. 33My lord the king should not be
concerned about the report that all the king's
sons are dead. Only Amnon is dead."
34Meanwhile, Absalom had fled.
Now the man standing watch looked up
and saw many people on the road west of
him, coming down the side of the hill. The
watchman went and told the king, "I see men
in the direction of Horonaim, on the side of
the hill." [a]
35Jonadab said to the king, "See, the king's
sons are here; it has happened just as your servant said."
36As he finished speaking, the king's sons
came in, wailing loudly. The king, too, and all
his servants wept very bitterly.
37Absalom fled and went to Talmai son of
Ammihud, the king of Geshur. But King David mourned for his son every day.
38After Absalom fled and went to Geshur,
he stayed there three years. 39And the spirit of
the king [b] longed to go to Absalom, for he was
consoled concerning Amnon's death.

Absalom Returns to Jerusalem

14 Joab son of Zeruiah knew that the king's
heart longed for Absalom. 2So Joab sent
someone to Tekoa and had a wise woman brought from there. He said to her, "Pretend you are in mourning. Dress in mourning
clothes, and don't use any cosmetic lotions.
Act like a woman who has spent many days
grieving for the dead. 3Then go to the king
and speak these words to him." And Joab put
the words in her mouth.
4When the woman from Tekoa went [c] to
the king, she fell with her face to the ground
to pay him honor, and she said, "Help me,
O king!"
5The king asked her, "What is troubling
you?"
She said, "I am indeed a widow; my husband is dead. 6I your servant had two sons.
They got into a fight with each other in the
field, and no one was there to separate them.
One struck the other and killed him. 7Now
the whole clan has risen up against your servant; they say, 'Hand over the one who struck
his brother down, so that we may put him
to death for the life of his brother whom he
killed; then we will get rid of the heir as well.'
They would put out the only burning coal I
have left, leaving my husband neither name
nor descendant on the face of the earth."
8The king said to the woman, "Go home,
and I will issue an order in your behalf."
9But the woman from Tekoa said to him,
"My lord the king, let the blame rest on me
and on my father's family, and let the king and
his throne be without guilt."
10The king replied, "If anyone says anything to you, bring him to me, and he will not
bother you again."
11She said, "Then let the king invoke the
LORD his God to prevent the avenger of blood
from adding to the destruction, so that my
son will not be destroyed."
"As surely as the LORD lives," he said, "not
one hair of your son's head will fall to the
ground."
12Then the woman said, "Let your servant
speak a word to my lord the king."
"Speak," he replied.
13The woman said, "Why then have you
devised a thing like this against the people of
God? When the king says this, does he not
convict himself, for the king has not brought
back his banished son? 14Like water spilled

---

[a] 34 Septuagint; Hebrew does not have this sentence. [b] 39 Dead Sea Scrolls and some Septuagint manuscripts; Masoretic Text *But the spirit of David the king* [c] 4 Many Hebrew manuscripts, Septuagint, Vulgate and Syriac; most Hebrew manuscripts *spoke*

MONDAY
READ 2 SAMUEL 14:1–24

FINDING A WAY TO RECONCILE

> **"Like water spilled on the ground, which cannot be recovered, so we must die. But God does not take away life; instead, he devises ways so that a banished person may not remain estranged from him."**
>
> — 2 SAMUEL 14:14

As we see in 2 Samuel 13, a terrible rift opened in David's family after David's affair with Bathsheba and murder of her husband. David's son Amnon raped his half sister Tamar. When Absalom, Tamar's full brother, realized that their father wasn't going to discipline Amnon in any way, he took matters into his own hands and killed his half brother. Then Absalom fled the country.

Three long years went by. Finally, David's commander, Joab, sent a messenger to the king. The woman told David a story of how, after one of her two sons had killed the other, her clan rose up to avenge the death. When David offered to protect the living son, the woman said that David was convicting himself by failing to restore his banished son. "[God] devises ways so that a banished person may not remain estranged from him," the woman from Tekoa said.

Like families, marriages too can be ripped apart by misunderstanding, arguments and betrayals. Perhaps a couple faces the agony of an affair. Whatever the reason, sometimes a marriage begins to unravel. Some couples actually live apart, while others remain under the same roof but are emotionally distant. Sadly, some couples, after repeated efforts to work things out, and after much counseling, prayer and soul searching, cannot find a way to bridge the gap and end up divorcing.

If a couple does divorce, it is a good idea to learn some healthy ways to interact. This is particularly necessary if there are children. If one person remarries, contact with the former spouse will be sticky and should only be done with full disclosure and with the blessing of the new spouse.

Even if a couple doesn't have children, we are children of God, and he has promised us that he devises ways so that we will not have to remain banished from others, particularly those who have deeply hurt us. Although a couple may be divorced, they may still strive to love each other again through Christ. We aren't told in 2 Samuel 14 exactly how to do that. But as Christians we know we are commanded to forgive others of wrongdoing, even as God has forgiven us. Letting go of hate and anger can only help us by halting inner erosion. It also frees us to learn ways to live in peace and harmony with others so that the world around us will know that we are Christians by our love.

David was convicted by the woman of Tekoa to allow his son Absalom to come back to Jerusalem. But he still wouldn't see him. That proved tragic for both of them; David almost lost the kingdom to his angry son, and Absalom lost his life in the resulting battle.

How much better it is to tune in to God's ways, which make it possible for us to love each other even when there is a breakdown in the relationship. For through Christ and the indwelling of his Spirit, these things are possible. As 2 Corinthians 5:18 tells us, "All this is from God, who reconciled us to himself through Christ and gave us the ministry of reconciliation."

—JOHN R. THROOP

let's talk

- ✦ What are some causes of estrangement in marriage? How is estrangement different from disagreement?
- ✦ What are some of the best ways to find common ground with each other? How do our shared experiences and our faith help us to start over?
- ✦ If one or both of us have been divorced, should communication with a former spouse take place in our situation? If so, what is the best way to do this?

FOR YOUR NEXT DEVOTIONAL READING, TURN TO PAGE 348.

on the ground, which cannot be recovered,
so we must die. But God does not take away
life; instead, he devises ways so that a banished person may not remain estranged from
him.
15"And now I have come to say this to my
lord the king because the people have made
me afraid. Your servant thought, 'I will speak
to the king; perhaps he will do what his servant asks. 16Perhaps the king will agree to
deliver his servant from the hand of the man
who is trying to cut off both me and my son
from the inheritance God gave us.'
17"And now your servant says, 'May the
word of my lord the king bring me rest, for
my lord the king is like an angel of God in
discerning good and evil. May the LORD your
God be with you.' "
18Then the king said to the woman, "Do
not keep from me the answer to what I am
going to ask you."
"Let my lord the king speak," the woman
said.
19The king asked, "Isn't the hand of Joab
with you in all this?"
The woman answered, "As surely as you
live, my lord the king, no one can turn to the
right or to the left from anything my lord the
king says. Yes, it was your servant Joab who
instructed me to do this and who put all these
words into the mouth of your servant. 20Your
servant Joab did this to change the present situation. My lord has wisdom like that of an
angel of God—he knows everything that happens in the land."
21The king said to Joab, "Very well, I will
do it. Go, bring back the young man Absalom."
22Joab fell with his face to the ground to
pay him honor, and he blessed the king. Joab
said, "Today your servant knows that he has
found favor in your eyes, my lord the king,
because the king has granted his servant's request."
23Then Joab went to Geshur and brought
Absalom back to Jerusalem. 24But the king
said, "He must go to his own house; he must
not see my face." So Absalom went to his own
house and did not see the face of the king.
25In all Israel there was not a man so highly
praised for his handsome appearance as Absalom. From the top of his head to the sole of
his foot there was no blemish in him. 26When-
ever he cut the hair of his head—he used to
cut his hair from time to time when it became
too heavy for him—he would weigh it, and
its weight was two hundred shekels[a] by the
royal standard.
27Three sons and a daughter were born to
Absalom. The daughter's name was Tamar,
and she became a beautiful woman.
28Absalom lived two years in Jerusalem
without seeing the king's face. 29Then Absalom sent for Joab in order to send him to the
king, but Joab refused to come to him. So he
sent a second time, but he refused to come.
30Then he said to his servants, "Look, Joab's
field is next to mine, and he has barley there.
Go and set it on fire." So Absalom's servants
set the field on fire.
31Then Joab did go to Absalom's house and
he said to him, "Why have your servants set
my field on fire?"
32Absalom said to Joab, "Look, I sent word
to you and said, 'Come here so I can send you
to the king to ask, "Why have I come from
Geshur? It would be better for me if I were
still there!" ' Now then, I want to see the king's
face, and if I am guilty of anything, let him
put me to death."
33So Joab went to the king and told him
this. Then the king summoned Absalom, and
he came in and bowed down with his face
to the ground before the king. And the king
kissed Absalom.

Absalom's Conspiracy

15 In the course of time, Absalom provided himself with a chariot and horses and
with fifty men to run ahead of him. 2He
would get up early and stand by the side of
the road leading to the city gate. Whenever
anyone came with a complaint to be placed
before the king for a decision, Absalom would
call out to him, "What town are you from?"
He would answer, "Your servant is from one
of the tribes of Israel." 3Then Absalom would
say to him, "Look, your claims are valid and
proper, but there is no representative of the
king to hear you." 4And Absalom would add,
"If only I were appointed judge in the land!
Then everyone who has a complaint or case
could come to me and I would see that he gets
justice."
5Also, whenever anyone approached him to
bow down before him, Absalom would reach
out his hand, take hold of him and kiss him.
6Absalom behaved in this way toward all the
Israelites who came to the king asking for jus-

a 26 That is, about 5 pounds (about 2.3 kilograms)

tice, and so he stole the hearts of the men of
Israel.
7At the end of four[a] years, Absalom said
to the king, "Let me go to Hebron and fulfill
a vow I made to the LORD. 8While your servant was living at Geshur in Aram, I made this
vow: 'If the LORD takes me back to Jerusalem,
I will worship the LORD in Hebron.[b]' "
9The king said to him, "Go in peace." So he
went to Hebron.
10Then Absalom sent secret messengers
throughout the tribes of Israel to say, "As soon
as you hear the sound of the trumpets, then
say, 'Absalom is king in Hebron.' " 11Two hundred men from Jerusalem had accompanied
Absalom. They had been invited as guests and
went quite innocently, knowing nothing about
the matter. 12While Absalom was offering sacrifices, he also sent for Ahithophel the Gilonite, David's counselor, to come from Giloh,
his hometown. And so the conspiracy gained
strength, and Absalom's following kept on increasing.

David Flees

13A messenger came and told David, "The
hearts of the men of Israel are with Absalom."
14Then David said to all his officials who
were with him in Jerusalem, "Come! We must
flee, or none of us will escape from Absalom.
We must leave immediately, or he will move
quickly to overtake us and bring ruin upon us
and put the city to the sword."
15The king's officials answered him, "Your
servants are ready to do whatever our lord the
king chooses."
16The king set out, with his entire household following him; but he left ten concubines to take care of the palace. 17So the king
set out, with all the people following him,
and they halted at a place some distance away.
18All his men marched past him, along with
all the Kerethites and Pelethites; and all the
six hundred Gittites who had accompanied
him from Gath marched before the king.
19The king said to Ittai the Gittite, "Why
should you come along with us? Go back and
stay with King Absalom. You are a foreigner, an exile from your homeland. 20You came
only yesterday. And today shall I make you
wander about with us, when I do not know
where I am going? Go back, and take your
countrymen. May kindness and faithfulness
be with you."
21But Ittai replied to the king, "As surely as
the LORD lives, and as my lord the king lives,
wherever my lord the king may be, whether it means life or death, there will your servant be."
22David said to Ittai, "Go ahead, march
on." So Ittai the Gittite marched on with all
his men and the families that were with him.
23The whole countryside wept aloud as all
the people passed by. The king also crossed the
Kidron Valley, and all the people moved on
toward the desert.
24Zadok was there, too, and all the Levites
who were with him were carrying the ark of
the covenant of God. They set down the ark of
God, and Abiathar offered sacrifices[c] until all
the people had finished leaving the city.
25Then the king said to Zadok, "Take the
ark of God back into the city. If I find favor in
the LORD's eyes, he will bring me back and let
me see it and his dwelling place again. 26But
if he says, 'I am not pleased with you,' then I
am ready; let him do to me whatever seems
good to him."
27The king also said to Zadok the priest,
"Aren't you a seer? Go back to the city in
peace, with your son Ahimaaz and Jonathan
son of Abiathar. You and Abiathar take your
two sons with you. 28I will wait at the fords
in the desert until word comes from you to
inform me." 29So Zadok and Abiathar took
the ark of God back to Jerusalem and stayed
there.
30But David continued up the Mount of
Olives, weeping as he went; his head was covered and he was barefoot. All the people with
him covered their heads too and were weeping
as they went up. 31Now David had been told,
"Ahithophel is among the conspirators with
Absalom." So David prayed, "O LORD, turn
Ahithophel's counsel into foolishness."
32When David arrived at the summit,
where people used to worship God, Hushai
the Arkite was there to meet him, his robe
torn and dust on his head. 33David said to
him, "If you go with me, you will be a burden
to me. 34But if you return to the city and say
to Absalom, 'I will be your servant, O king; I
was your father's servant in the past, but now
I will be your servant,' then you can help me
by frustrating Ahithophel's advice. 35Won't
the priests Zadok and Abiathar be there with
you? Tell them anything you hear in the king's
palace. 36Their two sons, Ahimaaz son of Zadok and Jonathan son of Abiathar, are there

[a] *7* Some Septuagint manuscripts, Syriac and Josephus; Hebrew *forty* [b] *8* Some Septuagint manuscripts; Hebrew does not have *in Hebron.* [c] *24* Or *Abiathar went up*

with them. Send them to me with anything
you hear."
37So David's friend Hushai arrived at Jerusalem as Absalom was entering the city.

David and Ziba

16 When David had gone a short distance
beyond the summit, there was Ziba, the
steward of Mephibosheth, waiting to
meet him. He had a string of donkeys saddled
and loaded with two hundred loaves of bread,
a hundred cakes of raisins, a hundred cakes of
figs and a skin of wine.
2The king asked Ziba, "Why have you
brought these?"
Ziba answered, "The donkeys are for the
king's household to ride on, the bread and
fruit are for the men to eat, and the wine is
to refresh those who become exhausted in the
desert."
3The king then asked, "Where is your master's grandson?"
Ziba said to him, "He is staying in Jerusalem, because he thinks, 'Today the house of
Israel will give me back my grandfather's kingdom.' "
4Then the king said to Ziba, "All that belonged to Mephibosheth is now yours."
"I humbly bow," Ziba said. "May I find favor in your eyes, my lord the king."

Shimei Curses David

5As King David approached Bahurim, a
man from the same clan as Saul's family came
out from there. His name was Shimei son
of Gera, and he cursed as he came out. 6He
pelted David and all the king's officials with
stones, though all the troops and the special
guard were on David's right and left. 7As he
cursed, Shimei said, "Get out, get out, you
man of blood, you scoundrel! 8The LORD has
repaid you for all the blood you shed in the
household of Saul, in whose place you have
reigned. The LORD has handed the kingdom
over to your son Absalom. You have come to
ruin because you are a man of blood!"
9Then Abishai son of Zeruiah said to the
king, "Why should this dead dog curse my
lord the king? Let me go over and cut off his
head."
10But the king said, "What do you and I
have in common, you sons of Zeruiah? If he is
cursing because the LORD said to him, 'Curse
David,' who can ask, 'Why do you do this?' "
11David then said to Abishai and all his
officials, "My son, who is of my own flesh,
is trying to take my life. How much more,
then, this Benjamite! Leave him alone; let him
curse, for the LORD has told him to. 12It may
be that the LORD will see my distress and repay
me with good for the cursing I am receiving
today."
13So David and his men continued along
the road while Shimei was going along the
hillside opposite him, cursing as he went and
throwing stones at him and showering him
with dirt. 14The king and all the people with
him arrived at their destination exhausted.
And there he refreshed himself.

The Advice of Ahithophel and Hushai

15Meanwhile, Absalom and all the men
of Israel came to Jerusalem, and Ahithophel
was with him. 16Then Hushai the Arkite, David's friend, went to Absalom and said to him,
"Long live the king! Long live the king!"
17Absalom asked Hushai, "Is this the love
you show your friend? Why didn't you go with
your friend?"
18Hushai said to Absalom, "No, the one
chosen by the LORD, by these people, and
by all the men of Israel—his I will be, and I
will remain with him. 19Furthermore, whom
should I serve? Should I not serve the son? Just
as I served your father, so I will serve you."
20Absalom said to Ahithophel, "Give us
your advice. What should we do?"
21Ahithophel answered, "Lie with your father's concubines whom he left to take care of
the palace. Then all Israel will hear that you
have made yourself a stench in your father's
nostrils, and the hands of everyone with you
will be strengthened." 22So they pitched a
tent for Absalom on the roof, and he lay with
his father's concubines in the sight of all Israel.
23Now in those days the advice Ahithophel
gave was like that of one who inquires of God.
That was how both David and Absalom regarded all of Ahithophel's advice.
17 Ahithophel said to Absalom, "I would[a]
choose twelve thousand men and set out
tonight in pursuit of David. 2I would[b]
attack him while he is weary and weak. I
would[b] strike him with terror, and then all
the people with him will flee. I would[b] strike
down only the king 3and bring all the people
back to you. The death of the man you seek
will mean the return of all; all the people will

---

[a] 1 Or *Let me* [b] 2 Or *will*

be unharmed." 4This plan seemed good to Absalom and to all the elders of Israel.

5But Absalom said, "Summon also Hushai
the Arkite, so we can hear what he has to say."
6When Hushai came to him, Absalom said,
"Ahithophel has given this advice. Should we
do what he says? If not, give us your opinion."

7Hushai replied to Absalom, "The advice
Ahithophel has given is not good this time.
8You know your father and his men; they are
fighters, and as fierce as a wild bear robbed
of her cubs. Besides, your father is an experienced fighter; he will not spend the night with
the troops. 9Even now, he is hidden in a cave
or some other place. If he should attack your
troops first,[a] whoever hears about it will say,
'There has been a slaughter among the troops
who follow Absalom.' 10Then even the bravest
soldier, whose heart is like the heart of a lion,
will melt with fear, for all Israel knows that
your father is a fighter and that those with him
are brave.

11"So I advise you: Let all Israel, from Dan
to Beersheba—as numerous as the sand on
the seashore—be gathered to you, with you
yourself leading them into battle. 12Then we
will attack him wherever he may be found,
and we will fall on him as dew settles on the
ground. Neither he nor any of his men will be
left alive. 13If he withdraws into a city, then
all Israel will bring ropes to that city, and we
will drag it down to the valley until not even a
piece of it can be found."

14Absalom and all the men of Israel said,
"The advice of Hushai the Arkite is better
than that of Ahithophel." For the LORD had
determined to frustrate the good advice of
Ahithophel in order to bring disaster on Absalom.

15Hushai told Zadok and Abiathar, the
priests, "Ahithophel has advised Absalom and
the elders of Israel to do such and such, but
I have advised them to do so and so. 16Now
send a message immediately and tell David,
'Do not spend the night at the fords in the
desert; cross over without fail, or the king
and all the people with him will be swallowed up.' "

17Jonathan and Ahimaaz were staying at
En Rogel. A servant girl was to go and inform
them, and they were to go and tell King David, for they could not risk being seen entering
the city. 18But a young man saw them and told
Absalom. So the two of them left quickly and
went to the house of a man in Bahurim. He
had a well in his courtyard, and they climbed
down into it. 19His wife took a covering and
spread it out over the opening of the well and
scattered grain over it. No one knew anything
about it.

20When Absalom's men came to the woman at the house, they asked, "Where are Ahimaaz and Jonathan?"

The woman answered them, "They crossed
over the brook."[b] The men searched but found
no one, so they returned to Jerusalem.

21After the men had gone, the two climbed
out of the well and went to inform King David. They said to him, "Set out and cross the
river at once; Ahithophel has advised such and
such against you." 22So David and all the people with him set out and crossed the Jordan.
By daybreak, no one was left who had not
crossed the Jordan.

23When Ahithophel saw that his advice
had not been followed, he saddled his donkey
and set out for his house in his hometown.
He put his house in order and then hanged
himself. So he died and was buried in his father's tomb.

24David went to Mahanaim, and Absalom
crossed the Jordan with all the men of Israel. 25Absalom had appointed Amasa over the
army in place of Joab. Amasa was the son of
a man named Jether,[c] an Israelite[d] who had
married Abigail,[e] the daughter of Nahash and
sister of Zeruiah the mother of Joab. 26The Israelites and Absalom camped in the land of
Gilead.

27When David came to Mahanaim, Shobi
son of Nahash from Rabbah of the Ammonites, and Makir son of Ammiel from Lo Debar, and Barzillai the Gileadite from Rogelim
28brought bedding and bowls and articles of
pottery. They also brought wheat and barley,
flour and roasted grain, beans and lentils,[f]
29honey and curds, sheep, and cheese from
cows' milk for David and his people to eat.
For they said, "The people have become hungry and tired and thirsty in the desert."

Absalom's Death

18 David mustered the men who were with
him and appointed over them commanders of thousands and commanders

[a] 9 Or *When some of the men fall at the first attack* [b] 20 Or *"They passed by the sheep pen toward the water."* [c] 25 Hebrew *Ithra,* a variant of *Jether* [d] 25 Hebrew and some Septuagint manuscripts; other Septuagint manuscripts (see also 1 Chron. 2:17) *Ishmaelite* or *Jezreelite* [e] 25 Hebrew *Abigal,* a variant of *Abigail* [f] 28 Most Septuagint manuscripts and Syriac; Hebrew *lentils, and roasted grain*

of hundreds. 2David sent the troops out—a third under the command of Joab, a third under Joab's brother Abishai son of Zeruiah, and a third under Ittai the Gittite. The king told the troops, "I myself will surely march out with you."

3But the men said, "You must not go out; if we are forced to flee, they won't care about us. Even if half of us die, they won't care; but you are worth ten thousand of us.[a] It would be better now for you to give us support from the city."

4The king answered, "I will do whatever seems best to you."

So the king stood beside the gate while all the men marched out in units of hundreds and of thousands. 5The king commanded Joab, Abishai and Ittai, "Be gentle with the young man Absalom for my sake." And all the troops heard the king giving orders concerning Absalom to each of the commanders.

6The army marched into the field to fight Israel, and the battle took place in the forest of Ephraim. 7There the army of Israel was defeated by David's men, and the casualties that day were great—twenty thousand men. 8The battle spread out over the whole countryside, and the forest claimed more lives that day than the sword.

9Now Absalom happened to meet David's men. He was riding his mule, and as the mule went under the thick branches of a large oak, Absalom's head got caught in the tree. He was left hanging in midair, while the mule he was riding kept on going.

10When one of the men saw this, he told Joab, "I just saw Absalom hanging in an oak tree."

11Joab said to the man who had told him this, "What! You saw him? Why didn't you strike him to the ground right there? Then I would have had to give you ten shekels[b] of silver and a warrior's belt."

12But the man replied, "Even if a thousand shekels[c] were weighed out into my hands, I would not lift my hand against the king's son. In our hearing the king commanded you and Abishai and Ittai, 'Protect the young man Absalom for my sake.[d]' 13And if I had put my life in jeopardy[e]—and nothing is hidden from the king—you would have kept your distance from me."

14Joab said, "I'm not going to wait like this for you." So he took three javelins in his hand and plunged them into Absalom's heart while Absalom was still alive in the oak tree. 15And ten of Joab's armor-bearers surrounded Absalom, struck him and killed him.

16Then Joab sounded the trumpet, and the troops stopped pursuing Israel, for Joab halted them. 17They took Absalom, threw him into a big pit in the forest and piled up a large heap of rocks over him. Meanwhile, all the Israelites fled to their homes.

18During his lifetime Absalom had taken a pillar and erected it in the King's Valley as a monument to himself, for he thought, "I have no son to carry on the memory of my name." He named the pillar after himself, and it is called Absalom's Monument to this day.

David Mourns

19Now Ahimaaz son of Zadok said, "Let me run and take the news to the king that the Lord has delivered him from the hand of his enemies."

20"You are not the one to take the news today," Joab told him. "You may take the news another time, but you must not do so today, because the king's son is dead."

21Then Joab said to a Cushite, "Go, tell the king what you have seen." The Cushite bowed down before Joab and ran off.

22Ahimaaz son of Zadok again said to Joab, "Come what may, please let me run behind the Cushite."

But Joab replied, "My son, why do you want to go? You don't have any news that will bring you a reward."

23He said, "Come what may, I want to run."

So Joab said, "Run!" Then Ahimaaz ran by way of the plain[f] and outran the Cushite.

24While David was sitting between the inner and outer gates, the watchman went up to the roof of the gateway by the wall. As he looked out, he saw a man running alone. 25The watchman called out to the king and reported it.

The king said, "If he is alone, he must have good news." And the man came closer and closer.

26Then the watchman saw another man running, and he called down to the gatekeeper, "Look, another man running alone!"

---

[a] *3* Two Hebrew manuscripts, some Septuagint manuscripts and Vulgate; most Hebrew manuscripts *care; for now there are ten thousand like us* [b] *11* That is, about 4 ounces (about 115 grams) [c] *12* That is, about 25 pounds (about 11 kilograms) [d] *12* A few Hebrew manuscripts, Septuagint, Vulgate and Syriac; most Hebrew manuscripts may be translated *Absalom, whoever you may be.* [e] *13* Or *Otherwise, if I had acted treacherously toward him* [f] *23* That is, the plain of the Jordan

The king said, "He must be bringing good news, too."

[27]The watchman said, "It seems to me that the first one runs like Ahimaaz son of Zadok."

"He's a good man," the king said. "He comes with good news."

[28]Then Ahimaaz called out to the king, "All is well!" He bowed down before the king with his face to the ground and said, "Praise be to the LORD your God! He has delivered up the men who lifted their hands against my lord the king."

[29]The king asked, "Is the young man Absalom safe?"

Ahimaaz answered, "I saw great confusion just as Joab was about to send the king's servant and me, your servant, but I don't know what it was."

[30]The king said, "Stand aside and wait here." So he stepped aside and stood there.

[31]Then the Cushite arrived and said, "My lord the king, hear the good news! The LORD has delivered you today from all who rose up against you."

[32]The king asked the Cushite, "Is the young man Absalom safe?"

The Cushite replied, "May the enemies of my lord the king and all who rise up to harm you be like that young man."

[33]The king was shaken. He went up to the room over the gateway and wept. As he went, he said: "O my son Absalom! My son, my son Absalom! If only I had died instead of you—O Absalom, my son, my son!"

19 Joab was told, "The king is weeping and mourning for Absalom." [2]And for the whole army the victory that day was turned into mourning, because on that day the troops heard it said, "The king is grieving for his son." [3]The men stole into the city that day as men steal in who are ashamed when they flee from battle. [4]The king covered his face and cried aloud, "O my son Absalom! O Absalom, my son, my son!"

[5]Then Joab went into the house to the king and said, "Today you have humiliated all your men, who have just saved your life and the lives of your sons and daughters and the lives of your wives and concubines. [6]You love those who hate you and hate those who love you. You have made it clear today that the commanders and their men mean nothing to you. I see that you would be pleased if Absalom were alive today and all of us were dead. [7]Now go out and encourage your men. I swear by the LORD that if you don't go out, not a man will be left with you by nightfall. This will be worse for you than all the calamities that have come upon you from your youth till now."

[8]So the king got up and took his seat in the gateway. When the men were told, "The king is sitting in the gateway," they all came before him.

David Returns to Jerusalem

Meanwhile, the Israelites had fled to their homes. [9]Throughout the tribes of Israel, the people were all arguing with each other, saying, "The king delivered us from the hand of our enemies; he is the one who rescued us from the hand of the Philistines. But now he has fled the country because of Absalom; [10]and Absalom, whom we anointed to rule over us, has died in battle. So why do you say nothing about bringing the king back?"

[11]King David sent this message to Zadok and Abiathar, the priests: "Ask the elders of Judah, 'Why should you be the last to bring the king back to his palace, since what is being said throughout Israel has reached the king at his quarters? [12]You are my brothers, my own flesh and blood. So why should you be the last to bring back the king?' [13]And say to Amasa, 'Are you not my own flesh and blood? May God deal with me, be it ever so severely, if from now on you are not the commander of my army in place of Joab.' "

[14]He won over the hearts of all the men of Judah as though they were one man. They sent word to the king, "Return, you and all your men." [15]Then the king returned and went as far as the Jordan.

Now the men of Judah had come to Gilgal to go out and meet the king and bring him across the Jordan. [16]Shimei son of Gera, the Benjamite from Bahurim, hurried down with the men of Judah to meet King David. [17]With him were a thousand Benjamites, along with Ziba, the steward of Saul's household, and his fifteen sons and twenty servants. They rushed to the Jordan, where the king was. [18]They crossed at the ford to take the king's household over and to do whatever he wished.

When Shimei son of Gera crossed the Jordan, he fell prostrate before the king [19]and said to him, "May my lord not hold me guilty. Do not remember how your servant did wrong on the day my lord the king left Jerusalem. May the king put it out of his mind. [20]For I your servant know that I have sinned, but today I have come here as the first of the whole house

of Joseph to come down and meet my lord
the king."
[21]Then Abishai son of Zeruiah said,
"Shouldn't Shimei be put to death for this? He
cursed the LORD's anointed."
[22]David replied, "What do you and I have
in common, you sons of Zeruiah? This day
you have become my adversaries! Should anyone be put to death in Israel today? Do I not
know that today I am king over Israel?" [23]So
the king said to Shimei, "You shall not die."
And the king promised him on oath.
[24]Mephibosheth, Saul's grandson, also went
down to meet the king. He had not taken care
of his feet or trimmed his mustache or washed
his clothes from the day the king left until the
day he returned safely. [25]When he came from
Jerusalem to meet the king, the king asked
him, "Why didn't you go with me, Mephibosheth?"
[26]He said, "My lord the king, since I your
servant am lame, I said, 'I will have my donkey saddled and will ride on it, so I can go
with the king.' But Ziba my servant betrayed
me. [27]And he has slandered your servant to
my lord the king. My lord the king is like
an angel of God; so do whatever pleases you.
[28]All my grandfather's descendants deserved
nothing but death from my lord the king,
but you gave your servant a place among
those who eat at your table. So what right
do I have to make any more appeals to the
king?"
[29]The king said to him, "Why say more? I
order you and Ziba to divide the fields."
[30]Mephibosheth said to the king, "Let him
take everything, now that my lord the king has
arrived home safely."
[31]Barzillai the Gileadite also came down
from Rogelim to cross the Jordan with the king
and to send him on his way from there. [32]Now
Barzillai was a very old man, eighty years of
age. He had provided for the king during his
stay in Mahanaim, for he was a very wealthy
man. [33]The king said to Barzillai, "Cross over
with me and stay with me in Jerusalem, and I
will provide for you."
[34]But Barzillai answered the king, "How
many more years will I live, that I should go
up to Jerusalem with the king? [35]I am now
eighty years old. Can I tell the difference between what is good and what is not? Can
your servant taste what he eats and drinks?
Can I still hear the voices of men and women
singers? Why should your servant be an added burden to my lord the king? [36]Your servant will cross over the Jordan with the king
for a short distance, but why should the king
reward me in this way? [37]Let your servant return, that I may die in my own town near
the tomb of my father and mother. But here
is your servant Kimham. Let him cross over
with my lord the king. Do for him whatever
pleases you."
[38]The king said, "Kimham shall cross over
with me, and I will do for him whatever pleases you. And anything you desire from me I
will do for you."
[39]So all the people crossed the Jordan, and
then the king crossed over. The king kissed
Barzillai and gave him his blessing, and Barzillai returned to his home.
[40]When the king crossed over to Gilgal,
Kimham crossed with him. All the troops of
Judah and half the troops of Israel had taken
the king over.
[41]Soon all the men of Israel were coming
to the king and saying to him, "Why did our
brothers, the men of Judah, steal the king
away and bring him and his household across
the Jordan, together with all his men?"
[42]All the men of Judah answered the men of
Israel, "We did this because the king is closely related to us. Why are you angry about it?
Have we eaten any of the king's provisions?
Have we taken anything for ourselves?"
[43]Then the men of Israel answered the men
of Judah, "We have ten shares in the king; and
besides, we have a greater claim on David than
you have. So why do you treat us with contempt? Were we not the first to speak of bringing back our king?"
But the men of Judah responded even more
harshly than the men of Israel.

Sheba Rebels Against David

20 Now a troublemaker named Sheba son
of Bicri, a Benjamite, happened to be
there. He sounded the trumpet and
shouted,

"We have no share in David,
no part in Jesse's son!
Every man to his tent, O Israel!"

[2]So all the men of Israel deserted David to
follow Sheba son of Bicri. But the men of Judah stayed by their king all the way from the
Jordan to Jerusalem.
[3]When David returned to his palace in Jerusalem, he took the ten concubines he had
left to take care of the palace and put them in
a house under guard. He provided for them,
but did not lie with them. They were kept in

confinement till the day of their death, living as widows.

[4]Then the king said to Amasa, "Summon the men of Judah to come to me within three days, and be here yourself." [5]But when Amasa went to summon Judah, he took longer than the time the king had set for him.

[6]David said to Abishai, "Now Sheba son of Bicri will do us more harm than Absalom did. Take your master's men and pursue him, or he will find fortified cities and escape from us." [7]So Joab's men and the Kerethites and Pelethites and all the mighty warriors went out under the command of Abishai. They marched out from Jerusalem to pursue Sheba son of Bicri.

[8]While they were at the great rock in Gibeon, Amasa came to meet them. Joab was wearing his military tunic, and strapped over it at his waist was a belt with a dagger in its sheath. As he stepped forward, it dropped out of its sheath.

[9]Joab said to Amasa, "How are you, my brother?" Then Joab took Amasa by the beard with his right hand to kiss him. [10]Amasa was not on his guard against the dagger in Joab's hand, and Joab plunged it into his belly, and his intestines spilled out on the ground. Without being stabbed again, Amasa died. Then Joab and his brother Abishai pursued Sheba son of Bicri.

[11]One of Joab's men stood beside Amasa and said, "Whoever favors Joab, and whoever is for David, let him follow Joab!" [12]Amasa lay wallowing in his blood in the middle of the road, and the man saw that all the troops came to a halt there. When he realized that everyone who came up to Amasa stopped, he dragged him from the road into a field and threw a garment over him. [13]After Amasa had been removed from the road, all the men went on with Joab to pursue Sheba son of Bicri.

[14]Sheba passed through all the tribes of Israel to Abel Beth Maacah[a] and through the entire region of the Berites, who gathered together and followed him. [15]All the troops with Joab came and besieged Sheba in Abel Beth Maacah. They built a siege ramp up to the city, and it stood against the outer fortifications. While they were battering the wall to bring it down, [16]a wise woman called from the city, "Listen! Listen! Tell Joab to come here so I can speak to him." [17]He went toward her, and she asked, "Are you Joab?"

"I am," he answered.

She said, "Listen to what your servant has to say."

"I'm listening," he said.

[18]She continued, "Long ago they used to say, 'Get your answer at Abel,' and that settled it. [19]We are the peaceful and faithful in Israel. You are trying to destroy a city that is a mother in Israel. Why do you want to swallow up the LORD's inheritance?"

[20]"Far be it from me!" Joab replied, "Far be it from me to swallow up or destroy! [21]That is not the case. A man named Sheba son of Bicri, from the hill country of Ephraim, has lifted up his hand against the king, against David. Hand over this one man, and I'll withdraw from the city."

The woman said to Joab, "His head will be thrown to you from the wall."

[22]Then the woman went to all the people with her wise advice, and they cut off the head of Sheba son of Bicri and threw it to Joab. So he sounded the trumpet, and his men dispersed from the city, each returning to his home. And Joab went back to the king in Jerusalem.

[23]Joab was over Israel's entire army; Benaiah son of Jehoiada was over the Kerethites and Pelethites; [24]Adoniram[b] was in charge of forced labor; Jehoshaphat son of Ahilud was recorder; [25]Sheva was secretary; Zadok and Abiathar were priests; [26]and Ira the Jairite was David's priest.

The Gibeonites Avenged

21 During the reign of David, there was a famine for three successive years; so David sought the face of the LORD. The LORD said, "It is on account of Saul and his blood-stained house; it is because he put the Gibeonites to death."

[2]The king summoned the Gibeonites and spoke to them. (Now the Gibeonites were not a part of Israel but were survivors of the Amorites; the Israelites had sworn to ⌞spare⌟ them, but Saul in his zeal for Israel and Judah had tried to annihilate them.) [3]David asked the Gibeonites, "What shall I do for you? How shall I make amends so that you will bless the LORD's inheritance?"

[4]The Gibeonites answered him, "We have no right to demand silver or gold from Saul or his family, nor do we have the right to put anyone in Israel to death."

---

[a] *14* Or *Abel, even Beth Maacah*; also in verse 15 [b] *24* Some Septuagint manuscripts (see also 1 Kings 4:6 and 5:14); Hebrew *Adoram*

"What do you want me to do for you?" David asked.
5They answered the king, "As for the man
who destroyed us and plotted against us so
that we have been decimated and have no
place anywhere in Israel, 6let seven of his male
descendants be given to us to be killed and exposed before the LORD at Gibeah of Saul—the
LORD's chosen one."
So the king said, "I will give them to you."
7The king spared Mephibosheth son of
Jonathan, the son of Saul, because of the
oath before the LORD between David and
Jonathan son of Saul. 8But the king took
Armoni and Mephibosheth, the two sons of
Aiah's daughter Rizpah, whom she had borne
to Saul, together with the five sons of Saul's
daughter Merab,[a] whom she had borne to
Adriel son of Barzillai the Meholathite. 9He
handed them over to the Gibeonites, who
killed and exposed them on a hill before the
LORD. All seven of them fell together; they
were put to death during the first days of the
harvest, just as the barley harvest was beginning.
10Rizpah daughter of Aiah took sackcloth
and spread it out for herself on a rock. From
the beginning of the harvest till the rain
poured down from the heavens on the bodies,
she did not let the birds of the air touch them
by day or the wild animals by night. 11When
David was told what Aiah's daughter Rizpah,
Saul's concubine, had done, 12he went and
took the bones of Saul and his son Jonathan
from the citizens of Jabesh Gilead. (They had
taken them secretly from the public square at
Beth Shan, where the Philistines had hung
them after they struck Saul down on Gilboa.)
13David brought the bones of Saul and his son
Jonathan from there, and the bones of those
who had been killed and exposed were gathered up.
14They buried the bones of Saul and his son
Jonathan in the tomb of Saul's father Kish, at
Zela in Benjamin, and did everything the king
commanded. After that, God answered prayer
in behalf of the land.

Wars Against the Philistines

15Once again there was a battle between
the Philistines and Israel. David went down
with his men to fight against the Philistines,
and he became exhausted. 16And Ishbi-Be-
nob, one of the descendants of Rapha, whose
bronze spearhead weighed three hundred
shekels[b] and who was armed with a new
⌊sword⌋, said he would kill David. 17But
Abishai son of Zeruiah came to David's rescue; he struck the Philistine down and killed
him. Then David's men swore to him, saying, "Never again will you go out with us to
battle, so that the lamp of Israel will not be
extinguished."
18In the course of time, there was another battle with the Philistines, at Gob. At that
time Sibbecai the Hushathite killed Saph, one
of the descendants of Rapha.
19In another battle with the Philistines at
Gob, Elhanan son of Jaare-Oregim[c] the Beth-
lehemite killed Goliath[d] the Gittite, who had
a spear with a shaft like a weaver's rod.
20In still another battle, which took place
at Gath, there was a huge man with six fingers on each hand and six toes on each foot—
twenty-four in all. He also was descended
from Rapha. 21When he taunted Israel, Jonathan son of Shimeah, David's brother, killed
him.
22These four were descendants of Rapha in
Gath, and they fell at the hands of David and
his men.

David's Song of Praise

22 David sang to the LORD the words of
this song when the LORD delivered him
from the hand of all his enemies and
from the hand of Saul. 2He said:

"The LORD is my rock, my fortress and my
deliverer;
3 my God is my rock, in whom I take
refuge,
my shield and the horn[e] of my
salvation.
He is my stronghold, my refuge and my
savior—
from violent men you save me.
4I call to the LORD, who is worthy of
praise,
and I am saved from my enemies.

5"The waves of death swirled about me;
the torrents of destruction
overwhelmed me.
6The cords of the grave[f] coiled around
me;
the snares of death confronted me.
7In my distress I called to the LORD;
I called out to my God.

[a] *8* Two Hebrew manuscripts, some Septuagint manuscripts and Syriac (see also 1 Samuel 18:19); most Hebrew and Septuagint manuscripts *Michal* [b] *16* That is, about 7 1/2 pounds (about 3.5 kilograms) [c] *19* Or *son of Jair the weaver* [d] *19* Hebrew and Septuagint; 1 Chron. 20:5 *son of Jair killed Lahmi the brother of Goliath* [e] *3* *Horn* here symbolizes strength. [f] *6* Hebrew *Sheol*

From his temple he heard my voice;
my cry came to his ears.
8 "The earth trembled and quaked,
the foundations of the heavens[a] shook;
they trembled because he was angry.
9 Smoke rose from his nostrils;
consuming fire came from his mouth,
burning coals blazed out of it.
10 He parted the heavens and came down;
dark clouds were under his feet.
11 He mounted the cherubim and flew;
he soared[b] on the wings of the wind.
12 He made darkness his canopy around him—
the dark[c] rain clouds of the sky.
13 Out of the brightness of his presence
bolts of lightning blazed forth.
14 The LORD thundered from heaven;
the voice of the Most High resounded.
15 He shot arrows and scattered ⌊the enemies⌋,
bolts of lightning and routed them.
16 The valleys of the sea were exposed
and the foundations of the earth laid bare
at the rebuke of the LORD,
at the blast of breath from his nostrils.
17 "He reached down from on high and took hold of me;
he drew me out of deep waters.
18 He rescued me from my powerful enemy,
from my foes, who were too strong for me.
19 They confronted me in the day of my disaster,
but the LORD was my support.
20 He brought me out into a spacious place;
he rescued me because he delighted in me.
21 "The LORD has dealt with me according to my righteousness;
according to the cleanness of my hands he has rewarded me.
22 For I have kept the ways of the LORD;
I have not done evil by turning from my God.
23 All his laws are before me;
I have not turned away from his decrees.
24 I have been blameless before him
and have kept myself from sin.
25 The LORD has rewarded me according to my righteousness,
according to my cleanness[d] in his sight.
26 "To the faithful you show yourself faithful,
to the blameless you show yourself blameless,
27 to the pure you show yourself pure,
but to the crooked you show yourself shrewd.
28 You save the humble,
but your eyes are on the haughty to bring them low.
29 You are my lamp, O LORD;
the LORD turns my darkness into light.
30 With your help I can advance against a troop[e];
with my God I can scale a wall.
31 "As for God, his way is perfect;
the word of the LORD is flawless.
He is a shield
for all who take refuge in him.
32 For who is God besides the LORD?
And who is the Rock except our God?
33 It is God who arms me with strength[f]
and makes my way perfect.
34 He makes my feet like the feet of a deer;
he enables me to stand on the heights.
35 He trains my hands for battle;
my arms can bend a bow of bronze.
36 You give me your shield of victory;
you stoop down to make me great.
37 You broaden the path beneath me,
so that my ankles do not turn.
38 "I pursued my enemies and crushed them;
I did not turn back till they were destroyed.
39 I crushed them completely, and they could not rise;
they fell beneath my feet.
40 You armed me with strength for battle;
you made my adversaries bow at my feet.
41 You made my enemies turn their backs in flight,
and I destroyed my foes.
42 They cried for help, but there was no one to save them—

---

[a] 8 Hebrew; Vulgate and Syriac (see also Psalm 18:7) *mountains* [b] 11 Many Hebrew manuscripts (see also Psalm 18:10); most Hebrew manuscripts *appeared* [c] 12 Septuagint and Vulgate (see also Psalm 18:11); Hebrew *massed* [d] 25 Hebrew; Septuagint and Vulgate (see also Psalm 18:24) *to the cleanness of my hands* [e] 30 Or *can run through a barricade* [f] 33 Dead Sea Scrolls, some Septuagint manuscripts, Vulgate and Syriac (see also Psalm 18:32); Masoretic Text *who is my strong refuge*

to the LORD, but he did not answer.
43 I beat them as fine as the dust of the
earth;
I pounded and trampled them like
mud in the streets.

44 "You have delivered me from the attacks
of my people;
you have preserved me as the head of
nations.
People I did not know are subject to me,
45 and foreigners come cringing to me;
as soon as they hear me, they obey me.
46 They all lose heart;
they come trembling[a] from their
strongholds.

47 "The LORD lives! Praise be to my Rock!
Exalted be God, the Rock, my Savior!
48 He is the God who avenges me,
who puts the nations under me,
49 who sets me free from my enemies.
You exalted me above my foes;
from violent men you rescued me.
50 Therefore I will praise you, O LORD,
among the nations;
I will sing praises to your name.
51 He gives his king great victories;
he shows unfailing kindness to his
anointed,
to David and his descendants forever."

The Last Words of David

23 These are the last words of David:

"The oracle of David son of Jesse,
the oracle of the man exalted by the
Most High,
the man anointed by the God of Jacob,
Israel's singer of songs[b]:

2 "The Spirit of the LORD spoke through
me;
his word was on my tongue.
3 The God of Israel spoke,
the Rock of Israel said to me:
'When one rules over men in
righteousness,
when he rules in the fear of God,
4 he is like the light of morning at sunrise
on a cloudless morning,
like the brightness after rain
that brings the grass from the earth.'

5 "Is not my house right with God?
Has he not made with me an
everlasting covenant,
arranged and secured in every part?
Will he not bring to fruition my salvation
and grant me my every desire?
6 But evil men are all to be cast aside like
thorns,
which are not gathered with the hand.
7 Whoever touches thorns
uses a tool of iron or the shaft of a
spear;
they are burned up where they lie."

David's Mighty Men

8 These are the names of David's mighty
men:
Josheb-Basshebeth,[c] a Tahkemonite,[d] was
chief of the Three; he raised his spear against
eight hundred men, whom he killed[e] in one
encounter.
9 Next to him was Eleazar son of Dodai the
Ahohite. As one of the three mighty men, he
was with David when they taunted the Philistines gathered ⌞at Pas Dammim⌟[f] for battle. Then the men of Israel retreated, 10 but he
stood his ground and struck down the Philistines till his hand grew tired and froze to the
sword. The LORD brought about a great victory that day. The troops returned to Eleazar,
but only to strip the dead.
11 Next to him was Shammah son of Agee
the Hararite. When the Philistines banded together at a place where there was a field full
of lentils, Israel's troops fled from them. 12 But
Shammah took his stand in the middle of the
field. He defended it and struck the Philistines down, and the LORD brought about a
great victory.
13 During harvest time, three of the thirty
chief men came down to David at the cave
of Adullam, while a band of Philistines was
encamped in the Valley of Rephaim. 14 At
that time David was in the stronghold, and
the Philistine garrison was at Bethlehem.
15 David longed for water and said, "Oh,
that someone would get me a drink of water
from the well near the gate of Bethlehem!"
16 So the three mighty men broke through
the Philistine lines, drew water from the well
near the gate of Bethlehem and carried it
back to David. But he refused to drink it;
instead, he poured it out before the LORD.
17 "Far be it from me, O LORD, to do this!"

[a] *46* Some Septuagint manuscripts and Vulgate (see also Psalm 18:45); Masoretic Text *they arm themselves.* [b] *1* Or *Israel's beloved singer* [c] *8* Hebrew; some Septuagint manuscripts suggest *Ish-Bosheth,* that is, *Esh-Baal* (see also 1 Chron. 11:11 *Jashobeam*). [d] *8* Probably a variant of *Hacmonite* (see 1 Chron. 11:11) [e] *8* Some Septuagint manuscripts (see also 1 Chron. 11:11); Hebrew and other Septuagint manuscripts *Three; it was Adino the Eznite who killed eight hundred men* [f] *9* See 1 Chron. 11:13; Hebrew *gathered there.*

TUESDAY

READ 2 SAMUEL 23:13–17

SACRIFICING FOR EACH OTHER

Having a healthy marriage requires sacrifices. Maybe you are living on a tight budget because your spouse decided to go to graduate school. Maybe you've moved far away from friends and family for your spouse's job. Or maybe you've let go of a personal dream so that the two of you can build new dreams together. We make these sacrifices because we know that the loss is tempered by an even greater gain.

It's ironic, then, that we tend to be resistant to sacrificing for God. Where we might not hesitate—at least not for long—to make a change for the sake of our spouses, how many of us are willing to make the kind of deep, life-altering changes that will help us become the people God created us to be?

The story of David's mighty men provides a good example of people willing to risk everything for a person they cared about. David's men put themselves in tremendous danger just to bring David a drink of water from the well near Bethlehem's gate, where as a boy he had likely quenched his thirst many times. When they returned, David recognized that he was unworthy of such devotion. So he poured out their hard-won water on the ground as an offering to God. While we don't know how the men responded to David's action, it's likely that they held David in even higher esteem because of his faithfulness, humility and devotion to the Lord.

After reading this story, one wonders, Would the mighty men have risked their lives if God had been doing the asking? Would we?

I wouldn't think twice about jumping in front of a moving car to save my husband, or jumping in front of a train to save my children. But I have gotten pretty good at thinking once or twice or even four times about doing the things God has asked me to do. I have found lots of good excuses for not serving the poor, not tending to the needs of orphans and widows. I have justified not seeking justice and mercy for those who are oppressed. I am perfectly willing to make the sacrifices necessary for a solid marriage and family, but for a solid life of following God? Well . . .

It's frighteningly easy to make an idol of marriage. This relationship between a man and woman is a good gift from God that needs protecting and nurturing. Like David's warriors, we can devote ourselves to the cause at hand—in our case it's marriage—because it is noble and worthy. But when we are more devoted to our marriage than to God, we have lost sight of God's real desire for us—that we be people of love, compassion and mercy, people who put everything aside and follow our Lord.

—CARLA BARNHILL

David longed for water . . . so the three mighty men broke through the Philistine lines, drew water from the well near the gate of Bethlehem and carried it back to David.

— 2 SAMUEL 23:15–16

let's *talk*

✦ Where have we sensed God leading us that we've resisted going? How can we devote ourselves to God with the same trust and passion that we have for each other?

✦ What are some sacrifices we have made for each other in marriage? How have we determined whether the sacrifice is worthwhile? Do we both feel good about the decision-making process we have developed? If not, how can we make it work better for both of us?

✦ How can we become more deeply involved in God's kingdom work? Can we give more time or money to a ministry? Are there other resources we can offer to our community to show God's love and care to the hurting?

FOR YOUR NEXT DEVOTIONAL READING, TURN TO PAGE 353.

he said. "Is it not the blood of men who went at the risk of their lives?" And David would not drink it.

Such were the exploits of the three mighty men.

18Abishai the brother of Joab son of Zeruiah was chief of the Three.[a] He raised his
spear against three hundred men, whom he
killed, and so he became as famous as the
Three. 19Was he not held in greater honor
than the Three? He became their commander, even though he was not included among
them.

20Benaiah son of Jehoiada was a valiant
fighter from Kabzeel, who performed great
exploits. He struck down two of Moab's best
men. He also went down into a pit on a snowy
day and killed a lion. 21And he struck down a
huge Egyptian. Although the Egyptian had a
spear in his hand, Benaiah went against him
with a club. He snatched the spear from the
Egyptian's hand and killed him with his own
spear. 22Such were the exploits of Benaiah son
of Jehoiada; he too was as famous as the three
mighty men. 23He was held in greater honor
than any of the Thirty, but he was not included among the Three. And David put him in
charge of his bodyguard.

24Among the Thirty were:
Asahel the brother of Joab,
Elhanan son of Dodo from Bethlehem,
25Shammah the Harodite,
Elika the Harodite,
26Helez the Paltite,
Ira son of Ikkesh from Tekoa,
27Abiezer from Anathoth,
Mebunnai[b] the Hushathite,
28Zalmon the Ahohite,
Maharai the Netophathite,
29Heled[c] son of Baanah the Netophathite,
Ithai son of Ribai from Gibeah in Benjamin,
30Benaiah the Pirathonite,
Hiddai[d] from the ravines of Gaash,
31Abi-Albon the Arbathite,
Azmaveth the Barhumite,
32Eliahba the Shaalbonite,
the sons of Jashen,
Jonathan 33son of[e] Shammah the Hararite,
Ahiam son of Sharar[f] the Hararite,
34Eliphelet son of Ahasbai the Maacathite,
Eliam son of Ahithophel the Gilonite,
35Hezro the Carmelite,
Paarai the Arbite,
36Igal son of Nathan from Zobah,
the son of Hagri,[g]
37Zelek the Ammonite,
Naharai the Beerothite, the armor-bearer of Joab son of Zeruiah,
38Ira the Ithrite,
Gareb the Ithrite
39and Uriah the Hittite.
There were thirty-seven in all.

David Counts the Fighting Men

24 Again the anger of the LORD burned
against Israel, and he incited David
against them, saying, "Go and take a
census of Israel and Judah."

2So the king said to Joab and the army
commanders[h] with him, "Go throughout the
tribes of Israel from Dan to Beersheba and enroll the fighting men, so that I may know how
many there are."

3But Joab replied to the king, "May the
LORD your God multiply the troops a hundred times over, and may the eyes of my lord
the king see it. But why does my lord the king
want to do such a thing?"

4The king's word, however, overruled Joab
and the army commanders; so they left the
presence of the king to enroll the fighting men
of Israel.

5After crossing the Jordan, they camped
near Aroer, south of the town in the gorge,
and then went through Gad and on to Jazer.
6They went to Gilead and the region of Tah-
tim Hodshi, and on to Dan Jaan and around
toward Sidon. 7Then they went toward the
fortress of Tyre and all the towns of the Hivites and Canaanites. Finally, they went on to
Beersheba in the Negev of Judah.

8After they had gone through the entire
land, they came back to Jerusalem at the end
of nine months and twenty days.

9Joab reported the number of the fighting
men to the king: In Israel there were eight
hundred thousand able-bodied men who

---

[a] *18* Most Hebrew manuscripts (see also 1 Chron. 11:20); two Hebrew manuscripts and Syriac *Thirty* [b] *27* Hebrew; some Septuagint manuscripts (see also 1 Chron. 11:29) *Sibbecai* [c] *29* Some Hebrew manuscripts and Vulgate (see also 1 Chron. 11:30); most Hebrew manuscripts *Heleb* [d] *30* Hebrew; some Septuagint manuscripts (see also 1 Chron. 11:32) *Hurai* [e] *33* Some Septuagint manuscripts (see also 1 Chron. 11:34); Hebrew does not have *son of.* [f] *33* Hebrew; some Septuagint manuscripts (see also 1 Chron. 11:35) *Sacar* [g] *36* Some Septuagint manuscripts (see also 1 Chron. 11:38); Hebrew *Haggadi* [h] *2* Septuagint (see also verse 4 and 1 Chron. 21:2); Hebrew *Joab the army commander*

could handle a sword, and in Judah five hundred thousand.
10David was conscience-stricken after he
had counted the fighting men, and he said
to the LORD, "I have sinned greatly in what
I have done. Now, O LORD, I beg you, take
away the guilt of your servant. I have done a
very foolish thing."
11Before David got up the next morning,
the word of the LORD had come to Gad the
prophet, David's seer: 12"Go and tell David,
'This is what the LORD says: I am giving you
three options. Choose one of them for me to
carry out against you.' "
13So Gad went to David and said to him,
"Shall there come upon you three[a] years of
famine in your land? Or three months of fleeing from your enemies while they pursue you?
Or three days of plague in your land? Now
then, think it over and decide how I should
answer the one who sent me."
14David said to Gad, "I am in deep distress.
Let us fall into the hands of the LORD, for his
mercy is great; but do not let me fall into the
hands of men."
15So the LORD sent a plague on Israel from
that morning until the end of the time designated, and seventy thousand of the people from Dan to Beersheba died. 16When
the angel stretched out his hand to destroy
Jerusalem, the LORD was grieved because of
the calamity and said to the angel who was
afflicting the people, "Enough! Withdraw
your hand." The angel of the LORD was then
at the threshing floor of Araunah the Jebusite.
17When David saw the angel who was striking down the people, he said to the LORD, "I
am the one who has sinned and done wrong.
These are but sheep. What have they done?
Let your hand fall upon me and my family."

David Builds an Altar

18On that day Gad went to David and
said to him, "Go up and build an altar to the
LORD on the threshing floor of Araunah the
Jebusite." 19So David went up, as the LORD
had commanded through Gad. 20When
Araunah looked and saw the king and his
men coming toward him, he went out and
bowed down before the king with his face to
the ground.
21Araunah said, "Why has my lord the king
come to his servant?"
"To buy your threshing floor," David
answered, "so I can build an altar to the
LORD, that the plague on the people may be
stopped."
22Araunah said to David, "Let my lord the
king take whatever pleases him and offer it
up. Here are oxen for the burnt offering, and
here are threshing sledges and ox yokes for the
wood. 23O king, Araunah gives all this to the
king." Araunah also said to him, "May the
LORD your God accept you."
24But the king replied to Araunah, "No, I
insist on paying you for it. I will not sacrifice
to the LORD my God burnt offerings that cost
me nothing."
So David bought the threshing floor and
the oxen and paid fifty shekels[b] of silver for
them. 25David built an altar to the LORD there
and sacrificed burnt offerings and fellowship
offerings.[c] Then the LORD answered prayer in
behalf of the land, and the plague on Israel
was stopped.

---

a 13 Septuagint (see also 1 Chron. 21:12); Hebrew *seven* *b 24* That is, about 1 1/4 pounds (about 0.6 kilogram) *c 25* Traditionally *peace offerings*

1 KINGS

1 Kings

QUICK FACTS

AUTHOR Unknown

AUDIENCE All Israel

DATE Probably during the Babylonian exile, around 550 B.C.

SETTING The time of Israel's kings, subsequent to David

Before David died, Adonijah, likely David's oldest surviving son, tried to grab the throne. But David had planned that his son Solomon, whose mother was Bathsheba, would be his successor. Having his father's favor, Solomon began his reign in a blaze of glory. God gave the young king what he asked for: wisdom—*plus* what he did not ask for: wealth, honor and the promise of a long life.

Solomon expanded the borders of Israel from Egypt to the Euphrates River, built a glorious temple for the Lord and "was greater in riches and wisdom than all the other kings of the earth" (1 Kings 10:23). But during his 40-year reign, Solomon also made critical mistakes. He burdened the people with taxes and conscription and allowed his foreign wives, many of whom he married as part of political alliances, to turn his heart toward their pagan gods.

God disciplined Solomon by sending adversaries against him, including Jeroboam, one of Solomon's own officials, who later ripped 10 tribes away from Solomon's successor, Rehoboam, and split the kingdom. But the real damage came later, when the kings who followed, and their kingdoms, continually struggled with the devastating effects of idolatry.

Solomon's story serves as a powerful lesson for couples: No matter how great our blessings—each other's love, supportive families, successful jobs, lovely houses—we still need to put our focus on God and his glory.

Adonijah Sets Himself Up as King

1 When King David was old and well advanced in years, he could not keep warm
even when they put covers over him. 2So
his servants said to him, "Let us look for a
young virgin to attend the king and take care
of him. She can lie beside him so that our lord
the king may keep warm."
3Then they searched throughout Israel for a
beautiful girl and found Abishag, a Shunammite, and brought her to the king. 4The girl
was very beautiful; she took care of the king
and waited on him, but the king had no intimate relations with her.
5Now Adonijah, whose mother was Haggith, put himself forward and said, "I will be
king." So he got chariots and horses[a] ready,
with fifty men to run ahead of him. 6(His father had never interfered with him by asking,
"Why do you behave as you do?" He was also
very handsome and was born next after Absalom.)
7Adonijah conferred with Joab son of Zeruiah and with Abiathar the priest, and they
gave him their support. 8But Zadok the priest,
Benaiah son of Jehoiada, Nathan the prophet,
Shimei and Rei[b] and David's special guard did
not join Adonijah.
9Adonijah then sacrificed sheep, cattle and
fattened calves at the Stone of Zoheleth near
En Rogel. He invited all his brothers, the
king's sons, and all the men of Judah who were
royal officials, 10but he did not invite Nathan
the prophet or Benaiah or the special guard or
his brother Solomon.
11Then Nathan asked Bathsheba, Solomon's
mother, "Have you not heard that Adonijah,
the son of Haggith, has become king without
our lord David's knowing it? 12Now then, let
me advise you how you can save your own life
and the life of your son Solomon. 13Go in to
King David and say to him, 'My lord the king,
did you not swear to me your servant: "Surely
Solomon your son shall be king after me, and
he will sit on my throne"? Why then has Adonijah become king?' 14While you are still there
talking to the king, I will come in and confirm
what you have said."
15So Bathsheba went to see the aged king in
his room, where Abishag the Shunammite was
attending him. 16Bathsheba bowed low and
knelt before the king.
"What is it you want?" the king asked.
17She said to him, "My lord, you yourself
swore to me your servant by the LORD your
God: 'Solomon your son shall be king after
me, and he will sit on my throne.' 18But now
Adonijah has become king, and you, my lord
the king, do not know about it. 19He has sacrificed great numbers of cattle, fattened calves,
and sheep, and has invited all the king's sons,
Abiathar the priest and Joab the commander
of the army, but he has not invited Solomon
your servant. 20My lord the king, the eyes of
all Israel are on you, to learn from you who
will sit on the throne of my lord the king after
him. 21Otherwise, as soon as my lord the king
is laid to rest with his fathers, I and my son
Solomon will be treated as criminals."
22While she was still speaking with the
king, Nathan the prophet arrived. 23And they
told the king, "Nathan the prophet is here."
So he went before the king and bowed with
his face to the ground.
24Nathan said, "Have you, my lord the
king, declared that Adonijah shall be king after you, and that he will sit on your throne?
25Today he has gone down and sacrificed great
numbers of cattle, fattened calves, and sheep.
He has invited all the king's sons, the commanders of the army and Abiathar the priest.
Right now they are eating and drinking with
him and saying, 'Long live King Adonijah!'
26But me your servant, and Zadok the priest,
and Benaiah son of Jehoiada, and your servant
Solomon he did not invite. 27Is this something
my lord the king has done without letting his
servants know who should sit on the throne of
my lord the king after him?"

David Makes Solomon King

28Then King David said, "Call in Bathsheba." So she came into the king's presence and
stood before him.
29The king then took an oath: "As surely as
the LORD lives, who has delivered me out of
every trouble, 30I will surely carry out today
what I swore to you by the LORD, the God
of Israel: Solomon your son shall be king after me, and he will sit on my throne in my
place."
31Then Bathsheba bowed low with her face
to the ground and, kneeling before the king,
said, "May my lord King David live forever!"
32King David said, "Call in Zadok the priest,
Nathan the prophet and Benaiah son of Jehoiada." When they came before the king, 33he said
to them: "Take your lord's servants with you
and set Solomon my son on my own mule and
take him down to Gihon. 34There have Zadok

[a] 5 Or *charioteers* [b] 8 Or *and his friends*

WEDNESDAY
READ 1 KINGS 1:5–30

'FESSING UP

Now Adonijah, whose mother was Haggith, put himself forward and said, "I will be king." So he got chariots and horses ready, with fifty men to run ahead of him.

— 1 Kings 1:5

When David was close to death, his son Adonijah made his move to take over the kingdom. Although this was a pivotal moment in David and Adonijah's relationship, and in the story of Israel, the two failed to communicate about what was really transpiring.

Isn't that usually the way we handle life? We can talk with the people close to us—our kids, our spouse, our friends—about politics, the weather, vacation plans, the TV show to which we're addicted. But in the midst of major transitions, we sometimes fail to talk things through with people who matter most to us.

It's like Brian, who came home from work one day and told his wife he had made the final cut for a new, exciting job. Great news! Except that Brian had been in conversation with a headhunter for months but never mentioned it to his wife.

Or like Heather and Chris, who turned up at Thanksgiving dinner with two adopted children to introduce to their parents, siblings and cousins. Heather and Chris hadn't shared their struggles with infertility with their families, so the children were a shock.

I was once in a Bible study that opened with 45 minutes of Scripture study and then moved into an hour of share-and-prayer time. What we usually talked about was whose prize camellias had been attacked by vicious beetles. Or whose neighbor's daughter's best friend's boyfriend was struggling with depression. There was something off about our discussions, but what? One day, near the end of share-and-prayer time, Lizzie announced that she and her family would be moving across the country. It was a decision she and her husband had been wrestling with for about six months, and they wanted to let us know what they'd decided.

Flash! I could finally express that vague dissatisfaction about prayer-and-share time that had been rattling my insides. We had spent six months praying for camellias. Meanwhile, we hadn't prayed for Lizzie's discernment because we had had no idea there was anything to discern. "Come to think of it," another friend said to me later that day, "Lizzie seemed a bit preoccupied, don't you think?" But none of us had made any inquiries.

It's easy to avoid conversations about important things. But when we neglect to share our pivotal points in life with others, especially our spouse, we are really saying, "I am keeping this for myself. I am not willing to give you my whole self. Not the parts that really matter."

It's like refusing to bring our pivotal points to God. We may say we love him, and we may be doing our best to obey his commands. But when we withhold some of the things we are struggling with, what we are really saying is, "You can have everything else, but not this. Here, where it really matters, I'll find my own way and do as I please."

—LAUREN WINNER

let's talk

- ✦ When have we failed to talk to each other about an important decision? Why did we choose to keep it to ourself? What was the result?
- ✦ Has there ever been an occasion when one of us has noticed the other in the midst of change but chosen not to talk about it? Why?
- ✦ What happens when we do ask each other, "What's going on? Why are you choosing what you're choosing?"

FOR YOUR NEXT DEVOTIONAL READING, TURN TO PAGE 366.

the priest and Nathan the prophet anoint him
king over Israel. Blow the trumpet and shout,
'Long live King Solomon!' 35Then you are to
go up with him, and he is to come and sit on
my throne and reign in my place. I have appointed him ruler over Israel and Judah."
36Benaiah son of Jehoiada answered the
king, "Amen! May the LORD, the God of my
lord the king, so declare it. 37As the LORD was
with my lord the king, so may he be with Solomon to make his throne even greater than
the throne of my lord King David!"
38So Zadok the priest, Nathan the prophet,
Benaiah son of Jehoiada, the Kerethites and
the Pelethites went down and put Solomon on
King David's mule and escorted him to Gihon.
39Zadok the priest took the horn of oil from
the sacred tent and anointed Solomon. Then
they sounded the trumpet and all the people
shouted, "Long live King Solomon!" 40And all
the people went up after him, playing flutes
and rejoicing greatly, so that the ground shook
with the sound.
41Adonijah and all the guests who were
with him heard it as they were finishing their
feast. On hearing the sound of the trumpet,
Joab asked, "What's the meaning of all the
noise in the city?"
42Even as he was speaking, Jonathan son
of Abiathar the priest arrived. Adonijah said,
"Come in. A worthy man like you must be
bringing good news."
43"Not at all!" Jonathan answered. "Our
lord King David has made Solomon king.
44The king has sent with him Zadok the
priest, Nathan the prophet, Benaiah son of Jehoiada, the Kerethites and the Pelethites, and
they have put him on the king's mule, 45and
Zadok the priest and Nathan the prophet have
anointed him king at Gihon. From there they
have gone up cheering, and the city resounds
with it. That's the noise you hear. 46More-
over, Solomon has taken his seat on the royal
throne. 47Also, the royal officials have come
to congratulate our lord King David, saying,
'May your God make Solomon's name more
famous than yours and his throne greater than
yours!' And the king bowed in worship on his
bed 48and said, 'Praise be to the LORD, the
God of Israel, who has allowed my eyes to see
a successor on my throne today.' "
49At this, all Adonijah's guests rose in alarm
and dispersed. 50But Adonijah, in fear of Solomon, went and took hold of the horns of the
altar. 51Then Solomon was told, "Adonijah is
afraid of King Solomon and is clinging to the
horns of the altar. He says, 'Let King Solomon
swear to me today that he will not put his servant to death with the sword.' "
52Solomon replied, "If he shows himself to
be a worthy man, not a hair of his head will fall
to the ground; but if evil is found in him, he
will die." 53Then King Solomon sent men, and
they brought him down from the altar. And
Adonijah came and bowed down to King Solomon, and Solomon said, "Go to your home."

David's Charge to Solomon

2 When the time drew near for David to die,
he gave a charge to Solomon his son.
2"I am about to go the way of all the earth,"
he said. "So be strong, show yourself a man,
3and observe what the LORD your God requires: Walk in his ways, and keep his decrees
and commands, his laws and requirements, as
written in the Law of Moses, so that you may
prosper in all you do and wherever you go,
4and that the LORD may keep his promise to
me: 'If your descendants watch how they live,
and if they walk faithfully before me with all
their heart and soul, you will never fail to have
a man on the throne of Israel.'
5"Now you yourself know what Joab son of
Zeruiah did to me—what he did to the two
commanders of Israel's armies, Abner son of
Ner and Amasa son of Jether. He killed them,
shedding their blood in peacetime as if in
battle, and with that blood stained the belt
around his waist and the sandals on his feet.
6Deal with him according to your wisdom,
but do not let his gray head go down to the
grave[a] in peace.
7"But show kindness to the sons of Barzillai
of Gilead and let them be among those who
eat at your table. They stood by me when I
fled from your brother Absalom.
8"And remember, you have with you Shimei son of Gera, the Benjamite from Bahurim,
who called down bitter curses on me the day
I went to Mahanaim. When he came down
to meet me at the Jordan, I swore to him by
the LORD: 'I will not put you to death by the
sword.' 9But now, do not consider him innocent. You are a man of wisdom; you will know
what to do to him. Bring his gray head down
to the grave in blood."
10Then David rested with his fathers and
was buried in the City of David. 11He had
reigned forty years over Israel—seven years
in Hebron and thirty-three in Jerusalem. 12So

[a] 6 Hebrew *Sheol*; also in verse 9

Solomon sat on the throne of his father David, and his rule was firmly established.

Solomon's Throne Established

[13]Now Adonijah, the son of Haggith, went
to Bathsheba, Solomon's mother. Bathsheba
asked him, "Do you come peacefully?"

He answered, "Yes, peacefully." [14]Then he
added, "I have something to say to you."

"You may say it," she replied.

[15]"As you know," he said, "the kingdom was
mine. All Israel looked to me as their king. But
things changed, and the kingdom has gone to
my brother; for it has come to him from the
LORD. [16]Now I have one request to make of
you. Do not refuse me."

"You may make it," she said.

[17]So he continued, "Please ask King Solomon—he will not refuse you—to give me Abishag the Shunammite as my wife."

[18]"Very well," Bathsheba replied, "I will
speak to the king for you."

[19]When Bathsheba went to King Solomon
to speak to him for Adonijah, the king stood
up to meet her, bowed down to her and sat
down on his throne. He had a throne brought
for the king's mother, and she sat down at his
right hand.

[20]"I have one small request to make of you,"
she said. "Do not refuse me."

The king replied, "Make it, my mother; I
will not refuse you."

[21]So she said, "Let Abishag the Shunammite be given in marriage to your brother Adonijah."

[22]King Solomon answered his mother,
"Why do you request Abishag the Shunammite for Adonijah? You might as well request
the kingdom for him—after all, he is my older brother—yes, for him and for Abiathar the
priest and Joab son of Zeruiah!"

[23]Then King Solomon swore by the LORD:
"May God deal with me, be it ever so severely, if Adonijah does not pay with his life for
this request! [24]And now, as surely as the LORD
lives—he who has established me securely on
the throne of my father David and has founded a dynasty for me as he promised—Adonijah shall be put to death today!" [25]So King
Solomon gave orders to Benaiah son of Jehoiada, and he struck down Adonijah and he
died.

[26]To Abiathar the priest the king said, "Go
back to your fields in Anathoth. You deserve
to die, but I will not put you to death now,
because you carried the ark of the Sovereign
LORD before my father David and shared
all my father's hardships." [27]So Solomon removed Abiathar from the priesthood of the
LORD, fulfilling the word the LORD had spoken at Shiloh about the house of Eli.

[28]When the news reached Joab, who had
conspired with Adonijah though not with
Absalom, he fled to the tent of the LORD and
took hold of the horns of the altar. [29]King Solomon was told that Joab had fled to the tent of
the LORD and was beside the altar. Then Solomon ordered Benaiah son of Jehoiada, "Go,
strike him down!"

[30]So Benaiah entered the tent of the LORD
and said to Joab, "The king says, 'Come out!' "

But he answered, "No, I will die here."

Benaiah reported to the king, "This is how
Joab answered me."

[31]Then the king commanded Benaiah, "Do
as he says. Strike him down and bury him, and
so clear me and my father's house of the guilt
of the innocent blood that Joab shed. [32]The
LORD will repay him for the blood he shed, because without the knowledge of my father David he attacked two men and killed them with
the sword. Both of them—Abner son of Ner,
commander of Israel's army, and Amasa son
of Jether, commander of Judah's army—were
better men and more upright than he. [33]May
the guilt of their blood rest on the head of Joab
and his descendants forever. But on David and
his descendants, his house and his throne, may
there be the LORD's peace forever."

[34]So Benaiah son of Jehoiada went up and
struck down Joab and killed him, and he was
buried on his own land[a] in the desert. [35]The
king put Benaiah son of Jehoiada over the
army in Joab's position and replaced Abiathar
with Zadok the priest.

[36]Then the king sent for Shimei and said to
him, "Build yourself a house in Jerusalem and
live there, but do not go anywhere else. [37]The
day you leave and cross the Kidron Valley, you
can be sure you will die; your blood will be on
your own head."

[38]Shimei answered the king, "What you say
is good. Your servant will do as my lord the
king has said." And Shimei stayed in Jerusalem for a long time.

[39]But three years later, two of Shimei's
slaves ran off to Achish son of Maacah, king
of Gath, and Shimei was told, "Your slaves are
in Gath." [40]At this, he saddled his donkey and
went to Achish at Gath in search of his slaves.

---

a 34 Or *buried in his tomb*

So Shimei went away and brought the slaves
back from Gath.
[41]When Solomon was told that Shimei
had gone from Jerusalem to Gath and had
returned, [42]the king summoned Shimei and
said to him, "Did I not make you swear by the
LORD and warn you, 'On the day you leave
to go anywhere else, you can be sure you will
die'? At that time you said to me, 'What you
say is good. I will obey.' [43]Why then did you
not keep your oath to the LORD and obey the
command I gave you?"
[44]The king also said to Shimei, "You know
in your heart all the wrong you did to my father David. Now the LORD will repay you for
your wrongdoing. [45]But King Solomon will
be blessed, and David's throne will remain secure before the LORD forever."
[46]Then the king gave the order to Benaiah
son of Jehoiada, and he went out and struck
Shimei down and killed him.
The kingdom was now firmly established in
Solomon's hands.

Solomon Asks for Wisdom

3 Solomon made an alliance with Pharaoh
king of Egypt and married his daughter.
He brought her to the City of David until
he finished building his palace and the temple
of the LORD, and the wall around Jerusalem.
[2]The people, however, were still sacrificing at
the high places, because a temple had not yet
been built for the Name of the LORD. [3]Solo-
mon showed his love for the LORD by walking
according to the statutes of his father David,
except that he offered sacrifices and burned incense on the high places.
[4]The king went to Gibeon to offer sacrifices, for that was the most important high
place, and Solomon offered a thousand burnt
offerings on that altar. [5]At Gibeon the LORD
appeared to Solomon during the night in a
dream, and God said, "Ask for whatever you
want me to give you."
[6]Solomon answered, "You have shown great
kindness to your servant, my father David,
because he was faithful to you and righteous
and upright in heart. You have continued this
great kindness to him and have given him a
son to sit on his throne this very day.
[7]"Now, O LORD my God, you have made
your servant king in place of my father David. But I am only a little child and do not
know how to carry out my duties. [8]Your servant is here among the people you have chosen, a great people, too numerous to count or
number. [9]So give your servant a discerning
heart to govern your people and to distinguish
between right and wrong. For who is able to
govern this great people of yours?"
[10]The Lord was pleased that Solomon had
asked for this. [11]So God said to him, "Since
you have asked for this and not for long life
or wealth for yourself, nor have asked for the
death of your enemies but for discernment in
administering justice, [12]I will do what you have
asked. I will give you a wise and discerning
heart, so that there will never have been anyone
like you, nor will there ever be. [13]Moreover, I
will give you what you have not asked for—
both riches and honor—so that in your lifetime
you will have no equal among kings. [14]And if
you walk in my ways and obey my statutes and
commands as David your father did, I will give
you a long life." [15]Then Solomon awoke—and
he realized it had been a dream.
He returned to Jerusalem, stood before the
ark of the Lord's covenant and sacrificed burnt
offerings and fellowship offerings.[a] Then he
gave a feast for all his court.

A Wise Ruling

[16]Now two prostitutes came to the king and
stood before him. [17]One of them said, "My
lord, this woman and I live in the same house.
I had a baby while she was there with me.
[18]The third day after my child was born, this
woman also had a baby. We were alone; there
was no one in the house but the two of us.
[19]"During the night this woman's son died
because she lay on him. [20]So she got up in the
middle of the night and took my son from my
side while I your servant was asleep. She put
him by her breast and put her dead son by my
breast. [21]The next morning, I got up to nurse
my son—and he was dead! But when I looked
at him closely in the morning light, I saw that
it wasn't the son I had borne."
[22]The other woman said, "No! The living
one is my son; the dead one is yours."
But the first one insisted, "No! The dead
one is yours; the living one is mine." And so
they argued before the king.
[23]The king said, "This one says, 'My son is
alive and your son is dead,' while that one says,
'No! Your son is dead and mine is alive.' "
[24]Then the king said, "Bring me a sword." So
they brought a sword for the king. [25]He then
gave an order: "Cut the living child in two and
give half to one and half to the other."

a 15 Traditionally *peace offerings*

26 The woman whose son was alive was
filled with compassion for her son and said to
the king, "Please, my lord, give her the living
baby! Don't kill him!"
But the other said, "Neither I nor you shall
have him. Cut him in two!"
27 Then the king gave his ruling: "Give the
living baby to the first woman. Do not kill
him; she is his mother."
28 When all Israel heard the verdict the king
had given, they held the king in awe, because
they saw that he had wisdom from God to administer justice.

Solomon's Officials and Governors

4 So King Solomon ruled over all Israel.
2 And these were his chief officials:

Azariah son of Zadok—the priest;
3 Elihoreph and Ahijah, sons of Shisha—
secretaries;
Jehoshaphat son of Ahilud—recorder;
4 Benaiah son of Jehoiada—commander in
chief;
Zadok and Abiathar—priests;
5 Azariah son of Nathan—in charge of the
district officers;
Zabud son of Nathan—a priest and personal adviser to the king;
6 Ahishar—in charge of the palace;
Adoniram son of Abda—in charge of
forced labor.

7 Solomon also had twelve district governors
over all Israel, who supplied provisions for the
king and the royal household. Each one had
to provide supplies for one month in the year.
8 These are their names:

Ben-Hur—in the hill country of
Ephraim;
9 Ben-Deker—in Makaz, Shaalbim, Beth
Shemesh and Elon Bethhanan;
10 Ben-Hesed—in Arubboth (Socoh and all
the land of Hepher were his);
11 Ben-Abinadab—in Naphoth Dor[a] (he
was married to Taphath daughter of
Solomon);
12 Baana son of Ahilud—in Taanach and
Megiddo, and in all of Beth Shan next
to Zarethan below Jezreel, from Beth
Shan to Abel Meholah across to Jokmeam;
13 Ben-Geber—in Ramoth Gilead (the settlements of Jair son of Manasseh in
Gilead were his, as well as the district
of Argob in Bashan and its sixty large
walled cities with bronze gate bars);
14 Ahinadab son of Iddo—in Mahanaim;
15 Ahimaaz—in Naphtali (he had married
Basemath daughter of Solomon);
16 Baana son of Hushai—in Asher and in
Aloth;
17 Jehoshaphat son of Paruah—in Issachar;
18 Shimei son of Ela—in Benjamin;
19 Geber son of Uri—in Gilead (the country
of Sihon king of the Amorites and the
country of Og king of Bashan). He was
the only governor over the district.

Solomon's Daily Provisions

20 The people of Judah and Israel were as
numerous as the sand on the seashore; they
ate, they drank and they were happy.
21 And
Solomon ruled over all the kingdoms from the
River[b] to the land of the Philistines, as far as
the border of Egypt. These countries brought
tribute and were Solomon's subjects all his
life.
22 Solomon's daily provisions were thirty
cors[c] of fine flour and sixty cors[d] of meal,
23 ten
head of stall-fed cattle, twenty of pasture-fed
cattle and a hundred sheep and goats, as well as
deer, gazelles, roebucks and choice fowl.
24 For
he ruled over all the kingdoms west of the River, from Tiphsah to Gaza, and had peace on all
sides.
25 During Solomon's lifetime Judah and
Israel, from Dan to Beersheba, lived in safety,
each man under his own vine and fig tree.
26 Solomon had four[e] thousand stalls for
chariot horses, and twelve thousand horses.[f]
27 The district officers, each in his month,
supplied provisions for King Solomon and all
who came to the king's table. They saw to it
that nothing was lacking.
28 They also brought
to the proper place their quotas of barley and
straw for the chariot horses and the other
horses.

Solomon's Wisdom

29 God gave Solomon wisdom and very
great insight, and a breadth of understanding as measureless as the sand on the seashore.
30 Solomon's wisdom was greater than the wisdom of all the men of the East, and greater
than all the wisdom of Egypt.
31 He was wiser
than any other man, including Ethan the Ezrahite—wiser than Heman, Calcol and Darda, the sons of Mahol. And his fame spread to

[a] 11 Or *in the heights of Dor* [b] 21 That is, the Euphrates; also in verse 24 [c] 22 That is, probably about 185 bushels (about 6.6 kiloliters) [d] 22 That is, probably about 375 bushels (about 13.2 kiloliters) [e] 26 Some Septuagint manuscripts (see also 2 Chron. 9:25); Hebrew *forty* [f] 26 Or *charioteers*

all the surrounding nations. 32He spoke three
thousand proverbs and his songs numbered a
thousand and five. 33He described plant life,
from the cedar of Lebanon to the hyssop that
grows out of walls. He also taught about animals and birds, reptiles and fish. 34Men of all
nations came to listen to Solomon's wisdom,
sent by all the kings of the world, who had
heard of his wisdom.

Preparations for Building the Temple

5 When Hiram king of Tyre heard that Solomon had been anointed king to succeed
his father David, he sent his envoys to Solomon, because he had always been on friendly terms with David. 2Solomon sent back this
message to Hiram:

> 3"You know that because of the wars
> waged against my father David from all
> sides, he could not build a temple for
> the Name of the LORD his God until the
> LORD put his enemies under his feet. 4But
> now the LORD my God has given me rest
> on every side, and there is no adversary
> or disaster. 5I intend, therefore, to build
> a temple for the Name of the LORD my
> God, as the LORD told my father David,
> when he said, 'Your son whom I will put
> on the throne in your place will build the
> temple for my Name.'
>
> 6"So give orders that cedars of Leba-
> non be cut for me. My men will work
> with yours, and I will pay you for your
> men whatever wages you set. You know
> that we have no one so skilled in felling
> timber as the Sidonians."

7When Hiram heard Solomon's message, he
was greatly pleased and said, "Praise be to the
LORD today, for he has given David a wise son
to rule over this great nation."
8So Hiram sent word to Solomon:

> "I have received the message you sent
> me and will do all you want in providing
> the cedar and pine logs. 9My men will
> haul them down from Lebanon to the
> sea, and I will float them in rafts by sea to
> the place you specify. There I will separate
> them and you can take them away. And
> you are to grant my wish by providing
> food for my royal household."

10In this way Hiram kept Solomon supplied with all the cedar and pine logs he
wanted, 11and Solomon gave Hiram twenty thousand cors[a] of wheat as food for his
household, in addition to twenty thousand
baths[b,c] of pressed olive oil. Solomon continued to do this for Hiram year after year. 12The
LORD gave Solomon wisdom, just as he had
promised him. There were peaceful relations
between Hiram and Solomon, and the two of
them made a treaty.
13King Solomon conscripted laborers from
all Israel—thirty thousand men. 14He sent
them off to Lebanon in shifts of ten thousand
a month, so that they spent one month in Lebanon and two months at home. Adoniram was
in charge of the forced labor. 15Solomon had
seventy thousand carriers and eighty thousand
stonecutters in the hills, 16as well as thirty-
three hundred[d] foremen who supervised the
project and directed the workmen. 17At the
king's command they removed from the quarry large blocks of quality stone to provide a
foundation of dressed stone for the temple.
18The craftsmen of Solomon and Hiram and
the men of Gebal[e] cut and prepared the timber and stone for the building of the temple.

Solomon Builds the Temple

6 In the four hundred and eightieth[f] year after the Israelites had come out of Egypt, in
the fourth year of Solomon's reign over Israel, in the month of Ziv, the second month,
he began to build the temple of the LORD.
2The temple that King Solomon built for
the LORD was sixty cubits long, twenty wide
and thirty high.[g] 3The portico at the front
of the main hall of the temple extended the
width of the temple, that is twenty cubits,[h]
and projected ten cubits[i] from the front of the
temple. 4He made narrow clerestory windows
in the temple. 5Against the walls of the main
hall and inner sanctuary he built a structure
around the building, in which there were side
rooms. 6The lowest floor was five cubits[j] wide,
the middle floor six cubits[k] and the third floor
seven.[l] He made offset ledges around the outside of the temple so that nothing would be
inserted into the temple walls.
7In building the temple, only blocks dressed
at the quarry were used, and no hammer, chis-

[a] *11* That is, probably about 125,000 bushels (about 4,400 kiloliters) [b] *11* Septuagint (see also 2 Chron. 2:10); Hebrew *twenty cors* [c] *11* That is, about 115,000 gallons (about 440 kiloliters) [d] *16* Hebrew; some Septuagint manuscripts (see also 2 Chron. 2:2,18) *thirty-six hundred* [e] *18* That is, Byblos [f] *1* Hebrew; Septuagint *four hundred and fortieth* [g] *2* That is, about 90 feet (about 27 meters) long and 30 feet (about 9 meters) wide and 45 feet (about 13.5 meters) high [h] *3* That is, about 30 feet (about 9 meters) [i] *3* That is, about 15 feet (about 4.5 meters) [j] *6* That is, about 7 1/2 feet (about 2.3 meters); also in verses 10 and 24 [k] *6* That is, about 9 feet (about 2.7 meters) [l] *6* That is, about 10 1/2 feet (about 3.1 meters)

el or any other iron tool was heard at the temple site while it was being built.
8The entrance to the lowest[a] floor was on
the south side of the temple; a stairway led up
to the middle level and from there to the third.
9So he built the temple and completed it, roofing it with beams and cedar planks. 10And he
built the side rooms all along the temple. The
height of each was five cubits, and they were
attached to the temple by beams of cedar.
11The word of the LORD came to Solomon:
12"As for this temple you are building, if you
follow my decrees, carry out my regulations and
keep all my commands and obey them, I will
fulfill through you the promise I gave to David
your father. 13And I will live among the Israelites and will not abandon my people Israel."
14So Solomon built the temple and completed it. 15He lined its interior walls with cedar boards, paneling them from the floor of
the temple to the ceiling, and covered the floor
of the temple with planks of pine. 16He par-
titioned off twenty cubits[b] at the rear of the
temple with cedar boards from floor to ceiling to form within the temple an inner sanctuary, the Most Holy Place. 17The main hall
in front of this room was forty cubits[c] long.
18The inside of the temple was cedar, carved
with gourds and open flowers. Everything was
cedar; no stone was to be seen.
19He prepared the inner sanctuary within
the temple to set the ark of the covenant of the
LORD there. 20The inner sanctuary was twenty
cubits long, twenty wide and twenty high.[d]
He overlaid the inside with pure gold, and he
also overlaid the altar of cedar. 21Solomon covered the inside of the temple with pure gold,
and he extended gold chains across the front
of the inner sanctuary, which was overlaid
with gold. 22So he overlaid the whole interior
with gold. He also overlaid with gold the altar
that belonged to the inner sanctuary.
23In the inner sanctuary he made a pair
of cherubim of olive wood, each ten cubits[e]
high. 24One wing of the first cherub was five
cubits long, and the other wing five cubits—
ten cubits from wing tip to wing tip. 25The
second cherub also measured ten cubits, for
the two cherubim were identical in size and
shape. 26The height of each cherub was ten cubits. 27He placed the cherubim inside the innermost room of the temple, with their wings
spread out. The wing of one cherub touched
one wall, while the wing of the other touched
the other wall, and their wings touched each
other in the middle of the room. 28He overlaid
the cherubim with gold.
29On the walls all around the temple, in
both the inner and outer rooms, he carved
cherubim, palm trees and open flowers. 30He
also covered the floors of both the inner and
outer rooms of the temple with gold.
31For the entrance of the inner sanctuary
he made doors of olive wood with five-sided
jambs. 32And on the two olive wood doors he
carved cherubim, palm trees and open flowers,
and overlaid the cherubim and palm trees with
beaten gold. 33In the same way he made four-
sided jambs of olive wood for the entrance to
the main hall. 34He also made two pine doors,
each having two leaves that turned in sockets.
35He carved cherubim, palm trees and open
flowers on them and overlaid them with gold
hammered evenly over the carvings.
36And he built the inner courtyard of three
courses of dressed stone and one course of
trimmed cedar beams.
37The foundation of the temple of the LORD
was laid in the fourth year, in the month of Ziv.
38In the eleventh year in the month of Bul, the
eighth month, the temple was finished in all
its details according to its specifications. He
had spent seven years building it.

Solomon Builds His Palace

7 It took Solomon thirteen years, however,
to complete the construction of his palace.
2He built the Palace of the Forest of Lebanon a hundred cubits long, fifty wide and thirty high,[f] with four rows of cedar columns supporting trimmed cedar beams. 3It was roofed
with cedar above the beams that rested on the
columns—forty-five beams, fifteen to a row.
4Its windows were placed high in sets of three,
facing each other. 5All the doorways had rectangular frames; they were in the front part in
sets of three, facing each other.[g]
6He made a colonnade fifty cubits long and
thirty wide.[h] In front of it was a portico, and
in front of that were pillars and an overhanging roof.
7He built the throne hall, the Hall of Justice, where he was to judge, and he covered
it with cedar from floor to ceiling.[i] 8And the

[a] 8 Septuagint; Hebrew *middle* [b] 16 That is, about 30 feet (about 9 meters) [c] 17 That is, about 60 feet (about 18 meters) [d] 20 That is, about 30 feet (about 9 meters) long, wide and high [e] 23 That is, about 15 feet (about 4.5 meters) [f] 2 That is, about 150 feet (about 46 meters) long, 75 feet (about 23 meters) wide and 45 feet (about 13.5 meters) high [g] 5 The meaning of the Hebrew for this verse is uncertain. [h] 6 That is, about 75 feet (about 23 meters) long and 45 feet (about 13.5 meters) wide [i] 7 Vulgate and Syriac; Hebrew *floor*

palace in which he was to live, set farther back, was similar in design. Solomon also made a palace like this hall for Pharaoh's daughter, whom he had married.

9All these structures, from the outside to the great courtyard and from foundation to eaves, were made of blocks of high-grade stone cut to size and trimmed with a saw on their inner and outer faces. 10The foundations were laid with large stones of good quality, some measuring ten cubits[a] and some eight.[b] 11Above were high-grade stones, cut to size, and cedar beams. 12The great courtyard was surrounded by a wall of three courses of dressed stone and one course of trimmed cedar beams, as was the inner courtyard of the temple of the LORD with its portico.

The Temple's Furnishings

13King Solomon sent to Tyre and brought Huram,[c] 14whose mother was a widow from the tribe of Naphtali and whose father was a man of Tyre and a craftsman in bronze. Huram was highly skilled and experienced in all kinds of bronze work. He came to King Solomon and did all the work assigned to him.

15He cast two bronze pillars, each eighteen cubits high and twelve cubits around,[d] by line. 16He also made two capitals of cast bronze to set on the tops of the pillars; each capital was five cubits[e] high. 17A network of interwoven chains festooned the capitals on top of the pillars, seven for each capital. 18He made pomegranates in two rows[f] encircling each network to decorate the capitals on top of the pillars.[g] He did the same for each capital. 19The capitals on top of the pillars in the portico were in the shape of lilies, four cubits[h] high. 20On the capitals of both pillars, above the bowl-shaped part next to the network, were the two hundred pomegranates in rows all around. 21He erected the pillars at the portico of the temple. The pillar to the south he named Jakin[i] and the one to the north Boaz.[j] 22The capitals on top were in the shape of lilies. And so the work on the pillars was completed.

23He made the Sea of cast metal, circular in shape, measuring ten cubits[a] from rim to rim and five cubits high. It took a line of thirty cubits[k] to measure around it. 24Below the rim, gourds encircled it—ten to a cubit. The gourds were cast in two rows in one piece with the Sea.

25The Sea stood on twelve bulls, three facing north, three facing west, three facing south and three facing east. The Sea rested on top of them, and their hindquarters were toward the center. 26It was a handbreadth[l] in thickness, and its rim was like the rim of a cup, like a lily blossom. It held two thousand baths.[m]

27He also made ten movable stands of bronze; each was four cubits long, four wide and three high.[n] 28This is how the stands were made: They had side panels attached to uprights. 29On the panels between the uprights were lions, bulls and cherubim—and on the uprights as well. Above and below the lions and bulls were wreaths of hammered work. 30Each stand had four bronze wheels with bronze axles, and each had a basin resting on four supports, cast with wreaths on each side. 31On the inside of the stand there was an opening that had a circular frame one cubit[o] deep. This opening was round, and with its basework it measured a cubit and a half.[p] Around its opening there was engraving. The panels of the stands were square, not round. 32The four wheels were under the panels, and the axles of the wheels were attached to the stand. The diameter of each wheel was a cubit and a half. 33The wheels were made like chariot wheels; the axles, rims, spokes and hubs were all of cast metal.

34Each stand had four handles, one on each corner, projecting from the stand. 35At the top of the stand there was a circular band half a cubit[q] deep. The supports and panels were attached to the top of the stand. 36He engraved cherubim, lions and palm trees on the surfaces of the supports and on the panels, in every available space, with wreaths all around. 37This is the way he made the ten stands. They were all cast in the same molds and were identical in size and shape.

38He then made ten bronze basins, each holding forty baths[r] and measuring four cu-

[a] *10,23* That is, about 15 feet (about 4.5 meters) [b] *10* That is, about 12 feet (about 3.6 meters) [c] *13* Hebrew *Hiram,* a variant of *Huram;* also in verses 40 and 45 [d] *15* That is, about 27 feet (about 8.1 meters) high and 18 feet (about 5.4 meters) around [e] *16* That is, about 7 1/2 feet (about 2.3 meters); also in verse 23 [f] *18* Two Hebrew manuscripts and Septuagint; most Hebrew manuscripts *made the pillars, and there were two rows* [g] *18* Many Hebrew manuscripts and Syriac; most Hebrew manuscripts *pomegranates* [h] *19* That is, about 6 feet (about 1.8 meters); also in verse 38 [i] *21* *Jakin* probably means *he establishes.* [j] *21* *Boaz* probably means *in him is strength.* [k] *23* That is, about 45 feet (about 13.5 meters) [l] *26* That is, about 3 inches (about 8 centimeters) [m] *26* That is, probably about 11,500 gallons (about 44 kiloliters); the Septuagint does not have this sentence. [n] *27* That is, about 6 feet (about 1.8 meters) long and wide and about 4 1/2 feet (about 1.3 meters) high [o] *31* That is, about 1 1/2 feet (about 0.5 meter) [p] *31* That is, about 2 1/4 feet (about 0.7 meter); also in verse 32 [q] *35* That is, about 3/4 foot (about 0.2 meter) [r] *38* That is, about 230 gallons (about 880 liters)

bits across, one basin to go on each of the
ten stands. 39He placed five of the stands on
the south side of the temple and five on the
north. He placed the Sea on the south side, at
the southeast corner of the temple. 40He also
made the basins and shovels and sprinkling
bowls.
So Huram finished all the work he had undertaken for King Solomon in the temple of
the LORD:

41 the two pillars;
the two bowl-shaped capitals on top of
the pillars;
the two sets of network decorating the
two bowl-shaped capitals on top of the
pillars;
42 the four hundred pomegranates for the
two sets of network (two rows of
pomegranates for each network, decorating the bowl-shaped capitals on top
of the pillars);
43 the ten stands with their ten basins;
44 the Sea and the twelve bulls under it;
45 the pots, shovels and sprinkling bowls.

All these objects that Huram made for King
Solomon for the temple of the LORD were of
burnished bronze. 46The king had them cast
in clay molds in the plain of the Jordan between Succoth and Zarethan. 47Solomon left
all these things unweighed, because there were
so many; the weight of the bronze was not determined.
48Solomon also made all the furnishings
that were in the LORD's temple:

the golden altar;
the golden table on which was the bread
of the Presence;
49 the lampstands of pure gold (five on the
right and five on the left, in front of
the inner sanctuary);
the gold floral work and lamps and
tongs;
50 the pure gold basins, wick trimmers,
sprinkling bowls, dishes and censers;
and the gold sockets for the doors of the
innermost room, the Most Holy Place,
and also for the doors of the main hall
of the temple.

51When all the work King Solomon had
done for the temple of the LORD was finished,
he brought in the things his father David had
dedicated—the silver and gold and the furnishings—and he placed them in the treasuries of the LORD's temple.

The Ark Brought to the Temple

8 Then King Solomon summoned into his
presence at Jerusalem the elders of Israel,
all the heads of the tribes and the chiefs of
the Israelite families, to bring up the ark of
the LORD's covenant from Zion, the City of
David. 2All the men of Israel came together to
King Solomon at the time of the festival in the
month of Ethanim, the seventh month.
3When all the elders of Israel had arrived,
the priests took up the ark, 4and they brought
up the ark of the LORD and the Tent of Meeting and all the sacred furnishings in it. The
priests and Levites carried them up, 5and King
Solomon and the entire assembly of Israel that
had gathered about him were before the ark,
sacrificing so many sheep and cattle that they
could not be recorded or counted.
6The priests then brought the ark of the
LORD's covenant to its place in the inner sanctuary of the temple, the Most Holy Place, and
put it beneath the wings of the cherubim.
7The cherubim spread their wings over the
place of the ark and overshadowed the ark and
its carrying poles. 8These poles were so long
that their ends could be seen from the Holy
Place in front of the inner sanctuary, but not
from outside the Holy Place; and they are still
there today. 9There was nothing in the ark
except the two stone tablets that Moses had
placed in it at Horeb, where the LORD made
a covenant with the Israelites after they came
out of Egypt.
10When the priests withdrew from the Holy
Place, the cloud filled the temple of the LORD.
11And the priests could not perform their service because of the cloud, for the glory of the
LORD filled his temple.
12Then Solomon said, "The LORD has said
that he would dwell in a dark cloud; 13I have
indeed built a magnificent temple for you, a
place for you to dwell forever."
14While the whole assembly of Israel was
standing there, the king turned around and
blessed them. 15Then he said:

"Praise be to the LORD, the God of Israel, who with his own hand has fulfilled
what he promised with his own mouth
to my father David. For he said, 16'Since
the day I brought my people Israel out
of Egypt, I have not chosen a city in any
tribe of Israel to have a temple built for
my Name to be there, but I have chosen
David to rule my people Israel.'
17"My father David had it in his heart
to build a temple for the Name of the

LORD, the God of Israel. 18But the LORD
said to my father David, 'Because it was
in your heart to build a temple for my
Name, you did well to have this in your
heart. 19Nevertheless, you are not the one
to build the temple, but your son, who
is your own flesh and blood—he is the
one who will build the temple for my
Name.'
20"The LORD has kept the promise he
made: I have succeeded David my father
and now I sit on the throne of Israel, just
as the LORD promised, and I have built
the temple for the Name of the LORD,
the God of Israel. 21I have provided a
place there for the ark, in which is the
covenant of the LORD that he made with
our fathers when he brought them out of
Egypt."

Solomon's Prayer of Dedication

22Then Solomon stood before the altar of
the LORD in front of the whole assembly of
Israel, spread out his hands toward heaven
23and said:

"O LORD, God of Israel, there is no
God like you in heaven above or on earth
below—you who keep your covenant of
love with your servants who continue
wholeheartedly in your way. 24You have
kept your promise to your servant David
my father; with your mouth you have
promised and with your hand you have
fulfilled it—as it is today.
25"Now LORD, God of Israel, keep for
your servant David my father the promises you made to him when you said, 'You
shall never fail to have a man to sit before
me on the throne of Israel, if only your
sons are careful in all they do to walk before me as you have done.' 26And now,
O God of Israel, let your word that you
promised your servant David my father
come true.
27"But will God really dwell on earth?
The heavens, even the highest heaven,
cannot contain you. How much less this
temple I have built! 28Yet give attention
to your servant's prayer and his plea for
mercy, O LORD my God. Hear the cry
and the prayer that your servant is praying in your presence this day. 29May
your eyes be open toward this temple
night and day, this place of which you
said, 'My Name shall be there,' so that
you will hear the prayer your servant
prays toward this place. 30Hear the supplication of your servant and of your
people Israel when they pray toward this
place. Hear from heaven, your dwelling
place, and when you hear, forgive.
31"When a man wrongs his neighbor
and is required to take an oath and he
comes and swears the oath before your
altar in this temple, 32then hear from
heaven and act. Judge between your servants, condemning the guilty and bringing down on his own head what he has
done. Declare the innocent not guilty,
and so establish his innocence.
33"When your people Israel have been
defeated by an enemy because they have
sinned against you, and when they turn
back to you and confess your name, praying and making supplication to you in
this temple, 34then hear from heaven and
forgive the sin of your people Israel and
bring them back to the land you gave to
their fathers.
35"When the heavens are shut up and
there is no rain because your people have
sinned against you, and when they pray
toward this place and confess your name
and turn from their sin because you have
afflicted them, 36then hear from heaven
and forgive the sin of your servants, your
people Israel. Teach them the right way to
live, and send rain on the land you gave
your people for an inheritance.
37"When famine or plague comes to
the land, or blight or mildew, locusts or
grasshoppers, or when an enemy besieges
them in any of their cities, whatever disaster or disease may come, 38and when
a prayer or plea is made by any of your
people Israel—each one aware of the
afflictions of his own heart, and spreading out his hands toward this temple—
39then hear from heaven, your dwelling
place. Forgive and act; deal with each
man according to all he does, since you
know his heart (for you alone know the
hearts of all men), 40so that they will fear
you all the time they live in the land you
gave our fathers.
41"As for the foreigner who does not
belong to your people Israel but has
come from a distant land because of your
name— 42for men will hear of your great
name and your mighty hand and your
outstretched arm—when he comes and
prays toward this temple, 43then hear
from heaven, your dwelling place, and

do whatever the foreigner asks of you,
so that all the peoples of the earth may
know your name and fear you, as do
your own people Israel, and may know
that this house I have built bears your
Name.
44“When your people go to war against
their enemies, wherever you send them,
and when they pray to the LORD toward
the city you have chosen and the temple
I have built for your Name, 45then hear
from heaven their prayer and their plea,
and uphold their cause.
46“When they sin against you—for
there is no one who does not sin—and
you become angry with them and give
them over to the enemy, who takes them
captive to his own land, far away or near;
47and if they have a change of heart in
the land where they are held captive, and
repent and plead with you in the land
of their conquerors and say, ‘We have
sinned, we have done wrong, we have
acted wickedly’; 48and if they turn back
to you with all their heart and soul in
the land of their enemies who took them
captive, and pray to you toward the land
you gave their fathers, toward the city
you have chosen and the temple I have
built for your Name; 49then from heaven,
your dwelling place, hear their prayer and
their plea, and uphold their cause. 50And
forgive your people, who have sinned
against you; forgive all the offenses they
have committed against you, and cause
their conquerors to show them mercy;
51for they are your people and your inheritance, whom you brought out of
Egypt, out of that iron-smelting furnace.
52“May your eyes be open to your servant’s plea and to the plea of your people
Israel, and may you listen to them whenever they cry out to you. 53For you sin-
gled them out from all the nations of the
world to be your own inheritance, just as
you declared through your servant Moses
when you, O Sovereign LORD, brought
our fathers out of Egypt.”

54When Solomon had finished all these
prayers and supplications to the LORD, he rose
from before the altar of the LORD, where he
had been kneeling with his hands spread out
toward heaven. 55He stood and blessed the
whole assembly of Israel in a loud voice, saying:

56“Praise be to the LORD, who has
given rest to his people Israel just as he
promised. Not one word has failed of all
the good promises he gave through his
servant Moses. 57May the LORD our God
be with us as he was with our fathers; may
he never leave us nor forsake us. 58May
he turn our hearts to him, to walk in all
his ways and to keep the commands, decrees and regulations he gave our fathers.
59And may these words of mine, which I
have prayed before the LORD, be near to
the LORD our God day and night, that he
may uphold the cause of his servant and
the cause of his people Israel according
to each day’s need, 60so that all the peoples of the earth may know that the LORD
is God and that there is no other. 61But
your hearts must be fully committed to
the LORD our God, to live by his decrees
and obey his commands, as at this time.”

The Dedication of the Temple

62Then the king and all Israel with him offered sacrifices before the LORD. 63Solomon
offered a sacrifice of fellowship offerings[a] to
the LORD: twenty-two thousand cattle and
a hundred and twenty thousand sheep and
goats. So the king and all the Israelites dedicated the temple of the LORD.
64On that same day the king consecrated
the middle part of the courtyard in front of
the temple of the LORD, and there he offered
burnt offerings, grain offerings and the fat of
the fellowship offerings, because the bronze altar before the LORD was too small to hold the
burnt offerings, the grain offerings and the fat
of the fellowship offerings.
65So Solomon observed the festival at that
time, and all Israel with him—a vast assembly, people from Lebo[b] Hamath to the Wadi
of Egypt. They celebrated it before the LORD
our God for seven days and seven days more,
fourteen days in all. 66On the following day
he sent the people away. They blessed the king
and then went home, joyful and glad in heart
for all the good things the LORD had done for
his servant David and his people Israel.

The LORD Appears to Solomon

9 When Solomon had finished building the
temple of the LORD and the royal palace,
and had achieved all he had desired to do,
2the LORD appeared to him a second time, as

[a] 63 Traditionally *peace offerings*; also in verse 64 [b] 65 Or *from the entrance to*

he had appeared to him at Gibeon. 3The LORD said to him:

"I have heard the prayer and plea you have made before me; I have consecrated this temple, which you have built, by putting my Name there forever. My eyes and my heart will always be there.

4"As for you, if you walk before me in integrity of heart and uprightness, as David your father did, and do all I command and observe my decrees and laws, 5I will establish your royal throne over Israel forever, as I promised David your father when I said, 'You shall never fail to have a man on the throne of Israel.'

6"But if you[a] or your sons turn away from me and do not observe the commands and decrees I have given you[a] and go off to serve other gods and worship them, 7then I will cut off Israel from the land I have given them and will reject this temple I have consecrated for my Name. Israel will then become a byword and an object of ridicule among all peoples. 8And though this temple is now imposing, all who pass by will be appalled and will scoff and say, 'Why has the LORD done such a thing to this land and to this temple?' 9People will answer, 'Because they have forsaken the LORD their God, who brought their fathers out of Egypt, and have embraced other gods, worshiping and serving them—that is why the LORD brought all this disaster on them.' "

Solomon's Other Activities

10At the end of twenty years, during which Solomon built these two buildings—the temple of the LORD and the royal palace— 11King Solomon gave twenty towns in Galilee to Hiram king of Tyre, because Hiram had supplied him with all the cedar and pine and gold he wanted. 12But when Hiram went from Tyre to see the towns that Solomon had given him, he was not pleased with them. 13"What kind of towns are these you have given me, my brother?" he asked. And he called them the Land of Cabul,[b] a name they have to this day. 14Now Hiram had sent to the king 120 talents[c] of gold.

15Here is the account of the forced labor King Solomon conscripted to build the LORD's temple, his own palace, the supporting terraces,[d] the wall of Jerusalem, and Hazor, Megiddo and Gezer. 16(Pharaoh king of Egypt had attacked and captured Gezer. He had set it on fire. He killed its Canaanite inhabitants and then gave it as a wedding gift to his daughter, Solomon's wife. 17And Solomon rebuilt Gezer.) He built up Lower Beth Horon, 18Baalath, and Tadmor[e] in the desert, within his land, 19as well as all his store cities and the towns for his chariots and for his horses[f]—whatever he desired to build in Jerusalem, in Lebanon and throughout all the territory he ruled.

20All the people left from the Amorites, Hittites, Perizzites, Hivites and Jebusites (these peoples were not Israelites), 21that is, their descendants remaining in the land, whom the Israelites could not exterminate[g]—these Solomon conscripted for his slave labor force, as it is to this day. 22But Solomon did not make slaves of any of the Israelites; they were his fighting men, his government officials, his officers, his captains, and the commanders of his chariots and charioteers. 23They were also the chief officials in charge of Solomon's projects—550 officials supervising the men who did the work.

24After Pharaoh's daughter had come up from the City of David to the palace Solomon had built for her, he constructed the supporting terraces.

25Three times a year Solomon sacrificed burnt offerings and fellowship offerings[h] on the altar he had built for the LORD, burning incense before the LORD along with them, and so fulfilled the temple obligations.

26King Solomon also built ships at Ezion Geber, which is near Elath in Edom, on the shore of the Red Sea.[i] 27And Hiram sent his men—sailors who knew the sea—to serve in the fleet with Solomon's men. 28They sailed to Ophir and brought back 420 talents[j] of gold, which they delivered to King Solomon.

The Queen of Sheba Visits Solomon

10 When the queen of Sheba heard about the fame of Solomon and his relation to the name of the LORD, she came to test him with hard questions. 2Arriving at Jerusalem with a very great caravan—with camels carrying spices, large quantities of gold, and precious stones—she came to Solomon and

[a] 6 The Hebrew is plural. [b] 13 *Cabul* sounds like the Hebrew for *good-for-nothing.* [c] 14 That is, about 4 1/2 tons (about 4 metric tons) [d] 15 Or *the Millo*; also in verse 24 [e] 18 The Hebrew may also be read *Tamar.* [f] 19 Or *charioteers* [g] 21 The Hebrew term refers to the irrevocable giving over of things or persons to the LORD, often by totally destroying them. [h] 25 Traditionally *peace offerings* [i] 26 Hebrew *Yam Suph*; that is, Sea of Reeds [j] 28 That is, about 16 tons (about 14.5 metric tons)

talked with him about all that she had on
her mind. 3Solomon answered all her questions; nothing was too hard for the king to
explain to her. 4When the queen of Sheba saw
all the wisdom of Solomon and the palace he
had built, 5the food on his table, the seating
of his officials, the attending servants in their
robes, his cupbearers, and the burnt offerings
he made at[a] the temple of the LORD, she was
overwhelmed.
6She said to the king, "The report I heard
in my own country about your achievements
and your wisdom is true. 7But I did not believe these things until I came and saw with
my own eyes. Indeed, not even half was told
me; in wisdom and wealth you have far exceeded the report I heard. 8How happy your
men must be! How happy your officials, who
continually stand before you and hear your
wisdom! 9Praise be to the LORD your God,
who has delighted in you and placed you on
the throne of Israel. Because of the LORD's
eternal love for Israel, he has made you king,
to maintain justice and righteousness."
10And she gave the king 120 talents[b] of
gold, large quantities of spices, and precious
stones. Never again were so many spices
brought in as those the queen of Sheba gave
to King Solomon.
11(Hiram's ships brought gold from Ophir;
and from there they brought great cargoes of
almugwood[c] and precious stones. 12The king
used the almugwood to make supports for the
temple of the LORD and for the royal palace,
and to make harps and lyres for the musicians.
So much almugwood has never been imported
or seen since that day.)
13King Solomon gave the queen of Sheba
all she desired and asked for, besides what he
had given her out of his royal bounty. Then
she left and returned with her retinue to her
own country.

Solomon's Splendor

14The weight of the gold that Solomon received yearly was 666 talents,[d] 15not including the revenues from merchants and traders
and from all the Arabian kings and the governors of the land.
16King Solomon made two hundred large
shields of hammered gold; six hundred bekas[e]
of gold went into each shield. 17He also made
three hundred small shields of hammered
gold, with three minas[f] of gold in each shield.
The king put them in the Palace of the Forest
of Lebanon.
18Then the king made a great throne inlaid
with ivory and overlaid with fine gold. 19The
throne had six steps, and its back had a rounded top. On both sides of the seat were armrests, with a lion standing beside each of them.
20Twelve lions stood on the six steps, one at
either end of each step. Nothing like it had
ever been made for any other kingdom. 21All
King Solomon's goblets were gold, and all the
household articles in the Palace of the Forest of Lebanon were pure gold. Nothing was
made of silver, because silver was considered
of little value in Solomon's days. 22The king
had a fleet of trading ships[g] at sea along with
the ships of Hiram. Once every three years it
returned, carrying gold, silver and ivory, and
apes and baboons.
23King Solomon was greater in riches and
wisdom than all the other kings of the earth.
24The whole world sought audience with Solomon to hear the wisdom God had put in his
heart. 25Year after year, everyone who came
brought a gift—articles of silver and gold,
robes, weapons and spices, and horses and
mules.
26Solomon accumulated chariots and horses; he had fourteen hundred chariots and
twelve thousand horses,[h] which he kept in
the chariot cities and also with him in Jerusalem. 27The king made silver as common in
Jerusalem as stones, and cedar as plentiful as
sycamore-fig trees in the foothills. 28Solomon's
horses were imported from Egypt[i] and from
Kue[j]—the royal merchants purchased them
from Kue. 29They imported a chariot from
Egypt for six hundred shekels[k] of silver, and
a horse for a hundred and fifty.[l] They also exported them to all the kings of the Hittites
and of the Arameans.

Solomon's Wives

11 King Solomon, however, loved many
foreign women besides Pharaoh's daughter—Moabites, Ammonites, Edomites,
Sidonians and Hittites. 2They were from nations about which the LORD had told the Israelites, "You must not intermarry with them,
because they will surely turn your hearts after
their gods." Nevertheless, Solomon held fast
to them in love. 3He had seven hundred wives

[a] *5* Or *the ascent by which he went up to* [b] *10* That is, about 4 1/2 tons (about 4 metric tons) [c] *11* Probably a variant of *algumwood*; also in verse 12 [d] *14* That is, about 25 tons (about 23 metric tons) [e] *16* That is, about 7 1/2 pounds (about 3.5 kilograms) [f] *17* That is, about 3 3/4 pounds (about 1.7 kilograms) [g] *22* Hebrew *of ships of Tarshish* [h] *26* Or *charioteers* [i] *28* Or possibly *Muzur*, a region in Cilicia; also in verse 29 [j] *28* Probably *Cilicia* [k] *29* That is, about 15 pounds (about 7 kilograms) [l] *29* That is, about 3 3/4 pounds (about 1.7 kilograms)

THURSDAY
READ 1 KINGS 11:1–13

LOOKING TOGETHER IN THE SAME DIRECTION

> **As Solomon grew old, his wives turned his heart after other gods, and his heart was not fully devoted to the LORD his God, as the heart of David his father had been.**
>
> — 1 Kings 11:4

Tony came to me looking for ammunition against his parents. Of course, he didn't put it that way. All he told me was that he loved Raisa and wanted to get married. Could I talk with his parents about it and help them see the light? The sticking point for the parents, according to Tony, was Raisa's lack of Christian commitment.

I met with Tony and Raisa. At first, things were very pleasant, and we found few of the typical red flags that might flutter in unsound marriages. Then we got into the religion thing. I wanted to know how deep their commitment to God flowed in each of their hearts and whether the waters would mingle fresh or stagnant.

Raisa's spirituality burbled nicely but quickly ran out of fizz. Oh, she said she believed in God, but it didn't take long to discover that Santa Claus and Grandpa Nick and "my best friend" all seemed like different faces for whatever "God" might be. Tony was uneasy about Raisa's lack of spiritual depth, but he thought they could work it out. They were two nice people, and a nice little religion was what they wanted.

I cautioned Tony and Raisa about the need for a deeper calling. During dating we often wear blinders, I said, even though we ought to keep our eyes wide open. Seemingly little things that irk us during courtship quickly become gaping and untreatable sores during marriage, particularly if they have roots that reach to the heart. Our initial love song may seem to be some variation of "I Only Have Eyes for You," but, as C. S. Lewis put it, a better marriage song might be "Looking Together in the Same Direction." We grow weary of gazing at each other's diminishing attractions after the wedding festivities, and if there is little of the deeper stuff to keep pulling us along on the same path, we may start wandering.

In spite of his wisdom, Solomon didn't learn that lesson, and his marriages eventually destroyed not only him but also his family and his country. Solomon's son Rehoboam proved to be a silly, self-absorbed ruler. As a result, the vast majority of Israelites walked away from Rehoboam in an election of contempt. In the end, Solomon converted none of his wives through marriage, while they, on the other hand, "led him astray" (1 Kings 11:3).

And Tony and Raisa? When I urged them to take a class in basic Christianity with me, they bolted and eloped. A year later they separated. Two years later they were divorced. Now their daughter has no church community and no religion. What little faith Tony once professed is also gone.

—WAYNE BROUWER

let's talk

- ✦ In spite of the increasing openness of our culture toward various kinds of spirituality, why might marrying someone of another faith still be considered a bad decision?
- ✦ Suppose a friend told us that she was trying to lead a non-believing friend to Christ. Suppose that she later told us that she was seriously dating this man. What questions would we ask to help her think through the spiritual foundations of her relationship? How would we advise her?
- ✦ In what ways does spiritual commitment become more of an issue in marriage than it was in dating? What level of shared religious perspective would we agree is essential to starting off a marriage?

FOR YOUR NEXT DEVOTIONAL READING, TURN TO PAGE 371.

of royal birth and three hundred concubines,
and his wives led him astray. 4As Solomon
grew old, his wives turned his heart after other
gods, and his heart was not fully devoted to
the LORD his God, as the heart of David his
father had been. 5He followed Ashtoreth the
goddess of the Sidonians, and Molech[a] the
detestable god of the Ammonites. 6So Solomon did evil in the eyes of the LORD; he did
not follow the LORD completely, as David his
father had done.
7On a hill east of Jerusalem, Solomon built
a high place for Chemosh the detestable god
of Moab, and for Molech the detestable god of
the Ammonites. 8He did the same for all his
foreign wives, who burned incense and offered
sacrifices to their gods.
9The LORD became angry with Solomon
because his heart had turned away from the
LORD, the God of Israel, who had appeared
to him twice. 10Although he had forbidden
Solomon to follow other gods, Solomon did
not keep the LORD's command. 11So the LORD
said to Solomon, "Since this is your attitude
and you have not kept my covenant and my
decrees, which I commanded you, I will most
certainly tear the kingdom away from you and
give it to one of your subordinates. 12Never-
theless, for the sake of David your father, I will
not do it during your lifetime. I will tear it
out of the hand of your son. 13Yet I will not
tear the whole kingdom from him, but will
give him one tribe for the sake of David my
servant and for the sake of Jerusalem, which
I have chosen."

Solomon's Adversaries

14Then the LORD raised up against Solomon an adversary, Hadad the Edomite, from
the royal line of Edom. 15Earlier when David
was fighting with Edom, Joab the commander of the army, who had gone up to bury the
dead, had struck down all the men in Edom.
16Joab and all the Israelites stayed there for six
months, until they had destroyed all the men
in Edom. 17But Hadad, still only a boy, fled to
Egypt with some Edomite officials who had
served his father. 18They set out from Midian and went to Paran. Then taking men from
Paran with them, they went to Egypt, to Pharaoh king of Egypt, who gave Hadad a house
and land and provided him with food.
19Pharaoh was so pleased with Hadad that
he gave him a sister of his own wife, Queen
Tahpenes, in marriage. 20The sister of Tahpenes bore him a son named Genubath, whom
Tahpenes brought up in the royal palace. There
Genubath lived with Pharaoh's own children.
21While he was in Egypt, Hadad heard that
David rested with his fathers and that Joab the
commander of the army was also dead. Then
Hadad said to Pharaoh, "Let me go, that I
may return to my own country."
22"What have you lacked here that you
want to go back to your own country?" Pharaoh asked.
"Nothing," Hadad replied, "but do let
me go!"
23And God raised up against Solomon another adversary, Rezon son of Eliada, who
had fled from his master, Hadadezer king of
Zobah. 24He gathered men around him and
became the leader of a band of rebels when
David destroyed the forces[b] ⌞of Zobah⌟; the
rebels went to Damascus, where they settled
and took control. 25Rezon was Israel's adversary as long as Solomon lived, adding to the
trouble caused by Hadad. So Rezon ruled in
Aram and was hostile toward Israel.

Jeroboam Rebels Against Solomon

26Also, Jeroboam son of Nebat rebelled
against the king. He was one of Solomon's officials, an Ephraimite from Zeredah, and his
mother was a widow named Zeruah.
27Here is the account of how he rebelled
against the king: Solomon had built the supporting terraces[c] and had filled in the gap in
the wall of the city of David his father. 28Now
Jeroboam was a man of standing, and when
Solomon saw how well the young man did his
work, he put him in charge of the whole labor
force of the house of Joseph.
29About that time Jeroboam was going out
of Jerusalem, and Ahijah the prophet of Shiloh met him on the way, wearing a new cloak.
The two of them were alone out in the country,
30and Ahijah took hold of the new cloak he was
wearing and tore it into twelve pieces. 31Then
he said to Jeroboam, "Take ten pieces for yourself, for this is what the LORD, the God of Israel, says: 'See, I am going to tear the kingdom
out of Solomon's hand and give you ten tribes.
32But for the sake of my servant David and the
city of Jerusalem, which I have chosen out of
all the tribes of Israel, he will have one tribe.
33I will do this because they have[d] forsaken me
and worshiped Ashtoreth the goddess of the

[a] 5 Hebrew *Milcom*; also in verse 33 [b] 24 Hebrew *destroyed them* [c] 27 Or *the Millo* [d] 33 Hebrew; Septuagint, Vulgate and Syriac *because he has*

Sidonians, Chemosh the god of the Moabites,
and Molech the god of the Ammonites, and
have not walked in my ways, nor done what
is right in my eyes, nor kept my statutes and
laws as David, Solomon's father, did.
34" 'But I will not take the whole kingdom
out of Solomon's hand; I have made him ruler
all the days of his life for the sake of David my
servant, whom I chose and who observed my
commands and statutes. 35I will take the kingdom from his son's hands and give you ten
tribes. 36I will give one tribe to his son so that
David my servant may always have a lamp before me in Jerusalem, the city where I chose to
put my Name. 37However, as for you, I will
take you, and you will rule over all that your
heart desires; you will be king over Israel. 38If
you do whatever I command you and walk in
my ways and do what is right in my eyes by
keeping my statutes and commands, as David
my servant did, I will be with you. I will build
you a dynasty as enduring as the one I built
for David and will give Israel to you. 39I will
humble David's descendants because of this,
but not forever.' "
40Solomon tried to kill Jeroboam, but Jeroboam fled to Egypt, to Shishak the king, and
stayed there until Solomon's death.

Solomon's Death

41As for the other events of Solomon's
reign—all he did and the wisdom he displayed—are they not written in the book of
the annals of Solomon? 42Solomon reigned in
Jerusalem over all Israel forty years. 43Then he
rested with his fathers and was buried in the
city of David his father. And Rehoboam his
son succeeded him as king.

Israel Rebels Against Rehoboam

12 Rehoboam went to Shechem, for all the
Israelites had gone there to make him
king. 2When Jeroboam son of Nebat
heard this (he was still in Egypt, where he had
fled from King Solomon), he returned from[a]
Egypt. 3So they sent for Jeroboam, and he and
the whole assembly of Israel went to Rehoboam and said to him: 4"Your father put a heavy
yoke on us, but now lighten the harsh labor
and the heavy yoke he put on us, and we will
serve you."
5Rehoboam answered, "Go away for three
days and then come back to me." So the people went away.
6Then King Rehoboam consulted the elders
who had served his father Solomon during his
lifetime. "How would you advise me to answer these people?" he asked.
7They replied, "If today you will be a servant to these people and serve them and give
them a favorable answer, they will always be
your servants."
8But Rehoboam rejected the advice the elders gave him and consulted the young men
who had grown up with him and were serving him. 9He asked them, "What is your advice? How should we answer these people who
say to me, 'Lighten the yoke your father put
on us'?"
10The young men who had grown up with
him replied, "Tell these people who have said
to you, 'Your father put a heavy yoke on us,
but make our yoke lighter'—tell them, 'My
little finger is thicker than my father's waist.
11My father laid on you a heavy yoke; I will
make it even heavier. My father scourged you
with whips; I will scourge you with scorpions.' "
12Three days later Jeroboam and all the
people returned to Rehoboam, as the king
had said, "Come back to me in three days."
13The king answered the people harshly. Rejecting the advice given him by the elders,
14he followed the advice of the young men
and said, "My father made your yoke heavy; I
will make it even heavier. My father scourged
you with whips; I will scourge you with scorpions." 15So the king did not listen to the people, for this turn of events was from the LORD,
to fulfill the word the LORD had spoken to
Jeroboam son of Nebat through Ahijah the
Shilonite.
16When all Israel saw that the king refused
to listen to them, they answered the king:

"What share do we have in David,
 what part in Jesse's son?
To your tents, O Israel!
 Look after your own house, O David!"

So the Israelites went home. 17But as for the
Israelites who were living in the towns of Judah, Rehoboam still ruled over them.
18King Rehoboam sent out Adoniram,[b]
who was in charge of forced labor, but all Israel stoned him to death. King Rehoboam,
however, managed to get into his chariot and
escape to Jerusalem. 19So Israel has been in
rebellion against the house of David to this
day.
20When all the Israelites heard that Jerobo-

[a] 2 Or *he remained in* [b] 18 Some Septuagint manuscripts and Syriac (see also 1 Kings 4:6 and 5:14); Hebrew *Adoram*

am had returned, they sent and called him to
the assembly and made him king over all Israel. Only the tribe of Judah remained loyal to
the house of David.
21When Rehoboam arrived in Jerusalem,
he mustered the whole house of Judah and
the tribe of Benjamin—a hundred and eighty
thousand fighting men—to make war against
the house of Israel and to regain the kingdom
for Rehoboam son of Solomon.
22But this word of God came to Shemaiah
the man of God: 23"Say to Rehoboam son of
Solomon king of Judah, to the whole house
of Judah and Benjamin, and to the rest of the
people, 24'This is what the LORD says: Do not
go up to fight against your brothers, the Israelites. Go home, every one of you, for this is
my doing.' " So they obeyed the word of the
LORD and went home again, as the LORD had
ordered.

Golden Calves at Bethel and Dan

25Then Jeroboam fortified Shechem in the
hill country of Ephraim and lived there. From
there he went out and built up Peniel. [a]
26Jeroboam thought to himself, "The kingdom will now likely revert to the house of David. 27If these people go up to offer sacrifices
at the temple of the LORD in Jerusalem, they
will again give their allegiance to their lord,
Rehoboam king of Judah. They will kill me
and return to King Rehoboam."
28After seeking advice, the king made two
golden calves. He said to the people, "It is too
much for you to go up to Jerusalem. Here are
your gods, O Israel, who brought you up out
of Egypt." 29One he set up in Bethel, and the
other in Dan. 30And this thing became a sin;
the people went even as far as Dan to worship
the one there.
31Jeroboam built shrines on high places and
appointed priests from all sorts of people, even
though they were not Levites. 32He instituted a festival on the fifteenth day of the eighth
month, like the festival held in Judah, and
offered sacrifices on the altar. This he did in
Bethel, sacrificing to the calves he had made.
And at Bethel he also installed priests at the
high places he had made. 33On the fifteenth
day of the eighth month, a month of his own
choosing, he offered sacrifices on the altar he
had built at Bethel. So he instituted the festival for the Israelites and went up to the altar
to make offerings.

The Man of God From Judah

13 By the word of the LORD a man of God
came from Judah to Bethel, as Jeroboam was standing by the altar to make
an offering. 2He cried out against the altar by
the word of the LORD: "O altar, altar! This
is what the LORD says: 'A son named Josiah
will be born to the house of David. On you
he will sacrifice the priests of the high places who now make offerings here, and human
bones will be burned on you.' " 3That same
day the man of God gave a sign: "This is the
sign the LORD has declared: The altar will be
split apart and the ashes on it will be poured
out."
4When King Jeroboam heard what the man
of God cried out against the altar at Bethel,
he stretched out his hand from the altar and
said, "Seize him!" But the hand he stretched
out toward the man shriveled up, so that he
could not pull it back. 5Also, the altar was split
apart and its ashes poured out according to the
sign given by the man of God by the word of
the LORD.
6Then the king said to the man of God,
"Intercede with the LORD your God and pray
for me that my hand may be restored." So the
man of God interceded with the LORD, and
the king's hand was restored and became as it
was before.
7The king said to the man of God, "Come
home with me and have something to eat, and
I will give you a gift."
8But the man of God answered the king,
"Even if you were to give me half your possessions, I would not go with you, nor would I
eat bread or drink water here. 9For I was commanded by the word of the LORD: 'You must
not eat bread or drink water or return by the
way you came.' " 10So he took another road
and did not return by the way he had come
to Bethel.
11Now there was a certain old prophet living in Bethel, whose sons came and told him
all that the man of God had done there that
day. They also told their father what he had
said to the king. 12Their father asked them,
"Which way did he go?" And his sons showed
him which road the man of God from Judah
had taken. 13So he said to his sons, "Saddle the
donkey for me." And when they had saddled
the donkey for him, he mounted it 14and rode
after the man of God. He found him sitting
under an oak tree and asked, "Are you the man
of God who came from Judah?"

---

[a] 25 Hebrew *Penuel*, a variant of *Peniel*

"I am," he replied.
15 So the prophet said to him, "Come home
with me and eat."
16 The man of God said, "I cannot turn back
and go with you, nor can I eat bread or drink
water with you in this place. 17 I have been told
by the word of the LORD: 'You must not eat
bread or drink water there or return by the
way you came.' "
18 The old prophet answered, "I too am a
prophet, as you are. And an angel said to me
by the word of the LORD: 'Bring him back
with you to your house so that he may eat
bread and drink water.' " (But he was lying to
him.) 19 So the man of God returned with him
and ate and drank in his house.
20 While they were sitting at the table, the
word of the LORD came to the old prophet
who had brought him back. 21 He cried out to
the man of God who had come from Judah,
"This is what the LORD says: 'You have defied the word of the LORD and have not kept
the command the LORD your God gave you.
22 You came back and ate bread and drank water in the place where he told you not to eat or
drink. Therefore your body will not be buried
in the tomb of your fathers.' "
23 When the man of God had finished
eating and drinking, the prophet who had
brought him back saddled his donkey for
him. 24 As he went on his way, a lion met him
on the road and killed him, and his body was
thrown down on the road, with both the donkey and the lion standing beside it. 25 Some
people who passed by saw the body thrown
down there, with the lion standing beside the
body, and they went and reported it in the city
where the old prophet lived.
26 When the prophet who had brought him
back from his journey heard of it, he said, "It
is the man of God who defied the word of the
LORD. The LORD has given him over to the
lion, which has mauled him and killed him, as
the word of the LORD had warned him."
27 The prophet said to his sons, "Saddle the
donkey for me," and they did so. 28 Then he
went out and found the body thrown down
on the road, with the donkey and the lion
standing beside it. The lion had neither eat-
en the body nor mauled the donkey. 29 So
the prophet picked up the body of the man
of God, laid it on the donkey, and brought
it back to his own city to mourn for him and
bury him. 30 Then he laid the body in his own
tomb, and they mourned over him and said,
"Oh, my brother!"
31 After burying him, he said to his sons,
"When I die, bury me in the grave where the
man of God is buried; lay my bones beside his
bones. 32 For the message he declared by the
word of the LORD against the altar in Bethel
and against all the shrines on the high places
in the towns of Samaria will certainly come
true."
33 Even after this, Jeroboam did not change
his evil ways, but once more appointed priests
for the high places from all sorts of people.
Anyone who wanted to become a priest he
consecrated for the high places. 34 This was the
sin of the house of Jeroboam that led to its
downfall and to its destruction from the face
of the earth.

Ahijah's Prophecy Against Jeroboam

14 At that time Abijah son of Jeroboam became ill, 2 and Jeroboam said to his wife,
"Go, disguise yourself, so you won't be
recognized as the wife of Jeroboam. Then go
to Shiloh. Ahijah the prophet is there—the
one who told me I would be king over this
people. 3 Take ten loaves of bread with you,
some cakes and a jar of honey, and go to him.
He will tell you what will happen to the boy."
4 So Jeroboam's wife did what he said and went
to Ahijah's house in Shiloh.
Now Ahijah could not see; his sight was
gone because of his age. 5 But the LORD had
told Ahijah, "Jeroboam's wife is coming to ask
you about her son, for he is ill, and you are to
give her such and such an answer. When she
arrives, she will pretend to be someone else."
6 So when Ahijah heard the sound of her
footsteps at the door, he said, "Come in, wife
of Jeroboam. Why this pretense? I have been
sent to you with bad news. 7 Go, tell Jeroboam that this is what the LORD, the God of
Israel, says: 'I raised you up from among the
people and made you a leader over my people Israel. 8 I tore the kingdom away from the
house of David and gave it to you, but you
have not been like my servant David, who
kept my commands and followed me with all
his heart, doing only what was right in my
eyes. 9 You have done more evil than all who
lived before you. You have made for yourself
other gods, idols made of metal; you have
provoked me to anger and thrust me behind
your back.
10 " 'Because of this, I am going to bring disaster on the house of Jeroboam. I will cut off
from Jeroboam every last male in Israel—slave
or free. I will burn up the house of Jeroboam
as one burns dung, until it is all gone. 11 Dogs
will eat those belonging to Jeroboam who die

FRIDAY

READ 1 KINGS 14:1–18

CHEATING TOGETHER

Jeroboam was in a predicament. He had served the great Israelite ruler Solomon as an official in the department of public works. Encouraged by the words of Ahijah the prophet that he would one day be king, Jeroboam rebelled against Solomon, resulting in his exile to Egypt (see 1 Kings 11:26–40). When Solomon died and Rehoboam took over, Jeroboam returned from Egypt and seized the opportunity to lure away most of the kingdom.

At that time Abijah son of Jeroboam became ill, and Jeroboam said to his wife, "Go, disguise yourself, so you won't be recognized as the wife of Jeroboam. Then go to Shiloh. Ahijah the prophet is there—the one who told me I would be king over this people."

— 1 KINGS 14:1–2

let's talk

✦ Are we playing games of deception right now? What might we lose through them?

✦ How can we keep one another morally committed to what is right? Should we schedule regular opportunities for accountability checks? What would we ask each other?

✦ In what areas are we most vulnerable to temptation or sin? What do we need most from each other to strengthen these vulnerable places?

Originally, Jeroboam's main goal was to help the Israelites find a better government than the one offered by Solomon and his self-absorbed son. But, along the way, power corrupted Jeroboam; he did things to ensure his tenacious leadership while minimizing God's influence.

Now Jeroboam's son was sick. So the king began weaving a web of deception, enlisting his wife to dress like someone else and feign piety before Ahijah to manipulate him into giving a good report on their son. Rather than seeking God's guidance, the couple tried to use the prophet like a good-luck charm. Things turned out very badly for them as a result.

Marriage binds husband and wife into a unity that changes both of them. While individual identities shouldn't be crushed as "two become one," it is also true that we cannot remain isolated or independent from one another. But in the fusing that takes place, both good and bad things can happen.

When we share our lives well, we can strengthen our mate's resolve, nurture our spouse's well-being and encourage each other's gifts. Unfortunately, we can also have a negative impact on each other. We can entice our partner into supporting our mistakes and sins. We can ask our spouse to cover up for us when the phone rings and we don't wish to be found. We can lie for our mate in public settings. We can manipulate our spouse into falsifying tax returns or hiding assets.

Marriage makes us complicit in the morality of our mate. That is an important reason to choose wisely before we wed and to build upon a strong moral center in our relationship after we are joined. Great businesses don't collapse overnight through some minor accounting error; their foundations slowly erode as leaders make each other complicit in deceptive schemes. So it is in marriages. While we can win for a while as we help each other cheat on the truth, in the long run we build a kingdom of facades in which we can neither trust our partner's face nor clearly see our own.

On the other hand, when we learn from mistakes like those of Jeroboam and his wife, we can build a complicity of goodness that our children and friends will admire someday when they help us celebrate our silver and golden wedding anniversaries.

—WAYNE BROUWER

FOR YOUR NEXT DEVOTIONAL READING, TURN TO PAGE 374.

in the city, and the birds of the air will feed
on those who die in the country. The LORD
has spoken!'
12"As for you, go back home. When you set
foot in your city, the boy will die. 13All Israel
will mourn for him and bury him. He is the
only one belonging to Jeroboam who will be
buried, because he is the only one in the house
of Jeroboam in whom the LORD, the God of
Israel, has found anything good.
14"The LORD will raise up for himself a king
over Israel who will cut off the family of Jeroboam. This is the day! What? Yes, even now.[a]
15And the LORD will strike Israel, so that it
will be like a reed swaying in the water. He
will uproot Israel from this good land that he
gave to their forefathers and scatter them beyond the River,[b] because they provoked the
LORD to anger by making Asherah poles.[c]
16And he will give Israel up because of the sins
Jeroboam has committed and has caused Israel
to commit."
17Then Jeroboam's wife got up and left
and went to Tirzah. As soon as she stepped
over the threshold of the house, the boy died.
18They buried him, and all Israel mourned for
him, as the LORD had said through his servant
the prophet Ahijah.
19The other events of Jeroboam's reign,
his wars and how he ruled, are written in the
book of the annals of the kings of Israel. 20He
reigned for twenty-two years and then rested
with his fathers. And Nadab his son succeeded
him as king.

Rehoboam King of Judah

21Rehoboam son of Solomon was king in
Judah. He was forty-one years old when he became king, and he reigned seventeen years in
Jerusalem, the city the LORD had chosen out
of all the tribes of Israel in which to put his
Name. His mother's name was Naamah; she
was an Ammonite.
22Judah did evil in the eyes of the LORD.
By the sins they committed they stirred up
his jealous anger more than their fathers had
done. 23They also set up for themselves high
places, sacred stones and Asherah poles on every high hill and under every spreading tree.
24There were even male shrine prostitutes in
the land; the people engaged in all the detestable practices of the nations the LORD had
driven out before the Israelites.
25In the fifth year of King Rehoboam, Shishak king of Egypt attacked Jerusalem. 26He
carried off the treasures of the temple of the
LORD and the treasures of the royal palace.
He took everything, including all the gold
shields Solomon had made. 27So King Rehoboam made bronze shields to replace them
and assigned these to the commanders of
the guard on duty at the entrance to the royal palace. 28Whenever the king went to the
LORD's temple, the guards bore the shields,
and afterward they returned them to the
guardroom.
29As for the other events of Rehoboam's
reign, and all he did, are they not written in
the book of the annals of the kings of Judah?
30There was continual warfare between Rehoboam and Jeroboam. 31And Rehoboam rested
with his fathers and was buried with them in
the City of David. His mother's name was Naamah; she was an Ammonite. And Abijah[d] his
son succeeded him as king.

Abijah King of Judah

15 In the eighteenth year of the reign of
Jeroboam son of Nebat, Abijah[e] became
king of Judah, 2and he reigned in Jerusalem three years. His mother's name was Maacah daughter of Abishalom.[f]
3He committed all the sins his father had
done before him; his heart was not fully devoted to the LORD his God, as the heart of
David his forefather had been. 4Nevertheless,
for David's sake the LORD his God gave him a
lamp in Jerusalem by raising up a son to succeed him and by making Jerusalem strong.
5For David had done what was right in the
eyes of the LORD and had not failed to keep
any of the LORD's commands all the days of
his life—except in the case of Uriah the Hittite.
6There was war between Rehoboam[g] and
Jeroboam throughout ⌞Abijah's⌟ lifetime. 7As
for the other events of Abijah's reign, and all
he did, are they not written in the book of the
annals of the kings of Judah? There was war
between Abijah and Jeroboam. 8And Abijah
rested with his fathers and was buried in the
City of David. And Asa his son succeeded him
as king.

Asa King of Judah

9In the twentieth year of Jeroboam king

---

a 14 The meaning of the Hebrew for this sentence is uncertain. *b 15* That is, the Euphrates *c 15* That is, symbols of the goddess Asherah; here and elsewhere in 1 Kings *d 31* Some Hebrew manuscripts and Septuagint (see also 2 Chron. 12:16); most Hebrew manuscripts *Abijam* *e 1* Some Hebrew manuscripts and Septuagint (see also 2 Chron. 12:16); most Hebrew manuscripts *Abijam*; also in verses 7 and 8 *f 2* A variant of *Absalom*; also in verse 10 *g 6* Most Hebrew manuscripts; some Hebrew manuscripts and Syriac *Abijam* (that is, Abijah)

of Israel, Asa became king of Judah, 10and
he reigned in Jerusalem forty-one years. His
grandmother's name was Maacah daughter of
Abishalom.

11Asa did what was right in the eyes of the
LORD, as his father David had done. 12He expelled the male shrine prostitutes from the
land and got rid of all the idols his fathers had
made. 13He even deposed his grandmother
Maacah from her position as queen mother,
because she had made a repulsive Asherah
pole. Asa cut the pole down and burned it
in the Kidron Valley. 14Although he did not
remove the high places, Asa's heart was fully committed to the LORD all his life. 15He
brought into the temple of the LORD the silver
and gold and the articles that he and his father
had dedicated.

16There was war between Asa and Baasha
king of Israel throughout their reigns. 17Baa-
sha king of Israel went up against Judah and
fortified Ramah to prevent anyone from leaving or entering the territory of Asa king of Judah.

18Asa then took all the silver and gold that
was left in the treasuries of the LORD's temple
and of his own palace. He entrusted it to his
officials and sent them to Ben-Hadad son of
Tabrimmon, the son of Hezion, the king of
Aram, who was ruling in Damascus. 19"Let
there be a treaty between me and you," he
said, "as there was between my father and
your father. See, I am sending you a gift of
silver and gold. Now break your treaty with
Baasha king of Israel so he will withdraw
from me."

20Ben-Hadad agreed with King Asa and
sent the commanders of his forces against
the towns of Israel. He conquered Ijon, Dan,
Abel Beth Maacah and all Kinnereth in addition to Naphtali. 21When Baasha heard this,
he stopped building Ramah and withdrew
to Tirzah. 22Then King Asa issued an order
to all Judah—no one was exempt—and they
carried away from Ramah the stones and timber Baasha had been using there. With them
King Asa built up Geba in Benjamin, and also
Mizpah.

23As for all the other events of Asa's reign,
all his achievements, all he did and the cities he built, are they not written in the book
of the annals of the kings of Judah? In his
old age, however, his feet became diseased.
24Then Asa rested with his fathers and was
buried with them in the city of his father David. And Jehoshaphat his son succeeded him
as king.

Nadab King of Israel

25Nadab son of Jeroboam became king of
Israel in the second year of Asa king of Judah,
and he reigned over Israel two years. 26He did
evil in the eyes of the LORD, walking in the
ways of his father and in his sin, which he had
caused Israel to commit.

27Baasha son of Ahijah of the house of Issachar plotted against him, and he struck him
down at Gibbethon, a Philistine town, while
Nadab and all Israel were besieging it. 28Baa-
sha killed Nadab in the third year of Asa king
of Judah and succeeded him as king.

29As soon as he began to reign, he killed
Jeroboam's whole family. He did not leave Jeroboam anyone that breathed, but destroyed
them all, according to the word of the LORD
given through his servant Ahijah the Shilonite— 30because of the sins Jeroboam had
committed and had caused Israel to commit,
and because he provoked the LORD, the God
of Israel, to anger.

31As for the other events of Nadab's reign,
and all he did, are they not written in the book
of the annals of the kings of Israel? 32There
was war between Asa and Baasha king of Israel
throughout their reigns.

Baasha King of Israel

33In the third year of Asa king of Judah, Baasha son of Ahijah became king of all Israel
in Tirzah, and he reigned twenty-four years.
34He did evil in the eyes of the LORD, walking
in the ways of Jeroboam and in his sin, which
he had caused Israel to commit.

16 Then the word of the LORD came to
Jehu son of Hanani against Baasha: 2"I
lifted you up from the dust and made
you leader of my people Israel, but you walked
in the ways of Jeroboam and caused my people Israel to sin and to provoke me to anger by
their sins. 3So I am about to consume Baasha
and his house, and I will make your house like
that of Jeroboam son of Nebat. 4Dogs will eat
those belonging to Baasha who die in the city,
and the birds of the air will feed on those who
die in the country."

5As for the other events of Baasha's reign,
what he did and his achievements, are they
not written in the book of the annals of the
kings of Israel? 6Baasha rested with his fathers
and was buried in Tirzah. And Elah his son
succeeded him as king.

7Moreover, the word of the LORD came
through the prophet Jehu son of Hanani to
Baasha and his house, because of all the evil he
had done in the eyes of the LORD, provoking

WEEKEND

dealing with temptation

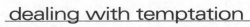

I have always had lots of guy friends. I know this bothers my husband, and I don't want him to feel uneasy about this, but I also don't want to sever all ties with my opposite-sex friends. What should I do?

You are wise to take your husband's feelings into consideration on this matter. It says that you care deeply about him and your relationship. But your strong desire to maintain relationships that trouble him makes us wonder: Which relationship is more important to you, the relationships with your male friends or the relationship with your husband?

Assuming you say it's your husband, we offer a few suggestions on how to enjoy your friendships with other men while making it very clear that you prize, above all other relationships, the one you have with your husband.

For starters, don't trust yourself. Sexual feelings are, in great part, biological, and at times sexual desire can rush in when we aren't prepared for it. Never assume that you (or any of your friends) are in complete control of these feelings—especially if you and your husband are not getting along well.

Second, stay clear of friendships if the other man is in a weak marriage and is hungry for love. You may have compassion for his suffering, but the chemistry makes boundary issues too precarious.

Third, think through the setting in which you meet. Some settings are more sexual than others, and you need to stay clear of them. Just the two of you at a candlelight dinner, for example, is not a good idea under any circumstances.

Fourth, fill your spouse in every time you meet your opposite-sex friend. Keep him informed of where you went and what you talked about. If you find yourself being protective or secretive, that is a danger sign.

Fifth, never allow any form of physical contact to take place in a private setting. If you do show affection, do it in front of others.

Finally, draw the line if you need to. If you feel that the relationship has potential to become something more than a friendship, remember how precious your marriage is to you and set strict boundaries on the friendship.

—DR. LES PARROTT III AND DR. LESLIE PARROTT

Whenever I feel particularly vulnerable to sexual temptation, I find it helpful to review the following effects that my action could have:

—Grieving the Lord who redeemed me.
—One day having to look Jesus, the Righteous Judge, in the face and giving an account of my actions.
—Inflicting untold hurt on my loyal wife and losing her respect and trust.
—Destroying credibility with my children and nullifying efforts to teach them to obey God.
—Perhaps losing my wife and my children forever.
—Losing self-respect.
—Forming memories and flashbacks that could plague future intimacy with my wife.
—Forfeiting years of witnessing to others.
—Heaping endless difficulty on the person with whom I committed adultery.
—Possibly causing pregnancy and a child as a lifelong reminder of my sin.

—RANDY ALCORN

responding to temptation

HOW ARE WE DOING?

What's the best way to flee temptation in the following situations? Test yourself by choosing one of the options.

1. You've been running with neighbors before work in the morning. Gradually the group whittles down to you and a very attractive neighbor, who is also married. When she suggests lunch, you:
   a. See if she prefers Italian or Thai
   b. Agree lunch would be great and suggest including your spouses
   c. Adapt your exercise program so that more people are involved
2. A coworker has been flirting with you. Next time it happens, you:
   a. Scream, "Stop or I'll press sexual harassment charges!"
   b. Suggest dinner so you can speak in private about the flirting
   c. Talk about your spouse often and lovingly, hoping the flirt will get the hint
3. Some good friends are having marital problems. The husband calls you periodically, needing to vent. You:
   a. Continue to be a good friend by listening to his problems
   b. Empathize by letting him in on some of your struggles
   c. Suggest that it might be more appropriate for him to talk to a counselor
4. An attractive neighbor is mowing the lawn with his shirt off. His gorgeous wife is sunning in a bikini. You:
   a. Watch from an upstairs window
   b. Introduce yourselves, since they look like fun people
   c. Buy new curtains for that side of the house

Answers: Not sure if you answered each question correctly? Check with your spouse.

let's make a DATE

FANTASY ADVENTURE

Have date night in a local bookstore. Linger over a latte in the coffee shop. Browse the travel section for fascinating travel destinations. If you could travel anywhere, where would it be? How would you spend your time there? Share your fantasy vacation with your spouse and talk about what the two of you would do there together.

FOR YOUR NEXT DEVOTIONAL READING, TURN TO PAGE 378.

LESSONS FROM THE *Bible*

Examine the following Scripture passages. Find a couple of ways these people fought temptation.

1. Joseph with Potiphar's wife (Genesis 39:1–12)
2. A young man encouraged to avoid temptation (Proverbs 5:1–23)

him to anger by the things he did, and becoming like the house of Jeroboam—and also
because he destroyed it.

Elah King of Israel

8In the twenty-sixth year of Asa king of Judah, Elah son of Baasha became king of Israel,
and he reigned in Tirzah two years.
9Zimri, one of his officials, who had command of half his chariots, plotted against him.
Elah was in Tirzah at the time, getting drunk
in the home of Arza, the man in charge of the
palace at Tirzah. 10Zimri came in, struck him
down and killed him in the twenty-seventh
year of Asa king of Judah. Then he succeeded
him as king.
11As soon as he began to reign and was seated on the throne, he killed off Baasha's whole
family. He did not spare a single male, whether relative or friend. 12So Zimri destroyed the
whole family of Baasha, in accordance with
the word of the Lord spoken against Baasha
through the prophet Jehu— 13because of all
the sins Baasha and his son Elah had committed and had caused Israel to commit, so that
they provoked the Lord, the God of Israel, to
anger by their worthless idols.
14As for the other events of Elah's reign, and
all he did, are they not written in the book of
the annals of the kings of Israel?

Zimri King of Israel

15In the twenty-seventh year of Asa king
of Judah, Zimri reigned in Tirzah seven days.
The army was encamped near Gibbethon, a
Philistine town. 16When the Israelites in the
camp heard that Zimri had plotted against
the king and murdered him, they proclaimed
Omri, the commander of the army, king over
Israel that very day there in the camp. 17Then
Omri and all the Israelites with him withdrew
from Gibbethon and laid siege to Tirzah.
18When Zimri saw that the city was taken, he
went into the citadel of the royal palace and
set the palace on fire around him. So he died,
19because of the sins he had committed, doing
evil in the eyes of the Lord and walking in the
ways of Jeroboam and in the sin he had committed and had caused Israel to commit.
20As for the other events of Zimri's reign,
and the rebellion he carried out, are they not
written in the book of the annals of the kings
of Israel?

Omri King of Israel

21Then the people of Israel were split into
two factions; half supported Tibni son of Ginath for king, and the other half supported
Omri. 22But Omri's followers proved stronger
than those of Tibni son of Ginath. So Tibni
died and Omri became king.
23In the thirty-first year of Asa king of
Judah, Omri became king of Israel, and he
reigned twelve years, six of them in Tirzah.
24He bought the hill of Samaria from Shemer
for two talents[a] of silver and built a city on the
hill, calling it Samaria, after Shemer, the name
of the former owner of the hill.
25But Omri did evil in the eyes of the Lord
and sinned more than all those before him.
26He walked in all the ways of Jeroboam son
of Nebat and in his sin, which he had caused
Israel to commit, so that they provoked the
Lord, the God of Israel, to anger by their
worthless idols.
27As for the other events of Omri's reign,
what he did and the things he achieved, are
they not written in the book of the annals of
the kings of Israel? 28Omri rested with his fathers and was buried in Samaria. And Ahab
his son succeeded him as king.

Ahab Becomes King of Israel

29In the thirty-eighth year of Asa king of Judah, Ahab son of Omri became king of Israel,
and he reigned in Samaria over Israel twenty-two years. 30Ahab son of Omri did more
evil in the eyes of the Lord than any of those
before him. 31He not only considered it trivial
to commit the sins of Jeroboam son of Nebat,
but he also married Jezebel daughter of Eth-
baal king of the Sidonians, and began to serve
Baal and worship him. 32He set up an altar for
Baal in the temple of Baal that he built in Samaria. 33Ahab also made an Asherah pole and
did more to provoke the Lord, the God of
Israel, to anger than did all the kings of Israel
before him.
34In Ahab's time, Hiel of Bethel rebuilt Jericho. He laid its foundations at the cost of his
firstborn son Abiram, and he set up its gates at
the cost of his youngest son Segub, in accordance with the word of the Lord spoken by
Joshua son of Nun.

Elijah Fed by Ravens

17 Now Elijah the Tishbite, from Tishbe[b]
in Gilead, said to Ahab, "As the Lord,
the God of Israel, lives, whom I serve,

[a] *24* That is, about 150 pounds (about 70 kilograms) [b] *1* Or *Tishbite, of the settlers*

there will be neither dew nor rain in the next few years except at my word."

2Then the word of the LORD came to Elijah: 3"Leave here, turn eastward and hide in the Kerith Ravine, east of the Jordan. 4You will drink from the brook, and I have ordered the ravens to feed you there."

5So he did what the LORD had told him. He went to the Kerith Ravine, east of the Jordan, and stayed there. 6The ravens brought him bread and meat in the morning and bread and meat in the evening, and he drank from the brook.

The Widow at Zarephath

7Some time later the brook dried up because there had been no rain in the land. 8Then the word of the LORD came to him: 9"Go at once to Zarephath of Sidon and stay there. I have commanded a widow in that place to supply you with food." 10So he went to Zarephath. When he came to the town gate, a widow was there gathering sticks. He called to her and asked, "Would you bring me a little water in a jar so I may have a drink?" 11As she was going to get it, he called, "And bring me, please, a piece of bread."

12"As surely as the LORD your God lives," she replied, "I don't have any bread—only a handful of flour in a jar and a little oil in a jug. I am gathering a few sticks to take home and make a meal for myself and my son, that we may eat it—and die."

13Elijah said to her, "Don't be afraid. Go home and do as you have said. But first make a small cake of bread for me from what you have and bring it to me, and then make something for yourself and your son. 14For this is what the LORD, the God of Israel, says: 'The jar of flour will not be used up and the jug of oil will not run dry until the day the LORD gives rain on the land.' "

15She went away and did as Elijah had told her. So there was food every day for Elijah and for the woman and her family. 16For the jar of flour was not used up and the jug of oil did not run dry, in keeping with the word of the LORD spoken by Elijah.

17Some time later the son of the woman who owned the house became ill. He grew worse and worse, and finally stopped breathing. 18She said to Elijah, "What do you have against me, man of God? Did you come to remind me of my sin and kill my son?"

19"Give me your son," Elijah replied. He took him from her arms, carried him to the upper room where he was staying, and laid him on his bed. 20Then he cried out to the LORD, "O LORD my God, have you brought tragedy also upon this widow I am staying with, by causing her son to die?" 21Then he stretched himself out on the boy three times and cried to the LORD, "O LORD my God, let this boy's life return to him!"

22The LORD heard Elijah's cry, and the boy's life returned to him, and he lived. 23Elijah picked up the child and carried him down from the room into the house. He gave him to his mother and said, "Look, your son is alive!"

24Then the woman said to Elijah, "Now I know that you are a man of God and that the word of the LORD from your mouth is the truth."

Elijah and Obadiah

18 After a long time, in the third year, the word of the LORD came to Elijah: "Go and present yourself to Ahab, and I will send rain on the land." 2So Elijah went to present himself to Ahab.

Now the famine was severe in Samaria, 3and Ahab had summoned Obadiah, who was in charge of his palace. (Obadiah was a devout believer in the LORD. 4While Jezebel was killing off the LORD's prophets, Obadiah had taken a hundred prophets and hidden them in two caves, fifty in each, and had supplied them with food and water.) 5Ahab had said to Obadiah, "Go through the land to all the springs and valleys. Maybe we can find some grass to keep the horses and mules alive so we will not have to kill any of our animals." 6So they divided the land they were to cover, Ahab going in one direction and Obadiah in another.

7As Obadiah was walking along, Elijah met him. Obadiah recognized him, bowed down to the ground, and said, "Is it really you, my lord Elijah?"

8"Yes," he replied. "Go tell your master, 'Elijah is here.' "

9"What have I done wrong," asked Obadiah, "that you are handing your servant over to Ahab to be put to death? 10As surely as the LORD your God lives, there is not a nation or kingdom where my master has not sent someone to look for you. And whenever a nation or kingdom claimed you were not there, he made them swear they could not find you. 11But now you tell me to go to my master and say, 'Elijah is here.' 12I don't know where the Spirit of the LORD may carry you when I leave you. If I go and tell Ahab and he doesn't

MONDAY
READ 1 KINGS 17:7–24

WHY, GOD?

She said to Elijah, "What do you have against me, man of God? Did you come to remind me of my sin and kill my son?"

— 1 KINGS 17:18

let's talk

- What is our personal response to suffering? Do we blame God for difficulties in our lives and see him as judging our sin?
- What characteristics of God do we see displayed in the story of Elijah and the widow?
- When we consider a difficult situation we're facing right now, what are some lessons we're learning about God through it?

A man I knew couldn't get over being angry with God after his dad died. "Why did God do this to me?" my friend asked. I listened while he railed about how unfair God had been to take his dad. He felt God had injured him as a judgment, and he couldn't understand the scales God was using to measure his guilt for whatever crime he might have committed.

While I felt compassion for my friend's suffering, I couldn't help wonder why he felt God was punishing him. Yet the widow in 1 Kings essentially told Elijah the same thing. "Did you come to remind me of my sin and kill my son?"

When God asked Elijah to go to Zarephath in the non-Israelite area of Sidon, Elijah had already been schooled by God's miraculous provision. So when he met the widow, he didn't question God's ability to use her last drop of oil and flour to fix an ongoing supply of food for the two of them and her son. And as long as the flour and the oil kept producing bread, the God whom Elijah represented seemed like a pretty good guy to the widow.

Then the unthinkable occurred: the widow's son died. Suddenly, Elijah no longer represented God as provider; now he was God's messenger of judgment. The age-old question, "Why would a good God allow this bad thing to happen to me?" became the widow's knee-jerk response to crisis.

Recently, a friend called me at dawn in a state of panic. Her nine-year-old son had just been diagnosed with a brain tumor. With her son's life hanging in the balance, all this young mom could do was beg everyone she knew to pray, then watch and wait while God worked a miracle. If she had overlooked God before this incident, he was front and center to her now. As the curtain went up and her drama unfolded, all eyes were on God, the One who holds life in his hands.

We can't know for sure why God chose to revive the widow's young son through Elijah's prayers. Was God simply reminding his audience—the widow and Elijah—that he could bring life from death? Since sin brings death and judgment, perhaps God allowed the boy to die to awaken this reality in his mother. The boy's resurrection then signified the new life we receive when we are forgiven and our relationship to God is restored.

Though we can't know God's purposes in choosing death for some and healing for others, Elijah and the widow and her son remind us of one basic truth about God: When suffering comes, God uses the experience to display his mercy, power and glory—and to bring us closer to him.

—MARIAN V. LIAUTAUD

FOR YOUR NEXT DEVOTIONAL READING, TURN TO PAGE 381.

find you, he will kill me. Yet I your servant
have worshiped the LORD since my youth.
[13]Haven't you heard, my lord, what I did
while Jezebel was killing the prophets of the
LORD? I hid a hundred of the LORD's prophets
in two caves, fifty in each, and supplied them
with food and water. [14]And now you tell me
to go to my master and say, 'Elijah is here.' He
will kill me!"
[15]Elijah said, "As the LORD Almighty lives,
whom I serve, I will surely present myself to
Ahab today."

Elijah on Mount Carmel

[16]So Obadiah went to meet Ahab and told
him, and Ahab went to meet Elijah. [17]When
he saw Elijah, he said to him, "Is that you, you
troubler of Israel?"
[18]"I have not made trouble for Israel," Elijah replied. "But you and your father's family
have. You have abandoned the LORD's commands and have followed the Baals. [19]Now
summon the people from all over Israel to
meet me on Mount Carmel. And bring the
four hundred and fifty prophets of Baal and
the four hundred prophets of Asherah, who
eat at Jezebel's table."
[20]So Ahab sent word throughout all Israel
and assembled the prophets on Mount Carmel. [21]Elijah went before the people and said,
"How long will you waver between two opinions? If the LORD is God, follow him; but if
Baal is God, follow him."
But the people said nothing.
[22]Then Elijah said to them, "I am the only
one of the LORD's prophets left, but Baal has
four hundred and fifty prophets. [23]Get two
bulls for us. Let them choose one for themselves, and let them cut it into pieces and put
it on the wood but not set fire to it. I will prepare the other bull and put it on the wood but
not set fire to it. [24]Then you call on the name
of your god, and I will call on the name of
the LORD. The god who answers by fire—he
is God."
Then all the people said, "What you say is
good."
[25]Elijah said to the prophets of Baal,
"Choose one of the bulls and prepare it first,
since there are so many of you. Call on the
name of your god, but do not light the fire."
[26]So they took the bull given them and prepared it.
Then they called on the name of Baal from
morning till noon. "O Baal, answer us!" they
shouted. But there was no response; no one
answered. And they danced around the altar
they had made.
[27]At noon Elijah began to taunt them.
"Shout louder!" he said. "Surely he is a god!
Perhaps he is deep in thought, or busy, or traveling. Maybe he is sleeping and must be awakened." [28]So they shouted louder and slashed
themselves with swords and spears, as was
their custom, until their blood flowed. [29]Mid-
day passed, and they continued their frantic
prophesying until the time for the evening
sacrifice. But there was no response, no one
answered, no one paid attention.
[30]Then Elijah said to all the people, "Come
here to me." They came to him, and he repaired the altar of the LORD, which was in ruins. [31]Elijah took twelve stones, one for each
of the tribes descended from Jacob, to whom
the word of the LORD had come, saying, "Your
name shall be Israel." [32]With the stones he
built an altar in the name of the LORD, and he
dug a trench around it large enough to hold
two seahs[a] of seed. [33]He arranged the wood,
cut the bull into pieces and laid it on the
wood. Then he said to them, "Fill four large
jars with water and pour it on the offering and
on the wood."
[34]"Do it again," he said, and they did it
again.
"Do it a third time," he ordered, and they
did it the third time. [35]The water ran down
around the altar and even filled the trench.
[36]At the time of sacrifice, the prophet Elijah
stepped forward and prayed: "O LORD, God
of Abraham, Isaac and Israel, let it be known
today that you are God in Israel and that I am
your servant and have done all these things at
your command. [37]Answer me, O LORD, answer me, so these people will know that you,
O LORD, are God, and that you are turning
their hearts back again."
[38]Then the fire of the LORD fell and burned
up the sacrifice, the wood, the stones and
the soil, and also licked up the water in the
trench.
[39]When all the people saw this, they fell
prostrate and cried, "The LORD—he is God!
The LORD—he is God!"
[40]Then Elijah commanded them, "Seize
the prophets of Baal. Don't let anyone get
away!" They seized them, and Elijah had
them brought down to the Kishon Valley and
slaughtered there.
[41]And Elijah said to Ahab, "Go, eat and

a *32* That is, probably about 13 quarts (about 15 liters)

drink, for there is the sound of a heavy rain."
42So Ahab went off to eat and drink, but Elijah climbed to the top of Carmel, bent down
to the ground and put his face between his
knees.
43"Go and look toward the sea," he told his
servant. And he went up and looked.
"There is nothing there," he said.
Seven times Elijah said, "Go back."
44The seventh time the servant reported, "A
cloud as small as a man's hand is rising from
the sea."
So Elijah said, "Go and tell Ahab, 'Hitch
up your chariot and go down before the rain
stops you.' "
45Meanwhile, the sky grew black with
clouds, the wind rose, a heavy rain came on
and Ahab rode off to Jezreel. 46The power of
the LORD came upon Elijah and, tucking his
cloak into his belt, he ran ahead of Ahab all
the way to Jezreel.

Elijah Flees to Horeb

19 Now Ahab told Jezebel everything Elijah had done and how he had killed all
the prophets with the sword. 2So Jezebel sent a messenger to Elijah to say, "May the
gods deal with me, be it ever so severely, if by
this time tomorrow I do not make your life
like that of one of them."
3Elijah was afraid[a] and ran for his life.
When he came to Beersheba in Judah, he
left his servant there, 4while he himself went
a day's journey into the desert. He came to a
broom tree, sat down under it and prayed that
he might die. "I have had enough, LORD," he
said. "Take my life; I am no better than my
ancestors." 5Then he lay down under the tree
and fell asleep.
All at once an angel touched him and said,
"Get up and eat." 6He looked around, and
there by his head was a cake of bread baked
over hot coals, and a jar of water. He ate and
drank and then lay down again.
7The angel of the LORD came back a second
time and touched him and said, "Get up and
eat, for the journey is too much for you." 8So
he got up and ate and drank. Strengthened
by that food, he traveled forty days and forty
nights until he reached Horeb, the mountain
of God. 9There he went into a cave and spent
the night.

The LORD Appears to Elijah

And the word of the LORD came to him:
"What are you doing here, Elijah?"
10He replied, "I have been very zealous for
the LORD God Almighty. The Israelites have
rejected your covenant, broken down your altars, and put your prophets to death with the
sword. I am the only one left, and now they
are trying to kill me too."
11The LORD said, "Go out and stand on the
mountain in the presence of the LORD, for the
LORD is about to pass by."
Then a great and powerful wind tore the
mountains apart and shattered the rocks
before the LORD, but the LORD was not in
the wind. After the wind there was an earthquake, but the LORD was not in the earthquake. 12After the earthquake came a fire,
but the LORD was not in the fire. And after
the fire came a gentle whisper. 13When Elijah heard it, he pulled his cloak over his face
and went out and stood at the mouth of the
cave.
Then a voice said to him, "What are you
doing here, Elijah?"
14He replied, "I have been very zealous for
the LORD God Almighty. The Israelites have
rejected your covenant, broken down your altars, and put your prophets to death with the
sword. I am the only one left, and now they
are trying to kill me too."
15The LORD said to him, "Go back the way
you came, and go to the Desert of Damascus. When you get there, anoint Hazael king
over Aram. 16Also, anoint Jehu son of Nimshi king over Israel, and anoint Elisha son of
Shaphat from Abel Meholah to succeed you
as prophet. 17Jehu will put to death any who
escape the sword of Hazael, and Elisha will
put to death any who escape the sword of
Jehu. 18Yet I reserve seven thousand in Israel—all whose knees have not bowed down to
Baal and all whose mouths have not kissed
him."

The Call of Elisha

19So Elijah went from there and found
Elisha son of Shaphat. He was plowing with
twelve yoke of oxen, and he himself was driving the twelfth pair. Elijah went up to him
and threw his cloak around him. 20Elisha then
left his oxen and ran after Elijah. "Let me kiss
my father and mother good-by," he said, "and
then I will come with you."

[a] 3 Or *Elijah saw*

TUESDAY
READ 1 KINGS 19:1–18

WHEN LIFE'S TOO HARD

Scott was away on business when his mother suffered a near-fatal heart attack. He cut his trip short and went to the hospital, where he stayed at his mother's side for weeks.

Amy understood that Scott's mother was dying, but she was at home alone with two preschoolers and a newborn baby. She felt like she was slowly being strangled. She wasn't eating or sleeping. She became so overwhelmed that late one night when she was talking by phone with Scott, she lost her temper (or, as she tells it, her mind).

"This has to stop now!" Amy yelled at Scott. "I don't care if your mom is dying; you act like you love her more than you love me. I need you to come home now!"

While Amy isn't proud of that moment, months later she can still recall the frustration and tension she felt as she tried to do it all alone.

Perhaps those were some of the emotions Elijah felt as he sat alone under the broom bush in the desert. Facing certain death, there was nowhere to turn, no one to help him. At that moment, the prophet just wanted to die.

We've all felt at times as if life is just too hard to go on. We want to give up on our self, our marriage, perhaps even our life. No matter how strong our faith, we can still reach a breaking point.

So what did Elijah do in this desperate situation? He went to sleep. It would have seemed much more spiritual for him to have stayed awake all night praying or offering a sacrifice to God, but Elijah laid down and slept. He was so tired that an angel had to wake him and encourage him to eat. Then did the prophet get up and do some great spiritual act? No. He slept again.

Sometimes we forget that we're humans who break down under stress. Sleep can be wonderfully restorative when we're burned out by circumstances. Once Elijah took care of his physical needs, he was able to follow God's lead. He walked 40 days and nights to Horeb. There, at a distance from his problems, well rested and fed, Elijah once again heard God's voice.

Decisions made out of fatigue and frustration are rarely our best decisions. So before you act, get some R & R (rest and recreation). Restoring your body will give you the energy to renew your mind and the clarity to hear God's voice.

After Amy had a chance to catch up on her sleep, she realized Scott needed to be with his mom. She was able to take on the challenges that once seemed so overwhelming. And she was more helpful to Scott.

The same is true for you. When you're feeling overwhelmed, like Elijah, take time to sleep, eat and calm down. Then listen for God's voice.

—JENNIFER SCHUCHMANN

FOR YOUR NEXT DEVOTIONAL READING, TURN TO PAGE 393.

"I have had enough, LORD," [Elijah] said. "Take my life; I am no better than my ancestors."

— 1 KINGS 19:4

let's talk

- What does verse 8 say about what strengthened Elijah? Look at Elijah's state of mind before, and then after, he slept and ate. What changed?
- Have we ever looked for spiritual food or rest when maybe what we needed most was physical food or rest? How does each kind of nourishment strengthen and sustain us?
- How can we prioritize our schedules and activities so that we don't neglect our physical needs for food and rest?

"Go back," Elijah replied. "What have I
done to you?"
21 So Elisha left him and went back. He
took his yoke of oxen and slaughtered them.
He burned the plowing equipment to cook
the meat and gave it to the people, and they
ate. Then he set out to follow Elijah and became his attendant.

Ben-Hadad Attacks Samaria

20 Now Ben-Hadad king of Aram mustered his entire army. Accompanied by
thirty-two kings with their horses and
chariots, he went up and besieged Samaria and attacked it. 2 He sent messengers into
the city to Ahab king of Israel, saying, "This is
what Ben-Hadad says: 3 'Your silver and gold
are mine, and the best of your wives and children are mine.' "
4 The king of Israel answered, "Just as you
say, my lord the king. I and all I have are
yours."
5 The messengers came again and said,
"This is what Ben-Hadad says: 'I sent to demand your silver and gold, your wives and
your children. 6 But about this time tomorrow
I am going to send my officials to search your
palace and the houses of your officials. They
will seize everything you value and carry it
away.' "
7 The king of Israel summoned all the elders
of the land and said to them, "See how this
man is looking for trouble! When he sent for
my wives and my children, my silver and my
gold, I did not refuse him."
8 The elders and the people all answered,
"Don't listen to him or agree to his demands."
9 So he replied to Ben-Hadad's messengers,
"Tell my lord the king, 'Your servant will do
all you demanded the first time, but this demand I cannot meet.' " They left and took the
answer back to Ben-Hadad.
10 Then Ben-Hadad sent another message to
Ahab: "May the gods deal with me, be it ever
so severely, if enough dust remains in Samaria
to give each of my men a handful."
11 The king of Israel answered, "Tell him:
'One who puts on his armor should not boast
like one who takes it off.' "
12 Ben-Hadad heard this message while he
and the kings were drinking in their tents,[a]
and he ordered his men: "Prepare to attack."
So they prepared to attack the city.

Ahab Defeats Ben-Hadad

13 Meanwhile a prophet came to Ahab king
of Israel and announced, "This is what the
LORD says: 'Do you see this vast army? I will
give it into your hand today, and then you will
know that I am the LORD.' "
14 "But who will do this?" asked Ahab.
The prophet replied, "This is what the
LORD says: 'The young officers of the provincial commanders will do it.' "
"And who will start the battle?" he asked.
The prophet answered, "You will."
15 So Ahab summoned the young officers of
the provincial commanders, 232 men. Then
he assembled the rest of the Israelites, 7,000 in
all. 16 They set out at noon while Ben-Hadad
and the 32 kings allied with him were in their
tents getting drunk. 17 The young officers of
the provincial commanders went out first.
Now Ben-Hadad had dispatched scouts,
who reported, "Men are advancing from Samaria."
18 He said, "If they have come out for peace,
take them alive; if they have come out for war,
take them alive."
19 The young officers of the provincial commanders marched out of the city with the army
behind them 20 and each one struck down his
opponent. At that, the Arameans fled, with
the Israelites in pursuit. But Ben-Hadad king
of Aram escaped on horseback with some of
his horsemen. 21 The king of Israel advanced
and overpowered the horses and chariots and
inflicted heavy losses on the Arameans.
22 Afterward, the prophet came to the king of
Israel and said, "Strengthen your position and
see what must be done, because next spring
the king of Aram will attack you again."
23 Meanwhile, the officials of the king of
Aram advised him, "Their gods are gods of the
hills. That is why they were too strong for us.
But if we fight them on the plains, surely we
will be stronger than they. 24 Do this: Remove
all the kings from their commands and replace
them with other officers. 25 You must also raise
an army like the one you lost—horse for horse
and chariot for chariot—so we can fight Israel
on the plains. Then surely we will be stronger
than they." He agreed with them and acted accordingly.
26 The next spring Ben-Hadad mustered
the Arameans and went up to Aphek to fight
against Israel. 27 When the Israelites were also
mustered and given provisions, they marched
out to meet them. The Israelites camped oppo-

---

[a] *12* Or *in Succoth*; also in verse 16

site them like two small flocks of goats, while
the Arameans covered the countryside.
28The man of God came up and told the
king of Israel, "This is what the LORD says:
'Because the Arameans think the LORD is a
god of the hills and not a god of the valleys,
I will deliver this vast army into your hands,
and you will know that I am the LORD.' "
29For seven days they camped opposite
each other, and on the seventh day the battle
was joined. The Israelites inflicted a hundred
thousand casualties on the Aramean foot soldiers in one day. 30The rest of them escaped
to the city of Aphek, where the wall collapsed
on twenty-seven thousand of them. And Ben-
Hadad fled to the city and hid in an inner
room.
31His officials said to him, "Look, we have
heard that the kings of the house of Israel are
merciful. Let us go to the king of Israel with
sackcloth around our waists and ropes around
our heads. Perhaps he will spare your life."
32Wearing sackcloth around their waists
and ropes around their heads, they went to
the king of Israel and said, "Your servant Ben-
Hadad says: 'Please let me live.' "
The king answered, "Is he still alive? He is
my brother."
33The men took this as a good sign and were
quick to pick up his word. "Yes, your brother
Ben-Hadad!" they said.
"Go and get him," the king said. When
Ben-Hadad came out, Ahab had him come up
into his chariot.
34"I will return the cities my father took
from your father," Ben-Hadad offered. "You
may set up your own market areas in Damascus, as my father did in Samaria."
⌞Ahab said,⌟ "On the basis of a treaty I will
set you free." So he made a treaty with him,
and let him go.

A Prophet Condemns Ahab

35By the word of the LORD one of the sons
of the prophets said to his companion, "Strike
me with your weapon," but the man refused.
36So the prophet said, "Because you have
not obeyed the LORD, as soon as you leave me
a lion will kill you." And after the man went
away, a lion found him and killed him.
37The prophet found another man and
said, "Strike me, please." So the man struck
him and wounded him. 38Then the prophet
went and stood by the road waiting for the
king. He disguised himself with his headband
down over his eyes. 39As the king passed by,
the prophet called out to him, "Your servant
went into the thick of the battle, and someone
came to me with a captive and said, 'Guard
this man. If he is missing, it will be your life
for his life, or you must pay a talent[a] of silver.'
40While your servant was busy here and there,
the man disappeared."
"That is your sentence," the king of Israel
said. "You have pronounced it yourself."
41Then the prophet quickly removed the
headband from his eyes, and the king of Israel
recognized him as one of the prophets. 42He
said to the king, "This is what the LORD says:
'You have set free a man I had determined
should die.[b] Therefore it is your life for his
life, your people for his people.' " 43Sullen and
angry, the king of Israel went to his palace in
Samaria.

Naboth's Vineyard

21 Some time later there was an incident
involving a vineyard belonging to Naboth the Jezreelite. The vineyard was in
Jezreel, close to the palace of Ahab king of Samaria. 2Ahab said to Naboth, "Let me have
your vineyard to use for a vegetable garden,
since it is close to my palace. In exchange I
will give you a better vineyard or, if you prefer,
I will pay you whatever it is worth."
3But Naboth replied, "The LORD forbid
that I should give you the inheritance of my
fathers."
4So Ahab went home, sullen and angry because Naboth the Jezreelite had said, "I will
not give you the inheritance of my fathers."
He lay on his bed sulking and refused to eat.
5His wife Jezebel came in and asked him,
"Why are you so sullen? Why won't you eat?"
6He answered her, "Because I said to Naboth the Jezreelite, 'Sell me your vineyard; or
if you prefer, I will give you another vineyard
in its place.' But he said, 'I will not give you
my vineyard.' "
7Jezebel his wife said, "Is this how you act
as king over Israel? Get up and eat! Cheer up.
I'll get you the vineyard of Naboth the Jezreelite."
8So she wrote letters in Ahab's name, placed
his seal on them, and sent them to the elders
and nobles who lived in Naboth's city with
him. 9In those letters she wrote:

"Proclaim a day of fasting and seat
Naboth in a prominent place among the

[a] *39* That is, about 75 pounds (about 34 kilograms) [b] *42* The Hebrew term refers to the irrevocable giving over of things or persons to the LORD, often by totally destroying them.

people. 10But seat two scoundrels opposite him and have them testify that he has
cursed both God and the king. Then take
him out and stone him to death."

11So the elders and nobles who lived in Naboth's city did as Jezebel directed in the letters
she had written to them. 12They proclaimed
a fast and seated Naboth in a prominent
place among the people. 13Then two scoundrels came and sat opposite him and brought
charges against Naboth before the people,
saying, "Naboth has cursed both God and the
king." So they took him outside the city and
stoned him to death. 14Then they sent word
to Jezebel: "Naboth has been stoned and is
dead."

15As soon as Jezebel heard that Naboth
had been stoned to death, she said to Ahab,
"Get up and take possession of the vineyard
of Naboth the Jezreelite that he refused to sell
you. He is no longer alive, but dead." 16When
Ahab heard that Naboth was dead, he got up
and went down to take possession of Naboth's
vineyard.

17Then the word of the LORD came to Elijah
the Tishbite: 18"Go down to meet Ahab king
of Israel, who rules in Samaria. He is now in
Naboth's vineyard, where he has gone to take
possession of it. 19Say to him, 'This is what the
LORD says: Have you not murdered a man and
seized his property?' Then say to him, 'This is
what the LORD says: In the place where dogs
licked up Naboth's blood, dogs will lick up
your blood—yes, yours!' "

20Ahab said to Elijah, "So you have found
me, my enemy!"

"I have found you," he answered, "because
you have sold yourself to do evil in the eyes of
the LORD. 21'I am going to bring disaster on
you. I will consume your descendants and cut
off from Ahab every last male in Israel—slave
or free. 22I will make your house like that of
Jeroboam son of Nebat and that of Baasha son
of Ahijah, because you have provoked me to
anger and have caused Israel to sin.'

23"And also concerning Jezebel the LORD
says: 'Dogs will devour Jezebel by the wall of[a]
Jezreel.'

24"Dogs will eat those belonging to Ahab
who die in the city, and the birds of the air will
feed on those who die in the country."

25(There was never a man like Ahab, who
sold himself to do evil in the eyes of the LORD,
urged on by Jezebel his wife. 26He behaved in
the vilest manner by going after idols, like the
Amorites the LORD drove out before Israel.)

27When Ahab heard these words, he tore
his clothes, put on sackcloth and fasted. He
lay in sackcloth and went around meekly.

28Then the word of the LORD came to Elijah the Tishbite: 29"Have you noticed how
Ahab has humbled himself before me? Because he has humbled himself, I will not bring
this disaster in his day, but I will bring it on his
house in the days of his son."

Micaiah Prophesies Against Ahab

22 For three years there was no war between Aram and Israel. 2But in the
third year Jehoshaphat king of Judah
went down to see the king of Israel. 3The king
of Israel had said to his officials, "Don't you
know that Ramoth Gilead belongs to us and
yet we are doing nothing to retake it from the
king of Aram?"

4So he asked Jehoshaphat, "Will you go
with me to fight against Ramoth Gilead?"

Jehoshaphat replied to the king of Israel, "I
am as you are, my people as your people, my
horses as your horses." 5But Jehoshaphat also
said to the king of Israel, "First seek the counsel of the LORD."

6So the king of Israel brought together the
prophets—about four hundred men—and
asked them, "Shall I go to war against Ramoth
Gilead, or shall I refrain?"

"Go," they answered, "for the Lord will give
it into the king's hand."

7But Jehoshaphat asked, "Is there not a
prophet of the LORD here whom we can inquire of?"

8The king of Israel answered Jehoshaphat,
"There is still one man through whom we can
inquire of the LORD, but I hate him because
he never prophesies anything good about me,
but always bad. He is Micaiah son of Imlah."

"The king should not say that," Jehoshaphat replied.

9So the king of Israel called one of his officials and said, "Bring Micaiah son of Imlah
at once."

10Dressed in their royal robes, the king of
Israel and Jehoshaphat king of Judah were sitting on their thrones at the threshing floor by
the entrance of the gate of Samaria, with all
the prophets prophesying before them. 11Now
Zedekiah son of Kenaanah had made iron
horns and he declared, "This is what the LORD

[a] 23 Most Hebrew manuscripts; a few Hebrew manuscripts, Vulgate and Syriac (see also 2 Kings 9:26) *the plot of ground at*

says: 'With these you will gore the Arameans
until they are destroyed.' "
12 All the other prophets were prophesying
the same thing. "Attack Ramoth Gilead and
be victorious," they said, "for the LORD will
give it into the king's hand."
13 The messenger who had gone to summon
Micaiah said to him, "Look, as one man the
other prophets are predicting success for the
king. Let your word agree with theirs, and
speak favorably."
14 But Micaiah said, "As surely as the LORD
lives, I can tell him only what the LORD
tells me."
15 When he arrived, the king asked him,
"Micaiah, shall we go to war against Ramoth
Gilead, or shall I refrain?"
"Attack and be victorious," he answered,
"for the LORD will give it into the king's
hand."
16 The king said to him, "How many times
must I make you swear to tell me nothing but
the truth in the name of the LORD?"
17 Then Micaiah answered, "I saw all Israel scattered on the hills like sheep without a
shepherd, and the LORD said, 'These people
have no master. Let each one go home in
peace.' "
18 The king of Israel said to Jehoshaphat,
"Didn't I tell you that he never prophesies
anything good about me, but only bad?"
19 Micaiah continued, "Therefore hear the
word of the LORD: I saw the LORD sitting on
his throne with all the host of heaven standing
around him on his right and on his left. 20 And
the LORD said, 'Who will entice Ahab into attacking Ramoth Gilead and going to his death
there?'
"One suggested this, and another that. 21 Finally, a spirit came forward, stood before the
LORD and said, 'I will entice him.'
22 " 'By what means?' the LORD asked.
" 'I will go out and be a lying spirit in the
mouths of all his prophets,' he said.
" 'You will succeed in enticing him,' said
the LORD. 'Go and do it.'
23 "So now the LORD has put a lying spirit in
the mouths of all these prophets of yours. The
LORD has decreed disaster for you."
24 Then Zedekiah son of Kenaanah went
up and slapped Micaiah in the face. "Which
way did the spirit from[a] the LORD go when he
went from me to speak to you?" he asked.
25 Micaiah replied, "You will find out on the
day you go to hide in an inner room."
26 The king of Israel then ordered, "Take
Micaiah and send him back to Amon the ruler
of the city and to Joash the king's son 27 and
say, 'This is what the king says: Put this fellow
in prison and give him nothing but bread and
water until I return safely.' "
28 Micaiah declared, "If you ever return
safely, the LORD has not spoken through me."
Then he added, "Mark my words, all you people!"

Ahab Killed at Ramoth Gilead

29 So the king of Israel and Jehoshaphat king
of Judah went up to Ramoth Gilead. 30 The
king of Israel said to Jehoshaphat, "I will enter
the battle in disguise, but you wear your royal
robes." So the king of Israel disguised himself
and went into battle.
31 Now the king of Aram had ordered his
thirty-two chariot commanders, "Do not fight
with anyone, small or great, except the king of
Israel." 32 When the chariot commanders saw
Jehoshaphat, they thought, "Surely this is the
king of Israel." So they turned to attack him,
but when Jehoshaphat cried out, 33 the chariot
commanders saw that he was not the king of
Israel and stopped pursuing him.
34 But someone drew his bow at random
and hit the king of Israel between the sections
of his armor. The king told his chariot driver,
"Wheel around and get me out of the fighting.
I've been wounded." 35 All day long the battle raged, and the king was propped up in his
chariot facing the Arameans. The blood from
his wound ran onto the floor of the chariot,
and that evening he died. 36 As the sun was setting, a cry spread through the army: "Every
man to his town; everyone to his land!"
37 So the king died and was brought to
Samaria, and they buried him there. 38 They
washed the chariot at a pool in Samaria (where
the prostitutes bathed),[b] and the dogs licked
up his blood, as the word of the LORD had
declared.
39 As for the other events of Ahab's reign,
including all he did, the palace he built and
inlaid with ivory, and the cities he fortified,
are they not written in the book of the annals
of the kings of Israel? 40 Ahab rested with his
fathers. And Ahaziah his son succeeded him
as king.

Jehoshaphat King of Judah

41 Jehoshaphat son of Asa became king of Judah in the fourth year of Ahab king of Israel.

[a] 24 Or *Spirit of* [b] 38 Or *Samaria and cleaned the weapons*

42Jehoshaphat was thirty-five years old when he
became king, and he reigned in Jerusalem twenty-five years. His mother's name was Azubah
daughter of Shilhi. 43In everything he walked
in the ways of his father Asa and did not stray
from them; he did what was right in the eyes
of the LORD. The high places, however, were
not removed, and the people continued to offer
sacrifices and burn incense there. 44Jehoshaphat
was also at peace with the king of Israel.

45As for the other events of Jehoshaphat's
reign, the things he achieved and his military
exploits, are they not written in the book of
the annals of the kings of Judah? 46He rid the
land of the rest of the male shrine prostitutes
who remained there even after the reign of his
father Asa. 47There was then no king in Edom;
a deputy ruled.

48Now Jehoshaphat built a fleet of trading
ships[a] to go to Ophir for gold, but they never
set sail—they were wrecked at Ezion Geber.
49At that time Ahaziah son of Ahab said to Jehoshaphat, "Let my men sail with your men,"
but Jehoshaphat refused.

50Then Jehoshaphat rested with his fathers
and was buried with them in the city of David his father. And Jehoram his son succeeded him.

Ahaziah King of Israel

51Ahaziah son of Ahab became king of Israel in Samaria in the seventeenth year of Jehoshaphat king of Judah, and he reigned over
Israel two years. 52He did evil in the eyes of
the LORD, because he walked in the ways of
his father and mother and in the ways of Jeroboam son of Nebat, who caused Israel to sin.
53He served and worshiped Baal and provoked
the LORD, the God of Israel, to anger, just as
his father had done.

[a] 48 Hebrew *of ships of Tarshish*

and as you live, I will not leave you." So the
two of them walked on.
[7]Fifty men of the company of the prophets
went and stood at a distance, facing the place
where Elijah and Elisha had stopped at the
Jordan. [8]Elijah took his cloak, rolled it up and
struck the water with it. The water divided to
the right and to the left, and the two of them
crossed over on dry ground.
[9]When they had crossed, Elijah said to Elisha, "Tell me, what can I do for you before I
am taken from you?"
"Let me inherit a double portion of your
spirit," Elisha replied.
[10]"You have asked a difficult thing," Elijah
said, "yet if you see me when I am taken from
you, it will be yours—otherwise not."
[11]As they were walking along and talking together, suddenly a chariot of fire and horses of
fire appeared and separated the two of them,
and Elijah went up to heaven in a whirlwind.
[12]Elisha saw this and cried out, "My father! My
father! The chariots and horsemen of Israel!"
And Elisha saw him no more. Then he took
hold of his own clothes and tore them apart.
[13]He picked up the cloak that had fallen
from Elijah and went back and stood on the
bank of the Jordan. [14]Then he took the cloak
that had fallen from him and struck the water
with it. "Where now is the LORD, the God of
Elijah?" he asked. When he struck the water,
it divided to the right and to the left, and he
crossed over.
[15]The company of the prophets from Jericho, who were watching, said, "The spirit of
Elijah is resting on Elisha." And they went to
meet him and bowed to the ground before
him. [16]"Look," they said, "we your servants
have fifty able men. Let them go and look for
your master. Perhaps the Spirit of the LORD
has picked him up and set him down on some
mountain or in some valley."
"No," Elisha replied, "do not send them."
[17]But they persisted until he was too
ashamed to refuse. So he said, "Send them."
And they sent fifty men, who searched for
three days but did not find him. [18]When they
returned to Elisha, who was staying in Jericho,
he said to them, "Didn't I tell you not to go?"

Healing of the Water

[19]The men of the city said to Elisha, "Look,
our lord, this town is well situated, as you can
see, but the water is bad and the land is unproductive."
[20]"Bring me a new bowl," he said, "and put
salt in it." So they brought it to him.
[21]Then he went out to the spring and threw
the salt into it, saying, "This is what the LORD
says: 'I have healed this water. Never again will
it cause death or make the land unproductive.' " [22]And the water has remained wholesome to this day, according to the word Elisha
had spoken.

Elisha Is Jeered

[23]From there Elisha went up to Bethel. As
he was walking along the road, some youths
came out of the town and jeered at him. "Go
on up, you baldhead!" they said. "Go on up,
you baldhead!" [24]He turned around, looked
at them and called down a curse on them in
the name of the LORD. Then two bears came
out of the woods and mauled forty-two of the
youths. [25]And he went on to Mount Carmel
and from there returned to Samaria.

Moab Revolts

3 Joram[a] son of Ahab became king of Israel in Samaria in the eighteenth year of Jehoshaphat king of Judah, and he reigned
twelve years. [2]He did evil in the eyes of the
LORD, but not as his father and mother had
done. He got rid of the sacred stone of Baal
that his father had made. [3]Nevertheless he
clung to the sins of Jeroboam son of Nebat,
which he had caused Israel to commit; he did
not turn away from them.
[4]Now Mesha king of Moab raised sheep, and
he had to supply the king of Israel with a hundred thousand lambs and with the wool of a
hundred thousand rams. [5]But after Ahab died,
the king of Moab rebelled against the king of
Israel. [6]So at that time King Joram set out from
Samaria and mobilized all Israel. [7]He also sent
this message to Jehoshaphat king of Judah:
"The king of Moab has rebelled against me.
Will you go with me to fight against Moab?"
"I will go with you," he replied. "I am as
you are, my people as your people, my horses
as your horses."
[8]"By what route shall we attack?" he asked.
"Through the Desert of Edom," he answered.
[9]So the king of Israel set out with the king
of Judah and the king of Edom. After a round-
about march of seven days, the army had no
more water for themselves or for the animals
with them.
[10]"What!" exclaimed the king of Israel.

---

[a] *1* Hebrew *Jehoram,* a variant of *Joram;* also in verse 6

"Has the LORD called us three kings together only to hand us over to Moab?"

11But Jehoshaphat asked, "Is there no prophet of the LORD here, that we may inquire of the LORD through him?"

An officer of the king of Israel answered, "Elisha son of Shaphat is here. He used to pour water on the hands of Elijah.[a]"

12Jehoshaphat said, "The word of the LORD is with him." So the king of Israel and Jehoshaphat and the king of Edom went down to him.

13Elisha said to the king of Israel, "What do we have to do with each other? Go to the prophets of your father and the prophets of your mother."

"No," the king of Israel answered, "because it was the LORD who called us three kings together to hand us over to Moab."

14Elisha said, "As surely as the LORD Almighty lives, whom I serve, if I did not have respect for the presence of Jehoshaphat king of Judah, I would not look at you or even notice you. 15But now bring me a harpist."

While the harpist was playing, the hand of the LORD came upon Elisha 16and he said, "This is what the LORD says: Make this valley full of ditches. 17For this is what the LORD says: You will see neither wind nor rain, yet this valley will be filled with water, and you, your cattle and your other animals will drink. 18This is an easy thing in the eyes of the LORD; he will also hand Moab over to you. 19You will overthrow every fortified city and every major town. You will cut down every good tree, stop up all the springs, and ruin every good field with stones."

20The next morning, about the time for offering the sacrifice, there it was—water flowing from the direction of Edom! And the land was filled with water.

21Now all the Moabites had heard that the kings had come to fight against them; so every man, young and old, who could bear arms was called up and stationed on the border. 22When they got up early in the morning, the sun was shining on the water. To the Moabites across the way, the water looked red—like blood. 23"That's blood!" they said. "Those kings must have fought and slaughtered each other. Now to the plunder, Moab!"

24But when the Moabites came to the camp of Israel, the Israelites rose up and fought them until they fled. And the Israelites invaded the land and slaughtered the Moabites. 25They destroyed the towns, and each man threw a stone on every good field until it was covered. They stopped up all the springs and cut down every good tree. Only Kir Hareseth was left with its stones in place, but men armed with slings surrounded it and attacked it as well.

26When the king of Moab saw that the battle had gone against him, he took with him seven hundred swordsmen to break through to the king of Edom, but they failed. 27Then he took his firstborn son, who was to succeed him as king, and offered him as a sacrifice on the city wall. The fury against Israel was great; they withdrew and returned to their own land.

The Widow's Oil

4 The wife of a man from the company of the prophets cried out to Elisha, "Your servant my husband is dead, and you know that he revered the LORD. But now his creditor is coming to take my two boys as his slaves."

2Elisha replied to her, "How can I help you? Tell me, what do you have in your house?"

"Your servant has nothing there at all," she said, "except a little oil."

3Elisha said, "Go around and ask all your neighbors for empty jars. Don't ask for just a few. 4Then go inside and shut the door behind you and your sons. Pour oil into all the jars, and as each is filled, put it to one side."

5She left him and afterward shut the door behind her and her sons. They brought the jars to her and she kept pouring. 6When all the jars were full, she said to her son, "Bring me another one."

But he replied, "There is not a jar left." Then the oil stopped flowing.

7She went and told the man of God, and he said, "Go, sell the oil and pay your debts. You and your sons can live on what is left."

The Shunammite's Son Restored to Life

8One day Elisha went to Shunem. And a well-to-do woman was there, who urged him to stay for a meal. So whenever he came by, he stopped there to eat. 9She said to her husband, "I know that this man who often comes our way is a holy man of God. 10Let's make a small room on the roof and put in it a bed and a table, a chair and a lamp for him. Then he can stay there whenever he comes to us."

11One day when Elisha came, he went up to his room and lay down there. 12He said to his servant Gehazi, "Call the Shunammite." So he called her, and she stood before him. 13Elisha said to him, "Tell her, 'You have gone to all

---

[a] *11* That is, he was Elijah's personal servant.

this trouble for us. Now what can be done for
you? Can we speak on your behalf to the king
or the commander of the army?’ ”
She replied, “I have a home among my own
people.”
14“What can be done for her?” Elisha
asked.
Gehazi said, “Well, she has no son and her
husband is old.”
15Then Elisha said, “Call her.” So he called
her, and she stood in the doorway. 16“About
this time next year,” Elisha said, “you will hold
a son in your arms.”
“No, my lord,” she objected. “Don’t mislead your servant, O man of God!”
17But the woman became pregnant, and
the next year about that same time she gave
birth to a son, just as Elisha had told her.
18The child grew, and one day he went out
to his father, who was with the reapers. 19“My
head! My head!” he said to his father.
His father told a servant, “Carry him to his
mother.” 20After the servant had lifted him up
and carried him to his mother, the boy sat on
her lap until noon, and then he died. 21She
went up and laid him on the bed of the man of
God, then shut the door and went out.
22She called her husband and said, “Please
send me one of the servants and a donkey so I
can go to the man of God quickly and return.”
23“Why go to him today?” he asked. “It’s
not the New Moon or the Sabbath.”
“It’s all right,” she said.
24She saddled the donkey and said to her
servant, “Lead on; don’t slow down for me unless I tell you.” 25So she set out and came to
the man of God at Mount Carmel.
When he saw her in the distance, the man
of God said to his servant Gehazi, “Look!
There’s the Shunammite! 26Run to meet her
and ask her, ‘Are you all right? Is your husband
all right? Is your child all right?’ ”
“Everything is all right,” she said.
27When she reached the man of God at the
mountain, she took hold of his feet. Gehazi
came over to push her away, but the man of
God said, “Leave her alone! She is in bitter distress, but the LORD has hidden it from me and
has not told me why.”
28“Did I ask you for a son, my lord?”
she said. “Didn’t I tell you, ‘Don’t raise my
hopes’?”
29Elisha said to Gehazi, “Tuck your cloak
into your belt, take my staff in your hand and
run. If you meet anyone, do not greet him,
and if anyone greets you, do not answer. Lay
my staff on the boy’s face.”
30But the child’s mother said, “As surely as
the LORD lives and as you live, I will not leave
you.” So he got up and followed her.
31Gehazi went on ahead and laid the staff
on the boy’s face, but there was no sound or
response. So Gehazi went back to meet Elisha
and told him, “The boy has not awakened.”
32When Elisha reached the house, there was
the boy lying dead on his couch. 33He went in,
shut the door on the two of them and prayed
to the LORD. 34Then he got on the bed and lay
upon the boy, mouth to mouth, eyes to eyes,
hands to hands. As he stretched himself out
upon him, the boy’s body grew warm. 35Elisha
turned away and walked back and forth in the
room and then got on the bed and stretched
out upon him once more. The boy sneezed
seven times and opened his eyes.
36Elisha summoned Gehazi and said, “Call
the Shunammite.” And he did. When she
came, he said, “Take your son.” 37She came
in, fell at his feet and bowed to the ground.
Then she took her son and went out.

Death in the Pot

38Elisha returned to Gilgal and there was a
famine in that region. While the company of
the prophets was meeting with him, he said
to his servant, “Put on the large pot and cook
some stew for these men.”
39One of them went out into the fields to
gather herbs and found a wild vine. He gathered some of its gourds and filled the fold of
his cloak. When he returned, he cut them up
into the pot of stew, though no one knew
what they were. 40The stew was poured out
for the men, but as they began to eat it, they
cried out, “O man of God, there is death in
the pot!” And they could not eat it.
41Elisha said, “Get some flour.” He put it
into the pot and said, “Serve it to the people
to eat.” And there was nothing harmful in the
pot.

Feeding of a Hundred

42A man came from Baal Shalishah, bringing the man of God twenty loaves of barley
bread baked from the first ripe grain, along
with some heads of new grain. “Give it to the
people to eat,” Elisha said.
43“How can I set this before a hundred
men?” his servant asked.
But Elisha answered, “Give it to the people
to eat. For this is what the LORD says: ‘They
will eat and have some left over.’ ” 44Then he
set it before them, and they ate and had some
left over, according to the word of the LORD.

Naaman Healed of Leprosy

5 Now Naaman was commander of the army
of the king of Aram. He was a great man in
the sight of his master and highly regarded,
because through him the LORD had given victory to Aram. He was a valiant soldier, but he
had leprosy.[a]
2Now bands from Aram had gone out
and had taken captive a young girl from Israel, and she served Naaman's wife. 3She said
to her mistress, "If only my master would see
the prophet who is in Samaria! He would cure
him of his leprosy."
4Naaman went to his master and told him
what the girl from Israel had said. 5"By all
means, go," the king of Aram replied. "I will
send a letter to the king of Israel." So Naaman
left, taking with him ten talents[b] of silver,
six thousand shekels[c] of gold and ten sets of
clothing. 6The letter that he took to the king
of Israel read: "With this letter I am sending
my servant Naaman to you so that you may
cure him of his leprosy."
7As soon as the king of Israel read the letter,
he tore his robes and said, "Am I God? Can
I kill and bring back to life? Why does this
fellow send someone to me to be cured of his
leprosy? See how he is trying to pick a quarrel
with me!"
8When Elisha the man of God heard that the
king of Israel had torn his robes, he sent him
this message: "Why have you torn your robes?
Have the man come to me and he will know
that there is a prophet in Israel." 9So Naaman
went with his horses and chariots and stopped
at the door of Elisha's house. 10Elisha sent a
messenger to say to him, "Go, wash yourself
seven times in the Jordan, and your flesh will
be restored and you will be cleansed."
11But Naaman went away angry and said, "I
thought that he would surely come out to me
and stand and call on the name of the LORD
his God, wave his hand over the spot and cure
me of my leprosy. 12Are not Abana and Phar-
par, the rivers of Damascus, better than any of
the waters of Israel? Couldn't I wash in them
and be cleansed?" So he turned and went off
in a rage.
13Naaman's servants went to him and said,
"My father, if the prophet had told you to do
some great thing, would you not have done
it? How much more, then, when he tells you,
'Wash and be cleansed'!" 14So he went down
and dipped himself in the Jordan seven times,
as the man of God had told him, and his flesh
was restored and became clean like that of a
young boy.
15Then Naaman and all his attendants went
back to the man of God. He stood before him
and said, "Now I know that there is no God
in all the world except in Israel. Please accept
now a gift from your servant."
16The prophet answered, "As surely as the
LORD lives, whom I serve, I will not accept a
thing." And even though Naaman urged him,
he refused.
17"If you will not," said Naaman, "please
let me, your servant, be given as much earth
as a pair of mules can carry, for your servant
will never again make burnt offerings and sacrifices to any other god but the LORD. 18But
may the LORD forgive your servant for this
one thing: When my master enters the temple of Rimmon to bow down and he is leaning on my arm and I bow there also—when I
bow down in the temple of Rimmon, may the
LORD forgive your servant for this."
19"Go in peace," Elisha said.
After Naaman had traveled some distance,
20Gehazi, the servant of Elisha the man of
God, said to himself, "My master was too easy
on Naaman, this Aramean, by not accepting
from him what he brought. As surely as the
LORD lives, I will run after him and get something from him."
21So Gehazi hurried after Naaman. When
Naaman saw him running toward him, he got
down from the chariot to meet him. "Is everything all right?" he asked.
22"Everything is all right," Gehazi answered.
"My master sent me to say, 'Two young men
from the company of the prophets have just
come to me from the hill country of Ephraim.
Please give them a talent[d] of silver and two
sets of clothing.' "
23"By all means, take two talents," said Naaman. He urged Gehazi to accept them, and
then tied up the two talents of silver in two
bags, with two sets of clothing. He gave them
to two of his servants, and they carried them
ahead of Gehazi. 24When Gehazi came to the
hill, he took the things from the servants and
put them away in the house. He sent the men
away and they left. 25Then he went in and
stood before his master Elisha.
"Where have you been, Gehazi?" Elisha
asked.

[a] *1* The Hebrew word was used for various diseases affecting the skin—not necessarily leprosy; also in verses 3, 6, 7, 11 and 27.
[b] *5* That is, about 750 pounds (about 340 kilograms) [c] *5* That is, about 150 pounds (about 70 kilograms) [d] *22* That is, about 75 pounds (about 34 kilograms)

WEDNESDAY
READ 2 KINGS 5:1–14

I'LL DO ANYTHING, BUT . . .

> **"Are not Abana and Pharpar, the rivers of Damascus, better than any of the waters of Israel? Couldn't I wash in them and be cleansed?"**
>
> — 2 Kings 5:12

Once my husband, Dan, and I sold everything we owned and took a year off to travel. During that time, we explored various cities to determine where to settle. We told God we were willing to go anywhere.

Until Daytona. If you've ever been to Daytona, Florida, during spring break, you might have a clue about why this did not seem like a good place for us to live. Years before, we had walked the beaches of Daytona while visiting my sister and her family. I still had a clear picture of beer-drinking college-age kids cruising the beaches in shorts and thong bikinis. After that experience, I filed Daytona under "Places Never to Return To."

Yet here we were, walking down some of the same streets that had turned me off before. As we passed by the deserted souvenir shops (it wasn't spring break this time), I remember thinking, "Oh, Lord, I'll live anywhere you want, just not Daytona." As soon as the thought formed, I stopped in my tracks. Did I just say, "I'll go anywhere, but . . ."?

Suddenly, it became clear that my devotion to God had limits. I would be obedient . . . to a point. Although I felt I trusted God with our future, I assumed he would lead us to a good place, not somewhere like Daytona. I wasn't being submissive; I was being a snob. Somehow, in my mind, Daytona was beneath me.

The great army commander Naaman had a similar revelation. Even though he desperately wanted to be healed, he questioned God's prescription for wellness that required a dip in the muddy Jordan River. Weren't the sparkling rivers of Damascus far better than the rivers of Israel?

Naaman's reaction to God's instructions revealed that a deeper cleansing needed to take place. God's ways are not our ways, and receiving his blessings means letting go of our preconceived ideas about how God will act. It means obeying his instructions, no matter how strange they seem.

Naaman's servants set him straight, reminding him what a simple thing God had asked of him. "If the prophet had told you to do some great thing, wouldn't you have done it?" they asked. "Why not this?" So Naaman gave up his objections, obeyed and was healed.

Similarly, after some backpedaling prayers, I agreed to take a closer look at Daytona. To my surprise, the city consisted of lovely tree-lined neighborhoods. Daytona offered much more than I had presumed. What blessings might God have in store for us if we were to live here?

Although I was grateful for what Daytona taught me, I breathed a sigh of relief when God gave us the green light to leave rather than settle there. Now, though, when I feel myself resisting God's call, all I have to do is remember Daytona.

—MARIAN V. LIAUTAUD

let's talk

- Was there a time when we said, "We'll do anything, Lord, but . . ."? What were the circumstances?
- Are there any areas of our lives we reserve for ourselves?
- When God calls us to do something, do we recognize his voice? How?

FOR YOUR NEXT DEVOTIONAL READING, TURN TO PAGE 396.

"Your servant didn't go anywhere," Gehazi answered.

26But Elisha said to him, "Was not my spirit with you when the man got down from his chariot to meet you? Is this the time to take money, or to accept clothes, olive groves, vineyards, flocks, herds, or menservants and maidservants? 27Naaman's leprosy will cling to you and to your descendants forever." Then Gehazi went from Elisha's presence and he was leprous, as white as snow.

An Axhead Floats

6 The company of the prophets said to Elisha, "Look, the place where we meet with you is too small for us. 2Let us go to the Jordan, where each of us can get a pole; and let us build a place there for us to live."

And he said, "Go."

3Then one of them said, "Won't you please come with your servants?"

"I will," Elisha replied. 4And he went with them.

They went to the Jordan and began to cut down trees. 5As one of them was cutting down a tree, the iron axhead fell into the water. "Oh, my lord," he cried out, "it was borrowed!"

6The man of God asked, "Where did it fall?" When he showed him the place, Elisha cut a stick and threw it there, and made the iron float. 7"Lift it out," he said. Then the man reached out his hand and took it.

Elisha Traps Blinded Arameans

8Now the king of Aram was at war with Israel. After conferring with his officers, he said, "I will set up my camp in such and such a place."

9The man of God sent word to the king of Israel: "Beware of passing that place, because the Arameans are going down there." 10So the king of Israel checked on the place indicated by the man of God. Time and again Elisha warned the king, so that he was on his guard in such places.

11This enraged the king of Aram. He summoned his officers and demanded of them, "Will you not tell me which of us is on the side of the king of Israel?"

12"None of us, my lord the king," said one of his officers, "but Elisha, the prophet who is in Israel, tells the king of Israel the very words you speak in your bedroom."

13"Go, find out where he is," the king ordered, "so I can send men and capture him." The report came back: "He is in Dothan." 14Then he sent horses and chariots and a strong force there. They went by night and surrounded the city.

15When the servant of the man of God got up and went out early the next morning, an army with horses and chariots had surrounded the city. "Oh, my lord, what shall we do?" the servant asked.

16"Don't be afraid," the prophet answered. "Those who are with us are more than those who are with them."

17And Elisha prayed, "O LORD, open his eyes so he may see." Then the LORD opened the servant's eyes, and he looked and saw the hills full of horses and chariots of fire all around Elisha.

18As the enemy came down toward him, Elisha prayed to the LORD, "Strike these people with blindness." So he struck them with blindness, as Elisha had asked.

19Elisha told them, "This is not the road and this is not the city. Follow me, and I will lead you to the man you are looking for." And he led them to Samaria.

20After they entered the city, Elisha said, "LORD, open the eyes of these men so they can see." Then the LORD opened their eyes and they looked, and there they were, inside Samaria.

21When the king of Israel saw them, he asked Elisha, "Shall I kill them, my father? Shall I kill them?"

22"Do not kill them," he answered. "Would you kill men you have captured with your own sword or bow? Set food and water before them so that they may eat and drink and then go back to their master." 23So he prepared a great feast for them, and after they had finished eating and drinking, he sent them away, and they returned to their master. So the bands from Aram stopped raiding Israel's territory.

Famine in Besieged Samaria

24Some time later, Ben-Hadad king of Aram mobilized his entire army and marched up and laid siege to Samaria. 25There was a great famine in the city; the siege lasted so long that a donkey's head sold for eighty shekels[a] of silver, and a quarter of a cab[b] of seed pods[c] for five shekels.[d]

26As the king of Israel was passing by on the wall, a woman cried to him, "Help me, my lord the king!"

27The king replied, "If the LORD does not

---

[a] 25 That is, about 2 pounds (about 1 kilogram) [b] 25 That is, probably about 1/2 pint (about 0.3 liter) [c] 25 Or *of doves' dung*
[d] 25 That is, about 2 ounces (about 55 grams)

help you, where can I get help for you? From
the threshing floor? From the winepress?"
28Then he asked her, "What's the matter?"
She answered, "This woman said to me,
'Give up your son so we may eat him today,
and tomorrow we'll eat my son.' 29So we
cooked my son and ate him. The next day I
said to her, 'Give up your son so we may eat
him,' but she had hidden him."
30When the king heard the woman's words,
he tore his robes. As he went along the wall,
the people looked, and there, underneath, he
had sackcloth on his body. 31He said, "May
God deal with me, be it ever so severely, if the
head of Elisha son of Shaphat remains on his
shoulders today!"
32Now Elisha was sitting in his house, and
the elders were sitting with him. The king
sent a messenger ahead, but before he arrived,
Elisha said to the elders, "Don't you see how
this murderer is sending someone to cut off
my head? Look, when the messenger comes,
shut the door and hold it shut against him.
Is not the sound of his master's footsteps behind him?"
33While he was still talking to them, the
messenger came down to him. And ⌞the king⌟
said, "This disaster is from the LORD. Why
should I wait for the LORD any longer?"
7 Elisha said, "Hear the word of the LORD.
This is what the LORD says: About this time
tomorrow, a seah[a] of flour will sell for a
shekel[b] and two seahs[c] of barley for a shekel
at the gate of Samaria."
2The officer on whose arm the king was
leaning said to the man of God, "Look, even
if the LORD should open the floodgates of the
heavens, could this happen?"
"You will see it with your own eyes," answered Elisha, "but you will not eat any
of it!"

The Siege Lifted

3Now there were four men with leprosy[d] at
the entrance of the city gate. They said to each
other, "Why stay here until we die? 4If we say,
'We'll go into the city'—the famine is there,
and we will die. And if we stay here, we will
die. So let's go over to the camp of the Arameans and surrender. If they spare us, we live; if
they kill us, then we die."
5At dusk they got up and went to the camp
of the Arameans. When they reached the edge
of the camp, not a man was there, 6for the
Lord had caused the Arameans to hear the
sound of chariots and horses and a great army,
so that they said to one another, "Look, the
king of Israel has hired the Hittite and Egyptian kings to attack us!" 7So they got up and
fled in the dusk and abandoned their tents
and their horses and donkeys. They left the
camp as it was and ran for their lives.
8The men who had leprosy reached the edge
of the camp and entered one of the tents. They
ate and drank, and carried away silver, gold
and clothes, and went off and hid them. They
returned and entered another tent and took
some things from it and hid them also.
9Then they said to each other, "We're not
doing right. This is a day of good news and
we are keeping it to ourselves. If we wait until
daylight, punishment will overtake us. Let's go
at once and report this to the royal palace."
10So they went and called out to the city
gatekeepers and told them, "We went into the
Aramean camp and not a man was there—not
a sound of anyone—only tethered horses and
donkeys, and the tents left just as they were."
11The gatekeepers shouted the news, and it
was reported within the palace.
12The king got up in the night and said to
his officers, "I will tell you what the Arameans
have done to us. They know we are starving;
so they have left the camp to hide in the countryside, thinking, 'They will surely come out,
and then we will take them alive and get into
the city.' "
13One of his officers answered, "Have some
men take five of the horses that are left in the
city. Their plight will be like that of all the Israelites left here—yes, they will only be like all
these Israelites who are doomed. So let us send
them to find out what happened."
14So they selected two chariots with their
horses, and the king sent them after the Aramean army. He commanded the drivers, "Go
and find out what has happened." 15They
followed them as far as the Jordan, and they
found the whole road strewn with the clothing and equipment the Arameans had thrown
away in their headlong flight. So the messengers returned and reported to the king. 16Then
the people went out and plundered the camp
of the Arameans. So a seah of flour sold for a
shekel, and two seahs of barley sold for a shekel, as the LORD had said.
17Now the king had put the officer on
whose arm he leaned in charge of the gate,

---

[a] *1* That is, probably about 7 quarts (about 7.3 liters); also in verses 16 and 18 [b] *1* That is, about 2/5 ounce (about 11 grams); also in verses 16 and 18 [c] *1* That is, probably about 13 quarts (about 15 liters); also in verses 16 and 18 [d] *3* The Hebrew word is used for various diseases affecting the skin—not necessarily leprosy; also in verse 8.

THURSDAY
READ 2 KINGS 7:1–16

SHARING STUFF

> **The men who had leprosy reached the edge of the camp and entered one of the tents. They ate and drank, and carried away silver, gold and clothes, and went off and hid them.**
>
> — 2 KINGS 7:8

let's talk

- If one of us gets a bonus check that the other knows nothing about, do we admit it quickly and willingly? How do we determine what it will be used for?
- What are our individual perspectives on giving? What are some ways we can be "rich toward God"?
- Are there some areas in our lives that we are reluctant to share with each other? Why?

My basic philosophy of money in marriage is simple: What's yours is mine, but what's mine is mine.

I'm working on that.

Early in our marriage, my husband and I pooled our paychecks and shared everything equally. When I stayed home to raise our kids, my husband handed me his paycheck, and I took care of the finances. What was his was also mine.

It's when I started earning money from writing and speaking and had to keep those earnings separate for tax purposes that I began thinking of money as mine, mine—all mine. The more I earned—I'm ashamed to admit—the more I didn't want to share it.

In 2 Kings 7, there was a famine in Samaria, and the city was under siege by the Arameans. Four lepers decided to surrender to the army that surrounded the city. Reasoning that they would either die of starvation inside the city or be killed by the Arameans while leaving it, they decided to take their chances. Maybe the enemy would take pity on them and spare them.

When the lepers went to the camp of the Arameans to surrender, they discovered the enemy had fled, leaving all of their food, clothing and treasures behind. The lepers helped themselves to the loot, stuffed themselves with food, then carried off as much stuff as they could and hid it.

But then their consciences bothered them. They said to each other, "We're not doing right. This is a day of good news and we are keeping it to ourselves" (2 Kings 7:9). So, they reported what they had discovered to their fellow countrymen, and everyone shared the bounty.

My conscience also bothers me when I hoard my money. I feel slimy and guilty, and those feelings block intimacy with my husband. I've had to go to him repeatedly and confess my selfishness and greed after hanging on to my earnings.

Jesus told a story about a rich man who, pleased with his abundance, decided to build bigger barns to store his stuff so he could sit back and enjoy it. However, God called the man foolish because that night he would die before he ever had a chance to benefit from his wealth. As Jesus said in Luke 12:21, "This is how it will be with anyone who stores up things for himself but is not rich toward God."

Keeping what is "mine" for myself might not kill me, but it will damage my relationships—both with God and with my husband. Because I want to do right, I now show my husband every check I get and every contract I receive. Together we decide what to do with the money. My husband has never denied me anything I've wanted to buy; I truly lack nothing.

Besides, it's better to be rich toward God, since what's ours is his anyway.

—NANCY KENNEDY

FOR YOUR NEXT DEVOTIONAL READING, TURN TO PAGE 401.

and the people trampled him in the gateway,
and he died, just as the man of God had foretold when the king came down to his house.
18It happened as the man of God had said to
the king: "About this time tomorrow, a seah of
flour will sell for a shekel and two seahs of barley for a shekel at the gate of Samaria."
19The officer had said to the man of God,
"Look, even if the LORD should open the
floodgates of the heavens, could this happen?"
The man of God had replied, "You will see it
with your own eyes, but you will not eat any
of it!" 20And that is exactly what happened to
him, for the people trampled him in the gateway, and he died.

The Shunammite's Land Restored

8 Now Elisha had said to the woman whose
son he had restored to life, "Go away with
your family and stay for a while wherever you can, because the LORD has decreed a
famine in the land that will last seven years."
2The woman proceeded to do as the man of
God said. She and her family went away and
stayed in the land of the Philistines seven
years.
3At the end of the seven years she came
back from the land of the Philistines and went
to the king to beg for her house and land. 4The
king was talking to Gehazi, the servant of the
man of God, and had said, "Tell me about all
the great things Elisha has done." 5Just as Gehazi was telling the king how Elisha had restored the dead to life, the woman whose son
Elisha had brought back to life came to beg
the king for her house and land.
Gehazi said, "This is the woman, my lord
the king, and this is her son whom Elisha restored to life." 6The king asked the woman
about it, and she told him.
Then he assigned an official to her case and
said to him, "Give back everything that belonged to her, including all the income from
her land from the day she left the country until now."

Hazael Murders Ben-Hadad

7Elisha went to Damascus, and Ben-Hadad king of Aram was ill. When the king was
told, "The man of God has come all the way
up here," 8he said to Hazael, "Take a gift with
you and go to meet the man of God. Consult
the LORD through him; ask him, 'Will I recover from this illness?' "
9Hazael went to meet Elisha, taking with
him as a gift forty camel-loads of all the finest
wares of Damascus. He went in and stood before him, and said, "Your son Ben-Hadad king
of Aram has sent me to ask, 'Will I recover
from this illness?' "
10Elisha answered, "Go and say to him,
'You will certainly recover'; but[a] the LORD has
revealed to me that he will in fact die." 11He
stared at him with a fixed gaze until Hazael
felt ashamed. Then the man of God began to
weep.
12"Why is my lord weeping?" asked Hazael.
"Because I know the harm you will do
to the Israelites," he answered. "You will set
fire to their fortified places, kill their young
men with the sword, dash their little children
to the ground, and rip open their pregnant
women."
13Hazael said, "How could your servant, a
mere dog, accomplish such a feat?"
"The LORD has shown me that you will become king of Aram," answered Elisha.
14Then Hazael left Elisha and returned to
his master. When Ben-Hadad asked, "What
did Elisha say to you?" Hazael replied, "He
told me that you would certainly recover."
15But the next day he took a thick cloth,
soaked it in water and spread it over the king's
face, so that he died. Then Hazael succeeded
him as king.

Jehoram King of Judah

16In the fifth year of Joram son of Ahab
king of Israel, when Jehoshaphat was king
of Judah, Jehoram son of Jehoshaphat began
his reign as king of Judah. 17He was thirty-
two years old when he became king, and he
reigned in Jerusalem eight years. 18He walked
in the ways of the kings of Israel, as the house
of Ahab had done, for he married a daughter
of Ahab. He did evil in the eyes of the LORD.
19Nevertheless, for the sake of his servant David, the LORD was not willing to destroy Judah. He had promised to maintain a lamp for
David and his descendants forever.
20In the time of Jehoram, Edom rebelled
against Judah and set up its own king. 21So
Jehoram[b] went to Zair with all his chariots.
The Edomites surrounded him and his chariot commanders, but he rose up and broke
through by night; his army, however, fled
back home. 22To this day Edom has been in
rebellion against Judah. Libnah revolted at the
same time.

[a] 10 The Hebrew may also be read *Go and say, 'You will certainly not recover,' for.* [b] 21 Hebrew *Joram,* a variant of *Jehoram*; also in verses 23 and 24

23As for the other events of Jehoram's reign,
and all he did, are they not written in the book
of the annals of the kings of Judah? 24Jehoram
rested with his fathers and was buried with
them in the City of David. And Ahaziah his
son succeeded him as king.

Ahaziah King of Judah

25In the twelfth year of Joram son of Ahab
king of Israel, Ahaziah son of Jehoram king
of Judah began to reign. 26Ahaziah was twenty-two years old when he became king, and
he reigned in Jerusalem one year. His mother's
name was Athaliah, a granddaughter of Omri
king of Israel. 27He walked in the ways of the
house of Ahab and did evil in the eyes of the
LORD, as the house of Ahab had done, for he
was related by marriage to Ahab's family.
28Ahaziah went with Joram son of Ahab to
war against Hazael king of Aram at Ramoth
Gilead. The Arameans wounded Joram; 29so
King Joram returned to Jezreel to recover
from the wounds the Arameans had inflicted
on him at Ramoth[a] in his battle with Hazael
king of Aram.
Then Ahaziah son of Jehoram king of Judah went down to Jezreel to see Joram son of
Ahab, because he had been wounded.

Jehu Anointed King of Israel

9 The prophet Elisha summoned a man from
the company of the prophets and said to
him, "Tuck your cloak into your belt, take
this flask of oil with you and go to Ramoth
Gilead. 2When you get there, look for Jehu
son of Jehoshaphat, the son of Nimshi. Go to
him, get him away from his companions and
take him into an inner room. 3Then take the
flask and pour the oil on his head and declare,
'This is what the LORD says: I anoint you king
over Israel.' Then open the door and run; don't
delay!"
4So the young man, the prophet, went to
Ramoth Gilead. 5When he arrived, he found
the army officers sitting together. "I have a
message for you, commander," he said.
"For which of us?" asked Jehu.
"For you, commander," he replied.
6Jehu got up and went into the house. Then
the prophet poured the oil on Jehu's head and
declared, "This is what the LORD, the God
of Israel, says: 'I anoint you king over the
LORD's people Israel. 7You are to destroy the
house of Ahab your master, and I will avenge
the blood of my servants the prophets and
the blood of all the LORD's servants shed by
Jezebel. 8The whole house of Ahab will perish. I will cut off from Ahab every last male in
Israel—slave or free. 9I will make the house
of Ahab like the house of Jeroboam son of
Nebat and like the house of Baasha son of
Ahijah. 10As for Jezebel, dogs will devour her
on the plot of ground at Jezreel, and no one
will bury her.' " Then he opened the door
and ran.
11When Jehu went out to his fellow officers, one of them asked him, "Is everything all
right? Why did this madman come to you?"
"You know the man and the sort of things
he says," Jehu replied.
12"That's not true!" they said. "Tell us."
Jehu said, "Here is what he told me: 'This
is what the LORD says: I anoint you king over
Israel.' "
13They hurried and took their cloaks and
spread them under him on the bare steps.
Then they blew the trumpet and shouted,
"Jehu is king!"

Jehu Kills Joram and Ahaziah

14So Jehu son of Jehoshaphat, the son of
Nimshi, conspired against Joram. (Now Joram and all Israel had been defending Ramoth
Gilead against Hazael king of Aram, 15but
King Joram[b] had returned to Jezreel to recover from the wounds the Arameans had inflicted on him in the battle with Hazael king of
Aram.) Jehu said, "If this is the way you feel,
don't let anyone slip out of the city to go and
tell the news in Jezreel." 16Then he got into his
chariot and rode to Jezreel, because Joram was
resting there and Ahaziah king of Judah had
gone down to see him.
17When the lookout standing on the tower in Jezreel saw Jehu's troops approaching, he
called out, "I see some troops coming."
"Get a horseman," Joram ordered. "Send
him to meet them and ask, 'Do you come in
peace?' "
18The horseman rode off to meet Jehu and
said, "This is what the king says: 'Do you
come in peace?' "
"What do you have to do with peace?" Jehu
replied. "Fall in behind me."
The lookout reported, "The messenger has
reached them, but he isn't coming back."
19So the king sent out a second horseman.
When he came to them he said, "This is what
the king says: 'Do you come in peace?' "

---

[a] 29 Hebrew *Ramah,* a variant of *Ramoth* [b] 15 Hebrew *Jehoram,* a variant of *Joram;* also in verses 17 and 21-24

Jehu replied, "What do you have to do with peace? Fall in behind me."

20 The lookout reported, "He has reached them, but he isn't coming back either. The driving is like that of Jehu son of Nimshi—he drives like a madman."

21 "Hitch up my chariot," Joram ordered. And when it was hitched up, Joram king of Israel and Ahaziah king of Judah rode out, each in his own chariot, to meet Jehu. They met him at the plot of ground that had belonged to Naboth the Jezreelite. 22 When Joram saw Jehu he asked, "Have you come in peace, Jehu?"

"How can there be peace," Jehu replied, "as long as all the idolatry and witchcraft of your mother Jezebel abound?"

23 Joram turned about and fled, calling out to Ahaziah, "Treachery, Ahaziah!"

24 Then Jehu drew his bow and shot Joram between the shoulders. The arrow pierced his heart and he slumped down in his chariot. 25 Jehu said to Bidkar, his chariot officer, "Pick him up and throw him on the field that belonged to Naboth the Jezreelite. Remember how you and I were riding together in chariots behind Ahab his father when the LORD made this prophecy about him: 26 'Yesterday I saw the blood of Naboth and the blood of his sons, declares the LORD, and I will surely make you pay for it on this plot of ground, declares the LORD.' [a] Now then, pick him up and throw him on that plot, in accordance with the word of the LORD."

27 When Ahaziah king of Judah saw what had happened, he fled up the road to Beth Haggan. [b] Jehu chased him, shouting, "Kill him too!" They wounded him in his chariot on the way up to Gur near Ibleam, but he escaped to Megiddo and died there. 28 His servants took him by chariot to Jerusalem and buried him with his fathers in his tomb in the City of David. 29 (In the eleventh year of Joram son of Ahab, Ahaziah had become king of Judah.)

Jezebel Killed

30 Then Jehu went to Jezreel. When Jezebel heard about it, she painted her eyes, arranged her hair and looked out of a window. 31 As Jehu entered the gate, she asked, "Have you come in peace, Zimri, you murderer of your master?" [c]

32 He looked up at the window and called out, "Who is on my side? Who?" Two or three eunuchs looked down at him. 33 "Throw her down!" Jehu said. So they threw her down, and some of her blood spattered the wall and the horses as they trampled her underfoot.

34 Jehu went in and ate and drank. "Take care of that cursed woman," he said, "and bury her, for she was a king's daughter." 35 But when they went out to bury her, they found nothing except her skull, her feet and her hands. 36 They went back and told Jehu, who said, "This is the word of the LORD that he spoke through his servant Elijah the Tishbite: On the plot of ground at Jezreel dogs will devour Jezebel's flesh. [d] 37 Jezebel's body will be like refuse on the ground in the plot at Jezreel, so that no one will be able to say, 'This is Jezebel.' "

Ahab's Family Killed

10 Now there were in Samaria seventy sons of the house of Ahab. So Jehu wrote letters and sent them to Samaria: to the officials of Jezreel, [e] to the elders and to the guardians of Ahab's children. He said, 2 "As soon as this letter reaches you, since your master's sons are with you and you have chariots and horses, a fortified city and weapons, 3 choose the best and most worthy of your master's sons and set him on his father's throne. Then fight for your master's house."

4 But they were terrified and said, "If two kings could not resist him, how can we?"

5 So the palace administrator, the city governor, the elders and the guardians sent this message to Jehu: "We are your servants and we will do anything you say. We will not appoint anyone as king; you do whatever you think best."

6 Then Jehu wrote them a second letter, saying, "If you are on my side and will obey me, take the heads of your master's sons and come to me in Jezreel by this time tomorrow."

Now the royal princes, seventy of them, were with the leading men of the city, who were rearing them. 7 When the letter arrived, these men took the princes and slaughtered all seventy of them. They put their heads in baskets and sent them to Jehu in Jezreel. 8 When the messenger arrived, he told Jehu, "They have brought the heads of the princes."

Then Jehu ordered, "Put them in two piles at the entrance of the city gate until morning."

9 The next morning Jehu went out. He stood

[a] *26* See 1 Kings 21:19. [b] *27* Or *fled by way of the garden house* [c] *31* Or *"Did Zimri have peace, who murdered his master?"*
[d] *36* See 1 Kings 21:23. [e] *1* Hebrew; some Septuagint manuscripts and Vulgate *of the city*

before all the people and said, "You are innocent. It was I who conspired against my master and killed him, but who killed all these? 10Know then, that not a word the LORD has spoken against the house of Ahab will fail. The LORD has done what he promised through his servant Elijah." 11So Jehu killed everyone in Jezreel who remained of the house of Ahab, as well as all his chief men, his close friends and his priests, leaving him no survivor.

12Jehu then set out and went toward Samaria. At Beth Eked of the Shepherds, 13he met some relatives of Ahaziah king of Judah and asked, "Who are you?"

They said, "We are relatives of Ahaziah, and we have come down to greet the families of the king and of the queen mother."

14"Take them alive!" he ordered. So they took them alive and slaughtered them by the well of Beth Eked—forty-two men. He left no survivor.

15After he left there, he came upon Jehonadab son of Recab, who was on his way to meet him. Jehu greeted him and said, "Are you in accord with me, as I am with you?"

"I am," Jehonadab answered.

"If so," said Jehu, "give me your hand." So he did, and Jehu helped him up into the chariot. 16Jehu said, "Come with me and see my zeal for the LORD." Then he had him ride along in his chariot.

17When Jehu came to Samaria, he killed all who were left there of Ahab's family; he destroyed them, according to the word of the LORD spoken to Elijah.

Ministers of Baal Killed

18Then Jehu brought all the people together and said to them, "Ahab served Baal a little; Jehu will serve him much. 19Now summon all the prophets of Baal, all his ministers and all his priests. See that no one is missing, because I am going to hold a great sacrifice for Baal. Anyone who fails to come will no longer live." But Jehu was acting deceptively in order to destroy the ministers of Baal.

20Jehu said, "Call an assembly in honor of Baal." So they proclaimed it. 21Then he sent word throughout Israel, and all the ministers of Baal came; not one stayed away. They crowded into the temple of Baal until it was full from one end to the other. 22And Jehu said to the keeper of the wardrobe, "Bring robes for all the ministers of Baal." So he brought out robes for them.

23Then Jehu and Jehonadab son of Recab went into the temple of Baal. Jehu said to the ministers of Baal, "Look around and see that no servants of the LORD are here with you—only ministers of Baal." 24So they went in to make sacrifices and burnt offerings. Now Jehu had posted eighty men outside with this warning: "If one of you lets any of the men I am placing in your hands escape, it will be your life for his life."

25As soon as Jehu had finished making the burnt offering, he ordered the guards and officers: "Go in and kill them; let no one escape." So they cut them down with the sword. The guards and officers threw the bodies out and then entered the inner shrine of the temple of Baal. 26They brought the sacred stone out of the temple of Baal and burned it. 27They demolished the sacred stone of Baal and tore down the temple of Baal, and people have used it for a latrine to this day.

28So Jehu destroyed Baal worship in Israel. 29However, he did not turn away from the sins of Jeroboam son of Nebat, which he had caused Israel to commit—the worship of the golden calves at Bethel and Dan.

30The LORD said to Jehu, "Because you have done well in accomplishing what is right in my eyes and have done to the house of Ahab all I had in mind to do, your descendants will sit on the throne of Israel to the fourth generation." 31Yet Jehu was not careful to keep the law of the LORD, the God of Israel, with all his heart. He did not turn away from the sins of Jeroboam, which he had caused Israel to commit.

32In those days the LORD began to reduce the size of Israel. Hazael overpowered the Israelites throughout their territory 33east of the Jordan in all the land of Gilead (the region of Gad, Reuben and Manasseh), from Aroer by the Arnon Gorge through Gilead to Bashan.

34As for the other events of Jehu's reign, all he did, and all his achievements, are they not written in the book of the annals of the kings of Israel?

35Jehu rested with his fathers and was buried in Samaria. And Jehoahaz his son succeeded him as king. 36The time that Jehu reigned over Israel in Samaria was twenty-eight years.

Athaliah and Joash

11 When Athaliah the mother of Ahaziah saw that her son was dead, she proceeded to destroy the whole royal family. 2But Jehosheba, the daughter of King Jehoram[a]

[a] 2 Hebrew *Joram,* a variant of *Jehoram*

F **FRIDAY**
READ 2 KINGS 11:1–16

FAMILY ABUSE AND RESCUE

Until a few years ago, I was only marginally aware of this emotionally powerful story about Joash. It is, after all, stuck in the middle of the long section of 1 and 2 Kings that many of us sometimes, um, skim.

At any rate, we read here about King Ahaziah's mother, Athaliah, who had begun killing off the royal family so that she could rule as queen. Jehosheba, Ahaziah's sister, saw what was going on and rescued Ahaziah's young son Joash, hiding him and his nurse at the temple. Joash remained there for six years, finally emerging when it was time for him to be crowned as king.

What first gripped me about this story was Athaliah, a wicked matriarch of fairy-tale proportions. Can't you just see her as the Wicked Witch of the West? Once I tore myself away from that specter, I noticed how complicated her family was. On the one hand, this group of relatives was truly dysfunctional (they were, after all, related to the infamous family of King Ahab and Queen Jezebel). They were so dysfunctional that a grandmother began killing off her own grandchildren—her own descendants!—so she could grab the throne. Athaliah makes my overbearing grandmother look like a wimp.

On the other hand, the family wasn't all bad. Joash's aunt, Jehosheba, intervened to rescue the little boy and hide him till he was old enough to be king. That's a powerful illustration of how families that contain violent and destructive kooks and abusers can also contain courageous and self-sacrificing heroes.

I can relate to the story of Joash because my own aunts played such a huge role in my growing-up years. While never in danger of being killed, I sometimes felt like I didn't fit in with my parents and sister. My aunts stepped into that gap to nurture me, to explain the weird Winner family mysteries to me, and to help me feel like I belonged. Now that I'm an adult, my aunts continue to be my cherished confidants.

My own aunts—not to mention Aunt Jehosheba—remind me what a blessing extended family can be. They help me understand how important it is not to get so focused on our nuclear families that we forget our wider kith and kin. For some of us, extended families may not be biological; they may be in-laws, neighbors, friends or church family.

I certainly hope my own little family is never as destructive and broken as Joash's. But I would be fooling myself to think that my husband and I are perfect parents or that we can do the job of raising our children by ourselves. We need others to help us do that. By looking outside the walls of our own home to our relatives and church family, Griff and I will help ensure that our own bad tendencies are caught, checked and corrected by others who love us and ours.

—LAUREN WINNER

But Jehosheba, the daughter of King Jehoram and sister of Ahaziah, took Joash son of Ahaziah and stole him away from among the royal princes, who were about to be murdered.

— 2 KINGS 11:2

let's *talk*

- Thinking about each other's families, what people are the dysfunctional or difficult ones? Who are the heroes? How do all of these people influence our marriage?
- Are we as a couple open to intervention, love, even rebuke from friends or extended family? If we have children, how do we encourage relationships between them and other adults in our family whom we love and trust?
- Have we ever acted as someone else's Jehosheba, stepping in to help the child of a friend or relative? What have we learned from that experience?

FOR YOUR NEXT DEVOTIONAL READING, TURN TO PAGE 408.

and sister of Ahaziah, took Joash son of Ahaziah and stole him away from among the royal
princes, who were about to be murdered. She
put him and his nurse in a bedroom to hide
him from Athaliah; so he was not killed. 3He
remained hidden with his nurse at the temple
of the LORD for six years while Athaliah ruled
the land.

4In the seventh year Jehoiada sent for the
commanders of units of a hundred, the Carites and the guards and had them brought to
him at the temple of the LORD. He made a
covenant with them and put them under oath
at the temple of the LORD. Then he showed
them the king's son. 5He commanded them,
saying, "This is what you are to do: You who
are in the three companies that are going on
duty on the Sabbath—a third of you guarding
the royal palace, 6a third at the Sur Gate, and
a third at the gate behind the guard, who take
turns guarding the temple— 7and you who
are in the other two companies that normally
go off Sabbath duty are all to guard the temple
for the king. 8Station yourselves around the
king, each man with his weapon in his hand.
Anyone who approaches your ranks[a] must be
put to death. Stay close to the king wherever
he goes."

9The commanders of units of a hundred
did just as Jehoiada the priest ordered. Each
one took his men—those who were going on
duty on the Sabbath and those who were going off duty—and came to Jehoiada the priest.
10Then he gave the commanders the spears and
shields that had belonged to King David and
that were in the temple of the LORD. 11The
guards, each with his weapon in his hand, stationed themselves around the king—near the
altar and the temple, from the south side to
the north side of the temple.

12Jehoiada brought out the king's son and
put the crown on him; he presented him with
a copy of the covenant and proclaimed him
king. They anointed him, and the people
clapped their hands and shouted, "Long live
the king!"

13When Athaliah heard the noise made
by the guards and the people, she went to
the people at the temple of the LORD. 14She
looked and there was the king, standing by the
pillar, as the custom was. The officers and the
trumpeters were beside the king, and all the
people of the land were rejoicing and blowing
trumpets. Then Athaliah tore her robes and
called out, "Treason! Treason!"

15Jehoiada the priest ordered the commanders of units of a hundred, who were in charge of
the troops: "Bring her out between the ranks[b]
and put to the sword anyone who follows her."
For the priest had said, "She must not be put
to death in the temple of the LORD." 16So they
seized her as she reached the place where the
horses enter the palace grounds, and there she
was put to death.

17Jehoiada then made a covenant between
the LORD and the king and people that they
would be the LORD's people. He also made a
covenant between the king and the people.
18All the people of the land went to the temple of Baal and tore it down. They smashed
the altars and idols to pieces and killed Mattan
the priest of Baal in front of the altars.

Then Jehoiada the priest posted guards at
the temple of the LORD. 19He took with him
the commanders of hundreds, the Carites, the
guards and all the people of the land, and together they brought the king down from the
temple of the LORD and went into the palace,
entering by way of the gate of the guards. The
king then took his place on the royal throne,
20and all the people of the land rejoiced. And
the city was quiet, because Athaliah had been
slain with the sword at the palace.

21Joash[c] was seven years old when he began
to reign.

Joash Repairs the Temple

12 In the seventh year of Jehu, Joash[d] became king, and he reigned in Jerusalem
forty years. His mother's name was Zibiah; she was from Beersheba. 2Joash did what
was right in the eyes of the LORD all the years
Jehoiada the priest instructed him. 3The high
places, however, were not removed; the people
continued to offer sacrifices and burn incense
there.

4Joash said to the priests, "Collect all the
money that is brought as sacred offerings to
the temple of the LORD—the money collected
in the census, the money received from personal vows and the money brought voluntarily to the temple. 5Let every priest receive the
money from one of the treasurers, and let it
be used to repair whatever damage is found
in the temple."

6But by the twenty-third year of King Joash
the priests still had not repaired the temple.

[a] 8 Or *approaches the precincts* [b] 15 Or *out from the precincts* [c] 21 Hebrew *Jehoash,* a variant of *Joash* [d] 1 Hebrew *Jehoash,* a variant of *Joash;* also in verses 2, 4, 6, 7 and 18

7Therefore King Joash summoned Jehoiada the priest and the other priests and asked
them, "Why aren't you repairing the damage
done to the temple? Take no more money
from your treasurers, but hand it over for repairing the temple." 8The priests agreed that
they would not collect any more money from
the people and that they would not repair the
temple themselves.
9Jehoiada the priest took a chest and bored
a hole in its lid. He placed it beside the altar, on the right side as one enters the temple of the LORD. The priests who guarded
the entrance put into the chest all the money
that was brought to the temple of the LORD.
10Whenever they saw that there was a large
amount of money in the chest, the royal secretary and the high priest came, counted the
money that had been brought into the temple
of the LORD and put it into bags. 11When the
amount had been determined, they gave the
money to the men appointed to supervise the
work on the temple. With it they paid those
who worked on the temple of the LORD—
the carpenters and builders, 12the masons
and stonecutters. They purchased timber and
dressed stone for the repair of the temple of
the LORD, and met all the other expenses of
restoring the temple.
13The money brought into the temple was
not spent for making silver basins, wick trimmers, sprinkling bowls, trumpets or any other articles of gold or silver for the temple of
the LORD; 14it was paid to the workmen, who
used it to repair the temple. 15They did not require an accounting from those to whom they
gave the money to pay the workers, because
they acted with complete honesty. 16The money from the guilt offerings and sin offerings
was not brought into the temple of the LORD;
it belonged to the priests.
17About this time Hazael king of Aram
went up and attacked Gath and captured it.
Then he turned to attack Jerusalem. 18But Joash king of Judah took all the sacred objects
dedicated by his fathers—Jehoshaphat, Jehoram and Ahaziah, the kings of Judah—and
the gifts he himself had dedicated and all the
gold found in the treasuries of the temple of
the LORD and of the royal palace, and he sent
them to Hazael king of Aram, who then withdrew from Jerusalem.
19As for the other events of the reign of Joash, and all he did, are they not written in the
book of the annals of the kings of Judah? 20His
officials conspired against him and assassinated him at Beth Millo, on the road down to
Silla. 21The officials who murdered him were
Jozabad son of Shimeath and Jehozabad son
of Shomer. He died and was buried with his
fathers in the City of David. And Amaziah his
son succeeded him as king.

Jehoahaz King of Israel

13 In the twenty-third year of Joash son
of Ahaziah king of Judah, Jehoahaz son
of Jehu became king of Israel in Samaria, and he reigned seventeen years. 2He did
evil in the eyes of the LORD by following the
sins of Jeroboam son of Nebat, which he had
caused Israel to commit, and he did not turn
away from them. 3So the LORD's anger burned
against Israel, and for a long time he kept
them under the power of Hazael king of Aram
and Ben-Hadad his son.
4Then Jehoahaz sought the LORD's favor,
and the LORD listened to him, for he saw how
severely the king of Aram was oppressing Israel. 5The LORD provided a deliverer for Israel,
and they escaped from the power of Aram. So
the Israelites lived in their own homes as they
had before. 6But they did not turn away from
the sins of the house of Jeroboam, which he
had caused Israel to commit; they continued
in them. Also, the Asherah pole[a] remained
standing in Samaria.
7Nothing had been left of the army of Jehoahaz except fifty horsemen, ten chariots
and ten thousand foot soldiers, for the king of
Aram had destroyed the rest and made them
like the dust at threshing time.
8As for the other events of the reign of Jehoahaz, all he did and his achievements, are
they not written in the book of the annals of
the kings of Israel? 9Jehoahaz rested with his
fathers and was buried in Samaria. And Jehoash[b] his son succeeded him as king.

Jehoash King of Israel

10In the thirty-seventh year of Joash king of
Judah, Jehoash son of Jehoahaz became king
of Israel in Samaria, and he reigned sixteen
years. 11He did evil in the eyes of the LORD
and did not turn away from any of the sins of
Jeroboam son of Nebat, which he had caused
Israel to commit; he continued in them.
12As for the other events of the reign of
Jehoash, all he did and his achievements, including his war against Amaziah king of Judah, are they not written in the book of the

[a] 6 That is, a symbol of the goddess Asherah; here and elsewhere in 2 Kings [b] 9 Hebrew *Joash*, a variant of *Jehoash*; also in verses 12-14 and 25

annals of the kings of Israel? 13Jehoash rested with his fathers, and Jeroboam succeeded him on the throne. Jehoash was buried in Samaria with the kings of Israel.

14Now Elisha was suffering from the illness from which he died. Jehoash king of Israel went down to see him and wept over him. "My father! My father!" he cried. "The chariots and horsemen of Israel!"

15Elisha said, "Get a bow and some arrows," and he did so. 16"Take the bow in your hands," he said to the king of Israel. When he had taken it, Elisha put his hands on the king's hands.

17"Open the east window," he said, and he opened it. "Shoot!" Elisha said, and he shot. "The LORD's arrow of victory, the arrow of victory over Aram!" Elisha declared. "You will completely destroy the Arameans at Aphek."

18Then he said, "Take the arrows," and the king took them. Elisha told him, "Strike the ground." He struck it three times and stopped. 19The man of God was angry with him and said, "You should have struck the ground five or six times; then you would have defeated Aram and completely destroyed it. But now you will defeat it only three times."

20Elisha died and was buried.

Now Moabite raiders used to enter the country every spring. 21Once while some Israelites were burying a man, suddenly they saw a band of raiders; so they threw the man's body into Elisha's tomb. When the body touched Elisha's bones, the man came to life and stood up on his feet.

22Hazael king of Aram oppressed Israel throughout the reign of Jehoahaz. 23But the LORD was gracious to them and had compassion and showed concern for them because of his covenant with Abraham, Isaac and Jacob. To this day he has been unwilling to destroy them or banish them from his presence.

24Hazael king of Aram died, and Ben-Hadad his son succeeded him as king. 25Then Jehoash son of Jehoahaz recaptured from Ben-Hadad son of Hazael the towns he had taken in battle from his father Jehoahaz. Three times Jehoash defeated him, and so he recovered the Israelite towns.

Amaziah King of Judah

14 In the second year of Jehoash[a] son of Jehoahaz king of Israel, Amaziah son of Joash king of Judah began to reign. 2He was twenty-five years old when he became king, and he reigned in Jerusalem twenty-nine years. His mother's name was Jehoaddin; she was from Jerusalem. 3He did what was right in the eyes of the LORD, but not as his father David had done. In everything he followed the example of his father Joash. 4The high places, however, were not removed; the people continued to offer sacrifices and burn incense there.

5After the kingdom was firmly in his grasp, he executed the officials who had murdered his father the king. 6Yet he did not put the sons of the assassins to death, in accordance with what is written in the Book of the Law of Moses where the LORD commanded: "Fathers shall not be put to death for their children, nor children put to death for their fathers; each is to die for his own sins."[b]

7He was the one who defeated ten thousand Edomites in the Valley of Salt and captured Sela in battle, calling it Joktheel, the name it has to this day.

8Then Amaziah sent messengers to Jehoash son of Jehoahaz, the son of Jehu, king of Israel, with the challenge: "Come, meet me face to face."

9But Jehoash king of Israel replied to Amaziah king of Judah: "A thistle in Lebanon sent a message to a cedar in Lebanon, 'Give your daughter to my son in marriage.' Then a wild beast in Lebanon came along and trampled the thistle underfoot. 10You have indeed defeated Edom and now you are arrogant. Glory in your victory, but stay at home! Why ask for trouble and cause your own downfall and that of Judah also?"

11Amaziah, however, would not listen, so Jehoash king of Israel attacked. He and Amaziah king of Judah faced each other at Beth Shemesh in Judah. 12Judah was routed by Israel, and every man fled to his home. 13Jehoash king of Israel captured Amaziah king of Judah, the son of Joash, the son of Ahaziah, at Beth Shemesh. Then Jehoash went to Jerusalem and broke down the wall of Jerusalem from the Ephraim Gate to the Corner Gate—a section about six hundred feet long.[c] 14He took all the gold and silver and all the articles found in the temple of the LORD and in the treasuries of the royal palace. He also took hostages and returned to Samaria.

15As for the other events of the reign of Jehoash, what he did and his achievements,

[a] *1* Hebrew *Joash,* a variant of *Jehoash*; also in verses 13, 23 and 27 [b] *6* Deut. 24:16 [c] *13* Hebrew *four hundred cubits* (about 180 meters)

including his war against Amaziah king of Judah, are they not written in the book of the
annals of the kings of Israel? 16Jehoash rested with his fathers and was buried in Samaria
with the kings of Israel. And Jeroboam his son
succeeded him as king.
17Amaziah son of Joash king of Judah lived
for fifteen years after the death of Jehoash son
of Jehoahaz king of Israel. 18As for the other
events of Amaziah's reign, are they not written in the book of the annals of the kings of
Judah?
19They conspired against him in Jerusalem,
and he fled to Lachish, but they sent men after him to Lachish and killed him there. 20He
was brought back by horse and was buried
in Jerusalem with his fathers, in the City of
David.
21Then all the people of Judah took Azariah,[a] who was sixteen years old, and made him
king in place of his father Amaziah. 22He was
the one who rebuilt Elath and restored it to
Judah after Amaziah rested with his fathers.

Jeroboam II King of Israel

23In the fifteenth year of Amaziah son of
Joash king of Judah, Jeroboam son of Jehoash
king of Israel became king in Samaria, and he
reigned forty-one years. 24He did evil in the
eyes of the LORD and did not turn away from
any of the sins of Jeroboam son of Nebat,
which he had caused Israel to commit. 25He
was the one who restored the boundaries of
Israel from Lebo[b] Hamath to the Sea of the
Arabah,[c] in accordance with the word of the
LORD, the God of Israel, spoken through his
servant Jonah son of Amittai, the prophet
from Gath Hepher.
26The LORD had seen how bitterly everyone
in Israel, whether slave or free, was suffering;
there was no one to help them. 27And since
the LORD had not said he would blot out the
name of Israel from under heaven, he saved
them by the hand of Jeroboam son of Jehoash.
28As for the other events of Jeroboam's reign,
all he did, and his military achievements, including how he recovered for Israel both Damascus and Hamath, which had belonged to
Yaudi,[d] are they not written in the book of the
annals of the kings of Israel? 29Jeroboam rested
with his fathers, the kings of Israel. And Zechariah his son succeeded him as king.

Azariah King of Judah

15 In the twenty-seventh year of Jeroboam
king of Israel, Azariah son of Amaziah
king of Judah began to reign. 2He was
sixteen years old when he became king, and
he reigned in Jerusalem fifty-two years. His
mother's name was Jecoliah; she was from Jerusalem. 3He did what was right in the eyes
of the LORD, just as his father Amaziah had
done. 4The high places, however, were not removed; the people continued to offer sacrifices
and burn incense there.
5The LORD afflicted the king with leprosy[e]
until the day he died, and he lived in a separate house.[f] Jotham the king's son had charge
of the palace and governed the people of the
land.
6As for the other events of Azariah's reign,
and all he did, are they not written in the book
of the annals of the kings of Judah? 7Azari-
ah rested with his fathers and was buried near
them in the City of David. And Jotham his
son succeeded him as king.

Zechariah King of Israel

8In the thirty-eighth year of Azariah king
of Judah, Zechariah son of Jeroboam became
king of Israel in Samaria, and he reigned six
months. 9He did evil in the eyes of the LORD,
as his fathers had done. He did not turn away
from the sins of Jeroboam son of Nebat, which
he had caused Israel to commit.
10Shallum son of Jabesh conspired against
Zechariah. He attacked him in front of the
people,[g] assassinated him and succeeded him
as king. 11The other events of Zechariah's reign
are written in the book of the annals of the
kings of Israel. 12So the word of the LORD spoken to Jehu was fulfilled: "Your descendants
will sit on the throne of Israel to the fourth
generation."[h]

Shallum King of Israel

13Shallum son of Jabesh became king in
the thirty-ninth year of Uzziah king of Judah,
and he reigned in Samaria one month. 14Then
Menahem son of Gadi went from Tirzah up to
Samaria. He attacked Shallum son of Jabesh in
Samaria, assassinated him and succeeded him
as king.
15The other events of Shallum's reign, and
the conspiracy he led, are written in the book
of the annals of the kings of Israel.
16At that time Menahem, starting out from

---

[a] *21* Also called *Uzziah* [b] *25* Or *from the entrance to* [c] *25* That is, the Dead Sea [d] *28* Or *Judah* [e] *5* The Hebrew word was used for various diseases affecting the skin—not necessarily leprosy. [f] *5* Or *in a house where he was relieved of responsibility* [g] *10* Hebrew; some Septuagint manuscripts *in Ibleam* [h] *12* 2 Kings 10:30

Tirzah, attacked Tiphsah and everyone in the city and its vicinity, because they refused to open their gates. He sacked Tiphsah and ripped open all the pregnant women.

Menahem King of Israel

17In the thirty-ninth year of Azariah king of Judah, Menahem son of Gadi became king of Israel, and he reigned in Samaria ten years. 18He did evil in the eyes of the LORD. During his entire reign he did not turn away from the sins of Jeroboam son of Nebat, which he had caused Israel to commit.

19Then Pul[a] king of Assyria invaded the land, and Menahem gave him a thousand talents[b] of silver to gain his support and strengthen his own hold on the kingdom. 20Menahem exacted this money from Israel. Every wealthy man had to contribute fifty shekels[c] of silver to be given to the king of Assyria. So the king of Assyria withdrew and stayed in the land no longer.

21As for the other events of Menahem's reign, and all he did, are they not written in the book of the annals of the kings of Israel? 22Menahem rested with his fathers. And Pekahiah his son succeeded him as king.

Pekahiah King of Israel

23In the fiftieth year of Azariah king of Judah, Pekahiah son of Menahem became king of Israel in Samaria, and he reigned two years. 24Pekahiah did evil in the eyes of the LORD. He did not turn away from the sins of Jeroboam son of Nebat, which he had caused Israel to commit. 25One of his chief officers, Pekah son of Remaliah, conspired against him. Taking fifty men of Gilead with him, he assassinated Pekahiah, along with Argob and Arieh, in the citadel of the royal palace at Samaria. So Pekah killed Pekahiah and succeeded him as king.

26The other events of Pekahiah's reign, and all he did, are written in the book of the annals of the kings of Israel.

Pekah King of Israel

27In the fifty-second year of Azariah king of Judah, Pekah son of Remaliah became king of Israel in Samaria, and he reigned twenty years. 28He did evil in the eyes of the LORD. He did not turn away from the sins of Jeroboam son of Nebat, which he had caused Israel to commit.

29In the time of Pekah king of Israel, Tiglath-Pileser king of Assyria came and took Ijon, Abel Beth Maacah, Janoah, Kedesh and Hazor. He took Gilead and Galilee, including all the land of Naphtali, and deported the people to Assyria. 30Then Hoshea son of Elah conspired against Pekah son of Remaliah. He attacked and assassinated him, and then succeeded him as king in the twentieth year of Jotham son of Uzziah.

31As for the other events of Pekah's reign, and all he did, are they not written in the book of the annals of the kings of Israel?

Jotham King of Judah

32In the second year of Pekah son of Remaliah king of Israel, Jotham son of Uzziah king of Judah began to reign. 33He was twenty-five years old when he became king, and he reigned in Jerusalem sixteen years. His mother's name was Jerusha daughter of Zadok. 34He did what was right in the eyes of the LORD, just as his father Uzziah had done. 35The high places, however, were not removed; the people continued to offer sacrifices and burn incense there. Jotham rebuilt the Upper Gate of the temple of the LORD.

36As for the other events of Jotham's reign, and what he did, are they not written in the book of the annals of the kings of Judah? 37(In those days the LORD began to send Rezin king of Aram and Pekah son of Remaliah against Judah.) 38Jotham rested with his fathers and was buried with them in the City of David, the city of his father. And Ahaz his son succeeded him as king.

Ahaz King of Judah

16 In the seventeenth year of Pekah son of Remaliah, Ahaz son of Jotham king of Judah began to reign. 2Ahaz was twenty years old when he became king, and he reigned in Jerusalem sixteen years. Unlike David his father, he did not do what was right in the eyes of the LORD his God. 3He walked in the ways of the kings of Israel and even sacrificed his son in[d] the fire, following the detestable ways of the nations the LORD had driven out before the Israelites. 4He offered sacrifices and burned incense at the high places, on the hilltops and under every spreading tree.

5Then Rezin king of Aram and Pekah son of Remaliah king of Israel marched up to fight against Jerusalem and besieged Ahaz, but they could not overpower him. 6At that time, Rezin king of Aram recovered Elath for Aram by

---

[a] *19* Also called *Tiglath-Pileser* [b] *19* That is, about 37 tons (about 34 metric tons) [c] *20* That is, about 1 1/4 pounds (about 0.6 kilogram) [d] *3* Or *even made his son pass through*

driving out the men of Judah. Edomites then
moved into Elath and have lived there to this
day.
7Ahaz sent messengers to say to Tiglath-Pileser king of Assyria, "I am your servant and
vassal. Come up and save me out of the hand
of the king of Aram and of the king of Israel, who are attacking me." 8And Ahaz took
the silver and gold found in the temple of the
LORD and in the treasuries of the royal palace
and sent it as a gift to the king of Assyria. 9The
king of Assyria complied by attacking Damascus and capturing it. He deported its inhabitants to Kir and put Rezin to death.
10Then King Ahaz went to Damascus to
meet Tiglath-Pileser king of Assyria. He saw
an altar in Damascus and sent to Uriah the
priest a sketch of the altar, with detailed plans
for its construction. 11So Uriah the priest
built an altar in accordance with all the plans
that King Ahaz had sent from Damascus
and finished it before King Ahaz returned.
12When the king came back from Damascus
and saw the altar, he approached it and presented offerings[a] on it. 13He offered up his
burnt offering and grain offering, poured out
his drink offering, and sprinkled the blood of
his fellowship offerings[b] on the altar. 14The
bronze altar that stood before the LORD he
brought from the front of the temple—from
between the new altar and the temple of the
LORD—and put it on the north side of the
new altar.
15King Ahaz then gave these orders to Uriah the priest: "On the large new altar, offer
the morning burnt offering and the evening
grain offering, the king's burnt offering and
his grain offering, and the burnt offering of all
the people of the land, and their grain offering
and their drink offering. Sprinkle on the altar
all the blood of the burnt offerings and sacrifices. But I will use the bronze altar for seeking
guidance." 16And Uriah the priest did just as
King Ahaz had ordered.
17King Ahaz took away the side panels and
removed the basins from the movable stands.
He removed the Sea from the bronze bulls
that supported it and set it on a stone base.
18He took away the Sabbath canopy[c] that had
been built at the temple and removed the royal entryway outside the temple of the LORD, in
deference to the king of Assyria.
19As for the other events of the reign of
Ahaz, and what he did, are they not written in
the book of the annals of the kings of Judah?
20Ahaz rested with his fathers and was buried
with them in the City of David. And Hezekiah his son succeeded him as king.

Hoshea Last King of Israel

17 In the twelfth year of Ahaz king of Judah, Hoshea son of Elah became king
of Israel in Samaria, and he reigned nine
years. 2He did evil in the eyes of the LORD,
but not like the kings of Israel who preceded him.
3Shalmaneser king of Assyria came up to attack Hoshea, who had been Shalmaneser's vassal and had paid him tribute. 4But the king of
Assyria discovered that Hoshea was a traitor,
for he had sent envoys to So[d] king of Egypt,
and he no longer paid tribute to the king of
Assyria, as he had done year by year. Therefore Shalmaneser seized him and put him in
prison. 5The king of Assyria invaded the entire
land, marched against Samaria and laid siege
to it for three years. 6In the ninth year of Hoshea, the king of Assyria captured Samaria and
deported the Israelites to Assyria. He settled
them in Halah, in Gozan on the Habor River
and in the towns of the Medes.

Israel Exiled Because of Sin

7All this took place because the Israelites
had sinned against the LORD their God, who
had brought them up out of Egypt from under the power of Pharaoh king of Egypt. They
worshiped other gods 8and followed the practices of the nations the LORD had driven out
before them, as well as the practices that the
kings of Israel had introduced. 9The Israelites
secretly did things against the LORD their God
that were not right. From watchtower to fortified city they built themselves high places
in all their towns. 10They set up sacred stones
and Asherah poles on every high hill and under every spreading tree. 11At every high place
they burned incense, as the nations whom
the LORD had driven out before them had
done. They did wicked things that provoked
the LORD to anger. 12They worshiped idols,
though the LORD had said, "You shall not do
this."[e] 13The LORD warned Israel and Judah
through all his prophets and seers: "Turn from
your evil ways. Observe my commands and
decrees, in accordance with the entire Law
that I commanded your fathers to obey and
that I delivered to you through my servants
the prophets."
14But they would not listen and were as

---

[a] 12 Or *and went up* [b] 13 Traditionally *peace offerings* [c] 18 Or *the dais of his throne* (see Septuagint) [d] 4 Or *to Sais, to the*; *So* is possibly an abbreviation for *Osorkon.* [e] 12 Exodus 20:4,5

WEEKEND

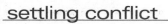

settling conflict

Conflict is not all the same. The rules are different for different kinds of conflict. If one of you comes home late without calling, for example, then confession and an apology are in order. But if you are disagreeing about where to go for dinner, no one should have to grovel as if he has committed a grievous sin!

Nevertheless, we run into couples who do exactly that. They feel that every conflict has a right and a wrong, and instead of trying to resolve the problem, they argue over which one of them is right. It is amazing how creative someone can get in defending the "righteousness" of her position when she might be talking about how the couple is going to spend a vacation! In most conflict there is not a right or wrong. Yet, some spouses can sound like a couple of attorneys in court.

Wherever you have two people, you will have conflicting desires. It is one of the things that make a relationship what it is. Two different people bring differences to the table. In fact, your differences are part of what brought you together. You complement each other . . . Normally, two giving people develop a pattern of give and take, and differences get negotiated. But sometimes they hit a stalemate. A few principles can help:

1. Avoid moralizing your preference. Make sure you realize that your desire is not a higher one than your spouse's. Do not try to win by making yours right and your spouse's wrong. These are preferences, not laws.
2. Empathize with and understand the importance of your spouse's desires. Avoid devaluing what your spouse wants. Stay away from statements that make it sound as if what she wants is less important than what you want. Her desires are just as real to her as yours are to you. Validate her desires as real and good.
3. Move to meet your spouse's desires before you meet your own. Seek to make sure that your spouse gets his or her desires met before yours are met, and you will avoid most arguments. In reality, this is not going to happen often, but your attitude is what is important.
4. If necessary, keep an account of yours, mine and ours. This system is valuable for couples with differing personalities who drift into unconscious patterns. If you keep an account, you will guard against the passive spouse becoming the perpetual loser. The more assertive will finally get some limits.
5. Make sure "we's" are agreed upon. When you both have to sacrifice for something, make sure that you are on the same page in wanting it and agreeing to it. Otherwise, make sure that you are freely giving in to the other person and will not carry a grudge or an emotional debt.

—DR. HENRY CLOUD AND DR. JOHN TOWNSEND

how you settle conflict

1. When you are wrong, you admit it to your partner:
   a. Within seconds
   b. Just as soon as cows produce root beer
   c. Usually before sunset
2. On your most recent vacation, you:
   a. Strolled sun-soaked beaches barefoot, then basked in the glow of each other's eyes
   b. Left messages on each other's answering machines
   c. Had to come home for a rest
3. Which of the following most accurately describes the frequency of your lovemaking?
   a. Tri-weekly
   b. Try weakly
   c. Try weekly
4. When you're watching TV together, who controls the remote?
   a. We do not watch television; we go for walks and talk about our feelings.
   b. I do.
   c. Whoever gets it first.
5. It's 12:30 A.M. and neither of you can sleep. Your spouse says, "Honey, I'm hungry. Would you get me a slice of cheese?" You say:
   a. "Is that all, sweetheart? How about a salad with croutons?"
   b. "Z-z-z."
   c. "Swiss or cheddar?"

How to score:

If you answered "a" more than four times, thanks for taking this quiz during your honeymoon.

If you found yourself gravitating to the "b" responses, find a soft pillow. You'll need it on the couch.

If you chose "c" five times, you've got a good thing going.

Collect ten bonus points if you also answered "a" more than once. Sounds like some flexibility, lots of laughter and a servant heart are keeping your marriage fresh. Now, break out the ginger ale. It's time to try weekly!

—PHIL CALLAWAY

HOW ARE WE DOING?

let's make a DATE

RESTAURANT ROTATION

Eat at several of your favorite restaurants in the same night. One spouse picks a favorite restaurant for appetizers. The other spouse picks a new restaurant for salads. Continue alternating restaurants for soup and, finally, the main entrée. Conclude your gastronomic tour with a restaurant you can both agree on for dessert. At the end of the night, you'll not only have a belly full of food but a head full of your partner's preferences.

FOR YOUR NEXT DEVOTIONAL READING, TURN TO PAGE 414.

LESSONS FROM THE *Bible*

Talk about how Jacob, Leah and Rachel dealt with conflict in Genesis 29:31—30:24.

stiff-necked as their fathers, who did not trust in the LORD their God. 15They rejected his decrees and the covenant he had made with their fathers and the warnings he had given them. They followed worthless idols and themselves became worthless. They imitated the nations around them although the LORD had ordered them, "Do not do as they do," and they did the things the LORD had forbidden them to do.

16They forsook all the commands of the LORD their God and made for themselves two idols cast in the shape of calves, and an Asherah pole. They bowed down to all the starry hosts, and they worshiped Baal. 17They sacrificed their sons and daughters in[a] the fire. They practiced divination and sorcery and sold themselves to do evil in the eyes of the LORD, provoking him to anger.

18So the LORD was very angry with Israel and removed them from his presence. Only the tribe of Judah was left, 19and even Judah did not keep the commands of the LORD their God. They followed the practices Israel had introduced. 20Therefore the LORD rejected all the people of Israel; he afflicted them and gave them into the hands of plunderers, until he thrust them from his presence.

21When he tore Israel away from the house of David, they made Jeroboam son of Nebat their king. Jeroboam enticed Israel away from following the LORD and caused them to commit a great sin. 22The Israelites persisted in all the sins of Jeroboam and did not turn away from them 23until the LORD removed them from his presence, as he had warned through all his servants the prophets. So the people of Israel were taken from their homeland into exile in Assyria, and they are still there.

Samaria Resettled

24The king of Assyria brought people from Babylon, Cuthah, Avva, Hamath and Sepharvaim and settled them in the towns of Samaria to replace the Israelites. They took over Samaria and lived in its towns. 25When they first lived there, they did not worship the LORD; so he sent lions among them and they killed some of the people. 26It was reported to the king of Assyria: "The people you deported and resettled in the towns of Samaria do not know what the god of that country requires. He has sent lions among them, which are killing them off, because the people do not know what he requires."

27Then the king of Assyria gave this order: "Have one of the priests you took captive from Samaria go back to live there and teach the people what the god of the land requires." 28So one of the priests who had been exiled from Samaria came to live in Bethel and taught them how to worship the LORD.

29Nevertheless, each national group made its own gods in the several towns where they settled, and set them up in the shrines the people of Samaria had made at the high places. 30The men from Babylon made Succoth Benoth, the men from Cuthah made Nergal, and the men from Hamath made Ashima; 31the Avvites made Nibhaz and Tartak, and the Sepharvites burned their children in the fire as sacrifices to Adrammelech and Anammelech, the gods of Sepharvaim. 32They worshiped the LORD, but they also appointed all sorts of their own people to officiate for them as priests in the shrines at the high places. 33They worshiped the LORD, but they also served their own gods in accordance with the customs of the nations from which they had been brought.

34To this day they persist in their former practices. They neither worship the LORD nor adhere to the decrees and ordinances, the laws and commands that the LORD gave the descendants of Jacob, whom he named Israel. 35When the LORD made a covenant with the Israelites, he commanded them: "Do not worship any other gods or bow down to them, serve them or sacrifice to them. 36But the LORD, who brought you up out of Egypt with mighty power and outstretched arm, is the one you must worship. To him you shall bow down and to him offer sacrifices. 37You must always be careful to keep the decrees and ordinances, the laws and commands he wrote for you. Do not worship other gods. 38Do not forget the covenant I have made with you, and do not worship other gods. 39Rather, worship the LORD your God; it is he who will deliver you from the hand of all your enemies."

40They would not listen, however, but persisted in their former practices. 41Even while these people were worshiping the LORD, they were serving their idols. To this day their children and grandchildren continue to do as their fathers did.

Hezekiah King of Judah

18 In the third year of Hoshea son of Elah king of Israel, Hezekiah son of Ahaz king of Judah began to reign. 2He was twen-

[a] 17 Or *They made their sons and daughters pass through*

ty-five years old when he became king, and he
reigned in Jerusalem twenty-nine years. His
mother's name was Abijah[a] daughter of Zechariah. 3He did what was right in the eyes of
the LORD, just as his father David had done.
4He removed the high places, smashed the sacred stones and cut down the Asherah poles.
He broke into pieces the bronze snake Moses
had made, for up to that time the Israelites
had been burning incense to it. (It was called[b]
Nehushtan.[c])

5Hezekiah trusted in the LORD, the God of
Israel. There was no one like him among all
the kings of Judah, either before him or after
him. 6He held fast to the LORD and did not
cease to follow him; he kept the commands
the LORD had given Moses. 7And the LORD
was with him; he was successful in whatever
he undertook. He rebelled against the king of
Assyria and did not serve him. 8From watchtower to fortified city, he defeated the Philistines, as far as Gaza and its territory.

9In King Hezekiah's fourth year, which was
the seventh year of Hoshea son of Elah king
of Israel, Shalmaneser king of Assyria marched
against Samaria and laid siege to it. 10At the
end of three years the Assyrians took it. So Samaria was captured in Hezekiah's sixth year,
which was the ninth year of Hoshea king of
Israel. 11The king of Assyria deported Israel
to Assyria and settled them in Halah, in Gozan on the Habor River and in towns of the
Medes. 12This happened because they had not
obeyed the LORD their God, but had violated his covenant—all that Moses the servant of
the LORD commanded. They neither listened
to the commands nor carried them out.

13In the fourteenth year of King Hezekiah's
reign, Sennacherib king of Assyria attacked
all the fortified cities of Judah and captured
them. 14So Hezekiah king of Judah sent this
message to the king of Assyria at Lachish: "I
have done wrong. Withdraw from me, and
I will pay whatever you demand of me." The
king of Assyria exacted from Hezekiah king
of Judah three hundred talents[d] of silver and
thirty talents[e] of gold. 15So Hezekiah gave
him all the silver that was found in the temple
of the LORD and in the treasuries of the royal
palace.

16At this time Hezekiah king of Judah
stripped off the gold with which he had covered the doors and doorposts of the temple of
the LORD, and gave it to the king of Assyria.

Sennacherib Threatens Jerusalem

17The king of Assyria sent his supreme commander, his chief officer and his field commander with a large army, from Lachish to
King Hezekiah at Jerusalem. They came up to
Jerusalem and stopped at the aqueduct of the
Upper Pool, on the road to the Washerman's
Field. 18They called for the king; and Eliakim
son of Hilkiah the palace administrator, Shebna the secretary, and Joah son of Asaph the
recorder went out to them.

19The field commander said to them, "Tell
Hezekiah:

" 'This is what the great king, the king
of Assyria, says: On what are you basing
this confidence of yours? 20You say you
have strategy and military strength—but
you speak only empty words. On whom
are you depending, that you rebel against
me? 21Look now, you are depending on
Egypt, that splintered reed of a staff,
which pierces a man's hand and wounds
him if he leans on it! Such is Pharaoh
king of Egypt to all who depend on him.
22And if you say to me, "We are depending on the LORD our God"—isn't he the
one whose high places and altars Hezekiah removed, saying to Judah and Jerusalem, "You must worship before this altar
in Jerusalem"?

23" 'Come now, make a bargain with
my master, the king of Assyria: I will give
you two thousand horses—if you can put
riders on them! 24How can you repulse
one officer of the least of my master's officials, even though you are depending
on Egypt for chariots and horsemen[f]?
25Furthermore, have I come to attack
and destroy this place without word
from the LORD? The LORD himself told
me to march against this country and destroy it.' "

26Then Eliakim son of Hilkiah, and Shebna
and Joah said to the field commander, "Please
speak to your servants in Aramaic, since we
understand it. Don't speak to us in Hebrew in
the hearing of the people on the wall."

27But the commander replied, "Was it only
to your master and you that my master sent
me to say these things, and not to the men
sitting on the wall—who, like you, will have
to eat their own filth and drink their own
urine?"

[a] *2* Hebrew *Abi,* a variant of *Abijah* [b] *4* Or *He called it* [c] *4* *Nehushtan* sounds like the Hebrew for *bronze* and *snake* and *unclean thing.* [d] *14* That is, about 11 tons (about 10 metric tons) [e] *14* That is, about 1 ton (about 1 metric ton) [f] *24* Or *charioteers*

28Then the commander stood and called out in Hebrew: "Hear the word of the great king, the king of Assyria! 29This is what the king says: Do not let Hezekiah deceive you. He cannot deliver you from my hand. 30Do not let Hezekiah persuade you to trust in the LORD when he says, 'The LORD will surely deliver us; this city will not be given into the hand of the king of Assyria.'

31"Do not listen to Hezekiah. This is what the king of Assyria says: Make peace with me and come out to me. Then every one of you will eat from his own vine and fig tree and drink water from his own cistern, 32until I come and take you to a land like your own, a land of grain and new wine, a land of bread and vineyards, a land of olive trees and honey. Choose life and not death!

"Do not listen to Hezekiah, for he is misleading you when he says, 'The LORD will deliver us.' 33Has the god of any nation ever delivered his land from the hand of the king of Assyria? 34Where are the gods of Hamath and Arpad? Where are the gods of Sepharvaim, Hena and Ivvah? Have they rescued Samaria from my hand? 35Who of all the gods of these countries has been able to save his land from me? How then can the LORD deliver Jerusalem from my hand?"

36But the people remained silent and said nothing in reply, because the king had commanded, "Do not answer him."

37Then Eliakim son of Hilkiah the palace administrator, Shebna the secretary and Joah son of Asaph the recorder went to Hezekiah, with their clothes torn, and told him what the field commander had said.

Jerusalem's Deliverance Foretold

19 When King Hezekiah heard this, he tore his clothes and put on sackcloth and went into the temple of the LORD. 2He sent Eliakim the palace administrator, Shebna the secretary and the leading priests, all wearing sackcloth, to the prophet Isaiah son of Amoz. 3They told him, "This is what Hezekiah says: This day is a day of distress and rebuke and disgrace, as when children come to the point of birth and there is no strength to deliver them. 4It may be that the LORD your God will hear all the words of the field commander, whom his master, the king of Assyria, has sent to ridicule the living God, and that he will rebuke him for the words the LORD your God has heard. Therefore pray for the remnant that still survives."

5When King Hezekiah's officials came to Isaiah, 6Isaiah said to them, "Tell your master, 'This is what the LORD says: Do not be afraid of what you have heard—those words with which the underlings of the king of Assyria have blasphemed me. 7Listen! I am going to put such a spirit in him that when he hears a certain report, he will return to his own country, and there I will have him cut down with the sword.' "

8When the field commander heard that the king of Assyria had left Lachish, he withdrew and found the king fighting against Libnah.

9Now Sennacherib received a report that Tirhakah, the Cushite[a] king ⌞of Egypt⌟, was marching out to fight against him. So he again sent messengers to Hezekiah with this word: 10"Say to Hezekiah king of Judah: Do not let the god you depend on deceive you when he says, 'Jerusalem will not be handed over to the king of Assyria.' 11Surely you have heard what the kings of Assyria have done to all the countries, destroying them completely. And will you be delivered? 12Did the gods of the nations that were destroyed by my forefathers deliver them: the gods of Gozan, Haran, Rezeph and the people of Eden who were in Tel Assar? 13Where is the king of Hamath, the king of Arpad, the king of the city of Sepharvaim, or of Hena or Ivvah?"

Hezekiah's Prayer

14Hezekiah received the letter from the messengers and read it. Then he went up to the temple of the LORD and spread it out before the LORD. 15And Hezekiah prayed to the LORD: "O LORD, God of Israel, enthroned between the cherubim, you alone are God over all the kingdoms of the earth. You have made heaven and earth. 16Give ear, O LORD, and hear; open your eyes, O LORD, and see; listen to the words Sennacherib has sent to insult the living God.

17"It is true, O LORD, that the Assyrian kings have laid waste these nations and their lands. 18They have thrown their gods into the fire and destroyed them, for they were not gods but only wood and stone, fashioned by men's hands. 19Now, O LORD our God, deliver us from his hand, so that all kingdoms on earth may know that you alone, O LORD, are God."

[a] 9 That is, from the upper Nile region

Isaiah Prophesies Sennacherib's Fall

20Then Isaiah son of Amoz sent a message
to Hezekiah: "This is what the LORD, the God
of Israel, says: I have heard your prayer concerning Sennacherib king of Assyria. 21This
is the word that the LORD has spoken against
him:

" 'The Virgin Daughter of Zion
despises you and mocks you.
The Daughter of Jerusalem
tosses her head as you flee.
22 Who is it you have insulted and
blasphemed?
Against whom have you raised your
voice
and lifted your eyes in pride?
Against the Holy One of Israel!
23 By your messengers
you have heaped insults on the Lord.
And you have said,
"With my many chariots
I have ascended the heights of the
mountains,
the utmost heights of Lebanon.
I have cut down its tallest cedars,
the choicest of its pines.
I have reached its remotest parts,
the finest of its forests.
24 I have dug wells in foreign lands
and drunk the water there.
With the soles of my feet
I have dried up all the streams of
Egypt."
25 " 'Have you not heard?
Long ago I ordained it.
In days of old I planned it;
now I have brought it to pass,
that you have turned fortified cities
into piles of stone.
26 Their people, drained of power,
are dismayed and put to shame.
They are like plants in the field,
like tender green shoots,
like grass sprouting on the roof,
scorched before it grows up.
27 " 'But I know where you stay
and when you come and go
and how you rage against me.
28 Because you rage against me
and your insolence has reached my ears,
I will put my hook in your nose
and my bit in your mouth,
and I will make you return
by the way you came.'

29"This will be the sign for you, O Hezekiah:

"This year you will eat what grows by
itself,
and the second year what springs from
that.
But in the third year sow and reap,
plant vineyards and eat their fruit.
30 Once more a remnant of the house of
Judah
will take root below and bear fruit
above.
31 For out of Jerusalem will come a remnant,
and out of Mount Zion a band of
survivors.

The zeal of the LORD Almighty will accomplish this.

32"Therefore this is what the LORD says
concerning the king of Assyria:

"He will not enter this city
or shoot an arrow here.
He will not come before it with shield
or build a siege ramp against it.
33 By the way that he came he will return;
he will not enter this city,
declares the LORD.
34 I will defend this city and save it,
for my sake and for the sake of David
my servant."

35That night the angel of the LORD went out
and put to death a hundred and eighty-five
thousand men in the Assyrian camp. When
the people got up the next morning—there
were all the dead bodies! 36So Sennacherib
king of Assyria broke camp and withdrew. He
returned to Nineveh and stayed there.
37One day, while he was worshiping in the
temple of his god Nisroch, his sons Adrammelech and Sharezer cut him down with the
sword, and they escaped to the land of Ararat. And Esarhaddon his son succeeded him
as king.

Hezekiah's Illness

20 In those days Hezekiah became ill and
was at the point of death. The prophet Isaiah son of Amoz went to him and
said, "This is what the LORD says: Put your
house in order, because you are going to die;
you will not recover."
2Hezekiah turned his face to the wall and
prayed to the LORD, 3"Remember, O LORD,
how I have walked before you faithfully and
with wholehearted devotion and have done

MONDAY
READ
2 KINGS 20:1–11; 21:1–15

WHEN TIME RUNS OUT

> **"Put your house in order, because you are going to die; you will not recover."**
>
> — 2 Kings 20:1

let's talk

- If we only had 15 years left with each other, how would we spend the time? What would be most important? Least important?
- Are we putting off doing something until a better time? What's preventing us from doing it now? What might be the consequences of putting it off?
- What lessons are we teaching others by the way we live?

If you knew you had 15 years to live, how would you spend your remaining time on Earth? Watching TV? Eating more ice cream? Spending more time with each other? Buying more stuff? Having a child?

King Hezekiah did the equivalent of all that. When he was told that he was about to die but then had that sentence amended to include 15 more years of life, he took his medicine, got out of bed and went back to work. He continued amassing storehouses of treasure. He was so happy with what he accumulated that he led tours through his massive collection to show off all his gold, silver, spices, fine oil and weapons.

And he had a son, Manasseh.

If Hezekiah had not lived those extra 15 years, the course of Israel's history would have been different. If he hadn't shown off everything he owned to the Babylonian messengers, for example, the Babylonians might not have returned later to empty those storehouses and carry off everything to their country.

As for his son, Manasseh, well, the boy became king when he was 12 years old and ruled for 55 years. During that time he undid all the good his father had done. He rebuilt the shrines on high places that Hezekiah had destroyed. He put up new altars to Baal and made an Asherah pole. He worshiped the sun, moon and stars and built an altar to them in the temple of the Lord. He even sacrificed his son to a false god. In short, he did such evil in the eyes of the Lord that God decided to wipe out Jerusalem and Judah and send the people into captivity.

The sins of our children aren't always a direct result of our parenting, but often they are. It's a pretty sure guess that Hezekiah didn't wisely use the time with his son during the final 15 years of his life. Time is easily squandered, yet it's impossible to get it back. Time is especially precious when children are involved, and it's sobering to know that they learn the value of time and of life by our example.

The Five for Fighting song "100 Years" reminds us of how fast our days go by. King Hezekiah could have meditated on these lyrics to gain perspective as he squandered his remaining years. The song describes how quickly our years pass: first the singer is just 15 years old with his whole life before him, but as the song progresses, he's 33 then 45 then 67. Finally, "67 is gone, the sun is getting high, we're moving on." Then the singer is 99 "for a moment." Hezekiah didn't realize how quickly his time would go. He wasted his brief time on Earth, and his son paid the price.

Unlike Hezekiah, we don't know how many days or years we have left together as husband and wife. We could live to celebrate our silver or gold anniversary. Or we could be separated in a few years by disease, disaster, divorce or death. Because we don't know how many days or years we have, we would do well to put our house in order and ask God to "teach us to number our days aright, that we may gain a heart of wisdom" (Psalm 90:12).

—NANCY KENNEDY

FOR YOUR NEXT DEVOTIONAL READING, TURN TO PAGE 428.

what is good in your eyes." And Hezekiah
wept bitterly.
4Before Isaiah had left the middle court, the
word of the LORD came to him: 5"Go back and
tell Hezekiah, the leader of my people, 'This is
what the LORD, the God of your father David,
says: I have heard your prayer and seen your
tears; I will heal you. On the third day from
now you will go up to the temple of the LORD.
6I will add fifteen years to your life. And I will
deliver you and this city from the hand of the
king of Assyria. I will defend this city for my
sake and for the sake of my servant David.' "
7Then Isaiah said, "Prepare a poultice of
figs." They did so and applied it to the boil,
and he recovered.
8Hezekiah had asked Isaiah, "What will be
the sign that the LORD will heal me and that
I will go up to the temple of the LORD on the
third day from now?"
9Isaiah answered, "This is the LORD's sign to
you that the LORD will do what he has promised: Shall the shadow go forward ten steps, or
shall it go back ten steps?"
10"It is a simple matter for the shadow to
go forward ten steps," said Hezekiah. "Rather,
have it go back ten steps."
11Then the prophet Isaiah called upon the
LORD, and the LORD made the shadow go
back the ten steps it had gone down on the
stairway of Ahaz.

Envoys From Babylon

12At that time Merodach-Baladan son of
Baladan king of Babylon sent Hezekiah letters
and a gift, because he had heard of Hezekiah's
illness. 13Hezekiah received the messengers
and showed them all that was in his storehouses—the silver, the gold, the spices and the fine
oil—his armory and everything found among
his treasures. There was nothing in his palace
or in all his kingdom that Hezekiah did not
show them.
14Then Isaiah the prophet went to King
Hezekiah and asked, "What did those men
say, and where did they come from?"
"From a distant land," Hezekiah replied.
"They came from Babylon."
15The prophet asked, "What did they see in
your palace?"
"They saw everything in my palace," Hezekiah said. "There is nothing among my treasures that I did not show them."
16Then Isaiah said to Hezekiah, "Hear the
word of the LORD: 17The time will surely come
when everything in your palace, and all that
your fathers have stored up until this day, will
be carried off to Babylon. Nothing will be left,
says the LORD. 18And some of your descendants, your own flesh and blood, that will be
born to you, will be taken away, and they will
become eunuchs in the palace of the king of
Babylon."
19"The word of the LORD you have spoken
is good," Hezekiah replied. For he thought,
"Will there not be peace and security in my
lifetime?"
20As for the other events of Hezekiah's
reign, all his achievements and how he made
the pool and the tunnel by which he brought
water into the city, are they not written in
the book of the annals of the kings of Judah?
21Hezekiah rested with his fathers. And Manasseh his son succeeded him as king.

Manasseh King of Judah

21 Manasseh was twelve years old when he
became king, and he reigned in Jerusalem fifty-five years. His mother's name
was Hephzibah. 2He did evil in the eyes of the
LORD, following the detestable practices of the
nations the LORD had driven out before the
Israelites. 3He rebuilt the high places his father Hezekiah had destroyed; he also erected
altars to Baal and made an Asherah pole, as
Ahab king of Israel had done. He bowed down
to all the starry hosts and worshiped them.
4He built altars in the temple of the LORD, of
which the LORD had said, "In Jerusalem I will
put my Name." 5In both courts of the temple
of the LORD, he built altars to all the starry
hosts. 6He sacrificed his own son in[a] the fire,
practiced sorcery and divination, and consulted mediums and spiritists. He did much evil in
the eyes of the LORD, provoking him to anger.
7He took the carved Asherah pole he had
made and put it in the temple, of which the
LORD had said to David and to his son Solomon, "In this temple and in Jerusalem, which
I have chosen out of all the tribes of Israel, I
will put my Name forever. 8I will not again
make the feet of the Israelites wander from
the land I gave their forefathers, if only they
will be careful to do everything I commanded
them and will keep the whole Law that my
servant Moses gave them." 9But the people did
not listen. Manasseh led them astray, so that
they did more evil than the nations the LORD
had destroyed before the Israelites.
10The LORD said through his servants the

[a] 6 Or *He made his own son pass through*

prophets: 11“Manasseh king of Judah has committed these detestable sins. He has done more evil than the Amorites who preceded him and has led Judah into sin with his idols. 12Therefore this is what the LORD, the God of Israel, says: I am going to bring such disaster on Jerusalem and Judah that the ears of everyone who hears of it will tingle. 13I will stretch out over Jerusalem the measuring line used against Samaria and the plumb line used against the house of Ahab. I will wipe out Jerusalem as one wipes a dish, wiping it and turning it upside down. 14I will forsake the remnant of my inheritance and hand them over to their enemies. They will be looted and plundered by all their foes, 15because they have done evil in my eyes and have provoked me to anger from the day their forefathers came out of Egypt until this day.”

16Moreover, Manasseh also shed so much innocent blood that he filled Jerusalem from end to end—besides the sin that he had caused Judah to commit, so that they did evil in the eyes of the LORD.

17As for the other events of Manasseh’s reign, and all he did, including the sin he committed, are they not written in the book of the annals of the kings of Judah? 18Manasseh rested with his fathers and was buried in his palace garden, the garden of Uzza. And Amon his son succeeded him as king.

Amon King of Judah

19Amon was twenty-two years old when he became king, and he reigned in Jerusalem two years. His mother’s name was Meshullemeth daughter of Haruz; she was from Jotbah. 20He did evil in the eyes of the LORD, as his father Manasseh had done. 21He walked in all the ways of his father; he worshiped the idols his father had worshiped, and bowed down to them. 22He forsook the LORD, the God of his fathers, and did not walk in the way of the LORD.

23Amon’s officials conspired against him and assassinated the king in his palace. 24Then the people of the land killed all who had plotted against King Amon, and they made Josiah his son king in his place.

25As for the other events of Amon’s reign, and what he did, are they not written in the book of the annals of the kings of Judah? 26He was buried in his grave in the garden of Uzza. And Josiah his son succeeded him as king.

The Book of the Law Found

22 Josiah was eight years old when he became king, and he reigned in Jerusalem thirty-one years. His mother’s name was Jedidah daughter of Adaiah; she was from Bozkath. 2He did what was right in the eyes of the LORD and walked in all the ways of his father David, not turning aside to the right or to the left.

3In the eighteenth year of his reign, King Josiah sent the secretary, Shaphan son of Azaliah, the son of Meshullam, to the temple of the LORD. He said: 4“Go up to Hilkiah the high priest and have him get ready the money that has been brought into the temple of the LORD, which the doorkeepers have collected from the people. 5Have them entrust it to the men appointed to supervise the work on the temple. And have these men pay the workers who repair the temple of the LORD— 6the carpenters, the builders and the masons. Also have them purchase timber and dressed stone to repair the temple. 7But they need not account for the money entrusted to them, because they are acting faithfully.”

8Hilkiah the high priest said to Shaphan the secretary, “I have found the Book of the Law in the temple of the LORD.” He gave it to Shaphan, who read it. 9Then Shaphan the secretary went to the king and reported to him: “Your officials have paid out the money that was in the temple of the LORD and have entrusted it to the workers and supervisors at the temple.” 10Then Shaphan the secretary informed the king, “Hilkiah the priest has given me a book.” And Shaphan read from it in the presence of the king.

11When the king heard the words of the Book of the Law, he tore his robes. 12He gave these orders to Hilkiah the priest, Ahikam son of Shaphan, Acbor son of Micaiah, Shaphan the secretary and Asaiah the king’s attendant: 13“Go and inquire of the LORD for me and for the people and for all Judah about what is written in this book that has been found. Great is the LORD’s anger that burns against us because our fathers have not obeyed the words of this book; they have not acted in accordance with all that is written there concerning us.”

14Hilkiah the priest, Ahikam, Acbor, Shaphan and Asaiah went to speak to the prophetess Huldah, who was the wife of Shallum son of Tikvah, the son of Harhas, keeper of the wardrobe. She lived in Jerusalem, in the Second District.

15She said to them, “This is what the LORD, the God of Israel, says: Tell the man who sent you to me, 16‘This is what the LORD says: I am going to bring disaster on this place and its people, according to everything written in the book the king of Judah has read. 17Because

they have forsaken me and burned incense to
other gods and provoked me to anger by all
the idols their hands have made,[a] my anger
will burn against this place and will not be
quenched.' 18Tell the king of Judah, who sent
you to inquire of the LORD, 'This is what the
LORD, the God of Israel, says concerning the
words you heard: 19Because your heart was
responsive and you humbled yourself before
the LORD when you heard what I have spoken against this place and its people, that they
would become accursed and laid waste, and
because you tore your robes and wept in my
presence, I have heard you, declares the LORD.
20Therefore I will gather you to your fathers,
and you will be buried in peace. Your eyes will
not see all the disaster I am going to bring on
this place.' "

So they took her answer back to the king.

Josiah Renews the Covenant

23 Then the king called together all the elders of Judah and Jerusalem. 2He went
up to the temple of the LORD with
the men of Judah, the people of Jerusalem,
the priests and the prophets—all the people
from the least to the greatest. He read in their
hearing all the words of the Book of the Covenant, which had been found in the temple
of the LORD. 3The king stood by the pillar
and renewed the covenant in the presence of
the LORD—to follow the LORD and keep his
commands, regulations and decrees with all
his heart and all his soul, thus confirming the
words of the covenant written in this book.
Then all the people pledged themselves to the
covenant.

4The king ordered Hilkiah the high priest,
the priests next in rank and the doorkeepers
to remove from the temple of the LORD all
the articles made for Baal and Asherah and all
the starry hosts. He burned them outside Jerusalem in the fields of the Kidron Valley and
took the ashes to Bethel. 5He did away with
the pagan priests appointed by the kings of
Judah to burn incense on the high places of
the towns of Judah and on those around Jerusalem—those who burned incense to Baal, to
the sun and moon, to the constellations and to
all the starry hosts. 6He took the Asherah pole
from the temple of the LORD to the Kidron
Valley outside Jerusalem and burned it there.
He ground it to powder and scattered the
dust over the graves of the common people.
7He also tore down the quarters of the male
shrine prostitutes, which were in the temple
of the LORD and where women did weaving
for Asherah.

8Josiah brought all the priests from the
towns of Judah and desecrated the high places,
from Geba to Beersheba, where the priests had
burned incense. He broke down the shrines[b]
at the gates—at the entrance to the Gate of
Joshua, the city governor, which is on the left
of the city gate. 9Although the priests of the
high places did not serve at the altar of the
LORD in Jerusalem, they ate unleavened bread
with their fellow priests.

10He desecrated Topheth, which was in the
Valley of Ben Hinnom, so no one could use
it to sacrifice his son or daughter in[c] the fire
to Molech. 11He removed from the entrance
to the temple of the LORD the horses that the
kings of Judah had dedicated to the sun. They
were in the court near the room of an official
named Nathan-Melech. Josiah then burned
the chariots dedicated to the sun.

12He pulled down the altars the kings of Judah had erected on the roof near the upper
room of Ahaz, and the altars Manasseh had
built in the two courts of the temple of the
LORD. He removed them from there, smashed
them to pieces and threw the rubble into the
Kidron Valley. 13The king also desecrated the
high places that were east of Jerusalem on the
south of the Hill of Corruption—the ones
Solomon king of Israel had built for Ashtoreth
the vile goddess of the Sidonians, for Chemosh the vile god of Moab, and for Molech[d]
the detestable god of the people of Ammon.
14Josiah smashed the sacred stones and cut
down the Asherah poles and covered the sites
with human bones.

15Even the altar at Bethel, the high place
made by Jeroboam son of Nebat, who had
caused Israel to sin—even that altar and high
place he demolished. He burned the high
place and ground it to powder, and burned
the Asherah pole also. 16Then Josiah looked
around, and when he saw the tombs that
were there on the hillside, he had the bones
removed from them and burned on the altar
to defile it, in accordance with the word of
the LORD proclaimed by the man of God who
foretold these things.

17The king asked, "What is that tombstone
I see?"

The men of the city said, "It marks the
tomb of the man of God who came from Ju-

[a] 17 Or *by everything they have done* [b] 8 Or *high places* [c] 10 Or *to make his son or daughter pass through* [d] 13 Hebrew *Milcom*

dah and pronounced against the altar of Bethel the very things you have done to it."
18"Leave it alone," he said. "Don't let anyone disturb his bones." So they spared his
bones and those of the prophet who had come
from Samaria.
19Just as he had done at Bethel, Josiah removed and defiled all the shrines at the high
places that the kings of Israel had built in the
towns of Samaria that had provoked the LORD
to anger. 20Josiah slaughtered all the priests of
those high places on the altars and burned human bones on them. Then he went back to
Jerusalem.
21The king gave this order to all the people: "Celebrate the Passover to the LORD your
God, as it is written in this Book of the Covenant." 22Not since the days of the judges
who led Israel, nor throughout the days of
the kings of Israel and the kings of Judah,
had any such Passover been observed. 23But
in the eighteenth year of King Josiah, this
Passover was celebrated to the LORD in Jerusalem.
24Furthermore, Josiah got rid of the mediums and spiritists, the household gods, the
idols and all the other detestable things seen in
Judah and Jerusalem. This he did to fulfill the
requirements of the law written in the book
that Hilkiah the priest had discovered in the
temple of the LORD. 25Neither before nor after
Josiah was there a king like him who turned
to the LORD as he did—with all his heart and
with all his soul and with all his strength, in
accordance with all the Law of Moses.
26Nevertheless, the LORD did not turn away
from the heat of his fierce anger, which burned
against Judah because of all that Manasseh had
done to provoke him to anger. 27So the LORD
said, "I will remove Judah also from my presence as I removed Israel, and I will reject Jerusalem, the city I chose, and this temple, about
which I said, 'There shall my Name be.'[a]"
28As for the other events of Josiah's reign,
and all he did, are they not written in the book
of the annals of the kings of Judah?
29While Josiah was king, Pharaoh Neco
king of Egypt went up to the Euphrates River to help the king of Assyria. King Josiah
marched out to meet him in battle, but Neco
faced him and killed him at Megiddo. 30Jo-
siah's servants brought his body in a chariot
from Megiddo to Jerusalem and buried him
in his own tomb. And the people of the land
took Jehoahaz son of Josiah and anointed him
and made him king in place of his father.

Jehoahaz King of Judah

31Jehoahaz was twenty-three years old when
he became king, and he reigned in Jerusalem
three months. His mother's name was Hamutal daughter of Jeremiah; she was from Libnah.
32He did evil in the eyes of the LORD, just as
his fathers had done. 33Pharaoh Neco put him
in chains at Riblah in the land of Hamath[b] so
that he might not reign in Jerusalem, and he
imposed on Judah a levy of a hundred talents[c]
of silver and a talent[d] of gold. 34Pharaoh Neco
made Eliakim son of Josiah king in place of his
father Josiah and changed Eliakim's name to
Jehoiakim. But he took Jehoahaz and carried
him off to Egypt, and there he died. 35Jehoi-
akim paid Pharaoh Neco the silver and gold
he demanded. In order to do so, he taxed the
land and exacted the silver and gold from the
people of the land according to their assessments.

Jehoiakim King of Judah

36Jehoiakim was twenty-five years old when
he became king, and he reigned in Jerusalem
eleven years. His mother's name was Zebidah
daughter of Pedaiah; she was from Rumah.
37And he did evil in the eyes of the LORD, just
as his fathers had done.

24 During Jehoiakim's reign, Nebuchadnezzar king of Babylon invaded the
land, and Jehoiakim became his vassal
for three years. But then he changed his mind
and rebelled against Nebuchadnezzar. 2The
LORD sent Babylonian,[e] Aramean, Moabite
and Ammonite raiders against him. He sent
them to destroy Judah, in accordance with the
word of the LORD proclaimed by his servants
the prophets. 3Surely these things happened
to Judah according to the LORD's command,
in order to remove them from his presence because of the sins of Manasseh and all he had
done, 4including the shedding of innocent
blood. For he had filled Jerusalem with innocent blood, and the LORD was not willing to
forgive.
5As for the other events of Jehoiakim's
reign, and all he did, are they not written in
the book of the annals of the kings of Judah?
6Jehoiakim rested with his fathers. And Jehoiachin his son succeeded him as king.
7The king of Egypt did not march out from
his own country again, because the king of

---

[a] 27 1 Kings 8:29 [b] 33 Hebrew; Septuagint (see also 2 Chron. 36:3) *Neco at Riblah in Hamath removed him* [c] 33 That is, about 3 3/4 tons (about 3.4 metric tons) [d] 33 That is, about 75 pounds (about 34 kilograms) [e] 2 Or *Chaldean*

Babylon had taken all his territory, from the
Wadi of Egypt to the Euphrates River.

Jehoiachin King of Judah

8 Jehoiachin was eighteen years old when
he became king, and he reigned in Jerusalem
three months. His mother's name was Ne-
hushta daughter of Elnathan; she was from Jerusalem. 9 He did evil in the eyes of the LORD,
just as his father had done.

10 At that time the officers of Nebuchadnezzar king of Babylon advanced on Jerusalem
and laid siege to it, 11 and Nebuchadnezzar
himself came up to the city while his officers
were besieging it. 12 Jehoiachin king of Judah,
his mother, his attendants, his nobles and his
officials all surrendered to him.

In the eighth year of the reign of the king
of Babylon, he took Jehoiachin prisoner.
13 As the LORD had declared, Nebuchadnezzar removed all the treasures from the temple
of the LORD and from the royal palace, and
took away all the gold articles that Solomon
king of Israel had made for the temple of the
LORD. 14 He carried into exile all Jerusalem:
all the officers and fighting men, and all the
craftsmen and artisans—a total of ten thousand. Only the poorest people of the land
were left.

15 Nebuchadnezzar took Jehoiachin captive
to Babylon. He also took from Jerusalem to
Babylon the king's mother, his wives, his officials and the leading men of the land. 16 The
king of Babylon also deported to Babylon
the entire force of seven thousand fighting
men, strong and fit for war, and a thousand
craftsmen and artisans. 17 He made Mattaniah, Jehoiachin's uncle, king in his place and
changed his name to Zedekiah.

Zedekiah King of Judah

18 Zedekiah was twenty-one years old when
he became king, and he reigned in Jerusalem
eleven years. His mother's name was Hamutal
daughter of Jeremiah; she was from Libnah.
19 He did evil in the eyes of the LORD, just as
Jehoiakim had done. 20 It was because of the
LORD's anger that all this happened to Jerusalem and Judah, and in the end he thrust them
from his presence.

The Fall of Jerusalem

Now Zedekiah rebelled against the king of
Babylon.

25 So in the ninth year of Zedekiah's
reign, on the tenth day of the tenth
month, Nebuchadnezzar king of Babylon marched against Jerusalem with his
whole army. He encamped outside the city
and built siege works all around it. 2 The city
was kept under siege until the eleventh year
of King Zedekiah. 3 By the ninth day of the
⌞fourth⌟[a] month the famine in the city had
become so severe that there was no food for
the people to eat. 4 Then the city wall was
broken through, and the whole army fled at
night through the gate between the two walls
near the king's garden, though the Babylonians[b] were surrounding the city. They fled
toward the Arabah,[c] 5 but the Babylonian[d]
army pursued the king and overtook him
in the plains of Jericho. All his soldiers were
separated from him and scattered, 6 and he
was captured. He was taken to the king of
Babylon at Riblah, where sentence was pronounced on him. 7 They killed the sons of
Zedekiah before his eyes. Then they put out
his eyes, bound him with bronze shackles and
took him to Babylon.

8 On the seventh day of the fifth month, in
the nineteenth year of Nebuchadnezzar king
of Babylon, Nebuzaradan commander of the
imperial guard, an official of the king of Babylon, came to Jerusalem. 9 He set fire to the
temple of the LORD, the royal palace and all
the houses of Jerusalem. Every important
building he burned down. 10 The whole Babylonian army, under the commander of the
imperial guard, broke down the walls around
Jerusalem. 11 Nebuzaradan the commander of
the guard carried into exile the people who remained in the city, along with the rest of the
populace and those who had gone over to the
king of Babylon. 12 But the commander left
behind some of the poorest people of the land
to work the vineyards and fields.

13 The Babylonians broke up the bronze pillars, the movable stands and the bronze Sea
that were at the temple of the LORD and they
carried the bronze to Babylon. 14 They also
took away the pots, shovels, wick trimmers,
dishes and all the bronze articles used in the
temple service. 15 The commander of the imperial guard took away the censers and sprinkling bowls—all that were made of pure gold
or silver.

16 The bronze from the two pillars, the Sea
and the movable stands, which Solomon had
made for the temple of the LORD, was more

---

[a] 3 See Jer. 52:6. [b] 4 Or *Chaldeans*; also in verses 13, 25 and 26 [c] 4 Or *the Jordan Valley* [d] 5 Or *Chaldean*; also in verses 10 and 24

than could be weighed. [17]Each pillar was twenty-seven feet[a] high. The bronze capital on top of one pillar was four and a half feet[b] high and was decorated with a network and pomegranates of bronze all around. The other pillar, with its network, was similar.

[18]The commander of the guard took as prisoners Seraiah the chief priest, Zephaniah the priest next in rank and the three doorkeepers. [19]Of those still in the city, he took the officer in charge of the fighting men and five royal advisers. He also took the secretary who was chief officer in charge of conscripting the people of the land and sixty of his men who were found in the city. [20]Nebuzaradan the commander took them all and brought them to the king of Babylon at Riblah. [21]There at Riblah, in the land of Hamath, the king had them executed.

So Judah went into captivity, away from her land.

[22]Nebuchadnezzar king of Babylon appointed Gedaliah son of Ahikam, the son of Shaphan, to be over the people he had left behind in Judah. [23]When all the army officers and their men heard that the king of Babylon had appointed Gedaliah as governor, they came to Gedaliah at Mizpah—Ishmael son of Nethaniah, Johanan son of Kareah, Seraiah son of Tanhumeth the Netophathite, Jaazaniah the son of the Maacathite, and their men. [24]Gedaliah took an oath to reassure them and their men. "Do not be afraid of the Babylonian officials," he said. "Settle down in the land and serve the king of Babylon, and it will go well with you."

[25]In the seventh month, however, Ishmael son of Nethaniah, the son of Elishama, who was of royal blood, came with ten men and assassinated Gedaliah and also the men of Judah and the Babylonians who were with him at Mizpah. [26]At this, all the people from the least to the greatest, together with the army officers, fled to Egypt for fear of the Babylonians.

Jehoiachin Released

[27]In the thirty-seventh year of the exile of Jehoiachin king of Judah, in the year Evil-Merodach[c] became king of Babylon, he released Jehoiachin from prison on the twenty-seventh day of the twelfth month. [28]He spoke kindly to him and gave him a seat of honor higher than those of the other kings who were with him in Babylon. [29]So Jehoiachin put aside his prison clothes and for the rest of his life ate regularly at the king's table. [30]Day by day the king gave Jehoiachin a regular allowance as long as he lived.

[a] 17 Hebrew *eighteen cubits* (about 8.1 meters) [b] 17 Hebrew *three cubits* (about 1.3 meters) [c] 27 Also called *Amel-Marduk*

1 CHRONICLES

1 Chronicles

QUICK FACTS

AUTHOR Unknown, but possibly Ezra

AUDIENCE All Israel

DATE Likely between 450 and 400 B.C.

SETTING The book begins with Israel's genealogical records and then focuses on King David's reign, paralleling many of the events recorded in 2 Samuel.

Chronicles appears to review the history already covered in Samuel and Kings. (Each of these three accounts was originally one book before being divided into two volumes.) However, they have different emphases.

First, the books were written for different audiences. Samuel was written hundreds of years before Kings. And Kings was written about a hundred years before Chronicles to the people in exile who wondered how and why they had ended up in Babylon. Chronicles was intended for those who had returned from exile and wondered if and how they were connected with the Israel of the past. Furthermore, Samuel and Kings emphasize the political, prophetic and moral aspects of Israel's history, while Chronicles is more like a sermon series on the spiritual aspects of those events.

First Chronicles stresses Israel's genealogy, showing how God worked through both Israel's ancestors and the returning exiles. It also shows the primacy of worship through David's extensive preparations for building the temple: restoring the ark to Jerusalem; collecting building materials; organizing priests, Levites and other workers; drawing up detailed plans; and doing preliminary fundraising.

Planning for a wedding or a new house or a child are some of the more complicated tasks we take on as couples. But as Chronicles reminds us, God desires that we place him at the heart of all our plans.

Historical Records From Adam to Abraham

To Noah's Sons

1 Adam, Seth, Enosh, 2 Kenan, Mahalalel, Jared, 3 Enoch, Methuselah, Lamech, Noah.

4 The sons of Noah:[a]
Shem, Ham and Japheth.

The Japhethites

5 The sons[b] of Japheth:
Gomer, Magog, Madai, Javan, Tubal,
Meshech and Tiras.
6 The sons of Gomer:
Ashkenaz, Riphath[c] and Togarmah.
7 The sons of Javan:
Elishah, Tarshish, the Kittim and the
Rodanim.

The Hamites

8 The sons of Ham:
Cush, Mizraim,[d] Put and Canaan.
9 The sons of Cush:
Seba, Havilah, Sabta, Raamah and
Sabteca.
The sons of Raamah:
Sheba and Dedan.
10 Cush was the father[e] of
Nimrod, who grew to be a mighty
warrior on earth.
11 Mizraim was the father of
the Ludites, Anamites, Lehabites,
Naphtuhites, 12 Pathrusites, Casluhites
(from whom the Philistines came) and
Caphtorites.
13 Canaan was the father of
Sidon his firstborn,[f] and of the Hittites, 14 Jebusites, Amorites, Girgashites, 15 Hivites, Arkites, Sinites, 16 Ar-
vadites, Zemarites and Hamathites.

The Semites

17 The sons of Shem:
Elam, Asshur, Arphaxad, Lud and
Aram.
The sons of Aram:[g]
Uz, Hul, Gether and Meshech.
18 Arphaxad was the father of Shelah,
and Shelah the father of Eber.
19 Two sons were born to Eber:
One was named Peleg,[h] because in his
time the earth was divided; his brother
was named Joktan.
20 Joktan was the father of
Almodad, Sheleph, Hazarmaveth, Je-
rah, 21 Hadoram, Uzal, Diklah, 22 Obal,[i]
Abimael, Sheba, 23 Ophir, Havilah and
Jobab. All these were sons of Joktan.

24 Shem, Arphaxad,[j] Shelah,
25 Eber, Peleg, Reu,
26 Serug, Nahor, Terah
27 and Abram (that is, Abraham).

The Family of Abraham

28 The sons of Abraham:
Isaac and Ishmael.

Descendants of Hagar

29 These were their descendants:
Nebaioth the firstborn of Ishmael,
Kedar, Adbeel, Mibsam, 30 Mishma,
Dumah, Massa, Hadad, Tema, 31 Jetur,
Naphish and Kedemah. These were
the sons of Ishmael.

Descendants of Keturah

32 The sons born to Keturah, Abraham's
concubine:
Zimran, Jokshan, Medan, Midian,
Ishbak and Shuah.
The sons of Jokshan:
Sheba and Dedan.
33 The sons of Midian:
Ephah, Epher, Hanoch, Abida and El-
daah.
All these were descendants of Keturah.

Descendants of Sarah

34 Abraham was the father of Isaac.
The sons of Isaac:
Esau and Israel.

Esau's Sons

35 The sons of Esau:
Eliphaz, Reuel, Jeush, Jalam and Korah.
36 The sons of Eliphaz:
Teman, Omar, Zepho,[k] Gatam and
Kenaz;
by Timna: Amalek.[l]

---

[a] *4* Septuagint; Hebrew does not have this line. [b] *5* *Sons* may mean *descendants* or *successors* or *nations;* also in verses 6-10, 17 and 20. [c] *6* Many Hebrew manuscripts and Vulgate (see also Septuagint and Gen. 10:3); most Hebrew manuscripts *Diphath* [d] *8* That is, Egypt; also in verse 11 [e] *10* *Father* may mean *ancestor* or *predecessor* or *founder;* also in verses 11, 13, 18 and 20. [f] *13* Or *of the Sidonians, the foremost* [g] *17* One Hebrew manuscript and some Septuagint manuscripts (see also Gen. 10:23); most Hebrew manuscripts do not have this line. [h] *19* *Peleg* means *division.* [i] *22* Some Hebrew manuscripts and Syriac (see also Gen. 10:28); most Hebrew manuscripts *Ebal* [j] *24* Hebrew; some Septuagint manuscripts *Arphaxad, Cainan* (see also note at Gen. 11:10) [k] *36* Many Hebrew manuscripts, some Septuagint manuscripts and Syriac (see also Gen. 36:11); most Hebrew manuscripts *Zephi* [l] *36* Some Septuagint manuscripts (see also Gen. 36:12); Hebrew *Gatam, Kenaz, Timna and Amalek*

37 The sons of Reuel:
Nahath, Zerah, Shammah and Mizzah.

The People of Seir in Edom

38 The sons of Seir:
Lotan, Shobal, Zibeon, Anah, Dishon, Ezer and Dishan.
39 The sons of Lotan:
Hori and Homam. Timna was Lotan's sister.
40 The sons of Shobal:
Alvan,[a] Manahath, Ebal, Shepho and Onam.
The sons of Zibeon:
Aiah and Anah.
41 The son of Anah:
Dishon.
The sons of Dishon:
Hemdan,[b] Eshban, Ithran and Keran.
42 The sons of Ezer:
Bilhan, Zaavan and Akan.[c]
The sons of Dishan[d]:
Uz and Aran.

The Rulers of Edom

43 These were the kings who reigned in Edom before any Israelite king reigned[e]:
Bela son of Beor, whose city was named Dinhabah.
44 When Bela died, Jobab son of Zerah from Bozrah succeeded him as king.
45 When Jobab died, Husham from the land of the Temanites succeeded him as king.
46 When Husham died, Hadad son of Bedad, who defeated Midian in the country of Moab, succeeded him as king. His city was named Avith.
47 When Hadad died, Samlah from Masrekah succeeded him as king.
48 When Samlah died, Shaul from Rehoboth on the river[f] succeeded him as king.
49 When Shaul died, Baal-Hanan son of Acbor succeeded him as king.
50 When Baal-Hanan died, Hadad succeeded him as king. His city was named Pau,[g] and his wife's name was Mehetabel daughter of Matred, the daughter of Me-Zahab.
51 Hadad also died.
The chiefs of Edom were:
Timna, Alvah, Jetheth,
52 Oholibamah, Elah, Pinon,
53 Kenaz, Teman, Mibzar,
54 Magdiel and Iram. These were the chiefs of Edom.

Israel's Sons

2 These were the sons of Israel:
Reuben, Simeon, Levi, Judah, Issachar, Zebulun,
2 Dan, Joseph, Benjamin, Naphtali, Gad and Asher.

Judah

To Hezron's Sons

3 The sons of Judah:
Er, Onan and Shelah. These three were born to him by a Canaanite woman, the daughter of Shua. Er, Judah's firstborn, was wicked in the LORD's sight; so the LORD put him to death.
4 Tamar, Judah's daughter-in-law, bore him Perez and Zerah. Judah had five sons in all.

5 The sons of Perez:
Hezron and Hamul.
6 The sons of Zerah:
Zimri, Ethan, Heman, Calcol and Darda[h]—five in all.
7 The son of Carmi:
Achar,[i] who brought trouble on Israel by violating the ban on taking devoted things.[j]
8 The son of Ethan:
Azariah.
9 The sons born to Hezron were:
Jerahmeel, Ram and Caleb.[k]

From Ram Son of Hezron

10 Ram was the father of
Amminadab, and Amminadab the father of Nahshon, the leader of the people of Judah.
11 Nahshon was the father of Salmon,[l] Salmon the father of Boaz,
12 Boaz the father of Obed and Obed the father of Jesse.
13 Jesse was the father of

---

[a] *40* Many Hebrew manuscripts and some Septuagint manuscripts (see also Gen. 36:23); most Hebrew manuscripts *Alian* [b] *41* Many Hebrew manuscripts and some Septuagint manuscripts (see also Gen. 36:26); most Hebrew manuscripts *Hamran* [c] *42* Many Hebrew and Septuagint manuscripts (see also Gen. 36:27); most Hebrew manuscripts *Zaavan, Jaakan* [d] *42* Hebrew *Dishon,* a variant of *Dishan* [e] *43* Or *before an Israelite king reigned over them* [f] *48* Possibly the Euphrates [g] *50* Many Hebrew manuscripts, some Septuagint manuscripts, Vulgate and Syriac (see also Gen. 36:39); most Hebrew manuscripts *Pai* [h] *6* Many Hebrew manuscripts, some Septuagint manuscripts and Syriac (see also 1 Kings 4:31); most Hebrew manuscripts *Dara* [i] *7* *Achar* means *trouble*; *Achar* is called *Achan* in Joshua. [j] *7* The Hebrew term refers to the irrevocable giving over of things or persons to the LORD, often by totally destroying them. [k] *9* Hebrew *Kelubai,* a variant of *Caleb* [l] *11* Septuagint (see also Ruth 4:21); Hebrew *Salma*

Eliab his firstborn; the second son
was Abinadab, the third Shimea,
14 the fourth Nethanel, the fifth Rad-
dai, 15 the sixth Ozem and the seventh
David. 16 Their sisters were Zeruiah
and Abigail. Zeruiah's three sons were
Abishai, Joab and Asahel. 17 Abigail
was the mother of Amasa, whose father was Jether the Ishmaelite.

Caleb Son of Hezron

18 Caleb son of Hezron had children by his
wife Azubah (and by Jerioth). These
were her sons: Jesher, Shobab and
Ardon. 19 When Azubah died, Caleb
married Ephrath, who bore him Hur.
20 Hur was the father of Uri, and Uri
the father of Bezalel.

21 Later, Hezron lay with the daughter of
Makir the father of Gilead (he had
married her when he was sixty years
old), and she bore him Segub. 22 Segub
was the father of Jair, who controlled
twenty-three towns in Gilead. 23 (But
Geshur and Aram captured Havvoth
Jair,[a] as well as Kenath with its surrounding settlements—sixty towns.)
All these were descendants of Makir
the father of Gilead.

24 After Hezron died in Caleb Ephrathah,
Abijah the wife of Hezron bore him
Ashhur the father[b] of Tekoa.

Jerahmeel Son of Hezron

25 The sons of Jerahmeel the firstborn of Hezron:
Ram his firstborn, Bunah, Oren,
Ozem and[c] Ahijah. 26 Jerahmeel had
another wife, whose name was Atarah;
she was the mother of Onam.

27 The sons of Ram the firstborn of Jerahmeel:
Maaz, Jamin and Eker.

28 The sons of Onam:
Shammai and Jada.

The sons of Shammai:
Nadab and Abishur.

29 Abishur's wife was named Abihail, who bore him Ahban and Molid.

30 The sons of Nadab:
Seled and Appaim. Seled died without children.

31 The son of Appaim:
Ishi, who was the father of Sheshan.
Sheshan was the father of Ahlai.

32 The sons of Jada, Shammai's brother:
Jether and Jonathan. Jether died without children.

33 The sons of Jonathan:
Peleth and Zaza.

These were the descendants of Jerahmeel.

34 Sheshan had no sons—only daughters.
He had an Egyptian servant named
Jarha. 35 Sheshan gave his daughter in
marriage to his servant Jarha, and she
bore him Attai.

36 Attai was the father of Nathan,
Nathan the father of Zabad,
37 Zabad the father of Ephlal,
Ephlal the father of Obed,
38 Obed the father of Jehu,
Jehu the father of Azariah,
39 Azariah the father of Helez,
Helez the father of Eleasah,
40 Eleasah the father of Sismai,
Sismai the father of Shallum,
41 Shallum the father of Jekamiah,
and Jekamiah the father of Elishama.

The Clans of Caleb

42 The sons of Caleb the brother of Jerahmeel:
Mesha his firstborn, who was the father of Ziph, and his son Mareshah,[d] who was the father of Hebron.

43 The sons of Hebron:
Korah, Tappuah, Rekem and Shema.
44 Shema was the father of Raham, and
Raham the father of Jorkeam. Rekem
was the father of Shammai. 45 The son
of Shammai was Maon, and Maon was
the father of Beth Zur.

46 Caleb's concubine Ephah was the mother of Haran, Moza and Gazez. Haran was the father of Gazez.

47 The sons of Jahdai:
Regem, Jotham, Geshan, Pelet, Ephah and Shaaph.

48 Caleb's concubine Maacah was the mother of Sheber and Tirhanah. 49 She also
gave birth to Shaaph the father of
Madmannah and to Sheva the father of Macbenah and Gibea. Caleb's
daughter was Acsah. 50 These were the
descendants of Caleb.

The sons of Hur the firstborn of Ephrathah:

---

[a] 23 Or *captured the settlements of Jair* [b] 24 *Father* may mean *civic leader* or *military leader*; also in verses 42, 45, 49-52 and possibly elsewhere. [c] 25 Or *Oren and Ozem, by* [d] 42 The meaning of the Hebrew for this phrase is uncertain.

Shobal the father of Kiriath Jearim,
51 Salma the father of Bethlehem, and
Hareph the father of Beth Gader.
52 The descendants of Shobal the father of
Kiriath Jearim were:
Haroeh, half the Manahathites, 53 and
the clans of Kiriath Jearim: the Ithrites,
Puthites, Shumathites and Mishraites.
From these descended the Zorathites
and Eshtaolites.
54 The descendants of Salma:
Bethlehem, the Netophathites, Atroth
Beth Joab, half the Manahathites, the
Zorites, 55 and the clans of scribes[a] who
lived at Jabez: the Tirathites, Shime-
athites and Sucathites. These are the
Kenites who came from Hammath,
the father of the house of Recab.[b]

The Sons of David

3 These were the sons of David born to him
in Hebron:
The firstborn was Amnon the son of
Ahinoam of Jezreel;
the second, Daniel the son of Abigail
of Carmel;
2 the third, Absalom the son of Maacah
daughter of Talmai king of Geshur;
the fourth, Adonijah the son of Haggith;
3 the fifth, Shephatiah the son of Abital;
and the sixth, Ithream, by his wife Eglah.
4 These six were born to David in Hebron, where he reigned seven years and
six months.
David reigned in Jerusalem thirty-three years,
5 and these were the children born to him
there:
Shammua,[c] Shobab, Nathan and Solomon. These four were by Bathsheba[d]
daughter of Ammiel. 6 There were also
Ibhar, Elishua,[e] Eliphelet, 7 Nogah,
Nepheg, Japhia, 8 Elishama, Eliada and
Eliphelet—nine in all. 9 All these were
the sons of David, besides his sons by
his concubines. And Tamar was their
sister.

The Kings of Judah

10 Solomon's son was Rehoboam,
Abijah his son,
Asa his son,
Jehoshaphat his son,
11 Jehoram[f] his son,
Ahaziah his son,
Joash his son,
12 Amaziah his son,
Azariah his son,
Jotham his son,
13 Ahaz his son,
Hezekiah his son,
Manasseh his son,
14 Amon his son,
Josiah his son.
15 The sons of Josiah:
Johanan the firstborn,
Jehoiakim the second son,
Zedekiah the third,
Shallum the fourth.
16 The successors of Jehoiakim:
Jehoiachin[g] his son,
and Zedekiah.

The Royal Line After the Exile

17 The descendants of Jehoiachin the captive:
Shealtiel his son, 18 Malkiram, Pedaiah,
Shenazzar, Jekamiah, Hoshama and
Nedabiah.
19 The sons of Pedaiah:
Zerubbabel and Shimei.
The sons of Zerubbabel:
Meshullam and Hananiah.
Shelomith was their sister.
20 There were also five others:
Hashubah, Ohel, Berekiah, Hasadiah
and Jushab-Hesed.
21 The descendants of Hananiah:
Pelatiah and Jeshaiah, and the sons of
Rephaiah, of Arnan, of Obadiah and
of Shecaniah.
22 The descendants of Shecaniah:
Shemaiah and his sons:
Hattush, Igal, Bariah, Neariah and
Shaphat—six in all.
23 The sons of Neariah:
Elioenai, Hizkiah and Azrikam—three
in all.
24 The sons of Elioenai:
Hodaviah, Eliashib, Pelaiah, Akkub,
Johanan, Delaiah and Anani—seven
in all.

---

[a] 55 Or *of the Sopherites* [b] 55 Or *father of Beth Recab* [c] 5 Hebrew *Shimea,* a variant of *Shammua* [d] 5 One Hebrew manuscript and Vulgate (see also Septuagint and 2 Samuel 11:3); most Hebrew manuscripts *Bathshua* [e] 6 Two Hebrew manuscripts (see also 2 Samuel 5:15 and 1 Chron. 14:5); most Hebrew manuscripts *Elishama* [f] 11 Hebrew *Joram,* a variant of *Jehoram* [g] 16 Hebrew *Jeconiah,* a variant of *Jehoiachin;* also in verse 17

Other Clans of Judah

4 The descendants of Judah:
Perez, Hezron, Carmi, Hur and Shobal.
2 Reaiah son of Shobal was the father of Jahath, and Jahath the father of Ahumai and Lahad. These were the clans of the Zorathites.
3 These were the sons[a] of Etam:
Jezreel, Ishma and Idbash. Their sister was named Hazzelelponi. 4 Penuel was the father of Gedor, and Ezer the father of Hushah.
These were the descendants of Hur, the firstborn of Ephrathah and father[b] of Bethlehem.
5 Ashhur the father of Tekoa had two wives, Helah and Naarah.
6 Naarah bore him Ahuzzam, Hepher, Temeni and Haahashtari. These were the descendants of Naarah.
7 The sons of Helah:
Zereth, Zohar, Ethnan, 8 and Koz, who was the father of Anub and Hazzobebah and of the clans of Aharhel son of Harum.

9 Jabez was more honorable than his brothers. His mother had named him Jabez,[c] saying, "I gave birth to him in pain." 10 Jabez cried out to the God of Israel, "Oh, that you would bless me and enlarge my territory! Let your hand be with me, and keep me from harm so that I will be free from pain." And God granted his request.

11 Kelub, Shuhah's brother, was the father of Mehir, who was the father of Eshton.
12 Eshton was the father of Beth Rapha, Paseah and Tehinnah the father of Ir Nahash.[d] These were the men of Recah.

13 The sons of Kenaz:
Othniel and Seraiah.
The sons of Othniel:
Hathath and Meonothai.[e] 14 Meonothai was the father of Ophrah.
Seraiah was the father of Joab,
the father of Ge Harashim.[f] It was called this because its people were craftsmen.
15 The sons of Caleb son of Jephunneh:
Iru, Elah and Naam.
The son of Elah:
Kenaz.
16 The sons of Jehallelel:
Ziph, Ziphah, Tiria and Asarel.
17 The sons of Ezrah:
Jether, Mered, Epher and Jalon. One of Mered's wives gave birth to Miriam, Shammai and Ishbah the father of Eshtemoa. 18 (His Judean wife gave birth to Jered the father of Gedor, Heber the father of Soco, and Jekuthiel the father of Zanoah.) These were the children of Pharaoh's daughter Bithiah, whom Mered had married.
19 The sons of Hodiah's wife, the sister of Naham:
the father of Keilah the Garmite, and Eshtemoa the Maacathite.
20 The sons of Shimon:
Amnon, Rinnah, Ben-Hanan and Tilon.
The descendants of Ishi:
Zoheth and Ben-Zoheth.
21 The sons of Shelah son of Judah:
Er the father of Lecah, Laadah the father of Mareshah and the clans of the linen workers at Beth Ashbea, 22 Jokim, the men of Cozeba, and Joash and Saraph, who ruled in Moab and Jashubi Lehem. (These records are from ancient times.) 23 They were the potters who lived at Netaim and Gederah; they stayed there and worked for the king.

Simeon

24 The descendants of Simeon:
Nemuel, Jamin, Jarib, Zerah and Shaul;
25 Shallum was Shaul's son, Mibsam his son and Mishma his son.
26 The descendants of Mishma:
Hammuel his son, Zaccur his son and Shimei his son.

27 Shimei had sixteen sons and six daughters, but his brothers did not have many children; so their entire clan did not become as
numerous as the people of Judah. 28 They lived
in Beersheba, Moladah, Hazar Shual, 29 Bilhah, Ezem, Tolad, 30 Bethuel, Hormah, Ziklag, 31 Beth Marcaboth, Hazar Susim, Beth
Biri and Shaaraim. These were their towns
until the reign of David. 32 Their surrounding
villages were Etam, Ain, Rimmon, Token and
Ashan—five towns— 33 and all the villages

---

[a] 3 Some Septuagint manuscripts (see also Vulgate); Hebrew *father* [b] 4 *Father* may mean *civic leader* or *military leader*; also in verses 12, 14, 17, 18 and possibly elsewhere. [c] 9 *Jabez* sounds like the Hebrew for *pain.* [d] 12 Or *of the city of Nahash* [e] 13 Some Septuagint manuscripts and Vulgate; Hebrew does not have *and Meonothai.* [f] 14 *Ge Harashim* means *valley of craftsmen.*

around these towns as far as Baalath.[a] These
were their settlements. And they kept a genealogical record.

34 Meshobab, Jamlech, Joshah son of Amaziah, 35 Joel, Jehu son of Joshibiah, the
son of Seraiah, the son of Asiel, 36 also
Elioenai, Jaakobah, Jeshohaiah, Asaiah,
Adiel, Jesimiel, Benaiah, 37 and Ziza son
of Shiphi, the son of Allon, the son of Jedaiah, the son of Shimri, the son of Shemaiah.

38 The men listed above by name were leaders
of their clans. Their families increased greatly,
39 and they went to the outskirts of Gedor to
the east of the valley in search of pasture for
their flocks. 40 They found rich, good pasture,
and the land was spacious, peaceful and quiet.
Some Hamites had lived there formerly.

41 The men whose names were listed came
in the days of Hezekiah king of Judah. They
attacked the Hamites in their dwellings and
also the Meunites who were there and completely destroyed[b] them, as is evident to this
day. Then they settled in their place, because
there was pasture for their flocks. 42 And five
hundred of these Simeonites, led by Pelatiah, Neariah, Rephaiah and Uzziel, the sons of
Ishi, invaded the hill country of Seir. 43 They
killed the remaining Amalekites who had escaped, and they have lived there to this day.

Reuben

5 The sons of Reuben the firstborn of Israel (he was the firstborn, but when he defiled his father's marriage bed, his rights
as firstborn were given to the sons of Joseph
son of Israel; so he could not be listed in the
genealogical record in accordance with his
birthright, 2 and though Judah was the strongest of his brothers and a ruler came from
him, the rights of the firstborn belonged to
Joseph)— 3 the sons of Reuben the firstborn
of Israel:

Hanoch, Pallu, Hezron and Carmi.

4 The descendants of Joel:

Shemaiah his son, Gog his son,
Shimei his son, 5 Micah his son,
Reaiah his son, Baal his son,
6 and Beerah his son, whom Tiglath-Pi-
leser[c] king of Assyria took into exile.
Beerah was a leader of the Reubenites.

7 Their relatives by clans, listed according
to their genealogical records:

Jeiel the chief, Zechariah, 8 and Bela
son of Azaz, the son of Shema, the son
of Joel. They settled in the area from
Aroer to Nebo and Baal Meon. 9 To
the east they occupied the land up to
the edge of the desert that extends to
the Euphrates River, because their livestock had increased in Gilead.

10 During Saul's reign they waged war
against the Hagrites, who were defeated
at their hands; they occupied the dwellings of the Hagrites throughout the entire region east of Gilead.

Gad

11 The Gadites lived next to them in Bashan, as far as Salecah:

12 Joel was the chief, Shapham the second, then Janai and Shaphat, in Bashan.

13 Their relatives, by families, were:

Michael, Meshullam, Sheba, Jorai, Ja-
can, Zia and Eber—seven in all.

14 These were the sons of Abihail son of
Huri, the son of Jaroah, the son of Gilead, the son of Michael, the son of Je-
shishai, the son of Jahdo, the son of
Buz.

15 Ahi son of Abdiel, the son of Guni,
was head of their family.

16 The Gadites lived in Gilead, in Bashan
and its outlying villages, and on all the
pasturelands of Sharon as far as they
extended.

17 All these were entered in the genealogical
records during the reigns of Jotham king of
Judah and Jeroboam king of Israel.

18 The Reubenites, the Gadites and the
half-tribe of Manasseh had 44,760 men ready
for military service—able-bodied men who
could handle shield and sword, who could
use a bow, and who were trained for battle.
19 They waged war against the Hagrites, Jetur,
Naphish and Nodab. 20 They were helped in
fighting them, and God handed the Hagrites
and all their allies over to them, because they
cried out to him during the battle. He answered their prayers, because they trusted in
him. 21 They seized the livestock of the Hagrites—fifty thousand camels, two hundred fifty thousand sheep and two thousand donkeys.
They also took one hundred thousand people
captive, 22 and many others fell slain, because

[a] *33* Some Septuagint manuscripts (see also Joshua 19:8); Hebrew *Baal* [b] *41* The Hebrew term refers to the irrevocable giving over of things or persons to the LORD, often by totally destroying them. [c] *6* Hebrew *Tilgath-Pilneser,* a variant of *Tiglath-Pileser;* also in verse 26

TUESDAY
READ 1 CHRONICLES 5:1–2

FINDING FORGIVENESS

[Reuben] was the firstborn, but when he defiled his father's marriage bed, his rights as firstborn were given to the sons of Joseph son of Israel; so he could not be listed in the genealogical record in accordance with his birthright.

— 1 Chronicles 5:1

In the midst of Israel's genealogy, the important detail about Reuben sleeping with his father's concubine Bilhah is mentioned almost in passing. The incident is first reported in Genesis 35:22. But Scripture is never redundant. Inherent in the repetition is a lesson about how sin's consequences keep cropping up.

We have a bit of a conundrum regarding the consequences of sin. If we repent of sin, we are truly, wholly forgiven by God. Our scarlet souls are washed as clean as the whitest snow. Yet sinful actions can cast a shadow for years. Sometimes we overemphasize the effects of sin and forget about forgiveness. Other times we distort the importance of forgiveness, concluding that since we're forgiven, we can keep indulging in sinful behavior.

That conundrum is critically important in marriage. None of us is a perfect spouse. We do wrongs, sometimes grave wrongs, against each other. We withhold the truth or tell each other lies. We let small resentments build and fester. We use sex as a weapon. We focus on our jobs or our kids at the expense of our marriage.

Of course, these wrongs give us an opportunity to repent and be forgiven. And when our spouse wrongs us, we can speak God's forgiveness to our beloved. But in marriage, we also see, as Reuben saw, that our sinful behaviors have consequences that sometimes last for years—if not a lifetime.

For example, early in her marriage, Joan had an affair. She broke it off and in the presence of a minister told her husband, Henry, about her betrayal. Henry could have divorced his wife. Instead, his forgiveness came in small cupfuls—not all at once; but it was forgiveness. Today, they have an admirable marriage.

Yet Joan's infidelity was not without consequences. For a year or two after her affair, Henry didn't want to have sex with her. And years later, in the heat of anger, he couldn't help lashing out at her by raking through the coals of her affair.

But the most lasting consequence, Joan says, is inside herself. "I live with the awareness that I'm capable of this terrible sin," she said. "Henry trusts me, but I don't trust myself."

Henry also lives with the consequences. However, through grace, he's learning how to love beyond the loss. While shopping for a gift for their tenth wedding anniversary, Henry said, "Joan and I both wish we could go back and undo not just her affair but countless smaller ways we've sinned against each other. Yet we also recognize that God has used even our most grievous mistakes to draw us closer to one another and to him.

"We have the marriage we have because God has brought us through trials. And though I regret the trials, I wouldn't want a different marriage."

Those words, says Joan, were the very best anniversary present ever.

—LAUREN WINNER

let's talk

- When have we wronged each other? How did we come to forgiveness?
- In what ways have sins against each other cast shadows on our marriage? How are we dealing with the consequences?
- Does forgiving mean forgetting what we've done to hurt each other? Should we consciously try to forget? Why or why not?

FOR YOUR NEXT DEVOTIONAL READING, TURN TO PAGE 438.

the battle was God's. And they occupied the land until the exile.

The Half-Tribe of Manasseh

23 The people of the half-tribe of Manas-
seh were numerous; they settled in the land from Bashan to Baal Hermon, that is, to Senir (Mount Hermon).

24 These were the heads of their families:
Epher, Ishi, Eliel, Azriel, Jeremiah, Hodaviah and Jahdiel. They were brave warriors, famous
men, and heads of their families. 25 But they
were unfaithful to the God of their fathers and prostituted themselves to the gods of the peoples of the land, whom God had destroyed
before them. 26 So the God of Israel stirred
up the spirit of Pul king of Assyria (that is, Tiglath-Pileser king of Assyria), who took the Reubenites, the Gadites and the half-tribe of Manasseh into exile. He took them to Halah, Habor, Hara and the river of Gozan, where they are to this day.

Levi

6 The sons of Levi:
Gershon, Kohath and Merari.
2 The sons of Kohath:
Amram, Izhar, Hebron and Uzziel.
3 The children of Amram:
Aaron, Moses and Miriam.
The sons of Aaron:
Nadab, Abihu, Eleazar and Ithamar.
4 Eleazar was the father of Phinehas,
Phinehas the father of Abishua,
5 Abishua the father of Bukki,
Bukki the father of Uzzi,
6 Uzzi the father of Zerahiah,
Zerahiah the father of Meraioth,
7 Meraioth the father of Amariah,
Amariah the father of Ahitub,
8 Ahitub the father of Zadok,
Zadok the father of Ahimaaz,
9 Ahimaaz the father of Azariah,
Azariah the father of Johanan,
10 Johanan the father of Azariah (it was he who served as priest in the temple Solomon built in Jerusalem),
11 Azariah the father of Amariah,
Amariah the father of Ahitub,
12 Ahitub the father of Zadok,
Zadok the father of Shallum,
13 Shallum the father of Hilkiah,
Hilkiah the father of Azariah,
14 Azariah the father of Seraiah,
and Seraiah the father of Jehozadak.
15 Jehozadak was deported when the LORD sent Judah and Jerusalem into exile by the hand of Nebuchadnezzar.

16 The sons of Levi:
Gershon,[a] Kohath and Merari.
17 These are the names of the sons of Gershon:
Libni and Shimei.
18 The sons of Kohath:
Amram, Izhar, Hebron and Uzziel.
19 The sons of Merari:
Mahli and Mushi.
These are the clans of the Levites listed according to their fathers:
20 Of Gershon:
Libni his son, Jehath his son,
Zimmah his son, 21 Joah his son,
Iddo his son, Zerah his son
and Jeatherai his son.
22 The descendants of Kohath:
Amminadab his son, Korah his son,
Assir his son, 23 Elkanah his son,
Ebiasaph his son, Assir his son,
24 Tahath his son, Uriel his son,
Uzziah his son and Shaul his son.
25 The descendants of Elkanah:
Amasai, Ahimoth,
26 Elkanah his son,[b] Zophai his son,
Nahath his son, 27 Eliab his son,
Jeroham his son, Elkanah his son
and Samuel his son.[c]
28 The sons of Samuel:
Joel[d] the firstborn
and Abijah the second son.
29 The descendants of Merari:
Mahli, Libni his son,
Shimei his son, Uzzah his son,
30 Shimea his son, Haggiah his son
and Asaiah his son.

The Temple Musicians

31 These are the men David put in charge of the music in the house of the LORD after
the ark came to rest there. 32 They ministered
with music before the tabernacle, the Tent of Meeting, until Solomon built the temple of the LORD in Jerusalem. They performed their duties according to the regulations laid down for them.

33 Here are the men who served, together with their sons:

---

a 16 Hebrew *Gershom,* a variant of *Gershon;* also in verses 17, 20, 43, 62 and 71 *b 26* Some Hebrew manuscripts, Septuagint and Syriac; most Hebrew manuscripts *Ahimoth 26and Elkanah. The sons of Elkanah:* *c 27* Some Septuagint manuscripts (see also 1 Samuel 1:19,20 and 1 Chron. 6:33,34); Hebrew does not have *and Samuel his son.* *d 28* Some Septuagint manuscripts and Syriac (see also 1 Samuel 8:2 and 1 Chron. 6:33); Hebrew does not have *Joel.*

From the Kohathites:
Heman, the musician,
the son of Joel, the son of Samuel,
34 the son of Elkanah, the son of Jeroham,
the son of Eliel, the son of Toah,
35 the son of Zuph, the son of Elkanah,
the son of Mahath, the son of Amasai,
36 the son of Elkanah, the son of Joel,
the son of Azariah, the son of Zephaniah,
37 the son of Tahath, the son of Assir,
the son of Ebiasaph, the son of Korah,
38 the son of Izhar, the son of Kohath,
the son of Levi, the son of Israel;
39 and Heman's associate Asaph, who served at his right hand:
Asaph son of Berekiah, the son of Shimea,
40 the son of Michael, the son of Baaseiah,[a]
the son of Malkijah, 41 the son of Ethni,
the son of Zerah, the son of Adaiah,
42 the son of Ethan, the son of Zimmah,
the son of Shimei, 43 the son of Jahath,
the son of Gershon, the son of Levi;
44 and from their associates, the Merarites, at his left hand:
Ethan son of Kishi, the son of Abdi,
the son of Malluch, 45 the son of Hashabiah,
the son of Amaziah, the son of Hilkiah,
46 the son of Amzi, the son of Bani,
the son of Shemer, 47 the son of Mahli,
the son of Mushi, the son of Merari,
the son of Levi.

48 Their fellow Levites were assigned to all the other duties of the tabernacle, the house of God.
49 But Aaron and his descendants were the ones who presented offerings on the altar of burnt offering and on the altar of incense in connection with all that was done in the Most Holy Place, making atonement for Israel, in accordance with all that Moses the servant of God had commanded.

50 These were the descendants of Aaron:
Eleazar his son, Phinehas his son,
Abishua his son, 51 Bukki his son,
Uzzi his son, Zerahiah his son,
52 Meraioth his son, Amariah his son,
Ahitub his son, 53 Zadok his son
and Ahimaaz his son.

54 These were the locations of their settlements allotted as their territory (they were assigned to the descendants of Aaron who were from the Kohathite clan, because the first lot was for them):

55 They were given Hebron in Judah with its surrounding pasturelands.
56 But the fields and villages around the city were given to Caleb son of Jephunneh.
57 So the descendants of Aaron were given Hebron (a city of refuge), and Libnah,[b] Jattir, Eshtemoa,
58 Hilen, Debir,
59 Ashan, Juttah[c] and Beth Shemesh, together with their pasturelands.
60 And from the tribe of Benjamin they were given Gibeon,[d] Geba, Alemeth and Anathoth, together with their pasturelands.

These towns, which were distributed among the Kohathite clans, were thirteen in all.

61 The rest of Kohath's descendants were allotted ten towns from the clans of half the tribe of Manasseh.

62 The descendants of Gershon, clan by clan, were allotted thirteen towns from the tribes of Issachar, Asher and Naphtali, and from the part of the tribe of Manasseh that is in Bashan.

63 The descendants of Merari, clan by clan, were allotted twelve towns from the tribes of Reuben, Gad and Zebulun.

64 So the Israelites gave the Levites these towns and their pasturelands.
65 From the tribes of Judah, Simeon and Benjamin they allotted the previously named towns.

66 Some of the Kohathite clans were given as their territory towns from the tribe of Ephraim.

67 In the hill country of Ephraim they were given Shechem (a city of refuge), and Gezer,[e]
68 Jokmeam, Beth Horon,
69 Aijalon and Gath Rimmon, together with their pasturelands.

70 And from half the tribe of Manasseh the Israelites gave Aner and Bileam, together with their pasturelands, to the rest of the Kohathite clans.

71 The Gershonites received the following:
From the clan of the half-tribe of Manasseh
they received Golan in Bashan and also

[a] 40 Most Hebrew manuscripts; some Hebrew manuscripts, one Septuagint manuscript and Syriac *Maaseiah* [b] 57 See Joshua 21:13; Hebrew *given the cities of refuge: Hebron, Libnah.* [c] 59 Syriac (see also Septuagint and Joshua 21:16); Hebrew does not have *Juttah.* [d] 60 See Joshua 21:17; Hebrew does not have *Gibeon.* [e] 67 See Joshua 21:21; Hebrew *given the cities of refuge: Shechem, Gezer.*

Ashtaroth, together with their pasturelands;
72 from the tribe of Issachar
they received Kedesh, Daberath, 73 Ramoth and Anem, together with their pasturelands;
74 from the tribe of Asher
they received Mashal, Abdon, 75 Hukok and Rehob, together with their pasturelands;
76 and from the tribe of Naphtali
they received Kedesh in Galilee, Hammon and Kiriathaim, together with their pasturelands.

77 The Merarites (the rest of the Levites) received the following:
From the tribe of Zebulun
they received Jokneam, Kartah,[a] Rimmono and Tabor, together with their pasturelands;
78 from the tribe of Reuben across the Jordan east of Jericho
they received Bezer in the desert, Jahzah, 79 Kedemoth and Mephaath, together with their pasturelands;
80 and from the tribe of Gad
they received Ramoth in Gilead, Mahanaim, 81 Heshbon and Jazer, together with their pasturelands.

Issachar

7 The sons of Issachar:
Tola, Puah, Jashub and Shimron—four in all.
2 The sons of Tola:
Uzzi, Rephaiah, Jeriel, Jahmai, Ibsam and Samuel—heads of their families. During the reign of David, the descendants of Tola listed as fighting men in their genealogy numbered 22,600.
3 The son of Uzzi:
Izrahiah.
The sons of Izrahiah:
Michael, Obadiah, Joel and Isshiah. All five of them were chiefs. 4 According to their family genealogy, they had 36,000 men ready for battle, for they had many wives and children.
5 The relatives who were fighting men belonging to all the clans of Issachar, as listed in their genealogy, were 87,000 in all.

Benjamin

6 Three sons of Benjamin:
Bela, Beker and Jediael.
7 The sons of Bela:
Ezbon, Uzzi, Uzziel, Jerimoth and Iri, heads of families—five in all. Their genealogical record listed 22,034 fighting men.
8 The sons of Beker:
Zemirah, Joash, Eliezer, Elioenai, Omri, Jeremoth, Abijah, Anathoth and Alemeth. All these were the sons of Beker. 9 Their genealogical record listed the heads of families and 20,200 fighting men.
10 The son of Jediael:
Bilhan.
The sons of Bilhan:
Jeush, Benjamin, Ehud, Kenaanah, Zethan, Tarshish and Ahishahar. 11 All these sons of Jediael were heads of families. There were 17,200 fighting men ready to go out to war.
12 The Shuppites and Huppites were the descendants of Ir, and the Hushites the descendants of Aher.

Naphtali

13 The sons of Naphtali:
Jahziel, Guni, Jezer and Shillem[b]—the descendants of Bilhah.

Manasseh

14 The descendants of Manasseh:
Asriel was his descendant through his Aramean concubine. She gave birth to Makir the father of Gilead. 15 Makir took a wife from among the Huppites and Shuppites. His sister's name was Maacah.
Another descendant was named Zelophehad, who had only daughters.
16 Makir's wife Maacah gave birth to a son and named him Peresh. His brother was named Sheresh, and his sons were Ulam and Rakem.
17 The son of Ulam:
Bedan.
These were the sons of Gilead son of Makir, the son of Manasseh. 18 His sister Hammoleketh gave birth to Ishhod, Abiezer and Mahlah.
19 The sons of Shemida were:
Ahian, Shechem, Likhi and Aniam.

[a] 77 See Septuagint and Joshua 21:34; Hebrew does not have *Jokneam, Kartah.* [b] 13 Some Hebrew and Septuagint manuscripts (see also Gen. 46:24 and Num. 26:49); most Hebrew manuscripts *Shallum*

Ephraim

20 The descendants of Ephraim:
Shuthelah, Bered his son,
Tahath his son, Eleadah his son,
Tahath his son, 21 Zabad his son
and Shuthelah his son.
Ezer and Elead were killed by the native-born men of Gath, when they went
down to seize their livestock. 22 Their father Ephraim mourned for them many
days, and his relatives came to comfort
him. 23 Then he lay with his wife again,
and she became pregnant and gave birth
to a son. He named him Beriah,[a] because
there had been misfortune in his family.
24 His daughter was Sheerah, who built
Lower and Upper Beth Horon as well as
Uzzen Sheerah.
25 Rephah was his son, Resheph his son,[b]
Telah his son, Tahan his son,
26 Ladan his son, Ammihud his son,
Elishama his son, 27 Nun his son
and Joshua his son.
28 Their lands and settlements included
Bethel and its surrounding villages, Naaran to
the east, Gezer and its villages to the west, and
Shechem and its villages all the way to Ayyah
and its villages. 29 Along the borders of Manasseh were Beth Shan, Taanach, Megiddo
and Dor, together with their villages. The descendants of Joseph son of Israel lived in these
towns.

Asher

30 The sons of Asher:
Imnah, Ishvah, Ishvi and Beriah. Their
sister was Serah.
31 The sons of Beriah:
Heber and Malkiel, who was the father
of Birzaith.
32 Heber was the father of Japhlet, Shomer
and Hotham and of their sister Shua.
33 The sons of Japhlet:
Pasach, Bimhal and Ashvath.
These were Japhlet's sons.
34 The sons of Shomer:
Ahi, Rohgah,[c] Hubbah and Aram.
35 The sons of his brother Helem:
Zophah, Imna, Shelesh and Amal.
36 The sons of Zophah:
Suah, Harnepher, Shual, Beri, Imrah,
37 Bezer, Hod, Shamma, Shilshah, Ithran[d] and Beera.
38 The sons of Jether:
Jephunneh, Pispah and Ara.
39 The sons of Ulla:
Arah, Hanniel and Rizia.
40 All these were descendants of Asher—
heads of families, choice men, brave warriors
and outstanding leaders. The number of men
ready for battle, as listed in their genealogy,
was 26,000.

The Genealogy of Saul the Benjamite

8 Benjamin was the father of Bela his firstborn,
Ashbel the second son, Aharah the
third,
2 Nohah the fourth and Rapha the
fifth.
3 The sons of Bela were:
Addar, Gera, Abihud,[e] 4 Abishua, Naaman, Ahoah, 5 Gera, Shephuphan and
Huram.
6 These were the descendants of Ehud, who
were heads of families of those living
in Geba and were deported to Manahath:
7 Naaman, Ahijah, and Gera, who deported them and who was the father
of Uzza and Ahihud.
8 Sons were born to Shaharaim in Moab after he had divorced his wives Hushim
and Baara. 9 By his wife Hodesh he had
Jobab, Zibia, Mesha, Malcam, 10 Jeuz,
Sakia and Mirmah. These were his
sons, heads of families. 11 By Hushim
he had Abitub and Elpaal.
12 The sons of Elpaal:
Eber, Misham, Shemed (who built
Ono and Lod with its surrounding villages), 13 and Beriah and Shema, who
were heads of families of those living
in Aijalon and who drove out the inhabitants of Gath.
14 Ahio, Shashak, Jeremoth, 15 Zebadiah,
Arad, Eder, 16 Michael, Ishpah and
Joha were the sons of Beriah.
17 Zebadiah, Meshullam, Hizki, Heber,
18 Ishmerai, Izliah and Jobab were the
sons of Elpaal.
19 Jakim, Zicri, Zabdi, 20 Elienai, Zillethai,
Eliel, 21 Adaiah, Beraiah and Shimrath
were the sons of Shimei.
22 Ishpan, Eber, Eliel, 23 Abdon, Zicri, Hanan, 24 Hananiah, Elam, Anthothijah,
25 Iphdeiah and Penuel were the sons
of Shashak.
26 Shamsherai, Shehariah, Athaliah, 27 Jaare-

[a] 23 *Beriah* sounds like the Hebrew for *misfortune.* [b] 25 Some Septuagint manuscripts; Hebrew does not have *his son.* [c] 34 Or *of his brother Shomer: Rohgah* [d] 37 Possibly a variant of *Jether* [e] 3 Or *Gera the father of Ehud*

shiah, Elijah and Zicri were the sons
of Jeroham.
28 All these were heads of families, chiefs as
listed in their genealogy, and they lived in Jerusalem.

29 Jeiel[a] the father[b] of Gibeon lived in Gibeon.
His wife's name was Maacah, 30 and his
firstborn son was Abdon, followed by
Zur, Kish, Baal, Ner,[c] Nadab, 31 Gedor, Ahio, Zeker 32 and Mikloth, who
was the father of Shimeah. They too
lived near their relatives in Jerusalem.
33 Ner was the father of Kish, Kish the father of Saul, and Saul the father of
Jonathan, Malki-Shua, Abinadab and
Esh-Baal.[d]
34 The son of Jonathan:
Merib-Baal,[e] who was the father of
Micah.
35 The sons of Micah:
Pithon, Melech, Tarea and Ahaz.
36 Ahaz was the father of Jehoaddah, Jehoaddah was the father of Alemeth,
Azmaveth and Zimri, and Zimri was
the father of Moza. 37 Moza was the
father of Binea; Raphah was his son,
Eleasah his son and Azel his son.
38 Azel had six sons, and these were their
names:
Azrikam, Bokeru, Ishmael, Sheariah,
Obadiah and Hanan. All these were
the sons of Azel.
39 The sons of his brother Eshek:
Ulam his firstborn, Jeush the second
son and Eliphelet the third. 40 The
sons of Ulam were brave warriors who
could handle the bow. They had many
sons and grandsons—150 in all.
All these were the descendants of Benjamin.

9 All Israel was listed in the genealogies recorded in the book of the kings of Israel.

The People in Jerusalem

The people of Judah were taken captive to
Babylon because of their unfaithfulness. 2 Now
the first to resettle on their own property in
their own towns were some Israelites, priests,
Levites and temple servants.
3 Those from Judah, from Benjamin, and
from Ephraim and Manasseh who lived in Jerusalem were:
4 Uthai son of Ammihud, the son of Omri,
the son of Imri, the son of Bani, a descendant of Perez son of Judah.
5 Of the Shilonites:
Asaiah the firstborn and his sons.
6 Of the Zerahites:
Jeuel.
The people from Judah numbered
690.
7 Of the Benjamites:
Sallu son of Meshullam, the son of
Hodaviah, the son of Hassenuah;
8 Ibneiah son of Jeroham; Elah son of
Uzzi, the son of Micri; and Meshullam
son of Shephatiah, the son of Reuel,
the son of Ibnijah.
9 The people from Benjamin, as listed
in their genealogy, numbered 956. All
these men were heads of their families.
10 Of the priests:
Jedaiah; Jehoiarib; Jakin;
11 Azariah son of Hilkiah, the son of
Meshullam, the son of Zadok, the
son of Meraioth, the son of Ahitub,
the official in charge of the house of
God;
12 Adaiah son of Jeroham, the son of
Pashhur, the son of Malkijah; and Ma-
asai son of Adiel, the son of Jahzerah,
the son of Meshullam, the son of Me-
shillemith, the son of Immer.
13 The priests, who were heads of families, numbered 1,760. They were able
men, responsible for ministering in the
house of God.
14 Of the Levites:
Shemaiah son of Hasshub, the son
of Azrikam, the son of Hashabiah, a
Merarite; 15 Bakbakkar, Heresh, Galal
and Mattaniah son of Mica, the son of
Zicri, the son of Asaph; 16 Obadiah son
of Shemaiah, the son of Galal, the son
of Jeduthun; and Berekiah son of Asa,
the son of Elkanah, who lived in the
villages of the Netophathites.
17 The gatekeepers:
Shallum, Akkub, Talmon, Ahiman
and their brothers, Shallum their chief
18 being stationed at the King's Gate on
the east, up to the present time. These
were the gatekeepers belonging to the

[a] 29 Some Septuagint manuscripts (see also 1 Chron. 9:35); Hebrew does not have *Jeiel.* [b] 29 *Father* may mean *civic leader* or *military leader.* [c] 30 Some Septuagint manuscripts (see also 1 Chron. 9:36); Hebrew does not have *Ner.* [d] 33 Also known as *Ish-Bosheth*
[e] 34 Also known as *Mephibosheth*

camp of the Levites. 19 Shallum son
of Kore, the son of Ebiasaph, the son
of Korah, and his fellow gatekeepers
from his family (the Korahites) were
responsible for guarding the thresholds of the Tent[a] just as their fathers
had been responsible for guarding the
entrance to the dwelling of the LORD.
20 In earlier times Phinehas son of Eleazar was in charge of the gatekeepers,
and the LORD was with him. 21 Zechariah son of Meshelemiah was the gatekeeper at the entrance to the Tent of
Meeting.

22 Altogether, those chosen to be gatekeepers at the thresholds numbered 212. They
were registered by genealogy in their villages.
The gatekeepers had been assigned to their positions of trust by David and Samuel the seer.
23 They and their descendants were in charge of
guarding the gates of the house of the LORD—
the house called the Tent. 24 The gatekeepers
were on the four sides: east, west, north and
south. 25 Their brothers in their villages had to
come from time to time and share their duties
for seven-day periods. 26 But the four principal
gatekeepers, who were Levites, were entrusted with the responsibility for the rooms and
treasuries in the house of God. 27 They would
spend the night stationed around the house
of God, because they had to guard it; and
they had charge of the key for opening it each
morning.

28 Some of them were in charge of the articles used in the temple service; they counted
them when they were brought in and when
they were taken out. 29 Others were assigned
to take care of the furnishings and all the other articles of the sanctuary, as well as the flour
and wine, and the oil, incense and spices.
30 But some of the priests took care of mixing
the spices. 31 A Levite named Mattithiah, the
firstborn son of Shallum the Korahite, was
entrusted with the responsibility for baking
the offering bread. 32 Some of their Kohathite
brothers were in charge of preparing for every
Sabbath the bread set out on the table.

33 Those who were musicians, heads of Levite families, stayed in the rooms of the temple
and were exempt from other duties because
they were responsible for the work day and
night.

34 All these were heads of Levite families,
chiefs as listed in their genealogy, and they
lived in Jerusalem.

The Genealogy of Saul

35 Jeiel the father[b] of Gibeon lived in Gibeon.
His wife's name was Maacah, 36 and his
firstborn son was Abdon, followed by
Zur, Kish, Baal, Ner, Nadab, 37 Gedor,
Ahio, Zechariah and Mikloth. 38 Mikloth was the father of Shimeam. They
too lived near their relatives in Jerusalem.

39 Ner was the father of Kish, Kish the fa-
ther of Saul, and Saul the father of
Jonathan, Malki-Shua, Abinadab and
Esh-Baal.[c]

40 The son of Jonathan:
Merib-Baal,[d] who was the father of
Micah.

41 The sons of Micah:
Pithon, Melech, Tahrea and Ahaz.[e]
42 Ahaz was the father of Jadah, Jadah[f]
was the father of Alemeth, Azmaveth
and Zimri, and Zimri was the father of
Moza. 43 Moza was the father of Binea;
Rephaiah was his son, Eleasah his son
and Azel his son.

44 Azel had six sons, and these were their
names:
Azrikam, Bokeru, Ishmael, Sheariah,
Obadiah and Hanan. These were the
sons of Azel.

Saul Takes His Life

10 Now the Philistines fought against Israel; the Israelites fled before them, and
many fell slain on Mount Gilboa. 2 The
Philistines pressed hard after Saul and his
sons, and they killed his sons Jonathan, Abinadab and Malki-Shua. 3 The fighting grew fierce
around Saul, and when the archers overtook
him, they wounded him.

4 Saul said to his armor-bearer, "Draw your
sword and run me through, or these uncircumcised fellows will come and abuse me."

But his armor-bearer was terrified and
would not do it; so Saul took his own sword
and fell on it. 5 When the armor-bearer saw
that Saul was dead, he too fell on his sword
and died. 6 So Saul and his three sons died, and
all his house died together.

7 When all the Israelites in the valley saw
that the army had fled and that Saul and his

[a] *19* That is, the temple; also in verses 21 and 23 [b] *35* *Father* may mean *civic leader* or *military leader.* [c] *39* Also known as *Ish-Bosheth* [d] *40* Also known as *Mephibosheth* [e] *41* Vulgate and Syriac (see also Septuagint and 1 Chron. 8:35); Hebrew does not have *and Ahaz.* [f] *42* Some Hebrew manuscripts and Septuagint (see also 1 Chron. 8:36); most Hebrew manuscripts *Jarah, Jarah*

sons had died, they abandoned their towns and fled. And the Philistines came and occupied them.

8The next day, when the Philistines came to strip the dead, they found Saul and his sons fallen on Mount Gilboa. 9They stripped him and took his head and his armor, and sent messengers throughout the land of the Philistines to proclaim the news among their idols and their people. 10They put his armor in the temple of their gods and hung up his head in the temple of Dagon.

11When all the inhabitants of Jabesh Gilead heard of everything the Philistines had done to Saul, 12all their valiant men went and took the bodies of Saul and his sons and brought them to Jabesh. Then they buried their bones under the great tree in Jabesh, and they fasted seven days.

13Saul died because he was unfaithful to the LORD; he did not keep the word of the LORD and even consulted a medium for guidance, 14and did not inquire of the LORD. So the LORD put him to death and turned the kingdom over to David son of Jesse.

David Becomes King Over Israel

11 All Israel came together to David at Hebron and said, "We are your own flesh and blood. 2In the past, even while Saul was king, you were the one who led Israel on their military campaigns. And the LORD your God said to you, 'You will shepherd my people Israel, and you will become their ruler.' "

3When all the elders of Israel had come to King David at Hebron, he made a compact with them at Hebron before the LORD, and they anointed David king over Israel, as the LORD had promised through Samuel.

David Conquers Jerusalem

4David and all the Israelites marched to Jerusalem (that is, Jebus). The Jebusites who lived there 5said to David, "You will not get in here." Nevertheless, David captured the fortress of Zion, the City of David.

6David had said, "Whoever leads the attack on the Jebusites will become commander-in-chief." Joab son of Zeruiah went up first, and so he received the command.

7David then took up residence in the fortress, and so it was called the City of David. 8He built up the city around it, from the supporting terraces[a] to the surrounding wall, while Joab restored the rest of the city. 9And David became more and more powerful, because the LORD Almighty was with him.

David's Mighty Men

10These were the chiefs of David's mighty men—they, together with all Israel, gave his kingship strong support to extend it over the whole land, as the LORD had promised—11this is the list of David's mighty men:

Jashobeam,[b] a Hacmonite, was chief of the officers[c]; he raised his spear against three hundred men, whom he killed in one encounter.

12Next to him was Eleazar son of Dodai the Ahohite, one of the three mighty men. 13He was with David at Pas Dammim when the Philistines gathered there for battle. At a place where there was a field full of barley, the troops fled from the Philistines. 14But they took their stand in the middle of the field. They defended it and struck the Philistines down, and the LORD brought about a great victory.

15Three of the thirty chiefs came down to David to the rock at the cave of Adullam, while a band of Philistines was encamped in the Valley of Rephaim. 16At that time David was in the stronghold, and the Philistine garrison was at Bethlehem. 17David longed for water and said, "Oh, that someone would get me a drink of water from the well near the gate of Bethlehem!" 18So the Three broke through the Philistine lines, drew water from the well near the gate of Bethlehem and carried it back to David. But he refused to drink it; instead, he poured it out before the LORD. 19"God forbid that I should do this!" he said. "Should I drink the blood of these men who went at the risk of their lives?" Because they risked their lives to bring it back, David would not drink it.

Such were the exploits of the three mighty men.

20Abishai the brother of Joab was chief of the Three. He raised his spear against three hundred men, whom he killed, and so he became as famous as the Three. 21He was doubly honored above the Three and became their commander, even though he was not included among them.

22Benaiah son of Jehoiada was a valiant fighter from Kabzeel, who performed great exploits. He struck down two of Mo-

[a] 8 Or *the Millo* [b] 11 Possibly a variant of *Jashob-Baal* [c] 11 Or *Thirty*; some Septuagint manuscripts *Three* (see also 2 Samuel 23:8)

ab's best men. He also went down into a pit
on a snowy day and killed a lion. 23 And he
struck down an Egyptian who was seven and
a half feet[a] tall. Although the Egyptian had a
spear like a weaver's rod in his hand, Benaiah
went against him with a club. He snatched
the spear from the Egyptian's hand and killed
him with his own spear. 24 Such were the exploits of Benaiah son of Jehoiada; he too was
as famous as the three mighty men. 25 He was
held in greater honor than any of the Thirty,
but he was not included among the Three.
And David put him in charge of his bodyguard.

26 The mighty men were:
Asahel the brother of Joab,
Elhanan son of Dodo from Bethlehem,
27 Shammoth the Harorite,
Helez the Pelonite,
28 Ira son of Ikkesh from Tekoa,
Abiezer from Anathoth,
29 Sibbecai the Hushathite,
Ilai the Ahohite,
30 Maharai the Netophathite,
Heled son of Baanah the Netophathite,
31 Ithai son of Ribai from Gibeah in Benjamin,
Benaiah the Pirathonite,
32 Hurai from the ravines of Gaash,
Abiel the Arbathite,
33 Azmaveth the Baharumite,
Eliahba the Shaalbonite,
34 the sons of Hashem the Gizonite,
Jonathan son of Shagee the Hararite,
35 Ahiam son of Sacar the Hararite,
Eliphal son of Ur,
36 Hepher the Mekerathite,
Ahijah the Pelonite,
37 Hezro the Carmelite,
Naarai son of Ezbai,
38 Joel the brother of Nathan,
Mibhar son of Hagri,
39 Zelek the Ammonite,
Naharai the Berothite, the armor-bearer of Joab son of Zeruiah,
40 Ira the Ithrite,
Gareb the Ithrite,
41 Uriah the Hittite,
Zabad son of Ahlai,
42 Adina son of Shiza the Reubenite, who was chief of the Reubenites, and the thirty with him,
43 Hanan son of Maacah,
Joshaphat the Mithnite,
44 Uzzia the Ashterathite,
Shama and Jeiel the sons of Hotham the Aroerite,
45 Jediael son of Shimri,
his brother Joha the Tizite,
46 Eliel the Mahavite,
Jeribai and Joshaviah the sons of Elnaam,
Ithmah the Moabite,
47 Eliel, Obed and Jaasiel the Mezobaite.

Warriors Join David

12 These were the men who came to David
at Ziklag, while he was banished from
the presence of Saul son of Kish (they
were among the warriors who helped him
in battle; 2 they were armed with bows and
were able to shoot arrows or to sling stones
right-handed or left-handed; they were kinsmen of Saul from the tribe of Benjamin):

3 Ahiezer their chief and Joash the sons
of Shemaah the Gibeathite; Jeziel and
Pelet the sons of Azmaveth; Beracah,
Jehu the Anathothite, 4 and Ishmaiah
the Gibeonite, a mighty man among the
Thirty, who was a leader of the Thirty;
Jeremiah, Jahaziel, Johanan, Jozabad the
Gederathite, 5 Eluzai, Jerimoth, Bealiah,
Shemariah and Shephatiah the Haru-
phite; 6 Elkanah, Isshiah, Azarel, Joezer
and Jashobeam the Korahites; 7 and Jo-
elah and Zebadiah the sons of Jeroham
from Gedor.

8 Some Gadites defected to David at his
stronghold in the desert. They were brave warriors, ready for battle and able to handle the
shield and spear. Their faces were the faces of
lions, and they were as swift as gazelles in the
mountains.

9 Ezer was the chief,
Obadiah the second in command, Eliab the third,
10 Mishmannah the fourth, Jeremiah the fifth,
11 Attai the sixth, Eliel the seventh,
12 Johanan the eighth, Elzabad the ninth,
13 Jeremiah the tenth and Macbannai the eleventh.

14 These Gadites were army commanders;
the least was a match for a hundred, and the
greatest for a thousand. 15 It was they who
crossed the Jordan in the first month when it
was overflowing all its banks, and they put to

[a] 23 Hebrew *five cubits* (about 2.3 meters)

flight everyone living in the valleys, to the east
and to the west.
16Other Benjamites and some men from
Judah also came to David in his stronghold.
17David went out to meet them and said to
them, "If you have come to me in peace, to
help me, I am ready to have you unite with
me. But if you have come to betray me to my
enemies when my hands are free from violence, may the God of our fathers see it and
judge you."
18Then the Spirit came upon Amasai, chief
of the Thirty, and he said:

"We are yours, O David!
  We are with you, O son of Jesse!
Success, success to you,
  and success to those who help you,
    for your God will help you."

So David received them and made them
leaders of his raiding bands.
19Some of the men of Manasseh defected
to David when he went with the Philistines
to fight against Saul. (He and his men did
not help the Philistines because, after consul-
tation, their rulers sent him away. They said,
"It will cost us our heads if he deserts to his
master Saul.") 20When David went to Ziklag,
these were the men of Manasseh who defected
to him: Adnah, Jozabad, Jediael, Michael, Jozabad, Elihu and Zillethai, leaders of units of
a thousand in Manasseh. 21They helped David against raiding bands, for all of them were
brave warriors, and they were commanders in
his army. 22Day after day men came to help
David, until he had a great army, like the army
of God.[a]

Others Join David at Hebron

23These are the numbers of the men armed
for battle who came to David at Hebron to
turn Saul's kingdom over to him, as the LORD
had said:

24 men of Judah, carrying shield and spear—6,800 armed for battle;
25 men of Simeon, warriors ready for battle—7,100;
26 men of Levi—4,600, 27including Jehoiada, leader of the family of Aaron, with 3,700 men, 28and Zadok, a brave young warrior, with 22 officers from his family;
29 men of Benjamin, Saul's kinsmen—3,000, most of whom had remained loyal to Saul's house until then;
30 men of Ephraim, brave warriors, famous in their own clans—20,800;
31 men of half the tribe of Manasseh, designated by name to come and make David king—18,000;
32 men of Issachar, who understood the times and knew what Israel should do—200 chiefs, with all their relatives under their command;
33 men of Zebulun, experienced soldiers prepared for battle with every type of weapon, to help David with undivided loyalty—50,000;
34 men of Naphtali—1,000 officers, together with 37,000 men carrying shields and spears;
35 men of Dan, ready for battle—28,600;
36 men of Asher, experienced soldiers prepared for battle—40,000;
37 and from east of the Jordan, men of Reuben, Gad and the half-tribe of Manasseh, armed with every type of weapon—120,000.

38All these were fighting men who volunteered to serve in the ranks. They came to
Hebron fully determined to make David king
over all Israel. All the rest of the Israelites were
also of one mind to make David king. 39The
men spent three days there with David, eating
and drinking, for their families had supplied
provisions for them. 40Also, their neighbors
from as far away as Issachar, Zebulun and
Naphtali came bringing food on donkeys,
camels, mules and oxen. There were plentiful
supplies of flour, fig cakes, raisin cakes, wine,
oil, cattle and sheep, for there was joy in Israel.

Bringing Back the Ark

13 David conferred with each of his officers,
the commanders of thousands and commanders of hundreds. 2He then said to
the whole assembly of Israel, "If it seems good
to you and if it is the will of the LORD our
God, let us send word far and wide to the rest
of our brothers throughout the territories of
Israel, and also to the priests and Levites who
are with them in their towns and pasturelands,
to come and join us. 3Let us bring the ark of
our God back to us, for we did not inquire
of[b] it[c] during the reign of Saul." 4The whole
assembly agreed to do this, because it seemed
right to all the people.
5So David assembled all the Israelites, from
the Shihor River in Egypt to Lebo[d] Hamath,

[a] 22 Or *a great and mighty army* [b] 3 Or *we neglected* [c] 3 Or *him* [d] 5 Or *to the entrance to*

WEDNESDAY
READ
1 CHRONICLES 12:23–40

LEANING ON EACH OTHER

> **Men of Issachar . . . understood the times and knew what Israel should do.**
>
> — 1 Chronicles 12:32

let's talk

- How do we, like the men of Issachar, "understand the times" and know what to do? What equips us to do that?
- In what ways have we fully determined to help each other be victorious? How does that help? What is the result?
- What trenches are we currently walking through together?

In coming to David to make him their king, many men volunteered to join his ranks, including the men of Issachar who "understood the times and knew what Israel should do."

On the day Dan asked me to marry him, essentially he was joining my ranks, and I his. I'll never forget the first time I realized that Dan's role as husband included serving as my "commander in chief." I was struggling with a difficult relationship in my life, and I poured my heart out to Dan. He could easily have sided with me, especially because I was feeding him plenty of bitterness bullets. Instead, he gently said, "Mar, you just need to keep loving." Dan knew, based on his own experience of being forgiven and loved unconditionally by Christ, that love was the only ammunition I needed for my strained relationship. Dan's simple yet thoughtful words gave me the direction and encouragement I needed to persevere.

This incident might seem insignificant because of its simplicity. For me, however, it was a pivotal moment in which I realized that being husband and wife carried the weight of going into battle together (i.e., doing life together). Through his own walk with the Lord, Dan understood the times—the difficult struggle I was facing with this adversary of mine—and he knew what I needed to do.

Time and again, my spouse has proven to be my most reliable adviser. From helping me weigh different job opportunities to sorting out the challenging issues of raising a family, no one is more in my camp than my husband is. Every time I see Dan pick up his Bible, I know that he, like the men of Issachar, is training himself to understand the times and learning how to respond. When we pray together at night and bring our needs to God, I'm reassured that we are working together toward victory.

David must have been overwhelmed by the incredible number of men who came to him at Hebron to turn Saul's kingdom over to him. Yet knowing they were fully determined to make him king, David could be confident that his troops had his best interests (and Israel's) at heart.

Even in our little army of two, I've been moved by Dan's commitment to help me become more like Christ. Of all the roles we fill in marriage—lover, friend, companion, provider—none is so profound as coming alongside each other and walking through the trenches of difficulty. David had his multitudes; I have Dan. And together, we're working toward victory.

—MARIAN V. LIAUTAUD

FOR YOUR NEXT DEVOTIONAL READING, TURN TO PAGE 443.

to bring the ark of God from Kiriath Jearim.
6David and all the Israelites with him went to
Baalah of Judah (Kiriath Jearim) to bring up
from there the ark of God the LORD, who is
enthroned between the cherubim—the ark
that is called by the Name.
7They moved the ark of God from Abinadab's house on a new cart, with Uzzah and
Ahio guiding it. 8David and all the Israelites
were celebrating with all their might before
God, with songs and with harps, lyres, tambourines, cymbals and trumpets.
9When they came to the threshing floor of
Kidon, Uzzah reached out his hand to steady
the ark, because the oxen stumbled. 10The
LORD's anger burned against Uzzah, and he
struck him down because he had put his hand
on the ark. So he died there before God.
11Then David was angry because the LORD's
wrath had broken out against Uzzah, and to
this day that place is called Perez Uzzah.[a]
12David was afraid of God that day and
asked, "How can I ever bring the ark of God
to me?" 13He did not take the ark to be with
him in the City of David. Instead, he took it
aside to the house of Obed-Edom the Gittite.
14The ark of God remained with the family
of Obed-Edom in his house for three months,
and the LORD blessed his household and everything he had.

David's House and Family

14 Now Hiram king of Tyre sent messengers to David, along with cedar logs,
stonemasons and carpenters to build
a palace for him. 2And David knew that the
LORD had established him as king over Israel
and that his kingdom had been highly exalted
for the sake of his people Israel.
3In Jerusalem David took more wives and
became the father of more sons and daughters.
4These are the names of the children born to
him there: Shammua, Shobab, Nathan, Solomon, 5Ibhar, Elishua, Elpelet, 6Nogah, Nepheg, Japhia, 7Elishama, Beeliada[b] and Eliphelet.

David Defeats the Philistines

8When the Philistines heard that David had
been anointed king over all Israel, they went
up in full force to search for him, but David
heard about it and went out to meet them.
9Now the Philistines had come and raided
the Valley of Rephaim; 10so David inquired
of God: "Shall I go and attack the Philistines?
Will you hand them over to me?"
The LORD answered him, "Go, I will hand
them over to you."
11So David and his men went up to Baal
Perazim, and there he defeated them. He
said, "As waters break out, God has broken
out against my enemies by my hand." So that
place was called Baal Perazim.[c] 12The Philistines had abandoned their gods there, and David gave orders to burn them in the fire.
13Once more the Philistines raided the valley; 14so David inquired of God again, and
God answered him, "Do not go straight up,
but circle around them and attack them in
front of the balsam trees. 15As soon as you
hear the sound of marching in the tops of the
balsam trees, move out to battle, because that
will mean God has gone out in front of you to
strike the Philistine army." 16So David did as
God commanded him, and they struck down
the Philistine army, all the way from Gibeon
to Gezer.
17So David's fame spread throughout every
land, and the LORD made all the nations fear
him.

The Ark Brought to Jerusalem

15 After David had constructed buildings
for himself in the City of David, he prepared a place for the ark of God and
pitched a tent for it. 2Then David said, "No
one but the Levites may carry the ark of God,
because the LORD chose them to carry the ark
of the LORD and to minister before him forever."
3David assembled all Israel in Jerusalem to
bring up the ark of the LORD to the place he
had prepared for it. 4He called together the
descendants of Aaron and the Levites:
5 From the descendants of Kohath,
Uriel the leader and 120 relatives;
6 from the descendants of Merari,
Asaiah the leader and 220 relatives;
7 from the descendants of Gershon,[d]
Joel the leader and 130 relatives;
8 from the descendants of Elizaphan,
Shemaiah the leader and 200 relatives;
9 from the descendants of Hebron,
Eliel the leader and 80 relatives;
10 from the descendants of Uzziel,
Amminadab the leader and 112 relatives.
11Then David summoned Zadok and Abiathar the priests, and Uriel, Asaiah, Joel, She-

[a] 11 *Perez Uzzah* means *outbreak against Uzzah.* [b] 7 A variant of *Eliada* [c] 11 *Baal Perazim* means *the lord who breaks out.*
[d] 7 Hebrew *Gershom,* a variant of *Gershon*

maiah, Eliel and Amminadab the Levites.
12He said to them, "You are the heads of the
Levitical families; you and your fellow Levites
are to consecrate yourselves and bring up the
ark of the LORD, the God of Israel, to the place
I have prepared for it. 13It was because you,
the Levites, did not bring it up the first time
that the LORD our God broke out in anger
against us. We did not inquire of him about
how to do it in the prescribed way." 14So the
priests and Levites consecrated themselves in
order to bring up the ark of the LORD, the
God of Israel. 15And the Levites carried the
ark of God with the poles on their shoulders,
as Moses had commanded in accordance with
the word of the LORD.

16David told the leaders of the Levites to
appoint their brothers as singers to sing joyful
songs, accompanied by musical instruments:
lyres, harps and cymbals.

17So the Levites appointed Heman son of
Joel; from his brothers, Asaph son of Berekiah;
and from their brothers the Merarites, Ethan
son of Kushaiah; 18and with them their brothers next in rank: Zechariah,[a] Jaaziel, Shemiramoth, Jehiel, Unni, Eliab, Benaiah, Maaseiah,
Mattithiah, Eliphelehu, Mikneiah, Obed-
Edom and Jeiel,[b] the gatekeepers.

19The musicians Heman, Asaph and Ethan
were to sound the bronze cymbals; 20Zecha-
riah, Aziel, Shemiramoth, Jehiel, Unni, Eliab, Maaseiah and Benaiah were to play the
lyres according to *alamoth,*[c] 21and Mattithiah, Eliphelehu, Mikneiah, Obed-Edom, Jeiel
and Azaziah were to play the harps, directing according to *sheminith.*[c] 22Kenaniah the
head Levite was in charge of the singing; that
was his responsibility because he was skillful
at it.

23Berekiah and Elkanah were to be doorkeepers for the ark. 24Shebaniah, Joshaphat,
Nethanel, Amasai, Zechariah, Benaiah and Eliezer the priests were to blow trumpets before
the ark of God. Obed-Edom and Jehiah were
also to be doorkeepers for the ark.

25So David and the elders of Israel and the
commanders of units of a thousand went to
bring up the ark of the covenant of the LORD
from the house of Obed-Edom, with rejoicing. 26Because God had helped the Levites
who were carrying the ark of the covenant of
the LORD, seven bulls and seven rams were
sacrificed. 27Now David was clothed in a
robe of fine linen, as were all the Levites who
were carrying the ark, and as were the singers, and Kenaniah, who was in charge of the
singing of the choirs. David also wore a linen
ephod. 28So all Israel brought up the ark of
the covenant of the LORD with shouts, with
the sounding of rams' horns and trumpets,
and of cymbals, and the playing of lyres and
harps.

29As the ark of the covenant of the LORD
was entering the City of David, Michal daughter of Saul watched from a window. And when
she saw King David dancing and celebrating,
she despised him in her heart.

16 They brought the ark of God and set it
inside the tent that David had pitched
for it, and they presented burnt offerings and fellowship offerings[d] before God.
2After David had finished sacrificing the
burnt offerings and fellowship offerings, he
blessed the people in the name of the LORD.
3Then he gave a loaf of bread, a cake of dates
and a cake of raisins to each Israelite man and
woman.

4He appointed some of the Levites to minister before the ark of the LORD, to make petition, to give thanks, and to praise the LORD,
the God of Israel: 5Asaph was the chief, Zechariah second, then Jeiel, Shemiramoth, Jehiel,
Mattithiah, Eliab, Benaiah, Obed-Edom and
Jeiel. They were to play the lyres and harps,
Asaph was to sound the cymbals, 6and Benaiah and Jahaziel the priests were to blow the
trumpets regularly before the ark of the covenant of God.

David's Psalm of Thanks

7That day David first committed to Asaph
and his associates this psalm of thanks to the
LORD:

8 Give thanks to the LORD, call on his
name;
make known among the nations what
he has done.
9 Sing to him, sing praise to him;
tell of all his wonderful acts.
10 Glory in his holy name;
let the hearts of those who seek the
LORD rejoice.
11 Look to the LORD and his strength;
seek his face always.
12 Remember the wonders he has done,
his miracles, and the judgments he
pronounced,

---

[a] *18* Three Hebrew manuscripts and most Septuagint manuscripts (see also verse 20 and 1 Chron. 16:5); most Hebrew manuscripts *Zechariah son and* or *Zechariah, Ben and* [b] *18* Hebrew; Septuagint (see also verse 21) *Jeiel and Azaziah* [c] *20* Probably a musical term [d] *1* Traditionally *peace offerings*; also in verse 2

13 O descendants of Israel his servant,
O sons of Jacob, his chosen ones.

14 He is the LORD our God;
his judgments are in all the earth.
15 He remembers[a] his covenant forever,
the word he commanded, for a
thousand generations,
16 the covenant he made with Abraham,
the oath he swore to Isaac.
17 He confirmed it to Jacob as a decree,
to Israel as an everlasting covenant:
18 "To you I will give the land of Canaan
as the portion you will inherit."

19 When they were but few in number,
few indeed, and strangers in it,
20 they[b] wandered from nation to nation,
from one kingdom to another.
21 He allowed no man to oppress them;
for their sake he rebuked kings:
22 "Do not touch my anointed ones;
do my prophets no harm."

23 Sing to the LORD, all the earth;
proclaim his salvation day after day.
24 Declare his glory among the nations,
his marvelous deeds among all
peoples.
25 For great is the LORD and most worthy of
praise;
he is to be feared above all gods.
26 For all the gods of the nations are idols,
but the LORD made the heavens.
27 Splendor and majesty are before him;
strength and joy in his dwelling place.
28 Ascribe to the LORD, O families of
nations,
ascribe to the LORD glory and
strength,
29 ascribe to the LORD the glory due his
name.
Bring an offering and come before him;
worship the LORD in the splendor of
his[c] holiness.
30 Tremble before him, all the earth!
The world is firmly established; it
cannot be moved.
31 Let the heavens rejoice, let the earth be
glad;
let them say among the nations, "The
LORD reigns!"
32 Let the sea resound, and all that is in it;
let the fields be jubilant, and everything
in them!
33 Then the trees of the forest will sing,
they will sing for joy before the LORD,
for he comes to judge the earth.

34 Give thanks to the LORD, for he is good;
his love endures forever.
35 Cry out, "Save us, O God our Savior;
gather us and deliver us from the
nations,
that we may give thanks to your holy
name,
that we may glory in your praise."
36 Praise be to the LORD, the God of Israel,
from everlasting to everlasting.

Then all the people said "Amen" and "Praise
the LORD."

37 David left Asaph and his associates before the ark of the covenant of the LORD to
minister there regularly, according to each
day's requirements. 38 He also left Obed-Edom
and his sixty-eight associates to minister with
them. Obed-Edom son of Jeduthun, and also
Hosah, were gatekeepers.
39 David left Zadok the priest and his fellow priests before the tabernacle of the LORD
at the high place in Gibeon 40 to present
burnt offerings to the LORD on the altar of
burnt offering regularly, morning and evening, in accordance with everything written
in the Law of the LORD, which he had given
Israel. 41 With them were Heman and Jeduthun and the rest of those chosen and designated by name to give thanks to the LORD,
"for his love endures forever." 42 Heman and
Jeduthun were responsible for the sounding
of the trumpets and cymbals and for the playing of the other instruments for sacred song.
The sons of Jeduthun were stationed at the
gate.
43 Then all the people left, each for his own
home, and David returned home to bless his
family.

God's Promise to David

17 After David was settled in his palace,
he said to Nathan the prophet, "Here
I am, living in a palace of cedar, while
the ark of the covenant of the LORD is under
a tent."
2 Nathan replied to David, "Whatever you
have in mind, do it, for God is with you."
3 That night the word of God came to Nathan, saying:

[a] 15 Some Septuagint manuscripts (see also Psalm 105:8); Hebrew *Remember* [b] 18-20 One Hebrew manuscript, Septuagint and Vulgate (see also Psalm 105:12); most Hebrew manuscripts *inherit, / [19]though you are but few in number, / few indeed, and strangers in it." / [20]They* [c] 29 Or *LORD with the splendor of*

4“Go and tell my servant David, ‘This is what the LORD says: You are not the one to build me a house to dwell in. 5I have not dwelt in a house from the day I brought Israel up out of Egypt to this day. I have moved from one tent site to another, from one dwelling place to another. 6Wherever I have moved with all the Israelites, did I ever say to any of their leaders[a] whom I commanded to shepherd my people, “Why have you not built me a house of cedar?” ’

7“Now then, tell my servant David, ‘This is what the LORD Almighty says: I took you from the pasture and from following the flock, to be ruler over my people Israel. 8I have been with you wherever you have gone, and I have cut off all your enemies from before you. Now I will make your name like the names of the greatest men of the earth. 9And I will provide a place for my people Israel and will plant them so that they can have a home of their own and no longer be disturbed. Wicked people will not oppress them anymore, as they did at the beginning 10and have done ever since the time I appointed leaders over my people Israel. I will also subdue all your enemies.

“ ‘I declare to you that the LORD will build a house for you: 11When your days are over and you go to be with your fathers, I will raise up your offspring to succeed you, one of your own sons, and I will establish his kingdom. 12He is the one who will build a house for me, and I will establish his throne forever. 13I will be his father, and he will be my son. I will never take my love away from him, as I took it away from your predecessor. 14I will set him over my house and my kingdom forever; his throne will be established forever.’ ”

15Nathan reported to David all the words of this entire revelation.

David's Prayer

16Then King David went in and sat before the LORD, and he said:

“Who am I, O LORD God, and what is my family, that you have brought me this far? 17And as if this were not enough in your sight, O God, you have spoken about the future of the house of your servant. You have looked on me as though I were the most exalted of men, O LORD God.

18“What more can David say to you for honoring your servant? For you know your servant, 19O LORD. For the sake of your servant and according to your will, you have done this great thing and made known all these great promises.

20“There is no one like you, O LORD, and there is no God but you, as we have heard with our own ears. 21And who is like your people Israel—the one nation on earth whose God went out to redeem a people for himself, and to make a name for yourself, and to perform great and awesome wonders by driving out nations from before your people, whom you redeemed from Egypt? 22You made your people Israel your very own forever, and you, O LORD, have become their God.

23“And now, LORD, let the promise you have made concerning your servant and his house be established forever. Do as you promised, 24so that it will be established and that your name will be great forever. Then men will say, ‘The LORD Almighty, the God over Israel, is Israel's God!’ And the house of your servant David will be established before you.

25“You, my God, have revealed to your servant that you will build a house for him. So your servant has found courage to pray to you. 26O LORD, you are God! You have promised these good things to your servant. 27Now you have been pleased to bless the house of your servant, that it may continue forever in your sight; for you, O LORD, have blessed it, and it will be blessed forever.”

David's Victories

18 In the course of time, David defeated the Philistines and subdued them, and he took Gath and its surrounding villages from the control of the Philistines.

2David also defeated the Moabites, and they became subject to him and brought tribute.

3Moreover, David fought Hadadezer king of Zobah, as far as Hamath, when he went to establish his control along the Euphrates River. 4David captured a thousand of his chariots, seven thousand charioteers and twenty

[a] 6 Traditionally *judges*; also in verse 10

DEALING WITH REJECTION

> **"Go and tell my servant David, 'This is what the LORD says: You are not the one to build me a house to dwell in.' "**
>
> — 1 CHRONICLES 17:4

let's talk

- When have we experienced a situation like David's—wanting to do something for God, but finding ourselves passed over? How did we react?
- Did we share these feelings of disappointment with each other or did we keep them to ourselves?
- When have we sensed God redirecting our desires as a couple? What was the outcome? What did we learn?

I don't know about you, but I've had moments when I've felt like David after God rejected his offer to build the temple. There have been times when I've wanted to do something that I thought would honor God—and I haven't been allowed to do it.

My friends Sharon and Ken spent several years of their marriage feeling rejected as potential parents. They both love children and strongly believe that one of the central purposes of Christian marriage is creating a home where children can be loved and nurtured. "Be fruitful and multiply seems like a basic instruction," Sharon said. "We couldn't wait to get to it!"

Indeed, Sharon and Ken began trying to conceive in the days immediately after their wedding. Six months went by. No pregnancy. After 14 months, my friends sought medical help. They soon learned that they would probably never conceive a baby.

Sharon went into a depression that seemed unrelenting. Friends and relatives urged her to consider adoption, but she couldn't think about that. Everyone else's pregnancy seemed like a personal rebuke. Sharon tried to be happy when others got pregnant, but she couldn't fake it. She was jealous and sad and angry, wondering why she was being punished with infertility.

Then, one day in a bookstore, she found herself reading a book about adoption. She bought the book. She started searching the Web for adoption agencies. And she began thinking about how, through Jesus Christ, she had been adopted into the family of God.

Something began shifting inside. "The still, small voice of the Holy Spirit became a little less small, maybe," Sharon said. "Or maybe I just got the wax out of my ears."

Sharon and Ken are now advancing through the adoption process. "We still grieve the biological children we won't have," Sharon said. "But we are very excited about adopting a child."

Marriage so often is the vessel through which God reshapes our desires and gives us new, unexpected channels in which to glorify him. We think we've been called to stay home with the kids, but then our husband gets laid off and we have to go back to work. Or we plan to serve God in our town but then find ourselves moving across the country. Indeed, we thought we were called to serve God as a single person, but, lo and behold, we're planning our wedding.

Those turnings can be challenging. But we can rest easy knowing that it is God who is doing the turning, and he will use this seeming rejection to keep us on our knees before him and to open us up to his plans for us.

—LAUREN WINNER

FOR YOUR NEXT DEVOTIONAL READING, TURN TO PAGE 447.

thousand foot soldiers. He hamstrung all but
a hundred of the chariot horses.
5When the Arameans of Damascus came to
help Hadadezer king of Zobah, David struck
down twenty-two thousand of them. 6He put
garrisons in the Aramean kingdom of Damascus, and the Arameans became subject to him
and brought tribute. The LORD gave David
victory everywhere he went.
7David took the gold shields carried by the
officers of Hadadezer and brought them to Jerusalem. 8From Tebah[a] and Cun, towns that
belonged to Hadadezer, David took a great
quantity of bronze, which Solomon used to
make the bronze Sea, the pillars and various
bronze articles.
9When Tou king of Hamath heard that David had defeated the entire army of Hadadezer king of Zobah, 10he sent his son Hadoram
to King David to greet him and congratulate
him on his victory in battle over Hadadezer,
who had been at war with Tou. Hadoram
brought all kinds of articles of gold and silver
and bronze.
11King David dedicated these articles to the
LORD, as he had done with the silver and gold
he had taken from all these nations: Edom
and Moab, the Ammonites and the Philistines, and Amalek.
12Abishai son of Zeruiah struck down
eighteen thousand Edomites in the Valley of
Salt. 13He put garrisons in Edom, and all the
Edomites became subject to David. The LORD
gave David victory everywhere he went.

David's Officials

14David reigned over all Israel, doing what
was just and right for all his people. 15Joab son
of Zeruiah was over the army; Jehoshaphat
son of Ahilud was recorder; 16Zadok son of
Ahitub and Ahimelech[b] son of Abiathar were
priests; Shavsha was secretary; 17Benaiah son
of Jehoiada was over the Kerethites and Pelethites; and David's sons were chief officials at
the king's side.

The Battle Against the Ammonites

19 In the course of time, Nahash king of
the Ammonites died, and his son succeeded him as king. 2David thought, "I
will show kindness to Hanun son of Nahash,
because his father showed kindness to me." So
David sent a delegation to express his sympathy to Hanun concerning his father.
When David's men came to Hanun in the
land of the Ammonites to express sympathy
to him, 3the Ammonite nobles said to Hanun,
"Do you think David is honoring your father
by sending men to you to express sympathy?
Haven't his men come to you to explore and
spy out the country and overthrow it?" 4So
Hanun seized David's men, shaved them, cut
off their garments in the middle at the buttocks, and sent them away.
5When someone came and told David
about the men, he sent messengers to meet
them, for they were greatly humiliated. The
king said, "Stay at Jericho till your beards have
grown, and then come back."
6When the Ammonites realized that they
had become a stench in David's nostrils, Hanun and the Ammonites sent a thousand talents[c] of silver to hire chariots and charioteers
from Aram Naharaim,[d] Aram Maacah and
Zobah. 7They hired thirty-two thousand chariots and charioteers, as well as the king of Maacah with his troops, who came and camped
near Medeba, while the Ammonites were
mustered from their towns and moved out for
battle.
8On hearing this, David sent Joab out with
the entire army of fighting men. 9The Ammonites came out and drew up in battle formation at the entrance to their city, while the
kings who had come were by themselves in the
open country.
10Joab saw that there were battle lines in
front of him and behind him; so he selected
some of the best troops in Israel and deployed
them against the Arameans. 11He put the rest
of the men under the command of Abishai his
brother, and they were deployed against the
Ammonites. 12Joab said, "If the Arameans are
too strong for me, then you are to rescue me;
but if the Ammonites are too strong for you,
then I will rescue you. 13Be strong and let us
fight bravely for our people and the cities of
our God. The LORD will do what is good in
his sight."
14Then Joab and the troops with him advanced to fight the Arameans, and they fled
before him. 15When the Ammonites saw that
the Arameans were fleeing, they too fled before his brother Abishai and went inside the
city. So Joab went back to Jerusalem.
16After the Arameans saw that they had been
routed by Israel, they sent messengers and had
Arameans brought from beyond the River,[e]

[a] 8 Hebrew *Tibhath*, a variant of *Tebah* [b] 16 Some Hebrew manuscripts, Vulgate and Syriac (see also 2 Samuel 8:17); most Hebrew manuscripts *Abimelech* [c] 6 That is, about 37 tons (about 34 metric tons) [d] 6 That is, Northwest Mesopotamia [e] 16 That is, the Euphrates

with Shophach the commander of Hadadezer's army leading them.
17When David was told of this, he gathered
all Israel and crossed the Jordan; he advanced
against them and formed his battle lines opposite them. David formed his lines to meet the
Arameans in battle, and they fought against
him. 18But they fled before Israel, and David killed seven thousand of their charioteers
and forty thousand of their foot soldiers. He
also killed Shophach the commander of their
army.
19When the vassals of Hadadezer saw that
they had been defeated by Israel, they made
peace with David and became subject to
him.
So the Arameans were not willing to help
the Ammonites anymore.

The Capture of Rabbah

20 In the spring, at the time when kings go
off to war, Joab led out the armed forces.
He laid waste the land of the Ammonites and went to Rabbah and besieged it, but
David remained in Jerusalem. Joab attacked
Rabbah and left it in ruins. 2David took the
crown from the head of their king[a]—its
weight was found to be a talent[b] of gold, and
it was set with precious stones—and it was
placed on David's head. He took a great quantity of plunder from the city 3and brought
out the people who were there, consigning
them to labor with saws and with iron picks
and axes. David did this to all the Ammonite towns. Then David and his entire army returned to Jerusalem.

War With the Philistines

4In the course of time, war broke out with
the Philistines, at Gezer. At that time Sibbecai
the Hushathite killed Sippai, one of the descendants of the Rephaites, and the Philistines
were subjugated.
5In another battle with the Philistines, Elhanan son of Jair killed Lahmi the brother of
Goliath the Gittite, who had a spear with a
shaft like a weaver's rod.
6In still another battle, which took place at
Gath, there was a huge man with six fingers on
each hand and six toes on each foot—twenty-
four in all. He also was descended from Rapha. 7When he taunted Israel, Jonathan son of
Shimea, David's brother, killed him.
8These were descendants of Rapha in Gath,
and they fell at the hands of David and his
men.

David Numbers the Fighting Men

21 Satan rose up against Israel and incited
David to take a census of Israel. 2So David said to Joab and the commanders of
the troops, "Go and count the Israelites from
Beersheba to Dan. Then report back to me so
that I may know how many there are."
3But Joab replied, "May the LORD multiply
his troops a hundred times over. My lord the
king, are they not all my lord's subjects? Why
does my lord want to do this? Why should he
bring guilt on Israel?"
4The king's word, however, overruled Joab;
so Joab left and went throughout Israel and
then came back to Jerusalem. 5Joab reported
the number of the fighting men to David: In
all Israel there were one million one hundred
thousand men who could handle a sword, including four hundred and seventy thousand
in Judah.
6But Joab did not include Levi and Benjamin in the numbering, because the king's
command was repulsive to him. 7This command was also evil in the sight of God; so he
punished Israel.
8Then David said to God, "I have sinned
greatly by doing this. Now, I beg you, take
away the guilt of your servant. I have done a
very foolish thing."
9The LORD said to Gad, David's seer, 10"Go
and tell David, 'This is what the LORD says: I
am giving you three options. Choose one of
them for me to carry out against you.' "
11So Gad went to David and said to him,
"This is what the LORD says: 'Take your choice:
12three years of famine, three months of being swept away[c] before your enemies, with
their swords overtaking you, or three days of
the sword of the LORD—days of plague in the
land, with the angel of the LORD ravaging every part of Israel.' Now then, decide how I
should answer the one who sent me."
13David said to Gad, "I am in deep distress.
Let me fall into the hands of the LORD, for his
mercy is very great; but do not let me fall into
the hands of men."
14So the LORD sent a plague on Israel, and
seventy thousand men of Israel fell dead.
15And God sent an angel to destroy Jerusalem. But as the angel was doing so, the LORD
saw it and was grieved because of the calamity
and said to the angel who was destroying the

---

[a] *2* Or *of Milcom,* that is, Molech [b] *2* That is, about 75 pounds (about 34 kilograms) [c] *12* Hebrew; Septuagint and Vulgate (see also 2 Samuel 24:13) *of fleeing*

people, "Enough! Withdraw your hand." The
angel of the LORD was then standing at the
threshing floor of Araunah[a] the Jebusite.
16David looked up and saw the angel of
the LORD standing between heaven and earth,
with a drawn sword in his hand extended over
Jerusalem. Then David and the elders, clothed
in sackcloth, fell facedown.
17David said to God, "Was it not I who ordered the fighting men to be counted? I am
the one who has sinned and done wrong.
These are but sheep. What have they done?
O LORD my God, let your hand fall upon me
and my family, but do not let this plague remain on your people."
18Then the angel of the LORD ordered Gad
to tell David to go up and build an altar to the
LORD on the threshing floor of Araunah the
Jebusite. 19So David went up in obedience to
the word that Gad had spoken in the name of
the LORD.
20While Araunah was threshing wheat, he
turned and saw the angel; his four sons who
were with him hid themselves. 21Then David approached, and when Araunah looked
and saw him, he left the threshing floor and
bowed down before David with his face to the
ground.
22David said to him, "Let me have the site
of your threshing floor so I can build an altar to the LORD, that the plague on the people may be stopped. Sell it to me at the full
price."
23Araunah said to David, "Take it! Let my
lord the king do whatever pleases him. Look,
I will give the oxen for the burnt offerings, the
threshing sledges for the wood, and the wheat
for the grain offering. I will give all this."
24But King David replied to Araunah, "No,
I insist on paying the full price. I will not take
for the LORD what is yours, or sacrifice a burnt
offering that costs me nothing."
25So David paid Araunah six hundred shekels[b] of gold for the site. 26David built an altar
to the LORD there and sacrificed burnt offerings and fellowship offerings.[c] He called on
the LORD, and the LORD answered him with
fire from heaven on the altar of burnt offering.
27Then the LORD spoke to the angel, and
he put his sword back into its sheath. 28At
that time, when David saw that the LORD had
answered him on the threshing floor of Araunah the Jebusite, he offered sacrifices there.
29The tabernacle of the LORD, which Moses
had made in the desert, and the altar of burnt
offering were at that time on the high place at
Gibeon. 30But David could not go before it to
inquire of God, because he was afraid of the
sword of the angel of the LORD.

22 Then David said, "The house of the
LORD God is to be here, and also the
altar of burnt offering for Israel."

Preparations for the Temple

2So David gave orders to assemble the
aliens living in Israel, and from among them
he appointed stonecutters to prepare dressed
stone for building the house of God. 3He provided a large amount of iron to make nails for
the doors of the gateways and for the fittings,
and more bronze than could be weighed. 4He
also provided more cedar logs than could be
counted, for the Sidonians and Tyrians had
brought large numbers of them to David.
5David said, "My son Solomon is young
and inexperienced, and the house to be built
for the LORD should be of great magnificence
and fame and splendor in the sight of all the
nations. Therefore I will make preparations
for it." So David made extensive preparations
before his death.
6Then he called for his son Solomon and
charged him to build a house for the LORD,
the God of Israel. 7David said to Solomon:
"My son, I had it in my heart to build a house
for the Name of the LORD my God. 8But this
word of the LORD came to me: 'You have shed
much blood and have fought many wars. You
are not to build a house for my Name, because
you have shed much blood on the earth in my
sight. 9But you will have a son who will be
a man of peace and rest, and I will give him
rest from all his enemies on every side. His
name will be Solomon,[d] and I will grant Israel
peace and quiet during his reign. 10He is the
one who will build a house for my Name. He
will be my son, and I will be his father. And I
will establish the throne of his kingdom over
Israel forever.'
11"Now, my son, the LORD be with you,
and may you have success and build the house
of the LORD your God, as he said you would.
12May the LORD give you discretion and understanding when he puts you in command
over Israel, so that you may keep the law of the
LORD your God. 13Then you will have success
if you are careful to observe the decrees and

[a] *15* Hebrew *Ornan,* a variant of *Araunah;* also in verses 18-28 [b] *25* That is, about 15 pounds (about 7 kilograms) [c] *26* Traditionally *peace offerings* [d] *9* *Solomon* sounds like and may be derived from the Hebrew for *peace.*

F

FRIDAY

READ 1 CHRONICLES 22:2–19

BUILDING OUR RELATIONSHIP

> **Then you will have success if you are careful to observe the decrees and laws that the LORD gave Moses for Israel. Be strong and courageous. Do not be afraid or discouraged.**
>
> — 1 CHRONICLES 22:13

let's talk

- How has our love for each other and for God deepened as a result of persevering through struggles in our marriage?
- Which one of us needs the most help now, and how can the other best provide that help?
- What can we do today to build a strong marriage relationship?

"Marriage is a most remarkable and courageous human act," says Ernest Boyer in *A Way in the World* (HarperSanFrancisco, 1984). "It's the promise of two human beings to share life together on all levels, physical, economic, and spiritual. It's a promise made despite the certainty of death, the certainty of change, and the uncertainty of everything else. There is nothing else we might choose to do that is quite like this act, nothing so foolish or so profound."

Why do so many of us enter into this "foolish and profound" commitment when we realize that it is such a difficult thing to unify two separate individuals? Why do we assume we will have success when we know that others fail?

Before his death, David shared his vision for building a temple for the Lord with his son Solomon, to whom God had entrusted this sacred task. David had spent countless hours collecting and preparing all of the materials his son would need to build a house worthy of the Lord. Then David told Solomon that if he was careful to observe the laws of the Lord, he would have success.

Likewise we, too, need to take great care in preparing for the construction of a marriage. Marriage is like a temple—a magnificent living, breathing house for the Lord. When we stand at the altar exchanging wedding vows, we're essentially agreeing to erect a temple in which to honor God. By following God's plan for marriage—loving, honoring, and remaining faithful to each other—we will have success in honoring him. When we're strong and courageous, we'll be able to overcome obstacles and persevere.

Sounds easy. But it's not.

When Dan and I were preparing to get married, we spent an entire year budgeting, envisioning, and getting quotes on bands, caterers, cakes and invitations—planning all of the elements that go into making a wedding day a success. Soon after we walked down the aisle as Mr. and Mrs., we realized we would need to apply that same kind of care to building our relationship for a lifetime, not just planning for a day.

Marriages often include struggles. Changes in career aspirations, guilty feelings over past mistakes, conflicts in other relationships—these and a myriad of other situations present many opportunities to be either the afflicted or the comforter within marriage. In these periods the one doing the supporting may begin to think, "I am not being helped by this person, only held back." But because of that foolish, extraordinary vow of marriage, he or she keeps going.

Through the ordinary pains and sharing of day-to-day life, marital love matures into a love that models God's own love for us. It is in this temple we call marriage that God profoundly manifests himself, giving us the tools we need to be successful as husband and wife.

—MARIAN V. LIAUTAUD

FOR YOUR NEXT DEVOTIONAL READING, TURN TO PAGE 454.

laws that the LORD gave Moses for Israel. Be
strong and courageous. Do not be afraid or
discouraged.
14 "I have taken great pains to provide for
the temple of the LORD a hundred thousand
talents[a] of gold, a million talents[b] of silver,
quantities of bronze and iron too great to be
weighed, and wood and stone. And you may
add to them. 15 You have many workmen:
stonecutters, masons and carpenters, as well as
men skilled in every kind of work 16 in gold
and silver, bronze and iron—craftsmen beyond number. Now begin the work, and the
LORD be with you."
17 Then David ordered all the leaders of Israel to help his son Solomon. 18 He said to them,
"Is not the LORD your God with you? And has
he not granted you rest on every side? For he
has handed the inhabitants of the land over to
me, and the land is subject to the LORD and
to his people. 19 Now devote your heart and
soul to seeking the LORD your God. Begin to
build the sanctuary of the LORD God, so that
you may bring the ark of the covenant of the
LORD and the sacred articles belonging to God
into the temple that will be built for the Name
of the LORD."

The Levites

23 When David was old and full of years,
he made his son Solomon king over Israel.
2 He also gathered together all the leaders of
Israel, as well as the priests and Levites. 3 The
Levites thirty years old or more were counted,
and the total number of men was thirty-eight
thousand. 4 David said, "Of these, twenty-four
thousand are to supervise the work of the temple of the LORD and six thousand are to be
officials and judges. 5 Four thousand are to be
gatekeepers and four thousand are to praise
the LORD with the musical instruments I have
provided for that purpose."
6 David divided the Levites into groups corresponding to the sons of Levi: Gershon, Kohath and Merari.

Gershonites

7 Belonging to the Gershonites:
Ladan and Shimei.
8 The sons of Ladan:
Jehiel the first, Zetham and Joel—
three in all.
9 The sons of Shimei:
Shelomoth, Haziel and Haran—three
in all.
These were the heads of the families of
Ladan.
10 And the sons of Shimei:
Jahath, Ziza,[c] Jeush and Beriah.
These were the sons of Shimei—four
in all.
11 Jahath was the first and Ziza the second, but Jeush and Beriah did not
have many sons; so they were counted
as one family with one assignment.

Kohathites

12 The sons of Kohath:
Amram, Izhar, Hebron and Uzziel—
four in all.
13 The sons of Amram:
Aaron and Moses.
Aaron was set apart, he and his descendants forever, to consecrate the most
holy things, to offer sacrifices before
the LORD, to minister before him and
to pronounce blessings in his name
forever. 14 The sons of Moses the man
of God were counted as part of the
tribe of Levi.
15 The sons of Moses:
Gershom and Eliezer.
16 The descendants of Gershom:
Shubael was the first.
17 The descendants of Eliezer:
Rehabiah was the first.
Eliezer had no other sons, but the sons
of Rehabiah were very numerous.
18 The sons of Izhar:
Shelomith was the first.
19 The sons of Hebron:
Jeriah the first, Amariah the second,
Jahaziel the third and Jekameam the
fourth.
20 The sons of Uzziel:
Micah the first and Isshiah the second.

Merarites

21 The sons of Merari:
Mahli and Mushi.
The sons of Mahli:
Eleazar and Kish.
22 Eleazar died without having sons: he
had only daughters. Their cousins, the
sons of Kish, married them.
23 The sons of Mushi:

[a] *14* That is, about 3,750 tons (about 3,450 metric tons) [b] *14* That is, about 37,500 tons (about 34,500 metric tons)
[c] *10* One Hebrew manuscript, Septuagint and Vulgate (see also verse 11); most Hebrew manuscripts *Zina*

Mahli, Eder and Jerimoth—three in
all.

24 These were the descendants of Levi by
their families—the heads of families as they
were registered under their names and counted individually, that is, the workers twenty
years old or more who served in the temple
of the LORD. 25 For David had said, "Since the
LORD, the God of Israel, has granted rest to
his people and has come to dwell in Jerusalem
forever, 26 the Levites no longer need to carry
the tabernacle or any of the articles used in its
service." 27 According to the last instructions
of David, the Levites were counted from those
twenty years old or more.

28 The duty of the Levites was to help Aaron's descendants in the service of the temple
of the LORD: to be in charge of the courtyards,
the side rooms, the purification of all sacred
things and the performance of other duties
at the house of God. 29 They were in charge
of the bread set out on the table, the flour
for the grain offerings, the unleavened wafers,
the baking and the mixing, and all measurements of quantity and size. 30 They were also
to stand every morning to thank and praise
the LORD. They were to do the same in the
evening 31 and whenever burnt offerings were
presented to the LORD on Sabbaths and at
New Moon festivals and at appointed feasts.
They were to serve before the LORD regularly in the proper number and in the way prescribed for them.

32 And so the Levites carried out their responsibilities for the Tent of Meeting, for the
Holy Place and, under their brothers the descendants of Aaron, for the service of the temple of the LORD.

The Divisions of Priests

24 These were the divisions of the sons of
Aaron:
The sons of Aaron were Nadab, Abihu,
Eleazar and Ithamar. 2 But Nadab and Abihu died before their father did, and they had
no sons; so Eleazar and Ithamar served as the
priests. 3 With the help of Zadok a descendant of Eleazar and Ahimelech a descendant
of Ithamar, David separated them into divisions for their appointed order of ministering. 4 A larger number of leaders were found
among Eleazar's descendants than among
Ithamar's, and they were divided accordingly: sixteen heads of families from Eleazar's
descendants and eight heads of families from
Ithamar's descendants. 5 They divided them
impartially by drawing lots, for there were
officials of the sanctuary and officials of God
among the descendants of both Eleazar and
Ithamar.

6 The scribe Shemaiah son of Nethanel, a
Levite, recorded their names in the presence of
the king and of the officials: Zadok the priest,
Ahimelech son of Abiathar and the heads of
families of the priests and of the Levites—one
family being taken from Eleazar and then one
from Ithamar.

7 The first lot fell to Jehoiarib,
the second to Jedaiah,
8 the third to Harim,
the fourth to Seorim,
9 the fifth to Malkijah,
the sixth to Mijamin,
10 the seventh to Hakkoz,
the eighth to Abijah,
11 the ninth to Jeshua,
the tenth to Shecaniah,
12 the eleventh to Eliashib,
the twelfth to Jakim,
13 the thirteenth to Huppah,
the fourteenth to Jeshebeab,
14 the fifteenth to Bilgah,
the sixteenth to Immer,
15 the seventeenth to Hezir,
the eighteenth to Happizzez,
16 the nineteenth to Pethahiah,
the twentieth to Jehezkel,
17 the twenty-first to Jakin,
the twenty-second to Gamul,
18 the twenty-third to Delaiah
and the twenty-fourth to Maaziah.

19 This was their appointed order of ministering when they entered the temple of the
LORD, according to the regulations prescribed
for them by their forefather Aaron, as the
LORD, the God of Israel, had commanded
him.

The Rest of the Levites

20 As for the rest of the descendants of Levi:
from the sons of Amram: Shubael;
from the sons of Shubael: Jehdeiah.
21 As for Rehabiah, from his sons:
Isshiah was the first.
22 From the Izharites: Shelomoth;
from the sons of Shelomoth: Jahath.
23 The sons of Hebron: Jeriah the first,[a]

---

[a] 23 Two Hebrew manuscripts and some Septuagint manuscripts (see also 1 Chron. 23:19); most Hebrew manuscripts *The sons of Jeriah:*

Amariah the second, Jahaziel the third
and Jekameam the fourth.
24 The son of Uzziel: Micah;
from the sons of Micah: Shamir.
25 The brother of Micah: Isshiah;
from the sons of Isshiah: Zechariah.
26 The sons of Merari: Mahli and Mushi.
The son of Jaaziah: Beno.
27 The sons of Merari:
from Jaaziah: Beno, Shoham, Zaccur
and Ibri.
28 From Mahli: Eleazar, who had no sons.
29 From Kish: the son of Kish:
Jerahmeel.
30 And the sons of Mushi: Mahli, Eder and
Jerimoth.

These were the Levites, according to their
families. 31 They also cast lots, just as their
brothers the descendants of Aaron did, in the
presence of King David and of Zadok, Ahimelech, and the heads of families of the priests
and of the Levites. The families of the oldest
brother were treated the same as those of the
youngest.

The Singers

25 David, together with the commanders
of the army, set apart some of the sons
of Asaph, Heman and Jeduthun for the
ministry of prophesying, accompanied by
harps, lyres and cymbals. Here is the list of the
men who performed this service:

2 From the sons of Asaph:
Zaccur, Joseph, Nethaniah and Asarelah.
The sons of Asaph were under the supervision of Asaph, who prophesied under
the king's supervision.
3 As for Jeduthun, from his sons:
Gedaliah, Zeri, Jeshaiah, Shimei,[a] Hashabiah and Mattithiah, six in all, under the
supervision of their father Jeduthun, who
prophesied, using the harp in thanking
and praising the LORD.
4 As for Heman, from his sons:
Bukkiah, Mattaniah, Uzziel, Shubael and
Jerimoth; Hananiah, Hanani, Eliathah,
Giddalti and Romamti-Ezer; Joshbekashah, Mallothi, Hothir and Mahazioth.
5 All these were sons of Heman the king's
seer. They were given him through the
promises of God to exalt him.[b] God gave
Heman fourteen sons and three daughters.

6 All these men were under the supervision
of their fathers for the music of the temple of
the LORD, with cymbals, lyres and harps, for
the ministry at the house of God. Asaph, Jeduthun and Heman were under the supervision
of the king. 7 Along with their relatives—all
of them trained and skilled in music for the
LORD—they numbered 288. 8 Young and old
alike, teacher as well as student, cast lots for
their duties.

9 The first lot, which was for Asaph,
fell to Joseph,
his sons and relatives,[c] 12[d]
the second to Gedaliah,
he and his relatives and sons, 12
10 the third to Zaccur,
his sons and relatives, 12
11 the fourth to Izri,[e]
his sons and relatives, 12
12 the fifth to Nethaniah,
his sons and relatives, 12
13 the sixth to Bukkiah,
his sons and relatives, 12
14 the seventh to Jesarelah,[f]
his sons and relatives, 12
15 the eighth to Jeshaiah,
his sons and relatives, 12
16 the ninth to Mattaniah,
his sons and relatives, 12
17 the tenth to Shimei,
his sons and relatives, 12
18 the eleventh to Azarel,[g]
his sons and relatives, 12
19 the twelfth to Hashabiah,
his sons and relatives, 12
20 the thirteenth to Shubael,
his sons and relatives, 12
21 the fourteenth to Mattithiah,
his sons and relatives, 12
22 the fifteenth to Jerimoth,
his sons and relatives, 12
23 the sixteenth to Hananiah,
his sons and relatives, 12
24 the seventeenth to Joshbekashah,
his sons and relatives, 12
25 the eighteenth to Hanani,
his sons and relatives, 12
26 the nineteenth to Mallothi,
his sons and relatives, 12
27 the twentieth to Eliathah,
his sons and relatives, 12
28 the twenty-first to Hothir,
his sons and relatives, 12

---

[a] 3 One Hebrew manuscript and some Septuagint manuscripts (see also verse 17); most Hebrew manuscripts do not have *Shimei.*
[b] 5 Hebrew *exalt the horn* [c] 9 See Septuagint; Hebrew does not have *his sons and relatives.* [d] 9 See the total in verse 7; Hebrew does not have *twelve.* [e] 11 A variant of *Zeri* [f] 14 A variant of *Asarelah* [g] 18 A variant of *Uzziel*

29 the twenty-second to Giddalti,
his sons and relatives, 12
30 the twenty-third to Mahazioth,
his sons and relatives, 12
31 the twenty-fourth to Romamti-Ezer,
his sons and relatives, 12

The Gatekeepers

26 The divisions of the gatekeepers:
From the Korahites: Meshelemiah
son of Kore, one of the sons of Asaph.
2 Meshelemiah had sons:
Zechariah the firstborn,
Jediael the second,
Zebadiah the third,
Jathniel the fourth,
3 Elam the fifth,
Jehohanan the sixth
and Eliehoenai the seventh.
4 Obed-Edom also had sons:
Shemaiah the firstborn,
Jehozabad the second,
Joah the third,
Sacar the fourth,
Nethanel the fifth,
5 Ammiel the sixth,
Issachar the seventh
and Peullethai the eighth.
(For God had blessed Obed-Edom.)

6 His son Shemaiah also had sons, who
were leaders in their father's family
because they were very capable men.
7 The sons of Shemaiah: Othni, Repha-
el, Obed and Elzabad; his relatives Elihu and Semakiah were also able men.
8 All these were descendants of Obed-
Edom; they and their sons and their
relatives were capable men with the
strength to do the work—descendants
of Obed-Edom, 62 in all.
9 Meshelemiah had sons and relatives, who
were able men—18 in all.

10 Hosah the Merarite had sons: Shimri the
first (although he was not the firstborn, his father had appointed him
the first), 11 Hilkiah the second, Tabali-
ah the third and Zechariah the fourth.
The sons and relatives of Hosah were
13 in all.

12 These divisions of the gatekeepers,
through their chief men, had duties for ministering in the temple of the LORD, just as
their relatives had. 13 Lots were cast for each
gate, according to their families, young and
old alike.

14 The lot for the East Gate fell to Shelemiah.[a] Then lots were cast for his son Zechariah, a wise counselor, and the lot for the North
Gate fell to him. 15 The lot for the South Gate
fell to Obed-Edom, and the lot for the storehouse fell to his sons. 16 The lots for the West
Gate and the Shalleketh Gate on the upper
road fell to Shuppim and Hosah.

Guard was alongside of guard: 17 There were
six Levites a day on the east, four a day on the
north, four a day on the south and two at a
time at the storehouse. 18 As for the court to
the west, there were four at the road and two
at the court itself.

19 These were the divisions of the gatekeepers who were descendants of Korah and Merari.

The Treasurers and Other Officials

20 Their fellow Levites were[b] in charge of
the treasuries of the house of God and the
treasuries for the dedicated things.

21 The descendants of Ladan, who were Gershonites through Ladan and who were heads
of families belonging to Ladan the Gershonite, were Jehieli, 22 the sons of Jehieli, Zetham
and his brother Joel. They were in charge of
the treasuries of the temple of the LORD.

23 From the Amramites, the Izharites, the
Hebronites and the Uzzielites:

24 Shubael, a descendant of Gershom son
of Moses, was the officer in charge of
the treasuries. 25 His relatives through
Eliezer: Rehabiah his son, Jeshaiah his
son, Joram his son, Zicri his son and
Shelomith his son. 26 Shelomith and
his relatives were in charge of all the
treasuries for the things dedicated by
King David, by the heads of families
who were the commanders of thousands and commanders of hundreds,
and by the other army commanders.
27 Some of the plunder taken in battle they dedicated for the repair of the
temple of the LORD. 28 And everything
dedicated by Samuel the seer and by
Saul son of Kish, Abner son of Ner
and Joab son of Zeruiah, and all the
other dedicated things were in the care
of Shelomith and his relatives.
29 From the Izharites: Kenaniah and his
sons were assigned duties away from

[a] 14 A variant of *Meshelemiah* [b] 20 Septuagint; Hebrew *As for the Levites, Ahijah was*

the temple, as officials and judges over
Israel.
30 From the Hebronites: Hashabiah and
his relatives—seventeen hundred able
men—were responsible in Israel west
of the Jordan for all the work of the
LORD and for the king's service. 31 As
for the Hebronites, Jeriah was their
chief according to the genealogical
records of their families. In the fortieth year of David's reign a search was
made in the records, and capable men
among the Hebronites were found at
Jazer in Gilead. 32 Jeriah had twenty-
seven hundred relatives, who were able
men and heads of families, and King
David put them in charge of the Reubenites, the Gadites and the half-tribe
of Manasseh for every matter pertain-
ing to God and for the affairs of the
king.

Army Divisions

27 This is the list of the Israelites—heads of
families, commanders of thousands and
commanders of hundreds, and their
officers, who served the king in all that concerned the army divisions that were on duty
month by month throughout the year. Each
division consisted of 24,000 men.

2 In charge of the first division, for the first
month, was Jashobeam son of Zabdi-
el. There were 24,000 men in his division. 3 He was a descendant of Perez and
chief of all the army officers for the first
month.
4 In charge of the division for the second
month was Dodai the Ahohite; Mikloth
was the leader of his division. There were
24,000 men in his division.
5 The third army commander, for the third
month, was Benaiah son of Jehoiada
the priest. He was chief and there were
24,000 men in his division. 6 This was
the Benaiah who was a mighty man
among the Thirty and was over the Thirty. His son Ammizabad was in charge of
his division.
7 The fourth, for the fourth month, was Asahel the brother of Joab; his son Zebadiah was his successor. There were 24,000
men in his division.
8 The fifth, for the fifth month, was the commander Shamhuth the Izrahite. There
were 24,000 men in his division.
9 The sixth, for the sixth month, was Ira the
son of Ikkesh the Tekoite. There were
24,000 men in his division.
10 The seventh, for the seventh month, was
Helez the Pelonite, an Ephraimite. There
were 24,000 men in his division.
11 The eighth, for the eighth month, was Sibbecai the Hushathite, a Zerahite. There
were 24,000 men in his division.
12 The ninth, for the ninth month, was Abiezer the Anathothite, a Benjamite. There
were 24,000 men in his division.
13 The tenth, for the tenth month, was Maharai the Netophathite, a Zerahite. There
were 24,000 men in his division.
14 The eleventh, for the eleventh month, was
Benaiah the Pirathonite, an Ephraimite.
There were 24,000 men in his division.
15 The twelfth, for the twelfth month, was
Heldai the Netophathite, from the family of Othniel. There were 24,000 men in
his division.

Officers of the Tribes

16 The officers over the tribes of Israel:

over the Reubenites: Eliezer son of Zicri;
over the Simeonites: Shephatiah son of
Maacah;
17 over Levi: Hashabiah son of Kemuel;
over Aaron: Zadok;
18 over Judah: Elihu, a brother of David;
over Issachar: Omri son of Michael;
19 over Zebulun: Ishmaiah son of Obadiah;
over Naphtali: Jerimoth son of Azriel;
20 over the Ephraimites: Hoshea son of Azaziah;
over half the tribe of Manasseh: Joel son
of Pedaiah;
21 over the half-tribe of Manasseh in Gilead:
Iddo son of Zechariah;
over Benjamin: Jaasiel son of Abner;
22 over Dan: Azarel son of Jeroham.

These were the officers over the tribes of Israel.

23 David did not take the number of the men
twenty years old or less, because the LORD had
promised to make Israel as numerous as the
stars in the sky. 24 Joab son of Zeruiah began to
count the men but did not finish. Wrath came
on Israel on account of this numbering, and
the number was not entered in the book[a] of
the annals of King David.

---

a 24 Septuagint; Hebrew *number*

The King's Overseers

25Azmaveth son of Adiel was in charge of
the royal storehouses.
Jonathan son of Uzziah was in charge of
the storehouses in the outlying districts, in the
towns, the villages and the watchtowers.
26Ezri son of Kelub was in charge of the
field workers who farmed the land.
27Shimei the Ramathite was in charge of
the vineyards.
Zabdi the Shiphmite was in charge of the
produce of the vineyards for the wine vats.
28Baal-Hanan the Gederite was in charge of
the olive and sycamore-fig trees in the western
foothills.
Joash was in charge of the supplies of olive oil.
29Shitrai the Sharonite was in charge of the
herds grazing in Sharon.
Shaphat son of Adlai was in charge of the
herds in the valleys.
30Obil the Ishmaelite was in charge of the
camels.
Jehdeiah the Meronothite was in charge of
the donkeys.
31Jaziz the Hagrite was in charge of the
flocks.
All these were the officials in charge of King
David's property.

32Jonathan, David's uncle, was a counselor,
a man of insight and a scribe. Jehiel son of
Hacmoni took care of the king's sons.
33Ahithophel was the king's counselor.
Hushai the Arkite was the king's friend.
34Ahithophel was succeeded by Jehoiada son
of Benaiah and by Abiathar.
Joab was the commander of the royal
army.

David's Plans for the Temple

28 David summoned all the officials of Israel to assemble at Jerusalem: the officers
over the tribes, the commanders of the
divisions in the service of the king, the commanders of thousands and commanders of
hundreds, and the officials in charge of all the
property and livestock belonging to the king
and his sons, together with the palace officials,
the mighty men and all the brave warriors.
2King David rose to his feet and said: "Listen to me, my brothers and my people. I had
it in my heart to build a house as a place of rest
for the ark of the covenant of the LORD, for
the footstool of our God, and I made plans to
build it. 3But God said to me, 'You are not to
build a house for my Name, because you are a
warrior and have shed blood.'
4"Yet the LORD, the God of Israel, chose
me from my whole family to be king over
Israel forever. He chose Judah as leader, and
from the house of Judah he chose my family, and from my father's sons he was pleased
to make me king over all Israel. 5Of all my
sons—and the LORD has given me many—
he has chosen my son Solomon to sit on the
throne of the kingdom of the LORD over Israel. 6He said to me: 'Solomon your son is the
one who will build my house and my courts,
for I have chosen him to be my son, and I
will be his father. 7I will establish his kingdom forever if he is unswerving in carrying
out my commands and laws, as is being done
at this time.'
8"So now I charge you in the sight of all
Israel and of the assembly of the LORD, and
in the hearing of our God: Be careful to follow all the commands of the LORD your God,
that you may possess this good land and pass
it on as an inheritance to your descendants
forever.
9"And you, my son Solomon, acknowledge the God of your father, and serve him
with wholehearted devotion and with a willing mind, for the LORD searches every heart
and understands every motive behind the
thoughts. If you seek him, he will be found
by you; but if you forsake him, he will reject
you forever. 10Consider now, for the LORD has
chosen you to build a temple as a sanctuary.
Be strong and do the work."
11Then David gave his son Solomon the
plans for the portico of the temple, its buildings, its storerooms, its upper parts, its inner
rooms and the place of atonement. 12He gave
him the plans of all that the Spirit had put
in his mind for the courts of the temple of
the LORD and all the surrounding rooms, for
the treasuries of the temple of God and for
the treasuries for the dedicated things. 13He
gave him instructions for the divisions of the
priests and Levites, and for all the work of
serving in the temple of the LORD, as well
as for all the articles to be used in its service.
14He designated the weight of gold for all the
gold articles to be used in various kinds of
service, and the weight of silver for all the
silver articles to be used in various kinds of
service: 15the weight of gold for the gold
lampstands and their lamps, with the weight
for each lampstand and its lamps; and the
weight of silver for each silver lampstand and
its lamps, according to the use of each lamp-

WEEKEND

praying together

Just a few months after we were married, as a favor to some friends, Lisa and I agreed to swap beds with another couple. They had a waterbed and wanted to move into an upper apartment where waterbeds weren't allowed. Because we lived in a basement apartment, the weight of the waterbed didn't matter, and Lisa and I decided to give our friends a break.

It was an act of charity we soon lived to regret.

Most difficult for me was that throughout all my years of singleness, I enjoyed sleeping alone. Somewhat to my dismay, I learned that Lisa is a cuddler. It took me months to learn how to sleep with someone touching me.

With the waterbed, it got even worse. When one of us moved, it was like trying to sleep on top of a tsunami. I hated it. To make matters more complicated, Lisa has a tendency to drift toward my side of the bed, pushing me over further and further. One night I awoke with my cheek mashed against the wooden frame of the bed.

"This is ridiculous," I thought, so I got out of bed and went over to the other side, slipping in next to Lisa so that I'd have three-fourths of the bed free. You can guess what happened. I awoke early the next morning with my face smashed against the *other* side. "This bed has *got* to go," I insisted.

Just as difficult for me as learning to sleep as a married man was learning to pray as a married man. Overnight everything changed. My usual rituals and spiritual habits just didn't seem to fit my life anymore. I had to find new ones.

I was not alone in finding it more difficult to pray as a married man. Martin Luther confessed to the same dilemma. Verse 7 of 1 Peter 3 explains why: "Husbands, in the same way be considerate as you live with your wives, and treat them with respect as the weaker partner and as heirs with you of the gracious gift of life, so that nothing will hinder your prayers."

When Peter says that men must be considerate of their wives and treat them with respect *so that nothing will hinder their prayers*, he's directly connecting our attitude toward our wives with the fundamental Christian discipline.

I will never again be able to approach prayer as if I were a single man. God sees me, in one sense through my wife. This means that if I want to grow as a married pray-er, I can't pretend that I'm a celibate monk. I can't parrot the practices of medieval scholars who addressed single men and women in their pursuit of God.

Much Christian teaching has gotten this backwards. We're told that if we want to have a stronger marriage, we should improve our prayer lives. But Peter tells us that *we should improve our marriages so that we can improve our prayer lives*. Instead of prayer being the tool that will refine my marriage, Peter tells me that marriage is the tool that will refine my prayers!

—GARY THOMAS

how do you work as a team?

Getting married means that many formerly single activities must now be done as a team. Rate yourself 1, 2, or 3 (1 being great, 2 being OK, 3 being "we're working on it") on the following items.

1. Sleeping together: Do you share the bed and the sheets equally? Is one of you a blanket hog? Or does one of you regularly find yourself being pushed toward the edge of the bed?
2. Holiday traditions: How have you worked out holiday traditions, like decorations, food, gift giving and spending time with extended family?
3. Scheduling personal activities: Do you consult each other before accepting invitations? When making plans with your friends, do you involve each other in the planning?
4. Household chores: Are you both satisfied with the division of labor inside and outside of the house? Does it bother you when he folds the towels in thirds and she folds them in half?
5. Future dreams: When thinking about the future, do you do it alone, only with each other, or some of both?
6. Resolving disputes: Do you both accept responsibility when something goes wrong? Is one spouse more likely to apologize than the other?
7. Driving: When traveling together, who drives and who is the passenger? Do you get directions from a map, stop and ask for help when you get lost, or just wing it? When one serves as navigator, does the other trust the directions?
8. Bathroom: Do you work as a team to give each person space and time?
9. Prayer: Do you and your spouse regularly pray together? Do you alternate who prays out loud, or does one of you usually take the lead? Do you actively seek to resolve marital problems so that they don't hinder your prayer life?

HOW ARE WE DOING?

let's make a DATE

OUR PRAYER GROUP

Read or sing a Christian song or hymn that expresses something you're feeling. Then read a verse or two from the Bible that you selected especially for your partner. Ask your spouse to list three things he or she would like you to pray for. Then add your own items to the list. Pray out loud, but also spend time praying together in silence for each other. Post the list where you'll see it every day, and continue to pray for your partner.

FOR YOUR NEXT DEVOTIONAL READING, TURN TO PAGE 465.

LESSONS FROM THE *Bible*

What can you learn about prayer from Zechariah and Elizabeth in Luke 1:5–25?

stand; 16the weight of gold for each table for consecrated bread; the weight of silver for the silver tables; 17the weight of pure gold for the forks, sprinkling bowls and pitchers; the weight of gold for each gold dish; the weight of silver for each silver dish; 18and the weight of the refined gold for the altar of incense. He also gave him the plan for the chariot, that is, the cherubim of gold that spread their wings and shelter the ark of the covenant of the LORD.

19"All this," David said, "I have in writing from the hand of the LORD upon me, and he gave me understanding in all the details of the plan."

20David also said to Solomon his son, "Be strong and courageous, and do the work. Do not be afraid or discouraged, for the LORD God, my God, is with you. He will not fail you or forsake you until all the work for the service of the temple of the LORD is finished. 21The divisions of the priests and Levites are ready for all the work on the temple of God, and every willing man skilled in any craft will help you in all the work. The officials and all the people will obey your every command."

Gifts for Building the Temple

29 Then King David said to the whole assembly: "My son Solomon, the one whom God has chosen, is young and inexperienced. The task is great, because this palatial structure is not for man but for the LORD God. 2With all my resources I have provided for the temple of my God—gold for the gold work, silver for the silver, bronze for the bronze, iron for the iron and wood for the wood, as well as onyx for the settings, turquoise,[a] stones of various colors, and all kinds of fine stone and marble—all of these in large quantities. 3Besides, in my devotion to the temple of my God I now give my personal treasures of gold and silver for the temple of my God, over and above everything I have provided for this holy temple: 4three thousand talents[b] of gold (gold of Ophir) and seven thousand talents[c] of refined silver, for the overlaying of the walls of the buildings, 5for the gold work and the silver work, and for all the work to be done by the craftsmen. Now, who is willing to consecrate himself today to the LORD?"

6Then the leaders of families, the officers of the tribes of Israel, the commanders of thousands and commanders of hundreds, and the officials in charge of the king's work gave willingly. 7They gave toward the work on the temple of God five thousand talents[d] and ten thousand darics[e] of gold, ten thousand talents[f] of silver, eighteen thousand talents[g] of bronze and a hundred thousand talents[h] of iron. 8Any who had precious stones gave them to the treasury of the temple of the LORD in the custody of Jehiel the Gershonite. 9The people rejoiced at the willing response of their leaders, for they had given freely and wholeheartedly to the LORD. David the king also rejoiced greatly.

David's Prayer

10David praised the LORD in the presence of the whole assembly, saying,

"Praise be to you, O LORD,
  God of our father Israel,
  from everlasting to everlasting.
11 Yours, O LORD, is the greatness and the power
  and the glory and the majesty and the splendor,
  for everything in heaven and earth is yours.
Yours, O LORD, is the kingdom;
  you are exalted as head over all.
12 Wealth and honor come from you;
  you are the ruler of all things.
In your hands are strength and power
  to exalt and give strength to all.
13 Now, our God, we give you thanks,
  and praise your glorious name.

14"But who am I, and who are my people, that we should be able to give as generously as this? Everything comes from you, and we have given you only what comes from your hand. 15We are aliens and strangers in your sight, as were all our forefathers. Our days on earth are like a shadow, without hope. 16O LORD our God, as for all this abundance that we have provided for building you a temple for your Holy Name, it comes from your hand, and all of it belongs to you. 17I know, my God, that you test the heart and are pleased with integrity. All these things have I given willingly and with honest intent. And now I have seen with joy how willingly your people who are here have given to you. 18O LORD, God of our fa-

[a] *2* The meaning of the Hebrew for this word is uncertain. [b] *4* That is, about 110 tons (about 100 metric tons) [c] *4* That is, about 260 tons (about 240 metric tons) [d] *7* That is, about 190 tons (about 170 metric tons) [e] *7* That is, about 185 pounds (about 84 kilograms) [f] *7* That is, about 375 tons (about 345 metric tons) [g] *7* That is, about 675 tons (about 610 metric tons) [h] *7* That is, about 3,750 tons (about 3,450 metric tons)

thers Abraham, Isaac and Israel, keep this desire in the hearts of your people forever, and keep their hearts loyal to you. [19]And give my son Solomon the wholehearted devotion to keep your commands, requirements and decrees and to do everything to build the palatial structure for which I have provided."

[20]Then David said to the whole assembly, "Praise the LORD your God." So they all praised the LORD, the God of their fathers; they bowed low and fell prostrate before the LORD and the king.

Solomon Acknowledged as King

[21]The next day they made sacrifices to the LORD and presented burnt offerings to him: a thousand bulls, a thousand rams and a thousand male lambs, together with their drink offerings, and other sacrifices in abundance for all Israel. [22]They ate and drank with great joy in the presence of the LORD that day.

Then they acknowledged Solomon son of David as king a second time, anointing him before the LORD to be ruler and Zadok to be priest. [23]So Solomon sat on the throne of the LORD as king in place of his father David. He prospered and all Israel obeyed him. [24]All the officers and mighty men, as well as all of King David's sons, pledged their submission to King Solomon.

[25]The LORD highly exalted Solomon in the sight of all Israel and bestowed on him royal splendor such as no king over Israel ever had before.

The Death of David

[26]David son of Jesse was king over all Israel. [27]He ruled over Israel forty years—seven in Hebron and thirty-three in Jerusalem. [28]He died at a good old age, having enjoyed long life, wealth and honor. His son Solomon succeeded him as king.

[29]As for the events of King David's reign, from beginning to end, they are written in the records of Samuel the seer, the records of Nathan the prophet and the records of Gad the seer, [30]together with the details of his reign and power, and the circumstances that surrounded him and Israel and the kingdoms of all the other lands.

2 CHRONICLES

QUICK FACTS

AUTHOR Unknown, but possibly Ezra

AUDIENCE All Israel

DATE Likely between 450 and 400 B.C.

SETTING The book covers the time from Solomon's reign (970 B.C.) to Cyrus's decree encouraging the exiles to return to Judah (538 B.C.), paralleling many of the events of 1 and 2 Kings.

After Solomon built and dedicated the temple, he stood before the people and prayed a prayer of dedication. He praised God and then recited God's rules for holy living in relation to the temple. Soon thereafter, the Lord appeared to Solomon and said, "I have heard your prayer and have chosen this place for myself as a temple" (2 Chronicles 7:12). The Lord went on to promise that if the people would humbly continue to seek him, he would continue to bless them. But if the people turned away from him and worshiped other gods, they would be uprooted from the land and the temple would be destroyed.

Solomon's own infidelity to God resulted in a schism; the kingdom was divided into the northern kingdom of Israel and the southern kingdom of Judah. As a result, the northern kingdom no longer worshiped at the temple. Rather than encouraging people to worship God in Judah, Jeroboam I, the king of Israel, set up alternate places of worship (with calf idols) and appointed his own priests—and Jeroboam's successors failed to turn from his idolatrous ways. Judah was also attracted to idol worship. Despite repeated attempts to remove them, pagan altars, high places, sacred stones and Asherah poles proliferated the kingdom like a viral epidemic. Even Josiah's attempts to revive temple worship faded in the wickedness of his successors. So Jerusalem fell to invaders. The temple was emptied of its valuables and burned.

We no longer have one temple in which to worship. But where two or three people come together in Jesus' name, he promises to be with them (see Matthew 18:20). This promise serves as unbeatable encouragement for couples to pray, read Scripture and share devotional time together.

Solomon Asks for Wisdom

1 Solomon son of David established himself
firmly over his kingdom, for the LORD his
God was with him and made him exceedingly great.
2Then Solomon spoke to all Israel—to the
commanders of thousands and commanders of hundreds, to the judges and to all the
leaders in Israel, the heads of families— 3and
Solomon and the whole assembly went to
the high place at Gibeon, for God's Tent of
Meeting was there, which Moses the LORD's
servant had made in the desert. 4Now David
had brought up the ark of God from Kiriath
Jearim to the place he had prepared for it, because he had pitched a tent for it in Jerusalem.
5But the bronze altar that Bezalel son of Uri,
the son of Hur, had made was in Gibeon in
front of the tabernacle of the LORD; so Solomon and the assembly inquired of him there.
6Solomon went up to the bronze altar before
the LORD in the Tent of Meeting and offered a
thousand burnt offerings on it.
7That night God appeared to Solomon and
said to him, "Ask for whatever you want me
to give you."
8Solomon answered God, "You have shown
great kindness to David my father and have
made me king in his place. 9Now, LORD God,
let your promise to my father David be confirmed, for you have made me king over a people who are as numerous as the dust of the
earth. 10Give me wisdom and knowledge, that
I may lead this people, for who is able to govern this great people of yours?"
11God said to Solomon, "Since this is your
heart's desire and you have not asked for
wealth, riches or honor, nor for the death of
your enemies, and since you have not asked
for a long life but for wisdom and knowledge
to govern my people over whom I have made
you king, 12therefore wisdom and knowledge
will be given you. And I will also give you
wealth, riches and honor, such as no king who
was before you ever had and none after you
will have."
13Then Solomon went to Jerusalem from
the high place at Gibeon, from before the Tent
of Meeting. And he reigned over Israel.
14Solomon accumulated chariots and horses; he had fourteen hundred chariots and
twelve thousand horses,[a] which he kept in the
chariot cities and also with him in Jerusalem.
15The king made silver and gold as common
in Jerusalem as stones, and cedar as plentiful
as sycamore-fig trees in the foothills. 16Solo-
mon's horses were imported from Egypt[b] and
from Kue[c]—the royal merchants purchased
them from Kue. 17They imported a chariot
from Egypt for six hundred shekels[d] of silver,
and a horse for a hundred and fifty.[e] They also
exported them to all the kings of the Hittites
and of the Arameans.

Preparations for Building the Temple

2 Solomon gave orders to build a temple for
the Name of the LORD and a royal palace
for himself. 2He conscripted seventy thousand men as carriers and eighty thousand as
stonecutters in the hills and thirty-six hundred
as foremen over them.
3Solomon sent this message to Hiram[f] king
of Tyre:

"Send me cedar logs as you did for my
father David when you sent him cedar
to build a palace to live in. 4Now I am
about to build a temple for the Name of
the LORD my God and to dedicate it to
him for burning fragrant incense before
him, for setting out the consecrated bread
regularly, and for making burnt offerings
every morning and evening and on Sabbaths and New Moons and at the appointed feasts of the LORD our God. This
is a lasting ordinance for Israel.
5"The temple I am going to build will
be great, because our God is greater than
all other gods. 6But who is able to build
a temple for him, since the heavens, even
the highest heavens, cannot contain him?
Who then am I to build a temple for
him, except as a place to burn sacrifices
before him?
7"Send me, therefore, a man skilled to
work in gold and silver, bronze and iron,
and in purple, crimson and blue yarn,
and experienced in the art of engraving,
to work in Judah and Jerusalem with my
skilled craftsmen, whom my father David
provided.
8"Send me also cedar, pine and algum[g]
logs from Lebanon, for I know that your
men are skilled in cutting timber there.
My men will work with yours 9to provide
me with plenty of lumber, because the
temple I build must be large and mag-

a *14* Or *charioteers* *b* *16* Or possibly *Muzur,* a region in Cilicia; also in verse 17 *c* *16* Probably Cilicia *d* *17* That is, about 15 pounds (about 7 kilograms) *e* *17* That is, about 3 3/4 pounds (about 1.7 kilograms) *f* *3* Hebrew *Huram,* a variant of *Hiram;* also in verses 11 and 12 *g* *8* Probably a variant of *almug;* possibly juniper

nificent. 10I will give your servants, the
woodsmen who cut the timber, twenty
thousand cors[a] of ground wheat, twenty thousand cors of barley, twenty thousand baths[b] of wine and twenty thousand
baths of olive oil."

11Hiram king of Tyre replied by letter to
Solomon:

"Because the LORD loves his people, he
has made you their king."

12And Hiram added:

"Praise be to the LORD, the God of Israel, who made heaven and earth! He has
given King David a wise son, endowed
with intelligence and discernment, who
will build a temple for the LORD and a
palace for himself.
13"I am sending you Huram-Abi, a
man of great skill, 14whose mother was
from Dan and whose father was from
Tyre. He is trained to work in gold and
silver, bronze and iron, stone and wood,
and with purple and blue and crimson
yarn and fine linen. He is experienced
in all kinds of engraving and can execute
any design given to him. He will work
with your craftsmen and with those of
my lord, David your father.
15"Now let my lord send his servants
the wheat and barley and the olive oil
and wine he promised, 16and we will cut
all the logs from Lebanon that you need
and will float them in rafts by sea down
to Joppa. You can then take them up to
Jerusalem."

17Solomon took a census of all the aliens
who were in Israel, after the census his father
David had taken; and they were found to be
153,600. 18He assigned 70,000 of them to be
carriers and 80,000 to be stonecutters in the
hills, with 3,600 foremen over them to keep
the people working.

Solomon Builds the Temple

3 Then Solomon began to build the temple of
the LORD in Jerusalem on Mount Moriah,
where the LORD had appeared to his father
David. It was on the threshing floor of Araunah[c] the Jebusite, the place provided by David.
2He began building on the second day of the
second month in the fourth year of his reign.
3The foundation Solomon laid for building
the temple of God was sixty cubits long and
twenty cubits wide[d] (using the cubit of the old
standard). 4The portico at the front of the temple was twenty cubits[e] long across the width of
the building and twenty cubits[f] high.
He overlaid the inside with pure gold. 5He
paneled the main hall with pine and covered
it with fine gold and decorated it with palm
tree and chain designs. 6He adorned the temple with precious stones. And the gold he used
was gold of Parvaim. 7He overlaid the ceiling
beams, doorframes, walls and doors of the
temple with gold, and he carved cherubim on
the walls.
8He built the Most Holy Place, its length
corresponding to the width of the temple—
twenty cubits long and twenty cubits wide.
He overlaid the inside with six hundred talents[g] of fine gold. 9The gold nails weighed fifty shekels.[h] He also overlaid the upper parts
with gold.
10In the Most Holy Place he made a pair of
sculptured cherubim and overlaid them with
gold. 11The total wingspan of the cherubim
was twenty cubits. One wing of the first cherub was five cubits[i] long and touched the temple wall, while its other wing, also five cubits
long, touched the wing of the other cherub.
12Similarly one wing of the second cherub was
five cubits long and touched the other temple
wall, and its other wing, also five cubits long,
touched the wing of the first cherub. 13The
wings of these cherubim extended twenty cubits. They stood on their feet, facing the main
hall.[j]
14He made the curtain of blue, purple and
crimson yarn and fine linen, with cherubim
worked into it.
15In the front of the temple he made two
pillars, which ⌞together⌟ were thirty-five cubits[k]
long, each with a capital on top measuring five
cubits. 16He made interwoven chains[l] and put
them on top of the pillars. He also made a
hundred pomegranates and attached them to
the chains. 17He erected the pillars in the front
of the temple, one to the south and one to the
north. The one to the south he named Jakin[m]
and the one to the north Boaz.[n]

[a] *10* That is, probably about 125,000 bushels (about 4,400 kiloliters) [b] *10* That is, probably about 115,000 gallons (about 440 kiloliters) [c] *1* Hebrew *Ornan,* a variant of *Araunah* [d] *3* That is, about 90 feet (about 27 meters) long and 30 feet (about 9 meters) wide [e] *4* That is, about 30 feet (about 9 meters); also in verses 8, 11 and 13 [f] *4* Some Septuagint and Syriac manuscripts; Hebrew *and a hundred and twenty* [g] *8* That is, about 23 tons (about 21 metric tons) [h] *9* That is, about 1 1/4 pounds (about 0.6 kilogram) [i] *11* That is, about 7 1/2 feet (about 2.3 meters); also in verse 15 [j] *13* Or *facing inward* [k] *15* That is, about 52 feet (about 16 meters) [l] *16* Or possibly *made chains in the inner sanctuary;* the meaning of the Hebrew for this phrase is uncertain. [m] *17* *Jakin* probably means *he establishes.* [n] *17* *Boaz* probably means *in him is strength.*

The Temple's Furnishings

4 He made a bronze altar twenty cubits long,
twenty cubits wide and ten cubits high.[a]
2He made the Sea of cast metal, circular in
shape, measuring ten cubits from rim to rim
and five cubits[b] high. It took a line of thirty
cubits[c] to measure around it. 3Below the rim,
figures of bulls encircled it—ten to a cubit.[d]
The bulls were cast in two rows in one piece
with the Sea.

4The Sea stood on twelve bulls, three facing north, three facing west, three facing
south and three facing east. The Sea rested
on top of them, and their hindquarters were
toward the center. 5It was a handbreadth[e] in
thickness, and its rim was like the rim of a
cup, like a lily blossom. It held three thousand baths.[f]

6He then made ten basins for washing and
placed five on the south side and five on the
north. In them the things to be used for the
burnt offerings were rinsed, but the Sea was to
be used by the priests for washing.

7He made ten gold lampstands according
to the specifications for them and placed them
in the temple, five on the south side and five
on the north.

8He made ten tables and placed them in the
temple, five on the south side and five on the
north. He also made a hundred gold sprinkling bowls.

9He made the courtyard of the priests, and
the large court and the doors for the court,
and overlaid the doors with bronze. 10He
placed the Sea on the south side, at the southeast corner.

11He also made the pots and shovels and
sprinkling bowls.

So Huram finished the work he had undertaken for King Solomon in the temple of
God:

12 the two pillars;
the two bowl-shaped capitals on top of
the pillars;
the two sets of network decorating the
two bowl-shaped capitals on top of the
pillars;
13 the four hundred pomegranates for the
two sets of network (two rows of
pomegranates for each network, decorating the bowl-shaped capitals on top
of the pillars);
14 the stands with their basins;
15 the Sea and the twelve bulls under it;
16 the pots, shovels, meat forks and all related articles.

All the objects that Huram-Abi made for
King Solomon for the temple of the LORD
were of polished bronze. 17The king had them
cast in clay molds in the plain of the Jordan
between Succoth and Zarethan.[g] 18All these
things that Solomon made amounted to so
much that the weight of the bronze was not
determined.

19Solomon also made all the furnishings
that were in God's temple:

the golden altar;
the tables on which was the bread of the
Presence;
20 the lampstands of pure gold with their
lamps, to burn in front of the inner
sanctuary as prescribed;
21 the gold floral work and lamps and tongs
(they were solid gold);
22 the pure gold wick trimmers, sprinkling
bowls, dishes and censers; and the gold
doors of the temple: the inner doors to
the Most Holy Place and the doors of
the main hall.

5 When all the work Solomon had done for
the temple of the LORD was finished, he
brought in the things his father David had
dedicated—the silver and gold and all the furnishings—and he placed them in the treasuries of God's temple.

The Ark Brought to the Temple

2Then Solomon summoned to Jerusalem
the elders of Israel, all the heads of the tribes
and the chiefs of the Israelite families, to bring
up the ark of the LORD's covenant from Zion,
the City of David. 3And all the men of Israel
came together to the king at the time of the
festival in the seventh month.

4When all the elders of Israel had arrived,
the Levites took up the ark, 5and they brought
up the ark and the Tent of Meeting and all the
sacred furnishings in it. The priests, who were
Levites, carried them up; 6and King Solomon
and the entire assembly of Israel that had gathered about him were before the ark, sacrificing
so many sheep and cattle that they could not
be recorded or counted.

7The priests then brought the ark of the
LORD's covenant to its place in the inner sanc-

[a] *1* That is, about 30 feet (about 9 meters) long and wide, and about 15 feet (about 4.5 meters) high [b] *2* That is, about 7 1/2 feet (about 2.3 meters) [c] *2* That is, about 45 feet (about 13.5 meters) [d] *3* That is, about 1 1/2 feet (about 0.5 meter) [e] *5* That is, about 3 inches (about 8 centimeters) [f] *5* That is, about 17,500 gallons (about 66 kiloliters) [g] *17* Hebrew *Zeredatha,* a variant of *Zarethan*

tuary of the temple, the Most Holy Place, and put it beneath the wings of the cherubim. 8The cherubim spread their wings over the place of the ark and covered the ark and its carrying poles. 9These poles were so long that their ends, extending from the ark, could be seen from in front of the inner sanctuary, but not from outside the Holy Place; and they are still there today. 10There was nothing in the ark except the two tablets that Moses had placed in it at Horeb, where the LORD made a covenant with the Israelites after they came out of Egypt.

11The priests then withdrew from the Holy Place. All the priests who were there had consecrated themselves, regardless of their divisions. 12All the Levites who were musicians—Asaph, Heman, Jeduthun and their sons and relatives—stood on the east side of the altar, dressed in fine linen and playing cymbals, harps and lyres. They were accompanied by 120 priests sounding trumpets. 13The trumpeters and singers joined in unison, as with one voice, to give praise and thanks to the LORD. Accompanied by trumpets, cymbals and other instruments, they raised their voices in praise to the LORD and sang:

"He is good;
his love endures forever."

Then the temple of the LORD was filled with a cloud, 14and the priests could not perform their service because of the cloud, for the glory of the LORD filled the temple of God.

6 Then Solomon said, "The LORD has said that he would dwell in a dark cloud; 2I have built a magnificent temple for you, a place for you to dwell forever."

3While the whole assembly of Israel was standing there, the king turned around and blessed them. 4Then he said:

"Praise be to the LORD, the God of Israel, who with his hands has fulfilled what he promised with his mouth to my father David. For he said, 5'Since the day I brought my people out of Egypt, I have not chosen a city in any tribe of Israel to have a temple built for my Name to be there, nor have I chosen anyone to be the leader over my people Israel. 6But now I have chosen Jerusalem for my Name to be there, and I have chosen David to rule my people Israel.'

7"My father David had it in his heart to build a temple for the Name of the LORD, the God of Israel. 8But the LORD said to my father David, 'Because it was in your heart to build a temple for my Name, you did well to have this in your heart. 9Nevertheless, you are not the one to build the temple, but your son, who is your own flesh and blood—he is the one who will build the temple for my Name.'

10"The LORD has kept the promise he made. I have succeeded David my father and now I sit on the throne of Israel, just as the LORD promised, and I have built the temple for the Name of the LORD, the God of Israel. 11There I have placed the ark, in which is the covenant of the LORD that he made with the people of Israel."

Solomon's Prayer of Dedication

12Then Solomon stood before the altar of the LORD in front of the whole assembly of Israel and spread out his hands. 13Now he had made a bronze platform, five cubits[a] long, five cubits wide and three cubits[b] high, and had placed it in the center of the outer court. He stood on the platform and then knelt down before the whole assembly of Israel and spread out his hands toward heaven. 14He said:

"O LORD, God of Israel, there is no God like you in heaven or on earth—you who keep your covenant of love with your servants who continue wholeheartedly in your way. 15You have kept your promise to your servant David my father; with your mouth you have promised and with your hand you have fulfilled it—as it is today.

16"Now LORD, God of Israel, keep for your servant David my father the promises you made to him when you said, 'You shall never fail to have a man to sit before me on the throne of Israel, if only your sons are careful in all they do to walk before me according to my law, as you have done.' 17And now, O LORD, God of Israel, let your word that you promised your servant David come true.

18"But will God really dwell on earth with men? The heavens, even the highest heavens, cannot contain you. How much less this temple I have built! 19Yet give attention to your servant's prayer and his plea for mercy, O LORD my God. Hear

a 13 That is, about 7 1/2 feet (about 2.3 meters) b 13 That is, about 4 1/2 feet (about 1.3 meters)

the cry and the prayer that your servant
is praying in your presence. 20May your
eyes be open toward this temple day and
night, this place of which you said you
would put your Name there. May you
hear the prayer your servant prays toward this place. 21Hear the supplications
of your servant and of your people Israel
when they pray toward this place. Hear
from heaven, your dwelling place; and
when you hear, forgive.

22"When a man wrongs his neighbor
and is required to take an oath and he
comes and swears the oath before your altar in this temple, 23then hear from heav-
en and act. Judge between your servants,
repaying the guilty by bringing down on
his own head what he has done. Declare
the innocent not guilty and so establish
his innocence.

24"When your people Israel have been
defeated by an enemy because they have
sinned against you and when they turn
back and confess your name, praying
and making supplication before you in
this temple, 25then hear from heaven and
forgive the sin of your people Israel and
bring them back to the land you gave to
them and their fathers.

26"When the heavens are shut up and
there is no rain because your people have
sinned against you, and when they pray
toward this place and confess your name
and turn from their sin because you have
afflicted them, 27then hear from heaven
and forgive the sin of your servants, your
people Israel. Teach them the right way to
live, and send rain on the land you gave
your people for an inheritance.

28"When famine or plague comes to
the land, or blight or mildew, locusts or
grasshoppers, or when enemies besiege
them in any of their cities, whatever disaster or disease may come, 29and when
a prayer or plea is made by any of your
people Israel—each one aware of his afflictions and pains, and spreading out his
hands toward this temple— 30then hear
from heaven, your dwelling place. Forgive, and deal with each man according
to all he does, since you know his heart
(for you alone know the hearts of men),
31so that they will fear you and walk in
your ways all the time they live in the
land you gave our fathers.

32"As for the foreigner who does not
belong to your people Israel but has
come from a distant land because of your
great name and your mighty hand and
your outstretched arm—when he comes
and prays toward this temple, 33then
hear from heaven, your dwelling place,
and do whatever the foreigner asks of
you, so that all the peoples of the earth
may know your name and fear you, as do
your own people Israel, and may know
that this house I have built bears your
Name.

34"When your people go to war
against their enemies, wherever you send
them, and when they pray to you toward
this city you have chosen and the temple
I have built for your Name, 35then hear
from heaven their prayer and their plea,
and uphold their cause.

36"When they sin against you—for
there is no one who does not sin—and
you become angry with them and give
them over to the enemy, who takes them
captive to a land far away or near; 37and
if they have a change of heart in the land
where they are held captive, and repent
and plead with you in the land of their
captivity and say, 'We have sinned, we
have done wrong and acted wickedly';
38and if they turn back to you with all
their heart and soul in the land of their
captivity where they were taken, and pray
toward the land you gave their fathers, toward the city you have chosen and toward
the temple I have built for your Name;
39then from heaven, your dwelling place,
hear their prayer and their pleas, and uphold their cause. And forgive your people, who have sinned against you.

40"Now, my God, may your eyes
be open and your ears attentive to the
prayers offered in this place.

41 "Now arise, O Lord God, and come
to your resting place,
you and the ark of your might.
May your priests, O Lord God, be
clothed with salvation,
may your saints rejoice in your
goodness.
42 O Lord God, do not reject your
anointed one.
Remember the great love
promised to David your
servant."

The Dedication of the Temple

7 When Solomon finished praying, fire
came down from heaven and consumed
the burnt offering and the sacrifices, and
the glory of the LORD filled the temple. [2]The
priests could not enter the temple of the LORD
because the glory of the LORD filled it. [3]When
all the Israelites saw the fire coming down and
the glory of the LORD above the temple, they
knelt on the pavement with their faces to the
ground, and they worshiped and gave thanks
to the LORD, saying,

"He is good;
his love endures forever."

[4]Then the king and all the people offered sacrifices before the LORD. [5]And King Solomon offered a sacrifice of twenty-two thousand head
of cattle and a hundred and twenty thousand
sheep and goats. So the king and all the people dedicated the temple of God. [6]The priests
took their positions, as did the Levites with
the LORD's musical instruments, which King
David had made for praising the LORD and
which were used when he gave thanks, saying,
"His love endures forever." Opposite the Levites, the priests blew their trumpets, and all
the Israelites were standing.

[7]Solomon consecrated the middle part of
the courtyard in front of the temple of the
LORD, and there he offered burnt offerings
and the fat of the fellowship offerings,[a] because the bronze altar he had made could not
hold the burnt offerings, the grain offerings
and the fat portions.

[8]So Solomon observed the festival at that
time for seven days, and all Israel with him—a
vast assembly, people from Lebo[b] Hamath to
the Wadi of Egypt. [9]On the eighth day they
held an assembly, for they had celebrated the
dedication of the altar for seven days and the
festival for seven days more. [10]On the twenty-third day of the seventh month he sent the
people to their homes, joyful and glad in heart
for the good things the LORD had done for
David and Solomon and for his people Israel.

The LORD Appears to Solomon

[11]When Solomon had finished the temple
of the LORD and the royal palace, and had succeeded in carrying out all he had in mind to
do in the temple of the LORD and in his own
palace, [12]the LORD appeared to him at night
and said:

"I have heard your prayer and have
chosen this place for myself as a temple
for sacrifices.

[13]"When I shut up the heavens so that
there is no rain, or command locusts to
devour the land or send a plague among
my people, [14]if my people, who are called
by my name, will humble themselves and
pray and seek my face and turn from
their wicked ways, then will I hear from
heaven and will forgive their sin and will
heal their land. [15]Now my eyes will be
open and my ears attentive to the prayers
offered in this place. [16]I have chosen and
consecrated this temple so that my Name
may be there forever. My eyes and my
heart will always be there.

[17]"As for you, if you walk before me as
David your father did, and do all I command, and observe my decrees and laws,
[18]I will establish your royal throne, as I
covenanted with David your father when
I said, 'You shall never fail to have a man
to rule over Israel.'

[19]"But if you[c] turn away and forsake
the decrees and commands I have given
you[c] and go off to serve other gods and
worship them, [20]then I will uproot Israel
from my land, which I have given them,
and will reject this temple I have consecrated for my Name. I will make it a
byword and an object of ridicule among
all peoples. [21]And though this temple is
now so imposing, all who pass by will
be appalled and say, 'Why has the LORD
done such a thing to this land and to
this temple?' [22]People will answer, 'Because they have forsaken the LORD, the
God of their fathers, who brought them
out of Egypt, and have embraced other
gods, worshiping and serving them—
that is why he brought all this disaster on
them.' "

Solomon's Other Activities

8 At the end of twenty years, during which
Solomon built the temple of the LORD and
his own palace, [2]Solomon rebuilt the villages that Hiram[d] had given him, and settled
Israelites in them. [3]Solomon then went to Hamath Zobah and captured it. [4]He also built
up Tadmor in the desert and all the store cities
he had built in Hamath. [5]He rebuilt Upper
Beth Horon and Lower Beth Horon as fortified cities, with walls and with gates and bars,

[a] 7 Traditionally *peace offerings* [b] 8 Or *from the entrance to* [c] 19 The Hebrew is plural. [d] 2 Hebrew *Huram,* a variant of *Hiram;* also in verse 18

MONDAY

READ

2 CHRONICLES 6:12–42; 7:11–22

NO ROOM FOR PRIDE

According to Rudyard Kipling's tale "How the Camel Got Its Hump," at the dawn of creation God gave each animal a job to do. Working together, the animals prepared the new world for the coming of humankind.

One animal refused to work. Whenever others asked the camel for his help, he just said, "Humph!" and walked away. When God saw what was happening, he collected all of the haughty camel's humphs. One day he dumped them onto the camel's back. That, said Kipling, is how the camel got its hump.

When Solomon dedicated the temple, he prayed for God's blessing on a nation that included more than a few camel-like souls. Acknowledging that God's people would not always live faithfully or fully love God in return, Solomon pleaded with God to be gracious, to forgive his errant children and to continue working at the relationship. God responded with divine honesty. He said he would indeed be gracious, loving and forgiving to his people. But there was a condition: They must humble themselves and turn from their wicked ways.

We know that Solomon and God were concerned about Israel's humility and obedience. We need to consider that for ourselves too, both in national and personal ways. Take marriage, for instance. A spouse who truly loves us energizes us to be the best we can be. But a prideful, self-centered mate can soil the relationship with cancerous self-love.

"If my people, who are called by my name, will humble themselves and pray and seek my face and turn from their wicked ways, then will I hear from heaven and will forgive their sin and will heal their land."

— 2 CHRONICLES 7:14

let's talk

- How do we determine what is harmful to our relationship? What do we use as our rationale?
- Is it possible to take offense at something one of us says or does when none is intended? How do we get through such misunderstandings?
- How do we cultivate a spirit of humility in our relationship with God and with each other? How do we become each other's source of self-esteem and affirmation?

Ancient Greeks told the story of Narcissus, an exceptionally handsome young man. One day Narcissus paused at a pool and bent to drink. Before his lips broke the mirrored surface, however, the lad caught sight of a face staring up at him. Narcissus was entranced by the soulful eyes, the marvelous nose, the chiseled chin. Caught in his reverie of self-love, Narcissus stared at his own reflection until he finally fell famished to his death.

The point is clear: The moment self-love becomes our highest priority, we lose the ability to contribute to our relationships. We lose the power to live authentically. We become so absorbed in ourselves that we fail to respond in love and obedience to others and to God. Even when we mess up, our pride makes us unwilling to ask for forgiveness and unwilling to accept it.

No marriage can survive if both partners are in love with the same person. That's why Paul, in Ephesians 5:21, urged both husband and wife to "submit to one another out of reverence for Christ." A strong relationship starts with submission before God and grows best in the garden of humble respect for one another.

—WAYNE BROUWER

FOR YOUR NEXT DEVOTIONAL READING, TURN TO PAGE 469.

6as well as Baalath and all his store cities, and
all the cities for his chariots and for his horses[a]—whatever he desired to build in Jerusalem, in Lebanon and throughout all the territory he ruled.
7All the people left from the Hittites, Amorites, Perizzites, Hivites and Jebusites (these
peoples were not Israelites), 8that is, their descendants remaining in the land, whom the
Israelites had not destroyed—these Solomon
conscripted for his slave labor force, as it is to
this day. 9But Solomon did not make slaves of
the Israelites for his work; they were his fighting men, commanders of his captains, and
commanders of his chariots and charioteers.
10They were also King Solomon's chief officials—two hundred and fifty officials supervising the men.
11Solomon brought Pharaoh's daughter up
from the City of David to the palace he had
built for her, for he said, "My wife must not
live in the palace of David king of Israel, because the places the ark of the LORD has entered are holy."
12On the altar of the LORD that he had built
in front of the portico, Solomon sacrificed
burnt offerings to the LORD, 13according to
the daily requirement for offerings commanded by Moses for Sabbaths, New Moons and
the three annual feasts—the Feast of Unleavened Bread, the Feast of Weeks and the Feast of
Tabernacles. 14In keeping with the ordinance
of his father David, he appointed the divisions
of the priests for their duties, and the Levites
to lead the praise and to assist the priests according to each day's requirement. He also
appointed the gatekeepers by divisions for the
various gates, because this was what David the
man of God had ordered. 15They did not de-
viate from the king's commands to the priests
or to the Levites in any matter, including that
of the treasuries.
16All Solomon's work was carried out, from
the day the foundation of the temple of the
LORD was laid until its completion. So the
temple of the LORD was finished.
17Then Solomon went to Ezion Geber and
Elath on the coast of Edom. 18And Hiram
sent him ships commanded by his own officers, men who knew the sea. These, with Solomon's men, sailed to Ophir and brought back
four hundred and fifty talents[b] of gold, which
they delivered to King Solomon.

The Queen of Sheba Visits Solomon

9 When the queen of Sheba heard of Solomon's fame, she came to Jerusalem to test
him with hard questions. Arriving with
a very great caravan—with camels carrying
spices, large quantities of gold, and precious
stones—she came to Solomon and talked
with him about all she had on her mind. 2Sol-
omon answered all her questions; nothing was
too hard for him to explain to her. 3When
the queen of Sheba saw the wisdom of Solomon, as well as the palace he had built, 4the
food on his table, the seating of his officials,
the attending servants in their robes, the cupbearers in their robes and the burnt offerings
he made at[c] the temple of the LORD, she was
overwhelmed.
5She said to the king, "The report I heard in
my own country about your achievements and
your wisdom is true. 6But I did not believe
what they said until I came and saw with my
own eyes. Indeed, not even half the greatness
of your wisdom was told me; you have far exceeded the report I heard. 7How happy your
men must be! How happy your officials, who
continually stand before you and hear your
wisdom! 8Praise be to the LORD your God,
who has delighted in you and placed you on
his throne as king to rule for the LORD your
God. Because of the love of your God for Israel and his desire to uphold them forever, he
has made you king over them, to maintain justice and righteousness."
9Then she gave the king 120 talents[d] of
gold, large quantities of spices, and precious
stones. There had never been such spices as
those the queen of Sheba gave to King Solomon.
10(The men of Hiram and the men of Solomon brought gold from Ophir; they also
brought algumwood[e] and precious stones.
11The king used the algumwood to make steps
for the temple of the LORD and for the royal
palace, and to make harps and lyres for the
musicians. Nothing like them had ever been
seen in Judah.)
12King Solomon gave the queen of Sheba all she desired and asked for; he gave her
more than she had brought to him. Then she
left and returned with her retinue to her own
country.

Solomon's Splendor

13The weight of the gold that Solomon received yearly was 666 talents,[f] 14not includ-

[a] *6* Or *charioteers* [b] *18* That is, about 17 tons (about 16 metric tons) [c] *4* Or *the ascent by which he went up to* [d] *9* That is, about 4 1/2 tons (about 4 metric tons) [e] *10* Probably a variant of *almugwood* [f] *13* That is, about 25 tons (about 23 metric tons)

ing the revenues brought in by merchants and
traders. Also all the kings of Arabia and the
governors of the land brought gold and silver
to Solomon.
15King Solomon made two hundred large
shields of hammered gold; six hundred bekas[a] of hammered gold went into each shield.
16He also made three hundred small shields of
hammered gold, with three hundred bekas[b] of
gold in each shield. The king put them in the
Palace of the Forest of Lebanon.
17Then the king made a great throne inlaid
with ivory and overlaid with pure gold. 18The
throne had six steps, and a footstool of gold was
attached to it. On both sides of the seat were
armrests, with a lion standing beside each of
them. 19Twelve lions stood on the six steps, one
at either end of each step. Nothing like it had
ever been made for any other kingdom. 20All
King Solomon's goblets were gold, and all the
household articles in the Palace of the Forest of
Lebanon were pure gold. Nothing was made of
silver, because silver was considered of little value in Solomon's day. 21The king had a fleet of
trading ships[c] manned by Hiram's[d] men. Once
every three years it returned, carrying gold, silver and ivory, and apes and baboons.
22King Solomon was greater in riches and
wisdom than all the other kings of the earth.
23All the kings of the earth sought audience
with Solomon to hear the wisdom God had
put in his heart. 24Year after year, everyone
who came brought a gift—articles of silver
and gold, and robes, weapons and spices, and
horses and mules.
25Solomon had four thousand stalls for
horses and chariots, and twelve thousand
horses,[e] which he kept in the chariot cities
and also with him in Jerusalem. 26He ruled
over all the kings from the River[f] to the land
of the Philistines, as far as the border of Egypt.
27The king made silver as common in Jerusalem as stones, and cedar as plentiful as sycamore-fig trees in the foothills. 28Solomon's
horses were imported from Egypt[g] and from
all other countries.

Solomon's Death

29As for the other events of Solomon's reign,
from beginning to end, are they not written
in the records of Nathan the prophet, in the
prophecy of Ahijah the Shilonite and in the
visions of Iddo the seer concerning Jeroboam
son of Nebat? 30Solomon reigned in Jerusalem over all Israel forty years. 31Then he rested
with his fathers and was buried in the city of
David his father. And Rehoboam his son succeeded him as king.

Israel Rebels Against Rehoboam

10 Rehoboam went to Shechem, for all
the Israelites had gone there to make
him king. 2When Jeroboam son of Nebat heard this (he was in Egypt, where he had
fled from King Solomon), he returned from
Egypt. 3So they sent for Jeroboam, and he and
all Israel went to Rehoboam and said to him:
4"Your father put a heavy yoke on us, but now
lighten the harsh labor and the heavy yoke he
put on us, and we will serve you."
5Rehoboam answered, "Come back to me
in three days." So the people went away.
6Then King Rehoboam consulted the elders
who had served his father Solomon during his
lifetime. "How would you advise me to answer these people?" he asked.
7They replied, "If you will be kind to these
people and please them and give them a favorable answer, they will always be your servants."
8But Rehoboam rejected the advice the elders gave him and consulted the young men
who had grown up with him and were serving him. 9He asked them, "What is your advice? How should we answer these people who
say to me, 'Lighten the yoke your father put
on us'?"
10The young men who had grown up with
him replied, "Tell the people who have said to
you, 'Your father put a heavy yoke on us, but
make our yoke lighter'—tell them, 'My little
finger is thicker than my father's waist. 11My
father laid on you a heavy yoke; I will make
it even heavier. My father scourged you with
whips; I will scourge you with scorpions.' "
12Three days later Jeroboam and all the
people returned to Rehoboam, as the king
had said, "Come back to me in three days."
13The king answered them harshly. Rejecting
the advice of the elders, 14he followed the advice of the young men and said, "My father
made your yoke heavy; I will make it even
heavier. My father scourged you with whips;
I will scourge you with scorpions." 15So the
king did not listen to the people, for this turn
of events was from God, to fulfill the word the
LORD had spoken to Jeroboam son of Nebat
through Ahijah the Shilonite.

---

[a] *15* That is, about 7 1/2 pounds (about 3.5 kilograms) [b] *16* That is, about 3 3/4 pounds (about 1.7 kilograms) [c] *21* Hebrew *of ships that could go to Tarshish* [d] *21* Hebrew *Huram,* a variant of *Hiram* [e] *25* Or *charioteers* [f] *26* That is, the Euphrates [g] *28* Or possibly *Muzur,* a region in Cilicia

16When all Israel saw that the king refused
to listen to them, they answered the king:

"What share do we have in David,
what part in Jesse's son?
To your tents, O Israel!
Look after your own house, O David!"

So all the Israelites went home. 17But as for
the Israelites who were living in the towns of
Judah, Rehoboam still ruled over them.
18King Rehoboam sent out Adoniram,[a]
who was in charge of forced labor, but the Israelites stoned him to death. King Rehoboam,
however, managed to get into his chariot and
escape to Jerusalem. 19So Israel has been in rebellion against the house of David to this day.

11 When Rehoboam arrived in Jerusalem,
he mustered the house of Judah and
Benjamin—a hundred and eighty thousand fighting men—to make war against Israel
and to regain the kingdom for Rehoboam.
2But this word of the LORD came to Shemaiah the man of God: 3"Say to Rehoboam son
of Solomon king of Judah and to all the Israelites in Judah and Benjamin, 4'This is what
the LORD says: Do not go up to fight against
your brothers. Go home, every one of you, for
this is my doing.'" So they obeyed the words
of the LORD and turned back from marching
against Jeroboam.

Rehoboam Fortifies Judah

5Rehoboam lived in Jerusalem and built
up towns for defense in Judah: 6Bethlehem,
Etam, Tekoa, 7Beth Zur, Soco, Adullam,
8Gath, Mareshah, Ziph, 9Adoraim, Lachish,
Azekah, 10Zorah, Aijalon and Hebron. These
were fortified cities in Judah and Benjamin.
11He strengthened their defenses and put
commanders in them, with supplies of food,
olive oil and wine. 12He put shields and spears
in all the cities, and made them very strong.
So Judah and Benjamin were his.
13The priests and Levites from all their districts throughout Israel sided with him. 14The
Levites even abandoned their pasturelands
and property, and came to Judah and Jerusalem because Jeroboam and his sons had rejected them as priests of the LORD. 15And he
appointed his own priests for the high places
and for the goat and calf idols he had made.
16Those from every tribe of Israel who set their
hearts on seeking the LORD, the God of Israel,
followed the Levites to Jerusalem to offer sacrifices to the LORD, the God of their fathers.
17They strengthened the kingdom of Judah
and supported Rehoboam son of Solomon
three years, walking in the ways of David and
Solomon during this time.

Rehoboam's Family

18Rehoboam married Mahalath, who was
the daughter of David's son Jerimoth and
of Abihail, the daughter of Jesse's son Eliab.
19She bore him sons: Jeush, Shemariah and
Zaham. 20Then he married Maacah daughter of Absalom, who bore him Abijah, Attai,
Ziza and Shelomith. 21Rehoboam loved Maacah daughter of Absalom more than any of
his other wives and concubines. In all, he had
eighteen wives and sixty concubines, twenty-
eight sons and sixty daughters.
22Rehoboam appointed Abijah son of Maacah to be the chief prince among his brothers,
in order to make him king. 23He acted wisely, dispersing some of his sons throughout the
districts of Judah and Benjamin, and to all the
fortified cities. He gave them abundant provisions and took many wives for them.

Shishak Attacks Jerusalem

12 After Rehoboam's position as king was
established and he had become strong,
he and all Israel[b] with him abandoned
the law of the LORD. 2Because they had been
unfaithful to the LORD, Shishak king of Egypt
attacked Jerusalem in the fifth year of King Rehoboam. 3With twelve hundred chariots and
sixty thousand horsemen and the innumerable troops of Libyans, Sukkites and Cushites[c]
that came with him from Egypt, 4he captured
the fortified cities of Judah and came as far as
Jerusalem.
5Then the prophet Shemaiah came to Rehoboam and to the leaders of Judah who had
assembled in Jerusalem for fear of Shishak,
and he said to them, "This is what the LORD
says, 'You have abandoned me; therefore, I
now abandon you to Shishak.'"
6The leaders of Israel and the king humbled
themselves and said, "The LORD is just."
7When the LORD saw that they humbled
themselves, this word of the LORD came to
Shemaiah: "Since they have humbled themselves, I will not destroy them but will soon
give them deliverance. My wrath will not be
poured out on Jerusalem through Shishak.
8They will, however, become subject to him,
so that they may learn the difference between

[a] *18* Hebrew *Hadoram,* a variant of *Adoniram* [b] *1* That is, Judah, as frequently in 2 Chronicles [c] *3* That is, people from the upper Nile region

TUESDAY
READ 2 CHRONICLES 12:1–12

REMEMBERING GOD IN THE GOOD TIMES

> **After Rehoboam's position as king was established and he had become strong, he and all Israel with him abandoned the law of the LORD.**
> — 2 CHRONICLES 12:1

let's talk

- How has marriage increased our dependence on God? How has marriage dulled our dependence on God?
- What are the dangers of being strong, of seemingly "making it"? What strengths tempt us to believe that we are self-sufficient?
- When we start forgetting about God, what do we do? How can we intentionally cultivate daily routines that lead us to God?

Rehoboam's folly of abandoning the Lord after becoming king isn't so unusual. It's what we humans have been doing ever since the fall. Marriage, in particular, is a relationship in which we risk repeating Rehoboam's mistake. When things are going well, when we're strong as a couple, it's easy to forget about spending time with God.

Sometimes marriage itself is the strength that draws us away from God. Those of us who live in Christian communities that place great emphasis on marrying—and marrying young—run the risk of thinking that marriage is the highest good. We think it's the shiniest prize, the most desirable trophy in life. So during our single years, we spend many nights talking to God, regaling him with our desires. We cry out to him when the object of our affections spurns us, or we praise him after we've gone on a promising date.

Then we get married. And, poof!, there's no need for God anymore. He's finally given us what we wanted and, well, we find that we don't need him quite so much now.

Or maybe our relationship with God was vibrant in the early years of our marriage when we were broke and our social life revolved around potlucks. We didn't know what the future held—if we'd find meaningful work or if we'd live in one place for more than two years.

And then one day we turn around and realize we've segued into all the trappings of middle-class adulthood. We own a house. We both have great jobs, complete with Christmas bonuses. Our kids start talking at 18 months old and are clearly geniuses. We start reading financial magazines more than Scripture. Of course we take the kids to church, but that day-to-day sense of relying on God? Um, no, not really. That has slipped into the past, just like the potlucks.

One of the wonderful things about marriage is that we have someone to turn to, someone to help us, someone we can rely on. And yet the attendant danger is the temptation to forget the One on whom we must truly rely and who alone is trustworthy.

My husband, who is reading over my shoulder, says that if our marriage has been blissful, it has also been hellish, and surely in the hellish moments we know whom to turn to. He's right, of course. I know that my dependence on God has never seemed as real as in the moments when my marriage seemed dead on the vine. That's when I've felt most keenly that only God can revive it.

The hope is that we don't have to hit the nadir of married life to remember our dependence on God. At best, all our strengths—our good marriages, our fine houses, our fulfilling jobs—direct us back to God. These strengths are only strong when they send us to our knees in humility, thanksgiving and praise, and when they send us out into the world to share our abundance with others.

—LAUREN WINNER

FOR YOUR NEXT DEVOTIONAL READING, TURN TO PAGE 473.

serving me and serving the kings of other
lands."
9When Shishak king of Egypt attacked Jerusalem, he carried off the treasures of the temple of the LORD and the treasures of the royal
palace. He took everything, including the gold
shields Solomon had made. 10So King Rehoboam made bronze shields to replace them
and assigned these to the commanders of the
guard on duty at the entrance to the royal palace. 11Whenever the king went to the LORD's
temple, the guards went with him, bearing the
shields, and afterward they returned them to
the guardroom.
12Because Rehoboam humbled himself, the
LORD's anger turned from him, and he was
not totally destroyed. Indeed, there was some
good in Judah.
13King Rehoboam established himself firmly in Jerusalem and continued as king. He was
forty-one years old when he became king, and
he reigned seventeen years in Jerusalem, the
city the LORD had chosen out of all the tribes
of Israel in which to put his Name. His mother's name was Naamah; she was an Ammonite.
14He did evil because he had not set his heart
on seeking the LORD.
15As for the events of Rehoboam's reign,
from beginning to end, are they not written
in the records of Shemaiah the prophet and of
Iddo the seer that deal with genealogies? There
was continual warfare between Rehoboam and
Jeroboam. 16Rehoboam rested with his fathers
and was buried in the City of David. And Abijah his son succeeded him as king.

Abijah King of Judah

13 In the eighteenth year of the reign of Jeroboam, Abijah became king of Judah,
2and he reigned in Jerusalem three years.
His mother's name was Maacah,[a] a daughter[b]
of Uriel of Gibeah.

There was war between Abijah and Jeroboam. 3Abijah went into battle with a force of
four hundred thousand able fighting men, and
Jeroboam drew up a battle line against him
with eight hundred thousand able troops.
4Abijah stood on Mount Zemaraim, in the
hill country of Ephraim, and said, "Jeroboam
and all Israel, listen to me! 5Don't you know
that the LORD, the God of Israel, has given
the kingship of Israel to David and his descendants forever by a covenant of salt? 6Yet
Jeroboam son of Nebat, an official of Solomon son of David, rebelled against his master.
7Some worthless scoundrels gathered around
him and opposed Rehoboam son of Solomon
when he was young and indecisive and not
strong enough to resist them.
8"And now you plan to resist the kingdom
of the LORD, which is in the hands of David's
descendants. You are indeed a vast army and
have with you the golden calves that Jeroboam
made to be your gods. 9But didn't you drive
out the priests of the LORD, the sons of Aaron, and the Levites, and make priests of your
own as the peoples of other lands do? Whoever comes to consecrate himself with a young
bull and seven rams may become a priest of
what are not gods.
10"As for us, the LORD is our God, and we
have not forsaken him. The priests who serve
the LORD are sons of Aaron, and the Levites
assist them. 11Every morning and evening
they present burnt offerings and fragrant incense to the LORD. They set out the bread
on the ceremonially clean table and light the
lamps on the gold lampstand every evening.
We are observing the requirements of the
LORD our God. But you have forsaken him.
12God is with us; he is our leader. His priests
with their trumpets will sound the battle cry
against you. Men of Israel, do not fight against
the LORD, the God of your fathers, for you
will not succeed."
13Now Jeroboam had sent troops around
to the rear, so that while he was in front of
Judah the ambush was behind them. 14Judah
turned and saw that they were being attacked
at both front and rear. Then they cried out
to the LORD. The priests blew their trumpets
15and the men of Judah raised the battle cry.
At the sound of their battle cry, God routed
Jeroboam and all Israel before Abijah and Judah. 16The Israelites fled before Judah, and
God delivered them into their hands. 17Abijah
and his men inflicted heavy losses on them, so
that there were five hundred thousand casualties among Israel's able men. 18The men of
Israel were subdued on that occasion, and the
men of Judah were victorious because they relied on the LORD, the God of their fathers.
19Abijah pursued Jeroboam and took
from him the towns of Bethel, Jeshanah and
Ephron, with their surrounding villages. 20Jer-
oboam did not regain power during the time
of Abijah. And the LORD struck him down
and he died.
21But Abijah grew in strength. He married

---

[a] 2 Most Septuagint manuscripts and Syriac (see also 2 Chron. 11:20 and 1 Kings 15:2); Hebrew *Micaiah* [b] 2 Or *granddaughter*

fourteen wives and had twenty-two sons and
sixteen daughters.
22The other events of Abijah's reign, what
he did and what he said, are written in the
annotations of the prophet Iddo.

14 And Abijah rested with his fathers and
was buried in the City of David. Asa his
son succeeded him as king, and in his
days the country was at peace for ten years.

Asa King of Judah

2Asa did what was good and right in the
eyes of the LORD his God. 3He removed the
foreign altars and the high places, smashed
the sacred stones and cut down the Asherah
poles.[a] 4He commanded Judah to seek the
LORD, the God of their fathers, and to obey
his laws and commands. 5He removed the
high places and incense altars in every town
in Judah, and the kingdom was at peace under
him. 6He built up the fortified cities of Judah,
since the land was at peace. No one was at war
with him during those years, for the LORD
gave him rest.
7"Let us build up these towns," he said to
Judah, "and put walls around them, with towers, gates and bars. The land is still ours, because we have sought the LORD our God; we
sought him and he has given us rest on every
side." So they built and prospered.
8Asa had an army of three hundred thousand men from Judah, equipped with large
shields and with spears, and two hundred and
eighty thousand from Benjamin, armed with
small shields and with bows. All these were
brave fighting men.
9Zerah the Cushite marched out against
them with a vast army[b] and three hundred
chariots, and came as far as Mareshah. 10Asa
went out to meet him, and they took up battle positions in the Valley of Zephathah near
Mareshah.
11Then Asa called to the LORD his God
and said, "LORD, there is no one like you to
help the powerless against the mighty. Help
us, O LORD our God, for we rely on you, and
in your name we have come against this vast
army. O LORD, you are our God; do not let
man prevail against you."
12The LORD struck down the Cushites before Asa and Judah. The Cushites fled, 13and
Asa and his army pursued them as far as Gerar.
Such a great number of Cushites fell that they
could not recover; they were crushed before
the LORD and his forces. The men of Judah
carried off a large amount of plunder. 14They
destroyed all the villages around Gerar, for
the terror of the LORD had fallen upon them.
They plundered all these villages, since there
was much booty there. 15They also attacked
the camps of the herdsmen and carried off
droves of sheep and goats and camels. Then
they returned to Jerusalem.

Asa's Reform

15 The Spirit of God came upon Azariah
son of Oded. 2He went out to meet Asa
and said to him, "Listen to me, Asa and
all Judah and Benjamin. The LORD is with you
when you are with him. If you seek him, he
will be found by you, but if you forsake him,
he will forsake you. 3For a long time Israel
was without the true God, without a priest
to teach and without the law. 4But in their
distress they turned to the LORD, the God of
Israel, and sought him, and he was found by
them. 5In those days it was not safe to travel about, for all the inhabitants of the lands
were in great turmoil. 6One nation was being
crushed by another and one city by another,
because God was troubling them with every
kind of distress. 7But as for you, be strong
and do not give up, for your work will be rewarded."
8When Asa heard these words and the
prophecy of Azariah son of[c] Oded the prophet, he took courage. He removed the detestable
idols from the whole land of Judah and Benjamin and from the towns he had captured in
the hills of Ephraim. He repaired the altar of
the LORD that was in front of the portico of
the LORD's temple.
9Then he assembled all Judah and Benjamin and the people from Ephraim, Manasseh
and Simeon who had settled among them, for
large numbers had come over to him from Israel when they saw that the LORD his God was
with him.
10They assembled at Jerusalem in the third
month of the fifteenth year of Asa's reign. 11At
that time they sacrificed to the LORD seven
hundred head of cattle and seven thousand
sheep and goats from the plunder they had
brought back. 12They entered into a covenant
to seek the LORD, the God of their fathers,
with all their heart and soul. 13All who would
not seek the LORD, the God of Israel, were to
be put to death, whether small or great, man

[a] 3 That is, symbols of the goddess Asherah; here and elsewhere in 2 Chronicles [b] 9 Hebrew *with an army of a thousand thousands* or *with an army of thousands upon thousands* [c] 8 Vulgate and Syriac (see also Septuagint and verse 1); Hebrew does not have *Azariah son of.*

or woman. 14They took an oath to the LORD
with loud acclamation, with shouting and
with trumpets and horns. 15All Judah rejoiced
about the oath because they had sworn it
wholeheartedly. They sought God eagerly, and
he was found by them. So the LORD gave them
rest on every side.

16King Asa also deposed his grandmother
Maacah from her position as queen mother,
because she had made a repulsive Asherah
pole. Asa cut the pole down, broke it up and
burned it in the Kidron Valley. 17Although he
did not remove the high places from Israel,
Asa's heart was fully committed ⌞to the LORD⌟
all his life. 18He brought into the temple of
God the silver and gold and the articles that
he and his father had dedicated.

19There was no more war until the thirty-
fifth year of Asa's reign.

Asa's Last Years

16 In the thirty-sixth year of Asa's reign Baasha king of Israel went up against Judah
and fortified Ramah to prevent anyone
from leaving or entering the territory of Asa
king of Judah.

2Asa then took the silver and gold out of
the treasuries of the LORD's temple and of his
own palace and sent it to Ben-Hadad king of
Aram, who was ruling in Damascus. 3"Let
there be a treaty between me and you," he
said, "as there was between my father and your
father. See, I am sending you silver and gold.
Now break your treaty with Baasha king of Israel so he will withdraw from me."

4Ben-Hadad agreed with King Asa and
sent the commanders of his forces against the
towns of Israel. They conquered Ijon, Dan,
Abel Maim[a] and all the store cities of Naphtali. 5When Baasha heard this, he stopped
building Ramah and abandoned his work.
6Then King Asa brought all the men of Judah,
and they carried away from Ramah the stones
and timber Baasha had been using. With them
he built up Geba and Mizpah.

7At that time Hanani the seer came to Asa
king of Judah and said to him: "Because you
relied on the king of Aram and not on the
LORD your God, the army of the king of Aram
has escaped from your hand. 8Were not the
Cushites[b] and Libyans a mighty army with
great numbers of chariots and horsemen[c]?
Yet when you relied on the LORD, he delivered them into your hand. 9For the eyes of the
LORD range throughout the earth to strength-
en those whose hearts are fully committed to
him. You have done a foolish thing, and from
now on you will be at war."

10Asa was angry with the seer because of
this; he was so enraged that he put him in prison. At the same time Asa brutally oppressed
some of the people.

11The events of Asa's reign, from beginning
to end, are written in the book of the kings of
Judah and Israel. 12In the thirty-ninth year of
his reign Asa was afflicted with a disease in his
feet. Though his disease was severe, even in his
illness he did not seek help from the LORD,
but only from the physicians. 13Then in the
forty-first year of his reign Asa died and rested with his fathers. 14They buried him in the
tomb that he had cut out for himself in the
City of David. They laid him on a bier covered
with spices and various blended perfumes, and
they made a huge fire in his honor.

Jehoshaphat King of Judah

17 Jehoshaphat his son succeeded him as
king and strengthened himself against
Israel. 2He stationed troops in all the
fortified cities of Judah and put garrisons in
Judah and in the towns of Ephraim that his
father Asa had captured.

3The LORD was with Jehoshaphat because
in his early years he walked in the ways his
father David had followed. He did not consult the Baals 4but sought the God of his father and followed his commands rather than
the practices of Israel. 5The LORD established
the kingdom under his control; and all Judah
brought gifts to Jehoshaphat, so that he had
great wealth and honor. 6His heart was devoted to the ways of the LORD; furthermore,
he removed the high places and the Asherah
poles from Judah.

7In the third year of his reign he sent his officials Ben-Hail, Obadiah, Zechariah, Nethanel and Micaiah to teach in the towns of Judah.
8With them were certain Levites—Shemaiah,
Nethaniah, Zebadiah, Asahel, Shemiramoth,
Jehonathan, Adonijah, Tobijah and Tob-Ado-
nijah—and the priests Elishama and Jehoram.
9They taught throughout Judah, taking with
them the Book of the Law of the LORD; they
went around to all the towns of Judah and
taught the people.

10The fear of the LORD fell on all the kingdoms of the lands surrounding Judah, so that
they did not make war with Jehoshaphat.
11Some Philistines brought Jehoshaphat gifts

[a] 4 Also known as *Abel Beth Maacah* [b] 8 That is, people from the upper Nile region [c] 8 Or *charioteers*

IN SICKNESS AND IN HEALTH

When we exchange marriage vows, we promise that we will be faithful to each other "in sickness and in health." Sickness can mean a brief illness, a chronic condition or a difficult disease. It is easy enough to stand by a healthy person who requires very little physical care. When a spouse faces a long-term disease, however, the story changes in fundamental ways.

In the thirty-ninth year of his reign Asa was afflicted with a disease in his feet. Though his disease was severe, even in his illness he did not seek help from the LORD, but only from the physicians.

— 2 CHRONICLES 16:12

Asa had been king of Judah for 39 years when he was "afflicted with a disease in his feet." The symptoms no doubt were painful and the treatment options limited. This leader of Judah could have done what many believers do during an illness; he could have prayed to the Lord, and asked others—his wife, his friends and his advisers—to pray. Instead, he did what many people who think they have it all under control do: He bought the best medical services he could find. Sounds like many people today; instead of taking the opportunity to lean on God's strength and look to him during an illness, many people rely only on human medical advances and treatments.

let's talk

- ✦ What is the difference between making demands on God to take a certain action and seeking God's will for direction and provision?
- ✦ How can we help each other deal with the multiple challenges of illness? What's helpful and what's not?
- ✦ Who in our families or among our friends have been godly heroes in sickness? What are some lessons we can learn from them?

Second Chronicles 16:12 suggests that Asa had other options before him, and yet he chose to turn his back on God, even though he had faithfully trusted in the Lord for the first 36 years of his reign. Likewise, Christians know that Jesus himself is the Great Physician who cares for our spiritual and physical health. By trusting in him, we can learn what Jesus knew so well: Illness is physical, mental, emotional and spiritual, and healing needs to happen at all levels for grace and health to abound.

A friend of mine with cancer told me, "When I first faced my disease, I panicked. I couldn't pray, at least not consistently. So my wife prayed for me, for us and for our physicians. She invited our friends to pray too. She asked for God's guidance for the right physicians, for medical options—you name it. Then I could begin to pray again."

My friend said that when he first heard he had cancer, his first thought was about the "till death do us part" line from his marriage vows. Later, his wife's prayer support helped him to once again concentrate on "in sickness and in health." He is in remission from cancer today.

Not every disease we get is healed. And helping a spouse with a debilitating, long-term illness is a struggle and, at times, an overwhelming challenge. But God is sovereign and his will is done—even in sickness.

What's more, God can transform our times of suffering and pain into times of blessing. When a couple seeks help from the Lord when dealing with sickness, divine direction, grace and health can fill hearts and minds with hope—and make marriages stronger.

—JOHN R. THROOP

FOR YOUR NEXT DEVOTIONAL READING, TURN TO PAGE 476.

and silver as tribute, and the Arabs brought
him flocks: seven thousand seven hundred
rams and seven thousand seven hundred
goats.
12 Jehoshaphat became more and more
powerful; he built forts and store cities in Judah 13 and had large supplies in the towns of
Judah. He also kept experienced fighting men
in Jerusalem. 14 Their enrollment by families
was as follows:

From Judah, commanders of units
of 1,000:
Adnah the commander, with 300,000
fighting men;
15 next, Jehohanan the commander, with
280,000;
16 next, Amasiah son of Zicri, who volunteered himself for the service of
the LORD, with 200,000.
17 From Benjamin:
Eliada, a valiant soldier, with 200,000
men armed with bows and shields;
18 next, Jehozabad, with 180,000 men
armed for battle.

19 These were the men who served the king, besides those he stationed in the fortified cities
throughout Judah.

Micaiah Prophesies Against Ahab

18 Now Jehoshaphat had great wealth and
honor, and he allied himself with Ahab
by marriage. 2 Some years later he went
down to visit Ahab in Samaria. Ahab slaughtered many sheep and cattle for him and the
people with him and urged him to attack Ramoth Gilead. 3 Ahab king of Israel asked Jehoshaphat king of Judah, "Will you go with
me against Ramoth Gilead?"
Jehoshaphat replied, "I am as you are, and
my people as your people; we will join you
in the war." 4 But Jehoshaphat also said to the
king of Israel, "First seek the counsel of the
LORD."
5 So the king of Israel brought together the
prophets—four hundred men—and asked
them, "Shall we go to war against Ramoth
Gilead, or shall I refrain?"
"Go," they answered, "for God will give it
into the king's hand."
6 But Jehoshaphat asked, "Is there not a
prophet of the LORD here whom we can inquire of?"
7 The king of Israel answered Jehoshaphat,
"There is still one man through whom we can
inquire of the LORD, but I hate him because
he never prophesies anything good about me,
but always bad. He is Micaiah son of Imlah."
"The king should not say that," Jehoshaphat replied.
8 So the king of Israel called one of his officials and said, "Bring Micaiah son of Imlah
at once."
9 Dressed in their royal robes, the king of
Israel and Jehoshaphat king of Judah were
sitting on their thrones at the threshing floor
by the entrance to the gate of Samaria, with
all the prophets prophesying before them.
10 Now Zedekiah son of Kenaanah had made
iron horns, and he declared, "This is what the
LORD says: 'With these you will gore the Arameans until they are destroyed.' "
11 All the other prophets were prophesying
the same thing. "Attack Ramoth Gilead and
be victorious," they said, "for the LORD will
give it into the king's hand."
12 The messenger who had gone to summon
Micaiah said to him, "Look, as one man the
other prophets are predicting success for the
king. Let your word agree with theirs, and
speak favorably."
13 But Micaiah said, "As surely as the LORD
lives, I can tell him only what my God says."
14 When he arrived, the king asked him,
"Micaiah, shall we go to war against Ramoth
Gilead, or shall I refrain?"
"Attack and be victorious," he answered,
"for they will be given into your hand."
15 The king said to him, "How many times
must I make you swear to tell me nothing but
the truth in the name of the LORD?"
16 Then Micaiah answered, "I saw all Israel
scattered on the hills like sheep without a shepherd, and the LORD said, 'These people have
no master. Let each one go home in peace.' "
17 The king of Israel said to Jehoshaphat,
"Didn't I tell you that he never prophesies
anything good about me, but only bad?"
18 Micaiah continued, "Therefore hear the
word of the LORD: I saw the LORD sitting on
his throne with all the host of heaven standing
on his right and on his left. 19 And the LORD
said, 'Who will entice Ahab king of Israel into
attacking Ramoth Gilead and going to his
death there?'
"One suggested this, and another that. 20 Finally, a spirit came forward, stood before the
LORD and said, 'I will entice him.'
" 'By what means?' the LORD asked.
21 " 'I will go and be a lying spirit in the
mouths of all his prophets,' he said.
" 'You will succeed in enticing him,' said
the LORD. 'Go and do it.'

22“So now the LORD has put a lying spirit
in the mouths of these prophets of yours. The
LORD has decreed disaster for you.”
23Then Zedekiah son of Kenaanah went
up and slapped Micaiah in the face. “Which
way did the spirit from[a] the LORD go when he
went from me to speak to you?” he asked.
24Micaiah replied, “You will find out on the
day you go to hide in an inner room.”
25The king of Israel then ordered, “Take
Micaiah and send him back to Amon the ruler
of the city and to Joash the king’s son, 26and
say, ‘This is what the king says: Put this fellow
in prison and give him nothing but bread and
water until I return safely.’ ”
27Micaiah declared, “If you ever return
safely, the LORD has not spoken through me.”
Then he added, “Mark my words, all you people!”

Ahab Killed at Ramoth Gilead

28So the king of Israel and Jehoshaphat king
of Judah went up to Ramoth Gilead. 29The
king of Israel said to Jehoshaphat, “I will enter
the battle in disguise, but you wear your royal
robes.” So the king of Israel disguised himself
and went into battle.
30Now the king of Aram had ordered his
chariot commanders, “Do not fight with anyone, small or great, except the king of Israel.”
31When the chariot commanders saw Jehoshaphat, they thought, “This is the king of Israel.”
So they turned to attack him, but Jehoshaphat
cried out, and the LORD helped him. God
drew them away from him, 32for when the
chariot commanders saw that he was not the
king of Israel, they stopped pursuing him.
33But someone drew his bow at random
and hit the king of Israel between the sections
of his armor. The king told the chariot driver,
“Wheel around and get me out of the fighting.
I’ve been wounded.” 34All day long the battle
raged, and the king of Israel propped himself
up in his chariot facing the Arameans until
evening. Then at sunset he died.

19 When Jehoshaphat king of Judah returned safely to his palace in Jerusalem,
2Jehu the seer, the son of Hanani, went
out to meet him and said to the king, “Should
you help the wicked and love[b] those who hate
the LORD? Because of this, the wrath of the
LORD is upon you. 3There is, however, some
good in you, for you have rid the land of the
Asherah poles and have set your heart on seeking God.”

Jehoshaphat Appoints Judges

4Jehoshaphat lived in Jerusalem, and he
went out again among the people from Beersheba to the hill country of Ephraim and
turned them back to the LORD, the God of
their fathers. 5He appointed judges in the
land, in each of the fortified cities of Judah.
6He told them, “Consider carefully what you
do, because you are not judging for man but
for the LORD, who is with you whenever you
give a verdict. 7Now let the fear of the LORD
be upon you. Judge carefully, for with the
LORD our God there is no injustice or partiality or bribery.”
8In Jerusalem also, Jehoshaphat appointed
some of the Levites, priests and heads of Israelite families to administer the law of the LORD
and to settle disputes. And they lived in Jerusalem. 9He gave them these orders: “You must
serve faithfully and wholeheartedly in the fear
of the LORD. 10In every case that comes before you from your fellow countrymen who
live in the cities—whether bloodshed or other concerns of the law, commands, decrees or
ordinances—you are to warn them not to sin
against the LORD; otherwise his wrath will
come on you and your brothers. Do this, and
you will not sin.
11“Amariah the chief priest will be over you
in any matter concerning the LORD, and Zebadiah son of Ishmael, the leader of the tribe of
Judah, will be over you in any matter concerning the king, and the Levites will serve as officials before you. Act with courage, and may
the LORD be with those who do well.”

Jehoshaphat Defeats Moab and Ammon

20 After this, the Moabites and Ammonites with some of the Meunites[c] came
to make war on Jehoshaphat.
2Some men came and told Jehoshaphat, “A
vast army is coming against you from Edom,[d]
from the other side of the Sea.[e] It is already in
Hazazon Tamar” (that is, En Gedi). 3Alarmed,
Jehoshaphat resolved to inquire of the LORD,
and he proclaimed a fast for all Judah. 4The
people of Judah came together to seek help
from the LORD; indeed, they came from every
town in Judah to seek him.
5Then Jehoshaphat stood up in the assembly of Judah and Jerusalem at the temple of
the LORD in the front of the new courtyard
6and said:

“O LORD, God of our fathers, are you

[a] 23 Or *Spirit of* [b] 2 Or *and make alliances with* [c] 1 Some Septuagint manuscripts; Hebrew *Ammonites* [d] 2 One Hebrew manuscript; most Hebrew manuscripts, Septuagint and Vulgate *Aram* [e] 2 That is, the Dead Sea

THURSDAY
READ
2 CHRONICLES 20:1–30

WHEN YOU DON'T KNOW WHAT TO DO

My husband and I are both fix-it people. When faced with problems, we immediately go into crisis-intervention mode. We also tend to consider depending on God as a last resort rather than instinctively turning to him first.

However, sometimes not even our best efforts to fix things can change our circumstances. That's when we've learned that if we belong to God, our lives are not our own, and our battles aren't really ours, but his.

One situation that crystallized this lesson was when I learned that I was pregnant with our youngest daughter, and two weeks later my husband was laid off from his job. We had no health insurance, no savings, no income and no job prospects. We were powerless to fix this condition ourselves.

I remember thinking that either (1) God didn't exist and everything was spinning out of control, or (2) God not only existed but was in complete control and would take care of all of our needs. We might have to struggle, but he would be with us.

Still, as the baby inside of me grew and the bills piled up and my husband couldn't find a job, we were afraid.

Second Chronicles describes a time when the Israelites were afraid. A vast army had assembled to attack them. Powerless to defend themselves, they turned to the Lord for help. With King Jehoshaphat as their leader, they prayed, "We do not know what to do, but our eyes are upon you" (2 Chronicles 20:12).

Through a Levite named Jahaziel, the Spirit of the Lord told them, "Do not be afraid or discouraged because of this vast army. For the battle is not yours, but God's" (verse 15). The following day God set ambushes against the enemy armies and defeated them for the Israelites.

Our situation wasn't a battle against an army, but it was a battle nonetheless. We fought to trust God and to believe that he was able and willing to do more for us than we could ever dream or imagine or do for ourselves.

Space prohibits me from telling all that God did, but during that entire year of my husband's unemployment, through various odd jobs and the generosity of our church family, all of our bills were paid, including the baby's delivery cost.

More important, God used the hardships we went through as a strong testimony to our neighbors and friends, as well as to us. As we said repeatedly, "God did it." We realized that not only was the battle his but so, too, was the victory.

—NANCY KENNEDY

FOR YOUR NEXT DEVOTIONAL READING, TURN TO PAGE 481.

This is what the LORD says to you: "Do not be afraid or discouraged because of this vast army. For the battle is not yours, but God's."

— 2 CHRONICLES 20:15

let's talk

- When problems arise, what is our normal default mode for facing them?
- What good can result from bad things that happen to us?
- How has God fought our battles for us?

not the God who is in heaven? You rule
over all the kingdoms of the nations.
Power and might are in your hand, and
no one can withstand you. [7]O our God,
did you not drive out the inhabitants of
this land before your people Israel and
give it forever to the descendants of Abraham your friend? [8]They have lived in it
and have built in it a sanctuary for your
Name, saying, [9]'If calamity comes upon
us, whether the sword of judgment, or
plague or famine, we will stand in your
presence before this temple that bears
your Name and will cry out to you in
our distress, and you will hear us and
save us.'

[10]"But now here are men from Ammon, Moab and Mount Seir, whose
territory you would not allow Israel to
invade when they came from Egypt; so
they turned away from them and did not
destroy them. [11]See how they are repaying us by coming to drive us out of the
possession you gave us as an inheritance.
[12]O our God, will you not judge them?
For we have no power to face this vast
army that is attacking us. We do not
know what to do, but our eyes are upon
you."

[13]All the men of Judah, with their wives
and children and little ones, stood there before the LORD.

[14]Then the Spirit of the LORD came upon
Jahaziel son of Zechariah, the son of Benaiah,
the son of Jeiel, the son of Mattaniah, a Levite
and descendant of Asaph, as he stood in the
assembly.

[15]He said: "Listen, King Jehoshaphat and
all who live in Judah and Jerusalem! This is
what the LORD says to you: 'Do not be afraid
or discouraged because of this vast army. For
the battle is not yours, but God's. [16]Tomorrow
march down against them. They will be climbing up by the Pass of Ziz, and you will find
them at the end of the gorge in the Desert of
Jeruel. [17]You will not have to fight this battle.
Take up your positions; stand firm and see the
deliverance the LORD will give you, O Judah
and Jerusalem. Do not be afraid; do not be
discouraged. Go out to face them tomorrow,
and the LORD will be with you.' "

[18]Jehoshaphat bowed with his face to the
ground, and all the people of Judah and Jerusalem fell down in worship before the LORD.
[19]Then some Levites from the Kohathites and
Korahites stood up and praised the LORD, the
God of Israel, with a very loud voice.

[20]Early in the morning they left for the
Desert of Tekoa. As they set out, Jehoshaphat
stood and said, "Listen to me, Judah and people of Jerusalem! Have faith in the LORD your
God and you will be upheld; have faith in his
prophets and you will be successful." [21]After
consulting the people, Jehoshaphat appointed
men to sing to the LORD and to praise him for
the splendor of his[a] holiness as they went out
at the head of the army, saying:

"Give thanks to the LORD,
for his love endures forever."

[22]As they began to sing and praise, the
LORD set ambushes against the men of Ammon and Moab and Mount Seir who were invading Judah, and they were defeated. [23]The
men of Ammon and Moab rose up against the
men from Mount Seir to destroy and annihilate them. After they finished slaughtering
the men from Seir, they helped to destroy one
another.

[24]When the men of Judah came to the place
that overlooks the desert and looked toward
the vast army, they saw only dead bodies lying
on the ground; no one had escaped. [25]So Jehoshaphat and his men went to carry off their
plunder, and they found among them a great
amount of equipment and clothing[b] and also
articles of value—more than they could take
away. There was so much plunder that it took
three days to collect it. [26]On the fourth day
they assembled in the Valley of Beracah, where
they praised the LORD. This is why it is called
the Valley of Beracah[c] to this day.

[27]Then, led by Jehoshaphat, all the men of
Judah and Jerusalem returned joyfully to Jerusalem, for the LORD had given them cause
to rejoice over their enemies. [28]They entered
Jerusalem and went to the temple of the LORD
with harps and lutes and trumpets.

[29]The fear of God came upon all the kingdoms of the countries when they heard how
the LORD had fought against the enemies of
Israel. [30]And the kingdom of Jehoshaphat was
at peace, for his God had given him rest on
every side.

The End of Jehoshaphat's Reign

[31]So Jehoshaphat reigned over Judah. He
was thirty-five years old when he became king
of Judah, and he reigned in Jerusalem twen-

[a] 21 Or *him with the splendor of* [b] 25 Some Hebrew manuscripts and Vulgate; most Hebrew manuscripts *corpses* [c] 26 *Beracah* means *praise.*

ty-five years. His mother's name was Azubah
daughter of Shilhi. 32He walked in the ways
of his father Asa and did not stray from them;
he did what was right in the eyes of the LORD.
33The high places, however, were not removed,
and the people still had not set their hearts on
the God of their fathers.

34The other events of Jehoshaphat's reign,
from beginning to end, are written in the annals of Jehu son of Hanani, which are recorded in the book of the kings of Israel.

35Later, Jehoshaphat king of Judah made an
alliance with Ahaziah king of Israel, who was
guilty of wickedness. 36He agreed with him to
construct a fleet of trading ships.[a] After these
were built at Ezion Geber, 37Eliezer son of
Dodavahu of Mareshah prophesied against Jehoshaphat, saying, "Because you have made an
alliance with Ahaziah, the LORD will destroy
what you have made." The ships were wrecked
and were not able to set sail to trade.[b]

21 Then Jehoshaphat rested with his fathers and was buried with them in the
City of David. And Jehoram his son
succeeded him as king. 2Jehoram's brothers,
the sons of Jehoshaphat, were Azariah, Jehiel, Zechariah, Azariahu, Michael and Shephatiah. All these were sons of Jehoshaphat king
of Israel.[c] 3Their father had given them many
gifts of silver and gold and articles of value,
as well as fortified cities in Judah, but he had
given the kingdom to Jehoram because he was
his firstborn son.

Jehoram King of Judah

4When Jehoram established himself firmly
over his father's kingdom, he put all his brothers to the sword along with some of the princes of Israel. 5Jehoram was thirty-two years old
when he became king, and he reigned in Jerusalem eight years. 6He walked in the ways of
the kings of Israel, as the house of Ahab had
done, for he married a daughter of Ahab. He
did evil in the eyes of the LORD. 7Nevertheless,
because of the covenant the LORD had made
with David, the LORD was not willing to destroy the house of David. He had promised to
maintain a lamp for him and his descendants
forever.

8In the time of Jehoram, Edom rebelled
against Judah and set up its own king. 9So Jehoram went there with his officers and all his
chariots. The Edomites surrounded him and
his chariot commanders, but he rose up and
broke through by night. 10To this day Edom
has been in rebellion against Judah.

Libnah revolted at the same time, because
Jehoram had forsaken the LORD, the God of
his fathers. 11He had also built high places on
the hills of Judah and had caused the people
of Jerusalem to prostitute themselves and had
led Judah astray.

12Jehoram received a letter from Elijah the
prophet, which said:

> "This is what the LORD, the God of your
> father David, says: 'You have not walked
> in the ways of your father Jehoshaphat
> or of Asa king of Judah. 13But you have
> walked in the ways of the kings of Israel,
> and you have led Judah and the people
> of Jerusalem to prostitute themselves, just
> as the house of Ahab did. You have also
> murdered your own brothers, members
> of your father's house, men who were bet-
> ter than you. 14So now the LORD is about
> to strike your people, your sons, your
> wives and everything that is yours, with
> a heavy blow. 15You yourself will be very
> ill with a lingering disease of the bowels,
> until the disease causes your bowels to
> come out.' "

16The LORD aroused against Jehoram the
hostility of the Philistines and of the Arabs
who lived near the Cushites. 17They attacked
Judah, invaded it and carried off all the goods
found in the king's palace, together with his
sons and wives. Not a son was left to him except Ahaziah,[d] the youngest.

18After all this, the LORD afflicted Jehoram
with an incurable disease of the bowels. 19In
the course of time, at the end of the second
year, his bowels came out because of the disease, and he died in great pain. His people
made no fire in his honor, as they had for his
fathers.

20Jehoram was thirty-two years old when
he became king, and he reigned in Jerusalem
eight years. He passed away, to no one's regret,
and was buried in the City of David, but not
in the tombs of the kings.

Ahaziah King of Judah

22 The people of Jerusalem made Ahaziah, Jehoram's youngest son, king in his
place, since the raiders, who came with
the Arabs into the camp, had killed all the older sons. So Ahaziah son of Jehoram king of
Judah began to reign.

[a] 36 Hebrew *of ships that could go to Tarshish* [b] 37 Hebrew *sail for Tarshish* [c] 2 That is, Judah, as frequently in 2 Chronicles
[d] 17 Hebrew *Jehoahaz*, a variant of *Ahaziah*

2 Ahaziah was twenty-two[a] years old when
he became king, and he reigned in Jerusalem
one year. His mother's name was Athaliah, a
granddaughter of Omri.
3 He too walked in the ways of the house
of Ahab, for his mother encouraged him in
doing wrong. 4 He did evil in the eyes of the
LORD, as the house of Ahab had done, for after
his father's death they became his advisers, to
his undoing. 5 He also followed their counsel
when he went with Joram[b] son of Ahab king
of Israel to war against Hazael king of Aram
at Ramoth Gilead. The Arameans wounded
Joram; 6 so he returned to Jezreel to recover
from the wounds they had inflicted on him
at Ramoth[c] in his battle with Hazael king of
Aram.

Then Ahaziah[d] son of Jehoram king of Judah went down to Jezreel to see Joram son of Ahab because he had been wounded.

7 Through Ahaziah's visit to Joram, God
brought about Ahaziah's downfall. When
Ahaziah arrived, he went out with Joram to
meet Jehu son of Nimshi, whom the LORD
had anointed to destroy the house of Ahab.
8 While Jehu was executing judgment on the
house of Ahab, he found the princes of Judah and the sons of Ahaziah's relatives, who
had been attending Ahaziah, and he killed
them. 9 He then went in search of Ahaziah,
and his men captured him while he was hiding in Samaria. He was brought to Jehu and
put to death. They buried him, for they said,
"He was a son of Jehoshaphat, who sought the
LORD with all his heart." So there was no one
in the house of Ahaziah powerful enough to
retain the kingdom.

Athaliah and Joash

10 When Athaliah the mother of Ahaziah
saw that her son was dead, she proceeded to
destroy the whole royal family of the house
of Judah. 11 But Jehosheba,[e] the daughter of
King Jehoram, took Joash son of Ahaziah and
stole him away from among the royal princes
who were about to be murdered and put him
and his nurse in a bedroom. Because Jehosheba,[e] the daughter of King Jehoram and wife
of the priest Jehoiada, was Ahaziah's sister, she
hid the child from Athaliah so she could not
kill him. 12 He remained hidden with them at
the temple of God for six years while Athaliah
ruled the land.

23 In the seventh year Jehoiada showed his
strength. He made a covenant with the
commanders of units of a hundred: Azariah son of Jeroham, Ishmael son of Jehohanan, Azariah son of Obed, Maaseiah son of
Adaiah, and Elishaphat son of Zicri. 2 They
went throughout Judah and gathered the Levites and the heads of Israelite families from
all the towns. When they came to Jerusalem,
3 the whole assembly made a covenant with the
king at the temple of God.

Jehoiada said to them, "The king's son shall
reign, as the LORD promised concerning the
descendants of David. 4 Now this is what you
are to do: A third of you priests and Levites
who are going on duty on the Sabbath are
to keep watch at the doors, 5 a third of you
at the royal palace and a third at the Foundation Gate, and all the other men are to be
in the courtyards of the temple of the LORD.
6 No one is to enter the temple of the LORD
except the priests and Levites on duty; they
may enter because they are consecrated, but all
the other men are to guard what the LORD has
assigned to them.[f] 7 The Levites are to station
themselves around the king, each man with
his weapons in his hand. Anyone who enters
the temple must be put to death. Stay close to
the king wherever he goes."

8 The Levites and all the men of Judah did
just as Jehoiada the priest ordered. Each one
took his men—those who were going on duty
on the Sabbath and those who were going off
duty—for Jehoiada the priest had not released
any of the divisions. 9 Then he gave the commanders of units of a hundred the spears and
the large and small shields that had belonged
to King David and that were in the temple of
God. 10 He stationed all the men, each with his
weapon in his hand, around the king—near
the altar and the temple, from the south side
to the north side of the temple.

11 Jehoiada and his sons brought out the
king's son and put the crown on him; they
presented him with a copy of the covenant
and proclaimed him king. They anointed him
and shouted, "Long live the king!"

12 When Athaliah heard the noise of the
people running and cheering the king, she
went to them at the temple of the LORD.
13 She looked, and there was the king, standing by his pillar at the entrance. The officers
and the trumpeters were beside the king, and

[a] *2* Some Septuagint manuscripts and Syriac (see also 2 Kings 8:26); Hebrew *forty-two* [b] *5* Hebrew *Jehoram,* a variant of *Joram;* also in verses 6 and 7 [c] *6* Hebrew *Ramah,* a variant of *Ramoth* [d] *6* Some Hebrew manuscripts, Septuagint, Vulgate and Syriac (see also 2 Kings 8:29); most Hebrew manuscripts *Azariah* [e] *11* Hebrew *Jehoshabeath,* a variant of *Jehosheba* [f] *6* Or *to observe the LORD's command* ⌊*not to enter*⌋

all the people of the land were rejoicing and blowing trumpets, and singers with musical instruments were leading the praises. Then Athaliah tore her robes and shouted, "Treason! Treason!"

14Jehoiada the priest sent out the commanders of units of a hundred, who were in charge of the troops, and said to them: "Bring her out between the ranks[a] and put to the sword anyone who follows her." For the priest had said, "Do not put her to death at the temple of the LORD." 15So they seized her as she reached the entrance of the Horse Gate on the palace grounds, and there they put her to death.

16Jehoiada then made a covenant that he and the people and the king[b] would be the LORD's people. 17All the people went to the temple of Baal and tore it down. They smashed the altars and idols and killed Mattan the priest of Baal in front of the altars.

18Then Jehoiada placed the oversight of the temple of the LORD in the hands of the priests, who were Levites, to whom David had made assignments in the temple, to present the burnt offerings of the LORD as written in the Law of Moses, with rejoicing and singing, as David had ordered. 19He also stationed doorkeepers at the gates of the LORD's temple so that no one who was in any way unclean might enter.

20He took with him the commanders of hundreds, the nobles, the rulers of the people and all the people of the land and brought the king down from the temple of the LORD. They went into the palace through the Upper Gate and seated the king on the royal throne, 21and all the people of the land rejoiced. And the city was quiet, because Athaliah had been slain with the sword.

Joash Repairs the Temple

24 Joash was seven years old when he became king, and he reigned in Jerusalem forty years. His mother's name was Zibiah; she was from Beersheba. 2Joash did what was right in the eyes of the LORD all the years of Jehoiada the priest. 3Jehoiada chose two wives for him, and he had sons and daughters.

4Some time later Joash decided to restore the temple of the LORD. 5He called together the priests and Levites and said to them, "Go to the towns of Judah and collect the money due annually from all Israel, to repair the temple of your God. Do it now." But the Levites did not act at once.

6Therefore the king summoned Jehoiada the chief priest and said to him, "Why haven't you required the Levites to bring in from Judah and Jerusalem the tax imposed by Moses the servant of the LORD and by the assembly of Israel for the Tent of the Testimony?"

7Now the sons of that wicked woman Athaliah had broken into the temple of God and had used even its sacred objects for the Baals.

8At the king's command, a chest was made and placed outside, at the gate of the temple of the LORD. 9A proclamation was then issued in Judah and Jerusalem that they should bring to the LORD the tax that Moses the servant of God had required of Israel in the desert. 10All the officials and all the people brought their contributions gladly, dropping them into the chest until it was full. 11Whenever the chest was brought in by the Levites to the king's officials and they saw that there was a large amount of money, the royal secretary and the officer of the chief priest would come and empty the chest and carry it back to its place. They did this regularly and collected a great amount of money. 12The king and Jehoiada gave it to the men who carried out the work required for the temple of the LORD. They hired masons and carpenters to restore the LORD's temple, and also workers in iron and bronze to repair the temple.

13The men in charge of the work were diligent, and the repairs progressed under them. They rebuilt the temple of God according to its original design and reinforced it. 14When they had finished, they brought the rest of the money to the king and Jehoiada, and with it were made articles for the LORD's temple: articles for the service and for the burnt offerings, and also dishes and other objects of gold and silver. As long as Jehoiada lived, burnt offerings were presented continually in the temple of the LORD.

15Now Jehoiada was old and full of years, and he died at the age of a hundred and thirty. 16He was buried with the kings in the City of David, because of the good he had done in Israel for God and his temple.

The Wickedness of Joash

17After the death of Jehoiada, the officials of Judah came and paid homage to the king, and he listened to them. 18They abandoned the temple of the LORD, the God of their fa-

[a] 14 Or *out from the precincts* [b] 16 Or *covenant between* ⌊*the LORD*⌋ *and the people and the king that they* (see 2 Kings 11:17)

FRIDAY
READ 2 CHRONICLES 24:1–25

WHO INFLUENCES US?

Think about how other people have influenced your life. One couple I know, Brett and Kayla, were profoundly influenced by others. Brett had played multiple sports in high school and enjoyed a wonderful mentoring relationship with one of his coaches. But after he started playing sports in college, he found that it wasn't the game he cared about as much as it was his former coach, and he ended up dropping out of athletics. Similarly, Kayla became active in her church's women's ministries because of the great lessons she had learned from the women's leader in her previous church.

Influence is powerful. We often want to emulate good leaders and follow their examples. The high priest Jehoiada was a great influence on little King Joash, who was only seven years old when he became king. Joash needed some help ruling the kingdom, and Jehoiada stepped up as his helper and adviser. He chose two wives for Joash and helped Joash restore the temple in Jerusalem and resume worship of the Lord there.

Joash did what was right in the eyes of the LORD all the years of Jehoiada the priest.

— 2 CHRONICLES 24:2

let's talk

- Who has greatly influenced our lives as a couple? Did they teach us mostly *what* to think or *how* to think? Describe their approaches.
- How are leaders or role models helpful for us? How can they be negative influences? How can we turn negative influences into positive results?
- What are some good ways for us to blend the positive influences of others into our lives? How can their lessons shape our faith and our values?

Joash was heavily influenced by others—first by Jehoiada, who led him in the ways of God, and then, after Jehoiada died, by the officials of Judah, who abandoned God and worshiped other gods. When Jehoiada's son Zechariah spoke out against idol worship, warning the king and his people that God would forsake them because they had forsaken God, Joash and his leaders had Zechariah stoned to death.

Like Joash, we have people who have had a major impact on our lives, and we feel lost when they are no longer with us. We may even think that we need others to step in to fill that gap. But like Joash, depending too much on others can prevent us from learning to make critical decisions in our lives.

The best role of a parent, mentor, teacher or pastor is that of helping others to learn how to think for themselves. If Jehoiada had taught Joash to think for himself, the story of this king might have had a different ending. Instead of being led by others, Joash might have been a strong, decisive king who set before the people a lifelong pattern of trusting God for guidance and direction.

My friends James and Elaine relied on the leadership and guidance of key people until they were in a couples' group at church. The rule in that group was that everyone was expected to think about and discuss key issues and situations. The group then asked everyone to take one more step: Each couple was expected to reach their own conclusion on an issue, based on Scriptural guidelines, and explain to the group how they had come to that decision.

Learning and practicing that kind of decision making changed their marriage forever as James and Elaine learned how to think for themselves. Reaching their own conclusions on various issues became a lifelong pattern of learning God's lessons without leaning on others to do it for them.

—JOHN R. THROOP

FOR YOUR NEXT DEVOTIONAL READING, TURN TO PAGE 488.

thers, and worshiped Asherah poles and idols.
Because of their guilt, God's anger came upon
Judah and Jerusalem. 19Although the LORD
sent prophets to the people to bring them
back to him, and though they testified against
them, they would not listen.
20Then the Spirit of God came upon Zechariah son of Jehoiada the priest. He stood before
the people and said, "This is what God says:
'Why do you disobey the LORD's commands?
You will not prosper. Because you have forsak-
en the LORD, he has forsaken you.' "
21But they plotted against him, and by order of the king they stoned him to death in the
courtyard of the LORD's temple. 22King Joash
did not remember the kindness Zechariah's father Jehoiada had shown him but killed his
son, who said as he lay dying, "May the LORD
see this and call you to account."
23At the turn of the year,[a] the army of
Aram marched against Joash; it invaded Judah and Jerusalem and killed all the leaders of
the people. They sent all the plunder to their
king in Damascus. 24Although the Aramean army had come with only a few men, the
LORD delivered into their hands a much larger
army. Because Judah had forsaken the LORD,
the God of their fathers, judgment was executed on Joash. 25When the Arameans withdrew, they left Joash severely wounded. His
officials conspired against him for murdering
the son of Jehoiada the priest, and they killed
him in his bed. So he died and was buried in
the City of David, but not in the tombs of
the kings.
26Those who conspired against him were
Zabad,[b] son of Shimeath an Ammonite woman, and Jehozabad, son of Shimrith[c] a Moabite
woman. 27The account of his sons, the many
prophecies about him, and the record of the
restoration of the temple of God are written in
the annotations on the book of the kings. And
Amaziah his son succeeded him as king.

Amaziah King of Judah

25 Amaziah was twenty-five years old when
he became king, and he reigned in Jerusalem twenty-nine years. His mother's
name was Jehoaddin[d]; she was from Jerusalem. 2He did what was right in the eyes of
the LORD, but not wholeheartedly. 3After the
kingdom was firmly in his control, he executed
the officials who had murdered his father the
king. 4Yet he did not put their sons to death,
but acted in accordance with what is written
in the Law, in the Book of Moses, where the
LORD commanded: "Fathers shall not be put
to death for their children, nor children put
to death for their fathers; each is to die for his
own sins."[e]
5Amaziah called the people of Judah together
and assigned them according to their families
to commanders of thousands and commanders of hundreds for all Judah and Benjamin.
He then mustered those twenty years old or
more and found that there were three hundred
thousand men ready for military service, able
to handle the spear and shield. 6He also hired
a hundred thousand fighting men from Israel
for a hundred talents[f] of silver.
7But a man of God came to him and said,
"O king, these troops from Israel must not
march with you, for the LORD is not with
Israel—not with any of the people of Ephraim. 8Even if you go and fight courageously
in battle, God will overthrow you before the
enemy, for God has the power to help or to
overthrow."
9Amaziah asked the man of God, "But what
about the hundred talents I paid for these Israelite troops?"
The man of God replied, "The LORD can
give you much more than that."
10So Amaziah dismissed the troops who had
come to him from Ephraim and sent them
home. They were furious with Judah and left
for home in a great rage.
11Amaziah then marshaled his strength and
led his army to the Valley of Salt, where he
killed ten thousand men of Seir. 12The army of
Judah also captured ten thousand men alive,
took them to the top of a cliff and threw them
down so that all were dashed to pieces.
13Meanwhile the troops that Amaziah had
sent back and had not allowed to take part in
the war raided Judean towns from Samaria to
Beth Horon. They killed three thousand people and carried off great quantities of plunder.
14When Amaziah returned from slaughtering the Edomites, he brought back the gods
of the people of Seir. He set them up as his
own gods, bowed down to them and burned
sacrifices to them. 15The anger of the LORD
burned against Amaziah, and he sent a prophet to him, who said, "Why do you consult this
people's gods, which could not save their own
people from your hand?"
16While he was still speaking, the king said

[a] 23 Probably in the spring [b] 26 A variant of *Jozabad* [c] 26 A variant of *Shomer* [d] 1 Hebrew *Jehoaddan,* a variant of *Jehoaddin*
[e] 4 Deut. 24:16 [f] 6 That is, about 3 3/4 tons (about 3.4 metric tons); also in verse 9

to him, "Have we appointed you an adviser to the king? Stop! Why be struck down?"

So the prophet stopped but said, "I know that God has determined to destroy you, because you have done this and have not listened to my counsel."

17 After Amaziah king of Judah consulted his advisers, he sent this challenge to Jehoash[a] son of Jehoahaz, the son of Jehu, king of Israel: "Come, meet me face to face."

18 But Jehoash king of Israel replied to Amaziah king of Judah: "A thistle in Lebanon sent a message to a cedar in Lebanon, 'Give your daughter to my son in marriage.' Then a wild beast in Lebanon came along and trampled the thistle underfoot. 19 You say to yourself that you have defeated Edom, and now you are arrogant and proud. But stay at home! Why ask for trouble and cause your own downfall and that of Judah also?"

20 Amaziah, however, would not listen, for God so worked that he might hand them over to ⌞Jehoash⌟, because they sought the gods of Edom. 21 So Jehoash king of Israel attacked. He and Amaziah king of Judah faced each other at Beth Shemesh in Judah. 22 Judah was routed by Israel, and every man fled to his home. 23 Jehoash king of Israel captured Amaziah king of Judah, the son of Joash, the son of Ahaziah,[b] at Beth Shemesh. Then Jehoash brought him to Jerusalem and broke down the wall of Jerusalem from the Ephraim Gate to the Corner Gate—a section about six hundred feet[c] long. 24 He took all the gold and silver and all the articles found in the temple of God that had been in the care of Obed-Edom, together with the palace treasures and the hostages, and returned to Samaria.

25 Amaziah son of Joash king of Judah lived for fifteen years after the death of Jehoash son of Jehoahaz king of Israel. 26 As for the other events of Amaziah's reign, from beginning to end, are they not written in the book of the kings of Judah and Israel? 27 From the time that Amaziah turned away from following the LORD, they conspired against him in Jerusalem and he fled to Lachish, but they sent men after him to Lachish and killed him there. 28 He was brought back by horse and was buried with his fathers in the City of Judah.

Uzziah King of Judah

26 Then all the people of Judah took Uzziah,[d] who was sixteen years old, and made him king in place of his father Amaziah. 2 He was the one who rebuilt Elath and restored it to Judah after Amaziah rested with his fathers.

3 Uzziah was sixteen years old when he became king, and he reigned in Jerusalem fifty-two years. His mother's name was Jecoliah; she was from Jerusalem. 4 He did what was right in the eyes of the LORD, just as his father Amaziah had done. 5 He sought God during the days of Zechariah, who instructed him in the fear[e] of God. As long as he sought the LORD, God gave him success.

6 He went to war against the Philistines and broke down the walls of Gath, Jabneh and Ashdod. He then rebuilt towns near Ashdod and elsewhere among the Philistines. 7 God helped him against the Philistines and against the Arabs who lived in Gur Baal and against the Meunites. 8 The Ammonites brought tribute to Uzziah, and his fame spread as far as the border of Egypt, because he had become very powerful.

9 Uzziah built towers in Jerusalem at the Corner Gate, at the Valley Gate and at the angle of the wall, and he fortified them. 10 He also built towers in the desert and dug many cisterns, because he had much livestock in the foothills and in the plain. He had people working his fields and vineyards in the hills and in the fertile lands, for he loved the soil.

11 Uzziah had a well-trained army, ready to go out by divisions according to their numbers as mustered by Jeiel the secretary and Maaseiah the officer under the direction of Hananiah, one of the royal officials. 12 The total number of family leaders over the fighting men was 2,600. 13 Under their command was an army of 307,500 men trained for war, a powerful force to support the king against his enemies. 14 Uzziah provided shields, spears, helmets, coats of armor, bows and slingstones for the entire army. 15 In Jerusalem he made machines designed by skillful men for use on the towers and on the corner defenses to shoot arrows and hurl large stones. His fame spread far and wide, for he was greatly helped until he became powerful.

16 But after Uzziah became powerful, his pride led to his downfall. He was unfaithful

---

[a] *17* Hebrew *Joash,* a variant of *Jehoash*; also in verses 18, 21, 23 and 25 [b] *23* Hebrew *Jehoahaz,* a variant of *Ahaziah* [c] *23* Hebrew *four hundred cubits* (about 180 meters) [d] *1* Also called *Azariah* [e] *5* Many Hebrew manuscripts, Septuagint and Syriac; other Hebrew manuscripts *vision*

to the LORD his God, and entered the temple
of the LORD to burn incense on the altar of
incense. 17Azariah the priest with eighty other
courageous priests of the LORD followed him
in. 18They confronted him and said, "It is not
right for you, Uzziah, to burn incense to the
LORD. That is for the priests, the descendants
of Aaron, who have been consecrated to burn
incense. Leave the sanctuary, for you have
been unfaithful; and you will not be honored
by the LORD God."
19Uzziah, who had a censer in his hand
ready to burn incense, became angry. While
he was raging at the priests in their presence
before the incense altar in the LORD's temple,
leprosy[a] broke out on his forehead. 20When
Azariah the chief priest and all the other
priests looked at him, they saw that he had
leprosy on his forehead, so they hurried him
out. Indeed, he himself was eager to leave, because the LORD had afflicted him.
21King Uzziah had leprosy until the day he
died. He lived in a separate house[b]—leprous,
and excluded from the temple of the LORD.
Jotham his son had charge of the palace and
governed the people of the land.
22The other events of Uzziah's reign, from
beginning to end, are recorded by the prophet
Isaiah son of Amoz. 23Uzziah rested with his
fathers and was buried near them in a field for
burial that belonged to the kings, for people
said, "He had leprosy." And Jotham his son
succeeded him as king.

Jotham King of Judah

27 Jotham was twenty-five years old when
he became king, and he reigned in Jerusalem sixteen years. His mother's name
was Jerusha daughter of Zadok. 2He did what
was right in the eyes of the LORD, just as his
father Uzziah had done, but unlike him he did
not enter the temple of the LORD. The people,
however, continued their corrupt practices.
3Jotham rebuilt the Upper Gate of the temple
of the LORD and did extensive work on the
wall at the hill of Ophel. 4He built towns in
the Judean hills and forts and towers in the
wooded areas.
5Jotham made war on the king of the Ammonites and conquered them. That year the
Ammonites paid him a hundred talents[c] of
silver, ten thousand cors[d] of wheat and ten
thousand cors of barley. The Ammonites
brought him the same amount also in the second and third years.
6Jotham grew powerful because he walked
steadfastly before the LORD his God.
7The other events in Jotham's reign, including all his wars and the other things he did, are
written in the book of the kings of Israel and
Judah. 8He was twenty-five years old when he
became king, and he reigned in Jerusalem sixteen years. 9Jotham rested with his fathers and
was buried in the City of David. And Ahaz his
son succeeded him as king.

Ahaz King of Judah

28 Ahaz was twenty years old when he became king, and he reigned in Jerusalem
sixteen years. Unlike David his father,
he did not do what was right in the eyes of the
LORD. 2He walked in the ways of the kings of
Israel and also made cast idols for worshiping
the Baals. 3He burned sacrifices in the Valley of Ben Hinnom and sacrificed his sons in
the fire, following the detestable ways of the
nations the LORD had driven out before the
Israelites. 4He offered sacrifices and burned
incense at the high places, on the hilltops and
under every spreading tree.
5Therefore the LORD his God handed him
over to the king of Aram. The Arameans defeated him and took many of his people as
prisoners and brought them to Damascus.
He was also given into the hands of the
king of Israel, who inflicted heavy casualties
on him. 6In one day Pekah son of Remaliah
killed a hundred and twenty thousand soldiers in Judah—because Judah had forsaken
the LORD, the God of their fathers. 7Zicri,
an Ephraimite warrior, killed Maaseiah the
king's son, Azrikam the officer in charge of
the palace, and Elkanah, second to the king.
8The Israelites took captive from their kinsmen two hundred thousand wives, sons
and daughters. They also took a great deal
of plunder, which they carried back to Samaria.
9But a prophet of the LORD named Oded
was there, and he went out to meet the army
when it returned to Samaria. He said to them,
"Because the LORD, the God of your fathers,
was angry with Judah, he gave them into your
hand. But you have slaughtered them in a rage
that reaches to heaven. 10And now you intend
to make the men and women of Judah and Jerusalem your slaves. But aren't you also guilty

[a] 19 The Hebrew word was used for various diseases affecting the skin—not necessarily leprosy; also in verses 20, 21 and 23.
[b] 21 Or *in a house where he was relieved of responsibilities* [c] 5 That is, about 3 3/4 tons (about 3.4 metric tons) [d] 5 That is, probably about 62,000 bushels (about 2,200 kiloliters)

of sins against the LORD your God? 11Now listen to me! Send back your fellow countrymen you have taken as prisoners, for the LORD's fierce anger rests on you."

12Then some of the leaders in Ephraim—Azariah son of Jehohanan, Berekiah son of Meshillemoth, Jehizkiah son of Shallum, and Amasa son of Hadlai—confronted those who were arriving from the war. 13"You must not bring those prisoners here," they said, "or we will be guilty before the LORD. Do you intend to add to our sin and guilt? For our guilt is already great, and his fierce anger rests on Israel."

14So the soldiers gave up the prisoners and plunder in the presence of the officials and all the assembly. 15The men designated by name took the prisoners, and from the plunder they clothed all who were naked. They provided them with clothes and sandals, food and drink, and healing balm. All those who were weak they put on donkeys. So they took them back to their fellow countrymen at Jericho, the City of Palms, and returned to Samaria.

16At that time King Ahaz sent to the king[a] of Assyria for help. 17The Edomites had again come and attacked Judah and carried away prisoners, 18while the Philistines had raided towns in the foothills and in the Negev of Judah. They captured and occupied Beth Shemesh, Aijalon and Gederoth, as well as Soco, Timnah and Gimzo, with their surrounding villages. 19The LORD had humbled Judah because of Ahaz king of Israel,[b] for he had promoted wickedness in Judah and had been most unfaithful to the LORD. 20Tiglath-Pileser[c] king of Assyria came to him, but he gave him trouble instead of help. 21Ahaz took some of the things from the temple of the LORD and from the royal palace and from the princes and presented them to the king of Assyria, but that did not help him.

22In his time of trouble King Ahaz became even more unfaithful to the LORD. 23He offered sacrifices to the gods of Damascus, who had defeated him; for he thought, "Since the gods of the kings of Aram have helped them, I will sacrifice to them so they will help me." But they were his downfall and the downfall of all Israel.

24Ahaz gathered together the furnishings from the temple of God and took them away.[d] He shut the doors of the LORD's temple and set up altars at every street corner in Jerusalem. 25In every town in Judah he built high places to burn sacrifices to other gods and provoked the LORD, the God of his fathers, to anger.

26The other events of his reign and all his ways, from beginning to end, are written in the book of the kings of Judah and Israel. 27Ahaz rested with his fathers and was buried in the city of Jerusalem, but he was not placed in the tombs of the kings of Israel. And Hezekiah his son succeeded him as king.

Hezekiah Purifies the Temple

29 Hezekiah was twenty-five years old when he became king, and he reigned in Jerusalem twenty-nine years. His mother's name was Abijah daughter of Zechariah. 2He did what was right in the eyes of the LORD, just as his father David had done.

3In the first month of the first year of his reign, he opened the doors of the temple of the LORD and repaired them. 4He brought in the priests and the Levites, assembled them in the square on the east side 5and said: "Listen to me, Levites! Consecrate yourselves now and consecrate the temple of the LORD, the God of your fathers. Remove all defilement from the sanctuary. 6Our fathers were unfaithful; they did evil in the eyes of the LORD our God and forsook him. They turned their faces away from the LORD's dwelling place and turned their backs on him. 7They also shut the doors of the portico and put out the lamps. They did not burn incense or present any burnt offerings at the sanctuary to the God of Israel. 8Therefore, the anger of the LORD has fallen on Judah and Jerusalem; he has made them an object of dread and horror and scorn, as you can see with your own eyes. 9This is why our fathers have fallen by the sword and why our sons and daughters and our wives are in captivity. 10Now I intend to make a covenant with the LORD, the God of Israel, so that his fierce anger will turn away from us. 11My sons, do not be negligent now, for the LORD has chosen you to stand before him and serve him, to minister before him and to burn incense."

12Then these Levites set to work:

from the Kohathites,
Mahath son of Amasai and Joel son of Azariah;
from the Merarites,
Kish son of Abdi and Azariah son of Jehallelel;
from the Gershonites,

---

a 16 One Hebrew manuscript, Septuagint and Vulgate (see also 2 Kings 16:7); most Hebrew manuscripts *kings* *b* 19 That is, Judah, as frequently in 2 Chronicles *c* 20 Hebrew *Tilgath-Pilneser,* a variant of *Tiglath-Pileser* *d* 24 Or *and cut them up*

Joah son of Zimmah and Eden son of
Joah;
13 from the descendants of Elizaphan,
Shimri and Jeiel;
from the descendants of Asaph,
Zechariah and Mattaniah;
14 from the descendants of Heman,
Jehiel and Shimei;
from the descendants of Jeduthun,
Shemaiah and Uzziel.

15 When they had assembled their brothers and consecrated themselves, they went
in to purify the temple of the LORD, as the
king had ordered, following the word of the
LORD. 16 The priests went into the sanctuary
of the LORD to purify it. They brought out to
the courtyard of the LORD's temple everything
unclean that they found in the temple of the
LORD. The Levites took it and carried it out
to the Kidron Valley. 17 They began the consecration on the first day of the first month, and
by the eighth day of the month they reached
the portico of the LORD. For eight more days
they consecrated the temple of the LORD itself, finishing on the sixteenth day of the first
month.

18 Then they went in to King Hezekiah and
reported: "We have purified the entire temple
of the LORD, the altar of burnt offering with
all its utensils, and the table for setting out the
consecrated bread, with all its articles. 19 We
have prepared and consecrated all the articles
that King Ahaz removed in his unfaithfulness
while he was king. They are now in front of
the LORD's altar."

20 Early the next morning King Hezekiah gathered the city officials together and
went up to the temple of the LORD. 21 They
brought seven bulls, seven rams, seven male
lambs and seven male goats as a sin offering
for the kingdom, for the sanctuary and for Judah. The king commanded the priests, the descendants of Aaron, to offer these on the altar
of the LORD. 22 So they slaughtered the bulls,
and the priests took the blood and sprinkled
it on the altar; next they slaughtered the rams
and sprinkled their blood on the altar; then
they slaughtered the lambs and sprinkled their
blood on the altar. 23 The goats for the sin offering were brought before the king and the
assembly, and they laid their hands on them.
24 The priests then slaughtered the goats and
presented their blood on the altar for a sin offering to atone for all Israel, because the king
had ordered the burnt offering and the sin offering for all Israel.

25 He stationed the Levites in the temple of
the LORD with cymbals, harps and lyres in the
way prescribed by David and Gad the king's
seer and Nathan the prophet; this was commanded by the LORD through his prophets.
26 So the Levites stood ready with David's instruments, and the priests with their trumpets.

27 Hezekiah gave the order to sacrifice the
burnt offering on the altar. As the offering
began, singing to the LORD began also, accompanied by trumpets and the instruments
of David king of Israel. 28 The whole assembly
bowed in worship, while the singers sang and
the trumpeters played. All this continued until the sacrifice of the burnt offering was completed.

29 When the offerings were finished, the
king and everyone present with him knelt
down and worshiped. 30 King Hezekiah and
his officials ordered the Levites to praise the
LORD with the words of David and of Asaph
the seer. So they sang praises with gladness
and bowed their heads and worshiped.

31 Then Hezekiah said, "You have now dedicated yourselves to the LORD. Come and bring
sacrifices and thank offerings to the temple of
the LORD." So the assembly brought sacrifices
and thank offerings, and all whose hearts were
willing brought burnt offerings.

32 The number of burnt offerings the assembly brought was seventy bulls, a hundred rams
and two hundred male lambs—all of them
for burnt offerings to the LORD. 33 The animals consecrated as sacrifices amounted to six
hundred bulls and three thousand sheep and
goats. 34 The priests, however, were too few to
skin all the burnt offerings; so their kinsmen
the Levites helped them until the task was
finished and until other priests had been consecrated, for the Levites had been more con-
scientious in consecrating themselves than the
priests had been. 35 There were burnt offerings
in abundance, together with the fat of the fellowship offerings[a] and the drink offerings that
accompanied the burnt offerings.

So the service of the temple of the LORD
was reestablished. 36 Hezekiah and all the people rejoiced at what God had brought about
for his people, because it was done so quickly.

a 35 Traditionally *peace offerings*

Hezekiah Celebrates the Passover

30 Hezekiah sent word to all Israel and Judah and also wrote letters to Ephraim and Manasseh, inviting them to come to the temple of the LORD in Jerusalem and celebrate the Passover to the LORD, the God of Israel. [2]The king and his officials and the whole assembly in Jerusalem decided to celebrate the Passover in the second month. [3]They had not been able to celebrate it at the regular time because not enough priests had consecrated themselves and the people had not assembled in Jerusalem. [4]The plan seemed right both to the king and to the whole assembly. [5]They decided to send a proclamation throughout Israel, from Beersheba to Dan, calling the people to come to Jerusalem and celebrate the Passover to the LORD, the God of Israel. It had not been celebrated in large numbers according to what was written.

[6]At the king's command, couriers went throughout Israel and Judah with letters from the king and from his officials, which read:

> "People of Israel, return to the LORD, the God of Abraham, Isaac and Israel, that he may return to you who are left, who have escaped from the hand of the kings of Assyria. [7]Do not be like your fathers and brothers, who were unfaithful to the LORD, the God of their fathers, so that he made them an object of horror, as you see. [8]Do not be stiff-necked, as your fathers were; submit to the LORD. Come to the sanctuary, which he has consecrated forever. Serve the LORD your God, so that his fierce anger will turn away from you. [9]If you return to the LORD, then your brothers and your children will be shown compassion by their captors and will come back to this land, for the LORD your God is gracious and compassionate. He will not turn his face from you if you return to him."

[10]The couriers went from town to town in Ephraim and Manasseh, as far as Zebulun, but the people scorned and ridiculed them. [11]Nevertheless, some men of Asher, Manasseh and Zebulun humbled themselves and went to Jerusalem. [12]Also in Judah the hand of God was on the people to give them unity of mind to carry out what the king and his officials had ordered, following the word of the LORD.

[13]A very large crowd of people assembled in Jerusalem to celebrate the Feast of Unleavened Bread in the second month. [14]They removed the altars in Jerusalem and cleared away the incense altars and threw them into the Kidron Valley.

[15]They slaughtered the Passover lamb on the fourteenth day of the second month. The priests and the Levites were ashamed and consecrated themselves and brought burnt offerings to the temple of the LORD. [16]Then they took up their regular positions as prescribed in the Law of Moses the man of God. The priests sprinkled the blood handed to them by the Levites. [17]Since many in the crowd had not consecrated themselves, the Levites had to kill the Passover lambs for all those who were not ceremonially clean and could not consecrate ⌊their lambs⌋ to the LORD. [18]Although most of the many people who came from Ephraim, Manasseh, Issachar and Zebulun had not purified themselves, yet they ate the Passover, contrary to what was written. But Hezekiah prayed for them, saying, "May the LORD, who is good, pardon everyone [19]who sets his heart on seeking God—the LORD, the God of his fathers—even if he is not clean according to the rules of the sanctuary." [20]And the LORD heard Hezekiah and healed the people.

[21]The Israelites who were present in Jerusalem celebrated the Feast of Unleavened Bread for seven days with great rejoicing, while the Levites and priests sang to the LORD every day, accompanied by the LORD's instruments of praise.[a]

[22]Hezekiah spoke encouragingly to all the Levites, who showed good understanding of the service of the LORD. For the seven days they ate their assigned portion and offered fellowship offerings[b] and praised the LORD, the God of their fathers.

[23]The whole assembly then agreed to celebrate the festival seven more days; so for another seven days they celebrated joyfully. [24]Hezekiah king of Judah provided a thousand bulls and seven thousand sheep and goats for the assembly, and the officials provided them with a thousand bulls and ten thousand sheep and goats. A great number of priests consecrated themselves. [25]The entire assembly of Judah rejoiced, along with the priests and Levites and all who had assembled from Israel, including the aliens who had come from Israel and those who lived in Judah. [26]There was great joy in Jerusalem, for since the days of Solomon son of David king of Israel there had been noth-

---

a 21 *Or priests praised the LORD every day with resounding instruments belonging to the LORD* *b* 22 Traditionally *peace offerings*

WEEKEND

holiday negotiations

In starting a new life with your spouse, you'll want to keep many of the holiday rituals you've practiced since birth. Your significant other may have the same goal in mind but through different traditions.

"I usually eat a lot on holidays," says Mark Paulik, who lives in Park Ridge, Illinois, near both his parents and in-laws. "We spend Christmas Eve with one family and Christmas day with the other. But holidays like Easter and Thanksgiving can be tough on the waistline," he says, patting a paunch. "That's when we usually end up eating two full meals in both dining rooms. So by the time I get home, put a fork in me—I'm done."

Trying to outsmart the situation can backfire. You arrive late to the first house to avoid a meal, only to be served dessert. You can't exactly eat and run. So you end up visiting longer than you normally would. By the time you get to the next house, you find yourself staring at another piece of fruitcake—and embarking on a three-day sugar high.

So how do you handle the situation without insulting anyone? Be honest upfront. Let everyone know your situation and negotiate a compromise. Perhaps you can do lunch with one family and dinner with the other. No dessert for me today, thanks.

Dean Leftakes and his wife, Cleo, have three young children, so they could use a moving van to transport all the baby gear they need for a day with both families—even if they live just a few blocks away. So they had a better idea. "We invited both sides to our house," says Dean. "We're already equipped with everything the kids need, from electric swings to Nintendo, and everyone volunteers to bring their special recipes."

These solutions keep you on talking terms with both of your families. It may be better to give than to receive during the holidays, but when you spend New Year's Day, Easter, July 4, Thanksgiving and Christmas with your spouse's family and only seem to get Flag Day with yours, perhaps you should push for better sharing.

The Out-of-Towners.

As long as you have gas in your Leer jet, there's no reason why you can't visit both out-of-state families on the same day. But you're probably thinking, who has time to fill up the plane?

Traveling is stressful during any holiday season, not to mention expensive. And when both sides live far away, that can double the pressure to please everyone.

Most newlyweds can't afford two long-distance family visits in the same year. Even if you could afford it, you might not want to kiss that getaway vacation goodbye. If you also have to deal with stepfamilies, let's hope your frequent flyer mileage is adding up. So what's the solution? Most people alternate holidays with their families. If parents can visit you, all the better. But your parents may want to visit your other siblings, making multiple trips expensive for them as well.

So how about at your next gathering, break out into song with "I'm Dreaming of a White-sand Beach Christmas?" You can suggest combining a particular holiday with an exotic vacation. If you have children that other relatives want to get to know while you and your spouse do some sightseeing, who are you to get in their way?

If you're dealing with only one long-distance family, create a second holiday. Spend the day with the family you live closest to. Then a few days later, make your trip. It's still considered the holiday season and nobody will object, especially when gifts are at stake.

—CONRAD THEODORE

your holiday wish list

How well do you know your spouse when it comes to holiday traditions? Use these conversation starters to reveal hidden expectations about the holidays.

1. How did our families celebrate Christmas while we were growing up? Thanksgiving? Easter?
2. What holidays are especially important to our families? Why?
3. What traditions would we each like to keep as a part of our marriage and family?
4. If we could pick only one day a year to be with our families, which day would it be and why?
5. How would we feel if we couldn't be with our family on that day?
6. Do our parents or siblings have expectations about which holidays we will spend with them?
7. How do we truly feel about entertaining during the holidays? Does the thought of doing so energize us or drain us?
8. How long should relatives stay at our home?
9. Where will we stay while visiting each of our parents?
10. How long do you think we should stay as guests in our parents' homes?
11. When our families get together for the holidays, who does the cooking?
12. Whom do we buy for at Christmas?
13. Would we ever want to vacation with our family? Under what conditions?
14. How many times and when during the year should we travel?
15. Should those times be used to visit family, to vacation away from family, or both?

HOW ARE WE DOING?

let's make a DATE

COMPILATION CALENDAR

On this date, find a quiet café and sit at a table away from the crowd. Each of you bring a list of your family's important dates, such as birthdays and anniversaries. Be sure to include dates that are important to the two of you, such as the date you met and the anniversary of your wedding. Combine all the dates into a master calendar. When you get home, hang the calendar in a central location in your home as a reminder that you've joined families and that what is important to one spouse should be important to the other.

FOR YOUR NEXT DEVOTIONAL READING, TURN TO PAGE 499.

LESSONS FROM THE *Bible*

Read in Esther 9:20–22 about the origin of the festival of Purim, which Jewish people continue to celebrate today. What activities and attitudes are mentioned? What can we learn about celebrating holidays from this passage?

ing like this in Jerusalem. 27The priests and the Levites stood to bless the people, and God heard them, for their prayer reached heaven, his holy dwelling place.

31 When all this had ended, the Israelites who were there went out to the towns of Judah, smashed the sacred stones and cut down the Asherah poles. They destroyed the high places and the altars throughout Judah and Benjamin and in Ephraim and Manasseh. After they had destroyed all of them, the Israelites returned to their own towns and to their own property.

Contributions for Worship

2Hezekiah assigned the priests and Levites to divisions—each of them according to their duties as priests or Levites—to offer burnt offerings and fellowship offerings,[a] to minister, to give thanks and to sing praises at the gates of the LORD's dwelling. 3The king contributed from his own possessions for the morning and evening burnt offerings and for the burnt offerings on the Sabbaths, New Moons and appointed feasts as written in the Law of the LORD. 4He ordered the people living in Jerusalem to give the portion due the priests and Levites so they could devote themselves to the Law of the LORD. 5As soon as the order went out, the Israelites generously gave the firstfruits of their grain, new wine, oil and honey and all that the fields produced. They brought a great amount, a tithe of everything. 6The men of Israel and Judah who lived in the towns of Judah also brought a tithe of their herds and flocks and a tithe of the holy things dedicated to the LORD their God, and they piled them in heaps. 7They began doing this in the third month and finished in the seventh month. 8When Hezekiah and his officials came and saw the heaps, they praised the LORD and blessed his people Israel.

9Hezekiah asked the priests and Levites about the heaps; 10and Azariah the chief priest, from the family of Zadok, answered, "Since the people began to bring their contributions to the temple of the LORD, we have had enough to eat and plenty to spare, because the LORD has blessed his people, and this great amount is left over."

11Hezekiah gave orders to prepare storerooms in the temple of the LORD, and this was done. 12Then they faithfully brought in the contributions, tithes and dedicated gifts. Conaniah, a Levite, was in charge of these things, and his brother Shimei was next in rank. 13Jehiel, Azaziah, Nahath, Asahel, Jerimoth, Jozabad, Eliel, Ismakiah, Mahath and Benaiah were supervisors under Conaniah and Shimei his brother, by appointment of King Hezekiah and Azariah the official in charge of the temple of God.

14Kore son of Imnah the Levite, keeper of the East Gate, was in charge of the freewill offerings given to God, distributing the contributions made to the LORD and also the consecrated gifts. 15Eden, Miniamin, Jeshua, Shemaiah, Amariah and Shecaniah assisted him faithfully in the towns of the priests, distributing to their fellow priests according to their divisions, old and young alike.

16In addition, they distributed to the males three years old or more whose names were in the genealogical records—all who would enter the temple of the LORD to perform the daily duties of their various tasks, according to their responsibilities and their divisions. 17And they distributed to the priests enrolled by their families in the genealogical records and likewise to the Levites twenty years old or more, according to their responsibilities and their divisions. 18They included all the little ones, the wives, and the sons and daughters of the whole community listed in these genealogical records. For they were faithful in consecrating themselves.

19As for the priests, the descendants of Aaron, who lived on the farm lands around their towns or in any other towns, men were designated by name to distribute portions to every male among them and to all who were recorded in the genealogies of the Levites.

20This is what Hezekiah did throughout Judah, doing what was good and right and faithful before the LORD his God. 21In everything that he undertook in the service of God's temple and in obedience to the law and the commands, he sought his God and worked wholeheartedly. And so he prospered.

Sennacherib Threatens Jerusalem

32 After all that Hezekiah had so faithfully done, Sennacherib king of Assyria came and invaded Judah. He laid siege to the fortified cities, thinking to conquer them for himself. 2When Hezekiah saw that Sennacherib had come and that he intended to make war on Jerusalem, 3he consulted with his officials and military staff about blocking off the water from the springs outside the city, and they

[a] 2 Traditionally *peace offerings*

helped him. 4A large force of men assembled,
and they blocked all the springs and the stream
that flowed through the land. "Why should
the kings[a] of Assyria come and find plenty of
water?" they said. 5Then he worked hard repairing all the broken sections of the wall and
building towers on it. He built another wall
outside that one and reinforced the supporting
terraces[b] of the City of David. He also made
large numbers of weapons and shields.

6He appointed military officers over the
people and assembled them before him in the
square at the city gate and encouraged them
with these words: 7"Be strong and courageous.
Do not be afraid or discouraged because of the
king of Assyria and the vast army with him, for
there is a greater power with us than with him.
8With him is only the arm of flesh, but with
us is the LORD our God to help us and to fight
our battles." And the people gained confidence
from what Hezekiah the king of Judah said.

9Later, when Sennacherib king of Assyria
and all his forces were laying siege to Lachish,
he sent his officers to Jerusalem with this message for Hezekiah king of Judah and for all the
people of Judah who were there:

> 10"This is what Sennacherib king of
> Assyria says: On what are you basing your
> confidence, that you remain in Jerusalem
> under siege? 11When Hezekiah says, 'The
> LORD our God will save us from the hand
> of the king of Assyria,' he is misleading
> you, to let you die of hunger and thirst.
> 12Did not Hezekiah himself remove this
> god's high places and altars, saying to Ju-
> dah and Jerusalem, 'You must worship be-
> fore one altar and burn sacrifices on it'?
>
> 13"Do you not know what I and my
> fathers have done to all the peoples of the
> other lands? Were the gods of those na-
> tions ever able to deliver their land from
> my hand? 14Who of all the gods of these
> nations that my fathers destroyed has
> been able to save his people from me?
> How then can your god deliver you from
> my hand? 15Now do not let Hezekiah de-
> ceive you and mislead you like this. Do
> not believe him, for no god of any nation
> or kingdom has been able to deliver his
> people from my hand or the hand of my
> fathers. How much less will your god de-
> liver you from my hand!"

16Sennacherib's officers spoke further against
the LORD God and against his servant Hezekiah. 17The king also wrote letters insulting
the LORD, the God of Israel, and saying this
against him: "Just as the gods of the peoples
of the other lands did not rescue their people
from my hand, so the god of Hezekiah will not
rescue his people from my hand." 18Then they
called out in Hebrew to the people of Jerusalem who were on the wall, to terrify them and
make them afraid in order to capture the city.
19They spoke about the God of Jerusalem as
they did about the gods of the other peoples of
the world—the work of men's hands.

20King Hezekiah and the prophet Isaiah son
of Amoz cried out in prayer to heaven about
this. 21And the LORD sent an angel, who anni-
hilated all the fighting men and the leaders and
officers in the camp of the Assyrian king. So
he withdrew to his own land in disgrace. And
when he went into the temple of his god, some
of his sons cut him down with the sword.

22So the LORD saved Hezekiah and the people of Jerusalem from the hand of Sennacherib king of Assyria and from the hand of all
others. He took care of them[c] on every side.
23Many brought offerings to Jerusalem for the
LORD and valuable gifts for Hezekiah king of
Judah. From then on he was highly regarded
by all the nations.

Hezekiah's Pride, Success and Death

24In those days Hezekiah became ill and
was at the point of death. He prayed to the
LORD, who answered him and gave him a
miraculous sign. 25But Hezekiah's heart was
proud and he did not respond to the kindness
shown him; therefore the LORD's wrath was
on him and on Judah and Jerusalem. 26Then
Hezekiah repented of the pride of his heart,
as did the people of Jerusalem; therefore the
LORD's wrath did not come upon them during
the days of Hezekiah.

27Hezekiah had very great riches and honor,
and he made treasuries for his silver and gold
and for his precious stones, spices, shields and
all kinds of valuables. 28He also made buildings
to store the harvest of grain, new wine and oil;
and he made stalls for various kinds of cattle,
and pens for the flocks. 29He built villages and
acquired great numbers of flocks and herds, for
God had given him very great riches.

30It was Hezekiah who blocked the upper
outlet of the Gihon spring and channeled
the water down to the west side of the City
of David. He succeeded in everything he undertook. 31But when envoys were sent by the

---

[a] 4 Hebrew; Septuagint and Syriac *king* [b] 5 Or *the Millo* [c] 22 Hebrew; Septuagint and Vulgate *He gave them rest*

rulers of Babylon to ask him about the miraculous sign that had occurred in the land, God left him to test him and to know everything that was in his heart.

32The other events of Hezekiah's reign and his acts of devotion are written in the vision of the prophet Isaiah son of Amoz in the book of the kings of Judah and Israel.
33Hezekiah rested with his fathers and was buried on the hill where the tombs of David's descendants are. All Judah and the people of Jerusalem honored him when he died. And Manasseh his son succeeded him as king.

Manasseh King of Judah

33 Manasseh was twelve years old when he became king, and he reigned in Jerusalem fifty-five years.
2He did evil in the eyes of the LORD, following the detestable practices of the nations the LORD had driven out before the Israelites.
3He rebuilt the high places his father Hezekiah had demolished; he also erected altars to the Baals and made Asherah poles. He bowed down to all the starry hosts and worshiped them.
4He built altars in the temple of the LORD, of which the LORD had said, "My Name will remain in Jerusalem forever."
5In both courts of the temple of the LORD, he built altars to all the starry hosts.
6He sacrificed his sons in[a] the fire in the Valley of Ben Hinnom, practiced sorcery, divination and witchcraft, and consulted mediums and spiritists. He did much evil in the eyes of the LORD, provoking him to anger.

7He took the carved image he had made and put it in God's temple, of which God had said to David and to his son Solomon, "In this temple and in Jerusalem, which I have chosen out of all the tribes of Israel, I will put my Name forever.
8I will not again make the feet of the Israelites leave the land I assigned to your forefathers, if only they will be careful to do everything I commanded them concerning all the laws, decrees and ordinances given through Moses."
9But Manasseh led Judah and the people of Jerusalem astray, so that they did more evil than the nations the LORD had destroyed before the Israelites.

10The LORD spoke to Manasseh and his people, but they paid no attention.
11So the LORD brought against them the army commanders of the king of Assyria, who took Manasseh prisoner, put a hook in his nose, bound him with bronze shackles and took him to Babylon.
12In his distress he sought the favor of the LORD his God and humbled himself greatly before the God of his fathers.
13And when he prayed to him, the LORD was moved by his entreaty and listened to his plea; so he brought him back to Jerusalem and to his kingdom. Then Manasseh knew that the LORD is God.

14Afterward he rebuilt the outer wall of the City of David, west of the Gihon spring in the valley, as far as the entrance of the Fish Gate and encircling the hill of Ophel; he also made it much higher. He stationed military commanders in all the fortified cities in Judah.

15He got rid of the foreign gods and removed the image from the temple of the LORD, as well as all the altars he had built on the temple hill and in Jerusalem; and he threw them out of the city.
16Then he restored the altar of the LORD and sacrificed fellowship offerings[b] and thank offerings on it, and told Judah to serve the LORD, the God of Israel.
17The people, however, continued to sacrifice at the high places, but only to the LORD their God.

18The other events of Manasseh's reign, including his prayer to his God and the words the seers spoke to him in the name of the LORD, the God of Israel, are written in the annals of the kings of Israel.[c]
19His prayer and how God was moved by his entreaty, as well as all his sins and unfaithfulness, and the sites where he built high places and set up Asherah poles and idols before he humbled himself—all are written in the records of the seers.[d]
20Manasseh rested with his fathers and was buried in his palace. And Amon his son succeeded him as king.

Amon King of Judah

21Amon was twenty-two years old when he became king, and he reigned in Jerusalem two years.
22He did evil in the eyes of the LORD, as his father Manasseh had done. Amon worshiped and offered sacrifices to all the idols Manasseh had made.
23But unlike his father Manasseh, he did not humble himself before the LORD; Amon increased his guilt.

24Amon's officials conspired against him and assassinated him in his palace.
25Then the people of the land killed all who had plotted against King Amon, and they made Josiah his son king in his place.

Josiah's Reforms

34 Josiah was eight years old when he became king, and he reigned in Jerusalem thirty-one years.
2He did what was

[a] 6 Or *He made his sons pass through* [b] 16 Traditionally *peace offerings* [c] 18 That is, Judah, as frequently in 2 Chronicles
[d] 19 One Hebrew manuscript and Septuagint; most Hebrew manuscripts *of Hozai*

right in the eyes of the LORD and walked in the ways of his father David, not turning aside to the right or to the left.

[3]In the eighth year of his reign, while he was still young, he began to seek the God of his father David. In his twelfth year he began to purge Judah and Jerusalem of high places, Asherah poles, carved idols and cast images. [4]Under his direction the altars of the Baals were torn down; he cut to pieces the incense altars that were above them, and smashed the Asherah poles, the idols and the images. These he broke to pieces and scattered over the graves of those who had sacrificed to them. [5]He burned the bones of the priests on their altars, and so he purged Judah and Jerusalem. [6]In the towns of Manasseh, Ephraim and Simeon, as far as Naphtali, and in the ruins around them, [7]he tore down the altars and the Asherah poles and crushed the idols to powder and cut to pieces all the incense altars throughout Israel. Then he went back to Jerusalem.

[8]In the eighteenth year of Josiah's reign, to purify the land and the temple, he sent Shaphan son of Azaliah and Maaseiah the ruler of the city, with Joah son of Joahaz, the recorder, to repair the temple of the LORD his God.

[9]They went to Hilkiah the high priest and gave him the money that had been brought into the temple of God, which the Levites who were the doorkeepers had collected from the people of Manasseh, Ephraim and the entire remnant of Israel and from all the people of Judah and Benjamin and the inhabitants of Jerusalem. [10]Then they entrusted it to the men appointed to supervise the work on the LORD's temple. These men paid the workers who repaired and restored the temple. [11]They also gave money to the carpenters and builders to purchase dressed stone, and timber for joists and beams for the buildings that the kings of Judah had allowed to fall into ruin.

[12]The men did the work faithfully. Over them to direct them were Jahath and Obadiah, Levites descended from Merari, and Zechariah and Meshullam, descended from Kohath. The Levites—all who were skilled in playing musical instruments— [13]had charge of the laborers and supervised all the workers from job to job. Some of the Levites were secretaries, scribes and doorkeepers.

The Book of the Law Found

[14]While they were bringing out the money that had been taken into the temple of the LORD, Hilkiah the priest found the Book of the Law of the LORD that had been given through Moses. [15]Hilkiah said to Shaphan the secretary, "I have found the Book of the Law in the temple of the LORD." He gave it to Shaphan.

[16]Then Shaphan took the book to the king and reported to him: "Your officials are doing everything that has been committed to them. [17]They have paid out the money that was in the temple of the LORD and have entrusted it to the supervisors and workers." [18]Then Shaphan the secretary informed the king, "Hilkiah the priest has given me a book." And Shaphan read from it in the presence of the king.

[19]When the king heard the words of the Law, he tore his robes. [20]He gave these orders to Hilkiah, Ahikam son of Shaphan, Abdon son of Micah,[a] Shaphan the secretary and Asaiah the king's attendant: [21]"Go and inquire of the LORD for me and for the remnant in Israel and Judah about what is written in this book that has been found. Great is the LORD's anger that is poured out on us because our fathers have not kept the word of the LORD; they have not acted in accordance with all that is written in this book."

[22]Hilkiah and those the king had sent with him[b] went to speak to the prophetess Huldah, who was the wife of Shallum son of Tokhath,[c] the son of Hasrah,[d] keeper of the wardrobe. She lived in Jerusalem, in the Second District.

[23]She said to them, "This is what the LORD, the God of Israel, says: Tell the man who sent you to me, [24]'This is what the LORD says: I am going to bring disaster on this place and its people—all the curses written in the book that has been read in the presence of the king of Judah. [25]Because they have forsaken me and burned incense to other gods and provoked me to anger by all that their hands have made,[e] my anger will be poured out on this place and will not be quenched.' [26]Tell the king of Judah, who sent you to inquire of the LORD, 'This is what the LORD, the God of Israel, says concerning the words you heard: [27]Because your heart was responsive and you humbled yourself before God when you heard what he spoke against this place and its people, and because you humbled yourself before me and tore your robes and wept in my presence, I have heard you, declares the LORD. [28]Now I will gather you to your fathers, and you will be buried in peace. Your eyes will not see all the

---

[a] 20 Also called *Acbor son of Micaiah* [b] 22 One Hebrew manuscript, Vulgate and Syriac; most Hebrew manuscripts do not have *had sent with him.* [c] 22 Also called *Tikvah* [d] 22 Also called *Harhas* [e] 25 Or *by everything they have done*

disaster I am going to bring on this place and
on those who live here.' "
So they took her answer back to the king.
29 Then the king called together all the elders of Judah and Jerusalem. 30 He went up to
the temple of the LORD with the men of Judah, the people of Jerusalem, the priests and
the Levites—all the people from the least to
the greatest. He read in their hearing all the
words of the Book of the Covenant, which
had been found in the temple of the LORD.
31 The king stood by his pillar and renewed the
covenant in the presence of the LORD—to follow the LORD and keep his commands, regulations and decrees with all his heart and all his
soul, and to obey the words of the covenant
written in this book.
32 Then he had everyone in Jerusalem and
Benjamin pledge themselves to it; the people
of Jerusalem did this in accordance with the
covenant of God, the God of their fathers.
33 Josiah removed all the detestable idols
from all the territory belonging to the Israelites, and he had all who were present in Israel
serve the LORD their God. As long as he lived,
they did not fail to follow the LORD, the God
of their fathers.

Josiah Celebrates the Passover

35 Josiah celebrated the Passover to the
LORD in Jerusalem, and the Passover
lamb was slaughtered on the fourteenth
day of the first month. 2 He appointed the
priests to their duties and encouraged them in
the service of the LORD's temple. 3 He said to
the Levites, who instructed all Israel and who
had been consecrated to the LORD: "Put the
sacred ark in the temple that Solomon son of
David king of Israel built. It is not to be carried about on your shoulders. Now serve the
LORD your God and his people Israel. 4 Prepare yourselves by families in your divisions,
according to the directions written by David
king of Israel and by his son Solomon.
5 "Stand in the holy place with a group of
Levites for each subdivision of the families
of your fellow countrymen, the lay people.
6 Slaughter the Passover lambs, consecrate
yourselves and prepare ⌊the lambs⌋ for your
fellow countrymen, doing what the LORD
commanded through Moses."
7 Josiah provided for all the lay people who
were there a total of thirty thousand sheep and
goats for the Passover offerings, and also three
thousand cattle—all from the king's own possessions.
8 His officials also contributed voluntarily to
the people and the priests and Levites. Hilkiah, Zechariah and Jehiel, the administrators of
God's temple, gave the priests twenty-six hundred Passover offerings and three hundred cattle. 9 Also Conaniah along with Shemaiah and
Nethanel, his brothers, and Hashabiah, Jeiel
and Jozabad, the leaders of the Levites, provided five thousand Passover offerings and five
hundred head of cattle for the Levites.
10 The service was arranged and the priests
stood in their places with the Levites in their
divisions as the king had ordered. 11 The Passover lambs were slaughtered, and the priests
sprinkled the blood handed to them, while
the Levites skinned the animals. 12 They set
aside the burnt offerings to give them to the
subdivisions of the families of the people to
offer to the LORD, as is written in the Book
of Moses. They did the same with the cattle.
13 They roasted the Passover animals over the
fire as prescribed, and boiled the holy offerings
in pots, caldrons and pans and served them
quickly to all the people. 14 After this, they
made preparations for themselves and for the
priests, because the priests, the descendants of
Aaron, were sacrificing the burnt offerings and
the fat portions until nightfall. So the Levites
made preparations for themselves and for the
Aaronic priests.
15 The musicians, the descendants of Asaph,
were in the places prescribed by David, Asaph,
Heman and Jeduthun the king's seer. The
gatekeepers at each gate did not need to leave
their posts, because their fellow Levites made
the preparations for them.
16 So at that time the entire service of the
LORD was carried out for the celebration of
the Passover and the offering of burnt offerings on the altar of the LORD, as King Josiah
had ordered. 17 The Israelites who were present
celebrated the Passover at that time and observed the Feast of Unleavened Bread for sev-
en days. 18 The Passover had not been observed
like this in Israel since the days of the prophet
Samuel; and none of the kings of Israel had
ever celebrated such a Passover as did Josiah,
with the priests, the Levites and all Judah and
Israel who were there with the people of Jerusalem. 19 This Passover was celebrated in the
eighteenth year of Josiah's reign.

The Death of Josiah

20 After all this, when Josiah had set the
temple in order, Neco king of Egypt went
up to fight at Carchemish on the Euphrates,
and Josiah marched out to meet him in battle.
21 But Neco sent messengers to him, saying,

"What quarrel is there between you and me,
O king of Judah? It is not you I am attacking at this time, but the house with which I
am at war. God has told me to hurry; so stop
opposing God, who is with me, or he will destroy you."
22 Josiah, however, would not turn away
from him, but disguised himself to engage
him in battle. He would not listen to what
Neco had said at God's command but went to
fight him on the plain of Megiddo.
23 Archers shot King Josiah, and he told his
officers, "Take me away; I am badly wounded." 24 So they took him out of his chariot, put
him in the other chariot he had and brought
him to Jerusalem, where he died. He was buried in the tombs of his fathers, and all Judah
and Jerusalem mourned for him.
25 Jeremiah composed laments for Josiah,
and to this day all the men and women singers commemorate Josiah in the laments. These
became a tradition in Israel and are written in
the Laments.
26 The other events of Josiah's reign and his
acts of devotion, according to what is written
in the Law of the LORD— 27 all the events,
from beginning to end, are written in the book
36 of the kings of Israel and Judah. 1 And
the people of the land took Jehoahaz
son of Josiah and made him king in Jerusalem in place of his father.

Jehoahaz King of Judah

2 Jehoahaz[a] was twenty-three years old
when he became king, and he reigned in Jerusalem three months. 3 The king of Egypt
dethroned him in Jerusalem and imposed on
Judah a levy of a hundred talents[b] of silver and
a talent[c] of gold. 4 The king of Egypt made Eliakim, a brother of Jehoahaz, king over Judah
and Jerusalem and changed Eliakim's name to
Jehoiakim. But Neco took Eliakim's brother
Jehoahaz and carried him off to Egypt.

Jehoiakim King of Judah

5 Jehoiakim was twenty-five years old when
he became king, and he reigned in Jerusalem
eleven years. He did evil in the eyes of the
LORD his God. 6 Nebuchadnezzar king of Babylon attacked him and bound him with bronze
shackles to take him to Babylon. 7 Nebuchadnezzar also took to Babylon articles from the
temple of the LORD and put them in his temple[d] there.
8 The other events of Jehoiakim's reign, the
detestable things he did and all that was found
against him, are written in the book of the
kings of Israel and Judah. And Jehoiachin his
son succeeded him as king.

Jehoiachin King of Judah

9 Jehoiachin was eighteen[e] years old when
he became king, and he reigned in Jerusalem
three months and ten days. He did evil in the
eyes of the LORD. 10 In the spring, King Nebuchadnezzar sent for him and brought him to
Babylon, together with articles of value from
the temple of the LORD, and he made Jehoiachin's uncle,[f] Zedekiah, king over Judah and
Jerusalem.

Zedekiah King of Judah

11 Zedekiah was twenty-one years old when
he became king, and he reigned in Jerusalem
eleven years. 12 He did evil in the eyes of the
LORD his God and did not humble himself before Jeremiah the prophet, who spoke the word
of the LORD. 13 He also rebelled against King
Nebuchadnezzar, who had made him take an
oath in God's name. He became stiff-necked
and hardened his heart and would not turn to
the LORD, the God of Israel. 14 Furthermore,
all the leaders of the priests and the people
became more and more unfaithful, following
all the detestable practices of the nations and
defiling the temple of the LORD, which he had
consecrated in Jerusalem.

The Fall of Jerusalem

15 The LORD, the God of their fathers, sent
word to them through his messengers again
and again, because he had pity on his people
and on his dwelling place. 16 But they mocked
God's messengers, despised his words and
scoffed at his prophets until the wrath of the
LORD was aroused against his people and there
was no remedy. 17 He brought up against them
the king of the Babylonians,[g] who killed their
young men with the sword in the sanctuary,
and spared neither young man nor young
woman, old man or aged. God handed all of
them over to Nebuchadnezzar. 18 He carried
to Babylon all the articles from the temple of
God, both large and small, and the treasures
of the LORD's temple and the treasures of the
king and his officials. 19 They set fire to God's
temple and broke down the wall of Jerusalem;

---

[a] *2* Hebrew *Joahaz,* a variant of *Jehoahaz;* also in verse 4 [b] *3* That is, about 3 3/4 tons (about 3.4 metric tons) [c] *3* That is, about 75 pounds (about 34 kilograms) [d] *7* Or *palace* [e] *9* One Hebrew manuscript, some Septuagint manuscripts and Syriac (see also 2 Kings 24:8); most Hebrew manuscripts *eight* [f] *10* Hebrew *brother,* that is, relative (see 2 Kings 24:17) [g] *17* Or *Chaldeans*

they burned all the palaces and destroyed everything of value there.

20He carried into exile to Babylon the remnant, who escaped from the sword, and they became servants to him and his sons until the kingdom of Persia came to power. 21The land enjoyed its sabbath rests; all the time of its desolation it rested, until the seventy years were completed in fulfillment of the word of the LORD spoken by Jeremiah.

22In the first year of Cyrus king of Persia, in order to fulfill the word of the LORD spoken by Jeremiah, the LORD moved the heart of Cyrus king of Persia to make a proclamation throughout his realm and to put it in writing:

23"This is what Cyrus king of Persia says:

" 'The LORD, the God of heaven, has given me all the kingdoms of the earth and he has appointed me to build a temple for him at Jerusalem in Judah. Anyone of his people among you—may the LORD his God be with him, and let him go up.' "

EZRA

Ezra

QUICK FACTS

AUTHOR Unknown, but possibly Ezra

AUDIENCE All Israel

DATE Around 440 B.C.

SETTING The homecoming of exiles from Babylon

God did not abandon his exiled people. He had sent prophets to assure them that they would one day return to Canaan. Indeed, after Babylon was conquered by Persia, Cyrus the king allowed the Jews to return to Jerusalem.

Armed with gifts from neighbors, as well as items that previously had been plundered from the temple of the Lord, about 50,000 Jews traveled more than 700 miles to a city in ruins. The first thing they did was start rebuilding the temple.

The work halted for several years after neighboring peoples discouraged the exiles through tactics of intimidation. The work resumed when a later king, Darius, decreed, "Let the temple be rebuilt" (Ezra 6:3), and financed the work. Four years later, in 516 B.C., the temple was completed.

About 60 years later Ezra, a godly priest and teacher of the Law, led another group of exiles to Jerusalem and taught them how to live as God's people. He taught them the Law, led them in prayers of repentance and urged them to rid themselves of pagan practices, including wrongful marriages with non-Israelites.

As the exiles knew all too well, resettling is difficult. Today new jobs or transfers can lead us to unfamiliar places, where there are no friends or family to support us. But as many couples—including those who lived in Ezra's day—can attest, one of the best ways to adapt is to find a place to worship. You will always find a home in the family of God.

Cyrus Helps the Exiles to Return

1 In the first year of Cyrus king of Persia,
in order to fulfill the word of the LORD
spoken by Jeremiah, the LORD moved the
heart of Cyrus king of Persia to make a proclamation throughout his realm and to put it
in writing:

2 "This is what Cyrus king of Persia says:
" 'The LORD, the God of heaven, has
given me all the kingdoms of the earth
and he has appointed me to build a temple for him at Jerusalem in Judah. 3 Anyone of his people among you—may his
God be with him, and let him go up to
Jerusalem in Judah and build the temple
of the LORD, the God of Israel, the God
who is in Jerusalem. 4 And the people of
any place where survivors may now be
living are to provide him with silver and
gold, with goods and livestock, and with
freewill offerings for the temple of God in
Jerusalem.' "

5 Then the family heads of Judah and Benjamin, and the priests and Levites—everyone
whose heart God had moved—prepared to go
up and build the house of the LORD in Jerusalem. 6 All their neighbors assisted them with
articles of silver and gold, with goods and
livestock, and with valuable gifts, in addition
to all the freewill offerings. 7 Moreover, King
Cyrus brought out the articles belonging to
the temple of the LORD, which Nebuchadnezzar had carried away from Jerusalem and had
placed in the temple of his god.[a] 8 Cyrus king
of Persia had them brought by Mithredath the
treasurer, who counted them out to Sheshbazzar the prince of Judah.

9 This was the inventory:

	gold dishes	30
	silver dishes	1,000
	silver pans[b]	29
10	gold bowls	30
	matching silver bowls	410
	other articles	1,000

11 In all, there were 5,400 articles of gold
and of silver. Sheshbazzar brought all these
along when the exiles came up from Babylon
to Jerusalem.

The List of the Exiles Who Returned

2 Now these are the people of the province
who came up from the captivity of the exiles, whom Nebuchadnezzar king of Babylon had taken captive to Babylon (they returned to Jerusalem and Judah, each to his
own town, 2 in company with Zerubbabel,
Jeshua, Nehemiah, Seraiah, Reelaiah, Mordecai, Bilshan, Mispar, Bigvai, Rehum and Baanah):

The list of the men of the people of Israel:

3	the descendants of Parosh	2,172
4	of Shephatiah	372
5	of Arah	775
6	of Pahath-Moab (through the line of Jeshua and Joab)	2,812
7	of Elam	1,254
8	of Zattu	945
9	of Zaccai	760
10	of Bani	642
11	of Bebai	623
12	of Azgad	1,222
13	of Adonikam	666
14	of Bigvai	2,056
15	of Adin	454
16	of Ater (through Hezekiah)	98
17	of Bezai	323
18	of Jorah	112
19	of Hashum	223
20	of Gibbar	95

21	the men of Bethlehem	123
22	of Netophah	56
23	of Anathoth	128
24	of Azmaveth	42
25	of Kiriath Jearim,[c] Kephirah and Beeroth	743
26	of Ramah and Geba	621
27	of Micmash	122
28	of Bethel and Ai	223
29	of Nebo	52
30	of Magbish	156
31	of the other Elam	1,254
32	of Harim	320
33	of Lod, Hadid and Ono	725
34	of Jericho	345
35	of Senaah	3,630

36 The priests:

	the descendants of Jedaiah (through the family of Jeshua)	973
37	of Immer	1,052
38	of Pashhur	1,247
39	of Harim	1,017

40 The Levites:

[a] 7 Or *gods* [b] 9 The meaning of the Hebrew for this word is uncertain. [c] 25 See Septuagint (see also Neh. 7:29); Hebrew *Kiriath Arim.*

to the people of Sidon and Tyre, so that they
would bring cedar logs by sea from Lebanon
to Joppa, as authorized by Cyrus king of Persia.
8In the second month of the second year
after their arrival at the house of God in Jerusalem, Zerubbabel son of Shealtiel, Jeshua
son of Jozadak and the rest of their brothers
(the priests and the Levites and all who had returned from the captivity to Jerusalem) began
the work, appointing Levites twenty years of
age and older to supervise the building of the
house of the LORD. 9Jeshua and his sons and
brothers and Kadmiel and his sons (descendants of Hodaviah[a]) and the sons of Henadad
and their sons and brothers—all Levites—
joined together in supervising those working
on the house of God.
10When the builders laid the foundation of
the temple of the LORD, the priests in their
vestments and with trumpets, and the Levites
(the sons of Asaph) with cymbals, took their
places to praise the LORD, as prescribed by David king of Israel. 11With praise and thanksgiving they sang to the LORD:

"He is good;
his love to Israel endures forever."

And all the people gave a great shout of praise
to the LORD, because the foundation of the
house of the LORD was laid. 12But many of
the older priests and Levites and family heads,
who had seen the former temple, wept aloud
when they saw the foundation of this temple
being laid, while many others shouted for joy.
13No one could distinguish the sound of the
shouts of joy from the sound of weeping, because the people made so much noise. And the
sound was heard far away.

Opposition to the Rebuilding

4 When the enemies of Judah and Benjamin
heard that the exiles were building a temple
for the LORD, the God of Israel, 2they came
to Zerubbabel and to the heads of the families
and said, "Let us help you build because, like
you, we seek your God and have been sacrificing to him since the time of Esarhaddon king
of Assyria, who brought us here."
3But Zerubbabel, Jeshua and the rest of the
heads of the families of Israel answered, "You
have no part with us in building a temple to
our God. We alone will build it for the LORD,
the God of Israel, as King Cyrus, the king of
Persia, commanded us."
4Then the peoples around them set out
to discourage the people of Judah and make
them afraid to go on building.[b] 5They hired
counselors to work against them and frustrate
their plans during the entire reign of Cyrus
king of Persia and down to the reign of Darius
king of Persia.

Later Opposition Under Xerxes and Artaxerxes

6At the beginning of the reign of Xerxes,[c]
they lodged an accusation against the people
of Judah and Jerusalem.
7And in the days of Artaxerxes king of Persia, Bishlam, Mithredath, Tabeel and the rest
of his associates wrote a letter to Artaxerxes.
The letter was written in Aramaic script and
in the Aramaic language.[d,e]
8Rehum the commanding officer and
Shimshai the secretary wrote a letter against
Jerusalem to Artaxerxes the king as follows:

9Rehum the commanding officer and
Shimshai the secretary, together with the
rest of their associates—the judges and
officials over the men from Tripolis, Persia,[f] Erech and Babylon, the Elamites of
Susa, 10and the other people whom the
great and honorable Ashurbanipal[g] deported and settled in the city of Samaria
and elsewhere in Trans-Euphrates.

11(This is a copy of the letter they sent him.)

To King Artaxerxes,

From your servants, the men of Trans-
Euphrates:

12The king should know that the Jews
who came up to us from you have gone
to Jerusalem and are rebuilding that rebellious and wicked city. They are restoring the walls and repairing the foundations.

13Furthermore, the king should know
that if this city is built and its walls are restored, no more taxes, tribute or duty will
be paid, and the royal revenues will suffer. 14Now since we are under obligation
to the palace and it is not proper for us
to see the king dishonored, we are sending this message to inform the king, 15so
that a search may be made in the archives

---

[a] 9 Hebrew *Yehudah,* probably a variant of *Hodaviah* [b] 4 Or *and troubled them as they built* [c] 6 Hebrew *Ahasuerus,* a variant of Xerxes' Persian name [d] 7 Or *written in Aramaic and translated* [e] 7 The text of Ezra 4:8–6:18 is in Aramaic. [f] 9 Or *officials, magistrates and governors over the men from* [g] 10 Aramaic *Osnappar,* a variant of *Ashurbanipal*

of your predecessors. In these records
you will find that this city is a rebellious
city, troublesome to kings and provinces,
a place of rebellion from ancient times.
That is why this city was destroyed. 16We
inform the king that if this city is built
and its walls are restored, you will be left
with nothing in Trans-Euphrates.

17The king sent this reply:

To Rehum the commanding officer,
Shimshai the secretary and the rest of
their associates living in Samaria and elsewhere in Trans-Euphrates:

Greetings.

18The letter you sent us has been read
and translated in my presence. 19I issued
an order and a search was made, and it
was found that this city has a long history of revolt against kings and has been a
place of rebellion and sedition. 20Jerusa-
lem has had powerful kings ruling over
the whole of Trans-Euphrates, and taxes, tribute and duty were paid to them.
21Now issue an order to these men to
stop work, so that this city will not be
rebuilt until I so order. 22Be careful not
to neglect this matter. Why let this threat
grow, to the detriment of the royal interests?

23As soon as the copy of the letter of King
Artaxerxes was read to Rehum and Shimshai
the secretary and their associates, they went
immediately to the Jews in Jerusalem and
compelled them by force to stop.

24Thus the work on the house of God in
Jerusalem came to a standstill until the second
year of the reign of Darius king of Persia.

Tattenai's Letter to Darius

5 Now Haggai the prophet and Zechariah the
prophet, a descendant of Iddo, prophesied
to the Jews in Judah and Jerusalem in the
name of the God of Israel, who was over them.
2Then Zerubbabel son of Shealtiel and Jeshua son of Jozadak set to work to rebuild the
house of God in Jerusalem. And the prophets
of God were with them, helping them.
3At that time Tattenai, governor of
Trans-Euphrates, and Shethar-Bozenai and
their associates went to them and asked,
"Who authorized you to rebuild this temple
and restore this structure?" 4They also asked,
"What are the names of the men constructing
this building?"[a] 5But the eye of their God was
watching over the elders of the Jews, and they
were not stopped until a report could go to
Darius and his written reply be received.
6This is a copy of the letter that Tattenai,
governor of Trans-Euphrates, and Shethar-
Bozenai and their associates, the officials of
Trans-Euphrates, sent to King Darius. 7The
report they sent him read as follows:

To King Darius:

Cordial greetings.

8The king should know that we went
to the district of Judah, to the temple of
the great God. The people are building it
with large stones and placing the timbers
in the walls. The work is being carried on
with diligence and is making rapid progress under their direction.
9We questioned the elders and asked
them, "Who authorized you to rebuild
this temple and restore this structure?"
10We also asked them their names, so
that we could write down the names of
their leaders for your information.
11This is the answer they gave us:

"We are the servants of the God of
heaven and earth, and we are rebuilding the temple that was built many years
ago, one that a great king of Israel built
and finished. 12But because our fathers
angered the God of heaven, he handed
them over to Nebuchadnezzar the Chaldean, king of Babylon, who destroyed
this temple and deported the people to
Babylon.
13"However, in the first year of Cyrus
king of Babylon, King Cyrus issued a decree to rebuild this house of God. 14He
even removed from the temple[b] of Babylon the gold and silver articles of the
house of God, which Nebuchadnezzar
had taken from the temple in Jerusalem
and brought to the temple[b] in Babylon.
"Then King Cyrus gave them to a
man named Sheshbazzar, whom he had
appointed governor, 15and he told him,
'Take these articles and go and deposit
them in the temple in Jerusalem. And rebuild the house of God on its site.' 16So
this Sheshbazzar came and laid the foundations of the house of God in Jerusalem.

[a] 4 See Septuagint; Aramaic 4*We told them the names of the men constructing this building.* [b] 14 Or *palace*

From that day to the present it has been
under construction but is not yet finished."

17Now if it pleases the king, let a search
be made in the royal archives of Babylon
to see if King Cyrus did in fact issue a
decree to rebuild this house of God in
Jerusalem. Then let the king send us his
decision in this matter.

The Decree of Darius

6 King Darius then issued an order, and they
searched in the archives stored in the treasury at Babylon. 2A scroll was found in the
citadel of Ecbatana in the province of Media,
and this was written on it:

Memorandum:

3In the first year of King Cyrus, the
king issued a decree concerning the temple of God in Jerusalem:

Let the temple be rebuilt as a place
to present sacrifices, and let its foundations be laid. It is to be ninety feet[a] high
and ninety feet wide, 4with three courses
of large stones and one of timbers. The
costs are to be paid by the royal treasury.
5Also, the gold and silver articles of the
house of God, which Nebuchadnezzar
took from the temple in Jerusalem and
brought to Babylon, are to be returned to
their places in the temple in Jerusalem;
they are to be deposited in the house of
God.

6Now then, Tattenai, governor of
Trans-Euphrates, and Shethar-Bozenai
and you, their fellow officials of that
province, stay away from there. 7Do not
interfere with the work on this temple of
God. Let the governor of the Jews and
the Jewish elders rebuild this house of
God on its site.

8Moreover, I hereby decree what you
are to do for these elders of the Jews in
the construction of this house of God:

The expenses of these men are to be
fully paid out of the royal treasury, from
the revenues of Trans-Euphrates, so that
the work will not stop. 9Whatever is
needed—young bulls, rams, male lambs
for burnt offerings to the God of heaven,
and wheat, salt, wine and oil, as requested
by the priests in Jerusalem—must be giv-
en them daily without fail, 10so that they
may offer sacrifices pleasing to the God of
heaven and pray for the well-being of the
king and his sons.

11Furthermore, I decree that if anyone
changes this edict, a beam is to be pulled
from his house and he is to be lifted up
and impaled on it. And for this crime
his house is to be made a pile of rubble.
12May God, who has caused his Name to
dwell there, overthrow any king or people
who lifts a hand to change this decree or
to destroy this temple in Jerusalem.

I Darius have decreed it. Let it be carried out with diligence.

Completion and Dedication of the Temple

13Then, because of the decree King Darius
had sent, Tattenai, governor of Trans-Euphrates,
and Shethar-Bozenai and their associates carried it out with diligence. 14So the elders of the
Jews continued to build and prosper under the
preaching of Haggai the prophet and Zechariah, a descendant of Iddo. They finished building the temple according to the command of
the God of Israel and the decrees of Cyrus,
Darius and Artaxerxes, kings of Persia. 15The
temple was completed on the third day of the
month Adar, in the sixth year of the reign of
King Darius.

16Then the people of Israel—the priests, the
Levites and the rest of the exiles—celebrated
the dedication of the house of God with joy.
17For the dedication of this house of God they
offered a hundred bulls, two hundred rams,
four hundred male lambs and, as a sin offering
for all Israel, twelve male goats, one for each
of the tribes of Israel. 18And they installed the
priests in their divisions and the Levites in
their groups for the service of God at Jerusalem, according to what is written in the Book
of Moses.

The Passover

19On the fourteenth day of the first
month, the exiles celebrated the Passover.
20The priests and Levites had purified themselves and were all ceremonially clean. The
Levites slaughtered the Passover lamb for all
the exiles, for their brothers the priests and
for themselves. 21So the Israelites who had
returned from the exile ate it, together with
all who had separated themselves from the
unclean practices of their Gentile neighbors
in order to seek the LORD, the God of Israel.

---

a 3 Aramaic *sixty cubits* (about 27 meters)

22For seven days they celebrated with joy the
Feast of Unleavened Bread, because the LORD
had filled them with joy by changing the attitude of the king of Assyria, so that he assisted
them in the work on the house of God, the
God of Israel.

Ezra Comes to Jerusalem

7 After these things, during the reign of Artaxerxes king of Persia, Ezra son of Seraiah,
the son of Azariah, the son of Hilkiah, 2the
son of Shallum, the son of Zadok, the son of
Ahitub, 3the son of Amariah, the son of Azariah, the son of Meraioth, 4the son of Zerahiah,
the son of Uzzi, the son of Bukki, 5the son of
Abishua, the son of Phinehas, the son of Eleazar, the son of Aaron the chief priest— 6this
Ezra came up from Babylon. He was a teacher
well versed in the Law of Moses, which the
LORD, the God of Israel, had given. The king
had granted him everything he asked, for the
hand of the LORD his God was on him. 7Some
of the Israelites, including priests, Levites,
singers, gatekeepers and temple servants, also
came up to Jerusalem in the seventh year of
King Artaxerxes.

8Ezra arrived in Jerusalem in the fifth
month of the seventh year of the king. 9He
had begun his journey from Babylon on the
first day of the first month, and he arrived in
Jerusalem on the first day of the fifth month,
for the gracious hand of his God was on him.
10For Ezra had devoted himself to the study
and observance of the Law of the LORD, and
to teaching its decrees and laws in Israel.

King Artaxerxes' Letter to Ezra

11This is a copy of the letter King Artaxerxes
had given to Ezra the priest and teacher, a man
learned in matters concerning the commands
and decrees of the LORD for Israel:

12[a] Artaxerxes, king of kings,

To Ezra the priest, a teacher of the Law of
the God of heaven:

Greetings.

13Now I decree that any of the Israelites in my kingdom, including priests
and Levites, who wish to go to Jerusalem
with you, may go. 14You are sent by the
king and his seven advisers to inquire
about Judah and Jerusalem with regard
to the Law of your God, which is in your
hand. 15Moreover, you are to take with
you the silver and gold that the king and
his advisers have freely given to the God
of Israel, whose dwelling is in Jerusalem,
16together with all the silver and gold you
may obtain from the province of Babylon, as well as the freewill offerings of
the people and priests for the temple of
their God in Jerusalem. 17With this money be sure to buy bulls, rams and male
lambs, together with their grain offerings
and drink offerings, and sacrifice them
on the altar of the temple of your God in
Jerusalem.

18You and your brother Jews may then
do whatever seems best with the rest of
the silver and gold, in accordance with
the will of your God. 19Deliver to the
God of Jerusalem all the articles entrusted to you for worship in the temple of
your God. 20And anything else needed
for the temple of your God that you may
have occasion to supply, you may provide
from the royal treasury.

21Now I, King Artaxerxes, order all the
treasurers of Trans-Euphrates to provide
with diligence whatever Ezra the priest, a
teacher of the Law of the God of heaven,
may ask of you— 22up to a hundred talents[b] of silver, a hundred cors[c] of wheat,
a hundred baths[d] of wine, a hundred
baths[d] of olive oil, and salt without limit.
23Whatever the God of heaven has prescribed, let it be done with diligence for
the temple of the God of heaven. Why
should there be wrath against the realm
of the king and of his sons? 24You are also
to know that you have no authority to
impose taxes, tribute or duty on any of
the priests, Levites, singers, gatekeepers,
temple servants or other workers at this
house of God.

25And you, Ezra, in accordance with
the wisdom of your God, which you
possess, appoint magistrates and judges
to administer justice to all the people of
Trans-Euphrates—all who know the laws
of your God. And you are to teach any
who do not know them. 26Whoever does
not obey the law of your God and the law
of the king must surely be punished by
death, banishment, confiscation of property, or imprisonment.

27Praise be to the LORD, the God of our fa-

[a] 12 The text of Ezra 7:12-26 is in Aramaic. [b] 22 That is, about 3 3/4 tons (about 3.4 metric tons) [c] 22 That is, probably about 600 bushels (about 22 kiloliters) [d] 22 That is, probably about 600 gallons (about 2.2 kiloliters)

thers, who has put it into the king's heart to
bring honor to the house of the LORD in Jerusalem in this way
28and who has extended
his good favor to me before the king and his
advisers and all the king's powerful officials.
Because the hand of the LORD my God was on
me, I took courage and gathered leading men
from Israel to go up with me.

List of the Family Heads Returning With Ezra

8 These are the family heads and those registered with them who came up with me
from Babylon during the reign of King Artaxerxes:

2 of the descendants of Phinehas, Gershom;
of the descendants of Ithamar, Daniel;
of the descendants of David, Hattush
3 of
the descendants of Shecaniah;

of the descendants of Parosh, Zechariah, and with him were registered 150
men;
4 of the descendants of Pahath-Moab, Eliehoenai son of Zerahiah, and with him
200 men;
5 of the descendants of Zattu,[a] Shecaniah son of Jahaziel, and with him 300
men;
6 of the descendants of Adin, Ebed son of
Jonathan, and with him 50 men;
7 of the descendants of Elam, Jeshaiah son
of Athaliah, and with him 70 men;
8 of the descendants of Shephatiah, Zebadiah son of Michael, and with him 80
men;
9 of the descendants of Joab, Obadiah son
of Jehiel, and with him 218 men;
10 of the descendants of Bani,[b] Shelomith
son of Josiphiah, and with him 160
men;
11 of the descendants of Bebai, Zechariah
son of Bebai, and with him 28 men;
12 of the descendants of Azgad, Johanan son
of Hakkatan, and with him 110 men;
13 of the descendants of Adonikam, the last
ones, whose names were Eliphelet, Jeuel and Shemaiah, and with them 60
men;
14 of the descendants of Bigvai, Uthai and
Zaccur, and with them 70 men.

The Return to Jerusalem

15 I assembled them at the canal that flows
toward Ahava, and we camped there three
days. When I checked among the people and
the priests, I found no Levites there.
16 So I
summoned Eliezer, Ariel, Shemaiah, Elnathan, Jarib, Elnathan, Nathan, Zechariah
and Meshullam, who were leaders, and Joiarib and Elnathan, who were men of learning,
17 and I sent them to Iddo, the leader in
Casiphia. I told them what to say to Iddo
and his kinsmen, the temple servants in Casiphia, so that they might bring attendants to
us for the house of our God.
18 Because the
gracious hand of our God was on us, they
brought us Sherebiah, a capable man, from
the descendants of Mahli son of Levi, the son
of Israel, and Sherebiah's sons and brothers,
18 men;
19 and Hashabiah, together with Jeshaiah from the descendants of Merari, and
his brothers and nephews, 20 men.
20 They
also brought 220 of the temple servants—a
body that David and the officials had established to assist the Levites. All were registered
by name.

21 There, by the Ahava Canal, I proclaimed a
fast, so that we might humble ourselves before
our God and ask him for a safe journey for
us and our children, with all our possessions.
22 I was ashamed to ask the king for soldiers
and horsemen to protect us from enemies on
the road, because we had told the king, "The
gracious hand of our God is on everyone who
looks to him, but his great anger is against all
who forsake him."
23 So we fasted and peti-
tioned our God about this, and he answered
our prayer.

24 Then I set apart twelve of the leading
priests, together with Sherebiah, Hashabiah
and ten of their brothers,
25 and I weighed out
to them the offering of silver and gold and the
articles that the king, his advisers, his officials
and all Israel present there had donated for the
house of our God.
26 I weighed out to them
650 talents[c] of silver, silver articles weighing 100 talents,[d] 100 talents[d] of gold,
27 20
bowls of gold valued at 1,000 darics,[e] and two
fine articles of polished bronze, as precious as
gold.

28 I said to them, "You as well as these articles are consecrated to the LORD. The silver
and gold are a freewill offering to the LORD,
the God of your fathers.
29 Guard them care-
fully until you weigh them out in the chambers of the house of the LORD in Jerusalem before the leading priests and the Levites and the

[a] *5* Some Septuagint manuscripts (also 1 Esdras 8:32); Hebrew does not have *Zattu*. [b] *10* Some Septuagint manuscripts (also 1 Esdras 8:36); Hebrew does not have *Bani*. [c] *26* That is, about 25 tons (about 22 metric tons) [d] *26* That is, about 3 3/4 tons (about 3.4 metric tons) [e] *27* That is, about 19 pounds (about 8.5 kilograms)

TUESDAY
READ EZRA 8:15–32

FINDING PEACE IN A NEW PLACE

> **I was ashamed to ask the king for soldiers and horsemen to protect us from enemies on the road, because we had told the king, "The gracious hand of our God is on everyone who looks to him, but his great anger is against all who forsake him." So we fasted and petitioned our God about this, and he answered our prayer.**
>
> — Ezra 8:22–23

I was afraid when Griff and I moved from Charlottesville, Virginia, the town in which I had grown up, to Durham, North Carolina. Griff and I would be outside of the town that had nurtured us through months of friendship and dating, and through our first tempestuous year of marriage. How could we survive without people who knew us intimately and loved us well?

The answer to that question, of course, was that I had to anchor myself, not in people, but in God. As a result, God helped me to feel centered, even in those lonely first months in Durham. Part of that nurturing also happened through my marriage. Away from all our friends, Griff and I had to become better friends to one another. We had to rely on each other. And God turned a difficult move into a nuptial blessing.

Marriage is not always a comfort. At times, marriage can prompt fear instead of comfort, especially when it forces us to move out of our comfort zone. We may not have to move hundreds of miles away via a road infested with bandits, as Ezra and the Jewish exiles did, but we may be forced to travel a challenging emotional journey. We may find ourselves in a place without familiar landmarks when we discover that our spouse has been unfaithful or is flirting with pornography or has lost a great deal of money in a risky investment. Maybe our spouse distances himself emotionally due to depression. Maybe she is no longer supportive because she's struggling with cancer. As we travel this new terrain, we often feel afraid.

Occasionally I look around my house and my life, and I wonder, "When did I become this married lady with Christmas china? Where did my other self, which was so free, so unencumbered, go?" I realize that marriage is about dying to my former self so I may be transformed and remade in loving relationship with my spouse. I realize how marriage is like a school in which God teaches us how to become new creatures. But in that transformation, we can feel scared and stressed and sad.

Where do we go for help when we're afraid? Do we run to the shopping mall to buy something that makes us feel better about ourselves? I've tried that a few times, but it doesn't work. I end up feeling not only dissatisfied but guilty for having spent too much money. I've tried pouring myself into work as well. But overwork just makes me exhausted. And it doesn't solve the problem of fear.

The only true solution is turning to the One whom Ezra called on for protection from enemies on the journey. He and his fellow exiles fasted and prayed for God's help. And God's gracious hand was on them all the way back to Jerusalem.

—LAUREN WINNER

let's talk

- ✦ When have we been in a fearful situation, physically or emotionally? To what or whom did we look for help?
- ✦ In what ways has marriage pushed us into new, scary terrain? How have we found comfort in each other?
- ✦ Think about an occasion when we called upon God for help in a trying time. How did he respond?

FOR YOUR NEXT DEVOTIONAL READING, TURN TO PAGE 512.

family heads of Israel." 30Then the priests and Levites received the silver and gold and sacred articles that had been weighed out to be taken to the house of our God in Jerusalem.

31On the twelfth day of the first month we set out from the Ahava Canal to go to Jerusalem. The hand of our God was on us, and he protected us from enemies and bandits along the way. 32So we arrived in Jerusalem, where we rested three days.

33On the fourth day, in the house of our God, we weighed out the silver and gold and the sacred articles into the hands of Meremoth son of Uriah, the priest. Eleazar son of Phinehas was with him, and so were the Levites Jozabad son of Jeshua and Noadiah son of Binnui. 34Everything was accounted for by number and weight, and the entire weight was recorded at that time.

35Then the exiles who had returned from captivity sacrificed burnt offerings to the God of Israel: twelve bulls for all Israel, ninety-six rams, seventy-seven male lambs and, as a sin offering, twelve male goats. All this was a burnt offering to the LORD. 36They also delivered the king's orders to the royal satraps and to the governors of Trans-Euphrates, who then gave assistance to the people and to the house of God.

Ezra's Prayer About Intermarriage

9 After these things had been done, the leaders came to me and said, "The people of Israel, including the priests and the Levites, have not kept themselves separate from the neighboring peoples with their detestable practices, like those of the Canaanites, Hittites, Perizzites, Jebusites, Ammonites, Moabites, Egyptians and Amorites. 2They have taken some of their daughters as wives for themselves and their sons, and have mingled the holy race with the peoples around them. And the leaders and officials have led the way in this unfaithfulness."

3When I heard this, I tore my tunic and cloak, pulled hair from my head and beard and sat down appalled. 4Then everyone who trembled at the words of the God of Israel gathered around me because of this unfaithfulness of the exiles. And I sat there appalled until the evening sacrifice.

5Then, at the evening sacrifice, I rose from my self-abasement, with my tunic and cloak torn, and fell on my knees with my hands spread out to the LORD my God 6and prayed:

"O my God, I am too ashamed and disgraced to lift up my face to you, my God, because our sins are higher than our heads and our guilt has reached to the heavens. 7From the days of our forefathers until now, our guilt has been great. Because of our sins, we and our kings and our priests have been subjected to the sword and captivity, to pillage and humiliation at the hand of foreign kings, as it is today.

8"But now, for a brief moment, the LORD our God has been gracious in leaving us a remnant and giving us a firm place in his sanctuary, and so our God gives light to our eyes and a little relief in our bondage. 9Though we are slaves, our God has not deserted us in our bondage. He has shown us kindness in the sight of the kings of Persia: He has granted us new life to rebuild the house of our God and repair its ruins, and he has given us a wall of protection in Judah and Jerusalem.

10"But now, O our God, what can we say after this? For we have disregarded the commands 11you gave through your servants the prophets when you said: 'The land you are entering to possess is a land polluted by the corruption of its peoples. By their detestable practices they have filled it with their impurity from one end to the other. 12Therefore, do not give your daughters in marriage to their sons or take their daughters for your sons. Do not seek a treaty of friendship with them at any time, that you may be strong and eat the good things of the land and leave it to your children as an everlasting inheritance.'

13"What has happened to us is a result of our evil deeds and our great guilt, and yet, our God, you have punished us less than our sins have deserved and have given us a remnant like this. 14Shall we again break your commands and intermarry with the peoples who commit such detestable practices? Would you not be angry enough with us to destroy us, leaving us no remnant or survivor? 15O LORD, God of Israel, you are righteous! We are left this day as a remnant. Here we are before you in our guilt, though because of it not one of us can stand in your presence."

The People's Confession of Sin

10 While Ezra was praying and confessing, weeping and throwing himself
down before the house of God, a large
crowd of Israelites—men, women and children—gathered around him. They too wept
bitterly. 2Then Shecaniah son of Jehiel, one
of the descendants of Elam, said to Ezra, "We
have been unfaithful to our God by marrying foreign women from the peoples around
us. But in spite of this, there is still hope for
Israel. 3Now let us make a covenant before
our God to send away all these women and
their children, in accordance with the counsel of my lord and of those who fear the commands of our God. Let it be done according
to the Law. 4Rise up; this matter is in your
hands. We will support you, so take courage
and do it."

5So Ezra rose up and put the leading priests
and Levites and all Israel under oath to do
what had been suggested. And they took the
oath. 6Then Ezra withdrew from before the
house of God and went to the room of Jehohanan son of Eliashib. While he was there, he
ate no food and drank no water, because he
continued to mourn over the unfaithfulness
of the exiles.

7A proclamation was then issued throughout Judah and Jerusalem for all the exiles to
assemble in Jerusalem. 8Anyone who failed to
appear within three days would forfeit all his
property, in accordance with the decision of
the officials and elders, and would himself be
expelled from the assembly of the exiles.

9Within the three days, all the men of Judah and Benjamin had gathered in Jerusalem.
And on the twentieth day of the ninth month,
all the people were sitting in the square before
the house of God, greatly distressed by the occasion and because of the rain. 10Then Ezra
the priest stood up and said to them, "You
have been unfaithful; you have married foreign women, adding to Israel's guilt. 11Now
make confession to the LORD, the God of your
fathers, and do his will. Separate yourselves
from the peoples around you and from your
foreign wives."

12The whole assembly responded with a
loud voice: "You are right! We must do as you
say. 13But there are many people here and it is
the rainy season; so we cannot stand outside.
Besides, this matter cannot be taken care of in
a day or two, because we have sinned greatly in
this thing. 14Let our officials act for the whole
assembly. Then let everyone in our towns who
has married a foreign woman come at a set
time, along with the elders and judges of each
town, until the fierce anger of our God in this
matter is turned away from us." 15Only Jonathan son of Asahel and Jahzeiah son of Tikvah,
supported by Meshullam and Shabbethai the
Levite, opposed this.

16So the exiles did as was proposed. Ezra
the priest selected men who were family
heads, one from each family division, and all
of them designated by name. On the first day
of the tenth month they sat down to investigate the cases, 17and by the first day of the first
month they finished dealing with all the men
who had married foreign women.

Those Guilty of Intermarriage

18 Among the descendants of the priests,
the following had married foreign
women:

From the descendants of Jeshua son of
Jozadak, and his brothers: Maaseiah,
Eliezer, Jarib and Gedaliah. 19(They all
gave their hands in pledge to put away
their wives, and for their guilt they
each presented a ram from the flock as
a guilt offering.)

20 From the descendants of Immer:
Hanani and Zebadiah.

21 From the descendants of Harim:
Maaseiah, Elijah, Shemaiah, Jehiel and
Uzziah.

22 From the descendants of Pashhur:
Elioenai, Maaseiah, Ishmael, Nethanel, Jozabad and Elasah.

23 Among the Levites:

Jozabad, Shimei, Kelaiah (that is, Kelita), Pethahiah, Judah and Eliezer.

24 From the singers:
Eliashib.

From the gatekeepers:
Shallum, Telem and Uri.

25 And among the other Israelites:

From the descendants of Parosh:
Ramiah, Izziah, Malkijah, Mijamin,
Eleazar, Malkijah and Benaiah.

26 From the descendants of Elam:
Mattaniah, Zechariah, Jehiel, Abdi,
Jeremoth and Elijah.

27 From the descendants of Zattu:
Elioenai, Eliashib, Mattaniah, Jeremoth, Zabad and Aziza.

28 From the descendants of Bebai:

Jehohanan, Hananiah, Zabbai and Athlai.

29 From the descendants of Bani:
Meshullam, Malluch, Adaiah, Jashub, Sheal and Jeremoth.

30 From the descendants of Pahath-Moab:
Adna, Kelal, Benaiah, Maaseiah, Mattaniah, Bezalel, Binnui and Manasseh.

31 From the descendants of Harim:
Eliezer, Ishijah, Malkijah, Shemaiah, Shimeon, 32 Benjamin, Malluch and Shemariah.

33 From the descendants of Hashum:
Mattenai, Mattattah, Zabad, Eliphelet, Jeremai, Manasseh and Shimei.

34 From the descendants of Bani:
Maadai, Amram, Uel, 35 Benaiah, Bedeiah, Keluhi, 36 Vaniah, Meremoth, Eliashib, 37 Mattaniah, Mattenai and Jaasu.

38 From the descendants of Binnui:[a]
Shimei, 39 Shelemiah, Nathan, Adaiah, 40 Macnadebai, Shashai, Sharai, 41 Azarel, Shelemiah, Shemariah, 42 Shallum, Amariah and Joseph.

43 From the descendants of Nebo:
Jeiel, Mattithiah, Zabad, Zebina, Jaddai, Joel and Benaiah.

44 All these had married foreign women, and some of them had children by these wives.[b]

---

a 37,38 See Septuagint (also 1 Esdras 9:34); Hebrew *Jaasu* [38]*and Bani and Binnui,* *b* 44 Or *and they sent them away with their children*

NEHEMIAH

Nehemiah

QUICK FACTS

AUTHOR Unknown, but possibly Ezra or Nehemiah

AUDIENCE All Israel

DATE Around 430 B.C.

SETTING The rebuilding of the city wall of Jerusalem by the Jewish remnant despite harsh opposition

The temple was finished, but the wall of Jerusalem was still in ruins. Without walls of protection, the exiles who had returned were defenseless. Nehemiah, cupbearer to the Persian king, wept when he learned this news, and the king sent him to Jerusalem to rebuild the walls.

The challenges were great: motivating people who had given up, combating mean-spirited neighbors who opposed the project, organizing the workload and guarding against sabotage. And in the midst of the effort, Nehemiah had to confront social injustices against the poor who lived among the Jewish community. Nonetheless, under Nehemiah's administrative genius, the project was finished in less than two months.

Then the job of rebuilding the spiritual boundaries of the people began. Ezra's public reading of the Law caused the people to confess, repent and publicly declare that they would follow the Law of God. In the wake of this national revival, Jerusalem was repopulated, the temple was cleansed of unbelievers, Sabbath practices were reinstituted and the priesthood was purified.

The people needed that wall for their spiritual well-being. We too need walls to maintain a godly focus. When we separate ourselves from the unholy influences of the culture around us (pornography, infidelity, overspending, etc.), we are better able to follow Christ. Within the walls of God's protection, our marriages can thrive.

Nehemiah's Prayer

1 The words of Nehemiah son of Hacaliah:

In the month of Kislev in the twentieth
year, while I was in the citadel of Susa, [2]Ha-
nani, one of my brothers, came from Judah
with some other men, and I questioned them
about the Jewish remnant that survived the
exile, and also about Jerusalem.

[3]They said to me, "Those who survived the
exile and are back in the province are in great
trouble and disgrace. The wall of Jerusalem is
broken down, and its gates have been burned
with fire."

[4]When I heard these things, I sat down and
wept. For some days I mourned and fasted
and prayed before the God of heaven. [5]Then
I said:

> "O LORD, God of heaven, the great
> and awesome God, who keeps his cov-
> enant of love with those who love him
> and obey his commands, [6]let your ear
> be attentive and your eyes open to hear
> the prayer your servant is praying before
> you day and night for your servants, the
> people of Israel. I confess the sins we Is-
> raelites, including myself and my father's
> house, have committed against you. [7]We
> have acted very wickedly toward you. We
> have not obeyed the commands, decrees
> and laws you gave your servant Moses.
>
> [8]"Remember the instruction you gave
> your servant Moses, saying, 'If you are un-
> faithful, I will scatter you among the na-
> tions, [9]but if you return to me and obey
> my commands, then even if your exiled
> people are at the farthest horizon, I will
> gather them from there and bring them
> to the place I have chosen as a dwelling
> for my Name.'
>
> [10]"They are your servants and your
> people, whom you redeemed by your
> great strength and your mighty hand.
> [11]O Lord, let your ear be attentive to
> the prayer of this your servant and to the
> prayer of your servants who delight in re-
> vering your name. Give your servant suc-
> cess today by granting him favor in the
> presence of this man."

I was cupbearer to the king.

Artaxerxes Sends Nehemiah to Jerusalem

2 In the month of Nisan in the twentieth year
of King Artaxerxes, when wine was brought
for him, I took the wine and gave it to the
king. I had not been sad in his presence before; [2]so the king asked me, "Why does your
face look so sad when you are not ill? This can
be nothing but sadness of heart."

I was very much afraid, [3]but I said to the
king, "May the king live forever! Why should
my face not look sad when the city where my
fathers are buried lies in ruins, and its gates
have been destroyed by fire?"

[4]The king said to me, "What is it you
want?"

Then I prayed to the God of heaven, [5]and I
answered the king, "If it pleases the king and
if your servant has found favor in his sight, let
him send me to the city in Judah where my fathers are buried so that I can rebuild it."

[6]Then the king, with the queen sitting
beside him, asked me, "How long will your
journey take, and when will you get back?" It
pleased the king to send me; so I set a time.

[7]I also said to him, "If it pleases the
king, may I have letters to the governors of
Trans-Euphrates, so that they will provide me
safe-conduct until I arrive in Judah? [8]And may
I have a letter to Asaph, keeper of the king's
forest, so he will give me timber to make
beams for the gates of the citadel by the temple and for the city wall and for the residence
I will occupy?" And because the gracious hand
of my God was upon me, the king granted
my requests. [9]So I went to the governors of
Trans-Euphrates and gave them the king's letters. The king had also sent army officers and
cavalry with me.

[10]When Sanballat the Horonite and Tobiah
the Ammonite official heard about this, they
were very much disturbed that someone had
come to promote the welfare of the Israelites.

Nehemiah Inspects Jerusalem's Walls

[11]I went to Jerusalem, and after staying
there three days [12]I set out during the night
with a few men. I had not told anyone what
my God had put in my heart to do for Jerusalem. There were no mounts with me except
the one I was riding on.

[13]By night I went out through the Valley
Gate toward the Jackal[a] Well and the Dung
Gate, examining the walls of Jerusalem, which
had been broken down, and its gates, which
had been destroyed by fire. [14]Then I moved on

---

a 13 Or *Serpent* or *Fig*

WEDNESDAY
READ NEHEMIAH 1:1—2:18

REKINDLING OUR CONNECTION

> **Then I said to them, " . . . Come, let us rebuild the wall of Jerusalem, and we will no longer be in disgrace." . . . They replied, "Let us start rebuilding."**
>
> — NEHEMIAH 2:17–18

The wall around Jerusalem had been destroyed. Nehemiah recognized that Israel needed the protection of that wall, and, with the blessing of King Artaxerxes, he undertook the work of rebuilding it.

Our marriages also need structures to help safeguard us—to protect us from erosion, invaders and sometimes even our own bad impulses. What might our marriages need protection from, and what kinds of safeguards can we put in place?

Infidelity. Now there's an obvious (though not necessarily fatal) poison to a marriage. One way to protect our marriage from this threat is to intentionally include our spouse in any friendships we have with members of the opposite sex. Another has to do with technology: Husbands and wives who share email accounts and cell phones are a lot less likely to get into risky, tempting, secretive relationships than those who have separate accounts and phones.

Walls raised against infidelity will keep something bad out. But walls can also help us keep good things in. If you've been married for longer than a week, you've probably had moments when you've wondered where the ardor and intimacy you once felt for each other have gone. We can put up walls to help keep in the good feelings in our marriage.

For example, during their fifth year of marriage, Tucker and Gigi noticed that they had lost interest in each other's lives. So they made a commitment to daily ask one question about something the other cared about. "You know," explained Gigi, "something basic like, 'What are you thinking about that novel you're reading?' " That one simple discipline has gone a long way toward rekindling intimacy between them.

Parenting also poses special challenges to a marriage. Life easily becomes too child-centered, with mom and dad devoting all of their energy to being, well, mom and dad, and none to being husband and wife. Carving out regular time for each other away from the kids, budgeting money for a babysitter, and reminding kids that they're not always the center of attention are all fences we can put up to protect our relationship.

Finally, financial problems can wreak havoc on a marriage. The stress of carrying debt can fray even the strongest relationship. Some straightforward steps can help protect us: tithing, spending less than we make and never lying to each other about a financial crisis.

Marriages are fragile. Our society doesn't much to help us honor our vows. And the enemy loves to bring husbands and wives down. Just as King Artaxerxes blessed Nehemiah's building of a protective wall around Jerusalem, so too our King will bless the walls we lovingly lay to shore up our marriages.

—LAUREN WINNER

let's talk

- ✦ What outside forces threaten our intimacy? What fences can we put up to keep those forces at bay?
- ✦ What positive aspects of our marriage do we want to hold on to? What can we do to build walls around our marriage to help keep those good things in?
- ✦ Have we suffered a breach in the walls around our marriage? If so, what can we do to rebuild them?

FOR YOUR NEXT DEVOTIONAL READING, TURN TO PAGE 519.

toward the Fountain Gate and the King's Pool,
but there was not enough room for my mount
to get through; 15so I went up the valley by
night, examining the wall. Finally, I turned
back and reentered through the Valley Gate.
16The officials did not know where I had gone
or what I was doing, because as yet I had said
nothing to the Jews or the priests or nobles
or officials or any others who would be doing
the work.

17Then I said to them, "You see the trouble we are in: Jerusalem lies in ruins, and its
gates have been burned with fire. Come, let us
rebuild the wall of Jerusalem, and we will no
longer be in disgrace." 18I also told them about
the gracious hand of my God upon me and
what the king had said to me.

They replied, "Let us start rebuilding." So
they began this good work.

19But when Sanballat the Horonite, Tobiah
the Ammonite official and Geshem the Arab
heard about it, they mocked and ridiculed us.
"What is this you are doing?" they asked. "Are
you rebelling against the king?"

20I answered them by saying, "The God of
heaven will give us success. We his servants
will start rebuilding, but as for you, you have
no share in Jerusalem or any claim or historic
right to it."

Builders of the Wall

3 Eliashib the high priest and his fellow
priests went to work and rebuilt the Sheep
Gate. They dedicated it and set its doors in
place, building as far as the Tower of the Hundred, which they dedicated, and as far as the
Tower of Hananel. 2The men of Jericho built
the adjoining section, and Zaccur son of Imri
built next to them.

3The Fish Gate was rebuilt by the sons of
Hassenaah. They laid its beams and put its
doors and bolts and bars in place. 4Meremoth
son of Uriah, the son of Hakkoz, repaired the
next section. Next to him Meshullam son of
Berekiah, the son of Meshezabel, made repairs, and next to him Zadok son of Baana
also made repairs. 5The next section was repaired by the men of Tekoa, but their nobles
would not put their shoulders to the work under their supervisors.[a]

6The Jeshanah[b] Gate was repaired by Joiada son of Paseah and Meshullam son of Bes-
odeiah. They laid its beams and put its doors
and bolts and bars in place. 7Next to them,
repairs were made by men from Gibeon and
Mizpah—Melatiah of Gibeon and Jadon of
Meronoth—places under the authority of the
governor of Trans-Euphrates. 8Uzziel son of
Harhaiah, one of the goldsmiths, repaired the
next section; and Hananiah, one of the per-
fume-makers, made repairs next to that. They
restored[c] Jerusalem as far as the Broad Wall.
9Rephaiah son of Hur, ruler of a half-district
of Jerusalem, repaired the next section. 10Ad-
joining this, Jedaiah son of Harumaph made
repairs opposite his house, and Hattush son
of Hashabneiah made repairs next to him.
11Malkijah son of Harim and Hasshub son
of Pahath-Moab repaired another section
and the Tower of the Ovens. 12Shallum son
of Hallohesh, ruler of a half-district of Jerusalem, repaired the next section with the help of
his daughters.

13The Valley Gate was repaired by Hanun
and the residents of Zanoah. They rebuilt it
and put its doors and bolts and bars in place.
They also repaired five hundred yards[d] of the
wall as far as the Dung Gate.

14The Dung Gate was repaired by Malkijah son of Recab, ruler of the district of Beth
Hakkerem. He rebuilt it and put its doors and
bolts and bars in place.

15The Fountain Gate was repaired by Shal-
lun son of Col-Hozeh, ruler of the district of
Mizpah. He rebuilt it, roofing it over and putting its doors and bolts and bars in place. He
also repaired the wall of the Pool of Siloam,[e]
by the King's Garden, as far as the steps going
down from the City of David. 16Beyond him,
Nehemiah son of Azbuk, ruler of a half-district of Beth Zur, made repairs up to a point
opposite the tombs[f] of David, as far as the artificial pool and the House of the Heroes.

17Next to him, the repairs were made by the
Levites under Rehum son of Bani. Beside him,
Hashabiah, ruler of half the district of Keilah,
carried out repairs for his district. 18Next to
him, the repairs were made by their countrymen under Binnui[g] son of Henadad, ruler of the other half-district of Keilah. 19Next
to him, Ezer son of Jeshua, ruler of Mizpah,
repaired another section, from a point facing
the ascent to the armory as far as the angle.
20Next to him, Baruch son of Zabbai zealous-
ly repaired another section, from the angle to

[a] 5 Or *their Lord* or *the governor* [b] 6 Or *Old* [c] 8 Or *They left out part of* [d] 13 Hebrew *a thousand cubits* (about 450 meters)
[e] 15 Hebrew *Shelah,* a variant of *Shiloah,* that is, Siloam [f] 16 Hebrew; Septuagint, some Vulgate manuscripts and Syriac *tomb*
[g] 18 Two Hebrew manuscripts and Syriac (see also Septuagint and verse 24); most Hebrew manuscripts *Bavvai*

the entrance of the house of Eliashib the high
priest. [21]Next to him, Meremoth son of Uriah, the son of Hakkoz, repaired another section, from the entrance of Eliashib's house to
the end of it.
[22]The repairs next to him were made by the
priests from the surrounding region. [23]Beyond
them, Benjamin and Hasshub made repairs in
front of their house; and next to them, Azariah son of Maaseiah, the son of Ananiah,
made repairs beside his house. [24]Next to him,
Binnui son of Henadad repaired another section, from Azariah's house to the angle and the
corner, [25]and Palal son of Uzai worked opposite the angle and the tower projecting from
the upper palace near the court of the guard.
Next to him, Pedaiah son of Parosh [26]and the
temple servants living on the hill of Ophel
made repairs up to a point opposite the Water
Gate toward the east and the projecting tower.
[27]Next to them, the men of Tekoa repaired another section, from the great projecting tower
to the wall of Ophel.

[28]Above the Horse Gate, the priests made
repairs, each in front of his own house. [29]Next
to them, Zadok son of Immer made repairs
opposite his house. Next to him, Shemaiah
son of Shecaniah, the guard at the East Gate,
made repairs. [30]Next to him, Hananiah son of
Shelemiah, and Hanun, the sixth son of Za-
laph, repaired another section. Next to them,
Meshullam son of Berekiah made repairs opposite his living quarters. [31]Next to him, Malkijah, one of the goldsmiths, made repairs as
far as the house of the temple servants and
the merchants, opposite the Inspection Gate,
and as far as the room above the corner; [32]and
between the room above the corner and the
Sheep Gate the goldsmiths and merchants
made repairs.

Opposition to the Rebuilding

4 When Sanballat heard that we were rebuilding the wall, he became angry and was
greatly incensed. He ridiculed the Jews,
[2]and in the presence of his associates and the
army of Samaria, he said, "What are those feeble Jews doing? Will they restore their wall?
Will they offer sacrifices? Will they finish in
a day? Can they bring the stones back to life
from those heaps of rubble—burned as they
are?"
[3]Tobiah the Ammonite, who was at his
side, said, "What they are building—if even
a fox climbed up on it, he would break down
their wall of stones!"

[4]Hear us, O our God, for we are despised.
Turn their insults back on their own heads.
Give them over as plunder in a land of captivity. [5]Do not cover up their guilt or blot
out their sins from your sight, for they have
thrown insults in the face of[a] the builders.

[6]So we rebuilt the wall till all of it reached
half its height, for the people worked with all
their heart.
[7]But when Sanballat, Tobiah, the Arabs,
the Ammonites and the men of Ashdod heard
that the repairs to Jerusalem's walls had gone
ahead and that the gaps were being closed,
they were very angry. [8]They all plotted together to come and fight against Jerusalem and stir
up trouble against it. [9]But we prayed to our
God and posted a guard day and night to meet
this threat.
[10]Meanwhile, the people in Judah said,
"The strength of the laborers is giving out,
and there is so much rubble that we cannot
rebuild the wall."
[11]Also our enemies said, "Before they know
it or see us, we will be right there among
them and will kill them and put an end to the
work."
[12]Then the Jews who lived near them came
and told us ten times over, "Wherever you
turn, they will attack us."
[13]Therefore I stationed some of the people
behind the lowest points of the wall at the exposed places, posting them by families, with
their swords, spears and bows. [14]After I looked
things over, I stood up and said to the nobles,
the officials and the rest of the people, "Don't
be afraid of them. Remember the Lord, who is
great and awesome, and fight for your brothers, your sons and your daughters, your wives
and your homes."
[15]When our enemies heard that we were
aware of their plot and that God had frustrated it, we all returned to the wall, each to his
own work.
[16]From that day on, half of my men did the
work, while the other half were equipped with
spears, shields, bows and armor. The officers
posted themselves behind all the people of Judah [17]who were building the wall. Those who
carried materials did their work with one hand
and held a weapon in the other, [18]and each of
the builders wore his sword at his side as he

[a] 5 Or *have provoked you to anger before*

worked. But the man who sounded the trumpet stayed with me.
19Then I said to the nobles, the officials and
the rest of the people, "The work is extensive
and spread out, and we are widely separated
from each other along the wall. 20Wherever
you hear the sound of the trumpet, join us
there. Our God will fight for us!"
21So we continued the work with half the
men holding spears, from the first light of
dawn till the stars came out. 22At that time I
also said to the people, "Have every man and
his helper stay inside Jerusalem at night, so
they can serve us as guards by night and workmen by day." 23Neither I nor my brothers nor
my men nor the guards with me took off our
clothes; each had his weapon, even when he
went for water.[a]

Nehemiah Helps the Poor

5 Now the men and their wives raised a great
outcry against their Jewish brothers. 2Some
were saying, "We and our sons and daughters are numerous; in order for us to eat and
stay alive, we must get grain."
3Others were saying, "We are mortgaging
our fields, our vineyards and our homes to get
grain during the famine."
4Still others were saying, "We have had to
borrow money to pay the king's tax on our
fields and vineyards. 5Although we are of the
same flesh and blood as our countrymen and
though our sons are as good as theirs, yet we
have to subject our sons and daughters to slavery. Some of our daughters have already been
enslaved, but we are powerless, because our
fields and our vineyards belong to others."
6When I heard their outcry and these
charges, I was very angry. 7I pondered them
in my mind and then accused the nobles and
officials. I told them, "You are exacting usury from your own countrymen!" So I called
together a large meeting to deal with them
8and said: "As far as possible, we have bought
back our Jewish brothers who were sold to the
Gentiles. Now you are selling your brothers,
only for them to be sold back to us!" They
kept quiet, because they could find nothing
to say.
9So I continued, "What you are doing is
not right. Shouldn't you walk in the fear of
our God to avoid the reproach of our Gentile
enemies? 10I and my brothers and my men are
also lending the people money and grain. But
let the exacting of usury stop! 11Give back to
them immediately their fields, vineyards, olive groves and houses, and also the usury you
are charging them—the hundredth part of the
money, grain, new wine and oil."
12"We will give it back," they said. "And we
will not demand anything more from them.
We will do as you say."
Then I summoned the priests and made the
nobles and officials take an oath to do what
they had promised. 13I also shook out the
folds of my robe and said, "In this way may
God shake out of his house and possessions
every man who does not keep this promise. So
may such a man be shaken out and emptied!"
At this the whole assembly said, "Amen,"
and praised the LORD. And the people did as
they had promised.
14Moreover, from the twentieth year of
King Artaxerxes, when I was appointed to be
their governor in the land of Judah, until his
thirty-second year—twelve years—neither I
nor my brothers ate the food allotted to the
governor. 15But the earlier governors—those
preceding me—placed a heavy burden on
the people and took forty shekels[b] of silver
from them in addition to food and wine.
Their assistants also lorded it over the people. But out of reverence for God I did not
act like that. 16Instead, I devoted myself to
the work on this wall. All my men were assembled there for the work; we[c] did not acquire any land.
17Furthermore, a hundred and fifty Jews
and officials ate at my table, as well as those
who came to us from the surrounding nations.
18Each day one ox, six choice sheep and some
poultry were prepared for me, and every ten
days an abundant supply of wine of all kinds.
In spite of all this, I never demanded the food
allotted to the governor, because the demands
were heavy on these people.
19Remember me with favor, O my God, for
all I have done for these people.

Further Opposition to the Rebuilding

6 When word came to Sanballat, Tobiah,
Geshem the Arab and the rest of our enemies that I had rebuilt the wall and not
a gap was left in it—though up to that time I
had not set the doors in the gates— 2Sanballat
and Geshem sent me this message: "Come, let
us meet together in one of the villages[d] on the
plain of Ono."
But they were scheming to harm me; 3so
I sent messengers to them with this reply: "I

[a] *23* The meaning of the Hebrew for this clause is uncertain. [b] *15* That is, about 1 pound (about 0.5 kilogram) [c] *16* Most Hebrew manuscripts; some Hebrew manuscripts, Septuagint, Vulgate and Syriac *I* [d] *2* Or *in Kephirim*

am carrying on a great project and cannot go down. Why should the work stop while I leave it and go down to you?" 4Four times they sent me the same message, and each time I gave them the same answer.

5Then, the fifth time, Sanballat sent his aide to me with the same message, and in his hand was an unsealed letter 6in which was written:

> "It is reported among the nations—and Geshem[a] says it is true—that you and the Jews are plotting to revolt, and therefore you are building the wall. Moreover, according to these reports you are about to become their king 7and have even appointed prophets to make this proclamation about you in Jerusalem: 'There is a king in Judah!' Now this report will get back to the king; so come, let us confer together."

8I sent him this reply: "Nothing like what you are saying is happening; you are just making it up out of your head."

9They were all trying to frighten us, thinking, "Their hands will get too weak for the work, and it will not be completed."

⌞But I prayed,⌟ "Now strengthen my hands."

10One day I went to the house of Shemaiah son of Delaiah, the son of Mehetabel, who was shut in at his home. He said, "Let us meet in the house of God, inside the temple, and let us close the temple doors, because men are coming to kill you—by night they are coming to kill you."

11But I said, "Should a man like me run away? Or should one like me go into the temple to save his life? I will not go!" 12I realized that God had not sent him, but that he had prophesied against me because Tobiah and Sanballat had hired him. 13He had been hired to intimidate me so that I would commit a sin by doing this, and then they would give me a bad name to discredit me.

14Remember Tobiah and Sanballat, O my God, because of what they have done; remember also the prophetess Noadiah and the rest of the prophets who have been trying to intimidate me.

The Completion of the Wall

15So the wall was completed on the twenty-fifth of Elul, in fifty-two days. 16When all our enemies heard about this, all the surrounding nations were afraid and lost their self-confidence, because they realized that this work had been done with the help of our God.

17Also, in those days the nobles of Judah were sending many letters to Tobiah, and replies from Tobiah kept coming to them. 18For many in Judah were under oath to him, since he was son-in-law to Shecaniah son of Arah, and his son Jehohanan had married the daughter of Meshullam son of Berekiah. 19Moreover, they kept reporting to me his good deeds and then telling him what I said. And Tobiah sent letters to intimidate me.

7 After the wall had been rebuilt and I had set the doors in place, the gatekeepers and the singers and the Levites were appointed. 2I put in charge of Jerusalem my brother Hanani, along with[b] Hananiah the commander of the citadel, because he was a man of integrity and feared God more than most men do. 3I said to them, "The gates of Jerusalem are not to be opened until the sun is hot. While the gatekeepers are still on duty, have them shut the doors and bar them. Also appoint residents of Jerusalem as guards, some at their posts and some near their own houses."

The List of the Exiles Who Returned

4Now the city was large and spacious, but there were few people in it, and the houses had not yet been rebuilt. 5So my God put it into my heart to assemble the nobles, the officials and the common people for registration by families. I found the genealogical record of those who had been the first to return. This is what I found written there:

> 6These are the people of the province who came up from the captivity of the exiles whom Nebuchadnezzar king of Babylon had taken captive (they returned to Jerusalem and Judah, each to his own town, 7in company with Zerubbabel, Jeshua, Nehemiah, Azariah, Raamiah, Nahamani, Mordecai, Bilshan, Mispereth, Bigvai, Nehum and Baanah):

The list of the men of Israel:

8the descendants of Parosh	2,172
9of Shephatiah	372
10of Arah	652
11of Pahath-Moab (through the line of Jeshua and Joab)	2,818
12of Elam	1,254
13of Zattu	845
14of Zaccai	760

[a] 6 Hebrew *Gashmu,* a variant of *Geshem* [b] 2 Or *Hanani, that is,*

15 of Binnui 648
16 of Bebai 628
17 of Azgad 2,322
18 of Adonikam 667
19 of Bigvai 2,067
20 of Adin 655
21 of Ater (through Hezekiah) 98
22 of Hashum 328
23 of Bezai 324
24 of Hariph 112
25 of Gibeon 95

26 the men of Bethlehem and
Netophah 188
27 of Anathoth 128
28 of Beth Azmaveth 42
29 of Kiriath Jearim, Kephirah
and Beeroth 743
30 of Ramah and Geba 621
31 of Micmash 122
32 of Bethel and Ai 123
33 of the other Nebo 52
34 of the other Elam 1,254
35 of Harim 320
36 of Jericho 345
37 of Lod, Hadid and Ono 721
38 of Senaah 3,930

39 The priests:

the descendants of Jedaiah
(through the family of
Jeshua) 973
40 of Immer 1,052
41 of Pashhur 1,247
42 of Harim 1,017

43 The Levites:
the descendants of Jeshua (through
Kadmiel through the line of
Hodaviah) 74

44 The singers:
the descendants of Asaph 148

45 The gatekeepers:

the descendants of
Shallum, Ater, Talmon, Akkub,
Hatita and Shobai 138

46 The temple servants:

the descendants of
Ziha, Hasupha, Tabbaoth,
47 Keros, Sia, Padon,
48 Lebana, Hagaba, Shalmai,
49 Hanan, Giddel, Gahar,
50 Reaiah, Rezin, Nekoda,
51 Gazzam, Uzza, Paseah,
52 Besai, Meunim, Nephusim,
53 Bakbuk, Hakupha, Harhur,
54 Bazluth, Mehida, Harsha,
55 Barkos, Sisera, Temah,
56 Neziah and Hatipha

57 The descendants of the servants of Solomon:

the descendants of
Sotai, Sophereth, Perida,
58 Jaala, Darkon, Giddel,
59 Shephatiah, Hattil,
Pokereth-Hazzebaim and Amon

60 The temple servants and the
descendants of the servants
of Solomon 392

61 The following came up from the
towns of Tel Melah, Tel Harsha, Kerub,
Addon and Immer, but they could not
show that their families were descended
from Israel:

62 the descendants of
Delaiah, Tobiah and Nekoda 642

63 And from among the priests:

the descendants of
Hobaiah, Hakkoz and Barzillai (a
man who had married a daughter
of Barzillai the Gileadite and was
called by that name).

64 These searched for their family records, but they could not find them and so
were excluded from the priesthood as unclean. 65 The governor, therefore, ordered
them not to eat any of the most sacred
food until there should be a priest ministering with the Urim and Thummim.

66 The whole company numbered
42,360, 67 besides their 7,337 menservants and maidservants; and they also
had 245 men and women singers. 68 There
were 736 horses, 245 mules,[a] 69 435 camels and 6,720 donkeys.

70 Some of the heads of the families
contributed to the work. The governor
gave to the treasury 1,000 drachmas[b]
of gold, 50 bowls and 530 garments for
priests. 71 Some of the heads of the families gave to the treasury for the work
20,000 drachmas[c] of gold and 2,200

[a] *68* Some Hebrew manuscripts (see also Ezra 2:66); most Hebrew manuscripts do not have this verse. [b] *70* That is, about 19 pounds (about 8.5 kilograms) [c] *71* That is, about 375 pounds (about 170 kilograms); also in verse 72

minas[a] of silver. 72The total given by the
rest of the people was 20,000 drachmas
of gold, 2,000 minas[b] of silver and 67
garments for priests.
73The priests, the Levites, the gatekeepers, the singers and the temple servants,
along with certain of the people and the
rest of the Israelites, settled in their own
towns.

Ezra Reads the Law

8 When the seventh month came and the Israelites had settled in their towns, 1all the
people assembled as one man in the square
before the Water Gate. They told Ezra the
scribe to bring out the Book of the Law of
Moses, which the LORD had commanded for
Israel.
2So on the first day of the seventh month
Ezra the priest brought the Law before the assembly, which was made up of men and wom-
en and all who were able to understand. 3He
read it aloud from daybreak till noon as he
faced the square before the Water Gate in the
presence of the men, women and others who
could understand. And all the people listened
attentively to the Book of the Law.
4Ezra the scribe stood on a high wooden
platform built for the occasion. Beside him
on his right stood Mattithiah, Shema, Anaiah,
Uriah, Hilkiah and Maaseiah; and on his left
were Pedaiah, Mishael, Malkijah, Hashum,
Hashbaddanah, Zechariah and Meshullam.
5Ezra opened the book. All the people could
see him because he was standing above them;
and as he opened it, the people all stood up.
6Ezra praised the LORD, the great God; and
all the people lifted their hands and responded, "Amen! Amen!" Then they bowed down
and worshiped the LORD with their faces to
the ground.
7The Levites—Jeshua, Bani, Sherebiah, Jamin, Akkub, Shabbethai, Hodiah, Maaseiah,
Kelita, Azariah, Jozabad, Hanan and Pelaiah—instructed the people in the Law while
the people were standing there. 8They read
from the Book of the Law of God, making it
clear[c] and giving the meaning so that the people could understand what was being read.
9Then Nehemiah the governor, Ezra the
priest and scribe, and the Levites who were
instructing the people said to them all, "This
day is sacred to the LORD your God. Do not
mourn or weep." For all the people had been
weeping as they listened to the words of the
Law.
10Nehemiah said, "Go and enjoy choice
food and sweet drinks, and send some to those
who have nothing prepared. This day is sacred
to our Lord. Do not grieve, for the joy of the
LORD is your strength."
11The Levites calmed all the people, saying, "Be still, for this is a sacred day. Do not
grieve."
12Then all the people went away to eat and
drink, to send portions of food and to celebrate with great joy, because they now understood the words that had been made known
to them.
13On the second day of the month, the
heads of all the families, along with the priests
and the Levites, gathered around Ezra the
scribe to give attention to the words of the
Law. 14They found written in the Law, which
the LORD had commanded through Moses,
that the Israelites were to live in booths during the feast of the seventh month 15and that
they should proclaim this word and spread
it throughout their towns and in Jerusalem:
"Go out into the hill country and bring back
branches from olive and wild olive trees, and
from myrtles, palms and shade trees, to make
booths"—as it is written.[d]
16So the people went out and brought back
branches and built themselves booths on their
own roofs, in their courtyards, in the courts of
the house of God and in the square by the Water Gate and the one by the Gate of Ephraim.
17The whole company that had returned from
exile built booths and lived in them. From the
days of Joshua son of Nun until that day, the
Israelites had not celebrated it like this. And
their joy was very great.
18Day after day, from the first day to the
last, Ezra read from the Book of the Law of
God. They celebrated the feast for seven days,
and on the eighth day, in accordance with the
regulation, there was an assembly.

The Israelites Confess Their Sins

9 On the twenty-fourth day of the same
month, the Israelites gathered together,
fasting and wearing sackcloth and having
dust on their heads. 2Those of Israelite descent
had separated themselves from all foreigners. They stood in their places and confessed
their sins and the wickedness of their fathers.
3They stood where they were and read from
the Book of the Law of the LORD their God

---

[a] *71* That is, about 1 1/3 tons (about 1.2 metric tons) [b] *72* That is, about 1 1/4 tons (about 1.1 metric tons) [c] *8* Or *God, translating it*
[d] *15* See Lev. 23:37-40.

THURSDAY
READ NEHEMIAH 9:1–37

THE HEALING POWER OF REPENTANCE

> **On the twenty-fourth day of the same month, the Israelites gathered together, fasting and wearing sackcloth and having dust on their heads. Those of Israelite descent had separated themselves from all foreigners. They stood in their places and confessed their sins and the wickedness of their fathers.**
>
> — NEHEMIAH 9:1–2

In his book The Ragamuffin Gospel (Multnomah, 2000), Brennan Manning recalls the treatment program he went through to deal with his addiction to alcohol. The therapy included group sessions in which fellow strugglers sat in a circle and told how drinking was affecting their lives. One businessman, however, had come to the center under legal compulsion and didn't believe he had a problem.

The counselors had ways to deal with such denial. In the room was a small table with a speakerphone. A call was placed to the bartender who serviced the businessman's habit. "He drinks like a fish," the bartender said. "He's my best customer."

Embarrassed but not knuckling under, the man protested that he was always in control and had never hurt anyone. But in the next phone call, the man's wife told the group about the night her husband took their nine-year-old daughter to buy a pair of shoes. On the way home he stopped for a drink. He left the car running to keep out the subfreezing temperatures and locked the doors. "I'll be right back," he told his daughter.

Eight hours later he emerged to find the car's engine stilled, its windows frosted over, and its doors frozen shut. His daughter was comatose. Doctors had to amputate two of her fingers. Before his wife finished recounting the story, the man slid from his chair, whimpering. This, according to Manning, was the beginning of the man's healing.

Repentance, according to the Bible, is a change of heart, a turning of the mind. Ezra the priest led his people in Jerusalem to this sacred place. They had come through a tough time in their relationship with God and with one another. Until the Israelites stopped, reflected, confessed their sin, repented and changed their ways, they would be dragging their sins along with them wherever they went.

Marriages also need to come to this sacred place of repentance. Periodically, couples need to pull off the superhighway of busyness to examine themselves and determine where they're going. When people live so closely together, they can't help but hurt one another occasionally. Words are spoken in anger, promises are broken, tenderness is violated. Furthermore, the pace of married life, after the initial rush of the courtship and wedding, leads easily to the development of patterns of dysfunction and deception, resulting in suspicion-edged questions, such as, "What do you mean, where was I last night? Are you checking up on me?" Or "Were you really at the mall all that time? What did you buy?"

Each wedding anniversary ought to be a time of celebration. But it would also be beneficial to make that day an occasion for review, confession, repentance and forgiveness. Such healing exercises might be a prelude to the best moments of intimacy each year.

—WAYNE BROUWER

let's talk

- ✦ How can we lovingly help each other to be honest about personal failings?
- ✦ When does a demand for repentance become browbeating and nagging? How do we find a balance?
- ✦ When have we found healing through confession and repentance? How did we change our ways?

FOR YOUR NEXT DEVOTIONAL READING, TURN TO PAGE 529.

for a quarter of the day, and spent another
quarter in confession and in worshiping the
LORD their God. 4Standing on the stairs were
the Levites—Jeshua, Bani, Kadmiel, Shebaniah, Bunni, Sherebiah, Bani and Kenani—who
called with loud voices to the LORD their God.
5And the Levites—Jeshua, Kadmiel, Bani,
Hashabneiah, Sherebiah, Hodiah, Shebaniah
and Pethahiah—said: "Stand up and praise
the LORD your God, who is from everlasting
to everlasting.[a]"

"Blessed be your glorious name, and
may it be exalted above all blessing and
praise. 6You alone are the LORD. You
made the heavens, even the highest heavens, and all their starry host, the earth
and all that is on it, the seas and all that
is in them. You give life to everything,
and the multitudes of heaven worship
you.

7"You are the LORD God, who chose
Abram and brought him out of Ur of the
Chaldeans and named him Abraham.
8You found his heart faithful to you, and
you made a covenant with him to give to
his descendants the land of the Canaanites, Hittites, Amorites, Perizzites, Jebusites and Girgashites. You have kept your
promise because you are righteous.

9"You saw the suffering of our forefathers in Egypt; you heard their cry at the
Red Sea.[b] 10You sent miraculous signs
and wonders against Pharaoh, against
all his officials and all the people of his
land, for you knew how arrogantly the
Egyptians treated them. You made a
name for yourself, which remains to this
day. 11You divided the sea before them,
so that they passed through it on dry
ground, but you hurled their pursuers
into the depths, like a stone into mighty
waters. 12By day you led them with a pillar of cloud, and by night with a pillar of
fire to give them light on the way they
were to take.

13"You came down on Mount Sinai;
you spoke to them from heaven. You gave
them regulations and laws that are just
and right, and decrees and commands
that are good. 14You made known to
them your holy Sabbath and gave them
commands, decrees and laws through
your servant Moses. 15In their hunger
you gave them bread from heaven and in
their thirst you brought them water from
the rock; you told them to go in and take
possession of the land you had sworn
with uplifted hand to give them.

16"But they, our forefathers, became
arrogant and stiff-necked, and did not
obey your commands. 17They refused to
listen and failed to remember the miracles you performed among them. They
became stiff-necked and in their rebellion
appointed a leader in order to return to
their slavery. But you are a forgiving God,
gracious and compassionate, slow to anger and abounding in love. Therefore you
did not desert them, 18even when they
cast for themselves an image of a calf and
said, 'This is your god, who brought you
up out of Egypt,' or when they committed awful blasphemies.

19"Because of your great compassion
you did not abandon them in the desert.
By day the pillar of cloud did not cease to
guide them on their path, nor the pillar
of fire by night to shine on the way they
were to take. 20You gave your good Spirit
to instruct them. You did not withhold
your manna from their mouths, and you
gave them water for their thirst. 21For
forty years you sustained them in the desert; they lacked nothing, their clothes did
not wear out nor did their feet become
swollen.

22"You gave them kingdoms and nations, allotting to them even the remotest
frontiers. They took over the country of
Sihon[c] king of Heshbon and the country
of Og king of Bashan. 23You made their
sons as numerous as the stars in the sky,
and you brought them into the land that
you told their fathers to enter and possess. 24Their sons went in and took possession of the land. You subdued before
them the Canaanites, who lived in the
land; you handed the Canaanites over
to them, along with their kings and the
peoples of the land, to deal with them
as they pleased. 25They captured fortified
cities and fertile land; they took possession of houses filled with all kinds of
good things, wells already dug, vineyards,
olive groves and fruit trees in abundance.
They ate to the full and were well-nour-
ished; they reveled in your great goodness.

26"But they were disobedient and re-

---

[a] *5* Or *God for ever and ever* [b] *9* Hebrew *Yam Suph*; that is, Sea of Reeds [c] *22* One Hebrew manuscript and Septuagint; most Hebrew manuscripts *Sihon, that is, the country of the*

belled against you; they put your law
behind their backs. They killed your
prophets, who had admonished them
in order to turn them back to you; they
committed awful blasphemies. 27So you
handed them over to their enemies, who
oppressed them. But when they were oppressed they cried out to you. From heav-
en you heard them, and in your great
compassion you gave them deliverers,
who rescued them from the hand of their
enemies.

28"But as soon as they were at rest,
they again did what was evil in your
sight. Then you abandoned them to the
hand of their enemies so that they ruled
over them. And when they cried out to
you again, you heard from heaven, and
in your compassion you delivered them
time after time.

29"You warned them to return to your
law, but they became arrogant and disobeyed your commands. They sinned
against your ordinances, by which a man
will live if he obeys them. Stubbornly
they turned their backs on you, became
stiff-necked and refused to listen. 30For
many years you were patient with them.
By your Spirit you admonished them
through your prophets. Yet they paid no
attention, so you handed them over to
the neighboring peoples. 31But in your
great mercy you did not put an end to
them or abandon them, for you are a gracious and merciful God.

32"Now therefore, O our God, the
great, mighty and awesome God, who
keeps his covenant of love, do not let all
this hardship seem trifling in your eyes—
the hardship that has come upon us, upon
our kings and leaders, upon our priests
and prophets, upon our fathers and all
your people, from the days of the kings
of Assyria until today. 33In all that has
happened to us, you have been just; you
have acted faithfully, while we did wrong.
34Our kings, our leaders, our priests and
our fathers did not follow your law; they
did not pay attention to your commands
or the warnings you gave them. 35Even
while they were in their kingdom, enjoying your great goodness to them in the
spacious and fertile land you gave them,
they did not serve you or turn from their
evil ways.

36"But see, we are slaves today, slaves
in the land you gave our forefathers so
they could eat its fruit and the other good
things it produces. 37Because of our sins,
its abundant harvest goes to the kings
you have placed over us. They rule over
our bodies and our cattle as they please.
We are in great distress.

The Agreement of the People

38"In view of all this, we are making a binding agreement, putting it in writing, and our
leaders, our Levites and our priests are affixing
their seals to it."

10 Those who sealed it were:

Nehemiah the governor, the son of Hacaliah.

Zedekiah, 2Seraiah, Azariah, Jeremiah,
3Pashhur, Amariah, Malkijah,
4Hattush, Shebaniah, Malluch,
5Harim, Meremoth, Obadiah,
6Daniel, Ginnethon, Baruch,
7Meshullam, Abijah, Mijamin,
8Maaziah, Bilgai and Shemaiah.
These were the priests.

9The Levites:

Jeshua son of Azaniah, Binnui of the sons of Henadad, Kadmiel,
10and their associates: Shebaniah,
Hodiah, Kelita, Pelaiah, Hanan,
11Mica, Rehob, Hashabiah,
12Zaccur, Sherebiah, Shebaniah,
13Hodiah, Bani and Beninu.

14The leaders of the people:

Parosh, Pahath-Moab, Elam, Zattu, Bani,
15Bunni, Azgad, Bebai,
16Adonijah, Bigvai, Adin,
17Ater, Hezekiah, Azzur,
18Hodiah, Hashum, Bezai,
19Hariph, Anathoth, Nebai,
20Magpiash, Meshullam, Hezir,
21Meshezabel, Zadok, Jaddua,
22Pelatiah, Hanan, Anaiah,
23Hoshea, Hananiah, Hasshub,
24Hallohesh, Pilha, Shobek,
25Rehum, Hashabnah, Maaseiah,
26Ahiah, Hanan, Anan,
27Malluch, Harim and Baanah.

28"The rest of the people—priests,
Levites, gatekeepers, singers, temple servants and all who separated themselves
from the neighboring peoples for the
sake of the Law of God, together with

their wives and all their sons and daughters who are able to understand— 29all
these now join their brothers the nobles, and bind themselves with a curse
and an oath to follow the Law of God
given through Moses the servant of God
and to obey carefully all the commands,
regulations and decrees of the LORD our
Lord.

30"We promise not to give our daughters in marriage to the peoples around us
or take their daughters for our sons.

31"When the neighboring peoples
bring merchandise or grain to sell on the
Sabbath, we will not buy from them on
the Sabbath or on any holy day. Every
seventh year we will forgo working the
land and will cancel all debts.

32"We assume the responsibility for
carrying out the commands to give a
third of a shekel[a] each year for the service
of the house of our God: 33for the bread
set out on the table; for the regular grain
offerings and burnt offerings; for the offerings on the Sabbaths, New Moon festivals and appointed feasts; for the holy
offerings; for sin offerings to make atonement for Israel; and for all the duties of
the house of our God.

34"We—the priests, the Levites and
the people—have cast lots to determine
when each of our families is to bring to
the house of our God at set times each
year a contribution of wood to burn on
the altar of the LORD our God, as it is
written in the Law.

35"We also assume responsibility for
bringing to the house of the LORD each
year the firstfruits of our crops and of every fruit tree.

36"As it is also written in the Law, we
will bring the firstborn of our sons and of
our cattle, of our herds and of our flocks
to the house of our God, to the priests
ministering there.

37"Moreover, we will bring to the
storerooms of the house of our God, to
the priests, the first of our ground meal,
of our ⌞grain⌟ offerings, of the fruit of all
our trees and of our new wine and oil.
And we will bring a tithe of our crops to
the Levites, for it is the Levites who collect the tithes in all the towns where we
work. 38A priest descended from Aaron
is to accompany the Levites when they
receive the tithes, and the Levites are to
bring a tenth of the tithes up to the house
of our God, to the storerooms of the treasury. 39The people of Israel, including the
Levites, are to bring their contributions
of grain, new wine and oil to the storerooms where the articles for the sanctuary are kept and where the ministering
priests, the gatekeepers and the singers
stay.

"We will not neglect the house of our
God."

The New Residents of Jerusalem

11 Now the leaders of the people settled in
Jerusalem, and the rest of the people cast
lots to bring one out of every ten to live
in Jerusalem, the holy city, while the remaining nine were to stay in their own towns. 2The
people commended all the men who volunteered to live in Jerusalem.

3These are the provincial leaders who settled in Jerusalem (now some Israelites, priests,
Levites, temple servants and descendants of
Solomon's servants lived in the towns of Judah, each on his own property in the various
towns, 4while other people from both Judah
and Benjamin lived in Jerusalem):

From the descendants of Judah:

Athaiah son of Uzziah, the son of Zechariah, the son of Amariah, the son of
Shephatiah, the son of Mahalalel, a descendant of Perez; 5and Maaseiah son of
Baruch, the son of Col-Hozeh, the son
of Hazaiah, the son of Adaiah, the son of
Joiarib, the son of Zechariah, a descendant of Shelah. 6The descendants of Perez
who lived in Jerusalem totaled 468 able
men.

7From the descendants of Benjamin:

Sallu son of Meshullam, the son of Joed,
the son of Pedaiah, the son of Kolaiah,
the son of Maaseiah, the son of Ithiel,
the son of Jeshaiah, 8and his followers,
Gabbai and Sallai—928 men. 9Joel son
of Zicri was their chief officer, and Judah
son of Hassenuah was over the Second
District of the city.

10From the priests:

Jedaiah; the son of Joiarib; Jakin; 11Sera-
iah son of Hilkiah, the son of Meshullam, the son of Zadok, the son of Mera-

a 32 That is, about 1/8 ounce (about 4 grams)

ioth, the son of Ahitub, supervisor in the house of God, [12]and their associates, who carried on work for the temple—822 men; Adaiah son of Jeroham, the son of Pelaliah, the son of Amzi, the son of Zechariah, the son of Pashhur, the son of Malkijah, [13]and his associates, who were heads of families—242 men; Amashsai son of Azarel, the son of Ahzai, the son of Meshillemoth, the son of Immer, [14]and his[a] associates, who were able men—128. Their chief officer was Zabdiel son of Haggedolim.

[15]From the Levites:

Shemaiah son of Hasshub, the son of Azrikam, the son of Hashabiah, the son of Bunni; [16]Shabbethai and Jozabad, two of the heads of the Levites, who had charge of the outside work of the house of God; [17]Mattaniah son of Mica, the son of Zabdi, the son of Asaph, the director who led in thanksgiving and prayer; Bakbukiah, second among his associates; and Abda son of Shammua, the son of Galal, the son of Jeduthun. [18]The Levites in the holy city totaled 284.

[19]The gatekeepers:

Akkub, Talmon and their associates, who kept watch at the gates—172 men.

[20]The rest of the Israelites, with the priests and Levites, were in all the towns of Judah, each on his ancestral property.

[21]The temple servants lived on the hill of Ophel, and Ziha and Gishpa were in charge of them.

[22]The chief officer of the Levites in Jerusalem was Uzzi son of Bani, the son of Hashabiah, the son of Mattaniah, the son of Mica. Uzzi was one of Asaph's descendants, who were the singers responsible for the service of the house of God. [23]The singers were under the king's orders, which regulated their daily activity.

[24]Pethahiah son of Meshezabel, one of the descendants of Zerah son of Judah, was the king's agent in all affairs relating to the people.

[25]As for the villages with their fields, some of the people of Judah lived in Kiriath Arba and its surrounding settlements, in Dibon and its settlements, in Jekabzeel and its villages, [26]in Jeshua, in Moladah, in Beth Pelet, [27]in Hazar Shual, in Beersheba and its settlements, [28]in Ziklag, in Meconah and its settlements, [29]in En Rimmon, in Zorah, in Jarmuth, [30]Zanoah, Adullam and their villages, in Lachish and its fields, and in Azekah and its settlements. So they were living all the way from Beersheba to the Valley of Hinnom.

[31]The descendants of the Benjamites from Geba lived in Micmash, Aija, Bethel and its settlements, [32]in Anathoth, Nob and Ananiah, [33]in Hazor, Ramah and Gittaim, [34]in Hadid, Zeboim and Neballat, [35]in Lod and Ono, and in the Valley of the Craftsmen.

[36]Some of the divisions of the Levites of Judah settled in Benjamin.

Priests and Levites

12 These were the priests and Levites who returned with Zerubbabel son of Shealtiel and with Jeshua:

Seraiah, Jeremiah, Ezra,
[2]Amariah, Malluch, Hattush,
[3]Shecaniah, Rehum, Meremoth,
[4]Iddo, Ginnethon,[b] Abijah,
[5]Mijamin,[c] Moadiah, Bilgah,
[6]Shemaiah, Joiarib, Jedaiah,
[7]Sallu, Amok, Hilkiah and Jedaiah.

These were the leaders of the priests and their associates in the days of Jeshua.

[8]The Levites were Jeshua, Binnui, Kadmiel, Sherebiah, Judah, and also Mattaniah, who, together with his associates, was in charge of the songs of thanksgiving. [9]Bakbukiah and Unni, their associates, stood opposite them in the services.

[10]Jeshua was the father of Joiakim, Joiakim the father of Eliashib, Eliashib the father of Joiada, [11]Joiada the father of Jonathan, and Jonathan the father of Jaddua.

[12]In the days of Joiakim, these were the heads of the priestly families:

of Seraiah's family, Meraiah;
of Jeremiah's, Hananiah;
[13]of Ezra's, Meshullam;
of Amariah's, Jehohanan;
[14]of Malluch's, Jonathan;
of Shecaniah's,[d] Joseph;
[15]of Harim's, Adna;
of Meremoth's,[e] Helkai;
[16]of Iddo's, Zechariah;
of Ginnethon's, Meshullam;
[17]of Abijah's, Zicri;

---

[a] *14* Most Septuagint manuscripts; Hebrew *their* [b] *4* Many Hebrew manuscripts and Vulgate (see also Neh. 12:16); most Hebrew manuscripts *Ginnethoi* [c] *5* A variant of *Miniamin* [d] *14* Very many Hebrew manuscripts, some Septuagint manuscripts and Syriac (see also Neh. 12:3); most Hebrew manuscripts *Shebaniah's* [e] *15* Some Septuagint manuscripts (see also Neh. 12:3); Hebrew *Meraioth's*

of Miniamin's and of Moadiah's, Piltai;
18 of Bilgah's, Shammua;
of Shemaiah's, Jehonathan;
19 of Joiarib's, Mattenai;
of Jedaiah's, Uzzi;
20 of Sallu's, Kallai;
of Amok's, Eber;
21 of Hilkiah's, Hashabiah;
of Jedaiah's, Nethanel.

22 The family heads of the Levites in the
days of Eliashib, Joiada, Johanan and Jaddua,
as well as those of the priests, were recorded
in the reign of Darius the Persian. 23 The family heads among the descendants of Levi up
to the time of Johanan son of Eliashib were
recorded in the book of the annals. 24 And the
leaders of the Levites were Hashabiah, Sherebiah, Jeshua son of Kadmiel, and their associates, who stood opposite them to give praise
and thanksgiving, one section responding to
the other, as prescribed by David the man of
God.

25 Mattaniah, Bakbukiah, Obadiah, Meshullam, Talmon and Akkub were gatekeepers who guarded the storerooms at the gates.
26 They served in the days of Joiakim son of
Jeshua, the son of Jozadak, and in the days of
Nehemiah the governor and of Ezra the priest
and scribe.

Dedication of the Wall of Jerusalem

27 At the dedication of the wall of Jerusalem, the Levites were sought out from where
they lived and were brought to Jerusalem to
celebrate joyfully the dedication with songs
of thanksgiving and with the music of cymbals, harps and lyres. 28 The singers also were
brought together from the region around Jerusalem—from the villages of the Netophathites, 29 from Beth Gilgal, and from the area
of Geba and Azmaveth, for the singers had
built villages for themselves around Jerusalem.
30 When the priests and Levites had purified
themselves ceremonially, they purified the
people, the gates and the wall.

31 I had the leaders of Judah go up on top[a]
of the wall. I also assigned two large choirs to
give thanks. One was to proceed on top[b] of
the wall to the right, toward the Dung Gate.
32 Hoshaiah and half the leaders of Judah followed them, 33 along with Azariah, Ezra, Meshullam, 34 Judah, Benjamin, Shemaiah, Jeremiah, 35 as well as some priests with trumpets,
and also Zechariah son of Jonathan, the son
of Shemaiah, the son of Mattaniah, the son of
Micaiah, the son of Zaccur, the son of Asaph,
36 and his associates—Shemaiah, Azarel, Mil-
alai, Gilalai, Maai, Nethanel, Judah and Hanani—with musical instruments ⌊prescribed
by⌋ David the man of God. Ezra the scribe led
the procession. 37 At the Fountain Gate they
continued directly up the steps of the City of
David on the ascent to the wall and passed
above the house of David to the Water Gate
on the east.

38 The second choir proceeded in the opposite direction. I followed them on top[c] of the
wall, together with half the people—past the
Tower of the Ovens to the Broad Wall, 39 over
the Gate of Ephraim, the Jeshanah[d] Gate, the
Fish Gate, the Tower of Hananel and the Tower of the Hundred, as far as the Sheep Gate. At
the Gate of the Guard they stopped.

40 The two choirs that gave thanks then
took their places in the house of God; so did
I, together with half the officials, 41 as well as
the priests—Eliakim, Maaseiah, Miniamin,
Micaiah, Elioenai, Zechariah and Hananiah
with their trumpets— 42 and also Maaseiah,
Shemaiah, Eleazar, Uzzi, Jehohanan, Malkijah, Elam and Ezer. The choirs sang under
the direction of Jezrahiah. 43 And on that day
they offered great sacrifices, rejoicing because
God had given them great joy. The women
and children also rejoiced. The sound of
rejoicing in Jerusalem could be heard far
away.

44 At that time men were appointed to be
in charge of the storerooms for the contributions, firstfruits and tithes. From the fields
around the towns they were to bring into the
storerooms the portions required by the Law
for the priests and the Levites, for Judah was
pleased with the ministering priests and Levites. 45 They performed the service of their
God and the service of purification, as did
also the singers and gatekeepers, according
to the commands of David and his son Solomon. 46 For long ago, in the days of David and
Asaph, there had been directors for the singers
and for the songs of praise and thanksgiving
to God. 47 So in the days of Zerubbabel and
of Nehemiah, all Israel contributed the daily
portions for the singers and gatekeepers. They
also set aside the portion for the other Levites,
and the Levites set aside the portion for the
descendants of Aaron.

---

[a] 31 Or *go alongside* [b] 31 Or *proceed alongside* [c] 38 Or *them alongside* [d] 39 Or *Old*

Nehemiah's Final Reforms

13 On that day the Book of Moses was
read aloud in the hearing of the people
and there it was found written that no
Ammonite or Moabite should ever be admitted into the assembly of God, [2]because they
had not met the Israelites with food and water
but had hired Balaam to call a curse down on
them. (Our God, however, turned the curse
into a blessing.) [3]When the people heard this
law, they excluded from Israel all who were of
foreign descent.

[4]Before this, Eliashib the priest had been
put in charge of the storerooms of the house of
our God. He was closely associated with Tobiah, [5]and he had provided him with a large
room formerly used to store the grain offerings
and incense and temple articles, and also the
tithes of grain, new wine and oil prescribed for
the Levites, singers and gatekeepers, as well as
the contributions for the priests.

[6]But while all this was going on, I was not
in Jerusalem, for in the thirty-second year of
Artaxerxes king of Babylon I had returned
to the king. Some time later I asked his permission [7]and came back to Jerusalem. Here I
learned about the evil thing Eliashib had done
in providing Tobiah a room in the courts of
the house of God. [8]I was greatly displeased
and threw all Tobiah's household goods out of
the room. [9]I gave orders to purify the rooms,
and then I put back into them the equipment
of the house of God, with the grain offerings
and the incense.

[10]I also learned that the portions assigned
to the Levites had not been given to them, and
that all the Levites and singers responsible for
the service had gone back to their own fields.
[11]So I rebuked the officials and asked them,
"Why is the house of God neglected?" Then
I called them together and stationed them at
their posts.

[12]All Judah brought the tithes of grain,
new wine and oil into the storerooms. [13]I
put Shelemiah the priest, Zadok the scribe,
and a Levite named Pedaiah in charge of the
storerooms and made Hanan son of Zaccur,
the son of Mattaniah, their assistant, because
these men were considered trustworthy. They
were made responsible for distributing the
supplies to their brothers.

[14]Remember me for this, O my God, and
do not blot out what I have so faithfully done
for the house of my God and its services.

[15]In those days I saw men in Judah treading
winepresses on the Sabbath and bringing in
grain and loading it on donkeys, together with
wine, grapes, figs and all other kinds of loads.
And they were bringing all this into Jerusalem on the Sabbath. Therefore I warned them
against selling food on that day. [16]Men from
Tyre who lived in Jerusalem were bringing in
fish and all kinds of merchandise and selling
them in Jerusalem on the Sabbath to the people of Judah. [17]I rebuked the nobles of Judah
and said to them, "What is this wicked thing
you are doing—desecrating the Sabbath day?
[18]Didn't your forefathers do the same things,
so that our God brought all this calamity upon
us and upon this city? Now you are stirring up
more wrath against Israel by desecrating the
Sabbath."

[19]When evening shadows fell on the gates
of Jerusalem before the Sabbath, I ordered
the doors to be shut and not opened until
the Sabbath was over. I stationed some of my
own men at the gates so that no load could
be brought in on the Sabbath day. [20]Once or
twice the merchants and sellers of all kinds of
goods spent the night outside Jerusalem. [21]But
I warned them and said, "Why do you spend
the night by the wall? If you do this again,
I will lay hands on you." From that time on
they no longer came on the Sabbath. [22]Then
I commanded the Levites to purify themselves
and go and guard the gates in order to keep
the Sabbath day holy.

Remember me for this also, O my God,
and show mercy to me according to your great
love.

[23]Moreover, in those days I saw men of Judah who had married women from Ashdod,
Ammon and Moab. [24]Half of their children
spoke the language of Ashdod or the language
of one of the other peoples, and did not know
how to speak the language of Judah. [25]I rebuked them and called curses down on them.
I beat some of the men and pulled out their
hair. I made them take an oath in God's name
and said: "You are not to give your daughters
in marriage to their sons, nor are you to take
their daughters in marriage for your sons or
for yourselves. [26]Was it not because of marriages like these that Solomon king of Israel
sinned? Among the many nations there was
no king like him. He was loved by his God,
and God made him king over all Israel, but
even he was led into sin by foreign women.
[27]Must we hear now that you too are doing
all this terrible wickedness and are being
unfaithful to our God by marrying foreign
women?"

28One of the sons of Joiada son of Eliashib the high priest was son-in-law to Sanballat the Horonite. And I drove him away from me.

29Remember them, O my God, because they defiled the priestly office and the covenant of the priesthood and of the Levites.

30So I purified the priests and the Levites of everything foreign, and assigned them duties, each to his own task. 31I also made provision for contributions of wood at designated times, and for the firstfruits.

Remember me with favor, O my God.

ESTHER

Esther

QUICK FACTS

AUTHOR Unknown

AUDIENCE All Israel

DATE Sometime after the events described in the book, about 460 B.C.

SETTING Susa, one of the capitals of the Persian Empire, during a turbulent time for the Jews

The book of Esther tells the story of the near annihilation of the Jewish people. Haman, a Persian official, hated the Jews because Mordecai, a Jew, refused to kneel down and pay honor to him. So Haman persuaded King Xerxes to sign an order to kill all of Mordecai's people.

Only Mordecai's cousin, Esther, was in a position to counteract that order. Esther had become queen after the king's wife Vashti was deposed. Still, Esther feared the consequences of intervening for her people. It was true that the king favored her above all other women, but if Esther approached Xerxes without an invitation, she could be killed. When she told this to Mordecai, he responded: "Who knows but that you have come to royal position for such a time as this?" (Esther 4:14).

While Mordecai and all the Jews in Susa gathered to fast and pray for her, Esther went to the king, who responded with the scepter of grace. God then used Esther to save the Jews and kill Haman.

While Esther's union with King Xerxes is hardly a model for marriage, it does show how God can use us to influence our spouses for good and bless the lives of many others.

Queen Vashti Deposed

1 This is what happened during the time of Xerxes,[a] the Xerxes who ruled over 127 provinces stretching from India to Cush[b]: 2At that time King Xerxes reigned from his royal throne in the citadel of Susa, 3and in the third year of his reign he gave a banquet for all his nobles and officials. The military leaders of Persia and Media, the princes, and the nobles of the provinces were present.

4For a full 180 days he displayed the vast wealth of his kingdom and the splendor and glory of his majesty. 5When these days were over, the king gave a banquet, lasting seven days, in the enclosed garden of the king's palace, for all the people from the least to the greatest, who were in the citadel of Susa. 6The garden had hangings of white and blue linen, fastened with cords of white linen and purple material to silver rings on marble pillars. There were couches of gold and silver on a mosaic pavement of porphyry, marble, mother-of-pearl and other costly stones. 7Wine was served in goblets of gold, each one different from the other, and the royal wine was abundant, in keeping with the king's liberality. 8By the king's command each guest was allowed to drink in his own way, for the king instructed all the wine stewards to serve each man what he wished.

9Queen Vashti also gave a banquet for the women in the royal palace of King Xerxes.

10On the seventh day, when King Xerxes was in high spirits from wine, he commanded the seven eunuchs who served him—Mehuman, Biztha, Harbona, Bigtha, Abagtha, Zethar and Carcas— 11to bring before him Queen Vashti, wearing her royal crown, in order to display her beauty to the people and nobles, for she was lovely to look at. 12But when the attendants delivered the king's command, Queen Vashti refused to come. Then the king became furious and burned with anger.

13Since it was customary for the king to consult experts in matters of law and justice, he spoke with the wise men who understood the times 14and were closest to the king—Carshena, Shethar, Admatha, Tarshish, Meres, Marsena and Memucan, the seven nobles of Persia and Media who had special access to the king and were highest in the kingdom.

15"According to law, what must be done to Queen Vashti?" he asked. "She has not obeyed the command of King Xerxes that the eunuchs have taken to her."

16Then Memucan replied in the presence of the king and the nobles, "Queen Vashti has done wrong, not only against the king but also against all the nobles and the peoples of all the provinces of King Xerxes. 17For the queen's conduct will become known to all the women, and so they will despise their husbands and say, 'King Xerxes commanded Queen Vashti to be brought before him, but she would not come.' 18This very day the Persian and Median women of the nobility who have heard about the queen's conduct will respond to all the king's nobles in the same way. There will be no end of disrespect and discord.

19"Therefore, if it pleases the king, let him issue a royal decree and let it be written in the laws of Persia and Media, which cannot be repealed, that Vashti is never again to enter the presence of King Xerxes. Also let the king give her royal position to someone else who is better than she. 20Then when the king's edict is proclaimed throughout all his vast realm, all the women will respect their husbands, from the least to the greatest."

21The king and his nobles were pleased with this advice, so the king did as Memucan proposed. 22He sent dispatches to all parts of the kingdom, to each province in its own script and to each people in its own language, proclaiming in each people's tongue that every man should be ruler over his own household.

Esther Made Queen

2 Later when the anger of King Xerxes had subsided, he remembered Vashti and what she had done and what he had decreed about her. 2Then the king's personal attendants proposed, "Let a search be made for beautiful young virgins for the king. 3Let the king appoint commissioners in every province of his realm to bring all these beautiful girls into the harem at the citadel of Susa. Let them be placed under the care of Hegai, the king's eunuch, who is in charge of the women; and let beauty treatments be given to them. 4Then let the girl who pleases the king be queen instead of Vashti." This advice appealed to the king, and he followed it.

5Now there was in the citadel of Susa a Jew of the tribe of Benjamin, named Mordecai son of Jair, the son of Shimei, the son of Kish, 6who had been carried into exile from Jerusalem by Nebuchadnezzar king of Babylon, among those taken captive with Jehoiachin[c] king of Judah. 7Mordecai had a cousin named

---

[a] *1* Hebrew *Ahasuerus,* a variant of Xerxes' Persian name; here and throughout Esther [b] *1* That is, the upper Nile region
[c] *6* Hebrew *Jeconiah,* a variant of *Jehoiachin*

F **FRIDAY**
READ ESTHER 1:1–22

WHEN YOU HAVE TO SAY NO

King Xerxes, the military leader of the Medes and Persians, tried to fulfill his father's failed plan to conquer Greece. Darius had been defeated at Marathon in 490 B.C. and had died soon after. Xerxes amassed one of the largest armies ever and marched back toward Greece. His army managed to get around the Spartan forces at Thermopylae but went down outside Athens when the Persian fleet was sunk in the bay of Salamis.

Esther 1 records what may have been Xerxes' planning meeting for the military campaigns of 482–479 B.C.. During this lengthy meeting (lasting 180 days), the men feasted and drank extensively. At one point, Xerxes commanded his wife, Vashti, to appear before the assembled men. We are not told why Vashti refused, but given the circumstances and the rate at which we can assume the men were consuming alcohol, perhaps Vashti was afraid they would ask her to act immodestly—or worse.

Xerxes reacted like a spoiled child. He was furious that his order had not been obeyed. His advisers encouraged the king's stupidity. They proposed deposing Vashti as queen and banishing her from the presence of the king. Then they planned the first Miss Universe pageant to replace Vashti with someone more beautiful and (hopefully) more compliant.

"This very day the Persian and Median women of the nobility who have heard about the queen's conduct will respond to all the king's nobles in the same way. There will be no end of disrespect and discord."

— ESTHER 1:18

let's talk

- ✦ What iffy spots of moral behavior have caused disagreement in our marriage?
- ✦ Has one of us ever asked the other to do something morally questionable? How do we balance mutual submission to each other with saying no to behavior that compromises our integrity?
- ✦ How can we keep our relationship unified so that we avoid situations that cause conflict when our morals differ?

Enter Mordecai and Esther, two Jews who were still living in Persia. Although Mordecai may have also had a Hebrew name, his Babylonian name may betray the comfort his family had with Babylonian life; it is derived from Marduk, the god Nebuchadnezzar followed and to whom he dedicated Babylon, his capital.

Ultimately, Esther was chosen to be the new queen, placing her in a position to intervene at a time when her people were threatened. Esther and Mordecai were able to save the Jews, but the dire threat made to exterminate them as a people during that time made its mark. Perhaps it was an impetus for Ezra and Nehemiah to go back to Jerusalem to help the Jews there rebuild the city's walls and reclaim their spiritual foundations.

Within this story, Vashti often goes unrecognized as a heroine. Yet perhaps that should be acknowledged, particularly within the context of marriage. For while Vashti had been obedient to her husband in all things, there came a point when her moral fiber pulled taut and would not allow her to cross a line that required her to do something she knew was wrong.

In our marriages we need mutual submission and respect, as the apostle Paul wrote (see Ephesians 5:21–33). But we also need personal courage to say no to one another when decency is twisted or when obedience to little things would deny obedience to God's greater ways.

—WAYNE BROUWER

FOR YOUR NEXT DEVOTIONAL READING, TURN TO PAGE 532.

Hadassah, whom he had brought up because
she had neither father nor mother. This girl,
who was also known as Esther, was lovely in
form and features, and Mordecai had taken
her as his own daughter when her father and
mother died.
8When the king's order and edict had been
proclaimed, many girls were brought to the
citadel of Susa and put under the care of Hegai. Esther also was taken to the king's palace
and entrusted to Hegai, who had charge of
the harem. 9The girl pleased him and won his
favor. Immediately he provided her with her
beauty treatments and special food. He assigned to her seven maids selected from the
king's palace and moved her and her maids
into the best place in the harem.
10Esther had not revealed her nationality and family background, because Mordecai had forbidden her to do so. 11Every day
he walked back and forth near the courtyard
of the harem to find out how Esther was and
what was happening to her.
12Before a girl's turn came to go in to King
Xerxes, she had to complete twelve months of
beauty treatments prescribed for the women,
six months with oil of myrrh and six with perfumes and cosmetics. 13And this is how she
would go to the king: Anything she wanted
was given her to take with her from the harem to the king's palace. 14In the evening she
would go there and in the morning return to
another part of the harem to the care of Sha-
ashgaz, the king's eunuch who was in charge
of the concubines. She would not return to
the king unless he was pleased with her and
summoned her by name.
15When the turn came for Esther (the girl
Mordecai had adopted, the daughter of his
uncle Abihail) to go to the king, she asked for
nothing other than what Hegai, the king's eunuch who was in charge of the harem, suggested. And Esther won the favor of everyone who
saw her. 16She was taken to King Xerxes in the
royal residence in the tenth month, the month
of Tebeth, in the seventh year of his reign.
17Now the king was attracted to Esther
more than to any of the other women, and
she won his favor and approval more than any
of the other virgins. So he set a royal crown
on her head and made her queen instead of
Vashti. 18And the king gave a great banquet,
Esther's banquet, for all his nobles and officials. He proclaimed a holiday throughout the
provinces and distributed gifts with royal liberality.

Mordecai Uncovers a Conspiracy

19When the virgins were assembled a second time, Mordecai was sitting at the king's
gate. 20But Esther had kept secret her family
background and nationality just as Mordecai
had told her to do, for she continued to follow
Mordecai's instructions as she had done when
he was bringing her up.
21During the time Mordecai was sitting at
the king's gate, Bigthana[a] and Teresh, two of
the king's officers who guarded the doorway,
became angry and conspired to assassinate
King Xerxes. 22But Mordecai found out about
the plot and told Queen Esther, who in turn
reported it to the king, giving credit to Mordecai. 23And when the report was investigated
and found to be true, the two officials were
hanged on a gallows.[b] All this was recorded
in the book of the annals in the presence of
the king.

Haman's Plot to Destroy the Jews

3 After these events, King Xerxes honored
Haman son of Hammedatha, the Agagite, elevating him and giving him a seat of
honor higher than that of all the other nobles.
2All the royal officials at the king's gate knelt
down and paid honor to Haman, for the king
had commanded this concerning him. But
Mordecai would not kneel down or pay him
honor.
3Then the royal officials at the king's gate
asked Mordecai, "Why do you disobey the
king's command?" 4Day after day they spoke
to him but he refused to comply. Therefore
they told Haman about it to see whether Mordecai's behavior would be tolerated, for he had
told them he was a Jew.
5When Haman saw that Mordecai would
not kneel down or pay him honor, he was
enraged. 6Yet having learned who Mordecai's
people were, he scorned the idea of killing
only Mordecai. Instead Haman looked for a
way to destroy all Mordecai's people, the Jews,
throughout the whole kingdom of Xerxes.
7In the twelfth year of King Xerxes, in the
first month, the month of Nisan, they cast the
pur (that is, the lot) in the presence of Haman
to select a day and month. And the lot fell on[c]
the twelfth month, the month of Adar.
8Then Haman said to King Xerxes, "There
is a certain people dispersed and scattered

[a] 21 Hebrew *Bigthan*, a variant of *Bigthana* [b] 23 Or *were hung* (or *impaled*) *on poles*; similarly elsewhere in Esther [c] 7 Septuagint; Hebrew does not have *And the lot fell on.*

among the peoples in all the provinces of your kingdom whose customs are different from those of all other people and who do not obey the king's laws; it is not in the king's best interest to tolerate them. 9If it pleases the king, let a decree be issued to destroy them, and I will put ten thousand talents[a] of silver into the royal treasury for the men who carry out this business."

10So the king took his signet ring from his finger and gave it to Haman son of Hammedatha, the Agagite, the enemy of the Jews. 11"Keep the money," the king said to Haman, "and do with the people as you please."

12Then on the thirteenth day of the first month the royal secretaries were summoned. They wrote out in the script of each province and in the language of each people all Haman's orders to the king's satraps, the governors of the various provinces and the nobles of the various peoples. These were written in the name of King Xerxes himself and sealed with his own ring. 13Dispatches were sent by couriers to all the king's provinces with the order to destroy, kill and annihilate all the Jews—young and old, women and little children—on a single day, the thirteenth day of the twelfth month, the month of Adar, and to plunder their goods. 14A copy of the text of the edict was to be issued as law in every province and made known to the people of every nationality so they would be ready for that day.

15Spurred on by the king's command, the couriers went out, and the edict was issued in the citadel of Susa. The king and Haman sat down to drink, but the city of Susa was bewildered.

Mordecai Persuades Esther to Help

4 When Mordecai learned of all that had been done, he tore his clothes, put on sackcloth and ashes, and went out into the city, wailing loudly and bitterly. 2But he went only as far as the king's gate, because no one clothed in sackcloth was allowed to enter it. 3In every province to which the edict and order of the king came, there was great mourning among the Jews, with fasting, weeping and wailing. Many lay in sackcloth and ashes.

4When Esther's maids and eunuchs came and told her about Mordecai, she was in great distress. She sent clothes for him to put on instead of his sackcloth, but he would not accept them. 5Then Esther summoned Hathach, one of the king's eunuchs assigned to attend her, and ordered him to find out what was troubling Mordecai and why.

6So Hathach went out to Mordecai in the open square of the city in front of the king's gate. 7Mordecai told him everything that had happened to him, including the exact amount of money Haman had promised to pay into the royal treasury for the destruction of the Jews. 8He also gave him a copy of the text of the edict for their annihilation, which had been published in Susa, to show to Esther and explain it to her, and he told him to urge her to go into the king's presence to beg for mercy and plead with him for her people.

9Hathach went back and reported to Esther what Mordecai had said. 10Then she instructed him to say to Mordecai, 11"All the king's officials and the people of the royal provinces know that for any man or woman who approaches the king in the inner court without being summoned the king has but one law: that he be put to death. The only exception to this is for the king to extend the gold scepter to him and spare his life. But thirty days have passed since I was called to go to the king."

12When Esther's words were reported to Mordecai, 13he sent back this answer: "Do not think that because you are in the king's house you alone of all the Jews will escape. 14For if you remain silent at this time, relief and deliverance for the Jews will arise from another place, but you and your father's family will perish. And who knows but that you have come to royal position for such a time as this?"

15Then Esther sent this reply to Mordecai: 16"Go, gather together all the Jews who are in Susa, and fast for me. Do not eat or drink for three days, night or day. I and my maids will fast as you do. When this is done, I will go to the king, even though it is against the law. And if I perish, I perish."

17So Mordecai went away and carried out all of Esther's instructions.

Esther's Request to the King

5 On the third day Esther put on her royal robes and stood in the inner court of the palace, in front of the king's hall. The king was sitting on his royal throne in the hall, facing the entrance. 2When he saw Queen Esther standing in the court, he was pleased with her and held out to her the gold scepter that

a 9 That is, about 375 tons (about 345 metric tons)

love in the gender gap

WEEKEND

"You aren't really going to pack all those clothes, are you? This is a three-night trip, not three weeks. Besides, who cares how you look when you're camping?" I (Les) instantly regretted the words as they came out of my mouth. It was nearly midnight, and we were both a little testy. Early the next morning we were leaving for a weekend trip to a rustic camp near Santa Barbara.

"You can take what you want, and I take what I want," Leslie replied. "Just because you are content to wear the same pair of jeans for three days, don't expect me to do the same. Anyway, what about your laptop computer? Last time we flew back east we ended up lugging that thing all over the place, and you never even turned it on. So who is being frivolous about what he packs?"

"I like knowing my computer is there if I want to use it."

"Well, I like having these clothes if I want to wear them," Leslie replied.

"You're right," I confessed. "What seems essential to me can be incidental to you and vice versa. At times we are just so different."

Different indeed. In recent years researchers have discovered that women and men have different biological, psychological, and professional realities. Biologically, women have larger connections between the two hemispheres of their brains and a tendency toward superior verbal ability. Men's greater brain hemisphere separation may contribute a slight tendency toward abstract reasoning and a superior capacity to mentally rotate objects in space. Psychologically, women frequently find their sense of identity through relationship with others; men tend to find their sense of self through being separate. Professionally, men are often more focused on long-range goals; women are frequently more attentive to the process through which goals are achieved.

There is an inherent completeness when a man and woman marry. Our partner makes up for what we lack. When we are discouraged, they are hopeful. When we are stingy, they are generous. When we are weak, they are strong. Because we are male and female joined together, there is a wholeness. But our differences, if not understood and accepted, become a source of confusion rather than completeness.

Too often in marriage the fundamental differences between women and men are overlooked when we mistakenly assume that our partners are just like us—"what is good for me is good for you." We evaluate their behavior according to our feminine or masculine standards, never considering the vast differences between the sexes.

What a Husband Should Know About His Wife

- She needs to be cherished. If it came down to an evening with your buddies or a night with your wife, she needs to know you would choose her—not because you have to, but because you want to.
- She needs to be known. Being understood means having her feelings validated and accepted.
- She needs to be respected. When she is not respected, she feels insecure and loses her sense of self.

What a Wife Should Know About Her Husband

- He needs to be admired. He measures his worth through his achievements, big and small, and needs them to be recognized.
- He needs autonomy. When he is under stress, he requires a little space.
- He needs shared activity. Husbands place surprising importance on having their wives as recreational companions.

—DR. LES PARROTT III AND DR. LESLIE PARROTT

gender bias

Fill in the blanks below with "men" or "women," and have your spouse do the same. Discuss your answers. Do you both agree? Why or why not?

1. _______ are too emotional.
2. _______ aren't sensitive enough.
3. _______ get their identity from their friends.
4. _______ focus on achievement.
5. _______ like to shop.
6. _______ are afraid to ask for directions.
7. _______ don't do their fair share of the housework.
8. _______ talk too much.
9. _______ frequently deny their real power.
10. _______ are practical.
11. _______ don't listen.
12. _______ aren't pressured to provide the family's income.
13. _______ are afraid to be vulnerable.
14. _______ get their identity from their cars.
15. _______ can endure a lot of emotional pain.
16. _______ focus on relationships.
17. _______ are romantic.
18. _______ can endure a lot of physical pain.
19. _______ are too literal.
20. _______ put too much emphasis on appearance.

HOW ARE WE DOING?

let's make a DATE

ROLE REVERSAL

Try trading roles to see what it feels like to be in your mate's shoes. For an entire weekend, he parks in her spot, she parks in his. Exchange chores: If she usually cooks and he cleans up, this weekend he cooks and she cleans up. Do both of you have a favorite chair that you sit in? Who controls the remote? This weekend trade chairs and hand over the remote to the one who usually doesn't have it. While in the car, reverse who usually drives; the spouse who usually sits in the passenger seat should do the driving. If you're a talker, learn what it feels like to quietly listen while your spouse talks.

On Sunday night return to your regular roles and discuss what you learned while looking at life from your mate's point of view.

FOR YOUR NEXT DEVOTIONAL READING, TURN TO PAGE 535.

LESSONS FROM THE *Bible*

How did the men near them react when the women in the following passages broke some of the traditional female stereotypes of the times?

1. Deborah (Judges 4:1–10)
2. The wife of noble character (Proverbs 31:10–31)

was in his hand. So Esther approached and
touched the tip of the scepter.
[3]Then the king asked, "What is it, Queen
Esther? What is your request? Even up to half
the kingdom, it will be given you."
[4]"If it pleases the king," replied Esther, "let
the king, together with Haman, come today
to a banquet I have prepared for him."
[5]"Bring Haman at once," the king said, "so
that we may do what Esther asks."
So the king and Haman went to the banquet Esther had prepared. [6]As they were
drinking wine, the king again asked Esther,
"Now what is your petition? It will be given
you. And what is your request? Even up to half
the kingdom, it will be granted."
[7]Esther replied, "My petition and my request is this: [8]If the king regards me with favor
and if it pleases the king to grant my petition
and fulfill my request, let the king and Haman
come tomorrow to the banquet I will prepare
for them. Then I will answer the king's question."

Haman's Rage Against Mordecai

[9]Haman went out that day happy and in
high spirits. But when he saw Mordecai at the
king's gate and observed that he neither rose
nor showed fear in his presence, he was filled
with rage against Mordecai. [10]Nevertheless,
Haman restrained himself and went home.
Calling together his friends and Zeresh, his
wife, [11]Haman boasted to them about his vast
wealth, his many sons, and all the ways the
king had honored him and how he had elevated him above the other nobles and officials.
[12]"And that's not all," Haman added. "I'm the
only person Queen Esther invited to accompany the king to the banquet she gave. And
she has invited me along with the king tomorrow. [13]But all this gives me no satisfaction as
long as I see that Jew Mordecai sitting at the
king's gate."
[14]His wife Zeresh and all his friends said to
him, "Have a gallows built, seventy-five feet[a]
high, and ask the king in the morning to have
Mordecai hanged on it. Then go with the king
to the dinner and be happy." This suggestion
delighted Haman, and he had the gallows
built.

Mordecai Honored

6 That night the king could not sleep; so he
ordered the book of the chronicles, the record of his reign, to be brought in and read
to him. [2]It was found recorded there that Mordecai had exposed Bigthana and Teresh, two of
the king's officers who guarded the doorway,
who had conspired to assassinate King Xerxes.
[3]"What honor and recognition has Mordecai received for this?" the king asked.
"Nothing has been done for him," his attendants answered.
[4]The king said, "Who is in the court?" Now
Haman had just entered the outer court of
the palace to speak to the king about hanging Mordecai on the gallows he had erected
for him.
[5]His attendants answered, "Haman is
standing in the court."
"Bring him in," the king ordered.
[6]When Haman entered, the king asked
him, "What should be done for the man the
king delights to honor?"
Now Haman thought to himself, "Who is
there that the king would rather honor than
me?" [7]So he answered the king, "For the man
the king delights to honor, [8]have them bring
a royal robe the king has worn and a horse the
king has ridden, one with a royal crest placed
on its head. [9]Then let the robe and horse be entrusted to one of the king's most noble princes. Let them robe the man the king delights
to honor, and lead him on the horse through
the city streets, proclaiming before him, 'This
is what is done for the man the king delights
to honor!' "
[10]"Go at once," the king commanded Haman. "Get the robe and the horse and do just
as you have suggested for Mordecai the Jew,
who sits at the king's gate. Do not neglect anything you have recommended."
[11]So Haman got the robe and the horse. He
robed Mordecai, and led him on horseback
through the city streets, proclaiming before
him, "This is what is done for the man the
king delights to honor!"
[12]Afterward Mordecai returned to the
king's gate. But Haman rushed home, with
his head covered in grief, [13]and told Zeresh
his wife and all his friends everything that had
happened to him.
His advisers and his wife Zeresh said to
him, "Since Mordecai, before whom your
downfall has started, is of Jewish origin, you
cannot stand against him—you will surely
come to ruin!" [14]While they were still talking
with him, the king's eunuchs arrived and hurried Haman away to the banquet Esther had
prepared.

a *14* Hebrew *fifty cubits* (about 23 meters)

MONDAY
READ ESTHER 4:1—5:8

THE BEST WAY TO ASK

My friend is an amazing cook who can make the toughest piece of meat melt like butter in your mouth. Her best dish, however, is what I call her grace sandwich.

When they were first married, my friend's husband started going out for drinks with the guys after work. Sometimes he didn't come home until after midnight.

This upset my friend terribly, but she didn't know what to do about it. As a new Christian, she thought that being Christlike and submissive meant not speaking her mind to her spouse.

For the most part her husband was responsible and hard working; he treated her kindly and always paid their bills on time. He didn't go out drinking every night, but still, she worried about the situation.

A few months went by before my friend decided that she had to speak up, so she prepared her husband's favorite Italian food and left a note in his lunch box to come home early after work. He did, and they had a great feast, but she didn't say anything to him.

She cooked another great meal a week later and then again several days after that. That's when she delivered her message. As they sat on the front porch together after dinner, she handed her husband a "grace sandwich."

She said, "I love you and I'm glad you're my husband. When you're out drinking, especially when you're out late, I worry about you. I miss you and want you here."

She didn't hammer him over the head. She didn't nag, whine or issue an ultimatum. Instead, she sandwiched her message "I don't want you out drinking" between "I love you" and "I miss you," which he readily received. After that front-porch conversation, he came right home every night after work.

My friend said that she followed the example of Esther, who was also married to an unbeliever, the king of Persia. Esther, too, wanted to speak to her husband about a sensitive subject: reversing his edict to annihilate the Jews. To speak to the king without being invited was to risk death, but Esther took her chances and invited her husband to a feast—twice, in fact. Wisely and respectfully, she appealed to her husband's appetites, it would seem, and she won his favor, which eventually helped save the lives of her people.

"I prayed, I cooked, and then I spoke," my friend said. "I didn't save an entire nation, but I may have saved my marriage. I know I could've destroyed it if I had hit him with a frying pan instead!"

—NANCY KENNEDY

Esther replied, "My petition and my request is this: If the king regards me with favor and if it pleases the king to grant my petition and fulfill my request, let the king and Haman come tomorrow to the banquet I will prepare for them. Then I will answer the king's question."

— ESTHER 5:7–8

let's talk

- In our marriage, what are our usual methods of delivering sensitive messages or making requests? How effective are they?
- What are ways that we can change what isn't working to make our requests more like a grace sandwich?
- Is there something that needs to be said in our relationship? What's keeping us from saying it?

FOR YOUR NEXT DEVOTIONAL READING, TURN TO PAGE 541.

Haman Hanged

7 So the king and Haman went to dine with Queen Esther, 2and as they were drinking wine on that second day, the king again asked, "Queen Esther, what is your petition? It will be given you. What is your request? Even up to half the kingdom, it will be granted."

3Then Queen Esther answered, "If I have found favor with you, O king, and if it pleases your majesty, grant me my life—this is my petition. And spare my people—this is my request. 4For I and my people have been sold for destruction and slaughter and annihilation. If we had merely been sold as male and female slaves, I would have kept quiet, because no such distress would justify disturbing the king.[a]"

5King Xerxes asked Queen Esther, "Who is he? Where is the man who has dared to do such a thing?"

6Esther said, "The adversary and enemy is this vile Haman."

Then Haman was terrified before the king and queen. 7The king got up in a rage, left his wine and went out into the palace garden. But Haman, realizing that the king had already decided his fate, stayed behind to beg Queen Esther for his life.

8Just as the king returned from the palace garden to the banquet hall, Haman was falling on the couch where Esther was reclining.

The king exclaimed, "Will he even molest the queen while she is with me in the house?"

As soon as the word left the king's mouth, they covered Haman's face. 9Then Harbona, one of the eunuchs attending the king, said, "A gallows seventy-five feet[b] high stands by Haman's house. He had it made for Mordecai, who spoke up to help the king."

The king said, "Hang him on it!" 10So they hanged Haman on the gallows he had prepared for Mordecai. Then the king's fury subsided.

The King's Edict in Behalf of the Jews

8 That same day King Xerxes gave Queen Esther the estate of Haman, the enemy of the Jews. And Mordecai came into the presence of the king, for Esther had told how he was related to her. 2The king took off his signet ring, which he had reclaimed from Haman, and presented it to Mordecai. And Esther appointed him over Haman's estate.

3Esther again pleaded with the king, falling at his feet and weeping. She begged him to put an end to the evil plan of Haman the Agagite, which he had devised against the Jews. 4Then the king extended the gold scepter to Esther and she arose and stood before him.

5"If it pleases the king," she said, "and if he regards me with favor and thinks it the right thing to do, and if he is pleased with me, let an order be written overruling the dispatches that Haman son of Hammedatha, the Agagite, devised and wrote to destroy the Jews in all the king's provinces. 6For how can I bear to see disaster fall on my people? How can I bear to see the destruction of my family?"

7King Xerxes replied to Queen Esther and to Mordecai the Jew, "Because Haman attacked the Jews, I have given his estate to Esther, and they have hanged him on the gallows. 8Now write another decree in the king's name in behalf of the Jews as seems best to you, and seal it with the king's signet ring—for no document written in the king's name and sealed with his ring can be revoked."

9At once the royal secretaries were summoned—on the twenty-third day of the third month, the month of Sivan. They wrote out all Mordecai's orders to the Jews, and to the satraps, governors and nobles of the 127 provinces stretching from India to Cush.[c] These orders were written in the script of each province and the language of each people and also to the Jews in their own script and language. 10Mordecai wrote in the name of King Xerxes, sealed the dispatches with the king's signet ring, and sent them by mounted couriers, who rode fast horses especially bred for the king.

11The king's edict granted the Jews in every city the right to assemble and protect themselves; to destroy, kill and annihilate any armed force of any nationality or province that might attack them and their women and children; and to plunder the property of their enemies. 12The day appointed for the Jews to do this in all the provinces of King Xerxes was the thirteenth day of the twelfth month, the month of Adar. 13A copy of the text of the edict was to be issued as law in every province and made known to the people of every nationality so that the Jews would be ready on that day to avenge themselves on their enemies.

14The couriers, riding the royal horses, raced out, spurred on by the king's command. And the edict was also issued in the citadel of Susa.

---

[a] 4 Or *quiet, but the compensation our adversary offers cannot be compared with the loss the king would suffer* [b] 9 Hebrew *fifty cubits* (about 23 meters) [c] 9 That is, the upper Nile region

15Mordecai left the king's presence wearing royal garments of blue and white, a large
crown of gold and a purple robe of fine linen.
And the city of Susa held a joyous celebration.
16For the Jews it was a time of happiness and
joy, gladness and honor. 17In every province
and in every city, wherever the edict of the king
went, there was joy and gladness among the
Jews, with feasting and celebrating. And many
people of other nationalities became Jews because fear of the Jews had seized them.

Triumph of the Jews

9 On the thirteenth day of the twelfth
month, the month of Adar, the edict commanded by the king was to be carried
out. On this day the enemies of the Jews had
hoped to overpower them, but now the tables
were turned and the Jews got the upper hand
over those who hated them. 2The Jews assembled in their cities in all the provinces of King
Xerxes to attack those seeking their destruction. No one could stand against them, because the people of all the other nationalities
were afraid of them. 3And all the nobles of the
provinces, the satraps, the governors and the
king's administrators helped the Jews, because
fear of Mordecai had seized them. 4Mordecai
was prominent in the palace; his reputation
spread throughout the provinces, and he became more and more powerful.

5The Jews struck down all their enemies
with the sword, killing and destroying them,
and they did what they pleased to those who
hated them. 6In the citadel of Susa, the Jews
killed and destroyed five hundred men. 7They
also killed Parshandatha, Dalphon, Aspatha,
8Poratha, Adalia, Aridatha, 9Parmashta, Aris-
ai, Aridai and Vaizatha, 10the ten sons of Haman son of Hammedatha, the enemy of the
Jews. But they did not lay their hands on the
plunder.

11The number of those slain in the citadel
of Susa was reported to the king that same day.
12The king said to Queen Esther, "The Jews
have killed and destroyed five hundred men
and the ten sons of Haman in the citadel of
Susa. What have they done in the rest of the
king's provinces? Now what is your petition? It
will be given you. What is your request? It will
also be granted."

13"If it pleases the king," Esther answered,
"give the Jews in Susa permission to carry out
this day's edict tomorrow also, and let Haman's ten sons be hanged on gallows."

14So the king commanded that this be
done. An edict was issued in Susa, and they
hanged the ten sons of Haman. 15The Jews in
Susa came together on the fourteenth day of
the month of Adar, and they put to death in
Susa three hundred men, but they did not lay
their hands on the plunder.

16Meanwhile, the remainder of the Jews
who were in the king's provinces also assembled to protect themselves and get relief from
their enemies. They killed seventy-five thousand of them but did not lay their hands on
the plunder. 17This happened on the thirteenth day of the month of Adar, and on the
fourteenth they rested and made it a day of
feasting and joy.

Purim Celebrated

18The Jews in Susa, however, had assembled
on the thirteenth and fourteenth, and then on
the fifteenth they rested and made it a day of
feasting and joy.

19That is why rural Jews—those living in
villages—observe the fourteenth of the month
of Adar as a day of joy and feasting, a day for
giving presents to each other.

20Mordecai recorded these events, and he
sent letters to all the Jews throughout the
provinces of King Xerxes, near and far, 21to
have them celebrate annually the fourteenth
and fifteenth days of the month of Adar 22as
the time when the Jews got relief from their
enemies, and as the month when their sorrow
was turned into joy and their mourning into a
day of celebration. He wrote them to observe
the days as days of feasting and joy and giving
presents of food to one another and gifts to
the poor.

23So the Jews agreed to continue the celebration they had begun, doing what Mordecai had written to them. 24For Haman son
of Hammedatha, the Agagite, the enemy of
all the Jews, had plotted against the Jews to
destroy them and had cast the *pur* (that is,
the lot) for their ruin and destruction. 25But
when the plot came to the king's attention,[a]
he issued written orders that the evil scheme
Haman had devised against the Jews should
come back onto his own head, and that he
and his sons should be hanged on the gallows.
26(Therefore these days were called Purim,
from the word *pur*.) Because of everything
written in this letter and because of what they
had seen and what had happened to them,
27the Jews took it upon themselves to establish

---

[a] 25 Or *when Esther came before the king*

the custom that they and their descendants
and all who join them should without fail
observe these two days every year, in the way
prescribed and at the time appointed. 28These
days should be remembered and observed in
every generation by every family, and in every
province and in every city. And these days of
Purim should never cease to be celebrated by
the Jews, nor should the memory of them die
out among their descendants.

29So Queen Esther, daughter of Abihail,
along with Mordecai the Jew, wrote with full
authority to confirm this second letter concerning Purim. 30And Mordecai sent letters
to all the Jews in the 127 provinces of the
kingdom of Xerxes—words of goodwill and
assurance— 31to establish these days of Purim at their designated times, as Mordecai the
Jew and Queen Esther had decreed for them,
and as they had established for themselves
and their descendants in regard to their times
of fasting and lamentation. 32Esther's decree
confirmed these regulations about Purim, and
it was written down in the records.

The Greatness of Mordecai

10 King Xerxes imposed tribute throughout the empire, to its distant shores.
2And all his acts of power and might,
together with a full account of the greatness of
Mordecai to which the king had raised him,
are they not written in the book of the annals
of the kings of Media and Persia? 3Mordecai
the Jew was second in rank to King Xerxes,
preeminent among the Jews, and held in high
esteem by his many fellow Jews, because he
worked for the good of his people and spoke
up for the welfare of all the Jews.

JOB

Job

QUICK FACTS

AUTHOR Unknown

AUDIENCE God's people

DATE Unknown, though Job himself may have lived around 2,000 B.C. (the time of Abraham, Isaac and Jacob)

SETTING Uz, east of Canaan

Job had everything going for him: ten children, thousands of animals and a large number of servants. He was also such a good man that God bragged about him to Satan. Satan responded by asking, "Does Job fear God for nothing?" (Job 1:9). Take away his blessings and Job's obedience would go with it, Satan said.

So Job lost everything: his possessions, his children, his health and, as he later discovered, the respect of his friends. But he would not curse God and die, as his wife suggested. Nor would he accept his losses as punishment for something he had done wrong, as his friends argued. What he wanted to do was beg God to explain the reason for his circumstances. "If only I knew where to find him . . . I would state my case before him and fill my mouth with arguments," Job said (Job 23:3–4).

When God did appear, he stunned Job into silence by asking his own questions: "Where were you when I laid the earth's foundation? . . . Who marked off its dimensions? . . . Who shut up the sea behind doors?" (Job 38:4–5,8). In other words, Job was to let God be God.

Our God reigns—even when we suffer. We may not always know why we are assaulted by illness, infertility, financial difficulty or other problems in marriage. But like Job, we can trust God to be with us through the storm.

Prologue

1 In the land of Uz there lived a man whose
name was Job. This man was blameless and
upright; he feared God and shunned evil.
2He had seven sons and three daughters, 3and
he owned seven thousand sheep, three thousand camels, five hundred yoke of oxen and
five hundred donkeys, and had a large number
of servants. He was the greatest man among all
the people of the East.
4His sons used to take turns holding feasts
in their homes, and they would invite their
three sisters to eat and drink with them.
5When a period of feasting had run its course,
Job would send and have them purified. Early in the morning he would sacrifice a burnt
offering for each of them, thinking, "Perhaps
my children have sinned and cursed God in
their hearts." This was Job's regular custom.

Job's First Test

6One day the angels[a] came to present themselves before the LORD, and Satan[b] also came
with them. 7The LORD said to Satan, "Where
have you come from?"
Satan answered the LORD, "From roaming
through the earth and going back and forth
in it."
8Then the LORD said to Satan, "Have you
considered my servant Job? There is no one on
earth like him; he is blameless and upright, a
man who fears God and shuns evil."
9"Does Job fear God for nothing?" Satan
replied. 10"Have you not put a hedge around
him and his household and everything he has?
You have blessed the work of his hands, so that
his flocks and herds are spread throughout the
land. 11But stretch out your hand and strike
everything he has, and he will surely curse you
to your face."
12The LORD said to Satan, "Very well, then,
everything he has is in your hands, but on the
man himself do not lay a finger."
Then Satan went out from the presence of
the LORD.
13One day when Job's sons and daughters
were feasting and drinking wine at the oldest
brother's house, 14a messenger came to Job
and said, "The oxen were plowing and the
donkeys were grazing nearby, 15and the Sabeans attacked and carried them off. They put
the servants to the sword, and I am the only
one who has escaped to tell you!"
16While he was still speaking, another messenger came and said, "The fire of God fell
from the sky and burned up the sheep and the
servants, and I am the only one who has escaped to tell you!"
17While he was still speaking, another messenger came and said, "The Chaldeans formed
three raiding parties and swept down on your
camels and carried them off. They put the servants to the sword, and I am the only one who
has escaped to tell you!"
18While he was still speaking, yet another messenger came and said, "Your sons and
daughters were feasting and drinking wine at
the oldest brother's house, 19when suddenly
a mighty wind swept in from the desert and
struck the four corners of the house. It collapsed on them and they are dead, and I am
the only one who has escaped to tell you!"
20At this, Job got up and tore his robe and
shaved his head. Then he fell to the ground in
worship 21and said:

"Naked I came from my mother's womb,
  and naked I will depart.[c]
The LORD gave and the LORD has taken
    away;
  may the name of the LORD be praised."

22In all this, Job did not sin by charging
God with wrongdoing.

Job's Second Test

2 On another day the angels[a] came to present themselves before the LORD, and Satan also came with them to present himself before him. 2And the LORD said to Satan,
"Where have you come from?"
Satan answered the LORD, "From roaming
through the earth and going back and forth
in it."
3Then the LORD said to Satan, "Have you
considered my servant Job? There is no one
on earth like him; he is blameless and upright,
a man who fears God and shuns evil. And he
still maintains his integrity, though you incited me against him to ruin him without any
reason."
4"Skin for skin!" Satan replied. "A man will
give all he has for his own life. 5But stretch out
your hand and strike his flesh and bones, and
he will surely curse you to your face."
6The LORD said to Satan, "Very well, then,
he is in your hands; but you must spare his
life."
7So Satan went out from the presence of
the LORD and afflicted Job with painful sores
from the soles of his feet to the top of his head.

[a] 6,1 Hebrew *the sons of God* [b] 6 *Satan* means *accuser.* [c] 21 Or *will return there*

TUESDAY
READ JOB 2:1–10

BLESSING IN THE DARKNESS

> **His wife said to him, "Are you still holding on to your integrity? Curse God and die!"**
> — Job 2:9

let's talk

- What has been the most difficult time in our marriage?
- How did it affect our faith? Our relationship with each other?
- In what ways can suffering make a marriage stronger?

After 25 years of marriage, my normally easy-going, even-tempered husband fell into a depression that lasted more than a year. We called it "the darkness."

He worked (and lived) out of town at the time and was caring for two aunts, which taxed him physically, mentally and emotionally. Also, several of his friends had recently died, including his best friend since childhood.

My husband's weekend visits home grew less frequent, but when he was home, he stayed to himself. The husband I had known for more than half of my life wasn't the same one who now sat on the couch and stared at the television.

Even though it was my husband's depression, it affected me as well. He resisted any attempt at comfort; he didn't want my help or anyone else's. We suffered together—alone. He talked a lot about insurance, his pension and what to do if anything bad happened to him. He even suggested that we divorce, so I could find happiness with someone else. It tore me apart to watch the darkness swallow him. I felt helpless and, at times, hopeless.

Proverbs 13:12 says, "Hope deferred makes the heart sick." Our hearts were definitely sick during that dark time. I questioned God, saying, "Where are you? Why won't you do something?"

I pleaded for relief for my husband, for me and for our whole family. I never reached the "curse God and die" point that Job's wife did when it seemed like the gates of hell had opened and dumped calamity and sorrow on her husband and their family. But I often wondered if my husband's darkness would be our life from then on. I wondered how I could endure it.

The one thing that got me through that bleak time was the Word of God. I used to go down to the lake by our house and listen to the water lapping against the dock. A breeze would blow across my face and I'd recall Scripture: "I can do everything through him who gives me strength" (Philippians 4:13). "Who shall separate us from the love of Christ?" (Romans 8:35). "When you pass through the waters, I will be with you; and when you pass through the rivers, they will not sweep over you" (Isaiah 43:2).

Sometimes in the evenings, as my husband slept, I would put my hand on him and pray. Eventually, with the help of counseling and time, the darkness lifted.

That was more than eight years ago. Recently, my husband said that knowing that I wouldn't leave him, even when he told me that I should, was what stayed with him through the darkness and gave him hope.

It was a terrible time, but it was also good, he said. We are stronger for having gone through it together.

—NANCY KENNEDY

FOR YOUR NEXT DEVOTIONAL READING, TURN TO PAGE 545.

8Then Job took a piece of broken pottery and
scraped himself with it as he sat among the
ashes.
9His wife said to him, "Are you still holding
on to your integrity? Curse God and die!"
10He replied, "You are talking like a foolish[a] woman. Shall we accept good from God,
and not trouble?"
In all this, Job did not sin in what he said.

Job's Three Friends

11When Job's three friends, Eliphaz the
Temanite, Bildad the Shuhite and Zophar
the Naamathite, heard about all the troubles
that had come upon him, they set out from
their homes and met together by agreement
to go and sympathize with him and comfort
him. 12When they saw him from a distance,
they could hardly recognize him; they began
to weep aloud, and they tore their robes and
sprinkled dust on their heads. 13Then they sat
on the ground with him for seven days and
seven nights. No one said a word to him, because they saw how great his suffering was.

Job Speaks

3 After this, Job opened his mouth and
cursed the day of his birth. 2He said:

3"May the day of my birth perish,
and the night it was said, 'A boy is born!'
4That day—may it turn to darkness;
may God above not care about it;
may no light shine upon it.
5May darkness and deep shadow[b] claim it once more;
may a cloud settle over it;
may blackness overwhelm its light.
6That night—may thick darkness seize it;
may it not be included among the days of the year
nor be entered in any of the months.
7May that night be barren;
may no shout of joy be heard in it.
8May those who curse days[c] curse that day,
those who are ready to rouse Leviathan.
9May its morning stars become dark;
may it wait for daylight in vain
and not see the first rays of dawn,
10for it did not shut the doors of the womb on me
to hide trouble from my eyes.

11"Why did I not perish at birth,
and die as I came from the womb?
12Why were there knees to receive me
and breasts that I might be nursed?
13For now I would be lying down in peace;
I would be asleep and at rest
14with kings and counselors of the earth,
who built for themselves places now lying in ruins,
15with rulers who had gold,
who filled their houses with silver.
16Or why was I not hidden in the ground like a stillborn child,
like an infant who never saw the light of day?
17There the wicked cease from turmoil,
and there the weary are at rest.
18Captives also enjoy their ease;
they no longer hear the slave driver's shout.
19The small and the great are there,
and the slave is freed from his master.

20"Why is light given to those in misery,
and life to the bitter of soul,
21to those who long for death that does not come,
who search for it more than for hidden treasure,
22who are filled with gladness
and rejoice when they reach the grave?
23Why is life given to a man
whose way is hidden,
whom God has hedged in?
24For sighing comes to me instead of food;
my groans pour out like water.
25What I feared has come upon me;
what I dreaded has happened to me.
26I have no peace, no quietness;
I have no rest, but only turmoil."

Eliphaz

4 Then Eliphaz the Temanite replied:

2"If someone ventures a word with you,
will you be impatient?
But who can keep from speaking?
3Think how you have instructed many,
how you have strengthened feeble hands.
4Your words have supported those who stumbled;
you have strengthened faltering knees.
5But now trouble comes to you, and you are discouraged;
it strikes you, and you are dismayed.
6Should not your piety be your confidence
and your blameless ways your hope?

[a] *10* The Hebrew word rendered *foolish* denotes moral deficiency. [b] *5* Or *and the shadow of death* [c] *8* Or *the sea*

7 "Consider now: Who, being innocent, has
ever perished?
Where were the upright ever destroyed?
8 As I have observed, those who plow evil
and those who sow trouble reap it.
9 At the breath of God they are destroyed;
at the blast of his anger they perish.
10 The lions may roar and growl,
yet the teeth of the great lions are
broken.
11 The lion perishes for lack of prey,
and the cubs of the lioness are
scattered.

12 "A word was secretly brought to me,
my ears caught a whisper of it.
13 Amid disquieting dreams in the night,
when deep sleep falls on men,
14 fear and trembling seized me
and made all my bones shake.
15 A spirit glided past my face,
and the hair on my body stood on end.
16 It stopped,
but I could not tell what it was.
A form stood before my eyes,
and I heard a hushed voice:
17 'Can a mortal be more righteous than
God?
Can a man be more pure than his
Maker?
18 If God places no trust in his servants,
if he charges his angels with error,
19 how much more those who live in houses
of clay,
whose foundations are in the dust,
who are crushed more readily than a
moth!
20 Between dawn and dusk they are broken
to pieces;
unnoticed, they perish forever.
21 Are not the cords of their tent pulled up,
so that they die without wisdom?' [a]

5 "Call if you will, but who will answer you?
To which of the holy ones will you
turn?
2 Resentment kills a fool,
and envy slays the simple.
3 I myself have seen a fool taking root,
but suddenly his house was cursed.
4 His children are far from safety,
crushed in court without a defender.
5 The hungry consume his harvest,
taking it even from among thorns,
and the thirsty pant after his wealth.
6 For hardship does not spring from the soil,
nor does trouble sprout from the
ground.
7 Yet man is born to trouble
as surely as sparks fly upward.

8 "But if it were I, I would appeal to God;
I would lay my cause before him.
9 He performs wonders that cannot be
fathomed,
miracles that cannot be counted.
10 He bestows rain on the earth;
he sends water upon the countryside.
11 The lowly he sets on high,
and those who mourn are lifted to
safety.
12 He thwarts the plans of the crafty,
so that their hands achieve no success.
13 He catches the wise in their craftiness,
and the schemes of the wily are swept
away.
14 Darkness comes upon them in the
daytime;
at noon they grope as in the night.
15 He saves the needy from the sword in
their mouth;
he saves them from the clutches of the
powerful.
16 So the poor have hope,
and injustice shuts its mouth.

17 "Blessed is the man whom God corrects;
so do not despise the discipline of the
Almighty. [b]
18 For he wounds, but he also binds up;
he injures, but his hands also heal.
19 From six calamities he will rescue you;
in seven no harm will befall you.
20 In famine he will ransom you from death,
and in battle from the stroke of the
sword.
21 You will be protected from the lash of the
tongue,
and need not fear when destruction
comes.
22 You will laugh at destruction and famine,
and need not fear the beasts of the
earth.
23 For you will have a covenant with the
stones of the field,
and the wild animals will be at peace
with you.
24 You will know that your tent is secure;
you will take stock of your property
and find nothing missing.
25 You will know that your children will be
many,

[a] *21* Some interpreters end the quotation after verse 17. [b] *17* Hebrew *Shaddai*; here and throughout Job

and your descendants like the grass of
the earth.
26 You will come to the grave in full vigor,
like sheaves gathered in season.

27 "We have examined this, and it is true.
So hear it and apply it to yourself."

Job

6 Then Job replied:

2 "If only my anguish could be weighed
and all my misery be placed on the
scales!
3 It would surely outweigh the sand of the
seas—
no wonder my words have been
impetuous.
4 The arrows of the Almighty are in me,
my spirit drinks in their poison;
God's terrors are marshaled against me.
5 Does a wild donkey bray when it has
grass,
or an ox bellow when it has fodder?
6 Is tasteless food eaten without salt,
or is there flavor in the white of an egg[a]?
7 I refuse to touch it;
such food makes me ill.

8 "Oh, that I might have my request,
that God would grant what I hope for,
9 that God would be willing to crush me,
to let loose his hand and cut me off!
10 Then I would still have this consolation—
my joy in unrelenting pain—
that I had not denied the words of the
Holy One.

11 "What strength do I have, that I should
still hope?
What prospects, that I should be
patient?
12 Do I have the strength of stone?
Is my flesh bronze?
13 Do I have any power to help myself,
now that success has been driven from
me?

14 "A despairing man should have the
devotion of his friends,
even though he forsakes the fear of the
Almighty.
15 But my brothers are as undependable as
intermittent streams,
as the streams that overflow
16 when darkened by thawing ice
and swollen with melting snow,
17 but that cease to flow in the dry season,
and in the heat vanish from their
channels.
18 Caravans turn aside from their routes;
they go up into the wasteland and
perish.
19 The caravans of Tema look for water,
the traveling merchants of Sheba look
in hope.
20 They are distressed, because they had been
confident;
they arrive there, only to be
disappointed.
21 Now you too have proved to be of no help;
you see something dreadful and are
afraid.
22 Have I ever said, 'Give something on my
behalf,
pay a ransom for me from your wealth,
23 deliver me from the hand of the enemy,
ransom me from the clutches of the
ruthless'?

24 "Teach me, and I will be quiet;
show me where I have been wrong.
25 How painful are honest words!
But what do your arguments prove?
26 Do you mean to correct what I say,
and treat the words of a despairing man
as wind?
27 You would even cast lots for the fatherless
and barter away your friend.

28 "But now be so kind as to look at me.
Would I lie to your face?
29 Relent, do not be unjust;
reconsider, for my integrity is at stake.[b]
30 Is there any wickedness on my lips?
Can my mouth not discern malice?

7 "Does not man have hard service on
earth?
Are not his days like those of a hired
man?
2 Like a slave longing for the evening
shadows,
or a hired man waiting eagerly for his
wages,
3 so I have been allotted months of futility,
and nights of misery have been assigned
to me.
4 When I lie down I think, 'How long
before I get up?'
The night drags on, and I toss till
dawn.
5 My body is clothed with worms and scabs,
my skin is broken and festering.

[a] 6 The meaning of the Hebrew for this phrase is uncertain. [b] 29 Or *my righteousness still stands*

W

WEDNESDAY
READ JOB 6:11–30

UNFRIENDLY ADVICE

Have you ever wondered what married life would be like without friends? Although I find marriage the most rewarding human relationship, my life is enriched by the involvement and relationships my wife and I have with our friends. Our friends add a special dimension to our marriage. Not only do they allow us to share personal experiences, but they also encourage us and support us along the way.

But friends are not always a positive influence. Perhaps you and your spouse have experienced the interference of friends. Sometimes their influence is subtle, like when your buddies invite you to an activity, but your wife wants you to stay home and watch a movie with her. At other times they interfere in ways that threaten the health of your marriage. Perhaps you have friends who persist in giving advice that is consistently wrong. In such situations, it's difficult to know what to do with the advice. Following bad advice will lead to trouble, but ignoring it might result in a strained friendship. Sometimes, it's hard to know what to do. Do you protect your marriage or your friendship? Although the choice would seem clear, it's not always an easy one for married partners.

"A despairing man should have the devotion of his friends, even though he forsakes the fear of the Almighty."

— Job 6:14

let's *talk*

✦ When have we been given advice from friends that we knew was not good for us as a couple? How did we handle it?

✦ What are some reasons why people try interfering in our lives? Are they purposely trying to harm us? What difference does their motivation make in how we respond?

✦ Have we in any way withheld kindness or support from friends who we knew were going through some difficulty? How did we do that? What should we have done?

Job's friends made some mistaken assumptions about him. They tried to convince him that God was punishing him for some sin. Job argued with his friends to no avail; they persisted in blaming him for his misfortune. Job challenged them to show him his sin, saying, "Teach me, and I will be quiet; show me where I have been wrong" (Job 6:24). They couldn't do that, of course, so Job did the right thing: He looked not to his friends but to God for justification.

Here is where we need to emulate Job. We must weigh the advice of friends against what God says in his Word. And if their advice doesn't measure up, we must go on, like Job, to wait for God to speak. And when God does answer, we will be struck speechless with the power of the Almighty. Like Job, we will fall on our knees and confess, "Surely I spoke of things I did not understand, things too wonderful for me to know" (Job 42:3).

Christian couples don't need to worry about being friendless when they resist bad advice or disagree with a friend. Jesus told his disciples that his friends are those who do his will (see John 15:14). We are justified before God in Christ, who took our sin and bore its penalty on the cross and gave us his righteousness. In doing so he became both our friend and our Lord.

Be a friend to your spouse, and when those friends outside your marriage give bad advice, remind your spouse that because you are justified before God, you can listen to God's advice rather than that of friends. When bad advice comes from friends, the best response is to pray for those friends and seek God's leading. God's plan and will are for our good.

—ALLEN CURRY

FOR YOUR NEXT DEVOTIONAL READING, TURN TO PAGE 548.

6 "My days are swifter than a weaver's
shuttle,
and they come to an end without hope.
7 Remember, O God, that my life is but a
breath;
my eyes will never see happiness again.
8 The eye that now sees me will see me no
longer;
you will look for me, but I will be no
more.
9 As a cloud vanishes and is gone,
so he who goes down to the grave[a]
does not return.
10 He will never come to his house again;
his place will know him no more.

11 "Therefore I will not keep silent;
I will speak out in the anguish of my
spirit,
I will complain in the bitterness of my
soul.
12 Am I the sea, or the monster of the deep,
that you put me under guard?
13 When I think my bed will comfort me
and my couch will ease my complaint,
14 even then you frighten me with dreams
and terrify me with visions,
15 so that I prefer strangling and death,
rather than this body of mine.
16 I despise my life; I would not live forever.
Let me alone; my days have no
meaning.

17 "What is man that you make so much of
him,
that you give him so much attention,
18 that you examine him every morning
and test him every moment?
19 Will you never look away from me,
or let me alone even for an instant?
20 If I have sinned, what have I done to you,
O watcher of men?
Why have you made me your target?
Have I become a burden to you?[b]
21 Why do you not pardon my offenses
and forgive my sins?
For I will soon lie down in the dust;
you will search for me, but I will be no
more."

Bildad

8 Then Bildad the Shuhite replied:

2 "How long will you say such things?
Your words are a blustering wind.
3 Does God pervert justice?
Does the Almighty pervert what is
right?
4 When your children sinned against him,
he gave them over to the penalty of
their sin.
5 But if you will look to God
and plead with the Almighty,
6 if you are pure and upright,
even now he will rouse himself on your
behalf
and restore you to your rightful place.
7 Your beginnings will seem humble,
so prosperous will your future be.

8 "Ask the former generations
and find out what their fathers learned,
9 for we were born only yesterday and know
nothing,
and our days on earth are but a shadow.
10 Will they not instruct you and tell you?
Will they not bring forth words from
their understanding?
11 Can papyrus grow tall where there is no
marsh?
Can reeds thrive without water?
12 While still growing and uncut,
they wither more quickly than grass.
13 Such is the destiny of all who forget God;
so perishes the hope of the godless.
14 What he trusts in is fragile[c];
what he relies on is a spider's web.
15 He leans on his web, but it gives way;
he clings to it, but it does not hold.
16 He is like a well-watered plant in the
sunshine,
spreading its shoots over the garden;
17 it entwines its roots around a pile of rocks
and looks for a place among the stones.
18 But when it is torn from its spot,
that place disowns it and says, 'I never
saw you.'
19 Surely its life withers away,
and[d] from the soil other plants grow.

20 "Surely God does not reject a blameless
man
or strengthen the hands of evildoers.
21 He will yet fill your mouth with laughter
and your lips with shouts of joy.
22 Your enemies will be clothed in shame,
and the tents of the wicked will be no
more."

---

[a] 9 Hebrew *Sheol* [b] 20 A few manuscripts of the Masoretic Text, an ancient Hebrew scribal tradition and Septuagint; most manuscripts of the Masoretic Text *I have become a burden to myself.* [c] 14 The meaning of the Hebrew for this word is uncertain. [d] 19 Or *Surely all the joy it has / is that*

Job

9 Then Job replied:

2 "Indeed, I know that this is true.
But how can a mortal be righteous before God?
3 Though one wished to dispute with him,
he could not answer him one time out of a thousand.
4 His wisdom is profound, his power is vast.
Who has resisted him and come out unscathed?
5 He moves mountains without their knowing it
and overturns them in his anger.
6 He shakes the earth from its place
and makes its pillars tremble.
7 He speaks to the sun and it does not shine;
he seals off the light of the stars.
8 He alone stretches out the heavens
and treads on the waves of the sea.
9 He is the Maker of the Bear and Orion,
the Pleiades and the constellations of the south.
10 He performs wonders that cannot be fathomed,
miracles that cannot be counted.
11 When he passes me, I cannot see him;
when he goes by, I cannot perceive him.
12 If he snatches away, who can stop him?
Who can say to him, 'What are you doing?'
13 God does not restrain his anger;
even the cohorts of Rahab cowered at his feet.

14 "How then can I dispute with him?
How can I find words to argue with him?
15 Though I were innocent, I could not answer him;
I could only plead with my Judge for mercy.
16 Even if I summoned him and he responded,
I do not believe he would give me a hearing.
17 He would crush me with a storm
and multiply my wounds for no reason.
18 He would not let me regain my breath
but would overwhelm me with misery.
19 If it is a matter of strength, he is mighty!
And if it is a matter of justice, who will summon him[a]?
20 Even if I were innocent, my mouth would condemn me;
if I were blameless, it would pronounce me guilty.

21 "Although I am blameless,
I have no concern for myself;
I despise my own life.
22 It is all the same; that is why I say,
'He destroys both the blameless and the wicked.'
23 When a scourge brings sudden death,
he mocks the despair of the innocent.
24 When a land falls into the hands of the wicked,
he blindfolds its judges.
If it is not he, then who is it?

25 "My days are swifter than a runner;
they fly away without a glimpse of joy.
26 They skim past like boats of papyrus,
like eagles swooping down on their prey.
27 If I say, 'I will forget my complaint,
I will change my expression, and smile,'
28 I still dread all my sufferings,
for I know you will not hold me innocent.
29 Since I am already found guilty,
why should I struggle in vain?
30 Even if I washed myself with soap[b]
and my hands with washing soda,
31 you would plunge me into a slime pit
so that even my clothes would detest me.

32 "He is not a man like me that I might answer him,
that we might confront each other in court.
33 If only there were someone to arbitrate between us,
to lay his hand upon us both,
34 someone to remove God's rod from me,
so that his terror would frighten me no more.
35 Then I would speak up without fear of him,
but as it now stands with me, I cannot.

10 "I loathe my very life;
therefore I will give free rein to my complaint
and speak out in the bitterness of my soul.
2 I will say to God: Do not condemn me,

[a] 19 See Septuagint; Hebrew *me.* [b] 30 Or *snow*

THURSDAY
READ JOB 10:1–22

TURNING BITTERNESS TO JOY

Like Job, Martin knew what it was like to wish he was dead. Death seemed preferable to facing the wreck his marriage had become.

To tell the truth, things had been bad for years—a sort of dull bad. He and his wife, Charlene, had drifted apart. There was no emotional connection between them any more and even less of a sexual connection. Somehow Martin had made his peace with this—he and Charlene just went along, doing their stuff.

He *thought* he had made his peace with the situation. Now, Martin realized that he had been—what did their new counselor call it?—compartmentalizing. All along, he had felt a deep sadness about his marriage, but he had kept that locked up. Everything came to a head when Charlene had an affair in which she not only gave her body, but also her heart, to another man.

Martin knew that he had Biblical grounds to leave the marriage, but what he realized in the wake of the affair was that he still wanted to be married to Charlene. He wanted God to fix his marriage. At least, that's what he wanted on the days he didn't wake up wanting to die.

"I loathe my very life; therefore I will give free rein to my complaint and speak out in the bitterness of my soul."

— Job 10:1

let's talk

✦ Has there been a time when one of us has felt bitter disappointment in our marriage? What provoked that feeling? What did we do about it?

✦ Are there any areas in our marriage about which we feel a sense of bitterness right now? How can we best address these feelings? How can God help us?

✦ What are some ways God can turn bitterness to joy?

Hopefully, you've not been in a marriage quite as heartbreaking as Martin and Charlene's—and certainly your life has not been as tragic as Job's—but maybe you too have been so bitterly disappointed in your marriage that you've fantasized about checking out. Your spouse has failed to live up to your expectations. And perhaps even more disappointing, you've failed to live up to your own expectations. You haven't been the husband or wife you wanted to be. And that disjuncture between hope and reality is too much to bear.

Thankfully, you don't have to bear that disappointment alone. Christ bears it with you. Martin learned that. Initially he hesitated to follow Job's example to "give free rein to [his] complaint and speak out in the bitterness of [his] soul," since even voicing his hurt to God would have required being honest with himself, and Martin didn't want to face his pain. But one morning, sitting with his Bible—reading, yes, the book of Job—Martin cracked. All his feelings came pouring out. And God listened. That talk with God prompted lots of other conversations, sometimes very angry conversations, with Charlene, with their new counselor and with a trusted couple from church.

Martin says he's learned a lot in the past three years about himself and his wife, about forgiveness and reconciliation. But most important, he says, he has learned to be honest with God. "I now understand that nothing is gained by trying to keep my feelings from God," says Martin. "I'm always better off having laid it all out there before our God, who alone can turn our fiercest bitterness into love and joy."

—LAUREN WINNER

FOR YOUR NEXT DEVOTIONAL READING, TURN TO PAGE 555.

but tell me what charges you have
against me.
3 Does it please you to oppress me,
to spurn the work of your hands,
while you smile on the schemes of the
wicked?
4 Do you have eyes of flesh?
Do you see as a mortal sees?
5 Are your days like those of a mortal
or your years like those of a man,
6 that you must search out my faults
and probe after my sin—
7 though you know that I am not guilty
and that no one can rescue me from
your hand?

8 "Your hands shaped me and made me.
Will you now turn and destroy me?
9 Remember that you molded me like clay.
Will you now turn me to dust again?
10 Did you not pour me out like milk
and curdle me like cheese,
11 clothe me with skin and flesh
and knit me together with bones and
sinews?
12 You gave me life and showed me kindness,
and in your providence watched over
my spirit.

13 "But this is what you concealed in your
heart,
and I know that this was in your mind:
14 If I sinned, you would be watching me
and would not let my offense go
unpunished.
15 If I am guilty—woe to me!
Even if I am innocent, I cannot lift my
head,
for I am full of shame
and drowned in[a] my affliction.
16 If I hold my head high, you stalk me like a
lion
and again display your awesome power
against me.
17 You bring new witnesses against me
and increase your anger toward me;
your forces come against me wave upon
wave.

18 "Why then did you bring me out of the
womb?
I wish I had died before any eye saw
me.
19 If only I had never come into being,
or had been carried straight from the
womb to the grave!
20 Are not my few days almost over?
Turn away from me so I can have a
moment's joy
21 before I go to the place of no return,
to the land of gloom and deep
shadow,[b]
22 to the land of deepest night,
of deep shadow and disorder,
where even the light is like darkness."

Zophar

11 Then Zophar the Naamathite replied:

2 "Are all these words to go unanswered?
Is this talker to be vindicated?
3 Will your idle talk reduce men to silence?
Will no one rebuke you when you
mock?
4 You say to God, 'My beliefs are flawless
and I am pure in your sight.'
5 Oh, how I wish that God would speak,
that he would open his lips against you
6 and disclose to you the secrets of wisdom,
for true wisdom has two sides.
Know this: God has even forgotten
some of your sin.

7 "Can you fathom the mysteries of God?
Can you probe the limits of the
Almighty?
8 They are higher than the heavens—what
can you do?
They are deeper than the depths of the
grave[c]—what can you know?
9 Their measure is longer than the earth
and wider than the sea.

10 "If he comes along and confines you in
prison
and convenes a court, who can oppose
him?
11 Surely he recognizes deceitful men;
and when he sees evil, does he not take
note?
12 But a witless man can no more become
wise
than a wild donkey's colt can be born a
man.[d]

13 "Yet if you devote your heart to him
and stretch out your hands to him,
14 if you put away the sin that is in your
hand
and allow no evil to dwell in your tent,
15 then you will lift up your face without
shame;

[a] 15 Or *and aware of* [b] 21 Or *and the shadow of death*; also in verse 22 [c] 8 Hebrew *than Sheol* [d] 12 Or *wild donkey can be born tame*

you will stand firm and without fear.
16 You will surely forget your trouble,
recalling it only as waters gone by.
17 Life will be brighter than noonday,
and darkness will become like morning.
18 You will be secure, because there is hope;
you will look about you and take your rest in safety.
19 You will lie down, with no one to make you afraid,
and many will court your favor.
20 But the eyes of the wicked will fail,
and escape will elude them;
their hope will become a dying gasp."

Job

12 Then Job replied:

2 "Doubtless you are the people,
and wisdom will die with you!
3 But I have a mind as well as you;
I am not inferior to you.
Who does not know all these things?

4 "I have become a laughingstock to my friends,
though I called upon God and he answered—
a mere laughingstock, though righteous and blameless!
5 Men at ease have contempt for misfortune
as the fate of those whose feet are slipping.
6 The tents of marauders are undisturbed,
and those who provoke God are secure—
those who carry their god in their hands.[a]

7 "But ask the animals, and they will teach you,
or the birds of the air, and they will tell you;
8 or speak to the earth, and it will teach you,
or let the fish of the sea inform you.
9 Which of all these does not know
that the hand of the LORD has done this?
10 In his hand is the life of every creature
and the breath of all mankind.
11 Does not the ear test words
as the tongue tastes food?
12 Is not wisdom found among the aged?
Does not long life bring understanding?

13 "To God belong wisdom and power;
counsel and understanding are his.
14 What he tears down cannot be rebuilt;
the man he imprisons cannot be released.
15 If he holds back the waters, there is drought;
if he lets them loose, they devastate the land.
16 To him belong strength and victory;
both deceived and deceiver are his.
17 He leads counselors away stripped
and makes fools of judges.
18 He takes off the shackles put on by kings
and ties a loincloth[b] around their waist.
19 He leads priests away stripped
and overthrows men long established.
20 He silences the lips of trusted advisers
and takes away the discernment of elders.
21 He pours contempt on nobles
and disarms the mighty.
22 He reveals the deep things of darkness
and brings deep shadows into the light.
23 He makes nations great, and destroys them;
he enlarges nations, and disperses them.
24 He deprives the leaders of the earth of their reason;
he sends them wandering through a trackless waste.
25 They grope in darkness with no light;
he makes them stagger like drunkards.

13 "My eyes have seen all this,
my ears have heard and understood it.
2 What you know, I also know;
I am not inferior to you.
3 But I desire to speak to the Almighty
and to argue my case with God.
4 You, however, smear me with lies;
you are worthless physicians, all of you!
5 If only you would be altogether silent!
For you, that would be wisdom.
6 Hear now my argument;
listen to the plea of my lips.
7 Will you speak wickedly on God's behalf?
Will you speak deceitfully for him?
8 Will you show him partiality?
Will you argue the case for God?
9 Would it turn out well if he examined you?
Could you deceive him as you might deceive men?
10 He would surely rebuke you
if you secretly showed partiality.

---

[a] 6 Or *secure / in what God's hand brings them* [b] 18 Or *shackles of kings / and ties a belt*

11 Would not his splendor terrify you?
Would not the dread of him fall on you?
12 Your maxims are proverbs of ashes;
your defenses are defenses of clay.

13 "Keep silent and let me speak;
then let come to me what may.
14 Why do I put myself in jeopardy
and take my life in my hands?
15 Though he slay me, yet will I hope in him;
I will surely[a] defend my ways to his face.
16 Indeed, this will turn out for my deliverance,
for no godless man would dare come before him!
17 Listen carefully to my words;
let your ears take in what I say.
18 Now that I have prepared my case,
I know I will be vindicated.
19 Can anyone bring charges against me?
If so, I will be silent and die.

20 "Only grant me these two things, O God,
and then I will not hide from you:
21 Withdraw your hand far from me,
and stop frightening me with your terrors.
22 Then summon me and I will answer,
or let me speak, and you reply.
23 How many wrongs and sins have I committed?
Show me my offense and my sin.
24 Why do you hide your face
and consider me your enemy?
25 Will you torment a windblown leaf?
Will you chase after dry chaff?
26 For you write down bitter things against me
and make me inherit the sins of my youth.
27 You fasten my feet in shackles;
you keep close watch on all my paths
by putting marks on the soles of my feet.

28 "So man wastes away like something rotten,
like a garment eaten by moths.

14 "Man born of woman
is of few days and full of trouble.
2 He springs up like a flower and withers away;
like a fleeting shadow, he does not endure.
3 Do you fix your eye on such a one?
Will you bring him[b] before you for judgment?
4 Who can bring what is pure from the impure?
No one!
5 Man's days are determined;
you have decreed the number of his months
and have set limits he cannot exceed.
6 So look away from him and let him alone,
till he has put in his time like a hired man.

7 "At least there is hope for a tree:
If it is cut down, it will sprout again,
and its new shoots will not fail.
8 Its roots may grow old in the ground
and its stump die in the soil,
9 yet at the scent of water it will bud
and put forth shoots like a plant.
10 But man dies and is laid low;
he breathes his last and is no more.
11 As water disappears from the sea
or a riverbed becomes parched and dry,
12 so man lies down and does not rise;
till the heavens are no more, men will not awake
or be roused from their sleep.

13 "If only you would hide me in the grave[c]
and conceal me till your anger has passed!
If only you would set me a time
and then remember me!
14 If a man dies, will he live again?
All the days of my hard service
I will wait for my renewal[d] to come.
15 You will call and I will answer you;
you will long for the creature your hands have made.
16 Surely then you will count my steps
but not keep track of my sin.
17 My offenses will be sealed up in a bag;
you will cover over my sin.

18 "But as a mountain erodes and crumbles
and as a rock is moved from its place,
19 as water wears away stones
and torrents wash away the soil,
so you destroy man's hope.
20 You overpower him once for all, and he is gone;
you change his countenance and send him away.

---

[a] 15 Or *He will surely slay me; I have no hope — / yet I will* [b] 3 Septuagint, Vulgate and Syriac; Hebrew *me* [c] 13 Hebrew *Sheol*
[d] 14 Or *release*

21 If his sons are honored, he does not know it;
if they are brought low, he does not see it.
22 He feels but the pain of his own body
and mourns only for himself."

Eliphaz

15 Then Eliphaz the Temanite replied:

2 "Would a wise man answer with empty notions
or fill his belly with the hot east wind?
3 Would he argue with useless words,
with speeches that have no value?
4 But you even undermine piety
and hinder devotion to God.
5 Your sin prompts your mouth;
you adopt the tongue of the crafty.
6 Your own mouth condemns you, not mine;
your own lips testify against you.

7 "Are you the first man ever born?
Were you brought forth before the hills?
8 Do you listen in on God's council?
Do you limit wisdom to yourself?
9 What do you know that we do not know?
What insights do you have that we do not have?
10 The gray-haired and the aged are on our side,
men even older than your father.
11 Are God's consolations not enough for you,
words spoken gently to you?
12 Why has your heart carried you away,
and why do your eyes flash,
13 so that you vent your rage against God
and pour out such words from your mouth?

14 "What is man, that he could be pure,
or one born of woman, that he could be righteous?
15 If God places no trust in his holy ones,
if even the heavens are not pure in his eyes,
16 how much less man, who is vile and corrupt,
who drinks up evil like water!

17 "Listen to me and I will explain to you;
let me tell you what I have seen,
18 what wise men have declared,
hiding nothing received from their fathers
19 (to whom alone the land was given
when no alien passed among them):
20 All his days the wicked man suffers torment,
the ruthless through all the years stored up for him.
21 Terrifying sounds fill his ears;
when all seems well, marauders attack him.
22 He despairs of escaping the darkness;
he is marked for the sword.
23 He wanders about—food for vultures[a];
he knows the day of darkness is at hand.
24 Distress and anguish fill him with terror;
they overwhelm him, like a king poised to attack,
25 because he shakes his fist at God
and vaunts himself against the Almighty,
26 defiantly charging against him
with a thick, strong shield.

27 "Though his face is covered with fat
and his waist bulges with flesh,
28 he will inhabit ruined towns
and houses where no one lives,
houses crumbling to rubble.
29 He will no longer be rich and his wealth will not endure,
nor will his possessions spread over the land.
30 He will not escape the darkness;
a flame will wither his shoots,
and the breath of God's mouth will carry him away.
31 Let him not deceive himself by trusting what is worthless,
for he will get nothing in return.
32 Before his time he will be paid in full,
and his branches will not flourish.
33 He will be like a vine stripped of its unripe grapes,
like an olive tree shedding its blossoms.
34 For the company of the godless will be barren,
and fire will consume the tents of those who love bribes.
35 They conceive trouble and give birth to evil;
their womb fashions deceit."

---

a 23 Or *about, looking for food*

Job

16 Then Job replied:

2 "I have heard many things like these;
miserable comforters are you all!
3 Will your long-winded speeches never end?
What ails you that you keep on arguing?
4 I also could speak like you,
if you were in my place;
I could make fine speeches against you
and shake my head at you.
5 But my mouth would encourage you;
comfort from my lips would bring you relief.

6 "Yet if I speak, my pain is not relieved;
and if I refrain, it does not go away.
7 Surely, O God, you have worn me out;
you have devastated my entire household.
8 You have bound me—and it has become a witness;
my gauntness rises up and testifies against me.
9 God assails me and tears me in his anger
and gnashes his teeth at me;
my opponent fastens on me his piercing eyes.
10 Men open their mouths to jeer at me;
they strike my cheek in scorn
and unite together against me.
11 God has turned me over to evil men
and thrown me into the clutches of the wicked.
12 All was well with me, but he shattered me;
he seized me by the neck and crushed me.
He has made me his target;
13 his archers surround me.
Without pity, he pierces my kidneys
and spills my gall on the ground.
14 Again and again he bursts upon me;
he rushes at me like a warrior.

15 "I have sewed sackcloth over my skin
and buried my brow in the dust.
16 My face is red with weeping,
deep shadows ring my eyes;
17 yet my hands have been free of violence
and my prayer is pure.

18 "O earth, do not cover my blood;
may my cry never be laid to rest!
19 Even now my witness is in heaven;
my advocate is on high.
20 My intercessor is my friend[a]
as my eyes pour out tears to God;
21 on behalf of a man he pleads with God
as a man pleads for his friend.

22 "Only a few years will pass
before I go on the journey of no return.

17 1 My spirit is broken,
my days are cut short,
the grave awaits me.
2 Surely mockers surround me;
my eyes must dwell on their hostility.

3 "Give me, O God, the pledge you demand.
Who else will put up security for me?
4 You have closed their minds to understanding;
therefore you will not let them triumph.
5 If a man denounces his friends for reward,
the eyes of his children will fail.

6 "God has made me a byword to everyone,
a man in whose face people spit.
7 My eyes have grown dim with grief;
my whole frame is but a shadow.
8 Upright men are appalled at this;
the innocent are aroused against the ungodly.
9 Nevertheless, the righteous will hold to their ways,
and those with clean hands will grow stronger.

10 "But come on, all of you, try again!
I will not find a wise man among you.
11 My days have passed, my plans are shattered,
and so are the desires of my heart.
12 These men turn night into day;
in the face of darkness they say, 'Light is near.'
13 If the only home I hope for is the grave,[b]
if I spread out my bed in darkness,
14 if I say to corruption, 'You are my father,'
and to the worm, 'My mother' or 'My sister,'
15 where then is my hope?
Who can see any hope for me?
16 Will it go down to the gates of death[b]?
Will we descend together into the dust?"

---

[a] 20 Or *My friends treat me with scorn* [b] 13,16 Hebrew *Sheol*

Bildad

18 Then Bildad the Shuhite replied:

2 "When will you end these speeches?
Be sensible, and then we can talk.
3 Why are we regarded as cattle
and considered stupid in your sight?
4 You who tear yourself to pieces in your anger,
is the earth to be abandoned for your sake?
Or must the rocks be moved from their place?

5 "The lamp of the wicked is snuffed out;
the flame of his fire stops burning.
6 The light in his tent becomes dark;
the lamp beside him goes out.
7 The vigor of his step is weakened;
his own schemes throw him down.
8 His feet thrust him into a net
and he wanders into its mesh.
9 A trap seizes him by the heel;
a snare holds him fast.
10 A noose is hidden for him on the ground;
a trap lies in his path.
11 Terrors startle him on every side
and dog his every step.
12 Calamity is hungry for him;
disaster is ready for him when he falls.
13 It eats away parts of his skin;
death's firstborn devours his limbs.
14 He is torn from the security of his tent
and marched off to the king of terrors.
15 Fire resides[a] in his tent;
burning sulfur is scattered over his dwelling.
16 His roots dry up below
and his branches wither above.
17 The memory of him perishes from the earth;
he has no name in the land.
18 He is driven from light into darkness
and is banished from the world.
19 He has no offspring or descendants among his people,
no survivor where once he lived.
20 Men of the west are appalled at his fate;
men of the east are seized with horror.
21 Surely such is the dwelling of an evil man;
such is the place of one who knows not God."

Job

19 Then Job replied:

2 "How long will you torment me
and crush me with words?
3 Ten times now you have reproached me;
shamelessly you attack me.
4 If it is true that I have gone astray,
my error remains my concern alone.
5 If indeed you would exalt yourselves above me
and use my humiliation against me,
6 then know that God has wronged me
and drawn his net around me.

7 "Though I cry, 'I've been wronged!' I get no response;
though I call for help, there is no justice.
8 He has blocked my way so I cannot pass;
he has shrouded my paths in darkness.
9 He has stripped me of my honor
and removed the crown from my head.
10 He tears me down on every side till I am gone;
he uproots my hope like a tree.
11 His anger burns against me;
he counts me among his enemies.
12 His troops advance in force;
they build a siege ramp against me
and encamp around my tent.

13 "He has alienated my brothers from me;
my acquaintances are completely estranged from me.
14 My kinsmen have gone away;
my friends have forgotten me.
15 My guests and my maidservants count me a stranger;
they look upon me as an alien.
16 I summon my servant, but he does not answer,
though I beg him with my own mouth.
17 My breath is offensive to my wife;
I am loathsome to my own brothers.
18 Even the little boys scorn me;
when I appear, they ridicule me.
19 All my intimate friends detest me;
those I love have turned against me.
20 I am nothing but skin and bones;
I have escaped with only the skin of my teeth.[b]

21 "Have pity on me, my friends, have pity,
for the hand of God has struck me.
22 Why do you pursue me as God does?

[a] 15 Or *Nothing he had remains* [b] 20 Or *only my gums*

F FRIDAY

READ JOB 19:21–29

JOB'S HOPE

A teenager told me she thought her parents were about to divorce. She had heard her parents' nightly arguments and watched her mom turn away her tear-stained face when asked about the situation. The parents of many of this young woman's friends had divorced, so she assumed her parents were next.

The teen did not give me permission to talk to her parents about her fears. Yet I felt obligated to open a pastoral door for either the husband or the wife if it would allow them to get help and healing.

When an opportunity came to enter that home, I lingered in order to hint at the well-being of the marriage. Neither spouse did more than smile and spout platitudes, but a week later the husband called and said he wanted to talk.

He furtively slipped into my office. Any excuse to leave would have been welcome, but none presented itself. After moments of expansive quiet and several invitations to say what was on his mind, he finally began to talk.

He had always thought marriage would be wonderful, he said. His parents had been solid in their commitments, and his dating relationship with his wife had been marvelous. They had seemed to be a perfect match, sharing interests, passions and religious commitments.

But several years into their marriage, his wife was in an accident. She experienced a closed-head injury that altered her personality. She became suspicious, forgetful, impatient and abusive. What's more, she was an emotional chameleon. In public her negative symptoms disappeared. Even her sisters and parents had no idea of the ogre she could become. The husband's pleas for help were questioned and pushed aside. He felt very alone.

I listened as the hurting man wept, and I thought of Job, around whom unseen and unjust powers had swirled. Job was bewildered. So was this misunderstood husband. Neither man understood why bad things were happening. Each faced a murky future in an iffy marriage.

Yet I was amazed by this husband's testimony. When I asked him if he had considered divorce, he said, "Never! I made a vow and my wife needs to count on that, especially now. Even if she doesn't know that she needs me." He added, "I read about a note scratched into a basement in Paris during World War II: 'I believe in the sun even when it's not shining. I believe in love even when I can't feel it. I believe in God even when he is silent.' "

I was reminded of Job when he professed, "I know that my Redeemer lives, and that in the end he will stand upon the earth." Though Job was unable to see how, he was confident that neither loss nor pain nor death itself could stymie God's care for him.

If we are believers, there is no lament we can sing that does not have an Easter refrain. Trials and torments and troubles are part of our lives here, but they are not the whole story. Christ rose from the dead, and because he lives, we too shall live.

—WAYNE BROUWER

"I know that my Redeemer lives, and that in the end he will stand upon the earth."

— JOB 19:25

let's talk

- ✦ When have we felt plagued like Job? How has trouble affected our relationship?
- ✦ When life was good, Job offered daily sacrifices for himself and his family (see Job 1:5). What habits are we developing in good times that will help us through the tough times?
- ✦ Whom do we look to as models of endurance and hope? What have these people taught us? How might they serve as mentors?

FOR YOUR NEXT DEVOTIONAL READING, TURN TO PAGE 560.

Will you never get enough of my flesh?
23 "Oh, that my words were recorded,
that they were written on a scroll,
24 that they were inscribed with an iron tool
on[a] lead,
or engraved in rock forever!
25 I know that my Redeemer[b] lives,
and that in the end he will stand upon
the earth.[c]
26 And after my skin has been destroyed,
yet[d] in[e] my flesh I will see God;
27 I myself will see him
with my own eyes—I, and not another.
How my heart yearns within me!
28 "If you say, 'How we will hound him,
since the root of the trouble lies in
him,[f]
29 you should fear the sword yourselves;
for wrath will bring punishment by the
sword,
and then you will know that there is
judgment.[g]"

Zophar

20 Then Zophar the Naamathite replied:

2 "My troubled thoughts prompt me
to answer
because I am greatly disturbed.
3 I hear a rebuke that dishonors me,
and my understanding inspires me to
reply.
4 "Surely you know how it has been from of
old,
ever since man[h] was placed on the
earth,
5 that the mirth of the wicked is brief,
the joy of the godless lasts but a
moment.
6 Though his pride reaches to the heavens
and his head touches the clouds,
7 he will perish forever, like his own dung;
those who have seen him will say,
'Where is he?'
8 Like a dream he flies away, no more to be
found,
banished like a vision of the night.
9 The eye that saw him will not see him
again;
his place will look on him no more.
10 His children must make amends to the
poor;
his own hands must give back his
wealth.
11 The youthful vigor that fills his bones
will lie with him in the dust.

12 "Though evil is sweet in his mouth
and he hides it under his tongue,
13 though he cannot bear to let it go
and keeps it in his mouth,
14 yet his food will turn sour in his
stomach;
it will become the venom of serpents
within him.
15 He will spit out the riches he swallowed;
God will make his stomach vomit them
up.
16 He will suck the poison of serpents;
the fangs of an adder will kill him.
17 He will not enjoy the streams,
the rivers flowing with honey and
cream.
18 What he toiled for he must give back
uneaten;
he will not enjoy the profit from his
trading.
19 For he has oppressed the poor and left
them destitute;
he has seized houses he did not build.

20 "Surely he will have no respite from his
craving;
he cannot save himself by his treasure.
21 Nothing is left for him to devour;
his prosperity will not endure.
22 In the midst of his plenty, distress will
overtake him;
the full force of misery will come upon
him.
23 When he has filled his belly,
God will vent his burning anger against
him
and rain down his blows upon him.
24 Though he flees from an iron weapon,
a bronze-tipped arrow pierces him.
25 He pulls it out of his back,
the gleaming point out of his liver.
Terrors will come over him;
26 total darkness lies in wait for his
treasures.
A fire unfanned will consume him
and devour what is left in his tent.
27 The heavens will expose his guilt;
the earth will rise up against him.
28 A flood will carry off his house,

[a] 24 Or *and* [b] 25 Or *defender* [c] 25 Or *upon my grave* [d] 26 Or *And after I awake, / though this ⌞body⌟ has been destroyed, / then* [e] 26 Or */ apart from* [f] 28 Many Hebrew manuscripts, Septuagint and Vulgate; most Hebrew manuscripts *me* [g] 29 Or */ that you may come to know the Almighty* [h] 4 Or *Adam*

rushing waters[a] on the day of God's
wrath.
29 Such is the fate God allots the wicked,
the heritage appointed for them by
God."

Job

21 Then Job replied:

2 "Listen carefully to my words;
let this be the consolation you give me.
3 Bear with me while I speak,
and after I have spoken, mock on.

4 "Is my complaint directed to man?
Why should I not be impatient?
5 Look at me and be astonished;
clap your hand over your mouth.
6 When I think about this, I am terrified;
trembling seizes my body.
7 Why do the wicked live on,
growing old and increasing in power?
8 They see their children established around
them,
their offspring before their eyes.
9 Their homes are safe and free from fear;
the rod of God is not upon them.
10 Their bulls never fail to breed;
their cows calve and do not miscarry.
11 They send forth their children as a flock;
their little ones dance about.
12 They sing to the music of tambourine and
harp;
they make merry to the sound of the
flute.
13 They spend their years in prosperity
and go down to the grave[b] in peace.[c]
14 Yet they say to God, 'Leave us alone!
We have no desire to know your ways.
15 Who is the Almighty, that we should serve
him?
What would we gain by praying to
him?'
16 But their prosperity is not in their own
hands,
so I stand aloof from the counsel of the
wicked.

17 "Yet how often is the lamp of the wicked
snuffed out?
How often does calamity come upon
them,
the fate God allots in his anger?
18 How often are they like straw before the
wind,
like chaff swept away by a gale?
19 ⌊It is said,⌋ 'God stores up a man's
punishment for his sons.'
Let him repay the man himself, so that
he will know it!
20 Let his own eyes see his destruction;
let him drink of the wrath of the
Almighty.[d]
21 For what does he care about the family he
leaves behind
when his allotted months come to an
end?

22 "Can anyone teach knowledge to God,
since he judges even the highest?
23 One man dies in full vigor,
completely secure and at ease,
24 his body[e] well nourished,
his bones rich with marrow.
25 Another man dies in bitterness of soul,
never having enjoyed anything good.
26 Side by side they lie in the dust,
and worms cover them both.

27 "I know full well what you are thinking,
the schemes by which you would
wrong me.
28 You say, 'Where now is the great man's
house,
the tents where wicked men lived?'
29 Have you never questioned those who
travel?
Have you paid no regard to their
accounts—
30 that the evil man is spared from the day of
calamity,
that he is delivered from[f] the day of
wrath?
31 Who denounces his conduct to his face?
Who repays him for what he has done?
32 He is carried to the grave,
and watch is kept over his tomb.
33 The soil in the valley is sweet to him;
all men follow after him,
and a countless throng goes[g] before
him.

34 "So how can you console me with your
nonsense?
Nothing is left of your answers but
falsehood!"

[a] 28 Or *The possessions in his house will be carried off, / washed away* [b] 13 Hebrew *Sheol* [c] 13 Or *in an instant* [d] 17-20 Verses 17 and 18 may be taken as exclamations and 19 and 20 as declarations. [e] 24 The meaning of the Hebrew for this word is uncertain. [f] 30 Or *man is reserved for the day of calamity, / that he is brought forth to* [g] 33 Or */ as a countless throng went*

Eliphaz

22 Then Eliphaz the Temanite replied:

2 "Can a man be of benefit to God?
Can even a wise man benefit him?
3 What pleasure would it give the Almighty
if you were righteous?
What would he gain if your ways were
blameless?

4 "Is it for your piety that he rebukes you
and brings charges against you?
5 Is not your wickedness great?
Are not your sins endless?
6 You demanded security from your
brothers for no reason;
you stripped men of their clothing,
leaving them naked.
7 You gave no water to the weary
and you withheld food from the
hungry,
8 though you were a powerful man, owning
land—
an honored man, living on it.
9 And you sent widows away empty-handed
and broke the strength of the fatherless.
10 That is why snares are all around you,
why sudden peril terrifies you,
11 why it is so dark you cannot see,
and why a flood of water covers you.

12 "Is not God in the heights of heaven?
And see how lofty are the highest stars!
13 Yet you say, 'What does God know?
Does he judge through such darkness?
14 Thick clouds veil him, so he does not see
us
as he goes about in the vaulted
heavens.'
15 Will you keep to the old path
that evil men have trod?
16 They were carried off before their time,
their foundations washed away by a
flood.
17 They said to God, 'Leave us alone!
What can the Almighty do to us?'
18 Yet it was he who filled their houses with
good things,
so I stand aloof from the counsel of the
wicked.

19 "The righteous see their ruin and rejoice;
the innocent mock them, saying,
20 'Surely our foes are destroyed,
and fire devours their wealth.'

21 "Submit to God and be at peace with him;
in this way prosperity will come to you.
22 Accept instruction from his mouth
and lay up his words in your heart.
23 If you return to the Almighty, you will be
restored:
If you remove wickedness far from your
tent
24 and assign your nuggets to the dust,
your gold of Ophir to the rocks in the
ravines,
25 then the Almighty will be your gold,
the choicest silver for you.
26 Surely then you will find delight in the
Almighty
and will lift up your face to God.
27 You will pray to him, and he will hear you,
and you will fulfill your vows.
28 What you decide on will be done,
and light will shine on your ways.
29 When men are brought low and you say,
'Lift them up!'
then he will save the downcast.
30 He will deliver even one who is not
innocent,
who will be delivered through the
cleanness of your hands."

Job

23 Then Job replied:

2 "Even today my complaint is bitter;
his hand[a] is heavy in spite of[b] my
groaning.
3 If only I knew where to find him;
if only I could go to his dwelling!
4 I would state my case before him
and fill my mouth with arguments.
5 I would find out what he would answer
me,
and consider what he would say.
6 Would he oppose me with great power?
No, he would not press charges against
me.
7 There an upright man could present his
case before him,
and I would be delivered forever from
my judge.

8 "But if I go to the east, he is not there;
if I go to the west, I do not find him.
9 When he is at work in the north, I do not
see him;
when he turns to the south, I catch no
glimpse of him.
10 But he knows the way that I take;

---

[a] 2 Septuagint and Syriac; Hebrew / *the hand on me* [b] 2 Or *heavy on me in*

when he has tested me, I will come
forth as gold.
11 My feet have closely followed his steps;
I have kept to his way without turning
aside.
12 I have not departed from the commands
of his lips;
I have treasured the words of his mouth
more than my daily bread.

13 "But he stands alone, and who can oppose
him?
He does whatever he pleases.
14 He carries out his decree against me,
and many such plans he still has in
store.
15 That is why I am terrified before him;
when I think of all this, I fear him.
16 God has made my heart faint;
the Almighty has terrified me.
17 Yet I am not silenced by the darkness,
by the thick darkness that covers my
face.

24 "Why does the Almighty not set times
for judgment?
Why must those who know him look
in vain for such days?
2 Men move boundary stones;
they pasture flocks they have stolen.
3 They drive away the orphan's donkey
and take the widow's ox in pledge.
4 They thrust the needy from the path
and force all the poor of the land into
hiding.
5 Like wild donkeys in the desert,
the poor go about their labor of
foraging food;
the wasteland provides food for their
children.
6 They gather fodder in the fields
and glean in the vineyards of the
wicked.
7 Lacking clothes, they spend the night
naked;
they have nothing to cover themselves
in the cold.
8 They are drenched by mountain rains
and hug the rocks for lack of shelter.
9 The fatherless child is snatched from the
breast;
the infant of the poor is seized for a
debt.
10 Lacking clothes, they go about naked;
they carry the sheaves, but still go
hungry.
11 They crush olives among the terraces[a];
they tread the winepresses, yet suffer
thirst.
12 The groans of the dying rise from the city,
and the souls of the wounded cry out
for help.
But God charges no one with
wrongdoing.

13 "There are those who rebel against the
light,
who do not know its ways
or stay in its paths.
14 When daylight is gone, the murderer rises
up
and kills the poor and needy;
in the night he steals forth like a thief.
15 The eye of the adulterer watches for dusk;
he thinks, 'No eye will see me,'
and he keeps his face concealed.
16 In the dark, men break into houses,
but by day they shut themselves in;
they want nothing to do with the light.
17 For all of them, deep darkness is their
morning[b];
they make friends with the terrors of
darkness.[c]

18 "Yet they are foam on the surface of the
water;
their portion of the land is cursed,
so that no one goes to the vineyards.
19 As heat and drought snatch away the
melted snow,
so the grave[d] snatches away those who
have sinned.
20 The womb forgets them,
the worm feasts on them;
evil men are no longer remembered
but are broken like a tree.
21 They prey on the barren and childless
woman,
and to the widow show no kindness.
22 But God drags away the mighty by his
power;
though they become established, they
have no assurance of life.
23 He may let them rest in a feeling of
security,
but his eyes are on their ways.
24 For a little while they are exalted, and then
they are gone;

---

[a] 11 Or *olives between the millstones*; the meaning of the Hebrew for this word is uncertain. [b] 17 Or *them, their morning is like the shadow of death* [c] 17 Or *of the shadow of death* [d] 19 Hebrew *Sheol*

WEEKEND

your fantasy life

Is it wrong for a husband to fantasize as long as he doesn't commit adultery? Although I feel guilty about it, I find that fantasies stimulate me. Three psychiatrists have told me that fantasizing is perfectly normal and everybody does it.

Fantasizing about a woman other than your wife is a fancy title for old-fashioned "lust," which Jesus Christ equated with adultery (Matthew 5:28). The Bible has much to say about keeping our thought lives pure (Philippians 4:8) and "taking captive every thought to make it obedient to Christ" (2 Corinthians 10:5 [NASB]).

The mind is the doorway to the emotions or heart. If you think evil or lustful thoughts, they will make you feel lustful. As Proverbs 23:7 says, "For as he thinks within himself, so he is" [NASB]. Fantasizing will often cause a person to use his partner rather than love her; it tends to overstimulate, producing premature ejaculation, and it creates unreal expectations. Just because something is exciting doesn't make it right.

How can I learn to control my thought life?

Here are six steps to gaining control of your mind.

1. Confess all evil thinking as sin—1 John 1:9.
2. Keep in step with the Spirit—Galatians 5:16–25.
3. Ask God for victory over the habit—1 John 5:14–15.
4. Whenever possible, avoid all suggestive material, such as questionable movies, TV programs and pornography.
5. If you are married, think only of your wife or husband; if single, force your mind to think pure thoughts about all other people—Philippians 4:8.
6. Repeat the above steps when your mind digs up old lustful thought patterns.

It takes from thirty to sixty days to create new thought patterns, so don't expect success overnight and don't permit your mind an exception. Gradually you will find it easier to control your thoughts.

If sex starts in the mind, should a wife try to turn herself on by imagining sexually exciting things? Are such thoughts (if not including one's own husband) sinful?

Yes and no. Yes—it is perfectly all right for a wife to visualize herself being embraced and caressed by her husband. No—a wife should not picture herself in the arms of another man; that is lust, which is expressly forbidden by our Lord. "But I tell you that anyone who looks at a woman lustfully has already committed adultery with her in his heart" (Matthew 5:28).

I love my husband and am not at all infatuated by any other man; but during sex relations I have to fantasize some illicit relations with another man (never one I know). I am ashamed to tell my husband this. Is this sinful of me? Is it because my husband doesn't excite me enough, or what?

You have developed a bad mental habit. Transfer your thoughts to your husband. Visualize earlier lovemaking experiences with him, or better yet, make love in a softly lighted room, keep your eyes open, and concentrate on what you are doing.

How much sex or possible lust should be allowed to fill one's daily thinking?

None. Lust is like a disease—it will grow. Bring your mind into obedience to Christ (2 Corinthians 10:5) and root out *all* evil imaginations.

—TIM AND BEVERLY LAHAYE

is it lust or love?

HOW ARE WE DOING?

For each statement below consider whether the thought is lust or love. If you're unsure, discuss it with your spouse.

1. [Wife] While on a business trip, you flip on the TV and find a movie channel that's not X-rated but it's also not something you would feel comfortable watching in the presence of your spouse or your kids. You turn the television off and decide to go for a run. Are you operating out of love or lust?
2. [Husband] At the neighborhood pool you see a neighbor who appears to have had surgery to enhance her breasts. Later you consider how the same surgery could improve your wife's appearance. Are you operating out of love or lust?
3. [Wife] You're attracted to a coworker. You spend hours thinking about him. You know that's wrong. You consider telling the coworker because he is also a Christian, and you think that will help you both stay out of trouble. Are you operating out of love or lust?
4. [Husband] You flip through a magazine with pictures of hot models in swimsuits. You don't spend much time thinking about it until later that night when your spouse undresses and the images come rushing back to you. Mentally, you compare your spouse to the model. Are you operating out of love or lust?
5. [Wife] Watching TV, you see the young lovers kissing deeply then slowly peeling off each others' clothes. You try to remember when the last time your spouse was that excited over you, and, just for a minute, you picture yourself in the television scene. Are you operating out of love or lust?
6. [Husband] There are many tempting images on the Internet, and you and your spouse both know you're susceptible to them. Together you decide to install software that blocks your ability to go to those websites. Are you operating out of love or lust?

let's make a DATE

KISS ALBUM

This weekend kiss your spouse on camera. Take pictures of the two of you kissing in front of a waterfall, a breathtaking overlook or next to the "kiss-and-ride" sign at the airport. If you have children, take kissing pictures with each of them. Paste the photos into a book and label each picture with a word that best describes that memory. In the future, take kissing pictures at special events, scenic locations or while traveling. Each time you look through the album, remember the love you have for your family.

FOR YOUR NEXT DEVOTIONAL READING, TURN TO PAGE 563.

LESSONS FROM THE *Bible*

Take a look at these Scriptures to get a grip on your thought life.

1. Mark 9:42–48. What are the practical implications of this advice in marriage?
2. 1 Peter 2:11–12. Even though our thoughts are private, how might they be affecting our behaviors in ways that others pick up on? If unbelievers knew about our fantasies, how would it affect our testimony?

they are brought low and gathered up
like all others;
they are cut off like heads of grain.

25 "If this is not so, who can prove me false
and reduce my words to nothing?"

Bildad

25 Then Bildad the Shuhite replied:

2 "Dominion and awe belong to God;
he establishes order in the heights of
heaven.
3 Can his forces be numbered?
Upon whom does his light not rise?
4 How then can a man be righteous before
God?
How can one born of woman be pure?
5 If even the moon is not bright
and the stars are not pure in his eyes,
6 how much less man, who is but a
maggot—
a son of man, who is only a worm!"

Job

26 Then Job replied:

2 "How you have helped the powerless!
How you have saved the arm that is
feeble!
3 What advice you have offered to one
without wisdom!
And what great insight you have
displayed!
4 Who has helped you utter these words?
And whose spirit spoke from your
mouth?

5 "The dead are in deep anguish,
those beneath the waters and all that
live in them.
6 Death[a] is naked before God;
Destruction[b] lies uncovered.
7 He spreads out the northern ⌞skies⌟ over
empty space;
he suspends the earth over nothing.
8 He wraps up the waters in his clouds,
yet the clouds do not burst under their
weight.
9 He covers the face of the full moon,
spreading his clouds over it.
10 He marks out the horizon on the face of
the waters
for a boundary between light and
darkness.
11 The pillars of the heavens quake,
aghast at his rebuke.
12 By his power he churned up the sea;
by his wisdom he cut Rahab to pieces.
13 By his breath the skies became fair;
his hand pierced the gliding serpent.
14 And these are but the outer fringe of his
works;
how faint the whisper we hear of him!
Who then can understand the thunder
of his power?"

27 And Job continued his discourse:

2 "As surely as God lives, who has
denied me justice,
the Almighty, who has made me taste
bitterness of soul,
3 as long as I have life within me,
the breath of God in my nostrils,
4 my lips will not speak wickedness,
and my tongue will utter no deceit.
5 I will never admit you are in the right;
till I die, I will not deny my integrity.
6 I will maintain my righteousness and
never let go of it;
my conscience will not reproach me as
long as I live.

7 "May my enemies be like the wicked,
my adversaries like the unjust!
8 For what hope has the godless when he is
cut off,
when God takes away his life?
9 Does God listen to his cry
when distress comes upon him?
10 Will he find delight in the Almighty?
Will he call upon God at all times?

11 "I will teach you about the power of God;
the ways of the Almighty I will not
conceal.
12 You have all seen this yourselves.
Why then this meaningless talk?

13 "Here is the fate God allots to the wicked,
the heritage a ruthless man receives
from the Almighty:
14 However many his children, their fate is
the sword;
his offspring will never have enough to
eat.
15 The plague will bury those who survive
him,
and their widows will not weep for
them.
16 Though he heaps up silver like dust
and clothes like piles of clay,

[a] 6 Hebrew *Sheol* [b] 6 Hebrew *Abaddon*

and the old men rose to their feet;
9 the chief men refrained from speaking
and covered their mouths with their hands;
10 the voices of the nobles were hushed,
and their tongues stuck to the roof of their mouths.
11 Whoever heard me spoke well of me,
and those who saw me commended me,
12 because I rescued the poor who cried for help,
and the fatherless who had none to assist him.
13 The man who was dying blessed me;
I made the widow's heart sing.
14 I put on righteousness as my clothing;
justice was my robe and my turban.
15 I was eyes to the blind
and feet to the lame.
16 I was a father to the needy;
I took up the case of the stranger.
17 I broke the fangs of the wicked
and snatched the victims from their teeth.

18 "I thought, 'I will die in my own house,
my days as numerous as the grains of sand.
19 My roots will reach to the water,
and the dew will lie all night on my branches.
20 My glory will remain fresh in me,
the bow ever new in my hand.'

21 "Men listened to me expectantly,
waiting in silence for my counsel.
22 After I had spoken, they spoke no more;
my words fell gently on their ears.
23 They waited for me as for showers
and drank in my words as the spring rain.
24 When I smiled at them, they scarcely believed it;
the light of my face was precious to them.[a]
25 I chose the way for them and sat as their chief;
I dwelt as a king among his troops;
I was like one who comforts mourners.

30 "But now they mock me,
men younger than I,
whose fathers I would have disdained
to put with my sheep dogs.
2 Of what use was the strength of their hands to me,
since their vigor had gone from them?
3 Haggard from want and hunger,
they roamed[b] the parched land
in desolate wastelands at night.
4 In the brush they gathered salt herbs,
and their food[c] was the root of the broom tree.
5 They were banished from their fellow men,
shouted at as if they were thieves.
6 They were forced to live in the dry stream beds,
among the rocks and in holes in the ground.
7 They brayed among the bushes
and huddled in the undergrowth.
8 A base and nameless brood,
they were driven out of the land.

9 "And now their sons mock me in song;
I have become a byword among them.
10 They detest me and keep their distance;
they do not hesitate to spit in my face.
11 Now that God has unstrung my bow and afflicted me,
they throw off restraint in my presence.
12 On my right the tribe[a] attacks;
they lay snares for my feet,
they build their siege ramps against me.
13 They break up my road;
they succeed in destroying me—
without anyone's helping them.[d]
14 They advance as through a gaping breach;
amid the ruins they come rolling in.
15 Terrors overwhelm me;
my dignity is driven away as by the wind,
my safety vanishes like a cloud.

16 "And now my life ebbs away;
days of suffering grip me.
17 Night pierces my bones;
my gnawing pains never rest.
18 In his great power ⌊God⌋ becomes like clothing to me[e];
he binds me like the neck of my garment.
19 He throws me into the mud,
and I am reduced to dust and ashes.

20 "I cry out to you, O God, but you do not answer;
I stand up, but you merely look at me.
21 You turn on me ruthlessly;

a 24,12 The meaning of the Hebrew for this clause is uncertain. *b* 3 Or *gnawed* *c* 4 Or *fuel* *d* 13 Or *me. / 'No one can help him,' ⌊they say⌋.* *e* 18 Hebrew; Septuagint *⌊God⌋ grasps my clothing*

with the might of your hand you attack
me.
22 You snatch me up and drive me before the
wind;
you toss me about in the storm.
23 I know you will bring me down to death,
to the place appointed for all the living.

24 "Surely no one lays a hand on a broken
man
when he cries for help in his distress.
25 Have I not wept for those in trouble?
Has not my soul grieved for the poor?
26 Yet when I hoped for good, evil came;
when I looked for light, then came
darkness.
27 The churning inside me never stops;
days of suffering confront me.
28 I go about blackened, but not by the sun;
I stand up in the assembly and cry for
help.
29 I have become a brother of jackals,
a companion of owls.
30 My skin grows black and peels;
my body burns with fever.
31 My harp is tuned to mourning,
and my flute to the sound of wailing.

31 "I made a covenant with my eyes
not to look lustfully at a girl.
2 For what is man's lot from God above,
his heritage from the Almighty on
high?
3 Is it not ruin for the wicked,
disaster for those who do wrong?
4 Does he not see my ways
and count my every step?

5 "If I have walked in falsehood
or my foot has hurried after deceit—
6 let God weigh me in honest scales
and he will know that I am blameless—
7 if my steps have turned from the path,
if my heart has been led by my eyes,
or if my hands have been defiled,
8 then may others eat what I have sown,
and may my crops be uprooted.

9 "If my heart has been enticed by a woman,
or if I have lurked at my neighbor's
door,
10 then may my wife grind another man's
grain,
and may other men sleep with her.
11 For that would have been shameful,
a sin to be judged.
12 It is a fire that burns to Destruction[a];
it would have uprooted my harvest.

13 "If I have denied justice to my
menservants and maidservants
when they had a grievance against me,
14 what will I do when God confronts me?
What will I answer when called to
account?
15 Did not he who made me in the womb
make them?
Did not the same one form us both
within our mothers?

16 "If I have denied the desires of the poor
or let the eyes of the widow grow
weary,
17 if I have kept my bread to myself,
not sharing it with the fatherless—
18 but from my youth I reared him as would
a father,
and from my birth I guided the
widow—
19 if I have seen anyone perishing for lack of
clothing,
or a needy man without a garment,
20 and his heart did not bless me
for warming him with the fleece from
my sheep,
21 if I have raised my hand against the
fatherless,
knowing that I had influence in court,
22 then let my arm fall from the shoulder,
let it be broken off at the joint.
23 For I dreaded destruction from God,
and for fear of his splendor I could not
do such things.

24 "If I have put my trust in gold
or said to pure gold, 'You are my
security,'
25 if I have rejoiced over my great wealth,
the fortune my hands had gained,
26 if I have regarded the sun in its radiance
or the moon moving in splendor,
27 so that my heart was secretly enticed
and my hand offered them a kiss of
homage,
28 then these also would be sins to be judged,
for I would have been unfaithful to
God on high.

29 "If I have rejoiced at my enemy's
misfortune
or gloated over the trouble that came to
him—
30 I have not allowed my mouth to sin
by invoking a curse against his life—

[a] 12 Hebrew *Abaddon*

TUESDAY
READ JOB 31:1–40

JUST LOOKING

"I made a covenant with my eyes not to look lustfully at a girl."

— Job 31:1

let's talk

- What are the vulnerable areas for each of us in sexual or relational matters? What fences are we building to protect ourselves from such entanglements? Whom do we have as partners to keep us accountable?
- What temptations have we overcome? How might we celebrate these victories?
- What would be our testimony today if we stood in Job's spot? Would we cringe because we knew our troubles resulted from our own failures and faults? Or would we confidently maintain our innocence? In what areas?

"I catch my husband ogling other women when he thinks I don't see him," wrote a woman to columnist Dr. Diane Mandt Langberg in *Today's Christian Woman* (January/February 2000). "It makes me feel uncomfortable and inadequate, as though I'm not desirable enough for him. Should I accept it as a 'guy thing' or put my foot down and forbid it?"

The doctor's response was firm: "Yes, it's a 'guy thing,' but you need to talk to your guy about it," she said. "God wired men to notice pretty women (otherwise, your husband wouldn't have noticed you!). But this God-created response can be terribly twisted by sin. If your husband is looking at other women in a prolonged, lustful fashion, your discomfort is appropriate—and he is sinning before God, them and you."

It starts with just looking. It may be an action, a thought or a fantasy, but it is the kind of indulgence that can lead to crossing the line of morality into territory that is immoral and addictive, and possibly illegal. What's more, the harm caused by such sin is usually to more people than just the couple.

It's not only husbands who are tempted by this sin. For one woman, looking led to lingering too long and chatting with a trainer at a fitness club. She nearly walked away from her marriage and children and bankrupted a family business. For a pastor, looking at Internet porn led to an embarrassing incident that terminated his ministry. For a young businessman, looking led to entertaining clients at strip clubs. Eventually he lost his marriage, his home and his role as an elder in his church.

"Just looking" is hardly innocent. Job testified to that. In the midst of his suffering, when his life had become a fragile feather falling into a volcano, Job ruthlessly examined how he had lived his life. He couldn't find an obvious connection between his sin and his suffering, but he did understand the kind of looking that could lead to sin. His review of problem areas—looking with lust at a virgin, cheating in business, being enticed by his neighbor's wife, failing to see justice done to a servant, seeing others in need and failing to respond to them, being covetous or idolatrous—is also a challenge and warning to us.

Can we look without sinning? Perhaps, but not without considering this warning: Many sins— including envy, stealing, greed, pornography and adultery—often begin with "just looking."

—WAYNE BROUWER

FOR YOUR NEXT DEVOTIONAL READING, TURN TO PAGE 572.

31 if the men of my household have never said,
'Who has not had his fill of Job's meat?'—
32 but no stranger had to spend the night in the street,
for my door was always open to the traveler—
33 if I have concealed my sin as men do, [a]
by hiding my guilt in my heart
34 because I so feared the crowd
and so dreaded the contempt of the clans
that I kept silent and would not go outside—

35 ("Oh, that I had someone to hear me!
I sign now my defense—let the Almighty answer me;
let my accuser put his indictment in writing.
36 Surely I would wear it on my shoulder,
I would put it on like a crown.
37 I would give him an account of my every step;
like a prince I would approach him.)—

38 "if my land cries out against me
and all its furrows are wet with tears,
39 if I have devoured its yield without payment
or broken the spirit of its tenants,
40 then let briers come up instead of wheat
and weeds instead of barley."

The words of Job are ended.

Elihu

32 So these three men stopped answering
Job, because he was righteous in his
own eyes. 2 But Elihu son of Barakel
the Buzite, of the family of Ram, became very
angry with Job for justifying himself rather
than God. 3 He was also angry with the three
friends, because they had found no way to refute Job, and yet had condemned him. [b] 4 Now
Elihu had waited before speaking to Job because they were older than he. 5 But when he
saw that the three men had nothing more to
say, his anger was aroused.
6 So Elihu son of Barakel the Buzite said:

"I am young in years,
and you are old;
that is why I was fearful,
not daring to tell you what I know.
7 I thought, 'Age should speak;
advanced years should teach wisdom.'
8 But it is the spirit [c] in a man,
the breath of the Almighty, that gives him understanding.
9 It is not only the old [d] who are wise,
not only the aged who understand what is right.

10 "Therefore I say: Listen to me;
I too will tell you what I know.
11 I waited while you spoke,
I listened to your reasoning;
while you were searching for words,
12 I gave you my full attention.
But not one of you has proved Job wrong;
none of you has answered his arguments.
13 Do not say, 'We have found wisdom;
let God refute him, not man.'
14 But Job has not marshaled his words against me,
and I will not answer him with your arguments.

15 "They are dismayed and have no more to say;
words have failed them.
16 Must I wait, now that they are silent,
now that they stand there with no reply?
17 I too will have my say;
I too will tell what I know.
18 For I am full of words,
and the spirit within me compels me;
19 inside I am like bottled-up wine,
like new wineskins ready to burst.
20 I must speak and find relief;
I must open my lips and reply.
21 I will show partiality to no one,
nor will I flatter any man;
22 for if I were skilled in flattery,
my Maker would soon take me away.

33 "But now, Job, listen to my words;
pay attention to everything I say.
2 I am about to open my mouth;
my words are on the tip of my tongue.
3 My words come from an upright heart;
my lips sincerely speak what I know.
4 The Spirit of God has made me;
the breath of the Almighty gives me life.
5 Answer me then, if you can;
prepare yourself and confront me.
6 I am just like you before God;
I too have been taken from clay.

[a] 33 Or *as Adam did* [b] 3 Masoretic Text; an ancient Hebrew scribal tradition *Job, and so had condemned God* [c] 8 Or *Spirit*; also in verse 18 [d] 9 Or *many*; or *great*

7 No fear of me should alarm you,
nor should my hand be heavy upon you.

8 "But you have said in my hearing—
I heard the very words—
9 'I am pure and without sin;
I am clean and free from guilt.
10 Yet God has found fault with me;
he considers me his enemy.
11 He fastens my feet in shackles;
he keeps close watch on all my paths.'

12 "But I tell you, in this you are not right,
for God is greater than man.
13 Why do you complain to him
that he answers none of man's words[a]?
14 For God does speak—now one way, now another—
though man may not perceive it.
15 In a dream, in a vision of the night,
when deep sleep falls on men
as they slumber in their beds,
16 he may speak in their ears
and terrify them with warnings,
17 to turn man from wrongdoing
and keep him from pride,
18 to preserve his soul from the pit,[b]
his life from perishing by the sword.[c]
19 Or a man may be chastened on a bed of pain
with constant distress in his bones,
20 so that his very being finds food repulsive
and his soul loathes the choicest meal.
21 His flesh wastes away to nothing,
and his bones, once hidden, now stick out.
22 His soul draws near to the pit,[d]
and his life to the messengers of death.[e]

23 "Yet if there is an angel on his side
as a mediator, one out of a thousand,
to tell a man what is right for him,
24 to be gracious to him and say,
'Spare him from going down to the pit[f];
I have found a ransom for him'—
25 then his flesh is renewed like a child's;
it is restored as in the days of his youth.
26 He prays to God and finds favor with him,
he sees God's face and shouts for joy;
he is restored by God to his righteous state.
27 Then he comes to men and says,
'I sinned, and perverted what was right,
but I did not get what I deserved.
28 He redeemed my soul from going down to the pit,[g]
and I will live to enjoy the light.'

29 "God does all these things to a man—
twice, even three times—
30 to turn back his soul from the pit,[h]
that the light of life may shine on him.

31 "Pay attention, Job, and listen to me;
be silent, and I will speak.
32 If you have anything to say, answer me;
speak up, for I want you to be cleared.
33 But if not, then listen to me;
be silent, and I will teach you wisdom."

34

Then Elihu said:

2 "Hear my words, you wise men;
listen to me, you men of learning.
3 For the ear tests words
as the tongue tastes food.
4 Let us discern for ourselves what is right;
let us learn together what is good.

5 "Job says, 'I am innocent,
but God denies me justice.
6 Although I am right,
I am considered a liar;
although I am guiltless,
his arrow inflicts an incurable wound.'
7 What man is like Job,
who drinks scorn like water?
8 He keeps company with evildoers;
he associates with wicked men.
9 For he says, 'It profits a man nothing
when he tries to please God.'

10 "So listen to me, you men of understanding.
Far be it from God to do evil,
from the Almighty to do wrong.
11 He repays a man for what he has done;
he brings upon him what his conduct deserves.
12 It is unthinkable that God would do wrong,
that the Almighty would pervert justice.
13 Who appointed him over the earth?
Who put him in charge of the whole world?
14 If it were his intention

[a] 13 Or *that he does not answer for any of his actions* [b] 18 Or *preserve him from the grave* [c] 18 Or *from crossing the River*
[d] 22 Or *He draws near to the grave* [e] 22 Or *to the dead* [f] 24 Or *grave* [g] 28 Or *redeemed me from going down to the grave*
[h] 30 Or *turn him back from the grave*

and he withdrew his spirit[a] and
breath,
15 all mankind would perish together
and man would return to the dust.

16 "If you have understanding, hear this;
listen to what I say.
17 Can he who hates justice govern?
Will you condemn the just and mighty
One?
18 Is he not the One who says to kings, 'You
are worthless,'
and to nobles, 'You are wicked,'
19 who shows no partiality to princes
and does not favor the rich over the
poor,
for they are all the work of his hands?
20 They die in an instant, in the middle of
the night;
the people are shaken and they pass
away;
the mighty are removed without
human hand.

21 "His eyes are on the ways of men;
he sees their every step.
22 There is no dark place, no deep shadow,
where evildoers can hide.
23 God has no need to examine men
further,
that they should come before him for
judgment.
24 Without inquiry he shatters the mighty
and sets up others in their place.
25 Because he takes note of their deeds,
he overthrows them in the night and
they are crushed.
26 He punishes them for their wickedness
where everyone can see them,
27 because they turned from following him
and had no regard for any of his ways.
28 They caused the cry of the poor to come
before him,
so that he heard the cry of the needy.
29 But if he remains silent, who can
condemn him?
If he hides his face, who can see him?
Yet he is over man and nation alike,
30 to keep a godless man from ruling,
from laying snares for the people.

31 "Suppose a man says to God,
'I am guilty but will offend no more.
32 Teach me what I cannot see;
if I have done wrong, I will not do so
again.'
33 Should God then reward you on your
terms,
when you refuse to repent?
You must decide, not I;
so tell me what you know.

34 "Men of understanding declare,
wise men who hear me say to me,
35 'Job speaks without knowledge;
his words lack insight.'
36 Oh, that Job might be tested to the
utmost
for answering like a wicked man!
37 To his sin he adds rebellion;
scornfully he claps his hands among us
and multiplies his words against God."

35 Then Elihu said:

2 "Do you think this is just?
You say, 'I will be cleared by God.[b]'
3 Yet you ask him, 'What profit is it to
me,[c]
and what do I gain by not sinning?'

4 "I would like to reply to you
and to your friends with you.
5 Look up at the heavens and see;
gaze at the clouds so high above you.
6 If you sin, how does that affect him?
If your sins are many, what does that do
to him?
7 If you are righteous, what do you give to
him,
or what does he receive from your
hand?
8 Your wickedness affects only a man like
yourself,
and your righteousness only the sons of
men.

9 "Men cry out under a load of oppression;
they plead for relief from the arm of the
powerful.
10 But no one says, 'Where is God my
Maker,
who gives songs in the night,
11 who teaches more to us than to[d] the
beasts of the earth
and makes us wiser than[e] the birds of
the air?'
12 He does not answer when men cry out
because of the arrogance of the
wicked.
13 Indeed, God does not listen to their empty
plea;
the Almighty pays no attention to it.

[a] 14 Or *Spirit* [b] 2 Or *My righteousness is more than God's* [c] 3 Or *you* [d] 11 Or *teaches us by* [e] 11 Or *us wise by*

14 How much less, then, will he listen
when you say that you do not see him,
that your case is before him
and you must wait for him,
15 and further, that his anger never punishes
and he does not take the least notice of
wickedness.[a]
16 So Job opens his mouth with empty talk;
without knowledge he multiplies
words."

36 Elihu continued:

2 "Bear with me a little longer and I
will show you
that there is more to be said in God's
behalf.
3 I get my knowledge from afar;
I will ascribe justice to my Maker.
4 Be assured that my words are not false;
one perfect in knowledge is with you.

5 "God is mighty, but does not despise
men;
he is mighty, and firm in his purpose.
6 He does not keep the wicked alive
but gives the afflicted their rights.
7 He does not take his eyes off the
righteous;
he enthrones them with kings
and exalts them forever.
8 But if men are bound in chains,
held fast by cords of affliction,
9 he tells them what they have done—
that they have sinned arrogantly.
10 He makes them listen to correction
and commands them to repent of their
evil.
11 If they obey and serve him,
they will spend the rest of their days in
prosperity
and their years in contentment.
12 But if they do not listen,
they will perish by the sword[b]
and die without knowledge.

13 "The godless in heart harbor resentment;
even when he fetters them, they do not
cry for help.
14 They die in their youth,
among male prostitutes of the shrines.
15 But those who suffer he delivers in their
suffering;
he speaks to them in their affliction.
16 "He is wooing you from the jaws of
distress
to a spacious place free from
restriction,
to the comfort of your table laden with
choice food.
17 But now you are laden with the judgment
due the wicked;
judgment and justice have taken hold
of you.
18 Be careful that no one entices you by
riches;
do not let a large bribe turn you aside.
19 Would your wealth
or even all your mighty efforts
sustain you so you would not be in
distress?
20 Do not long for the night,
to drag people away from their
homes.[c]
21 Beware of turning to evil,
which you seem to prefer to affliction.

22 "God is exalted in his power.
Who is a teacher like him?
23 Who has prescribed his ways for him,
or said to him, 'You have done
wrong'?
24 Remember to extol his work,
which men have praised in song.
25 All mankind has seen it;
men gaze on it from afar.
26 How great is God—beyond our
understanding!
The number of his years is past finding
out.

27 "He draws up the drops of water,
which distill as rain to the streams[d];
28 the clouds pour down their moisture
and abundant showers fall on
mankind.
29 Who can understand how he spreads out
the clouds,
how he thunders from his pavilion?
30 See how he scatters his lightning about
him,
bathing the depths of the sea.
31 This is the way he governs[e] the nations
and provides food in abundance.
32 He fills his hands with lightning
and commands it to strike its mark.
33 His thunder announces the coming storm;
even the cattle make known its
approach.[f]

[a] 15 Symmachus, Theodotion and Vulgate; the meaning of the Hebrew for this word is uncertain. [b] 12 Or *will cross the River* [c] 20 The meaning of the Hebrew for verses 18-20 is uncertain. [d] 27 Or *distill from the mist as rain* [e] 31 Or *nourishes* [f] 33 Or *announces his coming— / the One zealous against evil*

WEDNESDAY
READ JOB 36:22–33

KEEPING GOD IN SIGHT

> **"God is exalted in his power . . . Remember to extol his work."**
> — JOB 36:22,24

let's talk

- What are some seasons when our marriage has felt especially focused on God? When have we felt focused everywhere *but* God?
- Where is our marriage focused right now?
- What are some things we can do to help direct our marriage toward God?

Our everyday lives can sometimes keep us from focusing on God. We can lose sight of God's grandeur through both suffering and joy. In our best, joy-filled moments, we, like Hannah, David, Mary and so many other faithful people we meet in the Bible, can turn to God. We can also turn to God in moments of great affliction, as we see Job do in the book of Job. But sometimes we get so consumed by our own experience that we forget to center on God during the good and bad times.

Marriage illustrates the point. Consider the overwhelming suffering we can experience when we betray or are betrayed by a spouse, when we fail or are failed by the one we love most, or when we simply run up against our own limitations in marriage. In our agony we can go to God. Or we can go to pornography, credit cards, wine, etc.

Marriage, of course, also brings great joy. Some moments of elation, such as having a baby, are big and dramatic. Some moments of elation are quieter: You've had a busy week at work, and you're sort of distracted; during dinner your husband says something sweet, and you look at him and your heart flip-flops and fills up with delight. Sometimes, in this joy, we praise God for that provision. Sometimes we don't.

Marriage helps us become new creatures. It helps us become the people we were meant to be: people who together love, praise and revere the Lord. But in the frenzy and busyness of married life, we can also forget that our primary task is to love God. Some nights it seems difficult just getting dinner on the table, laundry in the washing machine and our tired selves into bed.

So how can we keep our focus—and the focus of our marriage—on God?

Some simple disciplines can help. Prayer, of course, should be a priority. Pray before meals. Set aside one hour a week to sit with your spouse and pray. Say a prayer together at bedtime. In Orthodox Jewish prayer books, there are prayers that can be said after almost anything, even after having sex! How's that for keeping marital attention squarely on God?

Having a regular devotional time together can also help us to keep our eyes on God. Reading a devotional Bible like this one can help to prompt reflections on the connections between our marital life and our spiritual life. Or it can be helpful to read a novel that depicts Christian marriage well. (My current favorite is Wendell Berry's *Hannah Coulter*.)

Tithing also redirects us toward God. As much as I want to save every extra penny for a house (after all, I've been taught that owning a house is my middle-class marital right!), supporting God's house comes first.

Finally, our marriages are reshaped for God when we practice hospitality—opening our marital home to kith and kin, strangers and friends, so that we might, to borrow John Wesley's phrase, "shed our love abroad." Hospitality takes the focus off us and puts it on our brothers and sisters, in whom we are called to see God.

These practices can help transform our marriages into choirs of song, exalting God and extolling his work.

—LAUREN WINNER

FOR YOUR NEXT DEVOTIONAL READING, TURN TO PAGE 580.

37 "At this my heart pounds
and leaps from its place.
2 Listen! Listen to the roar of his voice,
to the rumbling that comes from his
mouth.
3 He unleashes his lightning beneath the
whole heaven
and sends it to the ends of the earth.
4 After that comes the sound of his roar;
he thunders with his majestic voice.
When his voice resounds,
he holds nothing back.
5 God's voice thunders in marvelous ways;
he does great things beyond our
understanding.
6 He says to the snow, 'Fall on the earth,'
and to the rain shower, 'Be a mighty
downpour.'
7 So that all men he has made may know his
work,
he stops every man from his labor.[a]
8 The animals take cover;
they remain in their dens.
9 The tempest comes out from its chamber,
the cold from the driving winds.
10 The breath of God produces ice,
and the broad waters become frozen.
11 He loads the clouds with moisture;
he scatters his lightning through them.
12 At his direction they swirl around
over the face of the whole earth
to do whatever he commands them.
13 He brings the clouds to punish men,
or to water his earth[b] and show his
love.

14 "Listen to this, Job;
stop and consider God's wonders.
15 Do you know how God controls the
clouds
and makes his lightning flash?
16 Do you know how the clouds hang poised,
those wonders of him who is perfect in
knowledge?
17 You who swelter in your clothes
when the land lies hushed under the
south wind,
18 can you join him in spreading out the
skies,
hard as a mirror of cast bronze?

19 "Tell us what we should say to him;
we cannot draw up our case because of
our darkness.
20 Should he be told that I want to speak?
Would any man ask to be swallowed
up?
21 Now no one can look at the sun,
bright as it is in the skies
after the wind has swept them clean.
22 Out of the north he comes in golden
splendor;
God comes in awesome majesty.
23 The Almighty is beyond our reach and
exalted in power;
in his justice and great righteousness,
he does not oppress.
24 Therefore, men revere him,
for does he not have regard for all the
wise in heart?[c]"

The Lord Speaks

38 Then the Lord answered Job out of the
storm. He said:

2 "Who is this that darkens my counsel
with words without knowledge?
3 Brace yourself like a man;
I will question you,
and you shall answer me.

4 "Where were you when I laid the earth's
foundation?
Tell me, if you understand.
5 Who marked off its dimensions? Surely
you know!
Who stretched a measuring line across
it?
6 On what were its footings set,
or who laid its cornerstone—
7 while the morning stars sang together
and all the angels[d] shouted for joy?

8 "Who shut up the sea behind doors
when it burst forth from the womb,
9 when I made the clouds its garment
and wrapped it in thick darkness,
10 when I fixed limits for it
and set its doors and bars in place,
11 when I said, 'This far you may come and
no farther;
here is where your proud waves halt'?

12 "Have you ever given orders to the
morning,
or shown the dawn its place,
13 that it might take the earth by the edges
and shake the wicked out of it?
14 The earth takes shape like clay under a
seal;

---

[a] 7 Or *I he fills all men with fear by his power* [b] 13 Or *to favor them* [c] 24 Or *for he does not have regard for any who think they are wise.* [d] 7 Hebrew *the sons of God*

its features stand out like those of a
garment.
15 The wicked are denied their light,
and their upraised arm is broken.

16 "Have you journeyed to the springs of the
sea
or walked in the recesses of the deep?
17 Have the gates of death been shown to
you?
Have you seen the gates of the shadow
of death[a]?
18 Have you comprehended the vast expanses
of the earth?
Tell me, if you know all this.

19 "What is the way to the abode of light?
And where does darkness reside?
20 Can you take them to their places?
Do you know the paths to their
dwellings?
21 Surely you know, for you were already
born!
You have lived so many years!

22 "Have you entered the storehouses of the
snow
or seen the storehouses of the hail,
23 which I reserve for times of trouble,
for days of war and battle?
24 What is the way to the place where the
lightning is dispersed,
or the place where the east winds are
scattered over the earth?
25 Who cuts a channel for the torrents of
rain,
and a path for the thunderstorm,
26 to water a land where no man lives,
a desert with no one in it,
27 to satisfy a desolate wasteland
and make it sprout with grass?
28 Does the rain have a father?
Who fathers the drops of dew?
29 From whose womb comes the ice?
Who gives birth to the frost from the
heavens
30 when the waters become hard as stone,
when the surface of the deep is frozen?

31 "Can you bind the beautiful[b] Pleiades?
Can you loose the cords of Orion?
32 Can you bring forth the constellations in
their seasons[c]
or lead out the Bear[d] with its cubs?
33 Do you know the laws of the heavens?
Can you set up ⌊God's[e]⌋ dominion over
the earth?

34 "Can you raise your voice to the clouds
and cover yourself with a flood of
water?
35 Do you send the lightning bolts on their
way?
Do they report to you, 'Here we are'?
36 Who endowed the heart[f] with wisdom
or gave understanding to the mind[f]?
37 Who has the wisdom to count the clouds?
Who can tip over the water jars of the
heavens
38 when the dust becomes hard
and the clods of earth stick together?

39 "Do you hunt the prey for the lioness
and satisfy the hunger of the lions
40 when they crouch in their dens
or lie in wait in a thicket?
41 Who provides food for the raven
when its young cry out to God
and wander about for lack of food?

39 "Do you know when the mountain
goats give birth?
Do you watch when the doe bears her
fawn?
2 Do you count the months till they bear?
Do you know the time they give birth?
3 They crouch down and bring forth their
young;
their labor pains are ended.
4 Their young thrive and grow strong in the
wilds;
they leave and do not return.

5 "Who let the wild donkey go free?
Who untied his ropes?
6 I gave him the wasteland as his home,
the salt flats as his habitat.
7 He laughs at the commotion in the town;
he does not hear a driver's shout.
8 He ranges the hills for his pasture
and searches for any green thing.

9 "Will the wild ox consent to serve you?
Will he stay by your manger at night?
10 Can you hold him to the furrow with a
harness?
Will he till the valleys behind you?
11 Will you rely on him for his great
strength?
Will you leave your heavy work to him?
12 Can you trust him to bring in your grain
and gather it to your threshing floor?

13 "The wings of the ostrich flap joyfully,

[a] 17 Or *gates of deep shadows* [b] 31 Or *the twinkling*; or *the chains of the* [c] 32 Or *the morning star in its season* [d] 32 Or *out Leo*
[e] 33 Or *his*; or *their* [f] 36 The meaning of the Hebrew for this word is uncertain.

but they cannot compare with the
pinions and feathers of the stork.
14 She lays her eggs on the ground
and lets them warm in the sand,
15 unmindful that a foot may crush them,
that some wild animal may trample
them.
16 She treats her young harshly, as if they
were not hers;
she cares not that her labor was in vain,
17 for God did not endow her with wisdom
or give her a share of good sense.
18 Yet when she spreads her feathers to run,
she laughs at horse and rider.

19 "Do you give the horse his strength
or clothe his neck with a flowing mane?
20 Do you make him leap like a locust,
striking terror with his proud snorting?
21 He paws fiercely, rejoicing in his strength,
and charges into the fray.
22 He laughs at fear, afraid of nothing;
he does not shy away from the sword.
23 The quiver rattles against his side,
along with the flashing spear and lance.
24 In frenzied excitement he eats up the
ground;
he cannot stand still when the trumpet
sounds.
25 At the blast of the trumpet he snorts,
'Aha!'
He catches the scent of battle from afar,
the shout of commanders and the
battle cry.

26 "Does the hawk take flight by your
wisdom
and spread his wings toward the south?
27 Does the eagle soar at your command
and build his nest on high?
28 He dwells on a cliff and stays there at
night;
a rocky crag is his stronghold.
29 From there he seeks out his food;
his eyes detect it from afar.
30 His young ones feast on blood,
and where the slain are, there is he."

40 The LORD said to Job:

2 "Will the one who contends with the
Almighty correct him?
Let him who accuses God answer him!"

3 Then Job answered the LORD:

4 "I am unworthy—how can I reply to you?
I put my hand over my mouth.
5 I spoke once, but I have no answer—
twice, but I will say no more."

6 Then the LORD spoke to Job out of the
storm:

7 "Brace yourself like a man;
I will question you,
and you shall answer me.

8 "Would you discredit my justice?
Would you condemn me to justify
yourself?
9 Do you have an arm like God's,
and can your voice thunder like his?
10 Then adorn yourself with glory and
splendor,
and clothe yourself in honor and
majesty.
11 Unleash the fury of your wrath,
look at every proud man and bring him
low,
12 look at every proud man and humble him,
crush the wicked where they stand.
13 Bury them all in the dust together;
shroud their faces in the grave.
14 Then I myself will admit to you
that your own right hand can save you.

15 "Look at the behemoth,[a]
which I made along with you
and which feeds on grass like an ox.
16 What strength he has in his loins,
what power in the muscles of his belly!
17 His tail[b] sways like a cedar;
the sinews of his thighs are close-knit.
18 His bones are tubes of bronze,
his limbs like rods of iron.
19 He ranks first among the works of God,
yet his Maker can approach him with
his sword.
20 The hills bring him their produce,
and all the wild animals play nearby.
21 Under the lotus plants he lies,
hidden among the reeds in the marsh.
22 The lotuses conceal him in their shadow;
the poplars by the stream surround
him.
23 When the river rages, he is not alarmed;
he is secure, though the Jordan should
surge against his mouth.
24 Can anyone capture him by the eyes,[c]
or trap him and pierce his nose?

41 "Can you pull in the leviathan[d] with a
fishhook
or tie down his tongue with a rope?

[a] *15* Possibly the hippopotamus or the elephant [b] *17* Possibly trunk [c] *24* Or *by a water hole* [d] *1* Possibly the crocodile

2 Can you put a cord through his nose
or pierce his jaw with a hook?
3 Will he keep begging you for mercy?
Will he speak to you with gentle words?
4 Will he make an agreement with you
for you to take him as your slave for life?
5 Can you make a pet of him like a bird
or put him on a leash for your girls?
6 Will traders barter for him?
Will they divide him up among the merchants?
7 Can you fill his hide with harpoons
or his head with fishing spears?
8 If you lay a hand on him,
you will remember the struggle and never do it again!
9 Any hope of subduing him is false;
the mere sight of him is overpowering.
10 No one is fierce enough to rouse him.
Who then is able to stand against me?
11 Who has a claim against me that I must pay?
Everything under heaven belongs to me.

12 "I will not fail to speak of his limbs,
his strength and his graceful form.
13 Who can strip off his outer coat?
Who would approach him with a bridle?
14 Who dares open the doors of his mouth,
ringed about with his fearsome teeth?
15 His back has[a] rows of shields
tightly sealed together;
16 each is so close to the next
that no air can pass between.
17 They are joined fast to one another;
they cling together and cannot be parted.
18 His snorting throws out flashes of light;
his eyes are like the rays of dawn.
19 Firebrands stream from his mouth;
sparks of fire shoot out.
20 Smoke pours from his nostrils
as from a boiling pot over a fire of reeds.
21 His breath sets coals ablaze,
and flames dart from his mouth.
22 Strength resides in his neck;
dismay goes before him.
23 The folds of his flesh are tightly joined;
they are firm and immovable.
24 His chest is hard as rock,
hard as a lower millstone.
25 When he rises up, the mighty are terrified;
they retreat before his thrashing.
26 The sword that reaches him has no effect,
nor does the spear or the dart or the javelin.
27 Iron he treats like straw
and bronze like rotten wood.
28 Arrows do not make him flee;
slingstones are like chaff to him.
29 A club seems to him but a piece of straw;
he laughs at the rattling of the lance.
30 His undersides are jagged potsherds,
leaving a trail in the mud like a threshing sledge.
31 He makes the depths churn like a boiling caldron
and stirs up the sea like a pot of ointment.
32 Behind him he leaves a glistening wake;
one would think the deep had white hair.
33 Nothing on earth is his equal—
a creature without fear.
34 He looks down on all that are haughty;
he is king over all that are proud."

Job

42 Then Job replied to the LORD:

2 "I know that you can do all things;
no plan of yours can be thwarted.
3 ⌊You asked,⌋ 'Who is this that obscures my counsel without knowledge?'
Surely I spoke of things I did not understand,
things too wonderful for me to know.

4 ⌊"You said,⌋ 'Listen now, and I will speak;
I will question you,
and you shall answer me.'
5 My ears had heard of you
but now my eyes have seen you.
6 Therefore I despise myself
and repent in dust and ashes."

Epilogue

7 After the LORD had said these things to
Job, he said to Eliphaz the Temanite, "I am
angry with you and your two friends, because
you have not spoken of me what is right, as
my servant Job has. 8 So now take seven bulls
and seven rams and go to my servant Job and
sacrifice a burnt offering for yourselves. My
servant Job will pray for you, and I will accept
his prayer and not deal with you according to
your folly. You have not spoken of me what

[a] 15 Or *His pride is his*

is right, as my servant Job has." 9So Eliphaz
the Temanite, Bildad the Shuhite and Zophar
the Naamathite did what the LORD told them;
and the LORD accepted Job's prayer.
10After Job had prayed for his friends, the
LORD made him prosperous again and gave
him twice as much as he had before. 11All his
brothers and sisters and everyone who had
known him before came and ate with him in
his house. They comforted and consoled him
over all the trouble the LORD had brought
upon him, and each one gave him a piece of
silver[a] and a gold ring.
12The LORD blessed the latter part of Job's
life more than the first. He had fourteen thousand sheep, six thousand camels, a thousand
yoke of oxen and a thousand donkeys. 13And
he also had seven sons and three daughters.
14The first daughter he named Jemimah, the
second Keziah and the third Keren-Happuch.
15Nowhere in all the land were there found
women as beautiful as Job's daughters, and
their father granted them an inheritance along
with their brothers.
16After this, Job lived a hundred and forty
years; he saw his children and their children to
the fourth generation. 17And so he died, old
and full of years.

---

a 11 Hebrew *him a kesitah*; a kesitah was a unit of money of unknown weight and value.

PSALMS

Psalms

QUICK FACTS

AUTHORS David, Asaph, the "Sons of Korah," Solomon, Heman, Ethan and Moses

AUDIENCE All Israel

DATE Between the time of Moses (about 1440 B.C.) and the time following the Babylonian captivity (after 538 B.C.)

SETTING Worship in God's temple

Appropriately, the Hebrew title for the book of Psalms is *tehillim,* which means "praises." Some people have called this collection the hymnbook of Israel because its words were (and still are) used in the context of public worship. While other books in the Bible focus on specific people and their actions, Psalms focuses on God. Much can be learned from experiencing these prayers as a form of worship.

Psalms also gives us an honest view of what a relationship with God looks like. The psalms reveal aspects of God's character and describe honest human emotions. Because it has several authors, and because those authors wrote under diverse circumstances, the collection reflects a range of human experience from joy to sadness, doubt to hope, guilt and shame to love and acceptance.

While this book provides married couples with a model for worship and prayer, it also offers examples of honest communication within the context of a loving relationship. Just as God longs for us to be honest with him, so we desire the kind of openness that can only be found in an intimate and committed relationship.

BOOK I

Psalms 1–41

Psalm 1

1 Blessed is the man
who does not walk in the counsel of the wicked
or stand in the way of sinners
or sit in the seat of mockers.
2 But his delight is in the law of the LORD,
and on his law he meditates day and night.
3 He is like a tree planted by streams of water,
which yields its fruit in season
and whose leaf does not wither.
Whatever he does prospers.

4 Not so the wicked!
They are like chaff
that the wind blows away.
5 Therefore the wicked will not stand in the judgment,
nor sinners in the assembly of the righteous.

6 For the LORD watches over the way of the righteous,
but the way of the wicked will perish.

Psalm 2

1 Why do the nations conspire[a]
and the peoples plot in vain?
2 The kings of the earth take their stand
and the rulers gather together
against the LORD
and against his Anointed One.[b]
3 "Let us break their chains," they say,
"and throw off their fetters."

4 The One enthroned in heaven laughs;
the Lord scoffs at them.
5 Then he rebukes them in his anger
and terrifies them in his wrath, saying,
6 "I have installed my King[c]
on Zion, my holy hill."
7 I will proclaim the decree of the LORD:

He said to me, "You are my Son[d];
today I have become your Father.[e]
8 Ask of me,
and I will make the nations your inheritance,
the ends of the earth your possession.
9 You will rule them with an iron scepter[f];
you will dash them to pieces like pottery."

10 Therefore, you kings, be wise;
be warned, you rulers of the earth.
11 Serve the LORD with fear
and rejoice with trembling.
12 Kiss the Son, lest he be angry
and you be destroyed in your way,
for his wrath can flare up in a moment.
Blessed are all who take refuge in him.

Psalm 3

A psalm of David. When he fled from his son Absalom.

1 O LORD, how many are my foes!
How many rise up against me!
2 Many are saying of me,
"God will not deliver him." *Selah*[g]
3 But you are a shield around me, O LORD;
you bestow glory on me and lift[h] up my head.
4 To the LORD I cry aloud,
and he answers me from his holy hill. *Selah*

5 I lie down and sleep;
I wake again, because the LORD sustains me.
6 I will not fear the tens of thousands
drawn up against me on every side.

7 Arise, O LORD!
Deliver me, O my God!
Strike all my enemies on the jaw;
break the teeth of the wicked.

8 From the LORD comes deliverance.
May your blessing be on your people. *Selah*

Psalm 4

For the director of music. With stringed instruments. A psalm of David.

1 Answer me when I call to you,
O my righteous God.
Give me relief from my distress;
be merciful to me and hear my prayer.

[a] *1* Hebrew; Septuagint *rage* [b] *2* Or *anointed one* [c] *6* Or *king* [d] *7* Or *son*; also in verse 12 [e] *7* Or *have begotten you* [f] *9* Or *will break them with a rod of iron* [g] *2* A word of uncertain meaning, occurring frequently in the Psalms; possibly a musical term
[h] *3* Or LORD, */ my Glorious One, who lifts*

SHAKY CHOICES

> **For the LORD watches over the way of the righteous, but the way of the wicked will perish.**
>
> — PSALM 1:6

When we lived in Alberta, we took visiting friends to see the Frank Slide. No, that isn't a water park. It's a 100-million-ton piece of Turtle Mountain that tumbled onto the mining town of Frank on April 29, 1903. At least 76 people were killed.

People of the nearby Blackfoot tribe, fearing the "mountain that walks," had warned settlers not to build there. But the coal seams promised quick profits. And the mine almost harvested itself as the tremors shook coal into the shafts. The earnings were too tempting to be blocked by superstitious warnings.

But then the mountain walked.

In this situation, it was the lure of easy money that brought an entire community into a danger zone. As Psalm 1 suggests, many choices that seem innocent or obvious early in the morning look quite different by nightfall.

Every choice we make affects our ultimate well-being and either brings us into a closer relationship with our Lord or turns us away from him. C. S. Lewis wrote that we come into this world as unfinished and somewhat neutral creatures, but that our little selections along the way gradually nudge us into becoming more heavenly or hellish creatures. These are the caricatures described in Psalm 1.

Psalm 1 belongs to the "wisdom psalms," songs meant to teach younger and newer members of the community how to live. None of us desires to be "the wicked" of verses 4–5. We all want to become the "blessed" ones of verses 1–3, he whose "delight is in the law of the LORD and on his law he meditates day and night." To do so, however, we have to make choices wiser than the one of settling at the base of a shaky mountain—where the gratification is immediate but the dangers threaten to bury us.

The principle carries over into marriage. The choice to say "I do" on our wedding day doesn't mean we will every day of our lives. The choices that illustrate our engagement and marriage vows have to be remade over and over again. Sacrifice, support, laughter, kindness and care are found in the little interactions of each new hour, from the beginning of the day to the end. Such decisions build a righteous marriage.

On the other hand, compromise, deceit, bitterness and alienation are also created in the moments that tumble through the weeks and months of marriage. And those unwise choices can shake the foundations of a relationship and bring upon it the disasters that Psalm 1 warns about.

When folks stand at the visitor center overlooking your relationship, what do they see?

—WAYNE BROUWER

let's *talk*

- Do we sometimes think that a choice is too trivial to make much difference? How do "minor" choices affect our marriage?
- What have been some rough spots in our relationship? What choices got us there? What decisions pulled us through?
- How can we live more deliberately each day?

FOR YOUR NEXT DEVOTIONAL READING, TURN TO PAGE 585.

2 How long, O men, will you turn my glory into shame[a]?
How long will you love delusions and seek false gods[b]? *Selah*
3 Know that the LORD has set apart the godly for himself;
the LORD will hear when I call to him.

4 In your anger do not sin;
when you are on your beds,
search your hearts and be silent. *Selah*
5 Offer right sacrifices
and trust in the LORD.

6 Many are asking, "Who can show us any good?"
Let the light of your face shine upon us, O LORD.
7 You have filled my heart with greater joy
than when their grain and new wine abound.
8 I will lie down and sleep in peace,
for you alone, O LORD,
make me dwell in safety.

Psalm 5

For the director of music. For flutes.
A psalm of David.

1 Give ear to my words, O LORD,
consider my sighing.
2 Listen to my cry for help,
my King and my God,
for to you I pray.
3 In the morning, O LORD, you hear my voice;
in the morning I lay my requests before you
and wait in expectation.

4 You are not a God who takes pleasure in evil;
with you the wicked cannot dwell.
5 The arrogant cannot stand in your presence;
you hate all who do wrong.
6 You destroy those who tell lies;
bloodthirsty and deceitful men
the LORD abhors.

7 But I, by your great mercy,
will come into your house;
in reverence will I bow down
toward your holy temple.
8 Lead me, O LORD, in your righteousness
because of my enemies—
make straight your way before me.
9 Not a word from their mouth can be trusted;
their heart is filled with destruction.
Their throat is an open grave;
with their tongue they speak deceit.
10 Declare them guilty, O God!
Let their intrigues be their downfall.
Banish them for their many sins,
for they have rebelled against you.

11 But let all who take refuge in you be glad;
let them ever sing for joy.
Spread your protection over them,
that those who love your name may rejoice in you.
12 For surely, O LORD, you bless the righteous;
you surround them with your favor as with a shield.

Psalm 6

For the director of music. With stringed instruments. According to *sheminith.*[c]
A psalm of David.

1 O LORD, do not rebuke me in your anger
or discipline me in your wrath.
2 Be merciful to me, LORD, for I am faint;
O LORD, heal me, for my bones are in agony.
3 My soul is in anguish.
How long, O LORD, how long?

4 Turn, O LORD, and deliver me;
save me because of your unfailing love.
5 No one remembers you when he is dead.
Who praises you from the grave[d]?

6 I am worn out from groaning;
all night long I flood my bed with weeping
and drench my couch with tears.
7 My eyes grow weak with sorrow;
they fail because of all my foes.

8 Away from me, all you who do evil,
for the LORD has heard my weeping.
9 The LORD has heard my cry for mercy;
the LORD accepts my prayer.
10 All my enemies will be ashamed and dismayed;
they will turn back in sudden disgrace.

[a] 2 Or *you dishonor my Glorious One* [b] 2 Or *seek lies* [c] Title: Probably a musical term [d] 5 Hebrew *Sheol*

Psalm 7

A *shiggaion*[a] of David, which he sang to the LORD concerning Cush, a Benjamite.

1 O LORD my God, I take refuge in you;
save and deliver me from all who pursue me,
2 or they will tear me like a lion
and rip me to pieces with no one to rescue me.

3 O LORD my God, if I have done this
and there is guilt on my hands—
4 if I have done evil to him who is at peace with me
or without cause have robbed my foe—
5 then let my enemy pursue and overtake me;
let him trample my life to the ground
and make me sleep in the dust. *Selah*

6 Arise, O LORD, in your anger;
rise up against the rage of my enemies.
Awake, my God; decree justice.
7 Let the assembled peoples gather around you.
Rule over them from on high;
8 let the LORD judge the peoples.
Judge me, O LORD, according to my righteousness,
according to my integrity, O Most High.
9 O righteous God,
who searches minds and hearts,
bring to an end the violence of the wicked
and make the righteous secure.

10 My shield[b] is God Most High,
who saves the upright in heart.
11 God is a righteous judge,
a God who expresses his wrath every day.
12 If he does not relent,
he[c] will sharpen his sword;
he will bend and string his bow.
13 He has prepared his deadly weapons;
he makes ready his flaming arrows.

14 He who is pregnant with evil
and conceives trouble gives birth to disillusionment.
15 He who digs a hole and scoops it out
falls into the pit he has made.
16 The trouble he causes recoils on himself;
his violence comes down on his own head.

17 I will give thanks to the LORD because of his righteousness
and will sing praise to the name of the LORD Most High.

Psalm 8

For the director of music. According to *gittith.*[d] A psalm of David.

1 O LORD, our Lord,
how majestic is your name in all the earth!

You have set your glory
above the heavens.
2 From the lips of children and infants
you have ordained praise[e]
because of your enemies,
to silence the foe and the avenger.

3 When I consider your heavens,
the work of your fingers,
the moon and the stars,
which you have set in place,
4 what is man that you are mindful of him,
the son of man that you care for him?
5 You made him a little lower than the heavenly beings[f]
and crowned him with glory and honor.

6 You made him ruler over the works of your hands;
you put everything under his feet:
7 all flocks and herds,
and the beasts of the field,
8 the birds of the air,
and the fish of the sea,
all that swim the paths of the seas.

9 O LORD, our Lord,
how majestic is your name in all the earth!

Psalm 9[g]

For the director of music. To ⌞the tune of⌟ "The Death of the Son." A psalm of David.

1 I will praise you, O LORD, with all my heart;
I will tell of all your wonders.
2 I will be glad and rejoice in you;

---

[a] Title: Probably a literary or musical term [b] 10 Or *sovereign* [c] 12 Or *If a man does not repent, / God* [d] Title: Probably a musical term [e] 2 Or *strength* [f] 5 Or *than God* [g] *Psalms 9 and 10 may have been originally a single acrostic poem, the stanzas of which begin with the successive letters of the Hebrew alphabet. In the Septuagint they constitute one psalm.*

I will sing praise to your name, O Most
High.

3 My enemies turn back;
they stumble and perish before you.
4 For you have upheld my right and my
cause;
you have sat on your throne, judging
righteously.
5 You have rebuked the nations and
destroyed the wicked;
you have blotted out their name for
ever and ever.
6 Endless ruin has overtaken the enemy,
you have uprooted their cities;
even the memory of them has
perished.

7 The LORD reigns forever;
he has established his throne for
judgment.
8 He will judge the world in righteousness;
he will govern the peoples with
justice.
9 The LORD is a refuge for the oppressed,
a stronghold in times of trouble.
10 Those who know your name will trust in
you,
for you, LORD, have never forsaken
those who seek you.

11 Sing praises to the LORD, enthroned in
Zion;
proclaim among the nations what he
has done.
12 For he who avenges blood remembers;
he does not ignore the cry of the
afflicted.

13 O LORD, see how my enemies persecute
me!
Have mercy and lift me up from the
gates of death,
14 that I may declare your praises
in the gates of the Daughter of Zion
and there rejoice in your salvation.
15 The nations have fallen into the pit they
have dug;
their feet are caught in the net they
have hidden.
16 The LORD is known by his justice;
the wicked are ensnared by the work of
their hands. *Higgaion.* [a] *Selah*
17 The wicked return to the grave, [b]
all the nations that forget God.
18 But the needy will not always be
forgotten,
nor the hope of the afflicted ever
perish.

19 Arise, O LORD, let not man triumph;
let the nations be judged in your
presence.
20 Strike them with terror, O LORD;
let the nations know they are but men.
Selah

Psalm 10 [c]

1 Why, O LORD, do you stand far off?
Why do you hide yourself in times of
trouble?

2 In his arrogance the wicked man hunts
down the weak,
who are caught in the schemes he
devises.
3 He boasts of the cravings of his heart;
he blesses the greedy and reviles the
LORD.
4 In his pride the wicked does not seek him;
in all his thoughts there is no room for
God.
5 His ways are always prosperous;
he is haughty and your laws are far
from him;
he sneers at all his enemies.
6 He says to himself, "Nothing will shake
me;
I'll always be happy and never have
trouble."
7 His mouth is full of curses and lies and
threats;
trouble and evil are under his tongue.
8 He lies in wait near the villages;
from ambush he murders the innocent,
watching in secret for his victims.
9 He lies in wait like a lion in cover;
he lies in wait to catch the helpless;
he catches the helpless and drags them
off in his net.
10 His victims are crushed, they collapse;
they fall under his strength.
11 He says to himself, "God has forgotten;
he covers his face and never sees."

12 Arise, LORD! Lift up your hand, O God.
Do not forget the helpless.
13 Why does the wicked man revile God?
Why does he say to himself,
"He won't call me to account"?

[a] 16 Or *Meditation*; possibly a musical notation [b] 17 Hebrew *Sheol* [c] *Psalms 9 and 10 may have been originally a single acrostic poem, the stanzas of which begin with the successive letters of the Hebrew alphabet. In the Septuagint they constitute one psalm.*

14 But you, O God, do see trouble and grief;
you consider it to take it in hand.
The victim commits himself to you;
you are the helper of the fatherless.
15 Break the arm of the wicked and evil man;
call him to account for his wickedness
that would not be found out.
16 The LORD is King for ever and ever;
the nations will perish from his land.
17 You hear, O LORD, the desire of the afflicted;
you encourage them, and you listen to their cry,
18 defending the fatherless and the oppressed,
in order that man, who is of the earth,
may terrify no more.

Psalm 11

For the director of music. Of David.

1 In the LORD I take refuge.
How then can you say to me:
"Flee like a bird to your mountain.
2 For look, the wicked bend their bows;
they set their arrows against the strings
to shoot from the shadows
at the upright in heart.
3 When the foundations are being destroyed,
what can the righteous do[a]?"

4 The LORD is in his holy temple;
the LORD is on his heavenly throne.
He observes the sons of men;
his eyes examine them.
5 The LORD examines the righteous,
but the wicked[b] and those who love violence
his soul hates.
6 On the wicked he will rain
fiery coals and burning sulfur;
a scorching wind will be their lot.

7 For the LORD is righteous,
he loves justice;
upright men will see his face.

Psalm 12

For the director of music. According to *sheminith*.[c] A psalm of David.

1 Help, LORD, for the godly are no more;
the faithful have vanished from among men.
2 Everyone lies to his neighbor;
their flattering lips speak with deception.

3 May the LORD cut off all flattering lips
and every boastful tongue
4 that says, "We will triumph with our tongues;
we own our lips[d]—who is our master?"

5 "Because of the oppression of the weak
and the groaning of the needy,
I will now arise," says the LORD.
"I will protect them from those who malign them."
6 And the words of the LORD are flawless,
like silver refined in a furnace of clay,
purified seven times.
7 O LORD, you will keep us safe
and protect us from such people forever.
8 The wicked freely strut about
when what is vile is honored among men.

Psalm 13

For the director of music. A psalm of David.

1 How long, O LORD? Will you forget me forever?
How long will you hide your face from me?
2 How long must I wrestle with my thoughts
and every day have sorrow in my heart?
How long will my enemy triumph over me?

3 Look on me and answer, O LORD my God.
Give light to my eyes, or I will sleep in death;
4 my enemy will say, "I have overcome him,"
and my foes will rejoice when I fall.

5 But I trust in your unfailing love;
my heart rejoices in your salvation.
6 I will sing to the LORD,
for he has been good to me.

---

a 3 Or *what is the Righteous One doing* *b* 5 Or *The LORD, the Righteous One, examines the wicked, /* *c* Title: Probably a musical term
d 4 Or */ our lips are our plowshares*

FRIDAY
READ PSALM 13:1–6

WHEN GOD HIDES

How long, O LORD? Will you forget me forever? How long will you hide your face from me?

— PSALM 13:1

let's talk

- ✦ What suffering have we known? How did it affect us? What was our relationship with God like at the time?
- ✦ How do we know that God cares for us today? What would we say as a testimony if asked to share our stories?
- ✦ What do we need from each other during stressful times? How can we best echo back to one another the confident testimonies of Psalm 13?

There are benefits to pastoral ministry. Recently a woman wrote about how thrilled her family was to receive their green cards for permanent residency in this country. We had prayed consistently for this family and supported them through their many struggles and setbacks. Now she shared her joy with her church family.

Of course, pastoral ministry also has tough times. Once I stood with a newly married wife as her husband yelled at her, calling her every name possible. He ripped her house keys out of her hands. Later, he replaced the locks on their house and boarded up the windows to prevent her from getting back in.

The ups and downs of pastoral ministry are echoed in Psalm 13. Among the delights of praise, we hear a litany of despair. Where is God when one of us gets a bad report from the doctor? Where is God when a marriage breaks under the stress of unemployment? Where is God when a spouse dies?

One of the hardest challenges I've faced is finding God in loss. I remember sitting with a mother in a hospital, praying for the recovery of her daughter. The daughter had been married only a year. While delivering the woman's baby, the doctor nicked something with his knife. Now the young woman was fighting for her life.

Her mother was inconsolable. When we prayed, she felt no peace. Within hours, her daughter was gone. After that, the mother stopped going to church. The young husband was angry and didn't know how to care for his baby alone. Where was God?

That question is often asked in suffering or loss. And often the only answer appears to be silence. The promises of Scripture fade in the agony of sorrow. The Holy Spirit seems to withdraw from hearts that grow chilly. Where is God when airplanes crash? Where is God when a spouse is unfaithful? Where is God when a baby dies? Where is God?

Psalm 13 echoes those concerns. In verse 1, the psalmist David asks God, "How long will you hide your face from me?" But this isn't the end of the psalm. Rather, the psalmist goes on to assure us that our God, who is enthroned on high, stoops low to see and hear and know us—even when we can't see his face and his words are like a foreign language to us.

"I trust in your unfailing love; my heart rejoices in your salvation," said David (Psalm 13:5). Likewise we continue to love and trust God, not for what we get out of it right now, but because it is the only way to make sense of this life. We trust in God, not because we always feel the wonder of his divine presence, but because there is truly no one else to turn to but God. And in time we will live to say, "He has been good to me" (Psalm 13:6).

—WAYNE BROUWER

FOR YOUR NEXT DEVOTIONAL READING, TURN TO PAGE 588.

Psalm 14

For the director of music. Of David.

1 The fool[a] says in his heart,
"There is no God."
They are corrupt, their deeds are vile;
there is no one who does good.

2 The LORD looks down from heaven
on the sons of men
to see if there are any who understand,
any who seek God.
3 All have turned aside,
they have together become corrupt;
there is no one who does good,
not even one.

4 Will evildoers never learn—
those who devour my people as men
eat bread
and who do not call on the LORD?
5 There they are, overwhelmed with dread,
for God is present in the company of
the righteous.
6 You evildoers frustrate the plans of the
poor,
but the LORD is their refuge.

7 Oh, that salvation for Israel would come
out of Zion!
When the LORD restores the fortunes of
his people,
let Jacob rejoice and Israel be glad!

Psalm 15

A psalm of David.

1 LORD, who may dwell in your sanctuary?
Who may live on your holy hill?

2 He whose walk is blameless
and who does what is righteous,
who speaks the truth from his heart
3 and has no slander on his tongue,
who does his neighbor no wrong
and casts no slur on his fellowman,
4 who despises a vile man
but honors those who fear the LORD,
who keeps his oath
even when it hurts,
5 who lends his money without usury
and does not accept a bribe against the
innocent.

He who does these things
will never be shaken.

Psalm 16

A *miktam*[b] of David.

1 Keep me safe, O God,
for in you I take refuge.

2 I said to the LORD, "You are my Lord;
apart from you I have no good thing."
3 As for the saints who are in the land,
they are the glorious ones in whom is
all my delight.[c]
4 The sorrows of those will increase
who run after other gods.
I will not pour out their libations of blood
or take up their names on my lips.

5 LORD, you have assigned me my portion
and my cup;
you have made my lot secure.
6 The boundary lines have fallen for me in
pleasant places;
surely I have a delightful inheritance.

7 I will praise the LORD, who counsels me;
even at night my heart instructs me.
8 I have set the LORD always before me.
Because he is at my right hand,
I will not be shaken.

9 Therefore my heart is glad and my tongue
rejoices;
my body also will rest secure,
10 because you will not abandon me to the
grave,[d]
nor will you let your Holy One[e] see
decay.
11 You have made[f] known to me the path of
life;
you will fill me with joy in your
presence,
with eternal pleasures at your right
hand.

Psalm 17

A prayer of David.

1 Hear, O LORD, my righteous plea;
listen to my cry.
Give ear to my prayer—
it does not rise from deceitful lips.
2 May my vindication come from you;
may your eyes see what is right.

3 Though you probe my heart and examine
me at night,

---

a 1 The Hebrew words rendered *fool* in Psalms denote one who is morally deficient. *b* Title: Probably a literary or musical term
c 3 Or *As for the pagan priests who are in the land / and the nobles in whom all delight, I said:* *d* 10 Hebrew *Sheol* *e* 10 Or *your faithful one* *f* 11 Or *You will make*

though you test me, you will find
nothing;
I have resolved that my mouth will not
sin.
4 As for the deeds of men—
by the word of your lips
I have kept myself
from the ways of the violent.
5 My steps have held to your paths;
my feet have not slipped.

6 I call on you, O God, for you will answer
me;
give ear to me and hear my prayer.
7 Show the wonder of your great love,
you who save by your right hand
those who take refuge in you from their
foes.
8 Keep me as the apple of your eye;
hide me in the shadow of your wings
9 from the wicked who assail me,
from my mortal enemies who surround
me.

10 They close up their callous hearts,
and their mouths speak with
arrogance.
11 They have tracked me down, they now
surround me,
with eyes alert, to throw me to the
ground.
12 They are like a lion hungry for prey,
like a great lion crouching in cover.

13 Rise up, O LORD, confront them, bring
them down;
rescue me from the wicked by your
sword.
14 O LORD, by your hand save me from such
men,
from men of this world whose reward is
in this life.

You still the hunger of those you cherish;
their sons have plenty,
and they store up wealth for their
children.
15 And I—in righteousness I will see your
face;
when I awake, I will be satisfied with
seeing your likeness.

Psalm 18

For the director of music. Of David the servant of the LORD. He sang to the LORD the words of this song when the LORD delivered him from the hand of all his enemies and from the hand of Saul. He said:

1 I love you, O LORD, my strength.
2 The LORD is my rock, my fortress and my
deliverer;
my God is my rock, in whom I take
refuge.
He is my shield and the horn[a] of my
salvation, my stronghold.
3 I call to the LORD, who is worthy of praise,
and I am saved from my enemies.

4 The cords of death entangled me;
the torrents of destruction
overwhelmed me.
5 The cords of the grave[b] coiled around me;
the snares of death confronted me.
6 In my distress I called to the LORD;
I cried to my God for help.
From his temple he heard my voice;
my cry came before him, into his ears.

7 The earth trembled and quaked,
and the foundations of the mountains
shook;
they trembled because he was angry.
8 Smoke rose from his nostrils;
consuming fire came from his mouth,
burning coals blazed out of it.
9 He parted the heavens and came down;
dark clouds were under his feet.
10 He mounted the cherubim and flew;
he soared on the wings of the wind.
11 He made darkness his covering, his canopy
around him—
the dark rain clouds of the sky.
12 Out of the brightness of his presence
clouds advanced,
with hailstones and bolts of lightning.
13 The LORD thundered from heaven;
the voice of the Most High resounded.[c]
14 He shot his arrows and scattered ⌊the
enemies⌋,
great bolts of lightning and routed
them.
15 The valleys of the sea were exposed
and the foundations of the earth laid
bare
at your rebuke, O LORD,

[a] 2 *Horn* here symbolizes strength. [b] 5 Hebrew *Sheol* [c] 13 Some Hebrew manuscripts and Septuagint (see also 2 Samuel 22:14); most Hebrew manuscripts *resounded, / amid hailstones and bolts of lightning*

WEEKEND

birth control

Is it right for Christians to practice birth control?

Virtually every couple practices some form of birth control; otherwise families would be much larger than they are. If couples do not use one or more of the scientific methods, they at least practice abstinence during the wife's most fertile time. However, this seems unfair to the wife, because that is the time when she would find lovemaking most enjoyable. Rather than cheat her out of the pleasure God designed for her to enjoy in marriage, it would be better to use a proven contraceptive.

Doesn't God's displeasure with Onan's spilling his seed on the ground indicate that He opposes birth control?

If that kind of reasoning were used to explain the slaying of Ananias and Sapphira in Acts 5, one could conclude that God opposes a person's selling his possessions and giving the return as an offering to Him. In both instances, however, God slew the people because they pretended to do one thing, but did another. In Genesis 38:8–10, we read that Onan cheated his brother out of his rightful heritage by refusing to father a child in his brother's name, as was the custom in his day. Thus it is wrong to use this isolated text to condemn the use of birth control.

Since withdrawal is the most natural method of birth control, is it okay?

It is not wrong to use the withdrawal method (coitus interruptus), but doctors tell us it is not effective. Most men think that if their ejaculation occurs outside of the vagina, their wife will not get pregnant. But that is not necessarily true. Preceding ejaculation, a man excretes a small amount of fluid that contains enough sperm to impregnate a woman. For that reason the withdrawal method is not a recommended procedure. In addition, it is almost impossible for the wife to reach orgasm when coitus interruptus is used.

Please suggest Scriptures on birth control. I have a friend who is going to have her seventh child—her fifth baby in five years. Her husband does not believe in birth control (except the rhythm method).

There is no clear-cut scriptural reference advocating birth control, nor is there one condemning it. The attitude of Christians is changing on this subject, and thus birth control is gaining much more acceptance. The Bible was written long before such methods were developed; consequently its silence cannot be used to prove either point.

As a counselor I cannot help but comment on the abject selfishness of the above-mentioned husband. He obviously does not have loving regard for his wife's health, energy, interests or person. There is certainly nothing wrong with a couple having seven or more children, but it should be a *mutually* agreed-upon decision.

Is sterilization for either man or woman really trusting the Lord?

God has designed our bodies for the propagation of the race. The question really is, when does a couple quit—after two, six or more children? Couples must answer that question for themselves with help from the Lord. We don't hesitate to have an infected appendix or gall bladder removed—is that "trusting the Lord"? We use modern science and medicine frequently; why shouldn't couples do the same with their reproductive organs once their families reach the size they feel they can effectively raise to serve Him?

—TIM AND BEVERLY LAHAYE

our thoughts on birth control

HOW ARE WE DOING?

Use these questions to work toward an informed, mutual decision on the details related to family planning.

1. How many children do you each want? Has the number changed for either of you since you got married? What are some of the reasons for the change?
2. If your numbers differ, how will you decide how many children to have?
3. How many children does God want you to have? How do you know?
4. Do you talk to God about his plans for your family, or do you just trust that he knows best and will take care of it?
5. What form of birth control do you each feel comfortable with?
6. What form of birth control do you each feel least comfortable with?
7. What kind of information do you have on different forms of contraception? Have you asked for medical advice? Biblical direction? Counsel from Christian mentor couples? Where else might you get reliable information on birth control?
8. Are you currently using birth control? How did you decide what to use?
9. What if you and your spouse had an agreed-upon number of children and one of them died? Would you want to have another one? How should this affect your choice of birth control?
10. If your spouse died and you remarried, would you want more children with your new partner? How should this decision affect your choice of birth control?

let's make a DATE

TIME WITH CHILDREN

Whether you already have children, are planning or trying to have children, or are not planning to have children at all, for this activity spend some time enjoying the blessing of children. Offer to take your neighbor's children to the park to give their parents a little free time. Take a niece or nephew to the zoo. Maybe you have a friend who is a single parent. Offer to come over and watch the kids so that the parent can run some errands or get away for coffee. The point is to enjoy the wonder and joy of spending time with little ones.

FOR YOUR NEXT DEVOTIONAL READING, TURN TO PAGE 592.

LESSONS FROM THE *Bible*

Overt examples of contraception in the Bible are uncommon. Most stories are of couples who desperately wanted children but couldn't have them because of infertility.

What do couples such as Zechariah and Elizabeth (see Luke 1:5–25) teach us about the deep yearning to have a child? Is this an innate desire that God implants within all of us? What about couples who chose not to have children? Why would a couple decide that? Are we considering this option?

at the blast of breath from your
nostrils.
16 He reached down from on high and took
hold of me;
he drew me out of deep waters.
17 He rescued me from my powerful enemy,
from my foes, who were too strong for
me.
18 They confronted me in the day of my
disaster,
but the LORD was my support.
19 He brought me out into a spacious place;
he rescued me because he delighted in
me.

20 The LORD has dealt with me according to
my righteousness;
according to the cleanness of my hands
he has rewarded me.
21 For I have kept the ways of the LORD;
I have not done evil by turning from
my God.
22 All his laws are before me;
I have not turned away from his
decrees.
23 I have been blameless before him
and have kept myself from sin.
24 The LORD has rewarded me according to
my righteousness,
according to the cleanness of my hands
in his sight.

25 To the faithful you show yourself faithful,
to the blameless you show yourself
blameless,
26 to the pure you show yourself pure,
but to the crooked you show yourself
shrewd.
27 You save the humble
but bring low those whose eyes are
haughty.
28 You, O LORD, keep my lamp burning;
my God turns my darkness into light.
29 With your help I can advance against a
troop[a];
with my God I can scale a wall.

30 As for God, his way is perfect;
the word of the LORD is flawless.
He is a shield
for all who take refuge in him.
31 For who is God besides the LORD?
And who is the Rock except our God?
32 It is God who arms me with strength
and makes my way perfect.
33 He makes my feet like the feet of a deer;
he enables me to stand on the heights.
34 He trains my hands for battle;
my arms can bend a bow of bronze.
35 You give me your shield of victory,
and your right hand sustains me;
you stoop down to make me great.
36 You broaden the path beneath me,
so that my ankles do not turn.

37 I pursued my enemies and overtook
them;
I did not turn back till they were
destroyed.
38 I crushed them so that they could not rise;
they fell beneath my feet.
39 You armed me with strength for battle;
you made my adversaries bow at my
feet.
40 You made my enemies turn their backs in
flight,
and I destroyed my foes.
41 They cried for help, but there was no one
to save them—
to the LORD, but he did not answer.
42 I beat them as fine as dust borne on the
wind;
I poured them out like mud in the
streets.

43 You have delivered me from the attacks of
the people;
you have made me the head of nations;
people I did not know are subject to
me.
44 As soon as they hear me, they obey me;
foreigners cringe before me.
45 They all lose heart;
they come trembling from their
strongholds.

46 The LORD lives! Praise be to my Rock!
Exalted be God my Savior!
47 He is the God who avenges me,
who subdues nations under me,
48 who saves me from my enemies.
You exalted me above my foes;
from violent men you rescued me.
49 Therefore I will praise you among the
nations, O LORD;
I will sing praises to your name.
50 He gives his king great victories;
he shows unfailing kindness to his
anointed,
to David and his descendants forever.

a *29* Or *can run through a barricade*

Psalm 19

For the director of music. A psalm of David.

1 The heavens declare the glory of God;
the skies proclaim the work of his hands.
2 Day after day they pour forth speech;
night after night they display knowledge.
3 There is no speech or language
where their voice is not heard. [a]
4 Their voice [b] goes out into all the earth,
their words to the ends of the world.

In the heavens he has pitched a tent for the sun,
5 which is like a bridegroom coming forth from his pavilion,
like a champion rejoicing to run his course.
6 It rises at one end of the heavens
and makes its circuit to the other;
nothing is hidden from its heat.

7 The law of the LORD is perfect,
reviving the soul.
The statutes of the LORD are trustworthy,
making wise the simple.
8 The precepts of the LORD are right,
giving joy to the heart.
The commands of the LORD are radiant,
giving light to the eyes.
9 The fear of the LORD is pure,
enduring forever.
The ordinances of the LORD are sure
and altogether righteous.
10 They are more precious than gold,
than much pure gold;
they are sweeter than honey,
than honey from the comb.
11 By them is your servant warned;
in keeping them there is great reward.

12 Who can discern his errors?
Forgive my hidden faults.
13 Keep your servant also from willful sins;
may they not rule over me.
Then will I be blameless,
innocent of great transgression.

14 May the words of my mouth and the meditation of my heart
be pleasing in your sight,
O LORD, my Rock and my Redeemer.

Psalm 20

For the director of music. A psalm of David.

1 May the LORD answer you when you are in distress;
may the name of the God of Jacob protect you.
2 May he send you help from the sanctuary
and grant you support from Zion.
3 May he remember all your sacrifices
and accept your burnt offerings. *Selah*
4 May he give you the desire of your heart
and make all your plans succeed.
5 We will shout for joy when you are victorious
and will lift up our banners in the name of our God.
May the LORD grant all your requests.

6 Now I know that the LORD saves his anointed;
he answers him from his holy heaven
with the saving power of his right hand.
7 Some trust in chariots and some in horses,
but we trust in the name of the LORD our God.
8 They are brought to their knees and fall,
but we rise up and stand firm.
9 O LORD, save the king!
Answer [c] us when we call!

Psalm 21

For the director of music. A psalm of David.

1 O LORD, the king rejoices in your strength.
How great is his joy in the victories you give!
2 You have granted him the desire of his heart
and have not withheld the request of his lips. *Selah*
3 You welcomed him with rich blessings
and placed a crown of pure gold on his head.
4 He asked you for life, and you gave it to him—
length of days, for ever and ever.
5 Through the victories you gave, his glory is great;
you have bestowed on him splendor and majesty.
6 Surely you have granted him eternal blessings

[a] 3 Or *They have no speech, there are no words; / no sound is heard from them* [b] 4 Septuagint, Jerome and Syriac; Hebrew *line*
[c] 9 Or *save! / O King, answer*

MONDAY
READ PSALM 20:1–9

TRUST AMID THE CHALLENGES

> **Some trust in chariots and some in horses, but we trust in the name of the LORD our God.**
> — PSALM 20:7

David, the writer of Psalm 20, trusted God because he had experienced God's deliverance in deadly encounters with various enemies. Even as a youth when he faced the giant Goliath, David said, "The LORD who delivered me from the paw of the lion and the paw of the bear will deliver me from the hand of this Philistine" (1 Samuel 17:37).

Trusting in the name of our God sounds like good advice, but how should husbands and wives trust God in the daily frustrations and concerns of married life? For example, newlyweds Tom and Emily have two small townhouses from their single days, some hefty credit card debt, two dogs (Tom's) and one child (Emily's). They want to sell both townhouses, buy a house while lowering their credit card debt, and, oh yeah, Emily's little girl is allergic to dogs.

Then, two months after the wedding, Tom loses his job. What does trusting the Lord look like to this couple? What does it look like to us?

First, trusting God no matter what happens to us isn't optional; it's essential. While drinking iced tea with an atheist friend, Tom and Emily said they were trusting God amid all their challenges. The friend responded, "Sounds pretty irresponsible to me." Instead of becoming defensive, Tom and Emily explained that the key word was *amid*. They didn't expect God to help them win the lottery or make their child's allergies disappear. They would simply follow a strategy based on their unshakable trust in God and his Word.

They would first pray, knowing God would give them wisdom and peace of mind while they waited. They would then wait patiently to see what God was doing. Then they would move ahead, trusting God to lead them.

While trusting God, they would also take sensible action. They would work hard to make their townhouses attractive to buyers. They would hire a good realtor to list the houses. They'd take a debt-control course offered by a Christian organization. They'd update Tom's work résumé and begin networking for job opportunities. And they'd give their dogs to a good friend.

Psalm 20 shows that many of us trust other things besides God when we experience difficulties. What are the "chariots and horses" we trust in instead of God? Do we trust in youth, looks, good health, a nice job with a 401(k), a great house or even our spouse? While all of these things may be good, and we may appreciate them as God's blessings, it's best not to count on them to deliver happiness and peace of mind. Only God can deliver that.

—MARY ANN JEFFREYS

FOR YOUR NEXT DEVOTIONAL READING, TURN TO PAGE 595.

let's talk

- In what ways has God shown us that he is worthy of our trust? In what ways has he helped us through difficulty?
- Why is it better to wait for God's leading rather than to try to solve things on our own?
- What part of trusting God—praying, waiting, moving ahead—do we find the hardest? What makes it so difficult?

and made him glad with the joy of your
presence.
7 For the king trusts in the LORD;
through the unfailing love of the Most
High
he will not be shaken.

8 Your hand will lay hold on all your
enemies;
your right hand will seize your foes.
9 At the time of your appearing
you will make them like a fiery
furnace.
In his wrath the LORD will swallow them
up,
and his fire will consume them.
10 You will destroy their descendants from
the earth,
their posterity from mankind.
11 Though they plot evil against you
and devise wicked schemes, they cannot
succeed;
12 for you will make them turn their backs
when you aim at them with drawn
bow.

13 Be exalted, O LORD, in your strength;
we will sing and praise your might.

Psalm 22

For the director of music. To ⌞the tune
of⌟ "The Doe of the Morning." A psalm
of David.

1 My God, my God, why have you forsaken
me?
Why are you so far from saving me,
so far from the words of my groaning?
2 O my God, I cry out by day, but you do
not answer,
by night, and am not silent.

3 Yet you are enthroned as the Holy One;
you are the praise of Israel.[a]
4 In you our fathers put their trust;
they trusted and you delivered them.
5 They cried to you and were saved;
in you they trusted and were not
disappointed.

6 But I am a worm and not a man,
scorned by men and despised by the
people.
7 All who see me mock me;
they hurl insults, shaking their heads:
8 "He trusts in the LORD;
let the LORD rescue him.
Let him deliver him,
since he delights in him."

9 Yet you brought me out of the womb;
you made me trust in you
even at my mother's breast.
10 From birth I was cast upon you;
from my mother's womb you have been
my God.
11 Do not be far from me,
for trouble is near
and there is no one to help.

12 Many bulls surround me;
strong bulls of Bashan encircle me.
13 Roaring lions tearing their prey
open their mouths wide against me.
14 I am poured out like water,
and all my bones are out of joint.
My heart has turned to wax;
it has melted away within me.
15 My strength is dried up like a potsherd,
and my tongue sticks to the roof of my
mouth;
you lay me[b] in the dust of death.
16 Dogs have surrounded me;
a band of evil men has encircled me,
they have pierced[c] my hands and my
feet.

17 I can count all my bones;
people stare and gloat over me.
18 They divide my garments among them
and cast lots for my clothing.

19 But you, O LORD, be not far off;
O my Strength, come quickly to help
me.
20 Deliver my life from the sword,
my precious life from the power of the
dogs.
21 Rescue me from the mouth of the lions;
save[d] me from the horns of the wild
oxen.

22 I will declare your name to my brothers;
in the congregation I will praise you.
23 You who fear the LORD, praise him!
All you descendants of Jacob, honor
him!
Revere him, all you descendants of
Israel!
24 For he has not despised or disdained
the suffering of the afflicted one;
he has not hidden his face from him
but has listened to his cry for help.

---

[a] 3 Or *Yet you are holy, / enthroned on the praises of Israel* [b] 15 Or */ I am laid* [c] 16 Some Hebrew manuscripts, Septuagint and Syriac; most Hebrew manuscripts */ like the lion,* [d] 21 Or */ you have heard*

25 From you comes the theme of my praise
in the great assembly;
before those who fear you[a] will I fulfill
my vows.
26 The poor will eat and be satisfied;
they who seek the LORD will praise
him—
may your hearts live forever!
27 All the ends of the earth
will remember and turn to the LORD,
and all the families of the nations
will bow down before him,
28 for dominion belongs to the LORD
and he rules over the nations.

29 All the rich of the earth will feast and
worship;
all who go down to the dust will kneel
before him—
those who cannot keep themselves
alive.
30 Posterity will serve him;
future generations will be told about
the Lord.
31 They will proclaim his righteousness
to a people yet unborn—
for he has done it.

Psalm 23

A psalm of David.

1 The LORD is my shepherd, I shall not be in
want.
2 He makes me lie down in green
pastures,
he leads me beside quiet waters,
3 he restores my soul.
He guides me in paths of righteousness
for his name's sake.
4 Even though I walk
through the valley of the shadow of
death,[b]
I will fear no evil,
for you are with me;
your rod and your staff,
they comfort me.

5 You prepare a table before me
in the presence of my enemies.
You anoint my head with oil;
my cup overflows.
6 Surely goodness and love will follow me
all the days of my life,
and I will dwell in the house of the LORD
forever.

Psalm 24

Of David. A psalm.

1 The earth is the LORD's, and everything in
it,
the world, and all who live in it;
2 for he founded it upon the seas
and established it upon the waters.

3 Who may ascend the hill of the LORD?
Who may stand in his holy place?
4 He who has clean hands and a pure
heart,
who does not lift up his soul to an idol
or swear by what is false.[c]
5 He will receive blessing from the LORD
and vindication from God his Savior.
6 Such is the generation of those who seek
him,
who seek your face, O God of Jacob.[d]
Selah

7 Lift up your heads, O you gates;
be lifted up, you ancient doors,
that the King of glory may come in.
8 Who is this King of glory?
The LORD strong and mighty,
the LORD mighty in battle.
9 Lift up your heads, O you gates;
lift them up, you ancient doors,
that the King of glory may come in.
10 Who is he, this King of glory?
The LORD Almighty—
he is the King of glory. *Selah*

Psalm 25[e]

Of David.

1 To you, O LORD, I lift up my soul;
2 in you I trust, O my God.
Do not let me be put to shame,
nor let my enemies triumph over me.
3 No one whose hope is in you
will ever be put to shame,
but they will be put to shame
who are treacherous without excuse.

4 Show me your ways, O LORD,
teach me your paths;
5 guide me in your truth and teach me,
for you are God my Savior,
and my hope is in you all day long.
6 Remember, O LORD, your great mercy
and love,
for they are from of old.

---

[a] 25 Hebrew *him* [b] 4 Or *through the darkest valley* [c] 4 Or *swear falsely* [d] 6 Two Hebrew manuscripts and Syriac (see also Septuagint); most Hebrew manuscripts *face, Jacob* [e] *This psalm is an acrostic poem, the verses of which begin with the successive letters of the Hebrew alphabet.*

T

TUESDAY
READ PSALM 25:1–22

EXORCISING THE PAST

Years ago I gathered with a group of about 30 godly men who had met to pray for three days. After many hours together before the Lord, men began to confess the sins and weaknesses that were keeping them from growing. One man in his mid-30s broke down and asked for prayer. "I was saved after college," he said. "Before that I slept with a number of women. Now I'm married and I love my wife, but I just can't get those images out of my mind. I don't know what to do!"

The sins of our past, whatever they are, affect our marriages. When we're dating, we naively assume that if we just communicate well, our marriage will be strong. But open communication doesn't solve every problem. Sin, past and present, has an enormous effect on our marriages. And that, according to Psalm 25, is an issue that should drive us to the Lord first.

In Psalm 25 David teaches us how to talk to God about past sins that still spread their poison in our lives. Sin, of course, is never general or vague. We sin in specific ways. Though this psalm speaks generally of sin, we each need to personalize it and plug into it the specific sins of our past as we process them through God's mercy.

This psalm, in its original Hebrew form, was an acrostic, with every couplet beginning with the next letter of the alphabet. It was a memory tool, but it was also a kind of A-B-C of dealing with past sins. It tells us how to think about God, what exactly to pray for, and what to trust God to do for us.

Notice that the concerns David prayed for were all rooted in the sins of his youth. In verses 1–3 he thought about the shame of being defeated by his enemies. He may have been thinking about his military or political enemies, but taken with later verses, he probably was thinking about what would happen if his enemies used his past sins to disgrace him. We should likewise pray that God will keep our past sins from being fodder for Satan or for others to shame us and those we love.

Verses 4–5 and 8–10 are a prayer that, having walked in sinful ways, we would now learn the right way to walk. Sin, of course, fouls up our spiritual sense of direction. We tend to react badly and to get off the right track, so we pray for God to teach us the ways we should go in life—the ways to think and the directions to pursue.

Then, in verses 6, 7 and 11, David sought God's forgiveness. We can do the same by remembering the kind of God we serve. All our hope for forgiveness and restoration depends on God's merciful and loving character.

Remember, as with all psalms, this is not only a passage to be studied but a prayer to be used—even sung—to God. This is spiritual medicine for us and our marriages.

—LEE ECLOV

FOR YOUR NEXT DEVOTIONAL READING, TURN TO PAGE 601.

Remember not the sins of my youth and my rebellious ways; according to your love remember me, for you are good, O LORD.

— PSALM 25:7

let's talk

- ✦ List the descriptions of God in this psalm. How does thinking about God's character this way change our prayers?
- ✦ Sin is always an issue between us and God, but as we peer into this very personal prayer, how can we help each other with the spiritual processes that we need to follow in order to find forgiveness and hope?
- ✦ When trying to solve problems caused by past sins, what goes wrong when we go to each other before we go to God?

7 Remember not the sins of my youth
and my rebellious ways;
according to your love remember me,
for you are good, O LORD.

8 Good and upright is the LORD;
therefore he instructs sinners in his ways.
9 He guides the humble in what is right
and teaches them his way.
10 All the ways of the LORD are loving and faithful
for those who keep the demands of his covenant.
11 For the sake of your name, O LORD,
forgive my iniquity, though it is great.
12 Who, then, is the man that fears the LORD?
He will instruct him in the way chosen for him.
13 He will spend his days in prosperity,
and his descendants will inherit the land.
14 The LORD confides in those who fear him;
he makes his covenant known to them.
15 My eyes are ever on the LORD,
for only he will release my feet from the snare.

16 Turn to me and be gracious to me,
for I am lonely and afflicted.
17 The troubles of my heart have multiplied;
free me from my anguish.
18 Look upon my affliction and my distress
and take away all my sins.
19 See how my enemies have increased
and how fiercely they hate me!
20 Guard my life and rescue me;
let me not be put to shame,
for I take refuge in you.
21 May integrity and uprightness protect me,
because my hope is in you.

22 Redeem Israel, O God,
from all their troubles!

Psalm 26

Of David.

1 Vindicate me, O LORD,
for I have led a blameless life;
I have trusted in the LORD
without wavering.
2 Test me, O LORD, and try me,
examine my heart and my mind;
3 for your love is ever before me,
and I walk continually in your truth.
4 I do not sit with deceitful men,
nor do I consort with hypocrites;
5 I abhor the assembly of evildoers
and refuse to sit with the wicked.
6 I wash my hands in innocence,
and go about your altar, O LORD,
7 proclaiming aloud your praise
and telling of all your wonderful deeds.
8 I love the house where you live, O LORD,
the place where your glory dwells.
9 Do not take away my soul along with sinners,
my life with bloodthirsty men,
10 in whose hands are wicked schemes,
whose right hands are full of bribes.
11 But I lead a blameless life;
redeem me and be merciful to me.

12 My feet stand on level ground;
in the great assembly I will praise the LORD.

Psalm 27

Of David.

1 The LORD is my light and my salvation—
whom shall I fear?
The LORD is the stronghold of my life—
of whom shall I be afraid?
2 When evil men advance against me
to devour my flesh,[a]
when my enemies and my foes attack me,
they will stumble and fall.
3 Though an army besiege me,
my heart will not fear;
though war break out against me,
even then will I be confident.

4 One thing I ask of the LORD,
this is what I seek:
that I may dwell in the house of the LORD
all the days of my life,
to gaze upon the beauty of the LORD
and to seek him in his temple.
5 For in the day of trouble
he will keep me safe in his dwelling;
he will hide me in the shelter of his tabernacle
and set me high upon a rock.

[a] 2 Or *to slander me*

6 Then my head will be exalted
above the enemies who surround me;
at his tabernacle will I sacrifice with shouts of joy;
I will sing and make music to the LORD.

7 Hear my voice when I call, O LORD;
be merciful to me and answer me.
8 My heart says of you, "Seek his[a] face!"
Your face, LORD, I will seek.
9 Do not hide your face from me,
do not turn your servant away in anger;
you have been my helper.
Do not reject me or forsake me,
O God my Savior.
10 Though my father and mother forsake me,
the LORD will receive me.
11 Teach me your way, O LORD;
lead me in a straight path
because of my oppressors.
12 Do not turn me over to the desire of my foes,
for false witnesses rise up against me,
breathing out violence.

13 I am still confident of this:
I will see the goodness of the LORD
in the land of the living.
14 Wait for the LORD;
be strong and take heart
and wait for the LORD.

Psalm 28

Of David.

1 To you I call, O LORD my Rock;
do not turn a deaf ear to me.
For if you remain silent,
I will be like those who have gone down to the pit.
2 Hear my cry for mercy
as I call to you for help,
as I lift up my hands
toward your Most Holy Place.

3 Do not drag me away with the wicked,
with those who do evil,
who speak cordially with their neighbors
but harbor malice in their hearts.
4 Repay them for their deeds
and for their evil work;
repay them for what their hands have done
and bring back upon them what they deserve.
5 Since they show no regard for the works of the LORD
and what his hands have done,
he will tear them down
and never build them up again.

6 Praise be to the LORD,
for he has heard my cry for mercy.
7 The LORD is my strength and my shield;
my heart trusts in him, and I am helped.
My heart leaps for joy
and I will give thanks to him in song.

8 The LORD is the strength of his people,
a fortress of salvation for his anointed one.
9 Save your people and bless your inheritance;
be their shepherd and carry them forever.

Psalm 29

A psalm of David.

1 Ascribe to the LORD, O mighty ones,
ascribe to the LORD glory and strength.
2 Ascribe to the LORD the glory due his name;
worship the LORD in the splendor of his[b] holiness.

3 The voice of the LORD is over the waters;
the God of glory thunders,
the LORD thunders over the mighty waters.
4 The voice of the LORD is powerful;
the voice of the LORD is majestic.
5 The voice of the LORD breaks the cedars;
the LORD breaks in pieces the cedars of Lebanon.
6 He makes Lebanon skip like a calf,
Sirion[c] like a young wild ox.
7 The voice of the LORD strikes
with flashes of lightning.
8 The voice of the LORD shakes the desert;
the LORD shakes the Desert of Kadesh.
9 The voice of the LORD twists the oaks[d]
and strips the forests bare.
And in his temple all cry, "Glory!"

10 The LORD sits[e] enthroned over the flood;
the LORD is enthroned as King forever.

---

[a] 8 Or *To you, O my heart, he has said, "Seek my* [b] 2 Or *LORD with the splendor of* [c] 6 That is, Mount Hermon [d] 9 Or *LORD makes the deer give birth* [e] 10 Or *sat*

11 The LORD gives strength to his people;
the LORD blesses his people with peace.

Psalm 30

A psalm. A song. For the dedication of the temple.[a] Of David.

1 I will exalt you, O LORD,
for you lifted me out of the depths
and did not let my enemies gloat over me.
2 O LORD my God, I called to you for help
and you healed me.
3 O LORD, you brought me up from the grave[b];
you spared me from going down into the pit.

4 Sing to the LORD, you saints of his;
praise his holy name.
5 For his anger lasts only a moment,
but his favor lasts a lifetime;
weeping may remain for a night,
but rejoicing comes in the morning.

6 When I felt secure, I said,
"I will never be shaken."
7 O LORD, when you favored me,
you made my mountain[c] stand firm;
but when you hid your face,
I was dismayed.

8 To you, O LORD, I called;
to the Lord I cried for mercy:
9 "What gain is there in my destruction,[d]
in my going down into the pit?
Will the dust praise you?
Will it proclaim your faithfulness?
10 Hear, O LORD, and be merciful to me;
O LORD, be my help."

11 You turned my wailing into dancing;
you removed my sackcloth and clothed me with joy,
12 that my heart may sing to you and not be silent.
O LORD my God, I will give you thanks forever.

Psalm 31

For the director of music. A psalm of David.

1 In you, O LORD, I have taken refuge;
let me never be put to shame;
deliver me in your righteousness.
2 Turn your ear to me,
come quickly to my rescue;
be my rock of refuge,
a strong fortress to save me.
3 Since you are my rock and my fortress,
for the sake of your name lead and guide me.
4 Free me from the trap that is set for me,
for you are my refuge.
5 Into your hands I commit my spirit;
redeem me, O LORD, the God of truth.

6 I hate those who cling to worthless idols;
I trust in the LORD.
7 I will be glad and rejoice in your love,
for you saw my affliction
and knew the anguish of my soul.
8 You have not handed me over to the enemy
but have set my feet in a spacious place.

9 Be merciful to me, O LORD, for I am in distress;
my eyes grow weak with sorrow,
my soul and my body with grief.
10 My life is consumed by anguish
and my years by groaning;
my strength fails because of my affliction,[e]
and my bones grow weak.
11 Because of all my enemies,
I am the utter contempt of my neighbors;
I am a dread to my friends—
those who see me on the street flee from me.
12 I am forgotten by them as though I were dead;
I have become like broken pottery.
13 For I hear the slander of many;
there is terror on every side;
they conspire against me
and plot to take my life.

14 But I trust in you, O LORD;
I say, "You are my God."
15 My times are in your hands;
deliver me from my enemies
and from those who pursue me.
16 Let your face shine on your servant;
save me in your unfailing love.
17 Let me not be put to shame, O LORD,
for I have cried out to you;
but let the wicked be put to shame
and lie silent in the grave.[b]
18 Let their lying lips be silenced,

[a] Title: Or *palace* [b] *3,17* Hebrew *Sheol* [c] *7* Or *hill country* [d] *9* Or *there if I am silenced* [e] *10* Or *guilt*

for with pride and contempt
they speak arrogantly against the righteous.

19 How great is your goodness,
which you have stored up for those who fear you,
which you bestow in the sight of men
on those who take refuge in you.
20 In the shelter of your presence you hide them
from the intrigues of men;
in your dwelling you keep them safe
from accusing tongues.

21 Praise be to the LORD,
for he showed his wonderful love to me
when I was in a besieged city.
22 In my alarm I said,
"I am cut off from your sight!"
Yet you heard my cry for mercy
when I called to you for help.

23 Love the LORD, all his saints!
The LORD preserves the faithful,
but the proud he pays back in full.
24 Be strong and take heart,
all you who hope in the LORD.

Psalm 32

Of David. A *maskil.* [a]

1 Blessed is he
whose transgressions are forgiven,
whose sins are covered.
2 Blessed is the man
whose sin the LORD does not count against him
and in whose spirit is no deceit.

3 When I kept silent,
my bones wasted away
through my groaning all day long.
4 For day and night
your hand was heavy upon me;
my strength was sapped
as in the heat of summer. *Selah*
5 Then I acknowledged my sin to you
and did not cover up my iniquity.
I said, "I will confess
my transgressions to the LORD"—
and you forgave
the guilt of my sin. *Selah*

6 Therefore let everyone who is godly pray to you
while you may be found;
surely when the mighty waters rise,
they will not reach him.
7 You are my hiding place;
you will protect me from trouble
and surround me with songs of deliverance. *Selah*

8 I will instruct you and teach you in the way you should go;
I will counsel you and watch over you.
9 Do not be like the horse or the mule,
which have no understanding
but must be controlled by bit and bridle
or they will not come to you.
10 Many are the woes of the wicked,
but the LORD's unfailing love
surrounds the man who trusts in him.

11 Rejoice in the LORD and be glad, you righteous;
sing, all you who are upright in heart!

Psalm 33

1 Sing joyfully to the LORD, you righteous;
it is fitting for the upright to praise him.
2 Praise the LORD with the harp;
make music to him on the ten-stringed lyre.
3 Sing to him a new song;
play skillfully, and shout for joy.

4 For the word of the LORD is right and true;
he is faithful in all he does.
5 The LORD loves righteousness and justice;
the earth is full of his unfailing love.

6 By the word of the LORD were the heavens made,
their starry host by the breath of his mouth.
7 He gathers the waters of the sea into jars [b];
he puts the deep into storehouses.
8 Let all the earth fear the LORD;
let all the people of the world revere him.
9 For he spoke, and it came to be;
he commanded, and it stood firm.
10 The LORD foils the plans of the nations;
he thwarts the purposes of the peoples.

[a] Title: Probably a literary or musical term [b] 7 Or *sea as into a heap*

11 But the plans of the LORD stand firm forever,
the purposes of his heart through all generations.

12 Blessed is the nation whose God is the LORD,
the people he chose for his inheritance.

13 From heaven the LORD looks down
and sees all mankind;
14 from his dwelling place he watches
all who live on earth—
15 he who forms the hearts of all,
who considers everything they do.
16 No king is saved by the size of his army;
no warrior escapes by his great strength.
17 A horse is a vain hope for deliverance;
despite all its great strength it cannot save.
18 But the eyes of the LORD are on those who fear him,
on those whose hope is in his unfailing love,
19 to deliver them from death
and keep them alive in famine.

20 We wait in hope for the LORD;
he is our help and our shield.
21 In him our hearts rejoice,
for we trust in his holy name.
22 May your unfailing love rest upon us, O LORD,
even as we put our hope in you.

Psalm 34[a]

Of David. When he pretended to be insane before Abimelech, who drove him away, and he left.

1 I will extol the LORD at all times;
his praise will always be on my lips.
2 My soul will boast in the LORD;
let the afflicted hear and rejoice.
3 Glorify the LORD with me;
let us exalt his name together.

4 I sought the LORD, and he answered me;
he delivered me from all my fears.
5 Those who look to him are radiant;
their faces are never covered with shame.
6 This poor man called, and the LORD heard him;
he saved him out of all his troubles.
7 The angel of the LORD encamps around those who fear him,
and he delivers them.

8 Taste and see that the LORD is good;
blessed is the man who takes refuge in him.
9 Fear the LORD, you his saints,
for those who fear him lack nothing.
10 The lions may grow weak and hungry,
but those who seek the LORD lack no good thing.

11 Come, my children, listen to me;
I will teach you the fear of the LORD.
12 Whoever of you loves life
and desires to see many good days,
13 keep your tongue from evil
and your lips from speaking lies.
14 Turn from evil and do good;
seek peace and pursue it.

15 The eyes of the LORD are on the righteous
and his ears are attentive to their cry;
16 the face of the LORD is against those who do evil,
to cut off the memory of them from the earth.

17 The righteous cry out, and the LORD hears them;
he delivers them from all their troubles.
18 The LORD is close to the brokenhearted
and saves those who are crushed in spirit.

19 A righteous man may have many troubles,
but the LORD delivers him from them all;
20 he protects all his bones,
not one of them will be broken.

21 Evil will slay the wicked;
the foes of the righteous will be condemned.
22 The LORD redeems his servants;
no one will be condemned who takes refuge in him.

Psalm 35

Of David.

1 Contend, O LORD, with those who contend with me;
fight against those who fight against me.

---

[a] This psalm is an acrostic poem, the verses of which begin with the successive letters of the Hebrew alphabet.

W

WEDNESDAY
READ
PSALMS 34:1–22; 56:1–13

COMFORT IN A TIME OF LOSS

> **The Lord is close to the brokenhearted and saves those who are crushed in spirit.**
>
> — Psalm 34:18

Gwen Voss was recovering from surgery on a Saturday morning in September 2005. Her mother, Kathy, was keeping her company. Gwen was 27, and she was to be married in a week. Then, suddenly, Gwen died. A blood clot broke loose and stopped her heart. Gwen's parents, sisters and her fiancé, Tim, were all believers. But Gwen's death was a shocking loss.

What are believers to do when hammered by loss? How do you manage the ransacked emotions such trouble brings? For the people of God, prayer is how we begin putting things back on the shelves; prayer is how we sweep up the broken glass; prayer is how we figure out what's left.

David was running from the fury of King Saul when he fell into the hands of the Philistines. The account of this event in 1 Samuel 21:10–15 is brief. David cleverly came up with the idea of pretending to be insane so the bad guys would let him go. You can almost picture him with a jaunty grin when he was freed. But his prayers and poems tell another story: The background of Psalm 56 is likely how David prayed when he thought his life was over, and the occasion of Psalm 34 is likely how he prayed once he was free. His prayers give us insight into how to pray when life threatens our very sanity.

let's talk

- How has the loss of a child, parent, sibling or friend affected us as a couple?
- David's exuberant praise in Psalm 34 doesn't come easy if we are suffering a terrible loss. How can this psalm help us even when we don't feel its joy?
- There is comfort in the promise of Psalm 34:18 that "the Lord is close to the brokenhearted," but what other assurances does this psalm give us about the Lord in a time of sorrow?

There are two basic parts of David's prayers. In the first part, David cried out to the Lord for mercy. *What* we cry out isn't as important as *that* we cry out and *whom* we cry out to (the Lord).

Kathy Voss also cried out to God for help in her time of loss. "That first year, there are times when you feel you can hardly breathe," she says. During that time, Kathy journaled her thoughts and prayers, meditated on Scripture and listened to Christian music. She and her husband posted Scripture passages around their home. It is how they cried out to the Lord.

In the second part of David's prayers, he resolved not to sin. He saw the wickedness in his pursuers but determined he would not sin himself. "Turn from evil and do good" (Psalm 34:14). There is a unique and powerful temptation to sin when our hearts are breaking or when we are terrified. But we can pray, "O Lord, I resolve before you not to sin, no matter what."

Standing like a mighty sentinel behind David's prayers was his trust that God would rescue him and that the day would come when he would rejoice in the Lord's deliverance—as he did in Psalm 34. His declaration that "the Lord is close to the brokenhearted" (Psalm 34:18) isn't only a promise of God's comforting presence; it is also a promise of God's rescue, for God "saves those who are crushed in spirit."

You may be deep in the fear and heartache of Psalm 56 right now. But as Thomas Moore once wrote, "Earth has no sorrow that heaven cannot heal." Learn the words and rhythms of Psalm 34 today. They will bolster your hope and feed your faith. And when the day of God's deliverance comes—whether in this world or in heaven—you will know the words to the perfect hymn!

—LEE ECLOV

FOR YOUR NEXT DEVOTIONAL READING, TURN TO PAGE 604.

2 Take up shield and buckler;
arise and come to my aid.
3 Brandish spear and javelin[a]
against those who pursue me.
Say to my soul,
"I am your salvation."

4 May those who seek my life
be disgraced and put to shame;
may those who plot my ruin
be turned back in dismay.
5 May they be like chaff before the wind,
with the angel of the LORD driving
them away;
6 may their path be dark and slippery,
with the angel of the LORD pursuing
them.
7 Since they hid their net for me without
cause
and without cause dug a pit for me,
8 may ruin overtake them by surprise—
may the net they hid entangle them,
may they fall into the pit, to their ruin.
9 Then my soul will rejoice in the LORD
and delight in his salvation.
10 My whole being will exclaim,
"Who is like you, O LORD?
You rescue the poor from those too strong
for them,
the poor and needy from those who rob
them."

11 Ruthless witnesses come forward;
they question me on things I know
nothing about.
12 They repay me evil for good
and leave my soul forlorn.
13 Yet when they were ill, I put on sackcloth
and humbled myself with fasting.
When my prayers returned to me
unanswered,
14 I went about mourning
as though for my friend or brother.
I bowed my head in grief
as though weeping for my mother.
15 But when I stumbled, they gathered in
glee;
attackers gathered against me when I
was unaware.
They slandered me without ceasing.
16 Like the ungodly they maliciously
mocked[b];
they gnashed their teeth at me.
17 O Lord, how long will you look on?
Rescue my life from their ravages,
my precious life from these lions.
18 I will give you thanks in the great
assembly;
among throngs of people I will praise
you.

19 Let not those gloat over me
who are my enemies without cause;
let not those who hate me without reason
maliciously wink the eye.
20 They do not speak peaceably,
but devise false accusations
against those who live quietly in the
land.
21 They gape at me and say, "Aha! Aha!
With our own eyes we have seen it."

22 O LORD, you have seen this; be not
silent.
Do not be far from me, O Lord.
23 Awake, and rise to my defense!
Contend for me, my God and Lord.
24 Vindicate me in your righteousness,
O LORD my God;
do not let them gloat over me.
25 Do not let them think, "Aha, just what we
wanted!"
or say, "We have swallowed him up."

26 May all who gloat over my distress
be put to shame and confusion;
may all who exalt themselves over me
be clothed with shame and disgrace.
27 May those who delight in my
vindication
shout for joy and gladness;
may they always say, "The LORD be
exalted,
who delights in the well-being of his
servant."
28 My tongue will speak of your
righteousness
and of your praises all day long.

Psalm 36

For the director of music. Of David the servant of the LORD.

1 An oracle is within my heart
concerning the sinfulness of the
wicked:[c]
There is no fear of God
before his eyes.
2 For in his own eyes he flatters himself
too much to detect or hate his sin.

---

[a] 3 Or *and block the way* [b] 16 Septuagint; Hebrew may mean *ungodly circle of mockers.* [c] 1 Or *heart: / Sin proceeds from the wicked.*

[3]The words of his mouth are wicked and
deceitful;
he has ceased to be wise and to do
good.
[4]Even on his bed he plots evil;
he commits himself to a sinful course
and does not reject what is wrong.

[5]Your love, O LORD, reaches to the
heavens,
your faithfulness to the skies.
[6]Your righteousness is like the mighty
mountains,
your justice like the great deep.
O LORD, you preserve both man and
beast.
[7] How priceless is your unfailing love!
Both high and low among men
find[a] refuge in the shadow of your
wings.
[8]They feast on the abundance of your
house;
you give them drink from your river of
delights.
[9]For with you is the fountain of life;
in your light we see light.

[10]Continue your love to those who know
you,
your righteousness to the upright in
heart.
[11]May the foot of the proud not come
against me,
nor the hand of the wicked drive me
away.
[12]See how the evildoers lie fallen—
thrown down, not able to rise!

Psalm 37[b]

Of David.

[1]Do not fret because of evil men
or be envious of those who do wrong;
[2]for like the grass they will soon wither,
like green plants they will soon die
away.

[3]Trust in the LORD and do good;
dwell in the land and enjoy safe
pasture.
[4]Delight yourself in the LORD
and he will give you the desires of your
heart.

[5]Commit your way to the LORD;
trust in him and he will do this:
[6]He will make your righteousness shine like
the dawn,
the justice of your cause like the
noonday sun.

[7]Be still before the LORD and wait patiently
for him;
do not fret when men succeed in their
ways,
when they carry out their wicked
schemes.
[8]Refrain from anger and turn from wrath;
do not fret—it leads only to evil.
[9]For evil men will be cut off,
but those who hope in the LORD will
inherit the land.

[10]A little while, and the wicked will be no
more;
though you look for them, they will
not be found.
[11]But the meek will inherit the land
and enjoy great peace.

[12]The wicked plot against the righteous
and gnash their teeth at them;
[13]but the Lord laughs at the wicked,
for he knows their day is coming.

[14]The wicked draw the sword
and bend the bow
to bring down the poor and needy,
to slay those whose ways are upright.
[15]But their swords will pierce their own
hearts,
and their bows will be broken.

[16]Better the little that the righteous have
than the wealth of many wicked;
[17]for the power of the wicked will be
broken,
but the LORD upholds the righteous.

[18]The days of the blameless are known to
the LORD,
and their inheritance will endure
forever.
[19]In times of disaster they will not wither;
in days of famine they will enjoy plenty.

[20]But the wicked will perish:
The LORD's enemies will be like the
beauty of the fields,
they will vanish—vanish like smoke.

[21]The wicked borrow and do not repay,
but the righteous give generously;

[a] 7 Or *love, O God! / Men find*; or *love! / Both heavenly beings and men / find* [b] *This psalm is an acrostic poem, the stanzas of which begin with the successive letters of the Hebrew alphabet.*

THURSDAY
READ PSALM 37:1–9

ANGER MANAGEMENT

> **Refrain from anger and turn from wrath.**
> — Psalm 37:8

let's talk

- What have been some past issues that have led to anger in our relationship?
- What types of situations currently make us so angry with each other that we trip into sin? What kinds of sin do we commit?
- How could each of us do a better job of handling our anger? Do we need to be more willing to express anger? To take a time-out?

Husbands and wives become angry at each other for many reasons, ranging from nitpicky differences that can annoy to major issues that can destroy. One key adjustment for any married couple going through a difficult time is learning how to deal with feelings, such as anger, and learning how to work together toward a solution that is mutually beneficial.

In the Bible, there are many instances in which people who loved one another became angry with each other. Think of Moses being furious with the people of Israel for making a golden calf, for example, or Paul being angry with John Mark for deserting him on their missionary journey. Anger is part of being human. Yet we often feel the need to place the cause of those feelings on other people: "What you did was so awful" or "You make me so mad."

Understanding how to handle anger is a key aspect of marital communication. One way to initiate conversation about a situation that has resulted in angry feelings is to simply talk about how you feel without blaming each other. I can gain more by saying, "I'm angry because I've been hurt by something like this before" or "I'm miffed because I miss our after-work talks" than by accusing my wife of wounding me or by purposely avoiding conversation about the problem.

The Bible stresses the importance of dealing with anger as clearly, quickly and lovingly as possible. Yet so often we can explode with heated words or seethe with cold silence, withdrawal or indifference. Unexpressed anger or poorly expressed anger can lead us to sin in word or deed. We may say things in anger that we might regret later or do things to cause emotional damage or even physical harm.

How do we prevent sin, pain and hurt from a sudden outburst of anger?

Early in our marriage when we got mad at each other, Cindy and I would blurt out things that were hurtful, thoughtless or ill timed. Eventually we learned how destructive that could be. We learned to follow the Biblical advice to search our hearts and become silent until our anger subsided. Now if we get angry at each other, we take a two-minute time-out before discussing a difficult issue. We take time to cool down, pray through the matter individually, and seek God's guidance. Then we come back to each other and find a way to say important and necessary things without causing emotional upheaval. We are learning how to be angry without sinning against each other (see Ephesians 4:26).

It's tough to take a time-out when we're mad—but if we do, and use that time in a prayerful way, we can work things through without sinning.

—JOHN R. THROOP

FOR YOUR NEXT DEVOTIONAL READING, TURN TO PAGE 611.

22 those the LORD blesses will inherit the land,
but those he curses will be cut off.

23 If the LORD delights in a man's way,
he makes his steps firm;
24 though he stumble, he will not fall,
for the LORD upholds him with his hand.

25 I was young and now I am old,
yet I have never seen the righteous forsaken
or their children begging bread.
26 They are always generous and lend freely;
their children will be blessed.

27 Turn from evil and do good;
then you will dwell in the land forever.
28 For the LORD loves the just
and will not forsake his faithful ones.

They will be protected forever,
but the offspring of the wicked will be cut off;
29 the righteous will inherit the land
and dwell in it forever.

30 The mouth of the righteous man utters wisdom,
and his tongue speaks what is just.
31 The law of his God is in his heart;
his feet do not slip.

32 The wicked lie in wait for the righteous,
seeking their very lives;
33 but the LORD will not leave them in their power
or let them be condemned when brought to trial.

34 Wait for the LORD
and keep his way.
He will exalt you to inherit the land;
when the wicked are cut off, you will see it.

35 I have seen a wicked and ruthless man
flourishing like a green tree in its native soil,
36 but he soon passed away and was no more;
though I looked for him, he could not be found.

37 Consider the blameless, observe the upright;
there is a future[a] for the man of peace.
38 But all sinners will be destroyed;
the future[b] of the wicked will be cut off.

39 The salvation of the righteous comes from the LORD;
he is their stronghold in time of trouble.
40 The LORD helps them and delivers them;
he delivers them from the wicked and saves them,
because they take refuge in him.

Psalm 38

A psalm of David. A petition.

1 O LORD, do not rebuke me in your anger
or discipline me in your wrath.
2 For your arrows have pierced me,
and your hand has come down upon me.
3 Because of your wrath there is no health in my body;
my bones have no soundness because of my sin.
4 My guilt has overwhelmed me
like a burden too heavy to bear.

5 My wounds fester and are loathsome
because of my sinful folly.
6 I am bowed down and brought very low;
all day long I go about mourning.
7 My back is filled with searing pain;
there is no health in my body.
8 I am feeble and utterly crushed;
I groan in anguish of heart.

9 All my longings lie open before you, O Lord;
my sighing is not hidden from you.
10 My heart pounds, my strength fails me;
even the light has gone from my eyes.
11 My friends and companions avoid me because of my wounds;
my neighbors stay far away.
12 Those who seek my life set their traps,
those who would harm me talk of my ruin;
all day long they plot deception.

13 I am like a deaf man, who cannot hear,
like a mute, who cannot open his mouth;
14 I have become like a man who does not hear,
whose mouth can offer no reply.
15 I wait for you, O LORD;
you will answer, O Lord my God.
16 For I said, "Do not let them gloat

[a] 37 Or *there will be posterity* [b] 38 Or *posterity*

or exalt themselves over me when my
foot slips."
17 For I am about to fall,
and my pain is ever with me.
18 I confess my iniquity;
I am troubled by my sin.
19 Many are those who are my vigorous
enemies;
those who hate me without reason are
numerous.
20 Those who repay my good with evil
slander me when I pursue what is
good.

21 O LORD, do not forsake me;
be not far from me, O my God.
22 Come quickly to help me,
O Lord my Savior.

Psalm 39

For the director of music. For Jeduthun.
A psalm of David.

1 I said, "I will watch my ways
and keep my tongue from sin;
I will put a muzzle on my mouth
as long as the wicked are in my
presence."
2 But when I was silent and still,
not even saying anything good,
my anguish increased.
3 My heart grew hot within me,
and as I meditated, the fire burned;
then I spoke with my tongue:

4 "Show me, O LORD, my life's end
and the number of my days;
let me know how fleeting is my life.
5 You have made my days a mere
handbreadth;
the span of my years is as nothing
before you.
Each man's life is but a breath. *Selah*
6 Man is a mere phantom as he goes to and
fro:
He bustles about, but only in vain;
he heaps up wealth, not knowing who
will get it.

7 "But now, Lord, what do I look for?
My hope is in you.
8 Save me from all my transgressions;
do not make me the scorn of fools.
9 I was silent; I would not open my mouth,
for you are the one who has done this.
10 Remove your scourge from me;
I am overcome by the blow of your
hand.
11 You rebuke and discipline men for their
sin;
you consume their wealth like a
moth—
each man is but a breath. *Selah*

12 "Hear my prayer, O LORD,
listen to my cry for help;
be not deaf to my weeping.
For I dwell with you as an alien,
a stranger, as all my fathers were.
13 Look away from me, that I may rejoice
again
before I depart and am no more."

Psalm 40

For the director of music. Of David.
A psalm.

1 I waited patiently for the LORD;
he turned to me and heard my cry.
2 He lifted me out of the slimy pit,
out of the mud and mire;
he set my feet on a rock
and gave me a firm place to stand.
3 He put a new song in my mouth,
a hymn of praise to our God.
Many will see and fear
and put their trust in the LORD.

4 Blessed is the man
who makes the LORD his trust,
who does not look to the proud,
to those who turn aside to false
gods.[a]
5 Many, O LORD my God,
are the wonders you have done.
The things you planned for us
no one can recount to you;
were I to speak and tell of them,
they would be too many to declare.

6 Sacrifice and offering you did not desire,
but my ears you have pierced[b, c];
burnt offerings and sin offerings
you did not require.
7 Then I said, "Here I am, I have come—
it is written about me in the scroll.[d]
8 I desire to do your will, O my God;
your law is within my heart."

9 I proclaim righteousness in the great
assembly;

[a] 4 Or *to falsehood* [b] 6 Hebrew; Septuagint *but a body you have prepared for me* (see also Symmachus and Theodotion)
[c] 6 Or *opened* [d] 7 Or *come / with the scroll written for me*

I do not seal my lips,
as you know, O LORD.
10 I do not hide your righteousness in my heart;
I speak of your faithfulness and salvation.
I do not conceal your love and your truth
from the great assembly.

11 Do not withhold your mercy from me, O LORD;
may your love and your truth always protect me.
12 For troubles without number surround me;
my sins have overtaken me, and I cannot see.
They are more than the hairs of my head,
and my heart fails within me.

13 Be pleased, O LORD, to save me;
O LORD, come quickly to help me.
14 May all who seek to take my life
be put to shame and confusion;
may all who desire my ruin
be turned back in disgrace.
15 May those who say to me, "Aha! Aha!"
be appalled at their own shame.
16 But may all who seek you
rejoice and be glad in you;
may those who love your salvation always say,
"The LORD be exalted!"

17 Yet I am poor and needy;
may the Lord think of me.
You are my help and my deliverer;
O my God, do not delay.

Psalm 41

For the director of music. A psalm of David.

1 Blessed is he who has regard for the weak;
the LORD delivers him in times of trouble.
2 The LORD will protect him and preserve his life;
he will bless him in the land
and not surrender him to the desire of his foes.
3 The LORD will sustain him on his sickbed
and restore him from his bed of illness.

4 I said, "O LORD, have mercy on me;
heal me, for I have sinned against you."
5 My enemies say of me in malice,
"When will he die and his name perish?"
6 Whenever one comes to see me,
he speaks falsely, while his heart gathers slander;
then he goes out and spreads it abroad.

7 All my enemies whisper together against me;
they imagine the worst for me, saying,
8 "A vile disease has beset him;
he will never get up from the place where he lies."
9 Even my close friend, whom I trusted,
he who shared my bread,
has lifted up his heel against me.

10 But you, O LORD, have mercy on me;
raise me up, that I may repay them.
11 I know that you are pleased with me,
for my enemy does not triumph over me.
12 In my integrity you uphold me
and set me in your presence forever.

13 Praise be to the LORD, the God of Israel,
from everlasting to everlasting.
Amen and Amen.

BOOK II

Psalms 42–72

Psalm 42[a]

For the director of music. A *maskil*[b] of the Sons of Korah.

1 As the deer pants for streams of water,
so my soul pants for you, O God.
2 My soul thirsts for God, for the living God.
When can I go and meet with God?
3 My tears have been my food
day and night,
while men say to me all day long,
"Where is your God?"
4 These things I remember
as I pour out my soul:
how I used to go with the multitude,
leading the procession to the house of God,
with shouts of joy and thanksgiving
among the festive throng.

5 Why are you downcast, O my soul?

[a] *In many Hebrew manuscripts Psalms 42 and 43 constitute one psalm.* [b] Title: Probably a literary or musical term

Why so disturbed within me?
Put your hope in God,
for I will yet praise him,
my Savior and 6my God.

My[a] soul is downcast within me;
therefore I will remember you
from the land of the Jordan,
the heights of Hermon—from Mount Mizar.
7 Deep calls to deep
in the roar of your waterfalls;
all your waves and breakers
have swept over me.

8 By day the LORD directs his love,
at night his song is with me—
a prayer to the God of my life.

9 I say to God my Rock,
"Why have you forgotten me?
Why must I go about mourning,
oppressed by the enemy?"
10 My bones suffer mortal agony
as my foes taunt me,
saying to me all day long,
"Where is your God?"

11 Why are you downcast, O my soul?
Why so disturbed within me?
Put your hope in God,
for I will yet praise him,
my Savior and my God.

Psalm 43[b]

1 Vindicate me, O God,
and plead my cause against an ungodly nation;
rescue me from deceitful and wicked men.
2 You are God my stronghold.
Why have you rejected me?
Why must I go about mourning,
oppressed by the enemy?
3 Send forth your light and your truth,
let them guide me;
let them bring me to your holy mountain,
to the place where you dwell.
4 Then will I go to the altar of God,
to God, my joy and my delight.
I will praise you with the harp,
O God, my God.

5 Why are you downcast, O my soul?
Why so disturbed within me?
Put your hope in God,
for I will yet praise him,
my Savior and my God.

Psalm 44

For the director of music. Of the Sons of Korah. A *maskil.*[c]

1 We have heard with our ears, O God;
our fathers have told us
what you did in their days,
in days long ago.
2 With your hand you drove out the nations
and planted our fathers;
you crushed the peoples
and made our fathers flourish.
3 It was not by their sword that they won the land,
nor did their arm bring them victory;
it was your right hand, your arm,
and the light of your face, for you loved them.

4 You are my King and my God,
who decrees[d] victories for Jacob.
5 Through you we push back our enemies;
through your name we trample our foes.
6 I do not trust in my bow,
my sword does not bring me victory;
7 but you give us victory over our enemies,
you put our adversaries to shame.
8 In God we make our boast all day long,
and we will praise your name forever.
Selah

9 But now you have rejected and humbled us;
you no longer go out with our armies.
10 You made us retreat before the enemy,
and our adversaries have plundered us.
11 You gave us up to be devoured like sheep
and have scattered us among the nations.
12 You sold your people for a pittance,
gaining nothing from their sale.

13 You have made us a reproach to our neighbors,
the scorn and derision of those around us.

[a] 5,6 A few Hebrew manuscripts, Septuagint and Syriac; most Hebrew manuscripts *praise him for his saving help. / 6O my God, my* [b] *In many Hebrew manuscripts Psalms 42 and 43 constitute one psalm.* [c] Title: Probably a literary or musical term [d] 4 Septuagint, Aquila and Syriac; Hebrew *King, O God; / command*

14 You have made us a byword among the nations;
the peoples shake their heads at us.
15 My disgrace is before me all day long,
and my face is covered with shame
16 at the taunts of those who reproach and revile me,
because of the enemy, who is bent on revenge.

17 All this happened to us,
though we had not forgotten you
or been false to your covenant.
18 Our hearts had not turned back;
our feet had not strayed from your path.
19 But you crushed us and made us a haunt for jackals
and covered us over with deep darkness.

20 If we had forgotten the name of our God
or spread out our hands to a foreign god,
21 would not God have discovered it,
since he knows the secrets of the heart?
22 Yet for your sake we face death all day long;
we are considered as sheep to be slaughtered.

23 Awake, O Lord! Why do you sleep?
Rouse yourself! Do not reject us forever.
24 Why do you hide your face
and forget our misery and oppression?

25 We are brought down to the dust;
our bodies cling to the ground.
26 Rise up and help us;
redeem us because of your unfailing love.

Psalm 45

For the director of music. To ⌞the tune of⌟ "Lilies." Of the Sons of Korah. A *maskil.* [a] A wedding song.

1 My heart is stirred by a noble theme
as I recite my verses for the king;
my tongue is the pen of a skillful writer.

2 You are the most excellent of men
and your lips have been anointed with grace,
since God has blessed you forever.
3 Gird your sword upon your side,
O mighty one;
clothe yourself with splendor and majesty.
4 In your majesty ride forth victoriously
in behalf of truth, humility and righteousness;
let your right hand display awesome deeds.
5 Let your sharp arrows pierce the hearts of the king's enemies;
let the nations fall beneath your feet.
6 Your throne, O God, will last for ever and ever;
a scepter of justice will be the scepter of your kingdom.
7 You love righteousness and hate wickedness;
therefore God, your God, has set you above your companions
by anointing you with the oil of joy.
8 All your robes are fragrant with myrrh and aloes and cassia;
from palaces adorned with ivory
the music of the strings makes you glad.
9 Daughters of kings are among your honored women;
at your right hand is the royal bride in gold of Ophir.

10 Listen, O daughter, consider and give ear:
Forget your people and your father's house.
11 The king is enthralled by your beauty;
honor him, for he is your lord.
12 The Daughter of Tyre will come with a gift, [b]
men of wealth will seek your favor.

13 All glorious is the princess within ⌞her chamber⌟;
her gown is interwoven with gold.
14 In embroidered garments she is led to the king;
her virgin companions follow her
and are brought to you.
15 They are led in with joy and gladness;
they enter the palace of the king.

16 Your sons will take the place of your fathers;
you will make them princes throughout the land.
17 I will perpetuate your memory through all generations;

---

[a] Title: Probably a literary or musical term [b] *12* Or *A Tyrian robe is among the gifts*

therefore the nations will praise you for
ever and ever.

Psalm 46

For the director of music. Of the Sons of Korah. According to *alamoth.*[a] A song.

1 God is our refuge and strength,
an ever-present help in trouble.
2 Therefore we will not fear, though the earth give way
and the mountains fall into the heart of the sea,
3 though its waters roar and foam
and the mountains quake with their surging. *Selah*

4 There is a river whose streams make glad the city of God,
the holy place where the Most High dwells.
5 God is within her, she will not fall;
God will help her at break of day.
6 Nations are in uproar, kingdoms fall;
he lifts his voice, the earth melts.

7 The LORD Almighty is with us;
the God of Jacob is our fortress. *Selah*

8 Come and see the works of the LORD,
the desolations he has brought on the earth.
9 He makes wars cease to the ends of the earth;
he breaks the bow and shatters the spear,
he burns the shields[b] with fire.
10 "Be still, and know that I am God;
I will be exalted among the nations,
I will be exalted in the earth."

11 The LORD Almighty is with us;
the God of Jacob is our fortress. *Selah*

Psalm 47

For the director of music. Of the Sons of Korah. A psalm.

1 Clap your hands, all you nations;
shout to God with cries of joy.
2 How awesome is the LORD Most High,
the great King over all the earth!
3 He subdued nations under us,
peoples under our feet.
4 He chose our inheritance for us,
the pride of Jacob, whom he loved. *Selah*

5 God has ascended amid shouts of joy,
the LORD amid the sounding of trumpets.
6 Sing praises to God, sing praises;
sing praises to our King, sing praises.

7 For God is the King of all the earth;
sing to him a psalm[c] of praise.
8 God reigns over the nations;
God is seated on his holy throne.
9 The nobles of the nations assemble
as the people of the God of Abraham,
for the kings[d] of the earth belong to God;
he is greatly exalted.

Psalm 48

A song. A psalm of the Sons of Korah.

1 Great is the LORD, and most worthy of praise,
in the city of our God, his holy mountain.
2 It is beautiful in its loftiness,
the joy of the whole earth.
Like the utmost heights of Zaphon[e] is Mount Zion,
the[f] city of the Great King.
3 God is in her citadels;
he has shown himself to be her fortress.

4 When the kings joined forces,
when they advanced together,
5 they saw ⌊her⌋ and were astounded;
they fled in terror.
6 Trembling seized them there,
pain like that of a woman in labor.
7 You destroyed them like ships of Tarshish
shattered by an east wind.

8 As we have heard,
so have we seen
in the city of the LORD Almighty,
in the city of our God:
God makes her secure forever. *Selah*

9 Within your temple, O God,
we meditate on your unfailing love.
10 Like your name, O God,
your praise reaches to the ends of the earth;

[a] Title: Probably a musical term [b] 9 Or *chariots* [c] 7 Or *a maskil* (probably a literary or musical term) [d] 9 Or *shields* [e] 2 *Zaphon* can refer to a sacred mountain or the direction north. [f] 2 Or *earth, / Mount Zion, on the northern side / of the*

F

FRIDAY
READ PSALM 46:1–11

HELP FOR A SHAKY MARRIAGE

What could shake the very foundation of your marriage?

For Rick and Amanda, it started with Rick's working too much. With each promotion, Rick spent more time on the road and less time with Amanda. But success at work left him empty. He bought things he couldn't afford to reward himself for his long hours away. Soon he and Amanda were arguing over money.

To pay the mounting bills, Amanda found a job. She also found a sympathetic friend at work and tried to heal her hurts with an affair. When Rick found out about the affair, he quietly made plans to divorce Amanda. Before the papers could be filed, however, Amanda got sick with a minor illness. But complications set in, and she was put into the hospital. More than once, the doctors told Rick that she wouldn't make it through the night.

That night Rick began to see things differently. He wanted to save the marriage, but he didn't know how. As Amanda's illness became progressively worse, she went into a coma. Rick feared for her life and spent every waking moment by her side.

God is our refuge and strength, an ever-present help in trouble.
— Psalm 46:1

let's talk

- This psalm inspired the hymn "A Mighty Fortress Is Our God." What spiritual fortresses can we build to protect our marriage in times of trials?
- Recognizing that God is our refuge and our strength during trials means understanding his character before trials occur. What is God really like? How does knowing who he is provide us with strength and refuge?
- When our world is shaken, how hard is it for us to believe that God is really in control?

In Psalm 46, we see the world being torn apart by cataclysmic disasters—mountains collapsing into the sea, earthquakes, floods and military conquests. But the author of this psalm tells us that we shouldn't fear. How could we not be afraid when faced with such terrifying events?

The psalmist tells us that through all of the turbulence, God is with us. God is our refuge and strength when problems shake our world. He has such awesome power that the world actually melts at the sound of his voice. God is in control and will be exalted.

As Amanda lay in the hospital, fighting to live, Rick was fired from his job. He had to sell their house and their car. But when everything he thought was important was stripped away, Rick found God was there through it all. When he heard God's voice, it was as if his earthly troubles melted away. Rick believed God was in control and that Amanda would live.

And she did.

Today Amanda is permanently disabled. She requires full-time care. Life will never be the same for this couple. But their marriage has withstood the worst threats possible. They now trust God daily for healing, forgiveness and the restoration of their marriage. They endured past trials and found that God was their refuge. They will face future trials knowing he is their strength. Their marriage has never been stronger.

Whatever long, dark nights you face as a couple, let this passage remind you that God is ever-present, the morning will come, and the battle has already been won.

—JENNIFER SCHUCHMANN

FOR YOUR NEXT DEVOTIONAL READING, TURN TO PAGE 616.

your right hand is filled with
righteousness.
11 Mount Zion rejoices,
the villages of Judah are glad
because of your judgments.

12 Walk about Zion, go around her,
count her towers,
13 consider well her ramparts,
view her citadels,
that you may tell of them to the next
generation.
14 For this God is our God for ever and
ever;
he will be our guide even to the end.

Psalm 49

For the director of music. Of the Sons
of Korah. A psalm.

1 Hear this, all you peoples;
listen, all who live in this world,
2 both low and high,
rich and poor alike:
3 My mouth will speak words of wisdom;
the utterance from my heart will give
understanding.
4 I will turn my ear to a proverb;
with the harp I will expound my
riddle:

5 Why should I fear when evil days come,
when wicked deceivers surround
me—
6 those who trust in their wealth
and boast of their great riches?
7 No man can redeem the life of another
or give to God a ransom for him—
8 the ransom for a life is costly,
no payment is ever enough—
9 that he should live on forever
and not see decay.

10 For all can see that wise men die;
the foolish and the senseless alike
perish
and leave their wealth to others.
11 Their tombs will remain their houses[a]
forever,
their dwellings for endless
generations,
though they had[b] named lands after
themselves.

12 But man, despite his riches, does not
endure;
he is[c] like the beasts that perish.

13 This is the fate of those who trust in
themselves,
and of their followers, who approve
their sayings. *Selah*
14 Like sheep they are destined for the
grave,[d]
and death will feed on them.
The upright will rule over them in the
morning;
their forms will decay in the grave,[d]
far from their princely mansions.
15 But God will redeem my life[e] from the
grave;
he will surely take me to himself. *Selah*

16 Do not be overawed when a man grows
rich,
when the splendor of his house
increases;
17 for he will take nothing with him when he
dies,
his splendor will not descend with him.
18 Though while he lived he counted himself
blessed—
and men praise you when you
prosper—
19 he will join the generation of his fathers,
who will never see the light ⌞of life⌟.

20 A man who has riches without
understanding
is like the beasts that perish.

Psalm 50

A psalm of Asaph.

1 The Mighty One, God, the LORD,
speaks and summons the earth
from the rising of the sun to the place
where it sets.
2 From Zion, perfect in beauty,
God shines forth.
3 Our God comes and will not be silent;
a fire devours before him,
and around him a tempest rages.
4 He summons the heavens above,
and the earth, that he may judge his
people:
5 "Gather to me my consecrated ones,
who made a covenant with me by
sacrifice."
6 And the heavens proclaim his
righteousness,
for God himself is judge. *Selah*

---

[a] *11* Septuagint and Syriac; Hebrew *In their thoughts their houses will remain* [b] *11* Or / *for they have* [c] *12* Hebrew; Septuagint and Syriac read verse 12 the same as verse 20. [d] *14* Hebrew *Sheol*; also in verse 15 [e] *15* Or *soul*

7 "Hear, O my people, and I will speak,
O Israel, and I will testify against you:
I am God, your God.
8 I do not rebuke you for your sacrifices
or your burnt offerings, which are ever before me.
9 I have no need of a bull from your stall
or of goats from your pens,
10 for every animal of the forest is mine,
and the cattle on a thousand hills.
11 I know every bird in the mountains,
and the creatures of the field are mine.
12 If I were hungry I would not tell you,
for the world is mine, and all that is in it.
13 Do I eat the flesh of bulls
or drink the blood of goats?
14 Sacrifice thank offerings to God,
fulfill your vows to the Most High,
15 and call upon me in the day of trouble;
I will deliver you, and you will honor me."

16 But to the wicked, God says:

"What right have you to recite my laws
or take my covenant on your lips?
17 You hate my instruction
and cast my words behind you.
18 When you see a thief, you join with him;
you throw in your lot with adulterers.
19 You use your mouth for evil
and harness your tongue to deceit.
20 You speak continually against your brother
and slander your own mother's son.
21 These things you have done and I kept silent;
you thought I was altogether[a] like you.
But I will rebuke you
and accuse you to your face.

22 "Consider this, you who forget God,
or I will tear you to pieces, with none to rescue:
23 He who sacrifices thank offerings honors me,
and he prepares the way
so that I may show him[b] the salvation of God."

Psalm 51

For the director of music. A psalm of David. When the prophet Nathan came to him after David had committed adultery with Bathsheba.

1 Have mercy on me, O God,
according to your unfailing love;
according to your great compassion
blot out my transgressions.
2 Wash away all my iniquity
and cleanse me from my sin.

3 For I know my transgressions,
and my sin is always before me.
4 Against you, you only, have I sinned
and done what is evil in your sight,
so that you are proved right when you speak
and justified when you judge.
5 Surely I was sinful at birth,
sinful from the time my mother conceived me.
6 Surely you desire truth in the inner parts[c];
you teach[d] me wisdom in the inmost place.

7 Cleanse me with hyssop, and I will be clean;
wash me, and I will be whiter than snow.
8 Let me hear joy and gladness;
let the bones you have crushed rejoice.
9 Hide your face from my sins
and blot out all my iniquity.

10 Create in me a pure heart, O God,
and renew a steadfast spirit within me.
11 Do not cast me from your presence
or take your Holy Spirit from me.
12 Restore to me the joy of your salvation
and grant me a willing spirit, to sustain me.

13 Then I will teach transgressors your ways,
and sinners will turn back to you.
14 Save me from bloodguilt, O God,
the God who saves me,
and my tongue will sing of your righteousness.
15 O Lord, open my lips,
and my mouth will declare your praise.

[a] 21 Or *thought the 'I AM' was* [b] 23 Or *and to him who considers his way / I will show* [c] 6 The meaning of the Hebrew for this phrase is uncertain. [d] 6 Or *you desired . . . / you taught*

16 You do not delight in sacrifice, or I would bring it;
you do not take pleasure in burnt offerings.
17 The sacrifices of God are[a] a broken spirit;
a broken and contrite heart,
O God, you will not despise.

18 In your good pleasure make Zion prosper;
build up the walls of Jerusalem.
19 Then there will be righteous sacrifices,
whole burnt offerings to delight you;
then bulls will be offered on your altar.

Psalm 52

For the director of music. A *maskil*[b] of David. When Doeg the Edomite had gone to Saul and told him: "David has gone to the house of Ahimelech."

1 Why do you boast of evil, you mighty man?
Why do you boast all day long,
you who are a disgrace in the eyes of God?
2 Your tongue plots destruction;
it is like a sharpened razor,
you who practice deceit.
3 You love evil rather than good,
falsehood rather than speaking the truth. *Selah*
4 You love every harmful word,
O you deceitful tongue!
5 Surely God will bring you down to everlasting ruin:
He will snatch you up and tear you from your tent;
he will uproot you from the land of the living. *Selah*
6 The righteous will see and fear;
they will laugh at him, saying,
7 "Here now is the man
who did not make God his stronghold
but trusted in his great wealth
and grew strong by destroying others!"

8 But I am like an olive tree
flourishing in the house of God;
I trust in God's unfailing love
for ever and ever.
9 I will praise you forever for what you have done;
in your name I will hope, for your name is good.
I will praise you in the presence of your saints.

Psalm 53

For the director of music. According to *mahalath.*[c] A *maskil*[b] of David.

1 The fool says in his heart,
"There is no God."
They are corrupt, and their ways are vile;
there is no one who does good.
2 God looks down from heaven
on the sons of men
to see if there are any who understand,
any who seek God.
3 Everyone has turned away,
they have together become corrupt;
there is no one who does good,
not even one.
4 Will the evildoers never learn—
those who devour my people as men eat bread
and who do not call on God?
5 There they were, overwhelmed with dread,
where there was nothing to dread.
God scattered the bones of those who attacked you;
you put them to shame, for God despised them.

6 Oh, that salvation for Israel would come out of Zion!
When God restores the fortunes of his people,
let Jacob rejoice and Israel be glad!

Psalm 54

For the director of music. With stringed instruments. A *maskil*[b] of David. When the Ziphites had gone to Saul and said, "Is not David hiding among us?"

1 Save me, O God, by your name;
vindicate me by your might.
2 Hear my prayer, O God;
listen to the words of my mouth.

3 Strangers are attacking me;
ruthless men seek my life—
men without regard for God. *Selah*
4 Surely God is my help;
the Lord is the one who sustains me.

[a] 17 Or *My sacrifice, O God, is* [b] Title: Probably a literary or musical term [c] Title: Probably a musical term

5 Let evil recoil on those who slander me;
in your faithfulness destroy them.

6 I will sacrifice a freewill offering to you;
I will praise your name, O LORD,
for it is good.
7 For he has delivered me from all my troubles,
and my eyes have looked in triumph on my foes.

Psalm 55

For the director of music. With stringed instruments. A *maskil*[a] of David.

1 Listen to my prayer, O God,
do not ignore my plea;
2 hear me and answer me.
My thoughts trouble me and I am distraught
3 at the voice of the enemy,
at the stares of the wicked;
for they bring down suffering upon me
and revile me in their anger.

4 My heart is in anguish within me;
the terrors of death assail me.
5 Fear and trembling have beset me;
horror has overwhelmed me.
6 I said, "Oh, that I had the wings of a dove!
I would fly away and be at rest—
7 I would flee far away
and stay in the desert; *Selah*
8 I would hurry to my place of shelter,
far from the tempest and storm."

9 Confuse the wicked, O Lord, confound their speech,
for I see violence and strife in the city.
10 Day and night they prowl about on its walls;
malice and abuse are within it.
11 Destructive forces are at work in the city;
threats and lies never leave its streets.

12 If an enemy were insulting me,
I could endure it;
if a foe were raising himself against me,
I could hide from him.
13 But it is you, a man like myself,
my companion, my close friend,
14 with whom I once enjoyed sweet fellowship
as we walked with the throng at the house of God.

15 Let death take my enemies by surprise;
let them go down alive to the grave,[b]
for evil finds lodging among them.

16 But I call to God,
and the LORD saves me.
17 Evening, morning and noon
I cry out in distress,
and he hears my voice.
18 He ransoms me unharmed
from the battle waged against me,
even though many oppose me.
19 God, who is enthroned forever,
will hear them and afflict them— *Selah*
men who never change their ways
and have no fear of God.

20 My companion attacks his friends;
he violates his covenant.
21 His speech is smooth as butter,
yet war is in his heart;
his words are more soothing than oil,
yet they are drawn swords.

22 Cast your cares on the LORD
and he will sustain you;
he will never let the righteous fall.
23 But you, O God, will bring down the wicked
into the pit of corruption;
bloodthirsty and deceitful men
will not live out half their days.

But as for me, I trust in you.

Psalm 56

For the director of music. To ⌞the tune of⌟ "A Dove on Distant Oaks." Of David. A *miktam.*[a] When the Philistines had seized him in Gath.

1 Be merciful to me, O God, for men hotly pursue me;
all day long they press their attack.
2 My slanderers pursue me all day long;
many are attacking me in their pride.

3 When I am afraid,
I will trust in you.
4 In God, whose word I praise,
in God I trust; I will not be afraid.
What can mortal man do to me?

5 All day long they twist my words;
they are always plotting to harm me.
6 They conspire, they lurk,
they watch my steps,
eager to take my life.

---

[a] Title: Probably a literary or musical term [b] *15* Hebrew *Sheol*

WEEKEND

budgeting

Mention "budget" to some people and they immediately bristle. *Why get an ulcer worrying about nickels and dimes*, they think to themselves. *I don't like to be tied down to numbers*.

If you fit into that category, take a deep breath. Budgets aren't as bad as you might think. The goal of a good budget is to give you more freedom. It is a plan of spending to assure that you get whatever it is you need and want.

The truth is, we all budget informally. If you want to buy a new wardrobe but do not have the money to do so and choose not to buy it on credit, then you are budgeting. To budget formally, however, is to deliberately gain better control over all of your financial life—so it doesn't control you.

You can think of budgeting very simply as slotting money for necessities and then divvying up money that is left over for other wants. How does this save you money? Consider shopping at a supermarket. It is estimated that the spontaneous food shopper spends approximately 15 percent more for food than the shopper who has planned a food budget and a shopping list of needed items. Without a specific limit, it is extremely easy to buy impulsively.

Create a budget by following these four basic steps:

1. Analyze past spending by keeping careful records for a month or two of everything you spend.
2. Determine fixed expenses such as rent or mortgage and any other contractual payments that must be made, even if they are infrequent, such as insurance and taxes. Include utilities (gas, electric, water), giving and debt repayment.
3. Determine flexible expenses, such as food, clothing and entertainment.
4. Balance your fixed plus flexible expenditures with your available income. If a surplus exists, apply it toward savings for a home, another big-ticket item or investments. If there is a deficit, reexamine your flexible expenditures. You can also reexamine fixed expenses with a view to reducing them in the future (by changing your standard of living).

The only way to make sure you are following your budget is by keeping records of what you spend. The ultimate way to maintain records is to write everything down. This can be accomplished by simply taking a moment to make entries in a date book or on a piece of scrap paper and then tally up your expenses every so often throughout the month to see where you stand.

A couple of thoughts to remember: The key to managing your money is keeping track of where it is going. Also, it is important to remember that budgets are used for a specified time and then updated to reflect changing circumstances. As dull and uninteresting as budget planning may seem, the couple that does not put time into planning and controlling their finances may face increasing monetary strain and eventually end up with finances controlling them.

Still not convinced that a budget is for you? You may be right. The truth is, budgets are not the answer for every couple. They sometimes become just another way to fail on a monthly basis. However, we recommend that you try budgeting at least short term. See how it works for you. Reevaluate after a few months and tinker with your plan until both of you are happy.

—DR. LES PARROTT III AND DR. LESLIE PARROTT

who manages the money?

HOW ARE WE DOING?

Often spouses enter a marriage with preconceived ideas of who should control the finances. Using the table below, if you believe the item in the left column should be done by the husband, put your initials in the middle column. If you believe it should be done by the wife, put your initials in the right column. If you believe both partners should be involved, put your initials in both columns. Then have your spouse take the quiz.

If you've been married a few years and have already divvied up the tasks, take this quiz and answer how you would ideally like the tasks to be completed.

Discuss which items you agree on and where you disagree. Use this as a guide for talking about your financial responsibilities.

WHO DOES WHAT	Husband	Wife
Pay the bills		
Balance the checkbook		
Make investment decisions		
Track expenses		
Set up the budget		
Enforce the budget		
Make big purchases		
Track investments		
Annually review credit report		
Calculate and pay taxes		
Make contributions to church and other non-profits		
Access the major checking account		
Access all checking accounts		
Open new lines of credit		
Take out a loan		
Borrow money from parents		
Be listed on the deed to the house or apartment lease		
Be listed on the car title		
Make alimony or child support payments		
Override the other partner's decisions		

let's make a DATE

RISKY GAMES

This weekend have fun while learning about your partner's tolerance for risk. Play a card game that requires betting (use candy instead of money) or a board game that requires players to take risks to get ahead. As you play, talk about your tolerances for risk and your needs for security. Who is more competitive? Who is willing to risk all to win all? Who is content to keep what they have? At the end of the game, the winner is the one who learns the most about their partner.

FOR YOUR NEXT DEVOTIONAL READING, TURN TO PAGE 621.

LESSONS FROM THE *Bible*

What can you learn about money from the following people in the Bible?

1. The poor widow (Luke 21:1–4)
2. Ananias and Sapphira (Acts 5:1–11)

7 On no account let them escape;
in your anger, O God, bring down the nations.
8 Record my lament;
list my tears on your scroll[a]—
are they not in your record?

9 Then my enemies will turn back
when I call for help.
By this I will know that God is for me.
10 In God, whose word I praise,
in the LORD, whose word I praise—
11 in God I trust; I will not be afraid.
What can man do to me?

12 I am under vows to you, O God;
I will present my thank offerings to you.
13 For you have delivered me[b] from death
and my feet from stumbling,
that I may walk before God
in the light of life.[c]

Psalm 57

For the director of music. ⌊To the tune of⌋ "Do Not Destroy." Of David. A *miktam.*[d] When he had fled from Saul into the cave.

1 Have mercy on me, O God, have mercy on me,
for in you my soul takes refuge.
I will take refuge in the shadow of your wings
until the disaster has passed.

2 I cry out to God Most High,
to God, who fulfills ⌊his purpose⌋ for me.
3 He sends from heaven and saves me,
rebuking those who hotly pursue me; *Selah*
God sends his love and his faithfulness.

4 I am in the midst of lions;
I lie among ravenous beasts—
men whose teeth are spears and arrows,
whose tongues are sharp swords.

5 Be exalted, O God, above the heavens;
let your glory be over all the earth.

6 They spread a net for my feet—
I was bowed down in distress.
They dug a pit in my path—
but they have fallen into it themselves. *Selah*

7 My heart is steadfast, O God,
my heart is steadfast;
I will sing and make music.
8 Awake, my soul!
Awake, harp and lyre!
I will awaken the dawn.

9 I will praise you, O Lord, among the nations;
I will sing of you among the peoples.
10 For great is your love, reaching to the heavens;
your faithfulness reaches to the skies.

11 Be exalted, O God, above the heavens;
let your glory be over all the earth.

Psalm 58

For the director of music. ⌊To the tune of⌋ "Do Not Destroy." Of David. A *miktam.*[d]

1 Do you rulers indeed speak justly?
Do you judge uprightly among men?
2 No, in your heart you devise injustice,
and your hands mete out violence on the earth.
3 Even from birth the wicked go astray;
from the womb they are wayward and speak lies.
4 Their venom is like the venom of a snake,
like that of a cobra that has stopped its ears,
5 that will not heed the tune of the charmer,
however skillful the enchanter may be.

6 Break the teeth in their mouths, O God;
tear out, O LORD, the fangs of the lions!
7 Let them vanish like water that flows away;
when they draw the bow, let their arrows be blunted.
8 Like a slug melting away as it moves along,
like a stillborn child, may they not see the sun.

9 Before your pots can feel ⌊the heat of⌋ the thorns—
whether they be green or dry—the wicked will be swept away.[e]
10 The righteous will be glad when they are avenged,

---

[a] 8 Or / *put my tears in your wineskin* [b] 13 Or *my soul* [c] 13 Or *the land of the living* [d] Title: Probably a literary or musical term
[e] 9 The meaning of the Hebrew for this verse is uncertain.

when they bathe their feet in the blood
of the wicked.
11 Then men will say,
"Surely the righteous still are rewarded;
surely there is a God who judges the
earth."

Psalm 59

For the director of music. ⌞To the tune of⌟ "Do Not Destroy." Of David. A *miktam.* [a] When Saul had sent men to watch David's house in order to kill him.

1 Deliver me from my enemies, O God;
protect me from those who rise up
against me.
2 Deliver me from evildoers
and save me from bloodthirsty men.

3 See how they lie in wait for me!
Fierce men conspire against me
for no offense or sin of mine, O LORD.
4 I have done no wrong, yet they are ready
to attack me.
Arise to help me; look on my plight!
5 O LORD God Almighty, the God of
Israel,
rouse yourself to punish all the
nations;
show no mercy to wicked traitors. *Selah*

6 They return at evening,
snarling like dogs,
and prowl about the city.
7 See what they spew from their mouths—
they spew out swords from their lips,
and they say, "Who can hear us?"
8 But you, O LORD, laugh at them;
you scoff at all those nations.

9 O my Strength, I watch for you;
you, O God, are my fortress, 10 my
loving God.

God will go before me
and will let me gloat over those who
slander me.
11 But do not kill them, O Lord our
shield, [b]
or my people will forget.
In your might make them wander about,
and bring them down.
12 For the sins of their mouths,
for the words of their lips,
let them be caught in their pride.
For the curses and lies they utter,
13 consume them in wrath,
consume them till they are no more.
Then it will be known to the ends of the
earth
that God rules over Jacob. *Selah*

14 They return at evening,
snarling like dogs,
and prowl about the city.
15 They wander about for food
and howl if not satisfied.
16 But I will sing of your strength,
in the morning I will sing of your
love;
for you are my fortress,
my refuge in times of trouble.

17 O my Strength, I sing praise to you;
you, O God, are my fortress, my loving
God.

Psalm 60

For the director of music. To ⌞the tune of⌟ "The Lily of the Covenant." A *miktam* [a] of David. For teaching. When he fought Aram Naharaim [c] and Aram Zobah, [d] and when Joab returned and struck down twelve thousand Edomites in the Valley of Salt.

1 You have rejected us, O God, and burst
forth upon us;
you have been angry—now restore us!
2 You have shaken the land and torn it
open;
mend its fractures, for it is quaking.
3 You have shown your people desperate
times;
you have given us wine that makes us
stagger.

4 But for those who fear you, you have
raised a banner
to be unfurled against the bow. *Selah*

5 Save us and help us with your right hand,
that those you love may be delivered.
6 God has spoken from his sanctuary:
"In triumph I will parcel out
Shechem
and measure off the Valley of Succoth.
7 Gilead is mine, and Manasseh is mine;
Ephraim is my helmet,
Judah my scepter.
8 Moab is my washbasin,
upon Edom I toss my sandal;
over Philistia I shout in triumph."

---

[a] Title: Probably a literary or musical term [b] *11* Or *sovereign* [c] Title: That is, Arameans of Northwest Mesopotamia [d] Title: That is, Arameans of central Syria

9 Who will bring me to the fortified city?
Who will lead me to Edom?
10 Is it not you, O God, you who have rejected us
and no longer go out with our armies?
11 Give us aid against the enemy,
for the help of man is worthless.
12 With God we will gain the victory,
and he will trample down our enemies.

Psalm 61

For the director of music. With stringed instruments. Of David.

1 Hear my cry, O God;
listen to my prayer.

2 From the ends of the earth I call to you,
I call as my heart grows faint;
lead me to the rock that is higher than I.
3 For you have been my refuge,
a strong tower against the foe.

4 I long to dwell in your tent forever
and take refuge in the shelter of your wings. *Selah*
5 For you have heard my vows, O God;
you have given me the heritage of those who fear your name.

6 Increase the days of the king's life,
his years for many generations.
7 May he be enthroned in God's presence forever;
appoint your love and faithfulness to protect him.

8 Then will I ever sing praise to your name
and fulfill my vows day after day.

Psalm 62

For the director of music. For Jeduthun. A psalm of David.

1 My soul finds rest in God alone;
my salvation comes from him.
2 He alone is my rock and my salvation;
he is my fortress, I will never be shaken.

3 How long will you assault a man?
Would all of you throw him down—
this leaning wall, this tottering fence?
4 They fully intend to topple him
from his lofty place;
they take delight in lies.
With their mouths they bless,
but in their hearts they curse. *Selah*
5 Find rest, O my soul, in God alone;
my hope comes from him.
6 He alone is my rock and my salvation;
he is my fortress, I will not be shaken.
7 My salvation and my honor depend on God[a];
he is my mighty rock, my refuge.
8 Trust in him at all times, O people;
pour out your hearts to him,
for God is our refuge. *Selah*

9 Lowborn men are but a breath,
the highborn are but a lie;
if weighed on a balance, they are nothing;
together they are only a breath.
10 Do not trust in extortion
or take pride in stolen goods;
though your riches increase,
do not set your heart on them.

11 One thing God has spoken,
two things have I heard:
that you, O God, are strong,
12 and that you, O Lord, are loving.
Surely you will reward each person
according to what he has done.

Psalm 63

A psalm of David. When he was in the Desert of Judah.

1 O God, you are my God,
earnestly I seek you;
my soul thirsts for you,
my body longs for you,
in a dry and weary land
where there is no water.

2 I have seen you in the sanctuary
and beheld your power and your glory.
3 Because your love is better than life,
my lips will glorify you.
4 I will praise you as long as I live,
and in your name I will lift up my hands.
5 My soul will be satisfied as with the richest of foods;
with singing lips my mouth will praise you.
6 On my bed I remember you;

---

[a] 7 Or / *God Most High is my salvation and my honor*

A ROCK AND A HARD PLACE

> **You have been my refuge, a strong tower against the foe.**
> — PSALM 61:3

let's talk

- How is our weakness most evident when trouble comes?
- How could we help each other pray more effectively in such times? How would paraphrasing Psalm 61 draw us to the Lord?
- How are we passing on to each other the spiritual heritage of God's protecting love?

A work team from our church heard about one family's harrowing experience during Hurricane Katrina in New Orleans. The floodwaters drove the family from their home into their small boat. The boat carried them downriver until they came to a bridge. The water was so high they could not pass under the bridge, and they were stranded. The family watched in horror as the river carried their house straight into the bridge, where it was smashed into kindling.

David, presumably the writer of this psalm, must have felt like that family when he prayed, "I call as my heart grows faint; lead me to the rock that is higher than I" (Psalm 61:2). We all have known times when we desperately wanted a safe place during some terrifying flood; some place high enough to give us a vantage point from which to make sense of what has happened and be safe no matter how punishing the storm.

During tumultuous times in marriage, whether the storm is about money or career, kids or health, we usually pray, "Lord, make it stop!" Like the storm-tossed disciples yelling at the sleeping Jesus, we frantically pray, "Don't you care if we drown?"

This prayer of David's does not ask God to make the storm stop. Instead it is a prayer for safety—a prayer that God himself would be the safe place no matter what happens. Every married couple needs this prayer. No matter how strong a marriage is, there are storms we cannot weather in our own strength. We need to be led to a rock higher than ourselves.

Stormy times shake our faith. To fortify his faith the psalmist stirred up his memory. He remembered times when God was like a strong tower for him (see verse 3), surrounding him like the walls of a castle, sheltering him from the reach of the foe.

Then he pictured God's tent (see verse 4). A tent seems like a flimsy shelter in a storm until we remember that God's tent was the tabernacle, the place where God's people worshiped him and where God's glory dwelled. The "shelter of your wings" suggests the very heart of the tabernacle, the ark of the covenant, where two great golden angels spread their wings over the atonement cover, or mercy seat, where blood was applied for the forgiveness of sin. There is no safer place in heaven or on earth for a person to be than in the shelter of God's wings, because there we are guarded by God's grace and power. There mercy drives back all threats and keeps our souls forever safe.

Finally, David reflected on his spiritual heritage (see verse 5). Since he had made vows of commitment to God, he knew he was guarded by the rock-solid promises of God's covenant. Like David, we can remember how God cared for our spiritual forefathers when they faced terrible times.

In the end, David the king asked God to provide an everlasting king, One who will always protect us with the love and faithfulness of God's presence (see verses 6–7). That, of course, is what we celebrate in Jesus, our King. That is why we praise God (see verse 8).

—LEE ECLOV

FOR YOUR NEXT DEVOTIONAL READING, TURN TO PAGE 622.

TUESDAY
READ PSALM 62:1–12

CAVES OF COMFORT

> **My soul finds rest in God alone; my salvation comes from him.**
> — Psalm 62:1

let's talk

- How long did it take for each of us to realize that the other was not perfect—that I wasn't the ideal spouse who could meet all of your needs and that you couldn't meet all of mine?
- What was the effect of that?
- Was there a time when, against our natural inclinations, we sought God and found comfort before turning to each other.

The psalmist David, generally assumed to be the writer of Psalm 62, had plenty of reasons to seek rest: He was forever being hunted down by King Saul, betrayed by so-called friends and attacked by enemy armies. Sometimes the beleaguered fugitive found rest in the caves of En Gedi, an oasis in the Judean desert. There David wrote many psalms, reminding himself—and us—that all man-made shelters are temporary and that true rest for the soul is only found in God.

To put flesh on the idea of resting in God, we might imagine how a little child looks for comfort when hurt or disappointed. The child runs to a parent, asking to be held and kissed, and is soothed by his mom or dad. Or consider what a spouse might say when the atmosphere in her marriage heats up because of what she has done or failed to do. "I'm going home to my mother!" she yells at her husband. We may laugh at that old threat, but what the woman is seeking is someone who accepts her and loves her, flaws and all. And the person who most exemplified that, up until marriage, was Mom.

It's not unusual for married couples to feel hurt, disappointed and unloved at times. We enter marriage with high expectations. We assume that our spouse will fulfill our needs for companionship, affirmation, fun, sex, children, unconditional love, support, completion. The list goes on. Sooner or later, being everything to another person becomes too big a job for a mere mortal. Only God is big enough, loving enough and giving enough to give us the mental, emotional and spiritual support we crave from our spouse.

Both individually and as a couple, we need to look to God through Jesus Christ for satisfaction of our deepest needs. J. I. Packer suggests that in times of great need we repeat to each other several times a day, "I am a child of God." Once we are reminded of that childlike relationship with God, we can listen with our spouse for comforting words from God by reading his Word together. By filling our emotional tanks from God's supply, not only do we become stronger individually but we are also better able to meet some of each other's marital expectations.

When my husband needs consolation, he retreats to his "cave," an abstract place of solitary comfort. I've sometimes made light of this cave, but maybe he's on to something. Like David, my husband, Grey, withdraws to find rest from life's challenges before tackling more of them. Even if he writes no poems or psalms in that retreat, Grey comes out refreshed, having found rest in the Lord. And our marriage benefits.

As a woman, I tend to want to talk things out with Grey when I'm troubled. But maybe I should pay more attention to David's example, first talking and listening to God to find the refreshment and understanding I crave before dumping my needs on my husband.

—MARY ANN JEFFREYS

FOR YOUR NEXT DEVOTIONAL READING, TURN TO PAGE 629.

I think of you through the watches of
the night.
7 Because you are my help,
I sing in the shadow of your wings.
8 My soul clings to you;
your right hand upholds me.

9 They who seek my life will be destroyed;
they will go down to the depths of the
earth.
10 They will be given over to the sword
and become food for jackals.

11 But the king will rejoice in God;
all who swear by God's name will praise
him,
while the mouths of liars will be
silenced.

Psalm 64

For the director of music. A psalm of David.

1 Hear me, O God, as I voice my
complaint;
protect my life from the threat of the
enemy.
2 Hide me from the conspiracy of the
wicked,
from that noisy crowd of evildoers.

3 They sharpen their tongues like swords
and aim their words like deadly
arrows.
4 They shoot from ambush at the innocent
man;
they shoot at him suddenly, without
fear.

5 They encourage each other in evil plans,
they talk about hiding their snares;
they say, "Who will see them[a]?"
6 They plot injustice and say,
"We have devised a perfect plan!"
Surely the mind and heart of man are
cunning.

7 But God will shoot them with arrows;
suddenly they will be struck down.
8 He will turn their own tongues against
them
and bring them to ruin;
all who see them will shake their heads
in scorn.

9 All mankind will fear;
they will proclaim the works of God
and ponder what he has done.

10 Let the righteous rejoice in the LORD
and take refuge in him;
let all the upright in heart praise him!

Psalm 65

For the director of music. A psalm of David.
A song.

1 Praise awaits[b] you, O God, in Zion;
to you our vows will be fulfilled.
2 O you who hear prayer,
to you all men will come.
3 When we were overwhelmed by sins,
you forgave[c] our transgressions.
4 Blessed are those you choose
and bring near to live in your courts!
We are filled with the good things of your
house,
of your holy temple.

5 You answer us with awesome deeds of
righteousness,
O God our Savior,
the hope of all the ends of the earth
and of the farthest seas,
6 who formed the mountains by your
power,
having armed yourself with strength,
7 who stilled the roaring of the seas,
the roaring of their waves,
and the turmoil of the nations.
8 Those living far away fear your wonders;
where morning dawns and evening
fades
you call forth songs of joy.

9 You care for the land and water it;
you enrich it abundantly.
The streams of God are filled with water
to provide the people with grain,
for so you have ordained it.[d]
10 You drench its furrows
and level its ridges;
you soften it with showers
and bless its crops.
11 You crown the year with your bounty,
and your carts overflow with
abundance.
12 The grasslands of the desert overflow;
the hills are clothed with gladness.
13 The meadows are covered with flocks
and the valleys are mantled with
grain;
they shout for joy and sing.

---

[a] 5 Or *us* [b] 1 Or *befits*; the meaning of the Hebrew for this word is uncertain. [c] 3 Or *made atonement for* [d] 9 Or *for that is how you prepare the land*

Psalm 66

For the director of music. A song. A psalm.

1 Shout with joy to God, all the earth!
2 Sing the glory of his name;
make his praise glorious!
3 Say to God, "How awesome are your deeds!
So great is your power
that your enemies cringe before you.
4 All the earth bows down to you;
they sing praise to you,
they sing praise to your name." *Selah*

5 Come and see what God has done,
how awesome his works in man's behalf!
6 He turned the sea into dry land,
they passed through the waters on foot—
come, let us rejoice in him.
7 He rules forever by his power,
his eyes watch the nations—
let not the rebellious rise up against him. *Selah*

8 Praise our God, O peoples,
let the sound of his praise be heard;
9 he has preserved our lives
and kept our feet from slipping.
10 For you, O God, tested us;
you refined us like silver.
11 You brought us into prison
and laid burdens on our backs.
12 You let men ride over our heads;
we went through fire and water,
but you brought us to a place of abundance.

13 I will come to your temple with burnt offerings
and fulfill my vows to you—
14 vows my lips promised and my mouth spoke
when I was in trouble.
15 I will sacrifice fat animals to you
and an offering of rams;
I will offer bulls and goats. *Selah*

16 Come and listen, all you who fear God;
let me tell you what he has done for me.
17 I cried out to him with my mouth;
his praise was on my tongue.
18 If I had cherished sin in my heart,
the Lord would not have listened;
19 but God has surely listened
and heard my voice in prayer.
20 Praise be to God,
who has not rejected my prayer
or withheld his love from me!

Psalm 67

For the director of music. With stringed instruments. A psalm. A song.

1 May God be gracious to us and bless us
and make his face shine upon us, *Selah*
2 that your ways may be known on earth,
your salvation among all nations.

3 May the peoples praise you, O God;
may all the peoples praise you.
4 May the nations be glad and sing for joy,
for you rule the peoples justly
and guide the nations of the earth. *Selah*
5 May the peoples praise you, O God;
may all the peoples praise you.

6 Then the land will yield its harvest,
and God, our God, will bless us.
7 God will bless us,
and all the ends of the earth will fear him.

Psalm 68

For the director of music. Of David.
A psalm. A song.

1 May God arise, may his enemies be scattered;
may his foes flee before him.
2 As smoke is blown away by the wind,
may you blow them away;
as wax melts before the fire,
may the wicked perish before God.
3 But may the righteous be glad
and rejoice before God;
may they be happy and joyful.

4 Sing to God, sing praise to his name,
extol him who rides on the clouds[a]—
his name is the LORD—
and rejoice before him.
5 A father to the fatherless, a defender of widows,
is God in his holy dwelling.
6 God sets the lonely in families,[b]
he leads forth the prisoners with singing;
but the rebellious live in a sun-scorched land.

---

[a] 4 Or / *prepare the way for him who rides through the deserts* [b] 6 Or *the desolate in a homeland*

7 When you went out before your people,
O God,
when you marched through the
wasteland, *Selah*
8 the earth shook,
the heavens poured down rain,
before God, the One of Sinai,
before God, the God of Israel.
9 You gave abundant showers, O God;
you refreshed your weary inheritance.
10 Your people settled in it,
and from your bounty, O God, you
provided for the poor.

11 The Lord announced the word,
and great was the company of those
who proclaimed it:
12 "Kings and armies flee in haste;
in the camps men divide the plunder.
13 Even while you sleep among the
campfires,[a]
the wings of ⌞my⌟ dove are sheathed
with silver,
its feathers with shining gold."
14 When the Almighty[b] scattered the kings
in the land,
it was like snow fallen on Zalmon.
15 The mountains of Bashan are majestic
mountains;
rugged are the mountains of Bashan.
16 Why gaze in envy, O rugged mountains,
at the mountain where God chooses to
reign,
where the LORD himself will dwell
forever?
17 The chariots of God are tens of thousands
and thousands of thousands;
the Lord ⌞has come⌟ from Sinai into his
sanctuary.
18 When you ascended on high,
you led captives in your train;
you received gifts from men,
even from[c] the rebellious—
that you,[d] O LORD God, might dwell
there.

19 Praise be to the Lord, to God our Savior,
who daily bears our burdens. *Selah*
20 Our God is a God who saves;
from the Sovereign LORD comes escape
from death.

21 Surely God will crush the heads of his
enemies,
the hairy crowns of those who go on in
their sins.
22 The Lord says, "I will bring them from
Bashan;
I will bring them from the depths of
the sea,
23 that you may plunge your feet in the
blood of your foes,
while the tongues of your dogs have
their share."

24 Your procession has come into view,
O God,
the procession of my God and King
into the sanctuary.
25 In front are the singers, after them the
musicians;
with them are the maidens playing
tambourines.
26 Praise God in the great congregation;
praise the LORD in the assembly of
Israel.
27 There is the little tribe of Benjamin,
leading them,
there the great throng of Judah's
princes,
and there the princes of Zebulun and
of Naphtali.

28 Summon your power, O God[e];
show us your strength, O God, as you
have done before.
29 Because of your temple at Jerusalem
kings will bring you gifts.
30 Rebuke the beast among the reeds,
the herd of bulls among the calves of
the nations.
Humbled, may it bring bars of silver.
Scatter the nations who delight in war.
31 Envoys will come from Egypt;
Cush[f] will submit herself to God.

32 Sing to God, O kingdoms of the earth,
sing praise to the Lord, *Selah*
33 to him who rides the ancient skies above,
who thunders with mighty voice.
34 Proclaim the power of God,
whose majesty is over Israel,
whose power is in the skies.
35 You are awesome, O God, in your
sanctuary;
the God of Israel gives power and
strength to his people.

Praise be to God!

---

[a] 13 Or *saddlebags* [b] 14 Hebrew *Shaddai* [c] 18 Or *gifts for men, / even* [d] 18 Or *they* [e] 28 Many Hebrew manuscripts, Septuagint and Syriac; most Hebrew manuscripts *Your God has summoned power for you* [f] 31 That is, the upper Nile region

Psalm 69

For the director of music. To ⌊the tune of⌋ "Lilies." Of David.

1 Save me, O God,
for the waters have come up to my neck.
2 I sink in the miry depths,
where there is no foothold.
I have come into the deep waters;
the floods engulf me.
3 I am worn out calling for help;
my throat is parched.
My eyes fail,
looking for my God.
4 Those who hate me without reason
outnumber the hairs of my head;
many are my enemies without cause,
those who seek to destroy me.
I am forced to restore
what I did not steal.

5 You know my folly, O God;
my guilt is not hidden from you.

6 May those who hope in you
not be disgraced because of me,
O Lord, the LORD Almighty;
may those who seek you
not be put to shame because of me,
O God of Israel.
7 For I endure scorn for your sake,
and shame covers my face.
8 I am a stranger to my brothers,
an alien to my own mother's sons;
9 for zeal for your house consumes me,
and the insults of those who insult you fall on me.
10 When I weep and fast,
I must endure scorn;
11 when I put on sackcloth,
people make sport of me.
12 Those who sit at the gate mock me,
and I am the song of the drunkards.

13 But I pray to you, O LORD,
in the time of your favor;
in your great love, O God,
answer me with your sure salvation.
14 Rescue me from the mire,
do not let me sink;
deliver me from those who hate me,
from the deep waters.
15 Do not let the floodwaters engulf me
or the depths swallow me up
or the pit close its mouth over me.

16 Answer me, O LORD, out of the goodness of your love;
in your great mercy turn to me.
17 Do not hide your face from your servant;
answer me quickly, for I am in trouble.
18 Come near and rescue me;
redeem me because of my foes.

19 You know how I am scorned, disgraced and shamed;
all my enemies are before you.
20 Scorn has broken my heart
and has left me helpless;
I looked for sympathy, but there was none,
for comforters, but I found none.
21 They put gall in my food
and gave me vinegar for my thirst.

22 May the table set before them become a snare;
may it become retribution and[a] a trap.
23 May their eyes be darkened so they cannot see,
and their backs be bent forever.
24 Pour out your wrath on them;
let your fierce anger overtake them.
25 May their place be deserted;
let there be no one to dwell in their tents.
26 For they persecute those you wound
and talk about the pain of those you hurt.
27 Charge them with crime upon crime;
do not let them share in your salvation.
28 May they be blotted out of the book of life
and not be listed with the righteous.

29 I am in pain and distress;
may your salvation, O God, protect me.

30 I will praise God's name in song
and glorify him with thanksgiving.
31 This will please the LORD more than an ox,
more than a bull with its horns and hoofs.
32 The poor will see and be glad—
you who seek God, may your hearts live!
33 The LORD hears the needy
and does not despise his captive people.

34 Let heaven and earth praise him,
the seas and all that move in them,

[a] 22 Or *snare / and their fellowship become*

35 for God will save Zion
and rebuild the cities of Judah.
Then people will settle there and possess it;
36 the children of his servants will inherit it,
and those who love his name will dwell there.

Psalm 70

For the director of music. Of David. A petition.

1 Hasten, O God, to save me;
O LORD, come quickly to help me.
2 May those who seek my life
be put to shame and confusion;
may all who desire my ruin
be turned back in disgrace.
3 May those who say to me, "Aha! Aha!"
turn back because of their shame.
4 But may all who seek you
rejoice and be glad in you;
may those who love your salvation always say,
"Let God be exalted!"

5 Yet I am poor and needy;
come quickly to me, O God.
You are my help and my deliverer;
O LORD, do not delay.

Psalm 71

1 In you, O LORD, I have taken refuge;
let me never be put to shame.
2 Rescue me and deliver me in your righteousness;
turn your ear to me and save me.
3 Be my rock of refuge,
to which I can always go;
give the command to save me,
for you are my rock and my fortress.
4 Deliver me, O my God, from the hand of the wicked,
from the grasp of evil and cruel men.

5 For you have been my hope, O Sovereign LORD,
my confidence since my youth.
6 From birth I have relied on you;
you brought me forth from my mother's womb.
I will ever praise you.
7 I have become like a portent to many,
but you are my strong refuge.
8 My mouth is filled with your praise,
declaring your splendor all day long.
9 Do not cast me away when I am old;
do not forsake me when my strength is gone.
10 For my enemies speak against me;
those who wait to kill me conspire together.
11 They say, "God has forsaken him;
pursue him and seize him,
for no one will rescue him."
12 Be not far from me, O God;
come quickly, O my God, to help me.
13 May my accusers perish in shame;
may those who want to harm me
be covered with scorn and disgrace.

14 But as for me, I will always have hope;
I will praise you more and more.
15 My mouth will tell of your righteousness,
of your salvation all day long,
though I know not its measure.
16 I will come and proclaim your mighty acts, O Sovereign LORD;
I will proclaim your righteousness, yours alone.
17 Since my youth, O God, you have taught me,
and to this day I declare your marvelous deeds.
18 Even when I am old and gray,
do not forsake me, O God,
till I declare your power to the next generation,
your might to all who are to come.

19 Your righteousness reaches to the skies, O God,
you who have done great things.
Who, O God, is like you?
20 Though you have made me see troubles, many and bitter,
you will restore my life again;
from the depths of the earth
you will again bring me up.
21 You will increase my honor
and comfort me once again.

22 I will praise you with the harp
for your faithfulness, O my God;
I will sing praise to you with the lyre,
O Holy One of Israel.
23 My lips will shout for joy
when I sing praise to you—
I, whom you have redeemed.
24 My tongue will tell of your righteous acts
all day long,
for those who wanted to harm me
have been put to shame and confusion.

Psalm 72

Of Solomon.

1 Endow the king with your justice,
O God,
the royal son with your righteousness.
2 He will[a] judge your people in
righteousness,
your afflicted ones with justice.
3 The mountains will bring prosperity to the
people,
the hills the fruit of righteousness.
4 He will defend the afflicted among the
people
and save the children of the needy;
he will crush the oppressor.

5 He will endure[b] as long as the sun,
as long as the moon, through all
generations.
6 He will be like rain falling on a mown
field,
like showers watering the earth.
7 In his days the righteous will flourish;
prosperity will abound till the moon is
no more.

8 He will rule from sea to sea
and from the River[c] to the ends of the
earth.[d]
9 The desert tribes will bow before him
and his enemies will lick the dust.
10 The kings of Tarshish and of distant
shores
will bring tribute to him;
the kings of Sheba and Seba
will present him gifts.
11 All kings will bow down to him
and all nations will serve him.

12 For he will deliver the needy who cry
out,
the afflicted who have no one to help.
13 He will take pity on the weak and the
needy
and save the needy from death.
14 He will rescue them from oppression and
violence,
for precious is their blood in his sight.

15 Long may he live!
May gold from Sheba be given him.
May people ever pray for him
and bless him all day long.
16 Let grain abound throughout the land;
on the tops of the hills may it sway.
Let its fruit flourish like Lebanon;
let it thrive like the grass of the field.
17 May his name endure forever;
may it continue as long as the sun.

All nations will be blessed through him,
and they will call him blessed.

18 Praise be to the LORD God, the God of
Israel,
who alone does marvelous deeds.
19 Praise be to his glorious name forever;
may the whole earth be filled with his
glory.
Amen and Amen.

20 This concludes the prayers of David son of
Jesse.

BOOK III

Psalms 73–89

Psalm 73

A psalm of Asaph.

1 Surely God is good to Israel,
to those who are pure in heart.

2 But as for me, my feet had almost
slipped;
I had nearly lost my foothold.
3 For I envied the arrogant
when I saw the prosperity of the
wicked.

4 They have no struggles;
their bodies are healthy and strong.[e]
5 They are free from the burdens common
to man;
they are not plagued by human ills.
6 Therefore pride is their necklace;
they clothe themselves with violence.
7 From their callous hearts comes iniquity[f];
the evil conceits of their minds know
no limits.
8 They scoff, and speak with malice;
in their arrogance they threaten
oppression.
9 Their mouths lay claim to heaven,
and their tongues take possession of the
earth.
10 Therefore their people turn to them
and drink up waters in abundance.[g]
11 They say, "How can God know?
Does the Most High have knowledge?"

a 2 Or *May he*; similarly in verses 3-11 and 17 *b* 5 Septuagint; Hebrew *You will be feared* *c* 8 That is, the Euphrates *d* 8 Or *the end of the land* *e* 4 With a different word division of the Hebrew; Masoretic Text *struggles at their death; / their bodies are healthy* *f* 7 Syriac (see also Septuagint); Hebrew *Their eyes bulge with fat* *g* 10 The meaning of the Hebrew for this verse is uncertain.

WEDNESDAY
READ PSALM 73:1–28

SLIPPING THROUGH ENVY

But as for me, my feet had almost slipped; I had nearly lost my foothold. For I envied the arrogant when I saw the prosperity of the wicked.

— PSALM 73:2–3

let's talk

- How can envy "rot" a person's "bones"?
- In what ways can envy and discontent erode a marriage?
- How can we as a couple learn to be content with what we have right now?

Years ago, I cleaned rich people's houses. The job was neither glamorous nor challenging, but I could work when my kids were in school and be home by the time they got off the bus. Not all of my clients were actually wealthy, but, to my way of thinking, anyone who could afford a weekly housecleaner was rich.

As I cleaned other people's toilets, scrubbed their expensive tile floors, waxed their heirloom furniture and washed the soft, Egyptian cotton linens that went on their oversized beds, I imagined people with perfect lives, people able to buy their way out of most every problem. Meanwhile, my family struggled financially, budgeting every gallon of milk. It was difficult not to envy the owners of those grand homes I scrubbed—and difficult not to resent our financial struggles.

Although I rarely saw most of the people I worked for, one woman was always home, and we would talk. She told me about family fights over future inheritances and about a grandchild's drug habit. She gave me bags of food to take home to my family and said she envied me because I seemed so happy and at peace.

At another house the homeowners were divorcing. At another, the owners were involved in occult practices. As I gained glimpses into the lives of the people in those homes, I began to realize that every family has its trials and struggles.

In Psalm 73, Asaph (or one of his descendants who functioned in his place as leader of one of the worshiping choirs at the temple) was perplexed. He knew that God was good to those who followed him, but Asaph forgot that when he considered the showy prosperity of those around him. "Why are they so strong and healthy?" he wondered. "Why don't they have to sweat for their food like I do? It's not fair!" He went on to complain, "When I tried to understand all this, it was oppressive to me" (Psalm 73:16).

Asaph felt gypped till he entered the sanctuary of God. Then he considered the spiritual end of the arrogant, the wicked, the proud and the calloused. "Surely you place them on slippery ground," he said to God. "You cast them down to ruin. How suddenly are they destroyed, completely swept away by terrors!" (verses 18–19).

When he envied the wicked, Asaph admitted, he was being senseless and ignorant. He was thinking only about ease and riches and the newest gadgets on the market. When he acknowledged that the world really had nothing that could satisfy the deepest longings that only God could fulfill, Asaph realized that he had more than the richest man he envied. God was "the strength of [his] heart and [his] portion forever" (verse 26). And that kind of peace could not be purchased with money.

Proverbs 14:30 tells us that "envy rots the bones." It can also erode the marital relationship. When discontentment, covetousness and wanting more muddies up a relationship, resentment of one another follows. Designer furniture is nicer than thrift-store bargains, but a couple that is content with what God provides and is strengthened through struggle is infinitely richer than a couple who has only money.

—NANCY KENNEDY

FOR YOUR NEXT DEVOTIONAL READING, TURN TO PAGE 640.

12 This is what the wicked are like—
always carefree, they increase in wealth.

13 Surely in vain have I kept my heart pure;
in vain have I washed my hands in innocence.
14 All day long I have been plagued;
I have been punished every morning.

15 If I had said, "I will speak thus,"
I would have betrayed your children.
16 When I tried to understand all this,
it was oppressive to me
17 till I entered the sanctuary of God;
then I understood their final destiny.

18 Surely you place them on slippery ground;
you cast them down to ruin.
19 How suddenly are they destroyed,
completely swept away by terrors!
20 As a dream when one awakes,
so when you arise, O Lord,
you will despise them as fantasies.
21 When my heart was grieved
and my spirit embittered,
22 I was senseless and ignorant;
I was a brute beast before you.

23 Yet I am always with you;
you hold me by my right hand.
24 You guide me with your counsel,
and afterward you will take me into glory.
25 Whom have I in heaven but you?
And earth has nothing I desire besides you.
26 My flesh and my heart may fail,
but God is the strength of my heart
and my portion forever.

27 Those who are far from you will perish;
you destroy all who are unfaithful to you.
28 But as for me, it is good to be near God.
I have made the Sovereign LORD my refuge;
I will tell of all your deeds.

Psalm 74

A *maskil*[a] of Asaph.

1 Why have you rejected us forever, O God?
Why does your anger smolder against the sheep of your pasture?
2 Remember the people you purchased of old,
the tribe of your inheritance, whom you redeemed—
Mount Zion, where you dwelt.
3 Turn your steps toward these everlasting ruins,
all this destruction the enemy has brought on the sanctuary.

4 Your foes roared in the place where you met with us;
they set up their standards as signs.
5 They behaved like men wielding axes
to cut through a thicket of trees.
6 They smashed all the carved paneling
with their axes and hatchets.
7 They burned your sanctuary to the ground;
they defiled the dwelling place of your Name.
8 They said in their hearts, "We will crush them completely!"
They burned every place where God was worshiped in the land.
9 We are given no miraculous signs;
no prophets are left,
and none of us knows how long this will be.

10 How long will the enemy mock you, O God?
Will the foe revile your name forever?
11 Why do you hold back your hand, your right hand?
Take it from the folds of your garment and destroy them!

12 But you, O God, are my king from of old;
you bring salvation upon the earth.
13 It was you who split open the sea by your power;
you broke the heads of the monster in the waters.
14 It was you who crushed the heads of Leviathan
and gave him as food to the creatures of the desert.
15 It was you who opened up springs and streams;
you dried up the ever flowing rivers.
16 The day is yours, and yours also the night;
you established the sun and moon.
17 It was you who set all the boundaries of the earth;
you made both summer and winter.

[a] Title: Probably a literary or musical term

18 Remember how the enemy has mocked
you, O LORD,
how foolish people have reviled your
name.
19 Do not hand over the life of your dove to
wild beasts;
do not forget the lives of your afflicted
people forever.
20 Have regard for your covenant,
because haunts of violence fill the dark
places of the land.
21 Do not let the oppressed retreat in
disgrace;
may the poor and needy praise your
name.

22 Rise up, O God, and defend your cause;
remember how fools mock you all day
long.
23 Do not ignore the clamor of your
adversaries,
the uproar of your enemies, which rises
continually.

Psalm 75

For the director of music. ⌊To the tune of⌋ "Do Not Destroy." A psalm of Asaph. A song.

1 We give thanks to you, O God,
we give thanks, for your Name is near;
men tell of your wonderful deeds.

2 You say, "I choose the appointed time;
it is I who judge uprightly.
3 When the earth and all its people quake,
it is I who hold its pillars firm. *Selah*
4 To the arrogant I say, 'Boast no more,'
and to the wicked, 'Do not lift up your
horns.
5 Do not lift your horns against heaven;
do not speak with outstretched neck.' "

6 No one from the east or the west
or from the desert can exalt a man.
7 But it is God who judges:
He brings one down, he exalts
another.
8 In the hand of the LORD is a cup
full of foaming wine mixed with
spices;
he pours it out, and all the wicked of the
earth
drink it down to its very dregs.

9 As for me, I will declare this forever;
I will sing praise to the God of Jacob.

10 I will cut off the horns of all the wicked,
but the horns of the righteous will be
lifted up.

Psalm 76

For the director of music. With stringed instruments. A psalm of Asaph. A song.

1 In Judah God is known;
his name is great in Israel.
2 His tent is in Salem,
his dwelling place in Zion.
3 There he broke the flashing arrows,
the shields and the swords, the weapons
of war. *Selah*

4 You are resplendent with light,
more majestic than mountains rich
with game.
5 Valiant men lie plundered,
they sleep their last sleep;
not one of the warriors
can lift his hands.
6 At your rebuke, O God of Jacob,
both horse and chariot lie still.
7 You alone are to be feared.
Who can stand before you when you
are angry?
8 From heaven you pronounced
judgment,
and the land feared and was quiet—
9 when you, O God, rose up to judge,
to save all the afflicted of the land. *Selah*
10 Surely your wrath against men brings you
praise,
and the survivors of your wrath are
restrained.[a]

11 Make vows to the LORD your God and
fulfill them;
let all the neighboring lands
bring gifts to the One to be feared.
12 He breaks the spirit of rulers;
he is feared by the kings of the earth.

Psalm 77

For the director of music. For Jeduthun. Of Asaph. A psalm.

1 I cried out to God for help;
I cried out to God to hear me.
2 When I was in distress, I sought the
Lord;
at night I stretched out untiring hands
and my soul refused to be comforted.

a 10 Or *Surely the wrath of men brings you praise, / and with the remainder of wrath you arm yourself*

3 I remembered you, O God, and I
groaned;
I mused, and my spirit grew
faint. *Selah*
4 You kept my eyes from closing;
I was too troubled to speak.
5 I thought about the former days,
the years of long ago;
6 I remembered my songs in the night.
My heart mused and my spirit
inquired:

7 "Will the Lord reject forever?
Will he never show his favor again?
8 Has his unfailing love vanished forever?
Has his promise failed for all time?
9 Has God forgotten to be merciful?
Has he in anger withheld his
compassion?" *Selah*

10 Then I thought, "To this I will appeal:
the years of the right hand of the Most
High."
11 I will remember the deeds of the LORD;
yes, I will remember your miracles of
long ago.
12 I will meditate on all your works
and consider all your mighty deeds.

13 Your ways, O God, are holy.
What god is so great as our God?
14 You are the God who performs miracles;
you display your power among the
peoples.
15 With your mighty arm you redeemed your
people,
the descendants of Jacob and Joseph.
Selah

16 The waters saw you, O God,
the waters saw you and writhed;
the very depths were convulsed.
17 The clouds poured down water,
the skies resounded with thunder;
your arrows flashed back and forth.
18 Your thunder was heard in the
whirlwind,
your lightning lit up the world;
the earth trembled and quaked.
19 Your path led through the sea,
your way through the mighty waters,
though your footprints were not seen.

20 You led your people like a flock
by the hand of Moses and Aaron.

Psalm 78

A *maskil*[a] of Asaph.

1 O my people, hear my teaching;
listen to the words of my mouth.
2 I will open my mouth in parables,
I will utter hidden things, things from
of old—
3 what we have heard and known,
what our fathers have told us.
4 We will not hide them from their
children;
we will tell the next generation
the praiseworthy deeds of the LORD,
his power, and the wonders he has
done.

5 He decreed statutes for Jacob
and established the law in Israel,
which he commanded our forefathers
to teach their children,
6 so the next generation would know
them,
even the children yet to be born,
and they in turn would tell their
children.
7 Then they would put their trust in God
and would not forget his deeds
but would keep his commands.
8 They would not be like their
forefathers—
a stubborn and rebellious generation,
whose hearts were not loyal to God,
whose spirits were not faithful to him.

9 The men of Ephraim, though armed with
bows,
turned back on the day of battle;
10 they did not keep God's covenant
and refused to live by his law.
11 They forgot what he had done,
the wonders he had shown them.
12 He did miracles in the sight of their
fathers
in the land of Egypt, in the region of
Zoan.
13 He divided the sea and led them through;
he made the water stand firm like a
wall.
14 He guided them with the cloud by day
and with light from the fire all night.
15 He split the rocks in the desert
and gave them water as abundant as the
seas;
16 he brought streams out of a rocky crag
and made water flow down like rivers.

[a] Title: Probably a literary or musical term

17 But they continued to sin against him,
rebelling in the desert against the Most High.
18 They willfully put God to the test
by demanding the food they craved.
19 They spoke against God, saying,
"Can God spread a table in the desert?
20 When he struck the rock, water gushed out,
and streams flowed abundantly.
But can he also give us food?
Can he supply meat for his people?"
21 When the LORD heard them, he was very angry;
his fire broke out against Jacob,
and his wrath rose against Israel,
22 for they did not believe in God
or trust in his deliverance.
23 Yet he gave a command to the skies above
and opened the doors of the heavens;
24 he rained down manna for the people to eat,
he gave them the grain of heaven.
25 Men ate the bread of angels;
he sent them all the food they could eat.
26 He let loose the east wind from the heavens
and led forth the south wind by his power.
27 He rained meat down on them like dust,
flying birds like sand on the seashore.
28 He made them come down inside their camp,
all around their tents.
29 They ate till they had more than enough,
for he had given them what they craved.
30 But before they turned from the food they craved,
even while it was still in their mouths,
31 God's anger rose against them;
he put to death the sturdiest among them,
cutting down the young men of Israel.

32 In spite of all this, they kept on sinning;
in spite of his wonders, they did not believe.
33 So he ended their days in futility
and their years in terror.
34 Whenever God slew them, they would seek him;
they eagerly turned to him again.
35 They remembered that God was their Rock,
that God Most High was their Redeemer.
36 But then they would flatter him with their mouths,
lying to him with their tongues;
37 their hearts were not loyal to him,
they were not faithful to his covenant.
38 Yet he was merciful;
he forgave their iniquities
and did not destroy them.
Time after time he restrained his anger
and did not stir up his full wrath.
39 He remembered that they were but flesh,
a passing breeze that does not return.

40 How often they rebelled against him in the desert
and grieved him in the wasteland!
41 Again and again they put God to the test;
they vexed the Holy One of Israel.
42 They did not remember his power—
the day he redeemed them from the oppressor,
43 the day he displayed his miraculous signs in Egypt,
his wonders in the region of Zoan.
44 He turned their rivers to blood;
they could not drink from their streams.
45 He sent swarms of flies that devoured them,
and frogs that devastated them.
46 He gave their crops to the grasshopper,
their produce to the locust.
47 He destroyed their vines with hail
and their sycamore-figs with sleet.
48 He gave over their cattle to the hail,
their livestock to bolts of lightning.
49 He unleashed against them his hot anger,
his wrath, indignation and hostility—
a band of destroying angels.
50 He prepared a path for his anger;
he did not spare them from death
but gave them over to the plague.
51 He struck down all the firstborn of Egypt,
the firstfruits of manhood in the tents of Ham.
52 But he brought his people out like a flock;
he led them like sheep through the desert.
53 He guided them safely, so they were unafraid;
but the sea engulfed their enemies.
54 Thus he brought them to the border of his holy land,

to the hill country his right hand had
taken.
55 He drove out nations before them
and allotted their lands to them as an
inheritance;
he settled the tribes of Israel in their
homes.

56 But they put God to the test
and rebelled against the Most High;
they did not keep his statutes.
57 Like their fathers they were disloyal and
faithless,
as unreliable as a faulty bow.
58 They angered him with their high places;
they aroused his jealousy with their
idols.
59 When God heard them, he was very
angry;
he rejected Israel completely.
60 He abandoned the tabernacle of Shiloh,
the tent he had set up among men.
61 He sent ⌊the ark of⌋ his might into
captivity,
his splendor into the hands of the
enemy.
62 He gave his people over to the sword;
he was very angry with his inheritance.
63 Fire consumed their young men,
and their maidens had no wedding
songs;
64 their priests were put to the sword,
and their widows could not weep.

65 Then the Lord awoke as from sleep,
as a man wakes from the stupor of
wine.
66 He beat back his enemies;
he put them to everlasting shame.
67 Then he rejected the tents of Joseph,
he did not choose the tribe of Ephraim;
68 but he chose the tribe of Judah,
Mount Zion, which he loved.
69 He built his sanctuary like the heights,
like the earth that he established
forever.
70 He chose David his servant
and took him from the sheep pens;
71 from tending the sheep he brought him
to be the shepherd of his people Jacob,
of Israel his inheritance.
72 And David shepherded them with
integrity of heart;
with skillful hands he led them.

Psalm 79

A psalm of Asaph.

1 O God, the nations have invaded your
inheritance;
they have defiled your holy temple,
they have reduced Jerusalem to rubble.
2 They have given the dead bodies of your
servants
as food to the birds of the air,
the flesh of your saints to the beasts of
the earth.
3 They have poured out blood like water
all around Jerusalem,
and there is no one to bury the dead.
4 We are objects of reproach to our
neighbors,
of scorn and derision to those around
us.

5 How long, O LORD? Will you be angry
forever?
How long will your jealousy burn like
fire?
6 Pour out your wrath on the nations
that do not acknowledge you,
on the kingdoms
that do not call on your name;
7 for they have devoured Jacob
and destroyed his homeland.
8 Do not hold against us the sins of the
fathers;
may your mercy come quickly to meet
us,
for we are in desperate need.

9 Help us, O God our Savior,
for the glory of your name;
deliver us and forgive our sins
for your name's sake.
10 Why should the nations say,
"Where is their God?"
Before our eyes, make known among the
nations
that you avenge the outpoured blood of
your servants.
11 May the groans of the prisoners come
before you;
by the strength of your arm
preserve those condemned to die.

12 Pay back into the laps of our neighbors
seven times
the reproach they have hurled at you,
O Lord.
13 Then we your people, the sheep of your
pasture,
will praise you forever;

from generation to generation
we will recount your praise.

Psalm 80

For the director of music. To ⌊the tune of⌋ "The Lilies of the Covenant." Of Asaph. A psalm.

1 Hear us, O Shepherd of Israel,
you who lead Joseph like a flock;
you who sit enthroned between the cherubim, shine forth
2 before Ephraim, Benjamin and Manasseh.
Awaken your might;
come and save us.

3 Restore us, O God;
make your face shine upon us,
that we may be saved.

4 O LORD God Almighty,
how long will your anger smolder
against the prayers of your people?
5 You have fed them with the bread of tears;
you have made them drink tears by the bowlful.
6 You have made us a source of contention to our neighbors,
and our enemies mock us.

7 Restore us, O God Almighty;
make your face shine upon us,
that we may be saved.

8 You brought a vine out of Egypt;
you drove out the nations and planted it.
9 You cleared the ground for it,
and it took root and filled the land.
10 The mountains were covered with its shade,
the mighty cedars with its branches.
11 It sent out its boughs to the Sea,[a]
its shoots as far as the River.[b]

12 Why have you broken down its walls
so that all who pass by pick its grapes?
13 Boars from the forest ravage it
and the creatures of the field feed on it.
14 Return to us, O God Almighty!
Look down from heaven and see!
Watch over this vine,
15 the root your right hand has planted,
the son[c] you have raised up for yourself.

16 Your vine is cut down, it is burned with fire;
at your rebuke your people perish.
17 Let your hand rest on the man at your right hand,
the son of man you have raised up for yourself.
18 Then we will not turn away from you;
revive us, and we will call on your name.

19 Restore us, O LORD God Almighty;
make your face shine upon us,
that we may be saved.

Psalm 81

For the director of music. According to *gittith.*[d] Of Asaph.

1 Sing for joy to God our strength;
shout aloud to the God of Jacob!
2 Begin the music, strike the tambourine,
play the melodious harp and lyre.

3 Sound the ram's horn at the New Moon,
and when the moon is full, on the day of our Feast;
4 this is a decree for Israel,
an ordinance of the God of Jacob.
5 He established it as a statute for Joseph
when he went out against Egypt,
where we heard a language we did not understand.[e]

6 He says, "I removed the burden from their shoulders;
their hands were set free from the basket.
7 In your distress you called and I rescued you,
I answered you out of a thundercloud;
I tested you at the waters of Meribah.
Selah

8 "Hear, O my people, and I will warn you—
if you would but listen to me, O Israel!
9 You shall have no foreign god among you;
you shall not bow down to an alien god.
10 I am the LORD your God,
who brought you up out of Egypt.
Open wide your mouth and I will fill it.

11 "But my people would not listen to me;
Israel would not submit to me.

---

a 11 Probably the Mediterranean *b 11* That is, the Euphrates *c 15* Or *branch* *d* Title: Probably a musical term *e 5* Or */ and we heard a voice we had not known*

12 So I gave them over to their stubborn hearts
to follow their own devices.

13 "If my people would but listen to me,
if Israel would follow my ways,
14 how quickly would I subdue their enemies
and turn my hand against their foes!
15 Those who hate the LORD would cringe before him,
and their punishment would last forever.
16 But you would be fed with the finest of wheat;
with honey from the rock I would satisfy you."

Psalm 82

A psalm of Asaph.

1 God presides in the great assembly;
he gives judgment among the "gods":

2 "How long will you[a] defend the unjust
and show partiality to the wicked? *Selah*
3 Defend the cause of the weak and fatherless;
maintain the rights of the poor and oppressed.
4 Rescue the weak and needy;
deliver them from the hand of the wicked.

5 "They know nothing, they understand nothing.
They walk about in darkness;
all the foundations of the earth are shaken.

6 "I said, 'You are "gods";
you are all sons of the Most High.'
7 But you will die like mere men;
you will fall like every other ruler."

8 Rise up, O God, judge the earth,
for all the nations are your inheritance.

Psalm 83

A song. A psalm of Asaph.

1 O God, do not keep silent;
be not quiet, O God, be not still.
2 See how your enemies are astir,
how your foes rear their heads.
3 With cunning they conspire against your people;
they plot against those you cherish.
4 "Come," they say, "let us destroy them as a nation,
that the name of Israel be remembered no more."

5 With one mind they plot together;
they form an alliance against you—
6 the tents of Edom and the Ishmaelites,
of Moab and the Hagrites,
7 Gebal,[b] Ammon and Amalek,
Philistia, with the people of Tyre.
8 Even Assyria has joined them
to lend strength to the descendants of Lot. *Selah*

9 Do to them as you did to Midian,
as you did to Sisera and Jabin at the river Kishon,
10 who perished at Endor
and became like refuse on the ground.
11 Make their nobles like Oreb and Zeeb,
all their princes like Zebah and Zalmunna,
12 who said, "Let us take possession
of the pasturelands of God."

13 Make them like tumbleweed, O my God,
like chaff before the wind.
14 As fire consumes the forest
or a flame sets the mountains ablaze,
15 so pursue them with your tempest
and terrify them with your storm.
16 Cover their faces with shame
so that men will seek your name,
O LORD.

17 May they ever be ashamed and dismayed;
may they perish in disgrace.
18 Let them know that you, whose name is the LORD—
that you alone are the Most High over all the earth.

Psalm 84

For the director of music. According to *gittith*.[c] Of the Sons of Korah. A psalm.

1 How lovely is your dwelling place,
O LORD Almighty!
2 My soul yearns, even faints,
for the courts of the LORD;
my heart and my flesh cry out
for the living God.

3 Even the sparrow has found a home,
and the swallow a nest for herself,
where she may have her young—

[a] 2 The Hebrew is plural. [b] 7 That is, Byblos [c] Title: Probably a musical term

a place near your altar,
O LORD Almighty, my King and my God.
4 Blessed are those who dwell in your house;
they are ever praising you. *Selah*
5 Blessed are those whose strength is in you,
who have set their hearts on pilgrimage.
6 As they pass through the Valley of Baca,
they make it a place of springs;
the autumn rains also cover it with pools.[a]
7 They go from strength to strength,
till each appears before God in Zion.

8 Hear my prayer, O LORD God Almighty;
listen to me, O God of Jacob. *Selah*
9 Look upon our shield,[b] O God;
look with favor on your anointed one.

10 Better is one day in your courts
than a thousand elsewhere;
I would rather be a doorkeeper in the house of my God
than dwell in the tents of the wicked.
11 For the LORD God is a sun and shield;
the LORD bestows favor and honor;
no good thing does he withhold
from those whose walk is blameless.

12 O LORD Almighty,
blessed is the man who trusts in you.

Psalm 85

For the director of music. Of the Sons of Korah. A psalm.

1 You showed favor to your land, O LORD;
you restored the fortunes of Jacob.
2 You forgave the iniquity of your people
and covered all their sins. *Selah*
3 You set aside all your wrath
and turned from your fierce anger.

4 Restore us again, O God our Savior,
and put away your displeasure toward us.
5 Will you be angry with us forever?
Will you prolong your anger through all generations?
6 Will you not revive us again,
that your people may rejoice in you?
7 Show us your unfailing love, O LORD,
and grant us your salvation.

8 I will listen to what God the LORD will say;
he promises peace to his people, his saints—
but let them not return to folly.
9 Surely his salvation is near those who fear him,
that his glory may dwell in our land.

10 Love and faithfulness meet together;
righteousness and peace kiss each other.
11 Faithfulness springs forth from the earth,
and righteousness looks down from heaven.
12 The LORD will indeed give what is good,
and our land will yield its harvest.
13 Righteousness goes before him
and prepares the way for his steps.

Psalm 86

A prayer of David.

1 Hear, O LORD, and answer me,
for I am poor and needy.
2 Guard my life, for I am devoted to you.
You are my God; save your servant
who trusts in you.
3 Have mercy on me, O Lord,
for I call to you all day long.
4 Bring joy to your servant,
for to you, O Lord,
I lift up my soul.

5 You are forgiving and good, O Lord,
abounding in love to all who call to you.
6 Hear my prayer, O LORD;
listen to my cry for mercy.
7 In the day of my trouble I will call to you,
for you will answer me.

8 Among the gods there is none like you, O Lord;
no deeds can compare with yours.
9 All the nations you have made
will come and worship before you, O Lord;
they will bring glory to your name.
10 For you are great and do marvelous deeds;
you alone are God.

11 Teach me your way, O LORD,
and I will walk in your truth;
give me an undivided heart,
that I may fear your name.
12 I will praise you, O Lord my God, with all my heart;
I will glorify your name forever.
13 For great is your love toward me;

[a] 6 Or *blessings* [b] 9 Or *sovereign*

you have delivered me from the depths
of the grave.[a]
14 The arrogant are attacking me, O God;
a band of ruthless men seeks my life—
men without regard for you.
15 But you, O Lord, are a compassionate and
gracious God,
slow to anger, abounding in love and
faithfulness.
16 Turn to me and have mercy on me;
grant your strength to your servant
and save the son of your maidservant.[b]
17 Give me a sign of your goodness,
that my enemies may see it and be put
to shame,
for you, O LORD, have helped me and
comforted me.

Psalm 87

Of the Sons of Korah. A psalm. A song.

1 He has set his foundation on the holy
mountain;
2 the LORD loves the gates of Zion
more than all the dwellings of Jacob.
3 Glorious things are said of you,
O city of God: *Selah*
4 "I will record Rahab[c] and Babylon
among those who acknowledge me—
Philistia too, and Tyre, along with
Cush[d]—
and will say, 'This[e] one was born in
Zion.' "
5 Indeed, of Zion it will be said,
"This one and that one were born in
her,
and the Most High himself will
establish her."
6 The LORD will write in the register of the
peoples:
"This one was born in Zion." *Selah*
7 As they make music they will sing,
"All my fountains are in you."

Psalm 88

A song. A psalm of the Sons of Korah.
For the director of music. According to
mahalath leannoth.[f] A *maskil*[g]
of Heman the Ezrahite.

1 O LORD, the God who saves me,
day and night I cry out before you.
2 May my prayer come before you;
turn your ear to my cry.
3 For my soul is full of trouble
and my life draws near the grave.[a]
4 I am counted among those who go down
to the pit;
I am like a man without strength.
5 I am set apart with the dead,
like the slain who lie in the grave,
whom you remember no more,
who are cut off from your care.

6 You have put me in the lowest pit,
in the darkest depths.
7 Your wrath lies heavily upon me;
you have overwhelmed me with all
your waves. *Selah*
8 You have taken from me my closest friends
and have made me repulsive to them.
I am confined and cannot escape;
9 my eyes are dim with grief.

I call to you, O LORD, every day;
I spread out my hands to you.
10 Do you show your wonders to the dead?
Do those who are dead rise up and
praise you? *Selah*
11 Is your love declared in the grave,
your faithfulness in Destruction[h]?
12 Are your wonders known in the place of
darkness,
or your righteous deeds in the land of
oblivion?

13 But I cry to you for help, O LORD;
in the morning my prayer comes before
you.
14 Why, O LORD, do you reject me
and hide your face from me?
15 From my youth I have been afflicted and
close to death;
I have suffered your terrors and am in
despair.
16 Your wrath has swept over me;
your terrors have destroyed me.
17 All day long they surround me like a
flood;
they have completely engulfed me.
18 You have taken my companions and loved
ones from me;
the darkness is my closest friend.

[a] *13,3* Hebrew *Sheol* [b] *16* Or *save your faithful son* [c] *4* A poetic name for Egypt [d] *4* That is, the upper Nile region [e] *4* Or *"O Rahab and Babylon, / Philistia, Tyre and Cush, / I will record concerning those who acknowledge me: / 'This* [f] Title: Possibly a tune, "The Suffering of Affliction" [g] Title: Probably a literary or musical term [h] *11* Hebrew *Abaddon*

Psalm 89

A *maskil*[a] of Ethan the Ezrahite.

1 I will sing of the LORD's great love
forever;
with my mouth I will make your
faithfulness known through all
generations.
2 I will declare that your love stands firm
forever,
that you established your faithfulness in
heaven itself.
3 You said, "I have made a covenant with
my chosen one,
I have sworn to David my servant,
4 'I will establish your line forever
and make your throne firm through all
generations.' " *Selah*
5 The heavens praise your wonders,
O LORD,
your faithfulness too, in the assembly of
the holy ones.
6 For who in the skies above can compare
with the LORD?
Who is like the LORD among the
heavenly beings?
7 In the council of the holy ones God is
greatly feared;
he is more awesome than all who
surround him.
8 O LORD God Almighty, who is like you?
You are mighty, O LORD, and your
faithfulness surrounds you.
9 You rule over the surging sea;
when its waves mount up, you still
them.
10 You crushed Rahab like one of the slain;
with your strong arm you scattered
your enemies.
11 The heavens are yours, and yours also the
earth;
you founded the world and all that is
in it.
12 You created the north and the south;
Tabor and Hermon sing for joy at your
name.
13 Your arm is endued with power;
your hand is strong, your right hand
exalted.
14 Righteousness and justice are the
foundation of your throne;
love and faithfulness go before you.
15 Blessed are those who have learned to
acclaim you,
who walk in the light of your presence,
O LORD.
16 They rejoice in your name all day long;
they exult in your righteousness.
17 For you are their glory and strength,
and by your favor you exalt our horn.[b]
18 Indeed, our shield[c] belongs to the LORD,
our king to the Holy One of Israel.

19 Once you spoke in a vision,
to your faithful people you said:
"I have bestowed strength on a warrior;
I have exalted a young man from
among the people.
20 I have found David my servant;
with my sacred oil I have anointed
him.
21 My hand will sustain him;
surely my arm will strengthen him.
22 No enemy will subject him to tribute;
no wicked man will oppress him.
23 I will crush his foes before him
and strike down his adversaries.
24 My faithful love will be with him,
and through my name his horn[d] will
be exalted.
25 I will set his hand over the sea,
his right hand over the rivers.
26 He will call out to me, 'You are my Father,
my God, the Rock my Savior.'
27 I will also appoint him my firstborn,
the most exalted of the kings of the
earth.
28 I will maintain my love to him forever,
and my covenant with him will never
fail.
29 I will establish his line forever,
his throne as long as the heavens
endure.

30 "If his sons forsake my law
and do not follow my statutes,
31 if they violate my decrees
and fail to keep my commands,
32 I will punish their sin with the rod,
their iniquity with flogging;
33 but I will not take my love from him,
nor will I ever betray my faithfulness.
34 I will not violate my covenant
or alter what my lips have uttered.
35 Once for all, I have sworn by my
holiness—
and I will not lie to David—

[a] Title: Probably a literary or musical term [b] 17 *Horn* here symbolizes strong one. [c] 18 Or *sovereign* [d] 24 *Horn* here symbolizes strength.

THURSDAY
READ PSALM 89:1–52

HOLDING OUT HOPE

How long, O LORD? Will you hide yourself forever? . . . O Lord, where is your former great love, which in your faithfulness you swore to David?

— PSALM 89:46,49

let's talk

- What hopes did we bring to our relationship? Have our hopes materialized? How have we thanked God?
- When have we sung laments? Why? Do others share our pain and frustration? How?
- Are we stumbling in our faith? What might be the cause? Are there things we need to confess and repent of?

An ancient painting at Karnak in Upper Egypt shows a man of royal bearing being led by Pharaoh Sheshonk to the god Amun. The man appears humiliated, beaten. On his hand is a ring bearing the title "King of Judah."

The man was Rehoboam, son of King Solomon. Solomon had vastly extended Israel's territory, making gold and silver as abundant as the stones that paved Jerusalem's streets. But in the fifth year of Rehoboam's reign (see 1 Kings 14:25), the walls of Jerusalem were breached, the gold was removed from the temple and the young king was mocked in front of the austere idols of Egypt.

What was the sense in all of this? Where was justice? And where was God?

We can't be sure of the identity of Ethan the Ezrahite, the ascribed author of Psalm 89. Perhaps he wrote this psalm in response to this event in the life of Rehoboam. Or the occasion may have come more than 300 years later with the attack on Jerusalem by the Babylonians and the exile of King Jehoiachin (see 2 Kings 24:8–17). At any rate, the psalmist was depressed and mystified as he asked, "O Lord, where is your former great love, which in your faithfulness you swore to David?" (Psalm 89:49).

The first half of the psalm reflects on God's promises to David and his royal lineage. But beginning at verse 38, Ethan's tone changes: "You have cut short the days of his youth; you have covered him with a mantle of shame" (verse 45).

Ethan's psalm resonates with some of us with regard to our marriages. Every couple that celebrates a wedding echoes the enthusiasm of the first 37 verses: "God's love endures forever and will shine through our lives!" But too many relationships run into hard times. For example, one couple we know struggled through decades of infidelity. She partied with her friends from work, and he cozied up to other women while on business trips. When the couple finally decided to call it quits, she realized she was pregnant. Unsure of what to do, they put parting on hold. During that time, they fell in love all over again.

Some years later I was part of their 25th anniversary celebration in a rented hall. When the couple stood to thank the large gathering of friends for coming, the tears flowed. They confessed sins. They told of their early hopes and wayward paths. They spoke of losing faith and questioning God's promises.

Then they revealed why all of us had been invited to the party. Each of us, they said, had kept faith in God for them even while they had lost courage and confidence. They had tried, failed, prayed and grown bitter. But we had wrestled with God on their behalf, using both praise and lament, similar to the way Ethan had in Psalm 89.

That night we laughed together in the great joy of God's promises—and we wept together over the pain of lost opportunities and faded hopes. And as we lingered over final good wishes, we recognized that life in all its shades is a faith journey.

—WAYNE BROUWER

FOR YOUR NEXT DEVOTIONAL READING, TURN TO PAGE 644.

36 that his line will continue forever
and his throne endure before me like the sun;
37 it will be established forever like the moon,
the faithful witness in the sky." *Selah*

38 But you have rejected, you have spurned,
you have been very angry with your anointed one.
39 You have renounced the covenant with your servant
and have defiled his crown in the dust.
40 You have broken through all his walls
and reduced his strongholds to ruins.
41 All who pass by have plundered him;
he has become the scorn of his neighbors.
42 You have exalted the right hand of his foes;
you have made all his enemies rejoice.
43 You have turned back the edge of his sword
and have not supported him in battle.
44 You have put an end to his splendor
and cast his throne to the ground.
45 You have cut short the days of his youth;
you have covered him with a mantle of shame. *Selah*

46 How long, O LORD? Will you hide yourself forever?
How long will your wrath burn like fire?
47 Remember how fleeting is my life.
For what futility you have created all men!
48 What man can live and not see death,
or save himself from the power of the grave[a]? *Selah*
49 O Lord, where is your former great love,
which in your faithfulness you swore to David?
50 Remember, Lord, how your servant has[b] been mocked,
how I bear in my heart the taunts of all the nations,
51 the taunts with which your enemies have mocked, O LORD,
with which they have mocked every step of your anointed one.

52 Praise be to the LORD forever!
Amen and Amen.

BOOK IV

Psalms 90–106

Psalm 90

A prayer of Moses the man of God.

1 Lord, you have been our dwelling place
throughout all generations.
2 Before the mountains were born
or you brought forth the earth and the world,
from everlasting to everlasting you are God.

3 You turn men back to dust,
saying, "Return to dust, O sons of men."
4 For a thousand years in your sight
are like a day that has just gone by,
or like a watch in the night.
5 You sweep men away in the sleep of death;
they are like the new grass of the morning—
6 though in the morning it springs up new,
by evening it is dry and withered.

7 We are consumed by your anger
and terrified by your indignation.
8 You have set our iniquities before you,
our secret sins in the light of your presence.
9 All our days pass away under your wrath;
we finish our years with a moan.
10 The length of our days is seventy years—
or eighty, if we have the strength;
yet their span[c] is but trouble and sorrow,
for they quickly pass, and we fly away.

11 Who knows the power of your anger?
For your wrath is as great as the fear that is due you.
12 Teach us to number our days aright,
that we may gain a heart of wisdom.

13 Relent, O LORD! How long will it be?
Have compassion on your servants.
14 Satisfy us in the morning with your unfailing love,
that we may sing for joy and be glad all our days.
15 Make us glad for as many days as you have afflicted us,
for as many years as we have seen trouble.
16 May your deeds be shown to your servants,
your splendor to their children.

[a] 48 Hebrew *Sheol* [b] 50 Or *your servants have* [c] 10 Or *yet the best of them*

17 May the favor[a] of the Lord our God rest upon us;
establish the work of our hands for us—
yes, establish the work of our hands.

Psalm 91

1 He who dwells in the shelter of the Most High
will rest in the shadow of the Almighty.[b]
2 I will say[c] of the LORD, "He is my refuge and my fortress,
my God, in whom I trust."

3 Surely he will save you from the fowler's snare
and from the deadly pestilence.
4 He will cover you with his feathers,
and under his wings you will find refuge;
his faithfulness will be your shield and rampart.
5 You will not fear the terror of night,
nor the arrow that flies by day,
6 nor the pestilence that stalks in the darkness,
nor the plague that destroys at midday.
7 A thousand may fall at your side,
ten thousand at your right hand,
but it will not come near you.
8 You will only observe with your eyes
and see the punishment of the wicked.

9 If you make the Most High your dwelling—
even the LORD, who is my refuge—
10 then no harm will befall you,
no disaster will come near your tent.
11 For he will command his angels concerning you
to guard you in all your ways;
12 they will lift you up in their hands,
so that you will not strike your foot against a stone.
13 You will tread upon the lion and the cobra;
you will trample the great lion and the serpent.

14 "Because he loves me," says the LORD, "I will rescue him;
I will protect him, for he acknowledges my name.
15 He will call upon me, and I will answer him;
I will be with him in trouble,
I will deliver him and honor him.
16 With long life will I satisfy him
and show him my salvation."

Psalm 92

A psalm. A song. For the Sabbath day.

1 It is good to praise the LORD
and make music to your name, O Most High,
2 to proclaim your love in the morning
and your faithfulness at night,
3 to the music of the ten-stringed lyre
and the melody of the harp.

4 For you make me glad by your deeds, O LORD;
I sing for joy at the works of your hands.
5 How great are your works, O LORD,
how profound your thoughts!
6 The senseless man does not know,
fools do not understand,
7 that though the wicked spring up like grass
and all evildoers flourish,
they will be forever destroyed.

8 But you, O LORD, are exalted forever.

9 For surely your enemies, O LORD,
surely your enemies will perish;
all evildoers will be scattered.
10 You have exalted my horn[d] like that of a wild ox;
fine oils have been poured upon me.
11 My eyes have seen the defeat of my adversaries;
my ears have heard the rout of my wicked foes.

12 The righteous will flourish like a palm tree,
they will grow like a cedar of Lebanon;
13 planted in the house of the LORD,
they will flourish in the courts of our God.
14 They will still bear fruit in old age,
they will stay fresh and green,
15 proclaiming, "The LORD is upright;
he is my Rock, and there is no wickedness in him."

Psalm 93

1 The LORD reigns, he is robed in majesty;
the LORD is robed in majesty
and is armed with strength.

---

[a] *17* Or *beauty* [b] *1* Hebrew *Shaddai* [c] *2* Or *He says* [d] *10* *Horn* here symbolizes strength.

The world is firmly established;
it cannot be moved.
2 Your throne was established long ago;
you are from all eternity.

3 The seas have lifted up, O LORD,
the seas have lifted up their voice;
the seas have lifted up their pounding waves.
4 Mightier than the thunder of the great waters,
mightier than the breakers of the sea—
the LORD on high is mighty.

5 Your statutes stand firm;
holiness adorns your house
for endless days, O LORD.

Psalm 94

1 O LORD, the God who avenges,
O God who avenges, shine forth.
2 Rise up, O Judge of the earth;
pay back to the proud what they deserve.
3 How long will the wicked, O LORD,
how long will the wicked be jubilant?

4 They pour out arrogant words;
all the evildoers are full of boasting.
5 They crush your people, O LORD;
they oppress your inheritance.
6 They slay the widow and the alien;
they murder the fatherless.
7 They say, "The LORD does not see;
the God of Jacob pays no heed."
8 Take heed, you senseless ones among the people;
you fools, when will you become wise?
9 Does he who implanted the ear not hear?
Does he who formed the eye not see?
10 Does he who disciplines nations not punish?
Does he who teaches man lack knowledge?
11 The LORD knows the thoughts of man;
he knows that they are futile.

12 Blessed is the man you discipline, O LORD,
the man you teach from your law;
13 you grant him relief from days of trouble,
till a pit is dug for the wicked.
14 For the LORD will not reject his people;
he will never forsake his inheritance.
15 Judgment will again be founded on righteousness,
and all the upright in heart will follow it.

16 Who will rise up for me against the wicked?
Who will take a stand for me against evildoers?
17 Unless the LORD had given me help,
I would soon have dwelt in the silence of death.
18 When I said, "My foot is slipping,"
your love, O LORD, supported me.
19 When anxiety was great within me,
your consolation brought joy to my soul.

20 Can a corrupt throne be allied with you—
one that brings on misery by its decrees?
21 They band together against the righteous
and condemn the innocent to death.
22 But the LORD has become my fortress,
and my God the rock in whom I take refuge.
23 He will repay them for their sins
and destroy them for their wickedness;
the LORD our God will destroy them.

Psalm 95

1 Come, let us sing for joy to the LORD;
let us shout aloud to the Rock of our salvation.
2 Let us come before him with thanksgiving
and extol him with music and song.
3 For the LORD is the great God,
the great King above all gods.
4 In his hand are the depths of the earth,
and the mountain peaks belong to him.
5 The sea is his, for he made it,
and his hands formed the dry land.

6 Come, let us bow down in worship,
let us kneel before the LORD our Maker;
7 for he is our God
and we are the people of his pasture,
the flock under his care.

Today, if you hear his voice,
8 do not harden your hearts as you did at Meribah,[a]
as you did that day at Massah[b] in the desert,
9 where your fathers tested and tried me,
though they had seen what I did.

---

[a] 8 *Meribah* means *quarreling.* [b] 8 *Massah* means *testing.*

F **FRIDAY**
READ PSALM 95:1–11

CUE CARDS FOR PRAISE

> **Come, let us sing for joy to the LORD; let us shout aloud to the Rock of our salvation.**
>
> — PSALM 95:1

Imagine meeting someone famous and having to keep that news to yourself. Or what if you had pictures of your first child and no one to show them to? Praise and thanksgiving beg for company; joining with other voices makes the worship so much sweeter!

Psalm 95 tells us to find companions as we praise: "Come, let us sing . . . let us shout . . . let us bow down . . . let us kneel before the LORD our Maker" (Psalm 95:1,6). Marriage gives us a companion in praise—someone to share all the exciting details, someone to cheer and sing and laugh with before the Lord.

Psalms is our songbook; the psalms, our cue cards for praising God. Psalm 95 puts words in our mouths to express the joy in our hearts. And if our songs have gone all mumbly and dull, this psalm helps us rejuvenate our singing together.

This song has four stanzas that give us a structure for our praise. Verses 1–2 have us on our feet, singing at the tops of our voices to our champion, the Lord. The reason for such exuberance is described in the second stanza, in verses 3–5. We worship by picturing great mountains, pounding seas and majestic sunsets. And we come away ready to trust our mountain-moving God, our sea-parting Savior, our world-holding King.

As a couple we can praise God in a similar way, but we sing this kind of praise best when we gather with God's people in church. Don't miss such celebrations!

The third stanza, verses 6–7a, is an entirely different kind of melody; it is soft and thoughtful. This music bows our heads and brings us to our knees. We sing softly that the great God who made us is the Good Shepherd who feeds and leads us, who guards and guides our lives.

Try worshiping as a couple by recounting God's provision—your first apartment, for example, or unexpected money when things were very tight. Praising God for his "shepherd care" is important for our future as a couple and as a family, for it is how we learn to trust God to guide us through the next dark valley or be our protection in a troubled tomorrow.

Psalm 95 ends in a minor key (verses 7b–11), reminding us of what happens when we fail to let worship shape our will and our ways. Israel had sung songs about God's greatness and care when he had miraculously delivered them from Egypt and provided for them in the desert. But later, when God didn't come through for them as quickly as they wanted, the people lost faith in the God they had sung about, and they ended up being prohibited from entering the promised land, the place where God intended to give them "rest" (verse 11).

What a great reminder to keep our marriages full of praise—praise that is both exuberant and humble. When we worship God in our times of triumph, it prepares us to trust God in our times of struggle and prevents us from hardening our hearts toward him.

—LEE ECLOV

let's *talk*

- ✦ How does worshiping God as a couple help us spiritually? How can worshiping together have the kind of variety and breadth that we see in this psalm?
- ✦ How do we worship together with other believers? What could we do to worship more effectively with them?
- ✦ When might we be most tempted to "harden [our] hearts" and not trust God? How can we use worship times to fortify ourselves against such temptations?

FOR YOUR NEXT DEVOTIONAL READING, TURN TO PAGE 648.

10 For forty years I was angry with that
generation;
I said, "They are a people whose hearts
go astray,
and they have not known my ways."
11 So I declared on oath in my anger,
"They shall never enter my rest."

Psalm 96

1 Sing to the LORD a new song;
sing to the LORD, all the earth.
2 Sing to the LORD, praise his name;
proclaim his salvation day after day.
3 Declare his glory among the nations,
his marvelous deeds among all peoples.

4 For great is the LORD and most worthy of
praise;
he is to be feared above all gods.
5 For all the gods of the nations are idols,
but the LORD made the heavens.
6 Splendor and majesty are before him;
strength and glory are in his sanctuary.

7 Ascribe to the LORD, O families of
nations,
ascribe to the LORD glory and strength.
8 Ascribe to the LORD the glory due his
name;
bring an offering and come into his
courts.
9 Worship the LORD in the splendor of his[a]
holiness;
tremble before him, all the earth.
10 Say among the nations, "The LORD
reigns."
The world is firmly established, it
cannot be moved;
he will judge the peoples with equity.
11 Let the heavens rejoice, let the earth be
glad;
let the sea resound, and all that is in it;
12 let the fields be jubilant, and everything
in them.
Then all the trees of the forest will sing for
joy;
13 they will sing before the LORD, for he
comes,
he comes to judge the earth.
He will judge the world in righteousness
and the peoples in his truth.

Psalm 97

1 The LORD reigns, let the earth be glad;
let the distant shores rejoice.
2 Clouds and thick darkness surround him;
righteousness and justice are the
foundation of his throne.
3 Fire goes before him
and consumes his foes on every side.
4 His lightning lights up the world;
the earth sees and trembles.
5 The mountains melt like wax before the
LORD,
before the Lord of all the earth.
6 The heavens proclaim his righteousness,
and all the peoples see his glory.

7 All who worship images are put to shame,
those who boast in idols—
worship him, all you gods!
8 Zion hears and rejoices
and the villages of Judah are glad
because of your judgments, O LORD.
9 For you, O LORD, are the Most High over
all the earth;
you are exalted far above all gods.

10 Let those who love the LORD hate evil,
for he guards the lives of his faithful
ones
and delivers them from the hand of the
wicked.
11 Light is shed upon the righteous
and joy on the upright in heart.
12 Rejoice in the LORD, you who are
righteous,
and praise his holy name.

Psalm 98

A psalm.

1 Sing to the LORD a new song,
for he has done marvelous things;
his right hand and his holy arm
have worked salvation for him.
2 The LORD has made his salvation known
and revealed his righteousness to the
nations.
3 He has remembered his love
and his faithfulness to the house of
Israel;
all the ends of the earth have seen
the salvation of our God.

4 Shout for joy to the LORD, all the earth,
burst into jubilant song with music;
5 make music to the LORD with the harp,
with the harp and the sound of singing,
6 with trumpets and the blast of the ram's
horn—

---

a 9 Or *LORD with the splendor of*

shout for joy before the LORD, the
King.

7 Let the sea resound, and everything in it,
the world, and all who live in it.
8 Let the rivers clap their hands,
let the mountains sing together for joy;
9 let them sing before the LORD,
for he comes to judge the earth.
He will judge the world in righteousness
and the peoples with equity.

Psalm 99

1 The LORD reigns,
let the nations tremble;
he sits enthroned between the cherubim,
let the earth shake.
2 Great is the LORD in Zion;
he is exalted over all the nations.
3 Let them praise your great and awesome
name—
he is holy.

4 The King is mighty, he loves justice—
you have established equity;
in Jacob you have done
what is just and right.
5 Exalt the LORD our God
and worship at his footstool;
he is holy.

6 Moses and Aaron were among his priests,
Samuel was among those who called on
his name;
they called on the LORD
and he answered them.
7 He spoke to them from the pillar of cloud;
they kept his statutes and the decrees he
gave them.

8 O LORD our God,
you answered them;
you were to Israel[a] a forgiving God,
though you punished their misdeeds.[b]
9 Exalt the LORD our God
and worship at his holy mountain,
for the LORD our God is holy.

Psalm 100

A psalm. For giving thanks.

1 Shout for joy to the LORD, all the earth.
2 Worship the LORD with gladness;
come before him with joyful songs.
3 Know that the LORD is God.
It is he who made us, and we are his[c];
we are his people, the sheep of his
pasture.

4 Enter his gates with thanksgiving
and his courts with praise;
give thanks to him and praise his name.
5 For the LORD is good and his love endures
forever;
his faithfulness continues through all
generations.

Psalm 101

Of David. A psalm.

1 I will sing of your love and justice;
to you, O LORD, I will sing praise.
2 I will be careful to lead a blameless life—
when will you come to me?

I will walk in my house
with blameless heart.
3 I will set before my eyes
no vile thing.

The deeds of faithless men I hate;
they will not cling to me.
4 Men of perverse heart shall be far from
me;
I will have nothing to do with evil.

5 Whoever slanders his neighbor in secret,
him will I put to silence;
whoever has haughty eyes and a proud
heart,
him will I not endure.

6 My eyes will be on the faithful in the land,
that they may dwell with me;
he whose walk is blameless
will minister to me.

7 No one who practices deceit
will dwell in my house;
no one who speaks falsely
will stand in my presence.

8 Every morning I will put to silence
all the wicked in the land;
I will cut off every evildoer
from the city of the LORD.

Psalm 102

A prayer of an afflicted man. When
he is faint and pours out his lament
before the LORD.

1 Hear my prayer, O LORD;
let my cry for help come to you.
2 Do not hide your face from me

---

[a] 8 Hebrew *them* [b] 8 Or / *an avenger of the wrongs done to them* [c] 3 Or *and not we ourselves*

when I am in distress.
Turn your ear to me;
when I call, answer me quickly.
3 For my days vanish like smoke;
my bones burn like glowing embers.
4 My heart is blighted and withered like grass;
I forget to eat my food.
5 Because of my loud groaning
I am reduced to skin and bones.
6 I am like a desert owl,
like an owl among the ruins.
7 I lie awake; I have become
like a bird alone on a roof.
8 All day long my enemies taunt me;
those who rail against me use my name as a curse.
9 For I eat ashes as my food
and mingle my drink with tears
10 because of your great wrath,
for you have taken me up and thrown me aside.
11 My days are like the evening shadow;
I wither away like grass.

12 But you, O LORD, sit enthroned forever;
your renown endures through all generations.
13 You will arise and have compassion on Zion,
for it is time to show favor to her;
the appointed time has come.
14 For her stones are dear to your servants;
her very dust moves them to pity.
15 The nations will fear the name of the LORD,
all the kings of the earth will revere your glory.
16 For the LORD will rebuild Zion
and appear in his glory.
17 He will respond to the prayer of the destitute;
he will not despise their plea.

18 Let this be written for a future generation,
that a people not yet created may praise the LORD:
19 "The LORD looked down from his sanctuary on high,
from heaven he viewed the earth,
20 to hear the groans of the prisoners
and release those condemned to death."
21 So the name of the LORD will be declared in Zion
and his praise in Jerusalem
22 when the peoples and the kingdoms
assemble to worship the LORD.
23 In the course of my life[a] he broke my strength;
he cut short my days.
24 So I said:
"Do not take me away, O my God, in the midst of my days;
your years go on through all generations.
25 In the beginning you laid the foundations of the earth,
and the heavens are the work of your hands.
26 They will perish, but you remain;
they will all wear out like a garment.
Like clothing you will change them
and they will be discarded.
27 But you remain the same,
and your years will never end.
28 The children of your servants will live in your presence;
their descendants will be established before you."

Psalm 103

Of David.

1 Praise the LORD, O my soul;
all my inmost being, praise his holy name.
2 Praise the LORD, O my soul,
and forget not all his benefits—
3 who forgives all your sins
and heals all your diseases,
4 who redeems your life from the pit
and crowns you with love and compassion,
5 who satisfies your desires with good things
so that your youth is renewed like the eagle's.

6 The LORD works righteousness
and justice for all the oppressed.

7 He made known his ways to Moses,
his deeds to the people of Israel:
8 The LORD is compassionate and gracious,
slow to anger, abounding in love.
9 He will not always accuse,
nor will he harbor his anger forever;
10 he does not treat us as our sins deserve
or repay us according to our iniquities.
11 For as high as the heavens are above the earth,

---

[a] 23 Or *By his power*

WEEKEND

choosing a church

We moved to a new city recently, so we're looking for a church home that we both appreciate. We've shopped around a little bit, but so far we haven't found a church where we both want to get involved. What suggestions do you have for choosing a church together?

Finding a church you both feel good about and want to offer your time and resources to is vital to the spiritual health of your marriage. The following guidelines may help you in that process.

1. Be a good consumer. Many couples choose a church because of its location or its architecture or any number of superficial reasons. Instead focus on finding a church that shows true signs of health. In *A Faith That Hurts, a Faith That Heals*, Stephen Arterburn and Jack Felton describe a healthy church as one that is not controlling, blaming, delusional, distrustful, and so on. Make a list of what you want in a church and shop around.

2. Remember, there is no perfect church. Once you have made a list of what you are looking for in a church, you may still shop around and come up empty if you don't remind yourself that no church is perfect. Every church is going to have deficits. Even the spectacularly successful Jerusalem church in the book of Acts had occasional problems, and yours won't be better than that. So don't waste your time looking for perfection.

3. Attend church regularly. Once you have settled into a church home, make worship a consistent part of your life together. Don't fall into the weekly debate of "Shall we go or not?" Instead, think of church attendance as a necessary fueling station for your soul. Just as your automobile needs to be refilled with gasoline, so your relationship with God needs to be tuned up at church.

4. Support your church financially. If you are attending a church regularly, you should contribute to its ongoing ministry in your life and marriage. That means tithing your income. Make this a regular part of your budget and pay it just as you would any other expense. Supporting the work of the church not only helps the church, it helps you and your marriage to invest in something important too.

5. Try to find one area where you can serve together. Many Christian couples arrive at church and head off in separate directions. While you may certainly have some independent realms of service, try to get involved in a ministry as a couple. Whether teaching a class, singing together in the choir, or co-directing an outreach ministry, look for something that brings you together in the house of God.

6. Maintain a healthy balance. While it is valuable to find a place of service together, it is equally important not to overdo it. We have seen couples get so involved in their church that they lose touch with each other. You need to have time in your week that is just for you. If you find that church activities keep you from having family time together, you know you have crossed the line and it's time to realign your priorities.

7. Don't bad-mouth the church. Since no church, no matter how great, is perfect, you don't need to spend time griping about this and that. You don't even need to point out the flaws together. You can think critically about your church and its actions, but you don't need to nitpick. Make it a practice to discuss problems you see only with those in the church who can make a difference, and work from the assumption that fellow members and leaders are well meaning. If you gripe about a problem, you should be the first one volunteering to make an improvement.

—DR. LES PARROTT III AND DR. LESLIE PARROTT

church shopping

Sit down together and decide what is important for each of you in a church. Use the questions below to guide (but not limit) your thinking.

1. What did we like about churches we've attended before?
2. What denominational or theological criteria are important to us?
3. In what activities and leadership positions would we like to serve?
4. What kind of worship music do we prefer? What will we tolerate?
5. What prevents or distracts us from worshiping within a service? Is this a real hindrance or just baggage from a previous experience?
6. How would we like to worship in the future? As a couple, while the kids are in the nursery or attending Sunday school, or as a family?
7. What services would we be most likely to attend regularly?
8. Do we agree with the church's giving priorities regarding missions and helping hurting people? Are these the kinds of activities we'd like to support on our own?
9. Does the congregation seem open and accepting of new people?
10. What kind of additional teaching or training is available?

HOW ARE WE DOING?

let's make a DATE

WORSHIP SUNDAES

This week, pick up all the fixings for an old-fashioned ice cream sundae to enjoy on Sunday after worshiping with each other at church. Be sure to include sauces, fruits, nuts, sprinkles and plenty of whipped cream. But instead of eating your own creation, spoon-feed it to your spouse and have him or her do the same with you. Then talk about what you enjoyed most at the church service.

FOR YOUR NEXT DEVOTIONAL READING, TURN TO PAGE 652.

LESSONS FROM THE *Bible*

Galatians 5:22–23 describes the "fruit of the Spirit." Read this passage and then answer the following questions:

1. In what ways can a church exhibit the fruit of the Spirit?
2. How can a church help develop the fruit of the Spirit in us individually and as a couple?

so great is his love for those who fear
him;
12 as far as the east is from the west,
so far has he removed our transgressions
from us.
13 As a father has compassion on his
children,
so the LORD has compassion on those
who fear him;
14 for he knows how we are formed,
he remembers that we are dust.
15 As for man, his days are like grass,
he flourishes like a flower of the field;
16 the wind blows over it and it is gone,
and its place remembers it no more.
17 But from everlasting to everlasting
the LORD's love is with those who fear
him,
and his righteousness with their
children's children—
18 with those who keep his covenant
and remember to obey his precepts.

19 The LORD has established his throne in
heaven,
and his kingdom rules over all.

20 Praise the LORD, you his angels,
you mighty ones who do his bidding,
who obey his word.
21 Praise the LORD, all his heavenly hosts,
you his servants who do his will.
22 Praise the LORD, all his works
everywhere in his dominion.

Praise the LORD, O my soul.

Psalm 104

1 Praise the LORD, O my soul.

O LORD my God, you are very great;
you are clothed with splendor and
majesty.
2 He wraps himself in light as with a
garment;
he stretches out the heavens like a tent
3 and lays the beams of his upper
chambers on their waters.
He makes the clouds his chariot
and rides on the wings of the wind.
4 He makes winds his messengers,[a]
flames of fire his servants.

5 He set the earth on its foundations;
it can never be moved.
6 You covered it with the deep as with a
garment;
the waters stood above the
mountains.
7 But at your rebuke the waters fled,
at the sound of your thunder they took
to flight;
8 they flowed over the mountains,
they went down into the valleys,
to the place you assigned for them.
9 You set a boundary they cannot cross;
never again will they cover the earth.

10 He makes springs pour water into the
ravines;
it flows between the mountains.
11 They give water to all the beasts of the
field;
the wild donkeys quench their thirst.
12 The birds of the air nest by the waters;
they sing among the branches.
13 He waters the mountains from his upper
chambers;
the earth is satisfied by the fruit of his
work.
14 He makes grass grow for the cattle,
and plants for man to cultivate—
bringing forth food from the earth:
15 wine that gladdens the heart of man,
oil to make his face shine,
and bread that sustains his heart.
16 The trees of the LORD are well watered,
the cedars of Lebanon that he planted.
17 There the birds make their nests;
the stork has its home in the pine
trees.
18 The high mountains belong to the wild
goats;
the crags are a refuge for the coneys.[b]

19 The moon marks off the seasons,
and the sun knows when to go down.
20 You bring darkness, it becomes night,
and all the beasts of the forest prowl.
21 The lions roar for their prey
and seek their food from God.
22 The sun rises, and they steal away;
they return and lie down in their dens.
23 Then man goes out to his work,
to his labor until evening.

24 How many are your works, O LORD!
In wisdom you made them all;
the earth is full of your creatures.
25 There is the sea, vast and spacious,
teeming with creatures beyond
number—
living things both large and small.
26 There the ships go to and fro,

a 4 Or *angels* *b* 18 That is, the hyrax or rock badger

and the leviathan, which you formed to
frolic there.

27 These all look to you
to give them their food at the proper
time.
28 When you give it to them,
they gather it up;
when you open your hand,
they are satisfied with good things.
29 When you hide your face,
they are terrified;
when you take away their breath,
they die and return to the dust.
30 When you send your Spirit,
they are created,
and you renew the face of the earth.

31 May the glory of the LORD endure forever;
may the LORD rejoice in his works—
32 he who looks at the earth, and it trembles,
who touches the mountains, and they
smoke.

33 I will sing to the LORD all my life;
I will sing praise to my God as long as I
live.
34 May my meditation be pleasing to him,
as I rejoice in the LORD.
35 But may sinners vanish from the earth
and the wicked be no more.

Praise the LORD, O my soul.

Praise the LORD. [a]

Psalm 105

1 Give thanks to the LORD, call on his
name;
make known among the nations what
he has done.
2 Sing to him, sing praise to him;
tell of all his wonderful acts.
3 Glory in his holy name;
let the hearts of those who seek the
LORD rejoice.
4 Look to the LORD and his strength;
seek his face always.

5 Remember the wonders he has done,
his miracles, and the judgments he
pronounced,
6 O descendants of Abraham his servant,
O sons of Jacob, his chosen ones.
7 He is the LORD our God;
his judgments are in all the earth.

8 He remembers his covenant forever,
the word he commanded, for a
thousand generations,
9 the covenant he made with Abraham,
the oath he swore to Isaac.
10 He confirmed it to Jacob as a decree,
to Israel as an everlasting covenant:
11 "To you I will give the land of Canaan
as the portion you will inherit."

12 When they were but few in number,
few indeed, and strangers in it,
13 they wandered from nation to nation,
from one kingdom to another.
14 He allowed no one to oppress them;
for their sake he rebuked kings:
15 "Do not touch my anointed ones;
do my prophets no harm."
16 He called down famine on the land
and destroyed all their supplies of
food;
17 and he sent a man before them—
Joseph, sold as a slave.
18 They bruised his feet with shackles,
his neck was put in irons,
19 till what he foretold came to pass,
till the word of the LORD proved him
true.
20 The king sent and released him,
the ruler of peoples set him free.
21 He made him master of his household,
ruler over all he possessed,
22 to instruct his princes as he pleased
and teach his elders wisdom.

23 Then Israel entered Egypt;
Jacob lived as an alien in the land of
Ham.
24 The LORD made his people very fruitful;
he made them too numerous for their
foes,
25 whose hearts he turned to hate his people,
to conspire against his servants.
26 He sent Moses his servant,
and Aaron, whom he had chosen.
27 They performed his miraculous signs
among them,
his wonders in the land of Ham.
28 He sent darkness and made the land
dark—
for had they not rebelled against his
words?
29 He turned their waters into blood,
causing their fish to die.
30 Their land teemed with frogs,
which went up into the bedrooms of
their rulers.

a 35 Hebrew *Hallelu Yah*; in the Septuagint this line stands at the beginning of Psalm 105.

LET'S CELEBRATE!

When Americans were recently asked what they were most thankful for, 61 percent said family, 20 percent said children, and about 7 percent said God. It is surely appropriate to be grateful to God for marriage and family. But people who are not particularly thankful for God himself are not only blind, they are poor.

Psalm 105 is a sweeping saga of praise that recalls how God kept his covenant to Israel by delivering his people from bondage and bringing them into the promised land. The heart of Psalm 105 is also the basis for Israel's praise: God keeps his promises. "He remembers his covenant forever . . . the covenant he made with Abraham . . . 'To you I will give the land of Canaan' " (verses 8–11).

As Christian couples we can surely thank God for our marriages and families, but our praise should go deeper than that as we celebrate God's eternal covenant extended to us his people. To the Jews, God promised the land of Canaan; to his church, God promises the new Jerusalem and an eternal life of fulfilled promises.

Give thanks to the LORD, call on his name; make known among the nations what he has done.

— PSALM 105:1

let's talk

- **Let's find a song of praise and sing it together (even if we sing poorly). Then let's tell each other at least three of God's "wonderful acts" in our lives.**
- **How have we seen God preserve our relationship through hard or dangerous times?**
- **What are some of God's blessings that we have enjoyed as a couple as a result of our salvation in Christ?**

According to Psalm 105, God's promises to Israel were fulfilled in three ways. These three aspects of God's faithfulness are still true today for those who have trusted in his promises. They are the reasons for our thankful hearts.

First, we thank God for preserving us as his people when we are in trouble. Verses 12–25 point out how God guarded his vulnerable people. Even while they were slaves for many years in Egypt, God was preserving and protecting the people of Israel.

As couples, we too remember hard times—frightening times— when it seemed we were in great danger or when we suffered deep sorrow. Yet God, true to his word, was guarding and protecting us during that time.

Second, we thank God for his victorious salvation. Verses 26–41 recall how Israel saw Egypt crushed by the ten plagues and Pharaoh and his army drowned in the Red Sea, and then how God provided for his people in the desert.

We see a far greater victory in the death and resurrection of Christ on our behalf. A Christian couple is bonded by this great deliverance of our covenant-keeping God. We rejoice together with all God's people as we sing of our eternal salvation.

Third, verses 42–45 remind God's people to celebrate the extravagant blessings that come with God's gift of salvation.

As a married couple, bonded by our own covenant with God and one another, we can be extravagantly thankful and joyful. We can celebrate together the deep benefits of our relationship with God. It is fine to thank God for our families and health, but our greatest joy is in God's salvation.

—LEE ECLOV

FOR YOUR NEXT DEVOTIONAL READING, TURN TO PAGE 659.

31 He spoke, and there came swarms of flies,
and gnats throughout their country.
32 He turned their rain into hail,
with lightning throughout their land;
33 he struck down their vines and fig trees
and shattered the trees of their country.
34 He spoke, and the locusts came,
grasshoppers without number;
35 they ate up every green thing in their land,
ate up the produce of their soil.
36 Then he struck down all the firstborn in their land,
the firstfruits of all their manhood.

37 He brought out Israel, laden with silver and gold,
and from among their tribes no one faltered.
38 Egypt was glad when they left,
because dread of Israel had fallen on them.
39 He spread out a cloud as a covering,
and a fire to give light at night.
40 They asked, and he brought them quail
and satisfied them with the bread of heaven.
41 He opened the rock, and water gushed out;
like a river it flowed in the desert.

42 For he remembered his holy promise
given to his servant Abraham.
43 He brought out his people with rejoicing,
his chosen ones with shouts of joy;
44 he gave them the lands of the nations,
and they fell heir to what others had toiled for—
45 that they might keep his precepts
and observe his laws.

Praise the LORD.[a]

Psalm 106

1 Praise the LORD.[b]

Give thanks to the LORD, for he is good;
his love endures forever.
2 Who can proclaim the mighty acts of the LORD
or fully declare his praise?
3 Blessed are they who maintain justice,
who constantly do what is right.
4 Remember me, O LORD, when you show favor to your people,
come to my aid when you save them,
5 that I may enjoy the prosperity of your chosen ones,
that I may share in the joy of your nation
and join your inheritance in giving praise.

6 We have sinned, even as our fathers did;
we have done wrong and acted wickedly.
7 When our fathers were in Egypt,
they gave no thought to your miracles;
they did not remember your many kindnesses,
and they rebelled by the sea, the Red Sea.[c]
8 Yet he saved them for his name's sake,
to make his mighty power known.
9 He rebuked the Red Sea, and it dried up;
he led them through the depths as through a desert.
10 He saved them from the hand of the foe;
from the hand of the enemy he redeemed them.
11 The waters covered their adversaries;
not one of them survived.
12 Then they believed his promises
and sang his praise.

13 But they soon forgot what he had done
and did not wait for his counsel.
14 In the desert they gave in to their craving;
in the wasteland they put God to the test.
15 So he gave them what they asked for,
but sent a wasting disease upon them.

16 In the camp they grew envious of Moses
and of Aaron, who was consecrated to the LORD.
17 The earth opened up and swallowed Dathan;
it buried the company of Abiram.
18 Fire blazed among their followers;
a flame consumed the wicked.

19 At Horeb they made a calf
and worshiped an idol cast from metal.
20 They exchanged their Glory
for an image of a bull, which eats grass.
21 They forgot the God who saved them,
who had done great things in Egypt,
22 miracles in the land of Ham
and awesome deeds by the Red Sea.
23 So he said he would destroy them—
had not Moses, his chosen one,

[a] 45 Hebrew *Hallelu Yah* [b] 1 Hebrew *Hallelu Yah*; also in verse 48 [c] 7 Hebrew *Yam Suph*; that is, Sea of Reeds; also in verses 9 and 22

stood in the breach before him
to keep his wrath from destroying them.

24 Then they despised the pleasant land;
they did not believe his promise.
25 They grumbled in their tents
and did not obey the LORD.
26 So he swore to them with uplifted hand
that he would make them fall in the desert,
27 make their descendants fall among the nations
and scatter them throughout the lands.

28 They yoked themselves to the Baal of Peor
and ate sacrifices offered to lifeless gods;
29 they provoked the LORD to anger by their wicked deeds,
and a plague broke out among them.
30 But Phinehas stood up and intervened,
and the plague was checked.
31 This was credited to him as righteousness
for endless generations to come.

32 By the waters of Meribah they angered the LORD,
and trouble came to Moses because of them;
33 for they rebelled against the Spirit of God,
and rash words came from Moses' lips.[a]

34 They did not destroy the peoples
as the LORD had commanded them,
35 but they mingled with the nations
and adopted their customs.
36 They worshiped their idols,
which became a snare to them.
37 They sacrificed their sons
and their daughters to demons.
38 They shed innocent blood,
the blood of their sons and daughters,
whom they sacrificed to the idols of Canaan,
and the land was desecrated by their blood.
39 They defiled themselves by what they did;
by their deeds they prostituted themselves.

40 Therefore the LORD was angry with his people
and abhorred his inheritance.
41 He handed them over to the nations,
and their foes ruled over them.
42 Their enemies oppressed them
and subjected them to their power.
43 Many times he delivered them,
but they were bent on rebellion
and they wasted away in their sin.

44 But he took note of their distress
when he heard their cry;
45 for their sake he remembered his covenant
and out of his great love he relented.
46 He caused them to be pitied
by all who held them captive.

47 Save us, O LORD our God,
and gather us from the nations,
that we may give thanks to your holy name
and glory in your praise.

48 Praise be to the LORD, the God of Israel,
from everlasting to everlasting.
Let all the people say, "Amen!"

Praise the LORD.

BOOK V

Psalms 107–150

Psalm 107

1 Give thanks to the LORD, for he is good;
his love endures forever.
2 Let the redeemed of the LORD say this—
those he redeemed from the hand of the foe,
3 those he gathered from the lands,
from east and west, from north and south.[b]

4 Some wandered in desert wastelands,
finding no way to a city where they could settle.
5 They were hungry and thirsty,
and their lives ebbed away.
6 Then they cried out to the LORD in their trouble,
and he delivered them from their distress.
7 He led them by a straight way
to a city where they could settle.
8 Let them give thanks to the LORD for his unfailing love
and his wonderful deeds for men,
9 for he satisfies the thirsty
and fills the hungry with good things.

10 Some sat in darkness and the deepest gloom,
prisoners suffering in iron chains,

[a] 33 Or *against his spirit, / and rash words came from his lips* [b] 3 Hebrew *north and the sea*

11 for they had rebelled against the words of God
and despised the counsel of the Most High.
12 So he subjected them to bitter labor;
they stumbled, and there was no one to help.
13 Then they cried to the LORD in their trouble,
and he saved them from their distress.
14 He brought them out of darkness and the deepest gloom
and broke away their chains.
15 Let them give thanks to the LORD for his unfailing love
and his wonderful deeds for men,
16 for he breaks down gates of bronze
and cuts through bars of iron.

17 Some became fools through their rebellious ways
and suffered affliction because of their iniquities.
18 They loathed all food
and drew near the gates of death.
19 Then they cried to the LORD in their trouble,
and he saved them from their distress.
20 He sent forth his word and healed them;
he rescued them from the grave.
21 Let them give thanks to the LORD for his unfailing love
and his wonderful deeds for men.
22 Let them sacrifice thank offerings
and tell of his works with songs of joy.

23 Others went out on the sea in ships;
they were merchants on the mighty waters.
24 They saw the works of the LORD,
his wonderful deeds in the deep.
25 For he spoke and stirred up a tempest
that lifted high the waves.
26 They mounted up to the heavens and went down to the depths;
in their peril their courage melted away.
27 They reeled and staggered like drunken men;
they were at their wits' end.
28 Then they cried out to the LORD in their trouble,
and he brought them out of their distress.
29 He stilled the storm to a whisper;
the waves of the sea were hushed.
30 They were glad when it grew calm,
and he guided them to their desired haven.
31 Let them give thanks to the LORD for his unfailing love
and his wonderful deeds for men.
32 Let them exalt him in the assembly of the people
and praise him in the council of the elders.

33 He turned rivers into a desert,
flowing springs into thirsty ground,
34 and fruitful land into a salt waste,
because of the wickedness of those who lived there.
35 He turned the desert into pools of water
and the parched ground into flowing springs;
36 there he brought the hungry to live,
and they founded a city where they could settle.
37 They sowed fields and planted vineyards
that yielded a fruitful harvest;
38 he blessed them, and their numbers greatly increased,
and he did not let their herds diminish.

39 Then their numbers decreased, and they were humbled
by oppression, calamity and sorrow;
40 he who pours contempt on nobles
made them wander in a trackless waste.
41 But he lifted the needy out of their affliction
and increased their families like flocks.
42 The upright see and rejoice,
but all the wicked shut their mouths.

43 Whoever is wise, let him heed these things
and consider the great love of the LORD.

Psalm 108

A song. A psalm of David.

1 My heart is steadfast, O God;
I will sing and make music with all my soul.
2 Awake, harp and lyre!
I will awaken the dawn.
3 I will praise you, O LORD, among the nations;
I will sing of you among the peoples.
4 For great is your love, higher than the heavens;
your faithfulness reaches to the skies.

5 Be exalted, O God, above the heavens,
and let your glory be over all the earth.

6 Save us and help us with your right hand,
that those you love may be delivered.
7 God has spoken from his sanctuary:
"In triumph I will parcel out Shechem
and measure off the Valley of Succoth.
8 Gilead is mine, Manasseh is mine;
Ephraim is my helmet,
Judah my scepter.
9 Moab is my washbasin,
upon Edom I toss my sandal;
over Philistia I shout in triumph."

10 Who will bring me to the fortified city?
Who will lead me to Edom?
11 Is it not you, O God, you who have
rejected us
and no longer go out with our armies?
12 Give us aid against the enemy,
for the help of man is worthless.
13 With God we will gain the victory,
and he will trample down our enemies.

Psalm 109

For the director of music. Of David.
A psalm.

1 O God, whom I praise,
do not remain silent,
2 for wicked and deceitful men
have opened their mouths against me;
they have spoken against me with lying
tongues.
3 With words of hatred they surround me;
they attack me without cause.
4 In return for my friendship they accuse
me,
but I am a man of prayer.
5 They repay me evil for good,
and hatred for my friendship.

6 Appoint[a] an evil man[b] to oppose him;
let an accuser[c] stand at his right hand.
7 When he is tried, let him be found
guilty,
and may his prayers condemn him.
8 May his days be few;
may another take his place of
leadership.
9 May his children be fatherless
and his wife a widow.
10 May his children be wandering beggars;
may they be driven[d] from their ruined
homes.
11 May a creditor seize all he has;
may strangers plunder the fruits of his
labor.
12 May no one extend kindness to him
or take pity on his fatherless children.
13 May his descendants be cut off,
their names blotted out from the next
generation.
14 May the iniquity of his fathers be
remembered before the LORD;
may the sin of his mother never be
blotted out.
15 May their sins always remain before the
LORD,
that he may cut off the memory of
them from the earth.

16 For he never thought of doing a
kindness,
but hounded to death the poor
and the needy and the brokenhearted.
17 He loved to pronounce a curse—
may it[e] come on him;
he found no pleasure in blessing—
may it be[f] far from him.
18 He wore cursing as his garment;
it entered into his body like water,
into his bones like oil.
19 May it be like a cloak wrapped about
him,
like a belt tied forever around him.
20 May this be the LORD's payment to my
accusers,
to those who speak evil of me.

21 But you, O Sovereign LORD,
deal well with me for your name's sake;
out of the goodness of your love,
deliver me.
22 For I am poor and needy,
and my heart is wounded within me.
23 I fade away like an evening shadow;
I am shaken off like a locust.
24 My knees give way from fasting;
my body is thin and gaunt.
25 I am an object of scorn to my accusers;
when they see me, they shake their
heads.

26 Help me, O LORD my God;
save me in accordance with your love.
27 Let them know that it is your hand,
that you, O LORD, have done it.
28 They may curse, but you will bless;
when they attack they will be put to
shame,

[a] 6 Or ⌞*They say:*⌟ *"Appoint* (with quotation marks at the end of verse 19) [b] 6 Or *the Evil One* [c] 6 Or *let Satan* [d] 10 Septuagint; Hebrew *sought* [e] 17 Or *curse, / and it has* [f] 17 Or *blessing, / and it is*

but your servant will rejoice.
29 My accusers will be clothed with disgrace
and wrapped in shame as in a cloak.

30 With my mouth I will greatly extol the
LORD;
in the great throng I will praise him.
31 For he stands at the right hand of the
needy one,
to save his life from those who
condemn him.

Psalm 110

Of David. A psalm.

1 The LORD says to my Lord:
"Sit at my right hand
until I make your enemies
a footstool for your feet."

2 The LORD will extend your mighty scepter
from Zion;
you will rule in the midst of your
enemies.
3 Your troops will be willing
on your day of battle.
Arrayed in holy majesty,
from the womb of the dawn
you will receive the dew of your
youth.[a]

4 The LORD has sworn
and will not change his mind:
"You are a priest forever,
in the order of Melchizedek."

5 The Lord is at your right hand;
he will crush kings on the day of his
wrath.
6 He will judge the nations, heaping up the
dead
and crushing the rulers of the whole
earth.
7 He will drink from a brook beside the
way[b];
therefore he will lift up his head.

Psalm 111[c]

1 Praise the LORD.[d]

I will extol the LORD with all my heart
in the council of the upright and in the
assembly.

2 Great are the works of the LORD;
they are pondered by all who delight in
them.
3 Glorious and majestic are his deeds,
and his righteousness endures forever.
4 He has caused his wonders to be
remembered;
the LORD is gracious and
compassionate.
5 He provides food for those who fear him;
he remembers his covenant forever.
6 He has shown his people the power of his
works,
giving them the lands of other nations.
7 The works of his hands are faithful and
just;
all his precepts are trustworthy.
8 They are steadfast for ever and ever,
done in faithfulness and uprightness.
9 He provided redemption for his people;
he ordained his covenant forever—
holy and awesome is his name.

10 The fear of the LORD is the beginning of
wisdom;
all who follow his precepts have good
understanding.
To him belongs eternal praise.

Psalm 112[c]

1 Praise the LORD.[d]

Blessed is the man who fears the LORD,
who finds great delight in his
commands.

2 His children will be mighty in the land;
the generation of the upright will be
blessed.
3 Wealth and riches are in his house,
and his righteousness endures forever.
4 Even in darkness light dawns for the
upright,
for the gracious and compassionate and
righteous man.[e]
5 Good will come to him who is generous
and lends freely,
who conducts his affairs with justice.
6 Surely he will never be shaken;
a righteous man will be remembered
forever.
7 He will have no fear of bad news;
his heart is steadfast, trusting in the
LORD.
8 His heart is secure, he will have no fear;

a 3 Or / *your young men will come to you like the dew* b 7 Or / *The One who grants succession will set him in authority* c *This psalm is an acrostic poem, the lines of which begin with the successive letters of the Hebrew alphabet.* d 1 Hebrew *Hallelu Yah* e 4 Or / *for ⌊the LORD⌋ is gracious and compassionate and righteous*

in the end he will look in triumph on
his foes.
9 He has scattered abroad his gifts to the
poor,
his righteousness endures forever;
his horn[a] will be lifted high in honor.

10 The wicked man will see and be vexed,
he will gnash his teeth and waste
away;
the longings of the wicked will come to
nothing.

Psalm 113

1 Praise the LORD.[b]

Praise, O servants of the LORD,
praise the name of the LORD.
2 Let the name of the LORD be praised,
both now and forevermore.
3 From the rising of the sun to the place
where it sets,
the name of the LORD is to be
praised.

4 The LORD is exalted over all the nations,
his glory above the heavens.
5 Who is like the LORD our God,
the One who sits enthroned on high,
6 who stoops down to look
on the heavens and the earth?

7 He raises the poor from the dust
and lifts the needy from the ash heap;
8 he seats them with princes,
with the princes of their people.
9 He settles the barren woman in her home
as a happy mother of children.

Praise the LORD.

Psalm 114

1 When Israel came out of Egypt,
the house of Jacob from a people of
foreign tongue,
2 Judah became God's sanctuary,
Israel his dominion.

3 The sea looked and fled,
the Jordan turned back;
4 the mountains skipped like rams,
the hills like lambs.

5 Why was it, O sea, that you fled,
O Jordan, that you turned back,
6 you mountains, that you skipped like
rams,
you hills, like lambs?

7 Tremble, O earth, at the presence of the
Lord,
at the presence of the God of Jacob,
8 who turned the rock into a pool,
the hard rock into springs of water.

Psalm 115

1 Not to us, O LORD, not to us
but to your name be the glory,
because of your love and faithfulness.

2 Why do the nations say,
"Where is their God?"
3 Our God is in heaven;
he does whatever pleases him.
4 But their idols are silver and gold,
made by the hands of men.
5 They have mouths, but cannot speak,
eyes, but they cannot see;
6 they have ears, but cannot hear,
noses, but they cannot smell;
7 they have hands, but cannot feel,
feet, but they cannot walk;
nor can they utter a sound with their
throats.
8 Those who make them will be like them,
and so will all who trust in them.

9 O house of Israel, trust in the LORD—
he is their help and shield.
10 O house of Aaron, trust in the LORD—
he is their help and shield.
11 You who fear him, trust in the LORD—
he is their help and shield.

12 The LORD remembers us and will bless
us:
He will bless the house of Israel,
he will bless the house of Aaron,
13 he will bless those who fear the LORD—
small and great alike.

14 May the LORD make you increase,
both you and your children.
15 May you be blessed by the LORD,
the Maker of heaven and earth.

16 The highest heavens belong to the LORD,
but the earth he has given to man.
17 It is not the dead who praise the LORD,
those who go down to silence;
18 it is we who extol the LORD,
both now and forevermore.

Praise the LORD.[c]

---

[a] 9 *Horn* here symbolizes dignity. [b] 1 Hebrew *Hallelu Yah*; also in verse 9 [c] 18 Hebrew *Hallelu Yah*

KIDS: BLESSED TROUBLES

He settles the barren woman in her home as a happy mother of children.

— PSALM 113:9

let's talk

- What are some ways that children (ours or others') have blessed our marriage?
- If we have children, what are some ways that they have put stress on our relationship?
- What are some things we can do to strengthen our marriage while we're struggling with the stresses of parenting?

When you hold your newborn baby for the first time and she smiles at you or blows a bubble, you forget about the hours you just spent in intense labor. You forget about the swollen ankles and heartburn of the past few months. All you know is that God heard your request for a baby and has blessed the two of you with a child of your own.

But then that baby throws up on your shoulder and refuses to sleep at night. She turns four and won't wear socks. She turns six and brings head lice home from school. She only eats grapes and cheese for weeks on end, won't change her underwear without a battle, and loves making up songs about toilets that burp.

When you don't have children, parenthood sounds idyllic. You envision babies cooing and preschoolers holding your hand. You imagine your child drawing you pictures, handing you flowers, kissing your nose and giggling at your jokes.

Certainly there are such moments, but there are also nights without sleep, hours of tedium and tension, trips to the emergency room, tantrums in the mall.

It's been said that the trouble with children is that when they're not a lump in your throat, they're a pain in your neck. In those trying times it's tempting to grab your spouse's hand and turn and run. It's either that or turn on each other.

Many times while raising our two daughters, my husband and I admitted that God's "blessing" of children felt more like a "curse," or at least a practical joke. We went through anorexia, car accidents, broken friendships and romances, bad grades, pierced noses and Skittles-colored hair.

We laughed and worried, felt like screaming, cried, prayed and laughed some more—but in the end we never regretted any of the heartaches our children caused because those hard times bonded us to them and to each other.

It seems to me that the greatest blessing of raising children lies in the struggle and difficulty, because it's during those end-of-ourselves times that we as parents discover God's sufficiency. When we feel at our wit's end, we find strength in his wisdom.

God's promise for parents is this: "I can do everything through him who gives me strength" (Philippians 4:13) and "My grace is sufficient for you, for my power is made perfect in weakness" (2 Corinthians 12:9).

We don't know what we are doing most of the time as parents, but thank God that he does! When it comes to raising children, happiness is knowing that God gives his grace, strength and mercy to those who most know they need it.

—NANCY KENNEDY

FOR YOUR NEXT DEVOTIONAL READING, TURN TO PAGE 667.

Psalm 116

1 I love the LORD, for he heard my voice;
he heard my cry for mercy.
2 Because he turned his ear to me,
I will call on him as long as I live.

3 The cords of death entangled me,
the anguish of the grave[a] came upon me;
I was overcome by trouble and sorrow.
4 Then I called on the name of the LORD:
"O LORD, save me!"

5 The LORD is gracious and righteous;
our God is full of compassion.
6 The LORD protects the simplehearted;
when I was in great need, he saved me.

7 Be at rest once more, O my soul,
for the LORD has been good to you.

8 For you, O LORD, have delivered my soul from death,
my eyes from tears,
my feet from stumbling,
9 that I may walk before the LORD
in the land of the living.
10 I believed; therefore[b] I said,
"I am greatly afflicted."
11 And in my dismay I said,
"All men are liars."

12 How can I repay the LORD
for all his goodness to me?
13 I will lift up the cup of salvation
and call on the name of the LORD.
14 I will fulfill my vows to the LORD
in the presence of all his people.

15 Precious in the sight of the LORD
is the death of his saints.
16 O LORD, truly I am your servant;
I am your servant, the son of your maidservant[c];
you have freed me from my chains.

17 I will sacrifice a thank offering to you
and call on the name of the LORD.
18 I will fulfill my vows to the LORD
in the presence of all his people,
19 in the courts of the house of the LORD—
in your midst, O Jerusalem.

Praise the LORD.[d]

Psalm 117

1 Praise the LORD, all you nations;
extol him, all you peoples.
2 For great is his love toward us,
and the faithfulness of the LORD endures forever.

Praise the LORD.[d]

Psalm 118

1 Give thanks to the LORD, for he is good;
his love endures forever.

2 Let Israel say:
"His love endures forever."
3 Let the house of Aaron say:
"His love endures forever."
4 Let those who fear the LORD say:
"His love endures forever."

5 In my anguish I cried to the LORD,
and he answered by setting me free.
6 The LORD is with me; I will not be afraid.
What can man do to me?
7 The LORD is with me; he is my helper.
I will look in triumph on my enemies.

8 It is better to take refuge in the LORD
than to trust in man.
9 It is better to take refuge in the LORD
than to trust in princes.

10 All the nations surrounded me,
but in the name of the LORD I cut them off.
11 They surrounded me on every side,
but in the name of the LORD I cut them off.
12 They swarmed around me like bees,
but they died out as quickly as burning thorns;
in the name of the LORD I cut them off.
13 I was pushed back and about to fall,
but the LORD helped me.
14 The LORD is my strength and my song;
he has become my salvation.

15 Shouts of joy and victory
resound in the tents of the righteous:
"The LORD's right hand has done mighty things!
16 The LORD's right hand is lifted high;
the LORD's right hand has done mighty things!"

17 I will not die but live,
and will proclaim what the LORD has done.
18 The LORD has chastened me severely,
but he has not given me over to death.

[a] 3 Hebrew *Sheol* [b] 10 Or *believed even when* [c] 16 Or *servant, your faithful son* [d] 19,2 Hebrew *Hallelu Yah*

19 Open for me the gates of righteousness;
I will enter and give thanks to the LORD.
20 This is the gate of the LORD
through which the righteous may enter.
21 I will give you thanks, for you answered me;
you have become my salvation.

22 The stone the builders rejected
has become the capstone;
23 the LORD has done this,
and it is marvelous in our eyes.
24 This is the day the LORD has made;
let us rejoice and be glad in it.

25 O LORD, save us;
O LORD, grant us success.
26 Blessed is he who comes in the name of the LORD.
From the house of the LORD we bless you.[a]
27 The LORD is God,
and he has made his light shine upon us.
With boughs in hand, join in the festal procession
up[b] to the horns of the altar.

28 You are my God, and I will give you thanks;
you are my God, and I will exalt you.

29 Give thanks to the LORD, for he is good;
his love endures forever.

Psalm 119[c]

א Aleph

1 Blessed are they whose ways are blameless,
who walk according to the law of the LORD.
2 Blessed are they who keep his statutes
and seek him with all their heart.
3 They do nothing wrong;
they walk in his ways.
4 You have laid down precepts
that are to be fully obeyed.
5 Oh, that my ways were steadfast
in obeying your decrees!
6 Then I would not be put to shame
when I consider all your commands.
7 I will praise you with an upright heart
as I learn your righteous laws.
8 I will obey your decrees;
do not utterly forsake me.

ב Beth

9 How can a young man keep his way pure?
By living according to your word.
10 I seek you with all my heart;
do not let me stray from your commands.
11 I have hidden your word in my heart
that I might not sin against you.
12 Praise be to you, O LORD;
teach me your decrees.
13 With my lips I recount
all the laws that come from your mouth.
14 I rejoice in following your statutes
as one rejoices in great riches.
15 I meditate on your precepts
and consider your ways.
16 I delight in your decrees;
I will not neglect your word.

ג Gimel

17 Do good to your servant, and I will live;
I will obey your word.
18 Open my eyes that I may see
wonderful things in your law.
19 I am a stranger on earth;
do not hide your commands from me.
20 My soul is consumed with longing
for your laws at all times.
21 You rebuke the arrogant, who are cursed
and who stray from your commands.
22 Remove from me scorn and contempt,
for I keep your statutes.
23 Though rulers sit together and slander me,
your servant will meditate on your decrees.
24 Your statutes are my delight;
they are my counselors.

ד Daleth

25 I am laid low in the dust;
preserve my life according to your word.
26 I recounted my ways and you answered me;
teach me your decrees.
27 Let me understand the teaching of your precepts;
then I will meditate on your wonders.
28 My soul is weary with sorrow;
strengthen me according to your word.

---

[a] 26 The Hebrew is plural. [b] 27 Or *Bind the festal sacrifice with ropes / and take it* [c] *This psalm is an acrostic poem; the verses of each stanza begin with the same letter of the Hebrew alphabet.*

29 Keep me from deceitful ways;
be gracious to me through your law.
30 I have chosen the way of truth;
I have set my heart on your laws.
31 I hold fast to your statutes, O LORD;
do not let me be put to shame.
32 I run in the path of your commands,
for you have set my heart free.

ה He

33 Teach me, O LORD, to follow your decrees;
then I will keep them to the end.
34 Give me understanding, and I will keep your law
and obey it with all my heart.
35 Direct me in the path of your commands,
for there I find delight.
36 Turn my heart toward your statutes
and not toward selfish gain.
37 Turn my eyes away from worthless things;
preserve my life according to your word.[a]
38 Fulfill your promise to your servant,
so that you may be feared.
39 Take away the disgrace I dread,
for your laws are good.
40 How I long for your precepts!
Preserve my life in your righteousness.

ו Waw

41 May your unfailing love come to me, O LORD,
your salvation according to your promise;
42 then I will answer the one who taunts me,
for I trust in your word.
43 Do not snatch the word of truth from my mouth,
for I have put my hope in your laws.
44 I will always obey your law,
for ever and ever.
45 I will walk about in freedom,
for I have sought out your precepts.
46 I will speak of your statutes before kings
and will not be put to shame,
47 for I delight in your commands
because I love them.
48 I lift up my hands to[b] your commands, which I love,
and I meditate on your decrees.

ז Zayin

49 Remember your word to your servant,
for you have given me hope.
50 My comfort in my suffering is this:
Your promise preserves my life.
51 The arrogant mock me without restraint,
but I do not turn from your law.
52 I remember your ancient laws, O LORD,
and I find comfort in them.
53 Indignation grips me because of the wicked,
who have forsaken your law.
54 Your decrees are the theme of my song
wherever I lodge.
55 In the night I remember your name, O LORD,
and I will keep your law.
56 This has been my practice:
I obey your precepts.

ח Heth

57 You are my portion, O LORD;
I have promised to obey your words.
58 I have sought your face with all my heart;
be gracious to me according to your promise.
59 I have considered my ways
and have turned my steps to your statutes.
60 I will hasten and not delay
to obey your commands.
61 Though the wicked bind me with ropes,
I will not forget your law.
62 At midnight I rise to give you thanks
for your righteous laws.
63 I am a friend to all who fear you,
to all who follow your precepts.
64 The earth is filled with your love, O LORD;
teach me your decrees.

ט Teth

65 Do good to your servant
according to your word, O LORD.
66 Teach me knowledge and good judgment,
for I believe in your commands.
67 Before I was afflicted I went astray,
but now I obey your word.
68 You are good, and what you do is good;
teach me your decrees.
69 Though the arrogant have smeared me with lies,
I keep your precepts with all my heart.
70 Their hearts are callous and unfeeling,
but I delight in your law.

---

[a] 37 Two manuscripts of the Masoretic Text and Dead Sea Scrolls; most manuscripts of the Masoretic Text *life in your way*
[b] 48 Or *for*

71 It was good for me to be afflicted
so that I might learn your decrees.
72 The law from your mouth is more precious to me
than thousands of pieces of silver and gold.

י Yodh

73 Your hands made me and formed me;
give me understanding to learn your commands.
74 May those who fear you rejoice when they see me,
for I have put my hope in your word.
75 I know, O LORD, that your laws are righteous,
and in faithfulness you have afflicted me.
76 May your unfailing love be my comfort,
according to your promise to your servant.
77 Let your compassion come to me that I may live,
for your law is my delight.
78 May the arrogant be put to shame for wronging me without cause;
but I will meditate on your precepts.
79 May those who fear you turn to me,
those who understand your statutes.
80 May my heart be blameless toward your decrees,
that I may not be put to shame.

כ Kaph

81 My soul faints with longing for your salvation,
but I have put my hope in your word.
82 My eyes fail, looking for your promise;
I say, "When will you comfort me?"
83 Though I am like a wineskin in the smoke,
I do not forget your decrees.
84 How long must your servant wait?
When will you punish my persecutors?
85 The arrogant dig pitfalls for me,
contrary to your law.
86 All your commands are trustworthy;
help me, for men persecute me without cause.
87 They almost wiped me from the earth,
but I have not forsaken your precepts.
88 Preserve my life according to your love,
and I will obey the statutes of your mouth.

ל Lamedh

89 Your word, O LORD, is eternal;
it stands firm in the heavens.
90 Your faithfulness continues through all generations;
you established the earth, and it endures.
91 Your laws endure to this day,
for all things serve you.
92 If your law had not been my delight,
I would have perished in my affliction.
93 I will never forget your precepts,
for by them you have preserved my life.
94 Save me, for I am yours;
I have sought out your precepts.
95 The wicked are waiting to destroy me,
but I will ponder your statutes.
96 To all perfection I see a limit;
but your commands are boundless.

מ Mem

97 Oh, how I love your law!
I meditate on it all day long.
98 Your commands make me wiser than my enemies,
for they are ever with me.
99 I have more insight than all my teachers,
for I meditate on your statutes.
100 I have more understanding than the elders,
for I obey your precepts.
101 I have kept my feet from every evil path
so that I might obey your word.
102 I have not departed from your laws,
for you yourself have taught me.
103 How sweet are your words to my taste,
sweeter than honey to my mouth!
104 I gain understanding from your precepts;
therefore I hate every wrong path.

נ Nun

105 Your word is a lamp to my feet
and a light for my path.
106 I have taken an oath and confirmed it,
that I will follow your righteous laws.
107 I have suffered much;
preserve my life, O LORD, according to your word.
108 Accept, O LORD, the willing praise of my mouth,
and teach me your laws.
109 Though I constantly take my life in my hands,
I will not forget your law.
110 The wicked have set a snare for me,
but I have not strayed from your precepts.

111 Your statutes are my heritage forever;
they are the joy of my heart.
112 My heart is set on keeping your decrees
to the very end.

ס Samekh

113 I hate double-minded men,
but I love your law.
114 You are my refuge and my shield;
I have put my hope in your word.
115 Away from me, you evildoers,
that I may keep the commands of my God!
116 Sustain me according to your promise, and I will live;
do not let my hopes be dashed.
117 Uphold me, and I will be delivered;
I will always have regard for your decrees.
118 You reject all who stray from your decrees,
for their deceitfulness is in vain.
119 All the wicked of the earth you discard like dross;
therefore I love your statutes.
120 My flesh trembles in fear of you;
I stand in awe of your laws.

ע Ayin

121 I have done what is righteous and just;
do not leave me to my oppressors.
122 Ensure your servant's well-being;
let not the arrogant oppress me.
123 My eyes fail, looking for your salvation,
looking for your righteous promise.
124 Deal with your servant according to your love
and teach me your decrees.
125 I am your servant; give me discernment
that I may understand your statutes.
126 It is time for you to act, O LORD;
your law is being broken.
127 Because I love your commands
more than gold, more than pure gold,
128 and because I consider all your precepts right,
I hate every wrong path.

פ Pe

129 Your statutes are wonderful;
therefore I obey them.
130 The unfolding of your words gives light;
it gives understanding to the simple.
131 I open my mouth and pant,
longing for your commands.
132 Turn to me and have mercy on me,
as you always do to those who love your name.
133 Direct my footsteps according to your word;
let no sin rule over me.
134 Redeem me from the oppression of men,
that I may obey your precepts.
135 Make your face shine upon your servant
and teach me your decrees.
136 Streams of tears flow from my eyes,
for your law is not obeyed.

צ Tsadhe

137 Righteous are you, O LORD,
and your laws are right.
138 The statutes you have laid down are righteous;
they are fully trustworthy.
139 My zeal wears me out,
for my enemies ignore your words.
140 Your promises have been thoroughly tested,
and your servant loves them.
141 Though I am lowly and despised,
I do not forget your precepts.
142 Your righteousness is everlasting
and your law is true.
143 Trouble and distress have come upon me,
but your commands are my delight.
144 Your statutes are forever right;
give me understanding that I may live.

ק Qoph

145 I call with all my heart; answer me, O LORD,
and I will obey your decrees.
146 I call out to you; save me
and I will keep your statutes.
147 I rise before dawn and cry for help;
I have put my hope in your word.
148 My eyes stay open through the watches of the night,
that I may meditate on your promises.
149 Hear my voice in accordance with your love;
preserve my life, O LORD, according to your laws.
150 Those who devise wicked schemes are near,
but they are far from your law.
151 Yet you are near, O LORD,
and all your commands are true.
152 Long ago I learned from your statutes
that you established them to last forever.

ר Resh

153 Look upon my suffering and deliver me,
for I have not forgotten your law.
154 Defend my cause and redeem me;
preserve my life according to your promise.

155 Salvation is far from the wicked,
for they do not seek out your decrees.
156 Your compassion is great, O LORD;
preserve my life according to your laws.
157 Many are the foes who persecute me,
but I have not turned from your statutes.
158 I look on the faithless with loathing,
for they do not obey your word.
159 See how I love your precepts;
preserve my life, O LORD, according to your love.
160 All your words are true;
all your righteous laws are eternal.

ש Sin and Shin

161 Rulers persecute me without cause,
but my heart trembles at your word.
162 I rejoice in your promise
like one who finds great spoil.
163 I hate and abhor falsehood
but I love your law.
164 Seven times a day I praise you
for your righteous laws.
165 Great peace have they who love your law,
and nothing can make them stumble.
166 I wait for your salvation, O LORD,
and I follow your commands.
167 I obey your statutes,
for I love them greatly.
168 I obey your precepts and your statutes,
for all my ways are known to you.

ת Taw

169 May my cry come before you, O LORD;
give me understanding according to your word.
170 May my supplication come before you;
deliver me according to your promise.
171 May my lips overflow with praise,
for you teach me your decrees.
172 May my tongue sing of your word,
for all your commands are righteous.
173 May your hand be ready to help me,
for I have chosen your precepts.
174 I long for your salvation, O LORD,
and your law is my delight.
175 Let me live that I may praise you,
and may your laws sustain me.
176 I have strayed like a lost sheep.
Seek your servant,
for I have not forgotten your commands.

Psalm 120

A song of ascents.

1 I call on the LORD in my distress,
and he answers me.
2 Save me, O LORD, from lying lips
and from deceitful tongues.
3 What will he do to you,
and what more besides, O deceitful tongue?
4 He will punish you with a warrior's sharp arrows,
with burning coals of the broom tree.

5 Woe to me that I dwell in Meshech,
that I live among the tents of Kedar!
6 Too long have I lived
among those who hate peace.
7 I am a man of peace;
but when I speak, they are for war.

Psalm 121

A song of ascents.

1 I lift up my eyes to the hills—
where does my help come from?
2 My help comes from the LORD,
the Maker of heaven and earth.
3 He will not let your foot slip—
he who watches over you will not slumber;
4 indeed, he who watches over Israel
will neither slumber nor sleep.
5 The LORD watches over you—
the LORD is your shade at your right hand;
6 the sun will not harm you by day,
nor the moon by night.

7 The LORD will keep you from all harm—
he will watch over your life;
8 the LORD will watch over your coming and going
both now and forevermore.

Psalm 122

A song of ascents. Of David.

1 I rejoiced with those who said to me,
"Let us go to the house of the LORD."
2 Our feet are standing
in your gates, O Jerusalem.

3 Jerusalem is built like a city
that is closely compacted together.
4 That is where the tribes go up,
the tribes of the LORD,
to praise the name of the LORD
according to the statute given to Israel.
5 There the thrones for judgment stand,
the thrones of the house of David.

6 Pray for the peace of Jerusalem:
"May those who love you be secure.
7 May there be peace within your walls
and security within your citadels."
8 For the sake of my brothers and friends,
I will say, "Peace be within you."
9 For the sake of the house of the LORD our God,
I will seek your prosperity.

Psalm 123

A song of ascents.

1 I lift up my eyes to you,
to you whose throne is in heaven.
2 As the eyes of slaves look to the hand of their master,
as the eyes of a maid look to the hand of her mistress,
so our eyes look to the LORD our God,
till he shows us his mercy.

3 Have mercy on us, O LORD, have mercy on us,
for we have endured much contempt.
4 We have endured much ridicule from the proud,
much contempt from the arrogant.

Psalm 124

A song of ascents. Of David.

1 If the LORD had not been on our side—
let Israel say—
2 if the LORD had not been on our side
when men attacked us,
3 when their anger flared against us,
they would have swallowed us alive;
4 the flood would have engulfed us,
the torrent would have swept over us,
5 the raging waters
would have swept us away.

6 Praise be to the LORD,
who has not let us be torn by their teeth.
7 We have escaped like a bird
out of the fowler's snare;
the snare has been broken,
and we have escaped.
8 Our help is in the name of the LORD,
the Maker of heaven and earth.

Psalm 125

A song of ascents.

1 Those who trust in the LORD are like Mount Zion,
which cannot be shaken but endures forever.
2 As the mountains surround Jerusalem,
so the LORD surrounds his people
both now and forevermore.

3 The scepter of the wicked will not remain
over the land allotted to the righteous,
for then the righteous might use
their hands to do evil.

4 Do good, O LORD, to those who are good,
to those who are upright in heart.
5 But those who turn to crooked ways
the LORD will banish with the evildoers.

Peace be upon Israel.

Psalm 126

A song of ascents.

1 When the LORD brought back the captives to[a] Zion,
we were like men who dreamed.[b]
2 Our mouths were filled with laughter,
our tongues with songs of joy.
Then it was said among the nations,
"The LORD has done great things for them."
3 The LORD has done great things for us,
and we are filled with joy.

4 Restore our fortunes,[c] O LORD,
like streams in the Negev.
5 Those who sow in tears
will reap with songs of joy.
6 He who goes out weeping,
carrying seed to sow,
will return with songs of joy,
carrying sheaves with him.

Psalm 127

A song of ascents. Of Solomon.

1 Unless the LORD builds the house,
its builders labor in vain.
Unless the LORD watches over the city,
the watchmen stand guard in vain.
2 In vain you rise early
and stay up late,

[a] 1 Or *LORD restored the fortunes of* [b] 1 Or *men restored to health* [c] 4 Or *Bring back our captives*

or go to my bed—
4 I will allow no sleep to my eyes,
no slumber to my eyelids,
5 till I find a place for the LORD,
a dwelling for the Mighty One of Jacob."

6 We heard it in Ephrathah,
we came upon it in the fields of Jaar[a]: [b]
7 "Let us go to his dwelling place;
let us worship at his footstool—
8 arise, O LORD, and come to your resting place,
you and the ark of your might.
9 May your priests be clothed with righteousness;
may your saints sing for joy."

10 For the sake of David your servant,
do not reject your anointed one.

11 The LORD swore an oath to David,
a sure oath that he will not revoke:
"One of your own descendants
I will place on your throne—
12 if your sons keep my covenant
and the statutes I teach them,
then their sons will sit
on your throne for ever and ever."

13 For the LORD has chosen Zion,
he has desired it for his dwelling:
14 "This is my resting place for ever and ever;
here I will sit enthroned, for I have desired it—
15 I will bless her with abundant provisions;
her poor will I satisfy with food.
16 I will clothe her priests with salvation,
and her saints will ever sing for joy.

17 "Here I will make a horn[c] grow for David
and set up a lamp for my anointed one.
18 I will clothe his enemies with shame,
but the crown on his head will be resplendent."

Psalm 133

A song of ascents. Of David.

1 How good and pleasant it is
when brothers live together in unity!
2 It is like precious oil poured on the head,
running down on the beard,
running down on Aaron's beard,
down upon the collar of his robes.
3 It is as if the dew of Hermon
were falling on Mount Zion.
For there the LORD bestows his blessing,
even life forevermore.

Psalm 134

A song of ascents.

1 Praise the LORD, all you servants of the LORD
who minister by night in the house of the LORD.
2 Lift up your hands in the sanctuary
and praise the LORD.

3 May the LORD, the Maker of heaven and earth,
bless you from Zion.

Psalm 135

1 Praise the LORD.[d]

Praise the name of the LORD;
praise him, you servants of the LORD,
2 you who minister in the house of the LORD,
in the courts of the house of our God.

3 Praise the LORD, for the LORD is good;
sing praise to his name, for that is pleasant.
4 For the LORD has chosen Jacob to be his own,
Israel to be his treasured possession.

5 I know that the LORD is great,
that our Lord is greater than all gods.
6 The LORD does whatever pleases him,
in the heavens and on the earth,
in the seas and all their depths.
7 He makes clouds rise from the ends of the earth;
he sends lightning with the rain
and brings out the wind from his storehouses.

8 He struck down the firstborn of Egypt,
the firstborn of men and animals.
9 He sent his signs and wonders into your midst, O Egypt,
against Pharaoh and all his servants.
10 He struck down many nations
and killed mighty kings—
11 Sihon king of the Amorites,
Og king of Bashan
and all the kings of Canaan—

[a] 6 That is, Kiriath Jearim [b] 6 Or *heard of it in Ephrathah, / we found it in the fields of Jaar.* (And no quotes around verses 7-9)
[c] *17 Horn* here symbolizes strong one, that is, king. [d] *1* Hebrew *Hallelu Yah*; also in verses 3 and 21

12 and he gave their land as an inheritance,
an inheritance to his people Israel.

13 Your name, O LORD, endures forever,
your renown, O LORD, through all generations.
14 For the LORD will vindicate his people
and have compassion on his servants.

15 The idols of the nations are silver and gold,
made by the hands of men.
16 They have mouths, but cannot speak,
eyes, but they cannot see;
17 they have ears, but cannot hear,
nor is there breath in their mouths.
18 Those who make them will be like them,
and so will all who trust in them.

19 O house of Israel, praise the LORD;
O house of Aaron, praise the LORD;
20 O house of Levi, praise the LORD;
you who fear him, praise the LORD.
21 Praise be to the LORD from Zion,
to him who dwells in Jerusalem.

Praise the LORD.

Psalm 136

1 Give thanks to the LORD, for he is good.
His love endures forever.
2 Give thanks to the God of gods.
His love endures forever.
3 Give thanks to the Lord of lords:
His love endures forever.

4 to him who alone does great wonders,
His love endures forever.
5 who by his understanding made the heavens,
His love endures forever.
6 who spread out the earth upon the waters,
His love endures forever.
7 who made the great lights—
His love endures forever.
8 the sun to govern the day,
His love endures forever.
9 the moon and stars to govern the night;
His love endures forever.

10 to him who struck down the firstborn of Egypt
His love endures forever.
11 and brought Israel out from among them
His love endures forever.
12 with a mighty hand and outstretched arm;
His love endures forever.
13 to him who divided the Red Sea[a] asunder
His love endures forever.
14 and brought Israel through the midst of it,
His love endures forever.
15 but swept Pharaoh and his army into the Red Sea;
His love endures forever.

16 to him who led his people through the desert,
His love endures forever.
17 who struck down great kings,
His love endures forever.
18 and killed mighty kings—
His love endures forever.
19 Sihon king of the Amorites
His love endures forever.
20 and Og king of Bashan—
His love endures forever.
21 and gave their land as an inheritance,
His love endures forever.
22 an inheritance to his servant Israel;
His love endures forever.

23 to the One who remembered us in our low estate
His love endures forever.
24 and freed us from our enemies,
His love endures forever.
25 and who gives food to every creature.
His love endures forever.

26 Give thanks to the God of heaven.
His love endures forever.

Psalm 137

1 By the rivers of Babylon we sat and wept
when we remembered Zion.
2 There on the poplars
we hung our harps,
3 for there our captors asked us for songs,
our tormentors demanded songs of joy;
they said, "Sing us one of the songs of Zion!"

4 How can we sing the songs of the LORD
while in a foreign land?
5 If I forget you, O Jerusalem,
may my right hand forget ⌊its skill⌋.
6 May my tongue cling to the roof of my mouth
if I do not remember you,
if I do not consider Jerusalem
my highest joy.

[a] 13 Hebrew *Yam Suph*; that is, Sea of Reeds; also in verse 15

7 Remember, O LORD, what the Edomites did
on the day Jerusalem fell.
"Tear it down," they cried,
"tear it down to its foundations!"
8 O Daughter of Babylon, doomed to destruction,
happy is he who repays you
for what you have done to us—
9 he who seizes your infants
and dashes them against the rocks.

Psalm 138

Of David.

1 I will praise you, O LORD, with all my heart;
before the "gods" I will sing your praise.
2 I will bow down toward your holy temple
and will praise your name
for your love and your faithfulness,
for you have exalted above all things
your name and your word.
3 When I called, you answered me;
you made me bold and stouthearted.

4 May all the kings of the earth praise you, O LORD,
when they hear the words of your mouth.
5 May they sing of the ways of the LORD,
for the glory of the LORD is great.

6 Though the LORD is on high, he looks upon the lowly,
but the proud he knows from afar.
7 Though I walk in the midst of trouble,
you preserve my life;
you stretch out your hand against the anger of my foes,
with your right hand you save me.
8 The LORD will fulfill ⌊his purpose⌋ for me;
your love, O LORD, endures forever—
do not abandon the works of your hands.

Psalm 139

For the director of music. Of David. A psalm.

1 O LORD, you have searched me
and you know me.
2 You know when I sit and when I rise;
you perceive my thoughts from afar.
3 You discern my going out and my lying down;
you are familiar with all my ways.
4 Before a word is on my tongue
you know it completely, O LORD.

5 You hem me in—behind and before;
you have laid your hand upon me.
6 Such knowledge is too wonderful for me,
too lofty for me to attain.

7 Where can I go from your Spirit?
Where can I flee from your presence?
8 If I go up to the heavens, you are there;
if I make my bed in the depths,[a] you are there.
9 If I rise on the wings of the dawn,
if I settle on the far side of the sea,
10 even there your hand will guide me,
your right hand will hold me fast.

11 If I say, "Surely the darkness will hide me
and the light become night around me,"
12 even the darkness will not be dark to you;
the night will shine like the day,
for darkness is as light to you.

13 For you created my inmost being;
you knit me together in my mother's womb.
14 I praise you because I am fearfully and wonderfully made;
your works are wonderful,
I know that full well.
15 My frame was not hidden from you
when I was made in the secret place.
When I was woven together in the depths of the earth,
16 your eyes saw my unformed body.
All the days ordained for me
were written in your book
before one of them came to be.

17 How precious to[b] me are your thoughts, O God!
How vast is the sum of them!
18 Were I to count them,
they would outnumber the grains of sand.
When I awake,
I am still with you.

19 If only you would slay the wicked, O God!
Away from me, you bloodthirsty men!
20 They speak of you with evil intent;
your adversaries misuse your name.
21 Do not I hate those who hate you, O LORD,
and abhor those who rise up against you?

---

[a] 8 Hebrew *Sheol* [b] 17 Or *concerning*

THURSDAY
READ PSALM 139:1–24

WHO ARE WE, ANYWAY?

> **For you created my inmost being; you knit me together in my mother's womb. I praise you because I am fearfully and wonderfully made.**
>
> — PSALM 139:13–14

When were you first surprised to discover that your spouse was not like you? It's still a wonder to me how two people can be so different as my husband Grey and I are, and yet we're still together!

God, however, is not surprised. He deliberately made each of us unique and according to his divine blueprint. He knows us intimately. The psalmist expressed a longing we all have to be known and to be loved for who we are. Perhaps that's why God brought my husband and me together—to complete and nurture each other.

Walter Wangerin tells a story about the wonder of spousal differences in *As for Me and My House* (Thomas Nelson Publishers, 1987):

> In our little apartment in St. Louis, Thanne went to bed at precisely nine o'clock every night. No matter the difference of the days, some harder and some easier. No matter how marvelous our conversations were, she cut talk short to get her sleep. And she always showered first. And she always laid her clothes out neatly! Thanne's prearranged, punctilious life seemed to me a compulsive, cold routine.
>
> I, on the other hand, was to her a stunning mess, so unpredictable as to be unreliable. And how, in the name of cleanly godliness, could I contrive to strew dirty socks through every room of the apartment?
>
> What had I married? A machine?
>
> What had she married? An adolescent?

In my marriage I'm the messy one, and Grey is the neatnik. That used to cause hurts and arguments. But I've learned to recognize the limits of his tolerance: I can safely leave stuff where it doesn't belong for two days, but not three. And Grey uses humor to get his point across, saying, "When the cleaning lady comes, just tell her we're getting ready for a garage sale."

We don't have a cleaning lady.

Wangerin expresses these everyday differences in a deeper way:

> In marriage, idealization will surely run upon realization. The question is not how we might avoid this crisis, because we can't. The question, rather, is what work is required to meet the crisis and to grow by it? For if we think that this revelation of the real spouse is the final truth of our mate and our marriage—and that we've made a dreadful mistake, therefore—then we will move to alienation, one from the other. But if we take this as a natural step in the process of growing together, we may, with clear sight, move toward acceptance and accommodation of each other.

—MARY ANN JEFFREYS

let's talk

- ✦ What differences have sparked conflict between us?
- ✦ How have we handled those times of conflict—with anger, irritation, interest, humor?
- ✦ What is the long-term effect of working through these differences? How have we learned from each other?
- ✦ In what ways have our differences strengthened our relationship?

FOR YOUR NEXT DEVOTIONAL READING, TURN TO PAGE 680.

22 I have nothing but hatred for them;
I count them my enemies.

23 Search me, O God, and know my heart;
test me and know my anxious thoughts.
24 See if there is any offensive way in me,
and lead me in the way everlasting.

Psalm 140

For the director of music. A psalm of David.

1 Rescue me, O LORD, from evil men;
protect me from men of violence,
2 who devise evil plans in their hearts
and stir up war every day.
3 They make their tongues as sharp as a serpent's;
the poison of vipers is on their lips.
Selah

4 Keep me, O LORD, from the hands of the wicked;
protect me from men of violence
who plan to trip my feet.
5 Proud men have hidden a snare for me;
they have spread out the cords of their net
and have set traps for me along my path.
Selah

6 O LORD, I say to you, "You are my God."
Hear, O LORD, my cry for mercy.
7 O Sovereign LORD, my strong deliverer,
who shields my head in the day of battle—
8 do not grant the wicked their desires, O LORD;
do not let their plans succeed,
or they will become proud.
Selah

9 Let the heads of those who surround me
be covered with the trouble their lips have caused.
10 Let burning coals fall upon them;
may they be thrown into the fire,
into miry pits, never to rise.
11 Let slanderers not be established in the land;
may disaster hunt down men of violence.

12 I know that the LORD secures justice for the poor
and upholds the cause of the needy.
13 Surely the righteous will praise your name
and the upright will live before you.

Psalm 141

A psalm of David.

1 O LORD, I call to you; come quickly to me.
Hear my voice when I call to you.
2 May my prayer be set before you like incense;
may the lifting up of my hands be like the evening sacrifice.

3 Set a guard over my mouth, O LORD;
keep watch over the door of my lips.
4 Let not my heart be drawn to what is evil,
to take part in wicked deeds
with men who are evildoers;
let me not eat of their delicacies.

5 Let a righteous man[a] strike me—it is a kindness;
let him rebuke me—it is oil on my head.
My head will not refuse it.

Yet my prayer is ever against the deeds of evildoers;
6 their rulers will be thrown down from the cliffs,
and the wicked will learn that my words were well spoken.
7 ⌞They will say,⌟ "As one plows and breaks up the earth,
so our bones have been scattered at the mouth of the grave.[b]"

8 But my eyes are fixed on you, O Sovereign LORD;
in you I take refuge—do not give me over to death.
9 Keep me from the snares they have laid for me,
from the traps set by evildoers.
10 Let the wicked fall into their own nets,
while I pass by in safety.

Psalm 142

A *maskil*[c] of David. When he was in the cave. A prayer.

1 I cry aloud to the LORD;
I lift up my voice to the LORD for mercy.
2 I pour out my complaint before him;
before him I tell my trouble.

3 When my spirit grows faint within me,
it is you who know my way.
In the path where I walk
men have hidden a snare for me.

[a] 5 Or *Let the Righteous One* [b] 7 Hebrew *Sheol* [c] Title: Probably a literary or musical term

4 Look to my right and see;
no one is concerned for me.
I have no refuge;
no one cares for my life.

5 I cry to you, O LORD;
I say, "You are my refuge,
my portion in the land of the living."
6 Listen to my cry,
for I am in desperate need;
rescue me from those who pursue me,
for they are too strong for me.
7 Set me free from my prison,
that I may praise your name.

Then the righteous will gather about me
because of your goodness to me.

Psalm 143

A psalm of David.

1 O LORD, hear my prayer,
listen to my cry for mercy;
in your faithfulness and righteousness
come to my relief.
2 Do not bring your servant into judgment,
for no one living is righteous before you.

3 The enemy pursues me,
he crushes me to the ground;
he makes me dwell in darkness
like those long dead.
4 So my spirit grows faint within me;
my heart within me is dismayed.

5 I remember the days of long ago;
I meditate on all your works
and consider what your hands have done.
6 I spread out my hands to you;
my soul thirsts for you like a parched land. *Selah*

7 Answer me quickly, O LORD;
my spirit fails.
Do not hide your face from me
or I will be like those who go down to the pit.
8 Let the morning bring me word of your unfailing love,
for I have put my trust in you.
Show me the way I should go,
for to you I lift up my soul.
9 Rescue me from my enemies, O LORD,
for I hide myself in you.
10 Teach me to do your will,
for you are my God;
may your good Spirit
lead me on level ground.

11 For your name's sake, O LORD, preserve my life;
in your righteousness, bring me out of trouble.
12 In your unfailing love, silence my enemies;
destroy all my foes,
for I am your servant.

Psalm 144

Of David.

1 Praise be to the LORD my Rock,
who trains my hands for war,
my fingers for battle.
2 He is my loving God and my fortress,
my stronghold and my deliverer,
my shield, in whom I take refuge,
who subdues peoples[a] under me.

3 O LORD, what is man that you care for him,
the son of man that you think of him?
4 Man is like a breath;
his days are like a fleeting shadow.

5 Part your heavens, O LORD, and come down;
touch the mountains, so that they smoke.
6 Send forth lightning and scatter ⌞the enemies⌟;
shoot your arrows and rout them.
7 Reach down your hand from on high;
deliver me and rescue me
from the mighty waters,
from the hands of foreigners
8 whose mouths are full of lies,
whose right hands are deceitful.

9 I will sing a new song to you, O God;
on the ten-stringed lyre I will make music to you,
10 to the One who gives victory to kings,
who delivers his servant David from the deadly sword.

11 Deliver me and rescue me
from the hands of foreigners
whose mouths are full of lies,
whose right hands are deceitful.

12 Then our sons in their youth
will be like well-nurtured plants,
and our daughters will be like pillars
carved to adorn a palace.

---

a *2* Many manuscripts of the Masoretic Text, Dead Sea Scrolls, Aquila, Jerome and Syriac; most manuscripts of the Masoretic Text *subdues my people*

13 Our barns will be filled
with every kind of provision.
Our sheep will increase by thousands,
by tens of thousands in our fields;
14 our oxen will draw heavy loads. [a]
There will be no breaching of walls,
no going into captivity,
no cry of distress in our streets.

15 Blessed are the people of whom this is true;
blessed are the people whose God is the
LORD.

Psalm 145 [b]

A psalm of praise. Of David.

1 I will exalt you, my God the King;
I will praise your name for ever and
ever.
2 Every day I will praise you
and extol your name for ever and ever.

3 Great is the LORD and most worthy of
praise;
his greatness no one can fathom.
4 One generation will commend your works
to another;
they will tell of your mighty acts.
5 They will speak of the glorious splendor of
your majesty,
and I will meditate on your wonderful
works. [c]
6 They will tell of the power of your
awesome works,
and I will proclaim your great deeds.
7 They will celebrate your abundant
goodness
and joyfully sing of your righteousness.

8 The LORD is gracious and compassionate,
slow to anger and rich in love.
9 The LORD is good to all;
he has compassion on all he has made.
10 All you have made will praise you, O LORD;
your saints will extol you.
11 They will tell of the glory of your kingdom
and speak of your might,
12 so that all men may know of your mighty
acts
and the glorious splendor of your
kingdom.
13 Your kingdom is an everlasting kingdom,
and your dominion endures through all
generations.

The LORD is faithful to all his promises
and loving toward all he has made. [d]
14 The LORD upholds all those who fall
and lifts up all who are bowed down.
15 The eyes of all look to you,
and you give them their food at the
proper time.
16 You open your hand
and satisfy the desires of every living
thing.

17 The LORD is righteous in all his ways
and loving toward all he has made.
18 The LORD is near to all who call on him,
to all who call on him in truth.
19 He fulfills the desires of those who fear
him;
he hears their cry and saves them.
20 The LORD watches over all who love him,
but all the wicked he will destroy.

21 My mouth will speak in praise of the LORD.
Let every creature praise his holy name
for ever and ever.

Psalm 146

1 Praise the LORD. [e]

Praise the LORD, O my soul.
2 I will praise the LORD all my life;
I will sing praise to my God as long as I
live.

3 Do not put your trust in princes,
in mortal men, who cannot save.
4 When their spirit departs, they return to
the ground;
on that very day their plans come to
nothing.

5 Blessed is he whose help is the God of
Jacob,
whose hope is in the LORD his God,
6 the Maker of heaven and earth,
the sea, and everything in them—
the LORD, who remains faithful forever.
7 He upholds the cause of the oppressed
and gives food to the hungry.
The LORD sets prisoners free,
8 the LORD gives sight to the blind,
the LORD lifts up those who are bowed
down,
the LORD loves the righteous.
9 The LORD watches over the alien

---

[a] *14* Or *our chieftains will be firmly established* [b] *This psalm is an acrostic poem, the verses of which (including verse 13b) begin with the successive letters of the Hebrew alphabet.* [c] *5* Dead Sea Scrolls and Syriac (see also Septuagint); Masoretic Text *On the glorious splendor of your majesty / and on your wonderful works I will meditate* [d] *13* One manuscript of the Masoretic Text, Dead Sea Scrolls and Syriac (see also Septuagint); most manuscripts of the Masoretic Text do not have the last two lines of verse 13. [e] *1* Hebrew *Hallelu Yah*; also in verse 10

and sustains the fatherless and the
widow,
but he frustrates the ways of the wicked.

10 The LORD reigns forever,
your God, O Zion, for all generations.
Praise the LORD.

Psalm 147

1 Praise the LORD. [a]

How good it is to sing praises to our God,
how pleasant and fitting to praise him!

2 The LORD builds up Jerusalem;
he gathers the exiles of Israel.
3 He heals the brokenhearted
and binds up their wounds.
4 He determines the number of the stars
and calls them each by name.
5 Great is our Lord and mighty in power;
his understanding has no limit.
6 The LORD sustains the humble
but casts the wicked to the ground.

7 Sing to the LORD with thanksgiving;
make music to our God on the harp.
8 He covers the sky with clouds;
he supplies the earth with rain
and makes grass grow on the hills.
9 He provides food for the cattle
and for the young ravens when they
call.

10 His pleasure is not in the strength of the
horse,
nor his delight in the legs of a man;
11 the LORD delights in those who fear him,
who put their hope in his unfailing love.

12 Extol the LORD, O Jerusalem;
praise your God, O Zion,
13 for he strengthens the bars of your gates
and blesses your people within you.
14 He grants peace to your borders
and satisfies you with the finest of
wheat.
15 He sends his command to the earth;
his word runs swiftly.
16 He spreads the snow like wool
and scatters the frost like ashes.
17 He hurls down his hail like pebbles.
Who can withstand his icy blast?
18 He sends his word and melts them;
he stirs up his breezes, and the waters
flow.

19 He has revealed his word to Jacob,
his laws and decrees to Israel.
20 He has done this for no other nation;
they do not know his laws.

Praise the LORD.

Psalm 148

1 Praise the LORD. [b]

Praise the LORD from the heavens,
praise him in the heights above.
2 Praise him, all his angels,
praise him, all his heavenly hosts.
3 Praise him, sun and moon,
praise him, all you shining stars.
4 Praise him, you highest heavens
and you waters above the skies.
5 Let them praise the name of the LORD,
for he commanded and they were
created.
6 He set them in place for ever and ever;
he gave a decree that will never pass
away.

7 Praise the LORD from the earth,
you great sea creatures and all ocean
depths,
8 lightning and hail, snow and clouds,
stormy winds that do his bidding,
9 you mountains and all hills,
fruit trees and all cedars,
10 wild animals and all cattle,
small creatures and flying birds,
11 kings of the earth and all nations,
you princes and all rulers on earth,
12 young men and maidens,
old men and children.

13 Let them praise the name of the LORD,
for his name alone is exalted;
his splendor is above the earth and the
heavens.
14 He has raised up for his people a horn, [c]
the praise of all his saints,
of Israel, the people close to his heart.

Praise the LORD.

Psalm 149

1 Praise the LORD. [d]

Sing to the LORD a new song,
his praise in the assembly of the saints.

2 Let Israel rejoice in their Maker;

[a] *1* Hebrew *Hallelu Yah*; also in verse 20 [b] *1* Hebrew *Hallelu Yah*; also in verse 14 [c] *14* *Horn* here symbolizes strong one, that is, king. [d] *1* Hebrew *Hallelu Yah*; also in verse 9

let the people of Zion be glad in their
King.
3 Let them praise his name with dancing
and make music to him with
tambourine and harp.
4 For the LORD takes delight in his people;
he crowns the humble with salvation.
5 Let the saints rejoice in this honor
and sing for joy on their beds.

6 May the praise of God be in their mouths
and a double-edged sword in their hands,
7 to inflict vengeance on the nations
and punishment on the peoples,
8 to bind their kings with fetters,
their nobles with shackles of iron,
9 to carry out the sentence written against
them.
This is the glory of all his saints.

Praise the LORD.

Psalm 150

1 Praise the LORD.[a]

Praise God in his sanctuary;
praise him in his mighty heavens.
2 Praise him for his acts of power;
praise him for his surpassing
greatness.
3 Praise him with the sounding of the
trumpet,
praise him with the harp and lyre,
4 praise him with tambourine and
dancing,
praise him with the strings and flute,
5 praise him with the clash of cymbals,
praise him with resounding cymbals.
6 Let everything that has breath praise the
LORD.

Praise the LORD.

---

a *1* Hebrew *Hallelu Yah*; also in verse 6

PROVERBS

Proverbs

QUICK FACTS

AUTHOR Primarily King Solomon

AUDIENCE All Israel

DATE Solomon wrote most of the proverbs during his reign (970 to 930 B.C.), but the book wasn't fully compiled until around 700 B.C.

SETTING Written during Solomon's wiser days, before he became caught up in materialism and idolatry

The book of Proverbs is a priceless collection of practical wisdom about everyday experiences. While many of the proverbs describe the typical consequences of a specific action or character quality, they are not to be taken as iron-clad promises or guarantees. Rather, they are pithy guidelines, general principles that, when appropriately applied, lead to reverence for God, respect for his ways and a blessed life.

The book of Proverbs tells us that wisdom is more than just being smart. If we want to live a godly life, we need moral discernment, clarity of mind and the discipline to do what is right. Proverbs reminds us that God will direct the paths of those who trust him.

The book also provides wise counsel for couples learning to share life together. It gives practical advice on child rearing, money management, work and giving. In life and in marriage, Proverbs is a source of practical guidance that will help us to be faithful and wise people of God.

Prologue: Purpose and Theme

1 The proverbs of Solomon son of David, king of Israel:

2 for attaining wisdom and discipline;
for understanding words of insight;
3 for acquiring a disciplined and prudent life,
doing what is right and just and fair;
4 for giving prudence to the simple,
knowledge and discretion to the young—
5 let the wise listen and add to their learning,
and let the discerning get guidance—
6 for understanding proverbs and parables,
the sayings and riddles of the wise.

7 The fear of the LORD is the beginning of knowledge,
but fools[a] despise wisdom and discipline.

Exhortations to Embrace Wisdom

Warning Against Enticement

8 Listen, my son, to your father's instruction
and do not forsake your mother's teaching.
9 They will be a garland to grace your head
and a chain to adorn your neck.

10 My son, if sinners entice you,
do not give in to them.
11 If they say, "Come along with us;
let's lie in wait for someone's blood,
let's waylay some harmless soul;
12 let's swallow them alive, like the grave,[b]
and whole, like those who go down to the pit;
13 we will get all sorts of valuable things
and fill our houses with plunder;
14 throw in your lot with us,
and we will share a common purse"—
15 my son, do not go along with them,
do not set foot on their paths;
16 for their feet rush into sin,
they are swift to shed blood.
17 How useless to spread a net
in full view of all the birds!
18 These men lie in wait for their own blood;
they waylay only themselves!
19 Such is the end of all who go after ill-gotten gain;
it takes away the lives of those who get it.

Warning Against Rejecting Wisdom

20 Wisdom calls aloud in the street,
she raises her voice in the public squares;
21 at the head of the noisy streets[c] she cries out,
in the gateways of the city she makes her speech:

22 "How long will you simple ones[d] love your simple ways?
How long will mockers delight in mockery
and fools hate knowledge?
23 If you had responded to my rebuke,
I would have poured out my heart to you
and made my thoughts known to you.
24 But since you rejected me when I called
and no one gave heed when I stretched out my hand,
25 since you ignored all my advice
and would not accept my rebuke,
26 I in turn will laugh at your disaster;
I will mock when calamity overtakes you—
27 when calamity overtakes you like a storm,
when disaster sweeps over you like a whirlwind,
when distress and trouble overwhelm you.

28 "Then they will call to me but I will not answer;
they will look for me but will not find me.
29 Since they hated knowledge
and did not choose to fear the LORD,
30 since they would not accept my advice
and spurned my rebuke,
31 they will eat the fruit of their ways
and be filled with the fruit of their schemes.
32 For the waywardness of the simple will kill them,
and the complacency of fools will destroy them;
33 but whoever listens to me will live in safety
and be at ease, without fear of harm."

[a] 7 The Hebrew words rendered *fool* in Proverbs, and often elsewhere in the Old Testament, denote one who is morally deficient.
[b] 12 Hebrew *Sheol* [c] 21 Hebrew; Septuagint / *on the tops of the walls* [d] 22 The Hebrew word rendered *simple* in Proverbs generally denotes one without moral direction and inclined to evil.

FRIDAY
READ PROVERBS 1:1–19

MARRY WISDOM

My father was a great teacher. When I was young, he drilled me on his favorite proverb: "Hindsight is better than foresight, but never as good as insight." As a child I was more intrigued by the fascinating twist of the words than by the wisdom it communicated. Time, however, has taught me the truth of this proverb (even though it isn't one of those found in the Bible): We see farther into the past than into the future, but those who are aware of how things fit into God's grand scheme are truly wise.

The book of Proverbs is the heart of Old Testament Wisdom Literature. Even though Proverbs does not lend itself to theological outlines, a clear understanding of the book's structure helps us to better understand it. Before the collections of proverbs fashioned in the definition of the English term (short, pithy sayings) begin in chapter 10, chapters 1–9 form a cohesive, well-developed introductory series of lectures. Although the words are addressed to a "son," this is more of a literary device than a reference to a historical person.

Both *wisdom* and *folly* in the Hebrew language are feminine nouns. So the writer of this section used these words to evoke possible partners for a masculine addressee. Throughout Proverbs 1–9, both Wisdom and Folly take turns declaring their attractions in a series of personified mating overtures. The speeches are biased in favor of Wisdom, of course, for this is the thesis stated in Proverbs 1:7.

The goal of Proverbs 1–9 is to show us how godly wisdom merges with real life. Along the way we get principles for building strong marriages, families and work relationships. The proverbs of chapters 10–31 are word pictures that describe the furnishings scattered throughout Wisdom's house. When we marry Wisdom, we begin to surround ourselves with her sayings, perspectives, tools and visual aids.

These words of introduction and the proverbs that follow are meant to be applied to all dimensions of life. But they resonate clearly with dating and marriage relationships. It is from our fathers and mothers that we first learn what marriage is like. If the lessons of marriage are taught well by parents who have lingered long in Wisdom's house, we gain invaluable perspectives on how to respect others, to enjoy the give-and-take of domestic living, and to create an environment of hospitality in which to bring children and friends.

The reverse is also true. Our parents are prone to sin and often tempted by Folly. So we may need to unlearn some of their bad lessons, such as deception, lack of discipline, immodesty or infidelity. But that mixed bag of instruction should only remind us that true wisdom, after all, is gained first from God.

—WAYNE BROUWER

FOR YOUR NEXT DEVOTIONAL READING, TURN TO PAGE 684.

Listen, my son, to your father's instruction and do not forsake your mother's teaching.

— Proverbs 1:8

let's talk

- ✦ What lessons from our parents are healthy for our relationship?
- ✦ What bad relationship habits did we learn from them? How should we do things differently? Where do we learn wisdom that transcends parental teachings?
- ✦ How will we model wisdom for our children? What are some good things they will learn about marriage from us?

Moral Benefits of Wisdom

2 My son, if you accept my words
and store up my commands within
you,
2 turning your ear to wisdom
and applying your heart to
understanding,
3 and if you call out for insight
and cry aloud for understanding,
4 and if you look for it as for silver
and search for it as for hidden treasure,
5 then you will understand the fear of the
LORD
and find the knowledge of God.
6 For the LORD gives wisdom,
and from his mouth come knowledge
and understanding.
7 He holds victory in store for the upright,
he is a shield to those whose walk is
blameless,
8 for he guards the course of the just
and protects the way of his faithful
ones.

9 Then you will understand what is right
and just
and fair—every good path.
10 For wisdom will enter your heart,
and knowledge will be pleasant to your
soul.
11 Discretion will protect you,
and understanding will guard you.
12 Wisdom will save you from the ways of
wicked men,
from men whose words are perverse,
13 who leave the straight paths
to walk in dark ways,
14 who delight in doing wrong
and rejoice in the perverseness of evil,
15 whose paths are crooked
and who are devious in their ways.

16 It will save you also from the adulteress,
from the wayward wife with her
seductive words,
17 who has left the partner of her youth
and ignored the covenant she made
before God.[a]
18 For her house leads down to death
and her paths to the spirits of the dead.
19 None who go to her return
or attain the paths of life.

20 Thus you will walk in the ways of good
men
and keep to the paths of the righteous.
21 For the upright will live in the land,
and the blameless will remain in it;
22 but the wicked will be cut off from the
land,
and the unfaithful will be torn from it.

Further Benefits of Wisdom

3 My son, do not forget my teaching,
but keep my commands in your heart,
2 for they will prolong your life many years
and bring you prosperity.

3 Let love and faithfulness never leave you;
bind them around your neck,
write them on the tablet of your heart.
4 Then you will win favor and a good name
in the sight of God and man.

5 Trust in the LORD with all your heart
and lean not on your own
understanding;
6 in all your ways acknowledge him,
and he will make your paths straight.[b]

7 Do not be wise in your own eyes;
fear the LORD and shun evil.
8 This will bring health to your body
and nourishment to your bones.

9 Honor the LORD with your wealth,
with the firstfruits of all your crops;
10 then your barns will be filled to
overflowing,
and your vats will brim over with new
wine.

11 My son, do not despise the LORD's
discipline
and do not resent his rebuke,
12 because the LORD disciplines those he
loves,
as a father[c] the son he delights in.

13 Blessed is the man who finds wisdom,
the man who gains understanding,
14 for she is more profitable than silver
and yields better returns than gold.
15 She is more precious than rubies;
nothing you desire can compare with
her.
16 Long life is in her right hand;
in her left hand are riches and honor.
17 Her ways are pleasant ways,
and all her paths are peace.
18 She is a tree of life to those who embrace
her;
those who lay hold of her will be
blessed.

[a] 17 Or *covenant of her God* [b] 6 Or *will direct your paths* [c] 12 Hebrew; Septuagint / *and he punishes*

19 By wisdom the LORD laid the earth's
foundations,
by understanding he set the heavens in
place;
20 by his knowledge the deeps were divided,
and the clouds let drop the dew.

21 My son, preserve sound judgment and
discernment,
do not let them out of your sight;
22 they will be life for you,
an ornament to grace your neck.
23 Then you will go on your way in safety,
and your foot will not stumble;
24 when you lie down, you will not be
afraid;
when you lie down, your sleep will be
sweet.
25 Have no fear of sudden disaster
or of the ruin that overtakes the
wicked,
26 for the LORD will be your confidence
and will keep your foot from being
snared.

27 Do not withhold good from those who
deserve it,
when it is in your power to act.
28 Do not say to your neighbor,
"Come back later; I'll give it
tomorrow"—
when you now have it with you.

29 Do not plot harm against your neighbor,
who lives trustfully near you.
30 Do not accuse a man for no reason—
when he has done you no harm.

31 Do not envy a violent man
or choose any of his ways,
32 for the LORD detests a perverse man
but takes the upright into his
confidence.

33 The LORD's curse is on the house of the
wicked,
but he blesses the home of the
righteous.
34 He mocks proud mockers
but gives grace to the humble.
35 The wise inherit honor,
but fools he holds up to shame.

Wisdom Is Supreme

4 Listen, my sons, to a father's instruction;
pay attention and gain understanding.
2 I give you sound learning,
so do not forsake my teaching.
3 When I was a boy in my father's house,
still tender, and an only child of my
mother,
4 he taught me and said,
"Lay hold of my words with all your
heart;
keep my commands and you will live.
5 Get wisdom, get understanding;
do not forget my words or swerve from
them.
6 Do not forsake wisdom, and she will
protect you;
love her, and she will watch over you.
7 Wisdom is supreme; therefore get
wisdom.
Though it cost all you have,[a] get
understanding.
8 Esteem her, and she will exalt you;
embrace her, and she will honor you.
9 She will set a garland of grace on your
head
and present you with a crown of
splendor."

10 Listen, my son, accept what I say,
and the years of your life will be
many.
11 I guide you in the way of wisdom
and lead you along straight paths.
12 When you walk, your steps will not be
hampered;
when you run, you will not stumble.
13 Hold on to instruction, do not let it go;
guard it well, for it is your life.
14 Do not set foot on the path of the wicked
or walk in the way of evil men.
15 Avoid it, do not travel on it;
turn from it and go on your way.
16 For they cannot sleep till they do evil;
they are robbed of slumber till they
make someone fall.
17 They eat the bread of wickedness
and drink the wine of violence.

18 The path of the righteous is like the first
gleam of dawn,
shining ever brighter till the full light of
day.
19 But the way of the wicked is like deep
darkness;
they do not know what makes them
stumble.

20 My son, pay attention to what I say;
listen closely to my words.
21 Do not let them out of your sight,
keep them within your heart;

[a] 7 Or *Whatever else you get*

deciding as a team

When it comes to making decisions, do you and your spouse work together or work against each other? Look at the statements below. Circle the word that best describes you, and put a box around the word that best describes your spouse. Then take a few minutes to talk about how you currently make decisions and how you'd like to make them in the future.

1. When making decisions, it's more important for me to be (right, heard).
2. I like to make decisions (quickly, slowly, after much research).
3. When forced to live with a decision I wasn't a part of, I feel (angry, relieved).
4. If I don't know what to do, I (talk to my friends, pray, eat).
5. When I'm stuck on making a decision, I (continue to research it, flip a coin).
6. I find when making a tough choice that it's good for me (to talk about it, to go off on my own and think about it).
7. Mistakes were made in the past because I (didn't think through the consequences, waited too long to make the decision).
8. After I make a decision, I (am content to live with it, often obsess over whether it was the right thing, learn from whatever happens).
9. I make decisions based on what I (feel, think) is right.
10. When making decisions, I (welcome, resent) outside advice.

HOW ARE WE DOING?

date

let's make a DATE

DESSERT ON ME

Go for a late night dessert at a favorite bakery or restaurant. Each of you should order a dessert and beverage for the other. While eating your partner's pick, think about what it feels like to live with a decision made without your input—even if it's only chocolate cake. Discuss what factors you each used in picking out the dessert. Then, based on your partner's feedback, discuss how you'd order the same or different next time. (After the discussion, you can always switch plates.)

FOR YOUR NEXT DEVOTIONAL READING, TURN TO PAGE 687.

LESSONS FROM THE *Bible*

What do the following passages say about various ways that God guides decision making?

1. Through Scripture (Psalm 119:104–105)
2. Through circumstances (Acts 6:1–6)
3. Through supernatural direction (Acts 18:5–11)
4. Through prayer (James 1:5–6)

14 who plots evil with deceit in his heart—
he always stirs up dissension.
15 Therefore disaster will overtake him in an instant;
he will suddenly be destroyed—without remedy.

16 There are six things the LORD hates,
seven that are detestable to him:
17 haughty eyes,
a lying tongue,
hands that shed innocent blood,
18 a heart that devises wicked schemes,
feet that are quick to rush into evil,
19 a false witness who pours out lies
and a man who stirs up dissension among brothers.

Warning Against Adultery

20 My son, keep your father's commands
and do not forsake your mother's teaching.
21 Bind them upon your heart forever;
fasten them around your neck.
22 When you walk, they will guide you;
when you sleep, they will watch over you;
when you awake, they will speak to you.
23 For these commands are a lamp,
this teaching is a light,
and the corrections of discipline
are the way to life,
24 keeping you from the immoral woman,
from the smooth tongue of the wayward wife.
25 Do not lust in your heart after her beauty
or let her captivate you with her eyes,
26 for the prostitute reduces you to a loaf of bread,
and the adulteress preys upon your very life.
27 Can a man scoop fire into his lap
without his clothes being burned?
28 Can a man walk on hot coals
without his feet being scorched?
29 So is he who sleeps with another man's wife;
no one who touches her will go unpunished.

30 Men do not despise a thief if he steals
to satisfy his hunger when he is starving.
31 Yet if he is caught, he must pay sevenfold,
though it costs him all the wealth of his house.
32 But a man who commits adultery lacks judgment;
whoever does so destroys himself.
33 Blows and disgrace are his lot,
and his shame will never be wiped away;
34 for jealousy arouses a husband's fury,
and he will show no mercy when he takes revenge.
35 He will not accept any compensation;
he will refuse the bribe, however great it is.

Warning Against the Adulteress

7 My son, keep my words
and store up my commands within you.
2 Keep my commands and you will live;
guard my teachings as the apple of your eye.
3 Bind them on your fingers;
write them on the tablet of your heart.
4 Say to wisdom, "You are my sister,"
and call understanding your kinsman;
5 they will keep you from the adulteress,
from the wayward wife with her seductive words.

6 At the window of my house
I looked out through the lattice.
7 I saw among the simple,
I noticed among the young men,
a youth who lacked judgment.
8 He was going down the street near her corner,
walking along in the direction of her house
9 at twilight, as the day was fading,
as the dark of night set in.

10 Then out came a woman to meet him,
dressed like a prostitute and with crafty intent.
11 (She is loud and defiant,
her feet never stay at home;
12 now in the street, now in the squares,
at every corner she lurks.)
13 She took hold of him and kissed him
and with a brazen face she said:

14 "I have fellowship offerings[a] at home;
today I fulfilled my vows.
15 So I came out to meet you;
I looked for you and have found you!
16 I have covered my bed

---

[a] 14 Traditionally *peace offerings*

PLAYING WITH FIRE

In the movie *Unfaithful*, a married woman meets a younger man by chance on a Manhattan street. She is drawn to him and over the course of time begins an affair with him. Her husband finds out, and when he confronts his wife's lover, the husband kills him. This tangled story shows the destruction and ruin that an affair can have on a couple.

It's a deeply disturbing movie, portraying how a seemingly normal and average couple can become drawn into a web of lies and deception through random circumstances. And the wife's adultery is at the heart of the web.

Even without events escalating into murder, as portrayed in the movie, adultery is still devastating. Recent statistics cited by the Associated Press state that 22 percent of married men and 14 percent of married women admit to having had at least one extramarital affair. The statistics are shocking, but they alone fail to portray the overwhelming fallout from infidelity: broken trust, hurt, shame, anger, bitterness, guilt, shattered families—sometimes even murder and suicide.

Adultery is a valid reason God gives for divorce (see Matthew 19:3–9). It's a sin that isn't easily forgiven and is seldom forgotten by the injured spouse. The writer of Proverbs offers stern warnings against adultery. "Can a man scoop fire into his lap without his clothes being burned? Can a man walk on hot coals without his feet being scorched?" (Proverbs 6:27–28). According to Proverbs 6:32, a person who commits adultery lacks judgment and destroys himself (or herself).

This Scripture warns that this sin, when committed in secrecy, can rarely be kept quiet, and when it does become known, the adulterer will have to face the fury of the betrayed spouse. "Jealousy arouses a husband's fury, and he will show no mercy when he takes revenge," says Proverbs 6:34. The adulterer will experience disgrace and the kind of shame that will never be wiped away, and will have to live with a guilty conscience for the rest of their life. And, even if the betrayed spouse decides to stay, the adulterer will have to prove their love and faithfulness for the rest of their marriage.

Even a casual flirtation can reap a lifetime of consequences. Ask those who have lost their spouses, children, friends, self-respect—even jobs—because of infidelity, and they will tell you, often with tears, how the years of regret were not worth the momentary pleasure.

It's human nature to be tempted, and while temptation isn't sin, giving in to it is. When you are attracted to someone other than your spouse, pull away from the fire or it could burn your marriage to death.

—NANCY KENNEDY

FOR YOUR NEXT DEVOTIONAL READING, TURN TO PAGE 690.

Can a man scoop fire into his lap without his clothes being burned?

— PROVERBS 6:27

let's talk

- ✦ What are the consequences of adultery? What people are hurt by it? In what ways are they hurt?
- ✦ Most infidelity begins by accident rather than by design. How can we be on guard when an accidental encounter seems to be leading to something more?
- ✦ Many affairs begin because of unmet emotional needs. What needs do we each have that might not be met at this time? What could we do to help correct that?

with colored linens from Egypt.
17 I have perfumed my bed
with myrrh, aloes and cinnamon.
18 Come, let's drink deep of love till morning;
let's enjoy ourselves with love!
19 My husband is not at home;
he has gone on a long journey.
20 He took his purse filled with money
and will not be home till full moon."

21 With persuasive words she led him astray;
she seduced him with her smooth talk.
22 All at once he followed her
like an ox going to the slaughter,
like a deer[a] stepping into a noose[b]
23 till an arrow pierces his liver,
like a bird darting into a snare,
little knowing it will cost him his life.

24 Now then, my sons, listen to me;
pay attention to what I say.
25 Do not let your heart turn to her ways
or stray into her paths.
26 Many are the victims she has brought down;
her slain are a mighty throng.
27 Her house is a highway to the grave,[c]
leading down to the chambers of death.

Wisdom's Call

8 Does not wisdom call out?
Does not understanding raise her voice?
2 On the heights along the way,
where the paths meet, she takes her stand;
3 beside the gates leading into the city,
at the entrances, she cries aloud:
4 "To you, O men, I call out;
I raise my voice to all mankind.
5 You who are simple, gain prudence;
you who are foolish, gain understanding.
6 Listen, for I have worthy things to say;
I open my lips to speak what is right.
7 My mouth speaks what is true,
for my lips detest wickedness.
8 All the words of my mouth are just;
none of them is crooked or perverse.
9 To the discerning all of them are right;
they are faultless to those who have knowledge.
10 Choose my instruction instead of silver,
knowledge rather than choice gold,
11 for wisdom is more precious than rubies,
and nothing you desire can compare with her.

12 "I, wisdom, dwell together with prudence;
I possess knowledge and discretion.
13 To fear the LORD is to hate evil;
I hate pride and arrogance,
evil behavior and perverse speech.
14 Counsel and sound judgment are mine;
I have understanding and power.
15 By me kings reign
and rulers make laws that are just;
16 by me princes govern,
and all nobles who rule on earth.[d]
17 I love those who love me,
and those who seek me find me.
18 With me are riches and honor,
enduring wealth and prosperity.
19 My fruit is better than fine gold;
what I yield surpasses choice silver.
20 I walk in the way of righteousness,
along the paths of justice,
21 bestowing wealth on those who love me
and making their treasuries full.

22 "The LORD brought me forth as the first of his works,[e,f]
before his deeds of old;
23 I was appointed[g] from eternity,
from the beginning, before the world began.
24 When there were no oceans, I was given birth,
when there were no springs abounding with water;
25 before the mountains were settled in place,
before the hills, I was given birth,
26 before he made the earth or its fields
or any of the dust of the world.
27 I was there when he set the heavens in place,
when he marked out the horizon on the face of the deep,
28 when he established the clouds above
and fixed securely the fountains of the deep,
29 when he gave the sea its boundary
so the waters would not overstep his command,
and when he marked out the foundations of the earth.
30 Then I was the craftsman at his side.
I was filled with delight day after day,

[a] 22 Syriac (see also Septuagint); Hebrew *fool* [b] 22 The meaning of the Hebrew for this line is uncertain. [c] 27 Hebrew *Sheol*
[d] 16 Many Hebrew manuscripts and Septuagint; most Hebrew manuscripts *and nobles—all righteous rulers* [e] 22 Or *way*; or *dominion* [f] 22 Or *The LORD possessed me at the beginning of his work*; or *The LORD brought me forth at the beginning of his work*
[g] 23 Or *fashioned*

rejoicing always in his presence,
31 rejoicing in his whole world
and delighting in mankind.

32 "Now then, my sons, listen to me;
blessed are those who keep my ways.
33 Listen to my instruction and be wise;
do not ignore it.
34 Blessed is the man who listens to me,
watching daily at my doors,
waiting at my doorway.
35 For whoever finds me finds life
and receives favor from the LORD.
36 But whoever fails to find me harms himself;
all who hate me love death."

Invitations of Wisdom and of Folly

9 Wisdom has built her house;
she has hewn out its seven pillars.
2 She has prepared her meat and mixed her wine;
she has also set her table.
3 She has sent out her maids, and she calls
from the highest point of the city.
4 "Let all who are simple come in here!"
she says to those who lack judgment.
5 "Come, eat my food
and drink the wine I have mixed.
6 Leave your simple ways and you will live;
walk in the way of understanding.

7 "Whoever corrects a mocker invites insult;
whoever rebukes a wicked man incurs abuse.
8 Do not rebuke a mocker or he will hate you;
rebuke a wise man and he will love you.
9 Instruct a wise man and he will be wiser still;
teach a righteous man and he will add to his learning.

10 "The fear of the LORD is the beginning of wisdom,
and knowledge of the Holy One is understanding.
11 For through me your days will be many,
and years will be added to your life.
12 If you are wise, your wisdom will reward you;
if you are a mocker, you alone will suffer."

13 The woman Folly is loud;
she is undisciplined and without knowledge.
14 She sits at the door of her house,
on a seat at the highest point of the city,
15 calling out to those who pass by,
who go straight on their way.
16 "Let all who are simple come in here!"
she says to those who lack judgment.
17 "Stolen water is sweet;
food eaten in secret is delicious!"
18 But little do they know that the dead are there,
that her guests are in the depths of the grave.[a]

Proverbs of Solomon

10 The proverbs of Solomon:

A wise son brings joy to his father,
but a foolish son grief to his mother.
2 Ill-gotten treasures are of no value,
but righteousness delivers from death.

3 The LORD does not let the righteous go hungry
but he thwarts the craving of the wicked.

4 Lazy hands make a man poor,
but diligent hands bring wealth.

5 He who gathers crops in summer is a wise son,
but he who sleeps during harvest is a disgraceful son.

6 Blessings crown the head of the righteous,
but violence overwhelms the mouth of the wicked.[b]

7 The memory of the righteous will be a blessing,
but the name of the wicked will rot.

8 The wise in heart accept commands,
but a chattering fool comes to ruin.
9 The man of integrity walks securely,
but he who takes crooked paths will be found out.

10 He who winks maliciously causes grief,
and a chattering fool comes to ruin.

11 The mouth of the righteous is a fountain of life,
but violence overwhelms the mouth of the wicked.

---

[a] 18 Hebrew *Sheol* [b] 6 Or *but the mouth of the wicked conceals violence*; also in verse 11

TUESDAY
READ PROVERBS 10:1–32

HOLD YOUR TONGUE

When words are many, sin is not absent, but he who holds his tongue is wise.
— PROVERBS 10:19

Some married friends of ours pick at each other all the time. Every point of conversation between them becomes a sparring match. For example, Melissa told me one day, "We just painted our kitchen a honey-gold color."

"No, Melissa, it's not honey-gold; it's ochre," said Eric, butting into our conversation.

"What's ochre anyway? A crayon color maybe, but not the color of our kitchen," Melissa responded.

"What, are you color-blind? Everyone knows what ochre is, and ochre is definitely the color of our kitchen!"

Stuck in the middle of too many "discussions" like this, you wish you could just reach over and turn off the spigot of useless words that flow from these friends. Granted, their disputes don't qualify as verbal abuse, but, over time, these petty disagreements appear to be fraying the fabric of their marriage.

Proverbs 10:19 warns us that using too many words can be an indication that sin is lurking. We may talk too much to cover our fear that our spouse is becoming too independent and doesn't need our advice. Maybe we've done something wrong and are diverting attention by sniping at our mate. Regardless, a marriage can become threadbare from too many petty arguments that lead to demeaning remarks.

Another couple I know, Todd and Kimberly, argue so much that their marriage has unraveled. Todd is particularly vicious in verbally attacking his wife. One particularly damaging comment—"You are so dumb"—cut Kimberly so deep that she walked away stunned. She may have had some choice words picked out in her mind, but she used great discretion in not speaking them aloud.

Why is holding our tongue so hard to do? Matthew 12:34 tells us that the mouth speaks from the overflow of our heart. If this is true, then what do most of the words we say indicate about our love—or lack of love—for our spouse?

Open, straightforward communication is vitally important to a thriving marriage, but sometimes it's better to stay silent until you've calmed down emotionally, thought through an issue, and prayed for God's guidance before discussing it with your spouse.

The next time you find yourself about to enter into a verbal match with your mate, check the condition of your heart. Is it brimming over with love, patience, gentleness and the other qualities that comprise the fruit of the Spirit (see Galatians 5:22–23), or is it boiling over with anger, resentment and hurt? What, then, will your words be like—will they be loving and affirming, or toxic and poisonous? Until you know, it's best to heed the advice of Proverbs 10:19: Be wise and hold your tongue.

—MARIAN V. LIAUTAUD

let's talk

- ✦ In what ways does talking too much affect our relationship? When have we said too much about an issue? What happened as a result?
- ✦ How would holding our tongue help us avoid sin? Does silence always indicate wisdom, or is it sometimes another way we choose to punish each other? When does silence become deadly?
- ✦ Here's a question for each of us to think about: What does the pattern of my speech usually say to you about the overflow of my heart?

FOR YOUR NEXT DEVOTIONAL READING, TURN TO PAGE 698.

[12] The wicked desire the plunder of evil men,
but the root of the righteous flourishes.

[13] An evil man is trapped by his sinful talk,
but a righteous man escapes trouble.

[14] From the fruit of his lips a man is filled with good things
as surely as the work of his hands rewards him.

[15] The way of a fool seems right to him,
but a wise man listens to advice.

[16] A fool shows his annoyance at once,
but a prudent man overlooks an insult.

[17] A truthful witness gives honest testimony,
but a false witness tells lies.

[18] Reckless words pierce like a sword,
but the tongue of the wise brings healing.

[19] Truthful lips endure forever,
but a lying tongue lasts only a moment.

[20] There is deceit in the hearts of those who plot evil,
but joy for those who promote peace.

[21] No harm befalls the righteous,
but the wicked have their fill of trouble.

[22] The LORD detests lying lips,
but he delights in men who are truthful.

[23] A prudent man keeps his knowledge to himself,
but the heart of fools blurts out folly.

[24] Diligent hands will rule,
but laziness ends in slave labor.

[25] An anxious heart weighs a man down,
but a kind word cheers him up.

[26] A righteous man is cautious in friendship,[a]
but the way of the wicked leads them astray.

[27] The lazy man does not roast[b] his game,
but the diligent man prizes his possessions.

[28] In the way of righteousness there is life;
along that path is immortality.

13 A wise son heeds his father's instruction,
but a mocker does not listen to rebuke.

[2] From the fruit of his lips a man enjoys good things,
but the unfaithful have a craving for violence.

[3] He who guards his lips guards his life,
but he who speaks rashly will come to ruin.

[4] The sluggard craves and gets nothing,
but the desires of the diligent are fully satisfied.

[5] The righteous hate what is false,
but the wicked bring shame and disgrace.

[6] Righteousness guards the man of integrity,
but wickedness overthrows the sinner.

[7] One man pretends to be rich, yet has nothing;
another pretends to be poor, yet has great wealth.

[8] A man's riches may ransom his life,
but a poor man hears no threat.

[9] The light of the righteous shines brightly,
but the lamp of the wicked is snuffed out.

[10] Pride only breeds quarrels,
but wisdom is found in those who take advice.

[11] Dishonest money dwindles away,
but he who gathers money little by little makes it grow.

[12] Hope deferred makes the heart sick,
but a longing fulfilled is a tree of life.

[13] He who scorns instruction will pay for it,
but he who respects a command is rewarded.

[14] The teaching of the wise is a fountain of life,
turning a man from the snares of death.

[15] Good understanding wins favor,
but the way of the unfaithful is hard.[c]

[16] Every prudent man acts out of knowledge,
but a fool exposes his folly.

[17] A wicked messenger falls into trouble,
but a trustworthy envoy brings healing.

a 26 Or *man is a guide to his neighbor* *b* 27 The meaning of the Hebrew for this word is uncertain. *c* 15 Or *unfaithful does not endure*

18 He who ignores discipline comes to
poverty and shame,
but whoever heeds correction is
honored.

19 A longing fulfilled is sweet to the soul,
but fools detest turning from evil.

20 He who walks with the wise grows wise,
but a companion of fools suffers harm.

21 Misfortune pursues the sinner,
but prosperity is the reward of the
righteous.

22 A good man leaves an inheritance for his
children's children,
but a sinner's wealth is stored up for the
righteous.

23 A poor man's field may produce abundant
food,
but injustice sweeps it away.

24 He who spares the rod hates his son,
but he who loves him is careful to
discipline him.

25 The righteous eat to their hearts' content,
but the stomach of the wicked goes
hungry.

14 The wise woman builds her house,
but with her own hands the foolish one
tears hers down.

2 He whose walk is upright fears the LORD,
but he whose ways are devious despises
him.

3 A fool's talk brings a rod to his back,
but the lips of the wise protect them.

4 Where there are no oxen, the manger is
empty,
but from the strength of an ox comes
an abundant harvest.

5 A truthful witness does not deceive,
but a false witness pours out lies.

6 The mocker seeks wisdom and finds
none,
but knowledge comes easily to the
discerning.

7 Stay away from a foolish man,
for you will not find knowledge on his
lips.

8 The wisdom of the prudent is to give
thought to their ways,
but the folly of fools is deception.

9 Fools mock at making amends for sin,
but goodwill is found among the
upright.

10 Each heart knows its own bitterness,
and no one else can share its joy.

11 The house of the wicked will be
destroyed,
but the tent of the upright will
flourish.

12 There is a way that seems right to a man,
but in the end it leads to death.

13 Even in laughter the heart may ache,
and joy may end in grief.

14 The faithless will be fully repaid for their
ways,
and the good man rewarded for his.

15 A simple man believes anything,
but a prudent man gives thought to his
steps.

16 A wise man fears the LORD and shuns
evil,
but a fool is hotheaded and reckless.

17 A quick-tempered man does foolish
things,
and a crafty man is hated.

18 The simple inherit folly,
but the prudent are crowned with
knowledge.

19 Evil men will bow down in the presence of
the good,
and the wicked at the gates of the
righteous.

20 The poor are shunned even by their
neighbors,
but the rich have many friends.

21 He who despises his neighbor sins,
but blessed is he who is kind to the
needy.

22 Do not those who plot evil go astray?
But those who plan what is good find[a]
love and faithfulness.

23 All hard work brings a profit,
but mere talk leads only to poverty.

24 The wealth of the wise is their crown,
but the folly of fools yields folly.

25 A truthful witness saves lives,
but a false witness is deceitful.

---

[a] 22 Or *show*

26 He who fears the LORD has a secure
fortress,
and for his children it will be a refuge.

27 The fear of the LORD is a fountain of life,
turning a man from the snares of
death.

28 A large population is a king's glory,
but without subjects a prince is ruined.

29 A patient man has great understanding,
but a quick-tempered man displays
folly.

30 A heart at peace gives life to the body,
but envy rots the bones.

31 He who oppresses the poor shows
contempt for their Maker,
but whoever is kind to the needy
honors God.

32 When calamity comes, the wicked are
brought down,
but even in death the righteous have a
refuge.

33 Wisdom reposes in the heart of the
discerning
and even among fools she lets herself be
known.[a]

34 Righteousness exalts a nation,
but sin is a disgrace to any people.

35 A king delights in a wise servant,
but a shameful servant incurs his
wrath.

15 A gentle answer turns away wrath,
but a harsh word stirs up anger.

2 The tongue of the wise commends
knowledge,
but the mouth of the fool gushes folly.

3 The eyes of the LORD are everywhere,
keeping watch on the wicked and the
good.

4 The tongue that brings healing is a tree of
life,
but a deceitful tongue crushes the
spirit.

5 A fool spurns his father's discipline,
but whoever heeds correction shows
prudence.

6 The house of the righteous contains great
treasure,
but the income of the wicked brings
them trouble.

7 The lips of the wise spread knowledge;
not so the hearts of fools.

8 The LORD detests the sacrifice of the
wicked,
but the prayer of the upright pleases
him.

9 The LORD detests the way of the wicked
but he loves those who pursue
righteousness.

10 Stern discipline awaits him who leaves the
path;
he who hates correction will die.

11 Death and Destruction[b] lie open before
the LORD—
how much more the hearts of men!

12 A mocker resents correction;
he will not consult the wise.

13 A happy heart makes the face cheerful,
but heartache crushes the spirit.

14 The discerning heart seeks knowledge,
but the mouth of a fool feeds on folly.

15 All the days of the oppressed are
wretched,
but the cheerful heart has a continual
feast.

16 Better a little with the fear of the LORD
than great wealth with turmoil.

17 Better a meal of vegetables where there is
love
than a fattened calf with hatred.

18 A hot-tempered man stirs up dissension,
but a patient man calms a quarrel.

19 The way of the sluggard is blocked with
thorns,
but the path of the upright is a
highway.

20 A wise son brings joy to his father,
but a foolish man despises his mother.

21 Folly delights a man who lacks judgment,
but a man of understanding keeps a
straight course.

22 Plans fail for lack of counsel,
but with many advisers they succeed.

23 A man finds joy in giving an apt reply—
and how good is a timely word!

[a] 33 Hebrew; Septuagint and Syriac / *but in the heart of fools she is not known* [b] 11 Hebrew *Sheol and Abaddon*

24 The path of life leads upward for the wise
to keep him from going down to the grave. [a]

25 The LORD tears down the proud man's house
but he keeps the widow's boundaries intact.

26 The LORD detests the thoughts of the wicked,
but those of the pure are pleasing to him.

27 A greedy man brings trouble to his family,
but he who hates bribes will live.

28 The heart of the righteous weighs its answers,
but the mouth of the wicked gushes evil.

29 The LORD is far from the wicked
but he hears the prayer of the righteous.

30 A cheerful look brings joy to the heart,
and good news gives health to the bones.

31 He who listens to a life-giving rebuke
will be at home among the wise.

32 He who ignores discipline despises himself,
but whoever heeds correction gains understanding.

33 The fear of the LORD teaches a man wisdom, [b]
and humility comes before honor.

16 To man belong the plans of the heart,
but from the LORD comes the reply of the tongue.

2 All a man's ways seem innocent to him,
but motives are weighed by the LORD.

3 Commit to the LORD whatever you do,
and your plans will succeed.

4 The LORD works out everything for his own ends—
even the wicked for a day of disaster.

5 The LORD detests all the proud of heart.
Be sure of this: They will not go unpunished.

6 Through love and faithfulness sin is atoned for;
through the fear of the LORD a man avoids evil.

7 When a man's ways are pleasing to the LORD,
he makes even his enemies live at peace with him.

8 Better a little with righteousness
than much gain with injustice.

9 In his heart a man plans his course,
but the LORD determines his steps.

10 The lips of a king speak as an oracle,
and his mouth should not betray justice.

11 Honest scales and balances are from the LORD;
all the weights in the bag are of his making.

12 Kings detest wrongdoing,
for a throne is established through righteousness.

13 Kings take pleasure in honest lips;
they value a man who speaks the truth.

14 A king's wrath is a messenger of death,
but a wise man will appease it.

15 When a king's face brightens, it means life;
his favor is like a rain cloud in spring.

16 How much better to get wisdom than gold,
to choose understanding rather than silver!

17 The highway of the upright avoids evil;
he who guards his way guards his life.

18 Pride goes before destruction,
a haughty spirit before a fall.

19 Better to be lowly in spirit and among the oppressed
than to share plunder with the proud.

20 Whoever gives heed to instruction prospers,
and blessed is he who trusts in the LORD.

21 The wise in heart are called discerning,
and pleasant words promote instruction. [c]

[a] 24 Hebrew *Sheol* [b] 33 Or *Wisdom teaches the fear of the LORD* [c] 21 Or *words make a man persuasive*

22 Understanding is a fountain of life to
those who have it,
but folly brings punishment to fools.

23 A wise man's heart guides his mouth,
and his lips promote instruction.[a]

24 Pleasant words are a honeycomb,
sweet to the soul and healing to the
bones.

25 There is a way that seems right to a man,
but in the end it leads to death.

26 The laborer's appetite works for him;
his hunger drives him on.

27 A scoundrel plots evil,
and his speech is like a scorching fire.

28 A perverse man stirs up dissension,
and a gossip separates close friends.

29 A violent man entices his neighbor
and leads him down a path that is not
good.

30 He who winks with his eye is plotting
perversity;
he who purses his lips is bent on evil.

31 Gray hair is a crown of splendor;
it is attained by a righteous life.

32 Better a patient man than a warrior,
a man who controls his temper than
one who takes a city.

33 The lot is cast into the lap,
but its every decision is from the
LORD.

17 Better a dry crust with peace and quiet
than a house full of feasting,[b] with
strife.

2 A wise servant will rule over a disgraceful
son,
and will share the inheritance as one of
the brothers.

3 The crucible for silver and the furnace for
gold,
but the LORD tests the heart.

4 A wicked man listens to evil lips;
a liar pays attention to a malicious
tongue.

5 He who mocks the poor shows contempt
for their Maker;
whoever gloats over disaster will not go
unpunished.

6 Children's children are a crown to the
aged,
and parents are the pride of their
children.

7 Arrogant[c] lips are unsuited to a fool—
how much worse lying lips to a ruler!

8 A bribe is a charm to the one who
gives it;
wherever he turns, he succeeds.

9 He who covers over an offense promotes
love,
but whoever repeats the matter
separates close friends.

10 A rebuke impresses a man of discernment
more than a hundred lashes a fool.

11 An evil man is bent only on rebellion;
a merciless official will be sent against
him.

12 Better to meet a bear robbed of her cubs
than a fool in his folly.

13 If a man pays back evil for good,
evil will never leave his house.

14 Starting a quarrel is like breaching a dam;
so drop the matter before a dispute
breaks out.

15 Acquitting the guilty and condemning the
innocent—
the LORD detests them both.

16 Of what use is money in the hand of a
fool,
since he has no desire to get wisdom?

17 A friend loves at all times,
and a brother is born for adversity.

18 A man lacking in judgment strikes hands
in pledge
and puts up security for his neighbor.

19 He who loves a quarrel loves sin;
he who builds a high gate invites
destruction.

20 A man of perverse heart does not
prosper;
he whose tongue is deceitful falls into
trouble.

21 To have a fool for a son brings grief;
there is no joy for the father of a fool.

22 A cheerful heart is good medicine,
but a crushed spirit dries up the bones.

---

a 23 Or *mouth / and makes his lips persuasive* b 1 Hebrew *sacrifices* c 7 Or *Eloquent*

PEACE AT THE TABLE

> **Better a dry crust with peace and quiet than a house full of feasting, with strife.**
>
> — PROVERBS 17:1

let's talk

- What are some things we can do to unwind before eating a meal together?
- What happens when we don't take time to decompress before having dinner?
- What is peace and quiet to each of us? What steps can we take to move from a tension-filled meal to a peaceful dinner that feeds our bodies and our relationship?

When a married couple has a meal together, husband and wife often need to share more than a piece of bread. They may have big issues, major decisions or upsetting developments to talk through. Each may be wrestling with work challenges, children's activities, home repairs, finances or other emotional, physical or psychological demands. But there's a huge difference between sharing peace of mind and giving someone a piece of one's mind.

As this proverb says, it is sweet for a couple to find peace and quiet together, even if there is only a dry crust of bread to share. Somehow a scanty meal can be incredibly satisfying when a husband and wife also enjoy a great conversation—or maybe even blessed peace and quietness together. However, if a spirit of sharing and togetherness is missing when breaking bread at the table, then spiritual and emotional indigestion can occur. Depending on one's attitude, a lavish and beautifully prepared meal can be filled with strife.

Everyone at some time faces stress at work and at home. Sometimes we make mistakes and bring problems on ourselves, and sometimes things happen to us that push us past our limits. A spouse can be a handy target for venting such frustration, especially at the end of a long day. But wait! Short term, we need a prayerful approach to calm down and recharge when coming together at the end of the day. The same thing must happen long term as we pray for peace, serenity and contentment in marriage.

How can a married couple find genuine peace together when eating a meal? Some couples give each other space after coming home from work at the end of the day. For example, my wife takes time before dinner to change into comfortable clothes, stretch, relax, get a cold soda and sit down with a sudoku puzzle.

Me? I take the dogs for a walk (when the children were younger, they came along) before I begin making dinner. After a few minutes, Cindy joins me in the kitchen, and we start catching up on the day, weaving the important issues into longer conversations. If we are upset or tense about something that happened, we spend some time reconnecting for a short time before sharing that with each other. We do not serve anger as the first course of our meal together.

Meeting and greeting each other in love before getting into issues feeds the soul as well as the body. After all, issues will always be there. We have to bring the right spirit and the right frame of mind into the conversation so that we will look forward to breaking bread together at the table, no matter how meager the meal.

—JOHN R. THROOP

FOR YOUR NEXT DEVOTIONAL READING, TURN TO PAGE 702.

23 A wicked man accepts a bribe in secret
to pervert the course of justice.

24 A discerning man keeps wisdom in view,
but a fool's eyes wander to the ends of the earth.

25 A foolish son brings grief to his father
and bitterness to the one who bore him.

26 It is not good to punish an innocent man,
or to flog officials for their integrity.

27 A man of knowledge uses words with restraint,
and a man of understanding is even-tempered.

28 Even a fool is thought wise if he keeps silent,
and discerning if he holds his tongue.

18 An unfriendly man pursues selfish ends;
he defies all sound judgment.

2 A fool finds no pleasure in understanding
but delights in airing his own opinions.

3 When wickedness comes, so does contempt,
and with shame comes disgrace.

4 The words of a man's mouth are deep waters,
but the fountain of wisdom is a bubbling brook.

5 It is not good to be partial to the wicked
or to deprive the innocent of justice.

6 A fool's lips bring him strife,
and his mouth invites a beating.

7 A fool's mouth is his undoing,
and his lips are a snare to his soul.

8 The words of a gossip are like choice morsels;
they go down to a man's inmost parts.

9 One who is slack in his work
is brother to one who destroys.

10 The name of the LORD is a strong tower;
the righteous run to it and are safe.

11 The wealth of the rich is their fortified city;
they imagine it an unscalable wall.

12 Before his downfall a man's heart is proud,
but humility comes before honor.

13 He who answers before listening—
that is his folly and his shame.

14 A man's spirit sustains him in sickness,
but a crushed spirit who can bear?

15 The heart of the discerning acquires knowledge;
the ears of the wise seek it out.

16 A gift opens the way for the giver
and ushers him into the presence of the great.

17 The first to present his case seems right,
till another comes forward and questions him.

18 Casting the lot settles disputes
and keeps strong opponents apart.

19 An offended brother is more unyielding than a fortified city,
and disputes are like the barred gates of a citadel.

20 From the fruit of his mouth a man's stomach is filled;
with the harvest from his lips he is satisfied.

21 The tongue has the power of life and death,
and those who love it will eat its fruit.

22 He who finds a wife finds what is good
and receives favor from the LORD.

23 A poor man pleads for mercy,
but a rich man answers harshly.

24 A man of many companions may come to ruin,
but there is a friend who sticks closer than a brother.

19 Better a poor man whose walk is blameless
than a fool whose lips are perverse.

2 It is not good to have zeal without knowledge,
nor to be hasty and miss the way.

3 A man's own folly ruins his life,
yet his heart rages against the LORD.

4 Wealth brings many friends,
but a poor man's friend deserts him.

5 A false witness will not go unpunished,

and he who pours out lies will not go free.

6 Many curry favor with a ruler,
and everyone is the friend of a man who gives gifts.

7 A poor man is shunned by all his relatives—
how much more do his friends avoid him!
Though he pursues them with pleading,
they are nowhere to be found. [a]

8 He who gets wisdom loves his own soul;
he who cherishes understanding prospers.

9 A false witness will not go unpunished,
and he who pours out lies will perish.

10 It is not fitting for a fool to live in luxury—
how much worse for a slave to rule over princes!

11 A man's wisdom gives him patience;
it is to his glory to overlook an offense.

12 A king's rage is like the roar of a lion,
but his favor is like dew on the grass.

13 A foolish son is his father's ruin,
and a quarrelsome wife is like a constant dripping.

14 Houses and wealth are inherited from parents,
but a prudent wife is from the LORD.

15 Laziness brings on deep sleep,
and the shiftless man goes hungry.

16 He who obeys instructions guards his life,
but he who is contemptuous of his ways will die.

17 He who is kind to the poor lends to the LORD,
and he will reward him for what he has done.

18 Discipline your son, for in that there is hope;
do not be a willing party to his death.

19 A hot-tempered man must pay the penalty;
if you rescue him, you will have to do it again.

20 Listen to advice and accept instruction,
and in the end you will be wise.

21 Many are the plans in a man's heart,
but it is the LORD's purpose that prevails.

22 What a man desires is unfailing love [b];
better to be poor than a liar.

23 The fear of the LORD leads to life:
Then one rests content, untouched by trouble.

24 The sluggard buries his hand in the dish;
he will not even bring it back to his mouth!

25 Flog a mocker, and the simple will learn prudence;
rebuke a discerning man, and he will gain knowledge.

26 He who robs his father and drives out his mother
is a son who brings shame and disgrace.

27 Stop listening to instruction, my son,
and you will stray from the words of knowledge.

28 A corrupt witness mocks at justice,
and the mouth of the wicked gulps down evil.

29 Penalties are prepared for mockers,
and beatings for the backs of fools.

20 Wine is a mocker and beer a brawler;
whoever is led astray by them is not wise.

2 A king's wrath is like the roar of a lion;
he who angers him forfeits his life.

3 It is to a man's honor to avoid strife,
but every fool is quick to quarrel.

4 A sluggard does not plow in season;
so at harvest time he looks but finds nothing.

5 The purposes of a man's heart are deep waters,
but a man of understanding draws them out.

6 Many a man claims to have unfailing love,
but a faithful man who can find?

[a] 7 The meaning of the Hebrew for this sentence is uncertain. [b] 22 Or *A man's greed is his shame*

7 The righteous man leads a blameless
life;
blessed are his children after him.

8 When a king sits on his throne to judge,
he winnows out all evil with his eyes.

9 Who can say, "I have kept my heart
pure;
I am clean and without sin"?

10 Differing weights and differing
measures—
the LORD detests them both.

11 Even a child is known by his actions,
by whether his conduct is pure and
right.

12 Ears that hear and eyes that see—
the LORD has made them both.

13 Do not love sleep or you will grow poor;
stay awake and you will have food to
spare.

14 "It's no good, it's no good!" says the
buyer;
then off he goes and boasts about his
purchase.

15 Gold there is, and rubies in abundance,
but lips that speak knowledge are a rare
jewel.

16 Take the garment of one who puts up
security for a stranger;
hold it in pledge if he does it for a
wayward woman.

17 Food gained by fraud tastes sweet to a
man,
but he ends up with a mouth full of
gravel.

18 Make plans by seeking advice;
if you wage war, obtain guidance.

19 A gossip betrays a confidence;
so avoid a man who talks too much.

20 If a man curses his father or mother,
his lamp will be snuffed out in pitch
darkness.

21 An inheritance quickly gained at the
beginning
will not be blessed at the end.

22 Do not say, "I'll pay you back for this
wrong!"
Wait for the LORD, and he will deliver
you.

23 The LORD detests differing weights,
and dishonest scales do not please him.

24 A man's steps are directed by the LORD.
How then can anyone understand his
own way?

25 It is a trap for a man to dedicate
something rashly
and only later to consider his vows.

26 A wise king winnows out the wicked;
he drives the threshing wheel over
them.

27 The lamp of the LORD searches the spirit
of a man[a];
it searches out his inmost being.

28 Love and faithfulness keep a king safe;
through love his throne is made secure.

29 The glory of young men is their strength,
gray hair the splendor of the old.

30 Blows and wounds cleanse away evil,
and beatings purge the inmost being.

21 The king's heart is in the hand of the
LORD;
he directs it like a watercourse wherever
he pleases.

2 All a man's ways seem right to him,
but the LORD weighs the heart.

3 To do what is right and just
is more acceptable to the LORD than
sacrifice.

4 Haughty eyes and a proud heart,
the lamp of the wicked, are sin!

5 The plans of the diligent lead to profit
as surely as haste leads to poverty.

6 A fortune made by a lying tongue
is a fleeting vapor and a deadly snare.[b]

7 The violence of the wicked will drag them
away,
for they refuse to do what is right.

8 The way of the guilty is devious,
but the conduct of the innocent is
upright.

9 Better to live on a corner of the roof
than share a house with a quarrelsome
wife.

---

[a] 27 Or *The spirit of man is the LORD's lamp* [b] 6 Some Hebrew manuscripts, Septuagint and Vulgate; most Hebrew manuscripts *vapor for those who seek death*

THURSDAY
READ PROVERBS 21:1–31

LET'S STOP BICKERING

> **Better to live on a corner of the roof than share a house with a quarrelsome wife.**
>
> — Proverbs 21:9

In the late 1940s a popular radio show featured John and Blanche Bickerson, who argued about everything: John's snoring, his job, his love of bourbon, Blanche's housekeeping and her out-of-control spending. Here's a typical Bickerson exchange:

"John, you used to be so considerate. Since we got married, you don't have any sympathy at all."

"I have too. I've got everybody's sympathy."

"You'd better say you're sorry for that, John."

"Okay, I'm sorry."

"You are not."

"I am too. I'm the sorriest man that was ever born."

It's one thing for a couple to engage in a disagreement or argue about something specific—that's part of living with another person. But it's something completely different to continuously criticize one another: "You're such a slob." "You're always negative." "I wouldn't have to nag if you'd just do what I ask."

The Bickersons may have been funny, but in real life there's nothing amusing about a husband and wife who constantly pick at each other. Bickering erodes respect and eats away at a relationship. Plus, it's plain old sin, which has no place in a marriage.

I'm ashamed to admit this, but early in our marriage my husband and I got into the habit of bickering, and not just when we were alone. Eventually, a friend leveled with me. She said she and her husband had repeatedly declined dinner invitations to our house because of our constant sniping at each other.

That stung! But it was enough to get us to stop. We stopped arguing in public, and we called a moratorium on it at home. We realized squabbling with each other was like termites destroying a house: It was a continual chomping away at our relationship that would eventually lead to destruction. Instead, we had to make a conscious effort to be kind and considerate of each other.

Proverbs 17:19 says, "He who loves a quarrel loves sin." Proverbs 19:13 warns, "A quarrelsome wife is like a constant dripping." And Proverbs 17:14 states, "Starting a quarrel is like breaching a dam." Constant arguing unleashes a flood of trouble, beginning with spouting words that you may later regret.

Proverbs 21:9 says it's, "Better to live on a corner of the roof than share a house with a quarrelsome wife." The workshop in the garage or an office in the basement might do as well. Or maybe just the other bedroom. Anyway you look at it, a quarrelsome person invites distance. Choose to treat each other with kindness and respect instead, and see how much you enjoy each other's company.

—NANCY KENNEDY

let's talk

- ✦ How do we feel when we see another couple quarreling? What's our opinion of their relationship?
- ✦ Why do we quarrel with each other? What are some emotions that fuel bickering?
- ✦ If we have slipped into the habit of picking at each other, either when we are alone or with others, what are some ways we might break out of this vicious cycle?

FOR YOUR NEXT DEVOTIONAL READING, TURN TO PAGE 708.

[10] The wicked man craves evil;
his neighbor gets no mercy from him.

[11] When a mocker is punished, the simple
gain wisdom;
when a wise man is instructed, he gets
knowledge.

[12] The Righteous One[a] takes note of the
house of the wicked
and brings the wicked to ruin.

[13] If a man shuts his ears to the cry of the
poor,
he too will cry out and not be
answered.

[14] A gift given in secret soothes anger,
and a bribe concealed in the cloak
pacifies great wrath.

[15] When justice is done, it brings joy to the
righteous
but terror to evildoers.

[16] A man who strays from the path of
understanding
comes to rest in the company of the
dead.

[17] He who loves pleasure will become poor;
whoever loves wine and oil will never
be rich.

[18] The wicked become a ransom for the
righteous,
and the unfaithful for the upright.

[19] Better to live in a desert
than with a quarrelsome and ill-
tempered wife.

[20] In the house of the wise are stores of
choice food and oil,
but a foolish man devours all he has.

[21] He who pursues righteousness and love
finds life, prosperity[b] and honor.

[22] A wise man attacks the city of the
mighty
and pulls down the stronghold in
which they trust.

[23] He who guards his mouth and his tongue
keeps himself from calamity.

[24] The proud and arrogant man—"Mocker"
is his name;
he behaves with overweening pride.

[25] The sluggard's craving will be the death of
him,
because his hands refuse to work.

[26] All day long he craves for more,
but the righteous give without
sparing.

[27] The sacrifice of the wicked is
detestable—
how much more so when brought with
evil intent!

[28] A false witness will perish,
and whoever listens to him will be
destroyed forever.[c]

[29] A wicked man puts up a bold front,
but an upright man gives thought to
his ways.

[30] There is no wisdom, no insight, no plan
that can succeed against the LORD.

[31] The horse is made ready for the day of
battle,
but victory rests with the LORD.

22 A good name is more desirable than
great riches;
to be esteemed is better than silver or
gold.

[2] Rich and poor have this in common:
The LORD is the Maker of them all.

[3] A prudent man sees danger and takes
refuge,
but the simple keep going and suffer
for it.

[4] Humility and the fear of the LORD
bring wealth and honor and life.

[5] In the paths of the wicked lie thorns and
snares,
but he who guards his soul stays far
from them.

[6] Train[d] a child in the way he should go,
and when he is old he will not turn
from it.

[7] The rich rule over the poor,
and the borrower is servant to the
lender.

[8] He who sows wickedness reaps trouble,
and the rod of his fury will be
destroyed.

[9] A generous man will himself be blessed,
for he shares his food with the poor.

[10] Drive out the mocker, and out goes strife;
quarrels and insults are ended.

---

[a] 12 Or *The righteous man* [b] 21 Or *righteousness* [c] 28 Or / *but the words of an obedient man will live on* [d] 6 Or *Start*

11 He who loves a pure heart and whose
speech is gracious
will have the king for his friend.
12 The eyes of the LORD keep watch over
knowledge,
but he frustrates the words of the
unfaithful.

13 The sluggard says, "There is a lion
outside!"
or, "I will be murdered in the
streets!"

14 The mouth of an adulteress is a deep
pit;
he who is under the LORD's wrath will
fall into it.
15 Folly is bound up in the heart of a
child,
but the rod of discipline will drive it far
from him.
16 He who oppresses the poor to increase his
wealth
and he who gives gifts to the rich—
both come to poverty.

Sayings of the Wise

17 Pay attention and listen to the sayings of
the wise;
apply your heart to what I teach,
18 for it is pleasing when you keep them in
your heart
and have all of them ready on your
lips.
19 So that your trust may be in the LORD,
I teach you today, even you.
20 Have I not written thirty[a] sayings for
you,
sayings of counsel and knowledge,
21 teaching you true and reliable words,
so that you can give sound answers
to him who sent you?

22 Do not exploit the poor because they are
poor
and do not crush the needy in court,
23 for the LORD will take up their case
and will plunder those who plunder
them.

24 Do not make friends with a hot-tempered
man,
do not associate with one easily
angered,
25 or you may learn his ways
and get yourself ensnared.

26 Do not be a man who strikes hands in
pledge
or puts up security for debts;
27 if you lack the means to pay,
your very bed will be snatched from
under you.

28 Do not move an ancient boundary stone
set up by your forefathers.

29 Do you see a man skilled in his work?
He will serve before kings;
he will not serve before obscure men.

23 When you sit to dine with a ruler,
note well what[b] is before you,
2 and put a knife to your throat
if you are given to gluttony.
3 Do not crave his delicacies,
for that food is deceptive.

4 Do not wear yourself out to get rich;
have the wisdom to show restraint.
5 Cast but a glance at riches, and they are
gone,
for they will surely sprout wings
and fly off to the sky like an eagle.

6 Do not eat the food of a stingy man,
do not crave his delicacies;
7 for he is the kind of man
who is always thinking about the
cost.[c]
"Eat and drink," he says to you,
but his heart is not with you.
8 You will vomit up the little you have
eaten
and will have wasted your
compliments.

9 Do not speak to a fool,
for he will scorn the wisdom of your
words.

10 Do not move an ancient boundary stone
or encroach on the fields of the
fatherless,
11 for their Defender is strong;
he will take up their case against you.

12 Apply your heart to instruction
and your ears to words of
knowledge.

13 Do not withhold discipline from a child;
if you punish him with the rod, he will
not die.

---

[a] 20 Or *not formerly written*; or *not written excellent* [b] 1 Or *who* [c] 7 Or *for as he thinks within himself, / so he is*; or *for as he puts on a feast, / so he is*

14 Punish him with the rod
and save his soul from death.[a]

15 My son, if your heart is wise,
then my heart will be glad;
16 my inmost being will rejoice
when your lips speak what is right.

17 Do not let your heart envy sinners,
but always be zealous for the fear of the LORD.
18 There is surely a future hope for you,
and your hope will not be cut off.

19 Listen, my son, and be wise,
and keep your heart on the right path.
20 Do not join those who drink too much wine
or gorge themselves on meat,
21 for drunkards and gluttons become poor,
and drowsiness clothes them in rags.

22 Listen to your father, who gave you life,
and do not despise your mother when she is old.
23 Buy the truth and do not sell it;
get wisdom, discipline and understanding.
24 The father of a righteous man has great joy;
he who has a wise son delights in him.
25 May your father and mother be glad;
may she who gave you birth rejoice!

26 My son, give me your heart
and let your eyes keep to my ways,
27 for a prostitute is a deep pit
and a wayward wife is a narrow well.
28 Like a bandit she lies in wait,
and multiplies the unfaithful among men.

29 Who has woe? Who has sorrow?
Who has strife? Who has complaints?
Who has needless bruises? Who has bloodshot eyes?
30 Those who linger over wine,
who go to sample bowls of mixed wine.
31 Do not gaze at wine when it is red,
when it sparkles in the cup,
when it goes down smoothly!
32 In the end it bites like a snake
and poisons like a viper.
33 Your eyes will see strange sights
and your mind imagine confusing things.
34 You will be like one sleeping on the high seas,
lying on top of the rigging.
35 "They hit me," you will say, "but I'm not hurt!
They beat me, but I don't feel it!
When will I wake up
so I can find another drink?"

24 Do not envy wicked men,
do not desire their company;
2 for their hearts plot violence,
and their lips talk about making trouble.

3 By wisdom a house is built,
and through understanding it is established;
4 through knowledge its rooms are filled
with rare and beautiful treasures.

5 A wise man has great power,
and a man of knowledge increases strength;
6 for waging war you need guidance,
and for victory many advisers.

7 Wisdom is too high for a fool;
in the assembly at the gate he has nothing to say.

8 He who plots evil
will be known as a schemer.
9 The schemes of folly are sin,
and men detest a mocker.

10 If you falter in times of trouble,
how small is your strength!

11 Rescue those being led away to death;
hold back those staggering toward slaughter.
12 If you say, "But we knew nothing about this,"
does not he who weighs the heart perceive it?
Does not he who guards your life know it?
Will he not repay each person
according to what he has done?

13 Eat honey, my son, for it is good;
honey from the comb is sweet to your taste.
14 Know also that wisdom is sweet to your soul;

a 14 Hebrew *Sheol*

if you find it, there is a future hope for
you,
and your hope will not be cut off.

15 Do not lie in wait like an outlaw against a
righteous man's house,
do not raid his dwelling place;
16 for though a righteous man falls seven
times, he rises again,
but the wicked are brought down by
calamity.

17 Do not gloat when your enemy falls;
when he stumbles, do not let your heart
rejoice,
18 or the LORD will see and disapprove
and turn his wrath away from him.

19 Do not fret because of evil men
or be envious of the wicked,
20 for the evil man has no future hope,
and the lamp of the wicked will be
snuffed out.

21 Fear the LORD and the king, my son,
and do not join with the rebellious,
22 for those two will send sudden destruction
upon them,
and who knows what calamities they
can bring?

Further Sayings of the Wise

23 These also are sayings of the wise:

To show partiality in judging is not
good:
24 Whoever says to the guilty, "You are
innocent"—
peoples will curse him and nations
denounce him.
25 But it will go well with those who convict
the guilty,
and rich blessing will come upon
them.

26 An honest answer
is like a kiss on the lips.

27 Finish your outdoor work
and get your fields ready;
after that, build your house.

28 Do not testify against your neighbor
without cause,
or use your lips to deceive.
29 Do not say, "I'll do to him as he has done
to me;
I'll pay that man back for what he
did."

30 I went past the field of the sluggard,
past the vineyard of the man who lacks
judgment;
31 thorns had come up everywhere,
the ground was covered with
weeds,
and the stone wall was in ruins.
32 I applied my heart to what I observed
and learned a lesson from what I
saw:
33 A little sleep, a little slumber,
a little folding of the hands to
rest—
34 and poverty will come on you like a
bandit
and scarcity like an armed man.[a]

More Proverbs of Solomon

25 These are more proverbs of Solomon,
copied by the men of Hezekiah king of
Judah:

2 It is the glory of God to conceal a
matter;
to search out a matter is the glory of
kings.

3 As the heavens are high and the earth is
deep,
so the hearts of kings are
unsearchable.

4 Remove the dross from the silver,
and out comes material for[b] the
silversmith;
5 remove the wicked from the king's
presence,
and his throne will be established
through righteousness.

6 Do not exalt yourself in the king's
presence,
and do not claim a place among great
men;
7 it is better for him to say to you, "Come
up here,"
than for him to humiliate you before a
nobleman.

What you have seen with your eyes
8 do not bring[c] hastily to court,
for what will you do in the end
if your neighbor puts you to
shame?

---

[a] 34 Or *like a vagrant / and scarcity like a beggar* [b] 4 Or *comes a vessel from* [c] 7,8 Or *nobleman / on whom you had set your eyes. / [8]Do not go*

[9]If you argue your case with a
neighbor,
do not betray another man's
confidence,
[10]or he who hears it may shame you
and you will never lose your bad
reputation.

[11]A word aptly spoken
is like apples of gold in settings of
silver.

[12]Like an earring of gold or an ornament of
fine gold
is a wise man's rebuke to a listening
ear.

[13]Like the coolness of snow at harvest time
is a trustworthy messenger to those
who send him;
he refreshes the spirit of his masters.

[14]Like clouds and wind without rain
is a man who boasts of gifts he does not
give.

[15]Through patience a ruler can be
persuaded,
and a gentle tongue can break a
bone.

[16]If you find honey, eat just enough—
too much of it, and you will vomit.
[17]Seldom set foot in your neighbor's
house—
too much of you, and he will hate
you.

[18]Like a club or a sword or a sharp arrow
is the man who gives false testimony
against his neighbor.

[19]Like a bad tooth or a lame foot
is reliance on the unfaithful in times of
trouble.
[20]Like one who takes away a garment on a
cold day,
or like vinegar poured on soda,
is one who sings songs to a heavy
heart.

[21]If your enemy is hungry, give him food to
eat;
if he is thirsty, give him water to
drink.
[22]In doing this, you will heap burning coals
on his head,
and the LORD will reward you.

[23]As a north wind brings rain,
so a sly tongue brings angry looks.

[24]Better to live on a corner of the roof
than share a house with a quarrelsome
wife.

[25]Like cold water to a weary soul
is good news from a distant land.

[26]Like a muddied spring or a polluted
well
is a righteous man who gives way to the
wicked.

[27]It is not good to eat too much honey,
nor is it honorable to seek one's own
honor.

[28]Like a city whose walls are broken down
is a man who lacks self-control.

26 Like snow in summer or rain in
harvest,
honor is not fitting for a fool.

[2]Like a fluttering sparrow or a darting
swallow,
an undeserved curse does not come to
rest.

[3]A whip for the horse, a halter for the
donkey,
and a rod for the backs of fools!

[4]Do not answer a fool according to his
folly,
or you will be like him yourself.
[5]Answer a fool according to his folly,
or he will be wise in his own eyes.
[6]Like cutting off one's feet or drinking
violence
is the sending of a message by the hand
of a fool.
[7]Like a lame man's legs that hang limp
is a proverb in the mouth of a fool.
[8]Like tying a stone in a sling
is the giving of honor to a fool.
[9]Like a thornbush in a drunkard's hand
is a proverb in the mouth of a fool.
[10]Like an archer who wounds at random
is he who hires a fool or any
passer-by.

[11]As a dog returns to its vomit,
so a fool repeats his folly.

[12]Do you see a man wise in his own eyes?
There is more hope for a fool than for
him.

FRIDAY

READ PROVERBS 25:1–28

HAND ME AN APPLE OF LOVE

> **A word aptly spoken is like apples of gold in settings of silver.**
>
> — PROVERBS 25:11

Remember how easy it was to whisper sweet nothings to each other back when you were dating? How effortlessly you could wax eloquently about your beloved? Now you're married, and, if you're anything like most couples, you not only skip the sweet talk but you might have whole days during which the only words you exchange involve what time you'll be home and why you need to stop at the store after work.

It's funny how our words are one of the first things we take for granted in marriage. Once we've promised to love and cherish each other forever, we quickly fall into the habit of rarely mentioning that love again. We assume the other person just knows how we feel. But even those couples who exchange "I love you" on a regular basis can neglect the other words that often do more to keep a couple connected than even expressions of love. Words like "Thank you," "I appreciate you," "You did a great job," "I support your decision," "It's good to talk to you," "You're a great dad," "You're very funny"—these are the golden apples that make a relationship sparkle.

Finding each other's love languages has taken my husband and me a few years to iron out. One way I feel love is through words of affirmation. I need to be told how someone feels about me. I need them to tell me—as well as show me—that they care about me, notice me and value me.

My husband, on the other hand, is a touch guy (is there another kind?), so he tends to show me love through a hug or a little kiss on the cheek or by snuggling up with me on the couch. While I enjoy the affection, I still need him to tell me why he loves me—and tell me often. Words matter to me, and over time we've found a good balance of kind words and tender touches.

The book of Proverbs is a wonderful gift of wisdom. Deceptively simple verses like Proverbs 25:11 pack a cartload of insight into just a few well-chosen words. Comparing thoughtful words, or "a word aptly spoken," to a lovely centerpiece, as this proverb seems to do, reminds us that when it comes to nurturing the relationships that make a house a home, the things we say are as important as the things we do.

Yes, it feels good to hear "I love you" on a regular basis, but it's often those other expressions that tell us we are noticed, cared for, respected and valued. So toss your spouse a golden apple of words and watch how your marriage picks up the shine.

—CARLA BARNHILL

let's talk

- ✦ What things have we said to each other—both good and not so good—that we still remember? What has been the impact of those words on the way we feel about each other?
- ✦ Let's take some time to tell each other how we feel about each other, focusing on what we see in each other rather than what we get from each other (for example, "You have a great sense of humor" rather than "You make me laugh").
- ✦ Let's make a commitment to toss each other at least one golden apple each day. If it helps, we could keep a bowl of apples on the kitchen table as a reminder to offer each other "a word aptly spoken."

FOR YOUR NEXT DEVOTIONAL READING, TURN TO PAGE 710.

[13] The sluggard says, "There is a lion in the road,
a fierce lion roaming the streets!"
[14] As a door turns on its hinges,
so a sluggard turns on his bed.
[15] The sluggard buries his hand in the dish;
he is too lazy to bring it back to his mouth.
[16] The sluggard is wiser in his own eyes
than seven men who answer discreetly.

[17] Like one who seizes a dog by the ears
is a passer-by who meddles in a quarrel not his own.
[18] Like a madman shooting
firebrands or deadly arrows
[19] is a man who deceives his neighbor
and says, "I was only joking!"
[20] Without wood a fire goes out;
without gossip a quarrel dies down.
[21] As charcoal to embers and as wood to fire,
so is a quarrelsome man for kindling strife.
[22] The words of a gossip are like choice morsels;
they go down to a man's inmost parts.
[23] Like a coating of glaze[a] over earthenware
are fervent lips with an evil heart.
[24] A malicious man disguises himself with his lips,
but in his heart he harbors deceit.
[25] Though his speech is charming, do not believe him,
for seven abominations fill his heart.
[26] His malice may be concealed by deception,
but his wickedness will be exposed in the assembly.
[27] If a man digs a pit, he will fall into it;
if a man rolls a stone, it will roll back on him.
[28] A lying tongue hates those it hurts,
and a flattering mouth works ruin.

27 Do not boast about tomorrow,
for you do not know what a day may bring forth.
[2] Let another praise you, and not your own mouth;
someone else, and not your own lips.
[3] Stone is heavy and sand a burden,
but provocation by a fool is heavier than both.
[4] Anger is cruel and fury overwhelming,
but who can stand before jealousy?
[5] Better is open rebuke
than hidden love.
[6] Wounds from a friend can be trusted,
but an enemy multiplies kisses.
[7] He who is full loathes honey,
but to the hungry even what is bitter tastes sweet.
[8] Like a bird that strays from its nest
is a man who strays from his home.
[9] Perfume and incense bring joy to the heart,
and the pleasantness of one's friend springs from his earnest counsel.
[10] Do not forsake your friend and the friend of your father,
and do not go to your brother's house when disaster strikes you—
better a neighbor nearby than a brother far away.
[11] Be wise, my son, and bring joy to my heart;
then I can answer anyone who treats me with contempt.
[12] The prudent see danger and take refuge,
but the simple keep going and suffer for it.
[13] Take the garment of one who puts up security for a stranger;
hold it in pledge if he does it for a wayward woman.
[14] If a man loudly blesses his neighbor early in the morning,
it will be taken as a curse.
[15] A quarrelsome wife is like
a constant dripping on a rainy day;
[16] restraining her is like restraining the wind
or grasping oil with the hand.

[a] 23 With a different word division of the Hebrew; Masoretic Text *of silver dross*

WEEKEND

family values

To define what makes a family a family, examine your marriage relationship for the values and goals that bring you stability. In other words, define the meaning of your family by defining your values as a couple. What is important to you as a couple? What are your shared passions? What are you aiming for beyond yourselves?

In defining your marriage's goals and values, consider the necessary ingredients of married love, such as respect, encouragement, kindness, patience and humility. Often these are the same values you want to pass on to your children, and as such they become part of the parenting mission.

Parenting is one of the most important tasks we face, yet the plethora of parenting approaches and techniques is enough to spin any marriage out of control. Take a father who was raised in a permissive environment where he learned by natural consequences, and add a mother who was reared in a militaristic home where "yes, ma'am" and "yes, sir" were required responses to every parental command; the result is a complete confusion of values. While not all couples share such divergent parenting backgrounds, each spouse brings his or her experiences and perspectives to parenting. Finding a united approach can be difficult for any couple, but it's well worth the effort.

In today's world, there is no one right way to define a family when it comes to work. We're surrounded by many models: two-career couples, stay-at-home moms, Mr. Moms, part-time everything. While the opportunities are staggering, there are a few principles to consider when making a decision for your family mission regarding work.

1. Children need their parents. Research has shown that a child's environment from birth to age 3 helps determine brain structure and the ability to learn. A 1994 Carnegie Corporation report finds that brain development before age 1 is more rapid and extensive, more vulnerable to environmental influence, and longer lasting than previously realized. Further, the environment affects the number of brain cells, connections among them, and the way connections are wired. Early stress has a negative impact on the brain development.

The choices you make about work should be considered with the developmental needs of each child in mind. Both father and mother have a responsibility to put their child's needs before their jobs and outside activities during these foundational years.

2. Take a seasonal approach. When making decisions about work, remember that the stage of raising young children is just that: a stage. We can "sequence" our work lives, narrowing the scope of our pursuits to give priority to children when they are young.

3. Include homework in your mission analysis. When making decisions regarding work, it's easy to look only outside the home. Yet work in the home can be as distracting as work done away. Often stay-at-home moms believe their focus is their children, when in actuality they've allowed housework and volunteer work to overtake their lives. It's also common for a couple to share the role of breadwinning and yet assume household chores belong to the woman. In effect, that leaves her doing two jobs.

Take care to review the hours spent in home businesses, housekeeping, business commuting and extracurricular activities to assess what your focus should be during these child-rearing years.

A mission statement is an expression of belief. So formulate a mission statement, after careful and prayerful thought and [after] processing who you are and what really matters to you as a family. Over time, as your family grows and changes, that definition will need adjustment.

—ELISA MORGAN AND CAROL KUYKENDALL

what's your family mission?

You may not be ready to write your mission statement yet, but you can get started on it by discussing the following questions.

1. What makes our family unique?
2. What do we value as a couple?
3. What do we value as a family?
4. What traditions or rituals are unique to our family?
5. How do we define work and responsibilities in our family?
6. What priority does our marriage have? How do we live this out?
7. What is the goal of our parenting?
8. What is our parenting approach? What techniques do we believe in?
9. What are our hopes and dreams for our children?
10. What qualities do we hope our children will have?

HOW ARE WE DOING?

let's make a DATE

FAMILY DATE

This weekend have the kids plan a date for you. You may end up eating at your favorite restaurant and seeing that movie you've both wanted to see. Or you might end up with a video of their favorite cartoon. Regardless of the activity, remind the kids that they can't go along. Be a good sport about whatever they choose and enjoy the time away. (If they pick a Disney movie and cheeseburger Happy Meals, use that time to talk about how you can stretch the kids' idea of a good time to think about others' needs.)

FOR YOUR NEXT DEVOTIONAL READING, TURN TO PAGE 714.

LESSONS FROM THE *Bible*

Jesus redefined the notion of family in Matthew 12:46–50.

1. How did Jesus define family? What was the context of his response?
2. Was Jesus clear on his mission? Why or why not?

17 As iron sharpens iron,
so one man sharpens another.

18 He who tends a fig tree will eat its fruit,
and he who looks after his master will be honored.

19 As water reflects a face,
so a man's heart reflects the man.

20 Death and Destruction[a] are never satisfied,
and neither are the eyes of man.

21 The crucible for silver and the furnace for gold,
but man is tested by the praise he receives.

22 Though you grind a fool in a mortar,
grinding him like grain with a pestle,
you will not remove his folly from him.

23 Be sure you know the condition of your flocks,
give careful attention to your herds;
24 for riches do not endure forever,
and a crown is not secure for all generations.
25 When the hay is removed and new growth appears
and the grass from the hills is gathered in,
26 the lambs will provide you with clothing,
and the goats with the price of a field.
27 You will have plenty of goats' milk
to feed you and your family
and to nourish your servant girls.

28 The wicked man flees though no one pursues,
but the righteous are as bold as a lion.

2 When a country is rebellious, it has many rulers,
but a man of understanding and knowledge maintains order.

3 A ruler[b] who oppresses the poor
is like a driving rain that leaves no crops.

4 Those who forsake the law praise the wicked,
but those who keep the law resist them.

5 Evil men do not understand justice,
but those who seek the LORD understand it fully.

6 Better a poor man whose walk is blameless
than a rich man whose ways are perverse.

7 He who keeps the law is a discerning son,
but a companion of gluttons disgraces his father.

8 He who increases his wealth by exorbitant interest
amasses it for another, who will be kind to the poor.

9 If anyone turns a deaf ear to the law,
even his prayers are detestable.

10 He who leads the upright along an evil path
will fall into his own trap,
but the blameless will receive a good inheritance.

11 A rich man may be wise in his own eyes,
but a poor man who has discernment sees through him.

12 When the righteous triumph, there is great elation;
but when the wicked rise to power, men go into hiding.

13 He who conceals his sins does not prosper,
but whoever confesses and renounces them finds mercy.

14 Blessed is the man who always fears the LORD,
but he who hardens his heart falls into trouble.

15 Like a roaring lion or a charging bear
is a wicked man ruling over a helpless people.

16 A tyrannical ruler lacks judgment,
but he who hates ill-gotten gain will enjoy a long life.

17 A man tormented by the guilt of murder
will be a fugitive till death;
let no one support him.

18 He whose walk is blameless is kept safe,

---

[a] 20 Hebrew *Sheol and Abaddon* [b] 3 Or *A poor man*

but he whose ways are perverse will
suddenly fall.

19 He who works his land will have abundant
food,
but the one who chases fantasies will
have his fill of poverty.

20 A faithful man will be richly blessed,
but one eager to get rich will not go
unpunished.

21 To show partiality is not good—
yet a man will do wrong for a piece of
bread.

22 A stingy man is eager to get rich
and is unaware that poverty awaits
him.

23 He who rebukes a man will in the end
gain more favor
than he who has a flattering tongue.

24 He who robs his father or mother
and says, "It's not wrong"—
he is partner to him who destroys.

25 A greedy man stirs up dissension,
but he who trusts in the LORD will
prosper.

26 He who trusts in himself is a fool,
but he who walks in wisdom is kept
safe.

27 He who gives to the poor will lack
nothing,
but he who closes his eyes to them
receives many curses.

28 When the wicked rise to power, people go
into hiding;
but when the wicked perish, the
righteous thrive.

29 A man who remains stiff-necked after
many rebukes
will suddenly be destroyed—without
remedy.

2 When the righteous thrive, the people
rejoice;
when the wicked rule, the people
groan.

3 A man who loves wisdom brings joy to his
father,
but a companion of prostitutes
squanders his wealth.

4 By justice a king gives a country
stability,
but one who is greedy for bribes tears it
down.

5 Whoever flatters his neighbor
is spreading a net for his feet.

6 An evil man is snared by his own sin,
but a righteous one can sing and be
glad.

7 The righteous care about justice for the
poor,
but the wicked have no such concern.

8 Mockers stir up a city,
but wise men turn away anger.

9 If a wise man goes to court with a fool,
the fool rages and scoffs, and there is no
peace.

10 Bloodthirsty men hate a man of integrity
and seek to kill the upright.

11 A fool gives full vent to his anger,
but a wise man keeps himself under
control.

12 If a ruler listens to lies,
all his officials become wicked.

13 The poor man and the oppressor have this
in common:
The LORD gives sight to the eyes of
both.

14 If a king judges the poor with fairness,
his throne will always be secure.

15 The rod of correction imparts wisdom,
but a child left to himself disgraces his
mother.

16 When the wicked thrive, so does sin,
but the righteous will see their
downfall.

17 Discipline your son, and he will give you
peace;
he will bring delight to your soul.

18 Where there is no revelation, the people
cast off restraint;
but blessed is he who keeps the law.

19 A servant cannot be corrected by mere
words;
though he understands, he will not
respond.

20 Do you see a man who speaks in haste?
There is more hope for a fool than for
him.

MONDAY
READ PROVERBS 29:1–27

THE DELIGHTS OF DISCIPLINE

> **The rod of correction imparts wisdom, but a child left to himself disgraces his mother . . . Discipline your son, and he will give you peace; he will bring delight to your soul.**
>
> — PROVERBS 29:15,17

Once, a four-year-old girl cracked a tree limb across my son's face, leaving a large, painful welt. When my husband, Dan, informed the little girl's mother about what had happened, all she said was, "Oh, well, Stephanie has a problem with sticks." The girl was not disciplined for what she had done.

Another time, a friend of ours overheard his eight-year-old son use bad language. The father took the boy aside and explained the privileges he would be losing for swearing. Then the dad carried out the discipline. His son's speech quickly became more positive.

Differing views on methods of discipline, as well as challenging situations involving our own children, our spouses and others, make disciplining a daunting task for many parents. And yet the rewards of discipline are clear. Proverbs 29 says that if we impart wisdom to our children in discipline, we will find peace and the delights we desire. Those are pretty good payoffs for some front-end investments.

I'll admit there are times when I'm too tired to deal with an unruly child or I'm not up for a tussle with one of my sons over how I discipline him. But I've learned that disciplining at the moment when it's needed reaps long-term dividends.

Dan and I have always felt strongly about not allowing our boys to physically hurt each other. In our rough-and-tumble family of four boys, we've worked hard to help our boys develop the skills necessary to work out their conflicts without resorting to blows. But it has been worth it; in the 19 years we have been raising these boys, we've rarely had to break up physical altercations.

We haven't addressed other issues quite as well. When we've not been consistent, like enforcing a bedtime routine, we've paid dearly. For years, bedtime equaled bedlam in our house. Even though Dan and I agreed on how to punish the boys if they didn't go to bed on time, I often failed to enforce the consequences. That invariably led to confusion for the kids.

It wasn't until I was working at night and physically out of the house at bedtime that Dan was able to get a consistent routine going with the boys. Once I saw the benefits of Dan's good disciplining—kids who went to bed earlier and with fewer hassles—I realized that my inconsistency was merely stalling the process of receiving the "peace" I desired.

Discipline is a pay-now or pay-later plan. It always costs you something; it's just a question of when. You can invest your time and energy as opportunities present themselves, or you can wait till later, tacking on additional "fines" of disgrace and conflict—as well as forfeiting years of "peace" and "delight." The choice is yours.

—MARIAN V. LIAUTAUD

let's *talk*

- ✦ How did each of our parents discipline us when we were growing up? How did those styles differ? What was effective and what was not?
- ✦ What kinds of disciplinary approaches will we, or do we, use with our kids—time-outs, loss of privileges, delayed privileges, spankings? Are we in agreement?
- ✦ What new ways of discipline might we consider using? Who will take the lead in this?

FOR YOUR NEXT DEVOTIONAL READING, TURN TO PAGE 720.

21 If a man pampers his servant from youth,
he will bring grief[a] in the end.
22 An angry man stirs up dissension,
and a hot-tempered one commits many sins.
23 A man's pride brings him low,
but a man of lowly spirit gains honor.
24 The accomplice of a thief is his own enemy;
he is put under oath and dare not testify.
25 Fear of man will prove to be a snare,
but whoever trusts in the LORD is kept safe.
26 Many seek an audience with a ruler,
but it is from the LORD that man gets justice.
27 The righteous detest the dishonest;
the wicked detest the upright.

Sayings of Agur

30 The sayings of Agur son of Jakeh—an oracle[b]:

This man declared to Ithiel,
to Ithiel and to Ucal:[c]

2 "I am the most ignorant of men;
I do not have a man's understanding.
3 I have not learned wisdom,
nor have I knowledge of the Holy One.
4 Who has gone up to heaven and come down?
Who has gathered up the wind in the hollow of his hands?
Who has wrapped up the waters in his cloak?
Who has established all the ends of the earth?
What is his name, and the name of his son?
Tell me if you know!

5 "Every word of God is flawless;
he is a shield to those who take refuge in him.
6 Do not add to his words,
or he will rebuke you and prove you a liar.

7 "Two things I ask of you, O LORD;
do not refuse me before I die:
8 Keep falsehood and lies far from me;
give me neither poverty nor riches,
but give me only my daily bread.
9 Otherwise, I may have too much and disown you
and say, 'Who is the LORD?'
Or I may become poor and steal,
and so dishonor the name of my God.

10 "Do not slander a servant to his master,
or he will curse you, and you will pay for it.

11 "There are those who curse their fathers
and do not bless their mothers;
12 those who are pure in their own eyes
and yet are not cleansed of their filth;
13 those whose eyes are ever so haughty,
whose glances are so disdainful;
14 those whose teeth are swords
and whose jaws are set with knives
to devour the poor from the earth,
the needy from among mankind.

15 "The leech has two daughters.
'Give! Give!' they cry.

"There are three things that are never satisfied,
four that never say, 'Enough!':
16 the grave,[d] the barren womb,
land, which is never satisfied with water,
and fire, which never says, 'Enough!'

17 "The eye that mocks a father,
that scorns obedience to a mother,
will be pecked out by the ravens of the valley,
will be eaten by the vultures.

18 "There are three things that are too amazing for me,
four that I do not understand:
19 the way of an eagle in the sky,
the way of a snake on a rock,
the way of a ship on the high seas,
and the way of a man with a maiden.

20 "This is the way of an adulteress:
She eats and wipes her mouth
and says, 'I've done nothing wrong.'

[a] *21* The meaning of the Hebrew for this word is uncertain. [b] *1* Or *Jakeh of Massa* [c] *1* Masoretic Text; with a different word division of the Hebrew *declared, "I am weary, O God; / I am weary, O God, and faint.* [d] *16* Hebrew *Sheol*

21 "Under three things the earth trembles,
under four it cannot bear up:
22 a servant who becomes king,
a fool who is full of food,
23 an unloved woman who is married,
and a maidservant who displaces her mistress.

24 "Four things on earth are small,
yet they are extremely wise:
25 Ants are creatures of little strength,
yet they store up their food in the summer;
26 coneys[a] are creatures of little power,
yet they make their home in the crags;
27 locusts have no king,
yet they advance together in ranks;
28 a lizard can be caught with the hand,
yet it is found in kings' palaces.

29 "There are three things that are stately in their stride,
four that move with stately bearing:
30 a lion, mighty among beasts,
who retreats before nothing;
31 a strutting rooster, a he-goat,
and a king with his army around him.[b]

32 "If you have played the fool and exalted yourself,
or if you have planned evil,
clap your hand over your mouth!
33 For as churning the milk produces butter,
and as twisting the nose produces blood,
so stirring up anger produces strife."

Sayings of King Lemuel

31 The sayings of King Lemuel—an oracle[c] his mother taught him:

2 "O my son, O son of my womb,
O son of my vows,[d]
3 do not spend your strength on women,
your vigor on those who ruin kings.

4 "It is not for kings, O Lemuel—
not for kings to drink wine,
not for rulers to crave beer,
5 lest they drink and forget what the law decrees,
and deprive all the oppressed of their rights.
6 Give beer to those who are perishing,
wine to those who are in anguish;
7 let them drink and forget their poverty
and remember their misery no more.
8 "Speak up for those who cannot speak for themselves,
for the rights of all who are destitute.
9 Speak up and judge fairly;
defend the rights of the poor and needy."

Epilogue: The Wife of Noble Character

10 [e] A wife of noble character who can find?
She is worth far more than rubies.
11 Her husband has full confidence in her
and lacks nothing of value.
12 She brings him good, not harm,
all the days of her life.
13 She selects wool and flax
and works with eager hands.
14 She is like the merchant ships,
bringing her food from afar.
15 She gets up while it is still dark;
she provides food for her family
and portions for her servant girls.
16 She considers a field and buys it;
out of her earnings she plants a vineyard.
17 She sets about her work vigorously;
her arms are strong for her tasks.
18 She sees that her trading is profitable,
and her lamp does not go out at night.
19 In her hand she holds the distaff
and grasps the spindle with her fingers.
20 She opens her arms to the poor
and extends her hands to the needy.
21 When it snows, she has no fear for her household;
for all of them are clothed in scarlet.
22 She makes coverings for her bed;
she is clothed in fine linen and purple.
23 Her husband is respected at the city gate,
where he takes his seat among the elders of the land.
24 She makes linen garments and sells them,
and supplies the merchants with sashes.
25 She is clothed with strength and dignity;
she can laugh at the days to come.
26 She speaks with wisdom,
and faithful instruction is on her tongue.

[a] *26* That is, the hyrax or rock badger [b] *31* Or *king secure against revolt* [c] *1* Or *of Lemuel king of Massa, which* [d] *2* Or */ the answer to my prayers* [e] *10* Verses 10-31 are an acrostic, each verse beginning with a successive letter of the Hebrew alphabet.

27 She watches over the affairs of her household
and does not eat the bread of idleness.
28 Her children arise and call her blessed;
her husband also, and he praises her:
29 "Many women do noble things,
but you surpass them all."
30 Charm is deceptive, and beauty is fleeting;
but a woman who fears the LORD is to be praised.
31 Give her the reward she has earned,
and let her works bring her praise at the city gate.

ECCLESIASTES

Ecclesiastes

QUICK FACTS

AUTHOR "The Teacher," who was probably King Solomon

AUDIENCE All Israel

DATE Most likely near the end of Solomon's life (930 B.C.)

SETTING In the twilight of his life, the wise Teacher reflected on the human experience.

On the surface, Ecclesiastes is perhaps the most pessimistic book in the Bible. It was most likely written by King Solomon in his later years, after he had accumulated many wives and wandered from God's ways. It describes the emptiness of life without God. It is a book filled with questions, many of which we still ask today: Why work so hard when everything we earn is given away when we die? Why are riches and possessions so unsatisfying? Is there anything under the sun that can fill our hearts?

Solomon, renowned for his wisdom and wealth, found that apart from God, everything in life is meaningless. In his search for meaning, Solomon found that, separate from God, wisdom, wealth and pleasure are worthless and that a person's efforts to find happiness will fail if God isn't his or her strength and focus. So Solomon encourages us to give ourselves to God while we are young so that our whole life and all of our work can have meaning in him.

Marriage without God is also meaningless. Working through relationship issues can be frustrating and at times appears to be not worth the effort. However, Ecclesiastes is a reminder that we need to look to God—not our spouse—for true happiness. He is the only source of everything we need. Once we are armed with this truth, we can then nurture hope, healing and joy in our relationships.

Everything Is Meaningless

1 The words of the Teacher,[a] son of David,
king in Jerusalem:

2 "Meaningless! Meaningless!"
says the Teacher.
"Utterly meaningless!
Everything is meaningless."
3 What does man gain from all his labor
at which he toils under the sun?
4 Generations come and generations go,
but the earth remains forever.
5 The sun rises and the sun sets,
and hurries back to where it rises.
6 The wind blows to the south
and turns to the north;
round and round it goes,
ever returning on its course.
7 All streams flow into the sea,
yet the sea is never full.
To the place the streams come from,
there they return again.
8 All things are wearisome,
more than one can say.
The eye never has enough of seeing,
nor the ear its fill of hearing.
9 What has been will be again,
what has been done will be done again;
there is nothing new under the sun.
10 Is there anything of which one can say,
"Look! This is something new"?
It was here already, long ago;
it was here before our time.
11 There is no remembrance of men of old,
and even those who are yet to come
will not be remembered
by those who follow.

Wisdom Is Meaningless

12 I, the Teacher, was king over Israel in
Jerusalem. 13 I devoted myself to study and
to explore by wisdom all that is done under
heaven. What a heavy burden God has laid on
men! 14 I have seen all the things that are done
under the sun; all of them are meaningless, a
chasing after the wind.

15 What is twisted cannot be straightened;
what is lacking cannot be counted.

16 I thought to myself, "Look, I have grown
and increased in wisdom more than anyone
who has ruled over Jerusalem before me; I
have experienced much of wisdom and knowledge." 17 Then I applied myself to the understanding of wisdom, and also of madness and
folly, but I learned that this, too, is a chasing
after the wind.

18 For with much wisdom comes much
sorrow;
the more knowledge, the more grief.

Pleasures Are Meaningless

2 I thought in my heart, "Come now, I will
test you with pleasure to find out what is
good." But that also proved to be meaningless. 2 "Laughter," I said, "is foolish. And what
does pleasure accomplish?" 3 I tried cheering
myself with wine, and embracing folly—my
mind still guiding me with wisdom. I wanted
to see what was worthwhile for men to do under heaven during the few days of their lives.

4 I undertook great projects: I built houses for myself and planted vineyards. 5 I made
gardens and parks and planted all kinds of
fruit trees in them. 6 I made reservoirs to water groves of flourishing trees. 7 I bought male
and female slaves and had other slaves who
were born in my house. I also owned more
herds and flocks than anyone in Jerusalem before me. 8 I amassed silver and gold for myself,
and the treasure of kings and provinces. I acquired men and women singers, and a harem[b]
as well—the delights of the heart of man. 9 I
became greater by far than anyone in Jerusalem before me. In all this my wisdom stayed
with me.

10 I denied myself nothing my eyes desired;
I refused my heart no pleasure.
My heart took delight in all my work,
and this was the reward for all my
labor.
11 Yet when I surveyed all that my hands had
done
and what I had toiled to achieve,
everything was meaningless, a chasing
after the wind;
nothing was gained under the sun.

Wisdom and Folly Are Meaningless

12 Then I turned my thoughts to consider
wisdom,
and also madness and folly.
What more can the king's successor do
than what has already been done?
13 I saw that wisdom is better than folly,
just as light is better than darkness.
14 The wise man has eyes in his head,
while the fool walks in the darkness;
but I came to realize

[a] *1* Or *leader of the assembly*; also in verses 2 and 12 [b] *8* The meaning of the Hebrew for this phrase is uncertain.

TUESDAY

READ ECCLESIASTES 1:1–11

RECYCLING MARRIAGE ADVICE

We learned that I was pregnant with our first child on our first wedding anniversary. I remember feeling like we were the first-ever couple to have that experience. We went to Bangor, Maine, to celebrate and told our amazing news to everyone we met—waitresses, the hotel clerk, the barber who cut my husband's hair.

Those people must have thought we were terribly young and naive to think that our situation was something unique, but we *were* young and naive. Besides, our situation was unique to us. We had never before had a first anniversary or a first pregnancy. Or both at the same time.

Now that we are older, we know, like the writer of Ecclesiastes, that there truly is nothing new under the sun. Couples have conceived children in the first year of marriage for tens of thousands of years. Couples continue to have their first big fight, paint the living room the wrong color, get sick, have in-law problems, overspend on their first big purchase, lose their jobs.

But unless you know that what you're facing as a young married couple is common to other married couples, you may panic at the first sign of trouble. It's therefore important to make friends with older, wiser, "been there, done that" couples so you can observe them, listen to their stories, learn from their mistakes and benefit from their wisdom.

I well remember Mr. and Mrs. Boody, who often had us over for dinner in our first years of marriage. Old enough to be our parents, they would answer our questions about life, marriage and how to raise our daughter.

I was a new Christian at the time, and Mrs. Boody helped me to not be overbearing or obnoxious as I tried to share my faith with my non-believing husband. Mr. Boody befriended my husband as they talked sports and grilled bear steaks in their backyard. This older, mentoring couple also prayed for us. Thirty years later, we still appreciate their influence in our lives.

Just as having mentor couples is invaluable, so is passing along our own experiences to other younger couples. The Bible tells us that as we go through hardships, God comforts us so that we can comfort others who are facing similar trials (see 2 Corinthians 1:3–4). Being a "been there, done that" resource for someone else—saying, "This is how God's grace saw us through our hard time"—comforts others. It also reinforces our own faith. We've had a few younger couples sit at our table, baring their souls to us about troubles that once troubled us.

There's nothing new under the sun, but there are always new opportunities to share what we've learned and to learn from others. It's the gift that keeps on giving.

—NANCY KENNEDY

What has been will be again, what has been done will be done again; there is nothing new under the sun.

— ECCLESIASTES 1:9

let's *talk*

- Who do we think of as role models for our marriage? What qualities do we admire about their relationship?
- Are we currently facing a difficult or challenging situation? Could we benefit from having a mentoring couple?
- To whom could we be mentors? How would we initiate such a relationship? What would we have to offer?

FOR YOUR NEXT DEVOTIONAL READING, TURN TO PAGE 722.

that the same fate overtakes them both.
15Then I thought in my heart,

"The fate of the fool will overtake me also.
What then do I gain by being wise?"
I said in my heart,
"This too is meaningless."
16 For the wise man, like the fool, will not be long remembered;
in days to come both will be forgotten.
Like the fool, the wise man too must die!

Toil Is Meaningless

17So I hated life, because the work that is
done under the sun was grievous to me. All of
it is meaningless, a chasing after the wind. 18I
hated all the things I had toiled for under the
sun, because I must leave them to the one who
comes after me. 19And who knows whether he
will be a wise man or a fool? Yet he will have
control over all the work into which I have
poured my effort and skill under the sun. This
too is meaningless. 20So my heart began to despair over all my toilsome labor under the sun.
21For a man may do his work with wisdom,
knowledge and skill, and then he must leave
all he owns to someone who has not worked
for it. This too is meaningless and a great misfortune. 22What does a man get for all the toil
and anxious striving with which he labors under the sun? 23All his days his work is pain
and grief; even at night his mind does not rest.
This too is meaningless.
24A man can do nothing better than to eat
and drink and find satisfaction in his work.
This too, I see, is from the hand of God, 25for
without him, who can eat or find enjoyment?
26To the man who pleases him, God gives wisdom, knowledge and happiness, but to the
sinner he gives the task of gathering and storing up wealth to hand it over to the one who
pleases God. This too is meaningless, a chasing
after the wind.

A Time for Everything

3 There is a time for everything,
and a season for every activity under heaven:

2 a time to be born and a time to die,
a time to plant and a time to uproot,
3 a time to kill and a time to heal,
a time to tear down and a time to build,
4 a time to weep and a time to laugh,
a time to mourn and a time to dance,
5 a time to scatter stones and a time to gather them,
a time to embrace and a time to refrain,
6 a time to search and a time to give up,
a time to keep and a time to throw away,
7 a time to tear and a time to mend,
a time to be silent and a time to speak,
8 a time to love and a time to hate,
a time for war and a time for peace.

9What does the worker gain from his toil?
10I have seen the burden God has laid on men.
11He has made everything beautiful in its time.
He has also set eternity in the hearts of men;
yet they cannot fathom what God has done
from beginning to end. 12I know that there is
nothing better for men than to be happy and
do good while they live. 13That everyone may
eat and drink, and find satisfaction in all his
toil—this is the gift of God. 14I know that everything God does will endure forever; nothing can be added to it and nothing taken from
it. God does it so that men will revere him.

15 Whatever is has already been,
and what will be has been before;
and God will call the past to account.[a]

16And I saw something else under the sun:

In the place of judgment—wickedness was there,
in the place of justice—wickedness was there.

17I thought in my heart,

"God will bring to judgment
both the righteous and the wicked,
for there will be a time for every activity,
a time for every deed."

18I also thought, "As for men, God tests
them so that they may see that they are like
the animals. 19Man's fate is like that of the
animals; the same fate awaits them both: As
one dies, so dies the other. All have the same
breath[b]; man has no advantage over the animal. Everything is meaningless. 20All go to the
same place; all come from dust, and to dust all
return. 21Who knows if the spirit of man rises
upward and if the spirit of the animal[c] goes
down into the earth?"
22So I saw that there is nothing better for
a man than to enjoy his work, because that is
his lot. For who can bring him to see what will
happen after him?

---

a 15 Or *God calls back the past* *b* 19 Or *spirit* *c* 21 Or *Who knows the spirit of man, which rises upward, or the spirit of the animal, which*

WEDNESDAY
READ
ECCLESIASTES 2:12–26

WHAT WILL WE LEAVE THEM?

I hated all the things I had toiled for under the sun, because I must leave them to the one who comes after me.

— Ecclesiastes 2:18

Many people work hard all their lives, hoping to leave their children a big inheritance. Others have qualms about handing over wealth to kids who might trash the treasure. Solomon had his own reservations. He despaired at the thought of his son wasting all that he had worked for. All his kingdom building would be meaningless if his heir failed to rule wisely.

Anyone would cringe at the thought of sweating a lifetime to provide resources for children only to have them squandered. How should Solomon—or anyone attempting to leave an inheritance—balance the desire to accumulate wealth against the risk of having it squandered by those who inherit it?

One way is to teach children, early on, ways of responsibly handling money. For example, my husband's father spends time with his children, teaching them the investment strategies he has learned over the years. By sharing principles of how to build a financial base, as well as his personal values for doing so, Dan's dad is assuring himself that his children know the value of money and how to use it wisely. He is reducing the chance that they will make poor financial decisions after his death. That's the difference between leaving an inheritance and leaving a legacy.

Some parents I know decided to send their kids to a Christian elementary school. They felt that the instruction their kids received justified the financial sacrifice on their part. In recent years, their children have become independent and are challenging the spiritual beliefs they have been taught. That hurts the parents, who can't help wondering why they spent all that money on Christian education and Bible camps. Along with Solomon, they're tempted to declare that sacrifice "meaningless."

Other parents believe differently. As one mom said recently, "Kids always come back to what they know. They may drift for a time, but that base has been formed and in their own time, they will return to it." That's the essence of Proverbs 22:6, of course, which we cling to: "Train a child in the way he should go, and when he is old he will not turn from it."

Our lives are fleeting, as the writer of Ecclesiastes notes. We toil to produce a legacy for our children that will last, something that says, "This is what I valued during my life and want to pass on to you." Such work is never meaningless.

—MARIAN V. LIAUTAUD

let's talk

- ✦ How do we feel about leaving an inheritance? What kind of inheritance do we want to leave others in terms of money, property and spiritual lessons?
- ✦ If we unexpectedly received an inheritance of $50,000 from a wealthy relative, what would we do with the money? Would our use of that money please the person who gave us the money? Would it please the Lord?
- ✦ What will our children and our children's children say about us some day? How will they describe our attitude toward money?

FOR YOUR NEXT DEVOTIONAL READING, TURN TO PAGE 724.

Oppression, Toil, Friendlessness

4 Again I looked and saw all the oppression
that was taking place under the sun:

I saw the tears of the oppressed—
and they have no comforter;
power was on the side of their
oppressors—
and they have no comforter.
2 And I declared that the dead,
who had already died,
are happier than the living,
who are still alive.
3 But better than both
is he who has not yet been,
who has not seen the evil
that is done under the sun.

4 And I saw that all labor and all achievement spring from man's envy of his neighbor.
This too is meaningless, a chasing after the
wind.

5 The fool folds his hands
and ruins himself.
6 Better one handful with tranquillity
than two handfuls with toil
and chasing after the wind.

7 Again I saw something meaningless under
the sun:

8 There was a man all alone;
he had neither son nor brother.
There was no end to his toil,
yet his eyes were not content with his
wealth.
"For whom am I toiling," he asked,
"and why am I depriving myself of
enjoyment?"
This too is meaningless—
a miserable business!

9 Two are better than one,
because they have a good return for
their work:
10 If one falls down,
his friend can help him up.
But pity the man who falls
and has no one to help him up!
11 Also, if two lie down together, they will
keep warm.
But how can one keep warm alone?
12 Though one may be overpowered,
two can defend themselves.
A cord of three strands is not quickly
broken.

Advancement Is Meaningless

13 Better a poor but wise youth than an old
but foolish king who no longer knows how
to take warning. 14 The youth may have come
from prison to the kingship, or he may have
been born in poverty within his kingdom. 15 I
saw that all who lived and walked under the
sun followed the youth, the king's successor.
16 There was no end to all the people who were
before them. But those who came later were
not pleased with the successor. This too is
meaningless, a chasing after the wind.

Stand in Awe of God

5 Guard your steps when you go to the house
of God. Go near to listen rather than to offer the sacrifice of fools, who do not know
that they do wrong.

2 Do not be quick with your mouth,
do not be hasty in your heart
to utter anything before God.
God is in heaven
and you are on earth,
so let your words be few.
3 As a dream comes when there are many
cares,
so the speech of a fool when there are
many words.

4 When you make a vow to God, do not delay in fulfilling it. He has no pleasure in fools;
fulfill your vow. 5 It is better not to vow than to
make a vow and not fulfill it. 6 Do not let your
mouth lead you into sin. And do not protest
to the ⌊temple⌋ messenger, "My vow was a
mistake." Why should God be angry at what
you say and destroy the work of your hands?
7 Much dreaming and many words are meaningless. Therefore stand in awe of God.

Riches Are Meaningless

8 If you see the poor oppressed in a district,
and justice and rights denied, do not be surprised at such things; for one official is eyed by
a higher one, and over them both are others
higher still. 9 The increase from the land is taken
by all; the king himself profits from the fields.

10 Whoever loves money never has money
enough;
whoever loves wealth is never satisfied
with his income.
This too is meaningless.

11 As goods increase,
so do those who consume them.
And what benefit are they to the owner
except to feast his eyes on them?

THREE CORDS OF LOVE

A cord of three strands is not quickly broken.

— ECCLESIASTES 4:12

let's talk

- What friends do we have as a couple who are centered in Christ? What friends help us grow in faith?
- Which of the three strands mentioned above is strongest in our marriage? Which is weakest?
- How can we begin a ministry of prayer?

A jeweler was showing his friend some precious stones in his store. One caught the friend's attention because it *wasn't* beautiful. It was lusterless. When he commented on it, the jeweler picked up the stone and simply held it a moment. When he opened his hand, the stone was beautiful. "It's an opal," the jeweler explained. "It's what we call a sympathetic jewel. It takes the warmth of a person's touch to bring out its beauty."

Christian marriage is a treasure, especially if it is warmed in the grip of mutual love for Christ and love for each other. Ecclesiastes 4:12 says, "A cord of three strands is not quickly broken." I see three "cords," or principles, that make a Christian marriage strong.

The first cord is having strong friendships and a support structure of friends and family. The Teacher observes a man who is all alone. He works and works, but when he looks around he sees no one with whom to share the fruits of his labors. "His eyes were not content with his wealth," yet the man continues to toil on alone (see verse 8).

There is a quality in Christ-centered relationships that is deeply satisfying. We feel more *complete* for having spent time with someone we love. That time together needs to involve time together and time together in Christ. If we simply toil and work, what is it all worth? What do we find at the end of our lives? Only shared ministry and shared priorities that focus on Christ make life meaningful.

A second cord that strengthens a Christian relationship is a shared commitment to ministry. The Teacher tells us that "two are better than one, because they have a good return for their work" (verse 9). When we work together, we magnify our resources, strengthen and encourage each other to do more to help others and further God's kingdom. By pooling the gifts God has given us, we gain a stake in one another's work for the Lord.

The third cord of strength is praying for one another. The Teacher reminds us that "if one falls down, his friend can help him up" (verse 10). We can take this teaching in a physical sense and think of ways we can help each other when we are working or laboring together. But we can also take this teaching to remind us to help each other mentally and spiritually. One way to do this is to pray for each other continually. When we pray for one another, our times together are marked by joy and refreshment.

The apostle Paul often asked for prayer from his friends and coworkers. In Romans 15:30, he urges the Roman believers to "join me in my struggle by praying to God for me." One of the ministries we can have as a couple is to pray for our friends and then track the outcomes with them. Our friendships grow strong when we pray for each other. So do our marriages. Like the opal, we are sympathetic jewels.

—LEE ECLOV

FOR YOUR NEXT DEVOTIONAL READING, TURN TO PAGE 729.

12 The sleep of a laborer is sweet,
whether he eats little or much,
but the abundance of a rich man
permits him no sleep.

13 I have seen a grievous evil under the sun:

wealth hoarded to the harm of its owner,
14 or wealth lost through some
misfortune,
so that when he has a son
there is nothing left for him.
15 Naked a man comes from his mother's
womb,
and as he comes, so he departs.
He takes nothing from his labor
that he can carry in his hand.

16 This too is a grievous evil:

As a man comes, so he departs,
and what does he gain,
since he toils for the wind?
17 All his days he eats in darkness,
with great frustration, affliction and
anger.

18 Then I realized that it is good and proper for a man to eat and drink, and to find
satisfaction in his toilsome labor under the
sun during the few days of life God has giv-
en him—for this is his lot. 19 Moreover, when
God gives any man wealth and possessions,
and enables him to enjoy them, to accept his
lot and be happy in his work—this is a gift
of God. 20 He seldom reflects on the days of
his life, because God keeps him occupied with
gladness of heart.

6 I have seen another evil under the sun, and
it weighs heavily on men: 2 God gives a man
wealth, possessions and honor, so that he
lacks nothing his heart desires, but God does
not enable him to enjoy them, and a stranger enjoys them instead. This is meaningless, a
grievous evil.

3 A man may have a hundred children and
live many years; yet no matter how long he
lives, if he cannot enjoy his prosperity and
does not receive proper burial, I say that a
stillborn child is better off than he. 4 It comes
without meaning, it departs in darkness, and
in darkness its name is shrouded. 5 Though it
never saw the sun or knew anything, it has
more rest than does that man— 6 even if he
lives a thousand years twice over but fails to
enjoy his prosperity. Do not all go to the same
place?

7 All man's efforts are for his mouth,
yet his appetite is never satisfied.
8 What advantage has a wise man
over a fool?
What does a poor man gain
by knowing how to conduct himself
before others?
9 Better what the eye sees
than the roving of the appetite.
This too is meaningless,
a chasing after the wind.

10 Whatever exists has already been named,
and what man is has been known;
no man can contend
with one who is stronger than he.
11 The more the words,
the less the meaning,
and how does that profit anyone?

12 For who knows what is good for a man
in life, during the few and meaningless days
he passes through like a shadow? Who can tell
him what will happen under the sun after he
is gone?

Wisdom

7 A good name is better than fine perfume,
and the day of death better than the
day of birth.
2 It is better to go to a house of mourning
than to go to a house of feasting,
for death is the destiny of every man;
the living should take this to heart.
3 Sorrow is better than laughter,
because a sad face is good for the
heart.
4 The heart of the wise is in the house of
mourning,
but the heart of fools is in the house of
pleasure.
5 It is better to heed a wise man's rebuke
than to listen to the song of fools.
6 Like the crackling of thorns under the
pot,
so is the laughter of fools.
This too is meaningless.

7 Extortion turns a wise man into a fool,
and a bribe corrupts the heart.

8 The end of a matter is better than its
beginning,
and patience is better than pride.
9 Do not be quickly provoked in your spirit,
for anger resides in the lap of fools.

10 Do not say, "Why were the old days better
than these?"
For it is not wise to ask such questions.

11 Wisdom, like an inheritance, is a good thing
and benefits those who see the sun.
12 Wisdom is a shelter
as money is a shelter,
but the advantage of knowledge is this:
that wisdom preserves the life of its possessor.

13 Consider what God has done:

Who can straighten
what he has made crooked?
14 When times are good, be happy;
but when times are bad, consider:
God has made the one
as well as the other.
Therefore, a man cannot discover
anything about his future.

15 In this meaningless life of mine I have seen both of these:

a righteous man perishing in his righteousness,
and a wicked man living long in his wickedness.
16 Do not be overrighteous,
neither be overwise—
why destroy yourself?
17 Do not be overwicked,
and do not be a fool—
why die before your time?
18 It is good to grasp the one
and not let go of the other.
The man who fears God will avoid all ⌊extremes⌋.[a]
19 Wisdom makes one wise man more powerful
than ten rulers in a city.

20 There is not a righteous man on earth
who does what is right and never sins.

21 Do not pay attention to every word people say,
or you may hear your servant cursing you—
22 for you know in your heart
that many times you yourself have cursed others.

23 All this I tested by wisdom and I said,

"I am determined to be wise"—
but this was beyond me.
24 Whatever wisdom may be,
it is far off and most profound—
who can discover it?
25 So I turned my mind to understand,
to investigate and to search out wisdom and the scheme of things
and to understand the stupidity of wickedness
and the madness of folly.
26 I find more bitter than death
the woman who is a snare,
whose heart is a trap
and whose hands are chains.
The man who pleases God will escape her,
but the sinner she will ensnare.

27 "Look," says the Teacher,[b] "this is what I have discovered:

"Adding one thing to another to discover the scheme of things—
28 while I was still searching
but not finding—
I found one ⌊upright⌋ man among a thousand,
but not one ⌊upright⌋ woman among them all.
29 This only have I found:
God made mankind upright,
but men have gone in search of many schemes."

8 Who is like the wise man?
Who knows the explanation of things?
Wisdom brightens a man's face
and changes its hard appearance.

Obey the King

2 Obey the king's command, I say, because
you took an oath before God. 3 Do not be in
a hurry to leave the king's presence. Do not
stand up for a bad cause, for he will do whatever he pleases. 4 Since a king's word is supreme, who can say to him, "What are you
doing?"

5 Whoever obeys his command will come to no harm,
and the wise heart will know the proper time and procedure.
6 For there is a proper time and procedure for every matter,
though a man's misery weighs heavily upon him.

7 Since no man knows the future,
who can tell him what is to come?
8 No man has power over the wind to contain it[c];

---

[a] 18 Or *will follow them both* [b] 27 Or *leader of the assembly* [c] 8 Or *over his spirit to retain it*

so no one has power over the day of his
death.
As no one is discharged in time of war,
so wickedness will not release those
who practice it.

9All this I saw, as I applied my mind to everything done under the sun. There is a time
when a man lords it over others to his own[a]
hurt. 10Then too, I saw the wicked buried—
those who used to come and go from the holy
place and receive praise[b] in the city where they
did this. This too is meaningless.
11When the sentence for a crime is not
quickly carried out, the hearts of the people
are filled with schemes to do wrong. 12Al-
though a wicked man commits a hundred
crimes and still lives a long time, I know that
it will go better with God-fearing men, who
are reverent before God. 13Yet because the
wicked do not fear God, it will not go well
with them, and their days will not lengthen
like a shadow.
14There is something else meaningless that
occurs on earth: righteous men who get what
the wicked deserve, and wicked men who get
what the righteous deserve. This too, I say, is
meaningless. 15So I commend the enjoyment
of life, because nothing is better for a man under the sun than to eat and drink and be glad.
Then joy will accompany him in his work all
the days of the life God has given him under
the sun.
16When I applied my mind to know wisdom and to observe man's labor on earth—his
eyes not seeing sleep day or night— 17then I
saw all that God has done. No one can comprehend what goes on under the sun. Despite
all his efforts to search it out, man cannot discover its meaning. Even if a wise man claims
he knows, he cannot really comprehend it.

A Common Destiny for All

9 So I reflected on all this and concluded
that the righteous and the wise and what
they do are in God's hands, but no man
knows whether love or hate awaits him. 2All
share a common destiny—the righteous and
the wicked, the good and the bad,[c] the clean
and the unclean, those who offer sacrifices and
those who do not.

As it is with the good man,
so with the sinner;
as it is with those who take oaths,
so with those who are afraid to take
them.

3This is the evil in everything that happens
under the sun: The same destiny overtakes all.
The hearts of men, moreover, are full of evil
and there is madness in their hearts while they
live, and afterward they join the dead. 4Any-
one who is among the living has hope[d]—even
a live dog is better off than a dead lion!

5For the living know that they will die,
but the dead know nothing;
they have no further reward,
and even the memory of them is
forgotten.
6Their love, their hate
and their jealousy have long since
vanished;
never again will they have a part
in anything that happens under the
sun.

7Go, eat your food with gladness, and drink
your wine with a joyful heart, for it is now that
God favors what you do. 8Always be clothed
in white, and always anoint your head with
oil. 9Enjoy life with your wife, whom you
love, all the days of this meaningless life that
God has given you under the sun—all your
meaningless days. For this is your lot in life
and in your toilsome labor under the sun.
10Whatever your hand finds to do, do it with
all your might, for in the grave,[e] where you
are going, there is neither working nor planning nor knowledge nor wisdom.

11I have seen something else under the
sun:

The race is not to the swift
or the battle to the strong,
nor does food come to the wise
or wealth to the brilliant
or favor to the learned;
but time and chance happen to them all.

12Moreover, no man knows when his hour
will come:

As fish are caught in a cruel net,
or birds are taken in a snare,
so men are trapped by evil times
that fall unexpectedly upon them.

Wisdom Better Than Folly

13I also saw under the sun this example of
wisdom that greatly impressed me: 14There

a 9 Or *to their* b 10 Some Hebrew manuscripts and Septuagint (Aquila); most Hebrew manuscripts *and are forgotten* c 2 Septuagint (Aquila), Vulgate and Syriac; Hebrew does not have *and the bad.* d 4 Or *What then is to be chosen? With all who live, there is hope*
e 10 Hebrew *Sheol*

was once a small city with only a few people
in it. And a powerful king came against it, surrounded it and built huge siegeworks against
it. 15Now there lived in that city a man poor
but wise, and he saved the city by his wisdom.
But nobody remembered that poor man. 16So
I said, "Wisdom is better than strength." But
the poor man's wisdom is despised, and his
words are no longer heeded.

17 The quiet words of the wise are more to be heeded
than the shouts of a ruler of fools.
18 Wisdom is better than weapons of war,
but one sinner destroys much good.

10 As dead flies give perfume a bad smell,
so a little folly outweighs wisdom and honor.
2 The heart of the wise inclines to the right,
but the heart of the fool to the left.
3 Even as he walks along the road,
the fool lacks sense
and shows everyone how stupid he is.
4 If a ruler's anger rises against you,
do not leave your post;
calmness can lay great errors to rest.

5 There is an evil I have seen under the sun,
the sort of error that arises from a ruler:
6 Fools are put in many high positions,
while the rich occupy the low ones.
7 I have seen slaves on horseback,
while princes go on foot like slaves.

8 Whoever digs a pit may fall into it;
whoever breaks through a wall may be bitten by a snake.
9 Whoever quarries stones may be injured by them;
whoever splits logs may be endangered by them.

10 If the ax is dull
and its edge unsharpened,
more strength is needed
but skill will bring success.

11 If a snake bites before it is charmed,
there is no profit for the charmer.

12 Words from a wise man's mouth are gracious,
but a fool is consumed by his own lips.
13 At the beginning his words are folly;
at the end they are wicked madness—
14 and the fool multiplies words.

No one knows what is coming—
who can tell him what will happen after him?

15 A fool's work wearies him;
he does not know the way to town.

16 Woe to you, O land whose king was a servant[a]
and whose princes feast in the morning.
17 Blessed are you, O land whose king is of noble birth
and whose princes eat at a proper time—
for strength and not for drunkenness.

18 If a man is lazy, the rafters sag;
if his hands are idle, the house leaks.

19 A feast is made for laughter,
and wine makes life merry,
but money is the answer for everything.

20 Do not revile the king even in your thoughts,
or curse the rich in your bedroom,
because a bird of the air may carry your words,
and a bird on the wing may report what you say.

Bread Upon the Waters

11 Cast your bread upon the waters,
for after many days you will find it again.
2 Give portions to seven, yes to eight,
for you do not know what disaster may come upon the land.

3 If clouds are full of water,
they pour rain upon the earth.
Whether a tree falls to the south or to the north,
in the place where it falls, there will it lie.
4 Whoever watches the wind will not plant;
whoever looks at the clouds will not reap.
5 As you do not know the path of the wind,
or how the body is formed[b] in a mother's womb,
so you cannot understand the work of God,
the Maker of all things.

[a] 16 Or *king is a child* [b] 5 Or *know how life (or the spirit) / enters the body being formed*

FRIDAY
READ
ECCLESIASTES 12:1–14

WHEN TROUBLE DIVIDES US

Remember your Creator in the days of your youth, before the days of trouble come and the years approach when you will say, "I find no pleasure in them."

— ECCLESIASTES 12:1

There are days—sometimes many of them—when it is hard to remember what it was about your spouse that you once found so lovable. Most of us expect a few waves on the voyage to marital bliss. We might even find humor in our spouse's foibles and failings. But what happens when those waves swell into crushing tsunamis? What do we do when a spouse falls into a depression, when infertility becomes the only topic of conversation, or when one of us loses a job?

In his first year of teaching, my husband walked into a war zone. He taught fourth-grade boys with severe emotional and behavioral problems. Between their physical aggression, verbal hostility and profound inability to control their inappropriate behavior, these young boys sucked the spirit out of my husband. He would come home exhausted, unable to offer our family much of anything.

For the first few months, I remained sympathetic. But as the year went on, I came to resent his job—and his desire to do it—for the toll it was taking on our relationship and our children. That year I lived with Jim at his worst—his most depressed, most damaged, most disillusioned self. There were days when I truly wondered if I could sustain our marriage with him doing that kind of work.

Yet in the midst of all this awfulness, God kept showing me the things I loved about Jim: his heart for broken people, his strength of character, his resilience and tenderness. It would have been easy for me to miss the good Jim was trying to accomplish because of the overwhelming nature of the bad it brought with it. It certainly wasn't my strength that kept our family together during this time; it was God's.

Look carefully at Ecclesiastes 12:1. It doesn't say, "Remember your Creator just in case the days of trouble come." It says trouble *will* come. It comes to everyone sooner or later. That's not a reason to despair but a reason to shore up our reserves. Like a cruise ship equipped with lifeboats, we need to be prepared for the hard times by treasuring the good.

So spend some time remembering your dating days. Flip through the photos from your honeymoon. Tell each other what you admire about each other and why that will never change. Then, when trouble comes, you'll have a trustworthy life raft to hold you up as you make your way to the calm shore on the other side.

—CARLA BARNHILL

let's *talk*

- ✦ Was there a time in our marriage when it was hard to remember what we loved about each other? What got us through that time?
- ✦ How can the memory of that success help us get through the next relational rough patch?
- ✦ Let's plan a project together—creating a photo album, a compilation CD, a computer slideshow—that tells the story of our life together. When we hit a difficult season, we'll revisit this project to help us remember what holds us together.

FOR YOUR NEXT DEVOTIONAL READING, TURN TO PAGE 730.

WEEKEND

finding fulfillment

Those of us who have been married for a while tend to forget the "single ruse." By that I mean the tendency on the part of some (certainly not all) single young people to think that what they really need is to find "the one." Once their life mate is found, they assume, everything else will fall into place. Their loneliness, their insecurity, their worries about their own significance—all this and more will somehow mystically melt away in the fire of marital passion.

And, for a very short season, this might appear to be the case. Infatuation can be an intoxicating drug that temporarily covers up any number of inner weaknesses.

But marriage is a spotlight showing us that our search for another human being to "complete" us is misguided. When disillusionment breaks through, we have one of two choices: Dump our spouse and become infatuated with somebody new, or seek to understand the message behind the disillusionment—that we should seek our significance, meaning and purpose in our Creator rather than in another human being.

Approached in the right way, marriage can cause us to reevaluate our dependency on other humans for our spiritual nourishment, and direct us to nurture our relationship with God instead. No human being can love us the way we long to be loved; it is just not possible for another human to reach and alleviate the spiritual ache that God has placed in all of us.

We need to remind ourselves of the ridiculousness of looking for something from other humans that only God can provide. Our close friends have a son named Nolan. When he was just four years old, he saw me carrying some rather large boxes and asked me, in all sincerity, "Gary are you the strongest, or is God strongest?"

His dad laughed a little *too* hard at that one. And of course we adults think it's absurd to compare our physical strength with God's. But how many of us "adults" have then turned around and asked, perhaps unconsciously, "Are you going to fulfill me, or will God fulfill me?" For some reason, *that* question doesn't sound as absurd to us as the one about physical strength, but it should!

I believe that much of the dissatisfaction we experience in marriage comes from expecting too much from it. I have a rather outdated computer—so I know there are some things I simply can't do with it; there's just not enough memory or processing power to run certain programs or combine certain tasks. It's not that I have a *bad* computer; it's just that I can't reasonably expect more from it than it has the power to give.

In the same way, some of us ask too much of marriage. We want to get the largest portion of our life's fulfillment from our relationship with our spouse. That's asking too much. Yes, without a doubt there should be moments of happiness, meaning and a general sense of fulfillment. But my wife can't be God, and I was created with a spirit that craves God. Anything less than God, and I'll feel an ache.

—GARY THOMAS

where are you looking?

Finding fulfillment means knowing where to look for it. Where would you look to find the following?

HOW ARE WE DOING?

1. To buy a new outfit, I would go . . .
2. To find my car keys, I would look . . .
3. I found my best friend . . .
4. To eat a great pizza, I would go . . .
5. To find my high school yearbook, I would look . . .
6. I found love and appreciation when . . .
7. To find my birth certificate, I would look . . .
8. To call someone who would care, I would dial . . .
9. To find an extra $20, I would look . . .
10. To find my car in the parking lot of the mall, I would . . .
11. I found you . . .
12. To find my mother when I came home from school, I looked . . .
13. To get a great haircut, I would go . . .
14. To find the specials not listed on the menu, I would . . .
15. To find my lost cell phone, I would look . . .
16. The best place to relax is . . .
17. For answers to my prayers, I would . . .
18. To find the last page I read in my book, I would . . .
19. To learn more about my in-laws, I would . . .
20. To find the one who can fill me up completely, I would look . . .

let's make a DATE

TAKE A DIP INTO THE PAST

To find out more about each other, invite your in-laws over for dinner and interview them. Take notes by hand or record via audio or video. Both of you should be interviewers and create questions that ask about your in-laws' lives. What were the most interesting things they did together? Where did they go to school? How did they meet and fall in love? What were their expectations about marriage? Where did they look for fulfillment? What were some of the lessons they learned about being happy together? How did they get through times of difficulty? What advice would they give to you about finding fulfillment as a couple? When you're finished, take a few photos too.

A gift idea: Write up the interview as a "celebrity bio" or love story and present a copy to the folks on their anniversary. Be sure to save a second copy for the grandkids!

FOR YOUR NEXT DEVOTIONAL READING, TURN TO PAGE 735.

LESSONS FROM THE *Bible*

When Abram and Sarai wanted to find fulfillment, where did they look? See Genesis 16.

6 Sow your seed in the morning,
and at evening let not your hands be idle,
for you do not know which will succeed,
whether this or that,
or whether both will do equally well.

Remember Your Creator While Young

7 Light is sweet,
and it pleases the eyes to see the sun.
8 However many years a man may live,
let him enjoy them all.
But let him remember the days of darkness,
for they will be many.
Everything to come is meaningless.

9 Be happy, young man, while you are young,
and let your heart give you joy in the days of your youth.
Follow the ways of your heart
and whatever your eyes see,
but know that for all these things
God will bring you to judgment.
10 So then, banish anxiety from your heart
and cast off the troubles of your body,
for youth and vigor are meaningless.

12 Remember your Creator
in the days of your youth,
before the days of trouble come
and the years approach when you will say,
"I find no pleasure in them"—
2 before the sun and the light
and the moon and the stars grow dark,
and the clouds return after the rain;
3 when the keepers of the house tremble,
and the strong men stoop,
when the grinders cease because they are few,
and those looking through the windows grow dim;
4 when the doors to the street are closed
and the sound of grinding fades;
when men rise up at the sound of birds,
but all their songs grow faint;
5 when men are afraid of heights
and of dangers in the streets;
when the almond tree blossoms
and the grasshopper drags himself along
and desire no longer is stirred.
Then man goes to his eternal home
and mourners go about the streets.

6 Remember him—before the silver cord is severed,
or the golden bowl is broken;
before the pitcher is shattered at the spring,
or the wheel broken at the well,
7 and the dust returns to the ground it came from,
and the spirit returns to God who gave it.

8 "Meaningless! Meaningless!" says the Teacher.[a]
"Everything is meaningless!"

The Conclusion of the Matter

9 Not only was the Teacher wise, but also he
imparted knowledge to the people. He pondered and searched out and set in order many
proverbs. 10 The Teacher searched to find just
the right words, and what he wrote was upright and true.
11 The words of the wise are like goads,
their collected sayings like firmly embedded
nails—given by one Shepherd. 12 Be warned,
my son, of anything in addition to them.

Of making many books there is no end, and much study wearies the body.

13 Now all has been heard;
here is the conclusion of the matter:
Fear God and keep his commandments,
for this is the whole ⌊duty⌋ of man.
14 For God will bring every deed into judgment,
including every hidden thing,
whether it is good or evil.

[a] 8 Or *the leader of the assembly*; also in verses 9 and 10

SONG OF SONGS

Song of Songs

QUICK FACTS

AUTHOR Probably King Solomon

AUDIENCE All Israel

DATE Most likely early in Solomon's reign, around 965 B.C.

SETTING A storybook romance and steamy dialogue between two passionate lovers

Song of Songs is a series of expressive love poems celebrating the relationship of a man and a woman. The passionate exchanges between the lovers, who longingly admire each other's bodies and charming delights, are often erotic in nature.

With its romantic and sexual imagery, Song of Songs is not your typical book of the Bible, but its lessons about love are priceless. The lovers' exchanges remind us of the ways in which love can be both pleasurable and painful in its openness, honesty and vulnerability. Consequently, it needs to be protected with a "seal" of ownership through the vows of marriage (see Song of Songs 8:6–7).

God created love and sex for our enjoyment, but he also expects us to enjoy them wisely. This book encourages husbands and wives to keep the flames of love burning with purpose, passion and commitment.

1 Solomon's Song of Songs.

Beloved [a]

2 Let him kiss me with the kisses of his
mouth—
for your love is more delightful than
wine.
3 Pleasing is the fragrance of your perfumes;
your name is like perfume poured out.
No wonder the maidens love you!
4 Take me away with you—let us hurry!
Let the king bring me into his chambers.

Friends

We rejoice and delight in you [b];
we will praise your love more than
wine.

Beloved

How right they are to adore you!

5 Dark am I, yet lovely,
O daughters of Jerusalem,
dark like the tents of Kedar,
like the tent curtains of Solomon. [c]
6 Do not stare at me because I am dark,
because I am darkened by the sun.
My mother's sons were angry with me
and made me take care of the
vineyards;
my own vineyard I have neglected.
7 Tell me, you whom I love, where you
graze your flock
and where you rest your sheep at
midday.
Why should I be like a veiled woman
beside the flocks of your friends?

Friends

8 If you do not know, most beautiful of
women,
follow the tracks of the sheep
and graze your young goats
by the tents of the shepherds.

Lover

9 I liken you, my darling, to a mare
harnessed to one of the chariots of
Pharaoh.
10 Your cheeks are beautiful with earrings,
your neck with strings of jewels.
11 We will make you earrings of gold,
studded with silver.

Beloved

12 While the king was at his table,
my perfume spread its fragrance.
13 My lover is to me a sachet of myrrh
resting between my breasts.
14 My lover is to me a cluster of henna
blossoms
from the vineyards of En Gedi.

Lover

15 How beautiful you are, my darling!
Oh, how beautiful!
Your eyes are doves.

Beloved

16 How handsome you are, my lover!
Oh, how charming!
And our bed is verdant.

Lover

17 The beams of our house are cedars;
our rafters are firs.

Beloved [d]

2 I am a rose [e] of Sharon,
a lily of the valleys.

Lover

2 Like a lily among thorns
is my darling among the maidens.

Beloved

3 Like an apple tree among the trees of the
forest
is my lover among the young men.
I delight to sit in his shade,
and his fruit is sweet to my taste.
4 He has taken me to the banquet hall,
and his banner over me is love.
5 Strengthen me with raisins,
refresh me with apples,
for I am faint with love.
6 His left arm is under my head,
and his right arm embraces me.
7 Daughters of Jerusalem, I charge you
by the gazelles and by the does of the
field:
Do not arouse or awaken love
until it so desires.

8 Listen! My lover!
Look! Here he comes,
leaping across the mountains,
bounding over the hills.

---

a Primarily on the basis of the gender of the Hebrew pronouns used, male and female speakers are indicated in the margins by the captions *Lover* and *Beloved* respectively. The words of others are marked *Friends*. In some instances the divisions and their captions are debatable. *b* 4 The Hebrew is masculine singular. *c* 5 Or *Salma* *d* Or *Lover* *e* 1 Possibly a member of the crocus family

MONDAY
READ
SONG OF SONGS 1:1–17

PROLONGING THE PASSION

"*Stuck on each* other like Super Glue" is the best way I can describe the behavior of Andrea and Kevin, two friends of ours who came to visit us a few weeks after their wedding. It seemed as if every second of the day Andrea and Kevin were touching each other—holding hands during breakfast, nestling together on the couch, walking shoulder-to-shoulder around the neighborhood, playing footsie during church. And in those rare moments when they weren't physically connected in some way, they were gazing longingly at each other.

While the king was at his table, my perfume spread its fragrance. My lover is to me a sachet of myrrh resting between my breasts.

— Song of Songs 1:12–13

let's talk

- What are the symbols of romance and passion in our relationship? What do they communicate?
- When have we felt the strongest physical and emotional yearning for each other?
- What are our favorite sexual memories together so far? How can we continue to cultivate and grow the passion in our love life?

Recalling the early stages of courtship and marriage might evoke images of romance: bouquets of flowers, candlelight dinners, kisses in the starlight. But in this love poem from Song of Songs, the author creates a remarkable vision using the idea of fragrance to symbolically capture the essence of passionate love.

This love scene opens with the king reclining at his table, while his beloved is some distance away. She describes her love and desire for him as a powerful perfume permeating the room. But the next image is unforgettable: She describes her beloved as a "sachet of myrrh resting between my breasts." We imagine her descending to his couch, drawing his head to her chest, right against her heart. This image visually communicates their interdependence and longing for intimacy.

In the next verse, the woman compares her beloved to a valuable shrub in the desert oasis of En Gedi. This is not merely an expression of physical passion—she is declaring that he is an oasis to her in a dry, barren land. He is renewal! He is life!

These Biblical lovers represent the epitome of God's plan for marital intimacy: passionate love that is both physical and emotional. Like Andrea and Kevin, who couldn't get enough of each other, Song of Songs vibrantly portrays the strong feelings and desires that characterize the initial stage of courtship and marriage.

But what about the rest of marriage? The good news is that God created sexuality for all stages of marriage. Sure, the "Super Glue phase" will eventually pass, but couples who are intentional about celebrating God's good gift of sexuality can continue to discover deeper and more meaningful bonds of marital love throughout the changing stages of married life: The excitement of physical intimacy between newlyweds. The wonder at the miracle of "one flesh" when a child is born. The deepening physical connection developed in the ups and downs of parenting, career moves and changing bodies. The quiet intimacy of holding hands. A loving gaze and a confident kiss as time passes. The quiet sense of knowing each other more truly than any other human being on Earth.

The awesome, growing bond God intends for your marriage is more constant than gravity, more compelling than magnetism and far more powerful than Super Glue.

—DAVID AND KELLI TRUJILLO

FOR YOUR NEXT DEVOTIONAL READING, TURN TO PAGE 737.

9 My lover is like a gazelle or a young stag.
Look! There he stands behind our wall,
gazing through the windows,
peering through the lattice.
10 My lover spoke and said to me,
"Arise, my darling,
my beautiful one, and come with me.
11 See! The winter is past;
the rains are over and gone.
12 Flowers appear on the earth;
the season of singing has come,
the cooing of doves
is heard in our land.
13 The fig tree forms its early fruit;
the blossoming vines spread their fragrance.
Arise, come, my darling;
my beautiful one, come with me."

Lover

14 My dove in the clefts of the rock,
in the hiding places on the mountainside,
show me your face,
let me hear your voice;
for your voice is sweet,
and your face is lovely.
15 Catch for us the foxes,
the little foxes
that ruin the vineyards,
our vineyards that are in bloom.

Beloved

16 My lover is mine and I am his;
he browses among the lilies.
17 Until the day breaks
and the shadows flee,
turn, my lover,
and be like a gazelle
or like a young stag
on the rugged hills.[a]

3 All night long on my bed
I looked for the one my heart loves;
I looked for him but did not find him.
2 I will get up now and go about the city,
through its streets and squares;
I will search for the one my heart loves.
So I looked for him but did not find him.
3 The watchmen found me
as they made their rounds in the city.
"Have you seen the one my heart loves?"
4 Scarcely had I passed them
when I found the one my heart loves.
I held him and would not let him go
till I had brought him to my mother's house,
to the room of the one who conceived me.
5 Daughters of Jerusalem, I charge you
by the gazelles and by the does of the field:
Do not arouse or awaken love
until it so desires.
6 Who is this coming up from the desert
like a column of smoke,
perfumed with myrrh and incense
made from all the spices of the merchant?
7 Look! It is Solomon's carriage,
escorted by sixty warriors,
the noblest of Israel,
8 all of them wearing the sword,
all experienced in battle,
each with his sword at his side,
prepared for the terrors of the night.
9 King Solomon made for himself the carriage;
he made it of wood from Lebanon.
10 Its posts he made of silver,
its base of gold.
Its seat was upholstered with purple,
its interior lovingly inlaid
by[b] the daughters of Jerusalem.
11 Come out, you daughters of Zion,
and look at King Solomon wearing the crown,
the crown with which his mother crowned him
on the day of his wedding,
the day his heart rejoiced.

Lover

4 How beautiful you are, my darling!
Oh, how beautiful!
Your eyes behind your veil are doves.
Your hair is like a flock of goats
descending from Mount Gilead.
2 Your teeth are like a flock of sheep just shorn,
coming up from the washing.
Each has its twin;
not one of them is alone.
3 Your lips are like a scarlet ribbon;
your mouth is lovely.
Your temples behind your veil
are like the halves of a pomegranate.
4 Your neck is like the tower of David,

[a] 17 *Or the hills of Bether* [b] 10 *Or its inlaid interior a gift of love / from*

TUESDAY
READ
SONG OF SONGS 2:1–17

OUR PESKY LITTLE VARMINTS

> **Catch for us the foxes, the little foxes that ruin the vineyards, our vineyards that are in bloom.**
> — SONG OF SONGS 2:15

Most of what you read in the Bible is applicable to marriage only in that it is part of the story of how we are to live as God's people. But Song of Songs 2:15 is so completely about marriage! The wise author, for all his poetic talk about his lover, nails the biggest issue in marriage with this perfect image of how quickly a relationship can come unraveled.

My husband and I will go to our graves arguing about photographs. We have a digital camera, but nearly every picture we take with it is either too blurry or too washed out by the flash. I think it's a problem with the auto focus. Jim is convinced it's not the camera that's causing the problem but rather "user error" (which, in this case, means "Carla"). We have become so entrenched in this disagreement that we can't look at other people's pictures without bringing up the poor quality of ours.

This is the kind of stuff the Song of Songs is talking about here. It's not always the big things—money or kids or the house—that destroy a marriage; it's the little stuff. A friend of mine whose parents divorced when he was young says he remembers the night his dad left. The last thing he heard was an argument between his parents about orange juice.

Of course orange juice wasn't the problem. But how easy it is to lose sight of the real issues in our marriage and focus instead on why the dishes didn't get washed, why that bill didn't get paid or why the pictures are so out of focus. Instead of addressing the core problem, we feud over the meaningless stuff. And that meaningless stuff is what eats away at the tender vines of respect, love and trust on which healthy marriages grow.

The ugly truth is that it's easier to talk about those little foxes because it helps us avoid facing our own failures and weaknesses. I'd rather argue about the state of our camera than think about why I don't like taking instructions from my husband. It's easier to complain about how poorly he loaded the dishwasher than dig into how worn out I feel as a stay-at-home mom constantly cleaning up after three messy kids.

It's easy to get distracted by those little foxes and ignore the work it takes to tend to the bigger weeds and varmints that threaten a marriage. But in the end, tending to the beautiful vineyard of a marriage is worth all the time and trouble it takes to keep the critters out.

—CARLA BARNHILL

let's *talk*

- ✦ Experts say every couple has ten irresolvable issues. Do we have that many? How can knowing that it's normal to have some disagreements that will never be resolved free us to let go of some of those ongoing arguments?
- ✦ What are the top three "little foxes" in our marriage? What are the greater issues hiding behind those foxes?
- ✦ Let's talk about what might be at the heart of some of our bickering. If we find there are deeper issues that are just too hard to deal with, who might we ask to help us deal with them?

FOR YOUR NEXT DEVOTIONAL READING, TURN TO PAGE 740.

built with elegance[a];
on it hang a thousand shields,
all of them shields of warriors.
5 Your two breasts are like two fawns,
like twin fawns of a gazelle
that browse among the lilies.
6 Until the day breaks
and the shadows flee,
I will go to the mountain of myrrh
and to the hill of incense.
7 All beautiful you are, my darling;
there is no flaw in you.

8 Come with me from Lebanon, my bride,
come with me from Lebanon.
Descend from the crest of Amana,
from the top of Senir, the summit of Hermon,
from the lions' dens
and the mountain haunts of the leopards.
9 You have stolen my heart, my sister, my bride;
you have stolen my heart
with one glance of your eyes,
with one jewel of your necklace.
10 How delightful is your love, my sister, my bride!
How much more pleasing is your love than wine,
and the fragrance of your perfume than any spice!
11 Your lips drop sweetness as the honeycomb, my bride;
milk and honey are under your tongue.
The fragrance of your garments is like that of Lebanon.
12 You are a garden locked up, my sister, my bride;
you are a spring enclosed, a sealed fountain.
13 Your plants are an orchard of pomegranates
with choice fruits,
with henna and nard,
14 nard and saffron,
calamus and cinnamon,
with every kind of incense tree,
with myrrh and aloes
and all the finest spices.
15 You are[b] a garden fountain,
a well of flowing water
streaming down from Lebanon.

Beloved

16 Awake, north wind,
and come, south wind!
Blow on my garden,
that its fragrance may spread abroad.
Let my lover come into his garden
and taste its choice fruits.

Lover

5 I have come into my garden, my sister, my bride;
I have gathered my myrrh with my spice.
I have eaten my honeycomb and my honey;
I have drunk my wine and my milk.

Friends

Eat, O friends, and drink;
drink your fill, O lovers.

Beloved

2 I slept but my heart was awake.
Listen! My lover is knocking:
"Open to me, my sister, my darling,
my dove, my flawless one.
My head is drenched with dew,
my hair with the dampness of the night."
3 I have taken off my robe—
must I put it on again?
I have washed my feet—
must I soil them again?
4 My lover thrust his hand through the latch-opening;
my heart began to pound for him.
5 I arose to open for my lover,
and my hands dripped with myrrh,
my fingers with flowing myrrh,
on the handles of the lock.
6 I opened for my lover,
but my lover had left; he was gone.
My heart sank at his departure.[c]
I looked for him but did not find him.
I called him but he did not answer.
7 The watchmen found me
as they made their rounds in the city.
They beat me, they bruised me;
they took away my cloak,
those watchmen of the walls!
8 O daughters of Jerusalem, I charge you—
if you find my lover,
what will you tell him?
Tell him I am faint with love.

[a] 4 The meaning of the Hebrew for this word is uncertain. [b] 15 Or *I am* (spoken by the *Beloved*) [c] 6 Or *heart had gone out to him when he spoke*

Friends

9 How is your beloved better than others,
most beautiful of women?
How is your beloved better than others,
that you charge us so?

Beloved

10 My lover is radiant and ruddy,
outstanding among ten thousand.
11 His head is purest gold;
his hair is wavy
and black as a raven.
12 His eyes are like doves
by the water streams,
washed in milk,
mounted like jewels.
13 His cheeks are like beds of spice
yielding perfume.
His lips are like lilies
dripping with myrrh.
14 His arms are rods of gold
set with chrysolite.
His body is like polished ivory
decorated with sapphires.[a]
15 His legs are pillars of marble
set on bases of pure gold.
His appearance is like Lebanon,
choice as its cedars.
16 His mouth is sweetness itself;
he is altogether lovely.
This is my lover, this my friend,
O daughters of Jerusalem.

Friends

6 Where has your lover gone,
most beautiful of women?
Which way did your lover turn,
that we may look for him with you?

Beloved

2 My lover has gone down to his garden,
to the beds of spices,
to browse in the gardens
and to gather lilies.
3 I am my lover's and my lover is mine;
he browses among the lilies.

Lover

4 You are beautiful, my darling, as Tirzah,
lovely as Jerusalem,
majestic as troops with banners.
5 Turn your eyes from me;
they overwhelm me.
Your hair is like a flock of goats
descending from Gilead.
6 Your teeth are like a flock of sheep
coming up from the washing.
Each has its twin,
not one of them is alone.
7 Your temples behind your veil
are like the halves of a pomegranate.
8 Sixty queens there may be,
and eighty concubines,
and virgins beyond number;
9 but my dove, my perfect one, is unique,
the only daughter of her mother,
the favorite of the one who bore her.
The maidens saw her and called her
blessed;
the queens and concubines praised
her.

Friends

10 Who is this that appears like the dawn,
fair as the moon, bright as the sun,
majestic as the stars in procession?

Lover

11 I went down to the grove of nut trees
to look at the new growth in the
valley,
to see if the vines had budded
or the pomegranates were in bloom.
12 Before I realized it,
my desire set me among the royal
chariots of my people.[b]

Friends

13 Come back, come back, O Shulammite;
come back, come back, that we may
gaze on you!

Lover

Why would you gaze on the Shulammite
as on the dance of Mahanaim?

7 How beautiful your sandaled feet,
O prince's daughter!
Your graceful legs are like jewels,
the work of a craftsman's hands.
2 Your navel is a rounded goblet
that never lacks blended wine.
Your waist is a mound of wheat
encircled by lilies.
3 Your breasts are like two fawns,
twins of a gazelle.
4 Your neck is like an ivory tower.
Your eyes are the pools of Heshbon
by the gate of Bath Rabbim.
Your nose is like the tower of Lebanon
looking toward Damascus.

---

a 14 Or *lapis lazuli* *b* 12 Or *among the chariots of Amminadab*; or *among the chariots of the people of the prince*

WEDNESDAY

READ

SONG OF SONGS 7:1—8:7

FUELING THE FIRE OF LOVE

> **Place me like a seal over your heart, like a seal on your arm; for love is as strong as death, its jealousy unyielding as the grave. It burns like blazing fire, like a mighty flame.**
>
> — Song of Songs 8:6

let's talk

- Whose relationships have been inspiring examples for us of marital passion and commitment? What is inspiring about them?
- What would it look like in practical terms for us to put a "seal" on each other?
- How has passion led to deepened commitment in our relationship? How has our loving commitment to each other increased our passion?

Right before we exchanged rings in our wedding ceremony, something totally unexpected happened: a fire broke out! A decorative candle had burned too low and ignited a wreath of artificial leaves. Within seconds, we had a small fireball on our hands. After a few moments of confusion, a wedding guest ran down the aisle and put out the flames with a fire extinguisher, temporarily obscuring the altar with white fog.

This unplanned interruption in our ceremony was humorous for some and horrifying for others. But it dramatically paired two powerful images—fire and the exchanging of rings—that symbolize two significant ideas about marriage: passion and commitment.

At the climax of Solomon's love poem in Song of Songs, passion and commitment are intimately connected, with one naturally resulting from the other. Because of the woman's passionate desire for her lover, she made the ultimate request. She asked to claim Solomon as her own by placing her seal on his heart and arm.

In Biblical times, seals were used to indicate ownership, so Solomon's lover was "staking her claim" on her husband. But since this is a love poem with symbolic language, we can conclude that the bride was not just asking for physical or social ownership; she was making a claim on everything her bridegroom was and did. She wanted all of him—not just ownership in an outward sense, but also fidelity in his inner man.

The way we love in marriage is substantially different from the way we love other people or things. We say we "love" ice cream or our new house or our pet, but that love can't compare with the love and commitment we feel for our spouse. The bride in Song of Songs said such love is "as strong as death" (Song of Songs 8:6); it is permanent, unrelenting and final. And within this framework of ultimate commitment, her passion for her husband burned as a "mighty flame."

Popular movies and TV shows imply that passion and commitment are mutually exclusive. True sexual passion, they suggest, happens between couples who barely know each other but are irresistibly attracted to each other. Committed married couples, on the other hand, are supposedly sexually boring and passionless. What a contrast to the image of marriage that God shows us in Song of Songs, where the bride and bridegroom burned with such passion. Such love only burns brighter within the solidarity of lifelong devotion. It's the kind of strong, unyielding love that extends beyond our outward actions to the deepest core of our being.

Unlike the climactic fireball in our wedding ceremony that was quickly snuffed out, passion paired with commitment is so strong that nothing can extinguish it—not temptation, discouragement, conflict, intrusive in-laws, financial hard times, tragedy or spiritual attacks. Unlike the short-lived expressions of passion lauded in our society, God's plan for marriage is an enduring flame of passion that lasts all the years of our life together.

—DAVID AND KELLI TRUJILLO

FOR YOUR NEXT DEVOTIONAL READING, TURN TO PAGE 744.

5 Your head crowns you like Mount Carmel.
Your hair is like royal tapestry;
the king is held captive by its tresses.
6 How beautiful you are and how pleasing,
O love, with your delights!
7 Your stature is like that of the palm,
and your breasts like clusters of fruit.
8 I said, "I will climb the palm tree;
I will take hold of its fruit."
May your breasts be like the clusters of the vine,
the fragrance of your breath like apples,
9 and your mouth like the best wine.

Beloved

May the wine go straight to my lover,
flowing gently over lips and teeth.[a]
10 I belong to my lover,
and his desire is for me.
11 Come, my lover, let us go to the countryside,
let us spend the night in the villages.[b]
12 Let us go early to the vineyards
to see if the vines have budded,
if their blossoms have opened,
and if the pomegranates are in bloom—
there I will give you my love.
13 The mandrakes send out their fragrance,
and at our door is every delicacy,
both new and old,
that I have stored up for you, my lover.

8 If only you were to me like a brother,
who was nursed at my mother's breasts!
Then, if I found you outside,
I would kiss you,
and no one would despise me.
2 I would lead you
and bring you to my mother's house—
she who has taught me.
I would give you spiced wine to drink,
the nectar of my pomegranates.
3 His left arm is under my head
and his right arm embraces me.
4 Daughters of Jerusalem, I charge you:
Do not arouse or awaken love
until it so desires.

Friends

5 Who is this coming up from the desert
leaning on her lover?

Beloved

Under the apple tree I roused you;
there your mother conceived you,
there she who was in labor gave you birth.
6 Place me like a seal over your heart,
like a seal on your arm;
for love is as strong as death,
its jealousy[c] unyielding as the grave.[d]
It burns like blazing fire,
like a mighty flame.[e]
7 Many waters cannot quench love;
rivers cannot wash it away.
If one were to give
all the wealth of his house for love,
it[f] would be utterly scorned.

Friends

8 We have a young sister,
and her breasts are not yet grown.
What shall we do for our sister
for the day she is spoken for?
9 If she is a wall,
we will build towers of silver on her.
If she is a door,
we will enclose her with panels of cedar.

Beloved

10 I am a wall,
and my breasts are like towers.
Thus I have become in his eyes
like one bringing contentment.
11 Solomon had a vineyard in Baal Hamon;
he let out his vineyard to tenants.
Each was to bring for its fruit
a thousand shekels[g] of silver.
12 But my own vineyard is mine to give;
the thousand shekels are for you, O Solomon,
and two hundred[h] are for those who tend its fruit.

Lover

13 You who dwell in the gardens
with friends in attendance,
let me hear your voice!

Beloved

14 Come away, my lover,
and be like a gazelle
or like a young stag
on the spice-laden mountains.

---

[a] 9 Septuagint, Aquila, Vulgate and Syriac; Hebrew *lips of sleepers* [b] 11 Or *henna bushes* [c] 6 Or *ardor* [d] 6 Hebrew *Sheol* [e] 6 Or / *like the very flame of the LORD* [f] 7 Or *he* [g] 11 That is, about 25 pounds (about 11.5 kilograms); also in verse 12 [h] 12 That is, about 5 pounds (about 2.3 kilograms)

ISAIAH

Isaiah

QUICK FACTS

AUTHOR Isaiah

AUDIENCE The people of Judah and Israel

DATE Between 740 and 680 B.C.

SETTING The stormy period of the expansion of the Assyrian Empire, during which Israel was conquered and Judah was threatened

Isaiah, who was a prophet of God and influential in the king's court, was called to deliver a message of both judgment and mercy to his fellow Israelites. Though he likely spent most of his life in Jerusalem, Isaiah predicted judgment upon the northern kingdom of Israel as well as the southern kingdom of Judah—and upon the surrounding nations. But Isaiah also delivered a message of hope for those who cried out to God for mercy and forgiveness.

With powerful images— such as a person covered with open sores, cities burned by fire and fields stripped by foreigners (see Isaiah 1:6–7)—the prophet encouraged those who would be broken, conquered and seemingly abandoned not to give up hope, because the Messiah would be coming. In time, the Lord's servant would not only suffer and die for his people, but he would also redeem them and reign over them in glorious fulfillment of God's promises.

Isaiah's words of warning, judgment and consolation offer us many insights in regard to marriage. The book of Isaiah shows how sin separates us from God—and each other. It reminds us that difficult times may be necessary to bring us to repentance. But even in the most painful times, we have a Savior who intercedes for us so that we might be restored and blessed in him.

1 The vision concerning Judah and Jerusalem that Isaiah son of Amoz saw during the reigns of Uzziah, Jotham, Ahaz and Hezekiah, kings of Judah.

A Rebellious Nation

2 Hear, O heavens! Listen, O earth!
For the LORD has spoken:
"I reared children and brought them up,
but they have rebelled against me.
3 The ox knows his master,
the donkey his owner's manger,
but Israel does not know,
my people do not understand."

4 Ah, sinful nation,
a people loaded with guilt,
a brood of evildoers,
children given to corruption!
They have forsaken the LORD;
they have spurned the Holy One of Israel
and turned their backs on him.

5 Why should you be beaten anymore?
Why do you persist in rebellion?
Your whole head is injured,
your whole heart afflicted.
6 From the sole of your foot to the top of your head
there is no soundness—
only wounds and welts
and open sores,
not cleansed or bandaged
or soothed with oil.

7 Your country is desolate,
your cities burned with fire;
your fields are being stripped by foreigners
right before you,
laid waste as when overthrown by strangers.
8 The Daughter of Zion is left
like a shelter in a vineyard,
like a hut in a field of melons,
like a city under siege.
9 Unless the LORD Almighty
had left us some survivors,
we would have become like Sodom,
we would have been like Gomorrah.

10 Hear the word of the LORD,
you rulers of Sodom;
listen to the law of our God,
you people of Gomorrah!
11 "The multitude of your sacrifices—
what are they to me?" says the LORD.
"I have more than enough of burnt offerings,
of rams and the fat of fattened animals;
I have no pleasure
in the blood of bulls and lambs and goats.
12 When you come to appear before me,
who has asked this of you,
this trampling of my courts?
13 Stop bringing meaningless offerings!
Your incense is detestable to me.
New Moons, Sabbaths and convocations—
I cannot bear your evil assemblies.
14 Your New Moon festivals and your appointed feasts
my soul hates.
They have become a burden to me;
I am weary of bearing them.
15 When you spread out your hands in prayer,
I will hide my eyes from you;
even if you offer many prayers,
I will not listen.
Your hands are full of blood;
16 wash and make yourselves clean.
Take your evil deeds
out of my sight!
Stop doing wrong,
17 learn to do right!
Seek justice,
encourage the oppressed. [a]
Defend the cause of the fatherless,
plead the case of the widow.

18 "Come now, let us reason together,"
says the LORD.
"Though your sins are like scarlet,
they shall be as white as snow;
though they are red as crimson,
they shall be like wool.
19 If you are willing and obedient,
you will eat the best from the land;
20 but if you resist and rebel,
you will be devoured by the sword."
For the mouth of the LORD has spoken.

21 See how the faithful city
has become a harlot!
She once was full of justice;
righteousness used to dwell in her—
but now murderers!
22 Your silver has become dross,
your choice wine is diluted with water.
23 Your rulers are rebels,

a 17 Or / *rebuke the oppressor*

THURSDAY
READ ISAIAH 1:1–20

THE BEST WAY TO LIVE

> **"If you are willing and obedient, you will eat the best from the land; but if you resist and rebel, you will be devoured by the sword."**
>
> — ISAIAH 1:19–20

let's talk

- In what ways are we willing to live for the Lord and each other? What are some easy ways to do that? How can those ways be difficult?
- How do husbands and wives become resistant to each other? Do we see a pattern of resistance in our marriage? What might we do to overcome that?
- What does the combination of willingness and obedience between husband and wife teach children about marriage? What are some hard lessons we've learned when we've been resistant to God's ways?

Ben and Beth were neighbors of Luke and Trish. Their kids frequently played together. But the two Christian couples were as different from each other as night and day. Ben and Beth bought expensive cars, furniture and clothes. They traveled often. They seemed to be happy on the outside, but they argued a lot, especially when they had too much to drink.

Luke and Trish also had a Christian upbringing, but they prioritized their lives so that they had time for spiritual growth. They didn't have much money, but they enjoyed life together and had fun with their children. Of course, this didn't guarantee them a perfect marriage. They argued at times, but they worked hard to communicate and had a shared foundation in their faith. Luke and Trish went to church regularly and had lots of friends there. It was evident that they were growing together in their walk with God.

Isaiah 1:19–20 offers both a promise and a warning to couples. If we are willing and obedient to God, we will "eat the best from the land"; if we resist and rebel, we will be "devoured by the sword." For the people of Israel, there were always two elements of a relationship with God: inner character and outer action. One had an impact on the other.

That same principle can be applied in marriage. A willingness to live out the marriage commitment plus actions that demonstrate obedience to God's Word most often result in a life of inner peace and joy. But resistance to God's call to faithfulness plus rebellion against a godly life often result in disaster.

How are we to be obedient to God and to each other in marriage? As Luke and Trish discovered, obedience becomes crucial in tough times, when it is easy to resist each other and act out of anger. When Luke lost his job, for example, the couple chose to trust God for his provision and support each other rather than to be angry and embittered. In time, Luke found a good job with better work hours. Through the ordeal their marriage became stronger as they trusted God and each other.

How different things went for Ben and Beth when Ben lost his job. Ben and Beth became increasingly angry about the situation. Instead of turning to God and fellow Christians for support during this hard time, the couple became impatient with each other and began to blame each other for their problems. Eventually they became so stuck in the blame game that their marriage ended in divorce.

As Isaiah 1 tells us, those who ignore and rebel against God's commands become restless and unfulfilled. When trouble comes and they succumb to anger and bitterness, their world and marriage can fall to pieces. But couples who walk together in the Lord reach for him and for each other when rough patches come. In so doing they find help, happiness and peace.

—JOHN R. THROOP

FOR YOUR NEXT DEVOTIONAL READING, TURN TO PAGE 748.

companions of thieves;
they all love bribes
and chase after gifts.
They do not defend the cause of the fatherless;
the widow's case does not come before them.
24 Therefore the Lord, the LORD Almighty,
the Mighty One of Israel, declares:
"Ah, I will get relief from my foes
and avenge myself on my enemies.
25 I will turn my hand against you;
I will thoroughly purge away your dross
and remove all your impurities.
26 I will restore your judges as in days of old,
your counselors as at the beginning.
Afterward you will be called
the City of Righteousness,
the Faithful City."
27 Zion will be redeemed with justice,
her penitent ones with righteousness.
28 But rebels and sinners will both be broken,
and those who forsake the LORD will perish.
29 "You will be ashamed because of the sacred oaks
in which you have delighted;
you will be disgraced because of the gardens
that you have chosen.
30 You will be like an oak with fading leaves,
like a garden without water.
31 The mighty man will become tinder
and his work a spark;
both will burn together,
with no one to quench the fire."

The Mountain of the LORD

2 This is what Isaiah son of Amoz saw concerning Judah and Jerusalem:

2 In the last days
the mountain of the LORD's temple will be established
as chief among the mountains;
it will be raised above the hills,
and all nations will stream to it.
3 Many peoples will come and say,
"Come, let us go up to the mountain of the LORD,
to the house of the God of Jacob.
He will teach us his ways,
so that we may walk in his paths."
The law will go out from Zion,
the word of the LORD from Jerusalem.
4 He will judge between the nations
and will settle disputes for many peoples.
They will beat their swords into plowshares
and their spears into pruning hooks.
Nation will not take up sword against nation,
nor will they train for war anymore.

5 Come, O house of Jacob,
let us walk in the light of the LORD.

The Day of the LORD

6 You have abandoned your people,
the house of Jacob.
They are full of superstitions from the East;
they practice divination like the Philistines
and clasp hands with pagans.
7 Their land is full of silver and gold;
there is no end to their treasures.
Their land is full of horses;
there is no end to their chariots.
8 Their land is full of idols;
they bow down to the work of their hands,
to what their fingers have made.
9 So man will be brought low
and mankind humbled—
do not forgive them.[a]

10 Go into the rocks,
hide in the ground
from dread of the LORD
and the splendor of his majesty!
11 The eyes of the arrogant man will be humbled
and the pride of men brought low;
the LORD alone will be exalted in that day.

12 The LORD Almighty has a day in store
for all the proud and lofty,
for all that is exalted
(and they will be humbled),
13 for all the cedars of Lebanon, tall and lofty,
and all the oaks of Bashan,
14 for all the towering mountains
and all the high hills,
15 for every lofty tower
and every fortified wall,
16 for every trading ship[b]
and every stately vessel.

[a] 9 Or *not raise them up* [b] 16 Hebrew *every ship of Tarshish*

17 The arrogance of man will be brought low
and the pride of men humbled;
the LORD alone will be exalted in that day,
18 and the idols will totally disappear.

19 Men will flee to caves in the rocks
and to holes in the ground
from dread of the LORD
and the splendor of his majesty,
when he rises to shake the earth.
20 In that day men will throw away
to the rodents and bats
their idols of silver and idols of gold,
which they made to worship.
21 They will flee to caverns in the rocks
and to the overhanging crags
from dread of the LORD
and the splendor of his majesty,
when he rises to shake the earth.

22 Stop trusting in man,
who has but a breath in his nostrils.
Of what account is he?

Judgment on Jerusalem and Judah

3 See now, the Lord,
the LORD Almighty,
is about to take from Jerusalem and Judah
both supply and support:
all supplies of food and all supplies of
water,
2 the hero and warrior,
the judge and prophet,
the soothsayer and elder,
3 the captain of fifty and man of rank,
the counselor, skilled craftsman and
clever enchanter.

4 I will make boys their officials;
mere children will govern them.
5 People will oppress each other—
man against man, neighbor against
neighbor.
The young will rise up against the old,
the base against the honorable.

6 A man will seize one of his brothers
at his father's home, and say,
"You have a cloak, you be our leader;
take charge of this heap of ruins!"
7 But in that day he will cry out,
"I have no remedy.
I have no food or clothing in my house;
do not make me the leader of the
people."

8 Jerusalem staggers,
Judah is falling;
their words and deeds are against the
LORD,
defying his glorious presence.
9 The look on their faces testifies against
them;
they parade their sin like Sodom;
they do not hide it.
Woe to them!
They have brought disaster upon
themselves.

10 Tell the righteous it will be well with
them,
for they will enjoy the fruit of their
deeds.
11 Woe to the wicked! Disaster is upon them!
They will be paid back for what their
hands have done.

12 Youths oppress my people,
women rule over them.
O my people, your guides lead you astray;
they turn you from the path.

13 The LORD takes his place in court;
he rises to judge the people.
14 The LORD enters into judgment
against the elders and leaders of his
people:
"It is you who have ruined my vineyard;
the plunder from the poor is in your
houses.
15 What do you mean by crushing my people
and grinding the faces of the poor?"
declares the Lord,
the LORD Almighty.

16 The LORD says,
"The women of Zion are haughty,
walking along with outstretched necks,
flirting with their eyes,
tripping along with mincing steps,
with ornaments jingling on their
ankles.
17 Therefore the Lord will bring sores on the
heads of the women of Zion;
the LORD will make their scalps bald."

18 In that day the Lord will snatch away
their finery: the bangles and headbands and
crescent necklaces, 19 the earrings and bracelets
and veils, 20 the headdresses and ankle chains
and sashes, the perfume bottles and charms,
21 the signet rings and nose rings, 22 the fine
robes and the capes and cloaks, the purses
23 and mirrors, and the linen garments and ti-
aras and shawls.

24 Instead of fragrance there will be a stench;
instead of a sash, a rope;

instead of well-dressed hair, baldness;
instead of fine clothing, sackcloth;
instead of beauty, branding.
25 Your men will fall by the sword,
your warriors in battle.
26 The gates of Zion will lament and mourn;
destitute, she will sit on the ground.

4 1 In that day seven women
will take hold of one man
and say, "We will eat our own food
and provide our own clothes;
only let us be called by your name.
Take away our disgrace!"

The Branch of the LORD

2 In that day the Branch of the LORD will
be beautiful and glorious, and the fruit of the
land will be the pride and glory of the survivors in Israel. 3 Those who are left in Zion,
who remain in Jerusalem, will be called holy,
all who are recorded among the living in Jerusalem. 4 The Lord will wash away the filth of
the women of Zion; he will cleanse the blood-
stains from Jerusalem by a spirit[a] of judgment
and a spirit[a] of fire. 5 Then the LORD will create over all of Mount Zion and over those who
assemble there a cloud of smoke by day and a
glow of flaming fire by night; over all the glory
will be a canopy. 6 It will be a shelter and shade
from the heat of the day, and a refuge and hiding place from the storm and rain.

The Song of the Vineyard

5 I will sing for the one I love
a song about his vineyard:
My loved one had a vineyard
on a fertile hillside.
2 He dug it up and cleared it of stones
and planted it with the choicest vines.
He built a watchtower in it
and cut out a winepress as well.
Then he looked for a crop of good grapes,
but it yielded only bad fruit.

3 "Now you dwellers in Jerusalem and men
of Judah,
judge between me and my vineyard.
4 What more could have been done for my
vineyard
than I have done for it?
When I looked for good grapes,
why did it yield only bad?
5 Now I will tell you
what I am going to do to my vineyard:
I will take away its hedge,
and it will be destroyed;
I will break down its wall,
and it will be trampled.
6 I will make it a wasteland,
neither pruned nor cultivated,
and briers and thorns will grow there.
I will command the clouds
not to rain on it."

7 The vineyard of the LORD Almighty
is the house of Israel,
and the men of Judah
are the garden of his delight.
And he looked for justice, but saw
bloodshed;
for righteousness, but heard cries of
distress.

Woes and Judgments

8 Woe to you who add house to house
and join field to field
till no space is left
and you live alone in the land.

9 The LORD Almighty has declared in my
hearing:

"Surely the great houses will become
desolate,
the fine mansions left without
occupants.
10 A ten-acre[b] vineyard will produce only a
bath[c] of wine,
a homer[d] of seed only an ephah[e] of
grain."

11 Woe to those who rise early in the
morning
to run after their drinks,
who stay up late at night
till they are inflamed with wine.
12 They have harps and lyres at their
banquets,
tambourines and flutes and wine,
but they have no regard for the deeds of
the LORD,
no respect for the work of his hands.
13 Therefore my people will go into exile
for lack of understanding;
their men of rank will die of hunger
and their masses will be parched with
thirst.
14 Therefore the grave[f] enlarges its appetite
and opens its mouth without limit;

---

[a] 4 Or *the Spirit* [b] 10 Hebrew *ten-yoke,* that is, the land plowed by 10 yoke of oxen in one day [c] 10 That is, probably about 6 gallons (about 22 liters) [d] 10 That is, probably about 6 bushels (about 220 liters) [e] 10 That is, probably about 3/5 bushel (about 22 liters) [f] 14 Hebrew *Sheol*

FRIDAY

READ ISAIAH 5:1–7

TENDING OUR MARRIAGE

> **"What more could have been done for my vineyard than I have done for it?"**
>
> — ISAIAH 5:4

let's talk

- When we reflect on our life together (how we met, our courtship and our engagement), where do we see God's guidance, protection and nurturing?
- If we, as God's people, are compared to a vineyard, how might we ensure the growth of good fruit within our marriage? What types of fruit do we most want to produce as a couple?
- What habits or behaviors have we fallen into that could spoil the fruit of our marriage? What steps can we take to stop those damaging patterns?

When I was young, I attended the wedding of an extended family member. I don't remember much about the ceremony, dancing or food. But I do remember the terrible fight at the reception. In front of all the guests, a woman screamed at her husband, broke down in tears and hid in a corner while her friends consoled her. The man yelled back, threatened to hit her, then stormed out of the building with his friends. He did not return that night.

It might shock you to learn that I'm describing the bride and groom. But it probably will not surprise you to learn that their marriage lasted less than a month.

In Isaiah 5, God addressed the people of Israel and described himself as the owner of a vineyard and Israel as the vineyard. He had chosen a prime location for his grapevines, nurtured the soil and protected the land from harm. But in the end, the crop of grapes was no good. So he asked, "What more could have been done for my vineyard than I have done for it?"

The farmer had done everything right; there was no reason why the crop should not have flourished. But the painful message soon became clear: Israel had failed despite God's efforts to ensure her success. Though the people kept up elaborate rituals of worship, those were meaningless to God because the people neglected to do what he truly valued: caring for orphans, widows and the poor. As a result, they managed to spoil the harvest that God had nurtured.

God offers this same nurturing care today for your marriage. Even before you met your spouse, God was preparing the soil, removing the stones and building a watchtower. God placed you in a cultivated land, ready to produce good fruit. But in this vineyard, the Farmer doesn't do all the work; you must also do your part.

More and more Christian couples today are producing bad marital fruit, spoiling their relationship despite God the Farmer's efforts. Some couples, like the couple mentioned earlier, manage to kill their vine before it even takes hold.

In the end, a marriage will be judged not by the strength of its passion or by its ceremonial promises, but by the fruit it produces. The Farmer is there to weed, water and cultivate. But we must also take practical steps that will help our marriage reflect authentic devotion to each other and a true love for God and his values.

We can choose to forgive quickly and resist resentment. We can serve each other in purposeful ways throughout the day. We can encourage each other with words of love and by praying for each other. We can invite strong Christian couples to mentor us in spiritual growth. We can minister to others in need. By authentically reflecting God's values in our relationship, we can do our part to nourish our marriage vineyard and produce a harvest of good fruit.

—DAVID AND KELLI TRUJILLO

FOR YOUR NEXT DEVOTIONAL READING, TURN TO PAGE 752.

into it will descend their nobles and
masses
with all their brawlers and revelers.
15 So man will be brought low
and mankind humbled,
the eyes of the arrogant humbled.
16 But the LORD Almighty will be exalted by
his justice,
and the holy God will show himself
holy by his righteousness.
17 Then sheep will graze as in their own
pasture;
lambs will feed[a] among the ruins of the
rich.

18 Woe to those who draw sin along with
cords of deceit,
and wickedness as with cart ropes,
19 to those who say, "Let God hurry,
let him hasten his work
so we may see it.
Let it approach,
let the plan of the Holy One of Israel
come,
so we may know it."

20 Woe to those who call evil good
and good evil,
who put darkness for light
and light for darkness,
who put bitter for sweet
and sweet for bitter.

21 Woe to those who are wise in their own
eyes
and clever in their own sight.

22 Woe to those who are heroes at drinking
wine
and champions at mixing drinks,
23 who acquit the guilty for a bribe,
but deny justice to the innocent.
24 Therefore, as tongues of fire lick up straw
and as dry grass sinks down in the
flames,
so their roots will decay
and their flowers blow away like dust;
for they have rejected the law of the LORD
Almighty
and spurned the word of the Holy One
of Israel.
25 Therefore the LORD's anger burns against
his people;
his hand is raised and he strikes them
down.
The mountains shake,
and the dead bodies are like refuse in
the streets.

Yet for all this, his anger is not turned
away,
his hand is still upraised.

26 He lifts up a banner for the distant nations,
he whistles for those at the ends of the
earth.
Here they come,
swiftly and speedily!
27 Not one of them grows tired or stumbles,
not one slumbers or sleeps;
not a belt is loosened at the waist,
not a sandal thong is broken.
28 Their arrows are sharp,
all their bows are strung;
their horses' hoofs seem like flint,
their chariot wheels like a whirlwind.
29 Their roar is like that of the lion,
they roar like young lions;
they growl as they seize their prey
and carry it off with no one to rescue.
30 In that day they will roar over it
like the roaring of the sea.
And if one looks at the land,
he will see darkness and distress;
even the light will be darkened by the
clouds.

Isaiah's Commission

6 In the year that King Uzziah died, I saw the
Lord seated on a throne, high and exalted,
and the train of his robe filled the temple.
2 Above him were seraphs, each with six wings:
With two wings they covered their faces, with
two they covered their feet, and with two they
were flying. 3 And they were calling to one another:

"Holy, holy, holy is the LORD Almighty;
the whole earth is full of his glory."

4 At the sound of their voices the doorposts
and thresholds shook and the temple was
filled with smoke.
5 "Woe to me!" I cried. "I am ruined! For I
am a man of unclean lips, and I live among a
people of unclean lips, and my eyes have seen
the King, the LORD Almighty."
6 Then one of the seraphs flew to me with
a live coal in his hand, which he had taken
with tongs from the altar. 7 With it he touched
my mouth and said, "See, this has touched
your lips; your guilt is taken away and your
sin atoned for."

[a] 17 Septuagint; Hebrew / *strangers will eat*

8Then I heard the voice of the Lord saying, "Whom shall I send? And who will go
for us?"
And I said, "Here am I. Send me!"
9He said, "Go and tell this people:

" 'Be ever hearing, but never
understanding;
be ever seeing, but never perceiving.'
10 Make the heart of this people calloused;
make their ears dull
and close their eyes.[a]
Otherwise they might see with their eyes,
hear with their ears,
understand with their hearts,
and turn and be healed."

11Then I said, "For how long, O Lord?"
And he answered:

"Until the cities lie ruined
and without inhabitant,
until the houses are left deserted
and the fields ruined and ravaged,
12 until the LORD has sent everyone far
away
and the land is utterly forsaken.
13 And though a tenth remains in the land,
it will again be laid waste.
But as the terebinth and oak
leave stumps when they are cut down,
so the holy seed will be the stump in
the land."

The Sign of Immanuel

7 When Ahaz son of Jotham, the son of Uzziah, was king of Judah, King Rezin of
Aram and Pekah son of Remaliah king of
Israel marched up to fight against Jerusalem,
but they could not overpower it.
2Now the house of David was told, "Aram
has allied itself with[b] Ephraim"; so the hearts
of Ahaz and his people were shaken, as the
trees of the forest are shaken by the wind.
3Then the LORD said to Isaiah, "Go out,
you and your son Shear-Jashub,[c] to meet Ahaz
at the end of the aqueduct of the Upper Pool,
on the road to the Washerman's Field. 4Say
to him, 'Be careful, keep calm and don't be
afraid. Do not lose heart because of these two
smoldering stubs of firewood—because of the
fierce anger of Rezin and Aram and of the son
of Remaliah. 5Aram, Ephraim and Remaliah's
son have plotted your ruin, saying, 6"Let us
invade Judah; let us tear it apart and divide it
among ourselves, and make the son of Tabeel
king over it." 7Yet this is what the Sovereign
LORD says:

" 'It will not take place,
it will not happen,
8 for the head of Aram is Damascus,
and the head of Damascus is only
Rezin.
Within sixty-five years
Ephraim will be too shattered to be a
people.
9 The head of Ephraim is Samaria,
and the head of Samaria is only
Remaliah's son.
If you do not stand firm in your faith,
you will not stand at all.' "

10Again the LORD spoke to Ahaz, 11"Ask
the LORD your God for a sign, whether in the
deepest depths or in the highest heights."
12But Ahaz said, "I will not ask; I will not
put the LORD to the test."
13Then Isaiah said, "Hear now, you house
of David! Is it not enough to try the patience
of men? Will you try the patience of my God
also? 14Therefore the Lord himself will give
you[d] a sign: The virgin will be with child and
will give birth to a son, and[e] will call him Immanuel.[f] 15He will eat curds and honey when
he knows enough to reject the wrong and
choose the right. 16But before the boy knows
enough to reject the wrong and choose the
right, the land of the two kings you dread will
be laid waste. 17The LORD will bring on you
and on your people and on the house of your
father a time unlike any since Ephraim broke
away from Judah—he will bring the king of
Assyria."
18In that day the LORD will whistle for flies
from the distant streams of Egypt and for bees
from the land of Assyria. 19They will all come
and settle in the steep ravines and in the crevices in the rocks, on all the thornbushes and
at all the water holes. 20In that day the Lord
will use a razor hired from beyond the River[g]—the king of Assyria—to shave your head
and the hair of your legs, and to take off your
beards also. 21In that day, a man will keep alive
a young cow and two goats. 22And because of
the abundance of the milk they give, he will
have curds to eat. All who remain in the land
will eat curds and honey. 23In that day, in every
place where there were a thousand vines worth

[a] 9,10 Hebrew; Septuagint *'You will be ever hearing, but never understanding; / you will be ever seeing, but never perceiving.' / [10]This people's heart has become calloused; / they hardly hear with their ears, / and they have closed their eyes* [b] 2 Or *has set up camp in*
[c] 3 *Shear-Jashub* means *a remnant will return.* [d] 14 The Hebrew is plural. [e] 14 Masoretic Text; Dead Sea Scrolls *and he* or *and they*
[f] 14 *Immanuel* means *God with us.* [g] 20 That is, the Euphrates

a thousand silver shekels,[a] there will be only
briers and thorns. 24 Men will go there with
bow and arrow, for the land will be covered
with briers and thorns. 25 As for all the hills
once cultivated by the hoe, you will no longer
go there for fear of the briers and thorns; they
will become places where cattle are turned
loose and where sheep run.

Assyria, the LORD's Instrument

8 The LORD said to me, "Take a large scroll
and write on it with an ordinary pen: Maher-Shalal-Hash-Baz.[b] 2 And I will call in
Uriah the priest and Zechariah son of Jebere-
kiah as reliable witnesses for me."
3 Then I went to the prophetess, and she
conceived and gave birth to a son. And the
LORD said to me, "Name him Maher-Shalal-Hash-Baz. 4 Before the boy knows how to
say 'My father' or 'My mother,' the wealth of
Damascus and the plunder of Samaria will be
carried off by the king of Assyria."
5 The LORD spoke to me again:

6 "Because this people has rejected
the gently flowing waters of Shiloah
and rejoices over Rezin
and the son of Remaliah,
7 therefore the Lord is about to bring
against them
the mighty floodwaters of the River[c]—
the king of Assyria with all his pomp.
It will overflow all its channels,
run over all its banks
8 and sweep on into Judah, swirling over it,
passing through it and reaching up to
the neck.
Its outspread wings will cover the breadth
of your land,
O Immanuel[d]!"

9 Raise the war cry,[e] you nations, and be
shattered!
Listen, all you distant lands.
Prepare for battle, and be shattered!
Prepare for battle, and be shattered!
10 Devise your strategy, but it will be
thwarted;
propose your plan, but it will not stand,
for God is with us.[f]

Fear God

11 The LORD spoke to me with his strong
hand upon me, warning me not to follow the
way of this people. He said:

12 "Do not call conspiracy
everything that these people call
conspiracy[g];
do not fear what they fear,
and do not dread it.
13 The LORD Almighty is the one you are to
regard as holy,
he is the one you are to fear,
he is the one you are to dread,
14 and he will be a sanctuary;
but for both houses of Israel he will be
a stone that causes men to stumble
and a rock that makes them fall.
And for the people of Jerusalem he will be
a trap and a snare.
15 Many of them will stumble;
they will fall and be broken,
they will be snared and captured."

16 Bind up the testimony
and seal up the law among my
disciples.
17 I will wait for the LORD,
who is hiding his face from the house
of Jacob.
I will put my trust in him.

18 Here am I, and the children the LORD has
given me. We are signs and symbols in Israel from the LORD Almighty, who dwells on
Mount Zion.
19 When men tell you to consult mediums
and spiritists, who whisper and mutter, should
not a people inquire of their God? Why consult the dead on behalf of the living? 20 To the
law and to the testimony! If they do not speak
according to this word, they have no light
of dawn. 21 Distressed and hungry, they will
roam through the land; when they are famished, they will become enraged and, looking
upward, will curse their king and their God.
22 Then they will look toward the earth and see
only distress and darkness and fearful gloom,
and they will be thrust into utter darkness.

To Us a Child Is Born

9 Nevertheless, there will be no more gloom
for those who were in distress. In the past
he humbled the land of Zebulun and the
land of Naphtali, but in the future he will
honor Galilee of the Gentiles, by the way of
the sea, along the Jordan—

2 The people walking in darkness
have seen a great light;

---

a 23 That is, about 25 pounds (about 11.5 kilograms) b 1 *Maher-Shalal-Hash-Baz* means *quick to the plunder, swift to the spoil*; also in verse 3. c 7 That is, the Euphrates d 8 *Immanuel* means *God with us.* e 9 Or *Do your worst* f 10 Hebrew *Immanuel* g 12 Or *Do not call for a treaty / every time these people call for a treaty*

WEEKEND

hold the talk

The usual way to solve problems in your relationship is to talk about them. But there can also be power and wisdom in not talking—in biding your time, walking away, or simply shutting up and getting on with things.

We've provided a capsule summary of seven times in every relationship in which silence is not only golden, but necessary.

Stop Talking . . .	By Saying . . .
When one of you isn't ready.	"I need to talk to you when you're ready; will you have some time before dinner?"
When you've said it a million times.	"I'm not going to talk about that subject for the next six months."
When you need time to think.	"That's interesting. Let me think about it."
When one of you is being unreasonable.	"I am going to give you some space right now."
When you've forgotten the problem you were talking about.	"Let's cool down for awhile."
When you're spewing advice.	"I know you didn't ask for my advice, but can I tell you what I'm thinking?"
When you're talking to avoid doing.	"Enough said, let's do this."

William Penn, the founder of Pennsylvania, was imprisoned during the fifteenth century for his Quaker beliefs. While in prison, he wrote something that sparked a thought in us. "True silence," he said, "is like rest for the mind." Indeed. And we would add that silence is to conversation what sleep is to the body. A moment of quiet reflection at the right time nourishes and refreshes the spirit of Love Talk.

Lest we be misunderstood, we want to underscore the value of talk. Having said that, we can then identify specific times and places where conversation is not necessary and is even hurtful in a relationship. The overarching goal, of course, is to bring about more productive, meaningful and intimate conversations between the two of you when it's truly time to talk.

—DR. LES PARROTT III AND DR. LESLIE PARROTT

when should you clam up?

HOW ARE WE DOING?

Discuss the situations below. Which situations beg for more conversation and which for silence? When you disagree about what should happen in the situations below, use that as an opportunity for discussion so that the next time you have a difficult communication situation, you'll know whether to speak up or wait it out.

1. The in-laws are coming for a visit next week and you need to know what to serve for dinner, but your spouse is trying to find a lost deposit slip to prove your checking account isn't overdrawn.
2. You've been married for a couple of years but your spouse still won't wipe down the walls after taking a shower. Should you remind him again?
3. You're about to be late for an important event, and your spouse still isn't ready, partly because one of the kids isn't feeling good and partly because the sitter arrived late. Is this the time to lecture her on why it's important to be on time?
4. You want to go on a cruise for Christmas. Your spouse wants to visit family in the Midwest. This will be the fourth year for this same conversation. Should you have this discussion again?
5. Your application for a mortgage was denied, and you want to talk about the next step, but when you bring up the subject, your spouse goes ballistic about your latest shopping trip. Do you continue the conversation?
6. Your spouse is unhappy with the pastor at your current church. It is the church you grew up in and have attended all your life. You've been arguing about the topic all week. Should you bring up the subject this weekend?
7. Over dinner at your parent's house, you remember that your spouse promised you that the two of you would talk about her cutting back on overtime at work. Is this a good time for this dialogue?

let's make a DATE

SILENCE IN THE BEDROOM

Light a few candles and invite your spouse to join you for a silent retreat. Once you cross into the bedroom, don't speak. If your spouse tries to say something, even softly, put your finger to your lips. You can point, use gestures or make noises, but no talking. See what develops.

FOR YOUR NEXT DEVOTIONAL READING, TURN TO PAGE 758.

LESSONS FROM THE Bible

Which of these situations called for talk? Which called for silence?

1. Moses and Zipporah (Exodus 4:24–26)
2. David and Michal (2 Samuel 6:12–22)
3. Job and his wife (Job 1–2)

on those living in the land of the shadow
of death[a]
a light has dawned.
3 You have enlarged the nation
and increased their joy;
they rejoice before you
as people rejoice at the harvest,
as men rejoice
when dividing the plunder.
4 For as in the day of Midian's defeat,
you have shattered
the yoke that burdens them,
the bar across their shoulders,
the rod of their oppressor.
5 Every warrior's boot used in battle
and every garment rolled in blood
will be destined for burning,
will be fuel for the fire.
6 For to us a child is born,
to us a son is given,
and the government will be on his
shoulders.
And he will be called
Wonderful Counselor,[b] Mighty God,
Everlasting Father, Prince of Peace.
7 Of the increase of his government and
peace
there will be no end.
He will reign on David's throne
and over his kingdom,
establishing and upholding it
with justice and righteousness
from that time on and forever.
The zeal of the LORD Almighty
will accomplish this.

The LORD's Anger Against Israel

8 The Lord has sent a message against Jacob;
it will fall on Israel.
9 All the people will know it—
Ephraim and the inhabitants of
Samaria—
who say with pride
and arrogance of heart,
10 "The bricks have fallen down,
but we will rebuild with dressed stone;
the fig trees have been felled,
but we will replace them with cedars."
11 But the LORD has strengthened Rezin's
foes against them
and has spurred their enemies on.
12 Arameans from the east and Philistines
from the west
have devoured Israel with open mouth.

Yet for all this, his anger is not turned
away,
his hand is still upraised.

13 But the people have not returned to him
who struck them,
nor have they sought the LORD
Almighty.
14 So the LORD will cut off from Israel both
head and tail,
both palm branch and reed in a single
day;
15 the elders and prominent men are the
head,
the prophets who teach lies are the tail.
16 Those who guide this people mislead
them,
and those who are guided are led astray.
17 Therefore the Lord will take no pleasure in
the young men,
nor will he pity the fatherless and
widows,
for everyone is ungodly and wicked,
every mouth speaks vileness.

Yet for all this, his anger is not turned away,
his hand is still upraised.

18 Surely wickedness burns like a fire;
it consumes briers and thorns,
it sets the forest thickets ablaze,
so that it rolls upward in a column of
smoke.
19 By the wrath of the LORD Almighty
the land will be scorched
and the people will be fuel for the fire;
no one will spare his brother.
20 On the right they will devour,
but still be hungry;
on the left they will eat,
but not be satisfied.
Each will feed on the flesh of his own
offspring[c]:
21 Manasseh will feed on Ephraim, and
Ephraim on Manasseh;
together they will turn against Judah.

Yet for all this, his anger is not turned
away,
his hand is still upraised.

10 Woe to those who make unjust laws,
to those who issue oppressive decrees,
2 to deprive the poor of their rights
and withhold justice from the
oppressed of my people,
making widows their prey

[a] 2 Or *land of darkness* [b] 6 Or *Wonderful, Counselor* [c] 20 Or *arm*

and robbing the fatherless.
3 What will you do on the day of reckoning,
when disaster comes from afar?
To whom will you run for help?
Where will you leave your riches?
4 Nothing will remain but to cringe among the captives
or fall among the slain.

Yet for all this, his anger is not turned away,
his hand is still upraised.

God's Judgment on Assyria

5 "Woe to the Assyrian, the rod of my anger,
in whose hand is the club of my wrath!
6 I send him against a godless nation,
I dispatch him against a people who anger me,
to seize loot and snatch plunder,
and to trample them down like mud in the streets.
7 But this is not what he intends,
this is not what he has in mind;
his purpose is to destroy,
to put an end to many nations.
8 'Are not my commanders all kings?' he says.
9 'Has not Calno fared like Carchemish?
Is not Hamath like Arpad,
and Samaria like Damascus?
10 As my hand seized the kingdoms of the idols,
kingdoms whose images excelled those of Jerusalem and Samaria—
11 shall I not deal with Jerusalem and her images
as I dealt with Samaria and her idols?' "

12 When the Lord has finished all his work
against Mount Zion and Jerusalem, he will
say, "I will punish the king of Assyria for the
willful pride of his heart and the haughty look
in his eyes. 13 For he says:

" 'By the strength of my hand I have done this,
and by my wisdom, because I have understanding.
I removed the boundaries of nations,
I plundered their treasures;
like a mighty one I subdued[a] their kings.
14 As one reaches into a nest,
so my hand reached for the wealth of the nations;
as men gather abandoned eggs,
so I gathered all the countries;
not one flapped a wing,
or opened its mouth to chirp.' "

15 Does the ax raise itself above him who swings it,
or the saw boast against him who uses it?
As if a rod were to wield him who lifts it up,
or a club brandish him who is not wood!
16 Therefore, the Lord, the LORD Almighty,
will send a wasting disease upon his sturdy warriors;
under his pomp a fire will be kindled
like a blazing flame.
17 The Light of Israel will become a fire,
their Holy One a flame;
in a single day it will burn and consume
his thorns and his briers.
18 The splendor of his forests and fertile fields
it will completely destroy,
as when a sick man wastes away.
19 And the remaining trees of his forests will be so few
that a child could write them down.

The Remnant of Israel

20 In that day the remnant of Israel,
the survivors of the house of Jacob,
will no longer rely on him
who struck them down
but will truly rely on the LORD,
the Holy One of Israel.
21 A remnant will return,[b] a remnant of Jacob
will return to the Mighty God.
22 Though your people, O Israel, be like the sand by the sea,
only a remnant will return.
Destruction has been decreed,
overwhelming and righteous.
23 The Lord, the LORD Almighty, will carry out
the destruction decreed upon the whole land.

24 Therefore, this is what the Lord, the LORD
Almighty, says:

"O my people who live in Zion,
do not be afraid of the Assyrians,
who beat you with a rod
and lift up a club against you, as Egypt did.

[a] 13 Or / *I subdued the mighty,* [b] 21 Hebrew *shear-jashub*; also in verse 22

25 Very soon my anger against you will end
and my wrath will be directed to their destruction."

26 The LORD Almighty will lash them with a whip,
as when he struck down Midian at the rock of Oreb;
and he will raise his staff over the waters,
as he did in Egypt.
27 In that day their burden will be lifted from your shoulders,
their yoke from your neck;
the yoke will be broken
because you have grown so fat.[a]

28 They enter Aiath;
they pass through Migron;
they store supplies at Micmash.
29 They go over the pass, and say,
"We will camp overnight at Geba."
Ramah trembles;
Gibeah of Saul flees.
30 Cry out, O Daughter of Gallim!
Listen, O Laishah!
Poor Anathoth!
31 Madmenah is in flight;
the people of Gebim take cover.
32 This day they will halt at Nob;
they will shake their fist
at the mount of the Daughter of Zion,
at the hill of Jerusalem.

33 See, the Lord, the LORD Almighty,
will lop off the boughs with great power.
The lofty trees will be felled,
the tall ones will be brought low.
34 He will cut down the forest thickets with an ax;
Lebanon will fall before the Mighty One.

The Branch From Jesse

11 A shoot will come up from the stump of Jesse;
from his roots a Branch will bear fruit.
2 The Spirit of the LORD will rest on him—
the Spirit of wisdom and of understanding,
the Spirit of counsel and of power,
the Spirit of knowledge and of the fear of the LORD—
3 and he will delight in the fear of the LORD.

He will not judge by what he sees with his eyes,
or decide by what he hears with his ears;
4 but with righteousness he will judge the needy,
with justice he will give decisions for the poor of the earth.
He will strike the earth with the rod of his mouth;
with the breath of his lips he will slay the wicked.
5 Righteousness will be his belt
and faithfulness the sash around his waist.

6 The wolf will live with the lamb,
the leopard will lie down with the goat,
the calf and the lion and the yearling[b] together;
and a little child will lead them.
7 The cow will feed with the bear,
their young will lie down together,
and the lion will eat straw like the ox.
8 The infant will play near the hole of the cobra,
and the young child put his hand into the viper's nest.
9 They will neither harm nor destroy
on all my holy mountain,
for the earth will be full of the knowledge of the LORD
as the waters cover the sea.

10 In that day the Root of Jesse will stand as
a banner for the peoples; the nations will rally
to him, and his place of rest will be glorious.
11 In that day the Lord will reach out his hand a
second time to reclaim the remnant that is left
of his people from Assyria, from Lower Egypt,
from Upper Egypt,[c] from Cush,[d] from Elam,
from Babylonia,[e] from Hamath and from the
islands of the sea.

12 He will raise a banner for the nations
and gather the exiles of Israel;
he will assemble the scattered people of Judah
from the four quarters of the earth.
13 Ephraim's jealousy will vanish,
and Judah's enemies[f] will be cut off;
Ephraim will not be jealous of Judah,
nor Judah hostile toward Ephraim.
14 They will swoop down on the slopes of Philistia to the west;
together they will plunder the people to the east.

[a] 27 Hebrew; Septuagint *broken / from your shoulders* [b] 6 Hebrew; Septuagint *lion will feed* [c] 11 Hebrew *from Pathros* [d] 11 That is, the upper Nile region [e] 11 Hebrew *Shinar* [f] 13 Or *hostility*

They will lay hands on Edom and Moab,
and the Ammonites will be subject to them.
15 The LORD will dry up
the gulf of the Egyptian sea;
with a scorching wind he will sweep his hand
over the Euphrates River.[a]
He will break it up into seven streams
so that men can cross over in sandals.
16 There will be a highway for the remnant of his people
that is left from Assyria,
as there was for Israel
when they came up from Egypt.

Songs of Praise

12 In that day you will say:

"I will praise you, O LORD.
Although you were angry with me,
your anger has turned away
and you have comforted me.
2 Surely God is my salvation;
I will trust and not be afraid.
The LORD, the LORD, is my strength and my song;
he has become my salvation."
3 With joy you will draw water
from the wells of salvation.
4 In that day you will say:
"Give thanks to the LORD, call on his name;
make known among the nations what he has done,
and proclaim that his name is exalted.
5 Sing to the LORD, for he has done glorious things;
let this be known to all the world.
6 Shout aloud and sing for joy, people of Zion,
for great is the Holy One of Israel
among you."

A Prophecy Against Babylon

13 An oracle concerning Babylon that Isaiah son of Amoz saw:

2 Raise a banner on a bare hilltop,
shout to them;
beckon to them
to enter the gates of the nobles.
3 I have commanded my holy ones;
I have summoned my warriors to carry out my wrath—
those who rejoice in my triumph.
4 Listen, a noise on the mountains,
like that of a great multitude!
Listen, an uproar among the kingdoms,
like nations massing together!
The LORD Almighty is mustering
an army for war.
5 They come from faraway lands,
from the ends of the heavens—
the LORD and the weapons of his wrath—
to destroy the whole country.
6 Wail, for the day of the LORD is near;
it will come like destruction from the Almighty.[b]
7 Because of this, all hands will go limp,
every man's heart will melt.
8 Terror will seize them,
pain and anguish will grip them;
they will writhe like a woman in labor.
They will look aghast at each other,
their faces aflame.
9 See, the day of the LORD is coming
—a cruel day, with wrath and fierce anger—
to make the land desolate
and destroy the sinners within it.
10 The stars of heaven and their constellations
will not show their light.
The rising sun will be darkened
and the moon will not give its light.
11 I will punish the world for its evil,
the wicked for their sins.
I will put an end to the arrogance of the haughty
and will humble the pride of the ruthless.
12 I will make man scarcer than pure gold,
more rare than the gold of Ophir.
13 Therefore I will make the heavens tremble;
and the earth will shake from its place
at the wrath of the LORD Almighty,
in the day of his burning anger.
14 Like a hunted gazelle,
like sheep without a shepherd,
each will return to his own people,
each will flee to his native land.
15 Whoever is captured will be thrust through;
all who are caught will fall by the sword.

[a] 15 Hebrew *the River* [b] 6 Hebrew *Shaddai*

MONDAY
READ ISAIAH 12:1–6

WHEN TO GIVE UP ANGER

Tyler could not get over his anger at Deb for ruining their finances. He had brought a little family money into the marriage, and Deb decided to borrow some of it to give to friends and family members who needed it. The problem: She never told Tyler that she had taken the money.

Then Tyler saw the bank statement. He became very angry, not because Deb took the money, but because she hadn't talked to him about it first. It didn't help when she said that the money was hers as much as his.

Tyler's anger turned from hot to cold over time, but it never really went away. Eventually it caused emotional distance from his wife and suspicion of everything she did with money. He questioned her about every penny she spent, while withholding from her bank statements, tax returns, investment paperwork and other information about finances. The more he mistrusted Deb, the more deceptive she became about money.

Meanwhile, the marital relationship suffered. Deb withdrew into the more welcoming arms of her family, and Tyler buried himself in his work, spending more time away from his wife. Neither husband nor wife turned to each other or to the Lord to find a way to reconcile.

Husbands and wives may find good justification for being angry with each other. But they can be childish and destructive in holding on to that anger. Isaiah tells us that the Lord is righteously angry when his own children, whom he loves, offend him. He is holy and just in that anger. But at a certain point, God chooses to give up his anger. When his people turn to him with a repentant heart, he forgives them and welcomes them back into his arms. God demonstrates that the party "in the right" has to take steps to forgive the offender to begin the process of reconciliation.

Tyler and Deb learned how that worked, but not before they had each suffered much pain. In the emotional distance of their relationship, Tyler found comfort in a coworker and had an affair with her. When Deb learned about the infidelity, she was furious. She was as righteous in her anger against her husband as he had once been against her for cleaning out their savings account.

The couple didn't want to end the marriage however. After much counseling and prayer, Tyler asked his wife for forgiveness for cheating on her, for keeping her at a distance, for nitpicking about money and for holding on to his anger. Likewise, Deb agreed to give up her anger against Tyler for having an affair. She also asked his forgiveness for spending so much time with her family and for being secretive about money.

God, the ultimate forgiver, became their salvation and their defense. It was and is a difficult process, but in giving up their anger, this couple could once more learn to trust, love and comfort each other.

—JOHN R. THROOP

FOR YOUR NEXT DEVOTIONAL READING, TURN TO PAGE 765.

"I will praise you, O LORD. Although you were angry with me, your anger has turned away and you have comforted me."

— ISAIAH 12:1

let's talk

- What are some reasons why we hang on to anger in marriage?
- What are some steps involved in rebuilding trust after it has been broken?
- How do we avoid giving in to destructive anger in our relationship? What happens if one of us holds on to a grudge?

16 Their infants will be dashed to pieces
before their eyes;
their houses will be looted and their
wives ravished.

17 See, I will stir up against them the
Medes,
who do not care for silver
and have no delight in gold.
18 Their bows will strike down the young
men;
they will have no mercy on infants
nor will they look with compassion on
children.
19 Babylon, the jewel of kingdoms,
the glory of the Babylonians'[a] pride,
will be overthrown by God
like Sodom and Gomorrah.
20 She will never be inhabited
or lived in through all generations;
no Arab will pitch his tent there,
no shepherd will rest his flocks there.
21 But desert creatures will lie there,
jackals will fill her houses;
there the owls will dwell,
and there the wild goats will leap
about.
22 Hyenas will howl in her strongholds,
jackals in her luxurious palaces.
Her time is at hand,
and her days will not be prolonged.

14 The LORD will have compassion on
Jacob;
once again he will choose Israel
and will settle them in their own land.
Aliens will join them
and unite with the house of Jacob.
2 Nations will take them
and bring them to their own place.
And the house of Israel will possess the
nations
as menservants and maidservants in the
LORD's land.
They will make captives of their captors
and rule over their oppressors.

3 On the day the LORD gives you relief from
suffering and turmoil and cruel bondage, 4 you
will take up this taunt against the king of Babylon:

How the oppressor has come to an end!
How his fury[b] has ended!
5 The LORD has broken the rod of the
wicked,
the scepter of the rulers,
6 which in anger struck down peoples
with unceasing blows,
and in fury subdued nations
with relentless aggression.
7 All the lands are at rest and at peace;
they break into singing.
8 Even the pine trees and the cedars of
Lebanon
exult over you and say,
"Now that you have been laid low,
no woodsman comes to cut us down."

9 The grave[c] below is all astir
to meet you at your coming;
it rouses the spirits of the departed to greet
you—
all those who were leaders in the world;
it makes them rise from their thrones—
all those who were kings over the
nations.
10 They will all respond,
they will say to you,
"You also have become weak, as we are;
you have become like us."
11 All your pomp has been brought down to
the grave,
along with the noise of your harps;
maggots are spread out beneath you
and worms cover you.

12 How you have fallen from heaven,
O morning star, son of the dawn!
You have been cast down to the earth,
you who once laid low the nations!
13 You said in your heart,
"I will ascend to heaven;
I will raise my throne
above the stars of God;
I will sit enthroned on the mount of
assembly,
on the utmost heights of the sacred
mountain.[d]
14 I will ascend above the tops of the clouds;
I will make myself like the Most High."
15 But you are brought down to the grave,
to the depths of the pit.

16 Those who see you stare at you,
they ponder your fate:
"Is this the man who shook the earth
and made kingdoms tremble,
17 the man who made the world a desert,
who overthrew its cities
and would not let his captives go
home?"

---

[a] *19* Or *Chaldeans'* [b] *4* Dead Sea Scrolls, Septuagint and Syriac; the meaning of the word in the Masoretic Text is uncertain.
[c] *9* Hebrew *Sheol*; also in verses 11 and 15 [d] *13* Or *the north*; Hebrew *Zaphon*

18 All the kings of the nations lie in state,
each in his own tomb.
19 But you are cast out of your tomb
like a rejected branch;
you are covered with the slain,
with those pierced by the sword,
those who descend to the stones of the pit.
Like a corpse trampled underfoot,
20 you will not join them in burial,
for you have destroyed your land
and killed your people.

The offspring of the wicked
will never be mentioned again.
21 Prepare a place to slaughter his sons
for the sins of their forefathers;
they are not to rise to inherit the land
and cover the earth with their cities.
22 "I will rise up against them,"
declares the LORD Almighty.
"I will cut off from Babylon her name and survivors,
her offspring and descendants,"
declares the LORD.
23 "I will turn her into a place for owls
and into swampland;
I will sweep her with the broom of destruction,"
declares the LORD Almighty.

A Prophecy Against Assyria

24 The LORD Almighty has sworn,
"Surely, as I have planned, so it will be,
and as I have purposed, so it will stand.
25 I will crush the Assyrian in my land;
on my mountains I will trample him down.
His yoke will be taken from my people,
and his burden removed from their shoulders."
26 This is the plan determined for the whole world;
this is the hand stretched out over all nations.
27 For the LORD Almighty has purposed, and who can thwart him?
His hand is stretched out, and who can turn it back?

A Prophecy Against the Philistines

28 This oracle came in the year King Ahaz died:

29 Do not rejoice, all you Philistines,
that the rod that struck you is broken;
from the root of that snake will spring up a viper,
its fruit will be a darting, venomous serpent.
30 The poorest of the poor will find pasture,
and the needy will lie down in safety.
But your root I will destroy by famine;
it will slay your survivors.
31 Wail, O gate! Howl, O city!
Melt away, all you Philistines!
A cloud of smoke comes from the north,
and there is not a straggler in its ranks.
32 What answer shall be given
to the envoys of that nation?
"The LORD has established Zion,
and in her his afflicted people will find refuge."

A Prophecy Against Moab

15 An oracle concerning Moab:

Ar in Moab is ruined,
destroyed in a night!
Kir in Moab is ruined,
destroyed in a night!
2 Dibon goes up to its temple,
to its high places to weep;
Moab wails over Nebo and Medeba.
Every head is shaved
and every beard cut off.
3 In the streets they wear sackcloth;
on the roofs and in the public squares
they all wail,
prostrate with weeping.
4 Heshbon and Elealeh cry out,
their voices are heard all the way to Jahaz.
Therefore the armed men of Moab cry out,
and their hearts are faint.

5 My heart cries out over Moab;
her fugitives flee as far as Zoar,
as far as Eglath Shelishiyah.
They go up the way to Luhith,
weeping as they go;
on the road to Horonaim
they lament their destruction.
6 The waters of Nimrim are dried up
and the grass is withered;
the vegetation is gone
and nothing green is left.
7 So the wealth they have acquired and stored up
they carry away over the Ravine of the Poplars.

8 Their outcry echoes along the border of
Moab;
their wailing reaches as far as Eglaim,
their lamentation as far as Beer Elim.
9 Dimon's[a] waters are full of blood,
but I will bring still more upon
Dimon[a]—
a lion upon the fugitives of Moab
and upon those who remain in the land.

16 Send lambs as tribute
to the ruler of the land,
from Sela, across the desert,
to the mount of the Daughter of Zion.
2 Like fluttering birds
pushed from the nest,
so are the women of Moab
at the fords of the Arnon.

3 "Give us counsel,
render a decision.
Make your shadow like night—
at high noon.
Hide the fugitives,
do not betray the refugees.
4 Let the Moabite fugitives stay with you;
be their shelter from the destroyer."

The oppressor will come to an end,
and destruction will cease;
the aggressor will vanish from the land.
5 In love a throne will be established;
in faithfulness a man will sit on it—
one from the house[b] of David—
one who in judging seeks justice
and speeds the cause of righteousness.

6 We have heard of Moab's pride—
her overweening pride and conceit,
her pride and her insolence—
but her boasts are empty.
7 Therefore the Moabites wail,
they wail together for Moab.
Lament and grieve
for the men[c] of Kir Hareseth.
8 The fields of Heshbon wither,
the vines of Sibmah also.
The rulers of the nations
have trampled down the choicest vines,
which once reached Jazer
and spread toward the desert.
Their shoots spread out
and went as far as the sea.
9 So I weep, as Jazer weeps,
for the vines of Sibmah.
O Heshbon, O Elealeh,
I drench you with tears!
The shouts of joy over your ripened fruit
and over your harvests have been
stilled.
10 Joy and gladness are taken away from the
orchards;
no one sings or shouts in the vineyards;
no one treads out wine at the presses,
for I have put an end to the shouting.
11 My heart laments for Moab like a harp,
my inmost being for Kir Hareseth.
12 When Moab appears at her high place,
she only wears herself out;
when she goes to her shrine to pray,
it is to no avail.

13 This is the word the LORD has already spoken concerning Moab. 14 But now the LORD
says: "Within three years, as a servant bound
by contract would count them, Moab's splendor and all her many people will be despised,
and her survivors will be very few and feeble."

An Oracle Against Damascus

17 An oracle concerning Damascus:

"See, Damascus will no longer be a city
but will become a heap of ruins.
2 The cities of Aroer will be deserted
and left to flocks, which will lie down,
with no one to make them afraid.
3 The fortified city will disappear from
Ephraim,
and royal power from Damascus;
the remnant of Aram will be
like the glory of the Israelites,"
declares the LORD Almighty.

4 "In that day the glory of Jacob will fade;
the fat of his body will waste away.
5 It will be as when a reaper gathers the
standing grain
and harvests the grain with his arm—
as when a man gleans heads of grain
in the Valley of Rephaim.
6 Yet some gleanings will remain,
as when an olive tree is beaten,
leaving two or three olives on the topmost
branches,
four or five on the fruitful boughs,"
declares the LORD, the God
of Israel.

7 In that day men will look to their Maker
and turn their eyes to the Holy One of
Israel.

a 9 Masoretic Text; Dead Sea Scrolls, some Septuagint manuscripts and Vulgate *Dibon* b 5 Hebrew *tent* c 7 Or "*raisin cakes*," a wordplay

8 They will not look to the altars,
the work of their hands,
and they will have no regard for the
Asherah poles [a]
and the incense altars their fingers have
made.

9 In that day their strong cities, which they
left because of the Israelites, will be like places
abandoned to thickets and undergrowth. And
all will be desolation.

10 You have forgotten God your Savior;
you have not remembered the Rock,
your fortress.
Therefore, though you set out the finest
plants
and plant imported vines,
11 though on the day you set them out, you
make them grow,
and on the morning when you plant
them, you bring them to bud,
yet the harvest will be as nothing
in the day of disease and incurable
pain.

12 Oh, the raging of many nations—
they rage like the raging sea!
Oh, the uproar of the peoples—
they roar like the roaring of great
waters!
13 Although the peoples roar like the roar of
surging waters,
when he rebukes them they flee far
away,
driven before the wind like chaff on the
hills,
like tumbleweed before a gale.
14 In the evening, sudden terror!
Before the morning, they are gone!
This is the portion of those who loot us,
the lot of those who plunder us.

A Prophecy Against Cush

18 Woe to the land of whirring wings [b]
along the rivers of Cush, [c]
2 which sends envoys by sea
in papyrus boats over the water.

Go, swift messengers,
to a people tall and smooth-skinned,
to a people feared far and wide,
an aggressive nation of strange speech,
whose land is divided by rivers.

3 All you people of the world,
you who live on the earth,
when a banner is raised on the mountains,
you will see it,
and when a trumpet sounds,
you will hear it.
4 This is what the LORD says to me:
"I will remain quiet and will look on
from my dwelling place,
like shimmering heat in the sunshine,
like a cloud of dew in the heat of
harvest."
5 For, before the harvest, when the blossom
is gone
and the flower becomes a ripening
grape,
he will cut off the shoots with pruning
knives,
and cut down and take away the
spreading branches.
6 They will all be left to the mountain birds
of prey
and to the wild animals;
the birds will feed on them all summer,
the wild animals all winter.

7 At that time gifts will be brought to the
LORD Almighty

from a people tall and smooth-skinned,
from a people feared far and wide,
an aggressive nation of strange speech,
whose land is divided by rivers—

the gifts will be brought to Mount Zion, the
place of the Name of the LORD Almighty.

A Prophecy About Egypt

19 An oracle concerning Egypt:

See, the LORD rides on a swift cloud
and is coming to Egypt.
The idols of Egypt tremble before him,
and the hearts of the Egyptians melt
within them.

2 "I will stir up Egyptian against Egyptian—
brother will fight against brother,
neighbor against neighbor,
city against city,
kingdom against kingdom.
3 The Egyptians will lose heart,
and I will bring their plans to nothing;
they will consult the idols and the spirits
of the dead,
the mediums and the spiritists.
4 I will hand the Egyptians over
to the power of a cruel master,
and a fierce king will rule over them,"
declares the Lord, the LORD Almighty.

---

[a] *8* That is, symbols of the goddess Asherah [b] *1* Or *of locusts* [c] *1* That is, the upper Nile region

5 The waters of the river will dry up,
and the riverbed will be parched and dry.
6 The canals will stink;
the streams of Egypt will dwindle and dry up.
The reeds and rushes will wither,
7 also the plants along the Nile,
at the mouth of the river.
Every sown field along the Nile
will become parched, will blow away and be no more.
8 The fishermen will groan and lament,
all who cast hooks into the Nile;
those who throw nets on the water
will pine away.
9 Those who work with combed flax will despair,
the weavers of fine linen will lose hope.
10 The workers in cloth will be dejected,
and all the wage earners will be sick at heart.

11 The officials of Zoan are nothing but fools;
the wise counselors of Pharaoh give senseless advice.
How can you say to Pharaoh,
"I am one of the wise men,
a disciple of the ancient kings"?

12 Where are your wise men now?
Let them show you and make known
what the LORD Almighty
has planned against Egypt.
13 The officials of Zoan have become fools,
the leaders of Memphis[a] are deceived;
the cornerstones of her peoples
have led Egypt astray.
14 The LORD has poured into them
a spirit of dizziness;
they make Egypt stagger in all that she does,
as a drunkard staggers around in his vomit.
15 There is nothing Egypt can do—
head or tail, palm branch or reed.

16 In that day the Egyptians will be like
women. They will shudder with fear at the
uplifted hand that the LORD Almighty raises
against them. 17 And the land of Judah will
bring terror to the Egyptians; everyone to
whom Judah is mentioned will be terrified,
because of what the LORD Almighty is planning against them.
18 In that day five cities in Egypt will speak
the language of Canaan and swear allegiance
to the LORD Almighty. One of them will be
called the City of Destruction.[b]
19 In that day there will be an altar to the
LORD in the heart of Egypt, and a monument
to the LORD at its border. 20 It will be a sign
and witness to the LORD Almighty in the land
of Egypt. When they cry out to the LORD because of their oppressors, he will send them a
savior and defender, and he will rescue them.
21 So the LORD will make himself known to
the Egyptians, and in that day they will acknowledge the LORD. They will worship with
sacrifices and grain offerings; they will make
vows to the LORD and keep them. 22 The LORD
will strike Egypt with a plague; he will strike
them and heal them. They will turn to the
LORD, and he will respond to their pleas and
heal them.
23 In that day there will be a highway from
Egypt to Assyria. The Assyrians will go to
Egypt and the Egyptians to Assyria. The Egyptians and Assyrians will worship together. 24 In
that day Israel will be the third, along with
Egypt and Assyria, a blessing on the earth.
25 The LORD Almighty will bless them, saying, "Blessed be Egypt my people, Assyria my
handiwork, and Israel my inheritance."

A Prophecy Against Egypt and Cush

20 In the year that the supreme commander, sent by Sargon king of Assyria, came
to Ashdod and attacked and captured
it— 2 at that time the LORD spoke through
Isaiah son of Amoz. He said to him, "Take off
the sackcloth from your body and the sandals
from your feet." And he did so, going around
stripped and barefoot.
3 Then the LORD said, "Just as my servant
Isaiah has gone stripped and barefoot for three
years, as a sign and portent against Egypt and
Cush,[c] 4 so the king of Assyria will lead away
stripped and barefoot the Egyptian captives
and Cushite exiles, young and old, with buttocks bared—to Egypt's shame. 5 Those who
trusted in Cush and boasted in Egypt will be
afraid and put to shame. 6 In that day the people who live on this coast will say, 'See what
has happened to those we relied on, those we
fled to for help and deliverance from the king
of Assyria! How then can we escape?' "

[a] *13* Hebrew *Noph* [b] *18* Most manuscripts of the Masoretic Text; some manuscripts of the Masoretic Text, Dead Sea Scrolls and Vulgate *City of the Sun* (that is, Heliopolis) [c] *3* That is, the upper Nile region; also in verse 5

A Prophecy Against Babylon

21 An oracle concerning the Desert by the Sea:

Like whirlwinds sweeping through the southland,
an invader comes from the desert,
from a land of terror.

2 A dire vision has been shown to me:
The traitor betrays, the looter takes loot.
Elam, attack! Media, lay siege!
I will bring to an end all the groaning she caused.

3 At this my body is racked with pain,
pangs seize me, like those of a woman in labor;
I am staggered by what I hear,
I am bewildered by what I see.
4 My heart falters,
fear makes me tremble;
the twilight I longed for
has become a horror to me.
5 They set the tables,
they spread the rugs,
they eat, they drink!
Get up, you officers,
oil the shields!

6 This is what the Lord says to me:

"Go, post a lookout
and have him report what he sees.
7 When he sees chariots
with teams of horses,
riders on donkeys
or riders on camels,
let him be alert,
fully alert."
8 And the lookout[a] shouted,

"Day after day, my lord, I stand on the watchtower;
every night I stay at my post.
9 Look, here comes a man in a chariot
with a team of horses.
And he gives back the answer:
'Babylon has fallen, has fallen!
All the images of its gods
lie shattered on the ground!' "
10 O my people, crushed on the threshing floor,
I tell you what I have heard
from the LORD Almighty,
from the God of Israel.

A Prophecy Against Edom

11 An oracle concerning Dumah[b]:

Someone calls to me from Seir,
"Watchman, what is left of the night?
Watchman, what is left of the night?"
12 The watchman replies,
"Morning is coming, but also the night.
If you would ask, then ask;
and come back yet again."

A Prophecy Against Arabia

13 An oracle concerning Arabia:

You caravans of Dedanites,
who camp in the thickets of Arabia,
14 bring water for the thirsty;
you who live in Tema,
bring food for the fugitives.
15 They flee from the sword,
from the drawn sword,
from the bent bow
and from the heat of battle.

16 This is what the Lord says to me: "Within
one year, as a servant bound by contract would
count it, all the pomp of Kedar will come to
an end. 17 The survivors of the bowmen, the
warriors of Kedar, will be few." The LORD, the
God of Israel, has spoken.

A Prophecy About Jerusalem

22 An oracle concerning the Valley of Vision:

What troubles you now,
that you have all gone up on the roofs,
2 O town full of commotion,
O city of tumult and revelry?
Your slain were not killed by the sword,
nor did they die in battle.
3 All your leaders have fled together;
they have been captured without using the bow.
All you who were caught were taken prisoner together,
having fled while the enemy was still far away.
4 Therefore I said, "Turn away from me;
let me weep bitterly.
Do not try to console me
over the destruction of my people."

5 The Lord, the LORD Almighty, has a day
of tumult and trampling and terror
in the Valley of Vision,
a day of battering down walls

---

a 8 Dead Sea Scrolls and Syriac; Masoretic Text *A lion*   *b* 11 *Dumah* means *silence* or *stillness,* a wordplay on *Edom.*

TUESDAY

READ ISAIAH 22:1–4

A ROOFTOP VIEW OF US

The roofs of houses in ancient Israel were mostly flat, allowing families to find an elevated retreat away from the bustle of life. People also used the upper floor space for other things: spreading harvested crops to dry and cure, and creating a place for visiting travelers. They also found the raised platform a great lookout. They could keep tabs on their neighbors in peacetime and, in wartime, mark the progress of battle.

That is the scene Isaiah's words call to mind. Social ills and religious failings were eating away at Israel like subsurface cancer. One day soon there would be a divine reckoning, for God's patience would no longer stay the punishing onslaught. If the citizens would use their rooftop lookouts to see things that needed to be changed and challenged during times of relative peace, they would not have to witness the shame and destruction brought about by malingering sins. The warning was clear: Use your rooftop now, while you can, rather than be forced to use it by circumstances beyond your control.

What troubles you now, that you have all gone up on the roofs?

— Isaiah 22:1

let's *talk*

- ✦ Let's spend some time getting a rooftop perspective on our relationship. What needs rebuilding, restoration or reconciliation?
- ✦ What steps will we take to develop a better way of relating?
- ✦ When was the last time we prayed out loud for each other? When will we do it again? What should we pray for?

That's a good word for marriages too. A friend once told me that he and his wife committed on their wedding night to each say a short prayer of blessing on the other person after they got into bed at night. "Then," he said, "we kiss and go to sleep."

"Every night?" I asked incredulously, knowing how some folks tend to overstate.

"Every night!" he replied. "We don't always feel like doing it. Sometimes we're really upset with each other, and now and again we feel like we're drifting apart. But when we force ourselves to go through this ritual, we see things from a better perspective."

"When we pray for God's blessing on each other, we see each other again like we did at the start," he explained. He would remember wanting to date his wife because he found her fascinating, beautiful and full of life. She would remember how he became her shelter, her rock, her stability. "And when someone sees us that way, we become like that for each other again," he said.

I have thought about adding my friend's bedtime routine to my own marriage, but it has never quite stuck. Maybe my wife and I are too tired or preoccupied most nights. But I keep my friend's idea in mind, and I pray for my wife regularly, remembering why we connected in the first place. It's like going up on a rooftop and seeing things the way they were and are and ought to be.

—WAYNE BROUWER

FOR YOUR NEXT DEVOTIONAL READING, TURN TO PAGE 770.

and of crying out to the mountains.
6 Elam takes up the quiver,
with her charioteers and horses;
Kir uncovers the shield.
7 Your choicest valleys are full of chariots,
and horsemen are posted at the city gates;
8 the defenses of Judah are stripped away.

And you looked in that day
to the weapons in the Palace of the Forest;
9 you saw that the City of David
had many breaches in its defenses;
you stored up water
in the Lower Pool.
10 You counted the buildings in Jerusalem
and tore down houses to strengthen the wall.
11 You built a reservoir between the two walls
for the water of the Old Pool,
but you did not look to the One who made it,
or have regard for the One who planned it long ago.

12 The Lord, the LORD Almighty,
called you on that day
to weep and to wail,
to tear out your hair and put on sackcloth.
13 But see, there is joy and revelry,
slaughtering of cattle and killing of sheep,
eating of meat and drinking of wine!
"Let us eat and drink," you say,
"for tomorrow we die!"

14 The LORD Almighty has revealed this in
my hearing: "Till your dying day this sin will
not be atoned for," says the Lord, the LORD
Almighty.

15 This is what the Lord, the LORD Almighty, says:

"Go, say to this steward,
to Shebna, who is in charge of the palace:
16 What are you doing here and who gave you permission
to cut out a grave for yourself here,
hewing your grave on the height
and chiseling your resting place in the rock?

17 "Beware, the LORD is about to take firm hold of you
and hurl you away, O you mighty man.
18 He will roll you up tightly like a ball
and throw you into a large country.
There you will die
and there your splendid chariots will remain—
you disgrace to your master's house!
19 I will depose you from your office,
and you will be ousted from your position.

20 "In that day I will summon my servant,
Eliakim son of Hilkiah. 21 I will clothe him
with your robe and fasten your sash around
him and hand your authority over to him. He
will be a father to those who live in Jerusalem
and to the house of Judah. 22 I will place on his
shoulder the key to the house of David; what
he opens no one can shut, and what he shuts
no one can open. 23 I will drive him like a peg
into a firm place; he will be a seat[a] of honor
for the house of his father. 24 All the glory of
his family will hang on him: its offspring and
offshoots—all its lesser vessels, from the bowls
to all the jars.

25 "In that day," declares the LORD Almighty,
"the peg driven into the firm place will give
way; it will be sheared off and will fall, and
the load hanging on it will be cut down." The
LORD has spoken.

A Prophecy About Tyre

23 An oracle concerning Tyre:

Wail, O ships of Tarshish!
For Tyre is destroyed
and left without house or harbor.
From the land of Cyprus[b]
word has come to them.

2 Be silent, you people of the island
and you merchants of Sidon,
whom the seafarers have enriched.
3 On the great waters
came the grain of the Shihor;
the harvest of the Nile[c] was the revenue of Tyre,
and she became the marketplace of the nations.

4 Be ashamed, O Sidon, and you, O fortress of the sea,
for the sea has spoken:
"I have neither been in labor nor given birth;

a 23 Or *throne* *b* 1 Hebrew *Kittim* *c* 2,3 Masoretic Text; one Dead Sea Scroll *Sidon, / who cross over the sea; / your envoys* [3]*are on the great waters. / The grain of the Shihor, / the harvest of the Nile,*

I have neither reared sons nor brought
up daughters."
5 When word comes to Egypt,
they will be in anguish at the report
from Tyre.

6 Cross over to Tarshish;
wail, you people of the island.
7 Is this your city of revelry,
the old, old city,
whose feet have taken her
to settle in far-off lands?
8 Who planned this against Tyre,
the bestower of crowns,
whose merchants are princes,
whose traders are renowned in the
earth?
9 The LORD Almighty planned it,
to bring low the pride of all glory
and to humble all who are renowned
on the earth.

10 Till [a] your land as along the Nile,
O Daughter of Tarshish,
for you no longer have a harbor.
11 The LORD has stretched out his hand over
the sea
and made its kingdoms tremble.
He has given an order concerning
Phoenicia [b]
that her fortresses be destroyed.
12 He said, "No more of your reveling,
O Virgin Daughter of Sidon, now
crushed!

"Up, cross over to Cyprus [c];
even there you will find no rest."
13 Look at the land of the Babylonians, [d]
this people that is now of no account!
The Assyrians have made it
a place for desert creatures;
they raised up their siege towers,
they stripped its fortresses bare
and turned it into a ruin.

14 Wail, you ships of Tarshish;
your fortress is destroyed!

15 At that time Tyre will be forgotten for
seventy years, the span of a king's life. But at
the end of these seventy years, it will happen
to Tyre as in the song of the prostitute:

16 "Take up a harp, walk through the city,
O prostitute forgotten;
play the harp well, sing many a song,
so that you will be remembered."

17 At the end of seventy years, the LORD
will deal with Tyre. She will return to her hire
as a prostitute and will ply her trade with all
the kingdoms on the face of the earth. 18 Yet
her profit and her earnings will be set apart
for the LORD; they will not be stored up or
hoarded. Her profits will go to those who live
before the LORD, for abundant food and fine
clothes.

The LORD's Devastation of the Earth

24 See, the LORD is going to lay waste the
earth
and devastate it;
he will ruin its face
and scatter its inhabitants—
2 it will be the same
for priest as for people,
for master as for servant,
for mistress as for maid,
for seller as for buyer,
for borrower as for lender,
for debtor as for creditor.
3 The earth will be completely laid waste
and totally plundered.
The LORD has spoken this word.

4 The earth dries up and withers,
the world languishes and withers,
the exalted of the earth languish.
5 The earth is defiled by its people;
they have disobeyed the laws,
violated the statutes
and broken the everlasting covenant.
6 Therefore a curse consumes the earth;
its people must bear their guilt.
Therefore earth's inhabitants are burned
up,
and very few are left.
7 The new wine dries up and the vine
withers;
all the merrymakers groan.
8 The gaiety of the tambourines is stilled,
the noise of the revelers has stopped,
the joyful harp is silent.
9 No longer do they drink wine with a
song;
the beer is bitter to its drinkers.
10 The ruined city lies desolate;
the entrance to every house is barred.
11 In the streets they cry out for wine;
all joy turns to gloom,
all gaiety is banished from the earth.
12 The city is left in ruins,
its gate is battered to pieces.

[a] 10 Dead Sea Scrolls and some Septuagint manuscripts; Masoretic Text *Go through* [b] 11 Hebrew *Canaan* [c] 12 Hebrew *Kittim*
[d] 13 Or *Chaldeans*

13 So will it be on the earth
and among the nations,
as when an olive tree is beaten,
or as when gleanings are left after the grape harvest.
14 They raise their voices, they shout for joy;
from the west they acclaim the LORD's majesty.
15 Therefore in the east give glory to the LORD;
exalt the name of the LORD, the God of Israel,
in the islands of the sea.
16 From the ends of the earth we hear singing:
"Glory to the Righteous One."

But I said, "I waste away, I waste away!
Woe to me!
The treacherous betray!
With treachery the treacherous betray!"
17 Terror and pit and snare await you,
O people of the earth.
18 Whoever flees at the sound of terror
will fall into a pit;
whoever climbs out of the pit
will be caught in a snare.

The floodgates of the heavens are opened,
the foundations of the earth shake.
19 The earth is broken up,
the earth is split asunder,
the earth is thoroughly shaken.
20 The earth reels like a drunkard,
it sways like a hut in the wind;
so heavy upon it is the guilt of its rebellion
that it falls—never to rise again.

21 In that day the LORD will punish
the powers in the heavens above
and the kings on the earth below.
22 They will be herded together
like prisoners bound in a dungeon;
they will be shut up in prison
and be punished[a] after many days.
23 The moon will be abashed, the sun ashamed;
for the LORD Almighty will reign
on Mount Zion and in Jerusalem,
and before its elders, gloriously.

Praise to the LORD

25 O LORD, you are my God;
I will exalt you and praise your name,
for in perfect faithfulness
you have done marvelous things,
things planned long ago.
2 You have made the city a heap of rubble,
the fortified town a ruin,
the foreigners' stronghold a city no more;
it will never be rebuilt.
3 Therefore strong peoples will honor you;
cities of ruthless nations will revere you.
4 You have been a refuge for the poor,
a refuge for the needy in his distress,
a shelter from the storm
and a shade from the heat.
For the breath of the ruthless
is like a storm driving against a wall
5 and like the heat of the desert.
You silence the uproar of foreigners;
as heat is reduced by the shadow of a cloud,
so the song of the ruthless is stilled.

6 On this mountain the LORD Almighty will prepare
a feast of rich food for all peoples,
a banquet of aged wine—
the best of meats and the finest of wines.
7 On this mountain he will destroy
the shroud that enfolds all peoples,
the sheet that covers all nations;
8 he will swallow up death forever.
The Sovereign LORD will wipe away the tears
from all faces;
he will remove the disgrace of his people
from all the earth.
The LORD has spoken.

9 In that day they will say,
"Surely this is our God;
we trusted in him, and he saved us.
This is the LORD, we trusted in him;
let us rejoice and be glad in his salvation."

10 The hand of the LORD will rest on this mountain;
but Moab will be trampled under him
as straw is trampled down in the manure.
11 They will spread out their hands in it,
as a swimmer spreads out his hands to swim.
God will bring down their pride
despite the cleverness[b] of their hands.
12 He will bring down your high fortified walls

a 22 Or *released* *b* 11 The meaning of the Hebrew for this word is uncertain.

and lay them low;
he will bring them down to the ground,
to the very dust.

A Song of Praise

26 In that day this song will be sung in the land of Judah:

We have a strong city;
God makes salvation
its walls and ramparts.
2 Open the gates
that the righteous nation may enter,
the nation that keeps faith.
3 You will keep in perfect peace
him whose mind is steadfast,
because he trusts in you.
4 Trust in the LORD forever,
for the LORD, the LORD, is the Rock
eternal.
5 He humbles those who dwell on high,
he lays the lofty city low;
he levels it to the ground
and casts it down to the dust.
6 Feet trample it down—
the feet of the oppressed,
the footsteps of the poor.

7 The path of the righteous is level;
O upright One, you make the way of
the righteous smooth.
8 Yes, LORD, walking in the way of your
laws, [a]
we wait for you;
your name and renown
are the desire of our hearts.
9 My soul yearns for you in the night;
in the morning my spirit longs for
you.
When your judgments come upon the
earth,
the people of the world learn
righteousness.
10 Though grace is shown to the wicked,
they do not learn righteousness;
even in a land of uprightness they go on
doing evil
and regard not the majesty of the
LORD.
11 O LORD, your hand is lifted high,
but they do not see it.
Let them see your zeal for your people and
be put to shame;
let the fire reserved for your enemies
consume them.

12 LORD, you establish peace for us;
all that we have accomplished you have
done for us.
13 O LORD, our God, other lords besides you
have ruled over us,
but your name alone do we honor.
14 They are now dead, they live no more;
those departed spirits do not rise.
You punished them and brought them to
ruin;
you wiped out all memory of them.
15 You have enlarged the nation, O LORD;
you have enlarged the nation.
You have gained glory for yourself;
you have extended all the borders of the
land.

16 LORD, they came to you in their distress;
when you disciplined them,
they could barely whisper a prayer. [b]
17 As a woman with child and about to give
birth
writhes and cries out in her pain,
so were we in your presence, O LORD.
18 We were with child, we writhed in pain,
but we gave birth to wind.
We have not brought salvation to the
earth;
we have not given birth to people of
the world.

19 But your dead will live;
their bodies will rise.
You who dwell in the dust,
wake up and shout for joy.
Your dew is like the dew of the morning;
the earth will give birth to her dead.

20 Go, my people, enter your rooms
and shut the doors behind you;
hide yourselves for a little while
until his wrath has passed by.
21 See, the LORD is coming out of his
dwelling
to punish the people of the earth for
their sins.
The earth will disclose the blood shed
upon her;
she will conceal her slain no longer.

Deliverance of Israel

27 In that day,

the LORD will punish with his sword,
his fierce, great and powerful sword,
Leviathan the gliding serpent,
Leviathan the coiling serpent;

[a] 8 Or *judgments* [b] 16 The meaning of the Hebrew for this clause is uncertain.

WEDNESDAY
READ ISAIAH 27:1–6

BLOOMS OF LOVE

"Sing about a fruitful vineyard: I, the LORD, watch over it; I water it continually. I guard it day and night so that no one may harm it."

— ISAIAH 27:2–3

let's talk

- What are some ways we "water" our relationship daily?
- When have we set aside a large chunk of time for our marriage? What fruitfulness have we seen from that effort?
- Can we share fruit with others because of our marriage?

My husband makes our yard look good. Both of his thumbs must be green, because we have an explosion of color around our house. I have flowers in the house virtually the whole year round. In the late winter David forces early daffodils and tulips in our little greenhouse. That's followed by a constant parade of garden flowers—irises, peonies, poppies, roses, dahlias, asters and the like—until the first freeze in late fall.

Gardening takes a lot of work. David regularly waters our flowers. Sometimes he takes a minute or two to quickly yank up a pile of weeds. Other times he'll set aside a whole morning or afternoon for yard work and for making a mysterious concoction of fish guts, mouthwash and dish soap that he sprays over his plants so that the bugs and bunnies will leave them alone. His blooms look good enough for the county fair.

It's a blessing for me that my husband cares as much for cultivating the fruitfulness of our marriage as he cares for cultivating the fruitfulness of our garden. Some of this cultivation takes place in a couple of minutes of "pulling weeds," making sure we're on the same page on financial decisions or parenting issues. We build our relationship in daily courtesies, affection, attention and joint prayer. Sometimes we give a whole evening (date night!) to marriage cultivation.

In Isaiah 27, God talks about cultivating the fruitful garden that is his chosen people. He keeps an eye on that garden. He waters it. He makes sure that nothing can harm it. His intention to go beyond protection and provision to fruitfulness is evident.

David and I like to share our garden blooms. This year flowers from our garden helped make a glorious, enormous Easter cross of flowers for our church sanctuary. Flowers from our garden end up on coworkers' desks, neighbors' kitchen counters and sickroom bedside tables. People walking their dogs wander up our driveway to get a glimpse into the backyard.

We don't want to be stingy with the fruit of our marriage either. The point of cultivating our marriage goes beyond simply protecting ourselves and our togetherness. We want our marriage to bear fruit. Some of the fruit it's now bearing is the secure, God-directed home environment that we're creating for our children. But our marriage bears fruit in our careers too; neither of us would have the creativity and energy required for work if we were emotionally drained by a damaged marital relationship. Our marriage also bears fruit in our church family life, as we live a testimony of faithfulness before others and as our support for each other enables us to serve in various ways.

David and I are determined to take time, whether it's five minutes or five evenings, to cultivate a marriage that keeps bearing fruit.

—ANNETTE LAPLACA

FOR YOUR NEXT DEVOTIONAL READING, TURN TO PAGE 775.

he will slay the monster of the sea.

2 In that day—

"Sing about a fruitful vineyard:
3 I, the LORD, watch over it;
I water it continually.
I guard it day and night
so that no one may harm it.
4 I am not angry.
If only there were briers and thorns
confronting me!
I would march against them in battle;
I would set them all on fire.
5 Or else let them come to me for refuge;
let them make peace with me,
yes, let them make peace with me."

6 In days to come Jacob will take root,
Israel will bud and blossom
and fill all the world with fruit.

7 Has ⌞the LORD⌟ struck her
as he struck down those who struck
her?
Has she been killed
as those were killed who killed her?
8 By warfare[a] and exile you contend with
her—
with his fierce blast he drives her out,
as on a day the east wind blows.
9 By this, then, will Jacob's guilt be atoned
for,
and this will be the full fruitage of the
removal of his sin:
When he makes all the altar stones
to be like chalk stones crushed to
pieces,
no Asherah poles[b] or incense altars
will be left standing.
10 The fortified city stands desolate,
an abandoned settlement, forsaken like
the desert;
there the calves graze,
there they lie down;
they strip its branches bare.
11 When its twigs are dry, they are broken off
and women come and make fires with
them.
For this is a people without
understanding;
so their Maker has no compassion on
them,
and their Creator shows them no favor.

12 In that day the LORD will thresh from the
flowing Euphrates[c] to the Wadi of Egypt, and
you, O Israelites, will be gathered up one by
one. 13 And in that day a great trumpet will
sound. Those who were perishing in Assyria
and those who were exiled in Egypt will come
and worship the LORD on the holy mountain
in Jerusalem.

Woe to Ephraim

28 Woe to that wreath, the pride of
Ephraim's drunkards,
to the fading flower, his glorious beauty,
set on the head of a fertile valley—
to that city, the pride of those laid low
by wine!
2 See, the Lord has one who is powerful and
strong.
Like a hailstorm and a destructive
wind,
like a driving rain and a flooding
downpour,
he will throw it forcefully to the
ground.
3 That wreath, the pride of Ephraim's
drunkards,
will be trampled underfoot.
4 That fading flower, his glorious beauty,
set on the head of a fertile valley,
will be like a fig ripe before harvest—
as soon as someone sees it and takes it
in his hand,
he swallows it.

5 In that day the LORD Almighty
will be a glorious crown,
a beautiful wreath
for the remnant of his people.
6 He will be a spirit of justice
to him who sits in judgment,
a source of strength
to those who turn back the battle at the
gate.

7 And these also stagger from wine
and reel from beer:
Priests and prophets stagger from beer
and are befuddled with wine;
they reel from beer,
they stagger when seeing visions,
they stumble when rendering decisions.
8 All the tables are covered with vomit
and there is not a spot without filth.

9 "Who is it he is trying to teach?
To whom is he explaining his message?
To children weaned from their milk,
to those just taken from the breast?

[a] *8* See Septuagint; the meaning of the Hebrew for this word is uncertain. [b] *9* That is, symbols of the goddess Asherah [c] *12* Hebrew *River*

10 For it is:
Do and do, do and do,
rule on rule, rule on rule[a];
a little here, a little there."
11 Very well then, with foreign lips and strange tongues
God will speak to this people,
12 to whom he said,
"This is the resting place, let the weary rest";
and, "This is the place of repose"—
but they would not listen.
13 So then, the word of the LORD to them will become:
Do and do, do and do,
rule on rule, rule on rule;
a little here, a little there—
so that they will go and fall backward,
be injured and snared and captured.

14 Therefore hear the word of the LORD, you scoffers
who rule this people in Jerusalem.
15 You boast, "We have entered into a covenant with death,
with the grave[b] we have made an agreement.
When an overwhelming scourge sweeps by,
it cannot touch us,
for we have made a lie our refuge
and falsehood[c] our hiding place."

16 So this is what the Sovereign LORD says:

"See, I lay a stone in Zion,
a tested stone,
a precious cornerstone for a sure foundation;
the one who trusts will never be dismayed.
17 I will make justice the measuring line
and righteousness the plumb line;
hail will sweep away your refuge, the lie,
and water will overflow your hiding place.
18 Your covenant with death will be annulled;
your agreement with the grave will not stand.
When the overwhelming scourge sweeps by,
you will be beaten down by it.
19 As often as it comes it will carry you away;
morning after morning, by day and by night,
it will sweep through."

The understanding of this message
will bring sheer terror.
20 The bed is too short to stretch out on,
the blanket too narrow to wrap around you.
21 The LORD will rise up as he did at Mount Perazim,
he will rouse himself as in the Valley of Gibeon—
to do his work, his strange work,
and perform his task, his alien task.
22 Now stop your mocking,
or your chains will become heavier;
the Lord, the LORD Almighty, has told me
of the destruction decreed against the whole land.

23 Listen and hear my voice;
pay attention and hear what I say.
24 When a farmer plows for planting, does he plow continually?
Does he keep on breaking up and harrowing the soil?
25 When he has leveled the surface,
does he not sow caraway and scatter cummin?
Does he not plant wheat in its place,[d]
barley in its plot,[d]
and spelt in its field?
26 His God instructs him
and teaches him the right way.

27 Caraway is not threshed with a sledge,
nor is a cartwheel rolled over cummin;
caraway is beaten out with a rod,
and cummin with a stick.
28 Grain must be ground to make bread;
so one does not go on threshing it forever.
Though he drives the wheels of his threshing cart over it,
his horses do not grind it.
29 All this also comes from the LORD Almighty,
wonderful in counsel and magnificent in wisdom.

Woe to David's City

29 Woe to you, Ariel, Ariel,
the city where David settled!
Add year to year
and let your cycle of festivals go on.
2 Yet I will besiege Ariel;
she will mourn and lament,

[a] *10* Hebrew / *sav lasav sav lasav* / *kav lakav kav lakav* (possibly meaningless sounds; perhaps a mimicking of the prophet's words); also in verse 13 [b] *15* Hebrew *Sheol*; also in verse 18 [c] *15* Or *false gods* [d] *25* The meaning of the Hebrew for this word is uncertain.

she will be to me like an altar hearth. [a]
3 I will encamp against you all around;
I will encircle you with towers
and set up my siege works against you.
4 Brought low, you will speak from the ground;
your speech will mumble out of the dust.
Your voice will come ghostlike from the earth;
out of the dust your speech will whisper.

5 But your many enemies will become like fine dust,
the ruthless hordes like blown chaff.
Suddenly, in an instant,
6 the LORD Almighty will come
with thunder and earthquake and great noise,
with windstorm and tempest and flames of a devouring fire.
7 Then the hordes of all the nations that fight against Ariel,
that attack her and her fortress and besiege her,
will be as it is with a dream,
with a vision in the night—
8 as when a hungry man dreams that he is eating,
but he awakens, and his hunger remains;
as when a thirsty man dreams that he is drinking,
but he awakens faint, with his thirst unquenched.
So will it be with the hordes of all the nations
that fight against Mount Zion.

9 Be stunned and amazed,
blind yourselves and be sightless;
be drunk, but not from wine,
stagger, but not from beer.
10 The LORD has brought over you a deep sleep:
He has sealed your eyes (the prophets);
he has covered your heads (the seers).

11 For you this whole vision is nothing but
words sealed in a scroll. And if you give the
scroll to someone who can read, and say to him,
"Read this, please," he will answer, "I can't; it is
sealed." 12 Or if you give the scroll to someone
who cannot read, and say, "Read this, please,"
he will answer, "I don't know how to read."

13 The Lord says:
"These people come near to me with their mouth
and honor me with their lips,
but their hearts are far from me.
Their worship of me
is made up only of rules taught by men. [b]
14 Therefore once more I will astound these people
with wonder upon wonder;
the wisdom of the wise will perish,
the intelligence of the intelligent will vanish."
15 Woe to those who go to great depths
to hide their plans from the LORD,
who do their work in darkness and think,
"Who sees us? Who will know?"
16 You turn things upside down,
as if the potter were thought to be like the clay!
Shall what is formed say to him who formed it,
"He did not make me"?
Can the pot say of the potter,
"He knows nothing"?

17 In a very short time, will not Lebanon be turned into a fertile field
and the fertile field seem like a forest?
18 In that day the deaf will hear the words of the scroll,
and out of gloom and darkness
the eyes of the blind will see.
19 Once more the humble will rejoice in the LORD;
the needy will rejoice in the Holy One of Israel.
20 The ruthless will vanish,
the mockers will disappear,
and all who have an eye for evil will be cut down—
21 those who with a word make a man out to be guilty,
who ensnare the defender in court
and with false testimony deprive the innocent of justice.

22 Therefore this is what the LORD, who redeemed Abraham, says to the house of Jacob:

"No longer will Jacob be ashamed;
no longer will their faces grow pale.
23 When they see among them their children,
the work of my hands,

[a] 2 The Hebrew for *altar hearth* sounds like the Hebrew for *Ariel.* [b] 13 Hebrew; Septuagint *They worship me in vain; / their teachings are but rules taught by men*

they will keep my name holy;
they will acknowledge the holiness of the Holy One of Jacob,
and will stand in awe of the God of Israel.
24 Those who are wayward in spirit will gain understanding;
those who complain will accept instruction."

Woe to the Obstinate Nation

30 "Woe to the obstinate children,"
declares the LORD,
"to those who carry out plans that are not mine,
forming an alliance, but not by my Spirit,
heaping sin upon sin;
2 who go down to Egypt
without consulting me;
who look for help to Pharaoh's protection,
to Egypt's shade for refuge.
3 But Pharaoh's protection will be to your shame,
Egypt's shade will bring you disgrace.
4 Though they have officials in Zoan
and their envoys have arrived in Hanes,
5 everyone will be put to shame
because of a people useless to them,
who bring neither help nor advantage,
but only shame and disgrace."

6 An oracle concerning the animals of the Negev:

Through a land of hardship and distress,
of lions and lionesses,
of adders and darting snakes,
the envoys carry their riches on donkeys' backs,
their treasures on the humps of camels,
to that unprofitable nation,
7 to Egypt, whose help is utterly useless.
Therefore I call her
Rahab the Do-Nothing.

8 Go now, write it on a tablet for them,
inscribe it on a scroll,
that for the days to come
it may be an everlasting witness.
9 These are rebellious people, deceitful children,
children unwilling to listen to the LORD's instruction.
10 They say to the seers,
"See no more visions!"
and to the prophets,
"Give us no more visions of what is right!
Tell us pleasant things,
prophesy illusions.
11 Leave this way,
get off this path,
and stop confronting us
with the Holy One of Israel!"

12 Therefore, this is what the Holy One of Israel says:

"Because you have rejected this message,
relied on oppression
and depended on deceit,
13 this sin will become for you
like a high wall, cracked and bulging,
that collapses suddenly, in an instant.
14 It will break in pieces like pottery,
shattered so mercilessly
that among its pieces not a fragment will be found
for taking coals from a hearth
or scooping water out of a cistern."

15 This is what the Sovereign LORD, the Holy One of Israel, says:

"In repentance and rest is your salvation,
in quietness and trust is your strength,
but you would have none of it.
16 You said, 'No, we will flee on horses.'
Therefore you will flee!
You said, 'We will ride off on swift horses.'
Therefore your pursuers will be swift!
17 A thousand will flee
at the threat of one;
at the threat of five
you will all flee away,
till you are left
like a flagstaff on a mountaintop,
like a banner on a hill."

18 Yet the LORD longs to be gracious to you;
he rises to show you compassion.
For the LORD is a God of justice.
Blessed are all who wait for him!

19 O people of Zion, who live in Jerusalem,
you will weep no more. How gracious he will
be when you cry for help! As soon as he hears,
he will answer you. 20 Although the Lord gives
you the bread of adversity and the water of
affliction, your teachers will be hidden no
more; with your own eyes you will see them.
21 Whether you turn to the right or to the left,
your ears will hear a voice behind you, saying, "This is the way; walk in it." 22 Then you
will defile your idols overlaid with silver and
your images covered with gold; you will throw

THURSDAY
READ ISAIAH 30:1–33

WHEN PLANS DON'T WORK OUT

> **"In repentance and rest is your salvation, in quietness and trust is your strength, but you would have none of it."**
>
> — Isaiah 30:15

let's talk

- When we see plans falling apart in our marriage, why is it hard for us to practice "repentance and rest"?
- How do we typically try to run away from trouble? What are the results?
- In what ways do we currently need the Lord's compassion and grace in our home? What would it mean to have God's voice quietly guiding us or his rain watering our efforts?

Mark and Courtney figured they could afford the timeshare condo if they were careful, so after the sales pitch during the free weekend at the resort, they signed up. And when some friends told them about a home-based business opportunity a few months later, they signed up for that too. But the meetings and appointments conflicted with their small group at church. What's more, their church friends started feeling more like potential customers than brothers and sisters. As business partners, Mark and Courtney started arguing more. And they chafed under the pressure to use the condo.

This fictional couple isn't so different from the nation of Israel in Isaiah's day. People wanted the good life, so they made big plans and developed friendships with other countries to help them get ahead (see Isaiah 30:1–2). But it wasn't long before the wheels came off those efforts, not just because of bad plans or foolish friendships. The real issue was that they were ignoring God and his plans for them.

It doesn't occur to some Christian couples to submit their plans to God. They make purchases, choose jobs or make time commitments without ever consulting the Lord. They may figure that as long as a decision isn't flat-out wicked, God leaves it up to them. But that's not how a relationship with God works.

God calls such people "obstinate" (Isaiah 30:1). Plans made without him and alliances formed to replace him are symptoms of hard hearts and stiff necks. When turmoil finally erupts in marriages, families or churches, the people involved are likely to turn on each other or hatch still more prayerless plans and relationships.

A couple like Mark and Courtney might try still more moneymaking schemes. Or they might end up in marriage counseling. But neither of those options turns them to God. Verses 16–17 tell us we can't outrun God. If we keep running from him, we will, in the end, be left forlorn and defeated.

God requires two responses when people's stubbornness has gotten them into trouble: repentance and rest. Repentance means turning from our sinful behavior; rest means learning to wait patiently until God acts. Resting in God means trusting him to do for us what we should not be doing for ourselves.

Amazingly, even when his people have been obstinate, God wants to be good to them. Verse 18 says, "Yet the Lord longs to be gracious to you." He does that by giving us a kind of internal GPS (global positioning system), whispering to us the direction we should take at each of life's crossroads. God also is good to us by blessing what we do, like sending the Israelites rain for their crops and enriching their harvest (see verse 23). Perhaps chief among our blessings is fearlessness in facing the future. Verse 29 says that when God's terrible day of judgment comes, those who have relied on repentance and are resting in him will sing; their hearts will rejoice!

—LEE ECLOV

FOR YOUR NEXT DEVOTIONAL READING, TURN TO PAGE 784.

them away like a menstrual cloth and say to
them, "Away with you!"

23He will also send you rain for the seed you
sow in the ground, and the food that comes
from the land will be rich and plentiful. In
that day your cattle will graze in broad meadows. 24The oxen and donkeys that work the
soil will eat fodder and mash, spread out with
fork and shovel. 25In the day of great slaughter, when the towers fall, streams of water will
flow on every high mountain and every lofty
hill. 26The moon will shine like the sun, and
the sunlight will be seven times brighter, like
the light of seven full days, when the LORD
binds up the bruises of his people and heals
the wounds he inflicted.

27 See, the Name of the LORD comes from afar,
with burning anger and dense clouds of smoke;
his lips are full of wrath,
and his tongue is a consuming fire.
28 His breath is like a rushing torrent,
rising up to the neck.
He shakes the nations in the sieve of destruction;
he places in the jaws of the peoples
a bit that leads them astray.
29 And you will sing
as on the night you celebrate a holy festival;
your hearts will rejoice
as when people go up with flutes
to the mountain of the LORD,
to the Rock of Israel.
30 The LORD will cause men to hear his majestic voice
and will make them see his arm coming down
with raging anger and consuming fire,
with cloudburst, thunderstorm and hail.
31 The voice of the LORD will shatter Assyria;
with his scepter he will strike them down.
32 Every stroke the LORD lays on them
with his punishing rod
will be to the music of tambourines and harps,
as he fights them in battle with the blows of his arm.
33 Topheth has long been prepared;
it has been made ready for the king.
Its fire pit has been made deep and wide,
with an abundance of fire and wood;
the breath of the LORD,
like a stream of burning sulfur,
sets it ablaze.

Woe to Those Who Rely on Egypt

31 Woe to those who go down to Egypt for help,
who rely on horses,
who trust in the multitude of their chariots
and in the great strength of their horsemen,
but do not look to the Holy One of Israel,
or seek help from the LORD.
2 Yet he too is wise and can bring disaster;
he does not take back his words.
He will rise up against the house of the wicked,
against those who help evildoers.
3 But the Egyptians are men and not God;
their horses are flesh and not spirit.
When the LORD stretches out his hand,
he who helps will stumble,
he who is helped will fall;
both will perish together.

4This is what the LORD says to me:

"As a lion growls,
a great lion over his prey—
and though a whole band of shepherds
is called together against him,
he is not frightened by their shouts
or disturbed by their clamor—
so the LORD Almighty will come down
to do battle on Mount Zion and on its heights.
5 Like birds hovering overhead,
the LORD Almighty will shield Jerusalem;
he will shield it and deliver it,
he will 'pass over' it and will rescue it."

6Return to him you have so greatly revolted
against, O Israelites. 7For in that day every one
of you will reject the idols of silver and gold
your sinful hands have made.

8 "Assyria will fall by a sword that is not of man;
a sword, not of mortals, will devour them.
They will flee before the sword
and their young men will be put to forced labor.
9 Their stronghold will fall because of terror;
at sight of the battle standard their commanders will panic,"
declares the LORD,
whose fire is in Zion,
whose furnace is in Jerusalem.

The Kingdom of Righteousness

32 See, a king will reign in righteousness
and rulers will rule with justice.
2 Each man will be like a shelter from the wind
and a refuge from the storm,
like streams of water in the desert
and the shadow of a great rock in a thirsty land.

3 Then the eyes of those who see will no longer be closed,
and the ears of those who hear will listen.
4 The mind of the rash will know and understand,
and the stammering tongue will be fluent and clear.
5 No longer will the fool be called noble
nor the scoundrel be highly respected.
6 For the fool speaks folly,
his mind is busy with evil:
He practices ungodliness
and spreads error concerning the LORD;
the hungry he leaves empty
and from the thirsty he withholds water.
7 The scoundrel's methods are wicked,
he makes up evil schemes
to destroy the poor with lies,
even when the plea of the needy is just.
8 But the noble man makes noble plans,
and by noble deeds he stands.

The Women of Jerusalem

9 You women who are so complacent,
rise up and listen to me;
you daughters who feel secure,
hear what I have to say!
10 In little more than a year
you who feel secure will tremble;
the grape harvest will fail,
and the harvest of fruit will not come.
11 Tremble, you complacent women;
shudder, you daughters who feel secure!
Strip off your clothes,
put sackcloth around your waists.
12 Beat your breasts for the pleasant fields,
for the fruitful vines
13 and for the land of my people,
a land overgrown with thorns and briers—
yes, mourn for all houses of merriment
and for this city of revelry.
14 The fortress will be abandoned,
the noisy city deserted;
citadel and watchtower will become a wasteland forever,
the delight of donkeys, a pasture for flocks,
15 till the Spirit is poured upon us from on high,
and the desert becomes a fertile field,
and the fertile field seems like a forest.
16 Justice will dwell in the desert
and righteousness live in the fertile field.
17 The fruit of righteousness will be peace;
the effect of righteousness will be quietness and confidence forever.
18 My people will live in peaceful dwelling places,
in secure homes,
in undisturbed places of rest.
19 Though hail flattens the forest
and the city is leveled completely,
20 how blessed you will be,
sowing your seed by every stream,
and letting your cattle and donkeys range free.

Distress and Help

33 Woe to you, O destroyer,
you who have not been destroyed!
Woe to you, O traitor,
you who have not been betrayed!
When you stop destroying,
you will be destroyed;
when you stop betraying,
you will be betrayed.

2 O LORD, be gracious to us;
we long for you.
Be our strength every morning,
our salvation in time of distress.
3 At the thunder of your voice, the peoples flee;
when you rise up, the nations scatter.
4 Your plunder, O nations, is harvested as by young locusts;
like a swarm of locusts men pounce on it.

5 The LORD is exalted, for he dwells on high;
he will fill Zion with justice and righteousness.
6 He will be the sure foundation for your times,
a rich store of salvation and wisdom and knowledge;
the fear of the LORD is the key to this treasure.[a]

[a] 6 Or *is a treasure from him*

7 Look, their brave men cry aloud in the streets;
the envoys of peace weep bitterly.
8 The highways are deserted,
no travelers are on the roads.
The treaty is broken,
its witnesses[a] are despised,
no one is respected.
9 The land mourns[b] and wastes away,
Lebanon is ashamed and withers;
Sharon is like the Arabah,
and Bashan and Carmel drop their leaves.

10 "Now will I arise," says the LORD.
"Now will I be exalted;
now will I be lifted up.
11 You conceive chaff,
you give birth to straw;
your breath is a fire that consumes you.
12 The peoples will be burned as if to lime;
like cut thornbushes they will be set ablaze."

13 You who are far away, hear what I have done;
you who are near, acknowledge my power!
14 The sinners in Zion are terrified;
trembling grips the godless:
"Who of us can dwell with the consuming fire?
Who of us can dwell with everlasting burning?"
15 He who walks righteously
and speaks what is right,
who rejects gain from extortion
and keeps his hand from accepting bribes,
who stops his ears against plots of murder
and shuts his eyes against contemplating evil—
16 this is the man who will dwell on the heights,
whose refuge will be the mountain fortress.
His bread will be supplied,
and water will not fail him.

17 Your eyes will see the king in his beauty
and view a land that stretches afar.
18 In your thoughts you will ponder the former terror:
"Where is that chief officer?
Where is the one who took the revenue?
Where is the officer in charge of the towers?"
19 You will see those arrogant people no more,
those people of an obscure speech,
with their strange, incomprehensible tongue.

20 Look upon Zion, the city of our festivals;
your eyes will see Jerusalem,
a peaceful abode, a tent that will not be moved;
its stakes will never be pulled up,
nor any of its ropes broken.
21 There the LORD will be our Mighty One.
It will be like a place of broad rivers and streams.
No galley with oars will ride them,
no mighty ship will sail them.
22 For the LORD is our judge,
the LORD is our lawgiver,
the LORD is our king;
it is he who will save us.

23 Your rigging hangs loose:
The mast is not held secure,
the sail is not spread.
Then an abundance of spoils will be divided
and even the lame will carry off plunder.
24 No one living in Zion will say, "I am ill";
and the sins of those who dwell there will be forgiven.

Judgment Against the Nations

34 Come near, you nations, and listen;
pay attention, you peoples!
Let the earth hear, and all that is in it,
the world, and all that comes out of it!
2 The LORD is angry with all nations;
his wrath is upon all their armies.
He will totally destroy[c] them,
he will give them over to slaughter.
3 Their slain will be thrown out,
their dead bodies will send up a stench;
the mountains will be soaked with their blood.
4 All the stars of the heavens will be dissolved
and the sky rolled up like a scroll;
all the starry host will fall
like withered leaves from the vine,
like shriveled figs from the fig tree.

5 My sword has drunk its fill in the heavens;
see, it descends in judgment on Edom,

[a] 8 Dead Sea Scrolls; Masoretic Text / *the cities* [b] 9 Or *dries up* [c] 2 The Hebrew term refers to the irrevocable giving over of things or persons to the LORD, often by totally destroying them; also in verse 5.

the people I have totally destroyed.
6 The sword of the LORD is bathed in blood,
it is covered with fat—
the blood of lambs and goats,
fat from the kidneys of rams.
For the LORD has a sacrifice in Bozrah
and a great slaughter in Edom.
7 And the wild oxen will fall with them,
the bull calves and the great bulls.
Their land will be drenched with blood,
and the dust will be soaked with fat.

8 For the LORD has a day of vengeance,
a year of retribution, to uphold Zion's
cause.
9 Edom's streams will be turned into pitch,
her dust into burning sulfur;
her land will become blazing pitch!
10 It will not be quenched night and day;
its smoke will rise forever.
From generation to generation it will lie
desolate;
no one will ever pass through it again.
11 The desert owl[a] and screech owl[a] will
possess it;
the great owl[a] and the raven will nest
there.
God will stretch out over Edom
the measuring line of chaos
and the plumb line of desolation.
12 Her nobles will have nothing there to be
called a kingdom,
all her princes will vanish away.
13 Thorns will overrun her citadels,
nettles and brambles her strongholds.
She will become a haunt for jackals,
a home for owls.
14 Desert creatures will meet with hyenas,
and wild goats will bleat to each other;
there the night creatures will also repose
and find for themselves places of rest.
15 The owl will nest there and lay eggs,
she will hatch them, and care for her
young under the shadow of her
wings;
there also the falcons will gather,
each with its mate.

16 Look in the scroll of the LORD and read:

None of these will be missing,
not one will lack her mate.
For it is his mouth that has given the
order,
and his Spirit will gather them together.
17 He allots their portions;
his hand distributes them by measure.
They will possess it forever
and dwell there from generation to
generation.

Joy of the Redeemed

35 The desert and the parched land will
be glad;
the wilderness will rejoice and blossom.
Like the crocus, 2 it will burst into bloom;
it will rejoice greatly and shout for joy.
The glory of Lebanon will be given to it,
the splendor of Carmel and Sharon;
they will see the glory of the LORD,
the splendor of our God.

3 Strengthen the feeble hands,
steady the knees that give way;
4 say to those with fearful hearts,
"Be strong, do not fear;
your God will come,
he will come with vengeance;
with divine retribution
he will come to save you."

5 Then will the eyes of the blind be opened
and the ears of the deaf unstopped.
6 Then will the lame leap like a deer,
and the mute tongue shout for joy.
Water will gush forth in the wilderness
and streams in the desert.
7 The burning sand will become a pool,
the thirsty ground bubbling springs.
In the haunts where jackals once lay,
grass and reeds and papyrus will grow.

8 And a highway will be there;
it will be called the Way of Holiness.
The unclean will not journey on it;
it will be for those who walk in that
Way;
wicked fools will not go about on it.[b]
9 No lion will be there,
nor will any ferocious beast get up on
it;
they will not be found there.
But only the redeemed will walk there,
10 and the ransomed of the LORD will
return.
They will enter Zion with singing;
everlasting joy will crown their heads.
Gladness and joy will overtake them,
and sorrow and sighing will flee away.

Sennacherib Threatens Jerusalem

36 In the fourteenth year of King Hezekiah's reign, Sennacherib king of Assyria
attacked all the fortified cities of Judah

a 11 The precise identification of these birds is uncertain. b 8 Or / *the simple will not stray from it*

and captured them. 2Then the king of Assyria
sent his field commander with a large army
from Lachish to King Hezekiah at Jerusalem.
When the commander stopped at the aqueduct of the Upper Pool, on the road to the
Washerman's Field, 3Eliakim son of Hilkiah
the palace administrator, Shebna the secretary,
and Joah son of Asaph the recorder went out
to him.
4The field commander said to them, "Tell
Hezekiah,

" 'This is what the great king, the king
of Assyria, says: On what are you basing
this confidence of yours? 5You say you
have strategy and military strength—but
you speak only empty words. On whom
are you depending, that you rebel against
me? 6Look now, you are depending on
Egypt, that splintered reed of a staff,
which pierces a man's hand and wounds
him if he leans on it! Such is Pharaoh
king of Egypt to all who depend on him.
7And if you say to me, "We are depending on the LORD our God"—isn't he the
one whose high places and altars Hezekiah removed, saying to Judah and Jerusalem, "You must worship before this
altar"?
8" 'Come now, make a bargain with my
master, the king of Assyria: I will give you
two thousand horses—if you can put riders on them! 9How then can you repulse
one officer of the least of my master's officials, even though you are depending on
Egypt for chariots and horsemen? 10Fur-
thermore, have I come to attack and destroy this land without the LORD? The
LORD himself told me to march against
this country and destroy it.' "

11Then Eliakim, Shebna and Joah said to
the field commander, "Please speak to your
servants in Aramaic, since we understand it.
Don't speak to us in Hebrew in the hearing of
the people on the wall."
12But the commander replied, "Was it only
to your master and you that my master sent
me to say these things, and not to the men
sitting on the wall—who, like you, will have
to eat their own filth and drink their own
urine?"
13Then the commander stood and called
out in Hebrew, "Hear the words of the great
king, the king of Assyria! 14This is what the
king says: Do not let Hezekiah deceive you.
He cannot deliver you! 15Do not let Hezekiah
persuade you to trust in the LORD when he
says, 'The LORD will surely deliver us; this city
will not be given into the hand of the king of
Assyria.'
16"Do not listen to Hezekiah. This is what
the king of Assyria says: Make peace with me
and come out to me. Then every one of you
will eat from his own vine and fig tree and
drink water from his own cistern, 17until I
come and take you to a land like your own—a
land of grain and new wine, a land of bread
and vineyards.
18"Do not let Hezekiah mislead you when
he says, 'The LORD will deliver us.' Has the
god of any nation ever delivered his land from
the hand of the king of Assyria? 19Where are
the gods of Hamath and Arpad? Where are the
gods of Sepharvaim? Have they rescued Samaria from my hand? 20Who of all the gods of
these countries has been able to save his land
from me? How then can the LORD deliver Jerusalem from my hand?"
21But the people remained silent and said
nothing in reply, because the king had commanded, "Do not answer him."
22Then Eliakim son of Hilkiah the palace
administrator, Shebna the secretary, and Joah
son of Asaph the recorder went to Hezekiah,
with their clothes torn, and told him what the
field commander had said.

Jerusalem's Deliverance Foretold

37 When King Hezekiah heard this, he
tore his clothes and put on sackcloth
and went into the temple of the LORD.
2He sent Eliakim the palace administrator,
Shebna the secretary, and the leading priests,
all wearing sackcloth, to the prophet Isaiah
son of Amoz. 3They told him, "This is what
Hezekiah says: This day is a day of distress and
rebuke and disgrace, as when children come to
the point of birth and there is no strength to
deliver them. 4It may be that the LORD your
God will hear the words of the field commander, whom his master, the king of Assyria,
has sent to ridicule the living God, and that he
will rebuke him for the words the LORD your
God has heard. Therefore pray for the remnant that still survives."
5When King Hezekiah's officials came to
Isaiah, 6Isaiah said to them, "Tell your master, 'This is what the LORD says: Do not be
afraid of what you have heard—those words
with which the underlings of the king of Assyria have blasphemed me. 7Listen! I am going
to put a spirit in him so that when he hears a
certain report, he will return to his own coun-

try, and there I will have him cut down with
the sword.' "
8When the field commander heard that the
king of Assyria had left Lachish, he withdrew
and found the king fighting against Libnah.
9Now Sennacherib received a report that
Tirhakah, the Cushite[a] king ⌊of Egypt⌋, was
marching out to fight against him. When he
heard it, he sent messengers to Hezekiah with
this word: 10"Say to Hezekiah king of Judah:
Do not let the god you depend on deceive you
when he says, 'Jerusalem will not be handed
over to the king of Assyria.' 11Surely you have
heard what the kings of Assyria have done to
all the countries, destroying them completely.
And will you be delivered? 12Did the gods of
the nations that were destroyed by my forefathers deliver them—the gods of Gozan, Haran, Rezeph and the people of Eden who were
in Tel Assar? 13Where is the king of Hamath,
the king of Arpad, the king of the city of Sepharvaim, or of Hena or Ivvah?"

Hezekiah's Prayer

14Hezekiah received the letter from the
messengers and read it. Then he went up to
the temple of the LORD and spread it out before the LORD. 15And Hezekiah prayed to the
LORD: 16"O LORD Almighty, God of Israel,
enthroned between the cherubim, you alone
are God over all the kingdoms of the earth.
You have made heaven and earth. 17Give ear,
O LORD, and hear; open your eyes, O LORD,
and see; listen to all the words Sennacherib has
sent to insult the living God.
18"It is true, O LORD, that the Assyrian
kings have laid waste all these peoples and
their lands. 19They have thrown their gods
into the fire and destroyed them, for they were
not gods but only wood and stone, fashioned
by human hands. 20Now, O LORD our God,
deliver us from his hand, so that all kingdoms
on earth may know that you alone, O LORD,
are God.[b]"

Sennacherib's Fall

21Then Isaiah son of Amoz sent a message
to Hezekiah: "This is what the LORD, the God
of Israel, says: Because you have prayed to me
concerning Sennacherib king of Assyria, 22this
is the word the LORD has spoken against him:

"The Virgin Daughter of Zion
  despises and mocks you.
The Daughter of Jerusalem
  tosses her head as you flee.
23Who is it you have insulted and
    blasphemed?
  Against whom have you raised your
    voice
and lifted your eyes in pride?
  Against the Holy One of Israel!
24By your messengers
  you have heaped insults on the Lord.
And you have said,
  'With my many chariots
I have ascended the heights of the
    mountains,
  the utmost heights of Lebanon.
I have cut down its tallest cedars,
  the choicest of its pines.
I have reached its remotest heights,
  the finest of its forests.
25I have dug wells in foreign lands[c]
  and drunk the water there.
With the soles of my feet
  I have dried up all the streams of
    Egypt.'

26"Have you not heard?
  Long ago I ordained it.
In days of old I planned it;
  now I have brought it to pass,
that you have turned fortified cities
  into piles of stone.
27Their people, drained of power,
  are dismayed and put to shame.
They are like plants in the field,
  like tender green shoots,
like grass sprouting on the roof,
  scorched[d] before it grows up.

28"But I know where you stay
  and when you come and go
  and how you rage against me.
29Because you rage against me
  and because your insolence has reached
    my ears,
I will put my hook in your nose
  and my bit in your mouth,
and I will make you return
  by the way you came.

30"This will be the sign for you, O Hezekiah:

"This year you will eat what grows by
    itself,
  and the second year what springs from
    that.

[a] 9 That is, from the upper Nile region [b] 20 Dead Sea Scrolls (see also 2 Kings 19:19); Masoretic Text *alone are the LORD* [c] 25 Dead Sea Scrolls (see also 2 Kings 19:24); Masoretic Text does not have *in foreign lands.* [d] 27 Some manuscripts of the Masoretic Text, Dead Sea Scrolls and some Septuagint manuscripts (see also 2 Kings 19:26); most manuscripts of the Masoretic Text *roof / and terraced fields*

But in the third year sow and reap,
plant vineyards and eat their fruit.
31 Once more a remnant of the house of Judah
will take root below and bear fruit above.
32 For out of Jerusalem will come a remnant,
and out of Mount Zion a band of survivors.
The zeal of the LORD Almighty
will accomplish this.

33 "Therefore this is what the LORD says
concerning the king of Assyria:

"He will not enter this city
or shoot an arrow here.
He will not come before it with shield
or build a siege ramp against it.
34 By the way that he came he will return;
he will not enter this city,"
declares the LORD.
35 "I will defend this city and save it,
for my sake and for the sake of David my servant!"

36 Then the angel of the LORD went out and
put to death a hundred and eighty-five thousand men in the Assyrian camp. When the
people got up the next morning—there were
all the dead bodies! 37 So Sennacherib king
of Assyria broke camp and withdrew. He returned to Nineveh and stayed there.
38 One day, while he was worshiping in the
temple of his god Nisroch, his sons Adrammelech and Sharezer cut him down with the
sword, and they escaped to the land of Ararat. And Esarhaddon his son succeeded him
as king.

Hezekiah's Illness

38 In those days Hezekiah became ill and
was at the point of death. The prophet Isaiah son of Amoz went to him and
said, "This is what the LORD says: Put your
house in order, because you are going to die;
you will not recover."
2 Hezekiah turned his face to the wall and
prayed to the LORD, 3 "Remember, O LORD,
how I have walked before you faithfully and
with wholehearted devotion and have done
what is good in your eyes." And Hezekiah
wept bitterly.
4 Then the word of the LORD came to Isaiah: 5 "Go and tell Hezekiah, 'This is what the
LORD, the God of your father David, says: I
have heard your prayer and seen your tears; I
will add fifteen years to your life. 6 And I will
deliver you and this city from the hand of the
king of Assyria. I will defend this city.
7 " 'This is the LORD's sign to you that the
LORD will do what he has promised: 8 I will
make the shadow cast by the sun go back the
ten steps it has gone down on the stairway of
Ahaz.' " So the sunlight went back the ten
steps it had gone down.

9 A writing of Hezekiah king of Judah after
his illness and recovery:

10 I said, "In the prime of my life
must I go through the gates of death[a]
and be robbed of the rest of my years?"
11 I said, "I will not again see the LORD,
the LORD, in the land of the living;
no longer will I look on mankind,
or be with those who now dwell in this world.[b]
12 Like a shepherd's tent my house
has been pulled down and taken from me.
Like a weaver I have rolled up my life,
and he has cut me off from the loom;
day and night you made an end of me.
13 I waited patiently till dawn,
but like a lion he broke all my bones;
day and night you made an end of me.
14 I cried like a swift or thrush,
I moaned like a mourning dove.
My eyes grew weak as I looked to the heavens.
I am troubled; O Lord, come to my aid!"

15 But what can I say?
He has spoken to me, and he himself has done this.
I will walk humbly all my years
because of this anguish of my soul.
16 Lord, by such things men live;
and my spirit finds life in them too.
You restored me to health
and let me live.
17 Surely it was for my benefit
that I suffered such anguish.
In your love you kept me
from the pit of destruction;
you have put all my sins
behind your back.
18 For the grave[a] cannot praise you,
death cannot sing your praise;
those who go down to the pit
cannot hope for your faithfulness.
19 The living, the living—they praise you,

a 10,18 Hebrew *Sheol* *b* 11 A few Hebrew manuscripts; most Hebrew manuscripts *in the place of cessation*

as I am doing today;
fathers tell their children
about your faithfulness.

20 The LORD will save me,
and we will sing with stringed instruments
all the days of our lives
in the temple of the LORD.

21 Isaiah had said, "Prepare a poultice of figs and apply it to the boil, and he will recover."
22 Hezekiah had asked, "What will be the sign that I will go up to the temple of the LORD?"

Envoys From Babylon

39 At that time Merodach-Baladan son of Baladan king of Babylon sent Hezekiah letters and a gift, because he had heard of his illness and recovery.
2 Hezekiah received the envoys gladly and showed them what was in his storehouses—the silver, the gold, the spices, the fine oil, his entire armory and everything found among his treasures. There was nothing in his palace or in all his kingdom that Hezekiah did not show them.
3 Then Isaiah the prophet went to King Hezekiah and asked, "What did those men say, and where did they come from?"

"From a distant land," Hezekiah replied. "They came to me from Babylon."
4 The prophet asked, "What did they see in your palace?"

"They saw everything in my palace," Hezekiah said. "There is nothing among my treasures that I did not show them."
5 Then Isaiah said to Hezekiah, "Hear the word of the LORD Almighty:
6 The time will surely come when everything in your palace, and all that your fathers have stored up until this day, will be carried off to Babylon. Nothing will be left, says the LORD.
7 And some of your descendants, your own flesh and blood who will be born to you, will be taken away, and they will become eunuchs in the palace of the king of Babylon."
8 "The word of the LORD you have spoken is good," Hezekiah replied. For he thought, "There will be peace and security in my lifetime."

Comfort for God's People

40 Comfort, comfort my people,
says your God.
2 Speak tenderly to Jerusalem,
and proclaim to her
that her hard service has been completed,
that her sin has been paid for,
that she has received from the LORD's hand
double for all her sins.

3 A voice of one calling:
"In the desert prepare
the way for the LORD[a];
make straight in the wilderness
a highway for our God.[b]
4 Every valley shall be raised up,
every mountain and hill made low;
the rough ground shall become level,
the rugged places a plain.
5 And the glory of the LORD will be revealed,
and all mankind together will see it.
For the mouth of the LORD has spoken."

6 A voice says, "Cry out."
And I said, "What shall I cry?"

"All men are like grass,
and all their glory is like the flowers of the field.
7 The grass withers and the flowers fall,
because the breath of the LORD blows on them.
Surely the people are grass.
8 The grass withers and the flowers fall,
but the word of our God stands forever."

9 You who bring good tidings to Zion,
go up on a high mountain.
You who bring good tidings to Jerusalem,[c]
lift up your voice with a shout,
lift it up, do not be afraid;
say to the towns of Judah,
"Here is your God!"
10 See, the Sovereign LORD comes with power,
and his arm rules for him.
See, his reward is with him,
and his recompense accompanies him.
11 He tends his flock like a shepherd:
He gathers the lambs in his arms
and carries them close to his heart;
he gently leads those that have young.

12 Who has measured the waters in the hollow of his hand,
or with the breadth of his hand marked off the heavens?

---

[a] 3 Or *A voice of one calling in the desert: / "Prepare the way for the LORD* [b] 3 Hebrew; Septuagint *make straight the paths of our God*
[c] 9 Or *O Zion, bringer of good tidings, / go up on a high mountain. / O Jerusalem, bringer of good tidings*

F

FRIDAY

READ ISAIAH 40:1–31

FUEL FOR THE LONG RUN

More weddings at which I tie the knot result in strong marriages than end in divorce. Maybe that's because I won't officiate unless both partners can openly declare their trust in God. I also insist that they go through significant premarriage counseling. Still, one couple lasted a mere 14 weeks because he didn't match up to her romantic ideals and she way overspent his budget. Another marriage survived for a decade before it was asphyxiated by his hyper-controlling tendencies.

But what scares me more is when a couple calls it quits after 20, 30 or 40 years. Once you get past the "11th-year-fear," shouldn't some deep interconnectedness set in to provide stability for the onslaught of the years? Shouldn't it be like the old John Deere tractor that I farmed with as a boy, which took more work to get going than to keep running? I would strain to turn the massive flywheel over the first time, but once the magnets caught, the pistons popped and the flywheel gained momentum, it almost took an act of God to kill the thing!

God isn't in the business of killing a good thing. As Isaiah notes, he "gives strength to the weary and increases the power of the weak" (Isaiah 40:29). Even in marriage? Especially in marriage, since God thought that one up in the first place. Still, how do we find the grace to run the race of relationship and not trip along the way?

> **Even youths grow tired and weary, and young men stumble and fall; but those who hope in the LORD will renew their strength. They will soar on wings like eagles; they will run and not grow weary, they will walk and not be faint.**
>
> — ISAIAH 40:30–31

let's talk

- What do we depend on God for in our relationship? How do we express that dependency?
- Where do we need God's help right now? Where are we stumbling or fainting? What should we ask for to recover our courage?
- Who around us has gone through rough places and survived? What can we learn from them? How might we gain new insights from their experiences?

Isaiah 40 isn't about magic. Its opening verses recall the stumbling and sinfulness of God's people. They speak also about the warm and compassionate heart of God. The rest of the chapter breathes a reminder to seek God's care. Marriages, like careers or characters, aren't made overnight. They happen when folks dig in for the long run and keep their eyes on the prize.

Psychiatrist M. Scott Peck said that the scariest people aren't those who have quirky personalities or relational scars. The most threatening folk, he wrote in *People of the Lie*, are those who don't believe in a power beyond themselves. When people stop praying and assume an attitude of belligerent self-sufficiency, said Peck, they shrink the world to their perspective and seek to control it according to their whims. The result is always horrifying.

Marriages that go the distance are inevitably built on trust—in God and in each other. It's as an 81-year-old man told me from his oversized chair. Slapping his hands on the armrests, he said, "We're 60 years married this week and mighty proud of our family. But it's not us that did it; it's the grace of God."

—WAYNE BROUWER

FOR YOUR NEXT DEVOTIONAL READING, TURN TO PAGE 790.

Who has held the dust of the earth in a
basket,
or weighed the mountains on the scales
and the hills in a balance?
13 Who has understood the mind[a] of the
LORD,
or instructed him as his counselor?
14 Whom did the LORD consult to enlighten
him,
and who taught him the right way?
Who was it that taught him knowledge
or showed him the path of
understanding?

15 Surely the nations are like a drop in a
bucket;
they are regarded as dust on the scales;
he weighs the islands as though they
were fine dust.
16 Lebanon is not sufficient for altar fires,
nor its animals enough for burnt
offerings.
17 Before him all the nations are as nothing;
they are regarded by him as worthless
and less than nothing.

18 To whom, then, will you compare God?
What image will you compare him to?
19 As for an idol, a craftsman casts it,
and a goldsmith overlays it with gold
and fashions silver chains for it.
20 A man too poor to present such an offering
selects wood that will not rot.
He looks for a skilled craftsman
to set up an idol that will not topple.

21 Do you not know?
Have you not heard?
Has it not been told you from the
beginning?
Have you not understood since the
earth was founded?
22 He sits enthroned above the circle of the
earth,
and its people are like grasshoppers.
He stretches out the heavens like a canopy,
and spreads them out like a tent to live
in.
23 He brings princes to naught
and reduces the rulers of this world to
nothing.
24 No sooner are they planted,
no sooner are they sown,
no sooner do they take root in the
ground,
than he blows on them and they wither,
and a whirlwind sweeps them away like
chaff.

25 "To whom will you compare me?
Or who is my equal?" says the Holy
One.
26 Lift your eyes and look to the heavens:
Who created all these?
He who brings out the starry host one by
one,
and calls them each by name.
Because of his great power and mighty
strength,
not one of them is missing.

27 Why do you say, O Jacob,
and complain, O Israel,
"My way is hidden from the LORD;
my cause is disregarded by my God"?
28 Do you not know?
Have you not heard?
The LORD is the everlasting God,
the Creator of the ends of the earth.
He will not grow tired or weary,
and his understanding no one can
fathom.
29 He gives strength to the weary
and increases the power of the weak.
30 Even youths grow tired and weary,
and young men stumble and fall;
31 but those who hope in the LORD
will renew their strength.
They will soar on wings like eagles;
they will run and not grow weary,
they will walk and not be faint.

The Helper of Israel

41 "Be silent before me, you islands!
Let the nations renew their strength!
Let them come forward and speak;
let us meet together at the place of
judgment.

2 "Who has stirred up one from the east,
calling him in righteousness to his
service[b]?
He hands nations over to him
and subdues kings before him.
He turns them to dust with his sword,
to windblown chaff with his bow.
3 He pursues them and moves on
unscathed,
by a path his feet have not traveled
before.
4 Who has done this and carried it through,
calling forth the generations from the
beginning?

---

[a] *13* Or *Spirit*; or *spirit* [b] *2* Or / *whom victory meets at every step*

I, the LORD—with the first of them
and with the last—I am he."

5 The islands have seen it and fear;
the ends of the earth tremble.
They approach and come forward;
6 each helps the other
and says to his brother, "Be strong!"
7 The craftsman encourages the goldsmith,
and he who smooths with the hammer
spurs on him who strikes the anvil.
He says of the welding, "It is good."
He nails down the idol so it will not topple.

8 "But you, O Israel, my servant,
Jacob, whom I have chosen,
you descendants of Abraham my friend,
9 I took you from the ends of the earth,
from its farthest corners I called you.
I said, 'You are my servant';
I have chosen you and have not rejected you.
10 So do not fear, for I am with you;
do not be dismayed, for I am your God.
I will strengthen you and help you;
I will uphold you with my righteous right hand.

11 "All who rage against you
will surely be ashamed and disgraced;
those who oppose you
will be as nothing and perish.
12 Though you search for your enemies,
you will not find them.
Those who wage war against you
will be as nothing at all.
13 For I am the LORD, your God,
who takes hold of your right hand
and says to you, Do not fear;
I will help you.
14 Do not be afraid, O worm Jacob,
O little Israel,
for I myself will help you," declares the LORD,
your Redeemer, the Holy One of Israel.
15 "See, I will make you into a threshing sledge,
new and sharp, with many teeth.
You will thresh the mountains and crush them,
and reduce the hills to chaff.
16 You will winnow them, the wind will pick them up,
and a gale will blow them away.
But you will rejoice in the LORD
and glory in the Holy One of Israel.

17 "The poor and needy search for water,
but there is none;
their tongues are parched with thirst.
But I the LORD will answer them;
I, the God of Israel, will not forsake them.
18 I will make rivers flow on barren heights,
and springs within the valleys.
I will turn the desert into pools of water,
and the parched ground into springs.
19 I will put in the desert
the cedar and the acacia, the myrtle and the olive.
I will set pines in the wasteland,
the fir and the cypress together,
20 so that people may see and know,
may consider and understand,
that the hand of the LORD has done this,
that the Holy One of Israel has created it.

21 "Present your case," says the LORD.
"Set forth your arguments," says Jacob's King.
22 "Bring in ⌊your idols⌋ to tell us
what is going to happen.
Tell us what the former things were,
so that we may consider them
and know their final outcome.
Or declare to us the things to come,
23 tell us what the future holds,
so we may know that you are gods.
Do something, whether good or bad,
so that we will be dismayed and filled with fear.
24 But you are less than nothing
and your works are utterly worthless;
he who chooses you is detestable.

25 "I have stirred up one from the north, and he comes—
one from the rising sun who calls on my name.
He treads on rulers as if they were mortar,
as if he were a potter treading the clay.
26 Who told of this from the beginning, so we could know,
or beforehand, so we could say, 'He was right'?
No one told of this,
no one foretold it,
no one heard any words from you.
27 I was the first to tell Zion, 'Look, here they are!'
I gave to Jerusalem a messenger of good tidings.
28 I look but there is no one—
no one among them to give counsel,

no one to give answer when I ask them.
29 See, they are all false!
Their deeds amount to nothing;
their images are but wind and
confusion.

The Servant of the LORD

42 "Here is my servant, whom I uphold,
my chosen one in whom I delight;
I will put my Spirit on him
and he will bring justice to the nations.
2 He will not shout or cry out,
or raise his voice in the streets.
3 A bruised reed he will not break,
and a smoldering wick he will not snuff
out.
In faithfulness he will bring forth justice;
4 he will not falter or be discouraged
till he establishes justice on earth.
In his law the islands will put their
hope."

5 This is what God the LORD says—
he who created the heavens and stretched
them out,
who spread out the earth and all that
comes out of it,
who gives breath to its people,
and life to those who walk on it:
6 "I, the LORD, have called you in
righteousness;
I will take hold of your hand.
I will keep you and will make you
to be a covenant for the people
and a light for the Gentiles,
7 to open eyes that are blind,
to free captives from prison
and to release from the dungeon those
who sit in darkness.

8 "I am the LORD; that is my name!
I will not give my glory to another
or my praise to idols.
9 See, the former things have taken place,
and new things I declare;
before they spring into being
I announce them to you."

Song of Praise to the LORD

10 Sing to the LORD a new song,
his praise from the ends of the earth,
you who go down to the sea, and all that
is in it,
you islands, and all who live in them.
11 Let the desert and its towns raise their
voices;
let the settlements where Kedar lives
rejoice.
Let the people of Sela sing for joy;
let them shout from the mountaintops.
12 Let them give glory to the LORD
and proclaim his praise in the islands.
13 The LORD will march out like a mighty
man,
like a warrior he will stir up his zeal;
with a shout he will raise the battle cry
and will triumph over his enemies.

14 "For a long time I have kept silent,
I have been quiet and held myself back.
But now, like a woman in childbirth,
I cry out, I gasp and pant.
15 I will lay waste the mountains and hills
and dry up all their vegetation;
I will turn rivers into islands
and dry up the pools.
16 I will lead the blind by ways they have not
known,
along unfamiliar paths I will guide
them;
I will turn the darkness into light before
them
and make the rough places smooth.
These are the things I will do;
I will not forsake them.
17 But those who trust in idols,
who say to images, 'You are our gods,'
will be turned back in utter shame.

Israel Blind and Deaf

18 "Hear, you deaf;
look, you blind, and see!
19 Who is blind but my servant,
and deaf like the messenger I send?
Who is blind like the one committed to
me,
blind like the servant of the LORD?
20 You have seen many things, but have paid
no attention;
your ears are open, but you hear
nothing."
21 It pleased the LORD
for the sake of his righteousness
to make his law great and glorious.
22 But this is a people plundered and looted,
all of them trapped in pits
or hidden away in prisons.
They have become plunder,
with no one to rescue them;
they have been made loot,
with no one to say, "Send them back."

23 Which of you will listen to this
or pay close attention in time to come?
24 Who handed Jacob over to become loot,
and Israel to the plunderers?

Was it not the LORD,
against whom we have sinned?
For they would not follow his ways;
they did not obey his law.
25 So he poured out on them his burning anger,
the violence of war.
It enveloped them in flames, yet they did not understand;
it consumed them, but they did not take it to heart.

Israel's Only Savior

43 But now, this is what the LORD says—
he who created you, O Jacob,
he who formed you, O Israel:
"Fear not, for I have redeemed you;
I have summoned you by name; you are mine.
2 When you pass through the waters,
I will be with you;
and when you pass through the rivers,
they will not sweep over you.
When you walk through the fire,
you will not be burned;
the flames will not set you ablaze.
3 For I am the LORD, your God,
the Holy One of Israel, your Savior;
I give Egypt for your ransom,
Cush [a] and Seba in your stead.
4 Since you are precious and honored in my sight,
and because I love you,
I will give men in exchange for you,
and people in exchange for your life.
5 Do not be afraid, for I am with you;
I will bring your children from the east
and gather you from the west.
6 I will say to the north, 'Give them up!'
and to the south, 'Do not hold them back.'
Bring my sons from afar
and my daughters from the ends of the earth—
7 everyone who is called by my name,
whom I created for my glory,
whom I formed and made."

8 Lead out those who have eyes but are blind,
who have ears but are deaf.
9 All the nations gather together
and the peoples assemble.
Which of them foretold this
and proclaimed to us the former things?
Let them bring in their witnesses to prove they were right,
so that others may hear and say, "It is true."
10 "You are my witnesses," declares the LORD,
"and my servant whom I have chosen,
so that you may know and believe me
and understand that I am he.
Before me no god was formed,
nor will there be one after me.
11 I, even I, am the LORD,
and apart from me there is no savior.
12 I have revealed and saved and proclaimed—
I, and not some foreign god among you.
You are my witnesses," declares the LORD,
"that I am God.
13 Yes, and from ancient days I am he.
No one can deliver out of my hand.
When I act, who can reverse it?"

God's Mercy and Israel's Unfaithfulness

14 This is what the LORD says—
your Redeemer, the Holy One of Israel:
"For your sake I will send to Babylon
and bring down as fugitives all the Babylonians, [b]
in the ships in which they took pride.
15 I am the LORD, your Holy One,
Israel's Creator, your King."

16 This is what the LORD says—
he who made a way through the sea,
a path through the mighty waters,
17 who drew out the chariots and horses,
the army and reinforcements together,
and they lay there, never to rise again,
extinguished, snuffed out like a wick:
18 "Forget the former things;
do not dwell on the past.
19 See, I am doing a new thing!
Now it springs up; do you not perceive it?
I am making a way in the desert
and streams in the wasteland.
20 The wild animals honor me,
the jackals and the owls,
because I provide water in the desert
and streams in the wasteland,
to give drink to my people, my chosen,
21 the people I formed for myself
that they may proclaim my praise.
22 "Yet you have not called upon me, O Jacob,
you have not wearied yourselves for me, O Israel.

[a] 3 That is, the upper Nile region [b] 14 Or *Chaldeans*

23 You have not brought me sheep for burnt
offerings,
nor honored me with your sacrifices.
I have not burdened you with grain
offerings
nor wearied you with demands for
incense.
24 You have not bought any fragrant calamus
for me,
or lavished on me the fat of your
sacrifices.
But you have burdened me with your sins
and wearied me with your offenses.

25 "I, even I, am he who blots out
your transgressions, for my own sake,
and remembers your sins no more.
26 Review the past for me,
let us argue the matter together;
state the case for your innocence.
27 Your first father sinned;
your spokesmen rebelled against me.
28 So I will disgrace the dignitaries of your
temple,
and I will consign Jacob to destruction[a]
and Israel to scorn.

Israel the Chosen

44 "But now listen, O Jacob, my servant,
Israel, whom I have chosen.
2 This is what the LORD says—
he who made you, who formed you in
the womb,
and who will help you:
Do not be afraid, O Jacob, my servant,
Jeshurun, whom I have chosen.
3 For I will pour water on the thirsty land,
and streams on the dry ground;
I will pour out my Spirit on your
offspring,
and my blessing on your descendants.
4 They will spring up like grass in a meadow,
like poplar trees by flowing streams.
5 One will say, 'I belong to the LORD';
another will call himself by the name of
Jacob;
still another will write on his hand, 'The
LORD's,'
and will take the name Israel.

The LORD, Not Idols

6 "This is what the LORD says—
Israel's King and Redeemer, the LORD
Almighty:
I am the first and I am the last;
apart from me there is no God.
7 Who then is like me? Let him proclaim it.
Let him declare and lay out before me
what has happened since I established my
ancient people,
and what is yet to come—
yes, let him foretell what will come.
8 Do not tremble, do not be afraid.
Did I not proclaim this and foretell it
long ago?
You are my witnesses. Is there any God
besides me?
No, there is no other Rock; I know not
one."

9 All who make idols are nothing,
and the things they treasure are
worthless.
Those who would speak up for them are
blind;
they are ignorant, to their own shame.
10 Who shapes a god and casts an idol,
which can profit him nothing?
11 He and his kind will be put to shame;
craftsmen are nothing but men.
Let them all come together and take their
stand;
they will be brought down to terror and
infamy.

12 The blacksmith takes a tool
and works with it in the coals;
he shapes an idol with hammers,
he forges it with the might of his arm.
He gets hungry and loses his strength;
he drinks no water and grows faint.
13 The carpenter measures with a line
and makes an outline with a marker;
he roughs it out with chisels
and marks it with compasses.
He shapes it in the form of man,
of man in all his glory,
that it may dwell in a shrine.
14 He cut down cedars,
or perhaps took a cypress or oak.
He let it grow among the trees of the
forest,
or planted a pine, and the rain made it
grow.
15 It is man's fuel for burning;
some of it he takes and warms himself,
he kindles a fire and bakes bread.
But he also fashions a god and worships it;
he makes an idol and bows down to it.
16 Half of the wood he burns in the fire;
over it he prepares his meal,
he roasts his meat and eats his fill.

[a] 28 The Hebrew term refers to the irrevocable giving over of things or persons to the LORD, often by totally destroying them.

WEEKEND

working with our expectations

Sometimes at our Marriage Alive seminars we ask the participants what their expectations were for the weekend. Often we get unexpected answers: One couple came because babysitting was offered. Another couple came because they thought the weekend was tax deductible! But the Harrisons, a couple in their sixties, had another reason. They had paid the registration for their son and daughter-in-law. At the last minute the younger couple couldn't attend, and the Harrisons didn't want to lose their investment, so they came instead.

We start marriage with stars in our eyes and a belief that our future mate is going to meet all our needs and expectations. Then when the honeymoon is over, our hormones settle down and we get into an everyday rut, marriage may not be quite what we anticipated.

Plus, our expectations may be different. A group of teenagers were questioned about what they wanted in a mate when they married. One boy said he wanted an "old-fashioned" wife just like his mom, one who would find cleaning the house, cooking, washing, and ironing his clothes creative and exciting. A girl in the same group said she wanted to have an exciting career as well as five children, and she was sure that her husband would share home responsibilities fifty-fifty. We looked at each other and thought, if these two get together, they're going to need more than our book and seminar!

What were your expectations before marriage? Here's what others have said:

"The main reason I got married was for sex."

"I expected my mate to meet my needs—to be a lot like me."

"What I wanted in a marriage was romance!"

"I was looking for security and love, someone I could trust and lean on."

"I wanted peace and harmony and to know that when we went to bed at night, everything was okay,"

Obviously, some of these people were shocked when their spouses didn't live up to their expectations. Dr. Selma Miller, former president of the Association of Marriage and Family Counselors, says, "The most common cause of marriage problems is that the partners' needs are in conflict, but they can't discuss the conflict because they don't know one exists. They only know that they are miserable."

Susie and Tom's marriage exploded after fifteen years. Unspoken expectations torpedoed their relationship. Tom wanted Susie to replace his best pal whom he'd lost in the Vietnam War. Susie wanted Tom to love and baby her as her dad used to do. They did not fulfill each other's expectations; they didn't even know what those expectations were.

It's important that we talk about our expectations. It's hard enough to meet expectations when we know what they are, but it is almost impossible when we don't know what our partner expects.

—DAVID AND CLAUDIA ARP

expectation survey

HOW ARE WE DOING?

Let's look at seven areas of expectations in marriage. Rank them in order of their importance to you (1 for very important; 7 for unimportant) and what you think your spouse would say. Then compare your lists.

1. Security—the knowledge of permanence in a relationship and of financial and material well-being.

My Rank_______ What I Think You'll Say______

2. Companionship—having a friend who goes through all the joys and sorrows of life with me, a soul partner; having common areas of interest.

My Rank_______ What I Think You'll Say______

3. Sex—the oneness that comes through physical intimacy in marriage; the initiation and enjoyment of a growing love relationship.

My Rank_______ What I Think You'll Say______

4. Understanding and tenderness—experiencing regularly the touch, the kiss, the winks across the room that say, "I love you," "I care" and "I'm thinking of you."

My Rank_______ What I Think You'll Say______

5. Encouragement—having someone verbally support and appreciate my work and efforts in my profession, at home, with the children and so on.

My Rank_______ What I Think You'll Say______

6. Intellectual closeness—discussing and growing together in common areas of intellectual thought.

My Rank_______ What I Think You'll Say______

7. Mutual activity—doing things together, such as politics, sports, church work, hobbies.

My Rank_______ What I Think You'll Say______

let's make a DATE

date

DO THE UNEXPECTED!

This weekend ask your spouse for a date. Decide on a time and then make your plan. Your job is to do something unexpected. Perhaps you don't cook, so you surprise your spouse by making dinner. Maybe you surprise your spouse with tickets to a concert or sporting event. Perhaps you stay in and do something unexpected in the bedroom. Whatever you do, the goal is to break out of your usual mold and surprise your spouse. Then schedule another surprise date that the other person gets to plan.

FOR YOUR NEXT DEVOTIONAL READING, TURN TO PAGE 795.

LESSONS FROM THE *Bible*

Read 2 Corinthians 8:1–15. This passage talks about collecting money for the distressed Christians in Jerusalem, but several principles here apply to a marriage as well.

1. How can you give to your partner beyond his or her expectations?
2. Would it be fair to say that in marriage "the goal is equality" (verse 14)?
3. How can you be sure that the one who has much doesn't have too much and the one who has little doesn't have too little in your marriage?

He also warms himself and says,
"Ah! I am warm; I see the fire."
17 From the rest he makes a god, his idol;
he bows down to it and worships.
He prays to it and says,
"Save me; you are my god."
18 They know nothing, they understand nothing;
their eyes are plastered over so they cannot see,
and their minds closed so they cannot understand.
19 No one stops to think,
no one has the knowledge or understanding to say,
"Half of it I used for fuel;
I even baked bread over its coals,
I roasted meat and I ate.
Shall I make a detestable thing from what is left?
Shall I bow down to a block of wood?"
20 He feeds on ashes, a deluded heart misleads him;
he cannot save himself, or say,
"Is not this thing in my right hand a lie?"

21 "Remember these things, O Jacob,
for you are my servant, O Israel.
I have made you, you are my servant;
O Israel, I will not forget you.
22 I have swept away your offenses like a cloud,
your sins like the morning mist.
Return to me,
for I have redeemed you."

23 Sing for joy, O heavens, for the LORD has done this;
shout aloud, O earth beneath.
Burst into song, you mountains,
you forests and all your trees,
for the LORD has redeemed Jacob,
he displays his glory in Israel.

Jerusalem to Be Inhabited

24 "This is what the LORD says—
your Redeemer, who formed you in the womb:

I am the LORD,
who has made all things,
who alone stretched out the heavens,
who spread out the earth by myself,
25 who foils the signs of false prophets
and makes fools of diviners,
who overthrows the learning of the wise
and turns it into nonsense,
26 who carries out the words of his servants
and fulfills the predictions of his messengers,

who says of Jerusalem, 'It shall be inhabited,'
of the towns of Judah, 'They shall be built,'
and of their ruins, 'I will restore them,'
27 who says to the watery deep, 'Be dry,
and I will dry up your streams,'
28 who says of Cyrus, 'He is my shepherd
and will accomplish all that I please;
he will say of Jerusalem, "Let it be rebuilt,"
and of the temple, "Let its foundations be laid." '

45 "This is what the LORD says to his anointed,
to Cyrus, whose right hand I take hold of
to subdue nations before him
and to strip kings of their armor,
to open doors before him
so that gates will not be shut:
2 I will go before you
and will level the mountains[a];
I will break down gates of bronze
and cut through bars of iron.
3 I will give you the treasures of darkness,
riches stored in secret places,
so that you may know that I am the LORD,
the God of Israel, who summons you by name.
4 For the sake of Jacob my servant,
of Israel my chosen,
I summon you by name
and bestow on you a title of honor,
though you do not acknowledge me.
5 I am the LORD, and there is no other;
apart from me there is no God.
I will strengthen you,
though you have not acknowledged me,
6 so that from the rising of the sun
to the place of its setting
men may know there is none besides me.
I am the LORD, and there is no other.
7 I form the light and create darkness,
I bring prosperity and create disaster;
I, the LORD, do all these things.

[a] 2 Dead Sea Scrolls and Septuagint; the meaning of the word in the Masoretic Text is uncertain.

8 "You heavens above, rain down
righteousness;
let the clouds shower it down.
Let the earth open wide,
let salvation spring up,
let righteousness grow with it;
I, the LORD, have created it.

9 "Woe to him who quarrels with his
Maker,
to him who is but a potsherd among
the potsherds on the ground.
Does the clay say to the potter,
'What are you making?'
Does your work say,
'He has no hands'?
10 Woe to him who says to his father,
'What have you begotten?'
or to his mother,
'What have you brought to birth?'

11 "This is what the LORD says—
the Holy One of Israel, and its Maker:
Concerning things to come,
do you question me about my children,
or give me orders about the work of my
hands?
12 It is I who made the earth
and created mankind upon it.
My own hands stretched out the heavens;
I marshaled their starry hosts.
13 I will raise up Cyrus[a] in my
righteousness:
I will make all his ways straight.
He will rebuild my city
and set my exiles free,
but not for a price or reward,
says the LORD Almighty."

14 This is what the LORD says:

"The products of Egypt and the
merchandise of Cush,[b]
and those tall Sabeans—
they will come over to you
and will be yours;
they will trudge behind you,
coming over to you in chains.
They will bow down before you
and plead with you, saying,
'Surely God is with you, and there is no
other;
there is no other god.' "

15 Truly you are a God who hides himself,
O God and Savior of Israel.
16 All the makers of idols will be put to
shame and disgraced;
they will go off into disgrace together.
17 But Israel will be saved by the LORD
with an everlasting salvation;
you will never be put to shame or
disgraced,
to ages everlasting.

18 For this is what the LORD says—
he who created the heavens,
he is God;
he who fashioned and made the earth,
he founded it;
he did not create it to be empty,
but formed it to be inhabited—
he says:
"I am the LORD,
and there is no other.
19 I have not spoken in secret,
from somewhere in a land of
darkness;
I have not said to Jacob's descendants,
'Seek me in vain.'
I, the LORD, speak the truth;
I declare what is right.

20 "Gather together and come;
assemble, you fugitives from the
nations.
Ignorant are those who carry about idols
of wood,
who pray to gods that cannot save.
21 Declare what is to be, present it—
let them take counsel together.
Who foretold this long ago,
who declared it from the distant past?
Was it not I, the LORD?
And there is no God apart from me,
a righteous God and a Savior;
there is none but me.

22 "Turn to me and be saved,
all you ends of the earth;
for I am God, and there is no other.
23 By myself I have sworn,
my mouth has uttered in all integrity
a word that will not be revoked:
Before me every knee will bow;
by me every tongue will swear.
24 They will say of me, 'In the LORD alone
are righteousness and strength.' "
All who have raged against him
will come to him and be put to shame.
25 But in the LORD all the descendants of
Israel
will be found righteous and will exult.

[a] *13* Hebrew *him* [b] *14* That is, the upper Nile region

Gods of Babylon

46 Bel bows down, Nebo stoops low;
their idols are borne by beasts of burden.[a]
The images that are carried about are burdensome,
a burden for the weary.
2 They stoop and bow down together;
unable to rescue the burden,
they themselves go off into captivity.

3 "Listen to me, O house of Jacob,
all you who remain of the house of Israel,
you whom I have upheld since you were conceived,
and have carried since your birth.
4 Even to your old age and gray hairs
I am he, I am he who will sustain you.
I have made you and I will carry you;
I will sustain you and I will rescue you.

5 "To whom will you compare me or count me equal?
To whom will you liken me that we may be compared?
6 Some pour out gold from their bags
and weigh out silver on the scales;
they hire a goldsmith to make it into a god,
and they bow down and worship it.
7 They lift it to their shoulders and carry it;
they set it up in its place, and there it stands.
From that spot it cannot move.
Though one cries out to it, it does not answer;
it cannot save him from his troubles.

8 "Remember this, fix it in mind,
take it to heart, you rebels.
9 Remember the former things, those of long ago;
I am God, and there is no other;
I am God, and there is none like me.
10 I make known the end from the beginning,
from ancient times, what is still to come.
I say: My purpose will stand,
and I will do all that I please.
11 From the east I summon a bird of prey;
from a far-off land, a man to fulfill my purpose.
What I have said, that will I bring about;
what I have planned, that will I do.
12 Listen to me, you stubborn-hearted,
you who are far from righteousness.
13 I am bringing my righteousness near,
it is not far away;
and my salvation will not be delayed.
I will grant salvation to Zion,
my splendor to Israel.

The Fall of Babylon

47 "Go down, sit in the dust,
Virgin Daughter of Babylon;
sit on the ground without a throne,
Daughter of the Babylonians.[b]
No more will you be called
tender or delicate.
2 Take millstones and grind flour;
take off your veil.
Lift up your skirts, bare your legs,
and wade through the streams.
3 Your nakedness will be exposed
and your shame uncovered.
I will take vengeance;
I will spare no one."

4 Our Redeemer—the LORD Almighty is his name—
is the Holy One of Israel.

5 "Sit in silence, go into darkness,
Daughter of the Babylonians;
no more will you be called
queen of kingdoms.
6 I was angry with my people
and desecrated my inheritance;
I gave them into your hand,
and you showed them no mercy.
Even on the aged
you laid a very heavy yoke.
7 You said, 'I will continue forever—
the eternal queen!'
But you did not consider these things
or reflect on what might happen.

8 "Now then, listen, you wanton creature,
lounging in your security
and saying to yourself,
'I am, and there is none besides me.
I will never be a widow
or suffer the loss of children.'
9 Both of these will overtake you
in a moment, on a single day:
loss of children and widowhood.
They will come upon you in full measure,
in spite of your many sorceries
and all your potent spells.
10 You have trusted in your wickedness
and have said, 'No one sees me.'
Your wisdom and knowledge mislead you

---

[a] 1 Or *are but beasts and cattle* [b] 1 Or *Chaldeans*; also in verse 5

M

MONDAY

READ ISAIAH 47:1–15

PUTTING AWAY THE "WHAT IFS"

> **"Disaster will come upon you, and you will not know how to conjure it away. A calamity will fall upon you that you cannot ward off with a ransom; a catastrophe you cannot foresee will suddenly come upon you."**
>
> — Isaiah 47:11

let's talk

- Which of us tends to be a worrier? What issues trouble us the most?
- How has God shown himself faithful to us in the past? How can we use that knowledge to keep the "what ifs" at bay?
- What aspects of God's character help us to trust him with our future?

Maybe it's just me, but I have a hard time not playing the "what if" game. What if my daughter never gets any better at reading? What if my son continues to rebel? What if my husband gets sick and dies? What if one of our children is abused? What if my kids grow up and don't follow Christ?

You've probably played the "what if" game yourself now and then. It's hard not to fall into the "what if" trap because bad stuff does happen to good people, and suffering does come to Christians. Everybody knows someone struggling through a divorce or battling cancer. Most people live with a daily awareness that hard stuff could possibly be just around the corner.

In Isaiah 47, God lambasted the people of wicked Babylon, telling them that a terrible destruction would certainly befall them, and it would be just too bad for them because they had cut themselves off from the source of hope. They had been so confident that they were in charge of their own well-being that they had given no thought or allegiance or devotion to their Creator. God warned them that when their day of trouble came, they would have no way out.

But what about us—modern-day believers living by faith in a world where anything can happen and usually does? Do we have hope?

We do. The best way I've found to put away the "what if" game is to remember that God's Word emphasizes that God is sovereign and good. God's sovereignty means he is completely in charge of everything that happens in this world and beyond it; nothing can happen to us without his hand controlling the entire situation. God's goodness includes his constant, faithful love for me and my family and his promise that in all things (even things that look very bad) he is working for my good because I love him and have been called according to his purpose (see Romans 8:28). Whether it's by God's miraculous intervention and provision or by his ability to shape my desires and will, God will have his holy way.

People whose marriages are dedicated to Christ also have the promise of God's constant presence through the Advocate, the Holy Spirit (see John 14:15–31). When hard things happen to us, we are not alone! We have not, like the Babylonians, trusted our own street smarts or cleverness to make our way in this world. We move ahead in intimate partnership with God to see him glorified and his purposes achieved.

David and I have struggled through some hard times, and we sometimes look ahead and shiver in anticipation of our children becoming adults in a dangerous world. We know this side of heaven is often a difficult place to be, and our family is not catastrophe-proof any more than the family next door. But we put our hope in our good and sovereign God. That enables us to step into the future with faith.

—ANNETTE LAPLACA

FOR YOUR NEXT DEVOTIONAL READING, TURN TO PAGE 800.

when you say to yourself,
'I am, and there is none besides me.'
11 Disaster will come upon you,
and you will not know how to conjure it away.
A calamity will fall upon you
that you cannot ward off with a ransom;
a catastrophe you cannot foresee
will suddenly come upon you.
12 "Keep on, then, with your magic spells
and with your many sorceries,
which you have labored at since childhood.
Perhaps you will succeed,
perhaps you will cause terror.
13 All the counsel you have received has only worn you out!
Let your astrologers come forward,
those stargazers who make predictions month by month,
let them save you from what is coming upon you.
14 Surely they are like stubble;
the fire will burn them up.
They cannot even save themselves
from the power of the flame.
Here are no coals to warm anyone;
here is no fire to sit by.
15 That is all they can do for you—
these you have labored with
and trafficked with since childhood.
Each of them goes on in his error;
there is not one that can save you.

Stubborn Israel

48 "Listen to this, O house of Jacob,
you who are called by the name of Israel
and come from the line of Judah,
you who take oaths in the name of the LORD
and invoke the God of Israel—
but not in truth or righteousness—
2 you who call yourselves citizens of the holy city
and rely on the God of Israel—
the LORD Almighty is his name:
3 I foretold the former things long ago,
my mouth announced them and I made them known;
then suddenly I acted, and they came to pass.
4 For I knew how stubborn you were;
the sinews of your neck were iron,
your forehead was bronze.
5 Therefore I told you these things long ago;
before they happened I announced them to you
so that you could not say,
'My idols did them;
my wooden image and metal god ordained them.'
6 You have heard these things; look at them all.
Will you not admit them?
"From now on I will tell you of new things,
of hidden things unknown to you.
7 They are created now, and not long ago;
you have not heard of them before today.
So you cannot say,
'Yes, I knew of them.'
8 You have neither heard nor understood;
from of old your ear has not been open.
Well do I know how treacherous you are;
you were called a rebel from birth.
9 For my own name's sake I delay my wrath;
for the sake of my praise I hold it back from you,
so as not to cut you off.
10 See, I have refined you, though not as silver;
I have tested you in the furnace of affliction.
11 For my own sake, for my own sake, I do this.
How can I let myself be defamed?
I will not yield my glory to another.

Israel Freed

12 "Listen to me, O Jacob,
Israel, whom I have called:
I am he;
I am the first and I am the last.
13 My own hand laid the foundations of the earth,
and my right hand spread out the heavens;
when I summon them,
they all stand up together.
14 "Come together, all of you, and listen:
Which of ⌞the idols⌟ has foretold these things?
The LORD's chosen ally
will carry out his purpose against Babylon;
his arm will be against the Babylonians.[a]

---

[a] 14 Or *Chaldeans*; also in verse 20

15 I, even I, have spoken;
yes, I have called him.
I will bring him,
and he will succeed in his mission.

16 "Come near me and listen to this:

"From the first announcement I have not spoken in secret;
at the time it happens, I am there."

And now the Sovereign LORD has sent me,
with his Spirit.

17 This is what the LORD says—
your Redeemer, the Holy One of Israel:
"I am the LORD your God,
who teaches you what is best for you,
who directs you in the way you should go.
18 If only you had paid attention to my commands,
your peace would have been like a river,
your righteousness like the waves of the sea.
19 Your descendants would have been like the sand,
your children like its numberless grains;
their name would never be cut off
nor destroyed from before me."

20 Leave Babylon,
flee from the Babylonians!
Announce this with shouts of joy
and proclaim it.
Send it out to the ends of the earth;
say, "The LORD has redeemed his servant Jacob."
21 They did not thirst when he led them through the deserts;
he made water flow for them from the rock;
he split the rock
and water gushed out.

22 "There is no peace," says the LORD, "for the wicked."

The Servant of the LORD

49 Listen to me, you islands;
hear this, you distant nations:
Before I was born the LORD called me;
from my birth he has made mention of my name.
2 He made my mouth like a sharpened sword,
in the shadow of his hand he hid me;
he made me into a polished arrow
and concealed me in his quiver.
3 He said to me, "You are my servant,
Israel, in whom I will display my splendor."
4 But I said, "I have labored to no purpose;
I have spent my strength in vain and for nothing.
Yet what is due me is in the LORD's hand,
and my reward is with my God."

5 And now the LORD says—
he who formed me in the womb to be his servant
to bring Jacob back to him
and gather Israel to himself,
for I am honored in the eyes of the LORD
and my God has been my strength—
6 he says:
"It is too small a thing for you to be my servant
to restore the tribes of Jacob
and bring back those of Israel I have kept.
I will also make you a light for the Gentiles,
that you may bring my salvation to the ends of the earth."

7 This is what the LORD says—
the Redeemer and Holy One of Israel—
to him who was despised and abhorred by the nation,
to the servant of rulers:
"Kings will see you and rise up,
princes will see and bow down,
because of the LORD, who is faithful,
the Holy One of Israel, who has chosen you."

Restoration of Israel

8 This is what the LORD says:

"In the time of my favor I will answer you,
and in the day of salvation I will help you;
I will keep you and will make you
to be a covenant for the people,
to restore the land
and to reassign its desolate inheritances,
9 to say to the captives, 'Come out,'
and to those in darkness, 'Be free!'

"They will feed beside the roads
and find pasture on every barren hill.
10 They will neither hunger nor thirst,
nor will the desert heat or the sun beat upon them.
He who has compassion on them will guide them
and lead them beside springs of water.

11 I will turn all my mountains into roads,
and my highways will be raised up.
12 See, they will come from afar—
some from the north, some from the west,
some from the region of Aswan.[a]"

13 Shout for joy, O heavens;
rejoice, O earth;
burst into song, O mountains!
For the LORD comforts his people
and will have compassion on his afflicted ones.

14 But Zion said, "The LORD has forsaken me,
the Lord has forgotten me."

15 "Can a mother forget the baby at her breast
and have no compassion on the child she has borne?
Though she may forget,
I will not forget you!
16 See, I have engraved you on the palms of my hands;
your walls are ever before me.
17 Your sons hasten back,
and those who laid you waste depart from you.
18 Lift up your eyes and look around;
all your sons gather and come to you.
As surely as I live," declares the LORD,
"you will wear them all as ornaments;
you will put them on, like a bride.

19 "Though you were ruined and made desolate
and your land laid waste,
now you will be too small for your people,
and those who devoured you will be far away.
20 The children born during your bereavement
will yet say in your hearing,
'This place is too small for us;
give us more space to live in.'
21 Then you will say in your heart,
'Who bore me these?
I was bereaved and barren;
I was exiled and rejected.
Who brought these up?
I was left all alone,
but these—where have they come from?' "

22 This is what the Sovereign LORD says:

"See, I will beckon to the Gentiles,
I will lift up my banner to the peoples;
they will bring your sons in their arms
and carry your daughters on their shoulders.
23 Kings will be your foster fathers,
and their queens your nursing mothers.
They will bow down before you with their faces to the ground;
they will lick the dust at your feet.
Then you will know that I am the LORD;
those who hope in me will not be disappointed."

24 Can plunder be taken from warriors,
or captives rescued from the fierce[b]?

25 But this is what the LORD says:

"Yes, captives will be taken from warriors,
and plunder retrieved from the fierce;
I will contend with those who contend with you,
and your children I will save.
26 I will make your oppressors eat their own flesh;
they will be drunk on their own blood, as with wine.
Then all mankind will know
that I, the LORD, am your Savior,
your Redeemer, the Mighty One of Jacob."

Israel's Sin and the Servant's Obedience

50 This is what the LORD says:

"Where is your mother's certificate of divorce
with which I sent her away?
Or to which of my creditors
did I sell you?
Because of your sins you were sold;
because of your transgressions your mother was sent away.
2 When I came, why was there no one?
When I called, why was there no one to answer?
Was my arm too short to ransom you?
Do I lack the strength to rescue you?
By a mere rebuke I dry up the sea,
I turn rivers into a desert;
their fish rot for lack of water
and die of thirst.

[a] 12 Dead Sea Scrolls; Masoretic Text *Sinim* [b] 24 Dead Sea Scrolls, Vulgate and Syriac (see also Septuagint and verse 25); Masoretic Text *righteous*

3 I clothe the sky with darkness
and make sackcloth its covering."
4 The Sovereign LORD has given me an
instructed tongue,
to know the word that sustains the
weary.
He wakens me morning by morning,
wakens my ear to listen like one being
taught.
5 The Sovereign LORD has opened my ears,
and I have not been rebellious;
I have not drawn back.
6 I offered my back to those who beat me,
my cheeks to those who pulled out my
beard;
I did not hide my face
from mocking and spitting.
7 Because the Sovereign LORD helps me,
I will not be disgraced.
Therefore have I set my face like flint,
and I know I will not be put to shame.
8 He who vindicates me is near.
Who then will bring charges against
me?
Let us face each other!
Who is my accuser?
Let him confront me!
9 It is the Sovereign LORD who helps me.
Who is he that will condemn me?
They will all wear out like a garment;
the moths will eat them up.

10 Who among you fears the LORD
and obeys the word of his servant?
Let him who walks in the dark,
who has no light,
trust in the name of the LORD
and rely on his God.
11 But now, all you who light fires
and provide yourselves with flaming
torches,
go, walk in the light of your fires
and of the torches you have set ablaze.
This is what you shall receive from my
hand:
You will lie down in torment.

Everlasting Salvation for Zion

51 "Listen to me, you who pursue
righteousness
and who seek the LORD:
Look to the rock from which you were cut
and to the quarry from which you were
hewn;
2 look to Abraham, your father,
and to Sarah, who gave you birth.
When I called him he was but one,
and I blessed him and made him
many.
3 The LORD will surely comfort Zion
and will look with compassion on all
her ruins;
he will make her deserts like Eden,
her wastelands like the garden of the
LORD.
Joy and gladness will be found in her,
thanksgiving and the sound of
singing.

4 "Listen to me, my people;
hear me, my nation:
The law will go out from me;
my justice will become a light to the
nations.
5 My righteousness draws near speedily,
my salvation is on the way,
and my arm will bring justice to the
nations.
The islands will look to me
and wait in hope for my arm.
6 Lift up your eyes to the heavens,
look at the earth beneath;
the heavens will vanish like smoke,
the earth will wear out like a garment
and its inhabitants die like flies.
But my salvation will last forever,
my righteousness will never fail.

7 "Hear me, you who know what is right,
you people who have my law in your
hearts:
Do not fear the reproach of men
or be terrified by their insults.
8 For the moth will eat them up like a
garment;
the worm will devour them like wool.
But my righteousness will last forever,
my salvation through all generations."

9 Awake, awake! Clothe yourself with
strength,
O arm of the LORD;
awake, as in days gone by,
as in generations of old.
Was it not you who cut Rahab to pieces,
who pierced that monster through?
10 Was it not you who dried up the sea,
the waters of the great deep,
who made a road in the depths of the sea
so that the redeemed might cross over?
11 The ransomed of the LORD will return.
They will enter Zion with singing;
everlasting joy will crown their heads.
Gladness and joy will overtake them,
and sorrow and sighing will flee away.

FACING OUR FEARS

> **"I, even I, am he who comforts you. Who are you that you fear mortal men, the sons of men, who are but grass, that you forget the Lord your Maker, who stretched out the heavens and laid the foundations of the earth?"**
>
> — Isaiah 51:12–13

There are so many things to worry about when we first marry: finding the right jobs, having enough money to pay the bills, deciding when to buy a house, deciding whether or not to have kids, determining what to do about intrusive in-laws. Couples wrestle with fears even when they deeply love each other.

In the beginning years of marriage, we don't have enough history together to have a sense of how things are going to work out—even when things are working fairly well. We can't see the big picture in our married life. We can't see the forest for the trees, the branches, the leaves. When we have such a limited view of life together, it's easy to become fearful about the future.

Isaiah notes that one reason we have such fears is that we, like the children of Israel, have lost sight of the Lord our Maker, who created all that we have and all that we are. Isaiah 51:12–13 assures us that God wants to deliver us from such fears because we belong to him. Isaiah says that God set the heavens in place and laid the foundations of the earth. He can set the pieces of married life in place. And he can guide us into the future.

Bill and Teresa wrestled with fears. Bill was so fearful of not having enough money that he couldn't bear the thought of dipping into savings to purchase a house. Meantime, Teresa struggled with fears about time management: How could she work fulltime, finish a master's degree that could get her a better job and maintain her relationship with Bill? Both partners in this marriage became so stressed that they could hardly function. They became cowering prisoners to fear.

When they recognized how the fun had gone out of their relationship, Bill and Teresa resolved to do three things together. First, they prayed for God's guidance for their overall life plan: What was God's mission for them as a Christian couple? Did that mean buying a house? Finishing a degree? Second, they talked frankly about money: How much did they need to invest? How could they cut back on spending to save for essentials, such as a house? Finally, they prayed about their use of time: How much time could they spend developing themselves professionally and spiritually while also having fun together?

It's easy for fear to enter into married life and cripple a relationship, but God doesn't want that for us. When we are most uncertain of our own ability to handle the future, we can find freedom from fear by remembering the One "who stretched out the heavens and laid the foundations of the earth" and who longs to comfort us.

—JOHN R. THROOP

let's talk

- ✦ What causes us to be afraid in our relationship?
- ✦ Why is it a good thing to be covered by "the shadow of [God's] hand" (Isaiah 51:16)? What happens when we feel like his hand is not on us?
- ✦ Why is it important to seek God's guidance on a life plan for our marriage? How do we know that he is revealing it to us as a couple?

FOR YOUR NEXT DEVOTIONAL READING, TURN TO PAGE 808.

12 "I, even I, am he who comforts you.
Who are you that you fear mortal men,
the sons of men, who are but grass,
13 that you forget the LORD your Maker,
who stretched out the heavens
and laid the foundations of the earth,
that you live in constant terror every day
because of the wrath of the oppressor,
who is bent on destruction?
For where is the wrath of the oppressor?
14 The cowering prisoners will soon be set free;
they will not die in their dungeon,
nor will they lack bread.
15 For I am the LORD your God,
who churns up the sea so that its waves roar—
the LORD Almighty is his name.
16 I have put my words in your mouth
and covered you with the shadow of my hand—
I who set the heavens in place,
who laid the foundations of the earth,
and who say to Zion, 'You are my people.' "

The Cup of the LORD's Wrath

17 Awake, awake!
Rise up, O Jerusalem,
you who have drunk from the hand of the LORD
the cup of his wrath,
you who have drained to its dregs
the goblet that makes men stagger.
18 Of all the sons she bore
there was none to guide her;
of all the sons she reared
there was none to take her by the hand.
19 These double calamities have come upon you—
who can comfort you?—
ruin and destruction, famine and sword—
who can[a] console you?
20 Your sons have fainted;
they lie at the head of every street,
like antelope caught in a net.
They are filled with the wrath of the LORD
and the rebuke of your God.

21 Therefore hear this, you afflicted one,
made drunk, but not with wine.
22 This is what your Sovereign LORD says,
your God, who defends his people:
"See, I have taken out of your hand
the cup that made you stagger;
from that cup, the goblet of my wrath,
you will never drink again.
23 I will put it into the hands of your tormentors,
who said to you,
'Fall prostrate that we may walk over you.'
And you made your back like the ground,
like a street to be walked over."

52 Awake, awake, O Zion,
clothe yourself with strength.
Put on your garments of splendor,
O Jerusalem, the holy city.
The uncircumcised and defiled
will not enter you again.
2 Shake off your dust;
rise up, sit enthroned, O Jerusalem.
Free yourself from the chains on your neck,
O captive Daughter of Zion.

3 For this is what the LORD says:

"You were sold for nothing,
and without money you will be redeemed."

4 For this is what the Sovereign LORD says:

"At first my people went down to Egypt to live;
lately, Assyria has oppressed them.

5 "And now what do I have here?" declares the LORD.

"For my people have been taken away for nothing,
and those who rule them mock,[b]"
declares the LORD.
"And all day long
my name is constantly blasphemed.
6 Therefore my people will know my name;
therefore in that day they will know
that it is I who foretold it.
Yes, it is I."

7 How beautiful on the mountains
are the feet of those who bring good news,
who proclaim peace,
who bring good tidings,
who proclaim salvation,
who say to Zion,
"Your God reigns!"
8 Listen! Your watchmen lift up their voices;
together they shout for joy.

---

[a] *19* Dead Sea Scrolls, Septuagint, Vulgate and Syriac; Masoretic Text / *how can I wail*
[b] *5* Dead Sea Scrolls and Vulgate; Masoretic Text

When the LORD returns to Zion,
they will see it with their own eyes.
9 Burst into songs of joy together,
you ruins of Jerusalem,
for the LORD has comforted his people,
he has redeemed Jerusalem.
10 The LORD will lay bare his holy arm
in the sight of all the nations,
and all the ends of the earth will see
the salvation of our God.

11 Depart, depart, go out from there!
Touch no unclean thing!
Come out from it and be pure,
you who carry the vessels of the LORD.
12 But you will not leave in haste
or go in flight;
for the LORD will go before you,
the God of Israel will be your rear guard.

The Suffering and Glory of the Servant

13 See, my servant will act wisely[a];
he will be raised and lifted up and highly exalted.
14 Just as there were many who were appalled at him[b]—
his appearance was so disfigured beyond that of any man
and his form marred beyond human likeness—
15 so will he sprinkle many nations,[c]
and kings will shut their mouths because of him.
For what they were not told, they will see,
and what they have not heard, they will understand.

53 Who has believed our message
and to whom has the arm of the LORD been revealed?
2 He grew up before him like a tender shoot,
and like a root out of dry ground.
He had no beauty or majesty to attract us to him,
nothing in his appearance that we should desire him.
3 He was despised and rejected by men,
a man of sorrows, and familiar with suffering.
Like one from whom men hide their faces
he was despised, and we esteemed him not.

4 Surely he took up our infirmities
and carried our sorrows,
yet we considered him stricken by God,
smitten by him, and afflicted.
5 But he was pierced for our transgressions,
he was crushed for our iniquities;
the punishment that brought us peace was upon him,
and by his wounds we are healed.
6 We all, like sheep, have gone astray,
each of us has turned to his own way;
and the LORD has laid on him
the iniquity of us all.

7 He was oppressed and afflicted,
yet he did not open his mouth;
he was led like a lamb to the slaughter,
and as a sheep before her shearers is silent,
so he did not open his mouth.
8 By oppression[d] and judgment he was taken away.
And who can speak of his descendants?
For he was cut off from the land of the living;
for the transgression of my people he was stricken.[e]
9 He was assigned a grave with the wicked,
and with the rich in his death,
though he had done no violence,
nor was any deceit in his mouth.

10 Yet it was the LORD's will to crush him
and cause him to suffer,
and though the LORD makes[f] his life a guilt offering,
he will see his offspring and prolong his days,
and the will of the LORD will prosper in his hand.
11 After the suffering of his soul,
he will see the light ⌞of life⌟[g] and be satisfied[h];
by his knowledge[i] my righteous servant will justify many,
and he will bear their iniquities.
12 Therefore I will give him a portion among the great,[j]
and he will divide the spoils with the strong,[k]

---

[a] 13 Or *will prosper* [b] 14 Hebrew *you* [c] 15 Hebrew; Septuagint *so will many nations marvel at him* [d] 8 Or *From arrest*
[e] 8 Or *away. / Yet who of his generation considered / that he was cut off from the land of the living / for the transgression of my people, to whom the blow was due?* [f] 10 Hebrew *though you make* [g] 11 Dead Sea Scrolls (see also Septuagint); Masoretic Text does not have *the light ⌞of life⌟*. [h] 11 Or (with Masoretic Text) *11He will see the result of the suffering of his soul / and be satisfied* [i] 11 Or *by knowledge of him* [j] 12 Or *many* [k] 12 Or *numerous*

because he poured out his life unto death,
and was numbered with the transgressors.
For he bore the sin of many,
and made intercession for the transgressors.

The Future Glory of Zion

54 "Sing, O barren woman,
you who never bore a child;
burst into song, shout for joy,
you who were never in labor;
because more are the children of the desolate woman
than of her who has a husband,"
says the LORD.
2 "Enlarge the place of your tent,
stretch your tent curtains wide,
do not hold back;
lengthen your cords,
strengthen your stakes.
3 For you will spread out to the right and to the left;
your descendants will dispossess nations
and settle in their desolate cities.

4 "Do not be afraid; you will not suffer shame.
Do not fear disgrace; you will not be humiliated.
You will forget the shame of your youth
and remember no more the reproach of your widowhood.
5 For your Maker is your husband—
the LORD Almighty is his name—
the Holy One of Israel is your Redeemer;
he is called the God of all the earth.
6 The LORD will call you back
as if you were a wife deserted and distressed in spirit—
a wife who married young,
only to be rejected," says your God.
7 "For a brief moment I abandoned you,
but with deep compassion I will bring you back.
8 In a surge of anger
I hid my face from you for a moment,
but with everlasting kindness
I will have compassion on you,"
says the LORD your Redeemer.

9 "To me this is like the days of Noah,
when I swore that the waters of Noah would never again cover the earth.
So now I have sworn not to be angry with you,
never to rebuke you again.
10 Though the mountains be shaken
and the hills be removed,
yet my unfailing love for you will not be shaken
nor my covenant of peace be removed,"
says the LORD, who has compassion on you.

11 "O afflicted city, lashed by storms and not comforted,
I will build you with stones of turquoise,[a]
your foundations with sapphires.[b]
12 I will make your battlements of rubies,
your gates of sparkling jewels,
and all your walls of precious stones.
13 All your sons will be taught by the LORD,
and great will be your children's peace.
14 In righteousness you will be established:
Tyranny will be far from you;
you will have nothing to fear.
Terror will be far removed;
it will not come near you.
15 If anyone does attack you, it will not be my doing;
whoever attacks you will surrender to you.

16 "See, it is I who created the blacksmith
who fans the coals into flame
and forges a weapon fit for its work.
And it is I who have created the destroyer to work havoc;
17 no weapon forged against you will prevail,
and you will refute every tongue that accuses you.
This is the heritage of the servants of the LORD,
and this is their vindication from me,"
declares the LORD.

Invitation to the Thirsty

55 "Come, all you who are thirsty,
come to the waters;
and you who have no money,
come, buy and eat!
Come, buy wine and milk
without money and without cost.
2 Why spend money on what is not bread,
and your labor on what does not satisfy?

[a] 11 The meaning of the Hebrew for this word is uncertain. [b] 11 Or *lapis lazuli*

Listen, listen to me, and eat what is good,
and your soul will delight in the richest of fare.
3 Give ear and come to me;
hear me, that your soul may live.
I will make an everlasting covenant with you,
my faithful love promised to David.
4 See, I have made him a witness to the peoples,
a leader and commander of the peoples.
5 Surely you will summon nations you know not,
and nations that do not know you will hasten to you,
because of the LORD your God,
the Holy One of Israel,
for he has endowed you with splendor."
6 Seek the LORD while he may be found;
call on him while he is near.
7 Let the wicked forsake his way
and the evil man his thoughts.
Let him turn to the LORD, and he will have mercy on him,
and to our God, for he will freely pardon.

8 "For my thoughts are not your thoughts,
neither are your ways my ways,"
declares the LORD.
9 "As the heavens are higher than the earth,
so are my ways higher than your ways
and my thoughts than your thoughts.
10 As the rain and the snow
come down from heaven,
and do not return to it
without watering the earth
and making it bud and flourish,
so that it yields seed for the sower and bread for the eater,
11 so is my word that goes out from my mouth:
It will not return to me empty,
but will accomplish what I desire
and achieve the purpose for which I sent it.
12 You will go out in joy
and be led forth in peace;
the mountains and hills
will burst into song before you,
and all the trees of the field
will clap their hands.
13 Instead of the thornbush will grow the pine tree,
and instead of briers the myrtle will grow.
This will be for the LORD's renown,
for an everlasting sign,
which will not be destroyed."

Salvation for Others

56 This is what the LORD says:

"Maintain justice
and do what is right,
for my salvation is close at hand
and my righteousness will soon be revealed.
2 Blessed is the man who does this,
the man who holds it fast,
who keeps the Sabbath without desecrating it,
and keeps his hand from doing any evil."

3 Let no foreigner who has bound himself to the LORD say,
"The LORD will surely exclude me from his people."
And let not any eunuch complain,
"I am only a dry tree."
4 For this is what the LORD says:

"To the eunuchs who keep my Sabbaths,
who choose what pleases me
and hold fast to my covenant—
5 to them I will give within my temple and its walls
a memorial and a name
better than sons and daughters;
I will give them an everlasting name
that will not be cut off.
6 And foreigners who bind themselves to the LORD
to serve him,
to love the name of the LORD,
and to worship him,
all who keep the Sabbath without desecrating it
and who hold fast to my covenant—
7 these I will bring to my holy mountain
and give them joy in my house of prayer.
Their burnt offerings and sacrifices
will be accepted on my altar;
for my house will be called
a house of prayer for all nations."
8 The Sovereign LORD declares—
he who gathers the exiles of Israel:
"I will gather still others to them
besides those already gathered."

God's Accusation Against the Wicked

9 Come, all you beasts of the field,

come and devour, all you beasts of the
forest!
10 Israel's watchmen are blind,
they all lack knowledge;
they are all mute dogs,
they cannot bark;
they lie around and dream,
they love to sleep.
11 They are dogs with mighty appetites;
they never have enough.
They are shepherds who lack
understanding;
they all turn to their own way,
each seeks his own gain.
12 "Come," each one cries, "let me get wine!
Let us drink our fill of beer!
And tomorrow will be like today,
or even far better."

57 The righteous perish,
and no one ponders it in his heart;
devout men are taken away,
and no one understands
that the righteous are taken away
to be spared from evil.
2 Those who walk uprightly
enter into peace;
they find rest as they lie in death.

3 "But you—come here, you sons of a
sorceress,
you offspring of adulterers and
prostitutes!
4 Whom are you mocking?
At whom do you sneer
and stick out your tongue?
Are you not a brood of rebels,
the offspring of liars?
5 You burn with lust among the oaks
and under every spreading tree;
you sacrifice your children in the ravines
and under the overhanging crags.
6 ⌊The idols⌋ among the smooth stones of
the ravines are your portion;
they, they are your lot.
Yes, to them you have poured out drink
offerings
and offered grain offerings.
In the light of these things, should I
relent?
7 You have made your bed on a high and
lofty hill;
there you went up to offer your
sacrifices.
8 Behind your doors and your doorposts
you have put your pagan symbols.
Forsaking me, you uncovered your bed,
you climbed into it and opened it
wide;
you made a pact with those whose beds
you love,
and you looked on their nakedness.
9 You went to Molech[a] with olive oil
and increased your perfumes.
You sent your ambassadors[b] far away;
you descended to the grave[c] itself!
10 You were wearied by all your ways,
but you would not say, 'It is hopeless.'
You found renewal of your strength,
and so you did not faint.

11 "Whom have you so dreaded and feared
that you have been false to me,
and have neither remembered me
nor pondered this in your hearts?
Is it not because I have long been silent
that you do not fear me?
12 I will expose your righteousness and your
works,
and they will not benefit you.
13 When you cry out for help,
let your collection ⌊of idols⌋ save you!
The wind will carry all of them off,
a mere breath will blow them away.
But the man who makes me his refuge
will inherit the land
and possess my holy mountain."

Comfort for the Contrite

14 And it will be said:

"Build up, build up, prepare the road!
Remove the obstacles out of the way of
my people."
15 For this is what the high and lofty One
says—
he who lives forever, whose name is
holy:
"I live in a high and holy place,
but also with him who is contrite and
lowly in spirit,
to revive the spirit of the lowly
and to revive the heart of the contrite.
16 I will not accuse forever,
nor will I always be angry,
for then the spirit of man would grow
faint before me—
the breath of man that I have created.
17 I was enraged by his sinful greed;
I punished him, and hid my face in
anger,
yet he kept on in his willful ways.

a 9 Or *to the king* b 9 Or *idols* c 9 Hebrew *Sheol*

18 I have seen his ways, but I will heal him;
I will guide him and restore comfort to him,
19 creating praise on the lips of the mourners in Israel.
Peace, peace, to those far and near,"
says the LORD. "And I will heal them."
20 But the wicked are like the tossing sea,
which cannot rest,
whose waves cast up mire and mud.
21 "There is no peace," says my God, "for the wicked."

True Fasting

58 "Shout it aloud, do not hold back.
Raise your voice like a trumpet.
Declare to my people their rebellion
and to the house of Jacob their sins.
2 For day after day they seek me out;
they seem eager to know my ways,
as if they were a nation that does what is right
and has not forsaken the commands of its God.
They ask me for just decisions
and seem eager for God to come near them.
3 'Why have we fasted,' they say,
'and you have not seen it?
Why have we humbled ourselves,
and you have not noticed?'

"Yet on the day of your fasting, you do as you please
and exploit all your workers.
4 Your fasting ends in quarreling and strife,
and in striking each other with wicked fists.
You cannot fast as you do today
and expect your voice to be heard on high.
5 Is this the kind of fast I have chosen,
only a day for a man to humble himself?
Is it only for bowing one's head like a reed
and for lying on sackcloth and ashes?
Is that what you call a fast,
a day acceptable to the LORD?
6 "Is not this the kind of fasting I have chosen:
to loose the chains of injustice
and untie the cords of the yoke,
to set the oppressed free
and break every yoke?
7 Is it not to share your food with the hungry
and to provide the poor wanderer with shelter—
when you see the naked, to clothe him,
and not to turn away from your own flesh and blood?
8 Then your light will break forth like the dawn,
and your healing will quickly appear;
then your righteousness[a] will go before you,
and the glory of the LORD will be your rear guard.
9 Then you will call, and the LORD will answer;
you will cry for help, and he will say:
Here am I.

"If you do away with the yoke of oppression,
with the pointing finger and malicious talk,
10 and if you spend yourselves in behalf of the hungry
and satisfy the needs of the oppressed,
then your light will rise in the darkness,
and your night will become like the noonday.
11 The LORD will guide you always;
he will satisfy your needs in a sun-scorched land
and will strengthen your frame.
You will be like a well-watered garden,
like a spring whose waters never fail.
12 Your people will rebuild the ancient ruins
and will raise up the age-old foundations;
you will be called Repairer of Broken Walls,
Restorer of Streets with Dwellings.
13 "If you keep your feet from breaking the Sabbath
and from doing as you please on my holy day,
if you call the Sabbath a delight
and the LORD's holy day honorable,
and if you honor it by not going your own way
and not doing as you please or speaking idle words,
14 then you will find your joy in the LORD,
and I will cause you to ride on the heights of the land

[a] 8 Or *your righteous One*

and to feast on the inheritance of your
father Jacob."
The mouth of the LORD
has spoken.

Sin, Confession and Redemption

59 Surely the arm of the LORD is not too
short to save,
nor his ear too dull to hear.
2 But your iniquities have separated
you from your God;
your sins have hidden his face from you,
so that he will not hear.
3 For your hands are stained with blood,
your fingers with guilt.
Your lips have spoken lies,
and your tongue mutters wicked
things.
4 No one calls for justice;
no one pleads his case with integrity.
They rely on empty arguments and speak
lies;
they conceive trouble and give birth to
evil.
5 They hatch the eggs of vipers
and spin a spider's web.
Whoever eats their eggs will die,
and when one is broken, an adder is
hatched.
6 Their cobwebs are useless for clothing;
they cannot cover themselves with what
they make.
Their deeds are evil deeds,
and acts of violence are in their hands.
7 Their feet rush into sin;
they are swift to shed innocent blood.
Their thoughts are evil thoughts;
ruin and destruction mark their ways.
8 The way of peace they do not know;
there is no justice in their paths.
They have turned them into crooked
roads;
no one who walks in them will know
peace.

9 So justice is far from us,
and righteousness does not reach us.
We look for light, but all is darkness;
for brightness, but we walk in deep
shadows.
10 Like the blind we grope along the wall,
feeling our way like men without eyes.
At midday we stumble as if it were
twilight;
among the strong, we are like the dead.
11 We all growl like bears;
we moan mournfully like doves.
We look for justice, but find none;
for deliverance, but it is far away.
12 For our offenses are many in your sight,
and our sins testify against us.
Our offenses are ever with us,
and we acknowledge our iniquities:
13 rebellion and treachery against the LORD,
turning our backs on our God,
fomenting oppression and revolt,
uttering lies our hearts have conceived.
14 So justice is driven back,
and righteousness stands at a distance;
truth has stumbled in the streets,
honesty cannot enter.
15 Truth is nowhere to be found,
and whoever shuns evil becomes a prey.

The LORD looked and was displeased
that there was no justice.
16 He saw that there was no one,
he was appalled that there was no one
to intervene;
so his own arm worked salvation for him,
and his own righteousness sustained
him.
17 He put on righteousness as his breastplate,
and the helmet of salvation on his head;
he put on the garments of vengeance
and wrapped himself in zeal as in a
cloak.
18 According to what they have done,
so will he repay
wrath to his enemies
and retribution to his foes;
he will repay the islands their due.
19 From the west, men will fear the name of
the LORD,
and from the rising of the sun, they will
revere his glory.
For he will come like a pent-up flood
that the breath of the LORD drives
along.[a]

20 "The Redeemer will come to Zion,
to those in Jacob who repent of their
sins,"
declares the LORD.

21 "As for me, this is my covenant with
them," says the LORD. "My Spirit, who is on
you, and my words that I have put in your
mouth will not depart from your mouth, or
from the mouths of your children, or from the
mouths of their descendants from this time on
and forever," says the LORD.

---

[a] 19 Or *When the enemy comes in like a flood, / the Spirit of the LORD will put him to flight*

WEDNESDAY
READ ISAIAH 59:1–21

WHEN LIFE ISN'T FAIR

That's not fair! That's what I said when my bride informed me that since we had agreed that my job would be to take out the garbage, it was also my job to put a new garbage bag in the trash can. "That's an entirely different job," I protested. I thought I had a rather keen sense of justice.

In marriage, we each have a code of justice in our heads, a detailed (though often unspoken) contract of responsibilities and rights. But in a Christian marriage there are issues of justice we often ignore.

One of the great benefits of a Christian marriage is helping one another see the truth about ourselves that we are prone to miss. We can help each other see ourselves by facing the mirror of Isaiah 59, a chapter that is all about justice. (The word "justice" appears six times.)

Injustice is often most vivid to us when we read about racism, sexism, the torture of prisoners of war or the victimization of the poor. But sin of every kind is essentially injustice. Sinners are always unjust people. In all sin there is something deeply unfair, and there is always a victim who has been denied justice.

As you read through Isaiah 59, you will notice four consequences of the injustice of sin. The first is that sin separates us from God (verses 1–2). Sin is the reason why God isn't answering your calls; why he keeps putting your prayers on hold with elevator music in the background. The second consequence is that sin harms others. Innocent blood is shed by acts of violence (verse 7). People are hurt and hurt badly.

A third consequence is that those who deny justice to others will be deprived of justice themselves (verses 9–11). "What goes around comes around," as they say. "You reap what you sow." The fourth consequence is that God himself comes as avenging Judge (verses 15–19). He refuses to look on injustice without getting involved.

Since God's own people have not been agents of justice, God takes matters into his own hands. He dresses for justice, not in the black robe of a judge, but as a warrior wearing righteousness, salvation, vengeance and zeal.

But there is a surprise about this warrior God. Though he is dressed for righteous wrath, he offers to redeem any who will repent (verse 20). Not only that, but when we—like the Israelites—repent of our sin, God will make a spiritual covenant with us and renew us with his Spirit and put his righteous words in our mouths (verse 21). So not only can we be redeemed from our sin, but we can be agents of justice in our marriages and in the society around us.

—LEE ECLOV

The LORD looked and was displeased that there was no justice. He saw that there was no one, he was appalled that there was no one to intervene; so his own arm worked salvation for him, and his own righteousness sustained him.

— ISAIAH 59:15–16

let's talk

- When have we recently sensed that our sin separated us from God? What may have led to that? How did we get through that time?
- What specific sins of injustice are detailed in verses 12–13? Are these the kinds of things we would have described as injustice? How does our understanding of injustice need to change?
- How many reasons can we find in this chapter to praise God?

FOR YOUR NEXT DEVOTIONAL READING, TURN TO PAGE 818.

The Glory of Zion

60 "Arise, shine, for your light has come,
and the glory of the LORD rises upon you.
2 See, darkness covers the earth
and thick darkness is over the peoples,
but the LORD rises upon you
and his glory appears over you.
3 Nations will come to your light,
and kings to the brightness of your dawn.

4 "Lift up your eyes and look about you:
All assemble and come to you;
your sons come from afar,
and your daughters are carried on the arm.
5 Then you will look and be radiant,
your heart will throb and swell with joy;
the wealth on the seas will be brought to you,
to you the riches of the nations will come.
6 Herds of camels will cover your land,
young camels of Midian and Ephah.
And all from Sheba will come,
bearing gold and incense
and proclaiming the praise of the LORD.
7 All Kedar's flocks will be gathered to you,
the rams of Nebaioth will serve you;
they will be accepted as offerings on my altar,
and I will adorn my glorious temple.

8 "Who are these that fly along like clouds,
like doves to their nests?
9 Surely the islands look to me;
in the lead are the ships of Tarshish,[a]
bringing your sons from afar,
with their silver and gold,
to the honor of the LORD your God,
the Holy One of Israel,
for he has endowed you with splendor.

10 "Foreigners will rebuild your walls,
and their kings will serve you.
Though in anger I struck you,
in favor I will show you compassion.
11 Your gates will always stand open,
they will never be shut, day or night,
so that men may bring you the wealth of the nations—
their kings led in triumphal procession.
12 For the nation or kingdom that will not serve you will perish;
it will be utterly ruined.

13 "The glory of Lebanon will come to you,
the pine, the fir and the cypress together,
to adorn the place of my sanctuary;
and I will glorify the place of my feet.
14 The sons of your oppressors will come bowing before you;
all who despise you will bow down at your feet
and will call you the City of the LORD,
Zion of the Holy One of Israel.

15 "Although you have been forsaken and hated,
with no one traveling through,
I will make you the everlasting pride
and the joy of all generations.
16 You will drink the milk of nations
and be nursed at royal breasts.
Then you will know that I, the LORD, am your Savior,
your Redeemer, the Mighty One of Jacob.
17 Instead of bronze I will bring you gold,
and silver in place of iron.
Instead of wood I will bring you bronze,
and iron in place of stones.
I will make peace your governor
and righteousness your ruler.
18 No longer will violence be heard in your land,
nor ruin or destruction within your borders,
but you will call your walls Salvation
and your gates Praise.
19 The sun will no more be your light by day,
nor will the brightness of the moon shine on you,
for the LORD will be your everlasting light,
and your God will be your glory.
20 Your sun will never set again,
and your moon will wane no more;
the LORD will be your everlasting light,
and your days of sorrow will end.
21 Then will all your people be righteous
and they will possess the land forever.
They are the shoot I have planted,
the work of my hands,
for the display of my splendor.
22 The least of you will become a thousand,
the smallest a mighty nation.
I am the LORD;
in its time I will do this swiftly."

a 9 Or *the trading ships*

The Year of the LORD's Favor

61 The Spirit of the Sovereign LORD is on me,
because the LORD has anointed me
to preach good news to the poor.
He has sent me to bind up the brokenhearted,
to proclaim freedom for the captives
and release from darkness for the prisoners,[a]
2 to proclaim the year of the LORD's favor
and the day of vengeance of our God,
to comfort all who mourn,
3 and provide for those who grieve in Zion—
to bestow on them a crown of beauty
instead of ashes,
the oil of gladness
instead of mourning,
and a garment of praise
instead of a spirit of despair.
They will be called oaks of righteousness,
a planting of the LORD
for the display of his splendor.

4 They will rebuild the ancient ruins
and restore the places long devastated;
they will renew the ruined cities
that have been devastated for generations.
5 Aliens will shepherd your flocks;
foreigners will work your fields and vineyards.
6 And you will be called priests of the LORD,
you will be named ministers of our God.
You will feed on the wealth of nations,
and in their riches you will boast.

7 Instead of their shame
my people will receive a double portion,
and instead of disgrace
they will rejoice in their inheritance;
and so they will inherit a double portion in their land,
and everlasting joy will be theirs.

8 "For I, the LORD, love justice;
I hate robbery and iniquity.
In my faithfulness I will reward them
and make an everlasting covenant with them.
9 Their descendants will be known among the nations
and their offspring among the peoples.
All who see them will acknowledge
that they are a people the LORD has blessed."

10 I delight greatly in the LORD;
my soul rejoices in my God.
For he has clothed me with garments of salvation
and arrayed me in a robe of righteousness,
as a bridegroom adorns his head like a priest,
and as a bride adorns herself with her jewels.
11 For as the soil makes the sprout come up
and a garden causes seeds to grow,
so the Sovereign LORD will make righteousness and praise
spring up before all nations.

Zion's New Name

62 For Zion's sake I will not keep silent,
for Jerusalem's sake I will not remain quiet,
till her righteousness shines out like the dawn,
her salvation like a blazing torch.
2 The nations will see your righteousness,
and all kings your glory;
you will be called by a new name
that the mouth of the LORD will bestow.
3 You will be a crown of splendor in the LORD's hand,
a royal diadem in the hand of your God.
4 No longer will they call you Deserted,
or name your land Desolate.
But you will be called Hephzibah,[b]
and your land Beulah[c];
for the LORD will take delight in you,
and your land will be married.
5 As a young man marries a maiden,
so will your sons[d] marry you;
as a bridegroom rejoices over his bride,
so will your God rejoice over you.

6 I have posted watchmen on your walls, O Jerusalem;
they will never be silent day or night.
You who call on the LORD,
give yourselves no rest,
7 and give him no rest till he establishes Jerusalem
and makes her the praise of the earth.

8 The LORD has sworn by his right hand
and by his mighty arm:

---

[a] 1 Hebrew; Septuagint *the blind* [b] 4 *Hephzibah* means *my delight is in her.* [c] 4 *Beulah* means *married.* [d] 5 Or *Builder*

"Never again will I give your grain
as food for your enemies,
and never again will foreigners drink the new wine
for which you have toiled;
9 but those who harvest it will eat it
and praise the LORD,
and those who gather the grapes will drink it
in the courts of my sanctuary."

10 Pass through, pass through the gates!
Prepare the way for the people.
Build up, build up the highway!
Remove the stones.
Raise a banner for the nations.

11 The LORD has made proclamation
to the ends of the earth:
"Say to the Daughter of Zion,
'See, your Savior comes!
See, his reward is with him,
and his recompense accompanies him.' "
12 They will be called the Holy People,
the Redeemed of the LORD;
and you will be called Sought After,
the City No Longer Deserted.

God's Day of Vengeance and Redemption

63 Who is this coming from Edom,
from Bozrah, with his garments stained crimson?
Who is this, robed in splendor,
striding forward in the greatness of his strength?

"It is I, speaking in righteousness,
mighty to save."

2 Why are your garments red,
like those of one treading the winepress?

3 "I have trodden the winepress alone;
from the nations no one was with me.
I trampled them in my anger
and trod them down in my wrath;
their blood spattered my garments,
and I stained all my clothing.
4 For the day of vengeance was in my heart,
and the year of my redemption has come.
5 I looked, but there was no one to help,
I was appalled that no one gave support;
so my own arm worked salvation for me,
and my own wrath sustained me.
6 I trampled the nations in my anger;
in my wrath I made them drunk
and poured their blood on the ground."

Praise and Prayer

7 I will tell of the kindnesses of the LORD,
the deeds for which he is to be praised,
according to all the LORD has done for us—
yes, the many good things he has done
for the house of Israel,
according to his compassion and many kindnesses.
8 He said, "Surely they are my people,
sons who will not be false to me";
and so he became their Savior.
9 In all their distress he too was distressed,
and the angel of his presence saved them.
In his love and mercy he redeemed them;
he lifted them up and carried them
all the days of old.
10 Yet they rebelled
and grieved his Holy Spirit.
So he turned and became their enemy
and he himself fought against them.

11 Then his people recalled[a] the days of old,
the days of Moses and his people—
where is he who brought them through the sea,
with the shepherd of his flock?
Where is he who set
his Holy Spirit among them,
12 who sent his glorious arm of power
to be at Moses' right hand,
who divided the waters before them,
to gain for himself everlasting renown,
13 who led them through the depths?
Like a horse in open country,
they did not stumble;
14 like cattle that go down to the plain,
they were given rest by the Spirit of the LORD.
This is how you guided your people
to make for yourself a glorious name.

15 Look down from heaven and see
from your lofty throne, holy and glorious.
Where are your zeal and your might?
Your tenderness and compassion are withheld from us.
16 But you are our Father,
though Abraham does not know us
or Israel acknowledge us;

a 11 Or *But may he recall*

you, O LORD, are our Father,
our Redeemer from of old is your name.
17 Why, O LORD, do you make us wander from your ways
and harden our hearts so we do not revere you?
Return for the sake of your servants,
the tribes that are your inheritance.
18 For a little while your people possessed your holy place,
but now our enemies have trampled down your sanctuary.
19 We are yours from of old;
but you have not ruled over them,
they have not been called by your name. [a]

64 Oh, that you would rend the heavens and come down,
that the mountains would tremble before you!
2 As when fire sets twigs ablaze
and causes water to boil,
come down to make your name known to your enemies
and cause the nations to quake before you!
3 For when you did awesome things that we did not expect,
you came down, and the mountains trembled before you.
4 Since ancient times no one has heard,
no ear has perceived,
no eye has seen any God besides you,
who acts on behalf of those who wait for him.
5 You come to the help of those who gladly do right,
who remember your ways.
But when we continued to sin against them,
you were angry.
How then can we be saved?
6 All of us have become like one who is unclean,
and all our righteous acts are like filthy rags;
we all shrivel up like a leaf,
and like the wind our sins sweep us away.
7 No one calls on your name
or strives to lay hold of you;
for you have hidden your face from us
and made us waste away because of our sins.
8 Yet, O LORD, you are our Father.
We are the clay, you are the potter;
we are all the work of your hand.
9 Do not be angry beyond measure, O LORD;
do not remember our sins forever.
Oh, look upon us, we pray,
for we are all your people.
10 Your sacred cities have become a desert;
even Zion is a desert, Jerusalem a desolation.
11 Our holy and glorious temple, where our fathers praised you,
has been burned with fire,
and all that we treasured lies in ruins.
12 After all this, O LORD, will you hold yourself back?
Will you keep silent and punish us beyond measure?

Judgment and Salvation

65 "I revealed myself to those who did not ask for me;
I was found by those who did not seek me.
To a nation that did not call on my name,
I said, 'Here am I, here am I.'
2 All day long I have held out my hands
to an obstinate people,
who walk in ways not good,
pursuing their own imaginations—
3 a people who continually provoke me
to my very face,
offering sacrifices in gardens
and burning incense on altars of brick;
4 who sit among the graves
and spend their nights keeping secret vigil;
who eat the flesh of pigs,
and whose pots hold broth of unclean meat;
5 who say, 'Keep away; don't come near me,
for I am too sacred for you!'
Such people are smoke in my nostrils,
a fire that keeps burning all day.
6 "See, it stands written before me:
I will not keep silent but will pay back in full;
I will pay it back into their laps—

[a] 19 Or *We are like those you have never ruled, / like those never called by your name*

7 both your sins and the sins of your
fathers,"
says the LORD.
"Because they burned sacrifices on the
mountains
and defied me on the hills,
I will measure into their laps
the full payment for their former
deeds."

8 This is what the LORD says:

"As when juice is still found in a cluster of
grapes
and men say, 'Don't destroy it,
there is yet some good in it,'
so will I do in behalf of my servants;
I will not destroy them all.
9 I will bring forth descendants from Jacob,
and from Judah those who will possess
my mountains;
my chosen people will inherit them,
and there will my servants live.
10 Sharon will become a pasture for flocks,
and the Valley of Achor a resting place
for herds,
for my people who seek me.

11 "But as for you who forsake the LORD
and forget my holy mountain,
who spread a table for Fortune
and fill bowls of mixed wine for
Destiny,
12 I will destine you for the sword,
and you will all bend down for the
slaughter;
for I called but you did not answer,
I spoke but you did not listen.
You did evil in my sight
and chose what displeases me."

13 Therefore this is what the Sovereign LORD
says:

"My servants will eat,
but you will go hungry;
my servants will drink,
but you will go thirsty;
my servants will rejoice,
but you will be put to shame.
14 My servants will sing
out of the joy of their hearts,
but you will cry out
from anguish of heart
and wail in brokenness of spirit.
15 You will leave your name
to my chosen ones as a curse;
the Sovereign LORD will put you to death,
but to his servants he will give another
name.
16 Whoever invokes a blessing in the land
will do so by the God of truth;
he who takes an oath in the land
will swear by the God of truth.
For the past troubles will be forgotten
and hidden from my eyes.

New Heavens and a New Earth

17 "Behold, I will create
new heavens and a new earth.
The former things will not be
remembered,
nor will they come to mind.
18 But be glad and rejoice forever
in what I will create,
for I will create Jerusalem to be a delight
and its people a joy.
19 I will rejoice over Jerusalem
and take delight in my people;
the sound of weeping and of crying
will be heard in it no more.

20 "Never again will there be in it
an infant who lives but a few days,
or an old man who does not live out his
years;
he who dies at a hundred
will be thought a mere youth;
he who fails to reach[a] a hundred
will be considered accursed.
21 They will build houses and dwell in them;
they will plant vineyards and eat their
fruit.
22 No longer will they build houses and
others live in them,
or plant and others eat.
For as the days of a tree,
so will be the days of my people;
my chosen ones will long enjoy
the works of their hands.
23 They will not toil in vain
or bear children doomed to misfortune;
for they will be a people blessed by the
LORD,
they and their descendants with them.
24 Before they call I will answer;
while they are still speaking I will hear.
25 The wolf and the lamb will feed together,
and the lion will eat straw like the ox,
but dust will be the serpent's food.
They will neither harm nor destroy
on all my holy mountain,"
says the LORD.

a 20 Or */ the sinner who reaches*

Judgment and Hope

66 This is what the LORD says:

"Heaven is my throne,
and the earth is my footstool.
Where is the house you will build for me?
Where will my resting place be?
2 Has not my hand made all these things,
and so they came into being?"
declares the LORD.

"This is the one I esteem:
he who is humble and contrite in spirit,
and trembles at my word.
3 But whoever sacrifices a bull
is like one who kills a man,
and whoever offers a lamb,
like one who breaks a dog's neck;
whoever makes a grain offering
is like one who presents pig's blood,
and whoever burns memorial incense,
like one who worships an idol.
They have chosen their own ways,
and their souls delight in their abominations;
4 so I also will choose harsh treatment for them
and will bring upon them what they dread.
For when I called, no one answered,
when I spoke, no one listened.
They did evil in my sight
and chose what displeases me."
5 Hear the word of the LORD,
you who tremble at his word:
"Your brothers who hate you,
and exclude you because of my name, have said,
'Let the LORD be glorified,
that we may see your joy!'
Yet they will be put to shame.
6 Hear that uproar from the city,
hear that noise from the temple!
It is the sound of the LORD
repaying his enemies all they deserve.

7 "Before she goes into labor,
she gives birth;
before the pains come upon her,
she delivers a son.
8 Who has ever heard of such a thing?
Who has ever seen such things?
Can a country be born in a day
or a nation be brought forth in a moment?
Yet no sooner is Zion in labor
than she gives birth to her children.
9 Do I bring to the moment of birth
and not give delivery?" says the LORD.
"Do I close up the womb
when I bring to delivery?" says your God.
10 "Rejoice with Jerusalem and be glad for her,
all you who love her;
rejoice greatly with her,
all you who mourn over her.
11 For you will nurse and be satisfied
at her comforting breasts;
you will drink deeply
and delight in her overflowing abundance."

12 For this is what the LORD says:

"I will extend peace to her like a river,
and the wealth of nations like a flooding stream;
you will nurse and be carried on her arm
and dandled on her knees.
13 As a mother comforts her child,
so will I comfort you;
and you will be comforted over Jerusalem."

14 When you see this, your heart will rejoice
and you will flourish like grass;
the hand of the LORD will be made known to his servants,
but his fury will be shown to his foes.
15 See, the LORD is coming with fire,
and his chariots are like a whirlwind;
he will bring down his anger with fury,
and his rebuke with flames of fire.
16 For with fire and with his sword
the LORD will execute judgment upon all men,
and many will be those slain by the LORD.

17 "Those who consecrate and purify themselves to go into the gardens, following the one
in the midst of[a] those who eat the flesh of pigs
and rats and other abominable things—they
will meet their end together," declares the
LORD.
18 "And I, because of their actions and their
imaginations, am about to come[b] and gather
all nations and tongues, and they will come
and see my glory.
19 "I will set a sign among them, and I will
send some of those who survive to the na-

[a] 17 Or *gardens behind one of your temples, and* [b] 18 The meaning of the Hebrew for this clause is uncertain.

tions—to Tarshish, to the Libyans[a] and Lydians (famous as archers), to Tubal and Greece, and to the distant islands that have not heard of my fame or seen my glory. They will proclaim my glory among the nations.
20And they will bring all your brothers, from all the nations, to my holy mountain in Jerusalem as an offering to the LORD—on horses, in chariots and wagons, and on mules and camels," says the LORD. "They will bring them, as the Israelites bring their grain offerings, to the temple of the LORD in ceremonially clean vessels.
21And I will select some of them also to be priests and Levites," says the LORD.

22"As the new heavens and the new earth that I make will endure before me," declares the LORD, "so will your name and descendants endure.
23From one New Moon to another and from one Sabbath to another, all mankind will come and bow down before me," says the LORD.
24"And they will go out and look upon the dead bodies of those who rebelled against me; their worm will not die, nor will their fire be quenched, and they will be loathsome to all mankind."

[a] 19 Some Septuagint manuscripts *Put* (Libyans); Hebrew *Pul*

JEREMIAH

Jeremiah

QUICK FACTS

AUTHOR Jeremiah

AUDIENCE The people of Judah

DATE Jeremiah wrote from 626 B.C. through sometime after the fall of Jerusalem in 586 B.C.

SETTING Just before God allowed Babylon to sweep Judah away

The book of Jeremiah is named for the prophet whose story fills its pages. Jeremiah, who was a priest, was called to proclaim a miserable message to his beloved nation: God had given Judah many warnings, but like their sister nation, Israel, the people had ignored him. Now the inevitable was coming. Babylon was going to capture Judah, and it would be best for the people to surrender to save their lives.

This message, addressed to a people whose national status as God's chosen people defined them, caused the prophet to be regarded as a defeatist and a traitor. Many leaders of Judah wanted the prophet put to death. But Jeremiah continued to prophesy, even though the message made him feel such despair that he wished he hadn't been born (see Jeremiah 15:10; 20:14–18).

For 40 years Jeremiah was faithful to God's call, standing for the truth when those around him fervently opposed him. At the same time, God was faithful to his prophet. As Jeremiah discovered, we will find that God meets all our needs. When the glitter disappears from our marriage, we too have the assurance of knowing that God rewards faithfulness and is the power that sustains us.

1 The words of Jeremiah son of Hilkiah, one
of the priests at Anathoth in the territory of
Benjamin. 2 The word of the LORD came to
him in the thirteenth year of the reign of Josiah son of Amon king of Judah, 3 and through
the reign of Jehoiakim son of Josiah king of
Judah, down to the fifth month of the eleventh year of Zedekiah son of Josiah king of
Judah, when the people of Jerusalem went
into exile.

The Call of Jeremiah

4 The word of the LORD came to me, saying,

5 "Before I formed you in the womb I
knew[a] you,
before you were born I set you apart;
I appointed you as a prophet to the
nations."

6 "Ah, Sovereign LORD," I said, "I do not
know how to speak; I am only a child."
7 But the LORD said to me, "Do not say, 'I
am only a child.' You must go to everyone I
send you to and say whatever I command you.
8 Do not be afraid of them, for I am with you
and will rescue you," declares the LORD.
9 Then the LORD reached out his hand and
touched my mouth and said to me, "Now, I
have put my words in your mouth. 10 See, today I appoint you over nations and kingdoms
to uproot and tear down, to destroy and overthrow, to build and to plant."
11 The word of the LORD came to me: "What
do you see, Jeremiah?"
"I see the branch of an almond tree," I replied.
12 The LORD said to me, "You have seen correctly, for I am watching[b] to see that my word
is fulfilled."
13 The word of the LORD came to me again:
"What do you see?"
"I see a boiling pot, tilting away from the
north," I answered.
14 The LORD said to me, "From the north
disaster will be poured out on all who live in
the land. 15 I am about to summon all the peoples of the northern kingdoms," declares the
LORD.

"Their kings will come and set up their
thrones
in the entrance of the gates of
Jerusalem;
they will come against all her surrounding
walls
and against all the towns of Judah.
16 I will pronounce my judgments on my
people
because of their wickedness in forsaking
me,
in burning incense to other gods
and in worshiping what their hands
have made.

17 "Get yourself ready! Stand up and say to
them whatever I command you. Do not be
terrified by them, or I will terrify you before
them. 18 Today I have made you a fortified
city, an iron pillar and a bronze wall to stand
against the whole land—against the kings of
Judah, its officials, its priests and the people of
the land. 19 They will fight against you but will
not overcome you, for I am with you and will
rescue you," declares the LORD.

Israel Forsakes God

2 The word of the LORD came to me: 2 "Go
and proclaim in the hearing of Jerusalem:

" 'I remember the devotion of your youth,
how as a bride you loved me
and followed me through the desert,
through a land not sown.
3 Israel was holy to the LORD,
the firstfruits of his harvest;
all who devoured her were held guilty,
and disaster overtook them,' "
declares the LORD.

4 Hear the word of the LORD, O house of
Jacob,
all you clans of the house of Israel.

5 This is what the LORD says:

"What fault did your fathers find in me,
that they strayed so far from me?
They followed worthless idols
and became worthless themselves.
6 They did not ask, 'Where is the LORD,
who brought us up out of Egypt
and led us through the barren wilderness,
through a land of deserts and rifts,
a land of drought and darkness,[c]
a land where no one travels and no one
lives?'
7 I brought you into a fertile land
to eat its fruit and rich produce.
But you came and defiled my land
and made my inheritance detestable.
8 The priests did not ask,
'Where is the LORD?'

---

[a] 5 Or *chose* [b] 12 The Hebrew for *watching* sounds like the Hebrew for *almond tree.* [c] 6 Or *and the shadow of death*

THURSDAY
READ JEREMIAH 1:1–5

OUR "CATS IN THE HATS" STORY

> **"Before I formed you in the womb I knew you."**
> — JEREMIAH 1:5

let's talk

- What are the "cats in the hats" of how we met? What were the necessary connections that had to be made for us to have fallen in love and married?
- In what ways does knowing that God has brought the two of us together assure us that he will be with us through the rest of our time together?
- How do God's sovereignty and human responsibility work together here?

In the Dr. Seuss book *The Cat in the Hat Comes Back*, the cat eats pink cake in the bathtub, wipes the pink tub ring with Mother's white dress, wipes the gooey dress on the wall, and then on Dad's $10 shoes, the rug and Dad's bed. Eventually, the pink mess ends up in the snow, and only a tiny creature called a VOOM can clean it up.

Likewise, in marriage one thing can lead to another, which leads to another, and to still another until seemingly no one can figure out how everything got to where it is, let alone where it's leading. That's when you have, according to my mom, a case of "cats in the hats."

It boggles my mind to think of all the "cats in the hats" that have gone on continuously throughout history, especially in relationships. I was thinking about my daughter and son-in-law the other day and how "cats in the hats" brought them together in ways that seemed as bizarre as the critters in the Seuss book.

Craig had maxed out his credit cards by the time he got out of the army after his first enlistment, so he moved back home to live with his parents. His parents lived less than a mile from us, but we had not met each other. Because Craig didn't have a car, he had to find a job within walking distance, which meant working at either McDonald's or Burger King. He chose to work at McDonald's, which is where he met a coworker, my daughter, Alison.

They started dating and fell in love. But the story gets better. When the two started dating, Craig started coming to church with us. Because he came to church, he started listening to the sermons and asking questions. Eventually, what he learned was so convincing that he came to faith in Christ.

Now think of taking away any of the "cats" in this story. What if Craig had stayed in the army to pay off his debts? What if Alison had worked at Burger King instead of McDonald's? What if we didn't live so close to Craig's parents? What if we weren't believers? Take away one of the "cats" and Alison and Craig might not have met and fallen in love. Craig might not have become a Christian. The two might not have married.

But this "cats in the hats" story worked out well. Craig and Alison married and are debt free today. They have a daughter, Caroline, who will see how the "cats in the hats" story works out in her own life some day.

There is no need for her or her parents—or us—to fear seemingly unrelated things that happen to us. Because God is sovereign, knowing us even before we were formed in the womb, there are no accidents of birth or career or place of residence or relationship or commitment. He takes our choices (even those we made in sin and rebellion), which he knew about before time began, and weaves them all into a tremendously intricate, grand design to expand his great kingdom.

And not even a VOOM can change it.

—NANCY KENNEDY

FOR YOUR NEXT DEVOTIONAL READING, TURN TO PAGE 821.

Those who deal with the law did not know
me;
the leaders rebelled against me.
The prophets prophesied by Baal,
following worthless idols.

9 "Therefore I bring charges against you
again,"
declares the LORD.
"And I will bring charges against your
children's children.
10 Cross over to the coasts of Kittim[a] and
look,
send to Kedar[b] and observe closely;
see if there has ever been anything like
this:
11 Has a nation ever changed its gods?
(Yet they are not gods at all.)
But my people have exchanged their[c]
Glory
for worthless idols.
12 Be appalled at this, O heavens,
and shudder with great horror,"
declares the LORD.
13 "My people have committed two sins:
They have forsaken me,
the spring of living water,
and have dug their own cisterns,
broken cisterns that cannot hold water.
14 Is Israel a servant, a slave by birth?
Why then has he become plunder?
15 Lions have roared;
they have growled at him.
They have laid waste his land;
his towns are burned and deserted.
16 Also, the men of Memphis[d] and Tahpanhes
have shaved the crown of your head.[e]
17 Have you not brought this on yourselves
by forsaking the LORD your God
when he led you in the way?
18 Now why go to Egypt
to drink water from the Shihor[f]?
And why go to Assyria
to drink water from the River[g]?
19 Your wickedness will punish you;
your backsliding will rebuke you.
Consider then and realize
how evil and bitter it is for you
when you forsake the LORD your God
and have no awe of me,"
declares the Lord,
the LORD Almighty.

20 "Long ago you broke off your yoke
and tore off your bonds;
you said, 'I will not serve you!'
Indeed, on every high hill
and under every spreading tree
you lay down as a prostitute.
21 I had planted you like a choice vine
of sound and reliable stock.
How then did you turn against me
into a corrupt, wild vine?
22 Although you wash yourself with soda
and use an abundance of soap,
the stain of your guilt is still before
me,"
declares the Sovereign LORD.
23 "How can you say, 'I am not defiled;
I have not run after the Baals'?
See how you behaved in the valley;
consider what you have done.
You are a swift she-camel
running here and there,
24 a wild donkey accustomed to the desert,
sniffing the wind in her craving—
in her heat who can restrain her?
Any males that pursue her need not tire
themselves;
at mating time they will find her.
25 Do not run until your feet are bare
and your throat is dry.
But you said, 'It's no use!
I love foreign gods,
and I must go after them.'

26 "As a thief is disgraced when he is caught,
so the house of Israel is disgraced—
they, their kings and their officials,
their priests and their prophets.
27 They say to wood, 'You are my father,'
and to stone, 'You gave me birth.'
They have turned their backs to me
and not their faces;
yet when they are in trouble, they say,
'Come and save us!'
28 Where then are the gods you made for
yourselves?
Let them come if they can save you
when you are in trouble!
For you have as many gods
as you have towns, O Judah.

29 "Why do you bring charges against me?
You have all rebelled against me,"
declares the LORD.
30 "In vain I punished your people;
they did not respond to correction.
Your sword has devoured your prophets
like a ravening lion.

[a] *10* That is, Cyprus and western coastlands [b] *10* The home of Bedouin tribes in the Syro-Arabian desert [c] *11* Masoretic Text; an ancient Hebrew scribal tradition *my* [d] *16* Hebrew *Noph* [e] *16* Or *have cracked your skull* [f] *18* That is, a branch of the Nile [g] *18* That is, the Euphrates

31 "You of this generation, consider the
word of the LORD:

"Have I been a desert to Israel
or a land of great darkness?
Why do my people say, 'We are free to
roam;
we will come to you no more'?
32 Does a maiden forget her jewelry,
a bride her wedding ornaments?
Yet my people have forgotten me,
days without number.
33 How skilled you are at pursuing love!
Even the worst of women can learn
from your ways.
34 On your clothes men find
the lifeblood of the innocent poor,
though you did not catch them
breaking in.
Yet in spite of all this
35 you say, 'I am innocent;
he is not angry with me.'
But I will pass judgment on you
because you say, 'I have not sinned.'
36 Why do you go about so much,
changing your ways?
You will be disappointed by Egypt
as you were by Assyria.
37 You will also leave that place
with your hands on your head,
for the LORD has rejected those you trust;
you will not be helped by them.

3 "If a man divorces his wife
and she leaves him and marries another
man,
should he return to her again?
Would not the land be completely
defiled?
But you have lived as a prostitute with
many lovers—
would you now return to me?"
declares the LORD.
2 "Look up to the barren heights and see.
Is there any place where you have not
been ravished?
By the roadside you sat waiting for lovers,
sat like a nomad[a] in the desert.
You have defiled the land
with your prostitution and wickedness.
3 Therefore the showers have been withheld,
and no spring rains have fallen.
Yet you have the brazen look of a
prostitute;
you refuse to blush with shame.
4 Have you not just called to me:
'My Father, my friend from my youth,
5 will you always be angry?
Will your wrath continue forever?'
This is how you talk,
but you do all the evil you can."

Unfaithful Israel

6 During the reign of King Josiah, the LORD
said to me, "Have you seen what faithless Israel has done? She has gone up on every high hill
and under every spreading tree and has committed adultery there. 7 I thought that after she
had done all this she would return to me but
she did not, and her unfaithful sister Judah
saw it. 8 I gave faithless Israel her certificate of
divorce and sent her away because of all her
adulteries. Yet I saw that her unfaithful sister
Judah had no fear; she also went out and committed adultery. 9 Because Israel's immorality
mattered so little to her, she defiled the land
and committed adultery with stone and wood.
10 In spite of all this, her unfaithful sister Judah
did not return to me with all her heart, but
only in pretense," declares the LORD.
11 The LORD said to me, "Faithless Israel is
more righteous than unfaithful Judah. 12 Go,
proclaim this message toward the north:

" 'Return, faithless Israel,' declares the
LORD,
'I will frown on you no longer,
for I am merciful,' declares the LORD,
'I will not be angry forever.
13 Only acknowledge your guilt—
you have rebelled against the LORD
your God,
you have scattered your favors to foreign
gods
under every spreading tree,
and have not obeyed me,' "
declares the LORD.

14 "Return, faithless people," declares the
LORD, "for I am your husband. I will choose
you—one from a town and two from a clan—
and bring you to Zion. 15 Then I will give you
shepherds after my own heart, who will lead
you with knowledge and understanding. 16 In
those days, when your numbers have increased
greatly in the land," declares the LORD, "men
will no longer say, 'The ark of the covenant of
the LORD.' It will never enter their minds or
be remembered; it will not be missed, nor will
another one be made. 17 At that time they will
call Jerusalem The Throne of the LORD, and all
nations will gather in Jerusalem to honor the

[a] 2 *Or an Arab*

FRIDAY
READ JEREMIAH 2:1—3:5

THE BIG RESULT OF A LITTLE INDEPENDENCE

A while back, a man who had attended our Bible study stepped down from his responsibilities at church and moved out of his house. He left his wife and children and moved in with a gay lover. Our church was stunned, and our close-knit Bible study group was numb with shock. We hadn't seen this coming.

Yet the clues were there. With the 20/20 vision that hindsight provides, his wife and I identified numerous tiny infidelities that had led to the ultimate big one. He had often made unilateral decisions, not taking his wife's feelings or viewpoints into consideration. He often had kept his thoughts and feelings to himself. He certainly had not made a practice of humbly confessing his weaknesses or sins to his wife. His spending of time and money reflected a determination to primarily please himself, not to lay down his life for his family (see 1 John 3:16).

The prophet Jeremiah was called the "weeping prophet" because he often openly expressed his sorrow over the spiritual and moral condition of the faithless people of Judah and their impending destruction. God was long-suffering, but the people would suffer his coming judgment.

Judah's infidelity showed up in numerous acts of disobedience. The people had fallen into idolatry, immorality and injustice. Personal and social corruption was prevalent. The Israelites fulfilled their religious obligations, but their hearts weren't in the right place. Prophets, priests, nobility and common citizens were all guilty. God viewed his people's many acts of independence (rather than God-dependence) as tantamount to adultery, an ultimate breaking of relationship with him.

Most of us can't imagine how we would ever get to the point of entering into a sexual relationship outside our marriage. And yet adultery happens all the time, almost as often with Christians as with non-believers. And it usually begins with little acts of unfaithfulness that build gradually into bigger ones until suddenly one day we realize we're up to our necks in a full-blown affair.

So if we want to safeguard the purity of our marriage, we've got to be on guard against small acts of faithlessness. We've got to ask ourselves questions, such as: Are my decisions to spend money at the mall based primarily on my own self-interests or are they made for the good of my spouse and family? Do I think more about myself than I do about my spouse in making plans for the evening or weekend? How important are the needs of my family in deciding whether or not to take on more work?

If, with God's help, I refuse to take any baby steps of independence that distance me from my spouse, then I may never take that giant step of adultery. I'm not so overconfident as to say, "Sexual infidelity could never happen to us." Instead, I humbly say, "Lord, protect my daily faithfulness in every way, both to you and to my spouse."

—ANNETTE LAPLACA

"You have lived as a prostitute with many lovers—would you now return to me?" declares the LORD.

— JEREMIAH 3:1

let's talk

- When have we been totally surprised by someone's unfaithfulness?
- If we act as our own "fidelity police," can we identify ways we've each acted independently or without consideration for each other?
- How can everyday choices lead to lifelong sexual faithfulness?

FOR YOUR NEXT DEVOTIONAL READING, TURN TO PAGE 826.

name of the LORD. No longer will they follow the stubbornness of their evil hearts. 18In
those days the house of Judah will join the
house of Israel, and together they will come
from a northern land to the land I gave your
forefathers as an inheritance.

19"I myself said,

" 'How gladly would I treat you like sons
and give you a desirable land,
the most beautiful inheritance of any nation.'
I thought you would call me 'Father'
and not turn away from following me.
20 But like a woman unfaithful to her husband,
so you have been unfaithful to me,
O house of Israel,"
declares the LORD.

21 A cry is heard on the barren heights,
the weeping and pleading of the people of Israel,
because they have perverted their ways
and have forgotten the LORD their God.

22 "Return, faithless people;
I will cure you of backsliding."

"Yes, we will come to you,
for you are the LORD our God.
23 Surely the ⌊idolatrous⌋ commotion on the hills
and mountains is a deception;
surely in the LORD our God
is the salvation of Israel.
24 From our youth shameful gods have consumed
the fruits of our fathers' labor—
their flocks and herds,
their sons and daughters.
25 Let us lie down in our shame,
and let our disgrace cover us.
We have sinned against the LORD our God,
both we and our fathers;
from our youth till this day
we have not obeyed the LORD our God."

4 "If you will return, O Israel,
return to me,"
declares the LORD.
"If you put your detestable idols out of my sight
and no longer go astray,
2 and if in a truthful, just and righteous way
you swear, 'As surely as the LORD lives,'
then the nations will be blessed by him
and in him they will glory."

3This is what the LORD says to the men of
Judah and to Jerusalem:

"Break up your unplowed ground
and do not sow among thorns.
4 Circumcise yourselves to the LORD,
circumcise your hearts,
you men of Judah and people of Jerusalem,
or my wrath will break out and burn like fire
because of the evil you have done—
burn with no one to quench it.

Disaster From the North

5 "Announce in Judah and proclaim in Jerusalem and say:
'Sound the trumpet throughout the land!'
Cry aloud and say:
'Gather together!
Let us flee to the fortified cities!'
6 Raise the signal to go to Zion!
Flee for safety without delay!
For I am bringing disaster from the north,
even terrible destruction."

7 A lion has come out of his lair;
a destroyer of nations has set out.
He has left his place
to lay waste your land.
Your towns will lie in ruins
without inhabitant.
8 So put on sackcloth,
lament and wail,
for the fierce anger of the LORD
has not turned away from us.

9 "In that day," declares the LORD,
"the king and the officials will lose heart,
the priests will be horrified,
and the prophets will be appalled."

10Then I said, "Ah, Sovereign LORD, how
completely you have deceived this people and
Jerusalem by saying, 'You will have peace,'
when the sword is at our throats."

11At that time this people and Jerusalem will
be told, "A scorching wind from the barren
heights in the desert blows toward my people,
but not to winnow or cleanse; 12a wind too
strong for that comes from me.[a] Now I pronounce my judgments against them."

[a] 12 Or *comes at my command*

13 Look! He advances like the clouds,
his chariots come like a whirlwind,
his horses are swifter than eagles.
Woe to us! We are ruined!
14 O Jerusalem, wash the evil from your heart and be saved.
How long will you harbor wicked thoughts?
15 A voice is announcing from Dan,
proclaiming disaster from the hills of Ephraim.
16 "Tell this to the nations,
proclaim it to Jerusalem:
'A besieging army is coming from a distant land,
raising a war cry against the cities of Judah.
17 They surround her like men guarding a field,
because she has rebelled against me,' "
declares the LORD.
18 "Your own conduct and actions
have brought this upon you.
This is your punishment.
How bitter it is!
How it pierces to the heart!"

19 Oh, my anguish, my anguish!
I writhe in pain.
Oh, the agony of my heart!
My heart pounds within me,
I cannot keep silent.
For I have heard the sound of the trumpet;
I have heard the battle cry.
20 Disaster follows disaster;
the whole land lies in ruins.
In an instant my tents are destroyed,
my shelter in a moment.
21 How long must I see the battle standard
and hear the sound of the trumpet?

22 "My people are fools;
they do not know me.
They are senseless children;
they have no understanding.
They are skilled in doing evil;
they know not how to do good."

23 I looked at the earth,
and it was formless and empty;
and at the heavens,
and their light was gone.
24 I looked at the mountains,
and they were quaking;
all the hills were swaying.
25 I looked, and there were no people;
every bird in the sky had flown away.
26 I looked, and the fruitful land was a desert;
all its towns lay in ruins
before the LORD, before his fierce anger.

27 This is what the LORD says:

"The whole land will be ruined,
though I will not destroy it completely.
28 Therefore the earth will mourn
and the heavens above grow dark,
because I have spoken and will not relent,
I have decided and will not turn back."

29 At the sound of horsemen and archers
every town takes to flight.
Some go into the thickets;
some climb up among the rocks.
All the towns are deserted;
no one lives in them.

30 What are you doing, O devastated one?
Why dress yourself in scarlet
and put on jewels of gold?
Why shade your eyes with paint?
You adorn yourself in vain.
Your lovers despise you;
they seek your life.

31 I hear a cry as of a woman in labor,
a groan as of one bearing her first child—
the cry of the Daughter of Zion gasping for breath,
stretching out her hands and saying,
"Alas! I am fainting;
my life is given over to murderers."

Not One Is Upright

5 "Go up and down the streets of Jerusalem,
look around and consider,
search through her squares.
If you can find but one person
who deals honestly and seeks the truth,
I will forgive this city.
2 Although they say, 'As surely as the LORD lives,'
still they are swearing falsely."
3 O LORD, do not your eyes look for truth?
You struck them, but they felt no pain;
you crushed them, but they refused correction.
They made their faces harder than stone
and refused to repent.
4 I thought, "These are only the poor;
they are foolish,
for they do not know the way of the LORD,
the requirements of their God.

5 So I will go to the leaders
and speak to them;
surely they know the way of the LORD,
the requirements of their God."
But with one accord they too had broken off the yoke
and torn off the bonds.
6 Therefore a lion from the forest will attack them,
a wolf from the desert will ravage them,
a leopard will lie in wait near their towns
to tear to pieces any who venture out,
for their rebellion is great
and their backslidings many.

7 "Why should I forgive you?
Your children have forsaken me
and sworn by gods that are not gods.
I supplied all their needs,
yet they committed adultery
and thronged to the houses of prostitutes.
8 They are well-fed, lusty stallions,
each neighing for another man's wife.
9 Should I not punish them for this?"
declares the LORD.
"Should I not avenge myself
on such a nation as this?

10 "Go through her vineyards and ravage them,
but do not destroy them completely.
Strip off her branches,
for these people do not belong to the LORD.
11 The house of Israel and the house of Judah
have been utterly unfaithful to me,"
declares the LORD.

12 They have lied about the LORD;
they said, "He will do nothing!
No harm will come to us;
we will never see sword or famine.
13 The prophets are but wind
and the word is not in them;
so let what they say be done to them."

14 Therefore this is what the LORD God Almighty says:
"Because the people have spoken these words,
I will make my words in your mouth a fire
and these people the wood it consumes.
15 O house of Israel," declares the LORD,
"I am bringing a distant nation against you—
an ancient and enduring nation,
a people whose language you do not know,
whose speech you do not understand.
16 Their quivers are like an open grave;
all of them are mighty warriors.
17 They will devour your harvests and food,
devour your sons and daughters;
they will devour your flocks and herds,
devour your vines and fig trees.
With the sword they will destroy
the fortified cities in which you trust.

18 "Yet even in those days," declares the
LORD, "I will not destroy you completely.
19 And when the people ask, 'Why has the
LORD our God done all this to us?' you will
tell them, 'As you have forsaken me and served
foreign gods in your own land, so now you
will serve foreigners in a land not your own.'

20 "Announce this to the house of Jacob
and proclaim it in Judah:
21 Hear this, you foolish and senseless people,
who have eyes but do not see,
who have ears but do not hear:
22 Should you not fear me?" declares the LORD.
"Should you not tremble in my presence?
I made the sand a boundary for the sea,
an everlasting barrier it cannot cross.
The waves may roll, but they cannot prevail;
they may roar, but they cannot cross it.
23 But these people have stubborn and rebellious hearts;
they have turned aside and gone away.
24 They do not say to themselves,
'Let us fear the LORD our God,
who gives autumn and spring rains in season,
who assures us of the regular weeks of harvest.'
25 Your wrongdoings have kept these away;
your sins have deprived you of good.

26 "Among my people are wicked men
who lie in wait like men who snare birds
and like those who set traps to catch men.
27 Like cages full of birds,
their houses are full of deceit;
they have become rich and powerful
28 and have grown fat and sleek.
Their evil deeds have no limit;

they do not plead the case of the
fatherless to win it,
they do not defend the rights of the
poor.
29 Should I not punish them for this?"
declares the LORD.
"Should I not avenge myself
on such a nation as this?

30 "A horrible and shocking thing
has happened in the land:
31 The prophets prophesy lies,
the priests rule by their own authority,
and my people love it this way.
But what will you do in the end?

Jerusalem Under Siege

6 "Flee for safety, people of Benjamin!
Flee from Jerusalem!
Sound the trumpet in Tekoa!
Raise the signal over Beth Hakkerem!
For disaster looms out of the north,
even terrible destruction.
2 I will destroy the Daughter of Zion,
so beautiful and delicate.
3 Shepherds with their flocks will come
against her;
they will pitch their tents around her,
each tending his own portion."

4 "Prepare for battle against her!
Arise, let us attack at noon!
But, alas, the daylight is fading,
and the shadows of evening grow long.
5 So arise, let us attack at night
and destroy her fortresses!"

6 This is what the LORD Almighty says:

"Cut down the trees
and build siege ramps against
Jerusalem.
This city must be punished;
it is filled with oppression.
7 As a well pours out its water,
so she pours out her wickedness.
Violence and destruction resound in her;
her sickness and wounds are ever before
me.
8 Take warning, O Jerusalem,
or I will turn away from you
and make your land desolate
so no one can live in it."

9 This is what the LORD Almighty says:

"Let them glean the remnant of Israel
as thoroughly as a vine;
pass your hand over the branches again,
like one gathering grapes."
10 To whom can I speak and give warning?
Who will listen to me?
Their ears are closed[a]
so they cannot hear.
The word of the LORD is offensive to
them;
they find no pleasure in it.
11 But I am full of the wrath of the LORD,
and I cannot hold it in.

"Pour it out on the children in the street
and on the young men gathered
together;
both husband and wife will be caught in
it,
and the old, those weighed down with
years.
12 Their houses will be turned over to others,
together with their fields and their
wives,
when I stretch out my hand
against those who live in the land,"
declares the LORD.
13 "From the least to the greatest,
all are greedy for gain;
prophets and priests alike,
all practice deceit.
14 They dress the wound of my people
as though it were not serious.
'Peace, peace,' they say,
when there is no peace.
15 Are they ashamed of their loathsome
conduct?
No, they have no shame at all;
they do not even know how to blush.
So they will fall among the fallen;
they will be brought down when I
punish them,"
says the LORD.

16 This is what the LORD says:

"Stand at the crossroads and look;
ask for the ancient paths,
ask where the good way is, and walk in it,
and you will find rest for your souls.
But you said, 'We will not walk in it.'
17 I appointed watchmen over you and said,
'Listen to the sound of the trumpet!'
But you said, 'We will not listen.'
18 Therefore hear, O nations;
observe, O witnesses,
what will happen to them.
19 Hear, O earth:

[a] 10 Hebrew *uncircumcised*

WEEKEND

warning signs

Warning signs of trouble reveal themselves at whatever your stage of life may be. Many people have an idealistic view of marriage and are often "blindsided" by the problems that lead to divorce. Newlyweds are often astounded by the conflict that comes early in their marriage. After the wedding, a period of adjustment sets in, and the charm and enchantment of dating and courtship is only a blurred recollection.

After six months of marriage, half of all couples witness dramatic increases in the frequency of arguments. They're often surprised at how critical they have become of each other. Doubts emerge. They wonder if they really married the right person. How can couples caught in the sudden horror of this disenchantment be helped to grow through it? One way is to first celebrate the areas of strength in your relationship. For instance, one couple we worked with, Heather and Pete, agreed on their basic religious beliefs. They both felt their faith was important to their relationship, so when they argued, they could stop and pray for wisdom.

On the other hand, this same couple admitted that many of their conflicts were over money, a typical area of dispute among newlyweds. They asked us how we argue. I replied, "Our relationship is always more important than the issue in dispute, so we want to be in consensus on any decision, especially involving money. If we can't resolve an issue, we'll just postpone making a decision about it."

It turns out Heather and Pete's arguments about money weren't really solely about money. When I asked them to describe their conflicts, Pete admitted that he got angry at the way Heather spent her time. She wasn't working—they had agreed on her staying home—but he felt that she was spending too much time on petty activities. She got defensive because she saw herself as always being busy taking care of everything that needed to get done at home. When they explored this tension further, the source of Pete's anger finally came into focus.

"I kill myself at work but lose respect for Heather when she uses all her time on errands and little things that don't matter. I'm working to free her to do what's important and creative. She's good at writing—she should be doing that instead of all these petty little things."

Finally, here was the source of his anger. And Heather was hearing his point of view as for the first time.

"He's never said that before," she said softly. "He's right. I really do want to write . . . I guess I've been procrastinating." This was a special moment for this couple. From this point on, I knew they'd be successful in working out their disputes.

—MICHAEL J. MCMANUS

are we in trouble?

HOW ARE WE DOING?

Certain behaviors in a marriage relationship can alert you to potential long-term conflict.

1. ____*Ugly arguments.* Disagreements are natural, but they don't have to be ugly. There are ways to resolve conflict that are healthy and can actually strengthen a relationship.
2. ____*Being overly critical of each other.* When a spouse lacks the self-confidence to demand respect from a mate, one of two things will happen—both negative. Either the weaker person will placate the bully, or the bully will lose so much respect for the other person that he or she will find someone else to respect and will push for a divorce. Also, if one of the partners shows poor self-esteem or feels ignored, abandoned or betrayed by the other partner, serious trouble lies ahead.
3. ____*Money disputes.* Financial disagreements cause serious problems in a marriage. Married couples should resolve how to spend money and on what, asking such questions as: How much of a mortgage can we honestly take on without feeling "house-poor"? Can we use credit cards without stacking up monthly finance charges? Can we pay our bills in full and on time, or is our debt out of control? How much money are we giving back to God?
4. ____*Unresolved questions about children.* Do we share similar ideas of family planning? Will we have children? If so, how many and when? Will one of us stay home with them while the other spouse works, or will both parents work? Who will take care of the kids? If we can't discuss these issues without one of us blowing up or walking out, we have a problem.

If you checked any of the warning signs listed here, seek help through counseling or a mentor couple at church before the situation becomes critical. Whether you're discussing money or children, try to let each of your conversations be a gateway to understanding your mate, not to getting your own way. Affirm each other in your differences, and spend time praying together about the areas where you don't agree. And leave lots of time to celebrate the love you share!

let's make a DATE

PLANNING A DATE

Even if you're having trouble, take some time to be together—just the two of you—and have some fun. Get your calendars out and nail down an evening or a whole day for the two of you. If you have kids, make plans to farm them out to family or friends.

Decide how much you can spend on the date and how far you are willing to travel. Then decide what you want to do on that special evening or day. Each of you should think of three suggestions for a great date. Write each on a slip of paper, then put all the suggestions in a jar.

The week before your date, draw out one of the slips. Make arrangements. While you're out, try to put your troubles aside. Agree there will be no arguments, no disruptions, no touchy subjects. Pretend you're two teenagers again and in love. Act goofy. Flirt with each other. Remind each other of what first attracted you to each other.

The next week, draw out another slip and plan the next date.

FOR YOUR NEXT DEVOTIONAL READING, TURN TO PAGE 831.

LESSONS FROM THE *Bible*

Read the story of Ananias and Sapphira in Acts 5:1–11. Do you think this couple made a mutual agreement about how to handle the money from the sale of their property, or did one make the decision and the other simply fall in line with it? Should couples discuss major decisions and come to a consensus? What happens when they don't?

I am bringing disaster on this people,
the fruit of their schemes,
because they have not listened to my words
and have rejected my law.
20 What do I care about incense from Sheba
or sweet calamus from a distant land?
Your burnt offerings are not acceptable;
your sacrifices do not please me."

21 Therefore this is what the LORD says:

"I will put obstacles before this people.
Fathers and sons alike will stumble over
them;
neighbors and friends will perish."

22 This is what the LORD says:

"Look, an army is coming
from the land of the north;
a great nation is being stirred up
from the ends of the earth.
23 They are armed with bow and spear;
they are cruel and show no mercy.
They sound like the roaring sea
as they ride on their horses;
they come like men in battle formation
to attack you, O Daughter of Zion."

24 We have heard reports about them,
and our hands hang limp.
Anguish has gripped us,
pain like that of a woman in labor.
25 Do not go out to the fields
or walk on the roads,
for the enemy has a sword,
and there is terror on every side.
26 O my people, put on sackcloth
and roll in ashes;
mourn with bitter wailing
as for an only son,
for suddenly the destroyer
will come upon us.

27 "I have made you a tester of metals
and my people the ore,
that you may observe
and test their ways.
28 They are all hardened rebels,
going about to slander.
They are bronze and iron;
they all act corruptly.
29 The bellows blow fiercely
to burn away the lead with fire,
but the refining goes on in vain;
the wicked are not purged out.
30 They are called rejected silver,
because the LORD has rejected them."

False Religion Worthless

7 This is the word that came to Jeremiah from
the LORD: 2 "Stand at the gate of the LORD's
house and there proclaim this message:
" 'Hear the word of the LORD, all you people of Judah who come through these gates to
worship the LORD. 3 This is what the LORD Almighty, the God of Israel, says: Reform your
ways and your actions, and I will let you live
in this place. 4 Do not trust in deceptive words
and say, "This is the temple of the LORD, the
temple of the LORD, the temple of the LORD!"
5 If you really change your ways and your actions and deal with each other justly, 6 if you
do not oppress the alien, the fatherless or the
widow and do not shed innocent blood in this
place, and if you do not follow other gods to
your own harm, 7 then I will let you live in this
place, in the land I gave your forefathers for
ever and ever. 8 But look, you are trusting in
deceptive words that are worthless.
9 " 'Will you steal and murder, commit
adultery and perjury,[a] burn incense to Baal
and follow other gods you have not known,
10 and then come and stand before me in this
house, which bears my Name, and say, "We are
safe"—safe to do all these detestable things?
11 Has this house, which bears my Name, become a den of robbers to you? But I have been
watching! declares the LORD.
12 " 'Go now to the place in Shiloh where
I first made a dwelling for my Name, and see
what I did to it because of the wickedness of
my people Israel. 13 While you were doing all
these things, declares the LORD, I spoke to
you again and again, but you did not listen;
I called you, but you did not answer. 14 Therefore, what I did to Shiloh I will now do to
the house that bears my Name, the temple you
trust in, the place I gave to you and your fathers. 15 I will thrust you from my presence,
just as I did all your brothers, the people of
Ephraim.'
16 "So do not pray for this people nor offer
any plea or petition for them; do not plead
with me, for I will not listen to you. 17 Do you
not see what they are doing in the towns of
Judah and in the streets of Jerusalem? 18 The
children gather wood, the fathers light the fire,
and the women knead the dough and make
cakes of bread for the Queen of Heaven. They
pour out drink offerings to other gods to provoke me to anger. 19 But am I the one they
are provoking? declares the LORD. Are they

[a] 9 Or *and swear by false gods*

not rather harming themselves, to their own
shame?

20“ ‘Therefore this is what the Sovereign
LORD says: My anger and my wrath will be
poured out on this place, on man and beast,
on the trees of the field and on the fruit of
the ground, and it will burn and not be
quenched.

21“ ‘This is what the LORD Almighty, the
God of Israel, says: Go ahead, add your burnt
offerings to your other sacrifices and eat the
meat yourselves! 22For when I brought your
forefathers out of Egypt and spoke to them, I
did not just give them commands about burnt
offerings and sacrifices, 23but I gave them this
command: Obey me, and I will be your God
and you will be my people. Walk in all the
ways I command you, that it may go well with
you. 24But they did not listen or pay attention;
instead, they followed the stubborn inclinations of their evil hearts. They went backward
and not forward. 25From the time your forefathers left Egypt until now, day after day, again
and again I sent you my servants the prophets.
26But they did not listen to me or pay attention. They were stiff-necked and did more evil
than their forefathers.’

27“When you tell them all this, they will
not listen to you; when you call to them, they
will not answer. 28Therefore say to them, ‘This
is the nation that has not obeyed the LORD
its God or responded to correction. Truth has
perished; it has vanished from their lips. 29Cut
off your hair and throw it away; take up a lament on the barren heights, for the LORD has
rejected and abandoned this generation that is
under his wrath.

The Valley of Slaughter

30“ ‘The people of Judah have done evil in
my eyes, declares the LORD. They have set up
their detestable idols in the house that bears
my Name and have defiled it. 31They have built
the high places of Topheth in the Valley of Ben
Hinnom to burn their sons and daughters in
the fire—something I did not command, nor
did it enter my mind. 32So beware, the days
are coming, declares the LORD, when people
will no longer call it Topheth or the Valley of
Ben Hinnom, but the Valley of Slaughter, for
they will bury the dead in Topheth until there
is no more room. 33Then the carcasses of this
people will become food for the birds of the
air and the beasts of the earth, and there will
be no one to frighten them away. 34I will bring
an end to the sounds of joy and gladness and
to the voices of bride and bridegroom in the
towns of Judah and the streets of Jerusalem,
for the land will become desolate.

8 “ ‘At that time, declares the LORD, the
bones of the kings and officials of Judah,
the bones of the priests and prophets, and
the bones of the people of Jerusalem will be removed from their graves. 2They will be exposed
to the sun and the moon and all the stars of
the heavens, which they have loved and served
and which they have followed and consulted
and worshiped. They will not be gathered up
or buried, but will be like refuse lying on the
ground. 3Wherever I banish them, all the survivors of this evil nation will prefer death to
life, declares the LORD Almighty.’

Sin and Punishment

4“Say to them, ‘This is what the LORD says:

“ ‘When men fall down, do they not get
up?
When a man turns away, does he not
return?
5 Why then have these people turned away?
Why does Jerusalem always turn away?
They cling to deceit;
they refuse to return.
6 I have listened attentively,
but they do not say what is right.
No one repents of his wickedness,
saying, “What have I done?”
Each pursues his own course
like a horse charging into battle.
7 Even the stork in the sky
knows her appointed seasons,
and the dove, the swift and the thrush
observe the time of their migration.
But my people do not know
the requirements of the LORD.
8 “ ‘How can you say, “We are wise,
for we have the law of the LORD,”
when actually the lying pen of the scribes
has handled it falsely?
9 The wise will be put to shame;
they will be dismayed and trapped.
Since they have rejected the word of the
LORD,
what kind of wisdom do they have?
10 Therefore I will give their wives to other
men
and their fields to new owners.
From the least to the greatest,
all are greedy for gain;
prophets and priests alike,
all practice deceit.
11 They dress the wound of my people
as though it were not serious.

"Peace, peace," they say,
when there is no peace.
12 Are they ashamed of their loathsome conduct?
No, they have no shame at all;
they do not even know how to blush.
So they will fall among the fallen;
they will be brought down when they are punished,
says the LORD.

13 " 'I will take away their harvest,
declares the LORD.
There will be no grapes on the vine.
There will be no figs on the tree,
and their leaves will wither.
What I have given them
will be taken from them.[a]' "

14 "Why are we sitting here?
Gather together!
Let us flee to the fortified cities
and perish there!
For the LORD our God has doomed us to perish
and given us poisoned water to drink,
because we have sinned against him.
15 We hoped for peace
but no good has come,
for a time of healing
but there was only terror.
16 The snorting of the enemy's horses
is heard from Dan;
at the neighing of their stallions
the whole land trembles.
They have come to devour
the land and everything in it,
the city and all who live there."

17 "See, I will send venomous snakes among you,
vipers that cannot be charmed,
and they will bite you,"
declares the LORD.

18 O my Comforter[b] in sorrow,
my heart is faint within me.
19 Listen to the cry of my people
from a land far away:
"Is the LORD not in Zion?
Is her King no longer there?"

"Why have they provoked me to anger with their images,
with their worthless foreign idols?"

20 "The harvest is past,
the summer has ended,
and we are not saved."

21 Since my people are crushed, I am crushed;
I mourn, and horror grips me.
22 Is there no balm in Gilead?
Is there no physician there?
Why then is there no healing
for the wound of my people?

9 1 Oh, that my head were a spring of water
and my eyes a fountain of tears!
I would weep day and night
for the slain of my people.
2 Oh, that I had in the desert
a lodging place for travelers,
so that I might leave my people
and go away from them;
for they are all adulterers,
a crowd of unfaithful people.

3 "They make ready their tongue
like a bow, to shoot lies;
it is not by truth
that they triumph[c] in the land.
They go from one sin to another;
they do not acknowledge me,"
declares the LORD.

4 "Beware of your friends;
do not trust your brothers.
For every brother is a deceiver,[d]
and every friend a slanderer.
5 Friend deceives friend,
and no one speaks the truth.
They have taught their tongues to lie;
they weary themselves with sinning.
6 You[e] live in the midst of deception;
in their deceit they refuse to acknowledge me,"
declares the LORD.

7 Therefore this is what the LORD Almighty says:

"See, I will refine and test them,
for what else can I do
because of the sin of my people?
8 Their tongue is a deadly arrow;
it speaks with deceit.
With his mouth each speaks cordially to his neighbor,
but in his heart he sets a trap for him.
9 Should I not punish them for this?"
declares the LORD.
"Should I not avenge myself
on such a nation as this?"

[a] 13 The meaning of the Hebrew for this sentence is uncertain. [b] 18 The meaning of the Hebrew for this word is uncertain.
[c] 3 Or *lies; / they are not valiant for truth* [d] 4 Or *a deceiving Jacob* [e] 6 That is, Jeremiah (the Hebrew is singular)

MONDAY
READ JEREMIAH 9:1–11

MAKING FRIENDS WITH TRUTH

"Beware of your friends; do not trust your brothers. For every brother is a deceiver, and every friend a slanderer. Friend deceives friend, and no one speaks the truth."

— Jeremiah 9:4–5

Need a handy excuse for wiggling out of a pinch? Try an alibi club. According to a recent article in the *New York Times* ("For Liars and Loafers, Cell Phones Offer an Alibi" by Matt Richtel), alibi networks are emerging in the United States, Europe and parts of Asia. Kenny Hall used the club to help him cheat on his girlfriend. His text message via cell phone went out to 3,400 club members. Within minutes, a complete stranger offered to phone Hall's girlfriend with an alibi.

Lying is hardly new. Jeremiah lived among a people who were supposed to be dedicated to the Lord. But they were so mired in deceit that Jeremiah had all but given up hope that they would ever again know God.

God, too, was fed up with Judah and accused them of creating a culture of lies. In this climate, the people couldn't trust anyone, not even their friends. Their society had become so sinful that friends were deceiving friends.

Our marriages exist in a culture not so different from Judah's in Jeremiah's day. Sometimes people we know and trust may actually be treacherous. It's hard to think of most people we know as liars, and obviously many good people aren't. Yet in our culture, lying can become a kind of benign "dialect." The old Seinfeld TV show offered countless episodes built around the ordinary, everyday, self-promoting lies common in our culture. People laughed in response because the stories struck so close to home. But where friend deceives friend, God says, "Beware!"

Lies aren't always intended to be malicious and harmful, but they are still dangerous. Beyond the little "white lies" that many people tell are deeper, cultural lies about the existence of God, what is right and wrong, and what is okay and not okay in marriage.

For Christians, marriage must be a truthful environment. The apostle Paul encouraged his readers to speak "the truth in love" (Ephesians 4:15). For when husband and wife, who are connected mind, body and soul, become like "friends who deceive friends," the very rock on which the marriage is built crumbles. The closer the relationship, the greater is the damage caused by deceit, whether it's withholding the truth, shading it or outright lying.

As married couples, we need to choose our friends carefully. God can guide us when we're developing close friendships as we pray and seek his wisdom. And as in any relationship, we are called to model truthfulness to our friends. Truth is a beacon to others.

We should also choose to be part of a church that heralds the Bible's truth and where "speaking the truth in love" is the heartbeat of communication.

Above all, we must guard our own hearts. We are all prone to believe and tell lies, even to ourselves, and we daily face a tempter who is the "father of lies" (John 8:44).

—LEE ECLOV

let's *talk*

- ✦ When have subtle lies affected our marriage?
- ✦ How might the exaggerations or insinuations of friends (whether they realize they are lying or not) be affecting us right now?
- ✦ If we sense that certain friends aren't being truthful with us, what should we do? Does it make a difference if the friends are Christians or non-Christians?

FOR YOUR NEXT DEVOTIONAL READING, TURN TO PAGE 840.

10 I will weep and wail for the mountains
and take up a lament concerning the desert pastures.
They are desolate and untraveled,
and the lowing of cattle is not heard.
The birds of the air have fled
and the animals are gone.

11 "I will make Jerusalem a heap of ruins,
a haunt of jackals;
and I will lay waste the towns of Judah
so no one can live there."

12 What man is wise enough to understand
this? Who has been instructed by the LORD
and can explain it? Why has the land been ruined and laid waste like a desert that no one
can cross?
13 The LORD said, "It is because they have
forsaken my law, which I set before them; they
have not obeyed me or followed my law. 14 Instead, they have followed the stubbornness of
their hearts; they have followed the Baals, as
their fathers taught them." 15 Therefore, this is
what the LORD Almighty, the God of Israel,
says: "See, I will make this people eat bitter
food and drink poisoned water. 16 I will scatter them among nations that neither they nor
their fathers have known, and I will pursue
them with the sword until I have destroyed
them."

17 This is what the LORD Almighty says:

"Consider now! Call for the wailing
women to come;
send for the most skillful of them.
18 Let them come quickly
and wail over us
till our eyes overflow with tears
and water streams from our eyelids.
19 The sound of wailing is heard from Zion:
'How ruined we are!
How great is our shame!
We must leave our land
because our houses are in ruins.' "

20 Now, O women, hear the word of the LORD;
open your ears to the words of his mouth.
Teach your daughters how to wail;
teach one another a lament.
21 Death has climbed in through our windows
and has entered our fortresses;
it has cut off the children from the streets
and the young men from the public squares.

22 Say, "This is what the LORD declares:

" 'The dead bodies of men will lie
like refuse on the open field,
like cut grain behind the reaper,
with no one to gather them.' "

23 This is what the LORD says:

"Let not the wise man boast of his wisdom
or the strong man boast of his strength
or the rich man boast of his riches,
24 but let him who boasts boast about this:
that he understands and knows me,
that I am the LORD, who exercises kindness,
justice and righteousness on earth,
for in these I delight,"
declares the LORD.

25 "The days are coming," declares the
LORD, "when I will punish all who are circumcised only in the flesh— 26 Egypt, Judah,
Edom, Ammon, Moab and all who live in the
desert in distant places.[a] For all these nations
are really uncircumcised, and even the whole
house of Israel is uncircumcised in heart."

God and Idols

10 Hear what the LORD says to you,
O house of Israel. 2 This is what the
LORD says:

"Do not learn the ways of the nations
or be terrified by signs in the sky,
though the nations are terrified by them.
3 For the customs of the peoples are worthless;
they cut a tree out of the forest,
and a craftsman shapes it with his chisel.
4 They adorn it with silver and gold;
they fasten it with hammer and nails
so it will not totter.
5 Like a scarecrow in a melon patch,
their idols cannot speak;
they must be carried
because they cannot walk.
Do not fear them;
they can do no harm
nor can they do any good."

6 No one is like you, O LORD;
you are great,
and your name is mighty in power.

a 26 Or *desert and who clip the hair by their foreheads*

[7] Who should not revere you,
O King of the nations?
This is your due.
Among all the wise men of the nations
and in all their kingdoms,
there is no one like you.
[8] They are all senseless and foolish;
they are taught by worthless wooden idols.
[9] Hammered silver is brought from Tarshish
and gold from Uphaz.
What the craftsman and goldsmith have made
is then dressed in blue and purple—
all made by skilled workers.
[10] But the LORD is the true God;
he is the living God, the eternal King.
When he is angry, the earth trembles;
the nations cannot endure his wrath.

[11] "Tell them this: 'These gods, who did
not make the heavens and the earth, will perish from the earth and from under the heavens.' "[a]

[12] But God made the earth by his power;
he founded the world by his wisdom
and stretched out the heavens by his understanding.
[13] When he thunders, the waters in the heavens roar;
he makes clouds rise from the ends of the earth.
He sends lightning with the rain
and brings out the wind from his storehouses.

[14] Everyone is senseless and without knowledge;
every goldsmith is shamed by his idols.
His images are a fraud;
they have no breath in them.
[15] They are worthless, the objects of mockery;
when their judgment comes, they will perish.
[16] He who is the Portion of Jacob is not like these,
for he is the Maker of all things,
including Israel, the tribe of his inheritance—
the LORD Almighty is his name.

Coming Destruction

[17] Gather up your belongings to leave the land,
you who live under siege.
[18] For this is what the LORD says:
"At this time I will hurl out
those who live in this land;
I will bring distress on them
so that they may be captured."

[19] Woe to me because of my injury!
My wound is incurable!
Yet I said to myself,
"This is my sickness, and I must endure it."
[20] My tent is destroyed;
all its ropes are snapped.
My sons are gone from me and are no more;
no one is left now to pitch my tent
or to set up my shelter.
[21] The shepherds are senseless
and do not inquire of the LORD;
so they do not prosper
and all their flock is scattered.
[22] Listen! The report is coming—
a great commotion from the land of the north!
It will make the towns of Judah desolate,
a haunt of jackals.

Jeremiah's Prayer

[23] I know, O LORD, that a man's life is not his own;
it is not for man to direct his steps.
[24] Correct me, LORD, but only with justice—
not in your anger,
lest you reduce me to nothing.
[25] Pour out your wrath on the nations
that do not acknowledge you,
on the peoples who do not call on your name.
For they have devoured Jacob;
they have devoured him completely
and destroyed his homeland.

The Covenant Is Broken

11 This is the word that came to Jeremiah
from the LORD: [2] "Listen to the terms of
this covenant and tell them to the people
of Judah and to those who live in Jerusalem.
[3] Tell them that this is what the LORD, the God
of Israel, says: 'Cursed is the man who does
not obey the terms of this covenant— [4] the
terms I commanded your forefathers when I
brought them out of Egypt, out of the iron-
smelting furnace.' I said, 'Obey me and do everything I command you, and you will be my
people, and I will be your God. [5] Then I will
fulfill the oath I swore to your forefathers, to

[a] 11 The text of this verse is in Aramaic.

give them a land flowing with milk and honey'—the land you possess today."
I answered, "Amen, LORD."
6 The LORD said to me, "Proclaim all these
words in the towns of Judah and in the streets
of Jerusalem: 'Listen to the terms of this covenant and follow them. 7 From the time I
brought your forefathers up from Egypt until
today, I warned them again and again, saying,
"Obey me." 8 But they did not listen or pay
attention; instead, they followed the stubbornness of their evil hearts. So I brought on
them all the curses of the covenant I had commanded them to follow but that they did not
keep.' "
9 Then the LORD said to me, "There is a conspiracy among the people of Judah and those
who live in Jerusalem. 10 They have returned
to the sins of their forefathers, who refused to
listen to my words. They have followed other
gods to serve them. Both the house of Israel
and the house of Judah have broken the covenant I made with their forefathers. 11 Therefore this is what the LORD says: 'I will bring on
them a disaster they cannot escape. Although
they cry out to me, I will not listen to them.
12 The towns of Judah and the people of Jerusalem will go and cry out to the gods to whom
they burn incense, but they will not help them
at all when disaster strikes. 13 You have as many
gods as you have towns, O Judah; and the altars you have set up to burn incense to that
shameful god Baal are as many as the streets
of Jerusalem.'
14 "Do not pray for this people nor offer any
plea or petition for them, because I will not
listen when they call to me in the time of their
distress.

15 "What is my beloved doing in my temple
as she works out her evil schemes with many?
Can consecrated meat avert ⌊your punishment⌋?
When you engage in your wickedness,
then you rejoice.[a]"

16 The LORD called you a thriving olive tree
with fruit beautiful in form.
But with the roar of a mighty storm
he will set it on fire,
and its branches will be broken.

17 The LORD Almighty, who planted you, has
decreed disaster for you, because the house of
Israel and the house of Judah have done evil
and provoked me to anger by burning incense
to Baal.

Plot Against Jeremiah

18 Because the LORD revealed their plot to
me, I knew it, for at that time he showed me
what they were doing. 19 I had been like a gentle lamb led to the slaughter; I did not realize
that they had plotted against me, saying,

"Let us destroy the tree and its fruit;
let us cut him off from the land of the living,
that his name be remembered no more."
20 But, O LORD Almighty, you who judge righteously
and test the heart and mind,
let me see your vengeance upon them,
for to you I have committed my cause.

21 "Therefore this is what the LORD says
about the men of Anathoth who are seeking
your life and saying, 'Do not prophesy in
the name of the LORD or you will die by our
hands'— 22 therefore this is what the LORD Almighty says: 'I will punish them. Their young
men will die by the sword, their sons and
daughters by famine. 23 Not even a remnant
will be left to them, because I will bring disaster on the men of Anathoth in the year of their
punishment.' "

Jeremiah's Complaint

12 You are always righteous, O LORD,
when I bring a case before you.
Yet I would speak with you about your justice:
Why does the way of the wicked prosper?
Why do all the faithless live at ease?
2 You have planted them, and they have taken root;
they grow and bear fruit.
You are always on their lips
but far from their hearts.
3 Yet you know me, O LORD;
you see me and test my thoughts about you.
Drag them off like sheep to be butchered!
Set them apart for the day of slaughter!
4 How long will the land lie parched[b]
and the grass in every field be withered?
Because those who live in it are wicked,
the animals and birds have perished.

[a] 15 Or *Could consecrated meat avert your punishment? / Then you would rejoice* [b] 4 Or *land mourn*

Moreover, the people are saying,
"He will not see what happens to us."

God's Answer

5 "If you have raced with men on foot
and they have worn you out,
how can you compete with horses?
If you stumble in safe country,[a]
how will you manage in the thickets
by[b] the Jordan?
6 Your brothers, your own family—
even they have betrayed you;
they have raised a loud cry against you.
Do not trust them,
though they speak well of you.

7 "I will forsake my house,
abandon my inheritance;
I will give the one I love
into the hands of her enemies.
8 My inheritance has become to me
like a lion in the forest.
She roars at me;
therefore I hate her.
9 Has not my inheritance become to me
like a speckled bird of prey
that other birds of prey surround and
attack?
Go and gather all the wild beasts;
bring them to devour.
10 Many shepherds will ruin my vineyard
and trample down my field;
they will turn my pleasant field
into a desolate wasteland.
11 It will be made a wasteland,
parched and desolate before me;
the whole land will be laid waste
because there is no one who cares.
12 Over all the barren heights in the desert
destroyers will swarm,
for the sword of the LORD will devour
from one end of the land to the other;
no one will be safe.
13 They will sow wheat but reap thorns;
they will wear themselves out but gain
nothing.
So bear the shame of your harvest
because of the LORD's fierce anger."

14 This is what the LORD says: "As for all my
wicked neighbors who seize the inheritance
I gave my people Israel, I will uproot them
from their lands and I will uproot the house
of Judah from among them. 15 But after I uproot them, I will again have compassion and
will bring each of them back to his own inheritance and his own country. 16 And if they
learn well the ways of my people and swear
by my name, saying, 'As surely as the LORD
lives'—even as they once taught my people to
swear by Baal—then they will be established
among my people. 17 But if any nation does
not listen, I will completely uproot and destroy it," declares the LORD.

A Linen Belt

13 This is what the LORD said to me: "Go
and buy a linen belt and put it around
your waist, but do not let it touch water." 2 So I bought a belt, as the LORD directed,
and put it around my waist.
3 Then the word of the LORD came to me a
second time: 4 "Take the belt you bought and
are wearing around your waist, and go now
to Perath[c] and hide it there in a crevice in the
rocks." 5 So I went and hid it at Perath, as the
LORD told me.
6 Many days later the LORD said to me, "Go
now to Perath and get the belt I told you to
hide there." 7 So I went to Perath and dug up
the belt and took it from the place where I had
hidden it, but now it was ruined and completely useless.
8 Then the word of the LORD came to me:
9 "This is what the LORD says: 'In the same way
I will ruin the pride of Judah and the great
pride of Jerusalem. 10 These wicked people,
who refuse to listen to my words, who follow
the stubbornness of their hearts and go after
other gods to serve and worship them, will be
like this belt—completely useless! 11 For as a
belt is bound around a man's waist, so I bound
the whole house of Israel and the whole house
of Judah to me,' declares the LORD, 'to be my
people for my renown and praise and honor.
But they have not listened.'

Wineskins

12 "Say to them: 'This is what the LORD, the
God of Israel, says: Every wineskin should be
filled with wine.' And if they say to you, 'Don't
we know that every wineskin should be filled
with wine?' 13 then tell them, 'This is what the
LORD says: I am going to fill with drunkenness all who live in this land, including the
kings who sit on David's throne, the priests,
the prophets and all those living in Jerusalem.
14 I will smash them one against the other, fathers and sons alike, declares the LORD. I will
allow no pity or mercy or compassion to keep
me from destroying them.' "

[a] 5 Or *If you put your trust in a land of safety* [b] 5 Or *the flooding of* [c] 4 Or possibly *the Euphrates*; also in verses 5-7

Threat of Captivity

15 Hear and pay attention,
do not be arrogant,
for the LORD has spoken.
16 Give glory to the LORD your God
before he brings the darkness,
before your feet stumble
on the darkening hills.
You hope for light,
but he will turn it to thick darkness
and change it to deep gloom.
17 But if you do not listen,
I will weep in secret
because of your pride;
my eyes will weep bitterly,
overflowing with tears,
because the LORD's flock will be taken
captive.

18 Say to the king and to the queen mother,
"Come down from your thrones,
for your glorious crowns
will fall from your heads."
19 The cities in the Negev will be shut up,
and there will be no one to open them.
All Judah will be carried into exile,
carried completely away.

20 Lift up your eyes and see
those who are coming from the north.
Where is the flock that was entrusted to
you,
the sheep of which you boasted?
21 What will you say when ⌊the LORD⌋ sets
over you
those you cultivated as your special
allies?
Will not pain grip you
like that of a woman in labor?
22 And if you ask yourself,
"Why has this happened to me?"—
it is because of your many sins
that your skirts have been torn off
and your body mistreated.
23 Can the Ethiopian[a] change his skin
or the leopard its spots?
Neither can you do good
who are accustomed to doing evil.

24 "I will scatter you like chaff
driven by the desert wind.
25 This is your lot,
the portion I have decreed for you,"
declares the LORD,
"because you have forgotten me
and trusted in false gods.
26 I will pull up your skirts over your face
that your shame may be seen—
27 your adulteries and lustful neighings,
your shameless prostitution!
I have seen your detestable acts
on the hills and in the fields.
Woe to you, O Jerusalem!
How long will you be unclean?"

Drought, Famine, Sword

14 This is the word of the LORD to Jeremiah concerning the drought:

2 "Judah mourns,
her cities languish;
they wail for the land,
and a cry goes up from Jerusalem.
3 The nobles send their servants for water;
they go to the cisterns
but find no water.
They return with their jars unfilled;
dismayed and despairing,
they cover their heads.
4 The ground is cracked
because there is no rain in the land;
the farmers are dismayed
and cover their heads.
5 Even the doe in the field
deserts her newborn fawn
because there is no grass.
6 Wild donkeys stand on the barren heights
and pant like jackals;
their eyesight fails
for lack of pasture."

7 Although our sins testify against us,
O LORD, do something for the sake of
your name.
For our backsliding is great;
we have sinned against you.
8 O Hope of Israel,
its Savior in times of distress,
why are you like a stranger in the land,
like a traveler who stays only a night?
9 Why are you like a man taken by surprise,
like a warrior powerless to save?
You are among us, O LORD,
and we bear your name;
do not forsake us!

10 This is what the LORD says about this people:

"They greatly love to wander;
they do not restrain their feet.
So the LORD does not accept them;
he will now remember their wickedness
and punish them for their sins."

[a] 23 Hebrew *Cushite* (probably a person from the upper Nile region)

[11]Then the LORD said to me, "Do not pray
for the well-being of this people. [12]Although
they fast, I will not listen to their cry; though
they offer burnt offerings and grain offerings,
I will not accept them. Instead, I will destroy
them with the sword, famine and plague."

[13]But I said, "Ah, Sovereign LORD, the
prophets keep telling them, 'You will not see
the sword or suffer famine. Indeed, I will give
you lasting peace in this place.' "

[14]Then the LORD said to me, "The prophets
are prophesying lies in my name. I have not sent
them or appointed them or spoken to them.
They are prophesying to you false visions, divinations, idolatries[a] and the delusions of their
own minds. [15]Therefore, this is what the LORD
says about the prophets who are prophesying in
my name: I did not send them, yet they are saying, 'No sword or famine will touch this land.'
Those same prophets will perish by sword and
famine. [16]And the people they are prophesying
to will be thrown out into the streets of Jerusalem because of the famine and sword. There
will be no one to bury them or their wives,
their sons or their daughters. I will pour out on
them the calamity they deserve.

[17]"Speak this word to them:

" 'Let my eyes overflow with tears
night and day without ceasing;
for my virgin daughter—my people—
has suffered a grievous wound,
a crushing blow.
[18]If I go into the country,
I see those slain by the sword;
if I go into the city,
I see the ravages of famine.
Both prophet and priest
have gone to a land they know not.' "

[19]Have you rejected Judah completely?
Do you despise Zion?
Why have you afflicted us
so that we cannot be healed?
We hoped for peace
but no good has come,
for a time of healing
but there is only terror.
[20]O LORD, we acknowledge our wickedness
and the guilt of our fathers;
we have indeed sinned against you.
[21]For the sake of your name do not despise
us;
do not dishonor your glorious throne.
Remember your covenant with us
and do not break it.
[22]Do any of the worthless idols of the
nations bring rain?
Do the skies themselves send down
showers?
No, it is you, O LORD our God.
Therefore our hope is in you,
for you are the one who does all this.

15 Then the LORD said to me: "Even if Moses and Samuel were to stand before me,
my heart would not go out to this people. Send them away from my presence! Let
them go! [2]And if they ask you, 'Where shall we
go?' tell them, 'This is what the LORD says:

" 'Those destined for death, to death;
those for the sword, to the sword;
those for starvation, to starvation;
those for captivity, to captivity.'

[3]"I will send four kinds of destroyers against
them," declares the LORD, "the sword to kill
and the dogs to drag away and the birds of
the air and the beasts of the earth to devour
and destroy. [4]I will make them abhorrent to
all the kingdoms of the earth because of what
Manasseh son of Hezekiah king of Judah did
in Jerusalem.

[5]"Who will have pity on you, O Jerusalem?
Who will mourn for you?
Who will stop to ask how you are?
[6]You have rejected me," declares the LORD.
"You keep on backsliding.
So I will lay hands on you and destroy
you;
I can no longer show compassion.
[7]I will winnow them with a winnowing
fork
at the city gates of the land.
I will bring bereavement and destruction
on my people,
for they have not changed their ways.
[8]I will make their widows more numerous
than the sand of the sea.
At midday I will bring a destroyer
against the mothers of their young
men;
suddenly I will bring down on them
anguish and terror.
[9]The mother of seven will grow faint
and breathe her last.
Her sun will set while it is still day;
she will be disgraced and humiliated.
I will put the survivors to the sword
before their enemies,"
declares the LORD.

[a] 14 Or *visions, worthless divinations*

10 Alas, my mother, that you gave me birth,
a man with whom the whole land
strives and contends!
I have neither lent nor borrowed,
yet everyone curses me.

11 The LORD said,

"Surely I will deliver you for a good
purpose;
surely I will make your enemies plead
with you
in times of disaster and times of
distress.
12 "Can a man break iron—
iron from the north—or bronze?
13 Your wealth and your treasures
I will give as plunder, without charge,
because of all your sins
throughout your country.
14 I will enslave you to your enemies
in[a] a land you do not know,
for my anger will kindle a fire
that will burn against you."

15 You understand, O LORD;
remember me and care for me.
Avenge me on my persecutors.
You are long-suffering—do not take me
away;
think of how I suffer reproach for your
sake.
16 When your words came, I ate them;
they were my joy and my heart's
delight,
for I bear your name,
O LORD God Almighty.
17 I never sat in the company of revelers,
never made merry with them;
I sat alone because your hand was on me
and you had filled me with indignation.
18 Why is my pain unending
and my wound grievous and incurable?
Will you be to me like a deceptive brook,
like a spring that fails?

19 Therefore this is what the LORD says:

"If you repent, I will restore you
that you may serve me;
if you utter worthy, not worthless, words,
you will be my spokesman.
Let this people turn to you,
but you must not turn to them.
20 I will make you a wall to this people,
a fortified wall of bronze;
they will fight against you
but will not overcome you,
for I am with you
to rescue and save you,"
declares the LORD.
21 "I will save you from the hands of the
wicked
and redeem you from the grasp of the
cruel."

Day of Disaster

16 Then the word of the LORD came to me:
2 "You must not marry and have sons
or daughters in this place." 3 For this is
what the LORD says about the sons and daughters born in this land and about the women
who are their mothers and the men who are
their fathers: 4 "They will die of deadly diseases. They will not be mourned or buried but
will be like refuse lying on the ground. They
will perish by sword and famine, and their
dead bodies will become food for the birds of
the air and the beasts of the earth."
5 For this is what the LORD says: "Do not
enter a house where there is a funeral meal; do
not go to mourn or show sympathy, because
I have withdrawn my blessing, my love and
my pity from this people," declares the LORD.
6 "Both high and low will die in this land. They
will not be buried or mourned, and no one
will cut himself or shave his head for them.
7 No one will offer food to comfort those who
mourn for the dead—not even for a father or
a mother—nor will anyone give them a drink
to console them.
8 "And do not enter a house where there is
feasting and sit down to eat and drink. 9 For
this is what the LORD Almighty, the God of
Israel, says: Before your eyes and in your days
I will bring an end to the sounds of joy and
gladness and to the voices of bride and bridegroom in this place.
10 "When you tell these people all this and
they ask you, 'Why has the LORD decreed
such a great disaster against us? What wrong
have we done? What sin have we committed against the LORD our God?' 11 then say to
them, 'It is because your fathers forsook me,'
declares the LORD, 'and followed other gods
and served and worshiped them. They forsook
me and did not keep my law. 12 But you have
behaved more wickedly than your fathers. See
how each of you is following the stubbornness
of his evil heart instead of obeying me. 13 So
I will throw you out of this land into a land
neither you nor your fathers have known, and

[a] 14 Some Hebrew manuscripts, Septuagint and Syriac (see also Jer. 17:4); most Hebrew manuscripts *I will cause your enemies to bring you / into*

there you will serve other gods day and night,
for I will show you no favor.'
14"However, the days are coming," declares
the LORD, "when men will no longer say, 'As
surely as the LORD lives, who brought the Israelites up out of Egypt,' 15but they will say,
'As surely as the LORD lives, who brought the
Israelites up out of the land of the north and
out of all the countries where he had banished
them.' For I will restore them to the land I
gave their forefathers.
16"But now I will send for many fishermen," declares the LORD, "and they will catch
them. After that I will send for many hunt-
ers, and they will hunt them down on every
mountain and hill and from the crevices of the
rocks. 17My eyes are on all their ways; they are
not hidden from me, nor is their sin concealed
from my eyes. 18I will repay them double for
their wickedness and their sin, because they
have defiled my land with the lifeless forms
of their vile images and have filled my inheritance with their detestable idols."

19 O LORD, my strength and my fortress,
my refuge in time of distress,
to you the nations will come
from the ends of the earth and say,
"Our fathers possessed nothing but false gods,
worthless idols that did them no good.
20 Do men make their own gods?
Yes, but they are not gods!"

21 "Therefore I will teach them—
this time I will teach them
my power and might.
Then they will know
that my name is the LORD.

17 "Judah's sin is engraved with an iron tool,
inscribed with a flint point,
on the tablets of their hearts
and on the horns of their altars.
2 Even their children remember
their altars and Asherah poles[a]
beside the spreading trees
and on the high hills.
3 My mountain in the land
and your[b] wealth and all your treasures
I will give away as plunder,
together with your high places,
because of sin throughout your country.
4 Through your own fault you will lose
the inheritance I gave you.
I will enslave you to your enemies
in a land you do not know,
for you have kindled my anger,
and it will burn forever."

5This is what the LORD says:

"Cursed is the one who trusts in man,
who depends on flesh for his strength
and whose heart turns away from the LORD.
6 He will be like a bush in the wastelands;
he will not see prosperity when it comes.
He will dwell in the parched places of the desert,
in a salt land where no one lives.

7 "But blessed is the man who trusts in the LORD,
whose confidence is in him.
8 He will be like a tree planted by the water
that sends out its roots by the stream.
It does not fear when heat comes;
its leaves are always green.
It has no worries in a year of drought
and never fails to bear fruit."

9 The heart is deceitful above all things
and beyond cure.
Who can understand it?

10 "I the LORD search the heart
and examine the mind,
to reward a man according to his conduct,
according to what his deeds deserve."

11 Like a partridge that hatches eggs it did not lay
is the man who gains riches by unjust means.
When his life is half gone, they will desert him,
and in the end he will prove to be a fool.

12 A glorious throne, exalted from the beginning,
is the place of our sanctuary.
13 O LORD, the hope of Israel,
all who forsake you will be put to shame.
Those who turn away from you will be written in the dust
because they have forsaken the LORD,
the spring of living water.

14 Heal me, O LORD, and I will be healed;
save me and I will be saved,

[a] 2 That is, symbols of the goddess Asherah [b] 2,3 Or *hills / [3]and the mountains of the land. / Your*

PRESERVING OUR ASSETS

> **Cursed is the one . . . whose heart turns away from the LORD . . . But blessed is the man who trusts in the LORD.**
>
> — JEREMIAH 17:5,7

The island nation of Nauru is a tiny dot in the Pacific. It's just over eight square miles of heat and humidity almost directly on the equator. Whaling ships began stopping at the island in 1798. Captain John Fearn named the place Pleasant Island.

Nauru's subsequent history proved anything but pleasant. Deserters from the ships vied for control with the indigenous Micronesian and Polynesian peoples, and law and order melted as islanders traded food for alcohol and firearms from passing ships. A decade of bloodshed reduced the population to less than a thousand by 1888.

In 1900 Albert Ellis discovered that the island was essentially a big phosphorus rock. Within years the place became little more than a strip mine. The yield was enormous, but government and company corruption wasted most of the profits. When the minerals and money ran out, Nauru became a tax haven for corrupt businesses and nations, then a refugee detention center for Australia. "The Nauruans literally sold off their homeland for a pot of wealth, which is now lost," said a reporter.

Since the time of Esau, humans have displayed an eerie ability to trade their most priceless assets for temporary baubles. As Esau gave up his birthright for a pot of stew, so women and men today give up their bodies for late-night promises of love. Athletes invest in body-destroying drugs for a single headline on the sports page. Spouses fixate on the Internet late into the night, honoring images more than interaction with their mates.

Jeremiah wrote with prophetic sorrow about people in his country who traded their surety in Almighty God for the worthless altars and Asherah poles of false gods. Like the people of Nauru, they became like a withered bush in the wastelands through years of poor choices and loser deals. But there is hope, according to Jeremiah. When people and societies worship the true God and honor him with their lives, God will transform them from a withered bush into a well-watered, fruitful tree.

Good marriages, like good economies and productive orchards, take years to build. Though they too can be eroded and exploited and laid waste by poor choices, all is not lost. Like the children of Judah, Christian marriages can be turned around and restored if husbands and wives repent of their ways, ask forgiveness of the Lord, sink their roots deep into his promises and live according to his commands. As Jeremiah 17:8 says, "He will be like a tree planted by the water that . . . never fails to bear fruit."

—WAYNE BROUWER

let's *talk*

- ✦ What pictures and paintings hang on the walls of our home? What do they say about us and our priorities?
- ✦ What are some ways in which people sell themselves cheaply? What about us? How do we compromise our relationship? What are some danger points in our relationship?
- ✦ What habits can we begin or continue that will help paint a better picture of our relationship? How can we make that happen?

FOR YOUR NEXT DEVOTIONAL READING, TURN TO PAGE 852.

for you are the one I praise.
15 They keep saying to me,
"Where is the word of the LORD?
Let it now be fulfilled!"
16 I have not run away from being your
shepherd;
you know I have not desired the day of
despair.
What passes my lips is open before
you.
17 Do not be a terror to me;
you are my refuge in the day of
disaster.
18 Let my persecutors be put to shame,
but keep me from shame;
let them be terrified,
but keep me from terror.
Bring on them the day of disaster;
destroy them with double destruction.

Keeping the Sabbath Holy

19 This is what the LORD said to me: "Go
and stand at the gate of the people, through
which the kings of Judah go in and out; stand
also at all the other gates of Jerusalem. 20 Say
to them, 'Hear the word of the LORD, O kings
of Judah and all people of Judah and everyone
living in Jerusalem who come through these
gates. 21 This is what the LORD says: Be careful not to carry a load on the Sabbath day or
bring it through the gates of Jerusalem. 22 Do
not bring a load out of your houses or do any
work on the Sabbath, but keep the Sabbath
day holy, as I commanded your forefathers.
23 Yet they did not listen or pay attention; they
were stiff-necked and would not listen or respond to discipline. 24 But if you are careful
to obey me, declares the LORD, and bring no
load through the gates of this city on the Sabbath, but keep the Sabbath day holy by not
doing any work on it, 25 then kings who sit on
David's throne will come through the gates
of this city with their officials. They and their
officials will come riding in chariots and on
horses, accompanied by the men of Judah and
those living in Jerusalem, and this city will be
inhabited forever. 26 People will come from the
towns of Judah and the villages around Jerusalem, from the territory of Benjamin and the
western foothills, from the hill country and
the Negev, bringing burnt offerings and sacrifices, grain offerings, incense and thank offerings to the house of the LORD. 27 But if you
do not obey me to keep the Sabbath day holy
by not carrying any load as you come through
the gates of Jerusalem on the Sabbath day,
then I will kindle an unquenchable fire in the
gates of Jerusalem that will consume her fortresses.' "

At the Potter's House

18 This is the word that came to Jeremiah from the LORD: 2 "Go down to the
potter's house, and there I will give you
my message." 3 So I went down to the potter's
house, and I saw him working at the wheel.
4 But the pot he was shaping from the clay was
marred in his hands; so the potter formed it
into another pot, shaping it as seemed best to
him.

5 Then the word of the LORD came to me:
6 "O house of Israel, can I not do with you as
this potter does?" declares the LORD. "Like
clay in the hand of the potter, so are you in my
hand, O house of Israel. 7 If at any time I announce that a nation or kingdom is to be uprooted, torn down and destroyed, 8 and if that
nation I warned repents of its evil, then I will
relent and not inflict on it the disaster I had
planned. 9 And if at another time I announce
that a nation or kingdom is to be built up and
planted, 10 and if it does evil in my sight and
does not obey me, then I will reconsider the
good I had intended to do for it.

11 "Now therefore say to the people of Judah
and those living in Jerusalem, 'This is what the
LORD says: Look! I am preparing a disaster for
you and devising a plan against you. So turn
from your evil ways, each one of you, and reform your ways and your actions.' 12 But they
will reply, 'It's no use. We will continue with
our own plans; each of us will follow the stubbornness of his evil heart.' "

13 Therefore this is what the LORD says:

"Inquire among the nations:
Who has ever heard anything like this?
A most horrible thing has been done
by Virgin Israel.
14 Does the snow of Lebanon
ever vanish from its rocky slopes?
Do its cool waters from distant sources
ever cease to flow?[a]
15 Yet my people have forgotten me;
they burn incense to worthless idols,
which made them stumble in their ways
and in the ancient paths.
They made them walk in bypaths
and on roads not built up.
16 Their land will be laid waste,

---

a 14 The meaning of the Hebrew for this sentence is uncertain.

an object of lasting scorn;
all who pass by will be appalled
and will shake their heads.
17 Like a wind from the east,
I will scatter them before their
enemies;
I will show them my back and not my face
in the day of their disaster."

18 They said, "Come, let's make plans against
Jeremiah; for the teaching of the law by the
priest will not be lost, nor will counsel from
the wise, nor the word from the prophets. So
come, let's attack him with our tongues and
pay no attention to anything he says."

19 Listen to me, O LORD;
hear what my accusers are saying!
20 Should good be repaid with evil?
Yet they have dug a pit for me.
Remember that I stood before you
and spoke in their behalf
to turn your wrath away from them.
21 So give their children over to famine;
hand them over to the power of the
sword.
Let their wives be made childless and
widows;
let their men be put to death,
their young men slain by the sword in
battle.
22 Let a cry be heard from their houses
when you suddenly bring invaders
against them,
for they have dug a pit to capture me
and have hidden snares for my feet.
23 But you know, O LORD,
all their plots to kill me.
Do not forgive their crimes
or blot out their sins from your sight.
Let them be overthrown before you;
deal with them in the time of your
anger.

19 This is what the LORD says: "Go and buy
a clay jar from a potter. Take along some
of the elders of the people and of the
priests 2 and go out to the Valley of Ben Hinnom, near the entrance of the Potsherd Gate.
There proclaim the words I tell you, 3 and say,
'Hear the word of the LORD, O kings of Judah and people of Jerusalem. This is what
the LORD Almighty, the God of Israel, says:
Listen! I am going to bring a disaster on this
place that will make the ears of everyone who
hears of it tingle. 4 For they have forsaken me
and made this a place of foreign gods; they
have burned sacrifices in it to gods that neither
they nor their fathers nor the kings of Judah
ever knew, and they have filled this place with
the blood of the innocent. 5 They have built
the high places of Baal to burn their sons in
the fire as offerings to Baal—something I did
not command or mention, nor did it enter my
mind. 6 So beware, the days are coming, declares the LORD, when people will no longer
call this place Topheth or the Valley of Ben
Hinnom, but the Valley of Slaughter.

7 " 'In this place I will ruin [a] the plans of Judah and Jerusalem. I will make them fall by
the sword before their enemies, at the hands of
those who seek their lives, and I will give their
carcasses as food to the birds of the air and
the beasts of the earth. 8 I will devastate this
city and make it an object of scorn; all who
pass by will be appalled and will scoff because
of all its wounds. 9 I will make them eat the
flesh of their sons and daughters, and they will
eat one another's flesh during the stress of the
siege imposed on them by the enemies who
seek their lives.'

10 "Then break the jar while those who go
with you are watching, 11 and say to them,
'This is what the LORD Almighty says: I will
smash this nation and this city just as this potter's jar is smashed and cannot be repaired.
They will bury the dead in Topheth until there
is no more room. 12 This is what I will do to
this place and to those who live here, declares
the LORD. I will make this city like Topheth.
13 The houses in Jerusalem and those of the
kings of Judah will be defiled like this place,
Topheth—all the houses where they burned
incense on the roofs to all the starry hosts and
poured out drink offerings to other gods.' "

14 Jeremiah then returned from Topheth,
where the LORD had sent him to prophesy,
and stood in the court of the LORD's temple
and said to all the people, 15 "This is what the
LORD Almighty, the God of Israel, says: 'Listen! I am going to bring on this city and the
villages around it every disaster I pronounced
against them, because they were stiff-necked
and would not listen to my words.' "

Jeremiah and Pashhur

20 When the priest Pashhur son of Immer, the chief officer in the temple of
the LORD, heard Jeremiah prophesying
these things, 2 he had Jeremiah the prophet beaten and put in the stocks at the Upper

[a] 7 The Hebrew for *ruin* sounds like the Hebrew for *jar* (see verses 1 and 10).

18 Therefore this is what the LORD says about
Jehoiakim son of Josiah king of Judah:

"They will not mourn for him:
'Alas, my brother! Alas, my sister!'
They will not mourn for him:
'Alas, my master! Alas, his splendor!'
19 He will have the burial of a donkey—
dragged away and thrown
outside the gates of Jerusalem."

20 "Go up to Lebanon and cry out,
let your voice be heard in Bashan,
cry out from Abarim,
for all your allies are crushed.
21 I warned you when you felt secure,
but you said, 'I will not listen!'
This has been your way from your youth;
you have not obeyed me.
22 The wind will drive all your shepherds away,
and your allies will go into exile.
Then you will be ashamed and disgraced
because of all your wickedness.
23 You who live in 'Lebanon,[a]'
who are nestled in cedar buildings,
how you will groan when pangs come upon you,
pain like that of a woman in labor!

24 "As surely as I live," declares the LORD,
"even if you, Jehoiachin[b] son of Jehoiakim
king of Judah, were a signet ring on my right
hand, I would still pull you off. 25 I will hand
you over to those who seek your life, those you
fear—to Nebuchadnezzar king of Babylon
and to the Babylonians.[c] 26 I will hurl you and
the mother who gave you birth into another
country, where neither of you was born, and
there you both will die. 27 You will never come
back to the land you long to return to."

28 Is this man Jehoiachin a despised, broken pot,
an object no one wants?
Why will he and his children be hurled out,
cast into a land they do not know?
29 O land, land, land,
hear the word of the LORD!
30 This is what the LORD says:
"Record this man as if childless,
a man who will not prosper in his lifetime,
for none of his offspring will prosper,
none will sit on the throne of David
or rule anymore in Judah."

The Righteous Branch

23 "Woe to the shepherds who are destroying and scattering the sheep of my
pasture!" declares the LORD. 2 Therefore
this is what the LORD, the God of Israel, says
to the shepherds who tend my people: "Because you have scattered my flock and driv-
en them away and have not bestowed care on
them, I will bestow punishment on you for
the evil you have done," declares the LORD.
3 "I myself will gather the remnant of my flock
out of all the countries where I have driven
them and will bring them back to their pasture, where they will be fruitful and increase
in number. 4 I will place shepherds over them
who will tend them, and they will no longer
be afraid or terrified, nor will any be missing,"
declares the LORD.

5 "The days are coming," declares the LORD,
"when I will raise up to David[d] a righteous Branch,
a King who will reign wisely
and do what is just and right in the land.
6 In his days Judah will be saved
and Israel will live in safety.
This is the name by which he will be called:
The LORD Our Righteousness.

7 "So then, the days are coming," declares the
LORD, "when people will no longer say, 'As
surely as the LORD lives, who brought the Israelites up out of Egypt,' 8 but they will say,
'As surely as the LORD lives, who brought the
descendants of Israel up out of the land of the
north and out of all the countries where he
had banished them.' Then they will live in
their own land."

Lying Prophets

9 Concerning the prophets:

My heart is broken within me;
all my bones tremble.
I am like a drunken man,
like a man overcome by wine,
because of the LORD
and his holy words.
10 The land is full of adulterers;
because of the curse[e] the land lies parched[f]
and the pastures in the desert are withered.

[a] 23 That is, the palace in Jerusalem (see 1 Kings 7:2) [b] 24 Hebrew *Coniah,* a variant of *Jehoiachin;* also in verse 28
[c] 25 Or *Chaldeans* [d] 5 Or *up from David's line* [e] 10 Or *because of these things* [f] 10 Or *land mourns*

The ⌞prophets⌟ follow an evil course
and use their power unjustly.

11 "Both prophet and priest are godless;
even in my temple I find their wickedness,"
declares the LORD.
12 "Therefore their path will become slippery;
they will be banished to darkness
and there they will fall.
I will bring disaster on them
in the year they are punished,"
declares the LORD.

13 "Among the prophets of Samaria
I saw this repulsive thing:
They prophesied by Baal
and led my people Israel astray.
14 And among the prophets of Jerusalem
I have seen something horrible:
They commit adultery and live a lie.
They strengthen the hands of evildoers,
so that no one turns from his wickedness.
They are all like Sodom to me;
the people of Jerusalem are like Gomorrah."

15 Therefore, this is what the LORD Almighty says concerning the prophets:

"I will make them eat bitter food
and drink poisoned water,
because from the prophets of Jerusalem
ungodliness has spread throughout the land."

16 This is what the LORD Almighty says:

"Do not listen to what the prophets are prophesying to you;
they fill you with false hopes.
They speak visions from their own minds,
not from the mouth of the LORD.
17 They keep saying to those who despise me,
'The LORD says: You will have peace.'
And to all who follow the stubbornness of their hearts
they say, 'No harm will come to you.'
18 But which of them has stood in the council of the LORD
to see or to hear his word?
Who has listened and heard his word?
19 See, the storm of the LORD
will burst out in wrath,
a whirlwind swirling down
on the heads of the wicked.
20 The anger of the LORD will not turn back
until he fully accomplishes
the purposes of his heart.
In days to come
you will understand it clearly.
21 I did not send these prophets,
yet they have run with their message;
I did not speak to them,
yet they have prophesied.
22 But if they had stood in my council,
they would have proclaimed my words to my people
and would have turned them from their evil ways
and from their evil deeds.

23 "Am I only a God nearby,"
declares the LORD,
"and not a God far away?
24 Can anyone hide in secret places
so that I cannot see him?"
declares the LORD.
"Do not I fill heaven and earth?"
declares the LORD.

25 "I have heard what the prophets say who
prophesy lies in my name. They say, 'I had a
dream! I had a dream!' 26 How long will this
continue in the hearts of these lying prophets, who prophesy the delusions of their own
minds? 27 They think the dreams they tell one
another will make my people forget my name,
just as their fathers forgot my name through
Baal worship. 28 Let the prophet who has a
dream tell his dream, but let the one who has
my word speak it faithfully. For what has straw
to do with grain?" declares the LORD. 29 "Is not
my word like fire," declares the LORD, "and
like a hammer that breaks a rock in pieces?

30 "Therefore," declares the LORD, "I am
against the prophets who steal from one another words supposedly from me. 31 Yes," declares the LORD, "I am against the prophets
who wag their own tongues and yet declare,
'The LORD declares.' 32 Indeed, I am against
those who prophesy false dreams," declares
the LORD. "They tell them and lead my people astray with their reckless lies, yet I did not
send or appoint them. They do not benefit
these people in the least," declares the LORD.

False Oracles and False Prophets

33 "When these people, or a prophet or a
priest, ask you, 'What is the oracle[a] of the
LORD?' say to them, 'What oracle?[b] I will for-

[a] 33 Or *burden* (see Septuagint and Vulgate) [b] 33 Hebrew; Septuagint and Vulgate '*You are the burden.* (The Hebrew for *oracle* and *burden* is the same.)

sake you, declares the LORD.' 34If a prophet
or a priest or anyone else claims, 'This is the
oracle of the LORD,' I will punish that man
and his household. 35This is what each of
you keeps on saying to his friend or relative:
'What is the LORD's answer?' or 'What has the
LORD spoken?' 36But you must not mention
'the oracle of the LORD' again, because every
man's own word becomes his oracle and so
you distort the words of the living God, the
LORD Almighty, our God. 37This is what you
keep saying to a prophet: 'What is the LORD's
answer to you?' or 'What has the LORD spoken?' 38Although you claim, 'This is the oracle of the LORD,' this is what the LORD says:
You used the words, 'This is the oracle of the
LORD,' even though I told you that you must
not claim, 'This is the oracle of the LORD.'
39Therefore, I will surely forget you and cast
you out of my presence along with the city
I gave to you and your fathers. 40I will bring
upon you everlasting disgrace—everlasting
shame that will not be forgotten."

Two Baskets of Figs

24 After Jehoiachin[a] son of Jehoiakim king
of Judah and the officials, the craftsmen and the artisans of Judah were carried into exile from Jerusalem to Babylon by
Nebuchadnezzar king of Babylon, the LORD
showed me two baskets of figs placed in front
of the temple of the LORD. 2One basket had
very good figs, like those that ripen early; the
other basket had very poor figs, so bad they
could not be eaten.

3Then the LORD asked me, "What do you
see, Jeremiah?"

"Figs," I answered. "The good ones are very
good, but the poor ones are so bad they cannot be eaten."

4Then the word of the LORD came to me:
5"This is what the LORD, the God of Israel,
says: 'Like these good figs, I regard as good the
exiles from Judah, whom I sent away from this
place to the land of the Babylonians.[b] 6My
eyes will watch over them for their good, and
I will bring them back to this land. I will build
them up and not tear them down; I will plant
them and not uproot them. 7I will give them
a heart to know me, that I am the LORD. They
will be my people, and I will be their God, for
they will return to me with all their heart.

8" 'But like the poor figs, which are so bad
they cannot be eaten,' says the LORD, 'so will
I deal with Zedekiah king of Judah, his officials and the survivors from Jerusalem, whether they remain in this land or live in Egypt.
9I will make them abhorrent and an offense
to all the kingdoms of the earth, a reproach
and a byword, an object of ridicule and cursing, wherever I banish them. 10I will send the
sword, famine and plague against them until they are destroyed from the land I gave to
them and their fathers.' "

Seventy Years of Captivity

25 The word came to Jeremiah concerning all the people of Judah in the fourth
year of Jehoiakim son of Josiah king
of Judah, which was the first year of Nebuchadnezzar king of Babylon. 2So Jeremiah the
prophet said to all the people of Judah and to
all those living in Jerusalem: 3For twenty-three
years—from the thirteenth year of Josiah son
of Amon king of Judah until this very day—
the word of the LORD has come to me and I
have spoken to you again and again, but you
have not listened.

4And though the LORD has sent all his servants the prophets to you again and again, you
have not listened or paid any attention. 5They
said, "Turn now, each of you, from your evil
ways and your evil practices, and you can stay
in the land the LORD gave to you and your fathers for ever and ever. 6Do not follow other
gods to serve and worship them; do not provoke me to anger with what your hands have
made. Then I will not harm you."

7"But you did not listen to me," declares
the LORD, "and you have provoked me with
what your hands have made, and you have
brought harm to yourselves."

8Therefore the LORD Almighty says this:
"Because you have not listened to my words,
9I will summon all the peoples of the north
and my servant Nebuchadnezzar king of Babylon," declares the LORD, "and I will bring
them against this land and its inhabitants
and against all the surrounding nations. I will
completely destroy[c] them and make them an
object of horror and scorn, and an everlasting
ruin. 10I will banish from them the sounds of
joy and gladness, the voices of bride and bridegroom, the sound of millstones and the light
of the lamp. 11This whole country will become
a desolate wasteland, and these nations will
serve the king of Babylon seventy years.

12"But when the seventy years are fulfilled,

[a] *1* Hebrew *Jeconiah,* a variant of *Jehoiachin* [b] *5* Or *Chaldeans* [c] *9* The Hebrew term refers to the irrevocable giving over of things or persons to the LORD, often by totally destroying them.

I will punish the king of Babylon and his nation, the land of the Babylonians,[a] for their
guilt," declares the LORD, "and will make it
desolate forever. 13I will bring upon that land
all the things I have spoken against it, all that
are written in this book and prophesied by
Jeremiah against all the nations. 14They themselves will be enslaved by many nations and
great kings; I will repay them according to
their deeds and the work of their hands."

The Cup of God's Wrath

15This is what the LORD, the God of Israel, said to me: "Take from my hand this cup
filled with the wine of my wrath and make
all the nations to whom I send you drink it.
16When they drink it, they will stagger and go
mad because of the sword I will send among
them."

17So I took the cup from the LORD's hand
and made all the nations to whom he sent me
drink it: 18Jerusalem and the towns of Judah,
its kings and officials, to make them a ruin
and an object of horror and scorn and cursing,
as they are today; 19Pharaoh king of Egypt,
his attendants, his officials and all his people,
20and all the foreign people there; all the kings
of Uz; all the kings of the Philistines (those
of Ashkelon, Gaza, Ekron, and the people left
at Ashdod); 21Edom, Moab and Ammon; 22all
the kings of Tyre and Sidon; the kings of the
coastlands across the sea; 23Dedan, Tema, Buz
and all who are in distant places[b]; 24all the
kings of Arabia and all the kings of the foreign
people who live in the desert; 25all the kings
of Zimri, Elam and Media; 26and all the kings
of the north, near and far, one after the other—all the kingdoms on the face of the earth.
And after all of them, the king of Sheshach[c]
will drink it too.

27"Then tell them, 'This is what the LORD
Almighty, the God of Israel, says: Drink, get
drunk and vomit, and fall to rise no more because of the sword I will send among you.'
28But if they refuse to take the cup from your
hand and drink, tell them, 'This is what the
LORD Almighty says: You must drink it! 29See,
I am beginning to bring disaster on the city
that bears my Name, and will you indeed go
unpunished? You will not go unpunished, for
I am calling down a sword upon all who live
on the earth, declares the LORD Almighty.'

30"Now prophesy all these words against
them and say to them:

"'The LORD will roar from on high;
he will thunder from his holy dwelling
and roar mightily against his land.
He will shout like those who tread the
grapes,
shout against all who live on the earth.
31The tumult will resound to the ends of the
earth,
for the LORD will bring charges against
the nations;
he will bring judgment on all mankind
and put the wicked to the sword,'"
declares the LORD.

32This is what the LORD Almighty says:

"Look! Disaster is spreading
from nation to nation;
a mighty storm is rising
from the ends of the earth."

33At that time those slain by the LORD will be
everywhere—from one end of the earth to the
other. They will not be mourned or gathered
up or buried, but will be like refuse lying on
the ground.

34Weep and wail, you shepherds;
roll in the dust, you leaders of the flock.
For your time to be slaughtered has come;
you will fall and be shattered like fine
pottery.
35The shepherds will have nowhere to flee,
the leaders of the flock no place to
escape.
36Hear the cry of the shepherds,
the wailing of the leaders of the flock,
for the LORD is destroying their pasture.
37The peaceful meadows will be laid waste
because of the fierce anger of the LORD.
38Like a lion he will leave his lair,
and their land will become desolate
because of the sword[d] of the oppressor
and because of the LORD's fierce anger.

Jeremiah Threatened With Death

26 Early in the reign of Jehoiakim son of Josiah king of Judah, this word came from
the LORD: 2"This is what the LORD says:
Stand in the courtyard of the LORD's house
and speak to all the people of the towns of Judah who come to worship in the house of the
LORD. Tell them everything I command you;
do not omit a word. 3Perhaps they will listen
and each will turn from his evil way. Then I
will relent and not bring on them the disaster

[a] 12 Or *Chaldeans* [b] 23 Or *who clip the hair by their foreheads* [c] 26 *Sheshach* is a cryptogram for Babylon. [d] 38 Some Hebrew manuscripts and Septuagint (see also Jer. 46:16 and 50:16); most Hebrew manuscripts *anger*

I was planning because of the evil they have done. [4]Say to them, 'This is what the LORD says: If you do not listen to me and follow my law, which I have set before you, [5]and if you do not listen to the words of my servants the prophets, whom I have sent to you again and again (though you have not listened), [6]then I will make this house like Shiloh and this city an object of cursing among all the nations of the earth.' "

[7]The priests, the prophets and all the people heard Jeremiah speak these words in the house of the LORD. [8]But as soon as Jeremiah finished telling all the people everything the LORD had commanded him to say, the priests, the prophets and all the people seized him and said, "You must die! [9]Why do you prophesy in the LORD's name that this house will be like Shiloh and this city will be desolate and deserted?" And all the people crowded around Jeremiah in the house of the LORD.

[10]When the officials of Judah heard about these things, they went up from the royal palace to the house of the LORD and took their places at the entrance of the New Gate of the LORD's house. [11]Then the priests and the prophets said to the officials and all the people, "This man should be sentenced to death because he has prophesied against this city. You have heard it with your own ears!"

[12]Then Jeremiah said to all the officials and all the people: "The LORD sent me to prophesy against this house and this city all the things you have heard. [13]Now reform your ways and your actions and obey the LORD your God. Then the LORD will relent and not bring the disaster he has pronounced against you. [14]As for me, I am in your hands; do with me whatever you think is good and right. [15]Be assured, however, that if you put me to death, you will bring the guilt of innocent blood on yourselves and on this city and on those who live in it, for in truth the LORD has sent me to you to speak all these words in your hearing."

[16]Then the officials and all the people said to the priests and the prophets, "This man should not be sentenced to death! He has spoken to us in the name of the LORD our God."

[17]Some of the elders of the land stepped forward and said to the entire assembly of people, [18]"Micah of Moresheth prophesied in the days of Hezekiah king of Judah. He told all the people of Judah, 'This is what the LORD Almighty says:

" 'Zion will be plowed like a field,
Jerusalem will become a heap of rubble,
the temple hill a mound overgrown
with thickets.' [a]

[19]"Did Hezekiah king of Judah or anyone else in Judah put him to death? Did not Hezekiah fear the LORD and seek his favor? And did not the LORD relent, so that he did not bring the disaster he pronounced against them? We are about to bring a terrible disaster on ourselves!"

[20](Now Uriah son of Shemaiah from Kiriath Jearim was another man who prophesied in the name of the LORD; he prophesied the same things against this city and this land as Jeremiah did. [21]When King Jehoiakim and all his officers and officials heard his words, the king sought to put him to death. But Uriah heard of it and fled in fear to Egypt. [22]King Jehoiakim, however, sent Elnathan son of Acbor to Egypt, along with some other men. [23]They brought Uriah out of Egypt and took him to King Jehoiakim, who had him struck down with a sword and his body thrown into the burial place of the common people.)

[24]Furthermore, Ahikam son of Shaphan supported Jeremiah, and so he was not handed over to the people to be put to death.

Judah to Serve Nebuchadnezzar

27 Early in the reign of Zedekiah [b] son of Josiah king of Judah, this word came to Jeremiah from the LORD: [2]This is what the LORD said to me: "Make a yoke out of straps and crossbars and put it on your neck. [3]Then send word to the kings of Edom, Moab, Ammon, Tyre and Sidon through the envoys who have come to Jerusalem to Zedekiah king of Judah. [4]Give them a message for their masters and say, 'This is what the LORD Almighty, the God of Israel, says: "Tell this to your masters: [5]With my great power and outstretched arm I made the earth and its people and the animals that are on it, and I give it to anyone I please. [6]Now I will hand all your countries over to my servant Nebuchadnezzar king of Babylon; I will make even the wild animals subject to him. [7]All nations will serve him and his son and his grandson until the time for his land comes; then many nations and great kings will subjugate him.

a *18* Micah 3:12 *b* *1* A few Hebrew manuscripts and Syriac (see also Jer. 27:3,12 and 28:1); most Hebrew manuscripts *Jehoiakim* (Most Septuagint manuscripts do not have this verse.)

8" ' "If, however, any nation or kingdom will not serve Nebuchadnezzar king of Babylon or bow its neck under his yoke, I will punish that nation with the sword, famine and plague, declares the LORD, until I destroy it by his hand. 9So do not listen to your prophets, your diviners, your interpreters of dreams, your mediums or your sorcerers who tell you, 'You will not serve the king of Babylon.' 10They prophesy lies to you that will only serve to remove you far from your lands; I will banish you and you will perish. 11But if any nation will bow its neck under the yoke of the king of Babylon and serve him, I will let that nation remain in its own land to till it and to live there, declares the LORD." ' "

12I gave the same message to Zedekiah king of Judah. I said, "Bow your neck under the yoke of the king of Babylon; serve him and his people, and you will live. 13Why will you and your people die by the sword, famine and plague with which the LORD has threatened any nation that will not serve the king of Babylon? 14Do not listen to the words of the prophets who say to you, 'You will not serve the king of Babylon,' for they are prophesying lies to you. 15'I have not sent them,' declares the LORD. 'They are prophesying lies in my name. Therefore, I will banish you and you will perish, both you and the prophets who prophesy to you.' "

16Then I said to the priests and all these people, "This is what the LORD says: Do not listen to the prophets who say, 'Very soon now the articles from the LORD's house will be brought back from Babylon.' They are prophesying lies to you. 17Do not listen to them. Serve the king of Babylon, and you will live. Why should this city become a ruin? 18If they are prophets and have the word of the LORD, let them plead with the LORD Almighty that the furnishings remaining in the house of the LORD and in the palace of the king of Judah and in Jerusalem not be taken to Babylon. 19For this is what the LORD Almighty says about the pillars, the Sea, the movable stands and the other furnishings that are left in this city, 20which Nebuchadnezzar king of Babylon did not take away when he carried Jehoiachin[a] son of Jehoiakim king of Judah into exile from Jerusalem to Babylon, along with all the nobles of Judah and Jerusalem— 21yes, this is what the LORD Almighty, the God of Israel, says about the things that are left in the house of the LORD and in the palace of the king of Judah and in Jerusalem: 22'They will be taken to Babylon and there they will remain until the day I come for them,' declares the LORD. 'Then I will bring them back and restore them to this place.' "

The False Prophet Hananiah

28 In the fifth month of that same year, the fourth year, early in the reign of Zedekiah king of Judah, the prophet Hananiah son of Azzur, who was from Gibeon, said to me in the house of the LORD in the presence of the priests and all the people: 2"This is what the LORD Almighty, the God of Israel, says: 'I will break the yoke of the king of Babylon. 3Within two years I will bring back to this place all the articles of the LORD's house that Nebuchadnezzar king of Babylon removed from here and took to Babylon. 4I will also bring back to this place Jehoiachin[a] son of Jehoiakim king of Judah and all the other exiles from Judah who went to Babylon,' declares the LORD, 'for I will break the yoke of the king of Babylon.' "

5Then the prophet Jeremiah replied to the prophet Hananiah before the priests and all the people who were standing in the house of the LORD. 6He said, "Amen! May the LORD do so! May the LORD fulfill the words you have prophesied by bringing the articles of the LORD's house and all the exiles back to this place from Babylon. 7Nevertheless, listen to what I have to say in your hearing and in the hearing of all the people: 8From early times the prophets who preceded you and me have prophesied war, disaster and plague against many countries and great kingdoms. 9But the prophet who prophesies peace will be recognized as one truly sent by the LORD only if his prediction comes true."

10Then the prophet Hananiah took the yoke off the neck of the prophet Jeremiah and broke it, 11and he said before all the people, "This is what the LORD says: 'In the same way will I break the yoke of Nebuchadnezzar king of Babylon off the neck of all the nations within two years.' " At this, the prophet Jeremiah went on his way.

12Shortly after the prophet Hananiah had broken the yoke off the neck of the prophet Jeremiah, the word of the LORD came to Jeremiah: 13"Go and tell Hananiah, 'This is what the LORD says: You have broken a wooden yoke, but in its place you will get a yoke of iron. 14This is what the LORD Almighty, the

[a] 20,4 Hebrew *Jeconiah,* a variant of *Jehoiachin*

God of Israel, says: I will put an iron yoke on
the necks of all these nations to make them
serve Nebuchadnezzar king of Babylon, and
they will serve him. I will even give him control over the wild animals.' "
15Then the prophet Jeremiah said to Hananiah the prophet, "Listen, Hananiah! The
LORD has not sent you, yet you have persuaded this nation to trust in lies. 16Therefore,
this is what the LORD says: 'I am about to remove you from the face of the earth. This very
year you are going to die, because you have
preached rebellion against the LORD.' "
17In the seventh month of that same year,
Hananiah the prophet died.

A Letter to the Exiles

29 This is the text of the letter that the
prophet Jeremiah sent from Jerusalem
to the surviving elders among the exiles and to the priests, the prophets and all the
other people Nebuchadnezzar had carried into
exile from Jerusalem to Babylon. 2(This was
after King Jehoiachin[a] and the queen mother,
the court officials and the leaders of Judah and
Jerusalem, the craftsmen and the artisans had
gone into exile from Jerusalem.) 3He entrusted the letter to Elasah son of Shaphan and to
Gemariah son of Hilkiah, whom Zedekiah
king of Judah sent to King Nebuchadnezzar
in Babylon. It said:

4This is what the LORD Almighty, the
God of Israel, says to all those I carried
into exile from Jerusalem to Babylon:
5"Build houses and settle down; plant gardens and eat what they produce. 6Marry
and have sons and daughters; find wives
for your sons and give your daughters in
marriage, so that they too may have sons
and daughters. Increase in number there;
do not decrease. 7Also, seek the peace
and prosperity of the city to which I have
carried you into exile. Pray to the LORD
for it, because if it prospers, you too will
prosper." 8Yes, this is what the LORD Almighty, the God of Israel, says: "Do not
let the prophets and diviners among you
deceive you. Do not listen to the dreams
you encourage them to have. 9They are
prophesying lies to you in my name. I
have not sent them," declares the LORD.
10This is what the LORD says: "When
seventy years are completed for Babylon,
I will come to you and fulfill my gracious
promise to bring you back to this place.
11For I know the plans I have for you,"
declares the LORD, "plans to prosper you
and not to harm you, plans to give you
hope and a future. 12Then you will call
upon me and come and pray to me, and I
will listen to you. 13You will seek me and
find me when you seek me with all your
heart. 14I will be found by you," declares
the LORD, "and will bring you back from
captivity.[b] I will gather you from all the
nations and places where I have banished
you," declares the LORD, "and will bring
you back to the place from which I carried you into exile."
15You may say, "The LORD has raised
up prophets for us in Babylon," 16but this
is what the LORD says about the king who
sits on David's throne and all the people
who remain in this city, your countrymen
who did not go with you into exile—
17yes, this is what the LORD Almighty
says: "I will send the sword, famine and
plague against them and I will make them
like poor figs that are so bad they cannot
be eaten. 18I will pursue them with the
sword, famine and plague and will make
them abhorrent to all the kingdoms of the
earth and an object of cursing and horror,
of scorn and reproach, among all the nations where I drive them. 19For they have
not listened to my words," declares the
LORD, "words that I sent to them again
and again by my servants the prophets.
And you exiles have not listened either,"
declares the LORD.
20Therefore, hear the word of the
LORD, all you exiles whom I have sent
away from Jerusalem to Babylon. 21This
is what the LORD Almighty, the God of
Israel, says about Ahab son of Kolaiah
and Zedekiah son of Maaseiah, who are
prophesying lies to you in my name: "I
will hand them over to Nebuchadnezzar
king of Babylon, and he will put them to
death before your very eyes. 22Because of
them, all the exiles from Judah who are
in Babylon will use this curse: 'The LORD
treat you like Zedekiah and Ahab, whom
the king of Babylon burned in the fire.'
23For they have done outrageous things
in Israel; they have committed adultery
with their neighbors' wives and in my
name have spoken lies, which I did not
tell them to do. I know it and am a witness to it," declares the LORD.

---

[a] 2 Hebrew *Jeconiah,* a variant of *Jehoiachin* [b] 14 Or *will restore your fortunes*

RULES FOR RELOCATION

My first congregation consisted mostly of immigrants who had left the Netherlands after World War II, sensing that their homeland was no longer the world they'd been born into and loved as children. Foreign occupation, betrayal within communities, collapse of the economy and even religious infighting within churches had turned everything upside down. Glowing promises of a better life lured them to Canada.

By the time I was called to be their pastor, most of the immigrants who had arrived penniless had prospered. But wealth had come at a price. Families were torn apart; some children hadn't seen their parents in Holland for decades. Almost every household had lost a child to illness or a farm accident. And there were heartbreaking reports of children who had given up the faith and left the church.

Jeremiah addressed a similar situation regarding a group of Israelites who had been taken as captives to Babylon in 597 B.C. The word to them from the Lord, the prophet said, was to live as though their situation was permanent, not temporary. Since God had shown Jeremiah that the whole nation was about to be destroyed (which indeed came to pass in 586), these exiles were to hunker down for the long haul. They should build houses and plant gardens; they should marry and encourage their children to marry.

Jeremiah's letter to the exiles is still good advice today. In North America, the average person experiences seven career changes and 12 moves in his or her adult lifetime. With such a mobile lifestyle, it's easy to lose religious anchors, family life or even marriage commitments.

While we shift vagabond-like through the changes of our years, we may think that our old ways, culture, customs and religion don't match our hopes and dreams in our new location. Yet we need to remember that we are all exiles, pilgrims in a foreign land. And wherever we are, God tells us to make the most of our experience, to be full, engaged members of our community and to put our whole hearts into our world.

So move, relocate, take a job transfer, if you will. But when you do, settle down and make the most of it. No matter where you end up, whether it's a town of friendly neighbors or one of hard-to-get-to-know strangers, pray for your city or town. Pray for the people next door. Get to know them and pray for their peace and prosperity.

"Build houses and settle down; plant gardens and eat what they produce. Marry and have sons and daughters; . . . Also, seek the peace and prosperity of the city to which I have carried you into exile. Pray to the LORD for it, because if it prospers, you too will prosper."

— JEREMIAH 29:5–7

let's talk

- Do we feel like settlers, exiles or nomads where we are? What have been some of the results of our moves and relocations? What traditions of faith and family do we carry with us and which have we discarded?
- What have we lost? Who have we left behind? What do we need to recover?
- What have we gained? Where have we made an impact? How have we spread peace?

—WAYNE BROUWER

FOR YOUR NEXT DEVOTIONAL READING, TURN TO PAGE 855.

Message to Shemaiah

[24]Tell Shemaiah the Nehelamite, [25]"This
is what the LORD Almighty, the God of Israel, says: You sent letters in your own name to
all the people in Jerusalem, to Zephaniah son
of Maaseiah the priest, and to all the other
priests. You said to Zephaniah, [26]'The LORD
has appointed you priest in place of Jehoiada to be in charge of the house of the LORD;
you should put any madman who acts like a
prophet into the stocks and neck-irons. [27]So
why have you not reprimanded Jeremiah from
Anathoth, who poses as a prophet among you?
[28]He has sent this message to us in Babylon:
It will be a long time. Therefore build houses
and settle down; plant gardens and eat what
they produce.' "

[29]Zephaniah the priest, however, read the
letter to Jeremiah the prophet. [30]Then the
word of the LORD came to Jeremiah: [31]"Send
this message to all the exiles: 'This is what the
LORD says about Shemaiah the Nehelamite:
Because Shemaiah has prophesied to you,
even though I did not send him, and has led
you to believe a lie, [32]this is what the LORD
says: I will surely punish Shemaiah the Nehelamite and his descendants. He will have no
one left among this people, nor will he see the
good things I will do for my people, declares
the LORD, because he has preached rebellion
against me.' "

Restoration of Israel

30 This is the word that came to Jeremiah from the LORD: [2]"This is what the
LORD, the God of Israel, says: 'Write
in a book all the words I have spoken to you.
[3]The days are coming,' declares the LORD,
'when I will bring my people Israel and Judah
back from captivity[a] and restore them to the
land I gave their forefathers to possess,' says
the LORD."

[4]These are the words the LORD spoke concerning Israel and Judah: [5]"This is what the
LORD says:

" 'Cries of fear are heard—
terror, not peace.
[6]Ask and see:
Can a man bear children?
Then why do I see every strong man
with his hands on his stomach like a
woman in labor,
every face turned deathly pale?
[7]How awful that day will be!
None will be like it.
It will be a time of trouble for Jacob,
but he will be saved out of it.

[8]" 'In that day,' declares the LORD
Almighty,
'I will break the yoke off their necks
and will tear off their bonds;
no longer will foreigners enslave them.
[9]Instead, they will serve the LORD their
God
and David their king,
whom I will raise up for them.

[10]" 'So do not fear, O Jacob my servant;
do not be dismayed, O Israel,'
declares the LORD.
'I will surely save you out of a distant
place,
your descendants from the land of their
exile.
Jacob will again have peace and security,
and no one will make him afraid.
[11]I am with you and will save you,'
declares the LORD.
'Though I completely destroy all the
nations
among which I scatter you,
I will not completely destroy you.
I will discipline you but only with
justice;
I will not let you go entirely
unpunished.'

[12]"This is what the LORD says:

" 'Your wound is incurable,
your injury beyond healing.
[13]There is no one to plead your cause,
no remedy for your sore,
no healing for you.
[14]All your allies have forgotten you;
they care nothing for you.
I have struck you as an enemy would
and punished you as would the cruel,
because your guilt is so great
and your sins so many.
[15]Why do you cry out over your wound,
your pain that has no cure?
Because of your great guilt and many sins
I have done these things to you.

[16]" 'But all who devour you will be
devoured;
all your enemies will go into exile.
Those who plunder you will be
plundered;
all who make spoil of you I will
despoil.

[a] 3 Or *will restore the fortunes of my people Israel and Judah*

17 But I will restore you to health
and heal your wounds,'
declares the LORD,
'because you are called an outcast,
Zion for whom no one cares.'

18 "This is what the LORD says:

" 'I will restore the fortunes of Jacob's tents
and have compassion on his dwellings;
the city will be rebuilt on her ruins,
and the palace will stand in its proper place.
19 From them will come songs of thanksgiving
and the sound of rejoicing.
I will add to their numbers,
and they will not be decreased;
I will bring them honor,
and they will not be disdained.
20 Their children will be as in days of old,
and their community will be established before me;
I will punish all who oppress them.
21 Their leader will be one of their own;
their ruler will arise from among them.
I will bring him near and he will come close to me,
for who is he who will devote himself
to be close to me?'
declares the LORD.
22 " 'So you will be my people,
and I will be your God.' "

23 See, the storm of the LORD
will burst out in wrath,
a driving wind swirling down
on the heads of the wicked.
24 The fierce anger of the LORD will not turn back
until he fully accomplishes
the purposes of his heart.
In days to come
you will understand this.

31 "At that time," declares the LORD, "I will be the God of all the clans of Israel, and they will be my people."

2 This is what the LORD says:

"The people who survive the sword
will find favor in the desert;
I will come to give rest to Israel."

3 The LORD appeared to us in the past,[a] saying:

"I have loved you with an everlasting love;
I have drawn you with loving-kindness.
4 I will build you up again
and you will be rebuilt, O Virgin Israel.
Again you will take up your tambourines
and go out to dance with the joyful.
5 Again you will plant vineyards
on the hills of Samaria;
the farmers will plant them
and enjoy their fruit.
6 There will be a day when watchmen cry out
on the hills of Ephraim,
'Come, let us go up to Zion,
to the LORD our God.' "

7 This is what the LORD says:

"Sing with joy for Jacob;
shout for the foremost of the nations.
Make your praises heard, and say,
'O LORD, save your people,
the remnant of Israel.'
8 See, I will bring them from the land of the north
and gather them from the ends of the earth.
Among them will be the blind and the lame,
expectant mothers and women in labor;
a great throng will return.
9 They will come with weeping;
they will pray as I bring them back.
I will lead them beside streams of water
on a level path where they will not stumble,
because I am Israel's father,
and Ephraim is my firstborn son.

10 "Hear the word of the LORD, O nations;
proclaim it in distant coastlands:
'He who scattered Israel will gather them
and will watch over his flock like a shepherd.'
11 For the LORD will ransom Jacob
and redeem them from the hand of those stronger than they.
12 They will come and shout for joy on the heights of Zion;
they will rejoice in the bounty of the LORD—
the grain, the new wine and the oil,
the young of the flocks and herds.
They will be like a well-watered garden,
and they will sorrow no more.
13 Then maidens will dance and be glad,
young men and old as well.

[a] 3 Or *LORD has appeared to us from afar*

THURSDAY
READ JEREMIAH 31:1–14

WHEN PROMISES AREN'T ENOUGH

We often talk about marriage as a commitment. There's nothing wrong with that, but to be honest, there are times when commitment isn't enough.

When we talk about commitment, we're really talking about intention: I intend to do the thing I said I would do. But even our best intentions are only as good as our follow through. How many times have you made a promise to do something—work as a volunteer, serve on a committee, meet for lunch—only to break that commitment when something else came up or other priorities surfaced? We can mean it when we make a promise. We can fully believe we will show up. And we can feel horrible when we have to back out. But no matter what the reason, no matter how badly we feel, it's very easy to break a commitment.

That's why marriage calls for a different kind of promise.

God's love for Israel wasn't based on a commitment but on covenant love. God didn't just intend to stick with the nation of Israel; God followed through. And God's intention didn't change even when the Israelites turned their backs on him through terrible sin and selfishness.

We read Jeremiah 31:3 and see it as a wonderful assurance of God's unending love. And it is. Yet it is far more profound than that. The people of Israel would reject God, turn their backs on him and refuse to trust him. They would break God's heart. God's response to that would be anger, yes, but not vengeance. And it would be followed by unfailing kindness.

In the face of betrayal, rejection and mistrust, the last thing we want to give in return is our love. But covenant love is precisely what is needed in order for a broken marriage to heal.

Still, covenant love is no doormat. When my friend Jake developed a drug addiction, his wife, Bess, had a choice to make: bail out or hang on. With God's help, Bess decided to stay and help Jake through the long, painful process of recovery and redemption. The couple went through years of counseling. They talked about painful issues that made both of them squirm. There were times when they lived apart to protect their young children from Jake's lifestyle.

Bess's commitment wavered daily, but her belief that she had entered a covenant with Jake helped her stick with him in his darkest moments. That covenant love gave Bess the ability to see Jake through a lens of compassion and mercy, like the lens through which God sees us. Their marriage hasn't fully recovered, but they both know they will make it because their covenant has been tested and has held fast.

Covenant love involves tremendous risk. We may be disappointed at times in marriage. We may feel abandoned. We may even have to remove ourselves from a damaging situation in order to preserve our covenant. But sharing the kind of love that goes deeper than a promise means living that love out every day, no matter what.

—CARLA BARNHILL

FOR YOUR NEXT DEVOTIONAL READING, TURN TO PAGE 859.

The LORD appeared to us in the past, saying: "I have loved you with an everlasting love; I have drawn you with loving-kindness."

— JEREMIAH 31:3

let's *talk*

- Is there something each of us believes would make us end our marriage? Let's talk now about how we could hold on to covenant love in the midst of that situation.
- If our marriage has suffered a blow, what are we doing to get ourselves on track? How are repentance and forgiveness crucial to covenant love?
- What does unfailing love look like in our marriage? How can we show each other covenant love?

I will turn their mourning into gladness;
I will give them comfort and joy
instead of sorrow.
14 I will satisfy the priests with abundance,
and my people will be filled with my
bounty,"
declares the LORD.

15 This is what the LORD says:

"A voice is heard in Ramah,
mourning and great weeping,
Rachel weeping for her children
and refusing to be comforted,
because her children are no more."

16 This is what the LORD says:

"Restrain your voice from weeping
and your eyes from tears,
for your work will be rewarded,"
declares the LORD.
"They will return from the land of the
enemy.
17 So there is hope for your future,"
declares the LORD.
"Your children will return to their own
land.

18 "I have surely heard Ephraim's moaning:
'You disciplined me like an unruly calf,
and I have been disciplined.
Restore me, and I will return,
because you are the LORD my God.
19 After I strayed,
I repented;
after I came to understand,
I beat my breast.
I was ashamed and humiliated
because I bore the disgrace of my
youth.'
20 Is not Ephraim my dear son,
the child in whom I delight?
Though I often speak against him,
I still remember him.
Therefore my heart yearns for him;
I have great compassion for him,"
declares the LORD.

21 "Set up road signs;
put up guideposts.
Take note of the highway,
the road that you take.
Return, O Virgin Israel,
return to your towns.
22 How long will you wander,
O unfaithful daughter?
The LORD will create a new thing on
earth—
a woman will surround[a] a man."

23 This is what the LORD Almighty, the God
of Israel, says: "When I bring them back from
captivity,[b] the people in the land of Judah and
in its towns will once again use these words:
'The LORD bless you, O righteous dwelling,
O sacred mountain.' 24 People will live together in Judah and all its towns—farmers and
those who move about with their flocks. 25 I
will refresh the weary and satisfy the faint."
26 At this I awoke and looked around. My
sleep had been pleasant to me.
27 "The days are coming," declares the
LORD, "when I will plant the house of Israel and the house of Judah with the offspring
of men and of animals. 28 Just as I watched
over them to uproot and tear down, and to
overthrow, destroy and bring disaster, so I will
watch over them to build and to plant," declares the LORD. 29 "In those days people will
no longer say,

'The fathers have eaten sour grapes,
and the children's teeth are set on edge.'

30 Instead, everyone will die for his own sin;
whoever eats sour grapes—his own teeth will
be set on edge.

31 "The time is coming," declares the LORD,
"when I will make a new covenant
with the house of Israel
and with the house of Judah.
32 It will not be like the covenant
I made with their forefathers
when I took them by the hand
to lead them out of Egypt,
because they broke my covenant,
though I was a husband to[c] them,[d]"
declares the LORD.
33 "This is the covenant I will make with the
house of Israel
after that time," declares the LORD.
"I will put my law in their minds
and write it on their hearts.
I will be their God,
and they will be my people.
34 No longer will a man teach his neighbor,
or a man his brother, saying, 'Know the
LORD,'
because they will all know me,
from the least of them to the greatest,"
declares the LORD.
"For I will forgive their wickedness

[a] 22 Or *will go about* (*seeking*); or *will protect* [b] 23 Or *I restore their fortunes* [c] 32 Hebrew; Septuagint and Syriac / *and I turned away from* [d] 32 Or *was their master*

and will remember their sins no more."

35This is what the LORD says,

he who appoints the sun
to shine by day,
who decrees the moon and stars
to shine by night,
who stirs up the sea
so that its waves roar—
the LORD Almighty is his name:
36"Only if these decrees vanish from my
sight,"
declares the LORD,
"will the descendants of Israel ever cease
to be a nation before me."

37This is what the LORD says:

"Only if the heavens above can be
measured
and the foundations of the earth below
be searched out
will I reject all the descendants of Israel
because of all they have done,"
declares the LORD.

38"The days are coming," declares the LORD,
"when this city will be rebuilt for me from the
Tower of Hananel to the Corner Gate. 39The
measuring line will stretch from there straight
to the hill of Gareb and then turn to Goah.
40The whole valley where dead bodies and ashes are thrown, and all the terraces out to the
Kidron Valley on the east as far as the corner
of the Horse Gate, will be holy to the LORD.
The city will never again be uprooted or demolished."

Jeremiah Buys a Field

32 This is the word that came to Jeremiah from the LORD in the tenth year of
Zedekiah king of Judah, which was
the eighteenth year of Nebuchadnezzar. 2The
army of the king of Babylon was then besieging Jerusalem, and Jeremiah the prophet was
confined in the courtyard of the guard in the
royal palace of Judah.
3Now Zedekiah king of Judah had imprisoned him there, saying, "Why do you prophesy as you do? You say, 'This is what the LORD
says: I am about to hand this city over to the
king of Babylon, and he will capture it. 4Zed-
ekiah king of Judah will not escape out of the
hands of the Babylonians[a] but will certainly
be handed over to the king of Babylon, and
will speak with him face to face and see him
with his own eyes. 5He will take Zedekiah to
Babylon, where he will remain until I deal with
him, declares the LORD. If you fight against
the Babylonians, you will not succeed.' "
6Jeremiah said, "The word of the LORD
came to me: 7Hanamel son of Shallum your
uncle is going to come to you and say, 'Buy
my field at Anathoth, because as nearest relative it is your right and duty to buy it.'
8"Then, just as the LORD had said, my cousin Hanamel came to me in the courtyard of
the guard and said, 'Buy my field at Anathoth
in the territory of Benjamin. Since it is your
right to redeem it and possess it, buy it for
yourself.'
"I knew that this was the word of the
LORD; 9so I bought the field at Anathoth
from my cousin Hanamel and weighed out
for him seventeen shekels[b] of silver. 10I signed
and sealed the deed, had it witnessed, and
weighed out the silver on the scales. 11I took
the deed of purchase—the sealed copy containing the terms and conditions, as well as
the unsealed copy— 12and I gave this deed
to Baruch son of Neriah, the son of Mahseiah, in the presence of my cousin Hanamel
and of the witnesses who had signed the deed
and of all the Jews sitting in the courtyard of
the guard.
13"In their presence I gave Baruch these instructions: 14'This is what the LORD Almighty,
the God of Israel, says: Take these documents,
both the sealed and unsealed copies of the
deed of purchase, and put them in a clay jar so
they will last a long time. 15For this is what the
LORD Almighty, the God of Israel, says: Houses, fields and vineyards will again be bought
in this land.'
16"After I had given the deed of purchase to
Baruch son of Neriah, I prayed to the LORD:

17"Ah, Sovereign LORD, you have made
the heavens and the earth by your great
power and outstretched arm. Nothing
is too hard for you. 18You show love to
thousands but bring the punishment for
the fathers' sins into the laps of their children after them. O great and powerful
God, whose name is the LORD Almighty,
19great are your purposes and mighty are
your deeds. Your eyes are open to all the
ways of men; you reward everyone according to his conduct and as his deeds deserve. 20You performed miraculous signs
and wonders in Egypt and have continued them to this day, both in Israel and
among all mankind, and have gained the

---

[a] 4 Or *Chaldeans*; also in verses 5, 24, 25, 28, 29 and 43 [b] 9 That is, about 7 ounces (about 200 grams)

renown that is still yours. 21 You brought your people Israel out of Egypt with signs and wonders, by a mighty hand and an outstretched arm and with great terror. 22 You gave them this land you had sworn to give their forefathers, a land flowing with milk and honey. 23 They came in and took possession of it, but they did not obey you or follow your law; they did not do what you commanded them to do. So you brought all this disaster upon them.

24 "See how the siege ramps are built up to take the city. Because of the sword, famine and plague, the city will be handed over to the Babylonians who are attacking it. What you said has happened, as you now see. 25 And though the city will be handed over to the Babylonians, you, O Sovereign LORD, say to me, 'Buy the field with silver and have the transaction witnessed.' "

26 Then the word of the LORD came to Jeremiah: 27 "I am the LORD, the God of all mankind. Is anything too hard for me? 28 Therefore, this is what the LORD says: I am about to hand this city over to the Babylonians and to Nebuchadnezzar king of Babylon, who will capture it. 29 The Babylonians who are attacking this city will come in and set it on fire; they will burn it down, along with the houses where the people provoked me to anger by burning incense on the roofs to Baal and by pouring out drink offerings to other gods.

30 "The people of Israel and Judah have done nothing but evil in my sight from their youth; indeed, the people of Israel have done nothing but provoke me with what their hands have made, declares the LORD. 31 From the day it was built until now, this city has so aroused my anger and wrath that I must remove it from my sight. 32 The people of Israel and Judah have provoked me by all the evil they have done—they, their kings and officials, their priests and prophets, the men of Judah and the people of Jerusalem. 33 They turned their backs to me and not their faces; though I taught them again and again, they would not listen or respond to discipline. 34 They set up their abominable idols in the house that bears my Name and defiled it. 35 They built high places for Baal in the Valley of Ben Hinnom to sacrifice their sons and daughters[a] to Molech, though I never commanded, nor did it enter my mind, that they should do such a detestable thing and so make Judah sin.

36 "You are saying about this city, 'By the sword, famine and plague it will be handed over to the king of Babylon'; but this is what the LORD, the God of Israel, says: 37 I will surely gather them from all the lands where I banish them in my furious anger and great wrath; I will bring them back to this place and let them live in safety. 38 They will be my people, and I will be their God. 39 I will give them singleness of heart and action, so that they will always fear me for their own good and the good of their children after them. 40 I will make an everlasting covenant with them: I will never stop doing good to them, and I will inspire them to fear me, so that they will never turn away from me. 41 I will rejoice in doing them good and will assuredly plant them in this land with all my heart and soul.

42 "This is what the LORD says: As I have brought all this great calamity on this people, so I will give them all the prosperity I have promised them. 43 Once more fields will be bought in this land of which you say, 'It is a desolate waste, without men or animals, for it has been handed over to the Babylonians.' 44 Fields will be bought for silver, and deeds will be signed, sealed and witnessed in the territory of Benjamin, in the villages around Jerusalem, in the towns of Judah and in the towns of the hill country, of the western foothills and of the Negev, because I will restore their fortunes,[b] declares the LORD."

Promise of Restoration

33 While Jeremiah was still confined in the courtyard of the guard, the word of the LORD came to him a second time: 2 "This is what the LORD says, he who made the earth, the LORD who formed it and established it—the LORD is his name: 3 'Call to me and I will answer you and tell you great and unsearchable things you do not know.' 4 For this is what the LORD, the God of Israel, says about the houses in this city and the royal palaces of Judah that have been torn down to be used against the siege ramps and the sword 5 in the fight with the Babylonians[c]: 'They will be filled with the dead bodies of the men I will slay in my anger and wrath. I will hide my face from this city because of all its wickedness.

6 " 'Nevertheless, I will bring health and healing to it; I will heal my people and will let them enjoy abundant peace and security. 7 I will bring Judah and Israel back from cap-

[a] 35 Or *to make their sons and daughters pass through ⌞the fire⌟* [b] 44 Or *will bring them back from captivity* [c] 5 Or *Chaldeans*

COMING TO TERMS WITH THE PAST

A pastor friend told the story of a couple who had come to him for counseling. The couple had been married 40 or so years, and they were both plagued with guilt. They hadn't become Christians until their later years, and, prior to that, they had both lived sexually immoral lives. Although they had been faithful to each other during their marriage, their past dips into immorality were now making them feel guilty for enjoying sex with each other.

"I will heal my people and will let them enjoy abundant peace and security."

— Jeremiah 33:6

let's talk

- ✦ What are some things from the past that each of us are still struggling with?
- ✦ How are they affecting our marriage?
- ✦ How can we talk about those struggles in a way that builds up our marriage?

The pastor thought for a moment, then asked the couple to name their favorite hymn. They both said at the same time, "It Is Well With My Soul." So the pastor told them to go home and either listen to or sing the hymn every night before they went to bed.

A week later the couple returned to the pastor's office. They told him that they had felt foolish at first, but they had sung their favorite hymn together each night. The wife blushed and the husband got teary eyed as he told the pastor, "When we got to the part that says, 'My sin, oh the bliss of this glorious thought! My sin not in part but the whole, is nailed to the cross and I bear it no more. Praise the Lord, praise the Lord, O, my soul!' well . . . after all these years we feel fresh and squeaky clean and new all over again."

Throughout the Bible, God's relationship with Israel was tested over and over by Israel's sin. The book of Jeremiah talks about the horrible result of that sin. When the prophet received the prophecy recorded in chapter 33, Jerusalem was under siege from the invading Babylonians. Soon God would allow his people to be carried away from their land into captivity and their land to be destroyed. Like the couple who wrestled with memories of past sins, the Israelites would live with heartrending images of how their unfaithfulness to God had resulted in the burning and pillaging of their land. Their city would be filled with dead bodies.

But the story doesn't end there. The prophet went on to say that because of God's immense love, God would heal Israel's pain, cleanse the people from their sin, and restore them to abundant peace and security. "Then this city will bring me renown, joy, praise and honor before all nations on earth that hear of all the good things I do for it," God said (Jeremiah 33:9).

Likewise, God does not want us to be forever burdened with our past sins. "If anyone is in Christ, he is a new creation; the old has gone, the new has come!" says 2 Corinthians 5:17. And Romans 6:4 promises, "We were therefore buried with him . . . in order that, just as Christ was raised from the dead through the glory of the Father, we too may live a new life."

So too is the promise for our marriages, which so often bend under the load of sins, both past and present. We must be honest with ourselves, with the Lord and with each other about memories or habits or activities that may be eroding our relationship and then deal with them. But we can do so in the joy of knowing that in Christ we can find forgiveness, restoration and a new start.

—NANCY KENNEDY

FOR YOUR NEXT DEVOTIONAL READING, TURN TO PAGE 866.

tivity[a] and will rebuild them as they were before. 8 I will cleanse them from all the sin they have committed against me and will forgive all their sins of rebellion against me. 9 Then this city will bring me renown, joy, praise and honor before all nations on earth that hear of all the good things I do for it; and they will be in awe and will tremble at the abundant prosperity and peace I provide for it.'

10 "This is what the LORD says: 'You say about this place, "It is a desolate waste, without men or animals." Yet in the towns of Judah and the streets of Jerusalem that are deserted, inhabited by neither men nor animals, there will be heard once more 11 the sounds of joy and gladness, the voices of bride and bridegroom, and the voices of those who bring thank offerings to the house of the LORD, saying,

"Give thanks to the LORD Almighty,
for the LORD is good;
his love endures forever."

For I will restore the fortunes of the land as they were before,' says the LORD.

12 "This is what the LORD Almighty says: 'In this place, desolate and without men or animals—in all its towns there will again be pastures for shepherds to rest their flocks. 13 In the towns of the hill country, of the western foothills and of the Negev, in the territory of Benjamin, in the villages around Jerusalem and in the towns of Judah, flocks will again pass under the hand of the one who counts them,' says the LORD.

14 " 'The days are coming,' declares the LORD, 'when I will fulfill the gracious promise I made to the house of Israel and to the house of Judah.

15 " 'In those days and at that time
I will make a righteous Branch sprout
from David's line;
he will do what is just and right in the land.
16 In those days Judah will be saved
and Jerusalem will live in safety.
This is the name by which it[b] will be called:
The LORD Our Righteousness.'

17 For this is what the LORD says: 'David will never fail to have a man to sit on the throne of the house of Israel, 18 nor will the priests, who are Levites, ever fail to have a man to stand before me continually to offer burnt offerings, to burn grain offerings and to present sacrifices.' "

19 The word of the LORD came to Jeremiah: 20 "This is what the LORD says: 'If you can break my covenant with the day and my covenant with the night, so that day and night no longer come at their appointed time, 21 then my covenant with David my servant—and my covenant with the Levites who are priests ministering before me—can be broken and David will no longer have a descendant to reign on his throne. 22 I will make the descendants of David my servant and the Levites who minister before me as countless as the stars of the sky and as measureless as the sand on the seashore.' "

23 The word of the LORD came to Jeremiah: 24 "Have you not noticed that these people are saying, 'The LORD has rejected the two kingdoms[c] he chose'? So they despise my people and no longer regard them as a nation. 25 This is what the LORD says: 'If I have not established my covenant with day and night and the fixed laws of heaven and earth, 26 then I will reject the descendants of Jacob and David my servant and will not choose one of his sons to rule over the descendants of Abraham, Isaac and Jacob. For I will restore their fortunes[d] and have compassion on them.' "

Warning to Zedekiah

34 While Nebuchadnezzar king of Babylon and all his army and all the kingdoms and peoples in the empire he ruled were fighting against Jerusalem and all its surrounding towns, this word came to Jeremiah from the LORD: 2 "This is what the LORD, the God of Israel, says: Go to Zedekiah king of Judah and tell him, 'This is what the LORD says: I am about to hand this city over to the king of Babylon, and he will burn it down. 3 You will not escape from his grasp but will surely be captured and handed over to him. You will see the king of Babylon with your own eyes, and he will speak with you face to face. And you will go to Babylon.

4 " 'Yet hear the promise of the LORD, O Zedekiah king of Judah. This is what the LORD says concerning you: You will not die by the sword; 5 you will die peacefully. As people made a funeral fire in honor of your fathers, the former kings who preceded you, so they will make a fire in your honor and lament, "Alas, O master!" I myself make this promise, declares the LORD.' "

[a] 7 Or *will restore the fortunes of Judah and Israel* [b] 16 Or *he* [c] 24 Or *families* [d] 26 Or *will bring them back from captivity*

6 Then Jeremiah the prophet told all this to Zedekiah king of Judah, in Jerusalem, 7 while the army of the king of Babylon was fighting against Jerusalem and the other cities of Judah that were still holding out—Lachish and Azekah. These were the only fortified cities left in Judah.

Freedom for Slaves

8 The word came to Jeremiah from the LORD after King Zedekiah had made a covenant with all the people in Jerusalem to proclaim freedom for the slaves. 9 Everyone was to free his Hebrew slaves, both male and female; no one was to hold a fellow Jew in bondage. 10 So all the officials and people who entered into this covenant agreed that they would free their male and female slaves and no longer hold them in bondage. They agreed, and set them free. 11 But afterward they changed their minds and took back the slaves they had freed and enslaved them again.

12 Then the word of the LORD came to Jeremiah: 13 "This is what the LORD, the God of Israel, says: I made a covenant with your forefathers when I brought them out of Egypt, out of the land of slavery. I said, 14 'Every seventh year each of you must free any fellow Hebrew who has sold himself to you. After he has served you six years, you must let him go free.' [a] Your fathers, however, did not listen to me or pay attention to me. 15 Recently you repented and did what is right in my sight: Each of you proclaimed freedom to his countrymen. You even made a covenant before me in the house that bears my Name. 16 But now you have turned around and profaned my name; each of you has taken back the male and female slaves you had set free to go where they wished. You have forced them to become your slaves again.

17 "Therefore, this is what the LORD says: You have not obeyed me; you have not proclaimed freedom for your fellow countrymen. So I now proclaim 'freedom' for you, declares the LORD—'freedom' to fall by the sword, plague and famine. I will make you abhorrent to all the kingdoms of the earth. 18 The men who have violated my covenant and have not fulfilled the terms of the covenant they made before me, I will treat like the calf they cut in two and then walked between its pieces. 19 The leaders of Judah and Jerusalem, the court officials, the priests and all the people of the land who walked between the pieces of the calf, 20 I will hand over to their enemies who seek their lives. Their dead bodies will become food for the birds of the air and the beasts of the earth.

21 "I will hand Zedekiah king of Judah and his officials over to their enemies who seek their lives, to the army of the king of Babylon, which has withdrawn from you. 22 I am going to give the order, declares the LORD, and I will bring them back to this city. They will fight against it, take it and burn it down. And I will lay waste the towns of Judah so no one can live there."

The Recabites

35 This is the word that came to Jeremiah from the LORD during the reign of Jehoiakim son of Josiah king of Judah: 2 "Go to the Recabite family and invite them to come to one of the side rooms of the house of the LORD and give them wine to drink."

3 So I went to get Jaazaniah son of Jeremiah, the son of Habazziniah, and his brothers and all his sons—the whole family of the Recabites. 4 I brought them into the house of the LORD, into the room of the sons of Hanan son of Igdaliah the man of God. It was next to the room of the officials, which was over that of Maaseiah son of Shallum the doorkeeper. 5 Then I set bowls full of wine and some cups before the men of the Recabite family and said to them, "Drink some wine."

6 But they replied, "We do not drink wine, because our forefather Jonadab son of Recab gave us this command: 'Neither you nor your descendants must ever drink wine. 7 Also you must never build houses, sow seed or plant vineyards; you must never have any of these things, but must always live in tents. Then you will live a long time in the land where you are nomads.' 8 We have obeyed everything our forefather Jonadab son of Recab commanded us. Neither we nor our wives nor our sons and daughters have ever drunk wine 9 or built houses to live in or had vineyards, fields or crops. 10 We have lived in tents and have fully obeyed everything our forefather Jonadab commanded us. 11 But when Nebuchadnezzar king of Babylon invaded this land, we said, 'Come, we must go to Jerusalem to escape the Babylonian [b] and Aramean armies.' So we have remained in Jerusalem."

12 Then the word of the LORD came to Jeremiah, saying: 13 "This is what the LORD Almighty, the God of Israel, says: Go and tell

[a] *14* Deut. 15:12 [b] *11* Or *Chaldean*

the men of Judah and the people of Jerusalem, ‘Will you not learn a lesson and obey my
words?’ declares the LORD. 14‘Jonadab son of
Recab ordered his sons not to drink wine and
this command has been kept. To this day they
do not drink wine, because they obey their
forefather’s command. But I have spoken to
you again and again, yet you have not obeyed
me. 15Again and again I sent all my servants
the prophets to you. They said, “Each of you
must turn from your wicked ways and reform your actions; do not follow other gods
to serve them. Then you will live in the land I
have given to you and your fathers.” But you
have not paid attention or listened to me.
16The descendants of Jonadab son of Recab
have carried out the command their forefather gave them, but these people have not
obeyed me.’

17“Therefore, this is what the LORD God Almighty, the God of Israel, says: ‘Listen! I am
going to bring on Judah and on everyone living in Jerusalem every disaster I pronounced
against them. I spoke to them, but they did
not listen; I called to them, but they did not
answer.’ ”

18Then Jeremiah said to the family of the
Recabites, “This is what the LORD Almighty,
the God of Israel, says: ‘You have obeyed the
command of your forefather Jonadab and have
followed all his instructions and have done everything he ordered.’ 19Therefore, this is what
the LORD Almighty, the God of Israel, says:
‘Jonadab son of Recab will never fail to have a
man to serve me.’ ”

Jehoiakim Burns Jeremiah’s Scroll

36 In the fourth year of Jehoiakim son of
Josiah king of Judah, this word came to
Jeremiah from the LORD: 2“Take a scroll
and write on it all the words I have spoken to
you concerning Israel, Judah and all the other
nations from the time I began speaking to you
in the reign of Josiah till now. 3Perhaps when
the people of Judah hear about every disaster I
plan to inflict on them, each of them will turn
from his wicked way; then I will forgive their
wickedness and their sin.”

4So Jeremiah called Baruch son of Neriah,
and while Jeremiah dictated all the words the
LORD had spoken to him, Baruch wrote them
on the scroll. 5Then Jeremiah told Baruch, “I
am restricted; I cannot go to the LORD’s temple. 6So you go to the house of the LORD on a
day of fasting and read to the people from the
scroll the words of the LORD that you wrote as
I dictated. Read them to all the people of Judah who come in from their towns. 7Perhaps
they will bring their petition before the LORD,
and each will turn from his wicked ways, for
the anger and wrath pronounced against this
people by the LORD are great.”

8Baruch son of Neriah did everything Jeremiah the prophet told him to do; at the
LORD’s temple he read the words of the LORD
from the scroll. 9In the ninth month of the
fifth year of Jehoiakim son of Josiah king of
Judah, a time of fasting before the LORD was
proclaimed for all the people in Jerusalem and
those who had come from the towns of Judah.
10From the room of Gemariah son of Shaphan
the secretary, which was in the upper courtyard at the entrance of the New Gate of the
temple, Baruch read to all the people at the
LORD’s temple the words of Jeremiah from the
scroll.

11When Micaiah son of Gemariah, the son
of Shaphan, heard all the words of the LORD
from the scroll, 12he went down to the secretary’s room in the royal palace, where all the
officials were sitting: Elishama the secretary,
Delaiah son of Shemaiah, Elnathan son of Acbor, Gemariah son of Shaphan, Zedekiah son
of Hananiah, and all the other officials. 13Af-
ter Micaiah told them everything he had heard
Baruch read to the people from the scroll, 14all
the officials sent Jehudi son of Nethaniah, the
son of Shelemiah, the son of Cushi, to say to
Baruch, “Bring the scroll from which you have
read to the people and come.” So Baruch son
of Neriah went to them with the scroll in his
hand. 15They said to him, “Sit down, please,
and read it to us.”

So Baruch read it to them. 16When they
heard all these words, they looked at each other in fear and said to Baruch, “We must report
all these words to the king.” 17Then they asked
Baruch, “Tell us, how did you come to write
all this? Did Jeremiah dictate it?”

18“Yes,” Baruch replied, “he dictated all
these words to me, and I wrote them in ink
on the scroll.”

19Then the officials said to Baruch, “You
and Jeremiah, go and hide. Don’t let anyone
know where you are.”

20After they put the scroll in the room of
Elishama the secretary, they went to the king
in the courtyard and reported everything to
him. 21The king sent Jehudi to get the scroll,
and Jehudi brought it from the room of Elishama the secretary and read it to the king and
all the officials standing beside him. 22It was
the ninth month and the king was sitting in
the winter apartment, with a fire burning in

will not escape from their hands but will be
captured by the king of Babylon; and this city
will[a] be burned down."
24Then Zedekiah said to Jeremiah, "Do not
let anyone know about this conversation, or
you may die. 25If the officials hear that I talked
with you, and they come to you and say, 'Tell
us what you said to the king and what the king
said to you; do not hide it from us or we will
kill you,' 26then tell them, 'I was pleading with
the king not to send me back to Jonathan's
house to die there.' "
27All the officials did come to Jeremiah and
question him, and he told them everything
the king had ordered him to say. So they said
no more to him, for no one had heard his conversation with the king.
28And Jeremiah remained in the courtyard
of the guard until the day Jerusalem was captured.

The Fall of Jerusalem

39 This is how Jerusalem was taken: 1In the
ninth year of Zedekiah king of Judah, in
the tenth month, Nebuchadnezzar king
of Babylon marched against Jerusalem with
his whole army and laid siege to it. 2And on
the ninth day of the fourth month of Zedekiah's eleventh year, the city wall was broken
through. 3Then all the officials of the king of
Babylon came and took seats in the Middle
Gate: Nergal-Sharezer of Samgar, Nebo-Sar-
sekim[b] a chief officer, Nergal-Sharezer a high
official and all the other officials of the king of
Babylon. 4When Zedekiah king of Judah and
all the soldiers saw them, they fled; they left
the city at night by way of the king's garden,
through the gate between the two walls, and
headed toward the Arabah.[c]
5But the Babylonian[d] army pursued them
and overtook Zedekiah in the plains of Jericho. They captured him and took him to
Nebuchadnezzar king of Babylon at Riblah
in the land of Hamath, where he pronounced
sentence on him. 6There at Riblah the king of
Babylon slaughtered the sons of Zedekiah before his eyes and also killed all the nobles of
Judah. 7Then he put out Zedekiah's eyes and
bound him with bronze shackles to take him
to Babylon.
8The Babylonians[e] set fire to the royal palace and the houses of the people and broke
down the walls of Jerusalem. 9Nebuzaradan
commander of the imperial guard carried into
exile to Babylon the people who remained in
the city, along with those who had gone over
to him, and the rest of the people. 10But Nebuzaradan the commander of the guard left behind in the land of Judah some of the poor
people, who owned nothing; and at that time
he gave them vineyards and fields.
11Now Nebuchadnezzar king of Babylon had given these orders about Jeremiah
through Nebuzaradan commander of the imperial guard: 12"Take him and look after him;
don't harm him but do for him whatever he
asks." 13So Nebuzaradan the commander of
the guard, Nebushazban a chief officer, Nergal-Sharezer a high official and all the other
officers of the king of Babylon 14sent and had
Jeremiah taken out of the courtyard of the
guard. They turned him over to Gedaliah son
of Ahikam, the son of Shaphan, to take him
back to his home. So he remained among his
own people.
15While Jeremiah had been confined in the
courtyard of the guard, the word of the LORD
came to him: 16"Go and tell Ebed-Melech the
Cushite, 'This is what the LORD Almighty, the
God of Israel, says: I am about to fulfill my
words against this city through disaster, not
prosperity. At that time they will be fulfilled
before your eyes. 17But I will rescue you on
that day, declares the LORD; you will not be
handed over to those you fear. 18I will save
you; you will not fall by the sword but will
escape with your life, because you trust in me,
declares the LORD.' "

Jeremiah Freed

40 The word came to Jeremiah from the
LORD after Nebuzaradan commander
of the imperial guard had released him
at Ramah. He had found Jeremiah bound in
chains among all the captives from Jerusalem
and Judah who were being carried into exile to Babylon. 2When the commander of the
guard found Jeremiah, he said to him, "The
LORD your God decreed this disaster for this
place. 3And now the LORD has brought it
about; he has done just as he said he would.
All this happened because you people sinned
against the LORD and did not obey him.
4But today I am freeing you from the chains
on your wrists. Come with me to Babylon,
if you like, and I will look after you; but if
you do not want to, then don't come. Look,
the whole country lies before you; go wherever you please." 5However, before Jeremiah turned to go,[f] Nebuzaradan added, "Go

---

[a] 23 Or *and you will cause this city to* [b] 3 Or *Nergal-Sharezer, Samgar-Nebo, Sarsekim* [c] 4 Or *the Jordan Valley* [d] 5 Or *Chaldean*
[e] 8 Or *Chaldeans* [f] 5 Or *Jeremiah answered*

WEEKEND

spicing up sex

My husband often initiates sex in the morning. We both work, and between getting myself ready and getting our toddler ready for daycare, there just isn't time to accommodate his needs. And don't even suggest getting up earlier—we're already waking up at the crack of dawn! Once we put our son to bed in the evening, I'm more than willing, but alas, my hubby usually falls asleep the minute his head hits the pillow. Help!

Most couples have some of the same problems, including Melissa and me. I'm more of a night person, so getting up early for lovemaking is unthinkable. But Melissa turns into a pumpkin at sunset and has a hard time being romantic. For us, help has come from three sources: communication, compromise and creative scheduling.

Communication: Understanding each other's feelings is essential in all aspects of marriage, but especially with sex. Either of you could easily interpret the other's preference as a rejection. Talk about how the dilemma is affecting your deep desires for connectedness. It's important for your common concern about intimacy to form the foundation for finding a solution.

Compromise: Finding ways to meet your spouse's needs is one of the most powerful expressions of love. It's also commanded in Scripture: Jesus said the second greatest commandment is to love your neighbor like yourself (Mark 12:31). A spouse qualifies as a "neighbor." Negotiations about when to have sex are built on this principle of love.

Creative scheduling: Some conflict requires thinking outside the box. First, commit to working as a team to create a new pattern, with both of you willing to be flexible in your thinking. Next, set aside some time, maybe a day or weekend, when the two of you can get away together to relax, talk and be romantic. In that context brainstorm how your schedules look and where you could make changes that might create space for lovemaking. That might mean giving up something else in your lives.

My husband and I have been married twenty-five years and we say and do the same old thing over and over in the bedroom. I'm not sure how to change things—but I'm bored, which makes me not interested in sex. Any ideas?

Sex is much too enticing, exhilarating and erotic for any couple to sink into monotony. So try something new. Since most men long for their mate to have an unquenchable desire for them sexually, seduce him. Kidnap him for a romantic getaway, wear a sexy teddy, say sexy things ("I need your body!"), touch him in erotic areas, go to bed naked, invade his shower, write him love notes, make unexpected phone calls inviting him to make love with you.

If he shows any life, tell him how much you like that!

We hope you're getting the message. You have power to change the same ole rut you're in. You don't have to wait for your husband to wake up. He may not have an inkling that he has a woman starved for sexual excitement!

—LOUIS AND MELISSA MCBURNEY

let's talk sex!

The bedroom may not be the best place to talk about sex, so use these questions as a way to begin a dialogue with your spouse before you hit the sack.

1. Am I as spontaneous about sex now as when I first got married? Why or why not?
2. What are the top three things that interfere with our sex life? What can I do to guard against them interfering in the future?
3. How can I make foreplay last all day?
4. Would I like to have more or less sex?
5. Would I be willing to schedule sex?
6. What part of our sex life do I like best?
7. Are there specific aspects of our sex life that I find difficult or troubling?
8. Would outside help (such as a book or counseling) help us with any aspect of our sex life?
9. Did having children change our sex life?
10. Do I regularly pray for our sex life?

HOW ARE WE DOING?

let's make a DATE

SPICE IT UP

Make a date to go out to a restaurant you've never tried before. Order something for yourself that you think the other might like. Compare notes. Did you like what you got, or would you prefer to trade? Now talk a bit about your lovemaking—is it time to try something different? What do you each prefer? Can you share?

FOR YOUR NEXT DEVOTIONAL READING, TURN TO PAGE 871.

LESSONS FROM THE *Bible*

In Song of Songs the lovers compare each other to a lily, a blossoming vine, a dove, a gazelle and a young stag. How can the following verses give you ideas about how to be more creative with your lover?

1. Song of Songs 1:2–4
2. Song of Songs 2:2–13

back to Gedaliah son of Ahikam, the son of Shaphan, whom the king of Babylon has appointed over the towns of Judah, and live with him among the people, or go anywhere else you please."

Then the commander gave him provisions and a present and let him go. 6So Jeremiah went to Gedaliah son of Ahikam at Mizpah and stayed with him among the people who were left behind in the land.

Gedaliah Assassinated

7When all the army officers and their men who were still in the open country heard that the king of Babylon had appointed Gedaliah son of Ahikam as governor over the land and had put him in charge of the men, women and children who were the poorest in the land and who had not been carried into exile to Babylon, 8they came to Gedaliah at Mizpah—Ishmael son of Nethaniah, Johanan and Jonathan the sons of Kareah, Seraiah son of Tanhumeth, the sons of Ephai the Netophathite, and Jaazaniah[a] the son of the Maacathite, and their men. 9Gedaliah son of Ahikam, the son of Shaphan, took an oath to reassure them and their men. "Do not be afraid to serve the Babylonians,[b]" he said. "Settle down in the land and serve the king of Babylon, and it will go well with you. 10I myself will stay at Mizpah to represent you before the Babylonians who come to us, but you are to harvest the wine, summer fruit and oil, and put them in your storage jars, and live in the towns you have taken over."

11When all the Jews in Moab, Ammon, Edom and all the other countries heard that the king of Babylon had left a remnant in Judah and had appointed Gedaliah son of Ahikam, the son of Shaphan, as governor over them, 12they all came back to the land of Judah, to Gedaliah at Mizpah, from all the countries where they had been scattered. And they harvested an abundance of wine and summer fruit.

13Johanan son of Kareah and all the army officers still in the open country came to Gedaliah at Mizpah 14and said to him, "Don't you know that Baalis king of the Ammonites has sent Ishmael son of Nethaniah to take your life?" But Gedaliah son of Ahikam did not believe them.

15Then Johanan son of Kareah said privately to Gedaliah in Mizpah, "Let me go and kill Ishmael son of Nethaniah, and no one will know it. Why should he take your life and cause all the Jews who are gathered around you to be scattered and the remnant of Judah to perish?"

16But Gedaliah son of Ahikam said to Johanan son of Kareah, "Don't do such a thing! What you are saying about Ishmael is not true."

41 In the seventh month Ishmael son of Nethaniah, the son of Elishama, who was of royal blood and had been one of the king's officers, came with ten men to Gedaliah son of Ahikam at Mizpah. While they were eating together there, 2Ishmael son of Nethaniah and the ten men who were with him got up and struck down Gedaliah son of Ahikam, the son of Shaphan, with the sword, killing the one whom the king of Babylon had appointed as governor over the land. 3Ishmael also killed all the Jews who were with Gedaliah at Mizpah, as well as the Babylonian[c] soldiers who were there.

4The day after Gedaliah's assassination, before anyone knew about it, 5eighty men who had shaved off their beards, torn their clothes and cut themselves came from Shechem, Shiloh and Samaria, bringing grain offerings and incense with them to the house of the LORD. 6Ishmael son of Nethaniah went out from Mizpah to meet them, weeping as he went. When he met them, he said, "Come to Gedaliah son of Ahikam." 7When they went into the city, Ishmael son of Nethaniah and the men who were with him slaughtered them and threw them into a cistern. 8But ten of them said to Ishmael, "Don't kill us! We have wheat and barley, oil and honey, hidden in a field." So he let them alone and did not kill them with the others. 9Now the cistern where he threw all the bodies of the men he had killed along with Gedaliah was the one King Asa had made as part of his defense against Baasha king of Israel. Ishmael son of Nethaniah filled it with the dead.

10Ishmael made captives of all the rest of the people who were in Mizpah—the king's daughters along with all the others who were left there, over whom Nebuzaradan commander of the imperial guard had appointed Gedaliah son of Ahikam. Ishmael son of Nethaniah took them captive and set out to cross over to the Ammonites.

11When Johanan son of Kareah and all the army officers who were with him heard about all the crimes Ishmael son of Nethani-

[a] 8 Hebrew *Jezaniah,* a variant of *Jaazaniah* [b] 9 Or *Chaldeans;* also in verse 10 [c] 3 Or *Chaldean*

ah had committed, [12]they took all their men
and went to fight Ishmael son of Nethaniah.
They caught up with him near the great pool
in Gibeon. [13]When all the people Ishmael had
with him saw Johanan son of Kareah and the
army officers who were with him, they were
glad. [14]All the people Ishmael had taken captive at Mizpah turned and went over to Johanan son of Kareah. [15]But Ishmael son of
Nethaniah and eight of his men escaped from
Johanan and fled to the Ammonites.

Flight to Egypt

[16]Then Johanan son of Kareah and all the
army officers who were with him led away all
the survivors from Mizpah whom he had recovered from Ishmael son of Nethaniah after
he had assassinated Gedaliah son of Ahikam:
the soldiers, women, children and court officials he had brought from Gibeon. [17]And they
went on, stopping at Geruth Kimham near
Bethlehem on their way to Egypt [18]to escape
the Babylonians.[a] They were afraid of them
because Ishmael son of Nethaniah had killed
Gedaliah son of Ahikam, whom the king of
Babylon had appointed as governor over the
land.

42 Then all the army officers, including Johanan son of Kareah and Jezaniah[b] son
of Hoshaiah, and all the people from the
least to the greatest approached [2]Jeremiah the
prophet and said to him, "Please hear our petition and pray to the LORD your God for this
entire remnant. For as you now see, though we
were once many, now only a few are left. [3]Pray
that the LORD your God will tell us where we
should go and what we should do."

[4]"I have heard you," replied Jeremiah the
prophet. "I will certainly pray to the LORD
your God as you have requested; I will tell you
everything the LORD says and will keep nothing back from you."

[5]Then they said to Jeremiah, "May the LORD
be a true and faithful witness against us if we
do not act in accordance with everything the
LORD your God sends you to tell us. [6]Whether
it is favorable or unfavorable, we will obey the
LORD our God, to whom we are sending you,
so that it will go well with us, for we will obey
the LORD our God."

[7]Ten days later the word of the LORD came
to Jeremiah. [8]So he called together Johanan
son of Kareah and all the army officers who
were with him and all the people from the
least to the greatest. [9]He said to them, "This
is what the LORD, the God of Israel, to whom
you sent me to present your petition, says: [10]'If
you stay in this land, I will build you up and
not tear you down; I will plant you and not
uproot you, for I am grieved over the disaster
I have inflicted on you. [11]Do not be afraid of
the king of Babylon, whom you now fear. Do
not be afraid of him, declares the LORD, for I
am with you and will save you and deliver you
from his hands. [12]I will show you compassion
so that he will have compassion on you and
restore you to your land.'

[13]"However, if you say, 'We will not stay in
this land,' and so disobey the LORD your God,
[14]and if you say, 'No, we will go and live in
Egypt, where we will not see war or hear the
trumpet or be hungry for bread,' [15]then hear
the word of the LORD, O remnant of Judah.
This is what the LORD Almighty, the God of
Israel, says: 'If you are determined to go to
Egypt and you do go to settle there, [16]then the
sword you fear will overtake you there, and the
famine you dread will follow you into Egypt,
and there you will die. [17]Indeed, all who are
determined to go to Egypt to settle there will
die by the sword, famine and plague; not one
of them will survive or escape the disaster I
will bring on them.' [18]This is what the LORD
Almighty, the God of Israel, says: 'As my anger
and wrath have been poured out on those who
lived in Jerusalem, so will my wrath be poured
out on you when you go to Egypt. You will be
an object of cursing and horror, of condemnation and reproach; you will never see this
place again.'

[19]"O remnant of Judah, the LORD has told
you, 'Do not go to Egypt.' Be sure of this: I
warn you today [20]that you made a fatal mistake[c] when you sent me to the LORD your
God and said, 'Pray to the LORD our God for
us; tell us everything he says and we will do it.'
[21]I have told you today, but you still have not
obeyed the LORD your God in all he sent me
to tell you. [22]So now, be sure of this: You will
die by the sword, famine and plague in the
place where you want to go to settle."

43 When Jeremiah finished telling the
people all the words of the LORD their
God—everything the LORD had sent
him to tell them— [2]Azariah son of Hoshaiah
and Johanan son of Kareah and all the arrogant men said to Jeremiah, "You are lying! The
LORD our God has not sent you to say, 'You
must not go to Egypt to settle there.' [3]But
Baruch son of Neriah is inciting you against us

[a] *18* Or *Chaldeans* [b] *1* Hebrew; Septuagint (see also 43:2) *Azariah* [c] *20* Or *you erred in your hearts*

to hand us over to the Babylonians,[a] so they
may kill us or carry us into exile to Babylon."
4So Johanan son of Kareah and all the
army officers and all the people disobeyed
the LORD's command to stay in the land of
Judah. 5Instead, Johanan son of Kareah and
all the army officers led away all the remnant
of Judah who had come back to live in the
land of Judah from all the nations where they
had been scattered. 6They also led away all
the men, women and children and the king's
daughters whom Nebuzaradan commander
of the imperial guard had left with Gedaliah
son of Ahikam, the son of Shaphan, and Jeremiah the prophet and Baruch son of Neriah.
7So they entered Egypt in disobedience to the
LORD and went as far as Tahpanhes.
8In Tahpanhes the word of the LORD came
to Jeremiah: 9"While the Jews are watching,
take some large stones with you and bury them
in clay in the brick pavement at the entrance
to Pharaoh's palace in Tahpanhes. 10Then say
to them, 'This is what the LORD Almighty, the
God of Israel, says: I will send for my servant
Nebuchadnezzar king of Babylon, and I will
set his throne over these stones I have buried
here; he will spread his royal canopy above
them. 11He will come and attack Egypt, bringing death to those destined for death, captivity
to those destined for captivity, and the sword
to those destined for the sword. 12He[b] will set
fire to the temples of the gods of Egypt; he will
burn their temples and take their gods captive.
As a shepherd wraps his garment around him,
so will he wrap Egypt around himself and depart from there unscathed. 13There in the temple of the sun[c] in Egypt he will demolish the
sacred pillars and will burn down the temples
of the gods of Egypt.' "

Disaster Because of Idolatry

44 This word came to Jeremiah concerning
all the Jews living in Lower Egypt—in
Migdol, Tahpanhes and Memphis[d]—
and in Upper Egypt[e]: 2"This is what the LORD
Almighty, the God of Israel, says: You saw the
great disaster I brought on Jerusalem and on
all the towns of Judah. Today they lie deserted and in ruins 3because of the evil they have
done. They provoked me to anger by burning incense and by worshiping other gods that
neither they nor you nor your fathers ever
knew. 4Again and again I sent my servants the
prophets, who said, 'Do not do this detestable
thing that I hate!' 5But they did not listen or
pay attention; they did not turn from their
wickedness or stop burning incense to other
gods. 6Therefore, my fierce anger was poured
out; it raged against the towns of Judah and
the streets of Jerusalem and made them the
desolate ruins they are today.
7"Now this is what the LORD God Almighty, the God of Israel, says: Why bring
such great disaster on yourselves by cutting off
from Judah the men and women, the children
and infants, and so leave yourselves without
a remnant? 8Why provoke me to anger with
what your hands have made, burning incense to other gods in Egypt, where you have
come to live? You will destroy yourselves and
make yourselves an object of cursing and reproach among all the nations on earth. 9Have
you forgotten the wickedness committed by
your fathers and by the kings and queens of
Judah and the wickedness committed by you
and your wives in the land of Judah and the
streets of Jerusalem? 10To this day they have
not humbled themselves or shown reverence,
nor have they followed my law and the decrees
I set before you and your fathers.
11"Therefore, this is what the LORD Almighty, the God of Israel, says: I am determined to bring disaster on you and to destroy
all Judah. 12I will take away the remnant of
Judah who were determined to go to Egypt
to settle there. They will all perish in Egypt;
they will fall by the sword or die from famine. From the least to the greatest, they will
die by sword or famine. They will become an
object of cursing and horror, of condemnation
and reproach. 13I will punish those who live in
Egypt with the sword, famine and plague, as I
punished Jerusalem. 14None of the remnant of
Judah who have gone to live in Egypt will escape or survive to return to the land of Judah,
to which they long to return and live; none
will return except a few fugitives."
15Then all the men who knew that their
wives were burning incense to other gods,
along with all the women who were present—a
large assembly—and all the people living in
Lower and Upper Egypt,[f] said to Jeremiah,
16"We will not listen to the message you have
spoken to us in the name of the LORD! 17We
will certainly do everything we said we would:
We will burn incense to the Queen of Heaven
and will pour out drink offerings to her just as
we and our fathers, our kings and our officials
did in the towns of Judah and in the streets of
Jerusalem. At that time we had plenty of food

[a] 3 Or *Chaldeans* [b] 12 Or *I* [c] 13 Or *in Heliopolis* [d] 1 Hebrew *Noph* [e] 1 Hebrew *in Pathros* [f] 15 Hebrew *in Egypt and Pathros*

M **MONDAY**
READ JEREMIAH 44:1–30

NO MORE BLAME GAME

Joe and Annie struggled with financial problems, family disagreements and work issues. Yet they learned to dance around problems in a kind of blame game, saying: "It's her fault!" "It's his fault!" They both sidestepped taking responsibility for making mistakes, doing wrong or harming others. Meanwhile, their problems got worse.

The blame game has been going on for a long time. During King Manasseh's reign in Israel, husbands and wives enjoyed prosperity. But by the time of King Josiah, those benefits had disappeared. People wanted the good times to return. Instead of appealing to the God of Israel, however, the people placed their trust in other gods. The women, in particular, worshiped Ishtar, the goddess of sexual love and fertility. They poured out food and drink offerings to her, hoping that the Queen of Heaven would help them prosper.

Yet when the prophet Jeremiah berated the Jews who had fled to Egypt after the fall of Jerusalem for their faithlessness to the Lord, the women danced away from responsibility, passing it off on their husbands. It is true that in those days a religious vow made by a married woman had to be confirmed by her husband. Still, it wasn't right for the women to shift the responsibility for their sins to their husbands.

"When we burned incense to the Queen of Heaven and poured out drink offerings to her, did not our husbands know that we were making cakes like her image and pouring out drink offerings to her?"

— JEREMIAH 44:19

let's talk

- **How do we play the blame game?**
- **How am I responsible for the sins you commit? How do we each contribute to the behavior of the other? How can we repent of sin together?**
- **Is there ever a time when one of us is 100 percent responsible, while the other is blameless? What about a 90–10 split in responsibility? 50–50? Does it matter?**

The men played the blame game too. They said that when things had gone well, they had brought offerings of thanks to the Queen of Heaven. But when they had stopped doing that, the blessings had dried up. So they intended to keep right on worshiping the Queen of Heaven. Indirectly, of course, they were blaming the God of Israel for not taking care of them.

Jeremiah didn't let anyone off the hook. He held both men and women responsible for worshiping false gods rather than the one true God.

In marriage we are responsible for our actions, both individually and as a couple. If a husband lies on a tax return, for example, and the wife finds out, she is obligated before God to confront her husband about his dishonesty. Likewise, if a wife takes part in spreading gossip about someone in the neighborhood, her husband needs to confront her.

Yes, in each example, the one who sins is primarily responsible for that sin. But because we are in covenant relationship with each other and have become "one flesh," we also have the responsibility to help each other live right before God. Without being overly self-righteous or condemning, we need to understand the full extent of each other's sin, forgive what can be forgiven, work to loosen the grip of that sin, and hold each other accountable.

—JOHN R. THROOP

FOR YOUR NEXT DEVOTIONAL READING, TURN TO PAGE 889.

and were well off and suffered no harm. 18But
ever since we stopped burning incense to the
Queen of Heaven and pouring out drink offerings to her, we have had nothing and have
been perishing by sword and famine."
19The women added, "When we burned incense to the Queen of Heaven and poured out
drink offerings to her, did not our husbands
know that we were making cakes like her image and pouring out drink offerings to her?"
20Then Jeremiah said to all the people,
both men and women, who were answering
him, 21"Did not the LORD remember and
think about the incense burned in the towns
of Judah and the streets of Jerusalem by you
and your fathers, your kings and your officials and the people of the land? 22When the
LORD could no longer endure your wicked actions and the detestable things you did, your
land became an object of cursing and a desolate waste without inhabitants, as it is today.
23Because you have burned incense and have
sinned against the LORD and have not obeyed
him or followed his law or his decrees or his
stipulations, this disaster has come upon you,
as you now see."
24Then Jeremiah said to all the people, including the women, "Hear the word of the
LORD, all you people of Judah in Egypt. 25This
is what the LORD Almighty, the God of Israel,
says: You and your wives have shown by your
actions what you promised when you said,
'We will certainly carry out the vows we made
to burn incense and pour out drink offerings
to the Queen of Heaven.'
"Go ahead then, do what you promised!
Keep your vows! 26But hear the word of the
LORD, all Jews living in Egypt: 'I swear by my
great name,' says the LORD, 'that no one from
Judah living anywhere in Egypt will ever again
invoke my name or swear, "As surely as the
Sovereign LORD lives." 27For I am watching
over them for harm, not for good; the Jews
in Egypt will perish by sword and famine until they are all destroyed. 28Those who escape
the sword and return to the land of Judah
from Egypt will be very few. Then the whole
remnant of Judah who came to live in Egypt
will know whose word will stand—mine or
theirs.
29" 'This will be the sign to you that I will
punish you in this place,' declares the LORD,
'so that you will know that my threats of harm
against you will surely stand.' 30This is what
the LORD says: 'I am going to hand Pharaoh
Hophra king of Egypt over to his enemies
who seek his life, just as I handed Zedekiah
king of Judah over to Nebuchadnezzar king
of Babylon, the enemy who was seeking his
life.' "

A Message to Baruch

45 This is what Jeremiah the prophet told
Baruch son of Neriah in the fourth year
of Jehoiakim son of Josiah king of Judah, after Baruch had written on a scroll the
words Jeremiah was then dictating: 2"This is
what the LORD, the God of Israel, says to you,
Baruch: 3You said, 'Woe to me! The LORD has
added sorrow to my pain; I am worn out with
groaning and find no rest.' "
4⌞The LORD said,⌟ "Say this to him: 'This
is what the LORD says: I will overthrow what
I have built and uproot what I have planted,
throughout the land. 5Should you then seek
great things for yourself? Seek them not. For
I will bring disaster on all people, declares the
LORD, but wherever you go I will let you escape with your life.' "

A Message About Egypt

46 This is the word of the LORD that came
to Jeremiah the prophet concerning the
nations:

2Concerning Egypt:

This is the message against the army of
Pharaoh Neco king of Egypt, which was defeated at Carchemish on the Euphrates River by Nebuchadnezzar king of Babylon in the
fourth year of Jehoiakim son of Josiah king of
Judah:

3"Prepare your shields, both large and
small,
and march out for battle!
4Harness the horses,
mount the steeds!
Take your positions
with helmets on!
Polish your spears,
put on your armor!
5What do I see?
They are terrified,
they are retreating,
their warriors are defeated.
They flee in haste
without looking back,
and there is terror on every side,"
declares the LORD.

6"The swift cannot flee
nor the strong escape.
In the north by the River Euphrates
they stumble and fall.

7 "Who is this that rises like the Nile,
like rivers of surging waters?
8 Egypt rises like the Nile,
like rivers of surging waters.
She says, 'I will rise and cover the earth;
I will destroy cities and their people.'
9 Charge, O horses!
Drive furiously, O charioteers!
March on, O warriors—
men of Cush[a] and Put who carry shields,
men of Lydia who draw the bow.
10 But that day belongs to the Lord, the LORD Almighty—
a day of vengeance, for vengeance on his foes.
The sword will devour till it is satisfied,
till it has quenched its thirst with blood.
For the Lord, the LORD Almighty, will offer sacrifice
in the land of the north by the River Euphrates.

11 "Go up to Gilead and get balm,
O Virgin Daughter of Egypt.
But you multiply remedies in vain;
there is no healing for you.
12 The nations will hear of your shame;
your cries will fill the earth.
One warrior will stumble over another;
both will fall down together."

13 This is the message the LORD spoke to Jeremiah the prophet about the coming of Nebuchadnezzar king of Babylon to attack Egypt:

14 "Announce this in Egypt, and proclaim it in Migdol;
proclaim it also in Memphis[b] and Tahpanhes:
'Take your positions and get ready,
for the sword devours those around you.'
15 Why will your warriors be laid low?
They cannot stand, for the LORD will push them down.
16 They will stumble repeatedly;
they will fall over each other.
They will say, 'Get up, let us go back
to our own people and our native lands,
away from the sword of the oppressor.'
17 There they will exclaim,
'Pharaoh king of Egypt is only a loud noise;
he has missed his opportunity.'

18 "As surely as I live," declares the King,
whose name is the LORD Almighty,
"one will come who is like Tabor among the mountains,
like Carmel by the sea.
19 Pack your belongings for exile,
you who live in Egypt,
for Memphis will be laid waste
and lie in ruins without inhabitant.

20 "Egypt is a beautiful heifer,
but a gadfly is coming
against her from the north.
21 The mercenaries in her ranks
are like fattened calves.
They too will turn and flee together,
they will not stand their ground,
for the day of disaster is coming upon them,
the time for them to be punished.
22 Egypt will hiss like a fleeing serpent
as the enemy advances in force;
they will come against her with axes,
like men who cut down trees.
23 They will chop down her forest,"
declares the LORD,
"dense though it be.
They are more numerous than locusts,
they cannot be counted.
24 The Daughter of Egypt will be put to shame,
handed over to the people of the north."

25 The LORD Almighty, the God of Israel,
says: "I am about to bring punishment on
Amon god of Thebes,[c] on Pharaoh, on Egypt
and her gods and her kings, and on those who
rely on Pharaoh. 26 I will hand them over to
those who seek their lives, to Nebuchadnezzar
king of Babylon and his officers. Later, however, Egypt will be inhabited as in times past,"
declares the LORD.

27 "Do not fear, O Jacob my servant;
do not be dismayed, O Israel.
I will surely save you out of a distant place,
your descendants from the land of their exile.
Jacob will again have peace and security,
and no one will make him afraid.
28 Do not fear, O Jacob my servant,
for I am with you," declares the LORD.
"Though I completely destroy all the nations
among which I scatter you,

[a] 9 That is, the upper Nile region [b] 14 Hebrew *Noph*; also in verse 19 [c] 25 Hebrew *No*

I will not completely destroy you.
I will discipline you but only with justice;
I will not let you go entirely
unpunished."

A Message About the Philistines

47 This is the word of the LORD that came to Jeremiah the prophet concerning the Philistines before Pharaoh attacked Gaza:

2 This is what the LORD says:

"See how the waters are rising in the north;
they will become an overflowing torrent.
They will overflow the land and everything in it,
the towns and those who live in them.
The people will cry out;
all who dwell in the land will wail
3 at the sound of the hoofs of galloping steeds,
at the noise of enemy chariots
and the rumble of their wheels.
Fathers will not turn to help their children;
their hands will hang limp.
4 For the day has come
to destroy all the Philistines
and to cut off all survivors
who could help Tyre and Sidon.
The LORD is about to destroy the Philistines,
the remnant from the coasts of Caphtor.[a]
5 Gaza will shave her head in mourning;
Ashkelon will be silenced.
O remnant on the plain,
how long will you cut yourselves?
6 " 'Ah, sword of the LORD,' ⌊you cry,⌋
'how long till you rest?
Return to your scabbard;
cease and be still.'
7 But how can it rest
when the LORD has commanded it,
when he has ordered it
to attack Ashkelon and the coast?"

A Message About Moab

48 Concerning Moab:

This is what the LORD Almighty, the God of Israel, says:

"Woe to Nebo, for it will be ruined.
Kiriathaim will be disgraced and captured;
the stronghold[b] will be disgraced and shattered.
2 Moab will be praised no more;
in Heshbon[c] men will plot her downfall:
'Come, let us put an end to that nation.'
You too, O Madmen,[d] will be silenced;
the sword will pursue you.
3 Listen to the cries from Horonaim,
cries of great havoc and destruction.
4 Moab will be broken;
her little ones will cry out.[e]
5 They go up the way to Luhith,
weeping bitterly as they go;
on the road down to Horonaim
anguished cries over the destruction are heard.
6 Flee! Run for your lives;
become like a bush[f] in the desert.
7 Since you trust in your deeds and riches,
you too will be taken captive,
and Chemosh will go into exile,
together with his priests and officials.
8 The destroyer will come against every town,
and not a town will escape.
The valley will be ruined
and the plateau destroyed,
because the LORD has spoken.
9 Put salt on Moab,
for she will be laid waste[g];
her towns will become desolate,
with no one to live in them.

10 "A curse on him who is lax in doing the LORD's work!
A curse on him who keeps his sword from bloodshed!

11 "Moab has been at rest from youth,
like wine left on its dregs,
not poured from one jar to another—
she has not gone into exile.
So she tastes as she did,
and her aroma is unchanged.
12 But days are coming,"
declares the LORD,
"when I will send men who pour from jars,
and they will pour her out;
they will empty her jars

[a] 4 That is, Crete [b] 1 Or / *Misgab* [c] 2 The Hebrew for *Heshbon* sounds like the Hebrew for *plot.* [d] 2 The name of the Moabite town Madmen sounds like the Hebrew for *be silenced.* [e] 4 Hebrew; Septuagint / *proclaim it to Zoar* [f] 6 Or *like Aroer* [g] 9 Or *Give wings to Moab, / for she will fly away*

and smash her jugs.
13 Then Moab will be ashamed of
Chemosh,
as the house of Israel was ashamed
when they trusted in Bethel.

14 "How can you say, 'We are warriors,
men valiant in battle'?
15 Moab will be destroyed and her towns
invaded;
her finest young men will go down in
the slaughter,"
declares the King, whose name is the
LORD Almighty.
16 "The fall of Moab is at hand;
her calamity will come quickly.
17 Mourn for her, all who live around her,
all who know her fame;
say, 'How broken is the mighty scepter,
how broken the glorious staff!'

18 "Come down from your glory
and sit on the parched ground,
O inhabitants of the Daughter of
Dibon,
for he who destroys Moab
will come up against you
and ruin your fortified cities.
19 Stand by the road and watch,
you who live in Aroer.
Ask the man fleeing and the woman
escaping,
ask them, 'What has happened?'
20 Moab is disgraced, for she is shattered.
Wail and cry out!
Announce by the Arnon
that Moab is destroyed.
21 Judgment has come to the plateau—
to Holon, Jahzah and Mephaath,
22 to Dibon, Nebo and Beth Diblathaim,
23 to Kiriathaim, Beth Gamul and Beth
Meon,
24 to Kerioth and Bozrah—
to all the towns of Moab, far and near.
25 Moab's horn[a] is cut off;
her arm is broken,"
declares the LORD.

26 "Make her drunk,
for she has defied the LORD.
Let Moab wallow in her vomit;
let her be an object of ridicule.
27 Was not Israel the object of your ridicule?
Was she caught among thieves,
that you shake your head in scorn
whenever you speak of her?
28 Abandon your towns and dwell among the
rocks,
you who live in Moab.
Be like a dove that makes its nest
at the mouth of a cave.

29 "We have heard of Moab's pride—
her overweening pride and conceit,
her pride and arrogance
and the haughtiness of her heart.
30 I know her insolence but it is futile,"
declares the LORD,
"and her boasts accomplish nothing.
31 Therefore I wail over Moab,
for all Moab I cry out,
I moan for the men of Kir Hareseth.
32 I weep for you, as Jazer weeps,
O vines of Sibmah.
Your branches spread as far as the sea;
they reached as far as the sea of Jazer.
The destroyer has fallen
on your ripened fruit and grapes.
33 Joy and gladness are gone
from the orchards and fields of
Moab.
I have stopped the flow of wine from the
presses;
no one treads them with shouts of joy.
Although there are shouts,
they are not shouts of joy.

34 "The sound of their cry rises
from Heshbon to Elealeh and Jahaz,
from Zoar as far as Horonaim and Eglath
Shelishiyah,
for even the waters of Nimrim are dried
up.
35 In Moab I will put an end
to those who make offerings on the
high places
and burn incense to their gods,"
declares the LORD.
36 "So my heart laments for Moab like a
flute;
it laments like a flute for the men of
Kir Hareseth.
The wealth they acquired is gone.
37 Every head is shaved
and every beard cut off;
every hand is slashed
and every waist is covered with
sackcloth.
38 On all the roofs in Moab
and in the public squares
there is nothing but mourning,
for I have broken Moab

---

[a] 25 *Horn* here symbolizes strength.

like a jar that no one wants,"
declares the LORD.
39 "How shattered she is! How they wail!
How Moab turns her back in shame!
Moab has become an object of ridicule,
an object of horror to all those around her."
40 This is what the LORD says:

"Look! An eagle is swooping down,
spreading its wings over Moab.
41 Kerioth[a] will be captured
and the strongholds taken.
In that day the hearts of Moab's warriors
will be like the heart of a woman in labor.
42 Moab will be destroyed as a nation
because she defied the LORD.
43 Terror and pit and snare await you,
O people of Moab,"
declares the LORD.
44 "Whoever flees from the terror
will fall into a pit,
whoever climbs out of the pit
will be caught in a snare;
for I will bring upon Moab
the year of her punishment,"
declares the LORD.

45 "In the shadow of Heshbon
the fugitives stand helpless,
for a fire has gone out from Heshbon,
a blaze from the midst of Sihon;
it burns the foreheads of Moab,
the skulls of the noisy boasters.
46 Woe to you, O Moab!
The people of Chemosh are destroyed;
your sons are taken into exile
and your daughters into captivity.
47 "Yet I will restore the fortunes of Moab
in days to come,"
declares the LORD.

Here ends the judgment on Moab.

A Message About Ammon

49 Concerning the Ammonites:

This is what the LORD says:

"Has Israel no sons?
Has she no heirs?
Why then has Molech[b] taken possession of Gad?
Why do his people live in its towns?
2 But the days are coming,"
declares the LORD,
"when I will sound the battle cry
against Rabbah of the Ammonites;
it will become a mound of ruins,
and its surrounding villages will be set on fire.
Then Israel will drive out
those who drove her out,"
says the LORD.
3 "Wail, O Heshbon, for Ai is destroyed!
Cry out, O inhabitants of Rabbah!
Put on sackcloth and mourn;
rush here and there inside the walls,
for Molech will go into exile,
together with his priests and officials.
4 Why do you boast of your valleys,
boast of your valleys so fruitful?
O unfaithful daughter,
you trust in your riches and say,
'Who will attack me?'
5 I will bring terror on you
from all those around you,"
declares the Lord,
the LORD Almighty.
"Every one of you will be driven away,
and no one will gather the fugitives.

6 "Yet afterward, I will restore the fortunes
of the Ammonites,"
declares the LORD.

A Message About Edom

7 Concerning Edom:

This is what the LORD Almighty says:

"Is there no longer wisdom in Teman?
Has counsel perished from the prudent?
Has their wisdom decayed?
8 Turn and flee, hide in deep caves,
you who live in Dedan,
for I will bring disaster on Esau
at the time I punish him.
9 If grape pickers came to you,
would they not leave a few grapes?
If thieves came during the night,
would they not steal only as much as they wanted?
10 But I will strip Esau bare;
I will uncover his hiding places,
so that he cannot conceal himself.
His children, relatives and neighbors will perish,
and he will be no more.

[a] 41 Or *The cities* [b] 1 Or *their king*; Hebrew *malcam*; also in verse 3

[11]Leave your orphans; I will protect their lives.
Your widows too can trust in me."

[12]This is what the LORD says: "If those who
do not deserve to drink the cup must drink it,
why should you go unpunished? You will not
go unpunished, but must drink it. [13]I swear by
myself," declares the LORD, "that Bozrah will
become a ruin and an object of horror, of reproach and of cursing; and all its towns will be
in ruins forever."

[14]I have heard a message from the LORD:
An envoy was sent to the nations to say,
"Assemble yourselves to attack it!
Rise up for battle!"

[15]"Now I will make you small among the nations,
despised among men.
[16]The terror you inspire
and the pride of your heart have deceived you,
you who live in the clefts of the rocks,
who occupy the heights of the hill.
Though you build your nest as high as the eagle's,
from there I will bring you down,"
declares the LORD.
[17]"Edom will become an object of horror;
all who pass by will be appalled and will scoff
because of all its wounds.
[18]As Sodom and Gomorrah were overthrown,
along with their neighboring towns,"
says the LORD,
"so no one will live there;
no man will dwell in it.

[19]"Like a lion coming up from Jordan's thickets
to a rich pastureland,
I will chase Edom from its land in an instant.
Who is the chosen one I will appoint for this?
Who is like me and who can challenge me?
And what shepherd can stand against me?"
[20]Therefore, hear what the LORD has planned against Edom,
what he has purposed against those who live in Teman:
The young of the flock will be dragged away;
he will completely destroy their pasture because of them.
[21]At the sound of their fall the earth will tremble;
their cry will resound to the Red Sea.[a]
[22]Look! An eagle will soar and swoop down,
spreading its wings over Bozrah.
In that day the hearts of Edom's warriors
will be like the heart of a woman in labor.

A Message About Damascus

[23]Concerning Damascus:

"Hamath and Arpad are dismayed,
for they have heard bad news.
They are disheartened,
troubled like[b] the restless sea.
[24]Damascus has become feeble,
she has turned to flee
and panic has gripped her;
anguish and pain have seized her,
pain like that of a woman in labor.
[25]Why has the city of renown not been abandoned,
the town in which I delight?
[26]Surely, her young men will fall in the streets;
all her soldiers will be silenced in that day,"
declares the LORD Almighty.
[27]"I will set fire to the walls of Damascus;
it will consume the fortresses of Ben-Hadad."

A Message About Kedar and Hazor

[28]Concerning Kedar and the kingdoms of
Hazor, which Nebuchadnezzar king of Babylon attacked:

This is what the LORD says:

"Arise, and attack Kedar
and destroy the people of the East.
[29]Their tents and their flocks will be taken;
their shelters will be carried off
with all their goods and camels.
Men will shout to them,
'Terror on every side!'
[30]"Flee quickly away!
Stay in deep caves, you who live in Hazor,"
declares the LORD.

[a] 21 Hebrew *Yam Suph*; that is, Sea of Reeds [b] 23 Hebrew *on* or *by*

"Nebuchadnezzar king of Babylon has
plotted against you;
he has devised a plan against you.

31 "Arise and attack a nation at ease,
which lives in confidence,"
declares the LORD,
"a nation that has neither gates nor bars;
its people live alone.
32 Their camels will become plunder,
and their large herds will be booty.
I will scatter to the winds those who are in
distant places[a]
and will bring disaster on them from
every side,"
declares the LORD.
33 "Hazor will become a haunt of jackals,
a desolate place forever.
No one will live there;
no man will dwell in it."

A Message About Elam

34 This is the word of the LORD that came to
Jeremiah the prophet concerning Elam, early
in the reign of Zedekiah king of Judah:
35 This is what the LORD Almighty says:

"See, I will break the bow of Elam,
the mainstay of their might.
36 I will bring against Elam the four winds
from the four quarters of the heavens;
I will scatter them to the four winds,
and there will not be a nation
where Elam's exiles do not go.
37 I will shatter Elam before their foes,
before those who seek their lives;
I will bring disaster upon them,
even my fierce anger,"
declares the LORD.
"I will pursue them with the sword
until I have made an end of them.
38 I will set my throne in Elam
and destroy her king and officials,"
declares the LORD.

39 "Yet I will restore the fortunes of Elam
in days to come,"
declares the LORD.

A Message About Babylon

50 This is the word the LORD spoke through
Jeremiah the prophet concerning Babylon and the land of the Babylonians[b]:

2 "Announce and proclaim among the
nations,
lift up a banner and proclaim it;
keep nothing back, but say,
'Babylon will be captured;
Bel will be put to shame,
Marduk filled with terror.
Her images will be put to shame
and her idols filled with terror.'
3 A nation from the north will attack her
and lay waste her land.
No one will live in it;
both men and animals will flee away.

4 "In those days, at that time,"
declares the LORD,
"the people of Israel and the people of
Judah together
will go in tears to seek the LORD their
God.
5 They will ask the way to Zion
and turn their faces toward it.
They will come and bind themselves to the
LORD
in an everlasting covenant
that will not be forgotten.

6 "My people have been lost sheep;
their shepherds have led them astray
and caused them to roam on the
mountains.
They wandered over mountain and hill
and forgot their own resting place.
7 Whoever found them devoured them;
their enemies said, 'We are not guilty,
for they sinned against the LORD, their
true pasture,
the LORD, the hope of their fathers.'

8 "Flee out of Babylon;
leave the land of the Babylonians,
and be like the goats that lead the flock.
9 For I will stir up and bring against
Babylon
an alliance of great nations from the
land of the north.
They will take up their positions against
her,
and from the north she will be
captured.
Their arrows will be like skilled warriors
who do not return empty-handed.
10 So Babylonia[c] will be plundered;
all who plunder her will have their fill,"
declares the LORD.

11 "Because you rejoice and are glad,
you who pillage my inheritance,
because you frolic like a heifer threshing
grain

[a] 32 Or *who clip the hair by their foreheads* [b] 1 Or *Chaldeans*; also in verses 8, 25, 35 and 45 [c] 10 Or *Chaldea*

and neigh like stallions,
12 your mother will be greatly ashamed;
she who gave you birth will be disgraced.
She will be the least of the nations—
a wilderness, a dry land, a desert.
13 Because of the LORD's anger she will not be inhabited
but will be completely desolate.
All who pass Babylon will be horrified and scoff
because of all her wounds.

14 "Take up your positions around Babylon,
all you who draw the bow.
Shoot at her! Spare no arrows,
for she has sinned against the LORD.
15 Shout against her on every side!
She surrenders, her towers fall,
her walls are torn down.
Since this is the vengeance of the LORD,
take vengeance on her;
do to her as she has done to others.
16 Cut off from Babylon the sower,
and the reaper with his sickle at harvest.
Because of the sword of the oppressor
let everyone return to his own people,
let everyone flee to his own land.

17 "Israel is a scattered flock
that lions have chased away.
The first to devour him
was the king of Assyria;
the last to crush his bones
was Nebuchadnezzar king of Babylon."

18 Therefore this is what the LORD Almighty, the God of Israel, says:

"I will punish the king of Babylon and his land
as I punished the king of Assyria.
19 But I will bring Israel back to his own pasture
and he will graze on Carmel and Bashan;
his appetite will be satisfied
on the hills of Ephraim and Gilead.
20 In those days, at that time,"
declares the LORD,
"search will be made for Israel's guilt,
but there will be none,
and for the sins of Judah,
but none will be found,
for I will forgive the remnant I spare.

21 "Attack the land of Merathaim
and those who live in Pekod.
Pursue, kill and completely destroy[a] them,"
declares the LORD.
"Do everything I have commanded you.
22 The noise of battle is in the land,
the noise of great destruction!
23 How broken and shattered
is the hammer of the whole earth!
How desolate is Babylon
among the nations!
24 I set a trap for you, O Babylon,
and you were caught before you knew it;
you were found and captured
because you opposed the LORD.
25 The LORD has opened his arsenal
and brought out the weapons of his wrath,
for the Sovereign LORD Almighty has work to do
in the land of the Babylonians.
26 Come against her from afar.
Break open her granaries;
pile her up like heaps of grain.
Completely destroy her
and leave her no remnant.
27 Kill all her young bulls;
let them go down to the slaughter!
Woe to them! For their day has come,
the time for them to be punished.
28 Listen to the fugitives and refugees from Babylon
declaring in Zion
how the LORD our God has taken vengeance,
vengeance for his temple.

29 "Summon archers against Babylon,
all those who draw the bow.
Encamp all around her;
let no one escape.
Repay her for her deeds;
do to her as she has done.
For she has defied the LORD,
the Holy One of Israel.
30 Therefore, her young men will fall in the streets;
all her soldiers will be silenced in that day,"
declares the LORD.
31 "See, I am against you, O arrogant one,"
declares the Lord, the LORD Almighty,

a 21 The Hebrew term refers to the irrevocable giving over of things or persons to the LORD, often by totally destroying them; also in verse 26.

"for your day has come,
the time for you to be punished.
32 The arrogant one will stumble and fall
and no one will help her up;
I will kindle a fire in her towns
that will consume all who are around
her."

33 This is what the LORD Almighty says:

"The people of Israel are oppressed,
and the people of Judah as well.
All their captors hold them fast,
refusing to let them go.
34 Yet their Redeemer is strong;
the LORD Almighty is his name.
He will vigorously defend their cause
so that he may bring rest to their land,
but unrest to those who live in
Babylon.

35 "A sword against the Babylonians!"
declares the LORD—
"against those who live in Babylon
and against her officials and wise men!
36 A sword against her false prophets!
They will become fools.
A sword against her warriors!
They will be filled with terror.
37 A sword against her horses and chariots
and all the foreigners in her ranks!
They will become women.
A sword against her treasures!
They will be plundered.
38 A drought on [a] her waters!
They will dry up.
For it is a land of idols,
idols that will go mad with terror.

39 "So desert creatures and hyenas will live
there,
and there the owl will dwell.
It will never again be inhabited
or lived in from generation to
generation.
40 As God overthrew Sodom and Gomorrah
along with their neighboring towns,"
declares the LORD,
"so no one will live there;
no man will dwell in it.
41 "Look! An army is coming from the north;
a great nation and many kings
are being stirred up from the ends of
the earth.
42 They are armed with bows and spears;
they are cruel and without mercy.
They sound like the roaring sea
as they ride on their horses;
they come like men in battle formation
to attack you, O Daughter of Babylon.
43 The king of Babylon has heard reports
about them,
and his hands hang limp.
Anguish has gripped him,
pain like that of a woman in labor.
44 Like a lion coming up from Jordan's
thickets
to a rich pastureland,
I will chase Babylon from its land in an
instant.
Who is the chosen one I will appoint
for this?
Who is like me and who can challenge
me?
And what shepherd can stand against
me?"
45 Therefore, hear what the LORD has
planned against Babylon,
what he has purposed against the land
of the Babylonians:
The young of the flock will be dragged
away;
he will completely destroy their pasture
because of them.
46 At the sound of Babylon's capture the
earth will tremble;
its cry will resound among the nations.

51 This is what the LORD says:

"See, I will stir up the spirit of a
destroyer
against Babylon and the people of Leb
Kamai. [b]
2 I will send foreigners to Babylon
to winnow her and to devastate her
land;
they will oppose her on every side
in the day of her disaster.
3 Let not the archer string his bow,
nor let him put on his armor.
Do not spare her young men;
completely destroy [c] her army.
4 They will fall down slain in Babylon, [d]
fatally wounded in her streets.
5 For Israel and Judah have not been
forsaken
by their God, the LORD Almighty,
though their land [e] is full of guilt

[a] 38 Or *A sword against* [b] 1 *Leb Kamai* is a cryptogram for Chaldea, that is, Babylonia. [c] 3 The Hebrew term refers to the irrevocable giving over of things or persons to the LORD, often by totally destroying them. [d] 4 Or *Chaldea* [e] 5 Or *| and the land of the Babylonians|*

before the Holy One of Israel.

6 "Flee from Babylon!
Run for your lives!
Do not be destroyed because of her sins.
It is time for the LORD's vengeance;
he will pay her what she deserves.
7 Babylon was a gold cup in the LORD's hand;
she made the whole earth drunk.
The nations drank her wine;
therefore they have now gone mad.
8 Babylon will suddenly fall and be broken.
Wail over her!
Get balm for her pain;
perhaps she can be healed.

9 " 'We would have healed Babylon,
but she cannot be healed;
let us leave her and each go to his own land,
for her judgment reaches to the skies,
it rises as high as the clouds.'

10 " 'The LORD has vindicated us;
come, let us tell in Zion
what the LORD our God has done.'

11 "Sharpen the arrows,
take up the shields!
The LORD has stirred up the kings of the Medes,
because his purpose is to destroy Babylon.
The LORD will take vengeance,
vengeance for his temple.
12 Lift up a banner against the walls of Babylon!
Reinforce the guard,
station the watchmen,
prepare an ambush!
The LORD will carry out his purpose,
his decree against the people of Babylon.
13 You who live by many waters
and are rich in treasures,
your end has come,
the time for you to be cut off.
14 The LORD Almighty has sworn by himself:
I will surely fill you with men, as with a swarm of locusts,
and they will shout in triumph over you.

15 "He made the earth by his power;
he founded the world by his wisdom
and stretched out the heavens by his understanding.
16 When he thunders, the waters in the heavens roar;
he makes clouds rise from the ends of the earth.
He sends lightning with the rain
and brings out the wind from his storehouses.

17 "Every man is senseless and without knowledge;
every goldsmith is shamed by his idols.
His images are a fraud;
they have no breath in them.
18 They are worthless, the objects of mockery;
when their judgment comes, they will perish.
19 He who is the Portion of Jacob is not like these,
for he is the Maker of all things,
including the tribe of his inheritance—
the LORD Almighty is his name.

20 "You are my war club,
my weapon for battle—
with you I shatter nations,
with you I destroy kingdoms,
21 with you I shatter horse and rider,
with you I shatter chariot and driver,
22 with you I shatter man and woman,
with you I shatter old man and youth,
with you I shatter young man and maiden,
23 with you I shatter shepherd and flock,
with you I shatter farmer and oxen,
with you I shatter governors and officials.

24 "Before your eyes I will repay Babylon and all who live in Babylonia[a] for all the wrong they have done in Zion," declares the LORD.

25 "I am against you, O destroying mountain,
you who destroy the whole earth,"
declares the LORD.
"I will stretch out my hand against you,
roll you off the cliffs,
and make you a burned-out mountain.
26 No rock will be taken from you for a cornerstone,
nor any stone for a foundation,
for you will be desolate forever,"
declares the LORD.

27 "Lift up a banner in the land!

---

[a] 24 Or *Chaldea*; also in verse 35

Blow the trumpet among the nations!
Prepare the nations for battle against her;
summon against her these kingdoms:
Ararat, Minni and Ashkenaz.
Appoint a commander against her;
send up horses like a swarm of locusts.
28 Prepare the nations for battle against
her—
the kings of the Medes,
their governors and all their officials,
and all the countries they rule.
29 The land trembles and writhes,
for the LORD's purposes against
Babylon stand—
to lay waste the land of Babylon
so that no one will live there.
30 Babylon's warriors have stopped fighting;
they remain in their strongholds.
Their strength is exhausted;
they have become like women.
Her dwellings are set on fire;
the bars of her gates are broken.
31 One courier follows another
and messenger follows messenger
to announce to the king of Babylon
that his entire city is captured,
32 the river crossings seized,
the marshes set on fire,
and the soldiers terrified."

33 This is what the LORD Almighty, the God of Israel, says:

"The Daughter of Babylon is like a
threshing floor
at the time it is trampled;
the time to harvest her will soon come."

34 "Nebuchadnezzar king of Babylon has
devoured us,
he has thrown us into confusion,
he has made us an empty jar.
Like a serpent he has swallowed us
and filled his stomach with our
delicacies,
and then has spewed us out.
35 May the violence done to our flesh[a] be
upon Babylon,"
say the inhabitants of Zion.
"May our blood be on those who live in
Babylonia,"
says Jerusalem.

36 Therefore, this is what the LORD says:

"See, I will defend your cause
and avenge you;
I will dry up her sea
and make her springs dry.
37 Babylon will be a heap of ruins,
a haunt of jackals,
an object of horror and scorn,
a place where no one lives.
38 Her people all roar like young lions,
they growl like lion cubs.
39 But while they are aroused,
I will set out a feast for them
and make them drunk,
so that they shout with laughter—
then sleep forever and not awake,"
declares the LORD.

40 "I will bring them down
like lambs to the slaughter,
like rams and goats.

41 "How Sheshach[b] will be captured,
the boast of the whole earth seized!
What a horror Babylon will be
among the nations!
42 The sea will rise over Babylon;
its roaring waves will cover her.
43 Her towns will be desolate,
a dry and desert land,
a land where no one lives,
through which no man travels.
44 I will punish Bel in Babylon
and make him spew out what he has
swallowed.
The nations will no longer stream to him.
And the wall of Babylon will fall.

45 "Come out of her, my people!
Run for your lives!
Run from the fierce anger of the LORD.
46 Do not lose heart or be afraid
when rumors are heard in the land;
one rumor comes this year, another the
next,
rumors of violence in the land
and of ruler against ruler.
47 For the time will surely come
when I will punish the idols of
Babylon;
her whole land will be disgraced
and her slain will all lie fallen within
her.
48 Then heaven and earth and all that is in
them
will shout for joy over Babylon,
for out of the north
destroyers will attack her,"
declares the LORD.

49 "Babylon must fall because of Israel's slain,
just as the slain in all the earth

[a] 35 Or *done to us and to our children* [b] 41 *Sheshach* is a cryptogram for Babylon.

have fallen because of Babylon.
50 You who have escaped the sword,
leave and do not linger!
Remember the LORD in a distant land,
and think on Jerusalem."

51 "We are disgraced,
for we have been insulted
and shame covers our faces,
because foreigners have entered
the holy places of the LORD's house."

52 "But days are coming," declares the LORD,
"when I will punish her idols,
and throughout her land
the wounded will groan.
53 Even if Babylon reaches the sky
and fortifies her lofty stronghold,
I will send destroyers against her,"
declares the LORD.

54 "The sound of a cry comes from Babylon,
the sound of great destruction
from the land of the Babylonians.[a]
55 The LORD will destroy Babylon;
he will silence her noisy din.
Waves ⌊of enemies⌋ will rage like great waters;
the roar of their voices will resound.
56 A destroyer will come against Babylon;
her warriors will be captured,
and their bows will be broken.
For the LORD is a God of retribution;
he will repay in full.
57 I will make her officials and wise men drunk,
her governors, officers and warriors as well;
they will sleep forever and not awake,"
declares the King, whose name is the LORD Almighty.

58 This is what the LORD Almighty says:

"Babylon's thick wall will be leveled
and her high gates set on fire;
the peoples exhaust themselves for nothing,
the nations' labor is only fuel for the flames."

59 This is the message Jeremiah gave to the
staff officer Seraiah son of Neriah, the son of
Mahseiah, when he went to Babylon with
Zedekiah king of Judah in the fourth year of
his reign. 60 Jeremiah had written on a scroll
about all the disasters that would come upon
Babylon—all that had been recorded concerning Babylon. 61 He said to Seraiah, "When
you get to Babylon, see that you read all these
words aloud. 62 Then say, 'O LORD, you have
said you will destroy this place, so that neither
man nor animal will live in it; it will be desolate forever.' 63 When you finish reading this
scroll, tie a stone to it and throw it into the
Euphrates. 64 Then say, 'So will Babylon sink
to rise no more because of the disaster I will
bring upon her. And her people will fall.' "

The words of Jeremiah end here.

The Fall of Jerusalem

52 Zedekiah was twenty-one years old
when he became king, and he reigned
in Jerusalem eleven years. His mother's
name was Hamutal daughter of Jeremiah; she
was from Libnah. 2 He did evil in the eyes of
the LORD, just as Jehoiakim had done. 3 It was
because of the LORD's anger that all this happened to Jerusalem and Judah, and in the end
he thrust them from his presence.

Now Zedekiah rebelled against the king of Babylon.

4 So in the ninth year of Zedekiah's reign, on
the tenth day of the tenth month, Nebuchadnezzar king of Babylon marched against Jerusalem with his whole army. They camped outside the city and built siege works all around
it. 5 The city was kept under siege until the
eleventh year of King Zedekiah.

6 By the ninth day of the fourth month the
famine in the city had become so severe that
there was no food for the people to eat. 7 Then
the city wall was broken through, and the
whole army fled. They left the city at night
through the gate between the two walls near
the king's garden, though the Babylonians[b]
were surrounding the city. They fled toward
the Arabah,[c] 8 but the Babylonian[d] army pursued King Zedekiah and overtook him in the
plains of Jericho. All his soldiers were separated from him and scattered, 9 and he was captured.

He was taken to the king of Babylon at Riblah in the land of Hamath, where he pronounced sentence on him. 10 There at Riblah
the king of Babylon slaughtered the sons of
Zedekiah before his eyes; he also killed all the
officials of Judah. 11 Then he put out Zedekiah's eyes, bound him with bronze shackles and
took him to Babylon, where he put him in
prison till the day of his death.

12 On the tenth day of the fifth month,
in the nineteenth year of Nebuchadnezzar

[a] 54 Or *Chaldeans* [b] 7 Or *Chaldeans*; also in verse 17 [c] 7 Or *the Jordan Valley* [d] 8 Or *Chaldean*; also in verse 14

king of Babylon, Nebuzaradan commander
of the imperial guard, who served the king
of Babylon, came to Jerusalem. [13]He set fire
to the temple of the LORD, the royal palace
and all the houses of Jerusalem. Every important building he burned down. [14]The whole
Babylonian army under the commander of
the imperial guard broke down all the walls
around Jerusalem. [15]Nebuzaradan the commander of the guard carried into exile some of
the poorest people and those who remained in
the city, along with the rest of the craftsmen[a]
and those who had gone over to the king of
Babylon. [16]But Nebuzaradan left behind the
rest of the poorest people of the land to work
the vineyards and fields.

[17]The Babylonians broke up the bronze pillars, the movable stands and the bronze Sea
that were at the temple of the LORD and they
carried all the bronze to Babylon. [18]They also
took away the pots, shovels, wick trimmers,
sprinkling bowls, dishes and all the bronze articles used in the temple service. [19]The commander of the imperial guard took away the
basins, censers, sprinkling bowls, pots, lampstands, dishes and bowls used for drink offerings—all that were made of pure gold or
silver.

[20]The bronze from the two pillars, the Sea
and the twelve bronze bulls under it, and the
movable stands, which King Solomon had
made for the temple of the LORD, was more
than could be weighed. [21]Each of the pillars
was eighteen cubits high and twelve cubits in
circumference[b]; each was four fingers thick,
and hollow. [22]The bronze capital on top of
the one pillar was five cubits[c] high and was
decorated with a network and pomegranates
of bronze all around. The other pillar, with
its pomegranates, was similar. [23]There were
ninety-six pomegranates on the sides; the total
number of pomegranates above the surrounding network was a hundred.

[24]The commander of the guard took as prisoners Seraiah the chief priest, Zephaniah the
priest next in rank and the three doorkeepers.
[25]Of those still in the city, he took the officer in charge of the fighting men, and seven
royal advisers. He also took the secretary who
was chief officer in charge of conscripting the
people of the land and sixty of his men who
were found in the city. [26]Nebuzaradan the
commander took them all and brought them
to the king of Babylon at Riblah. [27]There at
Riblah, in the land of Hamath, the king had
them executed.

So Judah went into captivity, away from her
land. [28]This is the number of the people Nebuchadnezzar carried into exile:

in the seventh year, 3,023 Jews;
[29] in Nebuchadnezzar's eighteenth year,
832 people from Jerusalem;
[30] in his twenty-third year,
745 Jews taken into exile by Nebuzaradan the commander of the imperial
guard.
There were 4,600 people in all.

Jehoiachin Released

[31]In the thirty-seventh year of the exile of
Jehoiachin king of Judah, in the year Evil-Merodach[d] became king of Babylon, he released
Jehoiachin king of Judah and freed him from
prison on the twenty-fifth day of the twelfth
month. [32]He spoke kindly to him and gave
him a seat of honor higher than those of the
other kings who were with him in Babylon.
[33]So Jehoiachin put aside his prison clothes
and for the rest of his life ate regularly at the
king's table. [34]Day by day the king of Babylon
gave Jehoiachin a regular allowance as long as
he lived, till the day of his death.

[a] *15* Or *populace* [b] *21* That is, about 27 feet (about 8.1 meters) high and 18 feet (about 5.4 meters) in circumference [c] *22* That is, about 7 1/2 feet (about 2.3 meters) [d] *31* Also called *Amel-Marduk*

LAMENTATIONS

Lamentations

QUICK FACTS

AUTHOR Unknown, but quite possibly Jeremiah

AUDIENCE All who mourned Jerusalem's destruction

DATE Shortly after the fall of Jerusalem in 586 B.C.

SETTING The Babylonians had destroyed Jerusalem and had either killed or taken away its inhabitants as captives.

The book of Lamentations was likely written by the prophet Jeremiah (2 Chronicles 35:25 mentions that he composed laments), who was an eyewitness to the fall of Jerusalem. The book contains five poems or songs. The first four are laments and the last is a prayer. The vivid descriptions indicate a heart that was breaking over the complete ruin of the city, the temple and Judah's people under the conquering Babylonians. It describes great national sorrow.

Lamentations was obviously written shortly after the fall of Jerusalem because the horrible details were still fresh in the author's mind. The book begins by likening the great city to a widowed and shamed queen. Fittingly, the book ends in a prayer for mercy. Although the author clearly admitted despair at Judah's captivity, he concluded that God alone rules all things and has the power to restore. In these few brief lines we see a glimmer of hope.

For those of us struggling with difficulties in marriage, we can be assured that God listens to our honest prayers and is in control of our situations. As we put our trust in God, he will sustain us.

1 [a]How deserted lies the city,
once so full of people!
How like a widow is she,
who once was great among the nations!
She who was queen among the provinces
has now become a slave.

2 Bitterly she weeps at night,
tears are upon her cheeks.
Among all her lovers
there is none to comfort her.
All her friends have betrayed her;
they have become her enemies.

3 After affliction and harsh labor,
Judah has gone into exile.
She dwells among the nations;
she finds no resting place.
All who pursue her have overtaken her
in the midst of her distress.

4 The roads to Zion mourn,
for no one comes to her appointed
feasts.
All her gateways are desolate,
her priests groan,
her maidens grieve,
and she is in bitter anguish.

5 Her foes have become her masters;
her enemies are at ease.
The LORD has brought her grief
because of her many sins.
Her children have gone into exile,
captive before the foe.

6 All the splendor has departed
from the Daughter of Zion.
Her princes are like deer
that find no pasture;
in weakness they have fled
before the pursuer.

7 In the days of her affliction and
wandering
Jerusalem remembers all the treasures
that were hers in days of old.
When her people fell into enemy hands,
there was no one to help her.
Her enemies looked at her
and laughed at her destruction.

8 Jerusalem has sinned greatly
and so has become unclean.
All who honored her despise her,
for they have seen her nakedness;
she herself groans
and turns away.

9 Her filthiness clung to her skirts;
she did not consider her future.
Her fall was astounding;
there was none to comfort her.
"Look, O LORD, on my affliction,
for the enemy has triumphed."

10 The enemy laid hands
on all her treasures;
she saw pagan nations
enter her sanctuary—
those you had forbidden
to enter your assembly.

11 All her people groan
as they search for bread;
they barter their treasures for food
to keep themselves alive.
"Look, O LORD, and consider,
for I am despised."

12 "Is it nothing to you, all you who pass by?
Look around and see.
Is any suffering like my suffering
that was inflicted on me,
that the LORD brought on me
in the day of his fierce anger?

13 "From on high he sent fire,
sent it down into my bones.
He spread a net for my feet
and turned me back.
He made me desolate,
faint all the day long.

14 "My sins have been bound into a yoke[b];
by his hands they were woven together.
They have come upon my neck
and the Lord has sapped my strength.
He has handed me over
to those I cannot withstand.

15 "The Lord has rejected
all the warriors in my midst;
he has summoned an army against me
to[c] crush my young men.
In his winepress the Lord has trampled
the Virgin Daughter of Judah.

16 "This is why I weep
and my eyes overflow with tears.
No one is near to comfort me,
no one to restore my spirit.
My children are destitute
because the enemy has prevailed."

17 Zion stretches out her hands,
but there is no one to comfort her.
The LORD has decreed for Jacob

[a] This chapter is an acrostic poem, the verses of which begin with the successive letters of the Hebrew alphabet. [b] 14 Most Hebrew manuscripts; Septuagint *He kept watch over my sins* [c] 15 Or *has set a time for me / when he will*

that his neighbors become his foes;
Jerusalem has become
an unclean thing among them.

18 "The LORD is righteous,
yet I rebelled against his command.
Listen, all you peoples;
look upon my suffering.
My young men and maidens
have gone into exile.

19 "I called to my allies
but they betrayed me.
My priests and my elders
perished in the city
while they searched for food
to keep themselves alive.

20 "See, O LORD, how distressed I am!
I am in torment within,
and in my heart I am disturbed,
for I have been most rebellious.
Outside, the sword bereaves;
inside, there is only death.

21 "People have heard my groaning,
but there is no one to comfort me.
All my enemies have heard of my distress;
they rejoice at what you have done.
May you bring the day you have
announced
so they may become like me.

22 "Let all their wickedness come before
you;
deal with them
as you have dealt with me
because of all my sins.
My groans are many
and my heart is faint."

2 [a]How the Lord has covered the Daughter
of Zion
with the cloud of his anger[b]!
He has hurled down the splendor of Israel
from heaven to earth;
he has not remembered his footstool
in the day of his anger.

2 Without pity the Lord has swallowed up
all the dwellings of Jacob;
in his wrath he has torn down
the strongholds of the Daughter of
Judah.
He has brought her kingdom and its
princes
down to the ground in dishonor.

3 In fierce anger he has cut off
every horn[c] of Israel.
He has withdrawn his right hand
at the approach of the enemy.
He has burned in Jacob like a flaming fire
that consumes everything around it.

4 Like an enemy he has strung his bow;
his right hand is ready.
Like a foe he has slain
all who were pleasing to the eye;
he has poured out his wrath like fire
on the tent of the Daughter of Zion.

5 The Lord is like an enemy;
he has swallowed up Israel.
He has swallowed up all her palaces
and destroyed her strongholds.
He has multiplied mourning and
lamentation
for the Daughter of Judah.

6 He has laid waste his dwelling like a
garden;
he has destroyed his place of meeting.
The LORD has made Zion forget
her appointed feasts and her Sabbaths;
in his fierce anger he has spurned
both king and priest.

7 The Lord has rejected his altar
and abandoned his sanctuary.
He has handed over to the enemy
the walls of her palaces;
they have raised a shout in the house of
the LORD
as on the day of an appointed feast.

8 The LORD determined to tear down
the wall around the Daughter of Zion.
He stretched out a measuring line
and did not withhold his hand from
destroying.
He made ramparts and walls lament;
together they wasted away.

9 Her gates have sunk into the ground;
their bars he has broken and destroyed.
Her king and her princes are exiled among
the nations,
the law is no more,
and her prophets no longer find
visions from the LORD.

10 The elders of the Daughter of Zion
sit on the ground in silence;
they have sprinkled dust on their heads
and put on sackcloth.

---

[a] This chapter is an acrostic poem, the verses of which begin with the successive letters of the Hebrew alphabet. [b] *1* Or *How the Lord in his anger / has treated the Daughter of Zion with contempt* [c] *3* Or / *all the strength*; or *every king*; *horn* here symbolizes strength.

The young women of Jerusalem
have bowed their heads to the ground.

11 My eyes fail from weeping,
I am in torment within,
my heart is poured out on the ground
because my people are destroyed,
because children and infants faint
in the streets of the city.

12 They say to their mothers,
"Where is bread and wine?"
as they faint like wounded men
in the streets of the city,
as their lives ebb away
in their mothers' arms.

13 What can I say for you?
With what can I compare you,
O Daughter of Jerusalem?
To what can I liken you,
that I may comfort you,
O Virgin Daughter of Zion?
Your wound is as deep as the sea.
Who can heal you?

14 The visions of your prophets
were false and worthless;
they did not expose your sin
to ward off your captivity.
The oracles they gave you
were false and misleading.

15 All who pass your way
clap their hands at you;
they scoff and shake their heads
at the Daughter of Jerusalem:
"Is this the city that was called
the perfection of beauty,
the joy of the whole earth?"

16 All your enemies open their mouths
wide against you;
they scoff and gnash their teeth
and say, "We have swallowed her up.
This is the day we have waited for;
we have lived to see it."

17 The LORD has done what he planned;
he has fulfilled his word,
which he decreed long ago.
He has overthrown you without pity,
he has let the enemy gloat over you,
he has exalted the horn[a] of your foes.

18 The hearts of the people
cry out to the Lord.
O wall of the Daughter of Zion,
let your tears flow like a river
day and night;
give yourself no relief,
your eyes no rest.

19 Arise, cry out in the night,
as the watches of the night begin;
pour out your heart like water
in the presence of the Lord.
Lift up your hands to him
for the lives of your children,
who faint from hunger
at the head of every street.

20 "Look, O LORD, and consider:
Whom have you ever treated like this?
Should women eat their offspring,
the children they have cared for?
Should priest and prophet be killed
in the sanctuary of the Lord?

21 "Young and old lie together
in the dust of the streets;
my young men and maidens
have fallen by the sword.
You have slain them in the day of your anger;
you have slaughtered them without pity.

22 "As you summon to a feast day,
so you summoned against me terrors on every side.
In the day of the LORD's anger
no one escaped or survived;
those I cared for and reared,
my enemy has destroyed."

3 [b]I am the man who has seen affliction
by the rod of his wrath.
2 He has driven me away and made me walk
in darkness rather than light;
3 indeed, he has turned his hand against me
again and again, all day long.

4 He has made my skin and my flesh grow old
and has broken my bones.
5 He has besieged me and surrounded me
with bitterness and hardship.
6 He has made me dwell in darkness
like those long dead.

7 He has walled me in so I cannot escape;
he has weighed me down with chains.
8 Even when I call out or cry for help,
he shuts out my prayer.

a 17 *Horn* here symbolizes strength. *b* This chapter is an acrostic poem; the verses of each stanza begin with the successive letters of the Hebrew alphabet, and the verses within each stanza begin with the same letter.

TUESDAY
READ
LAMENTATIONS 3:1–33

FOR BETTER, FOR WORSE, FORGIVE

Because of the LORD's great love we are not consumed, for his compassions never fail. They are new every morning; great is your faithfulness.

— LAMENTATIONS 3:22–23

let's talk

- How have the two of us dealt with failure in our marriage?
- What did we do right? What did we do wrong? If we could do it over, how would we change the way we handled it?
- Could my hardness of heart be as much of a barrier to healing as some offense you may have committed against me?

When we married, we vowed to stay together "for better or for worse." But how many of us actually knew what that meant when we said our vows?

We imagined the "better" as romantic walks on moonlit nights, sharing a bowl of popcorn and a movie, kissing in the kitchen. Those things were fun to think about.

But what about the "worse"? Did we imagine online affairs, secret addictions, blatant animosity? What if your spouse says, "I don't want to go to church anymore. I only went with you while we were dating because I didn't want to lose you"? That's not so fun to think about, yet sadly it's something that many people deal with.

In *Boundaries in Marriage*, Dr. Henry Cloud says that the reality of every marriage is that the person you love the most and have committed your life to is an imperfect being, guaranteed to hurt and fail you in many ways, sometimes seriously.

The question is, What do you do about it? Do you kick your spouse to the curb? Issue threats and ultimatums? Drag your spouse onto the stage of a daytime talk show?

Throughout Scripture, Israel is depicted as God's wayward bride, always wandering, always committing adultery with other gods. Yet God never completely severed the relationship. He stood by while Israel suffered the consequences of her sin, but he continued to love her and continued in his willingness to forgive. He pleaded with her to return to him—"Return, faithless Israel . . . I will frown on you no longer, for I am merciful" (Jeremiah 3:12) and "Return, faithless people, . . . for I am your husband" (Jeremiah 3:14).

Here in Lamentations 3:22–23, the prophet Jeremiah (likely the writer of Lamentations) looked to the Lord's great love, compassion and faithfulness even in the aftermath of the destruction of his nation.

When things go from better to worse in marriage, Cloud says that nothing has to permanently destroy a relationship. "No failure is larger than grace," he writes. No hurt exists that is beyond forgiveness or that "love cannot heal." He says that hardness of heart, much more than failure, is the true relationship killer.

When things go wrong in marriage, we are called to forgive as the Lord has forgiven us (see Colossians 3:13). We can do this by remembering that no sin (besides blaspheming against the Holy Spirit) is beyond God's forgiveness, and thus no sin is beyond our forgiveness (see Mark 3:28–29).

When failure enters a marriage, it's better to choose to heal the relationship than to satisfy the need to be right or get even. Because of God's great love and faithfulness, we can do whatever it takes to work through even the "worse" that comes our way.

—NANCY KENNEDY

FOR YOUR NEXT DEVOTIONAL READING, TURN TO PAGE 892.

9 He has barred my way with blocks of stone;
he has made my paths crooked.

10 Like a bear lying in wait,
like a lion in hiding,
11 he dragged me from the path and mangled me
and left me without help.
12 He drew his bow
and made me the target for his arrows.

13 He pierced my heart
with arrows from his quiver.
14 I became the laughingstock of all my people;
they mock me in song all day long.
15 He has filled me with bitter herbs
and sated me with gall.

16 He has broken my teeth with gravel;
he has trampled me in the dust.
17 I have been deprived of peace;
I have forgotten what prosperity is.
18 So I say, "My splendor is gone
and all that I had hoped from the LORD."

19 I remember my affliction and my wandering,
the bitterness and the gall.
20 I well remember them,
and my soul is downcast within me.
21 Yet this I call to mind
and therefore I have hope:

22 Because of the LORD's great love we are not consumed,
for his compassions never fail.
23 They are new every morning;
great is your faithfulness.
24 I say to myself, "The LORD is my portion;
therefore I will wait for him."

25 The LORD is good to those whose hope is in him,
to the one who seeks him;
26 it is good to wait quietly
for the salvation of the LORD.
27 It is good for a man to bear the yoke
while he is young.

28 Let him sit alone in silence,
for the LORD has laid it on him.
29 Let him bury his face in the dust—
there may yet be hope.
30 Let him offer his cheek to one who would strike him,
and let him be filled with disgrace.

31 For men are not cast off
by the Lord forever.
32 Though he brings grief, he will show compassion,
so great is his unfailing love.
33 For he does not willingly bring affliction
or grief to the children of men.

34 To crush underfoot
all prisoners in the land,
35 to deny a man his rights
before the Most High,
36 to deprive a man of justice—
would not the Lord see such things?

37 Who can speak and have it happen
if the Lord has not decreed it?
38 Is it not from the mouth of the Most High
that both calamities and good things come?
39 Why should any living man complain
when punished for his sins?

40 Let us examine our ways and test them,
and let us return to the LORD.
41 Let us lift up our hearts and our hands
to God in heaven, and say:
42 "We have sinned and rebelled
and you have not forgiven.

43 "You have covered yourself with anger and pursued us;
you have slain without pity.
44 You have covered yourself with a cloud
so that no prayer can get through.
45 You have made us scum and refuse
among the nations.

46 "All our enemies have opened their mouths
wide against us.
47 We have suffered terror and pitfalls,
ruin and destruction."
48 Streams of tears flow from my eyes
because my people are destroyed.

49 My eyes will flow unceasingly,
without relief,
50 until the LORD looks down
from heaven and sees.
51 What I see brings grief to my soul
because of all the women of my city.

52 Those who were my enemies without cause
hunted me like a bird.
53 They tried to end my life in a pit
and threw stones at me;
54 the waters closed over my head,
and I thought I was about to be cut off.

55 I called on your name, O LORD,
from the depths of the pit.

56 You heard my plea: "Do not close your
ears
to my cry for relief."
57 You came near when I called you,
and you said, "Do not fear."

58 O Lord, you took up my case;
you redeemed my life.
59 You have seen, O LORD, the wrong done
to me.
Uphold my cause!
60 You have seen the depth of their
vengeance,
all their plots against me.

61 O LORD, you have heard their insults,
all their plots against me—
62 what my enemies whisper and mutter
against me all day long.
63 Look at them! Sitting or standing,
they mock me in their songs.

64 Pay them back what they deserve,
O LORD,
for what their hands have done.
65 Put a veil over their hearts,
and may your curse be on them!
66 Pursue them in anger and destroy them
from under the heavens of the LORD.

4 [a]How the gold has lost its luster,
the fine gold become dull!
The sacred gems are scattered
at the head of every street.

2 How the precious sons of Zion,
once worth their weight in gold,
are now considered as pots of clay,
the work of a potter's hands!

3 Even jackals offer their breasts
to nurse their young,
but my people have become heartless
like ostriches in the desert.

4 Because of thirst the infant's tongue
sticks to the roof of its mouth;
the children beg for bread,
but no one gives it to them.

5 Those who once ate delicacies
are destitute in the streets.
Those nurtured in purple
now lie on ash heaps.

6 The punishment of my people
is greater than that of Sodom,
which was overthrown in a moment
without a hand turned to help her.

7 Their princes were brighter than snow
and whiter than milk,
their bodies more ruddy than rubies,
their appearance like sapphires.[b]

8 But now they are blacker than soot;
they are not recognized in the streets.
Their skin has shriveled on their bones;
it has become as dry as a stick.

9 Those killed by the sword are better off
than those who die of famine;
racked with hunger, they waste away
for lack of food from the field.

10 With their own hands compassionate
women
have cooked their own children,
who became their food
when my people were destroyed.

11 The LORD has given full vent to his
wrath;
he has poured out his fierce anger.
He kindled a fire in Zion
that consumed her foundations.

12 The kings of the earth did not believe,
nor did any of the world's people,
that enemies and foes could enter
the gates of Jerusalem.

13 But it happened because of the sins of her
prophets
and the iniquities of her priests,
who shed within her
the blood of the righteous.

14 Now they grope through the streets
like men who are blind.
They are so defiled with blood
that no one dares to touch their
garments.

15 "Go away! You are unclean!" men cry to
them.
"Away! Away! Don't touch us!"
When they flee and wander about,
people among the nations say,
"They can stay here no longer."

16 The LORD himself has scattered them;
he no longer watches over them.
The priests are shown no honor,
the elders no favor.

17 Moreover, our eyes failed,
looking in vain for help;
from our towers we watched
for a nation that could not save us.

[a] This chapter is an acrostic poem, the verses of which begin with the successive letters of the Hebrew alphabet. [b] 7 Or *lapis lazuli*

WEDNESDAY
READ
LAMENTATIONS 4:1–22

WHEN LOVE FADES

Not so long ago, my husband and I were at a restaurant on one of our precious few dates. We ordered our food, then stared at each other, each at a loss for conversation. Finally Jim said, "So, should we talk about our loveless marriage?" I laughed, but I knew he was only half joking.

It wasn't that we were any less committed to each other or that either of us wanted our marriage to end, but we had reached the point where we were more like business partners than life partners. The toll of raising young children, balancing two careers, getting involved in our new church and moving to a new state had left us with little energy or interest in each other. The luster of our relationship was gone, and even the dullness was starting to fade into indifference.

How the gold has lost its luster, the fine gold become dull! The sacred gems are scattered at the head of every street.

— Lamentations 4:1

let's talk

- How would we describe our marriage? Are we business partners? Roommates? Lovers? What do we expect each other to be?
- If our love has lost its shine, what might we do to restore its brightness?
- What was the first thing we noticed about each other? How is that still evident today?

The author of Lamentations (likely the prophet Jeremiah) wrote in a state of deep despondency. He was stunned by what had become of God's chosen people. He had seen their sins—their corruption, greed and violence; and then he had witnessed their destruction at the hands of the conquering Babylonians. He laid out his sorrow before God, and it's clear he mourned the situation with every fiber of his being. The whole book of Lamentations tells of Jeremiah's grief, not only over the loss of his dreams for the nation of Israel, but over the nation itself. He was like a parent whose child had committed a terrible crime; he was angry, humiliated and broken.

Yet woven throughout Jeremiah's lament is a thread of hope. Even in the face of his pain, the prophet knew God was present and active and would bring something good out of the mess the people had created. It couldn't have been easy to maintain that hope. Most of the book of Lamentations is pretty bleak, but it's not the end of the story. We know that God remained faithful to Israel. We know that God one day brought redemption through the Messiah. We know Jeremiah's hope wasn't in vain.

That hope is the key to helping a marriage survive when we've made a mess of things. And marriage is rife with potential messes! There's nothing like living with someone to bring all our faults to the surface. My husband is—how can I put this—a slob. And I can be a nag. Together, these lovely traits make for some ridiculously heated arguments. And that's just one of many arenas in which our familiarity has bred contempt.

Every couple goes through seasons of dullness, boredom, even disinterest. But whether we've done something blatantly hurtful or simply grown tired of each other, we need to look for the glint of love that remains. That's where we'll find hope.

Of course it takes work to clean up our messes. There will be emotional work as we seek to be the people we need to be in marriage. There will be spiritual work as we seek forgiveness and offer grace. And there will be physical work as we remember the power of touch and the value of intimacy. Restoration can be difficult, but it's never impossible. God is alive in every marriage, ready to help restore the beautiful gleam of love.

—Carla Barnhill

FOR YOUR NEXT DEVOTIONAL READING, TURN TO PAGE 896.

18 Men stalked us at every step,
so we could not walk in our streets.
Our end was near, our days were numbered,
for our end had come.

19 Our pursuers were swifter
than eagles in the sky;
they chased us over the mountains
and lay in wait for us in the desert.

20 The LORD's anointed, our very life breath,
was caught in their traps.
We thought that under his shadow
we would live among the nations.

21 Rejoice and be glad, O Daughter of
Edom,
you who live in the land of Uz.
But to you also the cup will be passed;
you will be drunk and stripped naked.

22 O Daughter of Zion, your punishment
will end;
he will not prolong your exile.
But, O Daughter of Edom, he will punish
your sin
and expose your wickedness.

5 Remember, O LORD, what has happened
to us;
look, and see our disgrace.
2 Our inheritance has been turned over to
aliens,
our homes to foreigners.
3 We have become orphans and fatherless,
our mothers like widows.
4 We must buy the water we drink;
our wood can be had only at a price.
5 Those who pursue us are at our heels;
we are weary and find no rest.
6 We submitted to Egypt and Assyria
to get enough bread.
7 Our fathers sinned and are no more,
and we bear their punishment.
8 Slaves rule over us,
and there is none to free us from their
hands.
9 We get our bread at the risk of our lives
because of the sword in the desert.
10 Our skin is hot as an oven,
feverish from hunger.
11 Women have been ravished in Zion,
and virgins in the towns of Judah.
12 Princes have been hung up by their hands;
elders are shown no respect.
13 Young men toil at the millstones;
boys stagger under loads of wood.
14 The elders are gone from the city gate;
the young men have stopped their
music.
15 Joy is gone from our hearts;
our dancing has turned to mourning.
16 The crown has fallen from our head.
Woe to us, for we have sinned!
17 Because of this our hearts are faint,
because of these things our eyes grow
dim
18 for Mount Zion, which lies desolate,
with jackals prowling over it.
19 You, O LORD, reign forever;
your throne endures from generation to
generation.
20 Why do you always forget us?
Why do you forsake us so long?
21 Restore us to yourself, O LORD, that we
may return;
renew our days as of old
22 unless you have utterly rejected us
and are angry with us beyond measure.

EZEKIEL

Ezekiel

QUICK FACTS

AUTHOR Ezekiel

AUDIENCE Ezekiel's fellow Jewish exiles in Babylon

DATE Between 593 and 571 B.C.

SETTING The priest Ezekiel prophesied to his fellow Jews who were taken as prisoners to Babylon in 597 B.C.

Ezekiel, a member of a priestly family familiar with Jerusalem and its temple, was taken captive to Babylon along with about 10,000 of his fellow Jews in 597 B.C. (see 2 Kings 24:10–14), 11 years before the eventual fall of Jerusalem. Ezekiel, whose name means "God strengthens," was dramatically appointed by God as a watchman and spokesman to this group of exiles.

The prophet preached repentance and judgment to a rebellious people who repeatedly turned to idolatry, blending in with their pagan neighbors. But to those who listened, Ezekiel was a consoler, reassuring them of a just God who longed to welcome them back into the fold. He even hinted at the conversion of people outside the nation of Israel.

In chapter 16, God eloquently spoke through Ezekiel as a husband would speak to an unfaithful wife. Although he clearly stated her sin, he also offered her grace because of the covenant he had made with his beloved nation. What a tangible lesson: God shows us what grace and forgiveness look like so that we can extend those qualities to others.

The Living Creatures and the Glory of the LORD

1 In the[a] thirtieth year, in the fourth month on the fifth day, while I was among the exiles by the Kebar River, the heavens were opened and I saw visions of God.

2On the fifth of the month—it was the fifth year of the exile of King Jehoiachin— 3the word of the LORD came to Ezekiel the priest, the son of Buzi,[b] by the Kebar River in the land of the Babylonians.[c] There the hand of the LORD was upon him.

4I looked, and I saw a windstorm coming out of the north—an immense cloud with flashing lightning and surrounded by brilliant light. The center of the fire looked like glowing metal, 5and in the fire was what looked like four living creatures. In appearance their form was that of a man, 6but each of them had four faces and four wings. 7Their legs were straight; their feet were like those of a calf and gleamed like burnished bronze. 8Under their wings on their four sides they had the hands of a man. All four of them had faces and wings, 9and their wings touched one another. Each one went straight ahead; they did not turn as they moved.

10Their faces looked like this: Each of the four had the face of a man, and on the right side each had the face of a lion, and on the left the face of an ox; each also had the face of an eagle. 11Such were their faces. Their wings were spread out upward; each had two wings, one touching the wing of another creature on either side, and two wings covering its body. 12Each one went straight ahead. Wherever the spirit would go, they would go, without turning as they went. 13The appearance of the living creatures was like burning coals of fire or like torches. Fire moved back and forth among the creatures; it was bright, and lightning flashed out of it. 14The creatures sped back and forth like flashes of lightning.

15As I looked at the living creatures, I saw a wheel on the ground beside each creature with its four faces. 16This was the appearance and structure of the wheels: They sparkled like chrysolite, and all four looked alike. Each appeared to be made like a wheel intersecting a wheel. 17As they moved, they would go in any one of the four directions the creatures faced; the wheels did not turn about[d] as the creatures went. 18Their rims were high and awesome, and all four rims were full of eyes all around.

19When the living creatures moved, the wheels beside them moved; and when the living creatures rose from the ground, the wheels also rose. 20Wherever the spirit would go, they would go, and the wheels would rise along with them, because the spirit of the living creatures was in the wheels. 21When the creatures moved, they also moved; when the creatures stood still, they also stood still; and when the creatures rose from the ground, the wheels rose along with them, because the spirit of the living creatures was in the wheels.

22Spread out above the heads of the living creatures was what looked like an expanse, sparkling like ice, and awesome. 23Under the expanse their wings were stretched out one toward the other, and each had two wings covering its body. 24When the creatures moved, I heard the sound of their wings, like the roar of rushing waters, like the voice of the Almighty,[e] like the tumult of an army. When they stood still, they lowered their wings.

25Then there came a voice from above the expanse over their heads as they stood with lowered wings. 26Above the expanse over their heads was what looked like a throne of sapphire,[f] and high above on the throne was a figure like that of a man. 27I saw that from what appeared to be his waist up he looked like glowing metal, as if full of fire, and that from there down he looked like fire; and brilliant light surrounded him. 28Like the appearance of a rainbow in the clouds on a rainy day, so was the radiance around him.

This was the appearance of the likeness of the glory of the LORD. When I saw it, I fell facedown, and I heard the voice of one speaking.

Ezekiel's Call

2 He said to me, "Son of man, stand up on your feet and I will speak to you." 2As he spoke, the Spirit came into me and raised me to my feet, and I heard him speaking to me.

3He said: "Son of man, I am sending you to the Israelites, to a rebellious nation that has rebelled against me; they and their fathers have been in revolt against me to this very day. 4The people to whom I am sending you are obstinate and stubborn. Say to them, 'This is what the Sovereign LORD says.' 5And whether they listen or fail to listen—for they are a rebellious house—they will know that a prophet has been among them. 6And you, son of man,

[a] *1* Or ⌊*my*⌋ [b] *3* Or *Ezekiel son of Buzi the priest* [c] *3* Or *Chaldeans* [d] *17* Or *aside* [e] *24* Hebrew *Shaddai* [f] *26* Or *lapis lazuli*

THURSDAY
READ EZEKIEL 2:1–10

CALLED TO SPEAK

> **And you, son of man, do not be afraid of them or their words . . . You must speak my words to them, whether they listen or fail to listen, for they are rebellious.**
> — Ezekiel 2:6–7

We are called to be prophets, speaking the words of life to people around us, whether they listen or fail to listen. But that's a big order. It's much more comfortable to talk to people who are like us and who share our Christian faith and values.

When Mel and Vanessa visited his parents, his brothers, sisters and cousins made fun of the young couple and were critical of their beliefs. In addition, the behavior at those gatherings made Mel and Vanessa uncomfortable. Heavy drinking, foul language and embarrassing comments made the young couple wish they had stayed home.

So Mel and Vanessa learned to not say much at the family events they did attend. And they avoided most family gatherings at holidays and special events, pleading busyness. It was better, they decided, to be criticized for not coming to the folks' house for Christmas or birthdays than to be scratched, stung or bitten at those events.

In the book of Ezekiel, the Lord told the prophet, "Do not be afraid of them or their words." But when others' speech is like briers, thorns and scorpions, it's easy to become fearful or silent or—worse yet—to become like them to fit in.

From Ezekiel's experience, we learn that when encountering such difficulties in the family, at work or in the community, the first step is to find strength and security in God. Yes, unbelievers can be cruel to believers today just as they were in Ezekiel's time and in Jesus' day. They can ignore us, insult us for our faith or attack us verbally because we stand for something they reject. They can speak unkind words to us. But rather than keeping our mouths shut and slinking off, we can learn how to respond to such words.

The first thing we can do is hold on to God and not be afraid. Second, we can respond, not by counterattacking those who attack us, but by caring for them and demonstrating God's love for them. As God said to Ezekiel, "You must speak my words to them."

Mel and Vanessa slowly learned how to interact with Mel's family. When family members were negative about their commitment to Christ, the couple didn't respond with anger or retaliation. Rather, they chose to speak winsomely about matters of faith, sharing the great things God had done for them. They also did loving things for Mel's family. For example, Vanessa helped care for Mel's grandmother when she developed Alzheimer's disease and had to go to a nursing home. Mel volunteered to tutor a brother's child who was having reading problems in school. Because Christ was evident in their actions, people in their family were slowly won over to Christ.

As believers, we know that right words and actions work together to convict, convince and communicate with others. If our marriages are God-honoring, people can look at us and see how relationships can work. What we say and do can then become words of life to unbelievers.

—JOHN R. THROOP

let's *talk*

- Are there certain words we feel called to speak to others? Are we to condemn, explain, witness or teach?
- If we are the only Christian couple in the midst of unbelievers, do we keep quiet about our faith or talk about it? What are some ways to share our beliefs in such situations?
- Why are some family members hard to witness to? How can we reach out effectively to bring them to Christ?

FOR YOUR NEXT DEVOTIONAL READING, TURN TO PAGE 911.

do not be afraid of them or their words. Do
not be afraid, though briers and thorns are all
around you and you live among scorpions. Do
not be afraid of what they say or terrified by
them, though they are a rebellious house. 7You
must speak my words to them, whether they
listen or fail to listen, for they are rebellious.
8But you, son of man, listen to what I say to
you. Do not rebel like that rebellious house;
open your mouth and eat what I give you."
9Then I looked, and I saw a hand stretched
out to me. In it was a scroll, 10which he un-
rolled before me. On both sides of it were
written words of lament and mourning and
woe.

3 And he said to me, "Son of man, eat what
is before you, eat this scroll; then go and
speak to the house of Israel." 2So I opened
my mouth, and he gave me the scroll to eat.
3Then he said to me, "Son of man, eat this
scroll I am giving you and fill your stomach
with it." So I ate it, and it tasted as sweet as
honey in my mouth.
4He then said to me: "Son of man, go now
to the house of Israel and speak my words to
them. 5You are not being sent to a people of
obscure speech and difficult language, but to
the house of Israel— 6not to many peoples of
obscure speech and difficult language, whose
words you cannot understand. Surely if I had
sent you to them, they would have listened to
you. 7But the house of Israel is not willing to
listen to you because they are not willing to
listen to me, for the whole house of Israel is
hardened and obstinate. 8But I will make you
as unyielding and hardened as they are. 9I will
make your forehead like the hardest stone,
harder than flint. Do not be afraid of them or
terrified by them, though they are a rebellious
house."
10And he said to me, "Son of man, listen
carefully and take to heart all the words I speak
to you. 11Go now to your countrymen in exile
and speak to them. Say to them, 'This is what
the Sovereign LORD says,' whether they listen
or fail to listen."
12Then the Spirit lifted me up, and I heard
behind me a loud rumbling sound—May the
glory of the LORD be praised in his dwelling
place!— 13the sound of the wings of the living creatures brushing against each other and
the sound of the wheels beside them, a loud
rumbling sound. 14The Spirit then lifted me
up and took me away, and I went in bitterness
and in the anger of my spirit, with the strong
hand of the LORD upon me. 15I came to the
exiles who lived at Tel Abib near the Kebar
River. And there, where they were living, I sat
among them for seven days—overwhelmed.

Warning to Israel

16At the end of seven days the word of the
LORD came to me: 17"Son of man, I have made
you a watchman for the house of Israel; so hear
the word I speak and give them warning from
me. 18When I say to a wicked man, 'You will
surely die,' and you do not warn him or speak
out to dissuade him from his evil ways in order to save his life, that wicked man will die
for[a] his sin, and I will hold you accountable
for his blood. 19But if you do warn the wicked
man and he does not turn from his wickedness
or from his evil ways, he will die for his sin;
but you will have saved yourself.
20"Again, when a righteous man turns from
his righteousness and does evil, and I put a
stumbling block before him, he will die. Since
you did not warn him, he will die for his sin.
The righteous things he did will not be remembered, and I will hold you accountable
for his blood. 21But if you do warn the righteous man not to sin and he does not sin, he
will surely live because he took warning, and
you will have saved yourself."
22The hand of the LORD was upon me
there, and he said to me, "Get up and go out
to the plain, and there I will speak to you."
23So I got up and went out to the plain. And
the glory of the LORD was standing there, like
the glory I had seen by the Kebar River, and I
fell facedown.
24Then the Spirit came into me and raised
me to my feet. He spoke to me and said: "Go,
shut yourself inside your house. 25And you,
son of man, they will tie with ropes; you will
be bound so that you cannot go out among
the people. 26I will make your tongue stick to
the roof of your mouth so that you will be silent and unable to rebuke them, though they
are a rebellious house. 27But when I speak to
you, I will open your mouth and you shall say
to them, 'This is what the Sovereign LORD
says.' Whoever will listen let him listen, and
whoever will refuse let him refuse; for they are
a rebellious house.

Siege of Jerusalem Symbolized

4 "Now, son of man, take a clay tablet, put
it in front of you and draw the city of Jerusalem on it. 2Then lay siege to it: Erect

---

a *18* Or *in*; also in verses 19 and 20

siege works against it, build a ramp up to it,
set up camps against it and put battering rams
around it. 3Then take an iron pan, place it as
an iron wall between you and the city and
turn your face toward it. It will be under siege,
and you shall besiege it. This will be a sign to
the house of Israel.
4"Then lie on your left side and put the sin
of the house of Israel upon yourself.[a] You are
to bear their sin for the number of days you
lie on your side. 5I have assigned you the same
number of days as the years of their sin. So for
390 days you will bear the sin of the house
of Israel.
6"After you have finished this, lie down
again, this time on your right side, and bear
the sin of the house of Judah. I have assigned
you 40 days, a day for each year. 7Turn your
face toward the siege of Jerusalem and with
bared arm prophesy against her. 8I will tie you
up with ropes so that you cannot turn from
one side to the other until you have finished
the days of your siege.
9"Take wheat and barley, beans and lentils,
millet and spelt; put them in a storage jar and
use them to make bread for yourself. You are
to eat it during the 390 days you lie on your
side. 10Weigh out twenty shekels[b] of food to
eat each day and eat it at set times. 11Also measure out a sixth of a hin[c] of water and drink
it at set times. 12Eat the food as you would a
barley cake; bake it in the sight of the people,
using human excrement for fuel." 13The LORD
said, "In this way the people of Israel will eat
defiled food among the nations where I will
drive them."
14Then I said, "Not so, Sovereign LORD!
I have never defiled myself. From my youth
until now I have never eaten anything found
dead or torn by wild animals. No unclean
meat has ever entered my mouth."
15"Very well," he said, "I will let you bake
your bread over cow manure instead of human
excrement."
16He then said to me: "Son of man, I will
cut off the supply of food in Jerusalem. The
people will eat rationed food in anxiety and
drink rationed water in despair, 17for food and
water will be scarce. They will be appalled at
the sight of each other and will waste away because of[d] their sin.

5 "Now, son of man, take a sharp sword and
use it as a barber's razor to shave your head
and your beard. Then take a set of scales
and divide up the hair. 2When the days of
your siege come to an end, burn a third of
the hair with fire inside the city. Take a third
and strike it with the sword all around the
city. And scatter a third to the wind. For I will
pursue them with drawn sword. 3But take a
few strands of hair and tuck them away in the
folds of your garment. 4Again, take a few of
these and throw them into the fire and burn
them up. A fire will spread from there to the
whole house of Israel.
5"This is what the Sovereign LORD says: This
is Jerusalem, which I have set in the center of
the nations, with countries all around her. 6Yet
in her wickedness she has rebelled against my
laws and decrees more than the nations and
countries around her. She has rejected my laws
and has not followed my decrees.
7"Therefore this is what the Sovereign LORD
says: You have been more unruly than the nations around you and have not followed my
decrees or kept my laws. You have not even[e]
conformed to the standards of the nations
around you.
8"Therefore this is what the Sovereign LORD
says: I myself am against you, Jerusalem, and
I will inflict punishment on you in the sight
of the nations. 9Because of all your detestable
idols, I will do to you what I have never done
before and will never do again. 10Therefore
in your midst fathers will eat their children,
and children will eat their fathers. I will inflict
punishment on you and will scatter all your
survivors to the winds. 11Therefore as surely
as I live, declares the Sovereign LORD, because
you have defiled my sanctuary with all your
vile images and detestable practices, I myself
will withdraw my favor; I will not look on you
with pity or spare you. 12A third of your people will die of the plague or perish by famine
inside you; a third will fall by the sword outside your walls; and a third I will scatter to the
winds and pursue with drawn sword.
13"Then my anger will cease and my wrath
against them will subside, and I will be
avenged. And when I have spent my wrath
upon them, they will know that I the LORD
have spoken in my zeal.
14"I will make you a ruin and a reproach
among the nations around you, in the sight of
all who pass by. 15You will be a reproach and a
taunt, a warning and an object of horror to the
nations around you when I inflict punishment
on you in anger and in wrath and with sting-
ing rebuke. I the LORD have spoken. 16When
I shoot at you with my deadly and destructive

---

[a] *4* Or *your side* [b] *10* That is, about 8 ounces (about 0.2 kilogram) [c] *11* That is, about 2/3 quart (about 0.6 liter) [d] *17* Or *away in*
[e] *7* Most Hebrew manuscripts; some Hebrew manuscripts and Syriac *You have*

arrows of famine, I will shoot to destroy you.
I will bring more and more famine upon you
and cut off your supply of food. 17I will send
famine and wild beasts against you, and they
will leave you childless. Plague and bloodshed
will sweep through you, and I will bring the
sword against you. I the LORD have spoken."

A Prophecy Against the Mountains of Israel

6 The word of the LORD came to me: 2"Son
of man, set your face against the mountains of Israel; prophesy against them 3and
say: 'O mountains of Israel, hear the word of
the Sovereign LORD. This is what the Sovereign LORD says to the mountains and hills, to
the ravines and valleys: I am about to bring
a sword against you, and I will destroy your
high places. 4Your altars will be demolished
and your incense altars will be smashed; and
I will slay your people in front of your idols.
5I will lay the dead bodies of the Israelites in
front of their idols, and I will scatter your
bones around your altars. 6Wherever you live,
the towns will be laid waste and the high places demolished, so that your altars will be laid
waste and devastated, your idols smashed and
ruined, your incense altars broken down, and
what you have made wiped out. 7Your people
will fall slain among you, and you will know
that I am the LORD.

8" 'But I will spare some, for some of you
will escape the sword when you are scattered
among the lands and nations. 9Then in the
nations where they have been carried captive,
those who escape will remember me—how I
have been grieved by their adulterous hearts,
which have turned away from me, and by
their eyes, which have lusted after their idols.
They will loathe themselves for the evil they
have done and for all their detestable practices. 10And they will know that I am the LORD; I
did not threaten in vain to bring this calamity
on them.

11" 'This is what the Sovereign LORD says:
Strike your hands together and stamp your
feet and cry out "Alas!" because of all the
wicked and detestable practices of the house
of Israel, for they will fall by the sword, famine and plague. 12He that is far away will die
of the plague, and he that is near will fall by
the sword, and he that survives and is spared
will die of famine. So will I spend my wrath
upon them. 13And they will know that I am
the LORD, when their people lie slain among
their idols around their altars, on every high
hill and on all the mountaintops, under every spreading tree and every leafy oak—places where they offered fragrant incense to all
their idols. 14And I will stretch out my hand
against them and make the land a desolate
waste from the desert to Diblah[a]—wherever
they live. Then they will know that I am the
LORD.' "

The End Has Come

7 The word of the LORD came to me: 2"Son
of man, this is what the Sovereign LORD
says to the land of Israel: The end! The end
has come upon the four corners of the land.
3The end is now upon you and I will unleash
my anger against you. I will judge you according to your conduct and repay you for all your
detestable practices. 4I will not look on you
with pity or spare you; I will surely repay you
for your conduct and the detestable practices
among you. Then you will know that I am the
LORD.

5"This is what the Sovereign LORD says:
Disaster! An unheard-of[b] disaster is coming.
6The end has come! The end has come! It has
roused itself against you. It has come! 7Doom
has come upon you—you who dwell in the
land. The time has come, the day is near; there
is panic, not joy, upon the mountains. 8I am
about to pour out my wrath on you and spend
my anger against you; I will judge you according to your conduct and repay you for all your
detestable practices. 9I will not look on you
with pity or spare you; I will repay you in accordance with your conduct and the detestable practices among you. Then you will know
that it is I the LORD who strikes the blow.

10"The day is here! It has come! Doom has
burst forth, the rod has budded, arrogance has
blossomed! 11Violence has grown into[c] a rod
to punish wickedness; none of the people will
be left, none of that crowd—no wealth, nothing of value. 12The time has come, the day has
arrived. Let not the buyer rejoice nor the seller grieve, for wrath is upon the whole crowd.
13The seller will not recover the land he has
sold as long as both of them live, for the vision
concerning the whole crowd will not be re-
versed. Because of their sins, not one of them
will preserve his life. 14Though they blow the
trumpet and get everything ready, no one will
go into battle, for my wrath is upon the whole
crowd.

15"Outside is the sword, inside are plague
and famine; those in the country will die by

[a] 14 Most Hebrew manuscripts; a few Hebrew manuscripts *Riblah* [b] 5 Most Hebrew manuscripts; some Hebrew manuscripts and Syriac *Disaster after* [c] 11 Or *The violent one has become*

the sword, and those in the city will be devoured by famine and plague. 16All who survive and escape will be in the mountains,
moaning like doves of the valleys, each because of his sins. 17Every hand will go limp,
and every knee will become as weak as water.
18They will put on sackcloth and be clothed
with terror. Their faces will be covered with
shame and their heads will be shaved. 19They
will throw their silver into the streets, and
their gold will be an unclean thing. Their silver and gold will not be able to save them in
the day of the LORD's wrath. They will not satisfy their hunger or fill their stomachs with it,
for it has made them stumble into sin. 20They
were proud of their beautiful jewelry and used
it to make their detestable idols and vile images. Therefore I will turn these into an unclean thing for them. 21I will hand it all over as
plunder to foreigners and as loot to the wicked
of the earth, and they will defile it. 22I will
turn my face away from them, and they will
desecrate my treasured place; robbers will enter it and desecrate it.

23"Prepare chains, because the land is full
of bloodshed and the city is full of violence.
24I will bring the most wicked of the nations
to take possession of their houses; I will put
an end to the pride of the mighty, and their
sanctuaries will be desecrated. 25When terror
comes, they will seek peace, but there will be
none. 26Calamity upon calamity will come,
and rumor upon rumor. They will try to get
a vision from the prophet; the teaching of
the law by the priest will be lost, as will the
counsel of the elders. 27The king will mourn,
the prince will be clothed with despair, and
the hands of the people of the land will tremble. I will deal with them according to their
conduct, and by their own standards I will
judge them. Then they will know that I am
the LORD."

Idolatry in the Temple

8 In the sixth year, in the sixth month on the
fifth day, while I was sitting in my house
and the elders of Judah were sitting before
me, the hand of the Sovereign LORD came
upon me there. 2I looked, and I saw a figure
like that of a man.[a] From what appeared to
be his waist down he was like fire, and from
there up his appearance was as bright as glowing metal. 3He stretched out what looked like
a hand and took me by the hair of my head.
The Spirit lifted me up between earth and
heaven and in visions of God he took me to
Jerusalem, to the entrance to the north gate of
the inner court, where the idol that provokes
to jealousy stood. 4And there before me was
the glory of the God of Israel, as in the vision
I had seen in the plain.

5Then he said to me, "Son of man, look toward the north." So I looked, and in the entrance north of the gate of the altar I saw this
idol of jealousy.

6And he said to me, "Son of man, do you
see what they are doing—the utterly detestable things the house of Israel is doing here,
things that will drive me far from my sanctuary? But you will see things that are even more
detestable."

7Then he brought me to the entrance to the
court. I looked, and I saw a hole in the wall.
8He said to me, "Son of man, now dig into
the wall." So I dug into the wall and saw a
doorway there.

9And he said to me, "Go in and see the
wicked and detestable things they are doing
here." 10So I went in and looked, and I saw
portrayed all over the walls all kinds of crawling things and detestable animals and all the
idols of the house of Israel. 11In front of them
stood seventy elders of the house of Israel, and
Jaazaniah son of Shaphan was standing among
them. Each had a censer in his hand, and a fragrant cloud of incense was rising.

12He said to me, "Son of man, have you
seen what the elders of the house of Israel are
doing in the darkness, each at the shrine of his
own idol? They say, 'The LORD does not see us;
the LORD has forsaken the land.' " 13Again, he
said, "You will see them doing things that are
even more detestable."

14Then he brought me to the entrance to
the north gate of the house of the LORD, and I
saw women sitting there, mourning for Tam-
muz. 15He said to me, "Do you see this, son
of man? You will see things that are even more
detestable than this."

16He then brought me into the inner court
of the house of the LORD, and there at the entrance to the temple, between the portico and
the altar, were about twenty-five men. With
their backs toward the temple of the LORD and
their faces toward the east, they were bowing
down to the sun in the east.

17He said to me, "Have you seen this, son
of man? Is it a trivial matter for the house of
Judah to do the detestable things they are doing here? Must they also fill the land with vi-

[a] 2 Or *saw a fiery figure*

olence and continually provoke me to anger?
Look at them putting the branch to their nose!
18Therefore I will deal with them in anger; I
will not look on them with pity or spare them.
Although they shout in my ears, I will not listen to them."

Idolaters Killed

9 Then I heard him call out in a loud voice,
"Bring the guards of the city here, each
with a weapon in his hand." 2And I saw
six men coming from the direction of the
upper gate, which faces north, each with a
deadly weapon in his hand. With them was
a man clothed in linen who had a writing kit
at his side. They came in and stood beside the
bronze altar.

3Now the glory of the God of Israel went
up from above the cherubim, where it had
been, and moved to the threshold of the temple. Then the LORD called to the man clothed
in linen who had the writing kit at his side
4and said to him, "Go throughout the city of
Jerusalem and put a mark on the foreheads of
those who grieve and lament over all the detestable things that are done in it."

5As I listened, he said to the others, "Follow him through the city and kill, without
showing pity or compassion. 6Slaughter old
men, young men and maidens, women and
children, but do not touch anyone who has
the mark. Begin at my sanctuary." So they began with the elders who were in front of the
temple.

7Then he said to them, "Defile the temple
and fill the courts with the slain. Go!" So they
went out and began killing throughout the
city. 8While they were killing and I was left
alone, I fell facedown, crying out, "Ah, Sovereign LORD! Are you going to destroy the entire
remnant of Israel in this outpouring of your
wrath on Jerusalem?"

9He answered me, "The sin of the house of
Israel and Judah is exceedingly great; the land
is full of bloodshed and the city is full of injustice. They say, 'The LORD has forsaken the
land; the LORD does not see.' 10So I will not
look on them with pity or spare them, but I
will bring down on their own heads what they
have done."

11Then the man in linen with the writing
kit at his side brought back word, saying, "I
have done as you commanded."

The Glory Departs From the Temple

10 I looked, and I saw the likeness of a
throne of sapphire[a] above the expanse
that was over the heads of the cherubim.
2The LORD said to the man clothed in linen,
"Go in among the wheels beneath the cherubim. Fill your hands with burning coals from
among the cherubim and scatter them over
the city." And as I watched, he went in.

3Now the cherubim were standing on the
south side of the temple when the man went
in, and a cloud filled the inner court. 4Then
the glory of the LORD rose from above the
cherubim and moved to the threshold of the
temple. The cloud filled the temple, and the
court was full of the radiance of the glory of
the LORD. 5The sound of the wings of the
cherubim could be heard as far away as the
outer court, like the voice of God Almighty[b]
when he speaks.

6When the LORD commanded the man
in linen, "Take fire from among the wheels,
from among the cherubim," the man went in
and stood beside a wheel. 7Then one of the
cherubim reached out his hand to the fire that
was among them. He took up some of it and
put it into the hands of the man in linen, who
took it and went out. 8(Under the wings of the
cherubim could be seen what looked like the
hands of a man.)

9I looked, and I saw beside the cherubim
four wheels, one beside each of the cherubim; the wheels sparkled like chrysolite. 10As
for their appearance, the four of them looked
alike; each was like a wheel intersecting a
wheel. 11As they moved, they would go in
any one of the four directions the cherubim
faced; the wheels did not turn about[c] as the
cherubim went. The cherubim went in whatever direction the head faced, without turning
as they went. 12Their entire bodies, including their backs, their hands and their wings,
were completely full of eyes, as were their four
wheels. 13I heard the wheels being called "the
whirling wheels." 14Each of the cherubim had
four faces: One face was that of a cherub, the
second the face of a man, the third the face of
a lion, and the fourth the face of an eagle.

15Then the cherubim rose upward. These
were the living creatures I had seen by the
Kebar River. 16When the cherubim moved,
the wheels beside them moved; and when the
cherubim spread their wings to rise from the
ground, the wheels did not leave their side.
17When the cherubim stood still, they also

[a] *1* Or *lapis lazuli* [b] *5* Hebrew *El-Shaddai* [c] *11* Or *aside*

stood still; and when the cherubim rose, they
rose with them, because the spirit of the living
creatures was in them.
18 Then the glory of the LORD departed from
over the threshold of the temple and stopped
above the cherubim. 19 While I watched, the
cherubim spread their wings and rose from
the ground, and as they went, the wheels went
with them. They stopped at the entrance to
the east gate of the LORD's house, and the glory of the God of Israel was above them.
20 These were the living creatures I had seen
beneath the God of Israel by the Kebar River,
and I realized that they were cherubim. 21 Each
had four faces and four wings, and under their
wings was what looked like the hands of a
man. 22 Their faces had the same appearance as
those I had seen by the Kebar River. Each one
went straight ahead.

Judgment on Israel's Leaders

11 Then the Spirit lifted me up and brought
me to the gate of the house of the LORD
that faces east. There at the entrance
to the gate were twenty-five men, and I saw
among them Jaazaniah son of Azzur and Pelatiah son of Benaiah, leaders of the people.
2 The LORD said to me, "Son of man, these
are the men who are plotting evil and giving
wicked advice in this city. 3 They say, 'Will it
not soon be time to build houses?[a] This city is
a cooking pot, and we are the meat.' 4 Therefore prophesy against them; prophesy, son of
man."
5 Then the Spirit of the LORD came upon me,
and he told me to say: "This is what the LORD
says: That is what you are saying, O house of
Israel, but I know what is going through your
mind. 6 You have killed many people in this
city and filled its streets with the dead.
7 "Therefore this is what the Sovereign LORD
says: The bodies you have thrown there are the
meat and this city is the pot, but I will drive
you out of it. 8 You fear the sword, and the
sword is what I will bring against you, declares
the Sovereign LORD. 9 I will drive you out of
the city and hand you over to foreigners and
inflict punishment on you. 10 You will fall by
the sword, and I will execute judgment on you
at the borders of Israel. Then you will know
that I am the LORD. 11 This city will not be a
pot for you, nor will you be the meat in it; I
will execute judgment on you at the borders
of Israel. 12 And you will know that I am the
LORD, for you have not followed my decrees
or kept my laws but have conformed to the
standards of the nations around you."
13 Now as I was prophesying, Pelatiah son of
Benaiah died. Then I fell facedown and cried
out in a loud voice, "Ah, Sovereign LORD!
Will you completely destroy the remnant of
Israel?"
14 The word of the LORD came to me:
15 "Son of man, your brothers—your brothers
who are your blood relatives[b] and the whole
house of Israel—are those of whom the people of Jerusalem have said, 'They are[c] far away
from the LORD; this land was given to us as
our possession.'

Promised Return of Israel

16 "Therefore say: 'This is what the Sovereign LORD says: Although I sent them far away
among the nations and scattered them among
the countries, yet for a little while I have been
a sanctuary for them in the countries where
they have gone.'
17 "Therefore say: 'This is what the Sovereign LORD says: I will gather you from the nations and bring you back from the countries
where you have been scattered, and I will give
you back the land of Israel again.'
18 "They will return to it and remove all its
vile images and detestable idols. 19 I will give
them an undivided heart and put a new spirit
in them; I will remove from them their heart
of stone and give them a heart of flesh. 20 Then
they will follow my decrees and be careful to
keep my laws. They will be my people, and I
will be their God. 21 But as for those whose
hearts are devoted to their vile images and detestable idols, I will bring down on their own
heads what they have done, declares the Sovereign LORD."
22 Then the cherubim, with the wheels beside them, spread their wings, and the glory of
the God of Israel was above them. 23 The glory
of the LORD went up from within the city and
stopped above the mountain east of it. 24 The
Spirit lifted me up and brought me to the exiles in Babylonia[d] in the vision given by the
Spirit of God.
Then the vision I had seen went up from
me, 25 and I told the exiles everything the
LORD had shown me.

The Exile Symbolized

12 The word of the LORD came to me:
2 "Son of man, you are living among a
rebellious people. They have eyes to see

[a] 3 Or *This is not the time to build houses.* [b] 15 Or *are in exile with you* (see Septuagint and Syriac) [c] 15 Or *those to whom the people of Jerusalem have said, 'Stay* [d] 24 Or *Chaldea*

but do not see and ears to hear but do not
hear, for they are a rebellious people.
3“Therefore, son of man, pack your belongings for exile and in the daytime, as they
watch, set out and go from where you are to
another place. Perhaps they will understand,
though they are a rebellious house. 4During
the daytime, while they watch, bring out your
belongings packed for exile. Then in the evening, while they are watching, go out like
those who go into exile. 5While they watch,
dig through the wall and take your belongings
out through it. 6Put them on your shoulder
as they are watching and carry them out at
dusk. Cover your face so that you cannot see
the land, for I have made you a sign to the
house of Israel.”
7So I did as I was commanded. During the
day I brought out my things packed for exile.
Then in the evening I dug through the wall
with my hands. I took my belongings out at
dusk, carrying them on my shoulders while
they watched.
8In the morning the word of the LORD
came to me: 9“Son of man, did not that rebellious house of Israel ask you, ‘What are you
doing?’
10“Say to them, ‘This is what the Sovereign
LORD says: This oracle concerns the prince in
Jerusalem and the whole house of Israel who
are there.’ 11Say to them, ‘I am a sign to you.’
“As I have done, so it will be done to them.
They will go into exile as captives.
12“The prince among them will put his
things on his shoulder at dusk and leave, and
a hole will be dug in the wall for him to go
through. He will cover his face so that he cannot see the land. 13I will spread my net for
him, and he will be caught in my snare; I
will bring him to Babylonia, the land of the
Chaldeans, but he will not see it, and there he
will die. 14I will scatter to the winds all those
around him—his staff and all his troops—and
I will pursue them with drawn sword.
15“They will know that I am the LORD,
when I disperse them among the nations and
scatter them through the countries. 16But I
will spare a few of them from the sword, famine and plague, so that in the nations where
they go they may acknowledge all their detestable practices. Then they will know that I am
the LORD.”
17The word of the LORD came to me:
18“Son of man, tremble as you eat your food,
and shudder in fear as you drink your water.
19Say to the people of the land: ‘This is what
the Sovereign LORD says about those living in
Jerusalem and in the land of Israel: They will
eat their food in anxiety and drink their water
in despair, for their land will be stripped of
everything in it because of the violence of all
who live there. 20The inhabited towns will be
laid waste and the land will be desolate. Then
you will know that I am the LORD.’ ”
21The word of the LORD came to me: 22“Son
of man, what is this proverb you have in the
land of Israel: ‘The days go by and every vision
comes to nothing’? 23Say to them, ‘This is what
the Sovereign LORD says: I am going to put an
end to this proverb, and they will no longer
quote it in Israel.’ Say to them, ‘The days are
near when every vision will be fulfilled. 24For
there will be no more false visions or flattering
divinations among the people of Israel. 25But I
the LORD will speak what I will, and it shall be
fulfilled without delay. For in your days, you
rebellious house, I will fulfill whatever I say,
declares the Sovereign LORD.’ ”
26The word of the LORD came to me: 27“Son
of man, the house of Israel is saying, ‘The vision he sees is for many years from now, and
he prophesies about the distant future.’
28“Therefore say to them, ‘This is what the
Sovereign LORD says: None of my words will
be delayed any longer; whatever I say will be
fulfilled, declares the Sovereign LORD.’ ”

False Prophets Condemned

13 The word of the LORD came to me:
2“Son of man, prophesy against the
prophets of Israel who are now prophesying. Say to those who prophesy out of
their own imagination: ‘Hear the word of
the LORD! 3This is what the Sovereign LORD
says: Woe to the foolish[a] prophets who follow
their own spirit and have seen nothing! 4Your
prophets, O Israel, are like jackals among ruins. 5You have not gone up to the breaks in the
wall to repair it for the house of Israel so that it
will stand firm in the battle on the day of the
LORD. 6Their visions are false and their divinations a lie. They say, “The LORD declares,”
when the LORD has not sent them; yet they expect their words to be fulfilled. 7Have you not
seen false visions and uttered lying divinations
when you say, “The LORD declares,” though I
have not spoken?
8“ ‘Therefore this is what the Sovereign
LORD says: Because of your false words and
lying visions, I am against you, declares the

[a] 3 Or *wicked*

Sovereign LORD. [9]My hand will be against the
prophets who see false visions and utter lying
divinations. They will not belong to the council of my people or be listed in the records of
the house of Israel, nor will they enter the land
of Israel. Then you will know that I am the
Sovereign LORD.

[10]" 'Because they lead my people astray,
saying, "Peace," when there is no peace, and
because, when a flimsy wall is built, they cover
it with whitewash, [11]therefore tell those who
cover it with whitewash that it is going to fall.
Rain will come in torrents, and I will send
hailstones hurtling down, and violent winds
will burst forth. [12]When the wall collapses,
will people not ask you, "Where is the whitewash you covered it with?"

[13]" 'Therefore this is what the Sovereign
LORD says: In my wrath I will unleash a violent wind, and in my anger hailstones and
torrents of rain will fall with destructive fury.
[14]I will tear down the wall you have covered
with whitewash and will level it to the ground
so that its foundation will be laid bare. When
it[a] falls, you will be destroyed in it; and you
will know that I am the LORD. [15]So I will
spend my wrath against the wall and against
those who covered it with whitewash. I will
say to you, "The wall is gone and so are those
who whitewashed it, [16]those prophets of Israel
who prophesied to Jerusalem and saw visions
of peace for her when there was no peace, declares the Sovereign LORD." '

[17]"Now, son of man, set your face against
the daughters of your people who prophesy out of their own imagination. Prophesy against them [18]and say, 'This is what the
Sovereign LORD says: Woe to the women who
sew magic charms on all their wrists and make
veils of various lengths for their heads in order
to ensnare people. Will you ensnare the lives
of my people but preserve your own? [19]You
have profaned me among my people for a few
handfuls of barley and scraps of bread. By lying to my people, who listen to lies, you have
killed those who should not have died and
have spared those who should not live.

[20]" 'Therefore this is what the Sovereign
LORD says: I am against your magic charms
with which you ensnare people like birds and
I will tear them from your arms; I will set free
the people that you ensnare like birds. [21]I will
tear off your veils and save my people from
your hands, and they will no longer fall prey
to your power. Then you will know that I am
the LORD. [22]Because you disheartened the
righteous with your lies, when I had brought
them no grief, and because you encouraged
the wicked not to turn from their evil ways
and so save their lives, [23]therefore you will no
longer see false visions or practice divination.
I will save my people from your hands. And
then you will know that I am the LORD.' "

Idolaters Condemned

14 Some of the elders of Israel came to me
and sat down in front of me. [2]Then the
word of the LORD came to me: [3]"Son
of man, these men have set up idols in their
hearts and put wicked stumbling blocks before their faces. Should I let them inquire of
me at all? [4]Therefore speak to them and tell
them, 'This is what the Sovereign LORD says:
When any Israelite sets up idols in his heart
and puts a wicked stumbling block before his
face and then goes to a prophet, I the LORD
will answer him myself in keeping with his
great idolatry. [5]I will do this to recapture the
hearts of the people of Israel, who have all deserted me for their idols.'

[6]"Therefore say to the house of Israel, 'This
is what the Sovereign LORD says: Repent! Turn
from your idols and renounce all your detestable practices!

[7]" 'When any Israelite or any alien living
in Israel separates himself from me and sets
up idols in his heart and puts a wicked stumbling block before his face and then goes to
a prophet to inquire of me, I the LORD will
answer him myself. [8]I will set my face against
that man and make him an example and a byword. I will cut him off from my people. Then
you will know that I am the LORD.

[9]" 'And if the prophet is enticed to utter a
prophecy, I the LORD have enticed that prophet, and I will stretch out my hand against him
and destroy him from among my people Israel. [10]They will bear their guilt—the prophet will be as guilty as the one who consults
him. [11]Then the people of Israel will no longer
stray from me, nor will they defile themselves
anymore with all their sins. They will be my
people, and I will be their God, declares the
Sovereign LORD.' "

Judgment Inescapable

[12]The word of the LORD came to me:
[13]"Son of man, if a country sins against me
by being unfaithful and I stretch out my hand
against it to cut off its food supply and send

---

a 14 Or *the city*

famine upon it and kill its men and their animals, 14even if these three men—Noah, Daniel[a] and Job—were in it, they could save only
themselves by their righteousness, declares the
Sovereign LORD.
15"Or if I send wild beasts through that
country and they leave it childless and it becomes desolate so that no one can pass through
it because of the beasts, 16as surely as I live, declares the Sovereign LORD, even if these three
men were in it, they could not save their own
sons or daughters. They alone would be saved,
but the land would be desolate.
17"Or if I bring a sword against that country and say, 'Let the sword pass throughout the
land,' and I kill its men and their animals, 18as
surely as I live, declares the Sovereign LORD,
even if these three men were in it, they could
not save their own sons or daughters. They
alone would be saved.
19"Or if I send a plague into that land and
pour out my wrath upon it through bloodshed, killing its men and their animals, 20as
surely as I live, declares the Sovereign LORD,
even if Noah, Daniel and Job were in it, they
could save neither son nor daughter. They
would save only themselves by their righteousness.
21"For this is what the Sovereign LORD
says: How much worse will it be when I send
against Jerusalem my four dreadful judgments—sword and famine and wild beasts
and plague—to kill its men and their animals!
22Yet there will be some survivors—sons and
daughters who will be brought out of it. They
will come to you, and when you see their conduct and their actions, you will be consoled
regarding the disaster I have brought upon Jerusalem—every disaster I have brought upon
it. 23You will be consoled when you see their
conduct and their actions, for you will know
that I have done nothing in it without cause,
declares the Sovereign LORD."

Jerusalem, A Useless Vine

15 The word of the LORD came to me: 2"Son
of man, how is the wood of a vine better than that of a branch on any of the
trees in the forest? 3Is wood ever taken from
it to make anything useful? Do they make
pegs from it to hang things on? 4And after it
is thrown on the fire as fuel and the fire burns
both ends and chars the middle, is it then useful for anything? 5If it was not useful for anything when it was whole, how much less can it
be made into something useful when the fire
has burned it and it is charred?
6"Therefore this is what the Sovereign
LORD says: As I have given the wood of the
vine among the trees of the forest as fuel for
the fire, so will I treat the people living in Jerusalem. 7I will set my face against them. Although they have come out of the fire, the fire
will yet consume them. And when I set my
face against them, you will know that I am the
LORD. 8I will make the land desolate because
they have been unfaithful, declares the Sovereign LORD."

An Allegory of Unfaithful Jerusalem

16 The word of the LORD came to me:
2"Son of man, confront Jerusalem with
her detestable practices 3and say, 'This
is what the Sovereign LORD says to Jerusalem:
Your ancestry and birth were in the land of
the Canaanites; your father was an Amorite
and your mother a Hittite. 4On the day you
were born your cord was not cut, nor were
you washed with water to make you clean,
nor were you rubbed with salt or wrapped in
cloths. 5No one looked on you with pity or
had compassion enough to do any of these
things for you. Rather, you were thrown out
into the open field, for on the day you were
born you were despised.
6" 'Then I passed by and saw you kicking
about in your blood, and as you lay there in
your blood I said to you, "Live!"[b] 7I made you
grow like a plant of the field. You grew up and
developed and became the most beautiful of
jewels.[c] Your breasts were formed and your
hair grew, you who were naked and bare.
8" 'Later I passed by, and when I looked
at you and saw that you were old enough for
love, I spread the corner of my garment over
you and covered your nakedness. I gave you
my solemn oath and entered into a covenant
with you, declares the Sovereign LORD, and
you became mine.
9" 'I bathed[d] you with water and washed
the blood from you and put ointments on
you. 10I clothed you with an embroidered
dress and put leather sandals on you. I dressed
you in fine linen and covered you with costly
garments. 11I adorned you with jewelry: I put
bracelets on your arms and a necklace around
your neck, 12and I put a ring on your nose,
earrings on your ears and a beautiful crown

[a] 14 Or *Danel*; the Hebrew spelling may suggest a person other than the prophet Daniel; also in verse 20. [b] 6 A few Hebrew manuscripts, Septuagint and Syriac; most Hebrew manuscripts *"Live!" And as you lay there in your blood I said to you, "Live!"*
[c] 7 Or *became mature* [d] 9 Or *I had bathed*

on your head. 13So you were adorned with
gold and silver; your clothes were of fine linen
and costly fabric and embroidered cloth. Your
food was fine flour, honey and olive oil. You
became very beautiful and rose to be a queen.
14And your fame spread among the nations on
account of your beauty, because the splendor
I had given you made your beauty perfect, declares the Sovereign LORD.

15" 'But you trusted in your beauty and
used your fame to become a prostitute. You
lavished your favors on anyone who passed by
and your beauty became his.[a] 16You took some
of your garments to make gaudy high places,
where you carried on your prostitution. Such
things should not happen, nor should they
ever occur. 17You also took the fine jewelry I
gave you, the jewelry made of my gold and
silver, and you made for yourself male idols
and engaged in prostitution with them. 18And
you took your embroidered clothes to put
on them, and you offered my oil and incense
before them. 19Also the food I provided for
you—the fine flour, olive oil and honey I gave
you to eat—you offered as fragrant incense before them. That is what happened, declares the
Sovereign LORD.

20" 'And you took your sons and daughters
whom you bore to me and sacrificed them as
food to the idols. Was your prostitution not
enough? 21You slaughtered my children and
sacrificed them[b] to the idols. 22In all your detestable practices and your prostitution you
did not remember the days of your youth,
when you were naked and bare, kicking about
in your blood.

23" 'Woe! Woe to you, declares the Sovereign LORD. In addition to all your other wickedness, 24you built a mound for yourself and
made a lofty shrine in every public square.
25At the head of every street you built your
lofty shrines and degraded your beauty, offering your body with increasing promiscuity
to anyone who passed by. 26You engaged in
prostitution with the Egyptians, your lustful
neighbors, and provoked me to anger with
your increasing promiscuity. 27So I stretched
out my hand against you and reduced your
territory; I gave you over to the greed of your
enemies, the daughters of the Philistines, who
were shocked by your lewd conduct. 28You engaged in prostitution with the Assyrians too,
because you were insatiable; and even after
that, you still were not satisfied. 29Then you
increased your promiscuity to include Babylonia,[c] a land of merchants, but even with this
you were not satisfied.

30" 'How weak-willed you are, declares the
Sovereign LORD, when you do all these things,
acting like a brazen prostitute! 31When you
built your mounds at the head of every street
and made your lofty shrines in every public
square, you were unlike a prostitute, because
you scorned payment.

32" 'You adulterous wife! You prefer strangers to your own husband! 33Every prostitute
receives a fee, but you give gifts to all your
lovers, bribing them to come to you from everywhere for your illicit favors. 34So in your
prostitution you are the opposite of others; no
one runs after you for your favors. You are the
very opposite, for you give payment and none
is given to you.

35" 'Therefore, you prostitute, hear the
word of the LORD! 36This is what the Sovereign LORD says: Because you poured out your
wealth[d] and exposed your nakedness in your
promiscuity with your lovers, and because of
all your detestable idols, and because you gave
them your children's blood, 37therefore I am
going to gather all your lovers, with whom
you found pleasure, those you loved as well
as those you hated. I will gather them against
you from all around and will strip you in front
of them, and they will see all your nakedness.
38I will sentence you to the punishment of
women who commit adultery and who shed
blood; I will bring upon you the blood vengeance of my wrath and jealous anger. 39Then
I will hand you over to your lovers, and they
will tear down your mounds and destroy
your lofty shrines. They will strip you of your
clothes and take your fine jewelry and leave
you naked and bare. 40They will bring a mob
against you, who will stone you and hack you
to pieces with their swords. 41They will burn
down your houses and inflict punishment on
you in the sight of many women. I will put a
stop to your prostitution, and you will no longer pay your lovers. 42Then my wrath against
you will subside and my jealous anger will
turn away from you; I will be calm and no
longer angry.

43" 'Because you did not remember the
days of your youth but enraged me with all
these things, I will surely bring down on your
head what you have done, declares the Sovereign LORD. Did you not add lewdness to all
your other detestable practices?

44" 'Everyone who quotes proverbs will

---

a 15 Most Hebrew manuscripts; one Hebrew manuscript (see some Septuagint manuscripts) *by. Such a thing should not happen*
b 21 Or *and made them pass through ⌞the fire⌟* c 29 Or *Chaldea* d 36 Or *lust*

quote this proverb about you: "Like mother, like daughter." 45You are a true daughter
of your mother, who despised her husband
and her children; and you are a true sister of
your sisters, who despised their husbands and
their children. Your mother was a Hittite and
your father an Amorite. 46Your older sister was
Samaria, who lived to the north of you with
her daughters; and your younger sister, who
lived to the south of you with her daughters,
was Sodom. 47You not only walked in their
ways and copied their detestable practices, but
in all your ways you soon became more depraved than they. 48As surely as I live, declares
the Sovereign LORD, your sister Sodom and
her daughters never did what you and your
daughters have done.
49" 'Now this was the sin of your sister Sodom: She and her daughters were arrogant,
overfed and unconcerned; they did not help
the poor and needy. 50They were haughty and
did detestable things before me. Therefore I
did away with them as you have seen. 51Sa-
maria did not commit half the sins you did.
You have done more detestable things than
they, and have made your sisters seem righteous by all these things you have done. 52Bear
your disgrace, for you have furnished some
justification for your sisters. Because your sins
were more vile than theirs, they appear more
righteous than you. So then, be ashamed and
bear your disgrace, for you have made your
sisters appear righteous.
53" 'However, I will restore the fortunes of
Sodom and her daughters and of Samaria and
her daughters, and your fortunes along with
them, 54so that you may bear your disgrace
and be ashamed of all you have done in giving
them comfort. 55And your sisters, Sodom with
her daughters and Samaria with her daughters,
will return to what they were before; and you
and your daughters will return to what you
were before. 56You would not even mention
your sister Sodom in the day of your pride,
57before your wickedness was uncovered. Even
so, you are now scorned by the daughters of
Edom[a] and all her neighbors and the daughters of the Philistines—all those around you
who despise you. 58You will bear the consequences of your lewdness and your detestable
practices, declares the LORD.
59" 'This is what the Sovereign LORD says:
I will deal with you as you deserve, because
you have despised my oath by breaking the
covenant. 60Yet I will remember the covenant
I made with you in the days of your youth,
and I will establish an everlasting covenant
with you. 61Then you will remember your
ways and be ashamed when you receive your
sisters, both those who are older than you and
those who are younger. I will give them to you
as daughters, but not on the basis of my covenant with you. 62So I will establish my covenant with you, and you will know that I am
the LORD. 63Then, when I make atonement for
you for all you have done, you will remember
and be ashamed and never again open your
mouth because of your humiliation, declares
the Sovereign LORD.' "

Two Eagles and a Vine

17 The word of the LORD came to me:
2"Son of man, set forth an allegory and
tell the house of Israel a parable. 3Say to
them, 'This is what the Sovereign LORD says:
A great eagle with powerful wings, long feathers and full plumage of varied colors came to
Lebanon. Taking hold of the top of a cedar,
4he broke off its topmost shoot and carried it
away to a land of merchants, where he planted
it in a city of traders.
5" 'He took some of the seed of your land
and put it in fertile soil. He planted it like a
willow by abundant water, 6and it sprouted
and became a low, spreading vine. Its branches turned toward him, but its roots remained
under it. So it became a vine and produced
branches and put out leafy boughs.
7" 'But there was another great eagle with
powerful wings and full plumage. The vine
now sent out its roots toward him from the
plot where it was planted and stretched out its
branches to him for water. 8It had been planted in good soil by abundant water so that it
would produce branches, bear fruit and become a splendid vine.'
9"Say to them, 'This is what the Sovereign
LORD says: Will it thrive? Will it not be uprooted and stripped of its fruit so that it withers? All its new growth will wither. It will not
take a strong arm or many people to pull it up
by the roots. 10Even if it is transplanted, will it
thrive? Will it not wither completely when the
east wind strikes it—wither away in the plot
where it grew?' "
11Then the word of the LORD came to me:
12"Say to this rebellious house, 'Do you not
know what these things mean?' Say to them:
'The king of Babylon went to Jerusalem and
carried off her king and her nobles, bringing

[a] 57 Many Hebrew manuscripts and Syriac; most Hebrew manuscripts, Septuagint and Vulgate *Aram*

them back with him to Babylon. 13 Then he
took a member of the royal family and made a
treaty with him, putting him under oath. He
also carried away the leading men of the land,
14 so that the kingdom would be brought low,
unable to rise again, surviving only by keeping
his treaty. 15 But the king rebelled against him
by sending his envoys to Egypt to get horses and a large army. Will he succeed? Will he
who does such things escape? Will he break
the treaty and yet escape?

16 " 'As surely as I live, declares the Sovereign LORD, he shall die in Babylon, in the land
of the king who put him on the throne, whose
oath he despised and whose treaty he broke.
17 Pharaoh with his mighty army and great
horde will be of no help to him in war, when
ramps are built and siege works erected to destroy many lives. 18 He despised the oath by
breaking the covenant. Because he had given
his hand in pledge and yet did all these things,
he shall not escape.

19 " 'Therefore this is what the Sovereign
LORD says: As surely as I live, I will bring
down on his head my oath that he despised
and my covenant that he broke. 20 I will spread
my net for him, and he will be caught in my
snare. I will bring him to Babylon and execute
judgment upon him there because he was unfaithful to me. 21 All his fleeing troops will fall
by the sword, and the survivors will be scattered to the winds. Then you will know that I
the LORD have spoken.

22 " 'This is what the Sovereign LORD says: I
myself will take a shoot from the very top of
a cedar and plant it; I will break off a tender
sprig from its topmost shoots and plant it on a
high and lofty mountain. 23 On the mountain
heights of Israel I will plant it; it will produce
branches and bear fruit and become a splendid
cedar. Birds of every kind will nest in it; they
will find shelter in the shade of its branches.
24 All the trees of the field will know that I the
LORD bring down the tall tree and make the
low tree grow tall. I dry up the green tree and
make the dry tree flourish.

" 'I the LORD have spoken, and I will
do it.' "

The Soul Who Sins Will Die

18 The word of the LORD came to me:
2 "What do you people mean by quoting
this proverb about the land of Israel:

" 'The fathers eat sour grapes,
and the children's teeth are set on edge'?

3 "As surely as I live, declares the Sovereign
LORD, you will no longer quote this proverb
in Israel. 4 For every living soul belongs to me,
the father as well as the son—both alike belong to me. The soul who sins is the one who
will die.

5 "Suppose there is a righteous man
who does what is just and right.
6 He does not eat at the mountain shrines
or look to the idols of the house of
Israel.
He does not defile his neighbor's wife
or lie with a woman during her period.
7 He does not oppress anyone,
but returns what he took in pledge for
a loan.
He does not commit robbery
but gives his food to the hungry
and provides clothing for the naked.
8 He does not lend at usury
or take excessive interest.[a]
He withholds his hand from doing wrong
and judges fairly between man and
man.
9 He follows my decrees
and faithfully keeps my laws.
That man is righteous;
he will surely live,
declares the Sovereign LORD.

10 "Suppose he has a violent son, who sheds
blood or does any of these other things[b]
11 (though the father has done none of them):

"He eats at the mountain shrines.
He defiles his neighbor's wife.
12 He oppresses the poor and needy.
He commits robbery.
He does not return what he took in
pledge.
He looks to the idols.
He does detestable things.
13 He lends at usury and takes excessive
interest.

Will such a man live? He will not! Because he
has done all these detestable things, he will
surely be put to death and his blood will be
on his own head.

14 "But suppose this son has a son who sees
all the sins his father commits, and though he
sees them, he does not do such things:

15 "He does not eat at the mountain shrines
or look to the idols of the house of
Israel.
He does not defile his neighbor's wife.

---

[a] 8 Or *take interest*; similarly in verses 13 and 17 [b] 10 Or *things to a brother*

16He does not oppress anyone
or require a pledge for a loan.
He does not commit robbery
but gives his food to the hungry
and provides clothing for the naked.
17He withholds his hand from sin[a]
and takes no usury or excessive interest.
He keeps my laws and follows my
decrees.

He will not die for his father's sin; he will surely live. 18But his father will die for his own
sin, because he practiced extortion, robbed his
brother and did what was wrong among his
people.
19"Yet you ask, 'Why does the son not share
the guilt of his father?' Since the son has done
what is just and right and has been careful to
keep all my decrees, he will surely live. 20The
soul who sins is the one who will die. The son
will not share the guilt of the father, nor will
the father share the guilt of the son. The righteousness of the righteous man will be credited to him, and the wickedness of the wicked
will be charged against him.
21"But if a wicked man turns away from all
the sins he has committed and keeps all my
decrees and does what is just and right, he will
surely live; he will not die. 22None of the offenses he has committed will be remembered
against him. Because of the righteous things
he has done, he will live. 23Do I take any pleasure in the death of the wicked? declares the
Sovereign Lord. Rather, am I not pleased
when they turn from their ways and live?
24"But if a righteous man turns from his
righteousness and commits sin and does the
same detestable things the wicked man does,
will he live? None of the righteous things he
has done will be remembered. Because of the
unfaithfulness he is guilty of and because of
the sins he has committed, he will die.
25"Yet you say, 'The way of the Lord is not
just.' Hear, O house of Israel: Is my way unjust? Is it not your ways that are unjust? 26If
a righteous man turns from his righteousness
and commits sin, he will die for it; because of
the sin he has committed he will die. 27But if
a wicked man turns away from the wickedness
he has committed and does what is just and
right, he will save his life. 28Because he considers all the offenses he has committed and
turns away from them, he will surely live; he
will not die. 29Yet the house of Israel says, 'The
way of the Lord is not just.' Are my ways unjust, O house of Israel? Is it not your ways that
are unjust?
30"Therefore, O house of Israel, I will judge
you, each one according to his ways, declares
the Sovereign Lord. Repent! Turn away from
all your offenses; then sin will not be your
downfall. 31Rid yourselves of all the offenses
you have committed, and get a new heart and
a new spirit. Why will you die, O house of
Israel? 32For I take no pleasure in the death of
anyone, declares the Sovereign Lord. Repent
and live!

A Lament for Israel's Princes

19 "Take up a lament concerning the princes of Israel 2and say:

" 'What a lioness was your mother
among the lions!
She lay down among the young lions
and reared her cubs.
3She brought up one of her cubs,
and he became a strong lion.
He learned to tear the prey
and he devoured men.
4The nations heard about him,
and he was trapped in their pit.
They led him with hooks
to the land of Egypt.

5" 'When she saw her hope unfulfilled,
her expectation gone,
she took another of her cubs
and made him a strong lion.
6He prowled among the lions,
for he was now a strong lion.
He learned to tear the prey
and he devoured men.
7He broke down[b] their strongholds
and devastated their towns.
The land and all who were in it
were terrified by his roaring.
8Then the nations came against him,
those from regions round about.
They spread their net for him,
and he was trapped in their pit.
9With hooks they pulled him into a cage
and brought him to the king of
Babylon.
They put him in prison,
so his roar was heard no longer
on the mountains of Israel.

10" 'Your mother was like a vine in your
vineyard[c]

[a] *17* Septuagint (see also verse 8); Hebrew *from the poor* [b] *7* Targum (see Septuagint); Hebrew *He knew* [c] *10* Two Hebrew manuscripts; most Hebrew manuscripts *your blood*

planted by the water;
it was fruitful and full of branches
because of abundant water.
11 Its branches were strong,
fit for a ruler's scepter.
It towered high
above the thick foliage,
conspicuous for its height
and for its many branches.
12 But it was uprooted in fury
and thrown to the ground.
The east wind made it shrivel,
it was stripped of its fruit;
its strong branches withered
and fire consumed them.
13 Now it is planted in the desert,
in a dry and thirsty land.
14 Fire spread from one of its main[a] branches
and consumed its fruit.
No strong branch is left on it
fit for a ruler's scepter.'

This is a lament and is to be used as a lament."

Rebellious Israel

20 In the seventh year, in the fifth month
on the tenth day, some of the elders of
Israel came to inquire of the LORD, and
they sat down in front of me.
2Then the word of the LORD came to me:
3"Son of man, speak to the elders of Israel
and say to them, 'This is what the Sovereign
LORD says: Have you come to inquire of me?
As surely as I live, I will not let you inquire of
me, declares the Sovereign LORD.'
4"Will you judge them? Will you judge
them, son of man? Then confront them
with the detestable practices of their fathers
5and say to them: 'This is what the Sovereign
LORD says: On the day I chose Israel, I swore
with uplifted hand to the descendants of the
house of Jacob and revealed myself to them
in Egypt. With uplifted hand I said to them,
"I am the LORD your God." 6On that day I
swore to them that I would bring them out
of Egypt into a land I had searched out for
them, a land flowing with milk and honey,
the most beautiful of all lands. 7And I said to
them, "Each of you, get rid of the vile images
you have set your eyes on, and do not defile
yourselves with the idols of Egypt. I am the
LORD your God."
8" 'But they rebelled against me and would
not listen to me; they did not get rid of the vile
images they had set their eyes on, nor did they
forsake the idols of Egypt. So I said I would
pour out my wrath on them and spend my
anger against them in Egypt. 9But for the sake
of my name I did what would keep it from
being profaned in the eyes of the nations they
lived among and in whose sight I had revealed
myself to the Israelites by bringing them out
of Egypt. 10Therefore I led them out of Egypt
and brought them into the desert. 11I gave
them my decrees and made known to them
my laws, for the man who obeys them will live
by them. 12Also I gave them my Sabbaths as
a sign between us, so they would know that I
the LORD made them holy.
13" 'Yet the people of Israel rebelled against
me in the desert. They did not follow my decrees but rejected my laws—although the man
who obeys them will live by them—and they
utterly desecrated my Sabbaths. So I said I
would pour out my wrath on them and destroy them in the desert. 14But for the sake
of my name I did what would keep it from
being profaned in the eyes of the nations in
whose sight I had brought them out. 15Also
with uplifted hand I swore to them in the desert that I would not bring them into the land
I had given them—a land flowing with milk
and honey, most beautiful of all lands—16because they rejected my laws and did not follow my decrees and desecrated my Sabbaths.
For their hearts were devoted to their idols.
17Yet I looked on them with pity and did not
destroy them or put an end to them in the
desert. 18I said to their children in the desert,
"Do not follow the statutes of your fathers or
keep their laws or defile yourselves with their
idols. 19I am the LORD your God; follow my
decrees and be careful to keep my laws. 20Keep
my Sabbaths holy, that they may be a sign between us. Then you will know that I am the
LORD your God."
21" 'But the children rebelled against me:
They did not follow my decrees, they were not
careful to keep my laws—although the man
who obeys them will live by them—and they
desecrated my Sabbaths. So I said I would
pour out my wrath on them and spend my
anger against them in the desert. 22But I withheld my hand, and for the sake of my name I
did what would keep it from being profaned
in the eyes of the nations in whose sight I had
brought them out. 23Also with uplifted hand
I swear to them in the desert that I would
disperse them among the nations and scatter
them through the countries, 24because they

[a] 14 Or *from under its*

FRIDAY
READ EZEKIEL 20:1–29

PARENTAL LESSONS TO AVOID

> **"Do not follow the statutes of your fathers or keep their laws or defile yourselves with their idols. I am the LORD your God; follow my decrees and be careful to keep my laws."**
> — EZEKIEL 20:18–19

Most children follow the example of their parents. Even as we move into adulthood and marriage, it is natural to mirror our parents' attitudes and actions. Following their examples can be positive and productive. But what some parents teach can also be difficult and destructive, or somewhere in between.

Jim and Jolene wrestled with the lessons each had learned in their dysfunctional families. When they gave their lives and their marriage to Jesus Christ, they found themselves on a healthier path. But the lessons each had learned from parents and other family members required a lot of sifting. As the couple grew in Christ, they learned three important lessons that the people of Israel also had to learn. The prophet Ezekiel provided specific directions:

First, do not follow the rules (written and unwritten) of sinful parents. Their destructive behavior, broken relationships and spiritual emptiness can lead to death. That was Jim's experience. He had witnessed drunkenness, abuse and betrayal in his parents' relationship, and as a teen Jim followed their example as he got into drugs, alcohol and trouble with the law.

Even religious parents can provide poor examples to follow. Jolene often went to church with her family and took part in a youth group. But her mother was judgmental, and her father was preoccupied with his own life. Neither one modeled for Jolene how to behave in a long-term relationship.

Second, do everything you can to pattern your lives and relationship after Christ and his followers. Before meeting each other, Jim and Jolene had become believers. Yet they had to learn how to live as authentic Christians in marriage. They learned as much as they could from Christ's teachings and example as well as from godly couples in church.

Third, keep the Sabbath. It's easy to organize life around each other, your jobs, recreational activities, house and yard upkeep, or caring for the kids. But as God says in Ezekiel 20:20, we must keep the Sabbaths holy, "that they may be a sign between us." When our lives conform to the pattern suggested to us by Scripture, setting aside a day to worship God with other believers and letting everything else line up after that, then, as Ezekiel said, we will know God is our Lord.

—JOHN R. THROOP

let's *talk*

- ✦ What were some of the lessons our parents taught us about being a husband or wife? How did they model good behavior? Not-so-good behavior?
- ✦ What are some practical and productive ways we can follow the commands of Christ to build a spiritual life as a couple and together glorify him?
- ✦ In a time-challenged world, what are some ways we can keep the Sabbath together? How can we worship and obey God together?

FOR YOUR NEXT DEVOTIONAL READING, TURN TO PAGE 916.

had not obeyed my laws but had rejected my
decrees and desecrated my Sabbaths, and their
eyes ⌊lusted⌋ after their fathers' idols. 25I also
gave them over to statutes that were not good
and laws they could not live by; 26I let them
become defiled through their gifts—the sacrifice of every firstborn[a]—that I might fill them
with horror so they would know that I am the
LORD.'

27"Therefore, son of man, speak to the people of Israel and say to them, 'This is what the
Sovereign LORD says: In this also your fathers
blasphemed me by forsaking me: 28When I
brought them into the land I had sworn to
give them and they saw any high hill or any
leafy tree, there they offered their sacrifices,
made offerings that provoked me to anger,
presented their fragrant incense and poured
out their drink offerings. 29Then I said to
them: What is this high place you go to?' " (It
is called Bamah[b] to this day.)

Judgment and Restoration

30"Therefore say to the house of Israel: 'This
is what the Sovereign LORD says: Will you defile yourselves the way your fathers did and
lust after their vile images? 31When you offer
your gifts—the sacrifice of your sons in[c] the
fire—you continue to defile yourselves with
all your idols to this day. Am I to let you inquire of me, O house of Israel? As surely as I
live, declares the Sovereign LORD, I will not let
you inquire of me.

32" 'You say, "We want to be like the nations, like the peoples of the world, who serve
wood and stone." But what you have in mind
will never happen. 33As surely as I live, declares the Sovereign LORD, I will rule over
you with a mighty hand and an outstretched
arm and with outpoured wrath. 34I will bring
you from the nations and gather you from the
countries where you have been scattered—
with a mighty hand and an outstretched arm
and with outpoured wrath. 35I will bring you
into the desert of the nations and there, face
to face, I will execute judgment upon you.
36As I judged your fathers in the desert of the
land of Egypt, so I will judge you, declares the
Sovereign LORD. 37I will take note of you as
you pass under my rod, and I will bring you
into the bond of the covenant. 38I will purge
you of those who revolt and rebel against me.
Although I will bring them out of the land
where they are living, yet they will not enter
the land of Israel. Then you will know that I
am the LORD.

39" 'As for you, O house of Israel, this is
what the Sovereign LORD says: Go and serve
your idols, every one of you! But afterward you
will surely listen to me and no longer profane
my holy name with your gifts and idols. 40For
on my holy mountain, the high mountain of
Israel, declares the Sovereign LORD, there in
the land the entire house of Israel will serve
me, and there I will accept them. There I will
require your offerings and your choice gifts,[d]
along with all your holy sacrifices. 41I will accept you as fragrant incense when I bring you
out from the nations and gather you from the
countries where you have been scattered, and
I will show myself holy among you in the sight
of the nations. 42Then you will know that I
am the LORD, when I bring you into the land
of Israel, the land I had sworn with uplifted
hand to give to your fathers. 43There you will
remember your conduct and all the actions by
which you have defiled yourselves, and you
will loathe yourselves for all the evil you have
done. 44You will know that I am the LORD,
when I deal with you for my name's sake and
not according to your evil ways and your corrupt practices, O house of Israel, declares the
Sovereign LORD.' "

Prophecy Against the South

45The word of the LORD came to me:
46"Son of man, set your face toward the south;
preach against the south and prophesy against
the forest of the southland. 47Say to the southern forest: 'Hear the word of the LORD. This
is what the Sovereign LORD says: I am about
to set fire to you, and it will consume all your
trees, both green and dry. The blazing flame
will not be quenched, and every face from
south to north will be scorched by it. 48Every-
one will see that I the LORD have kindled it; it
will not be quenched.' "

49Then I said, "Ah, Sovereign LORD! They
are saying of me, 'Isn't he just telling parables?' "

Babylon, God's Sword of Judgment

21 The word of the LORD came to me:
2"Son of man, set your face against Jerusalem and preach against the sanctuary.
Prophesy against the land of Israel 3and say to
her: 'This is what the LORD says: I am against
you. I will draw my sword from its scabbard
and cut off from you both the righteous and

[a] 26 Or *—making every firstborn pass through ⌊the fire⌋* [b] 29 *Bamah* means *high place.* [c] 31 Or *—making your sons pass through*
[d] 40 Or *and the gifts of your firstfruits*

the wicked. 4Because I am going to cut off the
righteous and the wicked, my sword will be
unsheathed against everyone from south to
north. 5Then all people will know that I the
LORD have drawn my sword from its scabbard;
it will not return again.'
6"Therefore groan, son of man! Groan before them with broken heart and bitter grief.
7And when they ask you, 'Why are you groaning?' you shall say, 'Because of the news that
is coming. Every heart will melt and every
hand go limp; every spirit will become faint
and every knee become as weak as water.' It is
coming! It will surely take place, declares the
Sovereign LORD."
8The word of the LORD came to me: 9"Son
of man, prophesy and say, 'This is what the
Lord says:

" 'A sword, a sword,
 sharpened and polished—
10 sharpened for the slaughter,
 polished to flash like lightning!

" 'Shall we rejoice in the scepter of my son
⌞Judah⌟? The sword despises every such stick.

11 " 'The sword is appointed to be polished,
 to be grasped with the hand;
it is sharpened and polished,
 made ready for the hand of the slayer.
12 Cry out and wail, son of man,
 for it is against my people;
 it is against all the princes of Israel.
They are thrown to the sword
 along with my people.
Therefore beat your breast.

13" 'Testing will surely come. And what if
the scepter ⌞of Judah⌟, which the sword despises, does not continue? declares the Sovereign
LORD.'

14 "So then, son of man, prophesy
 and strike your hands together.
Let the sword strike twice,
 even three times.
It is a sword for slaughter—
 a sword for great slaughter,
 closing in on them from every side.
15 So that hearts may melt
 and the fallen be many,
I have stationed the sword for slaughter[a]
 at all their gates.
Oh! It is made to flash like lightning,
 it is grasped for slaughter.
16 O sword, slash to the right,
 then to the left,
 wherever your blade is turned.
17 I too will strike my hands together,
 and my wrath will subside.
I the LORD have spoken."

18The word of the LORD came to me:
19"Son of man, mark out two roads for the
sword of the king of Babylon to take, both
starting from the same country. Make a sign-
post where the road branches off to the city.
20Mark out one road for the sword to come
against Rabbah of the Ammonites and another against Judah and fortified Jerusalem. 21For
the king of Babylon will stop at the fork in
the road, at the junction of the two roads, to
seek an omen: He will cast lots with arrows,
he will consult his idols, he will examine the
liver. 22Into his right hand will come the lot
for Jerusalem, where he is to set up battering rams, to give the command to slaughter,
to sound the battle cry, to set battering rams
against the gates, to build a ramp and to erect
siege works. 23It will seem like a false omen to
those who have sworn allegiance to him, but
he will remind them of their guilt and take
them captive.
24"Therefore this is what the Sovereign
LORD says: 'Because you people have brought
to mind your guilt by your open rebellion, revealing your sins in all that you do—because
you have done this, you will be taken captive.
25" 'O profane and wicked prince of Israel,
whose day has come, whose time of punishment has reached its climax, 26this is what the
Sovereign LORD says: Take off the turban, remove the crown. It will not be as it was: The
lowly will be exalted and the exalted will be
brought low. 27A ruin! A ruin! I will make it
a ruin! It will not be restored until he comes
to whom it rightfully belongs; to him I will
give it.'
28"And you, son of man, prophesy and say,
'This is what the Sovereign LORD says about
the Ammonites and their insults:

" 'A sword, a sword,
 drawn for the slaughter,
polished to consume
 and to flash like lightning!
29 Despite false visions concerning you
 and lying divinations about you,
it will be laid on the necks
 of the wicked who are to be slain,
whose day has come,
 whose time of punishment has reached
 its climax.

---
a 15 Septuagint; the meaning of the Hebrew for this word is uncertain.

30 Return the sword to its scabbard.
  In the place where you were created,
in the land of your ancestry,
  I will judge you.
31 I will pour out my wrath upon you
  and breathe out my fiery anger against
    you;
I will hand you over to brutal men,
  men skilled in destruction.
32 You will be fuel for the fire,
  your blood will be shed in your land,
you will be remembered no more;
  for I the LORD have spoken.' "

Jerusalem's Sins

22 The word of the LORD came to me:
2 "Son of man, will you judge her? Will
you judge this city of bloodshed? Then
confront her with all her detestable practices
3 and say: 'This is what the Sovereign LORD
says: O city that brings on herself doom by
shedding blood in her midst and defiles herself
by making idols, 4 you have become guilty because of the blood you have shed and have become defiled by the idols you have made. You
have brought your days to a close, and the end
of your years has come. Therefore I will make
you an object of scorn to the nations and a
laughingstock to all the countries. 5 Those who
are near and those who are far away will mock
you, O infamous city, full of turmoil.

6 " 'See how each of the princes of Israel
who are in you uses his power to shed blood.
7 In you they have treated father and mother
with contempt; in you they have oppressed
the alien and mistreated the fatherless and the
widow. 8 You have despised my holy things
and desecrated my Sabbaths. 9 In you are slanderous men bent on shedding blood; in you
are those who eat at the mountain shrines and
commit lewd acts. 10 In you are those who
dishonor their fathers' bed; in you are those
who violate women during their period, when
they are ceremonially unclean. 11 In you one
man commits a detestable offense with his
neighbor's wife, another shamefully defiles his
daughter-in-law, and another violates his sister, his own father's daughter. 12 In you men
accept bribes to shed blood; you take usury
and excessive interest[a] and make unjust gain
from your neighbors by extortion. And you
have forgotten me, declares the Sovereign
LORD.

13 " 'I will surely strike my hands together
at the unjust gain you have made and at the
blood you have shed in your midst. 14 Will
your courage endure or your hands be strong
in the day I deal with you? I the LORD have
spoken, and I will do it. 15 I will disperse you
among the nations and scatter you through
the countries; and I will put an end to your
uncleanness. 16 When you have been defiled[b]
in the eyes of the nations, you will know that
I am the LORD.' "

17 Then the word of the LORD came to me:
18 "Son of man, the house of Israel has become
dross to me; all of them are the copper, tin,
iron and lead left inside a furnace. They are
but the dross of silver. 19 Therefore this is what
the Sovereign LORD says: 'Because you have
all become dross, I will gather you into Jerusalem. 20 As men gather silver, copper, iron, lead
and tin into a furnace to melt it with a fiery
blast, so will I gather you in my anger and my
wrath and put you inside the city and melt
you. 21 I will gather you and I will blow on you
with my fiery wrath, and you will be melted
inside her. 22 As silver is melted in a furnace,
so you will be melted inside her, and you will
know that I the LORD have poured out my
wrath upon you.' "

23 Again the word of the LORD came to me:
24 "Son of man, say to the land, 'You are a land
that has had no rain or showers[c] in the day of
wrath.' 25 There is a conspiracy of her princes[d]
within her like a roaring lion tearing its prey;
they devour people, take treasures and precious
things and make many widows within her.
26 Her priests do violence to my law and profane my holy things; they do not distinguish
between the holy and the common; they teach
that there is no difference between the unclean
and the clean; and they shut their eyes to the
keeping of my Sabbaths, so that I am profaned
among them. 27 Her officials within her are
like wolves tearing their prey; they shed blood
and kill people to make unjust gain. 28 Her
prophets whitewash these deeds for them by
false visions and lying divinations. They say,
'This is what the Sovereign LORD says'—when
the LORD has not spoken. 29 The people of the
land practice extortion and commit robbery;
they oppress the poor and needy and mistreat
the alien, denying them justice.

30 "I looked for a man among them who
would build up the wall and stand before me
in the gap on behalf of the land so I would not
have to destroy it, but I found none. 31 So I
will pour out my wrath on them and consume
them with my fiery anger, bringing down on

[a] *12* Or *usury and interest* [b] *16* Or *When I have allotted you your inheritance* [c] *24* Septuagint; Hebrew *has not been cleansed or rained on* [d] *25* Septuagint; Hebrew *prophets*

their own heads all they have done, declares the Sovereign LORD.”

Two Adulterous Sisters

23 The word of the LORD came to me: 2“Son of man, there were two women, daughters of the same mother. 3They became prostitutes in Egypt, engaging in prostitution from their youth. In that land their breasts were fondled and their virgin bosoms caressed. 4The older was named Oholah, and her sister was Oholibah. They were mine and gave birth to sons and daughters. Oholah is Samaria, and Oholibah is Jerusalem.

5“Oholah engaged in prostitution while she was still mine; and she lusted after her lovers, the Assyrians—warriors 6clothed in blue, governors and commanders, all of them handsome young men, and mounted horsemen. 7She gave herself as a prostitute to all the elite of the Assyrians and defiled herself with all the idols of everyone she lusted after. 8She did not give up the prostitution she began in Egypt, when during her youth men slept with her, caressed her virgin bosom and poured out their lust upon her.

9“Therefore I handed her over to her lovers, the Assyrians, for whom she lusted. 10They stripped her naked, took away her sons and daughters and killed her with the sword. She became a byword among women, and punishment was inflicted on her.

11“Her sister Oholibah saw this, yet in her lust and prostitution she was more depraved than her sister. 12She too lusted after the Assyrians—governors and commanders, warriors in full dress, mounted horsemen, all handsome young men. 13I saw that she too defiled herself; both of them went the same way.

14“But she carried her prostitution still further. She saw men portrayed on a wall, figures of Chaldeans[a] portrayed in red, 15with belts around their waists and flowing turbans on their heads; all of them looked like Babylonian chariot officers, natives of Chaldea.[b] 16As soon as she saw them, she lusted after them and sent messengers to them in Chaldea. 17Then the Babylonians came to her, to the bed of love, and in their lust they defiled her. After she had been defiled by them, she turned away from them in disgust. 18When she carried on her prostitution openly and exposed her nakedness, I turned away from her in disgust, just as I had turned away from her sister. 19Yet she became more and more promiscuous as she recalled the days of her youth, when she was a prostitute in Egypt. 20There she lusted after her lovers, whose genitals were like those of donkeys and whose emission was like that of horses. 21So you longed for the lewdness of your youth, when in Egypt your bosom was caressed and your young breasts fondled.[c]

22“Therefore, Oholibah, this is what the Sovereign LORD says: I will stir up your lovers against you, those you turned away from in disgust, and I will bring them against you from every side— 23the Babylonians and all the Chaldeans, the men of Pekod and Shoa and Koa, and all the Assyrians with them, handsome young men, all of them governors and commanders, chariot officers and men of high rank, all mounted on horses. 24They will come against you with weapons,[d] chariots and wagons and with a throng of people; they will take up positions against you on every side with large and small shields and with helmets. I will turn you over to them for punishment, and they will punish you according to their standards. 25I will direct my jealous anger against you, and they will deal with you in fury. They will cut off your noses and your ears, and those of you who are left will fall by the sword. They will take away your sons and daughters, and those of you who are left will be consumed by fire. 26They will also strip you of your clothes and take your fine jewelry. 27So I will put a stop to the lewdness and prostitution you began in Egypt. You will not look on these things with longing or remember Egypt anymore.

28“For this is what the Sovereign LORD says: I am about to hand you over to those you hate, to those you turned away from in disgust. 29They will deal with you in hatred and take away everything you have worked for. They will leave you naked and bare, and the shame of your prostitution will be exposed. Your lewdness and promiscuity 30have brought this upon you, because you lusted after the nations and defiled yourself with their idols. 31You have gone the way of your sister; so I will put her cup into your hand.

32“This is what the Sovereign LORD says:

“You will drink your sister’s cup,
  a cup large and deep;
it will bring scorn and derision,
  for it holds so much.

---

[a] 14 Or *Babylonians* [b] 15 Or *Babylonia*; also in verse 16 [c] 21 Syriac (see also verse 3); Hebrew *caressed because of your young breasts*
[d] 24 The meaning of the Hebrew for this word is uncertain.

WEEKEND

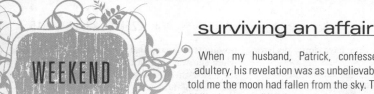

surviving an affair

When my husband, Patrick, confessed he'd committed adultery, his revelation was as unbelievable as if someone had told me the moon had fallen from the sky. The man who told me he'd lived a secret life of sexual sin seemed so different from the man to whom I'd been married for nine years.

My rage, disillusionment and confusion were intense. Yet Pat was so broken, so willing to do whatever it took to break free from his sexual addiction, that, despite my anger and hurt, I agreed to go through counseling with him.

There came a moment during counseling when I thought our marriage would end. I was five months pregnant, and we had a four-year-old daughter. Our counselor sat with me one night and said, "Connie, you have to accept the possibility Patrick might not break free of this addiction." That was the worst night of my life. Only my confidence in God gave me the courage to hold on.

But as the months went by, Pat found the strength to change, and our marriage was slowly, painfully restored. I discovered I needed God's grace as much as Pat did. And I had to choose to remember that if God could forgive Pat's wrongs, I could, too. Today, thanks to God's love and power, our life together is better than ever before.

As I share my story of hurt and hope, women often reveal the terrible traumas their husbands have put them through: infidelity, bankruptcy, depression, and rebellion against God. But you can't fix your husband; you can only pray for him. When you come to the end of yourself, God will come through.

I've learned that, as a Christian, forgiveness isn't optional. But I don't think we ever forget the pain. Suffering teaches us deep truths about God's grace and love.

A few years ago, Pat surprised me by planting tulip bulbs in our flowerbeds. For many months—before beautiful tulips bloomed everywhere—all I saw was dirt pelted by rain. That's just like life. Sometimes all we see is the dirt watered by our tears. But God promises to bring back our joy (Isaiah 61:1–3). If you are hurting right now, trust God to bring blossoms of joy out of the dirt of your despair. He brought joy and laughter back into our lives; he can do it for you, too.

How to Handle Tough Times

1. Stay connected. When I felt weak or angry, I'd call my Christian friends for prayer. They kept me on track and boosted my faith.

2. Soak it up. As I recovered from my broken heart, I found it essential to stay immersed in God's Word.

3. Be good to yourself. Go to the movies. Laugh. Eat well. If you don't take care of yourself, you'll be less able to care for your husband.

4. Take note. Remember, God won't waste your pain! Some day he'll use you to encourage somebody else who's going through a tough time.

—CONNIE NEAL WITH JANE JOHNSON STRUCK

signs of an affair

These are a list of warning signs that alert a person that their spouse is having an affair. Go over the list individually, if that would be more comfortable for you. Or read through the list together and determine if any questions prompt a need for discussion. Is there anything that you need to do differently to keep your lives transparent and keep each other from suspicion?

1. Does your spouse have a friend of the opposite sex? How much time does he or she spend with that person? What do they do together?
2. What person of the opposite sex does your spouse admire the most? Talk about repeatedly?
3. Whom does he spend time talking to on the phone? Does he lower his voice or hang up when you enter the room?
4. Are there any indications that your spouse might have a secret life?
5. Do you have access to your spouse all the time, or are there portions of the day when she is unaccounted for?
6. Do you have access to your spouse's mail, specifically things like credit card statements and cell phone records?
7. Are you always completely honest with each other? Are there times your spouse appears to be lying?
8. Have you told your spouse you don't want to hear the truth if it is upsetting?
9. Have you picked up a sexually transmitted disease that you can't explain?
10. Are you concerned that your spouse is having an affair, but they won't admit it?
11. Do you really want to know if your spouse is cheating?

—CINDY CROSBY

HOW ARE WE DOING?

let's make a DATE

CONNECTION TIME

Develop a list of things you can do weekly, monthly and yearly to keep the two of you connected and to help affair-proof your marriage. For example, you may plan a weekly coffee date to catch up on your schedules, a monthly "serious talk" to air concerns, or a yearly seminar or couples retreat with your church. Whatever you decide, make your time together a priority.

FOR YOUR NEXT DEVOTIONAL READING, TURN TO PAGE 920.

LESSONS FROM THE *Bible*

What are some lessons we can learn about infidelity from the following people in the Bible?

1. Potiphar and his wife (Genesis 39:1–20)
2. David and Bathsheba (2 Samuel 11:1—12:13)

[33] You will be filled with drunkenness and sorrow,
the cup of ruin and desolation,
the cup of your sister Samaria.
[34] You will drink it and drain it dry;
you will dash it to pieces
and tear your breasts.

I have spoken, declares the Sovereign LORD.

[35] "Therefore this is what the Sovereign
LORD says: Since you have forgotten me and
thrust me behind your back, you must bear
the consequences of your lewdness and prostitution."
[36] The LORD said to me: "Son of man, will
you judge Oholah and Oholibah? Then confront them with their detestable practices,
[37] for they have committed adultery and blood
is on their hands. They committed adultery
with their idols; they even sacrificed their
children, whom they bore to me,[a] as food for
them. [38] They have also done this to me: At
that same time they defiled my sanctuary and
desecrated my Sabbaths. [39] On the very day
they sacrificed their children to their idols,
they entered my sanctuary and desecrated it.
That is what they did in my house.
[40] "They even sent messengers for men who
came from far away, and when they arrived
you bathed yourself for them, painted your
eyes and put on your jewelry. [41] You sat on an
elegant couch, with a table spread before it on
which you had placed the incense and oil that
belonged to me.
[42] "The noise of a carefree crowd was around
her; Sabeans[b] were brought from the desert
along with men from the rabble, and they put
bracelets on the arms of the woman and her
sister and beautiful crowns on their heads.
[43] Then I said about the one worn out by adultery, 'Now let them use her as a prostitute, for
that is all she is.' [44] And they slept with her. As
men sleep with a prostitute, so they slept with
those lewd women, Oholah and Oholibah.
[45] But righteous men will sentence them to the
punishment of women who commit adultery
and shed blood, because they are adulterous
and blood is on their hands.
[46] "This is what the Sovereign LORD says:
Bring a mob against them and give them over
to terror and plunder. [47] The mob will stone
them and cut them down with their swords;
they will kill their sons and daughters and
burn down their houses.
[48] "So I will put an end to lewdness in the
land, that all women may take warning and
not imitate you. [49] You will suffer the penalty
for your lewdness and bear the consequences
of your sins of idolatry. Then you will know
that I am the Sovereign LORD."

The Cooking Pot

24 In the ninth year, in the tenth month
on the tenth day, the word of the LORD
came to me: [2] "Son of man, record this
date, this very date, because the king of Babylon has laid siege to Jerusalem this very day.
[3] Tell this rebellious house a parable and say
to them: 'This is what the Sovereign LORD
says:

" 'Put on the cooking pot; put it on
and pour water into it.
[4] Put into it the pieces of meat,
all the choice pieces—the leg and the shoulder.
Fill it with the best of these bones;
[5] take the pick of the flock.
Pile wood beneath it for the bones;
bring it to a boil
and cook the bones in it.

[6] " 'For this is what the Sovereign LORD says:

" 'Woe to the city of bloodshed,
to the pot now encrusted,
whose deposit will not go away!
Empty it piece by piece
without casting lots for them.

[7] " 'For the blood she shed is in her midst:
She poured it on the bare rock;
she did not pour it on the ground,
where the dust would cover it.
[8] To stir up wrath and take revenge
I put her blood on the bare rock,
so that it would not be covered.

[9] " 'Therefore this is what the Sovereign LORD
says:

" 'Woe to the city of bloodshed!
I, too, will pile the wood high.
[10] So heap on the wood
and kindle the fire.
Cook the meat well,
mixing in the spices;
and let the bones be charred.
[11] Then set the empty pot on the coals
till it becomes hot and its copper glows
so its impurities may be melted
and its deposit burned away.
[12] It has frustrated all efforts;

---

[a] 37 *Or even made the children they bore to me pass through the fire* [b] 42 *Or drunkards*

its heavy deposit has not been removed,
not even by fire.

13" 'Now your impurity is lewdness. Because I tried to cleanse you but you would not be cleansed from your impurity, you will not be clean again until my wrath against you has subsided.

14" 'I the LORD have spoken. The time has come for me to act. I will not hold back; I will not have pity, nor will I relent. You will be judged according to your conduct and your actions, declares the Sovereign LORD.' "

Ezekiel's Wife Dies

15The word of the LORD came to me: 16"Son of man, with one blow I am about to take away from you the delight of your eyes. Yet do not lament or weep or shed any tears. 17Groan quietly; do not mourn for the dead. Keep your turban fastened and your sandals on your feet; do not cover the lower part of your face or eat the customary food ⌊of mourners⌋."

18So I spoke to the people in the morning, and in the evening my wife died. The next morning I did as I had been commanded.

19Then the people asked me, "Won't you tell us what these things have to do with us?"

20So I said to them, "The word of the LORD came to me: 21Say to the house of Israel, 'This is what the Sovereign LORD says: I am about to desecrate my sanctuary—the stronghold in which you take pride, the delight of your eyes, the object of your affection. The sons and daughters you left behind will fall by the sword. 22And you will do as I have done. You will not cover the lower part of your face or eat the customary food ⌊of mourners⌋. 23You will keep your turbans on your heads and your sandals on your feet. You will not mourn or weep but will waste away because of[a] your sins and groan among yourselves. 24Ezekiel will be a sign to you; you will do just as he has done. When this happens, you will know that I am the Sovereign LORD.'

25"And you, son of man, on the day I take away their stronghold, their joy and glory, the delight of their eyes, their heart's desire, and their sons and daughters as well— 26on that day a fugitive will come to tell you the news. 27At that time your mouth will be opened; you will speak with him and will no longer be silent. So you will be a sign to them, and they will know that I am the LORD."

A Prophecy Against Ammon

25 The word of the LORD came to me: 2"Son of man, set your face against the Ammonites and prophesy against them. 3Say to them, 'Hear the word of the Sovereign LORD. This is what the Sovereign LORD says: Because you said "Aha!" over my sanctuary when it was desecrated and over the land of Israel when it was laid waste and over the people of Judah when they went into exile, 4therefore I am going to give you to the people of the East as a possession. They will set up their camps and pitch their tents among you; they will eat your fruit and drink your milk. 5I will turn Rabbah into a pasture for camels and Ammon into a resting place for sheep. Then you will know that I am the LORD. 6For this is what the Sovereign LORD says: Because you have clapped your hands and stamped your feet, rejoicing with all the malice of your heart against the land of Israel, 7therefore I will stretch out my hand against you and give you as plunder to the nations. I will cut you off from the nations and exterminate you from the countries. I will destroy you, and you will know that I am the LORD.' "

A Prophecy Against Moab

8"This is what the Sovereign LORD says: 'Because Moab and Seir said, "Look, the house of Judah has become like all the other nations," 9therefore I will expose the flank of Moab, beginning at its frontier towns—Beth Jeshimoth, Baal Meon and Kiriathaim—the glory of that land. 10I will give Moab along with the Ammonites to the people of the East as a possession, so that the Ammonites will not be remembered among the nations; 11and I will inflict punishment on Moab. Then they will know that I am the LORD.' "

A Prophecy Against Edom

12"This is what the Sovereign LORD says: 'Because Edom took revenge on the house of Judah and became very guilty by doing so, 13therefore this is what the Sovereign LORD says: I will stretch out my hand against Edom and kill its men and their animals. I will lay it waste, and from Teman to Dedan they will fall by the sword. 14I will take vengeance on Edom by the hand of my people Israel, and they will deal with Edom in accordance with my anger and my wrath; they will know my vengeance, declares the Sovereign LORD.' "

---

[a] 23 Or *away in*

MONDAY
READ EZEKIEL 24:15–27

LESSONS OF LOSS

> **"With one blow I am about to take away from you the delight of your eyes."**
>
> — EZEKIEL 24:16

let's talk

- What do we learn about the consequences of sin from this story?
- What do we learn about God from this story?
- What could we do to help each other be more sensitive to sin in our lives? How can we encourage each other to walk closer with the Lord?

The Holmes and Rahe Life Stress Scale lists 43 stressful life events and the value of each. At 100 points, the death of a spouse tops the list of life stresses.

No wonder. As James D. Berkeley so poignantly wrote in "Called into Crisis" (*Christianity Today*, 1989), "Gone is the dear companion, the keeper of books, the vacation partner, the purchaser of groceries, the maker of dinner or the fixer of cars. Gone is the one who shares sunsets or midnight diaperings or pet jokes or holiday traditions. Gone. In one final moment, it's all gone, to be replaced by grief, a miserable substitute."

Now imagine this: The Lord speaks to you directly and says that he is about to take away "the delight of your eyes." If that's not terrible enough, you are not to mourn. No crying. No black clothes. No sign whatsoever that you are grieving. If you must groan, keep that to yourself. Carry on as if nothing happened, and do it in the public eye.

That is the dark assignment God gave to the prophet Ezekiel as he was proclaiming God's message to fellow Israelites who had been exiled to Babylon prior to the fall of Jerusalem. At first, you might think this demand unworthy of a loving God, but it actually illustrates the profound ache in the heart of God because his people simply would not take seriously his warnings about their sin (see Ezekiel 24:13–14).

God's point was that his people were going to be overwhelmed by their losses. They would lose the temple where they worshiped God—"the stronghold in which you take pride, the delight of your eyes, the object of your affection" (verse 21). Not only that, but they would also lose their sons and daughters who had remained in Jerusalem.

Incredibly, they would not mourn—at least not in the typical way. Verse 23 tells us that the people had become so numbed to sin and its consequences that they could only groan when sin finally made them "waste away" (a Hebrew word that could also mean "rot"). They would have to live with the knowledge that their home country's destruction had been foretold by the prophets and judgment was to be expected.

Now, if you were to lose as much as these Israelites lost, what would your grief be like? If you knew that not only your children but virtually all the children of the next generation would be lost, how would you feel?

God uses marriage to help us grasp the intimacy, emotion and treasure of our relationship with him. If we sense that we (like Israel) could not grieve because of our remorse, the reason may well be that sin has dulled our senses to what matters in life. We have forgotten that our relationship with God must be more deeply loving and devoted than a spouse's. Our response, of course, should not be to try to feel sadder about loss but rather to deal with the soul-deadening sin in our lives.

One of God's great gifts to us is our life's partner. This sad story in Ezekiel reminds us how we need to help one another keep hot and bright our love for the Lord our God, as well as for each other.

—LEE ECLOV

FOR YOUR NEXT DEVOTIONAL READING, TURN TO PAGE 933.

A Prophecy Against Philistia

15"This is what the Sovereign LORD says: 'Because the Philistines acted in vengeance and took revenge with malice in their hearts, and with ancient hostility sought to destroy Judah, 16therefore this is what the Sovereign LORD says: I am about to stretch out my hand against the Philistines, and I will cut off the Kerethites and destroy those remaining along the coast. 17I will carry out great vengeance on them and punish them in my wrath. Then they will know that I am the LORD, when I take vengeance on them.' "

A Prophecy Against Tyre

26 In the eleventh year, on the first day of the month, the word of the LORD came to me: 2"Son of man, because Tyre has said of Jerusalem, 'Aha! The gate to the nations is broken, and its doors have swung open to me; now that she lies in ruins I will prosper,' 3therefore this is what the Sovereign LORD says: I am against you, O Tyre, and I will bring many nations against you, like the sea casting up its waves. 4They will destroy the walls of Tyre and pull down her towers; I will scrape away her rubble and make her a bare rock. 5Out in the sea she will become a place to spread fishnets, for I have spoken, declares the Sovereign LORD. She will become plunder for the nations, 6and her settlements on the mainland will be ravaged by the sword. Then they will know that I am the LORD.

7"For this is what the Sovereign LORD says: From the north I am going to bring against Tyre Nebuchadnezzar[a] king of Babylon, king of kings, with horses and chariots, with horsemen and a great army. 8He will ravage your settlements on the mainland with the sword; he will set up siege works against you, build a ramp up to your walls and raise his shields against you. 9He will direct the blows of his battering rams against your walls and demolish your towers with his weapons. 10His horses will be so many that they will cover you with dust. Your walls will tremble at the noise of the war horses, wagons and chariots when he enters your gates as men enter a city whose walls have been broken through. 11The hoofs of his horses will trample all your streets; he will kill your people with the sword, and your strong pillars will fall to the ground. 12They will plunder your wealth and loot your merchandise; they will break down your walls and demolish your fine houses and throw your stones, timber and rubble into the sea. 13I will put an end to your noisy songs, and the music of your harps will be heard no more. 14I will make you a bare rock, and you will become a place to spread fishnets. You will never be rebuilt, for I the LORD have spoken, declares the Sovereign LORD.

15"This is what the Sovereign LORD says to Tyre: Will not the coastlands tremble at the sound of your fall, when the wounded groan and the slaughter takes place in you? 16Then all the princes of the coast will step down from their thrones and lay aside their robes and take off their embroidered garments. Clothed with terror, they will sit on the ground, trembling every moment, appalled at you. 17Then they will take up a lament concerning you and say to you:

" 'How you are destroyed, O city of
renown,
peopled by men of the sea!
You were a power on the seas,
you and your citizens;
you put your terror
on all who lived there.
18Now the coastlands tremble
on the day of your fall;
the islands in the sea
are terrified at your collapse.'

19"This is what the Sovereign LORD says: When I make you a desolate city, like cities no longer inhabited, and when I bring the ocean depths over you and its vast waters cover you, 20then I will bring you down with those who go down to the pit, to the people of long ago. I will make you dwell in the earth below, as in ancient ruins, with those who go down to the pit, and you will not return or take your place[b] in the land of the living. 21I will bring you to a horrible end and you will be no more. You will be sought, but you will never again be found, declares the Sovereign LORD."

A Lament for Tyre

27 The word of the LORD came to me: 2"Son of man, take up a lament concerning Tyre. 3Say to Tyre, situated at the gateway to the sea, merchant of peoples on many coasts, 'This is what the Sovereign LORD says:

" 'You say, O Tyre,
"I am perfect in beauty."

a 7 Hebrew *Nebuchadrezzar,* of which *Nebuchadnezzar* is a variant; here and often in Ezekiel and Jeremiah *b* 20 Septuagint; Hebrew *return, and I will give glory*

4 Your domain was on the high seas;
your builders brought your beauty to perfection.
5 They made all your timbers
of pine trees from Senir[a];
they took a cedar from Lebanon
to make a mast for you.
6 Of oaks from Bashan
they made your oars;
of cypress wood[b] from the coasts of Cyprus[c]
they made your deck, inlaid with ivory.
7 Fine embroidered linen from Egypt was your sail
and served as your banner;
your awnings were of blue and purple
from the coasts of Elishah.
8 Men of Sidon and Arvad were your oarsmen;
your skilled men, O Tyre, were aboard
as your seamen.
9 Veteran craftsmen of Gebal[d] were on board
as shipwrights to caulk your seams.
All the ships of the sea and their sailors
came alongside to trade for your wares.

10 " 'Men of Persia, Lydia and Put
served as soldiers in your army.
They hung their shields and helmets on your walls,
bringing you splendor.
11 Men of Arvad and Helech
manned your walls on every side;
men of Gammad
were in your towers.
They hung their shields around your walls;
they brought your beauty to perfection.

12 " 'Tarshish did business with you because
of your great wealth of goods; they exchanged
silver, iron, tin and lead for your merchandise.
13 " 'Greece, Tubal and Meshech traded
with you; they exchanged slaves and articles of
bronze for your wares.
14 " 'Men of Beth Togarmah exchanged
work horses, war horses and mules for your
merchandise.
15 " 'The men of Rhodes[e] traded with you,
and many coastlands were your customers;
they paid you with ivory tusks and ebony.
16 " 'Aram[f] did business with you because
of your many products; they exchanged turquoise, purple fabric, embroidered work, fine
linen, coral and rubies for your merchandise.
17 " 'Judah and Israel traded with you; they
exchanged wheat from Minnith and confec-
tions,[g] honey, oil and balm for your wares.
18 " 'Damascus, because of your many products and great wealth of goods, did business
with you in wine from Helbon and wool from
Zahar.
19 " 'Danites and Greeks from Uzal bought
your merchandise; they exchanged wrought
iron, cassia and calamus for your wares.
20 " 'Dedan traded in saddle blankets with
you.
21 " 'Arabia and all the princes of Kedar were
your customers; they did business with you in
lambs, rams and goats.
22 " 'The merchants of Sheba and Raamah
traded with you; for your merchandise they
exchanged the finest of all kinds of spices and
precious stones, and gold.
23 " 'Haran, Canneh and Eden and merchants of Sheba, Asshur and Kilmad traded
with you. 24 In your marketplace they traded
with you beautiful garments, blue fabric, embroidered work and multicolored rugs with
cords twisted and tightly knotted.

25 " 'The ships of Tarshish serve
as carriers for your wares.
You are filled with heavy cargo
in the heart of the sea.
26 Your oarsmen take you
out to the high seas.
But the east wind will break you to pieces
in the heart of the sea.
27 Your wealth, merchandise and wares,
your mariners, seamen and shipwrights,
your merchants and all your soldiers,
and everyone else on board
will sink into the heart of the sea
on the day of your shipwreck.
28 The shorelands will quake
when your seamen cry out.
29 All who handle the oars
will abandon their ships;
the mariners and all the seamen
will stand on the shore.
30 They will raise their voice
and cry bitterly over you;
they will sprinkle dust on their heads
and roll in ashes.
31 They will shave their heads because of you
and will put on sackcloth.

---

[a] *5* That is, Hermon [b] *6* Targum; the Masoretic Text has a different division of the consonants. [c] *6* Hebrew *Kittim* [d] *9* That is, Byblos [e] *15* Septuagint; Hebrew *Dedan* [f] *16* Most Hebrew manuscripts; some Hebrew manuscripts and Syriac *Edom*
[g] *17* The meaning of the Hebrew for this word is uncertain.

They will weep over you with anguish of soul
and with bitter mourning.
32 As they wail and mourn over you,
they will take up a lament concerning you:
"Who was ever silenced like Tyre,
surrounded by the sea?"
33 When your merchandise went out on the seas,
you satisfied many nations;
with your great wealth and your wares
you enriched the kings of the earth.
34 Now you are shattered by the sea
in the depths of the waters;
your wares and all your company
have gone down with you.
35 All who live in the coastlands
are appalled at you;
their kings shudder with horror
and their faces are distorted with fear.
36 The merchants among the nations hiss at you;
you have come to a horrible end
and will be no more.' "

A Prophecy Against the King of Tyre

28 The word of the LORD came to me:
2 "Son of man, say to the ruler of Tyre,
'This is what the Sovereign LORD says:

" 'In the pride of your heart
you say, "I am a god;
I sit on the throne of a god
in the heart of the seas."
But you are a man and not a god,
though you think you are as wise as a god.
3 Are you wiser than Daniel[a]?
Is no secret hidden from you?
4 By your wisdom and understanding
you have gained wealth for yourself
and amassed gold and silver
in your treasuries.
5 By your great skill in trading
you have increased your wealth,
and because of your wealth
your heart has grown proud.

6 " 'Therefore this is what the Sovereign
LORD says:

" 'Because you think you are wise,
as wise as a god,
7 I am going to bring foreigners against you,
the most ruthless of nations;
they will draw their swords against your beauty and wisdom
and pierce your shining splendor.
8 They will bring you down to the pit,
and you will die a violent death
in the heart of the seas.
9 Will you then say, "I am a god,"
in the presence of those who kill you?
You will be but a man, not a god,
in the hands of those who slay you.
10 You will die the death of the uncircumcised
at the hands of foreigners.

I have spoken, declares the Sovereign LORD.' "

11 The word of the LORD came to me: 12 "Son
of man, take up a lament concerning the king
of Tyre and say to him: 'This is what the Sovereign LORD says:

" 'You were the model of perfection,
full of wisdom and perfect in beauty.
13 You were in Eden,
the garden of God;
every precious stone adorned you:
ruby, topaz and emerald,
chrysolite, onyx and jasper,
sapphire,[b] turquoise and beryl.[c]
Your settings and mountings[d] were made of gold;
on the day you were created they were prepared.
14 You were anointed as a guardian cherub,
for so I ordained you.
You were on the holy mount of God;
you walked among the fiery stones.
15 You were blameless in your ways
from the day you were created
till wickedness was found in you.
16 Through your widespread trade
you were filled with violence,
and you sinned.
So I drove you in disgrace from the mount of God,
and I expelled you, O guardian cherub,
from among the fiery stones.
17 Your heart became proud
on account of your beauty,
and you corrupted your wisdom
because of your splendor.
So I threw you to the earth;
I made a spectacle of you before kings.
18 By your many sins and dishonest trade
you have desecrated your sanctuaries.

[a] 3 Or *Danel*; the Hebrew spelling may suggest a person other than the prophet Daniel. [b] 13 Or *lapis lazuli* [c] 13 The precise identification of some of these precious stones is uncertain. [d] 13 The meaning of the Hebrew for this phrase is uncertain.

So I made a fire come out from you,
and it consumed you,
and I reduced you to ashes on the ground
in the sight of all who were watching.
19 All the nations who knew you
are appalled at you;
you have come to a horrible end
and will be no more.' "

A Prophecy Against Sidon

20 The word of the LORD came to me: 21 "Son
of man, set your face against Sidon; prophesy
against her 22 and say: 'This is what the Sovereign LORD says:

" 'I am against you, O Sidon,
and I will gain glory within you.
They will know that I am the LORD,
when I inflict punishment on her
and show myself holy within her.
23 I will send a plague upon her
and make blood flow in her streets.
The slain will fall within her,
with the sword against her on every
side.
Then they will know that I am the LORD.

24 " 'No longer will the people of Israel have
malicious neighbors who are painful briers
and sharp thorns. Then they will know that I
am the Sovereign LORD.
25 " 'This is what the Sovereign LORD says:
When I gather the people of Israel from the
nations where they have been scattered, I will
show myself holy among them in the sight
of the nations. Then they will live in their
own land, which I gave to my servant Jacob.
26 They will live there in safety and will build
houses and plant vineyards; they will live in
safety when I inflict punishment on all their
neighbors who maligned them. Then they will
know that I am the LORD their God.' "

A Prophecy Against Egypt

29 In the tenth year, in the tenth month on
the twelfth day, the word of the LORD
came to me: 2 "Son of man, set your face
against Pharaoh king of Egypt and prophesy
against him and against all Egypt. 3 Speak to
him and say: 'This is what the Sovereign LORD
says:

" 'I am against you, Pharaoh king of
Egypt,
you great monster lying among your
streams.
You say, "The Nile is mine;
I made it for myself."
4 But I will put hooks in your jaws
and make the fish of your streams stick
to your scales.
I will pull you out from among your
streams,
with all the fish sticking to your scales.
5 I will leave you in the desert,
you and all the fish of your streams.
You will fall on the open field
and not be gathered or picked up.
I will give you as food
to the beasts of the earth and the birds
of the air.

6 Then all who live in Egypt will know that I
am the LORD.

" 'You have been a staff of reed for the
house of Israel. 7 When they grasped you with
their hands, you splintered and you tore open
their shoulders; when they leaned on you, you
broke and their backs were wrenched.[a]
8 " 'Therefore this is what the Sovereign
LORD says: I will bring a sword against you
and kill your men and their animals. 9 Egypt
will become a desolate wasteland. Then they
will know that I am the LORD.
" 'Because you said, "The Nile is mine; I
made it," 10 therefore I am against you and
against your streams, and I will make the land
of Egypt a ruin and a desolate waste from Migdol to Aswan, as far as the border of Cush.[b]
11 No foot of man or animal will pass through
it; no one will live there for forty years. 12 I will
make the land of Egypt desolate among devastated lands, and her cities will lie desolate forty
years among ruined cities. And I will disperse
the Egyptians among the nations and scatter
them through the countries.
13 " 'Yet this is what the Sovereign LORD
says: At the end of forty years I will gather the
Egyptians from the nations where they were
scattered. 14 I will bring them back from captivity and return them to Upper Egypt,[c] the
land of their ancestry. There they will be a lowly kingdom. 15 It will be the lowliest of kingdoms and will never again exalt itself above
the other nations. I will make it so weak that it
will never again rule over the nations. 16 Egypt
will no longer be a source of confidence for
the people of Israel but will be a reminder of
their sin in turning to her for help. Then they
will know that I am the Sovereign LORD.' "

[a] 7 Syriac (see also Septuagint and Vulgate); Hebrew *and you caused their backs to stand* [b] 10 That is, the upper Nile region
[c] 14 Hebrew *to Pathros*

17In the twenty-seventh year, in the first
month on the first day, the word of the LORD
came to me: 18"Son of man, Nebuchadnezzar king of Babylon drove his army in a hard
campaign against Tyre; every head was rubbed
bare and every shoulder made raw. Yet he and
his army got no reward from the campaign he
led against Tyre. 19Therefore this is what the
Sovereign LORD says: I am going to give Egypt
to Nebuchadnezzar king of Babylon, and he
will carry off its wealth. He will loot and plunder the land as pay for his army. 20I have given
him Egypt as a reward for his efforts because
he and his army did it for me, declares the
Sovereign LORD.

21"On that day I will make a horn[a] grow
for the house of Israel, and I will open your
mouth among them. Then they will know that
I am the LORD."

A Lament for Egypt

30 The word of the LORD came to me:
2"Son of man, prophesy and say: 'This
is what the Sovereign LORD says:

" 'Wail and say,
"Alas for that day!"
3For the day is near,
the day of the LORD is near—
a day of clouds,
a time of doom for the nations.
4A sword will come against Egypt,
and anguish will come upon Cush.[b]
When the slain fall in Egypt,
her wealth will be carried away
and her foundations torn down.

5Cush and Put, Lydia and all Arabia, Libya[c]
and the people of the covenant land will fall
by the sword along with Egypt.

6" 'This is what the LORD says:

" 'The allies of Egypt will fall
and her proud strength will fail.
From Migdol to Aswan
they will fall by the sword within
her,
declares the Sovereign LORD.
7" 'They will be desolate
among desolate lands,
and their cities will lie
among ruined cities.
8Then they will know that I am the LORD,
when I set fire to Egypt
and all her helpers are crushed.

9" 'On that day messengers will go out
from me in ships to frighten Cush out of her
complacency. Anguish will take hold of them
on the day of Egypt's doom, for it is sure to
come.

10" 'This is what the Sovereign LORD says:

" 'I will put an end to the hordes of Egypt
by the hand of Nebuchadnezzar king of
Babylon.
11He and his army—the most ruthless of
nations—
will be brought in to destroy the land.
They will draw their swords against Egypt
and fill the land with the slain.
12I will dry up the streams of the Nile
and sell the land to evil men;
by the hand of foreigners
I will lay waste the land and everything
in it.
I the LORD have spoken.

13" 'This is what the Sovereign LORD says:

" 'I will destroy the idols
and put an end to the images in
Memphis.[d]
No longer will there be a prince in Egypt,
and I will spread fear throughout the
land.
14I will lay waste Upper Egypt,[e]
set fire to Zoan
and inflict punishment on Thebes.[f]
15I will pour out my wrath on Pelusium,[g]
the stronghold of Egypt,
and cut off the hordes of Thebes.
16I will set fire to Egypt;
Pelusium will writhe in agony.
Thebes will be taken by storm;
Memphis will be in constant distress.
17The young men of Heliopolis[h] and
Bubastis[i]
will fall by the sword,
and the cities themselves will go into
captivity.
18Dark will be the day at Tahpanhes
when I break the yoke of Egypt;
there her proud strength will come to
an end.
She will be covered with clouds,
and her villages will go into captivity.
19So I will inflict punishment on Egypt,
and they will know that I am the
LORD.' "

---

[a] *21* *Horn* here symbolizes strength. [b] *4* That is, the upper Nile region; also in verses 5 and 9 [c] *5* Hebrew *Cub* [d] *13* Hebrew *Noph*; also in verse 16 [e] *14* Hebrew *waste Pathros* [f] *14* Hebrew *No*; also in verses 15 and 16 [g] *15* Hebrew *Sin*; also in verse 16 [h] *17* Hebrew *Awen* (or *On*) [i] *17* Hebrew *Pi Beseth*

[20]In the eleventh year, in the first month
on the seventh day, the word of the LORD
came to me: [21]"Son of man, I have broken
the arm of Pharaoh king of Egypt. It has not
been bound up for healing or put in a splint so
as to become strong enough to hold a sword.
[22]Therefore this is what the Sovereign LORD
says: I am against Pharaoh king of Egypt. I
will break both his arms, the good arm as well
as the broken one, and make the sword fall
from his hand. [23]I will disperse the Egyptians
among the nations and scatter them through
the countries. [24]I will strengthen the arms of
the king of Babylon and put my sword in his
hand, but I will break the arms of Pharaoh,
and he will groan before him like a mortally
wounded man. [25]I will strengthen the arms of
the king of Babylon, but the arms of Pharaoh
will fall limp. Then they will know that I am
the LORD, when I put my sword into the hand
of the king of Babylon and he brandishes it
against Egypt. [26]I will disperse the Egyptians
among the nations and scatter them through
the countries. Then they will know that I am
the LORD."

A Cedar in Lebanon

31 In the eleventh year, in the third month
on the first day, the word of the LORD
came to me: [2]"Son of man, say to Pharaoh king of Egypt and to his hordes:

" 'Who can be compared with you in
majesty?
[3]Consider Assyria, once a cedar in
Lebanon,
with beautiful branches overshadowing
the forest;
it towered on high,
its top above the thick foliage.
[4]The waters nourished it,
deep springs made it grow tall;
their streams flowed
all around its base
and sent their channels
to all the trees of the field.
[5]So it towered higher
than all the trees of the field;
its boughs increased
and its branches grew long,
spreading because of abundant waters.
[6]All the birds of the air
nested in its boughs,
all the beasts of the field
gave birth under its branches;
all the great nations
lived in its shade.
[7]It was majestic in beauty,
with its spreading boughs,
for its roots went down
to abundant waters.
[8]The cedars in the garden of God
could not rival it,
nor could the pine trees
equal its boughs,
nor could the plane trees
compare with its branches—
no tree in the garden of God
could match its beauty.
[9]I made it beautiful
with abundant branches,
the envy of all the trees of Eden
in the garden of God.

[10]" 'Therefore this is what the Sovereign
LORD says: Because it towered on high, lifting
its top above the thick foliage, and because it
was proud of its height, [11]I handed it over to
the ruler of the nations, for him to deal with
according to its wickedness. I cast it aside,
[12]and the most ruthless of foreign nations
cut it down and left it. Its boughs fell on the
mountains and in all the valleys; its branches
lay broken in all the ravines of the land. All
the nations of the earth came out from under
its shade and left it. [13]All the birds of the air
settled on the fallen tree, and all the beasts of
the field were among its branches. [14]Therefore
no other trees by the waters are ever to tower
proudly on high, lifting their tops above the
thick foliage. No other trees so well-watered
are ever to reach such a height; they are all destined for death, for the earth below, among
mortal men, with those who go down to the
pit.

[15]" 'This is what the Sovereign LORD says:
On the day it was brought down to the grave[a]
I covered the deep springs with mourning
for it; I held back its streams, and its abundant waters were restrained. Because of it I
clothed Lebanon with gloom, and all the trees
of the field withered away. [16]I made the nations tremble at the sound of its fall when I
brought it down to the grave with those who
go down to the pit. Then all the trees of Eden,
the choicest and best of Lebanon, all the trees
that were well-watered, were consoled in the
earth below. [17]Those who lived in its shade, its
allies among the nations, had also gone down
to the grave with it, joining those killed by the
sword.

[18]" 'Which of the trees of Eden can be com-

[a] *15* Hebrew *Sheol*; also in verses 16 and 17

pared with you in splendor and majesty? Yet you, too, will be brought down with the trees of Eden to the earth below; you will lie among the uncircumcised, with those killed by the sword.

" 'This is Pharaoh and all his hordes, declares the Sovereign LORD.' "

A Lament for Pharaoh

32 In the twelfth year, in the twelfth month on the first day, the word of the LORD came to me: 2"Son of man, take up a lament concerning Pharaoh king of Egypt and say to him:

" 'You are like a lion among the nations;
you are like a monster in the seas
thrashing about in your streams,
churning the water with your feet
and muddying the streams.

3" 'This is what the Sovereign LORD says:

" 'With a great throng of people
I will cast my net over you,
and they will haul you up in my net.
4 I will throw you on the land
and hurl you on the open field.
I will let all the birds of the air settle on you
and all the beasts of the earth gorge themselves on you.
5 I will spread your flesh on the mountains
and fill the valleys with your remains.
6 I will drench the land with your flowing blood
all the way to the mountains,
and the ravines will be filled with your flesh.
7 When I snuff you out, I will cover the heavens
and darken their stars;
I will cover the sun with a cloud,
and the moon will not give its light.
8 All the shining lights in the heavens
I will darken over you;
I will bring darkness over your land,
declares the Sovereign LORD.
9 I will trouble the hearts of many peoples
when I bring about your destruction among the nations,
among[a] lands you have not known.
10 I will cause many peoples to be appalled at you,
and their kings will shudder with horror because of you
when I brandish my sword before them.
On the day of your downfall
each of them will tremble
every moment for his life.

11" 'For this is what the Sovereign LORD says:

" 'The sword of the king of Babylon
will come against you.
12 I will cause your hordes to fall
by the swords of mighty men—
the most ruthless of all nations.
They will shatter the pride of Egypt,
and all her hordes will be overthrown.
13 I will destroy all her cattle
from beside abundant waters
no longer to be stirred by the foot of man
or muddied by the hoofs of cattle.
14 Then I will let her waters settle
and make her streams flow like oil,
declares the Sovereign LORD.
15 When I make Egypt desolate
and strip the land of everything in it,
when I strike down all who live there,
then they will know that I am the LORD.'

16"This is the lament they will chant for her. The daughters of the nations will chant it; for Egypt and all her hordes they will chant it, declares the Sovereign LORD."

17In the twelfth year, on the fifteenth day of the month, the word of the LORD came to me:
18"Son of man, wail for the hordes of Egypt and consign to the earth below both her and the daughters of mighty nations, with those who go down to the pit.
19Say to them, 'Are you more favored than others? Go down and be laid among the uncircumcised.'
20They will fall among those killed by the sword. The sword is drawn; let her be dragged off with all her hordes.
21From within the grave[b] the mighty leaders will say of Egypt and her allies, 'They have come down and they lie with the uncircumcised, with those killed by the sword.'

22"Assyria is there with her whole army; she is surrounded by the graves of all her slain, all who have fallen by the sword.
23Their graves are in the depths of the pit and her army lies around her grave. All who had spread terror in the land of the living are slain, fallen by the sword.

24"Elam is there, with all her hordes around

[a] 9 Hebrew; Septuagint *bring you into captivity among the nations, / to*
[b] 21 Hebrew *Sheol*; also in verse 27

her grave. All of them are slain, fallen by the
sword. All who had spread terror in the land
of the living went down uncircumcised to
the earth below. They bear their shame with
those who go down to the pit. 25A bed is made
for her among the slain, with all her hordes
around her grave. All of them are uncircumcised, killed by the sword. Because their terror
had spread in the land of the living, they bear
their shame with those who go down to the
pit; they are laid among the slain.

26"Meshech and Tubal are there, with all
their hordes around their graves. All of them
are uncircumcised, killed by the sword because they spread their terror in the land of the
living. 27Do they not lie with the other uncircumcised warriors who have fallen, who went
down to the grave with their weapons of war,
whose swords were placed under their heads?
The punishment for their sins rested on their
bones, though the terror of these warriors had
stalked through the land of the living.

28"You too, O Pharaoh, will be broken and
will lie among the uncircumcised, with those
killed by the sword.

29"Edom is there, her kings and all her
princes; despite their power, they are laid with
those killed by the sword. They lie with the
uncircumcised, with those who go down to
the pit.

30"All the princes of the north and all the
Sidonians are there; they went down with
the slain in disgrace despite the terror caused
by their power. They lie uncircumcised with
those killed by the sword and bear their shame
with those who go down to the pit.

31"Pharaoh—he and all his army—will see
them and he will be consoled for all his hordes
that were killed by the sword, declares the
Sovereign LORD. 32Although I had him spread
terror in the land of the living, Pharaoh and all
his hordes will be laid among the uncircumcised, with those killed by the sword, declares
the Sovereign LORD."

Ezekiel a Watchman

33 The word of the LORD came to me:
2"Son of man, speak to your countrymen and say to them: 'When I bring the
sword against a land, and the people of the
land choose one of their men and make him
their watchman, 3and he sees the sword coming against the land and blows the trumpet
to warn the people, 4then if anyone hears the
trumpet but does not take warning and the
sword comes and takes his life, his blood will
be on his own head. 5Since he heard the sound
of the trumpet but did not take warning, his
blood will be on his own head. If he had taken
warning, he would have saved himself. 6But if
the watchman sees the sword coming and does
not blow the trumpet to warn the people and
the sword comes and takes the life of one of
them, that man will be taken away because of
his sin, but I will hold the watchman accountable for his blood.'

7"Son of man, I have made you a watchman
for the house of Israel; so hear the word I speak
and give them warning from me. 8When I say
to the wicked, 'O wicked man, you will surely die,' and you do not speak out to dissuade
him from his ways, that wicked man will die
for[a] his sin, and I will hold you accountable
for his blood. 9But if you do warn the wicked
man to turn from his ways and he does not
do so, he will die for his sin, but you will have
saved yourself.

10"Son of man, say to the house of Israel,
'This is what you are saying: "Our offenses and
sins weigh us down, and we are wasting away
because of[b] them. How then can we live?" '
11Say to them, 'As surely as I live, declares
the Sovereign LORD, I take no pleasure in the
death of the wicked, but rather that they turn
from their ways and live. Turn! Turn from
your evil ways! Why will you die, O house of
Israel?'

12"Therefore, son of man, say to your countrymen, 'The righteousness of the righteous
man will not save him when he disobeys, and
the wickedness of the wicked man will not
cause him to fall when he turns from it. The
righteous man, if he sins, will not be allowed
to live because of his former righteousness.'
13If I tell the righteous man that he will surely live, but then he trusts in his righteousness
and does evil, none of the righteous things
he has done will be remembered; he will die
for the evil he has done. 14And if I say to the
wicked man, 'You will surely die,' but he then
turns away from his sin and does what is just
and right— 15if he gives back what he took in
pledge for a loan, returns what he has stolen,
follows the decrees that give life, and does no
evil, he will surely live; he will not die. 16None
of the sins he has committed will be remembered against him. He has done what is just
and right; he will surely live.

17"Yet your countrymen say, 'The way of
the Lord is not just.' But it is their way that

[a] 8 Or *in*; also in verse 9 [b] 10 Or *away in*

is not just. 18If a righteous man turns from his
righteousness and does evil, he will die for it.
19And if a wicked man turns away from his
wickedness and does what is just and right, he
will live by doing so. 20Yet, O house of Israel,
you say, 'The way of the Lord is not just.' But
I will judge each of you according to his own
ways."

Jerusalem's Fall Explained

21In the twelfth year of our exile, in the
tenth month on the fifth day, a man who had
escaped from Jerusalem came to me and said,
"The city has fallen!" 22Now the evening before the man arrived, the hand of the LORD
was upon me, and he opened my mouth before the man came to me in the morning. So
my mouth was opened and I was no longer
silent.
23Then the word of the LORD came to me:
24"Son of man, the people living in those ruins in the land of Israel are saying, 'Abraham
was only one man, yet he possessed the land.
But we are many; surely the land has been giv-
en to us as our possession.' 25Therefore say to
them, 'This is what the Sovereign LORD says:
Since you eat meat with the blood still in it
and look to your idols and shed blood, should
you then possess the land? 26You rely on your
sword, you do detestable things, and each of
you defiles his neighbor's wife. Should you
then possess the land?'
27"Say this to them: 'This is what the Sovereign LORD says: As surely as I live, those who
are left in the ruins will fall by the sword, those
out in the country I will give to the wild animals to be devoured, and those in strongholds
and caves will die of a plague. 28I will make the
land a desolate waste, and her proud strength
will come to an end, and the mountains of Israel will become desolate so that no one will
cross them. 29Then they will know that I am
the LORD, when I have made the land a desolate waste because of all the detestable things
they have done.'
30"As for you, son of man, your countrymen are talking together about you by the
walls and at the doors of the houses, saying to
each other, 'Come and hear the message that
has come from the LORD.' 31My people come
to you, as they usually do, and sit before you
to listen to your words, but they do not put
them into practice. With their mouths they
express devotion, but their hearts are greedy
for unjust gain. 32Indeed, to them you are
nothing more than one who sings love songs
with a beautiful voice and plays an instrument
well, for they hear your words but do not put
them into practice.
33"When all this comes true—and it surely
will—then they will know that a prophet has
been among them."

Shepherds and Sheep

34 The word of the LORD came to me:
2"Son of man, prophesy against the
shepherds of Israel; prophesy and say to
them: 'This is what the Sovereign LORD says:
Woe to the shepherds of Israel who only take
care of themselves! Should not shepherds take
care of the flock? 3You eat the curds, clothe
yourselves with the wool and slaughter the
choice animals, but you do not take care of
the flock. 4You have not strengthened the
weak or healed the sick or bound up the injured. You have not brought back the strays
or searched for the lost. You have ruled them
harshly and brutally. 5So they were scattered
because there was no shepherd, and when
they were scattered they became food for all
the wild animals. 6My sheep wandered over
all the mountains and on every high hill. They
were scattered over the whole earth, and no
one searched or looked for them.
7" 'Therefore, you shepherds, hear the word
of the LORD: 8As surely as I live, declares the
Sovereign LORD, because my flock lacks a
shepherd and so has been plundered and has
become food for all the wild animals, and
because my shepherds did not search for my
flock but cared for themselves rather than for
my flock, 9therefore, O shepherds, hear the
word of the LORD: 10This is what the Sovereign LORD says: I am against the shepherds and
will hold them accountable for my flock. I will
remove them from tending the flock so that
the shepherds can no longer feed themselves. I
will rescue my flock from their mouths, and it
will no longer be food for them.
11" 'For this is what the Sovereign LORD
says: I myself will search for my sheep and
look after them. 12As a shepherd looks after
his scattered flock when he is with them, so
will I look after my sheep. I will rescue them
from all the places where they were scattered
on a day of clouds and darkness. 13I will bring
them out from the nations and gather them
from the countries, and I will bring them into
their own land. I will pasture them on the
mountains of Israel, in the ravines and in all
the settlements in the land. 14I will tend them
in a good pasture, and the mountain heights
of Israel will be their grazing land. There they
will lie down in good grazing land, and there

they will feed in a rich pasture on the mountains of Israel. 15I myself will tend my sheep
and have them lie down, declares the Sovereign LORD. 16I will search for the lost and
bring back the strays. I will bind up the injured and strengthen the weak, but the sleek
and the strong I will destroy. I will shepherd
the flock with justice.
17" 'As for you, my flock, this is what the
Sovereign LORD says: I will judge between
one sheep and another, and between rams and
goats. 18Is it not enough for you to feed on
the good pasture? Must you also trample the
rest of your pasture with your feet? Is it not
enough for you to drink clear water? Must you
also muddy the rest with your feet? 19Must
my flock feed on what you have trampled and
drink what you have muddied with your feet?
20" 'Therefore this is what the Sovereign
LORD says to them: See, I myself will judge between the fat sheep and the lean sheep. 21Be-
cause you shove with flank and shoulder, butting all the weak sheep with your horns until
you have driven them away, 22I will save my
flock, and they will no longer be plundered. I
will judge between one sheep and another. 23I
will place over them one shepherd, my servant
David, and he will tend them; he will tend
them and be their shepherd. 24I the LORD will
be their God, and my servant David will be
prince among them. I the LORD have spoken.
25" 'I will make a covenant of peace with
them and rid the land of wild beasts so that
they may live in the desert and sleep in the forests in safety. 26I will bless them and the places
surrounding my hill.[a] I will send down showers in season; there will be showers of blessing.
27The trees of the field will yield their fruit and
the ground will yield its crops; the people will
be secure in their land. They will know that I
am the LORD, when I break the bars of their
yoke and rescue them from the hands of those
who enslaved them. 28They will no longer be
plundered by the nations, nor will wild animals devour them. They will live in safety, and
no one will make them afraid. 29I will provide
for them a land renowned for its crops, and
they will no longer be victims of famine in the
land or bear the scorn of the nations. 30Then
they will know that I, the LORD their God, am
with them and that they, the house of Israel,
are my people, declares the Sovereign LORD.
31You my sheep, the sheep of my pasture, are
people, and I am your God, declares the Sovereign LORD.' "

A Prophecy Against Edom

35 The word of the LORD came to me:
2"Son of man, set your face against
Mount Seir; prophesy against it 3and
say: 'This is what the Sovereign LORD says: I
am against you, Mount Seir, and I will stretch
out my hand against you and make you a desolate waste. 4I will turn your towns into ruins
and you will be desolate. Then you will know
that I am the LORD.
5" 'Because you harbored an ancient hostility and delivered the Israelites over to the
sword at the time of their calamity, the time
their punishment reached its climax, 6there-
fore as surely as I live, declares the Sovereign
LORD, I will give you over to bloodshed and it
will pursue you. Since you did not hate bloodshed, bloodshed will pursue you. 7I will make
Mount Seir a desolate waste and cut off from
it all who come and go. 8I will fill your mountains with the slain; those killed by the sword
will fall on your hills and in your valleys and in
all your ravines. 9I will make you desolate forever; your towns will not be inhabited. Then
you will know that I am the LORD.
10" 'Because you have said, "These two nations and countries will be ours and we will
take possession of them," even though I the
LORD was there, 11therefore as surely as I live,
declares the Sovereign LORD, I will treat you
in accordance with the anger and jealousy you
showed in your hatred of them and I will make
myself known among them when I judge you.
12Then you will know that I the LORD have
heard all the contemptible things you have
said against the mountains of Israel. You said,
"They have been laid waste and have been giv-
en over to us to devour." 13You boasted against
me and spoke against me without restraint,
and I heard it. 14This is what the Sovereign
LORD says: While the whole earth rejoices, I
will make you desolate. 15Because you rejoiced
when the inheritance of the house of Israel became desolate, that is how I will treat you. You
will be desolate, O Mount Seir, you and all
of Edom. Then they will know that I am the
LORD.' "

A Prophecy to the Mountains of Israel

36 "Son of man, prophesy to the mountains of Israel and say, 'O mountains of
Israel, hear the word of the LORD. 2This
is what the Sovereign LORD says: The enemy
said of you, "Aha! The ancient heights have
become our possession." ' 3Therefore prophe-

[a] 26 Or *I will make them and the places surrounding my hill a blessing*

sy and say, 'This is what the Sovereign LORD
says: Because they ravaged and hounded you
from every side so that you became the possession of the rest of the nations and the object of
people's malicious talk and slander, 4therefore,
O mountains of Israel, hear the word of the
Sovereign LORD: This is what the Sovereign
LORD says to the mountains and hills, to the
ravines and valleys, to the desolate ruins and
the deserted towns that have been plundered
and ridiculed by the rest of the nations around
you— 5this is what the Sovereign LORD says:
In my burning zeal I have spoken against the
rest of the nations, and against all Edom, for
with glee and with malice in their hearts they
made my land their own possession so that
they might plunder its pastureland.' 6Therefore
prophesy concerning the land of Israel and say
to the mountains and hills, to the ravines and
valleys: 'This is what the Sovereign LORD says:
I speak in my jealous wrath because you have
suffered the scorn of the nations. 7Therefore
this is what the Sovereign LORD says: I swear
with uplifted hand that the nations around
you will also suffer scorn.

8" 'But you, O mountains of Israel, will
produce branches and fruit for my people
Israel, for they will soon come home. 9I am
concerned for you and will look on you with
favor; you will be plowed and sown, 10and I
will multiply the number of people upon you,
even the whole house of Israel. The towns will
be inhabited and the ruins rebuilt. 11I will increase the number of men and animals upon
you, and they will be fruitful and become numerous. I will settle people on you as in the
past and will make you prosper more than before. Then you will know that I am the LORD.
12I will cause people, my people Israel, to walk
upon you. They will possess you, and you will
be their inheritance; you will never again deprive them of their children.

13" 'This is what the Sovereign LORD says:
Because people say to you, "You devour men
and deprive your nation of its children,"
14therefore you will no longer devour men or
make your nation childless, declares the Sovereign LORD. 15No longer will I make you hear
the taunts of the nations, and no longer will
you suffer the scorn of the peoples or cause
your nation to fall, declares the Sovereign
LORD.' "

16Again the word of the LORD came to me:
17"Son of man, when the people of Israel were
living in their own land, they defiled it by
their conduct and their actions. Their conduct
was like a woman's monthly uncleanness in
my sight. 18So I poured out my wrath on them
because they had shed blood in the land and
because they had defiled it with their idols. 19I
dispersed them among the nations, and they
were scattered through the countries; I judged
them according to their conduct and their actions. 20And wherever they went among the
nations they profaned my holy name, for it
was said of them, 'These are the LORD's people, and yet they had to leave his land.' 21I had
concern for my holy name, which the house of
Israel profaned among the nations where they
had gone.

22"Therefore say to the house of Israel, 'This
is what the Sovereign LORD says: It is not for
your sake, O house of Israel, that I am going
to do these things, but for the sake of my holy
name, which you have profaned among the
nations where you have gone. 23I will show
the holiness of my great name, which has
been profaned among the nations, the name
you have profaned among them. Then the nations will know that I am the LORD, declares
the Sovereign LORD, when I show myself holy
through you before their eyes.

24" 'For I will take you out of the nations;
I will gather you from all the countries and
bring you back into your own land. 25I will
sprinkle clean water on you, and you will be
clean; I will cleanse you from all your impurities and from all your idols. 26I will give you
a new heart and put a new spirit in you; I will
remove from you your heart of stone and give
you a heart of flesh. 27And I will put my Spirit in you and move you to follow my decrees
and be careful to keep my laws. 28You will
live in the land I gave your forefathers; you
will be my people, and I will be your God.
29I will save you from all your uncleanness. I
will call for the grain and make it plentiful and
will not bring famine upon you. 30I will increase the fruit of the trees and the crops of the
field, so that you will no longer suffer disgrace
among the nations because of famine. 31Then
you will remember your evil ways and wicked
deeds, and you will loathe yourselves for your
sins and detestable practices. 32I want you to
know that I am not doing this for your sake,
declares the Sovereign LORD. Be ashamed and
disgraced for your conduct, O house of Israel!

33" 'This is what the Sovereign LORD says:
On the day I cleanse you from all your sins, I
will resettle your towns, and the ruins will be
rebuilt. 34The desolate land will be cultivated
instead of lying desolate in the sight of all who
pass through it. 35They will say, "This land
that was laid waste has become like the gar-

den of Eden; the cities that were lying in ruins,
desolate and destroyed, are now fortified and
inhabited." 36Then the nations around you
that remain will know that I the LORD have
rebuilt what was destroyed and have replanted
what was desolate. I the LORD have spoken,
and I will do it.'
37"This is what the Sovereign LORD says:
Once again I will yield to the plea of the house
of Israel and do this for them: I will make their
people as numerous as sheep, 38as numerous
as the flocks for offerings at Jerusalem during
her appointed feasts. So will the ruined cities
be filled with flocks of people. Then they will
know that I am the LORD."

The Valley of Dry Bones

37 The hand of the LORD was upon me,
and he brought me out by the Spirit
of the LORD and set me in the middle
of a valley; it was full of bones. 2He led me
back and forth among them, and I saw a great
many bones on the floor of the valley, bones
that were very dry. 3He asked me, "Son of
man, can these bones live?"
I said, "O Sovereign LORD, you alone
know."
4Then he said to me, "Prophesy to these
bones and say to them, 'Dry bones, hear the
word of the LORD! 5This is what the Sovereign
LORD says to these bones: I will make breath[a]
enter you, and you will come to life. 6I will
attach tendons to you and make flesh come
upon you and cover you with skin; I will put
breath in you, and you will come to life. Then
you will know that I am the LORD.' "
7So I prophesied as I was commanded. And
as I was prophesying, there was a noise, a rattling sound, and the bones came together,
bone to bone. 8I looked, and tendons and flesh
appeared on them and skin covered them, but
there was no breath in them.
9Then he said to me, "Prophesy to the
breath; prophesy, son of man, and say to it,
'This is what the Sovereign LORD says: Come
from the four winds, O breath, and breathe
into these slain, that they may live.' " 10So I
prophesied as he commanded me, and breath
entered them; they came to life and stood up
on their feet—a vast army.
11Then he said to me: "Son of man, these
bones are the whole house of Israel. They say,
'Our bones are dried up and our hope is gone;
we are cut off.' 12Therefore prophesy and say
to them: 'This is what the Sovereign LORD
says: O my people, I am going to open your
graves and bring you up from them; I will
bring you back to the land of Israel. 13Then
you, my people, will know that I am the
LORD, when I open your graves and bring you
up from them. 14I will put my Spirit in you
and you will live, and I will settle you in your
own land. Then you will know that I the LORD
have spoken, and I have done it, declares the
LORD.' "

One Nation Under One King

15The word of the LORD came to me:
16"Son of man, take a stick of wood and write
on it, 'Belonging to Judah and the Israelites
associated with him.' Then take another stick
of wood, and write on it, 'Ephraim's stick, belonging to Joseph and all the house of Israel associated with him.' 17Join them together
into one stick so that they will become one in
your hand.
18"When your countrymen ask you, 'Won't
you tell us what you mean by this?' 19say to
them, 'This is what the Sovereign LORD says: I
am going to take the stick of Joseph—which is
in Ephraim's hand—and of the Israelite tribes
associated with him, and join it to Judah's
stick, making them a single stick of wood, and
they will become one in my hand.' 20Hold before their eyes the sticks you have written on
21and say to them, 'This is what the Sovereign
LORD says: I will take the Israelites out of the
nations where they have gone. I will gather
them from all around and bring them back
into their own land. 22I will make them one
nation in the land, on the mountains of Israel. There will be one king over all of them
and they will never again be two nations or
be divided into two kingdoms. 23They will no
longer defile themselves with their idols and
vile images or with any of their offenses, for
I will save them from all their sinful backsliding,[b] and I will cleanse them. They will be my
people, and I will be their God.
24" 'My servant David will be king over
them, and they will all have one shepherd.
They will follow my laws and be careful to
keep my decrees. 25They will live in the land I
gave to my servant Jacob, the land where your
fathers lived. They and their children and their
children's children will live there forever, and
David my servant will be their prince forever.
26I will make a covenant of peace with them; it
will be an everlasting covenant. I will establish
them and increase their numbers, and I will

---

[a] 5 The Hebrew for this word can also mean *wind* or *spirit* (see verses 6-14). [b] 23 Many Hebrew manuscripts (see also Septuagint); most Hebrew manuscripts *all their dwelling places where they sinned*

T

TUESDAY
EZEKIEL 37:1–14

BRINGING MARRIAGE BACK TO LIFE

> **"This is what the Sovereign LORD says to these bones: I will make breath enter you, and you will come to life."**
>
> — EZEKIEL 37:5

let's talk

- Has our marriage ever felt like a valley of dry bones? What caused the dryness?
- Whom do we know whose marriage appeared broken but was ultimately revitalized? How did that happen?
- Are we in trouble in our marriage? What parts of us feel like they're dying? What would it take to revive those dead spots?

Forget about sitting quietly with your Bible on your knees, letting your eyes skim Ezekiel 37:1–14. Read the story of the valley of dry bones aloud to one another. Hearing those words spoken never fails to give me chills.

In our lives, we don't have to look very hard for dry bones. Sometimes even a marriage feels like a valley of dry bones. Maybe it was deceit or some sort of betrayal that desiccated your marriage. Or maybe it was something less dramatic and more ordinary: the nagging sense that after all these years, your spouse doesn't really know you. The fear that you haven't become the person you wanted to be in this marriage. Maybe disappointment that this isn't what you expected of marriage. Maybe just plain boredom.

Kelli, who was with me in church on the eve of Easter, can testify about the dry bones of marriage. Her marriage was rocky from the start. She and her husband increasingly seemed interested in different things. Sex felt like a chore. When she was honest with herself, Kelli had to admit that she no longer cared if the marriage failed or succeeded.

One day, over coffee, Kelli talked about her problems to Jenny, an acquaintance from work. Mostly Jenny just listened. Then she asked Kelli what she really wanted from marriage and what she would do if she had a magic wand. Kelli realized, right there in Starbucks, that what she wanted most was to fix her marriage.

"Well, we don't have magic wands in this world," replied Jenny, "but we do have the power of an awesome God, and I believe that God wants to restore your marriage."

That conversation at Starbucks happened three years ago. Kelli says that the process of resurrecting her marriage has been slow. "We're not finished yet because God's not finished with us yet," she says. "And this really is God. We couldn't have saved our marriage alone, just like we can't save ourselves."

Ezekiel 37 reminds us that we don't have to breathe life back into dead bones by ourselves. We don't have the power to do that. Ezekiel is very clear: It is the Lord who splits open our graves and brings us up from them. It is the Lord who attaches tendons and flesh to our dry, bare bones. And it is the Lord who puts his Spirit in us so that we might live.

Of course, we have some responsibility to live out God's promises of resurrection. We can live out God's work by ordering our marriages around practices like prayer and Scripture study, by carving out time to spend alone with our spouse, by risking honest conversations about our struggles. Kelli and her husband sought God's healing power in the company of a skilled counselor. God shows up in all these places. God can even use an afternoon chat at Starbucks to say to our dry bones, "Live!"

—LAUREN WINNER

FOR YOUR NEXT DEVOTIONAL READING, TURN TO PAGE 948.

put my sanctuary among them forever. 27My
dwelling place will be with them; I will be
their God, and they will be my people. 28Then
the nations will know that I the LORD make
Israel holy, when my sanctuary is among them
forever.' "

A Prophecy Against Gog

38 The word of the LORD came to me:
2"Son of man, set your face against
Gog, of the land of Magog, the chief
prince of[a] Meshech and Tubal; prophesy
against him 3and say: 'This is what the Sovereign LORD says: I am against you, O Gog,
chief prince of[b] Meshech and Tubal. 4I will
turn you around, put hooks in your jaws and
bring you out with your whole army—your
horses, your horsemen fully armed, and a
great horde with large and small shields, all of
them brandishing their swords. 5Persia, Cush[c]
and Put will be with them, all with shields and
helmets, 6also Gomer with all its troops, and
Beth Togarmah from the far north with all its
troops—the many nations with you.

7" 'Get ready; be prepared, you and all the
hordes gathered about you, and take command of them. 8After many days you will be
called to arms. In future years you will invade
a land that has recovered from war, whose
people were gathered from many nations to
the mountains of Israel, which had long been
desolate. They had been brought out from the
nations, and now all of them live in safety.
9You and all your troops and the many nations
with you will go up, advancing like a storm;
you will be like a cloud covering the land.

10" 'This is what the Sovereign LORD says:
On that day thoughts will come into your
mind and you will devise an evil scheme. 11You
will say, "I will invade a land of unwalled villages; I will attack a peaceful and unsuspecting
people—all of them living without walls and
without gates and bars. 12I will plunder and
loot and turn my hand against the resettled
ruins and the people gathered from the nations, rich in livestock and goods, living at the
center of the land." 13Sheba and Dedan and
the merchants of Tarshish and all her villages[d]
will say to you, "Have you come to plunder?
Have you gathered your hordes to loot, to carry off silver and gold, to take away livestock
and goods and to seize much plunder?" '

14"Therefore, son of man, prophesy and say
to Gog: 'This is what the Sovereign LORD says:
In that day, when my people Israel are living in
safety, will you not take notice of it? 15You will
come from your place in the far north, you
and many nations with you, all of them riding
on horses, a great horde, a mighty army. 16You
will advance against my people Israel like a
cloud that covers the land. In days to come, O
Gog, I will bring you against my land, so that
the nations may know me when I show myself
holy through you before their eyes.

17" 'This is what the Sovereign LORD says:
Are you not the one I spoke of in former days
by my servants the prophets of Israel? At that
time they prophesied for years that I would
bring you against them. 18This is what will
happen in that day: When Gog attacks the
land of Israel, my hot anger will be aroused,
declares the Sovereign LORD. 19In my zeal and
fiery wrath I declare that at that time there
shall be a great earthquake in the land of Israel. 20The fish of the sea, the birds of the air, the
beasts of the field, every creature that moves
along the ground, and all the people on the
face of the earth will tremble at my presence.
The mountains will be overturned, the cliffs
will crumble and every wall will fall to the
ground. 21I will summon a sword against Gog
on all my mountains, declares the Sovereign
LORD. Every man's sword will be against his
brother. 22I will execute judgment upon him
with plague and bloodshed; I will pour down
torrents of rain, hailstones and burning sulfur
on him and on his troops and on the many
nations with him. 23And so I will show my
greatness and my holiness, and I will make
myself known in the sight of many nations.
Then they will know that I am the LORD.'

39 "Son of man, prophesy against Gog and
say: 'This is what the Sovereign LORD
says: I am against you, O Gog, chief
prince of[e] Meshech and Tubal. 2I will turn
you around and drag you along. I will bring
you from the far north and send you against
the mountains of Israel. 3Then I will strike
your bow from your left hand and make your
arrows drop from your right hand. 4On the
mountains of Israel you will fall, you and all
your troops and the nations with you. I will
give you as food to all kinds of carrion birds
and to the wild animals. 5You will fall in the
open field, for I have spoken, declares the Sovereign LORD. 6I will send fire on Magog and
on those who live in safety in the coastlands,
and they will know that I am the LORD.

[a] *2* Or *the prince of Rosh,* [b] *3* Or *Gog, prince of Rosh,* [c] *5* That is, the upper Nile region [d] *13* Or *her strong lions* [e] *1* Or *Gog, prince of Rosh,*

7“ ‘I will make known my holy name
among my people Israel. I will no longer let
my holy name be profaned, and the nations
will know that I the LORD am the Holy One
in Israel. 8It is coming! It will surely take place,
declares the Sovereign LORD. This is the day I
have spoken of.

9“ ‘Then those who live in the towns of
Israel will go out and use the weapons for
fuel and burn them up—the small and large
shields, the bows and arrows, the war clubs
and spears. For seven years they will use them
for fuel. 10They will not need to gather wood
from the fields or cut it from the forests, because they will use the weapons for fuel. And
they will plunder those who plundered them
and loot those who looted them, declares the
Sovereign LORD.

11“ ‘On that day I will give Gog a burial
place in Israel, in the valley of those who travel
east toward[a] the Sea.[b] It will block the way of
travelers, because Gog and all his hordes will
be buried there. So it will be called the Valley
of Hamon Gog.[c]

12“ ‘For seven months the house of Israel
will be burying them in order to cleanse the
land. 13All the people of the land will bury
them, and the day I am glorified will be a
memorable day for them, declares the Sovereign LORD.

14“ ‘Men will be regularly employed to
cleanse the land. Some will go throughout
the land and, in addition to them, others will
bury those that remain on the ground. At the
end of the seven months they will begin their
search. 15As they go through the land and one
of them sees a human bone, he will set up a
marker beside it until the gravediggers have
buried it in the Valley of Hamon Gog. 16(Also
a town called Hamonah[d] will be there.) And
so they will cleanse the land.’

17“Son of man, this is what the Sovereign
LORD says: Call out to every kind of bird and
all the wild animals: ‘Assemble and come together from all around to the sacrifice I am
preparing for you, the great sacrifice on the
mountains of Israel. There you will eat flesh
and drink blood. 18You will eat the flesh of
mighty men and drink the blood of the princes of the earth as if they were rams and lambs,
goats and bulls—all of them fattened animals
from Bashan. 19At the sacrifice I am preparing
for you, you will eat fat till you are glutted
and drink blood till you are drunk. 20At my
table you will eat your fill of horses and riders,
mighty men and soldiers of every kind,’ declares the Sovereign LORD.

21“I will display my glory among the nations, and all the nations will see the punishment I inflict and the hand I lay upon them.
22From that day forward the house of Israel will know that I am the LORD their God.
23And the nations will know that the people
of Israel went into exile for their sin, because
they were unfaithful to me. So I hid my face
from them and handed them over to their enemies, and they all fell by the sword. 24I dealt
with them according to their uncleanness and
their offenses, and I hid my face from them.

25“Therefore this is what the Sovereign
LORD says: I will now bring Jacob back from
captivity[e] and will have compassion on all the
people of Israel, and I will be zealous for my
holy name. 26They will forget their shame and
all the unfaithfulness they showed toward me
when they lived in safety in their land with
no one to make them afraid. 27When I have
brought them back from the nations and have
gathered them from the countries of their enemies, I will show myself holy through them
in the sight of many nations. 28Then they
will know that I am the LORD their God, for
though I sent them into exile among the nations, I will gather them to their own land, not
leaving any behind. 29I will no longer hide my
face from them, for I will pour out my Spirit
on the house of Israel, declares the Sovereign
LORD.”

The New Temple Area

40 In the twenty-fifth year of our exile, at
the beginning of the year, on the tenth
of the month, in the fourteenth year after the fall of the city—on that very day the
hand of the LORD was upon me and he took
me there. 2In visions of God he took me to
the land of Israel and set me on a very high
mountain, on whose south side were some
buildings that looked like a city. 3He took
me there, and I saw a man whose appearance
was like bronze; he was standing in the gateway with a linen cord and a measuring rod in
his hand. 4The man said to me, “Son of man,
look with your eyes and hear with your ears
and pay attention to everything I am going
to show you, for that is why you have been
brought here. Tell the house of Israel everything you see.”

[a] 11 Or *of* [b] 11 That is, the Dead Sea [c] 11 *Hamon Gog* means *hordes of Gog.* [d] 16 *Hamonah* means *horde.* [e] 25 Or *now restore the fortunes of Jacob*

The East Gate to the Outer Court

5I saw a wall completely surrounding the
temple area. The length of the measuring rod
in the man's hand was six long cubits, each of
which was a cubit[a] and a handbreadth.[b] He
measured the wall; it was one measuring rod
thick and one rod high.

6Then he went to the gate facing east. He
climbed its steps and measured the threshold
of the gate; it was one rod deep.[c] 7The alcoves
for the guards were one rod long and one rod
wide, and the projecting walls between the alcoves were five cubits thick. And the threshold
of the gate next to the portico facing the temple was one rod deep.

8Then he measured the portico of the gateway; 9it[d] was eight cubits deep and its jambs
were two cubits thick. The portico of the gateway faced the temple.

10Inside the east gate were three alcoves on
each side; the three had the same measurements, and the faces of the projecting walls on
each side had the same measurements. 11Then
he measured the width of the entrance to the
gateway; it was ten cubits and its length was
thirteen cubits. 12In front of each alcove was
a wall one cubit high, and the alcoves were six
cubits square. 13Then he measured the gateway from the top of the rear wall of one alcove
to the top of the opposite one; the distance
was twenty-five cubits from one parapet opening to the opposite one. 14He measured along
the faces of the projecting walls all around the
inside of the gateway—sixty cubits. The measurement was up to the portico[e] facing the
courtyard.[f] 15The distance from the entrance
of the gateway to the far end of its portico was
fifty cubits. 16The alcoves and the projecting
walls inside the gateway were surmounted by
narrow parapet openings all around, as was
the portico; the openings all around faced inward. The faces of the projecting walls were
decorated with palm trees.

The Outer Court

17Then he brought me into the outer court.
There I saw some rooms and a pavement that
had been constructed all around the court;
there were thirty rooms along the pavement.
18It abutted the sides of the gateways and was
as wide as they were long; this was the lower
pavement. 19Then he measured the distance
from the inside of the lower gateway to the
outside of the inner court; it was a hundred
cubits on the east side as well as on the north.

The North Gate

20Then he measured the length and width
of the gate facing north, leading into the outer
court. 21Its alcoves—three on each side—its
projecting walls and its portico had the same
measurements as those of the first gateway. It
was fifty cubits long and twenty-five cubits
wide. 22Its openings, its portico and its palm
tree decorations had the same measurements
as those of the gate facing east. Seven steps
led up to it, with its portico opposite them.
23There was a gate to the inner court facing
the north gate, just as there was on the east.
He measured from one gate to the opposite
one; it was a hundred cubits.

The South Gate

24Then he led me to the south side and I
saw a gate facing south. He measured its jambs
and its portico, and they had the same measurements as the others. 25The gateway and
its portico had narrow openings all around,
like the openings of the others. It was fifty cubits long and twenty-five cubits wide. 26Sev-
en steps led up to it, with its portico opposite
them; it had palm tree decorations on the faces of the projecting walls on each side. 27The
inner court also had a gate facing south, and
he measured from this gate to the outer gate
on the south side; it was a hundred cubits.

Gates to the Inner Court

28Then he brought me into the inner court
through the south gate, and he measured the
south gate; it had the same measurements as
the others. 29Its alcoves, its projecting walls
and its portico had the same measurements as
the others. The gateway and its portico had
openings all around. It was fifty cubits long
and twenty-five cubits wide. 30(The porticoes
of the gateways around the inner court were
twenty-five cubits wide and five cubits deep.)
31Its portico faced the outer court; palm trees
decorated its jambs, and eight steps led up
to it.

32Then he brought me to the inner court
on the east side, and he measured the gateway;
it had the same measurements as the others.
33Its alcoves, its projecting walls and its portico had the same measurements as the others.

---

[a] *5* The common cubit was about 1 1/2 feet (about 0.5 meter). [b] *5* That is, about 3 inches (about 8 centimeters) [c] *6* Septuagint; Hebrew *deep, the first threshold, one rod deep* [d] *8,9* Many Hebrew manuscripts, Septuagint, Vulgate and Syriac; most Hebrew manuscripts *gateway facing the temple; it was one rod deep. 9Then he measured the portico of the gateway; it* [e] *14* Septuagint; Hebrew *projecting wall* [f] *14* The meaning of the Hebrew for this verse is uncertain.

The gateway and its portico had openings all around. It was fifty cubits long and twenty-five cubits wide. 34Its portico faced the outer court; palm trees decorated the jambs on either side, and eight steps led up to it.

35Then he brought me to the north gate and measured it. It had the same measurements as the others, 36as did its alcoves, its projecting walls and its portico, and it had openings all around. It was fifty cubits long and twenty-five cubits wide. 37Its portico[a] faced the outer court; palm trees decorated the jambs on either side, and eight steps led up to it.

The Rooms for Preparing Sacrifices

38A room with a doorway was by the portico in each of the inner gateways, where the burnt offerings were washed. 39In the portico of the gateway were two tables on each side, on which the burnt offerings, sin offerings and guilt offerings were slaughtered. 40By the outside wall of the portico of the gateway, near the steps at the entrance to the north gateway were two tables, and on the other side of the steps were two tables. 41So there were four tables on one side of the gateway and four on the other—eight tables in all—on which the sacrifices were slaughtered. 42There were also four tables of dressed stone for the burnt offerings, each a cubit and a half long, a cubit and a half wide and a cubit high. On them were placed the utensils for slaughtering the burnt offerings and the other sacrifices. 43And double-pronged hooks, each a handbreadth long, were attached to the wall all around. The tables were for the flesh of the offerings.

Rooms for the Priests

44Outside the inner gate, within the inner court, were two rooms, one[b] at the side of the north gate and facing south, and another at the side of the south[c] gate and facing north. 45He said to me, "The room facing south is for the priests who have charge of the temple, 46and the room facing north is for the priests who have charge of the altar. These are the sons of Zadok, who are the only Levites who may draw near to the LORD to minister before him."

47Then he measured the court: It was square—a hundred cubits long and a hundred cubits wide. And the altar was in front of the temple.

The Temple

48He brought me to the portico of the temple and measured the jambs of the portico; they were five cubits wide on either side. The width of the entrance was fourteen cubits and its projecting walls were[d] three cubits wide on either side. 49The portico was twenty cubits wide, and twelve[e] cubits from front to back. It was reached by a flight of stairs,[f] and there were pillars on each side of the jambs.

41 Then the man brought me to the outer sanctuary and measured the jambs; the width of the jambs was six cubits[g] on each side.[h] 2The entrance was ten cubits wide, and the projecting walls on each side of it were five cubits wide. He also measured the outer sanctuary; it was forty cubits long and twenty cubits wide.

3Then he went into the inner sanctuary and measured the jambs of the entrance; each was two cubits wide. The entrance was six cubits wide, and the projecting walls on each side of it were seven cubits wide. 4And he measured the length of the inner sanctuary; it was twenty cubits, and its width was twenty cubits across the end of the outer sanctuary. He said to me, "This is the Most Holy Place."

5Then he measured the wall of the temple; it was six cubits thick, and each side room around the temple was four cubits wide. 6The side rooms were on three levels, one above another, thirty on each level. There were ledges all around the wall of the temple to serve as supports for the side rooms, so that the supports were not inserted into the wall of the temple. 7The side rooms all around the temple were wider at each successive level. The structure surrounding the temple was built in ascending stages, so that the rooms widened as one went upward. A stairway went up from the lowest floor to the top floor through the middle floor.

8I saw that the temple had a raised base all around it, forming the foundation of the side rooms. It was the length of the rod, six long cubits. 9The outer wall of the side rooms was five cubits thick. The open area between the side rooms of the temple 10and the ⌞priests'⌟ rooms was twenty cubits wide all around the temple. 11There were entrances to the side rooms from the open area, one on the north and another on the south; and the base adjoining the open area was five cubits wide all around.

12The building facing the temple courtyard

---

[a] 37 Septuagint (see also verses 31 and 34); Hebrew *jambs* [b] 44 Septuagint; Hebrew *were rooms for singers, which were* [c] 44 Septuagint; Hebrew *east* [d] 48 Septuagint; Hebrew *entrance was* [e] 49 Septuagint; Hebrew *eleven* [f] 49 Hebrew; Septuagint *Ten steps led up to it* [g] 1 The common cubit was about 1 1/2 feet (about 0.5 meter). [h] 1 One Hebrew manuscript and Septuagint; most Hebrew manuscripts *side, the width of the tent*

on the west side was seventy cubits wide. The wall of the building was five cubits thick all around, and its length was ninety cubits.

[13]Then he measured the temple; it was a hundred cubits long, and the temple courtyard and the building with its walls were also a hundred cubits long. [14]The width of the temple courtyard on the east, including the front of the temple, was a hundred cubits.

[15]Then he measured the length of the building facing the courtyard at the rear of the temple, including its galleries on each side; it was a hundred cubits.

The outer sanctuary, the inner sanctuary and the portico facing the court, [16]as well as the thresholds and the narrow windows and galleries around the three of them—everything beyond and including the threshold was covered with wood. The floor, the wall up to the windows, and the windows were covered. [17]In the space above the outside of the entrance to the inner sanctuary and on the walls at regular intervals all around the inner and outer sanctuary [18]were carved cherubim and palm trees. Palm trees alternated with cherubim. Each cherub had two faces: [19]the face of a man toward the palm tree on one side and the face of a lion toward the palm tree on the other. They were carved all around the whole temple. [20]From the floor to the area above the entrance, cherubim and palm trees were carved on the wall of the outer sanctuary.

[21]The outer sanctuary had a rectangular doorframe, and the one at the front of the Most Holy Place was similar. [22]There was a wooden altar three cubits high and two cubits square[a]; its corners, its base[b] and its sides were of wood. The man said to me, "This is the table that is before the LORD." [23]Both the outer sanctuary and the Most Holy Place had double doors. [24]Each door had two leaves—two hinged leaves for each door. [25]And on the doors of the outer sanctuary were carved cherubim and palm trees like those carved on the walls, and there was a wooden overhang on the front of the portico. [26]On the sidewalls of the portico were narrow windows with palm trees carved on each side. The side rooms of the temple also had overhangs.

Rooms for the Priests

42 Then the man led me northward into the outer court and brought me to the rooms opposite the temple courtyard and opposite the outer wall on the north side. [2]The building whose door faced north was a hundred cubits[c] long and fifty cubits wide. [3]Both in the section twenty cubits from the inner court and in the section opposite the pavement of the outer court, gallery faced gallery at the three levels. [4]In front of the rooms was an inner passageway ten cubits wide and a hundred cubits[d] long. Their doors were on the north. [5]Now the upper rooms were narrower, for the galleries took more space from them than from the rooms on the lower and middle floors of the building. [6]The rooms on the third floor had no pillars, as the courts had; so they were smaller in floor space than those on the lower and middle floors. [7]There was an outer wall parallel to the rooms and the outer court; it extended in front of the rooms for fifty cubits. [8]While the row of rooms on the side next to the outer court was fifty cubits long, the row on the side nearest the sanctuary was a hundred cubits long. [9]The lower rooms had an entrance on the east side as one enters them from the outer court.

[10]On the south side[e] along the length of the wall of the outer court, adjoining the temple courtyard and opposite the outer wall, were rooms [11]with a passageway in front of them. These were like the rooms on the north; they had the same length and width, with similar exits and dimensions. Similar to the doorways on the north [12]were the doorways of the rooms on the south. There was a doorway at the beginning of the passageway that was parallel to the corresponding wall extending eastward, by which one enters the rooms.

[13]Then he said to me, "The north and south rooms facing the temple courtyard are the priests' rooms, where the priests who approach the LORD will eat the most holy offerings. There they will put the most holy offerings—the grain offerings, the sin offerings and the guilt offerings—for the place is holy. [14]Once the priests enter the holy precincts, they are not to go into the outer court until they leave behind the garments in which they minister, for these are holy. They are to put on other clothes before they go near the places that are for the people."

[15]When he had finished measuring what was inside the temple area, he led me out by the east gate and measured the area all around: [16]He measured the east side with the mea-

[a] 22 Septuagint; Hebrew *long* [b] 22 Septuagint; Hebrew *length* [c] 2 The common cubit was about 1 1/2 feet (about 0.5 meter).
[d] 4 Septuagint and Syriac; Hebrew *and one cubit* [e] 10 Septuagint; Hebrew *Eastward*

suring rod; it was five hundred cubits.[a] 17He measured the north side; it was five hundred cubits[b] by the measuring rod. 18He measured the south side; it was five hundred cubits by the measuring rod. 19Then he turned to the west side and measured; it was five hundred cubits by the measuring rod. 20So he measured the area on all four sides. It had a wall around it, five hundred cubits long and five hundred cubits wide, to separate the holy from the common.

The Glory Returns to the Temple

43 Then the man brought me to the gate facing east, 2and I saw the glory of the God of Israel coming from the east. His voice was like the roar of rushing waters, and the land was radiant with his glory. 3The vision I saw was like the vision I had seen when he[c] came to destroy the city and like the visions I had seen by the Kebar River, and I fell facedown. 4The glory of the LORD entered the temple through the gate facing east. 5Then the Spirit lifted me up and brought me into the inner court, and the glory of the LORD filled the temple.

6While the man was standing beside me, I heard someone speaking to me from inside the temple. 7He said: "Son of man, this is the place of my throne and the place for the soles of my feet. This is where I will live among the Israelites forever. The house of Israel will never again defile my holy name—neither they nor their kings—by their prostitution[d] and the lifeless idols[e] of their kings at their high places. 8When they placed their threshold next to my threshold and their doorposts beside my doorposts, with only a wall between me and them, they defiled my holy name by their detestable practices. So I destroyed them in my anger. 9Now let them put away from me their prostitution and the lifeless idols of their kings, and I will live among them forever.

10"Son of man, describe the temple to the people of Israel, that they may be ashamed of their sins. Let them consider the plan, 11and if they are ashamed of all they have done, make known to them the design of the temple—its arrangement, its exits and entrances—its whole design and all its regulations[f] and laws. Write these down before them so that they may be faithful to its design and follow all its regulations.

12"This is the law of the temple: All the surrounding area on top of the mountain will be most holy. Such is the law of the temple.

The Altar

13"These are the measurements of the altar in long cubits, that cubit being a cubit[g] and a handbreadth[h]: Its gutter is a cubit deep and a cubit wide, with a rim of one span[i] around the edge. And this is the height of the altar: 14From the gutter on the ground up to the lower ledge it is two cubits high and a cubit wide, and from the smaller ledge up to the larger ledge it is four cubits high and a cubit wide. 15The altar hearth is four cubits high, and four horns project upward from the hearth. 16The altar hearth is square, twelve cubits long and twelve cubits wide. 17The upper ledge also is square, fourteen cubits long and fourteen cubits wide, with a rim of half a cubit and a gutter of a cubit all around. The steps of the altar face east."

18Then he said to me, "Son of man, this is what the Sovereign LORD says: These will be the regulations for sacrificing burnt offerings and sprinkling blood upon the altar when it is built: 19You are to give a young bull as a sin offering to the priests, who are Levites, of the family of Zadok, who come near to minister before me, declares the Sovereign LORD. 20You are to take some of its blood and put it on the four horns of the altar and on the four corners of the upper ledge and all around the rim, and so purify the altar and make atonement for it. 21You are to take the bull for the sin offering and burn it in the designated part of the temple area outside the sanctuary.

22"On the second day you are to offer a male goat without defect for a sin offering, and the altar is to be purified as it was purified with the bull. 23When you have finished purifying it, you are to offer a young bull and a ram from the flock, both without defect. 24You are to offer them before the LORD, and the priests are to sprinkle salt on them and sacrifice them as a burnt offering to the LORD.

25"For seven days you are to provide a male goat daily for a sin offering; you are also to provide a young bull and a ram from the flock, both without defect. 26For seven days they are

---

[a] *16* See Septuagint of verse 17; Hebrew *rods*; also in verses 18 and 19. [b] *17* Septuagint; Hebrew *rods* [c] *3* Some Hebrew manuscripts and Vulgate; most Hebrew manuscripts *I* [d] *7* Or *their spiritual adultery*; also in verse 9 [e] *7* Or *the corpses*; also in verse 9
[f] *11* Some Hebrew manuscripts and Septuagint; most Hebrew manuscripts *regulations and its whole design* [g] *13* The common cubit was about 1 1/2 feet (about 0.5 meter). [h] *13* That is, about 3 inches (about 8 centimeters) [i] *13* That is, about 9 inches (about 22 centimeters)

to make atonement for the altar and cleanse it; thus they will dedicate it. 27At the end of these days, from the eighth day on, the priests are to present your burnt offerings and fellowship offerings[a] on the altar. Then I will accept you, declares the Sovereign LORD."

The Prince, the Levites, the Priests

44 Then the man brought me back to the outer gate of the sanctuary, the one facing east, and it was shut. 2The LORD said to me, "This gate is to remain shut. It must not be opened; no one may enter through it. It is to remain shut because the LORD, the God of Israel, has entered through it. 3The prince himself is the only one who may sit inside the gateway to eat in the presence of the LORD. He is to enter by way of the portico of the gateway and go out the same way."

4Then the man brought me by way of the north gate to the front of the temple. I looked and saw the glory of the LORD filling the temple of the LORD, and I fell facedown.

5The LORD said to me, "Son of man, look carefully, listen closely and give attention to everything I tell you concerning all the regulations regarding the temple of the LORD. Give attention to the entrance of the temple and all the exits of the sanctuary. 6Say to the rebellious house of Israel, 'This is what the Sovereign LORD says: Enough of your detestable practices, O house of Israel! 7In addition to all your other detestable practices, you brought foreigners uncircumcised in heart and flesh into my sanctuary, desecrating my temple while you offered me food, fat and blood, and you broke my covenant. 8Instead of carrying out your duty in regard to my holy things, you put others in charge of my sanctuary. 9This is what the Sovereign LORD says: No foreigner uncircumcised in heart and flesh is to enter my sanctuary, not even the foreigners who live among the Israelites.

10" 'The Levites who went far from me when Israel went astray and who wandered from me after their idols must bear the consequences of their sin. 11They may serve in my sanctuary, having charge of the gates of the temple and serving in it; they may slaughter the burnt offerings and sacrifices for the people and stand before the people and serve them. 12But because they served them in the presence of their idols and made the house of Israel fall into sin, therefore I have sworn with uplifted hand that they must bear the consequences of their sin, declares the Sovereign LORD. 13They are not to come near to serve me as priests or come near any of my holy things or my most holy offerings; they must bear the shame of their detestable practices. 14Yet I will put them in charge of the duties of the temple and all the work that is to be done in it.

15" 'But the priests, who are Levites and descendants of Zadok and who faithfully carried out the duties of my sanctuary when the Israelites went astray from me, are to come near to minister before me; they are to stand before me to offer sacrifices of fat and blood, declares the Sovereign LORD. 16They alone are to enter my sanctuary; they alone are to come near my table to minister before me and perform my service.

17" 'When they enter the gates of the inner court, they are to wear linen clothes; they must not wear any woolen garment while ministering at the gates of the inner court or inside the temple. 18They are to wear linen turbans on their heads and linen undergarments around their waists. They must not wear anything that makes them perspire. 19When they go out into the outer court where the people are, they are to take off the clothes they have been ministering in and are to leave them in the sacred rooms, and put on other clothes, so that they do not consecrate the people by means of their garments.

20" 'They must not shave their heads or let their hair grow long, but they are to keep the hair of their heads trimmed. 21No priest is to drink wine when he enters the inner court. 22They must not marry widows or divorced women; they may marry only virgins of Israelite descent or widows of priests. 23They are to teach my people the difference between the holy and the common and show them how to distinguish between the unclean and the clean.

24" 'In any dispute, the priests are to serve as judges and decide it according to my ordinances. They are to keep my laws and my decrees for all my appointed feasts, and they are to keep my Sabbaths holy.

25" 'A priest must not defile himself by going near a dead person; however, if the dead person was his father or mother, son or daughter, brother or unmarried sister, then he may defile himself. 26After he is cleansed, he must wait seven days. 27On the day he goes into the inner court of the sanctuary to minister in the

[a] 27 Traditionally *peace offerings*

sanctuary, he is to offer a sin offering for himself, declares the Sovereign LORD.

28“ ‘I am to be the only inheritance the priests have. You are to give them no possession in Israel; I will be their possession. 29They will eat the grain offerings, the sin offerings and the guilt offerings; and everything in Israel devoted[a] to the LORD will belong to them. 30The best of all the firstfruits and of all your special gifts will belong to the priests. You are to give them the first portion of your ground meal so that a blessing may rest on your household. 31The priests must not eat anything, bird or animal, found dead or torn by wild animals.

Division of the Land

45 “ ‘When you allot the land as an inheritance, you are to present to the LORD a portion of the land as a sacred district, 25,000 cubits long and 20,000[b] cubits wide; the entire area will be holy. 2Of this, a section 500 cubits square is to be for the sanctuary, with 50 cubits around it for open land. 3In the sacred district, measure off a section 25,000 cubits[c] long and 10,000 cubits[d] wide. In it will be the sanctuary, the Most Holy Place. 4It will be the sacred portion of the land for the priests, who minister in the sanctuary and who draw near to minister before the LORD. It will be a place for their houses as well as a holy place for the sanctuary. 5An area 25,000 cubits long and 10,000 cubits wide will belong to the Levites, who serve in the temple, as their possession for towns to live in.[e]

6“ ‘You are to give the city as its property an area 5,000 cubits wide and 25,000 cubits long, adjoining the sacred portion; it will belong to the whole house of Israel.

7“ ‘The prince will have the land bordering each side of the area formed by the sacred district and the property of the city. It will extend westward from the west side and eastward from the east side, running lengthwise from the western to the eastern border parallel to one of the tribal portions. 8This land will be his possession in Israel. And my princes will no longer oppress my people but will allow the house of Israel to possess the land according to their tribes.

9“ ‘This is what the Sovereign LORD says: You have gone far enough, O princes of Israel! Give up your violence and oppression and do what is just and right. Stop dispossessing my people, declares the Sovereign LORD. 10You are to use accurate scales, an accurate ephah[f] and an accurate bath.[g] 11The ephah and the bath are to be the same size, the bath containing a tenth of a homer[h] and the ephah a tenth of a homer; the homer is to be the standard measure for both. 12The shekel[i] is to consist of twenty gerahs. Twenty shekels plus twenty-five shekels plus fifteen shekels equal one mina.[j]

Offerings and Holy Days

13“ ‘This is the special gift you are to offer: a sixth of an ephah from each homer of wheat and a sixth of an ephah from each homer of barley. 14The prescribed portion of oil, measured by the bath, is a tenth of a bath from each cor (which consists of ten baths or one homer, for ten baths are equivalent to a homer). 15Also one sheep is to be taken from every flock of two hundred from the well-watered pastures of Israel. These will be used for the grain offerings, burnt offerings and fellowship offerings[k] to make atonement for the people, declares the Sovereign LORD. 16All the people of the land will participate in this special gift for the use of the prince in Israel. 17It will be the duty of the prince to provide the burnt offerings, grain offerings and drink offerings at the festivals, the New Moons and the Sabbaths—at all the appointed feasts of the house of Israel. He will provide the sin offerings, grain offerings, burnt offerings and fellowship offerings to make atonement for the house of Israel.

18“ ‘This is what the Sovereign LORD says: In the first month on the first day you are to take a young bull without defect and purify the sanctuary. 19The priest is to take some of the blood of the sin offering and put it on the doorposts of the temple, on the four corners of the upper ledge of the altar and on the gateposts of the inner court. 20You are to do the same on the seventh day of the month for anyone who sins unintentionally or through ignorance; so you are to make atonement for the temple.

21“ ‘In the first month on the fourteenth day you are to observe the Passover, a feast lasting seven days, during which you shall eat bread made without yeast. 22On that day the prince is to provide a bull as a sin offering for him-

---

[a] 29 The Hebrew term refers to the irrevocable giving over of things or persons to the LORD. [b] 1 Septuagint (see also verses 3 and 5 and 48:9); Hebrew *10,000* [c] 3 That is, about 7 miles (about 12 kilometers) [d] 3 That is, about 3 miles (about 5 kilometers) [e] 5 Septuagint; Hebrew *temple; they will have as their possession 20 rooms* [f] 10 An ephah was a dry measure. [g] 10 A bath was a liquid measure. [h] 11 A homer was a dry measure. [i] 12 A shekel weighed about 2/5 ounce (about 11.5 grams). [j] 12 That is, 60 shekels; the common mina was 50 shekels. [k] 15 Traditionally *peace offerings*; also in verse 17

self and for all the people of the land. 23 Every
day during the seven days of the Feast he is
to provide seven bulls and seven rams without
defect as a burnt offering to the LORD, and a
male goat for a sin offering. 24 He is to provide
as a grain offering an ephah for each bull and
an ephah for each ram, along with a hin[a] of
oil for each ephah.

25 " 'During the seven days of the Feast,
which begins in the seventh month on the fifteenth day, he is to make the same provision
for sin offerings, burnt offerings, grain offerings and oil.

46 " 'This is what the Sovereign LORD says:
The gate of the inner court facing east
is to be shut on the six working days,
but on the Sabbath day and on the day of the
New Moon it is to be opened. 2 The prince is
to enter from the outside through the portico
of the gateway and stand by the gatepost. The
priests are to sacrifice his burnt offering and
his fellowship offerings.[b] He is to worship at
the threshold of the gateway and then go out,
but the gate will not be shut until evening.
3 On the Sabbaths and New Moons the people
of the land are to worship in the presence of
the LORD at the entrance to that gateway. 4 The
burnt offering the prince brings to the LORD
on the Sabbath day is to be six male lambs and
a ram, all without defect. 5 The grain offering
given with the ram is to be an ephah,[c] and the
grain offering with the lambs is to be as much
as he pleases, along with a hin[a] of oil for each
ephah. 6 On the day of the New Moon he is
to offer a young bull, six lambs and a ram, all
without defect. 7 He is to provide as a grain
offering one ephah with the bull, one ephah
with the ram, and with the lambs as much as
he wants to give, along with a hin of oil with
each ephah. 8 When the prince enters, he is to
go in through the portico of the gateway, and
he is to come out the same way.

9 " 'When the people of the land come before the LORD at the appointed feasts, whoever
enters by the north gate to worship is to go
out the south gate; and whoever enters by the
south gate is to go out the north gate. No one
is to return through the gate by which he entered, but each is to go out the opposite gate.
10 The prince is to be among them, going in
when they go in and going out when they go
out.

11 " 'At the festivals and the appointed feasts,
the grain offering is to be an ephah with a bull,
an ephah with a ram, and with the lambs as
much as one pleases, along with a hin of oil
for each ephah. 12 When the prince provides
a freewill offering to the LORD—whether a
burnt offering or fellowship offerings—the
gate facing east is to be opened for him. He
shall offer his burnt offering or his fellowship
offerings as he does on the Sabbath day. Then
he shall go out, and after he has gone out, the
gate will be shut.

13 " 'Every day you are to provide a year-old
lamb without defect for a burnt offering to the
LORD; morning by morning you shall provide
it. 14 You are also to provide with it morning
by morning a grain offering, consisting of a
sixth of an ephah with a third of a hin of oil to
moisten the flour. The presenting of this grain
offering to the LORD is a lasting ordinance.
15 So the lamb and the grain offering and the
oil shall be provided morning by morning for
a regular burnt offering.

16 " 'This is what the Sovereign LORD says:
If the prince makes a gift from his inheritance
to one of his sons, it will also belong to his descendants; it is to be their property by inheritance. 17 If, however, he makes a gift from his
inheritance to one of his servants, the servant
may keep it until the year of freedom; then it
will revert to the prince. His inheritance belongs to his sons only; it is theirs. 18 The prince
must not take any of the inheritance of the
people, driving them off their property. He
is to give his sons their inheritance out of his
own property, so that none of my people will
be separated from his property.' "

19 Then the man brought me through the
entrance at the side of the gate to the sacred
rooms facing north, which belonged to the
priests, and showed me a place at the western
end. 20 He said to me, "This is the place where
the priests will cook the guilt offering and the
sin offering and bake the grain offering, to
avoid bringing them into the outer court and
consecrating the people."

21 He then brought me to the outer court
and led me around to its four corners, and
I saw in each corner another court. 22 In the
four corners of the outer court were enclosed[d]
courts, forty cubits long and thirty cubits
wide; each of the courts in the four corners
was the same size. 23 Around the inside of each
of the four courts was a ledge of stone, with
places for fire built all around under the ledge.
24 He said to me, "These are the kitchens where

---

[a] *24,5* That is, probably about 4 quarts (about 4 liters) [b] *2* Traditionally *peace offerings*; also in verse 12 [c] *5* That is, probably about 3/5 bushel (about 22 liters) [d] *22* The meaning of the Hebrew for this word is uncertain.

those who minister at the temple will cook the
sacrifices of the people."

The River From the Temple

47 The man brought me back to the entrance of the temple, and I saw water
coming out from under the threshold
of the temple toward the east (for the temple
faced east). The water was coming down from
under the south side of the temple, south of
the altar. 2He then brought me out through
the north gate and led me around the outside
to the outer gate facing east, and the water was
flowing from the south side.
3As the man went eastward with a measuring line in his hand, he measured off a thousand cubits[a] and then led me through water
that was ankle-deep. 4He measured off another thousand cubits and led me through water
that was knee-deep. He measured off another
thousand and led me through water that was
up to the waist. 5He measured off another
thousand, but now it was a river that I could
not cross, because the water had risen and was
deep enough to swim in—a river that no one
could cross. 6He asked me, "Son of man, do
you see this?"
Then he led me back to the bank of the river. 7When I arrived there, I saw a great number of trees on each side of the river. 8He said
to me, "This water flows toward the eastern region and goes down into the Arabah,[b] where
it enters the Sea.[c] When it empties into the
Sea,[c] the water there becomes fresh. 9Swarms
of living creatures will live wherever the river flows. There will be large numbers of fish,
because this water flows there and makes the
salt water fresh; so where the river flows everything will live. 10Fishermen will stand along
the shore; from En Gedi to En Eglaim there
will be places for spreading nets. The fish will
be of many kinds—like the fish of the Great
Sea.[d] 11But the swamps and marshes will not
become fresh; they will be left for salt. 12Fruit
trees of all kinds will grow on both banks of
the river. Their leaves will not wither, nor will
their fruit fail. Every month they will bear, because the water from the sanctuary flows to
them. Their fruit will serve for food and their
leaves for healing."

The Boundaries of the Land

13This is what the Sovereign LORD says:
"These are the boundaries by which you are to
divide the land for an inheritance among the
twelve tribes of Israel, with two portions for
Joseph. 14You are to divide it equally among
them. Because I swore with uplifted hand to
give it to your forefathers, this land will become your inheritance.

15"This is to be the boundary of the land:

"On the north side it will run from the
Great Sea by the Hethlon road past
Lebo[e] Hamath to Zedad, 16Berothah[f]
and Sibraim (which lies on the border
between Damascus and Hamath), as far
as Hazer Hatticon, which is on the border of Hauran. 17The boundary will extend from the sea to Hazar Enan,[g] along
the northern border of Damascus, with
the border of Hamath to the north. This
will be the north boundary.
18"On the east side the boundary will run between Hauran and Damascus, along the
Jordan between Gilead and the land of
Israel, to the eastern sea and as far as Tamar.[h] This will be the east boundary.
19"On the south side it will run from Tamar
as far as the waters of Meribah Kadesh,
then along the Wadi ⌞of Egypt⌟ to the
Great Sea. This will be the south boundary.
20"On the west side, the Great Sea will be the
boundary to a point opposite Lebo[i] Hamath. This will be the west boundary.

21"You are to distribute this land among
yourselves according to the tribes of Israel. 22You are to allot it as an inheritance for
yourselves and for the aliens who have settled
among you and who have children. You are to
consider them as native-born Israelites; along
with you they are to be allotted an inheritance
among the tribes of Israel. 23In whatever tribe
the alien settles, there you are to give him his
inheritance," declares the Sovereign LORD.

The Division of the Land

48 "These are the tribes, listed by name:
At the northern frontier, Dan will have
one portion; it will follow the Hethlon
road to Lebo[j] Hamath; Hazar Enan and the
northern border of Damascus next to Hamath
will be part of its border from the east side to
the west side.

---

[a] 3 That is, about 1,500 feet (about 450 meters) [b] 8 Or *the Jordan Valley* [c] 8 That is, the Dead Sea [d] 10 That is, the Mediterranean; also in verses 15, 19 and 20 [e] 15 Or *past the entrance to* [f] 15,16 See Septuagint and Ezekiel 48:1; Hebrew *road to go into Zedad, 16Hamath, Berothah* [g] 17 Hebrew *Enon*, a variant of *Enan* [h] 18 Septuagint and Syriac; Hebrew *Israel. You will measure to the eastern sea* [i] 20 Or *opposite the entrance to* [j] 1 Or *to the entrance to*

2“Asher will have one portion; it will border
the territory of Dan from east to west.
3“Naphtali will have one portion; it will
border the territory of Asher from east to
west.
4“Manasseh will have one portion; it will
border the territory of Naphtali from east to
west.
5“Ephraim will have one portion; it will
border the territory of Manasseh from east to
west.
6“Reuben will have one portion; it will
border the territory of Ephraim from east to
west.
7“Judah will have one portion; it will border the territory of Reuben from east to west.
8“Bordering the territory of Judah from east
to west will be the portion you are to present
as a special gift. It will be 25,000 cubits[a] wide,
and its length from east to west will equal one
of the tribal portions; the sanctuary will be in
the center of it.
9“The special portion you are to offer to the
LORD will be 25,000 cubits long and 10,000
cubits[b] wide. 10This will be the sacred portion
for the priests. It will be 25,000 cubits long on
the north side, 10,000 cubits wide on the west
side, 10,000 cubits wide on the east side and
25,000 cubits long on the south side. In the
center of it will be the sanctuary of the LORD.
11This will be for the consecrated priests, the
Zadokites, who were faithful in serving me
and did not go astray as the Levites did when
the Israelites went astray. 12It will be a special
gift to them from the sacred portion of the
land, a most holy portion, bordering the territory of the Levites.
13“Alongside the territory of the priests, the
Levites will have an allotment 25,000 cubits
long and 10,000 cubits wide. Its total length
will be 25,000 cubits and its width 10,000 cubits. 14They must not sell or exchange any of
it. This is the best of the land and must not
pass into other hands, because it is holy to the
LORD.
15“The remaining area, 5,000 cubits wide
and 25,000 cubits long, will be for the common use of the city, for houses and for pastureland. The city will be in the center of it
16and will have these measurements: the north
side 4,500 cubits, the south side 4,500 cubits,
the east side 4,500 cubits, and the west side
4,500 cubits. 17The pastureland for the city
will be 250 cubits on the north, 250 cubits on
the south, 250 cubits on the east, and 250 cubits on the west. 18What remains of the area,
bordering on the sacred portion and running
the length of it, will be 10,000 cubits on the
east side and 10,000 cubits on the west side.
Its produce will supply food for the workers of
the city. 19The workers from the city who farm
it will come from all the tribes of Israel. 20The
entire portion will be a square, 25,000 cubits
on each side. As a special gift you will set aside
the sacred portion, along with the property of
the city.
21“What remains on both sides of the area
formed by the sacred portion and the city
property will belong to the prince. It will extend eastward from the 25,000 cubits of the
sacred portion to the eastern border, and westward from the 25,000 cubits to the western
border. Both these areas running the length of
the tribal portions will belong to the prince,
and the sacred portion with the temple sanctuary will be in the center of them. 22So the
property of the Levites and the property of
the city will lie in the center of the area that
belongs to the prince. The area belonging to
the prince will lie between the border of Judah
and the border of Benjamin.
23“As for the rest of the tribes: Benjamin
will have one portion; it will extend from the
east side to the west side.
24“Simeon will have one portion; it will
border the territory of Benjamin from east to
west.
25“Issachar will have one portion; it will
border the territory of Simeon from east to
west.
26“Zebulun will have one portion; it will
border the territory of Issachar from east to
west.
27“Gad will have one portion; it will border
the territory of Zebulun from east to west.
28“The southern boundary of Gad will run
south from Tamar to the waters of Meribah
Kadesh, then along the Wadi ⌊of Egypt⌋ to the
Great Sea.[c]
29“This is the land you are to allot as an
inheritance to the tribes of Israel, and these
will be their portions,” declares the Sovereign
LORD.

The Gates of the City

30“These will be the exits of the city: Beginning on the north side, which is 4,500 cubits
long, 31the gates of the city will be named after the tribes of Israel. The three gates on the

[a] 8 That is, about 7 miles (about 12 kilometers) [b] 9 That is, about 3 miles (about 5 kilometers) [c] 28 That is, the Mediterranean

north side will be the gate of Reuben, the gate of Judah and the gate of Levi.

32 "On the east side, which is 4,500 cubits long, will be three gates: the gate of Joseph, the gate of Benjamin and the gate of Dan.

33 "On the south side, which measures 4,500 cubits, will be three gates: the gate of Simeon, the gate of Issachar and the gate of Zebulun.

34 "On the west side, which is 4,500 cubits long, will be three gates: the gate of Gad, the gate of Asher and the gate of Naphtali.

35 "The distance all around will be 18,000 cubits.

"And the name of the city from that time on will be:

THE LORD IS THERE."

DANIEL

Daniel

QUICK FACTS

AUTHOR Daniel

AUDIENCE Jewish exiles in Babylon and all of God's people

DATE About 530 B.C.

SETTING The Jews were captives in Babylon.

Daniel was part of the first group of captives taken from Jerusalem to Babylon in 605 B.C. Although he eventually became a high-ranking government official, he is first described as a young man who stuck to his principles against the challenges of notoriously cruel pagan rulers.

When King Nebuchadnezzar was disturbed by a dream, he demanded that someone recount the dream and explain its meaning. Only Daniel could do so, and, as a result, the king made Daniel one of his highest officials. Although he had close contact with several rulers, Daniel faithfully gave the credit and his allegiance to God alone, even when he knew it would cause him to be thrown to the lions.

At the end of the book, God gave Daniel a remarkable look into the future, to a time when God will bring all troubles to a close and establish his eternal reign over all kings and nations. With this perspective, we can learn from Daniel how to remain faithful to God and our spouses, no matter what the circumstances. We can also be confident that God guides and protects those who honor him.

Daniel's Training in Babylon

1 In the third year of the reign of Jehoiakim
king of Judah, Nebuchadnezzar king of
Babylon came to Jerusalem and besieged it.
2And the Lord delivered Jehoiakim king of Judah into his hand, along with some of the articles from the temple of God. These he carried
off to the temple of his god in Babylonia[a] and
put in the treasure house of his god.
3Then the king ordered Ashpenaz, chief of
his court officials, to bring in some of the Israelites from the royal family and the nobility— 4young men without any physical defect,
handsome, showing aptitude for every kind of
learning, well informed, quick to understand,
and qualified to serve in the king's palace. He
was to teach them the language and literature of the Babylonians.[b] 5The king assigned
them a daily amount of food and wine from
the king's table. They were to be trained for
three years, and after that they were to enter
the king's service.
6Among these were some from Judah: Daniel, Hananiah, Mishael and Azariah. 7The
chief official gave them new names: to Daniel, the name Belteshazzar; to Hananiah, Shadrach; to Mishael, Meshach; and to Azariah,
Abednego.
8But Daniel resolved not to defile himself
with the royal food and wine, and he asked
the chief official for permission not to defile
himself this way. 9Now God had caused the
official to show favor and sympathy to Daniel, 10but the official told Daniel, "I am afraid
of my lord the king, who has assigned your[c]
food and drink. Why should he see you looking worse than the other young men your age?
The king would then have my head because
of you."
11Daniel then said to the guard whom
the chief official had appointed over Daniel,
Hananiah, Mishael and Azariah, 12"Please
test your servants for ten days: Give us nothing but vegetables to eat and water to drink.
13Then compare our appearance with that of
the young men who eat the royal food, and
treat your servants in accordance with what
you see." 14So he agreed to this and tested
them for ten days.
15At the end of the ten days they looked
healthier and better nourished than any of the
young men who ate the royal food. 16So the
guard took away their choice food and the
wine they were to drink and gave them vegetables instead.
17To these four young men God gave
knowledge and understanding of all kinds of
literature and learning. And Daniel could understand visions and dreams of all kinds.
18At the end of the time set by the king
to bring them in, the chief official presented
them to Nebuchadnezzar. 19The king talked
with them, and he found none equal to Daniel, Hananiah, Mishael and Azariah; so they
entered the king's service. 20In every matter
of wisdom and understanding about which
the king questioned them, he found them ten
times better than all the magicians and enchanters in his whole kingdom.
21And Daniel remained there until the first
year of King Cyrus.

Nebuchadnezzar's Dream

2 In the second year of his reign, Nebuchadnezzar had dreams; his mind was troubled
and he could not sleep. 2So the king summoned the magicians, enchanters, sorcerers
and astrologers[d] to tell him what he had
dreamed. When they came in and stood before the king, 3he said to them, "I have had a
dream that troubles me and I want to know
what it means.[e]"
4Then the astrologers answered the king in
Aramaic,[f] "O king, live forever! Tell your servants the dream, and we will interpret it."
5The king replied to the astrologers, "This
is what I have firmly decided: If you do not
tell me what my dream was and interpret it, I
will have you cut into pieces and your houses
turned into piles of rubble. 6But if you tell me
the dream and explain it, you will receive from
me gifts and rewards and great honor. So tell
me the dream and interpret it for me."
7Once more they replied, "Let the king
tell his servants the dream, and we will interpret it."
8Then the king answered, "I am certain that
you are trying to gain time, because you realize that this is what I have firmly decided:
9If you do not tell me the dream, there is just
one penalty for you. You have conspired to
tell me misleading and wicked things, hoping
the situation will change. So then, tell me the
dream, and I will know that you can interpret
it for me."
10The astrologers answered the king, "There
is not a man on earth who can do what the

[a] 2 Hebrew *Shinar* [b] 4 Or *Chaldeans* [c] 10 The Hebrew for *your* and *you* in this verse is plural. [d] 2 Or *Chaldeans*; also in verses 4, 5 and 10 [e] 3 Or *was* [f] 4 The text from here through chapter 7 is in Aramaic.

WEDNESDAY
READ DANIEL 1:1–21

EATING RIGHT TOGETHER

If someone asked you if being married has changed you, you might have to admit, "Well, yes. My spouse helps me see things differently. She tells me when I'm messing up or getting out of line. He encourages me to try new things. She is helping me become a better person." So says Will Willimon, dean of Duke University Chapel in Durham, North Carolina (*Marriage Partnership*, Spring 1990).

Personal change, so important in marriage, is also a theme in the Old Testament. For example, in Exodus and Leviticus we read about a huge group of people, most of whom had been slaves all of their lives, who were taught how to become a holy people, dedicated to God. They had to change all kinds of attitudes and behaviors prior to their entry into the land that had been promised to them. Moses offered God's holiness plan to his people in laws that covered almost every aspect of life, from how to offer a sacrifice to God right down to changes in their dietary habits.

Those laws carried over to Babylon too, where God's children were taken captive because of their repeated sin and unfaithfulness. So it's a bit refreshing, in all that darkness, to learn about Daniel and his friends—good Jewish boys who were unwilling to give up their holy eating habits while being trained to serve in the king's palace. They politely refused to defile themselves with royal food and wine, choosing instead a simple diet of vegetables and water. And God honored them by making them look healthier and more nourished after ten days than those who ate the king's food.

God wasn't just being fussy in insisting that these young men eat only foods that were prepared according to Jewish dietary laws. He was showing them—and us—how to make a connection between spirit and body, between diet and health. He was teaching them how to be holy in every part of life.

Couples face big changes when they start eating together every day. They may face another huge adjustment if they have to adapt their eating habits to lose weight, lower cholesterol, control blood sugar or simply promote good health. Choosing what to eat—fried or broiled chicken, oatmeal or Cocoa Puffs, potato chips or vegetables—may be one of the most subtle yet important changes we have to make to sustain a long life together.

Daniel and his friends risked a king's wrath and possible death for choosing the way of holiness and health. What are we willing to give up to live right before God in every part of our lives, right down to what we put in our mouths?

—JOHN R. THROOP

"Please test your servants for ten days: Give us nothing but vegetables to eat and water to drink."

— DANIEL 1:12

let's talk

- How did dietary restrictions strengthen the relationship between God and his people?
- How has our relationship with God affected our marriage relationship in regard to personal habits, such as eating, exercising, getting enough sleep?
- Has being married to each other made each of us a better person—whether in diet or any other part of life? How?

FOR YOUR NEXT DEVOTIONAL READING, TURN TO PAGE 951.

king asks! No king, however great and mighty,
has ever asked such a thing of any magician or
enchanter or astrologer. 11What the king asks
is too difficult. No one can reveal it to the king
except the gods, and they do not live among
men."
12This made the king so angry and furious
that he ordered the execution of all the wise
men of Babylon. 13So the decree was issued
to put the wise men to death, and men were
sent to look for Daniel and his friends to put
them to death.
14When Arioch, the commander of the
king's guard, had gone out to put to death the
wise men of Babylon, Daniel spoke to him
with wisdom and tact. 15He asked the king's
officer, "Why did the king issue such a harsh
decree?" Arioch then explained the matter to
Daniel. 16At this, Daniel went in to the king
and asked for time, so that he might interpret
the dream for him.
17Then Daniel returned to his house and
explained the matter to his friends Hananiah, Mishael and Azariah. 18He urged them to
plead for mercy from the God of heaven concerning this mystery, so that he and his friends
might not be executed with the rest of the wise
men of Babylon. 19During the night the mystery was revealed to Daniel in a vision. Then
Daniel praised the God of heaven 20and said:

"Praise be to the name of God for ever and
ever;
wisdom and power are his.
21 He changes times and seasons;
he sets up kings and deposes them.
He gives wisdom to the wise
and knowledge to the discerning.
22 He reveals deep and hidden things;
he knows what lies in darkness,
and light dwells with him.
23 I thank and praise you, O God of my
fathers:
You have given me wisdom and power,
you have made known to me what we
asked of you,
you have made known to us the dream
of the king."

Daniel Interprets the Dream

24Then Daniel went to Arioch, whom the
king had appointed to execute the wise men
of Babylon, and said to him, "Do not execute
the wise men of Babylon. Take me to the king,
and I will interpret his dream for him."
25Arioch took Daniel to the king at once
and said, "I have found a man among the exiles from Judah who can tell the king what his
dream means."
26The king asked Daniel (also called Belteshazzar), "Are you able to tell me what I saw in
my dream and interpret it?"
27Daniel replied, "No wise man, enchanter, magician or diviner can explain to the king
the mystery he has asked about, 28but there
is a God in heaven who reveals mysteries. He
has shown King Nebuchadnezzar what will
happen in days to come. Your dream and the
visions that passed through your mind as you
lay on your bed are these:
29"As you were lying there, O king, your
mind turned to things to come, and the revealer of mysteries showed you what is going
to happen. 30As for me, this mystery has been
revealed to me, not because I have greater wisdom than other living men, but so that you,
O king, may know the interpretation and that
you may understand what went through your
mind.
31"You looked, O king, and there before
you stood a large statue—an enormous, daz-
zling statue, awesome in appearance. 32The
head of the statue was made of pure gold, its
chest and arms of silver, its belly and thighs of
bronze, 33its legs of iron, its feet partly of iron
and partly of baked clay. 34While you were
watching, a rock was cut out, but not by human hands. It struck the statue on its feet of
iron and clay and smashed them. 35Then the
iron, the clay, the bronze, the silver and the
gold were broken to pieces at the same time
and became like chaff on a threshing floor in
the summer. The wind swept them away without leaving a trace. But the rock that struck
the statue became a huge mountain and filled
the whole earth.
36"This was the dream, and now we will interpret it to the king. 37You, O king, are the
king of kings. The God of heaven has given
you dominion and power and might and glory; 38in your hands he has placed mankind
and the beasts of the field and the birds of the
air. Wherever they live, he has made you ruler
over them all. You are that head of gold.
39"After you, another kingdom will rise, inferior to yours. Next, a third kingdom, one of
bronze, will rule over the whole earth. 40Fi-
nally, there will be a fourth kingdom, strong
as iron—for iron breaks and smashes everything—and as iron breaks things to pieces, so
it will crush and break all the others. 41Just as
you saw that the feet and toes were partly of
baked clay and partly of iron, so this will be
a divided kingdom; yet it will have some of

the strength of iron in it, even as you saw iron
mixed with clay. 42As the toes were partly iron
and partly clay, so this kingdom will be partly
strong and partly brittle. 43And just as you saw
the iron mixed with baked clay, so the people
will be a mixture and will not remain united,
any more than iron mixes with clay.

44"In the time of those kings, the God of
heaven will set up a kingdom that will never
be destroyed, nor will it be left to another people. It will crush all those kingdoms and bring
them to an end, but it will itself endure forever. 45This is the meaning of the vision of the
rock cut out of a mountain, but not by human
hands—a rock that broke the iron, the bronze,
the clay, the silver and the gold to pieces.

"The great God has shown the king what
will take place in the future. The dream is true
and the interpretation is trustworthy."

46Then King Nebuchadnezzar fell prostrate
before Daniel and paid him honor and ordered that an offering and incense be presented to him. 47The king said to Daniel, "Surely
your God is the God of gods and the Lord of
kings and a revealer of mysteries, for you were
able to reveal this mystery."

48Then the king placed Daniel in a high
position and lavished many gifts on him. He
made him ruler over the entire province of
Babylon and placed him in charge of all its
wise men. 49Moreover, at Daniel's request the
king appointed Shadrach, Meshach and Abednego administrators over the province of Babylon, while Daniel himself remained at the
royal court.

The Image of Gold and the Fiery Furnace

3 King Nebuchadnezzar made an image of
gold, ninety feet high and nine feet[a] wide,
and set it up on the plain of Dura in the
province of Babylon. 2He then summoned the
satraps, prefects, governors, advisers, treasurers, judges, magistrates and all the other provincial officials to come to the dedication of
the image he had set up. 3So the satraps, prefects, governors, advisers, treasurers, judges,
magistrates and all the other provincial officials assembled for the dedication of the image that King Nebuchadnezzar had set up, and
they stood before it.

4Then the herald loudly proclaimed, "This
is what you are commanded to do, O peoples,
nations and men of every language: 5As soon
as you hear the sound of the horn, flute, zither, lyre, harp, pipes and all kinds of music, you
must fall down and worship the image of gold
that King Nebuchadnezzar has set up. 6Who-
ever does not fall down and worship will immediately be thrown into a blazing furnace."

7Therefore, as soon as they heard the sound
of the horn, flute, zither, lyre, harp and all
kinds of music, all the peoples, nations and
men of every language fell down and worshiped the image of gold that King Nebuchadnezzar had set up.

8At this time some astrologers[b] came forward and denounced the Jews. 9They said to
King Nebuchadnezzar, "O king, live forever!
10You have issued a decree, O king, that everyone who hears the sound of the horn, flute,
zither, lyre, harp, pipes and all kinds of music
must fall down and worship the image of gold,
11and that whoever does not fall down and
worship will be thrown into a blazing furnace.
12But there are some Jews whom you have set
over the affairs of the province of Babylon—
Shadrach, Meshach and Abednego—who pay
no attention to you, O king. They neither
serve your gods nor worship the image of gold
you have set up."

13Furious with rage, Nebuchadnezzar summoned Shadrach, Meshach and Abednego.
So these men were brought before the king,
14and Nebuchadnezzar said to them, "Is it
true, Shadrach, Meshach and Abednego, that
you do not serve my gods or worship the image of gold I have set up? 15Now when you
hear the sound of the horn, flute, zither, lyre,
harp, pipes and all kinds of music, if you are
ready to fall down and worship the image I
made, very good. But if you do not worship it,
you will be thrown immediately into a blazing
furnace. Then what god will be able to rescue
you from my hand?"

16Shadrach, Meshach and Abednego replied to the king, "O Nebuchadnezzar, we do
not need to defend ourselves before you in
this matter. 17If we are thrown into the blazing furnace, the God we serve is able to save
us from it, and he will rescue us from your
hand, O king. 18But even if he does not, we
want you to know, O king, that we will not
serve your gods or worship the image of gold
you have set up."

19Then Nebuchadnezzar was furious with
Shadrach, Meshach and Abednego, and his attitude toward them changed. He ordered the
furnace heated seven times hotter than usual
20and commanded some of the strongest soldiers in his army to tie up Shadrach, Meshach

---

[a] *1* Aramaic *sixty cubits high and six cubits wide* (about 27 meters high and 2.7 meters wide) [b] *8* Or *Chaldeans*

messengers, the holy ones declare the
verdict, so that the living may know that
the Most High is sovereign over the kingdoms of men and gives them to anyone
he wishes and sets over them the lowliest
of men.'
[18]"This is the dream that I, King Nebuchadnezzar, had. Now, Belteshazzar, tell
me what it means, for none of the wise
men in my kingdom can interpret it for
me. But you can, because the spirit of the
holy gods is in you."

Daniel Interprets the Dream

[19]Then Daniel (also called Belteshazzar) was greatly perplexed for a time, and
his thoughts terrified him. So the king
said, "Belteshazzar, do not let the dream
or its meaning alarm you."

Belteshazzar answered, "My lord, if
only the dream applied to your enemies and its meaning to your adversaries! [20]The tree you saw, which grew large
and strong, with its top touching the sky,
visible to the whole earth, [21]with beautiful leaves and abundant fruit, providing
food for all, giving shelter to the beasts
of the field, and having nesting places
in its branches for the birds of the air—
[22]you, O king, are that tree! You have become great and strong; your greatness has
grown until it reaches the sky, and your
dominion extends to distant parts of the
earth.
[23]"You, O king, saw a messenger, a
holy one, coming down from heaven and
saying, 'Cut down the tree and destroy
it, but leave the stump, bound with iron
and bronze, in the grass of the field, while
its roots remain in the ground. Let him
be drenched with the dew of heaven; let
him live like the wild animals, until seven
times pass by for him.'
[24]"This is the interpretation, O king,
and this is the decree the Most High has
issued against my lord the king: [25]You
will be driven away from people and will
live with the wild animals; you will eat
grass like cattle and be drenched with the
dew of heaven. Seven times will pass by
for you until you acknowledge that the
Most High is sovereign over the kingdoms of men and gives them to anyone
he wishes. [26]The command to leave the
stump of the tree with its roots means
that your kingdom will be restored to
you when you acknowledge that Heaven
rules. [27]Therefore, O king, be pleased to
accept my advice: Renounce your sins by
doing what is right, and your wickedness
by being kind to the oppressed. It may be
that then your prosperity will continue."

The Dream Is Fulfilled

[28]All this happened to King Nebuchadnezzar. [29]Twelve months later, as the
king was walking on the roof of the royal
palace of Babylon, [30]he said, "Is not this
the great Babylon I have built as the royal
residence, by my mighty power and for
the glory of my majesty?"
[31]The words were still on his lips when
a voice came from heaven, "This is what
is decreed for you, King Nebuchadnezzar:
Your royal authority has been taken from
you. [32]You will be driven away from people and will live with the wild animals;
you will eat grass like cattle. Seven times
will pass by for you until you acknowledge that the Most High is sovereign over
the kingdoms of men and gives them to
anyone he wishes."
[33]Immediately what had been said
about Nebuchadnezzar was fulfilled. He
was driven away from people and ate
grass like cattle. His body was drenched
with the dew of heaven until his hair
grew like the feathers of an eagle and his
nails like the claws of a bird.
[34]At the end of that time, I, Nebuchadnezzar, raised my eyes toward heav-
en, and my sanity was restored. Then I
praised the Most High; I honored and
glorified him who lives forever.

His dominion is an eternal dominion;
his kingdom endures from generation
to generation.
[35]All the peoples of the earth
are regarded as nothing.
He does as he pleases
with the powers of heaven
and the peoples of the earth.
No one can hold back his hand
or say to him: "What have you done?"

[36]At the same time that my sanity was
restored, my honor and splendor were returned to me for the glory of my kingdom. My advisers and nobles sought me
out, and I was restored to my throne and
became even greater than before. [37]Now
I, Nebuchadnezzar, praise and exalt and
glorify the King of heaven, because every-

thing he does is right and all his ways are
just. And those who walk in pride he is
able to humble.

The Writing on the Wall

5 King Belshazzar gave a great banquet for
a thousand of his nobles and drank wine
with them. 2While Belshazzar was drinking his wine, he gave orders to bring in the
gold and silver goblets that Nebuchadnezzar
his father[a] had taken from the temple in Jerusalem, so that the king and his nobles, his
wives and his concubines might drink from
them. 3So they brought in the gold goblets
that had been taken from the temple of God
in Jerusalem, and the king and his nobles, his
wives and his concubines drank from them.
4As they drank the wine, they praised the gods
of gold and silver, of bronze, iron, wood and
stone.

5Suddenly the fingers of a human hand appeared and wrote on the plaster of the wall,
near the lampstand in the royal palace. The
king watched the hand as it wrote. 6His face
turned pale and he was so frightened that his
knees knocked together and his legs gave way.

7The king called out for the enchanters, astrologers[b] and diviners to be brought and said
to these wise men of Babylon, "Whoever reads
this writing and tells me what it means will be
clothed in purple and have a gold chain placed
around his neck, and he will be made the third
highest ruler in the kingdom."

8Then all the king's wise men came in, but
they could not read the writing or tell the king
what it meant. 9So King Belshazzar became
even more terrified and his face grew more
pale. His nobles were baffled.

10The queen,[c] hearing the voices of the
king and his nobles, came into the banquet
hall. "O king, live forever!" she said. "Don't
be alarmed! Don't look so pale! 11There is a
man in your kingdom who has the spirit of
the holy gods in him. In the time of your father he was found to have insight and intelligence and wisdom like that of the gods. King
Nebuchadnezzar your father—your father the
king, I say—appointed him chief of the magicians, enchanters, astrologers and diviners.
12This man Daniel, whom the king called Belteshazzar, was found to have a keen mind and
knowledge and understanding, and also the
ability to interpret dreams, explain riddles and
solve difficult problems. Call for Daniel, and
he will tell you what the writing means."

13So Daniel was brought before the king,
and the king said to him, "Are you Daniel,
one of the exiles my father the king brought
from Judah? 14I have heard that the spirit of
the gods is in you and that you have insight,
intelligence and outstanding wisdom. 15The
wise men and enchanters were brought before
me to read this writing and tell me what it
means, but they could not explain it. 16Now
I have heard that you are able to give interpretations and to solve difficult problems. If
you can read this writing and tell me what it
means, you will be clothed in purple and have
a gold chain placed around your neck, and
you will be made the third highest ruler in the
kingdom."

17Then Daniel answered the king, "You
may keep your gifts for yourself and give your
rewards to someone else. Nevertheless, I will
read the writing for the king and tell him what
it means.

18"O king, the Most High God gave your
father Nebuchadnezzar sovereignty and greatness and glory and splendor. 19Because of the
high position he gave him, all the peoples and
nations and men of every language dreaded
and feared him. Those the king wanted to put
to death, he put to death; those he wanted to
spare, he spared; those he wanted to promote,
he promoted; and those he wanted to humble,
he humbled. 20But when his heart became arrogant and hardened with pride, he was deposed from his royal throne and stripped of
his glory. 21He was driven away from people
and given the mind of an animal; he lived
with the wild donkeys and ate grass like cattle;
and his body was drenched with the dew of
heaven, until he acknowledged that the Most
High God is sovereign over the kingdoms of
men and sets over them anyone he wishes.

22"But you his son,[d] O Belshazzar, have not
humbled yourself, though you knew all this.
23Instead, you have set yourself up against the
Lord of heaven. You had the goblets from his
temple brought to you, and you and your nobles, your wives and your concubines drank
wine from them. You praised the gods of silver and gold, of bronze, iron, wood and stone,
which cannot see or hear or understand. But
you did not honor the God who holds in his
hand your life and all your ways. 24Therefore
he sent the hand that wrote the inscription.

25"This is the inscription that was written:

MENE, MENE, TEKEL, PARSIN[e]

---

[a] 2 Or *ancestor*; or *predecessor*; also in verses 11, 13 and 18 [b] 7 Or *Chaldeans*; also in verse 11 [c] 10 Or *queen mother*
[d] 22 Or *descendant*; or *successor* [e] 25 Aramaic *UPARSIN* (that is, *AND PARSIN*)

26"This is what these words mean:

Mene[a]: God has numbered the days of your reign and brought it to an end.
27 *Tekel*[b]: You have been weighed on the scales and found wanting.
28 *Peres*[c]: Your kingdom is divided and given to the Medes and Persians."

29Then at Belshazzar's command, Daniel was clothed in purple, a gold chain was placed around his neck, and he was proclaimed the third highest ruler in the kingdom.

30That very night Belshazzar, king of the Babylonians,[d] was slain, 31and Darius the Mede took over the kingdom, at the age of sixty-two.

Daniel in the Den of Lions

6 It pleased Darius to appoint 120 satraps to rule throughout the kingdom, 2with three administrators over them, one of whom was Daniel. The satraps were made accountable to them so that the king might not suffer loss. 3Now Daniel so distinguished himself among the administrators and the satraps by his exceptional qualities that the king planned to set him over the whole kingdom. 4At this, the administrators and the satraps tried to find grounds for charges against Daniel in his conduct of government affairs, but they were unable to do so. They could find no corruption in him, because he was trustworthy and neither corrupt nor negligent. 5Finally these men said, "We will never find any basis for charges against this man Daniel unless it has something to do with the law of his God."

6So the administrators and the satraps went as a group to the king and said: "O King Darius, live forever! 7The royal administrators, prefects, satraps, advisers and governors have all agreed that the king should issue an edict and enforce the decree that anyone who prays to any god or man during the next thirty days, except to you, O king, shall be thrown into the lions' den. 8Now, O king, issue the decree and put it in writing so that it cannot be altered—in accordance with the laws of the Medes and Persians, which cannot be repealed." 9So King Darius put the decree in writing.

10Now when Daniel learned that the decree had been published, he went home to his upstairs room where the windows opened toward Jerusalem. Three times a day he got down on his knees and prayed, giving thanks to his God, just as he had done before. 11Then these men went as a group and found Daniel praying and asking God for help. 12So they went to the king and spoke to him about his royal decree: "Did you not publish a decree that during the next thirty days anyone who prays to any god or man except to you, O king, would be thrown into the lions' den?"

The king answered, "The decree stands—in accordance with the laws of the Medes and Persians, which cannot be repealed."

13Then they said to the king, "Daniel, who is one of the exiles from Judah, pays no attention to you, O king, or to the decree you put in writing. He still prays three times a day." 14When the king heard this, he was greatly distressed; he was determined to rescue Daniel and made every effort until sundown to save him.

15Then the men went as a group to the king and said to him, "Remember, O king, that according to the law of the Medes and Persians no decree or edict that the king issues can be changed."

16So the king gave the order, and they brought Daniel and threw him into the lions' den. The king said to Daniel, "May your God, whom you serve continually, rescue you!"

17A stone was brought and placed over the mouth of the den, and the king sealed it with his own signet ring and with the rings of his nobles, so that Daniel's situation might not be changed. 18Then the king returned to his palace and spent the night without eating and without any entertainment being brought to him. And he could not sleep.

19At the first light of dawn, the king got up and hurried to the lions' den. 20When he came near the den, he called to Daniel in an anguished voice, "Daniel, servant of the living God, has your God, whom you serve continually, been able to rescue you from the lions?"

21Daniel answered, "O king, live forever! 22My God sent his angel, and he shut the mouths of the lions. They have not hurt me, because I was found innocent in his sight. Nor have I ever done any wrong before you, O king."

23The king was overjoyed and gave orders to lift Daniel out of the den. And when Daniel

[a] 26 *Mene* can mean *numbered* or *mina* (a unit of money). [b] 27 *Tekel* can mean *weighed* or *shekel.* [c] 28 *Peres* (the singular of *Parsin*) can mean *divided* or *Persia* or *a half mina* or *a half shekel.* [d] 30 Or *Chaldeans*

FRIDAY

READ DANIEL 6:1–28

HOLY HABITS UNDER PRESSURE

Some years ago a major research firm conducted a survey to determine what people would be willing to do for ten million dollars. The results were astounding:

3 percent would put their children up for adoption
7 percent would kill a stranger
16 percent would divorce their spouses
25 percent would leave their families

We all apparently have our selling price. It might be ten million dollars or only a bottle of wine. Our selling price is linked to our identity; the deeper our character, the higher our selling price.

Daniel was a foreigner in a strange land, and there were many officials who wished to define his identity for him. Yet he tenaciously clung to the rituals that helped define his truest self as a child of God. Daniel would not sell himself short, even when the pressure was on. He continued to get down on his knees three times a day, giving thanks to God, even when he knew the penalty for doing so was being torn apart by hungry lions. He knew that without God he was nothing.

When a ship is built, each part has a voice of its own. As seamen walk through the new ship, they can almost hear the creaking whispers: "I am a rivet!" "I am a sheet of steel!" "I am a propeller!" "I am a beam!" For a while these little voices sing their individual songs, proudly independent and fiercely self-protective.

But then a storm blows in on the high seas. The waves toss, the gales hurl and the rains beat. If the parts of the ship tried to withstand the pummeling independent from one another, each would be lost. On the bridge, however, stands the captain. He issues orders that take all of the little voices and bring them together for a larger purpose. By the time the vessel has weathered the storm, sailors sense a new and deeper song echoing from stem to stern: "I am a ship!"

Our Captain calls each of us, especially in marriage, to a greater purpose than furthering ourselves. Answering that call is a top priority for our lives, as Daniel knew. Those who hear the Captain's call are able to sail true and straight. And those who have that strong sense of service and self-awareness are able to give out of that fullness to the Lord, to marriage and to others.

—WAYNE BROUWER

FOR YOUR NEXT DEVOTIONAL READING, TURN TO PAGE 960.

Now when Daniel learned that the decree had been published, he went home to his upstairs room where the windows opened toward Jerusalem. Three times a day he got down on his knees and prayed, giving thanks to his God, just as he had done before.

— DANIEL 6:10

let's *talk*

✦ What kind of home life might have created in Daniel the strength of character he displayed for a lifetime, even in adverse conditions?

✦ What habits of faith and its expressions are routine and meaningless in our lives? Which ritual practices do we do mainly for others?

✦ What habits might be good to develop to grow our relationship?

was lifted from the den, no wound was found
on him, because he had trusted in his God.
24 At the king's command, the men who had
falsely accused Daniel were brought in and
thrown into the lions' den, along with their
wives and children. And before they reached
the floor of the den, the lions overpowered
them and crushed all their bones.
25 Then King Darius wrote to all the peoples, nations and men of every language
throughout the land:

"May you prosper greatly!

26 "I issue a decree that in every part of
my kingdom people must fear and reverence the God of Daniel.

"For he is the living God
and he endures forever;
his kingdom will not be destroyed,
his dominion will never end.
27 He rescues and he saves;
he performs signs and wonders
in the heavens and on the earth.
He has rescued Daniel
from the power of the lions."

28 So Daniel prospered during the reign of
Darius and the reign of Cyrus[a] the Persian.

Daniel's Dream of Four Beasts

7 In the first year of Belshazzar king of Babylon, Daniel had a dream, and visions
passed through his mind as he was lying
on his bed. He wrote down the substance of
his dream.
2 Daniel said: "In my vision at night I
looked, and there before me were the four
winds of heaven churning up the great sea.
3 Four great beasts, each different from the
others, came up out of the sea.
4 "The first was like a lion, and it had the
wings of an eagle. I watched until its wings
were torn off and it was lifted from the ground
so that it stood on two feet like a man, and the
heart of a man was given to it.
5 "And there before me was a second beast,
which looked like a bear. It was raised up on
one of its sides, and it had three ribs in its
mouth between its teeth. It was told, 'Get up
and eat your fill of flesh!'
6 "After that, I looked, and there before me
was another beast, one that looked like a leopard. And on its back it had four wings like
those of a bird. This beast had four heads, and
it was given authority to rule.
7 "After that, in my vision at night I
looked, and there before me was a fourth
beast—terrifying and frightening and very
powerful. It had large iron teeth; it crushed
and devoured its victims and trampled underfoot whatever was left. It was different from all
the former beasts, and it had ten horns.
8 "While I was thinking about the horns,
there before me was another horn, a little one,
which came up among them; and three of the
first horns were uprooted before it. This horn
had eyes like the eyes of a man and a mouth
that spoke boastfully.
9 "As I looked,

"thrones were set in place,
and the Ancient of Days took his seat.
His clothing was as white as snow;
the hair of his head was white like
wool.
His throne was flaming with fire,
and its wheels were all ablaze.
10 A river of fire was flowing,
coming out from before him.
Thousands upon thousands attended him;
ten thousand times ten thousand stood
before him.
The court was seated,
and the books were opened.

11 "Then I continued to watch because of
the boastful words the horn was speaking. I
kept looking until the beast was slain and its
body destroyed and thrown into the blazing
fire. 12 (The other beasts had been stripped of
their authority, but were allowed to live for a
period of time.)
13 "In my vision at night I looked, and there
before me was one like a son of man, coming
with the clouds of heaven. He approached the
Ancient of Days and was led into his presence.
14 He was given authority, glory and sovereign
power; all peoples, nations and men of every
language worshiped him. His dominion is an
everlasting dominion that will not pass away,
and his kingdom is one that will never be destroyed.

The Interpretation of the Dream

15 "I, Daniel, was troubled in spirit, and
the visions that passed through my mind disturbed me. 16 I approached one of those standing there and asked him the true meaning of
all this.
"So he told me and gave me the interpretation of these things: 17 'The four great beasts

[a] 28 Or *Darius, that is, the reign of Cyrus*

are four kingdoms that will rise from the earth. [18]But the saints of the Most High will receive the kingdom and will possess it forever—yes, for ever and ever.'

[19]"Then I wanted to know the true meaning of the fourth beast, which was different from all the others and most terrifying, with its iron teeth and bronze claws—the beast that crushed and devoured its victims and trampled underfoot whatever was left. [20]I also wanted to know about the ten horns on its head and about the other horn that came up, before which three of them fell—the horn that looked more imposing than the others and that had eyes and a mouth that spoke boastfully. [21]As I watched, this horn was waging war against the saints and defeating them, [22]until the Ancient of Days came and pronounced judgment in favor of the saints of the Most High, and the time came when they possessed the kingdom.

[23]"He gave me this explanation: 'The fourth beast is a fourth kingdom that will appear on earth. It will be different from all the other kingdoms and will devour the whole earth, trampling it down and crushing it. [24]The ten horns are ten kings who will come from this kingdom. After them another king will arise, different from the earlier ones; he will subdue three kings. [25]He will speak against the Most High and oppress his saints and try to change the set times and the laws. The saints will be handed over to him for a time, times and half a time.[a]

[26]" 'But the court will sit, and his power will be taken away and completely destroyed forever. [27]Then the sovereignty, power and greatness of the kingdoms under the whole heaven will be handed over to the saints, the people of the Most High. His kingdom will be an everlasting kingdom, and all rulers will worship and obey him.'

[28]"This is the end of the matter. I, Daniel, was deeply troubled by my thoughts, and my face turned pale, but I kept the matter to myself."

Daniel's Vision of a Ram and a Goat

8 In the third year of King Belshazzar's reign, I, Daniel, had a vision, after the one that had already appeared to me. [2]In my vision I saw myself in the citadel of Susa in the province of Elam; in the vision I was beside the Ulai Canal. [3]I looked up, and there before me was a ram with two horns, standing beside the canal, and the horns were long. One of the horns was longer than the other but grew up later. [4]I watched the ram as he charged toward the west and the north and the south. No animal could stand against him, and none could rescue from his power. He did as he pleased and became great.

[5]As I was thinking about this, suddenly a goat with a prominent horn between his eyes came from the west, crossing the whole earth without touching the ground. [6]He came toward the two-horned ram I had seen standing beside the canal and charged at him in great rage. [7]I saw him attack the ram furiously, striking the ram and shattering his two horns. The ram was powerless to stand against him; the goat knocked him to the ground and trampled on him, and none could rescue the ram from his power. [8]The goat became very great, but at the height of his power his large horn was broken off, and in its place four prominent horns grew up toward the four winds of heaven.

[9]Out of one of them came another horn, which started small but grew in power to the south and to the east and toward the Beautiful Land. [10]It grew until it reached the host of the heavens, and it threw some of the starry host down to the earth and trampled on them. [11]It set itself up to be as great as the Prince of the host; it took away the daily sacrifice from him, and the place of his sanctuary was brought low. [12]Because of rebellion, the host ⌊of the saints⌋[b] and the daily sacrifice were given over to it. It prospered in everything it did, and truth was thrown to the ground.

[13]Then I heard a holy one speaking, and another holy one said to him, "How long will it take for the vision to be fulfilled—the vision concerning the daily sacrifice, the rebellion that causes desolation, and the surrender of the sanctuary and of the host that will be trampled underfoot?"

[14]He said to me, "It will take 2,300 evenings and mornings; then the sanctuary will be reconsecrated."

The Interpretation of the Vision

[15]While I, Daniel, was watching the vision and trying to understand it, there before me stood one who looked like a man. [16]And I heard a man's voice from the Ulai calling, "Gabriel, tell this man the meaning of the vision."

[17]As he came near the place where I was standing, I was terrified and fell prostrate.

[a] 25 Or *for a year, two years and half a year* [b] 12 Or *rebellion, the armies*

"Son of man," he said to me, "understand that
the vision concerns the time of the end."
18While he was speaking to me, I was in a
deep sleep, with my face to the ground. Then
he touched me and raised me to my feet.
19He said: "I am going to tell you what
will happen later in the time of wrath, because the vision concerns the appointed time
of the end.[a] 20The two-horned ram that you
saw represents the kings of Media and Persia. 21The shaggy goat is the king of Greece,
and the large horn between his eyes is the first
king. 22The four horns that replaced the one
that was broken off represent four kingdoms
that will emerge from his nation but will not
have the same power.
23"In the latter part of their reign, when
rebels have become completely wicked, a
stern-faced king, a master of intrigue, will
arise. 24He will become very strong, but not
by his own power. He will cause astounding
devastation and will succeed in whatever he
does. He will destroy the mighty men and the
holy people. 25He will cause deceit to prosper,
and he will consider himself superior. When
they feel secure, he will destroy many and take
his stand against the Prince of princes. Yet he
will be destroyed, but not by human power.
26"The vision of the evenings and mornings
that has been given you is true, but seal up the
vision, for it concerns the distant future."
27I, Daniel, was exhausted and lay ill for
several days. Then I got up and went about the
king's business. I was appalled by the vision; it
was beyond understanding.

Daniel's Prayer

9 In the first year of Darius son of Xerxes[b]
(a Mede by descent), who was made ruler
over the Babylonian[c] kingdom— 2in the
first year of his reign, I, Daniel, understood
from the Scriptures, according to the word of
the LORD given to Jeremiah the prophet, that
the desolation of Jerusalem would last seventy
years. 3So I turned to the Lord God and pleaded with him in prayer and petition, in fasting,
and in sackcloth and ashes.
4I prayed to the LORD my God and confessed:

"O Lord, the great and awesome God,
who keeps his covenant of love with all
who love him and obey his commands,
5we have sinned and done wrong. We
have been wicked and have rebelled; we
have turned away from your commands
and laws. 6We have not listened to your
servants the prophets, who spoke in your
name to our kings, our princes and our
fathers, and to all the people of the land.
7"Lord, you are righteous, but this day
we are covered with shame—the men of
Judah and people of Jerusalem and all Israel, both near and far, in all the countries
where you have scattered us because of
our unfaithfulness to you. 8O LORD, we
and our kings, our princes and our fathers
are covered with shame because we have
sinned against you. 9The Lord our God
is merciful and forgiving, even though
we have rebelled against him; 10we have
not obeyed the LORD our God or kept
the laws he gave us through his servants
the prophets. 11All Israel has transgressed
your law and turned away, refusing to
obey you.
"Therefore the curses and sworn judgments written in the Law of Moses, the
servant of God, have been poured out
on us, because we have sinned against
you. 12You have fulfilled the words spoken against us and against our rulers by
bringing upon us great disaster. Under
the whole heaven nothing has ever been
done like what has been done to Jerusalem. 13Just as it is written in the Law of
Moses, all this disaster has come upon
us, yet we have not sought the favor of
the LORD our God by turning from our
sins and giving attention to your truth.
14The LORD did not hesitate to bring the
disaster upon us, for the LORD our God
is righteous in everything he does; yet we
have not obeyed him.
15"Now, O Lord our God, who
brought your people out of Egypt with a
mighty hand and who made for yourself
a name that endures to this day, we have
sinned, we have done wrong. 16O Lord,
in keeping with all your righteous acts,
turn away your anger and your wrath
from Jerusalem, your city, your holy hill.
Our sins and the iniquities of our fathers
have made Jerusalem and your people an
object of scorn to all those around us.
17"Now, our God, hear the prayers and
petitions of your servant. For your sake,
O Lord, look with favor on your desolate sanctuary. 18Give ear, O God, and
hear; open your eyes and see the desolation of the city that bears your Name. We

[a] *19* Or *because the end will be at the appointed time* [b] *1* Hebrew *Ahasuerus* [c] *1* Or *Chaldean*

WEEKEND

the Bible on sex

God is the creator of sex. He set our human drives in motion, not to torture men and women, but to bring them enjoyment and fulfillment. Keep in mind how it all came about. Adam was unfulfilled in the Garden of Eden. Although he lived in the world's most beautiful garden, surrounded by tame animals of every sort, he had no companionship with his own kind. God then took some flesh from Adam and performed another creative miracle—woman—similar to man in every respect except her physical reproductive system. Instead of being opposites they were complementary to each other.

For further proof that God approves lovemaking between married partners, consider the beautiful story that explains its origin. Of all God's creations only the human being was made "in the image of God" (Genesis 1:27). This in itself makes humans the unique living creatures on the earth. The next verse further states, "God blessed them and said to them, 'Be fruitful and increase in number'" (verse 28). Then He delivered His personal comment regarding all His creation: "God saw all that he had made, and it was very good" (verse 31).

Genesis 2 affords a more detailed description of God's creation of Adam and Eve, including the statement that God Himself brought Eve to Adam (verse 22), evidently to introduce them formally and give them the command to be fruitful. Then it beautifully describes their innocence with these words: "The man and his wife were both naked, and they felt no shame" (verse 25). Adam and Eve knew no shame on that occasion for three reasons: they were introduced by a holy and righteous God who commanded them to make love; their minds were not preconditioned to guilt, for no prohibitions concerning the act of marriage had yet been given; and no other people were around to observe their intimate relations.

Interestingly enough, the best lovemaking in the world is not limited to beautiful people with perfectly sculpted bodies. It is at its best when two healthy lovers, more interested in satisfying their partner's needs than their own, approach their marriage bed without guilt. That is why virtue is the best preparation for marriage, and why faithfulness throughout the relationship is so enriching. God's plan was for one man and one woman to share the ecstasy of that experience only with each other.

Some people have the strange idea that anything spiritually acceptable to God cannot be enjoyable. In recent years we have found great success in counseling married couples to pray together regularly. The book *How to Be Happy Though Married* describes a particular method for conversational prayer that we have found most helpful, and we frequently suggest this procedure because of its variety and practicality. Through the years many couples have tried it and reported remarkable results.

One emotional, outgoing young wife who exclaimed that prayer had changed their relationship also confided, "The main reason I was reluctant to pray with my husband before going to bed was that I feared it would hinder lovemaking. But to my amazement, I found we were so emotionally close after prayer that it set the stage for loving." Her experience is not rare; in fact, we have found no reason why a couple cannot pray before or after a spirited time of loving. However, most couples find themselves so relaxed afterward that all they want to do is sleep—the sleep of contentment.

—TIM AND BEVERLY LAHAYE

can you talk about sex?

We get ideas about sex from our parents, our church upbringing, the Bible and many other sources. Occasionally people learn to feel guilty about certain aspects of sex. This guilt causes them to keep things bottled up inside, fearful of expressing their thoughts or needs to their partner. Are you comfortable talking about sex? Take this quiz, and then discuss your responses with your spouse. Are you comfortable or uncomfortable . . .

1. Talking to my spouse about my sexual needs
2. Discussing what gets me excited sexually
3. Talking to my spouse about sexual problems
4. Conversing about sex in general
5. Letting my spouse initiate sex
6. Asking my spouse what is uncomfortable sexually for him or her
7. Discussing my anatomy with my doctor or other healthcare professional
8. Praying before sex
9. Initiating foreplay
10. Talking about sex after sex
11. Telling my spouse what I don't like sexually
12. Talking to a pastor or marriage counselor about sexual problems
13. Asking my spouse what is pleasurable to him or her
14. Hearing about my spouse's past sexual behavior
15. Discussing birth control options
16. Talking about sex with my kids

HOW ARE WE DOING?

date

let's make a DATE

BREAKFAST IN BED

Who says you can only make love at night? Set an alarm for early on a Saturday morning. While your spouse makes breakfast, set the mood in the bedroom by putting on music, lighting a few candles or changing into something your partner finds appealing. When the food is ready, take turns feeding each other in bed . . . then feeding each others' sexual needs. Bon appétit!

FOR YOUR NEXT DEVOTIONAL READING, TURN TO PAGE 963.

LESSONS FROM THE *Bible*

What can we learn about sexual interaction from the following couples? Is it all about procreation, or are romance, pleasuring each other and foreplay involved as well? How does fidelity and trust affect lovemaking?

1. Adam and Eve (Genesis 2:22–25)
2. The two lovers (Song of Songs 7:1–13)

do not make requests of you because we
are righteous, but because of your great
mercy. 19 O Lord, listen! O Lord, forgive! O Lord, hear and act! For your sake,
O my God, do not delay, because your
city and your people bear your Name."

The Seventy "Sevens"

20 While I was speaking and praying, confessing my sin and the sin of my people Israel and making my request to the LORD my
God for his holy hill— 21 while I was still in
prayer, Gabriel, the man I had seen in the earlier vision, came to me in swift flight about the
time of the evening sacrifice. 22 He instructed
me and said to me, "Daniel, I have now come
to give you insight and understanding. 23 As
soon as you began to pray, an answer was giv-
en, which I have come to tell you, for you are
highly esteemed. Therefore, consider the message and understand the vision:

24 "Seventy 'sevens'[a] are decreed for your
people and your holy city to finish[b] transgression, to put an end to sin, to atone for wickedness, to bring in everlasting righteousness,
to seal up vision and prophecy and to anoint
the most holy.[c]

25 "Know and understand this: From the
issuing of the decree[d] to restore and rebuild
Jerusalem until the Anointed One,[e] the ruler,
comes, there will be seven 'sevens,' and sixty-
two 'sevens.' It will be rebuilt with streets and
a trench, but in times of trouble. 26 After the
sixty-two 'sevens,' the Anointed One will be
cut off and will have nothing.[f] The people of
the ruler who will come will destroy the city
and the sanctuary. The end will come like a
flood: War will continue until the end, and
desolations have been decreed. 27 He will confirm a covenant with many for one 'seven.'[g] In
the middle of the 'seven'[g] he will put an end
to sacrifice and offering. And on a wing ⌊of
the temple⌋ he will set up an abomination that
causes desolation, until the end that is decreed
is poured out on him.[h]"[i]

Daniel's Vision of a Man

10 In the third year of Cyrus king of Persia,
a revelation was given to Daniel (who
was called Belteshazzar). Its message was
true and it concerned a great war.[j] The understanding of the message came to him in a
vision.

2 At that time I, Daniel, mourned for three
weeks. 3 I ate no choice food; no meat or wine
touched my lips; and I used no lotions at all
until the three weeks were over.

4 On the twenty-fourth day of the first
month, as I was standing on the bank of the
great river, the Tigris, 5 I looked up and there
before me was a man dressed in linen, with a
belt of the finest gold around his waist. 6 His
body was like chrysolite, his face like lightning, his eyes like flaming torches, his arms
and legs like the gleam of burnished bronze,
and his voice like the sound of a multitude.

7 I, Daniel, was the only one who saw the
vision; the men with me did not see it, but
such terror overwhelmed them that they fled
and hid themselves. 8 So I was left alone, gazing at this great vision; I had no strength left,
my face turned deathly pale and I was helpless.
9 Then I heard him speaking, and as I listened
to him, I fell into a deep sleep, my face to the
ground.

10 A hand touched me and set me trembling
on my hands and knees. 11 He said, "Daniel,
you who are highly esteemed, consider carefully the words I am about to speak to you,
and stand up, for I have now been sent to
you." And when he said this to me, I stood
up trembling.

12 Then he continued, "Do not be afraid,
Daniel. Since the first day that you set your
mind to gain understanding and to humble
yourself before your God, your words were
heard, and I have come in response to them.
13 But the prince of the Persian kingdom resisted me twenty-one days. Then Michael, one
of the chief princes, came to help me, because
I was detained there with the king of Persia.
14 Now I have come to explain to you what will
happen to your people in the future, for the
vision concerns a time yet to come."

15 While he was saying this to me, I bowed
with my face toward the ground and was
speechless. 16 Then one who looked like a
man[k] touched my lips, and I opened my
mouth and began to speak. I said to the one
standing before me, "I am overcome with anguish because of the vision, my lord, and I am
helpless. 17 How can I, your servant, talk with
you, my lord? My strength is gone and I can
hardly breathe."

18 Again the one who looked like a man
touched me and gave me strength. 19 "Do not

---

[a] *24* Or *'weeks'*; also in verses 25 and 26 [b] *24* Or *restrain* [c] *24* Or *Most Holy Place*; or *most holy One* [d] *25* Or *word* [e] *25* Or *an anointed one*; also in verse 26 [f] *26* Or *off and will have no one*; or *off, but not for himself* [g] *27* Or *'week'* [h] *27* Or *it* [i] *27* Or *And one who causes desolation will come upon the pinnacle of the abominable ⌊temple⌋, until the end that is decreed is poured out on the desolated ⌊city⌋* [j] *1* Or *true and burdensome* [k] *16* Most manuscripts of the Masoretic Text; one manuscript of the Masoretic Text, Dead Sea Scrolls and Septuagint *Then something that looked like a man's hand*

MONDAY
READ DANIEL 10:1—11:1

WHY SOME PRAYERS GO UNANSWERED

> **"Since the first day that you set your mind to gain understanding and to humble yourself before your God, your words were heard, and I have come in response to them."**
>
> — DANIEL 10:12

The Rinards noticed Chuck walking past their house to the little church in the next block. Chuck was only going to church to earn the Boy Scout's "God and Country Award"; as soon as the boy got the award, they knew he would quit going. But the Rinards decided to pray for Chuck. They prayed for a long time for his salvation, never knowing what happened.

Is there something for which you as a couple have been praying for a long time without receiving an answer? One man who prayed over a lifelong battle with sin wrote, "I can't tell you why a prayer prayed for ten years is answered on the 1,000th request when God has met the first 999 with silence."

Daniel 10 suggests one reason for the delay. Daniel was given a troubling, mysterious vision from the Lord, but he didn't understand what it meant. Daniel asked God to tell him what the vision meant, but no answer came. A week passed, then two, then three. For 21 days Daniel struggled in prayer over the tumultuous things he had seen but couldn't decipher.

Then finally he received a visitor, a mighty heavenly man who, though probably an angel, bore a striking resemblance to Christ as described in Revelation 1:12–16. The visitor explained to the trembling Daniel why the answer was so long in coming. This message was so important, so world changing, that the mighty, demonic "prince of the Persian kingdom" (Daniel 10:13) had resisted the visitor for 21 days.

We most likely have not received any visions of angelic visitors, but as we read about the spiritual battle detaining Daniel's messenger, we do get a glimpse of what happens "behind the curtain" in the unseen world of principalities and powers when we pray.

Our prayers seek to wrestle away from Satan something he desperately wants to control. Prayers that say to the Lord, "Your kingdom come, your will be done" are prayers that the devil will resist. When there is a delay, it is not because the request is too difficult or because the enemy is too strong, but because God is overcoming a web of satanic lies and control. Though the wait may be agonizing, our prayers somehow become part of the Almighty's weapons in pushing back the borders of his kingdom.

Chuck Sackett did a little yard work for the Rinards, but he never knew that the old couple was praying for him. Twelve years later, Chuck was converted and eventually became a pastor. While serving his first church in Indiana, he learned that Mr. and Mrs. Rinard were nearby in a nursing home. Out of respect for the family, Chuck and his wife decided to visit the couple. "I'll never forget what they said," Chuck said. "They asked, 'Do you remember when you used to walk to that little church? We've not missed one day since, praying that God would do something in your life.' "

There was no other Christian influence in Chuck Sackett's young life, so far as he knows, except for the unceasing, persistent prayers of the Rinards. As Daniel 10 suggests, their words were heard and God responded to them in his time.

—LEE ECLOV

let's talk

- What are we praying for that Satan is bound to resist?
- What lends potency to our prayers?
- What are some issues that God may be prompting us to pray for that would stymie the kingdom of darkness?

FOR YOUR NEXT DEVOTIONAL READING, TURN TO PAGE 969.

be afraid, O man highly esteemed," he said.
"Peace! Be strong now; be strong."
When he spoke to me, I was strengthened
and said, "Speak, my lord, since you have giv-
en me strength."
20 So he said, "Do you know why I have
come to you? Soon I will return to fight against
the prince of Persia, and when I go, the prince
of Greece will come; 21 but first I will tell you
what is written in the Book of Truth. (No one
supports me against them except Michael,
11 your prince. 1 And in the first year of Darius the Mede, I took my stand to support and protect him.)

The Kings of the South and the North

2 "Now then, I tell you the truth: Three
more kings will appear in Persia, and then a
fourth, who will be far richer than all the others. When he has gained power by his wealth,
he will stir up everyone against the kingdom
of Greece. 3 Then a mighty king will appear,
who will rule with great power and do as he
pleases. 4 After he has appeared, his empire
will be broken up and parceled out toward the
four winds of heaven. It will not go to his descendants, nor will it have the power he exercised, because his empire will be uprooted and
given to others.
5 "The king of the South will become strong,
but one of his commanders will become even
stronger than he and will rule his own kingdom with great power. 6 After some years, they
will become allies. The daughter of the king of
the South will go to the king of the North to
make an alliance, but she will not retain her
power, and he and his power[a] will not last. In
those days she will be handed over, together
with her royal escort and her father[b] and the
one who supported her.
7 "One from her family line will arise to take
her place. He will attack the forces of the king
of the North and enter his fortress; he will
fight against them and be victorious. 8 He will
also seize their gods, their metal images and
their valuable articles of silver and gold and
carry them off to Egypt. For some years he will
leave the king of the North alone. 9 Then the
king of the North will invade the realm of the
king of the South but will retreat to his own
country. 10 His sons will prepare for war and
assemble a great army, which will sweep on
like an irresistible flood and carry the battle as
far as his fortress.
11 "Then the king of the South will march
out in a rage and fight against the king of the
North, who will raise a large army, but it will
be defeated. 12 When the army is carried off,
the king of the South will be filled with pride
and will slaughter many thousands, yet he will
not remain triumphant. 13 For the king of the
North will muster another army, larger than
the first; and after several years, he will advance with a huge army fully equipped.
14 "In those times many will rise against the
king of the South. The violent men among
your own people will rebel in fulfillment of the
vision, but without success. 15 Then the king of
the North will come and build up siege ramps
and will capture a fortified city. The forces of
the South will be powerless to resist; even their
best troops will not have the strength to stand.
16 The invader will do as he pleases; no one will
be able to stand against him. He will establish
himself in the Beautiful Land and will have
the power to destroy it. 17 He will determine
to come with the might of his entire kingdom
and will make an alliance with the king of the
South. And he will give him a daughter in
marriage in order to overthrow the kingdom,
but his plans[c] will not succeed or help him.
18 Then he will turn his attention to the coastlands and will take many of them, but a commander will put an end to his insolence and
will turn his insolence back upon him. 19 After
this, he will turn back toward the fortresses of
his own country but will stumble and fall, to
be seen no more.
20 "His successor will send out a tax collector to maintain the royal splendor. In a few
years, however, he will be destroyed, yet not in
anger or in battle.
21 "He will be succeeded by a contemptible
person who has not been given the honor of
royalty. He will invade the kingdom when its
people feel secure, and he will seize it through
intrigue. 22 Then an overwhelming army will
be swept away before him; both it and a
prince of the covenant will be destroyed. 23 After coming to an agreement with him, he will
act deceitfully, and with only a few people he
will rise to power. 24 When the richest provinces feel secure, he will invade them and will
achieve what neither his fathers nor his forefathers did. He will distribute plunder, loot and
wealth among his followers. He will plot the
overthrow of fortresses—but only for a time.
25 "With a large army he will stir up his
strength and courage against the king of the
South. The king of the South will wage war

[a] *6* Or *offspring* [b] *6* Or *child* (see Vulgate and Syriac) [c] *17* Or *but she*

with a large and very powerful army, but he
will not be able to stand because of the plots
devised against him. 26 Those who eat from
the king's provisions will try to destroy him;
his army will be swept away, and many will
fall in battle. 27 The two kings, with their
hearts bent on evil, will sit at the same table
and lie to each other, but to no avail, because
an end will still come at the appointed time.
28 The king of the North will return to his own
country with great wealth, but his heart will
be set against the holy covenant. He will take
action against it and then return to his own
country.

29 “At the appointed time he will invade the
South again, but this time the outcome will
be different from what it was before. 30 Ships
of the western coastlands[a] will oppose him,
and he will lose heart. Then he will turn back
and vent his fury against the holy covenant.
He will return and show favor to those who
forsake the holy covenant.

31 “His armed forces will rise up to desecrate
the temple fortress and will abolish the daily
sacrifice. Then they will set up the abomination that causes desolation. 32 With flattery
he will corrupt those who have violated the
covenant, but the people who know their God
will firmly resist him.

33 “Those who are wise will instruct many,
though for a time they will fall by the sword or
be burned or captured or plundered. 34 When
they fall, they will receive a little help, and
many who are not sincere will join them.
35 Some of the wise will stumble, so that they
may be refined, purified and made spotless
until the time of the end, for it will still come
at the appointed time.

The King Who Exalts Himself

36 “The king will do as he pleases. He will
exalt and magnify himself above every god and
will say unheard-of things against the God of
gods. He will be successful until the time of
wrath is completed, for what has been determined must take place. 37 He will show no regard for the gods of his fathers or for the one
desired by women, nor will he regard any god,
but will exalt himself above them all. 38 Instead
of them, he will honor a god of fortresses; a
god unknown to his fathers he will honor with
gold and silver, with precious stones and costly
gifts. 39 He will attack the mightiest fortresses
with the help of a foreign god and will greatly honor those who acknowledge him. He will
make them rulers over many people and will
distribute the land at a price.[b]

40 “At the time of the end the king of the
South will engage him in battle, and the king
of the North will storm out against him with
chariots and cavalry and a great fleet of ships.
He will invade many countries and sweep
through them like a flood. 41 He will also invade the Beautiful Land. Many countries will
fall, but Edom, Moab and the leaders of Ammon will be delivered from his hand. 42 He
will extend his power over many countries;
Egypt will not escape. 43 He will gain control
of the treasures of gold and silver and all the
riches of Egypt, with the Libyans and Nubi-
ans in submission. 44 But reports from the east
and the north will alarm him, and he will set
out in a great rage to destroy and annihilate
many. 45 He will pitch his royal tents between
the seas at[c] the beautiful holy mountain. Yet
he will come to his end, and no one will help
him.

The End Times

12 “At that time Michael, the great prince
who protects your people, will arise.
There will be a time of distress such as
has not happened from the beginning of nations until then. But at that time your people—everyone whose name is found written
in the book—will be delivered. 2 Multitudes
who sleep in the dust of the earth will awake:
some to everlasting life, others to shame and
everlasting contempt. 3 Those who are wise[d]
will shine like the brightness of the heavens,
and those who lead many to righteousness,
like the stars for ever and ever. 4 But you, Daniel, close up and seal the words of the scroll
until the time of the end. Many will go here
and there to increase knowledge.”

5 Then I, Daniel, looked, and there before
me stood two others, one on this bank of the
river and one on the opposite bank. 6 One of
them said to the man clothed in linen, who
was above the waters of the river, “How long
will it be before these astonishing things are
fulfilled?”

7 The man clothed in linen, who was above
the waters of the river, lifted his right hand
and his left hand toward heaven, and I heard
him swear by him who lives forever, saying,
“It will be for a time, times and half a time.[e]
When the power of the holy people has been

---

[a] 30 Hebrew *of Kittim* [b] 39 Or *land for a reward* [c] 45 Or *the sea and* [d] 3 Or *who impart wisdom* [e] 7 Or *a year, two years and half a year*

finally broken, all these things will be completed."
8I heard, but I did not understand. So I
asked, "My lord, what will the outcome of all
this be?"
9He replied, "Go your way, Daniel, because the words are closed up and sealed until
the time of the end. 10Many will be purified,
made spotless and refined, but the wicked will
continue to be wicked. None of the wicked
will understand, but those who are wise will
understand.
11"From the time that the daily sacrifice is
abolished and the abomination that causes
desolation is set up, there will be 1,290 days.
12Blessed is the one who waits for and reaches
the end of the 1,335 days.
13"As for you, go your way till the end. You
will rest, and then at the end of the days you
will rise to receive your allotted inheritance."

HOSEA

Hosea

QUICK FACTS

AUTHOR Hosea

AUDIENCE The northern kingdom of Israel and all of God's people

DATE About 715 B.C.

SETTING Just prior to the end of the northern kingdom, which fell to the Assyrians in 722 B.C.

Hosea prophesied to Israel (also referred to as Ephraim, its largest tribe) during the same time Isaiah was prophesying to Judah. Neither nation had yet been conquered, but both were teetering on the edge of destruction. Remarkably, God commanded Hosea to marry a promiscuous woman, Gomer, to demonstrate how the Lord cared for his people. The book chronicles one heartbreaking scene after another, including Gomer leaving Hosea for other men while he continued to forgive her and woo her back home.

Hosea's story is a powerful symbol of Israel's repeated infidelity to God. After vowing to worship God alone, Israel embraced Baal and the other gods of Canaan until God allowed Israel to be taken into exile. Although the book of Hosea warns of the consequences of sin, it also vividly illustrates how destructive sin is to those who embrace it.

Throughout the story, God presents himself as a tender and faithful lover, who yearns over his people, and, in chapter 11, as a parent who gently lifts his little child to his cheek. As we follow God's example, we know that, while we cannot excuse the sins of our spouse, we can extend grace whenever possible and love them by wanting the best for them.

1 The word of the LORD that came to Hosea
son of Beeri during the reigns of Uzziah,
Jotham, Ahaz and Hezekiah, kings of Judah, and during the reign of Jeroboam son of
Jehoash[a] king of Israel:

Hosea's Wife and Children

2 When the LORD began to speak through
Hosea, the LORD said to him, "Go, take to
yourself an adulterous wife and children of
unfaithfulness, because the land is guilty of the
vilest adultery in departing from the LORD."
3 So he married Gomer daughter of Diblaim,
and she conceived and bore him a son.

4 Then the LORD said to Hosea, "Call him
Jezreel, because I will soon punish the house
of Jehu for the massacre at Jezreel, and I will
put an end to the kingdom of Israel. 5 In that
day I will break Israel's bow in the Valley of
Jezreel."

6 Gomer conceived again and gave birth
to a daughter. Then the LORD said to Hosea,
"Call her Lo-Ruhamah,[b] for I will no longer
show love to the house of Israel, that I should
at all forgive them. 7 Yet I will show love to the
house of Judah; and I will save them—not by
bow, sword or battle, or by horses and horsemen, but by the LORD their God."

8 After she had weaned Lo-Ruhamah, Gomer had another son. 9 Then the LORD said,
"Call him Lo-Ammi,[c] for you are not my people, and I am not your God.

10 "Yet the Israelites will be like the sand
on the seashore, which cannot be measured
or counted. In the place where it was said to
them, 'You are not my people,' they will be
called 'sons of the living God.' 11 The people of
Judah and the people of Israel will be reunit-
ed, and they will appoint one leader and will
come up out of the land, for great will be the
day of Jezreel.

2 "Say of your brothers, 'My people,' and of
your sisters, 'My loved one.'

Israel Punished and Restored

2 "Rebuke your mother, rebuke her,
for she is not my wife,
and I am not her husband.
Let her remove the adulterous look from her face
and the unfaithfulness from between her breasts.
3 Otherwise I will strip her naked
and make her as bare as on the day she was born;
I will make her like a desert,
turn her into a parched land,
and slay her with thirst.
4 I will not show my love to her children,
because they are the children of adultery.
5 Their mother has been unfaithful
and has conceived them in disgrace.
She said, 'I will go after my lovers,
who give me my food and my water,
my wool and my linen, my oil and my drink.'
6 Therefore I will block her path with thornbushes;
I will wall her in so that she cannot find her way.
7 She will chase after her lovers but not catch them;
she will look for them but not find them.
Then she will say,
'I will go back to my husband as at first,
for then I was better off than now.'
8 She has not acknowledged that I was the one
who gave her the grain, the new wine and oil,
who lavished on her the silver and gold—
which they used for Baal.

9 "Therefore I will take away my grain when it ripens,
and my new wine when it is ready.
I will take back my wool and my linen,
intended to cover her nakedness.
10 So now I will expose her lewdness
before the eyes of her lovers;
no one will take her out of my hands.
11 I will stop all her celebrations:
her yearly festivals, her New Moons,
her Sabbath days—all her appointed feasts.
12 I will ruin her vines and her fig trees,
which she said were her pay from her lovers;
I will make them a thicket,
and wild animals will devour them.
13 I will punish her for the days
she burned incense to the Baals;
she decked herself with rings and jewelry,
and went after her lovers,
but me she forgot,"
declares the LORD.

---

[a] *1* Hebrew *Joash,* a variant of *Jehoash* [b] *6* *Lo-Ruhamah* means *not loved.* [c] *9* *Lo-Ammi* means *not my people.*

TUESDAY
READ HOSEA 1:1–11

WORKING WITH OUR FLAWS

When the LORD began to speak through Hosea, the LORD said to him, "Go, take to yourself an adulterous wife and children of unfaithfulness, because the land is guilty of the vilest adultery in departing from the LORD."

— HOSEA 1:2

let's talk

- How does God's faithfulness to us work itself out in our marriage?
- What flaws did we sense in each other before we got married?
- What flaws did we discover in each other after we married? How have we reacted to them over time? If the flaws have been corrected, what has contributed most to the change?

Hosea's marriage to Gomer is a most troubling nuptial tale. The Lord told Hosea to marry a promiscuous woman; she bore him three children who, if their names are any indication, were trouble; and though Gomer repeatedly committed adultery, the Lord instructed Hosea to forgive her again and again and continue being faithful to her.

The narrative of this marriage, told in Hosea 1 and 3, is interrupted by the account of God's marriage to Israel in Hosea 2. That interruption is an important message for all marriages, because God's faithfulness to us is central to our ability to be faithful to one another. I only know how to love my husband because of God's love for me.

What was it like for Hosea to marry someone who he knew would be habitually unfaithful? Did he find it impossibly difficult to obey that command? Or did Hosea actually find some freedom amid Gomer's sin, knowing that he couldn't possibly change her tendency to wander and that only God could heal her?

Most of us go into marriage thinking that we can fix our beloved once we've exchanged vows. In the catchy but completely misguided words of a song from *Guys and Dolls*, "Marry the man today and change his ways tomorrow!" After a week or month of marriage, we discover more things about our spouse that we don't like. We may even stumble across deep, dark hurts we never knew were there. And try as we might, our attempts to change our spouse usually fail. All my nagging won't get my husband to zip up his jeans before throwing them in the wash. And nothing my friend Tom says to his wife will make her quit drinking; she'll keep at it until something terrible forces her to recognize that she's an alcoholic and needs to quit.

The truth is, you're not just married to someone with flaws. You're married to a sinful person. And your spouse is married to a sinful person. No amount of determination or hard work on your part is going to change that.

Still, God sometimes uses us to change our spouses. As Proverbs 27:17 reminds us, we may shape each other "as iron sharpens iron." Indeed, marriage is a means by which God transforms us into people who are loving, patient and forgiving. Imagine how Gomer felt when her husband reconciled with her and said, "You are to live with me many days" (Hosea 3:3). I imagine that Gomer was able to change, in part, because her husband forgave her, loved her and welcomed her home.

Even if we are part of someone else's transformation, it is finally God, not us, who effects the change. I am thankful that I am not married to someone who will betray me as Gomer betrayed Hosea. But something about Hosea embracing Gomer helps me to realize that I am a sinful person married to another sinful person. I am not called to change my husband; nor he, me. We are called to love and forgive each other. And we can rest assured that our broken, holy, hard, blessed marriage is one of the tools God is using to change us both.

—LAUREN WINNER

FOR YOUR NEXT DEVOTIONAL READING, TURN TO PAGE 971.

14 "Therefore I am now going to allure her;
I will lead her into the desert
and speak tenderly to her.
15 There I will give her back her vineyards,
and will make the Valley of Achor[a] a door of hope.
There she will sing[b] as in the days of her youth,
as in the day she came up out of Egypt.

16 "In that day," declares the LORD,
"you will call me 'my husband';
you will no longer call me 'my master.[c]'
17 I will remove the names of the Baals from her lips;
no longer will their names be invoked.
18 In that day I will make a covenant for them
with the beasts of the field and the birds of the air
and the creatures that move along the ground.
Bow and sword and battle
I will abolish from the land,
so that all may lie down in safety.
19 I will betroth you to me forever;
I will betroth you in[d] righteousness and justice,
in[e] love and compassion.
20 I will betroth you in faithfulness,
and you will acknowledge the LORD.

21 "In that day I will respond,"
declares the LORD—
"I will respond to the skies,
and they will respond to the earth;
22 and the earth will respond to the grain,
the new wine and oil,
and they will respond to Jezreel.[f]
23 I will plant her for myself in the land;
I will show my love to the one I called 'Not my loved one.[g]'
I will say to those called 'Not my people,[h]'
'You are my people';
and they will say, 'You are my God.' "

Hosea's Reconciliation With His Wife

3 The LORD said to me, "Go, show your love
to your wife again, though she is loved by
another and is an adulteress. Love her as the
LORD loves the Israelites, though they turn to
other gods and love the sacred raisin cakes."
2 So I bought her for fifteen shekels[i] of silver and about a homer and a lethek[j] of barley.
3 Then I told her, "You are to live with[k] me
many days; you must not be a prostitute or be
intimate with any man, and I will live with[k]
you."
4 For the Israelites will live many days without king or prince, without sacrifice or sacred
stones, without ephod or idol. 5 Afterward the
Israelites will return and seek the LORD their
God and David their king. They will come
trembling to the LORD and to his blessings in
the last days.

The Charge Against Israel

4 Hear the word of the LORD, you Israelites,
because the LORD has a charge to bring
against you who live in the land:
"There is no faithfulness, no love,
no acknowledgment of God in the land.
2 There is only cursing,[l] lying and murder,
stealing and adultery;
they break all bounds,
and bloodshed follows bloodshed.
3 Because of this the land mourns,[m]
and all who live in it waste away;
the beasts of the field and the birds of the air
and the fish of the sea are dying.

4 "But let no man bring a charge,
let no man accuse another,
for your people are like those
who bring charges against a priest.
5 You stumble day and night,
and the prophets stumble with you.
So I will destroy your mother—
6 my people are destroyed from lack of knowledge.
"Because you have rejected knowledge,
I also reject you as my priests;
because you have ignored the law of your God,
I also will ignore your children.
7 The more the priests increased,
the more they sinned against me;
they exchanged[n] their[o] Glory for something disgraceful.
8 They feed on the sins of my people
and relish their wickedness.
9 And it will be: Like people, like priests.
I will punish both of them for their ways
and repay them for their deeds.

---

[a] 15 *Achor* means *trouble.* [b] 15 Or *respond* [c] 16 Hebrew *baal* [d] 19 Or *with*; also in verse 20 [e] 19 Or *with* [f] 22 *Jezreel* means *God plants.* [g] 23 Hebrew *Lo-Ruhamah* [h] 23 Hebrew *Lo-Ammi* [i] 2 That is, about 6 ounces (about 170 grams) [j] 2 That is, probably about 10 bushels (about 330 liters) [k] 3 Or *wait for* [l] 2 That is, to pronounce a curse upon [m] 3 Or *dries up* [n] 7 Syriac and an ancient Hebrew scribal tradition; Masoretic Text *I will exchange* [o] 7 Masoretic Text; an ancient Hebrew scribal tradition *my*

FORGIVING AGAIN

The Lord said to me, "Go, show your love to your wife again, though she is loved by another and is an adulteress."

— Hosea 3:1

let's talk

- How might someone argue against giving a sinning spouse undeserved forgiveness and restoration? Why does it seem wrong to be so forgiving?
- Put yourself in Gomer's place in this passage. What would Hosea's love do even to her hardened heart?
- When we think of showing each other such mercy, especially when trust has been violated in some way, what would hinder us? How can we pray so that we might become more like the Lover of our souls?

Bryan Chapell wrote about a woman with an emotional problem who periodically stole from her own family and gambled away the money. Every time she emptied her husband's savings, he forgave her and took her back. Even when she gave up and tried to kill herself, he refused to let her go.

"I asked this husband once why he didn't end this marriage, in spite of pressure from many friends and family to do so," Chapell wrote. "His words were courageous and simple: 'She is a good mother most of the time, and my children need her. But more than that, they need to know the love of their God. How can they know of a Father in heaven who forgives them if their own father won't forgive their mother?' "

That husband was like Hosea. We've already seen in the book of Hosea how God told Hosea to marry Gomer, a promiscuous woman who was certain to be unfaithful to him. Hosea 3 tells us what happened next.

One of the cornerstones of marriage is trust and faithfulness. When that is gone, a marriage covenant is deeply injured. Likewise, we who have put our faith in Christ have entered into a covenant with the Lord. He is our husband and we, the church, are his bride. It was the same with Israel in the Old Testament. But over the generations, God's chosen people abandoned him and gave themselves to other gods. Here in Hosea God wooed his profoundly unfaithful people back to his love. He wanted them, even though they had not wanted him.

In this amazing story, we marvel at the intensity of God's love for us, his people. In Hosea's day, God's people, like Gomer, were practically worthless (15 shekels of silver is half the price of a slave), yet God would buy his people back—and us as well—at enormous cost. Romans 5:8 tells us that Jesus (who was betrayed for 30 pieces of silver) gave up his life for us while we were still sinners.

Like the husband with the gambling-addicted wife and like Hosea with the adulteress wife, many married people know the pain caused by a spouse who has violated their trust or compromised their love. When trust is damaged badly enough, and when sinful acts pile up, there is a sense in which a sinning spouse's "value" goes down. Such people demean and diminish themselves when they sin and are unfaithful.

But when we forgive our spouse, whether the offense is small or great, we add value back to them. When we "pay" something precious from within ourselves to receive them back with no strings attached, and when we love and adore them regardless, we follow the example of God, our Bridegroom. Sometimes even relatively small offenses can be very hard to forgive, but, whether the offense is great or small, grace—undeserved and unreserved—and forgiveness are how we show the character of our Father in heaven.

—LEE ECLOV

FOR YOUR NEXT DEVOTIONAL READING, TURN TO PAGE 978.

10 "They will eat but not have enough;
they will engage in prostitution but not increase,
because they have deserted the LORD
to give themselves 11 to prostitution,
to old wine and new,
which take away the understanding 12 of my people.
They consult a wooden idol
and are answered by a stick of wood.
A spirit of prostitution leads them astray;
they are unfaithful to their God.
13 They sacrifice on the mountaintops
and burn offerings on the hills,
under oak, poplar and terebinth,
where the shade is pleasant.
Therefore your daughters turn to prostitution
and your daughters-in-law to adultery.

14 "I will not punish your daughters
when they turn to prostitution,
nor your daughters-in-law
when they commit adultery,
because the men themselves consort with harlots
and sacrifice with shrine prostitutes—
a people without understanding will come to ruin!

15 "Though you commit adultery, O Israel,
let not Judah become guilty.

"Do not go to Gilgal;
do not go up to Beth Aven.[a]
And do not swear, 'As surely as the LORD lives!'
16 The Israelites are stubborn,
like a stubborn heifer.
How then can the LORD pasture them
like lambs in a meadow?
17 Ephraim is joined to idols;
leave him alone!
18 Even when their drinks are gone,
they continue their prostitution;
their rulers dearly love shameful ways.
19 A whirlwind will sweep them away,
and their sacrifices will bring them shame.

Judgment Against Israel

5 "Hear this, you priests!
Pay attention, you Israelites!
Listen, O royal house!
This judgment is against you:
You have been a snare at Mizpah,
a net spread out on Tabor.
2 The rebels are deep in slaughter.
I will discipline all of them.
3 I know all about Ephraim;
Israel is not hidden from me.
Ephraim, you have now turned to prostitution;
Israel is corrupt.

4 "Their deeds do not permit them
to return to their God.
A spirit of prostitution is in their heart;
they do not acknowledge the LORD.
5 Israel's arrogance testifies against them;
the Israelites, even Ephraim, stumble in their sin;
Judah also stumbles with them.
6 When they go with their flocks and herds
to seek the LORD,
they will not find him;
he has withdrawn himself from them.
7 They are unfaithful to the LORD;
they give birth to illegitimate children.
Now their New Moon festivals
will devour them and their fields.

8 "Sound the trumpet in Gibeah,
the horn in Ramah.
Raise the battle cry in Beth Aven[a];
lead on, O Benjamin.
9 Ephraim will be laid waste
on the day of reckoning.
Among the tribes of Israel
I proclaim what is certain.
10 Judah's leaders are like those
who move boundary stones.
I will pour out my wrath on them
like a flood of water.
11 Ephraim is oppressed,
trampled in judgment,
intent on pursuing idols.[b]
12 I am like a moth to Ephraim,
like rot to the people of Judah.

13 "When Ephraim saw his sickness,
and Judah his sores,
then Ephraim turned to Assyria,
and sent to the great king for help.
But he is not able to cure you,
not able to heal your sores.
14 For I will be like a lion to Ephraim,
like a great lion to Judah.
I will tear them to pieces and go away;
I will carry them off, with no one to rescue them.
15 Then I will go back to my place

a 15,8 *Beth Aven* means *house of wickedness* (a name for Bethel, which means *house of God*). *b* 11 The meaning of the Hebrew for this word is uncertain.

until they admit their guilt.
And they will seek my face;
in their misery they will earnestly seek
me."

Israel Unrepentant

6 "Come, let us return to the LORD.
He has torn us to pieces
but he will heal us;
he has injured us
but he will bind up our wounds.
2 After two days he will revive us;
on the third day he will restore us,
that we may live in his presence.
3 Let us acknowledge the LORD;
let us press on to acknowledge him.
As surely as the sun rises,
he will appear;
he will come to us like the winter rains,
like the spring rains that water the
earth."

4 "What can I do with you, Ephraim?
What can I do with you, Judah?
Your love is like the morning mist,
like the early dew that disappears.
5 Therefore I cut you in pieces with my
prophets,
I killed you with the words of my
mouth;
my judgments flashed like lightning
upon you.
6 For I desire mercy, not sacrifice,
and acknowledgment of God rather
than burnt offerings.
7 Like Adam,[a] they have broken the
covenant—
they were unfaithful to me there.
8 Gilead is a city of wicked men,
stained with footprints of blood.
9 As marauders lie in ambush for a man,
so do bands of priests;
they murder on the road to Shechem,
committing shameful crimes.
10 I have seen a horrible thing
in the house of Israel.
There Ephraim is given to prostitution
and Israel is defiled.

11 "Also for you, Judah,
a harvest is appointed.

"Whenever I would restore the fortunes of
my people,
7 1 whenever I would heal Israel,
the sins of Ephraim are exposed
and the crimes of Samaria revealed.
They practice deceit,
thieves break into houses,
bandits rob in the streets;
2 but they do not realize
that I remember all their evil deeds.
Their sins engulf them;
they are always before me.

3 "They delight the king with their
wickedness,
the princes with their lies.
4 They are all adulterers,
burning like an oven
whose fire the baker need not stir
from the kneading of the dough till it
rises.
5 On the day of the festival of our king
the princes become inflamed with
wine,
and he joins hands with the mockers.
6 Their hearts are like an oven;
they approach him with intrigue.
Their passion smolders all night;
in the morning it blazes like a flaming
fire.
7 All of them are hot as an oven;
they devour their rulers.
All their kings fall,
and none of them calls on me.

8 "Ephraim mixes with the nations;
Ephraim is a flat cake not turned over.
9 Foreigners sap his strength,
but he does not realize it.
His hair is sprinkled with gray,
but he does not notice.
10 Israel's arrogance testifies against him,
but despite all this
he does not return to the LORD his God
or search for him.

11 "Ephraim is like a dove,
easily deceived and senseless—
now calling to Egypt,
now turning to Assyria.
12 When they go, I will throw my net over
them;
I will pull them down like birds of the
air.
When I hear them flocking together,
I will catch them.
13 Woe to them,
because they have strayed from me!
Destruction to them,
because they have rebelled against me!
I long to redeem them
but they speak lies against me.

[a] 7 Or *As at Adam*; or *Like men*

14 They do not cry out to me from their hearts
but wail upon their beds.
They gather together[a] for grain and new wine
but turn away from me.
15 I trained them and strengthened them,
but they plot evil against me.
16 They do not turn to the Most High;
they are like a faulty bow.
Their leaders will fall by the sword
because of their insolent words.
For this they will be ridiculed
in the land of Egypt.

Israel to Reap the Whirlwind

8 "Put the trumpet to your lips!
An eagle is over the house of the LORD
because the people have broken my covenant
and rebelled against my law.
2 Israel cries out to me,
'O our God, we acknowledge you!'
3 But Israel has rejected what is good;
an enemy will pursue him.
4 They set up kings without my consent;
they choose princes without my approval.
With their silver and gold
they make idols for themselves
to their own destruction.
5 Throw out your calf-idol, O Samaria!
My anger burns against them.
How long will they be incapable of purity?
6 They are from Israel!
This calf—a craftsman has made it;
it is not God.
It will be broken in pieces,
that calf of Samaria.

7 "They sow the wind
and reap the whirlwind.
The stalk has no head;
it will produce no flour.
Were it to yield grain,
foreigners would swallow it up.
8 Israel is swallowed up;
now she is among the nations
like a worthless thing.
9 For they have gone up to Assyria
like a wild donkey wandering alone.
Ephraim has sold herself to lovers.
10 Although they have sold themselves
among the nations,
I will now gather them together.
They will begin to waste away
under the oppression of the mighty king.
11 "Though Ephraim built many altars for sin offerings,
these have become altars for sinning.
12 I wrote for them the many things of my law,
but they regarded them as something alien.
13 They offer sacrifices given to me
and they eat the meat,
but the LORD is not pleased with them.
Now he will remember their wickedness
and punish their sins:
They will return to Egypt.
14 Israel has forgotten his Maker
and built palaces;
Judah has fortified many towns.
But I will send fire upon their cities
that will consume their fortresses."

Punishment for Israel

9 Do not rejoice, O Israel;
do not be jubilant like the other nations.
For you have been unfaithful to your God;
you love the wages of a prostitute
at every threshing floor.
2 Threshing floors and winepresses will not feed the people;
the new wine will fail them.
3 They will not remain in the LORD's land;
Ephraim will return to Egypt
and eat unclean[b] food in Assyria.
4 They will not pour out wine offerings to the LORD,
nor will their sacrifices please him.
Such sacrifices will be to them like the bread of mourners;
all who eat them will be unclean.
This food will be for themselves;
it will not come into the temple of the LORD.

5 What will you do on the day of your appointed feasts,
on the festival days of the LORD?
6 Even if they escape from destruction,
Egypt will gather them,
and Memphis will bury them.
Their treasures of silver will be taken over by briers,
and thorns will overrun their tents.
7 The days of punishment are coming,
the days of reckoning are at hand.

---

[a] *14* Most Hebrew manuscripts; some Hebrew manuscripts and Septuagint *They slash themselves* [b] *3* That is, ceremonially unclean

Let Israel know this.
Because your sins are so many
and your hostility so great,
the prophet is considered a fool,
the inspired man a maniac.
8 The prophet, along with my God,
is the watchman over Ephraim,[a]
yet snares await him on all his paths,
and hostility in the house of his God.
9 They have sunk deep into corruption,
as in the days of Gibeah.
God will remember their wickedness
and punish them for their sins.

10 "When I found Israel,
it was like finding grapes in the desert;
when I saw your fathers,
it was like seeing the early fruit on the fig tree.
But when they came to Baal Peor,
they consecrated themselves to that shameful idol
and became as vile as the thing they loved.
11 Ephraim's glory will fly away like a bird—
no birth, no pregnancy, no conception.
12 Even if they rear children,
I will bereave them of every one.
Woe to them
when I turn away from them!
13 I have seen Ephraim, like Tyre,
planted in a pleasant place.
But Ephraim will bring out
their children to the slayer."

14 Give them, O LORD—
what will you give them?
Give them wombs that miscarry
and breasts that are dry.
15 "Because of all their wickedness in Gilgal,
I hated them there.
Because of their sinful deeds,
I will drive them out of my house.
I will no longer love them;
all their leaders are rebellious.
16 Ephraim is blighted,
their root is withered,
they yield no fruit.
Even if they bear children,
I will slay their cherished offspring."

17 My God will reject them
because they have not obeyed him;
they will be wanderers among the nations.

10 Israel was a spreading vine;
he brought forth fruit for himself.
As his fruit increased,
he built more altars;
as his land prospered,
he adorned his sacred stones.
2 Their heart is deceitful,
and now they must bear their guilt.
The LORD will demolish their altars
and destroy their sacred stones.

3 Then they will say, "We have no king
because we did not revere the LORD.
But even if we had a king,
what could he do for us?"
4 They make many promises,
take false oaths
and make agreements;
therefore lawsuits spring up
like poisonous weeds in a plowed field.
5 The people who live in Samaria fear
for the calf-idol of Beth Aven.[b]
Its people will mourn over it,
and so will its idolatrous priests,
those who had rejoiced over its splendor,
because it is taken from them into exile.
6 It will be carried to Assyria
as tribute for the great king.
Ephraim will be disgraced;
Israel will be ashamed of its wooden idols.[c]
7 Samaria and its king will float away
like a twig on the surface of the waters.
8 The high places of wickedness[d] will be destroyed—
it is the sin of Israel.
Thorns and thistles will grow up
and cover their altars.
Then they will say to the mountains,
"Cover us!"
and to the hills, "Fall on us!"

9 "Since the days of Gibeah, you have sinned, O Israel,
and there you have remained.[e]
Did not war overtake
the evildoers in Gibeah?
10 When I please, I will punish them;
nations will be gathered against them
to put them in bonds for their double sin.
11 Ephraim is a trained heifer
that loves to thresh;
so I will put a yoke
on her fair neck.

[a] 8 Or *The prophet is the watchman over Ephraim, / the people of my God* [b] 5 *Beth Aven* means *house of wickedness* (a name for Bethel, which means *house of God*). [c] 6 Or *its counsel* [d] 8 Hebrew *aven,* a reference to Beth Aven (a derogatory name for Bethel) [e] 9 Or *there a stand was taken*

I will drive Ephraim,
Judah must plow,
and Jacob must break up the ground.
12 Sow for yourselves righteousness,
reap the fruit of unfailing love,
and break up your unplowed ground;
for it is time to seek the LORD,
until he comes
and showers righteousness on you.
13 But you have planted wickedness,
you have reaped evil,
you have eaten the fruit of deception.
Because you have depended on your own strength
and on your many warriors,
14 the roar of battle will rise against your people,
so that all your fortresses will be devastated—
as Shalman devastated Beth Arbel on the day of battle,
when mothers were dashed to the ground with their children.
15 Thus will it happen to you, O Bethel,
because your wickedness is great.
When that day dawns,
the king of Israel will be completely destroyed.

God's Love for Israel

11 "When Israel was a child, I loved him,
and out of Egypt I called my son.
2 But the more I[a] called Israel,
the further they went from me.[b]
They sacrificed to the Baals
and they burned incense to images.
3 It was I who taught Ephraim to walk,
taking them by the arms;
but they did not realize
it was I who healed them.
4 I led them with cords of human kindness,
with ties of love;
I lifted the yoke from their neck
and bent down to feed them.

5 "Will they not return to Egypt
and will not Assyria rule over them
because they refuse to repent?
6 Swords will flash in their cities,
will destroy the bars of their gates
and put an end to their plans.
7 My people are determined to turn from me.
Even if they call to the Most High,
he will by no means exalt them.

8 "How can I give you up, Ephraim?
How can I hand you over, Israel?
How can I treat you like Admah?
How can I make you like Zeboiim?
My heart is changed within me;
all my compassion is aroused.
9 I will not carry out my fierce anger,
nor will I turn and devastate Ephraim.
For I am God, and not man—
the Holy One among you.
I will not come in wrath.[c]
10 They will follow the LORD;
he will roar like a lion.
When he roars,
his children will come trembling from the west.
11 They will come trembling
like birds from Egypt,
like doves from Assyria.
I will settle them in their homes,"
declares the LORD.

Israel's Sin

12 Ephraim has surrounded me with lies,
the house of Israel with deceit.
And Judah is unruly against God,
even against the faithful Holy One.
12 1 Ephraim feeds on the wind;
he pursues the east wind all day
and multiplies lies and violence.
He makes a treaty with Assyria
and sends olive oil to Egypt.
2 The LORD has a charge to bring against Judah;
he will punish Jacob[d] according to his ways
and repay him according to his deeds.
3 In the womb he grasped his brother's heel;
as a man he struggled with God.
4 He struggled with the angel and overcame him;
he wept and begged for his favor.
He found him at Bethel
and talked with him there—
5 the LORD God Almighty,
the LORD is his name of renown!
6 But you must return to your God;
maintain love and justice,
and wait for your God always.

7 The merchant uses dishonest scales;
he loves to defraud.
8 Ephraim boasts,
"I am very rich; I have become wealthy.

[a] 2 Some Septuagint manuscripts; Hebrew *they* [b] 2 Septuagint; Hebrew *them* [c] 9 Or *come against any city* [d] 2 *Jacob* means *he grasps the heel* (figuratively, *he deceives*).

With all my wealth they will not find in
me
any iniquity or sin."

9 "I am the LORD your God,
⌊who brought you⌋ out of[a] Egypt;
I will make you live in tents again,
as in the days of your appointed feasts.
10 I spoke to the prophets,
gave them many visions
and told parables through them."

11 Is Gilead wicked?
Its people are worthless!
Do they sacrifice bulls in Gilgal?
Their altars will be like piles of stones
on a plowed field.
12 Jacob fled to the country of Aram[b];
Israel served to get a wife,
and to pay for her he tended sheep.
13 The LORD used a prophet to bring Israel
up from Egypt,
by a prophet he cared for him.
14 But Ephraim has bitterly provoked him to
anger;
his Lord will leave upon him the guilt
of his bloodshed
and will repay him for his contempt.

The LORD's Anger Against Israel

13 When Ephraim spoke, men trembled;
he was exalted in Israel.
But he became guilty of Baal worship
and died.
2 Now they sin more and more;
they make idols for themselves from
their silver,
cleverly fashioned images,
all of them the work of craftsmen.
It is said of these people,
"They offer human sacrifice
and kiss[c] the calf-idols."
3 Therefore they will be like the morning
mist,
like the early dew that disappears,
like chaff swirling from a threshing
floor,
like smoke escaping through a window.

4 "But I am the LORD your God,
⌊who brought you⌋ out of[d] Egypt.
You shall acknowledge no God but me,
no Savior except me.
5 I cared for you in the desert,
in the land of burning heat.
6 When I fed them, they were satisfied;
when they were satisfied, they became
proud;
then they forgot me.
7 So I will come upon them like a lion,
like a leopard I will lurk by the path.
8 Like a bear robbed of her cubs,
I will attack them and rip them open.
Like a lion I will devour them;
a wild animal will tear them apart.

9 "You are destroyed, O Israel,
because you are against me, against
your helper.
10 Where is your king, that he may save you?
Where are your rulers in all your towns,
of whom you said,
'Give me a king and princes'?
11 So in my anger I gave you a king,
and in my wrath I took him away.
12 The guilt of Ephraim is stored up,
his sins are kept on record.
13 Pains as of a woman in childbirth come to
him,
but he is a child without wisdom;
when the time arrives,
he does not come to the opening of the
womb.

14 "I will ransom them from the power of the
grave[e];
I will redeem them from death.
Where, O death, are your plagues?
Where, O grave,[e] is your destruction?
"I will have no compassion,
15 even though he thrives among his
brothers.
An east wind from the LORD will come,
blowing in from the desert;
his spring will fail
and his well dry up.
His storehouse will be plundered
of all its treasures.
16 The people of Samaria must bear their
guilt,
because they have rebelled against their
God.
They will fall by the sword;
their little ones will be dashed to the
ground,
their pregnant women ripped open."

Repentance to Bring Blessing

14 Return, O Israel, to the LORD your
God.
Your sins have been your downfall!

---

[a] 9 Or *God / ever since you were in* [b] 12 That is, Northwest Mesopotamia [c] 2 Or *"Men who sacrifice / kiss* [d] 4 Or *God / ever since you were in* [e] 14 Hebrew *Sheol*

THURSDAY
READ HOSEA 14:1–9

INCHING TOWARD RESTORATION

Return, O Israel, to the LORD your God. Your sins have been your downfall!

— HOSEA 14:1

let's talk

- What marriage breakdowns have we experienced among our friends or family? What were the outcomes?
- What causes some marriages to fail? What allows others to survive?
- In what ways are we learning the disciplines of repentance and reconciliation? How do God's words through Hosea apply to our relationship as it exists right now?

A gracious couple in their senior years seemed absolutely right for each other. They deferred to one another in conversation, yet often finished each other's sentences. They enjoyed taking early evening walks, usually holding hands. They traveled some, golfed a bit and appeared to have the same tastes in food and fun. They shared coffee dates and Bible studies with friends. Their marriage appeared to be textbook perfect.

It wasn't. I took the husband home several times when he was utterly drunk. Once he totaled his car after slamming it into a building, and he could only slobber pathetic apologies. One day, after watching him in a public setting and being suspicious that he was trying to drive under the influence, I called the police and had him arrested.

His wife was exhausted from his childish alcoholic tantrums, hiding their dysfunctional relationship, and working part-time to cover expenses for booze, broken things and high-risk car insurance. He made things worse by becoming religiously self-righteous and loudly attacking heresies and social ills, as well as berating women who didn't mind "their place" as obedient servants. Finally, with quiet shame his wife filed for divorce.

None of us who knew about this man's self-destructiveness imagined that this couple's marriage could be saved. Yet it was. Friends stood by both of them. They got the husband into a substance-abuse program. He repented and made a slow series of amends to his wife and family. And by the grace of God, the couple found reconciliation and renewal.

In truth, their marriage is a retelling of Hosea's religious soap opera. The book of Hosea tells an amazing story of tender love between Israel and God, couched in the language of youthful passions and tender promises. It also describes Israel's abysmal failure to be faithful to that love and God's repeated pleas for her to come to her senses and return home to him.

Unfortunately, Hosea would never see God's desire for marriage reconciliation with Israel become reality. Israel would take spiritual adultery and prostitution too far and be removed from her homeland. Still, Hosea's story lingers in Scripture as a testimony of God's faithful love and as a model of how a spouse is to respond to a partner's repeated sin. Those who find a way to imitate God's patience and forgiveness may even experience the restoration of a marriage written off by others as compromised beyond reason and damaged beyond recovery.

Not every broken partnership can be saved. Nor should foolish, scandalous, hurtful or destructive behavior be forgiven simply to keep a religious pretense of marital faithfulness. Yet the best remedy for infidelity or other attacks on marriage is repentance, reconciliation and renewal. These, as Hosea indicates, are very much God's true desire.

—WAYNE BROUWER

FOR YOUR NEXT DEVOTIONAL READING, TURN TO PAGE 982.

2 Take words with you
and return to the Lord.
Say to him:
"Forgive all our sins
and receive us graciously,
that we may offer the fruit of our lips.[a]
3 Assyria cannot save us;
we will not mount war-horses.
We will never again say 'Our gods'
to what our own hands have made,
for in you the fatherless find
compassion."

4 "I will heal their waywardness
and love them freely,
for my anger has turned away from
them.
5 I will be like the dew to Israel;
he will blossom like a lily.
Like a cedar of Lebanon
he will send down his roots;
6 his young shoots will grow.
His splendor will be like an olive tree,
his fragrance like a cedar of
Lebanon.
7 Men will dwell again in his shade.
He will flourish like the grain.
He will blossom like a vine,
and his fame will be like the wine from
Lebanon.
8 O Ephraim, what more have I[b] to do with
idols?
I will answer him and care for him.
I am like a green pine tree;
your fruitfulness comes from me."

9 Who is wise? He will realize these things.
Who is discerning? He will understand
them.
The ways of the Lord are right;
the righteous walk in them,
but the rebellious stumble in them.

[a] 2 Or *offer our lips as sacrifices of bulls* [b] 8 Or *What more has Ephraim*

JOEL

Joel

QUICK FACTS

AUTHOR Joel

AUDIENCE The people of Judah

DATE Unknown

SETTING A time of idolatry and complacency in Judah

"*Repent* and return!" That's the theme of the book of Joel. The prophet Joel pleaded with the people of Judah. He offered dire warnings about "the day of the LORD," a time of fierce judgment on those who displease God. These warnings were filled with urgent calls to repent and turn away from sinful choices.

At the same time, Joel presented God's amazing grace. The prophet articulately described the faithfulness and power of God to renew and restore those who turn to him. He reminded the people of God's character and of the fact that God alone was the source of their future hope. He urged the people, "Return to the LORD your God, for he is gracious and compassionate, slow to anger and abounding in love" (Joel 2:13).

Joel's hammering refrain—"Look out! Think! Consider how your choices look to God, the Judge of all!"—is a strong recommendation to couples who have committed to live for God's glory and purposes. Christian couples who recognize the ramifications and importance of their decisions can be assured that even when they do falter, the Lord will remain committed to them.

1 The word of the LORD that came to Joel
son of Pethuel.

An Invasion of Locusts

2 Hear this, you elders;
listen, all who live in the land.
Has anything like this ever happened in
your days
or in the days of your forefathers?
3 Tell it to your children,
and let your children tell it to their
children,
and their children to the next
generation.
4 What the locust swarm has left
the great locusts have eaten;
what the great locusts have left
the young locusts have eaten;
what the young locusts have left
other locusts[a] have eaten.

5 Wake up, you drunkards, and weep!
Wail, all you drinkers of wine;
wail because of the new wine,
for it has been snatched from your lips.
6 A nation has invaded my land,
powerful and without number;
it has the teeth of a lion,
the fangs of a lioness.
7 It has laid waste my vines
and ruined my fig trees.
It has stripped off their bark
and thrown it away,
leaving their branches white.

8 Mourn like a virgin[b] in sackcloth
grieving for the husband[c] of her youth.
9 Grain offerings and drink offerings
are cut off from the house of the LORD.
The priests are in mourning,
those who minister before the LORD.
10 The fields are ruined,
the ground is dried up[d];
the grain is destroyed,
the new wine is dried up,
the oil fails.
11 Despair, you farmers,
wail, you vine growers;
grieve for the wheat and the barley,
because the harvest of the field is
destroyed.
12 The vine is dried up
and the fig tree is withered;
the pomegranate, the palm and the apple
tree—
all the trees of the field—are dried up.
Surely the joy of mankind
is withered away.

A Call to Repentance

13 Put on sackcloth, O priests, and mourn;
wail, you who minister before the altar.
Come, spend the night in sackcloth,
you who minister before my God;
for the grain offerings and drink offerings
are withheld from the house of your
God.
14 Declare a holy fast;
call a sacred assembly.
Summon the elders
and all who live in the land
to the house of the LORD your God,
and cry out to the LORD.

15 Alas for that day!
For the day of the LORD is near;
it will come like destruction from the
Almighty.[e]

16 Has not the food been cut off
before our very eyes—
joy and gladness
from the house of our God?
17 The seeds are shriveled
beneath the clods.[f]
The storehouses are in ruins,
the granaries have been broken down,
for the grain has dried up.
18 How the cattle moan!
The herds mill about
because they have no pasture;
even the flocks of sheep are suffering.

19 To you, O LORD, I call,
for fire has devoured the open pastures
and flames have burned up all the trees
of the field.
20 Even the wild animals pant for you;
the streams of water have dried up
and fire has devoured the open
pastures.

An Army of Locusts

2 Blow the trumpet in Zion;
sound the alarm on my holy hill.
Let all who live in the land tremble,
for the day of the LORD is coming.
It is close at hand—
2 a day of darkness and gloom,
a day of clouds and blackness.
Like dawn spreading across the mountains
a large and mighty army comes,

[a] 4 The precise meaning of the four Hebrew words used here for locusts is uncertain. [b] 8 Or *young woman* [c] 8 Or *betrothed*
[d] 10 Or *ground mourns* [e] 15 Hebrew *Shaddai* [f] 17 The meaning of the Hebrew for this word is uncertain.

FRIDAY
READ JOEL 2:1–32

FIGHTING OVER NOTHING

> **Be not afraid, O land; be glad and rejoice. Surely the LORD has done great things.**
>
> — JOEL 2:21

let's talk

- What are some of the great things God has done in our marriage?
- What are some small sins in our marriage that sometimes threaten to turn into big, destructive sins?
- How might inviting Jesus into our squabbles lead us to repentance? What might change as a result?

In the midst of calamity, of living with the consequences of sin, the prophet Joel reminds us not to be afraid, but rather to be glad and rejoice, for "the LORD has done great things." This is a great reminder for me in marriage.

Okay, my marriage doesn't usually feel like a calamity. But at times it has felt impossible . . . like a mistake . . . like a mess. It has felt, to borrow an image from Joel, like a horde of locusts has come in and taken over everything.

Our most recent rough patch was over nothing. I think the immediate cause was sleep deprivation and too many evening meetings at church and work. Griff and I just got stuck, like a needle on a broken record. For about three days, we couldn't exchange a pleasant word, let alone a loving one.

We had lost our sense of being a team. Each, I think, was thinking, "I'm contributing way more here." One of us was thinking, "I do way more housework," and the other was thinking, "I slog away at work for endless hours to pay the mortgage." And together we were concluding, "Why do I put up with this? I'm not getting anything out of it." There were moments in that three-day period when I seriously wondered if we would ever get through that horrible time. "This is how we'll be for the rest of forever," I thought.

Our dissatisfaction was not only superficial but also sinful. We were allowing ourselves to feel alienated from each other and to enjoy strangely delicious feelings of self-righteous annoyance. I felt a little superior; I'm sure Griff did too.

The prophet Joel told the people of Judah that unless they got their act together (that is, repented), God would destroy them just as locusts had destroyed their land.

At the time, I didn't think God was waiting around to unleash lightning bolts on our marriage. But unless Griff and I repented of our small sins—tetchiness, selfishness, anger—our small sins would quickly become large sins that could do serious harm to our marriage.

At times like that, I find it helpful to remember that the Lord has done great things. He has done great things in our marriage. He has gotten us through far worse patches than three days of clawing at each other. Remembering that I don't have to be in control and that I should cede that control to God, who has done great things, leads me to repent. After three days or three hours of tetchiness, repentance can be as simple and profound as acknowledging that if I let God into the situation, we won't feel so stuck.

For me, the beginning of repentance is as basic as picturing Jesus walking into the situation. Sometimes I do that when Griff and I are in the middle of a squabble. Sometimes, I can't get there until later, when I'm alone. Then I replay the scene, the tension and the annoyance, and I envision Jesus showing up. This is not just some imaginative exercise. It is a prayer, a plea for help. And the God who does great things answers.

—LAUREN WINNER

FOR YOUR NEXT DEVOTIONAL READING, TURN TO PAGE 990.

such as never was of old
nor ever will be in ages to come.

3 Before them fire devours,
behind them a flame blazes.
Before them the land is like the garden of Eden,
behind them, a desert waste—
nothing escapes them.
4 They have the appearance of horses;
they gallop along like cavalry.
5 With a noise like that of chariots
they leap over the mountaintops,
like a crackling fire consuming stubble,
like a mighty army drawn up for battle.

6 At the sight of them, nations are in anguish;
every face turns pale.
7 They charge like warriors;
they scale walls like soldiers.
They all march in line,
not swerving from their course.
8 They do not jostle each other;
each marches straight ahead.
They plunge through defenses
without breaking ranks.
9 They rush upon the city;
they run along the wall.
They climb into the houses;
like thieves they enter through the windows.

10 Before them the earth shakes,
the sky trembles,
the sun and moon are darkened,
and the stars no longer shine.
11 The LORD thunders
at the head of his army;
his forces are beyond number,
and mighty are those who obey his command.
The day of the LORD is great;
it is dreadful.
Who can endure it?

Rend Your Heart

12 "Even now," declares the LORD,
"return to me with all your heart,
with fasting and weeping and mourning."

13 Rend your heart
and not your garments.
Return to the LORD your God,
for he is gracious and compassionate,
slow to anger and abounding in love,
and he relents from sending calamity.
14 Who knows? He may turn and have pity
and leave behind a blessing—
grain offerings and drink offerings
for the LORD your God.

15 Blow the trumpet in Zion,
declare a holy fast,
call a sacred assembly.
16 Gather the people,
consecrate the assembly;
bring together the elders,
gather the children,
those nursing at the breast.
Let the bridegroom leave his room
and the bride her chamber.
17 Let the priests, who minister before the LORD,
weep between the temple porch and the altar.
Let them say, "Spare your people, O LORD.
Do not make your inheritance an object of scorn,
a byword among the nations.
Why should they say among the peoples,
'Where is their God?' "

The LORD's Answer

18 Then the LORD will be jealous for his land
and take pity on his people.

19 The LORD will reply[a] to them:

"I am sending you grain, new wine and oil,
enough to satisfy you fully;
never again will I make you
an object of scorn to the nations.

20 "I will drive the northern army far from you,
pushing it into a parched and barren land,
with its front columns going into the eastern sea[b]
and those in the rear into the western sea.[c]
And its stench will go up;
its smell will rise."

Surely he has done great things.[d]
21 Be not afraid, O land;
be glad and rejoice.
Surely the LORD has done great things.
22 Be not afraid, O wild animals,

[a] 18,19 Or *LORD was jealous . . . / and took pity . . . / [19]The LORD replied* [b] 20 That is, the Dead Sea [c] 20 That is, the Mediterranean
[d] 20 Or *rise. / Surely it has done great things."*

for the open pastures are becoming
green.
The trees are bearing their fruit;
the fig tree and the vine yield their
riches.
23 Be glad, O people of Zion,
rejoice in the LORD your God,
for he has given you
the autumn rains in righteousness.[a]
He sends you abundant showers,
both autumn and spring rains, as
before.
24 The threshing floors will be filled with
grain;
the vats will overflow with new wine
and oil.
25 "I will repay you for the years the locusts
have eaten—
the great locust and the young locust,
the other locusts and the locust
swarm[b]—
my great army that I sent among you.
26 You will have plenty to eat, until you are
full,
and you will praise the name of the
LORD your God,
who has worked wonders for you;
never again will my people be shamed.
27 Then you will know that I am in Israel,
that I am the LORD your God,
and that there is no other;
never again will my people be shamed.

The Day of the LORD

28 "And afterward,
I will pour out my Spirit on all people.
Your sons and daughters will prophesy,
your old men will dream dreams,
your young men will see visions.
29 Even on my servants, both men and
women,
I will pour out my Spirit in those days.
30 I will show wonders in the heavens
and on the earth,
blood and fire and billows of smoke.
31 The sun will be turned to darkness
and the moon to blood
before the coming of the great and
dreadful day of the LORD.
32 And everyone who calls
on the name of the LORD will be saved;
for on Mount Zion and in Jerusalem
there will be deliverance,
as the LORD has said,
among the survivors
whom the LORD calls.

The Nations Judged

3 "In those days and at that time,
when I restore the fortunes of Judah
and Jerusalem,
2 I will gather all nations
and bring them down to the Valley of
Jehoshaphat.[c]
There I will enter into judgment against
them
concerning my inheritance, my people
Israel,
for they scattered my people among the
nations
and divided up my land.
3 They cast lots for my people
and traded boys for prostitutes;
they sold girls for wine
that they might drink.

4 "Now what have you against me, O Tyre
and Sidon and all you regions of Philistia? Are
you repaying me for something I have done?
If you are paying me back, I will swiftly and
speedily return on your own heads what you
have done. 5 For you took my silver and my
gold and carried off my finest treasures to your
temples. 6 You sold the people of Judah and
Jerusalem to the Greeks, that you might send
them far from their homeland.
7 "See, I am going to rouse them out of the
places to which you sold them, and I will return on your own heads what you have done.
8 I will sell your sons and daughters to the people of Judah, and they will sell them to the
Sabeans, a nation far away." The LORD has
spoken.

9 Proclaim this among the nations:
Prepare for war!
Rouse the warriors!
Let all the fighting men draw near and
attack.
10 Beat your plowshares into swords
and your pruning hooks into spears.
Let the weakling say,
"I am strong!"
11 Come quickly, all you nations from every
side,
and assemble there.
Bring down your warriors, O LORD!
12 "Let the nations be roused;

[a] 23 Or / *the teacher for righteousness:* [b] 25 The precise meaning of the four Hebrew words used here for locusts is uncertain.
[c] 2 *Jehoshaphat* means *the LORD judges*; also in verse 12.

let them advance into the Valley of
Jehoshaphat,
for there I will sit
to judge all the nations on every side.
13 Swing the sickle,
for the harvest is ripe.
Come, trample the grapes,
for the winepress is full
and the vats overflow—
so great is their wickedness!"

14 Multitudes, multitudes
in the valley of decision!
For the day of the LORD is near
in the valley of decision.
15 The sun and moon will be darkened,
and the stars no longer shine.
16 The LORD will roar from Zion
and thunder from Jerusalem;
the earth and the sky will tremble.
But the LORD will be a refuge for his
people,
a stronghold for the people of Israel.

Blessings for God's People

17 "Then you will know that I, the LORD
your God,
dwell in Zion, my holy hill.
Jerusalem will be holy;
never again will foreigners invade her.

18 "In that day the mountains will drip new
wine,
and the hills will flow with milk;
all the ravines of Judah will run with
water.
A fountain will flow out of the LORD's
house
and will water the valley of acacias. [a]
19 But Egypt will be desolate,
Edom a desert waste,
because of violence done to the people of
Judah,
in whose land they shed innocent
blood.
20 Judah will be inhabited forever
and Jerusalem through all
generations.
21 Their bloodguilt, which I have not
pardoned,
I will pardon."

The LORD dwells in Zion!

---

[a] 18 Or *Valley of Shittim*

AMOS

Amos

QUICK FACTS

AUTHOR Amos

AUDIENCE The northern kingdom (Israel) and all of God's people

DATE About 760–750 B.C.

SETTING A time of great prosperity in Israel, when the people were guilty of idolatry, materialism, corruption and oppression of the poor

The book of Amos thunders with the threat of punishment. God was angry with the people of the northern kingdom of Israel, for they were breaking their covenant promises to him. The Lord sent Amos, a simple shepherd and farmer from Tekoa (not far from Jerusalem) in Judah, to deliver his messages of ferocious displeasure to Israel.

What made God so angry was that his chosen people went through the proper religious motions and claimed with their lips that they belonged to God, yet they worshiped idols and treated the needy with indifference and even violence. The punishment described by Amos made God seem harsh and negative, but the Lord's discipline had a positive purpose: the restoration and protection of his people and the renewal of their covenant relationship. God had to use tough love to get his people to wake up and reform.

God doesn't waver in hating sin. He is prepared to speak the tough truths we need to hear to bring us back to our commitment to honor him. This kind of courageous truth telling is part of our heritage as God's people. Even though such confrontations may be difficult and exhausting, we show true love for one another, particularly in marriage, by holding each other accountable to God's high standards for covenant relationships.

1 The words of Amos, one of the shepherds of Tekoa—what he saw concerning Israel two years before the earthquake, when Uzziah was king of Judah and Jeroboam son of Jehoash[a] was king of Israel.

2 He said:

"The LORD roars from Zion
and thunders from Jerusalem;
the pastures of the shepherds dry up,[b]
and the top of Carmel withers."

Judgment on Israel's Neighbors

3 This is what the LORD says:

"For three sins of Damascus,
even for four, I will not turn back ⌊my wrath⌋.
Because she threshed Gilead
with sledges having iron teeth,
4 I will send fire upon the house of Hazael
that will consume the fortresses of Ben-Hadad.
5 I will break down the gate of Damascus;
I will destroy the king who is in[c] the Valley of Aven[d]
and the one who holds the scepter in Beth Eden.
The people of Aram will go into exile to Kir,"
says the LORD.

6 This is what the LORD says:

"For three sins of Gaza,
even for four, I will not turn back ⌊my wrath⌋.
Because she took captive whole communities
and sold them to Edom,
7 I will send fire upon the walls of Gaza
that will consume her fortresses.
8 I will destroy the king[e] of Ashdod
and the one who holds the scepter in Ashkelon.
I will turn my hand against Ekron,
till the last of the Philistines is dead,"
says the Sovereign LORD.

9 This is what the LORD says:

"For three sins of Tyre,
even for four, I will not turn back ⌊my wrath⌋.
Because she sold whole communities of captives to Edom,
disregarding a treaty of brotherhood,
10 I will send fire upon the walls of Tyre
that will consume her fortresses."

11 This is what the LORD says:

"For three sins of Edom,
even for four, I will not turn back ⌊my wrath⌋.
Because he pursued his brother with a sword,
stifling all compassion,[f]
because his anger raged continually
and his fury flamed unchecked,
12 I will send fire upon Teman
that will consume the fortresses of Bozrah."

13 This is what the LORD says:

"For three sins of Ammon,
even for four, I will not turn back ⌊my wrath⌋.
Because he ripped open the pregnant women of Gilead
in order to extend his borders,
14 I will set fire to the walls of Rabbah
that will consume her fortresses
amid war cries on the day of battle,
amid violent winds on a stormy day.
15 Her king[g] will go into exile,
he and his officials together,"
says the LORD.

2 This is what the LORD says:

"For three sins of Moab,
even for four, I will not turn back ⌊my wrath⌋.
Because he burned, as if to lime,
the bones of Edom's king,
2 I will send fire upon Moab
that will consume the fortresses of Kerioth.[h]
Moab will go down in great tumult
amid war cries and the blast of the trumpet.
3 I will destroy her ruler
and kill all her officials with him,"
says the LORD.

4 This is what the LORD says:

"For three sins of Judah,
even for four, I will not turn back ⌊my wrath⌋.
Because they have rejected the law of the LORD
and have not kept his decrees,

[a] 1 Hebrew *Joash*, a variant of *Jehoash* [b] 2 Or *shepherds mourn* [c] 5 Or *the inhabitants of* [d] 5 *Aven* means *wickedness.*
[e] 8 Or *inhabitants* [f] 11 Or *sword / and destroyed his allies* [g] 15 Or / *Molech*; Hebrew *malcam* [h] 2 Or *of her cities*

because they have been led astray by false gods,[a]
the gods[b] their ancestors followed,
5 I will send fire upon Judah
that will consume the fortresses of Jerusalem."

Judgment on Israel

6 This is what the LORD says:

"For three sins of Israel,
even for four, I will not turn back ⌞my wrath⌟.
They sell the righteous for silver,
and the needy for a pair of sandals.
7 They trample on the heads of the poor
as upon the dust of the ground
and deny justice to the oppressed.
Father and son use the same girl
and so profane my holy name.
8 They lie down beside every altar
on garments taken in pledge.
In the house of their god
they drink wine taken as fines.

9 "I destroyed the Amorite before them,
though he was tall as the cedars
and strong as the oaks.
I destroyed his fruit above
and his roots below.

10 "I brought you up out of Egypt,
and I led you forty years in the desert
to give you the land of the Amorites.
11 I also raised up prophets from among your sons
and Nazirites from among your young men.
Is this not true, people of Israel?"
declares the LORD.
12 "But you made the Nazirites drink wine
and commanded the prophets not to prophesy.

13 "Now then, I will crush you
as a cart crushes when loaded with grain.
14 The swift will not escape,
the strong will not muster their strength,
and the warrior will not save his life.
15 The archer will not stand his ground,
the fleet-footed soldier will not get away,
and the horseman will not save his life.
16 Even the bravest warriors
will flee naked on that day,"
declares the LORD.

Witnesses Summoned Against Israel

3 Hear this word the LORD has spoken against you, O people of Israel—against the whole family I brought up out of Egypt:

2 "You only have I chosen
of all the families of the earth;
therefore I will punish you
for all your sins."

3 Do two walk together
unless they have agreed to do so?
4 Does a lion roar in the thicket
when he has no prey?
Does he growl in his den
when he has caught nothing?
5 Does a bird fall into a trap on the ground
where no snare has been set?
Does a trap spring up from the earth
when there is nothing to catch?
6 When a trumpet sounds in a city,
do not the people tremble?
When disaster comes to a city,
has not the LORD caused it?

7 Surely the Sovereign LORD does nothing
without revealing his plan
to his servants the prophets.

8 The lion has roared—
who will not fear?
The Sovereign LORD has spoken—
who can but prophesy?

9 Proclaim to the fortresses of Ashdod
and to the fortresses of Egypt:
"Assemble yourselves on the mountains of Samaria;
see the great unrest within her
and the oppression among her people."

10 "They do not know how to do right,"
declares the LORD,
"who hoard plunder and loot in their fortresses."

11 Therefore this is what the Sovereign LORD says:

"An enemy will overrun the land;
he will pull down your strongholds
and plunder your fortresses."

12 This is what the LORD says:

"As a shepherd saves from the lion's mouth
only two leg bones or a piece of an ear,
so will the Israelites be saved,
those who sit in Samaria

[a] 4 Or *by lies* [b] 4 Or *lies*

on the edge of their beds
and in Damascus on their couches.[a]"

13 "Hear this and testify against the house
of Jacob," declares the Lord, the LORD God
Almighty.

14 "On the day I punish Israel for her sins,
I will destroy the altars of Bethel;
the horns of the altar will be cut off
and fall to the ground.
15 I will tear down the winter house
along with the summer house;
the houses adorned with ivory will be destroyed
and the mansions will be demolished,"
declares the LORD.

Israel Has Not Returned to God

4 Hear this word, you cows of Bashan on Mount Samaria,
you women who oppress the poor and crush the needy
and say to your husbands, "Bring us some drinks!"
2 The Sovereign LORD has sworn by his holiness:
"The time will surely come
when you will be taken away with hooks,
the last of you with fishhooks.
3 You will each go straight out
through breaks in the wall,
and you will be cast out toward Harmon,[b]"
declares the LORD.

4 "Go to Bethel and sin;
go to Gilgal and sin yet more.
Bring your sacrifices every morning,
your tithes every three years.[c]
5 Burn leavened bread as a thank offering
and brag about your freewill offerings—
boast about them, you Israelites,
for this is what you love to do,"
declares the Sovereign LORD.

6 "I gave you empty stomachs[d] in every city
and lack of bread in every town,
yet you have not returned to me,"
declares the LORD.

7 "I also withheld rain from you
when the harvest was still three months away.
I sent rain on one town,
but withheld it from another.
One field had rain;
another had none and dried up.
8 People staggered from town to town for water
but did not get enough to drink,
yet you have not returned to me,"
declares the LORD.

9 "Many times I struck your gardens and vineyards,
I struck them with blight and mildew.
Locusts devoured your fig and olive trees,
yet you have not returned to me,"
declares the LORD.

10 "I sent plagues among you
as I did to Egypt.
I killed your young men with the sword,
along with your captured horses.
I filled your nostrils with the stench of your camps,
yet you have not returned to me,"
declares the LORD.

11 "I overthrew some of you
as I[e] overthrew Sodom and Gomorrah.
You were like a burning stick snatched from the fire,
yet you have not returned to me,"
declares the LORD.

12 "Therefore this is what I will do to you, Israel,
and because I will do this to you,
prepare to meet your God, O Israel."

13 He who forms the mountains,
creates the wind,
and reveals his thoughts to man,
he who turns dawn to darkness,
and treads the high places of the earth—
the LORD God Almighty is his name.

A Lament and Call to Repentance

5 Hear this word, O house of Israel, this lament I take up concerning you:

2 "Fallen is Virgin Israel,
never to rise again,
deserted in her own land,
with no one to lift her up."

3 This is what the Sovereign LORD says:

"The city that marches out a thousand strong for Israel
will have only a hundred left;

[a] 12 The meaning of the Hebrew for this line is uncertain. [b] 3 Masoretic Text; with a different word division of the Hebrew (see Septuagint) *out, O mountain of oppression* [c] 4 Or *tithes on the third day* [d] 6 Hebrew *you cleanness of teeth* [e] 11 Hebrew *God*

WEEKEND

marriage counseling

Sometimes it feels like we aren't doing very well as a couple, but I'm not sure how we compare to others. How do we know if we need professional help?

The fairy-tale marriage concludes with "and they lived happily ever after." In other words, once you find the right person, fall in love and marry, all your problems will be over. Of course, this is pure fiction. In real life, all married couples have problems. But how do you know if your problems are serious enough to get professional help?

There is no clear-cut answer to this question, but a good rule of thumb is that if you are bumping your heads up against the same troubling issue over and over, you can probably benefit from seeing an objective professional counselor with expertise in marital issues. Whether your struggles center around communication, in-laws, intimacy, money, sexuality, spiritual matters or conflict, a trained professional can save you years of frustration and lead you to a more fulfilling marriage.

Marriage counselors can also be a tremendous help for couples who want to enrich their relationship. You don't have to be in a crisis to seek help from a counselor. Since most of us have never learned how to relate intimately to another, there are many benefits to be derived from discovering what marriage is all about from a trained professional.

Some couples get into trouble because they believe that they can't do much to improve their marriage, or they simply don't take the time to find the kind of help they need. Don't fall into this trap. Recognizing that you may not be able to solve a problem on your own is a sign of health and maturity, not inferiority or weakness.

We are experiencing some turbulence right now and have decided to get professional help. How can we find a competent counselor?

Unfortunately, the large demand for marriage improvement programs has brought some untrained and unscrupulous people into the field of marriage counseling. However, there are several things you can do to ensure competent help.

Start with a referral from a physician, minister, nurse, teacher or even a trusted friend. Then, check the credentials of people who are recommended. The foremost organization for accrediting and certifying marriage counselors is the American Association of Marriage and Family Therapists.

Membership in the American Psychological Association (APA) indicates that the person has met the minimum training requirements and has agreed to abide by strict ethics in client relationships. Your local phone book usually lists members of national and/or state psychological associations. The American Association of Sex Educators and Counselors has established certification standards for sex therapists.

Each of the secular professional organizations mentioned above can be a good source of information, but they are in no way the last word on whether a particular counselor or therapist is competent. If you are looking for Christian counselors, these organizations are not going to identify them for you. We recommend several sources for finding competent Christian counselors. One is maintained by Focus on the Family in Colorado Springs. Call 719–531–3400 for the names of Christian counselors in your area. You might also check to see if the counselor you are considering is a member of the American Association of Christian Counselors or the Christian Association of Psychological Studies.

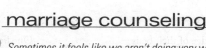

—DR. LES PARROTT III AND DR. LESLIE PARROTT

interviewing a counselor

Once you have several referrals, it is important to see which therapist is a good match for your situation. Before booking your first appointment, have a preliminary phone conversation and ask questions such as:

1. Are you certified or licensed?
2. Do you work with married couples on a regular basis?
3. What are your credentials (degrees)?
4. At what university did you earn your degrees?
5. What professional associations do you belong to?
6. How will you approach our particular issue?
7. How many sessions will we need?

If the phone interview sounds promising, schedule an in-person interview to better assess the number of sessions the counselor recommends. Both of you should feel comfortable working with the counselor. Follow your instincts.

HOW ARE WE DOING?

let's make a DATE

RELIVING HOW WE MET

Plan a date that pays tribute to the era you met. Download Billboard's number one song for that year to your iPod. Watch the movie that won the Academy Award for Best Picture that year. Rent a car that was new the year you met, and wear something that pays tribute to the hot fashion trend of the time. Build your date around reliving the first time you met. For a variation of this date, recreate the year your spouse was born.

FOR YOUR NEXT DEVOTIONAL READING, TURN TO PAGE 994.

LESSONS FROM THE *Bible*

Having trouble deciding whether you need marriage counseling? Compare your marriage to the descriptions in these passages. How do you measure up? In what ways could outside help move your marriage toward the ideal?

1. Ephesians 5:21–33
2. 1 Peter 3:1–12

the town that marches out a hundred
strong
will have only ten left."

4 This is what the LORD says to the house
of Israel:

"Seek me and live;
5 do not seek Bethel,
do not go to Gilgal,
do not journey to Beersheba.
For Gilgal will surely go into exile,
and Bethel will be reduced to
nothing.[a]"
6 Seek the LORD and live,
or he will sweep through the house of
Joseph like a fire;
it will devour,
and Bethel will have no one to quench
it.
7 You who turn justice into bitterness
and cast righteousness to the ground
8 (he who made the Pleiades and Orion,
who turns blackness into dawn
and darkens day into night,
who calls for the waters of the sea
and pours them out over the face of the
land—
the LORD is his name—
9 he flashes destruction on the stronghold
and brings the fortified city to ruin),
10 you hate the one who reproves in court
and despise him who tells the truth.

11 You trample on the poor
and force him to give you grain.
Therefore, though you have built stone
mansions,
you will not live in them;
though you have planted lush vineyards,
you will not drink their wine.
12 For I know how many are your offenses
and how great your sins.

You oppress the righteous and take bribes
and you deprive the poor of justice in
the courts.
13 Therefore the prudent man keeps quiet in
such times,
for the times are evil.

14 Seek good, not evil,
that you may live.
Then the LORD God Almighty will be with
you,
just as you say he is.
15 Hate evil, love good;
maintain justice in the courts.
Perhaps the LORD God Almighty will have
mercy
on the remnant of Joseph.

16 Therefore this is what the Lord, the LORD
God Almighty, says:

"There will be wailing in all the streets
and cries of anguish in every public
square.
The farmers will be summoned to weep
and the mourners to wail.
17 There will be wailing in all the vineyards,
for I will pass through your midst,"
says the LORD.

The Day of the LORD

18 Woe to you who long
for the day of the LORD!
Why do you long for the day of the
LORD?
That day will be darkness, not light.
19 It will be as though a man fled from a lion
only to meet a bear,
as though he entered his house
and rested his hand on the wall
only to have a snake bite him.
20 Will not the day of the LORD be darkness,
not light—
pitch-dark, without a ray of
brightness?

21 "I hate, I despise your religious feasts;
I cannot stand your assemblies.
22 Even though you bring me burnt offerings
and grain offerings,
I will not accept them.
Though you bring choice fellowship
offerings,[b]
I will have no regard for them.
23 Away with the noise of your songs!
I will not listen to the music of your
harps.
24 But let justice roll on like a river,
righteousness like a never-failing
stream!

25 "Did you bring me sacrifices and offerings
forty years in the desert, O house of
Israel?
26 You have lifted up the shrine of your
king,
the pedestal of your idols,
the star of your god[c]—

[a] 5 Or *grief*; or *wickedness*; Hebrew *aven*, a reference to Beth Aven (a derogatory name for Bethel) [b] 22 Traditionally *peace offerings*
[c] 26 Or *lifted up Sakkuth your king / and Kaiwan your idols, / your star-gods*; Septuagint *lifted up the shrine of Molech / and the star of your god Rephan, / their idols*

which you made for yourselves.
27 Therefore I will send you into exile beyond
Damascus,"
says the LORD, whose name is God
Almighty.

Woe to the Complacent

6 Woe to you who are complacent in Zion,
and to you who feel secure on Mount
Samaria,
you notable men of the foremost nation,
to whom the people of Israel come!
2 Go to Calneh and look at it;
go from there to great Hamath,
and then go down to Gath in Philistia.
Are they better off than your two
kingdoms?
Is their land larger than yours?
3 You put off the evil day
and bring near a reign of terror.
4 You lie on beds inlaid with ivory
and lounge on your couches.
You dine on choice lambs
and fattened calves.
5 You strum away on your harps like
David
and improvise on musical instruments.
6 You drink wine by the bowlful
and use the finest lotions,
but you do not grieve over the ruin of
Joseph.
7 Therefore you will be among the first to go
into exile;
your feasting and lounging will end.

The LORD Abhors the Pride of Israel

8 The Sovereign LORD has sworn by himself—the LORD God Almighty declares:

"I abhor the pride of Jacob
and detest his fortresses;
I will deliver up the city
and everything in it."

9 If ten men are left in one house, they too
will die. 10 And if a relative who is to burn the
bodies comes to carry them out of the house
and asks anyone still hiding there, "Is anyone
with you?" and he says, "No," then he will say,
"Hush! We must not mention the name of the
LORD."

11 For the LORD has given the command,
and he will smash the great house into
pieces
and the small house into bits.
12 Do horses run on the rocky crags?
Does one plow there with oxen?
But you have turned justice into poison
and the fruit of righteousness into
bitterness—
13 you who rejoice in the conquest of Lo
Debar[a]
and say, "Did we not take Karnaim[b] by
our own strength?"
14 For the LORD God Almighty declares,
"I will stir up a nation against you,
O house of Israel,
that will oppress you all the way
from Lebo[c] Hamath to the valley of the
Arabah."

Locusts, Fire and a Plumb Line

7 This is what the Sovereign LORD showed
me: He was preparing swarms of locusts after the king's share had been harvested and
just as the second crop was coming up. 2 When
they had stripped the land clean, I cried out,
"Sovereign LORD, forgive! How can Jacob survive? He is so small!"
3 So the LORD relented.
"This will not happen," the LORD said.
4 This is what the Sovereign LORD showed
me: The Sovereign LORD was calling for judgment by fire; it dried up the great deep and devoured the land. 5 Then I cried out, "Sovereign
LORD, I beg you, stop! How can Jacob survive?
He is so small!"
6 So the LORD relented.
"This will not happen either," the Sovereign
LORD said.

7 This is what he showed me: The Lord was
standing by a wall that had been built true
to plumb, with a plumb line in his hand.
8 And the LORD asked me, "What do you see,
Amos?"
"A plumb line," I replied.
Then the Lord said, "Look, I am setting
a plumb line among my people Israel; I will
spare them no longer.

9 "The high places of Isaac will be destroyed
and the sanctuaries of Israel will be
ruined;
with my sword I will rise against the
house of Jeroboam."

Amos and Amaziah

10 Then Amaziah the priest of Bethel sent
a message to Jeroboam king of Israel: "Amos
is raising a conspiracy against you in the very

---

[a] 13 *Lo Debar* means *nothing.* [b] 13 *Karnaim* means *horns; horn* here symbolizes strength. [c] 14 Or *from the entrance to*

GOING OUT OF OUR WAY

> **You will be among the first to go into exile; your feasting and lounging will end.**
>
> — Amos 6:7

let's talk

- What kinds of love and compassion do we find difficult to extend to others? Why?
- When have we been "bothered" to serve each other or a friend? What did that cost us? Was it worth the benefit we provided someone else? In what way?
- What caring and considerate gestures have others extended to us? How did they encourage us?

One day when David was out of town, I backed the car out of the drive and ran over some nails. The roof on our house had recently been replaced, and the roofers had thrown old shingles and nails onto the driveway and failed to clean up all the nails. Two of the tires were flat. Two flats plus only one spare minus one husband plus a house full of small children equaled a real mess. But then something beautiful happened.

When I called my neighbor for a ride, her self-employed husband dropped everything he was doing. He and his son put two spares (ours and theirs) on our van and took it away to have both tires replaced. They were back in a few hours and refused to let me pay for the new tires. Can you imagine such thoughtfulness? My van came back ready to drive with two new tires.

My neighbors showed the kind of love and compassion that was lacking in the people of Israel in Amos's day. In fact, God said that the people were the very opposite of helpful and kind; they were self-centered, complacent and lazy. God warned them that they would suffer divine justice for their lack of faithfulness to God and consideration for others.

It's important to God that we, his people, look after each other. Sometimes I find it's easy to be kind or extend a favor *if* it fits into my schedule or *if* it's something that doesn't cost me time, money, mess or bother. But how much love do those favors really require?

Recently my husband and I attended a family wedding. Some distant relative cornered my husband for what my sister-in-law called a "yak-a-thon." "Is David enjoying that conversation?" my sister-in-law asked me with a grin.

"No," I told her, "but he's trying to!" He really was too. He was giving the long-winded talker his close attention, and he was trying hard not to cut him short or slide away. I like that about David; he cares more about a person's feelings than about how bored or bothered he is by a rambling conversation.

My personal challenge is learning to welcome interruptions. With four kids, a busy schedule and a self-employed, at-home husband, my time is at a premium. I wake up each morning with a lengthy to-do list for the day imprinted on my mind. Sometimes it's hard for me to let that list go so that I can give my attention and time to someone—a visitor, a telephone caller, one of the kids—whose need shakes up my agenda.

In the book of Amos, the prophet called the people to account and deliberately reminded them of their selfishness. As a result, they, and we, are left with a strong reminder of how important it is to love and serve others.

My neighbors pleased God and deeply blessed me by taking care of my disabled van. David edified his yakking relative with kind attention. Being bothered for Christ's sake is ultimately more worthy than protecting a personal agenda.

—ANNETTE LAPLACA

FOR YOUR NEXT DEVOTIONAL READING, TURN TO PAGE 999.

heart of Israel. The land cannot bear all his
words. 11For this is what Amos is saying:

" 'Jeroboam will die by the sword,
and Israel will surely go into exile,
away from their native land.' "

12Then Amaziah said to Amos, "Get out,
you seer! Go back to the land of Judah. Earn
your bread there and do your prophesying
there. 13Don't prophesy anymore at Bethel,
because this is the king's sanctuary and the
temple of the kingdom."
14Amos answered Amaziah, "I was neither
a prophet nor a prophet's son, but I was a
shepherd, and I also took care of sycamore-fig
trees. 15But the LORD took me from tending
the flock and said to me, 'Go, prophesy to my
people Israel.' 16Now then, hear the word of
the LORD. You say,

" 'Do not prophesy against Israel,
and stop preaching against the house of Isaac.'

17"Therefore this is what the LORD says:

" 'Your wife will become a prostitute in the city,
and your sons and daughters will fall by the sword.
Your land will be measured and divided up,
and you yourself will die in a pagan[a] country.
And Israel will certainly go into exile,
away from their native land.' "

A Basket of Ripe Fruit

8 This is what the Sovereign LORD showed
me: a basket of ripe fruit. 2"What do you
see, Amos?" he asked.
"A basket of ripe fruit," I answered.
Then the LORD said to me, "The time is ripe
for my people Israel; I will spare them no longer.
3"In that day," declares the Sovereign LORD,
"the songs in the temple will turn to wailing.[b]
Many, many bodies—flung everywhere! Silence!"

4Hear this, you who trample the needy
and do away with the poor of the land,

5saying,

"When will the New Moon be over
that we may sell grain,
and the Sabbath be ended
that we may market wheat?"—
skimping the measure,
boosting the price
and cheating with dishonest scales,
6buying the poor with silver
and the needy for a pair of sandals,
selling even the sweepings with the wheat.

7The LORD has sworn by the Pride of Jacob:
"I will never forget anything they have done.

8"Will not the land tremble for this,
and all who live in it mourn?
The whole land will rise like the Nile;
it will be stirred up and then sink
like the river of Egypt.

9"In that day," declares the Sovereign LORD,

"I will make the sun go down at noon
and darken the earth in broad daylight.
10I will turn your religious feasts into mourning
and all your singing into weeping.
I will make all of you wear sackcloth
and shave your heads.
I will make that time like mourning for an only son
and the end of it like a bitter day.

11"The days are coming," declares the Sovereign LORD,
"when I will send a famine through the land—
not a famine of food or a thirst for water,
but a famine of hearing the words of the LORD.
12Men will stagger from sea to sea
and wander from north to east,
searching for the word of the LORD,
but they will not find it.

13"In that day

"the lovely young women and strong young men
will faint because of thirst.
14They who swear by the shame[c] of Samaria,
or say, 'As surely as your god lives, O Dan,'
or, 'As surely as the god[d] of Beersheba lives'—
they will fall,
never to rise again."

[a] 17 Hebrew *an unclean* [b] 3 Or *"the temple singers will wail* [c] 14 Or *by Ashima*; or *by the idol* [d] 14 Or *power*

Israel to Be Destroyed

9 I saw the Lord standing by the altar, and he said:

"Strike the tops of the pillars
so that the thresholds shake.
Bring them down on the heads of all the people;
those who are left I will kill with the sword.
Not one will get away,
none will escape.
2 Though they dig down to the depths of the grave,[a]
from there my hand will take them.
Though they climb up to the heavens,
from there I will bring them down.
3 Though they hide themselves on the top of Carmel,
there I will hunt them down and seize them.
Though they hide from me at the bottom of the sea,
there I will command the serpent to bite them.
4 Though they are driven into exile by their enemies,
there I will command the sword to slay them.
I will fix my eyes upon them
for evil and not for good."

5 The Lord, the LORD Almighty,
he who touches the earth and it melts,
and all who live in it mourn—
the whole land rises like the Nile,
then sinks like the river of Egypt—
6 he who builds his lofty palace[b] in the heavens
and sets its foundation[c] on the earth,
who calls for the waters of the sea
and pours them out over the face of the land—
the LORD is his name.

7 "Are not you Israelites
the same to me as the Cushites[d]?"
declares the LORD.
"Did I not bring Israel up from Egypt,
the Philistines from Caphtor[e]
and the Arameans from Kir?

8 "Surely the eyes of the Sovereign LORD
are on the sinful kingdom.
I will destroy it
from the face of the earth—
yet I will not totally destroy
the house of Jacob,"
declares the LORD.
9 "For I will give the command,
and I will shake the house of Israel
among all the nations
as grain is shaken in a sieve,
and not a pebble will reach the ground.
10 All the sinners among my people
will die by the sword,
all those who say,
'Disaster will not overtake or meet us.'

Israel's Restoration

11 "In that day I will restore
David's fallen tent.
I will repair its broken places,
restore its ruins,
and build it as it used to be,
12 so that they may possess the remnant of Edom
and all the nations that bear my name,[f]"
declares the LORD,
who will do these things.

13 "The days are coming," declares the LORD,

"when the reaper will be overtaken by the plowman
and the planter by the one treading grapes.
New wine will drip from the mountains
and flow from all the hills.
14 I will bring back my exiled[g] people Israel;
they will rebuild the ruined cities and live in them.
They will plant vineyards and drink their wine;
they will make gardens and eat their fruit.
15 I will plant Israel in their own land,
never again to be uprooted
from the land I have given them,"
says the LORD your God.

a 2 Hebrew *to Sheol* *b* 6 The meaning of the Hebrew for this phrase is uncertain. *c* 6 The meaning of the Hebrew for this word is uncertain. *d* 7 That is, people from the upper Nile region *e* 7 That is, Crete *f* 12 Hebrew; Septuagint *so that the remnant of men / and all the nations that bear my name may seek ⌞the Lord⌟* *g* 14 Or *will restore the fortunes of my*

OBADIAH

Obadiah

QUICK FACTS

AUTHOR Obadiah

AUDIENCE The Edomites and the people of Judah

DATE Probably during the Babylonian attacks on Jerusalem (605–586 B.C.)

SETTING The Edomites, who were descendants of Esau and related to the Israelites, were gloating over Israel's troubles.

When world events are violent and unsettling or when tragedy touches close to home, do you ever wonder, "Where is God? What in the world is he doing?" Obadiah has an answer: No matter what is going on or how grim the future looks, God's righteous purposes for this world will prevail. Behind the scenes, God is working for his people.

Obadiah described how Edom, Judah's wicked neighbor and relative (the people of Edom were descendants of Esau, and the people of Judah were descendants of Esau's brother Jacob), gloated as Judah fell and then looted them. Obadiah then prophesied how the same fate, and worse, would befall the Edomites. Obadiah pronounced God's fierce judgment on Edom, promising Israel that ultimately "the kingdom will be the LORD's" (Obadiah 21). Israel would one day be restored under God's permanent royal authority. God's people would be triumphant with him at the end of earthly time.

In a world plagued by war, terrorism, crime, addictions and broken relationships, sin often seems to be gaining so many strongholds that Christian couples cannot possibly hope for a victorious future. Obadiah tells us to keep trusting in our faithful, sovereign God. Those who belong to the Lord and cling to his promises and power will experience great victory.

1 The vision of Obadiah.

This is what the Sovereign LORD says about Edom—

We have heard a message from the LORD:
An envoy was sent to the nations to say,
"Rise, and let us go against her for battle"—

2 "See, I will make you small among the nations;
you will be utterly despised.
3 The pride of your heart has deceived you,
you who live in the clefts of the rocks[a]
and make your home on the heights,
you who say to yourself,
'Who can bring me down to the ground?'
4 Though you soar like the eagle
and make your nest among the stars,
from there I will bring you down,"
declares the LORD.
5 "If thieves came to you,
if robbers in the night—
Oh, what a disaster awaits you—
would they not steal only as much as they wanted?
If grape pickers came to you,
would they not leave a few grapes?
6 But how Esau will be ransacked,
his hidden treasures pillaged!
7 All your allies will force you to the border;
your friends will deceive and overpower you;
those who eat your bread will set a trap for you,[b]
but you will not detect it.

8 "In that day," declares the LORD,
"will I not destroy the wise men of Edom,
men of understanding in the mountains of Esau?
9 Your warriors, O Teman, will be terrified,
and everyone in Esau's mountains
will be cut down in the slaughter.
10 Because of the violence against your brother Jacob,
you will be covered with shame;
you will be destroyed forever.
11 On the day you stood aloof
while strangers carried off his wealth
and foreigners entered his gates
and cast lots for Jerusalem,
you were like one of them.
12 You should not look down on your brother
in the day of his misfortune,
nor rejoice over the people of Judah
in the day of their destruction,
nor boast so much
in the day of their trouble.
13 You should not march through the gates of my people
in the day of their disaster,
nor look down on them in their calamity
in the day of their disaster,
nor seize their wealth
in the day of their disaster.
14 You should not wait at the crossroads
to cut down their fugitives,
nor hand over their survivors
in the day of their trouble.

15 "The day of the LORD is near
for all nations.
As you have done, it will be done to you;
your deeds will return upon your own head.
16 Just as you drank on my holy hill,
so all the nations will drink continually;
they will drink and drink
and be as if they had never been.
17 But on Mount Zion will be deliverance;
it will be holy,
and the house of Jacob
will possess its inheritance.
18 The house of Jacob will be a fire
and the house of Joseph a flame;
the house of Esau will be stubble,
and they will set it on fire and consume it.
There will be no survivors
from the house of Esau."
The LORD has spoken.

19 People from the Negev will occupy
the mountains of Esau,
and people from the foothills will possess
the land of the Philistines.
They will occupy the fields of Ephraim and Samaria,
and Benjamin will possess Gilead.
20 This company of Israelite exiles who are in Canaan
will possess ⌞the land⌟ as far as Zarephath;
the exiles from Jerusalem who are in Sepharad
will possess the towns of the Negev.
21 Deliverers will go up on[c] Mount Zion
to govern the mountains of Esau.
And the kingdom will be the LORD's.

---

[a] 3 Or *of Sela* [b] 7 The meaning of the Hebrew for this clause is uncertain. [c] 21 Or *from*

TUESDAY
READ OBADIAH 1–21

NO MORE GLOATING

"You should not look down on your brother in the day of his misfortune, nor rejoice over the people of Judah in the day of their destruction."

— Obadiah 12

let's talk

- ✦ In what ways do we find that our individual ideas about justice or what's fair lead to resentments between us?
- ✦ How have we each needed God's forgiveness in the past?
- ✦ How does being forgiven help us extend grace to each other?

Humans have an innate sense of justice. Children continually demand that things be fair. We gravitate toward stories in which heroes triumph and the bad guys get what they deserve. But many places in Scripture warn God's people and others not to cherish their own sense of justice.

Although the book of Obadiah ends on a high note, pointing to the eventual triumph of Judah, the prophecy is almost all bad news. Through Obadiah, God was chastising the people of Edom, the descendants of Esau, who nurtured long-held animosities against the people of Israel. The Edomites looked on in glee while the Babylonians ransacked Jerusalem and carried the Hebrew people into captivity. They even joined in the looting. God said to the Edomites, "As you have done, it will be done to you; your deeds will return upon your own head" (Obadiah 15).

This warning to view one's own situation with humility is a recurrent theme in both the Old and New Testaments. That's what looking for the plank in your own eye instead of the speck of sawdust in someone else's eye is all about (see Matthew 7:3). That's what "Do not judge, and you will not be judged" means (Luke 6:37). The warning is that we should not be too glad when someone else gets what's coming to him or her because our own day of reckoning will come, and then we will long for God's mercy for ourselves.

The Edomites gloated over the Israelites in their day of trouble. While we might not admit to smiling over another person's downfall, we are prone to similar feelings. When others have wronged us, it's natural to gloat when circumstances seem to slap them down. This can even happen in marriage when there are unresolved issues between spouses. It's easy to focus on our own selfless actions and get up on our high horse, looking down on our spouse's more annoying behaviors. We might even feel pleased when our spouse gets his or her "comeuppance."

But God has called us to something much better than indulging our natural human reactions. He teaches us the only way to break these downward spiraling cycles of getting back at our enemy or rejoicing as they suffer: When we see ourselves clearly, we realize that we all need to be at the cross of Christ, asking forgiveness for our sinful choices and begging for God's grace.

So when your natural sense of justice begins to say, "Well, that serves him right!" or "Maybe she won't be so snooty now," don't listen. Recall your dependence on the mercy of God, and pray for God to replace your sinful desires with his gracious loving-kindness.

—ANNETTE LAPLACA

FOR YOUR NEXT DEVOTIONAL READING, TURN TO PAGE 1002.

JONAH

Jonah

QUICK FACTS

AUTHOR Jonah

AUDIENCE The northern kingdom (Israel) and all of God's people

DATE Probably about 750 B.C.

SETTING God sent reluctant Jonah to the despised city of Nineveh to preach repentance.

The book of Jonah is more than a story about a man who got swallowed by a big fish. It is a story that powerfully illustrates the mercy God shows to even the most sinful and hard-hearted people.

Despite God's command, Jonah felt no desire to bring God's call of repentance to Nineveh—the "great city" and future capital of the brutal, terrifying Assyrian Empire. During his three-day captivity in the belly of a fish, Jonah should have developed some personal understanding of God's mercy. Yet, because of the Ninevites' enmity against Israel, Jonah became angry when God forgave them. Jonah knew they didn't deserve God's grace, and it offended his sense of justice to see the Ninevites dodge God's judgment. Through the provision and destruction of a shade-giving plant, God patiently showed Jonah that his mercy is for everyone, even a runaway prophet.

We can all identify with Jonah's reluctance to forgive. But we are all called, like Jonah, to do God's work and to extend God's grace to others in a needy, sinful world.

Jonah Flees From the LORD

1 The word of the LORD came to Jonah son
of Amittai: 2"Go to the great city of Nineveh and preach against it, because its wickedness has come up before me."
3But Jonah ran away from the LORD and
headed for Tarshish. He went down to Joppa,
where he found a ship bound for that port. After paying the fare, he went aboard and sailed
for Tarshish to flee from the LORD.
4Then the LORD sent a great wind on the
sea, and such a violent storm arose that the
ship threatened to break up. 5All the sailors
were afraid and each cried out to his own god.
And they threw the cargo into the sea to light-
en the ship.
But Jonah had gone below deck, where
he lay down and fell into a deep sleep. 6The
captain went to him and said, "How can you
sleep? Get up and call on your god! Maybe he
will take notice of us, and we will not perish."
7Then the sailors said to each other, "Come,
let us cast lots to find out who is responsible
for this calamity." They cast lots and the lot
fell on Jonah.
8So they asked him, "Tell us, who is responsible for making all this trouble for us? What
do you do? Where do you come from? What is
your country? From what people are you?"
9He answered, "I am a Hebrew and I worship the LORD, the God of heaven, who made
the sea and the land."
10This terrified them and they asked, "What
have you done?" (They knew he was running
away from the LORD, because he had already
told them so.)
11The sea was getting rougher and rougher.
So they asked him, "What should we do to
you to make the sea calm down for us?"
12"Pick me up and throw me into the sea,"
he replied, "and it will become calm. I know
that it is my fault that this great storm has
come upon you."
13Instead, the men did their best to row
back to land. But they could not, for the sea
grew even wilder than before. 14Then they
cried to the LORD, "O LORD, please do not let
us die for taking this man's life. Do not hold
us accountable for killing an innocent man,
for you, O LORD, have done as you pleased."
15Then they took Jonah and threw him overboard, and the raging sea grew calm. 16At this
the men greatly feared the LORD, and they offered a sacrifice to the LORD and made vows
to him.
17But the LORD provided a great fish to
swallow Jonah, and Jonah was inside the fish
three days and three nights.

Jonah's Prayer

2 From inside the fish Jonah prayed to the
LORD his God. 2He said:

"In my distress I called to the LORD,
 and he answered me.
From the depths of the grave[a] I called for
  help,
 and you listened to my cry.
3You hurled me into the deep,
 into the very heart of the seas,
 and the currents swirled about me;
all your waves and breakers
 swept over me.
4I said, 'I have been banished
 from your sight;
yet I will look again
 toward your holy temple.'
5The engulfing waters threatened me,[b]
 the deep surrounded me;
 seaweed was wrapped around my
  head.
6To the roots of the mountains I sank
  down;
 the earth beneath barred me in
  forever.
But you brought my life up from the pit,
 O LORD my God.

7"When my life was ebbing away,
 I remembered you, LORD,
and my prayer rose to you,
 to your holy temple.

8"Those who cling to worthless idols
 forfeit the grace that could be theirs.
9But I, with a song of thanksgiving,
 will sacrifice to you.
What I have vowed I will make good.
 Salvation comes from the LORD."

10And the LORD commanded the fish, and
it vomited Jonah onto dry land.

Jonah Goes to Nineveh

3 Then the word of the LORD came to Jonah a second time: 2"Go to the great city
of Nineveh and proclaim to it the message
I give you."
3Jonah obeyed the word of the LORD and

[a] 2 Hebrew *Sheol* [b] 5 Or *waters were at my throat*

W

WEDNESDAY
READ JONAH 1:1–17

RUNNING FROM TROUBLE

But Jonah ran away from the LORD and headed for Tarshish.

— JONAH 1:3

let's talk

- Is there a current situation with our family that we'd like to run from? What might happen if we do? What does the Bible say about trying to avoid sticky issues, particularly within the family?
- Must we always interact with people who are difficult, regardless of how unreasonable they are?
- What are some good ways of handling tension with parents or in-laws that would be God-honoring?

We had taken our daughters on a cross-country flight to visit their grandparents. Although my mother-in-law had never particularly liked me, she had always managed to be civil. However, during this visit the "gloves came off." She criticized me almost from day one, and we were staying with her for two weeks—14 extremely long days.

To escape her barbs, I stayed to myself as much as possible, wrestling between wanting to protect myself and not wanting to be rude and thus giving her more reason to dislike me.

One night she exploded and unleashed years' worth of venom and anger toward me. In the middle of her outburst, my husband announced, "This is my wife, and you will not treat her this way. I'm taking my family and leaving."

Mentally, I was already packed and on a flight home, but something in me knew that God was calling us to stay. Even though everything in me wanted to flee, I told my husband that we couldn't leave and that I would be okay. He could trust me on this.

We did stay, and though things remained terribly tense, I was okay. God's grace was sufficient for every trial.

Less than six months later, my husband's mother unexpectedly died. That awful visit was the last time we ever saw her alive.

I understand wanting to run away from difficulty. The prophet Jonah moved fast in the opposite direction after God told him to go to Nineveh, the future capital city of Assyria, to preach to its people. The Assyrians, the dominant people of the time, were known for their wickedness in general and their cruelty in particular. Jonah couldn't stand the thought of the Ninevites receiving mercy and pardon, so he ran from the Lord and boarded a ship heading for Tarshish.

Eventually Jonah did go to Nineveh, but not until after he was thrown off the ship into a stormy sea and was saved from drowning by a big fish that later vomited him up on shore. After that fearful, disgusting ordeal, Jonah didn't hesitate when God told him a second time to go to Nineveh.

As a result, the Ninevites repented, and Israel had one less enemy to contend with for a while. In my encounter with my mother-in-law, we didn't do anything so dramatic as to spare a nation from God's wrath, but if we had run away from my mother-in-law, my husband might have been haunted by guilt for the rest of his life.

One thing we both do know: We did the right thing, and because of that, we have no regrets.

—NANCY KENNEDY

FOR YOUR NEXT DEVOTIONAL READING, TURN TO PAGE 1007.

went to Nineveh. Now Nineveh was a very
important city—a visit required three days.
4On the first day, Jonah started into the city.
He proclaimed: "Forty more days and Nineveh will be overturned." 5The Ninevites believed God. They declared a fast, and all of
them, from the greatest to the least, put on
sackcloth.

6When the news reached the king of Nineveh, he rose from his throne, took off his royal
robes, covered himself with sackcloth and sat
down in the dust. 7Then he issued a proclamation in Nineveh:

"By the decree of the king and his nobles:

Do not let any man or beast, herd or
flock, taste anything; do not let them eat
or drink. 8But let man and beast be covered with sackcloth. Let everyone call urgently on God. Let them give up their evil
ways and their violence. 9Who knows?
God may yet relent and with compassion
turn from his fierce anger so that we will
not perish."

10When God saw what they did and how
they turned from their evil ways, he had compassion and did not bring upon them the destruction he had threatened.

Jonah's Anger at the LORD's Compassion

4 But Jonah was greatly displeased and became angry. 2He prayed to the LORD,
"O LORD, is this not what I said when I
was still at home? That is why I was so quick
to flee to Tarshish. I knew that you are a gracious and compassionate God, slow to anger
and abounding in love, a God who relents
from sending calamity. 3Now, O LORD, take
away my life, for it is better for me to die than
to live."

4But the LORD replied, "Have you any right
to be angry?"

5Jonah went out and sat down at a place
east of the city. There he made himself a shelter, sat in its shade and waited to see what
would happen to the city. 6Then the LORD
God provided a vine and made it grow up over
Jonah to give shade for his head to ease his discomfort, and Jonah was very happy about the
vine. 7But at dawn the next day God provided a worm, which chewed the vine so that it
withered. 8When the sun rose, God provided
a scorching east wind, and the sun blazed on
Jonah's head so that he grew faint. He wanted
to die, and said, "It would be better for me to
die than to live."

9But God said to Jonah, "Do you have a
right to be angry about the vine?"

"I do," he said. "I am angry enough to
die."

10But the LORD said, "You have been concerned about this vine, though you did not
tend it or make it grow. It sprang up overnight
and died overnight. 11But Nineveh has more
than a hundred and twenty thousand people
who cannot tell their right hand from their
left, and many cattle as well. Should I not be
concerned about that great city?"

MICAH

Micah

QUICK FACTS

AUTHOR Micah

AUDIENCE The people of Judah and Israel

DATE Sometime between 750 and 686 B.C., during the ministries of Isaiah and Hosea

SETTING A time of political mayhem and corruption, when evil kings ruled

The prophet Micah lived during difficult times: God's people were corrupted by sin and did not follow his commands to care for others. The prophecies of Micah reminded the people that God would judge and that God would save. The character of God emerged as Micah denounced the things God hates, and the heart of God became clear as Micah proclaimed God's strong desire to restore and bless his wayward people.

Micah answered the question "What does a holy but loving God expect from us?" The answer seems startlingly simple: "To act justly and to love mercy and to walk humbly with your God" (Micah 6:8). In many ways, this is a summary of much of the teaching found in the New Testament. The reason God's demands upon us are so succinct is that he has already done so much for us. He has graciously purchased our salvation through the sacrifice of Jesus. By the gift of his Spirit, he enables us to live for him.

Dig into the prophet Micah's message to discover the righteous character and the tender heart of God. Acting justly, loving mercy and walking humbly with God could transform all your relationships—starting with the ones at home.

1 The word of the LORD that came to Micah of Moresheth during the reigns of Jotham, Ahaz and Hezekiah, kings of Judah—the vision he saw concerning Samaria and Jerusalem.

2 Hear, O peoples, all of you,
listen, O earth and all who are in it,
that the Sovereign LORD may witness against you,
the Lord from his holy temple.

Judgment Against Samaria and Jerusalem

3 Look! The LORD is coming from his dwelling place;
he comes down and treads the high places of the earth.
4 The mountains melt beneath him
and the valleys split apart,
like wax before the fire,
like water rushing down a slope.
5 All this is because of Jacob's transgression,
because of the sins of the house of Israel.
What is Jacob's transgression?
Is it not Samaria?
What is Judah's high place?
Is it not Jerusalem?

6 "Therefore I will make Samaria a heap of rubble,
a place for planting vineyards.
I will pour her stones into the valley
and lay bare her foundations.
7 All her idols will be broken to pieces;
all her temple gifts will be burned with fire;
I will destroy all her images.
Since she gathered her gifts from the wages of prostitutes,
as the wages of prostitutes they will again be used."

Weeping and Mourning

8 Because of this I will weep and wail;
I will go about barefoot and naked.
I will howl like a jackal
and moan like an owl.
9 For her wound is incurable;
it has come to Judah.
It[a] has reached the very gate of my people,
even to Jerusalem itself.
10 Tell it not in Gath[b];
weep not at all.[c]
In Beth Ophrah[d]
roll in the dust.
11 Pass on in nakedness and shame,
you who live in Shaphir.[e]
Those who live in Zaanan[f]
will not come out.
Beth Ezel is in mourning;
its protection is taken from you.
12 Those who live in Maroth[g] writhe in pain,
waiting for relief,
because disaster has come from the LORD,
even to the gate of Jerusalem.
13 You who live in Lachish,[h]
harness the team to the chariot.
You were the beginning of sin
to the Daughter of Zion,
for the transgressions of Israel
were found in you.
14 Therefore you will give parting gifts
to Moresheth Gath.
The town of Aczib[i] will prove deceptive
to the kings of Israel.
15 I will bring a conqueror against you
who live in Mareshah.[j]
He who is the glory of Israel
will come to Adullam.
16 Shave your heads in mourning
for the children in whom you delight;
make yourselves as bald as the vulture,
for they will go from you into exile.

Man's Plans and God's

2 Woe to those who plan iniquity,
to those who plot evil on their beds!
At morning's light they carry it out
because it is in their power to do it.
2 They covet fields and seize them,
and houses, and take them.
They defraud a man of his home,
a fellowman of his inheritance.

3 Therefore, the LORD says:

"I am planning disaster against this people,
from which you cannot save yourselves.
You will no longer walk proudly,
for it will be a time of calamity.
4 In that day men will ridicule you;
they will taunt you with this mournful song:
'We are utterly ruined;
my people's possession is divided up.
He takes it from me!
He assigns our fields to traitors.' "

---

[a] 9 Or *He* [b] 10 *Gath* sounds like the Hebrew for *tell.* [c] 10 Hebrew; Septuagint may suggest *not in Acco.* The Hebrew for *in Acco* sounds like the Hebrew for *weep.* [d] 10 *Beth Ophrah* means *house of dust.* [e] 11 *Shaphir* means *pleasant.* [f] 11 *Zaanan* sounds like the Hebrew for *come out.* [g] 12 *Maroth* sounds like the Hebrew for *bitter.* [h] 13 *Lachish* sounds like the Hebrew for *team.* [i] 14 *Aczib* means *deception.* [j] 15 *Mareshah* sounds like the Hebrew for *conqueror.*

5 Therefore you will have no one in the
assembly of the LORD
to divide the land by lot.

False Prophets

6 "Do not prophesy," their prophets say.
"Do not prophesy about these things;
disgrace will not overtake us."
7 Should it be said, O house of Jacob:
"Is the Spirit of the LORD angry?
Does he do such things?"

"Do not my words do good
to him whose ways are upright?
8 Lately my people have risen up
like an enemy.
You strip off the rich robe
from those who pass by without a care,
like men returning from battle.
9 You drive the women of my people
from their pleasant homes.
You take away my blessing
from their children forever.
10 Get up, go away!
For this is not your resting place,
because it is defiled,
it is ruined, beyond all remedy.
11 If a liar and deceiver comes and says,
'I will prophesy for you plenty of wine
and beer,'
he would be just the prophet for this
people!

Deliverance Promised

12 "I will surely gather all of you, O Jacob;
I will surely bring together the remnant
of Israel.
I will bring them together like sheep in a
pen,
like a flock in its pasture;
the place will throng with people.
13 One who breaks open the way will go up
before them;
they will break through the gate and go
out.
Their king will pass through before them,
the LORD at their head."

Leaders and Prophets Rebuked

3 Then I said,

"Listen, you leaders of Jacob,
you rulers of the house of Israel.
Should you not know justice,
2 you who hate good and love evil;
who tear the skin from my people
and the flesh from their bones;
3 who eat my people's flesh,
strip off their skin
and break their bones in pieces;
who chop them up like meat for the pan,
like flesh for the pot?"
4 Then they will cry out to the LORD,
but he will not answer them.
At that time he will hide his face from
them
because of the evil they have done.

5 This is what the LORD says:

"As for the prophets
who lead my people astray,
if one feeds them,
they proclaim 'peace';
if he does not,
they prepare to wage war against him.
6 Therefore night will come over you,
without visions,
and darkness, without divination.
The sun will set for the prophets,
and the day will go dark for them.
7 The seers will be ashamed
and the diviners disgraced.
They will all cover their faces
because there is no answer from God."

8 But as for me, I am filled with power,
with the Spirit of the LORD,
and with justice and might,
to declare to Jacob his transgression,
to Israel his sin.
9 Hear this, you leaders of the house of
Jacob,
you rulers of the house of Israel,
who despise justice
and distort all that is right;
10 who build Zion with bloodshed,
and Jerusalem with wickedness.
11 Her leaders judge for a bribe,
her priests teach for a price,
and her prophets tell fortunes for
money.
Yet they lean upon the LORD and say,
"Is not the LORD among us?
No disaster will come upon us."
12 Therefore because of you,
Zion will be plowed like a field,
Jerusalem will become a heap of rubble,
the temple hill a mound overgrown
with thickets.

THURSDAY
READ MICAH 3:1–12

DEALING WITH DOUBLETALK

> **Then they will cry out to the LORD, but he will not answer them. At that time he will hide his face from them because of the evil they have done.**
>
> — MICAH 3:4

When you live up-close and personal, as married couples do, it doesn't take long to see through each other's doubletalk. If he says, "Sure, I'll take on a good share of the housekeeping" but never picks up a mop or dust cloth and fails to put his dirty socks in the hamper, she's going to learn mighty quickly that his words are empty. If she says, "Of course I respect you, Darling" but doesn't forget her own agenda long enough to give him her attention, he will know her words don't mean a thing.

Actions speak so loudly that after a while people won't listen anymore to words they know to be empty. In Micah 3, the prophet warned that one day God would turn a deaf ear to the leaders in Judah. Instead of extending the mercy that is so characteristic of God, he would "listen" to their evil deeds rather than their cries for help. Micah pointed out the doubletalk of these rulers, who should have known and practiced justice but instead were oppressing the people. Likewise, the prophets were guilty of falsely proclaiming—for a fee—what people wanted to hear. God, who judges the hearts of humankind, knew that the leaders' actions, not their words, spoke the truth.

If we pattern our marital behavior after Jesus, our model for godly behavior, we will want to forgive each other "seventy-seven times," as Jesus instructed Peter to do in Matthew 18:22. We will want to offer unlimited fresh starts to those who have sinned against us. And yet, forgiving each other doesn't mean allowing wrong or sinful actions to continue. Genuine repentance is demonstrated through changed behavior that flows from a renewed heart and transformed attitudes.

So what kind of damage do we create if we say one thing with our lips and behave, again and again, in ways that contradict our spoken words? Eventually others will stop believing our words, promises and commitments and expect our words to be meaningless. Trust can be so abused, so broken, that others become deaf to what we speak and "listen" only to what's being done.

When I was little, we sang a song in Sunday school with a verse that went, "Oh, be careful little mouth what you say, for the Father up above is listening in love, so be careful little mouth what you say." I want my actions to back up the verbal promises I made to my husband on the day I vowed, "I do!" I don't ever want to violate that trust.

My spouse is watching and "listening" to my actions. So is God, who is the ultimate judge of all our hearts. And he will hold me accountable for the consistency of my words and behavior.

—ANNETTE LAPLACA

let's talk

- ✦ When have my actions failed to live up to my words—or my good intentions?
- ✦ Does living in close fellowship with each other help hold us accountable for what we say and do? Does that kind of closeness make us feel uncomfortably vulnerable?
- ✦ How does offering each other forgiveness balance itself with helping each other turn around negative behavior patterns?

FOR YOUR NEXT DEVOTIONAL READING, TURN TO PAGE 1010.

The Mountain of the LORD

4 In the last days
the mountain of the LORD's temple will be established
as chief among the mountains;
it will be raised above the hills,
and peoples will stream to it.

2 Many nations will come and say,

"Come, let us go up to the mountain of the LORD,
to the house of the God of Jacob.
He will teach us his ways,
so that we may walk in his paths."
The law will go out from Zion,
the word of the LORD from Jerusalem.
3 He will judge between many peoples
and will settle disputes for strong nations far and wide.
They will beat their swords into plowshares
and their spears into pruning hooks.
Nation will not take up sword against nation,
nor will they train for war anymore.
4 Every man will sit under his own vine
and under his own fig tree,
and no one will make them afraid,
for the LORD Almighty has spoken.
5 All the nations may walk
in the name of their gods;
we will walk in the name of the LORD
our God for ever and ever.

The LORD's Plan

6 "In that day," declares the LORD,

"I will gather the lame;
I will assemble the exiles
and those I have brought to grief.
7 I will make the lame a remnant,
those driven away a strong nation.
The LORD will rule over them in Mount Zion
from that day and forever.
8 As for you, O watchtower of the flock,
O stronghold[a] of the Daughter of Zion,
the former dominion will be restored to you;
kingship will come to the Daughter of Jerusalem."

9 Why do you now cry aloud—
have you no king?
Has your counselor perished,
that pain seizes you like that of a woman in labor?
10 Writhe in agony, O Daughter of Zion,
like a woman in labor,
for now you must leave the city
to camp in the open field.
You will go to Babylon;
there you will be rescued.
There the LORD will redeem you
out of the hand of your enemies.
11 But now many nations
are gathered against you.
They say, "Let her be defiled,
let our eyes gloat over Zion!"
12 But they do not know
the thoughts of the LORD;
they do not understand his plan,
he who gathers them like sheaves to the threshing floor.
13 "Rise and thresh, O Daughter of Zion,
for I will give you horns of iron;
I will give you hoofs of bronze
and you will break to pieces many nations."

You will devote their ill-gotten gains to the LORD,
their wealth to the Lord of all the earth.

A Promised Ruler From Bethlehem

5 Marshal your troops, O city of troops,[b]
for a siege is laid against us.
They will strike Israel's ruler
on the cheek with a rod.

2 "But you, Bethlehem Ephrathah,
though you are small among the clans[c] of Judah,
out of you will come for me
one who will be ruler over Israel,
whose origins[d] are from of old,
from ancient times.[e]"

3 Therefore Israel will be abandoned
until the time when she who is in labor gives birth
and the rest of his brothers return
to join the Israelites.

4 He will stand and shepherd his flock
in the strength of the LORD,
in the majesty of the name of the LORD his God.
And they will live securely, for then his greatness

[a] 8 Or *hill* [b] 1 Or *Strengthen your walls, O walled city* [c] 2 Or *rulers* [d] 2 Hebrew *goings out* [e] 2 Or *from days of eternity*

will reach to the ends of the earth.
5 And he will be their peace.

Deliverance and Destruction

When the Assyrian invades our land
and marches through our fortresses,
we will raise against him seven
shepherds,
even eight leaders of men.
6 They will rule[a] the land of Assyria with
the sword,
the land of Nimrod with drawn
sword.[b]
He will deliver us from the Assyrian
when he invades our land
and marches into our borders.
7 The remnant of Jacob will be
in the midst of many peoples
like dew from the LORD,
like showers on the grass,
which do not wait for man
or linger for mankind.
8 The remnant of Jacob will be among the
nations,
in the midst of many peoples,
like a lion among the beasts of the forest,
like a young lion among flocks of
sheep,
which mauls and mangles as it goes,
and no one can rescue.
9 Your hand will be lifted up in triumph
over your enemies,
and all your foes will be destroyed.

10 "In that day," declares the LORD,

"I will destroy your horses from among
you
and demolish your chariots.
11 I will destroy the cities of your land
and tear down all your strongholds.
12 I will destroy your witchcraft
and you will no longer cast spells.
13 I will destroy your carved images
and your sacred stones from among
you;
you will no longer bow down
to the work of your hands.
14 I will uproot from among you your
Asherah poles[c]
and demolish your cities.
15 I will take vengeance in anger and wrath
upon the nations that have not obeyed
me."

The LORD's Case Against Israel

6 Listen to what the LORD says:

"Stand up, plead your case before the
mountains;
let the hills hear what you have to say.
2 Hear, O mountains, the LORD's
accusation;
listen, you everlasting foundations of
the earth.
For the LORD has a case against his
people;
he is lodging a charge against Israel.

3 "My people, what have I done to you?
How have I burdened you? Answer me.
4 I brought you up out of Egypt
and redeemed you from the land of
slavery.
I sent Moses to lead you,
also Aaron and Miriam.
5 My people, remember
what Balak king of Moab counseled
and what Balaam son of Beor answered.
Remember ⌊your journey⌋ from Shittim to
Gilgal,
that you may know the righteous acts
of the LORD."

6 With what shall I come before the LORD
and bow down before the exalted God?
Shall I come before him with burnt
offerings,
with calves a year old?
7 Will the LORD be pleased with thousands
of rams,
with ten thousand rivers of oil?
Shall I offer my firstborn for my
transgression,
the fruit of my body for the sin of my
soul?
8 He has showed you, O man, what is good.
And what does the LORD require of
you?
To act justly and to love mercy
and to walk humbly with your God.

Israel's Guilt and Punishment

9 Listen! The LORD is calling to the city—
and to fear your name is wisdom—
"Heed the rod and the One who
appointed it.[d]
10 Am I still to forget, O wicked house,
your ill-gotten treasures
and the short ephah,[e] which is
accursed?

[a] 6 Or *crush* [b] 6 Or *Nimrod in its gates* [c] 14 That is, symbols of the goddess Asherah [d] 9 The meaning of the Hebrew for this line is uncertain. [e] 10 An ephah was a dry measure.

F

FRIDAY
READ MICAH 6:1–16

THE REALLY GOOD LIFE

He has showed you, O man, what is good.

— MICAH 6:8

let's talk

- How do we define the "good life"?
- In what ways can we show each other justice, mercy and humility? What do I treasure from you as acts of justice, mercy and kindness? What do you treasure from me? In what ways do these differ? In what ways are they the same?
- What areas do we specifically need to work on in our marriage to live according to Micah 6:8?

My friend Meg keeps a fuzzy blue sock filled with diamond rings, bracelets and earrings—all gifts from her husband—inside her top dresser drawer. She wears expensive clothes, which her husband insists she buy, and they're always taking trips to the Bahamas or Hawaii.

My friend is tanned, toned, her hair highlighted and her face lifted, but she's miserable. Although most people who know Meg and her high-profile husband envy their "good life," only Meg's closest friends know how much she hates it.

Most people associate the good life with a nice house, the latest electronic toys and sleek cars, but those things don't necessarily make life good. My friend would gladly give up everything she owns for a more fulfilling life.

In the community, Meg's husband is generous and giving and the life of every party. He does favors for everyone and is the first to make a showy donation to a cause. But at home, he's aloof, demanding, cutting and very controlling. With each new gift he tells my friend, "See how much I love you?" Outwardly, his life looks good, but he misses the mark when it comes to what God requires of him in loving his wife.

The Israelites were also guilty of making showy declarations of love for God, but those gifts were mere bribes. And God abhors such sacrifices. Micah told Israel that God was not impressed or pleased with the offerings of "thousands of rams" and "ten thousand rivers of oil" (Micah 6:7).

Instead, what God requires, what he says is good, is to act justly, with fairness and equity; to love mercy and kindness, to be steadfastly dependable, respectful and committed; and to walk humbly with God (see Micah 6:8).

So too in marriage spouses are called to live together sacrificially and with respect (see Ephesians 5:33). We are to "clothe [ourselves] with compassion, kindness, humility, gentleness and patience" (Colossians 3:12). We are to "keep [our] lives free from the love of money and be content with what [we] have" (Hebrews 13:5).

We are to "do nothing out of selfish ambition or vain conceit, but in humility consider others better than [ourselves]. Each of [us] should look not only to [our] own interests, but also to the interests of others." (Philippians 2:3–4).

The good life, according to Micah 6:8, is not diamonds stashed in fuzzy socks; it's doing what is good.

—NANCY KENNEDY

FOR YOUR NEXT DEVOTIONAL READING, TURN TO PAGE 1012.

[11] Shall I acquit a man with dishonest scales,
with a bag of false weights?
[12] Her rich men are violent;
her people are liars
and their tongues speak deceitfully.
[13] Therefore, I have begun to destroy you,
to ruin you because of your sins.
[14] You will eat but not be satisfied;
your stomach will still be empty.[a]
You will store up but save nothing,
because what you save I will give to the sword.
[15] You will plant but not harvest;
you will press olives but not use the oil on yourselves,
you will crush grapes but not drink the wine.
[16] You have observed the statutes of Omri
and all the practices of Ahab's house,
and you have followed their traditions.
Therefore I will give you over to ruin
and your people to derision;
you will bear the scorn of the nations.[b]"

Israel's Misery

7 What misery is mine!
I am like one who gathers summer fruit
at the gleaning of the vineyard;
there is no cluster of grapes to eat,
none of the early figs that I crave.
[2] The godly have been swept from the land;
not one upright man remains.
All men lie in wait to shed blood;
each hunts his brother with a net.
[3] Both hands are skilled in doing evil;
the ruler demands gifts,
the judge accepts bribes,
the powerful dictate what they desire—
they all conspire together.
[4] The best of them is like a brier,
the most upright worse than a thorn hedge.
The day of your watchmen has come,
the day God visits you.
Now is the time of their confusion.
[5] Do not trust a neighbor;
put no confidence in a friend.
Even with her who lies in your embrace
be careful of your words.
[6] For a son dishonors his father,
a daughter rises up against her mother,
a daughter-in-law against her mother-in-law—
a man's enemies are the members of his own household.

[7] But as for me, I watch in hope for the LORD,
I wait for God my Savior;
my God will hear me.

Israel Will Rise

[8] Do not gloat over me, my enemy!
Though I have fallen, I will rise.
Though I sit in darkness,
the LORD will be my light.
[9] Because I have sinned against him,
I will bear the LORD's wrath,
until he pleads my case
and establishes my right.
He will bring me out into the light;
I will see his righteousness.
[10] Then my enemy will see it
and will be covered with shame,
she who said to me,
"Where is the LORD your God?"
My eyes will see her downfall;
even now she will be trampled underfoot
like mire in the streets.

[11] The day for building your walls will come,
the day for extending your boundaries.
[12] In that day people will come to you
from Assyria and the cities of Egypt,
even from Egypt to the Euphrates
and from sea to sea
and from mountain to mountain.
[13] The earth will become desolate because of its inhabitants,
as the result of their deeds.

Prayer and Praise

[14] Shepherd your people with your staff,
the flock of your inheritance,
which lives by itself in a forest,
in fertile pasturelands.[c]
Let them feed in Bashan and Gilead
as in days long ago.

[15] "As in the days when you came out of Egypt,
I will show them my wonders."

[16] Nations will see and be ashamed,
deprived of all their power.
They will lay their hands on their mouths

---

[a] *14* The meaning of the Hebrew for this word is uncertain. [b] *16* Septuagint; Hebrew *scorn due my people* [c] *14* Or *in the middle of Carmel*

WEEKEND

finding happiness the second time around

Ask the question: Is marriage to a formerly adulterous or sinfully divorced person prohibited? Follow that up with: Is marriage to a murderer or liar or slanderer prohibited? There is no more biblical reason to believe that marrying anyone from the first group of sinners is prohibited any more than marrying someone from the second. Either God's cleansing cleanses or it does not.

That is why we are so often incorrect in speaking of the "guilty party" and the "innocent party" in considering remarriage. This language isn't biblical and must be used only with great care. While at the time of the divorce one party may have been guilty (of sinfully obtaining a divorce) and the other innocent of it, it is not proper to continue to speak of the repentant, forgiven person (whether his sin was committed before or after conversion) as the "guilty" party. In Christ, he is now innocent. Who are we to remember and hold that guilt against him when God does not?

Bottom line: there is no law in the Bible that says a divorced person must remain unmarried.

God allowed the marriage of David and Bathsheba to stand even though both of them had been guilty of adultery, and David, even of murder. No more sordid beginning to a marriage could be imagined. Yet, God blessed that marriage in time because forgiveness was granted, the past was cleansed, and the future was cleared for God's blessing (see 2 Samuel 12:13; Psalm 51:2). If this marriage, which *at its inception* was knee-deep in sin, could be blessed by God to the bringing forth of the Messiah, why do we say that persons who are forgiven and cleansed before marrying cannot expect God to bless their marriage because of sin in their past?

Now, someone will say that this makes forgiveness too easy and encourages divorce. I do not honor that argument any more than Paul did in Romans. Divorce, wrongly obtained, is *sin*—a heinous offense against God and man. I am not encouraging divorce any more than God encouraged robbery, adultery, homosexuality, lying and murder by declaring that such sins are totally forgiven in Christ and put into the past (1 Corinthians 6:11). A repentant sinner recognizes the serious nature of his offense and is not only grateful but produces fruit appropriate to repentance. In any discussion of divorce and remarriage we must be careful to preserve the integrity of two biblical truths:

1. Sin is heinous.
2. Grace is greater than the most heinous sin (Romans 5:20).

So, we have seen that remarriage after divorce is allowed in the Bible and that the guilty party—after forgiveness—is free to remarry.

Some have suggested that the wedding of a divorced person not take place in the church building. That is plainly wrong. First, it views the church building as something that it is not—a sanctuary (or an especially holy place). But more important, if a marriage is right, it is right *all the way*—and the church of Jesus Christ should say so. Nothing should be done to indicate in the slightest way that forgiveness is not complete. Jesus Christ saves! Let the white wedding gown symbolize the cleansing of the blood of Jesus Christ. Let there be no spot or wrinkle, or any such thing! Let us proclaim to all who will hear the overwhelming grace and amazing forgiveness of Jesus Christ in *every legitimate* way!

—JAY E. ADAMS

working through your past

If this is a second marriage for you or your spouse, work through these questions to ensure that you are free physically, emotionally and spiritually from your past marriage(s).

1. Have you freed yourself from all past obligations—emotionally, financially and physically?
2. Have you asked for forgiveness not only from God but from your former spouse, children, relatives and others involved?
3. Have you made all possible efforts at reconciliation?
4. Have you made all possible efforts to right wrongs regarding such matters as:
   a. voluntary repayment of unfairly obtained money, rights or property in a divorce settlement
   b. assuming obligations for child support?
5. Have you gone through counseling for sins in your life that may have contributed in some way to the divorce?
6. Have you uncovered any wrong attitudes or ideas about marriage or marriage partners that may have developed during your previous marriage?
7. Have you explored the idea of love as a way of giving, not getting?

HOW ARE WE DOING?

date

let's make a DATE

OVERCOMING OBSTACLES

Find a gym or recreation area that has a climbing wall. Fasten on a harness and race your mate to the top. If you live near an actual mountain, plan a day to hike or climb as high as you safely can. Or visit a nearby park and scope out a great climbing tree, one that is older with lots of thick branches. Climb up together and enjoy the view. Whatever activity you decide to do, take a moment afterward to reflect on the journey and to discuss the strength and hard work it took to reach your goal.

FOR YOUR NEXT DEVOTIONAL READING, TURN TO PAGE 1017.

LESSONS FROM THE *Bible*

What were some of the difficulties in the following marriages in which a man had more than one wife? In what ways are these relationships similar to couples that divorce and remarry? What kinds of problems do both experience? What are some ways to work out such problems?

1. Jacob, Leah and Rachel (Genesis 29:16—30:24)
2. Elkanah, Peninnah and Hannah (1 Samuel 1:1–8)

and their ears will become deaf.
17 They will lick dust like a snake,
like creatures that crawl on the ground.
They will come trembling out of their dens;
they will turn in fear to the LORD our God
and will be afraid of you.
18 Who is a God like you,
who pardons sin and forgives the transgression
of the remnant of his inheritance?
You do not stay angry forever
but delight to show mercy.
19 You will again have compassion on us;
you will tread our sins underfoot
and hurl all our iniquities into the depths of the sea.
20 You will be true to Jacob,
and show mercy to Abraham,
as you pledged on oath to our fathers
in days long ago.

NAHUM

Nahum

QUICK FACTS

AUTHOR Nahum

AUDIENCE The people of Judah

DATE Probably shortly before the fall of Nineveh in 612 B.C.

SETTING There was great apprehension in Judah because Assyria had just conquered the Egyptian city of Thebes (663 B.C.), and Judah appeared to be next. However, Assyria would fall in 612 B.C.

The book of Nahum reads like it was addressed to Assyria, represented by its capital city of Nineveh, which was the dominant world power at the time. But Nahum's message, in reality, was for the people of Judah. The Assyrians, known for their brutality, had previously conquered the northern kingdom of Israel and carried off its citizens to Assyria. Now the people of Judah were facing the threat of a similar fate. But Nineveh's rampage against the people of God would finally end, thanks to God's justice. Nineveh's impending destruction comforted its victims, who could now expect an end to their ordeal. Their time of cringing in fear of Nineveh's cruelty was over. They could watch with hope for God to render his verdict and set them free.

Nineveh was given opportunities to reform, most notably through the prophet Jonah, but the city persisted in its wickedness. God had finally run out of patience. The attack on Nineveh, Nahum predicted, would be relentless, overpowering and unsparing. The city of blood and lies would become a smoldering heap. Its fate would become an object lesson to those who seek to oppress and a comfort to those who languish under the heel of tyrants.

At times, pressures on a marriage can seem unrelenting, especially when trouble comes in twos and threes. Nahum is a reminder that oppression, whatever its source, will not prevail. Christian marriage is fueled by reliance on God. We can be confident that any problems that arise will be dealt with through God's goodness, grace, power and justice.

1 An oracle concerning Nineveh. The book of the vision of Nahum the Elkoshite.

The LORD's Anger Against Nineveh

2 The LORD is a jealous and avenging God;
the LORD takes vengeance and is filled with wrath.
The LORD takes vengeance on his foes
and maintains his wrath against his enemies.
3 The LORD is slow to anger and great in power;
the LORD will not leave the guilty unpunished.
His way is in the whirlwind and the storm,
and clouds are the dust of his feet.
4 He rebukes the sea and dries it up;
he makes all the rivers run dry.
Bashan and Carmel wither
and the blossoms of Lebanon fade.
5 The mountains quake before him
and the hills melt away.
The earth trembles at his presence,
the world and all who live in it.
6 Who can withstand his indignation?
Who can endure his fierce anger?
His wrath is poured out like fire;
the rocks are shattered before him.

7 The LORD is good,
a refuge in times of trouble.
He cares for those who trust in him,
8 but with an overwhelming flood
he will make an end of ⌊Nineveh⌋;
he will pursue his foes into darkness.

9 Whatever they plot against the LORD
he[a] will bring to an end;
trouble will not come a second time.
10 They will be entangled among thorns
and drunk from their wine;
they will be consumed like dry stubble.[b]
11 From you, ⌊O Nineveh,⌋ has one come forth
who plots evil against the LORD
and counsels wickedness.

12 This is what the LORD says:

"Although they have allies and are numerous,
they will be cut off and pass away.
Although I have afflicted you, ⌊O Judah,⌋
I will afflict you no more.
13 Now I will break their yoke from your neck
and tear your shackles away."
14 The LORD has given a command concerning you, ⌊Nineveh⌋:
"You will have no descendants to bear your name.
I will destroy the carved images and cast idols
that are in the temple of your gods.
I will prepare your grave,
for you are vile."

15 Look, there on the mountains,
the feet of one who brings good news,
who proclaims peace!
Celebrate your festivals, O Judah,
and fulfill your vows.
No more will the wicked invade you;
they will be completely destroyed.

Nineveh to Fall

2 An attacker advances against you, ⌊Nineveh⌋.
Guard the fortress,
watch the road,
brace yourselves,
marshal all your strength!

2 The LORD will restore the splendor of Jacob
like the splendor of Israel,
though destroyers have laid them waste
and have ruined their vines.

3 The shields of his soldiers are red;
the warriors are clad in scarlet.
The metal on the chariots flashes
on the day they are made ready;
the spears of pine are brandished.[c]
4 The chariots storm through the streets,
rushing back and forth through the squares.
They look like flaming torches;
they dart about like lightning.

5 He summons his picked troops,
yet they stumble on their way.
They dash to the city wall;
the protective shield is put in place.
6 The river gates are thrown open
and the palace collapses.
7 It is decreed[b] that ⌊the city⌋
be exiled and carried away.
Its slave girls moan like doves

[a] 9 Or *What do you foes plot against the LORD? / He* [b] *10,7* The meaning of the Hebrew for this verse is uncertain. [c] 3 Hebrew; Septuagint and Syriac / *the horsemen rush to and fro*

FINDING GOODNESS IN TROUBLE

> **The LORD is good, a refuge in times of trouble. He cares for those who trust in him.**
>
> — NAHUM 1:7

Christian contemporary music and preaching usually emphasize the tenderness of God—his extensive forgiveness, his selfless humility and his ultimate sacrifice. And it's no wonder. Can you imagine marketing the God described in Nahum, a book prophesying the demise of the Assyrian Empire, represented by its capital city of Nineveh? People would be more likely to run away than to come close to a God who is "jealous and avenging," whose "way is in the whirlwind and the storm," and whose "wrath is poured out like fire."

Nahum says, "The mountains quake before him and the hills melt away. The earth trembles at his presence." Who wouldn't quake before such a display of unequaled power? Yet Nahum claims, "The LORD is good." And that goodness makes all the difference! If such power were contained and controlled by ultimate evil, we would have no hope at all. But when the power that hurled a universe into place is wielded by ultimate goodness, the result is that we can trust this God and find refuge in him. As Nahum says, "The LORD is good, a refuge in times of trouble. He cares for those who trust in him."

let's talk

- ✦ When has Scripture surprised us with a terrifying glimpse into the power or wrath of God?
- ✦ How comfortable are we with these truths about God's power and justice? How can we reconcile the differing views of God we see in Scripture?
- ✦ When have we had to cling to the truth of God's goodness? What happened when we did that?

The question is, can we believe that promise enough to rest in it? I am determined to trust in God, no matter how terrifying he seems. I would rather be in the safe center of his love than out in front as the target of that terrifying storm of God's wrath. But having such trust isn't always easy.

When my father developed leukemia, went through horrific suffering, and finally died, I had to remind myself forcibly, "The LORD is good." When my husband quit his job and decided to work independently, I had no choice but to put the financial stress in God's hands, trusting that "the LORD is good." When I look at the sad and cruel state of so many marriages in today's world and begin to shudder at the future dangers my four children will face, I must tell myself again, "The LORD is good."

The Lord is my personal fortress, my security in an unstable, frightening world. His total goodness at the helm of the universe reassures me as I repeatedly realize how little control I have over what happens to me. I can't be in control of people and events, but I can trust in the everlasting beneficence of the One who *is* in control.

It's the Lord's goodness that allows me to draw near to him. "Who can withstand his indignation? Who can endure his fierce anger?" Nahum asks (Nahum 1:6). Not me! So I stand behind Jesus, who takes upon himself all the wrath of God that I deserve. And I'm safe in God's provision, because "he cares for those who trust in him."

—ANNETTE LAPLACA

FOR YOUR NEXT DEVOTIONAL READING, TURN TO PAGE 1022.

and beat upon their breasts.
8 Nineveh is like a pool,
and its water is draining away.
"Stop! Stop!" they cry,
but no one turns back.
9 Plunder the silver!
Plunder the gold!
The supply is endless,
the wealth from all its treasures!
10 She is pillaged, plundered, stripped!
Hearts melt, knees give way,
bodies tremble, every face grows pale.

11 Where now is the lions' den,
the place where they fed their young,
where the lion and lioness went,
and the cubs, with nothing to fear?
12 The lion killed enough for his cubs
and strangled the prey for his mate,
filling his lairs with the kill
and his dens with the prey.

13 "I am against you,"
declares the LORD Almighty.
"I will burn up your chariots in smoke,
and the sword will devour your young lions.
I will leave you no prey on the earth.
The voices of your messengers
will no longer be heard."

Woe to Nineveh

3 Woe to the city of blood,
full of lies,
full of plunder,
never without victims!
2 The crack of whips,
the clatter of wheels,
galloping horses
and jolting chariots!
3 Charging cavalry,
flashing swords
and glittering spears!
Many casualties,
piles of dead,
bodies without number,
people stumbling over the corpses—
4 all because of the wanton lust of a harlot,
alluring, the mistress of sorceries,
who enslaved nations by her prostitution
and peoples by her witchcraft.

5 "I am against you," declares the LORD Almighty.
"I will lift your skirts over your face.
I will show the nations your nakedness
and the kingdoms your shame.
6 I will pelt you with filth,
I will treat you with contempt
and make you a spectacle.
7 All who see you will flee from you and say,
'Nineveh is in ruins—who will mourn for her?'
Where can I find anyone to comfort you?"

8 Are you better than Thebes,[a]
situated on the Nile,
with water around her?
The river was her defense,
the waters her wall.
9 Cush[b] and Egypt were her boundless strength;
Put and Libya were among her allies.
10 Yet she was taken captive
and went into exile.
Her infants were dashed to pieces
at the head of every street.
Lots were cast for her nobles,
and all her great men were put in chains.
11 You too will become drunk;
you will go into hiding
and seek refuge from the enemy.

12 All your fortresses are like fig trees
with their first ripe fruit;
when they are shaken,
the figs fall into the mouth of the eater.
13 Look at your troops—
they are all women!
The gates of your land
are wide open to your enemies;
fire has consumed their bars.

14 Draw water for the siege,
strengthen your defenses!
Work the clay,
tread the mortar,
repair the brickwork!
15 There the fire will devour you;
the sword will cut you down
and, like grasshoppers, consume you.
Multiply like grasshoppers,
multiply like locusts!
16 You have increased the number of your merchants
till they are more than the stars of the sky,
but like locusts they strip the land
and then fly away.

---

a 8 Hebrew *No Amon* b 9 That is, the upper Nile region

17 Your guards are like locusts,
your officials like swarms of locusts
that settle in the walls on a cold
day—
but when the sun appears they fly away,
and no one knows where.
18 O king of Assyria, your shepherds[a]
slumber;
your nobles lie down to rest.
Your people are scattered on the
mountains
with no one to gather them.
19 Nothing can heal your wound;
your injury is fatal.
Everyone who hears the news about you
claps his hands at your fall,
for who has not felt
your endless cruelty?

a 18 Or *rulers*

HABAKKUK

Habakkuk

QUICK FACTS

AUTHOR Habakkuk

AUDIENCE The people of Judah

DATE About 605 B.C.

SETTING Babylon was poised to destroy Judah.

Habakkuk proclaimed the need to maintain faith in the goodness of God, even when we are driven to our knees asking for relief from intense affliction. Our faith greatly influences the quality of our lives while we wait for God to act on our behalf in response to our pleas. For Habakkuk, faithful waiting paid off in the justice of God's response.

In the face of violence, corruption and injustice among his own people, Habakkuk asked God why he seemed impotent to respond. When the Lord replied that he was about to bring judgment upon Judah through the invading Babylonians, the prophet grew even more perplexed. God then explained that the wicked Babylonians would themselves be destroyed in due time. This promise was sufficient for the chafing prophet, who celebrated God's power and mercy with a heartfelt prayer of devotion. In the event of great calamity, such as the destruction of fields and flocks, he would wait patiently and joyfully for God to act (see Habakkuk 3:16–18).

We, too, patiently wait for God to act in our lives. For example, weddings are beautiful days filled with the radiant promise of a new life together. But after the music fades and the honeymoon comes to an end, reality takes hold. There will be inevitable differences of opinion and perhaps financial difficulty, illness and loss. Like Habakkuk, wives and husbands should not shrink from these trials but embrace the challenges, ask the hard questions, and believe that God has the power to help them grow through times of testing.

1 The oracle that Habakkuk the prophet received.

Habakkuk's Complaint

2 How long, O LORD, must I call for help,
but you do not listen?
Or cry out to you, "Violence!"
but you do not save?
3 Why do you make me look at injustice?
Why do you tolerate wrong?
Destruction and violence are before me;
there is strife, and conflict abounds.
4 Therefore the law is paralyzed,
and justice never prevails.
The wicked hem in the righteous,
so that justice is perverted.

The LORD's Answer

5 "Look at the nations and watch—
and be utterly amazed.
For I am going to do something in your days
that you would not believe,
even if you were told.
6 I am raising up the Babylonians,[a]
that ruthless and impetuous people,
who sweep across the whole earth
to seize dwelling places not their own.
7 They are a feared and dreaded people;
they are a law to themselves
and promote their own honor.
8 Their horses are swifter than leopards,
fiercer than wolves at dusk.
Their cavalry gallops headlong;
their horsemen come from afar.
They fly like a vulture swooping to devour;
9 they all come bent on violence.
Their hordes[b] advance like a desert wind
and gather prisoners like sand.
10 They deride kings
and scoff at rulers.
They laugh at all fortified cities;
they build earthen ramps and capture them.
11 Then they sweep past like the wind and go on—
guilty men, whose own strength is their god."

Habakkuk's Second Complaint

12 O LORD, are you not from everlasting?
My God, my Holy One, we will not die.
O LORD, you have appointed them to execute judgment;
O Rock, you have ordained them to punish.
13 Your eyes are too pure to look on evil;
you cannot tolerate wrong.
Why then do you tolerate the treacherous?
Why are you silent while the wicked
swallow up those more righteous than themselves?
14 You have made men like fish in the sea,
like sea creatures that have no ruler.
15 The wicked foe pulls all of them up with hooks,
he catches them in his net,
he gathers them up in his dragnet;
and so he rejoices and is glad.
16 Therefore he sacrifices to his net
and burns incense to his dragnet,
for by his net he lives in luxury
and enjoys the choicest food.
17 Is he to keep on emptying his net,
destroying nations without mercy?

2 I will stand at my watch
and station myself on the ramparts;
I will look to see what he will say to me,
and what answer I am to give to this complaint.[c]

The LORD's Answer

2 Then the LORD replied:
"Write down the revelation
and make it plain on tablets
so that a herald[d] may run with it.
3 For the revelation awaits an appointed time;
it speaks of the end
and will not prove false.
Though it linger, wait for it;
it[e] will certainly come and will not delay.

4 "See, he is puffed up;
his desires are not upright—
but the righteous will live by his faith[f]—
5 indeed, wine betrays him;
he is arrogant and never at rest.
Because he is as greedy as the grave[g]
and like death is never satisfied,
he gathers to himself all the nations
and takes captive all the peoples.

[a] 6 Or *Chaldeans* [b] 9 The meaning of the Hebrew for this word is uncertain. [c] 1 Or *and what to answer when I am rebuked*
[d] 2 Or *so that whoever reads it* [e] 3 Or *Though he linger, wait for him; / he* [f] 4 Or *faithfulness* [g] 5 Hebrew *Sheol*

T

TUESDAY
READ HABAKKUK 1:1—2:1

RUNNING OUT OF HOPE

How long, O Lord, must I call for help, but you do not listen? Or cry out to you, "Violence!" but you do not save?

— Habakkuk 1:2

Not long ago a young couple asked if our elders would pray for them. He was a student and she was a teacher. She came home from school most days a wreck, not because of the students, but because of her colleagues, who were petty, vindictive and emotionally dangerous. Her husband wanted to go there and crack some heads. She couldn't quit—they needed the income—but she didn't feel she could go on. So they asked for prayer.

Habakkuk is a book for believers who face times when the bad guys are winning. This book was written around 600 B.C. for the people of Judah. It's obvious from the opening verses that this godly prophet had prayed often for relief from the violence and lawlessness around him, begging God for justice and for a revival among the people. Like many other prophets, Habakkuk had been pounding his pulpit, charging God's people to return to holy living. But no one was listening.

The answer to Habakkuk's prayers was definitely not what the prophet had in mind. God's judgment on his wicked people would come in the form of a crushing defeat at the hands of the Babylonians. Wickedness and oppression were rampant in Judah, to be sure, but the Babylonians were even more wicked and ruthless. Habakkuk was appalled and argued with God about using such sinful people to judge Judah.

Sometimes Christian couples find themselves in situations like Habakkuk's. They see sin running amok in their church, at work or in their home, and they are grieved. They long for godliness and righteousness. Perhaps you've prayed for such situations. Maybe you've lived through such seemingly hopeless circumstances.

The book of Habakkuk shows how godly people come to grips with God's seemingly dark and mysterious ways of achieving his purposes. One lesson we learn is that it is all right to complain to God about how he works. For example, in Habakkuk 1:13 Habakkuk raised a good point: How can the holy God use unholy people to achieve his purposes? As you think through such things, pray about your questions. Test God's character against his actions. But then, listen humbly as Habakkuk did (see Habakkuk 2:1).

Another lesson is that, in the end, we can trust God no matter what happens. Habakkuk's determination to trust God after making his complaints is one of the Bible's most eloquent statements (see Habakkuk 3:16–19). At a certain point, trust is all we can do.

One of the great benefits of a Christian marriage is that we can help each other hold fast to the Lord when everything is crumbling and nothing seems right. In talking and praying together through such times, we can find the faith to say, with Habakkuk, "Yet I will rejoice in the Lord, I will be joyful in God my Savior" (Habakkuk 3:18).

—LEE ECLOV

let's *talk*

- Are there situations that burden us because it seems that the wicked are winning and God is not intervening? How do such things affect us?
- Sometimes God responds to prayers for righteousness by changing things. Other times, like here in Habakkuk, things only seem to get worse. How should we pray when we see unrighteousness, especially among God's own people?
- How can we help each other trust God in such times?

FOR YOUR NEXT DEVOTIONAL READING, TURN TO PAGE 1027.

6 "Will not all of them taunt him with ridicule and scorn, saying,

" 'Woe to him who piles up stolen goods
and makes himself wealthy by extortion!
How long must this go on?'
7 Will not your debtors[a] suddenly arise?
Will they not wake up and make you tremble?
Then you will become their victim.
8 Because you have plundered many nations,
the peoples who are left will plunder you.
For you have shed man's blood;
you have destroyed lands and cities and everyone in them.

9 "Woe to him who builds his realm by unjust gain
to set his nest on high,
to escape the clutches of ruin!
10 You have plotted the ruin of many peoples,
shaming your own house and forfeiting your life.
11 The stones of the wall will cry out,
and the beams of the woodwork will echo it.

12 "Woe to him who builds a city with bloodshed
and establishes a town by crime!
13 Has not the LORD Almighty determined
that the people's labor is only fuel for the fire,
that the nations exhaust themselves for nothing?
14 For the earth will be filled with the knowledge of the glory of the LORD,
as the waters cover the sea.

15 "Woe to him who gives drink to his neighbors,
pouring it from the wineskin till they are drunk,
so that he can gaze on their naked bodies.
16 You will be filled with shame instead of glory.
Now it is your turn! Drink and be exposed[b]!
The cup from the LORD's right hand is coming around to you,
and disgrace will cover your glory.
17 The violence you have done to Lebanon will overwhelm you,
and your destruction of animals will terrify you.
For you have shed man's blood;
you have destroyed lands and cities and everyone in them.

18 "Of what value is an idol, since a man has carved it?
Or an image that teaches lies?
For he who makes it trusts in his own creation;
he makes idols that cannot speak.
19 Woe to him who says to wood, 'Come to life!'
Or to lifeless stone, 'Wake up!'
Can it give guidance?
It is covered with gold and silver;
there is no breath in it.
20 But the LORD is in his holy temple;
let all the earth be silent before him."

Habakkuk's Prayer

3 A prayer of Habakkuk the prophet. On *shigionoth.*[c]

2 LORD, I have heard of your fame;
I stand in awe of your deeds, O LORD.
Renew them in our day,
in our time make them known;
in wrath remember mercy.

3 God came from Teman,
the Holy One from Mount Paran.
Selah[d]
His glory covered the heavens
and his praise filled the earth.
4 His splendor was like the sunrise;
rays flashed from his hand,
where his power was hidden.
5 Plague went before him;
pestilence followed his steps.
6 He stood, and shook the earth;
he looked, and made the nations tremble.
The ancient mountains crumbled
and the age-old hills collapsed.
His ways are eternal.
7 I saw the tents of Cushan in distress,
the dwellings of Midian in anguish.

8 Were you angry with the rivers, O LORD?
Was your wrath against the streams?
Did you rage against the sea
when you rode with your horses

[a] 7 Or *creditors* [b] 16 Masoretic Text; Dead Sea Scrolls, Aquila, Vulgate and Syriac (see also Septuagint) *and stagger* [c] 1 Probably a literary or musical term [d] 3 A word of uncertain meaning; possibly a musical term; also in verses 9 and 13

and your victorious chariots?
9 You uncovered your bow,
you called for many arrows. *Selah*
You split the earth with rivers;
10 the mountains saw you and writhed.
Torrents of water swept by;
the deep roared
and lifted its waves on high.

11 Sun and moon stood still in the heavens
at the glint of your flying arrows,
at the lightning of your flashing spear.
12 In wrath you strode through the earth
and in anger you threshed the nations.
13 You came out to deliver your people,
to save your anointed one.
You crushed the leader of the land of wickedness,
you stripped him from head to foot. *Selah*
14 With his own spear you pierced his head
when his warriors stormed out to scatter us,
gloating as though about to devour
the wretched who were in hiding.
15 You trampled the sea with your horses,
churning the great waters.

16 I heard and my heart pounded,
my lips quivered at the sound;
decay crept into my bones,
and my legs trembled.
Yet I will wait patiently for the day of calamity
to come on the nation invading us.
17 Though the fig tree does not bud
and there are no grapes on the vines,
though the olive crop fails
and the fields produce no food,
though there are no sheep in the pen
and no cattle in the stalls,
18 yet I will rejoice in the LORD,
I will be joyful in God my Savior.

19 The Sovereign LORD is my strength;
he makes my feet like the feet of a deer,
he enables me to go on the heights.

For the director of music. On my stringed instruments.

ZEPHANIAH

Zephaniah

QUICK FACTS

AUTHOR Zephaniah

AUDIENCE The people of Judah

DATE Likely during the early years of the reign of King Josiah (640–609 B.C.)

SETTING Zephaniah's prophecy encouraged King Josiah to bring spiritual reform to Judah.

Zephaniah looked with anticipation to the day of the Lord, when God's judgment would come against the nations, including Judah. Only a remnant of God's people would escape the fury. While waiting for that day, the people were reminded that God was zealous for their worship and that they were safe in his care.

Zephaniah told the people that life would be grim when judgment came—but not for the faithful people whom God would conceal from the coming furor. On that fateful day, nations such as Philistia, Moab, Ammon, Cush and Assyria would be swept away with all their riches. The corrupt leaders of Jerusalem would be in the crosshairs too. They would be removed, leaving the city to the faithful remnant who would rejoice at the change of regime.

Zephaniah suggested two approaches to life as man and wife. The first way is steeped in pride; it leads to idolatry and a corrosion of marital unity. The second is far better. It is based on humility rather than status and selfishness. Humble, faithful partners create homes that are places of sanctuary, places that offer shelter from the storms outside and create a blessed harmony inside.

1 The word of the LORD that came to Zephaniah son of Cushi, the son of Gedaliah, the son of Amariah, the son of Hezekiah, during the reign of Josiah son of Amon king of Judah:

Warning of Coming Destruction

2 "I will sweep away everything
from the face of the earth,"
declares the LORD.
3 "I will sweep away both men and animals;
I will sweep away the birds of the air
and the fish of the sea.
The wicked will have only heaps of rubble[a]
when I cut off man from the face of the earth,"
declares the LORD.

Against Judah

4 "I will stretch out my hand against Judah
and against all who live in Jerusalem.
I will cut off from this place every remnant of Baal,
the names of the pagan and the idolatrous priests—
5 those who bow down on the roofs
to worship the starry host,
those who bow down and swear by the LORD
and who also swear by Molech,[b]
6 those who turn back from following the LORD
and neither seek the LORD nor inquire of him.
7 Be silent before the Sovereign LORD,
for the day of the LORD is near.
The LORD has prepared a sacrifice;
he has consecrated those he has invited.
8 On the day of the LORD's sacrifice
I will punish the princes
and the king's sons
and all those clad
in foreign clothes.
9 On that day I will punish
all who avoid stepping on the threshold,[c]
who fill the temple of their gods
with violence and deceit.

10 "On that day," declares the LORD,
"a cry will go up from the Fish Gate,
wailing from the New Quarter,
and a loud crash from the hills.
11 Wail, you who live in the market district[d];
all your merchants will be wiped out,
all who trade with[e] silver will be ruined.
12 At that time I will search Jerusalem with lamps
and punish those who are complacent,
who are like wine left on its dregs,
who think, 'The LORD will do nothing,
either good or bad.'
13 Their wealth will be plundered,
their houses demolished.
They will build houses
but not live in them;
they will plant vineyards
but not drink the wine.

The Great Day of the LORD

14 "The great day of the LORD is near—
near and coming quickly.
Listen! The cry on the day of the LORD will be bitter,
the shouting of the warrior there.
15 That day will be a day of wrath,
a day of distress and anguish,
a day of trouble and ruin,
a day of darkness and gloom,
a day of clouds and blackness,
16 a day of trumpet and battle cry
against the fortified cities
and against the corner towers.
17 I will bring distress on the people
and they will walk like blind men,
because they have sinned against the LORD.
Their blood will be poured out like dust
and their entrails like filth.
18 Neither their silver nor their gold
will be able to save them
on the day of the LORD's wrath.
In the fire of his jealousy
the whole world will be consumed,
for he will make a sudden end
of all who live in the earth."

2 Gather together, gather together,
O shameful nation,
2 before the appointed time arrives
and that day sweeps on like chaff,
before the fierce anger of the LORD comes upon you,
before the day of the LORD's wrath comes upon you.

---

[a] 3 The meaning of the Hebrew for this line is uncertain. [b] 5 Hebrew *Malcam,* that is, Milcom [c] 9 See 1 Samuel 5:5. [d] 11 Or *the Mortar* [e] 11 Or *in*

WEDNESDAY
READ ZEPHANIAH 2:1–3

KEEPING EACH OTHER ACCOUNTABLE

Seek the Lord, all you humble of the land, you who do what he commands. Seek righteousness, seek humility; perhaps you will be sheltered on the day of the Lord's anger.

— Zephaniah 2:3

According to the Bible, God created the universe as an act of love and enthusiasm. Earth, among the planets and stars, was to be home to creatures that reflected the characteristics of God and interacted with God in dynamic ways. Sin marred that relationship, but in love and forgiveness, God continued to reach out to his creatures.

In the early years, this relationship took the form of a covenant between God and Abraham's descendants. If the people were true to God, all nations would see that and be drawn into a restorative relationship with him. The cancer of sin could be cured.

During the reigns of King David and King Solomon, the nation of Israel experienced times of great prosperity, and the blessings of the covenant were dispersed among the nations. People like the queen of Sheba (see 1 Kings 10) came looking for the secret that made Israel special. In later years, however, Israel became as infected by evil as the nations around her.

The accountability clauses in the covenant between God and Israel at Mount Sinai included blessings for keeping the covenant and curses for not keeping it (see Leviticus 26). Throughout Israel's history, God urged his people to be faithful, warning them against breaking faith with him. Prophets such as Zephaniah sounded the alarm of imminent destruction, since recurring disobedience triggered the covenant's penalty clause. First Israel and then Judah were assaulted and carried off by unspeakably cruel nations.

There, in a foreign land, the Israelites lost their distinctiveness as the people of God. Most of them were absorbed into the nations around them. Though a remnant of Judah would be spared, never again would Israel return to the promised land.

Marriages, too, are covenant relationships with accountability clauses. Good marriages in which partners keep faith with each other and the Lord usually blossom with blessings that overflow to others, such as children and neighbors and church members. Conversely, bad marriages in which covenants are broken and trust is destroyed bring pain into countless lives. Some couples are riding the crest of blessing right now. Others are suffering the painful consequences of foolish and unfaithful acts.

Regardless of the circumstances, every married couple may have confidence in this: God is gracious. As Zephaniah reminds us, if we truly repent of our sin and humble ourselves before God, we will receive forgiveness, hope, reconciliation and healing. As we move toward restoration of our marriage commitments, we can be certain that God will walk with us, encouraging us all the way.

—WAYNE BROUWER

let's talk

- ✦ What vows did we make to each other on our wedding day? What are some promises that we've made to each other since then?
- ✦ Which vows and promises have we kept? Which have we failed to keep?
- ✦ What accountability clauses are implied in our relationship? What are some of the blessings of keeping our promises to each other? The curses of not? How does keeping them strengthen our relationship now and for the future?

FOR YOUR NEXT DEVOTIONAL READING, TURN TO PAGE 1038.

3 Seek the LORD, all you humble of the land,
you who do what he commands.
Seek righteousness, seek humility;
perhaps you will be sheltered
on the day of the LORD's anger.

Against Philistia

4 Gaza will be abandoned
and Ashkelon left in ruins.
At midday Ashdod will be emptied
and Ekron uprooted.
5 Woe to you who live by the sea,
O Kerethite people;
the word of the LORD is against you,
O Canaan, land of the Philistines.

"I will destroy you,
and none will be left."

6 The land by the sea, where the Kerethites[a] dwell,
will be a place for shepherds and sheep pens.
7 It will belong to the remnant of the house of Judah;
there they will find pasture.
In the evening they will lie down
in the houses of Ashkelon.
The LORD their God will care for them;
he will restore their fortunes.[b]

Against Moab and Ammon

8 "I have heard the insults of Moab
and the taunts of the Ammonites,
who insulted my people
and made threats against their land.
9 Therefore, as surely as I live,"
declares the LORD Almighty, the God of Israel,
"surely Moab will become like Sodom,
the Ammonites like Gomorrah—
a place of weeds and salt pits,
a wasteland forever.
The remnant of my people will plunder them;
the survivors of my nation will inherit their land."

10 This is what they will get in return for their pride,
for insulting and mocking the people of the LORD Almighty.
11 The LORD will be awesome to them
when he destroys all the gods of the land.
The nations on every shore will worship him,
every one in its own land.

Against Cush

12 "You too, O Cushites,[c]
will be slain by my sword."

Against Assyria

13 He will stretch out his hand against the north
and destroy Assyria,
leaving Nineveh utterly desolate
and dry as the desert.
14 Flocks and herds will lie down there,
creatures of every kind.
The desert owl and the screech owl
will roost on her columns.
Their calls will echo through the windows,
rubble will be in the doorways,
the beams of cedar will be exposed.
15 This is the carefree city
that lived in safety.
She said to herself,
"I am, and there is none besides me."
What a ruin she has become,
a lair for wild beasts!
All who pass by her scoff
and shake their fists.

The Future of Jerusalem

3 Woe to the city of oppressors,
rebellious and defiled!
2 She obeys no one,
she accepts no correction.
She does not trust in the LORD,
she does not draw near to her God.
3 Her officials are roaring lions,
her rulers are evening wolves,
who leave nothing for the morning.
4 Her prophets are arrogant;
they are treacherous men.
Her priests profane the sanctuary
and do violence to the law.
5 The LORD within her is righteous;
he does no wrong.
Morning by morning he dispenses his justice,
and every new day he does not fail,
yet the unrighteous know no shame.

6 "I have cut off nations;
their strongholds are demolished.
I have left their streets deserted,

[a] 6 The meaning of the Hebrew for this word is uncertain. [b] 7 Or *will bring back their captives* [c] 12 That is, people from the upper Nile region

with no one passing through.
Their cities are destroyed;
no one will be left—no one at all.
7 I said to the city,
'Surely you will fear me
and accept correction!'
Then her dwelling would not be cut off,
nor all my punishments come upon
her.
But they were still eager
to act corruptly in all they did.
8 Therefore wait for me," declares the LORD,
"for the day I will stand up to testify.[a]
I have decided to assemble the nations,
to gather the kingdoms
and to pour out my wrath on them—
all my fierce anger.
The whole world will be consumed
by the fire of my jealous anger.

9 "Then will I purify the lips of the peoples,
that all of them may call on the name
of the LORD
and serve him shoulder to shoulder.
10 From beyond the rivers of Cush[b]
my worshipers, my scattered people,
will bring me offerings.
11 On that day you will not be put to shame
for all the wrongs you have done to me,
because I will remove from this city
those who rejoice in their pride.
Never again will you be haughty
on my holy hill.
12 But I will leave within you
the meek and humble,
who trust in the name of the LORD.
13 The remnant of Israel will do no wrong;
they will speak no lies,
nor will deceit be found in their
mouths.
They will eat and lie down
and no one will make them afraid."

14 Sing, O Daughter of Zion;
shout aloud, O Israel!
Be glad and rejoice with all your heart,
O Daughter of Jerusalem!
15 The LORD has taken away your
punishment,
he has turned back your enemy.
The LORD, the King of Israel, is with you;
never again will you fear any harm.
16 On that day they will say to Jerusalem,
"Do not fear, O Zion;
do not let your hands hang limp.
17 The LORD your God is with you,
he is mighty to save.
He will take great delight in you,
he will quiet you with his love,
he will rejoice over you with singing."

18 "The sorrows for the appointed feasts
I will remove from you;
they are a burden and a reproach to
you.[c]
19 At that time I will deal
with all who oppressed you;
I will rescue the lame
and gather those who have been
scattered.
I will give them praise and honor
in every land where they were put to
shame.
20 At that time I will gather you;
at that time I will bring you home.
I will give you honor and praise
among all the peoples of the earth
when I restore your fortunes[d]
before your very eyes,"
says the LORD.

---

[a] 8 Septuagint and Syriac; Hebrew *will rise up to plunder* [b] 10 That is, the upper Nile region [c] 18 Or *"I will gather you who mourn for the appointed feasts; / your reproach is a burden to you* [d] 20 Or *I bring back your captives*

HAGGAI

Haggai

QUICK FACTS

AUTHOR Haggai

AUDIENCE The exiles who had returned to Judah

DATE 520 B.C.

SETTING The Persian King Cyrus allowed the Jews to return to Jerusalem to rebuild the temple. However, misplaced priorities and local opposition brought the work to a halt.

Haggai commanded the people of Jerusalem to undertake a building project, but with a new attitude. After returning home from exile, workers had laid the foundation for a new temple but then abandoned the job in favor of rebuilding their own homes. The selfishness of this behavior roused the ire of God, who always finishes what he starts.

While the leaders dragged their feet on the temple rebuilding, the people suffered the effects of a poor harvest. God, through Haggai, asked the people to realize the link between these two events. Restoring the temple to its former glory would invite God to return and bless their land. Two discerning leaders and a faithful remnant of the people made the connection and began the work again. They were then rewarded with the promise of God's favor.

The union of male and female lays the foundation for the temple known as marriage, but this does not mean that the workers can pack up their gear and stop building. The marriage temple will attain its full glory only with the continued, diligent labor of both partners through obedience to God and submission to each other.

A Call to Build the House of the LORD

1 In the second year of King Darius, on the
first day of the sixth month, the word of
the LORD came through the prophet Haggai to Zerubbabel son of Shealtiel, governor of
Judah, and to Joshua[a] son of Jehozadak, the
high priest:

2This is what the LORD Almighty says:
"These people say, 'The time has not yet come
for the LORD's house to be built.' "

3Then the word of the LORD came through
the prophet Haggai: 4"Is it a time for you
yourselves to be living in your paneled houses,
while this house remains a ruin?"

5Now this is what the LORD Almighty says:
"Give careful thought to your ways. 6You have
planted much, but have harvested little. You
eat, but never have enough. You drink, but
never have your fill. You put on clothes, but
are not warm. You earn wages, only to put
them in a purse with holes in it."

7This is what the LORD Almighty says: "Give
careful thought to your ways. 8Go up into
the mountains and bring down timber and
build the house, so that I may take pleasure
in it and be honored," says the LORD. 9"You
expected much, but see, it turned out to be
little. What you brought home, I blew away.
Why?" declares the LORD Almighty. "Because
of my house, which remains a ruin, while each
of you is busy with his own house. 10There-
fore, because of you the heavens have withheld
their dew and the earth its crops. 11I called for
a drought on the fields and the mountains, on
the grain, the new wine, the oil and whatever
the ground produces, on men and cattle, and
on the labor of your hands."

12Then Zerubbabel son of Shealtiel, Joshua son of Jehozadak, the high priest, and the
whole remnant of the people obeyed the voice
of the LORD their God and the message of
the prophet Haggai, because the LORD their
God had sent him. And the people feared the
LORD.

13Then Haggai, the LORD's messenger, gave
this message of the LORD to the people: "I am
with you," declares the LORD. 14So the LORD
stirred up the spirit of Zerubbabel son of Shealtiel, governor of Judah, and the spirit of
Joshua son of Jehozadak, the high priest, and
the spirit of the whole remnant of the people.
They came and began to work on the house of
the LORD Almighty, their God, 15on the twenty-fourth day of the sixth month in the second
year of King Darius.

The Promised Glory of the New House

2 On the twenty-first day of the seventh
month, the word of the LORD came through
the prophet Haggai: 2"Speak to Zerubbabel
son of Shealtiel, governor of Judah, to Joshua
son of Jehozadak, the high priest, and to the
remnant of the people. Ask them, 3'Who of
you is left who saw this house in its former
glory? How does it look to you now? Does it
not seem to you like nothing? 4But now be
strong, O Zerubbabel,' declares the LORD. 'Be
strong, O Joshua son of Jehozadak, the high
priest. Be strong, all you people of the land,'
declares the LORD, 'and work. For I am with
you,' declares the LORD Almighty. 5'This is
what I covenanted with you when you came
out of Egypt. And my Spirit remains among
you. Do not fear.'

6"This is what the LORD Almighty says: 'In
a little while I will once more shake the heavens and the earth, the sea and the dry land. 7I
will shake all nations, and the desired of all nations will come, and I will fill this house with
glory,' says the LORD Almighty. 8'The silver is
mine and the gold is mine,' declares the LORD
Almighty. 9'The glory of this present house
will be greater than the glory of the former
house,' says the LORD Almighty. 'And in this
place I will grant peace,' declares the LORD Almighty."

Blessings for a Defiled People

10On the twenty-fourth day of the ninth
month, in the second year of Darius, the
word of the LORD came to the prophet Haggai: 11"This is what the LORD Almighty says:
'Ask the priests what the law says: 12If a person carries consecrated meat in the fold of his
garment, and that fold touches some bread or
stew, some wine, oil or other food, does it become consecrated?' "

The priests answered, "No."

13Then Haggai said, "If a person defiled by
contact with a dead body touches one of these
things, does it become defiled?"

"Yes," the priests replied, "it becomes defiled."

14Then Haggai said, " 'So it is with this
people and this nation in my sight,' declares
the LORD. 'Whatever they do and whatever
they offer there is defiled.

15" 'Now give careful thought to this from

---

[a] *1* A variant of *Jeshua*; here and elsewhere in Haggai

this day on[a]—consider how things were before one stone was laid on another in the LORD's temple. [16]When anyone came to a heap of twenty measures, there were only ten. When anyone went to a wine vat to draw fifty measures, there were only twenty. [17]I struck all the work of your hands with blight, mildew and hail, yet you did not turn to me,' declares the LORD. [18]'From this day on, from this twenty-fourth day of the ninth month, give careful thought to the day when the foundation of the LORD's temple was laid. Give careful thought: [19]Is there yet any seed left in the barn? Until now, the vine and the fig tree, the pomegranate and the olive tree have not borne fruit.

" 'From this day on I will bless you.' "

Zerubbabel the LORD's Signet Ring

[20]The word of the LORD came to Haggai a second time on the twenty-fourth day of the month: [21]"Tell Zerubbabel governor of Judah that I will shake the heavens and the earth. [22]I will overturn royal thrones and shatter the power of the foreign kingdoms. I will overthrow chariots and their drivers; horses and their riders will fall, each by the sword of his brother.

[23]" 'On that day,' declares the LORD Almighty, 'I will take you, my servant Zerubbabel son of Shealtiel,' declares the LORD, 'and I will make you like my signet ring, for I have chosen you,' declares the LORD Almighty."

a 15 Or *to the days past*

ZECHARIAH

Zechariah

QUICK FACTS

AUTHOR Zechariah

AUDIENCE The exiles who had returned to Judah

DATE Between about 520 and 480 B.C.

SETTING Zechariah, like Haggai, encouraged the exiles who had returned to Judah from Babylon to complete the rebuilding of the temple.

Zechariah had a twofold purpose in his prophecy: the reconstruction of the temple in Jerusalem and the renewal of the relationship between God and his people. Zechariah reminded the people of what they had once had with God and also what a future with God would entail; only God could restore freedom, justice and prosperity. So God restated his standing offer to his wayward people: Return to me and I will return to you.

Through a series of dramatic visions, Zechariah received glimpses of the restored temple, which was to be the symbol of a revived people. With the temple in place, God would acknowledge his people and send them the long-promised Messiah to rule as King over the earth.

Married life moves within the framework of time. In the blink of an eye, we find ourselves transported to somewhere other than the here and now. Sometimes a backward look is tinged with nostalgia or regret, while a forward glance is bathed in hope or apprehension. Whichever direction we look, our understanding of both past and future becomes clearer and more hopeful within the context of our covenant with God and with each other.

A Call to Return to the LORD

1 In the eighth month of the second year of
Darius, the word of the LORD came to the
prophet Zechariah son of Berekiah, the son
of Iddo:
2"The LORD was very angry with your forefathers. 3Therefore tell the people: This is what
the LORD Almighty says: 'Return to me,' declares the LORD Almighty, 'and I will return to
you,' says the LORD Almighty. 4Do not be like
your forefathers, to whom the earlier prophets
proclaimed: This is what the LORD Almighty
says: 'Turn from your evil ways and your evil
practices.' But they would not listen or pay attention to me, declares the LORD. 5Where are
your forefathers now? And the prophets, do
they live forever? 6But did not my words and
my decrees, which I commanded my servants
the prophets, overtake your forefathers?
"Then they repented and said, 'The LORD
Almighty has done to us what our ways
and practices deserve, just as he determined
to do.' "

The Man Among the Myrtle Trees

7On the twenty-fourth day of the eleventh
month, the month of Shebat, in the second
year of Darius, the word of the LORD came
to the prophet Zechariah son of Berekiah, the
son of Iddo.
8During the night I had a vision—and
there before me was a man riding a red horse!
He was standing among the myrtle trees in
a ravine. Behind him were red, brown and
white horses.
9I asked, "What are these, my lord?"
The angel who was talking with me answered, "I will show you what they are."
10Then the man standing among the myrtle
trees explained, "They are the ones the LORD
has sent to go throughout the earth."
11And they reported to the angel of the
LORD, who was standing among the myrtle
trees, "We have gone throughout the earth and
found the whole world at rest and in peace."
12Then the angel of the LORD said, "LORD
Almighty, how long will you withhold mercy from Jerusalem and from the towns of Judah, which you have been angry with these
seventy years?" 13So the LORD spoke kind and
comforting words to the angel who talked
with me.
14Then the angel who was speaking to me
said, "Proclaim this word: This is what the
LORD Almighty says: 'I am very jealous for Jerusalem and Zion, 15but I am very angry with
the nations that feel secure. I was only a little
angry, but they added to the calamity.'
16"Therefore, this is what the LORD says: 'I
will return to Jerusalem with mercy, and there
my house will be rebuilt. And the measuring
line will be stretched out over Jerusalem,' declares the LORD Almighty.
17"Proclaim further: This is what the LORD
Almighty says: 'My towns will again overflow
with prosperity, and the LORD will again comfort Zion and choose Jerusalem.' "

Four Horns and Four Craftsmen

18Then I looked up—and there before me
were four horns! 19I asked the angel who was
speaking to me, "What are these?"
He answered me, "These are the horns that
scattered Judah, Israel and Jerusalem."
20Then the LORD showed me four craftsmen.
21I asked, "What are these coming to do?"
He answered, "These are the horns that
scattered Judah so that no one could raise his
head, but the craftsmen have come to terrify them and throw down these horns of the
nations who lifted up their horns against the
land of Judah to scatter its people."

A Man With a Measuring Line

2 Then I looked up—and there before me
was a man with a measuring line in his
hand! 2I asked, "Where are you going?"
He answered me, "To measure Jerusalem,
to find out how wide and how long it is."
3Then the angel who was speaking to me
left, and another angel came to meet him 4and
said to him: "Run, tell that young man, 'Jerusalem will be a city without walls because
of the great number of men and livestock in
it. 5And I myself will be a wall of fire around
it,' declares the LORD, 'and I will be its glory
within.'
6"Come! Come! Flee from the land of the
north," declares the LORD, "for I have scattered you to the four winds of heaven," declares the LORD.
7"Come, O Zion! Escape, you who live in
the Daughter of Babylon!" 8For this is what
the LORD Almighty says: "After he has honored me and has sent me against the nations
that have plundered you—for whoever touches you touches the apple of his eye— 9I will
surely raise my hand against them so that their
slaves will plunder them. [a] Then you will know
that the LORD Almighty has sent me.

---

[a] 8,9 Or *says after . . . eye:* 9"*I . . . plunder them.*"

10"Shout and be glad, O Daughter of Zion.
For I am coming, and I will live among you,"
declares the LORD. 11"Many nations will be
joined with the LORD in that day and will become my people. I will live among you and
you will know that the LORD Almighty has
sent me to you. 12The LORD will inherit Judah
as his portion in the holy land and will again
choose Jerusalem. 13Be still before the LORD,
all mankind, because he has roused himself
from his holy dwelling."

Clean Garments for the High Priest

3 Then he showed me Joshua[a] the high priest
standing before the angel of the LORD, and
Satan[b] standing at his right side to accuse
him. 2The LORD said to Satan, "The LORD rebuke you, Satan! The LORD, who has chosen
Jerusalem, rebuke you! Is not this man a burning stick snatched from the fire?"
3Now Joshua was dressed in filthy clothes
as he stood before the angel. 4The angel said
to those who were standing before him, "Take
off his filthy clothes."

Then he said to Joshua, "See, I have taken
away your sin, and I will put rich garments
on you."
5Then I said, "Put a clean turban on his
head." So they put a clean turban on his head
and clothed him, while the angel of the LORD
stood by.
6The angel of the LORD gave this charge
to Joshua: 7"This is what the LORD Almighty
says: 'If you will walk in my ways and keep my
requirements, then you will govern my house
and have charge of my courts, and I will give
you a place among these standing here.
8" 'Listen, O high priest Joshua and your
associates seated before you, who are men
symbolic of things to come: I am going to
bring my servant, the Branch. 9See, the stone
I have set in front of Joshua! There are sev-
en eyes[c] on that one stone, and I will engrave
an inscription on it,' says the LORD Almighty,
'and I will remove the sin of this land in a single day.
10" 'In that day each of you will invite his
neighbor to sit under his vine and fig tree,' declares the LORD Almighty."

The Gold Lampstand and the Two Olive Trees

4 Then the angel who talked with me returned and wakened me, as a man is wakened from his sleep. 2He asked me, "What
do you see?"

I answered, "I see a solid gold lampstand
with a bowl at the top and seven lights on it,
with seven channels to the lights. 3Also there
are two olive trees by it, one on the right of the
bowl and the other on its left."
4I asked the angel who talked with me,
"What are these, my lord?"
5He answered, "Do you not know what
these are?"

"No, my lord," I replied.
6So he said to me, "This is the word of the
LORD to Zerubbabel: 'Not by might nor by
power, but by my Spirit,' says the LORD Almighty.
7"What[d] are you, O mighty mountain? Before Zerubbabel you will become level ground.
Then he will bring out the capstone to shouts
of 'God bless it! God bless it!' "
8Then the word of the LORD came to me:
9"The hands of Zerubbabel have laid the foundation of this temple; his hands will also complete it. Then you will know that the LORD
Almighty has sent me to you.
10"Who despises the day of small things?
Men will rejoice when they see the plumb line
in the hand of Zerubbabel.

"(These seven are the eyes of the LORD,
which range throughout the earth.)"
11Then I asked the angel, "What are these
two olive trees on the right and the left of the
lampstand?"
12Again I asked him, "What are these two
olive branches beside the two gold pipes that
pour out golden oil?"
13He replied, "Do you not know what these
are?"

"No, my lord," I said.
14So he said, "These are the two who are
anointed to[e] serve the Lord of all the earth."

The Flying Scroll

5 I looked again—and there before me was
a flying scroll!
2He asked me, "What do you see?"

I answered, "I see a flying scroll, thirty feet
long and fifteen feet wide.[f]"
3And he said to me, "This is the curse that
is going out over the whole land; for according to what it says on one side, every thief
will be banished, and according to what it
says on the other, everyone who swears falsely will be banished. 4The LORD Almighty declares, 'I will send it out, and it will enter the
house of the thief and the house of him who
swears falsely by my name. It will remain in

---

a 1 A variant of *Jeshua*; here and elsewhere in Zechariah *b* 1 *Satan* means *accuser.* *c* 9 Or *facets* *d* 7 Or *Who* *e* 14 Or *two who bring oil and* *f* 2 Hebrew *twenty cubits long and ten cubits wide* (about 9 meters long and 4.5 meters wide)

his house and destroy it, both its timbers and its stones.' "

The Woman in a Basket

5Then the angel who was speaking to me came forward and said to me, "Look up and see what this is that is appearing."

6I asked, "What is it?"

He replied, "It is a measuring basket.[a]" And he added, "This is the iniquity[b] of the people throughout the land."

7Then the cover of lead was raised, and there in the basket sat a woman! 8He said, "This is wickedness," and he pushed her back into the basket and pushed the lead cover down over its mouth.

9Then I looked up—and there before me were two women, with the wind in their wings! They had wings like those of a stork, and they lifted up the basket between heaven and earth.

10"Where are they taking the basket?" I asked the angel who was speaking to me.

11He replied, "To the country of Babylonia[c] to build a house for it. When it is ready, the basket will be set there in its place."

Four Chariots

6 I looked up again—and there before me were four chariots coming out from between two mountains—mountains of bronze! 2The first chariot had red horses, the second black, 3the third white, and the fourth dappled—all of them powerful. 4I asked the angel who was speaking to me, "What are these, my lord?"

5The angel answered me, "These are the four spirits[d] of heaven, going out from standing in the presence of the Lord of the whole world. 6The one with the black horses is going toward the north country, the one with the white horses toward the west,[e] and the one with the dappled horses toward the south."

7When the powerful horses went out, they were straining to go throughout the earth. And he said, "Go throughout the earth!" So they went throughout the earth.

8Then he called to me, "Look, those going toward the north country have given my Spirit[f] rest in the land of the north."

A Crown for Joshua

9The word of the LORD came to me: 10"Take ⌞silver and gold⌟ from the exiles Heldai, Tobijah and Jedaiah, who have arrived from Babylon. Go the same day to the house of Josiah son of Zephaniah. 11Take the silver and gold and make a crown, and set it on the head of the high priest, Joshua son of Jehozadak. 12Tell him this is what the LORD Almighty says: 'Here is the man whose name is the Branch, and he will branch out from his place and build the temple of the LORD. 13It is he who will build the temple of the LORD, and he will be clothed with majesty and will sit and rule on his throne. And he will be a priest on his throne. And there will be harmony between the two.' 14The crown will be given to Heldai,[g] Tobijah, Jedaiah and Hen[h] son of Zephaniah as a memorial in the temple of the LORD. 15Those who are far away will come and help to build the temple of the LORD, and you will know that the LORD Almighty has sent me to you. This will happen if you diligently obey the LORD your God."

Justice and Mercy, Not Fasting

7 In the fourth year of King Darius, the word of the LORD came to Zechariah on the fourth day of the ninth month, the month of Kislev. 2The people of Bethel had sent Sharezer and Regem-Melech, together with their men, to entreat the LORD 3by asking the priests of the house of the LORD Almighty and the prophets, "Should I mourn and fast in the fifth month, as I have done for so many years?"

4Then the word of the LORD Almighty came to me: 5"Ask all the people of the land and the priests, 'When you fasted and mourned in the fifth and seventh months for the past seventy years, was it really for me that you fasted? 6And when you were eating and drinking, were you not just feasting for yourselves? 7Are these not the words the LORD proclaimed through the earlier prophets when Jerusalem and its surrounding towns were at rest and prosperous, and the Negev and the western foothills were settled?' "

8And the word of the LORD came again to Zechariah: 9"This is what the LORD Almighty says: 'Administer true justice; show mercy and compassion to one another. 10Do not oppress the widow or the fatherless, the alien or the poor. In your hearts do not think evil of each other.'

11"But they refused to pay attention; stubbornly they turned their backs and stopped up their ears. 12They made their hearts as hard as flint and would not listen to the law or to the

[a] 6 Hebrew *an ephah*; also in verses 7-11 [b] 6 Or *appearance* [c] 11 Hebrew *Shinar* [d] 5 Or *winds* [e] 6 Or *horses after them*
[f] 8 Or *spirit* [g] 14 Syriac; Hebrew *Helem* [h] 14 Or *and the gracious one, the*

words that the LORD Almighty had sent by
his Spirit through the earlier prophets. So the
LORD Almighty was very angry.
13"'When I called, they did not listen; so
when they called, I would not listen,' says the
LORD Almighty. 14'I scattered them with a
whirlwind among all the nations, where they
were strangers. The land was left so desolate
behind them that no one could come or go.
This is how they made the pleasant land desolate.'"

The LORD Promises to Bless Jerusalem

8 Again the word of the LORD Almighty
came to me. 2This is what the LORD Almighty says: "I am very jealous for Zion; I
am burning with jealousy for her."
3This is what the LORD says: "I will return
to Zion and dwell in Jerusalem. Then Jerusalem will be called the City of Truth, and the
mountain of the LORD Almighty will be called
the Holy Mountain."
4This is what the LORD Almighty says:
"Once again men and women of ripe old age
will sit in the streets of Jerusalem, each with
cane in hand because of his age. 5The city
streets will be filled with boys and girls playing there."
6This is what the LORD Almighty says: "It
may seem marvelous to the remnant of this
people at that time, but will it seem marvelous
to me?" declares the LORD Almighty.
7This is what the LORD Almighty says: "I
will save my people from the countries of the
east and the west. 8I will bring them back to
live in Jerusalem; they will be my people, and
I will be faithful and righteous to them as their
God."
9This is what the LORD Almighty says:
"You who now hear these words spoken by
the prophets who were there when the foundation was laid for the house of the LORD Almighty, let your hands be strong so that the
temple may be built. 10Before that time there
were no wages for man or beast. No one could
go about his business safely because of his enemy, for I had turned every man against his
neighbor. 11But now I will not deal with the
remnant of this people as I did in the past,"
declares the LORD Almighty.
12"The seed will grow well, the vine will
yield its fruit, the ground will produce its
crops, and the heavens will drop their dew.
I will give all these things as an inheritance
to the remnant of this people. 13As you have
been an object of cursing among the nations,
O Judah and Israel, so will I save you, and you
will be a blessing. Do not be afraid, but let
your hands be strong."
14This is what the LORD Almighty says: "Just
as I had determined to bring disaster upon you
and showed no pity when your fathers angered
me," says the LORD Almighty, 15"so now I have
determined to do good again to Jerusalem and
Judah. Do not be afraid. 16These are the things
you are to do: Speak the truth to each other,
and render true and sound judgment in your
courts; 17do not plot evil against your neighbor, and do not love to swear falsely. I hate all
this," declares the LORD.
18Again the word of the LORD Almighty
came to me. 19This is what the LORD Almighty
says: "The fasts of the fourth, fifth, seventh
and tenth months will become joyful and
glad occasions and happy festivals for Judah.
Therefore love truth and peace."
20This is what the LORD Almighty says:
"Many peoples and the inhabitants of many
cities will yet come, 21and the inhabitants of
one city will go to another and say, 'Let us
go at once to entreat the LORD and seek the
LORD Almighty. I myself am going.' 22And
many peoples and powerful nations will come
to Jerusalem to seek the LORD Almighty and
to entreat him."
23This is what the LORD Almighty says:
"In those days ten men from all languages
and nations will take firm hold of one Jew by
the hem of his robe and say, 'Let us go with
you, because we have heard that God is with
you.'"

Judgment on Israel's Enemies

An Oracle

9 The word of the LORD is against the land
of Hadrach
and will rest upon Damascus—
for the eyes of men and all the tribes of
Israel
are on the LORD—[a]
2 and upon Hamath too, which borders
on it,
and upon Tyre and Sidon, though they
are very skillful.
3 Tyre has built herself a stronghold;
she has heaped up silver like dust,
and gold like the dirt of the
streets.
4 But the Lord will take away her
possessions

[a] 1 Or *Damascus. / For the eye of the LORD is on all mankind, / as well as on the tribes of Israel,*

THURSDAY
READ ZECHARIAH 8:1–23

HOPE FOR THE FUTURE

Today my front porch is littered with badminton rackets and tattered birdies, sidewalk chalk, a pair of scissors, two paper airplanes and a big sticky spot (melted popsicle, I think). But I love our front porch, which my husband built. I love its wicker chairs and swing and its good view of neighboring homes and the handsome tree on our tiny property. We have lived in this house nine years, and this is where I picture David and me in our old age. Maybe, someday, the popsicles will be dropped by our future grandchildren.

The prophet Zechariah ministered to the exiles who had returned to Jerusalem not long before. The city was surely still just a shell of what it had been before it was destroyed by the Babylonians. The temple was yet to be rebuilt. But Zechariah assured the people of God's continued presence and protection. For a picture of ultimate well-being, the prophet described old people who were respected and peaceful, and children at play in the streets. His words came to the Israelites at a time when Jerusalem in beautiful tranquility must have seemed like an impossible dream.

Many families today live with relationship issues that are so painful that a future of peace and tranquility also seems like an impossible dream. Yet those of us who take God's Word as truth know that "all things are possible with God" (Mark 10:27) and that there is a promise of future good for those who love God.

Do you know couples with "back from the brink" stories—couples who came close to divorce but who managed to build their way back to mutual love and affection? I know a few, and each would testify that God and his power helped save their marriages.

For example, on the very night that my friend Abby was crying in her kitchen, working up the courage to take her two daughters and leave her hard-drinking husband, he walked into the room and told her, "We're going to church this Sunday. I've given my life back to God." The couple had plenty of old habits that had to be slowly and painfully eradicated and exchanged for patterns of love and respect, but each of them sought the Lord's wisdom and help.

This year their oldest daughter began her first year at a Christian college. Both she and her little sister enjoy good relationships with their parents in a home where kindness and love prevail. Abby and Geoff are at peace, and their children are enjoying the freedom it brings.

Turn on the news for ten minutes tonight if you need a reminder of war, violence and disappointment in the world. It's Christ alone who brings people out of the maelstrom of life to a quiet center of peace. It's obedience to God's Word that opens the door to peace and freedom. In the aftermath of destruction, the Israelites could find no other God in whom to put their hope and trust, and neither can we.

—ANNETTE LAPLACA

"Once again men and women of ripe old age will sit in the streets of Jerusalem, each with cane in hand because of his age. The city streets will be filled with boys and girls playing there."

— ZECHARIAH 8:4–5

let's talk

- ✦ Based on how things are going these days in our relationship, how do we imagine the future? Will we enjoy old age together? Will we smile at our grandchildren as they play?
- ✦ In what ways has obeying God brought us peace and tranquility in the past?
- ✦ How could our attempts to obey God more fully lead to a future of peace and freedom for our family?

FOR YOUR NEXT DEVOTIONAL READING, TURN TO PAGE 1045.

and destroy her power on the sea,
and she will be consumed by fire.
5 Ashkelon will see it and fear;
Gaza will writhe in agony,
and Ekron too, for her hope will wither.
Gaza will lose her king
and Ashkelon will be deserted.
6 Foreigners will occupy Ashdod,
and I will cut off the pride of the Philistines.
7 I will take the blood from their mouths,
the forbidden food from between their teeth.
Those who are left will belong to our God
and become leaders in Judah,
and Ekron will be like the Jebusites.
8 But I will defend my house
against marauding forces.
Never again will an oppressor overrun my people,
for now I am keeping watch.

The Coming of Zion's King

9 Rejoice greatly, O Daughter of Zion!
Shout, Daughter of Jerusalem!
See, your king[a] comes to you,
righteous and having salvation,
gentle and riding on a donkey,
on a colt, the foal of a donkey.
10 I will take away the chariots from Ephraim
and the war-horses from Jerusalem,
and the battle bow will be broken.
He will proclaim peace to the nations.
His rule will extend from sea to sea
and from the River[b] to the ends of the earth.[c]
11 As for you, because of the blood of my covenant with you,
I will free your prisoners from the waterless pit.
12 Return to your fortress, O prisoners of hope;
even now I announce that I will restore twice as much to you.
13 I will bend Judah as I bend my bow
and fill it with Ephraim.
I will rouse your sons, O Zion,
against your sons, O Greece,
and make you like a warrior's sword.

The LORD Will Appear

14 Then the LORD will appear over them;
his arrow will flash like lightning.
The Sovereign LORD will sound the trumpet;
he will march in the storms of the south,
15 and the LORD Almighty will shield them.
They will destroy
and overcome with slingstones.
They will drink and roar as with wine;
they will be full like a bowl
used for sprinkling[d] the corners of the altar.
16 The LORD their God will save them on that day
as the flock of his people.
They will sparkle in his land
like jewels in a crown.
17 How attractive and beautiful they will be!
Grain will make the young men thrive,
and new wine the young women.

The LORD Will Care for Judah

10 Ask the LORD for rain in the springtime;
it is the LORD who makes the storm clouds.
He gives showers of rain to men,
and plants of the field to everyone.
2 The idols speak deceit,
diviners see visions that lie;
they tell dreams that are false,
they give comfort in vain.
Therefore the people wander like sheep
oppressed for lack of a shepherd.

3 "My anger burns against the shepherds,
and I will punish the leaders;
for the LORD Almighty will care
for his flock, the house of Judah,
and make them like a proud horse in battle.
4 From Judah will come the cornerstone,
from him the tent peg,
from him the battle bow,
from him every ruler.
5 Together they[e] will be like mighty men
trampling the muddy streets in battle.
Because the LORD is with them,
they will fight and overthrow the horsemen.

6 "I will strengthen the house of Judah
and save the house of Joseph.
I will restore them
because I have compassion on them.

[a] 9 Or *King* [b] 10 That is, the Euphrates [c] 10 Or *the end of the land* [d] 15 Or *bowl, / like* [e] 4,5 Or *ruler, all of them together. / [5] They*

They will be as though
I had not rejected them,
for I am the LORD their God
and I will answer them.
7 The Ephraimites will become like mighty men,
and their hearts will be glad as with wine.
Their children will see it and be joyful;
their hearts will rejoice in the LORD.
8 I will signal for them
and gather them in.
Surely I will redeem them;
they will be as numerous as before.
9 Though I scatter them among the peoples,
yet in distant lands they will remember me.
They and their children will survive,
and they will return.
10 I will bring them back from Egypt
and gather them from Assyria.
I will bring them to Gilead and Lebanon,
and there will not be room enough for them.
11 They will pass through the sea of trouble;
the surging sea will be subdued
and all the depths of the Nile will dry up.
Assyria's pride will be brought down
and Egypt's scepter will pass away.
12 I will strengthen them in the LORD
and in his name they will walk,"
declares the LORD.

11 Open your doors, O Lebanon,
so that fire may devour your cedars!
2 Wail, O pine tree, for the cedar has fallen;
the stately trees are ruined!
Wail, oaks of Bashan;
the dense forest has been cut down!
3 Listen to the wail of the shepherds;
their rich pastures are destroyed!
Listen to the roar of the lions;
the lush thicket of the Jordan is ruined!

Two Shepherds

4 This is what the LORD my God says: "Pasture the flock marked for slaughter. 5 Their
buyers slaughter them and go unpunished.
Those who sell them say, 'Praise the LORD, I
am rich!' Their own shepherds do not spare
them. 6 For I will no longer have pity on the
people of the land," declares the LORD. "I will
hand everyone over to his neighbor and his
king. They will oppress the land, and I will not
rescue them from their hands."

7 So I pastured the flock marked for slaughter, particularly the oppressed of the flock.
Then I took two staffs and called one Favor
and the other Union, and I pastured the flock.
8 In one month I got rid of the three shepherds.

The flock detested me, and I grew weary of
them 9 and said, "I will not be your shepherd.
Let the dying die, and the perishing perish.
Let those who are left eat one another's flesh."

10 Then I took my staff called Favor and
broke it, revoking the covenant I had made
with all the nations. 11 It was revoked on that
day, and so the afflicted of the flock who were
watching me knew it was the word of the
LORD.

12 I told them, "If you think it best, give me
my pay; but if not, keep it." So they paid me
thirty pieces of silver.

13 And the LORD said to me, "Throw it to
the potter"—the handsome price at which
they priced me! So I took the thirty pieces of
silver and threw them into the house of the
LORD to the potter.

14 Then I broke my second staff called
Union, breaking the brotherhood between Judah and Israel.

15 Then the LORD said to me, "Take again
the equipment of a foolish shepherd. 16 For
I am going to raise up a shepherd over the
land who will not care for the lost, or seek the
young, or heal the injured, or feed the healthy,
but will eat the meat of the choice sheep, tearing off their hoofs.

17 "Woe to the worthless shepherd,
who deserts the flock!
May the sword strike his arm and his right eye!
May his arm be completely withered,
his right eye totally blinded!"

Jerusalem's Enemies to Be Destroyed

An Oracle

12 This is the word of the LORD concerning Israel. The LORD, who stretches out
the heavens, who lays the foundation
of the earth, and who forms the spirit of man
within him, declares: 2 "I am going to make
Jerusalem a cup that sends all the surrounding peoples reeling. Judah will be besieged as
well as Jerusalem. 3 On that day, when all the
nations of the earth are gathered against her, I
will make Jerusalem an immovable rock for all
the nations. All who try to move it will injure

themselves. 4On that day I will strike every
horse with panic and its rider with madness,"
declares the LORD. "I will keep a watchful eye
over the house of Judah, but I will blind all
the horses of the nations. 5Then the leaders
of Judah will say in their hearts, 'The people
of Jerusalem are strong, because the LORD Almighty is their God.'
6"On that day I will make the leaders of Judah like a firepot in a woodpile, like a flaming
torch among sheaves. They will consume right
and left all the surrounding peoples, but Jerusalem will remain intact in her place.
7"The LORD will save the dwellings of Judah first, so that the honor of the house of
David and of Jerusalem's inhabitants may not
be greater than that of Judah. 8On that day
the LORD will shield those who live in Jerusalem, so that the feeblest among them will be
like David, and the house of David will be like
God, like the Angel of the LORD going before
them. 9On that day I will set out to destroy all
the nations that attack Jerusalem.

Mourning for the One They Pierced

10"And I will pour out on the house of David and the inhabitants of Jerusalem a spirit[a]
of grace and supplication. They will look on[b]
me, the one they have pierced, and they will
mourn for him as one mourns for an only
child, and grieve bitterly for him as one grieves
for a firstborn son. 11On that day the weeping in Jerusalem will be great, like the weeping
of Hadad Rimmon in the plain of Megiddo.
12The land will mourn, each clan by itself,
with their wives by themselves: the clan of the
house of David and their wives, the clan of the
house of Nathan and their wives, 13the clan
of the house of Levi and their wives, the clan
of Shimei and their wives, 14and all the rest of
the clans and their wives.

Cleansing From Sin

13 "On that day a fountain will be opened
to the house of David and the inhabitants of Jerusalem, to cleanse them from
sin and impurity.
2"On that day, I will banish the names of
the idols from the land, and they will be remembered no more," declares the LORD Almighty. "I will remove both the prophets and
the spirit of impurity from the land. 3And if
anyone still prophesies, his father and mother,
to whom he was born, will say to him, 'You
must die, because you have told lies in the
LORD's name.' When he prophesies, his own
parents will stab him.
4"On that day every prophet will be
ashamed of his prophetic vision. He will not
put on a prophet's garment of hair in order
to deceive. 5He will say, 'I am not a prophet.
I am a farmer; the land has been my livelihood since my youth.[c]' 6If someone asks him,
'What are these wounds on your body[d]?' he
will answer, 'The wounds I was given at the
house of my friends.'

The Shepherd Struck, the Sheep Scattered

7 "Awake, O sword, against my shepherd,
against the man who is close to me!"
declares the LORD Almighty.
"Strike the shepherd,
and the sheep will be scattered,
and I will turn my hand against the
little ones.
8 In the whole land," declares the LORD,
"two-thirds will be struck down and
perish;
yet one-third will be left in it.
9 This third I will bring into the fire;
I will refine them like silver
and test them like gold.
They will call on my name
and I will answer them;
I will say, 'They are my people,'
and they will say, 'The LORD is our
God.' "

The LORD Comes and Reigns

14 A day of the LORD is coming when your
plunder will be divided among you.
2I will gather all the nations to Jerusalem
to fight against it; the city will be captured, the
houses ransacked, and the women raped. Half
of the city will go into exile, but the rest of the
people will not be taken from the city.
3Then the LORD will go out and fight
against those nations, as he fights in the day of
battle. 4On that day his feet will stand on the
Mount of Olives, east of Jerusalem, and the
Mount of Olives will be split in two from east
to west, forming a great valley, with half of
the mountain moving north and half moving
south. 5You will flee by my mountain valley,
for it will extend to Azel. You will flee as you
fled from the earthquake[e] in the days of Uzziah king of Judah. Then the LORD my God will
come, and all the holy ones with him.
6On that day there will be no light, no cold
or frost. 7It will be a unique day, without day-

[a] 10 Or *the Spirit* [b] 10 Or *to* [c] 5 Or *farmer; a man sold me in my youth* [d] 6 Or *wounds between your hands* [e] 5 Or [5]*My mountain valley will be blocked and will extend to Azel. It will be blocked as it was blocked because of the earthquake*

time or nighttime—a day known to the LORD.
When evening comes, there will be light.
8On that day living water will flow out from
Jerusalem, half to the eastern sea[a] and half to
the western sea,[b] in summer and in winter.
9The LORD will be king over the whole
earth. On that day there will be one LORD,
and his name the only name.
10The whole land, from Geba to Rimmon,
south of Jerusalem, will become like the Arabah. But Jerusalem will be raised up and remain in its place, from the Benjamin Gate to
the site of the First Gate, to the Corner Gate,
and from the Tower of Hananel to the royal
winepresses. 11It will be inhabited; never again
will it be destroyed. Jerusalem will be secure.
12This is the plague with which the LORD
will strike all the nations that fought against
Jerusalem: Their flesh will rot while they are
still standing on their feet, their eyes will rot in
their sockets, and their tongues will rot in their
mouths. 13On that day men will be stricken
by the LORD with great panic. Each man will
seize the hand of another, and they will attack
each other. 14Judah too will fight at Jerusalem.
The wealth of all the surrounding nations will
be collected—great quantities of gold and silver and clothing. 15A similar plague will strike
the horses and mules, the camels and donkeys,
and all the animals in those camps.
16Then the survivors from all the nations
that have attacked Jerusalem will go up year
after year to worship the King, the LORD Almighty, and to celebrate the Feast of Tabernacles. 17If any of the peoples of the earth do not
go up to Jerusalem to worship the King, the
LORD Almighty, they will have no rain. 18If
the Egyptian people do not go up and take
part, they will have no rain. The LORD[c] will
bring on them the plague he inflicts on the nations that do not go up to celebrate the Feast
of Tabernacles. 19This will be the punishment
of Egypt and the punishment of all the nations that do not go up to celebrate the Feast
of Tabernacles.
20On that day HOLY TO THE LORD will be
inscribed on the bells of the horses, and the
cooking pots in the LORD's house will be like
the sacred bowls in front of the altar. 21Every
pot in Jerusalem and Judah will be holy to the
LORD Almighty, and all who come to sacrifice
will take some of the pots and cook in them.
And on that day there will no longer be a Canaanite[d] in the house of the LORD Almighty.

---

[a] 8 That is, the Dead Sea [b] 8 That is, the Mediterranean [c] 18 Or *part, then the LORD* [d] 21 Or *merchant*

MALACHI

Malachi

QUICK FACTS

AUTHOR Malachi

AUDIENCE The people of Judah

DATE About 430 B.C.

SETTING Although the temple in Jerusalem and the city walls had been rebuilt, the Jews languished in their worship.

The book of Malachi is an appeal to guard against half-hearted living and give God our best, even in the "blah" times. The people of Judah were lethargic. They no longer had looming enemies to mobilize against, but they were also weary of waiting for the glorious future promised by the prophets—the day when God would exalt his people in the sight of the nations. The result was an unmotivated people whose passion for God had turned into indifference.

One sign of this lukewarm attitude was the poor quality of sacrifices that were being offered to God. The malaise even affected the priests, who had broken faith with God in the same manner as an unfaithful husband breaks faith with his wife. A jilted God finally announced that he would no longer accept blemished offerings from useless fires. He would not be robbed without consequence.

Similar to the experience of the people to which Malachi spoke, married life often has its "blah" times. We mow our lawns, pay our bills, help our kids with homework. It's easy to become lethargic and allow indifference to replace passion in our marriages. But we should not let a lukewarm attitude take root. To keep their marriages strong, husbands and wives need to give each other their best in their everyday lives—lives that are gifts from a bountiful and gracious God.

1 An oracle: The word of the LORD to Israel
through Malachi.[a]

Jacob Loved, Esau Hated

2"I have loved you," says the LORD.
"But you ask, 'How have you loved us?'
"Was not Esau Jacob's brother?" the LORD
says. "Yet I have loved Jacob, 3but Esau I have
hated, and I have turned his mountains into a
wasteland and left his inheritance to the desert jackals."
4Edom may say, "Though we have been
crushed, we will rebuild the ruins."
But this is what the LORD Almighty says:
"They may build, but I will demolish. They
will be called the Wicked Land, a people always under the wrath of the LORD. 5You will
see it with your own eyes and say, 'Great is
the LORD—even beyond the borders of Israel!'

Blemished Sacrifices

6"A son honors his father, and a servant his
master. If I am a father, where is the honor
due me? If I am a master, where is the respect
due me?" says the LORD Almighty. "It is you,
O priests, who show contempt for my name.
"But you ask, 'How have we shown contempt for your name?'
7"You place defiled food on my altar.
"But you ask, 'How have we defiled you?'
"By saying that the LORD's table is contemptible. 8When you bring blind animals for
sacrifice, is that not wrong? When you sacrifice crippled or diseased animals, is that not
wrong? Try offering them to your governor!
Would he be pleased with you? Would he accept you?" says the LORD Almighty.
9"Now implore God to be gracious to us.
With such offerings from your hands, will he
accept you?"—says the LORD Almighty.
10"Oh, that one of you would shut the
temple doors, so that you would not light
useless fires on my altar! I am not pleased
with you," says the LORD Almighty, "and
I will accept no offering from your hands.
11My name will be great among the nations,
from the rising to the setting of the sun. In
every place incense and pure offerings will be
brought to my name, because my name will
be great among the nations," says the LORD
Almighty.
12"But you profane it by saying of the Lord's
table, 'It is defiled,' and of its food, 'It is contemptible.' 13And you say, 'What a burden!'
and you sniff at it contemptuously," says the
LORD Almighty.
"When you bring injured, crippled or
diseased animals and offer them as sacrifices, should I accept them from your hands?"
says the LORD. 14"Cursed is the cheat who has
an acceptable male in his flock and vows to
give it, but then sacrifices a blemished animal
to the Lord. For I am a great king," says the
LORD Almighty, "and my name is to be feared
among the nations.

Admonition for the Priests

2 "And now this admonition is for you,
O priests. 2If you do not listen, and if you
do not set your heart to honor my name,"
says the LORD Almighty, "I will send a curse
upon you, and I will curse your blessings. Yes,
I have already cursed them, because you have
not set your heart to honor me.
3"Because of you I will rebuke[b] your descendants[c]; I will spread on your faces the offal from your festival sacrifices, and you will
be carried off with it. 4And you will know that
I have sent you this admonition so that my
covenant with Levi may continue," says the
LORD Almighty. 5"My covenant was with him,
a covenant of life and peace, and I gave them
to him; this called for reverence and he revered
me and stood in awe of my name. 6True instruction was in his mouth and nothing false
was found on his lips. He walked with me in
peace and uprightness, and turned many from
sin.
7"For the lips of a priest ought to preserve
knowledge, and from his mouth men should
seek instruction—because he is the messenger
of the LORD Almighty. 8But you have turned
from the way and by your teaching have
caused many to stumble; you have violated the
covenant with Levi," says the LORD Almighty.
9"So I have caused you to be despised and humiliated before all the people, because you
have not followed my ways but have shown
partiality in matters of the law."

Judah Unfaithful

10Have we not all one Father[d]? Did not
one God create us? Why do we profane the
covenant of our fathers by breaking faith with
one another?
11Judah has broken faith. A detestable thing
has been committed in Israel and in Jerusalem:
Judah has desecrated the sanctuary the LORD

[a] 1 *Malachi* means *my messenger.* [b] 3 Or *cut off* (see Septuagint) [c] 3 Or *will blight your grain* [d] 10 Or *father*

F

FRIDAY
READ MALACHI 2:10–16

HATING DIVORCE

> **"I hate divorce," says the LORD God of Israel . . . So guard yourself in your spirit, and do not break faith.**
>
> — MALACHI 2:16

let's *talk*

- What are we looking for in marriage? What do each of us hope to gain from it?
- Has either of us ever thought about separation or divorce? What was going on at the time? How did we get through that time?
- What is the outcome that God desires for marriage in general and our marriage in particular?

During an early morning bike ride, I met a good friend walking his dog. We traded pleasantries. Then I asked, "How are things going at home?"

I already knew the answer. We were too close for me to be unaware of his troubled marriage. His wife was a striking woman. Her smile was warm and lingered throughout conversations. She clung closely to her husband and gave every appearance of devotion. They appeared to be the perfect couple.

Yet at home she was angry and spiteful. She refused to let her husband sleep in their bed. She made cutting remarks about his family, insisting that they hated her. No matter how he tried to please her, she always expressed justification for her anger.

So when I asked, "How are things going at home?" I anticipated his usual shrug of hopelessness. What surprised me this particular morning, however, was his talk of divorce. His wife kept insisting that they separate; she even threatened divorce. But if she filed, people would blame her. So she was trying to force him to file, so he would get criticized for ending the marriage.

My friend knew that divorce would be the wrong answer for his marriage, and that it would not solve all his problems. Yet he longed for relief. "How much can a man take?" he asked wistfully. "Don't I deserve something better in my last years?"

I ached for him. Too well I knew the dark side of marriage far from the smiles, songs and celebrations of wedding days. Yet I could not sanction his divorce. I assured him of my prayers, but I also talked about misconceptions people have about marriage. We think we deserve happiness; we believe we must have fairy-tale endings; we are certain that romance is our right even if we have to find it outside our marriages.

I also reminded him of what God says in Malachi: "I hate divorce." The Israelites who had returned from exile in Babylon were struggling to reestablish themselves in Judah. The economy was depressed. Foreign powers tossed the little province back and forth like a plaything. During this time of discouragement and spiritual lethargy, the Israelites apparently were not only marrying foreign women who worshiped foreign gods but were also divorcing their Israelite wives in the process.

God is not out to ruin our fun. But using divorce to gain personal satisfaction erodes one of the foundational commitments upon which human identity and trust are built. I reminded my friend of that. Then I suggested that even if his marriage was stifling him, it was still providing safety for his wife, who was clearly having emotional difficulties. Perhaps part of the reason he needed to stay with her was to protect her from self-destruction.

I don't know that for sure. Nor do I condemn people who have gone through the pain of divorce. But God's words are pretty clear: He hates divorce. So must we.

—WAYNE BROUWER

FOR YOUR NEXT DEVOTIONAL READING, TURN TO PAGE 1048.

loves, by marrying the daughter of a foreign
god. 12As for the man who does this, whoever
he may be, may the LORD cut him off from
the tents of Jacob[a]—even though he brings
offerings to the LORD Almighty.
13Another thing you do: You flood the
LORD's altar with tears. You weep and wail
because he no longer pays attention to your
offerings or accepts them with pleasure from
your hands. 14You ask, "Why?" It is because
the LORD is acting as the witness between
you and the wife of your youth, because you
have broken faith with her, though she is
your partner, the wife of your marriage covenant.
15Has not ⌊the LORD⌋ made them one? In
flesh and spirit they are his. And why one?
Because he was seeking godly offspring.[b] So
guard yourself in your spirit, and do not break
faith with the wife of your youth.
16"I hate divorce," says the LORD God of
Israel, "and I hate a man's covering himself[c]
with violence as well as with his garment," says
the LORD Almighty.
So guard yourself in your spirit, and do not
break faith.

The Day of Judgment

17You have wearied the LORD with your
words.
"How have we wearied him?" you ask.
By saying, "All who do evil are good in the
eyes of the LORD, and he is pleased with them"
or "Where is the God of justice?"
3 "See, I will send my messenger, who will
prepare the way before me. Then suddenly the Lord you are seeking will come to
his temple; the messenger of the covenant,
whom you desire, will come," says the LORD
Almighty.
2But who can endure the day of his coming? Who can stand when he appears? For he
will be like a refiner's fire or a launderer's soap.
3He will sit as a refiner and purifier of silver;
he will purify the Levites and refine them like
gold and silver. Then the LORD will have men
who will bring offerings in righteousness, 4and
the offerings of Judah and Jerusalem will be
acceptable to the LORD, as in days gone by, as
in former years.
5"So I will come near to you for judgment.
I will be quick to testify against sorcerers,
adulterers and perjurers, against those who defraud laborers of their wages, who oppress the
widows and the fatherless, and deprive aliens
of justice, but do not fear me," says the LORD
Almighty.

Robbing God

6"I the LORD do not change. So you, O descendants of Jacob, are not destroyed. 7Ever
since the time of your forefathers you have
turned away from my decrees and have not
kept them. Return to me, and I will return to
you," says the LORD Almighty.
"But you ask, 'How are we to return?'
8"Will a man rob God? Yet you rob me.
"But you ask, 'How do we rob you?'
"In tithes and offerings. 9You are under a
curse—the whole nation of you—because
you are robbing me. 10Bring the whole tithe
into the storehouse, that there may be food
in my house. Test me in this," says the LORD
Almighty, "and see if I will not throw open the
floodgates of heaven and pour out so much
blessing that you will not have room enough
for it. 11I will prevent pests from devouring
your crops, and the vines in your fields will
not cast their fruit," says the LORD Almighty.
12"Then all the nations will call you blessed,
for yours will be a delightful land," says the
LORD Almighty.
13"You have said harsh things against me,"
says the LORD.
"Yet you ask, 'What have we said against
you?'
14"You have said, 'It is futile to serve God.
What did we gain by carrying out his requirements and going about like mourners before
the LORD Almighty? 15But now we call the
arrogant blessed. Certainly the evildoers prosper, and even those who challenge God escape.' "
16Then those who feared the LORD talked
with each other, and the LORD listened and
heard. A scroll of remembrance was written in
his presence concerning those who feared the
LORD and honored his name.
17"They will be mine," says the LORD Almighty, "in the day when I make up my treasured possession.[d] I will spare them, just as in
compassion a man spares his son who serves
him. 18And you will again see the distinction
between the righteous and the wicked, between those who serve God and those who
do not.

[a] 12 Or *12May the LORD cut off from the tents of Jacob anyone who gives testimony in behalf of the man who does this* [b] 15 Or *15But the one ⌊who is our father⌋ did not do this, not as long as life remained in him. And what was he seeking? An offspring from God* [c] 16 Or *his wife* [d] 17 Or *Almighty, "my treasured possession, in the day when I act*

The Day of the LORD

4 "Surely the day is coming; it will burn like
a furnace. All the arrogant and every evildoer will be stubble, and that day that is
coming will set them on fire," says the LORD
Almighty. "Not a root or a branch will be left
to them. 2But for you who revere my name,
the sun of righteousness will rise with healing
in its wings. And you will go out and leap like
calves released from the stall. 3Then you will
trample down the wicked; they will be ashes
under the soles of your feet on the day when I
do these things," says the LORD Almighty.
4"Remember the law of my servant Moses,
the decrees and laws I gave him at Horeb for
all Israel.
5"See, I will send you the prophet Elijah before that great and dreadful day of the LORD
comes. 6He will turn the hearts of the fathers
to their children, and the hearts of the children to their fathers; or else I will come and
strike the land with a curse."

WEEKEND

the Bible on divorce

The Bible recognizes and regulates divorce. Because divorce is a biblical concept, used and referred to frequently in the pages of the Bible, Christians must do all they can to understand it and teach what God says about it. Moreover, the church is required to apply to actual cases the Scriptural principles regarding divorce.

Some people believe that the Bible makes no provisions for divorce, but (rather) only condemns and denounces it. Yet Joseph (a just man) was not condemned for determining to divorce Mary (Matthew 1:19). So, there must be more to the divorce question than some think.

To begin with, let us be clear that neither is the Bible silent on the subject of divorce, nor does it always, under all circumstances, condemn divorce. That much must be established from the outset.

While God emphatically says, "I hate divorce" (Malachi 2:16), that statement must not be taken absolutely to mean that there is *nothing* about divorce that could be anything but detestable, because God, Himself, also tells us in Jeremiah 3:8, "[I gave faithless Israel her certificate of divorce and sent her away because of all her adulteries]."

If God Himself became involved in divorce proceedings with Israel, it is surely wrong to condemn all divorce. Obviously, from this passage (and the passage in Matthew 1) it is certain that divorce for some people under some circumstances is altogether proper and not the object of God's hatred.

It is altogether true that God hates divorce. But He neither hates all divorces in the same way nor hates every aspect of divorce. He hates what occasions *every* divorce—even the one that *He* gave to sinful Israel. He hates the results of divorce on children and to injured parties of divorce (yet even that did not stop Him from willing divorce in Ezra 10:11,44). And He hates divorces obtained on grounds that He has not sanctioned. But that leaves some things about divorce that He does not hate. He certainly does not condemn or hate divorce proceedings *per se*—i.e., as a process. Nor does He hate divorce when it is obtained according to the principles and regulations laid down in the Scriptures and which He followed in His dealings with unfaithful Israel.

When Jesus spoke about the unpardonable sin, He carefully assured us about the forgivability of other sins (Matthew 12:31). All other sins can be forgiven. And since obtaining a divorce for sinful reasons falls into that category, we must conclude that it too is a forgivable sin. The only sin that can never be forgiven is the sin of attributing the work of the *Holy* Spirit to an *unclean* spirit. Christ allows no one to call the Holy Spirit unclean! Only those unsaved persons, whose views and values are so turned around as to think that biblical holiness is sinful, could commit such a sin. Divorce can be forgiven by God. His church, therefore, dares do no less.

Your attitude must be biblical, no matter what the opinions of others.

When someone comes up to you and asks, "Did you know that Dave and Mabel are getting a divorce?" how do you respond? Do you gasp in shocked disbelief? Or, in deep concern, do you express a truly biblical attitude? Perhaps you could say something like, "I'm sorry to hear that. Do you think we can do something to help them work out their problems some other way?" Most people don't think that there is much hope when people have gone as far as divorce. There is still hope—take it from one who has seen scores of marriages at this point turn around again. In discussing the question, you may even say, "If we knew the facts, divorce, while always undesirable may be the only option open to them." Answers like these help others to look at the situation in a realistic, concerned, biblical way. They provide a proper response that focuses on data rather than emotions and feelings. Surely, even divorce can be discussed this way.

—JAY E. ADAMS

what we think about divorce

HOW ARE WE DOING?

First, answer the following questions separately. Try to find Biblical evidence for your beliefs about divorce. Then spend time together discussing divorce and remarriage.

1. The only Biblical grounds for divorce is marital infidelity.
2. If a partner has been unfaithful, it's best to end the marriage.
3. The person who files for divorce is guilty of ending the marriage.
4. There are two sides to every divorce; both partners are guilty of making a marriage fail.
5. Divorce will never be an option for us; we promised to stay together till we die.
6. We shouldn't even talk about divorce; it just plants the seed of its possibility.
7. If our marriage ends in divorce, we can never marry anyone else.

let's make a DATE

DINE WITH MARRIAGE EXPERTS

This weekend invite a married couple (preferably one that has been happily married for more than 15 or 20 years) to your house for dinner, or take them out to lunch after church. Ask them what has kept them together all these years. Find out some of their secrets to a happy marriage.

FOR YOUR NEXT DEVOTIONAL READING, TURN TO PAGE 1055.

LESSONS FROM THE *Bible*

What do these couples in Scripture teach us about divorce?

1. Hosea and Gomer (Hosea 3:1–3)
2. Joseph and Mary (Matthew 1:18–25)

THE NEW TESTAMENT

The New Testament

MATTHEW

Matthew

QUICK FACTS

AUTHOR Matthew, also called Levi

AUDIENCE Primarily Greek-speaking Jews

DATE Sometime between A.D. 50 and 80

SETTING Most likely written in Israel or perhaps Syrian Antioch

The author of this Gospel is not named, but the early church unanimously held that the writer was Matthew, a tax collector who became one of the 12 apostles. He wanted to show the Jewish converts in the early church that Jesus was the prophesied Messiah. Matthew quoted the Old Testament some 50 times, reassuring Jewish believers that they did not have to repudiate the Old Testament to accept the claims of Jesus but instead could recognize that their beloved Scriptures were fulfilled in him.

Many believe that Matthew also wrote his Gospel as a kind of instructional manual for Christian converts. It documents Jesus' life from his birth to his ascension into heaven and records Jesus' teaching on discipleship, missions, church discipline and the end of the age.

In this examination of Jesus' life and teachings are many insights into what it takes to make a relationship such as marriage work. Think of how we and our spouses will benefit as we hold Jesus up as our role model: as we seek to be meek, merciful and pure in heart; as we hunger and thirst for righteousness; and as we strive to be peacemakers (see Matthew 5:3–10).

The Genealogy of Jesus

1 A record of the genealogy of Jesus Christ
the son of David, the son of Abraham:

2 Abraham was the father of Isaac,
Isaac the father of Jacob,
Jacob the father of Judah and his brothers,
3 Judah the father of Perez and Zerah, whose mother was Tamar,
Perez the father of Hezron,
Hezron the father of Ram,
4 Ram the father of Amminadab,
Amminadab the father of Nahshon,
Nahshon the father of Salmon,
5 Salmon the father of Boaz, whose mother was Rahab,
Boaz the father of Obed, whose mother was Ruth,
Obed the father of Jesse,
6 and Jesse the father of King David.

David was the father of Solomon, whose mother had been Uriah's wife,
7 Solomon the father of Rehoboam,
Rehoboam the father of Abijah,
Abijah the father of Asa,
8 Asa the father of Jehoshaphat,
Jehoshaphat the father of Jehoram,
Jehoram the father of Uzziah,
9 Uzziah the father of Jotham,
Jotham the father of Ahaz,
Ahaz the father of Hezekiah,
10 Hezekiah the father of Manasseh,
Manasseh the father of Amon,
Amon the father of Josiah,
11 and Josiah the father of Jeconiah[a] and his brothers at the time of the exile to Babylon.

12 After the exile to Babylon:
Jeconiah was the father of Shealtiel,
Shealtiel the father of Zerubbabel,
13 Zerubbabel the father of Abiud,
Abiud the father of Eliakim,
Eliakim the father of Azor,
14 Azor the father of Zadok,
Zadok the father of Akim,
Akim the father of Eliud,
15 Eliud the father of Eleazar,
Eleazar the father of Matthan,
Matthan the father of Jacob,
16 and Jacob the father of Joseph, the husband of Mary, of whom was born Jesus, who is called Christ.

17 Thus there were fourteen generations in
all from Abraham to David, fourteen from
David to the exile to Babylon, and fourteen
from the exile to the Christ.[b]

The Birth of Jesus Christ

18 This is how the birth of Jesus Christ came
about: His mother Mary was pledged to be
married to Joseph, but before they came together, she was found to be with child through
the Holy Spirit. 19 Because Joseph her husband
was a righteous man and did not want to expose her to public disgrace, he had in mind to
divorce her quietly.
20 But after he had considered this, an angel
of the Lord appeared to him in a dream and
said, "Joseph son of David, do not be afraid to
take Mary home as your wife, because what is
conceived in her is from the Holy Spirit. 21 She
will give birth to a son, and you are to give
him the name Jesus,[c] because he will save his
people from their sins."
22 All this took place to fulfill what the Lord
had said through the prophet: 23 "The virgin
will be with child and will give birth to a son,
and they will call him Immanuel"[d]—which
means, "God with us."
24 When Joseph woke up, he did what the
angel of the Lord had commanded him and
took Mary home as his wife. 25 But he had no
union with her until she gave birth to a son.
And he gave him the name Jesus.

The Visit of the Magi

2 After Jesus was born in Bethlehem in Judea, during the time of King Herod, Magi[e]
from the east came to Jerusalem 2 and asked,
"Where is the one who has been born king of
the Jews? We saw his star in the east[f] and have
come to worship him."
3 When King Herod heard this he was disturbed, and all Jerusalem with him. 4 When he
had called together all the people's chief priests
and teachers of the law, he asked them where
the Christ[g] was to be born. 5 "In Bethlehem
in Judea," they replied, "for this is what the
prophet has written:

6 " 'But you, Bethlehem, in the land of Judah,
are by no means least among the rulers of Judah;
for out of you will come a ruler

---

[a] 11 That is, Jehoiachin; also in verse 12 [b] 17 Or *Messiah.* "The Christ" (Greek) and "the Messiah" (Hebrew) both mean "the Anointed One." [c] 21 *Jesus* is the Greek form of *Joshua,* which means *the Lord saves.* [d] 23 Isaiah 7:14 [e] 1 Traditionally *Wise Men* [f] 2 Or *star when it rose* [g] 4 Or *Messiah*

M **MONDAY**
READ MATTHEW 1:1–17

FITTING OUR PUZZLING PIECES TOGETHER

Salmon the father of Boaz, whose mother was Rahab, Boaz the father of Obed, whose mother was Ruth, Obed the father of Jesse, and Jesse the father of King David.

— MATTHEW 1:5–6

My husband and I live in Florida, where most everyone comes from somewhere else.

I'm originally from California; so are both of my parents. My grandparents all came from New York. Prior to that, my mother's family came from Ireland and Czechoslovakia, which isn't even a country anymore.

My father's people were Russian Jews who came to America through Toronto, Canada. That's all I know about my family's genealogy.

My husband's mother was Italian and his father was Irish, but they were born in New York, as was my husband. Our son-in-law is from Arkansas and is one-quarter Cherokee Indian. Mix this all together and that makes our granddaughter a pedigreed mutt.

As I look at the complicated genealogy of our family, I am struck by how life is one huge jigsaw puzzle. Each person we come into contact with somehow fits into this puzzle, perfectly interlocking to fulfill God's purpose of expanding his kingdom.

Still, it boggles my mind to think about how I left California at age 19 to join the Air Force the year after a boy named Barry Kennedy left New York to join the same branch of the military. We were stationed at the same base in northern Maine and assigned to the same unit. If either of us had joined the Navy or had gone into vinyl repair, there would be no us, no daughters Alison and Laura, no granddaughter Caroline.

Our spiritual legacy would be different as well. It was in the Air Force that I first heard the gospel and believed in Christ as my Savior. Out of my conversion came my sister's step into faith. Later my children and her children came to Christ. We're both still praying for the conversion of our husbands, our parents and our brothers. But we also have a cousin and a niece and a nephew who are believers. And my son-in-law came to faith in Christ after meeting my daughter.

As the jigsaw puzzle of the family of God expands, the picture of God's kingdom becomes increasingly clear and its fine details more known.

One of my favorite genealogies in the Bible is Matthew 1:1–6, especially verse 5, which mentions Rahab, a prostitute; Ruth, a young pagan widow; and David, a shepherd boy turned king. All were chosen by God to be integral pieces in the puzzlelike lineage of Jesus. How awesome to think that God also chooses us to extend his kingdom. How comforting to know that he uses imperfect people to do so.

—NANCY KENNEDY

let's *talk*

- How much do we know about our family trees? How far back can we trace our ethnic roots? What interesting, exciting or disconcerting things have we discovered about our ancestors?
- What about our spiritual roots? What spiritual heritage did we inherit from our ancestors? Who helped us come to this point in our faith journey?
- Decisions made today impact future generations. How does knowing that affect our goals and plans about raising children?

FOR YOUR NEXT DEVOTIONAL READING, TURN TO PAGE 1058.

who will be the shepherd of my people
Israel.'[a]"

7Then Herod called the Magi secretly and
found out from them the exact time the star
had appeared. 8He sent them to Bethlehem
and said, "Go and make a careful search for
the child. As soon as you find him, report to
me, so that I too may go and worship him."
9After they had heard the king, they went
on their way, and the star they had seen in
the east[b] went ahead of them until it stopped
over the place where the child was. 10When
they saw the star, they were overjoyed. 11On
coming to the house, they saw the child with
his mother Mary, and they bowed down and
worshiped him. Then they opened their treasures and presented him with gifts of gold and
of incense and of myrrh. 12And having been
warned in a dream not to go back to Herod,
they returned to their country by another
route.

The Escape to Egypt

13When they had gone, an angel of the Lord
appeared to Joseph in a dream. "Get up," he
said, "take the child and his mother and escape
to Egypt. Stay there until I tell you, for Herod
is going to search for the child to kill him."
14So he got up, took the child and his
mother during the night and left for Egypt,
15where he stayed until the death of Herod.
And so was fulfilled what the Lord had said
through the prophet: "Out of Egypt I called
my son."[c]
16When Herod realized that he had been
outwitted by the Magi, he was furious, and
he gave orders to kill all the boys in Bethlehem and its vicinity who were two years old
and under, in accordance with the time he had
learned from the Magi. 17Then what was said
through the prophet Jeremiah was fulfilled:

18"A voice is heard in Ramah,
weeping and great mourning,
Rachel weeping for her children
and refusing to be comforted,
because they are no more."[d]

The Return to Nazareth

19After Herod died, an angel of the Lord
appeared in a dream to Joseph in Egypt 20and
said, "Get up, take the child and his mother and go to the land of Israel, for those who
were trying to take the child's life are dead."
21So he got up, took the child and his
mother and went to the land of Israel. 22But
when he heard that Archelaus was reigning
in Judea in place of his father Herod, he was
afraid to go there. Having been warned in a
dream, he withdrew to the district of Galilee, 23and he went and lived in a town called
Nazareth. So was fulfilled what was said
through the prophets: "He will be called a
Nazarene."

John the Baptist Prepares the Way

3 In those days John the Baptist came,
preaching in the Desert of Judea 2and saying, "Repent, for the kingdom of heaven is
near." 3This is he who was spoken of through
the prophet Isaiah:

"A voice of one calling in the desert,
'Prepare the way for the Lord,
make straight paths for him.' "[e]

4John's clothes were made of camel's hair,
and he had a leather belt around his waist. His
food was locusts and wild honey. 5People went
out to him from Jerusalem and all Judea and
the whole region of the Jordan. 6Confessing
their sins, they were baptized by him in the
Jordan River.
7But when he saw many of the Pharisees
and Sadducees coming to where he was baptizing, he said to them: "You brood of vipers!
Who warned you to flee from the coming
wrath? 8Produce fruit in keeping with repentance. 9And do not think you can say to yourselves, 'We have Abraham as our father.' I tell
you that out of these stones God can raise up
children for Abraham. 10The ax is already at
the root of the trees, and every tree that does
not produce good fruit will be cut down and
thrown into the fire.
11"I baptize you with[f] water for repentance.
But after me will come one who is more powerful than I, whose sandals I am not fit to carry. He will baptize you with the Holy Spirit
and with fire. 12His winnowing fork is in his
hand, and he will clear his threshing floor,
gathering his wheat into the barn and burning
up the chaff with unquenchable fire."

The Baptism of Jesus

13Then Jesus came from Galilee to the Jordan to be baptized by John. 14But John tried
to deter him, saying, "I need to be baptized by
you, and do you come to me?"
15Jesus replied, "Let it be so now; it is prop-

[a] *6* Micah 5:2 [b] *9* Or *seen when it rose* [c] *15* Hosea 11:1 [d] *18* Jer. 31:15 [e] *3* Isaiah 40:3 [f] *11* Or *in*

er for us to do this to fulfill all righteousness."
Then John consented.
[16]As soon as Jesus was baptized, he went up
out of the water. At that moment heaven was
opened, and he saw the Spirit of God descending like a dove and lighting on him. [17]And a
voice from heaven said, "This is my Son,
whom I love; with him I am well pleased."

The Temptation of Jesus

4 Then Jesus was led by the Spirit into the
desert to be tempted by the devil. [2]After
fasting forty days and forty nights, he was
hungry. [3]The tempter came to him and said,
"If you are the Son of God, tell these stones to
become bread."
[4]Jesus answered, "It is written: 'Man does
not live on bread alone, but on every word
that comes from the mouth of God.'[a]"
[5]Then the devil took him to the holy city
and had him stand on the highest point of the
temple. [6]"If you are the Son of God," he said,
"throw yourself down. For it is written:

" 'He will command his angels concerning
you,
and they will lift you up in their hands,
so that you will not strike your foot
against a stone.'[b]"

[7]Jesus answered him, "It is also written: 'Do
not put the Lord your God to the test.'[c]"
[8]Again, the devil took him to a very high
mountain and showed him all the kingdoms
of the world and their splendor. [9]"All this I
will give you," he said, "if you will bow down
and worship me."
[10]Jesus said to him, "Away from me, Satan!
For it is written: 'Worship the Lord your God,
and serve him only.'[d]"
[11]Then the devil left him, and angels came
and attended him.

Jesus Begins to Preach

[12]When Jesus heard that John had been put
in prison, he returned to Galilee. [13]Leaving
Nazareth, he went and lived in Capernaum,
which was by the lake in the area of Zebulun and Naphtali— [14]to fulfill what was said
through the prophet Isaiah:

[15]"Land of Zebulun and land of Naphtali,
the way to the sea, along the Jordan,
Galilee of the Gentiles—
[16]the people living in darkness
have seen a great light;
on those living in the land of the shadow
of death
a light has dawned."[e]

[17]From that time on Jesus began to preach,
"Repent, for the kingdom of heaven is near."

The Calling of the First Disciples

[18]As Jesus was walking beside the Sea of
Galilee, he saw two brothers, Simon called Peter and his brother Andrew. They were casting
a net into the lake, for they were fishermen.
[19]"Come, follow me," Jesus said, "and I will
make you fishers of men." [20]At once they left
their nets and followed him.
[21]Going on from there, he saw two other
brothers, James son of Zebedee and his brother John. They were in a boat with their father
Zebedee, preparing their nets. Jesus called
them, [22]and immediately they left the boat
and their father and followed him.

Jesus Heals the Sick

[23]Jesus went throughout Galilee, teaching in their synagogues, preaching the good
news of the kingdom, and healing every disease and sickness among the people. [24]News
about him spread all over Syria, and people
brought to him all who were ill with various diseases, those suffering severe pain, the
demon-possessed, those having seizures, and
the paralyzed, and he healed them. [25]Large
crowds from Galilee, the Decapolis,[f] Jerusalem, Judea and the region across the Jordan
followed him.

The Beatitudes

5 Now when he saw the crowds, he went up
on a mountainside and sat down. His disciples came to him, [2]and he began to teach
them, saying:

[3]"Blessed are the poor in spirit,
for theirs is the kingdom of heaven.
[4]Blessed are those who mourn,
for they will be comforted.
[5]Blessed are the meek,
for they will inherit the earth.
[6]Blessed are those who hunger and thirst
for righteousness,
for they will be filled.
[7]Blessed are the merciful,
for they will be shown mercy.
[8]Blessed are the pure in heart,
for they will see God.
[9]Blessed are the peacemakers,

---

[a] *4* Deut. 8:3 [b] *6* Psalm 91:11,12 [c] *7* Deut. 6:16 [d] *10* Deut. 6:13 [e] *16* Isaiah 9:1,2 [f] *25* That is, the Ten Cities

TUESDAY
READ MATTHEW 4:1–11

CONFRONTING TEMPTATION

What do you think about when you think about heaven? My thoughts turn to streets of gold and many mansions. I think about seeing my father and my believing grandparents, who have gone ahead of me. I think of seeing Jesus face-to-face. But my favorite idea of heaven is that I won't sin there. I won't have to be sorry for what I do wrong or forgive anyone else's wrongs. I won't have to show the Lord such ugliness in myself ever again. I won't even be tempted to sin.

Jesus was tempted to sin, although—unlike us—he never succumbed to temptation. The most striking episode of Jesus resisting temptation is recorded in Matthew 4. After fasting for 40 days and nights, and when he was physically at his weakest, Jesus was approached by Satan. The devil wasted no time; he got right down to attacking the human motives that most often lead people to sin. First he struck at Jesus' longing to fulfill a physical drive; in this case, hunger. Then he said, "Prove you're who you say you are," striking a blow at Jesus' identity. Finally he showed Jesus the glories of all the kingdoms of the world, then said, "You can have all of this if you worship me!" But Jesus refused to give in.

"Away from me, Satan! For it is written: 'Worship the Lord your God, and serve him only.' "

—MATTHEW 4:10

let's *talk*

- Although we experience temptations in all three areas—physical drives, pride and materialism—which do we struggle with most?
- In what ways has God strengthened us to resist temptations in the past? What has helped us avoid sinful behavior?
- How can we help each other in our most vulnerable areas of temptation? What changes could we make in our lifestyle that might help us avoid temptation?

Every person alive is tempted in these same areas: physical needs, personal identity and personal possessions. For the most part, our culture tells us to satisfy our needs any way we can. But as God's people, we are taught to align our choices with God's ideas of how to control our physical drives, to see ourselves in relation to him, and to rightly handle our possessions.

The ways Jesus responded to temptation offer us good weapons for our own struggles to resist the lures of Satan. For example, Jesus consistently used Scripture to respond to Satan. When tempted to satisfy a physical drive, Jesus pointed out the importance of seeking satisfaction in God's Word rather than earthly food. And he responded to Satan's attempts to make him glorify himself or to own worldly possessions by, in essence, saying, "Don't give that place of priority to yourself (pride) or to things (your home, your toys, sports, shopping). You are to worship God, and serve him only."

Many married couples spend an inordinate amount of time chasing after promotions or experiences or possessions that only make them want more. How much better to seek satisfaction in the eternal word that "comes from the mouth of God" (Matthew 4:4). How much better to find satisfaction in relationship with the One in whom we find the kind of peace and love that will never fail. Worshiping God alone—not our stuff, our careers or even each other—is the only way that will work for our good and God's glory.

Until we get to heaven and don't have to deal with temptation ever again, our best weapon against sin is to know God through his Word and worship him only.

—ANNETTE LAPLACA

FOR YOUR NEXT DEVOTIONAL READING, TURN TO PAGE 1060.

for they will be called sons of God.
10 Blessed are those who are persecuted
because of righteousness,
for theirs is the kingdom of heaven.

11“Blessed are you when people insult you,
persecute you and falsely say all kinds of evil
against you because of me. 12Rejoice and be
glad, because great is your reward in heav-
en, for in the same way they persecuted the
prophets who were before you.

Salt and Light

13“You are the salt of the earth. But if the
salt loses its saltiness, how can it be made salty
again? It is no longer good for anything, except to be thrown out and trampled by men.
14“You are the light of the world. A city on
a hill cannot be hidden. 15Neither do people
light a lamp and put it under a bowl. Instead
they put it on its stand, and it gives light to
everyone in the house. 16In the same way, let
your light shine before men, that they may
see your good deeds and praise your Father in
heaven.

The Fulfillment of the Law

17“Do not think that I have come to abolish the Law or the Prophets; I have not come
to abolish them but to fulfill them. 18I tell
you the truth, until heaven and earth disappear, not the smallest letter, not the least
stroke of a pen, will by any means disappear
from the Law until everything is accomplished. 19Anyone who breaks one of the
least of these commandments and teaches
others to do the same will be called least in
the kingdom of heaven, but whoever practices and teaches these commands will be called
great in the kingdom of heaven. 20For I tell
you that unless your righteousness surpasses
that of the Pharisees and the teachers of the
law, you will certainly not enter the kingdom
of heaven.

Murder

21“You have heard that it was said to the
people long ago, ‘Do not murder,[a] and anyone who murders will be subject to judgment.’
22But I tell you that anyone who is angry
with his brother[b] will be subject to judgment. Again, anyone who says to his brother,
‘Raca,[c]’ is answerable to the Sanhedrin. But
anyone who says, ‘You fool!’ will be in danger
of the fire of hell.

23“Therefore, if you are offering your gift at
the altar and there remember that your brother has something against you, 24leave your gift
there in front of the altar. First go and be reconciled to your brother; then come and offer
your gift.
25“Settle matters quickly with your adversary who is taking you to court. Do it while
you are still with him on the way, or he may
hand you over to the judge, and the judge may
hand you over to the officer, and you may be
thrown into prison. 26I tell you the truth, you
will not get out until you have paid the last
penny.[d]

Adultery

27“You have heard that it was said, ‘Do
not commit adultery.’[e] 28But I tell you that
anyone who looks at a woman lustfully has
already committed adultery with her in his
heart. 29If your right eye causes you to sin,
gouge it out and throw it away. It is better
for you to lose one part of your body than
for your whole body to be thrown into hell.
30And if your right hand causes you to sin, cut
it off and throw it away. It is better for you to
lose one part of your body than for your whole
body to go into hell.

Divorce

31“It has been said, ‘Anyone who divorces
his wife must give her a certificate of divorce.’[f]
32But I tell you that anyone who divorces his
wife, except for marital unfaithfulness, causes
her to become an adulteress, and anyone who
marries the divorced woman commits adultery.

Oaths

33“Again, you have heard that it was said to
the people long ago, ‘Do not break your oath,
but keep the oaths you have made to the Lord.’
34But I tell you, Do not swear at all: either
by heaven, for it is God’s throne; 35or by the
earth, for it is his footstool; or by Jerusalem,
for it is the city of the Great King. 36And do
not swear by your head, for you cannot make
even one hair white or black. 37Simply let your
‘Yes’ be ‘Yes,’ and your ‘No,’ ‘No’; anything
beyond this comes from the evil one.

An Eye for an Eye

38“You have heard that it was said, ‘Eye for
eye, and tooth for tooth.’[g] 39But I tell you,
Do not resist an evil person. If someone strikes

[a] *21* Exodus 20:13 [b] *22* Some manuscripts *brother without cause* [c] *22* An Aramaic term of contempt [d] *26* Greek *kodrantes*
[e] *27* Exodus 20:14 [f] *31* Deut. 24:1 [g] *38* Exodus 21:24; Lev. 24:20; Deut. 19:21

WEDNESDAY
READ MATTHEW 5:17–48

TRUE RIGHTEOUSNESS

In the Norman Rockwell painting *Sunday Morning*, Dad sits unshaven in a chair. Passing behind him are his wife and three kids, dressed in their Sunday best, Bibles under their arms, obviously on their way to church. Dad slumps behind the Sunday paper with a guilty look, as his family marches by with their noses in the air.

Ironically, people who are determined to keep God's rules are far more likely to incur Christ's holy wrath than people who blatantly sin. The problem is that the people who are good at keeping rules—especially *God's* rules—are the people who are most likely to think they do *not* need a Savior because they are on God's spiritual honor roll.

"You have heard that it was said . . . But I tell you . . ."

— MATTHEW 5:27–28

let's talk

- How do we react when someone close to us acts self-righteously? In what areas are we most likely to feel self-righteous?
- After reading Matthew 5:17–48, how would we summarize what Jesus was saying?
- What can these verses prompt us to pray as a couple?

In our marriages, where our faults are constantly on display, self-righteousness is especially smelly. It is pretty easy to find areas in which our righteousness exceeds our spouse's, and when we point to that, we're in trouble with the Lord.

In the Sermon on the Mount, Jesus didn't throw out God's rules. In Matthew 5:17–20, he affirmed them down to the last comma. But then, through a series of examples, he showed the kind of righteousness God expects. Jesus offered a series of you-have-heard-it-said-but-I-tell-you statements in regard to the Old Testament law that pushed that law off its stone tablets and into the human heart.

In one sense, Jesus wants us to aspire to the higher, heart-deep righteousness that he described through these examples. But in another sense, he wants us to throw up our hands in dismay, saying, "If this is what God expects, then I'm in deep trouble! I can't be that good." That's exactly where Jesus wants us—ready for a Savior who alone can cleanse us from our deepest sins and ready for his Holy Spirit, who can empower us to live at the level of true righteousness.

Two of Jesus' examples deal directly with marriage issues: adultery and divorce. These are issues about which people are prone to draw precise lines to see how close to the line they can go and still consider themselves righteous. Jesus didn't offer much wiggle room. He noted that even a lustful look is deadly trouble, and divorce not only makes the man seeking the divorce an adulterer, assuming he marries another woman, but also puts the innocent wife and her future second husband in the impossible position of betraying the marriage covenant. (I don't think Jesus' point is that the wife and future husband are *guilty* of adultery, but they are forced by the self-righteous divorcer into a soul-damaging, covenant-breaking situation that they shouldn't have to face.)

True righteousness in marriage begins with hearts that are utterly faithful to one another, fed by God's faithfulness to us. We do not keep score to decide who is most holy. And we don't try to figure out how much wiggle room there is in Scripture for splitting up. Above all, we realize that soul-deep righteousness is beyond our reach without the forgiveness of Christ and the help of the Holy Spirit.

—LEE ECLOV

FOR YOUR NEXT DEVOTIONAL READING, TURN TO PAGE 1062.

you on the right cheek, turn to him the other
also. [40]And if someone wants to sue you and
take your tunic, let him have your cloak as
well. [41]If someone forces you to go one mile,
go with him two miles. [42]Give to the one who
asks you, and do not turn away from the one
who wants to borrow from you.

Love for Enemies

[43]"You have heard that it was said, 'Love
your neighbor[a] and hate your enemy.' [44]But
I tell you: Love your enemies[b] and pray for
those who persecute you, [45]that you may be
sons of your Father in heaven. He causes his
sun to rise on the evil and the good, and sends
rain on the righteous and the unrighteous. [46]If
you love those who love you, what reward will
you get? Are not even the tax collectors doing
that? [47]And if you greet only your brothers,
what are you doing more than others? Do not
even pagans do that? [48]Be perfect, therefore, as
your heavenly Father is perfect.

Giving to the Needy

6 "Be careful not to do your 'acts of righteousness' before men, to be seen by them.
If you do, you will have no reward from
your Father in heaven.

[2]"So when you give to the needy, do not
announce it with trumpets, as the hypocrites
do in the synagogues and on the streets, to
be honored by men. I tell you the truth, they
have received their reward in full. [3]But when
you give to the needy, do not let your left hand
know what your right hand is doing, [4]so that
your giving may be in secret. Then your Father, who sees what is done in secret, will reward you.

Prayer

[5]"And when you pray, do not be like the
hypocrites, for they love to pray standing in
the synagogues and on the street corners to be
seen by men. I tell you the truth, they have
received their reward in full. [6]But when you
pray, go into your room, close the door and
pray to your Father, who is unseen. Then your
Father, who sees what is done in secret, will
reward you. [7]And when you pray, do not keep
on babbling like pagans, for they think they
will be heard because of their many words.
[8]Do not be like them, for your Father knows
what you need before you ask him.

[9]"This, then, is how you should pray:

" 'Our Father in heaven,
hallowed be your name,
[10]your kingdom come,
your will be done
on earth as it is in heaven.
[11]Give us today our daily bread.
[12]Forgive us our debts,
as we also have forgiven our debtors.
[13]And lead us not into temptation,
but deliver us from the evil one.[c]'

[14]For if you forgive men when they sin against
you, your heavenly Father will also forgive
you. [15]But if you do not forgive men their
sins, your Father will not forgive your sins.

Fasting

[16]"When you fast, do not look somber as
the hypocrites do, for they disfigure their faces
to show men they are fasting. I tell you the
truth, they have received their reward in full.
[17]But when you fast, put oil on your head and
wash your face, [18]so that it will not be obvious
to men that you are fasting, but only to your
Father, who is unseen; and your Father, who
sees what is done in secret, will reward you.

Treasures in Heaven

[19]"Do not store up for yourselves treasures on earth, where moth and rust destroy,
and where thieves break in and steal. [20]But
store up for yourselves treasures in heaven,
where moth and rust do not destroy, and
where thieves do not break in and steal. [21]For
where your treasure is, there your heart will
be also.

[22]"The eye is the lamp of the body. If your
eyes are good, your whole body will be full of
light. [23]But if your eyes are bad, your whole
body will be full of darkness. If then the light
within you is darkness, how great is that darkness!

[24]"No one can serve two masters. Either he
will hate the one and love the other, or he will
be devoted to the one and despise the other.
You cannot serve both God and Money.

Do Not Worry

[25]"Therefore I tell you, do not worry about
your life, what you will eat or drink; or about
your body, what you will wear. Is not life more
important than food, and the body more important than clothes? [26]Look at the birds of
the air; they do not sow or reap or store away
in barns, and yet your heavenly Father feeds

[a] *43* Lev. 19:18 [b] *44* Some late manuscripts *enemies, bless those who curse you, do good to those who hate you* [c] *13* Or *from evil*; some late manuscripts *one, / for yours is the kingdom and the power and the glory forever. Amen.*

THURSDAY
READ MATTHEW 6:19–34

CHOOSING CONTENTMENT

> **"Do not store up for yourselves treasures on earth, where moth and rust destroy, and where thieves break in and steal. But store up for yourselves treasures in heaven . . . For where your treasure is, there your heart will be also."**
>
> — MATTHEW 6:19–21

All that we have comes from God: our spouses, children, families, friends and jobs. That includes our houses, property, furnishings, cars, clothes, family heirlooms and all other personal belongings. God gives us these good gifts for our use and enjoyment. There is nothing wrong with these things, but sometimes our attitudes toward our things can cause problems for us.

Throughout history, people have had the desire to get more stuff. But in our culture today, the media allows us to see how much we don't have. Because we are exposed to people in different social standings, we are more easily able to compare ourselves to others. In previous generations, people compared what they had with their family or neighbors (who probably had similar things); today we have TV shows that portray the lives and belongings of the megarich. And we still envy our friends and neighbors. When we begin to focus on what others have, we become tempted to live beyond our means. We become obsessed with material things. We become stressed as we work harder and longer in order to buy more stuff.

It is easy to wonder why others have more than we do, especially if we're struggling to keep up with payments on our house, cars and loans. We say, "Other people are just like us, but they have so much more than we do. It's not fair! Why doesn't God bless us like he does them? Why should we always have money problems?"

Maybe we become upset with our spouse and insist that we should do better than we are doing, or that our children should have the same opportunities that other children have. Jealousy, anger and ambition can eat away at a marriage when we think we should have more than we do.

But the stuff we want may not be what God has allotted to us. He has promised that he will provide all that we need but not necessarily all that we want. So one tough spiritual lesson we need to learn as married couples is to shape our wants to match God's allotment, not the other way around, and to choose, like Paul, to be content whatever our circumstances (see Philippians 4:11).

Finding contentment with God's allotment to us helps ease the stress of getting and spending. It lightens the load of acquiring more and more. And it may help us grow together as a couple as we learn to enjoy each other's company without the pressure of reaching for bigger and better toys, vacations, houses or recreational vehicles. When we begin to treasure each other, our hearts will be there also.

—JOHN R. THROOP

let's talk

- In what ways are we dissatisfied with what we have? What feeds into that?
- How do we deal with our desires for material things? What's the effect of that on our relationship?
- How would we define our allotment from God? What might it include? Is this a limited amount or does it increase over time?

FOR YOUR NEXT DEVOTIONAL READING, TURN TO PAGE 1064.

them. Are you not much more valuable than they? [27]Who of you by worrying can add a single hour to his life[a]?

[28]"And why do you worry about clothes? See how the lilies of the field grow. They do not labor or spin. [29]Yet I tell you that not even Solomon in all his splendor was dressed like one of these. [30]If that is how God clothes the grass of the field, which is here today and tomorrow is thrown into the fire, will he not much more clothe you, O you of little faith? [31]So do not worry, saying, 'What shall we eat?' or 'What shall we drink?' or 'What shall we wear?' [32]For the pagans run after all these things, and your heavenly Father knows that you need them. [33]But seek first his kingdom and his righteousness, and all these things will be given to you as well. [34]Therefore do not worry about tomorrow, for tomorrow will worry about itself. Each day has enough trouble of its own.

Judging Others

7 "Do not judge, or you too will be judged. [2]For in the same way you judge others, you will be judged, and with the measure you use, it will be measured to you.

[3]"Why do you look at the speck of sawdust in your brother's eye and pay no attention to the plank in your own eye? [4]How can you say to your brother, 'Let me take the speck out of your eye,' when all the time there is a plank in your own eye? [5]You hypocrite, first take the plank out of your own eye, and then you will see clearly to remove the speck from your brother's eye.

[6]"Do not give dogs what is sacred; do not throw your pearls to pigs. If you do, they may trample them under their feet, and then turn and tear you to pieces.

Ask, Seek, Knock

[7]"Ask and it will be given to you; seek and you will find; knock and the door will be opened to you. [8]For everyone who asks receives; he who seeks finds; and to him who knocks, the door will be opened.

[9]"Which of you, if his son asks for bread, will give him a stone? [10]Or if he asks for a fish, will give him a snake? [11]If you, then, though you are evil, know how to give good gifts to your children, how much more will your Father in heaven give good gifts to those who ask him! [12]So in everything, do to others what you would have them do to you, for this sums up the Law and the Prophets.

The Narrow and Wide Gates

[13]"Enter through the narrow gate. For wide is the gate and broad is the road that leads to destruction, and many enter through it. [14]But small is the gate and narrow the road that leads to life, and only a few find it.

A Tree and Its Fruit

[15]"Watch out for false prophets. They come to you in sheep's clothing, but inwardly they are ferocious wolves. [16]By their fruit you will recognize them. Do people pick grapes from thornbushes, or figs from thistles? [17]Likewise every good tree bears good fruit, but a bad tree bears bad fruit. [18]A good tree cannot bear bad fruit, and a bad tree cannot bear good fruit. [19]Every tree that does not bear good fruit is cut down and thrown into the fire. [20]Thus, by their fruit you will recognize them.

[21]"Not everyone who says to me, 'Lord, Lord,' will enter the kingdom of heaven, but only he who does the will of my Father who is in heaven. [22]Many will say to me on that day, 'Lord, Lord, did we not prophesy in your name, and in your name drive out demons and perform many miracles?' [23]Then I will tell them plainly, 'I never knew you. Away from me, you evildoers!'

The Wise and Foolish Builders

[24]"Therefore everyone who hears these words of mine and puts them into practice is like a wise man who built his house on the rock. [25]The rain came down, the streams rose, and the winds blew and beat against that house; yet it did not fall, because it had its foundation on the rock. [26]But everyone who hears these words of mine and does not put them into practice is like a foolish man who built his house on sand. [27]The rain came down, the streams rose, and the winds blew and beat against that house, and it fell with a great crash."

[28]When Jesus had finished saying these things, the crowds were amazed at his teaching, [29]because he taught as one who had authority, and not as their teachers of the law.

The Man With Leprosy

8 When he came down from the mountainside, large crowds followed him. [2]A man with leprosy[b] came and knelt before him

---

[a] 27 Or *single cubit to his height* [b] 2 The Greek word was used for various diseases affecting the skin—not necessarily leprosy.

FRIDAY
READ MATTHEW 7:1–5

AFFIRMATION EXPERIMENT

"Do not judge, or you too will be judged. For in the same way you judge others, you will be judged, and with the measure you use, it will be measured to you."

— MATTHEW 7:1–2

let's talk

- In what areas are we critical of each other? What brings out words of judgment in our relationship? How has this affected who we are together?
- When has our relationship blossomed with warmth? What kinds of things did we say to one another during those times?
- How can we bring out the best in each other? What practices will help accomplish that?

Years ago graduate students at an Ivy League college conducted an experiment. First they observed undergraduates until they found one of the most unkempt, most socially inept women on campus.

Then they drew up a schedule; each would spend a month getting close to the woman. They would "happen" to bump into her between classes. They would show up in line behind her in the dining hall. They would call her for lecture notes or assignment reminders. Moreover, when each was "on duty," he would compliment the woman, expressing delight in her voice, her talents, her insights, her clothes.

The first student performed well. In spite of his misgivings, he began to speak to the woman, finding ways to affirm her. By the end of the month he found his task less onerous as the young woman started to respond. She smiled occasionally, combed her hair more often, and paid more attention to how she dressed.

The second graduate student took the experiment a step further. He asked the undergrad out on an official date and spent the month showering her with gifts and compliments.

By the third month there was a new glow about the young woman, and the third researcher enjoyed her company more than he cared to admit. When the graduate students got together to share their experiences and laugh at the "progress" of their victim, the third student had to force chuckles through self-conscious embarrassment.

The fourth member of the group never got the chance to lavish attention on the young woman because by then she was engaged to the man assigned to her during the third month. What started as a cruel and belittling pastime for the students turned into a love story.

None of us would want such a trick played on us. Yet there is something instructive about its outcome. As Jesus noted, when we spend our days looking at others with critical eyes, we find ourselves more in a laboratory than in a relationship. But when we begin to respect and affirm others as men and women made in the image of God, we move back into the relational warmth of family.

The implications are obvious for marriage. People who live closely with one another are bound to chip away at each other's rough edges. We become experts in analysis and faultfinding, but we don't gain much by that besides divisiveness and pain.

Jesus' warning not to judge others doesn't mean we should be blind to the faults of our mates. But it reminds us to be caring more than critical, compassionate more than judgmental. Just as Christ lavishes grace upon us, we can extend loving grace to each other, rejoicing as we together blossom and grow beautiful in each other's eyes.

—WAYNE BROUWER

FOR YOUR NEXT DEVOTIONAL READING, TURN TO PAGE 1066.

and said, "Lord, if you are willing, you can
make me clean."
3 Jesus reached out his hand and touched
the man. "I am willing," he said. "Be clean!"
Immediately he was cured[a] of his leprosy.
4 Then Jesus said to him, "See that you don't
tell anyone. But go, show yourself to the priest
and offer the gift Moses commanded, as a testimony to them."

The Faith of the Centurion

5 When Jesus had entered Capernaum,
a centurion came to him, asking for help.
6 "Lord," he said, "my servant lies at home paralyzed and in terrible suffering."
7 Jesus said to him, "I will go and heal
him."
8 The centurion replied, "Lord, I do not deserve to have you come under my roof. But just
say the word, and my servant will be healed.
9 For I myself am a man under authority, with
soldiers under me. I tell this one, 'Go,' and he
goes; and that one, 'Come,' and he comes. I
say to my servant, 'Do this,' and he does it."
10 When Jesus heard this, he was astonished
and said to those following him, "I tell you the
truth, I have not found anyone in Israel with
such great faith. 11 I say to you that many will
come from the east and the west, and will take
their places at the feast with Abraham, Isaac
and Jacob in the kingdom of heaven. 12 But
the subjects of the kingdom will be thrown
outside, into the darkness, where there will be
weeping and gnashing of teeth."
13 Then Jesus said to the centurion, "Go! It
will be done just as you believed it would."
And his servant was healed at that very hour.

Jesus Heals Many

14 When Jesus came into Peter's house, he
saw Peter's mother-in-law lying in bed with
a fever. 15 He touched her hand and the fever
left her, and she got up and began to wait on
him.
16 When evening came, many who were demon-possessed were brought to him, and he
drove out the spirits with a word and healed
all the sick. 17 This was to fulfill what was spoken through the prophet Isaiah:

"He took up our infirmities
and carried our diseases."[b]

The Cost of Following Jesus

18 When Jesus saw the crowd around him,
he gave orders to cross to the other side of the
lake. 19 Then a teacher of the law came to him
and said, "Teacher, I will follow you wherever
you go."
20 Jesus replied, "Foxes have holes and birds
of the air have nests, but the Son of Man has
no place to lay his head."
21 Another disciple said to him, "Lord, first
let me go and bury my father."
22 But Jesus told him, "Follow me, and let
the dead bury their own dead."

Jesus Calms the Storm

23 Then he got into the boat and his disciples
followed him. 24 Without warning, a furious
storm came up on the lake, so that the waves
swept over the boat. But Jesus was sleeping.
25 The disciples went and woke him, saying,
"Lord, save us! We're going to drown!"
26 He replied, "You of little faith, why are
you so afraid?" Then he got up and rebuked
the winds and the waves, and it was completely calm.
27 The men were amazed and asked, "What
kind of man is this? Even the winds and the
waves obey him!"

The Healing of Two Demon-possessed Men

28 When he arrived at the other side in the
region of the Gadarenes,[c] two demon-possessed men coming from the tombs met him.
They were so violent that no one could pass
that way. 29 "What do you want with us, Son
of God?" they shouted. "Have you come here
to torture us before the appointed time?"
30 Some distance from them a large herd of
pigs was feeding. 31 The demons begged Jesus,
"If you drive us out, send us into the herd of
pigs."
32 He said to them, "Go!" So they came out
and went into the pigs, and the whole herd
rushed down the steep bank into the lake and
died in the water. 33 Those tending the pigs
ran off, went into the town and reported all
this, including what had happened to the demon-possessed men. 34 Then the whole town
went out to meet Jesus. And when they saw
him, they pleaded with him to leave their region.

Jesus Heals a Paralytic

9 Jesus stepped into a boat, crossed over
and came to his own town. 2 Some men
brought to him a paralytic, lying on a
mat. When Jesus saw their faith, he said to

[a] 3 Greek *made clean* [b] 17 Isaiah 53:4 [c] 28 Some manuscripts *Gergesenes*; others *Gerasenes*

WEEKEND

spiritual mismatch

Once Leslie and I got a phone call at 3:30 P.M. on Easter. Theresa was crying. "Holidays are always the worst," she said between sobs. "But today, he really went too far. He's been making fun of me, saying I'm weak, saying I believe ridiculous things, saying the church is just trying to get my money. I'm tired of defending myself. I don't know what to do anymore. Why won't he just let me believe what I want? Why does he have to ruin everything? It was bad enough having to go to Easter services by myself; why does he have to destroy the rest of my day too?"

Or consider Kathy. She said her anguish over her marital situation has only been amplified by her church and Christian friends who inadvertently make matters worse for her. "There's this underlying implication that if I would just be a better witness, if I'd just pray harder, if I'd just get him to come to Christmas services, if I'd give him the right book to read or tape to listen to, that somehow everything would work out," she said. "They don't come right out and say it, but I get the feeling that I'm the one at fault—and that hurts!"

Linda Davis, who lived for years in an unequally yoked marriage until her husband became a Christian, said the only lonelier plight for an unequally yoked person would be the death of her spouse. "I doubt, however, that even physical widowhood makes a woman feel as rejected and inadequate as does 'spiritual widowhood,' " she added. "The spiritual widow receives no flowers or sympathy cards. She simply grieves in silence for a union that never was."

It's all too easy to turn our primary attention away from God and to stay riveted on the plight of our mismatched marriage. But that keeps us bogged down in our troubles rather than lifting our eyes toward our Solution. There are at least seven reasons why we must continue to keep God first in our lives.

1. *He deserves our primary allegiance.* God is our creator who made us in his image, our Sustainer who keeps us alive, our Redeemer whose Son died for our sins, and our Father who adopted us as his children. We put God above all else because that's what he so obviously warrants by virtue of who he is and what he has done.

2. *This perspective recalibrates our life.* When we give God the reverence, honor and awe that he deserves as our First Love, then we realize that nobody—and no circumstances—can ultimately harm us.

3. *He will meet needs that our spouse never could.* It is fundamentally unfair to expect our marriage partner to fulfill needs that only God is truly capable of meeting. If our spouse could do that, we would no longer have any use for God!

4. *He empowers us to love our spouse when our spouse isn't very lovable.*

5. *He can create something good from the pain of our mismatch.* If we abide in Christ, he can use our experiences as an unequally yoked Christian to develop and mold our character in ways that never would have been possible without the struggles and difficulties we have faced.

6. *He will be our spouse when our earthly spouse is distant.* At those times when the conflict from your mismatch makes you feel like a spiritual widow—isolated, lonely and separated from your spouse by his icy attitude—God is there to comfort, encourage and reassure you.

7. *He loves our partner more than we do.*

—LEE AND LESLIE STROBEL

are you a match?

"Spiritual mismatch" is often used to describe the marriage between a believer and a non-believer, but there can also be spiritual mismatches between believers who just don't see things the same way. Consider the following statements. Discuss your answers together.

1. Money
   a. I've earned my money on my own, so I can spend it however I want.
   b. Everything I have is God's, so I am happy to give generously.
2. Weekends
   a. Keeping the Sabbath holy and attending worship on the weekends is a way for me to recharge my spiritual battery and honor God.
   b. Weekends are a great time to catch up on sleep, watch TV or hang out with friends.
3. Daily Quiet Time
   a. When I have time, I like to read short devotionals or inspirational stories.
   b. My daily quiet time involves prayer, praise, confession, reading God's Word and using a Greek lexicon.
4. Hospitality
   a. I like having a few friends over for drinks and a movie.
   b. Inviting other couples into our home is a way for us to better connect with them spiritually.
5. Bible Study
   a. I regularly read my Bible for guidance on how to live my life.
   b. Isn't that John 3:16 sign that they hold up at the game related somehow to the Bible?
6. Sharing My Faith
   a. Witnessing involves street corners, tracts, a bull horn and shouts of "Turn or Burn."
   b. Evangelism is a lifestyle and the best way to win people to Christ is to love them unconditionally.
7. Spiritual Growth
   a. It happens when it happens.
   b. It comes from intentional time alone with God, reading his Word and learning from other believers.

HOW ARE WE DOING?

let's make a DATE

TASTE TEST

Pick a favorite food that you're both passionate about. Perhaps a hamburger, Caesar salad, hot fudge sundae or sushi. Go to two or three different restaurants and order the same item at each restaurant. Which restaurant makes the best one? Discuss your opinions and see if you can reach a consensus.

FOR YOUR NEXT DEVOTIONAL READING, TURN TO PAGE 1070.

LESSONS FROM THE *Bible*

What might have kept the following couples apart? What brought them together?

1. Joseph and Asenath (Genesis 41:41–45)
2. Esther and King Xerxes (Esther 2:5–18)

the paralytic, "Take heart, son; your sins are
forgiven."
3At this, some of the teachers of the law said
to themselves, "This fellow is blaspheming!"
4Knowing their thoughts, Jesus said, "Why
do you entertain evil thoughts in your hearts?
5Which is easier: to say, 'Your sins are forgiv-
en,' or to say, 'Get up and walk'? 6But so that
you may know that the Son of Man has authority on earth to forgive sins . . ." Then he
said to the paralytic, "Get up, take your mat
and go home." 7And the man got up and went
home. 8When the crowd saw this, they were
filled with awe; and they praised God, who
had given such authority to men.

The Calling of Matthew

9As Jesus went on from there, he saw a man
named Matthew sitting at the tax collector's
booth. "Follow me," he told him, and Matthew got up and followed him.
10While Jesus was having dinner at Matthew's house, many tax collectors and "sinners" came and ate with him and his disciples.
11When the Pharisees saw this, they asked his
disciples, "Why does your teacher eat with tax
collectors and 'sinners'?"
12On hearing this, Jesus said, "It is not the
healthy who need a doctor, but the sick. 13But
go and learn what this means: 'I desire mercy,
not sacrifice.'[a] For I have not come to call the
righteous, but sinners."

Jesus Questioned About Fasting

14Then John's disciples came and asked
him, "How is it that we and the Pharisees fast,
but your disciples do not fast?"
15Jesus answered, "How can the guests of
the bridegroom mourn while he is with them?
The time will come when the bridegroom will
be taken from them; then they will fast.
16"No one sews a patch of unshrunk cloth
on an old garment, for the patch will pull
away from the garment, making the tear
worse. 17Neither do men pour new wine into
old wineskins. If they do, the skins will burst,
the wine will run out and the wineskins will
be ruined. No, they pour new wine into new
wineskins, and both are preserved."

A Dead Girl and a Sick Woman

18While he was saying this, a ruler came
and knelt before him and said, "My daughter
has just died. But come and put your hand on
her, and she will live." 19Jesus got up and went
with him, and so did his disciples.
20Just then a woman who had been subject
to bleeding for twelve years came up behind
him and touched the edge of his cloak. 21She
said to herself, "If I only touch his cloak, I will
be healed."
22Jesus turned and saw her. "Take heart,
daughter," he said, "your faith has healed
you." And the woman was healed from that
moment.
23When Jesus entered the ruler's house and
saw the flute players and the noisy crowd,
24he said, "Go away. The girl is not dead but
asleep." But they laughed at him. 25After the
crowd had been put outside, he went in and
took the girl by the hand, and she got up.
26News of this spread through all that region.

Jesus Heals the Blind and Mute

27As Jesus went on from there, two blind
men followed him, calling out, "Have mercy
on us, Son of David!"
28When he had gone indoors, the blind
men came to him, and he asked them, "Do
you believe that I am able to do this?"
"Yes, Lord," they replied.
29Then he touched their eyes and said, "According to your faith will it be done to you";
30and their sight was restored. Jesus warned
them sternly, "See that no one knows about
this." 31But they went out and spread the news
about him all over that region.
32While they were going out, a man who
was demon-possessed and could not talk was
brought to Jesus. 33And when the demon was
driven out, the man who had been mute spoke.
The crowd was amazed and said, "Nothing
like this has ever been seen in Israel."
34But the Pharisees said, "It is by the prince
of demons that he drives out demons."

The Workers Are Few

35Jesus went through all the towns and villages, teaching in their synagogues, preaching
the good news of the kingdom and healing
every disease and sickness. 36When he saw
the crowds, he had compassion on them, because they were harassed and helpless, like
sheep without a shepherd. 37Then he said to
his disciples, "The harvest is plentiful but the
workers are few. 38Ask the Lord of the harvest,
therefore, to send out workers into his harvest
field."

---

[a] *13* Hosea 6:6

Jesus Sends Out the Twelve

10 He called his twelve disciples to him and
gave them authority to drive out evil[a]
spirits and to heal every disease and sickness.
2 These are the names of the twelve apostles: first, Simon (who is called Peter) and his
brother Andrew; James son of Zebedee, and
his brother John; 3 Philip and Bartholomew;
Thomas and Matthew the tax collector; James
son of Alphaeus, and Thaddaeus; 4 Simon the
Zealot and Judas Iscariot, who betrayed him.
5 These twelve Jesus sent out with the following instructions: "Do not go among the Gentiles or enter any town of the Samaritans. 6 Go
rather to the lost sheep of Israel. 7 As you go,
preach this message: 'The kingdom of heaven
is near.' 8 Heal the sick, raise the dead, cleanse
those who have leprosy,[b] drive out demons.
Freely you have received, freely give. 9 Do not
take along any gold or silver or copper in your
belts; 10 take no bag for the journey, or extra
tunic, or sandals or a staff; for the worker is
worth his keep.
11 "Whatever town or village you enter,
search for some worthy person there and stay
at his house until you leave. 12 As you enter
the home, give it your greeting. 13 If the home
is deserving, let your peace rest on it; if it is
not, let your peace return to you. 14 If anyone
will not welcome you or listen to your words,
shake the dust off your feet when you leave that
home or town. 15 I tell you the truth, it will be
more bearable for Sodom and Gomorrah on
the day of judgment than for that town. 16 I
am sending you out like sheep among wolves.
Therefore be as shrewd as snakes and as innocent as doves.
17 "Be on your guard against men; they will
hand you over to the local councils and flog
you in their synagogues. 18 On my account
you will be brought before governors and
kings as witnesses to them and to the Gentiles. 19 But when they arrest you, do not worry about what to say or how to say it. At that
time you will be given what to say, 20 for it will
not be you speaking, but the Spirit of your Father speaking through you.
21 "Brother will betray brother to death, and
a father his child; children will rebel against
their parents and have them put to death.
22 All men will hate you because of me, but
he who stands firm to the end will be saved.
23 When you are persecuted in one place, flee
to another. I tell you the truth, you will not
finish going through the cities of Israel before
the Son of Man comes.
24 "A student is not above his teacher, nor a
servant above his master. 25 It is enough for the
student to be like his teacher, and the servant
like his master. If the head of the house has
been called Beelzebub,[c] how much more the
members of his household!
26 "So do not be afraid of them. There is
nothing concealed that will not be disclosed, or
hidden that will not be made known. 27 What
I tell you in the dark, speak in the daylight;
what is whispered in your ear, proclaim from
the roofs. 28 Do not be afraid of those who kill
the body but cannot kill the soul. Rather, be
afraid of the One who can destroy both soul
and body in hell. 29 Are not two sparrows sold
for a penny[d]? Yet not one of them will fall to
the ground apart from the will of your Father.
30 And even the very hairs of your head are all
numbered. 31 So don't be afraid; you are worth
more than many sparrows.
32 "Whoever acknowledges me before men,
I will also acknowledge him before my Father
in heaven. 33 But whoever disowns me before
men, I will disown him before my Father in
heaven.
34 "Do not suppose that I have come to
bring peace to the earth. I did not come to
bring peace, but a sword. 35 For I have come
to turn

" 'a man against his father,
a daughter against her mother,
a daughter-in-law against her mother-in-law—
36 a man's enemies will be the members of his own household.'[e]

37 "Anyone who loves his father or mother
more than me is not worthy of me; anyone
who loves his son or daughter more than me
is not worthy of me; 38 and anyone who does
not take his cross and follow me is not worthy of me. 39 Whoever finds his life will lose
it, and whoever loses his life for my sake will
find it.
40 "He who receives you receives me, and he
who receives me receives the one who sent me.
41 Anyone who receives a prophet because he is
a prophet will receive a prophet's reward, and
anyone who receives a righteous man because
he is a righteous man will receive a righteous
man's reward. 42 And if anyone gives even a
cup of cold water to one of these little ones

---

[a] *1* Greek *unclean* [b] *8* The Greek word was used for various diseases affecting the skin—not necessarily leprosy. [c] *25* Greek *Beezeboul* or *Beelzeboul* [d] *29* Greek *an assarion* [e] *36* Micah 7:6

MONDAY
READ MATTHEW 10:1–15

A WELCOMING HOUSEHOLD

"Whatever town or village you enter, search for some worthy person there and stay at his house until you leave."
— MATTHEW 10:11

let's talk

- In what ways are we good at entertaining others? In what ways could we use who we are and what we have to be more hospitable to people whom God sends our way?
- How does God's truth show through our efforts at hospitality?
- How do we personally welcome God's truth, as given in God's Word, into our home?

Jesus sent his disciples out to do God's work with empty hands and empty pockets, counting on the provision of people who would welcome them because of the truth they carried in their hearts and shared with their words. Jesus gave the disciples specific instructions about looking for "worthy" (Matthew 10:11) or "deserving" (verse 13) households that would welcome them, and about being a blessing in those places. He also gave them some pretty severe words about warning those who refused to welcome the workers or listen to their words. To "shake the dust off your feet" (verse 14) was tantamount to writing people off spiritually, waiving responsibility for God's future judgment upon them.

Whew! There's a warning here about hospitality, and it doesn't have much to do with perfectly vacuumed carpets, matched china or the correct number of forks to the left of the plate. What made a household "worthy" was the degree to which it welcomed those who offered the truth about Jesus.

David and I like to have friends and neighbors over, and our kids have met most of our church's missionaries over our dinner table at one time or another. David, who leaves the everyday cooking to me, likes to whip up gourmet masterpieces for guests. But obviously what's for dinner is less important than the attention we give our guests and their needs. Do they know we are Christians? Do our home, courtesies and lifestyle choices say, "This is a place where we love God's truth"? Do our words resonate with echoes from God's Word or with testimonies of our experience of God's goodness to us? Do we welcome stories of God's grace from our guests?

Believe me, we vacuum the rug and iron the tablecloth and even try for the correct number of forks—at least when we know guests are coming. Sometimes we light up the grill and haul out the paper plates and folding chairs. Sometimes, when the knock at the door is unexpected and the six of us have been home all day wreaking our usual havoc, we put pride in our pockets and open wide the door. In whatever way people come into our home, we want them to see that this is a place where they are welcome. It's a place where we're searching out God's truth and where others can find it too.

Jesus told the disciples to "let your peace rest" (verse 13) on the worthy household. When God's words are central to shaping the lifestyle of a family and the behavior of its members, peace is a natural byproduct. That peace, internal or between family members, is attractive to a world that struggles to find relief from discord. A knock on your door could come precisely because the world is hungry for what's growing in your "worthy" household.

So listen for the knock—and respond with the best you have to offer.

—ANNETTE LAPLACA

FOR YOUR NEXT DEVOTIONAL READING, TURN TO PAGE 1072.

because he is my disciple, I tell you the truth,
he will certainly not lose his reward."

Jesus and John the Baptist

11 After Jesus had finished instructing his
twelve disciples, he went on from there
to teach and preach in the towns of Galilee.[a]
2When John heard in prison what Christ
was doing, he sent his disciples 3to ask him,
"Are you the one who was to come, or should
we expect someone else?"
4Jesus replied, "Go back and report to John
what you hear and see: 5The blind receive
sight, the lame walk, those who have leprosy[b]
are cured, the deaf hear, the dead are raised,
and the good news is preached to the poor.
6Blessed is the man who does not fall away on
account of me."
7As John's disciples were leaving, Jesus began to speak to the crowd about John: "What
did you go out into the desert to see? A reed
swayed by the wind? 8If not, what did you
go out to see? A man dressed in fine clothes?
No, those who wear fine clothes are in kings'
palaces. 9Then what did you go out to see?
A prophet? Yes, I tell you, and more than a
prophet. 10This is the one about whom it is
written:

" 'I will send my messenger ahead of you,
who will prepare your way before you.'[c]

11I tell you the truth: Among those born of
women there has not risen anyone greater than John the Baptist; yet he who is least
in the kingdom of heaven is greater than he.
12From the days of John the Baptist until now,
the kingdom of heaven has been forcefully advancing, and forceful men lay hold of it. 13For
all the Prophets and the Law prophesied until
John. 14And if you are willing to accept it, he
is the Elijah who was to come. 15He who has
ears, let him hear.
16"To what can I compare this generation?
They are like children sitting in the marketplaces and calling out to others:

17" 'We played the flute for you,
and you did not dance;
we sang a dirge,
and you did not mourn.'

18For John came neither eating nor drinking,
and they say, 'He has a demon.' 19The Son of
Man came eating and drinking, and they say,
'Here is a glutton and a drunkard, a friend of
tax collectors and "sinners." ' But wisdom is
proved right by her actions."

Woe on Unrepentant Cities

20Then Jesus began to denounce the cities
in which most of his miracles had been performed, because they did not repent. 21"Woe
to you, Korazin! Woe to you, Bethsaida! If the
miracles that were performed in you had been
performed in Tyre and Sidon, they would
have repented long ago in sackcloth and ashes.
22But I tell you, it will be more bearable for
Tyre and Sidon on the day of judgment than
for you. 23And you, Capernaum, will you be
lifted up to the skies? No, you will go down
to the depths.[d] If the miracles that were performed in you had been performed in Sodom,
it would have remained to this day. 24But I tell
you that it will be more bearable for Sodom
on the day of judgment than for you."

Rest for the Weary

25At that time Jesus said, "I praise you, Father, Lord of heaven and earth, because you
have hidden these things from the wise and
learned, and revealed them to little children.
26Yes, Father, for this was your good pleasure.
27"All things have been committed to me by
my Father. No one knows the Son except the
Father, and no one knows the Father except
the Son and those to whom the Son chooses
to reveal him.
28"Come to me, all you who are weary and
burdened, and I will give you rest. 29Take my
yoke upon you and learn from me, for I am
gentle and humble in heart, and you will find
rest for your souls. 30For my yoke is easy and
my burden is light."

Lord of the Sabbath

12 At that time Jesus went through the
grainfields on the Sabbath. His disciples
were hungry and began to pick some
heads of grain and eat them. 2When the Pharisees saw this, they said to him, "Look! Your
disciples are doing what is unlawful on the
Sabbath."
3He answered, "Haven't you read what David did when he and his companions were
hungry? 4He entered the house of God, and
he and his companions ate the consecrated
bread—which was not lawful for them to do,
but only for the priests. 5Or haven't you read
in the Law that on the Sabbath the priests in

---

[a] *1* Greek *in their towns* [b] *5* The Greek word was used for various diseases affecting the skin—not necessarily leprosy. [c] *10* Mal. 3:1
[d] *23* Greek *Hades*

TUESDAY
READ MATTHEW 11:25–30

ELEMENTS OF A GOOD FIGHT

> **"Take my yoke upon you and learn from me, for I am gentle and humble in heart, and you will find rest for your souls."**
> — MATTHEW 11:29

let's talk

- How do we define *gentleness* and *humility* in our relationship?
- When have we seen these traits in each other? How have they provided feelings of rest and peace in our marriage?
- What attitudes and feelings do we most often demonstrate during conflicts? How would our conflicts change if we lived out Jesus' gentleness and humility?

According to a recent article in *Psychology Today*, the average married couple has one serious fight a month and innumerable squabbles. If that's the average, then Andrew and Monica were overachievers. This Christian couple spent every evening of their honeymoon fighting. They couldn't see eye to eye on anything, and both passionately defended their point of view, certain that the other was wrong. No matter that they were in a tropical paradise—this was *not* the restful, romantic getaway they'd been anticipating.

Can you count the number of fights you and your spouse have had? In those fights, have *you* ever been wrong? Of course not! How many times in the heat of the moment have you wished that God would play back the tape for your spouse so that you would be vindicated in plain sight, and your partner would have no choice but to beg for your forgiveness?

Self-righteousness feels good—until that gut-sinking moment when you find the missing sock in *your* drawer and discover that you have wrongly accused your spouse of losing it. In such moments, we face the awful truth of how desperately we need to take up Christ's invitation to "learn from me, for I am gentle and humble in heart" (Matthew 11:29). Jesus highlighted two main principles in Matthew 11:28–30.

Gentleness: We see gentleness illustrated in Jesus' welcoming demeanor, in his touch of blessing as he interacted with small children (see Matthew 19:13–15), in his deep caring and empathy toward a paralyzed man (see Matthew 9:2), and in his compassionate interaction with a woman caught in adultery (see John 8:1–11). With Jesus as our model, we can treat each other with gentleness—offering a warm and affirming touch or hug, empathizing with each other's feelings, choosing to speak calmly and tenderly to each other—even when we disagree.

Humility: When we're having a disagreement with our spouse, humility doesn't mean trying to act like we're wrong even though deep down we believe we're right. It means determining not to value our "rightness" so highly, understanding that our spouse is far more important than proving our point. Ultimately, we have Jesus' example to follow: Jesus, who was more "right" than any person in history, went to the cross for *our* sakes.

Andrew and Monica called their pastor to ask for counseling after just one week of marriage. Though they still have disagreements, they're learning how to handle conflict differently. And now, far away from the palm trees of their disastrous honeymoon, they're finally experiencing true "rest" as they learn from Jesus together.

—DAVID AND KELLI TRUJILLO

FOR YOUR NEXT DEVOTIONAL READING, TURN TO PAGE 1074.

the temple desecrate the day and yet are innocent? 6I tell you that one[a] greater than the
temple is here. 7If you had known what these
words mean, 'I desire mercy, not sacrifice,'[b]
you would not have condemned the innocent.
8For the Son of Man is Lord of the Sabbath."
9Going on from that place, he went into
their synagogue, 10and a man with a shriveled
hand was there. Looking for a reason to accuse
Jesus, they asked him, "Is it lawful to heal on
the Sabbath?"
11He said to them, "If any of you has a sheep
and it falls into a pit on the Sabbath, will you
not take hold of it and lift it out? 12How much
more valuable is a man than a sheep! Therefore
it is lawful to do good on the Sabbath."
13Then he said to the man, "Stretch out
your hand." So he stretched it out and it was
completely restored, just as sound as the other.
14But the Pharisees went out and plotted how
they might kill Jesus.

God's Chosen Servant

15Aware of this, Jesus withdrew from that
place. Many followed him, and he healed all
their sick, 16warning them not to tell who
he was. 17This was to fulfill what was spoken
through the prophet Isaiah:

18 "Here is my servant whom I have chosen,
the one I love, in whom I delight;
I will put my Spirit on him,
and he will proclaim justice to the
nations.
19 He will not quarrel or cry out;
no one will hear his voice in the streets.
20 A bruised reed he will not break,
and a smoldering wick he will not snuff
out,
till he leads justice to victory.
21 In his name the nations will put their
hope."[c]

Jesus and Beelzebub

22Then they brought him a demon-possessed man who was blind and mute, and
Jesus healed him, so that he could both talk
and see. 23All the people were astonished and
said, "Could this be the Son of David?"
24But when the Pharisees heard this, they
said, "It is only by Beelzebub,[d] the prince of
demons, that this fellow drives out demons."
25Jesus knew their thoughts and said to
them, "Every kingdom divided against itself
will be ruined, and every city or household divided against itself will not stand. 26If Satan
drives out Satan, he is divided against himself.
How then can his kingdom stand? 27And if I
drive out demons by Beelzebub, by whom do
your people drive them out? So then, they will
be your judges. 28But if I drive out demons by
the Spirit of God, then the kingdom of God
has come upon you.
29"Or again, how can anyone enter a strong
man's house and carry off his possessions unless he first ties up the strong man? Then he
can rob his house.
30"He who is not with me is against me,
and he who does not gather with me scatters.
31And so I tell you, every sin and blasphemy will be forgiven men, but the blasphemy
against the Spirit will not be forgiven. 32Any-
one who speaks a word against the Son of
Man will be forgiven, but anyone who speaks
against the Holy Spirit will not be forgiven,
either in this age or in the age to come.
33"Make a tree good and its fruit will be
good, or make a tree bad and its fruit will be
bad, for a tree is recognized by its fruit. 34You
brood of vipers, how can you who are evil say
anything good? For out of the overflow of
the heart the mouth speaks. 35The good man
brings good things out of the good stored up
in him, and the evil man brings evil things out
of the evil stored up in him. 36But I tell you
that men will have to give account on the day
of judgment for every careless word they have
spoken. 37For by your words you will be ac-
quitted, and by your words you will be condemned."

The Sign of Jonah

38Then some of the Pharisees and teachers
of the law said to him, "Teacher, we want to
see a miraculous sign from you."
39He answered, "A wicked and adulterous
generation asks for a miraculous sign! But
none will be given it except the sign of the
prophet Jonah. 40For as Jonah was three days
and three nights in the belly of a huge fish, so
the Son of Man will be three days and three
nights in the heart of the earth. 41The men of
Nineveh will stand up at the judgment with
this generation and condemn it; for they repented at the preaching of Jonah, and now
one[e] greater than Jonah is here. 42The Queen
of the South will rise at the judgment with this
generation and condemn it; for she came from
the ends of the earth to listen to Solomon's

[a] *6* Or *something*; also in verses 41 and 42 [b] *7* Hosea 6:6 [c] *21* Isaiah 42:1-4 [d] *24* Greek *Beezeboul* or *Beelzeboul*; also in verse 27
[e] *41* Or *something*; also in verse 42

WEDNESDAY
READ MATTHEW 12:22–37

THE POWER OF WORDS

> **"Out of the overflow of the heart the mouth speaks."**
>
> — Matthew 12:34

let's talk

- When we've said something we later regret, is it possible to take back those words or are they irretrievable? How can we diminish their impact?
- What words have we tended to hold on to and then used like weapons against each other months later? Why do we do that?
- What are some things we've said that later surprised and pleased us? How can we find ways to use each other's words for good?

What you feel inside often shapes the words that come out of your mouth. The reverse is true too. What you say shapes how you feel. When I tell my husband that I love him—even if I don't feel aflame with ardor that very second—I teach my heart to let go and love him just a little bit more.

It's like praising God. If we praise God even on the mornings when praise is our last inclination, our hearts eventually catch up to our words. On such days we find ourselves lifted out of darkness and filled once more with joy.

I didn't fully understand the power of my words to hurt someone until I got married. I like to argue, and I'm good at it—I enjoy the skill of braiding words into neat insults; I enjoy the power it gives me to flick nasty little sentences in another person's direction. I didn't realize the harm I was causing, though, until I had to share a bed with the person I had so cavalierly insulted.

It isn't surprising that the words we say to our spouse in haste or in anger sometimes lodge very deep. You might forget the exact words you said to your beloved earlier in the day when you were so frustrated—was it something about regretting the day you'd ever laid eyes on him?—but he probably remembers every word.

Sometimes, I am guilty of holding on to my husband's words too long. He says something caustic in the heat of anger, and I throw those words back in his face months later. I hold on to his words because I am petty and vindictive. I know that nothing hurts my husband more than to hear me dredge up something harsh that he once said to me. I put forward his used sentences as evidence in some phony argument. I trot out his old words to justify my own anger.

Of course, sometimes it's wonderful for your spouse to remember your words. You casually mention that you like lavender sheet spray, and on your birthday, you discover that he has bought it for you. Or you tell him, dreamily, how much you want another child, and then, after you've awakened and started to think about matters more rationally, he remembers.

Griff may remind me of something I said that surprised both of us. Next December, when I'm complaining endlessly about the long drive to Georgia to see his parents, and trying to bargain down our visit from seven days to five, he may remind me that during our last Christmas visit, I asked him if there wasn't some way we could possibly stay one day longer. Our words have the power not just to wound but also to knit us more deeply into the narrative of our marriage.

It was, after all, words that made us who we are—a married couple bound together by the vows we took. Foolishly, extravagantly, we let our mouths express what our hearts were full of: "I promise to love you forever . . . I do . . . I will." But it is the love of the Word made flesh that makes it possible for us to aspire to such daring promises.

—LAUREN WINNER

FOR YOUR NEXT DEVOTIONAL READING, TURN TO PAGE 1081.

wisdom, and now one greater than Solomon
is here.
43"When an evil[a] spirit comes out of a man,
it goes through arid places seeking rest and
does not find it. 44Then it says, 'I will return
to the house I left.' When it arrives, it finds
the house unoccupied, swept clean and put in
order. 45Then it goes and takes with it seven
other spirits more wicked than itself, and they
go in and live there. And the final condition of
that man is worse than the first. That is how it
will be with this wicked generation."

Jesus' Mother and Brothers

46While Jesus was still talking to the crowd,
his mother and brothers stood outside, wanting to speak to him. 47Someone told him,
"Your mother and brothers are standing outside, wanting to speak to you."[b]
48He replied to him, "Who is my mother,
and who are my brothers?" 49Pointing to his
disciples, he said, "Here are my mother and
my brothers. 50For whoever does the will of
my Father in heaven is my brother and sister
and mother."

The Parable of the Sower

13 That same day Jesus went out of the
house and sat by the lake. 2Such large
crowds gathered around him that he got
into a boat and sat in it, while all the people
stood on the shore. 3Then he told them many
things in parables, saying: "A farmer went out
to sow his seed. 4As he was scattering the seed,
some fell along the path, and the birds came
and ate it up. 5Some fell on rocky places, where
it did not have much soil. It sprang up quickly, because the soil was shallow. 6But when
the sun came up, the plants were scorched,
and they withered because they had no root.
7Other seed fell among thorns, which grew up
and choked the plants. 8Still other seed fell on
good soil, where it produced a crop—a hundred, sixty or thirty times what was sown. 9He
who has ears, let him hear."
10The disciples came to him and asked,
"Why do you speak to the people in parables?"
11He replied, "The knowledge of the secrets
of the kingdom of heaven has been given to
you, but not to them. 12Whoever has will be
given more, and he will have an abundance.
Whoever does not have, even what he has will
be taken from him. 13This is why I speak to
them in parables:

"Though seeing, they do not see;
though hearing, they do not hear or
understand.

14In them is fulfilled the prophecy of Isaiah:

" 'You will be ever hearing but never
understanding;
you will be ever seeing but never
perceiving.
15For this people's heart has become
calloused;
they hardly hear with their ears,
and they have closed their eyes.
Otherwise they might see with their eyes,
hear with their ears,
understand with their hearts
and turn, and I would heal them.'[c]

16But blessed are your eyes because they see,
and your ears because they hear. 17For I tell
you the truth, many prophets and righteous
men longed to see what you see but did not
see it, and to hear what you hear but did not
hear it.
18"Listen then to what the parable of the
sower means: 19When anyone hears the message about the kingdom and does not understand it, the evil one comes and snatches away
what was sown in his heart. This is the seed
sown along the path. 20The one who received
the seed that fell on rocky places is the man
who hears the word and at once receives it
with joy. 21But since he has no root, he lasts
only a short time. When trouble or persecution comes because of the word, he quickly
falls away. 22The one who received the seed
that fell among the thorns is the man who
hears the word, but the worries of this life
and the deceitfulness of wealth choke it, making it unfruitful. 23But the one who received
the seed that fell on good soil is the man who
hears the word and understands it. He produces a crop, yielding a hundred, sixty or thirty times what was sown."

The Parable of the Weeds

24Jesus told them another parable: "The
kingdom of heaven is like a man who sowed
good seed in his field. 25But while everyone
was sleeping, his enemy came and sowed weeds
among the wheat, and went away. 26When the
wheat sprouted and formed heads, then the
weeds also appeared.
27"The owner's servants came to him and
said, 'Sir, didn't you sow good seed in your
field? Where then did the weeds come from?'

---

[a] 43 Greek *unclean* [b] 47 Some manuscripts do not have verse 47. [c] 15 Isaiah 6:9,10

28“ ‘An enemy did this,’ he replied.
“The servants asked him, ‘Do you want us
to go and pull them up?’
29“ ‘No,’ he answered, ‘because while you
are pulling the weeds, you may root up the
wheat with them. 30Let both grow together until the harvest. At that time I will tell
the harvesters: First collect the weeds and tie
them in bundles to be burned; then gather the
wheat and bring it into my barn.’ ”

The Parables of the Mustard Seed and the Yeast

31He told them another parable: “The kingdom of heaven is like a mustard seed, which a
man took and planted in his field. 32Though
it is the smallest of all your seeds, yet when it
grows, it is the largest of garden plants and becomes a tree, so that the birds of the air come
and perch in its branches.”
33He told them still another parable: “The
kingdom of heaven is like yeast that a woman
took and mixed into a large amount[a] of flour
until it worked all through the dough.”
34Jesus spoke all these things to the crowd
in parables; he did not say anything to them
without using a parable. 35So was fulfilled
what was spoken through the prophet:

“I will open my mouth in parables,
I will utter things hidden since the
creation of the world.”[b]

The Parable of the Weeds Explained

36Then he left the crowd and went into the
house. His disciples came to him and said,
“Explain to us the parable of the weeds in the
field.”
37He answered, “The one who sowed the
good seed is the Son of Man. 38The field is the
world, and the good seed stands for the sons
of the kingdom. The weeds are the sons of the
evil one, 39and the enemy who sows them is
the devil. The harvest is the end of the age,
and the harvesters are angels.
40“As the weeds are pulled up and burned
in the fire, so it will be at the end of the age.
41The Son of Man will send out his angels,
and they will weed out of his kingdom everything that causes sin and all who do evil.
42They will throw them into the fiery furnace,
where there will be weeping and gnashing of
teeth. 43Then the righteous will shine like the
sun in the kingdom of their Father. He who
has ears, let him hear.

The Parables of the Hidden Treasure and the Pearl

44“The kingdom of heaven is like treasure
hidden in a field. When a man found it, he
hid it again, and then in his joy went and sold
all he had and bought that field.
45“Again, the kingdom of heaven is like a
merchant looking for fine pearls. 46When he
found one of great value, he went away and
sold everything he had and bought it.

The Parable of the Net

47“Once again, the kingdom of heaven is
like a net that was let down into the lake and
caught all kinds of fish. 48When it was full,
the fishermen pulled it up on the shore. Then
they sat down and collected the good fish in
baskets, but threw the bad away. 49This is how
it will be at the end of the age. The angels will
come and separate the wicked from the righteous 50and throw them into the fiery furnace,
where there will be weeping and gnashing of
teeth.
51“Have you understood all these things?”
Jesus asked.
“Yes,” they replied.
52He said to them, “Therefore every teacher of the law who has been instructed about
the kingdom of heaven is like the owner of a
house who brings out of his storeroom new
treasures as well as old.”

A Prophet Without Honor

53When Jesus had finished these parables, he moved on from there. 54Coming to
his hometown, he began teaching the people
in their synagogue, and they were amazed.
“Where did this man get this wisdom and
these miraculous powers?” they asked. 55“Isn’t
this the carpenter’s son? Isn’t his mother’s
name Mary, and aren’t his brothers James, Joseph, Simon and Judas? 56Aren’t all his sisters
with us? Where then did this man get all these
things?” 57And they took offense at him.
But Jesus said to them, “Only in his hometown and in his own house is a prophet without honor.”
58And he did not do many miracles there
because of their lack of faith.

John the Baptist Beheaded

14 At that time Herod the tetrarch heard
the reports about Jesus, 2and he said to
his attendants, “This is John the Baptist;

[a] 33 Greek *three satas* (probably about 1/2 bushel or 22 liters) [b] 35 Psalm 78:2

he has risen from the dead! That is why miraculous powers are at work in him."
3Now Herod had arrested John and bound
him and put him in prison because of Herodias, his brother Philip's wife, 4for John had
been saying to him: "It is not lawful for you to
have her." 5Herod wanted to kill John, but he
was afraid of the people, because they considered him a prophet.
6On Herod's birthday the daughter of Herodias danced for them and pleased Herod so
much 7that he promised with an oath to give
her whatever she asked. 8Prompted by her
mother, she said, "Give me here on a platter
the head of John the Baptist." 9The king was
distressed, but because of his oaths and his
dinner guests, he ordered that her request be
granted 10and had John beheaded in the prison. 11His head was brought in on a platter and
given to the girl, who carried it to her mother.
12John's disciples came and took his body and
buried it. Then they went and told Jesus.

Jesus Feeds the Five Thousand

13When Jesus heard what had happened, he
withdrew by boat privately to a solitary place. Hearing of this, the crowds followed him on
foot from the towns. 14When Jesus landed
and saw a large crowd, he had compassion on them and healed their sick.
15As evening approached, the disciples came to him and said, "This is a remote place, and it's already getting late. Send the crowds away, so they can go to the villages and buy themselves some food."
16Jesus replied, "They do not need to go away. You give them something to eat."
17"We have here only five loaves of bread and two fish," they answered.
18"Bring them here to me," he said. 19And
he directed the people to sit down on the grass. Taking the five loaves and the two fish and looking up to heaven, he gave thanks and broke the loaves. Then he gave them to the disciples, and the disciples gave them to the
people. 20They all ate and were satisfied, and
the disciples picked up twelve basketfuls of
broken pieces that were left over. 21The num-
ber of those who ate was about five thousand men, besides women and children.

Jesus Walks on the Water

22Immediately Jesus made the disciples get into the boat and go on ahead of him to the
other side, while he dismissed the crowd. 23Af-
ter he had dismissed them, he went up on a mountainside by himself to pray. When evening came, he was there alone, 24but the boat
was already a considerable distance[a] from land, buffeted by the waves because the wind was against it.
25During the fourth watch of the night Jesus went out to them, walking on the lake.
26When the disciples saw him walking on the lake, they were terrified. "It's a ghost," they said, and cried out in fear.
27But Jesus immediately said to them: "Take courage! It is I. Don't be afraid."
28"Lord, if it's you," Peter replied, "tell me to come to you on the water."
29"Come," he said.
Then Peter got down out of the boat, walked
on the water and came toward Jesus. 30But
when he saw the wind, he was afraid and, beginning to sink, cried out, "Lord, save me!"
31Immediately Jesus reached out his hand and caught him. "You of little faith," he said, "why did you doubt?"
32And when they climbed into the boat, the
wind died down. 33Then those who were in
the boat worshiped him, saying, "Truly you are the Son of God."
34When they had crossed over, they landed
at Gennesaret. 35And when the men of that
place recognized Jesus, they sent word to all the surrounding country. People brought all
their sick to him 36and begged him to let the
sick just touch the edge of his cloak, and all who touched him were healed.

Clean and Unclean

15 Then some Pharisees and teachers of the law came to Jesus from Jerusalem and
asked, 2"Why do your disciples break
the tradition of the elders? They don't wash their hands before they eat!"
3Jesus replied, "And why do you break the command of God for the sake of your tradition? 4For God said, 'Honor your father and
mother'[b] and 'Anyone who curses his father
or mother must be put to death.'[c] 5But you
say that if a man says to his father or mother, 'Whatever help you might otherwise have received from me is a gift devoted to God,' 6he
is not to 'honor his father[d]' with it. Thus you nullify the word of God for the sake of your
tradition. 7You hypocrites! Isaiah was right
when he prophesied about you:
8" 'These people honor me with their lips,
but their hearts are far from me.

[a] 24 Greek *many stadia* [b] 4 Exodus 20:12; Deut. 5:16 [c] 4 Exodus 21:17; Lev. 20:9 [d] 6 Some manuscripts *father or his mother*

9 They worship me in vain;
their teachings are but rules taught by
men.' [a]"

10 Jesus called the crowd to him and said,
"Listen and understand. 11 What goes into a
man's mouth does not make him 'unclean,'
but what comes out of his mouth, that is what
makes him 'unclean.' "
12 Then the disciples came to him and asked,
"Do you know that the Pharisees were offended when they heard this?"
13 He replied, "Every plant that my heavenly
Father has not planted will be pulled up by the
roots. 14 Leave them; they are blind guides. [b] If
a blind man leads a blind man, both will fall
into a pit."
15 Peter said, "Explain the parable to us."
16 "Are you still so dull?" Jesus asked them.
17 "Don't you see that whatever enters the
mouth goes into the stomach and then out of
the body? 18 But the things that come out of the
mouth come from the heart, and these make a
man 'unclean.' 19 For out of the heart come evil
thoughts, murder, adultery, sexual immorality,
theft, false testimony, slander. 20 These are what
make a man 'unclean'; but eating with unwashed hands does not make him 'unclean.' "

The Faith of the Canaanite Woman

21 Leaving that place, Jesus withdrew to
the region of Tyre and Sidon. 22 A Canaanite
woman from that vicinity came to him, crying
out, "Lord, Son of David, have mercy on me!
My daughter is suffering terribly from demon-
possession."
23 Jesus did not answer a word. So his disciples came to him and urged him, "Send her
away, for she keeps crying out after us."
24 He answered, "I was sent only to the lost
sheep of Israel."
25 The woman came and knelt before him.
"Lord, help me!" she said.
26 He replied, "It is not right to take the
children's bread and toss it to their dogs."
27 "Yes, Lord," she said, "but even the dogs
eat the crumbs that fall from their masters' table."
28 Then Jesus answered, "Woman, you have
great faith! Your request is granted." And her
daughter was healed from that very hour.

Jesus Feeds the Four Thousand

29 Jesus left there and went along the Sea of
Galilee. Then he went up on a mountainside
and sat down. 30 Great crowds came to him,
bringing the lame, the blind, the crippled, the
mute and many others, and laid them at his
feet; and he healed them. 31 The people were
amazed when they saw the mute speaking, the
crippled made well, the lame walking and the
blind seeing. And they praised the God of Israel.
32 Jesus called his disciples to him and said,
"I have compassion for these people; they have
already been with me three days and have
nothing to eat. I do not want to send them
away hungry, or they may collapse on the
way."
33 His disciples answered, "Where could we
get enough bread in this remote place to feed
such a crowd?"
34 "How many loaves do you have?" Jesus
asked.
"Seven," they replied, "and a few small
fish."
35 He told the crowd to sit down on the
ground. 36 Then he took the seven loaves and
the fish, and when he had given thanks, he
broke them and gave them to the disciples,
and they in turn to the people. 37 They all ate
and were satisfied. Afterward the disciples
picked up seven basketfuls of broken pieces that were left over. 38 The number of those
who ate was four thousand, besides women
and children. 39 After Jesus had sent the crowd
away, he got into the boat and went to the vicinity of Magadan.

The Demand for a Sign

16 The Pharisees and Sadducees came to
Jesus and tested him by asking him to
show them a sign from heaven.
2 He replied, [c] "When evening comes, you
say, 'It will be fair weather, for the sky is red,'
3 and in the morning, 'Today it will be stormy,
for the sky is red and overcast.' You know how
to interpret the appearance of the sky, but you
cannot interpret the signs of the times. 4 A
wicked and adulterous generation looks for a
miraculous sign, but none will be given it except the sign of Jonah." Jesus then left them
and went away.

The Yeast of the Pharisees and Sadducees

5 When they went across the lake, the disciples forgot to take bread. 6 "Be careful," Jesus
said to them. "Be on your guard against the
yeast of the Pharisees and Sadducees."

[a] 9 Isaiah 29:13 [b] 14 Some manuscripts *guides of the blind* [c] 2 Some early manuscripts do not have the rest of verse 2 and all of verse 3.

7They discussed this among themselves and
said, "It is because we didn't bring any bread."
8Aware of their discussion, Jesus asked,
"You of little faith, why are you talking among
yourselves about having no bread? 9Do you
still not understand? Don't you remember
the five loaves for the five thousand, and how
many basketfuls you gathered? 10Or the seven
loaves for the four thousand, and how many
basketfuls you gathered? 11How is it you don't
understand that I was not talking to you about
bread? But be on your guard against the yeast
of the Pharisees and Sadducees." 12Then they
understood that he was not telling them to
guard against the yeast used in bread, but
against the teaching of the Pharisees and Sadducees.

Peter's Confession of Christ

13When Jesus came to the region of Caesarea Philippi, he asked his disciples, "Who do
people say the Son of Man is?"
14They replied, "Some say John the Baptist;
others say Elijah; and still others, Jeremiah or
one of the prophets."
15"But what about you?" he asked. "Who
do you say I am?"
16Simon Peter answered, "You are the
Christ,[a] the Son of the living God."
17Jesus replied, "Blessed are you, Simon son
of Jonah, for this was not revealed to you by
man, but by my Father in heaven. 18And I tell
you that you are Peter,[b] and on this rock I will
build my church, and the gates of Hades[c] will
not overcome it.[d] 19I will give you the keys of
the kingdom of heaven; whatever you bind on
earth will be[e] bound in heaven, and whatever
you loose on earth will be[e] loosed in heaven."
20Then he warned his disciples not to tell anyone that he was the Christ.

Jesus Predicts His Death

21From that time on Jesus began to explain
to his disciples that he must go to Jerusalem
and suffer many things at the hands of the elders, chief priests and teachers of the law, and
that he must be killed and on the third day be
raised to life.
22Peter took him aside and began to rebuke
him. "Never, Lord!" he said. "This shall never
happen to you!"
23Jesus turned and said to Peter, "Get behind me, Satan! You are a stumbling block to
me; you do not have in mind the things of
God, but the things of men."
24Then Jesus said to his disciples, "If anyone would come after me, he must deny
himself and take up his cross and follow me.
25For whoever wants to save his life[f] will lose
it, but whoever loses his life for me will find
it. 26What good will it be for a man if he
gains the whole world, yet forfeits his soul?
Or what can a man give in exchange for his
soul? 27For the Son of Man is going to come
in his Father's glory with his angels, and then
he will reward each person according to what
he has done. 28I tell you the truth, some who
are standing here will not taste death before
they see the Son of Man coming in his kingdom."

The Transfiguration

17 After six days Jesus took with him Peter,
James and John the brother of James,
and led them up a high mountain by
themselves. 2There he was transfigured before them. His face shone like the sun, and his
clothes became as white as the light. 3Just then
there appeared before them Moses and Elijah,
talking with Jesus.
4Peter said to Jesus, "Lord, it is good for us
to be here. If you wish, I will put up three
shelters—one for you, one for Moses and one
for Elijah."
5While he was still speaking, a bright cloud
enveloped them, and a voice from the cloud
said, "This is my Son, whom I love; with him
I am well pleased. Listen to him!"
6When the disciples heard this, they fell
facedown to the ground, terrified. 7But Jesus
came and touched them. "Get up," he said.
"Don't be afraid." 8When they looked up, they
saw no one except Jesus.
9As they were coming down the mountain,
Jesus instructed them, "Don't tell anyone what
you have seen, until the Son of Man has been
raised from the dead."
10The disciples asked him, "Why then do
the teachers of the law say that Elijah must
come first?"
11Jesus replied, "To be sure, Elijah comes
and will restore all things. 12But I tell you, Elijah has already come, and they did not recognize him, but have done to him everything
they wished. In the same way the Son of Man
is going to suffer at their hands." 13Then the
disciples understood that he was talking to
them about John the Baptist.

---

[a] 16 Or *Messiah*; also in verse 20 [b] 18 *Peter* means *rock.* [c] 18 Or *hell* [d] 18 Or *not prove stronger than it* [e] 19 Or *have been*
[f] 25 The Greek word means either *life* or *soul*; also in verse 26.

The Healing of a Boy With a Demon

14 When they came to the crowd, a man approached Jesus and knelt before him. 15 "Lord, have mercy on my son," he said. "He has seizures and is suffering greatly. He often falls into the fire or into the water. 16 I brought him to your disciples, but they could not heal him."

17 "O unbelieving and perverse generation," Jesus replied, "how long shall I stay with you? How long shall I put up with you? Bring the boy here to me." 18 Jesus rebuked the demon, and it came out of the boy, and he was healed from that moment.

19 Then the disciples came to Jesus in private and asked, "Why couldn't we drive it out?"

20 He replied, "Because you have so little faith. I tell you the truth, if you have faith as small as a mustard seed, you can say to this mountain, 'Move from here to there' and it will move. Nothing will be impossible for you. [a]"

22 When they came together in Galilee, he said to them, "The Son of Man is going to be betrayed into the hands of men. 23 They will kill him, and on the third day he will be raised to life." And the disciples were filled with grief.

The Temple Tax

24 After Jesus and his disciples arrived in Capernaum, the collectors of the two-drachma tax came to Peter and asked, "Doesn't your teacher pay the temple tax[b]?"

25 "Yes, he does," he replied.

When Peter came into the house, Jesus was the first to speak. "What do you think, Simon?" he asked. "From whom do the kings of the earth collect duty and taxes—from their own sons or from others?"

26 "From others," Peter answered.

"Then the sons are exempt," Jesus said to him. 27 "But so that we may not offend them, go to the lake and throw out your line. Take the first fish you catch; open its mouth and you will find a four-drachma coin. Take it and give it to them for my tax and yours."

The Greatest in the Kingdom of Heaven

18 At that time the disciples came to Jesus and asked, "Who is the greatest in the kingdom of heaven?"

2 He called a little child and had him stand among them. 3 And he said: "I tell you the truth, unless you change and become like little children, you will never enter the kingdom of heaven. 4 Therefore, whoever humbles himself like this child is the greatest in the kingdom of heaven.

5 "And whoever welcomes a little child like this in my name welcomes me. 6 But if anyone causes one of these little ones who believe in me to sin, it would be better for him to have a large millstone hung around his neck and to be drowned in the depths of the sea.

7 "Woe to the world because of the things that cause people to sin! Such things must come, but woe to the man through whom they come! 8 If your hand or your foot causes you to sin, cut it off and throw it away. It is better for you to enter life maimed or crippled than to have two hands or two feet and be thrown into eternal fire. 9 And if your eye causes you to sin, gouge it out and throw it away. It is better for you to enter life with one eye than to have two eyes and be thrown into the fire of hell.

The Parable of the Lost Sheep

10 "See that you do not look down on one of these little ones. For I tell you that their angels in heaven always see the face of my Father in heaven. [c]

12 "What do you think? If a man owns a hundred sheep, and one of them wanders away, will he not leave the ninety-nine on the hills and go to look for the one that wandered off? 13 And if he finds it, I tell you the truth, he is happier about that one sheep than about the ninety-nine that did not wander off. 14 In the same way your Father in heaven is not willing that any of these little ones should be lost.

A Brother Who Sins Against You

15 "If your brother sins against you, [d] go and show him his fault, just between the two of you. If he listens to you, you have won your brother over. 16 But if he will not listen, take one or two others along, so that 'every matter may be established by the testimony of two or three witnesses.' [e] 17 If he refuses to listen to them, tell it to the church; and if he refuses to listen even to the church, treat him as you would a pagan or a tax collector.

18 "I tell you the truth, whatever you bind on earth will be[f] bound in heaven, and whatever you loose on earth will be[f] loosed in heaven.

---

[a] 20 Some manuscripts *you.* [21] *But this kind does not go out except by prayer and fasting.* [b] 24 Greek *the two drachmas* [c] 10 Some manuscripts *heaven.* [11] *The Son of Man came to save what was lost.* [d] 15 Some manuscripts do not have *against you.* [e] 16 Deut. 19:15 [f] 18 Or *have been*

THURSDAY
READ MATTHEW 18:1–14

OUR CUES TO KIDS

"If anyone causes one of these little ones who believe in me to sin, it would be better for him to have a large millstone hung around his neck and to be drowned in the depths of the sea."

— Matthew 18:6

The boy who was running up the stairs toward the church fellowship hall couldn't have been more than six years old. I was aiming for the same door, but he darted around me and grabbed the knob before I had a chance. From a door half open, squeezing through to his pals on the other side, he looked up at me and said, "You talk to God, don't you?"

I didn't recognize the boy. Maybe he was new to our church. But already he knew that I stood in front of the congregation on Sunday mornings and "talked to God." I was amazed. I was also reminded of how learning happens.

Dorothy Law Nolte said, "Children learn what they live." If a boy's parents find religion important, they take him to church. If a pastor there stands and "talks to God," a young listener begins to believe that what the preacher says is right and normal. If a family espouses values of kindness and joy and caring, the child begins to measure life by those criteria.

But the same is also true in reverse. In homes of criticism and nagging, souls shrink. Among immoral parents, children choose self-destructive, uncontrolled ways of living lives of self-gratification. Influenced by a culture without religious values, the seeds of spirituality in young hearts die or mutate into something evil.

Although Jesus was undoubtedly expanding his discussion of "little ones" beyond children to all "who believe in me" (Matthew 18:6), surely the context of the preceding verses indicates that Jesus was warning parents and church leaders to pay special attention to children in the community. Big people make choices all the time, and they must live with the consequences, good or ill. But little people are brought to life or death by the choices that big people make. Little ones take their cues and their destinies from the words and actions of role models around them. They can't help it. That's what it means to be a child.

Jesus' words in Matthew 18:6 seem harsh. Wearing a millstone around your neck is no way to win an Olympic medal. But communities that nurture children in spiritual matters are critical. Much of the thinking we see in hurting people today is the result of what was breathed into them as children by parents and teachers and community leaders. Morally, ethically and spiritually, many of these grown-up children are now "stumbling."

By contrast, people whose marriages are centered in Christ and who model what they profess in daily activities have a positive effect on children and start them off in the way they should go. Then, as Proverbs 1:9 promises, these wise teachings will be a garland to grace children's heads and adorn their lives.

—WAYNE BROUWER

let's talk

- What do we communicate through our lifestyle? What values are we displaying through mealtime conversations? Through our work and leisure habits? Through entertainment choices?
- What values do we wish to pass along to the young ones of our community? What will it take to make these values obvious to neighborhood children?
- How do we talk about God and church and religion? What do the children around us hear? What do they learn?

FOR YOUR NEXT DEVOTIONAL READING, TURN TO PAGE 1083.

19"Again, I tell you that if two of you on
earth agree about anything you ask for, it
will be done for you by my Father in heaven.
20For where two or three come together in my
name, there am I with them."

The Parable of the Unmerciful Servant

21Then Peter came to Jesus and asked,
"Lord, how many times shall I forgive my
brother when he sins against me? Up to sev-
en times?"

22Jesus answered, "I tell you, not seven
times, but seventy-seven times.[a]

23"Therefore, the kingdom of heaven is like
a king who wanted to settle accounts with
his servants. 24As he began the settlement, a
man who owed him ten thousand talents[b]
was brought to him. 25Since he was not able
to pay, the master ordered that he and his wife
and his children and all that he had be sold to
repay the debt.

26"The servant fell on his knees before him.
'Be patient with me,' he begged, 'and I will
pay back everything.' 27The servant's master
took pity on him, canceled the debt and let
him go.

28"But when that servant went out, he
found one of his fellow servants who owed
him a hundred denarii.[c] He grabbed him and
began to choke him. 'Pay back what you owe
me!' he demanded.

29"His fellow servant fell to his knees and
begged him, 'Be patient with me, and I will
pay you back.'

30"But he refused. Instead, he went off
and had the man thrown into prison until he
could pay the debt. 31When the other servants
saw what had happened, they were greatly distressed and went and told their master everything that had happened.

32"Then the master called the servant in.
'You wicked servant,' he said, 'I canceled all
that debt of yours because you begged me to.
33Shouldn't you have had mercy on your fellow servant just as I had on you?' 34In anger
his master turned him over to the jailers to
be tortured, until he should pay back all he
owed.

35"This is how my heavenly Father will treat
each of you unless you forgive your brother
from your heart."

Divorce

19 When Jesus had finished saying these
things, he left Galilee and went into the
region of Judea to the other side of the
Jordan. 2Large crowds followed him, and he
healed them there.

3Some Pharisees came to him to test him.
They asked, "Is it lawful for a man to divorce
his wife for any and every reason?"

4"Haven't you read," he replied, "that at the
beginning the Creator 'made them male and
female,'[d] 5and said, 'For this reason a man will
leave his father and mother and be united to
his wife, and the two will become one flesh'[e]?
6So they are no longer two, but one. Therefore what God has joined together, let man
not separate."

7"Why then," they asked, "did Moses command that a man give his wife a certificate of
divorce and send her away?"

8Jesus replied, "Moses permitted you to
divorce your wives because your hearts were
hard. But it was not this way from the beginning. 9I tell you that anyone who divorces his
wife, except for marital unfaithfulness, and
marries another woman commits adultery."

10The disciples said to him, "If this is the
situation between a husband and wife, it is
better not to marry."

11Jesus replied, "Not everyone can accept
this word, but only those to whom it has been
given. 12For some are eunuchs because they
were born that way; others were made that
way by men; and others have renounced marriage[f] because of the kingdom of heaven. The
one who can accept this should accept it."

The Little Children and Jesus

13Then little children were brought to Jesus
for him to place his hands on them and pray
for them. But the disciples rebuked those who
brought them.

14Jesus said, "Let the little children come to
me, and do not hinder them, for the kingdom
of heaven belongs to such as these." 15When
he had placed his hands on them, he went on
from there.

The Rich Young Man

16Now a man came up to Jesus and asked,
"Teacher, what good thing must I do to get
eternal life?"

17"Why do you ask me about what is good?"
Jesus replied. "There is only One who is good.

[a] 22 Or *seventy times seven* [b] 24 That is, millions of dollars [c] 28 That is, a few dollars [d] 4 Gen. 1:27 [e] 5 Gen. 2:24 [f] 12 Or *have made themselves eunuchs*

F

FRIDAY

READ MATTHEW 19:1–12

WHAT JESUS SAYS ABOUT DIVORCE

Some Pharisees came to [Jesus] to test him. They asked, "Is it lawful for a man to divorce his wife for any and every reason?"

— MATTHEW 19:3

When married people face dark times in their marriage, they may quietly sort through the ramifications of divorce. Knowing what the Bible says is critical in that process. But couples also need to figure out how to respond to friends and family who divorce. Do we need to know all the details in order to know who to support? Do we have to choose sides? What do we do when a friend divorces and then remarries? Should we go to the wedding?

As a pastor, I don't think there is any life situation harder to sort out than divorce. Every story is different. Every situation is painful. It isn't always easy to determine if there is a "guilty party." How to weave compassion, grace and righteousness together often confounds me. Christians who take the Bible seriously and who earnestly want to please the Lord don't always come to the same conclusions. But one thing is certain: We need to consider what Jesus has to say about divorce and remarriage, particularly in Matthew 19.

Divorces in Jesus' day make our "quickie" divorces of today look positively glacial. A man could divorce his wife, as verse 3 says, "for any and every reason," at least according to one school of Jewish thought. (Others took a stricter view.) As we are all wont to do, these Pharisees who questioned Jesus wanted to know exactly what reasons justified getting a divorce. But the question was loaded; these Pharisees apparently were among those who used the Law of Moses (specifically Deuteronomy 24:1–4) as proof that divorce for any reason was lawful.

Jesus' response was that Moses allowed divorce, not to give permission for divorce, but to solve the problem of marital infidelity. Something has to be done when sin utterly poisons the covenant relationship of marriage. Jesus said that sexual immorality (sure evidence of a hard heart) can so poison the covenant of marriage that the innocent party can be released from the marriage commitment.

While Matthew 19 can stir up as many questions as it answers, there are some inescapable conclusions: First, divorce is rarely a solution for followers of Jesus to consider. Rather, we are to cultivate marriages with the grace and truth of God so that they may shine forth the love of Jesus to the world around us. We are not to be like the Pharisees, who tried to push the limits of the law as far as it would go.

Second, we are to become marriage builders among our friends and family. We know how hard and even hopeless marriage can seem sometimes, but we are to be agents of grace and truth to these struggling friends, helping them find hope and help, praying with them and providing a haven away from the tension.

Third, we should affirm those who choose to remain single for the sake of the kingdom, as Jesus did in this passage. Singles don't need our sympathy; they deserve our respect! Those who remain single and single-mindedly serve Christ are models to us all.

—LEE ECLOV

FOR YOUR NEXT DEVOTIONAL READING, TURN TO PAGE 1086.

let's *talk*

- ✦ Whom do we know who has divorced or is going through a divorce right now? What makes divorce so complicated for Christians to respond to?
- ✦ What does repeated sexual immorality do to a marriage? When does the damage become irreparable? How do some couples recover from such sin?
- ✦ How could we honor a single person we know who serves God with undivided attention?

If you want to enter life, obey the commandments."

18"Which ones?" the man inquired.

Jesus replied, " 'Do not murder, do not commit adultery, do not steal, do not give false testimony, 19honor your father and mother,'[a] and 'love your neighbor as yourself.'[b]"

20"All these I have kept," the young man said. "What do I still lack?"

21Jesus answered, "If you want to be perfect, go, sell your possessions and give to the poor, and you will have treasure in heaven. Then come, follow me."

22When the young man heard this, he went away sad, because he had great wealth.

23Then Jesus said to his disciples, "I tell you the truth, it is hard for a rich man to enter the kingdom of heaven. 24Again I tell you, it is easier for a camel to go through the eye of a needle than for a rich man to enter the kingdom of God."

25When the disciples heard this, they were greatly astonished and asked, "Who then can be saved?"

26Jesus looked at them and said, "With man this is impossible, but with God all things are possible."

27Peter answered him, "We have left everything to follow you! What then will there be for us?"

28Jesus said to them, "I tell you the truth, at the renewal of all things, when the Son of Man sits on his glorious throne, you who have followed me will also sit on twelve thrones, judging the twelve tribes of Israel. 29And everyone who has left houses or brothers or sisters or father or mother[c] or children or fields for my sake will receive a hundred times as much and will inherit eternal life. 30But many who are first will be last, and many who are last will be first.

The Parable of the Workers in the Vineyard

20 "For the kingdom of heaven is like a landowner who went out early in the morning to hire men to work in his vineyard. 2He agreed to pay them a denarius for the day and sent them into his vineyard.

3"About the third hour he went out and saw others standing in the marketplace doing nothing. 4He told them, 'You also go and work in my vineyard, and I will pay you whatever is right.' 5So they went.

"He went out again about the sixth hour and the ninth hour and did the same thing. 6About the eleventh hour he went out and found still others standing around. He asked them, 'Why have you been standing here all day long doing nothing?'

7" 'Because no one has hired us,' they answered.

"He said to them, 'You also go and work in my vineyard.'

8"When evening came, the owner of the vineyard said to his foreman, 'Call the workers and pay them their wages, beginning with the last ones hired and going on to the first.'

9"The workers who were hired about the eleventh hour came and each received a denarius. 10So when those came who were hired first, they expected to receive more. But each one of them also received a denarius. 11When they received it, they began to grumble against the landowner. 12'These men who were hired last worked only one hour,' they said, 'and you have made them equal to us who have borne the burden of the work and the heat of the day.'

13"But he answered one of them, 'Friend, I am not being unfair to you. Didn't you agree to work for a denarius? 14Take your pay and go. I want to give the man who was hired last the same as I gave you. 15Don't I have the right to do what I want with my own money? Or are you envious because I am generous?'

16"So the last will be first, and the first will be last."

Jesus Again Predicts His Death

17Now as Jesus was going up to Jerusalem, he took the twelve disciples aside and said to them, 18"We are going up to Jerusalem, and the Son of Man will be betrayed to the chief priests and the teachers of the law. They will condemn him to death 19and will turn him over to the Gentiles to be mocked and flogged and crucified. On the third day he will be raised to life!"

A Mother's Request

20Then the mother of Zebedee's sons came to Jesus with her sons and, kneeling down, asked a favor of him.

21"What is it you want?" he asked.

She said, "Grant that one of these two sons of mine may sit at your right and the other at your left in your kingdom."

22"You don't know what you are asking," Jesus said to them. "Can you drink the cup I am going to drink?"

---

a *19* Exodus 20:12-16; Deut. 5:16-20 *b* *19* Lev. 19:18 *c* *29* Some manuscripts *mother or wife*

"We can," they answered.

23 Jesus said to them, "You will indeed drink from my cup, but to sit at my right or left is not for me to grant. These places belong to those for whom they have been prepared by my Father."

24 When the ten heard about this, they were indignant with the two brothers. 25 Jesus called them together and said, "You know that the rulers of the Gentiles lord it over them, and their high officials exercise authority over them. 26 Not so with you. Instead, whoever wants to become great among you must be your servant, 27 and whoever wants to be first must be your slave— 28 just as the Son of Man did not come to be served, but to serve, and to give his life as a ransom for many."

Two Blind Men Receive Sight

29 As Jesus and his disciples were leaving Jericho, a large crowd followed him. 30 Two blind men were sitting by the roadside, and when they heard that Jesus was going by, they shouted, "Lord, Son of David, have mercy on us!"

31 The crowd rebuked them and told them to be quiet, but they shouted all the louder, "Lord, Son of David, have mercy on us!"

32 Jesus stopped and called them. "What do you want me to do for you?" he asked.

33 "Lord," they answered, "we want our sight."

34 Jesus had compassion on them and touched their eyes. Immediately they received their sight and followed him.

The Triumphal Entry

21 As they approached Jerusalem and came to Bethphage on the Mount of Olives, Jesus sent two disciples, 2 saying to them, "Go to the village ahead of you, and at once you will find a donkey tied there, with her colt by her. Untie them and bring them to me. 3 If anyone says anything to you, tell him that the Lord needs them, and he will send them right away."

4 This took place to fulfill what was spoken through the prophet:

5 "Say to the Daughter of Zion,
'See, your king comes to you,
gentle and riding on a donkey,
on a colt, the foal of a donkey.' "[a]

6 The disciples went and did as Jesus had instructed them. 7 They brought the donkey and the colt, placed their cloaks on them, and Jesus sat on them. 8 A very large crowd spread their cloaks on the road, while others cut branches from the trees and spread them on the road. 9 The crowds that went ahead of him and those that followed shouted,

"Hosanna[b] to the Son of David!"

"Blessed is he who comes in the name of
the Lord!"[c]

"Hosanna[b] in the highest!"

10 When Jesus entered Jerusalem, the whole city was stirred and asked, "Who is this?"

11 The crowds answered, "This is Jesus, the prophet from Nazareth in Galilee."

Jesus at the Temple

12 Jesus entered the temple area and drove out all who were buying and selling there. He overturned the tables of the money changers and the benches of those selling doves. 13 "It is written," he said to them, " 'My house will be called a house of prayer,'[d] but you are making it a 'den of robbers.'[e]"

14 The blind and the lame came to him at the temple, and he healed them. 15 But when the chief priests and the teachers of the law saw the wonderful things he did and the children shouting in the temple area, "Hosanna to the Son of David," they were indignant.

16 "Do you hear what these children are saying?" they asked him.

"Yes," replied Jesus, "have you never read,

" 'From the lips of children and infants
you have ordained praise'[f]?"

17 And he left them and went out of the city to Bethany, where he spent the night.

The Fig Tree Withers

18 Early in the morning, as he was on his way back to the city, he was hungry. 19 Seeing a fig tree by the road, he went up to it but found nothing on it except leaves. Then he said to it, "May you never bear fruit again!" Immediately the tree withered.

20 When the disciples saw this, they were amazed. "How did the fig tree wither so quickly?" they asked.

21 Jesus replied, "I tell you the truth, if you have faith and do not doubt, not only can you do what was done to the fig tree, but also you can say to this mountain, 'Go, throw yourself

[a] *5* Zech. 9:9 [b] *9* A Hebrew expression meaning "Save!" which became an exclamation of praise; also in verse 15 [c] *9* Psalm 118:26
[d] *13* Isaiah 56:7 [e] *13* Jer. 7:11 [f] *16* Psalm 8:2

WEEKEND

marriage myths

Myth 1: *You'll Live Happily Ever After*

Tom and Laura came to see us just nine months after their wedding. They had swallowed the happily-ever-after myth whole and were now feeling queasy. "Before we got married we couldn't be apart from one another," Laura confided. "We did almost everything together, and I thought that's how it would be in our marriage." She paused for a moment. "But now Tom needs more space. It seems like he's not the guy I married."

Tom rolled his eyes as Laura continued: "He used to be so considerate and thoughtful before we were married—"

"Oh, and I am a total slouch now?" Tom interrupted.

"Of course not, you—or maybe we—are just different now."

Nervously twisting his wedding band, Tom looked at Laura: "Marriage isn't what I expected either. I didn't expect it to be a big honeymoon or anything; I just thought you would try to make life a little easier for me. Instead, when I come home from the office, all you want is to go out or—"

"I make dinner every night for you," Laura interrupted.

Surprised by their display of unrestrained emotion in front of us, they stopped silent and looked to us as if to say, "See, our marriage isn't what it's supposed to be."

Tom and Laura entered their marriage believing that happiness would abound. They had heard that marriage was hard work, but they didn't expect it to be a twenty-four-hour, seven-day-a-week job.

Their belief in a happily-ever-after marriage is one of the most widely held and destructive marriage myths. But it is only the tip of the iceberg. Every difficult marriage is plagued by a vast assortment of misconceptions about what marriage should be.

Myth 2: *We expect exactly the same things from marriage.*

The expectations you bring to your partnership can make or break your marriage. Don't miss out on the sterling moments of marriage because your ideals are out of sync with your partner's. Don't believe the myth that you and your partner automatically come with the same expectations for marriage. Instead, remember that the more openly you discuss your differing expectations, the more likely you are to create a vision of marriage that you agree on—and that is unique to the two of you.

Myth 3: *Everything good in our relationship will get better.*

It is an illusion that the romance in the beginning of a relationship will last forever. This may be hard to swallow (it was for us), but debunking the myth of eternal romance will do more than just about anything to help you build a lifelong happy marriage. Once you realize that your marriage is not a source of constant romance, you can appreciate the fleeting moments of romance for what they are—a very special experience.

Myth 4: *Everything bad in my life will disappear.*

Many people marry to avoid or escape unpleasantness. But no matter how glorious the institution of marriage, it is not a substitute for the difficult work of inner spiritual healing. Marriage does not erase personal pain or eliminate loneliness.

Myth 5: *My spouse will make me whole.*

Marriage is a God-given way to improve and hone our beings. Marriage challenges us to new heights and calls us to be the best person possible, but neither marriage nor our partner will magically make us whole.

—DR. LES PARROTT III AND DR. LESLIE PARROTT

HOW ARE WE DOING?

common myths

Discuss the following statements. See if you both agree that the statement is a myth. Have either of you ever believed the statement at some point in time? How about now?

1. If I marry my soul mate, we're guaranteed to have a great marriage.
2. I can't grow spiritually unless you're growing too.
3. If we love each other, sex will always be great.
4. Love means never having to say you're sorry.
5. We'll love all our children the same.
6. Now that we're married, I'll never be attracted to another person.
7. Marriage won't change my relationship with friends.
8. We'll always be sexually attracted to each other.
9. Having debt is okay as long as we keep up with the payments.
10. Being married will make me happy.
11. We don't need a budget.
12. You would never cheat on me.
13. Romance isn't necessary once we're married.
14. Our marriage will get easier after we have kids.
15. Since we both love the Lord, growing spiritually will come naturally.
16. You would never look at pornography.
17. A marriage can never recover from adultery.
18. I'll always be in love with you.
19. I don't have to tell everything to you; some things are better left private.
20. We don't need to get involved in church until after we have kids.

let's make a DATE

REWRITE THE FAIRY TALE

Go to or rent a romance movie. After watching it, name some of the myths implicit in the story. Then suggest some new endings for the movie that throw out the myths and deal with reality.

Ask some hard questions about the couple from the film. For example, what do you suppose happened to them once they got married: Did problems with their in-laws surface? Did they automatically fit into each other's worlds, or were there glaring differences? Did the "prince" continue to romance his bride once the wedding was over? How did he do that?

Was the "princess" forever after drop-dead gorgeous, no matter what the circumstances? What did she look like without the makeup, designer clothes and personal trainer? What might happen after the couple had kids?

FOR YOUR NEXT DEVOTIONAL READING, TURN TO PAGE 1091.

LESSONS FROM THE *Bible*

What myths might you assume about Isaac and Rebekah (read Genesis 24). What, in reality, do you imagine life was like for them? Then read what they experienced later in their marriage (see Genesis 26:34—28:9). Does this sound like the same couple?

into the sea,' and it will be done. 22If you believe, you will receive whatever you ask for in
prayer."

The Authority of Jesus Questioned

23Jesus entered the temple courts, and,
while he was teaching, the chief priests and
the elders of the people came to him. "By
what authority are you doing these things?"
they asked. "And who gave you this authority?"

24Jesus replied, "I will also ask you one
question. If you answer me, I will tell you
by what authority I am doing these things.
25John's baptism—where did it come from?
Was it from heaven, or from men?"

They discussed it among themselves and
said, "If we say, 'From heaven,' he will ask,
'Then why didn't you believe him?' 26But if we
say, 'From men'—we are afraid of the people,
for they all hold that John was a prophet."

27So they answered Jesus, "We don't
know."

Then he said, "Neither will I tell you by
what authority I am doing these things.

The Parable of the Two Sons

28"What do you think? There was a man
who had two sons. He went to the first and
said, 'Son, go and work today in the vineyard.'

29" 'I will not,' he answered, but later he
changed his mind and went.

30"Then the father went to the other son
and said the same thing. He answered, 'I will,
sir,' but he did not go.

31"Which of the two did what his father
wanted?"

"The first," they answered.

Jesus said to them, "I tell you the truth, the
tax collectors and the prostitutes are entering
the kingdom of God ahead of you. 32For John
came to you to show you the way of righteousness, and you did not believe him, but the tax
collectors and the prostitutes did. And even
after you saw this, you did not repent and believe him.

The Parable of the Tenants

33"Listen to another parable: There was a
landowner who planted a vineyard. He put a
wall around it, dug a winepress in it and built
a watchtower. Then he rented the vineyard to
some farmers and went away on a journey.
34When the harvest time approached, he sent
his servants to the tenants to collect his fruit.

35"The tenants seized his servants; they beat
one, killed another, and stoned a third. 36Then
he sent other servants to them, more than the
first time, and the tenants treated them the
same way. 37Last of all, he sent his son to
them. 'They will respect my son,' he said.

38"But when the tenants saw the son, they
said to each other, 'This is the heir. Come, let's
kill him and take his inheritance.' 39So they
took him and threw him out of the vineyard
and killed him.

40"Therefore, when the owner of the vineyard comes, what will he do to those tenants?"

41"He will bring those wretches to a wretched end," they replied, "and he will rent the
vineyard to other tenants, who will give him
his share of the crop at harvest time."

42Jesus said to them, "Have you never read
in the Scriptures:

" 'The stone the builders rejected
has become the capstone[a];
the Lord has done this,
and it is marvelous in our eyes'[b]?

43"Therefore I tell you that the kingdom of
God will be taken away from you and given to
a people who will produce its fruit. 44He who
falls on this stone will be broken to pieces, but
he on whom it falls will be crushed."[c]

45When the chief priests and the Pharisees
heard Jesus' parables, they knew he was talking
about them. 46They looked for a way to arrest
him, but they were afraid of the crowd because
the people held that he was a prophet.

The Parable of the Wedding Banquet

22 Jesus spoke to them again in parables,
saying: 2"The kingdom of heaven is like
a king who prepared a wedding banquet
for his son. 3He sent his servants to those who
had been invited to the banquet to tell them
to come, but they refused to come.

4"Then he sent some more servants and said,
'Tell those who have been invited that I have
prepared my dinner: My oxen and fattened
cattle have been butchered, and everything is
ready. Come to the wedding banquet.'

5"But they paid no attention and went
off—one to his field, another to his business.
6The rest seized his servants, mistreated them
and killed them. 7The king was enraged. He

---

[a] 42 Or *cornerstone* [b] 42 Psalm 118:22,23 [c] 44 Some manuscripts do not have verse 44.

sent his army and destroyed those murderers and burned their city.

8“Then he said to his servants, ‘The wedding banquet is ready, but those I invited did not deserve to come. 9Go to the street corners and invite to the banquet anyone you find.’ 10So the servants went out into the streets and gathered all the people they could find, both good and bad, and the wedding hall was filled with guests.

11“But when the king came in to see the guests, he noticed a man there who was not wearing wedding clothes. 12‘Friend,’ he asked, ‘how did you get in here without wedding clothes?’ The man was speechless.

13“Then the king told the attendants, ‘Tie him hand and foot, and throw him outside, into the darkness, where there will be weeping and gnashing of teeth.’

14“For many are invited, but few are chosen.”

Paying Taxes to Caesar

15Then the Pharisees went out and laid plans to trap him in his words. 16They sent their disciples to him along with the Herodians. “Teacher,” they said, “we know you are a man of integrity and that you teach the way of God in accordance with the truth. You aren’t swayed by men, because you pay no attention to who they are. 17Tell us then, what is your opinion? Is it right to pay taxes to Caesar or not?”

18But Jesus, knowing their evil intent, said, “You hypocrites, why are you trying to trap me? 19Show me the coin used for paying the tax.” They brought him a denarius, 20and he asked them, “Whose portrait is this? And whose inscription?”

21“Caesar’s,” they replied.

Then he said to them, “Give to Caesar what is Caesar’s, and to God what is God’s.”

22When they heard this, they were amazed. So they left him and went away.

Marriage at the Resurrection

23That same day the Sadducees, who say there is no resurrection, came to him with a question. 24“Teacher,” they said, “Moses told us that if a man dies without having children, his brother must marry the widow and have children for him. 25Now there were seven brothers among us. The first one married and died, and since he had no children, he left his wife to his brother. 26The same thing happened to the second and third brother, right on down to the seventh. 27Finally, the woman died. 28Now then, at the resurrection, whose wife will she be of the seven, since all of them were married to her?”

29Jesus replied, “You are in error because you do not know the Scriptures or the power of God. 30At the resurrection people will neither marry nor be given in marriage; they will be like the angels in heaven. 31But about the resurrection of the dead—have you not read what God said to you, 32‘I am the God of Abraham, the God of Isaac, and the God of Jacob’[a]? He is not the God of the dead but of the living.”

33When the crowds heard this, they were astonished at his teaching.

The Greatest Commandment

34Hearing that Jesus had silenced the Sadducees, the Pharisees got together. 35One of them, an expert in the law, tested him with this question: 36“Teacher, which is the greatest commandment in the Law?”

37Jesus replied: “ ‘Love the Lord your God with all your heart and with all your soul and with all your mind.’[b] 38This is the first and greatest commandment. 39And the second is like it: ‘Love your neighbor as yourself.’[c] 40All the Law and the Prophets hang on these two commandments.”

Whose Son Is the Christ?

41While the Pharisees were gathered together, Jesus asked them, 42“What do you think about the Christ[d]? Whose son is he?”

“The son of David,” they replied.

43He said to them, “How is it then that David, speaking by the Spirit, calls him ‘Lord’? For he says,

44“ ‘The Lord said to my Lord:
“Sit at my right hand
until I put your enemies
under your feet.” ’[e]

45If then David calls him ‘Lord,’ how can he be his son?” 46No one could say a word in reply, and from that day on no one dared to ask him any more questions.

Seven Woes

23 Then Jesus said to the crowds and to his disciples: 2“The teachers of the law and the Pharisees sit in Moses’ seat. 3So you must obey them and do everything they tell

[a] 32 Exodus 3:6 [b] 37 Deut. 6:5 [c] 39 Lev. 19:18 [d] 42 Or *Messiah* [e] 44 Psalm 110:1

you. But do not do what they do, for they do not practice what they preach. 4They tie up heavy loads and put them on men's shoulders, but they themselves are not willing to lift a finger to move them.

5"Everything they do is done for men to see: They make their phylacteries[a] wide and the tassels on their garments long; 6they love the place of honor at banquets and the most important seats in the synagogues; 7they love to be greeted in the marketplaces and to have men call them 'Rabbi.'

8"But you are not to be called 'Rabbi,' for you have only one Master and you are all brothers. 9And do not call anyone on earth 'father,' for you have one Father, and he is in heaven. 10Nor are you to be called 'teacher,' for you have one Teacher, the Christ.[b] 11The greatest among you will be your servant. 12For whoever exalts himself will be humbled, and whoever humbles himself will be exalted.

13"Woe to you, teachers of the law and Pharisees, you hypocrites! You shut the kingdom of heaven in men's faces. You yourselves do not enter, nor will you let those enter who are trying to.[c]

15"Woe to you, teachers of the law and Pharisees, you hypocrites! You travel over land and sea to win a single convert, and when he becomes one, you make him twice as much a son of hell as you are.

16"Woe to you, blind guides! You say, 'If anyone swears by the temple, it means nothing; but if anyone swears by the gold of the temple, he is bound by his oath.' 17You blind fools! Which is greater: the gold, or the temple that makes the gold sacred? 18You also say, 'If anyone swears by the altar, it means nothing; but if anyone swears by the gift on it, he is bound by his oath.' 19You blind men! Which is greater: the gift, or the altar that makes the gift sacred? 20Therefore, he who swears by the altar swears by it and by everything on it. 21And he who swears by the temple swears by it and by the one who dwells in it. 22And he who swears by heaven swears by God's throne and by the one who sits on it.

23"Woe to you, teachers of the law and Pharisees, you hypocrites! You give a tenth of your spices—mint, dill and cummin. But you have neglected the more important matters of the law—justice, mercy and faithfulness. You should have practiced the latter, without neglecting the former. 24You blind guides! You strain out a gnat but swallow a camel.

25"Woe to you, teachers of the law and Pharisees, you hypocrites! You clean the outside of the cup and dish, but inside they are full of greed and self-indulgence. 26Blind Pharisee! First clean the inside of the cup and dish, and then the outside also will be clean.

27"Woe to you, teachers of the law and Pharisees, you hypocrites! You are like whitewashed tombs, which look beautiful on the outside but on the inside are full of dead men's bones and everything unclean. 28In the same way, on the outside you appear to people as righteous but on the inside you are full of hypocrisy and wickedness.

29"Woe to you, teachers of the law and Pharisees, you hypocrites! You build tombs for the prophets and decorate the graves of the righteous. 30And you say, 'If we had lived in the days of our forefathers, we would not have taken part with them in shedding the blood of the prophets.' 31So you testify against yourselves that you are the descendants of those who murdered the prophets. 32Fill up, then, the measure of the sin of your forefathers!

33"You snakes! You brood of vipers! How will you escape being condemned to hell? 34Therefore I am sending you prophets and wise men and teachers. Some of them you will kill and crucify; others you will flog in your synagogues and pursue from town to town. 35And so upon you will come all the righteous blood that has been shed on earth, from the blood of righteous Abel to the blood of Zechariah son of Berekiah, whom you murdered between the temple and the altar. 36I tell you the truth, all this will come upon this generation.

37"O Jerusalem, Jerusalem, you who kill the prophets and stone those sent to you, how often I have longed to gather your children together, as a hen gathers her chicks under her wings, but you were not willing. 38Look, your house is left to you desolate. 39For I tell you, you will not see me again until you say, 'Blessed is he who comes in the name of the Lord.'[d]"

Signs of the End of the Age

24 Jesus left the temple and was walking away when his disciples came up to him to call his attention to its buildings. 2"Do you see all these things?" he asked. "I tell

[a] 5 That is, boxes containing Scripture verses, worn on forehead and arm [b] 10 Or *Messiah* [c] 13 Some manuscripts *to.* 14*Woe to you, teachers of the law and Pharisees, you hypocrites! You devour widows' houses and for a show make lengthy prayers. Therefore you will be punished more severely.* [d] 39 Psalm 118:26

M

MONDAY

READ MATTHEW 23:1–12

WHAT WE EXPECT OF EACH OTHER

> **"But do not do what they do, for they do not practice what they preach. They tie up heavy loads and put them on men's shoulders, but they themselves are not willing to lift a finger to move them."**
>
> — MATTHEW 23:3–4

let's talk

- What are some hidden expectations that each of us brought into our marriage? Which ones can we laugh about now?
- Which expectations have been more challenging to deal with? Why?
- In what ways have we surpassed each other's expectations? What are three surprising qualities or traits in each other that we could celebrate?

Every Thanksgiving, Corrie's dad cooked and carved the turkey. He was famous for his methodical technique of roasting the bird on the barbeque over hot coals—and the turkey was always the perfect combination of succulence and crispiness.

In Justin's family, his *mom* was the designated turkey chef. Each year, she stuffed a bird, rubbed it with herbs, oven baked it to perfection, then served it on an heirloom platter.

Fast-forward to Justin and Corrie's first Thanksgiving together: It was noon on Thursday, and a huge, raw bird sat on the counter in front of the newlyweds. Eyes locked in frustration, husband and wife each said, "What?! You expect *me* to make the turkey? I don't have a clue how to do it . . . and I don't *want* to! That's *your* job!" This wasn't just a minor misunderstanding—each was sorely disappointed that the other was failing to live up to expectations.

We all bring expectations into marriage: Who is responsible to do the cooking? Clean up the kitchen? Mow the lawn? Take out the trash? Take care of the bills and budgeting? Decorate the home? When some of those expectations aren't met, we can make a joke of it and move forward, creating a new definition of *normal.*

But some expectations run deep, like what our spiritual roles should be, how sexual intimacy should take place (and how often), how to deal with conflict, how much income is enough, when to have children, or how much daily verbal communication we should have. When these expectations aren't met, it's dangerously easy to cycle into a harsh, critical mindset that says, "My husband is a huge disappointment. How did I get trapped with this guy?" Or "She can't do anything. What did I ever see in her?"

Burdening our spouse with unrealistic expectations is a lot like what the Pharisees did to their religious followers. In sharp contrast to Jesus' invitation, "Come to me, all you who are weary and burdened, and I will give you rest" (Matthew 11:28), the Pharisees multiplied religious rules to a tedious extreme, creating a spiritual burden of crippling weight.

Your wife or husband will *never* be just like your mom, dad or the ideal image of a partner that you've formulated in your head. And measuring your spouse against those expectations won't lead to anything but frustration and discouragement.

The next time you find yourself squaring off with an unmet expectation, take a lesson from Justin and Corrie. After talking through their turkey problem, they came up with a unique solution. Now each time Thanksgiving rolls around, Justin and Corrie together prepare their *own* traditional entrée: turkey burgers.

—DAVID AND KELLI TRUJILLO

FOR YOUR NEXT DEVOTIONAL READING, TURN TO PAGE 1098.

you the truth, not one stone here will be left on another; every one will be thrown down."

[3]As Jesus was sitting on the Mount of Olives, the disciples came to him privately. "Tell us," they said, "when will this happen, and what will be the sign of your coming and of the end of the age?"

[4]Jesus answered: "Watch out that no one deceives you. [5]For many will come in my name, claiming, 'I am the Christ,[a]' and will deceive many. [6]You will hear of wars and rumors of wars, but see to it that you are not alarmed. Such things must happen, but the end is still to come. [7]Nation will rise against nation, and kingdom against kingdom. There will be famines and earthquakes in various places. [8]All these are the beginning of birth pains.

[9]"Then you will be handed over to be persecuted and put to death, and you will be hated by all nations because of me. [10]At that time many will turn away from the faith and will betray and hate each other, [11]and many false prophets will appear and deceive many people. [12]Because of the increase of wickedness, the love of most will grow cold, [13]but he who stands firm to the end will be saved. [14]And this gospel of the kingdom will be preached in the whole world as a testimony to all nations, and then the end will come.

[15]"So when you see standing in the holy place 'the abomination that causes desolation,'[b] spoken of through the prophet Daniel—let the reader understand— [16]then let those who are in Judea flee to the mountains. [17]Let no one on the roof of his house go down to take anything out of the house. [18]Let no one in the field go back to get his cloak. [19]How dreadful it will be in those days for pregnant women and nursing mothers! [20]Pray that your flight will not take place in winter or on the Sabbath. [21]For then there will be great distress, unequaled from the beginning of the world until now—and never to be equaled again. [22]If those days had not been cut short, no one would survive, but for the sake of the elect those days will be shortened. [23]At that time if anyone says to you, 'Look, here is the Christ!' or, 'There he is!' do not believe it. [24]For false Christs and false prophets will appear and perform great signs and miracles to deceive even the elect—if that were possible. [25]See, I have told you ahead of time.

[26]"So if anyone tells you, 'There he is, out in the desert,' do not go out; or, 'Here he is, in the inner rooms,' do not believe it. [27]For as lightning that comes from the east is visible even in the west, so will be the coming of the Son of Man. [28]Wherever there is a carcass, there the vultures will gather.

[29]"Immediately after the distress of those days

" 'the sun will be darkened,
  and the moon will not give its light;
the stars will fall from the sky,
  and the heavenly bodies will be shaken.'[c]

[30]"At that time the sign of the Son of Man will appear in the sky, and all the nations of the earth will mourn. They will see the Son of Man coming on the clouds of the sky, with power and great glory. [31]And he will send his angels with a loud trumpet call, and they will gather his elect from the four winds, from one end of the heavens to the other.

[32]"Now learn this lesson from the fig tree: As soon as its twigs get tender and its leaves come out, you know that summer is near. [33]Even so, when you see all these things, you know that it[d] is near, right at the door. [34]I tell you the truth, this generation[e] will certainly not pass away until all these things have happened. [35]Heaven and earth will pass away, but my words will never pass away.

The Day and Hour Unknown

[36]"No one knows about that day or hour, not even the angels in heaven, nor the Son,[f] but only the Father. [37]As it was in the days of Noah, so it will be at the coming of the Son of Man. [38]For in the days before the flood, people were eating and drinking, marrying and giving in marriage, up to the day Noah entered the ark; [39]and they knew nothing about what would happen until the flood came and took them all away. That is how it will be at the coming of the Son of Man. [40]Two men will be in the field; one will be taken and the other left. [41]Two women will be grinding with a hand mill; one will be taken and the other left.

[42]"Therefore keep watch, because you do not know on what day your Lord will come. [43]But understand this: If the owner of the house had known at what time of night the thief was coming, he would have kept watch and would not have let his house be broken into. [44]So you also must be ready, because the

---

[a] 5 Or *Messiah*; also in verse 23 [b] *15* Daniel 9:27; 11:31; 12:11 [c] *29* Isaiah 13:10; 34:4 [d] *33* Or *he* [e] *34* Or *race* [f] *36* Some manuscripts do not have *nor the Son.*

Son of Man will come at an hour when you do
not expect him.
45"Who then is the faithful and wise servant, whom the master has put in charge of
the servants in his household to give them
their food at the proper time? 46It will be good
for that servant whose master finds him doing
so when he returns. 47I tell you the truth, he
will put him in charge of all his possessions.
48But suppose that servant is wicked and says
to himself, 'My master is staying away a long
time,' 49and he then begins to beat his fellow
servants and to eat and drink with drunkards.
50The master of that servant will come on a
day when he does not expect him and at an
hour he is not aware of. 51He will cut him to
pieces and assign him a place with the hypocrites, where there will be weeping and gnashing of teeth.

The Parable of the Ten Virgins

25 "At that time the kingdom of heaven will
be like ten virgins who took their lamps
and went out to meet the bridegroom.
2Five of them were foolish and five were wise.
3The foolish ones took their lamps but did not
take any oil with them. 4The wise, however,
took oil in jars along with their lamps. 5The
bridegroom was a long time in coming, and
they all became drowsy and fell asleep.
6"At midnight the cry rang out: 'Here's the
bridegroom! Come out to meet him!'
7"Then all the virgins woke up and trimmed
their lamps. 8The foolish ones said to the wise,
'Give us some of your oil; our lamps are going out.'
9" 'No,' they replied, 'there may not be
enough for both us and you. Instead, go to
those who sell oil and buy some for yourselves.'
10"But while they were on their way to buy
the oil, the bridegroom arrived. The virgins
who were ready went in with him to the wedding banquet. And the door was shut.
11"Later the others also came. 'Sir! Sir!' they
said. 'Open the door for us!'
12"But he replied, 'I tell you the truth, I
don't know you.'
13"Therefore keep watch, because you do
not know the day or the hour.

The Parable of the Talents

14"Again, it will be like a man going on a
journey, who called his servants and entrusted
his property to them. 15To one he gave five
talents[a] of money, to another two talents,
and to another one talent, each according
to his ability. Then he went on his journey.
16The man who had received the five talents
went at once and put his money to work and
gained five more. 17So also, the one with the
two talents gained two more. 18But the man
who had received the one talent went off,
dug a hole in the ground and hid his master's
money.
19"After a long time the master of those
servants returned and settled accounts with
them. 20The man who had received the five
talents brought the other five. 'Master,' he
said, 'you entrusted me with five talents. See, I
have gained five more.'
21"His master replied, 'Well done, good
and faithful servant! You have been faithful
with a few things; I will put you in charge of
many things. Come and share your master's
happiness!'
22"The man with the two talents also came.
'Master,' he said, 'you entrusted me with two
talents; see, I have gained two more.'
23"His master replied, 'Well done, good
and faithful servant! You have been faithful
with a few things; I will put you in charge of
many things. Come and share your master's
happiness!'
24"Then the man who had received the one
talent came. 'Master,' he said, 'I knew that you
are a hard man, harvesting where you have
not sown and gathering where you have not
scattered seed. 25So I was afraid and went out
and hid your talent in the ground. See, here is
what belongs to you.'
26"His master replied, 'You wicked, lazy
servant! So you knew that I harvest where I
have not sown and gather where I have not
scattered seed? 27Well then, you should have
put my money on deposit with the bankers,
so that when I returned I would have received
it back with interest.
28" 'Take the talent from him and give it to
the one who has the ten talents. 29For everyone who has will be given more, and he will
have an abundance. Whoever does not have,
even what he has will be taken from him.
30And throw that worthless servant outside,
into the darkness, where there will be weeping
and gnashing of teeth.'

The Sheep and the Goats

31"When the Son of Man comes in his glory, and all the angels with him, he will sit on

a *15* A talent was worth more than a thousand dollars.

his throne in heavenly glory. 32All the nations
will be gathered before him, and he will separate the people one from another as a shepherd separates the sheep from the goats. 33He
will put the sheep on his right and the goats
on his left.

34"Then the King will say to those on his
right, 'Come, you who are blessed by my
Father; take your inheritance, the kingdom
prepared for you since the creation of the
world. 35For I was hungry and you gave me
something to eat, I was thirsty and you gave
me something to drink, I was a stranger and
you invited me in, 36I needed clothes and
you clothed me, I was sick and you looked
after me, I was in prison and you came to visit me.'

37"Then the righteous will answer him,
'Lord, when did we see you hungry and feed
you, or thirsty and give you something to
drink? 38When did we see you a stranger and
invite you in, or needing clothes and clothe
you? 39When did we see you sick or in prison
and go to visit you?'

40"The King will reply, 'I tell you the truth,
whatever you did for one of the least of these
brothers of mine, you did for me.'

41"Then he will say to those on his left,
'Depart from me, you who are cursed, into
the eternal fire prepared for the devil and his
angels. 42For I was hungry and you gave me
nothing to eat, I was thirsty and you gave me
nothing to drink, 43I was a stranger and you
did not invite me in, I needed clothes and you
did not clothe me, I was sick and in prison
and you did not look after me.'

44"They also will answer, 'Lord, when did
we see you hungry or thirsty or a stranger or
needing clothes or sick or in prison, and did
not help you?'

45"He will reply, 'I tell you the truth, whatever you did not do for one of the least of
these, you did not do for me.'

46"Then they will go away to eternal punishment, but the righteous to eternal life."

The Plot Against Jesus

26 When Jesus had finished saying all these
things, he said to his disciples, 2"As you
know, the Passover is two days away—
and the Son of Man will be handed over to be
crucified."

3Then the chief priests and the elders of
the people assembled in the palace of the high
priest, whose name was Caiaphas, 4and they
plotted to arrest Jesus in some sly way and kill
him. 5"But not during the Feast," they said,
"or there may be a riot among the people."

Jesus Anointed at Bethany

6While Jesus was in Bethany in the home
of a man known as Simon the Leper, 7a woman came to him with an alabaster jar of very
expensive perfume, which she poured on his
head as he was reclining at the table.

8When the disciples saw this, they were indignant. "Why this waste?" they asked. 9"This
perfume could have been sold at a high price
and the money given to the poor."

10Aware of this, Jesus said to them, "Why
are you bothering this woman? She has done
a beautiful thing to me. 11The poor you will
always have with you, but you will not always have me. 12When she poured this perfume on my body, she did it to prepare me
for burial. 13I tell you the truth, wherever
this gospel is preached throughout the world,
what she has done will also be told, in memory of her."

Judas Agrees to Betray Jesus

14Then one of the Twelve—the one called
Judas Iscariot—went to the chief priests 15and
asked, "What are you willing to give me if I
hand him over to you?" So they counted out
for him thirty silver coins. 16From then on Judas watched for an opportunity to hand him
over.

The Lord's Supper

17On the first day of the Feast of Unleavened Bread, the disciples came to Jesus and
asked, "Where do you want us to make preparations for you to eat the Passover?"

18He replied, "Go into the city to a certain man and tell him, 'The Teacher says: My
appointed time is near. I am going to celebrate the Passover with my disciples at your
house.' " 19So the disciples did as Jesus had directed them and prepared the Passover.

20When evening came, Jesus was reclining
at the table with the Twelve. 21And while they
were eating, he said, "I tell you the truth, one
of you will betray me."

22They were very sad and began to say to
him one after the other, "Surely not I, Lord?"

23Jesus replied, "The one who has dipped
his hand into the bowl with me will betray
me. 24The Son of Man will go just as it is written about him. But woe to that man who betrays the Son of Man! It would be better for
him if he had not been born."

[25]Then Judas, the one who would betray him, said, "Surely not I, Rabbi?"

Jesus answered, "Yes, it is you." [a]

[26]While they were eating, Jesus took bread, gave thanks and broke it, and gave it to his disciples, saying, "Take and eat; this is my body."

[27]Then he took the cup, gave thanks and offered it to them, saying, "Drink from it, all of you. [28]This is my blood of the [b] covenant, which is poured out for many for the forgiveness of sins. [29]I tell you, I will not drink of this fruit of the vine from now on until that day when I drink it anew with you in my Father's kingdom."

[30]When they had sung a hymn, they went out to the Mount of Olives.

Jesus Predicts Peter's Denial

[31]Then Jesus told them, "This very night you will all fall away on account of me, for it is written:

" 'I will strike the shepherd,
and the sheep of the flock will be scattered.' [c]

[32]But after I have risen, I will go ahead of you into Galilee."

[33]Peter replied, "Even if all fall away on account of you, I never will."

[34]"I tell you the truth," Jesus answered, "this very night, before the rooster crows, you will disown me three times."

[35]But Peter declared, "Even if I have to die with you, I will never disown you." And all the other disciples said the same.

Gethsemane

[36]Then Jesus went with his disciples to a place called Gethsemane, and he said to them, "Sit here while I go over there and pray." [37]He took Peter and the two sons of Zebedee along with him, and he began to be sorrowful and troubled. [38]Then he said to them, "My soul is overwhelmed with sorrow to the point of death. Stay here and keep watch with me."

[39]Going a little farther, he fell with his face to the ground and prayed, "My Father, if it is possible, may this cup be taken from me. Yet not as I will, but as you will."

[40]Then he returned to his disciples and found them sleeping. "Could you men not keep watch with me for one hour?" he asked Peter. [41]"Watch and pray so that you will not fall into temptation. The spirit is willing, but the body is weak."

[42]He went away a second time and prayed, "My Father, if it is not possible for this cup to be taken away unless I drink it, may your will be done."

[43]When he came back, he again found them sleeping, because their eyes were heavy. [44]So he left them and went away once more and prayed the third time, saying the same thing.

[45]Then he returned to the disciples and said to them, "Are you still sleeping and resting? Look, the hour is near, and the Son of Man is betrayed into the hands of sinners. [46]Rise, let us go! Here comes my betrayer!"

Jesus Arrested

[47]While he was still speaking, Judas, one of the Twelve, arrived. With him was a large crowd armed with swords and clubs, sent from the chief priests and the elders of the people. [48]Now the betrayer had arranged a signal with them: "The one I kiss is the man; arrest him." [49]Going at once to Jesus, Judas said, "Greetings, Rabbi!" and kissed him.

[50]Jesus replied, "Friend, do what you came for." [d]

Then the men stepped forward, seized Jesus and arrested him. [51]With that, one of Jesus' companions reached for his sword, drew it out and struck the servant of the high priest, cutting off his ear.

[52]"Put your sword back in its place," Jesus said to him, "for all who draw the sword will die by the sword. [53]Do you think I cannot call on my Father, and he will at once put at my disposal more than twelve legions of angels? [54]But how then would the Scriptures be fulfilled that say it must happen in this way?"

[55]At that time Jesus said to the crowd, "Am I leading a rebellion, that you have come out with swords and clubs to capture me? Every day I sat in the temple courts teaching, and you did not arrest me. [56]But this has all taken place that the writings of the prophets might be fulfilled." Then all the disciples deserted him and fled.

Before the Sanhedrin

[57]Those who had arrested Jesus took him to Caiaphas, the high priest, where the teachers of the law and the elders had assembled. [58]But Peter followed him at a distance, right up to the courtyard of the high priest. He en-

[a] 25 Or *"You yourself have said it"* [b] 28 Some manuscripts *the new* [c] 31 Zech. 13:7 [d] 50 Or *"Friend, why have you come?"*

tered and sat down with the guards to see the outcome.

59The chief priests and the whole Sanhedrin were looking for false evidence against Jesus so that they could put him to death. 60But they did not find any, though many false witnesses came forward.

Finally two came forward 61and declared, "This fellow said, 'I am able to destroy the temple of God and rebuild it in three days.' "

62Then the high priest stood up and said to Jesus, "Are you not going to answer? What is this testimony that these men are bringing against you?" 63But Jesus remained silent.

The high priest said to him, "I charge you under oath by the living God: Tell us if you are the Christ,[a] the Son of God."

64"Yes, it is as you say," Jesus replied. "But I say to all of you: In the future you will see the Son of Man sitting at the right hand of the Mighty One and coming on the clouds of heaven."

65Then the high priest tore his clothes and said, "He has spoken blasphemy! Why do we need any more witnesses? Look, now you have heard the blasphemy. 66What do you think?"

"He is worthy of death," they answered.

67Then they spit in his face and struck him with their fists. Others slapped him 68and said, "Prophesy to us, Christ. Who hit you?"

Peter Disowns Jesus

69Now Peter was sitting out in the courtyard, and a servant girl came to him. "You also were with Jesus of Galilee," she said.

70But he denied it before them all. "I don't know what you're talking about," he said.

71Then he went out to the gateway, where another girl saw him and said to the people there, "This fellow was with Jesus of Nazareth."

72He denied it again, with an oath: "I don't know the man!"

73After a little while, those standing there went up to Peter and said, "Surely you are one of them, for your accent gives you away."

74Then he began to call down curses on himself and he swore to them, "I don't know the man!"

Immediately a rooster crowed. 75Then Peter remembered the word Jesus had spoken: "Before the rooster crows, you will disown me three times." And he went outside and wept bitterly.

Judas Hangs Himself

27 Early in the morning, all the chief priests and the elders of the people came to the decision to put Jesus to death. 2They bound him, led him away and handed him over to Pilate, the governor.

3When Judas, who had betrayed him, saw that Jesus was condemned, he was seized with remorse and returned the thirty silver coins to the chief priests and the elders. 4"I have sinned," he said, "for I have betrayed innocent blood."

"What is that to us?" they replied. "That's your responsibility."

5So Judas threw the money into the temple and left. Then he went away and hanged himself.

6The chief priests picked up the coins and said, "It is against the law to put this into the treasury, since it is blood money." 7So they decided to use the money to buy the potter's field as a burial place for foreigners. 8That is why it has been called the Field of Blood to this day. 9Then what was spoken by Jeremiah the prophet was fulfilled: "They took the thirty silver coins, the price set on him by the people of Israel, 10and they used them to buy the potter's field, as the Lord commanded me."[b]

Jesus Before Pilate

11Meanwhile Jesus stood before the governor, and the governor asked him, "Are you the king of the Jews?"

"Yes, it is as you say," Jesus replied.

12When he was accused by the chief priests and the elders, he gave no answer. 13Then Pilate asked him, "Don't you hear the testimony they are bringing against you?" 14But Jesus made no reply, not even to a single charge—to the great amazement of the governor.

15Now it was the governor's custom at the Feast to release a prisoner chosen by the crowd. 16At that time they had a notorious prisoner, called Barabbas. 17So when the crowd had gathered, Pilate asked them, "Which one do you want me to release to you: Barabbas, or Jesus who is called Christ?" 18For he knew it was out of envy that they had handed Jesus over to him.

19While Pilate was sitting on the judge's seat, his wife sent him this message: "Don't have anything to do with that innocent man, for I have suffered a great deal today in a dream because of him."

20But the chief priests and the elders per-

[a] *63* Or *Messiah*; also in verse 68 [b] *10* See Zech. 11:12,13; Jer. 19:1-13; 32:6-9.

suaded the crowd to ask for Barabbas and to
have Jesus executed.
21“Which of the two do you want me to
release to you?” asked the governor.
“Barabbas,” they answered.
22“What shall I do, then, with Jesus who is
called Christ?” Pilate asked.
They all answered, “Crucify him!”
23“Why? What crime has he committed?”
asked Pilate.
But they shouted all the louder, “Crucify
him!”
24When Pilate saw that he was getting nowhere, but that instead an uproar was starting,
he took water and washed his hands in front
of the crowd. “I am innocent of this man’s
blood,” he said. “It is your responsibility!”
25All the people answered, “Let his blood
be on us and on our children!”
26Then he released Barabbas to them. But
he had Jesus flogged, and handed him over to
be crucified.

The Soldiers Mock Jesus

27Then the governor’s soldiers took Jesus
into the Praetorium and gathered the whole
company of soldiers around him. 28They
stripped him and put a scarlet robe on him,
29and then twisted together a crown of thorns
and set it on his head. They put a staff in his
right hand and knelt in front of him and
mocked him. “Hail, king of the Jews!” they
said. 30They spit on him, and took the staff
and struck him on the head again and again.
31After they had mocked him, they took off
the robe and put his own clothes on him.
Then they led him away to crucify him.

The Crucifixion

32As they were going out, they met a man
from Cyrene, named Simon, and they forced
him to carry the cross. 33They came to a place
called Golgotha (which means The Place of
the Skull). 34There they offered Jesus wine
to drink, mixed with gall; but after tasting
it, he refused to drink it. 35When they had
crucified him, they divided up his clothes by
casting lots.[a] 36And sitting down, they kept
watch over him there. 37Above his head they
placed the written charge against him: THIS IS
JESUS, THE KING OF THE JEWS. 38Two robbers
were crucified with him, one on his right and
one on his left. 39Those who passed by hurled
insults at him, shaking their heads 40and saying, “You who are going to destroy the temple and build it in three days, save yourself!
Come down from the cross, if you are the Son
of God!”
41In the same way the chief priests, the
teachers of the law and the elders mocked
him. 42“He saved others,” they said, “but he
can’t save himself! He’s the King of Israel! Let
him come down now from the cross, and we
will believe in him. 43He trusts in God. Let
God rescue him now if he wants him, for he
said, ‘I am the Son of God.’ ” 44In the same
way the robbers who were crucified with him
also heaped insults on him.

The Death of Jesus

45From the sixth hour until the ninth hour
darkness came over all the land. 46About the
ninth hour Jesus cried out in a loud voice, *“Eloi,
Eloi,*[b] *lama sabachthani?”*—which means, “My
God, my God, why have you forsaken me?”[c]
47When some of those standing there heard
this, they said, “He’s calling Elijah.”
48Immediately one of them ran and got a
sponge. He filled it with wine vinegar, put
it on a stick, and offered it to Jesus to drink.
49The rest said, “Now leave him alone. Let’s
see if Elijah comes to save him.”
50And when Jesus had cried out again in a
loud voice, he gave up his spirit.
51At that moment the curtain of the temple
was torn in two from top to bottom. The earth
shook and the rocks split. 52The tombs broke
open and the bodies of many holy people who
had died were raised to life. 53They came out
of the tombs, and after Jesus’ resurrection they
went into the holy city and appeared to many
people.
54When the centurion and those with him
who were guarding Jesus saw the earthquake
and all that had happened, they were terrified, and exclaimed, “Surely he was the Son[d]
of God!”
55Many women were there, watching from
a distance. They had followed Jesus from
Galilee to care for his needs. 56Among them
were Mary Magdalene, Mary the mother of
James and Joses, and the mother of Zebedee’s
sons.

The Burial of Jesus

57As evening approached, there came a rich
man from Arimathea, named Joseph, who had
himself become a disciple of Jesus. 58Going to
Pilate, he asked for Jesus’ body, and Pilate ordered that it be given to him. 59Joseph took

[a] 35 A few late manuscripts *lots that the word spoken by the prophet might be fulfilled: “They divided my garments among themselves and cast lots for my clothing”* (Psalm 22:18) [b] 46 Some manuscripts *Eli, Eli* [c] 46 Psalm 22:1 [d] 54 Or *a son*

TUESDAY
READ MATTHEW 27:11–26

TAKING YOUR ADVICE

Advice for every aspect of life abounds. Not all of it is good or even makes sense. For example, baseball legend Yogi Berra once said, "When you get to a fork in the road, take it." Huh?

In 1998, *Marriage Partnership* magazine offered some practical advice for married couples:

- Don't hog the blanket.
- Husbands, think twice before complimenting your wife's best friend on her new hairstyle.
- Wives, decide not to describe, in excruciating detail, every plot twist in your day.
- Stop fiddling with the thermostat.
- If you get up first, don't sing in the shower.
- Don't leave nail clippings anyplace but in the wastebasket.

While Pilate was sitting on the judge's seat, his wife sent him [a] message.

— MATTHEW 27:19

let's talk

- ✦ Whom do we usually turn to for advice?
- ✦ How willing are we to listen to each other's advice?
- ✦ Let's talk about an upcoming situation about which we need some wisdom or guidance. How does the advice we're considering check out against Scripture?

The problem with good advice is that sometimes we don't take it. That was the case with Pontius Pilate, Judea's Roman governor, as Jesus stood before him, waiting for judgment. Pilate had the authority to set Jesus free, and he knew the charges against the Jewish rabbi were bogus. However, the crowd clamored for blood, and Pilate feared their reaction if his judgment went against their desires. If anyone needed advice, it was Pilate.

Enter Mrs. Pilate. While Pilate sat on the judge's seat, his wife sent him a message: "Don't have anything to do with that innocent man, for I have suffered a great deal today in a dream because of him" (Matthew 27:19).

But Pilate didn't heed his wife's advice. In a display of supreme indecision, Pilate let the crowd decide Jesus' fate. When people clamored for Jesus' death, Pilate washed his hands, symbolizing his own innocence in the matter.

The Bible doesn't say much about Mrs. Pilate, her dream, or the reason why Pilate disregarded her advice and let the crowd decide Jesus' fate. Even so, God used Pilate's cowardice as part of his plan to bring about Christ's death on the cross, which provided the only means of our salvation.

Giving and taking advice has its merits and dangers. In marriage, it's wise to listen to a partner's advice but wiser still to test it against Scripture. Is there a Biblical principle for or against what's being proposed? Are there examples from Scripture that are helpful?

Besides holding advice up to Scripture, praying through a matter can give spiritual insight to a decision. If we bring our decisions to God in prayer—as a couple and as individuals—we can be sure God will guide us and provide us with the tools we need to make good decisions.

—NANCY KENNEDY

FOR YOUR NEXT DEVOTIONAL READING, TURN TO PAGE 1102.

the body, wrapped it in a clean linen cloth,
60and placed it in his own new tomb that he
had cut out of the rock. He rolled a big stone
in front of the entrance to the tomb and went
away. 61Mary Magdalene and the other Mary
were sitting there opposite the tomb.

The Guard at the Tomb

62The next day, the one after Preparation
Day, the chief priests and the Pharisees went
to Pilate. 63"Sir," they said, "we remember that
while he was still alive that deceiver said, 'After
three days I will rise again.' 64So give the order
for the tomb to be made secure until the third
day. Otherwise, his disciples may come and
steal the body and tell the people that he has
been raised from the dead. This last deception
will be worse than the first."

65"Take a guard," Pilate answered. "Go,
make the tomb as secure as you know how."
66So they went and made the tomb secure by
putting a seal on the stone and posting the
guard.

The Resurrection

28 After the Sabbath, at dawn on the first
day of the week, Mary Magdalene and
the other Mary went to look at the
tomb.

2There was a violent earthquake, for an
angel of the Lord came down from heaven
and, going to the tomb, rolled back the stone
and sat on it. 3His appearance was like lightning, and his clothes were white as snow. 4The
guards were so afraid of him that they shook
and became like dead men.

5The angel said to the women, "Do not
be afraid, for I know that you are looking for
Jesus, who was crucified. 6He is not here; he
has risen, just as he said. Come and see the
place where he lay. 7Then go quickly and tell
his disciples: 'He has risen from the dead and
is going ahead of you into Galilee. There you
will see him.' Now I have told you."

8So the women hurried away from the
tomb, afraid yet filled with joy, and ran to
tell his disciples. 9Suddenly Jesus met them.
"Greetings," he said. They came to him,
clasped his feet and worshiped him. 10Then
Jesus said to them, "Do not be afraid. Go and
tell my brothers to go to Galilee; there they
will see me."

The Guards' Report

11While the women were on their way,
some of the guards went into the city and
reported to the chief priests everything that
had happened. 12When the chief priests had
met with the elders and devised a plan, they
gave the soldiers a large sum of money, 13tell-
ing them, "You are to say, 'His disciples came
during the night and stole him away while we
were asleep.' 14If this report gets to the governor, we will satisfy him and keep you out
of trouble." 15So the soldiers took the money
and did as they were instructed. And this story
has been widely circulated among the Jews to
this very day.

The Great Commission

16Then the eleven disciples went to Galilee,
to the mountain where Jesus had told them
to go. 17When they saw him, they worshiped
him; but some doubted. 18Then Jesus came to
them and said, "All authority in heaven and
on earth has been given to me. 19Therefore
go and make disciples of all nations, baptizing them in[a] the name of the Father and of
the Son and of the Holy Spirit, 20and teaching
them to obey everything I have commanded
you. And surely I am with you always, to the
very end of the age."

---

a 19 Or *into*; see Acts 8:16; 19:5; Romans 6:3; 1 Cor. 1:13; 10:2 and Gal. 3:27.

MARK

Mark

QUICK FACTS

AUTHOR John Mark (early church sources tell us the apostle Peter relayed information to Mark for his Gospel)

AUDIENCE Mark wrote with Gentiles in mind, probably in the church at Rome

DATE Sometime between A.D. 50 and 70

SETTING Most likely written from Rome

Although the author of the Gospel of Mark is not named, early church records indicate it was John Mark. Acts 12:12 reports that the believers gathered at his mother's house to pray for the imprisoned apostle Peter. Mark had a close relationship with Peter, who almost certainly was the primary source for the book. Mark also traveled with Paul and Barnabas on their first missionary journey.

Mark's Gospel, which was likely written primarily to Gentile converts to Christianity in the church at Rome, frequently explains Jewish terms and customs. The book is practical and to the point; it reports events without spending a lot of time on interpretation. Mark's account begins with the incidents immediately preceding Jesus' public ministry and focuses on Jesus' suffering and our calling to count the cost and follow him. Perhaps the believers in Rome were facing persecution and Mark was preparing them to suffer by lifting up before them the life and example of Christ.

Chapter 7 highlights the importance of wholehearted commitment over merely following human tradition. Jesus made it clear that our motives are more important than acts done by simply going through the motions. This serves as a valuable lesson for marriage: We are called to give our hearts to God and to the person he has given us to love and cherish.

John the Baptist Prepares the Way

1 The beginning of the gospel about Jesus Christ, the Son of God.[a]

2 It is written in Isaiah the prophet:

"I will send my messenger ahead of you,
  who will prepare your way"[b]—
3 "a voice of one calling in the desert,
'Prepare the way for the Lord,
  make straight paths for him.' "[c]

4 And so John came, baptizing in the desert region and preaching a baptism of repentance for the forgiveness of sins. 5 The whole Judean countryside and all the people of Jerusalem went out to him. Confessing their sins, they were baptized by him in the Jordan River. 6 John wore clothing made of camel's hair, with a leather belt around his waist, and he ate locusts and wild honey. 7 And this was his message: "After me will come one more powerful than I, the thongs of whose sandals I am not worthy to stoop down and untie. 8 I baptize you with[d] water, but he will baptize you with the Holy Spirit."

The Baptism and Temptation of Jesus

9 At that time Jesus came from Nazareth in Galilee and was baptized by John in the Jordan. 10 As Jesus was coming up out of the water, he saw heaven being torn open and the Spirit descending on him like a dove. 11 And a voice came from heaven: "You are my Son, whom I love; with you I am well pleased."

12 At once the Spirit sent him out into the desert, 13 and he was in the desert forty days, being tempted by Satan. He was with the wild animals, and angels attended him.

The Calling of the First Disciples

14 After John was put in prison, Jesus went into Galilee, proclaiming the good news of God. 15 "The time has come," he said. "The kingdom of God is near. Repent and believe the good news!"

16 As Jesus walked beside the Sea of Galilee, he saw Simon and his brother Andrew casting a net into the lake, for they were fishermen. 17 "Come, follow me," Jesus said, "and I will make you fishers of men." 18 At once they left their nets and followed him.

19 When he had gone a little farther, he saw James son of Zebedee and his brother John in a boat, preparing their nets. 20 Without delay he called them, and they left their father Zebedee in the boat with the hired men and followed him.

Jesus Drives Out an Evil Spirit

21 They went to Capernaum, and when the Sabbath came, Jesus went into the synagogue and began to teach. 22 The people were amazed at his teaching, because he taught them as one who had authority, not as the teachers of the law. 23 Just then a man in their synagogue who was possessed by an evil[e] spirit cried out, 24 "What do you want with us, Jesus of Nazareth? Have you come to destroy us? I know who you are—the Holy One of God!"

25 "Be quiet!" said Jesus sternly. "Come out of him!" 26 The evil spirit shook the man violently and came out of him with a shriek.

27 The people were all so amazed that they asked each other, "What is this? A new teaching—and with authority! He even gives orders to evil spirits and they obey him." 28 News about him spread quickly over the whole region of Galilee.

Jesus Heals Many

29 As soon as they left the synagogue, they went with James and John to the home of Simon and Andrew. 30 Simon's mother-in-law was in bed with a fever, and they told Jesus about her. 31 So he went to her, took her hand and helped her up. The fever left her and she began to wait on them.

32 That evening after sunset the people brought to Jesus all the sick and demon-possessed. 33 The whole town gathered at the door, 34 and Jesus healed many who had various diseases. He also drove out many demons, but he would not let the demons speak because they knew who he was.

Jesus Prays in a Solitary Place

35 Very early in the morning, while it was still dark, Jesus got up, left the house and went off to a solitary place, where he prayed. 36 Simon and his companions went to look for him, 37 and when they found him, they exclaimed: "Everyone is looking for you!"

38 Jesus replied, "Let us go somewhere else—to the nearby villages—so I can preach there also. That is why I have come." 39 So he traveled throughout Galilee, preaching in their synagogues and driving out demons.

---

[a] *1* Some manuscripts do not have *the Son of God.* [b] *2* Mal. 3:1 [c] *3* Isaiah 40:3 [d] *8* Or *in* [e] *23* Greek *unclean*; also in verses 26 and 27

WEDNESDAY

READ MARK 1:1–20

"FOLLOW ME"

> **"Come, follow me," Jesus said, "and I will make you fishers of men."**
>
> — MARK 1:17

let's talk

- What are we each typically doing midmorning on a Monday? Can we picture Jesus coming along and saying, "Follow me"? How hard would it be to drop everything and go?
- When have we had to relinquish some personal plan or goal because it seemed that God had something different in mind? What made that experience difficult? What made it satisfying?
- Have we both responded to Christ's command to "Follow me"? If obeying God is a mutual goal, how can we encourage each other to meet it?

Imagine being busy about your work, whatever it is, and having someone come along and say, "Drop everything, and come with me—for good!" Can you imagine that you and your spouse would actually follow that command? Yet when Jesus spoke a similar command to Simon and Andrew, they dropped everything and went with him.

As Christ's disciples today, how life changing is his call to us, "Follow me"? It can be just as life changing for us as it was for Simon Peter and his brother, Andrew, even though the Lord may not call us to turn our backs on our life's work to become traveling evangelists.

That call, "Follow me," carries with it the command to stop following our own agenda, and that's extraordinarily countercultural in the twenty-first century. So many voices in our society tell us to "look out for number one." But Jesus says, "Get out of the driver's seat!" It seems unrealistic to relinquish our own plans and goals and dreams to serve somebody else, but that's what Jesus wants us to do.

The good news is that our best interests are safe in God's hands. He knows our plans, goals and dreams, and he knows better than we do what is ultimately best for us.

In some ways, it was easier for Simon Peter and Andrew to follow Christ than it is for me. They could literally and physically get up and follow Jesus, a visible and tangible human authority. The only way I've found that I can follow Jesus is to pursue God through his Word. The Holy Spirit is at work in every believer and is present with us as we dig into Scripture, helping us learn and apply his principles.

Also, for me, following Jesus means that, year after year I discover ideas and attitudes and behaviors in myself that need to be pulled into submission to God's Word. Apparently, this job will not be done until Christ brings me, thanks to his righteousness, into his presence in heaven. Then I'll be able to follow him, as Simon and Andrew did, with Jesus right in view.

In some ways, submitting to God has helped me to live in mutual submission with my husband, David. I've had to get comfortable being out of the driver's seat in my relationship with the Lord, and that has made it easier for me to share the navigational duties of marriage with David.

Those fisherman brothers had each other during their great adventure of following Jesus, and I'm glad I have David, who shares my goal to obey Christ's command as he continually says, "Follow me." Two are always better than one as we encourage each other to be faithful to the authority we mutually embrace: Jesus Christ.

—ANNETTE LAPLACA

FOR YOUR NEXT DEVOTIONAL READING, TURN TO PAGE 1104.

A Man With Leprosy

40 A man with leprosy[a] came to him and begged him on his knees, "If you are willing, you can make me clean."

41 Filled with compassion, Jesus reached out his hand and touched the man. "I am willing," he said. "Be clean!" 42 Immediately the leprosy left him and he was cured.

43 Jesus sent him away at once with a strong warning: 44 "See that you don't tell this to anyone. But go, show yourself to the priest and offer the sacrifices that Moses commanded for your cleansing, as a testimony to them." 45 Instead he went out and began to talk freely, spreading the news. As a result, Jesus could no longer enter a town openly but stayed outside in lonely places. Yet the people still came to him from everywhere.

Jesus Heals a Paralytic

2 A few days later, when Jesus again entered Capernaum, the people heard that he had come home. 2 So many gathered that there was no room left, not even outside the door, and he preached the word to them. 3 Some men came, bringing to him a paralytic, carried by four of them. 4 Since they could not get him to Jesus because of the crowd, they made an opening in the roof above Jesus and, after digging through it, lowered the mat the paralyzed man was lying on. 5 When Jesus saw their faith, he said to the paralytic, "Son, your sins are forgiven."

6 Now some teachers of the law were sitting there, thinking to themselves, 7 "Why does this fellow talk like that? He's blaspheming! Who can forgive sins but God alone?"

8 Immediately Jesus knew in his spirit that this was what they were thinking in their hearts, and he said to them, "Why are you thinking these things? 9 Which is easier: to say to the paralytic, 'Your sins are forgiven,' or to say, 'Get up, take your mat and walk'? 10 But that you may know that the Son of Man has authority on earth to forgive sins . . ." He said to the paralytic, 11 "I tell you, get up, take your mat and go home." 12 He got up, took his mat and walked out in full view of them all. This amazed everyone and they praised God, saying, "We have never seen anything like this!"

The Calling of Levi

13 Once again Jesus went out beside the lake. A large crowd came to him, and he began to teach them. 14 As he walked along, he saw Levi son of Alphaeus sitting at the tax collector's booth. "Follow me," Jesus told him, and Levi got up and followed him.

15 While Jesus was having dinner at Levi's house, many tax collectors and "sinners" were eating with him and his disciples, for there were many who followed him. 16 When the teachers of the law who were Pharisees saw him eating with the "sinners" and tax collectors, they asked his disciples: "Why does he eat with tax collectors and 'sinners'?"

17 On hearing this, Jesus said to them, "It is not the healthy who need a doctor, but the sick. I have not come to call the righteous, but sinners."

Jesus Questioned About Fasting

18 Now John's disciples and the Pharisees were fasting. Some people came and asked Jesus, "How is it that John's disciples and the disciples of the Pharisees are fasting, but yours are not?"

19 Jesus answered, "How can the guests of the bridegroom fast while he is with them? They cannot, so long as they have him with them. 20 But the time will come when the bridegroom will be taken from them, and on that day they will fast.

21 "No one sews a patch of unshrunk cloth on an old garment. If he does, the new piece will pull away from the old, making the tear worse. 22 And no one pours new wine into old wineskins. If he does, the wine will burst the skins, and both the wine and the wineskins will be ruined. No, he pours new wine into new wineskins."

Lord of the Sabbath

23 One Sabbath Jesus was going through the grainfields, and as his disciples walked along, they began to pick some heads of grain. 24 The Pharisees said to him, "Look, why are they doing what is unlawful on the Sabbath?"

25 He answered, "Have you never read what David did when he and his companions were hungry and in need? 26 In the days of Abiathar the high priest, he entered the house of God and ate the consecrated bread, which is lawful only for priests to eat. And he also gave some to his companions."

27 Then he said to them, "The Sabbath was made for man, not man for the Sabbath. 28 So the Son of Man is Lord even of the Sabbath."

---

a 40 The Greek word was used for various diseases affecting the skin—not necessarily leprosy.

THE BEST KIND OF SABBATH

Jesus often upset the religious establishment of his day. In Mark 2:23–28 he challenged the Pharisees' rules about what could and couldn't be done on the Sabbath. And there were lots of rules and lots of Jewish leaders watching and enforcing the rules.

Did you have rules growing up about what you could and couldn't do on Sunday, the day that Christians have traditionally viewed as the parallel of the Old Testament Jewish Saturday Sabbath (see Acts 20:7; 1 Corinthians 16:2)? Whatever your past, in marriage you have to merge two potentially conflicting sets of expectations. Instead of arguing over whose history is more meaningful, why not wipe both slates clean and create a fresh approach based on Jesus' statement that the Sabbath was made for us?

A good place to start might be with the premise that the Sabbath is a gift, not an obligation. So we don't *have to* do anything. With that lovely thought in mind, we might think of the Sabbath as dinner in a fine restaurant. On this special day we get to sort through a full menu of delights to feed our spirits, minds and bodies.

Then [Jesus] said to them, "The Sabbath was made for man, not man for the Sabbath."

— Mark 2:27

let's talk

- Do we view Sunday, or another day of the week, as a special "Sabbath" time in our weekly schedule? How have our experiences growing up influenced our expectations in this regard?
- In what ways could we better use God's gift of the Sabbath?
- What activities could we add to—or subtract from—our current Sabbath day to make this time more restful and renewing?

My husband and I choose to feed our spirits first. We spend Sunday mornings in worship by attending church. On occasion, this "meal" has served as an indicator of how things are going between us. If we're in an unresolved relational storm, one or both of us usually doesn't feel like going to church. But since we don't want to forego worship, we're more inclined to tackle the issue and resolve it before Sunday. Other times we go anyway, and the message heals our wounds.

Besides worship, church offers fellowship and service. One Sunday our adult discussion group picked up pizzas for lunch, then went to a halfway house to clean and decorate a couple of rooms for new residents. My friend Pat usually has a dozen people, including some newcomers, over for Sunday lunch. That is not something we do at our house, but we love being invited to Pat's.

After that main course of worship, fellowship and service, Grey and I decide what to do the rest of the day. There are lots of options. I love to phone my sisters or friends for a good, long chat. My husband digs into his stack of recreational reading materials or watches a football game on TV. We might take a nap.

What's your idea of physical renewal? Hiking, fishing, biking? The options are limitless. We like to go lake kayaking. And we've also learned that not every activity has to be done together. Our Sunday afternoons are a comfortable flow of activities that we do together and alone.

Unlike the Jewish religious zealots, who weren't allowed to do anything on their Sabbath—not even take a long walk—we are free to choose the activities that renew us and prepare us for the week ahead. For us, Sunday is God's gift.

—MARY ANN JEFFREYS

FOR YOUR NEXT DEVOTIONAL READING, TURN TO PAGE 1107.

3 Another time he went into the synagogue,
and a man with a shriveled hand was there.
2Some of them were looking for a reason
to accuse Jesus, so they watched him closely
to see if he would heal him on the Sabbath.
3Jesus said to the man with the shriveled hand,
"Stand up in front of everyone."
4Then Jesus asked them, "Which is lawful
on the Sabbath: to do good or to do evil, to
save life or to kill?" But they remained silent.
5He looked around at them in anger and,
deeply distressed at their stubborn hearts,
said to the man, "Stretch out your hand." He
stretched it out, and his hand was completely restored. 6Then the Pharisees went out and
began to plot with the Herodians how they
might kill Jesus.

Crowds Follow Jesus

7Jesus withdrew with his disciples to the
lake, and a large crowd from Galilee followed.
8When they heard all he was doing, many
people came to him from Judea, Jerusalem,
Idumea, and the regions across the Jordan and
around Tyre and Sidon. 9Because of the crowd
he told his disciples to have a small boat ready
for him, to keep the people from crowding
him. 10For he had healed many, so that those
with diseases were pushing forward to touch
him. 11Whenever the evil[a] spirits saw him,
they fell down before him and cried out, "You
are the Son of God." 12But he gave them strict
orders not to tell who he was.

The Appointing of the Twelve Apostles

13Jesus went up on a mountainside and
called to him those he wanted, and they came
to him. 14He appointed twelve—designating
them apostles[b]—that they might be with him
and that he might send them out to preach
15and to have authority to drive out demons.
16These are the twelve he appointed: Simon
(to whom he gave the name Peter); 17James
son of Zebedee and his brother John (to them
he gave the name Boanerges, which means
Sons of Thunder); 18Andrew, Philip, Bartholomew, Matthew, Thomas, James son of Alphaeus, Thaddaeus, Simon the Zealot 19and
Judas Iscariot, who betrayed him.

Jesus and Beelzebub

20Then Jesus entered a house, and again a
crowd gathered, so that he and his disciples
were not even able to eat. 21When his family
heard about this, they went to take charge of
him, for they said, "He is out of his mind."
22And the teachers of the law who came
down from Jerusalem said, "He is possessed
by Beelzebub[c]! By the prince of demons he is
driving out demons."
23So Jesus called them and spoke to them
in parables: "How can Satan drive out Satan?
24If a kingdom is divided against itself, that
kingdom cannot stand. 25If a house is divided
against itself, that house cannot stand. 26And
if Satan opposes himself and is divided, he
cannot stand; his end has come. 27In fact, no
one can enter a strong man's house and carry
off his possessions unless he first ties up the
strong man. Then he can rob his house. 28I
tell you the truth, all the sins and blasphemies
of men will be forgiven them. 29But whoever
blasphemes against the Holy Spirit will never
be forgiven; he is guilty of an eternal sin."
30He said this because they were saying,
"He has an evil spirit."

Jesus' Mother and Brothers

31Then Jesus' mother and brothers arrived.
Standing outside, they sent someone in to call
him. 32A crowd was sitting around him, and
they told him, "Your mother and brothers are
outside looking for you."
33"Who are my mother and my brothers?"
he asked.
34Then he looked at those seated in a circle
around him and said, "Here are my mother
and my brothers! 35Whoever does God's will
is my brother and sister and mother."

The Parable of the Sower

4 Again Jesus began to teach by the lake. The
crowd that gathered around him was so
large that he got into a boat and sat in it
out on the lake, while all the people were along
the shore at the water's edge. 2He taught them
many things by parables, and in his teaching
said: 3"Listen! A farmer went out to sow his
seed. 4As he was scattering the seed, some fell
along the path, and the birds came and ate it
up. 5Some fell on rocky places, where it did not
have much soil. It sprang up quickly, because
the soil was shallow. 6But when the sun came
up, the plants were scorched, and they withered because they had no root. 7Other seed fell
among thorns, which grew up and choked the
plants, so that they did not bear grain. 8Still
other seed fell on good soil. It came up, grew

---

[a] 11 Greek *unclean*; also in verse 30 [b] 14 Some manuscripts do not have *designating them apostles.* [c] 22 Greek *Beezeboul* or *Beelzeboul*

and produced a crop, multiplying thirty, sixty,
or even a hundred times."
9Then Jesus said, "He who has ears to hear,
let him hear."
10When he was alone, the Twelve and the
others around him asked him about the parables. 11He told them, "The secret of the kingdom of God has been given to you. But to
those on the outside everything is said in parables 12so that,

" 'they may be ever seeing but never
perceiving,
and ever hearing but never
understanding;
otherwise they might turn and be
forgiven!'[a]"

13Then Jesus said to them, "Don't you understand this parable? How then will you understand any parable? 14The farmer sows the
word. 15Some people are like seed along the
path, where the word is sown. As soon as they
hear it, Satan comes and takes away the word
that was sown in them. 16Others, like seed
sown on rocky places, hear the word and at
once receive it with joy. 17But since they have
no root, they last only a short time. When
trouble or persecution comes because of the
word, they quickly fall away. 18Still others, like
seed sown among thorns, hear the word; 19but
the worries of this life, the deceitfulness of
wealth and the desires for other things come
in and choke the word, making it unfruitful.
20Others, like seed sown on good soil, hear
the word, accept it, and produce a crop—thirty, sixty or even a hundred times what was
sown."

A Lamp on a Stand

21He said to them, "Do you bring in a lamp
to put it under a bowl or a bed? Instead, don't
you put it on its stand? 22For whatever is hidden is meant to be disclosed, and whatever
is concealed is meant to be brought out into
the open. 23If anyone has ears to hear, let him
hear."
24"Consider carefully what you hear," he
continued. "With the measure you use, it will
be measured to you—and even more. 25Who-
ever has will be given more; whoever does not
have, even what he has will be taken from
him."

The Parable of the Growing Seed

26He also said, "This is what the kingdom
of God is like. A man scatters seed on the
ground. 27Night and day, whether he sleeps or
gets up, the seed sprouts and grows, though
he does not know how. 28All by itself the soil
produces grain—first the stalk, then the head,
then the full kernel in the head. 29As soon as
the grain is ripe, he puts the sickle to it, because the harvest has come."

The Parable of the Mustard Seed

30Again he said, "What shall we say the
kingdom of God is like, or what parable shall
we use to describe it? 31It is like a mustard
seed, which is the smallest seed you plant in
the ground. 32Yet when planted, it grows and
becomes the largest of all garden plants, with
such big branches that the birds of the air can
perch in its shade."
33With many similar parables Jesus spoke
the word to them, as much as they could understand. 34He did not say anything to them
without using a parable. But when he was
alone with his own disciples, he explained everything.

Jesus Calms the Storm

35That day when evening came, he said
to his disciples, "Let us go over to the other
side." 36Leaving the crowd behind, they took
him along, just as he was, in the boat. There
were also other boats with him. 37A furious
squall came up, and the waves broke over the
boat, so that it was nearly swamped. 38Jesus
was in the stern, sleeping on a cushion. The
disciples woke him and said to him, "Teacher,
don't you care if we drown?"
39He got up, rebuked the wind and said to
the waves, "Quiet! Be still!" Then the wind
died down and it was completely calm.
40He said to his disciples, "Why are you so
afraid? Do you still have no faith?"
41They were terrified and asked each other,
"Who is this? Even the wind and the waves
obey him!"

The Healing of a Demon-possessed Man

5 They went across the lake to the region of
the Gerasenes.[b] 2When Jesus got out of the
boat, a man with an evil[c] spirit came from
the tombs to meet him. 3This man lived in the
tombs, and no one could bind him any more,
not even with a chain. 4For he had often been
chained hand and foot, but he tore the chains
apart and broke the irons on his feet. No one
was strong enough to subdue him. 5Night

---

[a] *12* Isaiah 6:9,10 [b] *1* Some manuscripts *Gadarenes*; other manuscripts *Gergesenes* [c] *2* Greek *unclean*; also in verses 8 and 13

FRIDAY

READ MARK 4:21–25

GIVING UP OUR SECRETS

Robert Louis Stevenson wrote, "The cruelest lies are often told in silence." Much in our world is deceptive and dishonest: the rhetoric of political campaigns, for example, or the propaganda of advertising, with its slanted facts and testimonials. In a time that makes us wary, we long for honesty that breeds trust and nurtures hope.

A woman once came to me for counseling. For the next two years, we wrestled through the difficulties in her life. She was living a lie, and she didn't even know it. Secrets had twisted her in so many ways that she couldn't even say what her problem was. But finally God got through to her, wrapped his healing around her hurting heart, and took the kinks out of her troubled dreams.

When we first started counseling, the woman hid her pain behind clever tales and false fronts. She talks differently today. Her yes means yes, and she knows why. She doesn't have to lie to God anymore, and she doesn't have to invent stories for others. The doors of her prison have swung open. She has found God. She has found herself. She is free of secrets, and the way she talks shows it.

Straight talk is important in marriage. It is easy to distort the truth when we are doing the "dating dance" and wooing one another. We parade partial truths in hopes that some of our deeper secrets will stay hidden. The tipping point comes when we enter into the deeper relational stage we call "engagement." An older term for that was *betrothal*, which literally means giving our troth, an earlier variation on the word *truth*. In other words, dating is playing games, but engagement, or betrothal, means we are now committing to truth. We are choosing to reveal more of ourselves so we can see each other wholly and love each other in wholesome ways.

The outcome of a good engagement is marriage, when, as Adam and Eve discovered, we find ways to be "naked and not ashamed" before each other. This is more than just undressing; it is the psychological honesty that allows us to meet one another in truth, peering into each other's souls without embarrassment or threat of one of us walking away.

There may be times when too much honesty harms a good relationship, but it is hard to know how secrets can be part of a healthy relationship. God does not turn away from us when the secrets of our hearts are brought into the healing light of divine grace. Nor should we turn from those who trust us with the intimacy of private faults, disappointments, needs and dreams. As Jesus reminds us in this brief parable about a lamp, "Whatever is hidden is meant to be disclosed, and whatever is concealed is meant to be brought out into the open." Especially in marriage.

—WAYNE BROUWER

"Whatever is hidden is meant to be disclosed, and whatever is concealed is meant to be brought out into the open."

— MARK 4:22

let's talk

- ✦ How well do we know each other? How much can we entrust to one another? How are knowing and trusting related?
- ✦ What do we know about each other that no one else knows? How have we used that secret information in healthy and nurturing ways? How have we abused it?
- ✦ Are there secrets we keep from one another? Do we need to become more open with one another? How might we do that?

FOR YOUR NEXT DEVOTIONAL READING, TURN TO PAGE 1110.

and day among the tombs and in the hills he
would cry out and cut himself with stones.
6When he saw Jesus from a distance, he
ran and fell on his knees in front of him. 7He
shouted at the top of his voice, "What do you
want with me, Jesus, Son of the Most High
God? Swear to God that you won't torture
me!" 8For Jesus had said to him, "Come out
of this man, you evil spirit!"
9Then Jesus asked him, "What is your
name?"
"My name is Legion," he replied, "for we
are many." 10And he begged Jesus again and
again not to send them out of the area.
11A large herd of pigs was feeding on the
nearby hillside. 12The demons begged Jesus,
"Send us among the pigs; allow us to go into
them." 13He gave them permission, and the
evil spirits came out and went into the pigs.
The herd, about two thousand in number,
rushed down the steep bank into the lake and
were drowned.
14Those tending the pigs ran off and reported this in the town and countryside, and the
people went out to see what had happened.
15When they came to Jesus, they saw the man
who had been possessed by the legion of demons, sitting there, dressed and in his right
mind; and they were afraid. 16Those who had
seen it told the people what had happened to
the demon-possessed man—and told about
the pigs as well. 17Then the people began to
plead with Jesus to leave their region.
18As Jesus was getting into the boat, the
man who had been demon-possessed begged
to go with him. 19Jesus did not let him, but
said, "Go home to your family and tell them
how much the Lord has done for you, and
how he has had mercy on you." 20So the man
went away and began to tell in the Decapolis[a]
how much Jesus had done for him. And all the
people were amazed.

A Dead Girl and a Sick Woman

21When Jesus had again crossed over by
boat to the other side of the lake, a large crowd
gathered around him while he was by the lake.
22Then one of the synagogue rulers, named Jairus, came there. Seeing Jesus, he fell at his feet
23and pleaded earnestly with him, "My little
daughter is dying. Please come and put your
hands on her so that she will be healed and
live." 24So Jesus went with him.
A large crowd followed and pressed around
him. 25And a woman was there who had been
subject to bleeding for twelve years. 26She had
suffered a great deal under the care of many
doctors and had spent all she had, yet instead
of getting better she grew worse. 27When she
heard about Jesus, she came up behind him
in the crowd and touched his cloak, 28be-
cause she thought, "If I just touch his clothes,
I will be healed." 29Immediately her bleeding
stopped and she felt in her body that she was
freed from her suffering.
30At once Jesus realized that power had gone
out from him. He turned around in the crowd
and asked, "Who touched my clothes?"
31"You see the people crowding against
you," his disciples answered, "and yet you can
ask, 'Who touched me?' "
32But Jesus kept looking around to see who
had done it. 33Then the woman, knowing
what had happened to her, came and fell at
his feet and, trembling with fear, told him the
whole truth. 34He said to her, "Daughter, your
faith has healed you. Go in peace and be freed
from your suffering."
35While Jesus was still speaking, some men
came from the house of Jairus, the synagogue
ruler. "Your daughter is dead," they said.
"Why bother the teacher any more?"
36Ignoring what they said, Jesus told the synagogue ruler, "Don't be afraid; just believe."
37He did not let anyone follow him except
Peter, James and John the brother of James.
38When they came to the home of the synagogue ruler, Jesus saw a commotion, with
people crying and wailing loudly. 39He went
in and said to them, "Why all this commotion
and wailing? The child is not dead but asleep."
40But they laughed at him.
After he put them all out, he took the child's
father and mother and the disciples who were
with him, and went in where the child was.
41He took her by the hand and said to her,
"Talitha koum!" (which means, "Little girl, I
say to you, get up!"). 42Immediately the girl
stood up and walked around (she was twelve
years old). At this they were completely astonished. 43He gave strict orders not to let anyone
know about this, and told them to give her
something to eat.

A Prophet Without Honor

6 Jesus left there and went to his hometown,
accompanied by his disciples. 2When the
Sabbath came, he began to teach in the
synagogue, and many who heard him were
amazed.

---

a 20 That is, the Ten Cities

"Where did this man get these things?" they asked. "What's this wisdom that has been given him, that he even does miracles! 3Isn't this the carpenter? Isn't this Mary's son and the brother of James, Joseph,[a] Judas and Simon? Aren't his sisters here with us?" And they took offense at him.

4Jesus said to them, "Only in his hometown, among his relatives and in his own house is a prophet without honor." 5He could not do any miracles there, except lay his hands on a few sick people and heal them. 6And he was amazed at their lack of faith.

Jesus Sends Out the Twelve

Then Jesus went around teaching from village to village. 7Calling the Twelve to him, he sent them out two by two and gave them authority over evil[b] spirits.

8These were his instructions: "Take nothing for the journey except a staff—no bread, no bag, no money in your belts. 9Wear sandals but not an extra tunic. 10Whenever you enter a house, stay there until you leave that town. 11And if any place will not welcome you or listen to you, shake the dust off your feet when you leave, as a testimony against them."

12They went out and preached that people should repent. 13They drove out many demons and anointed many sick people with oil and healed them.

John the Baptist Beheaded

14King Herod heard about this, for Jesus' name had become well known. Some were saying,[c] "John the Baptist has been raised from the dead, and that is why miraculous powers are at work in him."

15Others said, "He is Elijah."

And still others claimed, "He is a prophet, like one of the prophets of long ago."

16But when Herod heard this, he said, "John, the man I beheaded, has been raised from the dead!"

17For Herod himself had given orders to have John arrested, and he had him bound and put in prison. He did this because of Herodias, his brother Philip's wife, whom he had married. 18For John had been saying to Herod, "It is not lawful for you to have your brother's wife." 19So Herodias nursed a grudge against John and wanted to kill him. But she was not able to, 20because Herod feared John and protected him, knowing him to be a righteous and holy man. When Herod heard John, he was greatly puzzled[d]; yet he liked to listen to him.

21Finally the opportune time came. On his birthday Herod gave a banquet for his high officials and military commanders and the leading men of Galilee. 22When the daughter of Herodias came in and danced, she pleased Herod and his dinner guests.

The king said to the girl, "Ask me for anything you want, and I'll give it to you." 23And he promised her with an oath, "Whatever you ask I will give you, up to half my kingdom."

24She went out and said to her mother, "What shall I ask for?"

"The head of John the Baptist," she answered.

25At once the girl hurried in to the king with the request: "I want you to give me right now the head of John the Baptist on a platter."

26The king was greatly distressed, but because of his oaths and his dinner guests, he did not want to refuse her. 27So he immediately sent an executioner with orders to bring John's head. The man went, beheaded John in the prison, 28and brought back his head on a platter. He presented it to the girl, and she gave it to her mother. 29On hearing of this, John's disciples came and took his body and laid it in a tomb.

Jesus Feeds the Five Thousand

30The apostles gathered around Jesus and reported to him all they had done and taught. 31Then, because so many people were coming and going that they did not even have a chance to eat, he said to them, "Come with me by yourselves to a quiet place and get some rest."

32So they went away by themselves in a boat to a solitary place. 33But many who saw them leaving recognized them and ran on foot from all the towns and got there ahead of them. 34When Jesus landed and saw a large crowd, he had compassion on them, because they were like sheep without a shepherd. So he began teaching them many things.

35By this time it was late in the day, so his disciples came to him. "This is a remote place," they said, "and it's already very late. 36Send the people away so they can go to the surrounding countryside and villages and buy themselves something to eat."

37But he answered, "You give them something to eat."

They said to him, "That would take eight

---

[a] 3 Greek *Joses*, a variant of *Joseph* [b] 7 Greek *unclean* [c] 14 Some early manuscripts *He was saying* [d] 20 Some early manuscripts *he did many things*

WEEKEND

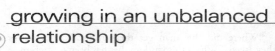

growing in an unbalanced relationship

What if you seem to care more about the future of your relationship than your spouse does? Maybe you have grown and changed since you married, but your spouse has not. Or your spouse has changed in a way that concerns or even frightens you. What if you are beginning to wonder if you married the wrong person? Where do you turn and what do you do in the midst of these painful questions?

Here are four suggestions for getting through this time:

1. *Do not lose hope.* All marriages go through transitions, and a husband and wife may not adapt to change at the same time or on the same level. It takes work and patience and prayer to regain a sense of balance in your relationship.

In *Getting the Love You Want*, Harville Hendrix describes how many modern marriages function as a box. You choose a mate, climb into your box together, settle in, then take a closer look at your box mate. If you like what you see, you stay in the box; if you don't, you climb out of the box and look around for another mate. Or you stay in the box together, tighten the lid, and put up with an unfulfilling, disappointing relationship for the rest of your lives.

Hendrix offers another solution: "Marriage is not a static state between two unchanging people. Marriage is a psychological and spiritual journey that begins in the ecstasy of attraction, meanders through a rocky stretch of self-discovery, and culminates in the creation of an intimate, joyful, lifelong union. Whether or not you realize the full potential of this vision depends not on your ability to attract the perfect mate, but on your willingness to acquire knowledge about hidden parts of your self."

The word *willingness* is the key here, because you or your mate may not be *willing* to put up with a less than perfect relationship. But many couples who have survived crises in their marriage will tell you that change didn't come by changing their mates but by changing themselves.

2. *Talk about it.* This is so obvious, yet many married people deny or suppress their concerns about commitment rather than talk to their mate. First, find a good time and a safe place to talk. Second, communicate your concerns honestly and clearly. And third, be willing to listen just as openly to your mate's response.

3. *Be strong.* In *Love Must Be Tough*, James Dobson addresses the problem of disrespect in marriages that are drifting toward divorce. He offers practical advice to the partner who desperately wants to hold the marriage together and advocates a loving toughness rather than pathetic pleading. He says begging or anger or guilt only lead to the other spouse's increased feelings of being trapped.

When love becomes an obligation rather than a privilege, the less committed spouse experiences an even greater desire to escape. Instead of trapping the partner, Dobson suggests using a stronger, more confident approach. He says open the cage door, pull back, and offer your partner some space. Often, your emotionally distant partner will respond by moving closer to you.

4. *Find help.* If you are in a one-sided marriage, resist the urge to downgrade your spouse or indulge in spouse bashing with a friend. Instead, channel your concerns in a direction where professional help is available. Help can be found in books and resources, but also through people in your community—a pastor, an older couple or person who will mentor you, or a counselor who comes with a good recommendation.

—ELISA MORGAN AND CAROL KUYKENDALL

have you tried everything?

HOW ARE WE DOING?

You're frustrated because you believe you are more committed to marriage than your spouse is. But have you really tried everything? Use this list to evaluate your options. Give yourself a "0" if you're unwilling to try this, a "3" if you think you might try it, and a "5" if you're a big believer in the idea. When finished, examine the lowest scoring items to see if there is room to try again, try in a new way or try harder.

1. I will to do whatever it takes to improve our marriage.
2. I have sought help through our pastor.
3. I have sought help through a recommended counselor.
4. I will never give up regardless of what happens.
5. I treat love like a privilege, not an obligation.
6. I have exhaustively investigated other resources that might help us.
7. I refuse to say anything negative about my spouse to friends and family.
8. I have taken my spouse away from daily distractions so we can focus on this issue.
9. I read books on the subject and try what they suggest.
10. I am willing to use tough love if necessary.
11. I have talked to my mate about the situation.
12. I have sought help through an older couple.
13. I have listened openly to my mate
14. I still have hope about the situation.
15. I am willing to change.

let's make a DATE

MAKE IT HAPPEN

What have you talked about doing but have never gotten around to completing? Maybe last year you talked about painting the dining room. Maybe when you were first married, you talked about saving for a special trip. Maybe you've been saying you want to have the new neighbors over for dinner. Whatever it is, put aside your excuses and take a step toward completing your project: Go to the store and get some paint chips. Go to your bank and open a vacation savings account and put $20.00 in it. Or make a phone call to your new neighbors. Decide together what project you want to accomplish and then do something, at least a first step, to make it happen.

FOR YOUR NEXT DEVOTIONAL READING, TURN TO PAGE 1112.

LESSONS FROM THE *Bible*

What do you learn about one-sided relationships from the following spouses? How did they work things out? Who helped them?

1. Leah (Genesis 29:16—30:21)
2. Hosea (Hosea 1:2–3; 3:1–3)

MONDAY
READ MARK 6:14–29

MISUSING OUR KIDS

> **[Herod] did this because of Herodias, his brother Philip's wife, whom he had married.**
> — MARK 6:17

let's talk

- Has either of us ever been used as a pawn in somebody else's plot or scheme? How did it make us feel?
- How do some parents use their children to get what they want? In what ways have we done something similar?
- What boundaries should we observe about communicating through our children?

This story reads like a soap opera: Herodias first married her uncle, (Herod) Philip. But while married to him, Philip's half brother, Herod (Antipas), persuaded her to leave her husband for him. Such a marriage was forbidden according to Jewish law (see Leviticus 18:16). However, there was no negative feedback regarding the union until John the Baptist began to speak out. When he proclaimed the Herod Antipas–Herodias marriage unlawful, Herod had John thrown into prison.

Meanwhile, the vengeful Herodias began to plot John's death. At Herod's birthday party, Herodias had her daughter dance for everyone, which pleased Herod so much that he told the girl she could have anything she wanted, up to half of his kingdom.

With prompting from Herodias, the girl asked for John's head on a platter. When she received it, she gave it to her mother.

When I read the story of Herodias and the way she used her daughter in her evil plot, I feel pretty confident that I would never use my child as a pawn like that to get my way. However, before I get too smug about it, I have to admit that I have used my children as pawns in other ways to get my husband to do things that I've wanted him to do. Or at least I've tried: "Go tell Dad that you and your sister want to go out to dinner tonight." Or "Ask Dad why he has to play golf today. Wouldn't he rather stay home with his family?" Or "Go tell Dad he should take us to the mall." And the one I'm most ashamed of: "Ask Dad why he doesn't go to church with us."

Now that my daughters are grown, I realize how unfair it was of me to put them in the position of being message bearers. It was pure cowardice and manipulation on my part, especially when I tried to use my children to guilt-trip their dad into joining us at church. (I've long since repented and told my children and my husband that I was sorry!)

Jesus said, "If anyone causes one of these little ones who believe in me to sin, it would be better for him to be thrown into the sea with a large millstone tied around his neck" (Mark 9:42). Though the term "little ones," in Jesus' thinking, included all believers, he gave a clear warning about misusing children.

God sometimes uses the innocent remarks and questions of children to touch their parents' hearts, and when that happens, it's a Holy Spirit thing. But when using kids is a me thing, it rarely works and almost always backfires. Worst of all, when I use my children for my own selfish end, no matter how good (or evil) the end may be, I'm teaching them how to one day use their children in the same way.

When that happens, just hand me a millstone and throw me off a boat, because that's what I deserve.

—NANCY KENNEDY

FOR YOUR NEXT DEVOTIONAL READING, TURN TO PAGE 1116.

months of a man's wages[a]! Are we to go and spend that much on bread and give it to them to eat?"

38"How many loaves do you have?" he asked. "Go and see."

When they found out, they said, "Five—and two fish."

39Then Jesus directed them to have all the people sit down in groups on the green grass. 40So they sat down in groups of hundreds and fifties. 41Taking the five loaves and the two fish and looking up to heaven, he gave thanks and broke the loaves. Then he gave them to his disciples to set before the people. He also divided the two fish among them all. 42They all ate and were satisfied, 43and the disciples picked up twelve basketfuls of broken pieces of bread and fish. 44The number of the men who had eaten was five thousand.

Jesus Walks on the Water

45Immediately Jesus made his disciples get into the boat and go on ahead of him to Bethsaida, while he dismissed the crowd. 46After leaving them, he went up on a mountainside to pray.

47When evening came, the boat was in the middle of the lake, and he was alone on land. 48He saw the disciples straining at the oars, because the wind was against them. About the fourth watch of the night he went out to them, walking on the lake. He was about to pass by them, 49but when they saw him walking on the lake, they thought he was a ghost. They cried out, 50because they all saw him and were terrified.

Immediately he spoke to them and said, "Take courage! It is I. Don't be afraid." 51Then he climbed into the boat with them, and the wind died down. They were completely amazed, 52for they had not understood about the loaves; their hearts were hardened.

53When they had crossed over, they landed at Gennesaret and anchored there. 54As soon as they got out of the boat, people recognized Jesus. 55They ran throughout that whole region and carried the sick on mats to wherever they heard he was. 56And wherever he went—into villages, towns or countryside—they placed the sick in the marketplaces. They begged him to let them touch even the edge of his cloak, and all who touched him were healed.

Clean and Unclean

7 The Pharisees and some of the teachers of the law who had come from Jerusalem gathered around Jesus and 2saw some of his disciples eating food with hands that were "unclean," that is, unwashed. 3(The Pharisees and all the Jews do not eat unless they give their hands a ceremonial washing, holding to the tradition of the elders. 4When they come from the marketplace they do not eat unless they wash. And they observe many other traditions, such as the washing of cups, pitchers and kettles.[b])

5So the Pharisees and teachers of the law asked Jesus, "Why don't your disciples live according to the tradition of the elders instead of eating their food with 'unclean' hands?"

6He replied, "Isaiah was right when he prophesied about you hypocrites; as it is written:

" 'These people honor me with their lips,
 but their hearts are far from me.
7They worship me in vain;
 their teachings are but rules taught by men.'[c]

8You have let go of the commands of God and are holding on to the traditions of men."

9And he said to them: "You have a fine way of setting aside the commands of God in order to observe[d] your own traditions! 10For Moses said, 'Honor your father and your mother,'[e] and, 'Anyone who curses his father or mother must be put to death.'[f] 11But you say that if a man says to his father or mother: 'Whatever help you might otherwise have received from me is Corban' (that is, a gift devoted to God), 12then you no longer let him do anything for his father or mother. 13Thus you nullify the word of God by your tradition that you have handed down. And you do many things like that."

14Again Jesus called the crowd to him and said, "Listen to me, everyone, and understand this. 15Nothing outside a man can make him 'unclean' by going into him. Rather, it is what comes out of a man that makes him 'unclean.'[g]"

17After he had left the crowd and entered the house, his disciples asked him about this parable. 18"Are you so dull?" he asked. "Don't you see that nothing that enters a man from the outside can make him 'unclean'? 19For it doesn't go into his heart but into his stom-

[a] 37 Greek *take two hundred denarii* [b] 4 Some early manuscripts *pitchers, kettles and dining couches* [c] 6,7 Isaiah 29:13 [d] 9 Some manuscripts *set up* [e] 10 Exodus 20:12; Deut. 5:16 [f] 10 Exodus 21:17; Lev. 20:9 [g] 15 Some early manuscripts *'unclean.' 16If anyone has ears to hear, let him hear.*

ach, and then out of his body." (In saying this,
Jesus declared all foods "clean.")
20He went on: "What comes out of a man is
what makes him 'unclean.' 21For from within,
out of men's hearts, come evil thoughts, sexual
immorality, theft, murder, adultery, 22greed,
malice, deceit, lewdness, envy, slander, arrogance and folly. 23All these evils come from
inside and make a man 'unclean.' "

The Faith of a Syrophoenician Woman

24Jesus left that place and went to the vicinity of Tyre.[a] He entered a house and did
not want anyone to know it; yet he could not
keep his presence secret. 25In fact, as soon
as she heard about him, a woman whose little daughter was possessed by an evil[b] spirit
came and fell at his feet. 26The woman was a
Greek, born in Syrian Phoenicia. She begged
Jesus to drive the demon out of her daughter.
27"First let the children eat all they want,"
he told her, "for it is not right to take the children's bread and toss it to their dogs."
28"Yes, Lord," she replied, "but even the dogs
under the table eat the children's crumbs."
29Then he told her, "For such a reply, you
may go; the demon has left your daughter."
30She went home and found her child lying
on the bed, and the demon gone.

The Healing of a Deaf and Mute Man

31Then Jesus left the vicinity of Tyre and
went through Sidon, down to the Sea of Galilee and into the region of the Decapolis.[c]
32There some people brought to him a man
who was deaf and could hardly talk, and they
begged him to place his hand on the man.
33After he took him aside, away from the
crowd, Jesus put his fingers into the man's
ears. Then he spit and touched the man's
tongue. 34He looked up to heaven and with
a deep sigh said to him, *"Ephphatha!"* (which
means, "Be opened!"). 35At this, the man's ears
were opened, his tongue was loosened and he
began to speak plainly.
36Jesus commanded them not to tell anyone. But the more he did so, the more they
kept talking about it. 37People were overwhelmed with amazement. "He has done everything well," they said. "He even makes the
deaf hear and the mute speak."

Jesus Feeds the Four Thousand

8 During those days another large crowd
gathered. Since they had nothing to eat,
Jesus called his disciples to him and said,
2"I have compassion for these people; they
have already been with me three days and have
nothing to eat. 3If I send them home hungry,
they will collapse on the way, because some of
them have come a long distance."
4His disciples answered, "But where in this
remote place can anyone get enough bread to
feed them?"
5"How many loaves do you have?" Jesus
asked.
"Seven," they replied.
6He told the crowd to sit down on the
ground. When he had taken the seven loaves
and given thanks, he broke them and gave
them to his disciples to set before the people,
and they did so. 7They had a few small fish as
well; he gave thanks for them also and told
the disciples to distribute them. 8The people
ate and were satisfied. Afterward the disciples
picked up seven basketfuls of broken pieces
that were left over. 9About four thousand men
were present. And having sent them away,
10he got into the boat with his disciples and
went to the region of Dalmanutha.
11The Pharisees came and began to question Jesus. To test him, they asked him for
a sign from heaven. 12He sighed deeply and
said, "Why does this generation ask for a miraculous sign? I tell you the truth, no sign will
be given to it." 13Then he left them, got back
into the boat and crossed to the other side.

The Yeast of the Pharisees and Herod

14The disciples had forgotten to bring
bread, except for one loaf they had with them
in the boat. 15"Be careful," Jesus warned them.
"Watch out for the yeast of the Pharisees and
that of Herod."
16They discussed this with one another and
said, "It is because we have no bread."
17Aware of their discussion, Jesus asked
them: "Why are you talking about having no
bread? Do you still not see or understand? Are
your hearts hardened? 18Do you have eyes but
fail to see, and ears but fail to hear? And don't
you remember? 19When I broke the five loaves
for the five thousand, how many basketfuls of
pieces did you pick up?"
"Twelve," they replied.
20"And when I broke the seven loaves for

[a] 24 Many early manuscripts *Tyre and Sidon* [b] 25 Greek *unclean* [c] 31 That is, the Ten Cities

spirit that has robbed him of speech. 18Whenever it seizes him, it throws him to the ground.
He foams at the mouth, gnashes his teeth and
becomes rigid. I asked your disciples to drive
out the spirit, but they could not."
19"O unbelieving generation," Jesus replied, "how long shall I stay with you? How
long shall I put up with you? Bring the boy
to me."
20So they brought him. When the spirit
saw Jesus, it immediately threw the boy into
a convulsion. He fell to the ground and rolled
around, foaming at the mouth.
21Jesus asked the boy's father, "How long
has he been like this?"
"From childhood," he answered. 22"It has
often thrown him into fire or water to kill
him. But if you can do anything, take pity on
us and help us."
23" 'If you can'?" said Jesus. "Everything is
possible for him who believes."
24Immediately the boy's father exclaimed, "I
do believe; help me overcome my unbelief!"
25When Jesus saw that a crowd was running
to the scene, he rebuked the evil[a] spirit. "You
deaf and mute spirit," he said, "I command
you, come out of him and never enter him
again."
26The spirit shrieked, convulsed him violently and came out. The boy looked so much
like a corpse that many said, "He's dead."
27But Jesus took him by the hand and lifted
him to his feet, and he stood up.
28After Jesus had gone indoors, his disciples
asked him privately, "Why couldn't we drive
it out?"
29He replied, "This kind can come out only
by prayer.[b]"
30They left that place and passed through
Galilee. Jesus did not want anyone to know
where they were, 31because he was teaching his
disciples. He said to them, "The Son of Man
is going to be betrayed into the hands of men.
They will kill him, and after three days he will
rise." 32But they did not understand what he
meant and were afraid to ask him about it.

Who Is the Greatest?

33They came to Capernaum. When he was
in the house, he asked them, "What were you
arguing about on the road?" 34But they kept
quiet because on the way they had argued
about who was the greatest.
35Sitting down, Jesus called the Twelve and
said, "If anyone wants to be first, he must be
the very last, and the servant of all."
36He took a little child and had him stand
among them. Taking him in his arms, he said
to them, 37"Whoever welcomes one of these
little children in my name welcomes me; and
whoever welcomes me does not welcome me
but the one who sent me."

Whoever Is Not Against Us Is for Us

38"Teacher," said John, "we saw a man driving out demons in your name and we told him
to stop, because he was not one of us."
39"Do not stop him," Jesus said. "No one
who does a miracle in my name can in the
next moment say anything bad about me,
40for whoever is not against us is for us. 41I
tell you the truth, anyone who gives you a cup
of water in my name because you belong to
Christ will certainly not lose his reward.

Causing to Sin

42"And if anyone causes one of these little ones who believe in me to sin, it would
be better for him to be thrown into the sea
with a large millstone tied around his neck.
43If your hand causes you to sin, cut it off. It is
better for you to enter life maimed than with
two hands to go into hell, where the fire never goes out.[c] 45And if your foot causes you to
sin, cut it off. It is better for you to enter life
crippled than to have two feet and be thrown
into hell.[d] 47And if your eye causes you to sin,
pluck it out. It is better for you to enter the
kingdom of God with one eye than to have
two eyes and be thrown into hell, 48where

" 'their worm does not die,
and the fire is not quenched.'[e]

49Everyone will be salted with fire.
50"Salt is good, but if it loses its saltiness,
how can you make it salty again? Have salt in
yourselves, and be at peace with each other."

Divorce

10 Jesus then left that place and went into
the region of Judea and across the Jordan. Again crowds of people came to
him, and as was his custom, he taught them.
2Some Pharisees came and tested him by
asking, "Is it lawful for a man to divorce his
wife?"
3"What did Moses command you?" he replied.

[a] 25 Greek *unclean* [b] 29 Some manuscripts *prayer and fasting* [c] 43 Some manuscripts *out,* [44]*where* / " *'their worm does not die, / and the fire is not quenched.'* [d] 45 Some manuscripts *hell,* [46]*where* / " *'their worm does not die, / and the fire is not quenched.'*
[e] 48 Isaiah 66:24

4 They said, "Moses permitted a man to
write a certificate of divorce and send her
away."
5 "It was because your hearts were hard that
Moses wrote you this law," Jesus replied. 6 "But
at the beginning of creation God 'made them
male and female.'[a] 7 'For this reason a man
will leave his father and mother and be united
to his wife,[b] 8 and the two will become one
flesh.'[c] So they are no longer two, but one.
9 Therefore what God has joined together, let
man not separate."
10 When they were in the house again, the
disciples asked Jesus about this. 11 He answered,
"Anyone who divorces his wife and marries another woman commits adultery against her.
12 And if she divorces her husband and marries
another man, she commits adultery."

The Little Children and Jesus

13 People were bringing little children to
Jesus to have him touch them, but the disciples rebuked them. 14 When Jesus saw this, he
was indignant. He said to them, "Let the little
children come to me, and do not hinder them,
for the kingdom of God belongs to such as
these. 15 I tell you the truth, anyone who will
not receive the kingdom of God like a little
child will never enter it." 16 And he took the
children in his arms, put his hands on them
and blessed them.

The Rich Young Man

17 As Jesus started on his way, a man ran
up to him and fell on his knees before him.
"Good teacher," he asked, "what must I do to
inherit eternal life?"
18 "Why do you call me good?" Jesus answered. "No one is good—except God alone.
19 You know the commandments: 'Do not
murder, do not commit adultery, do not steal,
do not give false testimony, do not defraud,
honor your father and mother.'[d]"
20 "Teacher," he declared, "all these I have
kept since I was a boy."
21 Jesus looked at him and loved him. "One
thing you lack," he said. "Go, sell everything
you have and give to the poor, and you will
have treasure in heaven. Then come, follow me."
22 At this the man's face fell. He went away
sad, because he had great wealth.
23 Jesus looked around and said to his disciples, "How hard it is for the rich to enter the
kingdom of God!"
24 The disciples were amazed at his words.
But Jesus said again, "Children, how hard it is[e]
to enter the kingdom of God! 25 It is easier for
a camel to go through the eye of a needle than
for a rich man to enter the kingdom of God."
26 The disciples were even more amazed, and
said to each other, "Who then can be saved?"
27 Jesus looked at them and said, "With man
this is impossible, but not with God; all things
are possible with God."
28 Peter said to him, "We have left everything to follow you!"
29 "I tell you the truth," Jesus replied, "no
one who has left home or brothers or sisters or mother or father or children or fields
for me and the gospel 30 will fail to receive a
hundred times as much in this present age
(homes, brothers, sisters, mothers, children
and fields—and with them, persecutions) and
in the age to come, eternal life. 31 But many
who are first will be last, and the last first."

Jesus Again Predicts His Death

32 They were on their way up to Jerusalem,
with Jesus leading the way, and the disciples
were astonished, while those who followed
were afraid. Again he took the Twelve aside
and told them what was going to happen to
him. 33 "We are going up to Jerusalem," he
said, "and the Son of Man will be betrayed to
the chief priests and teachers of the law. They
will condemn him to death and will hand him
over to the Gentiles, 34 who will mock him and
spit on him, flog him and kill him. Three days
later he will rise."

The Request of James and John

35 Then James and John, the sons of Zebedee, came to him. "Teacher," they said, "we
want you to do for us whatever we ask."
36 "What do you want me to do for you?"
he asked.
37 They replied, "Let one of us sit at your
right and the other at your left in your glory."
38 "You don't know what you are asking,"
Jesus said. "Can you drink the cup I drink or
be baptized with the baptism I am baptized
with?"
39 "We can," they answered.

Jesus said to them, "You will drink the cup
I drink and be baptized with the baptism I am
baptized with, 40 but to sit at my right or left
is not for me to grant. These places belong to
those for whom they have been prepared."
41 When the ten heard about this, they be-

---

[a] 6 Gen. 1:27 [b] 7 Some early manuscripts do not have *and be united to his wife.* [c] 8 Gen. 2:24 [d] 19 Exodus 20:12-16; Deut. 5:16-20 [e] 24 Some manuscripts *is for those who trust in riches*

WEDNESDAY
READ MARK 10:17–31

STRUGGLING WITH TOO MUCH MONEY

> **"It is easier for a camel to go through the eye of a needle than for a rich man to enter the kingdom of God."**
>
> — MARK 10:25

let's talk

- In what ways has the absence of money caused strain in our marriage? When has too much money caused problems?
- In what ways have we allowed money to drive a wedge between us?
- If wealth—money, cars, houses, stuff—is causing marital strain, what can we do about it? What could we give up to ease the stress?

Too little money can cause friction in a marriage. That's obvious. But can too *much* money also cause marital strain?

Yes. A therapist tells me that she sees unique problems in her wealthy clients. "Above a certain basic middle-class level, the more money you earn, the more important money becomes to you," she says. "I've never seen a wealthy couple for whom money isn't a source of real stress. You're working all the time to earn it. You resent working, and your spouse resents never seeing you. The more money you have, the more you look to money to provide you with security and joy. I think the wealthy have a difficult time delighting in the simple things of life."

If you're like me, you're thinking, "OK, if wealth is a great trial, let me risk living with it." On second thought, maybe not.

I think of Kara, who inherited enough money from her parents so that when she got married, she and her husband were able to buy a small house for cash. That sounds great, right? It was, except that every time the marriage hit a rough patch, Kara would find herself thinking, "What am *I* getting out of this marriage? Steve is getting a free roof over his head." It's hard enough to merge your finances with someone when you don't have much money. It's trickier when there's a $150,000 house in the mix.

Or consider how money affected Josie and Herb. At first, as struggling self-employed graphic artists, they weren't sure they could afford kids. Later, when they became established, they bought a house, then a lake house about two hours away. They talked about having kids again, and decided that children would increase expenses and decrease their productivity, which meant a drop in income. So they decided that they still couldn't afford kids.

Eventually Josie and Herb had a child. Now Josie wishes they'd had more. "We started too late," she says. "When we were struggling artists, we wouldn't really have noticed being slightly more broke. Once we had money, the money itself led us to postpone having kids."

Because I don't have the kind of money those couples struggle with, it would be easy to judge them and not examine myself. But I wonder, in what ways does the money Griff and I do have erode our marriage? Don't I sometimes resent his paycheck, which is small because he works for a non-profit company that builds apartments for homeless people? Haven't I adjusted to our current level of disposable income and wondered where we would have to cut back in order to have kids?

Wealth may distract us from enjoying the bounty of life that, as disciples of Jesus, we are privileged to experience right now. It's far better to live without money than without riches in Jesus.

—LAUREN WINNER

FOR YOUR NEXT DEVOTIONAL READING, TURN TO PAGE 1123.

came indignant with James and John. 42 Jesus
called them together and said, "You know
that those who are regarded as rulers of the
Gentiles lord it over them, and their high officials exercise authority over them. 43 Not so
with you. Instead, whoever wants to become
great among you must be your servant, 44 and
whoever wants to be first must be slave of all.
45 For even the Son of Man did not come to
be served, but to serve, and to give his life as a
ransom for many."

Blind Bartimaeus Receives His Sight

46 Then they came to Jericho. As Jesus and
his disciples, together with a large crowd, were
leaving the city, a blind man, Bartimaeus (that
is, the Son of Timaeus), was sitting by the
roadside begging. 47 When he heard that it was
Jesus of Nazareth, he began to shout, "Jesus,
Son of David, have mercy on me!"
48 Many rebuked him and told him to be
quiet, but he shouted all the more, "Son of
David, have mercy on me!"
49 Jesus stopped and said, "Call him."
So they called to the blind man, "Cheer up!
On your feet! He's calling you." 50 Throwing
his cloak aside, he jumped to his feet and came
to Jesus.
51 "What do you want me to do for you?"
Jesus asked him.
The blind man said, "Rabbi, I want to see."
52 "Go," said Jesus, "your faith has healed
you." Immediately he received his sight and
followed Jesus along the road.

The Triumphal Entry

11 As they approached Jerusalem and came
to Bethphage and Bethany at the Mount
of Olives, Jesus sent two of his disciples,
2 saying to them, "Go to the village ahead of
you, and just as you enter it, you will find a
colt tied there, which no one has ever ridden.
Untie it and bring it here. 3 If anyone asks you,
'Why are you doing this?' tell him, 'The Lord
needs it and will send it back here shortly.' "
4 They went and found a colt outside in
the street, tied at a doorway. As they untied
it, 5 some people standing there asked, "What
are you doing, untying that colt?" 6 They answered as Jesus had told them to, and the people let them go. 7 When they brought the colt
to Jesus and threw their cloaks over it, he sat
on it. 8 Many people spread their cloaks on the
road, while others spread branches they had
cut in the fields. 9 Those who went ahead and
those who followed shouted,

"Hosanna! [a]"

"Blessed is he who comes in the name of
the Lord!" [b]

10 "Blessed is the coming kingdom of our
father David!"

"Hosanna in the highest!"

11 Jesus entered Jerusalem and went to the
temple. He looked around at everything, but
since it was already late, he went out to Bethany with the Twelve.

Jesus Clears the Temple

12 The next day as they were leaving Bethany, Jesus was hungry. 13 Seeing in the distance
a fig tree in leaf, he went to find out if it had
any fruit. When he reached it, he found nothing but leaves, because it was not the season
for figs. 14 Then he said to the tree, "May no
one ever eat fruit from you again." And his
disciples heard him say it.
15 On reaching Jerusalem, Jesus entered
the temple area and began driving out those
who were buying and selling there. He overturned the tables of the money changers and
the benches of those selling doves, 16 and
would not allow anyone to carry merchandise
through the temple courts. 17 And as he taught
them, he said, "Is it not written:

" 'My house will be called
a house of prayer for all nations' [c]?

But you have made it 'a den of robbers.' [d]"
18 The chief priests and the teachers of the
law heard this and began looking for a way
to kill him, for they feared him, because the
whole crowd was amazed at his teaching.
19 When evening came, they [e] went out of
the city.

The Withered Fig Tree

20 In the morning, as they went along, they
saw the fig tree withered from the roots. 21 Peter remembered and said to Jesus, "Rabbi,
look! The fig tree you cursed has withered!"
22 "Have [f] faith in God," Jesus answered. 23 "I
tell you the truth, if anyone says to this mountain, 'Go, throw yourself into the sea,' and
does not doubt in his heart but believes that
what he says will happen, it will be done for
him. 24 Therefore I tell you, whatever you ask

[a] *9* A Hebrew expression meaning "Save!" which became an exclamation of praise; also in verse 10 [b] *9* Psalm 118:25,26
[c] *17* Isaiah 56:7 [d] *17* Jer. 7:11 [e] *19* Some early manuscripts *he* [f] *22* Some early manuscripts *If you have*

for in prayer, believe that you have received it, and it will be yours. 25And when you stand praying, if you hold anything against anyone, forgive him, so that your Father in heaven may forgive you your sins. [a]"

The Authority of Jesus Questioned

27They arrived again in Jerusalem, and while Jesus was walking in the temple courts, the chief priests, the teachers of the law and the elders came to him. 28"By what authority are you doing these things?" they asked. "And who gave you authority to do this?"

29Jesus replied, "I will ask you one question. Answer me, and I will tell you by what authority I am doing these things. 30John's baptism—was it from heaven, or from men? Tell me!"

31They discussed it among themselves and said, "If we say, 'From heaven,' he will ask, 'Then why didn't you believe him?' 32But if we say, 'From men' . . ." (They feared the people, for everyone held that John really was a prophet.)

33So they answered Jesus, "We don't know."

Jesus said, "Neither will I tell you by what authority I am doing these things."

The Parable of the Tenants

12 He then began to speak to them in parables: "A man planted a vineyard. He put a wall around it, dug a pit for the winepress and built a watchtower. Then he rented the vineyard to some farmers and went away on a journey. 2At harvest time he sent a servant to the tenants to collect from them some of the fruit of the vineyard. 3But they seized him, beat him and sent him away empty-handed. 4Then he sent another servant to them; they struck this man on the head and treated him shamefully. 5He sent still another, and that one they killed. He sent many others; some of them they beat, others they killed.

6"He had one left to send, a son, whom he loved. He sent him last of all, saying, 'They will respect my son.'

7"But the tenants said to one another, 'This is the heir. Come, let's kill him, and the inheritance will be ours.' 8So they took him and killed him, and threw him out of the vineyard.

9"What then will the owner of the vineyard do? He will come and kill those tenants and give the vineyard to others. 10Haven't you read this scripture:

" 'The stone the builders rejected
has become the capstone [b];
11 the Lord has done this,
and it is marvelous in our eyes' [c]?"

12Then they looked for a way to arrest him because they knew he had spoken the parable against them. But they were afraid of the crowd; so they left him and went away.

Paying Taxes to Caesar

13Later they sent some of the Pharisees and Herodians to Jesus to catch him in his words. 14They came to him and said, "Teacher, we know you are a man of integrity. You aren't swayed by men, because you pay no attention to who they are; but you teach the way of God in accordance with the truth. Is it right to pay taxes to Caesar or not? 15Should we pay or shouldn't we?"

But Jesus knew their hypocrisy. "Why are you trying to trap me?" he asked. "Bring me a denarius and let me look at it." 16They brought the coin, and he asked them, "Whose portrait is this? And whose inscription?"

"Caesar's," they replied.

17Then Jesus said to them, "Give to Caesar what is Caesar's and to God what is God's."

And they were amazed at him.

Marriage at the Resurrection

18Then the Sadducees, who say there is no resurrection, came to him with a question. 19"Teacher," they said, "Moses wrote for us that if a man's brother dies and leaves a wife but no children, the man must marry the widow and have children for his brother. 20Now there were seven brothers. The first one married and died without leaving any children. 21The second one married the widow, but he also died, leaving no child. It was the same with the third. 22In fact, none of the seven left any children. Last of all, the woman died too. 23At the resurrection [d] whose wife will she be, since the seven were married to her?"

24Jesus replied, "Are you not in error because you do not know the Scriptures or the power of God? 25When the dead rise, they will neither marry nor be given in marriage; they will be like the angels in heaven. 26Now about the dead rising—have you not read in the book of Moses, in the account of the bush, how God said to him, 'I am the God of Abraham, the

---

a 25 Some manuscripts *sins.* 26*But if you do not forgive, neither will your Father who is in heaven forgive your sins.* b 10 Or *cornerstone*
c 11 Psalm 118:22,23 d 23 Some manuscripts *resurrection, when men rise from the dead,*

God of Isaac, and the God of Jacob'[a]? 27He is not the God of the dead, but of the living. You are badly mistaken!"

The Greatest Commandment

28One of the teachers of the law came and heard them debating. Noticing that Jesus had given them a good answer, he asked him, "Of all the commandments, which is the most important?"

29"The most important one," answered Jesus, "is this: 'Hear, O Israel, the Lord our God, the Lord is one.[b] 30Love the Lord your God with all your heart and with all your soul and with all your mind and with all your strength.'[c] 31The second is this: 'Love your neighbor as yourself.'[d] There is no commandment greater than these."

32"Well said, teacher," the man replied. "You are right in saying that God is one and there is no other but him. 33To love him with all your heart, with all your understanding and with all your strength, and to love your neighbor as yourself is more important than all burnt offerings and sacrifices."

34When Jesus saw that he had answered wisely, he said to him, "You are not far from the kingdom of God." And from then on no one dared ask him any more questions.

Whose Son Is the Christ?

35While Jesus was teaching in the temple courts, he asked, "How is it that the teachers of the law say that the Christ[e] is the son of David? 36David himself, speaking by the Holy Spirit, declared:

" 'The Lord said to my Lord:
"Sit at my right hand
until I put your enemies
under your feet." '[f]

37David himself calls him 'Lord.' How then can he be his son?"

The large crowd listened to him with delight.

38As he taught, Jesus said, "Watch out for the teachers of the law. They like to walk around in flowing robes and be greeted in the marketplaces, 39and have the most important seats in the synagogues and the places of honor at banquets. 40They devour widows' houses and for a show make lengthy prayers. Such men will be punished most severely."

The Widow's Offering

41Jesus sat down opposite the place where the offerings were put and watched the crowd putting their money into the temple treasury. Many rich people threw in large amounts. 42But a poor widow came and put in two very small copper coins,[g] worth only a fraction of a penny.[h]

43Calling his disciples to him, Jesus said, "I tell you the truth, this poor widow has put more into the treasury than all the others. 44They all gave out of their wealth; but she, out of her poverty, put in everything—all she had to live on."

Signs of the End of the Age

13 As he was leaving the temple, one of his disciples said to him, "Look, Teacher! What massive stones! What magnificent buildings!"

2"Do you see all these great buildings?" replied Jesus. "Not one stone here will be left on another; every one will be thrown down."

3As Jesus was sitting on the Mount of Olives opposite the temple, Peter, James, John and Andrew asked him privately, 4"Tell us, when will these things happen? And what will be the sign that they are all about to be fulfilled?"

5Jesus said to them: "Watch out that no one deceives you. 6Many will come in my name, claiming, 'I am he,' and will deceive many. 7When you hear of wars and rumors of wars, do not be alarmed. Such things must happen, but the end is still to come. 8Nation will rise against nation, and kingdom against kingdom. There will be earthquakes in various places, and famines. These are the beginning of birth pains.

9"You must be on your guard. You will be handed over to the local councils and flogged in the synagogues. On account of me you will stand before governors and kings as witnesses to them. 10And the gospel must first be preached to all nations. 11Whenever you are arrested and brought to trial, do not worry beforehand about what to say. Just say whatever is given you at the time, for it is not you speaking, but the Holy Spirit.

12"Brother will betray brother to death, and a father his child. Children will rebel against their parents and have them put to death. 13All men will hate you because of me, but he who stands firm to the end will be saved.

---

[a] *26* Exodus 3:6 [b] *29* Or *the Lord our God is one Lord* [c] *30* Deut. 6:4,5 [d] *31* Lev. 19:18 [e] *35* Or *Messiah* [f] *36* Psalm 110:1
[g] *42* Greek *two lepta* [h] *42* Greek *kodrantes*

THURSDAY

READ MARK 12:28–34

IT'S NOT ABOUT ME

A few years ago during a shopping trip to the mall, my daughter spotted a T-shirt that read "It's all about me."

She held it out and said, "Mom, you should get this."

We both laughed, but she spoke the truth. It's always about *me.*

It's that way with many of us. We are experts at loving ourselves. We know what we like and what we don't like and will go to great lengths and sacrifice a lot to make sure our wants and needs are met.

Nobody has to teach us self-preservation. We don't need a "how to love yourself" seminar. Self-protection is instinctive, as natural as shopping.

Then we get married and suddenly there are two people who believe "It's all about me." That's either a recipe for conflict or an opportunity for learning what Jesus commands: "Love the Lord your God with all your heart and with all your soul and with all your mind and with all your strength" and "Love your neighbor as yourself" (Mark 12:30–31). The teacher of the law wisely responded that loving in this way "is more important than all burnt offerings and sacrifices" (verse 33); that is, loving sacrificially and personally is more important than offering mere gestures.

When it comes to loving my husband, I've never set fire to a bull as a sacrifice, but I have done some things out of sheer outward showiness. For example, I tell myself, and even my husband, that the new outfit I bought for myself is really for him, since it helps him feel good about having a well-dressed wife. But that's a blatant case of "It's all about me" run amok, and we both know it.

Likewise, what if my husband, who is a rabid football fan, presented me with the gift of a pigskin personally autographed by Joe Montana? That would be nice, but who's Joe Montana?

In either scenario, our offerings are for ourselves, not the other person. Instead, loving my husband as much as I love myself begins with becoming a student of him and discovering what love means to him. In our marriage, loving my husband means putting the hammer back in its spot in the garage after I use it, not complaining about whiskers in the bathroom sink, remembering to mail the electric bill, keeping my car clean and cooking veggies he likes (but I don't).

Likewise, my husband loves me by listening to me talk about my day without interrupting me, packing my lunch in the mornings before work, separating the laundry into whites and colors, and recycling his empty soda bottles.

Sure, we've loved each other by sitting with each other in the hospital and weathering storms together, but it's when we do the seemingly insignificant, everyday things for each other that we each feel most cherished. That's when we learn that love means "It's all about you."

—NANCY KENNEDY

"Love your neighbor as yourself."

— MARK 12:31

let's talk

- ✦ Expressions of love mean different things to different people. What does love mean to each of us?
- ✦ Discuss the ways I get it right in expressing love to you. How about how you get it right in showing love to me?
- ✦ What are some ways we can love each other better?

FOR YOUR NEXT DEVOTIONAL READING, TURN TO PAGE 1131.

14“When you see ‘the abomination that causes desolation’[a] standing where it[b] does not belong—let the reader understand—then let those who are in Judea flee to the mountains. 15Let no one on the roof of his house go down or enter the house to take anything out. 16Let no one in the field go back to get his cloak. 17How dreadful it will be in those days for pregnant women and nursing mothers! 18Pray that this will not take place in winter, 19because those will be days of distress unequaled from the beginning, when God created the world, until now—and never to be equaled again. 20If the Lord had not cut short those days, no one would survive. But for the sake of the elect, whom he has chosen, he has shortened them. 21At that time if anyone says to you, ‘Look, here is the Christ[c]!’ or, ‘Look, there he is!’ do not believe it. 22For false Christs and false prophets will appear and perform signs and miracles to deceive the elect—if that were possible. 23So be on your guard; I have told you everything ahead of time.

24“But in those days, following that distress,

“ ‘the sun will be darkened,
and the moon will not give its light;
25the stars will fall from the sky,
and the heavenly bodies will be
shaken.’[d]

26“At that time men will see the Son of Man coming in clouds with great power and glory. 27And he will send his angels and gather his elect from the four winds, from the ends of the earth to the ends of the heavens.

28“Now learn this lesson from the fig tree: As soon as its twigs get tender and its leaves come out, you know that summer is near. 29Even so, when you see these things happening, you know that it is near, right at the door. 30I tell you the truth, this generation[e] will certainly not pass away until all these things have happened. 31Heaven and earth will pass away, but my words will never pass away.

The Day and Hour Unknown

32“No one knows about that day or hour, not even the angels in heaven, nor the Son, but only the Father. 33Be on guard! Be alert[f]! You do not know when that time will come. 34It’s like a man going away: He leaves his house and puts his servants in charge, each with his assigned task, and tells the one at the door to keep watch.

35“Therefore keep watch because you do not know when the owner of the house will come back—whether in the evening, or at midnight, or when the rooster crows, or at dawn. 36If he comes suddenly, do not let him find you sleeping. 37What I say to you, I say to everyone: ‘Watch!’ ”

Jesus Anointed at Bethany

14 Now the Passover and the Feast of Unleavened Bread were only two days away, and the chief priests and the teachers of the law were looking for some sly way to arrest Jesus and kill him. 2“But not during the Feast,” they said, “or the people may riot.”

3While he was in Bethany, reclining at the table in the home of a man known as Simon the Leper, a woman came with an alabaster jar of very expensive perfume, made of pure nard. She broke the jar and poured the perfume on his head.

4Some of those present were saying indignantly to one another, “Why this waste of perfume? 5It could have been sold for more than a year’s wages[g] and the money given to the poor.” And they rebuked her harshly.

6“Leave her alone,” said Jesus. “Why are you bothering her? She has done a beautiful thing to me. 7The poor you will always have with you, and you can help them any time you want. But you will not always have me. 8She did what she could. She poured perfume on my body beforehand to prepare for my burial. 9I tell you the truth, wherever the gospel is preached throughout the world, what she has done will also be told, in memory of her.”

10Then Judas Iscariot, one of the Twelve, went to the chief priests to betray Jesus to them. 11They were delighted to hear this and promised to give him money. So he watched for an opportunity to hand him over.

The Lord’s Supper

12On the first day of the Feast of Unleavened Bread, when it was customary to sacrifice the Passover lamb, Jesus’ disciples asked him, “Where do you want us to go and make preparations for you to eat the Passover?”

13So he sent two of his disciples, telling them, “Go into the city, and a man carrying a jar of water will meet you. Follow him. 14Say to the owner of the house he enters, ‘The Teacher asks: Where is my guest room, where I may eat the Passover with my disciples?’ 15He will

a 14 Daniel 9:27; 11:31; 12:11 *b* 14 Or *he*; also in verse 29 *c* 21 Or *Messiah* *d* 25 Isaiah 13:10; 34:4 *e* 30 Or *race* *f* 33 Some manuscripts *alert and pray* *g* 5 Greek *than three hundred denarii*

show you a large upper room, furnished and ready. Make preparations for us there."

[16]The disciples left, went into the city and found things just as Jesus had told them. So they prepared the Passover.

[17]When evening came, Jesus arrived with the Twelve. [18]While they were reclining at the table eating, he said, "I tell you the truth, one of you will betray me—one who is eating with me."

[19]They were saddened, and one by one they said to him, "Surely not I?"

[20]"It is one of the Twelve," he replied, "one who dips bread into the bowl with me. [21]The Son of Man will go just as it is written about him. But woe to that man who betrays the Son of Man! It would be better for him if he had not been born."

[22]While they were eating, Jesus took bread, gave thanks and broke it, and gave it to his disciples, saying, "Take it; this is my body."

[23]Then he took the cup, gave thanks and offered it to them, and they all drank from it.

[24]"This is my blood of the[a] covenant, which is poured out for many," he said to them. [25]"I tell you the truth, I will not drink again of the fruit of the vine until that day when I drink it anew in the kingdom of God."

[26]When they had sung a hymn, they went out to the Mount of Olives.

Jesus Predicts Peter's Denial

[27]"You will all fall away," Jesus told them, "for it is written:

" 'I will strike the shepherd,
and the sheep will be scattered.'[b]

[28]But after I have risen, I will go ahead of you into Galilee."

[29]Peter declared, "Even if all fall away, I will not."

[30]"I tell you the truth," Jesus answered, "today—yes, tonight—before the rooster crows twice[c] you yourself will disown me three times."

[31]But Peter insisted emphatically, "Even if I have to die with you, I will never disown you." And all the others said the same.

Gethsemane

[32]They went to a place called Gethsemane, and Jesus said to his disciples, "Sit here while I pray." [33]He took Peter, James and John along with him, and he began to be deeply distressed and troubled. [34]"My soul is overwhelmed with sorrow to the point of death," he said to them. "Stay here and keep watch."

[35]Going a little farther, he fell to the ground and prayed that if possible the hour might pass from him. [36]"*Abba*,[d] Father," he said, "everything is possible for you. Take this cup from me. Yet not what I will, but what you will."

[37]Then he returned to his disciples and found them sleeping. "Simon," he said to Peter, "are you asleep? Could you not keep watch for one hour? [38]Watch and pray so that you will not fall into temptation. The spirit is willing, but the body is weak."

[39]Once more he went away and prayed the same thing. [40]When he came back, he again found them sleeping, because their eyes were heavy. They did not know what to say to him.

[41]Returning the third time, he said to them, "Are you still sleeping and resting? Enough! The hour has come. Look, the Son of Man is betrayed into the hands of sinners. [42]Rise! Let us go! Here comes my betrayer!"

Jesus Arrested

[43]Just as he was speaking, Judas, one of the Twelve, appeared. With him was a crowd armed with swords and clubs, sent from the chief priests, the teachers of the law, and the elders.

[44]Now the betrayer had arranged a signal with them: "The one I kiss is the man; arrest him and lead him away under guard." [45]Going at once to Jesus, Judas said, "Rabbi!" and kissed him. [46]The men seized Jesus and arrested him. [47]Then one of those standing near drew his sword and struck the servant of the high priest, cutting off his ear.

[48]"Am I leading a rebellion," said Jesus, "that you have come out with swords and clubs to capture me? [49]Every day I was with you, teaching in the temple courts, and you did not arrest me. But the Scriptures must be fulfilled." [50]Then everyone deserted him and fled.

[51]A young man, wearing nothing but a linen garment, was following Jesus. When they seized him, [52]he fled naked, leaving his garment behind.

Before the Sanhedrin

[53]They took Jesus to the high priest, and all the chief priests, elders and teachers of the law came together. [54]Peter followed him at a distance, right into the courtyard of the

[a] 24 Some manuscripts *the new* [b] 27 Zech. 13:7 [c] 30 Some early manuscripts do not have *twice.* [d] 36 Aramaic for *Father*

high priest. There he sat with the guards and warmed himself at the fire.

55The chief priests and the whole Sanhedrin were looking for evidence against Jesus so that they could put him to death, but they did not find any. 56Many testified falsely against him, but their statements did not agree.

57Then some stood up and gave this false testimony against him: 58"We heard him say, 'I will destroy this man-made temple and in three days will build another, not made by man.' " 59Yet even then their testimony did not agree.

60Then the high priest stood up before them and asked Jesus, "Are you not going to answer? What is this testimony that these men are bringing against you?" 61But Jesus remained silent and gave no answer.

Again the high priest asked him, "Are you the Christ,[a] the Son of the Blessed One?"

62"I am," said Jesus. "And you will see the Son of Man sitting at the right hand of the Mighty One and coming on the clouds of heaven."

63The high priest tore his clothes. "Why do we need any more witnesses?" he asked. 64"You have heard the blasphemy. What do you think?"

They all condemned him as worthy of death. 65Then some began to spit at him; they blindfolded him, struck him with their fists, and said, "Prophesy!" And the guards took him and beat him.

Peter Disowns Jesus

66While Peter was below in the courtyard, one of the servant girls of the high priest came by. 67When she saw Peter warming himself, she looked closely at him.

"You also were with that Nazarene, Jesus," she said.

68But he denied it. "I don't know or understand what you're talking about," he said, and went out into the entryway.[b]

69When the servant girl saw him there, she said again to those standing around, "This fellow is one of them." 70Again he denied it.

After a little while, those standing near said to Peter, "Surely you are one of them, for you are a Galilean."

71He began to call down curses on himself, and he swore to them, "I don't know this man you're talking about."

72Immediately the rooster crowed the second time.[c] Then Peter remembered the word Jesus had spoken to him: "Before the rooster crows twice[d] you will disown me three times." And he broke down and wept.

Jesus Before Pilate

15 Very early in the morning, the chief priests, with the elders, the teachers of the law and the whole Sanhedrin, reached a decision. They bound Jesus, led him away and handed him over to Pilate.

2"Are you the king of the Jews?" asked Pilate.

"Yes, it is as you say," Jesus replied.

3The chief priests accused him of many things. 4So again Pilate asked him, "Aren't you going to answer? See how many things they are accusing you of."

5But Jesus still made no reply, and Pilate was amazed.

6Now it was the custom at the Feast to release a prisoner whom the people requested. 7A man called Barabbas was in prison with the insurrectionists who had committed murder in the uprising. 8The crowd came up and asked Pilate to do for them what he usually did.

9"Do you want me to release to you the king of the Jews?" asked Pilate, 10knowing it was out of envy that the chief priests had handed Jesus over to him. 11But the chief priests stirred up the crowd to have Pilate release Barabbas instead.

12"What shall I do, then, with the one you call the king of the Jews?" Pilate asked them.

13"Crucify him!" they shouted.

14"Why? What crime has he committed?" asked Pilate.

But they shouted all the louder, "Crucify him!"

15Wanting to satisfy the crowd, Pilate released Barabbas to them. He had Jesus flogged, and handed him over to be crucified.

The Soldiers Mock Jesus

16The soldiers led Jesus away into the palace (that is, the Praetorium) and called together the whole company of soldiers. 17They put a purple robe on him, then twisted together a crown of thorns and set it on him. 18And they began to call out to him, "Hail, king of the Jews!" 19Again and again they struck him on the head with a staff and spit on him. Falling on their knees, they paid homage to him. 20And when they had mocked him, they took

[a] 61 Or *Messiah* [b] 68 Some early manuscripts *entryway and the rooster crowed* [c] 72 Some early manuscripts do not have *the second time.* [d] 72 Some early manuscripts do not have *twice.*

off the purple robe and put his own clothes on him. Then they led him out to crucify him.

The Crucifixion

21A certain man from Cyrene, Simon, the father of Alexander and Rufus, was passing by on his way in from the country, and they forced him to carry the cross. 22They brought Jesus to the place called Golgotha (which means The Place of the Skull). 23Then they offered him wine mixed with myrrh, but he did not take it. 24And they crucified him. Dividing up his clothes, they cast lots to see what each would get.

25It was the third hour when they crucified him. 26The written notice of the charge against him read: THE KING OF THE JEWS. 27They crucified two robbers with him, one on his right and one on his left.[a] 29Those who passed by hurled insults at him, shaking their heads and saying, "So! You who are going to destroy the temple and build it in three days, 30come down from the cross and save yourself!"

31In the same way the chief priests and the teachers of the law mocked him among themselves. "He saved others," they said, "but he can't save himself! 32Let this Christ,[b] this King of Israel, come down now from the cross, that we may see and believe." Those crucified with him also heaped insults on him.

The Death of Jesus

33At the sixth hour darkness came over the whole land until the ninth hour. 34And at the ninth hour Jesus cried out in a loud voice, *"Eloi, Eloi, lama sabachthani?"*—which means, "My God, my God, why have you forsaken me?"[c]

35When some of those standing near heard this, they said, "Listen, he's calling Elijah."

36One man ran, filled a sponge with wine vinegar, put it on a stick, and offered it to Jesus to drink. "Now leave him alone. Let's see if Elijah comes to take him down," he said.

37With a loud cry, Jesus breathed his last.

38The curtain of the temple was torn in two from top to bottom. 39And when the centurion, who stood there in front of Jesus, heard his cry and[d] saw how he died, he said, "Surely this man was the Son[e] of God!"

40Some women were watching from a distance. Among them were Mary Magdalene, Mary the mother of James the younger and of Joses, and Salome. 41In Galilee these women had followed him and cared for his needs. Many other women who had come up with him to Jerusalem were also there.

The Burial of Jesus

42It was Preparation Day (that is, the day before the Sabbath). So as evening approached, 43Joseph of Arimathea, a prominent member of the Council, who was himself waiting for the kingdom of God, went boldly to Pilate and asked for Jesus' body. 44Pilate was surprised to hear that he was already dead. Summoning the centurion, he asked him if Jesus had already died. 45When he learned from the centurion that it was so, he gave the body to Joseph. 46So Joseph bought some linen cloth, took down the body, wrapped it in the linen, and placed it in a tomb cut out of rock. Then he rolled a stone against the entrance of the tomb. 47Mary Magdalene and Mary the mother of Joses saw where he was laid.

The Resurrection

16 When the Sabbath was over, Mary Magdalene, Mary the mother of James, and Salome bought spices so that they might go to anoint Jesus' body. 2Very early on the first day of the week, just after sunrise, they were on their way to the tomb 3and they asked each other, "Who will roll the stone away from the entrance of the tomb?"

4But when they looked up, they saw that the stone, which was very large, had been rolled away. 5As they entered the tomb, they saw a young man dressed in a white robe sitting on the right side, and they were alarmed.

6"Don't be alarmed," he said. "You are looking for Jesus the Nazarene, who was crucified. He has risen! He is not here. See the place where they laid him. 7But go, tell his disciples and Peter, 'He is going ahead of you into Galilee. There you will see him, just as he told you.' "

8Trembling and bewildered, the women went out and fled from the tomb. They said nothing to anyone, because they were afraid.

[The earliest manuscripts and some other ancient witnesses do not have Mark 16:9-20.]

9When Jesus rose early on the first day of the week, he appeared first to Mary Magdalene, out of whom he had driven seven demons. 10She went and told those who had been with him and who were mourning and

---

[a] 27 Some manuscripts *left,* [28]*and the scripture was fulfilled which says, "He was counted with the lawless ones"* (Isaiah 53:12)
[b] 32 Or *Messiah* [c] 34 Psalm 22:1 [d] 39 Some manuscripts do not have *heard his cry and* [e] 39 Or *a son*

weeping. [11]When they heard that Jesus was alive and that she had seen him, they did not believe it.

[12]Afterward Jesus appeared in a different form to two of them while they were walking in the country. [13]These returned and reported it to the rest; but they did not believe them either.

[14]Later Jesus appeared to the Eleven as they were eating; he rebuked them for their lack of faith and their stubborn refusal to believe those who had seen him after he had risen.

[15]He said to them, "Go into all the world and preach the good news to all creation. [16]Whoever believes and is baptized will be saved, but whoever does not believe will be condemned. [17]And these signs will accompany those who believe: In my name they will drive out demons; they will speak in new tongues; [18]they will pick up snakes with their hands; and when they drink deadly poison, it will not hurt them at all; they will place their hands on sick people, and they will get well."

[19]After the Lord Jesus had spoken to them, he was taken up into heaven and he sat at the right hand of God. [20]Then the disciples went out and preached everywhere, and the Lord worked with them and confirmed his word by the signs that accompanied it.

LUKE

Luke

QUICK FACTS

AUTHOR Luke, a physician and Gentile Christian

AUDIENCE Specifically Theophilus, but also the whole world

DATE Probably about A.D. 60

SETTING Written from Rome or perhaps Caesarea, Achaia or Ephesus

The book of Luke gives us a more complete account of Jesus' life than any other Gospel. It is intended to be read alongside Luke's other account, the book of Acts, to give a comprehensive view of the beginnings of Christianity. Luke addressed his Gospel to Theophilus, a Gentile believer of high standing, and included information he felt every believer should know.

Luke was a Gentile physician and one of Paul's missionary companions. Although he was not an eyewitness to the events he recorded in his Gospel, he gathered his material from firsthand accounts of those who were there (see Luke 1:2–3). His Gospel reads like a modern biography, covering the details of Jesus' life from his birth to his ascension into heaven. Luke had a special interest in showing Jesus' concern for all people—Gentiles as well as Jews, women, children, the poor and the outcasts of society.

Jesus' life and teachings are also applicable to our daily walk as Christian husbands and wives. For example, Jesus' teaching on prayer (see chapter 11) is a helpful passage to focus on as we pray daily that God will transform us into Christ's image.

Introduction

1 Many have undertaken to draw up an
account of the things that have been fulfilled[a] among us, 2just as they were handed
down to us by those who from the first were
eyewitnesses and servants of the word. 3There-
fore, since I myself have carefully investigated everything from the beginning, it seemed
good also to me to write an orderly account
for you, most excellent Theophilus, 4so that
you may know the certainty of the things you
have been taught.

The Birth of John the Baptist Foretold

5In the time of Herod king of Judea there
was a priest named Zechariah, who belonged
to the priestly division of Abijah; his wife Elizabeth was also a descendant of Aaron. 6Both
of them were upright in the sight of God,
observing all the Lord's commandments and
regulations blamelessly. 7But they had no children, because Elizabeth was barren; and they
were both well along in years.

8Once when Zechariah's division was on
duty and he was serving as priest before God,
9he was chosen by lot, according to the custom of the priesthood, to go into the temple
of the Lord and burn incense. 10And when the
time for the burning of incense came, all the
assembled worshipers were praying outside.

11Then an angel of the Lord appeared to
him, standing at the right side of the altar of
incense. 12When Zechariah saw him, he was
startled and was gripped with fear. 13But the
angel said to him: "Do not be afraid, Zechariah; your prayer has been heard. Your wife Elizabeth will bear you a son, and you are to give
him the name John. 14He will be a joy and
delight to you, and many will rejoice because
of his birth, 15for he will be great in the sight
of the Lord. He is never to take wine or other fermented drink, and he will be filled with
the Holy Spirit even from birth.[b] 16Many of
the people of Israel will he bring back to the
Lord their God. 17And he will go on before
the Lord, in the spirit and power of Elijah, to
turn the hearts of the fathers to their children
and the disobedient to the wisdom of the righteous—to make ready a people prepared for
the Lord."

18Zechariah asked the angel, "How can I be
sure of this? I am an old man and my wife is
well along in years."

19The angel answered, "I am Gabriel. I
stand in the presence of God, and I have been
sent to speak to you and to tell you this good
news. 20And now you will be silent and not
able to speak until the day this happens, because you did not believe my words, which
will come true at their proper time."

21Meanwhile, the people were waiting for
Zechariah and wondering why he stayed so
long in the temple. 22When he came out, he
could not speak to them. They realized he had
seen a vision in the temple, for he kept making
signs to them but remained unable to speak.

23When his time of service was completed,
he returned home. 24After this his wife Elizabeth became pregnant and for five months
remained in seclusion. 25"The Lord has done
this for me," she said. "In these days he has
shown his favor and taken away my disgrace
among the people."

The Birth of Jesus Foretold

26In the sixth month, God sent the angel
Gabriel to Nazareth, a town in Galilee, 27to a
virgin pledged to be married to a man named
Joseph, a descendant of David. The virgin's
name was Mary. 28The angel went to her and
said, "Greetings, you who are highly favored!
The Lord is with you."

29Mary was greatly troubled at his words
and wondered what kind of greeting this
might be. 30But the angel said to her, "Do not
be afraid, Mary, you have found favor with
God. 31You will be with child and give birth
to a son, and you are to give him the name
Jesus. 32He will be great and will be called the
Son of the Most High. The Lord God will give
him the throne of his father David, 33and he
will reign over the house of Jacob forever; his
kingdom will never end."

34"How will this be," Mary asked the angel,
"since I am a virgin?"

35The angel answered, "The Holy Spirit will
come upon you, and the power of the Most
High will overshadow you. So the holy one to
be born will be called[c] the Son of God. 36Even
Elizabeth your relative is going to have a child
in her old age, and she who was said to be
barren is in her sixth month. 37For nothing is
impossible with God."

38"I am the Lord's servant," Mary answered.
"May it be to me as you have said." Then the
angel left her.

Mary Visits Elizabeth

39At that time Mary got ready and hurried
to a town in the hill country of Judea, 40where

[a] 1 Or *been surely believed* [b] 15 Or *from his mother's womb* [c] 35 Or *So the child to be born will be called holy,*

F

FRIDAY

READ LUKE 1:5–25,57–80

HAVING AND RAISING GOOD KIDS

The Second World War was thundering to a close when the young soldier stepped onto the troop carrier that would carry him from the United States to Europe. Halfway across the Atlantic, word arrived that an armistice had been signed. The war with Germany was over.

Of course, the ship could not turn around; there were clean-up operations to be done in Europe. So the ship kept going, and the young man did his duty.

After his tour was over, the soldier married his sweetheart back home. It took some time to find work, but they finally found employment at a farm. Growing a family was more important to them, though, than raising crops. Unfortunately, after years of trying, they learned they were not likely to have children.

They prayed that God would trump the doctor's word. Against human odds, a healthy baby girl was born in the fifth year of their marriage. A baby boy followed, then three more girls and another boy.

The couple had a good life on the farm, but none of their six children followed them into the family business. Instead, the four daughters became teachers in Christian schools. One son wed a doctor, and together they have been active in cross-cultural mission efforts; the other son became a pastor and Bible teacher.

To this day the postwar couple shrug when asked how it all came about. "We just begged God to give us kids," they say. "Then we learned to pray for our children every day."

I know. I'm their eldest son. And I'm only now beginning to realize how much my parents were like the infertile couple Elizabeth and Zechariah, who one day felt ecstasy as well as fear when God actually answered their prayers for a child. They could only vow to do their best and ask for God's help.

There is no magic formula for having kids, let alone having them turn out well. Many couples remain childless after years of agonizing prayer. And even miracle children, bathed in spiritual significance, carry with them no guarantees of piety. The old priest Zechariah and his wife celebrated the day of John's birth. But what did they think when their son lived like a wild man in the desert, provoking the wrath of Jewish leaders and priests with his scathing sermons and unorthodox baptisms? Were they alive when their son was imprisoned, then beheaded?

Should we stop asking for children because they bring pain into our lives? No. This story and others remind us that we live in a broken world in which we depend on one another for encouragement when the waiting is long or when children don't turn out the way we had hoped. With the help of others, and with God's encouragement and strength, we can have hope.

—WAYNE BROUWER

"Do not be afraid, Zechariah; your prayer has been heard. Your wife Elizabeth will bear you a son, and you are to give him the name John."

— LUKE 1:13

let's talk

✦ How do Christian couples spiritually prepare to have children? What are some requests we make of God? What happens when the waiting is long—where do we go for help?

✦ In what formal way do we declare that our children belong to God? How will these ceremonies be carried out? What part will our parents and friends play in them?

✦ What plans are we making to educate our children in the ways of the Lord? Who, besides us, is responsible for their ongoing instruction?

FOR YOUR NEXT DEVOTIONAL READING, TURN TO PAGE 1132.

WEEKEND

couple friends

Most couples never raise the question of how their friends affect their marriage. They assume, and often rightly so, that friends are a positive factor in both their personal and marital lives. Yet many couples' marriages are marred or threatened by so-called friends. The friend may not even be aware of the damage he or she is causing.

There are a number of other ways in which friends can be detrimental to your marriage. One is when a friend, whether same-sex or opposite, becomes your main confidant. That kind of sharing is what builds true and deep intimacy. When you confide your concerns and fears, your hopes and dreams, your struggles and temptations with a friend to the exclusion of your spouse, you forge your strongest bonds of intimacy with the friend. And that is potentially harmful for your marriage.

Another way in which friends can hurt your marriage is by consuming too much of your discretionary time. Couple time—the time you spend together connecting with each other and nurturing your relationship—is at a premium for most of us. Friends who expect or demand so much of your time that they deprive you of couple time are foes to your marriage.

Choose friends who help you feel better about yourself and make you a better mate. In the early years of her 11-year marriage, Melissa, whose parents divorced when she was 8, had little confidence in her ability to be a good wife. Her self-doubts tarnished the quality of her intimacy with her husband, John. It was only after she became good friends with Susan that Melissa began to change. Susan kept pointing out the ways in which Melissa was a great catch for any man, and the many ways she was a good wife. Susan helped Melissa feel good about her marriage. As Melissa's self-doubts receded, her marriage improved.

Hopefully, you have marriage-enhancing friends. If so, cherish them; if not, cultivate them. A good place to begin is to ask the following questions about current or potential friends:

- Do they enjoy the kind of activities and conversation that strengthen marriage?
- Do they make you feel better about your spouse?
- Do they respect and support your need for couple time?
- Do they celebrate marriage as a rich human experience?

If you have to say no to any of these questions, take care. Such friends could be foes of your marriage.

Where do you find friends who will enhance your marriage? Both individual and couple friends can be found in a variety of places: in church groups and classes; at marriage-enrichment weekends; at work, when you find a colleague who talks positively about his or her spouse and the joys of marriage; at local clubs where couples come together, such as book groups; at social events; at school gatherings such as the PTA; at Little League games where parents come to watch their children; and in the neighborhood where others live who are marriage and family oriented.

You may have to initiate the friendship by inviting a couple to dinner or to a church event. You may have to endure a few efforts that fall flat. But be persistent. Sooner or later your efforts will pay off with new, marriage-enhancing friends who will both enrich you personally and strengthen your bond with each other.

—JEANETTE C. AND ROBERT H. LAUER

looking for a friend

Spend a few minutes jotting down the characteristics of the ideal friend for your spouse. Ask your spouse to do the same for you. Use the following questions as a guide.

1. What kinds of things would your spouse and a friend enjoy doing together?
2. How much time could they realistically spend together without cutting into marriage time?
3. How much time might they spend on the phone?
4. What hobbies, music or movie tastes would they share?
5. How would the friend encourage your spouse?
6. How would the friend support your marriage?

Exchange lists with your spouse and explain why you wrote what you did. Discuss whether your partner has a friend who meets these criteria. If not, offer suggestions for developing such a friendship. Look for ways to affirm and support your partner's friendships while modeling friendship by being your spouse's best friend.

HOW ARE WE DOING?

let's make a DATE

EXPANDING FRIENDSHIPS

Plan a date when you can introduce your spouse to a new friend's spouse. Get together for a meal or an activity that gives everyone time to interact. Go to dinner, go bowling or host a game night at your house. Make sure your spouse doesn't feel left out by having private laughs with your pal. Instead make it your goal to focus conversation on interests or hobbies that the four of you can share. Just think, if the spouses hit it off, your partner may want to spend more time with you and your friends!

FOR YOUR NEXT DEVOTIONAL READING, TURN TO PAGE 1136.

LESSONS FROM THE *Bible*

Jesus was friends with three siblings, Mary, Martha and Lazarus (see Luke 10:38–42; John 11:1–44; 12:1–3). What can we learn about friendship from this example?

she entered Zechariah's home and greeted
Elizabeth. 41When Elizabeth heard Mary's
greeting, the baby leaped in her womb, and
Elizabeth was filled with the Holy Spirit. 42In
a loud voice she exclaimed: "Blessed are you
among women, and blessed is the child you
will bear! 43But why am I so favored, that the
mother of my Lord should come to me? 44As
soon as the sound of your greeting reached
my ears, the baby in my womb leaped for joy.
45Blessed is she who has believed that what the
Lord has said to her will be accomplished!"

Mary's Song

46And Mary said:

"My soul glorifies the Lord
47 and my spirit rejoices in God my
Savior,
48 for he has been mindful
of the humble state of his servant.
From now on all generations will call me
blessed,
49 for the Mighty One has done great
things for me—
holy is his name.
50 His mercy extends to those who fear him,
from generation to generation.
51 He has performed mighty deeds with his
arm;
he has scattered those who are proud in
their inmost thoughts.
52 He has brought down rulers from their
thrones
but has lifted up the humble.
53 He has filled the hungry with good things
but has sent the rich away empty.
54 He has helped his servant Israel,
remembering to be merciful
55 to Abraham and his descendants forever,
even as he said to our fathers."

56Mary stayed with Elizabeth for about
three months and then returned home.

The Birth of John the Baptist

57When it was time for Elizabeth to have
her baby, she gave birth to a son. 58Her neighbors and relatives heard that the Lord had
shown her great mercy, and they shared her
joy.

59On the eighth day they came to circumcise the child, and they were going to name
him after his father Zechariah, 60but his
mother spoke up and said, "No! He is to be
called John."

61They said to her, "There is no one among
your relatives who has that name."

62Then they made signs to his father, to
find out what he would like to name the child.
63He asked for a writing tablet, and to everyone's astonishment he wrote, "His name is
John." 64Immediately his mouth was opened
and his tongue was loosed, and he began to
speak, praising God. 65The neighbors were all
filled with awe, and throughout the hill country of Judea people were talking about all these
things. 66Everyone who heard this wondered
about it, asking, "What then is this child going to be?" For the Lord's hand was with him.

Zechariah's Song

67His father Zechariah was filled with the
Holy Spirit and prophesied:

68 "Praise be to the Lord, the God of Israel,
because he has come and has redeemed
his people.
69 He has raised up a horn[a] of salvation for
us
in the house of his servant David
70 (as he said through his holy prophets of
long ago),
71 salvation from our enemies
and from the hand of all who hate us—
72 to show mercy to our fathers
and to remember his holy covenant,
73 the oath he swore to our father
Abraham:
74 to rescue us from the hand of our enemies,
and to enable us to serve him without
fear
75 in holiness and righteousness before
him all our days.

76 And you, my child, will be called a
prophet of the Most High;
for you will go on before the Lord to
prepare the way for him,
77 to give his people the knowledge of
salvation
through the forgiveness of their sins,
78 because of the tender mercy of our God,
by which the rising sun will come to us
from heaven
79 to shine on those living in darkness
and in the shadow of death,
to guide our feet into the path of peace."

80And the child grew and became strong in
spirit; and he lived in the desert until he appeared publicly to Israel.

---

[a] 69 *Horn* here symbolizes strength.

The Birth of Jesus

2 In those days Caesar Augustus issued a decree that a census should be taken of the entire Roman world. 2(This was the first census that took place while Quirinius was governor of Syria.) 3And everyone went to his own town to register.

4So Joseph also went up from the town of Nazareth in Galilee to Judea, to Bethlehem the town of David, because he belonged to the house and line of David. 5He went there to register with Mary, who was pledged to be married to him and was expecting a child. 6While they were there, the time came for the baby to be born, 7and she gave birth to her firstborn, a son. She wrapped him in cloths and placed him in a manger, because there was no room for them in the inn.

The Shepherds and the Angels

8And there were shepherds living out in the fields nearby, keeping watch over their flocks at night. 9An angel of the Lord appeared to them, and the glory of the Lord shone around them, and they were terrified. 10But the angel said to them, "Do not be afraid. I bring you good news of great joy that will be for all the people. 11Today in the town of David a Savior has been born to you; he is Christ[a] the Lord. 12This will be a sign to you: You will find a baby wrapped in cloths and lying in a manger."

13Suddenly a great company of the heavenly host appeared with the angel, praising God and saying,

14"Glory to God in the highest,
and on earth peace to men on whom
his favor rests."

15When the angels had left them and gone into heaven, the shepherds said to one another, "Let's go to Bethlehem and see this thing that has happened, which the Lord has told us about."

16So they hurried off and found Mary and Joseph, and the baby, who was lying in the manger. 17When they had seen him, they spread the word concerning what had been told them about this child, 18and all who heard it were amazed at what the shepherds said to them. 19But Mary treasured up all these things and pondered them in her heart. 20The shepherds returned, glorifying and praising God for all the things they had heard and seen, which were just as they had been told.

Jesus Presented in the Temple

21On the eighth day, when it was time to circumcise him, he was named Jesus, the name the angel had given him before he had been conceived.

22When the time of their purification according to the Law of Moses had been completed, Joseph and Mary took him to Jerusalem to present him to the Lord 23(as it is written in the Law of the Lord, "Every firstborn male is to be consecrated to the Lord"[b]), 24and to offer a sacrifice in keeping with what is said in the Law of the Lord: "a pair of doves or two young pigeons."[c]

25Now there was a man in Jerusalem called Simeon, who was righteous and devout. He was waiting for the consolation of Israel, and the Holy Spirit was upon him. 26It had been revealed to him by the Holy Spirit that he would not die before he had seen the Lord's Christ. 27Moved by the Spirit, he went into the temple courts. When the parents brought in the child Jesus to do for him what the custom of the Law required, 28Simeon took him in his arms and praised God, saying:

29"Sovereign Lord, as you have promised,
you now dismiss[d] your servant in peace.
30For my eyes have seen your salvation,
31 which you have prepared in the sight of all people,
32a light for revelation to the Gentiles
and for glory to your people Israel."

33The child's father and mother marveled at what was said about him. 34Then Simeon blessed them and said to Mary, his mother: "This child is destined to cause the falling and rising of many in Israel, and to be a sign that will be spoken against, 35so that the thoughts of many hearts will be revealed. And a sword will pierce your own soul too."

36There was also a prophetess, Anna, the daughter of Phanuel, of the tribe of Asher. She was very old; she had lived with her husband seven years after her marriage, 37and then was a widow until she was eighty-four.[e] She never left the temple but worshiped night and day, fasting and praying. 38Coming up to them at that very moment, she gave thanks to God and spoke about the child to all who were looking forward to the redemption of Jerusalem.

39When Joseph and Mary had done everything required by the Law of the Lord, they returned to Galilee to their own town of Naza-

[a] *11* Or *Messiah.* "The Christ" (Greek) and "the Messiah" (Hebrew) both mean "the Anointed One"; also in verse 26.
[b] *23* Exodus 13:2,12 [c] *24* Lev. 12:8 [d] *29* Or *promised, / now dismiss* [e] *37* Or *widow for eighty-four years*

MONDAY
READ LUKE 2:1–20

OVERCOMING A ROCKY START

Paul and I married less than a year after we met. The aunts who had not met my fiancé were certain there was a baby on the way. By the time Brian was born five years later, the rumors had evaporated.

Mary and Joseph had no such grace period. True, they were engaged—which in those days was something like being married without living together—but sex during that time was definitely out of the question. So when the angel Gabriel told Mary she would have a baby before her wedding, she knew what that might cost her.

People would assume that she and Joseph had "done it," of course. Her parents—who are never mentioned in Scripture—would be so shamed that they'd send her off to relatives. And Joseph—what would this godly man think? Would he file for divorce (necessary in those days to nullify an engagement), citing Scriptural grounds of infidelity?

It was a rocky start. In addition to all the other adjustments young couples face, like stretching a budget, dealing with in-laws and outfitting a house, they had to deal with the averted faces of people who assumed the worst about them. How could they possibly explain an angel to skeptics?

The trip to Bethlehem might have offered a kind of relief from all that. True, the final weeks of pregnancy were a horrific time to travel. So too was giving birth in a filthy stable (likely in a cave), then allowing strangers rather than family and friends to gawk at the baby. Still, Mary could simply wonder at her newborn's eyes, his nose, his perfect little toes. "Child of my flesh, yet Son of the Most High!"

I once interviewed a lady in Mississippi who helped start the Garden Club Tours of antebellum homes after the Civil War. Though she was nearly a hundred years old, she refused to admit it. "A lady nevah gives huh age," she told me. Her daughter, who was pushing 80, said it was a cover-up. "Mama thinks if she gives her age, people will figure out that I was untimely born," she said.

The first year of marriage, they say, is the hardest. But adding an "untimely birth" to the mix of adjustments only adds to the difficulty. Like Mary and Joseph, we are troubled by the implications. We cringe at the thought of others judging us.

But like Mary and Joseph, the only way through such troubled times is to move forward in obedience, asking for God's help. If we have sinned, we must confess that sin and ask for forgiveness in Jesus Christ. Then we can live in the freedom of those washed clean by his blood, not like people covering up the sins of the past. What's more, we can trust God to take the junk of our lives—the blunders, the failures, the hurts, the disappointments and the oopses—and transform them into treasures that we, like Mary, may store up in our hearts and ponder.

—PHYLLIS TEN ELSHOF

FOR YOUR NEXT DEVOTIONAL READING, TURN TO PAGE 1139.

Mary treasured up all these things and pondered them in her heart.

— Luke 2:19

let's talk

✦ What are some things we have done together that have hurt or angered others? How did we deal with their disapproval—did we try to make things right or did we just ignore the problem?

✦ What guilt are we still carrying from the past? What will it take to move forward in the full freedom of forgiveness?

✦ What treasures have we accumulated together to ponder over in our hearts? In what ways are those worth more than all the sorrows that have pierced us (see Luke 2:35)?

reth. 40And the child grew and became strong;
he was filled with wisdom, and the grace of
God was upon him.

The Boy Jesus at the Temple

41Every year his parents went to Jerusalem
for the Feast of the Passover. 42When he was
twelve years old, they went up to the Feast,
according to the custom. 43After the Feast was
over, while his parents were returning home,
the boy Jesus stayed behind in Jerusalem, but
they were unaware of it. 44Thinking he was
in their company, they traveled on for a day.
Then they began looking for him among their
relatives and friends. 45When they did not
find him, they went back to Jerusalem to look
for him. 46After three days they found him in
the temple courts, sitting among the teachers,
listening to them and asking them questions.
47Everyone who heard him was amazed at his
understanding and his answers. 48When his
parents saw him, they were astonished. His
mother said to him, "Son, why have you treated us like this? Your father and I have been
anxiously searching for you."
49"Why were you searching for me?" he
asked. "Didn't you know I had to be in my Father's house?" 50But they did not understand
what he was saying to them.
51Then he went down to Nazareth with
them and was obedient to them. But his
mother treasured all these things in her heart.
52And Jesus grew in wisdom and stature, and
in favor with God and men.

John the Baptist Prepares the Way

3 In the fifteenth year of the reign of Tiberi-
us Caesar—when Pontius Pilate was governor of Judea, Herod tetrarch of Galilee, his
brother Philip tetrarch of Iturea and Traconi-
tis, and Lysanias tetrarch of Abilene— 2during
the high priesthood of Annas and Caiaphas,
the word of God came to John son of Zechariah in the desert. 3He went into all the country around the Jordan, preaching a baptism of
repentance for the forgiveness of sins. 4As is
written in the book of the words of Isaiah the
prophet:

"A voice of one calling in the desert,
'Prepare the way for the Lord,
make straight paths for him.
5Every valley shall be filled in,
every mountain and hill made low.
The crooked roads shall become straight,
the rough ways smooth.
6And all mankind will see God's
salvation.' "[a]

7John said to the crowds coming out to be
baptized by him, "You brood of vipers! Who
warned you to flee from the coming wrath?
8Produce fruit in keeping with repentance.
And do not begin to say to yourselves, 'We
have Abraham as our father.' For I tell you that
out of these stones God can raise up children
for Abraham. 9The ax is already at the root of
the trees, and every tree that does not produce
good fruit will be cut down and thrown into
the fire."
10"What should we do then?" the crowd
asked.
11John answered, "The man with two tunics should share with him who has none, and
the one who has food should do the same."
12Tax collectors also came to be baptized.
"Teacher," they asked, "what should we do?"
13"Don't collect any more than you are required to," he told them.
14Then some soldiers asked him, "And what
should we do?"
He replied, "Don't extort money and don't
accuse people falsely—be content with your
pay."
15The people were waiting expectantly and
were all wondering in their hearts if John
might possibly be the Christ.[b] 16John answered them all, "I baptize you with[c] water.
But one more powerful than I will come, the
thongs of whose sandals I am not worthy to
untie. He will baptize you with the Holy Spirit and with fire. 17His winnowing fork is in his
hand to clear his threshing floor and to gather
the wheat into his barn, but he will burn up
the chaff with unquenchable fire." 18And with
many other words John exhorted the people
and preached the good news to them.
19But when John rebuked Herod the tetrarch because of Herodias, his brother's wife,
and all the other evil things he had done,
20Herod added this to them all: He locked
John up in prison.

The Baptism and Genealogy of Jesus

21When all the people were being baptized, Jesus was baptized too. And as he was
praying, heaven was opened 22and the Holy
Spirit descended on him in bodily form like
a dove. And a voice came from heaven: "You
are my Son, whom I love; with you I am well
pleased."
23Now Jesus himself was about thirty years

[a] *6* Isaiah 40:3-5 [b] *15* Or *Messiah* [c] *16* Or *in*

old when he began his ministry. He was the son, so it was thought, of Joseph,

the son of Heli, 24the son of Matthat,
the son of Levi, the son of Melki,
the son of Jannai, the son of Joseph,
25 the son of Mattathias, the son of Amos,
the son of Nahum, the son of Esli,
the son of Naggai, 26the son of Maath,
the son of Mattathias, the son of Semein,
the son of Josech, the son of Joda,
27 the son of Joanan, the son of Rhesa,
the son of Zerubbabel, the son of Shealtiel,
the son of Neri, 28the son of Melki,
the son of Addi, the son of Cosam,
the son of Elmadam, the son of Er,
29 the son of Joshua, the son of Eliezer,
the son of Jorim, the son of Matthat,
the son of Levi, 30the son of Simeon,
the son of Judah, the son of Joseph,
the son of Jonam, the son of Eliakim,
31 the son of Melea, the son of Menna,
the son of Mattatha, the son of Nathan,
the son of David, 32the son of Jesse,
the son of Obed, the son of Boaz,
the son of Salmon,[a] the son of Nahshon,
33 the son of Amminadab, the son of Ram,[b]
the son of Hezron, the son of Perez,
the son of Judah, 34the son of Jacob,
the son of Isaac, the son of Abraham,
the son of Terah, the son of Nahor,
35 the son of Serug, the son of Reu,
the son of Peleg, the son of Eber,
the son of Shelah, 36the son of Cainan,
the son of Arphaxad, the son of Shem,
the son of Noah, the son of Lamech,
37 the son of Methuselah, the son of Enoch,
the son of Jared, the son of Mahalalel,
the son of Kenan, 38the son of Enosh,
the son of Seth, the son of Adam,
the son of God.

The Temptation of Jesus

4 Jesus, full of the Holy Spirit, returned from the Jordan and was led by the Spirit in the desert, 2where for forty days he was tempted by the devil. He ate nothing during those days, and at the end of them he was hungry.

3The devil said to him, "If you are the Son of God, tell this stone to become bread."

4Jesus answered, "It is written: 'Man does not live on bread alone.'[c]"

5The devil led him up to a high place and showed him in an instant all the kingdoms of the world. 6And he said to him, "I will give you all their authority and splendor, for it has been given to me, and I can give it to anyone I want to. 7So if you worship me, it will all be yours."

8Jesus answered, "It is written: 'Worship the Lord your God and serve him only.'[d]"

9The devil led him to Jerusalem and had him stand on the highest point of the temple. "If you are the Son of God," he said, "throw yourself down from here. 10For it is written:

" 'He will command his angels concerning you
to guard you carefully;
11 they will lift you up in their hands,
so that you will not strike your foot against a stone.'[e]"

12Jesus answered, "It says: 'Do not put the Lord your God to the test.'[f]"

13When the devil had finished all this tempting, he left him until an opportune time.

Jesus Rejected at Nazareth

14Jesus returned to Galilee in the power of the Spirit, and news about him spread through the whole countryside. 15He taught in their synagogues, and everyone praised him.

16He went to Nazareth, where he had been brought up, and on the Sabbath day he went into the synagogue, as was his custom. And he stood up to read. 17The scroll of the prophet Isaiah was handed to him. Unrolling it, he found the place where it is written:

18 "The Spirit of the Lord is on me,
because he has anointed me
to preach good news to the poor.
He has sent me to proclaim freedom for the prisoners
and recovery of sight for the blind,
to release the oppressed,
19 to proclaim the year of the Lord's favor."[g]

20Then he rolled up the scroll, gave it back to the attendant and sat down. The eyes of everyone in the synagogue were fastened on him,
21and he began by saying to them, "Today this scripture is fulfilled in your hearing."
22All spoke well of him and were amazed

[a] *32* Some early manuscripts *Sala* [b] *33* Some manuscripts *Amminadab, the son of Admin, the son of Arni*; other manuscripts vary widely. [c] *4* Deut. 8:3 [d] *8* Deut. 6:13 [e] *11* Psalm 91:11,12 [f] *12* Deut. 6:16 [g] *19* Isaiah 61:1,2

TUESDAY
READ LUKE 4:1–13

TESTING EACH OTHER

Jesus answered, "It says: 'Do not put the Lord your God to the test.' "

— LUKE 4:12

let's talk

- In what ways do we intentionally test each other? What in our relationship might be off-kilter that prompts such testing?
- In what ways have we tested God in our marriage? What feelings prompted us to test God? What was the result?
- Where is the line between trusting God's provision and testing him?

When Jesus was in the wilderness, Satan tempted him in various ways. One of those was his challenge to jump off the highest point of the temple. If Jesus was truly the Son of God, he wouldn't be harmed, Satan said, because God had promised to send angels to protect him. Satan's challenge was, "Check it out. See if God is true to his word."

Jesus' response, a direct quote from Scripture (Deuteronomy 6:16), was immediate: "Do not test the LORD your God."

We might wonder what's wrong with asking God to send angels to rescue us from falling. But the situation here was not that of falling by accident but of falling by design. Satan told Jesus to check out God's promise to protect him by purposely taking a risk. And in demanding that angels appear, Jesus would be asking God to show up on *his* terms.

We are all tempted at times to test God. We say things like "It's OK for my husband to quit his job to go back to school. God will provide the scholarships to do that." Or "We can't afford health insurance right now. God will keep us free of illness while we're not covered." Or "We're moving back to our hometown. God will provide jobs for us when we get there."

It's appropriate, of course, to trust God's bounty and provision. Yet, when we make assumptions without thoroughly praying through our decisions and hearing God's call, aren't we, in effect, putting God to the test, asking him to prove who he is by giving us what we want?

Sometimes in marriage we put our spouse to the test. When we go to a party and find ourselves enjoying conversation with a person of the opposite sex who is clearly flirting with us, we may be secretly putting our spouse to the test as we wonder, "Does he notice this man is attracted to me? Does he care?"

Sometimes I purposely leave the sink full of dirty dishes just to see what Griff will do. "Will he be the person I want him to be, responsible for his dishes and concerned about making a home that is tidy and hospitable? Or will he prove himself to be blind, indifferent and a slob?" That's a lot to ask from one round of breakfast dishes.

The inclination to test each other is a sign that something is out of order in our relationship. If we really believe someone is honest and true, we don't walk around testing that person. If I encourage someone who is flirting with me to see if it will make my husband jealous enough to show that he cares about me, something is already amiss in our relationship. Somehow, we're not communicating well. He's not telling me he cares about me in a way that I can hear, and I'm not listening to him carefully enough.

Likewise, there is no justification for putting God to the test. If I really believe that God is faithful and trustworthy, I can praise him for who he is instead of throwing tests at him to gauge whether he truly cares for me.

Jesus, who lives in the full realization of the faithfulness of the Father, says, "Don't test God." This is not just an instruction; it is also a statement of reassurance. We don't need to test God; Jesus has already proved God's love and care for us through his death and resurrection.

—LAUREN WINNER

FOR YOUR NEXT DEVOTIONAL READING, TURN TO PAGE 1141.

at the gracious words that came from his lips.
“Isn’t this Joseph’s son?” they asked.
23Jesus said to them, “Surely you will quote
this proverb to me: ‘Physician, heal yourself!
Do here in your hometown what we have
heard that you did in Capernaum.’ ”
24“I tell you the truth,” he continued, “no
prophet is accepted in his hometown. 25I assure you that there were many widows in Israel in Elijah’s time, when the sky was shut for
three and a half years and there was a severe
famine throughout the land. 26Yet Elijah was
not sent to any of them, but to a widow in
Zarephath in the region of Sidon. 27And there
were many in Israel with leprosy[a] in the time
of Elisha the prophet, yet not one of them was
cleansed—only Naaman the Syrian.”
28All the people in the synagogue were furious when they heard this. 29They got up,
drove him out of the town, and took him to
the brow of the hill on which the town was
built, in order to throw him down the cliff.
30But he walked right through the crowd and
went on his way.

Jesus Drives Out an Evil Spirit

31Then he went down to Capernaum, a
town in Galilee, and on the Sabbath began to
teach the people. 32They were amazed at his
teaching, because his message had authority.
33In the synagogue there was a man possessed by a demon, an evil[b] spirit. He cried
out at the top of his voice, 34“Ha! What do
you want with us, Jesus of Nazareth? Have you
come to destroy us? I know who you are—the
Holy One of God!”
35“Be quiet!” Jesus said sternly. “Come
out of him!” Then the demon threw the man
down before them all and came out without
injuring him.
36All the people were amazed and said to
each other, “What is this teaching? With authority and power he gives orders to evil spirits and they come out!” 37And the news about
him spread throughout the surrounding area.

Jesus Heals Many

38Jesus left the synagogue and went to the
home of Simon. Now Simon’s mother-in-law
was suffering from a high fever, and they asked
Jesus to help her. 39So he bent over her and
rebuked the fever, and it left her. She got up at
once and began to wait on them.
40When the sun was setting, the people
brought to Jesus all who had various kinds of
sickness, and laying his hands on each one, he
healed them. 41Moreover, demons came out
of many people, shouting, “You are the Son of
God!” But he rebuked them and would not allow them to speak, because they knew he was
the Christ.[c]
42At daybreak Jesus went out to a solitary
place. The people were looking for him and
when they came to where he was, they tried
to keep him from leaving them. 43But he said,
“I must preach the good news of the kingdom
of God to the other towns also, because that is
why I was sent.” 44And he kept on preaching
in the synagogues of Judea.[d]

The Calling of the First Disciples

5 One day as Jesus was standing by the Lake
of Gennesaret,[e] with the people crowding
around him and listening to the word of
God, 2he saw at the water’s edge two boats,
left there by the fishermen, who were washing
their nets. 3He got into one of the boats, the
one belonging to Simon, and asked him to put
out a little from shore. Then he sat down and
taught the people from the boat.
4When he had finished speaking, he said
to Simon, “Put out into deep water, and let
down[f] the nets for a catch.”
5Simon answered, “Master, we’ve worked
hard all night and haven’t caught anything.
But because you say so, I will let down the
nets.”
6When they had done so, they caught such
a large number of fish that their nets began to
break. 7So they signaled their partners in the
other boat to come and help them, and they
came and filled both boats so full that they
began to sink.
8When Simon Peter saw this, he fell at Jesus’
knees and said, “Go away from me, Lord; I am
a sinful man!” 9For he and all his companions
were astonished at the catch of fish they had
taken, 10and so were James and John, the sons
of Zebedee, Simon’s partners.
Then Jesus said to Simon, “Don’t be afraid;
from now on you will catch men.” 11So they
pulled their boats up on shore, left everything
and followed him.

The Man With Leprosy

12While Jesus was in one of the towns, a
man came along who was covered with leprosy.[g] When he saw Jesus, he fell with his face to

[a] 27 The Greek word was used for various diseases affecting the skin—not necessarily leprosy. [b] 33 Greek *unclean*; also in verse 36
[c] 41 Or *Messiah* [d] 44 Or *the land of the Jews*; some manuscripts *Galilee* [e] 1 That is, Sea of Galilee [f] 4 The Greek verb is plural.
[g] 12 The Greek word was used for various diseases affecting the skin—not necessarily leprosy.

BALANCING TOGETHER AND ALONE TIME

> **Yet the news about him spread all the more, so that crowds of people came to hear him and to be healed of their sicknesses. But Jesus often withdrew to lonely places and prayed.**
>
> — LUKE 5:15–16

When my husband and I got married, I couldn't imagine I would ever get sick of him. We couldn't wait to live together, to cook together, to watch TV together, to sleep together. For the first few months of our marriage, we would often look at each other and remind ourselves that neither of us had to go home; we *were* home.

That, however, was short-lived. Before the first year was over, I craved an evening alone—to go out by myself, read or go to bed early. It wasn't that I didn't love being with my husband; it was that I needed times of not being with him too. In our excitement over being together at last, we hadn't allowed much room for being apart.

The story of Jesus and the man with leprosy in Luke 5 is a powerful example of Jesus' ability to heal and change lives. It's not surprising that the people of Jesus' day were drawn to him, flocking to him in hopes of receiving the touch of his healing hand. Yet I believe we learn something else about Jesus in this story as well; he got tired. Not tired of helping people, but tired, period.

In his weariness, Jesus would pull away from the crowd and even from his friends to find a quiet place where he could rest his body and renew his spirit. Surely this was a necessity, not a luxury, for Jesus. He understood that making time to be alone with God wasn't selfish. And he didn't just do it so he could be a more effective minister to others. Jesus stepped away from the crowd because he needed to. This was Jesus at his most human—tired and in need of restoration.

We seem to have this idea that marriage, particularly a new marriage, should be all about togetherness. But when a couple spends all their free time together, something else suffers. Maybe old friends get pushed aside. Maybe quiet moments for personal reflection or prayer get overlooked. As great as it feels to be together, eventually we begin to feel the loss of other parts of our lives.

Early in our marriage, my husband and I decided to spend a Christmas apart. He went to his family's home and I went to mine. We had spent the two previous Christmases living far away from both sets of parents, and neither of us could bear to be the one to miss out for a third time. So the weekend before Christmas, we celebrated together, then headed for our respective hometowns. It was the perfect solution for us—after all, we decided, we see each other all the time.

But boy did we get questions! Were we getting along? Was this dumb plan his idea or mine? Did we regret our decision? There was no end to the speculation. That Christmas taught us two important lessons: (1) Sometimes the best thing we can do for our marriage is to take a little time for ourselves during the year, but (2) we should be together for Christmas.

Being together has obvious rewards. But being alone from time to time can be the key to keeping us in balance.

—CARLA BARNHILL

let's *talk*

- ✦ Do we feel we've found a good balance between couple time and alone time? If we don't have enough alone time, what are some ways we can find the alone time we need to restore our spirits?
- ✦ What are some of the emotional, physical and spiritual drains we face each day?
- ✦ How can we help each other so we don't get burned out by the busyness of life?

FOR YOUR NEXT DEVOTIONAL READING, TURN TO PAGE 1144.

the ground and begged him, "Lord, if you are willing, you can make me clean."

13 Jesus reached out his hand and touched the man. "I am willing," he said. "Be clean!" And immediately the leprosy left him.

14 Then Jesus ordered him, "Don't tell anyone, but go, show yourself to the priest and offer the sacrifices that Moses commanded for your cleansing, as a testimony to them."

15 Yet the news about him spread all the more, so that crowds of people came to hear him and to be healed of their sicknesses. 16 But Jesus often withdrew to lonely places and prayed.

Jesus Heals a Paralytic

17 One day as he was teaching, Pharisees and teachers of the law, who had come from every village of Galilee and from Judea and Jerusalem, were sitting there. And the power of the Lord was present for him to heal the sick. 18 Some men came carrying a paralytic on a mat and tried to take him into the house to lay him before Jesus. 19 When they could not find a way to do this because of the crowd, they went up on the roof and lowered him on his mat through the tiles into the middle of the crowd, right in front of Jesus.

20 When Jesus saw their faith, he said, "Friend, your sins are forgiven."

21 The Pharisees and the teachers of the law began thinking to themselves, "Who is this fellow who speaks blasphemy? Who can forgive sins but God alone?"

22 Jesus knew what they were thinking and asked, "Why are you thinking these things in your hearts? 23 Which is easier: to say, 'Your sins are forgiven,' or to say, 'Get up and walk'? 24 But that you may know that the Son of Man has authority on earth to forgive sins . . ." He said to the paralyzed man, "I tell you, get up, take your mat and go home." 25 Immediately he stood up in front of them, took what he had been lying on and went home praising God. 26 Everyone was amazed and gave praise to God. They were filled with awe and said, "We have seen remarkable things today."

The Calling of Levi

27 After this, Jesus went out and saw a tax collector by the name of Levi sitting at his tax booth. "Follow me," Jesus said to him, 28 and Levi got up, left everything and followed him.

29 Then Levi held a great banquet for Jesus at his house, and a large crowd of tax collectors and others were eating with them. 30 But the Pharisees and the teachers of the law who belonged to their sect complained to his disciples, "Why do you eat and drink with tax collectors and 'sinners'?"

31 Jesus answered them, "It is not the healthy who need a doctor, but the sick. 32 I have not come to call the righteous, but sinners to repentance."

Jesus Questioned About Fasting

33 They said to him, "John's disciples often fast and pray, and so do the disciples of the Pharisees, but yours go on eating and drinking."

34 Jesus answered, "Can you make the guests of the bridegroom fast while he is with them? 35 But the time will come when the bridegroom will be taken from them; in those days they will fast."

36 He told them this parable: "No one tears a patch from a new garment and sews it on an old one. If he does, he will have torn the new garment, and the patch from the new will not match the old. 37 And no one pours new wine into old wineskins. If he does, the new wine will burst the skins, the wine will run out and the wineskins will be ruined. 38 No, new wine must be poured into new wineskins. 39 And no one after drinking old wine wants the new, for he says, 'The old is better.' "

Lord of the Sabbath

6 One Sabbath Jesus was going through the grainfields, and his disciples began to pick some heads of grain, rub them in their hands and eat the kernels. 2 Some of the Pharisees asked, "Why are you doing what is unlawful on the Sabbath?"

3 Jesus answered them, "Have you never read what David did when he and his companions were hungry? 4 He entered the house of God, and taking the consecrated bread, he ate what is lawful only for priests to eat. And he also gave some to his companions." 5 Then Jesus said to them, "The Son of Man is Lord of the Sabbath."

6 On another Sabbath he went into the synagogue and was teaching, and a man was there whose right hand was shriveled. 7 The Pharisees and the teachers of the law were looking for a reason to accuse Jesus, so they watched him closely to see if he would heal on the Sabbath. 8 But Jesus knew what they were thinking and said to the man with the shriveled hand, "Get up and stand in front of everyone." So he got up and stood there.

9 Then Jesus said to them, "I ask you, which

is lawful on the Sabbath: to do good or to do
evil, to save life or to destroy it?"
10He looked around at them all, and then
said to the man, "Stretch out your hand." He
did so, and his hand was completely restored.
11But they were furious and began to discuss
with one another what they might do to Jesus.

The Twelve Apostles

12One of those days Jesus went out to a
mountainside to pray, and spent the night
praying to God. 13When morning came, he
called his disciples to him and chose twelve
of them, whom he also designated apostles:
14Simon (whom he named Peter), his brother Andrew, James, John, Philip, Bartholomew,
15Matthew, Thomas, James son of Alphaeus,
Simon who was called the Zealot, 16Judas son
of James, and Judas Iscariot, who became a
traitor.

Blessings and Woes

17He went down with them and stood on
a level place. A large crowd of his disciples
was there and a great number of people from
all over Judea, from Jerusalem, and from the
coast of Tyre and Sidon, 18who had come to
hear him and to be healed of their diseases.
Those troubled by evil[a] spirits were cured,
19and the people all tried to touch him, because power was coming from him and healing them all.
20Looking at his disciples, he said:

"Blessed are you who are poor,
for yours is the kingdom of God.
21 Blessed are you who hunger now,
for you will be satisfied.
Blessed are you who weep now,
for you will laugh.
22 Blessed are you when men hate you,
when they exclude you and insult you
and reject your name as evil,
because of the Son of Man.

23"Rejoice in that day and leap for joy, because great is your reward in heaven. For that
is how their fathers treated the prophets.

24 "But woe to you who are rich,
for you have already received your
comfort.
25 Woe to you who are well fed now,
for you will go hungry.
Woe to you who laugh now,
for you will mourn and weep.
26 Woe to you when all men speak well of
you,
for that is how their fathers treated the
false prophets.

Love for Enemies

27"But I tell you who hear me: Love your
enemies, do good to those who hate you,
28bless those who curse you, pray for those
who mistreat you. 29If someone strikes you on
one cheek, turn to him the other also. If someone takes your cloak, do not stop him from
taking your tunic. 30Give to everyone who
asks you, and if anyone takes what belongs to
you, do not demand it back. 31Do to others as
you would have them do to you.
32"If you love those who love you, what
credit is that to you? Even 'sinners' love those
who love them. 33And if you do good to those
who are good to you, what credit is that to
you? Even 'sinners' do that. 34And if you lend
to those from whom you expect repayment,
what credit is that to you? Even 'sinners' lend
to 'sinners,' expecting to be repaid in full. 35But
love your enemies, do good to them, and lend
to them without expecting to get anything
back. Then your reward will be great, and you
will be sons of the Most High, because he is
kind to the ungrateful and wicked. 36Be merciful, just as your Father is merciful.

Judging Others

37"Do not judge, and you will not be
judged. Do not condemn, and you will not be
condemned. Forgive, and you will be forgiven. 38Give, and it will be given to you. A good
measure, pressed down, shaken together and
running over, will be poured into your lap. For
with the measure you use, it will be measured
to you."
39He also told them this parable: "Can a
blind man lead a blind man? Will they not
both fall into a pit? 40A student is not above
his teacher, but everyone who is fully trained
will be like his teacher.
41"Why do you look at the speck of sawdust
in your brother's eye and pay no attention to
the plank in your own eye? 42How can you say
to your brother, 'Brother, let me take the speck
out of your eye,' when you yourself fail to see
the plank in your own eye? You hypocrite, first
take the plank out of your eye, and then you
will see clearly to remove the speck from your
brother's eye.

---

[a] 18 Greek *unclean*

THURSDAY
READ LUKE 6:27–42

MERCY TRIUMPHS OVER JUDGMENT

> **"With the measure you use, it will be measured to you."**
> — Luke 6:38

In my community, a local minister got involved in sexual sin. After the sin became known, the pastor confessed, resigned his position and willingly received counseling from the church elders. Before he moved away, his church family poured out their love and mercy on him. They told him, "Your sin violated the purity of Christ's church, but we are all sinners in need of forgiveness, and because you are contrite and seek restoration and wholeness, we will stand with you."

The minister left town knowing that he had been loved toward repentance. It was a beautiful thing to behold. I think it's an example of what Jesus was talking about in Luke 6:37–42. He started out by saying, "Do not judge . . . Do not condemn . . . Forgive, and you will be forgiven." He went on to say, "Why do you look at the speck of sawdust in your brother's eye and pay no attention to the plank in your own eye?" Knowing our hearts, Jesus was addressing our tendency to revel in other people's sin, measuring ourselves against them to boost our sense of moral superiority.

Judging is easy to do in marriage. Because we live in such intimacy with our spouse, we are all too aware of each other's shortcomings. Sometimes all we can see are each other's faults. That can send us on a downward spiral of judging and condemning and moral one-upmanship, which is exactly what Jesus said we're not to do. Judging results in separation and shame and self-protection. It creates walls and chasms and bad feelings all around. Even worse, it takes the pressure off being honest about our own faults and dealing with them.

Just before Jesus warned us not to judge, he talked about mercy. In Luke 6:36 he said, "Be merciful, just as your Father is merciful." Then, in the very next verse, he said, "Do not judge." James said, "Mercy triumphs over judgment" and "Judgment without mercy will be shown to anyone who has not been merciful" (James 2:13). No one but God knows how deeply another person struggles not to sin. Therefore, before considering another person's faults, we must first be aware that our own sin may be as great or even greater than theirs. Knowing we may come up short in any comparison may make us less inclined to judge them.

But understanding that we have received forgiveness and mercy through our Lord Jesus Christ is the ultimate reason why we can extend mercy to others who sin, especially the spouse we have vowed to love in sickness and in health, in good times and in bad times. Like the woman in Luke 7:36–50 who poured perfume on Jesus' feet, our response to having been forgiven much—even our judgmental, critical, negative faultfinding—should be to love much.

—NANCY KENNEDY

let's *talk*

- ✦ Let's be honest; when we hear of a Christian falling into sin, what are our first thoughts? In what ways do we judge that person?
- ✦ Meantime, what are some of the "planks" we're overlooking in our own eyes? How can we lovingly help each other spot those and deal with them?
- ✦ In our circle of friends or in our church, is there someone who could use some mercy? What are some ways we could help that person toward restoration.

FOR YOUR NEXT DEVOTIONAL READING, TURN TO PAGE 1149.

A Tree and Its Fruit

43“No good tree bears bad fruit, nor does
a bad tree bear good fruit. 44Each tree is recognized by its own fruit. People do not pick
figs from thornbushes, or grapes from briers.
45The good man brings good things out of the
good stored up in his heart, and the evil man
brings evil things out of the evil stored up in
his heart. For out of the overflow of his heart
his mouth speaks.

The Wise and Foolish Builders

46“Why do you call me, ‘Lord, Lord,’ and
do not do what I say? 47I will show you what
he is like who comes to me and hears my
words and puts them into practice. 48He is
like a man building a house, who dug down
deep and laid the foundation on rock. When a
flood came, the torrent struck that house but
could not shake it, because it was well built.
49But the one who hears my words and does
not put them into practice is like a man who
built a house on the ground without a foundation. The moment the torrent struck that
house, it collapsed and its destruction was
complete.”

The Faith of the Centurion

7 When Jesus had finished saying all this in
the hearing of the people, he entered Capernaum. 2There a centurion’s servant,
whom his master valued highly, was sick and
about to die. 3The centurion heard of Jesus
and sent some elders of the Jews to him, asking him to come and heal his servant. 4When
they came to Jesus, they pleaded earnestly with
him, “This man deserves to have you do this,
5because he loves our nation and has built our
synagogue.” 6So Jesus went with them.

He was not far from the house when the
centurion sent friends to say to him: “Lord,
don’t trouble yourself, for I do not deserve to
have you come under my roof. 7That is why I
did not even consider myself worthy to come
to you. But say the word, and my servant will
be healed. 8For I myself am a man under authority, with soldiers under me. I tell this one,
‘Go,’ and he goes; and that one, ‘Come,’ and
he comes. I say to my servant, ‘Do this,’ and
he does it.”

9When Jesus heard this, he was amazed at
him, and turning to the crowd following him,
he said, “I tell you, I have not found such great
faith even in Israel.” 10Then the men who had
been sent returned to the house and found the
servant well.

Jesus Raises a Widow’s Son

11Soon afterward, Jesus went to a town
called Nain, and his disciples and a large crowd
went along with him. 12As he approached the
town gate, a dead person was being carried
out—the only son of his mother, and she was
a widow. And a large crowd from the town was
with her. 13When the Lord saw her, his heart
went out to her and he said, “Don’t cry.”

14Then he went up and touched the coffin, and those carrying it stood still. He said,
“Young man, I say to you, get up!” 15The dead
man sat up and began to talk, and Jesus gave
him back to his mother.

16They were all filled with awe and praised
God. “A great prophet has appeared among
us,” they said. “God has come to help his people.” 17This news about Jesus spread throughout Judea[a] and the surrounding country.

Jesus and John the Baptist

18John’s disciples told him about all these
things. Calling two of them, 19he sent them to
the Lord to ask, “Are you the one who was to
come, or should we expect someone else?”

20When the men came to Jesus, they said,
“John the Baptist sent us to you to ask, ‘Are
you the one who was to come, or should we
expect someone else?’ ”

21At that very time Jesus cured many who
had diseases, sicknesses and evil spirits, and
gave sight to many who were blind. 22So he
replied to the messengers, “Go back and report to John what you have seen and heard:
The blind receive sight, the lame walk, those
who have leprosy[b] are cured, the deaf hear, the
dead are raised, and the good news is preached
to the poor. 23Blessed is the man who does not
fall away on account of me.”

24After John’s messengers left, Jesus began
to speak to the crowd about John: “What
did you go out into the desert to see? A reed
swayed by the wind? 25If not, what did you go
out to see? A man dressed in fine clothes? No,
those who wear expensive clothes and indulge
in luxury are in palaces. 26But what did you
go out to see? A prophet? Yes, I tell you, and
more than a prophet. 27This is the one about
whom it is written:

> “ ‘I will send my messenger ahead of you,
> who will prepare your way before you.’[c]

---

[a] 17 Or *the land of the Jews* [b] 22 The Greek word was used for various diseases affecting the skin—not necessarily leprosy.
[c] 27 Mal. 3:1

28I tell you, among those born of women
there is no one greater than John; yet the one
who is least in the kingdom of God is greater
than he."
29(All the people, even the tax collectors,
when they heard Jesus' words, acknowledged
that God's way was right, because they had
been baptized by John. 30But the Pharisees
and experts in the law rejected God's purpose
for themselves, because they had not been
baptized by John.)
31"To what, then, can I compare the people
of this generation? What are they like? 32They
are like children sitting in the marketplace and
calling out to each other:

" 'We played the flute for you,
and you did not dance;
we sang a dirge,
and you did not cry.'

33For John the Baptist came neither eating
bread nor drinking wine, and you say, 'He has
a demon.' 34The Son of Man came eating and
drinking, and you say, 'Here is a glutton and
a drunkard, a friend of tax collectors and "sinners." ' 35But wisdom is proved right by all her
children."

Jesus Anointed by a Sinful Woman

36Now one of the Pharisees invited Jesus to
have dinner with him, so he went to the Pharisee's house and reclined at the table. 37When
a woman who had lived a sinful life in that
town learned that Jesus was eating at the Pharisee's house, she brought an alabaster jar of
perfume, 38and as she stood behind him at his
feet weeping, she began to wet his feet with
her tears. Then she wiped them with her hair,
kissed them and poured perfume on them.
39When the Pharisee who had invited him
saw this, he said to himself, "If this man were
a prophet, he would know who is touching
him and what kind of woman she is—that she
is a sinner."
40Jesus answered him, "Simon, I have something to tell you."
"Tell me, teacher," he said.
41"Two men owed money to a certain moneylender. One owed him five hundred denarii,[a] and the other fifty. 42Neither of them had
the money to pay him back, so he canceled
the debts of both. Now which of them will
love him more?"
43Simon replied, "I suppose the one who
had the bigger debt canceled."
"You have judged correctly," Jesus said.
44Then he turned toward the woman and
said to Simon, "Do you see this woman? I
came into your house. You did not give me
any water for my feet, but she wet my feet
with her tears and wiped them with her hair.
45You did not give me a kiss, but this woman, from the time I entered, has not stopped
kissing my feet. 46You did not put oil on my
head, but she has poured perfume on my feet.
47Therefore, I tell you, her many sins have
been forgiven—for she loved much. But he
who has been forgiven little loves little."
48Then Jesus said to her, "Your sins are forgiven."
49The other guests began to say among
themselves, "Who is this who even forgives
sins?"
50Jesus said to the woman, "Your faith has
saved you; go in peace."

The Parable of the Sower

8 After this, Jesus traveled about from one
town and village to another, proclaiming
the good news of the kingdom of God.
The Twelve were with him, 2and also some
women who had been cured of evil spirits
and diseases: Mary (called Magdalene) from
whom seven demons had come out; 3Joan-
na the wife of Cuza, the manager of Herod's
household; Susanna; and many others. These
women were helping to support them out of
their own means.
4While a large crowd was gathering and
people were coming to Jesus from town after
town, he told this parable: 5"A farmer went
out to sow his seed. As he was scattering the
seed, some fell along the path; it was trampled
on, and the birds of the air ate it up. 6Some
fell on rock, and when it came up, the plants
withered because they had no moisture. 7Oth-
er seed fell among thorns, which grew up with
it and choked the plants. 8Still other seed fell
on good soil. It came up and yielded a crop, a
hundred times more than was sown."
When he said this, he called out, "He who
has ears to hear, let him hear."
9His disciples asked him what this parable
meant. 10He said, "The knowledge of the secrets of the kingdom of God has been given to
you, but to others I speak in parables, so that,

" 'though seeing, they may not see;
though hearing, they may not
understand.'[b]

[a] 41 A denarius was a coin worth about a day's wages. [b] 10 Isaiah 6:9

11“This is the meaning of the parable: The
seed is the word of God. 12Those along the
path are the ones who hear, and then the devil comes and takes away the word from their
hearts, so that they may not believe and be
saved. 13Those on the rock are the ones who
receive the word with joy when they hear
it, but they have no root. They believe for a
while, but in the time of testing they fall away.
14The seed that fell among thorns stands for
those who hear, but as they go on their way
they are choked by life’s worries, riches and
pleasures, and they do not mature. 15But the
seed on good soil stands for those with a noble
and good heart, who hear the word, retain it,
and by persevering produce a crop.

A Lamp on a Stand

16“No one lights a lamp and hides it in a
jar or puts it under a bed. Instead, he puts it
on a stand, so that those who come in can see
the light. 17For there is nothing hidden that
will not be disclosed, and nothing concealed
that will not be known or brought out into
the open. 18Therefore consider carefully how
you listen. Whoever has will be given more;
whoever does not have, even what he thinks
he has will be taken from him.”

Jesus’ Mother and Brothers

19Now Jesus’ mother and brothers came to
see him, but they were not able to get near
him because of the crowd. 20Someone told
him, “Your mother and brothers are standing
outside, wanting to see you.”

21He replied, “My mother and brothers are
those who hear God’s word and put it into
practice.”

Jesus Calms the Storm

22One day Jesus said to his disciples, “Let’s
go over to the other side of the lake.” So they
got into a boat and set out. 23As they sailed,
he fell asleep. A squall came down on the lake,
so that the boat was being swamped, and they
were in great danger.

24The disciples went and woke him, saying,
“Master, Master, we’re going to drown!”

He got up and rebuked the wind and the
raging waters; the storm subsided, and all was
calm. 25“Where is your faith?” he asked his
disciples.

In fear and amazement they asked one another, “Who is this? He commands even the
winds and the water, and they obey him.”

The Healing of a Demon-possessed Man

26They sailed to the region of the Gerasenes,[a] which is across the lake from Galilee.
27When Jesus stepped ashore, he was met by
a demon-possessed man from the town. For a
long time this man had not worn clothes or
lived in a house, but had lived in the tombs.
28When he saw Jesus, he cried out and fell
at his feet, shouting at the top of his voice,
“What do you want with me, Jesus, Son of the
Most High God? I beg you, don’t torture me!”
29For Jesus had commanded the evil[b] spirit
to come out of the man. Many times it had
seized him, and though he was chained hand
and foot and kept under guard, he had broken
his chains and had been driven by the demon
into solitary places.

30Jesus asked him, “What is your name?”

“Legion,” he replied, because many demons
had gone into him. 31And they begged him
repeatedly not to order them to go into the
Abyss.

32A large herd of pigs was feeding there on
the hillside. The demons begged Jesus to let
them go into them, and he gave them permission. 33When the demons came out of the
man, they went into the pigs, and the herd
rushed down the steep bank into the lake and
was drowned.

34When those tending the pigs saw what
had happened, they ran off and reported this
in the town and countryside, 35and the people went out to see what had happened. When
they came to Jesus, they found the man from
whom the demons had gone out, sitting at
Jesus’ feet, dressed and in his right mind; and
they were afraid. 36Those who had seen it told
the people how the demon-possessed man had
been cured. 37Then all the people of the region
of the Gerasenes asked Jesus to leave them, because they were overcome with fear. So he got
into the boat and left.

38The man from whom the demons had
gone out begged to go with him, but Jesus
sent him away, saying, 39“Return home and
tell how much God has done for you.” So the
man went away and told all over town how
much Jesus had done for him.

A Dead Girl and a Sick Woman

40Now when Jesus returned, a crowd welcomed him, for they were all expecting him.
41Then a man named Jairus, a ruler of the synagogue, came and fell at Jesus’ feet, pleading
with him to come to his house 42because his

---

[a] *26* Some manuscripts *Gadarenes*; other manuscripts *Gergesenes*; also in verse 37 [b] *29* Greek *unclean*

only daughter, a girl of about twelve, was dying.
As Jesus was on his way, the crowds almost
crushed him. 43And a woman was there who
had been subject to bleeding for twelve years,[a]
but no one could heal her. 44She came up behind him and touched the edge of his cloak,
and immediately her bleeding stopped.
45"Who touched me?" Jesus asked.
When they all denied it, Peter said, "Master, the people are crowding and pressing
against you."
46But Jesus said, "Someone touched me; I
know that power has gone out from me."
47Then the woman, seeing that she could
not go unnoticed, came trembling and fell at
his feet. In the presence of all the people, she
told why she had touched him and how she
had been instantly healed. 48Then he said to
her, "Daughter, your faith has healed you. Go
in peace."
49While Jesus was still speaking, someone
came from the house of Jairus, the synagogue
ruler. "Your daughter is dead," he said. "Don't
bother the teacher any more."
50Hearing this, Jesus said to Jairus, "Don't
be afraid; just believe, and she will be healed."
51When he arrived at the house of Jairus,
he did not let anyone go in with him except
Peter, John and James, and the child's father
and mother. 52Meanwhile, all the people were
wailing and mourning for her. "Stop wailing,"
Jesus said. "She is not dead but asleep."
53They laughed at him, knowing that she
was dead. 54But he took her by the hand and
said, "My child, get up!" 55Her spirit returned,
and at once she stood up. Then Jesus told
them to give her something to eat. 56Her parents were astonished, but he ordered them not
to tell anyone what had happened.

Jesus Sends Out the Twelve

9 When Jesus had called the Twelve together, he gave them power and authority to
drive out all demons and to cure diseases,
2and he sent them out to preach the kingdom
of God and to heal the sick. 3He told them:
"Take nothing for the journey—no staff, no
bag, no bread, no money, no extra tunic.
4Whatever house you enter, stay there until
you leave that town. 5If people do not welcome you, shake the dust off your feet when
you leave their town, as a testimony against
them." 6So they set out and went from village
to village, preaching the gospel and healing
people everywhere.
7Now Herod the tetrarch heard about all
that was going on. And he was perplexed,
because some were saying that John had
been raised from the dead, 8others that Elijah had appeared, and still others that one of
the prophets of long ago had come back to
life. 9But Herod said, "I beheaded John. Who,
then, is this I hear such things about?" And he
tried to see him.

Jesus Feeds the Five Thousand

10When the apostles returned, they reported to Jesus what they had done. Then he took
them with him and they withdrew by themselves to a town called Bethsaida, 11but the
crowds learned about it and followed him. He
welcomed them and spoke to them about the
kingdom of God, and healed those who needed healing.
12Late in the afternoon the Twelve came to
him and said, "Send the crowd away so they
can go to the surrounding villages and countryside and find food and lodging, because we
are in a remote place here."
13He replied, "You give them something to
eat."
They answered, "We have only five loaves
of bread and two fish—unless we go and buy
food for all this crowd." 14(About five thousand men were there.)
But he said to his disciples, "Have them
sit down in groups of about fifty each." 15The
disciples did so, and everybody sat down.
16Taking the five loaves and the two fish and
looking up to heaven, he gave thanks and
broke them. Then he gave them to the disciples to set before the people. 17They all ate
and were satisfied, and the disciples picked up
twelve basketfuls of broken pieces that were
left over.

Peter's Confession of Christ

18Once when Jesus was praying in private
and his disciples were with him, he asked
them, "Who do the crowds say I am?"
19They replied, "Some say John the Baptist; others say Elijah; and still others, that one
of the prophets of long ago has come back to
life."
20"But what about you?" he asked. "Who
do you say I am?"
Peter answered, "The Christ[b] of God."
21Jesus strictly warned them not to tell this

[a] 43 Many manuscripts *years, and she had spent all she had on doctors* [b] 20 Or *Messiah*

F

FRIDAY
READ LUKE 9:18–27

MEASURING OUR SUCCESS

Now and again I see mortality clinging to my steps like a lengthening shadow, and I am caught wondering why I am still here. A question chiseled in stone over the grave of a child recycles in my brain: "If I am so quickly done for, what on earth was I begun for?"

Life feeds that cynicism. Since people around us often cannot see our soul inside the material stuff with which we surround it, we are often beguiled into amassing possessions and accomplishments to proclaim our worth.

Yet all of those things can be stripped away from us in a matter of seconds. Recently I cried with a 30-something fellow who appeared to be a glowing testimony of success. He grew up in a close-knit family, has an athletic body and a movie-star face, married a beautiful and intelligent woman, lives in a luxurious home, and is buying a business that could become a multibillion-dollar corporation before he retires.

But now all the good looks and money mean nothing. A foolish action has fractured his marriage and torn him from his children. "Two weeks ago I thought I had it all. Now I don't know if I have anything," the man said. "I would trade everything to have my wife and children back."

His sad words made me think about Jesus' comment to his disciples. Jesus had set his sights on his future suffering in Jerusalem, and he was trying to prepare his friends for that reality. Jesus knew he would encounter denial, devastation and death. Rather than excusing his disciples from such painful experiences, Jesus warned them that they too would face some tough times. Indeed, it was a requirement of following him: "If anyone would come after me, he must deny himself and take up his cross daily and follow me" (Luke 9:23).

God meant for us to enjoy the marvelous beauty and material resources of our world. But Jesus wanted to make clear that we can't truly delight in possessions if they consume us while we are consuming them.

When Jesus made his pilgrimage to the cross, his disciples accompanied him to Jerusalem. True, they would all have their moments of quivering fright that sent them scrambling into hiding, yet they joined him as best they could. And eventually they all suffered great loss as they took up their crosses and followed him.

The greatest thing about courtship and marriage is that we don't have to go through life alone. We share our journey with another. We reaffirm the faith and values we have spoken about in the easy times so that when we have to slog through the swamp of despair or navigate the hard places of loss, we can encourage each other to put our feet in appropriate places and keep our eyes trained on our Savior, Jesus Christ. Together we can follow him.

—WAYNE BROUWER

FOR YOUR NEXT DEVOTIONAL READING, TURN TO PAGE 1154.

"What good is it for a man to gain the whole world, and yet lose or forfeit his very self?"
— LUKE 9:25

let's talk

- What are our 20-year goals? In what ways could those goals nurture or destroy our relationship? How would Jesus nudge us to change or clarify our plans?
- What is our net worth? How do we measure it? What questions can we ask to help us think through the true value of our possessions?
- What have we accumulated as a couple that we will pass on to our children? How might those things be a blessing? A hardship?

to anyone. 22And he said, "The Son of Man must suffer many things and be rejected by the elders, chief priests and teachers of the law, and he must be killed and on the third day be raised to life."

23Then he said to them all: "If anyone would come after me, he must deny himself and take up his cross daily and follow me. 24For whoever wants to save his life will lose it, but whoever loses his life for me will save it. 25What good is it for a man to gain the whole world, and yet lose or forfeit his very self? 26If anyone is ashamed of me and my words, the Son of Man will be ashamed of him when he comes in his glory and in the glory of the Father and of the holy angels. 27I tell you the truth, some who are standing here will not taste death before they see the kingdom of God."

The Transfiguration

28About eight days after Jesus said this, he took Peter, John and James with him and went up onto a mountain to pray. 29As he was praying, the appearance of his face changed, and his clothes became as bright as a flash of lightning. 30Two men, Moses and Elijah, 31appeared in glorious splendor, talking with Jesus. They spoke about his departure, which he was about to bring to fulfillment at Jerusalem. 32Peter and his companions were very sleepy, but when they became fully awake, they saw his glory and the two men standing with him. 33As the men were leaving Jesus, Peter said to him, "Master, it is good for us to be here. Let us put up three shelters—one for you, one for Moses and one for Elijah." (He did not know what he was saying.)

34While he was speaking, a cloud appeared and enveloped them, and they were afraid as they entered the cloud. 35A voice came from the cloud, saying, "This is my Son, whom I have chosen; listen to him." 36When the voice had spoken, they found that Jesus was alone. The disciples kept this to themselves, and told no one at that time what they had seen.

The Healing of a Boy With an Evil Spirit

37The next day, when they came down from the mountain, a large crowd met him. 38A man in the crowd called out, "Teacher, I beg you to look at my son, for he is my only child. 39A spirit seizes him and he suddenly screams; it throws him into convulsions so that he foams at the mouth. It scarcely ever leaves him and is destroying him. 40I begged your disciples to drive it out, but they could not."

41"O unbelieving and perverse generation," Jesus replied, "how long shall I stay with you and put up with you? Bring your son here."

42Even while the boy was coming, the demon threw him to the ground in a convulsion. But Jesus rebuked the evil[a] spirit, healed the boy and gave him back to his father. 43And they were all amazed at the greatness of God.

While everyone was marveling at all that Jesus did, he said to his disciples, 44"Listen carefully to what I am about to tell you: The Son of Man is going to be betrayed into the hands of men." 45But they did not understand what this meant. It was hidden from them, so that they did not grasp it, and they were afraid to ask him about it.

Who Will Be the Greatest?

46An argument started among the disciples as to which of them would be the greatest. 47Jesus, knowing their thoughts, took a little child and had him stand beside him. 48Then he said to them, "Whoever welcomes this little child in my name welcomes me; and whoever welcomes me welcomes the one who sent me. For he who is least among you all—he is the greatest."

49"Master," said John, "we saw a man driving out demons in your name and we tried to stop him, because he is not one of us."

50"Do not stop him," Jesus said, "for whoever is not against you is for you."

Samaritan Opposition

51As the time approached for him to be taken up to heaven, Jesus resolutely set out for Jerusalem. 52And he sent messengers on ahead, who went into a Samaritan village to get things ready for him; 53but the people there did not welcome him, because he was heading for Jerusalem. 54When the disciples James and John saw this, they asked, "Lord, do you want us to call fire down from heaven to destroy them[b]?" 55But Jesus turned and rebuked them, 56and[c] they went to another village.

The Cost of Following Jesus

57As they were walking along the road, a man said to him, "I will follow you wherever you go."

58Jesus replied, "Foxes have holes and birds of the air have nests, but the Son of Man has no place to lay his head."

---

[a] 42 Greek *unclean* [b] 54 Some manuscripts *them, even as Elijah did* [c] 55,56 Some manuscripts *them. And he said, "You do not know what kind of spirit you are of, for the Son of Man did not come to destroy men's lives, but to save them."* 56*And*

59 He said to another man, "Follow me."

But the man replied, "Lord, first let me go and bury my father."

60 Jesus said to him, "Let the dead bury their own dead, but you go and proclaim the kingdom of God."

61 Still another said, "I will follow you, Lord; but first let me go back and say good-by to my family."

62 Jesus replied, "No one who puts his hand to the plow and looks back is fit for service in the kingdom of God."

Jesus Sends Out the Seventy-two

10 After this the Lord appointed seventy-two[a] others and sent them two by two ahead of him to every town and place where he was about to go. 2 He told them, "The harvest is plentiful, but the workers are few. Ask the Lord of the harvest, therefore, to send out workers into his harvest field. 3 Go! I am sending you out like lambs among wolves. 4 Do not take a purse or bag or sandals; and do not greet anyone on the road.

5 "When you enter a house, first say, 'Peace to this house.' 6 If a man of peace is there, your peace will rest on him; if not, it will return to you. 7 Stay in that house, eating and drinking whatever they give you, for the worker deserves his wages. Do not move around from house to house.

8 "When you enter a town and are welcomed, eat what is set before you. 9 Heal the sick who are there and tell them, 'The kingdom of God is near you.' 10 But when you enter a town and are not welcomed, go into its streets and say, 11 'Even the dust of your town that sticks to our feet we wipe off against you. Yet be sure of this: The kingdom of God is near.' 12 I tell you, it will be more bearable on that day for Sodom than for that town.

13 "Woe to you, Korazin! Woe to you, Bethsaida! For if the miracles that were performed in you had been performed in Tyre and Sidon, they would have repented long ago, sitting in sackcloth and ashes. 14 But it will be more bearable for Tyre and Sidon at the judgment than for you. 15 And you, Capernaum, will you be lifted up to the skies? No, you will go down to the depths.[b]

16 "He who listens to you listens to me; he who rejects you rejects me; but he who rejects me rejects him who sent me."

17 The seventy-two returned with joy and said, "Lord, even the demons submit to us in your name."

18 He replied, "I saw Satan fall like lightning from heaven. 19 I have given you authority to trample on snakes and scorpions and to overcome all the power of the enemy; nothing will harm you. 20 However, do not rejoice that the spirits submit to you, but rejoice that your names are written in heaven."

21 At that time Jesus, full of joy through the Holy Spirit, said, "I praise you, Father, Lord of heaven and earth, because you have hidden these things from the wise and learned, and revealed them to little children. Yes, Father, for this was your good pleasure.

22 "All things have been committed to me by my Father. No one knows who the Son is except the Father, and no one knows who the Father is except the Son and those to whom the Son chooses to reveal him."

23 Then he turned to his disciples and said privately, "Blessed are the eyes that see what you see. 24 For I tell you that many prophets and kings wanted to see what you see but did not see it, and to hear what you hear but did not hear it."

The Parable of the Good Samaritan

25 On one occasion an expert in the law stood up to test Jesus. "Teacher," he asked, "what must I do to inherit eternal life?"

26 "What is written in the Law?" he replied. "How do you read it?"

27 He answered: " 'Love the Lord your God with all your heart and with all your soul and with all your strength and with all your mind'[c]; and, 'Love your neighbor as yourself.'[d]"

28 "You have answered correctly," Jesus replied. "Do this and you will live."

29 But he wanted to justify himself, so he asked Jesus, "And who is my neighbor?"

30 In reply Jesus said: "A man was going down from Jerusalem to Jericho, when he fell into the hands of robbers. They stripped him of his clothes, beat him and went away, leaving him half dead. 31 A priest happened to be going down the same road, and when he saw the man, he passed by on the other side. 32 So too, a Levite, when he came to the place and saw him, passed by on the other side. 33 But a Samaritan, as he traveled, came where the man was; and when he saw him, he took pity on him. 34 He went to him and bandaged his wounds, pouring on oil and wine. Then he put the man on his own donkey, took him to

---

[a] *1* Some manuscripts *seventy*; also in verse 17 [b] *15* Greek *Hades* [c] *27* Deut. 6:5 [d] *27* Lev. 19:18

an inn and took care of him. 35The next day he took out two silver coins[a] and gave them to the innkeeper. 'Look after him,' he said, 'and when I return, I will reimburse you for any extra expense you may have.'

36"Which of these three do you think was a neighbor to the man who fell into the hands of robbers?"

37The expert in the law replied, "The one who had mercy on him."

Jesus told him, "Go and do likewise."

At the Home of Martha and Mary

38As Jesus and his disciples were on their way, he came to a village where a woman named Martha opened her home to him. 39She had a sister called Mary, who sat at the Lord's feet listening to what he said. 40But Martha was distracted by all the preparations that had to be made. She came to him and asked, "Lord, don't you care that my sister has left me to do the work by myself? Tell her to help me!"

41"Martha, Martha," the Lord answered, "you are worried and upset about many things, 42but only one thing is needed.[b] Mary has chosen what is better, and it will not be taken away from her."

Jesus' Teaching on Prayer

11 One day Jesus was praying in a certain place. When he finished, one of his disciples said to him, "Lord, teach us to pray, just as John taught his disciples."

2He said to them, "When you pray, say:

" 'Father,[c]
hallowed be your name,
your kingdom come.[d]
3Give us each day our daily bread.
4Forgive us our sins,
for we also forgive everyone who sins against us.[e]
And lead us not into temptation.[f] "

5Then he said to them, "Suppose one of you has a friend, and he goes to him at midnight and says, 'Friend, lend me three loaves of bread, 6because a friend of mine on a journey has come to me, and I have nothing to set before him.'

7"Then the one inside answers, 'Don't bother me. The door is already locked, and my children are with me in bed. I can't get up and give you anything.' 8I tell you, though he will not get up and give him the bread because he is his friend, yet because of the man's boldness[g] he will get up and give him as much as he needs.

9"So I say to you: Ask and it will be given to you; seek and you will find; knock and the door will be opened to you. 10For everyone who asks receives; he who seeks finds; and to him who knocks, the door will be opened.

11"Which of you fathers, if your son asks for[h] a fish, will give him a snake instead? 12Or if he asks for an egg, will give him a scorpion? 13If you then, though you are evil, know how to give good gifts to your children, how much more will your Father in heaven give the Holy Spirit to those who ask him!"

Jesus and Beelzebub

14Jesus was driving out a demon that was mute. When the demon left, the man who had been mute spoke, and the crowd was amazed. 15But some of them said, "By Beelzebub,[i] the prince of demons, he is driving out demons." 16Others tested him by asking for a sign from heaven.

17Jesus knew their thoughts and said to them: "Any kingdom divided against itself will be ruined, and a house divided against itself will fall. 18If Satan is divided against himself, how can his kingdom stand? I say this because you claim that I drive out demons by Beelzebub. 19Now if I drive out demons by Beelzebub, by whom do your followers drive them out? So then, they will be your judges. 20But if I drive out demons by the finger of God, then the kingdom of God has come to you.

21"When a strong man, fully armed, guards his own house, his possessions are safe. 22But when someone stronger attacks and overpowers him, he takes away the armor in which the man trusted and divides up the spoils.

23"He who is not with me is against me, and he who does not gather with me, scatters.

24"When an evil[j] spirit comes out of a man, it goes through arid places seeking rest and does not find it. Then it says, 'I will return to the house I left.' 25When it arrives, it finds the house swept clean and put in order. 26Then it goes and takes seven other spirits more wicked than itself, and they go in and live there. And

[a] 35 Greek *two denarii* [b] 42 Some manuscripts *but few things are needed—or only one* [c] 2 Some manuscripts *Our Father in heaven* [d] 2 Some manuscripts *come. May your will be done on earth as it is in heaven.* [e] 4 Greek *everyone who is indebted to us* [f] 4 Some manuscripts *temptation but deliver us from the evil one* [g] 8 Or *persistence* [h] 11 Some manuscripts *for bread, will give him a stone; or if he asks for* [i] 15 Greek *Beezeboul* or *Beelzeboul*; also in verses 18 and 19 [j] 24 Greek *unclean*

the final condition of that man is worse than
the first."
27 As Jesus was saying these things, a woman
in the crowd called out, "Blessed is the mother
who gave you birth and nursed you."
28 He replied, "Blessed rather are those who
hear the word of God and obey it."

The Sign of Jonah

29 As the crowds increased, Jesus said, "This
is a wicked generation. It asks for a miraculous
sign, but none will be given it except the sign
of Jonah. 30 For as Jonah was a sign to the Ninevites, so also will the Son of Man be to this
generation. 31 The Queen of the South will rise
at the judgment with the men of this generation and condemn them; for she came from
the ends of the earth to listen to Solomon's
wisdom, and now one[a] greater than Solomon
is here. 32 The men of Nineveh will stand up at
the judgment with this generation and condemn it; for they repented at the preaching
of Jonah, and now one greater than Jonah is
here.

The Lamp of the Body

33 "No one lights a lamp and puts it in a
place where it will be hidden, or under a bowl.
Instead he puts it on its stand, so that those
who come in may see the light. 34 Your eye is
the lamp of your body. When your eyes are
good, your whole body also is full of light. But
when they are bad, your body also is full of
darkness. 35 See to it, then, that the light within you is not darkness. 36 Therefore, if your
whole body is full of light, and no part of it
dark, it will be completely lighted, as when the
light of a lamp shines on you."

Six Woes

37 When Jesus had finished speaking, a
Pharisee invited him to eat with him; so he
went in and reclined at the table. 38 But the
Pharisee, noticing that Jesus did not first wash
before the meal, was surprised.
39 Then the Lord said to him, "Now then,
you Pharisees clean the outside of the cup and
dish, but inside you are full of greed and wickedness. 40 You foolish people! Did not the one
who made the outside make the inside also?
41 But give what is inside ⌞the dish⌟[b] to the
poor, and everything will be clean for you.
42 "Woe to you Pharisees, because you give
God a tenth of your mint, rue and all other
kinds of garden herbs, but you neglect justice
and the love of God. You should have practiced the latter without leaving the former
undone.
43 "Woe to you Pharisees, because you love
the most important seats in the synagogues
and greetings in the marketplaces.
44 "Woe to you, because you are like un-
marked graves, which men walk over without
knowing it."
45 One of the experts in the law answered
him, "Teacher, when you say these things, you
insult us also."
46 Jesus replied, "And you experts in the law,
woe to you, because you load people down with
burdens they can hardly carry, and you yourselves will not lift one finger to help them.
47 "Woe to you, because you build tombs
for the prophets, and it was your forefathers
who killed them. 48 So you testify that you approve of what your forefathers did; they killed
the prophets, and you build their tombs.
49 Because of this, God in his wisdom said, 'I
will send them prophets and apostles, some
of whom they will kill and others they will
persecute.' 50 Therefore this generation will
be held responsible for the blood of all the
prophets that has been shed since the beginning of the world, 51 from the blood of Abel
to the blood of Zechariah, who was killed between the altar and the sanctuary. Yes, I tell
you, this generation will be held responsible
for it all.
52 "Woe to you experts in the law, because
you have taken away the key to knowledge.
You yourselves have not entered, and you have
hindered those who were entering."
53 When Jesus left there, the Pharisees and
the teachers of the law began to oppose him
fiercely and to besiege him with questions,
54 waiting to catch him in something he might
say.

Warnings and Encouragements

12 Meanwhile, when a crowd of many
thousands had gathered, so that they
were trampling on one another, Jesus
began to speak first to his disciples, saying:
"Be on your guard against the yeast of the
Pharisees, which is hypocrisy. 2 There is nothing concealed that will not be disclosed, or
hidden that will not be made known. 3 What
you have said in the dark will be heard in the
daylight, and what you have whispered in the
ear in the inner rooms will be proclaimed
from the roofs.

---

[a] 31 Or *something*; also in verse 32 [b] 41 Or *what you have*

WEEKEND

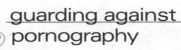

guarding against pornography

My husband sees nothing wrong with occasional pornography. He says he's not addicted; he just watches it as entertainment. I asked him how he'd feel if it were the other way around; if I were the one looking at porn. He says that would be OK. What should I do?

There are two issues at work here. The first is pornography. There's a potential for marital trust to erode whenever images of other individuals are introduced for sexual entertainment or arousal. We've seen hundreds of men and women who've slipped into disaster beginning with the infrequent, "innocent" use of pornography. If you're concerned that your husband would choose his occasional use of pornography over you, you need serious help with your relationship.

The second is how to deal with conflict in marriage. Being able to talk about your concerns and fears is important, but presenting those in an ultimatum is probably not the most effective way to say it. An ultimatum is a controlling style of communication that usually elicits a defensive response—an aggressive counterattack or passive withdrawal. Neither leads to resolution and connectedness.

An alternative is to make statements about your feelings or desires only, not your spouse's. Your husband needs to hear about your fears and your feelings of inadequacy or rejection. It's important for him to understand your desire to feel cherished, which is certainly more important than pornography. Let him know you want to be his playmate of a lifetime, and that you want to pleasure him in real, flesh and blood ways!

—LOUIS AND MELISSA MCBURNEY

If you struggle with sexual addiction or simply want to protect your family from the temptation of porn, consider these practical steps.

1. *Put up a safety net.* Keep all TVs and computers in the open, where the family gathers. If you must have cable television, install a filter or trap on your line to block out unwanted channels. Also, use an Internet filter or spam-blocking program on all computers in your home.

2. *Fortify your spirit.* Read your Bible regularly and memorize Scriptures that you can recite when tempted, such as Romans 6:13–14 and 1 Corinthians 6:19–20. Pray for strength (Philippians 4:13), and listen to Christian radio while doing mundane tasks.

3. *Get help.* If you're addicted to porn, find a Christian counselor who specializes in sexual addictions. Join a Christian support group for people with sexual addictions. Focus on the Family's Christian counselor referral service can recommend qualified counselors who specialize in sexual addictions; call 1–719–531–3400.

—TERESA COOK

do you have a problem?

HOW ARE WE DOING?

1. If you're curious about pornography but haven't looked for it, give yourself a 0.
2. If you've found some porn sites, give yourself a 1.
3. If you have checked out some of the sites, give yourself a 2.
4. If you regularly check out the sites to see what's new, give yourself a 3.
5. If you rearrange your schedule to view porn—for example, if you've ever stayed home while your wife went shopping or cancelled lunch plans so you could look at pornography—give yourself a 4.
6. If you can't go a day without looking at porn, give yourself a 5.

Now consider this. According to Craig Gross of XXXChurch.com, a ministry that exists to bring awareness, accountability and recovery to people involved with pornography, you can go from a 0 to a 5 in as little as three days.

—From the video *Porn Blvd*, produced by XXXChurch.com.

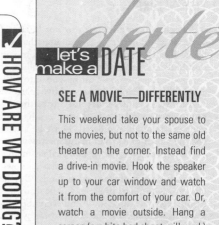

let's make a DATE

SEE A MOVIE—DIFFERENTLY

This weekend take your spouse to the movies, but not to the same old theater on the corner. Instead find a drive-in movie. Hook the speaker up to your car window and watch it from the comfort of your car. Or, watch a movie outside. Hang a screen (a white bed sheet will work) on the back of your house, borrow a projector and laptop, and show the movie. For a real visual experience, order 3-D glasses online (they're often free) and show a 3-D film. Or if you want the big picture, try visiting a local Imax theater.

FOR YOUR NEXT DEVOTIONAL READING, TURN TO PAGE 1157.

LESSONS FROM THE *Bible*

How did visual stimulation get Samson (Judges 14:1–3) and David (2 Samuel 11:1–5) in trouble?

4"I tell you, my friends, do not be afraid
of those who kill the body and after that can
do no more. 5But I will show you whom you
should fear: Fear him who, after the killing of
the body, has power to throw you into hell.
Yes, I tell you, fear him. 6Are not five sparrows
sold for two pennies[a]? Yet not one of them is
forgotten by God. 7Indeed, the very hairs of
your head are all numbered. Don't be afraid;
you are worth more than many sparrows.

8"I tell you, whoever acknowledges me before men, the Son of Man will also acknowledge him before the angels of God. 9But he
who disowns me before men will be disowned
before the angels of God. 10And everyone who
speaks a word against the Son of Man will be
forgiven, but anyone who blasphemes against
the Holy Spirit will not be forgiven.

11"When you are brought before synagogues, rulers and authorities, do not worry
about how you will defend yourselves or what
you will say, 12for the Holy Spirit will teach
you at that time what you should say."

The Parable of the Rich Fool

13Someone in the crowd said to him,
"Teacher, tell my brother to divide the inheritance with me."

14Jesus replied, "Man, who appointed me a
judge or an arbiter between you?" 15Then he
said to them, "Watch out! Be on your guard
against all kinds of greed; a man's life does not
consist in the abundance of his possessions."

16And he told them this parable: "The
ground of a certain rich man produced a good
crop. 17He thought to himself, 'What shall I
do? I have no place to store my crops.'

18"Then he said, 'This is what I'll do. I will
tear down my barns and build bigger ones, and
there I will store all my grain and my goods.
19And I'll say to myself, "You have plenty of
good things laid up for many years. Take life
easy; eat, drink and be merry." '

20"But God said to him, 'You fool! This
very night your life will be demanded from
you. Then who will get what you have prepared for yourself?'

21"This is how it will be with anyone who
stores up things for himself but is not rich toward God."

Do Not Worry

22Then Jesus said to his disciples: "Therefore I tell you, do not worry about your life,
what you will eat; or about your body, what
you will wear. 23Life is more than food, and
the body more than clothes. 24Consider the
ravens: They do not sow or reap, they have no
storeroom or barn; yet God feeds them. And
how much more valuable you are than birds!
25Who of you by worrying can add a single
hour to his life[b]? 26Since you cannot do this
very little thing, why do you worry about the
rest?

27"Consider how the lilies grow. They do
not labor or spin. Yet I tell you, not even Solomon in all his splendor was dressed like one
of these. 28If that is how God clothes the grass
of the field, which is here today, and tomorrow is thrown into the fire, how much more
will he clothe you, O you of little faith! 29And
do not set your heart on what you will eat or
drink; do not worry about it. 30For the pagan
world runs after all such things, and your Father knows that you need them. 31But seek
his kingdom, and these things will be given
to you as well.

32"Do not be afraid, little flock, for your
Father has been pleased to give you the kingdom. 33Sell your possessions and give to the
poor. Provide purses for yourselves that will
not wear out, a treasure in heaven that will not
be exhausted, where no thief comes near and
no moth destroys. 34For where your treasure
is, there your heart will be also.

Watchfulness

35"Be dressed ready for service and keep
your lamps burning, 36like men waiting for
their master to return from a wedding banquet, so that when he comes and knocks they
can immediately open the door for him. 37It
will be good for those servants whose master
finds them watching when he comes. I tell you
the truth, he will dress himself to serve, will
have them recline at the table and will come
and wait on them. 38It will be good for those
servants whose master finds them ready, even
if he comes in the second or third watch of the
night. 39But understand this: If the owner of
the house had known at what hour the thief
was coming, he would not have let his house
be broken into. 40You also must be ready, because the Son of Man will come at an hour
when you do not expect him."

41Peter asked, "Lord, are you telling this
parable to us, or to everyone?"

42The Lord answered, "Who then is the
faithful and wise manager, whom the master
puts in charge of his servants to give them

---

[a] 6 Greek *two assaria* [b] 25 Or *single cubit to his height*

MONDAY
READ LUKE 12:13–34

GIVING UP WORRY

> **"Do not be afraid, little flock, for your Father has been pleased to give you the kingdom."**
>
> — LUKE 12:32

let's talk

- Was there ever a time when we worried that God might not provide for us? What happened?
- As a couple, what is our greatest treasure?
- How can we loosen our grip on earthly things and begin to trust God more with our needs?

My friend DW operates a local homeless shelter. Until three years ago, he didn't draw a salary from the ministry. Even now, the ministry depends entirely on donations. Plus, DW has no health insurance or retirement plan.

DW trusted God for every penny to run the rescue mission and to meet his needs, including his need for a wife. He knew that any woman willing to be his wife would have to be willing to trust God to meet their needs as a couple.

Enter Kate. When she met DW, she was immediately attracted to him, particularly his passion for reaching out to people with the gospel. They dated long-distance for many months; then DW proposed. Because they lived in separate states, marrying DW meant that Kate would have to leave her job with a guaranteed salary, health insurance and a 401(k) plan. She wanted to say yes, but—

In Luke 12:32–34, Jesus cut to the heart of what holds many of us hostage: money and possessions. He wasn't just talking about greed or wanting riches for prestige, but about the false sense of security money can give. We tend to feel secure when our job provides generous benefits, including insurance, retirement savings and a bonus plan; when our house keeps escalating in value; and when our investments are growing. While it's true that God provides for his children through those means, his bounty is not limited to physical wealth.

In Luke 12:22–31, Jesus told his disciples not to worry like unbelievers do about what to wear, eat or drink. He said, "Do not worry about your life, what you will eat; or about your body, what you will wear. Life is more than food, and the body more than clothes" (verses 22–23). He then told his followers to sell their possessions and give the money to the poor so they could seek a treasure in heaven that would never fail. "For where your treasure is, there your heart will be also" (verse 34).

Jesus was using hyperbole here to make a point: Everything belongs to the Father and we can trust him to provide for us—even when our earthly resources run out. When we're downsized at work and forced to live off savings, when our car dies or refrigerator croaks, when we learn another baby is on the way, when we're asked to follow our heart even when it means giving up our usual way of earning a living—in all these situations we need not worry. God, who cares for the birds and flowers, cares for us even more.

When Kate turned down DW's proposal, he was disappointed, but he understood. "Not everybody is cut out to do what I do," he said. "It's scary to think of trusting God this much. But God has never failed me, and I know he never will."

As deep as Kate's fear was of letting go of her financial lifelines, God's grace reached deeper. After several months, she contacted DW and said that if he still wanted her, she was willing to live by faith as long as she could do it with him.

We aren't all expected to make such choices, but we are expected to find our treasure in God, not in stuff that can only fail us.

—NANCY KENNEDY

FOR YOUR NEXT DEVOTIONAL READING, TURN TO PAGE 1161.

their food allowance at the proper time? 43It will be good for that servant whom the master finds doing so when he returns. 44I tell you the truth, he will put him in charge of all his possessions. 45But suppose the servant says to himself, 'My master is taking a long time in coming,' and he then begins to beat the menservants and maidservants and to eat and drink and get drunk. 46The master of that servant will come on a day when he does not expect him and at an hour he is not aware of. He will cut him to pieces and assign him a place with the unbelievers.

47"That servant who knows his master's will and does not get ready or does not do what his master wants will be beaten with many blows. 48But the one who does not know and does things deserving punishment will be beaten with few blows. From everyone who has been given much, much will be demanded; and from the one who has been entrusted with much, much more will be asked.

Not Peace but Division

49"I have come to bring fire on the earth, and how I wish it were already kindled! 50But I have a baptism to undergo, and how distressed I am until it is completed! 51Do you think I came to bring peace on earth? No, I tell you, but division. 52From now on there will be five in one family divided against each other, three against two and two against three. 53They will be divided, father against son and son against father, mother against daughter and daughter against mother, mother-in-law against daughter-in-law and daughter-in-law against mother-in-law."

Interpreting the Times

54He said to the crowd: "When you see a cloud rising in the west, immediately you say, 'It's going to rain,' and it does. 55And when the south wind blows, you say, 'It's going to be hot,' and it is. 56Hypocrites! You know how to interpret the appearance of the earth and the sky. How is it that you don't know how to interpret this present time?

57"Why don't you judge for yourselves what is right? 58As you are going with your adversary to the magistrate, try hard to be reconciled to him on the way, or he may drag you off to the judge, and the judge turn you over to the officer, and the officer throw you into prison. 59I tell you, you will not get out until you have paid the last penny.[a]"

Repent or Perish

13 Now there were some present at that time who told Jesus about the Galileans whose blood Pilate had mixed with their sacrifices. 2Jesus answered, "Do you think that these Galileans were worse sinners than all the other Galileans because they suffered this way? 3I tell you, no! But unless you repent, you too will all perish. 4Or those eighteen who died when the tower in Siloam fell on them—do you think they were more guilty than all the others living in Jerusalem? 5I tell you, no! But unless you repent, you too will all perish."

6Then he told this parable: "A man had a fig tree, planted in his vineyard, and he went to look for fruit on it, but did not find any. 7So he said to the man who took care of the vineyard, 'For three years now I've been coming to look for fruit on this fig tree and haven't found any. Cut it down! Why should it use up the soil?'

8" 'Sir,' the man replied, 'leave it alone for one more year, and I'll dig around it and fertilize it. 9If it bears fruit next year, fine! If not, then cut it down.' "

A Crippled Woman Healed on the Sabbath

10On a Sabbath Jesus was teaching in one of the synagogues, 11and a woman was there who had been crippled by a spirit for eighteen years. She was bent over and could not straighten up at all. 12When Jesus saw her, he called her forward and said to her, "Woman, you are set free from your infirmity." 13Then he put his hands on her, and immediately she straightened up and praised God.

14Indignant because Jesus had healed on the Sabbath, the synagogue ruler said to the people, "There are six days for work. So come and be healed on those days, not on the Sabbath."

15The Lord answered him, "You hypocrites! Doesn't each of you on the Sabbath untie his ox or donkey from the stall and lead it out to give it water? 16Then should not this woman, a daughter of Abraham, whom Satan has kept bound for eighteen long years, be set free on the Sabbath day from what bound her?"

17When he said this, all his opponents were humiliated, but the people were delighted with all the wonderful things he was doing.

The Parables of the Mustard Seed and the Yeast

18Then Jesus asked, "What is the kingdom of God like? What shall I compare it to? 19It

c 59 Greek *lepton*

is like a mustard seed, which a man took and planted in his garden. It grew and became a tree, and the birds of the air perched in its branches."

20Again he asked, "What shall I compare the kingdom of God to? 21It is like yeast that a woman took and mixed into a large amount[a] of flour until it worked all through the dough."

The Narrow Door

22Then Jesus went through the towns and villages, teaching as he made his way to Jerusalem. 23Someone asked him, "Lord, are only a few people going to be saved?"

He said to them, 24"Make every effort to enter through the narrow door, because many, I tell you, will try to enter and will not be able to. 25Once the owner of the house gets up and closes the door, you will stand outside knocking and pleading, 'Sir, open the door for us.'

"But he will answer, 'I don't know you or where you come from.'

26"Then you will say, 'We ate and drank with you, and you taught in our streets.'

27"But he will reply, 'I don't know you or where you come from. Away from me, all you evildoers!'

28"There will be weeping there, and gnashing of teeth, when you see Abraham, Isaac and Jacob and all the prophets in the kingdom of God, but you yourselves thrown out. 29People will come from east and west and north and south, and will take their places at the feast in the kingdom of God. 30Indeed there are those who are last who will be first, and first who will be last."

Jesus' Sorrow for Jerusalem

31At that time some Pharisees came to Jesus and said to him, "Leave this place and go somewhere else. Herod wants to kill you."

32He replied, "Go tell that fox, 'I will drive out demons and heal people today and tomorrow, and on the third day I will reach my goal.' 33In any case, I must keep going today and tomorrow and the next day—for surely no prophet can die outside Jerusalem!

34"O Jerusalem, Jerusalem, you who kill the prophets and stone those sent to you, how often I have longed to gather your children together, as a hen gathers her chicks under her wings, but you were not willing! 35Look, your house is left to you desolate. I tell you, you will not see me again until you say, 'Blessed is he who comes in the name of the Lord.'[b]"

Jesus at a Pharisee's House

14 One Sabbath, when Jesus went to eat in the house of a prominent Pharisee, he was being carefully watched. 2There in front of him was a man suffering from dropsy. 3Jesus asked the Pharisees and experts in the law, "Is it lawful to heal on the Sabbath or not?" 4But they remained silent. So taking hold of the man, he healed him and sent him away.

5Then he asked them, "If one of you has a son[c] or an ox that falls into a well on the Sabbath day, will you not immediately pull him out?" 6And they had nothing to say.

7When he noticed how the guests picked the places of honor at the table, he told them this parable: 8"When someone invites you to a wedding feast, do not take the place of honor, for a person more distinguished than you may have been invited. 9If so, the host who invited both of you will come and say to you, 'Give this man your seat.' Then, humiliated, you will have to take the least important place. 10But when you are invited, take the lowest place, so that when your host comes, he will say to you, 'Friend, move up to a better place.' Then you will be honored in the presence of all your fellow guests. 11For everyone who exalts himself will be humbled, and he who humbles himself will be exalted."

12Then Jesus said to his host, "When you give a luncheon or dinner, do not invite your friends, your brothers or relatives, or your rich neighbors; if you do, they may invite you back and so you will be repaid. 13But when you give a banquet, invite the poor, the crippled, the lame, the blind, 14and you will be blessed. Although they cannot repay you, you will be repaid at the resurrection of the righteous."

The Parable of the Great Banquet

15When one of those at the table with him heard this, he said to Jesus, "Blessed is the man who will eat at the feast in the kingdom of God."

16Jesus replied: "A certain man was preparing a great banquet and invited many guests. 17At the time of the banquet he sent his servant to tell those who had been invited, 'Come, for everything is now ready.'

18"But they all alike began to make excuses.

[a] *21* Greek *three satas* (probably about 1/2 bushel or 22 liters) [b] *35* Psalm 118:26 [c] *5* Some manuscripts *donkey*

The first said, ‘I have just bought a field, and I must go and see it. Please excuse me.’

19“Another said, ‘I have just bought five yoke of oxen, and I’m on my way to try them out. Please excuse me.’

20“Still another said, ‘I just got married, so I can’t come.’

21“The servant came back and reported this to his master. Then the owner of the house became angry and ordered his servant, ‘Go out quickly into the streets and alleys of the town and bring in the poor, the crippled, the blind and the lame.’

22“ ‘Sir,’ the servant said, ‘what you ordered has been done, but there is still room.’

23“Then the master told his servant, ‘Go out to the roads and country lanes and make them come in, so that my house will be full. 24I tell you, not one of those men who were invited will get a taste of my banquet.’ ”

The Cost of Being a Disciple

25Large crowds were traveling with Jesus, and turning to them he said: 26“If anyone comes to me and does not hate his father and mother, his wife and children, his brothers and sisters—yes, even his own life—he cannot be my disciple. 27And anyone who does not carry his cross and follow me cannot be my disciple.

28“Suppose one of you wants to build a tower. Will he not first sit down and estimate the cost to see if he has enough money to complete it? 29For if he lays the foundation and is not able to finish it, everyone who sees it will ridicule him, 30saying, ‘This fellow began to build and was not able to finish.’

31“Or suppose a king is about to go to war against another king. Will he not first sit down and consider whether he is able with ten thousand men to oppose the one coming against him with twenty thousand? 32If he is not able, he will send a delegation while the other is still a long way off and will ask for terms of peace. 33In the same way, any of you who does not give up everything he has cannot be my disciple.

34“Salt is good, but if it loses its saltiness, how can it be made salty again? 35It is fit neither for the soil nor for the manure pile; it is thrown out.

“He who has ears to hear, let him hear.”

The Parable of the Lost Sheep

15 Now the tax collectors and “sinners” were all gathering around to hear him. 2But the Pharisees and the teachers of the law muttered, “This man welcomes sinners and eats with them.”

3Then Jesus told them this parable: 4“Suppose one of you has a hundred sheep and loses one of them. Does he not leave the ninety-nine in the open country and go after the lost sheep until he finds it? 5And when he finds it, he joyfully puts it on his shoulders 6and goes home. Then he calls his friends and neighbors together and says, ‘Rejoice with me; I have found my lost sheep.’ 7I tell you that in the same way there will be more rejoicing in heaven over one sinner who repents than over ninety-nine righteous persons who do not need to repent.

The Parable of the Lost Coin

8“Or suppose a woman has ten silver coins[a] and loses one. Does she not light a lamp, sweep the house and search carefully until she finds it? 9And when she finds it, she calls her friends and neighbors together and says, ‘Rejoice with me; I have found my lost coin.’ 10In the same way, I tell you, there is rejoicing in the presence of the angels of God over one sinner who repents.”

The Parable of the Lost Son

11Jesus continued: “There was a man who had two sons. 12The younger one said to his father, ‘Father, give me my share of the estate.’ So he divided his property between them.

13“Not long after that, the younger son got together all he had, set off for a distant country and there squandered his wealth in wild living. 14After he had spent everything, there was a severe famine in that whole country, and he began to be in need. 15So he went and hired himself out to a citizen of that country, who sent him to his fields to feed pigs. 16He longed to fill his stomach with the pods that the pigs were eating, but no one gave him anything.

17“When he came to his senses, he said, ‘How many of my father’s hired men have food to spare, and here I am starving to death! 18I will set out and go back to my father and say to him: Father, I have sinned against heaven and against you. 19I am no longer worthy to be called your son; make me like one of your hired men.’ 20So he got up and went to his father.

[a] 8 Greek *ten drachmas,* each worth about a day’s wages

arus, covered with sores 21and longing to eat
what fell from the rich man's table. Even the
dogs came and licked his sores.
22"The time came when the beggar died and
the angels carried him to Abraham's side. The
rich man also died and was buried. 23In hell,[a]
where he was in torment, he looked up and
saw Abraham far away, with Lazarus by his
side. 24So he called to him, 'Father Abraham,
have pity on me and send Lazarus to dip the
tip of his finger in water and cool my tongue,
because I am in agony in this fire.'
25"But Abraham replied, 'Son, remember
that in your lifetime you received your good
things, while Lazarus received bad things, but
now he is comforted here and you are in agony. 26And besides all this, between us and
you a great chasm has been fixed, so that those
who want to go from here to you cannot, nor
can anyone cross over from there to us.'
27"He answered, 'Then I beg you, father,
send Lazarus to my father's house, 28for I have
five brothers. Let him warn them, so that they
will not also come to this place of torment.'
29"Abraham replied, 'They have Moses and
the Prophets; let them listen to them.'
30" 'No, father Abraham,' he said, 'but if
someone from the dead goes to them, they
will repent.'
31"He said to him, 'If they do not listen to
Moses and the Prophets, they will not be convinced even if someone rises from the dead.' "

Sin, Faith, Duty

17 Jesus said to his disciples: "Things that
cause people to sin are bound to come,
but woe to that person through whom
they come. 2It would be better for him to
be thrown into the sea with a millstone tied
around his neck than for him to cause one of
these little ones to sin. 3So watch yourselves.
"If your brother sins, rebuke him, and if
he repents, forgive him. 4If he sins against
you seven times in a day, and seven times
comes back to you and says, 'I repent,' forgive him."
5The apostles said to the Lord, "Increase
our faith!"
6He replied, "If you have faith as small as
a mustard seed, you can say to this mulberry
tree, 'Be uprooted and planted in the sea,' and
it will obey you.
7"Suppose one of you had a servant plowing or looking after the sheep. Would he say
to the servant when he comes in from the
field, 'Come along now and sit down to eat'?
8Would he not rather say, 'Prepare my supper,
get yourself ready and wait on me while I eat
and drink; after that you may eat and drink'?
9Would he thank the servant because he did
what he was told to do? 10So you also, when
you have done everything you were told to
do, should say, 'We are unworthy servants; we
have only done our duty.' "

Ten Healed of Leprosy

11Now on his way to Jerusalem, Jesus traveled along the border between Samaria and
Galilee. 12As he was going into a village, ten
men who had leprosy[b] met him. They stood
at a distance 13and called out in a loud voice,
"Jesus, Master, have pity on us!"
14When he saw them, he said, "Go, show
yourselves to the priests." And as they went,
they were cleansed.
15One of them, when he saw he was healed,
came back, praising God in a loud voice.
16He threw himself at Jesus' feet and thanked
him—and he was a Samaritan.
17Jesus asked, "Were not all ten cleansed?
Where are the other nine? 18Was no one found
to return and give praise to God except this
foreigner?" 19Then he said to him, "Rise and
go; your faith has made you well."

The Coming of the Kingdom of God

20Once, having been asked by the Pharisees
when the kingdom of God would come, Jesus
replied, "The kingdom of God does not come
with your careful observation, 21nor will people say, 'Here it is,' or 'There it is,' because the
kingdom of God is within[c] you."
22Then he said to his disciples, "The time is
coming when you will long to see one of the
days of the Son of Man, but you will not see
it. 23Men will tell you, 'There he is!' or 'Here
he is!' Do not go running off after them. 24For
the Son of Man in his day[d] will be like the
lightning, which flashes and lights up the sky
from one end to the other. 25But first he must
suffer many things and be rejected by this generation.
26"Just as it was in the days of Noah, so also
will it be in the days of the Son of Man. 27Peo-
ple were eating, drinking, marrying and being
given in marriage up to the day Noah entered
the ark. Then the flood came and destroyed
them all.
28"It was the same in the days of Lot. People were eating and drinking, buying and sell-

[a] 23 Greek *Hades* [b] 12 The Greek word was used for various diseases affecting the skin—not necessarily leprosy. [c] 21 Or *among*
[d] 24 Some manuscripts do not have *in his day.*

WEDNESDAY
READ LUKE 17:1–10

GIVING FORGIVENESS A CHANCE

"If he sins against you seven times in a day, and seven times comes back to you and says, 'I repent,' forgive him." The apostles said to the Lord, "Increase our faith!"

— LUKE 17:4–5

My friend and her husband look through their wedding album together each year on their anniversary. My friend dreads the review because there, amid the pictures of happiness, is the visual reminder of an incident she still finds hard to forgive.

What brings back the anger and embarrassment of that day is the picture of my friend's husband smearing wedding cake over her face. He thought it was funny; she thought it was tacky and mean.

They bickered each time they saw that picture until my friend finally decided to accept her husband's apology and forgive him. "It doesn't mean what he did was right," she said. "Smearing cake in my face humiliated me in front of my friends and family. But I'm tired of carrying that anger around."

In Luke 17:4, Jesus tells us to forgive over and over again—time after time. Is he instructing us to be doormats and let others run over us? Or does he know something about forgiveness that will free us?

As we ponder our attitude toward forgiveness, we might say, "Easier said than done." A husband and wife can inflict pain on each other that scars their relationship for the rest of their lives. At the very least, a spouse can perpetuate annoyances and frustrations that make the other spouse blow up.

Jesus is not telling us that we need to condone behavior that hurts us. In fact, in Matthew 18:15–17, he gives instruction on confronting others with their sin. He doesn't expect us to say to the offender, "Hey, it's nothing; forget about it!"

Nor is he telling us to forgive only those people who ask for forgiveness. Jesus' own words on the cross asking the Father to pardon his executioners make that clear (see Luke 23:34).

Finally, Jesus is not telling us to ignore repeated sinful behavior by our spouse. After all, repeatedly forgiving wrong without confronting the reasons for it will ultimately kill trust in any relationship.

What Jesus *is* telling us is that denying forgiveness to the offender will ultimately hurt us more than it hurts them. For when we lug around a load of self-pity and bitterness and an attitude of martyrdom, we put a big roadblock of resentment between ourselves and the people who have hurt us. A future relationship with someone we refuse to forgive may become lost forever.

Still, it's difficult to forgive. That's why the disciples' response to Jesus—"Increase our faith!"—resounds with truth. It takes faith and trust to extend forgiveness to a spouse. And it takes faith and trust to accept that forgiveness and vow to work on the problems that caused the situation in the first place.

Only when we look at the One who forgives us of our sins can we put human forgiveness into perspective.

—VALERIE VAN KOOTEN

FOR YOUR NEXT DEVOTIONAL READING, TURN TO PAGE 1169.

let's *talk*

- ✦ Which is more difficult—to be the one who needs to forgive or to be the one who needs to be forgiven?
- ✦ Are there things in our marriage for which we need to forgive each other and move on? What makes such forgiveness difficult?
- ✦ How does looking at Jesus' forgiveness of our sins put our forgiveness of each other into perspective?

ing, planting and building. 29But the day Lot
left Sodom, fire and sulfur rained down from
heaven and destroyed them all.
30"It will be just like this on the day the Son
of Man is revealed. 31On that day no one who
is on the roof of his house, with his goods inside, should go down to get them. Likewise,
no one in the field should go back for anything. 32Remember Lot's wife! 33Whoever
tries to keep his life will lose it, and whoever
loses his life will preserve it. 34I tell you, on
that night two people will be in one bed; one
will be taken and the other left. 35Two wom-
en will be grinding grain together; one will be
taken and the other left.[a]"
37"Where, Lord?" they asked.
He replied, "Where there is a dead body,
there the vultures will gather."

The Parable of the Persistent Widow

18 Then Jesus told his disciples a parable
to show them that they should always
pray and not give up. 2He said: "In a
certain town there was a judge who neither
feared God nor cared about men. 3And there
was a widow in that town who kept coming to
him with the plea, 'Grant me justice against
my adversary.'
4"For some time he refused. But finally he
said to himself, 'Even though I don't fear God
or care about men, 5yet because this widow
keeps bothering me, I will see that she gets justice, so that she won't eventually wear me out
with her coming!' "
6And the Lord said, "Listen to what the unjust judge says. 7And will not God bring about
justice for his chosen ones, who cry out to him
day and night? Will he keep putting them off?
8I tell you, he will see that they get justice,
and quickly. However, when the Son of Man
comes, will he find faith on the earth?"

The Parable of the Pharisee and the Tax Collector

9To some who were confident of their own
righteousness and looked down on everybody
else, Jesus told this parable: 10"Two men went
up to the temple to pray, one a Pharisee and
the other a tax collector. 11The Pharisee stood
up and prayed about[b] himself: 'God, I thank
you that I am not like other men—robbers,
evildoers, adulterers—or even like this tax collector. 12I fast twice a week and give a tenth
of all I get.'
13"But the tax collector stood at a distance.
He would not even look up to heaven, but
beat his breast and said, 'God, have mercy on
me, a sinner.'
14"I tell you that this man, rather than the
other, went home justified before God. For
everyone who exalts himself will be humbled,
and he who humbles himself will be exalted."

The Little Children and Jesus

15People were also bringing babies to Jesus
to have him touch them. When the disciples saw this, they rebuked them. 16But Jesus
called the children to him and said, "Let the
little children come to me, and do not hinder them, for the kingdom of God belongs to
such as these. 17I tell you the truth, anyone
who will not receive the kingdom of God like
a little child will never enter it."

The Rich Ruler

18A certain ruler asked him, "Good teacher,
what must I do to inherit eternal life?"
19"Why do you call me good?" Jesus answered. "No one is good—except God alone.
20You know the commandments: 'Do not
commit adultery, do not murder, do not steal,
do not give false testimony, honor your father
and mother.'[c]"
21"All these I have kept since I was a boy,"
he said.
22When Jesus heard this, he said to him,
"You still lack one thing. Sell everything you
have and give to the poor, and you will have
treasure in heaven. Then come, follow me."
23When he heard this, he became very sad,
because he was a man of great wealth. 24Jesus
looked at him and said, "How hard it is for the
rich to enter the kingdom of God! 25Indeed, it
is easier for a camel to go through the eye of a
needle than for a rich man to enter the kingdom of God."
26Those who heard this asked, "Who then
can be saved?"
27Jesus replied, "What is impossible with
men is possible with God."
28Peter said to him, "We have left all we had
to follow you!"
29"I tell you the truth," Jesus said to them,
"no one who has left home or wife or brothers
or parents or children for the sake of the kingdom of God 30will fail to receive many times
as much in this age and, in the age to come,
eternal life."

---

[a] 35 Some manuscripts *left.* *36Two men will be in the field; one will be taken and the other left.* [b] 11 Or *to* [c] 20 Exodus 20:12-16; Deut. 5:16-20

Jesus Again Predicts His Death

31 Jesus took the Twelve aside and told
them, "We are going up to Jerusalem, and everything that is written by the prophets about
the Son of Man will be fulfilled. 32 He will be
handed over to the Gentiles. They will mock
him, insult him, spit on him, flog him and kill
him. 33 On the third day he will rise again."
34 The disciples did not understand any
of this. Its meaning was hidden from them,
and they did not know what he was talking
about.

A Blind Beggar Receives His Sight

35 As Jesus approached Jericho, a blind man
was sitting by the roadside begging. 36 When
he heard the crowd going by, he asked what
was happening. 37 They told him, "Jesus of
Nazareth is passing by."
38 He called out, "Jesus, Son of David, have
mercy on me!"
39 Those who led the way rebuked him and
told him to be quiet, but he shouted all the
more, "Son of David, have mercy on me!"
40 Jesus stopped and ordered the man to be
brought to him. When he came near, Jesus
asked him, 41 "What do you want me to do
for you?"
"Lord, I want to see," he replied.
42 Jesus said to him, "Receive your sight;
your faith has healed you." 43 Immediately he
received his sight and followed Jesus, praising
God. When all the people saw it, they also
praised God.

Zacchaeus the Tax Collector

19 Jesus entered Jericho and was passing
through. 2 A man was there by the name
of Zacchaeus; he was a chief tax collector and was wealthy. 3 He wanted to see who
Jesus was, but being a short man he could not,
because of the crowd. 4 So he ran ahead and
climbed a sycamore-fig tree to see him, since
Jesus was coming that way.
5 When Jesus reached the spot, he looked
up and said to him, "Zacchaeus, come down
immediately. I must stay at your house today."
6 So he came down at once and welcomed him
gladly.
7 All the people saw this and began to mutter, "He has gone to be the guest of a 'sinner.'"
8 But Zacchaeus stood up and said to the
Lord, "Look, Lord! Here and now I give half
of my possessions to the poor, and if I have
cheated anybody out of anything, I will pay
back four times the amount."
9 Jesus said to him, "Today salvation has
come to this house, because this man, too, is a
son of Abraham. 10 For the Son of Man came
to seek and to save what was lost."

The Parable of the Ten Minas

11 While they were listening to this, he went
on to tell them a parable, because he was near
Jerusalem and the people thought that the
kingdom of God was going to appear at once.
12 He said: "A man of noble birth went to a distant country to have himself appointed king
and then to return. 13 So he called ten of his
servants and gave them ten minas.[a] 'Put this
money to work,' he said, 'until I come back.'
14 "But his subjects hated him and sent a
delegation after him to say, 'We don't want
this man to be our king.'
15 "He was made king, however, and returned home. Then he sent for the servants to
whom he had given the money, in order to
find out what they had gained with it.
16 "The first one came and said, 'Sir, your
mina has earned ten more.'
17 " 'Well done, my good servant!' his master replied. 'Because you have been trustworthy in a very small matter, take charge of ten
cities.'
18 "The second came and said, 'Sir, your
mina has earned five more.'
19 "His master answered, 'You take charge
of five cities.'
20 "Then another servant came and said, 'Sir,
here is your mina; I have kept it laid away in
a piece of cloth. 21 I was afraid of you, because
you are a hard man. You take out what you did
not put in and reap what you did not sow.'
22 "His master replied, 'I will judge you by
your own words, you wicked servant! You
knew, did you, that I am a hard man, taking
out what I did not put in, and reaping what
I did not sow? 23 Why then didn't you put my
money on deposit, so that when I came back,
I could have collected it with interest?'
24 "Then he said to those standing by, 'Take
his mina away from him and give it to the one
who has ten minas.'
25 " 'Sir,' they said, 'he already has ten!'
26 "He replied, 'I tell you that to everyone
who has, more will be given, but as for the
one who has nothing, even what he has will be
taken away. 27 But those enemies of mine who

---

[a] *13* A mina was about three months' wages.

did not want me to be king over them—bring
them here and kill them in front of me.' "

The Triumphal Entry

28After Jesus had said this, he went on
ahead, going up to Jerusalem. 29As he approached Bethphage and Bethany at the hill
called the Mount of Olives, he sent two of his
disciples, saying to them, 30"Go to the village
ahead of you, and as you enter it, you will find
a colt tied there, which no one has ever ridden. Untie it and bring it here. 31If anyone
asks you, 'Why are you untying it?' tell him,
'The Lord needs it.' "

32Those who were sent ahead went and
found it just as he had told them. 33As they
were untying the colt, its owners asked them,
"Why are you untying the colt?"

34They replied, "The Lord needs it."

35They brought it to Jesus, threw their
cloaks on the colt and put Jesus on it. 36As
he went along, people spread their cloaks on
the road.

37When he came near the place where the
road goes down the Mount of Olives, the
whole crowd of disciples began joyfully to
praise God in loud voices for all the miracles
they had seen:

38 "Blessed is the king who comes in the
name of the Lord!"[a]

"Peace in heaven and glory in the highest!"

39Some of the Pharisees in the crowd said to
Jesus, "Teacher, rebuke your disciples!"

40"I tell you," he replied, "if they keep quiet, the stones will cry out."

41As he approached Jerusalem and saw the
city, he wept over it 42and said, "If you, even
you, had only known on this day what would
bring you peace—but now it is hidden from
your eyes. 43The days will come upon you
when your enemies will build an embank-
ment against you and encircle you and hem
you in on every side. 44They will dash you to
the ground, you and the children within your
walls. They will not leave one stone on another, because you did not recognize the time of
God's coming to you."

Jesus at the Temple

45Then he entered the temple area and began driving out those who were selling. 46"It
is written," he said to them, " 'My house will
be a house of prayer'[b]; but you have made it 'a
den of robbers.'[c]"

47Every day he was teaching at the temple.
But the chief priests, the teachers of the law
and the leaders among the people were trying to kill him. 48Yet they could not find any
way to do it, because all the people hung on
his words.

The Authority of Jesus Questioned

20 One day as he was teaching the people
in the temple courts and preaching the
gospel, the chief priests and the teachers
of the law, together with the elders, came up
to him. 2"Tell us by what authority you are
doing these things," they said. "Who gave you
this authority?"

3He replied, "I will also ask you a question.
Tell me, 4John's baptism—was it from heaven,
or from men?"

5They discussed it among themselves and
said, "If we say, 'From heaven,' he will ask,
'Why didn't you believe him?' 6But if we say,
'From men,' all the people will stone us, because they are persuaded that John was a
prophet."

7So they answered, "We don't know where
it was from."

8Jesus said, "Neither will I tell you by what
authority I am doing these things."

The Parable of the Tenants

9He went on to tell the people this parable:
"A man planted a vineyard, rented it to some
farmers and went away for a long time. 10At
harvest time he sent a servant to the tenants so
they would give him some of the fruit of the
vineyard. But the tenants beat him and sent
him away empty-handed. 11He sent another
servant, but that one also they beat and treated shamefully and sent away empty-handed.
12He sent still a third, and they wounded him
and threw him out.

13"Then the owner of the vineyard said,
'What shall I do? I will send my son, whom I
love; perhaps they will respect him.'

14"But when the tenants saw him, they
talked the matter over. 'This is the heir,' they
said. 'Let's kill him, and the inheritance will be
ours.' 15So they threw him out of the vineyard
and killed him.

"What then will the owner of the vineyard
do to them? 16He will come and kill those tenants and give the vineyard to others."

When the people heard this, they said,
"May this never be!"

17Jesus looked directly at them and asked,

---

a *38* Psalm 118:26 *b* *46* Isaiah 56:7 *c* *46* Jer. 7:11

"Then what is the meaning of that which is
written:

" 'The stone the builders rejected
has become the capstone[a]'[b]?

18Everyone who falls on that stone will be broken to pieces, but he on whom it falls will be
crushed."
19The teachers of the law and the chief
priests looked for a way to arrest him immediately, because they knew he had spoken this
parable against them. But they were afraid of
the people.

Paying Taxes to Caesar

20Keeping a close watch on him, they sent
spies, who pretended to be honest. They
hoped to catch Jesus in something he said so
that they might hand him over to the power
and authority of the governor. 21So the spies
questioned him: "Teacher, we know that you
speak and teach what is right, and that you do
not show partiality but teach the way of God
in accordance with the truth. 22Is it right for
us to pay taxes to Caesar or not?"
23He saw through their duplicity and said
to them, 24"Show me a denarius. Whose portrait and inscription are on it?"
25"Caesar's," they replied.
He said to them, "Then give to Caesar what
is Caesar's, and to God what is God's."
26They were unable to trap him in what he
had said there in public. And astonished by his
answer, they became silent.

The Resurrection and Marriage

27Some of the Sadducees, who say there is
no resurrection, came to Jesus with a question. 28"Teacher," they said, "Moses wrote for
us that if a man's brother dies and leaves a wife
but no children, the man must marry the widow and have children for his brother. 29Now
there were seven brothers. The first one married a woman and died childless. 30The second
31and then the third married her, and in the
same way the seven died, leaving no children.
32Finally, the woman died too. 33Now then, at
the resurrection whose wife will she be, since
the seven were married to her?"
34Jesus replied, "The people of this age marry and are given in marriage. 35But those who
are considered worthy of taking part in that
age and in the resurrection from the dead will
neither marry nor be given in marriage, 36and
they can no longer die; for they are like the
angels. They are God's children, since they are
children of the resurrection. 37But in the account of the bush, even Moses showed that
the dead rise, for he calls the Lord 'the God of
Abraham, and the God of Isaac, and the God
of Jacob.'[c] 38He is not the God of the dead,
but of the living, for to him all are alive."
39Some of the teachers of the law responded, "Well said, teacher!" 40And no one dared
to ask him any more questions.

Whose Son Is the Christ?

41Then Jesus said to them, "How is it that
they say the Christ[d] is the Son of David? 42Da-
vid himself declares in the Book of Psalms:

" 'The Lord said to my Lord:
"Sit at my right hand
43 until I make your enemies
a footstool for your feet." '[e]

44David calls him 'Lord.' How then can he be
his son?"
45While all the people were listening, Jesus
said to his disciples, 46"Beware of the teachers
of the law. They like to walk around in flowing robes and love to be greeted in the marketplaces and have the most important seats
in the synagogues and the places of honor at
banquets. 47They devour widows' houses and
for a show make lengthy prayers. Such men
will be punished most severely."

The Widow's Offering

21 As he looked up, Jesus saw the rich
putting their gifts into the temple treasury. 2He also saw a poor widow put
in two very small copper coins.[f] 3"I tell you
the truth," he said, "this poor widow has put
in more than all the others. 4All these people
gave their gifts out of their wealth; but she out
of her poverty put in all she had to live on."

Signs of the End of the Age

5Some of his disciples were remarking
about how the temple was adorned with beautiful stones and with gifts dedicated to God.
But Jesus said, 6"As for what you see here, the
time will come when not one stone will be left
on another; every one of them will be thrown
down."
7"Teacher," they asked, "when will these
things happen? And what will be the sign that
they are about to take place?"
8He replied: "Watch out that you are not
deceived. For many will come in my name,

a 17 Or *cornerstone* b 17 Psalm 118:22 c 37 Exodus 3:6 d 41 Or *Messiah* e 43 Psalm 110:1 f 2 Greek *two lepta*

THURSDAY
READ LUKE 20:27–40

MARRYING ONLY FOR A LIFETIME

> **"The people of this age marry and are given in marriage. But those who are considered worthy of taking part in that age and in the resurrection from the dead will neither marry nor be given in marriage, and they can no longer die; for they are like the angels."**
>
> — LUKE 20:34–36

One of my favorite things that my husband and I do together is travel. We've been to lots of places together. I have a framed picture of us taken on an island trip that includes this caption: "It doesn't matter where you go, it's who's beside you that counts."

I could be anywhere in the world, and as long as Dan and I are together, there's nowhere else I'd rather be.

I have taken great comfort in the thought that if Dan dies before me, I can endure a temporary layover in this world, knowing that one day I'll travel to heaven, and he'll be waiting at the gate for me. It's a nice idea. But as I read Luke 20, I'm wondering if it's true.

What if Dan and I are only married for this lifetime, and there's no possibility of being united in heaven as husband and wife? Doesn't the concept of a soul mate presume an eternal—no beginning, no end—kind of relationship? I have to be honest: If marriage is only for this lifetime, how can I believe that heaven is all it's cracked up to be—a place of eternal fulfillment? How can I be happy there without Dan?

For answers to those questions, I decided to consult the ultimate travel guide—the Bible. The first book of the Bible, Genesis, tells us that God created man and woman to be joined together as one in marriage to satisfy the deepest need for human intimacy. In so many ways, marriage mirrors the deeper hunger of our soul to know our Creator and to be known by him. Marriage, then, is simply a shadow of a deeper reality, much like the tabernacle was a symbol of the greater truth of God's presence with his people, and much like animal sacrifice foreshadowed the ultimate sacrifice God would make of his own Son, Jesus, on the cross.

The Bible refers to the church as Christ's bride. By living out fidelity, sacrificial love and purity in marriage, we're preparing ourselves for the reality of life with Christ. After we die, we will be married to Christ. He will be our bridegroom, and we will be his bride. When we love our mate the way we are supposed to, we live out our spiritual calling on earth to be holy. Marriage, then, is more than our need for a companion or soul mate. It is a path of sanctification that we travel before we pass into glory.

As much as I love Dan and strive to love him in a way that brings honor to God, it won't matter if we're not husband and wife anymore after we die and go to heaven. Rather than taking away the great blessing of marriage, Jesus is telling us that our marital relationships will be fulfilled, or brought to completion, in heaven. So the life I now live with Dan will be rewarded in full when I meet my new bridegroom, Jesus, at the gate.

—MARIAN V. LIAUTAUD

let's *talk*

- ✦ What are some of the purposes of marriage?
- ✦ What do we think heaven will be like, based on Luke 20:34–36?
- ✦ In what ways is our marriage making each of us more holy? How does it make us long for ultimate fulfillment in Christ?

FOR YOUR NEXT DEVOTIONAL READING, TURN TO PAGE 1174.

claiming, 'I am he,' and, 'The time is near.'
Do not follow them. [9]When you hear of wars
and revolutions, do not be frightened. These
things must happen first, but the end will not
come right away."

[10]Then he said to them: "Nation will rise
against nation, and kingdom against kingdom.
[11]There will be great earthquakes, famines and
pestilences in various places, and fearful events
and great signs from heaven.

[12]"But before all this, they will lay hands
on you and persecute you. They will deliver
you to synagogues and prisons, and you will
be brought before kings and governors, and all
on account of my name. [13]This will result in
your being witnesses to them. [14]But make up
your mind not to worry beforehand how you
will defend yourselves. [15]For I will give you
words and wisdom that none of your adversaries will be able to resist or contradict. [16]You
will be betrayed even by parents, brothers, relatives and friends, and they will put some of
you to death. [17]All men will hate you because
of me. [18]But not a hair of your head will perish. [19]By standing firm you will gain life.

[20]"When you see Jerusalem being surrounded by armies, you will know that its desolation
is near. [21]Then let those who are in Judea flee
to the mountains, let those in the city get out,
and let those in the country not enter the city.
[22]For this is the time of punishment in fulfillment of all that has been written. [23]How
dreadful it will be in those days for pregnant
women and nursing mothers! There will be
great distress in the land and wrath against this
people. [24]They will fall by the sword and will
be taken as prisoners to all the nations. Jerusalem will be trampled on by the Gentiles until
the times of the Gentiles are fulfilled.

[25]"There will be signs in the sun, moon and
stars. On the earth, nations will be in anguish
and perplexity at the roaring and tossing of
the sea. [26]Men will faint from terror, appre-
hensive of what is coming on the world, for
the heavenly bodies will be shaken. [27]At that
time they will see the Son of Man coming in
a cloud with power and great glory. [28]When
these things begin to take place, stand up and
lift up your heads, because your redemption is
drawing near."

[29]He told them this parable: "Look at the
fig tree and all the trees. [30]When they sprout
leaves, you can see for yourselves and know
that summer is near. [31]Even so, when you see
these things happening, you know that the
kingdom of God is near.

[32]"I tell you the truth, this generation[a] will
certainly not pass away until all these things
have happened. [33]Heaven and earth will pass
away, but my words will never pass away.

[34]"Be careful, or your hearts will be weighed
down with dissipation, drunkenness and the
anxieties of life, and that day will close on you
unexpectedly like a trap. [35]For it will come
upon all those who live on the face of the
whole earth. [36]Be always on the watch, and
pray that you may be able to escape all that is
about to happen, and that you may be able to
stand before the Son of Man."

[37]Each day Jesus was teaching at the temple, and each evening he went out to spend
the night on the hill called the Mount of Olives, [38]and all the people came early in the
morning to hear him at the temple.

Judas Agrees to Betray Jesus

22 Now the Feast of Unleavened Bread,
called the Passover, was approaching,
[2]and the chief priests and the teachers of
the law were looking for some way to get rid of
Jesus, for they were afraid of the people. [3]Then
Satan entered Judas, called Iscariot, one of the
Twelve. [4]And Judas went to the chief priests
and the officers of the temple guard and discussed with them how he might betray Jesus.
[5]They were delighted and agreed to give him
money. [6]He consented, and watched for an
opportunity to hand Jesus over to them when
no crowd was present.

The Last Supper

[7]Then came the day of Unleavened Bread
on which the Passover lamb had to be sacrificed. [8]Jesus sent Peter and John, saying, "Go
and make preparations for us to eat the Passover."

[9]"Where do you want us to prepare for it?"
they asked.

[10]He replied, "As you enter the city, a man
carrying a jar of water will meet you. Follow
him to the house that he enters, [11]and say to
the owner of the house, 'The Teacher asks:
Where is the guest room, where I may eat the
Passover with my disciples?' [12]He will show
you a large upper room, all furnished. Make
preparations there."

[13]They left and found things just as Jesus
had told them. So they prepared the Passover.

[14]When the hour came, Jesus and his apos-

[a] 32 Or *race*

tles reclined at the table. 15And he said to
them, "I have eagerly desired to eat this Passover with you before I suffer. 16For I tell you, I
will not eat it again until it finds fulfillment in
the kingdom of God."

17After taking the cup, he gave thanks and
said, "Take this and divide it among you. 18For
I tell you I will not drink again of the fruit of
the vine until the kingdom of God comes."

19And he took bread, gave thanks and
broke it, and gave it to them, saying, "This
is my body given for you; do this in remembrance of me."

20In the same way, after the supper he took
the cup, saying, "This cup is the new covenant
in my blood, which is poured out for you.
21But the hand of him who is going to betray
me is with mine on the table. 22The Son of
Man will go as it has been decreed, but woe to
that man who betrays him." 23They began to
question among themselves which of them it
might be who would do this.

24Also a dispute arose among them as to
which of them was considered to be greatest.
25Jesus said to them, "The kings of the Gentiles lord it over them; and those who exercise
authority over them call themselves Benefac-
tors. 26But you are not to be like that. Instead,
the greatest among you should be like the
youngest, and the one who rules like the one
who serves. 27For who is greater, the one who
is at the table or the one who serves? Is it not
the one who is at the table? But I am among
you as one who serves. 28You are those who
have stood by me in my trials. 29And I confer
on you a kingdom, just as my Father conferred
one on me, 30so that you may eat and drink at
my table in my kingdom and sit on thrones,
judging the twelve tribes of Israel.

31"Simon, Simon, Satan has asked to sift
you[a] as wheat. 32But I have prayed for you,
Simon, that your faith may not fail. And when
you have turned back, strengthen your brothers."

33But he replied, "Lord, I am ready to go
with you to prison and to death."

34Jesus answered, "I tell you, Peter, before
the rooster crows today, you will deny three
times that you know me."

35Then Jesus asked them, "When I sent you
without purse, bag or sandals, did you lack
anything?"

"Nothing," they answered.

36He said to them, "But now if you have a
purse, take it, and also a bag; and if you don't
have a sword, sell your cloak and buy one. 37It
is written: 'And he was numbered with the
transgressors'[b]; and I tell you that this must be
fulfilled in me. Yes, what is written about me
is reaching its fulfillment."

38The disciples said, "See, Lord, here are
two swords."

"That is enough," he replied.

Jesus Prays on the Mount of Olives

39Jesus went out as usual to the Mount of
Olives, and his disciples followed him. 40On
reaching the place, he said to them, "Pray that
you will not fall into temptation." 41He withdrew about a stone's throw beyond them, knelt
down and prayed, 42"Father, if you are willing,
take this cup from me; yet not my will, but
yours be done." 43An angel from heaven appeared to him and strengthened him. 44And
being in anguish, he prayed more earnestly,
and his sweat was like drops of blood falling
to the ground.[c]

45When he rose from prayer and went back
to the disciples, he found them asleep, exhausted from sorrow. 46"Why are you sleeping?" he asked them. "Get up and pray so that
you will not fall into temptation."

Jesus Arrested

47While he was still speaking a crowd came
up, and the man who was called Judas, one of
the Twelve, was leading them. He approached
Jesus to kiss him, 48but Jesus asked him, "Judas, are you betraying the Son of Man with
a kiss?"

49When Jesus' followers saw what was going to happen, they said, "Lord, should we
strike with our swords?" 50And one of them
struck the servant of the high priest, cutting
off his right ear.

51But Jesus answered, "No more of this!"
And he touched the man's ear and healed
him.

52Then Jesus said to the chief priests, the officers of the temple guard, and the elders, who
had come for him, "Am I leading a rebellion,
that you have come with swords and clubs?
53Every day I was with you in the temple
courts, and you did not lay a hand on me. But
this is your hour—when darkness reigns."

Peter Disowns Jesus

54Then seizing him, they led him away and
took him into the house of the high priest.
Peter followed at a distance. 55But when they

[a] *31* The Greek is plural. [b] *37* Isaiah 53:12 [c] *44* Some early manuscripts do not have verses 43 and 44.

had kindled a fire in the middle of the courtyard and had sat down together, Peter sat
down with them. 56A servant girl saw him
seated there in the firelight. She looked closely
at him and said, "This man was with him."
57But he denied it. "Woman, I don't know
him," he said.
58A little later someone else saw him and
said, "You also are one of them."
"Man, I am not!" Peter replied.
59About an hour later another asserted,
"Certainly this fellow was with him, for he is
a Galilean."
60Peter replied, "Man, I don't know what
you're talking about!" Just as he was speaking,
the rooster crowed. 61The Lord turned and
looked straight at Peter. Then Peter remembered the word the Lord had spoken to him:
"Before the rooster crows today, you will disown me three times." 62And he went outside
and wept bitterly.

The Guards Mock Jesus

63The men who were guarding Jesus began
mocking and beating him. 64They blindfolded him and demanded, "Prophesy! Who hit
you?" 65And they said many other insulting
things to him.

Jesus Before Pilate and Herod

66At daybreak the council of the elders of
the people, both the chief priests and teachers of the law, met together, and Jesus was led
before them. 67"If you are the Christ,[a]" they
said, "tell us."
Jesus answered, "If I tell you, you will not
believe me, 68and if I asked you, you would
not answer. 69But from now on, the Son of
Man will be seated at the right hand of the
mighty God."
70They all asked, "Are you then the Son of
God?"
He replied, "You are right in saying I am."
71Then they said, "Why do we need any
more testimony? We have heard it from his
own lips."
23 Then the whole assembly rose and led
him off to Pilate. 2And they began to
accuse him, saying, "We have found
this man subverting our nation. He opposes
payment of taxes to Caesar and claims to be
Christ,[b] a king."
3So Pilate asked Jesus, "Are you the king of
the Jews?"
"Yes, it is as you say," Jesus replied.
4Then Pilate announced to the chief priests
and the crowd, "I find no basis for a charge
against this man."
5But they insisted, "He stirs up the people
all over Judea[c] by his teaching. He started in
Galilee and has come all the way here."
6On hearing this, Pilate asked if the man
was a Galilean. 7When he learned that Jesus
was under Herod's jurisdiction, he sent him
to Herod, who was also in Jerusalem at that
time.
8When Herod saw Jesus, he was greatly
pleased, because for a long time he had been
wanting to see him. From what he had heard
about him, he hoped to see him perform some
miracle. 9He plied him with many questions,
but Jesus gave him no answer. 10The chief
priests and the teachers of the law were standing there, vehemently accusing him. 11Then
Herod and his soldiers ridiculed and mocked
him. Dressing him in an elegant robe, they
sent him back to Pilate. 12That day Herod and
Pilate became friends—before this they had
been enemies.
13Pilate called together the chief priests,
the rulers and the people, 14and said to them,
"You brought me this man as one who was
inciting the people to rebellion. I have examined him in your presence and have found no
basis for your charges against him. 15Neither
has Herod, for he sent him back to us; as you
can see, he has done nothing to deserve death.
16Therefore, I will punish him and then release him.[d]"
18With one voice they cried out, "Away with
this man! Release Barabbas to us!" 19(Barabbas
had been thrown into prison for an insurrection in the city, and for murder.)
20Wanting to release Jesus, Pilate appealed
to them again. 21But they kept shouting,
"Crucify him! Crucify him!"
22For the third time he spoke to them:
"Why? What crime has this man committed?
I have found in him no grounds for the death
penalty. Therefore I will have him punished
and then release him."
23But with loud shouts they insistently demanded that he be crucified, and their shouts
prevailed. 24So Pilate decided to grant their
demand. 25He released the man who had been
thrown into prison for insurrection and murder, the one they asked for, and surrendered
Jesus to their will.

[a] 67 Or *Messiah* [b] 2 Or *Messiah*; also in verses 35 and 39 [c] 5 Or *over the land of the Jews* [d] 16 Some manuscripts *him."* [17]*Now he was obliged to release one man to them at the Feast.*

The Crucifixion

26As they led him away, they seized Simon
from Cyrene, who was on his way in from the
country, and put the cross on him and made
him carry it behind Jesus. 27A large number of
people followed him, including women who
mourned and wailed for him. 28Jesus turned
and said to them, "Daughters of Jerusalem, do
not weep for me; weep for yourselves and for
your children. 29For the time will come when
you will say, 'Blessed are the barren women,
the wombs that never bore and the breasts
that never nursed!' 30Then

" 'they will say to the mountains, "Fall on
us!"
and to the hills, "Cover us!" ' [a]

31For if men do these things when the tree is
green, what will happen when it is dry?"
32Two other men, both criminals, were also
led out with him to be executed. 33When they
came to the place called the Skull, there they
crucified him, along with the criminals—one
on his right, the other on his left. 34Jesus said,
"Father, forgive them, for they do not know
what they are doing."[b] And they divided up
his clothes by casting lots.
35The people stood watching, and the rulers even sneered at him. They said, "He saved
others; let him save himself if he is the Christ
of God, the Chosen One."
36The soldiers also came up and mocked
him. They offered him wine vinegar 37and
said, "If you are the king of the Jews, save
yourself."
38There was a written notice above him,
which read: THIS IS THE KING OF THE JEWS.
39One of the criminals who hung there
hurled insults at him: "Aren't you the Christ?
Save yourself and us!"
40But the other criminal rebuked him.
"Don't you fear God," he said, "since you are
under the same sentence? 41We are punished
justly, for we are getting what our deeds deserve. But this man has done nothing wrong."
42Then he said, "Jesus, remember me when
you come into your kingdom.[c]"
43Jesus answered him, "I tell you the truth,
today you will be with me in paradise."

Jesus' Death

44It was now about the sixth hour, and darkness came over the whole land until the ninth
hour, 45for the sun stopped shining. And the
curtain of the temple was torn in two. 46Jesus
called out with a loud voice, "Father, into your
hands I commit my spirit." When he had said
this, he breathed his last.
47The centurion, seeing what had happened,
praised God and said, "Surely this was a righteous man." 48When all the people who had
gathered to witness this sight saw what took
place, they beat their breasts and went away.
49But all those who knew him, including the
women who had followed him from Galilee,
stood at a distance, watching these things.

Jesus' Burial

50Now there was a man named Joseph, a
member of the Council, a good and upright
man, 51who had not consented to their decision and action. He came from the Judean
town of Arimathea and he was waiting for
the kingdom of God. 52Going to Pilate, he
asked for Jesus' body. 53Then he took it down,
wrapped it in linen cloth and placed it in a
tomb cut in the rock, one in which no one had
yet been laid. 54It was Preparation Day, and
the Sabbath was about to begin.
55The women who had come with Jesus
from Galilee followed Joseph and saw the
tomb and how his body was laid in it. 56Then
they went home and prepared spices and perfumes. But they rested on the Sabbath in obedience to the commandment.

The Resurrection

24 On the first day of the week, very early in the morning, the women took
the spices they had prepared and went
to the tomb. 2They found the stone rolled
away from the tomb, 3but when they entered,
they did not find the body of the Lord Jesus.
4While they were wondering about this, suddenly two men in clothes that gleamed like
lightning stood beside them. 5In their fright
the women bowed down with their faces to
the ground, but the men said to them, "Why
do you look for the living among the dead?
6He is not here; he has risen! Remember how
he told you, while he was still with you in Galilee: 7'The Son of Man must be delivered into
the hands of sinful men, be crucified and on
the third day be raised again.' " 8Then they remembered his words.
9When they came back from the tomb,
they told all these things to the Eleven and to
all the others. 10It was Mary Magdalene, Joan-
na, Mary the mother of James, and the others
with them who told this to the apostles. 11But

[a] 30 Hosea 10:8 [b] 34 Some early manuscripts do not have this sentence. [c] 42 Some manuscripts *come with your kingly power*

F

FRIDAY
READ LUKE 24:1–35

APPRECIATING EACH OTHER

> **Then their eyes were opened and they recognized him, and he disappeared from their sight.**
> — LUKE 24:31

let's talk

- ✦ What attributes in each other have we sometimes taken for granted that others have helped us see?
- ✦ What qualities of Christ do I see working in you?
- ✦ What are some ways we can keep our eyes open, keeping Christ the central focus of our marriage?

My friend and her husband had been married for a few years, and though she still loved him dearly, the humdrum of day-to-day living had lulled her into taking him for granted. Sure, he was loving, steady and dependable, but the romance was gone.

Then at a yearly awards banquet at her husband's company, my friend was shocked and pleasantly surprised by the accolades heaped on her husband. Superiors spoke of him in glowing terms. Coworkers gushed about what a great guy he was. Even the custodian made a point of telling her what a likable man her husband was.

My friend found herself swelling with pride—and a little shame—wondering why she hadn't noticed this side of her husband. Did he act differently at work, or was she just not seeing what had been there the whole time?

Cleopas and his friend, who were walking to Emmaus two days after Jesus was crucified and buried, had a bit of the same problem. To be sure, they were depressed, tired and drained from what had happened in Jerusalem. A great teacher who had promised so much had been arrested, beaten, crucified and buried. Now his body was missing. Certainly they were not expecting that the man who joined them on the road was that very man—Jesus.

They didn't acknowledge Jesus as Messiah either—likely because they were disillusioned that the one they had expected to deliver their nation from Roman rule was now dead. "He was a prophet, powerful in word and deed before God and all the people," they said of Jesus (Luke 24:19). But they didn't have a clue that he was Savior of the world.

As we read this, we want to cry out, "How could you not see Jesus as Messiah after all the wonderful things he did? And how could you not recognize him as he explained the Scriptures to you and your hearts burned within you?" (see verse 32) But until they broke bread with Jesus and the Spirit of God opened their eyes, these men were blind to Jesus' true identity.

Isn't that the case with many of us today, in both marriage and our walk with Christ? Seeing Jesus as a living, vibrant presence in our lives comes before anything else, of course. Only when our eyes are focused on him as our Savior can we begin to truly appreciate a spouse who also believes in Christ. When we study the gracious attitudes and actions that Christ pours out on his church—loving, caring, cherishing, submitting even to death—we ask ourselves, "How does my spouse show these same attributes to me and to others? Have I shown appreciation for those Christlike qualities being lived out in him? Am I being Christlike to him?"

It's easy to become so self-absorbed that we fail to recognize the qualities and gifts of the person who is closest to us in life. In becoming blind to those attributes, however, we miss some great opportunities to build on each other's strengths.

Let's pray for open eyes before sickness, loss, separation—or accolades from others—force us to pay attention.

—VALERIE VAN KOOTEN

FOR YOUR NEXT DEVOTIONAL READING, TURN TO PAGE 1176.

they did not believe the women, because their words seemed to them like nonsense. [12]Peter, however, got up and ran to the tomb. Bending over, he saw the strips of linen lying by themselves, and he went away, wondering to himself what had happened.

On the Road to Emmaus

[13]Now that same day two of them were going to a village called Emmaus, about seven miles[a] from Jerusalem. [14]They were talking with each other about everything that had happened. [15]As they talked and discussed these things with each other, Jesus himself came up and walked along with them; [16]but they were kept from recognizing him.

[17]He asked them, "What are you discussing together as you walk along?"

They stood still, their faces downcast. [18]One of them, named Cleopas, asked him, "Are you only a visitor to Jerusalem and do not know the things that have happened there in these days?"

[19]"What things?" he asked.

"About Jesus of Nazareth," they replied. "He was a prophet, powerful in word and deed before God and all the people. [20]The chief priests and our rulers handed him over to be sentenced to death, and they crucified him; [21]but we had hoped that he was the one who was going to redeem Israel. And what is more, it is the third day since all this took place. [22]In addition, some of our women amazed us. They went to the tomb early this morning [23]but didn't find his body. They came and told us that they had seen a vision of angels, who said he was alive. [24]Then some of our companions went to the tomb and found it just as the women had said, but him they did not see."

[25]He said to them, "How foolish you are, and how slow of heart to believe all that the prophets have spoken! [26]Did not the Christ[b] have to suffer these things and then enter his glory?" [27]And beginning with Moses and all the Prophets, he explained to them what was said in all the Scriptures concerning himself.

[28]As they approached the village to which they were going, Jesus acted as if he were going farther. [29]But they urged him strongly, "Stay with us, for it is nearly evening; the day is almost over." So he went in to stay with them.

[30]When he was at the table with them, he took bread, gave thanks, broke it and began to give it to them. [31]Then their eyes were opened and they recognized him, and he disappeared from their sight. [32]They asked each other, "Were not our hearts burning within us while he talked with us on the road and opened the Scriptures to us?"

[33]They got up and returned at once to Jerusalem. There they found the Eleven and those with them, assembled together [34]and saying, "It is true! The Lord has risen and has appeared to Simon." [35]Then the two told what had happened on the way, and how Jesus was recognized by them when he broke the bread.

Jesus Appears to the Disciples

[36]While they were still talking about this, Jesus himself stood among them and said to them, "Peace be with you."

[37]They were startled and frightened, thinking they saw a ghost. [38]He said to them, "Why are you troubled, and why do doubts rise in your minds? [39]Look at my hands and my feet. It is I myself! Touch me and see; a ghost does not have flesh and bones, as you see I have."

[40]When he had said this, he showed them his hands and feet. [41]And while they still did not believe it because of joy and amazement, he asked them, "Do you have anything here to eat?" [42]They gave him a piece of broiled fish, [43]and he took it and ate it in their presence.

[44]He said to them, "This is what I told you while I was still with you: Everything must be fulfilled that is written about me in the Law of Moses, the Prophets and the Psalms."

[45]Then he opened their minds so they could understand the Scriptures. [46]He told them, "This is what is written: The Christ will suffer and rise from the dead on the third day, [47]and repentance and forgiveness of sins will be preached in his name to all nations, beginning at Jerusalem. [48]You are witnesses of these things. [49]I am going to send you what my Father has promised; but stay in the city until you have been clothed with power from on high."

The Ascension

[50]When he had led them out to the vicinity of Bethany, he lifted up his hands and blessed them. [51]While he was blessing them, he left them and was taken up into heaven. [52]Then they worshiped him and returned to Jerusalem with great joy. [53]And they stayed continually at the temple, praising God.

---

[a] *13* Greek *sixty stadia* (about 11 kilometers) [b] *26* Or *Messiah*; also in verse 46

WEEKEND

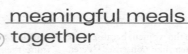

meaningful meals together

A leisurely meal gives a couple a way to rejoin their spirits. Think about it. What happens in your relationship when the two of you actually sit down without a scheduled appointment nipping at your heels?

We recently celebrated our twentieth wedding anniversary. Like most couples, we marked this milestone with a fancy meal—just the two of us. But this wasn't like any meal we had experienced before. We arrived at the five-star Herbfarm in the foothills of the Cascade Mountains at 6:00 p.m., and the meal did not end until after 11:00. No entertainment, no interludes, just five leisurely hours of a nine-course meal.

Occasionally we'd take a walk around the gardens between courses, but most of our time was spent talking about anything that came to mind. We basked in the time we had with no agenda other than to be together.

Granted, this is not the kind of meal we'd want all the time. It was highly unusual, to say the least. But it underscored for us the value that "slow food" brings to our relationship. Truth is, a slow approach to food strengthens any relationship. There is something in the nature of eating together that forms a bond between people. As Carl Honoré says in his book *In Praise of Slowness*, "It is no accident that the word *companion* is derived from the Latin words meaning 'with bread.' " Meals become meaningful when we share them with our spouse. As playwright Oscar Wilde once said, "After a good dinner one can forgive anybody, even one's own relations."

Babette's Feast, written by Isak Dinesen, is about a strict, dour, fundamentalist community in Denmark. Babette works as a cook for two elderly sisters who have no idea that she once was a chef to nobility in France. Babette's dream is to return to Paris, so every year she buys a lottery ticket hoping to win enough money to return. And every night her austere employers demand that she cook the same dreary meal of boiled fish and potatoes, because they say, Jesus commanded, "Take no thought of food and drink."

One day Babette wins the lottery. The prize is ten thousand francs, a small fortune. And because the anniversary of the founding of the community is approaching, Babette asks if she might prepare a French dinner for the entire village.

At first the townspeople refuse, saying, "It would be sin to indulge in such rich food." But Babette begs them, and finally they relent. Secretly the people vow not to enjoy the feast, believing God will not blame them for eating this sinful meal as long as they do not enjoy it.

Finally the big day comes, and the villagers gather to eat. The first course is an exquisite turtle soup. While the villagers usually eat in silence, a little conversation begins to emerge with each spoonful of soup. The atmosphere changes. Someone smiles. An arm comes up and drapes over a shoulder. Someone whispers, "After all, did not the Lord Jesus say, love one another?" By the time the main entrée of quail arrives, the austere, pleasure-fearing people are giggling and laughing and slurping and guffawing and praising God for their many years together.

This dour group is transformed into a loving community through the gift of a meal. One of the two sisters goes into the kitchen to thank Babette, saying, "Oh, how we will miss you when you return to Paris!" And Babette replies, "I will not be returning to Paris, because I have no money. I spent it all on the feast."

Babette's Feast reminds us that mealtimes are only as valuable as you make them. It's not enough to consume slow food if your heart isn't in it. But if you give it your best, and if your head and heart are fully immersed in your mealtime together, time will float by imperceptibly, and you'll wonder why so many couples sacrifice this gold mine of time with a measly meal of fast food.

—DR. LES PARROTT III AND DR. LESLIE PARROTT

do you have happy meals?

Talk through the following questions as a couple.

1. What were mealtimes like at your house as a kid, and how do those differ from what you have today? How has sharing meals affected your time together as a couple versus the kind of time your parents had together?
2. Are there specific topics you would like to declare off limits around the dinner table? Why or why not?
3. If you could press a magic button to make your mealtimes what you'd like them to be, what would happen? How much of your ideal could you make a reality by what you bring to the table—literally?
4. What is one thing you could give up to make sure you had more meals with your spouse?

HOW ARE WE DOING?

let's make a DATE

PRIORITY DINING

This weekend find a quiet place to have a slow meal and focused conversation. Bring your calendars. Between courses, compare schedules and set up appointments for meals together for the next month. For some couples, this may be as frequently as once a day; for others, even once a week will be hard to schedule. Push yourself and your spouse to make eating together a priority—but don't feel guilty if it doesn't work out every single day.

FOR YOUR NEXT DEVOTIONAL READING, TURN TO PAGE 1180.

LESSONS FROM THE *Bible*

Jesus' ministry spanned only three years, yet he took time to "recline at the table" with friends on a number of occasions. What can you learn about Jesus' priorities from the following passages?

1. Dinner at Matthew's home (Matthew 9:9–10)
2. Dinner with a Pharisee (Luke 7:36)
3. Dinner at Martha's home (Luke 10:38–42)

JOHN

John

QUICK FACTS

AUTHOR The apostle John

AUDIENCE Written to convince unbelievers, and assure believers, of who Jesus is

DATE Probably about A.D. 85–90

SETTING Shortly before John's exile to the island of Patmos (John's eyewitness account is presumably the last Gospel written)

While Matthew, Mark and Luke focused on Jesus' time in Galilee, John recorded primarily events that occurred in Judea. The other Gospel writers stressed the kingdom of God, but John emphasized Jesus himself and our need for him. John said he wrote his account "that you may believe that Jesus is the Christ, the Son of God, and that by believing you may have life in his name" (John 20:31).

New believers are often instructed to begin reading the Bible starting with the Gospel of John, because it is a powerful and straightforward argument for the deity of Jesus Christ. John's book is understandable to a new convert yet deep enough for the most accomplished scholar. The opening verses read like poetry, sparkling with enough mystery to invite a deeper plunge into the story.

John identified himself in this book as "the disciple whom Jesus loved." John explained in his later epistles that because God is love, we must love one another. As we realize more and more our Savior's love for us, we will have more and more love for our spouses. As we let Christ fill the cup of our own need, our love for Christ will overflow in love to those around us.

The Word Became Flesh

1 In the beginning was the Word, and the
Word was with God, and the Word was
God. 2He was with God in the beginning.
3Through him all things were made; without him nothing was made that has been
made. 4In him was life, and that life was the
light of men. 5The light shines in the darkness,
but the darkness has not understood[a] it.
6There came a man who was sent from God;
his name was John. 7He came as a witness to
testify concerning that light, so that through
him all men might believe. 8He himself was
not the light; he came only as a witness to the
light. 9The true light that gives light to every
man was coming into the world.[b]
10He was in the world, and though the
world was made through him, the world did
not recognize him. 11He came to that which
was his own, but his own did not receive him.
12Yet to all who received him, to those who
believed in his name, he gave the right to become children of God— 13children born not
of natural descent,[c] nor of human decision or
a husband's will, but born of God.
14The Word became flesh and made his
dwelling among us. We have seen his glory,
the glory of the One and Only,[d] who came
from the Father, full of grace and truth.
15John testifies concerning him. He cries
out, saying, "This was he of whom I said, 'He
who comes after me has surpassed me because
he was before me.' " 16From the fullness of
his grace we have all received one blessing after another. 17For the law was given through
Moses; grace and truth came through Jesus
Christ. 18No one has ever seen God, but God
the One and Only,[d,e] who is at the Father's
side, has made him known.

John the Baptist Denies Being the Christ

19Now this was John's testimony when
the Jews of Jerusalem sent priests and Levites
to ask him who he was. 20He did not fail to
confess, but confessed freely, "I am not the
Christ.[f]"
21They asked him, "Then who are you? Are
you Elijah?"
He said, "I am not."
"Are you the Prophet?"
He answered, "No."
22Finally they said, "Who are you? Give us
an answer to take back to those who sent us.
What do you say about yourself?"
23John replied in the words of Isaiah the
prophet, "I am the voice of one calling in
the desert, 'Make straight the way for the
Lord.' "[g]
24Now some Pharisees who had been sent
25questioned him, "Why then do you baptize
if you are not the Christ, nor Elijah, nor the
Prophet?"
26"I baptize with[h] water," John replied, "but
among you stands one you do not know. 27He
is the one who comes after me, the thongs of
whose sandals I am not worthy to untie."
28This all happened at Bethany on the other
side of the Jordan, where John was baptizing.

Jesus the Lamb of God

29The next day John saw Jesus coming toward him and said, "Look, the Lamb of God,
who takes away the sin of the world! 30This
is the one I meant when I said, 'A man who
comes after me has surpassed me because he
was before me.' 31I myself did not know him,
but the reason I came baptizing with water
was that he might be revealed to Israel."
32Then John gave this testimony: "I saw the
Spirit come down from heaven as a dove and
remain on him. 33I would not have known
him, except that the one who sent me to baptize with water told me, 'The man on whom
you see the Spirit come down and remain is
he who will baptize with the Holy Spirit.' 34I
have seen and I testify that this is the Son of
God."

Jesus' First Disciples

35The next day John was there again with
two of his disciples. 36When he saw Jesus passing by, he said, "Look, the Lamb of God!"
37When the two disciples heard him say
this, they followed Jesus. 38Turning around,
Jesus saw them following and asked, "What
do you want?"
They said, "Rabbi" (which means Teacher),
"where are you staying?"
39"Come," he replied, "and you will see."
So they went and saw where he was staying,
and spent that day with him. It was about the
tenth hour.
40Andrew, Simon Peter's brother, was one
of the two who heard what John had said and
who had followed Jesus. 41The first thing An-

[a] 5 Or *darkness, and the darkness has not overcome* [b] 9 Or *This was the true light that gives light to every man who comes into the world* [c] 13 Greek *of bloods* [d] *14,18* Or *the Only Begotten* [e] *18* Some manuscripts *but the only* (or *only begotten*) *Son* [f] *20* Or *Messiah.* "The Christ" (Greek) and "the Messiah" (Hebrew) both mean "the Anointed One"; also in verse 25. [g] *23* Isaiah 40:3 [h] *26* Or *in*; also in verses 31 and 33

MONDAY

READ JOHN 1:1–34

GIVING UP THE LEAD

> **"He who comes after me has surpassed me because he was before me."**
>
> — JOHN 1:15

let's talk

- When has one of us felt like we were taking a lesser role than the other? What were some of the difficulties of doing that? What lessons did we learn?
- If one of us consistently takes the lead in choosing where to eat dinner, what would happen if the other made that decision? Would there be tension? Relief?
- What are some ways we are messengers of Christ through our marriage? How do we direct others away from ourselves to him?

John the Baptist's purpose in life was to prepare the way for the Messiah. He knew his purpose and never considered himself greater than the one who came after him. When the Jewish leaders in Jerusalem sent priests and Levites to ask John who he was, John directed attention away from himself and to Jesus, saying, "He is the one who comes after me, the thongs of whose sandals I am not worthy to untie" (John 1:27).

John was born several months before Jesus. But in salvation history, Jesus came "before" John and had the greater ministry. John was willing to be a messenger so people would be drawn to Christ. He was a servant to the greatest servant of all.

In marriage, many of us find it hard to take a lesser place than our spouse. For example, I might feel slighted if a mutual friend spends most of the time talking to my spouse. Or if my spouse makes vacation plans without getting my approval, I might not be so enthusiastic about taking time off.

It's sometimes hard to be a servant to our spouse without feeling like we're losing ourselves. Yet God calls us to serve others. John modeled it for us by taking the lesser role of preparing others to meet Jesus, and Jesus modeled it for us by washing his disciples' feet.

How exactly does that work in marriage? According to Ephesians 5:21, believers are to "submit to one another." How that looks within marriage is then described: Women are told to submit to their husbands and men are told to love their wives just as Christ loved the church and gave himself up for her. Mutual submission is at the heart of this passage. We become servants to each other, not because we feel one person is superior to another, but because we yield in love to the other.

That's what Anna and Josh had to learn. Though both were gifted communicators, they had difficulty coordinating their work schedules, particularly after they had children. So for a time, Anna stayed home with the kids, working from home as an editor, while Josh worked full-time as a publisher. When Josh was laid off, however, and Anna found a great job working full-time as an editor, Josh agreed to freelance so he could be the primary caretaker of the kids. Through the process, both learned incredible lessons about themselves, their work and each other. When Josh griped about chauffeuring the kids all day, for example, Anna could relate. And when Anna talked about problems with coworkers, Josh could offer helpful encouragement. Meantime both looked for ways to help alleviate each other's stress.

We can take second place to each other in marriage without losing our sense of identity if we find our identity in Christ, the greatest servant of all, "who, being in very nature God, did not consider equality with God something to be grasped" (Philippians 2:6). Being a servant to each other teaches us to be more like Christ. And in him we find the joy of oneness in marriage.

—JOHN R. THROOP

FOR YOUR NEXT DEVOTIONAL READING, TURN TO PAGE 1183.

drew did was to find his brother Simon and tell him, "We have found the Messiah" (that is, the Christ). [42]And he brought him to Jesus.

Jesus looked at him and said, "You are Simon son of John. You will be called Cephas" (which, when translated, is Peter[a]).

Jesus Calls Philip and Nathanael

[43]The next day Jesus decided to leave for Galilee. Finding Philip, he said to him, "Follow me."

[44]Philip, like Andrew and Peter, was from the town of Bethsaida. [45]Philip found Nathanael and told him, "We have found the one Moses wrote about in the Law, and about whom the prophets also wrote—Jesus of Nazareth, the son of Joseph."

[46]"Nazareth! Can anything good come from there?" Nathanael asked.

"Come and see," said Philip.

[47]When Jesus saw Nathanael approaching, he said of him, "Here is a true Israelite, in whom there is nothing false."

[48]"How do you know me?" Nathanael asked.

Jesus answered, "I saw you while you were still under the fig tree before Philip called you."

[49]Then Nathanael declared, "Rabbi, you are the Son of God; you are the King of Israel."

[50]Jesus said, "You believe[b] because I told you I saw you under the fig tree. You shall see greater things than that." [51]He then added, "I tell you[c] the truth, you[c] shall see heaven open, and the angels of God ascending and descending on the Son of Man."

Jesus Changes Water to Wine

2 On the third day a wedding took place at Cana in Galilee. Jesus' mother was there, [2]and Jesus and his disciples had also been invited to the wedding. [3]When the wine was gone, Jesus' mother said to him, "They have no more wine."

[4]"Dear woman, why do you involve me?" Jesus replied. "My time has not yet come."

[5]His mother said to the servants, "Do whatever he tells you."

[6]Nearby stood six stone water jars, the kind used by the Jews for ceremonial washing, each holding from twenty to thirty gallons.[d]

[7]Jesus said to the servants, "Fill the jars with water"; so they filled them to the brim.

[8]Then he told them, "Now draw some out and take it to the master of the banquet."

They did so, [9]and the master of the banquet tasted the water that had been turned into wine. He did not realize where it had come from, though the servants who had drawn the water knew. Then he called the bridegroom aside [10]and said, "Everyone brings out the choice wine first and then the cheaper wine after the guests have had too much to drink; but you have saved the best till now."

[11]This, the first of his miraculous signs, Jesus performed at Cana in Galilee. He thus revealed his glory, and his disciples put their faith in him.

Jesus Clears the Temple

[12]After this he went down to Capernaum with his mother and brothers and his disciples. There they stayed for a few days.

[13]When it was almost time for the Jewish Passover, Jesus went up to Jerusalem. [14]In the temple courts he found men selling cattle, sheep and doves, and others sitting at tables exchanging money. [15]So he made a whip out of cords, and drove all from the temple area, both sheep and cattle; he scattered the coins of the money changers and overturned their tables. [16]To those who sold doves he said, "Get these out of here! How dare you turn my Father's house into a market!"

[17]His disciples remembered that it is written: "Zeal for your house will consume me."[e]

[18]Then the Jews demanded of him, "What miraculous sign can you show us to prove your authority to do all this?"

[19]Jesus answered them, "Destroy this temple, and I will raise it again in three days."

[20]The Jews replied, "It has taken forty-six years to build this temple, and you are going to raise it in three days?" [21]But the temple he had spoken of was his body. [22]After he was raised from the dead, his disciples recalled what he had said. Then they believed the Scripture and the words that Jesus had spoken.

[23]Now while he was in Jerusalem at the Passover Feast, many people saw the miraculous signs he was doing and believed in his name.[f] [24]But Jesus would not entrust himself to them, for he knew all men. [25]He did not need man's testimony about man, for he knew what was in a man.

[a] *42* Both *Cephas* (Aramaic) and *Peter* (Greek) mean *rock.* [b] *50* Or *Do you believe . . . ?* [c] *51* The Greek is plural. [d] *6* Greek *two to three metretes* (probably about 75 to 115 liters) [e] *17* Psalm 69:9 [f] *23* Or *and believed in him*

Jesus Teaches Nicodemus

3 Now there was a man of the Pharisees named Nicodemus, a member of the Jewish ruling council. 2He came to Jesus at night and said, "Rabbi, we know you are a teacher who has come from God. For no one could perform the miraculous signs you are doing if God were not with him."

3In reply Jesus declared, "I tell you the truth, no one can see the kingdom of God unless he is born again.[a]"

4"How can a man be born when he is old?" Nicodemus asked. "Surely he cannot enter a second time into his mother's womb to be born!"

5Jesus answered, "I tell you the truth, no one can enter the kingdom of God unless he is born of water and the Spirit. 6Flesh gives birth to flesh, but the Spirit[b] gives birth to spirit. 7You should not be surprised at my saying, 'You[c] must be born again.' 8The wind blows wherever it pleases. You hear its sound, but you cannot tell where it comes from or where it is going. So it is with everyone born of the Spirit."

9"How can this be?" Nicodemus asked.

10"You are Israel's teacher," said Jesus, "and do you not understand these things? 11I tell you the truth, we speak of what we know, and we testify to what we have seen, but still you people do not accept our testimony. 12I have spoken to you of earthly things and you do not believe; how then will you believe if I speak of heavenly things? 13No one has ever gone into heaven except the one who came from heaven—the Son of Man.[d] 14Just as Moses lifted up the snake in the desert, so the Son of Man must be lifted up, 15that everyone who believes in him may have eternal life.[e]

16"For God so loved the world that he gave his one and only Son,[f] that whoever believes in him shall not perish but have eternal life. 17For God did not send his Son into the world to condemn the world, but to save the world through him. 18Whoever believes in him is not condemned, but whoever does not believe stands condemned already because he has not believed in the name of God's one and only Son.[g] 19This is the verdict: Light has come into the world, but men loved darkness instead of light because their deeds were evil. 20Everyone who does evil hates the light, and will not come into the light for fear that his deeds will be exposed. 21But whoever lives by the truth comes into the light, so that it may be seen plainly that what he has done has been done through God."[h]

John the Baptist's Testimony About Jesus

22After this, Jesus and his disciples went out into the Judean countryside, where he spent some time with them, and baptized. 23Now John also was baptizing at Aenon near Salim, because there was plenty of water, and people were constantly coming to be baptized. 24(This was before John was put in prison.) 25An argument developed between some of John's disciples and a certain Jew[i] over the matter of ceremonial washing. 26They came to John and said to him, "Rabbi, that man who was with you on the other side of the Jordan—the one you testified about—well, he is baptizing, and everyone is going to him."

27To this John replied, "A man can receive only what is given him from heaven. 28You yourselves can testify that I said, 'I am not the Christ[j] but am sent ahead of him.' 29The bride belongs to the bridegroom. The friend who attends the bridegroom waits and listens for him, and is full of joy when he hears the bridegroom's voice. That joy is mine, and it is now complete. 30He must become greater; I must become less.

31"The one who comes from above is above all; the one who is from the earth belongs to the earth, and speaks as one from the earth. The one who comes from heaven is above all. 32He testifies to what he has seen and heard, but no one accepts his testimony. 33The man who has accepted it has certified that God is truthful. 34For the one whom God has sent speaks the words of God, for God[k] gives the Spirit without limit. 35The Father loves the Son and has placed everything in his hands. 36Whoever believes in the Son has eternal life, but whoever rejects the Son will not see life, for God's wrath remains on him."[l]

Jesus Talks With a Samaritan Woman

4 The Pharisees heard that Jesus was gaining and baptizing more disciples than John, 2although in fact it was not Jesus who baptized, but his disciples. 3When the Lord learned of this, he left Judea and went back once more to Galilee.

4Now he had to go through Samaria. 5So

[a] 3 Or *born from above*; also in verse 7 [b] 6 Or *but spirit* [c] 7 The Greek is plural. [d] 13 Some manuscripts *Man, who is in heaven* [e] 15 Or *believes may have eternal life in him* [f] 16 Or *his only begotten Son* [g] 18 Or *God's only begotten Son* [h] 21 Some interpreters end the quotation after verse 15. [i] 25 Some manuscripts *and certain Jews* [j] 28 Or *Messiah* [k] 34 Greek *he* [l] 36 Some interpreters end the quotation after verse 30.

TUESDAY
READ JOHN 3:1–21

EXPOSING THE SECRETS

A marriage rarely ends because of a single problem. Ask anyone who has been through a divorce, and they'll tell you that it wasn't one thing that led to the end of the marriage but a series of little betrayals that added up to a crisis.

No couple enters into marriage thinking about the ways they can hurt the other or chip away at the other person's trust. But that's exactly how marriages fracture. A little secret here, a little untruth there, and before long, the trust that holds a marriage together is gone. Broken trust doesn't always lead to divorce, but it certainly doesn't lead to a healthy marriage.

My friend Emma's marriage seemed solid. But one afternoon, she ran into a former college boyfriend at the mall. They grabbed a cup of coffee and then went their separate ways. When Emma got home, she decided not to tell her husband about seeing her former boyfriend, even though their time together had been perfectly innocent.

Over the next few weeks, Emma found herself thinking more about her old boyfriend. Eventually she called him to see if he wanted to meet again for coffee. Before long, she and this friend were seeing each other regularly—and, of course, secretly. While this covert relationship didn't become sexual, Emma was betraying her husband's trust. What had started as one small secret eventually became a big problem.

When Emma's guilt finally got the best of her, she told her husband about her relationship with the other man. She and her husband went through extensive, painful counseling and are working to heal their marriage. Yet significant damage was done. And all because one little secret led to another, and another . . .

John 3:20–21 is a good reminder for couples to not keep secrets. When we bring our actions into the light, we show our spouses that we trust them to love us in spite of the sometimes-ugly truth. And we allow God to heal wounds that tempt us to keep secrets in the first place. None of that healing can happen if we keep operating in the dark.

It's OK to have a little mystery in marriage. One of the joys of marriage is being surprised by the beautiful parts of your spouse that you didn't previously know about. But discovering each other through years of conversations and shared experiences isn't the same as keeping secrets or hiding our true selves from each other. A healthy, godly marriage involves risk. It involves a willingness to deal with little problems before they become big ones.

—CARLA BARNHILL

FOR YOUR NEXT DEVOTIONAL READING, TURN TO PAGE 1188.

Everyone who does evil hates the light, and will not come into the light for fear that his deeds will be exposed. But whoever lives by the truth comes into the light, so that it may be seen plainly that what he has done has been done through God.

— JOHN 3:20–21

let's *talk*

- What is our view on keeping secrets? Are there any secrets that are OK to keep? How can we create an environment in our marriage in which it's safe to talk about these secrets?
- What family secrets did we bring to our marriage? How can we diffuse the power of those secrets through good communication and trust?
- What secrets have we kept from each other? What have I done that you'd be angry about if you knew? How about what you've done? Are these little secrets so big that we should see a counselor?

he came to a town in Samaria called Sychar,
near the plot of ground Jacob had given to his
son Joseph. 6Jacob's well was there, and Jesus,
tired as he was from the journey, sat down by
the well. It was about the sixth hour.
7When a Samaritan woman came to draw
water, Jesus said to her, "Will you give me a
drink?" 8(His disciples had gone into the town
to buy food.)
9The Samaritan woman said to him, "You
are a Jew and I am a Samaritan woman. How
can you ask me for a drink?" (For Jews do not
associate with Samaritans.[a])
10Jesus answered her, "If you knew the gift
of God and who it is that asks you for a drink,
you would have asked him and he would have
given you living water."
11"Sir," the woman said, "you have nothing to draw with and the well is deep. Where
can you get this living water? 12Are you greater
than our father Jacob, who gave us the well
and drank from it himself, as did also his sons
and his flocks and herds?"
13Jesus answered, "Everyone who drinks
this water will be thirsty again, 14but whoever
drinks the water I give him will never thirst.
Indeed, the water I give him will become in
him a spring of water welling up to eternal
life."
15The woman said to him, "Sir, give me this
water so that I won't get thirsty and have to
keep coming here to draw water."
16He told her, "Go, call your husband and
come back."
17"I have no husband," she replied.
Jesus said to her, "You are right when you
say you have no husband. 18The fact is, you
have had five husbands, and the man you now
have is not your husband. What you have just
said is quite true."
19"Sir," the woman said, "I can see that you
are a prophet. 20Our fathers worshiped on this
mountain, but you Jews claim that the place
where we must worship is in Jerusalem."
21Jesus declared, "Believe me, woman, a
time is coming when you will worship the Father neither on this mountain nor in Jerusalem. 22You Samaritans worship what you do
not know; we worship what we do know, for
salvation is from the Jews. 23Yet a time is coming and has now come when the true worshipers will worship the Father in spirit and truth,
for they are the kind of worshipers the Father
seeks. 24God is spirit, and his worshipers must
worship in spirit and in truth."
25The woman said, "I know that Messiah"
(called Christ) "is coming. When he comes,
he will explain everything to us."
26Then Jesus declared, "I who speak to you
am he."

The Disciples Rejoin Jesus

27Just then his disciples returned and were
surprised to find him talking with a woman.
But no one asked, "What do you want?" or
"Why are you talking with her?"
28Then, leaving her water jar, the woman
went back to the town and said to the people,
29"Come, see a man who told me everything
I ever did. Could this be the Christ[b]?" 30They
came out of the town and made their way toward him.
31Meanwhile his disciples urged him, "Rabbi, eat something."
32But he said to them, "I have food to eat
that you know nothing about."
33Then his disciples said to each other,
"Could someone have brought him food?"
34"My food," said Jesus, "is to do the will
of him who sent me and to finish his work.
35Do you not say, 'Four months more and
then the harvest'? I tell you, open your eyes
and look at the fields! They are ripe for harvest. 36Even now the reaper draws his wages,
even now he harvests the crop for eternal life,
so that the sower and the reaper may be glad
together. 37Thus the saying 'One sows and another reaps' is true. 38I sent you to reap what
you have not worked for. Others have done
the hard work, and you have reaped the benefits of their labor."

Many Samaritans Believe

39Many of the Samaritans from that town
believed in him because of the woman's testimony, "He told me everything I ever did."
40So when the Samaritans came to him, they
urged him to stay with them, and he stayed
two days. 41And because of his words many
more became believers.
42They said to the woman, "We no longer
believe just because of what you said; now we
have heard for ourselves, and we know that
this man really is the Savior of the world."

Jesus Heals the Official's Son

43After the two days he left for Galilee.
44(Now Jesus himself had pointed out that a
prophet has no honor in his own country.)
45When he arrived in Galilee, the Galileans

---

[a] 9 Or *do not use dishes Samaritans have used* [b] 29 Or *Messiah*

welcomed him. They had seen all that he had
done in Jerusalem at the Passover Feast, for
they also had been there.
46 Once more he visited Cana in Galilee,
where he had turned the water into wine. And
there was a certain royal official whose son lay
sick at Capernaum. 47 When this man heard
that Jesus had arrived in Galilee from Judea,
he went to him and begged him to come and
heal his son, who was close to death.
48 "Unless you people see miraculous signs
and wonders," Jesus told him, "you will never
believe."
49 The royal official said, "Sir, come down
before my child dies."
50 Jesus replied, "You may go. Your son will
live."
The man took Jesus at his word and departed. 51 While he was still on the way, his
servants met him with the news that his boy
was living. 52 When he inquired as to the time
when his son got better, they said to him, "The
fever left him yesterday at the seventh hour."
53 Then the father realized that this was the
exact time at which Jesus had said to him,
"Your son will live." So he and all his household believed.
54 This was the second miraculous sign that
Jesus performed, having come from Judea to
Galilee.

The Healing at the Pool

5 Some time later, Jesus went up to Jerusalem
for a feast of the Jews. 2 Now there is in Jerusalem near the Sheep Gate a pool, which
in Aramaic is called Bethesda[a] and which is
surrounded by five covered colonnades. 3 Here
a great number of disabled people used to
lie—the blind, the lame, the paralyzed.[b] 5 One
who was there had been an invalid for thirty-
eight years. 6 When Jesus saw him lying there
and learned that he had been in this condition
for a long time, he asked him, "Do you want
to get well?"
7 "Sir," the invalid replied, "I have no one
to help me into the pool when the water is
stirred. While I am trying to get in, someone
else goes down ahead of me."
8 Then Jesus said to him, "Get up! Pick up
your mat and walk." 9 At once the man was
cured; he picked up his mat and walked.
The day on which this took place was a Sabbath, 10 and so the Jews said to the man who
had been healed, "It is the Sabbath; the law
forbids you to carry your mat."
11 But he replied, "The man who made
me well said to me, 'Pick up your mat and
walk.' "
12 So they asked him, "Who is this fellow
who told you to pick it up and walk?"
13 The man who was healed had no idea
who it was, for Jesus had slipped away into the
crowd that was there.
14 Later Jesus found him at the temple and
said to him, "See, you are well again. Stop sinning or something worse may happen to you."
15 The man went away and told the Jews that it
was Jesus who had made him well.

Life Through the Son

16 So, because Jesus was doing these things
on the Sabbath, the Jews persecuted him.
17 Jesus said to them, "My Father is always at
his work to this very day, and I, too, am working." 18 For this reason the Jews tried all the
harder to kill him; not only was he breaking
the Sabbath, but he was even calling God his
own Father, making himself equal with God.
19 Jesus gave them this answer: "I tell you
the truth, the Son can do nothing by himself;
he can do only what he sees his Father doing,
because whatever the Father does the Son also
does. 20 For the Father loves the Son and shows
him all he does. Yes, to your amazement he
will show him even greater things than these.
21 For just as the Father raises the dead and
gives them life, even so the Son gives life to
whom he is pleased to give it. 22 Moreover,
the Father judges no one, but has entrusted
all judgment to the Son, 23 that all may honor
the Son just as they honor the Father. He who
does not honor the Son does not honor the
Father, who sent him.
24 "I tell you the truth, whoever hears my
word and believes him who sent me has eternal life and will not be condemned; he has
crossed over from death to life. 25 I tell you
the truth, a time is coming and has now come
when the dead will hear the voice of the Son
of God and those who hear will live. 26 For as
the Father has life in himself, so he has granted
the Son to have life in himself. 27 And he has
given him authority to judge because he is the
Son of Man.
28 "Do not be amazed at this, for a time is
coming when all who are in their graves will
hear his voice 29 and come out—those who

[a] 2 Some manuscripts *Bethzatha*; other manuscripts *Bethsaida* [b] 3 Some manuscripts *paralyzed—and they waited for the moving of the waters.* *4 From time to time an angel of the Lord would come down and stir up the waters. The first one into the pool after each such disturbance would be cured of whatever disease he had.*

have done good will rise to live, and those who have done evil will rise to be condemned. 30By myself I can do nothing; I judge only as I hear, and my judgment is just, for I seek not to please myself but him who sent me.

Testimonies About Jesus

31"If I testify about myself, my testimony is not valid. 32There is another who testifies in my favor, and I know that his testimony about me is valid.

33"You have sent to John and he has testified to the truth. 34Not that I accept human testimony; but I mention it that you may be saved. 35John was a lamp that burned and gave light, and you chose for a time to enjoy his light.

36"I have testimony weightier than that of John. For the very work that the Father has given me to finish, and which I am doing, testifies that the Father has sent me. 37And the Father who sent me has himself testified concerning me. You have never heard his voice nor seen his form, 38nor does his word dwell in you, for you do not believe the one he sent. 39You diligently study[a] the Scriptures because you think that by them you possess eternal life. These are the Scriptures that testify about me, 40yet you refuse to come to me to have life.

41"I do not accept praise from men, 42but I know you. I know that you do not have the love of God in your hearts. 43I have come in my Father's name, and you do not accept me; but if someone else comes in his own name, you will accept him. 44How can you believe if you accept praise from one another, yet make no effort to obtain the praise that comes from the only God[b]?

45"But do not think I will accuse you before the Father. Your accuser is Moses, on whom your hopes are set. 46If you believed Moses, you would believe me, for he wrote about me. 47But since you do not believe what he wrote, how are you going to believe what I say?"

Jesus Feeds the Five Thousand

6 Some time after this, Jesus crossed to the far shore of the Sea of Galilee (that is, the Sea of Tiberias), 2and a great crowd of people followed him because they saw the miraculous signs he had performed on the sick. 3Then Jesus went up on a mountainside and sat down with his disciples. 4The Jewish Passover Feast was near.

5When Jesus looked up and saw a great crowd coming toward him, he said to Philip, "Where shall we buy bread for these people to eat?" 6He asked this only to test him, for he already had in mind what he was going to do.

7Philip answered him, "Eight months' wages[c] would not buy enough bread for each one to have a bite!"

8Another of his disciples, Andrew, Simon Peter's brother, spoke up, 9"Here is a boy with five small barley loaves and two small fish, but how far will they go among so many?"

10Jesus said, "Have the people sit down." There was plenty of grass in that place, and the men sat down, about five thousand of them. 11Jesus then took the loaves, gave thanks, and distributed to those who were seated as much as they wanted. He did the same with the fish.

12When they had all had enough to eat, he said to his disciples, "Gather the pieces that are left over. Let nothing be wasted." 13So they gathered them and filled twelve baskets with the pieces of the five barley loaves left over by those who had eaten.

14After the people saw the miraculous sign that Jesus did, they began to say, "Surely this is the Prophet who is to come into the world." 15Jesus, knowing that they intended to come and make him king by force, withdrew again to a mountain by himself.

Jesus Walks on the Water

16When evening came, his disciples went down to the lake, 17where they got into a boat and set off across the lake for Capernaum. By now it was dark, and Jesus had not yet joined them. 18A strong wind was blowing and the waters grew rough. 19When they had rowed three or three and a half miles,[d] they saw Jesus approaching the boat, walking on the water; and they were terrified. 20But he said to them, "It is I; don't be afraid." 21Then they were willing to take him into the boat, and immediately the boat reached the shore where they were heading.

22The next day the crowd that had stayed on the opposite shore of the lake realized that only one boat had been there, and that Jesus had not entered it with his disciples, but that they had gone away alone. 23Then some boats from Tiberias landed near the place where the people had eaten the bread after the Lord had given thanks. 24Once the crowd realized that neither Jesus nor his disciples were there, they

[a] 39 Or *Study diligently* (the imperative) [b] 44 Some early manuscripts *the Only One* [c] 7 Greek *two hundred denarii* [d] 19 Greek *rowed twenty-five or thirty stadia* (about 5 or 6 kilometers)

got into the boats and went to Capernaum in
search of Jesus.

Jesus the Bread of Life

25When they found him on the other side
of the lake, they asked him, "Rabbi, when did
you get here?"
26Jesus answered, "I tell you the truth, you
are looking for me, not because you saw miraculous signs but because you ate the loaves
and had your fill. 27Do not work for food that
spoils, but for food that endures to eternal
life, which the Son of Man will give you. On
him God the Father has placed his seal of approval."
28Then they asked him, "What must we do
to do the works God requires?"
29Jesus answered, "The work of God is this:
to believe in the one he has sent."
30So they asked him, "What miraculous
sign then will you give that we may see it and
believe you? What will you do? 31Our forefathers ate the manna in the desert; as it is
written: 'He gave them bread from heaven to
eat.'[a]"
32Jesus said to them, "I tell you the truth,
it is not Moses who has given you the bread
from heaven, but it is my Father who gives you
the true bread from heaven. 33For the bread of
God is he who comes down from heaven and
gives life to the world."
34"Sir," they said, "from now on give us this
bread."
35Then Jesus declared, "I am the bread of
life. He who comes to me will never go hungry, and he who believes in me will never be
thirsty. 36But as I told you, you have seen me
and still you do not believe. 37All that the Father gives me will come to me, and whoever
comes to me I will never drive away. 38For I
have come down from heaven not to do my
will but to do the will of him who sent me.
39And this is the will of him who sent me, that
I shall lose none of all that he has given me,
but raise them up at the last day. 40For my Father's will is that everyone who looks to the
Son and believes in him shall have eternal life,
and I will raise him up at the last day."
41At this the Jews began to grumble about
him because he said, "I am the bread that
came down from heaven." 42They said, "Is
this not Jesus, the son of Joseph, whose father
and mother we know? How can he now say, 'I
came down from heaven'?"
43"Stop grumbling among yourselves,"
Jesus answered. 44"No one can come to me
unless the Father who sent me draws him, and
I will raise him up at the last day. 45It is written in the Prophets: 'They will all be taught
by God.'[b] Everyone who listens to the Father
and learns from him comes to me. 46No one
has seen the Father except the one who is from
God; only he has seen the Father. 47I tell you
the truth, he who believes has everlasting life.
48I am the bread of life. 49Your forefathers ate
the manna in the desert, yet they died. 50But
here is the bread that comes down from heav-
en, which a man may eat and not die. 51I am
the living bread that came down from heaven.
If anyone eats of this bread, he will live forever. This bread is my flesh, which I will give for
the life of the world."
52Then the Jews began to argue sharply
among themselves, "How can this man give us
his flesh to eat?"
53Jesus said to them, "I tell you the truth,
unless you eat the flesh of the Son of Man
and drink his blood, you have no life in you.
54Whoever eats my flesh and drinks my blood
has eternal life, and I will raise him up at the
last day. 55For my flesh is real food and my
blood is real drink. 56Whoever eats my flesh
and drinks my blood remains in me, and I in
him. 57Just as the living Father sent me and
I live because of the Father, so the one who
feeds on me will live because of me. 58This is
the bread that came down from heaven. Your
forefathers ate manna and died, but he who
feeds on this bread will live forever." 59He said
this while teaching in the synagogue in Capernaum.

Many Disciples Desert Jesus

60On hearing it, many of his disciples said,
"This is a hard teaching. Who can accept it?"
61Aware that his disciples were grumbling
about this, Jesus said to them, "Does this offend you? 62What if you see the Son of Man
ascend to where he was before! 63The Spirit
gives life; the flesh counts for nothing. The
words I have spoken to you are spirit[c] and
they are life. 64Yet there are some of you who
do not believe." For Jesus had known from the
beginning which of them did not believe and
who would betray him. 65He went on to say,
"This is why I told you that no one can come
to me unless the Father has enabled him."
66From this time many of his disciples
turned back and no longer followed him.

---

a 31 Exodus 16:4; Neh. 9:15; Psalm 78:24,25 *b 45* Isaiah 54:13 *c 63* Or *Spirit*

WEDNESDAY
READ JOHN 6:25–59

MAKING THE MOST OF MEALS

> **"Do not work for food that spoils, but for food that endures to eternal life, which the Son of Man will give you."**
>
> — John 6:27

let's talk

- What mealtime habits are we developing? Why? How can we use our common need for food as an opportunity for renewing our relational and spiritual lives?
- Who are the spiritually and emotionally hungry among us, and how might they find a way to our table? What do they need, and how can we provide it?
- What might others glean from our meal besides food that meets their physical needs? What spiritual ingredients might also be offered?

When our daughters first learned in elementary school about the four food groups, our mealtime conversations changed abruptly. Suddenly every lunch or dinner had to be scrutinized for nutritional value and balance. Junk food was out!

Over the years since then, our daughters have returned to the troughs of sugars, trans fats, artificial flavors, hydrogenated oils and preservatives. We are, by and large, a healthy lot in our family, but there is so much convenience in convenience foods that we often grab something quick and not so healthy.

In John 6:27 Jesus tells us not to work for food that spoils but for food that endures. Just the day before, Jesus had provided fish and bread for about 5,000 men, plus women and children (see verses 5–13). Now he warned the people who had come back for another miracle meal to expend themselves for the right kind of food. We could spiritualize Jesus' instructions and not get too specific about applications, yet part of this teaching might literally apply to what's offered at our dinner table.

Few cravings are stronger than the need for food. Three meals a day aren't enough for many of us; we need to supplement those with snacks. During growth spurts the need is even more intense. I once found the teenage son of a friend draped over the open door of the refrigerator. "I am *so* tired of being hungry all the time," he said as his eyes grazed the leftovers.

While that kind of intense hunger may subside, the craving for food will not dissipate for most of us as long as we live. Jesus' teaching suggests that we should learn from such hunger. We must understand its incessant pleading, and then use it to channel our desires in ways that feed our spiritual nature along with our physical one.

The family meal is so important. Long before we could read the ingredient panels on food packages or had learned how to cook, many of us came to the dinner table and learned from our parents how to satisfy our appetites. We saw how they provided well-balanced, nutritional meals that came from the four food groups. We listened to the kind of table talk that fed our emotional needs and built up our relationships. And we heard them share their faith experiences in conversation, Bible reading and prayer.

Food brings us together as couples and families. But we can use mealtimes to feed more than our bodies. We can make the most of those times to connect, to catch up on each other's experiences from the day, and to build each other up. And when we have tasted what's offered on the table, we can reach for the true bread from heaven. For only when we feast on him will our appetite be forever satisfied.

—WAYNE BROUWER

FOR YOUR NEXT DEVOTIONAL READING, TURN TO PAGE 1191.

67“You do not want to leave too, do you?”
Jesus asked the Twelve.
68Simon Peter answered him, “Lord, to
whom shall we go? You have the words of eternal life. 69We believe and know that you are
the Holy One of God.”
70Then Jesus replied, “Have I not chosen
you, the Twelve? Yet one of you is a devil!”
71(He meant Judas, the son of Simon Iscariot,
who, though one of the Twelve, was later to
betray him.)

Jesus Goes to the Feast of Tabernacles

7 After this, Jesus went around in Galilee,
purposely staying away from Judea because
the Jews there were waiting to take his life.
2But when the Jewish Feast of Tabernacles was
near, 3Jesus’ brothers said to him, “You ought
to leave here and go to Judea, so that your disciples may see the miracles you do. 4No one
who wants to become a public figure acts in
secret. Since you are doing these things, show
yourself to the world.” 5For even his own
brothers did not believe in him.
6Therefore Jesus told them, “The right time
for me has not yet come; for you any time is
right. 7The world cannot hate you, but it hates
me because I testify that what it does is evil.
8You go to the Feast. I am not yet[a] going up
to this Feast, because for me the right time has
not yet come.” 9Having said this, he stayed in
Galilee.
10However, after his brothers had left for
the Feast, he went also, not publicly, but in secret. 11Now at the Feast the Jews were watching for him and asking, “Where is that man?”
12Among the crowds there was widespread
whispering about him. Some said, “He is a
good man.”
Others replied, “No, he deceives the people.” 13But no one would say anything publicly about him for fear of the Jews.

Jesus Teaches at the Feast

14Not until halfway through the Feast did
Jesus go up to the temple courts and begin
to teach. 15The Jews were amazed and asked,
“How did this man get such learning without
having studied?”
16Jesus answered, “My teaching is not my
own. It comes from him who sent me. 17If
anyone chooses to do God’s will, he will find
out whether my teaching comes from God or
whether I speak on my own. 18He who speaks
on his own does so to gain honor for himself,
but he who works for the honor of the one
who sent him is a man of truth; there is nothing false about him. 19Has not Moses given
you the law? Yet not one of you keeps the law.
Why are you trying to kill me?”
20“You are demon-possessed,” the crowd
answered. “Who is trying to kill you?”
21Jesus said to them, “I did one miracle,
and you are all astonished. 22Yet, because Moses gave you circumcision (though actually it
did not come from Moses, but from the patriarchs), you circumcise a child on the Sabbath.
23Now if a child can be circumcised on the
Sabbath so that the law of Moses may not be
broken, why are you angry with me for healing the whole man on the Sabbath? 24Stop
judging by mere appearances, and make a
right judgment.”

Is Jesus the Christ?

25At that point some of the people of Jerusalem began to ask, “Isn’t this the man they
are trying to kill? 26Here he is, speaking publicly, and they are not saying a word to him.
Have the authorities really concluded that he
is the Christ[b]? 27But we know where this man
is from; when the Christ comes, no one will
know where he is from.”
28Then Jesus, still teaching in the temple
courts, cried out, “Yes, you know me, and you
know where I am from. I am not here on my
own, but he who sent me is true. You do not
know him, 29but I know him because I am
from him and he sent me.”
30At this they tried to seize him, but no one
laid a hand on him, because his time had not
yet come. 31Still, many in the crowd put their
faith in him. They said, “When the Christ
comes, will he do more miraculous signs than
this man?”
32The Pharisees heard the crowd whispering
such things about him. Then the chief priests
and the Pharisees sent temple guards to arrest
him.
33Jesus said, “I am with you for only a short
time, and then I go to the one who sent me.
34You will look for me, but you will not find
me; and where I am, you cannot come.”
35The Jews said to one another, “Where
does this man intend to go that we cannot
find him? Will he go where our people live
scattered among the Greeks, and teach the
Greeks? 36What did he mean when he said,
‘You will look for me, but you will not find
me,’ and ‘Where I am, you cannot come’?”

---

[a] 8 Some early manuscripts do not have *yet.* [b] 26 Or *Messiah*; also in verses 27, 31, 41 and 42

37On the last and greatest day of the Feast,
Jesus stood and said in a loud voice, "If anyone is thirsty, let him come to me and drink.
38Whoever believes in me, as[a] the Scripture
has said, streams of living water will flow from
within him." 39By this he meant the Spirit,
whom those who believed in him were later
to receive. Up to that time the Spirit had not
been given, since Jesus had not yet been glorified.
40On hearing his words, some of the people
said, "Surely this man is the Prophet."
41Others said, "He is the Christ."
Still others asked, "How can the Christ
come from Galilee? 42Does not the Scripture
say that the Christ will come from David's
family[b] and from Bethlehem, the town where
David lived?" 43Thus the people were divided
because of Jesus. 44Some wanted to seize him,
but no one laid a hand on him.

Unbelief of the Jewish Leaders

45Finally the temple guards went back to
the chief priests and Pharisees, who asked
them, "Why didn't you bring him in?"
46"No one ever spoke the way this man
does," the guards declared.
47"You mean he has deceived you also?" the
Pharisees retorted. 48"Has any of the rulers or
of the Pharisees believed in him? 49No! But
this mob that knows nothing of the law—
there is a curse on them."
50Nicodemus, who had gone to Jesus earlier
and who was one of their own number, asked,
51"Does our law condemn anyone without
first hearing him to find out what he is doing?"
52They replied, "Are you from Galilee, too?
Look into it, and you will find that a prophet[c]
does not come out of Galilee."

[The earliest manuscripts and many other ancient witnesses do not have John 7:53-8:11.]

53Then each went to his own home.
8 But Jesus went to the Mount of Olives.
2At dawn he appeared again in the temple courts, where all the people gathered
around him, and he sat down to teach them.
3The teachers of the law and the Pharisees
brought in a woman caught in adultery. They
made her stand before the group 4and said to
Jesus, "Teacher, this woman was caught in the
act of adultery. 5In the Law Moses commanded us to stone such women. Now what do you
say?" 6They were using this question as a trap,
in order to have a basis for accusing him.
But Jesus bent down and started to write on
the ground with his finger. 7When they kept
on questioning him, he straightened up and
said to them, "If any one of you is without
sin, let him be the first to throw a stone at
her." 8Again he stooped down and wrote on
the ground.
9At this, those who heard began to go away
one at a time, the older ones first, until only
Jesus was left, with the woman still standing
there. 10Jesus straightened up and asked her,
"Woman, where are they? Has no one condemned you?"
11"No one, sir," she said.
"Then neither do I condemn you," Jesus declared. "Go now and leave your life of sin."

The Validity of Jesus' Testimony

12When Jesus spoke again to the people, he
said, "I am the light of the world. Whoever
follows me will never walk in darkness, but
will have the light of life."
13The Pharisees challenged him, "Here you
are, appearing as your own witness; your testimony is not valid."
14Jesus answered, "Even if I testify on my
own behalf, my testimony is valid, for I know
where I came from and where I am going.
But you have no idea where I come from or
where I am going. 15You judge by human
standards; I pass judgment on no one. 16But
if I do judge, my decisions are right, because
I am not alone. I stand with the Father, who
sent me. 17In your own Law it is written that
the testimony of two men is valid. 18I am one
who testifies for myself; my other witness is
the Father, who sent me."
19Then they asked him, "Where is your father?"
"You do not know me or my Father," Jesus
replied. "If you knew me, you would know
my Father also." 20He spoke these words while
teaching in the temple area near the place
where the offerings were put. Yet no one seized
him, because his time had not yet come.
21Once more Jesus said to them, "I am going away, and you will look for me, and you
will die in your sin. Where I go, you cannot
come."

---

[a] 37,38 Or / *If anyone is thirsty, let him come to me. / And let him drink,* 38*who believes in me. / As* [b] 42 Greek *seed* [c] 52 Two early manuscripts *the Prophet*

THURSDAY
READ JOHN 7:53—8:11

FINDING THE REAL CULPRIT

"If any one of you is without sin, let him be the first to throw a stone at her."

— JOHN 8:7

let's talk

- What is our usual way of confronting each other about a sin or bad habit?
- How is that hurtful or harmful to each other? To our relationship?
- Why is it best to wait till we have "a lump in our throat and tears in our eyes" before confronting each other about a sin? How does that affect what we say and how we say it?

As the oldest of four siblings, I was the family tattletale. Whenever my sister or one of my brothers did something wrong, I would muster up as much fake empathy and sympathy as I could, and then tell my mother, "I really hate to tell you this, but . . ." Then I'd stand back with secret glee while the sinner got his or her due.

Although I've long outgrown ratting on my siblings, that desire to be someone else's judge and jury still lives on in me, especially with regard to my husband. Sometimes he'll do or say something, and I'll wish that he were my brother and we were ten years old, so I could run to Mom and tattle on him.

Instead, I have to do the grown-up thing and tattle on him to God. "Did you see that?" I'll say. "Are you going to let him get away with that?" I don't even hide behind the phony "I hate to do this" bit. I want blood!

That's when God reminds me that I'm guilty of far worse, and that I should be thankful that he doesn't smite me with gnats in my teeth.

Wanting to point out people's sin and taking pleasure in their punishment is nothing new. According to this passage, the Pharisees brought a woman caught in adultery into the temple courts and tattled on her to Jesus. They made her stand in front of the crowd and broadcasted her sin. "In the Law Moses commanded us to stone such women," they said (John 8:5). In response, Jesus stooped down and wrote on the ground with his finger.

Then he told the accusers to go ahead and stone the woman, but the one who was without sin should be the first to throw a stone. Since none of them was sinless, they all put down their rocks and walked away. When only Jesus and the woman were left, Jesus neither winked at her sin nor condemned her as the Pharisees had hoped he would do. Instead, he told her to go and leave her life of sin (see verse 11).

In marriage, we're always bumping into each other's sin, and there's a real temptation to throw stones. That makes us feel better about our own shortcomings. Other times we look the other way and let a besetting sin continue because that's easier than confronting it. Both responses are unbiblical.

Long ago a friend said, "If the thought of pointing out your mate's sin gives you any sense of glee or smug self-satisfaction, then you had better wait until there's a lump in your throat and tears in your eyes."

That's great advice. When it comes to a spouse's sin, any words of confrontation must be prompted by a desire to help the other toward health, wholeness and spiritual restoration. The only rocks we should throw are the ones we toss at ourselves.

—NANCY KENNEDY

FOR YOUR NEXT DEVOTIONAL READING, TURN TO PAGE 1194.

22This made the Jews ask, "Will he kill himself? Is that why he says, 'Where I go, you cannot come'?"
23But he continued, "You are from below;
I am from above. You are of this world; I am
not of this world. 24I told you that you would
die in your sins; if you do not believe that I
am ⌞the one I claim to be⌟,[a] you will indeed
die in your sins."
25"Who are you?" they asked.
"Just what I have been claiming all along,"
Jesus replied. 26"I have much to say in judgment of you. But he who sent me is reliable,
and what I have heard from him I tell the
world."
27They did not understand that he was telling them about his Father. 28So Jesus said,
"When you have lifted up the Son of Man,
then you will know that I am ⌞the one I claim
to be⌟ and that I do nothing on my own but
speak just what the Father has taught me.
29The one who sent me is with me; he has
not left me alone, for I always do what pleases him." 30Even as he spoke, many put their
faith in him.

The Children of Abraham

31To the Jews who had believed him, Jesus
said, "If you hold to my teaching, you are
really my disciples. 32Then you will know the
truth, and the truth will set you free."
33They answered him, "We are Abraham's
descendants[b] and have never been slaves of
anyone. How can you say that we shall be set
free?"
34Jesus replied, "I tell you the truth, everyone who sins is a slave to sin. 35Now a slave
has no permanent place in the family, but a
son belongs to it forever. 36So if the Son sets
you free, you will be free indeed. 37I know you
are Abraham's descendants. Yet you are ready
to kill me, because you have no room for my
word. 38I am telling you what I have seen in
the Father's presence, and you do what you
have heard from your father.[c]"
39"Abraham is our father," they answered.
"If you were Abraham's children," said
Jesus, "then you would[d] do the things Abraham did. 40As it is, you are determined to kill
me, a man who has told you the truth that I
heard from God. Abraham did not do such
things. 41You are doing the things your own
father does."
"We are not illegitimate children," they
protested. "The only Father we have is God
himself."

The Children of the Devil

42Jesus said to them, "If God were your
Father, you would love me, for I came from
God and now am here. I have not come on my
own; but he sent me. 43Why is my language
not clear to you? Because you are unable to
hear what I say. 44You belong to your father,
the devil, and you want to carry out your father's desire. He was a murderer from the beginning, not holding to the truth, for there is
no truth in him. When he lies, he speaks his
native language, for he is a liar and the father
of lies. 45Yet because I tell the truth, you do
not believe me! 46Can any of you prove me
guilty of sin? If I am telling the truth, why
don't you believe me? 47He who belongs to
God hears what God says. The reason you do
not hear is that you do not belong to God."

The Claims of Jesus About Himself

48The Jews answered him, "Aren't we right
in saying that you are a Samaritan and demon-
possessed?"
49"I am not possessed by a demon," said
Jesus, "but I honor my Father and you dishonor me. 50I am not seeking glory for myself;
but there is one who seeks it, and he is the
judge. 51I tell you the truth, if anyone keeps
my word, he will never see death."
52At this the Jews exclaimed, "Now we
know that you are demon-possessed! Abraham
died and so did the prophets, yet you say that
if anyone keeps your word, he will never taste
death. 53Are you greater than our father Abraham? He died, and so did the prophets. Who
do you think you are?"
54Jesus replied, "If I glorify myself, my
glory means nothing. My Father, whom you
claim as your God, is the one who glorifies
me. 55Though you do not know him, I know
him. If I said I did not, I would be a liar like
you, but I do know him and keep his word.
56Your father Abraham rejoiced at the thought
of seeing my day; he saw it and was glad."
57"You are not yet fifty years old," the Jews
said to him, "and you have seen Abraham!"
58"I tell you the truth," Jesus answered,
"before Abraham was born, I am!" 59At this,
they picked up stones to stone him, but Jesus
hid himself, slipping away from the temple
grounds.

---

[a] 24 Or *I am he*; also in verse 28 [b] 33 Greek *seed*; also in verse 37 [c] 38 Or *presence. Therefore do what you have heard from the Father.* [d] 39 Some early manuscripts *"If you are Abraham's children," said Jesus, "then*

Jesus Heals a Man Born Blind

9 As he went along, he saw a man blind from
birth. 2His disciples asked him, "Rabbi,
who sinned, this man or his parents, that
he was born blind?"
3"Neither this man nor his parents sinned,"
said Jesus, "but this happened so that the work
of God might be displayed in his life. 4As long
as it is day, we must do the work of him who
sent me. Night is coming, when no one can
work. 5While I am in the world, I am the light
of the world."
6Having said this, he spit on the ground,
made some mud with the saliva, and put it on
the man's eyes. 7"Go," he told him, "wash in
the Pool of Siloam" (this word means Sent).
So the man went and washed, and came home
seeing.
8His neighbors and those who had formerly
seen him begging asked, "Isn't this the same
man who used to sit and beg?" 9Some claimed
that he was.
Others said, "No, he only looks like him."
But he himself insisted, "I am the man."
10"How then were your eyes opened?" they
demanded.
11He replied, "The man they call Jesus
made some mud and put it on my eyes. He
told me to go to Siloam and wash. So I went
and washed, and then I could see."
12"Where is this man?" they asked him.
"I don't know," he said.

The Pharisees Investigate the Healing

13They brought to the Pharisees the man
who had been blind. 14Now the day on which
Jesus had made the mud and opened the man's
eyes was a Sabbath. 15Therefore the Pharisees
also asked him how he had received his sight.
"He put mud on my eyes," the man replied,
"and I washed, and now I see."
16Some of the Pharisees said, "This man is
not from God, for he does not keep the Sabbath."
But others asked, "How can a sinner do
such miraculous signs?" So they were divided.
17Finally they turned again to the blind
man, "What have you to say about him? It was
your eyes he opened."
The man replied, "He is a prophet."
18The Jews still did not believe that he had
been blind and had received his sight until
they sent for the man's parents. 19"Is this your
son?" they asked. "Is this the one you say was
born blind? How is it that now he can see?"
20"We know he is our son," the parents
answered, "and we know he was born blind.
21But how he can see now, or who opened
his eyes, we don't know. Ask him. He is of
age; he will speak for himself." 22His parents
said this because they were afraid of the Jews,
for already the Jews had decided that anyone
who acknowledged that Jesus was the Christ[a]
would be put out of the synagogue. 23That was
why his parents said, "He is of age; ask him."
24A second time they summoned the man
who had been blind. "Give glory to God,[b]"
they said. "We know this man is a sinner."
25He replied, "Whether he is a sinner or
not, I don't know. One thing I do know. I was
blind but now I see!"
26Then they asked him, "What did he do to
you? How did he open your eyes?"
27He answered, "I have told you already
and you did not listen. Why do you want to
hear it again? Do you want to become his disciples, too?"
28Then they hurled insults at him and said,
"You are this fellow's disciple! We are disciples
of Moses! 29We know that God spoke to Moses, but as for this fellow, we don't even know
where he comes from."
30The man answered, "Now that is remarkable! You don't know where he comes from,
yet he opened my eyes. 31We know that God
does not listen to sinners. He listens to the
godly man who does his will. 32Nobody has
ever heard of opening the eyes of a man born
blind. 33If this man were not from God, he
could do nothing."
34To this they replied, "You were steeped
in sin at birth; how dare you lecture us!" And
they threw him out.

Spiritual Blindness

35Jesus heard that they had thrown him
out, and when he found him, he said, "Do
you believe in the Son of Man?"
36"Who is he, sir?" the man asked. "Tell me
so that I may believe in him."
37Jesus said, "You have now seen him; in
fact, he is the one speaking with you."
38Then the man said, "Lord, I believe," and
he worshiped him.
39Jesus said, "For judgment I have come
into this world, so that the blind will see and
those who see will become blind."
40Some Pharisees who were with him heard
him say this and asked, "What? Are we blind
too?"

---

a 22 Or *Messiah* *b* 24 A solemn charge to tell the truth (see Joshua 7:19)

FRIDAY
READ JOHN 9:1–41

RIGHTING WRONG ASSUMPTIONS

> **His disciples asked him, "Rabbi, who sinned, this man or his parents, that he was born blind?"**
>
> — JOHN 9:2

let's talk

- What preconceived notions did we have of each other when we first met? Were they correct or not?
- Why is it dangerous to make assumptions about a person or situation before knowing much about it? How do we find out what's really going on?
- When have our assumptions been proven wrong about others who were having a hard time? How did that change our response to them?

It's so easy to make assumptions. I remember a time I made a hasty conclusion and was proved wrong.

I was teaching a writing course for a local university, and on the first night, I strolled up the front sidewalk and noticed a man sitting on the bench outside, smoking a cigarette. He was dirty, missing most of his front teeth, and he didn't look too bright. His flannel shirt was torn, and his jeans were dirty. "He's probably homeless," I thought, moving on into the building.

As the students filed into class, I winced as I saw "Homeless" take a seat and pull a notebook out of his bag. "Oh, great," I thought. "He'll probably need remedial training; I bet he can't string two sentences together."

The man didn't say a word during that first class. At the end of the three hours, I collected some paragraphs I had assigned to the students earlier that evening in which they were to describe a childhood experience that had affected them as adults.

I skimmed through the assignments and gasped in disbelief. "Homeless" could write! His paper was eloquent and heart wrenching; in short, it was the best first paper I'd read from a student in years.

This man subsequently went on to publish a book of essays dealing with his childhood.

The people of Jesus' day were no different than I was. The man in John 9 must have had a rough life; because he had been born blind, people assumed he was being punished. Either he had sinned in the womb (or in a preexistent state) or else his condition was the result of the sin of his parents. Even Jesus' disciples bought into those assumptions!

That kind of thinking still pervades our society, even among Christians: If you'd had more faith, your parent could have been cured of cancer. If you'd been a better husband or wife, your spouse wouldn't have left you. On the flip side, those people over there have been so tremendously blessed; they must be doing something right.

We make judgments in marriage too. Assumptions about our spouse's motives, feelings or rationale for doing something—without speaking about it first—can be so wrong. Yet our misconceptions can escalate into angry words, hard feelings and cold wars without us ever knowing the truth.

Jesus' words in John 9:3 blow assumptions out of the water. "Neither this man nor his parents sinned, . . . but this happened so that the work of God might be displayed in his life." Likewise, God is working through our marriages and us, using various situations not to humble or exalt us but to reveal himself. He permits certain things to happen to us to teach us what it means to be his followers. So our assumptions may fall flat as we live out the works God displays in us.

We just need to be sure we open the Book before making judgments about what's inside others.

—VALERIE VAN KOOTEN

FOR YOUR NEXT DEVOTIONAL READING, TURN TO PAGE 1198.

41Jesus said, "If you were blind, you would not be guilty of sin; but now that you claim you can see, your guilt remains.

The Shepherd and His Flock

10 "I tell you the truth, the man who does not enter the sheep pen by the gate, but climbs in by some other way, is a thief and a robber. 2The man who enters by the gate is the shepherd of his sheep. 3The watchman opens the gate for him, and the sheep listen to his voice. He calls his own sheep by name and leads them out. 4When he has brought out all his own, he goes on ahead of them, and his sheep follow him because they know his voice. 5But they will never follow a stranger; in fact, they will run away from him because they do not recognize a stranger's voice." 6Jesus used this figure of speech, but they did not understand what he was telling them.

7Therefore Jesus said again, "I tell you the truth, I am the gate for the sheep. 8All who ever came before me were thieves and robbers, but the sheep did not listen to them. 9I am the gate; whoever enters through me will be saved.[a] He will come in and go out, and find pasture. 10The thief comes only to steal and kill and destroy; I have come that they may have life, and have it to the full.

11"I am the good shepherd. The good shepherd lays down his life for the sheep. 12The hired hand is not the shepherd who owns the sheep. So when he sees the wolf coming, he abandons the sheep and runs away. Then the wolf attacks the flock and scatters it. 13The man runs away because he is a hired hand and cares nothing for the sheep.

14"I am the good shepherd; I know my sheep and my sheep know me— 15just as the Father knows me and I know the Father—and I lay down my life for the sheep. 16I have other sheep that are not of this sheep pen. I must bring them also. They too will listen to my voice, and there shall be one flock and one shepherd. 17The reason my Father loves me is that I lay down my life—only to take it up again. 18No one takes it from me, but I lay it down of my own accord. I have authority to lay it down and authority to take it up again. This command I received from my Father."

19At these words the Jews were again divided. 20Many of them said, "He is demon-possessed and raving mad. Why listen to him?"

21But others said, "These are not the sayings of a man possessed by a demon. Can a demon open the eyes of the blind?"

The Unbelief of the Jews

22Then came the Feast of Dedication[b] at Jerusalem. It was winter, 23and Jesus was in the temple area walking in Solomon's Colonnade. 24The Jews gathered around him, saying, "How long will you keep us in suspense? If you are the Christ,[c] tell us plainly."

25Jesus answered, "I did tell you, but you do not believe. The miracles I do in my Father's name speak for me, 26but you do not believe because you are not my sheep. 27My sheep listen to my voice; I know them, and they follow me. 28I give them eternal life, and they shall never perish; no one can snatch them out of my hand. 29My Father, who has given them to me, is greater than all[d]; no one can snatch them out of my Father's hand. 30I and the Father are one."

31Again the Jews picked up stones to stone him, 32but Jesus said to them, "I have shown you many great miracles from the Father. For which of these do you stone me?"

33"We are not stoning you for any of these," replied the Jews, "but for blasphemy, because you, a mere man, claim to be God."

34Jesus answered them, "Is it not written in your Law, 'I have said you are gods'[e]? 35If he called them 'gods,' to whom the word of God came—and the Scripture cannot be broken— 36what about the one whom the Father set apart as his very own and sent into the world? Why then do you accuse me of blasphemy because I said, 'I am God's Son'? 37Do not believe me unless I do what my Father does. 38But if I do it, even though you do not believe me, believe the miracles, that you may know and understand that the Father is in me, and I in the Father." 39Again they tried to seize him, but he escaped their grasp.

40Then Jesus went back across the Jordan to the place where John had been baptizing in the early days. Here he stayed 41and many people came to him. They said, "Though John never performed a miraculous sign, all that John said about this man was true." 42And in that place many believed in Jesus.

The Death of Lazarus

11 Now a man named Lazarus was sick. He was from Bethany, the village of Mary and her sister Martha. 2This Mary, whose brother Lazarus now lay sick, was the

[a] 9 Or *kept safe* [b] 22 That is, Hanukkah [c] 24 Or *Messiah* [d] 29 Many early manuscripts *What my Father has given me is greater than all* [e] 34 Psalm 82:6

same one who poured perfume on the Lord and wiped his feet with her hair. [3]So the sisters sent word to Jesus, "Lord, the one you love is sick."

[4]When he heard this, Jesus said, "This sickness will not end in death. No, it is for God's glory so that God's Son may be glorified through it." [5]Jesus loved Martha and her sister and Lazarus. [6]Yet when he heard that Lazarus was sick, he stayed where he was two more days.

[7]Then he said to his disciples, "Let us go back to Judea."

[8]"But Rabbi," they said, "a short while ago the Jews tried to stone you, and yet you are going back there?"

[9]Jesus answered, "Are there not twelve hours of daylight? A man who walks by day will not stumble, for he sees by this world's light. [10]It is when he walks by night that he stumbles, for he has no light."

[11]After he had said this, he went on to tell them, "Our friend Lazarus has fallen asleep; but I am going there to wake him up."

[12]His disciples replied, "Lord, if he sleeps, he will get better." [13]Jesus had been speaking of his death, but his disciples thought he meant natural sleep.

[14]So then he told them plainly, "Lazarus is dead, [15]and for your sake I am glad I was not there, so that you may believe. But let us go to him."

[16]Then Thomas (called Didymus) said to the rest of the disciples, "Let us also go, that we may die with him."

Jesus Comforts the Sisters

[17]On his arrival, Jesus found that Lazarus had already been in the tomb for four days. [18]Bethany was less than two miles[a] from Jerusalem, [19]and many Jews had come to Martha and Mary to comfort them in the loss of their brother. [20]When Martha heard that Jesus was coming, she went out to meet him, but Mary stayed at home.

[21]"Lord," Martha said to Jesus, "if you had been here, my brother would not have died. [22]But I know that even now God will give you whatever you ask."

[23]Jesus said to her, "Your brother will rise again."

[24]Martha answered, "I know he will rise again in the resurrection at the last day."

[25]Jesus said to her, "I am the resurrection and the life. He who believes in me will live, even though he dies; [26]and whoever lives and believes in me will never die. Do you believe this?"

[27]"Yes, Lord," she told him, "I believe that you are the Christ,[b] the Son of God, who was to come into the world."

[28]And after she had said this, she went back and called her sister Mary aside. "The Teacher is here," she said, "and is asking for you." [29]When Mary heard this, she got up quickly and went to him. [30]Now Jesus had not yet entered the village, but was still at the place where Martha had met him. [31]When the Jews who had been with Mary in the house, comforting her, noticed how quickly she got up and went out, they followed her, supposing she was going to the tomb to mourn there.

[32]When Mary reached the place where Jesus was and saw him, she fell at his feet and said, "Lord, if you had been here, my brother would not have died."

[33]When Jesus saw her weeping, and the Jews who had come along with her also weeping, he was deeply moved in spirit and troubled. [34]"Where have you laid him?" he asked.

"Come and see, Lord," they replied.

[35]Jesus wept.

[36]Then the Jews said, "See how he loved him!"

[37]But some of them said, "Could not he who opened the eyes of the blind man have kept this man from dying?"

Jesus Raises Lazarus From the Dead

[38]Jesus, once more deeply moved, came to the tomb. It was a cave with a stone laid across the entrance. [39]"Take away the stone," he said.

"But, Lord," said Martha, the sister of the dead man, "by this time there is a bad odor, for he has been there four days."

[40]Then Jesus said, "Did I not tell you that if you believed, you would see the glory of God?"

[41]So they took away the stone. Then Jesus looked up and said, "Father, I thank you that you have heard me. [42]I knew that you always hear me, but I said this for the benefit of the people standing here, that they may believe that you sent me."

[43]When he had said this, Jesus called in a loud voice, "Lazarus, come out!" [44]The dead man came out, his hands and feet wrapped with strips of linen, and a cloth around his face.

---

[a] *18* Greek *fifteen stadia* (about 3 kilometers) [b] *27* Or *Messiah*

Jesus said to them, "Take off the grave clothes and let him go."

The Plot to Kill Jesus

45 Therefore many of the Jews who had come to visit Mary, and had seen what Jesus did, put their faith in him. 46 But some of them went to the Pharisees and told them what Jesus had done. 47 Then the chief priests and the Pharisees called a meeting of the Sanhedrin.

"What are we accomplishing?" they asked. "Here is this man performing many miraculous signs. 48 If we let him go on like this, everyone will believe in him, and then the Romans will come and take away both our place[a] and our nation."

49 Then one of them, named Caiaphas, who was high priest that year, spoke up, "You know nothing at all! 50 You do not realize that it is better for you that one man die for the people than that the whole nation perish."

51 He did not say this on his own, but as high priest that year he prophesied that Jesus would die for the Jewish nation, 52 and not only for that nation but also for the scattered children of God, to bring them together and make them one. 53 So from that day on they plotted to take his life.

54 Therefore Jesus no longer moved about publicly among the Jews. Instead he withdrew to a region near the desert, to a village called Ephraim, where he stayed with his disciples.

55 When it was almost time for the Jewish Passover, many went up from the country to Jerusalem for their ceremonial cleansing before the Passover. 56 They kept looking for Jesus, and as they stood in the temple area they asked one another, "What do you think? Isn't he coming to the Feast at all?" 57 But the chief priests and Pharisees had given orders that if anyone found out where Jesus was, he should report it so that they might arrest him.

Jesus Anointed at Bethany

12 Six days before the Passover, Jesus arrived at Bethany, where Lazarus lived, whom Jesus had raised from the dead. 2 Here a dinner was given in Jesus' honor. Martha served, while Lazarus was among those reclining at the table with him. 3 Then Mary took about a pint[b] of pure nard, an expensive perfume; she poured it on Jesus' feet and wiped his feet with her hair. And the house was filled with the fragrance of the perfume.

4 But one of his disciples, Judas Iscariot, who was later to betray him, objected, 5 "Why wasn't this perfume sold and the money given to the poor? It was worth a year's wages.[c]" 6 He did not say this because he cared about the poor but because he was a thief; as keeper of the money bag, he used to help himself to what was put into it.

7 "Leave her alone," Jesus replied. "⌊It was intended⌋ that she should save this perfume for the day of my burial. 8 You will always have the poor among you, but you will not always have me."

9 Meanwhile a large crowd of Jews found out that Jesus was there and came, not only because of him but also to see Lazarus, whom he had raised from the dead. 10 So the chief priests made plans to kill Lazarus as well, 11 for on account of him many of the Jews were going over to Jesus and putting their faith in him.

The Triumphal Entry

12 The next day the great crowd that had come for the Feast heard that Jesus was on his way to Jerusalem. 13 They took palm branches and went out to meet him, shouting,

> "Hosanna![d]"
>
> "Blessed is he who comes in the name of
> the Lord!"[e]
>
> "Blessed is the King of Israel!"

14 Jesus found a young donkey and sat upon it, as it is written,

> 15 "Do not be afraid, O Daughter of Zion;
> see, your king is coming,
> seated on a donkey's colt."[f]

16 At first his disciples did not understand all this. Only after Jesus was glorified did they realize that these things had been written about him and that they had done these things to him.

17 Now the crowd that was with him when he called Lazarus from the tomb and raised him from the dead continued to spread the word. 18 Many people, because they had heard that he had given this miraculous sign, went out to meet him. 19 So the Pharisees said to one another, "See, this is getting us nowhere. Look how the whole world has gone after him!"

Jesus Predicts His Death

20 Now there were some Greeks among those who went up to worship at the Feast.

---

a 48 Or *temple* *b* 3 Greek *a litra* (probably about 0.5 liter) *c* 5 Greek *three hundred denarii* *d* 13 A Hebrew expression meaning "Save!" which became an exclamation of praise *e* 13 Psalm 118:25,26 *f* 15 Zech. 9:9

WEEKEND

unwrap the gift of sex

Like many young married couples, we read our share of books about sex. We easily dismiss those authors who view sexual intercourse solely as a means of procreation and appreciate authors who acknowledge that God had designed human sexuality, in part at least, for married people's pleasure. Such authors describe sexual pleasure as a priceless gift spouses can give to one another—a gift, in fact, that they must give to one another.

The notion of sex as something we must give to our spouses is biblical. First Corinthians 7 teaches clearly that spouses must fulfill their "marital duty" to one another, and must not "deprive each other." According to this passage, a wife does not have authority over her own body; her husband does. Similarly, she has authority over his body. These verses are not-so-subtle reminders that we each owe our spouse a satisfying sexual relationship. We are, after all, our spouse's only sexual option. The commitment to marital fidelity, which every sincere Christian couple must make, means that if we don't find sexual fulfillment in our marriage, we'll go without it. It is as simple as that. Each of us must take our sexual responsibility seriously, and lovingly and enthusiastically do everything in our power to meet and fulfill our spouse's sexual needs and desires.

Putting too much emphasis on sex as something one does for his or her spouse can have a negative effect. For these people sex becomes one more obligation, one more task they need to perform to be a "good wife" or a "good husband." They forget that sex is something they should enjoy *for themselves*.

Some people don't enjoy sex because they don't enjoy their own sexuality. Some husbands and wives don't even view themselves as sexual beings. Sex is something they do, an out-of-character behavior they squeeze in at the end of a busy day rather than a natural extension of an important dimension of who they are. These people would become more interested and interesting sexual partners if they would give themselves permission to enjoy their sexuality, view their sexuality as an important part of their identity, and take delight in excelling sexually.

People who take a positive approach to their sexuality and commit themselves to developing their sexual skills just as they develop their other gifts and skills cultivate a sexual confidence that frees them to become active rather than passive participants in a sexual relationship. They become proactive sexually rather than merely reactive. And they bring tremendous pleasure to their spouses.

Fun sex doesn't start in the bedroom. It starts in the kitchen, during a private moment when a nonsexual touch slides over into the realm of the blatantly sexual. It begins with a playful suggestion of sexual intent, or a not-so-subtle sexual innuendo, or a well-placed flirtatious remark.

How spouses dress can heighten—or squelch—sexual desire. We know that for some people, dress truly makes little difference. Most spouses admit, however, that what their husband or wife wears affects their sexual interest.

Instead of taking your cues from Hollywood or from other couples, why not develop your own sexual style? Experiment. Explore new avenues of sexual expression. Above all, communicate. Talk openly, vulnerably, specifically and regularly about your sexual relationship. We have observed a direct correlation between a couple's level of sexual communication and their level of sexual fulfillment.

—BILL AND LYNNE HYBELS

what turns you on?

Decide whether the following scenarios are turn-ons or turn-offs for you and your mate.

1. Your spouse kisses you softly on the neck.
2. You come home from work and there are dirty dishes in the sink.
3. Your spouse calls you several times a day.
4. Your spouse leaves you a note with an enticing offer if you come home early.
5. You stay up all night to make cupcakes for your child's birthday party.
6. Your spouse compliments you on how you look.
7. Your spouse compliments you on what you've done.
8. Your spouse suggests, "No, you go take a nap. I'll handle things around here."
9. Your spouse loses ten pounds and starts exercising.
10. Your spouse surprises you with flowers.
11. You and your spouse get away for a weekend.
12. Your spouse quotes a poem.
13. Your spouse writes a poem for you.
14. Your spouse gives you an incredible back rub.
15. Your favorite sister and her kids visit for a week.
16. Your spouse gives you long, slow kisses.
17. Your spouse gives you fast, wet kisses.
18. Your spouse holds your hand in public.
19. One thing that turns you off (write in) ________ ____________.
20. One thing that turns you on (write in)_________ ______________.

HOW ARE WE DOING?

date

let's make a DATE

PLAN A ROMANTIC GETAWAY

Decide where is the most romantic place the two of you would like to go to and plan a trip there. Search for information on the Internet. Use pictures from travel magazines or brochures to find the ideal hotel location or mountain lodge retreat. Decide what activities the two of you would like to do in this romantic place. Long walks? Warm baths for two? Spend time talking about what each of you would like to do on a weekend just for the two of you. Estimate the cost and decide how you could make the trip happen.

If you really can't afford a trip, tell friends and family that you're going away, then lock the doors and turn off your phones. Take a couple of ideas from your planned vacation and recreate the perfect romantic weekend inside your own home.

FOR YOUR NEXT DEVOTIONAL READING, TURN TO PAGE 1201.

LESSONS FROM THE *Bible*

Check out the way these famous lovers in Song of Songs (4:1–15; 5:10–16) talked about each other. How would you describe your feelings for your spouse?

21 They came to Philip, who was from Bethsaida in Galilee, with a request. "Sir," they said, "we would like to see Jesus." 22 Philip went to tell Andrew; Andrew and Philip in turn told Jesus.

23 Jesus replied, "The hour has come for the Son of Man to be glorified. 24 I tell you the truth, unless a kernel of wheat falls to the ground and dies, it remains only a single seed. But if it dies, it produces many seeds. 25 The man who loves his life will lose it, while the man who hates his life in this world will keep it for eternal life. 26 Whoever serves me must follow me; and where I am, my servant also will be. My Father will honor the one who serves me.

27 "Now my heart is troubled, and what shall I say? 'Father, save me from this hour'? No, it was for this very reason I came to this hour. 28 Father, glorify your name!"

Then a voice came from heaven, "I have glorified it, and will glorify it again." 29 The crowd that was there and heard it said it had thundered; others said an angel had spoken to him.

30 Jesus said, "This voice was for your benefit, not mine. 31 Now is the time for judgment on this world; now the prince of this world will be driven out. 32 But I, when I am lifted up from the earth, will draw all men to myself." 33 He said this to show the kind of death he was going to die.

34 The crowd spoke up, "We have heard from the Law that the Christ[a] will remain forever, so how can you say, 'The Son of Man must be lifted up'? Who is this 'Son of Man'?"

35 Then Jesus told them, "You are going to have the light just a little while longer. Walk while you have the light, before darkness overtakes you. The man who walks in the dark does not know where he is going. 36 Put your trust in the light while you have it, so that you may become sons of light." When he had finished speaking, Jesus left and hid himself from them.

The Jews Continue in Their Unbelief

37 Even after Jesus had done all these miraculous signs in their presence, they still would not believe in him. 38 This was to fulfill the word of Isaiah the prophet:

"Lord, who has believed our message
 and to whom has the arm of the Lord
  been revealed?"[b]

39 For this reason they could not believe, because, as Isaiah says elsewhere:

40 "He has blinded their eyes
 and deadened their hearts,
so they can neither see with their eyes,
 nor understand with their hearts,
 nor turn—and I would heal them."[c]

41 Isaiah said this because he saw Jesus' glory and spoke about him.

42 Yet at the same time many even among the leaders believed in him. But because of the Pharisees they would not confess their faith for fear they would be put out of the synagogue; 43 for they loved praise from men more than praise from God.

44 Then Jesus cried out, "When a man believes in me, he does not believe in me only, but in the one who sent me. 45 When he looks at me, he sees the one who sent me. 46 I have come into the world as a light, so that no one who believes in me should stay in darkness.

47 "As for the person who hears my words but does not keep them, I do not judge him. For I did not come to judge the world, but to save it. 48 There is a judge for the one who rejects me and does not accept my words; that very word which I spoke will condemn him at the last day. 49 For I did not speak of my own accord, but the Father who sent me commanded me what to say and how to say it. 50 I know that his command leads to eternal life. So whatever I say is just what the Father has told me to say."

Jesus Washes His Disciples' Feet

13 It was just before the Passover Feast. Jesus knew that the time had come for him to leave this world and go to the Father. Having loved his own who were in the world, he now showed them the full extent of his love.[d]

2 The evening meal was being served, and the devil had already prompted Judas Iscariot, son of Simon, to betray Jesus. 3 Jesus knew that the Father had put all things under his power, and that he had come from God and was returning to God; 4 so he got up from the meal, took off his outer clothing, and wrapped a towel around his waist. 5 After that, he poured water into a basin and began to wash his disciples' feet, drying them with the towel that was wrapped around him.

6 He came to Simon Peter, who said to him, "Lord, are you going to wash my feet?"

---

[a] *34* Or *Messiah* [b] *38* Isaiah 53:1 [c] *40* Isaiah 6:10 [d] *1* Or *he loved them to the last*

MONDAY
READ JOHN 13:1–38

LOVING BEYOND FEELING

For most of my life, I have thought of *love* as a noun, not a verb. In our culture, marriage typically occurs as the result of two people falling in love and deciding that they want to spend the rest of their lives together. It's this intense feeling of love that prompts us to say "I do" and commit to all kinds of lofty promises, like remaining faithful, and honoring and respecting our mate in sickness and in health till death do us part. Unfortunately for too many people, once the feeling of love passes, so does the marriage.

Jesus turns this way of thinking on its ear. Instead of telling us to love others based on our feelings toward them, he commands us to love one another whether we feel love or not. He said in John 13:34, "As I have loved you, so you must love one another."

Jesus' love toward us isn't based on how he feels about us or what we feel about him. Nor is it based on what we deserve. It's based on actions that speak louder than the words "I love you." If you're looking for proof, just look at the cross. Jesus didn't stand at its foot and say, "You see this cross. I love you so much that I would die for you." He didn't make promises; he just did it. He died on the cross before we even realized we needed him to die for us. There is no greater love than that.

I confess that most of the time I dole out love to my husband, Dan, based on how he shows love to me, not on how God loves me. Instead, what if I started my day by focusing on how Jesus has loved me by sacrificing his life? What if I concentrated on Jesus' sacrifice that allows me to enjoy the fullness of all God intended for me? And then, what if I, in turn, loved Dan out of a heart of gratitude for what Christ has done for me? It's so simple and yet I'm only now beginning to grasp the concept of living according to God's love for me. And I can, at best, only implement it in stops and starts.

I want to love Dan better, but sometimes I get confused or bogged down in how exactly to do that. With so many self-help books out there, it's easy to get distracted from the main thing. But Jesus makes it all very clear. He said, "Love others as I have loved you."

How did Jesus love me? He gave his life for me. Although there was nothing I did to deserve it, he gave me all of himself. He sacrificed everything to wipe out the curse of my sin and create the only way back to God. If I could get my heart and my head in line with this basic but profound truth and get my actions to follow, I would never again have to wonder how to love Dan.

—MARIAN V. LIAUTAUD

"A new command I give you: Love one another. As I have loved you, so you must love one another."

— JOHN 13:34

let's *talk*

- Do we think of *love* as a noun or a verb? What's the difference? What changes could redefining the word make in our relationship?
- Why is it difficult to love each other sacrificially?
- What are some ways we might love each other as we think about Christ's sacrifice for us?

FOR YOUR NEXT DEVOTIONAL READING, TURN TO PAGE 1204.

7 Jesus replied, "You do not realize now what
I am doing, but later you will understand."
8 "No," said Peter, "you shall never wash my
feet."
Jesus answered, "Unless I wash you, you
have no part with me."
9 "Then, Lord," Simon Peter replied, "not
just my feet but my hands and my head as
well!"
10 Jesus answered, "A person who has had
a bath needs only to wash his feet; his whole
body is clean. And you are clean, though not
every one of you." 11 For he knew who was going to betray him, and that was why he said
not every one was clean.
12 When he had finished washing their feet,
he put on his clothes and returned to his place.
"Do you understand what I have done for
you?" he asked them. 13 "You call me 'Teacher' and 'Lord,' and rightly so, for that is what
I am. 14 Now that I, your Lord and Teacher,
have washed your feet, you also should wash
one another's feet. 15 I have set you an example
that you should do as I have done for you. 16 I
tell you the truth, no servant is greater than
his master, nor is a messenger greater than the
one who sent him. 17 Now that you know these
things, you will be blessed if you do them.

Jesus Predicts His Betrayal

18 "I am not referring to all of you; I know
those I have chosen. But this is to fulfill the
scripture: 'He who shares my bread has lifted
up his heel against me.'[a]
19 "I am telling you now before it happens,
so that when it does happen you will believe
that I am He. 20 I tell you the truth, whoever
accepts anyone I send accepts me; and whoever accepts me accepts the one who sent me."
21 After he had said this, Jesus was troubled
in spirit and testified, "I tell you the truth, one
of you is going to betray me."
22 His disciples stared at one another, at a
loss to know which of them he meant. 23 One
of them, the disciple whom Jesus loved, was
reclining next to him. 24 Simon Peter motioned
to this disciple and said, "Ask him which one
he means."
25 Leaning back against Jesus, he asked him,
"Lord, who is it?"
26 Jesus answered, "It is the one to whom
I will give this piece of bread when I have
dipped it in the dish." Then, dipping the piece
of bread, he gave it to Judas Iscariot, son of Simon. 27 As soon as Judas took the bread, Satan
entered into him.
"What you are about to do, do quickly,"
Jesus told him, 28 but no one at the meal understood why Jesus said this to him. 29 Since
Judas had charge of the money, some thought
Jesus was telling him to buy what was needed for the Feast, or to give something to the
poor. 30 As soon as Judas had taken the bread,
he went out. And it was night.

Jesus Predicts Peter's Denial

31 When he was gone, Jesus said, "Now is
the Son of Man glorified and God is glorified
in him. 32 If God is glorified in him,[b] God will
glorify the Son in himself, and will glorify him
at once.
33 "My children, I will be with you only a
little longer. You will look for me, and just as
I told the Jews, so I tell you now: Where I am
going, you cannot come.
34 "A new command I give you: Love one
another. As I have loved you, so you must love
one another. 35 By this all men will know that
you are my disciples, if you love one another."
36 Simon Peter asked him, "Lord, where are
you going?"
Jesus replied, "Where I am going, you cannot follow now, but you will follow later."
37 Peter asked, "Lord, why can't I follow you
now? I will lay down my life for you."
38 Then Jesus answered, "Will you really lay
down your life for me? I tell you the truth,
before the rooster crows, you will disown me
three times!

Jesus Comforts His Disciples

14 "Do not let your hearts be troubled.
Trust in God[c]; trust also in me. 2 In
my Father's house are many rooms; if it
were not so, I would have told you. I am going
there to prepare a place for you. 3 And if I go
and prepare a place for you, I will come back
and take you to be with me that you also may
be where I am. 4 You know the way to the place
where I am going."

Jesus the Way to the Father

5 Thomas said to him, "Lord, we don't know
where you are going, so how can we know the
way?"
6 Jesus answered, "I am the way and the truth
and the life. No one comes to the Father except through me. 7 If you really knew me, you

[a] *18* Psalm 41:9 [b] *32* Many early manuscripts do not have *If God is glorified in him.* [c] *1* Or *You trust in God*

would know[a] my Father as well. From now
on, you do know him and have seen him."
8Philip said, "Lord, show us the Father and
that will be enough for us."
9Jesus answered: "Don't you know me,
Philip, even after I have been among you such
a long time? Anyone who has seen me has seen
the Father. How can you say, 'Show us the Father'? 10Don't you believe that I am in the Father, and that the Father is in me? The words
I say to you are not just my own. Rather, it
is the Father, living in me, who is doing his
work. 11Believe me when I say that I am in
the Father and the Father is in me; or at least
believe on the evidence of the miracles themselves. 12I tell you the truth, anyone who has
faith in me will do what I have been doing.
He will do even greater things than these, because I am going to the Father. 13And I will do
whatever you ask in my name, so that the Son
may bring glory to the Father. 14You may ask
me for anything in my name, and I will do it.

Jesus Promises the Holy Spirit

15"If you love me, you will obey what I
command. 16And I will ask the Father, and
he will give you another Counselor to be with
you forever— 17the Spirit of truth. The world
cannot accept him, because it neither sees him
nor knows him. But you know him, for he
lives with you and will be[b] in you. 18I will not
leave you as orphans; I will come to you. 19Be-
fore long, the world will not see me anymore,
but you will see me. Because I live, you also
will live. 20On that day you will realize that
I am in my Father, and you are in me, and I
am in you. 21Whoever has my commands and
obeys them, he is the one who loves me. He
who loves me will be loved by my Father, and I
too will love him and show myself to him."
22Then Judas (not Judas Iscariot) said, "But,
Lord, why do you intend to show yourself to
us and not to the world?"
23Jesus replied, "If anyone loves me, he will
obey my teaching. My Father will love him,
and we will come to him and make our home
with him. 24He who does not love me will not
obey my teaching. These words you hear are
not my own; they belong to the Father who
sent me.
25"All this I have spoken while still with
you. 26But the Counselor, the Holy Spirit,
whom the Father will send in my name, will
teach you all things and will remind you of
everything I have said to you. 27Peace I leave
with you; my peace I give you. I do not give to
you as the world gives. Do not let your hearts
be troubled and do not be afraid.
28"You heard me say, 'I am going away and
I am coming back to you.' If you loved me,
you would be glad that I am going to the Father, for the Father is greater than I. 29I have
told you now before it happens, so that when
it does happen you will believe. 30I will not
speak with you much longer, for the prince of
this world is coming. He has no hold on me,
31but the world must learn that I love the Father and that I do exactly what my Father has
commanded me.
"Come now; let us leave.

The Vine and the Branches

15 "I am the true vine, and my Father is
the gardener. 2He cuts off every branch
in me that bears no fruit, while every
branch that does bear fruit he prunes[c] so that
it will be even more fruitful. 3You are already
clean because of the word I have spoken to
you. 4Remain in me, and I will remain in you.
No branch can bear fruit by itself; it must remain in the vine. Neither can you bear fruit
unless you remain in me.
5"I am the vine; you are the branches. If a
man remains in me and I in him, he will bear
much fruit; apart from me you can do nothing. 6If anyone does not remain in me, he is
like a branch that is thrown away and withers;
such branches are picked up, thrown into the
fire and burned. 7If you remain in me and my
words remain in you, ask whatever you wish,
and it will be given you. 8This is to my Father's
glory, that you bear much fruit, showing yourselves to be my disciples.
9"As the Father has loved me, so have I loved
you. Now remain in my love. 10If you obey
my commands, you will remain in my love,
just as I have obeyed my Father's commands
and remain in his love. 11I have told you this
so that my joy may be in you and that your
joy may be complete. 12My command is this:
Love each other as I have loved you. 13Greater
love has no one than this, that he lay down his
life for his friends. 14You are my friends if you
do what I command. 15I no longer call you
servants, because a servant does not know his
master's business. Instead, I have called you
friends, for everything that I learned from my
Father I have made known to you. 16You did
not choose me, but I chose you and appointed
you to go and bear fruit—fruit that will last.

[a] 7 Some early manuscripts *If you really have known me, you will know* [b] 17 Some early manuscripts *and is* [c] 2 The Greek for *prunes* also means *cleans.*

TUESDAY
READ JOHN 14:1–14

FROM HOUSE TO HOME

"In my Father's house are many rooms; if it were not so, I would have told you. I am going there to prepare a place for you."
— John 14:2

let's talk

- How can we keep the right perspective in this life, especially when we feel troubled and anxious about all of our responsibilities? How does looking toward heaven offer us a better perspective?
- Why do material possessions often take priority over spiritual promises? How can we confront this confusion in life?
- In what ways do we need to shift our priorities so that we can live close to Christ in the here and now?

We like living in nice houses with spacious rooms and tasteful furnishings. We also like the exciting challenge of upgrading periodically, either refurbishing our existing houses or moving to larger ones in better locations. Still, there's nothing that can compare to the home Jesus is preparing for us in heaven.

Heaven is a hard concept for us to grasp, partly because we live in the here and now, where we prefer to stay rather than face what precedes our passing into eternity (i.e., death). Also, most of us are not yet ready to let go of what we can now see and touch and feel—including our loving spouses, children and families—for something we can only accept by faith.

Jesus' disciples struggled with that tension as well. On one level they understood that Jesus was promising them a better place to live: his spacious Father's house. On another level they realized that the place he was preparing for them had more to do with faith than with sight. So they had questions.

Thomas asked, "Lord, we don't know where you are going, so how can we know the way?" Jesus' response was, "I am the way and the truth and the life. No one comes to the Father except through me." That left the disciples even more confused. "Lord, show us the Father and that will be enough for us," Philip said. "Anyone who has seen me has seen the Father," Jesus replied.

Nothing we have in this life can compare with the perfection and peace we will one day enjoy in our eternal home. Yet many of us spend huge amounts of time, money and effort on earthly things. We look, shop and spend, believing that what we have isn't enough. In short, our problems would dissipate if we just had "more."

Sometimes it takes a shake-up to help lift our eyes off of what we have and onto something far better. For example, Paul and Cindy, a fine Christian couple, had a wonderful house, designer clothes and expensive cars. They loved each other, but they were always looking for more stuff.

Then Paul had a heart attack. He survived, thanks to excellent medical care, a quadruple bypass, and the answered prayers of many people. But after Paul moved out of the intensive care unit and into a rehab unit, he and his wife talked a lot about their priorities. They realized that for all the stuff they had accumulated, they were still troubled, still wanting, still unhappy. Their eyes were so focused on the here and now that they were missing the joyful anticipation of eternity. "I guess I had to get flat on my back to look up and really trust in God," Paul said.

"We realized the life we had wasn't enough," Cindy said. "We needed Christ at the center of our lives—for now and all eternity."

We can have a good life here with each other in Christ, but living with Christ in eternity—ah, then we will truly be home!

—JOHN R. THROOP

FOR YOUR NEXT DEVOTIONAL READING, TURN TO PAGE 1207.

Then the Father will give you whatever you
ask in my name. 17This is my command: Love
each other.

The World Hates the Disciples

18“If the world hates you, keep in mind
that it hated me first. 19If you belonged to
the world, it would love you as its own. As
it is, you do not belong to the world, but I
have chosen you out of the world. That is why
the world hates you. 20Remember the words I
spoke to you: ‘No servant is greater than his
master.’ [a] If they persecuted me, they will persecute you also. If they obeyed my teaching,
they will obey yours also. 21They will treat you
this way because of my name, for they do not
know the One who sent me. 22If I had not
come and spoken to them, they would not be
guilty of sin. Now, however, they have no excuse for their sin. 23He who hates me hates
my Father as well. 24If I had not done among
them what no one else did, they would not
be guilty of sin. But now they have seen these
miracles, and yet they have hated both me
and my Father. 25But this is to fulfill what is
written in their Law: ‘They hated me without
reason.’ [b]

26“When the Counselor comes, whom I
will send to you from the Father, the Spirit
of truth who goes out from the Father, he will
testify about me. 27And you also must testify,
for you have been with me from the beginning.

16 “All this I have told you so that you will
not go astray. 2They will put you out of
the synagogue; in fact, a time is coming
when anyone who kills you will think he is
offering a service to God. 3They will do such
things because they have not known the Father
or me. 4I have told you this, so that when the
time comes you will remember that I warned
you. I did not tell you this at first because I
was with you.

The Work of the Holy Spirit

5“Now I am going to him who sent me,
yet none of you asks me, ‘Where are you going?’ 6Because I have said these things, you are
filled with grief. 7But I tell you the truth: It is
for your good that I am going away. Unless I
go away, the Counselor will not come to you;
but if I go, I will send him to you. 8When he
comes, he will convict the world of guilt [c] in
regard to sin and righteousness and judgment:
9in regard to sin, because men do not believe
in me; 10in regard to righteousness, because
I am going to the Father, where you can see
me no longer; 11and in regard to judgment,
because the prince of this world now stands
condemned.

12“I have much more to say to you, more
than you can now bear. 13But when he, the
Spirit of truth, comes, he will guide you into
all truth. He will not speak on his own; he will
speak only what he hears, and he will tell you
what is yet to come. 14He will bring glory to
me by taking from what is mine and making
it known to you. 15All that belongs to the Father is mine. That is why I said the Spirit will
take from what is mine and make it known
to you.

16“In a little while you will see me no more,
and then after a little while you will see me.”

The Disciples’ Grief Will Turn to Joy

17Some of his disciples said to one another, “What does he mean by saying, ‘In a little
while you will see me no more, and then after
a little while you will see me,’ and ‘Because I
am going to the Father’?” 18They kept asking,
“What does he mean by ‘a little while’? We
don’t understand what he is saying.”

19Jesus saw that they wanted to ask him
about this, so he said to them, “Are you asking
one another what I meant when I said, ‘In a
little while you will see me no more, and then
after a little while you will see me’? 20I tell you
the truth, you will weep and mourn while the
world rejoices. You will grieve, but your grief
will turn to joy. 21A woman giving birth to
a child has pain because her time has come;
but when her baby is born she forgets the anguish because of her joy that a child is born
into the world. 22So with you: Now is your
time of grief, but I will see you again and you
will rejoice, and no one will take away your
joy. 23In that day you will no longer ask me
anything. I tell you the truth, my Father will
give you whatever you ask in my name. 24Un-
til now you have not asked for anything in my
name. Ask and you will receive, and your joy
will be complete.

25“Though I have been speaking figuratively, a time is coming when I will no longer use
this kind of language but will tell you plainly
about my Father. 26In that day you will ask
in my name. I am not saying that I will ask
the Father on your behalf. 27No, the Father
himself loves you because you have loved me
and have believed that I came from God. 28I

[a] *20* John 13:16 [b] *25* Psalms 35:19; 69:4 [c] *8* Or *will expose the guilt of the world*

came from the Father and entered the world;
now I am leaving the world and going back to
the Father."
29 Then Jesus' disciples said, "Now you are
speaking clearly and without figures of speech.
30 Now we can see that you know all things
and that you do not even need to have anyone
ask you questions. This makes us believe that
you came from God."
31 "You believe at last!"[a] Jesus answered.
32 "But a time is coming, and has come, when
you will be scattered, each to his own home.
You will leave me all alone. Yet I am not alone,
for my Father is with me.
33 "I have told you these things, so that in
me you may have peace. In this world you will
have trouble. But take heart! I have overcome
the world."

Jesus Prays for Himself

17 After Jesus said this, he looked toward
heaven and prayed:

"Father, the time has come. Glorify
your Son, that your Son may glorify you.
2 For you granted him authority over all
people that he might give eternal life to
all those you have given him. 3 Now this is
eternal life: that they may know you, the
only true God, and Jesus Christ, whom
you have sent. 4 I have brought you glory on earth by completing the work you
gave me to do. 5 And now, Father, glorify
me in your presence with the glory I had
with you before the world began.

Jesus Prays for His Disciples

6 "I have revealed you[b] to those whom
you gave me out of the world. They were
yours; you gave them to me and they
have obeyed your word. 7 Now they know
that everything you have given me comes
from you. 8 For I gave them the words
you gave me and they accepted them.
They knew with certainty that I came
from you, and they believed that you sent
me. 9 I pray for them. I am not praying
for the world, but for those you have giv-
en me, for they are yours. 10 All I have is
yours, and all you have is mine. And glory has come to me through them. 11 I will
remain in the world no longer, but they
are still in the world, and I am coming
to you. Holy Father, protect them by the
power of your name—the name you gave
me—so that they may be one as we are
one. 12 While I was with them, I protected them and kept them safe by that name
you gave me. None has been lost except
the one doomed to destruction so that
Scripture would be fulfilled.
13 "I am coming to you now, but I say
these things while I am still in the world,
so that they may have the full measure of
my joy within them. 14 I have given them
your word and the world has hated them,
for they are not of the world any more
than I am of the world. 15 My prayer is
not that you take them out of the world
but that you protect them from the evil
one. 16 They are not of the world, even as
I am not of it. 17 Sanctify[c] them by the
truth; your word is truth. 18 As you sent
me into the world, I have sent them into
the world. 19 For them I sanctify myself,
that they too may be truly sanctified.

Jesus Prays for All Believers

20 "My prayer is not for them alone.
I pray also for those who will believe in
me through their message, 21 that all of
them may be one, Father, just as you are
in me and I am in you. May they also be
in us so that the world may believe that
you have sent me. 22 I have given them
the glory that you gave me, that they may
be one as we are one: 23 I in them and you
in me. May they be brought to complete
unity to let the world know that you sent
me and have loved them even as you have
loved me.
24 "Father, I want those you have given
me to be with me where I am, and to see
my glory, the glory you have given me because you loved me before the creation of
the world.
25 "Righteous Father, though the world
does not know you, I know you, and they
know that you have sent me. 26 I have
made you known to them, and will continue to make you known in order that
the love you have for me may be in them
and that I myself may be in them."

Jesus Arrested

18 When he had finished praying, Jesus left
with his disciples and crossed the Kidron Valley. On the other side there was
an olive grove, and he and his disciples went
into it.

[a] 31 Or *"Do you now believe?"* [b] 6 Greek *your name*; also in verse 26 [c] 17 Greek *hagiazo (set apart for sacred use* or *make holy)*; also in verse 19

WEDNESDAY
READ JOHN 17:1–26

TWO SHALL BECOME ONE

When I was a young teen, our pastor invited a group of us to distribute Bible studies in a nearby town. The Bible studies included the Gospel of John plus questions that challenged non-Christians to seek God's love in Jesus.

I went on those outings driven more by obligation than joy. If no one answered the door when we knocked, I was relieved. If someone slammed the door on us, I was thankful that I didn't have to carry on a conversation.

One day while I was out ringing doorbells, a man answered, and when I handed him the Bible study, he scanned the text of the Gospel for a few minutes. Then he spit out a question: "Have you actually read this?"

Actually, I had, because the Bible played a huge role in my family and in my personal life. But his question sent me back to the Gospel of John again, this time as if I had never read it before. I came away both discouraged and deeply renewed.

John's Gospel tells some of the most marvelous stories about Jesus—his nighttime encounter with Nicodemus in chapter 3, his visit with the Samaritan woman in chapter 4—but it also contains lengthy teachings that don't seem to work well as evangelistic tools. Jesus demanded that we eat his flesh and drink his blood in chapter 6; he accused some of being children of the devil in chapter 8; and he said that we have to "remain in" him in chapter 15.

While those who have walked with Jesus for a long time sense the rich philosophic significance of these passages, they appear to be mumbo jumbo to first-time readers. So too with this passage: "I have given them the glory that you gave me, that they may be one as we are one: I in them and you in me." These words speak of the kind of intimacy that can only happen between people who have been with each other for a long time.

In chapters 13–17, Jesus talked about his imminent departure and rued the trouble it would cause his friends. He urged them to trust the Holy Spirit, whom he would send them, and he cautioned them to remain in him even though he would be physically absent from them. He washed their feet and then offered a prayer requesting that the disciples be bound to him just as he is bound to his Father.

The longer we walk and talk with Jesus, the more we begin to grasp what unity with him really means. Similarly, the intimacy of a man and woman in marriage is only truly appreciated as we share our hearts and minds and souls over time.

Sometimes when I officiate at a wedding, either the bride or the groom has trouble slipping the wedding band on the other's finger. They become embarrassed, especially when guests snicker. I break the tension by saying that wedding rings seem to fit better the longer you wear them.

Likewise, true intimacy in marriage isn't instant; it fits better over time.

—WAYNE BROUWER

"I have given them the glory that you gave me, that they may be one as we are one: I in them and you in me. May they be brought to complete unity."

— JOHN 17:22–23

let's talk

- ✦ How has our relationship deepened and strengthened over time? What evidence can we point to that proves we are increasingly "becoming one"?
- ✦ How are we growing closer to God? How does intimacy with God bring us closer to one another?
- ✦ In what ways does our growing intimacy with each other open us up to others? In what ways does it cause us to become more private and exclusive?

FOR YOUR NEXT DEVOTIONAL READING, TURN TO PAGE 1215.

2Now Judas, who betrayed him, knew the place, because Jesus had often met there with his disciples. 3So Judas came to the grove, guiding a detachment of soldiers and some officials from the chief priests and Pharisees. They were carrying torches, lanterns and weapons.

4Jesus, knowing all that was going to happen to him, went out and asked them, "Who is it you want?"

5"Jesus of Nazareth," they replied.

"I am he," Jesus said. (And Judas the traitor was standing there with them.) 6When Jesus said, "I am he," they drew back and fell to the ground.

7Again he asked them, "Who is it you want?"

And they said, "Jesus of Nazareth."

8"I told you that I am he," Jesus answered. "If you are looking for me, then let these men go." 9This happened so that the words he had spoken would be fulfilled: "I have not lost one of those you gave me."[a]

10Then Simon Peter, who had a sword, drew it and struck the high priest's servant, cutting off his right ear. (The servant's name was Malchus.)

11Jesus commanded Peter, "Put your sword away! Shall I not drink the cup the Father has given me?"

Jesus Taken to Annas

12Then the detachment of soldiers with its commander and the Jewish officials arrested Jesus. They bound him 13and brought him first to Annas, who was the father-in-law of Caiaphas, the high priest that year. 14Caiaphas was the one who had advised the Jews that it would be good if one man died for the people.

Peter's First Denial

15Simon Peter and another disciple were following Jesus. Because this disciple was known to the high priest, he went with Jesus into the high priest's courtyard, 16but Peter had to wait outside at the door. The other disciple, who was known to the high priest, came back, spoke to the girl on duty there and brought Peter in.

17"You are not one of his disciples, are you?" the girl at the door asked Peter.

He replied, "I am not."

18It was cold, and the servants and officials stood around a fire they had made to keep warm. Peter also was standing with them, warming himself.

The High Priest Questions Jesus

19Meanwhile, the high priest questioned Jesus about his disciples and his teaching.

20"I have spoken openly to the world," Jesus replied. "I always taught in synagogues or at the temple, where all the Jews come together. I said nothing in secret. 21Why question me? Ask those who heard me. Surely they know what I said."

22When Jesus said this, one of the officials nearby struck him in the face. "Is this the way you answer the high priest?" he demanded.

23"If I said something wrong," Jesus replied, "testify as to what is wrong. But if I spoke the truth, why did you strike me?" 24Then Annas sent him, still bound, to Caiaphas the high priest.[b]

Peter's Second and Third Denials

25As Simon Peter stood warming himself, he was asked, "You are not one of his disciples, are you?"

He denied it, saying, "I am not."

26One of the high priest's servants, a relative of the man whose ear Peter had cut off, challenged him, "Didn't I see you with him in the olive grove?" 27Again Peter denied it, and at that moment a rooster began to crow.

Jesus Before Pilate

28Then the Jews led Jesus from Caiaphas to the palace of the Roman governor. By now it was early morning, and to avoid ceremonial uncleanness the Jews did not enter the palace; they wanted to be able to eat the Passover. 29So Pilate came out to them and asked, "What charges are you bringing against this man?"

30"If he were not a criminal," they replied, "we would not have handed him over to you."

31Pilate said, "Take him yourselves and judge him by your own law."

"But we have no right to execute anyone," the Jews objected. 32This happened so that the words Jesus had spoken indicating the kind of death he was going to die would be fulfilled.

33Pilate then went back inside the palace, summoned Jesus and asked him, "Are you the king of the Jews?"

34"Is that your own idea," Jesus asked, "or did others talk to you about me?"

---

[a] *9* John 6:39 [b] *24* Or *(Now Annas had sent him, still bound, to Caiaphas the high priest.)*

35“Am I a Jew?” Pilate replied. “It was your
people and your chief priests who handed you
over to me. What is it you have done?”

36Jesus said, “My kingdom is not of this
world. If it were, my servants would fight to
prevent my arrest by the Jews. But now my
kingdom is from another place.”

37“You are a king, then!” said Pilate.

Jesus answered, “You are right in saying I
am a king. In fact, for this reason I was born,
and for this I came into the world, to testify
to the truth. Everyone on the side of truth listens to me.”

38“What is truth?” Pilate asked. With this
he went out again to the Jews and said, “I find
no basis for a charge against him. 39But it is
your custom for me to release to you one prisoner at the time of the Passover. Do you want
me to release ‘the king of the Jews’?”

40They shouted back, “No, not him! Give
us Barabbas!” Now Barabbas had taken part
in a rebellion.

Jesus Sentenced to Be Crucified

19 Then Pilate took Jesus and had him
flogged. 2The soldiers twisted together a
crown of thorns and put it on his head.
They clothed him in a purple robe 3and went
up to him again and again, saying, “Hail, king
of the Jews!” And they struck him in the face.

4Once more Pilate came out and said to the
Jews, “Look, I am bringing him out to you to
let you know that I find no basis for a charge
against him.” 5When Jesus came out wearing
the crown of thorns and the purple robe, Pilate said to them, “Here is the man!”

6As soon as the chief priests and their officials saw him, they shouted, “Crucify! Crucify!”

But Pilate answered, “You take him and
crucify him. As for me, I find no basis for a
charge against him.”

7The Jews insisted, “We have a law, and according to that law he must die, because he
claimed to be the Son of God.”

8When Pilate heard this, he was even more
afraid, 9and he went back inside the palace.
“Where do you come from?” he asked Jesus,
but Jesus gave him no answer. 10“Do you refuse to speak to me?” Pilate said. “Don’t you
realize I have power either to free you or to
crucify you?”

11Jesus answered, “You would have no power over me if it were not given to you from
above. Therefore the one who handed me over
to you is guilty of a greater sin.”

12From then on, Pilate tried to set Jesus
free, but the Jews kept shouting, “If you let
this man go, you are no friend of Caesar. Anyone who claims to be a king opposes Caesar.”

13When Pilate heard this, he brought Jesus
out and sat down on the judge’s seat at a place
known as the Stone Pavement (which in Aramaic is Gabbatha). 14It was the day of Preparation of Passover Week, about the sixth hour.

“Here is your king,” Pilate said to the Jews.

15But they shouted, “Take him away! Take
him away! Crucify him!”

“Shall I crucify your king?” Pilate asked.

“We have no king but Caesar,” the chief
priests answered.

16Finally Pilate handed him over to them
to be crucified.

The Crucifixion

So the soldiers took charge of Jesus. 17Car-
rying his own cross, he went out to the place
of the Skull (which in Aramaic is called Golgotha). 18Here they crucified him, and with
him two others—one on each side and Jesus
in the middle.

19Pilate had a notice prepared and fastened
to the cross. It read: JESUS OF NAZARETH, THE
KING OF THE JEWS. 20Many of the Jews read
this sign, for the place where Jesus was crucified was near the city, and the sign was written in Aramaic, Latin and Greek. 21The chief
priests of the Jews protested to Pilate, “Do not
write ‘The King of the Jews,’ but that this man
claimed to be king of the Jews.”

22Pilate answered, “What I have written, I
have written.”

23When the soldiers crucified Jesus, they
took his clothes, dividing them into four
shares, one for each of them, with the under-
garment remaining. This garment was seam-
less, woven in one piece from top to bottom.

24“Let’s not tear it,” they said to one another. “Let’s decide by lot who will get it.”

This happened that the scripture might be
fulfilled which said,

> “They divided my garments among them
> and cast lots for my clothing.”[a]

So this is what the soldiers did.

25Near the cross of Jesus stood his mother,
his mother’s sister, Mary the wife of Clopas,
and Mary Magdalene. 26When Jesus saw his
mother there, and the disciple whom he loved

[a] *24* Psalm 22:18

standing nearby, he said to his mother, "Dear woman, here is your son," [27]and to the disciple, "Here is your mother." From that time on, this disciple took her into his home.

The Death of Jesus

[28]Later, knowing that all was now completed, and so that the Scripture would be fulfilled, Jesus said, "I am thirsty." [29]A jar of wine vinegar was there, so they soaked a sponge in it, put the sponge on a stalk of the hyssop plant, and lifted it to Jesus' lips. [30]When he had received the drink, Jesus said, "It is finished." With that, he bowed his head and gave up his spirit.

[31]Now it was the day of Preparation, and the next day was to be a special Sabbath. Because the Jews did not want the bodies left on the crosses during the Sabbath, they asked Pilate to have the legs broken and the bodies taken down. [32]The soldiers therefore came and broke the legs of the first man who had been crucified with Jesus, and then those of the other. [33]But when they came to Jesus and found that he was already dead, they did not break his legs. [34]Instead, one of the soldiers pierced Jesus' side with a spear, bringing a sudden flow of blood and water. [35]The man who saw it has given testimony, and his testimony is true. He knows that he tells the truth, and he testifies so that you also may believe. [36]These things happened so that the scripture would be fulfilled: "Not one of his bones will be broken," [a] [37]and, as another scripture says, "They will look on the one they have pierced." [b]

The Burial of Jesus

[38]Later, Joseph of Arimathea asked Pilate for the body of Jesus. Now Joseph was a disciple of Jesus, but secretly because he feared the Jews. With Pilate's permission, he came and took the body away. [39]He was accompanied by Nicodemus, the man who earlier had visited Jesus at night. Nicodemus brought a mixture of myrrh and aloes, about seventy-five pounds. [c] [40]Taking Jesus' body, the two of them wrapped it, with the spices, in strips of linen. This was in accordance with Jewish burial customs. [41]At the place where Jesus was crucified, there was a garden, and in the garden a new tomb, in which no one had ever been laid. [42]Because it was the Jewish day of Preparation and since the tomb was nearby, they laid Jesus there.

The Empty Tomb

20 Early on the first day of the week, while it was still dark, Mary Magdalene went to the tomb and saw that the stone had been removed from the entrance. [2]So she came running to Simon Peter and the other disciple, the one Jesus loved, and said, "They have taken the Lord out of the tomb, and we don't know where they have put him!"

[3]So Peter and the other disciple started for the tomb. [4]Both were running, but the other disciple outran Peter and reached the tomb first. [5]He bent over and looked in at the strips of linen lying there but did not go in. [6]Then Simon Peter, who was behind him, arrived and went into the tomb. He saw the strips of linen lying there, [7]as well as the burial cloth that had been around Jesus' head. The cloth was folded up by itself, separate from the linen. [8]Finally the other disciple, who had reached the tomb first, also went inside. He saw and believed. [9](They still did not understand from Scripture that Jesus had to rise from the dead.)

Jesus Appears to Mary Magdalene

[10]Then the disciples went back to their homes, [11]but Mary stood outside the tomb crying. As she wept, she bent over to look into the tomb [12]and saw two angels in white, seated where Jesus' body had been, one at the head and the other at the foot.

[13]They asked her, "Woman, why are you crying?"

"They have taken my Lord away," she said, "and I don't know where they have put him." [14]At this, she turned around and saw Jesus standing there, but she did not realize that it was Jesus.

[15]"Woman," he said, "why are you crying? Who is it you are looking for?"

Thinking he was the gardener, she said, "Sir, if you have carried him away, tell me where you have put him, and I will get him."

[16]Jesus said to her, "Mary."

She turned toward him and cried out in Aramaic, "Rabboni!" (which means Teacher).

[17]Jesus said, "Do not hold on to me, for I have not yet returned to the Father. Go instead to my brothers and tell them, 'I am returning to my Father and your Father, to my God and your God.' "

[18]Mary Magdalene went to the disciples with the news: "I have seen the Lord!" And she told them that he had said these things to her.

---

[a] *36* Exodus 12:46; Num. 9:12; Psalm 34:20 [b] *37* Zech. 12:10 [c] *39* Greek *a hundred litrai* (about 34 kilograms)

Jesus Appears to His Disciples

19On the evening of that first day of the
week, when the disciples were together, with
the doors locked for fear of the Jews, Jesus
came and stood among them and said, "Peace
be with you!" 20After he said this, he showed
them his hands and side. The disciples were
overjoyed when they saw the Lord.

21Again Jesus said, "Peace be with you! As
the Father has sent me, I am sending you."
22And with that he breathed on them and
said, "Receive the Holy Spirit. 23If you forgive
anyone his sins, they are forgiven; if you do
not forgive them, they are not forgiven."

Jesus Appears to Thomas

24Now Thomas (called Didymus), one of
the Twelve, was not with the disciples when
Jesus came. 25So the other disciples told him,
"We have seen the Lord!"

But he said to them, "Unless I see the nail
marks in his hands and put my finger where
the nails were, and put my hand into his side,
I will not believe it."

26A week later his disciples were in the
house again, and Thomas was with them.
Though the doors were locked, Jesus came and
stood among them and said, "Peace be with
you!" 27Then he said to Thomas, "Put your
finger here; see my hands. Reach out your
hand and put it into my side. Stop doubting
and believe."

28Thomas said to him, "My Lord and my
God!"

29Then Jesus told him, "Because you have
seen me, you have believed; blessed are those
who have not seen and yet have believed."

30Jesus did many other miraculous signs in
the presence of his disciples, which are not recorded in this book. 31But these are written
that you may[a] believe that Jesus is the Christ,
the Son of God, and that by believing you
may have life in his name.

Jesus and the Miraculous Catch of Fish

21 Afterward Jesus appeared again to his
disciples, by the Sea of Tiberias.[b] It happened this way: 2Simon Peter, Thomas
(called Didymus), Nathanael from Cana in
Galilee, the sons of Zebedee, and two other
disciples were together. 3"I'm going out to
fish," Simon Peter told them, and they said,
"We'll go with you." So they went out and
got into the boat, but that night they caught
nothing.

4Early in the morning, Jesus stood on the
shore, but the disciples did not realize that it
was Jesus.

5He called out to them, "Friends, haven't
you any fish?"

"No," they answered.

6He said, "Throw your net on the right side
of the boat and you will find some." When
they did, they were unable to haul the net in
because of the large number of fish.

7Then the disciple whom Jesus loved said to
Peter, "It is the Lord!" As soon as Simon Peter
heard him say, "It is the Lord," he wrapped his
outer garment around him (for he had taken
it off) and jumped into the water. 8The other
disciples followed in the boat, towing the net
full of fish, for they were not far from shore,
about a hundred yards.[c] 9When they landed,
they saw a fire of burning coals there with fish
on it, and some bread.

10Jesus said to them, "Bring some of the
fish you have just caught."

11Simon Peter climbed aboard and dragged
the net ashore. It was full of large fish, 153,
but even with so many the net was not torn.
12Jesus said to them, "Come and have breakfast." None of the disciples dared ask him,
"Who are you?" They knew it was the Lord.
13Jesus came, took the bread and gave it to
them, and did the same with the fish. 14This
was now the third time Jesus appeared to his
disciples after he was raised from the dead.

Jesus Reinstates Peter

15When they had finished eating, Jesus said
to Simon Peter, "Simon son of John, do you
truly love me more than these?"

"Yes, Lord," he said, "you know that I love
you."

Jesus said, "Feed my lambs."

16Again Jesus said, "Simon son of John, do
you truly love me?"

He answered, "Yes, Lord, you know that I
love you."

Jesus said, "Take care of my sheep."

17The third time he said to him, "Simon
son of John, do you love me?"

Peter was hurt because Jesus asked him
the third time, "Do you love me?" He said,
"Lord, you know all things; you know that I
love you."

Jesus said, "Feed my sheep. 18I tell you the
truth, when you were younger you dressed
yourself and went where you wanted; but
when you are old you will stretch out your

---

[a] *31* Some manuscripts *may continue to* [b] *1* That is, Sea of Galilee [c] *8* Greek *about two hundred cubits* (about 90 meters)

hands, and someone else will dress you and
lead you where you do not want to go."
19 Jesus said this to indicate the kind of death
by which Peter would glorify God. Then he
said to him, "Follow me!"

20 Peter turned and saw that the disciple
whom Jesus loved was following them. (This
was the one who had leaned back against Jesus
at the supper and had said, "Lord, who is going to betray you?") 21 When Peter saw him, he
asked, "Lord, what about him?"

22 Jesus answered, "If I want him to remain
alive until I return, what is that to you? You
must follow me." 23 Because of this, the rumor
spread among the brothers that this disciple
would not die. But Jesus did not say that he
would not die; he only said, "If I want him
to remain alive until I return, what is that to
you?"

24 This is the disciple who testifies to these
things and who wrote them down. We know
that his testimony is true.

25 Jesus did many other things as well. If every one of them were written down, I suppose
that even the whole world would not have
room for the books that would be written.

ACTS

Acts

QUICK FACTS

AUTHOR Luke, a physician and Gentile Christian

AUDIENCE Specifically Theophilus, whose name means "one who loves God," the same high official for whom the Gospel of Luke was written (see Luke 1:3)

DATE Probably around A.D. 63

SETTING Probably written in Rome (though Achaia, Ephesus and Caesarea have also been suggested) while the gospel was spreading to all parts of the Roman Empire

The book of Acts, a companion to the Gospel of Luke, is an account given to Theophilus, a Gentile believer of high standing, of how the church became established. As Paul's missionary companion, Luke had firsthand information from Paul as well as other disciples. He was also an eyewitness to much that occurred in the early church.

The book of Acts covers the activities of early Christians, especially Peter and Paul, as they spread the gospel. It also provides a broad outline of how the church was established from Jerusalem to Rome (see Acts 1:8). Luke describes how the church began as a group of Jewish converts and grew to embrace Gentiles as well as Jews.

However, the primary emphasis of Acts is the activity of the Holy Spirit. Luke demonstrated that Jesus is still alive and well, working through the Holy Spirit in believers. In fact, some have suggested the book be called "The Acts of the Holy Spirit."

Acts is an important book to incorporate into our married lives. As we rely on the Holy Spirit to conform us into Christ's image, we become better equipped to love and care for our spouses.

Jesus Taken Up Into Heaven

1 In my former book, Theophilus, I wrote
about all that Jesus began to do and to
teach 2until the day he was taken up to
heaven, after giving instructions through the
Holy Spirit to the apostles he had chosen. 3After
his suffering, he showed himself to these
men and gave many convincing proofs that he
was alive. He appeared to them over a period
of forty days and spoke about the kingdom of
God. 4On one occasion, while he was eating
with them, he gave them this command: "Do
not leave Jerusalem, but wait for the gift my
Father promised, which you have heard me
speak about. 5For John baptized with[a] water,
but in a few days you will be baptized with the
Holy Spirit."
6So when they met together, they asked
him, "Lord, are you at this time going to restore
the kingdom to Israel?"
7He said to them: "It is not for you to know
the times or dates the Father has set by his own
authority. 8But you will receive power when
the Holy Spirit comes on you; and you will
be my witnesses in Jerusalem, and in all Judea
and Samaria, and to the ends of the earth."
9After he said this, he was taken up before
their very eyes, and a cloud hid him from their
sight.
10They were looking intently up into the
sky as he was going, when suddenly two men
dressed in white stood beside them. 11"Men
of Galilee," they said, "why do you stand here
looking into the sky? This same Jesus, who has
been taken from you into heaven, will come
back in the same way you have seen him go
into heaven."

Matthias Chosen to Replace Judas

12Then they returned to Jerusalem from
the hill called the Mount of Olives, a Sabbath
day's walk[b] from the city. 13When they
arrived, they went upstairs to the room where
they were staying. Those present were Peter,
John, James and Andrew; Philip and Thomas,
Bartholomew and Matthew; James son of Alphaeus
and Simon the Zealot, and Judas son
of James. 14They all joined together constantly
in prayer, along with the women and Mary the
mother of Jesus, and with his brothers.
15In those days Peter stood up among the
believers[c] (a group numbering about a hundred
and twenty) 16and said, "Brothers, the
Scripture had to be fulfilled which the Holy
Spirit spoke long ago through the mouth of
David concerning Judas, who served as guide
for those who arrested Jesus— 17he was one of
our number and shared in this ministry."
18(With the reward he got for his wickedness,
Judas bought a field; there he fell headlong,
his body burst open and all his intestines
spilled out. 19Everyone in Jerusalem heard
about this, so they called that field in their language
Akeldama, that is, Field of Blood.)
20"For," said Peter, "it is written in the book
of Psalms,

> " 'May his place be deserted;
> let there be no one to dwell in it,'[d]

and,

> " 'May another take his place of
> leadership.'[e]

21Therefore it is necessary to choose one of the
men who have been with us the whole time
the Lord Jesus went in and out among us,
22beginning from John's baptism to the time
when Jesus was taken up from us. For one of
these must become a witness with us of his
resurrection."
23So they proposed two men: Joseph called
Barsabbas (also known as Justus) and Matthias.
24Then they prayed, "Lord, you know
everyone's heart. Show us which of these two
you have chosen 25to take over this apostolic
ministry, which Judas left to go where he belongs."
26Then they cast lots, and the lot fell
to Matthias; so he was added to the eleven
apostles.

The Holy Spirit Comes at Pentecost

2 When the day of Pentecost came, they were
all together in one place. 2Suddenly a sound
like the blowing of a violent wind came
from heaven and filled the whole house where
they were sitting. 3They saw what seemed to
be tongues of fire that separated and came to
rest on each of them. 4All of them were filled
with the Holy Spirit and began to speak in
other tongues[f] as the Spirit enabled them.
5Now there were staying in Jerusalem God-fearing
Jews from every nation under heaven.
6When they heard this sound, a crowd came
together in bewilderment, because each one
heard them speaking in his own language.
7Utterly amazed, they asked: "Are not all these
men who are speaking Galileans? 8Then how
is it that each of us hears them in his own native
language? 9Parthians, Medes and Elamites;
residents of Mesopotamia, Judea and

[a] 5 Or *in* [b] 12 That is, about 3/4 mile (about 1,100 meters) [c] 15 Greek *brothers* [d] 20 Psalm 69:25 [e] 20 Psalm 109:8
[f] 4 Or *languages*; also in verse 11

THURSDAY
READ ACTS 1:1–11

GIFTS OF WAITING

Some of the first words a toddler learns are *me* and *now*. From that point on, young children struggle to learn that they may not get everything they want or need and that they may have to wait a long time to get it.

After Jesus rose from the dead, he spent 40 days trying to help the disciples learn how to wait for God's timing so they could discern God's next steps for them. Even so, they asked, "Lord, are you at this time going to restore the kingdom to Israel?" In other words, "Could you do this for us *now*?"

They wanted it all, and they wanted it now!

Will and Sandy were faithful to each other and to God. They went to church and participated in various ministries. They tithed and helped people who were needy. But they also expected God to bless them for their faithfulness. So they prayed for a house, cars, jobs and bonuses, believing that God would provide everything. After all, Scripture promises "My God will meet all your needs according to his glorious riches in Christ Jesus" (Philippians 4:19).

Another couple at church, Greg and Carol, prayed sincerely for justice, peace, love and evangelistic victory. The problem was, they wanted those things now! They had little patience for the sluggishness of the church or the slow pace of ministry. They were convinced that God wanted to do great things in this world, and they sincerely wanted to glorify him in their social ministry and evangelism. But things were happening too slowly, and their patience was running thin. They became more critical of the church and less active in its work. And they felt increasingly more distance between themselves and God.

When they met together, they asked him, "Lord, are you at this time going to restore the kingdom to Israel?"

— Acts 1:6

let's talk

- ✦ What are some of the ways we have struggled with unanswered "now" requests we've made of the Lord? If we've had to wait to get specific prayers answered, what have we learned in that time of waiting?
- ✦ How do "now" requests we make of God become a challenge in marriage? What stresses do we put on each other during the waiting time? What do we learn by waiting?
- ✦ How do we learn to discern God's timing in directing our lives?

Jesus responded to his disciples' question, "Lord, are you at this time going to restore the kingdom to Israel?" by promising them the power of the Holy Spirit, so they could be his witnesses in Jerusalem, Judea and Samaria, and to the ends of the earth. Likewise, he responds to our requests—and to those of other couples—by directing us back to what empowers us: trust in the God who made us, redeemed us and gives us all things in his time.

Money problems, sickness and emotional difficulties stress a marriage. But nothing is quite so devastating as unmet expectations. The longer those go unfulfilled, the less tolerance spouses have for each other and the more tension builds. The only way to deal with the problem is for couples to be honest with each other, reset their priorities and then decide how best to meet those needs over time.

Likewise, as we continue to bring our needs to God, we can have faith and not lose heart when he fails to immediately provide what we need. For during the waiting time he may be giving us far better gifts than those we have asked for—gifts that can ease our selfishness, build our marriages and strengthen our families. As we wait and trust, we begin to experience love, joy, peace, patience, kindness, goodness, faithfulness, gentleness and self-control (see Galatians 5:22–23).

—JOHN R. THROOP

FOR YOUR NEXT DEVOTIONAL READING, TURN TO PAGE 1216.

FRIDAY
READ ACTS 1:12–26

PRAYING TOGETHER

> **They all joined together constantly in prayer.**
>
> — Acts 1:14

let's talk

- How regularly do we pray together? In what ways does our frequency of praying together affect our marriage?
- Why is praying together so important? What does it offer that we wouldn't gain by praying alone? Are there times when praying privately is better than praying together? When and why?
- What grace must we extend to each other when we pray? How can we encourage and affirm each other in prayer?

I don't remember when Dan and I started praying together, but I do recall that our first attempts felt awkward. For a long time we only prayed the Lord's Prayer out loud together. This was safe because we both knew the words to it.

Over time, and as each of us felt more comfortable being emotionally and spiritually naked with each other, we began to talk out loud to God as if he was the third person in our relationship. Now we try to pray out loud together daily. It's no longer awkward, and it has promoted spiritual intimacy. That was an unexpected bonus of being married to each other. No one had ever told us we could experience this kind of intimacy in our relationship.

Sometimes at night before we fall asleep, we pray out loud. In the darkness, I can listen to Dan's prayers and get a glimpse into the things he's grateful for as well as the issues that are troubling him. Hearing him pray reminds me that he's a work in progress, just as I am. It reminds me that my role in his life is to come alongside him, encourage him and support him. When I hear what's on his heart, I am reminded again and again of the reasons why I married him. Praying together sets us on the same track with each other and with God.

I met a couple once who were remarkably powerful and effective in their prayer life together. Like the disciples and other believers who joined together constantly in prayer, this couple brought all their needs, praises and requests to God, trusting that he would lead and guide them. They then patiently waited for God's answers.

In time God blessed this couple with a powerful ministry to special-needs orphans in China. The work keeps growing. This couple trusted God for everything, and, in turn, God entrusted them with the important work of caring for the least, which they are doing with all of their hearts.

It's one thing to say to your spouse, "I'll pray for your presentation today," as you grab your coffee and run out the door to work. It's another thing to grab your husband by the hand and say, "Let me pray with you before you go." Jesus promises us that whenever two or three come together in his name, he will also be there (see Matthew 18:20). Why not invite him into your marriage today through prayer?

—MARIAN V. LIAUTAUD

FOR YOUR NEXT DEVOTIONAL READING, TURN TO PAGE 1220.

Cappadocia, Pontus and Asia, 10Phrygia and
Pamphylia, Egypt and the parts of Libya near
Cyrene; visitors from Rome 11(both Jews and
converts to Judaism); Cretans and Arabs—we
hear them declaring the wonders of God in
our own tongues!" 12Amazed and perplexed,
they asked one another, "What does this
mean?"

13Some, however, made fun of them and
said, "They have had too much wine.[a]"

Peter Addresses the Crowd

14Then Peter stood up with the Eleven,
raised his voice and addressed the crowd: "Fellow Jews and all of you who live in Jerusalem,
let me explain this to you; listen carefully to
what I say. 15These men are not drunk, as you
suppose. It's only nine in the morning! 16No,
this is what was spoken by the prophet Joel:

17" 'In the last days, God says,
I will pour out my Spirit on all people.
Your sons and daughters will prophesy,
your young men will see visions,
your old men will dream dreams.
18Even on my servants, both men and
women,
I will pour out my Spirit in those days,
and they will prophesy.
19I will show wonders in the heaven above
and signs on the earth below,
blood and fire and billows of smoke.
20The sun will be turned to darkness
and the moon to blood
before the coming of the great and
glorious day of the Lord.
21And everyone who calls
on the name of the Lord will be
saved.'[b]

22"Men of Israel, listen to this: Jesus of Nazareth was a man accredited by God to you by
miracles, wonders and signs, which God did
among you through him, as you yourselves
know. 23This man was handed over to you
by God's set purpose and foreknowledge; and
you, with the help of wicked men,[c] put him to
death by nailing him to the cross. 24But God
raised him from the dead, freeing him from
the agony of death, because it was impossible
for death to keep its hold on him. 25David
said about him:

" 'I saw the Lord always before me.
Because he is at my right hand,
I will not be shaken.
26Therefore my heart is glad and my tongue
rejoices;
my body also will live in hope,
27because you will not abandon me to the
grave,
nor will you let your Holy One see
decay.
28You have made known to me the paths of
life;
you will fill me with joy in your
presence.'[d]

29"Brothers, I can tell you confidently that
the patriarch David died and was buried, and
his tomb is here to this day. 30But he was a
prophet and knew that God had promised
him on oath that he would place one of his
descendants on his throne. 31Seeing what was
ahead, he spoke of the resurrection of the
Christ,[e] that he was not abandoned to the
grave, nor did his body see decay. 32God has
raised this Jesus to life, and we are all witnesses
of the fact. 33Exalted to the right hand of God,
he has received from the Father the promised
Holy Spirit and has poured out what you now
see and hear. 34For David did not ascend to
heaven, and yet he said,

" 'The Lord said to my Lord:
"Sit at my right hand
35until I make your enemies
a footstool for your feet." '[f]

36"Therefore let all Israel be assured of this:
God has made this Jesus, whom you crucified,
both Lord and Christ."

37When the people heard this, they were
cut to the heart and said to Peter and the other apostles, "Brothers, what shall we do?"

38Peter replied, "Repent and be baptized,
every one of you, in the name of Jesus Christ
for the forgiveness of your sins. And you will
receive the gift of the Holy Spirit. 39The promise is for you and your children and for all who
are far off—for all whom the Lord our God
will call."

40With many other words he warned them;
and he pleaded with them, "Save yourselves
from this corrupt generation." 41Those who
accepted his message were baptized, and about
three thousand were added to their number
that day.

The Fellowship of the Believers

42They devoted themselves to the apostles'
teaching and to the fellowship, to the break-

a 13 Or *sweet wine* b 21 Joel 2:28-32 c 23 Or *of those not having the law* (that is, Gentiles) d 28 Psalm 16:8-11 e 31 Or *Messiah.* "The Christ" (Greek) and "the Messiah" (Hebrew) both mean "the Anointed One"; also in verse 36. f 35 Psalm 110:1

ing of bread and to prayer. 43Everyone was filled with awe, and many wonders and miraculous signs were done by the apostles. 44All the believers were together and had everything in common. 45Selling their possessions and goods, they gave to anyone as he had need. 46Every day they continued to meet together in the temple courts. They broke bread in their homes and ate together with glad and sincere hearts, 47praising God and enjoying the favor of all the people. And the Lord added to their number daily those who were being saved.

Peter Heals the Crippled Beggar

3 One day Peter and John were going up to the temple at the time of prayer—at three in the afternoon. 2Now a man crippled from birth was being carried to the temple gate called Beautiful, where he was put every day to beg from those going into the temple courts. 3When he saw Peter and John about to enter, he asked them for money. 4Peter looked straight at him, as did John. Then Peter said, "Look at us!" 5So the man gave them his attention, expecting to get something from them.

6Then Peter said, "Silver or gold I do not have, but what I have I give you. In the name of Jesus Christ of Nazareth, walk." 7Taking him by the right hand, he helped him up, and instantly the man's feet and ankles became strong. 8He jumped to his feet and began to walk. Then he went with them into the temple courts, walking and jumping, and praising God. 9When all the people saw him walking and praising God, 10they recognized him as the same man who used to sit begging at the temple gate called Beautiful, and they were filled with wonder and amazement at what had happened to him.

Peter Speaks to the Onlookers

11While the beggar held on to Peter and John, all the people were astonished and came running to them in the place called Solomon's Colonnade. 12When Peter saw this, he said to them: "Men of Israel, why does this surprise you? Why do you stare at us as if by our own power or godliness we had made this man walk? 13The God of Abraham, Isaac and Jacob, the God of our fathers, has glorified his servant Jesus. You handed him over to be killed, and you disowned him before Pilate, though he had decided to let him go. 14You disowned the Holy and Righteous One and asked that a murderer be released to you. 15You killed the author of life, but God raised him from the dead. We are witnesses of this. 16By faith in the name of Jesus, this man whom you see and know was made strong. It is Jesus' name and the faith that comes through him that has given this complete healing to him, as you can all see.

17"Now, brothers, I know that you acted in ignorance, as did your leaders. 18But this is how God fulfilled what he had foretold through all the prophets, saying that his Christ[a] would suffer. 19Repent, then, and turn to God, so that your sins may be wiped out, that times of refreshing may come from the Lord, 20and that he may send the Christ, who has been appointed for you—even Jesus. 21He must remain in heaven until the time comes for God to restore everything, as he promised long ago through his holy prophets. 22For Moses said, 'The Lord your God will raise up for you a prophet like me from among your own people; you must listen to everything he tells you. 23Anyone who does not listen to him will be completely cut off from among his people.'[b]

24"Indeed, all the prophets from Samuel on, as many as have spoken, have foretold these days. 25And you are heirs of the prophets and of the covenant God made with your fathers. He said to Abraham, 'Through your offspring all peoples on earth will be blessed.'[c] 26When God raised up his servant, he sent him first to you to bless you by turning each of you from your wicked ways."

Peter and John Before the Sanhedrin

4 The priests and the captain of the temple guard and the Sadducees came up to Peter and John while they were speaking to the people. 2They were greatly disturbed because the apostles were teaching the people and proclaiming in Jesus the resurrection of the dead. 3They seized Peter and John, and because it was evening, they put them in jail until the next day. 4But many who heard the message believed, and the number of men grew to about five thousand.

5The next day the rulers, elders and teachers of the law met in Jerusalem. 6Annas the high priest was there, and so were Caiaphas, John, Alexander and the other men of the high priest's family. 7They had Peter and John brought before them and began to question them: "By what power or what name did you do this?"

8Then Peter, filled with the Holy Spirit, said

[a] *18* Or *Messiah*; also in verse 20 [b] *23* Deut. 18:15,18,19 [c] *25* Gen. 22:18; 26:4

do you need closure?

Answer the following questions separately, then discuss your results together.

1. Do you agree that problems from the past can steal time from your present? How have you found that to be true?
2. How have those problems affected your spouse? You? In what ways is the pain of that unfinished business still evident today?
3. What are some sore spots in your marriage? Might any of that relate to unfinished business from the past?
4. Review some possible areas of unfinished business from the past, asking:
   a. Is there an incomplete task or failure that your mind keeps returning to?
   b. Are there things that you look back on and wish you could have done differently?
   c. Are there items on the list that you can't do anything about? Why or why not?
   d. What items on the list can you do something about? List one thing you can do for each of those items.

HOW ARE WE DOING?

date

let's make a DATE

WASH AWAY THE PAST

On a small slip of paper, write down something from the past that you'd like to forget. Talk about what you've written down. See what can be done to deal with this unfinished business. Until the issue is resolved (this may take a while), put the paper aside. When you've dealt with the issue, burn the paper then sprinkle the ashes in a river or stream. Watch the water carry away the remains of your paper.

Later find some fresh water: a hot tub or a bath at home (complete with scented candles and oils). Celebrate by writing something else on a piece of paper: a love letter to your spouse talking about your hopes for the future.

FOR YOUR NEXT DEVOTIONAL READING, TURN TO PAGE 1223.

LESSONS FROM THE *Bible*

Read Luke 9:62 and Philippians 3:4–14 for insight on dealing with the past.

1. What does Jesus say about letting go of the past?
2. What does Paul say about letting go of the past?
3. How do these verses apply to how you deal with the past?

and died. And great fear seized all who heard what had happened. 6Then the young men came forward, wrapped up his body, and carried him out and buried him.

7About three hours later his wife came in, not knowing what had happened. 8Peter asked her, "Tell me, is this the price you and Ananias got for the land?"

"Yes," she said, "that is the price."

9Peter said to her, "How could you agree to test the Spirit of the Lord? Look! The feet of the men who buried your husband are at the door, and they will carry you out also."

10At that moment she fell down at his feet and died. Then the young men came in and, finding her dead, carried her out and buried her beside her husband. 11Great fear seized the whole church and all who heard about these events.

The Apostles Heal Many

12The apostles performed many miraculous signs and wonders among the people. And all the believers used to meet together in Solomon's Colonnade. 13No one else dared join them, even though they were highly regarded by the people. 14Nevertheless, more and more men and women believed in the Lord and were added to their number. 15As a result, people brought the sick into the streets and laid them on beds and mats so that at least Peter's shadow might fall on some of them as he passed by. 16Crowds gathered also from the towns around Jerusalem, bringing their sick and those tormented by evil[a] spirits, and all of them were healed.

The Apostles Persecuted

17Then the high priest and all his associates, who were members of the party of the Sadducees, were filled with jealousy. 18They arrested the apostles and put them in the public jail. 19But during the night an angel of the Lord opened the doors of the jail and brought them out. 20"Go, stand in the temple courts," he said, "and tell the people the full message of this new life."

21At daybreak they entered the temple courts, as they had been told, and began to teach the people.

When the high priest and his associates arrived, they called together the Sanhedrin—the full assembly of the elders of Israel—and sent to the jail for the apostles. 22But on arriving at the jail, the officers did not find them there. So they went back and reported, 23"We found the jail securely locked, with the guards standing at the doors; but when we opened them, we found no one inside." 24On hearing this report, the captain of the temple guard and the chief priests were puzzled, wondering what would come of this.

25Then someone came and said, "Look! The men you put in jail are standing in the temple courts teaching the people." 26At that, the captain went with his officers and brought the apostles. They did not use force, because they feared that the people would stone them.

27Having brought the apostles, they made them appear before the Sanhedrin to be questioned by the high priest. 28"We gave you strict orders not to teach in this name," he said. "Yet you have filled Jerusalem with your teaching and are determined to make us guilty of this man's blood."

29Peter and the other apostles replied: "We must obey God rather than men! 30The God of our fathers raised Jesus from the dead—whom you had killed by hanging him on a tree. 31God exalted him to his own right hand as Prince and Savior that he might give repentance and forgiveness of sins to Israel. 32We are witnesses of these things, and so is the Holy Spirit, whom God has given to those who obey him."

33When they heard this, they were furious and wanted to put them to death. 34But a Pharisee named Gamaliel, a teacher of the law, who was honored by all the people, stood up in the Sanhedrin and ordered that the men be put outside for a little while. 35Then he addressed them: "Men of Israel, consider carefully what you intend to do to these men. 36Some time ago Theudas appeared, claiming to be somebody, and about four hundred men rallied to him. He was killed, all his followers were dispersed, and it all came to nothing. 37After him, Judas the Galilean appeared in the days of the census and led a band of people in revolt. He too was killed, and all his followers were scattered. 38Therefore, in the present case I advise you: Leave these men alone! Let them go! For if their purpose or activity is of human origin, it will fail. 39But if it is from God, you will not be able to stop these men; you will only find yourselves fighting against God."

40His speech persuaded them. They called the apostles in and had them flogged. Then

---

a 16 Greek *unclean*

MONDAY
READ ACTS 4:32—5:11

COLLABORATING IN SIN

With his wife's full knowledge [Ananias] kept back part of the money for himself, but brought the rest and put it at the apostles' feet.

— Acts 5:2

Julius and Ethel Rosenberg became notorious in the early 1950s for betraying the United States as spies. Usually when we read about spies, we learn about a surprised spouse who seemed to have no idea her husband was a traitor. But the Rosenbergs worked together. And they were both condemned to death for their treachery.

Ananias and Sapphira were traitors too. They betrayed the early church, and their resultant deaths shook the whole city of Jerusalem.

This couple lived in the heyday of the early church. God had magnetized the church through the bold witness and selfless generosity of new believers. People all over Jerusalem were drawn to this dynamic Christian community. Most of the believers, hearing about the selfless generosity of people like Barnabas (see Acts 4:36–37), rejoiced at the grace of God, but Ananias and Sapphira were evidently eaten up with jealousy and a craving for recognition. They wanted to look as saintly as Barnabas, but at a discount.

Ananias and Sapphira could have demagnetized the church with their selfishness. Though no one would have known what they were up to had God not intervened, this couple's sin would have compromised the spiritual integrity and power of the church.

The irony, of course, is that this husband and wife *were* generous. They sold property and gave part of the proceeds to the church. God would have blessed them for their generosity if they hadn't lied about it. But one couple's lies, out of a congregation of several thousand, posed such a danger that God had to strike them dead to preserve the faith of others.

This seems like a story of severe judgment, but it is actually a story of mercy. God showed mercy to the church and to the whole city by stopping a demagnetizing sin dead in its tracks. Had he not, the gospel would not have continued to spread so vigorously. I believe that God also showed mercy to Ananias and Sapphira. Some Bible teachers think that by ending their lives, God preserved their souls. They were Christians, after all, and it appears that before they could sin to the point of completely denying Christ, they were diverted by death.

Do you wonder how this couple first went wrong? How did the idea of deceiving the church take shape? Weren't they embarrassed to even broach the subject with one another? How were they so united that they sinned in sync?

It is possible that in the intimacy of marriage, Ananias and Sapphira were united and of one mind. That's a frightening responsibility in marriage. As we ponder this story, we see that we can encourage one another—even in sin. It's a sobering thought. But there is more at stake than ourselves. God's community is also at risk. Our actions as a couple affect not only ourselves but others as well.

—LEE ECLOV

let's *talk*

- ✦ What exactly were the sins of Ananias and Sapphira? Do you think they thought of their choices in terms of harming the church? How do you suppose they rationalized their behavior?
- ✦ In what ways can married partners hold each other accountable?
- ✦ Can we identify temptations to which we are especially vulnerable and which might cause us to one day collaborate in sin rather than in righteousness?

FOR YOUR NEXT DEVOTIONAL READING, TURN TO PAGE 1227.

they ordered them not to speak in the name of Jesus, and let them go.

41The apostles left the Sanhedrin, rejoicing because they had been counted worthy of suffering disgrace for the Name. 42Day after day, in the temple courts and from house to house, they never stopped teaching and proclaiming the good news that Jesus is the Christ.[a]

The Choosing of the Seven

6 In those days when the number of disciples was increasing, the Grecian Jews among them complained against the Hebraic Jews because their widows were being overlooked in the daily distribution of food. 2So the Twelve gathered all the disciples together and said, "It would not be right for us to neglect the ministry of the word of God in order to wait on tables. 3Brothers, choose seven men from among you who are known to be full of the Spirit and wisdom. We will turn this responsibility over to them 4and will give our attention to prayer and the ministry of the word."

5This proposal pleased the whole group. They chose Stephen, a man full of faith and of the Holy Spirit; also Philip, Procorus, Nicanor, Timon, Parmenas, and Nicolas from Antioch, a convert to Judaism. 6They presented these men to the apostles, who prayed and laid their hands on them.

7So the word of God spread. The number of disciples in Jerusalem increased rapidly, and a large number of priests became obedient to the faith.

Stephen Seized

8Now Stephen, a man full of God's grace and power, did great wonders and miraculous signs among the people. 9Opposition arose, however, from members of the Synagogue of the Freedmen (as it was called)—Jews of Cyrene and Alexandria as well as the provinces of Cilicia and Asia. These men began to argue with Stephen, 10but they could not stand up against his wisdom or the Spirit by whom he spoke.

11Then they secretly persuaded some men to say, "We have heard Stephen speak words of blasphemy against Moses and against God."

12So they stirred up the people and the elders and the teachers of the law. They seized Stephen and brought him before the Sanhedrin. 13They produced false witnesses, who testified, "This fellow never stops speaking against this holy place and against the law. 14For we have heard him say that this Jesus of Nazareth will destroy this place and change the customs Moses handed down to us."

15All who were sitting in the Sanhedrin looked intently at Stephen, and they saw that his face was like the face of an angel.

Stephen's Speech to the Sanhedrin

7 Then the high priest asked him, "Are these charges true?"

2To this he replied: "Brothers and fathers, listen to me! The God of glory appeared to our father Abraham while he was still in Mesopotamia, before he lived in Haran. 3'Leave your country and your people,' God said, 'and go to the land I will show you.'[b]

4"So he left the land of the Chaldeans and settled in Haran. After the death of his father, God sent him to this land where you are now living. 5He gave him no inheritance here, not even a foot of ground. But God promised him that he and his descendants after him would possess the land, even though at that time Abraham had no child. 6God spoke to him in this way: 'Your descendants will be strangers in a country not their own, and they will be enslaved and mistreated four hundred years. 7But I will punish the nation they serve as slaves,' God said, 'and afterward they will come out of that country and worship me in this place.'[c] 8Then he gave Abraham the covenant of circumcision. And Abraham became the father of Isaac and circumcised him eight days after his birth. Later Isaac became the father of Jacob, and Jacob became the father of the twelve patriarchs.

9"Because the patriarchs were jealous of Joseph, they sold him as a slave into Egypt. But God was with him 10and rescued him from all his troubles. He gave Joseph wisdom and enabled him to gain the goodwill of Pharaoh king of Egypt; so he made him ruler over Egypt and all his palace.

11"Then a famine struck all Egypt and Canaan, bringing great suffering, and our fathers could not find food. 12When Jacob heard that there was grain in Egypt, he sent our fathers on their first visit. 13On their second visit, Joseph told his brothers who he was, and Pharaoh learned about Joseph's family. 14After this, Joseph sent for his father Jacob and his whole family, seventy-five in all. 15Then Jacob went down to Egypt, where he and our fathers died. 16Their bodies were brought back to Shechem and placed in the tomb that Abraham had

[a] *42* Or *Messiah* [b] *3* Gen. 12:1 [c] *7* Gen. 15:13,14

bought from the sons of Hamor at Shechem
for a certain sum of money.
17 “As the time drew near for God to fulfill
his promise to Abraham, the number of our
people in Egypt greatly increased. 18 Then another king, who knew nothing about Joseph,
became ruler of Egypt. 19 He dealt treacherously with our people and oppressed our
forefathers by forcing them to throw out their
newborn babies so that they would die.
20 “At that time Moses was born, and he was
no ordinary child.[a] For three months he was
cared for in his father’s house. 21 When he was
placed outside, Pharaoh’s daughter took him
and brought him up as her own son. 22 Moses
was educated in all the wisdom of the Egyptians and was powerful in speech and action.
23 “When Moses was forty years old, he decided to visit his fellow Israelites. 24 He saw
one of them being mistreated by an Egyptian,
so he went to his defense and avenged him by
killing the Egyptian. 25 Moses thought that his
own people would realize that God was using
him to rescue them, but they did not. 26 The
next day Moses came upon two Israelites who
were fighting. He tried to reconcile them by
saying, ‘Men, you are brothers; why do you
want to hurt each other?’
27 “But the man who was mistreating the
other pushed Moses aside and said, ‘Who
made you ruler and judge over us? 28 Do you
want to kill me as you killed the Egyptian yesterday?’[b] 29 When Moses heard this, he fled to
Midian, where he settled as a foreigner and
had two sons.
30 “After forty years had passed, an angel appeared to Moses in the flames of a burning
bush in the desert near Mount Sinai. 31 When
he saw this, he was amazed at the sight. As he
went over to look more closely, he heard the
Lord’s voice: 32 ‘I am the God of your fathers,
the God of Abraham, Isaac and Jacob.’[c] Moses
trembled with fear and did not dare to look.
33 “Then the Lord said to him, ‘Take off
your sandals; the place where you are standing
is holy ground. 34 I have indeed seen the oppression of my people in Egypt. I have heard
their groaning and have come down to set
them free. Now come, I will send you back
to Egypt.’[d]
35 “This is the same Moses whom they had
rejected with the words, ‘Who made you ruler
and judge?’ He was sent to be their ruler and
deliverer by God himself, through the angel
who appeared to him in the bush. 36 He led
them out of Egypt and did wonders and miraculous signs in Egypt, at the Red Sea[e] and
for forty years in the desert.
37 “This is that Moses who told the Israelites,
‘God will send you a prophet like me from
your own people.’[f] 38 He was in the assembly
in the desert, with the angel who spoke to him
on Mount Sinai, and with our fathers; and he
received living words to pass on to us.
39 “But our fathers refused to obey him. Instead, they rejected him and in their hearts
turned back to Egypt. 40 They told Aaron,
‘Make us gods who will go before us. As for
this fellow Moses who led us out of Egypt—we
don’t know what has happened to him!’[g]
41 That was the time they made an idol in the
form of a calf. They brought sacrifices to it
and held a celebration in honor of what their
hands had made. 42 But God turned away and
gave them over to the worship of the heavenly
bodies. This agrees with what is written in the
book of the prophets:

“ ‘Did you bring me sacrifices and
offerings
forty years in the desert, O house of
Israel?
43 You have lifted up the shrine of Molech
and the star of your god Rephan,
the idols you made to worship.
Therefore I will send you into exile’[h]
beyond Babylon.

44 “Our forefathers had the tabernacle of
the Testimony with them in the desert. It had
been made as God directed Moses, according
to the pattern he had seen. 45 Having received
the tabernacle, our fathers under Joshua
brought it with them when they took the land
from the nations God drove out before them.
It remained in the land until the time of David, 46 who enjoyed God’s favor and asked that
he might provide a dwelling place for the God
of Jacob.[i] 47 But it was Solomon who built the
house for him.
48 “However, the Most High does not live in
houses made by men. As the prophet says:

49 “ ‘Heaven is my throne,
and the earth is my footstool.
What kind of house will you build for me?
says the Lord.
Or where will my resting place be?
50 Has not my hand made all these things?’[j]

51 “You stiff-necked people, with uncircumcised hearts and ears! You are just like your fa-

[a] 20 Or *was fair in the sight of God* [b] 28 Exodus 2:14 [c] 32 Exodus 3:6 [d] 34 Exodus 3:5,7,8,10 [e] 36 That is, Sea of Reeds
[f] 37 Deut. 18:15 [g] 40 Exodus 32:1 [h] 43 Amos 5:25-27 [i] 46 Some early manuscripts *the house of Jacob* [j] 50 Isaiah 66:1,2

thers: You always resist the Holy Spirit! 52 Was there ever a prophet your fathers did not persecute? They even killed those who predicted the coming of the Righteous One. And now you have betrayed and murdered him— 53 you who have received the law that was put into effect through angels but have not obeyed it."

The Stoning of Stephen

54 When they heard this, they were furious and gnashed their teeth at him. 55 But Stephen, full of the Holy Spirit, looked up to heaven and saw the glory of God, and Jesus standing at the right hand of God. 56 "Look," he said, "I see heaven open and the Son of Man standing at the right hand of God."

57 At this they covered their ears and, yelling at the top of their voices, they all rushed at him, 58 dragged him out of the city and began to stone him. Meanwhile, the witnesses laid their clothes at the feet of a young man named Saul.

59 While they were stoning him, Stephen prayed, "Lord Jesus, receive my spirit." 60 Then he fell on his knees and cried out, "Lord, do not hold this sin against them." When he had said this, he fell asleep.

8 And Saul was there, giving approval to his death.

The Church Persecuted and Scattered

On that day a great persecution broke out against the church at Jerusalem, and all except the apostles were scattered throughout Judea and Samaria. 2 Godly men buried Stephen and mourned deeply for him. 3 But Saul began to destroy the church. Going from house to house, he dragged off men and women and put them in prison.

Philip in Samaria

4 Those who had been scattered preached the word wherever they went. 5 Philip went down to a city in Samaria and proclaimed the Christ[a] there. 6 When the crowds heard Philip and saw the miraculous signs he did, they all paid close attention to what he said. 7 With shrieks, evil[b] spirits came out of many, and many paralytics and cripples were healed. 8 So there was great joy in that city.

Simon the Sorcerer

9 Now for some time a man named Simon had practiced sorcery in the city and amazed all the people of Samaria. He boasted that he was someone great, 10 and all the people, both high and low, gave him their attention and exclaimed, "This man is the divine power known as the Great Power." 11 They followed him because he had amazed them for a long time with his magic. 12 But when they believed Philip as he preached the good news of the kingdom of God and the name of Jesus Christ, they were baptized, both men and women. 13 Simon himself believed and was baptized. And he followed Philip everywhere, astonished by the great signs and miracles he saw.

14 When the apostles in Jerusalem heard that Samaria had accepted the word of God, they sent Peter and John to them. 15 When they arrived, they prayed for them that they might receive the Holy Spirit, 16 because the Holy Spirit had not yet come upon any of them; they had simply been baptized into[c] the name of the Lord Jesus. 17 Then Peter and John placed their hands on them, and they received the Holy Spirit.

18 When Simon saw that the Spirit was given at the laying on of the apostles' hands, he offered them money 19 and said, "Give me also this ability so that everyone on whom I lay my hands may receive the Holy Spirit."

20 Peter answered: "May your money perish with you, because you thought you could buy the gift of God with money! 21 You have no part or share in this ministry, because your heart is not right before God. 22 Repent of this wickedness and pray to the Lord. Perhaps he will forgive you for having such a thought in your heart. 23 For I see that you are full of bitterness and captive to sin."

24 Then Simon answered, "Pray to the Lord for me so that nothing you have said may happen to me."

25 When they had testified and proclaimed the word of the Lord, Peter and John returned to Jerusalem, preaching the gospel in many Samaritan villages.

Philip and the Ethiopian

26 Now an angel of the Lord said to Philip, "Go south to the road—the desert road—that goes down from Jerusalem to Gaza." 27 So he started out, and on his way he met an Ethiopian[d] eunuch, an important official in charge of all the treasury of Candace, queen of the Ethiopians. This man had gone to Jerusalem to worship, 28 and on his way home was sitting in his chariot reading the book of Isaiah the

---

[a] *5* Or *Messiah* [b] *7* Greek *unclean* [c] *16* Or *in* [d] *27* That is, from the upper Nile region

TUESDAY
READ ACTS 8:1–25

WHAT MONEY CAN'T BUY

When Simon saw that the Spirit was given at the laying on of the apostles' hands, he offered them money.

— Acts 8:18

I was reading a new book by a Christian author who pointed out how often we use the language of finance when we talk about relationships. We "value" a friend. We "invest in" a relationship. The author went on to say that we commonly use our love in the same way we use money: to get what we want.

I had to stop and check my own marriage relationship: Do I give/withhold courtesy, attention or affection to/from my husband, depending on whether David's behavior pleases or upsets me? In all honesty, I had to admit that sometimes my love is conditional toward him. Sometimes I do use love like money.

This is not the way of grace and mercy. This is not Christ's way. This is not kingdom behavior. God's love does not depend on my good behavior; there's no way I can earn his approval or salvation. Jesus gave his life for me, and God accepts me and welcomes me into his family because I trust Christ's work on my behalf.

Simon the Sorcerer failed to realize that some things in life are priceless. When he saw the powerful effects of the apostles' prayers, Simon wanted to buy what was in their "bag of tricks": "Give me also this ability so that everyone on whom I lay my hands may receive the Holy Spirit" (Acts 8:19). Peter's response was to rebuke Simon sternly, saying, "May your money perish with you, because you thought you could buy the gift of God with money!" Simon the Sorcerer hadn't figured out that the gifts of God are given by God's grace and goodness alone; they cannot be earned or bought.

I'm afraid my attempts to freely offer love and kindness to others, as Jesus would, will be a lifelong challenge for me. My consumer mentality seems too deeply rooted. But I want to love others without considering what they might think of me or what they might "owe" me. At home, that means choosing to love David through all my actions and attitudes, whether or not I think he's "earned" my affection.

Many times when one spouse behaves with grace and love toward an undeserving spouse, the spouse reciprocates with a renewed attempt to be gracious and loving, but there are no guarantees. In the end, I must choose to give my love freely, not in an attempt to manipulate my husband or get him to treat me well, but only because I want to please the Lord.

Money can't buy lasting love, and I don't want to use my love like money. In the end I'll be more gratified in receiving David's love and affection if I know I haven't manipulated his attention with a bag of tricks or with strategies of conditional love. My goal is to love him freely, the way God has loved me.

—ANNETTE LAPLACA

let's talk

- ✦ What gifts have we received from each other without asking for them? What was the result? Did we love and appreciate those gifts because they were more than what we had specifically asked for?
- ✦ In what ways have we given love to each other conditionally, like money, to get something for ourselves? Did that work or did it backfire? Who was most disappointed?
- ✦ Do we keep an account of the ways in which we fail to give to each other? How does that affect our relationship? What would happen if we only tallied what we do for each other?

FOR YOUR NEXT DEVOTIONAL READING, TURN TO PAGE 1230.

prophet. 29 The Spirit told Philip, "Go to that
chariot and stay near it."
30 Then Philip ran up to the chariot and
heard the man reading Isaiah the prophet.
"Do you understand what you are reading?"
Philip asked.
31 "How can I," he said, "unless someone explains it to me?" So he invited Philip to come
up and sit with him.
32 The eunuch was reading this passage of
Scripture:

"He was led like a sheep to the slaughter,
and as a lamb before the shearer is
silent,
so he did not open his mouth.
33 In his humiliation he was deprived of
justice.
Who can speak of his descendants?
For his life was taken from the earth."[a]

34 The eunuch asked Philip, "Tell me, please,
who is the prophet talking about, himself or
someone else?" 35 Then Philip began with that
very passage of Scripture and told him the
good news about Jesus.
36 As they traveled along the road, they came
to some water and the eunuch said, "Look,
here is water. Why shouldn't I be baptized?"[b]
38 And he gave orders to stop the chariot. Then
both Philip and the eunuch went down into
the water and Philip baptized him. 39 When
they came up out of the water, the Spirit of
the Lord suddenly took Philip away, and the
eunuch did not see him again, but went on his
way rejoicing. 40 Philip, however, appeared at
Azotus and traveled about, preaching the gospel in all the towns until he reached Caesarea.

Saul's Conversion

9 Meanwhile, Saul was still breathing out
murderous threats against the Lord's disciples. He went to the high priest 2 and asked
him for letters to the synagogues in Damascus,
so that if he found any there who belonged to
the Way, whether men or women, he might
take them as prisoners to Jerusalem. 3 As he
neared Damascus on his journey, suddenly a
light from heaven flashed around him. 4 He
fell to the ground and heard a voice say to
him, "Saul, Saul, why do you persecute me?"
5 "Who are you, Lord?" Saul asked.
"I am Jesus, whom you are persecuting,"
he replied. 6 "Now get up and go into the city,
and you will be told what you must do."
7 The men traveling with Saul stood there
speechless; they heard the sound but did not
see anyone. 8 Saul got up from the ground, but
when he opened his eyes he could see nothing.
So they led him by the hand into Damascus.
9 For three days he was blind, and did not eat
or drink anything.
10 In Damascus there was a disciple named
Ananias. The Lord called to him in a vision,
"Ananias!"
"Yes, Lord," he answered.
11 The Lord told him, "Go to the house of
Judas on Straight Street and ask for a man
from Tarsus named Saul, for he is praying.
12 In a vision he has seen a man named Ananias come and place his hands on him to restore
his sight."
13 "Lord," Ananias answered, "I have heard
many reports about this man and all the harm
he has done to your saints in Jerusalem. 14 And
he has come here with authority from the chief
priests to arrest all who call on your name."
15 But the Lord said to Ananias, "Go! This
man is my chosen instrument to carry my
name before the Gentiles and their kings and
before the people of Israel. 16 I will show him
how much he must suffer for my name."
17 Then Ananias went to the house and entered it. Placing his hands on Saul, he said,
"Brother Saul, the Lord—Jesus, who appeared
to you on the road as you were coming here—
has sent me so that you may see again and
be filled with the Holy Spirit." 18 Immediately, something like scales fell from Saul's eyes,
and he could see again. He got up and was
baptized, 19 and after taking some food, he re-
gained his strength.

Saul in Damascus and Jerusalem

Saul spent several days with the disciples in
Damascus. 20 At once he began to preach in
the synagogues that Jesus is the Son of God.
21 All those who heard him were astonished
and asked, "Isn't he the man who raised havoc in Jerusalem among those who call on this
name? And hasn't he come here to take them
as prisoners to the chief priests?" 22 Yet Saul
grew more and more powerful and baffled the
Jews living in Damascus by proving that Jesus
is the Christ.[c]
23 After many days had gone by, the Jews
conspired to kill him, 24 but Saul learned of
their plan. Day and night they kept close
watch on the city gates in order to kill him.
25 But his followers took him by night and

[a] 33 Isaiah 53:7,8 [b] 36 Some late manuscripts *baptized?"* [37] *Philip said, "If you believe with all your heart, you may." The eunuch answered, "I believe that Jesus Christ is the Son of God."* [c] 22 Or *Messiah*

lowered him in a basket through an opening
in the wall.
26When he came to Jerusalem, he tried to
join the disciples, but they were all afraid of
him, not believing that he really was a disciple. 27But Barnabas took him and brought
him to the apostles. He told them how Saul
on his journey had seen the Lord and that the
Lord had spoken to him, and how in Damascus he had preached fearlessly in the name of
Jesus. 28So Saul stayed with them and moved
about freely in Jerusalem, speaking boldly in
the name of the Lord. 29He talked and debated with the Grecian Jews, but they tried to kill
him. 30When the brothers learned of this, they
took him down to Caesarea and sent him off
to Tarsus.
31Then the church throughout Judea, Galilee and Samaria enjoyed a time of peace. It was
strengthened; and encouraged by the Holy
Spirit, it grew in numbers, living in the fear
of the Lord.

Aeneas and Dorcas

32As Peter traveled about the country, he
went to visit the saints in Lydda. 33There he
found a man named Aeneas, a paralytic who
had been bedridden for eight years. 34"Aeneas," Peter said to him, "Jesus Christ heals you.
Get up and take care of your mat." Immediately Aeneas got up. 35All those who lived in
Lydda and Sharon saw him and turned to the
Lord.
36In Joppa there was a disciple named Tabitha (which, when translated, is Dorcas[a]), who
was always doing good and helping the poor.
37About that time she became sick and died,
and her body was washed and placed in an upstairs room. 38Lydda was near Joppa; so when
the disciples heard that Peter was in Lydda,
they sent two men to him and urged him,
"Please come at once!"
39Peter went with them, and when he arrived he was taken upstairs to the room. All
the widows stood around him, crying and
showing him the robes and other clothing
that Dorcas had made while she was still with
them.
40Peter sent them all out of the room; then
he got down on his knees and prayed. Turning
toward the dead woman, he said, "Tabitha, get
up." She opened her eyes, and seeing Peter she
sat up. 41He took her by the hand and helped
her to her feet. Then he called the believers
and the widows and presented her to them
alive. 42This became known all over Joppa,
and many people believed in the Lord. 43Peter
stayed in Joppa for some time with a tanner
named Simon.

Cornelius Calls for Peter

10 At Caesarea there was a man named
Cornelius, a centurion in what was
known as the Italian Regiment. 2He and
all his family were devout and God-fearing; he
gave generously to those in need and prayed to
God regularly. 3One day at about three in the
afternoon he had a vision. He distinctly saw
an angel of God, who came to him and said,
"Cornelius!"
4Cornelius stared at him in fear. "What is
it, Lord?" he asked.
The angel answered, "Your prayers and gifts
to the poor have come up as a memorial offering before God. 5Now send men to Joppa to
bring back a man named Simon who is called
Peter. 6He is staying with Simon the tanner,
whose house is by the sea."
7When the angel who spoke to him had
gone, Cornelius called two of his servants
and a devout soldier who was one of his attendants. 8He told them everything that had
happened and sent them to Joppa.

Peter's Vision

9About noon the following day as they were
on their journey and approaching the city, Peter went up on the roof to pray. 10He became
hungry and wanted something to eat, and
while the meal was being prepared, he fell into
a trance. 11He saw heaven opened and something like a large sheet being let down to earth
by its four corners. 12It contained all kinds of
four-footed animals, as well as reptiles of the
earth and birds of the air. 13Then a voice told
him, "Get up, Peter. Kill and eat."
14"Surely not, Lord!" Peter replied. "I have
never eaten anything impure or unclean."
15The voice spoke to him a second time,
"Do not call anything impure that God has
made clean."
16This happened three times, and immediately the sheet was taken back to heaven.
17While Peter was wondering about the
meaning of the vision, the men sent by Cornelius found out where Simon's house was and
stopped at the gate. 18They called out, asking
if Simon who was known as Peter was staying
there.
19While Peter was still thinking about the

[a] *36* Both *Tabitha* (Aramaic) and *Dorcas* (Greek) mean *gazelle.*

WEDNESDAY
READ ACTS 10:1–48

LOVE WITHOUT BIAS

> **"Do not call anything impure that God has made clean."**
>
> — Acts 10:15

let's talk

- How do we love each other in unique ways?
- Within marriage, how might our focus on one another shut out or marginalize others? What lessons from Scripture should we keep in mind when we tend to do that?
- If Peter's vision were to come in our dreams tonight, what or who would be in the sheet? What would God be saying to us about including others?

The man wept as he told how his mother had treated each of her children in an equally rotten manner. One after another she had driven her children away. They had moved to other places just to escape her tirades about their tragic worthlessness. Even now, when her children return to celebrate her birthday or some other holiday, the mother only adds to their guilt by caustically reminding each about how they have abandoned her.

I admire this man and the way that he, in Christian faith, has chosen to remain close to his mother. He cares for her because she is his mother and because there is no one else left that she has not sadistically forced away with lacerating venom.

Like that cruel mother, judgment and prejudice often influence how we view others. We see it in Peter. Years of social training had identified the "OK" people and the "not OK" people, similar to how religious instruction shaped his views about animals for sacrifices. For Peter, some people were acceptable, some tolerable, some to be avoided altogether.

In situations where prejudice pulls our noses into the air and causes us, like my friend's mother, to become equal opportunity disdainers, that intolerance bites and hurts and destroys. But that can be counteracted with another form of prejudice: the discrimination of love, which chooses to care even when social convention says otherwise.

This is the lesson God taught Peter that day in Joppa when he showed Peter a net of animals and ordered him to kill and eat them. When Peter objected, saying he had never eaten anything impure or unclean, God told him not to call anything impure that God had made clean. This vision was an object lesson to show Peter that the Good News of Christ's sacrificial love is for all people, whether Jew or Gentile. This was a revelation to Peter, who had been taught to distance himself from non-Jews.

Although this passage is a wonderful story of equality, it also teaches us that sometimes there is a good side to discrimination. The beauty of family life is found precisely in its inequalities. In a family we learn that persons are to be loved uniquely, not equally. A wife does not love her husband because he is just one of the crowd that hangs around, but because he is uniquely her spouse. Nor does a father treat one child the same as another child. True love discriminates.

Parents who try to love all of their children in exactly the same way become frustrated to the point of incompetence. It is in the family that we learn to esteem each person greatly, not because each is a cloned pea in a pod, but because each is unique and different. It's the same in marriage; we learn to love each other uniquely, rejoicing in our differences and learning how those differences can enrich and enlarge our relationship.

—WAYNE BROUWER

FOR YOUR NEXT DEVOTIONAL READING, TURN TO PAGE 1236.

vision, the Spirit said to him, "Simon, three[a]
men are looking for you. 20So get up and go
downstairs. Do not hesitate to go with them,
for I have sent them."
21Peter went down and said to the men,
"I'm the one you're looking for. Why have you
come?"
22The men replied, "We have come from
Cornelius the centurion. He is a righteous and
God-fearing man, who is respected by all the
Jewish people. A holy angel told him to have
you come to his house so that he could hear
what you have to say." 23Then Peter invited
the men into the house to be his guests.

Peter at Cornelius's House

The next day Peter started out with them,
and some of the brothers from Joppa went
along. 24The following day he arrived in Caesarea. Cornelius was expecting them and had
called together his relatives and close friends.
25As Peter entered the house, Cornelius met
him and fell at his feet in reverence. 26But Peter made him get up. "Stand up," he said, "I
am only a man myself."
27Talking with him, Peter went inside and
found a large gathering of people. 28He said to
them: "You are well aware that it is against our
law for a Jew to associate with a Gentile or visit
him. But God has shown me that I should not
call any man impure or unclean. 29So when I
was sent for, I came without raising any objec-
tion. May I ask why you sent for me?"
30Cornelius answered: "Four days ago I
was in my house praying at this hour, at three
in the afternoon. Suddenly a man in shining
clothes stood before me 31and said, 'Cornelius,
God has heard your prayer and remembered
your gifts to the poor. 32Send to Joppa for Simon who is called Peter. He is a guest in the
home of Simon the tanner, who lives by the
sea.' 33So I sent for you immediately, and it
was good of you to come. Now we are all here
in the presence of God to listen to everything
the Lord has commanded you to tell us."
34Then Peter began to speak: "I now realize
how true it is that God does not show favoritism 35but accepts men from every nation who
fear him and do what is right. 36You know
the message God sent to the people of Israel,
telling the good news of peace through Jesus
Christ, who is Lord of all. 37You know what
has happened throughout Judea, beginning in
Galilee after the baptism that John preached—
38how God anointed Jesus of Nazareth with
the Holy Spirit and power, and how he went
around doing good and healing all who were
under the power of the devil, because God was
with him.
39"We are witnesses of everything he did
in the country of the Jews and in Jerusalem.
They killed him by hanging him on a tree,
40but God raised him from the dead on the
third day and caused him to be seen. 41He was
not seen by all the people, but by witnesses
whom God had already chosen—by us who
ate and drank with him after he rose from the
dead. 42He commanded us to preach to the
people and to testify that he is the one whom
God appointed as judge of the living and the
dead. 43All the prophets testify about him that
everyone who believes in him receives forgiveness of sins through his name."
44While Peter was still speaking these
words, the Holy Spirit came on all who heard
the message. 45The circumcised believers who
had come with Peter were astonished that the
gift of the Holy Spirit had been poured out
even on the Gentiles. 46For they heard them
speaking in tongues[b] and praising God.
Then Peter said, 47"Can anyone keep these
people from being baptized with water? They
have received the Holy Spirit just as we have."
48So he ordered that they be baptized in the
name of Jesus Christ. Then they asked Peter to
stay with them for a few days.

Peter Explains His Actions

11 The apostles and the brothers throughout Judea heard that the Gentiles also
had received the word of God. 2So when
Peter went up to Jerusalem, the circumcised
believers criticized him 3and said, "You went
into the house of uncircumcised men and ate
with them."
4Peter began and explained everything to
them precisely as it had happened: 5"I was
in the city of Joppa praying, and in a trance
I saw a vision. I saw something like a large
sheet being let down from heaven by its four
corners, and it came down to where I was. 6I
looked into it and saw four-footed animals of
the earth, wild beasts, reptiles, and birds of the
air. 7Then I heard a voice telling me, 'Get up,
Peter. Kill and eat.'
8"I replied, 'Surely not, Lord! Nothing impure or unclean has ever entered my mouth.'
9"The voice spoke from heaven a second
time, 'Do not call anything impure that God

---

[a] 19 One early manuscript *two*; other manuscripts do not have the number. [b] 46 Or *other languages*

has made clean.’ 10This happened three times, and then it was all pulled up to heaven again.

11“Right then three men who had been sent to me from Caesarea stopped at the house where I was staying. 12The Spirit told me to have no hesitation about going with them. These six brothers also went with me, and we entered the man’s house. 13He told us how he had seen an angel appear in his house and say, ‘Send to Joppa for Simon who is called Peter. 14He will bring you a message through which you and all your household will be saved.’

15“As I began to speak, the Holy Spirit came on them as he had come on us at the beginning. 16Then I remembered what the Lord had said: ‘John baptized with[a] water, but you will be baptized with the Holy Spirit.’ 17So if God gave them the same gift as he gave us, who believed in the Lord Jesus Christ, who was I to think that I could oppose God?”

18When they heard this, they had no further objections and praised God, saying, “So then, God has granted even the Gentiles repentance unto life.”

The Church in Antioch

19Now those who had been scattered by the persecution in connection with Stephen traveled as far as Phoenicia, Cyprus and Antioch, telling the message only to Jews. 20Some of them, however, men from Cyprus and Cyrene, went to Antioch and began to speak to Greeks also, telling them the good news about the Lord Jesus. 21The Lord’s hand was with them, and a great number of people believed and turned to the Lord.

22News of this reached the ears of the church at Jerusalem, and they sent Barnabas to Antioch. 23When he arrived and saw the evidence of the grace of God, he was glad and encouraged them all to remain true to the Lord with all their hearts. 24He was a good man, full of the Holy Spirit and faith, and a great number of people were brought to the Lord.

25Then Barnabas went to Tarsus to look for Saul, 26and when he found him, he brought him to Antioch. So for a whole year Barnabas and Saul met with the church and taught great numbers of people. The disciples were called Christians first at Antioch.

27During this time some prophets came down from Jerusalem to Antioch. 28One of them, named Agabus, stood up and through the Spirit predicted that a severe famine would spread over the entire Roman world. (This happened during the reign of Claudius.) 29The disciples, each according to his ability, decided to provide help for the brothers living in Judea. 30This they did, sending their gift to the elders by Barnabas and Saul.

Peter’s Miraculous Escape From Prison

12 It was about this time that King Herod arrested some who belonged to the church, intending to persecute them. 2He had James, the brother of John, put to death with the sword. 3When he saw that this pleased the Jews, he proceeded to seize Peter also. This happened during the Feast of Unleavened Bread. 4After arresting him, he put him in prison, handing him over to be guarded by four squads of four soldiers each. Herod intended to bring him out for public trial after the Passover.

5So Peter was kept in prison, but the church was earnestly praying to God for him.

6The night before Herod was to bring him to trial, Peter was sleeping between two soldiers, bound with two chains, and sentries stood guard at the entrance. 7Suddenly an angel of the Lord appeared and a light shone in the cell. He struck Peter on the side and woke him up. “Quick, get up!” he said, and the chains fell off Peter’s wrists.

8Then the angel said to him, “Put on your clothes and sandals.” And Peter did so. “Wrap your cloak around you and follow me,” the angel told him. 9Peter followed him out of the prison, but he had no idea that what the angel was doing was really happening; he thought he was seeing a vision. 10They passed the first and second guards and came to the iron gate leading to the city. It opened for them by itself, and they went through it. When they had walked the length of one street, suddenly the angel left him.

11Then Peter came to himself and said, “Now I know without a doubt that the Lord sent his angel and rescued me from Herod’s clutches and from everything the Jewish people were anticipating.”

12When this had dawned on him, he went to the house of Mary the mother of John, also called Mark, where many people had gathered and were praying. 13Peter knocked at the outer entrance, and a servant girl named Rhoda came to answer the door. 14When she recognized Peter’s voice, she was so overjoyed she ran back without opening it and exclaimed, “Peter is at the door!”

---

[a] 16 Or *in*

15“You’re out of your mind,” they told her.
When she kept insisting that it was so, they
said, “It must be his angel.”
16But Peter kept on knocking, and when
they opened the door and saw him, they were
astonished. 17Peter motioned with his hand
for them to be quiet and described how the
Lord had brought him out of prison. “Tell
James and the brothers about this,” he said,
and then he left for another place.
18In the morning, there was no small commotion among the soldiers as to what had become of Peter. 19After Herod had a thorough
search made for him and did not find him,
he cross-examined the guards and ordered that
they be executed.

Herod’s Death

Then Herod went from Judea to Caesarea and stayed there a while. 20He had been
quarreling with the people of Tyre and Sidon;
they now joined together and sought an audience with him. Having secured the support of
Blastus, a trusted personal servant of the king,
they asked for peace, because they depended
on the king’s country for their food supply.
21On the appointed day Herod, wearing
his royal robes, sat on his throne and delivered
a public address to the people. 22They shouted, “This is the voice of a god, not of a man.”
23Immediately, because Herod did not give
praise to God, an angel of the Lord struck him
down, and he was eaten by worms and died.
24But the word of God continued to increase and spread.
25When Barnabas and Saul had finished
their mission, they returned from[a] Jerusalem,
taking with them John, also called Mark.

Barnabas and Saul Sent Off

13 In the church at Antioch there were
prophets and teachers: Barnabas, Simeon called Niger, Lucius of Cyrene, Man-
aen (who had been brought up with Herod
the tetrarch) and Saul. 2While they were worshiping the Lord and fasting, the Holy Spirit
said, “Set apart for me Barnabas and Saul for
the work to which I have called them.” 3So
after they had fasted and prayed, they placed
their hands on them and sent them off.

On Cyprus

4The two of them, sent on their way by the
Holy Spirit, went down to Seleucia and sailed
from there to Cyprus. 5When they arrived at
Salamis, they proclaimed the word of God in
the Jewish synagogues. John was with them as
their helper.
6They traveled through the whole island
until they came to Paphos. There they met a
Jewish sorcerer and false prophet named Bar-
Jesus, 7who was an attendant of the proconsul,
Sergius Paulus. The proconsul, an intelligent
man, sent for Barnabas and Saul because he
wanted to hear the word of God. 8But Elymas
the sorcerer (for that is what his name means)
opposed them and tried to turn the proconsul from the faith. 9Then Saul, who was also
called Paul, filled with the Holy Spirit, looked
straight at Elymas and said, 10“You are a child
of the devil and an enemy of everything that
is right! You are full of all kinds of deceit and
trickery. Will you never stop perverting the
right ways of the Lord? 11Now the hand of the
Lord is against you. You are going to be blind,
and for a time you will be unable to see the
light of the sun.”
Immediately mist and darkness came over
him, and he groped about, seeking someone
to lead him by the hand. 12When the proconsul saw what had happened, he believed, for he
was amazed at the teaching about the Lord.

In Pisidian Antioch

13From Paphos, Paul and his companions
sailed to Perga in Pamphylia, where John left
them to return to Jerusalem. 14From Perga
they went on to Pisidian Antioch. On the
Sabbath they entered the synagogue and sat
down. 15After the reading from the Law and
the Prophets, the synagogue rulers sent word
to them, saying, “Brothers, if you have a message of encouragement for the people, please
speak.”
16Standing up, Paul motioned with his
hand and said: “Men of Israel and you Gentiles who worship God, listen to me! 17The
God of the people of Israel chose our fathers;
he made the people prosper during their stay
in Egypt, with mighty power he led them out
of that country, 18he endured their conduct[b]
for about forty years in the desert, 19he overthrew seven nations in Canaan and gave their
land to his people as their inheritance. 20All
this took about 450 years.
“After this, God gave them judges until the
time of Samuel the prophet. 21Then the people asked for a king, and he gave them Saul
son of Kish, of the tribe of Benjamin, who
ruled forty years. 22After removing Saul, he

[a] 25 Some manuscripts *to* [b] 18 Some manuscripts *and cared for them*

made David their king. He testified concerning him: 'I have found David son of Jesse a
man after my own heart; he will do everything
I want him to do.'

23"From this man's descendants God has
brought to Israel the Savior Jesus, as he promised. 24Before the coming of Jesus, John
preached repentance and baptism to all the people of Israel. 25As John was completing his work,
he said: 'Who do you think I am? I am not that
one. No, but he is coming after me, whose sandals I am not worthy to untie.'

26"Brothers, children of Abraham, and you
God-fearing Gentiles, it is to us that this message of salvation has been sent. 27The people
of Jerusalem and their rulers did not recognize
Jesus, yet in condemning him they fulfilled the
words of the prophets that are read every Sabbath. 28Though they found no proper ground
for a death sentence, they asked Pilate to have
him executed. 29When they had carried out
all that was written about him, they took him
down from the tree and laid him in a tomb.
30But God raised him from the dead, 31and
for many days he was seen by those who had
traveled with him from Galilee to Jerusalem.
They are now his witnesses to our people.

32"We tell you the good news: What God
promised our fathers 33he has fulfilled for us,
their children, by raising up Jesus. As it is written in the second Psalm:

> " 'You are my Son;
> today I have become your Father.[a]'[b]

34The fact that God raised him from the dead,
never to decay, is stated in these words:

> " 'I will give you the holy and sure
> blessings promised to David.'[c]

35So it is stated elsewhere:

> " 'You will not let your Holy One see
> decay.'[d]

36"For when David had served God's purpose in his own generation, he fell asleep; he
was buried with his fathers and his body decayed. 37But the one whom God raised from
the dead did not see decay.

38"Therefore, my brothers, I want you to
know that through Jesus the forgiveness of sins
is proclaimed to you. 39Through him everyone
who believes is justified from everything you
could not be justified from by the law of Moses. 40Take care that what the prophets have
said does not happen to you:

> 41" 'Look, you scoffers,
> wonder and perish,
> for I am going to do something in your
> days
> that you would never believe,
> even if someone told you.'[e]"

42As Paul and Barnabas were leaving the
synagogue, the people invited them to speak
further about these things on the next Sabbath. 43When the congregation was dismissed,
many of the Jews and devout converts to Judaism followed Paul and Barnabas, who talked
with them and urged them to continue in the
grace of God.

44On the next Sabbath almost the whole
city gathered to hear the word of the Lord.
45When the Jews saw the crowds, they were
filled with jealousy and talked abusively
against what Paul was saying.

46Then Paul and Barnabas answered them
boldly: "We had to speak the word of God to
you first. Since you reject it and do not consider yourselves worthy of eternal life, we now
turn to the Gentiles. 47For this is what the
Lord has commanded us:

> " 'I have made you[f] a light for the
> Gentiles,
> that you[f] may bring salvation to the
> ends of the earth.'[g]"

48When the Gentiles heard this, they were
glad and honored the word of the Lord; and all
who were appointed for eternal life believed.

49The word of the Lord spread through the
whole region. 50But the Jews incited the God-
fearing women of high standing and the leading men of the city. They stirred up persecution against Paul and Barnabas, and expelled
them from their region. 51So they shook the
dust from their feet in protest against them
and went to Iconium. 52And the disciples were
filled with joy and with the Holy Spirit.

In Iconium

14 At Iconium Paul and Barnabas went as
usual into the Jewish synagogue. There
they spoke so effectively that a great
number of Jews and Gentiles believed. 2But
the Jews who refused to believe stirred up the
Gentiles and poisoned their minds against the
brothers. 3So Paul and Barnabas spent considerable time there, speaking boldly for the
Lord, who confirmed the message of his grace
by enabling them to do miraculous signs and

[a] 33 Or *have begotten you* [b] 33 Psalm 2:7 [c] 34 Isaiah 55:3 [d] 35 Psalm 16:10 [e] 41 Hab. 1:5 [f] 47 The Greek is singular.
[g] 47 Isaiah 49:6

wonders. 4The people of the city were divided; some sided with the Jews, others with the
apostles. 5There was a plot afoot among the
Gentiles and Jews, together with their leaders,
to mistreat them and stone them. 6But they
found out about it and fled to the Lycaonian cities of Lystra and Derbe and to the surrounding country, 7where they continued to
preach the good news.

In Lystra and Derbe

8In Lystra there sat a man crippled in his
feet, who was lame from birth and had never
walked. 9He listened to Paul as he was speaking. Paul looked directly at him, saw that he
had faith to be healed 10and called out, "Stand
up on your feet!" At that, the man jumped up
and began to walk.

11When the crowd saw what Paul had done,
they shouted in the Lycaonian language, "The
gods have come down to us in human form!"
12Barnabas they called Zeus, and Paul they
called Hermes because he was the chief speaker. 13The priest of Zeus, whose temple was just
outside the city, brought bulls and wreaths to
the city gates because he and the crowd wanted to offer sacrifices to them.

14But when the apostles Barnabas and Paul
heard of this, they tore their clothes and rushed
out into the crowd, shouting: 15"Men, why are
you doing this? We too are only men, human
like you. We are bringing you good news, telling you to turn from these worthless things to
the living God, who made heaven and earth
and sea and everything in them. 16In the past,
he let all nations go their own way. 17Yet he
has not left himself without testimony: He
has shown kindness by giving you rain from
heaven and crops in their seasons; he provides
you with plenty of food and fills your hearts
with joy." 18Even with these words, they had
difficulty keeping the crowd from sacrificing
to them.

19Then some Jews came from Antioch and
Iconium and won the crowd over. They stoned
Paul and dragged him outside the city, thinking he was dead. 20But after the disciples had
gathered around him, he got up and went
back into the city. The next day he and Barnabas left for Derbe.

The Return to Antioch in Syria

21They preached the good news in that city
and won a large number of disciples. Then
they returned to Lystra, Iconium and Antioch,
22strengthening the disciples and encouraging
them to remain true to the faith. "We must go
through many hardships to enter the kingdom
of God," they said. 23Paul and Barnabas appointed elders[a] for them in each church and,
with prayer and fasting, committed them to
the Lord, in whom they had put their trust.
24After going through Pisidia, they came into
Pamphylia, 25and when they had preached the
word in Perga, they went down to Attalia.

26From Attalia they sailed back to Antioch,
where they had been committed to the grace
of God for the work they had now completed. 27On arriving there, they gathered the
church together and reported all that God had
done through them and how he had opened
the door of faith to the Gentiles. 28And they
stayed there a long time with the disciples.

The Council at Jerusalem

15 Some men came down from Judea to
Antioch and were teaching the brothers:
"Unless you are circumcised, according
to the custom taught by Moses, you cannot
be saved." 2This brought Paul and Barnabas
into sharp dispute and debate with them. So
Paul and Barnabas were appointed, along with
some other believers, to go up to Jerusalem to
see the apostles and elders about this question.
3The church sent them on their way, and as
they traveled through Phoenicia and Samaria,
they told how the Gentiles had been converted. This news made all the brothers very glad.
4When they came to Jerusalem, they were welcomed by the church and the apostles and elders, to whom they reported everything God
had done through them.

5Then some of the believers who belonged
to the party of the Pharisees stood up and
said, "The Gentiles must be circumcised and
required to obey the law of Moses."

6The apostles and elders met to consider
this question. 7After much discussion, Peter
got up and addressed them: "Brothers, you
know that some time ago God made a choice
among you that the Gentiles might hear from
my lips the message of the gospel and believe.
8God, who knows the heart, showed that he
accepted them by giving the Holy Spirit to
them, just as he did to us. 9He made no distinction between us and them, for he purified
their hearts by faith. 10Now then, why do you
try to test God by putting on the necks of the
disciples a yoke that neither we nor our fathers
have been able to bear? 11No! We believe it is

---

a 23 Or *Barnabas ordained elders*; or *Barnabas had elders elected*

THURSDAY

READ ACTS 15:1–35

BIG-STUFF CONFLICT

You may have times in your marriage when you find yourselves arguing a lot. During such times, it might be wise to heed the maxim "Don't sweat the small stuff." So often couples blow up over small issues such as taking out the garbage, what restaurant to go to or who's stealing the covers at night. These are minor issues, and with good communication and compromise, it can be fairly easy to resolve conflicts over the small stuff.

But what about the big stuff? What about when you and your spouse don't see eye to eye on important issues like money, church or child rearing? Such issues cut to the core of who we are, what we value and what we believe. These conflicts aren't so easily resolved.

The early Christians in the book of Acts had serious big-stuff conflict. Some Christians were telling new believers that they had to become converts to Judaism, which included being circumcised, in order to be saved. Paul and Barnabas vehemently disagreed, which led to some heated arguments (see Acts 15:1–2). This issue wasn't something that Paul and Barnabas could simply overlook or ignore for the sake of unity in the church. It dealt with the very heart of the gospel: what we must do to be saved.

This brought Paul and Barnabas into sharp dispute and debate with them.

— Acts 15:2

let's talk

✦ What are some examples of small stuff we've had big arguments about? How could we have resolved those issues more quickly and with less conflict?

✦ What are some of the bigger issues we disagree about? What are some ways we've attempted to resolve them?

✦ Which Biblical principle for conflict resolution outlined above comes easiest to us? Which is the biggest challenge? Why?

So Paul and Barnabas went to Jerusalem to debate the issue with other leaders of the church. The Jerusalem council, described in Acts 15, wasn't a simple, peaceful meeting; people on both sides of the issue experienced passionate emotions. Yet the leaders of the church were able to sort through the issue and come to a mutual decision. Their example serves as a powerful model for how we can deal with big-stuff conflicts in our marriages today. Check out the following principles:

1. They listened empathetically and with open minds. The leaders of the church heard both sides of the argument (see verses 4–5) and listened quietly instead of arguing or interrupting each other (see verse 12).

2. They sought God's guidance through Scripture and prayer. James relied on Amos 9 to discern God's will in the situation, and their prayerful attitude is revealed by the fact that their decision "seemed good to the Holy Spirit" as well as to them (verse 28). We too can rely on God's Word and seek the Holy Spirit's guidance through prayer (see Ephesians 6:17–18).

3. They found a way to agree. The council came to a decision that addressed the concerns of both sides: They required Gentile believers to follow four guidelines in areas that were particularly sensitive to Jews; but circumcision and formal conversion to Judaism were *not* a requirement for salvation (see Acts 15:19–21). To avoid misunderstanding, the decision was put in writing and sent to the churches via ambassadors who could answer any questions (see verses 22–30).

These are great steps to follow if you are working through big-stuff conflict.

—DAVID AND KELLI TRUJILLO

FOR YOUR NEXT DEVOTIONAL READING, TURN TO PAGE 1241.

through the grace of our Lord Jesus that we
are saved, just as they are."
12 The whole assembly became silent as they
listened to Barnabas and Paul telling about the
miraculous signs and wonders God had done
among the Gentiles through them. 13 When
they finished, James spoke up: "Brothers, listen to me. 14 Simon[a] has described to us how
God at first showed his concern by taking
from the Gentiles a people for himself. 15 The
words of the prophets are in agreement with
this, as it is written:

16 " 'After this I will return
and rebuild David's fallen tent.
Its ruins I will rebuild,
and I will restore it,
17 that the remnant of men may seek the
Lord,
and all the Gentiles who bear my name,
says the Lord, who does these things'[b]
18 that have been known for ages.[c]

19 "It is my judgment, therefore, that we
should not make it difficult for the Gentiles
who are turning to God. 20 Instead we should
write to them, telling them to abstain from
food polluted by idols, from sexual immorality, from the meat of strangled animals and
from blood. 21 For Moses has been preached in
every city from the earliest times and is read in
the synagogues on every Sabbath."

The Council's Letter to Gentile Believers

22 Then the apostles and elders, with the
whole church, decided to choose some of their
own men and send them to Antioch with Paul
and Barnabas. They chose Judas (called Barsabbas) and Silas, two men who were leaders
among the brothers. 23 With them they sent
the following letter:

The apostles and elders, your brothers,

To the Gentile believers in Antioch, Syria
and Cilicia:

Greetings.

24 We have heard that some went out
from us without our authorization and
disturbed you, troubling your minds
by what they said. 25 So we all agreed
to choose some men and send them to
you with our dear friends Barnabas and
Paul— 26 men who have risked their lives
for the name of our Lord Jesus Christ.
27 Therefore we are sending Judas and Silas to confirm by word of mouth what we
are writing. 28 It seemed good to the Holy
Spirit and to us not to burden you with
anything beyond the following requirements: 29 You are to abstain from food
sacrificed to idols, from blood, from the
meat of strangled animals and from sexual immorality. You will do well to avoid
these things.

Farewell.

30 The men were sent off and went down
to Antioch, where they gathered the church
together and delivered the letter. 31 The people read it and were glad for its encouraging
message. 32 Judas and Silas, who themselves
were prophets, said much to encourage and
strengthen the brothers. 33 After spending
some time there, they were sent off by the
brothers with the blessing of peace to return
to those who had sent them.[d] 35 But Paul and
Barnabas remained in Antioch, where they
and many others taught and preached the
word of the Lord.

Disagreement Between Paul and Barnabas

36 Some time later Paul said to Barnabas,
"Let us go back and visit the brothers in all
the towns where we preached the word of the
Lord and see how they are doing." 37 Barnabas wanted to take John, also called Mark,
with them, 38 but Paul did not think it wise
to take him, because he had deserted them
in Pamphylia and had not continued with
them in the work. 39 They had such a sharp
disagreement that they parted company. Barnabas took Mark and sailed for Cyprus, 40 but
Paul chose Silas and left, commended by the
brothers to the grace of the Lord. 41 He went
through Syria and Cilicia, strengthening the
churches.

Timothy Joins Paul and Silas

16 He came to Derbe and then to Lystra,
where a disciple named Timothy lived,
whose mother was a Jewess and a believer, but whose father was a Greek. 2 The brothers at Lystra and Iconium spoke well of him.
3 Paul wanted to take him along on the journey, so he circumcised him because of the Jews
who lived in that area, for they all knew that
his father was a Greek. 4 As they traveled from
town to town, they delivered the decisions
reached by the apostles and elders in Jerusa-

[a] 14 Greek *Simeon*, a variant of *Simon*; that is, Peter [b] 17 Amos 9:11,12 [c] 17,18 Some manuscripts *things'— / [18]known to the Lord for ages is his work* [d] 33 Some manuscripts *them, [34]but Silas decided to remain there*

lem for the people to obey. 5So the churches
were strengthened in the faith and grew daily
in numbers.

Paul's Vision of the Man of Macedonia

6Paul and his companions traveled throughout the region of Phrygia and Galatia, having
been kept by the Holy Spirit from preaching
the word in the province of Asia. 7When they
came to the border of Mysia, they tried to enter Bithynia, but the Spirit of Jesus would not
allow them to. 8So they passed by Mysia and
went down to Troas. 9During the night Paul
had a vision of a man of Macedonia standing
and begging him, "Come over to Macedonia
and help us." 10After Paul had seen the vision,
we got ready at once to leave for Macedonia,
concluding that God had called us to preach
the gospel to them.

Lydia's Conversion in Philippi

11From Troas we put out to sea and sailed
straight for Samothrace, and the next day on
to Neapolis. 12From there we traveled to Philippi, a Roman colony and the leading city
of that district of Macedonia. And we stayed
there several days.

13On the Sabbath we went outside the city
gate to the river, where we expected to find
a place of prayer. We sat down and began to
speak to the women who had gathered there.
14One of those listening was a woman named
Lydia, a dealer in purple cloth from the city
of Thyatira, who was a worshiper of God. The
Lord opened her heart to respond to Paul's
message. 15When she and the members of her
household were baptized, she invited us to her
home. "If you consider me a believer in the
Lord," she said, "come and stay at my house."
And she persuaded us.

Paul and Silas in Prison

16Once when we were going to the place of
prayer, we were met by a slave girl who had a
spirit by which she predicted the future. She
earned a great deal of money for her owners by
fortune-telling. 17This girl followed Paul and
the rest of us, shouting, "These men are servants of the Most High God, who are telling
you the way to be saved." 18She kept this up
for many days. Finally Paul became so troubled that he turned around and said to the
spirit, "In the name of Jesus Christ I command you to come out of her!" At that moment the spirit left her.

19When the owners of the slave girl realized
that their hope of making money was gone,
they seized Paul and Silas and dragged them
into the marketplace to face the authorities.
20They brought them before the magistrates
and said, "These men are Jews, and are throwing our city into an uproar 21by advocating
customs unlawful for us Romans to accept or
practice."

22The crowd joined in the attack against
Paul and Silas, and the magistrates ordered
them to be stripped and beaten. 23After they
had been severely flogged, they were thrown
into prison, and the jailer was commanded to
guard them carefully. 24Upon receiving such
orders, he put them in the inner cell and fastened their feet in the stocks.

25About midnight Paul and Silas were praying and singing hymns to God, and the other
prisoners were listening to them. 26Suddenly
there was such a violent earthquake that the
foundations of the prison were shaken. At
once all the prison doors flew open, and everybody's chains came loose. 27The jailer woke
up, and when he saw the prison doors open,
he drew his sword and was about to kill himself because he thought the prisoners had escaped. 28But Paul shouted, "Don't harm yourself! We are all here!"

29The jailer called for lights, rushed in and
fell trembling before Paul and Silas. 30He then
brought them out and asked, "Sirs, what must
I do to be saved?"

31They replied, "Believe in the Lord Jesus,
and you will be saved—you and your household." 32Then they spoke the word of the Lord
to him and to all the others in his house. 33At
that hour of the night the jailer took them
and washed their wounds; then immediately he and all his family were baptized. 34The
jailer brought them into his house and set a
meal before them; he was filled with joy because he had come to believe in God—he and
his whole family.

35When it was daylight, the magistrates sent
their officers to the jailer with the order: "Release those men." 36The jailer told Paul, "The
magistrates have ordered that you and Silas be
released. Now you can leave. Go in peace."

37But Paul said to the officers: "They beat
us publicly without a trial, even though we
are Roman citizens, and threw us into prison.
And now do they want to get rid of us quietly? No! Let them come themselves and escort
us out."

38The officers reported this to the magistrates, and when they heard that Paul and Silas were Roman citizens, they were alarmed.
39They came to appease them and escorted

them from the prison, requesting them to
leave the city. 40After Paul and Silas came
out of the prison, they went to Lydia's house,
where they met with the brothers and encouraged them. Then they left.

In Thessalonica

17 When they had passed through Am-
phipolis and Apollonia, they came to
Thessalonica, where there was a Jewish
synagogue. 2As his custom was, Paul went into
the synagogue, and on three Sabbath days he
reasoned with them from the Scriptures, 3ex-
plaining and proving that the Christ[a] had
to suffer and rise from the dead. "This Jesus
I am proclaiming to you is the Christ,[a]" he
said. 4Some of the Jews were persuaded and
joined Paul and Silas, as did a large number of
God-fearing Greeks and not a few prominent
women.

5But the Jews were jealous; so they rounded
up some bad characters from the marketplace,
formed a mob and started a riot in the city.
They rushed to Jason's house in search of Paul
and Silas in order to bring them out to the
crowd.[b] 6But when they did not find them,
they dragged Jason and some other brothers
before the city officials, shouting: "These men
who have caused trouble all over the world
have now come here, 7and Jason has welcomed
them into his house. They are all defying Caesar's decrees, saying that there is another king,
one called Jesus." 8When they heard this, the
crowd and the city officials were thrown into
turmoil. 9Then they made Jason and the others post bond and let them go.

In Berea

10As soon as it was night, the brothers sent
Paul and Silas away to Berea. On arriving there,
they went to the Jewish synagogue. 11Now the
Bereans were of more noble character than the
Thessalonians, for they received the message
with great eagerness and examined the Scriptures every day to see if what Paul said was
true. 12Many of the Jews believed, as did also
a number of prominent Greek women and
many Greek men.

13When the Jews in Thessalonica learned
that Paul was preaching the word of God
at Berea, they went there too, agitating the
crowds and stirring them up. 14The brothers
immediately sent Paul to the coast, but Silas
and Timothy stayed at Berea. 15The men who
escorted Paul brought him to Athens and then
left with instructions for Silas and Timothy to
join him as soon as possible.

In Athens

16While Paul was waiting for them in Athens, he was greatly distressed to see that the
city was full of idols. 17So he reasoned in the
synagogue with the Jews and the God-fearing
Greeks, as well as in the marketplace day by
day with those who happened to be there. 18A
group of Epicurean and Stoic philosophers
began to dispute with him. Some of them
asked, "What is this babbler trying to say?"
Others remarked, "He seems to be advocating foreign gods." They said this because Paul
was preaching the good news about Jesus and
the resurrection. 19Then they took him and
brought him to a meeting of the Areopagus,
where they said to him, "May we know what
this new teaching is that you are presenting?
20You are bringing some strange ideas to our
ears, and we want to know what they mean."
21(All the Athenians and the foreigners who
lived there spent their time doing nothing
but talking about and listening to the latest
ideas.)

22Paul then stood up in the meeting of the
Areopagus and said: "Men of Athens! I see that
in every way you are very religious. 23For as I
walked around and looked carefully at your
objects of worship, I even found an altar with
this inscription: TO AN UNKNOWN GOD. Now
what you worship as something unknown I
am going to proclaim to you.

24"The God who made the world and everything in it is the Lord of heaven and earth
and does not live in temples built by hands.
25And he is not served by human hands, as
if he needed anything, because he himself
gives all men life and breath and everything
else. 26From one man he made every nation of
men, that they should inhabit the whole earth;
and he determined the times set for them and
the exact places where they should live. 27God
did this so that men would seek him and perhaps reach out for him and find him, though
he is not far from each one of us. 28'For in
him we live and move and have our being.'
As some of your own poets have said, 'We are
his offspring.'

29"Therefore since we are God's offspring,
we should not think that the divine being is
like gold or silver or stone—an image made
by man's design and skill. 30In the past God
overlooked such ignorance, but now he com-

---

[a] 3 Or *Messiah* [b] 5 Or *the assembly of the people*

mands all people everywhere to repent. [31]For he has set a day when he will judge the world with justice by the man he has appointed. He has given proof of this to all men by raising him from the dead."

[32]When they heard about the resurrection of the dead, some of them sneered, but others said, "We want to hear you again on this subject." [33]At that, Paul left the Council. [34]A few men became followers of Paul and believed. Among them was Dionysius, a member of the Areopagus, also a woman named Damaris, and a number of others.

In Corinth

18 After this, Paul left Athens and went to Corinth. [2]There he met a Jew named Aquila, a native of Pontus, who had recently come from Italy with his wife Priscilla, because Claudius had ordered all the Jews to leave Rome. Paul went to see them, [3]and because he was a tentmaker as they were, he stayed and worked with them. [4]Every Sabbath he reasoned in the synagogue, trying to persuade Jews and Greeks.

[5]When Silas and Timothy came from Macedonia, Paul devoted himself exclusively to preaching, testifying to the Jews that Jesus was the Christ.[a] [6]But when the Jews opposed Paul and became abusive, he shook out his clothes in protest and said to them, "Your blood be on your own heads! I am clear of my responsibility. From now on I will go to the Gentiles."

[7]Then Paul left the synagogue and went next door to the house of Titius Justus, a worshiper of God. [8]Crispus, the synagogue ruler, and his entire household believed in the Lord; and many of the Corinthians who heard him believed and were baptized.

[9]One night the Lord spoke to Paul in a vision: "Do not be afraid; keep on speaking, do not be silent. [10]For I am with you, and no one is going to attack and harm you, because I have many people in this city." [11]So Paul stayed for a year and a half, teaching them the word of God.

[12]While Gallio was proconsul of Achaia, the Jews made a united attack on Paul and brought him into court. [13]"This man," they charged, "is persuading the people to worship God in ways contrary to the law."

[14]Just as Paul was about to speak, Gallio said to the Jews, "If you Jews were making a complaint about some misdemeanor or serious crime, it would be reasonable for me to listen to you. [15]But since it involves questions about words and names and your own law—settle the matter yourselves. I will not be a judge of such things." [16]So he had them ejected from the court. [17]Then they all turned on Sosthenes the synagogue ruler and beat him in front of the court. But Gallio showed no concern whatever.

Priscilla, Aquila and Apollos

[18]Paul stayed on in Corinth for some time. Then he left the brothers and sailed for Syria, accompanied by Priscilla and Aquila. Before he sailed, he had his hair cut off at Cenchrea because of a vow he had taken. [19]They arrived at Ephesus, where Paul left Priscilla and Aquila. He himself went into the synagogue and reasoned with the Jews. [20]When they asked him to spend more time with them, he declined. [21]But as he left, he promised, "I will come back if it is God's will." Then he set sail from Ephesus. [22]When he landed at Caesarea, he went up and greeted the church and then went down to Antioch.

[23]After spending some time in Antioch, Paul set out from there and traveled from place to place throughout the region of Galatia and Phrygia, strengthening all the disciples.

[24]Meanwhile a Jew named Apollos, a native of Alexandria, came to Ephesus. He was a learned man, with a thorough knowledge of the Scriptures. [25]He had been instructed in the way of the Lord, and he spoke with great fervor[b] and taught about Jesus accurately, though he knew only the baptism of John. [26]He began to speak boldly in the synagogue. When Priscilla and Aquila heard him, they invited him to their home and explained to him the way of God more adequately.

[27]When Apollos wanted to go to Achaia, the brothers encouraged him and wrote to the disciples there to welcome him. On arriving, he was a great help to those who by grace had believed. [28]For he vigorously refuted the Jews in public debate, proving from the Scriptures that Jesus was the Christ.

Paul in Ephesus

19 While Apollos was at Corinth, Paul took the road through the interior and arrived at Ephesus. There he found some disciples [2]and asked them, "Did you receive the Holy Spirit when[c] you believed?"

They answered, "No, we have not even heard that there is a Holy Spirit."

[a] 5 Or *Messiah;* also in verse 28 [b] 25 Or *with fervor in the Spirit* [c] 2 Or *after*

MINISTERING AS A TEAM

A couple in our church provides invaluable training for people who are planning to go into the ministry. Marshall and Chris show young couples how to love one another and how to raise their children wisely and well. They host a small group in their home in which they study and apply Scripture together. They talk through what it means to shape their homes around Christ, and how to do so while working in the church. Marshall and Chris share special meals with these couples and fuss over the kids.

Sounds great, doesn't it? But the work is draining. There are times when this mature couple would like a break from the emotional demands of such mentoring—even just a quiet night at home. Plus, it's hard to constantly be saying goodbye to families they've grown to love who are moving on in ministry. But Marshall and Chris mentor others because they believe in building the church.

The apostle Paul knew a couple like that, a couple who always worked together as a team. Their names were Aquila and Priscilla. And they understood the price of following Christ. Paul wrote about them in Romans 16:3, saying, "They risked their lives for me." Their initiative to live for others came from praying together and talking over ministry opportunities; it also came from a selfless love of other believers and, of course, their devotion to Jesus.

When Priscilla and Aquila heard [Apollos], they invited him to their home and explained to him the way of God more adequately.

— Acts 18:26

Let's talk

- What about Priscilla and Aquila's relationship appeals most to us?
- What couples do we know who have effective ministries together (whether in their home or beyond it)? What are some ministries that most appeal to us as a couple? Why?
- What steps might we take to expand or deepen our household ministry as a couple? Are we sensing that God wants us to open our home to others to perhaps lead a youth group, parent foster children, mentor engaged couples or host a neighborhood Bible study?

In more than 30 years of marriage, my wife and I have frequently invited people to stay in our home. Sometimes we offer a place to a student who is taking a two- or three-week class at Trinity Evangelical Seminary, which is near our home. Other times, we provide a place for someone who has nowhere else to go. Once we opened our home for 15 months to a young woman and her preschooler. Sometimes such commitments proved to be far more complicated than we had imagined; yet the rewards often exceeded our expectations.

Every ministry has its price and its privileges, and every ministry undertaken by a couple can be a challenge to their marriage. Learning to share the work, to complement one another's gifts, and to pray together through difficulties are not always easy.

Think about some of the issues Aquila and Priscilla must have talked about and prayed through together. They must have recognized and valued one another's natural and spiritual gifts and determined to work as a team. They were so good at working together that Scripture always mentions them as a team. They were such students of Scripture that they were able to make a significant contribution to the training of one of the church's most promising leaders: Apollos. And they had the gift of hospitality, for a church met regularly in their home (see 1 Corinthians 16:19). What a model for marriage!

—LEE ECLOV

FOR YOUR NEXT DEVOTIONAL READING, TURN TO PAGE 1246

3So Paul asked, "Then what baptism did
you receive?"
"John's baptism," they replied.
4Paul said, "John's baptism was a baptism
of repentance. He told the people to believe
in the one coming after him, that is, in Jesus."
5On hearing this, they were baptized into[a] the
name of the Lord Jesus. 6When Paul placed
his hands on them, the Holy Spirit came on
them, and they spoke in tongues[b] and prophesied. 7There were about twelve men in all.
8Paul entered the synagogue and spoke
boldly there for three months, arguing persua-
sively about the kingdom of God. 9But some
of them became obstinate; they refused to believe and publicly maligned the Way. So Paul
left them. He took the disciples with him and
had discussions daily in the lecture hall of Ty-
rannus. 10This went on for two years, so that
all the Jews and Greeks who lived in the province of Asia heard the word of the Lord.
11God did extraordinary miracles through
Paul, 12so that even handkerchiefs and aprons
that had touched him were taken to the sick,
and their illnesses were cured and the evil spirits left them.
13Some Jews who went around driving out
evil spirits tried to invoke the name of the Lord
Jesus over those who were demon-possessed.
They would say, "In the name of Jesus, whom
Paul preaches, I command you to come out."
14Seven sons of Sceva, a Jewish chief priest,
were doing this. 15⌊One day⌋ the evil spirit answered them, "Jesus I know, and I know about
Paul, but who are you?" 16Then the man who
had the evil spirit jumped on them and overpowered them all. He gave them such a beating that they ran out of the house naked and
bleeding.
17When this became known to the Jews and
Greeks living in Ephesus, they were all seized
with fear, and the name of the Lord Jesus was
held in high honor. 18Many of those who believed now came and openly confessed their
evil deeds. 19A number who had practiced sorcery brought their scrolls together and burned
them publicly. When they calculated the value
of the scrolls, the total came to fifty thousand
drachmas.[c] 20In this way the word of the Lord
spread widely and grew in power.
21After all this had happened, Paul decided
to go to Jerusalem, passing through Macedonia and Achaia. "After I have been there," he
said, "I must visit Rome also." 22He sent two
of his helpers, Timothy and Erastus, to Macedonia, while he stayed in the province of Asia
a little longer.

The Riot in Ephesus

23About that time there arose a great disturbance about the Way. 24A silversmith named
Demetrius, who made silver shrines of Artemis, brought in no little business for the
craftsmen. 25He called them together, along
with the workmen in related trades, and said:
"Men, you know we receive a good income
from this business. 26And you see and hear
how this fellow Paul has convinced and led
astray large numbers of people here in Ephesus and in practically the whole province
of Asia. He says that man-made gods are no
gods at all. 27There is danger not only that our
trade will lose its good name, but also that
the temple of the great goddess Artemis will
be discredited, and the goddess herself, who
is worshiped throughout the province of Asia
and the world, will be robbed of her divine
majesty."
28When they heard this, they were furious
and began shouting: "Great is Artemis of the
Ephesians!" 29Soon the whole city was in an
uproar. The people seized Gaius and Aristarchus, Paul's traveling companions from Macedonia, and rushed as one man into the theater.
30Paul wanted to appear before the crowd, but
the disciples would not let him. 31Even some
of the officials of the province, friends of Paul,
sent him a message begging him not to venture into the theater.
32The assembly was in confusion: Some
were shouting one thing, some another. Most
of the people did not even know why they
were there. 33The Jews pushed Alexander to
the front, and some of the crowd shouted instructions to him. He motioned for silence
in order to make a defense before the people.
34But when they realized he was a Jew, they all
shouted in unison for about two hours: "Great
is Artemis of the Ephesians!"
35The city clerk quieted the crowd and said:
"Men of Ephesus, doesn't all the world know
that the city of Ephesus is the guardian of the
temple of the great Artemis and of her image,
which fell from heaven? 36Therefore, since
these facts are undeniable, you ought to be
quiet and not do anything rash. 37You have
brought these men here, though they have
neither robbed temples nor blasphemed our
goddess. 38If, then, Demetrius and his fellow
craftsmen have a grievance against anybody,

---

[a] 5 Or *in* [b] 6 Or *other languages* [c] 19 A drachma was a silver coin worth about a day's wages.

the courts are open and there are proconsuls.
They can press charges. 39If there is anything
further you want to bring up, it must be settled in a legal assembly. 40As it is, we are in
danger of being charged with rioting because
of today's events. In that case we would not
be able to account for this commotion, since
there is no reason for it." 41After he had said
this, he dismissed the assembly.

Through Macedonia and Greece

20 When the uproar had ended, Paul sent
for the disciples and, after encouraging
them, said good-by and set out for Macedonia. 2He traveled through that area, speaking many words of encouragement to the people, and finally arrived in Greece, 3where he
stayed three months. Because the Jews made
a plot against him just as he was about to sail
for Syria, he decided to go back through Macedonia. 4He was accompanied by Sopater son
of Pyrrhus from Berea, Aristarchus and Se-
cundus from Thessalonica, Gaius from Derbe,
Timothy also, and Tychicus and Trophimus
from the province of Asia. 5These men went
on ahead and waited for us at Troas. 6But we
sailed from Philippi after the Feast of Unleavened Bread, and five days later joined the others at Troas, where we stayed seven days.

Eutychus Raised From the Dead at Troas

7On the first day of the week we came together to break bread. Paul spoke to the people and, because he intended to leave the next
day, kept on talking until midnight. 8There
were many lamps in the upstairs room where
we were meeting. 9Seated in a window was a
young man named Eutychus, who was sinking into a deep sleep as Paul talked on and
on. When he was sound asleep, he fell to the
ground from the third story and was picked
up dead. 10Paul went down, threw himself
on the young man and put his arms around
him. "Don't be alarmed," he said. "He's alive!"
11Then he went upstairs again and broke bread
and ate. After talking until daylight, he left.
12The people took the young man home alive
and were greatly comforted.

Paul's Farewell to the Ephesian Elders

13We went on ahead to the ship and sailed
for Assos, where we were going to take Paul
aboard. He had made this arrangement because he was going there on foot. 14When he
met us at Assos, we took him aboard and went
on to Mitylene. 15The next day we set sail
from there and arrived off Kios. The day after that we crossed over to Samos, and on the
following day arrived at Miletus. 16Paul had
decided to sail past Ephesus to avoid spending
time in the province of Asia, for he was in a
hurry to reach Jerusalem, if possible, by the
day of Pentecost.

17From Miletus, Paul sent to Ephesus for
the elders of the church. 18When they arrived,
he said to them: "You know how I lived the
whole time I was with you, from the first day I
came into the province of Asia. 19I served the
Lord with great humility and with tears, although I was severely tested by the plots of the
Jews. 20You know that I have not hesitated to
preach anything that would be helpful to you
but have taught you publicly and from house
to house. 21I have declared to both Jews and
Greeks that they must turn to God in repentance and have faith in our Lord Jesus.

22"And now, compelled by the Spirit, I am
going to Jerusalem, not knowing what will
happen to me there. 23I only know that in every city the Holy Spirit warns me that prison and hardships are facing me. 24However, I
consider my life worth nothing to me, if only
I may finish the race and complete the task the
Lord Jesus has given me—the task of testifying to the gospel of God's grace.

25"Now I know that none of you among
whom I have gone about preaching the kingdom will ever see me again. 26Therefore, I declare to you today that I am innocent of the
blood of all men. 27For I have not hesitated to
proclaim to you the whole will of God. 28Keep
watch over yourselves and all the flock of which
the Holy Spirit has made you overseers.[a] Be
shepherds of the church of God,[b] which he
bought with his own blood. 29I know that after I leave, savage wolves will come in among
you and will not spare the flock. 30Even from
your own number men will arise and distort
the truth in order to draw away disciples after
them. 31So be on your guard! Remember that
for three years I never stopped warning each of
you night and day with tears.

32"Now I commit you to God and to the
word of his grace, which can build you up and
give you an inheritance among all those who
are sanctified. 33I have not coveted anyone's
silver or gold or clothing. 34You yourselves
know that these hands of mine have supplied
my own needs and the needs of my companions. 35In everything I did, I showed you that

[a] 28 Traditionally *bishops* [b] 28 Many manuscripts *of the Lord*

by this kind of hard work we must help the weak, remembering the words the Lord Jesus himself said: 'It is more blessed to give than to receive.' "

36When he had said this, he knelt down with all of them and prayed. 37They all wept as they embraced him and kissed him. 38What grieved them most was his statement that they would never see his face again. Then they accompanied him to the ship.

On to Jerusalem

21 After we had torn ourselves away from them, we put out to sea and sailed straight to Cos. The next day we went to Rhodes and from there to Patara. 2We found a ship crossing over to Phoenicia, went on board and set sail. 3After sighting Cyprus and passing to the south of it, we sailed on to Syria. We landed at Tyre, where our ship was to unload its cargo. 4Finding the disciples there, we stayed with them seven days. Through the Spirit they urged Paul not to go on to Jerusalem. 5But when our time was up, we left and continued on our way. All the disciples and their wives and children accompanied us out of the city, and there on the beach we knelt to pray. 6After saying good-by to each other, we went aboard the ship, and they returned home.

7We continued our voyage from Tyre and landed at Ptolemais, where we greeted the brothers and stayed with them for a day. 8Leaving the next day, we reached Caesarea and stayed at the house of Philip the evangelist, one of the Seven. 9He had four unmarried daughters who prophesied.

10After we had been there a number of days, a prophet named Agabus came down from Judea. 11Coming over to us, he took Paul's belt, tied his own hands and feet with it and said, "The Holy Spirit says, 'In this way the Jews of Jerusalem will bind the owner of this belt and will hand him over to the Gentiles.' "

12When we heard this, we and the people there pleaded with Paul not to go up to Jerusalem. 13Then Paul answered, "Why are you weeping and breaking my heart? I am ready not only to be bound, but also to die in Jerusalem for the name of the Lord Jesus." 14When he would not be dissuaded, we gave up and said, "The Lord's will be done."

15After this, we got ready and went up to Jerusalem. 16Some of the disciples from Caesarea accompanied us and brought us to the home of Mnason, where we were to stay. He was a man from Cyprus and one of the early disciples.

Paul's Arrival at Jerusalem

17When we arrived at Jerusalem, the brothers received us warmly. 18The next day Paul and the rest of us went to see James, and all the elders were present. 19Paul greeted them and reported in detail what God had done among the Gentiles through his ministry.

20When they heard this, they praised God. Then they said to Paul: "You see, brother, how many thousands of Jews have believed, and all of them are zealous for the law. 21They have been informed that you teach all the Jews who live among the Gentiles to turn away from Moses, telling them not to circumcise their children or live according to our customs. 22What shall we do? They will certainly hear that you have come, 23so do what we tell you. There are four men with us who have made a vow. 24Take these men, join in their purification rites and pay their expenses, so that they can have their heads shaved. Then everybody will know there is no truth in these reports about you, but that you yourself are living in obedience to the law. 25As for the Gentile believers, we have written to them our decision that they should abstain from food sacrificed to idols, from blood, from the meat of strangled animals and from sexual immorality."

26The next day Paul took the men and purified himself along with them. Then he went to the temple to give notice of the date when the days of purification would end and the offering would be made for each of them.

Paul Arrested

27When the seven days were nearly over, some Jews from the province of Asia saw Paul at the temple. They stirred up the whole crowd and seized him, 28shouting, "Men of Israel, help us! This is the man who teaches all men everywhere against our people and our law and this place. And besides, he has brought Greeks into the temple area and defiled this holy place." 29(They had previously seen Trophimus the Ephesian in the city with Paul and assumed that Paul had brought him into the temple area.)

30The whole city was aroused, and the people came running from all directions. Seizing Paul, they dragged him from the temple, and immediately the gates were shut. 31While they were trying to kill him, news reached the commander of the Roman troops that the whole city of Jerusalem was in an uproar. 32He at once took some officers and soldiers and ran down to the crowd. When the rioters saw the commander and his soldiers, they stopped beating Paul.

33The commander came up and arrested him and ordered him to be bound with two chains. Then he asked who he was and what he had done. 34Some in the crowd shouted one thing and some another, and since the commander could not get at the truth because of the uproar, he ordered that Paul be taken into the barracks. 35When Paul reached the steps, the violence of the mob was so great he had to be carried by the soldiers. 36The crowd that followed kept shouting, "Away with him!"

Paul Speaks to the Crowd

37As the soldiers were about to take Paul into the barracks, he asked the commander, "May I say something to you?"

"Do you speak Greek?" he replied. 38"Aren't you the Egyptian who started a revolt and led four thousand terrorists out into the desert some time ago?"

39Paul answered, "I am a Jew, from Tarsus in Cilicia, a citizen of no ordinary city. Please let me speak to the people."

40Having received the commander's permission, Paul stood on the steps and motioned to the crowd. When they were all silent, he said

22

to them in Aramaic[a]: 1"Brothers and fathers, listen now to my defense."

2When they heard him speak to them in Aramaic, they became very quiet.

Then Paul said: 3"I am a Jew, born in Tarsus of Cilicia, but brought up in this city. Under Gamaliel I was thoroughly trained in the law of our fathers and was just as zealous for God as any of you are today. 4I persecuted the followers of this Way to their death, arresting both men and women and throwing them into prison, 5as also the high priest and all the Council can testify. I even obtained letters from them to their brothers in Damascus, and went there to bring these people as prisoners to Jerusalem to be punished.

6"About noon as I came near Damascus, suddenly a bright light from heaven flashed around me. 7I fell to the ground and heard a voice say to me, 'Saul! Saul! Why do you persecute me?'

8" 'Who are you, Lord?' I asked.

" 'I am Jesus of Nazareth, whom you are persecuting,' he replied. 9My companions saw the light, but they did not understand the voice of him who was speaking to me.

10" 'What shall I do, Lord?' I asked.

" 'Get up,' the Lord said, 'and go into Damascus. There you will be told all that you have been assigned to do.' 11My companions led me by the hand into Damascus, because the brilliance of the light had blinded me.

12"A man named Ananias came to see me. He was a devout observer of the law and highly respected by all the Jews living there. 13He stood beside me and said, 'Brother Saul, receive your sight!' And at that very moment I was able to see him.

14"Then he said: 'The God of our fathers has chosen you to know his will and to see the Righteous One and to hear words from his mouth. 15You will be his witness to all men of what you have seen and heard. 16And now what are you waiting for? Get up, be baptized and wash your sins away, calling on his name.'

17"When I returned to Jerusalem and was praying at the temple, I fell into a trance 18and saw the Lord speaking. 'Quick!' he said to me. 'Leave Jerusalem immediately, because they will not accept your testimony about me.'

19" 'Lord,' I replied, 'these men know that I went from one synagogue to another to imprison and beat those who believe in you. 20And when the blood of your martyr[b] Stephen was shed, I stood there giving my approval and guarding the clothes of those who were killing him.'

21"Then the Lord said to me, 'Go; I will send you far away to the Gentiles.' "

Paul the Roman Citizen

22The crowd listened to Paul until he said this. Then they raised their voices and shouted, "Rid the earth of him! He's not fit to live!"

23As they were shouting and throwing off their cloaks and flinging dust into the air, 24the commander ordered Paul to be taken into the barracks. He directed that he be flogged and questioned in order to find out why the people were shouting at him like this. 25As they stretched him out to flog him, Paul said to the centurion standing there, "Is it legal for you to flog a Roman citizen who hasn't even been found guilty?"

26When the centurion heard this, he went to the commander and reported it. "What are you going to do?" he asked. "This man is a Roman citizen."

27The commander went to Paul and asked, "Tell me, are you a Roman citizen?"

"Yes, I am," he answered.

28Then the commander said, "I had to pay a big price for my citizenship."

---

[a] 40 Or possibly *Hebrew*; also in 22:2 [b] 20 Or *witness*

WEEKEND

dual careers

We are both career minded. Before we even got married, we decided to respect one another's professional pursuits and support each other as a team. We now realize that our career pursuits can sometimes clash. So we are wondering—whose career should take priority?

In the age of the dual-income couple, relocation may mean dragging one spouse out of a job to satisfy another's advancement. It seems that one person's career will eventually call the couple to determine whose work will take priority. Granted, for many traditional couples that question is already settled. A couple with traditional gender-role values will see the husband as the primary provider and decision maker. But if you are asking the question of career priority, you are like the growing number of couples who are pursuing individual careers and struggling to find an answer to this quandary.

Of the twenty-two million people who packed up and moved for work in 1993, only two million were husbands going along with their wives. While that's double the number from 1980, it's a sluggish progression, considering the large number of women who have reached middle- and upper-management positions ripe for relocation assignments.

The issue comes down to what you, as a couple, value most. Once you determine what matters most to both of you, your decisions on how to allocate time and priorities fall more easily into place. So permit us to ask: Would your decision to move for work simply maximize your financial well being? A study by Mobil Corporation found that a man generally will follow his wife only if she earns at least 40 percent more than he does. Is that true of you? What about prestige and power? Is one of your goals to climb the corporate ladder? If so, does that mean that if your spouse is moving up faster than you, then his or her job takes precedence over yours?

Typically the priority gap can't be explained and settled by salary and stature alone. There is much more that goes into determining the actual balance of power in your relationship. You might find that one person's career takes precedence over the other's for a period of time and then, years into the marriage, the order of priority is exchanged.

Determining whose career should take priority is a personal journey for each couple. Sociologist Arlie Hochschild, author of *The Second Shift*, found that many people ideologically support the idea of egalitarian roles, yet in carrying out those roles and in valuing each other's careers, the principles get lost. What people say they believe about marital roles often contradicts what they seem to feel about them.

So to prioritize your respective careers you will need to do some soul-searching. You will need to be honest with each other and communicate your real feelings. Once you openly discuss your desires for your careers, you will eventually come close to balancing the power and respecting one another's goals. Remember, however, that it is a process for most couples.

The quick solution on this issue is rare, as we found in our own experience. Early in our marriage it became evident that both of us valued higher education and wanted to pursue advanced degrees. Each of us wanted to earn doctorates, not so much because we had individual career paths in mind, but because we wanted to stay on equal footing in our relationship. We had seen several examples of one-up-one-down relationships and decided that wasn't for us. With school bills, however, we had to take turns getting our degrees. We had a general plan, not a tidy step-by-step design, that brought us to where we are. And it took our first decade of marriage to achieve our shared dream of two doctorates. Like we said, prioritizing respective careers in marriage does not happen overnight.

—DR. LES PARROTT III AND DR. LESLIE PARROTT

dueling careers

Whose job is more important? Here are ten humorous ways to help you decide whose job is the most important at this time.

1. Both spouses should stay home from work until one of you gets fired. The one who still has the job is now the most important.
2. Move. If your spouse follows, yours is more important. If your spouse stays, his or her job is more important.
3. Ask your boss to duke it out with your spouse's boss.
4. Make a list of relevant criteria such as income, prestige, longevity, potential for advancement, flexibility, number of vacation days, health insurance, etc. Be sure to stack the list with criteria in which your job exceeds your spouse's.
5. Ask the kids, especially if they are under the age of three. Be sure to prep all week by bringing home candy and saying, "It's from my job."
6. Whose job is more convenient when you want to go out after work on a Friday night? Obviously that's the most important job.
7. Which spouse's job requires more travel? If that spouse is also accumulating more frequent flier miles and hotel points, that job is the most important.
8. Ask your mother. Ask his mother.
9. Examine each spouse's wardrobe. Whose job requires more "power suits"? Everyone knows you dress up for the important things—including jobs.
10. Flip a coin, throw a dice or, if you want to be Biblical about it, draw straws.

HOW ARE WE DOING?

date

let's make a DATE

PLAY HOOKY

Both of you take a half day off from work, maybe a Monday morning or a Friday afternoon. Go to the movies, have breakfast in bed or just hang out together while the kids are in school and you're not both exhausted from working. Enjoy your mini-vacation together.

FOR YOUR NEXT DEVOTIONAL READING, TURN TO PAGE 1249.

LESSONS FROM THE *Bible*

Read Mark 12:28–34 to see how Jesus handled a tough question. Then think about how Jesus' response relates to the topic of two-career marriages:

1. What is the most important principle when it comes to deciding whose job determines whether or not we move? Whose job takes priority when determining who will quit or reduce their work hours to take care of children?
2. How do our jobs enable us—or prevent us—from loving God above all and loving others.

"But I was born a citizen," Paul replied.
29Those who were about to question him
withdrew immediately. The commander himself was alarmed when he realized that he had
put Paul, a Roman citizen, in chains.

Before the Sanhedrin

30The next day, since the commander wanted to find out exactly why Paul was being
accused by the Jews, he released him and ordered the chief priests and all the Sanhedrin to
assemble. Then he brought Paul and had him
stand before them.

23 Paul looked straight at the Sanhedrin
and said, "My brothers, I have fulfilled
my duty to God in all good conscience
to this day." 2At this the high priest Ananias
ordered those standing near Paul to strike him
on the mouth. 3Then Paul said to him, "God
will strike you, you whitewashed wall! You sit
there to judge me according to the law, yet you
yourself violate the law by commanding that
I be struck!"
4Those who were standing near Paul said,
"You dare to insult God's high priest?"
5Paul replied, "Brothers, I did not realize that
he was the high priest; for it is written: 'Do not
speak evil about the ruler of your people.'[a]"
6Then Paul, knowing that some of them
were Sadducees and the others Pharisees,
called out in the Sanhedrin, "My brothers, I
am a Pharisee, the son of a Pharisee. I stand on
trial because of my hope in the resurrection of
the dead." 7When he said this, a dispute broke
out between the Pharisees and the Sadducees,
and the assembly was divided. 8(The Sadducees say that there is no resurrection, and that
there are neither angels nor spirits, but the
Pharisees acknowledge them all.)
9There was a great uproar, and some of the
teachers of the law who were Pharisees stood
up and argued vigorously. "We find nothing
wrong with this man," they said. "What if a
spirit or an angel has spoken to him?" 10The
dispute became so violent that the commander was afraid Paul would be torn to pieces by
them. He ordered the troops to go down and
take him away from them by force and bring
him into the barracks.
11The following night the Lord stood near
Paul and said, "Take courage! As you have testified about me in Jerusalem, so you must also
testify in Rome."

The Plot to Kill Paul

12The next morning the Jews formed a conspiracy and bound themselves with an oath
not to eat or drink until they had killed Paul.
13More than forty men were involved in this
plot. 14They went to the chief priests and elders and said, "We have taken a solemn oath
not to eat anything until we have killed Paul.
15Now then, you and the Sanhedrin petition
the commander to bring him before you on
the pretext of wanting more accurate information about his case. We are ready to kill him
before he gets here."
16But when the son of Paul's sister heard of
this plot, he went into the barracks and told
Paul.
17Then Paul called one of the centurions
and said, "Take this young man to the commander; he has something to tell him." 18So
he took him to the commander.
The centurion said, "Paul, the prisoner, sent
for me and asked me to bring this young man
to you because he has something to tell you."
19The commander took the young man by
the hand, drew him aside and asked, "What is
it you want to tell me?"
20He said: "The Jews have agreed to ask you
to bring Paul before the Sanhedrin tomorrow
on the pretext of wanting more accurate information about him. 21Don't give in to them,
because more than forty of them are waiting
in ambush for him. They have taken an oath
not to eat or drink until they have killed him.
They are ready now, waiting for your consent
to their request."
22The commander dismissed the young
man and cautioned him, "Don't tell anyone
that you have reported this to me."

Paul Transferred to Caesarea

23Then he called two of his centurions and
ordered them, "Get ready a detachment of two
hundred soldiers, seventy horsemen and two
hundred spearmen[b] to go to Caesarea at nine
tonight. 24Provide mounts for Paul so that he
may be taken safely to Governor Felix."
25He wrote a letter as follows:

26Claudius Lysias,

To His Excellency, Governor Felix:

Greetings.

27This man was seized by the Jews and
they were about to kill him, but I came

[a] 5 Exodus 22:28 [b] 23 The meaning of the Greek for this word is uncertain.

M

MONDAY

READ ACTS 23:12–22

HOW CAN I HELP?

Honey, I need your help . . ."

I sheepishly went on to explain my predicament. I was in a parking lot 30 minutes from home with our two-year-old in the car, and the front wheel had fallen off the car. Could David quit playing golf and come to help me?

Of course he did what any good husband would do: He packed up his clubs and drove over to assess the car situation and make arrangements with a mechanic.

That's what married folks *do*. They don't leave each other stranded. They stick together and help each other. They're family.

When the son of Paul's sister heard of this plot, he went into the barracks and told Paul.

— Acts 23:16

let's *talk*

- When have we needed each other's help? How did it feel to receive help? To provide help?
- When does helping each other come naturally? When is it tough? What's the difference?
- How would we rate our willingness to help each other in small ways? Our willingness to help in bigger, more courageous ways? How could we improve in these areas?

The apostle Paul's nephew helped out too, but his decision to help his uncle came at a much higher cost than quitting a golf game and driving 30 minutes out of his way. Paul's preaching had gotten Paul into a heap of trouble; a mob of men had banded together and formulated a plan to murder him. When Paul's nephew heard about the plot, he risked his life to warn Paul and report the matter to the commanding officer.

Paul's nephew wasn't just whistle-blowing; he was busting up a conspiracy ring straight out of a spy movie. This was one young man versus 40 thugs who were so vehement in their hatred of Paul that they had made a pact to fast until he was dead! Even the commanding officer sensed the danger and urged Paul's nephew to keep his actions secret.

We don't know for certain what motivated Paul's nephew to do what he did. It's possible that he was a believer in Christ and that he defended Paul as an act of faith. But even if the nephew wasn't a Jesus-follower, we can still learn something from his courage. He loved his uncle and was willing to put himself in grave danger to help him. That's what families do.

It's possible that, at some point in your life together, you'll be faced with a situation like this one—one that involves danger, risk or sacrifice; and you'll have an opportunity to make a heroic choice to help your spouse. But in everyday married life, often the tougher challenge comes by way of the thankless, humdrum, nondramatic opportunities you have to help your spouse and stick by him or her. It may be deciding to take over a household chore when your spouse is exhausted. It may mean listening, speaking words of encouragement or praying together when your spouse is discouraged. Perhaps it will mean giving up a night with friends to stay home and hang out. Or it may mean resolving to speak highly of your spouse when friends speak disparagingly about their own.

It isn't always thrilling to serve. There's no fanfare heralding your nonheroic choice to help behind the scenes and no movie soundtrack playing while you're up to your elbows in dirty dishes. But, hey, that's what married folks *do*.

—DAVID AND KELLI TRUJILLO

FOR YOUR NEXT DEVOTIONAL READING, TURN TO PAGE 1257.

with my troops and rescued him, for I
had learned that he is a Roman citizen.
28I wanted to know why they were accusing him, so I brought him to their Sanhedrin. 29I found that the accusation had
to do with questions about their law, but
there was no charge against him that deserved death or imprisonment. 30When
I was informed of a plot to be carried
out against the man, I sent him to you
at once. I also ordered his accusers to present to you their case against him.

31So the soldiers, carrying out their orders,
took Paul with them during the night and
brought him as far as Antipatris. 32The next
day they let the cavalry go on with him, while
they returned to the barracks. 33When the
cavalry arrived in Caesarea, they delivered the
letter to the governor and handed Paul over to
him. 34The governor read the letter and asked
what province he was from. Learning that he
was from Cilicia, 35he said, "I will hear your
case when your accusers get here." Then he ordered that Paul be kept under guard in Herod's palace.

The Trial Before Felix

24 Five days later the high priest Ananias
went down to Caesarea with some of
the elders and a lawyer named Tertullus,
and they brought their charges against Paul
before the governor. 2When Paul was called
in, Tertullus presented his case before Felix:
"We have enjoyed a long period of peace under you, and your foresight has brought about
reforms in this nation. 3Everywhere and in every way, most excellent Felix, we acknowledge
this with profound gratitude. 4But in order
not to weary you further, I would request that
you be kind enough to hear us briefly.

5"We have found this man to be a troublemaker, stirring up riots among the Jews all over
the world. He is a ringleader of the Nazarene
sect 6and even tried to desecrate the temple; so
we seized him. 8By[a] examining him yourself
you will be able to learn the truth about all
these charges we are bringing against him."

9The Jews joined in the accusation, assert-
ing that these things were true.

10When the governor motioned for him to
speak, Paul replied: "I know that for a number
of years you have been a judge over this nation; so I gladly make my defense. 11You can
easily verify that no more than twelve days ago
I went up to Jerusalem to worship. 12My accusers did not find me arguing with anyone at
the temple, or stirring up a crowd in the synagogues or anywhere else in the city. 13And they
cannot prove to you the charges they are now
making against me. 14However, I admit that I
worship the God of our fathers as a follower
of the Way, which they call a sect. I believe everything that agrees with the Law and that is
written in the Prophets, 15and I have the same
hope in God as these men, that there will be
a resurrection of both the righteous and the
wicked. 16So I strive always to keep my conscience clear before God and man.

17"After an absence of several years, I came
to Jerusalem to bring my people gifts for the
poor and to present offerings. 18I was ceremonially clean when they found me in the temple
courts doing this. There was no crowd with
me, nor was I involved in any disturbance.
19But there are some Jews from the province
of Asia, who ought to be here before you and
bring charges if they have anything against
me. 20Or these who are here should state what
crime they found in me when I stood before
the Sanhedrin— 21unless it was this one thing
I shouted as I stood in their presence: 'It is
concerning the resurrection of the dead that I
am on trial before you today.' "

22Then Felix, who was well acquainted with
the Way, adjourned the proceedings. "When
Lysias the commander comes," he said, "I will
decide your case." 23He ordered the centurion to keep Paul under guard but to give him
some freedom and permit his friends to take
care of his needs.

24Several days later Felix came with his
wife Drusilla, who was a Jewess. He sent for
Paul and listened to him as he spoke about
faith in Christ Jesus. 25As Paul discoursed on
righteousness, self-control and the judgment
to come, Felix was afraid and said, "That's
enough for now! You may leave. When I find
it convenient, I will send for you." 26At the
same time he was hoping that Paul would offer him a bribe, so he sent for him frequently
and talked with him.

27When two years had passed, Felix was
succeeded by Porcius Festus, but because Felix wanted to grant a favor to the Jews, he left
Paul in prison.

---

[a] 6-8 Some manuscripts *him and wanted to judge him according to our law. 7But the commander, Lysias, came and with the use of much force snatched him from our hands 8and ordered his accusers to come before you. By*

The Trial Before Festus

25 Three days after arriving in the province, Festus went up from Caesarea to Jerusalem, 2where the chief priests and Jewish leaders appeared before him and presented the charges against Paul. 3They urgently requested Festus, as a favor to them, to have Paul transferred to Jerusalem, for they were preparing an ambush to kill him along the way. 4Festus answered, "Paul is being held at Caesarea, and I myself am going there soon. 5Let some of your leaders come with me and press charges against the man there, if he has done anything wrong."

6After spending eight or ten days with them, he went down to Caesarea, and the next day he convened the court and ordered that Paul be brought before him. 7When Paul appeared, the Jews who had come down from Jerusalem stood around him, bringing many serious charges against him, which they could not prove.

8Then Paul made his defense: "I have done nothing wrong against the law of the Jews or against the temple or against Caesar."

9Festus, wishing to do the Jews a favor, said to Paul, "Are you willing to go up to Jerusalem and stand trial before me there on these charges?"

10Paul answered: "I am now standing before Caesar's court, where I ought to be tried. I have not done any wrong to the Jews, as you yourself know very well. 11If, however, I am guilty of doing anything deserving death, I do not refuse to die. But if the charges brought against me by these Jews are not true, no one has the right to hand me over to them. I appeal to Caesar!"

12After Festus had conferred with his council, he declared: "You have appealed to Caesar. To Caesar you will go!"

Festus Consults King Agrippa

13A few days later King Agrippa and Bernice arrived at Caesarea to pay their respects to Festus. 14Since they were spending many days there, Festus discussed Paul's case with the king. He said: "There is a man here whom Felix left as a prisoner. 15When I went to Jerusalem, the chief priests and elders of the Jews brought charges against him and asked that he be condemned.

16"I told them that it is not the Roman custom to hand over any man before he has faced his accusers and has had an opportunity to defend himself against their charges. 17When they came here with me, I did not delay the case, but convened the court the next day and ordered the man to be brought in. 18When his accusers got up to speak, they did not charge him with any of the crimes I had expected. 19Instead, they had some points of dispute with him about their own religion and about a dead man named Jesus who Paul claimed was alive. 20I was at a loss how to investigate such matters; so I asked if he would be willing to go to Jerusalem and stand trial there on these charges. 21When Paul made his appeal to be held over for the Emperor's decision, I ordered him held until I could send him to Caesar."

22Then Agrippa said to Festus, "I would like to hear this man myself."

He replied, "Tomorrow you will hear him."

Paul Before Agrippa

23The next day Agrippa and Bernice came with great pomp and entered the audience room with the high ranking officers and the leading men of the city. At the command of Festus, Paul was brought in. 24Festus said: "King Agrippa, and all who are present with us, you see this man! The whole Jewish community has petitioned me about him in Jerusalem and here in Caesarea, shouting that he ought not to live any longer. 25I found he had done nothing deserving of death, but because he made his appeal to the Emperor I decided to send him to Rome. 26But I have nothing definite to write to His Majesty about him. Therefore I have brought him before all of you, and especially before you, King Agrippa, so that as a result of this investigation I may have something to write. 27For I think it is unreasonable to send on a prisoner without specifying the charges against him."

26 Then Agrippa said to Paul, "You have permission to speak for yourself."

So Paul motioned with his hand and began his defense: 2"King Agrippa, I consider myself fortunate to stand before you today as I make my defense against all the accusations of the Jews, 3and especially so because you are well acquainted with all the Jewish customs and controversies. Therefore, I beg you to listen to me patiently.

4"The Jews all know the way I have lived ever since I was a child, from the beginning of my life in my own country, and also in Jerusalem. 5They have known me for a long time and can testify, if they are willing, that according to the strictest sect of our religion, I lived as a Pharisee. 6And now it is because of my hope in what God has promised our fathers that I am on trial today. 7This is the promise our twelve tribes are hoping to see fulfilled as they earnestly serve God day and night. O king, it is because of this hope that the Jews are accusing me. 8Why should any of you consider it incredible that God raises the dead?

9"I too was convinced that I ought to do all that was possible to oppose the name of Jesus of Nazareth. 10And that is just what I did in Jerusalem. On the authority of the chief priests I put many of the saints in prison, and when they were put to death, I cast my vote against them. 11Many a time I went from one synagogue to another to have them punished, and I tried to force them to blaspheme. In my obsession against them, I even went to foreign cities to persecute them.

12"On one of these journeys I was going to Damascus with the authority and commission of the chief priests. 13About noon, O king, as I was on the road, I saw a light from heaven, brighter than the sun, blazing around me and my companions. 14We all fell to the ground, and I heard a voice saying to me in Aramaic,[a] 'Saul, Saul, why do you persecute me? It is hard for you to kick against the goads.'

15"Then I asked, 'Who are you, Lord?'

" 'I am Jesus, whom you are persecuting,' the Lord replied. 16'Now get up and stand on your feet. I have appeared to you to appoint you as a servant and as a witness of what you have seen of me and what I will show you. 17I will rescue you from your own people and from the Gentiles. I am sending you to them 18to open their eyes and turn them from darkness to light, and from the power of Satan to God, so that they may receive forgiveness of sins and a place among those who are sanctified by faith in me.'

19"So then, King Agrippa, I was not disobedient to the vision from heaven. 20First to those in Damascus, then to those in Jerusalem and in all Judea, and to the Gentiles also, I preached that they should repent and turn to God and prove their repentance by their deeds. 21That is why the Jews seized me in the temple courts and tried to kill me. 22But I have had God's help to this very day, and so I stand here and testify to small and great alike. I am saying nothing beyond what the prophets and Moses said would happen— 23that the Christ[b] would suffer and, as the first to rise from the dead, would proclaim light to his own people and to the Gentiles."

24At this point Festus interrupted Paul's defense. "You are out of your mind, Paul!" he shouted. "Your great learning is driving you insane."

25"I am not insane, most excellent Festus," Paul replied. "What I am saying is true and reasonable. 26The king is familiar with these things, and I can speak freely to him. I am convinced that none of this has escaped his notice, because it was not done in a corner. 27King Agrippa, do you believe the prophets? I know you do."

28Then Agrippa said to Paul, "Do you think that in such a short time you can persuade me to be a Christian?"

29Paul replied, "Short time or long—I pray God that not only you but all who are listening to me today may become what I am, except for these chains."

30The king rose, and with him the governor and Bernice and those sitting with them. 31They left the room, and while talking with one another, they said, "This man is not doing anything that deserves death or imprisonment."

32Agrippa said to Festus, "This man could have been set free if he had not appealed to Caesar."

Paul Sails for Rome

27 When it was decided that we would sail for Italy, Paul and some other prisoners were handed over to a centurion named Julius, who belonged to the Imperial Regiment. 2We boarded a ship from Adramyttium about to sail for ports along the coast of the province of Asia, and we put out to sea. Aristarchus, a Macedonian from Thessalonica, was with us.

3The next day we landed at Sidon; and Julius, in kindness to Paul, allowed him to go to his friends so they might provide for his needs. 4From there we put out to sea again and passed to the lee of Cyprus because the winds were against us. 5When we had sailed across the open sea off the coast of Cilicia and Pamphylia, we landed at Myra in Lycia. 6There the centurion found an Alexandrian ship sailing for Italy and put us on board. 7We made slow headway for many days and had difficulty arriving off Cnidus. When the wind did not allow us to hold our course, we sailed to the lee of Crete, opposite Salmone. 8We moved along the coast with difficulty and came to a place called Fair Havens, near the town of Lasea.

9Much time had been lost, and sailing had

---

[a] 14 Or *Hebrew* [b] 23 Or *Messiah*

already become dangerous because by now it was after the Fast.[a] So Paul warned them, 10“Men, I can see that our voyage is going to be disastrous and bring great loss to ship and cargo, and to our own lives also.” 11But the centurion, instead of listening to what Paul said, followed the advice of the pilot and of the owner of the ship. 12Since the harbor was unsuitable to winter in, the majority decided that we should sail on, hoping to reach Phoenix and winter there. This was a harbor in Crete, facing both southwest and northwest.

The Storm

13When a gentle south wind began to blow, they thought they had obtained what they wanted; so they weighed anchor and sailed along the shore of Crete. 14Before very long, a wind of hurricane force, called the “northeaster,” swept down from the island. 15The ship was caught by the storm and could not head into the wind; so we gave way to it and were driven along. 16As we passed to the lee of a small island called Cauda, we were hardly able to make the lifeboat secure. 17When the men had hoisted it aboard, they passed ropes under the ship itself to hold it together. Fearing that they would run aground on the sandbars of Syrtis, they lowered the sea anchor and let the ship be driven along. 18We took such a violent battering from the storm that the next day they began to throw the cargo overboard. 19On the third day, they threw the ship’s tackle overboard with their own hands. 20When neither sun nor stars appeared for many days and the storm continued raging, we finally gave up all hope of being saved.

21After the men had gone a long time without food, Paul stood up before them and said: “Men, you should have taken my advice not to sail from Crete; then you would have spared yourselves this damage and loss. 22But now I urge you to keep up your courage, because not one of you will be lost; only the ship will be destroyed. 23Last night an angel of the God whose I am and whom I serve stood beside me 24and said, ‘Do not be afraid, Paul. You must stand trial before Caesar; and God has graciously given you the lives of all who sail with you.’ 25So keep up your courage, men, for I have faith in God that it will happen just as he told me. 26Nevertheless, we must run aground on some island.”

The Shipwreck

27On the fourteenth night we were still being driven across the Adriatic[b] Sea, when about midnight the sailors sensed they were approaching land. 28They took soundings and found that the water was a hundred and twenty feet[c] deep. A short time later they took soundings again and found it was ninety feet[d] deep. 29Fearing that we would be dashed against the rocks, they dropped four anchors from the stern and prayed for daylight. 30In an attempt to escape from the ship, the sailors let the lifeboat down into the sea, pretending they were going to lower some anchors from the bow. 31Then Paul said to the centurion and the soldiers, “Unless these men stay with the ship, you cannot be saved.” 32So the soldiers cut the ropes that held the lifeboat and let it fall away.

33Just before dawn Paul urged them all to eat. “For the last fourteen days,” he said, “you have been in constant suspense and have gone without food—you haven’t eaten anything. 34Now I urge you to take some food. You need it to survive. Not one of you will lose a single hair from his head.” 35After he said this, he took some bread and gave thanks to God in front of them all. Then he broke it and began to eat. 36They were all encouraged and ate some food themselves. 37Altogether there were 276 of us on board. 38When they had eaten as much as they wanted, they lightened the ship by throwing the grain into the sea.

39When daylight came, they did not recognize the land, but they saw a bay with a sandy beach, where they decided to run the ship aground if they could. 40Cutting loose the anchors, they left them in the sea and at the same time untied the ropes that held the rudders. Then they hoisted the foresail to the wind and made for the beach. 41But the ship struck a sandbar and ran aground. The bow stuck fast and would not move, and the stern was broken to pieces by the pounding of the surf.

42The soldiers planned to kill the prisoners to prevent any of them from swimming away and escaping. 43But the centurion wanted to spare Paul’s life and kept them from carrying out their plan. He ordered those who could swim to jump overboard first and get to land. 44The rest were to get there on planks or on pieces of the ship. In this way everyone reached land in safety.

[a] *9* That is, the Day of Atonement (Yom Kippur) [b] *27* In ancient times the name referred to an area extending well south of Italy.
[c] *28* Greek *twenty orguias* (about 37 meters) [d] *28* Greek *fifteen orguias* (about 27 meters)

Ashore on Malta

28 Once safely on shore, we found out
that the island was called Malta. 2The
islanders showed us unusual kindness.
They built a fire and welcomed us all because
it was raining and cold. 3Paul gathered a pile
of brushwood and, as he put it on the fire, a
viper, driven out by the heat, fastened itself on
his hand. 4When the islanders saw the snake
hanging from his hand, they said to each other, "This man must be a murderer; for though
he escaped from the sea, Justice has not allowed him to live." 5But Paul shook the snake
off into the fire and suffered no ill effects. 6The
people expected him to swell up or suddenly
fall dead, but after waiting a long time and
seeing nothing unusual happen to him, they
changed their minds and said he was a god.
7There was an estate nearby that belonged
to Publius, the chief official of the island. He
welcomed us to his home and for three days
entertained us hospitably. 8His father was
sick in bed, suffering from fever and dysen-
tery. Paul went in to see him and, after prayer,
placed his hands on him and healed him.
9When this had happened, the rest of the sick
on the island came and were cured. 10They
honored us in many ways and when we were
ready to sail, they furnished us with the supplies we needed.

Arrival at Rome

11After three months we put out to sea in
a ship that had wintered in the island. It was
an Alexandrian ship with the figurehead of the
twin gods Castor and Pollux. 12We put in at
Syracuse and stayed there three days. 13From
there we set sail and arrived at Rhegium. The
next day the south wind came up, and on the
following day we reached Puteoli. 14There we
found some brothers who invited us to spend
a week with them. And so we came to Rome.
15The brothers there had heard that we were
coming, and they traveled as far as the Forum
of Appius and the Three Taverns to meet us.
At the sight of these men Paul thanked God
and was encouraged. 16When we got to Rome,
Paul was allowed to live by himself, with a soldier to guard him.

Paul Preaches at Rome Under Guard

17Three days later he called together the
leaders of the Jews. When they had assembled,
Paul said to them: "My brothers, although
I have done nothing against our people or
against the customs of our ancestors, I was arrested in Jerusalem and handed over to the Romans. 18They examined me and wanted to release me, because I was not guilty of any crime
deserving death. 19But when the Jews objected, I was compelled to appeal to Caesar—not
that I had any charge to bring against my own
people. 20For this reason I have asked to see
you and talk with you. It is because of the hope
of Israel that I am bound with this chain."
21They replied, "We have not received any
letters from Judea concerning you, and none
of the brothers who have come from there
has reported or said anything bad about you.
22But we want to hear what your views are, for
we know that people everywhere are talking
against this sect."
23They arranged to meet Paul on a certain
day, and came in even larger numbers to the
place where he was staying. From morning till
evening he explained and declared to them the
kingdom of God and tried to convince them
about Jesus from the Law of Moses and from
the Prophets. 24Some were convinced by what
he said, but others would not believe. 25They
disagreed among themselves and began to leave
after Paul had made this final statement: "The
Holy Spirit spoke the truth to your forefathers
when he said through Isaiah the prophet:

26" 'Go to this people and say,
"You will be ever hearing but never
understanding;
you will be ever seeing but never
perceiving."
27 For this people's heart has become
calloused;
they hardly hear with their ears,
and they have closed their eyes.
Otherwise they might see with their eyes,
hear with their ears,
understand with their hearts
and turn, and I would heal them.' [a]

28"Therefore I want you to know that God's
salvation has been sent to the Gentiles, and
they will listen!" [b]
30For two whole years Paul stayed there in
his own rented house and welcomed all who
came to see him. 31Boldly and without hindrance he preached the kingdom of God and
taught about the Lord Jesus Christ.

---

a 27 Isaiah 6:9,10 *b 28* Some manuscripts *listen!" 29After he said this, the Jews left, arguing vigorously among themselves.*

ROMANS

Romans

QUICK FACTS

AUTHOR The apostle Paul

AUDIENCE Christians in Rome, most of whom were Gentiles

DATE About A.D. 57

SETTING Probably written from Corinth, regarding Paul's pending visit to Rome via Jerusalem

Paul wrote to Christian believers in Rome while he was on his third missionary journey. Since Paul couldn't come to Rome in person at that time, he wrote to them about the basics of the Christian faith. Although the book of Romans is warmly affectionate, it contains a great deal of doctrinal teaching. This book gives us valuable insights into Christian behavior, our sinful nature, the content of the gospel and the righteousness of God. It also explains in detail how Jews and Gentiles fit into God's plan.

The book of Romans contains important teaching to ground a new believer in Christ; it explains how we can be saved from sin, how we are justified by faith and how we can live in the power of the Holy Spirit. It also explains in detail the nature of God and how our relationship with him radically changes the way we live.

Paul prayed for the Roman Christians with great fervor and longed to see them (see Romans 1:9–11). His concern for them went beyond surface things; he desired that their lives be changed as they learned to follow Christ. We can follow Paul's example as we pray for our spouses with the same kind of fervor, longing for their spiritual welfare above all else.

1 Paul, a servant of Christ Jesus, called to be an apostle and set apart for the gospel of God— 2the gospel he promised beforehand through his prophets in the Holy Scriptures 3regarding his Son, who as to his human nature was a descendant of David, 4and who through the Spirit[a] of holiness was declared with power to be the Son of God[b] by his resurrection from the dead: Jesus Christ our Lord. 5Through him and for his name's sake, we received grace and apostleship to call people from among all the Gentiles to the obedience that comes from faith. 6And you also are among those who are called to belong to Jesus Christ.

7To all in Rome who are loved by God and called to be saints:

Grace and peace to you from God our Father and from the Lord Jesus Christ.

Paul's Longing to Visit Rome

8First, I thank my God through Jesus Christ for all of you, because your faith is being reported all over the world. 9God, whom I serve with my whole heart in preaching the gospel of his Son, is my witness how constantly I remember you 10in my prayers at all times; and I pray that now at last by God's will the way may be opened for me to come to you.

11I long to see you so that I may impart to you some spiritual gift to make you strong— 12that is, that you and I may be mutually encouraged by each other's faith. 13I do not want you to be unaware, brothers, that I planned many times to come to you (but have been prevented from doing so until now) in order that I might have a harvest among you, just as I have had among the other Gentiles.

14I am obligated both to Greeks and non-Greeks, both to the wise and the foolish. 15That is why I am so eager to preach the gospel also to you who are at Rome.

16I am not ashamed of the gospel, because it is the power of God for the salvation of everyone who believes: first for the Jew, then for the Gentile. 17For in the gospel a righteousness from God is revealed, a righteousness that is by faith from first to last,[c] just as it is written: "The righteous will live by faith."[d]

God's Wrath Against Mankind

18The wrath of God is being revealed from heaven against all the godlessness and wickedness of men who suppress the truth by their wickedness, 19since what may be known about God is plain to them, because God has made it plain to them. 20For since the creation of the world God's invisible qualities—his eternal power and divine nature—have been clearly seen, being understood from what has been made, so that men are without excuse.

21For although they knew God, they neither glorified him as God nor gave thanks to him, but their thinking became futile and their foolish hearts were darkened. 22Although they claimed to be wise, they became fools 23and exchanged the glory of the immortal God for images made to look like mortal man and birds and animals and reptiles.

24Therefore God gave them over in the sinful desires of their hearts to sexual impurity for the degrading of their bodies with one another. 25They exchanged the truth of God for a lie, and worshiped and served created things rather than the Creator—who is forever praised. Amen.

26Because of this, God gave them over to shameful lusts. Even their women exchanged natural relations for unnatural ones. 27In the same way the men also abandoned natural relations with women and were inflamed with lust for one another. Men committed indecent acts with other men, and received in themselves the due penalty for their perversion.

28Furthermore, since they did not think it worthwhile to retain the knowledge of God, he gave them over to a depraved mind, to do what ought not to be done. 29They have become filled with every kind of wickedness, evil, greed and depravity. They are full of envy, murder, strife, deceit and malice. They are gossips, 30slanderers, God-haters, insolent, arrogant and boastful; they invent ways of doing evil; they disobey their parents; 31they are senseless, faithless, heartless, ruthless. 32Although they know God's righteous decree that those who do such things deserve death, they not only continue to do these very things but also approve of those who practice them.

God's Righteous Judgment

2 You, therefore, have no excuse, you who pass judgment on someone else, for at whatever point you judge the other, you are condemning yourself, because you who pass judgment do the same things. 2Now we know that God's judgment against those who do such things is based on truth. 3So when you, a mere man, pass judgment on them and yet do

[a] 4 Or *who as to his spirit* [b] 4 Or *was appointed to be the Son of God with power* [c] 17 Or *is from faith to faith* [d] 17 Hab. 2:4

WHEN OUR PLANS DON'T WORK OUT

Sometimes, when I'm feeling defeated by my own spiritual mediocrity, I'll whine, "OK, so I'm not the apostle Paul. But he had a few advantages in his spiritual life."

The truth is, Paul faced the same struggles I face. Furthermore, God gives grace in equal measure to everyone. In Matthew 5:45 Jesus said, "[God] causes his sun to rise on the evil and the good, and sends rain on the righteous and the unrighteous." So because we're all on a level playing field, it's a good idea to see how Paul fared when he experienced disappointments, delayed answers to prayers, detours around his plans, suffering, shortages, deprivation—the kinds of things most marriages face today.

A husband and wife who had recently graduated from college had wonderful plans for their lives. They were going to move to their dream town in the Colorado mountains, get high-paying jobs in their fields of expertise, pay off their college loans, wait to start a family and enjoy being married.

But God's plans for them were different. The couple moved to a not-so-dreamy town, but it was one they could afford to live in. They did construction work and house cleaning while waiting, and waiting, for offers from companies they had applied to for those dream jobs. Then, surprise! She got pregnant. What would Paul say to them?

I long to see you so that I may impart to you some spiritual gift to make you strong—that is, that you and I may be mutually encouraged by each other's faith.

— ROMANS 1:11–12

let's talk

- What are some plans we have had for the future that still haven't been fulfilled? How might our lives have been less dependent on God had those personal dreams been fulfilled? How might our marriage have been different?
- In what ways is it wrong to plan for the future as a couple? In what ways is it wrong not to plan?
- What happens inside us when we are grateful to God when our plans don't work out?

He probably wouldn't serve up any platitudes like "We know that in all things God works for the good of those who love him" (Romans 8:28). Although that *is* true, Paul would understand this young couple's frustration in seeing none of their dreams coming true.

Instead, Paul might tell them a bit of his own story and some of the lessons he learned. He would want to be "mutually encouraged"—as he mentioned to the Christians in Rome (Romans 1:12)—humbly desiring both to minister *to* them and to be ministered to *by* them. He might talk about how, even in the midst of our trials, we can choose to thank God for his guidance in our lives. We can ask for wisdom to view God's unfolding plans for us as unexpected opportunities to serve him become available. We can remember that people are watching to see how we react to our challenges. We can grow and mature as we put faith to work in our lives.

This couple learned those lessons. When they talked with their parents about the coming baby, they said, "We are learning to trust God through all this. We're not sure why it's happening, but we're not moving an inch from God, and we'll just see what happens as these detours guide us down the road we're to travel."

What parents wouldn't be thrilled to hear their children express such faith and be encouraged in their own faith by such a testimony? Likewise, our heavenly Father is pleased to give us, his children, the best life possible as we trust him.

—MARY ANN JEFFREYS

FOR YOUR NEXT DEVOTIONAL READING, TURN TO PAGE 1259.

the same things, do you think you will escape God's judgment? [4]Or do you show contempt for the riches of his kindness, tolerance and patience, not realizing that God's kindness leads you toward repentance?

[5]But because of your stubbornness and your unrepentant heart, you are storing up wrath against yourself for the day of God's wrath, when his righteous judgment will be revealed. [6]God "will give to each person according to what he has done."[a] [7]To those who by persistence in doing good seek glory, honor and immortality, he will give eternal life. [8]But for those who are self-seeking and who reject the truth and follow evil, there will be wrath and anger. [9]There will be trouble and distress for every human being who does evil: first for the Jew, then for the Gentile; [10]but glory, honor and peace for everyone who does good: first for the Jew, then for the Gentile. [11]For God does not show favoritism.

[12]All who sin apart from the law will also perish apart from the law, and all who sin under the law will be judged by the law. [13]For it is not those who hear the law who are righteous in God's sight, but it is those who obey the law who will be declared righteous. [14](Indeed, when Gentiles, who do not have the law, do by nature things required by the law, they are a law for themselves, even though they do not have the law, [15]since they show that the requirements of the law are written on their hearts, their consciences also bearing witness, and their thoughts now accusing, now even defending them.) [16]This will take place on the day when God will judge men's secrets through Jesus Christ, as my gospel declares.

The Jews and the Law

[17]Now you, if you call yourself a Jew; if you rely on the law and brag about your relationship to God; [18]if you know his will and approve of what is superior because you are instructed by the law; [19]if you are convinced that you are a guide for the blind, a light for those who are in the dark, [20]an instructor of the foolish, a teacher of infants, because you have in the law the embodiment of knowledge and truth— [21]you, then, who teach others, do you not teach yourself? You who preach against stealing, do you steal? [22]You who say that people should not commit adultery, do you commit adultery? You who abhor idols, do you rob temples? [23]You who brag about the law, do you dishonor God by breaking the law? [24]As it is written: "God's name is blasphemed among the Gentiles because of you."[b]

[25]Circumcision has value if you observe the law, but if you break the law, you have become as though you had not been circumcised. [26]If those who are not circumcised keep the law's requirements, will they not be regarded as though they were circumcised? [27]The one who is not circumcised physically and yet obeys the law will condemn you who, even though you have the[c] written code and circumcision, are a lawbreaker.

[28]A man is not a Jew if he is only one outwardly, nor is circumcision merely outward and physical. [29]No, a man is a Jew if he is one inwardly; and circumcision is circumcision of the heart, by the Spirit, not by the written code. Such a man's praise is not from men, but from God.

God's Faithfulness

3 What advantage, then, is there in being a Jew, or what value is there in circumcision? [2]Much in every way! First of all, they have been entrusted with the very words of God.

[3]What if some did not have faith? Will their lack of faith nullify God's faithfulness? [4]Not at all! Let God be true, and every man a liar. As it is written:

> "So that you may be proved right when
> you speak
> and prevail when you judge."[d]

[5]But if our unrighteousness brings out God's righteousness more clearly, what shall we say? That God is unjust in bringing his wrath on us? (I am using a human argument.) [6]Certainly not! If that were so, how could God judge the world? [7]Someone might argue, "If my falsehood enhances God's truthfulness and so increases his glory, why am I still condemned as a sinner?" [8]Why not say—as we are being slanderously reported as saying and as some claim that we say—"Let us do evil that good may result"? Their condemnation is deserved.

No One Is Righteous

[9]What shall we conclude then? Are we any better[e]? Not at all! We have already made the charge that Jews and Gentiles alike are all under sin. [10]As it is written:

> "There is no one righteous, not even one;

[a] *6* Psalm 62:12; Prov. 24:12 [b] *24* Isaiah 52:5; Ezek. 36:22 [c] *27* Or *who, by means of a* [d] *4* Psalm 51:4 [e] *9* Or *worse*

WEDNESDAY
READ ROMANS 2:1–16

JUDGING OTHERS

I was silently fuming in the passenger seat as we drove home. My husband had made a remark about a friend's annoying habit, and it made me furious. I kept getting madder about the comment, thinking, "David is so judgmental! He has such a critical spirit! He is so self-righteous!"

I then mentally took inventory of all of my spouse's faults and failings, most notably—of course—his judgmental spirit. Eventually, when I could no longer bite my tongue, I let him have it.

The not-so-subtle irony here, of course, is that *I* was the one who was being judgmental! I had slipped into self-righteousness without realizing it.

The temptation to judge others is so appealing. It feeds our appetite for self-congratulation. It strokes our ego, assuring us that we are better than everyone else. And in marriage, this temptation is magnified as we view our spouse's faults, from big issues of sin right down to everyday infractions like neglecting to cap the toothpaste.

So when you, a mere man, pass judgment on them and yet do the same things, do you think you will escape God's judgment?

— ROMANS 2:3

let's talk

- ✦ Why is it tempting to be critical of others? What's the effect? Do we become less tolerant of ourselves when we fail?
- ✦ When are we most judgmental of each other? What situations tend to fuel that? What is usually the effect?
- ✦ How can we help each other grow in humility, grace and forgiveness toward each other?

We can learn a lesson about self-righteousness from the Jewish people described in Romans 2. Because they were God's chosen people, the Jews thought they were exempt from the judgment poured out by God on unbelieving Gentiles. And as Paul built his case against Gentile unbelievers in Romans 1:18–32, we can imagine the Jews standing back, nodding in agreement, and saying, "That's right. Give it to them, Paul! Dirty sinners!"

Then Paul set things straight by, in effect, saying to his own people, "You are even more guilty than those Gentiles, for you know God's law and still do the evil things they do." Paul went on to reveal a brutal reality: We are all on an even playing field. No one is exempt from God's wrath. All of us need a Savior. And yet, even when we profess Jesus as our Savior, we still struggle with sin.

Only when we come to terms with the theological reality that each of us is a sinner created and treasured by God will we understand that passing judgment on others is just plain wrong—first, because we're guilty of doing the same things and, second, because judgmentalism only adds to that sin. So Paul warned: "Do not think of yourself more highly than you ought, but rather think of yourself with sober judgment" (Romans 12:3).

The closer we get to people, the more we see their faults. Nowhere is that more evident than in marriage. The reality is that your spouse *is* a sinner saved by grace. He or she will mess up, fall, fail, forget you, neglect you, annoy you and overlook you. But *you* will do the same. So we must continually examine ourselves, measuring what we do against the yardstick of Scripture. With the help of the Holy Spirit, we battle pride, judgmentalism, self-righteousness and a critical spirit so that we may grow together in grace, forgiveness and humility.

—DAVID AND KELLI TRUJILLO

FOR YOUR NEXT DEVOTIONAL READING, TURN TO PAGE 1262.

11 there is no one who understands,
no one who seeks God.
12 All have turned away,
they have together become worthless;
there is no one who does good,
not even one."[a]
13 "Their throats are open graves;
their tongues practice deceit."[b]
"The poison of vipers is on their lips."[c]
14 "Their mouths are full of cursing and
bitterness."[d]
15 "Their feet are swift to shed blood;
16 ruin and misery mark their ways,
17 and the way of peace they do not know."[e]
18 "There is no fear of God before their
eyes."[f]

19 Now we know that whatever the law says,
it says to those who are under the law, so that
every mouth may be silenced and the whole
world held accountable to God. 20 Therefore
no one will be declared righteous in his sight
by observing the law; rather, through the law
we become conscious of sin.

Righteousness Through Faith

21 But now a righteousness from God, apart
from law, has been made known, to which the
Law and the Prophets testify. 22 This righteousness from God comes through faith in Jesus
Christ to all who believe. There is no difference, 23 for all have sinned and fall short of the
glory of God, 24 and are justified freely by his
grace through the redemption that came by
Christ Jesus. 25 God presented him as a sacrifice of atonement,[g] through faith in his blood.
He did this to demonstrate his justice, because
in his forbearance he had left the sins committed beforehand unpunished— 26 he did it
to demonstrate his justice at the present time,
so as to be just and the one who justifies those
who have faith in Jesus.

27 Where, then, is boasting? It is excluded.
On what principle? On that of observing the
law? No, but on that of faith. 28 For we maintain that a man is justified by faith apart from
observing the law. 29 Is God the God of Jews
only? Is he not the God of Gentiles too? Yes,
of Gentiles too, 30 since there is only one God,
who will justify the circumcised by faith and
the uncircumcised through that same faith.
31 Do we, then, nullify the law by this faith?
Not at all! Rather, we uphold the law.

Abraham Justified by Faith

4 What then shall we say that Abraham, our
forefather, discovered in this matter? 2 If,
in fact, Abraham was justified by works,
he had something to boast about—but not
before God. 3 What does the Scripture say?
"Abraham believed God, and it was credited
to him as righteousness."[h]

4 Now when a man works, his wages are not
credited to him as a gift, but as an obligation.
5 However, to the man who does not work but
trusts God who justifies the wicked, his faith
is credited as righteousness. 6 David says the
same thing when he speaks of the blessedness
of the man to whom God credits righteousness apart from works:

7 "Blessed are they
whose transgressions are forgiven,
whose sins are covered.
8 Blessed is the man
whose sin the Lord will never count
against him."[i]

9 Is this blessedness only for the circumcised, or also for the uncircumcised? We have
been saying that Abraham's faith was credited
to him as righteousness. 10 Under what circumstances was it credited? Was it after he was
circumcised, or before? It was not after, but
before! 11 And he received the sign of circumcision, a seal of the righteousness that he had
by faith while he was still uncircumcised. So
then, he is the father of all who believe but
have not been circumcised, in order that righteousness might be credited to them. 12 And he
is also the father of the circumcised who not
only are circumcised but who also walk in the
footsteps of the faith that our father Abraham
had before he was circumcised.

13 It was not through law that Abraham
and his offspring received the promise that
he would be heir of the world, but through
the righteousness that comes by faith. 14 For
if those who live by law are heirs, faith has no
value and the promise is worthless, 15 because
law brings wrath. And where there is no law
there is no transgression.

16 Therefore, the promise comes by faith, so
that it may be by grace and may be guaranteed
to all Abraham's offspring—not only to those
who are of the law but also to those who are of
the faith of Abraham. He is the father of us all.
17 As it is written: "I have made you a father of
many nations."[j] He is our father in the sight
of God, in whom he believed—the God who

a *12* Psalms 14:1-3; 53:1-3; Eccles. 7:20 *b* *13* Psalm 5:9 *c* *13* Psalm 140:3 *d* *14* Psalm 10:7 *e* *17* Isaiah 59:7,8 *f* *18* Psalm 36:1
g *25* *Or as the one who would turn aside his wrath, taking away sin* *h* *3* Gen. 15:6; also in verse 22 *i* *8* Psalm 32:1,2 *j* *17* Gen. 17:5

gives life to the dead and calls things that are
not as though they were.
[18]Against all hope, Abraham in hope believed and so became the father of many nations, just as it had been said to him, "So shall
your offspring be."[a] [19]Without weakening in
his faith, he faced the fact that his body was
as good as dead—since he was about a hundred years old—and that Sarah's womb was
also dead. [20]Yet he did not waver through
unbelief regarding the promise of God, but
was strengthened in his faith and gave glory
to God, [21]being fully persuaded that God had
power to do what he had promised. [22]This is
why "it was credited to him as righteousness."
[23]The words "it was credited to him" were
written not for him alone, [24]but also for us,
to whom God will credit righteousness—for
us who believe in him who raised Jesus our
Lord from the dead. [25]He was delivered over
to death for our sins and was raised to life for
our justification.

Peace and Joy

5 Therefore, since we have been justified
through faith, we[b] have peace with God
through our Lord Jesus Christ, [2]through
whom we have gained access by faith into this
grace in which we now stand. And we[b] rejoice in the hope of the glory of God. [3]Not
only so, but we[b] also rejoice in our sufferings,
because we know that suffering produces perseverance; [4]perseverance, character; and character, hope. [5]And hope does not disappoint
us, because God has poured out his love into
our hearts by the Holy Spirit, whom he has
given us.
[6]You see, at just the right time, when we
were still powerless, Christ died for the ungodly. [7]Very rarely will anyone die for a righteous
man, though for a good man someone might
possibly dare to die. [8]But God demonstrates
his own love for us in this: While we were still
sinners, Christ died for us.
[9]Since we have now been justified by his
blood, how much more shall we be saved
from God's wrath through him! [10]For if, when
we were God's enemies, we were reconciled to
him through the death of his Son, how much
more, having been reconciled, shall we be
saved through his life! [11]Not only is this so,
but we also rejoice in God through our Lord
Jesus Christ, through whom we have now received reconciliation.

Death Through Adam, Life Through Christ

[12]Therefore, just as sin entered the world
through one man, and death through sin, and
in this way death came to all men, because all
sinned— [13]for before the law was given, sin
was in the world. But sin is not taken into account when there is no law. [14]Nevertheless,
death reigned from the time of Adam to the
time of Moses, even over those who did not
sin by breaking a command, as did Adam,
who was a pattern of the one to come.
[15]But the gift is not like the trespass. For
if the many died by the trespass of the one
man, how much more did God's grace and the
gift that came by the grace of the one man,
Jesus Christ, overflow to the many! [16]Again,
the gift of God is not like the result of the one
man's sin: The judgment followed one sin and
brought condemnation, but the gift followed
many trespasses and brought justification.
[17]For if, by the trespass of the one man, death
reigned through that one man, how much
more will those who receive God's abundant
provision of grace and of the gift of righteousness reign in life through the one man, Jesus
Christ.
[18]Consequently, just as the result of one
trespass was condemnation for all men, so also
the result of one act of righteousness was justification that brings life for all men. [19]For just
as through the disobedience of the one man
the many were made sinners, so also through
the obedience of the one man the many will
be made righteous.
[20]The law was added so that the trespass
might increase. But where sin increased, grace
increased all the more, [21]so that, just as sin
reigned in death, so also grace might reign
through righteousness to bring eternal life
through Jesus Christ our Lord.

Dead to Sin, Alive in Christ

6 What shall we say, then? Shall we go on
sinning so that grace may increase? [2]By no
means! We died to sin; how can we live in
it any longer? [3]Or don't you know that all of
us who were baptized into Christ Jesus were
baptized into his death? [4]We were therefore
buried with him through baptism into death
in order that, just as Christ was raised from
the dead through the glory of the Father, we
too may live a new life.
[5]If we have been united with him like this
in his death, we will certainly also be united
with him in his resurrection. [6]For we know

a 18 Gen. 15:5 *b 1,2,3* Or *let us*

THURSDAY
READ ROMANS 5:1–11

THE REWARDS OF SUFFERING

Karen waited decades for someone as special as Wally to come along. She met him at the dealership where she bought her car. They dated for two years and then married. A few months after the wedding, Wally was diagnosed with cancer. The couple's plans to travel and lie on soft, sandy beaches evaporated. Instead, most of their time was taken up with doctor appointments, surgeries and chemotherapy.

Karen and Wally depended on God's strength and the support of friends to get through the hard times. They even leaned on their friends' faith when their own faith wavered.

Wally's final days on earth were rough. Yet Karen's love for her husband didn't waver. "As tragic and unfair and terrible as Wally's illness and dying were—he was a big, burly man and to see him waste away broke my heart—it was an incredible time," Karen said. She didn't want Wally to die in their bed, so Karen asked friends to transfer him to a hospital bed that she had set up in the living room. As they waited for their friends to come, Wally kept asking, "What time is it? What time are they coming to move me?"

Their friends came, cleaned Wally up and moved him into the living room, directly under a skylight. As they all gathered around the bed and started to pray, Wally and Karen's two dachshunds, Frank and Beans, scurried circles around the bed, their toenails scratching on the bare wood.

Not more than five minutes later, Wally died. As he did, the clouds overhead parted and two beams of light shot through the skylight.

"It was awesome," Karen said. "God came! I will always have that memory."

Jesus said that in this world we will have trouble, but because he has overcome the world, we can have hope in our sorrow and suffering (see John 16:33). As we see in Romans 5, pain, trials, heartache and loss are not the end for believers but a way through which God produces in us perseverance, which produces character, which produces hope—all of which lead us to eternal glory.

Days before he died, Wally said to Karen, "If I had known about the cancer, I never would have married you. It's not fair to you to have to take care of me like this."

Karen replied, "If I had known you would have cancer, I still would have married you because without that I wouldn't have learned how powerful God is. I don't regret one minute of it. Taking care of you has been my great honor."

Romans 5:5 tells us, "Hope does not disappoint us, because God has poured out his love into our hearts by the Holy Spirit, whom has he has given us." Karen will miss her husband—as we all will miss our spouses one day when we are separated by death—but that's not the end of the story. Wally's suffering is over; he is now pain-free. He is with Christ, who is watching over Karen. And one day both Karen and Wally, together with all the saints, will worship their Lord and Savior for all eternity.

—NANCY KENNEDY

We also rejoice in our sufferings, because we know that suffering produces perseverance; perseverance, character; and character, hope.

— Romans 5:3–4

let's talk

✦ Not all suffering involves illness and death. In what ways have we suffered since being married?

✦ What lessons has suffering taught us?

✦ How can suffering tear a couple apart? Bring them together?

FOR YOUR NEXT DEVOTIONAL READING, TURN TO PAGE 1265.

that our old self was crucified with him so that
the body of sin might be done away with,[a]
that we should no longer be slaves to sin—
7because anyone who has died has been freed
from sin.

8Now if we died with Christ, we believe
that we will also live with him. 9For we know
that since Christ was raised from the dead, he
cannot die again; death no longer has mastery
over him. 10The death he died, he died to sin
once for all; but the life he lives, he lives to
God.

11In the same way, count yourselves dead to
sin but alive to God in Christ Jesus. 12There-
fore do not let sin reign in your mortal body
so that you obey its evil desires. 13Do not offer
the parts of your body to sin, as instruments
of wickedness, but rather offer yourselves to
God, as those who have been brought from
death to life; and offer the parts of your body
to him as instruments of righteousness. 14For
sin shall not be your master, because you are
not under law, but under grace.

Slaves to Righteousness

15What then? Shall we sin because we
are not under law but under grace? By no
means! 16Don't you know that when you
offer yourselves to someone to obey him as
slaves, you are slaves to the one whom you
obey—whether you are slaves to sin, which
leads to death, or to obedience, which leads
to righteousness? 17But thanks be to God
that, though you used to be slaves to sin, you
wholeheartedly obeyed the form of teaching
to which you were entrusted. 18You have been
set free from sin and have become slaves to
righteousness.

19I put this in human terms because you
are weak in your natural selves. Just as you
used to offer the parts of your body in slavery to impurity and to ever-increasing wickedness, so now offer them in slavery to righteousness leading to holiness. 20When you
were slaves to sin, you were free from the
control of righteousness. 21What benefit did
you reap at that time from the things you
are now ashamed of? Those things result in
death! 22But now that you have been set free
from sin and have become slaves to God, the
benefit you reap leads to holiness, and the result is eternal life. 23For the wages of sin is
death, but the gift of God is eternal life in[b]
Christ Jesus our Lord.

An Illustration From Marriage

7 Do you not know, brothers—for I am
speaking to men who know the law—that
the law has authority over a man only as
long as he lives? 2For example, by law a married woman is bound to her husband as long
as he is alive, but if her husband dies, she is
released from the law of marriage. 3So then, if
she marries another man while her husband is
still alive, she is called an adulteress. But if her
husband dies, she is released from that law and
is not an adulteress, even though she marries
another man.

4So, my brothers, you also died to the law
through the body of Christ, that you might
belong to another, to him who was raised
from the dead, in order that we might bear
fruit to God. 5For when we were controlled by
the sinful nature,[c] the sinful passions aroused
by the law were at work in our bodies, so that
we bore fruit for death. 6But now, by dying to
what once bound us, we have been released
from the law so that we serve in the new way
of the Spirit, and not in the old way of the
written code.

Struggling With Sin

7What shall we say, then? Is the law sin?
Certainly not! Indeed I would not have known
what sin was except through the law. For I
would not have known what coveting really
was if the law had not said, "Do not covet."[d]
8But sin, seizing the opportunity afforded by
the commandment, produced in me every
kind of covetous desire. For apart from law,
sin is dead. 9Once I was alive apart from law;
but when the commandment came, sin sprang
to life and I died. 10I found that the very commandment that was intended to bring life
actually brought death. 11For sin, seizing the
opportunity afforded by the commandment,
deceived me, and through the commandment
put me to death. 12So then, the law is holy,
and the commandment is holy, righteous and
good.

13Did that which is good, then, become
death to me? By no means! But in order that
sin might be recognized as sin, it produced
death in me through what was good, so that
through the commandment sin might become
utterly sinful.

14We know that the law is spiritual; but I
am unspiritual, sold as a slave to sin. 15I do not
understand what I do. For what I want to do I
do not do, but what I hate I do. 16And if I do

[a] 6 Or *be rendered powerless* [b] 23 Or *through* [c] 5 Or *the flesh*; also in verse 25 [d] 7 Exodus 20:17; Deut. 5:21

what I do not want to do, I agree that the law
is good. 17As it is, it is no longer I myself who
do it, but it is sin living in me. 18I know that
nothing good lives in me, that is, in my sinful
nature.[a] For I have the desire to do what is
good, but I cannot carry it out. 19For what I
do is not the good I want to do; no, the evil
I do not want to do—this I keep on doing.
20Now if I do what I do not want to do, it is
no longer I who do it, but it is sin living in me
that does it.

21So I find this law at work: When I want to
do good, evil is right there with me. 22For in
my inner being I delight in God's law; 23but I
see another law at work in the members of my
body, waging war against the law of my mind
and making me a prisoner of the law of sin at
work within my members. 24What a wretched
man I am! Who will rescue me from this body
of death? 25Thanks be to God—through Jesus
Christ our Lord!

So then, I myself in my mind am a slave to
God's law, but in the sinful nature a slave to
the law of sin.

Life Through the Spirit

8 Therefore, there is now no condemnation
for those who are in Christ Jesus,[b] 2because
through Christ Jesus the law of the Spirit of
life set me free from the law of sin and death.
3For what the law was powerless to do in that
it was weakened by the sinful nature,[c] God
did by sending his own Son in the likeness of
sinful man to be a sin offering.[d] And so he
condemned sin in sinful man,[e] 4in order that
the righteous requirements of the law might
be fully met in us, who do not live according to the sinful nature but according to the
Spirit.

5Those who live according to the sinful
nature have their minds set on what that nature desires; but those who live in accordance
with the Spirit have their minds set on what
the Spirit desires. 6The mind of sinful man[f] is
death, but the mind controlled by the Spirit is
life and peace; 7the sinful mind[g] is hostile to
God. It does not submit to God's law, nor can
it do so. 8Those controlled by the sinful nature
cannot please God.

9You, however, are controlled not by the
sinful nature but by the Spirit, if the Spirit
of God lives in you. And if anyone does not
have the Spirit of Christ, he does not belong
to Christ. 10But if Christ is in you, your body
is dead because of sin, yet your spirit is alive
because of righteousness. 11And if the Spirit of
him who raised Jesus from the dead is living in
you, he who raised Christ from the dead will
also give life to your mortal bodies through his
Spirit, who lives in you.

12Therefore, brothers, we have an obligation—but it is not to the sinful nature, to live
according to it. 13For if you live according to
the sinful nature, you will die; but if by the
Spirit you put to death the misdeeds of the
body, you will live, 14because those who are
led by the Spirit of God are sons of God. 15For
you did not receive a spirit that makes you a
slave again to fear, but you received the Spirit
of sonship.[h] And by him we cry, "*Abba*,[i] Father." 16The Spirit himself testifies with our
spirit that we are God's children. 17Now if we
are children, then we are heirs—heirs of God
and co-heirs with Christ, if indeed we share in
his sufferings in order that we may also share
in his glory.

Future Glory

18I consider that our present sufferings are
not worth comparing with the glory that will
be revealed in us. 19The creation waits in eager
expectation for the sons of God to be revealed.
20For the creation was subjected to frustration,
not by its own choice, but by the will of the
one who subjected it, in hope 21that[j] the creation itself will be liberated from its bondage to
decay and brought into the glorious freedom
of the children of God.

22We know that the whole creation has
been groaning as in the pains of childbirth
right up to the present time. 23Not only so,
but we ourselves, who have the firstfruits of
the Spirit, groan inwardly as we wait eagerly
for our adoption as sons, the redemption of
our bodies. 24For in this hope we were saved.
But hope that is seen is no hope at all. Who
hopes for what he already has? 25But if we
hope for what we do not yet have, we wait for
it patiently.

26In the same way, the Spirit helps us in our
weakness. We do not know what we ought to
pray for, but the Spirit himself intercedes for us
with groans that words cannot express. 27And
he who searches our hearts knows the mind of
the Spirit, because the Spirit intercedes for the
saints in accordance with God's will.

---

[a] *18* Or *my flesh* [b] *1* Some later manuscripts *Jesus, who do not live according to the sinful nature but according to the Spirit,* [c] *3* Or *the flesh*; also in verses 4, 5, 8, 9, 12 and 13 [d] *3* Or *man, for sin* [e] *3* Or *in the flesh* [f] *6* Or *mind set on the flesh* [g] *7* Or the *mind set on the flesh* [h] *15* Or *adoption* [i] *15* Aramaic for *Father* [j] *20,21* Or *subjected it in hope.* [21]*For*

FRIDAY
READ ROMANS 8:1–17

COMING CLEAN WITH EACH OTHER

When Sheryl and Gary got engaged, they sat down and had some pretty frank conversations with one another. They discussed their families and their past relationships, trying to identify the ways their childhoods and dating histories might impinge on their present and future together.

What they didn't discuss—at least not adequately—was their financial history. In particular, Gary didn't tell his fiancée that, six years before, he had gotten into massive credit card debt. Gary figured he had dealt with the problem so it was behind him. Why bring up something that wasn't an issue anymore?

Of course, any time we find ourselves thinking along those lines, something more is going on. If the incident in question was truly in the past, we would feel OK sharing it. Failing to bring up credit card debt, porn use or an affair means the shame of it hasn't really left us but is still choking us as we try to keep it secret. Over time we become captive to our fears of being found out.

Gary managed to keep his financial past hidden from Sheryl for a few years, though he now says that, in hindsight, he can see that his inability to talk about money with Sheryl caused him to dodge conversations that were important for their financial future. Eventually, Gary had to talk about money and 'fess up to his past money mistakes and his deception when he and Sheryl tried to buy a house and were turned down for a loan because of Gary's bad credit rating.

It was hard, of course, to have those conversations. "It was much harder than if I'd told Sheryl about my credit card debt years before," Gary said. "Then we could have strategized together. And then I wouldn't have had to deal with both Sheryl's distress that we were having a hard time getting a mortgage and her even greater distress that I had, in effect, lied to her by not telling her the whole truth."

It can be hard—even terrifying—to reveal a long-buried secret to your spouse. You worry he'll be furious, that he'll judge you, that he'll be hurt. Indeed, your spouse might be hurt. She might be angry. She might be stunned. But put yourself in your spouse's shoes; if he was keeping something from you, you would want him to come clean, not only so that you could be in the know, but so that he could be freed from the chains of shame and secrecy.

Romans 8:14–15 tells us that we are no longer slaves to fear. As children of God, we live in the light of full disclosure, sure of forgiveness, pardon and restoration—in our relationship with God and with each other.

—LAUREN WINNER

Those who are led by the Spirit of God are sons of God. For you did not receive a spirit that makes you a slave again to fear.
— ROMANS 8:14–15

let's talk

- ✦ Is there a not-so-big issue one of us is keeping from the other? What is preventing full disclosure?
- ✦ Does envisioning God as truly present in our conversations make it easier to imagine starting a hard conversation with each other about that secret?
- ✦ Look back to the hard conversations we've had with each other. What have been the fruits of those discussions?

FOR YOUR NEXT DEVOTIONAL READING, TURN TO PAGE 1270.

More Than Conquerors

28 And we know that in all things God
works for the good of those who love him,[a]
who[b] have been called according to his purpose. 29 For those God foreknew he also predestined to be conformed to the likeness of
his Son, that he might be the firstborn among
many brothers. 30 And those he predestined,
he also called; those he called, he also justified;
those he justified, he also glorified.

31 What, then, shall we say in response to
this? If God is for us, who can be against us?
32 He who did not spare his own Son, but gave
him up for us all—how will he not also, along
with him, graciously give us all things? 33 Who
will bring any charge against those whom God
has chosen? It is God who justifies. 34 Who is
he that condemns? Christ Jesus, who died—
more than that, who was raised to life—is at
the right hand of God and is also interceding
for us. 35 Who shall separate us from the love
of Christ? Shall trouble or hardship or persecution or famine or nakedness or danger or
sword? 36 As it is written:

> "For your sake we face death all day long;
> we are considered as sheep to be
> slaughtered."[c]

37 No, in all these things we are more than conquerors through him who loved us. 38 For I am
convinced that neither death nor life, neither
angels nor demons,[d] neither the present nor
the future, nor any powers, 39 neither height
nor depth, nor anything else in all creation,
will be able to separate us from the love of
God that is in Christ Jesus our Lord.

God's Sovereign Choice

9 I speak the truth in Christ—I am not lying, my conscience confirms it in the Holy
Spirit— 2 I have great sorrow and unceasing
anguish in my heart. 3 For I could wish that I
myself were cursed and cut off from Christ for
the sake of my brothers, those of my own race,
4 the people of Israel. Theirs is the adoption as
sons; theirs the divine glory, the covenants, the
receiving of the law, the temple worship and
the promises. 5 Theirs are the patriarchs, and
from them is traced the human ancestry of
Christ, who is God over all, forever praised![e]
Amen.

6 It is not as though God's word had failed.
For not all who are descended from Israel are
Israel. 7 Nor because they are his descendants
are they all Abraham's children. On the contrary, "It is through Isaac that your offspring
will be reckoned."[f] 8 In other words, it is not
the natural children who are God's children,
but it is the children of the promise who are
regarded as Abraham's offspring. 9 For this was
how the promise was stated: "At the appointed time I will return, and Sarah will have a
son."[g]

10 Not only that, but Rebekah's children
had one and the same father, our father Isaac.
11 Yet, before the twins were born or had done
anything good or bad—in order that God's
purpose in election might stand: 12 not by
works but by him who calls—she was told,
"The older will serve the younger."[h] 13 Just as it
is written: "Jacob I loved, but Esau I hated."[i]

14 What then shall we say? Is God unjust?
Not at all! 15 For he says to Moses,

> "I will have mercy on whom I have mercy,
> and I will have compassion on whom I
> have compassion."[j]

16 It does not, therefore, depend on man's desire or effort, but on God's mercy. 17 For the
Scripture says to Pharaoh: "I raised you up
for this very purpose, that I might display my
power in you and that my name might be proclaimed in all the earth."[k] 18 Therefore God
has mercy on whom he wants to have mercy,
and he hardens whom he wants to harden.

19 One of you will say to me: "Then why
does God still blame us? For who resists his
will?" 20 But who are you, O man, to talk back
to God? "Shall what is formed say to him who
formed it, 'Why did you make me like this?' "[l]
21 Does not the potter have the right to make
out of the same lump of clay some pottery for
noble purposes and some for common use?

22 What if God, choosing to show his wrath
and make his power known, bore with great
patience the objects of his wrath—prepared
for destruction? 23 What if he did this to make
the riches of his glory known to the objects of
his mercy, whom he prepared in advance for
glory— 24 even us, whom he also called, not
only from the Jews but also from the Gentiles?
25 As he says in Hosea:

> "I will call them 'my people' who are not
> my people;
> and I will call her 'my loved one' who is
> not my loved one,"[m]

---

[a] *28* Some manuscripts *And we know that all things work together for good to those who love God* [b] *28* Or *works together with those who love him to bring about what is good—with those who* [c] *36* Psalm 44:22 [d] *38* Or *nor heavenly rulers* [e] *5* Or *Christ, who is over all. God be forever praised!* Or *Christ. God who is over all be forever praised!* [f] *7* Gen. 21:12 [g] *9* Gen. 18:10,14 [h] *12* Gen. 25:23 [i] *13* Mal. 1:2,3 [j] *15* Exodus 33:19 [k] *17* Exodus 9:16 [l] *20* Isaiah 29:16; 45:9 [m] *25* Hosea 2:23

26 and,

"It will happen that in the very place
where it was said to them,
'You are not my people,'
they will be called 'sons of the living
God.' "[a]

27 Isaiah cries out concerning Israel:

"Though the number of the Israelites be
like the sand by the sea,
only the remnant will be saved.
28 For the Lord will carry out
his sentence on earth with speed and
finality."[b]

29 It is just as Isaiah said previously:

"Unless the Lord Almighty
had left us descendants,
we would have become like Sodom,
we would have been like Gomorrah."[c]

Israel's Unbelief

30 What then shall we say? That the Gentiles, who did not pursue righteousness, have
obtained it, a righteousness that is by faith;
31 but Israel, who pursued a law of righteousness, has not attained it. 32 Why not? Because
they pursued it not by faith but as if it were
by works. They stumbled over the "stumbling
stone." 33 As it is written:

"See, I lay in Zion a stone that causes men
to stumble
and a rock that makes them fall,
and the one who trusts in him will never
be put to shame."[d]

10 Brothers, my heart's desire and prayer to
God for the Israelites is that they may
be saved. 2 For I can testify about them
that they are zealous for God, but their zeal is
not based on knowledge. 3 Since they did not
know the righteousness that comes from God
and sought to establish their own, they did
not submit to God's righteousness. 4 Christ is
the end of the law so that there may be righteousness for everyone who believes.

5 Moses describes in this way the righteousness that is by the law: "The man who does
these things will live by them."[e] 6 But the righteousness that is by faith says: "Do not say in
your heart, 'Who will ascend into heaven?'[f]"
(that is, to bring Christ down) 7 "or 'Who will
descend into the deep?'[g]" (that is, to bring
Christ up from the dead). 8 But what does
it say? "The word is near you; it is in your
mouth and in your heart,"[h] that is, the word
of faith we are proclaiming: 9 That if you confess with your mouth, "Jesus is Lord," and believe in your heart that God raised him from
the dead, you will be saved. 10 For it is with
your heart that you believe and are justified,
and it is with your mouth that you confess
and are saved. 11 As the Scripture says, "Anyone who trusts in him will never be put to
shame."[i] 12 For there is no difference between
Jew and Gentile—the same Lord is Lord of all
and richly blesses all who call on him, 13 for,
"Everyone who calls on the name of the Lord
will be saved."[j]

14 How, then, can they call on the one they
have not believed in? And how can they believe in the one of whom they have not
heard? And how can they hear without someone preaching to them? 15 And how can they
preach unless they are sent? As it is written,
"How beautiful are the feet of those who bring
good news!"[k]

16 But not all the Israelites accepted the good
news. For Isaiah says, "Lord, who has believed
our message?"[l] 17 Consequently, faith comes
from hearing the message, and the message is
heard through the word of Christ. 18 But I ask:
Did they not hear? Of course they did:

"Their voice has gone out into all the
earth,
their words to the ends of the world."[m]

19 Again I ask: Did Israel not understand? First,
Moses says,

"I will make you envious by those who are
not a nation;
I will make you angry by a nation that
has no understanding."[n]

20 And Isaiah boldly says,

"I was found by those who did not seek
me;
I revealed myself to those who did not
ask for me."[o]

21 But concerning Israel he says,

"All day long I have held out my hands
to a disobedient and obstinate
people."[p]

---

[a] *26* Hosea 1:10 [b] *28* Isaiah 10:22,23 [c] *29* Isaiah 1:9 [d] *33* Isaiah 8:14; 28:16 [e] *5* Lev. 18:5 [f] *6* Deut. 30:12 [g] *7* Deut. 30:13 [h] *8* Deut. 30:14 [i] *11* Isaiah 28:16 [j] *13* Joel 2:32 [k] *15* Isaiah 52:7 [l] *16* Isaiah 53:1 [m] *18* Psalm 19:4 [n] *19* Deut. 32:21 [o] *20* Isaiah 65:1 [p] *21* Isaiah 65:2

The Remnant of Israel

11 I ask then: Did God reject his people? By no means! I am an Israelite myself, a descendant of Abraham, from the tribe of Benjamin. 2 God did not reject his people, whom he foreknew. Don't you know what the Scripture says in the passage about Elijah—how he appealed to God against Israel: 3 "Lord, they have killed your prophets and torn down your altars; I am the only one left, and they are trying to kill me"[a]? 4 And what was God's answer to him? "I have reserved for myself seven thousand who have not bowed the knee to Baal."[b] 5 So too, at the present time there is a remnant chosen by grace. 6 And if by grace, then it is no longer by works; if it were, grace would no longer be grace.[c]

7 What then? What Israel sought so earnestly it did not obtain, but the elect did. The others were hardened, 8 as it is written:

> "God gave them a spirit of stupor,
> eyes so that they could not see
> and ears so that they could not hear,
> to this very day."[d]

9 And David says:

> "May their table become a snare and a trap,
> a stumbling block and a retribution for them.
> 10 May their eyes be darkened so they cannot see,
> and their backs be bent forever."[e]

Ingrafted Branches

11 Again I ask: Did they stumble so as to fall beyond recovery? Not at all! Rather, because of their transgression, salvation has come to the Gentiles to make Israel envious. 12 But if their transgression means riches for the world, and their loss means riches for the Gentiles, how much greater riches will their fullness bring!

13 I am talking to you Gentiles. Inasmuch as I am the apostle to the Gentiles, I make much of my ministry 14 in the hope that I may somehow arouse my own people to envy and save some of them. 15 For if their rejection is the reconciliation of the world, what will their acceptance be but life from the dead? 16 If the part of the dough offered as firstfruits is holy, then the whole batch is holy; if the root is holy, so are the branches.

17 If some of the branches have been broken off, and you, though a wild olive shoot, have been grafted in among the others and now share in the nourishing sap from the olive root, 18 do not boast over those branches. If you do, consider this: You do not support the root, but the root supports you. 19 You will say then, "Branches were broken off so that I could be grafted in." 20 Granted. But they were broken off because of unbelief, and you stand by faith. Do not be arrogant, but be afraid. 21 For if God did not spare the natural branches, he will not spare you either.

22 Consider therefore the kindness and sternness of God: sternness to those who fell, but kindness to you, provided that you continue in his kindness. Otherwise, you also will be cut off. 23 And if they do not persist in unbelief, they will be grafted in, for God is able to graft them in again. 24 After all, if you were cut out of an olive tree that is wild by nature, and contrary to nature were grafted into a cultivated olive tree, how much more readily will these, the natural branches, be grafted into their own olive tree!

All Israel Will Be Saved

25 I do not want you to be ignorant of this mystery, brothers, so that you may not be conceited: Israel has experienced a hardening in part until the full number of the Gentiles has come in. 26 And so all Israel will be saved, as it is written:

> "The deliverer will come from Zion;
> he will turn godlessness away from Jacob.
> 27 And this is[f] my covenant with them
> when I take away their sins."[g]

28 As far as the gospel is concerned, they are enemies on your account; but as far as election is concerned, they are loved on account of the patriarchs, 29 for God's gifts and his call are irrevocable. 30 Just as you who were at one time disobedient to God have now received mercy as a result of their disobedience, 31 so they too have now become disobedient in order that they too may now[h] receive mercy as a result of God's mercy to you. 32 For God has bound all men over to disobedience so that he may have mercy on them all.

---

[a] *3* 1 Kings 19:10,14 [b] *4* 1 Kings 19:18 [c] *6* Some manuscripts *be grace. But if by works, then it is no longer grace; if it were, work would no longer be work.* [d] *8* Deut. 29:4; Isaiah 29:10 [e] *10* Psalm 69:22,23 [f] *27* Or *will be* [g] *27* Isaiah 59:20,21; 27:9; Jer. 31:33,34
[h] *31* Some manuscripts do not have *now.*

Doxology

33 Oh, the depth of the riches of the wisdom
and[a] knowledge of God!
How unsearchable his judgments,
and his paths beyond tracing out!
34 "Who has known the mind of the Lord?
Or who has been his counselor?"[b]
35 "Who has ever given to God,
that God should repay him?"[c]
36 For from him and through him and to
him are all things.
To him be the glory forever! Amen.

Living Sacrifices

12 Therefore, I urge you, brothers, in view
of God's mercy, to offer your bodies as
living sacrifices, holy and pleasing to
God—this is your spiritual[d] act of worship.
2 Do not conform any longer to the pattern of
this world, but be transformed by the renewing of your mind. Then you will be able to
test and approve what God's will is—his good,
pleasing and perfect will.
3 For by the grace given me I say to every
one of you: Do not think of yourself more
highly than you ought, but rather think of
yourself with sober judgment, in accordance
with the measure of faith God has given you.
4 Just as each of us has one body with many
members, and these members do not all have
the same function, 5 so in Christ we who
are many form one body, and each member
belongs to all the others. 6 We have different gifts, according to the grace given us. If
a man's gift is prophesying, let him use it in
proportion to his[e] faith. 7 If it is serving, let
him serve; if it is teaching, let him teach; 8 if it
is encouraging, let him encourage; if it is contributing to the needs of others, let him give
generously; if it is leadership, let him govern
diligently; if it is showing mercy, let him do
it cheerfully.

Love

9 Love must be sincere. Hate what is evil;
cling to what is good. 10 Be devoted to one another in brotherly love. Honor one another
above yourselves. 11 Never be lacking in zeal,
but keep your spiritual fervor, serving the
Lord. 12 Be joyful in hope, patient in affliction,
faithful in prayer. 13 Share with God's people
who are in need. Practice hospitality.
14 Bless those who persecute you; bless and
do not curse. 15 Rejoice with those who rejoice;
mourn with those who mourn. 16 Live in harmony with one another. Do not be proud, but
be willing to associate with people of low position.[f] Do not be conceited.
17 Do not repay anyone evil for evil. Be careful to do what is right in the eyes of everybody.
18 If it is possible, as far as it depends on you,
live at peace with everyone. 19 Do not take revenge, my friends, but leave room for God's
wrath, for it is written: "It is mine to avenge;
I will repay,"[g] says the Lord. 20 On the contrary:

"If your enemy is hungry, feed him;
if he is thirsty, give him something to
drink.
In doing this, you will heap burning coals
on his head."[h]

21 Do not be overcome by evil, but overcome
evil with good.

Submission to the Authorities

13 Everyone must submit himself to the
governing authorities, for there is no
authority except that which God has established. The authorities that exist have been
established by God. 2 Consequently, he who
rebels against the authority is rebelling against
what God has instituted, and those who do so
will bring judgment on themselves. 3 For rulers hold no terror for those who do right, but
for those who do wrong. Do you want to be
free from fear of the one in authority? Then
do what is right and he will commend you.
4 For he is God's servant to do you good. But
if you do wrong, be afraid, for he does not
bear the sword for nothing. He is God's servant, an agent of wrath to bring punishment
on the wrongdoer. 5 Therefore, it is necessary
to submit to the authorities, not only because
of possible punishment but also because of
conscience.
6 This is also why you pay taxes, for the authorities are God's servants, who give their full
time to governing. 7 Give everyone what you
owe him: If you owe taxes, pay taxes; if revenue, then revenue; if respect, then respect; if
honor, then honor.

Love, for the Day Is Near

8 Let no debt remain outstanding, except
the continuing debt to love one another, for
he who loves his fellowman has fulfilled the
law. 9 The commandments, "Do not commit
adultery," "Do not murder," "Do not steal,"

---

[a] 33 Or *riches and the wisdom and the* [b] 34 Isaiah 40:13 [c] 35 Job 41:11 [d] 1 Or *reasonable* [e] 6 Or *in agreement with the*
[f] 16 Or *willing to do menial work* [g] 19 Deut. 32:35 [h] 20 Prov. 25:21,22

WEEKEND

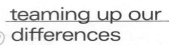

teaming up our differences

Two people can live together for many years and yet look at life from such different perspectives. Consider our friend who wrote us about her trip to Europe:

> I read over Ed's notes and thought we would combine our diaries, but now I wonder if we made the same trip. He remembers how far it is from Stockholm to wherever, what the money exchange was, what we had for breakfast, how many meals were on our own, and the address of every airline office in the four countries. I wrote about the things we did together—the places we visited and the interesting people we met. It really is true that opposites attract, and that God puts different people together to bring out the best in them. So if you want to know how far north or south we went, ask Ed. I have no idea!

Opposites do attract; however, the very characteristics that attracted you to your mate—his or her easygoing nature, never in a hurry, always has time for people—may later be an irritation to you. The trick is learning how to work with those differences so they help us operate as a team.

For the first eight years of our marriage we tried to change each other, and it didn't work. Dave didn't understand why I couldn't just laugh things off and not take life so seriously. I wanted Dave to be more introspective and analytical.

Then we made a job change that required us to take a battery of psychological tests. We still remember the day we took those tests. Dave nonchalantly checked off his answers while watching a football game on TV. I carefully thought through each answer and crosschecked them for consistency.

The next week a psychologist interviewed us. He sat at his desk, looking at our test results. "Dave, here are your strong points." As he listed them, Dave felt better and better. He went on, "Now here are the areas in which you are weak." That wasn't nearly as enjoyable for Dave to hear, but the psychologist was right on target!

Then he went through the same procedure with me, listing my strengths and weaknesses. Looking at both of us he said, "Dave and Claudia, here are the areas you agree on, and here are the areas in which you tend to have problems." His accuracy was uncanny. Then he gave us one of the most beneficial challenges of our lives: "You probably noticed, Dave, that your weak areas are Claudia's strengths, and Claudia, that your weak areas are Dave's strengths. If you will allow each other to operate in your areas of strengths and not be threatened by the other, you have the potential for building a great marriage partnership."

We would like to say that we went right out and applied his advice—but it didn't happen quite like that. It took time and practice, and at times it was awkward, but we took the doctor's challenge seriously.

Years later, we had the opportunity to retake the same battery of psychological tests and to sit down again with the same psychologist. We were surprised and pleased to learn that we had actually learned from each other. Our weak areas were not as weak. We were a stronger team. Work for unity in your diversity, and you, too, can be a strong marriage team. It will enrich your marriage—even your love life!

—DAVID AND CLAUDIA ARP

estimating your strengths

Look at these word pairs as a continuum. Which side of the continuum are you on? Which side is your spouse on? What does this suggest about how you could best work as a team?

1. Motivated by feelings
   Motivated by facts
2. Shy and introverted
   Outgoing and extraverted
3. Spontaneous
   Planner
4. Active and assertive
   Laid back and calm
5. Night owl
   Day lark
6. Time-oriented
   Event-oriented

More questions to help uncover your team strengths:

1. In what ways are you and your spouse alike?
2. Are there areas in which you are so much alike that it could be considered a weakness?
3. In what ways are you different?
4. How can your differences be used to balance you as a team?
5. Is there something new you would like to try or a risk you would like to take? What holds you back?
6. Do you like planning a vacation far in advance, or do you prefer to be more spontaneous? How can you combine those approaches to get the best experience?
7. Speaking of vacations, do you like going back to a place you've really enjoyed, or do you prefer to try something new each year? What are the advantages of revisiting the same place? The disadvantages?

HOW ARE WE DOING?

date

let's make a DATE

TRY SOMETHING NEW

Make a date for each spouse to try something new. Maybe it is something you can do together, like going for a hot-air balloon ride, or maybe it is something you have never done but always wanted to try, like rollerblading or painting or playing hockey. Whatever you both decide upon, you must go with your partner and support him or her while doing the activity. When you've completed both activities, have dinner or coffee together and talk about how it felt to try something new with support from your spouse.

FOR YOUR NEXT DEVOTIONAL READING, TURN TO PAGE 1273.

LESSONS FROM THE *Bible*

There is perhaps no better example of a couple working as a team than Mary and Joseph. How do these examples show them working as a team?

1. Mary's pregnancy (Matthew 1:18–25)
2. Jesus presented in the temple as a baby (Luke 2:21–40)
3. Jesus found at the temple as a boy (Luke 2:41–52)

"Do not covet,"[a] and whatever other commandment there may be, are summed up in
this one rule: "Love your neighbor as yourself."[b] 10Love does no harm to its neighbor.
Therefore love is the fulfillment of the law.

11And do this, understanding the present
time. The hour has come for you to wake
up from your slumber, because our salvation
is nearer now than when we first believed.
12The night is nearly over; the day is almost
here. So let us put aside the deeds of darkness
and put on the armor of light. 13Let us behave
decently, as in the daytime, not in orgies and
drunkenness, not in sexual immorality and
debauchery, not in dissension and jealousy.
14Rather, clothe yourselves with the Lord Jesus
Christ, and do not think about how to gratify
the desires of the sinful nature.[c]

The Weak and the Strong

14 Accept him whose faith is weak, without
passing judgment on disputable matters. 2One man's faith allows him to eat
everything, but another man, whose faith is
weak, eats only vegetables. 3The man who eats
everything must not look down on him who
does not, and the man who does not eat everything must not condemn the man who does,
for God has accepted him. 4Who are you to
judge someone else's servant? To his own master he stands or falls. And he will stand, for the
Lord is able to make him stand.

5One man considers one day more sacred
than another; another man considers every
day alike. Each one should be fully convinced
in his own mind. 6He who regards one day
as special, does so to the Lord. He who eats
meat, eats to the Lord, for he gives thanks to
God; and he who abstains, does so to the Lord
and gives thanks to God. 7For none of us lives
to himself alone and none of us dies to himself
alone. 8If we live, we live to the Lord; and if
we die, we die to the Lord. So, whether we live
or die, we belong to the Lord.

9For this very reason, Christ died and returned to life so that he might be the Lord
of both the dead and the living. 10You, then,
why do you judge your brother? Or why do
you look down on your brother? For we will
all stand before God's judgment seat. 11It is
written:

" 'As surely as I live,' says the Lord,
'every knee will bow before me;
every tongue will confess to God.' "[d]

12So then, each of us will give an account of
himself to God.

13Therefore let us stop passing judgment on
one another. Instead, make up your mind not
to put any stumbling block or obstacle in your
brother's way. 14As one who is in the Lord
Jesus, I am fully convinced that no food[e] is
unclean in itself. But if anyone regards something as unclean, then for him it is unclean.
15If your brother is distressed because of what
you eat, you are no longer acting in love. Do
not by your eating destroy your brother for
whom Christ died. 16Do not allow what you
consider good to be spoken of as evil. 17For
the kingdom of God is not a matter of eating
and drinking, but of righteousness, peace and
joy in the Holy Spirit, 18because anyone who
serves Christ in this way is pleasing to God
and approved by men.

19Let us therefore make every effort to do
what leads to peace and to mutual edification.
20Do not destroy the work of God for the sake
of food. All food is clean, but it is wrong for
a man to eat anything that causes someone
else to stumble. 21It is better not to eat meat
or drink wine or to do anything else that will
cause your brother to fall.

22So whatever you believe about these things
keep between yourself and God. Blessed is the
man who does not condemn himself by what
he approves. 23But the man who has doubts is
condemned if he eats, because his eating is not
from faith; and everything that does not come
from faith is sin.

15 We who are strong ought to bear with
the failings of the weak and not to please
ourselves. 2Each of us should please his
neighbor for his good, to build him up. 3For
even Christ did not please himself but, as it is
written: "The insults of those who insult you
have fallen on me."[f] 4For everything that was
written in the past was written to teach us, so
that through endurance and the encouragement of the Scriptures we might have hope.

5May the God who gives endurance and encouragement give you a spirit of unity among
yourselves as you follow Christ Jesus, 6so that
with one heart and mouth you may glorify the
God and Father of our Lord Jesus Christ.

7Accept one another, then, just as Christ accepted you, in order to bring praise to God.
8For I tell you that Christ has become a servant of the Jews[g] on behalf of God's truth, to
confirm the promises made to the patriarchs

---

[a] *9* Exodus 20:13-15,17; Deut. 5:17-19,21 [b] *9* Lev. 19:18 [c] *14* Or *the flesh* [d] *11* Isaiah 45:23 [e] *14* Or *that nothing* [f] *3* Psalm 69:9
[g] *8* Greek *circumcision*

M

MONDAY
READ ROMANS 13:1–14

CHOKING TO "DEBT"

Let no debt remain outstanding, except the continuing debt to love one another, for he who loves his fellowman has fulfilled the law.

— Romans 13:8

let's talk

- What does our lifestyle say to others about our view of debt? Of material things? Of love for our neighbors?
- What cultural messages about debt and materialism have each of us carried into our marriage?
- Do we have debt? How do we feel about our current debt load? How would freeing ourselves of debt allow us to better love our neighbors?

Matt and Lisa weren't sure what was more challenging—leaving the United States for five years or returning to it. While in Bolivia as relief workers, they lived in a rural farming community among Quechua Indians. There was no running water, no electricity and no doctor. Food consisted of whatever they grew or raised. But, despite the language differences and other cultural barriers, the couple soon felt like a loved and trusted part of that community.

Matt and Lisa basically had nothing during those five years of their marriage. Life was a challenge. Still, they were working together. Their goals were clear. And they loved their neighbors.

Their move back to the States was more difficult than they had imagined it would be. Sure, they had a house in the suburbs, good jobs and benefits such as health insurance. But their time-consuming jobs kept them apart. They had a big mortgage. They had to pay more than they were accustomed to paying for groceries and doctor visits. Worse, they got a crash course on a culture that promotes the maintenance of things rather than the love of neighbor.

Our stuff-centered culture tripped up this couple, but what does it do for married couples that have never experienced anything else?

The apostle Paul, in Romans 13, addresses the issue of what controls us. He warns believers to be responsible with their obligations, particularly to governmental authorities. Out of respect for what "God has established" (verse 1), we are to live as honest, responsible, upstanding citizens. Paul also says in verse 8, "Let no debt remain outstanding." Does this mean believers shouldn't take out loans for cars, houses or businesses? Does it mean paying cash rather than using credit cards?

Not necessarily. What Paul is probably warning against is biting off more than we can chew. He wants to prevent us from "choking to debt." It may mean that we buy a less expensive car with a more manageable loan. It may mean cutting up credit cards, buying less expensive clothes or toys, or forgoing restaurant meals.

But there is more. We are commanded to "let no debt remain outstanding, except the continuing debt to love one another" (verse 8). At the heart of financial planning is the question of whom we serve. Are our desires fueled by our culture or by the love of Christ? Do we serve ourselves or others?

When we become slaves to debt, we lose much of our freedom to serve others. In verse 11, Paul reminds us, "The hour has come for you to wake up from your slumber, because our salvation is nearer now than when we first believed." This is a warning to take a close look at the way we manage our assets. With wise planning, we can reduce our obligations to things that won't last and increase our debt to people for their eternal welfare.

—KYLE WHITE

FOR YOUR NEXT DEVOTIONAL READING, TURN TO PAGE 1274.

STUMBLING OVER SANTA

> **Let us stop passing judgment on one another. Instead, make up your mind not to put any stumbling block or obstacle in your brother's way.**
>
> — Romans 14:13

let's talk

- Name some of our practices that differ from those of other Christians. How do we regard their faith—as "weaker" or "stronger" than our own?
- In what ways have we relaxed our practices in response to the less-restricted behavior of other Christian couples? Do we feel guilty or freer?
- What are some ways we might alter our practices so we don't lead others to compromise their beliefs?

Jason and Amelia met in January and married in September. They each had a child from a previous marriage, but their children, both four-year-old girls, got along well. The four of them lived happily for the next three months—until Christmas approached.

One thing the couple hadn't discussed before they got married was Santa Claus. Jason had always made sure that his daughter knew that Christians celebrated the birth of Jesus at Christmas, but Santa was a part of the holiday too. Amelia, however, adamantly opposed the idea of including Santa Claus in any Christmas celebrations, believing that to include anything about Santa was a sin.

The Santa issue caused great turmoil in the new family. What should have been a time of joyful celebration turned into a daily bitter battle between the newlyweds.

In Romans 14:1—15:13, Paul addresses Christian liberty, or the freedom of believers to make their own decisions on matters not specifically spelled out in Scripture. For example, some believers thought it was OK to eat meat that had been sacrificed to an idol, while others felt it was sinful to do so. Likewise, some believers said the Sabbath and other special days of the Jewish calendar should be kept holy and dedicated to God, while others said every day was sacred and should be treated the same.

Paul said such differences were OK, but that one believer should not condemn another who believed differently, considering that person's faith inferior. "The man who eats everything must not look down on him who does not, and the man who does not eat everything must not condemn the man who does" (Romans 14:3). Furthermore, the person who felt less restricted should make every effort not to do something that would cause the other, more restricted person to violate his or her beliefs.

Amelia felt it was wrong to include Santa at Christmas, so according to Paul's advice, it would be better for her husband to exclude the jolly old man in the red furry suit from Christmas celebrations than to cause his wife to stumble by including Santa. That's what happened. After a phone call to their pastor, Jason decided that Santa wasn't worth risking his wife's personal beliefs or ruining the family's first holiday together. He announced, "This year we're going to focus on baby Jesus." The couple had a wonderful Christmas.

The following year, Amelia suggested they all go to the mall to see Santa. What happened? In seeing how her husband gave up his liberty to honor her beliefs, Amelia realized that she was free to honor his. She was able to watch their girls enjoy Santa as a fictional character without compromising her faith.

In marriage, not even the most compatible partners agree on everything, and in areas where one feels more restricted, it is the role of the less-restricted person to adapt so that his or her liberty won't be a stumbling block or an opportunity to judge. The goal is to honor each other, differences and all, and to live in peace.

—NANCY KENNEDY

FOR YOUR NEXT DEVOTIONAL READING, TURN TO PAGE 1277.

9so that the Gentiles may glorify God for his
mercy, as it is written:

> "Therefore I will praise you among the
> Gentiles;
> I will sing hymns to your name."[a]

10Again, it says,

> "Rejoice, O Gentiles, with his people."[b]

11And again,

> "Praise the Lord, all you Gentiles,
> and sing praises to him, all you
> peoples."[c]

12And again, Isaiah says,

> "The Root of Jesse will spring up,
> one who will arise to rule over the
> nations;
> the Gentiles will hope in him."[d]

13May the God of hope fill you with all joy
and peace as you trust in him, so that you may
overflow with hope by the power of the Holy
Spirit.

Paul the Minister to the Gentiles

14I myself am convinced, my brothers, that
you yourselves are full of goodness, complete
in knowledge and competent to instruct one
another. 15I have written you quite boldly
on some points, as if to remind you of them
again, because of the grace God gave me 16to
be a minister of Christ Jesus to the Gentiles
with the priestly duty of proclaiming the gospel of God, so that the Gentiles might become
an offering acceptable to God, sanctified by
the Holy Spirit.

17Therefore I glory in Christ Jesus in my
service to God. 18I will not venture to speak of
anything except what Christ has accomplished
through me in leading the Gentiles to obey
God by what I have said and done— 19by the
power of signs and miracles, through the power of the Spirit. So from Jerusalem all the way
around to Illyricum, I have fully proclaimed
the gospel of Christ. 20It has always been my
ambition to preach the gospel where Christ
was not known, so that I would not be building on someone else's foundation. 21Rather, as
it is written:

> "Those who were not told about him will
> see,
> and those who have not heard will
> understand."[e]

22This is why I have often been hindered from
coming to you.

Paul's Plan to Visit Rome

23But now that there is no more place for
me to work in these regions, and since I have
been longing for many years to see you, 24I
plan to do so when I go to Spain. I hope to
visit you while passing through and to have
you assist me on my journey there, after I have
enjoyed your company for a while. 25Now,
however, I am on my way to Jerusalem in the
service of the saints there. 26For Macedonia
and Achaia were pleased to make a contribution for the poor among the saints in Jerusalem. 27They were pleased to do it, and indeed
they owe it to them. For if the Gentiles have
shared in the Jews' spiritual blessings, they
owe it to the Jews to share with them their
material blessings. 28So after I have completed
this task and have made sure that they have
received this fruit, I will go to Spain and visit
you on the way. 29I know that when I come
to you, I will come in the full measure of the
blessing of Christ.

30I urge you, brothers, by our Lord Jesus
Christ and by the love of the Spirit, to join
me in my struggle by praying to God for me.
31Pray that I may be rescued from the unbelievers in Judea and that my service in Jerusalem may be acceptable to the saints there, 32so
that by God's will I may come to you with
joy and together with you be refreshed. 33The
God of peace be with you all. Amen.

Personal Greetings

16 I commend to you our sister Phoebe, a
servant[f] of the church in Cenchrea. 2I
ask you to receive her in the Lord in a
way worthy of the saints and to give her any
help she may need from you, for she has been
a great help to many people, including me.

3Greet Priscilla[g] and Aquila, my fellow
workers in Christ Jesus. 4They risked
their lives for me. Not only I but all the
churches of the Gentiles are grateful to
them.

5Greet also the church that meets at their
house.

Greet my dear friend Epenetus, who was
the first convert to Christ in the province of Asia.

6Greet Mary, who worked very hard for
you.

---

a 9 2 Samuel 22:50; Psalm 18:49 *b* 10 Deut. 32:43 *c* 11 Psalm 117:1 *d* 12 Isaiah 11:10 *e* 21 Isaiah 52:15 *f* 1 Or *deaconess*
g 3 Greek *Prisca*, a variant of *Priscilla*

7 Greet Andronicus and Junias, my relatives who have been in prison with me. They are outstanding among the apostles, and they were in Christ before I was.
8 Greet Ampliatus, whom I love in the Lord.
9 Greet Urbanus, our fellow worker in Christ, and my dear friend Stachys.
10 Greet Apelles, tested and approved in Christ.

Greet those who belong to the household of Aristobulus.
11 Greet Herodion, my relative.

Greet those in the household of Narcissus who are in the Lord.
12 Greet Tryphena and Tryphosa, those women who work hard in the Lord.

Greet my dear friend Persis, another woman who has worked very hard in the Lord.
13 Greet Rufus, chosen in the Lord, and his mother, who has been a mother to me, too.
14 Greet Asyncritus, Phlegon, Hermes, Patrobas, Hermas and the brothers with them.
15 Greet Philologus, Julia, Nereus and his sister, and Olympas and all the saints with them.
16 Greet one another with a holy kiss.

All the churches of Christ send greetings.

17 I urge you, brothers, to watch out for
those who cause divisions and put obstacles in
your way that are contrary to the teaching you
have learned. Keep away from them. 18 For
such people are not serving our Lord Christ,
but their own appetites. By smooth talk and
flattery they deceive the minds of naive people. 19 Everyone has heard about your obedience, so I am full of joy over you; but I want
you to be wise about what is good, and innocent about what is evil.

20 The God of peace will soon crush Satan
under your feet.

The grace of our Lord Jesus be with you.

21 Timothy, my fellow worker, sends his
greetings to you, as do Lucius, Jason and Sosipater, my relatives.

22 I, Tertius, who wrote down this letter,
greet you in the Lord.

23 Gaius, whose hospitality I and the whole
church here enjoy, sends you his greetings.

Erastus, who is the city's director of public works, and our brother Quartus send you their greetings. [a]

25 Now to him who is able to establish you
by my gospel and the proclamation of Jesus
Christ, according to the revelation of the
mystery hidden for long ages past, 26 but now
revealed and made known through the prophetic writings by the command of the eternal God, so that all nations might believe and
obey him— 27 to the only wise God be glory
forever through Jesus Christ! Amen.

[a] 23 Some manuscripts *their greetings.* [24] *May the grace of our Lord Jesus Christ be with all of you. Amen.*

WEDNESDAY

READ ROMANS 16:1–27

TUNE OUT TOKYO ROSE

I urge you, brothers, to watch out for those who cause divisions and put obstacles in your way that are contrary to the teaching you have learned. Keep away from them.

— Romans 16:17

During the Second World War, American servicemen were taunted over Radio Tokyo by a woman with a seductive voice they dubbed "Tokyo Rose." This temptress broadcasted propaganda to GIs in the midst of the war, trying to undermine their morale. Soldiers heard a sultry voice telling them that they were fighting a lost cause and that their significant others back home were cheating on them. Tokyo Rose encouraged the Americans to desert. It was later determined that Tokyo Rose was not one woman but several. But the name Tokyo Rose will forever be associated with misinformation, lies and divisiveness.

The early church dealt with its own Tokyo Rose. As the apostle Paul closed his letter to the church in Rome, he gave a final warning to watch out for divisive people. Paul didn't name the deceivers, but we can guess that they were smooth, smart and intriguing. Their messages sounded right, but they went against the basics of the gospel by adding rituals, rules and other obstacles to God's grace through Christ.

It's easy to see how those teachers could have divided the church. Paul's advice was simple: "Keep away from them." Believers were to keep away from not just the message but also the source! Paul encouraged the church to stick to the truth it had already learned about Jesus. As we see in Romans 16:19, Paul wanted new believers to be "wise" in focusing their energies on good things and to be "innocent" about deceptive additions to and subtractions from the gospel. They were not to give Tokyo Rose the time of day!

Marriage is holy ground in God's eyes; it is a metaphor of Christ's relationship with the church. But marriage is also contested ground. The enemy of Christ has a host of Tokyo Roses who question marriage's vows and commitments, undermine its strengths, and discourage its participants to the point of desertion.

Pop psychologists on morning talk shows advocate easy-out, self-centered marriages. Characters on television and in movies indulge in sexual attractions regardless of the cost to marriage. And bitter talk about marital discord fuels discussion around the copy machine at work. These pervasive messages, delivered so convincingly, can lead to dissatisfaction with God's gift of marriage. As we listen to others, we begin to probe our own relationship, asking questions such as "Don't I deserve more?" "How come my wife isn't more like *her*?" "Wouldn't life be easier if I were married to someone else?" "What's the point of putting up with a marriage that has lost its sexual energy?"

But wars like this can be won. We who are battling opposition in marriage need to remind ourselves of the Lord's good plan for us, identify our enemies, click off the Tokyo Roses, put on the armor of God, and jump back into the fray. Marriage is worth fighting for!

—KYLE WHITE

let's *talk*

- What are some Tokyo Roses that threaten our marriage? What sources of marital misinformation do we need to avoid? How would we do so?
- How can we regularly remind ourselves of the value of our marriage?
- What are some sources of truthful messages about marriage?

FOR YOUR NEXT DEVOTIONAL READING, TURN TO PAGE 1280.

1 CORINTHIANS

1 Corinthians

QUICK FACTS

AUTHOR The apostle Paul

AUDIENCE The church located in Corinth, a pagan cosmopolitan city in Greece

DATE About A.D. 55

SETTING Written from Ephesus to believers in the Corinthian church, which Paul started during his second missionary journey

As a major trading city in Greece, Corinth was rife with immorality. The problems faced by the Corinthian society at large spilled into the church at Corinth. In 1 Corinthians, Paul advised believers how to deal with sexual immorality, spiritual immaturity, divisions and schisms within the body, and the misuse of spiritual gifts—problems still common in the church today.

First Corinthians is a guidebook for propriety in congregational life and worship, dealing with an erring and unrepentant brother or sister in the Lord, and healing divisions that arise within a fellowship. Paul also counseled the Corinthian church on issues relating to marriage—whether to marry or stay single; how to deal with difficult situations, such as one spouse becoming a believer while the other remains an unbeliever; and appropriate behavior for those who are divorced or widowed. The book culminates in the famous passage on love in chapter 13 and the glorious truth of the resurrection in chapter 15.

This book, though written almost 2,000 years ago, deals with some everyday, down-to-earth issues that the church still wrestles with today. The implications are clear: God cares about his church, he cares about his people, and he cares about how we relate to each other.

1 Paul, called to be an apostle of Christ Jesus
by the will of God, and our brother Sosthenes,

2To the church of God in Corinth, to those
sanctified in Christ Jesus and called to be holy,
together with all those everywhere who call
on the name of our Lord Jesus Christ—their
Lord and ours:

3Grace and peace to you from God our Father and the Lord Jesus Christ.

Thanksgiving

4I always thank God for you because of his
grace given you in Christ Jesus. 5For in him
you have been enriched in every way—in all
your speaking and in all your knowledge—
6because our testimony about Christ was confirmed in you. 7Therefore you do not lack any
spiritual gift as you eagerly wait for our Lord
Jesus Christ to be revealed. 8He will keep you
strong to the end, so that you will be blameless on the day of our Lord Jesus Christ. 9God,
who has called you into fellowship with his
Son Jesus Christ our Lord, is faithful.

Divisions in the Church

10I appeal to you, brothers, in the name of
our Lord Jesus Christ, that all of you agree
with one another so that there may be no
divisions among you and that you may be
perfectly united in mind and thought. 11My
brothers, some from Chloe's household have
informed me that there are quarrels among
you. 12What I mean is this: One of you says,
"I follow Paul"; another, "I follow Apollos";
another, "I follow Cephas[a]"; still another, "I
follow Christ."
13Is Christ divided? Was Paul crucified for
you? Were you baptized into[b] the name of
Paul? 14I am thankful that I did not baptize
any of you except Crispus and Gaius, 15so no
one can say that you were baptized into my
name. 16(Yes, I also baptized the household of
Stephanas; beyond that, I don't remember if
I baptized anyone else.) 17For Christ did not
send me to baptize, but to preach the gospel—not with words of human wisdom, lest
the cross of Christ be emptied of its power.

Christ the Wisdom and Power of God

18For the message of the cross is foolishness
to those who are perishing, but to us who are
being saved it is the power of God. 19For it is
written:

"I will destroy the wisdom of the wise;
the intelligence of the intelligent I will
frustrate."[c]

20Where is the wise man? Where is the
scholar? Where is the philosopher of this age?
Has not God made foolish the wisdom of the
world? 21For since in the wisdom of God the
world through its wisdom did not know him,
God was pleased through the foolishness of
what was preached to save those who believe.
22Jews demand miraculous signs and Greeks
look for wisdom, 23but we preach Christ crucified: a stumbling block to Jews and foolishness to Gentiles, 24but to those whom God
has called, both Jews and Greeks, Christ the
power of God and the wisdom of God. 25For
the foolishness of God is wiser than man's
wisdom, and the weakness of God is stronger
than man's strength.
26Brothers, think of what you were when
you were called. Not many of you were wise
by human standards; not many were influential; not many were of noble birth. 27But
God chose the foolish things of the world to
shame the wise; God chose the weak things
of the world to shame the strong. 28He chose
the lowly things of this world and the despised
things—and the things that are not—to nullify the things that are, 29so that no one may
boast before him. 30It is because of him that
you are in Christ Jesus, who has become for
us wisdom from God—that is, our righteousness, holiness and redemption. 31Therefore, as
it is written: "Let him who boasts boast in the
Lord."[d]

2 When I came to you, brothers, I did not
come with eloquence or superior wisdom
as I proclaimed to you the testimony about
God.[e] 2For I resolved to know nothing while
I was with you except Jesus Christ and him
crucified. 3I came to you in weakness and fear,
and with much trembling. 4My message and
my preaching were not with wise and persuasive words, but with a demonstration of the
Spirit's power, 5so that your faith might not
rest on men's wisdom, but on God's power.

Wisdom From the Spirit

6We do, however, speak a message of wisdom among the mature, but not the wisdom
of this age or of the rulers of this age, who are
coming to nothing. 7No, we speak of God's
secret wisdom, a wisdom that has been hidden and that God destined for our glory be-

[a] *12* That is, Peter [b] *13* Or *in*; also in verse 15 [c] *19* Isaiah 29:14 [d] *31* Jer. 9:24 [e] *1* Some manuscripts *as I proclaimed to you God's mystery*

THURSDAY
READ
1 CORINTHIANS 1:1–9

REACHING FOR GRACE

Wouldn't we think it bizarre if a family struggled to eke out a living when all the while they had a huge sum of money in the bank or hidden under the floorboards? If they'd just dip into that stash, life would be a lot easier.

Well, we have a treasure that we, as married couples, can draw on in the everyday struggles, as well as in the major crises, of life. It's called "grace," and it's what will help us be strong today and keep us fortified to the end. That's the basis of Paul's statement to believers in 1 Corinthians 1:7–8. He's not merely giving us a motivational message to boost our faith. Verse 4 reveals the foundation on which that promise is made: We have all the gifts we need to keep us strong to the end because of God's grace given to us in Jesus.

In marriage, grace flows from God to a couple. Then, between a husband and wife, grace sustains, strengthens, washes and restores the relationship. For example, when a husband forgets his wife's birthday, she can pout and repeatedly remind him of his failure. Or she can say to her husband, "You know, because God covers my shortcomings with a big dose of grace, I can do the same for you." Or when I pull into the garage carelessly (like the other day), transferring paint and wood off the garage onto the car, my husband can choose to bestow grace on me. He may even make a joke of the incident, helping me to laugh rather than cry about the damage.

Therefore you do not lack any spiritual gift as you eagerly wait for our Lord Jesus Christ to be revealed. He will keep you strong to the end, so that you will be blameless on the day of our Lord Jesus Christ.

— 1 Corinthians 1:7–8

let's talk

- When have we tended to rely on our own strength, intelligence or money to solve our marital problems? How has that worked for us?
- When does relying on God's grace seem too passive? How does resting in his grace fit with personal responsibility in dealing with problem situations?
- How can God's grace help us when we feel we have reached the end of our rope in dealing with each other?

Perhaps the time when God's grace helps couples the most is when they are facing some difficulty. Instead of viewing a problem as something that separates them, they can draw on the power of God's grace and confront the problem together.

So how do we, practically speaking, apply God's grace? First, we recognize that we have this treasure. For example, when we are so cash-strapped that we can't afford to buy next week's groceries, my husband, in grace, might say to me, "Hey, hon, I just remembered we have a few savings bonds. Let's cash one of them in to get us through this tough spot."

Second, we reinforce that awareness of grace by reminding each other of the times God has helped us get through a difficult patch. When I lost a job, for example, Grey reminded me, "Honey, let's not forget how, when I lost my job, God gave us grace not to pick at each other when money got tight."

Third, we show gratitude for that grace. We express thanks to God in prayer. We tell each other how grateful we are for our marriage. We find ways to extend grace to others.

Could it be that some couples who have abandoned their marriages were trying to go it alone in their struggles? For all such couples, Jonah 2:8 warns: "Those who cling to worthless idols [ego, money, etc.] forfeit the grace that could be theirs." So claim grace to build a grace-filled marriage.

—MARY ANN JEFFREYS

FOR YOUR NEXT DEVOTIONAL READING, TURN TO PAGE 1281.

F

FRIDAY

READ

1 CORINTHIANS 1:10–17

GROWING THROUGH CONFLICT

During the first year of our marriage, my husband and I were good friends with a young couple. They were at that do-we-break-up-or-get-married crossroads, and we did what we could to support them as they struggled with their relationship. One evening, they stopped by our apartment to tell us they had decided to get serious about marriage. "Thank you for helping us with this," they said. "You've been a great example of people who fight all the time even though you really love each other."

It sounded like a backhanded compliment. But they came from homes in which arguments escalated into shouting matches, and parents left in anger and didn't come back. We had shown them a marriage in which two opinionated people managed to work through their differences—and differences are inevitable when two people try to make a life together—and still hold on to their connection.

A certain level of conflict in marriage means both partners feel free to speak their minds, can be honest about what they think and feel, and trust each other to stay committed despite occasional disagreements. First Corinthians 1:10 helps us understand the fine line between healthy conflict and hurtful discord.

Paul told the people in the church at Corinth to be perfectly united in mind and thought. But seriously, who could ever pull that off? It's important to understand that Paul wasn't suggesting that they agree on every detail of their lives. We see proof of that later in this letter; chapters 8–10 deal with gray areas such as whether or not it was OK to eat food that had been sacrificed to idols. Rather, Paul was talking about the big picture. "Look," he was saying, "you're never going to agree on all the details, but those details don't matter as much as you think they do. What matters is that you love God and that you help each other follow the way of Jesus."

Working out the details of married life naturally generates conflict. Why would we expect it to be otherwise? You take two people who grew up in different families with totally different sets of life experiences, expectations, hopes, ideas and beliefs, and, well, eventually someone's going to load the dishwasher the wrong way.

But the big picture of a healthy marriage is a different story. Two people, despite all the ways they differ from each other, have decided they want their lives to follow the way of Christ together. On that path the details and differences fade into the background to reveal the beautiful mystery of two becoming one. It doesn't mean their minds meld together. Or that only one person gets to have an opinion. Or that we pretend we don't argue. Instead, our unity comes as we, in Christ, daily and persistently strengthen the common bonds of love, respect and faith that make a marriage thrive.

—CARLA BARNHILL

I appeal to you, brothers, in the name of our Lord Jesus Christ, that all of you agree with one another so that there may be no divisions among you and that you may be perfectly united in mind and thought.

— 1 CORINTHIANS 1:10

let's *talk*

- ✦ What conflicts come up in our marriage? Which ones are big-picture issues? How do we manage those? Which are detail issues? How can we work together to avoid getting caught up in details that don't really matter?
- ✦ Do people think of us as a unified couple or as a couple who constantly argue? Which perception is accurate?
- ✦ Do we have too much or too little conflict? Let's talk about ways we might keep these things in balance. Could a Christian counselor help us develop better conflict management skills?

FOR YOUR NEXT DEVOTIONAL READING, TURN TO PAGE 1284.

fore time began. 8None of the rulers of this age understood it, for if they had, they would not have crucified the Lord of glory. 9However, as it is written:

> "No eye has seen,
> no ear has heard,
> no mind has conceived
> what God has prepared for those who love him"[a]—

10but God has revealed it to us by his Spirit.

The Spirit searches all things, even the deep things of God. 11For who among men knows the thoughts of a man except the man's spirit within him? In the same way no one knows the thoughts of God except the Spirit of God. 12We have not received the spirit of the world but the Spirit who is from God, that we may understand what God has freely given us. 13This is what we speak, not in words taught us by human wisdom but in words taught by the Spirit, expressing spiritual truths in spiritual words.[b] 14The man without the Spirit does not accept the things that come from the Spirit of God, for they are foolishness to him, and he cannot understand them, because they are spiritually discerned. 15The spiritual man makes judgments about all things, but he himself is not subject to any man's judgment:

> 16"For who has known the mind of the Lord
> that he may instruct him?"[c]

But we have the mind of Christ.

On Divisions in the Church

3 Brothers, I could not address you as spiritual but as worldly—mere infants in Christ. 2I gave you milk, not solid food, for you were not yet ready for it. Indeed, you are still not ready. 3You are still worldly. For since there is jealousy and quarreling among you, are you not worldly? Are you not acting like mere men? 4For when one says, "I follow Paul," and another, "I follow Apollos," are you not mere men?

5What, after all, is Apollos? And what is Paul? Only servants, through whom you came to believe—as the Lord has assigned to each his task. 6I planted the seed, Apollos watered it, but God made it grow. 7So neither he who plants nor he who waters is anything, but only God, who makes things grow. 8The man who plants and the man who waters have one purpose, and each will be rewarded according to his own labor. 9For we are God's fellow workers; you are God's field, God's building.

10By the grace God has given me, I laid a foundation as an expert builder, and someone else is building on it. But each one should be careful how he builds. 11For no one can lay any foundation other than the one already laid, which is Jesus Christ. 12If any man builds on this foundation using gold, silver, costly stones, wood, hay or straw, 13his work will be shown for what it is, because the Day will bring it to light. It will be revealed with fire, and the fire will test the quality of each man's work. 14If what he has built survives, he will receive his reward. 15If it is burned up, he will suffer loss; he himself will be saved, but only as one escaping through the flames.

16Don't you know that you yourselves are God's temple and that God's Spirit lives in you? 17If anyone destroys God's temple, God will destroy him; for God's temple is sacred, and you are that temple.

18Do not deceive yourselves. If any one of you thinks he is wise by the standards of this age, he should become a "fool" so that he may become wise. 19For the wisdom of this world is foolishness in God's sight. As it is written: "He catches the wise in their craftiness"[d]; 20and again, "The Lord knows that the thoughts of the wise are futile."[e] 21So then, no more boasting about men! All things are yours, 22whether Paul or Apollos or Cephas[f] or the world or life or death or the present or the future—all are yours, 23and you are of Christ, and Christ is of God.

Apostles of Christ

4 So then, men ought to regard us as servants of Christ and as those entrusted with the secret things of God. 2Now it is required that those who have been given a trust must prove faithful. 3I care very little if I am judged by you or by any human court; indeed, I do not even judge myself. 4My conscience is clear, but that does not make me innocent. It is the Lord who judges me. 5Therefore judge nothing before the appointed time; wait till the Lord comes. He will bring to light what is hidden in darkness and will expose the motives of men's hearts. At that time each will receive his praise from God.

6Now, brothers, I have applied these things to myself and Apollos for your benefit, so that you may learn from us the meaning of the

[a] 9 Isaiah 64:4 [b] 13 Or *Spirit, interpreting spiritual truths to spiritual men* [c] 16 Isaiah 40:13 [d] 19 Job 5:13 [e] 20 Psalm 94:11
[f] 22 That is, Peter

saying, "Do not go beyond what is written." Then you will not take pride in one man over against another. 7For who makes you different from anyone else? What do you have that you did not receive? And if you did receive it, why do you boast as though you did not?

8Already you have all you want! Already you have become rich! You have become kings—and that without us! How I wish that you really had become kings so that we might be kings with you! 9For it seems to me that God has put us apostles on display at the end of the procession, like men condemned to die in the arena. We have been made a spectacle to the whole universe, to angels as well as to men. 10We are fools for Christ, but you are so wise in Christ! We are weak, but you are strong! You are honored, we are dishonored! 11To this very hour we go hungry and thirsty, we are in rags, we are brutally treated, we are homeless. 12We work hard with our own hands. When we are cursed, we bless; when we are persecuted, we endure it; 13when we are slandered, we answer kindly. Up to this moment we have become the scum of the earth, the refuse of the world.

14I am not writing this to shame you, but to warn you, as my dear children. 15Even though you have ten thousand guardians in Christ, you do not have many fathers, for in Christ Jesus I became your father through the gospel. 16Therefore I urge you to imitate me. 17For this reason I am sending to you Timothy, my son whom I love, who is faithful in the Lord. He will remind you of my way of life in Christ Jesus, which agrees with what I teach everywhere in every church.

18Some of you have become arrogant, as if I were not coming to you. 19But I will come to you very soon, if the Lord is willing, and then I will find out not only how these arrogant people are talking, but what power they have. 20For the kingdom of God is not a matter of talk but of power. 21What do you prefer? Shall I come to you with a whip, or in love and with a gentle spirit?

Expel the Immoral Brother!

5 It is actually reported that there is sexual immorality among you, and of a kind that does not occur even among pagans: A man has his father's wife. 2And you are proud! Shouldn't you rather have been filled with grief and have put out of your fellowship the man who did this? 3Even though I am not physically present, I am with you in spirit. And I have already passed judgment on the one who did this, just as if I were present. 4When you are assembled in the name of our Lord Jesus and I am with you in spirit, and the power of our Lord Jesus is present, 5hand this man over to Satan, so that the sinful nature[a] may be destroyed and his spirit saved on the day of the Lord.

6Your boasting is not good. Don't you know that a little yeast works through the whole batch of dough? 7Get rid of the old yeast that you may be a new batch without yeast—as you really are. For Christ, our Passover lamb, has been sacrificed. 8Therefore let us keep the Festival, not with the old yeast, the yeast of malice and wickedness, but with bread without yeast, the bread of sincerity and truth.

9I have written you in my letter not to associate with sexually immoral people— 10not at all meaning the people of this world who are immoral, or the greedy and swindlers, or idolaters. In that case you would have to leave this world. 11But now I am writing you that you must not associate with anyone who calls himself a brother but is sexually immoral or greedy, an idolater or a slanderer, a drunkard or a swindler. With such a man do not even eat.

12What business is it of mine to judge those outside the church? Are you not to judge those inside? 13God will judge those outside. "Expel the wicked man from among you."[b]

Lawsuits Among Believers

6 If any of you has a dispute with another, dare he take it before the ungodly for judgment instead of before the saints? 2Do you not know that the saints will judge the world? And if you are to judge the world, are you not competent to judge trivial cases? 3Do you not know that we will judge angels? How much more the things of this life! 4Therefore, if you have disputes about such matters, appoint as judges even men of little account in the church![c] 5I say this to shame you. Is it possible that there is nobody among you wise enough to judge a dispute between believers? 6But instead, one brother goes to law against another—and this in front of unbelievers!

7The very fact that you have lawsuits among you means you have been completely defeated already. Why not rather be wronged? Why not

---

a 5 Or *that his body;* or *that the flesh* *b* 13 Deut. 17:7; 19:19; 21:21; 22:21,24; 24:7 *c* 4 Or *matters, do you appoint as judges men of little account in the church?*

WEEKEND

confidential matters

People sometimes feel the need to blow off steam or seek advice about their marriage. On the plus side, that can defuse an issue enough to prevent an unnecessary confrontation with a spouse. It can yield new perspectives or practical strategies for solving a problem. At times, unloading on a friend or relative can prevent a problem from escalating. As one husband said, "I get all worked up about something my wife does and then I talk to a few other guys and find out their wives do the same thing. Then I realize, 'This isn't a personal attack. It's just the way women are.' "

But venting also has a down side. It can diminish your motivation to actually solve the problem. What's more, it can be difficult to discern that fine line between sharing and being disloyal to your mate.

So before you open your mouth, here are a few questions to consider.

1. Is it premature to talk to someone else? Sometimes it's tempting to tell others about a problem before you've had a chance to cool off, pray about the problem, and work through it with your spouse. Ask yourself, "Will there be damaging consequences I can never undo if I share this information?"

2. What is my goal? Before you air negative feelings about your spouse, be sure you understand what you're trying to accomplish. If you're trying to get advice to solve a problem, make sure the problem really needs to be solved. There's nothing inherently wrong with seeking relief from negative emotions, as long as you don't make the problem worse in the process. But if, after challenging your own motivations, you realize that you're trying to get back at your spouse or you're unloading on a friend as a substitute for tackling an issue directly with your partner put a lid on that steam.

3. What are appropriate boundaries? The first rule is: Do no harm. This principle may mean different things in different situations. One woman going through a serious crisis in her marriage chose not to share her painful struggle with her parents and siblings. Her reasoning was simple: "If my marriage survives, I would not have given my family information about my husband that would affect how they see him for the rest of their lives. I don't want our marriage to have that kind of burden."

A good guideline to use is that the depth of revelation should be appropriate to the depth of the friendship. A friend of mine says that, with most people, she would never go beyond venting "little bursts of steam" about minor irritations in her marriage. "I might tell a friend how it bugs me that Todd collects so much junk," she says, "but I'd never share any painful problems unless it was with someone I trusted very deeply."

Another guideline: Try to talk about the problem instead of the person. There's no harm in occasional griping about irritations in your marriage as long as you're not labeling and judging your spouse in the process.

"Putting the marriage first has to be a conscious choice," says Maureen. She and her husband, Tom, have a ground rule: They never portray each other in a negative way. Maureen adds, "There are too many couples who make disparaging, pseudo-funny remarks that actually eat away at the foundation of marriage."

Is it a good idea to unload your marriage issues on someone else? It depends. If you just need to blow off some steam and you have a same-sex confidant who won't think any less of your spouse as a result, go for it. If you genuinely want help to solve a problem and have a wise marriage mentor, don't hesitate to seek advice.

But if you are developing a habit of ritual lament as a way to get even with your mate or as a substitute for working on your marriage problems, then consider a better alternative. Prayer, talking to your spouse directly, and examining your own role in the problem will do more to solve your dilemma.

—JANIS LONG HARRIS

is this confidant appropriate?

Use discernment when looking for a listening ear, and use this checklist to help evaluate potential confidants.

1. Can this person be trusted with confidential information?
2. Will this person keep this matter private?
3. Will this person respect my boundaries?
4. Will this person offer a mature perspective?
5. Will this person pray for me?
6. Is this person more experienced than I am?
7. Does this person value commitment in marriage?
8. Will this person keep me accountable without unjustly condemning me?
9. Is the confidant someone of the same sex or a married couple?
10. Is this person mature enough not to be negatively affected by my confidences?

HOW ARE WE DOING?

date

let's make a DATE

BLOW OFF SOME STEAM

One of the best ways to vent is through physical activity, so blow off some steam in a batting cage or on a racquetball court, bowling alley or golf course—then add a twist of humor. Instead of a real golf course, try a miniature one. At the batting cage, make the better spouse bat with his or her opposite hand. Buy two pairs of crazy socks to wear while bowling. Forget your real names; use pet names when scoring. And be sure to have incentives—each ball hit, par or strike earns a kiss. No keeping score—you're both winners!

FOR YOUR NEXT DEVOTIONAL READING, TURN TO PAGE 1286.

LESSONS FROM THE *Bible*

Take a look at 1 Chronicles 27:32–33 and discuss the following. David had two counselors and a confidant. How do you think those two roles differed in David's case? How do those two roles differ in the context of marriage? In what ways do we as a married couple need both counselors and confidants? Who might serve us in those roles?

MONDAY

READ

1 CORINTHIANS 3:1–23

HONORING OUR BODIES

In the first few days following my husband's open-heart surgery, I was struck by the sacredness of the human body. I also realized how much I loved every inch of my husband's flesh as he strained to breathe.

He's a good 12 inches taller than I am, outweighs me by 75 pounds and is strong as an ox. But in those first few days after surgery, he seemed so fragile.

I rigged up a chair for him to sit on in the shower while I bathed him and shampooed his hair. He couldn't lift his arms, so I helped him put on his shirt and blow-dried his hair. His incision had gotten infected, so his nurses taught me how to administer strong antibiotics through an intravenous line in his arm.

Before the surgery, when my husband was still strong and seemingly invincible, I'd often asked him to make a muscle so I could touch it. "That's my arm," I'd say, meaning that his arm and its muscle belonged to me and no one else. Likewise, when I would walk across the room, he'd good-naturedly toss a wadded up paper towel at me. "I can do that—that body's mine," he'd say.

Don't you know that you yourselves are God's temple and that God's Spirit lives in you?

— 1 Corinthians 3:16

let's talk

- ✦ What does each of us love about our own body? About the other's body?
- ✦ In what ways do we show that we honor each other's bodies?
- ✦ In what ways could we improve our health habits? How do we sabotage those efforts? How can we support and encourage each other in making healthy changes to our individual lifestyles?

The human body is indeed sacred because each one of us is made in God's image (see Genesis 1:26–27). Furthermore, as believers in whom God's Spirit dwells, we are God's "temples." Paul valued this concept so much that he used it twice in 1 Corinthians in relation to the church collectively (3:16–17) and to believers individually (6:19–20). As God's temples, we are to consider our bodies as holy places, set apart for his honor: "Do you not know that your body is a temple of the Holy Spirit, who is in you, whom you have received from God? You are not your own; you were bought at a price. Therefore honor God with your body" (1 Corinthians 6:19–20).

Marriage brings an additional dimension to the concept of the human body. When God made Adam and Eve, he said the two would become "one flesh" (Genesis 2:24). Jesus reiterated this in Matthew 19:5. That means that, in essence, my body no longer belongs solely to me; it also belongs to God and to my husband.

Therefore, I have a responsibility to honor my body for the sake of God, my husband and myself. For me, that means controlling what I eat (I struggle with my weight). It means exercising to keep myself healthy. It means not flaunting my sexuality before anyone other than my husband.

For my husband, it means quitting smoking. It means avoiding salt and caffeine and fat. It means taking daily walks to improve his cardiovascular system. It means finding ways to ease stress and put limits on work. And because we are two who have become one, it means helping each other struggle with lifestyle changes that will make our bodies strong and healthy.

We could have reacted to my husband's heart condition with a cavalier attitude: "Eat, drink, and be merry, for tomorrow we die." But I owe it to my spouse and to the God who made me in his image to care for my body as best I can—and to care for my husband's too.

—NANCY KENNEDY

FOR YOUR NEXT DEVOTIONAL READING, TURN TO PAGE 1288.

rather be cheated? 8Instead, you yourselves
cheat and do wrong, and you do this to your
brothers.
9Do you not know that the wicked will not
inherit the kingdom of God? Do not be deceived: Neither the sexually immoral nor idolaters nor adulterers nor male prostitutes nor
homosexual offenders 10nor thieves nor the
greedy nor drunkards nor slanderers nor swindlers will inherit the kingdom of God. 11And
that is what some of you were. But you were
washed, you were sanctified, you were justified
in the name of the Lord Jesus Christ and by
the Spirit of our God.

Sexual Immorality

12"Everything is permissible for me"—but
not everything is beneficial. "Everything is
permissible for me"—but I will not be mastered by anything. 13"Food for the stomach
and the stomach for food"—but God will destroy them both. The body is not meant for
sexual immorality, but for the Lord, and the
Lord for the body. 14By his power God raised
the Lord from the dead, and he will raise us
also. 15Do you not know that your bodies
are members of Christ himself? Shall I then
take the members of Christ and unite them
with a prostitute? Never! 16Do you not know
that he who unites himself with a prostitute
is one with her in body? For it is said, "The
two will become one flesh."[a] 17But he who
unites himself with the Lord is one with him
in spirit.
18Flee from sexual immorality. All other
sins a man commits are outside his body, but
he who sins sexually sins against his own body.
19Do you not know that your body is a temple of the Holy Spirit, who is in you, whom
you have received from God? You are not your
own; 20you were bought at a price. Therefore
honor God with your body.

Marriage

7 Now for the matters you wrote about: It is
good for a man not to marry.[b] 2But since
there is so much immorality, each man
should have his own wife, and each woman
her own husband. 3The husband should fulfill his marital duty to his wife, and likewise
the wife to her husband. 4The wife's body does
not belong to her alone but also to her husband. In the same way, the husband's body
does not belong to him alone but also to his
wife. 5Do not deprive each other except by
mutual consent and for a time, so that you
may devote yourselves to prayer. Then come
together again so that Satan will not tempt
you because of your lack of self-control. 6I
say this as a concession, not as a command. 7I
wish that all men were as I am. But each man
has his own gift from God; one has this gift,
another has that.
8Now to the unmarried and the widows I
say: It is good for them to stay unmarried, as
I am. 9But if they cannot control themselves,
they should marry, for it is better to marry
than to burn with passion.
10To the married I give this command (not
I, but the Lord): A wife must not separate
from her husband. 11But if she does, she must
remain unmarried or else be reconciled to her
husband. And a husband must not divorce his
wife.
12To the rest I say this (I, not the Lord): If
any brother has a wife who is not a believer
and she is willing to live with him, he must
not divorce her. 13And if a woman has a husband who is not a believer and he is willing to
live with her, she must not divorce him. 14For
the unbelieving husband has been sanctified
through his wife, and the unbelieving wife
has been sanctified through her believing husband. Otherwise your children would be unclean, but as it is, they are holy.
15But if the unbeliever leaves, let him do so.
A believing man or woman is not bound in
such circumstances; God has called us to live
in peace. 16How do you know, wife, whether
you will save your husband? Or, how do you
know, husband, whether you will save your
wife?
17Nevertheless, each one should retain the
place in life that the Lord assigned to him and
to which God has called him. This is the rule
I lay down in all the churches. 18Was a man
already circumcised when he was called? He
should not become uncircumcised. Was a man
uncircumcised when he was called? He should
not be circumcised. 19Circumcision is nothing
and uncircumcision is nothing. Keeping God's
commands is what counts. 20Each one should
remain in the situation which he was in when
God called him. 21Were you a slave when
you were called? Don't let it trouble you—although if you can gain your freedom, do so.
22For he who was a slave when he was called
by the Lord is the Lord's freedman; similarly,
he who was a free man when he was called is
Christ's slave. 23You were bought at a price;

---

[a] *16* Gen. 2:24 [b] *1* Or *"It is good for a man not to have sexual relations with a woman."*

TUESDAY
READ
1 CORINTHIANS 6:1–11

STAYING OUT OF COURT

The very fact that you have lawsuits among you means you have been completely defeated already. Why not rather be wronged? Why not rather be cheated?

— 1 Corinthians 6:7

let's talk

- What divorces have we witnessed among believers? What did we see in those marriages that may have contributed to the divorce? Did divorce solve anything, or is there still bitterness, anger, mistrust and hurt between the couple?
- How do we resolve our differences? Do we work through troublesome issues and settle them, or do the same issues keep surfacing? What might be at the heart of those disputes?
- At what point might we have to bring our difficulties to another couple, a counselor or a pastor for help?

Fifteen years ago, Ryan and Laura were young, newly married Christians. They had the same quirky sense of humor, and they both loved animals. They shared the gospel with friends and family. And they ministered together as musicians. Five years ago their marriage ended in a bitter divorce. They had some financial difficulties that led to anger, which led to resentment, which led to disconnection from the church, which led to infidelity, which led to separation, which led to divorce.

Today, Ryan and Laura only speak to each other through lawyers—and then, it seems, only to make accusations, argue about child support or schedule visitation for their two young boys. No one could have predicted this outcome.

Or could they? Of course, while most Christian couples occasionally fight, they don't end up in divorce court. But are there some below-the-surface attitudes that might predict such an outcome—self-centeredness, quarrelsomeness, vindictiveness, envy, impatience, pettiness, pride, scorekeeping, anger or avoidance of troublesome issues?

Some Christians say, "Life would be so much better for us if only we lived like people in the early church." Really? The church in Corinth was a mess. The culture surrounding the church was marked by pagan worship and immorality. And the church wasn't much different. In 1 Corinthians 6, Paul even had to warn believers about suing each other.

Paul chastised them, asking them what they would win in court if, along the way, they stopped being forgiving, patient, merciful and loving—in short, if they gave up their new identity in Christ.

So Paul urged believers—including us—to be willing to be wronged or cheated rather than bring our differences to lawyers in the judicial system. Divorce, he implied, means we have already been defeated. Instead, we must follow Jesus' instructions about settling disputes (see Matthew 18:15–17). If we are unable to work through our differences, we should bring in someone else—someone "wise enough to judge a dispute between believers" (1 Corinthians 6:5)—meaning, perhaps, a mentor couple or a pastor or a Christian counselor. If that fails, we might have to meet with church elders.

Throughout that process, we can trust that God will punish wrongdoing. Paul encourages us to stay out of secular court until we have exhausted the resources of the church to help us. And we can probably do that if we pattern our behavior on that of our crucified Lord and Savior Jesus Christ.

It's helpful to periodically examine our hearts for attitudes rooted in sin and ask for help purging those attitudes so we can act as new creatures in Christ. For as Paul assures us, "[we] were washed, [we] were sanctified, [we] were justified in the name of the Lord Jesus Christ and by the Spirit of our God" (1 Corinthians 6:11). That gives us power to work through most any differences—outside of court.

—KYLE WHITE

FOR YOUR NEXT DEVOTIONAL READING, TURN TO PAGE 1289.

WEDNESDAY
READ
1 CORINTHIANS 7:1–16

IS IT OK TO WITHHOLD SEX?

In 1 Corinthians 7:1-7, Paul addressed the sexual relationship between married couples. How could a single, celibate man who wrote on the profound and deep truths of Christ address such a personal issue between husband and wife?

Simply put, the church in Corinth asked him to do so. We can pick up the gist of their question in verse 1. I imagine the request went something like this: "Is it OK for one partner in a marriage to decide to be celibate for a time—perhaps because of a desire for heightened spirituality or because of a low libido?" In response, Paul laid down a principle of marriage that still works today: If you want to choose long-term celibacy, fine, but then it's better to stay single. Marriage without joyful, mutually satisfying sex is fertile ground in which Satan can plant seeds of infidelity.

Why did God give us the volatile, complex and mysterious gift of marital sexuality? We can't know for sure, but perhaps because—besides being fun, free, nurturing and procreating—marital sex works against selfishness, which many would agree is a strong contender for being "the root of all evil." Paul says spouses' bodies belong to each other.

A husband might not share the TV remote, some spouses keep separate checkbooks, but in the sexual relationship, there's no room for an I-can-do-whatever-I-want-or-don't-want attitude. And though Paul only said that we are not to unilaterally withhold God's magnificent gift of sex, he was speaking about more than physical intimacy. Spouses are not only to ensure that their sexual relationship is mutually satisfying, but they are also to act as guardians and protectors of each other's bodies.

If we apply Paul's basic principle that husband and wife share ownership of each other's bodies, lots of areas of mutual caring for those bodies come to mind. My husband has hypertension and needs to eat a low-salt diet. I like salt, but because I care for Grey's body, I use Mrs. Dash's salt-free seasoning.

We also encourage each other to exercise and eat healthy food. Grey knows that watching TV is not my idea of relaxing, so he'll turn it off (except during Bronco games) and suggest we take a ride into the mountains after lunch. Since, for men, sexual desire is sparked visually, I try to keep myself attractive and healthy for Grey. Women find emotional connection makes them desire their husbands sexually, so Grey does what he can to address my emotional needs before we make love.

Not only does this mutual giving reward us relationally and reflect God's best design for marriage, but the sex keeps getting better.

—MARY ANN JEFFREYS

The wife's body does not belong to her alone but also to her husband. In the same way, the husband's body does not belong to him alone but also to his wife.

— 1 CORINTHIANS 7:4

let's talk

✦ What did we know about sexual techniques before we married? What have we learned about pleasing each other sexually? What do we personally find most satisfying?

✦ What factors could make celibacy sound appealing to one of us? How does the other feel about that? When is celibacy good for our relationship? When is it not?

✦ Be honest: Has one of us ever withheld sex out of anger, revenge or selfishness? What was the effect? How can we work through issues without taking it out on our sex life?

FOR YOUR NEXT DEVOTIONAL READING, TURN TO PAGE 1292.

do not become slaves of men. 24Brothers, each
man, as responsible to God, should remain in
the situation God called him to.

25Now about virgins: I have no command
from the Lord, but I give a judgment as one
who by the Lord's mercy is trustworthy. 26Be-
cause of the present crisis, I think that it is
good for you to remain as you are. 27Are you
married? Do not seek a divorce. Are you unmarried? Do not look for a wife. 28But if you
do marry, you have not sinned; and if a virgin
marries, she has not sinned. But those who
marry will face many troubles in this life, and
I want to spare you this.

29What I mean, brothers, is that the time
is short. From now on those who have wives
should live as if they had none; 30those who
mourn, as if they did not; those who are happy, as if they were not; those who buy something, as if it were not theirs to keep; 31those
who use the things of the world, as if not en-
grossed in them. For this world in its present
form is passing away.

32I would like you to be free from concern.
An unmarried man is concerned about the
Lord's affairs—how he can please the Lord.
33But a married man is concerned about the
affairs of this world—how he can please his
wife— 34and his interests are divided. An unmarried woman or virgin is concerned about
the Lord's affairs: Her aim is to be devoted to
the Lord in both body and spirit. But a married woman is concerned about the affairs of
this world—how she can please her husband.
35I am saying this for your own good, not to
restrict you, but that you may live in a right
way in undivided devotion to the Lord.

36If anyone thinks he is acting improperly
toward the virgin he is engaged to, and if she is
getting along in years and he feels he ought to
marry, he should do as he wants. He is not sinning. They should get married. 37But the man
who has settled the matter in his own mind,
who is under no compulsion but has control
over his own will, and who has made up his
mind not to marry the virgin—this man also
does the right thing. 38So then, he who marries the virgin does right, but he who does not
marry her does even better. [a]

39A woman is bound to her husband as
long as he lives. But if her husband dies, she is
free to marry anyone she wishes, but he must
belong to the Lord. 40In my judgment, she is
happier if she stays as she is—and I think that
I too have the Spirit of God.

Food Sacrificed to Idols

8 Now about food sacrificed to idols: We
know that we all possess knowledge. [b]
Knowledge puffs up, but love builds up.
2The man who thinks he knows something
does not yet know as he ought to know. 3But
the man who loves God is known by God.

4So then, about eating food sacrificed to
idols: We know that an idol is nothing at all
in the world and that there is no God but one.
5For even if there are so-called gods, whether in heaven or on earth (as indeed there are
many "gods" and many "lords"), 6yet for us
there is but one God, the Father, from whom
all things came and for whom we live; and
there is but one Lord, Jesus Christ, through
whom all things came and through whom we
live.

7But not everyone knows this. Some people are still so accustomed to idols that when
they eat such food they think of it as having
been sacrificed to an idol, and since their conscience is weak, it is defiled. 8But food does
not bring us near to God; we are no worse if
we do not eat, and no better if we do.

9Be careful, however, that the exercise of
your freedom does not become a stumbling
block to the weak. 10For if anyone with a
weak conscience sees you who have this
knowledge eating in an idol's temple, won't he
be emboldened to eat what has been sacrificed
to idols? 11So this weak brother, for whom
Christ died, is destroyed by your knowledge.
12When you sin against your brothers in this
way and wound their weak conscience, you
sin against Christ. 13Therefore, if what I eat
causes my brother to fall into sin, I will never
eat meat again, so that I will not cause him
to fall.

The Rights of an Apostle

9 Am I not free? Am I not an apostle? Have I
not seen Jesus our Lord? Are you not the result of my work in the Lord? 2Even though
I may not be an apostle to others, surely I am
to you! For you are the seal of my apostleship
in the Lord.

3This is my defense to those who sit in judg-

---

[a] 36-38 Or [36]*If anyone thinks he is not treating his daughter properly, and if she is getting along in years, and he feels she ought to marry, he should do as he wants. He is not sinning. He should let her get married.* [37]*But the man who has settled the matter in his own mind, who is under no compulsion but has control over his own will, and who has made up his mind to keep the virgin unmarried—this man also does the right thing.* [38]*So then, he who gives his virgin in marriage does right, but he who does not give her in marriage does even better.*
[b] *1* Or *"We all possess knowledge," as you say*

ment on me. 4Don't we have the right to food
and drink? 5Don't we have the right to take a
believing wife along with us, as do the other
apostles and the Lord's brothers and Cephas[a]?
6Or is it only I and Barnabas who must work
for a living?

7Who serves as a soldier at his own expense?
Who plants a vineyard and does not eat of
its grapes? Who tends a flock and does not
drink of the milk? 8Do I say this merely from
a human point of view? Doesn't the Law say
the same thing? 9For it is written in the Law
of Moses: "Do not muzzle an ox while it is
treading out the grain."[b] Is it about oxen that
God is concerned? 10Surely he says this for us,
doesn't he? Yes, this was written for us, because
when the plowman plows and the thresher
threshes, they ought to do so in the hope of
sharing in the harvest. 11If we have sown spiritual seed among you, is it too much if we reap
a material harvest from you? 12If others have
this right of support from you, shouldn't we
have it all the more?

But we did not use this right. On the contrary, we put up with anything rather than
hinder the gospel of Christ. 13Don't you know
that those who work in the temple get their
food from the temple, and those who serve at
the altar share in what is offered on the altar?
14In the same way, the Lord has commanded
that those who preach the gospel should receive their living from the gospel.

15But I have not used any of these rights.
And I am not writing this in the hope that
you will do such things for me. I would rather
die than have anyone deprive me of this boast.
16Yet when I preach the gospel, I cannot boast,
for I am compelled to preach. Woe to me if
I do not preach the gospel! 17If I preach voluntarily, I have a reward; if not voluntarily, I
am simply discharging the trust committed to
me. 18What then is my reward? Just this: that
in preaching the gospel I may offer it free of
charge, and so not make use of my rights in
preaching it.

19Though I am free and belong to no man,
I make myself a slave to everyone, to win as
many as possible. 20To the Jews I became like
a Jew, to win the Jews. To those under the law
I became like one under the law (though I myself am not under the law), so as to win those
under the law. 21To those not having the law
I became like one not having the law (though
I am not free from God's law but am under
Christ's law), so as to win those not having the
law. 22To the weak I became weak, to win the
weak. I have become all things to all men so
that by all possible means I might save some.
23I do all this for the sake of the gospel, that I
may share in its blessings.

24Do you not know that in a race all the
runners run, but only one gets the prize? Run
in such a way as to get the prize. 25Everyone
who competes in the games goes into strict
training. They do it to get a crown that will
not last; but we do it to get a crown that will
last forever. 26Therefore I do not run like a
man running aimlessly; I do not fight like a
man beating the air. 27No, I beat my body and
make it my slave so that after I have preached
to others, I myself will not be disqualified for
the prize.

Warnings From Israel's History

10 For I do not want you to be ignorant
of the fact, brothers, that our forefathers were all under the cloud and that
they all passed through the sea. 2They were
all baptized into Moses in the cloud and in
the sea. 3They all ate the same spiritual food
4and drank the same spiritual drink; for they
drank from the spiritual rock that accompanied them, and that rock was Christ. 5Nev-
ertheless, God was not pleased with most of
them; their bodies were scattered over the
desert.

6Now these things occurred as examples[c] to
keep us from setting our hearts on evil things
as they did. 7Do not be idolaters, as some of
them were; as it is written: "The people sat
down to eat and drink and got up to indulge
in pagan revelry."[d] 8We should not commit
sexual immorality, as some of them did—and
in one day twenty-three thousand of them
died. 9We should not test the Lord, as some of
them did—and were killed by snakes. 10And
do not grumble, as some of them did—and
were killed by the destroying angel.

11These things happened to them as examples and were written down as warnings
for us, on whom the fulfillment of the ages
has come. 12So, if you think you are standing firm, be careful that you don't fall! 13No
temptation has seized you except what is
common to man. And God is faithful; he will
not let you be tempted beyond what you can
bear. But when you are tempted, he will also
provide a way out so that you can stand up
under it.

---

[a] 5 That is, Peter [b] 9 Deut. 25:4 [c] 6 Or *types*; also in verse 11 [d] 7 Exodus 32:6

THURSDAY
READ
1 CORINTHIANS 10:1–13

THE WAY OUT OF TEMPTATION

If you think you are standing firm, be careful that you don't fall! No temptation has seized you except what is common to man.

— 1 Corinthians 10:12–13

let's talk

- Have there been times in our marriage when one of us faced temptation and we weren't sure we could overcome it?
- Did we find the way out that God promised, or did we give in to temptation? What happened as a result?
- What are some of the temptations facing each of us today, and what strategies do we have in place to face them?

A friend who had a seemingly happy marriage was shocked when her husband admitted he was addicted to Internet pornography. "I didn't think this could happen to us," she said. "We love and serve the Lord. How could he get sucked into this awful stuff?"

How often we fall into the trap of believing that we could never be tempted to do something that would seriously damage our walk with God. After all, we're mature Christians. We know right from wrong.

Paul addressed that attitude in 1 Corinthians 10:12, saying that no matter how strong we are in the faith, we must never assume that we are above temptation. "If you think you are standing firm, be careful that you don't fall!" And Paul didn't accept the excuse that our situation is different from that of others and therefore our temptation is too hard to resist. For he said, "No temptation has seized you except what is common to man" (verse 13).

Sometimes pride sets us up for temptation. We think we are such good Christians that nothing bad will happen to us. We become like the arrogant people described in Psalm 10:6 who boasted, "Nothing will shake me . . . [I'll] never have trouble." But before we know it, the sin of thinking we're above temptation leads to the sin of pride, and we suddenly find ourselves confronted with the very problem, situation, emotion or person that we were certain would never tempt us. Proverbs 16:18 warns us that "pride goes before destruction, a haughty spirit before a fall."

When we're in the throes of temptation—and if we ultimately succumb to it—we often say, "It was just too much; it was too irresistible!" But Paul didn't buy that argument. He knew that even in the fiercest temptation, we know what is right and wrong, and we make the choice either to flee from sin or to indulge in it. Yet Paul didn't just abandon us with a warning against temptation. He said in 1 Corinthians 10:13, "God is faithful; he will not let you be tempted beyond what you can bear. But when you are tempted, he will also provide a way out so that you can stand up under it."

That puts the final nail in the argument, doesn't it? We're not tempted in any way that isn't common to others, we aren't tempted beyond what we can stand, and God promises us a way out of temptation. If we choose to give in to temptation and sin anyway, we can't say God didn't give us an exit strategy.

So many temptations face us as married couples—alcohol and drug addictions, gambling, flirting with a coworker, Internet friendships with the opposite sex, lying, overspending, gossip . . . and the list goes on. By remembering God's warning and his ultimate promise of deliverance, we can stand strong in the face of whatever temptation comes our way.

—VALERIE VAN KOOTEN

FOR YOUR NEXT DEVOTIONAL READING, TURN TO PAGE 1296.

Idol Feasts and the Lord's Supper

14Therefore, my dear friends, flee from idolatry. 15I speak to sensible people; judge for yourselves what I say. 16Is not the cup of thanksgiving for which we give thanks a participation in the blood of Christ? And is not the bread that we break a participation in the body of Christ? 17Because there is one loaf, we, who are many, are one body, for we all partake of the one loaf.

18Consider the people of Israel: Do not those who eat the sacrifices participate in the altar? 19Do I mean then that a sacrifice offered to an idol is anything, or that an idol is anything? 20No, but the sacrifices of pagans are offered to demons, not to God, and I do not want you to be participants with demons. 21You cannot drink the cup of the Lord and the cup of demons too; you cannot have a part in both the Lord's table and the table of demons. 22Are we trying to arouse the Lord's jealousy? Are we stronger than he?

The Believer's Freedom

23"Everything is permissible"—but not everything is beneficial. "Everything is permissible"—but not everything is constructive. 24Nobody should seek his own good, but the good of others.

25Eat anything sold in the meat market without raising questions of conscience, 26for, "The earth is the Lord's, and everything in it."[a]

27If some unbeliever invites you to a meal and you want to go, eat whatever is put before you without raising questions of conscience. 28But if anyone says to you, "This has been offered in sacrifice," then do not eat it, both for the sake of the man who told you and for conscience' sake[b]— 29the other man's conscience, I mean, not yours. For why should my freedom be judged by another's conscience? 30If I take part in the meal with thankfulness, why am I denounced because of something I thank God for?

31So whether you eat or drink or whatever you do, do it all for the glory of God. 32Do not cause anyone to stumble, whether Jews, Greeks or the church of God— 33even as I try to please everybody in every way. For I am not seeking my own good but the good of many, so that they may be saved.

11 1Follow my example, as I follow the example of Christ.

Propriety in Worship

2I praise you for remembering me in everything and for holding to the teachings,[c] just as I passed them on to you.

3Now I want you to realize that the head of every man is Christ, and the head of the woman is man, and the head of Christ is God. 4Every man who prays or prophesies with his head covered dishonors his head. 5And every woman who prays or prophesies with her head uncovered dishonors her head—it is just as though her head were shaved. 6If a woman does not cover her head, she should have her hair cut off; and if it is a disgrace for a woman to have her hair cut or shaved off, she should cover her head. 7A man ought not to cover his head,[d] since he is the image and glory of God; but the woman is the glory of man. 8For man did not come from woman, but woman from man; 9neither was man created for woman, but woman for man. 10For this reason, and because of the angels, the woman ought to have a sign of authority on her head.

11In the Lord, however, woman is not independent of man, nor is man independent of woman. 12For as woman came from man, so also man is born of woman. But everything comes from God. 13Judge for yourselves: Is it proper for a woman to pray to God with her head uncovered? 14Does not the very nature of things teach you that if a man has long hair, it is a disgrace to him, 15but that if a woman has long hair, it is her glory? For long hair is given to her as a covering. 16If anyone wants to be contentious about this, we have no other practice—nor do the churches of God.

The Lord's Supper

17In the following directives I have no praise for you, for your meetings do more harm than good. 18In the first place, I hear that when you come together as a church, there are divisions among you, and to some extent I believe it. 19No doubt there have to be differences among you to show which of you have God's approval. 20When you come together, it is not the Lord's Supper you eat, 21for as you

---

[a] 26 Psalm 24:1 [b] 28 Some manuscripts *conscience' sake, for "the earth is the Lord's and everything in it"* [c] 2 Or *traditions*
[d] 4-7 Or *4Every man who prays or prophesies with long hair dishonors his head. 5And every woman who prays or prophesies with no covering ⌞of hair⌟ on her head dishonors her head—she is just like one of the "shorn women." 6If a woman has no covering, let her be for now with short hair, but since it is a disgrace for a woman to have her hair shorn or shaved, she should grow it again. 7A man ought not to have long hair*

eat, each of you goes ahead without waiting for anybody else. One remains hungry, another gets drunk. 22Don't you have homes to eat and drink in? Or do you despise the church of God and humiliate those who have nothing? What shall I say to you? Shall I praise you for this? Certainly not!

23For I received from the Lord what I also passed on to you: The Lord Jesus, on the night he was betrayed, took bread, 24and when he had given thanks, he broke it and said, "This is my body, which is for you; do this in remembrance of me." 25In the same way, after supper he took the cup, saying, "This cup is the new covenant in my blood; do this, whenever you drink it, in remembrance of me." 26For whenever you eat this bread and drink this cup, you proclaim the Lord's death until he comes.

27Therefore, whoever eats the bread or drinks the cup of the Lord in an unworthy manner will be guilty of sinning against the body and blood of the Lord. 28A man ought to examine himself before he eats of the bread and drinks of the cup. 29For anyone who eats and drinks without recognizing the body of the Lord eats and drinks judgment on himself. 30That is why many among you are weak and sick, and a number of you have fallen asleep. 31But if we judged ourselves, we would not come under judgment. 32When we are judged by the Lord, we are being disciplined so that we will not be condemned with the world.

33So then, my brothers, when you come together to eat, wait for each other. 34If anyone is hungry, he should eat at home, so that when you meet together it may not result in judgment.

And when I come I will give further directions.

Spiritual Gifts

12 Now about spiritual gifts, brothers, I do not want you to be ignorant. 2You know that when you were pagans, somehow or other you were influenced and led astray to mute idols. 3Therefore I tell you that no one who is speaking by the Spirit of God says, "Jesus be cursed," and no one can say, "Jesus is Lord," except by the Holy Spirit.

4There are different kinds of gifts, but the same Spirit. 5There are different kinds of service, but the same Lord. 6There are different kinds of working, but the same God works all of them in all men.

7Now to each one the manifestation of the Spirit is given for the common good. 8To one there is given through the Spirit the message of wisdom, to another the message of knowledge by means of the same Spirit, 9to another faith by the same Spirit, to another gifts of healing by that one Spirit, 10to another miraculous powers, to another prophecy, to another distinguishing between spirits, to another speaking in different kinds of tongues,[a] and to still another the interpretation of tongues.[a] 11All these are the work of one and the same Spirit, and he gives them to each one, just as he determines.

One Body, Many Parts

12The body is a unit, though it is made up of many parts; and though all its parts are many, they form one body. So it is with Christ. 13For we were all baptized by[b] one Spirit into one body—whether Jews or Greeks, slave or free—and we were all given the one Spirit to drink.

14Now the body is not made up of one part but of many. 15If the foot should say, "Because I am not a hand, I do not belong to the body," it would not for that reason cease to be part of the body. 16And if the ear should say, "Because I am not an eye, I do not belong to the body," it would not for that reason cease to be part of the body. 17If the whole body were an eye, where would the sense of hearing be? If the whole body were an ear, where would the sense of smell be? 18But in fact God has arranged the parts in the body, every one of them, just as he wanted them to be. 19If they were all one part, where would the body be? 20As it is, there are many parts, but one body.

21The eye cannot say to the hand, "I don't need you!" And the head cannot say to the feet, "I don't need you!" 22On the contrary, those parts of the body that seem to be weaker are indispensable, 23and the parts that we think are less honorable we treat with special honor. And the parts that are unpresentable are treated with special modesty, 24while our presentable parts need no special treatment. But God has combined the members of the body and has given greater honor to the parts that lacked it, 25so that there should be no division in the body, but that its parts should have equal concern for each other. 26If one

a *10* Or *languages*; also in verse 28 *b* *13* Or *with*; or *in*

part suffers, every part suffers with it; if one
part is honored, every part rejoices with it.
27Now you are the body of Christ, and each
one of you is a part of it. 28And in the church
God has appointed first of all apostles, second
prophets, third teachers, then workers of miracles, also those having gifts of healing, those
able to help others, those with gifts of administration, and those speaking in different kinds
of tongues. 29Are all apostles? Are all prophets? Are all teachers? Do all work miracles?
30Do all have gifts of healing? Do all speak in
tongues[a]? Do all interpret? 31But eagerly desire[b] the greater gifts.

Love

And now I will show you the most excellent way.

13 If I speak in the tongues[c] of men and
of angels, but have not love, I am only a
resounding gong or a clanging cymbal.
2If I have the gift of prophecy and can fathom
all mysteries and all knowledge, and if I have
a faith that can move mountains, but have not
love, I am nothing. 3If I give all I possess to the
poor and surrender my body to the flames,[d]
but have not love, I gain nothing.
4Love is patient, love is kind. It does not
envy, it does not boast, it is not proud. 5It is
not rude, it is not self-seeking, it is not easily
angered, it keeps no record of wrongs. 6Love
does not delight in evil but rejoices with the
truth. 7It always protects, always trusts, always
hopes, always perseveres.
8Love never fails. But where there are
prophecies, they will cease; where there are
tongues, they will be stilled; where there is
knowledge, it will pass away. 9For we know
in part and we prophesy in part, 10but when
perfection comes, the imperfect disappears.
11When I was a child, I talked like a child, I
thought like a child, I reasoned like a child.
When I became a man, I put childish ways
behind me. 12Now we see but a poor reflection
as in a mirror; then we shall see face to face.
Now I know in part; then I shall know fully,
even as I am fully known.
13And now these three remain: faith, hope
and love. But the greatest of these is love.

Gifts of Prophecy and Tongues

14 Follow the way of love and eagerly desire spiritual gifts, especially the gift of
prophecy. 2For anyone who speaks in a
tongue[e] does not speak to men but to God.
Indeed, no one understands him; he utters
mysteries with his spirit.[f] 3But everyone who
prophesies speaks to men for their strengthening, encouragement and comfort. 4He who
speaks in a tongue edifies himself, but he who
prophesies edifies the church. 5I would like
every one of you to speak in tongues,[g] but
I would rather have you prophesy. He who
prophesies is greater than one who speaks
in tongues,[g] unless he interprets, so that the
church may be edified.
6Now, brothers, if I come to you and speak
in tongues, what good will I be to you, unless I bring you some revelation or knowledge
or prophecy or word of instruction? 7Even in
the case of lifeless things that make sounds,
such as the flute or harp, how will anyone
know what tune is being played unless there
is a distinction in the notes? 8Again, if the
trumpet does not sound a clear call, who will
get ready for battle? 9So it is with you. Unless you speak intelligible words with your
tongue, how will anyone know what you are
saying? You will just be speaking into the air.
10Undoubtedly there are all sorts of languages in the world, yet none of them is without
meaning. 11If then I do not grasp the meaning of what someone is saying, I am a foreigner to the speaker, and he is a foreigner to
me. 12So it is with you. Since you are eager to
have spiritual gifts, try to excel in gifts that
build up the church.
13For this reason anyone who speaks in a
tongue should pray that he may interpret
what he says. 14For if I pray in a tongue, my
spirit prays, but my mind is unfruitful. 15So
what shall I do? I will pray with my spirit, but
I will also pray with my mind; I will sing with
my spirit, but I will also sing with my mind.
16If you are praising God with your spirit,
how can one who finds himself among those
who do not understand[h] say "Amen" to your
thanksgiving, since he does not know what
you are saying? 17You may be giving thanks
well enough, but the other man is not edified.
18I thank God that I speak in tongues more
than all of you. 19But in the church I would
rather speak five intelligible words to instruct
others than ten thousand words in a tongue.
20Brothers, stop thinking like children. In
regard to evil be infants, but in your thinking
be adults. 21In the Law it is written:

[a] 30 Or *other languages* [b] 31 Or *But you are eagerly desiring* [c] 1 Or *languages* [d] 3 Some early manuscripts *body that I may boast*
[e] 2 Or *another language*; also in verses 4, 13, 14, 19, 26 and 27 [f] 2 Or *by the Spirit* [g] 5 Or *other languages*; also in verses 6, 18, 22, 23
and 39 [h] 16 Or *among the inquirers*

FRIDAY

READ

1 CORINTHIANS 13:1–13

LOVING BEYOND LIMITS

> **Love never fails.**
>
> — 1 CORINTHIANS 13:8

let's talk

- What is one verbal expression of love that is most like music to each of us?
- What one sacrifice of love is especially hard for each of us?
- What sacrifices do we make for each other that are especially meaningful?

Perhaps you've heard someone in a failed relationship say, "We always loved each other, but we just couldn't get along." They may have loved much, but they didn't know how to love well.

First Corinthians 13 is great counsel on how to love well in marriage. Loving well is the most essential ingredient for even the most spiritual people. For one thing, loving well brings music to our words (see verse 1). In times of trouble, we can be suspicious of the things our spouse says to us. If our actions don't show love, words of love will only clang in our hearts. But loving behavior makes even our most mundane conversations melodic.

Similarly, loving well adds muscle to our faith (see verse 2). It doesn't matter what kinds of obstacles we overcome or what kinds of insights we have; without acting in love toward those closest to us, even the greatest spiritual accomplishments turn to dust.

Finally, loving well brings value to our sacrifices (see verse 3). In marriage, we often sacrifice for our partner, but there can be a point at which we start keeping track of what those efforts cost us. When we love well, even the smallest sacrifices become treasures rather than points scored.

Verses 4–8 are practical reminders for marriage.

Verse 4: When he is thoughtless and inconsistent, "love is patient." When she hurts you, "love is kind." When other couples have what you want, love "does not envy." When you were right and he was wrong, love "does not boast." When you did a better job than she did, love "is not proud."

Verse 5: When you know your spouse hates it when you are habitually late, love "does not dishonor others." When no one thinks of you—your needs, your feelings, your desires or your rights—love "is not self-seeking." When you've had a long day and you're tired, or when she seems to be taking potshots at you, love "is not easily angered." When your spouse doesn't say "I'm sorry" for some offense, love "keeps no record of wrongs."

Verse 7: When he or she is taking a pounding from the world, your love, like a roof overhead, "protects." When you've been hurt or disappointed or betrayed, love "trusts." When no one notices how much you care or how often you cry, love "hopes." And when your love has been abused and questioned, when the door has been slammed in your face, when you've been completely ignored, love "perseveres."

Of course, if we're honest with one another, we have to admit that none of us measures up to the kind of love described in 1 Corinthians 13. No matter how *much* we love our spouse, loving *well* is too hard for us. That is why our relationship with Christ and the infilling of the Holy Spirit are so crucial. The Lord expects us to do our best—to throw our hearts and wills into all aspects of loving well. But when we've reached the limit of our ability, stunted by our sinfulness and weakness, we can pray for grace to do better. God can dial down our selfishness, release us from our insecurities and scorekeeping, and refresh our delight in our partner, so that we can begin to know the blessing of loving well.

—LEE ECLOV

FOR YOUR NEXT DEVOTIONAL READING, TURN TO PAGE 1298.

"Through men of strange tongues
  and through the lips of foreigners
I will speak to this people,
  but even then they will not listen
    to me,"[a]
      says the Lord.

[22]Tongues, then, are a sign, not for believers but for unbelievers; prophecy, however, is for believers, not for unbelievers. [23]So if the whole church comes together and everyone speaks in tongues, and some who do not understand[b] or some unbelievers come in, will they not say that you are out of your mind? [24]But if an unbeliever or someone who does not understand[c] comes in while everybody is prophesying, he will be convinced by all that he is a sinner and will be judged by all, [25]and the secrets of his heart will be laid bare. So he will fall down and worship God, exclaiming, "God is really among you!"

Orderly Worship

[26]What then shall we say, brothers? When you come together, everyone has a hymn, or a word of instruction, a revelation, a tongue or an interpretation. All of these must be done for the strengthening of the church. [27]If anyone speaks in a tongue, two—or at the most three—should speak, one at a time, and someone must interpret. [28]If there is no interpreter, the speaker should keep quiet in the church and speak to himself and God.

[29]Two or three prophets should speak, and the others should weigh carefully what is said. [30]And if a revelation comes to someone who is sitting down, the first speaker should stop. [31]For you can all prophesy in turn so that everyone may be instructed and encouraged. [32]The spirits of prophets are subject to the control of prophets. [33]For God is not a God of disorder but of peace.

As in all the congregations of the saints, [34]women should remain silent in the churches. They are not allowed to speak, but must be in submission, as the Law says. [35]If they want to inquire about something, they should ask their own husbands at home; for it is disgraceful for a woman to speak in the church.

[36]Did the word of God originate with you? Or are you the only people it has reached? [37]If anybody thinks he is a prophet or spiritually gifted, let him acknowledge that what I am writing to you is the Lord's command. [38]If he ignores this, he himself will be ignored.[d]

[39]Therefore, my brothers, be eager to prophesy, and do not forbid speaking in tongues. [40]But everything should be done in a fitting and orderly way.

The Resurrection of Christ

15 Now, brothers, I want to remind you of the gospel I preached to you, which you received and on which you have taken your stand. [2]By this gospel you are saved, if you hold firmly to the word I preached to you. Otherwise, you have believed in vain.

[3]For what I received I passed on to you as of first importance[e]: that Christ died for our sins according to the Scriptures, [4]that he was buried, that he was raised on the third day according to the Scriptures, [5]and that he appeared to Peter,[f] and then to the Twelve. [6]After that, he appeared to more than five hundred of the brothers at the same time, most of whom are still living, though some have fallen asleep. [7]Then he appeared to James, then to all the apostles, [8]and last of all he appeared to me also, as to one abnormally born.

[9]For I am the least of the apostles and do not even deserve to be called an apostle, because I persecuted the church of God. [10]But by the grace of God I am what I am, and his grace to me was not without effect. No, I worked harder than all of them—yet not I, but the grace of God that was with me. [11]Whether, then, it was I or they, this is what we preach, and this is what you believed.

The Resurrection of the Dead

[12]But if it is preached that Christ has been raised from the dead, how can some of you say that there is no resurrection of the dead? [13]If there is no resurrection of the dead, then not even Christ has been raised. [14]And if Christ has not been raised, our preaching is useless and so is your faith. [15]More than that, we are then found to be false witnesses about God, for we have testified about God that he raised Christ from the dead. But he did not raise him if in fact the dead are not raised. [16]For if the dead are not raised, then Christ has not been raised either. [17]And if Christ has not been raised, your faith is futile; you are still in your sins. [18]Then those also who have fallen asleep in Christ are lost. [19]If only for this life we have hope in Christ, we are to be pitied more than all men.

[20]But Christ has indeed been raised from

---

[a] *21* Isaiah 28:11,12 [b] *23* Or *some inquirers* [c] *24* Or *or some inquirer* [d] *38* Some manuscripts *If he is ignorant of this, let him be ignorant* [e] *3* Or *you at the first* [f] *5* Greek *Cephas*

WEEKEND

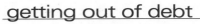

getting out of debt

We hate to admit it, but we started our marriage in significant debt. We spent more than we should have on our wedding and honeymoon, and then we both had pretty big school bills. We hate the financial burden we are under and want to get out of debt. How do we do it?

The huge amounts of debt most couples carry should probably come as no surprise since the gospel according to Madison Avenue is buy now and pay later. So couples take bank loans, borrow money from relatives, have past-due medical bills, and of course use the power of the plastic card. The problem with Madison Avenue's philosophy is that the debt of temporary freedom eventually puts us in financial prison. That's why Scripture speaks so directly about debt: "The rich rule over the poor, and the borrower is a [slave] to the lender" (Proverbs 22:7). The apostle Paul puts it this way: "You were bought at a price; do not become slaves of [human beings]" (1 Corinthians 7:23). By legally obligating ourselves to meet our debts, we lost the freedom of deciding where to spend our income. Most financial experts agree that the only reasons to go into debt are to buy a home, to finance a business, or to pay for an education.

So what do you do if you are carrying debt that is not healthy? We recommend starting with a written budget to help you analyze your spending pattern, plan ahead, and curb your impulsive spending. Next, determine whether there is anything you do not really need that might be sold to enable you to get out of debt more quickly. Are you living beyond your means by having a certain car, for example? The next step is to make a comprehensive list of everything you owe and the interest rate your creditors are charging for each debt. Pay off those charging the highest rate of interest first. Then establish a debt repayment schedule for each creditor by noting the monthly payment, the months remaining and the balance due. Put this in writing so you know exactly where you stand and where you have to go.

The next step may be to consider earning additional income. Earning a little additional income, even temporarily, may be a solution if you can do so without harming your marriage. Next, take special care not to accumulate new debt. This can be done by cutting up your credit cards. The little cards are dangerous. It has been shown that people spend approximately one-third more when they use credit cards rather than cash, probably because they feel they are not really spending money. Pay for things with cash or check. Along these same lines, delay your gratification and be content with what you have. If you persevere you will eventually become debt free. It is hard work to get there, but there is no magic involved, no special tricks—just discipline and perseverance. So don't give up. The freedom to be gained is worth the effort.

Once you have gotten out of debt, avoid getting back into it by saving money in an interest-bearing account for major purchases. Over the years, we all face major purchases such as buying an automobile, appliances or furniture. Prepare ahead by setting aside money for big-ticket items. You will then be able to pay cash for items that most people buy on credit.

—DR. LES PARROTT III AND DR. LESLIE PARROTT

HOW ARE WE DOING?

what is our debt load?

Do you know how much debt you are carrying as a couple? Write down your best guess ____________.

To find out the actual number, use the information below to calculate your total debt.

Item	Lender	Amount Owned	Interest Rate	Minimum Monthly Payment
Mortgage				
Home equity loan				
Car loans				
Student loans				
Furniture/ appliance loans				
Credit Card 1				
Credit Card 2				
Credit Card 3				
Store credit				
Personal loan				
Other				
Other				
Other				
Total				

What is your total income? ________________

Compare your total income to your total debt. What do you see?

let's make a DATE

CHEAP DATE

All this talk about money and budgets needn't make you stay home; use the opportunity to explore inexpensive dating opportunities. What can you do if you and your spouse each have $10? Check your local paper (free at the library) to find free concerts in the park, bookstore talks with authors, or do-it-yourself workshops by local experts. Consider local museums and zoos that have free hours, or a walking tour of an unfamiliar part of town. Have a dollar theater? Catch a previously run film while sharing popcorn and a soda. Or get a triple-thick chocolate milkshake at your favorite ice cream shop and ask for two straws. Remember, it's not the cost but the company that's important.

FOR YOUR NEXT DEVOTIONAL READING, TURN TO PAGE 1304.

LESSONS FROM THE *Bible*

Abraham insisted on paying for a piece of land on which to bury his wife, Sarah, even though the owner offered it to him for nothing (see Genesis 23:1–20). Why was it so critical for him to pay for this land? What things are we better off paying for than receiving as a gift?

The widow of a prophet in Elisha's day couldn't pay her debts. So the creditor was coming to take the widow's sons as slaves in payment (see 2 Kings 4:1–7). In what ways does debt enslave us today as married couples?

the dead, the firstfruits of those who have fall-
en asleep. 21For since death came through a
man, the resurrection of the dead comes also
through a man. 22For as in Adam all die, so in
Christ all will be made alive. 23But each in his
own turn: Christ, the firstfruits; then, when he
comes, those who belong to him. 24Then the
end will come, when he hands over the kingdom to God the Father after he has destroyed
all dominion, authority and power. 25For he
must reign until he has put all his enemies under his feet. 26The last enemy to be destroyed
is death. 27For he "has put everything under
his feet."[a] Now when it says that "everything"
has been put under him, it is clear that this
does not include God himself, who put everything under Christ. 28When he has done this,
then the Son himself will be made subject to
him who put everything under him, so that
God may be all in all.

29Now if there is no resurrection, what will
those do who are baptized for the dead? If the
dead are not raised at all, why are people baptized for them? 30And as for us, why do we
endanger ourselves every hour? 31I die every
day—I mean that, brothers—just as surely as
I glory over you in Christ Jesus our Lord. 32If
I fought wild beasts in Ephesus for merely human reasons, what have I gained? If the dead
are not raised,

"Let us eat and drink,
for tomorrow we die."[b]

33Do not be misled: "Bad company corrupts
good character." 34Come back to your senses
as you ought, and stop sinning; for there are
some who are ignorant of God—I say this to
your shame.

The Resurrection Body

35But someone may ask, "How are the
dead raised? With what kind of body will they
come?" 36How foolish! What you sow does
not come to life unless it dies. 37When you
sow, you do not plant the body that will be,
but just a seed, perhaps of wheat or of something else. 38But God gives it a body as he has
determined, and to each kind of seed he gives
its own body. 39All flesh is not the same: Men
have one kind of flesh, animals have another,
birds another and fish another. 40There are also
heavenly bodies and there are earthly bodies;
but the splendor of the heavenly bodies is one
kind, and the splendor of the earthly bodies is
another. 41The sun has one kind of splendor,
the moon another and the stars another; and
star differs from star in splendor.

42So will it be with the resurrection of the
dead. The body that is sown is perishable, it is
raised imperishable; 43it is sown in dishonor,
it is raised in glory; it is sown in weakness, it is
raised in power; 44it is sown a natural body, it
is raised a spiritual body.

If there is a natural body, there is also a
spiritual body. 45So it is written: "The first
man Adam became a living being"[c]; the last
Adam, a life-giving spirit. 46The spiritual did
not come first, but the natural, and after that
the spiritual. 47The first man was of the dust of
the earth, the second man from heaven. 48As
was the earthly man, so are those who are of
the earth; and as is the man from heaven, so
also are those who are of heaven. 49And just
as we have borne the likeness of the earthly
man, so shall we[d] bear the likeness of the man
from heaven.

50I declare to you, brothers, that flesh and
blood cannot inherit the kingdom of God, nor
does the perishable inherit the imperishable.
51Listen, I tell you a mystery: We will not all
sleep, but we will all be changed— 52in a flash,
in the twinkling of an eye, at the last trumpet.
For the trumpet will sound, the dead will be
raised imperishable, and we will be changed.
53For the perishable must clothe itself with the
imperishable, and the mortal with immortality. 54When the perishable has been clothed
with the imperishable, and the mortal with
immortality, then the saying that is written
will come true: "Death has been swallowed up
in victory."[e]

55"Where, O death, is your victory?
Where, O death, is your sting?"[f]

56The sting of death is sin, and the power of sin
is the law. 57But thanks be to God! He gives us
the victory through our Lord Jesus Christ.

58Therefore, my dear brothers, stand firm.
Let nothing move you. Always give yourselves fully to the work of the Lord, because
you know that your labor in the Lord is not
in vain.

The Collection for God's People

16 Now about the collection for God's people: Do what I told the Galatian churches to do. 2On the first day of every week,
each one of you should set aside a sum of
money in keeping with his income, saving it
up, so that when I come no collections will

[a] *27* Psalm 8:6 [b] *32* Isaiah 22:13 [c] *45* Gen. 2:7 [d] *49* Some early manuscripts *so let us* [e] *54* Isaiah 25:8 [f] *55* Hosea 13:14

have to be made. 3Then, when I arrive, I will
give letters of introduction to the men you approve and send them with your gift to Jerusalem. 4If it seems advisable for me to go also,
they will accompany me.

Personal Requests

5After I go through Macedonia, I will come
to you—for I will be going through Macedonia. 6Perhaps I will stay with you awhile, or
even spend the winter, so that you can help me
on my journey, wherever I go. 7I do not want
to see you now and make only a passing visit; I
hope to spend some time with you, if the Lord
permits. 8But I will stay on at Ephesus until
Pentecost, 9because a great door for effective
work has opened to me, and there are many
who oppose me.

10If Timothy comes, see to it that he has
nothing to fear while he is with you, for he is
carrying on the work of the Lord, just as I am.
11No one, then, should refuse to accept him.
Send him on his way in peace so that he may
return to me. I am expecting him along with
the brothers.

12Now about our brother Apollos: I strongly urged him to go to you with the brothers.
He was quite unwilling to go now, but he will
go when he has the opportunity.

13Be on your guard; stand firm in the faith;
be men of courage; be strong. 14Do everything
in love.

15You know that the household of Stephanas were the first converts in Achaia, and
they have devoted themselves to the service
of the saints. I urge you, brothers, 16to submit to such as these and to everyone who
joins in the work, and labors at it. 17I was
glad when Stephanas, Fortunatus and Achai-
cus arrived, because they have supplied what
was lacking from you. 18For they refreshed
my spirit and yours also. Such men deserve
recognition.

Final Greetings

19The churches in the province of Asia send
you greetings. Aquila and Priscilla[a] greet you
warmly in the Lord, and so does the church
that meets at their house. 20All the brothers
here send you greetings. Greet one another
with a holy kiss.

21I, Paul, write this greeting in my own
hand.

22If anyone does not love the Lord—a curse
be on him. Come, O Lord[b]!

23The grace of the Lord Jesus be with you.

24My love to all of you in Christ Jesus.
Amen.[c]

a 19 Greek *Prisca*, a variant of *Priscilla* *b* 22 In Aramaic the expression *Come, O Lord* is *Marana tha.* *c* 24 Some manuscripts do not have *Amen.*

2 CORINTHIANS

2 Corinthians

QUICK FACTS

AUTHOR The apostle Paul

AUDIENCE The church in Corinth

DATE About A.D. 55

SETTING False teachers in the church at Corinth were denying Paul's authority as an apostle.

After Paul wrote 1 Corinthians, he learned that a group of false teachers had come to Corinth presenting themselves as apostles. These troublemakers challenged, among others things, Paul's personal integrity and apostolic authority. As a result, Paul decided to visit the church—a visit which turned out to be "painful" and unsuccessful (see 2 Corinthians 2:1). That visit led Paul to write a severe letter "out of great distress and anguish of heart and with many tears" (2:4). Finally, Paul was relieved to hear that his severe letter had produced the desired results (see 7:5–16).

In 2 Corinthians, Paul defended himself as an apostle and reminded the Corinthian believers of his honorable actions while he had been with them. He also reminded them of the life-transforming message of salvation that he had brought to them, "the aroma of Christ among those who are being saved and those who are perishing" (2:15).

In our marriages, we too can become victims of troublemakers who question our personal integrity and who want to stir up divisions between us. Just as Paul urged the Corinthian church to have nothing to do with agitators, we are reminded to persevere with our spouses and not let those outside the relationship wreck that marital union.

1 Paul, an apostle of Christ Jesus by the will
of God, and Timothy our brother,

To the church of God in Corinth, together
with all the saints throughout Achaia:

[2]Grace and peace to you from God our Father and the Lord Jesus Christ.

The God of All Comfort

[3]Praise be to the God and Father of our
Lord Jesus Christ, the Father of compassion
and the God of all comfort, [4]who comforts
us in all our troubles, so that we can comfort
those in any trouble with the comfort we ourselves have received from God. [5]For just as the
sufferings of Christ flow over into our lives, so
also through Christ our comfort overflows. [6]If
we are distressed, it is for your comfort and
salvation; if we are comforted, it is for your
comfort, which produces in you patient endurance of the same sufferings we suffer. [7]And
our hope for you is firm, because we know
that just as you share in our sufferings, so also
you share in our comfort.

[8]We do not want you to be uninformed,
brothers, about the hardships we suffered in
the province of Asia. We were under great
pressure, far beyond our ability to endure, so
that we despaired even of life. [9]Indeed, in our
hearts we felt the sentence of death. But this
happened that we might not rely on ourselves
but on God, who raises the dead. [10]He has delivered us from such a deadly peril, and he will
deliver us. On him we have set our hope that
he will continue to deliver us, [11]as you help us
by your prayers. Then many will give thanks
on our[a] behalf for the gracious favor granted
us in answer to the prayers of many.

Paul's Change of Plans

[12]Now this is our boast: Our conscience
testifies that we have conducted ourselves
in the world, and especially in our relations
with you, in the holiness and sincerity that are
from God. We have done so not according to
worldly wisdom but according to God's grace.
[13]For we do not write you anything you cannot read or understand. And I hope that, [14]as
you have understood us in part, you will come
to understand fully that you can boast of us
just as we will boast of you in the day of the
Lord Jesus.

[15]Because I was confident of this, I planned
to visit you first so that you might benefit
twice. [16]I planned to visit you on my way to
Macedonia and to come back to you from
Macedonia, and then to have you send me on
my way to Judea. [17]When I planned this, did
I do it lightly? Or do I make my plans in a
worldly manner so that in the same breath I
say, "Yes, yes" and "No, no"?

[18]But as surely as God is faithful, our message to you is not "Yes" and "No." [19]For the
Son of God, Jesus Christ, who was preached
among you by me and Silas[b] and Timothy, was
not "Yes" and "No," but in him it has always
been "Yes." [20]For no matter how many promises God has made, they are "Yes" in Christ.
And so through him the "Amen" is spoken by
us to the glory of God. [21]Now it is God who
makes both us and you stand firm in Christ.
He anointed us, [22]set his seal of ownership on
us, and put his Spirit in our hearts as a deposit,
guaranteeing what is to come.

[23]I call God as my witness that it was in order to spare you that I did not return to Corinth. [24]Not that we lord it over your faith, but
we work with you for your joy, because it is by
2 faith you stand firm. [1]So I made up my
mind that I would not make another painful visit to you. [2]For if I grieve you, who
is left to make me glad but you whom I have
grieved? [3]I wrote as I did so that when I came
I should not be distressed by those who ought
to make me rejoice. I had confidence in all of
you, that you would all share my joy. [4]For I
wrote you out of great distress and anguish of
heart and with many tears, not to grieve you
but to let you know the depth of my love for
you.

Forgiveness for the Sinner

[5]If anyone has caused grief, he has not so
much grieved me as he has grieved all of you,
to some extent—not to put it too severely.
[6]The punishment inflicted on him by the majority is sufficient for him. [7]Now instead, you
ought to forgive and comfort him, so that he
will not be overwhelmed by excessive sorrow.
[8]I urge you, therefore, to reaffirm your love
for him. [9]The reason I wrote you was to see if
you would stand the test and be obedient in
everything. [10]If you forgive anyone, I also forgive him. And what I have forgiven—if there
was anything to forgive—I have forgiven in
the sight of Christ for your sake, [11]in order
that Satan might not outwit us. For we are not
unaware of his schemes.

[a] *11* Many manuscripts *your* [b] *19* Greek *Silvanus,* a variant of *Silas*

MONDAY
READ
2 CORINTHIANS 1:1–11

OPENING UP TO OTHERS

How do you define a good marriage? Most of us would answer by talking about how the relationship affects the people in it. Does the relationship help the husband and wife grow emotionally and spiritually? Is it creating a healthy environment in which to bring up children? When you really think about it, a good marriage isn't just good for the two people in the marriage and the family they create; it is good for everyone who gets drawn into its orbit.

When my husband was in seminary, he and a few other students lived with a professor and his wife. Rob and Julie, along with various students, lived in intentional community—eating together, holding weekly house meetings, divvying up the cooking and cleaning duties. They weren't just sharing a house; they were sharing their lives.

Rob and Julie chose to live with students because they believed their marriage was intended for something bigger than themselves. They opened their home to others so they could discover the beauty of community, the delicate balance of individual wants and communal needs, and the growth that comes from living with people who are in Christ and different from the world.

My husband and I got engaged while he was living in this community, and Rob and Julie proved to be incredible role models as we prepared for married life. Their example inspired us to open our home to people who need a place to stay, a meal to eat, friends to trust. And sure enough, today we spend many evenings in our living room listening to a friend share a dating struggle, talking through job options, or sorting out a faith issue. Rob and Julie taught us that marriage is God's gift, not only to us, but also to those around us.

Paul's letter to the Corinthians was written to a community, not an individual. In it Paul was offering a vision of what the church could be if people looked beyond their individual needs and started thinking of other people. His hope was that believers would share the love and compassion God had given them with everyone they met. Clearly, the church had problems, but Paul wanted believers to expand their vision and avoid letting interpersonal issues get in the way of their calling to reach out to others.

Naturally, developing a marriage that benefits others means making sure that the marriage benefits the couple as well. While Rob and Julie had a general open-door policy with students, they were also careful to save time for themselves. And there were parts of their lives they didn't share with others—the details of painful fights, the personal issues they struggled with, stories they shared with each other in confidence.

Married couples can extend their relationship by sharing the comfort, love and compassion they've been given. Doing so also develops a deeper marriage. The shared purpose of such a marriage mission bonds a couple like nothing else. Really, what could be better than bringing about the kingdom of God with your best friend?

—CARLA BARNHILL

FOR YOUR NEXT DEVOTIONAL READING, TURN TO PAGE 1306.

Praise be to the God and Father of our Lord Jesus Christ, the Father of compassion and the God of all comfort, who comforts us in all our troubles, so that we can comfort those in any trouble with the comfort we ourselves have received from God.

— 2 Corinthians 1:3–4

let's *talk*

✦ How have we been comforted or supported by another couple?

✦ How could we use our home, our time, our wisdom, our experiences to extend God's love to others? Let's talk about dreams or hopes we've had for reaching out to others. Are there ways we can live out those dreams as a couple?

✦ What barriers hold us back from inviting other people into our lives? How can we overcome some of those barriers together?

Ministers of the New Covenant

12Now when I went to Troas to preach the
gospel of Christ and found that the Lord had
opened a door for me, 13I still had no peace of
mind, because I did not find my brother Titus
there. So I said good-by to them and went on
to Macedonia.

14But thanks be to God, who always leads
us in triumphal procession in Christ and
through us spreads everywhere the fragrance
of the knowledge of him. 15For we are to God
the aroma of Christ among those who are being saved and those who are perishing. 16To
the one we are the smell of death; to the other,
the fragrance of life. And who is equal to such
a task? 17Unlike so many, we do not peddle
the word of God for profit. On the contrary,
in Christ we speak before God with sincerity,
like men sent from God.

3 Are we beginning to commend ourselves
again? Or do we need, like some people,
letters of recommendation to you or from
you? 2You yourselves are our letter, written
on our hearts, known and read by everybody.
3You show that you are a letter from Christ,
the result of our ministry, written not with
ink but with the Spirit of the living God, not
on tablets of stone but on tablets of human
hearts.

4Such confidence as this is ours through
Christ before God. 5Not that we are competent in ourselves to claim anything for ourselves, but our competence comes from God.
6He has made us competent as ministers of
a new covenant—not of the letter but of the
Spirit; for the letter kills, but the Spirit gives
life.

The Glory of the New Covenant

7Now if the ministry that brought death,
which was engraved in letters on stone, came
with glory, so that the Israelites could not look
steadily at the face of Moses because of its glory, fading though it was, 8will not the ministry of the Spirit be even more glorious? 9If
the ministry that condemns men is glorious,
how much more glorious is the ministry that
brings righteousness! 10For what was glorious
has no glory now in comparison with the surpassing glory. 11And if what was fading away
came with glory, how much greater is the glory of that which lasts!

12Therefore, since we have such a hope, we
are very bold. 13We are not like Moses, who
would put a veil over his face to keep the Israelites from gazing at it while the radiance was
fading away. 14But their minds were made dull,
for to this day the same veil remains when the
old covenant is read. It has not been removed,
because only in Christ is it taken away. 15Even
to this day when Moses is read, a veil covers
their hearts. 16But whenever anyone turns to
the Lord, the veil is taken away. 17Now the
Lord is the Spirit, and where the Spirit of the
Lord is, there is freedom. 18And we, who with
unveiled faces all reflect[a] the Lord's glory, are
being transformed into his likeness with ever-
increasing glory, which comes from the Lord,
who is the Spirit.

Treasures in Jars of Clay

4 Therefore, since through God's mercy we
have this ministry, we do not lose heart.
2Rather, we have renounced secret and
shameful ways; we do not use deception, nor
do we distort the word of God. On the contrary, by setting forth the truth plainly we
commend ourselves to every man's conscience
in the sight of God. 3And even if our gospel is
veiled, it is veiled to those who are perishing.
4The god of this age has blinded the minds of
unbelievers, so that they cannot see the light
of the gospel of the glory of Christ, who is
the image of God. 5For we do not preach ourselves, but Jesus Christ as Lord, and ourselves
as your servants for Jesus' sake. 6For God, who
said, "Let light shine out of darkness,"[b] made
his light shine in our hearts to give us the light
of the knowledge of the glory of God in the
face of Christ.

7But we have this treasure in jars of clay to
show that this all-surpassing power is from
God and not from us. 8We are hard pressed on
every side, but not crushed; perplexed, but not
in despair; 9persecuted, but not abandoned;
struck down, but not destroyed. 10We always
carry around in our body the death of Jesus,
so that the life of Jesus may also be revealed in
our body. 11For we who are alive are always being given over to death for Jesus' sake, so that
his life may be revealed in our mortal body.
12So then, death is at work in us, but life is at
work in you.

13It is written: "I believed; therefore I have
spoken."[c] With that same spirit of faith we
also believe and therefore speak, 14because we
know that the one who raised the Lord Jesus
from the dead will also raise us with Jesus
and present us with you in his presence. 15All
this is for your benefit, so that the grace that

---

a 18 Or *contemplate* *b 6* Gen. 1:3 *c 13* Psalm 116:10

TUESDAY
READ
2 CORINTHIANS 1:23—2:11

RESTORING AN ERRANT SPOUSE

The punishment inflicted on him by the majority is sufficient for him. Now instead, you ought to forgive and comfort him, so that he will not be overwhelmed by excessive sorrow.

— 2 CORINTHIANS 2:6–7

One Christian leaves her husband for another man. Another embezzles money. Fellow believers stir up division in the church. The Bible makes clear that in extreme cases of persistent, unrepentant sin, the church must discipline the offender (see Matthew 18:15–20).

In 1 Corinthians 5:1–5 Paul told the church in Corinth to deal with a sticky problem. A member of the church was having an affair with "his father's wife" (verse 1), likely his stepmother, which was an offense even to the jaded *unbelievers* in pagan Corinth. Paul said the man should be put out of the church until he repented. Imagine the turmoil that created! Yet church discipline is a crucial matter.

It's possible that the man discussed in 1 Corinthians 5:1–5 was the person Paul was referring to in 2 Corinthians 2:5–11. If so, the apostle had learned that the man had repented of his sin, and Paul was therefore guiding the church through the challenge of restoring the man to fellowship. Paul's advice is useful for us today as we deal with Christians who have repented of sin.

What situations in your marriage have required forgiveness and restoration? Have you suffered when a spouse lied to you or cheated on you? How did you react when your spouse repented?

Restoration is difficult. The sins of believers profoundly affect us (see what Paul said in 2 Corinthians 5:5 about grief). We are angry as we struggle with the pain of violated trust. And the situation is especially difficult when it is our spouse who has deeply hurt us.

The first step toward restoration begins when we reaffirm our love for the offender by extending forgiveness and comfort (see verses 7–8). No one can ever be sorry enough or do enough to pay off their sin. Forgiveness is all about grace. We do not extend love for our own sake; we do it in Jesus' name and for his sake. And we extend forgiveness and grace so the repentant sinner is not "overwhelmed by excessive sorrow" (verse 7).

If we've been badly hurt by someone, this step may require hard work on our part. Praying for God's grace in our weakness so that we may be merciful, just as our heavenly Father is merciful (see Luke 6:36) will help us take that step. It is important to remember that a situation like this is a spiritual minefield, for Satan will try to use the situation to destroy the heart of a church or marriage. If you leave sin unaddressed, Satan scores; but if you fail to restore a broken brother or sister, Satan also wins. The damage will be not only to the sinner but also to Christ and the church.

Extending grace strengthens believers, marriages and churches. One pastor wrote about the painful process of disciplining a man who was committing adultery and the equally painful process of helping the man's betrayed wife. After a long time, the man repented. The pastor wrote, "What a joy to announce to the church that discipline against this man had been lifted, and he was now restored to fellowship! People broke into applause at the wonder of God's work in restoring the man and his marriage."

—LEE ECLOV

let's talk

- Why is it difficult to forgive a believer who has profoundly and repeatedly sinned? In what ways do we feel betrayed?
- How could a repentant offender be lost if other believers failed to accept him or her back into fellowship? What could happen?
- How can we help each other extend the grace of forgiveness when someone has gone far away from the Lord and then returned to him?

FOR YOUR NEXT DEVOTIONAL READING, TURN TO PAGE 1308.

is reaching more and more people may cause
thanksgiving to overflow to the glory of God.
16Therefore we do not lose heart. Though
outwardly we are wasting away, yet inwardly
we are being renewed day by day. 17For our
light and momentary troubles are achieving
for us an eternal glory that far outweighs them
all. 18So we fix our eyes not on what is seen,
but on what is unseen. For what is seen is temporary, but what is unseen is eternal.

Our Heavenly Dwelling

5 Now we know that if the earthly tent we
live in is destroyed, we have a building from
God, an eternal house in heaven, not built
by human hands. 2Meanwhile we groan, longing to be clothed with our heavenly dwelling,
3because when we are clothed, we will not be
found naked. 4For while we are in this tent,
we groan and are burdened, because we do not
wish to be unclothed but to be clothed with
our heavenly dwelling, so that what is mortal
may be swallowed up by life. 5Now it is God
who has made us for this very purpose and has
given us the Spirit as a deposit, guaranteeing
what is to come.
6Therefore we are always confident and
know that as long as we are at home in the
body we are away from the Lord. 7We live by
faith, not by sight. 8We are confident, I say,
and would prefer to be away from the body
and at home with the Lord. 9So we make
it our goal to please him, whether we are at
home in the body or away from it. 10For we
must all appear before the judgment seat of
Christ, that each one may receive what is due
him for the things done while in the body,
whether good or bad.

The Ministry of Reconciliation

11Since, then, we know what it is to fear the
Lord, we try to persuade men. What we are
is plain to God, and I hope it is also plain to
your conscience. 12We are not trying to commend ourselves to you again, but are giving
you an opportunity to take pride in us, so that
you can answer those who take pride in what is
seen rather than in what is in the heart. 13If we
are out of our mind, it is for the sake of God;
if we are in our right mind, it is for you. 14For
Christ's love compels us, because we are convinced that one died for all, and therefore all
died. 15And he died for all, that those who live
should no longer live for themselves but for
him who died for them and was raised again.
16So from now on we regard no one from
a worldly point of view. Though we once regarded Christ in this way, we do so no longer. 17Therefore, if anyone is in Christ, he is
a new creation; the old has gone, the new has
come! 18All this is from God, who reconciled
us to himself through Christ and gave us the
ministry of reconciliation: 19that God was rec-
onciling the world to himself in Christ, not
counting men's sins against them. And he has
committed to us the message of reconciliation.
20We are therefore Christ's ambassadors, as
though God were making his appeal through
us. We implore you on Christ's behalf: Be reconciled to God. 21God made him who had no
sin to be sin[a] for us, so that in him we might
become the righteousness of God.

6 As God's fellow workers we urge you not to
receive God's grace in vain. 2For he says,

> "In the time of my favor I heard you,
> and in the day of salvation I helped
> you."[b]

I tell you, now is the time of God's favor, now
is the day of salvation.

Paul's Hardships

3We put no stumbling block in anyone's
path, so that our ministry will not be discredited. 4Rather, as servants of God we commend
ourselves in every way: in great endurance; in
troubles, hardships and distresses; 5in beatings, imprisonments and riots; in hard work,
sleepless nights and hunger; 6in purity, understanding, patience and kindness; in the Holy
Spirit and in sincere love; 7in truthful speech
and in the power of God; with weapons of
righteousness in the right hand and in the left;
8through glory and dishonor, bad report and
good report; genuine, yet regarded as impostors; 9known, yet regarded as unknown; dying, and yet we live on; beaten, and yet not
killed; 10sorrowful, yet always rejoicing; poor,
yet making many rich; having nothing, and
yet possessing everything.
11We have spoken freely to you, Corinthians, and opened wide our hearts to you. 12We
are not withholding our affection from you,
but you are withholding yours from us. 13As
a fair exchange—I speak as to my children—
open wide your hearts also.

Do Not Be Yoked With Unbelievers

14Do not be yoked together with unbelievers. For what do righteousness and wick-

---

[a] *21* Or *be a sin offering* [b] *2* Isaiah 49:8

WEDNESDAY
READ
2 CORINTHIANS 4:1–18

THE TRUTH ABOUT OUR RELATIONSHIP

"*There's a sucker* born every minute," said the great nineteenth-century huckster P. T. Barnum. A brilliant and shameless promoter, Barnum established a circus in 1871 that he billed as "The Greatest Show on Earth." Barnum's entire career was plagued with accusations of fraud and scandal. One of his working philosophies was that there was no such thing as bad press.

The apostle Paul wouldn't have agreed. He was well aware that there are naive people who are easily duped. However, Paul would have said that giving the gospel bad press hurts not only the followers of Christ but Christ himself.

As Paul wrote 2 Corinthians, he undoubtedly thought about the damaging effects of false teachers upon the new Christians in Corinth. In addition to the church's problems concerning disunity, spiritual arrogance, abuse of spiritual gifts and misunderstanding of basic Christian teachings, Paul's credibility as an apostle was being called into question by these false teachers. What right did he have to call himself an apostle when he had not been one of Jesus' chosen Twelve? How could he tell others to live a life of victory when he had experienced nothing but trouble, trial, suffering and pain? Why should believers follow him when all he did was criticize what they were doing?

We have renounced secret and shameful ways; we do not use deception, nor do we distort the word of God. On the contrary, by setting forth the truth plainly we commend ourselves to every man's conscience in the sight of God.

—2 Corinthians 4:2

let's talk

- ✦ Are there times when we've been tempted to give up on our marriage? What were some things that brought us to that point?
- ✦ In what ways have we been challenged to "speak the truth in love" to each other? To family and friends? To coworkers? How did that work out?
- ✦ What secrets or underhanded methods can tear a marriage apart? How does truth inevitably counteract them?

Paul did not lose heart however. Knowing that his hope was in Christ and not in the things of this world, Paul refused to give up, and he encouraged the believers in Corinth not to give up either. In addition, he rejected the underhanded methods that false teachers had been using to establish their authority. He set forth the truth plainly, even when it wasn't popular. Truth was his credibility.

As couples, we might also be tempted to lose heart. The world attacks our purity and commitments in marriage, scoffing at the roles God has given us in our relationship and tempting us to be less than truthful with our spouses and others whom we encounter on a daily basis.

But as Christians committed to our Lord Jesus Christ, we, like the apostle Paul, reject all shameful manipulation, deceitfulness and underhanded methods. We tell our spouses the truth about the people we are with, the money we spend and the ways we spend our free time. We witness to our coworkers through our honesty and the way we talk about the people we work with. We show Jesus to our friends and family by "speaking the truth in love" (Ephesians 4:15). In short, we refuse to give the gospel bad press.

The truth that we speak and live out will be our credibility in building up our marriages and in witnessing to those who don't yet know Christ, and it will help us share the Good News of Jesus Christ.

—VALERIE VAN KOOTEN

FOR YOUR NEXT DEVOTIONAL READING, TURN TO PAGE 1310.

edness have in common? Or what fellowship
can light have with darkness? 15What harmony is there between Christ and Belial[a]? What
does a believer have in common with an unbeliever? 16What agreement is there between
the temple of God and idols? For we are the
temple of the living God. As God has said:
"I will live with them and walk among them,
and I will be their God, and they will be my
people."[b]

17 "Therefore come out from them
and be separate,
says the Lord.
Touch no unclean thing,
and I will receive you."[c]
18 "I will be a Father to you,
and you will be my sons and daughters,
says the Lord Almighty."[d]

7 Since we have these promises, dear friends,
let us purify ourselves from everything that
contaminates body and spirit, perfecting
holiness out of reverence for God.

Paul's Joy

2Make room for us in your hearts. We have
wronged no one, we have corrupted no one,
we have exploited no one. 3I do not say this
to condemn you; I have said before that you
have such a place in our hearts that we would
live or die with you. 4I have great confidence
in you; I take great pride in you. I am greatly
encouraged; in all our troubles my joy knows
no bounds.

5For when we came into Macedonia, this
body of ours had no rest, but we were harassed
at every turn—conflicts on the outside, fears
within. 6But God, who comforts the downcast, comforted us by the coming of Titus,
7and not only by his coming but also by the
comfort you had given him. He told us about
your longing for me, your deep sorrow, your
ardent concern for me, so that my joy was
greater than ever.

8Even if I caused you sorrow by my letter, I
do not regret it. Though I did regret it—I see
that my letter hurt you, but only for a little
while— 9yet now I am happy, not because you
were made sorry, but because your sorrow led
you to repentance. For you became sorrowful as God intended and so were not harmed
in any way by us. 10Godly sorrow brings repentance that leads to salvation and leaves
no regret, but worldly sorrow brings death.
11See what this godly sorrow has produced in
you: what earnestness, what eagerness to clear
yourselves, what indignation, what alarm,
what longing, what concern, what readiness
to see justice done. At every point you have
proved yourselves to be innocent in this matter. 12So even though I wrote to you, it was
not on account of the one who did the wrong
or of the injured party, but rather that before
God you could see for yourselves how devoted to us you are. 13By all this we are encouraged.

In addition to our own encouragement, we
were especially delighted to see how happy Titus was, because his spirit has been refreshed
by all of you. 14I had boasted to him about
you, and you have not embarrassed me. But
just as everything we said to you was true, so
our boasting about you to Titus has proved to
be true as well. 15And his affection for you is
all the greater when he remembers that you
were all obedient, receiving him with fear and
trembling. 16I am glad I can have complete
confidence in you.

Generosity Encouraged

8 And now, brothers, we want you to know
about the grace that God has given the
Macedonian churches. 2Out of the most
severe trial, their overflowing joy and their
extreme poverty welled up in rich generosity. 3For I testify that they gave as much as
they were able, and even beyond their ability.
Entirely on their own, 4they urgently pleaded with us for the privilege of sharing in this
service to the saints. 5And they did not do as
we expected, but they gave themselves first to
the Lord and then to us in keeping with God's
will. 6So we urged Titus, since he had earlier
made a beginning, to bring also to completion this act of grace on your part. 7But just as
you excel in everything—in faith, in speech,
in knowledge, in complete earnestness and in
your love for us[e]—see that you also excel in
this grace of giving.

8I am not commanding you, but I want to
test the sincerity of your love by comparing it
with the earnestness of others. 9For you know
the grace of our Lord Jesus Christ, that though
he was rich, yet for your sakes he became poor,
so that you through his poverty might become
rich.

10And here is my advice about what is best
for you in this matter: Last year you were the
first not only to give but also to have the desire
to do so. 11Now finish the work, so that your

---

[a] *15* Greek *Beliar*, a variant of *Belial* [b] *16* Lev. 26:12; Jer. 32:38; Ezek. 37:27 [c] *17* Isaiah 52:11; Ezek. 20:34,41 [d] *18* 2 Samuel 7:14; 7:8
[e] *7* Some manuscripts *in our love for you*

THURSDAY

READ

2 CORINTHIANS 6:14—7:1

PURIFYING OURSELVES

The instruction in 2 Corinthians 7:1 feels flat-out intimidating. Who can purify themselves from everything that contaminates the body and spirit? For some of us, that feels so impossible that we just push it to the background and pray that we're covered by God's grace. For others, it feels so demanding that we exist in a constant state of guilt over our inability to live up to the perfect holiness we think is expected of us.

But this verse is a continuation of the passage that begins at 6:14—a passage in which Paul reminds believers of God's ancient promises to his people: "I will live with them and walk among them." "Touch no unclean thing, and I will receive you." "I will be a Father to you, and you will be my sons and daughters." These promises are about God, not believers. So when Paul talks about holiness and purity, he is reminding the church that God has loved them through the ages and has kept these promises through thick and thin. Now it's their turn to be the people God has called them to be. In essence, that call really isn't about perfection. It's about focusing our lives on God, not on ourselves.

So what does that have to do with marriage? Think about it: At the root of nearly every petty argument, every lingering disappointment, every hurtful word is a selfish desire to get our way, to meet some expectation, to prove a point. On a deeper level, it is often our individual struggles with those things that "contaminate the body and spirit" and that undermine marriages.

Jim and I have watched several dear friends go through painful divorces. Each was the result of one or both partners failing to move away from contaminants. Some were overt problems—addictions, affairs, abuse. But just as often, marriages crumbled because of stuff that was ignored or dismissed: a wife who preferred to spend time with her coworkers instead of her husband, a husband who shut down emotionally because he was afraid of his feelings, a couple that was so focused on their children that they became little more than business partners.

Overcoming selfishness starts with turning my focus away from myself and onto my partner. When I think about what I want from marriage, I end up irritated because the real thing rarely lives up to my *Glamour*-magazine version of romantic bliss. But when I think about Jim, about the love I know he wants from me, and how easy it is to make him feel cared for, it's a whole lot easier to be a selfless wife.

God has promised that we are not alone. We have his power, love and strength as we seek to build marriages and lives that glorify him.

—CARLA BARNHILL

Since we have these promises, dear friends, let us purify ourselves from everything that contaminates body and spirit, perfecting holiness out of reverence for God.

— 2 CORINTHIANS 7:1

let's talk

- ✦ What are some obvious contaminants in our marriage? (Issues such as addictions, affairs or abuse are too powerful to deal with on our own. In such instances, we need to get help right away from our pastor and/or a Christian counselor.)
- ✦ What other factors prevent us from focusing on each other? Busyness? Work? Kids? How could we turn our focus back onto each other?
- ✦ What habits get in the way of purifying our hearts and minds? Violent or lewd movies? Maintaining a friendship that interferes with our marriage? Let's take time alone to think about issues we need to deal with and then come back together to talk about them.

FOR YOUR NEXT DEVOTIONAL READING, TURN TO PAGE 1312.

ery pretension that sets itself up against the
knowledge of God, and we take captive every
thought to make it obedient to Christ. [6]And
we will be ready to punish every act of disobedience, once your obedience is complete.

[7]You are looking only on the surface of
things. [a] If anyone is confident that he belongs
to Christ, he should consider again that we belong to Christ just as much as he. [8]For even if
I boast somewhat freely about the authority
the Lord gave us for building you up rather
than pulling you down, I will not be ashamed
of it. [9]I do not want to seem to be trying to
frighten you with my letters. [10]For some say,
"His letters are weighty and forceful, but in
person he is unimpressive and his speaking
amounts to nothing." [11]Such people should
realize that what we are in our letters when
we are absent, we will be in our actions when
we are present.

[12]We do not dare to classify or compare ourselves with some who commend themselves.
When they measure themselves by themselves
and compare themselves with themselves, they
are not wise. [13]We, however, will not boast beyond proper limits, but will confine our boasting to the field God has assigned to us, a field
that reaches even to you. [14]We are not going
too far in our boasting, as would be the case if
we had not come to you, for we did get as far
as you with the gospel of Christ. [15]Neither do
we go beyond our limits by boasting of work
done by others. [b] Our hope is that, as your
faith continues to grow, our area of activity
among you will greatly expand, [16]so that we
can preach the gospel in the regions beyond
you. For we do not want to boast about work
already done in another man's territory. [17]But,
"Let him who boasts boast in the Lord." [c]
[18]For it is not the one who commends himself
who is approved, but the one whom the Lord
commends.

Paul and the False Apostles

11 I hope you will put up with a little of my
foolishness; but you are already doing
that. [2]I am jealous for you with a godly
jealousy. I promised you to one husband, to
Christ, so that I might present you as a pure
virgin to him. [3]But I am afraid that just as Eve
was deceived by the serpent's cunning, your
minds may somehow be led astray from your
sincere and pure devotion to Christ. [4]For if
someone comes to you and preaches a Jesus
other than the Jesus we preached, or if you
receive a different spirit from the one you received, or a different gospel from the one you
accepted, you put up with it easily enough.
[5]But I do not think I am in the least inferi-
or to those "super-apostles." [6]I may not be a
trained speaker, but I do have knowledge. We
have made this perfectly clear to you in every
way.

[7]Was it a sin for me to lower myself in order to elevate you by preaching the gospel of
God to you free of charge? [8]I robbed other
churches by receiving support from them so
as to serve you. [9]And when I was with you
and needed something, I was not a burden
to anyone, for the brothers who came from
Macedonia supplied what I needed. I have
kept myself from being a burden to you in
any way, and will continue to do so. [10]As surely as the truth of Christ is in me, nobody in
the regions of Achaia will stop this boasting
of mine. [11]Why? Because I do not love you?
God knows I do! [12]And I will keep on doing
what I am doing in order to cut the ground
from under those who want an opportunity
to be considered equal with us in the things
they boast about.

[13]For such men are false apostles, deceitful
workmen, masquerading as apostles of Christ.
[14]And no wonder, for Satan himself masquer-
ades as an angel of light. [15]It is not surprising,
then, if his servants masquerade as servants of
righteousness. Their end will be what their actions deserve.

Paul Boasts About His Sufferings

[16]I repeat: Let no one take me for a fool.
But if you do, then receive me just as you
would a fool, so that I may do a little boasting.
[17]In this self-confident boasting I am not talking as the Lord would, but as a fool. [18]Since
many are boasting in the way the world does,
I too will boast. [19]You gladly put up with
fools since you are so wise! [20]In fact, you even
put up with anyone who enslaves you or exploits you or takes advantage of you or pushes
himself forward or slaps you in the face. [21]To
my shame I admit that we were too weak for
that!

What anyone else dares to boast about—I
am speaking as a fool—I also dare to boast
about. [22]Are they Hebrews? So am I. Are they
Israelites? So am I. Are they Abraham's descendants? So am I. [23]Are they servants of Christ?

[a] 7 Or *Look at the obvious facts* [b] 13-15 Or *[13]We, however, will not boast about things that cannot be measured, but we will boast according to the standard of measurement that the God of measure has assigned us—a measurement that relates even to you. [14] . . . [15]Neither do we boast about things that cannot be measured in regard to the work done by others.* [c] 17 Jer. 9:24

WEEKEND

growing through illness

During our first year of marriage my wife and I encountered an unexpected challenge. Angela spent most of the year sick. Really sick.

Just as we were getting our apartment settled and becoming used to living with each other, she developed severe allergy and respiratory problems. For the next several months, this active woman who had hardly missed a day of work spent the majority of her time in bed. Angela was diagnosed with bronchitis eight times, pneumonia once, and a myriad of other allergic conditions in between.

Sickness is just one of many challenges that come into a marriage. Whether it's something drastic, such as a life-threatening disease, or something chronic, such as PMS, migraines or asthma attacks, here are seven things you can do to help your ill spouse.

1. Offer sympathy. Show you care. What your spouse needs and wants most during a tough time is your support. Don't be silent—that can communicate apathy. Express your sorrow at what your spouse is experiencing. Ask if you can get him anything—a cup of tea, a foot rub. Offer to pray with him.

2. Avoid blame. Your spouse's illness may require you to miss work, social outings or other events you consider important. Try to avoid compounding your mate's pain by acting as if it were her fault. Even shrugs or frowns can communicate disgust and leave your spouse feeling like a burden.

3. Be an advocate. When illness becomes severe, the world of medicine, physicians and insurance can be confusing. Try to accompany your spouse to important medical visits. You can be another set of eyes and ears, helping keep track of medicine dosages and precautions. What's more, your involvement sends an important signal that your sick spouse is not walking this road alone.

4. Be selfless. View your spouse's pain as an opportunity for servanthood. That may mean endless trips to the store, taking off work, performing household chores, or spending time at her bedside, ready to serve in whatever capacity she needs.

5. Help keep perspective. When you're really ill, it's easy to lose perspective. You may begin to wonder, *Is this going to last forever? Am I going to lose my job? Does the doctor really mean that?*

While you don't want to pretend everything's okay—that just bugs your mate!—you do want to focus on what's really happening and avoid the dangerous and alarming what-if games. Stay positive and upbeat so your ailing spouse can feed off that energy.

Sometimes you just need to have a good laugh. Retell some of your favorite stories or share something funny that happened at work. Proverbs 17:22 tells us that laughter can promote healing.

6. Stay connected. Everyone needs a support system, especially when going through a difficult time. You may be surprised at how people really want to help. Don't be too proud to ask for prayer, a babysitter or a meal.

7. Constantly affirm your love. During an illness—whether it's the flu, a headache or a serious disease—you see your loved one at his worst. Fatigue and medicinal side effects can make him moody and irritable. This is a good time to demonstrate unconditional love. An extra dose of patience, a kind word, a gentle touch, a sweet kiss, and a soft-spoken, "I'm here for you. I love you no matter what," go a long way to help your spouse feel better.

—DANIEL MICHAEL DARLING

MONDAY
READ
2 CORINTHIANS 12:1–10

MAKING SENSE OF THE PAIN

During one semester of my college years, everything seemed to conspire against me. Late one night I shared my fears and frustrations with my parents. They listened and prayed. Soon a letter arrived with a card on which Mom had copied a poem by Grant Tuller:

My life is but a weaving between my God and me
I do not choose the colors; He worketh steadily.
Oft times He weaveth sorrow, and I in foolish pride
Forget He sees the upper-, and I the under-side.
Not till the loom is silent and the shuttles cease to fly
Will God unroll the canvas and explain the reasons why
The dark threads are as needful in a skillful weaver's
hand
As the threads of gold and silver, in the pattern he has
planned.

Paul's letters to his congregation in Corinth are interwoven with threads of pain and joy. Sometimes Paul recounted his great apostolic calling and used it to persuade the church to accept his authority. Other times he wandered about in near despair, pleading with his fellow believers for support. In 2 Corinthians 12:1–10, Paul slid from ecstasy to entropy, ending up with reflections not unlike those of Tuller.

He could have been writing a journal entry about the relationship of any couple. We thrill when we first make eye contact. We find our days energized as we become engaged and plan for marriage, and our nights are vivid with passionate dreams of our lives together. When we marry and are happy with each other, we carry our partner along on the currents of victory.

But there are also pages in our relationships when days pass without a note, and those that finally appear are short and tear-stained. We feel the thorn of sickness. Lost opportunities. Foolish mistakes. Broken promises. Our elation bursts, our energy escapes, and darkness becomes our closest friend. What do we say then?

Perhaps, with Job, we need to be reminded that not all suffering comes from God, and that no suffering is beyond God's care. Perhaps, with Paul, we need to claim a larger perspective that prevents us from getting stuck too long in a slough of depression.

If today is the best day of your life, it won't last. Tonight might be an inch short of hopeless; it won't last either. Whatever has brought you to this moment is only part of the story of your life and relationship. The rest is yet to come. Put all of it—dark thorns and shining threads—into God's hands, and he will sustain you.

—WAYNE BROUWER

To keep me from becoming conceited . . . there was given me a thorn in my flesh, a messenger of Satan, to torment me.

— 2 CORINTHIANS 12:7

let's *talk*

- ✦ What are some victories we have shared? How can we celebrate those moments of glory? How can we show our appreciation to God?
- ✦ When have we felt the sting of some demonic "thorn in the flesh"? Is it a recurring pain for both of us? If so, how have we prayed for its removal? What is our sense of God's leading through this ongoing trauma?
- ✦ What are we learning from the troubles in our lives? Are we gaining strength, humility, kindness, grace? How will the grace of God be evident in our testimonies to others?

FOR YOUR NEXT DEVOTIONAL READING, TURN TO PAGE 1321.

already gave you a warning when I was with
you the second time. I now repeat it while absent: On my return I will not spare those who
sinned earlier or any of the others, 3since you
are demanding proof that Christ is speaking
through me. He is not weak in dealing with
you, but is powerful among you. 4For to be
sure, he was crucified in weakness, yet he lives
by God's power. Likewise, we are weak in him,
yet by God's power we will live with him to
serve you.

5Examine yourselves to see whether you
are in the faith; test yourselves. Do you not
realize that Christ Jesus is in you—unless,
of course, you fail the test? 6And I trust that
you will discover that we have not failed the
test. 7Now we pray to God that you will not
do anything wrong. Not that people will see
that we have stood the test but that you will
do what is right even though we may seem
to have failed. 8For we cannot do anything
against the truth, but only for the truth. 9We
are glad whenever we are weak but you are
strong; and our prayer is for your perfection.
10This is why I write these things when I am
absent, that when I come I may not have to
be harsh in my use of authority—the authority the Lord gave me for building you up, not
for tearing you down.

Final Greetings

11Finally, brothers, good-by. Aim for perfection, listen to my appeal, be of one mind,
live in peace. And the God of love and peace
will be with you.

12Greet one another with a holy kiss. 13All
the saints send their greetings.

14May the grace of the Lord Jesus Christ,
and the love of God, and the fellowship of the
Holy Spirit be with you all.

GALATIANS

Galatians

QUICK FACTS

AUTHOR The apostle Paul

AUDIENCE The churches in the region of Galatia

DATE Probably around A.D. 50

SETTING Judaizers were falsely telling Gentiles that they had to obey the Jewish laws to become Christians.

The book of Galatians shows Paul's exasperation with the churches in Galatia. He had worked very hard while he had been with the Galatian believers, convincing them that salvation in Christ comes through faith alone, not through works.

However, once Paul left, the Judaizers—Jewish Christians who believed that the rules of the Old Testament, particularly circumcision, were still binding for Jewish and Gentile Christians—moved in. The Judaizers convinced the Christians at Galatia that Paul was watering down the gospel, leaving out important Old Testament ceremonial practices to make it more palatable. And the believers seemed to buy it.

There is very little in this epistle that is warm and fuzzy—no compliments from Paul, no encouragement for the churches to continue what they were doing. Rather, the apostle despaired that his work with them may have been in vain: "You foolish Galatians! Who has bewitched you?" he asked (Galatians 3:1).

Sometimes our marriages also need correction. Maybe we're engaging in destructive practices within our relationship, or we've begun to take each other for granted. Maybe, like the churches in Galatia, we've let outsiders come into our marriage and persuade us of things that aren't healthy or true. Whatever it is, Paul's letter to the Galatians gives us a wake-up call to what is right and pleases the Lord.

1 Paul, an apostle—sent not from men nor
by man, but by Jesus Christ and God the
Father, who raised him from the dead—
2and all the brothers with me,

To the churches in Galatia:

3Grace and peace to you from God our
Father and the Lord Jesus Christ, 4who gave
himself for our sins to rescue us from the present evil age, according to the will of our God
and Father, 5to whom be glory for ever and
ever. Amen.

No Other Gospel

6I am astonished that you are so quickly deserting the one who called you by the
grace of Christ and are turning to a different
gospel— 7which is really no gospel at all. Evidently some people are throwing you into
confusion and are trying to pervert the gospel
of Christ. 8But even if we or an angel from
heaven should preach a gospel other than the
one we preached to you, let him be eternally
condemned! 9As we have already said, so now
I say again: If anybody is preaching to you a
gospel other than what you accepted, let him
be eternally condemned!

10Am I now trying to win the approval of
men, or of God? Or am I trying to please men?
If I were still trying to please men, I would not
be a servant of Christ.

Paul Called by God

11I want you to know, brothers, that the
gospel I preached is not something that man
made up. 12I did not receive it from any man,
nor was I taught it; rather, I received it by revelation from Jesus Christ.

13For you have heard of my previous way
of life in Judaism, how intensely I persecuted the church of God and tried to destroy it.
14I was advancing in Judaism beyond many
Jews of my own age and was extremely zealous for the traditions of my fathers. 15But
when God, who set me apart from birth[a]
and called me by his grace, was pleased 16to
reveal his Son in me so that I might preach
him among the Gentiles, I did not consult
any man, 17nor did I go up to Jerusalem to
see those who were apostles before I was, but
I went immediately into Arabia and later returned to Damascus.

18Then after three years, I went up to Jerusalem to get acquainted with Peter[b] and
stayed with him fifteen days. 19I saw none
of the other apostles—only James, the Lord's
brother. 20I assure you before God that what
I am writing you is no lie. 21Later I went to
Syria and Cilicia. 22I was personally unknown
to the churches of Judea that are in Christ.
23They only heard the report: "The man who
formerly persecuted us is now preaching the
faith he once tried to destroy." 24And they
praised God because of me.

Paul Accepted by the Apostles

2 Fourteen years later I went up again to Jerusalem, this time with Barnabas. I took
Titus along also. 2I went in response to a
revelation and set before them the gospel that
I preach among the Gentiles. But I did this
privately to those who seemed to be leaders,
for fear that I was running or had run my race
in vain. 3Yet not even Titus, who was with me,
was compelled to be circumcised, even though
he was a Greek. 4⌞This matter arose⌟ because
some false brothers had infiltrated our ranks
to spy on the freedom we have in Christ Jesus
and to make us slaves. 5We did not give in to
them for a moment, so that the truth of the
gospel might remain with you.

6As for those who seemed to be important—whatever they were makes no difference to me; God does not judge by external
appearance—those men added nothing to my
message. 7On the contrary, they saw that I had
been entrusted with the task of preaching the
gospel to the Gentiles,[c] just as Peter had been
to the Jews.[d] 8For God, who was at work in
the ministry of Peter as an apostle to the Jews,
was also at work in my ministry as an apostle
to the Gentiles. 9James, Peter[e] and John, those
reputed to be pillars, gave me and Barnabas
the right hand of fellowship when they recognized the grace given to me. They agreed that
we should go to the Gentiles, and they to the
Jews. 10All they asked was that we should continue to remember the poor, the very thing I
was eager to do.

Paul Opposes Peter

11When Peter came to Antioch, I opposed
him to his face, because he was clearly in
the wrong. 12Before certain men came from
James, he used to eat with the Gentiles. But
when they arrived, he began to draw back and
separate himself from the Gentiles because he
was afraid of those who belonged to the circumcision group. 13The other Jews joined him

[a] 15 Or *from my mother's womb* [b] 18 Greek *Cephas* [c] 7 Greek *uncircumcised* [d] 7 Greek *circumcised*; also in verses 8 and 9
[e] 9 Greek *Cephas*; also in verses 11 and 14

T

TUESDAY
READ GALATIANS 2:1–21

KNOWING WHEN TO CONFRONT

The Christian church was less than two decades old when serious doctrinal and leadership issues erupted. In his letter to the Galatians, Paul addressed the growing tension between Jewish and Gentile Christians within the church.

Paul spoke out against the Judaizers, Jewish Christians who believed that some practices from the Law of Moses were requirements for Gentiles who were becoming followers of Jesus. Paul was committed to helping Gentile converts fellowship with newfound Christian friends without worrying about ritual protocol and ethnic etiquette. Paul even went so far as to confront the apostle Peter (also referred to as Cephas) for buckling under the pressure of the Judaizers and separating himself from Gentiles, which went against what he knew to be right. Since Peter's actions were public, they called for a public reproof.

Sometimes conflict is inevitable and actually beneficial. Lawyers make their case in court by presenting differing viewpoints. Candidates campaign for office by laying out their differing political stances. Businesspeople wrestle through decisions around a boardroom table.

How do we find the strength to disagree gently and the fortitude to fight fearlessly for those things that really matter? One woman suggested a way at her golden wedding anniversary. She said, "When Frank and I got married, there were a number of things about him that I couldn't stand. But, for the sake of our relationship, I decided to make a list of ten things that I would forgive him for. That has saved our marriage quite a few times!"

There was laughter, of course, and a lot of knowing looks between spouses. A little later the matriarch was approached by a granddaughter whose own brief marriage was being tested. "Grandma," she said, "could you tell me what kinds of things you put on your list?"

"To tell you the truth," the grandmother replied, "I never had an actual list. But every time your grandfather did something I didn't like, I'd say to myself, 'He's lucky *that's* on the list!' "

No partner in a relationship should be a doormat that constantly bears with the bad behavior of the other. There are times to challenge and confront, and times to publicly point out errors and sins. What we can learn from Paul, however, is that our emphasis should be on sharing forgiveness and redemption in Jesus, which binds even grievous sinners in the family of God and links the hands of marriage partners in prayer when human bickering threatens to separate them.

—WAYNE BROUWER

When Peter came to Antioch, I opposed him to his face, because he was clearly in the wrong.

— GALATIANS 2:11

let's *talk*

- ✦ How can we be transparent with others, yet keep some things appropriately private?
- ✦ When have we confronted one another in public regarding differing viewpoints or even sinful actions? Was it helpful or not?
- ✦ Can we live peacefully with one another while still having the strength to confront? What do our children or friends know about the strength of our commitment to one another? What do we know about each other in that regard?

FOR YOUR NEXT DEVOTIONAL READING, TURN TO PAGE 1324.

in his hypocrisy, so that by their hypocrisy
even Barnabas was led astray.
14When I saw that they were not acting in
line with the truth of the gospel, I said to Peter in front of them all, "You are a Jew, yet you
live like a Gentile and not like a Jew. How is
it, then, that you force Gentiles to follow Jewish customs?
15"We who are Jews by birth and not 'Gentile sinners' 16know that a man is not justified by observing the law, but by faith in Jesus
Christ. So we, too, have put our faith in Christ
Jesus that we may be justified by faith in Christ
and not by observing the law, because by observing the law no one will be justified.
17"If, while we seek to be justified in
Christ, it becomes evident that we ourselves
are sinners, does that mean that Christ promotes sin? Absolutely not! 18If I rebuild what
I destroyed, I prove that I am a lawbreaker.
19For through the law I died to the law so
that I might live for God. 20I have been crucified with Christ and I no longer live, but
Christ lives in me. The life I live in the body,
I live by faith in the Son of God, who loved
me and gave himself for me. 21I do not set
aside the grace of God, for if righteousness
could be gained through the law, Christ died
for nothing!"[a]

Faith or Observance of the Law

3 You foolish Galatians! Who has bewitched
you? Before your very eyes Jesus Christ was
clearly portrayed as crucified. 2I would like
to learn just one thing from you: Did you receive the Spirit by observing the law, or by believing what you heard? 3Are you so foolish?
After beginning with the Spirit, are you now
trying to attain your goal by human effort?
4Have you suffered so much for nothing—if
it really was for nothing? 5Does God give you
his Spirit and work miracles among you because you observe the law, or because you believe what you heard?
6Consider Abraham: "He believed God,
and it was credited to him as righteousness."[b]
7Understand, then, that those who believe are
children of Abraham. 8The Scripture foresaw
that God would justify the Gentiles by faith,
and announced the gospel in advance to Abraham: "All nations will be blessed through
you."[c] 9So those who have faith are blessed
along with Abraham, the man of faith.
10All who rely on observing the law are under a curse, for it is written: "Cursed is everyone who does not continue to do everything
written in the Book of the Law."[d] 11Clearly
no one is justified before God by the law,
because, "The righteous will live by faith."[e]
12The law is not based on faith; on the contrary, "The man who does these things will
live by them."[f] 13Christ redeemed us from
the curse of the law by becoming a curse for
us, for it is written: "Cursed is everyone who
is hung on a tree."[g] 14He redeemed us in order that the blessing given to Abraham might
come to the Gentiles through Christ Jesus, so
that by faith we might receive the promise of
the Spirit.

The Law and the Promise

15Brothers, let me take an example from
everyday life. Just as no one can set aside or
add to a human covenant that has been duly
established, so it is in this case. 16The promises
were spoken to Abraham and to his seed. The
Scripture does not say "and to seeds," meaning
many people, but "and to your seed,"[h] meaning one person, who is Christ. 17What I mean
is this: The law, introduced 430 years later,
does not set aside the covenant previously established by God and thus do away with the
promise. 18For if the inheritance depends on
the law, then it no longer depends on a promise; but God in his grace gave it to Abraham
through a promise.
19What, then, was the purpose of the law? It
was added because of transgressions until the
Seed to whom the promise referred had come.
The law was put into effect through angels by
a mediator. 20A mediator, however, does not
represent just one party; but God is one.
21Is the law, therefore, opposed to the
promises of God? Absolutely not! For if a law
had been given that could impart life, then
righteousness would certainly have come by
the law. 22But the Scripture declares that the
whole world is a prisoner of sin, so that what
was promised, being given through faith in
Jesus Christ, might be given to those who believe.
23Before this faith came, we were held prisoners by the law, locked up until faith should
be revealed. 24So the law was put in charge to
lead us to Christ[i] that we might be justified
by faith. 25Now that faith has come, we are no
longer under the supervision of the law.

[a] *21* Some interpreters end the quotation after verse 14. [b] *6* Gen. 15:6 [c] *8* Gen. 12:3; 18:18; 22:18 [d] *10* Deut. 27:26 [e] *11* Hab. 2:4 [f] *12* Lev. 18:5 [g] *13* Deut. 21:23 [h] *16* Gen. 12:7; 13:15; 24:7 [i] *24* Or *charge until Christ came*

Sons of God

26You are all sons of God through faith in
Christ Jesus, 27for all of you who were baptized into Christ have clothed yourselves with
Christ. 28There is neither Jew nor Greek, slave
nor free, male nor female, for you are all one
in Christ Jesus. 29If you belong to Christ, then
you are Abraham's seed, and heirs according
to the promise.

4 What I am saying is that as long as the heir
is a child, he is no different from a slave,
although he owns the whole estate. 2He
is subject to guardians and trustees until the
time set by his father. 3So also, when we were
children, we were in slavery under the basic
principles of the world. 4But when the time
had fully come, God sent his Son, born of a
woman, born under law, 5to redeem those under law, that we might receive the full rights
of sons. 6Because you are sons, God sent the
Spirit of his Son into our hearts, the Spirit
who calls out, "*Abba*,[a] Father." 7So you are no
longer a slave, but a son; and since you are a
son, God has made you also an heir.

Paul's Concern for the Galatians

8Formerly, when you did not know God,
you were slaves to those who by nature are
not gods. 9But now that you know God—or
rather are known by God—how is it that you
are turning back to those weak and miserable principles? Do you wish to be enslaved by
them all over again? 10You are observing special days and months and seasons and years!
11I fear for you, that somehow I have wasted
my efforts on you.

12I plead with you, brothers, become like
me, for I became like you. You have done me
no wrong. 13As you know, it was because of
an illness that I first preached the gospel to
you. 14Even though my illness was a trial to
you, you did not treat me with contempt or
scorn. Instead, you welcomed me as if I were
an angel of God, as if I were Christ Jesus himself. 15What has happened to all your joy? I
can testify that, if you could have done so, you
would have torn out your eyes and given them
to me. 16Have I now become your enemy by
telling you the truth?

17Those people are zealous to win you over,
but for no good. What they want is to alienate
you ⌊from us⌋, so that you may be zealous for
them. 18It is fine to be zealous, provided the
purpose is good, and to be so always and not
just when I am with you. 19My dear children,
for whom I am again in the pains of childbirth
until Christ is formed in you, 20how I wish I
could be with you now and change my tone,
because I am perplexed about you!

Hagar and Sarah

21Tell me, you who want to be under the
law, are you not aware of what the law says?
22For it is written that Abraham had two sons,
one by the slave woman and the other by the
free woman. 23His son by the slave woman
was born in the ordinary way; but his son
by the free woman was born as the result of
a promise.

24These things may be taken figuratively, for
the women represent two covenants. One covenant is from Mount Sinai and bears children
who are to be slaves: This is Hagar. 25Now Hagar stands for Mount Sinai in Arabia and cor-
responds to the present city of Jerusalem, because she is in slavery with her children. 26But
the Jerusalem that is above is free, and she is
our mother. 27For it is written:

> "Be glad, O barren woman,
> who bears no children;
> break forth and cry aloud,
> you who have no labor pains;
> because more are the children of the
> desolate woman
> than of her who has a husband."[b]

28Now you, brothers, like Isaac, are children of promise. 29At that time the son born
in the ordinary way persecuted the son born
by the power of the Spirit. It is the same now.
30But what does the Scripture say? "Get rid
of the slave woman and her son, for the slave
woman's son will never share in the inheritance with the free woman's son."[c] 31There-
fore, brothers, we are not children of the slave
woman, but of the free woman.

Freedom in Christ

5 It is for freedom that Christ has set us free.
Stand firm, then, and do not let yourselves
be burdened again by a yoke of slavery.

2Mark my words! I, Paul, tell you that if you
let yourselves be circumcised, Christ will be of
no value to you at all. 3Again I declare to every man who lets himself be circumcised that
he is obligated to obey the whole law. 4You
who are trying to be justified by law have been
alienated from Christ; you have fallen away
from grace. 5But by faith we eagerly await
through the Spirit the righteousness for which

---

[a] *6* Aramaic for *Father* [b] *27* Isaiah 54:1 [c] *30* Gen. 21:10

CHILDREN OF PROMISE

She married a man who had rules for everything. She had to get up at a certain time, fix his breakfast a certain way, iron his shirts just the way he wanted and clean the house to his exacting standards. She did what he demanded, though her heart grew cold and resentful. She lived in fear of his rebuke if something wasn't right.

Then he died. After a couple of years, she met another man who loved her deeply and gently, and they married. More years passed, and one day she realized that she got up just as early as she used to so she could fix her husband breakfast just the way he liked it. And she ironed his shirts just so, and kept house meticulously. The second marriage looked like a repeat of her first, but this time she served her spouse gladly and without resentment. The difference was that her second husband loved her, and she chose to do things, even when he didn't demand them, because she delighted in him.

Abraham had two sons, one by the slave woman and the other by the free woman.

— GALATIANS 4:22

let's talk

- What do we love doing for each other simply because we know it is important to the other? What does it feel like when we serve each other in this way?
- What is something we'd like to do to please the Lord that we aren't doing very well right now?
- When are we more likely to be a Hagarite? A Sarahite?

Law and grace work like that. That is the point of the unusual allegory Paul used in Galatians 4:21–31. He recalled the story of Abraham. Hagar and Sarah were the mothers of Abraham's two children (see Genesis 16; 21), but Paul used the women as symbols to describe the two kinds of people in religion's family tree.

One branch, symbolized by Hagar, has a slave heritage and destiny in their relationship with God. The other branch, symbolized by Sarah, represents freedom in relationship with God. Those who believe they can, and must, keep all of God's rules to earn right standing with God are the "Hagarites." They are slaves to God's law. Those who live by faith in God's saving mercy and serve him out of love are "Sarahites." Believing that God has atoned for their sins through Jesus, they do not serve him out of pride or fear, but out of love and freedom.

In the account in Genesis, we read that Sarah gave birth to a son, Isaac. The baby was unique because Sarah, at age 90, was well beyond child-bearing years. He was, in a manner of speaking, a son born of faith more than of flesh. Paul, in his letter to the Galatians, used Isaac as an example, saying that those who walk by faith are the children of Sarah, the descendants of Isaac (see Galatians 4:27–28). The barren woman had children born of loving, trusting, grateful obedience, not of legalistic adherence to the rules.

Keeping God's rules is a good thing, of course. God's laws are good and right and are the very definition of what makes life work well. But our relationship with God cannot succeed if we think we please him with our goodness. He wants us to trust him, to be born by faith in Christ Jesus, and in that relationship to receive strength from the Holy Spirit to live right.

In a Christian marriage, we cannot do anything more loving than to help each other live in the freedom Jesus has given us. We can see better than anyone else when one of us is rule bound rather than living in God's grace. Furthermore, our grace-full service to each other in Christ is a wondrous witness to the world.

—LEE ECLOV

FOR YOUR NEXT DEVOTIONAL READING, TURN TO PAGE 1325.

THURSDAY

READ GALATIANS 5:1–26

FINDING FREEDOM IN MARRIAGE

> **You, my brothers, were called to be free. But do not use your freedom to indulge the sinful nature; rather, serve one another in love.**
>
> — GALATIANS 5:13

let's talk

- In what ways is personal freedom sacrificed in marriage?
- In what ways has marriage freed us to be happier, holier or more fulfilled?
- How can we help each other feel free to tell each other the truth, to do better next time and to find more joy in our relationship?

Back in the 1970s, a popular song celebrated relationships in the lyrics "You and me are free to be / you and me." The grammar isn't very good, but the all-American ideal of personal autonomy comes through loud and clear.

Most people in the United States grew up in search of self. We learned to identify our personal strengths. We chose for ourselves schools, jobs, friends, apartments and spouses. Americans love liberty; we love to flex our independence muscles.

But what has marriage done to my personal freedom or to my husband's, for that matter? Haven't we both sacrificed personal freedom, each for the other?

Yes, we have. In marriage, each of us has put the other's well-being and personal fulfillment before our own, and the result has been, to our surprise, a freedom more freeing than any we've ever known before.

The people of Israel had a relationship with God. Because of that he expected a lot of holy behavior from them. Yet the Old Testament records centuries of the Israelites' perpetual pattern of breaking away from God's commands followed by their repentance and a desire for a renewed relationship with him. When the people turned back to God, he responded by offering them the freedom that comes with his love: freedom to start again, freedom to be close to him again, freedom to do better next time.

Likewise, the Galatians had been freed from sin by Christ's death and resurrection. They had also been released from the legalistic restrictions that Jewish leaders were trying to impose on them, such as circumcision and other Old Testament practices. But that didn't give them license to do whatever they wanted. Rather, freedom in Christ so transformed their lives that they were free to live according to the Spirit's direction. They were to battle selfish indulgences such as sexual immorality, impurity, ambition and envy, and exhibit virtues such as love, joy, peace, patience, kindness, goodness and faithfulness. They were free from self so they could obey God and be close to him. They were also free to find joy in relationship with others.

That is what God does for us too. He says, "Put away your self, your own agenda, and serve me. I will take away your sin and give you a freedom better than any you have ever known."

The same daily grace of forgiveness that kept the Galatians free also keeps us free in marriage—free to tell each other the truth, free to hold each other accountable, free to extend forgiveness, free to make a new start when sin disrupts our relationship, free to do better next time, and free to find joy in serving each other in relationship.

I gave up a lot of my personal freedom to be me when I got married, but I'm daily receiving freedom (and encouragement and support) to be a better me in marriage and for God's glory.

—ANNETTE LAPLACA

FOR YOUR NEXT DEVOTIONAL READING, TURN TO PAGE 1327.

we hope. 6For in Christ Jesus neither circumcision nor uncircumcision has any value. The
only thing that counts is faith expressing itself
through love.
7You were running a good race. Who cut in
on you and kept you from obeying the truth?
8That kind of persuasion does not come from
the one who calls you. 9"A little yeast works
through the whole batch of dough." 10I am
confident in the Lord that you will take no
other view. The one who is throwing you
into confusion will pay the penalty, whoever
he may be. 11Brothers, if I am still preaching
circumcision, why am I still being persecuted? In that case the offense of the cross has
been abolished. 12As for those agitators, I wish
they would go the whole way and emasculate
themselves!
13You, my brothers, were called to be free.
But do not use your freedom to indulge the
sinful nature[a]; rather, serve one another in
love. 14The entire law is summed up in a single
command: "Love your neighbor as yourself."[b]
15If you keep on biting and devouring each
other, watch out or you will be destroyed by
each other.

Life by the Spirit

16So I say, live by the Spirit, and you will
not gratify the desires of the sinful nature.
17For the sinful nature desires what is contrary
to the Spirit, and the Spirit what is contrary
to the sinful nature. They are in conflict with
each other, so that you do not do what you
want. 18But if you are led by the Spirit, you
are not under law.
19The acts of the sinful nature are obvious:
sexual immorality, impurity and debauchery;
20idolatry and witchcraft; hatred, discord, jealousy, fits of rage, selfish ambition, dissensions,
factions 21and envy; drunkenness, orgies, and
the like. I warn you, as I did before, that those
who live like this will not inherit the kingdom
of God.
22But the fruit of the Spirit is love, joy,
peace, patience, kindness, goodness, faithfulness, 23gentleness and self-control. Against
such things there is no law. 24Those who belong to Christ Jesus have crucified the sinful
nature with its passions and desires. 25Since
we live by the Spirit, let us keep in step with
the Spirit. 26Let us not become conceited, provoking and envying each other.

Doing Good to All

6 Brothers, if someone is caught in a sin, you
who are spiritual should restore him gently. But watch yourself, or you also may be
tempted. 2Carry each other's burdens, and
in this way you will fulfill the law of Christ.
3If anyone thinks he is something when he
is nothing, he deceives himself. 4Each one
should test his own actions. Then he can take
pride in himself, without comparing himself
to somebody else, 5for each one should carry
his own load.
6Anyone who receives instruction in the
word must share all good things with his instructor.
7Do not be deceived: God cannot be
mocked. A man reaps what he sows. 8The one
who sows to please his sinful nature, from that
nature[c] will reap destruction; the one who
sows to please the Spirit, from the Spirit will
reap eternal life. 9Let us not become weary in
doing good, for at the proper time we will reap
a harvest if we do not give up. 10Therefore,
as we have opportunity, let us do good to all
people, especially to those who belong to the
family of believers.

Not Circumcision but a New Creation

11See what large letters I use as I write to
you with my own hand!
12Those who want to make a good impression outwardly are trying to compel you to
be circumcised. The only reason they do this
is to avoid being persecuted for the cross of
Christ. 13Not even those who are circumcised
obey the law, yet they want you to be circumcised that they may boast about your flesh.
14May I never boast except in the cross of our
Lord Jesus Christ, through which[d] the world
has been crucified to me, and I to the world.
15Neither circumcision nor uncircumcision
means anything; what counts is a new creation. 16Peace and mercy to all who follow this
rule, even to the Israel of God.
17Finally, let no one cause me trouble, for I
bear on my body the marks of Jesus.
18The grace of our Lord Jesus Christ be
with your spirit, brothers. Amen.

---

[a] *13* Or *the flesh*; also in verses 16, 17, 19 and 24 [b] *14* Lev. 19:18 [c] *8* Or *his flesh, from the flesh* [d] *14* Or *whom*

F

FRIDAY
READ GALATIANS 6:1–10

WHEN IS MY BURDEN YOURS?

Carry each other's burdens, and in this way you will fulfill the law of Christ.

— Galatians 6:2

let's talk

- ✦ What burdens have each of us had to shoulder in our marriage? What burdens have we weathered together?
- ✦ What are some practical ways we can help each other manage the burdens we are carrying right now?
- ✦ How can we help others who are struggling with marital problems? What are some cautions to exercise in doing that?

People who work with ocean-going ships will tell you that it's critical to check the way the cargo load is distributed in the vessel. If the cargo is too heavy, the ship will ride too low in the water and won't be able to travel at a good speed. If the load is too light, the ship will ride too high in the water and bob like a cork, especially when storms hit. The ship needs the proper amount of cargo for it to make the best progress across the ocean.

Life works like that for Christians too. When our burdens are too heavy, we can become so depressed and weary that we can hardly do our work, much less be a testimony of God's grace to others. When our burdens are too light, we find it difficult to empathize with others who are carrying a heavy load, or we find ourselves aimless and restless. We need the proper balance between load carrying and load sharing to progress in our Christian walk.

Paul knew this. By commanding us to share each other's burdens, he was echoing Jesus' words: "A new command I give you: Love one another" (John 13:34). The apostle warns us not to question the loads of others, thinking we're better than they are because we don't have their particular problems. "If anyone thinks he is something when he is nothing, he deceives himself," he said (Galatians 6:3). Instead, Paul tells us to examine ourselves, pick up our own loads and help others when we are called to do so.

When we look at problems in marriage, we see the same principle in place: If one spouse is sinking under a load of guilt, troubles or sin, while the other is bobbing around with seemingly no concern, anger and resentment will build. An unbalanced load will only stress and slow down the marital relationship. So to keep moving together in the right direction, we must remain firmly yoked together as we lovingly share each other's problems and do what we can to help each other deal with them.

But what do we do when our problems become too heavy for the two of us to carry? There may come a time when we need to look for help from others outside the marriage. When we feel overwhelmed by severe problems such as sexual addiction, alcohol abuse or clinical depression, it's time to get help. Going to a Christian doctor, counselor or pastor is not taking the easy way out—for some, admitting a problem in the marriage is an agonizing first step. But it is a necessary step for many couples that need help adjusting to life's problems, to a family crisis or simply to each other.

One caution: It is tempting to turn to friends, family and coworkers to vent our marital problems. This is rarely a good idea. Problems inside a marriage can almost never be solved by taking them outside the marriage, unless it's to a qualified professional. Letting too many people know about our marital struggles just burdens us with the responsibility of keeping others updated. It may force friends or family members to side with one spouse while distancing themselves from the other. And it will drain emotional energy from a marital relationship. Offering our spouses privacy within the marital relationship will keep trust in each other intact and will demonstrate our continued love and respect for each other as we learn better ways of sharing our load.

—VALERIE VAN KOOTEN

FOR YOUR NEXT DEVOTIONAL READING, TURN TO PAGE 1328.

WEEKEND

in-law issues

In-law conflicts are nothing new. Occurring in many forms, they tend to be ongoing issues that revolve around the couple as a whole. The first step toward finding a solution is to identify a specific problem. Here are five to consider.

1. Favoritism. Parents have an older, deeper relationship with their own child than with a new spouse, which is to be expected. However, when parental preference for one's own child over the spouse exists and is expressed, distance and hurt can result.

2. Intrusiveness. Some parents cross the line between responsibility and respect. They become too involved with their married children. Often such meddling leaves the younger couple feeling smothered or controlled.

3. Over-parenting. Some in-laws have difficulty letting go of their roles as parents. Instead of transitioning into an adult relationship with their married children, they offer unasked-for advice, criticism, or even withhold approval if they disagree with the younger couple's choices.

4. Emotional distance. Some parents have cold, disconnected relationships with their married children. They seem emotionally unavailable, self-absorbed, aloof or unfriendly. Although the younger couple wants more closeness, they find themselves rebuffed or ignored by the parents. Sometimes, unresolved issues or hurts account for this problem. But other times, it has more to do with the character of the in-laws. They may simply be distant folks. Regardless of the cause, it is a painful situation.

5. Dependence. Although we are told to care for our parents (1 Timothy 5:4), it may not be healthy to become involved in the problems of in-laws. For example, parents may try to have the younger couple referee their arguments or get them to take sides. They may want the couple to rescue a drug-addicted child they can't fix. Or they may be financially irresponsible and ask the couple to bail them out. Those are setups for future problems.

Consider these tips on how to create an open, working—if not wonderful—relationship with your in-laws.

Reality check. Find out if there really is a problem between you and your in-laws or if it's merely your perception. Sometimes we react to others based on our experiences. That can cloud judgment. For a better perspective, ask a trusted friend to observe and verify your perception of the situation.

Do a self-inventory. After you've identified the problem, ask yourself how you might be contributing to it. Jesus reminds us that we must deal with our own actions before we help correct others (Matthew 7:1–5).

Be direct. If you are avoiding dealing with your in-law problems, you may begin to withdraw emotionally from them. Instead, confront your in-laws gently but directly. Though it's good to involve your spouse, don't avoid dealing with the problem alone.

Choose your battles. End an issue by setting new limits or by simply adapting to it. If the conflict creates havoc in your marriage, you and your spouse may want to negotiate how you spend time with the parents. If the issue is simply annoying, then you may want to let it go and enjoy the healthier aspects of your relationship.

Strengthen your role as a spouse. Though you and your spouse love your parents, you should be more aligned with each other than with them. When a spouse isn't loyal to his or her mate, there may be a leaving-and-cleaving problem (Genesis 2:24). This problem is exhibited in behaviors such as requiring parental approval or respect, being afraid to confront parents, leaning on parents for support, being emotionally or financially dependent on parents, or feeling responsible for a parent's emotions. If your spouse struggles with these issues, express how you feel and how those actions affect your sense of safety as a couple.

—DR. JOHN TOWNSEND

how do you score on handling in-laws?

HOW ARE WE DOING?

1. Your in-laws come to visit. You:
   a. Have a to-do list
   b. Have a to-don't list
2. When speaking to your spouse about your in-laws, you:
   a. Tend to compliment
   b. Tend to criticize
3. You are with your in-laws when they do something that embarrasses you. You:
   a. Give your in-laws the benefit of the doubt
   b. Doubt the relationship is beneficial
4. The phone rings. It's your mother-in-law. You:
   a. Pick it up and say, "Hi, Mom!"
   b. Let the machine get it
5. When you say, "You're just like your mother" or "Your father always does that too," your spouse:
   a. Takes it as a compliment
   b. Takes it as a criticism
6. Your father-in-law is sick and needs full time care. You:
   a. Offer your house
   b. Offer to call a relative

Give yourself 1 point for each *"a"* answer.

Scoring:

5–6 points: You're a welcome addition to the family—and probably the favorite.

3–4 points: You've got room for improvement before the in-laws' next visit.

0–3 points: You're a real out-law. Stay clear until you can improve your attitude.

let's make a DATE

WESTERN FLING

Go on a date with your in-laws. Choose a western movie, attend a rodeo or eat at your favorite steak house. Promise your spouse that, at least for the night, you'll leave your out-laws at home and enjoy the evening with your in-laws.

FOR YOUR NEXT DEVOTIONAL READING, TURN TO PAGE 1332.

LESSONS FROM THE *Bible*

What can you learn from these in-law relationships?

1. Moses and Jethro (Exodus 18)
2. Ruth and Naomi (Ruth 1–4)
3. Peter and his mother-in-law (Matthew 8:14–15)

EPHESIANS

QUICK FACTS

AUTHOR The apostle Paul

AUDIENCE The church in Ephesus, a city that was located in modern-day Turkey

DATE About A.D. 60

SETTING Written from a Roman prison to encourage the Christians in Ephesus and likely other Christians in the surrounding area

The book of Ephesians ushers us into the mysterious things of God as it describes how Jesus builds a church that consists of sinners who have nothing to recommend them but his sacrifice. This is indeed a wonder, and Paul emphasized the diversity of those who have been called "to become a holy temple in the Lord" (Ephesians 2:21). Paul boldly stated that we—both Jews and Gentiles—were chosen before the creation of the world and are God's handiwork. Ephesians is filled with radical ideas for those who have tried to find eternal life through good works.

Just as a young man puts an engagement ring on the finger of the girl he loves and wants to marry, the Holy Spirit marks us with a seal of God's ownership (see Ephesians 1:13; 4:30). God loves us and wants us as his own. He wants us to live for him and him alone. Several chapters of Ephesians discuss what the Christian walk should look like and how a child of God can be a living witness in all spheres of life.

Just as the union of Christ with his church is a great mystery, so too is the love of a husband and wife (see Ephesians 5:21–33). Rightly done, our marriage relationship on earth will mirror the selfless love of Jesus and his bride, the church.

1 Paul, an apostle of Christ Jesus by the will
of God,

To the saints in Ephesus,[a] the faithful[b] in
Christ Jesus:

2Grace and peace to you from God our Father and the Lord Jesus Christ.

Spiritual Blessings in Christ

3Praise be to the God and Father of our
Lord Jesus Christ, who has blessed us in the
heavenly realms with every spiritual blessing
in Christ. 4For he chose us in him before the
creation of the world to be holy and blameless
in his sight. In love 5he[c] predestined us to be
adopted as his sons through Jesus Christ, in
accordance with his pleasure and will— 6to
the praise of his glorious grace, which he has
freely given us in the One he loves. 7In him we
have redemption through his blood, the forgiveness of sins, in accordance with the riches
of God's grace 8that he lavished on us with all
wisdom and understanding. 9And he[d] made
known to us the mystery of his will according to his good pleasure, which he purposed in
Christ, 10to be put into effect when the times
will have reached their fulfillment—to bring
all things in heaven and on earth together under one head, even Christ.

11In him we were also chosen,[e] having been
predestined according to the plan of him who
works out everything in conformity with the
purpose of his will, 12in order that we, who
were the first to hope in Christ, might be for
the praise of his glory. 13And you also were
included in Christ when you heard the word
of truth, the gospel of your salvation. Having believed, you were marked in him with
a seal, the promised Holy Spirit, 14who is a
deposit guaranteeing our inheritance until the
redemption of those who are God's possession—to the praise of his glory.

Thanksgiving and Prayer

15For this reason, ever since I heard about
your faith in the Lord Jesus and your love
for all the saints, 16I have not stopped giving thanks for you, remembering you in my
prayers. 17I keep asking that the God of our
Lord Jesus Christ, the glorious Father, may
give you the Spirit[f] of wisdom and revelation, so that you may know him better. 18I
pray also that the eyes of your heart may be
enlightened in order that you may know the
hope to which he has called you, the riches of
his glorious inheritance in the saints, 19and his
incomparably great power for us who believe.
That power is like the working of his mighty
strength, 20which he exerted in Christ when
he raised him from the dead and seated him
at his right hand in the heavenly realms, 21far
above all rule and authority, power and dominion, and every title that can be given, not
only in the present age but also in the one to
come. 22And God placed all things under his
feet and appointed him to be head over everything for the church, 23which is his body, the
fullness of him who fills everything in every
way.

Made Alive in Christ

2 As for you, you were dead in your transgressions and sins, 2in which you used to
live when you followed the ways of this
world and of the ruler of the kingdom of the
air, the spirit who is now at work in those who
are disobedient. 3All of us also lived among
them at one time, gratifying the cravings of
our sinful nature[g] and following its desires
and thoughts. Like the rest, we were by nature
objects of wrath. 4But because of his great love
for us, God, who is rich in mercy, 5made us
alive with Christ even when we were dead in
transgressions—it is by grace you have been
saved. 6And God raised us up with Christ and
seated us with him in the heavenly realms in
Christ Jesus, 7in order that in the coming ages
he might show the incomparable riches of his
grace, expressed in his kindness to us in Christ
Jesus. 8For it is by grace you have been saved,
through faith—and this not from yourselves,
it is the gift of God— 9not by works, so that
no one can boast. 10For we are God's work-
manship, created in Christ Jesus to do good
works, which God prepared in advance for us
to do.

One in Christ

11Therefore, remember that formerly you
who are Gentiles by birth and called "uncircumcised" by those who call themselves "the
circumcision" (that done in the body by the
hands of men)— 12remember that at that time
you were separate from Christ, excluded from
citizenship in Israel and foreigners to the covenants of the promise, without hope and without God in the world. 13But now in Christ
Jesus you who once were far away have been
brought near through the blood of Christ.

[a] *1* Some early manuscripts do not have *in Ephesus.* [b] *1* Or *believers who are* [c] *4,5* Or *sight in love.* [5]*He* [d] *8,9* Or *us. With all wisdom and understanding,* [9]*he* [e] *11* Or *were made heirs* [f] *17* Or *a spirit* [g] *3* Or *our flesh*

MONDAY
READ EPHESIANS 1:1–23

THANKFUL FOR EACH OTHER

> **I have not stopped giving thanks for you, remembering you in my prayers.**
>
> — EPHESIANS 1:16

let's talk

- What are we thankful for in each other? Since this is a time for building each other up personally, let's only mention positives without any qualifiers.
- What is it about our relationship that we as a couple are thankful for?
- Let's conduct a thanksgiving experiment of our own: Let's find others who need encouragement and tell them why we are thankful for them. Then let's compare notes on how they responded.

Paul began his letter to the Ephesians by addressing them as "the faithful in Christ Jesus" (Ephesians 1:1). Next, he told them that they had been chosen and adopted by God to be holy and blameless, and it was God's pleasure to have chosen them.

Paul said that God's grace had been lavished on them, they had been marked with the seal of the Holy Spirit, and they were God's possession. "For this reason," said Paul, "ever since I heard about your faith in the Lord Jesus and your love for all the saints, I have not stopped giving thanks for you, remembering you in my prayers" (Ephesians 1:15–16).

Imagine getting such a beautiful message from your spouse. How would you respond to his or her reminder of how precious you are to God because of your faith in Christ? How would you feel as your spouse expressed the things that he or she appreciates about you?

Imagine someone saying, "I'm continually giving thanks for you. Every time I think of you, I thank God for who you are and what you mean to me. My life is better because of you, and I remember you daily in my prayers."

If your spouse said that to you, you might hold your head a little higher, walk with a little more bounce in your step, smile more. You might be encouraged to try new things, take risks, be adventurous, be more generous.

Back when our girls were young and life was hectic, my husband and I found ourselves racing on a treadmill of busyness. We were tired and frazzled, and because we weren't taking time to cultivate our relationship, things became blah between us.

At the time I was in a women's Bible study group that was studying the book of Ephesians and how it relates to marriage and family. One morning the topic was thankfulness, and I decided to conduct an experiment. Later that evening as my husband raked leaves in the yard, I quietly picked up a rake and started working alongside him. As I did, I began telling him things for which I was thankful: how hard he worked for the family, how strong he was, that the bathroom he had just painted was beautiful, that I was glad to be his wife.

As I raked and talked, I noticed his posture change. Later, he said that I was a good wife and a good mom. I told him that he was a good husband.

My little experiment changed something in both of us that to this day has continued—a habit of being thankful for each other and saying so. It was so simple, yet so powerful.

Gratitude is perhaps one reason why our marriage has lasted so long. We do not stop giving thanks to God for him and for each other.

—NANCY KENNEDY

FOR YOUR NEXT DEVOTIONAL READING, TURN TO PAGE 1334.

14For he himself is our peace, who has made
the two one and has destroyed the barrier, the
dividing wall of hostility, 15by abolishing in
his flesh the law with its commandments and
regulations. His purpose was to create in himself one new man out of the two, thus making peace, 16and in this one body to reconcile
both of them to God through the cross, by
which he put to death their hostility. 17He
came and preached peace to you who were far
away and peace to those who were near. 18For
through him we both have access to the Father
by one Spirit.

19Consequently, you are no longer foreigners and aliens, but fellow citizens with God's
people and members of God's household,
20built on the foundation of the apostles and
prophets, with Christ Jesus himself as the chief
cornerstone. 21In him the whole building is
joined together and rises to become a holy
temple in the Lord. 22And in him you too are
being built together to become a dwelling in
which God lives by his Spirit.

Paul the Preacher to the Gentiles

3 For this reason I, Paul, the prisoner of
Christ Jesus for the sake of you Gentiles—
2Surely you have heard about the administration of God's grace that was given to me
for you, 3that is, the mystery made known
to me by revelation, as I have already written
briefly. 4In reading this, then, you will be able
to understand my insight into the mystery of
Christ, 5which was not made known to men
in other generations as it has now been revealed by the Spirit to God's holy apostles
and prophets. 6This mystery is that through
the gospel the Gentiles are heirs together
with Israel, members together of one body,
and sharers together in the promise in Christ
Jesus.

7I became a servant of this gospel by the gift
of God's grace given me through the working
of his power. 8Although I am less than the least
of all God's people, this grace was given me: to
preach to the Gentiles the unsearchable riches
of Christ, 9and to make plain to everyone the
administration of this mystery, which for ages
past was kept hidden in God, who created all
things. 10His intent was that now, through the
church, the manifold wisdom of God should
be made known to the rulers and authorities
in the heavenly realms, 11according to his eternal purpose which he accomplished in Christ
Jesus our Lord. 12In him and through faith in
him we may approach God with freedom and
confidence. 13I ask you, therefore, not to be
discouraged because of my sufferings for you,
which are your glory.

A Prayer for the Ephesians

14For this reason I kneel before the Father,
15from whom his whole family[a] in heaven
and on earth derives its name. 16I pray that
out of his glorious riches he may strengthen
you with power through his Spirit in your inner being, 17so that Christ may dwell in your
hearts through faith. And I pray that you,
being rooted and established in love, 18may
have power, together with all the saints, to
grasp how wide and long and high and deep
is the love of Christ, 19and to know this love
that surpasses knowledge—that you may be
filled to the measure of all the fullness of
God.

20Now to him who is able to do immea-
surably more than all we ask or imagine, according to his power that is at work within us,
21to him be glory in the church and in Christ
Jesus throughout all generations, for ever and
ever! Amen.

Unity in the Body of Christ

4 As a prisoner for the Lord, then, I urge you
to live a life worthy of the calling you have
received. 2Be completely humble and gentle; be patient, bearing with one another in
love. 3Make every effort to keep the unity of
the Spirit through the bond of peace. 4There
is one body and one Spirit—just as you were
called to one hope when you were called—
5one Lord, one faith, one baptism; 6one God
and Father of all, who is over all and through
all and in all.

7But to each one of us grace has been giv-
en as Christ apportioned it. 8This is why it[b]
says:

> "When he ascended on high,
> he led captives in his train
> and gave gifts to men."[c]

9(What does "he ascended" mean except that
he also descended to the lower, earthly regions[d]? 10He who descended is the very one
who ascended higher than all the heavens,
in order to fill the whole universe.) 11It was
he who gave some to be apostles, some to be
prophets, some to be evangelists, and some
to be pastors and teachers, 12to prepare God's
people for works of service, so that the body

---

[a] 15 Or *whom all fatherhood* [b] 8 Or *God* [c] 8 Psalm 68:18 [d] 9 Or *the depths of the earth*

TUESDAY
READ EPHESIANS 2:1–22

FINDING A PLACE FOR US

In our first three years of marriage, Jim and I moved 11 times. We hauled our Crate and Barrel boxes from Minnesota to California to Illinois and back to Minnesota again. Eventually, we just left the good dishes, the empty picture frames and the various knickknacks wrapped in boxes and only pulled out the essentials for living.

Although I didn't mind the moving, I got tired of constantly having to start over: getting the phone up and running, changing my driver's license, finding the closest Target, struggling to make new friends. Every move meant a time of loneliness as I attempted to connect with someone—anyone—to begin new friendships.

But, in truth, the physical moves involved in creating a life together are nothing compared to the emotional and spiritual upheaval marriage can bring. Becoming one with someone is no easy task, no matter how well you know each other and no matter how deeply you love each other. The transition from "me" to "we" changes everything—where you live, who your friends are, how you spend your money and free time, when you sleep, how you eat, everything. And all of this change can lead to a weird kind of loneliness; you feel almost like a foreigner in your own life.

Ephesians 2:19–20 is a balm for that feeling. It reminds us that we are more than husbands and wives. We are more than men and women. We are God's people. And because of that, we are integral members of God's family. What a beautiful way to understand ourselves and who we are! Even when we feel lonely or disconnected in the midst of transition and turmoil, we are part of the amazing story of God's love for his people. This is what Paul meant when he said that the household of God is built on the foundation of the apostles and prophets, as well as on Jesus himself. We are the next level, the next phase of God's incredible work in the world.

Understanding ourselves as part of the ongoing work of God can provide us with a new perspective on the ups and downs, the moves and shifts, that come with marriage. These changes open us up to what God has planned for us. They help us grow and change. A move to a new town offers a chance to touch—and be touched—by new friends. The accountability involved in sharing finances and time can prompt us to be better stewards of all God has given us. A spouse's hopes and dreams can dovetail into ours as we create bigger, better plans for bringing God's love to the world.

Yes, growth and change can be painful, but we have this promise: "[We] are being built together to become a dwelling in which God lives by his Spirit" (verse 22). If we welcome that, the process of building that dwelling will change us for the better.

—CARLA BARNHILL

You are no longer foreigners and aliens, but fellow citizens with God's people and members of God's household, built on the foundation of the apostles and prophets, with Christ Jesus himself as the chief cornerstone.
— EPHESIANS 2:19–20

let's *talk*

- ✦ What have been some surprises in our marriage? How did God use those events to shape us?
- ✦ What transitions are we experiencing right now—an impending move, a new child, a job change? How can we help each other handle those changes?
- ✦ What couple do we know who has gone through a similar transition? Let's make a date to talk with them about how to get through a potentially stressful time.

FOR YOUR NEXT DEVOTIONAL READING, TURN TO PAGE 1336.

of Christ may be built up 13until we all reach unity in the faith and in the knowledge of the Son of God and become mature, attaining to the whole measure of the fullness of Christ.

14Then we will no longer be infants, tossed back and forth by the waves, and blown here and there by every wind of teaching and by the cunning and craftiness of men in their deceitful scheming. 15Instead, speaking the truth in love, we will in all things grow up into him who is the Head, that is, Christ. 16From him the whole body, joined and held together by every supporting ligament, grows and builds itself up in love, as each part does its work.

Living as Children of Light

17So I tell you this, and insist on it in the Lord, that you must no longer live as the Gentiles do, in the futility of their thinking. 18They are darkened in their understanding and separated from the life of God because of the ignorance that is in them due to the hardening of their hearts. 19Having lost all sensitivity, they have given themselves over to sensuality so as to indulge in every kind of impurity, with a continual lust for more.

20You, however, did not come to know Christ that way. 21Surely you heard of him and were taught in him in accordance with the truth that is in Jesus. 22You were taught, with regard to your former way of life, to put off your old self, which is being corrupted by its deceitful desires; 23to be made new in the attitude of your minds; 24and to put on the new self, created to be like God in true righteousness and holiness.

25Therefore each of you must put off falsehood and speak truthfully to his neighbor, for we are all members of one body. 26"In your anger do not sin"[a]: Do not let the sun go down while you are still angry, 27and do not give the devil a foothold. 28He who has been stealing must steal no longer, but must work, doing something useful with his own hands, that he may have something to share with those in need.

29Do not let any unwholesome talk come out of your mouths, but only what is helpful for building others up according to their needs, that it may benefit those who listen. 30And do not grieve the Holy Spirit of God, with whom you were sealed for the day of redemption. 31Get rid of all bitterness, rage and anger, brawling and slander, along with every form of malice. 32Be kind and compassionate to one another, forgiving each other, just as in Christ God forgave you.

5 Be imitators of God, therefore, as dearly loved children 2and live a life of love, just as Christ loved us and gave himself up for us as a fragrant offering and sacrifice to God.

3But among you there must not be even a hint of sexual immorality, or of any kind of impurity, or of greed, because these are improper for God's holy people. 4Nor should there be obscenity, foolish talk or coarse joking, which are out of place, but rather thanksgiving. 5For of this you can be sure: No immoral, impure or greedy person—such a man is an idolater—has any inheritance in the kingdom of Christ and of God.[b] 6Let no one deceive you with empty words, for because of such things God's wrath comes on those who are disobedient. 7Therefore do not be partners with them.

8For you were once darkness, but now you are light in the Lord. Live as children of light 9(for the fruit of the light consists in all goodness, righteousness and truth) 10and find out what pleases the Lord. 11Have nothing to do with the fruitless deeds of darkness, but rather expose them. 12For it is shameful even to mention what the disobedient do in secret. 13But everything exposed by the light becomes visible, 14for it is light that makes everything visible. This is why it is said:

"Wake up, O sleeper,
  rise from the dead,
and Christ will shine on you."

15Be very careful, then, how you live—not as unwise but as wise, 16making the most of every opportunity, because the days are evil. 17Therefore do not be foolish, but understand what the Lord's will is. 18Do not get drunk on wine, which leads to debauchery. Instead, be filled with the Spirit. 19Speak to one another with psalms, hymns and spiritual songs. Sing and make music in your heart to the Lord, 20always giving thanks to God the Father for everything, in the name of our Lord Jesus Christ.

21Submit to one another out of reverence for Christ.

Wives and Husbands

22Wives, submit to your husbands as to the Lord. 23For the husband is the head of the wife as Christ is the head of the church, his body, of which he is the Savior. 24Now as the

---

[a] 26 Psalm 4:4 [b] 5 Or *kingdom of the Christ and God*

WEDNESDAY
READ EPHESIANS 4:17—5:2

HOW FORGIVENESS WORKS

> **Be kind and compassionate to one another, forgiving each other, just as in Christ God forgave you.**
>
> — Ephesians 4:32

let's talk

- ✦ What are some ways each of us quietly gets even after the other has inflicted hurt?
- ✦ Who gets injured when one of us holds a grudge against the other?
- ✦ What are some ways each of us could handle hurt more constructively?

Soon after marrying Grey, I was shocked to realize that he was adept at finding flaws in the meals I had worked so hard to plan, cook and present. After I lovingly presented one entrée to him, he said, "It could be hotter." After sweating over another meal, during a time when I was trying to be economical, he said, "This dish must have set us back a buck-fifty."

What would I do? Dump the meal in his lap? Go on strike? Cry in my napkin? Or would I laugh, let it go and accept the fact that I was not like his mother in the kitchen? In short, would I be willing to forgive him and move on?

Paul's instructions to the Ephesians to "be kind and compassionate to one another, forgiving each other" are still valid for us today. What's more, they are good advice for living in a peaceful and God-honoring marriage. As we adjust to living with each other, we'll inevitably face many little irritations and perhaps some big hurts. The sooner we get into the habit of forgiving each other, the happier we'll be.

So, how does forgiveness work? According to Lewis Smedes, author of *The Art of Forgiving* (Ballantine Books, 1997), when we forgive someone, we do three basic things:

First, we surrender our right to get even. "If you have been wronged, getting even is the natural impulse, but you resist that impulse," Smedes said.

Second, we revise our view of the person who hurt us. Smedes explained it this way: "When you've been deeply wounded by your spouse, you redraw your picture of that person, making him or her not primarily your husband or wife but rather 'the person who hurt me.' So in forgiving, you need to reconstruct that image and see the spouse as a flawed, weak human being—not much different from yourself—who hurt you as much out of weakness as out of ill will."

Third, we revise our feelings. "Gradually your feelings of rage are transformed into a desire for that person's blessing and for that person's change," Smedes said.

"This is a gradual process, of course," Smedes added. "God can forgive in a single swoosh, but we are finite, temporal creatures for whom almost everything takes time."

He's right about taking time to develop an attitude of forgiveness. But the alternative—harboring resentment and getting even—has never helped build a loving relationship. God's instructions worked for the Ephesians, and they still work for us today.

—MARY ANN JEFFREYS

FOR YOUR NEXT DEVOTIONAL READING, TURN TO PAGE 1338.

church submits to Christ, so also wives should
submit to their husbands in everything.
25Husbands, love your wives, just as Christ
loved the church and gave himself up for her
26to make her holy, cleansing[a] her by the
washing with water through the word, 27and
to present her to himself as a radiant church,
without stain or wrinkle or any other blemish, but holy and blameless. 28In this same
way, husbands ought to love their wives as
their own bodies. He who loves his wife loves
himself. 29After all, no one ever hated his own
body, but he feeds and cares for it, just as
Christ does the church— 30for we are members of his body. 31"For this reason a man will
leave his father and mother and be united to
his wife, and the two will become one flesh."[b]
32This is a profound mystery—but I am talking about Christ and the church. 33However,
each one of you also must love his wife as he
loves himself, and the wife must respect her
husband.

Children and Parents

6 Children, obey your parents in the Lord,
for this is right. 2"Honor your father and
mother"—which is the first commandment with a promise— 3"that it may go well
with you and that you may enjoy long life on
the earth."[c]
4Fathers, do not exasperate your children;
instead, bring them up in the training and instruction of the Lord.

Slaves and Masters

5Slaves, obey your earthly masters with respect and fear, and with sincerity of heart, just
as you would obey Christ. 6Obey them not
only to win their favor when their eye is on
you, but like slaves of Christ, doing the will
of God from your heart. 7Serve wholeheartedly, as if you were serving the Lord, not men,
8because you know that the Lord will reward
everyone for whatever good he does, whether
he is slave or free.
9And masters, treat your slaves in the same
way. Do not threaten them, since you know
that he who is both their Master and yours
is in heaven, and there is no favoritism with
him.

The Armor of God

10Finally, be strong in the Lord and in his
mighty power. 11Put on the full armor of
God so that you can take your stand against
the devil's schemes. 12For our struggle is not
against flesh and blood, but against the rulers,
against the authorities, against the powers of
this dark world and against the spiritual forces of evil in the heavenly realms. 13Therefore
put on the full armor of God, so that when
the day of evil comes, you may be able to
stand your ground, and after you have done
everything, to stand. 14Stand firm then, with
the belt of truth buckled around your waist,
with the breastplate of righteousness in place,
15and with your feet fitted with the readiness
that comes from the gospel of peace. 16In addition to all this, take up the shield of faith,
with which you can extinguish all the flaming
arrows of the evil one. 17Take the helmet of
salvation and the sword of the Spirit, which is
the word of God. 18And pray in the Spirit on
all occasions with all kinds of prayers and requests. With this in mind, be alert and always
keep on praying for all the saints.
19Pray also for me, that whenever I open
my mouth, words may be given me so that
I will fearlessly make known the mystery of
the gospel, 20for which I am an ambassador
in chains. Pray that I may declare it fearlessly,
as I should.

Final Greetings

21Tychicus, the dear brother and faithful
servant in the Lord, will tell you everything,
so that you also may know how I am and what
I am doing. 22I am sending him to you for this
very purpose, that you may know how we are,
and that he may encourage you.
23Peace to the brothers, and love with
faith from God the Father and the Lord Jesus
Christ. 24Grace to all who love our Lord Jesus
Christ with an undying love.

---

[a] 26 Or *having cleansed* [b] 31 Gen. 2:24 [c] 3 Deut. 5:16

THURSDAY

READ EPHESIANS 5:21–33

RULES OF ENGAGEMENT

Submit to one another out of reverence for Christ.

— Ephesians 5:21

let's *talk*

- How can seeing submission as a process help us deal with difficult issues in our marriage or perhaps even help us come to a consensus on the topic itself?
- Was there a time when we misused the concept of submission to get our way? What was the outcome of that approach?
- Let's write out some "rules of engagement" that we can use when we have tough decisions to make or conflicts to resolve. How can we make sure those rules are about process, not power?

It doesn't get much more controversial than this. In conversations about Christian marriage, Ephesians 5:21–33 gets hauled out and used to defend all kinds of ideas about who gets to do and say what in a marriage.

Entire books have been written on the issue of submission in marriage. Scholars have debated it. Well-meaning people have argued over it. Pastors have preached on it (and suffered the backlash from the congregation).

Yet for all its controversy, submission seems to be one of those issues that couples don't really talk about. Instead, it has become a self-selecting process: We tend to marry a person whose ideas about submission dovetail with our own. I don't know many couples who argue about, or come to the brink of divorce over, the topic of submission.

I do, however, know many couples who use their view on submission as an excuse to make really lousy decisions in their marriages. I know men who claim "headship" as an excuse for becoming overbearing and controlling, trampling their wives in the process. And I know women who wear their perception of submission like a veil behind which they can hide from responsibility and maturity, forcing their husbands to take on all the accountability in their marriages.

Perhaps we have misunderstood what submission is all about. We think of it as being an issue of *position*, of power. But, in truth, submission is about *process.*

Look at what is said—and isn't said—about submission in these verses. Ephesians 5:21–33 talks about mutuality and respect, about care and tenderness, about compassion, goodness and gentleness. It describes being Christlike in our marriages. This passage is about *how* we are to live together as husbands and wives.

When Paul wrote these words, most marriages were arranged by parents. So a husband and wife many times had little contact with each other before their wedding day. So when Paul told husbands and wives to build emotional and spiritual connections with each other, he was introducing a concept that would benefit the couple from the inception of their time together; mutual submission provided a foundation for the couple's life together. He was asking them to make their marriages reflections of the beautiful love between Christ and his church.

One's view on submission in marriage isn't about the outcome of a decision; it's about how that decision is made. It isn't about who is in charge; it's about how we treat each other. It isn't about hierarchy; it's about partnership. A godly marriage is two people working together to illustrate the love of God in their lives.

—CARLA BARNHILL

FOR YOUR NEXT DEVOTIONAL READING, TURN TO PAGE 1341.

PHILIPPIANS

Philippians

QUICK FACTS

AUTHOR The apostle Paul

AUDIENCE The church in Philippi (the first church in Europe)

DATE About A.D. 61

SETTING Written while Paul was under house arrest in Rome

It's hard to believe that a letter so full of commands to be joyful could have been written from prison. But that's where Paul was when this letter to the church at Philippi was written. Joy isn't happiness, Paul said. It isn't being glad when everything is going well for us. Joy is full-forward acceptance and contentment in whatever situation we find ourselves because God is in control and is doing what is best for us.

A gloomy Christian wins no converts. We can't attract others to the Lord if we're full of complaining, bitterness and rebellion. So Paul urged believers to think about things that are lovely, pure and true (see Philippians 4:8), and to live out joy in our daily walk. Only when we live for Christ will our lives be a joyful testament to others.

There are times in marriage when it can be difficult to be joyful. When the bills are overdue or we're tired of our spouse's bad habits or the in-laws are getting on our nerves, we can be grouchy and discontented. Paul, however, encourages us to see that joy is based on more than our circumstances. Our eternal hope in God is what leads us upward.

1 Paul and Timothy, servants of Christ Jesus,

To all the saints in Christ Jesus at Philippi,
together with the overseers[a] and deacons:

[2]Grace and peace to you from God our Father and the Lord Jesus Christ.

Thanksgiving and Prayer

[3]I thank my God every time I remember
you. [4]In all my prayers for all of you, I always
pray with joy [5]because of your partnership in
the gospel from the first day until now, [6]being
confident of this, that he who began a good
work in you will carry it on to completion until the day of Christ Jesus.
[7]It is right for me to feel this way about
all of you, since I have you in my heart; for
whether I am in chains or defending and confirming the gospel, all of you share in God's
grace with me. [8]God can testify how I long for
all of you with the affection of Christ Jesus.
[9]And this is my prayer: that your love may
abound more and more in knowledge and
depth of insight, [10]so that you may be able
to discern what is best and may be pure and
blameless until the day of Christ, [11]filled with
the fruit of righteousness that comes through
Jesus Christ—to the glory and praise of God.

Paul's Chains Advance the Gospel

[12]Now I want you to know, brothers, that
what has happened to me has really served to
advance the gospel. [13]As a result, it has become
clear throughout the whole palace guard[b] and
to everyone else that I am in chains for Christ.
[14]Because of my chains, most of the brothers
in the Lord have been encouraged to speak
the word of God more courageously and fearlessly.
[15]It is true that some preach Christ out of
envy and rivalry, but others out of goodwill.
[16]The latter do so in love, knowing that I am
put here for the defense of the gospel. [17]The
former preach Christ out of selfish ambition,
not sincerely, supposing that they can stir up
trouble for me while I am in chains.[c] [18]But
what does it matter? The important thing is
that in every way, whether from false motives
or true, Christ is preached. And because of
this I rejoice.
Yes, and I will continue to rejoice, [19]for I
know that through your prayers and the help
given by the Spirit of Jesus Christ, what has
happened to me will turn out for my deliverance.[d] [20]I eagerly expect and hope that I
will in no way be ashamed, but will have sufficient courage so that now as always Christ
will be exalted in my body, whether by life or
by death. [21]For to me, to live is Christ and
to die is gain. [22]If I am to go on living in the
body, this will mean fruitful labor for me. Yet
what shall I choose? I do not know! [23]I am
torn between the two: I desire to depart and
be with Christ, which is better by far; [24]but
it is more necessary for you that I remain in
the body. [25]Convinced of this, I know that I
will remain, and I will continue with all of
you for your progress and joy in the faith,
[26]so that through my being with you again
your joy in Christ Jesus will overflow on account of me.
[27]Whatever happens, conduct yourselves
in a manner worthy of the gospel of Christ.
Then, whether I come and see you or only hear
about you in my absence, I will know that you
stand firm in one spirit, contending as one
man for the faith of the gospel [28]without being frightened in any way by those who oppose you. This is a sign to them that they will
be destroyed, but that you will be saved—and
that by God. [29]For it has been granted to you
on behalf of Christ not only to believe on him,
but also to suffer for him, [30]since you are going through the same struggle you saw I had,
and now hear that I still have.

Imitating Christ's Humility

2 If you have any encouragement from being united with Christ, if any comfort from
his love, if any fellowship with the Spirit, if
any tenderness and compassion, [2]then make
my joy complete by being like-minded, having the same love, being one in spirit and purpose. [3]Do nothing out of selfish ambition or
vain conceit, but in humility consider others
better than yourselves. [4]Each of you should
look not only to your own interests, but also
to the interests of others.
[5]Your attitude should be the same as that
of Christ Jesus:

[6]Who, being in very nature[e] God,
did not consider equality with God
something to be grasped,
[7]but made himself nothing,
taking the very nature[f] of a servant,
being made in human likeness.
[8]And being found in appearance as a man,
he humbled himself

---

[a] *1* Traditionally *bishops* [b] *13* Or *whole palace* [c] *16,17* Some late manuscripts have verses 16 and 17 in reverse order.
[d] *19* Or *salvation* [e] *6* Or *in the form of* [f] *7* Or *the form*

GIVING OFF THE SCALE

> **Do nothing out of selfish ambition or vain conceit, but in humility consider others better than yourselves. Each of you should look not only to your own interests, but also to the interests of others.**
>
> — Philippians 2:3–4

let's *talk*

- In what ways do we treat our giving in marriage as pan-scale love? When have we felt cheated?
- How can we increase the level of generosity in our relationship? What gifts do each of us bring? How might they be used to strengthen our marriage?
- How can each of us invest more in our marriage without worrying about whether we're getting a good deal?

John Powell describes different kinds of relationships, including one he calls "pan-scale love." A pan scale is what Lady Justice carries. She stands blindfolded atop a courthouse with pans held by chains at both ends of a balance beam.

Powell says that many of us enter courtship or marriage with a pan-scale commitment. In the exhilaration of first falling in love, we give 100 percent of ourselves to our mate, and our end of the pan scale hangs heavy with love's offerings. For a week or a month or even a year, we don't check to see whether the pan scale is balanced because we assume our partner is also devoting 100 percent to the relationship.

But, says Powell, there comes a time when we begin to analyze which way the pan-scale balance beam is tipping. Invariably, as much as we love our spouse, we begin to recognize that he or she isn't investing quite as much as we are.

So we pull back a little. Maybe she doesn't pick up the clothes that he carelessly leaves in corners of the bedroom. Perhaps he doesn't offer a cheery "hello" and warm kiss when she walks in the door. Maybe she doesn't stop to pick up the dry cleaning or he forgets to gas up the car. This gradual lessening of giving doesn't usually mean coming up short on the scale of big things; rather, it's little cuts that over time begin adding up to the message: "I've been giving 100 percent to this relationship, and you're only offering 87 percent. If you won't put your full load of love on your end of the pan scale, I'm going to pull some of mine back to even things up."

The trouble is, such efforts at balancing the pan scale of love only backfire. Typically, when partners begin to notice that the scales aren't even, they each begin to think they are giving more than the other. The response is a subtle but progressive retaliatory cutback on a full deposit.

It may take a while, but if left unchecked, pan-scale love will eventually bankrupt a relationship. As I view my investments as overmatching my partner's, my mate, from another vantage point, feels similarly cheated. If we check the nuptial agreements and try to reclaim what we believe is rightfully ours, Lady Justice is left with empty scales.

How much better to be known, as the Philippians were, for their generosity. People in that church sensed Paul's needs and, without being asked, sent him gifts time after time. Paul regarded those surprises, their over-the-top giving, as "a fragrant offering, an acceptable sacrifice, pleasing to God" (Philippians 4:18). God asks each of us to bring him an offering according to what our heart prompts us to give, not one that matches what God gives us—that's impossible and we know it.

Likewise, we are to give to our partner in marriage—without weighing it against what's being offered on the other side, with humble thanks for each other, with sincere appreciation for each other, with gratitude for the opportunity to meet each other's needs without being asked. Then our giving will be an off-the-scale fragrant offering to each other, an acceptable sacrifice that is pleasing to God.

—WAYNE BROUWER

FOR YOUR NEXT DEVOTIONAL READING, TURN TO PAGE 1342.

WEEKEND

contentment

I once saw a cartoon in which a man is down on bended knee, saying, "I love you, Cindy. Will you marry me for a year or two?" The joke has an edge to it, of course, because it points to a frightening trend in our society. "Till death us do part" now has an addendum: "as long as I'm happy."

It's not that happiness is such a bad thing. Who doesn't like to feel happy? The Declaration of Independence proclaims "the pursuit of happiness" as one of the great American ideals, and most of us busy ourselves in the relentless pursuit of happiness.

For many Americans, the pursuit of self-fulfillment and personal happiness has become a religion. Even Christians have bought into this religion of self-actualization, pursuing God only because they see him as an agent for happiness. They want happiness, and they think they can use God to get it.

In our society, we tend to make choices based on what will bring us the most happiness. But in the Bible, God's concept of happiness is much better defined by the word *contentment*. Remember Paul saying, in essence, "No matter what circumstances I find myself in, I've learned to be content" (Philippians 4:11)?

It's amazing how whiny we can be. Sometimes I think we're a nation of self-pitying snivelers. Circumstances get us down, way down. And "way down" is a place where Christians, at least, don't have to stay. So how did Paul learn to be content whatever the circumstances? He tapped into the power source: "I can do [all this] through him who gives me strength" (Philippians 4:13). It's God who helps us choose love over personal happiness, fidelity over self-fulfillment, serving others over serving ourselves. It's God who provides contentment and even joy as we choose his way.

There are two weapons for being content when circumstances make us feel miserable. The first is to remember that *God is in control*. God has promised to do a "good work" in us, and to complete it (Philippians 1:6). When we're stuck in the muck of the moment, we need to keep our eyes on heaven; it puts things on earth into the correct perspective.

The second weapon is to *turn our obsession to satisfy ourselves into love for others*. Rather than focusing on others, too many Christians have bought into the cultural value of individualism. We think personal independence is so great that we no longer recognize the beauty and blessing of shared life. But Christianity is concerned with *interdependence*. God doesn't tell us to live for our own convenience. One reason he puts us in marriages is to help us find real satisfaction and real joy in serving others. Marriage is the first place in which we get to live out God's many commands for serving, accepting, encouraging, forgiving and submitting to one another.

I read in an airline magazine about a London jeweler who designed a ring with a band that doesn't go all the way around the finger. The symbolic meaning of the incomplete circle is that there's always a way out "if you're not happy."

Marriage was never meant to bend to our individual purposes. That's a shabby counterfeit of the real thing—the God-given opportunity to live out love and commitment to another human being for a lifetime. When we weigh the options, we can trade the pursuit of short-lived personal happiness for the contentment that grows when we shape our relationship God's way.

—GARY KINNAMAN WITH ANNETTE LAPLACA

HOW ARE WE DOING?

are we content?

Take this true or false quiz, then pass it to your partner. When you both finish, compare scores. Are you equally content? Why or why not? What can you do to increase your total contentment as a couple?

1. If I had a little more money, I'd be happier.
2. I've complained today about not having enough to wear.
3. If I could, I would change something about my body.
4. I've complained about my car this week.
5. I am sometimes envious of others.
6. At home, I often complain about my job.
7. At work, I often complain about my spouse or family.
8. I wish my lifestyle was more like that of friends, family members or coworkers.
9. I've complained about the weather several times this month.
10. I find few things to be thankful for in my life.
11. I tend to be unhappy with my hair or appearance.
12. I tend to find fault with others.
13. I am quick to find fault with myself.
14. My house would never be described as a peaceful haven.
15. In the past hour, I've daydreamed about getting something I didn't have.

Give yourself one point for every true answer.

1–3 points: You're so content, you probably don't even care what you scored on this quiz. Your joy comes from inside, not outside, validation.

4–8 points: You know what contentment is, but you occasionally let circumstances take away your joy.

9–12 points: You could invite more joy into your life by focusing on the things you are grateful for.

12–15 points: You are not happy about your life. Spend some time in prayer and with your spouse looking for ways you can find joy.

let's make a DATE

THE MOST GRATEFUL MATE

Plan a date night. Each of you bring a notebook along. Throughout the date, each of you should write down the things you are thankful for about your mate, your life together and even what you're enjoying on your date. At the end of the date, the person with the most things to be thankful for gets a back rub from the less-grateful spouse!

FOR YOUR NEXT DEVOTIONAL READING, TURN TO PAGE 1346.

LESSONS FROM THE *Bible*

The Bible talks about contentment in various areas of life. What can we learn from these teachings about being content and bringing contentment?

1. The relationship between contentment and our circumstances (Philippians 4:11–13)
2. Bringing contentment to our relationship (Song of Songs 8)

and became obedient to death—
even death on a cross!
9Therefore God exalted him to the highest
place
and gave him the name that is above
every name,
10that at the name of Jesus every knee
should bow,
in heaven and on earth and under the
earth,
11and every tongue confess that Jesus Christ
is Lord,
to the glory of God the Father.

Shining as Stars

12Therefore, my dear friends, as you have
always obeyed—not only in my presence, but
now much more in my absence—continue to
work out your salvation with fear and trembling, 13for it is God who works in you to will
and to act according to his good purpose.
14Do everything without complaining or
arguing, 15so that you may become blameless
and pure, children of God without fault in a
crooked and depraved generation, in which
you shine like stars in the universe 16as you
hold out[a] the word of life—in order that I
may boast on the day of Christ that I did not
run or labor for nothing. 17But even if I am
being poured out like a drink offering on the
sacrifice and service coming from your faith, I
am glad and rejoice with all of you. 18So you
too should be glad and rejoice with me.

Timothy and Epaphroditus

19I hope in the Lord Jesus to send Timothy
to you soon, that I also may be cheered when
I receive news about you. 20I have no one else
like him, who takes a genuine interest in your
welfare. 21For everyone looks out for his own
interests, not those of Jesus Christ. 22But you
know that Timothy has proved himself, because as a son with his father he has served
with me in the work of the gospel. 23I hope,
therefore, to send him as soon as I see how
things go with me. 24And I am confident in
the Lord that I myself will come soon.
25But I think it is necessary to send back to
you Epaphroditus, my brother, fellow worker
and fellow soldier, who is also your messenger,
whom you sent to take care of my needs. 26For
he longs for all of you and is distressed because
you heard he was ill. 27Indeed he was ill, and
almost died. But God had mercy on him, and
not on him only but also on me, to spare me
sorrow upon sorrow. 28Therefore I am all the
more eager to send him, so that when you see
him again you may be glad and I may have
less anxiety. 29Welcome him in the Lord with
great joy, and honor men like him, 30because
he almost died for the work of Christ, risking
his life to make up for the help you could not
give me.

No Confidence in the Flesh

3 Finally, my brothers, rejoice in the Lord!
It is no trouble for me to write the same
things to you again, and it is a safeguard
for you.
2Watch out for those dogs, those men who
do evil, those mutilators of the flesh. 3For
it is we who are the circumcision, we who
worship by the Spirit of God, who glory in
Christ Jesus, and who put no confidence in
the flesh— 4though I myself have reasons for
such confidence.
If anyone else thinks he has reasons to put
confidence in the flesh, I have more: 5circum-
cised on the eighth day, of the people of Israel,
of the tribe of Benjamin, a Hebrew of Hebrews; in regard to the law, a Pharisee; 6as for
zeal, persecuting the church; as for legalistic
righteousness, faultless.
7But whatever was to my profit I now consider loss for the sake of Christ. 8What is
more, I consider everything a loss compared
to the surpassing greatness of knowing Christ
Jesus my Lord, for whose sake I have lost all
things. I consider them rubbish, that I may
gain Christ 9and be found in him, not having a righteousness of my own that comes
from the law, but that which is through faith
in Christ—the righteousness that comes from
God and is by faith. 10I want to know Christ
and the power of his resurrection and the fellowship of sharing in his sufferings, becoming
like him in his death, 11and so, somehow, to
attain to the resurrection from the dead.

Pressing on Toward the Goal

12Not that I have already obtained all this,
or have already been made perfect, but I press
on to take hold of that for which Christ Jesus
took hold of me. 13Brothers, I do not consider myself yet to have taken hold of it. But
one thing I do: Forgetting what is behind and
straining toward what is ahead, 14I press on toward the goal to win the prize for which God
has called me heavenward in Christ Jesus.
15All of us who are mature should take such

[a] 16 Or *hold on to*

a view of things. And if on some point you think differently, that too God will make clear to you. 16Only let us live up to what we have already attained.

17Join with others in following my example, brothers, and take note of those who live according to the pattern we gave you. 18For, as I have often told you before and now say again even with tears, many live as enemies of the cross of Christ. 19Their destiny is destruction, their god is their stomach, and their glory is in their shame. Their mind is on earthly things. 20But our citizenship is in heaven. And we eagerly await a Savior from there, the Lord Jesus Christ, 21who, by the power that enables him to bring everything under his control, will transform our lowly bodies so that they will be like his glorious body.

4 Therefore, my brothers, you whom I love and long for, my joy and crown, that is how you should stand firm in the Lord, dear friends!

Exhortations

2I plead with Euodia and I plead with Syntyche to agree with each other in the Lord. 3Yes, and I ask you, loyal yokefellow,[a] help these women who have contended at my side in the cause of the gospel, along with Clement and the rest of my fellow workers, whose names are in the book of life.

4Rejoice in the Lord always. I will say it again: Rejoice! 5Let your gentleness be evident to all. The Lord is near. 6Do not be anxious about anything, but in everything, by prayer and petition, with thanksgiving, present your requests to God. 7And the peace of God, which transcends all understanding, will guard your hearts and your minds in Christ Jesus.

8Finally, brothers, whatever is true, whatever is noble, whatever is right, whatever is pure, whatever is lovely, whatever is admirable—if anything is excellent or praiseworthy—think about such things. 9Whatever you have learned or received or heard from me, or seen in me—put it into practice. And the God of peace will be with you.

Thanks for Their Gifts

10I rejoice greatly in the Lord that at last you have renewed your concern for me. Indeed, you have been concerned, but you had no opportunity to show it. 11I am not saying this because I am in need, for I have learned to be content whatever the circumstances. 12I know what it is to be in need, and I know what it is to have plenty. I have learned the secret of being content in any and every situation, whether well fed or hungry, whether living in plenty or in want. 13I can do everything through him who gives me strength.

14Yet it was good of you to share in my troubles. 15Moreover, as you Philippians know, in the early days of your acquaintance with the gospel, when I set out from Macedonia, not one church shared with me in the matter of giving and receiving, except you only; 16for even when I was in Thessalonica, you sent me aid again and again when I was in need. 17Not that I am looking for a gift, but I am looking for what may be credited to your account. 18I have received full payment and even more; I am amply supplied, now that I have received from Epaphroditus the gifts you sent. They are a fragrant offering, an acceptable sacrifice, pleasing to God. 19And my God will meet all your needs according to his glorious riches in Christ Jesus.

20To our God and Father be glory for ever and ever. Amen.

Final Greetings

21Greet all the saints in Christ Jesus. The brothers who are with me send greetings. 22All the saints send you greetings, especially those who belong to Caesar's household.

23The grace of the Lord Jesus Christ be with your spirit. Amen.[b]

---

[a] 3 Or *loyal Syzygus* [b] 23 Some manuscripts do not have *Amen*.

MONDAY

READ PHILIPPIANS 4:4–9

FINDING PEACE IN ANXIOUS TIMES

When we were in our late 20s, my friends and I discussed what would help us feel like adults. Some thought marriage would do the trick. Others that parenthood would move us into adulthood. We even wondered if the death of our parents would finally make us feel we had entered the grown-up ranks. But as we got married, had children and mourned parents, we realized that adulthood is marked by something far more universal: worry.

It's not so much that youth is worry-free—think back to the anxiety you felt over dating, homework, your future. But back then we found relief in knowing that the buck didn't stop with us. But there comes a time when there is no one else, nowhere to pass the buck. Responsibility rests squarely at our feet.

Once we take on the mantle of worry, it's almost impossible to set it aside. After all, life never stops throwing curveballs at us: a spouse loses a job, a child is injured, a parent gets sick. The future seems more uncertain every day, leaving us with nagging questions: Are we putting away enough money to retire? How will we pay the mortgage next month? We also worry about the world we live in: What can we do about the suffering we see? Will we ever live in peace with one another?

It's human to grow anxious about what lies ahead. That's why Paul gave the people of Philippi a message they needed to hear. They lived in a time of frequent disease, war and famine, so their future was tenuous and uncertain. But Paul wanted them to know that their lives were in the hands of a loving God who would give them peace.

Do not be anxious about anything, but in everything, by prayer and petition, with thanksgiving, present your requests to God. And the peace of God, which transcends all understanding, will guard your hearts and your minds in Christ Jesus.

— PHILIPPIANS 4:6–7

let's *talk*

- ✦ What do we worry about? What practical steps can we take to alleviate some of our worrying?
- ✦ What hurdles might be keeping us from trusting God to care for us in difficult times? How does our image of God affect our ability to trust him?
- ✦ Let's talk with a Christian who has gone through a difficult time to learn how that person felt God's presence and peace in the midst of it. How can their story help us worry less?

Notice that Paul didn't say, "God will make all the bad stuff go away." Instead, he promised believers that God would calm their fears and ease their spirits. He reminded them that they weren't in charge, that they could safely place their worries in the hands of someone far bigger than themselves and trust that God would walk with them through whatever troubles came their way.

I know a few people who have gone through terrible times—the death of a child, an unexpected divorce, a potentially fatal illness. All of them have said that even in the darkest, most difficult moments, they sensed God's presence. Their pain and heartache didn't go away, but they knew God was helping them stand up under it. They never lost the feeling that God was guarding their hearts.

Their experiences remind us that we can talk to God about the things that lie heavy on our hearts. We can ask for the peace God offers. We can thank God for caring, for shouldering our burdens, for giving us comfort and rest even in our most difficult times. Indeed, having a God like this transcends our understanding. All we can do is open our hearts and receive him.

—CARLA BARNHILL

FOR YOUR NEXT DEVOTIONAL READING, TURN TO PAGE 1349.

COLOSSIANS

Colossians

QUICK FACTS

AUTHOR The apostle Paul

AUDIENCE The church in Colossae (a city that was located in modern-day Turkey)

DATE About A.D. 60

SETTING Written while Paul was under house arrest in Rome to dispel false teachings in Colossae

When the apostle Paul wrote to the church at Colossae, he addressed some ideas that challenged the message of the gospel. Nearly 2,000 years later, Paul's short letter remains just as relevant, helping us battle cultural ideas and attitudes that run counter to the truth.

Many insist that truth is relative—that it depends on personal experiences or perspectives. "What's true for you is not necessarily true for me," some say. Colossians counteracts such views by presenting clear-cut absolutes: Jesus Christ is God's Son. He existed before creation. He created all things. He is the head of the church. He is the hope of glory.

Paul's letter reminds us that while human traditions and trendy philosophies can ensnare us, only the truth will set us free. Freedom in Christ means no more jumping through religious hoops; we don't have to be slaves to rules and regulations.

The book of Colossians shows how these truths affect us every day in our homes, our relationships and our work. Surprisingly, when we focus our heads and hearts on heaven, we see direct results here and now—on earth! That's great practical advice for wives, husbands, parents and children.

1 Paul, an apostle of Christ Jesus by the will
of God, and Timothy our brother,

2 To the holy and faithful[a] brothers in
Christ at Colosse:

Grace and peace to you from God our Father.[b]

Thanksgiving and Prayer

3 We always thank God, the Father of our
Lord Jesus Christ, when we pray for you, 4 because we have heard of your faith in Christ
Jesus and of the love you have for all the
saints— 5 the faith and love that spring from
the hope that is stored up for you in heaven
and that you have already heard about in the
word of truth, the gospel 6 that has come to
you. All over the world this gospel is bearing
fruit and growing, just as it has been doing
among you since the day you heard it and
understood God's grace in all its truth. 7 You
learned it from Epaphras, our dear fellow servant, who is a faithful minister of Christ on
our[c] behalf, 8 and who also told us of your love
in the Spirit.

9 For this reason, since the day we heard
about you, we have not stopped praying for
you and asking God to fill you with the knowledge of his will through all spiritual wisdom
and understanding. 10 And we pray this in order that you may live a life worthy of the Lord
and may please him in every way: bearing fruit
in every good work, growing in the knowledge
of God, 11 being strengthened with all power
according to his glorious might so that you
may have great endurance and patience, and
joyfully 12 giving thanks to the Father, who has
qualified you[d] to share in the inheritance of
the saints in the kingdom of light. 13 For he
has rescued us from the dominion of darkness
and brought us into the kingdom of the Son
he loves, 14 in whom we have redemption,[e] the
forgiveness of sins.

The Supremacy of Christ

15 He is the image of the invisible God, the
firstborn over all creation. 16 For by him all
things were created: things in heaven and on
earth, visible and invisible, whether thrones
or powers or rulers or authorities; all things
were created by him and for him. 17 He is before all things, and in him all things hold together. 18 And he is the head of the body, the
church; he is the beginning and the firstborn
from among the dead, so that in everything
he might have the supremacy. 19 For God was
pleased to have all his fullness dwell in him,
20 and through him to reconcile to himself all
things, whether things on earth or things in
heaven, by making peace through his blood,
shed on the cross.

21 Once you were alienated from God and
were enemies in your minds because of[f] your
evil behavior. 22 But now he has reconciled
you by Christ's physical body through death
to present you holy in his sight, without
blemish and free from accusation— 23 if you
continue in your faith, established and firm,
not moved from the hope held out in the gospel. This is the gospel that you heard and that
has been proclaimed to every creature under
heaven, and of which I, Paul, have become a
servant.

Paul's Labor for the Church

24 Now I rejoice in what was suffered for
you, and I fill up in my flesh what is still lacking in regard to Christ's afflictions, for the
sake of his body, which is the church. 25 I have
become its servant by the commission God
gave me to present to you the word of God
in its fullness— 26 the mystery that has been
kept hidden for ages and generations, but is
now disclosed to the saints. 27 To them God
has chosen to make known among the Gentiles the glorious riches of this mystery, which
is Christ in you, the hope of glory.

28 We proclaim him, admonishing and
teaching everyone with all wisdom, so that we
may present everyone perfect in Christ. 29 To
this end I labor, struggling with all his energy,
which so powerfully works in me.

2 I want you to know how much I am struggling for you and for those at Laodicea,
and for all who have not met me personally. 2 My purpose is that they may be encouraged in heart and united in love, so that they
may have the full riches of complete understanding, in order that they may know the
mystery of God, namely, Christ, 3 in whom
are hidden all the treasures of wisdom and
knowledge. 4 I tell you this so that no one
may deceive you by fine-sounding arguments.
5 For though I am absent from you in body, I
am present with you in spirit and delight to
see how orderly you are and how firm your
faith in Christ is.

---

[a] 2 Or *believing* [b] 2 Some manuscripts *Father and the Lord Jesus Christ* [c] 7 Some manuscripts *your* [d] 12 Some manuscripts *us*
[e] 14 A few late manuscripts *redemption through his blood* [f] 21 Or *minds, as shown by*

TUESDAY
READ COLOSSIANS 1:1–14

PRAYER NEEDED

For this reason, since the day we heard about you, we have not stopped praying for you.
— COLOSSIANS 1:9

let's talk

- What kinds of prayers do we pray for each other?
- Are friends or family members already praying for us and our marriage? Whom might we ask to be prayer partners with us?
- Let's compile a short prayer list for each other based on Colossians 1:10–12. We can stick it on a bathroom mirror, dashboard or some other well-frequented spot so that we will remember to pray for each other.

I often find myself sending up vague requests to the Lord regarding my husband: "Bless David today." "Help David in his work." "Be with David in all his decisions." Sometimes my prayers get more specific as I include details of his day: "Help him while he's teaching his class." "Give him creativity on this project." But lately I've been trying to pray for God to give David the things *God* wants him to have. The best way to find out what those things are is to keep my prayers anchored in God's Word.

The Christians at Colossae were blessed by the apostle Paul's intercession. In Colossians 1, Paul told them that he had "not stopped praying" for the Colossian believers. The actions and attitudes he asked God to give the Colossians provide a useful structure for how I can pray for my husband.

Paul's overarching goal for his believing friends was that they have a practical knowledge of God's will so that they would, as a result, "live a life worthy of the Lord and may please him in every way" (Colossians 1:10). This umbrella request seems to cover every aspect of life. So I'm praying that David and I will please God in our work, in our parenting, in our friendships and in our marriage.

Paul then offered a few specifics under the heading of pleasing God. He prayed that the believers would be fruitful in good work; grow in their knowledge of God; be strengthened with all power in order to have endurance and patience; and give God joyful thanks (see verses 10–12). What a great prayer list for someone you love!

Before my father died, he and my mother prayed together every night for David and me, for our marriage and for our children. That joint prayer time is one of the aspects of married life that my mom misses the most. I know she is still praying for David and me, and I know David's mother prays for us too. Like Paul interceding for the Colossian Christians, others are praying for us. We're thankful for that blessing!

In a world where couples staying together is no longer the norm, every married couple needs the prayer support of others. It would be invaluable to ask people to pray specifically for you and your spouse, whether those people are your parents, an older couple at church or friends from a Bible study. If you don't know what to ask your friends to pray for, borrow Paul's short list from Colossians 1:10–12 so that you and your spouse might "live a life worthy of the Lord and may please him in every way." That seems like the perfect place to begin.

—ANNETTE LAPLACA

FOR YOUR NEXT DEVOTIONAL READING, TURN TO PAGE 1351.

Freedom From Human Regulations Through Life With Christ

6So then, just as you received Christ Jesus
as Lord, continue to live in him, 7rooted and
built up in him, strengthened in the faith as
you were taught, and overflowing with thankfulness.
8See to it that no one takes you captive
through hollow and deceptive philosophy,
which depends on human tradition and the
basic principles of this world rather than on
Christ.
9For in Christ all the fullness of the Deity lives in bodily form, 10and you have been
given fullness in Christ, who is the head over
every power and authority. 11In him you were
also circumcised, in the putting off of the sinful nature,[a] not with a circumcision done by
the hands of men but with the circumcision
done by Christ, 12having been buried with
him in baptism and raised with him through
your faith in the power of God, who raised
him from the dead.
13When you were dead in your sins and in
the uncircumcision of your sinful nature,[b]
God made you[c] alive with Christ. He forgave
us all our sins, 14having canceled the written
code, with its regulations, that was against us
and that stood opposed to us; he took it away,
nailing it to the cross. 15And having disarmed
the powers and authorities, he made a public
spectacle of them, triumphing over them by
the cross.[d]
16Therefore do not let anyone judge you
by what you eat or drink, or with regard to
a religious festival, a New Moon celebration
or a Sabbath day. 17These are a shadow of the
things that were to come; the reality, however,
is found in Christ. 18Do not let anyone who
delights in false humility and the worship of
angels disqualify you for the prize. Such a person goes into great detail about what he has
seen, and his unspiritual mind puffs him up
with idle notions. 19He has lost connection
with the Head, from whom the whole body,
supported and held together by its ligaments
and sinews, grows as God causes it to grow.
20Since you died with Christ to the basic principles of this world, why, as though
you still belonged to it, do you submit to its
rules: 21"Do not handle! Do not taste! Do
not touch!"? 22These are all destined to perish with use, because they are based on human
commands and teachings. 23Such regulations
indeed have an appearance of wisdom, with
their self-imposed worship, their false humility and their harsh treatment of the body, but
they lack any value in restraining sensual indulgence.

Rules for Holy Living

3 Since, then, you have been raised with
Christ, set your hearts on things above,
where Christ is seated at the right hand of
God. 2Set your minds on things above, not
on earthly things. 3For you died, and your life
is now hidden with Christ in God. 4When
Christ, who is your[e] life, appears, then you
also will appear with him in glory.
5Put to death, therefore, whatever belongs
to your earthly nature: sexual immorality, impurity, lust, evil desires and greed, which is
idolatry. 6Because of these, the wrath of God
is coming.[f] 7You used to walk in these ways,
in the life you once lived. 8But now you must
rid yourselves of all such things as these: anger,
rage, malice, slander, and filthy language from
your lips. 9Do not lie to each other, since you
have taken off your old self with its practices
10and have put on the new self, which is being
renewed in knowledge in the image of its Creator. 11Here there is no Greek or Jew, circumcised or uncircumcised, barbarian, Scythian,
slave or free, but Christ is all, and is in all.
12Therefore, as God's chosen people, holy
and dearly loved, clothe yourselves with compassion, kindness, humility, gentleness and
patience. 13Bear with each other and forgive
whatever grievances you may have against
one another. Forgive as the Lord forgave you.
14And over all these virtues put on love, which
binds them all together in perfect unity.
15Let the peace of Christ rule in your hearts,
since as members of one body you were called
to peace. And be thankful. 16Let the word of
Christ dwell in you richly as you teach and
admonish one another with all wisdom, and
as you sing psalms, hymns and spiritual songs
with gratitude in your hearts to God. 17And
whatever you do, whether in word or deed,
do it all in the name of the Lord Jesus, giving
thanks to God the Father through him.

Rules for Christian Households

18Wives, submit to your husbands, as is fitting in the Lord.
19Husbands, love your wives and do not be
harsh with them.
20Children, obey your parents in everything, for this pleases the Lord.

---

[a] *11* Or *the flesh* [b] *13* Or *your flesh* [c] *13* Some manuscripts *us* [d] *15* Or *them in him* [e] *4* Some manuscripts *our* [f] *6* Some early manuscripts *coming on those who are disobedient*

WEDNESDAY
READ COLOSSIANS 3:1–17

A GUIDE FOR PEACEFUL LIVING

In our marriage, we have rules. The pillows in the closet—not the ones on the bed during the day—are to be used for sleeping. When not in use, the shower curtain is kept three-fourths closed. Don't buy printed paper towels or napkins—plain white only.

Most of the rules are mine, and my husband has learned that it goes well with him when he follows them. Also, he knows that these quirky, semineurotic things are important to me. He honors me when he follows my rules.

Likewise, I try not to leave the front door open, even if I'm going outside for only 30 seconds, because I know that the escaping heat or air-conditioning makes my husband nuts. In that way, I honor him.

Following each other's rules allows peace to rule in our marriage.

God has also given us rules—decrees and commands—that come with a promise. If we keep them, it will go well, not only with us, but with our children after us. Some of God's rules for general living that apply to marriage include:

1. Forgive grievances against one another. "Forgive as the Lord forgave you" (Colossians 3:13). How much has God forgiven us? Christ died for our laziness, sarcasm and failure to take out the trash, not just for murder and bank robbery.

2. Live with humility. "Clothe yourselves with humility toward one another" (1 Peter 5:5). Consider the other person as more important than yourself. Adopt the attitude "How can I serve you today?" not "How can you serve me?"

3. Walk together. Walk continually in God's truth, "in the light of [his] presence" (Psalm 89:15), "in the way of righteousness" (Proverbs 8:20), "in the way of understanding" (Proverbs 9:6), and in the footsteps of the faith. Walking together is good exercise.

4. Be committed to each other. Don't leave each other unless it's Biblically necessary and only as a last resort (see Matthew 19:3–9).

5. Give thanks for one another. "Give thanks in all circumstances" (1 Thessalonians 5:18). Appreciating each other, no matter what our faults, is a powerful peace builder.

Just before our oldest daughter got married, I asked her what she had learned about marriage from watching her dad and me. Forgiveness and staying together in spite of hard times topped her list. "I learned not to give up too quickly in difficult times because things usually turn around," she said. "I also learned that saying 'I'm sorry' isn't a weakness but a strength, that you don't have to spend a lot of money to have a good time, and that it makes Dad happy when you keep the front door closed."

It is, indeed, well with us.

—NANCY KENNEDY

Let the peace of Christ rule in your hearts, since as members of one body you were called to peace. And be thankful.

— COLOSSIANS 3:15

let's talk

- ✦ What are some of our rules in marriage? Why are they important to each of us?
- ✦ What did we learn about marriage from watching our parents?
- ✦ What are some Biblical commands that have generational effects? How can we begin now to affect our children and grandchildren?

FOR YOUR NEXT DEVOTIONAL READING, TURN TO PAGE 1355.

21 Fathers, do not embitter your children, or
they will become discouraged.
22 Slaves, obey your earthly masters in everything; and do it, not only when their eye
is on you and to win their favor, but with
sincerity of heart and reverence for the Lord.
23 Whatever you do, work at it with all your
heart, as working for the Lord, not for men,
24 since you know that you will receive an inheritance from the Lord as a reward. It is the
Lord Christ you are serving. 25 Anyone who
does wrong will be repaid for his wrong, and
there is no favoritism.

4 Masters, provide your slaves with what is
right and fair, because you know that you
also have a Master in heaven.

Further Instructions

2 Devote yourselves to prayer, being watchful and thankful. 3 And pray for us, too, that
God may open a door for our message, so that
we may proclaim the mystery of Christ, for
which I am in chains. 4 Pray that I may proclaim it clearly, as I should. 5 Be wise in the
way you act toward outsiders; make the most
of every opportunity. 6 Let your conversation
be always full of grace, seasoned with salt, so
that you may know how to answer everyone.

Final Greetings

7 Tychicus will tell you all the news about
me. He is a dear brother, a faithful minister
and fellow servant in the Lord. 8 I am sending
him to you for the express purpose that you
may know about our[a] circumstances and that
he may encourage your hearts. 9 He is coming
with Onesimus, our faithful and dear brother,
who is one of you. They will tell you everything that is happening here.
10 My fellow prisoner Aristarchus sends
you his greetings, as does Mark, the cousin
of Barnabas. (You have received instructions
about him; if he comes to you, welcome him.)
11 Jesus, who is called Justus, also sends greetings. These are the only Jews among my fellow
workers for the kingdom of God, and they
have proved a comfort to me. 12 Epaphras,
who is one of you and a servant of Christ
Jesus, sends greetings. He is always wrestling
in prayer for you, that you may stand firm in
all the will of God, mature and fully assured.
13 I vouch for him that he is working hard for
you and for those at Laodicea and Hierapolis.
14 Our dear friend Luke, the doctor, and Demas send greetings. 15 Give my greetings to the
brothers at Laodicea, and to Nympha and the
church in her house.
16 After this letter has been read to you, see
that it is also read in the church of the Laodi-
ceans and that you in turn read the letter from
Laodicea.
17 Tell Archippus: "See to it that you complete the work you have received in the Lord."
18 I, Paul, write this greeting in my own
hand. Remember my chains. Grace be with
you.

[a] 8 Some manuscripts *that he may know about your*

1 THESSALONIANS

1 Thessalonians

QUICK FACTS

AUTHOR The apostle Paul

AUDIENCE The church in Thessalonica (a city that was located in modern-day northern Greece)

DATE About A.D. 51

SETTING Written from Corinth to encourage the persecuted young Christians in Thessalonica

The believers who made up the fledgling church in the first-century city of Thessalonica lived under the shadow of the powerful Roman government and the pervasive Greek culture.

With such pressures, many believers may have been eager to exchange earth for heaven—Rome's kingdom for God's. But the Thessalonian believers were confused about when and how Jesus would return to earth. How would those who had already died be included in the second coming of Christ? Paul wrote this letter to explain what would happen in the end times and to clarify the believer's position in Christ. He offered both encouragement and perspective to believers: *encouragement* because of their faith and dedication to the gospel, and *perspective* regarding how they were to live on earth while waiting for Jesus' return.

Though Jesus' coming will be sudden and unexpected (see 1 Thessalonians 5:2,4), we can prepare for the end, confident of eternity with the Lord. Until then, we are to be alert and self-controlled.

While waiting, we are to resist unwholesome and sinful cultural influences, hold high to our standards, avoid sexual immorality, resist lustful passions, lead a quiet life (i.e., mind our own business) and work hard. This kind of living will win the respect of outsiders. It will also guard our homes and marriages through turbulent times.

1 Paul, Silas[a] and Timothy,

To the church of the Thessalonians in God
the Father and the Lord Jesus Christ:

Grace and peace to you.[b]

Thanksgiving for the Thessalonians' Faith

2We always thank God for all of you, mentioning you in our prayers. 3We continually
remember before our God and Father your
work produced by faith, your labor prompted
by love, and your endurance inspired by hope
in our Lord Jesus Christ.
4For we know, brothers loved by God, that
he has chosen you, 5because our gospel came
to you not simply with words, but also with
power, with the Holy Spirit and with deep con-
viction. You know how we lived among you
for your sake. 6You became imitators of us and
of the Lord; in spite of severe suffering, you
welcomed the message with the joy given by
the Holy Spirit. 7And so you became a model
to all the believers in Macedonia and Achaia.
8The Lord's message rang out from you not
only in Macedonia and Achaia—your faith in
God has become known everywhere. Therefore we do not need to say anything about it,
9for they themselves report what kind of reception you gave us. They tell how you turned
to God from idols to serve the living and true
God, 10and to wait for his Son from heaven,
whom he raised from the dead—Jesus, who
rescues us from the coming wrath.

Paul's Ministry in Thessalonica

2 You know, brothers, that our visit to you
was not a failure. 2We had previously suffered and been insulted in Philippi, as you
know, but with the help of our God we dared
to tell you his gospel in spite of strong opposition. 3For the appeal we make does not spring
from error or impure motives, nor are we trying to trick you. 4On the contrary, we speak
as men approved by God to be entrusted with
the gospel. We are not trying to please men
but God, who tests our hearts. 5You know we
never used flattery, nor did we put on a mask
to cover up greed—God is our witness. 6We
were not looking for praise from men, not
from you or anyone else.
As apostles of Christ we could have been
a burden to you, 7but we were gentle among
you, like a mother caring for her little children. 8We loved you so much that we were delighted to share with you not only the gospel
of God but our lives as well, because you had
become so dear to us. 9Surely you remember,
brothers, our toil and hardship; we worked
night and day in order not to be a burden to
anyone while we preached the gospel of God
to you.
10You are witnesses, and so is God, of how
holy, righteous and blameless we were among
you who believed. 11For you know that we
dealt with each of you as a father deals with
his own children, 12encouraging, comforting
and urging you to live lives worthy of God,
who calls you into his kingdom and glory.
13And we also thank God continually because, when you received the word of God,
which you heard from us, you accepted it not
as the word of men, but as it actually is, the
word of God, which is at work in you who believe. 14For you, brothers, became imitators of
God's churches in Judea, which are in Christ
Jesus: You suffered from your own countrymen the same things those churches suffered
from the Jews, 15who killed the Lord Jesus and
the prophets and also drove us out. They displease God and are hostile to all men 16in their
effort to keep us from speaking to the Gentiles
so that they may be saved. In this way they always heap up their sins to the limit. The wrath
of God has come upon them at last.[c]

Paul's Longing to See the Thessalonians

17But, brothers, when we were torn away
from you for a short time (in person, not in
thought), out of our intense longing we made
every effort to see you. 18For we wanted to
come to you—certainly I, Paul, did, again and
again—but Satan stopped us. 19For what is
our hope, our joy, or the crown in which we
will glory in the presence of our Lord Jesus
when he comes? Is it not you? 20Indeed, you
are our glory and joy.

3 So when we could stand it no longer, we
thought it best to be left by ourselves in Athens. 2We sent Timothy, who is our brother and God's fellow worker[d] in spreading the
gospel of Christ, to strengthen and encourage
you in your faith, 3so that no one would be
unsettled by these trials. You know quite well
that we were destined for them. 4In fact, when
we were with you, we kept telling you that we
would be persecuted. And it turned out that
way, as you well know. 5For this reason, when
I could stand it no longer, I sent to find out
about your faith. I was afraid that in some way

---

[a] *1* Greek *Silvanus*, a variant of *Silas* [b] *1* Some early manuscripts *you from God our Father and the Lord Jesus Christ* [c] *16* Or *them fully* [d] *2* Some manuscripts *brother and fellow worker*; other manuscripts *brother and God's servant*

THURSDAY

READ

1 THESSALONIANS 1:1–10

STAYING POWER

> **You became imitators of us and of the Lord; in spite of severe suffering, you welcomed the message with the joy given by the Holy Spirit.**
>
> — 1 THESSALONIANS 1:6

let's talk

- What couples do we look to as role models for our marriage?
- What problems have we weathered in our marriage that have allowed us to welcome Christ's message with joy?
- What can we do to strengthen the commitment we have to the Lord and to each other?

My in-laws recently celebrated their 50th wedding anniversary. As my husband's family gathered to help commemorate this special day, I looked around the room and was amazed at the composite number of years of marriage I saw before me.

There sat an aunt and uncle who had been together for 60 years. Over there were a cousin and his wife who had just celebrated 25 years of marriage. Younger newlyweds who had been together two or three years were there too. And there were engaged couples who observed this celebration of 50 years and hoped their own marriages would survive that long.

If I were to ask my in-laws if their 50 years together were totally happy, I know what the answer would be. They had raised six children, which wasn't always easy. They were farmers in a time when farming produced more debt than profit. For several years, they lived in a trailer on the yard of my father-in-law's parents. Talk about tension! Though their love for each other carried them through the years, my in-laws didn't necessarily consider those early years "the good old days" because of the many problems they experienced.

Today's marriages are tested also by challenges such as infidelity, unemployment, debt, pornography and the strain of raising children in an increasingly anti-Christian environment. Everywhere we look, we see depressing statistics about how few marriages actually stay together. According to the National Center for Health Statistics, 43 percent of first marriages begun in 2000 in the United States will, in all likelihood, end in divorce. The average American marriage lasts 7.8 years. Of all children under the age of 18 in America, 28 percent are living with a divorced parent.

It's not hard to find examples that confirm these dismal statistics. Celebrities who jump into marriage after just a few days together and then bail out soon after are sad reminders of how the world views this relationship in which we promise "till death do us part." Maybe that's why so many couples are choosing to live together instead of commit to marriage. Marriage doesn't last, we're told. If you have problems, bail out. Move on. Find someone else.

In our society, every day we remain committed to our spouse is a day of witness to others. Every day we take our marriage vows seriously is a day we live out what God intended marriage to be. That can be hard to do when marriage is stained by the sticky fingerprints of sin. "We're role models?" we might ask. "Our marriage is far from perfect!"

True, but the way you face the problems in your relationship is also a testimony. As imitators of Christ, we work through our difficulties in spite of pain. We live up to the commitments we made in our vows before the Lord. And, as Paul suggested, our marriages grow stronger as we welcome God's Word with the joy given by the Holy Spirit.

—VALERIE VAN KOOTEN

FOR YOUR NEXT DEVOTIONAL READING, TURN TO PAGE 1356.

FRIDAY
READ
1 THESSALONIANS 2:1–16

MODEL PARENTING

The apostle Paul gives us a beautiful model of the church: a family in which leaders think of themselves as loving parents who are called to care for and encourage those they lead.

But Paul's use of the analogy of parenthood in 1 Thessalonians 2 may have surprised some in the church. This was before the study of child development, so the parents of Paul's day probably didn't spend much time thinking about the emotional or spiritual needs of their kids.

So for Paul to say that he and his fellow missionaries, Silas and Timothy (see 1 Thessalonians 1:1), had acted like nurturing mothers and encouraging fathers was no doubt radical thinking for many. Paul assumed that a loving, caring parent doesn't just order a kid around and demand respect. Instead, a good parent is supportive, sets a good example, offers comfort and care when a child is struggling, and guides the child as parent and child each try to live lives "worthy of God."

Today some Christian parents believe that their most important role is to teach their children to be obedient and to respect authority. If they fail to do this, they think their children won't respect God's authority and will fall away from the faith. Such parenting can take on an air of infallibility, become harsh and demand absolute submission. In a family with this type of parenting style, children are punished for disrespecting parental authority or questioning a parent's God-given right to boss them around.

That is not the way God parents us. True, our heavenly Father asks for obedience to his commands—and he punishes those who persist in rebelling against him—but he is also compassionate, slow to anger and faithful to forgive. He doesn't demand our respect; he wins it by his loving care and mercy. God doesn't push us into obedience; he invites us to follow Jesus.

We want so badly to raise our children well that often, instead of graciously guiding our children toward abundant life with God, we fearfully pull them away from the evils of this fallen world. Instead of offering our children grace and guidance when they make mistakes, we pour shame and disappointment on them, hoping the guilt they feel will ward off future trouble. Parenting out of fear may work in the short run, but it does little to help our children become the hopeful, loving people God created them to be.

Parenting gives us an amazing opportunity to participate in the formation and training of another human being. Like Paul and his fellow church leaders, parents who offer their children encouragement, comfort, guidance and discipline are building the church of the future, the church that will continue to bring the love and grace of God to a hurting world.

—CARLA BARNHILL

FOR YOUR NEXT DEVOTIONAL READING, TURN TO PAGE 1358.

We were gentle among you, like a mother caring for her little children . . . we dealt with each of you as a father deals with his own children, encouraging, comforting and urging you to live lives worthy of God, who calls you into his kingdom and glory.

— 1 THESSALONIANS 2:7–8,11–12

let's talk

✦ What is our philosophy of parenting? What is the role of parents in the life of a child? How should parents handle disobedience and disrespect?

✦ How can we offer the kind of encouragement and comfort that Paul talked about to stepchildren or foster children who might still be getting to know us? How can we work together to help children in this type of situation adjust to a new family unit?

✦ How can we positively influence the kids we know who may not have a positive model of marriage and parenting?

the tempter might have tempted you and our
efforts might have been useless.

Timothy's Encouraging Report

6But Timothy has just now come to us
from you and has brought good news about
your faith and love. He has told us that you
always have pleasant memories of us and that
you long to see us, just as we also long to see
you. 7Therefore, brothers, in all our distress
and persecution we were encouraged about
you because of your faith. 8For now we really live, since you are standing firm in the
Lord. 9How can we thank God enough for
you in return for all the joy we have in the
presence of our God because of you? 10Night
and day we pray most earnestly that we may
see you again and supply what is lacking in
your faith.
11Now may our God and Father himself
and our Lord Jesus clear the way for us to
come to you. 12May the Lord make your love
increase and overflow for each other and for
everyone else, just as ours does for you. 13May
he strengthen your hearts so that you will be
blameless and holy in the presence of our God
and Father when our Lord Jesus comes with
all his holy ones.

Living to Please God

4 Finally, brothers, we instructed you how to
live in order to please God, as in fact you
are living. Now we ask you and urge you in
the Lord Jesus to do this more and more. 2For
you know what instructions we gave you by
the authority of the Lord Jesus.
3It is God's will that you should be sanctified: that you should avoid sexual immorality; 4that each of you should learn to control
his own body[a] in a way that is holy and honorable, 5not in passionate lust like the hea-
then, who do not know God; 6and that in
this matter no one should wrong his brother
or take advantage of him. The Lord will punish men for all such sins, as we have already
told you and warned you. 7For God did not
call us to be impure, but to live a holy life.
8Therefore, he who rejects this instruction
does not reject man but God, who gives you
his Holy Spirit.
9Now about brotherly love we do not need
to write to you, for you yourselves have been
taught by God to love each other. 10And in
fact, you do love all the brothers throughout
Macedonia. Yet we urge you, brothers, to do
so more and more.
11Make it your ambition to lead a quiet
life, to mind your own business and to work
with your hands, just as we told you, 12so that
your daily life may win the respect of outsiders and so that you will not be dependent on
anybody.

The Coming of the Lord

13Brothers, we do not want you to be ignorant about those who fall asleep, or to grieve
like the rest of men, who have no hope. 14We
believe that Jesus died and rose again and so
we believe that God will bring with Jesus those
who have fallen asleep in him. 15According to
the Lord's own word, we tell you that we who
are still alive, who are left till the coming of
the Lord, will certainly not precede those who
have fallen asleep. 16For the Lord himself will
come down from heaven, with a loud command, with the voice of the archangel and
with the trumpet call of God, and the dead in
Christ will rise first. 17After that, we who are
still alive and are left will be caught up together with them in the clouds to meet the Lord
in the air. And so we will be with the Lord
forever. 18Therefore encourage each other with
these words.

5 Now, brothers, about times and dates we
do not need to write to you, 2for you know
very well that the day of the Lord will come
like a thief in the night. 3While people are saying, "Peace and safety," destruction will come
on them suddenly, as labor pains on a pregnant woman, and they will not escape.
4But you, brothers, are not in darkness so
that this day should surprise you like a thief.
5You are all sons of the light and sons of the
day. We do not belong to the night or to the
darkness. 6So then, let us not be like others,
who are asleep, but let us be alert and self-controlled. 7For those who sleep, sleep at night,
and those who get drunk, get drunk at night.
8But since we belong to the day, let us be
self-controlled, putting on faith and love as
a breastplate, and the hope of salvation as a
helmet. 9For God did not appoint us to suffer wrath but to receive salvation through our
Lord Jesus Christ. 10He died for us so that,
whether we are awake or asleep, we may live
together with him. 11Therefore encourage one
another and build each other up, just as in fact
you are doing.

---

[a] 4 Or *learn to live with his own wife*; or *learn to acquire a wife*

WEEKEND

hope in hard times

I suppose there has never been a marriage between two honest, self-examining people that at some time has not reached a seemingly irredeemable low point. There have been moments in my own marriage when the wall between my wife and me seemed too high to hurdle, too thick to break. We found it hard to muster hope. It was not easy to be confident that somehow the barriers blocking our oneness could be removed.

Before the responsibilities of marriage will be regarded as inviting opportunities rather than pointless duties, the core of a person's attitude must shift from despair to hope. To effect this shift requires that we provide adequate answers to the tough questions.

In a world where *every* relationship is gnarled by the deforming effects of sin, nothing is needed more than an appreciation of the grace of God as a foundation for hope. To be fully persuaded that there is always reason to live responsibly no matter what may go wrong is indispensable to the Christian life.

Too many unhappy spouses claim promises that God never made as their foundation of hope. They trust that if they do all they can, God will change their spouses into the loving Christians they should be. But a reason to live *never* consists of a guarantee that "Things will get better" or that "God will save your husband and help him stop drinking." The hope of the Christian is far deeper than a mere change in someone else. The hope of the Christian is inescapably bound up in the grace of God.

It would be easy to quote a few verses from Hebrews (especially 6:18–19), and speak glowingly about the sure hope in Christ that serves as an anchor for our souls. But if you are plagued by chronic despair that results in a "Why bother" attitude, then prayerfully consider the following.

The Lord has not promised to put your marriage together for you. The hope of the Christian is *not* that one's spouse will change or that one's health will improve or that one's financial situation will become good. God does not promise or rearrange our worlds to suit our longings. He does promise to permit only those events that will further his purpose in our lives. Our responsibility is to respond to life's events in a manner that pleases the Lord, not to change our spouses into what we want. Even if we respond biblically, we have no guarantee that our spouses will respond in kind. Though they file for divorce or continue to drink or nag all the more, there is reason for us to persevere in obedience.

Certainly if both partners build on the foundation of hope and strive earnestly to live biblically, even the worst marriage can be turned around. Either way, there is reason to hope. This reason is bound up in the grace of God.

In God's presence, there is never cause for despair. Our spouses may not do what they should to restore our marriage to happy, fulfilling relationships. But if we remain faithful to God, pouring out our emotions before him, renewing our commitment to seek him, trusting him to guide us in our responses, then he will sustain us through our trials and provide rich fellowship with him. There is reason to go on. There is hope. God's grace is sufficient.

—DR. LARRY CRABB

identifying the tender spots

Most marriages eventually reach "a seemingly irredeemable low point." Answer the following questions to gain insight on your experience with these moments.

1. Have you ever felt a low point in your marriage? What was the situation?
2. Is some area of your marriage at a low point now? If so, describe the situation as objectively as you can. Focus on identifying your deep longings beneath the hurts and disillusionments.
3. Do you feel hope or despair about your relationship?
4. Reflect honestly: What change in each other would give you greater hope for the success of your marriage?
5. To what extent have you been quietly preoccupied (or perhaps unquietly occupied!) with each other in making this change? How has your preoccupation contributed to any despair you feel in your marriage?
6. If you feel despair, can you hope?
7. If you feel hope, how can you strengthen that hope?
8. What is your understanding of these statements: "The hope of the Christian is *not* that one's spouse will change or that one's health will improve or that one's financial situation will become good . . . There is reason to hope. This reason is bound up in the grace of God"?
9. Are you confident of God's presence in your life? Why or why not?
10. What choices do you face as you struggle with seeking relief from personal pain and depending obediently on the grace of God?
11. Are you prepared to obey God, even if your spouse will not?

HOW ARE WE DOING?

let's make a DATE

RECREATE YOUR FIRST DATE

Think about the first time you went out together. How did you first meet? Did you go out as a couple right away or were you "just friends" for awhile? What did you do on your first date? Where did you go? What did you eat? What did you talk about? What attracted you to each other and made you want to go out again?

Make a date with each other. Try to repeat some of the fun things you did when you were first dating. Think of what you still find attractive in each other. Talk about that. Then remind each other how you felt during those first times together and how those feelings have grown and changed over time.

FOR YOUR NEXT DEVOTIONAL READING, TURN TO PAGE 1360.

LESSONS FROM THE *Bible*

What was the desperate situation in Abigail's life in 1 Samuel 25? Up to this point in her obviously unhappy marriage, how do you think Abigail found hope and strength?

M

MONDAY

READ

1 THESSALONIANS 4:1–12

ON THE JOB FOR GOD

Attitudes about work generally run between two extremes. One extreme is the workaholic, with cell phone in one hand, BlackBerry in the other, and a computer open on their lap.

The other extreme is the person who views a job only as a necessary evil, a means to a paycheck. Leisure is the name of the game. This person exists for the weekends.

Neither extreme is Biblical.

Paul wrote to the Thessalonians concerning their attitude about work and the influence it had on their community. He told them to make it their ambition to lead a quiet life and to work with their hands "so that your daily life may win the respect of outsiders and so that you will not be dependent on anybody" (1 Thessalonians 4:12).

Some of the Thessalonian believers were hard workers, but others had become idle, and, with nothing to do, they had become busybodies. Paul told them in his second letter, "If a man will not work he shall not eat." (2 Thessalonians 3:10).

Dave McFadden, a pastor in New Mexico, told his congregation that the way we value work relates to more than our job. It affects how we approach our involvement in every area of life: marriage, family, friendships, church and community.

The apostle Paul told Timothy, "If anyone does not provide for his relatives . . . he has denied the faith and is worse than an unbeliever" (1 Timothy 5:8). But work goes beyond merely providing for our families, as important as that is. Our occupations are not just about earning a living; they are about how we live.

Whatever our job is, it is a vocation for the glory of God: A garbage collector helps make creation more beautiful for the glory of God. A mason or roofer builds for the glory of God. A teacher molds the minds of others for the glory of God. Our jobs, and our attitudes toward them, show others how we love God and strive to serve him in all we do.

The creation accounts in Genesis 1 and 2 show us that God called the first couple to exercise dominion over the earth in general and to work the Garden of Eden in particular. We are also called to work, and whether we have jobs outside the home or inside the home, work is good because it's from God. One of the best things we can do for each other in marriage is to hold our spouse's work in high esteem. We are to "spur one another on toward love and good deeds" (Hebrews 10:24), to bring out the best in each other, to build each other's self-respect and sense of worth. We are to help each other model Christlike behavior, which includes earning a living. Our Savior himself labored as a carpenter before beginning his ministry as a teacher.

"Instead of being a busybody, make your body busy by working with your own hands," McFadden said, "and as you endeavor to be a productive member of society, you will also be a productive member of the kingdom of God."

—NANCY KENNEDY

Make it your ambition to lead a quiet life, to mind your own business and to work with your hands, just as we told you.

— 1 THESSALONIANS 4:11

let's *talk*

- ✦ Growing up, what messages did each of us get from our families about work? Were we taught that work is honorable, right and fulfilling—or just something we have to do to pay the bills?
- ✦ What other messages have shaped our thoughts about work? When we are unhappy with our jobs, what may be feeding that dissatisfaction? How does lack of fulfillment on the job affect our relationship in marriage?
- ✦ In what ways can we view marriage as work? What are some of the responsibilities of marriage? The benefits? The bonuses?

FOR YOUR NEXT DEVOTIONAL READING, TURN TO PAGE 1364.

Final Instructions

12Now we ask you, brothers, to respect those who work hard among you, who are over you in the Lord and who admonish you. 13Hold them in the highest regard in love because of their work. Live in peace with each other. 14And we urge you, brothers, warn those who are idle, encourage the timid, help the weak, be patient with everyone. 15Make sure that nobody pays back wrong for wrong, but always try to be kind to each other and to everyone else.

16Be joyful always; 17pray continually; 18give thanks in all circumstances, for this is God's will for you in Christ Jesus.

19Do not put out the Spirit's fire; 20do not treat prophecies with contempt. 21Test everything. Hold on to the good. 22Avoid every kind of evil.

23May God himself, the God of peace, sanctify you through and through. May your whole spirit, soul and body be kept blameless at the coming of our Lord Jesus Christ. 24The one who calls you is faithful and he will do it.

25Brothers, pray for us. 26Greet all the brothers with a holy kiss. 27I charge you before the Lord to have this letter read to all the brothers.

28The grace of our Lord Jesus Christ be with you.

2 THESSALONIANS

2 Thessalonians

QUICK FACTS

AUTHOR The apostle Paul

AUDIENCE The church in Thessalonica (a city that was located in modern-day northern Greece)

DATE About A.D. 51 or 52, perhaps about six months after the writing of 1 Thessalonians

SETTING The Christians in Thessalonica thought that Christ would return immediately.

Shortly after writing his first letter to the Thessalonians, the apostle Paul wrote a second letter in which he elaborated on themes he had introduced earlier and confronted even more directly some difficult issues the church was facing.

Paul warned his readers that persecution and deception would precede the return of Christ. Yet believers were not to be alarmed or confused by such things, he said. Instead, they should hold steady in their commitment to the Lord, keeping a firm grip on all they had been taught.

Beyond these end-time challenges, however, Paul wrote 2 Thessalonians to expand his earlier advice about personal integrity. As we wait in eager anticipation of the Lord's coming, we should be even more committed to living responsible lives on earth. Paul's letter reminds us to fulfill our everyday obligations. We are not to live idle lives, for instance, existing off the generosity of others. Whoever refuses to work, Paul said, should not be permitted to eat (see 2 Thessalonians 3:10).

Paul's words have direct implications for couples today. Responsible, mature believers will live useful, productive lives, caring and providing for the needs of their families.

Warning Against Idleness

6In the name of the Lord Jesus Christ, we
command you, brothers, to keep away from
every brother who is idle and does not live
according to the teaching[a] you received from
us. 7For you yourselves know how you ought
to follow our example. We were not idle when
we were with you, 8nor did we eat anyone's
food without paying for it. On the contrary,
we worked night and day, laboring and toiling so that we would not be a burden to any
of you. 9We did this, not because we do not
have the right to such help, but in order to
make ourselves a model for you to follow.
10For even when we were with you, we gave
you this rule: "If a man will not work, he shall
not eat."

11We hear that some among you are idle.
They are not busy; they are busybodies. 12Such
people we command and urge in the Lord
Jesus Christ to settle down and earn the bread
they eat. 13And as for you, brothers, never tire
of doing what is right.

14If anyone does not obey our instruction
in this letter, take special note of him. Do not
associate with him, in order that he may feel
ashamed. 15Yet do not regard him as an enemy, but warn him as a brother.

Final Greetings

16Now may the Lord of peace himself give
you peace at all times and in every way. The
Lord be with all of you.

17I, Paul, write this greeting in my own
hand, which is the distinguishing mark in all
my letters. This is how I write.

18The grace of our Lord Jesus Christ be
with you all.

[a] 6 Or *tradition*

1 TIMOTHY

1 Timothy

QUICK FACTS

AUTHOR The apostle Paul

AUDIENCE Timothy, Paul's young protégé (and then, through him, the church at Ephesus)

DATE About A.D. 64, between Paul's first and second imprisonments in Rome

SETTING Timothy, the young pastor of the church of Ephesus, needed instructions from Paul on church leadership.

The apostle Paul wrote this letter to advise young Timothy, a minister whom he had personally mentored. He had given Timothy the daunting assignment of leading the new church at Ephesus. Timothy was facing major challenges, especially that of dealing with false teachers. And it appears that not everyone was eager to follow his leadership. Some likely considered him too young and inexperienced. Furthermore, as the son of a Greek father and a Jewish mother, Timothy was a potential target of criticism from both Greeks and Jews.

Paul reassured Timothy that he was well equipped for his leadership position because the Holy Spirit was at work in his life.

In the years since it was written, Paul's letter has made a profound impact on many church leaders. Its practical advice and spiritual insights have guided ministers on numerous issues: interacting with people, confronting false teachers, mentoring lay leaders, maintaining spiritual accountability, keeping proper decorum in worship, and much more.

1 Paul, an apostle of Christ Jesus by the command of God our Savior and of Christ
Jesus our hope,

2To Timothy my true son in the faith:

Grace, mercy and peace from God the Father and Christ Jesus our Lord.

Warning Against False Teachers of the Law

3As I urged you when I went into Macedonia, stay there in Ephesus so that you may
command certain men not to teach false doctrines any longer 4nor to devote themselves
to myths and endless genealogies. These promote controversies rather than God's work—
which is by faith. 5The goal of this command
is love, which comes from a pure heart and
a good conscience and a sincere faith. 6Some
have wandered away from these and turned to
meaningless talk. 7They want to be teachers
of the law, but they do not know what they
are talking about or what they so confidently
affirm.

8We know that the law is good if one uses
it properly. 9We also know that law[a] is made
not for the righteous but for lawbreakers and
rebels, the ungodly and sinful, the unholy and
irreligious; for those who kill their fathers or
mothers, for murderers, 10for adulterers and
perverts, for slave traders and liars and perjurers—and for whatever else is contrary to the
sound doctrine 11that conforms to the glorious gospel of the blessed God, which he entrusted to me.

The Lord's Grace to Paul

12I thank Christ Jesus our Lord, who has
given me strength, that he considered me
faithful, appointing me to his service. 13Even
though I was once a blasphemer and a perse-
cutor and a violent man, I was shown mercy because I acted in ignorance and unbelief.
14The grace of our Lord was poured out on me
abundantly, along with the faith and love that
are in Christ Jesus.

15Here is a trustworthy saying that deserves full acceptance: Christ Jesus came into
the world to save sinners—of whom I am the
worst. 16But for that very reason I was shown
mercy so that in me, the worst of sinners,
Christ Jesus might display his unlimited patience as an example for those who would believe on him and receive eternal life. 17Now to
the King eternal, immortal, invisible, the only
God, be honor and glory for ever and ever.
Amen.

18Timothy, my son, I give you this instruction in keeping with the prophecies once made
about you, so that by following them you may
fight the good fight, 19holding on to faith and
a good conscience. Some have rejected these
and so have shipwrecked their faith. 20Among
them are Hymenaeus and Alexander, whom I
have handed over to Satan to be taught not to
blaspheme.

Instructions on Worship

2 I urge, then, first of all, that requests,
prayers, intercession and thanksgiving be
made for everyone— 2for kings and all
those in authority, that we may live peaceful
and quiet lives in all godliness and holiness.
3This is good, and pleases God our Savior,
4who wants all men to be saved and to come
to a knowledge of the truth. 5For there is one
God and one mediator between God and
men, the man Christ Jesus, 6who gave himself
as a ransom for all men—the testimony given
in its proper time. 7And for this purpose I was
appointed a herald and an apostle—I am telling the truth, I am not lying—and a teacher of
the true faith to the Gentiles.

8I want men everywhere to lift up holy
hands in prayer, without anger or disputing.

9I also want women to dress modestly, with
decency and propriety, not with braided hair
or gold or pearls or expensive clothes, 10but
with good deeds, appropriate for women who
profess to worship God.

11A woman should learn in quietness and
full submission. 12I do not permit a woman
to teach or to have authority over a man; she
must be silent. 13For Adam was formed first,
then Eve. 14And Adam was not the one deceived; it was the woman who was deceived
and became a sinner. 15But women[b] will be
saved[c] through childbearing—if they continue in faith, love and holiness with propriety.

Overseers and Deacons

3 Here is a trustworthy saying: If anyone sets
his heart on being an overseer,[d] he desires
a noble task. 2Now the overseer must be
above reproach, the husband of but one wife,
temperate, self-controlled, respectable, hospitable, able to teach, 3not given to drunkenness, not violent but gentle, not quarrelsome,
not a lover of money. 4He must manage his

---

[a] 9 Or *that the law* [b] 15 Greek *she* [c] 15 Or *restored* [d] 1 Traditionally *bishop*; also in verse 2

DRESSING FOR GOD

I have an acquaintance who is the principal of a middle school in a large city. We were discussing dress codes at her school, the issue of school uniforms and what she did when her students dressed inappropriately.

"You want to know the truth?" she confided. "It's not so much the kids. It's their mothers!" I looked at her, not understanding. "These parents show up at conferences or PTA meetings, and I just want to say, 'Mom, go home and put on something decent!' It's no wonder their daughters don't know how to dress appropriately."

As we read Paul's words to Timothy in 1 Timothy 2:9–10, we might think that his advice was necessary 2,000 years ago but that we don't need it today. Think again. The call to dress modestly is relevant in every generation and to both genders.

Sure, fashions change. What was once considered shocking dress for women—a glimpse of an ankle, a showing of knees—is no longer cause for horror. Still, how the Christian dresses herself or himself in any time period may tell the world much about their relationship with their spouse and with God.

What is a woman saying when she wears clothing that is overtly sexual? At the very least, she's sharing something about her body that should be reserved for her husband alone. On the more extreme end, she may be broadcasting signals that she's available to someone other than her spouse.

What about a man who shows off his expensive watch or imported leather shoes? What message is he sending if he feels he has to wear the most up-to-date designer styles or if he's dressing to impress others with his expensive taste?

What do these choices about our appearance say about our relationship with God? What do they say about our priorities? Is our appearance more important than what's inside?

Our culture is all about self-promotion: "If you've got it, flaunt it." However, that goes directly against Paul's advice. He encourages women to forgo all the glitz and instead dress themselves "with good deeds, appropriate for women who profess to worship God." Those are worthy values to transmit to our daughters and sons and all those who come into contact with us.

Every person wants to look nice. Buying clothing that is appropriate for the situation and that flatters us is great. Keeping our appearance up-to-date is fine. True beauty, however, issues from internal character and deeds more than from external appearance.

And those qualities never go out of style.

—VALERIE VAN KOOTEN

FOR YOUR NEXT DEVOTIONAL READING, TURN TO PAGE 1370.

I also want women to dress modestly, with decency and propriety, not with braided hair or gold or pearls or expensive clothes, but with good deeds, appropriate for women who profess to worship God.

— 1 TIMOTHY 2:9–10

let's talk

- What may have been going on in the early church that made Paul feel the need to draw attention to modesty in dress?
- What are some of our boundaries in how we dress? What is OK with us regarding how a woman or man dresses? What would we consider to be a definite "no-no"?
- How does inner character and good deeds make us beautiful? How do we encourage that kind of beauty in each other?

own family well and see that his children obey him with proper respect. 5(If anyone does not know how to manage his own family, how can he take care of God's church?) 6He must not be a recent convert, or he may become conceited and fall under the same judgment as the devil. 7He must also have a good reputation with outsiders, so that he will not fall into disgrace and into the devil's trap.

8Deacons, likewise, are to be men worthy of respect, sincere, not indulging in much wine, and not pursuing dishonest gain. 9They must keep hold of the deep truths of the faith with a clear conscience. 10They must first be tested; and then if there is nothing against them, let them serve as deacons.

11In the same way, their wives[a] are to be women worthy of respect, not malicious talkers but temperate and trustworthy in everything.

12A deacon must be the husband of but one wife and must manage his children and his household well. 13Those who have served well gain an excellent standing and great assurance in their faith in Christ Jesus.

14Although I hope to come to you soon, I am writing you these instructions so that, 15if I am delayed, you will know how people ought to conduct themselves in God's household, which is the church of the living God, the pillar and foundation of the truth. 16Beyond all question, the mystery of godliness is great:

He[b] appeared in a body,[c]
  was vindicated by the Spirit,
was seen by angels,
  was preached among the nations,
was believed on in the world,
  was taken up in glory.

Instructions to Timothy

4 The Spirit clearly says that in later times some will abandon the faith and follow deceiving spirits and things taught by demons. 2Such teachings come through hypocritical liars, whose consciences have been seared as with a hot iron. 3They forbid people to marry and order them to abstain from certain foods, which God created to be received with thanksgiving by those who believe and who know the truth. 4For everything God created is good, and nothing is to be rejected if it is received with thanksgiving, 5because it is consecrated by the word of God and prayer.

6If you point these things out to the brothers, you will be a good minister of Christ Jesus, brought up in the truths of the faith and of the good teaching that you have followed. 7Have nothing to do with godless myths and old wives' tales; rather, train yourself to be godly. 8For physical training is of some value, but godliness has value for all things, holding promise for both the present life and the life to come.

9This is a trustworthy saying that deserves full acceptance 10(and for this we labor and strive), that we have put our hope in the living God, who is the Savior of all men, and especially of those who believe.

11Command and teach these things. 12Don't let anyone look down on you because you are young, but set an example for the believers in speech, in life, in love, in faith and in purity. 13Until I come, devote yourself to the public reading of Scripture, to preaching and to teaching. 14Do not neglect your gift, which was given you through a prophetic message when the body of elders laid their hands on you.

15Be diligent in these matters; give yourself wholly to them, so that everyone may see your progress. 16Watch your life and doctrine closely. Persevere in them, because if you do, you will save both yourself and your hearers.

Advice About Widows, Elders and Slaves

5 Do not rebuke an older man harshly, but exhort him as if he were your father. Treat younger men as brothers, 2older women as mothers, and younger women as sisters, with absolute purity.

3Give proper recognition to those widows who are really in need. 4But if a widow has children or grandchildren, these should learn first of all to put their religion into practice by caring for their own family and so repaying their parents and grandparents, for this is pleasing to God. 5The widow who is really in need and left all alone puts her hope in God and continues night and day to pray and to ask God for help. 6But the widow who lives for pleasure is dead even while she lives. 7Give the people these instructions, too, so that no one may be open to blame. 8If anyone does not provide for his relatives, and especially for his immediate family, he has denied the faith and is worse than an unbeliever.

9No widow may be put on the list of widows unless she is over sixty, has been faithful

[a] *11* Or *way, deaconesses* [b] *16* Some manuscripts *God* [c] *16* Or *in the flesh*

THURSDAY
READ 1 TIMOTHY 4:1–16

LEARNING FROM GOOD FRIENDS

While it is wise to seek counsel from others, particularly when you are new to marriage, it is also crucial to seek the right kind of counsel.

Imagine having the apostle Paul as your mentor and counselor. That's the wonderful privilege that Timothy experienced. Timothy had traveled with Paul on some of his missionary journeys, but eventually Timothy was charged with shepherding the church at Ephesus. It was there that he received this encouraging letter from his friend Paul. Paul knew Timothy needed some good advice on how to help those in his congregation. Thankfully, Timothy had Paul's wise, experienced counsel to guide him as he grew in discernment and faith.

Judicious counsel was especially important to me during the first year of my marriage. My parents had divorced when I was in grammar school, so I entered marriage with almost no idea of what a healthy marriage looked like. My scripts for marriage came from Hollywood, and we know how Hollywood tends to focus on steamy romances.

So in seeking wisdom for marriage, my parents and Hollywood were not the kind of advisers my husband and I needed to get through the problems and adjustments of making a life together. Griff's parents have been married for 30-plus years (quite happily, as far as I can tell), so Griff came into our marriage with a pretty strong picture of what a good marriage looks like. Still, we needed more counsel than that to build a great marriage.

Scripture directed us to God-fearing couples: Abraham and Sarah, who trusted that God would give them a child even when their bodies were too old to conceive; Moses' parents, who hid their baby for three months, under penalty of death, because they trusted God more than they feared a pharaoh; and Mary and Joseph, who left their homes, reputations and dreams to obey the directives of unearthly messengers of God.

Griff and I were also privileged to see up close the marriages of several God-fearing friends. Admittedly, one can never truly know the inside of another person's relationship, but one can come close when Christian friends are willing to show you, not the gussied-up, picture-perfect outsides of their marriages, but the messy, complicated insides.

We learned to fight well, in part, from watching how other married couples fight. We saw all sorts of different parenting styles played out in our friends' living rooms, and we made decisions about what would work best for us.

Today, when we stumble, as we inevitably do, we still look to other wiser and more experienced Christians for advice. How should we think about sex, birth control and pregnancy? When should we have a baby? Do I have to go with Griff every time he visits his family or is it OK for him to occasionally go by himself? What are the pros and cons of individual checking accounts? Believe it or not, these represent only a fraction of the questions we have brought to our mentor couples.

Newly married couples needn't do the hard work of adjusting to marriage by themselves. We have a community of faith to draw from to help us grow in godliness and give us hope.

—LAUREN WINNER

Command and teach these things. Don't let anyone look down on you because you are young, but set an example for the believers in speech, in life, in love, in faith and in purity.

— 1 TIMOTHY 4:11–12

let's talk

- ✦ When have we asked for advice from others before making a major decision in our marriage? Did we get wise or not-so-wise counsel? How could we tell the difference?
- ✦ How might our experience of marriage and parenting be transformed if we discussed some of our decisions with others in our community of faith?
- ✦ When have we invited a single person or newly married couple into our marriage, exposing not only the pretty parts but also the difficult, ugly, hard parts?

FOR YOUR NEXT DEVOTIONAL READING, TURN TO PAGE 1372.

to her husband,[a] [10]and is well known for her good deeds, such as bringing up children, showing hospitality, washing the feet of the saints, helping those in trouble and devoting herself to all kinds of good deeds.

[11]As for younger widows, do not put them on such a list. For when their sensual desires overcome their dedication to Christ, they want to marry. [12]Thus they bring judgment on themselves, because they have broken their first pledge. [13]Besides, they get into the habit of being idle and going about from house to house. And not only do they become idlers, but also gossips and busybodies, saying things they ought not to. [14]So I counsel younger widows to marry, to have children, to manage their homes and to give the enemy no opportunity for slander. [15]Some have in fact already turned away to follow Satan.

[16]If any woman who is a believer has widows in her family, she should help them and not let the church be burdened with them, so that the church can help those widows who are really in need.

[17]The elders who direct the affairs of the church well are worthy of double honor, especially those whose work is preaching and teaching. [18]For the Scripture says, "Do not muzzle the ox while it is treading out the grain,"[b] and "The worker deserves his wages."[c] [19]Do not entertain an accusation against an elder unless it is brought by two or three witnesses. [20]Those who sin are to be rebuked publicly, so that the others may take warning.

[21]I charge you, in the sight of God and Christ Jesus and the elect angels, to keep these instructions without partiality, and to do nothing out of favoritism.

[22]Do not be hasty in the laying on of hands, and do not share in the sins of others. Keep yourself pure.

[23]Stop drinking only water, and use a little wine because of your stomach and your frequent illnesses.

[24]The sins of some men are obvious, reaching the place of judgment ahead of them; the sins of others trail behind them. [25]In the same way, good deeds are obvious, and even those that are not cannot be hidden.

6 All who are under the yoke of slavery should consider their masters worthy of full respect, so that God's name and our teaching may not be slandered. [2]Those who have believing masters are not to show less respect for them because they are brothers. Instead, they are to serve them even better, because those who benefit from their service are believers, and dear to them. These are the things you are to teach and urge on them.

Love of Money

[3]If anyone teaches false doctrines and does not agree to the sound instruction of our Lord Jesus Christ and to godly teaching, [4]he is conceited and understands nothing. He has an unhealthy interest in controversies and quarrels about words that result in envy, strife, malicious talk, evil suspicions [5]and constant friction between men of corrupt mind, who have been robbed of the truth and who think that godliness is a means to financial gain.

[6]But godliness with contentment is great gain. [7]For we brought nothing into the world, and we can take nothing out of it. [8]But if we have food and clothing, we will be content with that. [9]People who want to get rich fall into temptation and a trap and into many foolish and harmful desires that plunge men into ruin and destruction. [10]For the love of money is a root of all kinds of evil. Some people, eager for money, have wandered from the faith and pierced themselves with many griefs.

Paul's Charge to Timothy

[11]But you, man of God, flee from all this, and pursue righteousness, godliness, faith, love, endurance and gentleness. [12]Fight the good fight of the faith. Take hold of the eternal life to which you were called when you made your good confession in the presence of many witnesses. [13]In the sight of God, who gives life to everything, and of Christ Jesus, who while testifying before Pontius Pilate made the good confession, I charge you [14]to keep this command without spot or blame until the appearing of our Lord Jesus Christ, [15]which God will bring about in his own time—God, the blessed and only Ruler, the King of kings and Lord of lords, [16]who alone is immortal and who lives in unapproachable light, whom no one has seen or can see. To him be honor and might forever. Amen.

[17]Command those who are rich in this present world not to be arrogant nor to put their hope in wealth, which is so uncertain, but to put their hope in God, who richly provides us with everything for our enjoyment. [18]Command them to do good, to be rich in good deeds, and to be generous and willing

---

[a] *9* Or *has had but one husband* [b] *18* Deut. 25:4 [c] *18* Luke 10:7

FRIDAY
READ 1 TIMOTHY 5:1–16

PROVIDING FOR THE FAMILY

Recently a friend recommended a course offered at her church titled "Financial Self-Defense." My first thought was that the church should offer another one called "Financial CPR" for those whose finances need complete resuscitation.

My husband and I are financial idiots. We continue to be thankful for those smarter than we are who are willing to step alongside us to walk us through mortgage paperwork and insurance headaches. In keeping with our simple financial minds, our financial goals are pretty simple: tithe and give offerings faithfully; get out—and stay out—of debt (I'm hoping we'll get there yet!); and take care of our family, including our parents, should that become necessary.

But, like most people, we have times of severe financial stress. One of the worst times was when our children were young and the furnace in our big, old house gave out for good. It was December, a time when it starts to get really cold in Illinois, where we live. And December is also a time when our bank account is emptier than usual because of Christmas spending.

If anyone does not provide for his relatives, and especially for his immediate family, he has denied the faith and is worse than an unbeliever.

— 1 Timothy 5:8

let's talk

- What financial goals do we share as a couple?
- Have we encountered difficulties in providing for our own household? How have we gotten help? In what ways has that assistance helped us become more discerning about handling money?
- How is financially providing for our family part of our calling as Christians?

Our furnace repairman was a deacon at our church, and he encouraged us to let our church help us pay for the furnace through the benevolent fund. It's an extremely humbling experience to lean on your Christian brothers and sisters this way, but we gratefully accepted the help. As recipients of that financial aid, we now are more keenly aware of the importance of giving to the benevolent fund at our church. We know what it feels like to need a cash rescue.

Generally, though, David and I work hard to provide for our children—by giving them, not a luxurious life, but a simple, safe and healthy one. This is a Biblical concept. The apostle Paul wrote that it is a shame for believers not to set a loving example by generously providing for their own households. The church plays a role in helping those who are alone in the world—those who are orphaned, widowed or abandoned. But Paul reminded Timothy that Christians who fail to take responsibility for their own families are worse than unbelievers. That's quite a reminder!

David and I need God's help to achieve our financial goals, and we're trusting God to help us be the ones to provide for the needs of our four kids and our parents. With God's help, we can keep his admonition in mind to care for our own household.

—ANNETTE LAPLACA

FOR YOUR NEXT DEVOTIONAL READING, TURN TO PAGE 1374.

to share. 19In this way they will lay up treasure for themselves as a firm foundation for
the coming age, so that they may take hold of
the life that is truly life.
20Timothy, guard what has been entrusted
to your care. Turn away from godless chatter
and the opposing ideas of what is falsely called
knowledge, 21which some have professed and
in so doing have wandered from the faith.

Grace be with you.

WEEKEND

blended families

My husband and I have been married five years and have a 3-year-old son. My husband also has a 12-year-old daughter from a previous marriage. I feel like I'm on the outside looking in when it comes to his daughter. When she stays with us, she's belligerent and disrespectful to me. Sometimes it seems as though my husband favors his daughter over me—or at least he doesn't stand up for me, as I believe he should. Help!

Your problem isn't uncommon. But let's think first about what it's like to be your stepdaughter. She can't have what she most wants in a family: her mom and dad under the same roof, happily married. You—more than anyone else—remind her of that loss. You're with her father, and he loves you, not her mother.

Your stepdaughter probably doesn't know what to do with her confusion, grief, anger and sadness. She may want you on the outside looking in when it comes to her relationship with her dad. If she can't have her mom there, she doesn't want you trying to take her place.

She also may be angry with her dad, and she takes it out on you to preserve her relationship with him. Your stepdaughter may also fear being preempted by you and your son, so she fights to keep you excluded.

Remember what it's like to be age 12, and try sympathizing with your stepdaughter's feelings. Try not to take her reactions personally; they're not about you but about what you represent.

Ask God to help you love your stepdaughter. Love her father as well. Talk to him about her disrespect, because he needs to help his daughter find more appropriate ways to express her feelings. Anger and sadness don't give her the right to be disrespectful.

—DR. DIANE MANDT LANGBERG

Many couples in remarriages find the problem isn't their spouse—but the children. One woman said, "I love my husband, but I wish I could divorce his kids." Trying to parent those children can bring intense conflict to the entire family. So what should you know and do? Realize:

- Stepfamilies (blended families) are born of loss. That's not always easy for the remarried couple to remember, but the children don't forget.
- Stepparents and stepchildren do not necessarily love each other, especially if there is another biological parent who influences the family.
- Because the parent-child bond existed before the couple bond, the child may feel pushed out of a special relationship with the biological parent and may fight the growth of intimacy between the new spouses.
- Conflicts over discipline can be huge. The blending spouse's parental values may differ. Spouses must talk as spouses, while parents talk as parents.

Tips for blending families:

- Pray over every aspect of your new family—expectations, boundaries, parenting.
- Try to put yourself in the child's place by thinking about the difficulty he or she may be forced to go through. Remember, the child didn't ask for the divorce or the parent's death.
- Make marriage your top priority. The best thing for your children is to see a strong marriage. They've experienced one family's disintegration; don't allow them to experience another.
- Give and receive grace, first from God, then from each other.

—SCOTTIE MAY

how are your stepparenting skills?

Take a look at the following statements. Decide if each statement is something you always do, sometimes do, or never do. Then compare notes with your spouse.

1. My spouse and I demonstrate a committed marriage to our children.
2. My words to my spouse are kind in front of the children.
3. When discussing financial issues, I don't let things get personal; I stick to business.
4. I only say positive things about my spouse's ex.
5. I pray daily for my spouse's ex.
6. I pray daily for my stepchildren.
7. I try not to contradict my spouse in front of the children.
8. I consider my stepchild's feelings.
9. I allow my spouse to manage the discipline of my stepchildren.
10. I seek outside counseling and support for blended-family issues.

HOW ARE WE DOING?

let's make a DATE

SKILLET NIGHT

Remember when Mom used to throw a few ingredients into a pan, and a half hour later dinner was ready? Make a date to try something like that with your spouse.

First, one person chooses a meat and a seasoning. Some ideas might be salt, Tabasco sauce, cream of mushroom soup, or other stuff you find in the cupboard. Next, the other person chooses a vegetable and a pasta, rice or other grain.

When it comes time to prepare dinner, combine all your ingredients, adding meats, vegetables and seasonings. While cooking together, discuss the unique flavors of each ingredient and how they will affect the taste. How does your skillet supper smell so far? Add in the pasta with enough liquid to soften it.

When the skillet dinner is nearly done, taste it and together decide what would improve the taste. When you sit down to eat, is your skillet dinner the most delicious thing you've ever cooked or is it barely edible? As you eat your blended meal, talk about how a variety of individual ingredients meld into something completely different.

FOR YOUR NEXT DEVOTIONAL READING, TURN TO PAGE 1378.

LESSONS FROM THE *Bible*

Jacob had children from four wives. His most loved son was Joseph, the firstborn of his beloved wife, Rachel. Jacob's obvious favoritism wreaked havoc in his family. Joseph's half brothers hated and resented him.

Read Genesis 37:1–36. How did Jacob's parenting mistakes affect his blended family? What could he have done differently?

2 TIMOTHY

2 Timothy

QUICK FACTS

AUTHOR The apostle Paul

AUDIENCE Timothy (and then, through him, the church at Ephesus)

DATE About A.D. 67

SETTING Written from a Roman dungeon shortly before Paul was martyred for his faith (this is Paul's last letter)

Paul wrote this second letter to Timothy from prison, shortly before his execution. Paul knew these were likely his last words to his young protégé. As a result, this letter seems more personal—and more urgent. One's last words often are.

Paul wanted to inspire Timothy to pick up the ministry where Paul himself was leaving off. He reminded Timothy of his godly heritage and recalled how the Holy Spirit had given him a gift for ministry. Paul knew that with such a strong spiritual foundation, Timothy could be expected to continue the work entrusted to him. He had what it took to stand up to ungodly teachers of false doctrine in those perilous days.

Paul's warnings are especially relevant for today. Some people claiming special authority from God take advantage of those who are ungrounded in the faith. As Paul cautioned Timothy to "keep your head in all situations" (2 Timothy 4:5), so should we. This is how we can deal with current fads and trends that seek to capture "itching ears" (2 Timothy 4:3) and dissuade us from building godly marriages.

1 Paul, an apostle of Christ Jesus by the will
of God, according to the promise of life
that is in Christ Jesus,

2To Timothy, my dear son:

Grace, mercy and peace from God the Father and Christ Jesus our Lord.

Encouragement to Be Faithful

3I thank God, whom I serve, as my forefathers did, with a clear conscience, as night and
day I constantly remember you in my prayers.
4Recalling your tears, I long to see you, so that
I may be filled with joy. 5I have been reminded
of your sincere faith, which first lived in your
grandmother Lois and in your mother Eunice
and, I am persuaded, now lives in you also.
6For this reason I remind you to fan into flame
the gift of God, which is in you through the
laying on of my hands. 7For God did not give
us a spirit of timidity, but a spirit of power, of
love and of self-discipline.

8So do not be ashamed to testify about our
Lord, or ashamed of me his prisoner. But join
with me in suffering for the gospel, by the
power of God, 9who has saved us and called
us to a holy life—not because of anything we
have done but because of his own purpose
and grace. This grace was given us in Christ
Jesus before the beginning of time, 10but it
has now been revealed through the appearing
of our Savior, Christ Jesus, who has destroyed
death and has brought life and immortality to
light through the gospel. 11And of this gospel
I was appointed a herald and an apostle and a
teacher. 12That is why I am suffering as I am.
Yet I am not ashamed, because I know whom
I have believed, and am convinced that he is
able to guard what I have entrusted to him
for that day.

13What you heard from me, keep as the
pattern of sound teaching, with faith and love
in Christ Jesus. 14Guard the good deposit that
was entrusted to you—guard it with the help
of the Holy Spirit who lives in us.

15You know that everyone in the province
of Asia has deserted me, including Phygelus
and Hermogenes.

16May the Lord show mercy to the household of Onesiphorus, because he often refreshed me and was not ashamed of my
chains. 17On the contrary, when he was in
Rome, he searched hard for me until he found
me. 18May the Lord grant that he will find
mercy from the Lord on that day! You know
very well in how many ways he helped me in
Ephesus.

2 You then, my son, be strong in the grace
that is in Christ Jesus. 2And the things
you have heard me say in the presence of
many witnesses entrust to reliable men who
will also be qualified to teach others. 3Endure
hardship with us like a good soldier of Christ
Jesus. 4No one serving as a soldier gets involved in civilian affairs—he wants to please
his commanding officer. 5Similarly, if anyone
competes as an athlete, he does not receive the
victor's crown unless he competes according to
the rules. 6The hardworking farmer should be
the first to receive a share of the crops. 7Reflect
on what I am saying, for the Lord will give you
insight into all this.

8Remember Jesus Christ, raised from the
dead, descended from David. This is my gospel, 9for which I am suffering even to the
point of being chained like a criminal. But
God's word is not chained. 10Therefore I endure everything for the sake of the elect, that
they too may obtain the salvation that is in
Christ Jesus, with eternal glory.

11Here is a trustworthy saying:

If we died with him,
  we will also live with him;
12if we endure,
  we will also reign with him.
If we disown him,
  he will also disown us;
13if we are faithless,
  he will remain faithful,
  for he cannot disown himself.

A Workman Approved by God

14Keep reminding them of these things.
Warn them before God against quarreling
about words; it is of no value, and only ruins those who listen. 15Do your best to present
yourself to God as one approved, a workman
who does not need to be ashamed and who
correctly handles the word of truth. 16Avoid
godless chatter, because those who indulge
in it will become more and more ungodly.
17Their teaching will spread like gangrene.
Among them are Hymenaeus and Philetus,
18who have wandered away from the truth.
They say that the resurrection has already tak-
en place, and they destroy the faith of some.
19Nevertheless, God's solid foundation stands
firm, sealed with this inscription: "The Lord
knows those who are his,"[a] and, "Everyone

a 19 Num. 16:5 (see Septuagint)

MONDAY

READ 2 TIMOTHY 2:14–26

AVOIDING GODLESS CHATTER

> **Avoid godless chatter, because those who indulge in it will become more and more ungodly.**
>
> — 2 TIMOTHY 2:16

When we were kids, my buddies and I did our version of scientific experiments on salamanders. If we cut off a piece of tail, the salamander would grow a new one. If we cut off a leg, the salamander would regenerate itself. No matter how we hacked away at the little lizards, they continued to survive, dropping a piece of dead flesh here or there, then regenerating as they slithered along.

I get that image in my mind when I read Paul's words in 2 Timothy 2:16. When we gossip, we're a lot like slimy salamanders, slinking around corners, depositing bits of rotting tissue, and growing new "tales" to carry us along.

"Godless chatter" is important to think about in all our relationships, but it holds special significance for marriages. The more we interact with each other, the more potential we have for either encouraging or discouraging each other. We can affirm each other's choices or erode each other's spirits with silly suspicions, nagging or doubts.

What is the antidote to godless chatter? Indiana University sociologist Dr. Donna Eder, after three years of investigation, said that a word spoken against another human being is not usually the starting point of gossip. Many negative judgments we make about other people are true: a man may indeed be "a slob," a girl may certainly show signs of "conceit," a driver may well make a "stupid" lane change. Our evaluation of these people is not, in and of itself, wrong. Nor does it constitute gossip.

After all, said Dr. Eder, the ability to be moral beings is what defines the soul of humanity over against the animal kingdom. If we are to understand the morality of our own lives, we must also be able to evaluate the ethical behavior of others.

But there are various ways to react to someone else's harsh assessment of another person: we can choose not to respond (in which case the matter most often dies); we can rebuff the negative judgment and argue about whose perception is accurate; or we can affirm the nasty chatter and add to it. It is only when a second person picks up the negative baton and starts running with it that gossip begins.

Godless chatter is an option, not a necessity. It begins when I take someone else's story and add weight to it. Likewise, it stops when I carry it no further. We have a choice in the matter, Paul said. And the choice begins at home. We can indulge in gossip and become more ungodly, or we can end it and extend grace instead of a critical spirit toward others, thereby growing in godliness with our gracious Savior, Jesus Christ, and with each other.

—WAYNE BROUWER

let's talk

- ✦ What happens when one of us repeats a nasty bit of information about someone? Does the other spread it or squelch it?
- ✦ How do we speak about each other to others? If we were to evaluate our comments or responses, from 1 (negative) to 10 (positive), what would be an average tally on a typical day?
- ✦ What are some fundamental rules of communication that we might adopt to make our talk more beneficial to the kingdom of God and to the health of our home?

FOR YOUR NEXT DEVOTIONAL READING, TURN TO PAGE 1380.

who confesses the name of the Lord must turn
away from wickedness."
20In a large house there are articles not
only of gold and silver, but also of wood and
clay; some are for noble purposes and some
for ignoble. 21If a man cleanses himself from
the latter, he will be an instrument for noble
purposes, made holy, useful to the Master and
prepared to do any good work.
22Flee the evil desires of youth, and pursue righteousness, faith, love and peace, along
with those who call on the Lord out of a pure
heart. 23Don't have anything to do with foolish and stupid arguments, because you know
they produce quarrels. 24And the Lord's servant must not quarrel; instead, he must be
kind to everyone, able to teach, not resentful.
25Those who oppose him he must gently instruct, in the hope that God will grant them
repentance leading them to a knowledge of
the truth, 26and that they will come to their
senses and escape from the trap of the devil,
who has taken them captive to do his will.

Godlessness in the Last Days

3 But mark this: There will be terrible times
in the last days. 2People will be lovers of
themselves, lovers of money, boastful,
proud, abusive, disobedient to their parents,
ungrateful, unholy, 3without love, unforgiv-
ing, slanderous, without self-control, brutal,
not lovers of the good, 4treacherous, rash,
conceited, lovers of pleasure rather than lovers of God— 5having a form of godliness but
denying its power. Have nothing to do with
them.
6They are the kind who worm their way
into homes and gain control over weak-willed
women, who are loaded down with sins and
are swayed by all kinds of evil desires, 7al-
ways learning but never able to acknowledge
the truth. 8Just as Jannes and Jambres opposed Moses, so also these men oppose the
truth—men of depraved minds, who, as far as
the faith is concerned, are rejected. 9But they
will not get very far because, as in the case of
those men, their folly will be clear to everyone.

Paul's Charge to Timothy

10You, however, know all about my teaching, my way of life, my purpose, faith, patience, love, endurance, 11persecutions, sufferings—what kinds of things happened to me in
Antioch, Iconium and Lystra, the persecutions
I endured. Yet the Lord rescued me from all of
them. 12In fact, everyone who wants to live a
godly life in Christ Jesus will be persecuted,
13while evil men and impostors will go from
bad to worse, deceiving and being deceived.
14But as for you, continue in what you have
learned and have become convinced of, because you know those from whom you learned
it, 15and how from infancy you have known
the holy Scriptures, which are able to make
you wise for salvation through faith in Christ
Jesus. 16All Scripture is God-breathed and is
useful for teaching, rebuking, correcting and
training in righteousness, 17so that the man of
God may be thoroughly equipped for every
good work.

4 In the presence of God and of Christ Jesus,
who will judge the living and the dead, and
in view of his appearing and his kingdom,
I give you this charge: 2Preach the Word; be
prepared in season and out of season; correct,
rebuke and encourage—with great patience
and careful instruction. 3For the time will
come when men will not put up with sound
doctrine. Instead, to suit their own desires,
they will gather around them a great number
of teachers to say what their itching ears want
to hear. 4They will turn their ears away from
the truth and turn aside to myths. 5But you,
keep your head in all situations, endure hardship, do the work of an evangelist, discharge
all the duties of your ministry.
6For I am already being poured out like
a drink offering, and the time has come for
my departure. 7I have fought the good fight,
I have finished the race, I have kept the faith.
8Now there is in store for me the crown of
righteousness, which the Lord, the righteous
Judge, will award to me on that day—and not
only to me, but also to all who have longed for
his appearing.

Personal Remarks

9Do your best to come to me quickly, 10for
Demas, because he loved this world, has deserted me and has gone to Thessalonica. Cres-
cens has gone to Galatia, and Titus to Dalma-
tia. 11Only Luke is with me. Get Mark and
bring him with you, because he is helpful to
me in my ministry. 12I sent Tychicus to Ephesus. 13When you come, bring the cloak that I
left with Carpus at Troas, and my scrolls, especially the parchments.
14Alexander the metalworker did me a
great deal of harm. The Lord will repay him
for what he has done. 15You too should be on
your guard against him, because he strongly
opposed our message.
16At my first defense, no one came to my

TUESDAY
READ 2 TIMOTHY 4:9–18

NO REASON TO PRETEND

Only Luke is with me. Get Mark and bring him with you, because he is helpful to me in my ministry.

— 2 TIMOTHY 4:11

let's talk

- ✦ God uses imperfect people. What imperfections of ours is he using to help others?
- ✦ Let's talk about some areas of strength and weakness in our marriage. How has God worked through our weaknesses?
- ✦ How can our marriage be a testimony to others? In what areas could we use help?

When a well-known pastor was exposed for his sexual immorality, his wife said to their church congregation, "For those of you who have been concerned that my marriage was so perfect that I could not possibly relate to women who are facing great difficulties, know that this will never again be the case."

It drew laughs, but probably also sighs of relief. A common misconception among unbelievers is that being a Christian means you have to be perfect, or at least close to perfect. Some believers even think this, and they feel uneasy or inadequate and thus keep their real selves hidden from others.

The late Michael Yaconelli addressed this issue in *Messy Spirituality*. He wrote, "There is no room for pretending in the spiritual life. Unfortunately, in many religious circles, there exists an unwritten rule. Pretend. Act like God is in control when you don't believe he is. Give the impression everything is okay in your life when it's not. Pretend you believe when you doubt; hide your imperfections; maintain the image of a perfect marriage with healthy and well-adjusted children when your family is like any other normal dysfunctional family."

The reality is that no one is perfect. Some of us have financial debt and wayward kids. Some of us are loud and obnoxious, ill mannered, inarticulate, self-centered or addicted. However, all of us who are born-again believers in Jesus have been forgiven, have been given Christ's righteousness and are increasingly being made more like him as time progresses. That's our hope!

The apostle Paul wrote in his second letter to Timothy that he wanted Mark to come to him and assist him. He said of Mark, "He is helpful to me in my ministry." It was not uncommon for Paul to commend a fellow worker, but what is amazing in this instance is that Paul and Mark had previously had a falling out. Mark (also known as John) had deserted Paul and Barnabas on their first missionary journey (see Acts 13:13). After Paul refused to take Mark on the second journey, Barnabas separated from Paul, taking Mark with him on a mission to Cyprus (see Acts 15:36–40).

Whatever the cause for Mark's desertion, he later proved himself. And Paul forgave him and welcomed him back. Mark overcame his shortcomings and ended up having a powerful ministry. He even has a Gospel attributed to him (the Gospel of Mark). Mark made mistakes, but he rose above them and didn't let them stop him from going on to be a leader in the early church.

In this life we will struggle with sin. Our marriages and families will never be perfect, but because of our relationship with Christ, we have a God who cares for us, a Savior who walks with us, and the Holy Spirit who gives us comfort, wisdom and power.

For our marriages and our lives to be a testimony to others, they don't need to be perfect, just authentic. That means letting others see our sin (they see it anyway) and also our repentance, our struggles and our dependence on Christ. That's the truest testimony we can give.

—NANCY KENNEDY

FOR YOUR NEXT DEVOTIONAL READING, TURN TO PAGE 1384.

support, but everyone deserted me. May it not
be held against them. [17]But the Lord stood at
my side and gave me strength, so that through
me the message might be fully proclaimed and
all the Gentiles might hear it. And I was delivered from the lion's mouth. [18]The Lord will
rescue me from every evil attack and will bring
me safely to his heavenly kingdom. To him be
glory for ever and ever. Amen.

Final Greetings

[19]Greet Priscilla[a] and Aquila and the
household of Onesiphorus. [20]Erastus stayed
in Corinth, and I left Trophimus sick in Miletus. [21]Do your best to get here before winter.
Eubulus greets you, and so do Pudens, Linus,
Claudia and all the brothers.

[22]The Lord be with your spirit. Grace be
with you.

a *19* Greek *Prisca,* a variant of *Priscilla*

TITUS

Titus

QUICK FACTS

AUTHOR The apostle Paul

AUDIENCE Titus, a Greek Christian (and then, through him, the believers in Crete)

DATE Probably about A.D. 64

SETTING Paul had left Titus in charge of the churches on the Mediterranean island of Crete.

Titus was no stranger to difficult situations in the church. He was present for some of the first controversies in Christianity. He accompanied Paul to Jerusalem for the earliest debates about circumcision, and he served as an intermediary to the church in Corinth after false teachers undermined Paul's authority there.

But Titus had his work cut out for him on the island of Crete. The churches there needed leaders, heresy was making inroads, and the values of the Cretan culture were seeping into the churches. Into this desperate situation Paul instructed Titus to work, not with great speeches in the marketplace, but in the homes of believers. Paul advised Titus to focus on character development, such as marital fidelity, gentleness, self-control and respect for authority.

Marriage can bring out the best and worst in a person. We all know how an under-the-breath comment can cause pain. And as dishonesty, selfishness and reckless living can kill a church, so too can they kill a marriage. Titus shows us that building up our character isn't optional; it is vital to the health of all our relationships, starting with marriage.

1 Paul, a servant of God and an apostle of Jesus Christ for the faith of God's elect and the knowledge of the truth that leads to godliness— [2]a faith and knowledge resting on the hope of eternal life, which God, who does not lie, promised before the beginning of time, [3]and at his appointed season he brought his word to light through the preaching entrusted to me by the command of God our Savior,

[4]To Titus, my true son in our common faith:

Grace and peace from God the Father and Christ Jesus our Savior.

Titus's Task on Crete

[5]The reason I left you in Crete was that you might straighten out what was left unfinished and appoint[a] elders in every town, as I directed you. [6]An elder must be blameless, the husband of but one wife, a man whose children believe and are not open to the charge of being wild and disobedient. [7]Since an overseer[b] is entrusted with God's work, he must be blameless—not overbearing, not quick-tempered, not given to drunkenness, not violent, not pursuing dishonest gain. [8]Rather he must be hospitable, one who loves what is good, who is self-controlled, upright, holy and disciplined. [9]He must hold firmly to the trustworthy message as it has been taught, so that he can encourage others by sound doctrine and refute those who oppose it.

[10]For there are many rebellious people, mere talkers and deceivers, especially those of the circumcision group. [11]They must be silenced, because they are ruining whole households by teaching things they ought not to teach—and that for the sake of dishonest gain. [12]Even one of their own prophets has said, "Cretans are always liars, evil brutes, lazy gluttons." [13]This testimony is true. Therefore, rebuke them sharply, so that they will be sound in the faith [14]and will pay no attention to Jewish myths or to the commands of those who reject the truth. [15]To the pure, all things are pure, but to those who are corrupted and do not believe, nothing is pure. In fact, both their minds and consciences are corrupted. [16]They claim to know God, but by their actions they deny him. They are detestable, disobedient and unfit for doing anything good.

What Must Be Taught to Various Groups

2 You must teach what is in accord with sound doctrine. [2]Teach the older men to be temperate, worthy of respect, self-controlled, and sound in faith, in love and in endurance.

[3]Likewise, teach the older women to be reverent in the way they live, not to be slanderers or addicted to much wine, but to teach what is good. [4]Then they can train the younger women to love their husbands and children, [5]to be self-controlled and pure, to be busy at home, to be kind, and to be subject to their husbands, so that no one will malign the word of God.

[6]Similarly, encourage the young men to be self-controlled. [7]In everything set them an example by doing what is good. In your teaching show integrity, seriousness [8]and soundness of speech that cannot be condemned, so that those who oppose you may be ashamed because they have nothing bad to say about us.

[9]Teach slaves to be subject to their masters in everything, to try to please them, not to talk back to them, [10]and not to steal from them, but to show that they can be fully trusted, so that in every way they will make the teaching about God our Savior attractive.

[11]For the grace of God that brings salvation has appeared to all men. [12]It teaches us to say "No" to ungodliness and worldly passions, and to live self-controlled, upright and godly lives in this present age, [13]while we wait for the blessed hope—the glorious appearing of our great God and Savior, Jesus Christ, [14]who gave himself for us to redeem us from all wickedness and to purify for himself a people that are his very own, eager to do what is good.

[15]These, then, are the things you should teach. Encourage and rebuke with all authority. Do not let anyone despise you.

Doing What Is Good

3 Remind the people to be subject to rulers and authorities, to be obedient, to be ready to do whatever is good, [2]to slander no one, to be peaceable and considerate, and to show true humility toward all men.

[3]At one time we too were foolish, disobedient, deceived and enslaved by all kinds of passions and pleasures. We lived in malice and envy, being hated and hating one another. [4]But when the kindness and love of God our Savior appeared, [5]he saved us, not be-

[a] 5 Or *ordain* [b] 7 Traditionally *bishop*

WEDNESDAY

READ TITUS 2:1–15

WHEN MENTORS FAIL

There's nothing sadder than watching a Christian couple stumble. Friends of ours are still reeling from the experience.

When Mikal and Char became engaged, they asked another couple at our church to mentor them. The two couples would get together for dinner every few weeks to talk about the realities of married life, discuss questions Mikal and Char had, and strengthen an already solid friendship with the understanding that Mikal and Char would continue to need support during their first year of marriage.

Shortly after Mikal and Char's wedding, their mentor couple announced that they were separating because of the husband's infidelity. This revelation truly came out of nowhere for Mikal and Char. They thought they knew this couple. They had shared their private fears and struggles with this couple. They had been as open and honest as they knew how to be and trusted that the other couple had done the same. But during all that time, the marriage they believed to be so solid was crumbling.

Needless to say, Mikal and Char were devastated.

Many of us know about the benefits of mentors and role models. Even when we don't have formal mentoring relationships, most of us can name a person or two whom we admire and learn from. And Titus 2 reminds us that mentoring isn't just a good idea; it's an essential element of Christian community. Paul was telling older women to mentor younger women, to teach them how to participate in godly living. But Paul also acknowledged that older women are not inherently paragons of virtue. They need to work on it.

Teach the older women to be reverent in the way they live . . . Then they can train the younger women to love their husbands and children, to be self-controlled and pure, to be busy at home, to be kind, and to be subject to their husbands, so that no one will malign the word of God.

— Titus 2:3–5

let's *talk*

- ✦ What are the benefits of meeting with a mentor couple? What couples have a marriage we could learn from? What people seem to have similar issues or personalities as ours? How honest could we be with another couple?
- ✦ How can we show other people a real marriage instead of a facade of perfection? How could that benefit us and others?
- ✦ What balance do we need between being open and maintaining trust and privacy in our relationship?

There's good advice here for both mentors and those they mentor. Mentors need to take care that they are living open and honest lives before they endeavor to help others. They don't have to have all the answers, but they do need to be aware of the questions.

We also need to have realistic expectations of our mentors. There's nothing like having the support of people who understand the challenges and frustrations of married life. Yet we have to remember that every marriage and every person is imperfect.

Thankfully, God is the master of using our imperfections for good. Rather than looking to other couples solely for advice on how to have model marriages, we can also look to each other for examples of grace in the midst of turmoil, forgiveness in the midst of failure, and trust in the midst of betrayal. Often, those who have struggled the most have the wisest perspective on how to help a marriage thrive when real life hits it hard. Those are the stories that can serve as a lifeline when circumstances threaten to pull our marriages under.

—CARLA BARNHILL

FOR YOUR NEXT DEVOTIONAL READING, TURN TO PAGE 1386.

cause of righteous things we had done, but
because of his mercy. He saved us through the
washing of rebirth and renewal by the Holy
Spirit, [6]whom he poured out on us generously through Jesus Christ our Savior, [7]so that,
having been justified by his grace, we might
become heirs having the hope of eternal life.
[8]This is a trustworthy saying. And I want you
to stress these things, so that those who have
trusted in God may be careful to devote themselves to doing what is good. These things are
excellent and profitable for everyone.

[9]But avoid foolish controversies and genealogies and arguments and quarrels about the
law, because these are unprofitable and useless.
[10]Warn a divisive person once; and then warn
him a second time. After that, have nothing
to do with him. [11]You may be sure that such
a man is warped and sinful; he is self-con-
demned.

Final Remarks

[12]As soon as I send Artemas or Tychicus to
you, do your best to come to me at Nicopolis,
because I have decided to winter there. [13]Do
everything you can to help Zenas the lawyer
and Apollos on their way and see that they
have everything they need. [14]Our people must
learn to devote themselves to doing what is
good, in order that they may provide for daily
necessities and not live unproductive lives.

[15]Everyone with me sends you greetings.
Greet those who love us in the faith.

Grace be with you all.

T **THURSDAY**
READ TITUS 3:1–11

OUR THIRST FOR SCANDAL

I have to admit it: I'm a scandalmonger. I have an insatiable appetite for having the scoop, the inside track, the story behind the story. I love knowing what no one else knows.

There's a sick kind of power in knowing about other people's problems. Maybe we're drawn to gossip and controversy because seeing what's wrong with others somehow makes us feel better about ourselves.

But then something strange happens: our perspective becomes skewed. I find that when I know too much about a conflict between spouses, that's all I can see. Or when I know one of my friends is fighting with a coworker, that's all we talk about. And in time, it isn't just my view of the people involved that gets messed up, but it's also my view of people in general. Not only do I not feel good about myself, but I don't feel good about *anyone*.

Dealing with false teachers was one of Paul's main concerns in his letter to Titus. Their effect upon the church was both doctrinal and relational. While there are some sins that hurt us as individuals, an unhealthy interest in controversies and quarrels tears apart communities. It pits us against each other. It makes us suspicious of each other. And Paul made it clear that we should stay clear of it.

An unhealthy interest in strife can also infect a marriage. Whether it's one partner's penchant for being an insider or the couple's tendency to argue about every little detail of life, we would do well to heed Paul's advice and break out of those destructive habits.

One couple I know—let's call them Carla and Jim—have a reputation among their friends as "the Bickersons." Sadly, there's a good deal of truth in that reputation. Jim and I are strong-willed, opinionated people who don't hesitate to tell each other when they're wrong, when they're doing something we wouldn't do or when they've made a mistake. Sometimes we catch ourselves before our bickering becomes a habit, but now and then we devolve into weeks of sniping and griping. Before long, we don't feel good about each other, our marriage or ourselves.

It's easy to focus our attention on the negative, whether it's in our partner, our marriage or our friends. But we have been created for something better. We are meant to shine God's light into the lives of others. Of course, there will be times when we must step into painful conversations to offer our love and support to friends who are struggling. But God's light illuminates the dark places. It offers the hope of rescue and renewal. And every time we join in slander, gossip or petty arguments, we dim that light a little.

That's a lesson we scandalmongers can't learn soon enough.

—CARLA BARNHILL

But avoid foolish controversies and genealogies and arguments and quarrels about the law, because these are unprofitable and useless.

— TITUS 3:9

let's *talk*

- In what ways do we indulge in scandalmongering? How do we harm ourselves or others by doing that?
- Let's set some boundaries regarding how we talk about our marital problems with friends. How much information is too much? Who are the people we both trust with this kind of information? What people are off limits?
- How can our marriage be a source of light for others? What are our strengths as a couple? What do we bring to our church and community that helps build it up rather than break it down?

FOR YOUR NEXT DEVOTIONAL READING, TURN TO PAGE 1389.

PHILEMON

Philemon

QUICK FACTS

AUTHOR The apostle Paul

AUDIENCE Philemon, who was a member of the Colossian church

DATE About A.D. 60

SETTING Paul wrote to his friend, Philemon, asking him to welcome back his runaway slave, Onesimus.

Onesimus, a slave, had run away from his owner, Philemon, who lived in Colossae. While in Rome, the runaway met Paul and was converted to Christianity. Paul wanted Onesimus to return to his master, but first he wrote a letter to Philemon to smooth the way.

Paul's diplomacy was flawless; while this was a personal letter, it was addressed to Philemon *and* the church that met in Philemon's house. Paul appealed to Philemon's character, mentioned his own situation (he was writing from prison), and drove his argument home by appealing to Christ's work in Philemon's life.

Paul's goal wasn't just to persuade Philemon to roll out the welcome mat for Onesimus. He actually urged Philemon to live out the principle that in Christ all people are equal; there is "neither slave nor free" (Galatians 3:28). For a slave owner it was unthinkable to welcome home a runaway slave as "a dear brother" (Philemon 16). Yet that is what Paul asked of Philemon.

In marriage we sometimes find ourselves a bit like Philemon; we think we have every earthly reason to feel self-righteous and withhold forgiveness from an errant spouse. But Jesus has leveled the playing field. As Paul taught, we all need grace, and we need to offer it to one another as God has offered it to us.

1Paul, a prisoner of Christ Jesus, and Timothy our brother,

To Philemon our dear friend and fellow
worker, 2to Apphia our sister, to Archippus
our fellow soldier and to the church that
meets in your home:

3Grace to you and peace from God our Father and the Lord Jesus Christ.

Thanksgiving and Prayer

4I always thank my God as I remember
you in my prayers, 5because I hear about your
faith in the Lord Jesus and your love for all
the saints. 6I pray that you may be active in
sharing your faith, so that you will have a full
understanding of every good thing we have in
Christ. 7Your love has given me great joy and
encouragement, because you, brother, have refreshed the hearts of the saints.

Paul's Plea for Onesimus

8Therefore, although in Christ I could be
bold and order you to do what you ought to
do, 9yet I appeal to you on the basis of love.
I then, as Paul—an old man and now also a
prisoner of Christ Jesus— 10I appeal to you
for my son Onesimus,[a] who became my son
while I was in chains. 11Formerly he was useless to you, but now he has become useful
both to you and to me.
12I am sending him—who is my very
heart—back to you. 13I would have liked to
keep him with me so that he could take your
place in helping me while I am in chains
for the gospel. 14But I did not want to do
anything without your consent, so that any
favor you do will be spontaneous and not
forced. 15Perhaps the reason he was separated from you for a little while was that you
might have him back for good— 16no longer as a slave, but better than a slave, as a
dear brother. He is very dear to me but even
dearer to you, both as a man and as a brother in the Lord.
17So if you consider me a partner, welcome
him as you would welcome me. 18If he has
done you any wrong or owes you anything,
charge it to me. 19I, Paul, am writing this
with my own hand. I will pay it back—not to
mention that you owe me your very self. 20I
do wish, brother, that I may have some benefit from you in the Lord; refresh my heart in
Christ. 21Confident of your obedience, I write
to you, knowing that you will do even more
than I ask.
22And one thing more: Prepare a guest
room for me, because I hope to be restored to
you in answer to your prayers.

23Epaphras, my fellow prisoner in Christ
Jesus, sends you greetings. 24And so do Mark,
Aristarchus, Demas and Luke, my fellow
workers.
25The grace of the Lord Jesus Christ be with
your spirit.

---

[a] 10 *Onesimus* means *useful.*

F

FRIDAY
READ PHILEMON 1–25

FINDING STRENGTH IN SUBMISSION

During the Reformation, when Martin Luther and Ulrich Zwingli were exchanging strong words about Biblical interpretations and ecclesiastical practices, Zwingli spent a troubled morning walking the mountain trails of his beloved Switzerland. From a distance he observed two goats making their way toward each other on a path barely stitched to the side of a cliff. It was obvious that these nimble creatures could not pass one another.

As the goats approached each other, each feinted a power move at the other in what looked like the beginning of a battle. In a surprise twist, however, one goat suddenly collapsed onto the narrow ledge so the other goat could walk over its back. Then each moved on.

Zwingli was impressed. Here was strength defined by submission. It allowed two opponents to survive a crisis so both could get on with more important things. Zwingli applied the lesson to his next encounter with Luther.

The same principle is evident in Paul's words to Philemon. Philemon's slave Onesimus had run away, met Paul in Rome and become a Christian. Now Paul was sending the slave back to his master, urging Philemon to receive Onesimus, not as mere property, but as a brother. Instead of butting heads with Philemon, Paul extended a hand of love. Was this a sign of weakness? Psychological manipulation?

Therefore, although in Christ I could be bold and order you to do what you ought to do, yet I appeal to you on the basis of love.

— Philemon 8–9

let's talk

- ✦ What do we tend to disagree about? What happens in our relationship whenever that topic comes up? How do our feelings get involved?
- ✦ When we disagree, does one of us generally dominate the other? What is dangerous about that? How could we change that pattern?
- ✦ How do we show our respect for one another when we disagree about something? If we videotaped one of our arguments and showed it to a friend or a marriage counselor, what would they say?

Both possibilities and a variety of others enter a marital relationship. Sometimes we badger one another. Sometimes, like goats poised for battle on a mountain trail, we come close to butting heads. Sometimes we spit and snarl and lash out. Sometimes we sit together and lovingly hash things out.

What is helpful and healthy in good relationships is honesty. Not just truthfulness that blurts out every last thought, but self-awareness that is not deceptive. It is as important that I learn to be honest with myself as it is to be truthful with my partner. If Paul was in touch with his own thoughts and feelings when he wrote to Philemon, he could state his case without deploying manipulative or subversive tactics. He could focus on Philemon's well-being and circumstances while maintaining his own perspective.

Too often we allow our emotions to derail relationships because we are blinded by excessive self-importance. The strength of our emotions, especially when we are at odds with each other, inflates our tendency for self-preservation and diminishes our sense of the other's importance in our lives. We need to keep relationships personal and issues impersonal as we build faithfulness with one another.

Disagreements are inevitable in any relationship. But the ways in which we work through them can bind us more tightly together in love. Paul's kindness to Philemon offers a very good example to follow.

—WAYNE BROUWER

FOR YOUR NEXT DEVOTIONAL READING, TURN TO PAGE 1392.

HEBREWS

Hebrews

QUICK FACTS

AUTHOR Unknown

AUDIENCE Hebrew Christians

DATE Sometime before the destruction of the temple in Jerusalem in A.D. 70

SETTING Jewish Christians were being persecuted, probably by both Jews and Romans, and were growing weary.

The book of Hebrews is about the supremacy of Christ over angels, over Moses, over the priests, over the sacrifices that were offered in the Jerusalem temple and over suffering. It was a timely message for its first audience, men and women who were under persecution for their faith, some of whom, the letter tells us, were walking away from their faith altogether.

For the Hebrew believers who were at their breaking point, the author provided strength to endure. He didn't tell them to run from their sufferings or go underground; he didn't tell them that their hardships weren't real. He simply reminded them of what they believed—that Christ is supreme. And he showed them how they were to live: imitating the faith of their spiritual mothers and fathers, and the faith of Jesus himself. The author concluded his letter with some very concrete instructions.

One of those instructions is this: "Marriage should be honored by all, and the marriage bed kept pure" (Hebrews 13:4). The author realized the temptation to neglect marriage during difficult times. But he also stressed the point that strong marriages build up faith. They are places of prayer, praise and encouragement when anxieties and insecurities run high.

The Son Superior to Angels

1 In the past God spoke to our forefathers
through the prophets at many times and in
various ways, 2but in these last days he has
spoken to us by his Son, whom he appointed heir of all things, and through whom he
made the universe. 3The Son is the radiance
of God's glory and the exact representation of
his being, sustaining all things by his powerful
word. After he had provided purification for
sins, he sat down at the right hand of the Majesty in heaven. 4So he became as much superior to the angels as the name he has inherited
is superior to theirs.

5For to which of the angels did God ever
say,

"You are my Son;
today I have become your Father[a]"[b]?

Or again,

"I will be his Father,
and he will be my Son"[c]?

6And again, when God brings his firstborn
into the world, he says,

"Let all God's angels worship him."[d]

7In speaking of the angels he says,

"He makes his angels winds,
his servants flames of fire."[e]

8But about the Son he says,

"Your throne, O God, will last for ever
and ever,
and righteousness will be the scepter of
your kingdom.
9You have loved righteousness and hated
wickedness;
therefore God, your God, has set you
above your companions
by anointing you with the oil of joy."[f]

10He also says,

"In the beginning, O Lord, you laid the
foundations of the earth,
and the heavens are the work of your
hands.
11They will perish, but you remain;
they will all wear out like a garment.
12You will roll them up like a robe;
like a garment they will be changed.
But you remain the same,
and your years will never end."[g]

13To which of the angels did God ever say,

"Sit at my right hand
until I make your enemies
a footstool for your feet"[h]?

14Are not all angels ministering spirits sent to
serve those who will inherit salvation?

Warning to Pay Attention

2 We must pay more careful attention, therefore, to what we have heard, so that we do
not drift away. 2For if the message spoken by
angels was binding, and every violation and disobedience received its just punishment, 3how
shall we escape if we ignore such a great salvation? This salvation, which was first announced
by the Lord, was confirmed to us by those who
heard him. 4God also testified to it by signs,
wonders and various miracles, and gifts of the
Holy Spirit distributed according to his will.

Jesus Made Like His Brothers

5It is not to angels that he has subjected the
world to come, about which we are speaking.
6But there is a place where someone has testified:

"What is man that you are mindful of
him,
the son of man that you care for him?
7You made him a little[i] lower than the
angels;
you crowned him with glory and honor
8 and put everything under his feet."[j]

In putting everything under him, God left
nothing that is not subject to him. Yet at present we do not see everything subject to him.
9But we see Jesus, who was made a little lower than the angels, now crowned with glory
and honor because he suffered death, so that
by the grace of God he might taste death for
everyone.

10In bringing many sons to glory, it was fitting that God, for whom and through whom
everything exists, should make the author
of their salvation perfect through suffering.
11Both the one who makes men holy and
those who are made holy are of the same family. So Jesus is not ashamed to call them brothers. 12He says,

"I will declare your name to my brothers;
in the presence of the congregation I
will sing your praises."[k]

[a] 5 Or *have begotten you* [b] 5 Psalm 2:7 [c] 5 2 Samuel 7:14; 1 Chron. 17:13 [d] 6 Deut. 32:43 (see Dead Sea Scrolls and Septuagint) [e] 7 Psalm 104:4 [f] 9 Psalm 45:6,7 [g] 12 Psalm 102:25-27 [h] 13 Psalm 110:1 [i] 7 Or *him for a little while*; also in verse 9 [j] 8 Psalm 8:4-6 [k] 12 Psalm 22:22

WEEKEND

time for us

Busy people rarely give their best to the ones they love. They serve leftovers. We're not talking about the kind that come from your fridge. We're talking about the emotional and relational leftovers—the ones that remain after the prime energy and attention has already been given to others. This is sometimes known as sunset fatigue. It's when we are too drained, too tired or too preoccupied to be fully present with the one we love the most. They get what's left over. And a marriage cannot survive on leftovers.

Here's a little trick we learned from our friend John Maxwell. He's one of the most productive men we know, but he makes a conscious effort to give his best time to his wife, Margaret. He told us, "Years ago when something exciting happened during the day, I'd share it with colleagues and friends. By the time I got home, I had little enthusiasm for sharing it with Margaret." He went on to say, "I purposely began keeping things to myself until I could share them with her first. That way she never got the leftovers." Of course, this goes for more than just sharing news from our own day. We give our best to our spouse when we give them attention and energy for the things they'd like to talk about as well.

One of the most difficult things some people ever have to do is say no. Yet this little word is one of your strongest weapons in the war against busyness. If you don't believe us, we've got to tell you that we've seen people literally collapse from fatigue, drown in depression, and develop debilitating illnesses because they never said no. Some physicians even call cancer "the disease of nice people."

Surgeon Bernie Siegel tells about one of his cancer patients who never said no. She began to improve after she finally told her boss that she could no longer work extra hours whenever he asked. She began to reclaim her time. Siegel said, "People who neglect their own needs are the ones who are most likely to become ill. For them the main problem often is learning to say no without feeling guilty."

If you suffer from the disease to please, treat it seriously and assert yourself. Begin by making a list of things that you have on your plate right now that you'd like to say no to. Discuss them with your spouse or someone else you respect. Chances are he or she can coach you on wielding the mighty power of this little word.

John Ortberg, author of *The Life You've Always Wanted*, writes about getting some spiritual direction from a wise friend shortly after moving to Chicago to become preaching pastor at the megasize Willow Creek Community Church. "I described [to my friend] the pace at which things tend to move in my current setting," John writes. "Then I asked, 'What do I need to do to be spiritually healthy?' "

After a quiet moment, his friend finally spoke: "You must ruthlessly eliminate hurry from your life."

Another long pause.

"Okay, I've written that one down," John had a lot to do, and he was talking to his friend long-distance, so, as he puts it, "I was anxious to cram as many units of spiritual wisdom into the least amount of time as possible."

"There is nothing else," his wise friend said. "You must ruthlessly eliminate hurry from your life."

That's it. His spiritual mentor could have given him a laundry list of things to do that would have aligned his spirit with the Almighty. But he didn't need to. There's nothing else but to eliminate hurry from your life.

—DR. LES PARROTT III AND DR. LESLIE PARROTT

HOW ARE WE DOING?

how busy are you?

1. What makes you feel most busy?
2. In what areas of your life do you most often feel that you must pedal faster and faster to keep up? Why?
3. Busyness can negatively affect four areas: your conversations, your love life, your ability to have fun and your spirituality. Which of these four areas is the most negatively affected by your busyness? In what ways?
4. What one thing can each of you do individually to battle busyness? How can you put it into practice?
5. What one thing can you do as a couple to battle busyness? How can you put it into practice?

let's make a DATE

A DATE OFF THE CLOCK

This weekend find something fun to do together that doesn't have a beginning or an ending. Get lost in an activity—walking around a lake, exploring a small town, checking out a flea market—without worrying about the time or how long you spend doing it. If you have children and have time constraints related to them, consider swapping babysitting with another busy couple. Then use your free time to forget about the clock for a few hours.

FOR YOUR NEXT DEVOTIONAL READING, TURN TO PAGE 1395.

LESSONS FROM THE *Bible*

Read 1 Peter 4:7–8.

1. How does recognizing that "the end of all things is near" affect our view of spending time together as a couple?
2. In what ways can we be "alert and of sober mind"? How will that help us pray together? Grow spiritually? Spend more time together?

13And again,

"I will put my trust in him."[a]

And again he says,

"Here am I, and the children God has
given me."[b]

14Since the children have flesh and blood,
he too shared in their humanity so that by his
death he might destroy him who holds the
power of death—that is, the devil— 15and free
those who all their lives were held in slavery by
their fear of death. 16For surely it is not angels
he helps, but Abraham's descendants. 17For
this reason he had to be made like his brothers
in every way, in order that he might become a
merciful and faithful high priest in service to
God, and that he might make atonement for[c]
the sins of the people. 18Because he himself
suffered when he was tempted, he is able to
help those who are being tempted.

Jesus Greater Than Moses

3 Therefore, holy brothers, who share in
the heavenly calling, fix your thoughts on
Jesus, the apostle and high priest whom we
confess. 2He was faithful to the one who appointed him, just as Moses was faithful in all
God's house. 3Jesus has been found worthy of
greater honor than Moses, just as the builder
of a house has greater honor than the house itself. 4For every house is built by someone, but
God is the builder of everything. 5Moses was
faithful as a servant in all God's house, testifying to what would be said in the future. 6But
Christ is faithful as a son over God's house.
And we are his house, if we hold on to our
courage and the hope of which we boast.

Warning Against Unbelief

7So, as the Holy Spirit says:

"Today, if you hear his voice,
8 do not harden your hearts
as you did in the rebellion,
during the time of testing in the desert,
9 where your fathers tested and tried me
and for forty years saw what I did.
10 That is why I was angry with that
generation,
and I said, 'Their hearts are always
going astray,
and they have not known my ways.'
11 So I declared on oath in my anger,
'They shall never enter my rest.' "[d]

12See to it, brothers, that none of you has a
sinful, unbelieving heart that turns away from
the living God. 13But encourage one another
daily, as long as it is called Today, so that none
of you may be hardened by sin's deceitfulness.
14We have come to share in Christ if we hold
firmly till the end the confidence we had at
first. 15As has just been said:

"Today, if you hear his voice,
do not harden your hearts
as you did in the rebellion."[e]

16Who were they who heard and rebelled?
Were they not all those Moses led out of
Egypt? 17And with whom was he angry for
forty years? Was it not with those who sinned,
whose bodies fell in the desert? 18And to
whom did God swear that they would never
enter his rest if not to those who disobeyed[f]?
19So we see that they were not able to enter,
because of their unbelief.

A Sabbath-Rest for the People of God

4 Therefore, since the promise of entering his
rest still stands, let us be careful that none
of you be found to have fallen short of it.
2For we also have had the gospel preached to
us, just as they did; but the message they heard
was of no value to them, because those who
heard did not combine it with faith.[g] 3Now
we who have believed enter that rest, just as
God has said,

"So I declared on oath in my anger,
'They shall never enter my rest.' "[h]

And yet his work has been finished since the
creation of the world. 4For somewhere he has
spoken about the seventh day in these words:
"And on the seventh day God rested from all
his work."[i] 5And again in the passage above he
says, "They shall never enter my rest."

6It still remains that some will enter that
rest, and those who formerly had the gospel
preached to them did not go in, because of
their disobedience. 7Therefore God again set a
certain day, calling it Today, when a long time
later he spoke through David, as was said before:

"Today, if you hear his voice,
do not harden your hearts."[e]

8For if Joshua had given them rest, God would
not have spoken later about another day.
9There remains, then, a Sabbath-rest for the

[a] 13 Isaiah 8:17 [b] 13 Isaiah 8:18 [c] 17 Or *and that he might turn aside God's wrath, taking away* [d] 11 Psalm 95:7-11
[e] 15,7 Psalm 95:7,8 [f] 18 Or *disbelieved* [g] 2 Many manuscripts *because they did not share in the faith of those who obeyed*
[h] 3 Psalm 95:11; also in verse 5 [i] 4 Gen. 2:2

MONDAY
READ HEBREWS 2:5–18

OUR LIFELINE IN TEMPTATION

In our society, there's a tendency to work alone, play alone and *be* alone. Our extended families live far from us. We don't know the neighbors who live just across the street. We tend not to make eye contact when we're on the bus or walking down the sidewalk.

In the 1990s, people began referring to our tendency to insulate ourselves at home as "cocooning." According to the last U.S. census, almost 20 percent of us work at home at least part of the time, something that was unheard of a generation ago. Restaurant take-outs continue to rise; we either pick up meals or have them delivered. We don't even have to leave our houses to see a movie; we can download what we want onto our computers, order them through cable television, or head to the home theater in our basements.

We're even ending our lives alone. A chaplain in a nursing home says he estimates 50 percent of the residents have no one at their bedside when they die.

So when troubles and temptations come our way, it's natural for us, even as couples, to cry out, "But you can't know what it's like! No one else is going through this!" It's true that everyone faces a unique set of problems. As couples, we face different problems than our friends or family members do.

However, the writer of Hebrews says we are not alone in our trials. There is someone who knows what we are going through because he has dealt with those troubles too. Our Lord Jesus Christ suffered hunger and thirst. He knew the pain of a friend's betrayal. He confronted Satan and temptation. He endured the excruciating pain of death on a cross.

When we as couples face the trials of marriage—discouragement, mounting debt, boredom, disenchantment with our spouse—Jesus is there. When we face the temptation of looking outside our marriage for validation, treating our spouse as a paycheck instead of as part of us, or doing our own thing rather than submitting to each other, Jesus is there.

Jesus understood our human struggles when he was on earth. But today, as he sits at the right hand of his heavenly Father, he can still fully relate to what we are going through. When he intercedes for us to the Father, he does so with the intimate knowledge of the kinds of struggles we face (see Hebrews 4:14–16; 7:23–25). And the best part is, through his sacrifice these issues have already been met and conquered.

We don't need to suffer alone, either as individuals or as a couple. There is a third person in our relationship who not only helps us but also empathizes with our pain. Jesus will carry our burdens.

—VALERIE VAN KOOTEN

Because [Jesus] himself suffered when he was tempted, he is able to help those who are being tempted.

— HEBREWS 2:18

let's talk

✦ How alone are we as a couple? What relationships are important to us and bind us to others in our church, neighborhood or workplace?

✦ What problems or temptations have we faced in our marriage? Have we tried to carry them alone, or have we brought them to Jesus?

✦ How does knowing that Jesus was fully human help us endure the problems we face individually and as a couple?

FOR YOUR NEXT DEVOTIONAL READING, TURN TO PAGE 1396.

TUESDAY
READ HEBREWS 4:1–16

AIRING THE SECRETS

> **Nothing in all creation is hidden from God's sight. Everything is uncovered and laid bare before the eyes of him to whom we must give account.**
>
> — Hebrews 4:13

let's talk

- When have we found a certain sin hiding in one of us? How did we discover it?
- How should we approach Bible reading and study so that God can show us the secrets of our hearts? How could we help each other?
- What is one area we each want to bring to Christ's throne of grace for help?

"*If there are* rats in a cellar you are most likely to see them if you go in very suddenly," wrote C. S. Lewis in *Mere Christianity.* "But the suddenness does not create the rats: it only prevents them from hiding." Lewis was writing about the ratlike secrets of our hearts that we can usually hide until some sudden provocation brings them out into the open. Lewis continued, "Apparently the rats of resentment and vindictiveness are always there in the cellar of my soul. [But] that cellar is out of reach of my conscious will. I can to some extent control my acts: I have no direct control over my temperament."

In a strong marriage, couples share secrets. But what about the secrets we keep from each other, as well as ourselves, and the lies we tell about what we're really like, what we treasure, what we hunger for?

Look at Hebrews 4:13. The rats within us cannot hide from God's sight. What's more, we must give full account for what God's eyes see.

As ominous as that sounds, baring secrets to each other in marriage is really good news. Rooting out our souls' vermin encourages healthier people and healthier marriages.

But what can you do if even *you* don't see the secrets of your heart? Hebrews 4 tells us three things we can do to expose our rats. First, verse 12 tells us that the Word of God uncovers secrets like a surgeon's scalpel exposes hidden cancer. When we read the Bible and look carefully at ourselves in its mirror (see James 1:23–25), we begin to see ourselves as we really are. God's ancient words speak frankly about our personal secrets. So as we regularly read Scripture, we see our hearts in its mirror.

God's word also comes to us in a living relationship with Jesus Christ. Through his Holy Spirit within us, Jesus prompts us to begin thinking more seriously about some fault or weakness, perhaps through a sermon we hear, a book we're reading or often through the insights of our spouse.

Second, verse 7 tells us that we are not to harden our hearts against God's message. When Israel heard the word of God, the people hardened their hearts against it (see Psalm 95:7–8). The rats stayed in their cellar. When God speaks to us of our sin, weakness or need, we are to welcome his words with soft, receptive hearts (see Psalm 139:23–24).

Even if we see our inward sin and yearn to change, that won't happen without the third step (see verses 14–16). Only Jesus Christ can exterminate the rats in our hearts. To begin with, he understands the frustration of tender hearts that want to be rid of sin and secrets but are helpless to do so. More than that, he invites us to his throne, where grace is freely dispensed to his loved ones. We receive mercy so that our sins can be forgiven, and we find grace to help us overcome them.

In marriage we often catch a glimpse of the rats in our *spouse's* cellar and take it upon ourselves to exterminate them. But such a job is usually out of our league. A better choice is to cultivate a relationship in which we tune in to the Word of God so we can help one another develop soft, sensitive hearts and pray with each other so that Jesus himself might cleanse the scurrying, disease-carrying secrets away.

—LEE ECLOV

FOR YOUR NEXT DEVOTIONAL READING, TURN TO PAGE 1399.

people of God; [10]for anyone who enters God's rest also rests from his own work, just as God did from his. [11]Let us, therefore, make every effort to enter that rest, so that no one will fall by following their example of disobedience.

[12]For the word of God is living and active. Sharper than any double-edged sword, it penetrates even to dividing soul and spirit, joints and marrow; it judges the thoughts and attitudes of the heart. [13]Nothing in all creation is hidden from God's sight. Everything is uncovered and laid bare before the eyes of him to whom we must give account.

Jesus the Great High Priest

[14]Therefore, since we have a great high priest who has gone through the heavens,[a] Jesus the Son of God, let us hold firmly to the faith we profess. [15]For we do not have a high priest who is unable to sympathize with our weaknesses, but we have one who has been tempted in every way, just as we are—yet was without sin. [16]Let us then approach the throne of grace with confidence, so that we may receive mercy and find grace to help us in our time of need.

5 Every high priest is selected from among men and is appointed to represent them in matters related to God, to offer gifts and sacrifices for sins. [2]He is able to deal gently with those who are ignorant and are going astray, since he himself is subject to weakness. [3]This is why he has to offer sacrifices for his own sins, as well as for the sins of the people.

[4]No one takes this honor upon himself; he must be called by God, just as Aaron was. [5]So Christ also did not take upon himself the glory of becoming a high priest. But God said to him,

> "You are my Son;
> today I have become your Father.[b]"[c]

[6]And he says in another place,

> "You are a priest forever,
> in the order of Melchizedek."[d]

[7]During the days of Jesus' life on earth, he offered up prayers and petitions with loud cries and tears to the one who could save him from death, and he was heard because of his reverent submission. [8]Although he was a son, he learned obedience from what he suffered [9]and, once made perfect, he became the source of eternal salvation for all who obey him [10]and was designated by God to be high priest in the order of Melchizedek.

Warning Against Falling Away

[11]We have much to say about this, but it is hard to explain because you are slow to learn. [12]In fact, though by this time you ought to be teachers, you need someone to teach you the elementary truths of God's word all over again. You need milk, not solid food! [13]Anyone who lives on milk, being still an infant, is not acquainted with the teaching about righteousness. [14]But solid food is for the mature, who by constant use have trained themselves to distinguish good from evil.

6 Therefore let us leave the elementary teachings about Christ and go on to maturity, not laying again the foundation of repentance from acts that lead to death,[e] and of faith in God, [2]instruction about baptisms, the laying on of hands, the resurrection of the dead, and eternal judgment. [3]And God permitting, we will do so.

[4]It is impossible for those who have once been enlightened, who have tasted the heavenly gift, who have shared in the Holy Spirit, [5]who have tasted the goodness of the word of God and the powers of the coming age, [6]if they fall away, to be brought back to repentance, because[f] to their loss they are crucifying the Son of God all over again and subjecting him to public disgrace.

[7]Land that drinks in the rain often falling on it and that produces a crop useful to those for whom it is farmed receives the blessing of God. [8]But land that produces thorns and thistles is worthless and is in danger of being cursed. In the end it will be burned.

[9]Even though we speak like this, dear friends, we are confident of better things in your case—things that accompany salvation. [10]God is not unjust; he will not forget your work and the love you have shown him as you have helped his people and continue to help them. [11]We want each of you to show this same diligence to the very end, in order to make your hope sure. [12]We do not want you to become lazy, but to imitate those who through faith and patience inherit what has been promised.

The Certainty of God's Promise

[13]When God made his promise to Abraham, since there was no one greater for him to swear by, he swore by himself, [14]saying, "I

---

[a] *14* Or *gone into heaven* [b] *5* Or *have begotten you* [c] *5* Psalm 2:7 [d] *6* Psalm 110:4 [e] *1* Or *from useless rituals* [f] *6* Or *repentance while*

will surely bless you and give you many descendants."[a] [15]And so after waiting patiently, Abraham received what was promised.

[16]Men swear by someone greater than themselves, and the oath confirms what is said and puts an end to all argument. [17]Because God wanted to make the unchanging nature of his purpose very clear to the heirs of what was promised, he confirmed it with an oath. [18]God did this so that, by two unchangeable things in which it is impossible for God to lie, we who have fled to take hold of the hope offered to us may be greatly encouraged. [19]We have this hope as an anchor for the soul, firm and secure. It enters the inner sanctuary behind the curtain, [20]where Jesus, who went before us, has entered on our behalf. He has become a high priest forever, in the order of Melchizedek.

Melchizedek the Priest

7 This Melchizedek was king of Salem and priest of God Most High. He met Abraham returning from the defeat of the kings and blessed him, [2]and Abraham gave him a tenth of everything. First, his name means "king of righteousness"; then also, "king of Salem" means "king of peace." [3]Without father or mother, without genealogy, without beginning of days or end of life, like the Son of God he remains a priest forever.

[4]Just think how great he was: Even the patriarch Abraham gave him a tenth of the plunder! [5]Now the law requires the descendants of Levi who become priests to collect a tenth from the people—that is, their brothers—even though their brothers are descended from Abraham. [6]This man, however, did not trace his descent from Levi, yet he collected a tenth from Abraham and blessed him who had the promises. [7]And without doubt the lesser person is blessed by the greater. [8]In the one case, the tenth is collected by men who die; but in the other case, by him who is declared to be living. [9]One might even say that Levi, who collects the tenth, paid the tenth through Abraham, [10]because when Melchizedek met Abraham, Levi was still in the body of his ancestor.

Jesus Like Melchizedek

[11]If perfection could have been attained through the Levitical priesthood (for on the basis of it the law was given to the people), why was there still need for another priest to come—one in the order of Melchizedek, not in the order of Aaron? [12]For when there is a change of the priesthood, there must also be a change of the law. [13]He of whom these things are said belonged to a different tribe, and no one from that tribe has ever served at the altar. [14]For it is clear that our Lord descended from Judah, and in regard to that tribe Moses said nothing about priests. [15]And what we have said is even more clear if another priest like Melchizedek appears, [16]one who has become a priest not on the basis of a regulation as to his ancestry but on the basis of the power of an indestructible life. [17]For it is declared:

"You are a priest forever,
  in the order of Melchizedek."[b]

[18]The former regulation is set aside because it was weak and useless [19](for the law made nothing perfect), and a better hope is introduced, by which we draw near to God.

[20]And it was not without an oath! Others became priests without any oath, [21]but he became a priest with an oath when God said to him:

"The Lord has sworn
  and will not change his mind:
'You are a priest forever.' "[b]

[22]Because of this oath, Jesus has become the guarantee of a better covenant.

[23]Now there have been many of those priests, since death prevented them from continuing in office; [24]but because Jesus lives forever, he has a permanent priesthood. [25]Therefore he is able to save completely[c] those who come to God through him, because he always lives to intercede for them.

[26]Such a high priest meets our need—one who is holy, blameless, pure, set apart from sinners, exalted above the heavens. [27]Unlike the other high priests, he does not need to offer sacrifices day after day, first for his own sins, and then for the sins of the people. He sacrificed for their sins once for all when he offered himself. [28]For the law appoints as high priests men who are weak; but the oath, which came after the law, appointed the Son, who has been made perfect forever.

The High Priest of a New Covenant

8 The point of what we are saying is this: We do have such a high priest, who sat down at the right hand of the throne of the Majesty

---

[a] *14* Gen. 22:17 [b] *17,21* Psalm 110:4 [c] *25* Or *forever*

WEDNESDAY
READ HEBREWS 5:11—6:12

OVERCOMING WEDDED BLAH

We do not want you to become lazy, but to imitate those who through faith and patience inherit what has been promised.

— Hebrews 6:12

let's talk

- ✦ Why are affection and romance important in marriage?
- ✦ How can laziness affect our feelings toward each other?
- ✦ What are ways that we can work through seasons of feeling blah toward one another?

Because no one had warned me, I was shocked the first time it happened, and then I panicked. We had only been married a few months, maybe a year (it was so long ago that I don't remember exactly), when I discovered that I was no longer wildly in love with my husband. I didn't feel much of anything. To me, he was just a hairy roommate. A nice guy and all, but . . .

I didn't tell anyone how I felt but resigned myself to a lifetime sentence of a passionless marriage, at least on my part. I felt trapped and bewildered, scared and guilty. I didn't think married people were supposed to feel "blah" toward their spouses, and I thought something was terribly wrong with me. I remember thinking, "Is this the end?"

After what seemed like decades (although it was probably more like days or weeks), my feelings of dullness and disinterest passed and once again the sight of my husband's biceps thrilled me. Crisis averted.

Fast-forward to the present. We've lived through and survived many seasons of feeling like roommates. My husband sometimes feels the same way about me. Maybe it's laziness, hormones, the weather or busyness. I don't know. I just know that I don't like it when it happens. Yet I also know that the blahs will pass. They always do. That said, I can't simply sit back and do nothing during such times.

In Hebrews 6:12, the writer admonished his readers not to become lazy. Prior to that, he told them to "show this same diligence to the very end, in order to make your hope sure" (Hebrews 6:11).

The writer was talking about matters of faith and being diligent in one's relationship with Christ. But the same principle can apply to marriage. You don't need diligence to get through easy times or even really hard times. You need diligence when you'd rather curl up with a book than your spouse.

In *A Celebration of Sex*, Douglas Rosenau tells those who feel out of love that God has given us a rational mind and the capacity to choose behaviors that lead to loving feelings. "Attitudes and behaviors are the basis of feeling in love and not some mysterious chemistry of feelings that you cannot control," he says.

Attitudes are fed by thoughts. So, whenever I recognize a season of blah feelings toward my husband, I immediately ask God to redirect my thoughts. I keep a running mental list of things I like and admire about him. Then I work on my behaviors: I consciously do something to move toward him, like make a favorite meal or talk to him while he's shaving—anything to connect.

Before long the blah feelings turn, not always to bliss, but to a deeper sense of contentment with the one I love.

—NANCY KENNEDY

FOR YOUR NEXT DEVOTIONAL READING, TURN TO PAGE 1402.

in heaven, 2and who serves in the sanctuary,
the true tabernacle set up by the Lord, not by
man.
3Every high priest is appointed to offer both
gifts and sacrifices, and so it was necessary for
this one also to have something to offer. 4If
he were on earth, he would not be a priest,
for there are already men who offer the gifts
prescribed by the law. 5They serve at a sanctuary that is a copy and shadow of what is in
heaven. This is why Moses was warned when
he was about to build the tabernacle: "See to
it that you make everything according to the
pattern shown you on the mountain."[a] 6But
the ministry Jesus has received is as superior to
theirs as the covenant of which he is mediator
is superior to the old one, and it is founded on
better promises.
7For if there had been nothing wrong with
that first covenant, no place would have been
sought for another. 8But God found fault with
the people and said[b]:

"The time is coming, declares the Lord,
when I will make a new covenant
with the house of Israel
and with the house of Judah.
9It will not be like the covenant
I made with their forefathers
when I took them by the hand
to lead them out of Egypt,
because they did not remain faithful to my
covenant,
and I turned away from them,
declares the Lord.
10This is the covenant I will make with the
house of Israel
after that time, declares the Lord.
I will put my laws in their minds
and write them on their hearts.
I will be their God,
and they will be my people.
11No longer will a man teach his neighbor,
or a man his brother, saying, 'Know the
Lord,'
because they will all know me,
from the least of them to the greatest.
12For I will forgive their wickedness
and will remember their sins no
more."[c]

13By calling this covenant "new," he has
made the first one obsolete; and what is obsolete and aging will soon disappear.

Worship in the Earthly Tabernacle

9 Now the first covenant had regulations
for worship and also an earthly sanctuary.
2A tabernacle was set up. In its first room
were the lampstand, the table and the consecrated bread; this was called the Holy Place.
3Behind the second curtain was a room called
the Most Holy Place, 4which had the golden
altar of incense and the gold-covered ark of
the covenant. This ark contained the gold jar
of manna, Aaron's staff that had budded, and
the stone tablets of the covenant. 5Above the
ark were the cherubim of the Glory, overshadowing the atonement cover.[d] But we cannot
discuss these things in detail now.
6When everything had been arranged like
this, the priests entered regularly into the
outer room to carry on their ministry. 7But
only the high priest entered the inner room,
and that only once a year, and never without blood, which he offered for himself and
for the sins the people had committed in ignorance. 8The Holy Spirit was showing by
this that the way into the Most Holy Place
had not yet been disclosed as long as the first
tabernacle was still standing. 9This is an illustration for the present time, indicating that
the gifts and sacrifices being offered were not
able to clear the conscience of the worshiper.
10They are only a matter of food and drink
and various ceremonial washings—external
regulations applying until the time of the
new order.

The Blood of Christ

11When Christ came as high priest of the
good things that are already here,[e] he went
through the greater and more perfect tabernacle that is not man-made, that is to say, not
a part of this creation. 12He did not enter by
means of the blood of goats and calves; but
he entered the Most Holy Place once for all
by his own blood, having obtained eternal redemption. 13The blood of goats and bulls and
the ashes of a heifer sprinkled on those who
are ceremonially unclean sanctify them so that
they are outwardly clean. 14How much more,
then, will the blood of Christ, who through
the eternal Spirit offered himself unblemished
to God, cleanse our consciences from acts that
lead to death,[f] so that we may serve the living God!
15For this reason Christ is the mediator of a
new covenant, that those who are called may
receive the promised eternal inheritance—

---

[a] 5 Exodus 25:40 [b] 8 Some manuscripts may be translated *fault and said to the people.* [c] 12 Jer. 31:31-34 [d] 5 Traditionally *the mercy seat* [e] 11 Some early manuscripts *are to come* [f] 14 Or *from useless rituals*

now that he has died as a ransom to set them
free from the sins committed under the first
covenant.
16 In the case of a will,[a] it is necessary to
prove the death of the one who made it, 17 because a will is in force only when somebody
has died; it never takes effect while the one
who made it is living. 18 This is why even the
first covenant was not put into effect without
blood. 19 When Moses had proclaimed every
commandment of the law to all the people,
he took the blood of calves, together with water, scarlet wool and branches of hyssop, and
sprinkled the scroll and all the people. 20 He
said, "This is the blood of the covenant, which
God has commanded you to keep."[b] 21 In the
same way, he sprinkled with the blood both
the tabernacle and everything used in its ceremonies. 22 In fact, the law requires that nearly
everything be cleansed with blood, and without the shedding of blood there is no forgiveness.
23 It was necessary, then, for the copies of
the heavenly things to be purified with these
sacrifices, but the heavenly things themselves
with better sacrifices than these. 24 For Christ
did not enter a man-made sanctuary that was
only a copy of the true one; he entered heaven
itself, now to appear for us in God's presence.
25 Nor did he enter heaven to offer himself
again and again, the way the high priest enters
the Most Holy Place every year with blood
that is not his own. 26 Then Christ would have
had to suffer many times since the creation
of the world. But now he has appeared once
for all at the end of the ages to do away with
sin by the sacrifice of himself. 27 Just as man
is destined to die once, and after that to face
judgment, 28 so Christ was sacrificed once to
take away the sins of many people; and he will
appear a second time, not to bear sin, but to
bring salvation to those who are waiting for
him.

Christ's Sacrifice Once for All

10 The law is only a shadow of the good
things that are coming—not the realities themselves. For this reason it can
never, by the same sacrifices repeated endlessly
year after year, make perfect those who draw
near to worship. 2 If it could, would they not
have stopped being offered? For the worshipers would have been cleansed once for all, and
would no longer have felt guilty for their sins.
3 But those sacrifices are an annual reminder of
sins, 4 because it is impossible for the blood of
bulls and goats to take away sins.
5 Therefore, when Christ came into the
world, he said:

"Sacrifice and offering you did not desire,
but a body you prepared for me;
6 with burnt offerings and sin offerings
you were not pleased.
7 Then I said, 'Here I am—it is written
about me in the scroll—
I have come to do your will,
O God.'"[c]

8 First he said, "Sacrifices and offerings, burnt
offerings and sin offerings you did not desire,
nor were you pleased with them" (although
the law required them to be made). 9 Then he
said, "Here I am, I have come to do your will."
He sets aside the first to establish the second.
10 And by that will, we have been made holy
through the sacrifice of the body of Jesus
Christ once for all.
11 Day after day every priest stands and performs his religious duties; again and again he
offers the same sacrifices, which can never take
away sins. 12 But when this priest had offered
for all time one sacrifice for sins, he sat down
at the right hand of God. 13 Since that time he
waits for his enemies to be made his footstool,
14 because by one sacrifice he has made perfect
forever those who are being made holy.
15 The Holy Spirit also testifies to us about
this. First he says:

16 "This is the covenant I will make with
them
after that time, says the Lord.
I will put my laws in their hearts,
and I will write them on their minds."[d]

17 Then he adds:

"Their sins and lawless acts
I will remember no more."[e]

18 And where these have been forgiven, there is
no longer any sacrifice for sin.

A Call to Persevere

19 Therefore, brothers, since we have confidence to enter the Most Holy Place by the
blood of Jesus, 20 by a new and living way
opened for us through the curtain, that is, his
body, 21 and since we have a great priest over
the house of God, 22 let us draw near to God
with a sincere heart in full assurance of faith,
having our hearts sprinkled to cleanse us from

[a] *16* Same Greek word as *covenant*; also in verse 17 [b] *20* Exodus 24:8 [c] *7* Psalm 40:6-8 (see Septuagint) [d] *16* Jer. 31:33
[e] *17* Jer. 31:34

THURSDAY
READ HEBREWS 10:1–39

TENDING EACH OTHER'S WOUNDS

The book of Hebrews was written to Christians who were facing persecution. Though evidently none of them had as yet been martyred because of their faith (see Hebrews 12:4), a number had been jailed or had their property confiscated (see Hebrews 10:34).

Most of the believers addressed in Hebrews had converted to Christianity from Judaism. Now, because of persecution, they were being pressured to return to Judaism. Some went along with the change, reasoning that the commandments and teachings of the Hebrew religion were the same as that of Christianity, but without Jesus.

The writer of Hebrews urged these believers to recognize that no faith is complete without Jesus. To turn away from Jesus is to cut out the very heart of Christianity.

Still, the threat of further persecution was real. Things would get very difficult for the believers. The writer of this letter responded to this threat by reminding his readers, first of all, that Jesus had endured hardships and persecution and therefore understood what they were going through. Jesus would provide them with divine assistance and encouragement, no matter how severe their suffering. Second, they could not make it on their own; they needed to help one another, precisely because of the tough times ahead.

Let us consider how we may spur one another on toward love and good deeds. Let us not give up meeting together, as some are in the habit of doing, but let us encourage one another.

— Hebrews 10:24–25

let's *talk*

- ✦ How do we encourage each other? When have we failed to do so?
- ✦ Am I more of a giver or a taker? How might each of us become better at offering encouragement to the other?
- ✦ What are we doing to encourage others? Do people sense strength radiating from our relationship—a strength that supports them as well? How does that happen?

That is good advice for spouses who need to encourage one another, particularly in times of crisis, such as financial hardship, relationship challenges, infertility issues or painful losses. No matter what happens or how badly we are hurt, the only way to triumph over trial is to be anchored in Christ and each other.

Years ago, anthropologist Margaret Mead was asked by a student what she considered to be the first sign of civilization in a culture. The student expected Mead to talk about fishhooks or clay pots or grinding stones. But no. Mead said that the first sign of civilization in an ancient culture was a femur (thighbone) that had been broken and then healed.

Mead explained that in the animal kingdom if you break your leg, you die. You cannot run from danger, get to the river for a drink or hunt for food. You are meat for prowling beasts. No animal survives a broken leg long enough for the bone to heal.

A broken femur that has healed is evidence that someone has taken time to stay with the one who fell, has bound up the wound, has carried the person to safety and has tended the person through recovery. Helping someone else through difficulty is where civilization starts, Mead said.

That sounds a lot like the gospel, doesn't it? Jesus died for our sins when we were still sinners. He is our comfort and salvation when we are broken and dying. He is our lifeline in suffering. Now, as the writer of Hebrews said, we get to do the same for one another.

—WAYNE BROUWER

FOR YOUR NEXT DEVOTIONAL READING, TURN TO PAGE 1404.

a guilty conscience and having our bodies
washed with pure water. 23Let us hold un-
swervingly to the hope we profess, for he who
promised is faithful. 24And let us consider
how we may spur one another on toward love
and good deeds. 25Let us not give up meeting
together, as some are in the habit of doing,
but let us encourage one another—and all the
more as you see the Day approaching.

26If we deliberately keep on sinning after
we have received the knowledge of the truth,
no sacrifice for sins is left, 27but only a fearful expectation of judgment and of raging fire
that will consume the enemies of God. 28Any-
one who rejected the law of Moses died without mercy on the testimony of two or three
witnesses. 29How much more severely do you
think a man deserves to be punished who has
trampled the Son of God under foot, who has
treated as an unholy thing the blood of the
covenant that sanctified him, and who has insulted the Spirit of grace? 30For we know him
who said, "It is mine to avenge; I will repay,"[a]
and again, "The Lord will judge his people."[b]
31It is a dreadful thing to fall into the hands of
the living God.

32Remember those earlier days after you
had received the light, when you stood your
ground in a great contest in the face of suffering. 33Sometimes you were publicly exposed
to insult and persecution; at other times you
stood side by side with those who were so
treated. 34You sympathized with those in
prison and joyfully accepted the confiscation of your property, because you knew that
you yourselves had better and lasting possessions.

35So do not throw away your confidence;
it will be richly rewarded. 36You need to persevere so that when you have done the will of
God, you will receive what he has promised.
37For in just a very little while,

"He who is coming will come and will not
delay.
38 But my righteous one[c] will live by
faith.
And if he shrinks back,
I will not be pleased with him."[d]

39But we are not of those who shrink back and
are destroyed, but of those who believe and
are saved.

By Faith

11 Now faith is being sure of what we hope
for and certain of what we do not see.
2This is what the ancients were commended for.

3By faith we understand that the universe
was formed at God's command, so that what
is seen was not made out of what was visible.

4By faith Abel offered God a better sacrifice
than Cain did. By faith he was commended
as a righteous man, when God spoke well of
his offerings. And by faith he still speaks, even
though he is dead.

5By faith Enoch was taken from this life, so
that he did not experience death; he could not
be found, because God had taken him away.
For before he was taken, he was commended
as one who pleased God. 6And without faith
it is impossible to please God, because anyone
who comes to him must believe that he exists
and that he rewards those who earnestly seek
him.

7By faith Noah, when warned about things
not yet seen, in holy fear built an ark to save
his family. By his faith he condemned the
world and became heir of the righteousness
that comes by faith.

8By faith Abraham, when called to go to a
place he would later receive as his inheritance,
obeyed and went, even though he did not
know where he was going. 9By faith he made
his home in the promised land like a stranger
in a foreign country; he lived in tents, as did
Isaac and Jacob, who were heirs with him of
the same promise. 10For he was looking forward to the city with foundations, whose ar-
chitect and builder is God.

11By faith Abraham, even though he was
past age—and Sarah herself was barren—was
enabled to become a father because he[e] considered him faithful who had made the promise. 12And so from this one man, and he as
good as dead, came descendants as numerous
as the stars in the sky and as countless as the
sand on the seashore.

13All these people were still living by faith
when they died. They did not receive the
things promised; they only saw them and welcomed them from a distance. And they admitted that they were aliens and strangers on
earth. 14People who say such things show that
they are looking for a country of their own.
15If they had been thinking of the country
they had left, they would have had opportuni-

[a] 30 Deut. 32:35 [b] 30 Deut. 32:36; Psalm 135:14 [c] 38 One early manuscript *But the righteous* [d] 38 Hab. 2:3,4 [e] 11 Or *By faith even Sarah, who was past age, was enabled to bear children because she*

FRIDAY

READ HEBREWS 11:1—12:3

CONQUERING FEARS IN MARRIAGE

Now faith is being sure of what we hope for and certain of what we do not see.

— Hebrews 11:1

let's talk

- What are the toughest choices or biggest risks we've ever had to take in our lives? In our marriage?
- What is our vision for our life together? What fears do we have? What hopes do we have?
- How can we help each other live like heroes of faith as we face fears and risks in the years to come?

It's scary to tell someone, "I love you." It's even more frightening to ask, "Will you marry me?"

Still even more terrifying is the answer: "Yes."

Think about the weak-in-the-knees words "I do" and what can follow them: buying a house, having children, moving the family to a different state, taking a new job . . . The list of intimidating, heart-pounding, fear-provoking aspects of marriage go on and on.

Responsibility really hit me when Kelli and I started having children. I thought, "Now, not only is my life inextricably linked to my wife's, and not only do I carry the responsibility of owning property, but now I am responsible for the well-being, provision and growth of other little human beings." What a scary thought!

It seems that in every new stage in life, the stakes get higher.

When you stop and think about it, though, *all* of the Christian life takes tremendous courage as we commit our lives to God and join others who are called to be God's people. Though we cannot see God, we can be confident of God's goodness, God's power, God's presence and God's wisdom. And yet we still must take that fearful first step of trust.

As Christians, we trust the unseen and base all our decisions about love and marriage on God's invisible reality and the promises he has made. To live the Christian life and to make choices (not only for me, but for my entire family) based on a God we can't see is tough. But the Bible tells us that this is the only wise choice to make.

As we look to Scripture for guidance, we can draw comfort and courage from heroes of faith such as Abel, Enoch, Noah, Abraham, Joseph, Moses and Rahab—people Søren Kierkegaard called the unsurpassed "Knights of Faith." After commending these and a few other Old Testament believers specifically (see Hebrews 11:4–31), the writer of Hebrews affirmed the many others who had faith to conquer kingdoms, administer justice, shut the mouths of lions and rout foreign armies (see Hebrews 11:32–38). These heroes weren't lauded because they were strong in themselves, but because they trusted God. They were weak as they considered the tasks ahead of them, but when they trusted God, he turned their weakness into strength.

Likewise we are to trust God as we face the risky and intimidating aspects of married life. For as Hebrews 12:1 assures us, we are surrounded by a great cloud of witnesses, and therefore we have the strength and courage to throw off everything that hinders us and move forward in love, confidence and trust. This is the unseen reality that makes sense of our choice to step forward into marriage despite our fears.

—DAVID AND KELLI TRUJILLO

FOR YOUR NEXT DEVOTIONAL READING, TURN TO PAGE 1406.

ty to return. 16Instead, they were longing for
a better country—a heavenly one. Therefore
God is not ashamed to be called their God, for
he has prepared a city for them.
17By faith Abraham, when God tested him,
offered Isaac as a sacrifice. He who had received
the promises was about to sacrifice his one and
only son, 18even though God had said to him,
"It is through Isaac that your offspring[a] will
be reckoned."[b] 19Abraham reasoned that God
could raise the dead, and figuratively speaking, he did receive Isaac back from death.
20By faith Isaac blessed Jacob and Esau in
regard to their future.
21By faith Jacob, when he was dying,
blessed each of Joseph's sons, and worshiped
as he leaned on the top of his staff.
22By faith Joseph, when his end was near,
spoke about the exodus of the Israelites from
Egypt and gave instructions about his bones.
23By faith Moses' parents hid him for three
months after he was born, because they saw
he was no ordinary child, and they were not
afraid of the king's edict.
24By faith Moses, when he had grown up,
refused to be known as the son of Pharaoh's
daughter. 25He chose to be mistreated along
with the people of God rather than to enjoy
the pleasures of sin for a short time. 26He regarded disgrace for the sake of Christ as of
greater value than the treasures of Egypt, because he was looking ahead to his reward. 27By
faith he left Egypt, not fearing the king's anger; he persevered because he saw him who is
invisible. 28By faith he kept the Passover and
the sprinkling of blood, so that the destroyer
of the firstborn would not touch the firstborn
of Israel.
29By faith the people passed through the
Red Sea[c] as on dry land; but when the Egyptians tried to do so, they were drowned.
30By faith the walls of Jericho fell, after the
people had marched around them for seven
days.
31By faith the prostitute Rahab, because she
welcomed the spies, was not killed with those
who were disobedient.[d]
32And what more shall I say? I do not have
time to tell about Gideon, Barak, Samson,
Jephthah, David, Samuel and the prophets,
33who through faith conquered kingdoms,
administered justice, and gained what was
promised; who shut the mouths of lions,
34quenched the fury of the flames, and escaped the edge of the sword; whose weakness was turned to strength; and who became
powerful in battle and routed foreign armies.
35Women received back their dead, raised to
life again. Others were tortured and refused
to be released, so that they might gain a better
resurrection. 36Some faced jeers and flogging,
while still others were chained and put in prison. 37They were stoned[e]; they were sawed in
two; they were put to death by the sword. They
went about in sheepskins and goatskins, destitute, persecuted and mistreated— 38the world
was not worthy of them. They wandered in
deserts and mountains, and in caves and holes
in the ground.
39These were all commended for their faith,
yet none of them received what had been
promised. 40God had planned something better for us so that only together with us would
they be made perfect.

God Disciplines His Sons

12 Therefore, since we are surrounded by
such a great cloud of witnesses, let us
throw off everything that hinders and
the sin that so easily entangles, and let us run
with perseverance the race marked out for
us. 2Let us fix our eyes on Jesus, the author
and perfecter of our faith, who for the joy set
before him endured the cross, scorning its
shame, and sat down at the right hand of the
throne of God. 3Consider him who endured
such opposition from sinful men, so that you
will not grow weary and lose heart.
4In your struggle against sin, you have not
yet resisted to the point of shedding your
blood. 5And you have forgotten that word of
encouragement that addresses you as sons:

"My son, do not make light of the Lord's
discipline,
and do not lose heart when he rebukes
you,
6because the Lord disciplines those he
loves,
and he punishes everyone he accepts as
a son."[f]

7Endure hardship as discipline; God is
treating you as sons. For what son is not disciplined by his father? 8If you are not disciplined (and everyone undergoes discipline),
then you are illegitimate children and not
true sons. 9Moreover, we have all had human
fathers who disciplined us and we respected them for it. How much more should we
submit to the Father of our spirits and live!

---

[a] 18 Greek *seed* [b] 18 Gen. 21:12 [c] 29 That is, Sea of Reeds [d] 31 Or *unbelieving* [e] 37 Some early manuscripts *stoned; they were put to the test;* [f] 6 Prov. 3:11,12

WEEKEND

children and marriage

Becoming a mom or dad changes who we are as individuals. For the wife, the change is both physical and emotional; her body is no longer her own but actually becomes womb, nest and food dispenser for a child. Her involuntary physical response to her child shocks her. Her milk flows at the sound of her child's cry, even in the middle of the shopping mall. At night, she bolts from deep sleep to complete consciousness when the baby whimpers. Instinctively, she reads the meaning of that cry, and adjusts her reaction accordingly. Her heart experiences an invasion of a new kind of consuming, protective love.

For the man, the change of identity is more gradual and often more external. On finding his wife pregnant, he alternately stoops under the heavy financial role that being a parent will require, and then struts with pride at his reproductive prowess. He will have a family! After witnessing the miraculous birth of his baby, he marvels at his response to both wife and child. The child promises him a future he'd never much considered. And his wife—wow! How incredible that she can do this "birth" thing! The instinctive hunter-gatherer part of him rises up to protect and provide for his new family.

Then he is struck with the reality of what he doesn't know and can't do. He wonders, "How does she know what cry means 'I'm wet' or 'I'm hungry'?" He concludes that his wife has some mysterious gift for parenthood that he lacks. As the years pass, he continues to explore his role as father, taking cues from his memories of his own father and other males around him, then testing out his assumptions on his own turf. Some attempts succeed; others are met with resistance from his wife. Sometimes a trickle of doubt runs through his mind as he wonders who he is becoming, and whether he has the stuff it takes to be both husband and father.

As alarming as the individual identity changes can be, the changes children bring to the husband and wife as a couple can be even more startling. Some of those changes:

- *Children mirror us.* In addition to giving us the opportunity to experience and express a rich, rewarding new kind of love, children can be like mirrors that reflect and reveal things about us to our selves and to our mates. Suddenly we see tenderness in a spouse we've never seen before. But we also come face-to-face with expressions of self-centeredness and confusing attitudes about male and female roles.
- *They bring family issues to the surface.* Issues concerning our family of origin continue throughout the lifetime of raising our children as the various ages and stages they go through continue to reveal unresolved issues from our own upbringing. In this way, children reveal us to ourselves at deeper and deeper levels.
- *They challenge our views about gender.* Gender differences, whether physiological, emotional, or otherwise, are reflected in how we relate to each other and to our world. But rather than stereotyping the differences or bashing them, we're wise to identify them in our own marriage relationship and respect them.
- *They broaden our personalities.* A schedule-oriented woman who delights in order and predictability and control usually discovers the need to be more flexible when she has a child. A stern, demanding man might soften with the presence of a newborn in his life. Children broaden the narrowness of our viewpoints, teach us about self-sacrifice, and stretch us to develop new aspects of our personalities.

—ELISA MORGAN AND CAROL KUYKENDALL

have children changed us?

Children bring great joy, but they also can make us feel tense, sad and inept. Talking about the changes together can help you to know that you're not alone in your feelings.

1. Since we've had a child, we make love:
   a. More often
   b. Less often
   c. Do what?
2. Future holiday plans include:
   a. Time off for rest and relaxation
   b. An intense time of spiritual growth
   c. Strategizing which grandmother gets to see the kids
3. Our date nights:
   a. Happen once a week if we can afford a sitter
   b. Include a little third person
   c. Date night? What's that?
4. A marriage retreat is:
   a. An opportunity to grow closer
   b. Something the church offers
   c. What happens when the baby sleeps late
5. Our biggest worry is:
   a. Loss of job
   b. Loss of limb
   c. Loss of child in the supermarket
6. Running errands means:
   a. Picking up dry cleaning
   b. Paying bills online
   c. Forty minutes of prep to get the child in a car seat before we can leave

HOW ARE WE DOING?

let's make a DATE

BE KIDS AGAIN

This weekend go to a museum, zoo or other fun spot without the kids. Spend as much time as you want at each exhibit or attraction. Stop at the gift shop on the way out and buy a postcard. When you get home, mail it to your spouse, thanking him or her for a great date.

FOR YOUR NEXT DEVOTIONAL READING, TURN TO PAGE 1409.

LESSONS FROM THE *Bible*

How do you suppose children changed the lives of the following couples? What were some of the lessons those couples might have learned?

1. Abraham and Sarah (Genesis 21:1–7)
2. Ruth and Boaz (Ruth 4:13–17)
3. Hannah and Elkanah (1 Samuel 1:1–20)

10Our fathers disciplined us for a little while as
they thought best; but God disciplines us for
our good, that we may share in his holiness.
11No discipline seems pleasant at the time, but
painful. Later on, however, it produces a harvest of righteousness and peace for those who
have been trained by it.

12Therefore, strengthen your feeble arms
and weak knees. 13"Make level paths for your
feet,"[a] so that the lame may not be disabled,
but rather healed.

Warning Against Refusing God

14Make every effort to live in peace with all
men and to be holy; without holiness no one
will see the Lord. 15See to it that no one misses
the grace of God and that no bitter root grows
up to cause trouble and defile many. 16See
that no one is sexually immoral, or is godless like Esau, who for a single meal sold his
inheritance rights as the oldest son. 17After-
ward, as you know, when he wanted to inherit
this blessing, he was rejected. He could bring
about no change of mind, though he sought
the blessing with tears.

18You have not come to a mountain that
can be touched and that is burning with fire;
to darkness, gloom and storm; 19to a trumpet blast or to such a voice speaking words
that those who heard it begged that no further word be spoken to them, 20because they
could not bear what was commanded: "If even
an animal touches the mountain, it must be
stoned."[b] 21The sight was so terrifying that
Moses said, "I am trembling with fear."[c]

22But you have come to Mount Zion, to the
heavenly Jerusalem, the city of the living God.
You have come to thousands upon thousands
of angels in joyful assembly, 23to the church
of the firstborn, whose names are written in
heaven. You have come to God, the judge of
all men, to the spirits of righteous men made
perfect, 24to Jesus the mediator of a new covenant, and to the sprinkled blood that speaks
a better word than the blood of Abel.

25See to it that you do not refuse him who
speaks. If they did not escape when they refused him who warned them on earth, how
much less will we, if we turn away from him
who warns us from heaven? 26At that time his
voice shook the earth, but now he has promised, "Once more I will shake not only the
earth but also the heavens."[d] 27The words
"once more" indicate the removing of what
can be shaken—that is, created things—so
that what cannot be shaken may remain.

28Therefore, since we are receiving a kingdom that cannot be shaken, let us be thankful,
and so worship God acceptably with reverence and awe, 29for our "God is a consuming
fire."[e]

Concluding Exhortations

13 Keep on loving each other as brothers.
2Do not forget to entertain strangers,
for by so doing some people have entertained angels without knowing it. 3Remember
those in prison as if you were their fellow prisoners, and those who are mistreated as if you
yourselves were suffering.

4Marriage should be honored by all, and the
marriage bed kept pure, for God will judge the
adulterer and all the sexually immoral. 5Keep
your lives free from the love of money and be
content with what you have, because God has
said,

> "Never will I leave you;
> never will I forsake you."[f]

6So we say with confidence,

> "The Lord is my helper; I will not be
> afraid.
> What can man do to me?"[g]

7Remember your leaders, who spoke the
word of God to you. Consider the outcome
of their way of life and imitate their faith.
8Jesus Christ is the same yesterday and today
and forever.

9Do not be carried away by all kinds of
strange teachings. It is good for our hearts to
be strengthened by grace, not by ceremonial
foods, which are of no value to those who eat
them. 10We have an altar from which those
who minister at the tabernacle have no right
to eat.

11The high priest carries the blood of animals into the Most Holy Place as a sin offering, but the bodies are burned outside the
camp. 12And so Jesus also suffered outside the
city gate to make the people holy through his
own blood. 13Let us, then, go to him outside
the camp, bearing the disgrace he bore. 14For
here we do not have an enduring city, but we
are looking for the city that is to come.

15Through Jesus, therefore, let us continually offer to God a sacrifice of praise—the fruit
of lips that confess his name. 16And do not

---

[a] 13 Prov. 4:26 [b] 20 Exodus 19:12,13 [c] 21 Deut. 9:19 [d] 26 Haggai 2:6 [e] 29 Deut. 4:24 [f] 5 Deut. 31:6 [g] 6 Psalm 118:6,7

MONDAY
READ HEBREWS 13:1–25

KEEPING MARRIAGE HOLY

Marriage should be honored by all, and the marriage bed kept pure, for God will judge the adulterer and all the sexually immoral.

— HEBREWS 13:4

I recently read about a Hollywood marriage in which the bride and groom promised to "love, honor and cherish as long as we still find each other attractive." If this weren't so sad, it would be funny. How long will each stay attractive? Will this marriage survive as the spouses age, get wrinkles and need dentures? Or will Botox and plastic surgery conquer all?

Odds are, this union is already in trouble.

Marriage is not something we enter into lightly, and it isn't something to be lightly discarded. The writer of Hebrews said that the state of marriage itself is to be honored by all.

Perhaps he wrote this in response to the beliefs of the Essenes, a Jewish sect that lived in a commune in the desert at the time the book of Hebrews was written. The Essenes believed they should remain celibate.

This passage contradicts such thinking. Marriage is valued as an honorable state to be revered by all. Even if our marriages, or those of our friends and family, aren't perfect, we should work to preserve them, encourage them and build them up.

Honoring each other may be difficult in a marriage that's being pulled apart at the seams. But no matter what challenge we are facing, we are instructed to keep our marriage in general, and our sex life ("the marriage bed") in particular, pure. Here are a few suggestions:

1. Be faithful to your spouse in word as well as deed. If things aren't going well in your marriage, carefully consider whom to share your burdens with. A professional or a friend who is available to mentor you are both good and safe places to share your pain and find encouragement.

2. Use common sense in relationships outside your marriage. If you are struggling in your marriage, you are particularly vulnerable. So set some boundaries regarding Internet use, office friendships or seemingly innocent meetings with members of the opposite sex. Be careful too whom you share your marital struggles with. Consider choosing a member of the same sex as a mentor or confidant.

3. Help preserve friends' and family members' marriages. When you attend a wedding as guests, you are giving your silent witness to the union—and you are also agreeing to assume responsibility for helping that couple keep their wedding vows. As you deal with challenges in your own marriage, you can, in turn, lend wisdom, help and encouragement to others who need advice or strength.

We're not in this alone. Hebrews 13:5 reminds us that God will always be with us: "Never will I leave you; never will I forsake you." By allowing just one "outsider" into the marriage—our Lord Jesus Christ—we set a firm foundation for keeping our marriages pure.

—VALERIE VAN KOOTEN

let's talk

✦ How do we balance the point in Hebrews 13:4 that "marriage should be honored by all" with Paul's encouragement for Christians to—like him—remain single (see 1 Corinthians 7:7–9,32–35)?

✦ What signs do we see that the world views marriage as something less than permanent?

✦ What are some boundaries we need to set in our marriage to keep us faithful to our vows?

FOR YOUR NEXT DEVOTIONAL READING, TURN TO PAGE 1413.

forget to do good and to share with others, for
with such sacrifices God is pleased.
17 Obey your leaders and submit to their
authority. They keep watch over you as men
who must give an account. Obey them so that
their work will be a joy, not a burden, for that
would be of no advantage to you.
18 Pray for us. We are sure that we have a
clear conscience and desire to live honorably
in every way. 19 I particularly urge you to pray
so that I may be restored to you soon.
20 May the God of peace, who through the
blood of the eternal covenant brought back
from the dead our Lord Jesus, that great Shepherd of the sheep, 21 equip you with everything
good for doing his will, and may he work in us
what is pleasing to him, through Jesus Christ,
to whom be glory for ever and ever. Amen.

22 Brothers, I urge you to bear with my
word of exhortation, for I have written you
only a short letter.
23 I want you to know that our brother Timothy has been released. If he arrives soon, I
will come with him to see you.
24 Greet all your leaders and all God's people. Those from Italy send you their greetings.
25 Grace be with you all.

JAMES

James

QUICK FACTS

AUTHOR James, the brother of Jesus and a leader of the early church in Jerusalem

AUDIENCE Jewish Christians scattered because of persecution

DATE Probably about A.D. 49

SETTING The former members of the Jerusalem church were scattered to various places because of persecution.

The book of James is about how to live the Christian life every day. It starts with instructions for how to live in the midst of trials and temptations, and it goes on to discuss several ways of putting faith into practice: listening before you act or speak, remembering to honor the poor, guarding your words, submitting yourselves completely to God and staying faithful—and prayerful—during times of trial.

The book of James is remarkably relevant to today's world, despite being written nearly 2,000 years ago. Then, as now, people blamed their shortcomings on God's lack of provision. Then, as now, people listened too slowly, spoke too quickly and were too easily angered. Then, as now, people exploited the poor, made plans with no consideration of God's will and dropped careless comments that caused incredible damage.

Nearly every paragraph in James's letter has wise principles that apply to marriage. Before we try to live out those principles in other relationships, let us align faith and deeds when we disagree with each other, when we make decisions about tomorrow and when we go through times of trial together.

1 James, a servant of God and of the Lord
Jesus Christ,

To the twelve tribes scattered among the
nations:

Greetings.

Trials and Temptations

2Consider it pure joy, my brothers, whenever you face trials of many kinds, 3because
you know that the testing of your faith develops perseverance. 4Perseverance must finish its work so that you may be mature and
complete, not lacking anything. 5If any of you
lacks wisdom, he should ask God, who gives
generously to all without finding fault, and it
will be given to him. 6But when he asks, he
must believe and not doubt, because he who
doubts is like a wave of the sea, blown and
tossed by the wind. 7That man should not
think he will receive anything from the Lord;
8he is a double-minded man, unstable in all
he does.
9The brother in humble circumstances
ought to take pride in his high position. 10But
the one who is rich should take pride in his
low position, because he will pass away like a
wild flower. 11For the sun rises with scorching
heat and withers the plant; its blossom falls
and its beauty is destroyed. In the same way,
the rich man will fade away even while he goes
about his business.
12Blessed is the man who perseveres under trial, because when he has stood the test,
he will receive the crown of life that God has
promised to those who love him.
13When tempted, no one should say, "God
is tempting me." For God cannot be tempted
by evil, nor does he tempt anyone; 14but each
one is tempted when, by his own evil desire,
he is dragged away and enticed. 15Then, after desire has conceived, it gives birth to sin;
and sin, when it is full-grown, gives birth to
death.
16Don't be deceived, my dear brothers.
17Every good and perfect gift is from above,
coming down from the Father of the heavenly
lights, who does not change like shifting shadows. 18He chose to give us birth through the
word of truth, that we might be a kind of firstfruits of all he created.

Listening and Doing

19My dear brothers, take note of this: Everyone should be quick to listen, slow to speak
and slow to become angry, 20for man's anger
does not bring about the righteous life that
God desires. 21Therefore, get rid of all moral
filth and the evil that is so prevalent and humbly accept the word planted in you, which can
save you.
22Do not merely listen to the word, and so
deceive yourselves. Do what it says. 23Anyone
who listens to the word but does not do what
it says is like a man who looks at his face in
a mirror 24and, after looking at himself, goes
away and immediately forgets what he looks
like. 25But the man who looks intently into
the perfect law that gives freedom, and continues to do this, not forgetting what he has
heard, but doing it—he will be blessed in
what he does.
26If anyone considers himself religious and
yet does not keep a tight rein on his tongue, he
deceives himself and his religion is worthless.
27Religion that God our Father accepts as pure
and faultless is this: to look after orphans and
widows in their distress and to keep oneself
from being polluted by the world.

Favoritism Forbidden

2 My brothers, as believers in our glorious
Lord Jesus Christ, don't show favoritism.
2Suppose a man comes into your meeting
wearing a gold ring and fine clothes, and a
poor man in shabby clothes also comes in. 3If
you show special attention to the man wearing fine clothes and say, "Here's a good seat
for you," but say to the poor man, "You stand
there" or "Sit on the floor by my feet," 4have
you not discriminated among yourselves and
become judges with evil thoughts?
5Listen, my dear brothers: Has not God
chosen those who are poor in the eyes of the
world to be rich in faith and to inherit the
kingdom he promised those who love him?
6But you have insulted the poor. Is it not the
rich who are exploiting you? Are they not the
ones who are dragging you into court? 7Are
they not the ones who are slandering the noble
name of him to whom you belong?
8If you really keep the royal law found in
Scripture, "Love your neighbor as yourself,"[a]
you are doing right. 9But if you show favoritism, you sin and are convicted by the law
as lawbreakers. 10For whoever keeps the whole
law and yet stumbles at just one point is guilty
of breaking all of it. 11For he who said, "Do
not commit adultery,"[b] also said, "Do not
murder."[c] If you do not commit adultery but

---

a 8 Lev. 19:18 *b 11* Exodus 20:14; Deut. 5:18 *c 11* Exodus 20:13; Deut. 5:17

TUESDAY

READ JAMES 1:19–27

PUTTING FEET TO FAITH

A group of boys at the high school where I used to teach decided to get together and help several female faculty and staff members who were single. Some of these women were widows, some were divorced and some had never married. All had talked on various occasions about how difficult it was to do the kinds of tasks that men traditionally do around the house.

The boys decided to pitch in and help where needed. They did minor car repairs, installed storm windows in the fall and helped haul heavy furniture. They transported children to activities when their mothers were busy. They even babysat in a pinch.

I was incredibly impressed by these boys' thoughtfulness. They didn't expect pay or even praise. They simply saw a need and filled it. They were witnesses to the entire school community as to what it means to be Jesus' hands and feet.

It's easy for us to give lip service to the idea of helping orphans and widows, but it's harder to put words into practice. Isn't that, however, the essence of what James teaches us when he says, "Faith by itself, if it is not accompanied by action, is dead" (James 2:17) and "As the body without the spirit is dead, so faith without works is dead" (James 2:26)?

Religion that God our Father accepts as pure and faultless is this: to look after orphans and widows in their distress and to keep oneself from being polluted by the world.

— JAMES 1:27

Let's *talk*

- ✦ Why did James link good works to faith? Why is faith meaningless without works?
- ✦ Who in our circle of family and acquaintances needs us in a practical way? What could we do for them, beginning now?
- ✦ Are there times when we have felt very much orphaned or widowed and another couple acted as Jesus' hands and feet to us? What did we learn from that experience?

How can we as couples practice the kind of religion that God accepts as pure and faultless? Here are a few ideas:

1. First, look within your own family. Are there mothers, sisters or aunts who are struggling to live alone or to raise a family on their own? What can you do to make it easier for them? Rake leaves? Shovel sidewalks? Bring the car in for repairs? Pick up the kids for a night out? Offer them tea and sympathy? Listen to their problems? Send them a gift card to help buy new winter snowsuits for the kids?

2. Look within your church family. What needs do people have who are alone in your congregation? Expand James's definition to include the widower, the divorced, the single adult, the mentally or physically challenged, the lonely. It may include the person whose spouse is in prison or never comes to church. How can you as a couple make a practical contribution to their lives? How can they see Jesus through you and your marriage?

3. Reach out into the world. Do you know your neighbors? Is there someone in your neighborhood who is alone? What can you do to help them? And what about in your city? Almost every city has organizations that are begging for adults to mentor a child. Many of these kids come from dysfunctional families or are missing the influence of one or both of their parents.

By caring for "the least of these" (Matthew 25:40), you and your spouse can show the world what it means to put the words of Jesus into action.

—VALERIE VAN KOOTEN

FOR YOUR NEXT DEVOTIONAL READING, TURN TO PAGE 1416.

do commit murder, you have become a lawbreaker.

12Speak and act as those who are going to be judged by the law that gives freedom, 13because judgment without mercy will be shown to anyone who has not been merciful. Mercy triumphs over judgment!

Faith and Deeds

14What good is it, my brothers, if a man claims to have faith but has no deeds? Can such faith save him? 15Suppose a brother or sister is without clothes and daily food. 16If one of you says to him, "Go, I wish you well; keep warm and well fed," but does nothing about his physical needs, what good is it? 17In the same way, faith by itself, if it is not accompanied by action, is dead.

18But someone will say, "You have faith; I have deeds."

Show me your faith without deeds, and I will show you my faith by what I do. 19You believe that there is one God. Good! Even the demons believe that—and shudder.

20You foolish man, do you want evidence that faith without deeds is useless[a]? 21Was not our ancestor Abraham considered righteous for what he did when he offered his son Isaac on the altar? 22You see that his faith and his actions were working together, and his faith was made complete by what he did. 23And the scripture was fulfilled that says, "Abraham believed God, and it was credited to him as righteousness,"[b] and he was called God's friend. 24You see that a person is justified by what he does and not by faith alone.

25In the same way, was not even Rahab the prostitute considered righteous for what she did when she gave lodging to the spies and sent them off in a different direction? 26As the body without the spirit is dead, so faith without deeds is dead.

Taming the Tongue

3 Not many of you should presume to be teachers, my brothers, because you know that we who teach will be judged more strictly. 2We all stumble in many ways. If anyone is never at fault in what he says, he is a perfect man, able to keep his whole body in check.

3When we put bits into the mouths of horses to make them obey us, we can turn the whole animal. 4Or take ships as an example. Although they are so large and are driven by strong winds, they are steered by a very small rudder wherever the pilot wants to go. 5Likewise the tongue is a small part of the body, but it makes great boasts. Consider what a great forest is set on fire by a small spark. 6The tongue also is a fire, a world of evil among the parts of the body. It corrupts the whole person, sets the whole course of his life on fire, and is itself set on fire by hell.

7All kinds of animals, birds, reptiles and creatures of the sea are being tamed and have been tamed by man, 8but no man can tame the tongue. It is a restless evil, full of deadly poison.

9With the tongue we praise our Lord and Father, and with it we curse men, who have been made in God's likeness. 10Out of the same mouth come praise and cursing. My brothers, this should not be. 11Can both fresh water and salt[c] water flow from the same spring? 12My brothers, can a fig tree bear olives, or a grapevine bear figs? Neither can a salt spring produce fresh water.

Two Kinds of Wisdom

13Who is wise and understanding among you? Let him show it by his good life, by deeds done in the humility that comes from wisdom. 14But if you harbor bitter envy and selfish ambition in your hearts, do not boast about it or deny the truth. 15Such "wisdom" does not come down from heaven but is earthly, unspiritual, of the devil. 16For where you have envy and selfish ambition, there you find disorder and every evil practice.

17But the wisdom that comes from heaven is first of all pure; then peace-loving, considerate, submissive, full of mercy and good fruit, impartial and sincere. 18Peacemakers who sow in peace raise a harvest of righteousness.

Submit Yourselves to God

4 What causes fights and quarrels among you? Don't they come from your desires that battle within you? 2You want something but don't get it. You kill and covet, but you cannot have what you want. You quarrel and fight. You do not have, because you do not ask God. 3When you ask, you do not receive, because you ask with wrong motives, that you may spend what you get on your pleasures.

4You adulterous people, don't you know that friendship with the world is hatred toward God? Anyone who chooses to be a friend of the world becomes an enemy of God. 5Or

---

[a] *20* Some early manuscripts *dead* [b] *23* Gen. 15:6 [c] *11* Greek *bitter* (see also verse 14)

do you think Scripture says without reason
that the spirit he caused to live in us envies
intensely?[a] 6But he gives us more grace. That
is why Scripture says:

"God opposes the proud
but gives grace to the humble."[b]

7Submit yourselves, then, to God. Resist
the devil, and he will flee from you. 8Come
near to God and he will come near to you.
Wash your hands, you sinners, and purify your
hearts, you double-minded. 9Grieve, mourn
and wail. Change your laughter to mourning
and your joy to gloom. 10Humble yourselves
before the Lord, and he will lift you up.
11Brothers, do not slander one another.
Anyone who speaks against his brother or
judges him speaks against the law and judges
it. When you judge the law, you are not keeping it, but sitting in judgment on it. 12There
is only one Lawgiver and Judge, the one who
is able to save and destroy. But you—who are
you to judge your neighbor?

Boasting About Tomorrow

13Now listen, you who say, "Today or tomorrow we will go to this or that city, spend a
year there, carry on business and make money." 14Why, you do not even know what will
happen tomorrow. What is your life? You are
a mist that appears for a little while and then
vanishes. 15Instead, you ought to say, "If it
is the Lord's will, we will live and do this or
that." 16As it is, you boast and brag. All such
boasting is evil. 17Anyone, then, who knows
the good he ought to do and doesn't do it,
sins.

Warning to Rich Oppressors

5 Now listen, you rich people, weep and wail
because of the misery that is coming upon
you. 2Your wealth has rotted, and moths
have eaten your clothes. 3Your gold and silver are corroded. Their corrosion will testify
against you and eat your flesh like fire. You
have hoarded wealth in the last days. 4Look!
The wages you failed to pay the workmen who
mowed your fields are crying out against you.
The cries of the harvesters have reached the
ears of the Lord Almighty. 5You have lived on
earth in luxury and self-indulgence. You have
fattened yourselves in the day of slaughter.[c]
6You have condemned and murdered innocent men, who were not opposing you.

Patience in Suffering

7Be patient, then, brothers, until the Lord's
coming. See how the farmer waits for the land
to yield its valuable crop and how patient he
is for the autumn and spring rains. 8You too,
be patient and stand firm, because the Lord's
coming is near. 9Don't grumble against each
other, brothers, or you will be judged. The
Judge is standing at the door!
10Brothers, as an example of patience in the
face of suffering, take the prophets who spoke
in the name of the Lord. 11As you know, we
consider blessed those who have persevered.
You have heard of Job's perseverance and have
seen what the Lord finally brought about. The
Lord is full of compassion and mercy.
12Above all, my brothers, do not swear—not
by heaven or by earth or by anything else. Let
your "Yes" be yes, and your "No," no, or you
will be condemned.

The Prayer of Faith

13Is any one of you in trouble? He should
pray. Is anyone happy? Let him sing songs of
praise. 14Is any one of you sick? He should call
the elders of the church to pray over him and
anoint him with oil in the name of the Lord.
15And the prayer offered in faith will make the
sick person well; the Lord will raise him up.
If he has sinned, he will be forgiven. 16There-
fore confess your sins to each other and pray
for each other so that you may be healed. The
prayer of a righteous man is powerful and effective.
17Elijah was a man just like us. He prayed
earnestly that it would not rain, and it did not
rain on the land for three and a half years.
18Again he prayed, and the heavens gave rain,
and the earth produced its crops.

19My brothers, if one of you should wander from the truth and someone should bring
him back, 20remember this: Whoever turns
a sinner from the error of his way will save
him from death and cover over a multitude
of sins.

---

[a] 5 Or *that God jealously longs for the spirit that he made to live in us*; or *that the Spirit he caused to live in us longs jealously*
[b] 6 Prov. 3:34 [c] 5 Or *yourselves as in a day of feasting*

WEDNESDAY
READ JAMES 5:1–12

CURE FOR THE CHRONIC GRUMBLER

> **Don't grumble against each other, brothers, or you will be judged.**
>
> — JAMES 5:9

let's talk

- Who are some chronic grumblers that we know? How do we feel when they start complaining?
- How does grumbling affect us in our relationship? Do we sometimes complain about each other to other people rather than talk with each other about the problems we need to discuss?
- If we are guilty of grumbling, what steps can we take to change?

A few years ago I was in a Bible study with a woman who, no matter what topic we were discussing, always used the time to complain about her husband. It made the rest of us uncomfortable. Every time I saw the woman's husband at church, I would remember the things she had said.

God takes a dim view of grumbling. After God miraculously rescued the Israelites out of slavery in Egypt and they were free in the wilderness, they started grumbling about everything—the lack of meat and certain foods, too little water. They didn't like Moses as their leader.

They were actually grumbling against the Lord, not Moses (see Exodus 16:6–8). Eventually God declared that the adults who left Egypt would not even set foot in the promised land because of their rebellious grumbling (see Numbers 14:26–32). It was a harsh sentence, but that's how grumbling and complaining can affect our attitudes and harden our hearts toward God.

I hate to admit this, but over the years I've been guilty of grumbling about my husband. What halted me was overhearing a former pastor's wife say to someone, "I hear so much bad stuff from women about their husbands that by the time I meet the guy, I already hate him."

When I heard that, I asked God to help me stop grumbling about my husband from that moment on. I don't want people who have never met my husband to hate him when they're introduced.

Grumbling against a spouse is disrespectful and factious. It pits spouses against each other, me versus you. I grumble to get people on my side so I can win. But I end up losing respect for my husband as well as for myself. And I don't really win anything except a momentary sense of being right. As Dr. Phil says, "Do you want to be right, or do you want to be happy?"

Besides, grumbling doesn't resolve anything. For example, if I grumble because my husband never takes out the trash, but I never ask him to do it or never tell him that I'm angry because he said he would and he didn't, then how is he supposed to know how I'm feeling? All I've done is make him look bad to someone else.

Actually, grumbling makes *me* look bad. It exposes my heart and reveals my exalted sense of self. I grumble because I feel entitled to better treatment.

The bottom line, though, is that grumbling against my spouse is grumbling against God. It's saying that God's gifts and provisions aren't good enough. Just ask the Israelites. When they thought they deserved meat instead of manna, God gave them meat along with judgment in the form of a severe plague, which caused many of them to die (see Numbers 11:4–34).

A good lesson to remember next time you're tempted to complain is this: It is possible to grumble our most precious relationships to death. Praise is a much happier alternative.

—NANCY KENNEDY

FOR YOUR NEXT DEVOTIONAL READING, TURN TO PAGE 1419.

1 PETER

1 Peter

QUICK FACTS

AUTHOR The apostle Peter

AUDIENCE Likely to Christians everywhere, but specifically to those scattered throughout Asia Minor (see 1 Peter 1:1)

DATE About A.D. 62–64, possibly written from Rome

SETTING Christians were being persecuted by the Romans during the reign of Nero.

Peter, who was a fisherman by trade, spent many years among smelly fish, torn and mended nets, and rough-hewn fishing boats. So Peter's epistles have a practical, real-life feel. When Peter encouraged believers to "[stand] firm in the faith" (1 Peter 5:9), he wasn't talking about a mystical, esoteric experience; he was talking about a faith that affects real decisions in real time. Peter explained what a relationship with God means in terms of our personal holiness and interactions with others—with both believers and nonbelievers, and specifically with spouses.

First Peter describes how faith perseveres under persecution and suffering. This letter helps believers who are struggling to understand where God is when they suffer persecution and why God allows them to endure such pain. It continually reminds them of the hope they have received in Christ, and the joy that comes from walking with God.

Faith becomes real in the nitty-gritty of financial stress, marital disagreements, parenting decisions, conflicts on the job, physical ailments, and problems with friends and neighbors. We need Peter's practical wisdom on how to trust and obey God in the real world of suffering, sorrow and sin.

1 Peter, an apostle of Jesus Christ,

To God's elect, strangers in the world, scattered throughout Pontus, Galatia, Cappadocia, Asia and Bithynia, 2who have been chosen according to the foreknowledge of God the Father, through the sanctifying work of the Spirit, for obedience to Jesus Christ and sprinkling by his blood:

Grace and peace be yours in abundance.

Praise to God for a Living Hope

3Praise be to the God and Father of our Lord Jesus Christ! In his great mercy he has given us new birth into a living hope through the resurrection of Jesus Christ from the dead, 4and into an inheritance that can never perish, spoil or fade—kept in heaven for you, 5who through faith are shielded by God's power until the coming of the salvation that is ready to be revealed in the last time. 6In this you greatly rejoice, though now for a little while you may have had to suffer grief in all kinds of trials. 7These have come so that your faith—of greater worth than gold, which perishes even though refined by fire—may be proved genuine and may result in praise, glory and honor when Jesus Christ is revealed. 8Though you have not seen him, you love him; and even though you do not see him now, you believe in him and are filled with an inexpressible and glorious joy, 9for you are receiving the goal of your faith, the salvation of your souls.

10Concerning this salvation, the prophets, who spoke of the grace that was to come to you, searched intently and with the greatest care, 11trying to find out the time and circumstances to which the Spirit of Christ in them was pointing when he predicted the sufferings of Christ and the glories that would follow. 12It was revealed to them that they were not serving themselves but you, when they spoke of the things that have now been told you by those who have preached the gospel to you by the Holy Spirit sent from heaven. Even angels long to look into these things.

Be Holy

13Therefore, prepare your minds for action; be self-controlled; set your hope fully on the grace to be given you when Jesus Christ is revealed. 14As obedient children, do not conform to the evil desires you had when you lived in ignorance. 15But just as he who called you is holy, so be holy in all you do; 16for it is written: "Be holy, because I am holy."[a]

17Since you call on a Father who judges each man's work impartially, live your lives as strangers here in reverent fear. 18For you know that it was not with perishable things such as silver or gold that you were redeemed from the empty way of life handed down to you from your forefathers, 19but with the precious blood of Christ, a lamb without blemish or defect. 20He was chosen before the creation of the world, but was revealed in these last times for your sake. 21Through him you believe in God, who raised him from the dead and glorified him, and so your faith and hope are in God.

22Now that you have purified yourselves by obeying the truth so that you have sincere love for your brothers, love one another deeply, from the heart.[b] 23For you have been born again, not of perishable seed, but of imperishable, through the living and enduring word of God. 24For,

"All men are like grass,
  and all their glory is like the flowers of the field;
the grass withers and the flowers fall,
25 but the word of the Lord stands forever."[c]

And this is the word that was preached to you.

2 Therefore, rid yourselves of all malice and all deceit, hypocrisy, envy, and slander of every kind. 2Like newborn babies, crave pure spiritual milk, so that by it you may grow up in your salvation, 3now that you have tasted that the Lord is good.

The Living Stone and a Chosen People

4As you come to him, the living Stone—rejected by men but chosen by God and precious to him— 5you also, like living stones, are being built into a spiritual house to be a holy priesthood, offering spiritual sacrifices acceptable to God through Jesus Christ. 6For in Scripture it says:

"See, I lay a stone in Zion,
  a chosen and precious cornerstone,
and the one who trusts in him
  will never be put to shame."[d]

7Now to you who believe, this stone is precious. But to those who do not believe,

[a] *16* Lev. 11:44,45; 19:2 [b] *22* Some early manuscripts *from a pure heart* [c] *25* Isaiah 40:6-8 [d] *6* Isaiah 28:16

THURSDAY
READ 1 PETER 1:1–25

IMITATING EACH OTHER

Peter was nearing the end of his life when he wrote the two epistles bearing his name. He wrote this, his first letter, to encourage believers in Christ Jesus as they suffered challenges, insults and persecution.

As he wrote, Peter thought of the words God had given to Moses at Mount Sinai for his covenant people, Israel: "I am the Lord your God; consecrate yourselves and be holy, because I am holy" (Leviticus 11:44). Among the many dimensions of this covenant relationship was a marital-type union. In effect, God was wedding himself to Israel and moving into her midst to reside in the tabernacle.

Most of us don't enjoy reading the book of Leviticus. It feels tedious and foreign, with a lot of attention paid to housekeeping, cooking and hygiene. That is not accidental. Newlyweds realize quickly that much of wedded bliss is spent in domestic engineering—who will cook, who will clean, will we squeeze or roll up the toothpaste tube, and the like. It is actually gratifying to think that God wants to be close enough to us to care about our daily health and well-being.

Perhaps that is why wives and husbands often begin to look more like one another over time. They spend so much time together; they eat the same meals, exercise together (or not), and influence each other's wardrobes. Yet marriage should never rob us of our individuality. A relationship in which one partner is manipulated into subservience at the expense of selfhood is not what God intends. Authentic love affirms the good in the other and truly seeks to serve. When love includes genuine give-and-take between husband and wife, each influences the other.

The point of 1 Peter 1:15–16 is that if we are married to God, we will begin to look more like God and act in ways that reflect God's character and values. Deep love imitates.

So it goes in a good marriage. There are words I acquired from my wife that I didn't think to use 25 years ago. There are dates scheduled in my wife's planner that she would never have thought important before we were married. Our tastes for foods have become much the same, and our expectations for vacations nicely match.

Probably the best imitation of love, as Peter noted, is the way we gain stabilizing depth in our relationships over time so that our baser inclinations are tamed. The longer we are married to God, the holier we become. The longer we are wed to our partner, the less likely we are to engage in secretive and self-destructive habits.

Marriage can't make flawed people perfect, but it can clean us up. As A. E. Housman put it: "When I was in love with you, then I was clean and brave; and miles around the wonder grew how well I did behave."

—WAYNE BROUWER

But just as he who called you is holy, so be holy in all you do; for it is written: "Be holy, because I am holy."

— 1 Peter 1:15–16

let's talk

- ✦ How have we influenced one another since we met? What good habits have we picked up from one another? What bad behaviors have we eased out of one another's lives?
- ✦ Are we more in tune with God now as a couple than we were as individuals? What habits of the heart have we grown?
- ✦ What does it mean for us to be holy? How might someone visiting our home sense an atmosphere of holiness? What visible evidence might show it? What practices might tell of it?

FOR YOUR NEXT DEVOTIONAL READING, TURN TO PAGE 1421.

"The stone the builders rejected
has become the capstone,[a]"[b]

[8]and,

"A stone that causes men to stumble
and a rock that makes them fall."[c]

They stumble because they disobey the message—which is also what they were destined
for.
[9]But you are a chosen people, a royal priesthood, a holy nation, a people belonging to
God, that you may declare the praises of him
who called you out of darkness into his wonderful light. [10]Once you were not a people,
but now you are the people of God; once you
had not received mercy, but now you have received mercy.
[11]Dear friends, I urge you, as aliens and
strangers in the world, to abstain from sinful desires, which war against your soul.
[12]Live such good lives among the pagans that,
though they accuse you of doing wrong, they
may see your good deeds and glorify God on
the day he visits us.

Submission to Rulers and Masters

[13]Submit yourselves for the Lord's sake to
every authority instituted among men: whether to the king, as the supreme authority, [14]or
to governors, who are sent by him to punish
those who do wrong and to commend those
who do right. [15]For it is God's will that by doing good you should silence the ignorant talk
of foolish men. [16]Live as free men, but do not
use your freedom as a cover-up for evil; live
as servants of God. [17]Show proper respect to
everyone: Love the brotherhood of believers,
fear God, honor the king.
[18]Slaves, submit yourselves to your masters with all respect, not only to those who are
good and considerate, but also to those who
are harsh. [19]For it is commendable if a man
bears up under the pain of unjust suffering
because he is conscious of God. [20]But how is
it to your credit if you receive a beating for
doing wrong and endure it? But if you suffer for doing good and you endure it, this is
commendable before God. [21]To this you were
called, because Christ suffered for you, leaving you an example, that you should follow
in his steps.

[22]"He committed no sin,
and no deceit was found in his
mouth."[d]

[23]When they hurled their insults at him, he
did not retaliate; when he suffered, he made
no threats. Instead, he entrusted himself to
him who judges justly. [24]He himself bore our
sins in his body on the tree, so that we might
die to sins and live for righteousness; by his
wounds you have been healed. [25]For you were
like sheep going astray, but now you have returned to the Shepherd and Overseer of your
souls.

Wives and Husbands

3 Wives, in the same way be submissive to
your husbands so that, if any of them do
not believe the word, they may be won
over without words by the behavior of their
wives, [2]when they see the purity and reverence
of your lives. [3]Your beauty should not come
from outward adornment, such as braided
hair and the wearing of gold jewelry and fine
clothes. [4]Instead, it should be that of your inner self, the unfading beauty of a gentle and
quiet spirit, which is of great worth in God's
sight. [5]For this is the way the holy women of
the past who put their hope in God used to
make themselves beautiful. They were submissive to their own husbands, [6]like Sarah, who
obeyed Abraham and called him her master.
You are her daughters if you do what is right
and do not give way to fear.
[7]Husbands, in the same way be considerate
as you live with your wives, and treat them
with respect as the weaker partner and as heirs
with you of the gracious gift of life, so that
nothing will hinder your prayers.

Suffering for Doing Good

[8]Finally, all of you, live in harmony with
one another; be sympathetic, love as brothers,
be compassionate and humble. [9]Do not repay
evil with evil or insult with insult, but with
blessing, because to this you were called so
that you may inherit a blessing. [10]For,

"Whoever would love life
and see good days
must keep his tongue from evil
and his lips from deceitful speech.
[11]He must turn from evil and do good;
he must seek peace and pursue it.
[12]For the eyes of the Lord are on the
righteous
and his ears are attentive to their prayer,
but the face of the Lord is against those
who do evil."[e]

---

[a] 7 Or *cornerstone* [b] 7 Psalm 118:22 [c] 8 Isaiah 8:14 [d] 22 Isaiah 53:9 [e] 12 Psalm 34:12-16

F

FRIDAY
READ 1 PETER 2:11—3:7

BEAUTY IN SUBMISSION

For many people, the word *submission* implies serving someone else hand and foot. Submission seems dehumanizing. We assume that such deference would sap a marriage of the mutual respect and service that a marriage ought to have to make it strong and vital.

In 1 Peter 3, Peter was addressing a specific situation: how the wives of unsaved husbands might influence them to become Christians. He counseled the women to be submissive, but he was thinking of the kind of submission that is deeply catalytic, a potent secret remedy for a lost loved one.

The secret of a Christian wife's submission is found in three phrases. The first is in verse 1: "in the same way." It refers back to the Christlike submission described in the previous verses (2:21–24). In the same way that Jesus trusted God to work redemptively through his submission, we can trust God to work through our submission.

The second key phrase is in verse 2: "when they see the purity and reverence of your lives." Purity and reverence ennoble a person; they are signs of spiritual strength. They are the marks of carefully guarded relationships with people and with God. Submission without purity and reverence has no potency, but when someone is the recipient of your humble submission and realizes that it springs not from his or her power over you but from your relationship with God, the person is changed by the experience.

The third important phrase is in verse 4: "a gentle and quiet spirit, which is of great worth in God's sight." A gentle and quiet spirit is the opposite of a fearful spirit. Wives of unsaved husbands in Peter's day had a lot to be afraid of, but those who learned to quiet their hearts in the promises of God took on an inner beauty that no dress or makeup could give them, a beauty that attracted others to Christ. The message, both then and now, is that while Christian wives serve their unsaved husbands, they are depending on God, and that is a transforming experience.

Notice that the goal is not a dominating husband, but a godly husband. God-shaped submission makes the people around us better, not worse. Furthermore, even if an unsaved husband never responds to Christ, the Christian wife may grow in such beautiful godliness that others will be attracted to Christ.

Peter didn't apply to believing husbands the same recipe for winning over an unsaved wife, but we can be assured that the principles are similar. Paul instructed Christians to "submit to one another out of reverence for Christ" (Ephesians 5:21). If a husband has an unsaved wife, his loving and sacrificial behavior toward her will show her a picture of Christ's love for the church (see Ephesians 5:25–32).

—LEE ECLOV

Wives, in the same way be submissive to your husbands so that, if any of them do not believe the word, they may be won over without words by the behavior of their wives, when they see the purity and reverence of your lives.

— 1 PETER 3:1–2

let's *talk*

- ✦ How can Christian submission as Peter described it actually empower rather than dehumanize us in marriage?
- ✦ How does fear sour submission (see 1 Peter 3:6)? What is it like to be around a fearfully submissive person?
- ✦ How does the purity and reverence of our lives change the character of submission?

FOR YOUR NEXT DEVOTIONAL READING, TURN TO PAGE 1422.

WEEKEND

sex and remarriage

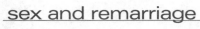

Usually, once a couple gets to the point of divorce, sex is no longer great, if it's there at all. So couples may enter remarriage believing their spouse is going to fulfill all their sexual desires. It becomes quite a jolt, then, when that doesn't happen.

If you and your spouse are struggling with intimacy issues, there's still hope. Here are eight things to help you get real about sex and remarriage.

1. Heed the effect of kids. The first time you were married, you didn't have children—the passion was free to flow whenever, however and wherever.

2. Guard your sex life. When my husband's daughter was living in our home, her bedroom was right next to ours. So for three years, we had little sex. The thought of a teenager sitting on her bed, listening through thin walls—you get the picture.

My husband and I had to become creative and make sex a priority. If the daughter went out with her friends or to visit her mother, bingo! Likewise, we'd make love very early in the morning while the daughter was still asleep, but very quietly.

3. Protect your thoughts. Many remarried spouses live with unspoken insecurity about their previous relationship. The reality is that you're probably thinking more about his ex than he is! Don't allow such thoughts to ruin what belongs to you and your marriage.

4. Talk about sex. Talk about what you like and dislike. Talk about your erogenous zones. Talk about the things that were turn-offs in your former marriage. (One caveat: don't talk about the things your former spouse did that you liked. Your current spouse doesn't need comparisons.)

5. Make foreplay an event. Greet each morning with affection. Hug each other. Call each other during the day. Lock eyes and hold that gaze for several seconds. Take a shower together. Take an interest in each other's day. Touch each other—a squeeze on the shoulder when you're walking past, a quick kiss on the neck. Hold hands just because.

6. Schedule sex. The unfortunate reality in remarriage when kids are around and careers are more established is that spontaneity goes out the window. If you want a sexual relationship with your spouse, you'll have to schedule sex. Pick a night, put it on the calendar, and stick to it. That way you know when it's a sex night and you can prepare for it.

7. Know when to seek counseling. Talking to a Christian sex therapist is essential if an ex had an affair. Trust has been lost. If your spouse does not want to have a sexual relationship, has an aversion to sex or struggles with sex, seek counseling to work through that.

8. Don't give up! If your sex life is still dragging, don't bury it yet. Start praying about it. That's what Janie did. She decided, "If God asks me to pray about everything else, I'm going to start praying about my sex life too." So every day she prayed for her husband. "I prayed that God would bless him and our sex life. That God would work a miracle there," Janie said.

Then she sat back and waited. "I started to see little sparks," she says. "They were small, but they were there." She readjusted her expectations and committed to praying daily for her sex life. "While it's still not earth-shattering sex, it's much better than it was," she says. "And we're enjoying each other much more now that I've let God worry about it."

—GINGER KOLBABA

MONDAY
READ 1 PETER 4:1–11

COVER ME WITH LOVE

We tend to throw the word *love* around pretty casually. We send our spouses off to work with a casual "Love you," toss in a little affection during a midday phone conversation or email, and offer a pleasant "Goodnight, I love you" before falling asleep. But what happens in between all those professions of love? Does the love you share with your spouse really "cover over [that is, bear with and forgive] a multitude of sins" (1 Peter 4:8)?

For many of us, it doesn't. We nag each other, criticize each other, bicker with each other. We complain about the dirty socks he leaves on the floor or the crusty dishes she leaves in the sink. We snap at each other, belittle each other and take out our frustrations on each other. We find it almost impossible to ignore all the ways our spouse drives us crazy.

Marriage experts say divorce is rarely the result of a single conflict. Rather, it's little grievances that, over time, add up to what feels like an intolerable situation. And if we're honest with ourselves, we can see why. There are days when I think, "If I have to trip over the shoes Jimmy's left by the door one more time . . ." When I'm feeling really crabby, those shoes—and what I think of as Jimmy's selfishness in leaving them where I'll trip over them—become the tipping point in the delicate balance of our marriage. Love goes out the window, and all I can think about is the ways he bugs me, how insensitive he is to my needs, and how little respect he shows for me when he leaves his stuff lying around.

Then I think about how ridiculous that is. Would I really end my marriage to an exceptional man because I tripped over his shoes? Of course not. Are those shoes really a subtle symbol of disrespect? Not in the least. And I think that's some of what 1 Peter 4:8 is getting at. The kind of love we are to have for others is the kind that "is not easily angered" (1 Corinthians 13:5). That's the kind of love I want from Jimmy, and it's what I want to offer him.

Of course, that's easy to say. In practice, allowing the love I have for Jimmy to "cover over a multitude of sins" would make me a far more patient, compassionate, grace-filled person than I am. But perhaps that's the point. Maybe the deep love Peter was talking about is intended to cover over not only Jimmy's sins but mine as well.

It's a mistake to use this passage as a weapon to wield over the head of my spouse, saying, "You're a loser, but I'm so loving that I'll pretend I don't notice." Instead, it's my sin that needs covering—my short fuse, my impossible expectations, my inability to see the good in my husband. The only thing that can cover over those powerful sins is the kind of love that comes from God.

When the love of God fills us, it flushes out selfishness, greed, disrespect and petty criticism. It's that deep love, the love that overrides our base instincts, that allows us to live well with our spouses.

—CARLA BARNHILL

Above all, love each other deeply, because love covers over a multitude of sins.

— 1 PETER 4:8

let's talk

✦ What are some of the little things that cause irritations in our marriage? What's really behind those issues? Let's talk honestly about the feelings and frustrations at the core of the petty issues that chip away at our marriage.

✦ What sinful impulses get in the way of fully accepting each other?

✦ What would it look like for us to let love "cover over" these sins?

FOR YOUR NEXT DEVOTIONAL READING, TURN TO PAGE 1429.

"God opposes the proud
but gives grace to the humble." [a]

6Humble yourselves, therefore, under God's mighty hand, that he may lift you up in due time. 7Cast all your anxiety on him because he cares for you.
8Be self-controlled and alert. Your enemy
the devil prowls around like a roaring lion
looking for someone to devour. 9Resist him,
standing firm in the faith, because you know that your brothers throughout the world are undergoing the same kind of sufferings.
10And the God of all grace, who called you to his eternal glory in Christ, after you have suffered a little while, will himself restore you
and make you strong, firm and steadfast. 11To
him be the power for ever and ever. Amen.

Final Greetings

12With the help of Silas, [b] whom I regard as a faithful brother, I have written to you briefly, encouraging you and testifying that this is the true grace of God. Stand fast in it.
13She who is in Babylon, chosen together with you, sends you her greetings, and so does
my son Mark. 14Greet one another with a kiss
of love.

Peace to all of you who are in Christ.

[a] 5 Prov. 3:34 [b] 12 Greek *Silvanus,* a variant of *Silas*

2 PETER

2 Peter

QUICK FACTS

AUTHOR The apostle Peter

AUDIENCE Probably the same people mentioned in 1 Peter 1:1

DATE About A.D. 67

SETTING Written shortly before Peter's death to warn believers about false teachers

Freedom is precious to all of us, particularly to those whose personal rights are restricted. Freedom in faith is critical as well. Of all the religions of the world, there is only one that offers salvation that is not dependent on the works of the believer to win God's approval. Only Christianity says that a Savior, Jesus Christ, has done it all—suffered, died, pardoned us from sin and brought us to favor with God. Through God's grace alone we are the blessed recipients of his gift. We are free.

Still, this freedom must not be abused. As 2 Peter tells us, we cannot use forgiveness of sin as a license to keep on sinning. Peter, in essence, tells believers who abuse freedom, "You should know better!" He reminds us that Jesus Christ is our strength and that our best remedy against failure is to keep growing in holiness through our relationship with him.

1 Simon Peter, a servant and apostle of Jesus Christ,

To those who through the righteousness of our God and Savior Jesus Christ have received a faith as precious as ours:

2Grace and peace be yours in abundance through the knowledge of God and of Jesus our Lord.

Making One's Calling and Election Sure

3His divine power has given us everything we need for life and godliness through our knowledge of him who called us by his own glory and goodness. 4Through these he has given us his very great and precious promises, so that through them you may participate in the divine nature and escape the corruption in the world caused by evil desires.

5For this very reason, make every effort to add to your faith goodness; and to goodness, knowledge; 6and to knowledge, self-control; and to self-control, perseverance; and to perseverance, godliness; 7and to godliness, brotherly kindness; and to brotherly kindness, love. 8For if you possess these qualities in increasing measure, they will keep you from being ineffective and unproductive in your knowledge of our Lord Jesus Christ. 9But if anyone does not have them, he is nearsighted and blind, and has forgotten that he has been cleansed from his past sins.

10Therefore, my brothers, be all the more eager to make your calling and election sure. For if you do these things, you will never fall, 11and you will receive a rich welcome into the eternal kingdom of our Lord and Savior Jesus Christ.

Prophecy of Scripture

12So I will always remind you of these things, even though you know them and are firmly established in the truth you now have. 13I think it is right to refresh your memory as long as I live in the tent of this body, 14because I know that I will soon put it aside, as our Lord Jesus Christ has made clear to me. 15And I will make every effort to see that after my departure you will always be able to remember these things.

16We did not follow cleverly invented stories when we told you about the power and coming of our Lord Jesus Christ, but we were eyewitnesses of his majesty. 17For he received honor and glory from God the Father when the voice came to him from the Majestic Glory, saying, "This is my Son, whom I love; with him I am well pleased."[a] 18We ourselves heard this voice that came from heaven when we were with him on the sacred mountain.

19And we have the word of the prophets made more certain, and you will do well to pay attention to it, as to a light shining in a dark place, until the day dawns and the morning star rises in your hearts. 20Above all, you must understand that no prophecy of Scripture came about by the prophet's own interpretation. 21For prophecy never had its origin in the will of man, but men spoke from God as they were carried along by the Holy Spirit.

False Teachers and Their Destruction

2 But there were also false prophets among the people, just as there will be false teachers among you. They will secretly introduce destructive heresies, even denying the sovereign Lord who bought them—bringing swift destruction on themselves. 2Many will follow their shameful ways and will bring the way of truth into disrepute. 3In their greed these teachers will exploit you with stories they have made up. Their condemnation has long been hanging over them, and their destruction has not been sleeping.

4For if God did not spare angels when they sinned, but sent them to hell,[b] putting them into gloomy dungeons[c] to be held for judgment; 5if he did not spare the ancient world when he brought the flood on its ungodly people, but protected Noah, a preacher of righteousness, and seven others; 6if he condemned the cities of Sodom and Gomorrah by burning them to ashes, and made them an example of what is going to happen to the ungodly; 7and if he rescued Lot, a righteous man, who was distressed by the filthy lives of lawless men 8(for that righteous man, living among them day after day, was tormented in his righteous soul by the lawless deeds he saw and heard)— 9if this is so, then the Lord knows how to rescue godly men from trials and to hold the unrighteous for the day of judgment, while continuing their punishment.[d] 10This is especially true of those who follow the corrupt desire of the sinful nature[e] and despise authority.

Bold and arrogant, these men are not afraid to slander celestial beings; 11yet even angels,

---

a *17* Matt. 17:5; Mark 9:7; Luke 9:35 *b* *4* Greek *Tartarus* *c* *4* Some manuscripts *into chains of darkness* *d* *9* Or *unrighteous for punishment until the day of judgment* *e* *10* Or *the flesh*

TUESDAY
READ 2 PETER 2:1–22

A PLACE FOR US

Lot obviously hadn't heard the realtors' mantra "Location, location, location." Though referred to as "righteous" in 2 Peter 2:7, Lot chose to live in Sodom—the polar opposite of Mayberry, USA—with his wife and two daughters. Genesis 13:12 says Lot "pitched his tents" there after he and his uncle Abraham parted company. Fortunately, God rescued Lot and his daughters before destroying Sodom.

[God] rescued Lot, a righteous man, who was distressed by the filthy lives of lawless men.
— 2 PETER 2:7

let's talk

- ✦ What "gray areas," morally speaking, are we participating in because it seems that everyone else is doing it? What TV shows or movies are we watching? How are we making financial decisions?
- ✦ How much time do we spend focused on knowing and serving God in our jobs, at home and in our leisure time?
- ✦ What is our strategy for making friends without compromising our Christian integrity?

What approach should a Christian husband and wife take when it comes to choosing where to settle? Some might choose to move into a gang-dominated neighborhood, hoping to season the area with their Christian worldview. Others want to live far away from that sort of atmosphere to protect their children from ungodly influences. Each couple has to weigh the challenges and opportunities. But whatever the choice, prayerfully consider how you can influence your neighborhood for Jesus.

Wherever you determine that God is calling you to live, there will be negative influences. If you choose to live in a neighborhood with high crime and poverty, you and your children will be influenced by the mindset of the disenfranchised. However, if you feel God calling you to a neighborhood with upwardly mobile families, you will deal with the attitudes of materialism, commercialism and selfishness that are at the core of a consumer-driven culture. How will you protect your family from harmful influences? Here are some ideas:

1. Focus on Jesus. Peter had power and charisma in the early church, but he never got a big head; he knew he was nothing without Jesus. Having witnessed Jesus' transfiguration, Peter knew that if he kept his focus on Jesus, he would not be corrupted by worldly influences. So, instead of watching and worrying about the corruption you see, spend more time building up your faith, being sure to . . .

2. Know yourselves. Peter knew his weaknesses. He remembered his denial of Jesus at Jesus' arrest. So he advises us to be aware and to practice virtue so we can "escape the corruption in the world" (2 Peter 1:4). Let's not be fooled into thinking we can do what unbelievers do and remain uncontaminated. It's true that we are to be the salt of the earth, but salt on rotting meat will not restore the meat. So it may be necessary to . . .

3. Be the outsider. Married couples naturally want friends; they want to fit in. But we can make a conscious decision that, if necessary to maintain integrity as followers of Jesus, we'll remain on the outside of groups that could lead us to compromise our standards.

Lot and his two daughters were rescued from destruction purely through God's mercy (his wife, you'll recall, turned into a pillar of salt). In many ways Lot was foolish. I think it's best to follow Peter's example.

—MARY ANN JEFFREYS

FOR YOUR NEXT DEVOTIONAL READING, TURN TO PAGE 1433.

although they are stronger and more powerful, do not bring slanderous accusations against such beings in the presence of the Lord. 12But these men blaspheme in matters they do not understand. They are like brute beasts, creatures of instinct, born only to be caught and destroyed, and like beasts they too will perish.

13They will be paid back with harm for the harm they have done. Their idea of pleasure is to carouse in broad daylight. They are blots and blemishes, reveling in their pleasures while they feast with you.[a] 14With eyes full of adultery, they never stop sinning; they seduce the unstable; they are experts in greed—an accursed brood! 15They have left the straight way and wandered off to follow the way of Balaam son of Beor, who loved the wages of wickedness. 16But he was rebuked for his wrongdoing by a donkey—a beast without speech—who spoke with a man's voice and restrained the prophet's madness.

17These men are springs without water and mists driven by a storm. Blackest darkness is reserved for them. 18For they mouth empty, boastful words and, by appealing to the lustful desires of sinful human nature, they entice people who are just escaping from those who live in error. 19They promise them freedom, while they themselves are slaves of depravity—for a man is a slave to whatever has mastered him. 20If they have escaped the corruption of the world by knowing our Lord and Savior Jesus Christ and are again entangled in it and overcome, they are worse off at the end than they were at the beginning. 21It would have been better for them not to have known the way of righteousness, than to have known it and then to turn their backs on the sacred command that was passed on to them. 22Of them the proverbs are true: "A dog returns to its vomit,"[b] and, "A sow that is washed goes back to her wallowing in the mud."

The Day of the Lord

3 Dear friends, this is now my second letter to you. I have written both of them as reminders to stimulate you to wholesome thinking. 2I want you to recall the words spoken in the past by the holy prophets and the command given by our Lord and Savior through your apostles.

3First of all, you must understand that in the last days scoffers will come, scoffing and following their own evil desires. 4They will say, "Where is this 'coming' he promised? Ever since our fathers died, everything goes on as it has since the beginning of creation." 5But they deliberately forget that long ago by God's word the heavens existed and the earth was formed out of water and by water. 6By these waters also the world of that time was deluged and destroyed. 7By the same word the present heavens and earth are reserved for fire, being kept for the day of judgment and destruction of ungodly men.

8But do not forget this one thing, dear friends: With the Lord a day is like a thousand years, and a thousand years are like a day. 9The Lord is not slow in keeping his promise, as some understand slowness. He is patient with you, not wanting anyone to perish, but everyone to come to repentance.

10But the day of the Lord will come like a thief. The heavens will disappear with a roar; the elements will be destroyed by fire, and the earth and everything in it will be laid bare.[c]

11Since everything will be destroyed in this way, what kind of people ought you to be? You ought to live holy and godly lives 12as you look forward to the day of God and speed its coming.[d] That day will bring about the destruction of the heavens by fire, and the elements will melt in the heat. 13But in keeping with his promise we are looking forward to a new heaven and a new earth, the home of righteousness.

14So then, dear friends, since you are looking forward to this, make every effort to be found spotless, blameless and at peace with him. 15Bear in mind that our Lord's patience means salvation, just as our dear brother Paul also wrote you with the wisdom that God gave him. 16He writes the same way in all his letters, speaking in them of these matters. His letters contain some things that are hard to understand, which ignorant and unstable people distort, as they do the other Scriptures, to their own destruction.

17Therefore, dear friends, since you already know this, be on your guard so that you may not be carried away by the error of lawless men and fall from your secure position. 18But grow in the grace and knowledge of our Lord and Savior Jesus Christ. To him be glory both now and forever! Amen.

---

[a] *13* Some manuscripts *in their love feasts* [b] *22* Prov. 26:11 [c] *10* Some manuscripts *be burned up* [d] *12* Or *as you wait eagerly for the day of God to come*

1 JOHN

1 John

QUICK FACTS

AUTHOR The apostle John, the beloved disciple and close friend of Jesus

AUDIENCE Likely to Christians everywhere, but specifically to those in and around Ephesus

DATE Between A.D. 85 and 95

SETTING Written by John in his old age to encourage fellow believers

Some people think truth is relative, that whatever they believe is OK as long as it works for them. So each person can choose whatever seems best to him or her from the cafeteria of life's religions and moral choices.

Christianity rejects such thinking. It says there is only one source of truth: God. God has created all things—the heavens, the earth and us. God has provided salvation for people who have sinned and fallen far short of God's glory. We can know God through Jesus Christ and we can know that we have eternal life through Christ.

Over and over the apostle John stressed in his first epistle that we can know God if we believe that Jesus is the Messiah, the Christ. In Jesus we can find true happiness, freedom from sin, protection from error and intimate fellowship with the Father, Son and Holy Spirit. What's more, true belief is evident by how we live. As we walk in the light of God's presence, his light shines in us, making us aware of our sin, our need to obey God's commands and our need to love one another.

In a culture of shifting values and slippery truths, married couples can find true joy only if they build their relationship on a firm foundation of truth, which God the Creator has revealed to us through his Son and his Word.

The Word of Life

1 That which was from the beginning, which
we have heard, which we have seen with
our eyes, which we have looked at and our
hands have touched—this we proclaim concerning the Word of life. 2The life appeared;
we have seen it and testify to it, and we proclaim to you the eternal life, which was with
the Father and has appeared to us. 3We proclaim to you what we have seen and heard,
so that you also may have fellowship with us.
And our fellowship is with the Father and
with his Son, Jesus Christ. 4We write this to
make our[a] joy complete.

Walking in the Light

5This is the message we have heard from
him and declare to you: God is light; in him
there is no darkness at all. 6If we claim to have
fellowship with him yet walk in the darkness,
we lie and do not live by the truth. 7But if we
walk in the light, as he is in the light, we have
fellowship with one another, and the blood of
Jesus, his Son, purifies us from all[b] sin.

8If we claim to be without sin, we deceive
ourselves and the truth is not in us. 9If we
confess our sins, he is faithful and just and
will forgive us our sins and purify us from all
unrighteousness. 10If we claim we have not
sinned, we make him out to be a liar and his
word has no place in our lives.

2 My dear children, I write this to you so
that you will not sin. But if anybody does
sin, we have one who speaks to the Father
in our defense—Jesus Christ, the Righteous
One. 2He is the atoning sacrifice for our sins,
and not only for ours but also for[c] the sins of
the whole world.

3We know that we have come to know him
if we obey his commands. 4The man who says,
"I know him," but does not do what he commands is a liar, and the truth is not in him.
5But if anyone obeys his word, God's love[d] is
truly made complete in him. This is how we
know we are in him: 6Whoever claims to live
in him must walk as Jesus did.

7Dear friends, I am not writing you a new
command but an old one, which you have had
since the beginning. This old command is the
message you have heard. 8Yet I am writing you
a new command; its truth is seen in him and
you, because the darkness is passing and the
true light is already shining.

9Anyone who claims to be in the light
but hates his brother is still in the darkness.
10Whoever loves his brother lives in the light,
and there is nothing in him[e] to make him
stumble. 11But whoever hates his brother is in
the darkness and walks around in the darkness; he does not know where he is going, because the darkness has blinded him.

12I write to you, dear children,
because your sins have been forgiven on
account of his name.
13I write to you, fathers,
because you have known him who is
from the beginning.
I write to you, young men,
because you have overcome the evil
one.
I write to you, dear children,
because you have known the Father.
14I write to you, fathers,
because you have known him who is
from the beginning.
I write to you, young men,
because you are strong,
and the word of God lives in you,
and you have overcome the evil one.

Do Not Love the World

15Do not love the world or anything in the
world. If anyone loves the world, the love of
the Father is not in him. 16For everything in
the world—the cravings of sinful man, the
lust of his eyes and the boasting of what he
has and does—comes not from the Father but
from the world. 17The world and its desires
pass away, but the man who does the will of
God lives forever.

Warning Against Antichrists

18Dear children, this is the last hour; and as
you have heard that the antichrist is coming,
even now many antichrists have come. This is
how we know it is the last hour. 19They went
out from us, but they did not really belong to
us. For if they had belonged to us, they would
have remained with us; but their going showed
that none of them belonged to us.

20But you have an anointing from the Holy
One, and all of you know the truth.[f] 21I do
not write to you because you do not know
the truth, but because you do know it and because no lie comes from the truth. 22Who is
the liar? It is the man who denies that Jesus is
the Christ. Such a man is the antichrist—he
denies the Father and the Son. 23No one who

---

[a] 4 Some manuscripts *your* [b] 7 Or *every* [c] 2 Or *He is the one who turns aside God's wrath, taking away our sins, and not only ours but also* [d] 5 Or *word, love for God* [e] 10 Or *it* [f] 20 Some manuscripts *and you know all things*

WEDNESDAY

READ 1 JOHN 1:5—2:2

WHAT THE MIRROR SHOWS

If we claim to have fellowship with him yet walk in the darkness, we lie and do not live by the truth. But if we walk in the light, as he is in the light, we have fellowship with one another, and the blood of Jesus, his Son, purifies us from all sin.

— 1 JOHN 1:6–7

let's talk

- ✦ What are some ways we fool ourselves into thinking that we have fellowship with God even when we "walk in the darkness" (live sinfully)?
- ✦ In practical terms, how do we "walk in the light"? What does that mean for us at work? At the gym? At home? While navigating traffic?
- ✦ What is our marriage like when we are both walking in the light? What improvements in conduct do we notice?

A man came down from the Carolina mountains one day. He was all dressed up and carrying his Bible. A friend saw him and asked, "Elias, what's happening? Where are you going all dressed up like that?"

"I'm heading for New Orleans," Elias said. "I've heard there's a lot of liquor and gamblin' and other interestin' trouble there."

The friend looked him over and said, "But Elias, why are you carrying your Bible under your arm?"

Elias answered, "Well, if it's as good as they say it is, I might just stay over until Sunday."

In 1 John 1:6–7, John was attacking the belief that our fellowship with God is not related to how we behave. So what if I lose my temper? So what if I mistreat my family and others? I'm spiritual. I pray. I go to church. I know my Bible. That's all that matters.

John's verdict is that those who think this way "lie and do not live out the truth." Truth isn't just something you believe; it is something you *do*. Christians *do* truth. The hypocrisy of not doing the truth is especially evident in our marriages and families.

Before a professional dance troupe appears on stage, they spend many hours rehearsing in a brightly lit room with a mirrored wall. Seeing themselves in action eliminates self-deception about their performance. Likewise, God's people must live their days in the light and before the mirror of Scripture and the Holy Spirit to face the truth and shape their lives accordingly.

First John 1:7 says there are benefits that come when we walk in the light. The first is: "We have fellowship with one another." The primary casualties of Christian hypocrisy are our relationships in the church and home, which begin to disintegrate as we lie to ourselves and God about what we're doing. People walking in darkness bump into each other, and it hurts.

But when we allow God's bright light to shine into our lives, we stop bruising each other because our actions are under God's control. We stop fighting over where to go because God's light reveals clearly how we're to follow.

The second great benefit of living truthfully is: "The blood of Jesus, his Son, purifies us from all sin." We began this walk of light when Jesus cleansed us from our sin. But the ongoing benefit of continuing to respond to the truth of God's Word and God's verdict about our day-to-day sins is that Jesus' blood continues to purify us from sin. The Greek word for *purify* is the origin of our English word *catharsis*, implying deep, inward cleansing. That's what the blood of Jesus does; it cleanses us.

The godliness of marriage is measured not by how spiritual we are but by how well we walk in the light. A man and woman who are close to God will be humble, kind, faithful, gentle, joyful, loving and, above all, honest. They will glory in walking in the light of God's presence together.

—LEE ECLOV

FOR YOUR NEXT DEVOTIONAL READING, TURN TO PAGE 1434.

THURSDAY
READ 1 JOHN 2:3–11

FINDING RELIEF FROM HATE

Whoever hates his brother is in the darkness and walks around in the darkness; he does not know where he is going, because the darkness has blinded him.

— 1 John 2:11

My friend Rachel has had a difficult life. Her father left her mother when Rachel was a little girl, leaving Rachel's mom a wreck. But while Rachel's mom struggled with this abandonment, Rachel seemed to handle it with shocking maturity.

For a while. Once Rachel hit young adulthood, she jumped into a series of unhealthy relationships with men. She started drinking heavily. She dropped out of college, unable to sustain the long-term commitment it took to complete her coursework. Clearly, Rachel's past was catching up with her.

Any amateur psychologist could see that Rachel was suffering from abandonment issues. She sought out relationships with men in an effort to fill the void left by her absent father. Alcohol became a way of numbing the pain. Because she saw someone she loved give up on his commitments, it was hard for her to stick with her own. Through years of therapy, Rachel made important connections between her childhood trauma and the poor choices she had made.

But the pain Rachel was dealing with didn't go away until she did something brave and, frankly, terrifying. She contacted her father. After nearly 20 years, Rachel told her father how much pain she had experienced because of his rejection. She told him how hard his leaving had been on her and her mother. And she told him that she forgave him.

Rachel believes that the real cause of her pain wasn't the choices her father had made, but the intense hatred she had for him. She felt stuck in it, tied to it, unable to move forward with her life because of the heavy weight of this hate. Once she talked to her dad, she knew she could let it go. He didn't change. He didn't really even apologize. But Rachel forgave him just the same.

Hate is a powerful force. It infects us in ways few other emotions can. When we are consumed with hate for someone, it eats away at our other relationships. And it doesn't matter who that hate is directed toward. Whether it's a parent, a coworker or a former spouse, harboring hatred for another person cripples *us*.

The image of hatred keeping us in the dark in 1 John 2:11 is a telling one. Think about what it's like to walk in a dark room. You crack your shin on the coffee table, trip over the rug, lose your sense of direction and walk into a wall.

The beauty of marriage is that you don't have to wander alone in the dark. If you're willing to open up about your feelings, allow your spouse to see the ugly parts of you, then your spouse can help you on your journey and act like a flashlight to guide you out of the darkness of hate toward the light of God's love and forgiveness.

—CARLA BARNHILL

let's talk

- ✦ What are some ways we've seen hate, anger or unresolved pain from the past infect our marriage? What steps can we take as a couple to deal with those issues and work toward healing?
- ✦ Do we have any unspoken grudges in our marriage that we need to work through?
- ✦ Are there other couples or family members that we don't like? If so, let's talk about how we treat those people. How can we be more Christlike in our relationships with people we don't like?

FOR YOUR NEXT DEVOTIONAL READING, TURN TO PAGE 1436.

denies the Son has the Father; whoever acknowledges the Son has the Father also.
24See that what you have heard from the
beginning remains in you. If it does, you
also will remain in the Son and in the Father.
25And this is what he promised us—even eternal life.
26I am writing these things to you about
those who are trying to lead you astray. 27As
for you, the anointing you received from him
remains in you, and you do not need anyone
to teach you. But as his anointing teaches you
about all things and as that anointing is real,
not counterfeit—just as it has taught you, remain in him.

Children of God

28And now, dear children, continue in him,
so that when he appears we may be confident
and unashamed before him at his coming.
29If you know that he is righteous, you
know that everyone who does what is right
has been born of him.
3 How great is the love the Father has lavished
on us, that we should be called children of
God! And that is what we are! The reason
the world does not know us is that it did not
know him. 2Dear friends, now we are children
of God, and what we will be has not yet been
made known. But we know that when he appears,[a] we shall be like him, for we shall see
him as he is. 3Everyone who has this hope in
him purifies himself, just as he is pure.
4Everyone who sins breaks the law; in fact,
sin is lawlessness. 5But you know that he appeared so that he might take away our sins.
And in him is no sin. 6No one who lives in
him keeps on sinning. No one who continues
to sin has either seen him or known him.
7Dear children, do not let anyone lead you
astray. He who does what is right is righteous,
just as he is righteous. 8He who does what
is sinful is of the devil, because the devil has
been sinning from the beginning. The reason
the Son of God appeared was to destroy the
devil's work. 9No one who is born of God will
continue to sin, because God's seed remains
in him; he cannot go on sinning, because he
has been born of God. 10This is how we know
who the children of God are and who the children of the devil are: Anyone who does not do
what is right is not a child of God; nor is anyone who does not love his brother.

Love One Another

11This is the message you heard from the
beginning: We should love one another. 12Do
not be like Cain, who belonged to the evil
one and murdered his brother. And why did
he murder him? Because his own actions were
evil and his brother's were righteous. 13Do not
be surprised, my brothers, if the world hates
you. 14We know that we have passed from
death to life, because we love our brothers.
Anyone who does not love remains in death.
15Anyone who hates his brother is a murderer,
and you know that no murderer has eternal
life in him.
16This is how we know what love is: Jesus
Christ laid down his life for us. And we ought
to lay down our lives for our brothers. 17If
anyone has material possessions and sees his
brother in need but has no pity on him, how
can the love of God be in him? 18Dear children, let us not love with words or tongue
but with actions and in truth. 19This then is
how we know that we belong to the truth, and
how we set our hearts at rest in his presence
20whenever our hearts condemn us. For God
is greater than our hearts, and he knows everything.
21Dear friends, if our hearts do not condemn us, we have confidence before God
22and receive from him anything we ask, because we obey his commands and do what
pleases him. 23And this is his command: to
believe in the name of his Son, Jesus Christ,
and to love one another as he commanded us.
24Those who obey his commands live in him,
and he in them. And this is how we know
that he lives in us: We know it by the Spirit
he gave us.

Test the Spirits

4 Dear friends, do not believe every spirit, but test the spirits to see whether they
are from God, because many false prophets have gone out into the world. 2This is how
you can recognize the Spirit of God: Every
spirit that acknowledges that Jesus Christ has
come in the flesh is from God, 3but every spirit that does not acknowledge Jesus is not from
God. This is the spirit of the antichrist, which
you have heard is coming and even now is already in the world.
4You, dear children, are from God and have
overcome them, because the one who is in you
is greater than the one who is in the world.
5They are from the world and therefore speak

---

[a] 2 Or *when it is made known*

FRIDAY
READ 1 JOHN 3:11–24

HOW TRUE LOVE BEHAVES

Art Linkletter once asked a little girl if she knew what *true love* was. She thought for a moment and then said, "*Love* is when your mommy reads you a bedtime story. *True love* is when she doesn't skip any pages."

The apostle John would have agreed. It's easy to pledge love in the heat of passion or during the quiet intimacy of a Valentine's Day dinner. But true love has to deal with short fuses, tired bodies, overextended commitments and inconvenient interruptions every day. And yet it keeps on giving.

The church at the end of the first century was wrestling with a philosophic aberration of Christian doctrine called Gnosticism. Gnosticism played up the spiritual nature of humanity and downplayed its physical nature. Some select people believed they had a spark of divinity trapped in their flesh. Only the religious elite had the secret information (*gnosis* means "knowledge") that would help them transcend their evil flesh. To them, Jesus was a heavenly visitor who came to this world like a ghostly apparition; he never actually became flesh and blood, for all flesh is evil and a divine spirit would never become human. Salvation consisted of secret chants and rituals that prepared one for release into the transcendent world. Gnostics ignored the physical needs of others and disdained those who did not share their secret inspiration.

Dear children, let us not love with words or tongue but with actions and in truth.

— 1 John 3:18

let's talk

- ✦ What is the romantic temperature of our relationship? Hot? Lukewarm? Frosty? How does each of us feel about that? Why?
- ✦ How do we express our love for one another in words? How do we express it in deeds and actions?
- ✦ What do we need to keep in mind in those times when we don't feel like loving? How can actions move our relationship forward when words become meaningless?

John wrote about the true Spirit of God, who helps us know that Jesus actually came in the flesh. The "true love" of God put Jesus into our world, not just to float around like a ghostly figure with meaningless chants and rituals, but to struggle with the world's problems and difficulties as a person of flesh and blood. Such true love helped those who were cold and hungry and in need of shelter. True love dug in and got dirty.

So it is in marriage. One couple I used to know never figured that out. The wife was addicted to romantic novels and TV soap operas. For her a constant flow of romantically charged passion was the only sure sign of love. When her husband came home from a hard day at his job too tired to court her, or when hours of cleaning or cooking took the fairy-tale bliss out of her week, she couldn't take it. Eventually she filed for divorce. She's probably still looking for that make-believe kind of happiness.

The apostle John urged the church to believe in a God who physically came into our world to be with us in our struggles. Furthermore, he calls us to imitate God's love by investing our energy in the day-to-day messiness of the real lives of others. We need to see others—especially our spouses—with our Father's eyes, touch them with our Savior's hands and be inspired by the Spirit's passion as we act out true love.

—WAYNE BROUWER

FOR YOUR NEXT DEVOTIONAL READING, TURN TO PAGE 1438.

from the viewpoint of the world, and the
world listens to them. [6]We are from God, and
whoever knows God listens to us; but whoever
is not from God does not listen to us. This is
how we recognize the Spirit[a] of truth and the
spirit of falsehood.

God's Love and Ours

[7]Dear friends, let us love one another, for
love comes from God. Everyone who loves has
been born of God and knows God. [8]Whoev-
er does not love does not know God, because
God is love. [9]This is how God showed his love
among us: He sent his one and only Son[b] into
the world that we might live through him.
[10]This is love: not that we loved God, but that
he loved us and sent his Son as an atoning sacrifice for[c] our sins. [11]Dear friends, since God
so loved us, we also ought to love one another.
[12]No one has ever seen God; but if we love one
another, God lives in us and his love is made
complete in us.

[13]We know that we live in him and he in us,
because he has given us of his Spirit. [14]And we
have seen and testify that the Father has sent
his Son to be the Savior of the world. [15]If anyone acknowledges that Jesus is the Son of God,
God lives in him and he in God. [16]And so we
know and rely on the love God has for us.

God is love. Whoever lives in love lives in
God, and God in him. [17]In this way, love is
made complete among us so that we will have
confidence on the day of judgment, because in
this world we are like him. [18]There is no fear
in love. But perfect love drives out fear, because fear has to do with punishment. The one
who fears is not made perfect in love.

[19]We love because he first loved us. [20]If anyone says, "I love God," yet hates his brother,
he is a liar. For anyone who does not love his
brother, whom he has seen, cannot love God,
whom he has not seen. [21]And he has given us
this command: Whoever loves God must also
love his brother.

Faith in the Son of God

5 Everyone who believes that Jesus is the
Christ is born of God, and everyone who
loves the father loves his child as well.
[2]This is how we know that we love the children of God: by loving God and carrying
out his commands. [3]This is love for God:
to obey his commands. And his commands
are not burdensome, [4]for everyone born of
God overcomes the world. This is the victory that has overcome the world, even our
faith. [5]Who is it that overcomes the world?
Only he who believes that Jesus is the Son
of God.

[6]This is the one who came by water and
blood—Jesus Christ. He did not come by water only, but by water and blood. And it is the
Spirit who testifies, because the Spirit is the
truth. [7]For there are three that testify: [8]the[d]
Spirit, the water and the blood; and the three
are in agreement. [9]We accept man's testimony,
but God's testimony is greater because it is the
testimony of God, which he has given about
his Son. [10]Anyone who believes in the Son of
God has this testimony in his heart. Anyone
who does not believe God has made him out
to be a liar, because he has not believed the testimony God has given about his Son. [11]And
this is the testimony: God has given us eternal
life, and this life is in his Son. [12]He who has
the Son has life; he who does not have the Son
of God does not have life.

Concluding Remarks

[13]I write these things to you who believe
in the name of the Son of God so that you
may know that you have eternal life. [14]This is
the confidence we have in approaching God:
that if we ask anything according to his will,
he hears us. [15]And if we know that he hears
us—whatever we ask—we know that we have
what we asked of him.

[16]If anyone sees his brother commit a sin
that does not lead to death, he should pray and
God will give him life. I refer to those whose
sin does not lead to death. There is a sin that
leads to death. I am not saying that he should
pray about that. [17]All wrongdoing is sin, and
there is sin that does not lead to death.

[18]We know that anyone born of God does
not continue to sin; the one who was born of
God keeps him safe, and the evil one cannot
harm him. [19]We know that we are children of
God, and that the whole world is under the
control of the evil one. [20]We know also that
the Son of God has come and has given us understanding, so that we may know him who is
true. And we are in him who is true—even in
his Son Jesus Christ. He is the true God and
eternal life.

[21]Dear children, keep yourselves from
idols.

---

[a] 6 Or *spirit* [b] 9 Or *his only begotten Son* [c] 10 Or *as the one who would turn aside his wrath, taking away* [d] 7,8 Late manuscripts of the Vulgate *testify in heaven: the Father, the Word and the Holy Spirit, and these three are one.* [8]*And there are three that testify on earth: the* (not found in any Greek manuscript before the fourteenth century)

WEEKEND

entertaining guests

It can be a happy time when loved ones come to call. But, in reality, it doesn't take long for the family ties that bind to feel restrictive. And marriages have a way of suffering from the tension. Some tips on surviving your house guests as a team:

1. Set some boundaries. Before your guests even step foot in your home, talk with your spouse about the visit. Discuss how you can make each other feel comfortable and less burdened by the invasion. If your spouse insists on specific boundaries, then respect them. This could mean bedtime by 10 p.m. or no "guest pets" in the house. Or you may decide on a guest-free zone, where the two of you can reconnect and unwind.

Make your kids comfortable. Determine that at least one parent, when not entertaining the guests, will be in charge of seeing to the kids' needs and feelings. Store their favorite toys and books in their rooms. Create a refuge for them in your room for those times when the strain of being without their routines overwhelms them.

2. Show a united front. If one of you is opposed to smoking in the house, for instance, together inform your guests that they will have to smoke outside. It's acceptable to set the tone of your home, especially when you and your partner support each other.

Ease up on your usual standards for a spotless house. By all means, work together to tidy up for comfort and cleanliness, but resist the urge to purge while your guests sit idly by. Accept the possibility that one of you may assume the lion's share of the chores, depending on which set of in-laws is visiting. If you fret and squabble over every soda can and dropped crumb, you'll send an unwelcome, unflattering message to your guests.

3. Work together. You can't do it all, so don't be afraid to ask your partner to help in the kitchen. If he's a wonderful breakfast chef, then put him in charge of the pancakes and eggs for your hungry crew. But try to plan meals that won't tether either of you to the kitchen. Prepare a tray of sliced cold cuts and cheeses, fruits and fresh veggies, or break out your crock-pot for a hot and easy meal at the end of the day.

Dote on each other in private moments. Offer a back massage or bring a bowl of ice cream to your spouse to enjoy at the end of a long day. Call a temporary truce and set aside any issues you may currently have in your marriage. Strive to be happy and "in the moment" with each other while you have visitors.

4. Invite your guests to be self-sufficient. Here are a few tips to inspire independence in your houseguests.

- Show your guests around the kitchen, show them how to make coffee, and invite them to help themselves from the pantry.
- Supply them with everything they need to strike out on their own: maps, sightseeing attractions, directions, phone numbers and a spare house key.
- Anticipate bathroom needs with extra towels, soap, shampoo and spare toothbrushes.
- Suggest they take a stroll around the block before dinner so you can prepare the meal without feeling like you're in a pressure cooker.

5. Finally, relax! Recognize that each of you is feeling the strain of house guests, but resolve not to blame the other for it. Do what you can to be a safe place for each other until things get back to normal. Above all, enjoy the time you have together with family!

—KERRI S. MABEE

how's your hospitality?

HOW ARE WE DOING?

1. I am happy to have guests over
   a. Anytime
   b. After I've picked up the dirty underwear
   c. The day my house appears in a photo shoot for Southern Living—in other words, never
2. Getting ready for guests in my home takes
   a. Years
   b. A few minutes
   c. I'm always ready
3. Having people over makes me feel
   a. Nervous and judged
   b. Happy
   c. Annoyed at the disruption
4. When cooking for company
   a. I can't do it; we'll go out
   b. I prepare for days ahead of time
   c. Whatever we have on hand will be fine
5. The people invited to my home are
   a. Guests
   b. Friends
   c. Family, regardless of whether we're related
6. My biggest fear of inviting people over is
   a. The condition of my house
   b. That they will stay too long
   c. That they will learn things about me I don't want them to know
7. Having people over is an opportunity for my spouse and me
   a. To argue over who cleans up
   b. To get to know each other better through the eyes of others
   c. To minister to other people

The correct answer is the one that you and your spouse agree on. If having people over is too stressful, find a way to scale back. Invite fewer people or serve snacks and watch a sporting event instead of offering a full-course dinner. Entertaining can be rewarding when you both agree.

let's make a DATE

PLAN A PARTY

Set aside time together and plan the ultimate party. Have each person determine who to invite, what food to serve, whether there will be a theme, who will do what. Use this conversation as a time to understand more about your spouse and what he or she likes and dislikes about entertaining. Then after you've dreamed big, find a way to downsize your ultimate party into a fabulous evening that you can manage. Then, just do it!

FOR YOUR NEXT DEVOTIONAL READING, TURN TO PAGE 1442.

LESSONS FROM THE *Bible*

What does the Bible teach us about hospitality in these passages?

1. Abraham serves three visitors (Genesis 18:1–8)
2. Lydia welcomes missionaries into her home (Acts 16:11–15)
3. Priscilla and Aquila provide hospitality to Apollos (Acts 18:24–28)
4. A challenge to believers from the writer of Hebrews (Hebrews 13:1–2)

2 JOHN

2 John

QUICK FACTS

AUTHOR The apostle John

AUDIENCE The "chosen lady and her children" (2 John 1), which refers either literally to a specific woman and her children or figuratively to a church and its members

DATE Between A.D. 85 and 95

SETTING Written from or near Ephesus to warn believers about traveling false teachers

During the first two centuries of Christianity, the gospel was taken from place to place by traveling evangelists and teachers. Believers opened their homes to these missionaries and gave them provisions for their journey when they left. Second John, in one way, serves as a counterpoint to 3 John. In 3 John, the apostle John addressed a problem in which a dictatorial leader in the church was refusing to provide hospitality for itinerant teachers sent out by John. In 2 John, the apostle focused on false teachers, about whom John told believers: "Do not take him into your house or welcome him" (2 John 10).

This instruction does not prohibit greeting or even inviting a person into one's home for conversation. John was warning against providing food and shelter, since this would be an investment in the "wicked work" (2 John 11) of false teachers and would give public approval. John urged believers to discern what is true no matter what false ideas are clamoring for attention.

We have a desperate need for such discernment because our world is rife with ideologies that conflict with one another. So as spouses we are to help each other grow in the love of Christ by discerning what is true and by living according to that truth.

1 The elder,

To the chosen lady and her children, whom
I love in the truth—and not I only, but also all
who know the truth— 2 because of the truth,
which lives in us and will be with us forever:

3 Grace, mercy and peace from God the Father and from Jesus Christ, the Father's Son,
will be with us in truth and love.

4 It has given me great joy to find some of
your children walking in the truth, just as the
Father commanded us. 5 And now, dear lady, I
am not writing you a new command but one
we have had from the beginning. I ask that we
love one another. 6 And this is love: that we
walk in obedience to his commands. As you
have heard from the beginning, his command
is that you walk in love.
7 Many deceivers, who do not acknowledge
Jesus Christ as coming in the flesh, have gone
out into the world. Any such person is the
deceiver and the antichrist. 8 Watch out that
you do not lose what you have worked for,
but that you may be rewarded fully. 9 Anyone who runs ahead and does not continue
in the teaching of Christ does not have God;
whoever continues in the teaching has both
the Father and the Son. 10 If anyone comes to
you and does not bring this teaching, do not
take him into your house or welcome him.
11 Anyone who welcomes him shares in his
wicked work.
12 I have much to write to you, but I do not
want to use paper and ink. Instead, I hope to
visit you and talk with you face to face, so that
our joy may be complete.

13 The children of your chosen sister send
their greetings.

M **MONDAY**
READ 2 JOHN 1–13

TRUTH WATCH

Have you ever thought of all the ways that ideas come into your home during a given day? I often listen to a morning radio show while I get breakfast ready for my kids. I read the kids' textbooks and school papers. I read the Bible. I read magazines. Family, friends and neighbors drop in or I talk with them on the phone. Many evenings my husband and I watch a DVD we've picked up at the library while we fold clothes and work on other projects. On Sundays and at least one other time during the week, we're all at church soaking up some good ideas. But no matter which day of the week it is, ideas keep coming at me, and most of the time I don't stop to analyze whether the ideas resonate with Christian truth or not.

In this, his second epistle, the apostle John expressed his joy and delight in the fact that some believers were "walking in the truth" (verse 4). John reminded them to examine what they heard, holding up the ideas they received against what they had been taught. John warned them to continue to keep the teaching of Christ at the forefront of their lives and to be on guard against deceptive false teachers. In fact, he said, "If anyone comes to you and does not bring this teaching, do not take him into your house or welcome him" (verse 10).

If you and your spouse don't already have a habit of talking about ideas and spiritual truths, it might seem strange to start now. But in no time flat, it'll make you laugh to think it was ever awkward. Discussions about what you think and believe can be incredibly stimulating. And you build intimacy by sharing the wisdom and reasoning that goes on inside your two separate heads.

David and I have been married long enough for me to pretty much know his opinion on topics. Sometimes when we're listening to someone speak, I'll hear something that doesn't sound quite right to me and look over at David. I can sense what he's thinking. Later we'll talk about the matter, especially if we feel our children may have absorbed teaching or instruction that we think isn't consistent with God's Word.

At night when we're both reading in bed, we'll sometimes read a passage aloud and discuss it. More recently, I was reading a book, getting more and more annoyed by some of its ideas. I felt better after I expressed to David why I thought the author's ideas sounded good but were really off base.

It's hard to compare the ideas that come into our "house" against the Scriptures unless we're regularly reading God's Word. Therefore, David and I are committed to keeping our noses in the Book. We know that all truth belongs to God, and everything else must be measured against it.

—ANNETTE LAPLACA

Anyone who runs ahead and does not continue in the teaching of Christ does not have God; whoever continues in the teaching has both the Father and the Son.

2 JOHN 9

let's *talk*

- ✦ What are the main sources of ideas that come into our home? What are some creative ways we might discuss those ideas with each other?
- ✦ Do we have a good foundation of Scriptural knowledge—enough to check the truth or accuracy of the ideas that come into our home? How could we gain more knowledge?
- ✦ In what ways do we examine the messages we hear (even Christian teachings), holding them up to Scripture to see if they're true? What do we do if we believe something isn't right?

FOR YOUR NEXT DEVOTIONAL READING, TURN TO PAGE 1449.

3 JOHN

3 John

QUICK FACTS

AUTHOR The apostle John

AUDIENCE John's "dear friend Gaius" (3 John 1)

DATE Between A.D. 85 and 95

SETTING Written from or near Ephesus to encourage believers to provide hospitality to traveling teachers

In 3 John the apostle introduced Demetrius to his godly friend Gaius. John urged Gaius to offer hospitality to this teacher and others, despite the opposition of a mean-spirited, self-centered church official named Diotrephes, who had refused to welcome other traveling ministers sent by John and had even excommunicated those who tried to do so.

The love of God urges us to make room in our lives and homes for others. Everything we have is a gift from God, so we must hold what we have loosely and share it. God's Word teaches us that people are eternal, not houses or food or belongings, so we must focus on souls who may be with us for eternity.

Cocooning, or hunkering down behind closed doors with one's family, is quite understandable today. Life's stresses can be overwhelming, so retreating to the family room is enticing as well as necessary. But we should not do so to the exclusion of others. The Scriptures consistently exhort us to show hospitality to others. When we welcome others into our homes, we often find ourselves energized and blessed as we work together for the truth.

[1]The elder,

To my dear friend Gaius, whom I love in
the truth.

[2]Dear friend, I pray that you may enjoy
good health and that all may go well with you,
even as your soul is getting along well. [3]It gave
me great joy to have some brothers come and
tell about your faithfulness to the truth and
how you continue to walk in the truth. [4]I have
no greater joy than to hear that my children
are walking in the truth.

[5]Dear friend, you are faithful in what you
are doing for the brothers, even though they
are strangers to you. [6]They have told the church
about your love. You will do well to send them
on their way in a manner worthy of God. [7]It
was for the sake of the Name that they went
out, receiving no help from the pagans. [8]We
ought therefore to show hospitality to such men
so that we may work together for the truth.

[9]I wrote to the church, but Diotrephes,
who loves to be first, will have nothing to do
with us. [10]So if I come, I will call attention
to what he is doing, gossiping maliciously
about us. Not satisfied with that, he refuses
to welcome the brothers. He also stops those
who want to do so and puts them out of the
church.

[11]Dear friend, do not imitate what is evil
but what is good. Anyone who does what is
good is from God. Anyone who does what
is evil has not seen God. [12]Demetrius is well
spoken of by everyone—and even by the truth
itself. We also speak well of him, and you
know that our testimony is true.

[13]I have much to write you, but I do not
want to do so with pen and ink. [14]I hope to
see you soon, and we will talk face to face.

Peace to you. The friends here send their
greetings. Greet the friends there by name.

JUDE

Jude

QUICK FACTS

AUTHOR Jude, the brother of Jesus and James

AUDIENCE An unspecified Christian audience

DATE Probably around A.D. 65

SETTING Written to warn against false teachers who were trying to lead people astray

The book of Jude is a call to arms against saboteurs who infiltrate the church to corrode it from within by contending that being saved by grace gives believers license to sin since their sins will no longer be held against them. These rebels brandish the weapons of false teaching, slander, dissension and selfishness, but in the end they will be overwhelmed by the truth of Christ. They will be consigned to the scrap heap of history, where they will be stacked up with other vanquished opponents of God.

In the time of Jude, false doctrines were burrowing their way into the early church, carried by rebellious people whose spirit was much like that of their Old Testament predecessors Cain, Korah and Balaam (see Jude 11). But Jude urged his readers to contend for the faith entrusted to them and to build themselves up through prayer, remain vigilant and shore up the faith of wavering fellow believers.

Our enemy, who specializes in divide-and-conquer tactics, can rattle Christian marriages. When one partner begins to veer from the truth and cozies up to dangerous ideas, the results can be catastrophic. Jude offers a warning to the stronger partner to fight back with mercy for the sinner to pluck him or her from disaster.

1Jude, a servant of Jesus Christ and a brother of James,

To those who have been called, who are
loved by God the Father and kept by[a] Jesus
Christ:

2Mercy, peace and love be yours in abundance.

The Sin and Doom of Godless Men

3Dear friends, although I was very eager to
write to you about the salvation we share, I
felt I had to write and urge you to contend
for the faith that was once for all entrusted to
the saints. 4For certain men whose condemnation was written about[b] long ago have secretly slipped in among you. They are godless
men, who change the grace of our God into a
license for immorality and deny Jesus Christ
our only Sovereign and Lord.

5Though you already know all this, I want to
remind you that the Lord[c] delivered his people
out of Egypt, but later destroyed those who did
not believe. 6And the angels who did not keep
their positions of authority but abandoned
their own home—these he has kept in darkness, bound with everlasting chains for judgment on the great Day. 7In a similar way, Sodom and Gomorrah and the surrounding towns
gave themselves up to sexual immorality and
perversion. They serve as an example of those
who suffer the punishment of eternal fire.

8In the very same way, these dreamers pollute their own bodies, reject authority and
slander celestial beings. 9But even the archangel Michael, when he was disputing with the
devil about the body of Moses, did not dare to
bring a slanderous accusation against him, but
said, "The Lord rebuke you!" 10Yet these men
speak abusively against whatever they do not
understand; and what things they do understand by instinct, like unreasoning animals—
these are the very things that destroy them.

11Woe to them! They have taken the way of
Cain; they have rushed for profit into Balaam's
error; they have been destroyed in Korah's rebellion.

12These men are blemishes at your love
feasts, eating with you without the slightest
qualm—shepherds who feed only themselves.
They are clouds without rain, blown along by
the wind; autumn trees, without fruit and uprooted—twice dead. 13They are wild waves of
the sea, foaming up their shame; wandering
stars, for whom blackest darkness has been reserved forever.

14Enoch, the seventh from Adam, prophesied about these men: "See, the Lord is coming
with thousands upon thousands of his holy
ones 15to judge everyone, and to convict all
the ungodly of all the ungodly acts they have
done in the ungodly way, and of all the harsh
words ungodly sinners have spoken against
him." 16These men are grumblers and fault-
finders; they follow their own evil desires; they
boast about themselves and flatter others for
their own advantage.

A Call to Persevere

17But, dear friends, remember what the
apostles of our Lord Jesus Christ foretold.
18They said to you, "In the last times there will
be scoffers who will follow their own ungodly
desires." 19These are the men who divide you,
who follow mere natural instincts and do not
have the Spirit.

20But you, dear friends, build yourselves up
in your most holy faith and pray in the Holy
Spirit. 21Keep yourselves in God's love as you
wait for the mercy of our Lord Jesus Christ to
bring you to eternal life.

22Be merciful to those who doubt; 23snatch
others from the fire and save them; to others
show mercy, mixed with fear—hating even the
clothing stained by corrupted flesh.

Doxology

24To him who is able to keep you from
falling and to present you before his glorious
presence without fault and with great joy—
25to the only God our Savior be glory, majesty,
power and authority, through Jesus Christ our
Lord, before all ages, now and forevermore!
Amen.

[a] *1* Or *for;* or *in* [b] *4* Or *men who were marked out for condemnation* [c] *5* Some early manuscripts *Jesus*

REVELATION

QUICK FACTS

AUTHOR The apostle John

AUDIENCE Likely Christians everywhere, but specifically those in seven churches in the Roman province of Asia (located in modern-day western Turkey)

DATE About A.D. 95

SETTING Describes a vision John had near the end of his life while exiled on the island of Patmos

Revelation is a stunning panorama of our world's end and how Jesus Christ will come again to reign over a new world. The earth will be wracked by a war to end all wars, one in which good and evil collide in the ultimate battle. In the end, a triumphant Christ will be united with all his faithful people who have ever lived.

This wild ride begins in relative calm, with the risen Jesus dictating letters of commendation—along with warnings in regard to faithfulness—to seven churches in Asia Minor. Then, hang on! Through a door into heaven, we see multitudes of men, beasts and angels. We hear trumpets and the thunder of horses' hooves. At the center of it all is a slain Lamb who will usher in a new day when God and his people will no longer be separated by distance or death.

When that happens, there's going to be a party—a sumptuous wedding celebration that will make the grandest of today's receptions seem puny. The guest list is written in the Lamb's book of life. Married people today can get on that list by inviting Christ into their lives, then asking him to stay and dwell within their marriages till one day they live with him in heaven.

Prologue

1 The revelation of Jesus Christ, which God
gave him to show his servants what must
soon take place. He made it known by
sending his angel to his servant John, 2 who testifies to everything he saw—that is, the word
of God and the testimony of Jesus Christ.
3 Blessed is the one who reads the words of this
prophecy, and blessed are those who hear it
and take to heart what is written in it, because
the time is near.

Greetings and Doxology

4 John,

To the seven churches in the province of
Asia:

Grace and peace to you from him who is,
and who was, and who is to come, and from
the seven spirits[a] before his throne, 5 and from
Jesus Christ, who is the faithful witness, the
firstborn from the dead, and the ruler of the
kings of the earth.

To him who loves us and has freed us from
our sins by his blood, 6 and has made us to be
a kingdom and priests to serve his God and
Father—to him be glory and power for ever
and ever! Amen.

7 Look, he is coming with the clouds,
  and every eye will see him,
even those who pierced him;
  and all the peoples of the earth will
    mourn because of him.
        So shall it be! Amen.

8 "I am the Alpha and the Omega," says the
Lord God, "who is, and who was, and who is
to come, the Almighty."

One Like a Son of Man

9 I, John, your brother and companion in
the suffering and kingdom and patient endurance that are ours in Jesus, was on the island
of Patmos because of the word of God and the
testimony of Jesus. 10 On the Lord's Day I was
in the Spirit, and I heard behind me a loud
voice like a trumpet, 11 which said: "Write on
a scroll what you see and send it to the sev-
en churches: to Ephesus, Smyrna, Pergamum,
Thyatira, Sardis, Philadelphia and Laodicea."
12 I turned around to see the voice that was
speaking to me. And when I turned I saw
seven golden lampstands, 13 and among the
lampstands was someone "like a son of man,"[b]
dressed in a robe reaching down to his feet
and with a golden sash around his chest. 14 His
head and hair were white like wool, as white as
snow, and his eyes were like blazing fire. 15 His
feet were like bronze glowing in a furnace, and
his voice was like the sound of rushing waters.
16 In his right hand he held seven stars, and
out of his mouth came a sharp double-edged
sword. His face was like the sun shining in all
its brilliance.

17 When I saw him, I fell at his feet as
though dead. Then he placed his right hand
on me and said: "Do not be afraid. I am the
First and the Last. 18 I am the Living One; I
was dead, and behold I am alive for ever and
ever! And I hold the keys of death and Hades.
19 "Write, therefore, what you have seen,
what is now and what will take place later. 20 The mystery of the seven stars that you
saw in my right hand and of the seven gold-
en lampstands is this: The seven stars are the
angels[c] of the seven churches, and the seven
lampstands are the seven churches.

To the Church in Ephesus

2 "To the angel[d] of the church in Ephesus
write:

These are the words of him who holds
the seven stars in his right hand and walks
among the seven golden lampstands: 2 I
know your deeds, your hard work and
your perseverance. I know that you cannot tolerate wicked men, that you have
tested those who claim to be apostles but
are not, and have found them false. 3 You
have persevered and have endured hardships for my name, and have not grown
weary.

4 Yet I hold this against you: You have
forsaken your first love. 5 Remember the
height from which you have fallen! Repent and do the things you did at first.
If you do not repent, I will come to you
and remove your lampstand from its
place. 6 But you have this in your favor:
You hate the practices of the Nicolaitans,
which I also hate.

7 He who has an ear, let him hear what
the Spirit says to the churches. To him
who overcomes, I will give the right to
eat from the tree of life, which is in the
paradise of God.

---

[a] *4* Or *the sevenfold Spirit* [b] *13* Daniel 7:13 [c] *20* Or *messengers* [d] *1* Or *messenger*; also in verses 8, 12 and 18

TUESDAY

READ REVELATION 2:1–7

FIRST LOVE

In his book *Sacred Marriage*, Gary Thomas tells about a businessman who sat next to a young man on an airplane. He asked the younger man whether he was traveling on business or pleasure.

"Pleasure," the young man replied. "I'm on my honeymoon."

"Your honeymoon?" the businessman asked, mystified. "Where's your wife?"

"Oh, she's a few rows back. The plane was full, so we couldn't get seats together."

The businessman said, "I'd be happy to change seats with her so that the two of you can be together."

"That's OK," the young man replied. "I've been talking to her all week."

Sometimes it doesn't take long for love to get road weary. It happens in marriage, and it happens in our relationship with Christ. In Jesus' message to the church at Ephesus, he commends them for their faithfulness under pressure. But pressure can take its toll.

Anyone who has been married a while knows that the pressures of life can cool "honeymoon love." It happens for Christians in our love for Jesus too. Sure, we're faithful to him, but sometimes there isn't much passion.

You have persevered and have endured hardships for my name, and have not grown weary. Yet I hold this against you: You have forsaken your first love.

—REVELATION 2:3–4

let's talk

- ✦ What do we remember about times when we were deeply in love with Jesus? What did it feel like? What did we do? How have things changed?
- ✦ Who do we know who seems to be deeply in love with Jesus now? How does being around that person affect us?
- ✦ Let's pray together, confessing to the Lord the ways in which our love for him and for each other has cooled. And let's ask God to help rekindle that first love for him and for each other.

Brennan Manning says that 100 years ago in the Deep South, people didn't refer to their conversion experiences as being "born again." Rather they said, "I have been seized by the power of a great affection." That's the kind of "first love" the Christians in Ephesus had lost. Maybe you have too.

We forget sometimes that what Jesus most wants from us is first love. He is our bridegroom, and we are his bride. He is unabashedly passionate about us. He's captivated with us. He thinks we're beautiful. He yearns for us to love him as passionately as he loves us.

Revelation 2:5 tells us how to recapture that kind of love. First, we need to "remember the height from which [we] have fallen." People sometimes describe their first love for Jesus as a mountaintop experience. Jesus tells us here to look back up the mountain.

Second, we need to "repent." That means we must not only confess our dulled love but also put our hearts back on the trail up the mountain, where we once loved Jesus passionately.

Third, we need to "do the things [we] did at first." We may be doing love-chilling things and failing to do love-warming things. To rekindle that first love, we should purposefully *do* the things we once did. When we do them, we will fall in love with Jesus again.

The same thing, of course, applies to marriage. If we have lost our first love for each other, we may need a temperature check. Are we spending enough time together? Doing fun things together? Lingering over dinner to talk through the day? Rekindling that love that once so powerfully attracted us to each other is worth all the effort we put into it—and more. It's priceless!

—LEE ECLOV

FOR YOUR NEXT DEVOTIONAL READING, TURN TO PAGE 1452.

To the Church in Smyrna

8“To the angel of the church in Smyrna write:

These are the words of him who is the
First and the Last, who died and came to
life again. 9I know your afflictions and
your poverty—yet you are rich! I know
the slander of those who say they are Jews
and are not, but are a synagogue of Satan.
10Do not be afraid of what you are about
to suffer. I tell you, the devil will put
some of you in prison to test you, and
you will suffer persecution for ten days.
Be faithful, even to the point of death,
and I will give you the crown of life.
11He who has an ear, let him hear what
the Spirit says to the churches. He who
overcomes will not be hurt at all by the
second death.

To the Church in Pergamum

12“To the angel of the church in Pergamum
write:

These are the words of him who has
the sharp, double-edged sword. 13I know
where you live—where Satan has his
throne. Yet you remain true to my name.
You did not renounce your faith in me,
even in the days of Antipas, my faithful
witness, who was put to death in your
city—where Satan lives.
14Nevertheless, I have a few things
against you: You have people there who
hold to the teaching of Balaam, who
taught Balak to entice the Israelites to sin
by eating food sacrificed to idols and by
committing sexual immorality. 15Like-
wise you also have those who hold to
the teaching of the Nicolaitans. 16Repent
therefore! Otherwise, I will soon come to
you and will fight against them with the
sword of my mouth.
17He who has an ear, let him hear
what the Spirit says to the churches. To
him who overcomes, I will give some of
the hidden manna. I will also give him a
white stone with a new name written on
it, known only to him who receives it.

To the Church in Thyatira

18“To the angel of the church in Thyatira
write:

These are the words of the Son of God,
whose eyes are like blazing fire and whose
feet are like burnished bronze. 19I know
your deeds, your love and faith, your service and perseverance, and that you are
now doing more than you did at first.
20Nevertheless, I have this against you:
You tolerate that woman Jezebel, who
calls herself a prophetess. By her teaching
she misleads my servants into sexual immorality and the eating of food sacrificed
to idols. 21I have given her time to repent
of her immorality, but she is unwilling.
22So I will cast her on a bed of suffering, and I will make those who commit
adultery with her suffer intensely, unless
they repent of her ways. 23I will strike her
children dead. Then all the churches will
know that I am he who searches hearts
and minds, and I will repay each of you
according to your deeds. 24Now I say to
the rest of you in Thyatira, to you who
do not hold to her teaching and have
not learned Satan's so-called deep secrets
(I will not impose any other burden on
you): 25Only hold on to what you have
until I come.
26To him who overcomes and does my
will to the end, I will give authority over
the nations—

27‘He will rule them with an iron
scepter;
he will dash them to pieces like
pottery’[a]—

just as I have received authority from my
Father. 28I will also give him the morning
star. 29He who has an ear, let him hear
what the Spirit says to the churches.

To the Church in Sardis

3 “To the angel[b] of the church in Sardis
write:

These are the words of him who holds
the seven spirits[c] of God and the seven
stars. I know your deeds; you have a reputation of being alive, but you are dead.
2Wake up! Strengthen what remains and
is about to die, for I have not found your
deeds complete in the sight of my God.
3Remember, therefore, what you have received and heard; obey it, and repent. But
if you do not wake up, I will come like a
thief, and you will not know at what time
I will come to you.
4Yet you have a few people in Sardis
who have not soiled their clothes. They

---

[a] *27* Psalm 2:9 [b] *1* Or *messenger;* also in verses 7 and 14 [c] *1* Or *the sevenfold Spirit*

will walk with me, dressed in white, for they are worthy. 5He who overcomes will, like them, be dressed in white. I will never blot out his name from the book of life, but will acknowledge his name before my Father and his angels. 6He who has an ear, let him hear what the Spirit says to the churches.

To the Church in Philadelphia

7"To the angel of the church in Philadelphia write:

These are the words of him who is holy and true, who holds the key of David. What he opens no one can shut, and what he shuts no one can open. 8I know your deeds. See, I have placed before you an open door that no one can shut. I know that you have little strength, yet you have kept my word and have not denied my name. 9I will make those who are of the synagogue of Satan, who claim to be Jews though they are not, but are liars—I will make them come and fall down at your feet and acknowledge that I have loved you. 10Since you have kept my command to endure patiently, I will also keep you from the hour of trial that is going to come upon the whole world to test those who live on the earth.

11I am coming soon. Hold on to what you have, so that no one will take your crown. 12Him who overcomes I will make a pillar in the temple of my God. Never again will he leave it. I will write on him the name of my God and the name of the city of my God, the new Jerusalem, which is coming down out of heaven from my God; and I will also write on him my new name. 13He who has an ear, let him hear what the Spirit says to the churches.

To the Church in Laodicea

14"To the angel of the church in Laodicea write:

These are the words of the Amen, the faithful and true witness, the ruler of God's creation. 15I know your deeds, that you are neither cold nor hot. I wish you were either one or the other! 16So, because you are lukewarm—neither hot nor cold—I am about to spit you out of my mouth. 17You say, 'I am rich; I have acquired wealth and do not need a thing.' But you do not realize that you are wretched, pitiful, poor, blind and naked. 18I counsel you to buy from me gold refined in the fire, so you can become rich; and white clothes to wear, so you can cover your shameful nakedness; and salve to put on your eyes, so you can see.

19Those whom I love I rebuke and discipline. So be earnest, and repent. 20Here I am! I stand at the door and knock. If anyone hears my voice and opens the door, I will come in and eat with him, and he with me.

21To him who overcomes, I will give the right to sit with me on my throne, just as I overcame and sat down with my Father on his throne. 22He who has an ear, let him hear what the Spirit says to the churches."

The Throne in Heaven

4 After this I looked, and there before me was a door standing open in heaven. And the voice I had first heard speaking to me like a trumpet said, "Come up here, and I will show you what must take place after this." 2At once I was in the Spirit, and there before me was a throne in heaven with someone sitting on it. 3And the one who sat there had the appearance of jasper and carnelian. A rainbow, resembling an emerald, encircled the throne. 4Surrounding the throne were twenty-four other thrones, and seated on them were twenty-four elders. They were dressed in white and had crowns of gold on their heads. 5From the throne came flashes of lightning, rumblings and peals of thunder. Before the throne, seven lamps were blazing. These are the seven spirits[a] of God. 6Also before the throne there was what looked like a sea of glass, clear as crystal.

In the center, around the throne, were four living creatures, and they were covered with eyes, in front and in back. 7The first living creature was like a lion, the second was like an ox, the third had a face like a man, the fourth was like a flying eagle. 8Each of the four living creatures had six wings and was covered with eyes all around, even under his wings. Day and night they never stop saying:

"Holy, holy, holy
is the Lord God Almighty,
who was, and is, and is to come."

---

a 5 Or *the sevenfold Spirit*

WEDNESDAY
READ REVELATION 3:14–22

MIDLOVE CORRECTION

My friend Danny is a big-shot public speaker, but his wife never lets him forget that he's still a guy who can't find his car keys without a little help. Whenever I start thinking I'm a smarty-pants writer who knows more than the average hack, I can count on my husband, Jimmy, to point out that I am a terrible speller and have benefited greatly from my computer's spell-checker.

Most of the time, I can laugh about my little quirks and foibles. But when it comes to big flaws, I just don't want to hear about them. I like thinking I'm practically perfect in every way, and I don't like it when Jimmy points out that I'm not. Even when he has my best interest in mind, I have a hard time accepting his constructive criticism.

But there are times—lots of them—when I need Jimmy's perspective whether I like it or not. When I'm being inflexible with the kids, when I'm so determined to be right that I won't listen to Jimmy's opinion, when I'm frustrated by a work issue but take it out on my family—that's when I need someone to call me to account. And because I trust Jimmy, I know he's not being cruel; he's being honest.

Of course, when it comes to critiquing a spouse, there's a fine line not to cross. To keep from sliding over that fine line, we need to look to the example God gives us of loving discipline and accountability.

In Revelation 3:19, the risen Christ told the believers in Laodicea that he rebukes and disciplines those he loves. This echoes Proverbs 3:11–12: "Do not despise the LORD's discipline and do not resent his rebuke, because the LORD disciplines those he loves." Every parent knows that to let a child do whatever he or she pleases is not good parenting; it's negligence. As our heavenly Father, God parents us by telling us how to live, allowing us to suffer the consequences when we choose to live outside of his commands, and offering us endless forgiveness when we realize how stupid we've been. It's a love that takes our humanity into account, a love that accepts us completely, a love that isn't willing to let us go even when we make terrible mistakes.

When we hold up a mirror for our spouses, we would do well to keep God's example in mind. At the heart of God's discipline is love. God doesn't rebuke us because he is embarrassed by something we've said. God doesn't reprimand us when we express an unpopular opinion. God corrects us when we've strayed from being the people he created us to be.

The best marriages are those in which couples trust each other enough to know that criticism is couched in love and concern. When Jimmy points to my stubbornness, I know he's doing it not only to help us get through a conflict but to help me see it for myself, so I can work on being more flexible. When I see Jimmy letting his anger get the best of him, I try to help him see that harsh words will cause more harm than good. Naturally we don't always appreciate the other person's criticism, but we have both grown and matured because of the other's willingness to say what needs to be said.

—CARLA BARNHILL

Those whom I love I rebuke and discipline. So be earnest, and repent.

— REVELATION 3:19

let's talk

✦ First, for each of us individually, how do I feel when you correct or criticize me? Next, let's talk about our motivations for offering rebukes. Are they offered in love, or are they attempts to hurt each other?

✦ Let's talk about ways we've helped each other grow and mature. What specific conversations or actions have helped us see ourselves differently?

✦ What are some areas that each of us might work on. Do we need to be more patient? More selfless? What else?

FOR YOUR NEXT DEVOTIONAL READING, TURN TO PAGE 1455.

9Whenever the living creatures give glory,
honor and thanks to him who sits on the
throne and who lives for ever and ever, 10the
twenty-four elders fall down before him who
sits on the throne, and worship him who lives
for ever and ever. They lay their crowns before
the throne and say:

11 "You are worthy, our Lord and God,
to receive glory and honor and power,
for you created all things,
and by your will they were created
and have their being."

The Scroll and the Lamb

5 Then I saw in the right hand of him who
sat on the throne a scroll with writing on
both sides and sealed with seven seals.
2And I saw a mighty angel proclaiming in a
loud voice, "Who is worthy to break the seals
and open the scroll?" 3But no one in heaven
or on earth or under the earth could open the
scroll or even look inside it. 4I wept and wept
because no one was found who was worthy to
open the scroll or look inside. 5Then one of
the elders said to me, "Do not weep! See, the
Lion of the tribe of Judah, the Root of David,
has triumphed. He is able to open the scroll
and its seven seals."

6Then I saw a Lamb, looking as if it had
been slain, standing in the center of the
throne, encircled by the four living creatures
and the elders. He had seven horns and seven
eyes, which are the seven spirits[a] of God sent
out into all the earth. 7He came and took the
scroll from the right hand of him who sat on
the throne. 8And when he had taken it, the
four living creatures and the twenty-four elders fell down before the Lamb. Each one had
a harp and they were holding golden bowls
full of incense, which are the prayers of the
saints. 9And they sang a new song:

"You are worthy to take the scroll
and to open its seals,
because you were slain,
and with your blood you purchased
men for God
from every tribe and language and
people and nation.
10 You have made them to be a kingdom and
priests to serve our God,
and they will reign on the earth."

11Then I looked and heard the voice of
many angels, numbering thousands upon
thousands, and ten thousand times ten thousand. They encircled the throne and the living
creatures and the elders. 12In a loud voice they
sang:

"Worthy is the Lamb, who was slain,
to receive power and wealth and wisdom
and strength
and honor and glory and praise!"

13Then I heard every creature in heaven and
on earth and under the earth and on the sea,
and all that is in them, singing:

"To him who sits on the throne and to the
Lamb
be praise and honor and glory and power,
for ever and ever!"

14The four living creatures said, "Amen," and
the elders fell down and worshiped.

The Seals

6 I watched as the Lamb opened the first of
the seven seals. Then I heard one of the four
living creatures say in a voice like thunder,
"Come!" 2I looked, and there before me was a
white horse! Its rider held a bow, and he was
given a crown, and he rode out as a conqueror
bent on conquest.

3When the Lamb opened the second seal, I
heard the second living creature say, "Come!"
4Then another horse came out, a fiery red one.
Its rider was given power to take peace from
the earth and to make men slay each other. To
him was given a large sword.

5When the Lamb opened the third seal, I
heard the third living creature say, "Come!" I
looked, and there before me was a black horse!
Its rider was holding a pair of scales in his
hand. 6Then I heard what sounded like a voice
among the four living creatures, saying, "A
quart[b] of wheat for a day's wages,[c] and three
quarts of barley for a day's wages,[c] and do not
damage the oil and the wine!"

7When the Lamb opened the fourth seal,
I heard the voice of the fourth living creature
say, "Come!" 8I looked, and there before me
was a pale horse! Its rider was named Death,
and Hades was following close behind him.
They were given power over a fourth of the
earth to kill by sword, famine and plague, and
by the wild beasts of the earth.

9When he opened the fifth seal, I saw under
the altar the souls of those who had been slain
because of the word of God and the testimony
they had maintained. 10They called out in a
loud voice, "How long, Sovereign Lord, holy

---

[a] 6 Or *the sevenfold Spirit* [b] 6 Greek *a choinix* (probably about a liter) [c] 6 Greek *a denarius*

and true, until you judge the inhabitants of
the earth and avenge our blood?" 11 Then each
of them was given a white robe, and they were
told to wait a little longer, until the number of
their fellow servants and brothers who were to
be killed as they had been was completed.

12 I watched as he opened the sixth seal.
There was a great earthquake. The sun turned
black like sackcloth made of goat hair, the
whole moon turned blood red, 13 and the stars
in the sky fell to earth, as late figs drop from a
fig tree when shaken by a strong wind. 14 The
sky receded like a scroll, rolling up, and every mountain and island was removed from
its place.

15 Then the kings of the earth, the princes, the generals, the rich, the mighty, and every slave and every free man hid in caves and
among the rocks of the mountains. 16 They
called to the mountains and the rocks, "Fall
on us and hide us from the face of him who
sits on the throne and from the wrath of the
Lamb! 17 For the great day of their wrath has
come, and who can stand?"

144,000 Sealed

7 After this I saw four angels standing at the
four corners of the earth, holding back the
four winds of the earth to prevent any wind
from blowing on the land or on the sea or on
any tree. 2 Then I saw another angel coming
up from the east, having the seal of the living
God. He called out in a loud voice to the four
angels who had been given power to harm the
land and the sea: 3 "Do not harm the land or
the sea or the trees until we put a seal on the
foreheads of the servants of our God." 4 Then
I heard the number of those who were sealed:
144,000 from all the tribes of Israel.

5 From the tribe of Judah 12,000 were
sealed,
from the tribe of Reuben 12,000,
from the tribe of Gad 12,000,
6 from the tribe of Asher 12,000,
from the tribe of Naphtali 12,000,
from the tribe of Manasseh 12,000,
7 from the tribe of Simeon 12,000,
from the tribe of Levi 12,000,
from the tribe of Issachar 12,000,
8 from the tribe of Zebulun 12,000,
from the tribe of Joseph 12,000,
from the tribe of Benjamin 12,000.

The Great Multitude in White Robes

9 After this I looked and there before me was
a great multitude that no one could count,
from every nation, tribe, people and language,
standing before the throne and in front of the
Lamb. They were wearing white robes and
were holding palm branches in their hands.
10 And they cried out in a loud voice:

"Salvation belongs to our God,
who sits on the throne,
and to the Lamb."

11 All the angels were standing around the
throne and around the elders and the four living creatures. They fell down on their faces before the throne and worshiped God, 12 saying:

"Amen!
Praise and glory
and wisdom and thanks and honor
and power and strength
be to our God for ever and ever.
Amen!"

13 Then one of the elders asked me, "These
in white robes—who are they, and where did
they come from?"

14 I answered, "Sir, you know."

And he said, "These are they who have
come out of the great tribulation; they have
washed their robes and made them white in
the blood of the Lamb. 15 Therefore,

"they are before the throne of God
and serve him day and night in his
temple;
and he who sits on the throne will spread
his tent over them.
16 Never again will they hunger;
never again will they thirst.
The sun will not beat upon them,
nor any scorching heat.
17 For the Lamb at the center of the throne
will be their shepherd;
he will lead them to springs of living
water.
And God will wipe away every tear from
their eyes."

The Seventh Seal and the Golden Censer

8 When he opened the seventh seal, there was
silence in heaven for about half an hour.

2 And I saw the seven angels who stand
before God, and to them were given seven
trumpets.

3 Another angel, who had a golden censer, came and stood at the altar. He was giv-
en much incense to offer, with the prayers of
all the saints, on the golden altar before the
throne. 4 The smoke of the incense, together
with the prayers of the saints, went up before

THURSDAY
READ REVELATION 8:1–5

THE SMOKE OF INCENSE

The smoke of the incense, together with the prayers of the saints, went up before God from the angel's hand.

— REVELATION 8:4

let's talk

- What is our practice of prayer, both as individuals and as a couple? Do we set aside a special time for prayer? How might we make praying together as regular as was the daily renewal of the smoldering incense in the tabernacle or temple?
- How do we sense God's continued presence and care between times of regular prayer together as a couple? How does the "smoke of the incense" linger and connect us with God even when we are apart from each other?
- Do we pray in the morning, at mealtimes, at bedtime or when sending each other off to work? How might we mark these times with new coals on the incense altar of our homes?

It helps to be acquainted with the Old Testament when reading Revelation, since many of its images and scenes are drawn from the Law and the Prophets. For example, the bowls of plagues in Revelation 16 are reminiscent of the plagues on Egypt recorded in the book of Exodus; the edible scroll in Revelation 10, the battle of the nations in Revelation 20 and the scenes of the new Jerusalem in Revelation 21 are based on words from Ezekiel the prophet. The beasts and images in Revelation 13 and the attacks of Satan the accuser in chapter 12 are based on scenes described in the book of Daniel. Furthermore, some images, such as the grand furnishings of the tabernacle mentioned in Revelation 8:3–5, come to life when viewed in their original context (see Exodus 35–40).

In his vision recorded in Revelation 8, John saw an altar and incense, which immediately remind us of the altar of incense that stood in the tabernacle (and later in the temple), along with the lampstand with seven lamps (see Exodus 25:31–40).

In Revelation, the altar, together with its aromatic smoke, is a symbol of the prayers of God's people that rise to God. In the temple, the earthly throne of God was the ark of the covenant, placed just behind the curtain that separated the Most Holy Place from the Holy Place. In Revelation, the smoke of the incense transfers our prayers from the earthly realm to that of the angels surrounding the throne of God (see also Revelation 5:8).

John wrote Revelation during a time of great persecution, so this vision of prayers ascending to the ear and heart of God was a comforting message for the church. People who wondered whether God saw their pain or listened to their cries were assured that God is always attentive to his people and cares about what they are going through. God cares. He hears. He sees.

Prayer is also critical in marriage. Like smoldering incense, sending up whiffs of smoke, the words we pray in hope and fear and helplessness, as well as in courage and faith, linger before God as an aromatic reminder of our dependence upon him and his willingness to care for us.

We need to pray often and together as couples, just as ancient priests daily renewed the incense altar fire. We may do so, trusting that what we say will swirl around the throne of God like the wisps of smoke that lingered day and night above the altar. In that confidence we come together, send each other off to work, turn off the lights at night and awaken each morning certain that we are not in this alone. Our relationship—like everything else in this world—belongs to God.

—WAYNE BROUWER

FOR YOUR NEXT DEVOTIONAL READING, TURN TO PAGE 1465.

God from the angel's hand. 5Then the angel took the censer, filled it with fire from the altar, and hurled it on the earth; and there came peals of thunder, rumblings, flashes of lightning and an earthquake.

The Trumpets

6Then the seven angels who had the seven trumpets prepared to sound them.

7The first angel sounded his trumpet, and there came hail and fire mixed with blood, and it was hurled down upon the earth. A third of the earth was burned up, a third of the trees were burned up, and all the green grass was burned up.

8The second angel sounded his trumpet, and something like a huge mountain, all ablaze, was thrown into the sea. A third of the sea turned into blood, 9a third of the living creatures in the sea died, and a third of the ships were destroyed.

10The third angel sounded his trumpet, and a great star, blazing like a torch, fell from the sky on a third of the rivers and on the springs of water— 11the name of the star is Wormwood.[a] A third of the waters turned bitter, and many people died from the waters that had become bitter.

12The fourth angel sounded his trumpet, and a third of the sun was struck, a third of the moon, and a third of the stars, so that a third of them turned dark. A third of the day was without light, and also a third of the night.

13As I watched, I heard an eagle that was flying in midair call out in a loud voice: "Woe! Woe! Woe to the inhabitants of the earth, because of the trumpet blasts about to be sounded by the other three angels!"

9 The fifth angel sounded his trumpet, and I saw a star that had fallen from the sky to the earth. The star was given the key to the shaft of the Abyss. 2When he opened the Abyss, smoke rose from it like the smoke from a gigantic furnace. The sun and sky were darkened by the smoke from the Abyss. 3And out of the smoke locusts came down upon the earth and were given power like that of scorpions of the earth. 4They were told not to harm the grass of the earth or any plant or tree, but only those people who did not have the seal of God on their foreheads. 5They were not given power to kill them, but only to torture them for five months. And the agony they suffered was like that of the sting of a scorpion when it strikes a man. 6During those days men will seek death, but will not find it; they will long to die, but death will elude them.

7The locusts looked like horses prepared for battle. On their heads they wore something like crowns of gold, and their faces resembled human faces. 8Their hair was like women's hair, and their teeth were like lions' teeth. 9They had breastplates like breastplates of iron, and the sound of their wings was like the thundering of many horses and chariots rushing into battle. 10They had tails and stings like scorpions, and in their tails they had power to torment people for five months. 11They had as king over them the angel of the Abyss, whose name in Hebrew is Abaddon, and in Greek, Apollyon.[b]

12The first woe is past; two other woes are yet to come.

13The sixth angel sounded his trumpet, and I heard a voice coming from the horns[c] of the golden altar that is before God. 14It said to the sixth angel who had the trumpet, "Release the four angels who are bound at the great river Euphrates." 15And the four angels who had been kept ready for this very hour and day and month and year were released to kill a third of mankind. 16The number of the mounted troops was two hundred million. I heard their number.

17The horses and riders I saw in my vision looked like this: Their breastplates were fiery red, dark blue, and yellow as sulfur. The heads of the horses resembled the heads of lions, and out of their mouths came fire, smoke and sulfur. 18A third of mankind was killed by the three plagues of fire, smoke and sulfur that came out of their mouths. 19The power of the horses was in their mouths and in their tails; for their tails were like snakes, having heads with which they inflict injury.

20The rest of mankind that were not killed by these plagues still did not repent of the work of their hands; they did not stop worshiping demons, and idols of gold, silver, bronze, stone and wood—idols that cannot see or hear or walk. 21Nor did they repent of their murders, their magic arts, their sexual immorality or their thefts.

The Angel and the Little Scroll

10 Then I saw another mighty angel coming down from heaven. He was robed in a cloud, with a rainbow above his head; his face was like the sun, and his legs were like fiery pillars. 2He was holding a little scroll,

[a] *11* That is, Bitterness [b] *11* *Abaddon* and *Apollyon* mean *Destroyer.* [c] *13* That is, projections

which lay open in his hand. He planted his
right foot on the sea and his left foot on the
land, 3and he gave a loud shout like the roar
of a lion. When he shouted, the voices of the
seven thunders spoke. 4And when the seven
thunders spoke, I was about to write; but I
heard a voice from heaven say, "Seal up what
the seven thunders have said and do not write
it down."
5Then the angel I had seen standing on the
sea and on the land raised his right hand to
heaven. 6And he swore by him who lives for
ever and ever, who created the heavens and
all that is in them, the earth and all that is in
it, and the sea and all that is in it, and said,
"There will be no more delay! 7But in the days
when the seventh angel is about to sound his
trumpet, the mystery of God will be accomplished, just as he announced to his servants
the prophets."
8Then the voice that I had heard from heav-
en spoke to me once more: "Go, take the scroll
that lies open in the hand of the angel who is
standing on the sea and on the land."
9So I went to the angel and asked him to
give me the little scroll. He said to me, "Take
it and eat it. It will turn your stomach sour,
but in your mouth it will be as sweet as honey." 10I took the little scroll from the angel's
hand and ate it. It tasted as sweet as honey in
my mouth, but when I had eaten it, my stomach turned sour. 11Then I was told, "You must
prophesy again about many peoples, nations,
languages and kings."

The Two Witnesses

11 I was given a reed like a measuring rod
and was told, "Go and measure the
temple of God and the altar, and count
the worshipers there. 2But exclude the outer
court; do not measure it, because it has been
given to the Gentiles. They will trample on the
holy city for 42 months. 3And I will give power to my two witnesses, and they will prophesy
for 1,260 days, clothed in sackcloth." 4These
are the two olive trees and the two lampstands
that stand before the Lord of the earth. 5If
anyone tries to harm them, fire comes from
their mouths and devours their enemies. This
is how anyone who wants to harm them must
die. 6These men have power to shut up the sky
so that it will not rain during the time they are
prophesying; and they have power to turn the
waters into blood and to strike the earth with
every kind of plague as often as they want.
7Now when they have finished their testimony, the beast that comes up from the
Abyss will attack them, and overpower and
kill them. 8Their bodies will lie in the street
of the great city, which is figuratively called
Sodom and Egypt, where also their Lord was
crucified. 9For three and a half days men from
every people, tribe, language and nation will
gaze on their bodies and refuse them burial.
10The inhabitants of the earth will gloat over
them and will celebrate by sending each other gifts, because these two prophets had tormented those who live on the earth.
11But after the three and a half days a breath
of life from God entered them, and they stood
on their feet, and terror struck those who saw
them. 12Then they heard a loud voice from
heaven saying to them, "Come up here." And
they went up to heaven in a cloud, while their
enemies looked on.
13At that very hour there was a severe earthquake and a tenth of the city collapsed. Seven
thousand people were killed in the earthquake,
and the survivors were terrified and gave glory
to the God of heaven.
14The second woe has passed; the third woe
is coming soon.

The Seventh Trumpet

15The seventh angel sounded his trumpet,
and there were loud voices in heaven, which
said:

"The kingdom of the world has become
the kingdom of our Lord and of
his Christ,
and he will reign for ever and ever."

16And the twenty-four elders, who were seated
on their thrones before God, fell on their faces
and worshiped God, 17saying:

"We give thanks to you, Lord God
Almighty,
the One who is and who was,
because you have taken your great power
and have begun to reign.
18The nations were angry;
and your wrath has come.
The time has come for judging the dead,
and for rewarding your servants the
prophets
and your saints and those who reverence
your name,
both small and great—
and for destroying those who destroy the
earth."

19Then God's temple in heaven was opened,
and within his temple was seen the ark of his
covenant. And there came flashes of lightning,

rumblings, peals of thunder, an earthquake
and a great hailstorm.

The Woman and the Dragon

12 A great and wondrous sign appeared
in heaven: a woman clothed with the
sun, with the moon under her feet and
a crown of twelve stars on her head. 2She was
pregnant and cried out in pain as she was about
to give birth. 3Then another sign appeared in
heaven: an enormous red dragon with seven
heads and ten horns and seven crowns on his
heads. 4His tail swept a third of the stars out
of the sky and flung them to the earth. The
dragon stood in front of the woman who was
about to give birth, so that he might devour
her child the moment it was born. 5She gave
birth to a son, a male child, who will rule all
the nations with an iron scepter. And her child
was snatched up to God and to his throne.
6The woman fled into the desert to a place
prepared for her by God, where she might be
taken care of for 1,260 days.

7And there was war in heaven. Michael and
his angels fought against the dragon, and the
dragon and his angels fought back. 8But he was
not strong enough, and they lost their place in
heaven. 9The great dragon was hurled down—
that ancient serpent called the devil, or Satan,
who leads the whole world astray. He was
hurled to the earth, and his angels with him.

10Then I heard a loud voice in heaven say:

"Now have come the salvation and the
power and the kingdom of our
God,
and the authority of his Christ.
For the accuser of our brothers,
who accuses them before our God day
and night,
has been hurled down.
11They overcame him
by the blood of the Lamb
and by the word of their testimony;
they did not love their lives so much
as to shrink from death.
12Therefore rejoice, you heavens
and you who dwell in them!
But woe to the earth and the sea,
because the devil has gone down to
you!
He is filled with fury,
because he knows that his time is
short."

13When the dragon saw that he had been
hurled to the earth, he pursued the woman
who had given birth to the male child. 14The
woman was given the two wings of a great
eagle, so that she might fly to the place prepared for her in the desert, where she would
be taken care of for a time, times and half a
time, out of the serpent's reach. 15Then from
his mouth the serpent spewed water like a river, to overtake the woman and sweep her away
with the torrent. 16But the earth helped the
woman by opening its mouth and swallowing
the river that the dragon had spewed out of his
mouth. 17Then the dragon was enraged at the
woman and went off to make war against the
rest of her offspring—those who obey God's
commandments and hold to the testimony of
13 Jesus. 1And the dragon[a] stood on the
shore of the sea.

The Beast out of the Sea

And I saw a beast coming out of the sea.
He had ten horns and seven heads, with ten
crowns on his horns, and on each head a blasphemous name. 2The beast I saw resembled a
leopard, but had feet like those of a bear and a
mouth like that of a lion. The dragon gave the
beast his power and his throne and great authority. 3One of the heads of the beast seemed
to have had a fatal wound, but the fatal wound
had been healed. The whole world was astonished and followed the beast. 4Men worshiped
the dragon because he had given authority to
the beast, and they also worshiped the beast
and asked, "Who is like the beast? Who can
make war against him?"

5The beast was given a mouth to utter proud
words and blasphemies and to exercise his authority for forty-two months. 6He opened his
mouth to blaspheme God, and to slander his
name and his dwelling place and those who
live in heaven. 7He was given power to make
war against the saints and to conquer them.
And he was given authority over every tribe,
people, language and nation. 8All inhabitants
of the earth will worship the beast—all whose
names have not been written in the book of
life belonging to the Lamb that was slain from
the creation of the world.[b]

9He who has an ear, let him hear.

10If anyone is to go into captivity,
into captivity he will go.
If anyone is to be killed[c] with the sword,
with the sword he will be killed.

---

[a] *1* Some late manuscripts *And I* [b] *8* Or *written from the creation of the world in the book of life belonging to the Lamb that was slain*
[c] *10* Some manuscripts *anyone kills*

This calls for patient endurance and faithfulness on the part of the saints.

The Beast out of the Earth

11Then I saw another beast, coming out of
the earth. He had two horns like a lamb, but
he spoke like a dragon. 12He exercised all the
authority of the first beast on his behalf, and
made the earth and its inhabitants worship
the first beast, whose fatal wound had been
healed. 13And he performed great and miraculous signs, even causing fire to come down
from heaven to earth in full view of men.
14Because of the signs he was given power to
do on behalf of the first beast, he deceived the
inhabitants of the earth. He ordered them to
set up an image in honor of the beast who was
wounded by the sword and yet lived. 15He
was given power to give breath to the image
of the first beast, so that it could speak and
cause all who refused to worship the image to
be killed. 16He also forced everyone, small and
great, rich and poor, free and slave, to receive
a mark on his right hand or on his forehead,
17so that no one could buy or sell unless he
had the mark, which is the name of the beast
or the number of his name.

18This calls for wisdom. If anyone has insight, let him calculate the number of the
beast, for it is man's number. His number is
666.

The Lamb and the 144,000

14 Then I looked, and there before me was
the Lamb, standing on Mount Zion,
and with him 144,000 who had his
name and his Father's name written on their
foreheads. 2And I heard a sound from heaven
like the roar of rushing waters and like a loud
peal of thunder. The sound I heard was like
that of harpists playing their harps. 3And they
sang a new song before the throne and before
the four living creatures and the elders. No
one could learn the song except the 144,000
who had been redeemed from the earth.
4These are those who did not defile themselves
with women, for they kept themselves pure.
They follow the Lamb wherever he goes. They
were purchased from among men and offered
as firstfruits to God and the Lamb. 5No lie was
found in their mouths; they are blameless.

The Three Angels

6Then I saw another angel flying in midair,
and he had the eternal gospel to proclaim to
those who live on the earth—to every nation,
tribe, language and people. 7He said in a loud
voice, "Fear God and give him glory, because
the hour of his judgment has come. Worship
him who made the heavens, the earth, the sea
and the springs of water."

8A second angel followed and said, "Fallen!
Fallen is Babylon the Great, which made all
the nations drink the maddening wine of her
adulteries."

9A third angel followed them and said in a
loud voice: "If anyone worships the beast and
his image and receives his mark on the forehead or on the hand, 10he, too, will drink of
the wine of God's fury, which has been poured
full strength into the cup of his wrath. He will
be tormented with burning sulfur in the presence of the holy angels and of the Lamb. 11And
the smoke of their torment rises for ever and
ever. There is no rest day or night for those
who worship the beast and his image, or for
anyone who receives the mark of his name."
12This calls for patient endurance on the part
of the saints who obey God's commandments
and remain faithful to Jesus.

13Then I heard a voice from heaven say,
"Write: Blessed are the dead who die in the
Lord from now on."

"Yes," says the Spirit, "they will rest from
their labor, for their deeds will follow them."

The Harvest of the Earth

14I looked, and there before me was a white
cloud, and seated on the cloud was one "like a
son of man" [a] with a crown of gold on his head
and a sharp sickle in his hand. 15Then another
angel came out of the temple and called in a
loud voice to him who was sitting on the cloud,
"Take your sickle and reap, because the time
to reap has come, for the harvest of the earth
is ripe." 16So he who was seated on the cloud
swung his sickle over the earth, and the earth
was harvested.

17Another angel came out of the temple in heaven, and he too had a sharp sickle. 18Still another angel, who had charge of
the fire, came from the altar and called in a
loud voice to him who had the sharp sickle,
"Take your sharp sickle and gather the clusters of grapes from the earth's vine, because its
grapes are ripe." 19The angel swung his sickle on the earth, gathered its grapes and threw
them into the great winepress of God's wrath.
20They were trampled in the winepress outside
the city, and blood flowed out of the press, ris-

a 14 Daniel 7:13

ing as high as the horses' bridles for a distance
of 1,600 stadia.[a]

Seven Angels With Seven Plagues

15 I saw in heaven another great and marvelous sign: seven angels with the sev-
en last plagues—last, because with
them God's wrath is completed. 2And I saw
what looked like a sea of glass mixed with fire
and, standing beside the sea, those who had
been victorious over the beast and his image
and over the number of his name. They held
harps given them by God 3and sang the song
of Moses the servant of God and the song of
the Lamb:

"Great and marvelous are your deeds,
  Lord God Almighty.
Just and true are your ways,
  King of the ages.
4 Who will not fear you, O Lord,
  and bring glory to your name?
For you alone are holy.
All nations will come
  and worship before you,
for your righteous acts have been
    revealed."

5After this I looked and in heaven the temple, that is, the tabernacle of the Testimony,
was opened. 6Out of the temple came the sev-
en angels with the seven plagues. They were
dressed in clean, shining linen and wore gold-
en sashes around their chests. 7Then one of the
four living creatures gave to the seven angels
seven golden bowls filled with the wrath of
God, who lives for ever and ever. 8And the
temple was filled with smoke from the glory
of God and from his power, and no one could
enter the temple until the seven plagues of the
seven angels were completed.

The Seven Bowls of God's Wrath

16 Then I heard a loud voice from the temple saying to the seven angels, "Go, pour
out the seven bowls of God's wrath on
the earth."

2The first angel went and poured out his
bowl on the land, and ugly and painful sores
broke out on the people who had the mark of
the beast and worshiped his image.

3The second angel poured out his bowl on
the sea, and it turned into blood like that of
a dead man, and every living thing in the sea
died.

4The third angel poured out his bowl on the
rivers and springs of water, and they became
blood. 5Then I heard the angel in charge of
the waters say:

"You are just in these judgments,
  you who are and who were, the Holy
    One,
  because you have so judged;
6 for they have shed the blood of your saints
    and prophets,
  and you have given them blood to
    drink as they deserve."

7And I heard the altar respond:

"Yes, Lord God Almighty,
  true and just are your judgments."

8The fourth angel poured out his bowl
on the sun, and the sun was given power to
scorch people with fire. 9They were seared by
the intense heat and they cursed the name of
God, who had control over these plagues, but
they refused to repent and glorify him.

10The fifth angel poured out his bowl on
the throne of the beast, and his kingdom was
plunged into darkness. Men gnawed their
tongues in agony 11and cursed the God of
heaven because of their pains and their sores,
but they refused to repent of what they had
done.

12The sixth angel poured out his bowl on
the great river Euphrates, and its water was
dried up to prepare the way for the kings from
the East. 13Then I saw three evil[b] spirits that
looked like frogs; they came out of the mouth
of the dragon, out of the mouth of the beast
and out of the mouth of the false prophet.
14They are spirits of demons performing miraculous signs, and they go out to the kings of
the whole world, to gather them for the battle
on the great day of God Almighty.

15"Behold, I come like a thief! Blessed is he
who stays awake and keeps his clothes with
him, so that he may not go naked and be
shamefully exposed."

16Then they gathered the kings together to
the place that in Hebrew is called Armaged-
don.

17The seventh angel poured out his bowl
into the air, and out of the temple came a loud
voice from the throne, saying, "It is done!"
18Then there came flashes of lightning, rumblings, peals of thunder and a severe earthquake. No earthquake like it has ever occurred
since man has been on earth, so tremendous
was the quake. 19The great city split into three

---

[a] *20* That is, about 180 miles (about 300 kilometers) [b] *13* Greek *unclean*

parts, and the cities of the nations collapsed.
God remembered Babylon the Great and gave
her the cup filled with the wine of the fury
of his wrath. 20 Every island fled away and
the mountains could not be found. 21 From
the sky huge hailstones of about a hundred
pounds each fell upon men. And they cursed
God on account of the plague of hail, because
the plague was so terrible.

The Woman on the Beast

17 One of the seven angels who had the sev-
en bowls came and said to me, "Come,
I will show you the punishment of the
great prostitute, who sits on many waters.
2 With her the kings of the earth committed
adultery and the inhabitants of the earth were
intoxicated with the wine of her adulteries."

3 Then the angel carried me away in the
Spirit into a desert. There I saw a woman sitting on a scarlet beast that was covered with
blasphemous names and had seven heads and
ten horns. 4 The woman was dressed in purple
and scarlet, and was glittering with gold, precious stones and pearls. She held a golden cup
in her hand, filled with abominable things and
the filth of her adulteries. 5 This title was written on her forehead:

MYSTERY
BABYLON THE GREAT
THE MOTHER OF PROSTITUTES
AND OF THE ABOMINATIONS OF THE EARTH.

6 I saw that the woman was drunk with the
blood of the saints, the blood of those who
bore testimony to Jesus.

When I saw her, I was greatly astonished.
7 Then the angel said to me: "Why are you astonished? I will explain to you the mystery of
the woman and of the beast she rides, which
has the seven heads and ten horns. 8 The beast,
which you saw, once was, now is not, and will
come up out of the Abyss and go to his destruction. The inhabitants of the earth whose
names have not been written in the book of
life from the creation of the world will be astonished when they see the beast, because he
once was, now is not, and yet will come.

9 "This calls for a mind with wisdom. The
seven heads are seven hills on which the woman sits. 10 They are also seven kings. Five have
fallen, one is, the other has not yet come; but
when he does come, he must remain for a little
while. 11 The beast who once was, and now is
not, is an eighth king. He belongs to the seven
and is going to his destruction.

12 "The ten horns you saw are ten kings who
have not yet received a kingdom, but who for
one hour will receive authority as kings along
with the beast. 13 They have one purpose and
will give their power and authority to the
beast. 14 They will make war against the Lamb,
but the Lamb will overcome them because he
is Lord of lords and King of kings—and with
him will be his called, chosen and faithful followers."

15 Then the angel said to me, "The waters
you saw, where the prostitute sits, are peoples,
multitudes, nations and languages. 16 The beast
and the ten horns you saw will hate the prostitute. They will bring her to ruin and leave
her naked; they will eat her flesh and burn
her with fire. 17 For God has put it into their
hearts to accomplish his purpose by agreeing
to give the beast their power to rule, until
God's words are fulfilled. 18 The woman you
saw is the great city that rules over the kings
of the earth."

The Fall of Babylon

18 After this I saw another angel coming
down from heaven. He had great authority, and the earth was illuminat-
ed by his splendor. 2 With a mighty voice he
shouted:

"Fallen! Fallen is Babylon the Great!
She has become a home for demons
and a haunt for every evil[a] spirit,
a haunt for every unclean and
detestable bird.
3 For all the nations have drunk
the maddening wine of her adulteries.
The kings of the earth committed adultery
with her,
and the merchants of the earth grew
rich from her excessive luxuries."

4 Then I heard another voice from heaven
say:

"Come out of her, my people,
so that you will not share in her sins,
so that you will not receive any of her
plagues;
5 for her sins are piled up to heaven,
and God has remembered her crimes.
6 Give back to her as she has given;
pay her back double for what she has
done.

---

a 2 Greek *unclean*

Mix her a double portion from her own cup.
7 Give her as much torture and grief
as the glory and luxury she gave herself.
In her heart she boasts,
'I sit as queen; I am not a widow,
and I will never mourn.'
8 Therefore in one day her plagues will overtake her:
death, mourning and famine.
She will be consumed by fire,
for mighty is the Lord God who judges her.

9 "When the kings of the earth who committed adultery with her and shared her luxury see the smoke of her burning, they will
weep and mourn over her. 10 Terrified at her
torment, they will stand far off and cry:

" 'Woe! Woe, O great city,
O Babylon, city of power!
In one hour your doom has come!'

11 "The merchants of the earth will weep and
mourn over her because no one buys their cargoes any more— 12 cargoes of gold, silver, precious stones and pearls; fine linen, purple, silk
and scarlet cloth; every sort of citron wood,
and articles of every kind made of ivory, costly wood, bronze, iron and marble; 13 cargoes
of cinnamon and spice, of incense, myrrh and
frankincense, of wine and olive oil, of fine
flour and wheat; cattle and sheep; horses and
carriages; and bodies and souls of men.
14 "They will say, 'The fruit you longed for
is gone from you. All your riches and splendor
have vanished, never to be recovered.' 15 The
merchants who sold these things and gained
their wealth from her will stand far off, terrified at her torment. They will weep and
mourn 16 and cry out:

" 'Woe! Woe, O great city,
dressed in fine linen, purple and scarlet,
and glittering with gold, precious stones and pearls!
17 In one hour such great wealth has been brought to ruin!'

"Every sea captain, and all who travel by
ship, the sailors, and all who earn their living from the sea, will stand far off. 18 When
they see the smoke of her burning, they will
exclaim, 'Was there ever a city like this great
city?' 19 They will throw dust on their heads,
and with weeping and mourning cry out:

" 'Woe! Woe, O great city,
where all who had ships on the sea
became rich through her wealth!
In one hour she has been brought to ruin!
20 Rejoice over her, O heaven!
Rejoice, saints and apostles and prophets!
God has judged her for the way she treated you.' "

21 Then a mighty angel picked up a boulder
the size of a large millstone and threw it into
the sea, and said:

"With such violence
the great city of Babylon will be thrown down,
never to be found again.
22 The music of harpists and musicians, flute players and trumpeters,
will never be heard in you again.
No workman of any trade
will ever be found in you again.
The sound of a millstone
will never be heard in you again.
23 The light of a lamp
will never shine in you again.
The voice of bridegroom and bride
will never be heard in you again.
Your merchants were the world's great men.
By your magic spell all the nations were led astray.
24 In her was found the blood of prophets and of the saints,
and of all who have been killed on the earth."

Hallelujah!

19 After this I heard what sounded like
the roar of a great multitude in heaven
shouting:

"Hallelujah!
Salvation and glory and power belong to our God,
2 for true and just are his judgments.
He has condemned the great prostitute
who corrupted the earth by her adulteries.
He has avenged on her the blood of his servants."

3 And again they shouted:

"Hallelujah!
The smoke from her goes up for ever and ever."

4 The twenty-four elders and the four living
creatures fell down and worshiped God, who
was seated on the throne. And they cried:

"Amen, Hallelujah!"

5Then a voice came from the throne, saying:

"Praise our God,
all you his servants,
you who fear him,
both small and great!"

6Then I heard what sounded like a great
multitude, like the roar of rushing waters and
like loud peals of thunder, shouting:

"Hallelujah!
For our Lord God Almighty reigns.
7Let us rejoice and be glad
and give him glory!
For the wedding of the Lamb has come,
and his bride has made herself ready.
8Fine linen, bright and clean,
was given her to wear."

(Fine linen stands for the righteous acts of the
saints.)

9Then the angel said to me, "Write: 'Blessed
are those who are invited to the wedding supper of the Lamb!' " And he added, "These are
the true words of God."
10At this I fell at his feet to worship him.
But he said to me, "Do not do it! I am a fellow servant with you and with your brothers
who hold to the testimony of Jesus. Worship
God! For the testimony of Jesus is the spirit
of prophecy."

The Rider on the White Horse

11I saw heaven standing open and there before me was a white horse, whose rider is called
Faithful and True. With justice he judges and
makes war. 12His eyes are like blazing fire, and
on his head are many crowns. He has a name
written on him that no one knows but he himself. 13He is dressed in a robe dipped in blood,
and his name is the Word of God. 14The armies of heaven were following him, riding on
white horses and dressed in fine linen, white
and clean. 15Out of his mouth comes a sharp
sword with which to strike down the nations.
"He will rule them with an iron scepter."[a] He
treads the winepress of the fury of the wrath of
God Almighty. 16On his robe and on his thigh
he has this name written:

KING OF KINGS AND LORD OF LORDS.

17And I saw an angel standing in the sun,
who cried in a loud voice to all the birds flying in midair, "Come, gather together for the
great supper of God, 18so that you may eat the
flesh of kings, generals, and mighty men, of
horses and their riders, and the flesh of all people, free and slave, small and great."
19Then I saw the beast and the kings of the
earth and their armies gathered together to
make war against the rider on the horse and
his army. 20But the beast was captured, and
with him the false prophet who had performed
the miraculous signs on his behalf. With these
signs he had deluded those who had received
the mark of the beast and worshiped his image. The two of them were thrown alive into
the fiery lake of burning sulfur. 21The rest of
them were killed with the sword that came out
of the mouth of the rider on the horse, and all
the birds gorged themselves on their flesh.

The Thousand Years

20 And I saw an angel coming down out of
heaven, having the key to the Abyss and
holding in his hand a great chain. 2He
seized the dragon, that ancient serpent, who is
the devil, or Satan, and bound him for a thousand years. 3He threw him into the Abyss, and
locked and sealed it over him, to keep him
from deceiving the nations anymore until
the thousand years were ended. After that, he
must be set free for a short time.
4I saw thrones on which were seated those
who had been given authority to judge. And I
saw the souls of those who had been beheaded because of their testimony for Jesus and
because of the word of God. They had not
worshiped the beast or his image and had not
received his mark on their foreheads or their
hands. They came to life and reigned with
Christ a thousand years. 5(The rest of the dead
did not come to life until the thousand years
were ended.) This is the first resurrection.
6Blessed and holy are those who have part in
the first resurrection. The second death has no
power over them, but they will be priests of
God and of Christ and will reign with him for
a thousand years.

Satan's Doom

7When the thousand years are over, Satan
will be released from his prison 8and will go
out to deceive the nations in the four corners
of the earth—Gog and Magog—to gather
them for battle. In number they are like the
sand on the seashore. 9They marched across
the breadth of the earth and surrounded the

[a] *15* Psalm 2:9

camp of God's people, the city he loves. But
fire came down from heaven and devoured
them. 10And the devil, who deceived them,
was thrown into the lake of burning sulfur,
where the beast and the false prophet had been
thrown. They will be tormented day and night
for ever and ever.

The Dead Are Judged

11Then I saw a great white throne and him
who was seated on it. Earth and sky fled from
his presence, and there was no place for them.
12And I saw the dead, great and small, standing before the throne, and books were opened.
Another book was opened, which is the book
of life. The dead were judged according to
what they had done as recorded in the books.
13The sea gave up the dead that were in it, and
death and Hades gave up the dead that were in
them, and each person was judged according
to what he had done. 14Then death and Hades were thrown into the lake of fire. The lake
of fire is the second death. 15If anyone's name
was not found written in the book of life, he
was thrown into the lake of fire.

The New Jerusalem

21 Then I saw a new heaven and a new
earth, for the first heaven and the first
earth had passed away, and there was no
longer any sea. 2I saw the Holy City, the new
Jerusalem, coming down out of heaven from
God, prepared as a bride beautifully dressed
for her husband. 3And I heard a loud voice
from the throne saying, "Now the dwelling of
God is with men, and he will live with them.
They will be his people, and God himself will
be with them and be their God. 4He will wipe
every tear from their eyes. There will be no
more death or mourning or crying or pain, for
the old order of things has passed away."

5He who was seated on the throne said, "I
am making everything new!" Then he said,
"Write this down, for these words are trustworthy and true."

6He said to me: "It is done. I am the Alpha and the Omega, the Beginning and the
End. To him who is thirsty I will give to drink
without cost from the spring of the water of
life. 7He who overcomes will inherit all this,
and I will be his God and he will be my son.
8But the cowardly, the unbelieving, the vile,
the murderers, the sexually immoral, those
who practice magic arts, the idolaters and all
liars—their place will be in the fiery lake of
burning sulfur. This is the second death."

9One of the seven angels who had the sev-
en bowls full of the seven last plagues came
and said to me, "Come, I will show you the
bride, the wife of the Lamb." 10And he carried
me away in the Spirit to a mountain great and
high, and showed me the Holy City, Jerusalem, coming down out of heaven from God.
11It shone with the glory of God, and its brilliance was like that of a very precious jewel,
like a jasper, clear as crystal. 12It had a great,
high wall with twelve gates, and with twelve
angels at the gates. On the gates were written the names of the twelve tribes of Israel.
13There were three gates on the east, three on
the north, three on the south and three on the
west. 14The wall of the city had twelve foundations, and on them were the names of the
twelve apostles of the Lamb.

15The angel who talked with me had a
measuring rod of gold to measure the city,
its gates and its walls. 16The city was laid out
like a square, as long as it was wide. He measured the city with the rod and found it to
be 12,000 stadia[a] in length, and as wide and
high as it is long. 17He measured its wall and
it was 144 cubits[b] thick,[c] by man's measurement, which the angel was using. 18The wall
was made of jasper, and the city of pure gold,
as pure as glass. 19The foundations of the city
walls were decorated with every kind of precious stone. The first foundation was jasper,
the second sapphire, the third chalcedony, the
fourth emerald, 20the fifth sardonyx, the sixth
carnelian, the seventh chrysolite, the eighth
beryl, the ninth topaz, the tenth chrysoprase,
the eleventh jacinth, and the twelfth amethyst.[d] 21The twelve gates were twelve pearls,
each gate made of a single pearl. The great
street of the city was of pure gold, like transparent glass.

22I did not see a temple in the city, because
the Lord God Almighty and the Lamb are its
temple. 23The city does not need the sun or
the moon to shine on it, for the glory of God
gives it light, and the Lamb is its lamp. 24The
nations will walk by its light, and the kings
of the earth will bring their splendor into it.
25On no day will its gates ever be shut, for
there will be no night there. 26The glory and
honor of the nations will be brought into it.
27Nothing impure will ever enter it, nor will
anyone who does what is shameful or deceit-

a 16 That is, about 1,400 miles (about 2,200 kilometers) *b 17* That is, about 200 feet (about 65 meters) *c 17* Or *high*
d 20 The precise identification of some of these precious stones is uncertain.

FRIDAY
READ REVELATION 21:1–27

FINDING THE BEST OF TIMES

> **He will wipe every tear from their eyes. There will be no more death or mourning or crying or pain, for the old order of things has passed away.**
>
> — REVELATION 21:4

let's talk

- What are some times when we felt the most togetherness? What helped fuel those times? When have we felt most alienated from each other? What brought us back together? What are some practical ways we can work together that will keep us close?
- Is either of us sometimes uncomfortable with too much intimacy? What do we do when we feel crowded into closeness? How do we get some space without offending each other?
- How does closeness and intimacy with God affect our relationship with each other?

Marriage can be like the days of the French Revolution, immortalized in the words of Charles Dickens in *A Tale of Two Cities*—"the best of times and the worst of times."

In the best times of marriage, we can't get enough of each other. We breeze through workdays, knowing we can be together afterward. We spoon our bodies in the night, delighting in how well we fit together. We cook special things for each other. We reach for each other's hands in church, show each other off to friends, get high at the sound of each other's voice on the phone.

We crave each other in the hard times too: when our parents decide to divorce, when a close friend is diagnosed with cancer, when one of us loses a job, when we have a miscarriage, when someone betrays us. We ease the hurt by holding each other tight and letting the tears fall, by reading passages of Scripture together, by linking hearts and hands in prayer. Somehow just being together fortifies us in the times when we ache and hurt.

In the worst of times, we lose each other. He flirts with a waitress, making his wife feel invisible. She goes on a spending spree at the mall, sabotaging the budget her husband so carefully worked out. He works late night after night; she spends too much time with friends. Even at church the togetherness is lost as she goes to choir, while he goes to Bible study. She has meetings that leave him sitting alone; he is so busy talking to others that he barely notices she's gone. Even when together, spouses can be alone. They stay home for the night, but he's upstairs watching a football game, while she's downstairs trotting on the treadmill. Or during dinner, she's replaying a work problem in her head, while he's reading the paper.

Whatever the reason, failing to connect becomes a kind of living death. The warmth, the passion, the closeness between us cools until it seems we're only going through the motions of marriage. Then something, somehow, prods us into reaching for each other again: Maybe it's a sermon that cuts truth like a knife into our hearts or a friend who begins asking questions about our relationship or a work associate whose problems become too personal. Then things can really heat up between us—this time with anger, accusations, threats and tears. The pain is excruciating, but if we work through it (sometimes with professional help), we can find each other again in a new kind of love, one that's forged in the fire and ashes of repentance and forgiveness. Then the tears we drop are ones of relief, gladness and joy.

One day we will stop crying for good. After we pass through the final vale of separation from each other, God himself will wipe our faces clean of tears. Then he will usher us into glory, where we will be so united with him, so one with him, that there will never again be a need for tears. The best times of marriage, in all their passion and delight, are a prelude to that.

—PHYLLIS TEN ELSHOF

FOR YOUR NEXT DEVOTIONAL READING, TURN TO PAGE 1466.

WEEKEND

unconditional love

Have you heard the old admonition to love your neighbor as yourself? This took on a fresh, new meaning when we applied it to our marriage. The keyword, neighbor, means the person closest to you. And for any married person, the person closest to you is your partner, the one with whom you chose to share life at its deepest and most intimate level. If we love our marriage partner as we love ourselves, we will have his or her best interests at heart. We will want to serve, and we will resist the urge to manipulate or pull power plays. We will have a relationship based on love and trust.

So many times marital conflict would be resolved if we just loved the other as we love ourselves. Too often we are "me" centered and want things to work out "my" way. But just the opposite approach is what promotes spiritual intimacy.

Central to our core-belief system is a commitment to accept and love each other unconditionally—not "I'll love you if . . . " but "I'll love you in spite of . . . " However, this is not easy to do, and many times we come up short. In "real time" it's not always easy to accept each other. Too often we react to surface issues—like the time I got my hair cut too short. It was much shorter than I had wanted and Dave's comment, "Makes you look older, doesn't it?" just made me furious!

It's not always easy to accept that extra ten pounds you wish your mate would lose or to be kind when you discover you spouse mailed your income tax forms without signing them, or have to economize because your partner blew a paycheck on a new computer printer. And then we all have little irritating habits such as leaving used tissues lying around, or neglecting to return rented videos or library books, or not hanging up clothes before going to bed at night. Yet our basic commitment to accept each other helps us to hang in there.

But in a spiritually intimate marriage, not only do we strive to accept one another; we also strive to love one another unconditionally. Two thousand years ago, Paul gave some good advice to the people of Corinth who were having trouble loving each other unconditionally. He reminded them that love is patient and kind. When you really love someone, you don't envy him or her or easily get angry. Your love forgives, so you do not keep track of wrongs or take note of the other's shortcomings.

It's hard to love like that. It's certainly not natural. In our experience, it's the spiritual dimension of life that empowers us to live out this kind of love with each other. We have to continually realize that love is a choice we can make.

Sometimes we give each other unconditional love in the hard times—like when Dave's migraine headache just wouldn't go away, and we had to cancel our dinner out. I chose to pamper Dave rather than complain. Or when I had a complicated root canal, and the dentist said, "Take a couple of aspirin when you get home and you'll be just fine." Who was he kidding? Not me! Through the throbbing pain that night, Dave chose to keep me supplied with ice packs and Jell-O™. At other times our unconditional love has been very conditional, but we keep trying.

—DAVID AND CLAUDIA ARP

what are our conditions?

HOW ARE WE DOING?

Unconditional love doesn't come naturally. Use the following questions to evaluate how well you're doing.

1. When my mate really messes things up:
   a. I forgive but I don't forget.
   b. I forgive immediately and never think of it again.
   c. I never forget.
2. My mate has a bad cold, and I've got a meeting at work.
   a. I'll reschedule the meeting. Staying home and taking care of my sweetie is more important than any meeting.
   b. If my spouse is staying home anyway, he might as well clean the house—it's not pneumonia, just a cold.
   c. I'll call my spouse between meetings to check on her and then I'll leave early to pick up chicken soup on the way home.
3. It's my spouse's birthday, and I know he or she would like a huge party, but the budget won't allow for it. So instead I:
   a. Ask friends to meet us in the park for a bring-your-own-picnic party.
   b. Tell my spouse we'll do something exciting next year.
   c. Save up to make sure I have enough for *my* birthday party.
4. When I come home after work, the house is a wreck. I:
   a. Leave it, thinking my spouse will get to it sooner or later.
   b. Go into overdrive cleaning so that my spouse won't have to do it.
   c. Pick up a few things while whining about how I'm the only one who does things around the house.

To find the correct answers, take the test again. This time respond with the answer you'd like your spouse to choose. Each answer that's the same is an example of loving your spouse as you love yourself.

let's make a DATE

WEATHER THE CONDITIONS

This weekend, brave the weather outside. Go sledding on a big hill. Put on snowshoes and go for a walk in the woods. Take a walk in the rain without an umbrella (dance and sing if you're brave enough). Or work up a sweat playing sports in the summer heat. What does it feel like to be kissed in the cold, rain, wind or heat? There's something about a change in body temperature that can make the ordinary more passionate.

FOR YOUR FIRST DEVOTIONAL READING, TURN TO PAGE 4.

LESSONS FROM THE *Bible*

Read the book of Ruth and answer the following questions:

1. How did Ruth demonstrate her unconditional love for Naomi?
2. How did Boaz demonstrate his love for Ruth?
3. What can you learn from this story about loving your spouse unconditionally?

ful, but only those whose names are written in
the Lamb's book of life.

The River of Life

22 Then the angel showed me the river of
the water of life, as clear as crystal, flowing from the throne of God and of the
Lamb 2down the middle of the great street of
the city. On each side of the river stood the
tree of life, bearing twelve crops of fruit, yielding its fruit every month. And the leaves of
the tree are for the healing of the nations. 3No
longer will there be any curse. The throne of
God and of the Lamb will be in the city, and
his servants will serve him. 4They will see his
face, and his name will be on their foreheads.
5There will be no more night. They will not
need the light of a lamp or the light of the sun,
for the Lord God will give them light. And
they will reign for ever and ever.
6The angel said to me, "These words are
trustworthy and true. The Lord, the God of
the spirits of the prophets, sent his angel to
show his servants the things that must soon
take place."

Jesus Is Coming

7"Behold, I am coming soon! Blessed is he
who keeps the words of the prophecy in this
book."

8I, John, am the one who heard and saw
these things. And when I had heard and seen
them, I fell down to worship at the feet of the
angel who had been showing them to me.
9But he said to me, "Do not do it! I am a fellow servant with you and with your brothers
the prophets and of all who keep the words of
this book. Worship God!"
10Then he told me, "Do not seal up the
words of the prophecy of this book, because
the time is near. 11Let him who does wrong
continue to do wrong; let him who is vile continue to be vile; let him who does right continue to do right; and let him who is holy continue to be holy."

12"Behold, I am coming soon! My reward is
with me, and I will give to everyone according
to what he has done. 13I am the Alpha and the
Omega, the First and the Last, the Beginning
and the End.
14"Blessed are those who wash their robes,
that they may have the right to the tree of life
and may go through the gates into the city.
15Outside are the dogs, those who practice
magic arts, the sexually immoral, the murderers, the idolaters and everyone who loves and
practices falsehood.
16"I, Jesus, have sent my angel to give you[a]
this testimony for the churches. I am the Root
and the Offspring of David, and the bright
Morning Star."

17The Spirit and the bride say, "Come!"
And let him who hears say, "Come!" Whoever
is thirsty, let him come; and whoever wishes,
let him take the free gift of the water of life.

18I warn everyone who hears the words of
the prophecy of this book: If anyone adds anything to them, God will add to him the plagues
described in this book. 19And if anyone takes
words away from this book of prophecy, God
will take away from him his share in the tree
of life and in the holy city, which are described
in this book.
20He who testifies to these things says, "Yes,
I am coming soon."
Amen. Come, Lord Jesus.
21The grace of the Lord Jesus be with God's
people. Amen.

---

a 16 The Greek is plural.

CONTENTS

Contents

WEIGHTS AND MEASURES

Weights and Measures

	Biblical Unit	Approximate American Equivalent	Approximate Metric Equivalent
WEIGHTS	talent (60 minas)	75 pounds	34 kilograms
	mina (50 shekels)	1 1/4 pounds	0.6 kilogram
	shekel (2 bekas)	2/5 ounce	11.5 grams
	pim (2/3 shekel)	1/3 ounce	9.5 grams
	beka (10 gerahs)	1/5 ounce	5.5 grams
	gerah	1/50 ounce	0.6 gram
LENGTH	cubit	18 inches	0.5 meter
	span	9 inches	23 centimeters
	handbreadth	3 inches	8 centimeters
CAPACITY			
Dry Measure	cor [homer] (10 ephahs)	6 bushels	220 liters
	lethek (5 ephahs)	3 bushels	110 liters
	ephah (10 omers)	3/5 bushel	22 liters
	seah (1/3 ephah)	7 quarts	7.7 liters
	omer (1/10 ephah)	2 quarts	2 liters
	cab (1/18 ephah)	1 quart	1 liter
Liquid Measure	bath (1 ephah)	6 gallons	22 liters
	hin (1/6 bath)	4 quarts	4 liters
	log (1/72 bath)	1/3 quart	0.3 liter

The figures of the table are calculated on the basis of a shekel equaling 11.5 grams, a cubit equaling 18 inches and an ephah equaling 22 liters. The quart referred to is either a dry quart (slightly larger than a liter) or a liquid quart (slightly smaller than a liter), whichever is applicable. The ton referred to in the footnotes is the American ton of 2,000 pounds. Since most readers are more familiar with dry measures being given in weight rather than capacity (bushel, quart), dry measures have been converted in the footnotes to approximate weights.

This table is based upon the best available information, but it is not intended to be mathematically precise; like the measurement equivalents in the footnotes, it merely gives approximate amounts and distances. Weights and measures differed somewhat at various times and places in the ancient world. There is uncertainty particularly about the ephah and the bath; further discoveries may shed more light on these units of capacity.

SUBJECT INDEX

ACKNOWLEDGEMENTS

Acknowledgements

The editor and publisher gratefully acknowledge the permission granted to reproduce the copyrighted material found within this Bible. Every effort has been made to trace copyright holders and to obtain their permission for the use of material under copyright. The publisher apologizes for any errors or omissions in the below list and would be grateful if notified of any corrections that should be incorporated in future reprints or editions of this book.

Page 24 Taken from *10 Great Dates to Energize Your Marriage* by David and Claudia Arp, pages 65–66,79. Copyright © 1997 by David and Claudia Arp. Published by Zondervan, Grand Rapids, MI. Used by permission.

Page 68 Taken from *Hidden Keys of a Loving, Lasting Marriage* by Gary Smalley, pages 175–176,177–178. Copyright © 1984,1988 by Gary Smalley. Published by Zondervan, Grand Rapids, MI. Used by permission.

Page 110 Taken from *The Act of Marriage*, Tim and Beverly LaHaye, pages 255–257,301. Copyright © 1998 by Zondervan. Published by Zondervan, Grand Rapids, MI. Used by permission.

Page 152 Taken from *Love Talk* by Drs. Les and Leslie Parrott, pages 73–74,76,77,78–79. Copyright © 2004 by Les and Leslie Parrott. Published by Zondervan, Grand Rapids, MI. Used by permission.

Page 202 Taken from *Sacred Marriage* by Gary Thomas, pages 13,26,262,263. Copyright © 2000 by Gary Thomas. Published by Zondervan, Grand Rapids, MI. Used by permission.

Page 234 Taken from *Love Talk* by Drs. Les and Leslie Parrott, pages 39–41. Copyright © 2004 by Les and Leslie Parrott. Published by Zondervan, Grand Rapids, MI. Used by permission.

Page 272 Taken from *Saving Your Marriage Before It Starts* by Dr. Les Parrott III and Dr. Leslie Parrott, pages 11–13. Copyright © 1995 by Les and Leslie Parrott. Published by Zondervan, Grand Rapids, MI. Used by permission.

Page 304 Taken from *Rock-Solid Marriage* by Robert and Rosemary Barnes, pages 53,55–56. Copyright © 1993 by Robert and Rosemary Barnes. Published by Zondervan, Grand Rapids, MI. Used by permission.

Page 332 Taken from "Preventing an Affair: How to Guard Your Relationship". by Dr. Tim and Julie Clinton, *Christian Parenting Today Magazine*, Sept/Oct 1998, page 14.

Page 374 Taken from *Questions Couples Ask* by Dr. Les Parrott III and Dr. Leslie Parrott, pages 121–122. Copyright © 1996 by Les and Leslie Parrott. Published by Zondervan, Grand Rapids, MI. Used by permission.
Taken from "The Real and Untold Cost: The Exorbitant Price of Sexual Sin" by Randy Alcorn, *Leadership Journal*, Summer 1996, page 52.

Page 408 Taken from *Boundaries in Marriage* by Dr. Henry Cloud and Dr. John Townsend, pages 170,183–189. Copyright © 1999 by Henry Cloud and John Townsend. Published by Zondervan, Grand Rapids, MI. Used by permission.

Page 409 Taken from information provided by Phil Callaway in *Marriage Partnership*, Fall 2000, page 57.

Page 454 Taken from *Sacred Marriage* by Gary Thomas, pages 73–74,75–76. Copyright © 2000 by Gary Thomas. Published by Zondervan, Grand Rapids, MI. Used by permission.

Page 488 Taken from "Holiday Negotiations" by Conrad Theodore, *Marriage Partnership*, Winter 2001, page 32.

Page 532 Taken from *Saving Your Marriage Before It Starts* by Dr. Les Parrott III and Dr. Leslie Parrott, pages 91–92,93,99–109. Copyright © 1995 by Les and Leslie Parrott. Published by Zondervan, Grand Rapids, MI. Used by permission.

Page 560 Taken from *The Act of Marriage*, Tim and Beverly LaHaye, pages 259–260. Copyright © 1998 by Zondervan. Published by Zondervan, Grand Rapids, MI. Used by permission.

Page 588 Taken from *The Act of Marriage*, Tim and Beverly LaHaye, pages 253–255. Copyright © 1998 by Zondervan. Published by Zondervan, Grand Rapids, MI. Used by permission.

Page 616 Taken from *Questions Couples Ask* by Dr. Les Parrott III and Dr. Leslie Parrott, pages 109–111. Copyright © 1996 by Les and Leslie Parrott. Published by Zondervan, Grand Rapids, MI. Used by permission.

Page 648 Taken from *Questions Couples Ask* by Dr. Les Parrott III and Dr. Leslie Parrott, pages 157–159. Copyright © 1996 by Les and Leslie Parrott. Published by Zondervan, Grand Rapids, MI. Used by permission.

Page 684 Taken from "Me vs. You" by Bob Moeller, *Marriage Partnership*, Spring 1999, page 38.

Page 710 Taken from *Children Change a Marriage* by Elisa Morgan and Carol Kuykendall, pages 141–147,150. Copyright © 1999 by MOPS International, Inc. Published by Zondervan, Grand Rapids, MI. Used by permission.

Page 730 Taken from *Sacred Marriage* by Gary Thomas, pages 82–83,25–26. Copyright © 2000 by Gary Thomas. Published by Zondervan, Grand Rapids, MI. Used by permission.

Page 752 Taken from *Love Talk* by Drs. Les and Leslie Parrott, pages 137–138,145–146. Copyright © 2004 by Les and Leslie Parrott. Published by Zondervan, Grand Rapids, MI. Used by permission.

Page 790 Taken from *10 Great Dates to Energize Your Marriage* by David and Claudia Arp, pages 123–125,205. Copyright © 1997 by David and Claudia Arp. Published by Zondervan, Grand Rapids, MI. Used by permission.

Page 826 Taken from *Insuring Marriage: 25 Proven Ways to Prevent Divorce* by Michael J. McManus, pages 16,19,20,60,61,62. Copyright © 1994 by Michael J. McManus. Published by Zondervan, Grand Rapids, MI. Used by permission.

Page 866 Taken from "Real Sex" by Louis and Melissa McBurney, *Marriage Partnership*, Fall 2004, page 62.

Page 916 Taken from "Surviving an Affair" by Connie Neal, as told to Jane Johnson Struck in *Today's Christian Woman*, March/April 1999, page 96.

Questions adapted from "What to Do If You Suspect Your Spouse Is Cheating" by Cindy Crosby, *Marriage Partnership*, Spring 2001, page 30.

Page 960 Taken from *The Act of Marriage*, Tim and Beverly LaHaye, pages 20–22. Copyright © 1998 by Zondervan. Published by Zondervan, Grand Rapids, MI. Used by permission.

Page 990 Taken from *Questions Couples Ask* by Dr. Les Parrott III and Dr. Leslie Parrott, pages 177–178,179–180. Copyright © 1996 by Les and Leslie Parrott. Published by Zondervan, Grand Rapids, MI. Used by permission.

Page 1012 Taken from *Marriage, Divorce, and Remarriage in the Bible* by Jay E. Adams, pages 94–96. Copyright © 1980 by Jay E. Adams. Published by Zondervan, Grand Rapids, MI. Used by permission.

CONTRIBUTOR BIOGRAPHIES

Jay E. Adams (PhD, University of Missouri), a retired pastor, is former director of advanced studies and professor of practical theology at Westminster Theological Seminary. He has written more than 50 books on pastoral ministry, preaching, counseling, Bible study and Christian living.

Randy Alcorn is founder of Eternal Perspective Ministries (EPM), which serves unreached, unfed, unborn, uneducated, unreconciled and unsupported people around the world. Alcorn is the author of 27 books, including *Heaven, The Purity Principle* and *Wait Until Then*.

David and Claudia Arp are founders and directors of Marriage Alive International, which helps empower churches to build better marriages and families. Their "Marriage Alive" seminars and "10 Great Dates" program are popular across the U.S. and Europe. The Arps have authored more than 30 books.

Robert and Rosemary Barnes: Robert Barnes is executive director of Sheridan House Family Ministries, the author of several books, host of the weekly *Family Time* radio program and writer of a newspaper column on family issues. Rosemary Barnes is a frequent speaker for national conferences. Together with her husband, Robert, she writes on marriage and family issues.

Carla Barnhill is the author of *The Myth of the Perfect Mother* and the former editor of *Christian Parenting Today* magazine. She is the mother of three and the wife of one (Jim). She and her family live in Minnesota.

Chris Blumhofer is an editor for BuildingChurchLeaders.com, a website of Christianity Today International, which trains and equips pastors and church leaders. He lives in the Chicago suburbs with his wife, Stephanie.

Wayne Brouwer teaches in the Religion Department at Hope College in Holland, Michigan, and has served as pastor in three congregations in the Christian Reformed denomination in Canada and the United States. Wayne has earned several master's degrees and a PhD in New Testament from McMaster University. He has written hundreds of articles in various publications and dozens of books. He is married and has three daughters.

Dr. Tim and Julie Clinton have authored more than 150 articles, chapters, notes and columns on Christian counseling, counselor education and development, marriage, family life and parenting issues, including the book *The Marriage You've Always Wanted*. Tim is coauthor of "*Baby Boomer Blues*" in Word's *Contemporary Christian Counselor* series and author of *Before a Bad Goodbye: How to Turn Your Marriage Around*. Julie Clinton is president of *Extraordinary Woman* Ministries. The Clintons have been married for 26 years and have two children: Megan and Zachary. The family resides in Forest, Virginia.

Dr. Henry Cloud and Dr. John Townsend are popular speakers and cohosts of the nationally broadcast *New Life Live!* radio program. They are also cofounders of Cloud-Townsend Clinic and Cloud-Townsend Resources. Their bestselling books include the Gold Medallion Award–winning *Boundaries*.

Teresa Cook is a pseudonym for a writer living in Mississippi.

Larry Crabb (PhD, University of Illinois) is a well-known speaker, author of numerous bestselling books and a distinguished scholar-in-residence at Colorado Christian University in Morrison, Colorado.

Allen D. Curry is Reaves Professor of Christian Education at Reformed Theological Seminary in Jackson, Mississippi. He and his wife, Marilyn, have two grown children and five grandchildren. Curry is the author of *The God We Love and Serve*. He has served as a pastor and worked several years at Great Commission Publications.

Daniel Michael Darling is a freelance writer and editor.

Lee A. Dean is a writer and editor from Plainwell, Michigan. He is a graduate of Grand Rapids Theological Seminary, a commissioned Stephen Minister and an ordained elder in the Reformed Church in America. He has served as an editor for Christianity Today International's Resources Department.

Richard Doebler is senior pastor of Gospel Tabernacle in Cloquet, Minnesota. He was editor and contributor to the *Quest Study Bible* and is a consulting editor for *Leadership*, a journal for pastors. He and his wife, Sharon, are the parents of three grown children: Nathan, Micah and Jennie.

Lee Eclov is senior pastor of Village Church of Lincolnshire, Illinois, a consulting editor for *Leadership Journal* and a regular contributor to PreachingToday.com. He is also an adjunct instructor at Trinity Evangelical Divinity School. He and his wife, Susan, have been married 35 years and have one son, Anders.

Janis Long Harris is a senior editor at Tyndale House Publishers. She has written numerous articles on marriage and family issues and several books, including *What Good Parents Have in Common: Thirteen Secrets for Success*. She and her husband have two children.

Bill and Lynne Hybels: Bill Hybels is the founding and senior pastor of Willow Creek Community Church in South Barrington, Illinois. He and his wife, Lynne, have authored and coauthored more than 20 books. Lynne Hybels has edited many books and has been involved in Willow Creek's ministry partnerships in Latin America. Currently she serves as an advocate for people affected by HIV/AIDS in Africa.

Mary Ann Jeffreys is a freelance writer and editor living in Golden, Colorado. She has been married for 35 years to Grey. They have two grown children. She was a contributing writer to the revised *Quest Study Bible*.

Nancy Kennedy is a staff writer and columnist for *Citrus County Chronicle* in Crystal River, Florida. She has been married to Barry since 1975 and has two grown daughters and one granddaughter. Her books include *Girl on a Swing, Lipstick Grace, When He Doesn't Believe* and *Move Over Victoria—I Know the Real Secret*. She is a retreat speaker for Christian women's groups.

Ginger Kolbaba is editor of *Marriage Partnership* magazine. She is also the author of *Surprised by Remarriage*.

Carol Kuykendall is director of special projects at MOPS International. She is the author of four books and coauthor of five more. She is a popular seminar and retreat speaker.

Tim and Beverly LaHaye: Tim LaHaye (DMin) is a noted author, minister, educator and nationally recognized speaker on Bible prophecy. He is president of Tim LaHaye Ministries (www.timlahaye.com) and founder of the Pre-Trib Research Center. He has written more than 40 books and coauthored books with his wife, Beverly. Beverly LaHaye is the founder and chairwoman of Concerned Women for America (www.cwfa.org) and shares a daily devotional commentary on the nationally syndicated radio show *Concerned Women Today*. She and her husband live in southern California.

Annette LaPlaca is a freelance editor and writer. She formerly was senior associate editor of *Marriage Partnership* magazine. She is the author of several books for children, teens and parents. She and her husband, David, have four children.

Jeanette G. and Robert H. Lauer are marriage experts with doctorates in sociology. They have written many books on marriage, including *The Play Solution*.

Marian V. Liautaud is editor of *Your Church Resources* for Christianity Today International. She is married and has four sons. She has edited and contributed to numerous books for Christianity Today International.

Kerri S. Mabee is a freelance author who has written for several magazines, including *Marriage Partnership*.

Scottie May, professor of Christian Formation and Ministry at Wheaton College in Wheaton, Illinois, is coauthor of *Children Matter: Celebrating Their Place in the Church, Family and Community*.

Louis and Melissa McBurney are marriage therapists and founders of Marble Retreat Center in Colorado. Louis McBurney is a psychiatrist and has written numerous articles dealing with the problems faced by ministers. He and Melissa coauthored *Real Questions, Real Answers About Sex*. They are currently leading Christian sessions for ministers and missionaries around the world.

Michael J. McManus writes a syndicated newspaper column, "Ethics and Religion," and codirects Marriage Preparation with his wife, Harriet, at Fourth Presbyterian Church in Bethesda, Maryland.

Bob Moeller is a pastor and author of three books on marriage, including *For Better, For Worse, For Keeps* and *Marriage Minutes: Inspirational Readings to Share with Your Spouse*.

Elisa Morgan is CEO of MOPS International, Inc., in Denver, Colorado. Her daily radio program, *MomSense*, is broadcast on more than 700 outlets nationwide. She is the author, editor or coauthor of numerous books, including *Children Change Your Marriage*.

Connie Neal is a writer, speaker and teacher specializing in the intersection of Christianity and pop culture. She has written several books including *MySpace for Moms and Dads: A Guide to Understanding the Risks and the Rewards*.

Drs. Les and Leslie Parrott are founders of RealRelationships.com and the Center for Relationship Development at Seattle Pacific University. Their bestselling books include *Love Talk, Your Time Starved Marriage* and the award-winning *Saving Your Marriage Before It Starts*. Their work has been featured in the *New York Times* and *USA Today*, and they have appeared on CNN, *Good Morning America* and *Oprah*.

JoHannah Reardon is an associate editor with ChristianBibleStudies.com, a division of Christianity Today International. She and her husband, a pastor, have three adult children and recently became grandparents.

Jennifer Schuchmann is a freelance writer who regularly writes for several publications of Christianity Today International. She is married and has one son. She is author of *Your Unforgettable Life*.

Gary Smalley is one of the country's best-known authors and speakers on family relationships. He is the award-winning, bestselling author or coauthor of 16 books, as well as several popular films and videos. His infomercial *Hidden Keys to Loving Relationships* has been viewed by television audiences all over the world.

Lee and Leslie Strobel: Lee Strobel has a journalism degree from the University of Missouri and a Master of Studies in Law degree from Yale Law School, was the award-winning legal editor of the *Chicago Tribune* and a spiritual skeptic until 1981. His books include four Gold Medallion Award winners and the 2005 Christian Book of the Year (coauthored with Garry Poole). Leslie Strobel has been involved in women's ministries and one-on-one mentoring in the churches where the Strobels have served.

Jane Johnson Struck is editor of *Today's Christian Woman* magazine. She and her husband have two adult daughters.

Phyllis Ten Elshof is editor of books and Bibles for the Resources Department of Christianity Today International, Carol Stream, Illinois. She is the author of *What Cancer Cannot Do*. She and her husband, Paul, have two children and four grandchildren.

Conrad Theodore is a freelance writer from Lake Forest, Illinois. He writes for several magazines, including *Marriage Partnership*.

Gary Thomas is author of several books, including *Sacred Marriage, Sacred Parenting, Sacred Pathways* and the Gold Medallion Award–winning *Authentic Faith*. He is an adjunct faculty member at Western Seminary in Portland, Oregon. His books and ministry focus on spiritual formation: how we can integrate Scripture, church history and the time-tested wisdom of the Christian classics into our modern experience of faith. Gary's speaking ministry has led him to speak across the United States, in six different countries and on numerous national television and radio programs, including *Focus on the Family* and *Family Life Today*.

John R. Throop is a management consultant for nonprofit and public agencies and churches. He is an ordained minister in the Episcopal Church. John is married, has two grown daughters and lives in the Midwest.

David and Kelli Trujillo live with their two young children in Indianapolis, Indiana. David teaches Bible, philosophy and film at a Christian high school. Kelli is a writer and editor; her latest book is *The Busy Mom's Guide to Spiritual Survival*. David and Kelli are coauthors of *Jesus the Life-Changer*.

Valerie Van Kooten is a freelance writer and lecturer from Pella, Iowa. She teaches technical writing at Central College. She is married, has three sons and works with junior high and high school youth at her church.

Kyle White is the founder and director of Neighbors' House, a nonprofit organization partnering with at-risk students and families in DeKalb, Illinois. He is married to Barb. They have two children.

Lauren F. Winner, former book editor for Beliefnet, is the author of *Girl Meets God, Mudhouse Sabbath* and *Real Sex: The Naked Truth about Chastity*. She has appeared on PBS's *Religion & Ethics Newsweekly* and has written for *The New York Times Book Review, The Washington Post Book World, Publishers Weekly* and *Christianity Today*. She has degrees from Columbia and Cambridge Universities and is working on her doctorate in the history of American religion. She lives in Durham, North Carolina, with her husband, Griff Gatewood.

COLOPHON

Colophon

COUPLES' DEVOTIONAL BIBLE

EDITORIAL
Amy Ballor
Natalie Block
Elaine Schulte
Shari Vanden Berg
Michael Vander Klipp

THEOLOGICAL REVIEW
Andrew Sloan, M. Div., Oral Roberts University

PRODUCTION MANAGEMENT
Phil Herich

ART DIRECTION
Jamie DeBruyn

CREATIVE DIRECTION
Ron Huizinga

COVER DESIGN
Jamie DeBruyn

INTERIOR DESIGN
Katherine Lloyd and Jamie DeBruyn

PROOFREADING
Peachtree Editorial and Proofreading Service, Peachtree City, GA

INTERIOR TYPESETTING
Blue Heron Bookcraft, Battle Ground, WA

GUARANTEE